NEST ANSERMET BELA BARTOK

FRANZ BOAS ALFREDO CASTELLA

L DAHLHAUS LUIGI DAL POLA

LUX E.M. FORSTER ALLEN FORTE

ONY VAN HOBOKEN ERICH MORITZ

MAURICIO KAGEL ILMARI KROHN

SURE ROLF LIEBERMANN SERGE

RTUR LUR'E EDWARD S. LOWINSKY

MARKEVITCH YEHUDI MENUHIN

RALD MOORE NICOLAS NABOKOV

TER PEARS GOFFREDO PETRASS

ILDEBRANDO PIZZETTI HENR

CAMILLE SAINT-SAËNS ALBERT

OGER SESSIONS RAVI SHANKAR

N MICHAEL TIPPETT PAUL VALÉRY

R VILLA-LOBOS EGON WELLESZ

KIS GUIDO ADLER HIGINI ANGLÈS

ACQUES BARZUN LUCIANO BERIO

RY COWELL FEDELE D'AMICO CARL

rilm

SPEAKING **OF MUSIC** MUSIC CONFERENCES, 1835-1966

RILM RETROSPECTIVE SERIES

FOUNDING EDITOR
Barry S. Brook

SERIES EDITOR
Barbara Dobbs Mackenzie

No. 1: *Thematic catalogues in music: An annotated bibliography* by Barry S. Brook (Stuyvesant, NY: Pendragon, 1972). Revised and updated by Barry S. Brook and Richard Viano (Stuyvesant, NY: Pendragon, 1997).

No. 2: *Thèses de doctorat en langue française relatives a la musique: Bibliographie commentée* by Jean Gribenski (Stuyvesant, NY: Pendragon, 1979). Out of print.

No. 3: *Guitar and vihuela: An annotated bibliography* by Meredith Alice McCutcheon (Stuyvesant, NY: Pendragon, 1985).

No. 4: *Speaking of music: Music conferences, 1835-1966,* edited by James R. Cowdery, Zdravko Blažeković, and Barry S. Brook (New York: RILM, 2004).

SPEAKING OF MUSIC

MUSIC CONFERENCES, 1835-1966

GENERAL EDITORS

JAMES R. COWDERY

ZDRAVKO BLAŽEKOVIĆ • BARRY S. BROOK

RÉPERTOIRE INTERNATIONAL DE LITTÉRATURE MUSICALE, NEW YORK

rilm

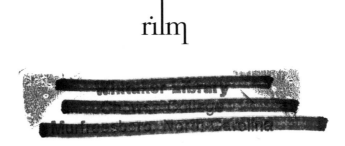

THE RÉPERTOIRE INTERNATIONAL DE LITTÉRATURE MUSICALE was founded in 1966. It is sponsored by the International Musicological Society and the International Association of Music Libraries, Archives and Documentation Centres and is governed by a Commission Internationale Mixte designated by the sponsors. The operation of the International Center is made possible through the very kind cooperation of The Graduate School of The City University of New York. RILM publications include *RILM Abstracts of Music Literature*, a continuously updated, international guide to writings on music, available in print, on CD-ROM, and online.

COMMISSION INTERNATIONALE MIXTE: Catherine Massip, president; Veslemöy Heintz, vice president; Dorothea Baumann, finance officer; Teresa Abejon, Chris Banks, H. Robert Cohen, Massimo Gentili-Tedeschi, Jane Hardie, Daniel Leech-Wilkinson, Suzanne Staral.

RILM is grateful for the support of THE ANDREW W. MELLON FOUNDATION. Without their generous grant this project would not have been possible.

RILM International Center

365 Fifth Avenue
New York, NY 10016
www.rilm.org

ISBN: 1-932765-00-X
ISSN: 1547-9390

Cover photograph reprinted with the permission of the National Anthropological Archives, Smithsonian Institution, Washington, D.C.

This volume was edited and produced on database and typesetting systems designed and built by Paul D. Petersen. Jacket and front matter design by Fred Gates. Printing by Port City Press, Baltimore, Maryland.

This book is printed on acid-free paper.

ABSTRACTORS

Michael Adelson
Ken Alboum
Michael Alterman
Daniel Anderson
James Donald Anderson
Laurie Appleby
Donna Arnold
Meredith E. Baker
André Balog
Carol K. Baron
Anthony F. Bavota
Warren A. Bebbington
John Berardi
Conrad T. Biel
Zdravko Blažeković
Marilyn S. Bliss
Ruth Block
David Bloom
Philip Brink
L. Poundie Burstein
Peter S. Bushnell
Chang Cho-Hee
Howard Cinnamon
Neill Clegg
Bill Clemmons
Karen Clute
Michael Collier
Arthur Comegno
Vivian Conejero
James R. Cowdery
Gregory D'Agostino
Sibylle Dahms
Albert Dlugasch
Brian Doherty
Leslie B. Dunner
Gary Eskow
Beverly Eskreis
Sylvia Eversole
Eric Ewazen
Murat Eyüboğlu
Terence Ford
Tina Frühauf

Scott Fruehwald
Katharine Fry
Gregory L. Fulkerson
David Gagné
Alan Garfield
Ronnie Gellis
William Gilmore
Joseph Giroux
June Goldenberg
Gray Dorothy
Alix Moyer Grunebaum
Jeanne Halley
Han Mi-Sook
Ralph Hartsock
Kevin James Harvey
David Hathwell
Ruth Herman
Barbara B. Heyman
Priscilla P. Hodges
Daniel Horn
Leonard Horowitz
Mary Lou Humphrey
Daven Jenkins
Nanette Jew
Christopher Johnson
Peter Kaliski
Helen-Ursula Katz
Alan Kingsley
Robert J. Kosovsky
Lee James Kotsambas
Orly Leah Krasner
Larry Laskowski
Gene W. Leonardi
Susan Levine
Joyce Z. Lindorff
José López-Calo
Allen Lott
Arthur Maisel
Meredith A. McCutcheon
James Melo
Meng Mei-Mei
John R. Metz

Judith Drogichen Meyer
Jeffrey Miller
Lisa Miller
Laurence Morell
John Gordon Morris
Miryam Moscovitz
Roy Nitzberg
Robert Noland
Marilyn Nonken
David Nussenbaum
Jenna Orkin
Rudolph Palmer
Elizabeth Parry
T. Pierce
Susan Poliniak
William Renwick
Daniel Rosenbaum
Helena Ross
Nathaniel Rudykoff
Barry Salwen
David Schiff
Joan Siegel
Carl Skoggard
Richard Slapsys
Alexander G. Smith
Jean W. Smith
Rollin Smith
John Stansell
Mark Stevens
Robert Taub
Jan Trojan
Jadranka Važanová
Edwin D. Wallace
Anthony Weinfeld
Anatole Wieck
Channan Willner
Elizabeth A. Wright
Yim Won-Bin
Tsipora Yosselevitch
You Jianning
Moshe Zorman

CONTENTS

Preface

We are now completing the editing and indexing of *RILM Retrospectives #3, Congress reports in music: An annotated bibliography*. . . . The work is divided into three parts: (1) systematic listing of the congress reports with tables of contents for each, (2) abstracts of the individual articles, and (3) indexes by author, subject, city, chronology, and sponsoring societies. . . . Much of our work has been completed. We have approximately 1500 abstracts, and the index is already underway.

In late 1978, the distinguished American musicologist Barry S. Brook (1918-1997) sent this optimistic letter to his many contacts among the world's music librarians. He could not have foreseen that this project would languish, not to be finished for another two and a half decades, nor that it would quadruple in size; and he could never have dreamed that its significance would grow far beyond the domain of bibliography. Reflecting myriad currents of thought—the twilight of Romanticism and the dawn of Modernism, the rise and fall of Marxism, and the advent of multiculturalism, to name just a few—this volume offers a fascinating window on intellectual history through the prism of music.

A farsighted innovator in bibliographic matters, Brook had established *Répertoire International de Littérature Musicale* (RILM) in 1966 under the joint sponsorship of the International Musicological Society and the International Association of Music Libraries, Archives, and Documentation Centers. This international bibliography aims at comprehensive coverage of writings on music published anywhere in the world, starting with publications from 1967. At the same time, Brook recognized the need for similar coverage of earlier materials; the *RILM Retrospectives* series is intended to fill this gap.

Pendragon Press published three volumes of the *Retrospectives* series. The first was Brook's *Thematic catalogues in music: An annotated bibliography* (1972; updated edition, 1997); the second was Jean Gribenski's *Thèses de doctorat en langue française relatives à la musique: Bibliographie commentée/French language dissertations in music: An annotated bibliography* (1979). In 1985, with the congress report project far from completion, *Guitar and vihuela: An annotated bibliography* by Meredith Alice McCutcheon became *RILM Retrospectives #3*. When Barry Brook died in 1997, those entrusted with sorting his papers found boxes of file cards and typed or handwritten lists, citations, and abstracts, in varying degrees of disorder: the congress report project. While this collection represented a great deal of diligent bibliographic work, it was unorganized, unwieldy, and certainly unpublishable. But whenever RILM's offices had moved, those boxes had been faithfully moved as well, and Brook's successors as Editor in Chief—Earl Terence Ford, Adam P.J. O'Connor, and Barbara Dobbs Mackenzie—had maintained the hope that somehow this daunting and enormous project would be completed. Finally, in 2001 the Andrew W. Mellon Foundation provided a generous grant toward that goal, enabling RILM to finish the job that Brook had begun a quarter-century earlier.

Brook's starting point was Marie Briquet's *La musique dans les congrès internationaux (1835-1939)* (Paris: Heugel, 1961), a compilation of citations of published congress reports. Brook intended (a) to enrich her citations with more complete lists of individual papers and with abstracts of all papers, (b) to add citations and abstracts for publications that Briquet missed, and (c)—the biggest challenge of all—to fill in the escalating number of such publications between Briquet's cutoff date of 1939 and the beginning of RILM's listings in 1967. He addressed these goals by soliciting citations and abstracts from his international contacts (the letter quoted above is from the final stage of this process) and from his students at the City University of New York Graduate Center. The materials he gathered became the contents of the dusty boxes that RILM refused to part with.

By the time we were ready to finish the project, another source had appeared: *A guide to international congress reports in musicology 1900-1975* by John Tyrrell and Rosemary Wise (New York: Garland, 1979), an explicit continuation of Briquet's bibliographic work. Yet another source for citations was *Appendix 1B: Conference reports* in volume 28 of the second edition of *The new Grove dictionary of music and musicians* (London: Macmillan, 2001), and a few additional citations came from Winifred Gregory's *International congresses and conferences, 1840-1937* (New York: H.W. Wilson, 1938; reprint Millwood, N.J.: Kraus, 1980). Serendipity was also a factor: For example, one of our editors happens to own an impressive collection of conference reports that are nearly impossible to find outside of Eastern Europe. In a few cases, volunteers from the world of music librarianship helped us by locating books and writing abstracts. We tried to fill in the gaps ourselves, borrowing the books whenever we could to ensure full and accurate citations and writing many of the abstracts. We are grateful to the many colleagues who have helped us; our long list of abstractors spans nearly three decades.

Of course, there are omissions. We are already aware of some of them, and we hope that our readers will call our attention to others. At some point we had to draw the line, reassuring ourselves—as all reference publishers must—that there can always be a second edition.

Unpublished papers

Some of these conference reports include references to papers that were presented at a particular conference but were not published in the report. In some cases, abstracts were published there in lieu of the full papers; in others, only the titles and authors were listed. We decided to include all examples of both of these cases. When the conference report includes only the title, author, and an abstract, we have provided the citation and the abstract (edited according to RILM's standards), accompanied by the indication "Summary of a paper". When the report includes only the title and author, with no abstract, we have provided the citation and, in place of an abstract, the indication "The conference report provides only a citation. Neither the text nor a summary of the paper was published here." Although the former points to a publication that provides minimal information on the paper's topic and the latter points to one that provides none beyond the title, these entries have been indexed to the extent possible.

Our rationale for including these entries is threefold. First, they contribute to a fuller picture of who was present and what took place at each conference. Also, they constitute biographical information about the authors, indicating where they were at a given moment, and what they were presenting or discussing. Finally, they provide potential aids to those researching the topics of these papers, since the reader is at least led to an author's name, and perhaps to a keyword, which may suggest further avenues of inquiry.

A window on intellectual history

As we worked on this project, we discovered that it was becoming much more than the sum of its parts: We began to realize that this collection of published papers illuminated matters of intellectual history in unforeseen ways. Here are a few observations; readers will no doubt make many more.

Conferences in musical life

As we point out in "Notes on using this book" (p. xvii–xix), entries are divided into classes as they are in RILM's other publications. We have moved our usual class 16, "Congress reports and symposium proceedings", to the front of this book and ordered it by year (secondarily by city); it therefore serves as an index by year as well as providing a full listing of all the conferences and papers covered here.

Patterns and currents emerge from a perusal of this section. For example, the changing nature and frequency of conferences over time can be tracked. The only 19th-century conferences devoted solely to music focused on Gregorian chant, and were held under the auspices of the Roman Catholic Church; otherwise, musical topics arose only in conferences devoted to history, folklore, psychology, or questions of public and private property. The first conferences devoted to miscellaneous studies in musicology were held in 1900, in Paris.

France's dominance in musicology gradually gave way to a preponderance of German work, mirrored by an increasing proportion of conferences in German-speaking countries; this trend becomes apparent by the mid-1920s, and conferences in general become more frequent. Their number declines during the social upheavals of the 1930s, and conferences with overt political agendas begin to appear. The picture becomes particularly bleak during World War II and its aftermath. In the 1950s, however, music conferences become more frequent than ever; for our time frame, the density of events peaks in 1963, with the presentation of some 600 papers on musical topics.

Other patterns in the role of conferences in musical life may be traced through two specialized indexes in this volume. **Conference locations** (p. 589–592) is organized geographically, showing where conferences were held and what their topics were; and **Conference sponsors** (p. 593–596) lists their sponsoring organizations and individuals by geographic affiliation, along with the conferences' years.

The advent of ethnomusicology

Before World War II, papers on non-Western and traditional Western musics largely came from the field of folklore—a rather woolly domain at that time, whose denizens ranged from wide-eyed dilettantes to rigorous collectors and cataloguers—or from the young sciences of ethnology, anthropology, and psychology. In the 1950s, attempts to synthesize the particular challenges and insights involved with all of these studies began to coalesce under the term "ethno-musicology" (so coined by Jaap Kunst; the hyphen was soon abandoned). Beginning around that time, several of the scholars involved were trying to define their field and its dynamics. The relative prominence of RILM classes 19 (**Universal perspectives**) and 31 (**Ethnomusicology: General**) in this volume attest to that process. (Metacultural topics that include consideration of Western classical music are in class 19; class 31 groups metacultural and intercultural topics—diffusion and acculturation, for example—that only involve traditional musics.) In this volume, the percentage of entries in classes 19 and 31 is more than twice that found in recent RILM volumes.

The social turmoil surrounding World War II is also reflected in the large proportion of ethnographic studies being done in Europe, often in response to explicit nationalist agendas. The preponderance of such studies in this period is reflected by the unusually large size of class 34 (**Ethnomusicology: Europe**) here. Again, the percentage of entries in class 34 in this volume is more than twice that found in recent RILM volumes.

By contrast, during our time period musical scholarship—be it termed musicology or ethnomusicology—had yet to embrace jazz and popular music. In this volume, classes 38 and 39 (**Jazz** and **Popular music**) comprise only a handful of entries; RILM's 1998 volume alone includes over 1300 entries on these topics.

The prism of music

From the abstract domain of philosophy to the concrete world of ethnography, music has long helped to illuminate general cultural attitudes and intellectual currents. The topics and approaches documented here illustrate a history of relationships between music and ideas; they also suggest developments that are less easily perceived, but no less compelling. These developments belong to more symbolic realms, such as those of affect and connotation.

The emergence of musicology, formalized in the first international music conferences in 1900, indicated the increasing importance of studying the history of Western music. Analyzing the achievements of master composers enhanced appreciation, and authenticity in performance practice became an issue. While pride in one's national compositional heritage was still a factor, the idea of a shared multinational foundation of aesthetics and practices was increasingly attractive and relevant.

Similarly, the importance of the social Darwinist perspective that inspired many early studies of non-Western musics—the notion of "primitive" cultures representing lower rungs of the evolutionary ladder—began to wane, as perceptions of world cultures broadened. Studying the music of other cultures increasingly involved an opening of the mind and spirit, and contributed to an expanded understanding of human potential that held implications for composers as well as for scholars.

As cultural perceptions widened, metacultural consciousness beckoned. Broad applications of theory and technology heralded liberation from the limitations of a culture-bound past. Microtonal musical instruments, for example, were not just mathematical exercises—they had an almost metaphysical import, promising to free us from the prison of equal temperament in a cleansing of music that mirrored a utopian cleansing of souls.

This volume documents an ever-expanding intellectual universe, not a straight line of progressive development. Looking back across the arc of history, we can begin to see how outlooks were formed, and we can assess the roles of the various currents and sidetracks that have shaped the disciplines that we pursue. The unique place of music in human life is salient at every turn.

James R. Cowdery

NOTES ON USING THIS BOOK

Speaking of Music is in two parts: (1) an **abstracts** section containing bibliographic citations and abstracts, and (2) an **index** section containing indexes of conference locations, conference sponsors, and combined authors and subjects.

This volume follows the editorial and formatting conventions of *RILM Abstracts of Music Literature*, which is a continuously updated, annotated, and indexed bibliography of writings on music from around the world; it is available in print, on CD-ROM, and online. More about *RILM Abstracts*, including contact and submission information, can be found online at www.rilm.org.

Non-Roman alphabets are not used, except for those that may be found in shelf marks. Romanizations conform to the standards approved by the International Organization for Standardization (ISO).

The abstracts section

Typography

Each entry begins with a boldface record number.

The two-letter code following the record number indicates the **document type,** or format of the source. The following document types appear in this volume:

Article
    ac in a collection of essays
    as in a symposium

Book
    bc collection of essays
    bm monograph
    bs symposium proceedings

Review
    rs of a symposium proceedings

Author surnames appear in capital letters, whether in the bibliographic citation (the "caption") or in the text of the abstract proper.

Titles of entries are in boldface, in the original language, followed by the title translation in square brackets.

Special features of the publication cited are abbreviated and shown in italics.

The following example is a complete entry with caption and abstract, and shows the different typefaces used.

3138 BARBEAU, Marius. **Migrations Sibériennes**
as   **en Amérique** [Siberian migrations in America],
         Miscellanea Paul Rivet octogenario dicata
         (México, D.F.: Universidad Nacional Autónoma
         de México, 1958) I, 17–48. *Illus., port.* In French.
         See no. 394 in this volume.
Explores evidence of the East Asian origins of the native populations of Alaska and British Columbia, including lamentation and funeral songs.

Arrangement of Entries

Entries are grouped by subject matter according to the classification scheme of *RILM Abstracts of Music Literature*, as reflected in the Contents. Within most classifications, entries are listed alphabetically by author. In cases where there is no named author or editor, the entry is listed by an appropriate subject heading appearing in square brackets.

Two classes are not listed by author:

- In **Chronology and Contents** (the first section in this volume), conferences are listed first by meeting year, and then by city.
- In class 4, **Catalogues for collections and exhibitions**, entries are listed by the city of the collection or exhibition.

Internal references

Right-arrows [→] appearing before a title indicate where a full entry for the item will be found in a different section of the volume. This reference allows an item to be represented in more than one place in the volume if the subject matter warrants a multiple (primary and secondary) classification.

A volume number at the end of the caption for an individual conference paper directs readers to the main entry for the conference proceedings volume in which it appears. The main entry, found in the **Chronology and Contents** section, lists the contents of the volume by author and title.

A reference to a record number in an abstract refers to directly related material in this book or in *RILM Abstracts of Music Literature*. For example, it may refer the reader to another edition of the work, or it may refer to a version of the item in another language. When such references point to another entry in this book, the words "no. [x] in this volume" are included; otherwise, they refer to entries in *RILM Abstracts*, as indicated by the superscript year preceding the number.

The index section

The **Conference Locations** index lists the conferences by country, city, topic, and date.

The **Conference Sponsors** index lists organizations and individuals indicated as sponsors in the published conference proceedings.

The **Authors and Subjects** index includes subject headings and names of authors, editors, translators, and other collaborators. Subject headings include genres, instruments, disciplines, geographic designations (countries, supranational regions, and continents), personal names, and general topics.

Typography

- An AUTHOR appears with the surname in capital letters.
- A **subject heading** appears in bold face.
- A *title* appears in italics.

Reference Numbers

The reference number at the end of each index entry comprises three elements: the number, the document type, and the classification. Together these elements indicate to the user the format of the publication (i.e., the document type) and the general subject matter (i.e., the classification). For example, the reference number

$$5909as^{77}$$

shows the entry's number in this volume (5909), the document type (as, article in a symposium proceedings), and the classification (77, Dramatic arts). Where no superscript appears, the number refers to an entry in the **Chronology and Contents** section.

An asterisk (*) preceding a reference number indicates that the item is a review of an author or editor's work. For example, the asterisk in the number

$$*145rs$$

listed under "ADLER, Guido" indicates that entry 145 is a review of a conference report edited by Adler.

Cross references

A *see* reference directs the user from a term that is not used to one that is used (**abstract music**, *see* **absolute music**).

A *see also* reference directs the user to related terms (**festivals**, *see also* **ceremonies; congresses, conferences,** symposia; societies, fraternities, associations, etc. headwords). As a rule, an item will not be indexed under two different headings connected by *see also* references.

Geographic headings

For the most part, countries, supranational regions, continents, and cities are designated by their present-day names. An exception has been made for the former Soviet Union: For general references to its territories in the period between 1917 and 1991, see **USSR**; for specific references to geographic entities within the Soviet Union (or for pre-Soviet Russia), see **Russia** or other states (e.g., **Latvia**). General references to the historic Yugoslavia (before 1991) are indexed under the headword **Slavic states** with the subheading "southern". Specific geographic references within the territory of the historic Yugoslavia are indexed under the corresponding successor states (e.g., **Croatia, Serbia and Montenegro, Slovenia**, etc). Similarly, items relating to the Austro-Hungarian Empire in general are indexed under **Europe** and the sub-heading "Austro-Hungarian Empire", while specific references to its cities or other geographic entities are indexed under the appropriate successor states. The same applies to Prussia, and so on. For former colonies see current geopolitical entities (e.g., for French Guinea, see **Guinea**).

Countries, supranational regions, and continents are in English; regions within a country are generally listed in that country's language; city names are also given in the original language. Generic designations (e.g., "West", "northern") are used when necessary. Places in Canada, China, and the United States of America are indexed by province or state where applicable.

> **Canada**, Ontario, Toronto
> **China**, Guangdong, Chaozhou region
> **Greece,** Athínai
> **Italy**, Venezia
> **Russia**, Moskva
> **United States of America**, South

Personal names

- Medieval and Renaissance names that consist of a forename and an associated place name (e.g., **Jacopo da Bologna**) appear under the forename.
- Honorifics, except those indicating sainthood or royalty, are omitted.
- Saints appear in the form **Francis of Assisi, Saint.**
- Popes are listed under their papal names, not their family names.
- Pseudonyms are not used as headings. *See* references direct the reader to the used form. However, pseudonyms are used in later fields.

Disciplines and concepts

In some cases, designations of disciplines and concepts are applied retroactively. For example, the activities of early musical folklorists and anthropologists are grouped with those of their successors under **ethnomusicology**, even though that term was not widely used before the 1950s.

Alphabetization

- Arrangement is by *word* order (an interword space takes precedence over any letter).
- Hyphenated words and names are alphabetized as separate words.
- Compound names and names beginning with a separate prefix are alphabetized as two words.
- Diacritics are ignored.
- Abbreviations are alphabetized as though the abbreviated spelling were a word.
- Numerals follow the letter Z.
- Personal names are alphabetized according to the International Federation of Library Associations and Institutions (IFLA) guidelines.

Surnames with prefixes are alphabetized as follows: American, British, Italian, and South African names are alphabetized under the prefix. Dutch and German names are alphabetized under the surname. French and Spanish names with article-only prefixes are listed under the article. French and Spanish names with preposition-only prefixes are listed under the surname. French names with both a preposition and an article are listed under the article; Spanish names with both a preposition and an article are listed under the surname.

de	[Dutch surname], see surname
de	[French surname], see surname
de'	[Italian surname], see De'
de	[Spanish surname], see surname
de la	[French surname], see La
de la	[Spanish surname], see surname
del	[Spanish surname], see surname
di	[Italian surname], see Di
du	[French surname], see Du
van	[Dutch/German surname], see surname
van der	[Dutch surname], see surname
von	[German surname], see surname

The following examples illustrate the main principles of alphabetization:

Augustine of Hippo, Saint
Beethoven, Ludwig van
D'Accone, Frank A.
Di Pasquale, Marco
Jacopo da Bologna
La Grange, Henry-Louis de
Laade, Wolfgang
Leo X, Pope
Louis XIV, King of France
Mendelssohn, Moses
Mendelssohn-Bartholdy, Felix
Ó Súilleabháin, Mícheál
Osthoff, Wolfgang
O'Sullivan, Donal
Oswald, Peter
Vega, Francisco de la

Abbreviations

anon.	anonymous	Ges.	Gesellschaft	no/s.	number/s
Arch.	Archiv, Archive, etc.	Inst.	Institut, Institute, etc.	op/p.	opus/es
Arh.	Arhiv	internat.	international	p.	page/s
Assoc.	Association, Associazione, etc.	Ist.	Istituto	r.	recto
		Lib.	Library	Soc.	Society, Società, etc.
Asoc.	Asociación	misc.	miscellaneous	U.	University, Univerzitet, etc.
b.	birth date	movt/s.	movement/s	U. Bibl.	Universitätsbibliothek, Universitetsbibliotek, etc.
Bibl.	Bibliotek, Biblioteca, etc.	Mun.	Municipal, Municipale, etc.		
c.	century	MS/S	manuscript/s	v.	verso
ca.	circa	Nac.	Nacional	vol/s.	volume/s
Col.	College, Collège, etc.	Nat.	National	vs.	versus
d.	death date	Naz.	Nazionale		

LIST OF PHOTOGRAPHS

Meeting of the International Association of Music Libraries (AIBM), Mainz, 1977.

Front row: Barry S. Brook (see nos. 528, 787, 1670, 1714, and 3734),

Harald Heckmann (see nos. 356, 589, 590, 591, and 3997).

Reproduced with permission of Claire Brook.

CHRONOLOGY AND CONTENTS

1835

1
bs
[Paris] [Ier] Congrès historique européen
[(First) European Conference on History]. Sponsored by the Institut Historique (Paris: P.H. Krabbe, 1836) 2 v. 480; 504 p. In French.

The conference was held from mid-November through mid-December 1835. The following contributions are cited separately: Auguste BOTTÉE DE TOULMON, **Histoire de l'art musical depuis l'ère chrétienne jusqu'à nos jours** [The history of music from the Christian era to our time] (951); LECOMTE, **Différence de la musique des Celtes et de celle des Grecs avec le chant ambrosien et mosarabique et celle du chant ambrosien et mosarbique avec le chant grégorien et celle du chant grégorien avec la musique du Moyen Age** [The difference between the music of the Celts and the Greeks and Ambrosian and Mozarabic chant, and that between Ambrosian and Mozarabic chant and Gregorian chant, and the difference between Gregorian chant and the music of the Middle Ages] (1036).

1838

2
bs
[Paris] Congrès historique [History conference] (Paris: A. Le Gallois, 1839) 448 p. In French.

The conference was held from 15 September through 17 October 1838. The following contribution is cited separately: Antoine-Amable-Élie ELWART, **Quelles sont les causes qui ont donné naissance à la musique religieuse? Pourquoi s'est-elle écartée de son but? Et quels seraient les moyens de l'y ramener?** [What gave birth to religious music? Why has it veered from its goal? How could it be brought back to it?] (6009).

1860

3
bs
[Paris] Congrès pour la restauration du plain-chant et de la musique d'église [Conference on the restoration of plainchant and church music]. Ed. by Joseph-Louis d' ORTIGUE, Adrien de LA FAGE, and Victor PELLETIER (Paris: De Mourgues, 1862) 130 p. In French.

The following contributions are cited separately: M. AVY, **Actes épiscopaux concernant la musique d'église: Deux observations** [Episcopal acts on church music: Two observations] (6155); BRUMARE (abbé), **Extrait d'une dissertation sur les moyens de restituer le plain-chant, se divisant en deux parties, l'une qui regarde la théorie et l'autre la pratique** [Extract of a dissertation on the means of restoring plainchant, divided into two parts: Theory and practice] (1923); P. DELORT, **Plan d'un enseignement pratique et général du plain-chant et de la musique d'église** [Method of practical and general teaching of plainchant and church music] (4514); Augustin GONTIER, **Extrait de la dissertation sur le plain-chant et son exécution** [Extract from the dissertation on plainchant and its performance] (1110); M. GROSJEAN, **De l'état actuel de la musique religieuse dans le diocèse de Saint-Dié** [The state of religious music in the diocese of Saint-Dié] (6243); J.-M.-Joseph JOUAN, **De l'instituteur primaire au point de vue de la propagation du plain-chant et de la musique religieuse** [The primary school teacher from the point of view of the propagation of plainchant and religious music] (4718); Aloys KUNC, **Du rhythme qui convient au plain-chant** [Appropriate rhythm for plainchant] (3705); Gabriel-Marie-Eugène de LA TOUR DE NOÉ, **Situation présente des églises des villes et des campagnes sous le rapport du chant et de la musique** [The state of chant and church music in cities and in the provinces] (2021) and **Véritable caractère de la musique d'église** [The true character of church music] (6278); Alfred LAIR DE BEAUVAIS, **De l'état actuel de la musique sacrée dans le diocèse de Bayeux** [The state of religious music in the diocese of Bayeux] (6280); A. LEMOINE, **Plain-chant, texte et exécution** [Plainchant: Text and performance] (1139); A.-Félix MARTINEAU, **De l'accompagnement du plain-chant** [The accompaniment of plainchant] (6297), **Du plain-chant dans le diocèse de Nantes** [Plainchant in the diocese of Nantes] (6298), **Enseignement du plain-chant et de la musique dans les séminaires du diocèse de Nantes** [Teaching of plainchant and music in the seminaries of the diocese of Nantes] (4594), **Le maître de chapelle** [The choirmaster] (6299), and **Maîtrise de la cathédrale de Nantes** [The choir school of the Nantes cathedral] (4735); M. MASSART, **Note sur l'état du chant dans la collégiale de Saint-Quentin** [The state of chant in the Collegiate church of Saint-Quentin] (6302); Octave POIX, **De l'enseignement du chant, de la musique et de l'orgue dans les écoles normales d'instituteurs, les séminaires et les maîtrises** [The teaching of chant, music, and organ in teachers' colleges, seminaries, and choir schools] (4841), **Maîtres de chapelle, organistes, orgues, sociétés chorales, cantiques** [Chapel masters, organists, organs, choral societies, hymns] (2068), and **Situation présente des églises et des campagnes du diocèse de Soissons, sous le rapport du chant et de la musique** [The state of chant and church music in the cities and the countryside of the diocese of Soissons] (2069); A. POPULUS, **De l'accompagnement du plain-chant** [The accompaniment of plainchant] (3710); F. RAILLARD, **De la restauration du chant grégorien** [The restoration of Gregorian chant] (6350); SÉGUY (abbé), **La musique d'église dans le diocèse de Valence** [Church music in the diocese of Valence] (6389); Charles-Victor VANSON, **Sur une association canoniquement érigée en la paroisse Saint-Pierre de Nancy pour l'exécution du chant dans les offices paroissiaux** [On a canonical association erected in the parish of Saint-Pierre in Nancy for the performance of chant in the parochial ceremonies] (6403); Alfred YUNG, **Note sur la musique d'église dans le diocèse de Verdun** [Church music in the diocese of Verdun] (6418).

1867

4
bs
[Saint-Brieuc] [Ier] Congrès celtique international [(First) International Congress on the Celts]. Sponsored by the Société d'Émulation des Côtes-du-Nord (Paris: Maisonneuve, 1867; Saint-Brieuc: Guyon Francisque, 1868) 2 v. xvi, 382 p. *Charts, diagr., maps.* In French.

The conference was held from 15 through 19 October 1867. The following contribution is cited separately: Eugène HALLÉGUEN, **Introduction à l'histoire littéraire de l'Armorique bretonne des Ve et VIe siècles jusqu'à nos jours** [Introduction to the literary history of Breton Armorica from the 5th and 6th century to the present] (2849).

1875

5
bs
[Nancy] Compte rendu du Ier Congrès international des américanistes [Proceedings of the First International Congress of Americanists] (Nancy: Crépin-Leblond, 1875) 2 v. 480, 478 p.; (reprint, Nendeln: Kraus, 1968). *Illus., music, bibliog., maps.* In French and English.

The following contribution is cited separately: Oscar COMETTANT, **La musique en Amérique avant la découverte de Christophe Colomb** [Music in America before Columbus's discovery] (3195).

1879

6
bs
[Brussels] Compte rendu du IIIᵉ Congrès international des américanistes [Proceedings of the Third International Congress of Americanists] (Bruxelles: C. Muquardt; Anatole Pamps, 1879) 2 v. 835 p.; (reprint, Nendeln: Kraus, 1968). *Maps.* In French, English, German, Italian, and Spanish.

The following contribution is cited separately: Marcos JIMÉNEZ DE LA ESPADA, **Cloches préhistoriques sud-américaines** [Prehistoric South American bells] (3651).

1881

7
bs
[Berlin] Verhandlungen des fünften Internationalen Orientalisten-Congresses [Proceedings of the Fifth International Congress of Orientalists]. Ed. by Christian Friedrich August DILLMANN (Berlin: A. Asher, 1882) 3 v. 1258 p. *Facs.* In German.

The conference was held in September 1881. The following contribution is cited separately: Spyridōn K. PAPAGEŌRGIOS, **Merkwürdige in der Synagogen von Corfu in Gebrauch befindliche Hymnen** [Curious hymns used in the synagogue of Corfu] (6086).

8
bs
[Madrid] Congreso Internacional de Americanistas: Cuarta reunion [International Congress of Americanists: Fourth meeting] (Madrid: M.G. Hernandez; Fortanet, 1881; 1882) 2 v. lxxxii, 416 p.; (reprint, Nendeln: Kraus, 1968). *Music.* In Spanish and French.

The conference was held from 18 through 22 September 1881. The following contribution is cited separately: Marcos JIMÉNEZ DE LA ESPADA, **Yaravíes quiteños** [Yaraví from Quito] (3203).

1882

9
bs
[Arezzo] Le Congrès européen d'Arezzo pour l'étude et l'amélioration du chant liturgique: Compte rendu non officiel, suivi d'un appendice bibliographique [European congress in Arezzo, for the study and improvement of liturgical chant: Unofficial conference proceedings, followed by a bibliographical appendix]. Ed. by Charles Étienne RUELLE (Paris: Firmin-Didot, 1884) 48 p. *Bibliog.* In French.

The conference is also cited as no. 10 in this volume.

10
bs
[Arezzo] Del congresso europeo di canto liturgico in Arezzo e della restaurazione del canto gregoriano: Memoria [Regarding the European congress on liturgical chant in Arezzo and the restoration of Gregorian chant: Recollections]. By Luigi NERICI (Lucca: author, 1882) 80 p. *Music.* In Italian.

The congress was held from 11 through 14 September 1882. The following contribution is cited separately: Antonius SCHMITT, **Propositions sur le chant grégorien, d'après les faits universellement admis pars les archéologues** [Propositions on Gregorian chant on the basis of facts that have been universally accepted by archaeologists] (6380).

1883

11
bs
[Leiden] Actes du sixième Congrès international des orientalistes [Proceedings of the Sixth International Congress of Orientalists]. Ed. by Michael Johan de GOEJE (Leiden: Brill, 1885) 4 v.; (reprint,

Nendeln: Kraus, 1972). *Illus., bibliog.* In French, Dutch, English, German, and Arabic.

The conference, which was held from 10 through 15 September 1883, was divided into six sections: (1) summary of proceedings; (2) Semitic studies; (3) Aryan studies; (4) African studies; (5) the Far East; and (6) Polynesia. The following contributions are cited separately: Jan Jakob Maria de GROOT, **Buddhist masses for the dead at Amoy: An ethnological essay** (6457); Jan Pieter Nicolaas LAND and ABŪ NAṢR MUḤAMMAD IBN MUḤAMMAD IBN ṬARKHĀN IBN UZALAGH AL-FĀRĀBĪ, **Recherches sur l'histoire de la gamme arabe** [Research on the history of the Arabic scale] (4090).

1885

12
bs
[Antwerp] Compte rendu du huitième Congrès de l'Association Littéraire et Artistique Internationale [Report of the Eighth Conference of the International Literary and Artistic Association], *Bulletin de l'Association Littéraire et Artistique Internationale* 2:3 (Oct 1885) 1–117. In French.

The report on the musical section of the conference, which was held from 19 through 25 September 1885, was published on pp. 92-97.

1889

13
bs
[Paris] [Iᵉ] Congrès international des traditions populaires [(First) International Folklore Congress]. Sponsored by the Ministère du Commerce, de l'Industrie et des Colonies. *Bibliothèque des Annales Économiques* (Paris: Société d'Éditions Scientifiques, 1891) 168 p. In French and English.

The congress was held during the Exposition Universelle, from 29 July to 2 August 1889.

1890

14
bs
[Paris] Congrès International des Américanistes: Compte rendu de la huitième session [International Congress of Americanists: Proceedings of the eighth meeting] (Paris: Leroux, 1892) 704 p.; (reprint, Nendeln: Kraus, 1968). *Illus.* In French, English, and Spanish.

The following contribution is cited separately: Raymond PILET, **Mélodies populaires des indiens du Guatemala** [Popular melodies of the Guatemalan Indians] (3213).

1891

15
bs
[Brussels] Annales de la Fédération Archéologique et Historique de Belgique. VII/1 [Annals of the Fédération Archeologique et Historique de Belgique. VII/1]. Ed. by Paul SAINTENOY and Victor JACQUES (Bruxelles: Goemaere, 1891). In French.

The following contribution is cited separately: Edmond vander STRAETEN, **Quels étaient les instruments de musique en usage dans les provinces Belges avant l'avènement de la maison de Bourgogne?** [What were the musical instruments used in the Belgian provinces before the coming of the House of Burgundy?] (1194).

1892

16
bs
[Brussels] **Annales de la Fédération Archéo-logique et Historique de Belgique. VII/2** [Annals of the Fédération Archéologique et Historique de Belgique. VII/2]. Ed. by Paul SAINTENOY and Victor JACQUES (Bruxelles: Goemaere, 1892). In French.
The following contribution is cited separately: Edmond vander STRAETEN, **Notes sur quelques instruments de musique en nature ou en figuration, trouvés dans la Gaule Belgo-Romaine** [Musical instruments, real or depicted, in actuality or in representation, from Belgo-Roman Gaul] (3280).

17
bs
[London] **International Congress of Experimental Psychology: Second session** (London: Williams & Norgate, 1892) 186 p.; (reprint, Nendeln: Kraus, 1974). In English, French, and German.
The following contribution is cited separately: Richard WALLASCHEK, **Natural selection and music** (5715).

1893

18
bs
[Chicago] **The International Folk-lore Congress of the World's Columbian Exposition. I.** Proceedings of the Third International Folk-lore Congress. Ed. by Helen Wheeler BASSETT and Frederick STARR. *Archives of the International Folk-lore Association* 1 (Chicago: Charles H. Sergel, 1898) 512 p.; (reprint, New York: Arno Press, 1980). ISBN 0-405-13327-8. *Illus., port., facs.*
The following contributions are cited separately: Andrejs JURJĀNS, **A study on the ligotnes: Popular songs of St. John's Eve** (2874); Friedrich S. KRAUSS, **Why national epics are composed: Some reflections illustrated by a song of guslars of Bosnia and Herzegovina** (2910); Washington MATTHEWS, **Some sacred objects of the Navajo rites** (3166); Vid VULETIĆ-VUKASOVIĆ, **A few notes on the songs of the Southern Slavs** (3113). Includes texts of songs sung at the Congress.

19
bs
[Chicago] **Memoirs of the International Congress of Anthropology.** Ed. by C. Staniland WAKE (Chicago: Schulte, 1894) 375 p. *Illus.*
The conference was held from 23 August through 2 September 1893. The following contributions are cited separately: John Comfort FILLMORE, **Primitive scales and rhythms** (3148); Alice Cunningham FLETCHER, **Love songs among the Omaha Indians** (3150).

1894

20
bs
[Geneva] **Actes du dixième Congrès international des orientalistes** [Proceedings of the Tenth International Congress of Orientalists] (Leiden: Brill, 1897). *Illus., maps.* In French, German, English, and Italian.
The conference was held from 4 through 12 September 1894. The following contributions are cited separately: H. HANLON, **The wedding customs and songs of Ladak** (2632); Jan Pieter Nicolaas LAND, **Note sur la musique de l'île de Java** [Note on the music of the island of Java] (2655).

1895

21
bs
[Niort] **La tradition en Poitou et Charentes: Art populaire, ethnographie, folk-lore, hagiographie, histoire** [Tradition in Poitou and Charentes: Folk art, ethnography, folklore, religion, and history]. Proceedings of the First Congress de la Société d'Ethnographie Nationale et d'Art Populaire.

Ed. by A. THEURIET, G. LAFENESTRE, G. PARIS, *et al.* (Paris: Librairie de la Tradition Nationale, 1897) xxi, 479 p.; (reprint, Poitiers: Le Bouquiniste, 1977; n.p.: Éditions du Bastion, 1999). ISBN 2-902170-0; 2-7455-0044-9. *Illus., music.* In French.
Includes the conferences of 24 March 1895 and 8 March 1896; an account of the Niort exhibition; the proceedings of the first conference of the Société d'Ethnographie Nationale et d'Art Populaire, held in Niort from 22 May through 22 June 1896; and the statutes of the Société d'Ethnographie Nationale. The following contributions are cited separately: Léo DESAIVRE, **La danse en Poitou** [Dance in Poitou] (4952); Auguste GAUD, **Rondes et chansons du Pays Melois** [Rounds and songs of the Le Mêle region] (2823); H. HANLON, **The wedding customs and songs of Ladak** (2632); Jan Pieter Nicolaas LAND, **Note sur la musique de l'île de Java** [Note on the music of the island of Java] (2655); Antonin LHOUMEAU, **La musique populaire à l'Église** [Folk music in the Church] (6286); Jean PHILLIPPE, **La chanson populaire en Poitou et dans la Haute-Bretagne** [Traditional songs in Poitou and Upper Brittany] (2999); Sylvain TRÉBUCQ, **Danses maraichines** [Maraichine dances] (5079) and **Les chansons de mariage en Vendée** [Wedding songs of the Vendée] (3088).

22
bs
[Rodez] **Congrès diocésain de musique religieuse et de plain-chant** [Diocesan congress of religious music and plainchant] (Rodez: Carrère, 1895) 175 p. *Illus.* In French.
The following contributions are cited separately: **L'étude du chant religieux** [The study of religious singing] (6191); **Lettre d'un organiste de campagne** [Letter from a country organist] (6190); **Si j'étais vicaire!** [If I were a vicar!] (6192); Charles BORDES, **De l'emploi de la musique figurée spécialement de la musique palestrinienne dans les offices liturgiques** [The use of figured-bass music, especially that of Palestrina's, in liturgical Offices] (6175); FORT (abbé), **Moyens pratiques de réorganisation du chant grégorien dans les paroisses rurales** [Practical means of reorganizing Gregorian chant in rural parishes] (6215); GRAVIER (canon), **Le cantique français: Son importance dans les exercices religieux et dans l'enseignement** [The French canticle: Its importance in religious practices and in teaching] (6242); Alexandre GUILMANT, **Du rôle de l'orgue dans les offices liturgiques** [The role of the organ in liturgical Offices] (6244); LAFFON (abbé), **Les livres liturgiques et les décrets du St-Siège** [The liturgical books and the decrees of St. Siège] (6279); LAMICHE (abbé), **Les débuts de l'organiste** [The beginnings of the organist] (3409); André MOCQUEREAU, **La psalmodie romaine et l'accent tonique latin** [Roman psalmody and the Latin tonic accent] (6308); POUNIAU (abbé), **Du chant dans les paroisses rurales** [Chant in rural parishes] (6340); SERVIÈRES (abbé), **A travers l'histoire du chant religieux** [Across the history of religious singing] (6391); VIGOUREL (abbé), **Du chant ecclésiastique** [On ecclesiastical singing] (6405).

1896

23
bs
[Ghent] **Fédération Archéologique et Historique de Belgique: Congrès de Gand** [Fédération Archéologique et Historique de Belgique: Ghent congress]. Proceedings of the 11th Congress of the Fédération Archéologique et Historique de Belgique; sponsored by the Cercle Archéologique et Historique de Gand. Ed. by Gabriel Edmond Guillaume VAN DEN GHEYN. *Annales de la Fédération Archéologique et Historique de Belgique* 11/2 (Gent: Siffer, 1897) 323 p. In French, Italian, German, Spanish, Latin, and English.
The conference was held from 2 through 5 August 1896. The following contribution is cited separately: César SNOECK, **Notes sur les instruments de musiques en usage dans les Flandres au Moyen Âge** [Musical instruments in Flanders during the Middle Ages] (1185).

⟶ **[Niort] La tradition en Poitou et Charentes: Art populaire, ethnographie, folk-lore, hagiographie, histoire** [Tradition in Poitou and Charentes: Folk art, ethnography, folklore, religion, and history]. See no. 21 in this volume.

1898

24
bs
[Brussels] Iᵉʳ Congrès international de l'art public [First International Congress of Public Art]. Sponsored by the Œuvre Nationale Belge and King Léopold II of Belgium (Liège: Bénard, 1900) 172 p. *Illus.* In French.
The conference was held from 24 through 29 September 1898. The following contributions are cited separately: Alexandre HALOT, **La musique envisagée au point de vue de l'art public: Ses bienfaits populaires** [Music seen from the point of view of public art: Its popular benefits] (4547); P. TEMPELS, **L'influence de l'art sur les mœurs et l'école primaire** [The influence of art on customs and the primary school] (4784).

25
bs
[Enghien] Annales de la Fédération Archéologique et Historique. III [Annals of the Fédération Archéologique et Historique. III]. Ed. by Ernest MATTHIEU (Enghien: Spinet, 1899). In French.
The following contribution is cited separately: Clément LYON, **Le musicien Philippe de Mons (de Monte): Est-il malinois ou montois?** [The musician Philippe de Monte: Was he from Mechelen or Mons?] (1375).

1900

26
bs
[Munich] Akten des fünften internationalen Kongresses katholischer Gelehrten/Compte rendu du Vᵉ Congrès scientifique international des catholiques [Proceedings of the Fifth International Congress of Catholic Scholars] (München: Herder, 1901). *Illus.* In German, French, and English; summary in Latin.
The conference was held from 24 through 28 September 1900. The following contributions are cited separately: Carl Jakob EISENRING, **Karl Greith: Der grösste schweizerische Kirchenmusiker** [Karl Greith: The greatest Swiss church musician] (1949); Franz Xaver HABERL, **Was ist im XIX. Jahrhundert für die Kenntnis altklassischer Werke kirchlicher Tonkunst geschehen** [Nineteenth-century contributions to our knowledge of the classic church music] (6247); Ambrosius KIENLE, **Über den Choral bei den Cisterciensern** [On the chant of the Cistercians] (6270); Dan MAC CREA, **Gregorian music in our churches** (6291); J. MOSER, **Klavierklang und Resonanzbodenkonstruktion** [Piano sound and soundboard construction] (3533); Andreas SCHMID, **Kirchengesang nach den Liturgikern des Mittelalters** [Church singing according to the liturgists of the Middle Ages] (6377).

27
bs
[Paris] Annales internationales d'histoire: Congrès de Paris, 1900. V: Histoire des sciences [International annals of history: Paris congress, 1900. V: History of the sciences] (Paris: Colin, 1901) 348 p.; (reprint, Nendeln: Kraus, 1972). *Illus., maps.* In French.
The conference was published in seven volumes over the course of two years: I: *Histoire générale et diplomatique* (1901); II: *Histoire comparée des institutions et du droit* (1902); III: *Histoire comparée de l'économie sociale* (1902); IV: *Histoire des affaires religieuses* (1902); V: *Histoire des sciences* (1901); VI: *Histoire comparée des littératures* (1901); VII: *Histoire des arts du dessin* (1902). The following contribution is cited separately: Paul TANNERY, **Lettres inédites adressées au Père Mersenne (celles de Pierre Trichet concernant la musique)** [Unpublished letters addressed to Father Mersenne (those of Pierre Trichet concerning music)] (1698).

28
bs
[Paris] Congrès international de l'éducation sociale. I: Rapports présentés; II: Compte rendu des séances [International Congress of Social Education. I: Reports; II. Proceedings] *Exposition Universelle de 1900* (Paris: Librairie Félix Alcan, 1901) xiv, 477 p. In French.
The conference was held from 26 through 30 September 1900. The following contribution is cited separately: Edmond BAILLY and Anna LAMPÉRIÈRE, **La musique et l'éducation sociale** [Music and social education] (4484).

29
bs
[Paris] Congrès international de musique: Iʳᵉ session—Exposition Universelle de 1900: Compte rendu, rapports, communications [International Congress of Music: First meeting—Exposition Universelle, 1900: Proceedings, reports, and papers] (Paris: conference, 1901) 64 p. *Music, charts, diagr.* In French.
The conference was held from 14 through 18 June 1900 in conjunction with the Exposition Universelle, Paris. Reports of the same meeting are cited as nos. 30 and 33 in this volume. The following contributions are cited separately: Ernest BAUDOT, **Avantages et inconvénients du tempérament au point de vue de la pratique musicale** [Advantages and disadvantages of temperament from the perspective of musical practice] (4049) and **Utilité d'un appareil enregistreur des mouvements des œuvres musicales** [The use of a device for registering the tempi of musical works] (3968); CANAT DE CHIZY, **Régularisation des indications et appareils métronomiques** [Regularization of metronomic indications and devices] (3976); Augustin CHÉRION, **Y a-t-il utilité à reconstituer les maîtrises? Dans le cas de l'affirmative, quels sont les moyens pratiques pour parvenir à cette reconstitution?** [Is it useful to reconstitute the choir schools? If so, what practical means are there to arrive at this reconstitution?] (4688); Jules COMBARIEU, **De l'évolution du drame lyrique** [On the evolution of lyric drama] (5122) and **L'état doit-il jouer dans les théâtres et concerts subventionnés un rôle de protecteur à l'égard des œuvres des maîtres tombés dans le domaine public?** [In subsidized theaters and concerts, should the state play the role of protector with regard to works that have come into the public domain?] (1938); Émile ERGO, **Réforme de l'enseignement et de la science de l'harmonie suivant le système des fonctions tonales du Dr. Hugo Riemann** [Reform of the teaching and science of harmony according to the system of tonal functions of Hugo Riemann] (4163); Alphonse FRÉMONT, **Régularisation des indications métronomiques** [Regularization of metronomic indications] (3993); Frédéric HELLOUIN, **Simplification de la notation musicale** [Simplification of musical notation] (3824); Vincent d' INDY, **De l'utilité des écoles de chefs d'orchestre et de la généralisation de l'étude de l'instrumentation** [On the usefulness of conducting schools and on the generalization of the study of instrumentation] (4558), **Emploi d'un signe distinctif, accompagnant les clefs de fa et de sol dans les partitions vocales et instrumentales pour les parties s'entendant à l'octave** [Use of a distinctive sign, accompanying the F and G clefs in vocal and instrumental scores, for parts heard at the octave] (3830), **Transformation des instruments dits simples en instruments chromatiques: Définition des instruments chromatiques** [Transformation of so-called simple instruments into chromatic instruments: Definition of chromatic instruments] (3255), and **Unification de l'orchestration des harmonies et fanfares** [Unification in the orchestration of *harmonies* and *fanfares*] (3788); Vincent d' INDY, Ernest BAUDOT, Théophile DUREAU, and Gabriel PARÈS, **Y a-t-il utilité à employer la note réelle dans l'écriture musicale?** [Is it useful to employ real pitches in musical notation?] (3831); Gustave LYON, **Généralisation de l'emploi du diapason normal: Étude des moyens de le rendre obligatoire** [Generalization of the use of *diapason normal*: A study of the means of making it compulsory] (4092); Victor-Charles MAHILLON, **Utilité de désigner les sons de l'échelle chromatique par des numéros** [The use of indicating the sounds of the chromatic scale by numbers] (3850); Paul MILLIET, **Étant donné l'influence que la critique peut exercer sur le développement de l'art musical, n'y a-t-il pas lieu d'émettre un vœu relatif à la manière dont elle s'exerce?** [Given the influence criticism can exercise on the development of the musical art, should not a standard be established with respect to the way it operates?] (5544); Henri RADIGUER, **La situation des chefs de musique militaire** [The situation of conductors of military music] (3270); Laurent de RILLÉ, Théophile DUREAU, Alfred BOUTIN, Wilhelm GRIMM, and F.R. ROBERT, **De l'utilité du développement des sociétés orphéoniques (chorales, symphonies, harmonies, fanfares), et des**

moyens d'améliorer leur répertoire [The importance of the development of music societies (choruses, symphonies, wind ensembles, brass bands) and the means of improving their repertoire] (2083).

30
bs
[Paris] Congrès international de musique de 1900: Commission de technique musicale [International Congress of Music, 1900: Commission of musical technique]. Ed. by F.R. ROBERT (Paris: Imprimerie de Chaix, 1902) 96 p. In French.

A report on the questionnaire of Gabriel PIERNÉ, which was presented to the participants by the Count Raoul CHANDON DE BRAILLES. Proceedings of the conference are cited as nos. 29 and 33 in this volume.

31
bs
[Paris] Congrès international des traditions populaires [International Folklore Congress] (Paris: E. Lechevalier, E. Leroux, J. Maisonneuve, 1902) x, 150 p. *Illus.* In French.

The following contributions are cited separately: Émile BLÉMONT, **La tradition poétique** [The poetic tradition] (5289); Léon PINEAU, **Les vieux chants populaires scandinaves** [The old traditional songs of Scandinavia] (3002); Stanislas PRATO, **Échantillon d'une étude comparée des chants populaires néo-grecs et des autres, européens et orientaux** [Examples from a study comparing neo-Greek traditional songs and others, European and Eastern] (3015); **Sur les applications du phonographe à l'étude des traditions populaires** [On the applications of the phonograph to the study of popular traditions] (2418); Northcote Whitridge THOMAS, **La danse totémique en Europe** [Totemic dance in Europe] (5077); Vid VULETIĆ-VUKASOVIĆ, **La moreška et le juge gras (le roi du village) dans l'île de Cuozola (Dalmatie)** [The moreška and the fat judge (the king of the village) on the island of Korčula (Dalmatia)] (5080).

32
bs
[Paris] Congrès international d'histoire de la musique: Documents, mémoires et vœux [International Conference of Music History: Documents, papers, and recommendations]. Sponsored by the Exposition Universelle de 1900. Ed. by Jules COMBARIEU (Solesmes: St. Pierre; Paris: Fischbacher, 1901) 318 p. *Music, index.* In French.

The conference was held at the Bibliothèque de l'Opéra, Paris, from 23 through 29 July 1900, as section 8 of the Congrès d'histoire comparée. The following contributions are cited separately: Pierre AUBRY, **La légende dorée du jongleur** [The golden legend of the jongleur] (5285); Marie BOBILLIER (Michel Brenet), **Un poète-musicien français du XVᵉ siècle: Eloy d'Amerval** [A French poet-musician of the 15th century: Eloy d'Amerval] (1238); Arnaldo BONAVENTURA, **Progrès et nationalité dans la musique** [Progress and nationality in music] (5431); Julián CARRILLO, **La nomenclature des sons** [The nomenclature of pitches] (4502); Oscar CHILESOTTI, **Musiciens français: Jean-Baptiste Besard et les luthistes du XVIᵉ siècle** [French musicians: Jean-Baptiste Besard and the lutenists of the 16th century] (1274); Jules COMBARIEU, **Le vandalisme musical** [Musical vandalism] (3675); Lionel Alexandre DAURIAC, **Le pensée musicale** [Musical thought] (5451); Hugo GAISSER, **L'origine du *tonus peregrinus*** [The origin of the *tonus peregrinus*] (1099) and **L'origine et la vraie nature du mode dit "chromatique oriental"** [The origin and the true nature of the mode known as "oriental chromatic"] (4077); Eduardo GARIEL, **De la nécessité de méthodiser l'enseignement de la musique en lui appliquant une base scientifique** [The necessity of systematizing the teaching of music by establishing it on scientific basis] (4536); Théodore GÉROLD, **De la valeur des petites notes d'agrément et d'expression** [Of the value of grace notes and ornament signs] (3741); Bartolomeo GRASSI LANDI, **Observations relatives à l'interprétation des notes neumatiques du chant grégorien** [Observations relative to the interpretation of neumatic notation of Gregorian chant] (3701) and **Observations sur le genre enharmonique** [Observations on the enharmonic genus] (4078); Frédéric HÉLOUIN, **Histoire du métronome en France** [The history of the metronome in France] (3999); Georges-Louis HOUDARD, **La notation neumatique** [Neumatic notation] (3827) and **La notation neumatique considérée dans son sens matériel extérieur** [The physical exterior meaning of neumatic notation] (3828); Georges HUMBERT, **Les principes naturels de l'évolution musicale** [The natural principles of the evolution of music] (973); Ilmari

KROHN, **De la mesure à 5 temps dans la musique populaire finnoise** [The five-beat measure in traditional Finnish music] (2912); Louis LALOY, **Le genre enharmonique des Grecs** [The Greek enharmonic genus] (4089); Paul LANDORMY, **Des moyens d'organiser, en France, une ligue pour la protection et le développement de l'art musical** [Of the means of organizing, in France, a league for the protection and development of the musical art] (2339); Adolf LINDGREN, **Contribution à l'histoire de la polonaise** [Contribution to the history of the polonaise] (4266); Alessandro LONGO, **Observations sur la valeur historique des compositions pour clavecin de Dominique Scarlatti** [Observations on the historical value of Domenico Scarlatti's compositions for harpsichord] (1607); Charles MEERENS, **Réforme du système musical** [Reform of the musical system] (2356); Hortense PARENT, **De l'enseignement élémentaire du piano en France au point de vue de la vulgarisation de la musique** [Elementary piano teaching in France from the point of view of the popularization of music] (4614); Élie POIRÉE, **Chant des sept voyelles: Analyse musicale** [Chant of the seven vowels: Musical analysis] (1037) and **Une nouvelle interprétation rythmique du second hymne à Apollon** [A new rhythmic interpretation of the second hymn to Apollo] (1038); Théodore REINACH, **L'harmonie des sphères** [The harmony of the spheres] (4104) and **Sur la transcription du premier hymne delphique** [On the transcription of the first Delphic hymn] (1040); Romain ROLLAND, **Notes sur l'*Orfeo* de Luigi Rossi, et sur les musiciens italiens à Paris, sous Mazarin** [Notes on the *Orfeo* of Luigi Rossi, and on Italian musicians in Paris under Mazarin] (1661); Émile RUELLE, **Le chant gnostico-magique des sept voyelles grecques** [Gnostic-magic chant of seven Greek vowels] (1042); Liborio SACCHETTI, **Le chant religieux de l'Église orthodoxe russe** [Religious chant of the Russian Orthodox Church] (1001); Camille SAINT-SAËNS, **Communication** (3868); John South SHEDLOCK, **Purcell et Bach** [Purcell and Bach] (1680); Jean-Baptiste THIBAUT, **Assimilation des êchoi byzantins et des modes latins avec les anciens tropes grecs** [Assimilation of Byzantine êchoi and Latin modes with ancient Greek tropes] (4119) and **Les notations byzantines** [Byzantine notations] (3875); Julien TIERSOT, **Des transformations de la tonalité et du rôle du dièze et du bémol depuis le Moyen Âge jusqu'au XVIIᵉ siècle: Résumé** [On the transformations of tonality and the role of the sharp and the flat from the Middle Ages to the 17th century: Abstract] (4121) and **Le premier hymne delphique** [The first Delphic hymn] (1044).

33
bs
[Paris] Exposition Universelle Internationale de 1900: Direction Générale de l'Exploitation—Congrès International de Musique [Exposition Universelle Internationale, 1900: Direction Générale de l'Exploitation—International Congress of Music]. Sponsored by the Ministère du Commerce, de l'Industrie, des Postes et des Télégraphes. By BAUDOIN LA LONDRE (Paris: Imprimerie Nationale, 1901) 15 p. In French.

Minutes and summaries of the conference held from 14 through 18 June 1900. Reports of the same meeting are cited as nos. 29 and 30 in this volume.

34
bs
[Paris] Mémoires de Musicologie sacrée, lus aux assises de musique religieuse [Papers on sacred music read at the sessions on religious music] (Paris: Schola Cantorum, n.d.) 104 p. *Music.* In French.

The conference was held from 27 through 29 September 1900 on the premises of the Schola Cantorum, Paris. The following contributions are cited separately: Pierre AUBRY, **Les jongleurs dans l'histoire: Saint-Julien-des-Ménétriers** [Minstrels in history: Saint-Julien-des-Ménétriers] (6152) and **Les raisons historiques du rythme oratoire** [The historical reasons for oratorical rhythm] (5917); J.A. CLERVAL, **La musique religieuse à Notre-Dame de Chartres** [Religious music at the Cathedral of Notre-Dame in Chartres] (6187); Amédée GASTOUÉ, **L'art grégorien: Les origines premières** [Gregorian art: The earliest origins] (1101); Jean PARISOT, **Essai d'application de mélodies orientales à des chants d'église** [Trying to match Eastern melodies to Church chants] (4452); André PIRRO, **Les formes de l'expression dans la musique de Heinrich Schütz** [Forms of expression in the music of Heinrich Schütz] (1645); Henri QUITTARD, **Carissimi et le XVIIᵉ siècle italien** [Carissimi and the Italian 17th century] (1652); Henri VILLETARD, **Recherche et étude de fragments de manuscrits de plain-chant** [Research and study of fragments of plainchant manuscripts] (6406).

35
bs

[Paris] Troisième Congrès international d'enseignement supérieur [Third International Congress of Higher Education]. Ed. by François PICAVET; pref. by Paul-Camille-Hippolyte BROUARDEL and Ferdinand LARNAUDE. *Bibliothèque internationale de l'enseignement supérieur* (Paris: A. Chevalier-Marescq, 1902) li, 591 p. In French.

The conference was held from 30 July through 4 August 1900. The following contribution is cited separately: Romain ROLLAND, **Que l'on doit faire une place à l'histoire de la musique dans l'histoire de l'art et dans l'enseignement universitaire** [There ought to be a place for music history in art history and in university education] (4844).

36
bs

[Paris] Iᵉʳ Congrès international de philosophie [First International Congress of Philosophy] *Bibliothèque du Congrès international de philosophie* (Paris: Colin, 1900-1903) 4 v. 460, 428, 688, 529 p.; (reprint, Nendeln: Kraus, 1968). *Illus., charts, diagr.* In French.

Another publication of the same conference is cited as no. 37.

37
bs

[Paris] [Iᵉʳ] Congrès international de philosophie: Procès-verbaux, sommaires [(First) International Congress of Philosophy: Proceedings and summaries]. Sponsored by the Ministère du Commerce, de l'Industrie, des Postes et des Télégraphes and Exposition Universelle of 1900. Ed. by Xavier LÉON (Paris: Imprimerie Nationale, 1901) 63 p. In French.

Minutes and summaries of the conference, held in Paris from 1 through 5 August 1900. The following contribution is cited separately in this volume: Charles DIMIER, **Prolégomènes à l'esthétique** [Prolegomena to aesthetics] (5454).

1901

38
bs

[Leipzig] IVᵉ Congrès international des éditeurs: Rapports [Fourth International Congress of Publishers: Reports]. Sponsored by the International Publishers' Association/Union Internationale des Éditeurs (Leipzig: F.A. Brockhaus, 1901) xviii, 172 p. In French.

The conference, which took place from 10 through 13 June 1901, is also cited as nos. 39 and 40 in this volume. The following contributions are cited separately: Arthur BOOSEY, **L'appropriation du droit d'auteur sur les œuvres musicales par les fabricants d'instruments mécaniques, tels que les éoliennes, etc.** [The appropriation of copyrights on musical works by manufacturers of mechanical instruments, such as aeolian instruments, etc.] (5950); Henry CLAYTON, **La subdivision territoriale du droit d'auteur** [The territorial subdivision of copyrights] (5954); Oskar von HASE, **Entente internationale entre les marchands de musique** [International agreement among music dealers] (5963); Henri HINRICHSEN, **Prix fort et rabais dans le commerce de la musique** [Full price and discounts in the sale of music] (5965).

39
bs

[Leipzig] Papers to be read. Proceedings of the Fourth International Congress of Publishers (Leipzig: F.A. Brockhaus, 1901) xiii, 138 p.

The conference is also cited as nos. 38 and 40 in this volume.

40
bs

[Leipzig] Report: June 10th, 13th, 1901. Proceedings of the Fourth International Congress of Publishers (Leipzig: F.A. Brockhaus, 1902) viii, 383 p.

The conference is also cited as nos. 38 and 39 in this volume.

1903

41
bs

[Dinant] Congrès de Dinant: Compte rendu [Congress of Dinant: Report]. Sponsored by the Société Archéologique de Namur. Ed. by Edmond de PIERPONT. *Annales de la Fédération Archéologique et Historique de Belgique* xvii (Namur: Wesmael-Charlier, 1904) 2 v. In French.

The conference was held from 10 through 12 September 1903. The following contribution is cited separately: Germain MÓRIN, **Les AOI de la Chanson de Roland** [The AOI of the *Chanson de Roland*] (5336).

42
bs

[Rome] Atti del Congresso internazionale di scienze storiche. VIII: Atti della sezione IV: Storia dell'arte musicale e drammatica [Acts of the International Congress of Historical Sciences. VIII: Section IV: History of musical and dramatic arts]. Proceedings of the Second International Congress of Historical Sciences (Roma: R. Accademia dei Lincei, 1905) xix, 362 p.; (reprint, Nendeln: Kraus, 1972). *Music.* In French, German, English, and Italian.

The following contributions are cited separately: Giorgio BARINI, **Sulla necessità di render completo e proficuo l'insegnamento della storia della musica negli istituti musicali, ponendo costantemente in relazione la produzione musicale con la storia civile e del costume e con le altre manifestazioni della vita intellettuale nel tempo in cui fiorirono i singoli compositori e si svolsero le varie forme musicali** [The necessity of making instruction in music history in musical institutions complete and useful, always relating musical production to civil and social history and the other manifestations of the intellectual life of the times in which individual composers thrived and various musical styles developed] (4488) and **Sulla opportunità di compilare una raccolta di indici e cataloghi dei codici musicali italiani esistenti negli archivi, nelle biblioteche e nelle collezioni pubbliche e private, per servire di base ad una serie di edizioni critiche delle opere dei nostri classici** [The opportunity of compiling a collection of indexes and catalogues of Italian musical codices existing in archives, libraries, and in public and private collections, to serve as a basis for a series of critical editions of our classical works] (518); Arnaldo BONAVENTURA, **Sull'ordinamento della musica e dei libri relativi nelle pubbliche biblioteche** [On the classification of music and music-related books in public libraries] (526); Alberto CAMETTI, **Un nuovo documento sulle origini di Giovanni Pierluigi da Palestrina: Il testamento di Jacobella Pierluigi (1527)** [A new document on the origins of Giovanni Pierluigi da Palestrina: The testament of Jacobella Pierluigi (1527)] (1265); Oscar CHILESOTTI, **Gli airs de court del Thesaurus harmonicus di J.B. Besard** [The *airs de court* of the *Thesaurus harmonicus* of J.B. Besard] (1272) and **Trascrizioni da un codice musicale di Vincenzo Galilei** [Transcriptions of a musical codex of Vincenzo Galilei] (1275); Alberto FAVARA, **Le melodie tradizionali di Val di Mazzara** [The traditional melodies of Val di Mazzara] (2812); P. Ugo GAÏSSER, **I canti ecclesiastici italo-greci** [Greco-Italian ecclesiastical songs] (6112); Antonio PAGLICCI-BROZZI, **Opportunità di raccogliere le antiche et tradizionali fanfare dei comuni italiani** [Opportunities for collecting the old and traditional fanfares of the Italian municipalities] (995); Giuseppe RADICIOTTI, **Teatro e musica in Roma nel secondo quarto del secolo XIX** [Theater and music in Rome during the second quarter of the 19th century] (5226); Felice RAMORINO, **Dell'opportunità di pubblicare in edizione critica gli scriptores musici latini** [The opportunity to publish the *scriptores musici latini* in a critical edition] (1039); Luigi RASI, **Della costruzione di un museo dell'arte drammatica italiana. I** [On the construction of a museum of Italian dramatic art. I] (5227) and **Della costruzione di un museo dell'arte drammatica italiana. II** [On the construction of a museum of Italian dramatic art. II] (5228); F. Alberto SALVAGNINI, **Francesco Caffi: Musicologo veneziano, (1778-1874)** [Francesco Caffi: Venetian musicologist (1778-1874)] (916); Pedro P. TRAVERSARI, **L'arte in America: Storia dell'arte musicale indigena e popolare** [Art in America: A history of native and popular music] (2543); Alessandro VESSELLA, **Sulla evoluzione storica della partitura di banda** [On the evolution of the score for band] (3640); Luigi Alberto VILLANIS, **Alcuni codici manoscritti di musica del secolo XVI** [Some musical codices from the 16th century] (1460); Giulio ZAMBIASI, **Sullo svolgimento storico-critico dei principii e criteri seguiti nel dare base scientifica alla** musica [On the historical-critical development of the principles and criteria following the given scientific basis of music] (3964).

1904

43
bs
[Berlin] Zweiter Musikpädagogischer Kongress: Vorträge und Referate [Second Music Pedagogy Congress: Lectures and reports]. Sponsored by the Musikpädagogischer Verband (Berlin: Klavier-Lehrer, 1904) 264 p. In German.
The conference was held from 6 through 8 October 1904. The following contributions are cited separately: Tony BANDMANN, **Welches sind die Grundfehler unserer heutigen Methodik?** [Which are the basic mistakes of our methods today?] (4487); Georg CAPELLEN, **Reformen auf dem Gebiet der Notenschrift** [Reforms in the area of notation] (3809) and **Reformen im musik-theoretischen Unterricht** [Reforms in music theory instruction] (4501); Siga GARSÓ, **Die Lehre des Kunstgesanges und das Bilden des losen Tones** [The theory of art singing and the development of a relaxed tone] (3300); W. HÄNSSEL, **Die Stimmbildung in der Volksschule** [Voice training in the Volksschule] (4701); Karl Raphael HENNIG, **Die Musikästhetik und ihre praktische Einführung** [Music aesthetics and its practical introduction] (4550); Robert HUCH, **Der Schulgesangunterricht auf Grundlage des blossen Intervallesens** [Classes in school singing based on the mere reading of intervals] (4712) and **Notenlese-Lehrmethode** [Teaching method for reading music] (4556); Richard KADEN, **Musikgeschichte und Formenlehre auf dem Seminar** [Music history and theory of musical form at the teacher-training institute] (4827); Maria LEO, **Die Pädagogik als Lehrgegenstand im Musiklehrer-Seminar** [Pedagogy as subject at the music teachers' seminar] (4832); Ina LÖHNER, **Psycho-physiologischer Musikunterricht** [Psychophysiological music instruction] (4588); Carl MENGEWEIN, **Die Ausbildung des musikalischen Gehörs** [The training of musical hearing] (4599); MÜLLER-LIEBENWALDE, **Referat zum Schulgesang-Unterricht** [Report on classes in school singing] (4746); Helene NÖRING, **Referat über die Arbeiten der Musiksektion zur Hebung des Schulgesang-Unterrichts** [Report on the work of the music divison in improving classes in school singing] (4750); Ludwig RIEMANN, **Die Notwendigkeit der Einführung der Akustik in den Lehrplan** [The need for the introduction of acoustics into the curriculum] (4634); Georg ROLLE, **Referat zur Reform des Schulgesang-Unterrichts** [Report on the reform of classes in school singing] (4762); Carlo SOMIGLI, **Aus welchen Werken soll die vollständige Ausbildung der Gesangsorgane erreicht werden?** [Which works should contribute to a comprehensive training of the voice?] (4649); Olga STIEGLITZ, **Die Musikästhetik und ihre praktische Einführung** [Music aesthetics and its practical introduction] (4652); Nana WEBER-BELL, **Gesangspädagogische Reformen** [Reforms in vocal pedagogy] (4670); Cornelie van ZANTEN, **Die Anforderungen des Examens für Kunstgesangspädagogik** [Examination requirements for vocal pedagogy] (4861) and **Referat zum Schulgesang in Holland** [Report on school singing in Holland] (4802).

44
bs
[Giessen] Bericht über den I. Kongress für Experimentelle Psychologie [Report on the First Congress for Experimental Psychology]. Sponsored by the Gesellschaft für Experimentelle Psychologie. Ed. by Robert SOMMER (Leipzig: Barth, 1904). In German.
The conference was held from 18 from 21 April 1904. The following contribution is cited separately: Hermann SIEBECK, **Über musikalische Einfühlung** [On musical empathy] (5597).

45
ap
[Leipzig] Bericht über die Verhandlungen des I. Kongresses der Internationalen Musikgesellschaft [Report on the proceedings of the First Congress of the International Musical Society], *Zeitschrift der Internationalen Musikgesellschaft* VI (1904-1905) 1–19. In German.
Includes the essay by Hermann KRETZSCHMAR, **Die Aufgaben der Internationalen Musikgesellschaft** [Tasks of the Internationale Musikgesellschaft].

46
bs
[Paris] Troisième Congrès de la Fédération des Artistes Musiciens de France (Deuxième Congrès international) [Third Congress of the Fédération des Artistes Musiciens de France (Second International Congress)] (Paris: Fédération des Artistes Musiciens de France, 1904) 157 p. In French.
The conference was held from 9 through 11 May 1904. The following contribution is cited separately: A. SEITZ, **Rapport sur la possibilité d'une confédération internationale** [Report on the possibility of an international federation] (5991).

47
bs
[Stuttgart] Internationaler Amerikanisten-Kongress: Vierzehnte Tagung [International Congress of Americanists: Fourteenth meeting] (Stuttgart: Kohlhammer, 1906) 3 v. 704 p.; (reprint, Nendeln: Kraus, 1968). *Illus., music.* In German, English, French, and Spanish.
The conference was held from 18 through 24 August 1904. The following contribution is cited separately: Karl SAPPER, **Sitten und Gebräuche der Pokonchi-Indianer** [Customs and traditions of the Pocomchi Indians] (3219).

1905

48
bs
[Algiers] Actes du XIVᵉ Congrès international des orientalistes. III: Langues musulmanes (arabe, persan et turc) [Proceedings of the 14th International Congress of Orientalists. III: Muslim languages (Arabic, Persian, and Turkic)] (Paris: Leroux, 1905) 3 v.; (reprint, Nendeln: Kraus, 1968) 4 v. *Bibliog.* In French, English, German, Italian, and Latin.
The following contribution is cited separately: Joseph DESPARMET, **La poésie arabe actuelle à Blida et sa métrique** [Contemporary Arab poetry in Blida, and its metrics] (5303).

49
bs
[Liège] IIIᵉ Congrès international de l'art public [The Third International Congress of Public Art]. Sponsored by the Exposition Internationale de Liège (Liège: n.p., 1905). *Illus.* In French.
The conference was held from 15 through 21 September 1905. The following contributions are cited separately: Florimond van DUYSE, **Chansons populaires** [Traditional songs] (2797); Alphonse GOSSET, **Le théâtre populaire** [Popular theater] (5820); Alexandre HALOT, **La bonne musique pour le peuple** [Good music for the public] (5410).

50
bs
[Strasbourg] Acta generalis cantus gregoriani studiosorum conventus, Argentinensis, 16-19 Aug. 1905/Bericht des internationalen Kongresses für gregorianischen Choralgesang/Compte rendu du Congrès international de plain-chant grégorien [Report of the International Congress of Gregorian Chant] (Strassburg: F.-X. Le Roux, 1905) lxviii, 176 p. In French, German, and Latin.
The conference was held from 16 through 19 August 1905. The following contributions are cited separately: Guerrino Ambrosio Maria AMELLI, **De Guidonis Aretini, eiusque asseclarum gestis, in conventibus internationalibus oratio Aretii, Romae et Argentinae** [Concerning the deeds of Guido d'Arezzo and his followers: Speech at the international meetings at Arezzo, Rome, and Strasbourg] (1052); Raphael ANDOYER, **Le rythme oratoire, principe de la méthode grégorienne** [Oratorical rhythm, principle of the Gregorian method] (3689); Alphonse-Gabriel FOUCAULT, **Simple observation sur le caractère du rythme grégorien dans la psalmodie** [Simple observation on the character of Gregorian rhythm in psalmody] (3698); Amédée GASTOUÉ, **Comment on peut s'inspirer des anciens pour l'accompagnement du chant romain** [How to take inspiration from the ancients in accompanying Gregorian chant] (1102) and **Sur l'intérêt de l'étude des traités du Moyen-Âge et de deux traités perdus** [On the reason for studying treatises of the Middle Ages and on two lost treatises] (1104); Michael HORN, **Die Choralfrage in Schule,**

im Lehrer- und Priesterseminar [The chant question in schools, in teacher training institutes, and in seminaries] (4555); Otto MARXER, **Untergang St. Gallischer Choralpflege im ausgehenden Mittelalter und in neuer Zeit** [The decline of the St. Gall chant tradition in the late Middle Ages and after] (988); François-Xavier MATHIAS, **Der Choral im Elsass** [Chant in Alsace] (1377) and **Die Choralbegleitung** [Chant accompaniment] (3708); Karl OTT, **Die Entwicklung des mailändischen Chorals** [The development of Ambrosian chant] (1152); Joseph POTHIER, **La catholicité du chant de l'église romaine** [The catholicity of the chant of the Roman church] (6339); Casiano ROJO, **Le chant grégorien en Espagne** [Gregorian chant in Spain] (6359); Peter WAGNER, **Der traditionelle Choralvortrag und seine geschichtliche Begründung** [Traditional chant performance and its historical foundation] (3720), **Ueber den traditionellen Choral** [On traditional chant] (1019), **Ueber die Zweckmässigkeit der Choralrestauration und ihre praktische Durchführung** [On the advisability of the chant revival and its practical realization] (6411), and **Wie müssen die Melodien der Vatikanischen Choralausgabe ausgeführt werden?** [How must the melodies of the Vatican edition of chant be performed?] (3881).

51 [Turin] **Relazioni** [Reports], *7° Congresso di musica*
as *sacra* (Torino: author, 1905) 77–102. In Italian. See no. 52 in this volume.
Records the contributions of several participants of the conference including remarks on Gregorian chant performance practice by Giulio BAS and Giovanni GROSSO; the technical requirements of organs by Luigi BOTTAZZO; the pedagogy of religious music by Raffaele CASIMIRI and Delfino THERMIGNON; observations regarding each of the three principal sections of the conference by Eduardo DAGNINO and Giovanni POLLERI; general remarks by Dino SINCERO; recommendations on propaganda and organization by Giovanni TEBALDINI; and on choirs by Giulio ZAMBIASI. (*André Balog*)

52 [Turin] **7° Congresso di musica sacra** [Seventh
bs Congress of Sacred Music]. Ed. by Marcello CAPRA (Torino: author, 1905) 108 p. In Italian.
The conference took place from 6 through 8 June 1905. The following contributions are cited separately: Giulio BAS, Luigi BOTTAZZO, Raffaele CASIMIRI, Eduardo DAGNINO, Giovanni B. GROSSO, Giovanni B. POLLERI, Sincero DINO, Giovanni TEBALDINI, Delfino THERMIGNON, and G. ZAMBIASI, **Relazioni** [Reports] (51); Antonio BERRONE, **Restaurazione della musica sacra secondo il** *Motu proprio* **di S.S. il Papa Pio X** [The restoration of sacred music according to the motu proprio of His Holiness Pope Pius X] (6165); Marcello CAPRA, **Breve cronaca del Congresso** [Brief chronicle of the congress] (6182); Filippo CRISPOLTI, **Il pensiero cattolico nella riforma delle arti colle sue necessarie attinenze alla musica sacra** [Catholic thinking regarding the reform of the arts and its inevitable bearing on sacred music] (6195); Alessandro GHIGNONI, **La musica sacra e religiosa del popolo** [Sacred and religious music of the people] (6236); A. NASONI, Giacomo SIZIA, and Giovanni TEBALDINI, **Considerandi, deliberazioni e voti esratti dai verbali e sinteticamente disposti** [Summaries of the considerations, deliberations, and votes of the congress] (6319); Stefano SCALA, **La stampa e la restaurazione della musica sacra** [The publishing and restoration of sacred music] (5987); A. SIMONETTI, **Il linguaggio della musica** [The language of music] (5598).

1906

53 [Basel] **Bericht über den zweiten Kongress der**
bs **Internationalen Musikgesellschaft** [Report of the Second Congress of the International Musical Society]. Ed. and forew. by Hermann KRETZSCHMAR, Oskar von HASE, and Max SEIFFERT (Leipzig: Breitkopf & Härtel, 1907) xxvii, 247 p. *Illus., music, charts, diagr.* In German, French, and English.
The conference was held from 25 through 27 September 1906. The following contributions are cited separately: Eduard BERNOULLI, **Über die Notation des Meistergesangs** [The notation of Meistergesang] (3806); Edward BUHLE, **Über den Stand der Instrumentenkunde** [The state of organology] (3246); Carl CLAUDIUS, **Die schwedische Nyckelharpa** [The Swedish nyckelharpa] (3558); Amédée GASTOUÉ, **Sur les orgines**

de la forme sequentia du VIIe-IXe siècles [The origins of the sequence from the 7th to the 9th century] (1103); Christian GEISLER, **Neue Notation für Gesangsmusik: Vereinfachte a cappella–Gesangsmethode für Schule und Volk—Eine Lösung des Grundgedanken Chevé's** [New notation for vocal music: A simplified a cappella method for school and lay singing—A solution based on Chevé's basic idea] (3821); Ernst GRAF, **Über den Stand der altgriechischen Musikforschung** [The state of research on ancient Greek music] (1031); Angul HAMMERICH, **Zur Frage nach dem Ursprung der Streichinstrumente** [The question of the origin of string instruments] (3577); Erich Moritz von HORNBOSTEL, **Über den gegenwärtigen Stand der vergleichenden Musikwissenschaft** [The current state of comparative musicology] (2437); Oswald KOLLER, **Wie könnte ein thematischer Katalog der Messen-, Motetten- und Madrigalliteratur des XV. und XVI. Jahrhunderts eingerichtet werden?** [How could we assemble a thematic catalogue of the Mass, motet, and madrigal literature of the 15th and 16th centuries?] (791); Ilmari KROHN, **Das akustische Harmonium der Universität zu Helsingfors** [The acoustic harmonium at Helsingin Yliopisto] (4085), **Über das lexikalische Ordnen von Volksmelodien** [The lexical ordering of traditional-music melodies] (792), **Zur Einheitlichkeit der Notenschlüssel** [The unification of clefs] (3839), and **Zweckmässige Notation von Psalmen und andern rezitativischen Gesängen** [A functional notation for psalms and other chant in recitation tones] (3840); Louis LALOY, **Notes sur la musique cambodgienne** [Notes on Cambodian music] (2654); Hugo LEICHTENTRITT, **Ältere Bildwerke als Quellen der musikgeschichtlichen Forschung** [Early sculptures as research sources for music history] (5384); Charles MACLEAN, **Questions of musical organization** (2350); Franz MARSCHNER, **Wertbegriff als Grundlage der Musikästhetik** [The concept of value as the foundation of musical aesthetics] (5534); Paul-Marie MASSON, **L'humanisme musical en France au XVIe siècle: La musique "mesurée à l'antique"** [Musical humanism in France in the 16th century: Music "mesurée à l'antique"] (1376); Paul MOOS, **Theodor Lipps als Musikästhetiker** [Theodor Lipps as a music aesthetician] (5550); Georg MÜNZER, **Zur Notation der Meistersinger** [The Meistersingers' notation] (3855); Karl NEF, **Zur Forschung über die ältere Instrumentalmusik** [Research on early instrumental music] (905); Alois OBRIST, **Die historische und künstlerische Bedeutung der Wiederbelebung altertümlicher Musikinstrumente** [The historical and artistic significance of the revival of old musical instruments] (3680); Alois OBRIST and Karl NEF, ed., **Dürfen oder sollen der Entwicklung der modernen Instrumentation Grenzen gezogen werden?** [Can and should limits be set to the development of modern instrumentation?] (3264) and **Sollen Musiker und Musikhistoriker die Entwicklung der Klavierspielapparate fördern, bekämpfen oder zu beeinflussen suchen?** [Should musicians and music historians try to support the development of keyboard playing apparatuses, combat them, or influence them?] (3661); Paul RUNGE, **Über die Notation des Meistergesangs** [The notation of Meistergesang] (3866); Arnold SCHERING, **Die freie Kadenz im Instrumentalkonzert des 18. Jahrhunderts** [The free cadenza in 18th-century instrumental concertos] (1672); Arnold SCHERING and Ludwig SCHIEDERMAIR, ed., **Die Anfänge des Oratoriums** [The beginnings of the oratorio] (1671); Ludwig SCHIEDERMAIR, **Die neapolitanische Oper des 18. Jahrhunderts** [Neapolitan opera of the 18th century] (1673) and **Über den Stand der Operngeschichte** [The state of historical research on opera] (5238); H. SCHMIDT, **Über die Registerausbildung der menschlichen Stimme: Methode Nehrlich-Schmidt** [Register training for the human voice: The Nehrlich-Schmidt method] (3319); Arthur SEIDL, **Hermann Abert: Die spätantike Musikästhetik und ihre Bedeutung für das Mittelalter** [Hermann Abert: The musical aesthetics of late antiquity and its significance for the Middle Ages] (5592) and **Läßt sich Ästhetik mit Aussicht auf Erfolg an Konservatorien lehren?** [Can aesthetics be taught in conservatories with a prospect of success?] (4893); Max SEIFFERT, **Zur Forschung über die ältere Klavier- und Orgelmusik** [Research on early keyboard and organ music] (923); Oscar G.T. SONNECK and Hermann SPRINGER, ed., **Bibliographie, Bibliothekswesen: Verhandlungen und Vorträge** [Bibliography and librarianship: Discussions and lectures] (686); Hermann SPRINGER, **Die musikalischen Blockdrucke des 15. und 16. Jahrhunderts** [Musical block printing in the 15th and 16th centuries] (5994) and **Über den Stand der musikalischen Bibliographie** [On the current state of musical bibliography] (690); Robert STAIGER, **Über die Notation des Meistergesangs** [The notation of Meistergesang] (3873); Carl STUMPF, **Vergleichende Musikforschung: Verhandlungen und Vorträge** [Comparative music research: Discussions and lectures] (2542) and **Vergleichende Musikforschung, Akustik, Tonpsychologie: Verhandlungen und Vorträge** [Comparative music research, acoustics, music psychology: Discussions and lectures] (2475); Adolf THÜRLINGS, **Die *soggetti cavati dalle vocali* in Huldigungskompositionen und die Herculesmesse des Lupus** [The *soggetti cavati dalle vocali* in Lupus's homage compositions and *Missa Hercules*] (1452); Peter WAGNER, **Über den gegenwärtigen Stand der mittelalterlichen Musikforschung** [The current state of research on medieval music] (1208); Stephan WITASEK, **Zur allgemeinen Analyse des musikalischen Genusses** [Toward a general analysis of musical pleasure] (5630); Johannes WOLF, ed., **Notationskunde: Verhandlungen und Vorträge** [The study of notation: Discussions and lectures] (3882); Johannes WOLF, **Über den Stand der Notationskunde** [The state of the study of notation] (3883). The conference is also cited as no. 54 in this volume.

54
bs
[Basel] Festschrift zum zweiten Kongreß der Internationalen Musikgesellschaft, verfaßt von Mitgliedern der Schweizerischen Landessektion und den Kongreßteilnehmern [Festschrift for the Second Congress of the International Musical Society, prepared by members of the Swiss national section and participants in the congress]. Sponsored by the Historisches Museum Basel (Basel: Reinhardt, 1906) 2 v. 156, vii, 74 p. *Illus., music.* In German.
The following contributions are cited separately: Eduard BERNOULLI, **Problem vokaler Kleinkunst aus dem 17. und beginnenden 18. Jahrhundert in der Schweiz** [The problem of minor vocal art from the end of the 17th and beginning of the 18th century in Switzerland] (1487); Mathis LUSSY, **De la culture du sentiment musical** [The cultivation of musical feeling] (5529); Karl NEF, **Katalog der Musikinstrumente im Historischen Museum zu Basel** [Catalogue of musical instruments in the Historisches Museum, Basel] (776); Adolf THÜRLINGS, ***Innsbruck, ich muss dich lassen* (Heinrich Isaac und Cosmas Alder)** [*Innsbruck, ich muss dich lassen* (Heinrich Isaac and Cosmas Alder)] (1451); Georg WALTER, **Verzeichnis von Werken der Mannheimer Symphoniker im Besitze der Universitäts-Bibliothek in Basel und der Allgemeinen Musikgesellschaft in Zürich** [Catalogue of works by the Mannheim symphonists in the collections of the Universitätsbibliothek Basel and the Allgemeine Musikgesellschaft Zurich] (775). The conference is also cited as no. 53 in this volume.

55
bs
[Milan] Congrès international des éditeurs: 5ᵉ session—Rapports [International Congress of Publishers: Proceedings of the fifth meeting]. Sponsored by the International Publishers' Association/Union Internationale des Éditeurs (Milano: Associazione Tipografico-Libraria Italiana, 1907) 237 p. In French.
The conference was held from 6 through 10 June 1906. The following contributions are cited separately: W. ENOCH, **Des instruments de musique mécaniques** [Mechanical musical instruments] (5959); Joseph WEINBERGER, **La réglementation internationale du droit d'exécution des œuvres musicales** [The international regulation of performing rights of musical works] (6000).

56
bs
[Quebec] Congrès international des américanistes: XVᵉ session [International Congress of Americanists: Fifteenth meeting] (Québec: Dussault & Proulx, 1907) 2 v.; (reprint, Nendeln: Kraus, 1968). *Illus., maps.* In French and English.
The conference was held from 10 through 15 September 1906. The following contributions are cited separately: John W. CHAPMAN, **Notes on the Tinneh tribe of Anvik, Alaska** (3142); Ernest GAGNON, **Les sauvages de l'Amérique et l'art musical** [The savages of America and the musical arts] (3151).

1907

57
bs
[Valladolid] Crónica del primer Congreso Nacional de Música Sagrada [Reports of the first Congreso Nacional de Música Sagrada] (Valladolid: A. Martín, 1908) 116 p. *Index.* In Spanish.
The following contributions are cited separately: Mariano BAIXAULI, **Necesidad del estudio de nuestra polifonía religiosa** [The necessity of

studying our religious polyphonic music] (6156); Casimiro GONZÁLEZ GARCÍA-VALLADOLID, **La música sagrada y los concilios españoles** [Religious music and the Spanish councils] (6240); J. JORGE, **La enseñanza del canto gregoriano en los seminarios** [The teaching of Gregorian chant in the seminaries] (6263); Felipe MERINO, **Importancia del estudio del canto gregoriano** [The importance of studying Gregorian chant] (4883); Federico OLMEDA, **La música sagrada en las parroquias** [Religious music in the parishes] (6327); Vicente RIPOLLÉS PÉREZ, **La cultura litúrgica-musical del clero** [The musical and liturgical culture of the clergy] (6354); Casiano ROJO, **Lección práctica de canto gregoriano** [A practical lesson on Gregorian chant] (6360); Miguel RUÉ, **Scholae cantorum** (4767); Gerardo María SALVANY, **Cómo se debe ejecutar el canto gregoriano y modo de promover la enseñanza de este canto, sobre todo en los seminarios** [The correct way to sing Gregorian chant and how to promote it, especially in the seminaries] (4892); Luciano SERRANO, **Los tres géneros de música sagrada y su situación canónica en el santuario** [The three genres of religious music and their canonical status in the churches] (6390); Luis VILLALBA, **La censura de la música religiosa** [Censorship in religious music] (2405); Francisco Pérez de VIÑASPRE Y ORTIZ, **Significado del *motu proprio*** [The significance of the motu proprio] (6407).

1908

58
bs
[Dresden] Kongresa kantareto (kun notoj): Eldonita de la Kvaro por la Kvara [Congress: Net of songs (with notes)—Given from the quartette to the fourth]. Report of the Fourth International Congress of Esperantists. Ed. and forew. by Marie HANKEL (Dresden: Boden, 1908) 26 p. In Esperanto.
A pamphlet of nine strophic songs, all in Esperanto. Some are based on previously composed melodies; one, for example, is by Mozart. Songs include: *La espero* (The hope), *La vojo* (The road), *Al la fratoj* (To the brothers), *Kanto de l'ligo* (Song of the league), *Kanto de studentoj* (Song of the students), *Paca kanto de la Esperantistoj* (Peace song of the Esperantists), *Venu Dresdenon!* (Come Dresden!), *Rozeto en herbejo* (Little rose in the meadow), and *La verda stelo* (The green star).

59
bs
[Frankfurt am Main] Bericht über den III. Kongress für experimentalle Psychologie [Report of the Third Congress for Experimental Psychology]. Sponsored by the Gesellschaft für Experimentelle Psychologie. Ed. by Friedrich SCHUMANN (Leipzig: Barth, 1909). In German.
The conference was held from 22 March through 5 April 1908. The following contribution is cited separately: Géza RÉVÉSZ, **Über Orthosymphonie: Eine merkwürdige parakustische Erscheinung** [On "orthosymphony": A strange para-acoustic phenomenon] (5696).

60
bs
[Madrid] Congrès international des éditeurs: VIᵉ session—Rapports [International Congress of Publishers: Sixth meeting—Proceedings]. Sponsored by the International Publishers' Association/Union Internationale des Éditeurs (Madrid: Asociación de la Librería de España, 1908) 298, ix, vii p. In French.
The conference was held from 26 through 30 May 1908. The following contributions are cited separately: Paul BERTRAND, **Les contrefaçons au Canada** [Counterfeiting in Canada] (5948); Paul BRETON, **La propriété artistique au Brésil** [Artistic property in Brazil] (5951); Louis DOTESIO, **La musique et les droits d'auteur** [Music and the rights of the author] (5957); W. ENOCH, **De la contrefaçon musicale en Europe (Belgique, Pays-Bas, Roumanie, Turquie, Grèce) et en Égypte** [On musical counterfeiting in Europe (Belgium, Low Countries, Romania, Turkey, Greece) and in Egypt] (5958) and **Instruments de musique mécanique** [Mechanical musical instruments] (3659); Émile LEDUC, **La protection des droits d'auteur dans les républiques latines de l'Amérique du Sud** [The protection of an author's rights in the Latin republics of South America] (5977) and **Les contrefaçons dans la République Argentine (et dans les États sud-américains de langue espagnole)** [Counterfeiting in the Argentine Republic (and in the Spanish-speaking South American states)] (5976); Ludwig VOLKMANN, **Conventions internationales pour les remises**

dans le commerce de la musique [International conventions for the sorting-out of the music business] (5999).

61
bs

[Vienna] **Verhandlungen des XVI. internationalen Amerikanisten-Kongresses** [Proceedings of the 16th International Congress of Americanists]. Ed. by Franz HEGER (Wien: A. Hartleben, 1910) 2 v. 660 p.; (reprint, Nendeln: Kraus, 1968). *Illus., port., bibliog.* In German, English, French, Spanish, and Italian.

The conference was held from 9 through 14 September 1908. The following contributions are cited separately: A.C. BRETON, **Survivals of ceremonial dances among Mexican Indians** (3194); C.V. HARTMANN, **The photographones** (5757); Konrad Theodor PREUSS, **Das Fest des Erwachens (Weinfest) bei den Cora-Indianern** [The festival of awakening (wine festival) among the Cora Indians] (3171); Richard WALLASCHEK, **Über den Wert phonographischer Aufnahmen von Gesängen der Naturvölker** [The value of phonographic recordings of the songs of primitive peoples] (2481).

62
rs

Review by Erich Moritz von HORNBOSTEL, *Zeitschrift der Internationalen Musikgesellschaft* 4 (1908-1909) 4–7. In German.

1909

63
bs

[Cairo] **Comptes rendus du Congrès international d'archéologie classique: 2ᵉ session** [Proceedings of the International Congress of Classical Archaeology: Second meeting] (Al-Qāhirah: Imprimerie Nationale, 1909) 316 p. In French.

The conference was held from 7 through 15 April 1909. The following contribution is cited separately: Valerios STAÏS, **Un instrument musical du tombeau à coupole de Menidi** [A musical instrument in the domed tomb of Menidi] (3604).

64
bs

[Liège] **Fédération Archéologique et Historique de Belgique: Annales du XXIᵉ congrès** [Fédération Archéologique et Historique de Belgique: Annals of the 21st congress]. Sponsored by the Société d'Art et d'Histoire du Diocèse de Liège and Institut Archéologique Liégeois. Ed. by Jacques BRASSINNE and Lucien RENARD-GRENSON (Liège: Poncelet, 1909). In French.

The conference was held from 31 July through 5 August 1909. The following contributions are cited separately: Paul BERGMANS, **De l'intérêt qu'il y aurait à dresser un inventaire général des instruments de musique anciens disséminés dans les musées et les collections privées de Belgique** [On the benefit of drawing up a general inventory of the early musical instruments scattered in the museums and private collections of Belgium] (3242) and **Le collegium musicum fondé à Hasselt au XVIᵉ siècle** [The Collegium Musicum founded at Hasselt in the 16th century] (1232); Charles van den BORREN, **Guillaume Dufay (avant 1400-1474): Son importance historique** [Guillaume Dufay (before 1400-1474): His historical importance] (1251); Georges DWELSHAUVERS, **La forme musicale, embryon de sonate, adoptée par Jean-Noël Hamal dans son opus I doit-elle être considerée comme une antériorité aux *Sonate a tre* de Stamitz?** [Should the musical form, embryo of sonata form, adopted by Jean-Noël Hamal in his opus 1, be considered an antecedent of the *Sonate a tre* by Stamic?] (4242) and **Programme des recherches à faire dans les fonds musicaux de la province de Liège** [Program of research to be done in music collections of the province of Liège] (867); Louis LAVOYE, **L'art musical belge pendant la Renaissance** [Belgian musical art during the Renaissance] (1363) and **Note sur la musique au pays de Liège aux Xᵉ, XIᵉ et XIIᵉ siècles** [On the music of the region of Liège in the 10th, 11th, and 12th centuries] (1137); Paul VITRY, **Le tombeau de Henry du Mont, musicien liégeois, établi en France au XVIIᵉ siècle** [The tomb of Henry du Mont, musician of Liège, established in France in the 17th century] (1708).

65
bs

[Vienna] **Haydn-Zentenarfeier** [Haydn centenary commemoration]. Proceedings of the Third Congress of the International Musical Society (Leipzig: Breitkopf & Härtel; Wien: Artaria, 1909) 690 p. *Illus., music, charts, diagr.* In German, French, English, and Italian.

The conference was held from 25 through 29 May 1909. The following contributions are cited separately: Hermann ABERT, **Zur Geschichte der Oper in Württemberg** [On the history of opera in Württemberg] (5094); William Arthur AIKIN, **Die Phonologie in der Gesangslehre** [Phonology in singing instruction] (3288); Otto ANDERSSON, **Altertümliche Tonarten in der Volksmusik mit besonderer Berücksichtigung der finnländischen** [The retention in traditional music of ancient tonalities, with particular attention to that of Finland] (2716) and **Altnordische Streichinstrumente** [Old Nordic string instruments] (3548); ANON. (a critic), **Musical criticism in England** (5422); Herbert ANTCLIFFE, **Inductive and comparative criticism as applied to the art of music** (5424); Amalie ARNHEIM, **Über das Musikleben in Bremen im 17. Jahrhundert** [On musical life in Bremen in the 17th century] (1481); Pierre AUBRY, **L'ars mensurabilis et les proses liturgiques au XIIIᵉ siècle** [Ars mensurabilis and liturgical prose in the 13th century] (1059); William BEHREND, **Musikalische Länderkunde Dänemarks** [Denmark's musical geography] (2282); Eduard BERNOULLI, **Hinweis auf gewisse Alterationszeichen in Drucken des 16. Jahrhunderts** [A note on certain accidental symbols in 16th-century prints] (3804) and **Über die Schweizerische Musikgesellschaft** [On the Schweizerische Musikgesellschaft] (862); Elsa BIENENFELD, **Neue Versuche zur Veränderung der klassichen Sinfonieform** [New attempts to modify the Classic symphonic form] (4233); Engbert BRANDSMA, **Über die Tonverhältnisse in der alten und neuen Musik** [Tonal relations in old and new music] (4052); Georgy CALMUS, **Das Théâtre de la Foire des Lesage (Paris 1712-1738) und seine Bedeutung für die Entwicklung der komischen Oper in Frankreich, England, und Deutschland** [The Théâtre de la Foire of Lesage (Paris 1712-1738) and its significance for the development of comic opera in France, England, and Germany] (1501); Gaetano CESARI, **Die Entwicklung der Monteverdischen Kammermusik** [The development of Monteverdi's chamber music] (1270); Oscar CHILESOTTI, **Le alterazioni cromatiche nel secolo XVIᵉ** [Chromatic alterations in the 16th century] (1273); Andrea D'ANGELI, **Novità, varietà, necessità del ritmo** [Novelty, variety, and necessity of rhythm] (3983); Mathilde DAUBRESSE, **Rapport sur l'enseignement musical en France** [Report on musical teaching in France] (4512); Lionel Alexandre DAURIAC, **Note sur l'inspiration musicale** [Note on musical inspiration] (5450); Jules ÉCORCHEVILLE, **Sur le catalogue du fond de musique ancienne de la Bibliothèque Nationale à Paris** [On the catalogue of the early music collection of the Bibliothèque Nationale in Paris] (716) and **Über die Lautenkommission** [On the commission on lute music] (3567); Walther Edmund EHRENHOFER, **Einheitliche Gestaltung des Spieltisches unter spezieller Berücksichtigung der Pedalfrage** [Uniform organization of the console with special consideration of the pedal question] (3357); Louis FLEURY, **De la situation économique des musiciens d'orchestre en France** [On the economic situation of French orchestra musicians] (1957); Hugo GAISSER, **Die acht Kirchentöne in der griechisch-albanesischen Überlieferung** [The eight church modes in Greek-Albanian transmission] (4076); Maurice GANDILLOT, **Base rationiste du système musical** [The rationist basis of the system of music] (5474); Riccardo GANDOLFI, **La cappella musicale della corte di Toscana: 1539-1859** [The music chapel of the Tuscan court: 1539-1859] (962); Christian GEISLER, **Der Schulgesang und die Notationsfrage** [School song and the question of notation] (3822); Hugo GOLD-SCHMIDT, **Die Reform der italienischen Oper des 18. Jahrhunderts und ihre Beziehungen zur musikalischen Ästhetik** [The reform of 18th-century Italian opera and its relation to musical aesthetics] (1765); Josef GÖTZ, **Die Fiedelmusik im der Iglauer Sprachinsel** [Fiddle music in the linguistic enclave of Jihlava] (3573) and **Stand der Volksliedforschung in Mähren und Schlesien** [The state of folk song research in Moravia and Silesia] (2836); George C. GOW, **Harmonic problems of to-day** (4173); Joseph GREGOR, **Die historische Dramaturgie in der Geschichte der Oper** [Historical dramaturgy in the history of opera] (5163); Robert HAAS, **Zur Frage der Orchesterbesetzungen in der zweiten Hälfte des 18. Jahrhunderts** [Instrumentation in the second half of the 18th century] (1773); Franz HABÖCK, **Der Gesangsunterricht in den Schulen** [Singing instruction in schools] (4545); William Henry HADOW, **Organization of musical life in England** (1977); Friedrich HAERPFER, **Erfahrungen über Aufstellung und Intonation von modernen Orgeln** [Experiments in the installation and tuning of modern organs] (3385); Angul HAMMERICH, **Bericht über eine alte griechische**

Lyra von Elfenbein aus der Mykenäzeit [Report on an ivory lyre from the Mycenaean period of ancient Greece] (3576); Carl Fredrik HENNERBERG, Die schwedischen Orgeln des Mittelalters [The Swedish organs of the Middle Ages] (3389) and Schwedische Haydn-Handschriften [Haydn autographs in Sweden] (1777); Alfred HEUSS, Einige grundlegende Begriffe für eine historische Darstellung der musikalischen Dynamik [Some basic concepts for a historical presentation of musical dynamics] (3678); Alfred Valentin HEUSS, Gedächtnisrede auf Händel [Memorial speech for Händel] (1577); Erich Moritz von HORNBOSTEL, Über Mehrstimmigkeit in der außereuropäischen Musik [On polyphony in non-European music] (2556); Otakar HOSTINSKÝ, Mitteilungen über das tschechische Volkslied in Böhmen und Mähren [Information on Czech traditional song in Bohemia and Moravia] (2859); Vincent d'INDY, De la sophistication de l'œuvre d'art par l'édition [The refinement of works of art in the editing process] (975) and Quand c'est formée la fugue telle qu'on enseigne actuellement dans les grands conservatoires de l'Europe? [When did the fugue as currently taught in the great European conservatories take shape?] (4260); Zdzisław JACHIMECKI, Südliche Einflüsse in der polnischen Musik [Southern influences in Polish music] (1582); Adolf KOCZIRZ, Über die Notwendigkeit eines einheitlichen, wissenschaftlichen und instrumentaltechnischen Forderungen entsprechenden Systems in der Übertragung von Lautentabulaturen [The need for a unified system that meets scientific and organological requirements for lute tablature transcription] (3904); Filaret KOLESSA, Über den melodischen und rhythmischen Aufbau der ukrainischen (kleinrussischen) rezitierenden Gesänge, der sogenannten Kosakenlieder [The melodic and rhythmic structure of Ukrainian (Little Russian) declamatory songs, the so-called Cossack songs] (2904); Ilmari KROHN, Reform der Taktbezeichnung [Reform of the barline] (3838) and Über die typischen Merkmale der finnischen Volksliedmelodien in den Abteilungen A I und A II [On typical features of Finnish folk song melodies in volumes A I and A II] (2913); Theodor KROYER, Zum Akzidentienproblem im Ausgang des 16. Jahrhunderts [On problems of accidentals at the end of the 16th century] (3841); Felix KRUEGER, Die psychologischen Grundlagen der Konsonanz und Dissonanz [The psychological foundations of consonance and dissonance] (5672); Ludvík KUBA, Einiges über das istro--dalmatinische Lied [Notes on Istrian-Dalmatian song] (2914); Lionel de LA LAURENCIE, Essai d'application des méthodes graphiques à l'étude de la bibliographie musicale [An application of graphic methods to the study of musical bibliography] (891); Armas LAUNIS, Die Pentatonik in den Melodien der Lappen [The pentatonic scale in the melodies of the Sámi people] (2924); Hugo LEICHTENTRITT, Zur Vortragspraxis des 17. Jahrhunderts [Performance practice in the 17th century] (3755); S. LEVYSOHN, Die Pflege der Haydnschen Musik in Dänemark [The cultivation of Haydn's music in Denmark] (2027); Evgenija LINĔVA, Über neue Methoden des Folklores in Rußland [On the new methods of folklore in Russia] (2444); Friedrich LUDWIG, Die mehrstimmige Musik des 11. und 12. Jahrhunderts [Polyphonic music of the 11th and 12th centuries] (1146); Gustave LYON, Utilité d'une numération logique des sons de l'échelle chromatique qui permette à première vue de se rendre compte de la note dont il s'agit et de l'octave où elle se trouve [Utility of a logical numeration of the sounds of the chromatic scale that allows one to realize at a glance what the note in question is and in what octave it is found] (3849); Alexander Campbell MACKENZIE, Gedächtnisrede auf Mendelssohn [Memorial speech for Mendelssohn-Bartholdy] (2032); Charles MALHERBE, La graphologie dans les écritures musicales [Graphology in musical composition] (3851), L'internationalisme dans la musique [Internationalism in music] (2352), and Observations relatives à l'établissement d'un catalogue des autographes musicaux dans les principales bibliothèques de l'Europe [Observations relative to the establishment of a catalogue of musical autographs in the principal libraries of Europe] (616); Josip MANTUANI, Über die Katalogisierung der katholischen liturgischen Texte [On the cataloguing of Roman Catholic liturgical texts] (617), Über die Katalogisierung des deutschen Liedes [On the cataloguing of German songs] (618), and Über die Umarbeitung von Riemanns Opernhandbuch [The revision of Riemann's Opern-Handbuch] (896); Franz MOISSL, Über die Notwendigkeit unterbehördlicher Durchführungsvorschriften zum motu propio vom 22 November 1903 [The necessity of regulations from the lesser hierarchy for the implementation of the motu proprio of 22 November 1903] (6309); Paul MOOS, Die Ästhetik des Rhythmus bei Theodor Lipps [The aesthetics of rhythm of Theodor Lipps] (5546); Hermann MÜLLER, Zur Urgeschichte des deutschen Kirchenliedes [On the early history of German hymns] (6318); Wilibald NAGEL, Kleine Beiträge zur Geschichte der Oper in Darmstadt [Small contributions to

the history of opera in Darmstadt] (1631); Manuel de OLIVEIRA-LIMA, La musique au Brésil au point de vue historique [Music in Brazil from a historical point of view] (994); Hans Wolfgang POLLAK, Ausrüstung der von Akademien und Gesellschaften zu entsendenden Reisenden, mit besonderer Rücksicht auf musikwissenschaftliche Zwecke [The preparation of field researchers from academic institutions and societies, with particular attention to musicological goals] (2460); Josef POMMER, Das Volkslied in Österreich: Unternehmen des k.k. Ministeriums für Kultus und Unterricht [Das Volkslied in Österreich: An undertaking of the Austro-Hungarian Ministry of Culture and Education] (3012) and Juchzer, Rufe und Almschreie aus den österreichischen Alpenländern [Yodels, calls, and Almschreie from the Austrian alpine countries] (3011); Felix ROSENTHAL, Die Musik als Eindruck. II [Music as impression. II] (5698); Poul Sophus RUNG-KELLER, Über Reform des Orgelbaues [On the reform of organ building] (3470); Paul RUNGE, Über die Notation des Meistergesanges: Berichtigung und Ergänzung des Referats auf dem Baseler Kongress 1906 [On the notation of Meistergesang: Correction and supplement to the report given at the Basel congress of 1906] (3865); Liborio SACCHETTI, Les principaux moments de l'histoire de la musique profane en Russie [The principal moments in the history of secular music in Russia] (1002); Adolf SANDBERGER, Neue Forschungen zu Caccini und Monteverdi [New research on Caccini and Monteverdi] (1667) and Richard Wagners Liebesverbot [Richard Wagner's Das Liebesverbot] (2091); Friedrich SANNEMANN, Grundsätze evangelischer Kirchenmusik [Principles of Protestant church music] (6445); Arnold SCHERING, Geschichtliches über das Verhältnis von Oper und Oratorium [Historical remarks on the relationship between opera and oratorio] (4284); Ludwig SCHIEDERMAIR, Bemerkungen zum musikhistorischen Unterricht an hohen und mittleren Schulen [Remarks on music history instruction in secondary schools] (4769); Wilhelm SCHMIDT, Über Musik und Gesänge der Karesau-Papuas, Deutsch-Neu-Guinea [On music and song of Karesau Island Papuans, German New Guinea] (3229); Eugen SCHMITZ, Das Verhältnis der Musikwissenschaft zur Populärliteratur und Musikkritik [The relationship of musicology to popular literature and music criticism] (921); Karl SCHNABL, Charakteristik der Kirchenmusik [Characteristic of church music] (6383); Alfred SCHNERICH, Die textlichen Versehen in den Messen Josef Haydns und deren Korrektur [Textual errors in the Masses of Joseph Haydn and their correction] (3918), Die Wiener Kirchenmusikvereine [Vienna church music associations] (6385), and Kirchenmusikalische Denkmalpflege [Preservation of monuments of church music] (6384); Rudolf SCHWARTZ, Zur Akzidentienfrage im 16. Jahrhundert [The use of accidentals in the 16th century] (1430); Albert SCHWEITZER, Die Reform unseres Orgelbaues auf Grund einer allgemeinen Umfrage bei Orgelspielern und Orgelbauern in deutschen und romanischen Ländern [The reform of our organ building based on a general survey of organ players and organ makers in German and Romance-language countries] (3478); Albert SCHWEITZER and François-Xavier MATHIAS, Internationales Regulativ für Orgelbau [International regulations for organ building] (3479); Alicja SIMON, Die Lautenmusikbestände der Königl. Bibliothek in Berlin [Lute music holdings of the Königliche Bibliothek, Berlin] (757); Arthur SOMERVELL, Musical education in England (4648); Oscar G.T. SONNECK, Das Musikleben Amerikas vom Standpunkte der musikalischen Länderkunde [America's musical life from the standpoint of musical geography] (2100); Hermann Wilhelm SPRINGER, Die internationale Verzeichnung der älteren Musikliteratur [The international cataloguing of early music literature] (823); Albert A. STANLEY, Music in American universities (4851); Adolf STÖHR, Das psychophysiologische Problem der Klangfarbe [The psycho-physiological problem of tone color] (5706); Richard Alexander STREATFEILD, Concert life in England (2395); Hjalmar THUREN, Über die folkloristische Sammlung in Kopenhagen [On the folklore collection in Copenhagen] (765); Peter WAGNER, Über gregorianischen Choral [On Gregorian chant] (6410); Karl WEINMANN, Alte und moderne Kirchenmusik: Historisch-kritische Bemerkungen zur Theorie und Praxis [Old and modern church music: Historical-critical remarks on theory and practice] (6413); Wilhelm WIDMANN, Einrichtung historischer Musikwerke für Aufführungen [The arrangement of historical musical works for performance] (3722); Johannes WOLF, Die Akzidentien im 15. und 16. Jahrhundert [Accidentals in the 15th and 16th centuries] (1470); Rudolf WUSTMANN, Über Bearbeitung älterer und ausländischer Gesangstexte [On the editing of older and foreign song texts] (3929); Giusto ZAMPIERI, I programmi d'insegnamento della storia della musica nel R. Conservatorio di Milano [The programs of instruction in music history at the Reale Conservatorio di Milano] (4903), La notazione della partitura d'orchestra secondo il sistema Giordano [The notation of orchestral scores according to the Giordano system] (3885), and L'insegnamento della teoria della musica e del solfeggio nel R. Conservatorio di Milano [The teaching of music theory and solfège in the Reale Conservatorio di Milano] (4902); Raimund ZODER, Über den Takt des Ländlers in Oberösterreich [On the meter of the Ländler in Upper Austria] (3126).

66
rs
Review by Hermann ABERT, *Zeitschrift der Internationalen Musikgesellschaft* 4 (1909-1910) 375–79. In German.

67
rs
Review by Albert Valentin HEUSS, *Zeitschrift der Internationalen Musikgesellschaft* 4 (1908-1909) 301–12. In German.

1910

68
bs
[Buenos Aires] Actas del XVIIº Congreso Internacional de Americanistas [Proceedings of the 17th International Congress of Americanists]. Ed. by Robert LEHMANN-NITSCHE (Buenos Aires: Coni, 1912) 676, 58, 49 p.; (reprint, Nendeln: Kraus, 1968). *Illus.* In Spanish.
The conference was held from 17 through 23 May 1910. The following contribution is cited separately: Tomás GUEVARA, **Folklore araucano: Proverbios y refránes** [The Araucano folklore: Proverbs and refránes] (3200).

1911

69
bs
[Bologna] Atti del IV Congresso internazionale di filosofia [Acts of the Fourth International Congress of Philosophy]. Sponsored by King Vittorio Emmanuele III of Italy. *Biblioteca di filosofia e di pedagogia* (Genova: A.F. Formíggini, 1911) 3 v. 367, 495, 685 p.; (reprint, Nendeln: Kraus, 1968). *Bibliog., index.* In Italian, English, French, and German.
The congress was held from 5 through 11 April 1911. The following contribution is cited separately: Fausto TORREFRANCA, **L'intuizione musicale quale sintesi a priori estetica** [Musical intuition as a priori aesthetic synthesis] (5617).

70
bs
[Innsbruck] Bericht über den IV. Kongress für Experimentelle Psychologie [Proceedings of the Fourth Congress for Experimental Psychology]. Sponsored by the Gesellschaft für Experimentelle Psychologie. Ed. by Friedrich SCHUMANN (Leipzig: Barth, 1911). In German.
The congress was held from 19 through 22 April 1911. The following contributions are cited separately: Géza RÉVÉSZ, **Über die hervorragenden akustischen Eigenschaften und musikalischen Fähigkeiten des siebenjährigen Komponisten Erwin Nyiregyházy** [The outstanding acoustic capacities and musical abilities of the seven-year-old composer Ervin Nyíregyházi] (5694); Carl STUMPF and Erich Moritz von HORNBOSTEL, **Über die Bedeutung ethnologischer Untersuchungen für die Psychologie und Ästhetik der Tonkunst** [The significance of ethnological studies for the psychology and aesthetics of music] (2476).

71
bs
[London] Report of the Fourth Congress of the International Musical Society. Ed. by Charles MACLEAN (London: Novello, 1912) viii, 427 p. *Illus., port., music, index, charts, diagr., tech. drawings.* In English, German, French, and Italian.
The congress was held from 29 May through 3 June 1911. The following contributions are cited separately: Guido ADLER, **Zur Periodisierung der Musikgeschichte** [On the periodization of music history] (857); Otto ANDERSSON, **The introduction of orchestral music into Finland** (1723) and **Violinists and dance-tunes among the Swedish population in Finland towards the middle of the XIX century** (2718); Herbert ANTCLIFFE, **Musical form and the symphonic poem** (4229); Amalie ARNHEIM, **Englische Suitenkomponisten des XVII. Jahrhunderts und ihre in Deutschland erschienenen Sammlungen** [English suite

composers of the 17th century, and German collections of their works] (1480); Eduard BERNOULLI, **Eine Handschrift mit rhythmisierten Meistersängermelodien** [A manuscript containing rhythmic Meistersinger melodien] (1235); Sándor de BERTHA, **Les Rhapsodies hongroises de Franz Liszt** [Franz Liszt's *Magyar rhapsodiák*] (1915); Heinrich BEWERUNGE, **The metrical cursus in the antiphon melodies of the Mass** (3970); Johannes BIEHLE, **Theorie des Kirchenbaues vom Standpunkte des Kirchenmusikers** [Architecture in Protestant churches from the standpoint of the church musician] (5803); Michel D. CALVOCORESSI, **Psychophysiology: The true road to necessary reforms in musical aesthetics** (5645); Julián CARILLO, **Sur la nécessité d'élever le niveau artistique de la musique militaire** [On the necessity of raising the artistic level of military music] (4865); William Hayman CUMMINGS, **Matthew Locke: Composer for the church and theatre** (1516); Edward CURLING, **Cherubini as a dramatic composer** (1737); Edward Joseph DENT, **Giuseppe Maria Buini** (1526); Félicien DURANT, **Instruments en cuivre omnitoniques à 6 pistons dépendants** [Omnitonic brass instruments with six dependent pistons] (3616); Jules ÉCORCHEVILLE, **L'internationalisme dans la musique** [Internationalism in music] (5457); Émile ERGO, **Des causes et des conséquences du manque d'unité dans plusieurs branches de la science musicale** [Causes and consequences of the lack of unity among branches of musicology] (869); Vito FEDELI, **L'insegnamento della composizione negli istituti musicali** [Composition teaching in musical institutes] (4870); Erwin FELBER, **Das Gesetz der Zahlenverschiebung in Märchen und Mythos und sein Einfluss auf die Skalenbildung** [The law of mutation of numbers in fairy tale and myth, and its influence on scale building] (4071) and **Die Musik in den Märchen und Mythen der verschiedenen Völker** [Music in the fairy tales and myths of various peoples] (5315); William Henry Grattan FLOOD, **Irish musical bibliography** (801); Walter Howard FRERE, **Key-relationships in early medieval music** (4169); Max FRIEDLAENDER, **German folk songs with reference to English and American folk songs** (2820); John Alexander FULLER-MAITLAND, **The interpretation of musical ornaments** (3740); Francis William GALPIN, **The origin of the clarsech or Irish harp** (3571); Maurice GANDILLOT, **Sur la langage musicale** [On musical language] (5475); Maurice GRIVEAU, **Le sens et l'expression de la musique pure** [Meaning and expression of pure music] (5483); Hermann GÜTTLER, **Die Pantomime W.A. Mozarts und ihre Aufführung** [Mozart's pantomime and its performance] (1770); William Henry HADOW, **The influence of secular idiom upon English church music** (6014); Angul HAMMERICH, **Musical relations between England and Denmark in the XVII century** (1574); Carl Fredrik HENNERBERG, **Einige Dokumente, den Abt Georg Joseph Vogler betreffend** [Documents relating to Abbé Georg Joseph Vogler] (1776); Charles KARLYLE, **International voice training** (4563); Frederick KEEL, **Some characteristics of British folk song** (2881); Filaret KOLESSA, **Ueber den rhythmischen Aufbau der ukrainischen (kleinrussischen) Volkslieder** [Rhythmic construction of Ukrainian (Little Russian) folk songs] (4008); Alexander KRAUS, **Italian inventions for instruments with a keyboard** (3525); Ilmari KROHN, **Ueber die Methode der musikalischen Analyse** [On the method of musical analysis] (3950); Lionel de LA LAURENCIE, **Les pastorales en musique au XVIIéme siècle en France avant Lully et leur influence sur l'opéra** [Musical pastorales in 17th-century France before Lully, and their influence on opera] (1596); Armas LAUNIS, **Ueber die Notwendigkeit einer ein Heitlichen Untersuchungsmethode der Volksmelodien** [The need for a uniform method for investigating traditional melodies] (4444); Evgenija LINÉVA, **Psalms and religious songs of the Russian sectarians in the Caucasus** (2931); François-Xavier MATHIAS, **Sujektivität und Objektivität in der katholischen Kirchenmusik** [Subjectivity and objectivity in Catholic church music] (6305); Tobias MATTHAY, **Principles of pianoforte teaching** (4595); Albert MAYER-REINACH, **Vorschläge zur Herausgabe von Vokalmusik des XV.-XVII. Jahrhunderts** [Proposals for editing vocal music of the 15th-17th centuries] (3907); William Gray MCNAUGHT, **Introductory to tonic sol-fa** (5680); Angel MENCHACA, **Nouveau système de notation musicale** [A new system of musical notation] (3853); Hermann MÜLLER, **Prinzipielles zur katholischen Kirchenmusik** [Principles of Catholic church music] (6317); Tobias NORLIND, **Die englische Lautenmusik zur Zeit Shakespeare's** [English lute music in the time of Shakespeare] (1389) and **Die polnischen Tänze ausserhalb Polens** [Polish dances outside Poland] (5042); Henryk OPIEN'SKI, **Les premiers opéras polonais et leur influence sur l'époque de la jeunesse de Chopin** [The first Polish operas and their influence on Chopin's youthful period] (2059); Icilio ORLANDINI, **Il dattilapero** [The finger stretcher] (5734); C. Hubert H. PARRY, **The meaning of ugliness in art** (5566); José

PEREIRA DE SAMPAIO, **Harmonium tessaradécatonique** [Tessaradecatonic harmonium] (3446); Geremia PIAZZANO, **Le fonotomo: Diviseur des sons** [The fonotomo: Divider of sounds] (4101); Jacques-Gabriel PROD'HOMME, **La musique et les musiciens en 1848** [Music and musicians in 1848] (2077); Henry PRUNIÈRES, **Notes sur les origines de l'ouverture française, 1640-1660** [Notes on the origin of the French overture, 1640-1660] (1647); Dorsan van REYSSCHOOT, **De quelques réformes dans la notation des partitions d'orchestre d'édition dite** *populaire* [Some reforms in the notation of orchestral scores in popular editions] (3863); Cecilio de RODA Y LOPEZ, **Les instruments de musique en Espagne au XIII**ᵐᵉ **siècle** [Musical instruments in Spain in the 13th century] (3272); Cyril Bradley ROOTHAM, **Choir-boy training** (4765); Melchior Ernst SACHS, **Das temperierte 19-tonsystem und eine dafür passende Schrift** [A system for dividing the octave into 19 tones, with appropriate notation] (4108); Friedrich SANNEMANN, **Ueber eine ungedruckte Sammlung deutscher Volkslieder mit ihren Singweisen in der Altmark und im Magdeburgischen aus Volksmunde gesammelt von Ludolf Parisius** [An unpublished collection of German traditional songs with their melodies collected from oral sources in the Altmark and Magdeburg districts by Ludolf Parisius] (3047); Daniel François SCHEURLEER, **Iconography of musical instruments** (5397); Max SEIFFERT, **Generalkatalog der in englischen öffenlichen und privaten Bibliotheken befindlichen älteren Musikalien bis 1800** [General catalogue of musical documents prior to the year 1800 contained in public and private libraries in England] (681) and **Neuausgabe der englischen Virginalmusik** [New editions of English virginal music] (3919); Stefan SIHLEANU, **De la musique populaire dans les pays roumains** [Traditional music in Romanian lands] (3059); Alicja SIMON, **Lute music in Berlin libraries** (758); Carlo SOMIGLI, **Les mécanismes laryngiens et les timbres vocaux** [Laryngeal mechanism and vocal sound quality] (3323); Oscar G.T. SONNECK, **Ciampi's** *Bertoldo, Bertoldino e Cacasenno*: **A contribution to the history of pasticcio** (5248); Friedrich SPIRO, **Ueber eine Revision der Beethoven-Gesamtausgabe** [On a revision of the complete works of Beethoven] (3921); Assia SPIRO-ROMBRO, **Proposals for improving elementary violin methods and hints for teaching the violin to children** (4779); Hermann SPRINGER, **Die jüngsten Fortschritte der Musikbibliographie** [The most recent advances in musical bibliography] (689); William Barclay SQUIRE, **Who was Benedictus?** (1439); Albert A. STANLEY, **Provincial music festivals in the United States** (2393) and **The value of a collection of musical instruments in universities** (4852); Fritz STEIN, **Mitteilungen über eine in Jena aufgefundene mutmassliche Jugendsymphonie Beethovens** [A youthful symphony allegedly by Beethoven discovered at Jena] (1868); Joseph SUMMERS, **Musical education in Australia, 1863-1911** (4855); Walter Hampden THELWALL, **Mathematical analysis of the tempered chromatic scale** (4118); Fausto TORREFRANCA, **La sonata italiana per cembalo nella prima metà del Settecento e i concerti di Giovanni Platti (1740)** [The Italian harpsichord sonata in the first half of the 18th century and the concertos of Giovanni Platti (1740)] (1705); Karl WEINMANN, **Zur Geschichte der Kirchenmusik im 17. und 18. Jahrhundert** [The history of church music in the 17th and 18th centuries] (1710); Egon WELLESZ, **Die Aussetzung des basso continuo in der italienischen Oper** [The realization of the basso continuo in Italian opera] (3777); Egon Stuart WILLFORT, **An encyclopædic method of pianoforte teaching** (4672); Julius WOITINEK, **Eine neuer Schultafel-Apparat für den Gesangs-Klassen Unterricht** [A new blackboard apparatus for teaching vocal classes] (4799); Johannes WOLF, **English influence on the evolution of music** (1024) and **Ueber Guitarren-Tabulaturen** [On guitar tablatures] (3884). English-language abstracts of all papers appear on p. 52-77.

72
rs
Review by Vito FEDELI, *Rivista musicale italiana* 4 (1911) 601-30. In Italian.

73
bs
[Mechelen] Fédération Archéologique et Historique de Belgique: Annales du XXIIᵉ **congrès. I: Documents et compte rendu; II: Rapports & mémoires** [Fédération Archéologique et Historique de Belgique: Annals of the 22nd congress. I: Documents and proceedings; II: Reports and memoranda]. Ed. by Hyacinthe J.B. CONINCKX. *Annales de la Fédération Archéologique et Historique de Belgique* 22 (Mechelen: Godenne, 1911) 2 v. 538, 917 p. *Illus., port., facs., music, them. cat., maps.* In French and Dutch.

The congress was held from 21 through 27 September 1911. The following contributions are cited separately: Raymond Joseph Justin van AERDE, **Les ménestrels communaux malinois et joueurs d'instruments divers, établis ou de passage à Malines de 1311 à 1790** [City minstrels of Mechelen and players of different instruments, established at or passing through Mechelen from 1311 to 1790] (938); H.-J.-L. BOEYNAEMS-PONTUS, **À propos du carillon** [On the carillon] (3644); Charles van den BORREN, **L'esthétique expressive de Guillaume Dufay dans ses rapports avec la technique musicale du XV**ᵉ **siècle** [The expressive aesthetic of Guillaume Dufay in relation to the musical technique of the 15th century] (1250); Gustave CAULLET, **L'origine malinoise de Philippe de Monte (Van den Berghe)** [The Mechelen origin of Philippe de Monte (Van den Berghe)] (1268) and **Simon: Maître de vièle (1313)** [Simon: Master of the vielle (1313)] (3556); Georges van DOORSLAER, **Connaît-on des documents relatifs au séjour de Jean-Ladislas Dussek à Malines?** [Are there any known documents relative to Jan Ladislav Dusík's stay in Mechelen?] (1745), **Connaît-on des documents relatifs au séjour de Jérôme Frescobaldi à Malines?** [Are there any known documents relating to Girolamo Frescobaldi's stay in Mechelen?] (1527), **Le carillon, son origine et son développement** [The carillon, its origin and development] (3648), and **Notes sur les facteurs d'orgues malinois** [Notes on the organ builders of Mechelen] (3349); Georges DWELSHAUVERS, **Programme des recherches faites ou à faire dans les fonds musicaux de la province de Liège** [Program of research done or to be done in the music collections of the province of Liège] (868); Gustave JORISSENNE, **Facteurs d'orgues dans le pays de Liège** [Organ builders in the Liège region] (3397); Theophiel PEETERS, **Oude Kempische liederen en dansen** [Old Kempish songs and dances] (2989).

74
bs
[Mons] Congrès international des Amitiés Françaises [International Congress of the Amitiés Françaises]. Ed. by Léon SOUGUENET (Mons: Libert, 1911) 344 p. In French.

The congress was held from 21 through 27 September 1911. The following contributions are cited separately: François ANDRÉ, **La vieille chanson française** [The old French chanson] (1220); Émile JENNISSEN, **La propagande en chantant** [Propaganda in singing] (2331); René VANDERHAEGE (René Lyr), **La musique en Wallonie** [Music in Wallonia] (1016).

75
bs
[Paris] Comptes rendus, rapports et vœux du Congrès parisien et régional de chant liturgique et de musique d'église [Proceedings, reports, and wishes of the Parisian and regional congress on liturgical chant and church music] (Paris: Schola Cantorum, 1912) 184 p. *Illus.* In French.

The conference was held from 12 through 15 June 1911. The following contributions are cited separately: Raphael ANDOYER, **Note sur la chant antégrégorien** [Note on pre-Gregorian chant] (1053); Léon BOUTROUX, **Quelques réflexions sur l'accompagnement du chant grégorien** [Some reflections on the accompaniment of Gregorian chant] (3693); F. BRUN, **Le cantique d'inspiration grégorienne** [Gregorian-inspired canticle] (6179); Camille COUILLAUT, **La réforme de la prononciation du latin** [Reforming Latin pronunciation] (5295); Amédée GASTOUÉ, **Les proses parisiennes du XII**ᵉ **siècle et l'œuvre d'Adam de Saint-Victor** [The Parisian prosae of the 12th century and the works of Adam de St. Victor] (6227); Pope PIUS X, *Motu proprio* **sur la musique sacrée** [Motu proprio on sacred music] (6337); Henry POIVET, *Una fides, unus cantus, una lingua* (6338); Henri QUITTARD, **Les anciennes orgues françaises** [Early French organs] (3450); Félix RAUGEL, **Le Congrès de musique religieuse de Paris (1860)** [The congress of religious music in Paris (1860)] (911); Gustave ROBERT DU BOTNEAU, **Une maîtrise grégorienne** [A Gregorian choir school] (6355); THINOT (abbé), **Les chœurs d'église de Reims** [Church choirs of Reims] (6399); Joseph-Marie TISSIER, **Chant liturgique et éducation chrétienne** [Liturgical singing and Christian education] (4658); Henri VILLETARD, **Odoranne de Sens et son œuvre musicale** [Odorannus de Sens and his musical oeuvre] (3960).

76
bs
[Rome] Rapport sur la musique contemporaine française [Report on contemporary French music]. Proceedings of the Congrès de Musique de l'Exposition Internationale; sponsored by the Section

d'Histoire Musicale de L'Institut Français de Florence. Ed. by Jules Philippe Louis ANGLAS; ed. and pref. by Paul-Marie MASSON (Roma: Armani & Stein, 1913) 167 p. *Bibliog.* In French.

Issued for the Congrès de Musique de l'Exposition Internationale, held from 4 through 11 April 1911. Separate edition of contributions to the section on French music. The following contributions are cited separately: Jules Philippe Louis ANGLAS, **La science des sons dans ses rapports avec la musique** [The science of sound in relation to music] (5800); Georges BAUDIN, **La législation** [Legislation] (5944); Marie BOBILLIER (Michel Brenet), **La musicologie** [Musicology] (864); Eugène de BRICQUEVILLE, **La facture instrumentale** [Instrument building] (3245); Gaston CARRAUD, **La musique symphonique** [Symphonic music] (1931); Jean HURÉ, **La musique religieuse et la musique chorale** [Religious music and choral music] (1988); Charles KOECHLIN, **La pédagogie musicale** [Music pedagogy] (4882); Charles LALO, **La philosophie de la musique** [Philosophy of music] (5518); Paul LANDORMY, **La musique de chambre** [Chamber music] (2024); Charles MALHERBE, **La musique dramatique** [Dramatic music] (2035); Paul-Marie MASSON, **Préface** [Preface] (2037).

77
bs
[Rouen] Congrès du Millénaire de la Normandie (911-1911) [Congress on the millennium of Normandy (911-1911)]. Ed. by Georges MONFLIER (Rouen: Léon Gy, 1912) 2 v. 631; 696 p. *Illus., music.* In French.

The following contributions are cited separately: Louis de FARCY, **La sonnerie de la cathédrale de Rouen** [The bells of the Rouen cathedral] (3649); Borghild HOLMSEN, **Les traces les plus anciennes de la musique en Norvège** [The oldest traces of music in Norway] (971); Paul-Louis ROBERT, **Boieldieu et *La dame blanche*** [Boieldieu and *La dame blanche*] (1846).

1912

78
bs
[Barcelona] Crónica y actas oficiales del tercer Congreso Nacional de Música Sagrada [Official report and proceedings of the third Congreso Nacional de Música Sagrada] (Barcelona: La Hormiga de Oro, 1913) xiv, 307 p. *Illus., port., index.* In Spanish.

The conference was held from 21 through 24 November 1912. The following contributions are cited separately: Juan BELDA, **Caracteres de la música orgánica litúrgica** [The characteristics of liturgical organ music] (6164); Vicente María GIBERT, **El canto gregoriano: Base y fuente de inspiración de la música orgánica** [The Gregorian chant: The basis and inspiration for organ music] (3374); Juan J. LAGUARDA Y FENORELLA, **La enseñanza de la música sagrada** [The teaching of religious music] (4580); Nemesio OTAÑO EGUINO, **Música litúrgica moderna** [Modern liturgical music] (6329); Felipe PEDRELL, **La música polifónica** [Polyphonic music] (1397); Luis ROMEU, **El canto gregoriano: Supremo modelo y fuente de inspiración de la música religiosa** [Gregorian chant: The ultimate model and inspiration for religious music] (6361); Miguel RUÉ, **Plan para los diversos cursos de enseñanza del canto gregoriano en los seminarios** [A plan for the various courses of Gregorian chant at seminaries] (4845); Mauro SABLAYROLLES, **Importancia de la enseñanza del canto gregoriano en los seminarios** [The importance of teaching Gregorian chant in seminaries] (4846); Gregori M. SUÑOL BAULINAS, **Características generales del canto gregoriano** [The general characteristics of Gregorian chant] (6393).

79
bs
[Berlin] Bericht über den V. Kongress für experimentelle Psychologie [Report on the Fifth Congress for Experimental Psychology. Sponsored by the Gesellschaft für Experimentelle Psychologie. Ed. by Friedrich SCHUMANN (Leipzig: Barth, 1912). In German.

The following contributions are cited separately: Wolfgang KÖHLER, **Akustische Untersuchungen** [Acoustic investigations] (5830); Charles Samuel MYERS, **Individuelle Unterschiede in der Auffassung von Tönen** [Individual differences in the concept of tones] (5684).

80
ap
[Paris] Le 5ᵉ Congrès de la Société Internationale de Musique [The Fifth Congress of the International Musical Society], *Revue musicale S.I.M.* X (July-Aug 1914) 1–32. *Illus., music.* In French.

Presents the proceedings of the congress, which met from 1 through 11 June 1912 in Paris. Included are the following accounts of papers: Gustave LYON, **La numérotation logique des notes de l'échelle chromatique** [The logical numbering of the notes of the chromatic scale], Georges-René-Marie MARAGE, **La voix humaine en action** [The human voice in action], and [Dr.] WOLFRUN, **La réforme des salles de concert** [Concert hall reform]. The program of the conference was published in the May 1914 issue of the same journal, pp.1-5.

81
ra
Review by J.P. BAKER, *Zeitschrift der Internationalen Musikgesellschaft* 4 (1913-1914) 268–74.

82
ra
Review by M. BRENET, *Le Correspondant* 4 (1914) 1192–205. In French.

83
ra
Review by J. CHANTAVOINE, *Musica* 4 (1914) 129–33. In French.

84
ra
Review by Félix RAUGEL, *Revue critique des idées et des livres* 4 (1914). In French.

85
ra
Review by J. WOLF, *Zeitschrift der Internationalen Musikgesellschaft* 4 (1913-1914) 260–68. In German.

1913

86
bs
[Berlin] Kongress für Ästhetik und allgemeine Kunstwissenschaft: Bericht [Congress for aesthetics and general studies of the arts: Report]. Ed. by Gustav Johannes von ALLESCH, Max DESSOIR, Curt GLASER, Werner WOLFFHEIM, and Oskar Konstantinen WULFF (Stuttgart: Enke, 1914). In German.

The following contributions are cited separately: Alfred GUTTMANN, **Kunst und Wissenschaft des Gesanges** [The art and science of singing] (3302); Alfred Valentin HEUSS, **Der geistige Zusammenhang zwischen Text und Musik im Strophenlied** [The intellectual connection between text and music in strophic song] (5320); Paul MOOS, **Über den gegenwärtigen Stand der Musikästhetik** [On the present status of music aesthetics] (5551); Charles Samuel MYERS, **Beitrag zum Studium der Anfänge der Musik** [Contribution to the study of the origins of music] (849); F. ÖHMANN, **Melodie und Akzent: Experimentelle Untersuchungen über ihre Beziehungen** [Melody and accent: Experimental investigations on their relationships] (4451); Anton PENKERT, **Die musikalische Formung von Witz und Humor** [The musical forming of wit and humor] (5567); Hugo RIEMANN, *Gignomenon* **und** *Gegonos* **beim Musikhören** [*Gignomenon* and *gegonos* in hearing music] (5574); Arnold SCHERING, **Zur Grundlegung der musikalische Hermeneutik** [On the foundation of musical hermeneutics] (5585); Eduard SIEVERS, **Demonstrationen zur Lehre von den klanglichen Konstanten in Rede und Musik** [Demonstration of the theory of sonic constants in speech and music] (5937); Justus Hermann WETZEL, **Dur und Moll im diatonischen Tonkreise** [Major and minor in the diatonic tonal circle] (4129).

87
bs
[Berlin] Vorträge und Referate [Contributions and papers]. Report of the International Congress of Music Pedagogy; sponsored by the Vorstande des Deutschen Musikpädagogischen Verbandes (Berlin: Deutscher Musikpädagogischer Verband, 1913) 478 p. In German.

The conference was held from 27 through 30 March 1913.

88
bs
[Budapest] Congrès international des éditeurs: Huitième session—Conclusion des rapports [The International Congress of Publishers: Eighth session—Conclusions]. Sponsored by the International Publishers' Association/Union Internationale des Éditeurs (Budapest: Athenaeum, 1913) 40 p. In French.

The conference was held from 1 through 5 June 1913. The following contribution is cited separately: Einar JESPERSEN, **Le maintien du prix fort ou prix du catalogue dans le commerce de la musique** [Maintaining full or catalogue prices in the sale of music] (5971).

89
bs
[Ghent] Annales du XXIIIe congrès [Annals of the 23rd congress]. Sponsored by the Fédération Archéologique et Historique de Belgique. Ed. by Gabriel van den GHEYN. *Annales de la Fédération Archéologique et Historique de Belgique* 23 (Gent: Siffer, 1914) 3 v. In French and German.

The following contributions are cited separately: Raymond Joseph Justin van AERDE, **Deux contrats de facteurs d'orgues belges inconnus jusqu'ici: XVIIe et XVIIIe siècles** [Two contracts of hitherto unknown Belgian organ builders: 17th and 18th centuries] (3333), **Les Tuerlinckx, facteurs d'instruments de musique à Malines, XVIIIe et XIXe siècles** [The Tuerlinckx family, makers of musical instruments in Mechelen, 18th and 19th centuries] (3609), and **Quelques documents inédits concernant la musique dans un village** [Some unpublished documents concerning music in a village] (1478); Amalie ARNHEIM, **Belgische Komponisten des 17. und 18. Jahrhunderts und ihre Beziehungen zu Deutschland** [Belgian composers of the 17th and 18th centuries and their relations with Germany] (1479); Paul BAYART, **Drogon de St. Winnoc et quelques autres composeurs d'offices liturgiques aux XIe et XIIe siècles** [Drogon of St. Winoc and some other composers of liturgical Offices in the 11th and 12th centuries] (1483); Louis KLEMANTASKI, **La musique flamande en Angleterre** [Flemish music in England] (977); Jacques-Gabriel PROD'HOMME, **Fétis, bibliothécaire du Conservatoire de Paris** [Fétis, librarian of the Paris Conservatoire] (2076) and **Lettres inédites de Le Sueur, Boieldieu et Cherubini au compositeur anversois Janssens** [Unpublished letters of Le Sueur, Boieldieu, and Cherubini to the Antwerp composer Janssens] (1840).

1914

90
bs
[Göttingen] Bericht über den VI. Kongress für Experimentelle Psychologie [Report on the Sixth Congress for Experimental Psychology]. Sponsored by the Gesellschaft für Experimentelle Psychologie. Ed. by Friedrich SCHUMANN (Leipzig: Barth, 1914) 351 p. In German.

The congress was held from 15 through 18 April 1914. The following contributions are cited separately: D. KATZ, **Über einige Versuche im Anschluss an die Tonwortmethode von Karl Eitz** [On some experiments following the solmization method of Carl Eitz] (5670); Géza RÉVÉSZ, **Neue Versuche über binaurale Tonmischung** [New research on binaural sound mixture] (5693) and **Über musikalische Begabung** [On musical talent] (5695); Carl STUMPF, **Über neuere Untersuchungen zur Tonlehre** [On new studies of musical acoustics] (5857).

1915

91
bs
[Washington, D.C.] Proceedings of the Nineteenth International Congress of Americanists. Ed. by Frederick Webb HODGE (Washington, D.C.: n.p., 1917) lvii, 649 p.; (reprint, Nendeln: Kraus, 1968). *Illus., bibliog., index, maps.* In English, French, German, and Spanish.

The congress was held from 27 through 31 December 1915. The following contributions are cited separately: Frances DENSMORE, **Recent developments in the study of Indian music** (3146); C. Alphonso SMITH, **Ballads surviving in the United States** (3177).

1919

92
bs
[Marseilles] Congrès français de la Syrie. III [French congress on Syria. III]. Sponsored by the Chambre de Commerce de Marseille. Ed. by Paul HUVELIN (Paris: Champion, 1919). *Illus., facs., maps.* In French.

The conference was held from 3 through 5 January 1919. It reported on economic, educational, medical, and cultural conditions as well as French interests in what are now Syria, Lebanon, and Israel. The following contribution is cited separately: Andre BITTAR, **La création d'un conservatoire de musique à Beyrouth** [The creation of a music conservatory in Beirut] (4864).

93
bs
[Tourcoing] La musique d'église: Compte rendu du Congrès de musique sacrée [Church music: Reports of the congress on religious music] (Tourcoing: Duvivier, 1920). *Music, charts, diagr.* In French.

The following contributions are cited separately: Winoc BARBRY, **Beauté musical et beauté liturgique** [Musical beauty and liturgical beauty] (6160); Louis BOYER, **La musique religieuse en Dordogne** [Religious music in Dordogne] (6178); Jules DELPORTE, **La restauration du chant unanime à l'Église: Question capitale** [The restoration of unison chant in the Church: Crucial question] (6202); A. DOUILLART, **La musique sacrée dans les institutions d'aveugles** [Sacred music in institutions for the blind] (2315); H. DUTOIT, **Tradition et progrès dans l'Église et dans l'art religieux** [Tradition and progress in the Church and in religious art] (6207); Amédée GASTOUÉ, **La musique polyphonique: Ses créateurs—L'école franco-belge au XVe siècle** [Polyphonic music: Its creators—The Franco-Belgian school in the 15th century] (1312); Louis GLORIEUX, **Excellence de la Messe solennelle** [Excellence of the solemn Mass] (6238) and **L'école pontificale de musique sacrée à Rome** [The Pontificio Istituto di Musica Sacra in Rome] (4877); J. de GUENYVEAU, **De la diction dans les écoles de chant** [On diction in chant schools] (4879); G. INRY, **L'état de la musique religieuse dans le diocèse de Rennes et spécialement à la Métropole** [The state of liturgical music in the diocese of Rennes and especially in the metropolitan area] (6258); H. JANSEN, **L'état de la musique d'église dans les Pays-Bas** [The state of church music in the Low Countries] (1992); Laurent JANSSENS, **Le chant officiel de l'Église** [The official chant of the Church] (6259); Joseph KREPS, **Le rôle unificateur de l'organiste liturgique** [The unifying role of the liturgical organist] (6275); Fernand de LA TOMBELLE, **Le répertoire moderne** [Modern repertoire] (6277); Auguste LE GUENNANT, **La crise du recrutement des chanteurs professionels d'Église** [The crisis of recruitment of professional singers of the Church] (6283); Léon MAHIEU, **La soumission à l'Église: Condition essentielle de la musique sacrée** [Submission to the Church: An essential condition of sacred music] (6292); MARTY, **Les journées grégoriennes de Lourdes** [The conference in Lourdes on Gregorian chant] (6301); François-Xavier MATHIAS, **La musique liturgique dans le cadre de l'enseignement supérieur** [Liturgical music in the framework of higher education] (4834); Clément MÉFRAY, **La formation vocale des garçons dans les écoles, catéchismes, patronages, maîtrises** [The vocal training of boys in schools, catechism class, youth clubs, and choir schools] (3314); André MOCQUEREAU, **Le rythme libre avant le chant grégorien: Un chapitre de son histoire** [Free rhythm before Gregorian chant: A chapter in its history] (4016); Jules van NUFFEL, **L'école interdiocésaine de Malines et la musique d'Église** [The Interdiocesaan Instituut voor Kerkmuziek in Mecheln and the music of the Catholic Church] (4836); Félix RAUGEL, **La cantique français** [The French canticle] (6351); Norbert ROUSSEAU, **Communication sur la notation nonantolienne** [Statement on Nonantolan notation] (3864); Gregori M. SUÑOL BAULINAS, **Association grégorianiste et cécilienne en Espagne** [Gregorian and Cecilian associations in Spain] (2396); Charles THELLIER DE PONCHEVILLE, **Le bienfait social de la liturgie** [The social benefit of the liturgy] (6398); Charles VANDEWALLE, **Organisation pratique des scholae grégoriennes** [Practical organization of the chant scholae] (4899).

1921

94
bs
[Paris] Actes du Congrès d'histoire de l'art [Proceedings of the Congress of Art History]. Sponsored by the Société de l'Histoire de l'Art Français. Pref. by André Paul Charles MICHEL (Paris: Presses Universitaires de France, 1923-1924) 4 v.; (reprint, Nendeln: Kraus, 1979). ISBN 3-262-01319-6. *Illus.,*

facs., music, bibliog., list of works, charts, diagr. In French, English, Italian, and Spanish.

The following contributions are cited separately: Eduard BERNOULLI, **Sur la notation de rythmes complexes dans deux imprimés du XVIe siècle** [On the notation of complex rhythms in two 16th-century books] (3805); Carlo Felice BOGHEN, **Bernardo Pasquini** (1491); L. BONELLI, **Les joueurs de flûte avignonnais au service de la République de Sienne au XVe siècle** [Avignon flutists in the service of the Republic of Siena during the 15th century] (1246); Gino BORGHEZIO, **Poésies latines et françaises mises en musique conservées dans un manuscrit inconnu de la Bibliothèque capitulaire d'Ivrée** [Latin and French poems set to music in an unknown manuscript in the Biblioteca Capitolare in Ivrea] (1247); Charles van den BORREN, **Deux recueils peu connus d'Orlande de Lassus** [Two little-known collections by Roland de Lassus] (1249); Luís de Freitas BRANCO, **Les contrepointistes de l'école d'Évora** [The Évora school of contrapuntists] (4143); Paul BRUNHOLD, **Un livre pièces de clavecin J.-F. d'Andrieu** [A book of harpsichord pieces by J.-F. Dandrieu] (1498); Guido CHIGI SARACINI, **Un musicien siennois du XVIIIe siècle: Azzolino Bernardino Della Ciaia, prêtre et chevalier de Saint-Étienne** [A Sienese musician of the 18th century: Azzolino Bernardino Della Ciaja, priest and knight of S. Stefano] (1506); John Alexander FULLER-MAITLAND, **Les influences réciproques internationales en musique** [International reciprocal influences in music] (2510); Amédée GASTOUÉ, **L'*Alarme* de Grimache (vers 1380-1390) et les chansons polyphoniques du Moyen Âge** [Grimace's *À l'arme* (around 1380-1390) and the polyphonic songs of the Middle Ages] (1100); Alberto GENTILI, **L'histoire de la théorie dans l'enseignement de la musique** [The history of theory in the teaching of music] (4540); Edward Burlingame HILL, **La musique aux États-Unis** [Music in the United States] (4345); René JOSZ and Ernest ROCHELLE, **Essai d'une théorie de l'évolution de l'art musical, conforme aux conceptions scientifiques modernes de l'évolution** [Essay on a theory of the evolution of the musical art according to modern scientific conceptions on evolution] (5503); Heikki KLEMETTI, **Aperçu de l'histoire musicale finlandaise** [Outline of Finnish musical history] (978); LOGOTHETI, **La contribution française à l'étude de la chanson populaire grecque** [The French contribution to the study of the Greek traditional song] (2934); Karl NEF, **L'influence de la musique française sur le développement de la suite** [The influence of French music on the development of the suite] (4274); Felipe PEDRELL, **Les échanges musicaux entre la France et la Catalogne au Moyen Âge: Le français Joan Brudieu, musicien catalan** [The musical exchanges between France and Catalonia during the Middle Ages: The Frenchman Joan Brudieu, Catalan musician] (1396); Marc PINCHERLE, **Autour d'une histoire de la harpe** [About a history of the harp] (3596); Henry PRUNIÈRES, **Un opéra de Paolo Lorenzani** [An opera by Paolo Lorenzani] (1648); Félix RAUGEL, **Josquin des Prés à la Collégiate de Saint-Quentin** [Josquin Desprez at the Saint-Quentin collegiate church] (1417) and **Le Chant de la Sibylle d'après un manuscrit du XIIe siècle, conservé aux Archives de l'Hérault** [The Chant of the Sybil after a 12th-century manuscript preserved at the archives of the Herault] (1165); Willian Barclay SQUIRE, **L'iconographie musical** [Musical iconography] (5398); André TESSIER, **Un document sur les répétitions du *Triomphe de l'Amour* à Saint-Germain-en-Laye (1681)** [A document about the rehearsals of *Le triomphe de l'Amour* at Saint Germain-en-Laye (1681)] (1699); Luigi TORRI, **La seule composition musicale connue de Jean d'Arras** [The only known musical composition by Jean d'Arras] (1203). The conference is also cited as no. 95 in this volume.

95 **[Paris] Actes du Congrès d'histoire de l'art: Compte rendu analytique** [Proceedings of the Congress of Art History: Analytic report]. Sponsored by the Société de l'Histoire de l'Art Français (Paris: Presses Universitaires de France, 1922) 239 p. In French.

The following contributions are cited separately: Giulio BAS, **Une composition d'Ockeghem conservée dans un manuscrit du Mont-Cassin** [A composition by Ockeghem preserved in a Monte Cassino manuscript] (1228); André COEUROY, **Gérard de Nerval et la diffusion du sentiment musical en France** [Gérard de Nerval and the diffusion of musical sentiment in France] (1937); Sem DRESDEN, **L'influence de la musique moderne française aux Pays-Bas** [The influence of modern French music in the Low Countries] (2157); Henry EXPERT, **Les imprimés d'Attaingnant conservés à la Bibliothèque Mazarine** [Attaingnant prints in the collections of the Bibliothèque Mazarine] (717); Wanda LANDOWSKA, **Bach et les clavecinistes français** [Bach and the French

harpsichordists] (1597); Paul-Marie MASSON, **La vie musicale en France, de 1695 à 1730, d'après les recueils périodiques de Ballard** [Musical life in France from 1695 to 1730, on the basis of Ballard's periodically issued collections] (1619); André PIRRO, **La musique sur les galères du roi** [Music on the royal galleys] (5903).

96 **[Strasbourg] Compte rendu du Congrès général de musique sacrée: Aperçu général des préliminaires et du congrès, discours et conférences** [Proceedings of the General Congress of Sacred Music: Overview of the preliminaries and of the congress, talks, and papers] (Strasbourg: Alsacien, 1922) xlviii, 310 p. *Music*. In French.

The conference was held from 26 through 31 July 1921. The following contributions are cited separately: Paul BAYART, **Les fins de la musique sacrée** [The goals of sacred music] (6163); Louis BOYER, **La musique moderne à l'église** [Modern music in church] (6177); F. BRUN, **Charles Bordes et son école** [Charles Bordes and his following] (1924); Emile CLAUSS, **L'Union Sainte-Cécile de Strasbourg** [The Union Sainte-Cécile of Strasbourg] (1936); E. COLLARD, **La musique palestrinienne** [The music of Palestrina] (6189); D.L. DAVID, **L'art dans la psalmodie** [Art in psalmody] (6197); Jules DELPORTE, **Le cantique populaire d'après les principes du *Motu proprio* et d'après la tradition** [The popular canticle according to the principles of the motu proprio and of the tradition] (6200); Amédée GASTOUÉ, **Essai sur le passé et l'avenir de la polyphonie sacrée** [Essay on the past and the future of sacred polyphony] (6225) and **Quelques aspects variés de la question grégorienne** [Various aspects of the Gregorian question] (6228); Lucie GASTOUÉ, **La formation pratique de la voix** [Practical formation of the voice] (3301); GLÉYO (church musician), **L'éducation de l'oreille** [Ear training] (4697); Clément MÉFRAY, **Fondation et organisation d'une maîtrise** [The foundation and organization of choir schools] (4598) and **La culture vocale** [Vocal training] (4597); Henri MULET, **Étude sur le rôle des mutations et la composition rationnelle du plein-jeu dans un grand-orgue** [The role of mutation stops and the rational composition of the full pleno in the grand organ] (3439) and **Les tendances néfastes et antireligieuses de l'orgue moderne** [Harmful and antireligious tendencies in the modern organ] (3440); Jean PARISOT, **De l'harmonisation du chant grégorien** [On the harmonization of Gregorian chant] (6332) and **La chant grégorien et les mélodies de la synagogue** [Gregorian chant and synagogue melodies] (6022); D. PIRIO, **Le chant d'église dans nos patronages de jeunes gens** [Religious song in our youth clubs] (2373); O.S.B. PRIEUR, **École d'orgue et de musique religieuse** [Organ and religious music education] (4625); RUFFIN, **Communication sur le Comité Charles Bordes** [Communication on the Charles Bordes committee] (2384); Antoine de SÉRENT, **Rapport sur l'enseignement du Latin liturgique** [Report on teaching liturgical Latin] (4645); Jean de VALOIS, **De la notation mouvement dans le chant grégorien** [The concept of tempo in Gregorian chant] (3718).

97 **[Turin] La vita musicale dell'Italia d'oggi** [Musical life in Italy today]. Proceedings of the first Congresso Italiano di Musica; sponsored by the *Rivista musicale italiana*, *Santa Cecilia*, and *Il pianoforte* (Torino: Fratelli Bocca, 1921). *Illus., charts, diagr., organ specification.* In Italian.

The following contributions are cited separately: Domenico ALALEONA, **Educazione musicale del popolo e sua organizzazione nella scuola e nella vita cittadina** [General musical education and its organization in schools and in city life] (4481); Giulio BAS, **Iniziazione musicale degli esecutori: Precedenza di un'adeguata preparazione artistica a qualsiasi studio tecnico** [The musical initiation of performers: The precedence of an adequate artistic preparation over technical studies] (4863); Attilio BRUGNOLI, **Proposta di riforma nell'indirizzo pedagogico e nell'ordinamento degli istituti musicali in Italia** [A proposal for reforming the pedagogical objectives and the regulations of musical institutions in Italy] (4498); Gaetano CESARI, **Critica musicale** [Music criticism] (2300); Edgardo CORIO, **Organizzazioni economiche fra musicisti e loro rapporti** [Economic organizations among musicians and their reports] (2308); Vincenzo DI DONATO, **L'industria della liuteria in Italia** [The string instrument industry in Italy] (3562); Giulio FARA, **Il folklore** [Folklore] (2809); Vito FEDELI, **La cultura musicale in Italia** [The musical culture in Italy] (4815) and **Musica da chiesa** [Church music] (2319); Luigi Ernesto FERRARIA, **L'educazione del senso ritmico col metodo

Jaques-Dalcroze: Ginnastica ritmica [Education of the rhythmic sense with the Dalcroze method—Rhythmic gymnastics] (4527); Alberto GASCO, **I diritti d'autore** [Copyrights] (5961), **Il teatro lirico in Italia** [Opera houses in Italy] (5155), and **La scenografia** [Scenography] (5154); Luigi PERRACHIO, **L'industria dei pianoforti in Italia** [The piano industry in Italy] (3538); Ildebrando PIZZETTI, **Gli istituti musicali italiani** [Italian musical institutions] (4621); Giulio SILVA, **L'arte del canto** [The art of song] (2391); Dino SINCERO, **L'arte e l'industria organaria** [The art and industry of the organ] (3480); Francesco VATIELLI, **L'edizione: Musica e letteratura musicale** [Publishing: Music and musical literature] (5996). Each article is followed by a panel discussion or a vote on resolutions presented or both.

1922

98
bs

[Metz] Congrès régional de liturgie et de musique sacrée [Regional conference on liturgy and sacred music]. Sponsored by the Association Française Sainte-Cécile (Moselle: Orphelins-Apprentis Guénange, 1923) 227 p. In French.

The following contributions are cited separately: Michael BARGILLIAT, **Du chant grégorien et de la musique religieuse dans les collèges et les séminaires** [Concerning Gregorian chant and religious music in colleges and seminaries] (4806); E. COLLARD, **Le cantique populaire** [The popular canticle] (6188); EVRARD (canon), **Rapport de M. le Chanoine Evrard** [Report by the canon Evrard] (6212); Amédée GASTOUÉ, **La musique religieuse française contemporaine** [Contemporary French religious music] (2166); Clement MÉFRAY and O.S.B. PRIEUR, **Conférence** [Presentation] (4739); Jean PARISOT, **L'accompagnement du chant grégorien** [Accompanying Gregorian Chant] (6331); S. SCHIES, **La question professionnelle des organistes** [The professional question of organists] (3473); **Séances d'études dans l'après-midi du Mardi 6 juin** [Study session on the afternoon of Tuesday, 6 June] (6151); Charles VANDEWALLE, **La schola paroissiale et le chant collectif** [The parish schola and congregational singing] (6402); François-Anatole WEYLAND, **Rapport de M. l'abbé Weyland** [Report by abbé Weyland] (6415).

99
bs

[Rio de Janeiro] Annaes do XX congresso internacional de americanistas [Annals of the 20th International Congress of Americanists]. Ed. by Léon Francisco R. CLÉROT and Paulo José Pires BRANDÃO (Rio de Janeiro: Imprensa Nacional, 1924) cix, 314 p.; (reprint, Nendeln: Kraus, 1968) 3 v. *Illus., facs., maps.* In Portuguese, English, French, German, and Spanish.

The congress was held from 20 through 30 August 1922. The following contribution is cited separately: Frances DENSMORE, **Rhythm in the music of the American Indian** (3985).

1923

100
bs

[Brussels] Compte rendu du Ve Congrès international des sciences historiques [Proceedings of the Fifth International Congress of Historical Sciences]. Ed. by Guillaume DES MAREZ and François Louis GANSHOF (Bruxelles: Weissenbruch, 1923) 552 p.; (reprint, Nendeln: Kraus, 1972). *Illus.* In French.

The conference was held from 8 through 15 April 1923. The following contributions are cited separately: Charles van den BORREN, **Quelques manuscripts de Gossec** [Autograph manuscripts of Gossec] (1730); Ernest CLOSSON, **Les instruments de musique disparus** [Vanished musical instruments] (3247); Arthur Jacob Hendrik CORNETTE, **Liszt: Le romantique** [Liszt: The romantic] (1939); Joseph KREPS, **Le développement des neumes** [The development of neumes] (3837); Lionel de LA LAURENCIE, **Les femmes et le luth en France aux XVIe et XVIIe siècle** [Women and the lute in France in the 16th and 17th centuries] (3586); Antonio TIRABASSI, **Notation mensurelle** [Mensural notation] (3878).

101
bs

[Leipzig] Bericht über den VIII. Kongress für experimentelle Psychologie [Report on the Eighth Congress for Experimental Psychology]. Sponsored by the Gesellschaft für Experimentelle Psychologie. Ed. by Karl BÜHLER (Jena: Fischer, 1924) 216 p. In German.

The conference was held from 18 through 21 April 1923. The following contribution is cited separately: A. JUHÁSZ, **Wiedererkennungsversuche auf musikalischem Gebiete** [Recognition experiments in music] (5669).

1924

102
bs

[Basel] Bericht über den musikwissenschaftlichen Kongreß in Basel [Report of the musicological congress in Basel]. Sponsored by the Neue Schweizerische Musikgesellschaft, Ortsgruppe Basel (Leipzig: Breitkopf & Härtel, 1925) vii, 399 p. *Facs., music, charts, diagr.* In German, French, Spanish, and Italian.

The conference, held from 26 through 29 September 1924, was convened in celebration of the 25th anniversary of the Neue Schweizerische Musikgesellschaft in Basel. The following contributions are cited separately: Hermann ABERT, **Grundprobleme der Operngeschichte** [Basic issues in opera history] (5093); Guido ADLER, **Internationalismus in der Tonkunst** [Internationalism in music] (937); Wilhelm ALTMANN, **Die Schaffung einer internationalen Bibliographie der Musikliteratur** [The creation of an international bibliography of music literature] (515); Higini ANGLÈS, **Cantors und Ministrers in den Diensten der Könige von Katalonien-Aragonien im 14. Jahrhundert** [Singers and minstrels in the service of the kings of Catalonia and Aragón in the 14th century] (1054); Gustav BECKING, **Zur Typologie des musikalischen Schaffens** [On the typology of musical works] (5428); Eduard BERNOULLI, **Dokumente zur Geschichte des Liedes und Tanzes aus dem 16. und 17. Jahrhundert** [Documents from the history of song and dance of the 16th and 17th centuries] (1234); Paul BOEPPLE, **Theoretisches und Praktisches zur Rythmik der neuesten Musik** [The theory and practice of rhythm in the newest music] (3971); Charles van den BORREN, **La musique pittoresque dans le manuscrit 222 C 22 de la Bibliothèque de Strasbourg (XVe siècle)** [The descriptive music in the manuscript 222 C 22 of the Bibliothèque de Strasbourg (15th century)] (1254); Gian BUNDI, **Ein musikhistorisches Kuriosum aus dem Oberengadin** [A historic musical curiosity from the Oberengadin] (1499); Antoine-Élisée CHERBULIEZ, **Über die Anwendung der Sieversschen Theorien auf die musikalische Interpretation** [The application of Sievers's theories to musical interpretation] (3935); Alexandre DENÉRÉAZ, **L'harmonie moderne et les phénomènes d'ordre "complémentaire"** [Modern harmony and the phenomena of the so-called complementary type] (5652); Hermann ERPF, **Einige Begriffe zur Harmonik der neueren Musik** [Some ideas about the harmony of new music] (4164); Wilhelm FISCHER, **Zur Chronologie der Klaviersuiten J.S. Bachs** [On the chronology of J.S. Bach's keyboard suites] (1551); Max FRIEDLAENDER, **Eigenleben von Volksliedmelodien** [The individual lives of folk-song melodies] (4428); Henri GAGNEBIN, **Divers courants qui se sont manifestes dans la musique suisse romande pendant les cinquante dernières années.** [Various currents in the music of French-speaking Switzerland during the last 50 years] (1961); Wolfgang GRAESER, **Joh. Seb. Bachs Kunst der Fuge** [Johann Sebastian Bach's *Die Kunst der Fuge*] (1563); Wilibald GURLITT, **Burgundische Chanson- und deutsche Liedkunst des 15. Jahrhunderts** [Burgundian chanson and the German art song during the 15th century] (4253); Fritz GYSI, **Über Zusammenhänge zwischen Ton und Farbe** [On the relationship between pitch and color] (5664); Toivo Elias HAAPANEN, **Denkmäler des gregorianischen Gesanges in Finnland** [Monuments of Gregorian chant in Finland] (6245); Jacques HANDSCHIN, **Über den Ursprung der Motette** [On the origin of the motet] (4255); Alfred Valentin HEUSS, **Das Orchestercrescendo bei Beethoven** [The orchestral crescendo in Beethoven] (4344); Erich Moritz von HORNBOSTEL, **Die Entstehung des Jodelns** [The rise of yodeling] (3306); Knud JEPPESEN, **Das *Sprunggesetz* des Palestrinastils bei betonten Viertelnoten (halben Taktzeiten): Eine vorläufige Mitteilung** [The *law of leaps* in the Palestrina style with respect to accented quarter-notes (in half-measures): A preliminary report] (4349); Ilmari KROHN, **Die Kirchentonarten** [The church modes] (4086); Theodor KROYER,

Die threnodische Bedeutung der Quart in der Mensuralmusik [The threnodic meaning of the fourth in mensural music] (4187); Hans MERSMANN, Beethovens Skizzen vom Standpunkt phänomenologischer Musikbetrachtung [Beethoven's sketches in the light of a phenomenological view of music] (1812); Hans Joachim MOSER, Musikalische Probleme des deutschen Minnesangs [Musical problems of the German Minnesang] (5337); Joseph MÜLLER-BLATTAU, Beethoven und die Variation [Beethoven and the variation] (4271) and Zum Verhältnis von Wort und Ton im 17. Jahrhundert [On the relationship between word and music in the 17th century] (1630); Karl NEF, Seb. Virdungs *Musica getutscht* [Sebastian Virdung's *Musica getutscht*] (5386); Friedrich NOACK, Die Tabulaturen der hessischen Landesbibliothek zu Darmstadt [The tablatures in the Hessische Landesbibliothek in Darmstadt] (3857); Yvonne RIHOUËT, Un motet de Moulu et ses diverses transcriptions pour orgue [A motet by Moulu and its various transcriptions for organ] (1420); Vicente RIPOLLÉS PÉREZ, Breves anotaciones a la Epístola Farçida de San Esteban [Brief annotations to the Epístola farçida of San Esteban] (1169); Curt SACHS, Die Musik im Rahmen der Schwesterkunste [Music in the milieu of the sister arts] (5395); Arnold SCHERING, Das Probleme einer Philosophie der Musikgeschichte [The problem of a philosophy of music history] (5583); Max SEIFFERT, Grundaufgaben der Musikwissenschaft und das Bückeburger Forschungsinstitut [Fundamental tasks of musicology and the Bückeburg Forschungsinstitut] (682); Robert SONDHEIMER, Sinfonien aus dem 18. Jahrhundert in den Basler Sammlungen Lucas Sarasin und Collegium Musicum [Eighteenth-century symphonies in the Lucas Sarasin and Collegium Musicum collections in Basel] (761); Hermann SPRINGER, Beziehungen zwischen Oper und Volksmusik im Settecento [Relationships between opera and traditional music in the 17th century] (1691); Antonio TIRABASSI, Histoire de l'harmonisation à partir de 1600 á 1750 [History of harmonization from 1600 to 1750] (3774); Ernst TOCH, Melodielehre [Melodic theory] (4467); Fausto TORREFRANCA, Influenza di alcuni musicisti Italiani vissuti a Londra su W.A. Mozart (1764-65) [Influence of some Italian musicians in London on W.A. Mozart (1764-65)] (1881); Max UNGER, Beethovens Handschrift [Beethoven's handwriting] (1884); Otto URSPRUNG, Der vokale Grundcharakter des diskantbetonten figurierten Stils [The basic vocal character of the figurative, discant-emphasized style] (4388); Theodor Wilhelm WERNER, Anmerkungen zur Motettenkunst Josquins [Notes concerning Josquin's motet compositions] (1466); Johannes WOLF, Altflämische Lieder 14.-15. Jahrhunderts und ihre rhythmische Lesung [Old Flemish songs of the 14th-15th centuries and their rhythmic interpretation] (1471). Another publication of the conference is cited as no. 103 in this volume.

103
bs

[Basel] Festschrift zum musikwissenschaftlichen Kongreß in Basel [Festschrift for the Basel musicological conference]. Sponsored by the Neue Schweizerische Musikgesellschaft, Ortsgruppe Basel, *Schweizer Jahrbuch für Musikwissenschaft/Annales suisses de musicologie/Annuario svizzero di musicologia* I (1924) 156 p. *Illus., port., music.* In German.

The conference, held from 26 through 29 September 1924, was convened in celebration of the 25th anniversary of the Neue Schweizerische Musikgesellschaft in Basel. The following contributions are cited separately: Eduard BERNOULLI, Der Archäologe Bianchini über Musikinstrumente in alten Volks- und Kultgebräuchen [The archaeologist Bianchini on music instruments in early folk and religious customs] (5740); Antoine-Élisée CHERBULIEZ, Zum Problem der religiösen Musik [The problem of religious music] (6004); Fritz GYSI, Alpine Darstellungen in der Musik [Alpine representations in music] (967); Jacques HANDSCHIN, Eine wenig beachtete Stilrichtung innerhalb der mittelalterlichen Mehrstimmigkeit [A little-noted stylistic tendency within medieval polyphony] (4341); Wilhelm MERIAN, Gregor Meyer (1381); Karl NEF, Kleine Beiträge zur Mozartforschung [Brief reports on Mozart research] (1824); Edgar REFARDT, Die Basler Choral-Inkunabeln [The Basel incunabula with choral notation] (749); Peter WAGNER, Das *Media vita* [The *Media vita*] (1206). Another publication of the conference is cited as no. 102 in this volume.

104
rs

Review by Adolf ABER, *Die Musikwelt* 4 (1924). In German.

105
rs

Review by Maurice CAUCHIE, *Revue de musicologie* 4 (1925) 174–76. In French.

106
rs

Review by Alfred EINSTEIN, *Zeitschrift für Musikwissenschaft* 4 (1924-1925) 107–10. In German.

107
rs

Review by Wilhelm HEINITZ, *Deutsche Tonkünstlerzeitung* 4 (1924) 390. In German.

108
rs

Review by A. HEUSS, *Zeitschrift für Musikwissenschaft* 4 (1924). In German.

109
rs

Review by Wilhelm MERIAN, *Schweizerische musikpädagogische Blätter* 4 (1925). In German.

110
rs

Review by MEYER, *Neue Musikzeitung* 4 (1925). In German.

111
rs

Review by Robert SONDHEIMER, *Rivista musicale italiana* 4 (1925) 652. In Italian.

112
rs

Review by Fausto TORREFRANCA, *Rivista musicale italiana* 4 (1925) 635–36. In Italian.

113
rs

Review by Max UNGER, *Der Auftakt* 4 (1924). In German.

114
bs

[Berlin] Zweiter Kongress für Ästhetik und allgemeine Kunstwissenschaft: Bericht [Second Congress for Aesthetics and General Studies of the Arts: Report]. Sponsored by the Gesellschaft für Ästhetik und Allgemeine Kunstwissenschaft. Ed. by Paul DESSOIR, *Zeitschrift für Ästhetik und allgemeine Kunstwissenschaft* XIX (1925) vi, 458 p. *Illus., music, index, charts, diagr., transcr., dance notation.* In German.

The congress was held from 16 through 18 October 1924. The following contributions are cited separately: Hermann ABERT, Geistlich und Weltlich in der Musik [The sacred and the secular in music] (5421); Heinrich JACOBY, Voraussetzungen und Grundlagen einer lebendigen Musikkultur [Prerequisites and foundations for a living musical culture] (5496); Rudolf von LABAN, Der Tanz als Eigenkunst [Dance as an art in its own right] (5013); Hans MERSMANN, Zur Phänomenologie der Musik [The phenomenology of music] (5541); Hans Joachim MOSER, Die Stilverwandtschaft zwischen der Musik und den anderen Künsten [Style relationships between music and the other arts] (4920); Georg SCHÜNEMANN, Beziehungen neuer Musik zu exotischer und frühmittelalterlicher Tonkunst [The relationships of new music to exotic and early medieval music] (2247); Alfred VIERKANDT, Prinzipienfragen der ethnologischen Kunstforschung [Fundamental questions of ethnologically oriented research on art] (855).

115
bs

[Bucharest] Compte rendu du premier Congrès international des études byzantines [Proceedings of the First International Congress of Byzantine Studies]. Ed. by Constantin MARINESCU. *Bulletin de la Section Historique* XI (1925) 96 p. (reprint, Nendeln: Kraus, 1978). *Illus., charts, diagr.* In French, German, and Italian.

The conference was held from 14 through 26 August 1924. The following contribution is cited separately: V.I. DRĂGHICEANU, Les coutumes d'enterrement des princes roumains [Burial customs of Romanian princes] (2796).

116
rs

Review by L. BRÉHIER, *Byzantion* 4 (1924) 734–44. In French.

117
rs

Review by A. BUSUISCEANU, *Bulletin of the International Committee of Historical Sciences* 4 (1926) 84–90. In French.

118
bs

[Göteborg] Congrès international des américanistes: Compte rendu de la XXIᵉ session, deuxième partie [International Congress of Americanists: Twenty-first meeting, second part] (Göteborg: Museum, 1925) 706 p.; (reprint, Nendeln: Kraus, 1968). *Illus., bibliog., maps.* In French, English, German, and Spanish.

Following the first meeting of the 21st congress in The Hague, the second meeting was held from 20 through 26 August 1924. The following contribution is cited separately: William THALBITZER, **Cultic games and festivals in Greenland** (3179).

1925

119
bs

[Bruges] Congrès jubilaire [Jubilee congress]. Proceedings of the 26th congress of the Fédération Archéologique et Historique de Belgique; sponsored by the Ministère des Sciences et des Arts, Ministère des Affaires Étrangères, and city of Bruges (Brugge: Gruuthuuse, 1925) 282 p. In French, English, and Italian.

The congress was held from 3 through 5 August 1925. The following contributions are cited separately: Paul BERGMANS, **L'imprimeur Gérard de Lisa, chantre maître de chapelle à Trevise (1463-1496)** [The printer Gerard de Lisa, cantor choirmaster at Treviso] (5946); Gino BORGHEZIO, **Un codice vaticano trecentesio di rime musicale** [A 14th-century Vatican codex of musical rhymes] (1066); Charles van den BORREN, **L'histoire de la musique dans l'enseignement universitaire** [The history of music in university teaching] (4809) and **Sur Benedictus de Opitiis et deux de ses œuvres recemment publiées en fac simile** [On Benedictus de Opitiis and two of his works recently published in facsimile] (1255); Alexandre DENÉRÉAZ, **De la musique à l'"Harmonie des spheres"** [From music to the "harmony of the spheres"] (5809); Georges van DOORSLAER, **Severin Cornet: Compositeur-maître de chapelle 1530-1582** [Séverin Cornet: Composer-choirmaster, 1530-1582] (1291); Rombaut van DOREN, **Le rôle joué par l'Abbay de Saint-Gall dans la diffusion du chant romain** [The role played by the abbey of St. Gallen in the diffusion of Roman chant] (6203); William Henry Grattan FLOOD, **Belgium's musical debt to Ireland** (2818); Joseph KREPS, **Aux sources de notre écriture musicale européenne: XXᵉ siècle (projections lumineuses)** [On the sources of our European musical writing: 20th century (slide projections)] (3836); Dragan PLAMENAC, **La chanson de L'homme armé et MS. VI.E.40 de la Bibliotèque Nationale de Naples** [The song *L'homme armé* and MS VI.E.40 of the Biblioteca Nazionale di Napoli] (1405); Robert PUGH, **Les Silbermann: Leur œuvre dans la région alsacienne (projections lumineuses)** [The Silbermanns: Their work in the Alsace region (slides)] (3449).

120
bs

[Leipzig] Bericht über den I. musikwissenschaftlichen Kongress der Deutschen Musikgesellschaft in Leipzig [Report on the First Musicological Conference of the Deutsche Musikgesellschaft in Leipzig] (Wiesbaden: Breitkopf & Härtel, 1926) 470 p. *Illus., facs., music, charts, diagr.* In German.

The conference was held from 4 through 8 June 1925. The following contributions are cited separately: Adolf ABER, **Das Problem der Stilbühne bei den Werken Richard Wagners** [*Stilbühne* and staging the works of Richard Wagner] (5091); Guido ADLER, **Das obligate Akkompagnement der Wiener Klassischen Schule** [Obbligato accompaniment in the Viennese Classic school] (1720); Wilhelm ALTMANN, **Die geschichtliche Entwicklung der Katalogisierung musikalischer Handschriften** [The historical development of the cataloguing of musical manuscripts] (514); Higini ANGLÈS, **Orgelmusik der Schola Hispanica vom XV. bis XVII. Jahrhundert** [Organ music of the Spanish school from the 15th to the 17th centuries] (3334); Adolphe APPIA, **Das Problem der Stilbühne den Werken Richard Wagners: Mitreferat** [*Stilbühne* and staging the works of Richard Wagner: A report] (5096); Willibrord BALLMANN, **Vom Wesen der liturgischen Musik** [On the nature of liturgical music] (6158); Karl BALTHASAR, **Kirchenmusik und neuere evangelische Liturgik** [Church music and the new Lutheran liturgy] (6424); Gustav BECKING, **Klassik und Romantik** [Classic and Romantic] (4312); Frank BENNEDIK, **Tonwort und Musikerziehung** [Solfège and music education] (4494); Hans Dagobert BRUGER, **Probleme der deutschen Lautenmusik des XVIII Jahrhunderts** [Topics in German lute music of the 18th century] (3553); Ernst BÜCKEN, **Zur Frage der Begrenzung und Benennung der Stilwandlung im 18. Jahrhundert** [Delimiting and naming the change in style of the 18th century] (1733); Werner DANCKERT, **Personale Typen des Melodiestils** [Personal types of melodic style] (4424); Hans DEINHARDT, **Übersetzungsfragen im besonderen Hinblick auf die Oper Mozarts** [Questions of translation, with a special view to the operas of Mozart] (5135); Arnold EBEL, **Einrichtung und Aufgaben der musikpädagogischen Organisation** [Organization and responsibilities of the music pedagogy association]

(4522); Paul EICKHOFF, **Die Bedeutung des Viertakters als herrschenden Prinzips in der griechisch-römischen Metrik und Rythmik** [The significance of four-four time as a governing principle in Greco-Roman meter and rhythm] (5310) and **Nach welchem Rhythmus müssen die Melodien der deutschen evangelischen Kirchenlieder gesungen werden?** [To which rhythms must the melodies of the German Protestant hymns be sung?] (5311); Peter EPSTEIN, **J.A. Herbsts geistliche Kompositionen** [J.A. Herbst's sacred compositions] (1542); Wilhelm FISCHER, **Zur Geschichte des Fugenthemas** [On the history of fugue subjects] (4427); Gotthold FROTSCHER, **Bachs Themenbildung unter dem Einfluß der Affektenlehre** [Bach's thematic construction under the influence of the affections doctrine] (4429) and **Ein Danziger Orgelbuch des 18. Jahrhunderts** [A Gdańsk organ book of the 18th century] (1554); Wilibald GURLITT, **Über Prinzipien und zur Geschichte der Registrierkunst in der alten Orgelmusik** [On the principles and history of registration in early organ music] (3382); Hermann GÜTTLER, **Die Monumentaloratorien des Königsberger Kantors Georg Riedel (1676-1738)** [The monumental oratorios of the Königsberg cantor Georg Riedel (1676-1738)] (1569); Fritz GYSI, **Mozart als Kritiker** [Mozart as critic] (1771); Robert HAAS, **Zur Bibliographie der Operntexte** [On the bibliography of opera librettos] (586); Alois HÁBA, **Welche Aufgaben bietet die Vierteltonmusik der Musikwissenschaft?** [What are the tasks quarter-tone music offers musicology?] (4080); Jacques HANDSCHIN, **Notizen über die Notre Dame Conductus** [Notes concerning Notre Dame conductus] (1114); Karl HASSE, **Palestrina, Schütz, Bach und Beethoven im Lichte der Stilwandlungen** [Palestrina, Schütz, Bach, and Beethoven in light of style transformations] (4343); Wilhelm HEINITZ, **Asymmetrien in Gebrauchstonleitern** [Asymmetries in functional scales] (4081); Alfred Valentin HEUSS, **Die genetische Methode, gezeigt an Lied und Arie** [The genetic method, demonstrated in song and aria] (4257); Hans Henny JAHNN, **Entstehung und Bedeutung der Kurvenmensur für die Labialstimmen der Orgel** [Origin and importance of non-linear scaling for the labial pipes of the organ] (3392); Knud JEPPESON, **Johann Joseph Fux und die moderne Kontrapunkttheorie** [Johann Joseph Fux and modern contrapuntal theory] (4183); Fritz JÖDE, **Wege zur Polyphonie in der Erziehung** [The role of polyphony in education] (4562); Lotte KALLENBACH-GRELLER, **Die Klangwerte der modernen Musik** [The sound values of modern music] (5504); Hermann KELLER, **Der Artikulationsstil der Bachschen Instrumentalwerke** [Articulation style in Bach's instrumental works] (3747); Gerhard von KEUSSLER, **Sinnestäuschungen und Musikästhetik** [Illusions and music aesthetics] (5506); Georg KINSKY, **Stand und Aufgaben der neueren Instrumentenkunde: Ein Bibliographischer Überblick** [The current state and the tasks of modern organology: A bibliographic survey] (817); Wilhelm KLATTE, **Stimmführung im homophonen Satz und Stufentheorie** [Voice-leading in homophonic music and harmonic theory] (4185); Ilmari KROHN, **Methode für Ausbildung zur Melodik** [Method for training in melodies] (4442); Josef KROMOLICKI, **Zum Stil des neuen Kirchenmusikalischen Schaffens** [On the style of new works of sacred music] (2195); Theodor KROYER, **Das Orgelbuch Cod.ms.153 der Münchener Universitäts-Bibliothek** [The organbook Cod.ms.153 of the Universitätsbibliothek, Munich] (1362); Eigel KRUTTGE, **Zur Musikgeschichte Westfalens** [On the music history of Westphalia] (818); Walter KÜHN, **Grundlinien zu einer Theorie der musikalischen Erziehung** [Fundamentals for a theory of music education] (4577); Wilhelm KURTHEN, **Liszt und Bruckner als Messenkomponisten** [Liszt and Bruckner as Mass composers] (2019) and **Zur Renaissancebewegung des 19. Jahrhunderts im Rheinlande** [On the Renaissance movement of the 19th century in the Rhineland] (2020); Robert LACHMANN, **Musik and Tonschrift des Nō** [Music and notation of noh] (2653); Franz LANDÉ, **Die Dissonanz als harmonisch-melodisches Mischgebilde** [Dissonance as a mixed harmonic-melodic structure] (4361); Josef LECHTHALER, **Die melodische Nachzeichnungstechnik in den kirchlichen Werken Alexander Uttendals** [The melodic imitation technique in the religious works of Alexander Utendal] (4361); Friedrich LUDWIG, **Die mehrstimmige Messe des 14. Jahrhunderts** [The polyphonic Mass in the 14th century] (1145); Hans MERSMANN, **Die Bedeutung der Substanzgemeinschaft für die Analyse von Instrumentalmusik: Ein Beitrag zur Methodik der Analyse** [The significance of shared substance for the analysis of instrumental music: A contribution to the analytic method] (4447) and **Die Lage der abendländischen Musik um 1900** [The situation of Western music around 1900] (2039); Kathi MEYER, **Zur musikalischen Wissenschaftslehre** [Music and scientific knowledge] (4601); Paul MIES, **Werdegang und Eigenschaften der Definition in der musikalischen Stilkunde** [The development and aspects of definition in the theory of musical style] (4373); Paul MOOS, **Beziehungen der** jüngsten Musikwissenschaft zur Ästhetik [The relationship of the new musicology to aesthetics] (5547); Hans Joachim MOSER, **Ziele und Wege der musikalischen Lokalforschung** [Goals and paths of regional music research] (901); Hermann MÜLLER, **Neue Bestrebungen auf dem Gebiete des katholischen deutschen Kirchenliedes** [New endeavors in the field of Catholic German hymns] (6316) and **Zur Editionstechnik bei Kirchenmusikwerken der klassischen Vokalperiode** [On the editing technique for vocal church music of the Classic period] (3910); Joseph MÜLLER-BLATTAU, **Die deutsche Kontrapunktlehre des 17. Jahrhunderts** [German contrapuntal theory in the 17th century] (4203); Richard MÜNNICH, **Die Behandlung musikästhetischer Probleme in der höheren Schule** [The handling of problems of musical aesthetics in high school] (4606); Paul NETTL, **Spuren des Wiener Liedes in der zweiten Hälfte des 17. Jahrhunderts** [Traces of the Vienna lied in the second half of the 17th century] (1635); Friedrich NOACK, **Die Opern von Christoph Graupner in Darmstadt** [The operas of Christoph Graupner in Darmstadt] (1637); Felix OBERBORBECK, **Schwäbische Reichsstädte als Träger deutscher Musikkultur im 18. Jahrhundert** [Swabian imperial cities as bearers of German music culture in the 18th century] (1639); Alfred OREL, **Zur Kompositionstechnik im Zeitalter der Trienter Codices** [On compositional technique in the age of the Trent Codices] (1391) and **Zur Quellenkunde für neuere Musikgeschichte** [On the information sources for more recent music history] (909); Edgar RABSCH, **Instrumentenkunde und vergleichende Musikwissenschaft in der Schule** [Knowledge of instruments and similar musical studies in school] (4628) and **Musikwissenschaft in der Schule: Zum Problem einer Musikbiologie** [Musicology in the school: On the problem of a music biology] (4629); Kurt RATTAY, **Die Musikkultur des deutschen Ostens im Zeitalter der Reformation** [The music culture of eastern German regions in the age of the Reformation] (1416); Heinrich SAMBETH, **Die Gregorianischen Melodien in den Werken Franz Liszts mit besonderer Berücksichtigung seiner Kirchenmusik Reformpläne** [The Gregorian melodies in the works of Franz Liszt with special consideration of his plans for the reform of church music] (2090); Oskar SCHÄFER, **Das musikalische sehen** [Musical seeing] (4110); Arnold SCHERING, **Musikwissenschaft und Kunst der Gegenwart** [Musicology and the art of today] (918) and **Zur Choralrhythmik** [On rhythm in the Protestant chorale] (4027); Ludwig SCHIEDERMAIR, **Die Musik des Rheinlandes** [Music of the Rhineland] (1004); Arnold SCHMITZ, **Beethovens Religiosität** [Beethoven and religion] (1856); Robert SONDHEIMER, **Anfänge des Wiener Stils in der Sinfonie des 18. Jahrhunderts** [Origins of the Viennese style in the 18th-century symphony] (1864); Hermann SPRINGER, **Wissenschaftliche und produktive Musikbibliographie** [Scholarly and productive music bibliography] (691); Rudolf STEGLICH, **Über das Formhören des Barock** [On hearing form in the Baroque] (4286); Hermann STEPHANI, **Das Verhältnis von reiner und pythagoreischer Stimmung als psychologisches Problem** [The relationship between pure and Pythagorean tuning as a psychological problem] (4116); Otto URSPRUNG, **Wirklich so viel griechische Einflüsse in der mittelalterlichen Musik?** [Really so much Greek influence on medieval music?] (1045); Peter WAGNER, **Germanisches und Romanisches im frühmittelalterlichen Kirchengesang** [Germanisms and Romanisms in the chant of the early Middle Ages] (1205); Karl WEINMANN, **Palestrina und das Oratorium des hl. Filippo Neri** [Palestrina and the oratory of St. Filippo Neri] (1464); Andreas WEISSENBÄCK, **Was bedeutet die neue liturgische Bewegung für die Kirchenmusik?** [What is the meaning of the new liturgical movement for church music?] (6414); Arno WERNER, **Die praktische Durchführung der lokalen Musikforschung in Sachsen-Thüringen** [Carrying out local music research in Saxe-Thuringia] (931); Theodor Wilhelm WERNER, **Aus der Frühzeit des unbegleiteten Männergesangs** [On the origins of the unaccompanied male vocal ensemble] (3329) and **Über innere Kriterien für die vokale oder instrumentale Bestimmung älterer Musik** [On the inner criteria for the vocal or instrumental determination of early music] (4293); Theodore WIEHMAYER, **Über die Grundfragen der musikalischen Rhythmik und Metrik** [On the basic questions of musical rhythm and meter] (4040); Johannes WOLF, **Über den Wert der Aufführungspraxis für die historische Erkenntnis** [On the value of performance practice for historical knowledge] (3723). The following papers presented at the conference were not submitted for publication: Joh. MÜLLER, **Bach-Psychologie** [Bach psychology]; Josef Maria MÜLLER-BLATTAU, **Das pädagogische Problem des Kontrapunktes und der Fuge** [The pedagogical problem of counterpoint and fugue]; Reinhold OPPEL, **Melodische und architektonische Gesetze bei Bach** [Melodic and architectonic principles in Bach]; Ludwig SCHIEDERMAIR, **Die Musik des Rheinlandes** [Music of the Rhineland]

121
bs

[Munich, 1925] Bericht über den IX. Kongress für experimentelle Psychologie [Report on the Ninth Congress for Experimental Psychology]. Sponsored by the Gesellschaft für Experimentelle Psychologie. Ed. by Karl BÜHLER (Jena: Fischer, 1925). *Illus., music.* In German.

The conference was held from 21 through 25 April 1925. The following contributions are cited separately: Fritz BREHMER, **Untersuchungen über Melodienauffassung und melodische Begabung des Kindes** [Investigations into the child's conception of melodies and the melodic talents of children] (4418); Richard WICKE, **Untersuchungen zur Gegensätzlichkeit von Dur und Moll** [Investigations on the opposition of major and minor] (4130).

1926

122
bs

[Freiburg im Breisgau] Bericht über die [I] Freiburger Tagung für Deutsche Orgelkunst [Report of the (first) Freiburg Tagung für Deutsche Orgelkunst]. Sponsored by the Universität Freiburg im Breisgau, Musikwissenschaftliches Institut. Ed. by Wilibald GURLITT (Augsburg: Bärenreiter, 1926) 173 p. *Illus., music, bibliog., charts, diagr., organ specification.* In German.

The conference was held from 27 through 30 July 1926. The following contributions are cited separately: Heinrich BESSELER, **Erläuterungen zu einer Vorführung ausgewählter Denkmäler der Musik des späten Mittelalters** [Commentary for a performance of selected monuments of late medieval music] (1064); Fidelis BÖSER, **Orgel und Liturgie** [Organ and liturgy] (6176); Hermann ERPF, **Orgel und zeitgenössische Musik** [The organ and contemporary music] (2161); Wilhelm FISCHER, **Die konzertierende Orgel im Orchester des 18. Jahrhunderts** [The concertante organ in the 18th-century orchestra] (3360); Ernst FLADE, **Gottfried Silbermann als Orgelbauer** [Gottfried Silbermann as organ builder] (3362); Gotthold FROTSCHER, **Zur Registrierkunst des 18. Jahrhunderts** [The art of registration in the 18th century] (3367); Wilibald GURLITT, **Die Wandlungen des Klangideals der Orgel im Lichte der Musikgeschichte** [Changes in the sound ideal of the organ in the light of music history] (3383); Karl HASSE, **Max Reger und die deutsche Orgelkunst** [Max Reger and German organ art] (3786); Hans Henny JAHNN, **Gesichtspunkte für die Wahl zweckmässiger Pfeifenmensuren** [Points of view in the choice of appropriate pipe measurements] (3393); Hermann JUNG, **Wege zu einem einheitlichen Aufbau von Disposition und Spieltisch** [Toward a unified construction of disposition and console] (3398); Hermann KELLER, **Die deutsche Orgelmusik nach Reger** [German organ music after Reger] (2189); Fritz LEHMANN, **Die neue Orgel als Instrument der Volksbildung** [The new organ as a means of mass education] (3410); Hans LUEDTKE, **Das Oskalyd als neuzeitliche Versuchsorgel** [The Oskalyd as a modern experimental organ] (3417); Joseph MÜLLER-BLATTAU, **Über Erziehung: Bildung und Fortbildung der Organisten** [Education: The training and further training of organists] (4884); Hermann MUND, **Geschichte und Bedeutung des Orgelgehäuses** [The history and significance of the organ case] (3442); Arnold SCHERING, **Zur Frage der Orgelmitwirkung in der Kirchenmusik des 15. Jahrhunderts** [The question of organ participation in church music of the 15th century] (6376); Oscar WALCKER, **Zur Geschichte der Orgelmensuren und ihrer Bedeutung für die Kunst des Orgelbaues** [The history of organ scaling and its significance for the art of organ building] (3500). Includes editions by Alfred SITTARD of chorale preludes by Heinrich SCHEIDEMANN (*Jesu, du wollest uns weisen*), Matthias WECKMANN (*Nun freut euch, lieven Christen gmein*), and Dietrich BUXTEHUDE (*Puer natus in Bethlehem*), performed by Sittard at the conference on the Praetorius-Orgel (Oscar Walcker and Wilibald Gurlitt, 1921) of the University's Musikwissenschaftliches Institut.

123
bs

[Geneva] Compte rendu du Ier Congrès du rythme [Proceedings of the First Congress on Rhythm]. Sponsored by the Institut de Rythmique de Genève. Ed. by Albert PFRIMMER (Genève: Institut Jaques-Dalcroze, 1926) 389 p. *Music, charts, diagr.* In French, German, and English.

The conference was held from 16 through 18 August 1926. The following contributions are cited separately: Wilhelm ALTWEGG, **Die Entwicklung des Rhythmus in Goethes Lyrik** [The development of rhythm in Goethe's lyric poetry] (5278) and **Die Rhythmen der deutschen Verskunst** [The rhythm of German verse] (5279); J. BÆRISWYL, **La gymnastique rythmique et l'école primaire** [Rhythmic gymnastics and the primary school] (4678); Charles BALLY, **Le rythme linguistique et sa signification sociale** [Lingustic rhythm and its social significance] (5918); Rafael BENEDITO, **Le rythme dans la pédagogie** [Rhythm in pedagogy] (4493); Charlotte BLENSDORF, **Rhythmische Erziehung im Kindergarten: Ausführungen im Anschluss an eine praktische Vorführung mit Kindern im Alter von 4 bis 6 Jahren** [Rhythmic education in kindergarten: Remarks following a practical demonstration with children aged 4 to 6] (4684); Joseph BOVET, **La liberté relative du rythme dans le chant grégorien** [The relative freedom of rhythm in Gregorian chant] (3972); Adrien BOVY, **Rythme et arts plastiques** [Rhythm and the plastic arts] (5376); Guido Lorenzo BREZZO, **Le rythme poétique et sa notation** [Poetic rhythm and its notation] (3807); Antoine-Élisée CHERBULIEZ, **L'unité du temps et sa division: Problème psychologique fondamental du rythme musical** [The unified beat and its divisions: A fundamental psychological problem of musical rhythm] (3981) and **Polyrythmique exotique** [Exotic polyrhythm] (3979); Lucien DAVID, **L'accent d'intensité et le geste dans l'expression rhythmique de la mélodie grégorienne** [The accent of intensity and gesture in the rhythmic expression of Gregorian melody] (3984); Alexandre DENÉRÉAZ, **Rythmes humains et rythmes cosmiques** [Human and cosmic rhythms] (5810); Maurice EMMANUEL, **Le rythme d'Euripide à Debussy** [Rhythm from Euripides to Debussy] (3987); Luigi Ernesto FERRARIA, **La rythmique en Italie** [Eurythmics in Italy] (4692); Oscar Louis FOREL, **Le rôle du rythme en physiologie et psycho-pathologie** [The role of rhythm in physiology and psycho-pathology] (5728); Fritz GIESE, **Körperrhythmus in Leben und Kunst der Völker** [Body rhythm in the life and art of peoples] (3995); Siegfried von GRASERN, **Das Wesen des Rhythmus** [The nature of rhythm] (3996); Gertrude A. INGHAM, **The place of Dalcroze eurhythmics in the school curriculum** (4716); Émile JAQUES-DALCROZE, **Rythmes d'hier, d'aujourd'hui et de demain et leur enseignement dans les écoles de musique** [Rhythms of yesterday, today, and tomorrow and their teaching in music schools] (4004) and **Une méthode d'éducation par et pour le rythme** [An educational method by and for rhythm] (4560); Joseph KREPS, **Le "nombre musical" chez saint Augustin et au Moyen Âge** [The musical number of St. Augustine and during the Middle Ages] (5834); Ernst LÉVY, **Métrique et rythmique: Definitions et bases** [Meter and rhythm: Definitions and foundations] (4009); Juan LLONGUERAS BADÍA, **La rythmique appliquée à la première éducation des aveugles** [Eurythmics as applied to the elementary education of the blind] (4727); Frank MARTIN, **La notation du rythme** [The notation of rhythm] (3852); R. MASÓ, **La rythmique dans l'enseignement primaire** [Eurythmics in elementary school education] (4736); L. NEF-LAVATER, **Les principaux mètres du vers français** [The principal meters of French verse] (5339); Henryk OPIEŃSKI, **Le rythme dans l'éxecution de la musique vocale** [Rhythm in the performance of vocal music] (3912); Albert PFRIMMER, **L'utilité de la méthode Jaques-Dalcroze pour le chef d'orchestre et les musiciens d'orchestre** [The utility of the Jaques-Dalcroze method for conductors and orchestral musicians] (4618); Edgar REFARDT, **Rhythmische Analysen** [Rhythmic analysis] (4020); Albert RHEINWALD, **Les rythmes de l'activité créatice** [The rhythms of creative activity] (5391); Jean RISLER, **Le rythme de la musique grecque** [The rhythm of Greek music] (4025); Nelly SCHINZ, **La rythmique Jaques-Dalcroze au jardin d'enfants** [The Dalcroze method in kindergarten] (4771); Mona SWANN, **Application de la rythmique à l'étude du "langage"** [The application of eurythmics to the study of language] (4782) and **The rhythms of English verse** (5363); Marco TREVES, **Le rythme dans les phénomènes de la vie** [Rhythm in the phenomena of life] (4037); Jean WALDSBURGER, **Les applications du rythme à l'organisation du travail professionnel** [The applications of rhythm to the organization of professional work] (5913); Léon WALTHER, **Le rythme dans le travail professionnel** [Rhythm in professional work] (5716); Léon WEBER-BAULER, **Le rôle du geste rythmé dans la pratique psychothérapique** [The role of the rhythmic gesture in psychotherapeutic practice] (5738).

124
rs
Review by F. MARTIN, *Revue musicale* 4 (1927) 265–68. In French.

125
bs
[Groningen] VIIIth International Congress of Psychology: Proceedings and papers. Ed. by Gerard HEYMANS (Groningen: Noordhoff, 1927) 451 p.; (reprint, Nendeln: Kraus, 1974).

The congress was held from 6 through 11 September 1926. The following contribution is cited separately: Llewellyn Wynn JONES, **Experimental studies in consonance and rhythm** (5668).

126
ap
[Lübeck] Congrès international de musicologie de l'Union Musicologique [International Musicological Congress of the Société Union Musicologique], *Zeitschrift für Musikwissenschaft* VIII (1925-1925) 381–82. In French.

The conference was held from 23 through 24 June 1926. Additional reports of the conference are cited as nos. 127 and 128 in this volume.

127
ap
[Lübeck] Congrès international de musicologie de l'Union Musicologique [International Musicological Congress of the Société Union Musicologique]. By Hermann ABERT, *Zeitschrift für Musikwissenschaft* 4 (1925-1926) 642–45. In German.

The conference was held from 23 through 24 June 1926. Additional reports of the conference are cited as nos. 126 and 128 in this volume.

128
ap
[Lübeck] Congrès international de musicologie de l'Union Musicologique [International Musicological Congress of the Société Union Musicologique]. By C.R. HENNINGS, *Die Harmonie* 4 (1926). In German.

The conference was held from 23 through 24 June 1926. Additional reports of the conference are cited as nos. 126 and 127 in this volume.

129
bs
[Paris] Compte rendu officiel du Congrès international du cinématographe [Official preoceedings of the International Congress of Cinematography]. Sponsored by the League of Nations, International Institute of Intellectual Cooperation (Paris: Chambre Syndicale Française de la Cinématographie, 1926) 173 p. In French.

The conference was held from 27 September through 3 October 1926.

130
bs
[Paris] Premier Congrès international des sociétés d'auteurs et compositeurs dramatiques [First International Congress of the Societies of Authors and Composers of Dramas]. Sponsored by the Confédération Internationale des Sociétés d'Auteurs et Compositeurs (Paris: conference, 1927) 168 p. In French.

At this meeting, the Confédération Internationale des Sociétés d'Auteurs et Compositeurs (CISAC) is created, which combines organizations in several countries and is mostly concerned with the administration of international copyright agreements.

1927

131
bs
[Belgrade] Deuxième Congrès international des études byzantines [Second International Congress on Byzantine Studies]. Sponsored by the International Association of Byzantine Studies. Ed. by Philaret GRANIĆ and Dragutin N. ANASTASIJEVIĆ (Beograd: Državna Štamparija, 1929) xxxi, 206 p.; (reprint, Nendeln: Kraus, 1978). *Facs.* In French, English, German, Russian, and Italian.

The conference was held from 11 through 16 April 1927. The following contributions are cited separately: Amédée GASTOUÉ, **Documents latins du moyen-âge sur le chant byzantins** [Latin documents from the Middle Ages on Byzantine chant] (6224); Jindrich KVĚT, **L'antiphonaire de Sedlec conservé à la Bibliothèque de l'Université de Prague** [The antiphonary of Sedlec kept at the library of the Univerzita Karlova v Praze] (5382).

132
rs

Review by Dragutin N. ANASTASIJEVIĆ, *Byzantion* 4 (1926) 547–48. In French.

133
rs

Review by N. VULIĆ, *Bulletin of the International Committee of Historical Sciences* 4 (1928) 533–36.

134
rs

Review in *Revue de musicologie* 4 (1927) 104–05. In French.

135
bs

[Berlin-Charlottenburg] Bericht über den Deutschen Kongreß für Kirchenmusik [Report on the Deutscher Kongreß für Kirchenmusik]. Sponsored by the Preußisches Ministerium für Wissenschaft, Kunst und Volksbildung and Staatliche Akademie für Kirchen- und Schulmusik in Charlottenburg (Kassel: Bärenreiter, 1928) 128 p. *Music.* In German.

The conference was held from 19 through 22 April 1927. The following contributions are cited separately: Paul GENNRICH, **Die gegenwärtigen Bedingungen für die Vorbildung unserer Kirchenmusiker** [Current conditions for the training of our church musicians] (4818); Richard GÖLZ, **Die heutige Lage der evangelischen Kirche auf dem Gebiete des Gottesdienstes** [The current situation of the Protestant church vis-à-vis the church service] (6434); Dominicus JOHNER, **Wie gelangen wir zu einem würdigen Vortrag des gregorianischen Chorals?** [How should we arrive at a worthy performance of Gregorian chant?] (6262); Josef LECHTHALER, **Der katholische Organist als Baumeister des liturgischen Gesamtkunstwerkes** [The Catholic organist as architect of the liturgical Gesamtkunstwerk] (6284); Hans Joachim MOSER, **Die Musikwissenschaft in der Ausbildung des Kirchenmusikers** [Musicology in the training of the church musician] (4605); Hermann MÜLLER, **Das katholische deutsche Kirchenlied** [The German Catholic hymn] (6315) and **Einiges über klassische kirchliche Polyphonie** [On classical church polyphony] (6314); Johannes PLATH, **Die liturgischen Aufgaben des Organisten und Chordirigenten** [The liturgical duties of the organist and choir director] (6443); Wolfgang REIMANN, **Die Orgel als Kult- und Konzertinstrument** [The organ as liturgical and as concert instrument] (3465); Julius SMEND, **Die notwendige Beziehung zwischen dem Kirchenmusiker und dem Vertreter des Predigtamts** [The necessary relation between the church musician and the person who holds the office of preacher] (6448); Peter WAGNER, **Ästhetik des gregorianischen Gesanges** [The aesthetics of Gregorian chant] (5623); Johannes WOLF, **Die Aufgaben des evangelischen Kirchenmusikers in geschichtlicher Beleuchtung** [The duties of the Lutheran church musician in a historical light] (6455).

136
bs

[Freiberg in Sachsen] Bericht über die dritte Tagung für Deutsche Orgelkunst [Report on the third Tagung für Deutsche Orgelkunst]. Sponsored by the Landesverein der Kirchenmusiker Sachsens. Ed. by Christhard MAHRENHOLZ; foreword by Julius SMEND (Kassel: Bärenreiter, 1928) 212 p. *Illus., music, charts, diagr., organ specification.* In German.

The meeting was held from 2 through 7 October 1927. The following contributions are cited separately: Friedrich BLUME, **Die Orgelbegleitung in der Musik des 17. Jahrhunderts** [Organ accompaniments in the music of the 17th century] (3731); Ernst FLADE, **Der Zukunftswert der Silbermannorgel** [The value to the future of the Silbermann organ] (3363); Gotthold FROTSCHER, **Kult-, Kirchen- und Konzertorgel** [Devotional, church, and concert organ] (3365); József GEYER, **Schwierigkeiten eines einheitlichen Aufbaues der Orgeldispositionen und des Orgelspieltisches** [Difficulties in achieving the uniform construction of organ dispositions and consoles] (3373); Wilibald GURLITT, **Die musikwissenschaftliche Bildung des Organisten** [The organist's training in musicology] (4880); Jacques HANDSCHIN, **Die Orgelbewegung in der Schweiz** [The Orgelbewegung in Switzerland] (1979); Karl HASSE, **Die geistigen und religiösen Grundlagen der Orgelmusik seit Bach** [The spiritual and religious foundations of organ music since Bach] (3388); Hans Henny JAHNN, **Monographie der Rohrflöte** [Monograph on the Rohrflöte] (3394); Hermann KELLER, **Der Spieltisch** [The console] (3399); Alfred LENK, **Etwas vom Rollschweller** [Something about the crescendo roller] (3411); Hans LÖFFLER, **J.S. Bach und die Orgeln seiner Zeit** [J.S. Bach and the organs of his time] (3414); Christhard MAHRENHOLZ, **Der**

gegenwärtige Stand der Orgelfrage im Lichte der Orgelgeschichte [The current state of the organ question in the light of organ history] (3419) and **Orgel und Liturgie** [Organ and liturgy] (6437); Arnold MENDELSSOHN, **Die Orgel im Gottesdienst** [The organ in church services] (6438); Hans Joachim MOSER, **Über deutsche Orgelkunst 1450-1500** [On the art of the German organ, 1450-1500] (3438); Hermann MUND, **Joachim Wagner, ein Altberliner Orgelbauer** [Joachim Wagner, an organ builder of old Berlin] (3443); Hermann Meinhard POPPEN, **Die Einstimmung der heutigen Orgel** [The tuning of the contemporary organ] (3448); Rudolf QUOIKA, **Gregorianischer Choral und Orgel** [Gregorian chant and the organ] (6024); Paul RUBARDT, **Arp Schnitger** (3469); Ernst SCHNORR VON CAROLSFELD, **Statistische Mitteilungen über die Orgeln im Bereich der Evangelisch-Lutherischen Landeskirche des Freistaates Sachsen** [Statistics on the organs in the jurisdiction of the Evangelical Lutheran Church of Saxony] (3476); Julius SMEND, **Die Synthese von Text und Ton im deutschen Choral und deren Bedeutung für das Orgelspiel** [The synthesis of text and music in the German chorale and its significance for organ playing] (5358); Joseph WÖRSCHING, **Beruf und Bedeutung des Organistenamtes für den Lehrstand und das deutsche Volk** [The vocation and significance of the position of organist for the teaching profession and for the German people] (2411); Erwin ZILLINGER, **Über die ästhetische Durchbildung der Organisten** [Completing the aesthetic training of organists] (4904). An edition of J.S. BACH's Pastorella in F major (BWV 590) by Günter RAMIN is appended.

137
bs

[Halle] Dritter Kongress für Ästhetik und allgemeine Kunstwissenschaft: Bericht [Third Congress for Aesthetics and General Art History: Report]. Sponsored by the Gesellschaft für Ästhetik und Allgemeine Kunstwissenschaft. By Wolfgang LIEPE (Stuttgart: Enke, 1927) 204 p. *Zeitschrift für Ästhetik und allgemeine Kunstwissenschaft* XXI (1927). In German.

The following contributions are cited separately: Otto BAENSCH, **Rhythmus in allgemein philosophischer Betrachung** [Rhythm as seen from a general philosophical perspective] (5425); Moritz BAUER, **Symbol in der Musik** [Symbol in music] (5426); Gerhard von KEUSSLER, **Rhythmus in der Musik** [Rhythm in music] (5505); Paul MOOS, **Symbol in der Musik** [Symbol in music] (5549); Alfred OREL, **Rhythmus in der Musik** [Rhythm in music] (5558); Arnold SCHERING, **Symbol in der Musik** [Symbol in music] (5584); Hermann Wolfgang von WALTERSHAUSEN, **Rhythmus in der Musik** [Rhythm in music] (5625).

138
bs

[Paris] Premier Congrès international du théâtre et premier Festival international d'art dramatique et lyrique, organisés par l'Union Française de la S.U.D.T. [First International Congress of Theater and First International Festival of Dramatic and Lyric Art, organized by the Union Française de la S.U.D.T.]. Sponsored by the Société Universelle du Théâtre (Paris: Les Cahiers du Théâtre, 1927) 3, 223, 23 p. *Illus.* In French.

The conference was held from 20 through 26 June 1927; parts of it were designated as "Compositeurs de musique".

139
rs

Review by J.J. BERNARD, *Les cahiers du théâtre* 4 (1927) 9. In French.

140
bs

[Rome] Deuxième Congrès international des sociétés d'auteurs et compositeurs [The Second International Congress of the Societies of Authors and Composers]. Sponsored by the Società Italiana degli Autori ed Editori (Paris: conference, 1927) 108 p. In French.

An annual meeting of the International Confederation of Societies of Authors and Composers (CISAC), which was formed in 1926.

141
bs

[Vienna] Beethoven-Zentenarfeier: Festbericht [Beethoven centenary: Presenation album]. Foreword by Guido ADLER (Wien: Otto Maass' Söhne, 1927) 83 p. *Illus., music, charts, diagr.* In German.

The conference, held from 26 through 31 March 1927, is also cited as nos. 142 and 147 in this volume. The following contributions are cited separately: Hermann ABERT, **Beethoven** (1719); **Beethoven und die Wiener Kultur seiner Zeit** [Beethoven and the Viennese culture of his time] (2404); Edward Joseph DENT, **Henry Purcell and his opera** *Dido and Aeneas* (5140); Romain ROLLAND, **An Beethoven: Dankgesang** [To Beethoven: Song of thanks] (1660).

142
bs
[Vienna] Beethoven-Zentenarfeier: Internationaler musikhistorischer Kongress [Beethoven centenary: International music-historical congress]. Sponsored by President Dr. Michael Hainisch. Ed. by Wilhelm FISCHER; pref. by Guido ADLER (Wien: Universal, 1927) 404 p. *Illus., music, list of works, charts, diagr., transcr.* In German and French.

The congress was held from 26 through 31 March 1927. It is also cited as nos. 141 and 147 in this volume. The following contributions are cited separately: Wilhelm ALTMANN, **Über thematische Kataloge** [On thematic catalogues] (783); Higini ANGLÈS, **Die mehrstimmige Musik in Spanien vor dem 15. Jahrhundert** [Polyphonic music in Spain before the 15th century] (1221); Paul BERGMANS, **Les carillons belges et la musique de carillon** [Belgian carillons and carillon music] (3643); Herbert BIEHLE, **Schuberts Lieder als Gesangsproblem** [Schubert's lieder as an issue for singers] (3782); Maurice CAUCHIE, **Les chansons à trois voix de Pierre Cléreau** [The three-voice chansons of Pierre Clereau] (1266); Ernest CLOSSON, **Les particularités flamandes de Beethoven** [Beethoven's Flemish characteristics] (1736); Alexandre DENÉRÉAZ, **Beethoven et les rythmes cosmiques** [Beethoven and cosmic rhythms] (4240); Otto Erich DEUTSCH, **Über bibliographische Aufnahme von Originalausgaben unserer Klassiker** [Bibliographic registration of the original editions of our classic composers] (550); Alfred EINSTEIN, **Beethoven und die Polyphonie** [Beethoven and polyphony] (4161); Erwin FELBER, **Die orientalischen Notationen und unsere Notenschriftreform** [Eastern notations and our notation reform] (3820); Karl Gustav FELLERER, **Der Stile antico in der katholischen Kirchenmusik des 18. Jahrhunderts** [The stile antico in Catholic church music of the 18th century] (1548); Karl GEIRINGER, **Gaudenzio Ferraris Engelkonzert im Dome von Saronno: Ein Beitrag zur Instrumentenkundes des 16. Jahrhunderts** [Gaudenzio Ferrari's angel concert in the cathedral of Saronno: A contribution to organology of the 16th century] (5380); Robert GEUTEBRÜCK, **Über die Mehrstimmigkeit im österreichischen Volksgesang** [On polyphony in Austrian traditional song] (2829); Otto GOMBOSI, **Quellenmäßige Belege über den Einfluß der Chansonkunst auf die deutsche Liedkunst in der zweiten Hälfte des 15. Jahrhunderts** [Source evidence of the influence of the chanson on German song in the second half of the 15th century] (1319); Wolfgang GRAESER, **Neue Bahnen in der Musikforschung** [New directions in music research] (5662); Melania GRAFCZYŃSKYA, **Die Polyphonie am Hofe der Jagellonen** [Polyphony at the Jagiellonian court] (1320); Wilibald GURLITT, **Robert Schumann in seinen Skizzen gegenüber Beethoven** [Robert Schumann in his sketches as compared with Beethoven] (1975); Hermann GÜTTLER, **Kant und sein musikalischer Umkreis** [Kant and his musical environment] (1769); Toivo Elias HAAPANEN, **Zur Verbreitung der romanischen und germanischen Tradition im gregorianischen Gesang** [On the spread of Roman and Germanic tradition in Gregorian chant] (878); Robert HAAS, **Die Erhaltung der musikalischen Meisterhandschriften** [The preservation of musical manuscripts of the masters] (585) and **Zum Kanon im** *Fidelio* [The *Fidelio* canon] (1772); Jacques HANDSCHIN, **Über frühes und spätes Mittelalter** [On the early and late Middle Ages] (1117); Karl HASSE, **Art und Wesen der Tonsprache Beethovens** [Beethoven's musical language as type and essence] (4342); Wilhelm HEINITZ, **Eine Studie zur dynamischen Schichtung in Beethovens Sonatenthemen** [A study of dynamic layering in Beethoven's sonata themes] (4432); Wilhelm HITZIG, **Bedeutung der Verlagsarchive für die Musikforschung** [The significance of publishing house archives for music research] (5968); Mihail IVANOV-BORECKIJ, **Ein Moskauer Skizzenbuch von Beethoven** [A Moscow sketchbook by Beethoven] (1783); Dezső JÁROSY, **Die historische Entwicklung der ungarischen Kirchenmusik** [The historic development of Hungarian church music] (1993); Knud JEPPESEN, **Die Textlegung in der Chansonmusik des späteren 15. Jahrhunderts** [Text underlay in the chanson of the late 15th century] (3903); Willi KAHL, **Geschichte, Kritik und Aufgaben der K.Ph.E. Bach-Forschung** [The history and tasks, and an assessment, of C.P.E. Bach research] (1786); Lotte KALLENBACH-GRELLER, **Die historischen Grundlagen der Vierteltöne** [The historical foundations of quarter tones] (4083); Lucjan KAMIEŃSKI, **Neue Beiträge zur Entwicklung der Polonaise bis Beethoven** [New contributions on the development of the polonaise up to Beethoven] (1788); Paul KAUFMANN, **Aus der Bonner Gesellschaft in Beethovens Jugendzeit** [Bonn society at the time of Beethoven's youth] (1790); Oskar KAUL, **Ausstrahlungen der Wiener Vorklassik nach Würzburg** [The influence of the Viennese pre-Classic in Würzburg] (1791); Karl Magnus KLIER, **Volkstümliche Querflöten und die Maultrommel in den österreichischen Alpen** [Popular transverse flutes and the jew's harp in the Austrian Alps] (3258); Hans KÖLTZSCH, **Das Gestaltungsproblem in der Instrumentalmusik Franz Schuberts** [Issues of form in Franz Schubert's instrumental music] (2011); Franz KOSCH, **Der Rhythmus im Choral der Solesmenser** [Rhythm in the chant of the Solesmes monks] (3702); Georg KOTEK, **Der Jodler in den österreichischen Alpen** [The yodel in the Austrian Alps] (2906); Ilmari KROHN, **Die Form des ersten Satzes der** *Mondscheinsonate* [The form of the first movement of the "Moonlight" sonata] (4263); Erwin KROLL, **E.T.A. Hoffmann und Beethoven** [E.T.A. Hoffmann and Beethoven] (1795); Robert LACHMANN, **Zur außereuropäischen Mehrstimmigkeit** [On non-European polyphony] (4188); Josef LECHTHALER, **Die stilistischen Strömungen in der Kirchenmusik der Nachkriegszeit** [Stylistic currents in the church music of the postwar period] (2198); Franz MARSCHNER, **Zählzeit, Tempo, und Ausdruck bei Beethoven** [Beat, tempo, and expression in Beethoven] (3761); Wilhelm MERIAN, **Das Verhältnis von Tabulaturtänzen des 16. Jahrhunderts zu vorhandenen Fassungen für mehrere Instrumente** [The relationship of 16th-century tablature dances to extant versions for several instruments] (1382); Hans MERSMANN, **Beethovens zyklisches Formprinzip** [Beethoven's principle of cyclic form] (4269); Kathi MEYER, **Über Melodiebildung in den geistlichen Spielen des früheren Mittelalters** [Melody formation in the religious plays of the early Middle Ages] (4448); Paul MIES, **Stilkundliche Probleme bei Beethoven** [Problems of stylistics in Beethoven's works] (4372); Karl Lothar MIKULICZ, **Skizzen zur III. und V. Symphonie und über die Notwendigkeit einer Gesamtausgabe der Skizzen Beethovens** [Sketches for the third and fifth symphonies, and on the need for a complete edition of Beethoven's sketches] (1814); Lluís MILLET, **La chanson populaire et l'art choral en Catalogne** [Traditional song and choral art in Catalonia] (2043); Paul MOOS, **Hermann Siebeck als Musikästhetiker** [Hermann Siebeck as aesthetician of music] (5548); Hans Joachim MOSER, **Paul Hofaimer als Orgelkomponist** [Paul Hofaimer as organ composer] (1385); José Vianna da MOTTA, **Beethoven in Portugal** [1820]; Hermann MÜLLER, **Beethovens** *Missa solemnis* **und das** *Motu proprio* **des Papstes Pius X. über Kirchenmusik** [Beethoven's *Missa solemnis* and Pope Pius X's motu proprio on church music] (6313); Siegfried NADEL, **Die Hauptprobleme der neueren Musikpsychologie** [Leading issues in recent music psychology] (5685); Wilibald NAGEL, **Beethoven der Romantiker?** [Beethoven the Romantic?] (1823); Paul NETTL, **Die Notwendigkeit einer Textbücherbibliographie** [The need for a bibliography of librettos] (636); Friedrich NOACK, **Landgraf Ernst Ludwig von Hessen-Darmstadt als Komponist** [Ernst Ludwig, Landgrave of Hessen-Darmstadt, as composer] (1636) and **Organisation und wissenschaftliche Nutzbarmachung der Arbeit in den Seminaren** [Organizing the work of academic departments and making it useful] (906); Henryk OPIEŃSKI, **Chopins Sonaten und ihr Verhältnis zum Beethovenschen Stil** [Chopin's sonatas and their relationship to the Beethoven style] (2058); Alfred OREL, **Zum Begriff der Wiener Klassik** [The concept of Viennese Classicism] (5559); Jacques-Gabriel PROD'HOMME, **Les débuts de Beethoven en France** [The early reception of Beethoven in France] (2075); Karl PRUSIK, **Das englische Madrigal um 1600** [The English madrigal around 1600] (1411); Francisco PUJOL PONS, **L'œuvre du** *Chansonnier populaire de la Catalogne* [The *Obra del cançoner popular de Catalunya*] (3017); Emil RIEGLER-DINU, **Das rumänische Volkslied und die Instrumentalmusik der Bauern** [Romanian traditional song and instrumental music of agricultural communities] (3029); Felix ROSENTHAL, **Auftakt und Abtakt in der Thematik Beethovens** [Upbeat and downbeat in Beethoven's themes] (4026); Karl August ROSENTHAL, **Zur Stilistik der Salzburger Kirchenmusik des 17. Jahrhunderts** [The style of Salzburg church music of the 17th century] (1662); Ludwig SCHIEDERMAIR, **Beethoven und das Rheinland** [Beethoven and the Rhineland] (1852); Josef SCHMIDT-PHISELDECK, **Datierung der Musikalien** [The dating of music materials] (675); Constantin SCHNEIDER, **Musikbibliographie in Österreich** [Music bibliography in Austria] (680) and **Zur Frühgeschichte der Oper in Salzburg (bis 1650)** [On the early history of opera in Salzburg (until 1650)] (1677); Alfred SCHNERICH, **Das konfessionelle Element bei Beethoven** [The denominational factor in Beethoven] (1857); Alicja SIMON, **Über einige** amerikanische Beethoven-Ausgaben [On some American Beethoven editions] (5992); Božidar ŠIROLA, **Haydn und Beethoven und ihre Stellung zur kroatischen Volksmusik** [Haydn and Beethoven and their relationship to Croatian traditional music] (1862); Hermann SPRINGER, **Aufgaben der Gesellschaft für Wissenschaftliche Musikbibliographie** [Tasks of the Gesellschaft für Wissenschaftliche Musikbibliographie] (688) and **Beethoven und die Musikkritik** [Beethoven and music criticism] (5603); Rudolf STEGLICH, **Über Dualismus der** *Taktqualität* **im Sonatensatz** [On the dualism of *Taktqualität* in sonata movements] (4032); Hermann STEPHANI, **Enharmonik (polare Harmonik) bei Beethoven** [Enharmonics (polar harmony) in Beethoven's works] (4219); Eugen Karl Gottfried TETZEL, **Rhythmus und Vortrag** [Rhythm and execution] (4036); Julien TIERSOT, **Les autographes de Beethoven à la Bibliothèque du Conservatoire de Paris** [Beethoven autographs in the Bibliothèque du Conservatoire, Paris] (766); Peter WAGNER, **Über den altspanischen, mozarabischen Kirchengesang** [The Old Spanish Mozarabic chant] (1207); Karl WEINMANN, **Beethovens Verhältnis zur Religion** [Beethoven's relationship to religion] (1894); Egon WELLESZ, **Die dramaturgische Bedeutung des** *Fidelio* [The dramaturgical significance of *Fidelio*] (5272); Arthur WILLNER, **Die innere Einheit der klassischen Symphonie** [The inner unity of the Classic symphony] (4294); Johannes WOLF, **Beethoven Kirchenmusiker?** [Beethoven: Church musician?] (1899); Fritz ZOBELEY, **Praktische Probleme der Musikbibliographie** [Practical problems of music bibliography] (703).

143
rs
Review by Guido ADLER, *Zeitschrift für Musikwissenschaft* 4 (1925-1926) 299–300. In German.

144
rs
Review by Guido ADLER, *Zeitschrift für Musikwissenschaft* 4 (1926-1927) 1–2. In German.

145
rs
Review by Alfred EINSTEIN, *Zeitschrift für Musikwissenschaft* 4 (1926-1927) 494–500. In German.

146
rs
Review in *Revue de musicologie* 4 (1927) 100–03. In French.

147
bs
[Vienna] Festschrift den Mitgliedern des Musikhistorischen Kongresses überreicht von der Leitenden Kommission der Denkmäler der Tonkunst in Österreich [Festschrift for the members of the music historical congress presented by the Governing Committee of the Denkmäler der Tonkunst in Österreich] *Studien z. Musikwissenschaft, Beheifte d. Denkmäler d. Tonkunst in Österreich* 14 (Wien: Universal, 1927) xvi, 320 p. *Illus., music.* In German.
The conference, held from 26 through 31 March 1927, is also cited as nos. 141 and 142 in this volume. The following contributions are cited separately: Friedrich BAYER, **Über den Gebrauch der Instrumente in den Kirchen- und Instrumentalwerken von W.A. Mozart** [On the use of instruments in church music and instrumental works by W.A. Mozart] (4297); Friedrich DEUTSCH, **Die Fugenarbeit in den Werken Beethovens** [Fugal technique in Beethoven's works] (4158); Franz KOSCH, **Florian Leopold Gassmann als Kirchenkomponist** [Florian Leopold Gassmann as composer of church music] (1794); Victor LUITHLEN, **Studie zu J. Brahms' Werken in Variationenform** [A study on variation forms in J. Brahms's works] (4368); Herbert NEURATH, **Das Violinkonzert in der Wiener klassischen Schule** [The violin concerto in the Viennese Classic school] (4275); Rudolf NÜTZLADER, **Salieri als Kirchenmusiker** [Salieri as church musician] (1828); Gertrude RIGLER, **Die Kammermusik Dittersdorfs** [Dittersdorf's chamber music] (4378); Karl August ROSENTHAL, **Über Vokalformen bei Mozart** [On Mozart's vocal forms] (4281); Victor URBANTSCHITSCH, **Die Entwicklung der Sonatenform bei Brahms** [The development of Brahms's sonata form] (4291); Hertha VOGL, **Zur Geschichte des Oratoriums in Wien von 1725 bis 1740** [The history of the oratorio in Vienna, 1725-1740] (1889); Andreas WEISSENBÄCK, **J.G. Albrechtsberger als Kirchenkomponist** [J.G. Albrechtsberger as composer of church music] (1895); Hans WLACH, **Die Oboe bei Beethoven** [The oboe in Beethoven's music] (4305).

1928

148
bs
[Berlin] Troisième Congrès international de la Confédération des Sociétés d'Auteurs et Com- positeurs [Third Congress of the International Confederation of Societies of Authors and Composers]. Sponsored by the Gesellschaft für Musikalische Aufführungs- und Mechanische Vervielfältigungsrechte (Paris: conference, 1928) 244 p. In French.
The conference was held from 16 through 23 April 1928. A discussion of the administrative policies of the societies.

149
bs
[New York] Proceedings of the Twenty-third International Congress of Americanists (New York: n.p., 1930) li, 944 p.; (reprint, Nendeln: Kraus, 1968).
The meeting was held from 17 through 22 September 1928. The following contributions are cited separately: George HERZOG, **Musical styles in North America** (3305); Truman MICHELSON, **Notes on Fox Gens festivals** (3169); I.D. STRELNIKOV, **La música y la danza de las tribus índias Kaa-Ohwua (Guaraní) y Botocudo** [The music and dance of the Guaraní and Botocudo Indian tribes] (5067).

150
ap
[New York] The Twenty-third International Congress of Americanists. By Franz BOAS, *Science* LXVIII/1764 (19 Oct 1928) 361–64.
Reports on the conference cited as no. 149 in this volume.

151
bs
[Oslo] VIᵉ Congrès international des sciences historiques [Sixth International Congress of Historical Sciences] (Roma: Loescher, 1928) xiv, 406 p.; (reprint, Nendeln: Kraus, 1978). In French.
The meeting was held from 14 through 18 August 1928. The following contribution is cited separately: Jean BONNEROT, **Saint-Saëns en Scandinavie en 1897** [Saint-Saëns in Scandinavia in 1897] (1921).

152
bs
[Prague] Art populaire: Travaux artistiques et scientifiques du Iᵉʳ Congrès international des arts populaires [Folk art: Artistic and scientific studies of the First International Congress of Popular Arts]. Sponsored by the Institut International de Coopération Intellectuelle. Intro. by Henri FOCILLON (Paris: Duchartre, 1931) 211 p. *Illus., music, bibliog., maps.* In French.
The conference was held from 7 through 13 October 1928. Vol. 2 includes abstracts relating to traditional music and dance. The following contributions are cited separately: Violet ALFORD, **Quelques danses du Pays Basque français** [Several dances of the French Basque region] (4927); U. ALLENDE, **La musique populaire chilienne** [Chilean traditional music] (3186); Ramon ARAMON I SERRA, **La "Danza" et la danse du cierge de Castelltersol** [The dansa and ball del ciri of Castelltersol] (4931); Ricardo del ARCO Y GARAY, **La jota aragonaise** [The Aragonese jota] (4933) and **Les couplets et les "Dances" dans le Haut-Aragon (Espagne)** [Couplets and the Dance in northern Aragón (Spain)] (4932); Béla BARTÓK, **Les recherches sur le folklore musical en Hongrie** [Music folklore research in Hungary] (2731); Rafael BENEDITO, **Le folklore musical à l'école** [Musical folklore in school] (4681); Nicola BORRELLI, **La tarentelle en Campanie** [The tarantella in Campania] (4940); Tiberiu BREDICEANU, **Historique et état actuel des recherches sur la musique populaire roumaine** [Historical and current research on Romanian traditional music] (2749); Elizabeth BURCHENAL, **Les danses populaires caractéristiques des États-Unis** [Typical traditional dances of the United States] (4942); Gonzalo CASTRILLO HERNÁNDEZ, **Le chant populaire de la vieille Castille** [The traditional song of old Castile] (2760); Jędrzej CIERNIAK, **Le théâtre populaire ancien et moderne en Pologne** [Historical and contemporary folk theater in Poland] (5119); Felisa de las CUEVAS, **Les chansons de noce dans la province de León** [Wedding songs of the province of León] (2782); Juan DOMÍNGUEZ BERRUETA, **Les couplets et la musique de la jota aragonaise** [The couplets and music of the jota of Aragón] (4953); Sixto María DURÁN, **La musique aborigène et populaire de l'Équateur** [Aboriginal and traditional music of Ecuador] (3198); Kiyomi FUJII, N. ORIGUCHI, and Yukichi KODERA, **Considérations sur la musique populaire au Japon** [Thoughts concerning traditional music in Japan] (2625); Pedro GRASES GONZÁLEZ, **Les danses du Panadés (Los bailes del Panadès)** [The dansas of Penedès] (4972); Antonio GUZMÁN, **Deux chansons de la**

province de Palencia [Two songs of the province of Palencia] (2840); Jiří HORÁK, L'état actuel de l'étude des chansons populaires en Tchécoslovaquie [The current state of research on traditional song in Czechoslovakia] (2858); Elsie HOUSTON, La musique, la danse et les cérémonies populaires du Brésil [Traditional music, dance, and ceremonies of Brazil] (3202); Douglas KENNEDY, Chants populaires anglais [English traditional songs] (2882) and La renaissance de la musique et de la danse populaire en Angleterre [The rebirth of traditional music and dance in England] (2888); Yukichi KODERA, Les kagura, les représentations populaires bouddhiques et les nouvelles représentations populaires au Japon [The kagura, traditional Buddhist performances, and contemporary folk theater in Japan] (5182); Yukichi KODERA, H. KITANO, and Nobuo ORIGUCHI, Les danses populaires japonaises [Japanese traditional dances] (5005); Filaret KOLESSA, Les formations anciennes et nouvelles dans les mélodies populaires ukrainiennes [Old and new formations in traditional Ukrainian songs] (2903); Ludvík KUBA, La danse slave: Ses principales formes et leur signification [Slavic dance: Its principal forms and their significance] (5008); Jaap KUNST, Quelques notes sur la musique javanaise moderne [Some notes on modern Javanese music] (2651); László LAJTHA, Les jeux et les danses populaires en Hongrie [Traditional games and dances in Hungary] (5015); E. LOUDON, Les cérémonies et les poèmes dansés des Indiens Pueblos [Ceremonies and danced poems of the Pueblo Indians] (3165); Casto MARTÍN GONZÁLEZ, Les chansons et les danses dans un village de Tolède [The songs and dances of a village in Toledo] (2948); Eduardo Fernando MARTÍNEZ TORNER, Bibliographie du folklore musical espagnole [Bibliography of Spanish musical folklore] (820); Juan MASOLIVER MARTÍNEZ, La "dance" de Híjar (province de Teruel) [The danza of Híjar (Teruel province)] (5030); Hans MERSMANN, Buts et méthode d'une étude musical des chants populaires [Goals and method of a musical study of traditional songs] (2957); Siegfried NADEL, Sur la structure des systèmes de gammes et le problème du cycle dans la musique primitive [On the scale structure and the cycle in primitive music] (3953); Daniel Luis ORTIZ DÍAZ, Refrains et chansons de la vallée de Iguña (Santander) [Refrains and songs of the Iguña Valley (Santander)] (2979); Hubert PERNOT, Chants et mélodies populaires: Résolution adoptée par le Congrès des arts populaires [Traditional songs and melodies: Resolution adopted by the Congress of Popular Arts] (2457); Mercedes PIERA GELABERT, La danse des gitanes du Vallès [The Ball de gitanes of El Valles] (5049); Konstantinos A. PSACHOS, Le chant populaire hellénique de l'antiquité à nos jours [Greek traditional song from antiquity to our day] (3016); Henriette RÉGNIER, Les danses populaires françaises [Traditional French dances] (5057); Friedrich REPP, La chanson populaire de l'îlot linguistique allemand de Spiz en Slovaquie [The traditional song of the German linguistic enclave of Spiš in Slovakia] (3026); Emil RIEGLER-DINU, La hora, la maquam et la chanson populaire de l'orient européen [The hora, the maqām, and Eastern European traditional song] (3027); Ole Mørk SANDVIK, La musique populaire norvégienne [Norwegian traditional music] (3045); Valerio SERRA Y BOLDÚ, Les goigs ou gozos, poèmes religieux chantés en Catalogne [The goigs or gozos, religious poems sung in Catalonia] (3056); Drahomíra STRÁNSKÁ, L'état actuel de la chanson populaire dans les Monts des Géants (Krkonose) [The current state of traditional song in the Riesengebirge (Krkonoše)] (3076); Noto SUROTO, Le caractère de la danse javanaise [The nature of Javanese dance] (5069); Hisao TANABE, Les études récentes concernant les instruments de musique de Japon [Recent studies on the musical instruments of Japan] (3281); Sándor TÉREY-KUTHY, La musique populaire dans la vie practique et dans l'enseignement [Traditional music in everyday life and in teaching] (4657); Bedřich VÁCLAVEK, Les chansons profanes tchèques devenues populaires [Secular Czech songs that have become folk songs] (3093); (Mme) VAN HOOGENHOUCK TULLEKEN, Le chant populaire au Canada [Traditional song in Canada] (3180); José ZALDÍVAR, Les danses populaires catalanes [Catalan traditional dances] (5083); Otákar ZICH, Les particularités rythmiques des danses populaires tchécoslovaques [The rhythmic characteristics of Czechoslovakian traditional dances] (5088); José Gonzalo ZULAICA Y ARREGUI (José Antonio de Donostia), La musique populaire basque [Traditional Basque music] (3131) and Les danses basques [Basque dances] (5090).

153
bs

[Prague] Congrès international des arts populaires/International congress of popular arts: Résumés (Paris: Institut international de coopération intellectuelle, 1928) 140 p. In French.

Presents papers and abstracts published on the occasion of the conference, which was held from 7 through 13 October 1928. The conference report is abstracted as no. 152 in this volume. The following contributions are cited separately: Violet ALFORD, Dances of the French Basque country (4926); Ramon ARAMON I SERRA, Danse et bal du cierge de Castelltersol [The dansa and ball del ciri of Castelltersol] (4930); Ricardo del ARCO Y GARAY, La jota aragonesa [The Aragonese jota] (2724) and Romances, couplets, danses et autres divertissements dans le Haut-Aragon [Romances, coplas, and other entertainments in upper Aragon] (2725); Béla BARTÓK, Les recherches sur le folklore musical en Hongrie [Music folklore research in Hungary] (2421); Rafael BENEDITO, Le folklore musical à l'école [Musical folklore in school] (4680); Nicola BORRELLI, La tarentelle en Campanie [The tarantella in Campania] (4939); Elizabeth BURCHENAL, Distinctive American country dances which exist in rural communities in the United States (4943); Gonzalo CASTRILLO HERNÁNDEZ, Modalité, forme, rythme et harmonie dans les chansons types de la vieille Castille [Modality, form, rhythm, and harmony in the song types of old Castile] (2761) and Notes bibliographiques pour l'étude du chant populaire en vielle Castille [Bibliographical notes toward the study of traditional song in old Castile] (800); Jędrzej CIERNIAK, Le théâtre populaire ancien et moderne en Pologne [Early and contemporary folk theater in Poland] (5120); Felisa de las CUEVAS, Les chansons de noce dans la province de Léon [Wedding songs of the province of León] (2781); Juan DOMÍNGUEZ BERRUETA, La jota aragonaise [The Aragonese jota] (2792); Kiyomi FUJII, Aperçu sur la chanson populaire au Japon [Survey of traditional song in Japan] (2624); Kiyomi FUJII, Nobuo ORIGUCHI, and Yukichi KODERA, Considérations sur la musique populaire au Japon [Thoughts concerning traditional music in Japan] (2626); Pedro GRASES GONZÁLEZ, Les danses du Panadés [The dances of Penedès] (4971); Antonio GUZMÁN, Deux chansons et deux danses populaires de la province de Palencia (2841); Jiří HORÁK, L'état actuel de l'étude des chansons populaires en Tchécoslovaquie [The current state of research on traditional song in Czechoslovakia] (2857); Julius JANICZEK (Walther Hensel), La mélodie et la chanson populaire allemande en Tchécoslovaquie [Melody and German traditional song in Czechoslovakia] (2870); Douglas KENNEDY, English folk-dance (5001), English folk music (2883), English folk songs (2884), English singing games (2885), and Folk-song and dance revival (2887); Yukichi KODERA, Les kagura, les représentations populaires bouddhiques et les nouvelles représentations populaires au Japon [The kagura, traditional Buddhist performances, and contemporary folk theater in Japan] (5181); Yukichi KODERA, H. KITANO, and Nobuo ORIGUCHI, Les danses populaires japonaises [Japanese traditional dances] (5006); Alexandre KOLESSA, Les motifs mythologiques solaires et lunaires dans les chansons de Noël ukrainiennes (2902); Filaret KOLESSA, Les formations anciennes et nouvelles dans les mélodies populaires ukrainiennes [Old and new formations in Ukrainian folk melodies] (4441); Ludvík KUBA, La danse slave: Ses principales formes et leur signification [Slavic dance: Its principal forms and their significance] (5007) and La préesthétique de la chanson populaire, sa source, son but, ses lois [The pre-aesthetics of traditional song, its source, goal, and laws] (2523); Le théâtre au Japon et ses relations avec l'art dramatique populaire [Japanese theater and its relations with traditional dramatic arts] (5123); Casto MARTÍN GONZÁLEZ, Détails folkloriques d'un village de Tolède: Chansons et danses [Folkloric details of a Toledan village: Songs and dances] (2949); Eduardo Fernando MARTÍNEZ TORNER, Bibliographie du folklore musical espagnole [Bibliography of Spanish musical folklore] (803); Juan MASOLIVER MARTÍNEZ, La danse de Híjar [The danza of Híjar] (5031); Siegfried NADEL, Le problème du cycle dans la musique populaire [The problem of the cycle in popular music] (4273) and Sur la structure des systèmes de gammes [On the structure of scale systems] (4096); Zdeněk NEJEDLÝ, Les études du prof. O. Hostinsky sur la chanson populaire tchèque [Professor O. Hostinský's research on Czech traditional song] (2452); Paul NETTL, La musique populaire du XVIIᵉ siècle en Autriche [Traditional music of the 17th century in Austria] (1634); Daniel Luis ORTIZ DÍAZ, Les refrains et chansons de la vallée de Iguna (Santander) [Refrains and songs of the Iguña valley (Santander)] (2978); Y. OZAWA, Le théâtre de marionnettes et d'ombres au Japon [The puppet and shadow theaters of Japan] (5219); Mercedes PIERA GELABERT, La danse des gitanes du Vallès [The Ball de gitanes of El Valles] (5050); Karel PLICKA, La musique pastorale et la chanson populaire slovaque [Shepherds' music and the Slovak traditional song] (3003); Friedrich REPP, La chanson populaire de l'îlot linguistique allemand de Spis en Slovaquie [The traditional song of the German linguistic enclave of Spiš in Slovakia] (3025);

Emil RIEGLER-DINU, **La hora, le maquam et la chanson populaire de l'orient européen** (3028) and **Primitivité, évolution et style de la chanson populaire** [Primitivity, evolution, and style of the traditional song] (2536); Antonio P. RIGAU, **Les fêtes de Saint-Roch sur la place Neuve de Barcelone** [The feast of Saint Roch on Plaça Nova, Barcelona] (3030); Valerio SERRA Y BOLDÚ, **Les goigs ou gozos, poèmes religieux chantés en Catalogne** [The goigs or gozos, religious poems sung in Catalonia] (3057); Drahomíra STRÁNSKÁ, **L'état actuel de la chanson populaire dans les montagnes des Géants (Krkonose)** [The current state of traditional song in the Riesengebirge (Krkonoše)] (3075); José SUBIRÁ, **La chanson et la danse populaires dans le Théatre espagnol du XVIIIᵉ siècle** [Traditional song and dance in the Spanish theater of the 18th century] (5253); Noto SUROTO, **Le caractère de la danse javanaise** [The nature of Javanese dance] (5070); Hisao TANABE, **Les études récentes concernant les instruments de musique de Japon** [Recent studies on the musical instruments of Japan] (3605) and **Note sur la musique japonaise** [Notes on Japanese music] (2697); Sándor TÉREY-KUTHY, **Projet d'archives internationales de la chanson et de la musique populaires** [Proposal for international archives of traditional song and music] (697); Pedro Pablo TRAVERSARI SALAZAR, **Les représentations dramatiques populaires de l'Equateur** [Traditional dramatic performance in Ecuador] (5261) and **Recherches sur la musique des Incas** (3221); Bedřich VÁCLAVEK, **Les chansons tchèques populaires** [Popularized Czech song] (3236); (Mme) VAN HOOGENHOUCK TULLEKEN, **Folk-song in Canada** (3181); José ZALDÍVAR, **Les danses populaires catalanes** [Catalan traditional dances] (5084); José Gonzalo ZULAICA Y ARREGUI (José Antonio de Donostia), **La musique basque** [Basque music] (3130) and **Les danses basques** [Basque dances] (5089).

154
bs
[Vienna, 1928] Bericht über den internationalen Kongress für Schubertforschung [Report on the International Congress for Schubert Research] (Augsburg: Benno Filser, 1929). *Illus., port., facs., music, charts, diagr.* In German.
The conference was held from 25 through 29 November 1928. The following contributions are cited separately: Ernst BÜCKEN, **Schubert und die Klassik** [Schubert and Classicism] (1927); Konstantin DANHELOVSKY, **Graf Ferdinand Troyer: Der Schubertmäzen** [Count Ferdinand Troyer: Schubert's patron] (1739); Ernst DECSEY, **Franz Schubert als Tanzmusiker** [Franz Schubert as dance musician] (1741); Otto Erich DEUTSCH, **Zum thematischen Katalog der Werke Schuberts** [On a thematic catalogue of Schubert's work] (551); Max FRIEDLAENDER, **Ansprache zur Einführung** [Inaugural address] (1959) and **Zur Handschriftenkunde Schuberts** [Schubert autography] (1960); Felix GÜNTHER, **Zur Darstellung Schubertscher Lieder** [On the interpretation of Schubert's lieder] (3785); Robert HAAS, **Schubertforschung und Meisterarchiv** [Schubert research and the Meisterarchiv] (1976); Alexander HAUSLEITHNER, **Franz Schuberts Gesänge für Männerstimmen** [Franz Schubert's songs for men's voices] (1775); Willi KAHL, **Schuberts lyrisches Klavierstück** [Schubert's lyrical piano music] (1997); Georg KINSKY, **Schuberthandschriften in deutschem Privatbesitz** [Schubert autographs in private possession in Germany] (731); Ernst KRENEK, **Franz Schubert und wir** [Franz Schubert and us] (2016); Robert LACH, **Schubert und die Volkslied** [Schubert and folk song] (2022); Joseph MARX, **Schuberts Lied** [Schubert's lied] (2036); Paul MIES, **Mehrfache Bearbeitung gleicher Texte bei Schubert** [Multiple settings of the same text by Schubert] (2041); Leopold NOWAK, **Franz Schuberts Kirchenmusik** [Franz Schubert's religious music] (2051); Alfred OREL, **Schubert und Wien** [Schubert and Vienna] (2061); Rudolf SCHWARTZ, **Zur Musikkultur der Renaissance** [The musical culture of the Renaissance] (1431); Paul STEFAN, **Schuberts geistige Haltung und Bedeutung** [Schubert's intellectuality and its significance] (2103); Edmond vander STRAETEN, **Schuberts Behandlung der Streichinstrumente mit besonder Berücksichtigung der Kammermusik** [Schubert's treatment of string instruments, with particular regard to his chamber music] (2105); Otto URSPRUNG, **Das Wesen des Kirchenstils** [The nature of the church style] (6401) and **Der kunst- und handelspolitische Gang der Musikdrucke von 1462-1600** [The development of artistic and commercial policy in music printing from 1462 to 1600] (5995); Otto VRIESLANDER, **Das organische in Schuberts Himmlischer Länge** [The organic in Schubert's heavenly length] (2122); Johannes WOLF, **Die Schuberthandschriften der Preussischen Staatsbibliothek in Berlin** [The Schubert manuscripts of the Preußische Staatsbibliothek in Berlin] (768).

155
bs
[Vitoria] Crónica del IV Congreso Nacional de Música Sagrada [Chronicle of the fourth Congreso Nacional de Música Sagrada] (Vitoria: Imprenta del Montepío Diocesano, 1930) 489 p. *Illus., port., music, index.* In Spanish.
The following contributions are cited separately: José ARTERO, **Pío X y su motu proprio en la historia musical de España** [Pius X and his motu proprio in Spain's musical history] (6150); Resurrección María AZKÚE, **La tradición en nuestra música popular y religiosa** [Tradition in our popular religious music] (2728); Juan Ruiz de LARRINAGA LARRAÑAGA, **Archivo musical de Aránzazu (Guipúzcoa)** [Musical archive of Aránzazu (Guipúzcoa)] (735); Francisco PÉREZ DE VIÑASPRE ORTIZ, **Consideraciones acerca de los polifonistas clásicos españoles** [Considerations concerning the great Spanish polyphonists] (1398); Germán PRADO PERAITA, **El canto litúrgico como medio de apostolado** [Liturgical chant as a medium for apostolate] (6341) and **Participación activa en el culto por medio del canto** [Active participation in the Mass through song] (6342); David PUJOL ROCA, **El canto litúrgico de los fieles** [The liturgical chant of the faithful] (6346); Vicente RIPOLLÉS PÉREZ, **Importancia de la polifonía en la liturgia y poder expresivo** [The use of polyphony in the liturgy and its expressive power] (6353); Casiano ROJO, **El arte y expresión en el canto gregoriano** [Art and expression in Gregorian chant] (1170); Joan Maria THOMÀS SABATER, **La música de órgano** [Organ music] (1700); José Gonzalo ZULAICA Y ARREGUI (José Antonio de Donostia), **La canción popular religiosa y artística** [Religious and artistic popular music] (3127).

1929

156
bs
[Barcelona] IV Congreso Internacional de Arqueología [Fourth International Congress of Archaeology] (Barcelona: Exposición Internacional, 1929). In Spanish.
The following contribution is cited separately: Blas TARACENA AGUIRRE, **Numancia** [Numantia] (5742).

157
bs
[Bologna] Mostra bibliografica musicale [Music bibliography fair]. Report of the First Congresso Internazionale di Bibliografia e Bibliofilia. Ed. by Francesco VATIELLI; pref. by Domenico FAVA (Bologna: Azzoguidi, 1929) 90 p. In Italian.
The conference and book fair was held at the Archiginnasio during June 1929.

158
bs
[Florence] Atti del I Congresso nazionale delle tradizioni popolari [Proceedings of the first Congresso nazionale delle tradizioni popolari]. Sponsored by the Comitato Nazionale per le Tradizioni Popolari (Firenze: Rinascimento del Libro, 1930). In Italian.
The following contributions are cited separately: Arnaldo BONAVENTURA, **L'archivio delle voci** [Archive of voices] (524); Giulio FARA, **La musica del popolo** [Music of the people] (2810); Vittorio SANTOLI, **Di una nuova raccolta di canti popolari toscani** [A new collection of popular Tuscan songs] (3048).

159
bs
[Madrid] Quatrième Congrès de la Confédération Internationale des Sociétés d'Auteurs et Compositeurs [The Fourth Congress of the International Confederation of Societies of Authors and Composers] (Paris: conference, 1929) 209 p. In French.
A discussion of the administrative policies of the societies. The congress was held from 20 through 25 May 1929.

160
bs
[New Haven] Ninth International Congress of Psychology. Ed. by James McKeen CATTELL (Princeton: Psychological Review Company, 1930); (reprint, Nendeln: Kraus, 1974).
The following contributions are cited separately: Christian Paul HEINLEIN, **The effect of the musical modes on amplitude of tapping**

and on the nature of pianoforte performance (5667); M.T. HOLLINSHEAD, **The vibrato in violin playing** (3580); William S. LARSON, **The role of musical aptitude in an instrumental music program in a public school** (4722); Joseph PETERSON and W.F. SMITH, **Habituation effects of the equally tempered musical scale** (5687); Carroll C. PRATT, **Schopenhauer's theory of music** (5569); Christian A. RUCKMICK, **Musical appreciation: A study of the higher emotions** (5579); Herbert Charles SANBORN, **The problem of music** (5580); Max SCHOEN, **The nature of the musical mind** (5700); Carl E. SEASHORE, **The role of experimental psychology in the science of art and music** (5702); Robert Holmes SEASHORE, **Individual differences in rhythmic motor coordinations** (5737); Hazel Martha STANTON, **Psychological tests: A factor in admission to the Eastman School of Music** (4896); Phillip Elwart VERNON, **The psychology of music: Its scope and methodology** (5714).

161
bs
[Rome; Venice] **Primo Congresso mondiale delle biblioteche e di bibliografia** [First World Conference on Libraries and Bibliography]. Sponsored by the Ministero della Educazione Nazionale: Direzione Generale delle Accademie e Biblioteche (Roma: Libreria dello Stato, 1931-1933) 6 v. 367,373,415,385,309 p. *Illus., facs., charts, diagr.* In Italian, English, German, French, and Spanish.

The following contributions are cited separately: Arnaldo BONAVENTURA, **L'ordinamento della musica nelle biblioteche italiane e le relazioni bibliografico-musicali con le altre nazioni** [The classification of music in Italian libraries and bibliographic-musical relations with other nations] (525); Otto Erich DEUTSCH, **Internationale Musikbibliographie der Erstdrucke** [International bibliography of musical first editions] (549); Guido GASPERINI, **Sulle collezioni musicali esistenti presso le pubbliche biblioteche e i loro rapporti con gli studi internazionali di musicologia** [On the existing music collections in public libraries and their relationships with international musicological study] (577); Vito RAELI, **Collezioni di libretti per musica: Statistica e catalogazione** [Collections of libretto for music: Statistics and cataloguing] (656); Fausto TORREFRANCA, **La bibliografia della musica theorica e la necessità di una bibliografia italiana a tutto l'Ottocento** [The bibliography of music theory and the necessity for an Italian bibliography for the entire 19th century] (824).

1930

162
bs
[Antwerp] **Congrès d'Anvers de la Fédération Archéologique et Historique de Belgique, 1930: XXVIIIᵉ session—Annales. II: Comptes rendus** [Antwerp congress of the Fédération Archéologique et Historique de Belgique, 1930: 28th meeting—Annals. II: Reports]. Ed. by Paul ROLLAND (Antwerpen: Resseler, 1931) 516 p. *Illus., charts, diagr.* In French and Dutch.

The following contributions are cited separately: Georges van DOORSLAER, **Aperçu sur la pratique de la musique vocale à Malines au XVᵉ siècle** [Survey of the performance of vocal music in Mechelen in the 15th century] (1289); Gerrit Cornelis Adrianus JUTEN, **Jacob Obrecht** (1351); René Bernard LENAERTS, **Nederlandsche polifoniese liederen uit de XVᵉ en XVIᵉ eeuwen** [Polyphonic songs of the Low Countries from the 15th and 16th centuries] (1366).

163
bs
[Athens] **IIIᵉ Congrès international des études byzantines** [Third International Congress of Byzantine Studies]. Sponsored by the International Association of Byzantine Studies. Ed. by Anastasios K. ORLANDOS (Athínai: Hestia, 1932) 423 p.; (reprint, Nendeln: Kraus, 1978). *Illus., bibliog.* In French and Greek.

The conference was held from 12 through 18 October 1930. The following contributions are cited separately: Sophia ANTONIADES, **La musique byzantine rendue par les ondes Martenot** [Byzantine music performed on the ondes martenot] (6106); Carsten HØEG, **L'état actuel de l'étude de la musique byzantine** [The current state of the study of Byzantine music]

(883); Melpo MERLIER, **Les particularités mélodiques de la chanson populaire grecque** [The melodic characteristics of Greek traditional song] (2956); A. PAPADĪMĪTRIOU, **Peri tis Eptanisō idiorrythmou byzantinis mousikis tis kaloumenis Kritikis** [Concerning the peculiarly rhythmed Byzantine music in the Ionian Islands, the so-called Cretan music] (1154); Konstantinos A. PSACHOS, **Histoire, art, parasémantique et tradition de la musique byzantine** [The history, art, parasemantics, and tradition of Byzantine music] (6129).

164
rs
Review by H. GRÉGOIRE, *Byzantion* 4 (1931) 509–16. In French.

165
rs
Review by V. GRUMEL, *Échos d'Orient* 4 (1931) 96–100. In French.

166
rs
Review by P. de JERPHANION, *Orientalia christiana* 4 (1930) 122–31. In Latin.

167
rs
Review by S.B. KOUGÉAS, *Bulletin of the International Committee of Historical Sciences* 4 (1931) 486–88.

168
rs
Review by G. ROUILLARD, *Bulletin de l'Association Guillaume Budé* 4 (1931) 3–10. In French.

169
bs
[Bonn] **Bericht über die I. Tagung der Internationalen Gesellschaft für Experimentelle Phonetik** [Report on the First Conference of the Internationale Gesellschaft für Experimentelle Phonetik]. Ed. and forew. by Paul MENZERATH (Bonn: Scheur, 1930) viii,124 p. In German, English, and French.

The conference was held from 10 through 14 June 1930. The following contributions are cited separately: R.T. BEATTY, **The sensation of pitch in listening to vibrato singing** (5640); Stephen JONES, **Two methods of measuring intonation** (5825); Franz KÖHLER, **Zur Abstammung Schuberts** [Schubert's ancestry] (2009); Hans KÖLTZSCH, **Schuberts Sonaten** [Schubert's sonatas] (2012); Robert Franz MÜLLER, **Der Körpergrösse Franz Schuberts: Eine Archivstudie** [Franz Schubert's height: An archival study] (2047); Jacques-Gabriel PROD'HOMME, **Les œuvres de Schubert en France** [The works of Schubert in France] (2078); E.W. SELMER, **Vorschläge zu Zeitnormungen bei Melodieaufnahmen** [Proposals for standardizing the time representation in intonation records] (5855).

170
bs
[Budapest] **Compte rendu du cinquième Congrès de la Confédération Internationale des Sociétés d'Auteurs et Compositeurs** [Fifth Congress of the International Confederation of Societies of Authors and Composers] (Paris: conference, 1930) 180 p. In French.

A discussion of the administrative policies of the societies.

171
ap
[Budapest] **1ᵉʳ Congrès international d'organologie** [The First International Congress of Organology], *Échos des sanctuaires de Sainte-Odile* II (1930) 113–28. In French.

Reports on the following contributions given at the conference held from 11 through 14 September 1930: Johannes BIEHLE, **Der Einbau der Orgel nach klanglicher und konfessioneller Zweckmässigkeit** [Installing the organ with respect to tonal and denominational usefulness]; József GEYER, **Organ problems in architecture**; Hans Henny JAHNN, **Architekt und Orgelarchitekt** [The architect and the organ architect]; and Gustave LYON, **La nouvelle salle Pleyel à Paris** [The new Pleyel room in Paris].

172
ap
[Frankfurt am Main] **Erste internationale Arbeits- und Festwoche für katholische Kirchenmusik.** By F. KOSCH, *Zeitschrift für Musikwissenschaft* (1930-1931) 152. In German.

Proceedings of the first international congress of sacred music, organized by the Internationale Gesellschaft für Erneuerung der Katholischen Kirchenmusik, held in Frankfurt am Main from 23 through 26 October 1930. Additional reviews are cited as nos. 173, 174, and 175.

173
ap
[Frankfurt am Main] Internationale Arbeits-woche für neue Kirchenmusik. By BERTEN, *Der Auftakt* 1 (1931). In German.

Review of the first international congress of sacred music, organized by the Internationale Gesellschaft für Erneuerung der Katholischen Kirchenmusik, held in Frankfurt am Main from 23 through 26 October 1930. Additional reviews are cited as nos. 172 , 174, and 175.

174
ap
[Frankfurt am Main] Internationale Fest-woche für katholische Kirchenmusik. By BERTEN, *Die Musikpflege* 10 (1930). In German.

Review of the first international congress of sacred music, organized by the Internationale Gesellschaft für Erneuerung der Katholischen Kirchenmusik, held in Frankfurt am Main from 23 through 26 October 1930. Additional reviews are cited as nos. 172 , 173, and 175.

175
ap
[Frankfurt am Main] La musica sacra catto-lica a Francoforte. By Fausto TORREFRANCA, *La rassegna musicale* (1930) 481. In Italian.

Review of the first international congress of sacred music, organized by the Internationale Gesellschaft für Erneuerung der Katholischen Kirchen-musik, held in Frankfurt am Main from 23 through 26 October 1930. Additional reviews are cited as nos. 172 , 173, and 174.

176
bs
[Hamburg] Verhandlungen des XXIV. internationalen Amerikanisten-Kongresses [Discussions of the 24th International Congress of Americanists]. Ed. by Rudolf GROSSMAN and Gustav Wilhelm Otto ANTZE (Hamburg: Friederichsen, De Gruyter, and Co., 1934) lxvi, 322 p.; (reprint, Nendeln: Kraus, 1968). *Illus., charts, diagr., maps.* In German, French, and English.

The congress was held from 7 through 13 September 1930. The following contributions are cited separately: L.C. van PANHUYS, **Quelques chan-sons et quelques danses dans la Guyane Néerlandaise** [Some songs and some dances in Dutch Guyana] (3210); František POSPÍŠIL, **The present condition of choreographic research in northern, central, and south-ern America** (5053).

177
bs
[Hamburg] Vierter Kongress für Ästhetik und allgemeine Kunstwissenschaft: Bericht [Fourth Congress for Aesthetics and General Art History: Re-port]. Sponsored by the Gesellschaft für Ästhetik und Allgemeine Kunstwissenschaft. Ed. by Hermann NOACK (Stuttgart: Enke, 1931). *Zeitschrift für Ästhetik und allgemeine Kunstwissenschaft* XXV (sup-plement 1931) 265 p. In German.

The conference was held from 7 through 9 October 1930. The following contributions are cited separately: Hans MERSMANN, **Zeit und Musik** [Time and music] (5540); Walter RIEZLER, **Das neue Raumgefühl in bildender Kunst und Musik** [The new feeling for space in graphic art and music] (5393); Max SCHNEIDER, **Raumtiefenhören in der Musik** [Spa-tial depth hearing in music] (5699); Wolfgang STECHOW, **Raum und Zeit in der graphischen und musikalischen Illustration** [Space and time in graphic and musical illustration] (5400).

178
bs
[Liège] Société Internationale de Musicologie: Premier Congrès Liège—Compte rendu/Inter-nationale Gesellschaft für Musikwissenschaft: Erster Kongress Lüttich—Kongressbericht/ International Society for Musical Research: First Congress Liège: Report (London: Plainsong and Mediaeval Music Society, 1930) 248 p. *Illus.* In English, French, and German.

The following contributions are cited separately: Higini ANGLÈS, **La polyphonie religieuse péninsulaire antérieure à la venue des musiciens Flamands en Espagne** [Religious polyphony of the Iberian Peninsula be-fore the arrival of Flemish musicians in Spain] (1223); Antoine AUDA, **Léonard Terry: Professeur, compositeur, chef d'orchestre et musicologue liégeois** [Léonard Terry: Professor, composer, orchestra con-ductor, and musicologist of Liège] (2280); Karel Philippus BERNET

KEMPERS, **Die wallonische und die französische Chanson in der ersten Hälfte des 16. Jahrhunderts** [The Wallonian and the French chan-son in the first half of the 16th century] (1233); Herbert BIEHLE, **Die textlichen Grundlagen als Gesangsproblem** [The text basis as a problem in song] (946); Charles van den BORREN, **Du rôle international de la Belgique dans l'histoire musicale** [The international role of Belgium in the history of music] (948); Maurice CAUCHIE, **Les psaumes de Janequin** [The psalms of Janequin] (1267); Clément CHARLIER, *L'écho: Périodique musical liégeois du XVIIIème* [*L'écho*: A musical periodical of Liège in the 18th century] (1734); Jules DELPORTE, **La Messe *Christus resurgens* de Louis van Pulaer (d. 1528)** [*Missa "Christus resurgens"* by Louis van Pullaer (d. 1528)] (1287); Georges van DOORSLAER, **Paul van Winde: Organiste à la Cour Impériale de Vienne (1598)** [Paul van Winde: Organist at the Viennese imperial court (1598)] (1290); Karl DREIMÜLLER, **Neue Neumenfunde** [New neume finds] (3819); Alfred EINSTEIN, **Filippo di Monte als Madrigalkomponist** [Philippe di Monte as madrigal composer] (1293); Karl Gustav FELLERER, **Das Partimentospiel: Eine Ausgabe des Organisten im 18. Jahrhundert** [The playing of partimento: A task of the 18th-century organist] (3359); Edmund Horace FELLOWES, **The English madrigal of the sixteenth century** (1304) and **The Ouseley Library at Tenbury** (718); Daniel FRYKLUND, **Eine schwedische Sammlung von Briefen von und an Fétis** [A Swedish collection of letters from and to Fétis] (1760); Wilibald GURLITT, **Ein Lütticher Beitrag zur Adam von Fulda-Frage** [A Liège contribution to the Adam von Fulda question] (1324) and **Franz-Joseph Fétis und seine Rolle in der Geschichte der Musikwissenschaft** [François-Joseph Fétis and his role in the history of musicology] (877); Hermann GÜTTLER, **Johann Reichardt: Ein preussischer Lautenist** [Johann Reichardt: A Prussian lutenist] (1768); Toivo Elias HAAPANEN, **Eine Introitsammlung in finnischen Sprache von Jahre 1605** [An In-troit collection in Finnish from 1605] (1570); Jacques HANDSCHIN, **Die Rolle der Nationen in der mittelaltenlicher Musikgeschichte** [The role of the nations in medieval music history] (1116) and **Zur Musikästhetik des 19. Jahrhunderts** [The aesthetics of music of the 19th century] (5486); Emil HARASZTI, **La question Tzigane-Hongroise au point de vue de l'histoire de la musique** [The Hungarian Gypsy issue from a musicologi-cal perspective] (2850); Rosamond E.M. HARDING, **The pianoforte from 1709-1851** (3519); Wilhelm HEINITZ, **Die Erfassung des subjectiv-motorischen Elements in der musikalischen Produktion des Primitiven** [A survey of subjective motoric elements in the musical pro-duction of primitive cultures] (5730); Knud JEPPESEN, **Die Mehrstimmige italienische Lauda am Anfang des 16. Jahrhunderts** [The polyphonic Italian lauda at the beginning of the 16th century] (1345); Ilmari KROHN, **Fr. Aug. Gevaerts Stellung zum gregorianischen Gesang** [François Auguste Gevaert's views on Gregorian chant] (4357); Louis LAVOYE, **Sur une pièce vocale à 4 voix d'un manuscrit de l'ancienne abbaye de Saint-Trond** [Concerning a four-voice piece in a manuscript from the old abbey of Sint-Truiden] (1364); René Bernard LENAERTS, **Le chanson polyphonique Néerlandaise aux 15e et 16e siècles** [The Netherlandish polyphonic chanson of the 15th and 16th centu-ries] (4363); Paul-Marie MASSON, **Beethoven et Rameau** [Beethoven and Rameau] (1809); François-Xavier MATHIAS, **Die Pragmatik der Orgelbaugeschichte des 18. Jahrhunderts im Lichte des Pariser Silbermann-Archivs** [The pragmatism of organ building in the 18th cen-tury in light of the Paris Silbermann archive] (3424); Carl-Allan MOBERG, **Zur Geschichte des schwedischen Kirchen-Gesangs** [On the history of Swedish church songs] (6440); Karl NEF, **Zur Geschichte der Passion** [On the history of the Passion] (1632); André PIRRO, **Remarques sur l'exécution musicale de la fin du 14e au milieu de 15e siècle** [Remarks on musical performance from the end of the 14th century to the middle of the 15th century] (1402); David PUJOL ROCA, **Les archives de musique de l'Abbaye de Montserrat** [The archives of music at the Abbey of Montserrat] (746); Alicja SIMON, **Grétry au Théâtre National de Varsovie** [Grétry at the Teatr Wielki in Warsaw] (1861); Leo SÖHNER, **Gregorianischen Choral und Orgel in Deutschland von 1500 bis 1700** [Gregorian chant and the organ in Germany, 1500-1700] (1437); José SUBIRÁ, **Le théâtre lyrique espagnol au 18e siècle** [The Spanish lyric theater in the 18th century] (5255); André TESSIER, **Quelques sources de l'école française de luth au XVIIe siècle** [Some sources of the French school of lute playing of the 17th century] (3606); John Brande TREND, **A note on Spanish madrigals** (5365); Max UNGER, **Die sogenannte Charakteristik der Tonarten** [The so-called key charateristics] (4223).

179
rs
Review by Jacques Samuel HANDSCHIN, *Zeitschrift für Musikwissenschaft* 4 (1930-1931) 29–33. In German.

180
rs
Review by Erich HERTZMANN, *Melos: Jahrbuch für zeit-genössische Musik* 4 (1930). In German.

181
rs
Review by Wilhelm MERIAN, *Bulletin de la Société Internationale de Musique* 4 (1930) 97–109. In German.

182
rs
Review by José SUBIRÁ, *Boletin musical* 4 (1930). In Spanish.

183
bs
[Prague] Procès-verbaux et documents [Minutes and documents]. Proceedings of the Fourth International Congress of Criticism; sponsored by the Ministerstvo Školství a Národní Osvěty. Ed. by Josef BARTOŠ (Praha: Státní Nakladatelství, 1931) 189 p. In French.
The following contributions are cited separately: O. BAUM, **Der Blinde als Kritiker** [The blind as critics] (5427); H. BLAZIAN, **La radiophonie en Roumanie** [Broadcasting in Romania] (2288); L. Dunton GREEN, **Situation actuelle de la critique en Angleterre** [The current situation of criticism in England] (5481); Frank WARSCHAUER, **Kritik neuer Gebiete** [Criticism of new areas] (5626).

184
rs
Review in *Deutsche Musikerzeitung* 4 (1931). In German.

185
rs
Review in *Mitteilungen des Verbandes Deutscher Musik-kritiker* 4 (1931). In German.

186
rs
Review in *Musikblätter des Anbruch* 4 (1931). In German.

187
rs
Review in *Tempo: A quarterly review of modern music* 4 (1931) 7. In German.

1931

188
bs
[Hamburg] Bericht über den XII. Kongreß der Deutschen Gesellschaft für Psychologie [Report of the 12th congress of the Deutsche Gesellschaft für Psychologie]. Ed. by Gustav KAFKA; pref. by Karl BÜHLER (Jena: Fischer, 1932) 480 p. *Illus., bibliog., charts, diagr.* In German.
The following contributions are cited separately: Alfred GUTTMANN, **Das Tempo und seine Variationsbreite** [Tempo and its range of variability] (5663); Albrecht LANGELÜDDEKE, **Über rhythmische Defekte** [Rhythmic defects] (5673).

189
bs
[Leiden] Actes du XVIIIᵉ Congrès international des orientalistes [Proceedings of the 18th International Congress of Orientalists] (Leiden: Brill, 1932) vi, 271 p.; (reprint, Nendeln: Kraus, 1974). In French, English, German, and Italian.
The meeting was held from 7 through 12 September 1931. The following contribution is cited separately: Evangeline Dora EDWARDS, **The establishment of schools of secular music by Ming Huang of the T'ang dynasty** (2656).

190
bs
[London] Compte rendu du sixième Congrès de la Confédération Internationale des Sociétés d'Auteurs et Compositeurs [The Sixth Congress of the International Confederation of the Societies of Authors and Composers]. Sponsored by the Performing Right Society (Paris: conference, 1931) 223 p. In French.
A discussion of the administrative policies of the societies.

191
bs
[Paris] Congrès international des éditeurs: Neuvième session [International Congress of Publishers: Ninth meeting]. Sponsored by the International Publishers' Association/Union Internationale des Éditeurs (Paris: Cercle de la Librairie, 1932) 265 p. *Charts, diagr.* In French.
The following contributions are cited separately: Carlo CLAUSETTI, **La diminution de la vente des éditions musicales et ses causes** [The decline of music publication sales and its causes] (5953); René DOMMANGE, **Le régime de la licence obligatoire en matière de reproduction musico-mécanique** [Mandatory licensing regulations concerning mechanically reproduced music] (5956); Oskar von HASE, **La vente et le prêt de matériel d'orchestre** [The sale and rental of orchestral equipment] (3252).

192
bs
[Paris] XVᵉ Congrès international d'anthropologie et d'archéologie préhistorique (suite); Vᵉ session de l'Institut International d'Anthropologie [15th International Congress of Anthropology and Prehistoric Archaelogy (sequel); 5th meeting of the International Institute of Anthropology] (Paris: Nourry, 1933) lxxxvii, 847 p. *Illus., charts, diagr.* In French.
The conference was held from 20 through 27 September 1931. The following contributions are cited separately: V. BUGIEL, **Quelles sont les premières phases de la poésie des peuples primitifs** [What are the first phases in the poetry of primitive peoples?] (5293); RIZA NUR, **Keuroghlou, poète populaire turc** [Köroğlu, Turkish traditional poet] (5345); Marie de VAUX-PHALIPAU, **Moeurs des Serbes de Lusace d'après les chansons populaires** [The customs of the Sorb people of Lusatia as seen in traditional songs] (3099); Divna VEKOVIĆ, **Chants populaires de femmes serbes** [Traditional songs of Serbian women] (5367). The first half of this congress and the fourth meeting of the Institut International d'Anthropologie took place in Portugal, 21-30 September 1930.

193
bs
[Salzburg] Bericht über die musikwissenschaftliche Tagung der Internationalen Stiftung Mozarteum [Report of the musicological meeting of the Internationale Stiftung Mozarteum]. Ed. by Erich SCHENK (Leipzig: Breitkopf & Härtel, 1932) xii, 312 p. *Music, bibliog., list of works, charts, diagr.* In German and Italian.
The conference was held from 2 through 5 August 1931. The following contributions are cited separately: Erdmann Werner BÖHME, **Mozart in der schönen Literatur** [Mozart in *belles lettres*] (5290); Antoine-Élisée CHERBULIEZ, **Stilkritischer Vergleich von Mozarts beiden g-moll Sinfonien von 1773 und 1788** [A stylistic comparison between Mozart's two G-minor symphonies, of 1773 and 1778] (4322), **Zur harmonischen Analyse der Einleitung von Mozarts C-Dur Streichquartett (K.V. 465)** [Harmonic analysis of the introduction to Mozart's C-major string quartet (K.465)] (4153), and **Zwei Passauer handschriftliche Klavierauszüge von Mozarts Figaro und Don Juan der Schwelger (1789)** [Two manuscript piano reductions from Passau of Mozart's *Figaro* and *Don Juan der Schwelger* (1789)] (1735); Werner DANCKERT, **Mozarts Menuettypen** [Mozart's minuet types] (4239); Hans ENGEL, **Mozarts Konzertwerke** [Mozart's concertos] (1748) and **Musiksoziologie und musikalische Volkskunde** [The sociology of music and musical folkore] (5880); Karl Gustav FELLERER, **Mozarts Litaneien** [Mozart's litanies] (4246); Wilhelm FISCHER, **Die Stetigkeit in Mozarts Schaffen** [The steadiness of Mozart's output] (1758); Robert HAAS, **Mozartforschung und Meisterarchiv** [Mozart research and the Meisterarchiv] (722); Oskar KAUL, **Zur Instrumentation Mozarts** [Mozart's instrumentation] (3746); Robert LACH, **Mozart und die Gegenwart** [Mozart and the present] (5516); Ernst LEWICKI, **Die Stimmcharaktere im** *Idomeneo* [Voice types of *Idomeneo*] (3757); Paul NETTL, **Mozarts Prager Kontertänze** [Mozart's Prague contredanses] (1826) and *Sethos* **und die freimauerische Grundlage der** *Zauberflöte* [*Sethos* and the Masonic foundation of *Die Zauberflöte*] (5212); Alfred OREL, **Mozart in der Kunstanschauung Franz Grillparzers** [Mozart in Franz Grillparzer's view of art] (5557); Bernhard PAUMGARTNER, **Zur Synthese der symphonischen Musik Mozarts** [The synthesis represented by Mozart's symphonic music] (1835); Erich SCHENK, **Mozarts mütterliche Familie** [Mozart's maternal relatives] (1851) and **Organisation der Mozartforschung** [The organization of Mozart research] (917); Ludwig SCHIEDERMAIR, **Das deutsche Mozartbild** [The German image of Mozart] (1853); Leo SCHRADE, **Mozart und die Romantiker** [Mozart and the Romantics] (5590); Rudolf STEGLICH, **Das Tempo als Problem der Mozartinterpretation** [Tempo as a problem in Mozart interpretation] (3769);

Fausto TORREFRANCA, **Mozart e il quartetto italiano** [Mozart and the Italian quartet] (1882); Lothar WALLERSTEIN, **Mozarts** *Idomeneo* **in der Wiener Bearbeitung** [Mozart's *Idomeneo* in the Vienna version] (3775).

1932

194
bs

[Amsterdam] Proceedings of the First International Congress of Phonetic Sciences: First meeting of the Internationale Arbeitsgemeinschaft für Phonologie *Archives néederlandaises de phonétique expérimentale* 8-9 (Harlem: J. Enschedé, 1933) 221 p. *Illus., port., bibliog.* In English, French, and German.

The following contributions are cited separately: Gustav BECKING, **Der musikalische Bau des montenegrinischen Volksepos** [The musical structure of the folk epic of Montenegro] (2736); Karel Philippus BERNET KEMPERS, **Das Entstehen von Tonsystemen** [The origin of tonal systems] (860); Erich FEUCHTWANGER, **Das Musische in der Sprache und seine Pathologie** [The artistic aspect of language and its pathology] (5655); Friedrich TRAUTWEIN, **Über elektrische Synthese von Sprachlauten und musikalischen Tönen (Instruments à ondes)** [On the electric synthesis of speech sound and musical notes (instruments *à ondes*)] (5940).

195
bs

[Brussels] La musique et le peuple: Rapports, suggestions, voeux [Music and the people: Reports, suggestions, wishes] (Bruxelles: Ministère des Sciences et des Arts, 1932) 112 p. In French.

The following contributions are cited separately: Arthur BOON, **La chanson populaire** [Folk song] (2741); Léopold CHARLIER, **Ce qui a été fait au pays de Liège pour l'éducation populaire par la musique** [What has been done in the area of Liège regarding music education of the populace] (4503); Ernest CLOSSON, **Folklore, radio et orphéons** [Folklore, radio, and choirs] (4508); Paul GILSON, **La musique et l'éducation des masses** [Music and the education of the masses] (4542); Georges HONINCKS, **Le rôle de la musique comme élément d'éducation populaire** [The role of music as an element of popular education] (4553); Emiel HULLEBROECK, **Comment faire chanter les vieilles chansons** [How to keep the old songs alive] (2868); **L'action de l'Orchestre Symphonique Populaire** [The activities of the Orchestre Symphonique Populaire] (2283); Alfred MAHY, **Le répertoire des sociétés d'amateurs** [The repertoire of amateur societies] (2351); Flor MIELANTS, **Les concerts "De Werker" d'Anvers** [The "De Werker" concerts in Antwerp] (2359); Louis PIÉRARD and Charles DEPASSE, **Avant-propos** [Opening remarks] (5902); Georges PITSCH, **Sur l'organisation de concerts de musique de chambre** [On the organization of chamber music concerts] (3682); Marcel POOT, **La radio et les sociétés instrumentales d'amateurs** [Radio and the amateur instrumental societies] (4915); A. PRÉVOST, **Éducation musicale populaire: Projet d'utilisation rationnelle de la musique du 1er Régiment de Guides** [Popular music education: A project for rational use of the music of the 1er Régiment de Guides] (4624); **Une manifestation d'art musical populaire à Frameries** [A demonstration of working people's musical art in Frameries] (2284).

196
bs

[Cairo] Recueil des travaux du Congrès de musique arabe [Collection of studies from the Congress on Arab Music]. Proceedings of the Mu'tamar al-Mūsīqá al-'Arabiyyah; sponsored by King Fu'ād of Egypt and the Ministry of Education. Intro. by Maḥmūd Aḥmad AL-ḤIFNĪ (Al-Qāhirah: Boulac, 1934) xii, 711 p. *Illus., port., music, discog., charts, diagr., transcr.* In French and Arabic.

The following contributions are cited separately: 'Alī AL-DARWĪSH, **Maqamates employés chez les Maures et spécialement en Tunisie** [Maqāmāt used among the Moors, particularly in Tunisia] (4042) and **Maqamates employés en Egypte et leur décomposition en genres** [Maqāmāt used in Egypt and their analysis into genres] (4043); Maḥmūd Aḥmad AL-ḤIFNĪ, **Commission de l'Enseignement** [The Commission on Pedagogy] (4480); Xavier Maurice COLLANGETTES, **Commission de l'Échelle Musicale** [The Commission on the Musical Scale] (4063);

Communications sur les rythmes [Communications on rhythms] (3982); Ali EL GAREM, **Rapport sur la composition** [Report on composition] (5312); François Rodolphe d' ERLANGER, **Rapport** [Report] (3941); Henry George FARMER, **Histoire abrégée de l'échelle de la musique arabe** [A short history of the scale in Arabic music] (4070) and **Rapport général sur les travaux de la Commission d'Histoire et des Manuscrits** [General report on the work of the Commission on History and Manuscripts] (870); Robert LACHMANN, **Commission de l'Enregistrement: Rapport** [The Commission on Recording: A report] (827); Curt SACHS, **Rapport général de la Commission des Instruments** [General report of the Commission on Instruments] (3273); Ali SAFAR, **Genres de composition musicale arabe employés en Egypte** [Arab musical genres practiced in Egypt] (2582); **Séances plénières de la semaine officiel du Congrès** [Plenary sessions of the conference's official week] (2296); Rauf YEKTA, **Commission des Modes, des Rythmes et de la Composition** [The Commission on Modes, Rhythms, and Composition] (3963). The proceedings of the conference are also published in Arabic under the title *Kitāb Mu'tamar al-Mūsīqá al-'Arabiyyah* (Cairo, 1933).

197
bs

[Liège] Congrès de Liège de la Fédération Archéologique et Historique de Belgique, 1932: XXIXᵉ session—Annales [Liège Congress of the Fédération Archéologique et Historique de Belgique, 1932: 29th meeting—Annals]. Ed. by Jules DUMONT and Paul HARSIN (Liège: n.p., 1932). In French.

The following contributions are cited separately: Charles van den BORREN, **Hugo et Arnold de Lantins** [Hugo and Arnold de Lantins] (1252); Roger BRAGARD, **André de Pape** (1256); Clément CHARLIER, **Un manuscrit musical mosan de 1728** [A 1728 music manuscript from the Meuse valley] (1504).

198
bs

[La Plata] Actas y trabajos científicos del XXVº Congreso Internacional de Americanistas [Proceedings and scholarly papers from the 25th International Congress of Americanists] (Buenos Aires: Coni; Universidad Nacional de La Plata, 1934) 2 v.; (reprint, Nendeln: Kraus, 1968). *Facs., music, bibliog., charts, diagr., maps.* In Spanish and English.

The following contributions are cited separately: Frances DENSMORE, **The music of the North American Indians** (3145); Carlos VEGA, **Escalas con semitonos en la música de los antiguos peruanos** [Scales with semitones in ancient Peruvian music] (4126) and **La flauta de Pan andina** [The Andean panpipe] (3639).

199
bs

[Strasbourg] Compte rendu du Congrès d'orgue tenu à l'Université de Strasbourg. IV [Report of the organ congress held at the Université de Strasbourg. IV]. Ed. by François-Xavier MATHIAS (Strasbourg: Société Strasbourgeoise de Librairie Sostralib, 1934) 265 p. *Illus., organ specification.* In French.

The following contributions are cited separately: Alexandre CELLIER, **Le rôle de l'orgue dans le culte protestant** [The role of the organ in the Protestant religion] (6429) and **L'improvisation** [Improvisation] (3673); Léon COUPLEUX, **L'orgue des ondes** [The bellows organ] (3347); R.P. DILLENSEGER, **La puissance organale mise en proportion avec le cubage des sanctuaires et des salles de concert** [The sound volume of organs in proportion to the area of churches and concert halls] (5812); Norbert DUFOURCQ, **Le grand orgue de la Chapelle de l'École Royale Militaire** [The great organ of the chapel of the École Royale Militaire] (3351); Theodore GÉROLD, **Strasbourg dans l'histoire de l'orgue** [Strasbourg in the history of the organ] (3370); József GEYER, **Fautes à éviter dans la disposition des jeux** [Mistakes to avoid in registration] (3371) and **Un orgue à 52 tuyaux, 4 jeux, sommier à coulisses, de l'an 228** [An organ with 52 pipes, four ranks, and slider chest, from the year 228] (3372); François-Xavier MATHIAS, **La continuité dans l'évolution de l'expression organale et ses conséquences pour la pédagogie musicale de l'heure présente** [Continuity in the evolution of expressivity in organ music and its consequences for current musical pedagogy] (3421), **L'emplacement des orgues dans les sanctuaires** [The placement of organs in churches] (3422), **L'orgue au service du culte catholique** [The role of the organ in the Catholic religion] (6303), **L'orgue dans la culture** musicale de tous les siècles [The organ in the musical culture of all centuries] (3423), **L'orgue dans l'antiquité chrétienne: Probabilité de sa part médiate et indirecte à l'évolution du chant cultuel, à partir du 5ᵉ siècle** [The organ in Christian antiquity: The probability that it played a mediate and indirect role in the evolution of liturgical chant from the 5th century onwards] (6019), and **L'orgue dans le culte** [The organ in the liturgy] (6304); Bérenger de MIRAMON FITZ-JAMES, André MARCHAL, Norbert DUFOURCQ, and V. GONZALEZ, **La doctrine parisienne de l'orgue** [The Parisian organ doctrine] (3435); André PIRRO, **Orgues et organistes de Haguenau de 1491 à 1525** [Organs and organists of Haguenau from 1491 to 1525] (1401) and **Orgues et organistes en Alsace et en Lorraine du XIVᵉ au XVIIIᵉ siècle** [Organs and organists in Alsace and in Lorraine from the 14th to the 18th century] (3447); Madame Pierre PIZOT-MONNIER, **De l'orgue dans le culte protestant** [The organ in the Protestant religion] (6442); Félix RAUGEL, **Les orgues de Bruckner** [The organs of Bruckner] (3463); E. RUPP, **Les sommiers et la traction de l'orgue** [The soundboards and action of the organ] (3471).

200
bs
[Vienna] Compte rendu du septième Congrès de la Confédération Internationale des Sociétés d'Auteurs et Compositeurs [Report of the Seventh Congress of the International Confederation of the Societies of Authors and Composers] (Paris: conference, 1932) 285 p. In French.
The conference was held from 6 through 11 June 1932. A discussion of the administrative policies of the societies.

201
rs
Review in *Der schaffende Musiker* 4 (1932) 26. In German.

1933

202
bs
[Copenhagen] Compte rendu du huitième Congrès de la Confédération Internationale des Sociétés d'Auteurs et Compositeurs [Report of the eighth Congress of the International Confederation of the Societies of Authors and Composers] (Paris: conference, 1934) 256 p. In French.
A discussion of the administrative policies of the societies. The conference was held from 29 May through 5 June 1933.

203
bs
[Florence] Atti del primo Congresso internazionale di musica [Proceedings of the First International Congress of Music] (Firenze: Le Monnier, 1935) 282 p. In Italian, French, English, and German.
The conference was held in conjunction with the first Maggio Musicale Fiorentino. The following contributions are cited separately: Paul BEKKER, **Organisation des Operntheaters** [The organization of opera theaters] (5103); Ferruccio BONAVIA, **L'opera in Inghilterra** [Opera in England] (5108); Alfredo CASELLA, **Scambi musicali** [Musical exchange] (2299); Gaetano CESARI, **Le funzione, i metodi, gli scopi della critica musicale** [The function, methods, and purposes of music criticism] (5441); André COEUROY, **Problèmes intérieurs et extérieurs de radio** [Radio's internal and external problems] (5747); Luigi COLACICCHI, **Il disco e la musica** [Records and music] (5748); Andrea DELLA CORTE, **Ricerca intorno alle "vicende degli stili del canto in rapporto alla cultura musicale e alla pedagogia stilistica"** [Developments in singing styles in relation to musical culture and pedagogy] (3294); Edward Joseph DENT, **International exchange in music** (2312); Carl EBERT, **Moderne Opernregie** [Modern opera direction] (5144); Alfred EINSTEIN, **Le tendenze attuali dell'opera tedesca** [Current trends in German opera] (5147); Herbert FLEISCHER, **Neue Musik und mechanische Musik** [New music and mechanical music] (3792); Leonhard FÜRST, **Prinzipien musikalischer Gestaltung im Tonfilm** [Principles of musical organization in the sound film] (5152); Guido Maria GATTI, **Dell'interpretazione musicale** [Musical interpretation] (5476); Ludwig KOCH, **Schallplattenmusik** [Recorded music] (5766); Adriano LUALDI, **Due nuove vie per la musica: Radio e film sonoro** [Two new roads for music: Radio and film with sound] (5198); Armand MACHABEY, **Rapport sur le théâtre musical en France** [Report on music theater in France] (5201); Basil MAINE, **Some effects of mechanized music** (2209); Massimo MILA, **Musica e ritmo nel cinematografo** [Music and rhythm in the

cinema] (5208); Robert-Aloys MOOSER, **Le contrôle de la critique musicale sur les auditions radiophoniques** [Music criticism as a way of monitoring radio programs] (5552); Guido PANNAIN, **La critica musicale come critica d'arte** [Music criticism as art criticism] (5562); Alfredo PARENTE, **Il problema dell'interpretazione musicale** [The problem of musical interpretation] (3681); Henry PRUNIÈRES, **Des rapports artistiques internationaux considérés du point de vue de la musique, de la musicologie et des musiciens** [International artistic relationships from the point of view of music, musicology, and musicians] (2378); Luigi RONGA, **Nuove tendenze nella critica musicale europea** [New tendencies in European music criticism] (5577); Hans ROSBAUD, **Probleme der Programmgestaltung und der künstlerisch-technischen Wiedergabe im deutschen Rundfunk** [Issues in programming and artistic and technical reproduction in German radio] (5784); Gastone ROSSI-DORIA, **Tendenze dell'odierno teatro musicale italiano** [Trends in today's Italian music theater] (5233); Boris de SCHLOEZER, **Comprendre la musique** [Understanding music] (5586); Roger SESSIONS, **L'opera negli Stati Uniti** [Opera in the United States] (5242); Paul STEFAN, **Ein Völkerbund der Musik** [A musical League of Nations] (2394); Émile VUILLERMOZ, **La musique mécanique et la culture musicale** [Mechanical music and musical culture] (4664).

204
rs
Review by Michel Dimitri CALVOCORESSI, *The musical times* 4 (1935) 898–99.

205
rs
Review by Henry PRUNIÈRES, *Revue musicale* 4 (1933) 64–68. In French.

206
rs
Review by P.A. SCHOLES, *The musical times* 4 (1933) 553–54.

207
bs
[Leipzig] Bericht über den XIII. Kongress der Deutschen Gesellschaft für Psychologie [Report on the 13th congress of the Deutsche Gesellschaft für Psychologie]. Ed. by Otto KLEMM (Jena: Fischer, 1934) 216 p. In German.
The meeting was held from 16 through 19 October 1933. The following contribution is cited separately: Julius BAHLE, **Die Gestaltübertragung im vokalen Schaffen zeitgenössischer Komponisten** [Shape translation in the vocal work of contemporary composers] (5637).

208
bs
[Stockholm] Congrès international d'histoire de l'art (XIIIᵉᵐᵉ) [Thirteenth International Congress of Art History] (Stockholm: A.B. Hasse, 1933) 268 p. *Charts, diagr.* In French.
The conference was held from 4 through 7 September 1933. The following contribution is cited separately: G.L. LUZZATO, **Essenza e funzione della critica d'arte** [Essence and function of art criticism] (5530).

209
bs
[Warsaw] VIIᵉ Congrès international des sciences historiques [Seventh International Congress of Historical Sciences] (Warszawa: conference, 1933) 2 v. v, 532 p.; (reprint, Nendeln: Kraus, 1972). *Illus.* In French, German, Italian, and English.
The meeting was held from 21 through 28 August 1933. The following contribution is cited separately: **Société des Historiens du Théâtre: Organisation internationale des recherches d'histoire théâtrale** [Société des Historiens du Théâtre: International organization for theater history research] (5247).

1934

210
bs
[Antwerp] Verhandelingen van het Muziekcongres [Proceedings of the music congress]. Proceedings of the Vlaamsche Muziekcongres I. Ed. by Jean Auguste STELLFELD (Antwerpen: Stad Antwerpen, 1935) 126 p. *Illus., port.* In Dutch.
The conference was held from 15 through 16 August 1934 on the occasion of the centenary of the birth of Peter Benoît. The following contributions are cited separately: Karel ALBERT, **Nationale elementen in het verloop der muziekgeschiedenis en hun beteekenis voor de huidige muziek** [Nationalist elements in the history of music and their meaning for music

today] (939); Charles van den BORREN, **Nationalistische strekkingen in de musiek** [Nationalist tendencies in music] (949); Maurits De BUCK, **De strijd van Benoit voor zijn kunstautonomie aan de Vlaamsche Muziekschool en aan het Koninklijk Vlaamsch Conservatorium te Antwerpen** [Benoît's battle for artistic autonomy at the Vlaamse Muziekschool and at the Koninklijk Vlaams Muziek Conservatorium in Antwerp] (1926); Marinus DE JONG, **Polyphonisten uit de 15ᵉ en 16ᵉ eeuw** [Polyphonists of the 15th and 16th centuries] (1285); Denijs DILLE, **Peter Benoit en de nieuwe muziek** [Peter Benoît and the new music] (1944); Jef HOREMANS, **Minder bekende lyrische drama's van Peter Benoit** [Lesser-known lyric dramas by Peter Benoît] (1986) and **Slotwoord** [Closing word] (2328); Emiel HULLEBROECK, **Het vraagstuk der auteursrechten** [The question of copyright] (5969); René Bernard LENAERTS, **Zestiende-eeuwse praalmuziek** [Sixteenth-century ceremonial music] (1368); Floris van der MUEREN, **Hoe komen we tot een geschiedenis der Vlaamsche muziek der 19ᵈᵉ eeuw?** [How to arrive at a history of Flemish music in the 19th century?] (904); Jules van NUFFEL, **De betrekkingen Benoit-Tinel** [The connections between Benoît and Tinel] (2054); Lodewijk ONTROP, **Bij de honderdste verjaring van Peter Benoit's geboortedag** [On the one hundredth anniversary of Peter Benoît's birth] (2057); André M. POLS, **De betrekkingen Benoit-Liszt** [The connections between Benoît and Liszt] (2070); Maurits SABBE, **De uitgave der werken van P. Benoit** [The publication of the works of Peter Benoît] (2087); J. De VEEN-HIEL, **Hiel-Benoit—Benoit-Hiel** [Hiel-Benoît—Benoît-Hiel] (2118); Prosper VERHEYDEN, **De muziekhandschriften van P. Benoit** [The music manuscripts of Peter Benoît] (2119).

211
ap

[Luxembourg] Internationaler orgelkongress in Luxembourg [The International Organ Congress in Luxembourg]. By G. KASCHNER, *Die Musik* XXVII (1934-1935) 60–62. In German.

The meeting was held from 30 August through 2 September 1934. Another report is cited as no. 212 in this volume.

212
ap

[Luxembourg] Luxembourg: Congrès internationale d'organologie [International Organ Congress in Luxembourg], *Revue de musicologie* (1934) 232. In French.

The meeting was held from 30 August to 2 September 1934. Another report is cited as no. 211 in this volume.

213
bs

[Prague] Actes du huitième Congrès international de philosophie [Proceedings of the Eighth International Congress of Philosophy] (Praha: conference, 1936) lxxii, 1103 p.; (reprint, Nendeln: Kraus, 1968). In French.

The conference was held from 2 through 7 September 1934. The following contribution is cited separately: Dimitrie CUCLIN, **Musique: Art, science, et philosophie** [Music: Art, science, and philosophy] (5444).

214
bs

[Recife] Estudos Afro-Brasileiros. I [Afro-Brazilian studies. I]. Proceedings of the first Congresso Afro-Brasileiro. Ed. by Gilberto FREYRE; pref. by Edgar ROQUETTE-PINTO (Rio de Janeiro: Ariel, 1935). *Port., facs., music, maps.* In Portuguese.

The following contribution is cited separately: Mário de ANDRADE, **A calunga dos maracatús** [The *calunga* of the maracatu] (4929).

215
bs

[Sofia] Actes du IVᵉ Congrès des études byzantines [Proceedings of the Fourth Congress of Byzantine Studies]. Sponsored by the International Association of Byzantine Studies. Ed. by Bogdan D. FILOV. *Izvestija na Bǎlgarskija Arheologičeski Institut* 9-10 (Sofija: Imprimerie de la Cour, 1935) 2 v. 342 p.; (reprint, Nendeln: Kraus, 1978). *Illus.* In French, German, Italian, and Russian.

The conference was held in September 1934. The following contribution is cited separately: Ioan Dumitru PETRESCU, **Les principes du chant d'église byzantin** [Principles of chant in the Byzantine church] (6126).

216
rs

Review by H. GRÉGOIRE, *Byzantion* 4 (1935) 259–81. In French.

217
rs

Review in *Bulletin of the International Committee of Historical Sciences* 4 (1934) 351–52.

218
bs

[Trent] Atti del III Congresso nazionale di arti e tradizioni popolari [Acts of the third Congresso nazionale di arti e tradizioni popolari]. Sponsored by the Comitato Nazionale Italiano per le Arti Popolari (Roma: Opera Nazionale Dopolavoro, 1936) 662 p. *Illus., maps.* In Italian.

The conference took place from 8 through 11 September 1934. The following contributions are cited separately: M. BARBI, **Poesia e musica popolare** [Poetry and traditional music] (5287); Cesare CARAVAGLIOS, **Metodi ed orientamenti nelle ricerche delle tradizioni popolari musicale** [Methods and orientations in the search for folk music traditions] (2425); Luigi COLACICCHI, **Canti popolari de Ciociaria** [Popular songs of Ciociaria] (2772); Giulio FARA, **Canzone popolare, canto del popolo etnofonia** [Popular songs, song of the ethnophonic people] (2807); Gavino GABRIEL, **Laofonografia** [Laophonography] (2432); R. GIRALDI, **La liuteria italiana come arte popolare** [Italian lute music as traditional art] (964); Fernando LIUZZI, **Della raccolta dei canti popolari a cura della commissione tecnica del Comitato Nazionale per le Arti Popolari** [On the collection of traditional songs edited by the technical commission of the Comitato Nazionale per le Arte Popolari] (2933); Renato LUNELLI, **La fisarmonica e il Trentino** [The accordion and Trentino] (3529); F.L. LUNGHI, **Sulla scheda Caravaglios per la raccolta dei canti popolari** [On the Caravaglios index for the collection of traditional songs] (614); M. MAFFIOLETTI, **L'aderenza spirituale ed espressiva della poesia alla musica nei canti del popolo italiano nel Risorgimento** [The spiritual and expressive adherence of the poetry to the music in Italian popular song of the Risorgimento] (2034); Giorgio NATALETTI, **I poeti a braccio della campagna romana** [The poets' contests of the Roman countryside] (2971) and **Il disco e il film sonoro nella ricerca e nelle trascrizioni della musica popolare** [The record and the sound film in the research and transcription of traditional music] (4922); R. PARTINI, **Elementi e sviluppi nel canto popolare** [Elements and development of traditional song] (2988); Mary TIBALDI CHIESA, **Canzoni popolari valdostane** [Traditional songs of Valle d'Aosta] (3081); Fausto TORREFRANCA, **Le prime villote a quattro e loro importanza storica ed estetica** [The first villottas in four voices and their historic and aesthetic importance] (1455).

219
bs

[Tübingen] Psychologie des Gemeinschaftslebens: Bericht über den XIV. Kongress der Deutschen Gesellschaft für Psychologie [The psychology of life in the community: Report on the 14th congress of the Deutsche Gesellschaft für Psychologie]. Ed. by Otto KLEMM (Jena: Fischer, 1935). In German.

The conference was held from 22 through 26 May 1934. The following contributions are cited separately: Julius BAHLE, **Persönlichkeit und Kunstwerk im zeitgenössischen Musikschaffen: Ein psychologisch-pädagogischer Beitrag zum Verständnis neuer Musik** [Personality and he work of art in contemporary composition: A psychological and pedagogical contribution to the understanding of new music] (5639); G.D. MALL, **Wirkungen der Musik auf verschiedene Persönlichkeitstypen** [The effects of music on different personality types] (5678); Heinrich SCHOLE, **Experimentelle Untersuchungen an höchsten und an kürzesten Tönen** [Experimental investigations into the highest and shortest tones] (5701); Albert WELLEK, **Zur Typologie der Musikalität der Deutschen Stämme** [A typology of musicality among the Germanic tribes] (5718).

1935

220
bs

[Brussels] Actes et travaux du Congrés international pour l'étude du XVIIIᵉᵐᵉ siècle en Belgique [Proceedings and works of the International Congress for the Study of the 18th century in Belgium]. Sponsored by the Société des Amis du Prince de Ligne.

Ed. by Félicien LEURIDANT (Bruxelles: Editions des Annales Prince de Ligne, 1936) 2 v. *Illus., port., charts, diagr.* In French.

The conference in honor of the 200th anniversary of the birth of Prince Charles-Joseph de Ligne (1735-1814) was held from 27 through 30 July 1935. The following contributions are cited separately: Martin LANSSENS, **Sur la musique nouvelle de *Colette et Lucas*: Comédie du Prince de Ligne** [On the new music for *Colette et Lucas*: A comedy by the Prince of Ligne] (1799); Louis LAVOYE, **Le théâtre musical liègeois au XVIIIe siècle** [Musical theater of Liège in the 18th century] (1600); Albert vander LINDEN, **La musique et la danse dans les Pays-Bas au XVIIIème siècle** [Music and dance in the Low Countries in the 18th century] (1606).

221 **[Brussels] XVIe Congrès international**
bs **d'anthropologie et d'archéologie préhistorique: VIe Assemblée générale de l'Institut International d'Anthropologie** [Sixteenth International Congress of Prehistoric Anthropology and Archaeology: Sixth General Assembly of the International Institute of Anthropology] (Bruxelles: Imprimerie Médicale et Scientifique, 1936) cii, 1162 p. In French.

The conference was held from 1 through 8 September 1935. The following contribution is cited separately: Ryuzo TORII, **Les gongs-cloches au Japan** [The gong-bells of Japan] (3656).

222 **[London] Proceedings of the Second Interna-**
bs **tional Congress of Phonetic Sciences.** Ed. by Daniel JONES and Dennis Butler FRY (Cambridge: Cambridge University Press, 1936) ix, 328 p. *Illus., port.* In English, German, and French.

The conference was held at University College from 22 through 26 July 1935. The following contributions are cited separately: Elena Garnett FORBES (Elena Garnetti), **The exercise of voice** (3297); Miles Laurence HANLEY, **Phonographic recording** (5756); Jean TARNEAUD, **Évolution de nos connaissances en pathologie vocale** [The evolution of our knowledge of vocal pathology] (3325).

223 **[Seville] Compte rendu du dixième Congrès de**
bs **la Confédération Internationale des Sociétés d'Auteurs et Compositeurs** [Proceedings of the Tenth Congress of the International Confederation of the Societies of Authors and Composers]. Sponsored by the Sociedad General de Autores y Editores (Paris: conference, 1935) 392 p. In French.

A discussion of the administrative policies of the societies. The conference was held from 6 through 11 May 1935.

1936

224 **[Barcelona] Congrés de la Societat Interna-**
bs **cional de Musicologia** [Congress of the International Musicological Society] (Barcelona: Casa de Caritat, 1936) 47 p. *Illus., port.* In Spanish, Catalan, French, German, and Italian.

The conference was held from 18 through 25 April 1936. The following contributions are cited separately: Higini ANGLÈS, **La polyphonie de la Court pontificale d'Avignon de la seconde moitié du XIVe siècle en Catalogne** [Polyphony at the papal court of Avignon during the second half of the 14th century in Catalonia] (6147) and **Nécessité d'un catalogue détaillé des manuscrits grégoriens du Moyen Age** [The necessity for a detailed catalogue of Gregorian manuscripts of the Middle Ages] (6145); Jesús BAL Y GAY, **La canción amorosa della corte de Castilla de fines del siglo XVI y principios del siglo XVII** [The love song at the court of Castile from the end of the 16th and the beginning of the 17th centuries] (1227); Josep BARBERÀ, **Supervivències gregues en la cançó popular catalana** [The survival of Greek elements in Catalan traditional song] (2730); Heinrich BESSELER, **Die Anfänge der musikalischen Neuzeit** [The beginnings of musical modernity] (1236); Marie-Louise BOËLLMANN, **La pénétration en France de la musique d'orgue de**

J.S. Bach au XIXe siècle [The dissemination of J.S. Bach's organ music in 19th-century France] (1920); Manfred F. BUKOFZER, **Zur Erklärung des *Lobetanz* in der schweizerischen Volksmusik** [Explanation of the *Lobetanz* in Swiss folk music] (2752) and **Zur Frage der Blasquinte in den exotischen Tonsystemen** [On the question of the blown fifth in exotic tone systems] (4055); Conrado del CAMPO, **La harmonización del canto popular** [The harmonization of traditional song] (4145); Antoine-Élisée CHERBULIEZ, **La canción popular en la Suiza Retica** [The traditional songs of the Rhaetia region of Switzerland] (2763) and **La sarabande, la chaconne, la passacaille et la folia dans l'œuvre de J.S. Bach** [The sarabande, the chaconne, the passacaille, and the folia in J.S. Bach's oeuvre] (1505); Patrice COIRAULT, **Quelques exemples de la parenté que montrent des timbres populaires aux XVIIe et XVIIIe siècles avec certaines de nos mélodies folkloriques** [Some examples of the kinship between popular *timbres* of the 17th and 18th centuries and our folkloric melodies] (2771); Norbert DUFOURCQ, **Le maître franco-espagnol Aristide Cavaillé-Coll et l'évolution de la musique d'orgue en France** [The Franco-Spanish master Aristide Cavaillé-Coll and the evolution of organ music in France] (3353); Alfred EINSTEIN, **Der Tempo-Wechsel im italienischen Madrigal** [Tempo changes in the Italian madrigal] (3986); Hans ENGEL, **Soziologische Betrachtung des Madrigales** [Sociological perspective on the madrigal] (5881); Giulio FARA, **Etnofonia e civiltà mediterranea: Le basi storia della musica** [Ethnophony and Mediterranean civilization: The bases of music history] (960); Karl Gustav FELLERER, **Modus und Melodie-Modell** [Mode and melody model] (4072); J. FRANQUESA, **Darreres troballes sobre el cant visigòtic** [The latest findings about Visigothic chant] (1097); Joseph GAJARD, **La restitution mélodique du chant grégorien** [The melodic reconstruction of Gregorian chant] (6220) and **L'interprétation du chant grégorien** [Performance of Gregorian chant] (6219); Amédée GASTOUÉ, **Les récitatifs liturgiques du codex espagnol Rés. F. 967 de la Bibliothèque du Conservatore Nationale [*sic*] de Musique à Paris** [The liturgical recitatives of the Spanish codex rés.F.967 at the library of the Conservatoire National de Musique in Paris] (6229); Thrasybulos Georges GEORGIADES, **Neue Quellen zur Theorie der englischen Mehrstimmigkeit bis Dunstable** [New sources for the theory of English polyphony until Dunstable] (4336); Theodore GÉROLD, **La musique à Strasbourg dans la première moitié du XVIe siècle** [Music in Strasbourg in the first half of the 16th century] (1313) and **La section d'orgue, au congrès de la S.I.M. à Vienne 1909, point de départ du mouvement organal actuel** [The organ section at the S.I.M. congress in Vienna in 1909: The departure point of the current organ movement] (3369); Walter GERSTENBERG, **Spanien in der deutschen Musikgeschichtsschreibung** [Spain in German music historiography] (876); Vicente Maria de GIBERT, **Les melodies de les cançons romanesques a Catalunya** [The melodies of Catalan romances] (2833); Wilibald GURLITT, **Neue Forschungen über Orgelmusik und Orgelbaukunst** [New research on organ music and the art of organ building] (3381); Jacques HANDSCHIN, **La notion de "qualité" dans la psychologie du son** [The concept of quality in the psychology of sound] (5665); Emil HARASZTI, **Le double aspect de l'art de François Liszt** [The double appearance of Franz Liszt's art] (1980); Kurt HUBER, **Zur Typologie des Volkslieds im mittel- und westeuropäischen Raum** [On folk-song typology in Central and Western Europe] (2866); Edgar ISTEL, **The work and personality of Felipe Pedrell** (1989); Knud JEPPESEN, **Eine musiktheoretische Korrespondenz des früheren Cinquecento** [A correspondence concerning music theory, from the early sixteenth century] (1346); Dominicus JOHNER, **Der Dialog im liturgischen Gesang** [Dialogue in liturgical chant] (6261); A. JOSÉ, **La canción popular burgalesa** [The traditional songs of Burgos] (2873); Macario Santiago KASTNER, **O estilo musical do Padre Manoel Rodriguez Coelho** [The musical style of Manuel Rodrigues Coelho] (1585); Hermann KELLER, **Die Aufgaben der Musikwissenschaft an den Hochschulen für Musik** [Musicological tasks at Musikhochschulen] (4828); Rezső KÓKAI, **Franz Liszt** (2010); Franz KOSCH, **Zum Choral der Franziskaner [*sic*] im XIII. Jahrhundert** [On the chant of the Franciscans in the 13th century] (1134); Emirto de LIMA, **Las flautas indígenas** [Indigenous flutes] (3628); Fernando LIUZZI, **Musica e poesia profana del secolo XIV nel ms. Vaticano-Rossiano 215** [Secular music and poetry from the 14th century in the Vatican manuscript Rossi 215] (1144) and **Un nuovo schedario di bibliografia musicale romana presso l'Istituto di Studi Romani** [A new index of Roman musical bibliography at the Istituto di Studi Romani] (740); Elizabeth Jeannette LUIN, **L'importanza della Stabat Mater del Pergolese nei paesi nordici prima della diffusione della *Matthäuspassion*** [The importance of Pergolesi's Stabat Mater in the Nordic countries before the propagation of the *Matthäuspassion*] (1614); Eduardo Fernando MARTÍNEZ TORNER, **Los ritmos en la música popular**

castellana [The rhythms of Spanish traditional music] (4014); Paul-Marie MASSON, **Le recueil madrilène des** *Canciones francesas para todos los instrumentos* **vers 1700** [The Madrid anthology *Canciones francesas para todos los instrumentos* from around 1700] (1810); François-Xavier MATHIAS, **La Société Internationale d'Orgue: Son activité au Congrès de Budapest (1930), Strasbourg (1932), Luxemburg (1934)** [The international society of the organ: Its activities at the congresses of Budapest (1930), Strasbourg (1932), Luxembourg (1934)] (3425); Melpo MERLIER, **Création à Athènes d'archives musicales de folklore** [Creation of traditional music archives in Athens] (622); Bérenger de MIRAMON, **Les plus récentes entreprises de la Société Française des Amies de l'Orgue** [The most recent undertakings of the Société Française des Amis de l'Orgue] (3434); F. MOCKERS, **La famille franco-suisse Mockers, complétant en France l'œuvre organale d'Aristide Cavaillé-Coll, en continuant celle de Jean André Silbermann (1712-1783)** [The Franco-Swiss Mockers family, completing the organ work of Aristide Cavaillé-Coll in France, and continuing that of Johann Andreas Silbermann (1712-1783)] (3436); Robert-Aloys MOOSER, **Un musicien espagnol en Russie à la fin du XVIIIᵉ siècle: Contribution à la biographie de Vincenç Martin i Soler et à la bibliographie de son œuvre** [A Spanish musician in Russia at the end of the 18th century: Contribution to the biography of Vicente Martín y Soler and to the bibliography of his oeuvre] (1818); Nemesio OTAÑO EGUINO, **La organería y los órganos del país vasco** [Organ building and organs in the Basque region] (3445) and **Notas sobre el folklore gallego** [Notes on Galician folklore] (2981); Dragan PLAMENAC, **La musique en Dalmatie et sur le littoral croate aux XVIᵉ et XVIIᵉ siècles** [Music in Dalmatia and coastal Croatia in the 16th and 17th centuries] (1408); David PUJOL ROCA, **Un libre manuscrit amb dotze misses de Pierre de Manchicourt, mestre de capella de Felip II** [A manuscript volume with twelve Masses by Pierre de Manchicourt, chapel master of Philip II] (1412); Emili PUJOL VILARRUBÍ, **La transcription de la tablature pour viuhela d'après la technique de l'instrument** [The transcription of the tablature for vihuela according to the technique of the instrument] (3862) and **Le sens instrumental dans la tablature** [Instrumental meaning in tablatures] (3861); Francisco PUJOL PONS, **Ritme i metrificació de les cançons populars catalanes** [The rhythm and metrics of Catalan traditional songs] (4019); Julian von PULIKOWSKI, **Probleme und Aufgaben der Musikgeschichte** [Problems and tasks in music history] (912); Josep RICART MATAS, **Els instruments musicals en la iconografia hispànica de l'Edat mitjana** [Musical instruments in Spanish iconography of the Middle Ages] (5392); Vicente RIPOLLÉS PÉREZ, **Los ministriles de los siglos XVI-XVII en la catedral de Valencia** [The ministriles of the cathedral of Valencia in the 16th and 17th centuries] (1421); Mauro SABLAYROLLES, **Un regard sur mon** *Iter hispanicum* [A look at my *Iter hispanicum*] (6371); Curt SACHS, **Problèmes qui se présentent dans l'exécution moderne de la polyphonie du Moyen Age** [Problems concerning the modern performances of medieval polyphony] (3714) and **Vers une préhistoire musicale** [Toward a musical prehistory] (915); Baltasar SAMPER, **El cant de les cançons de treballada a Mallorca** [The singing of work songs in Majorca] (3043); Marius SCHNEIDER, **Musikethnologische Kriterien zur Überschichtung von Kultur und Rasse in Afrika** [Ethnomusicological criteria for the overlap of cultures and races in Africa] (2588); A. SIMON, **Das musikwissenschaftliche Studium in der Gegenwart und seine Zukunftsmöglichkeiten** [The study of musicology today, and future possibilities] (924); José SUBIRÁ, **La música instrumental al servicio de las obras dramáticas declamadas** [Instrumental music at the service of dramatic declamations] (5254) and **Un fondo desconocido de música para guitarra** [An unknown stock of guitar music] (1871); Gregori M. SUÑOL BAULINAS, **État actuel des travaux sur le chant ambrosien** [State of research concerning Ambrosian chant] (1198) and **La modalitat del cant litúrgic llatí** [The modality of Latin liturgical chant] (4117); Joan Maria THOMÁS SABATER, **Jordi Bosch, le plus grand facteur espagnol d'orgues du XVIIIᵉ siècle** [Jordi Bosch: The greatest Spanish organ builder of the 18th century] (3496); Julien TIERSOT, **Les chansons populaires de la France et de la Catalogne** [Traditional songs of France and Catalonia] (3083); John Brande TREND, **The madrigal of Pedro Rimonte** (1456); Joaquín TURINA, **El cant populár andaluz** [Andalusian traditional song] (3092); Max UNGER, **Aus Beethovens Werkstatt** [From Beethoven's workshop] (1883); Otto URSPRUNG, **Spanische Musik der Vor-Reservata um 1500 und der Früh-Reservata** [Spanish music from before musica reservata, ca. 1500, and the beginnings of musica reservata] (1457); Guillaume de VAN, **Les neumes et le chant grégorien** [Neumes and the Gregorian chant] (3879); N. WALTER, **L'évolution de la musique d'orgue française au XIXᵉ siècle sous l'influence de la musique d'orgue de J.S.**

Bach [The evolution of French organ music in the 19th century under the influence of the organ music of J.S. Bach] (2124); Egon WELLESZ, **Stand der byzantinischen Forschung** [The state of Byzantine research] (6132); Johannes WOLF, **Ein angebliches Ramos-Manuskript in der Preussischen Staatsbibliothek** [An alleged manuscript of Ramos in the Preußische Staatsbibliothek] (1472); José Gonzalo ZULAICA Y ARREGUI (José Antonio de Donostia), **La música de Juan Anchieta, siglos XV-XVI** [The music of Juan de Anchieta (15th-16th century)] (1476).

225
rs
Review by Hans von ENGEL, *Archiv für Musikforschung* 4 (1936) 238–42. In German.

226
rs
Review by Knud JEPPESEN, *Acta musicologica* 4 (1936) 2–6.

227
rs
Review by Paul-Marie MASSON, *Revue de musicologie* 4 (1936) 113–123; 136. In French.

228
rs
Review by Nemesio OTAÑO EGUINO, *Razon y fe* 4 (1936) 452–75. In Spanish.

229
bs
[Berlin] Compte rendu du onzième Congrès de la Confédération Internationale des Sociétés d'Auteurs et Compositeurs [Eleventh Congress of the International Confederation of the Societies of Authors and Composers] (Paris: conference, 1936) 343 p. In French.
The conference took place from 28 September to 3 October 1936. A discussion of the administrative policies of the societies.

230
bs
[Chicago] Papers read at the Annual Meeting of the American Musicological Society. Sponsored by the Music Teachers National Association (New York: American Musicological Society, 1936) 95 p. *Music, charts, diagr.*
The following contributions are cited separately: Carl BRICKEN, **Some analytical approaches to musical criticism** (4395); Leland A. COON, **The distinction between clavichord and harpsichord music** (3510); Donald N. FERGUSON, **The relation of theory to musicology** (875); Otto KINKELDEY, **Changing relations within the field of musicology** (887); Hugo LEICHTENTRITT, **On the prologue in early opera** (5192); Otto ORTMANN, **The contribution of physiopsychology to musicology** (910); Helen Heffron ROBERTS, **The viewpoint of comparative musicology** (2464); Carleton Sprague SMITH, **The service of the library to musicology** (685); Harold SPIVACKE, **The place of acoustics in musicology** (926); Oliver STRUNK, **The historical aspect of musicology** (927); Benjamin Franklin SWALIN, **The Brahms violin concerto: A stylistic criticism** (4384); Roy Dickinson WELCH, **The bearing of aesthetics and criticism on musicology** (930).

231
bs
[Jena] Gefühl und Wille: Bericht über den XV. Kongress der Deutschen Gesellschaft für Psychologie [Feeling and will: Report of the 15th congress of the Deutsche Gesellschaft für Psychologie]. Ed. by Otto KLEMM (Jena: Fischer, 1937) vi, 290 p. *Illus.* In German.
The conference was held from 5 through 8 July 1936. The following contribution is cited separately: Julius BAHLE, **Gefühl und Wille im musikalischen Schaffen** [Feeling and will in musical creation] (5636).

232
bs
[Prague] L'éducation musicale trait d'union entre les peuples: Rapports et discours sur l'éducation musicale dans les divers pays [Music education and friendship between nations: Reports and discussions on music education in different countries]. Proceedings of the First International Congress on Music Education (Praha: Orbis, 1937) 240 p. In French.
The congress was held from 4 through 9 April 1936. The following contributions are cited separately: Emil ADAMIČ, **Yougoslavie** [Yugoslavia] (4478); Enrique AINAUD, **Espagne** [Spain] (4479); Karl von BALTZ, **Autriche** [Austria] (4486); Jorgen BENTZON, **Danemark** [Denmark] (4495); Constantin BRĂILOIU, **Roumanie** [Romania] (4496); George

BREAZUL, **Roumanie** [Romania] (4497); Edward Joseph DENT, **Grande-Bretagne** [Great Britain] (4515); Samuel FISCH, **Suisse** [Switzerland] (4528); W. GEHRELS, **Pays-Bas** [The Netherlands] (4537); Alois HÁBA, **Tchécoslovaquie** [Czechoslovakia] (4544); W. HELFERT, **Tchécoslovaquie** [Czechoslovakia] (4549); Lucie HICKENLOOPER (Olga Samaroff Stokowski), **États-Unis d'Amérique** [The United States of America] (4552); Mary IBBERSON, **Grande-Bretagne** [Great Britain] (4557); Émile JAQUES-DALCROZE, **Suisse** [Switzerland] (4561); Leo KESTENBERG, **Tchécoslovaquie** [Czechoslovakia] (4570); Sven KJELLSTRÖM, **Suède** [Sweden] (4571); Ernst KRENEK, **Autriche** [Austria] (4575); Anna LECHNER, **Autriche** [Austria] (4585); Juan LLONGUERAS BADÍA, **Espagne** [Spain] (4587); Rudolf MAYER, **Grande-Bretagne** [Great Britain] (4596); Miloje MILOJEVIĆ, **Yougoslavie** [Yugoslavia] (4602); Zdeněk NEJEDLÝ, **Tchécoslovaquie** [Czechoslovakia] (4607); Dobroslav OREL, **Tchécoslovaquie** [Czechoslovakia] (4610); W. PIOTROWSKI, **Pologne** [Poland] (4620); H.E. PRINGSHEIM, **Japon** [Japan] (4626); Herman REICHENBACH, **U.R.S.S.** [The Soviet Union] (4633); Jean Jules ROGER-DUCASSE, **France** [France] (4635); Curt SACHS, **France** [France] (4638); Carleton Sprague SMITH, **États-Unis d'Amérique** [The United States of America] (4646) and **Grande-Bretagne** [Great Britain] (4647); Frederick Benjamin STIVEN, **États-Unis d'Amérique** [The United States of America] (4653); Heitor VILLA-LOBOS, **Brésil** [Brazil] (4663).

233
bs
[Rome] Atti del V Congresso internazionale di studi bizantini [Proceedings of the Fifth International Congress of Byzantine Studies]. Sponsored by the International Association of Byzantine Studies. *Studi bizantini e neoellenici* 5-6 (Roma: Associazione Nazionale per gli Studi Bizantini, 1940) 2 v.; (reprint, Nendeln: Kraus, 1978). *Illus., facs., music, maps.* In Italian, French, German, Greek, and English.

The conference was held from 20 through 26 September 1936. The following contributions are cited separately: Dimitrie CUCLIN, **Le rôle du chant grégorien dans le passé jusqu'à nos jours et du chant byzantin dans l'avenir** [The role of Gregorian chant up to the present day and of Byzantine chant in the future] (956); Andrea D'ANGELI, **La musica bizantina o neogreca è il tramite fra la ellenica o classico e la gregoriana?** [Is Byzantine or neo-Greek music the path between the Hellenic or classical and the Gregorian?] (1028); Ioan Dumitru PETRESCU, **La lecture des manuscrits musicaux byzantins des Xe, XIe, XIIe siècles** [Reading Byzantine musical manuscripts of the 10th, 11th, and 12th centuries] (1158); Gregori M. SUÑOL BAULINAS, **Rapporti tra la musica bizantina e la musica latina liturgica, specialmente il canto ambrosiano** [Connections between Byzantine music and Latin liturgical music, especially Ambrosian chant] (1043); Henry Julius Wetenhall TILLYARD, **Neumes byzantins primitifs: Systéme Cioslin (sic)—Un nouveau principe de déchiffrement** [Primitive Byzantine neumes: The Coislin system—A new principle of decoding] (3877); Egon WELLESZ, **Lo stadio attuale delle ricerche nel campo della musica sacra bizantina** [The current state of research in the area of Byzantine religious music] (1213).

234
rs
Review by H. GRÉGOIRE, *Byzantion* 4 (1936) 377–81. In French.

235
rs
Review by H. GRÉGOIRE, *Byzantion* 4 (1937) 437–39. In French.

236
rs
Review by V. LAURENT, *Échos d'Orient* 4 (Jan-Mar 1937) 95–107. In French.

237
rs
Review by A. LEMAN, *Bulletin of the International Committee of Historical Sciences* 4 (1938) 437–39.

1937

238
bs
[Cremona] Congresso internazionale di liuteria: Celebrazioni stradivariane [International Congress on String Instrument Making: Celebrations of Stradivari]. Sponsored by the Federazione Nazionale Fascista degli Artigiani and Comitato per le Celebrazioni Stradivariane (Roma: Staderini, 1937) 34 p. In Italian.

The following contributions are cited separately: Michelangelo ABBADO, **Liuteria classica moderna e decadente** [Classic string instrument making: Modern and decadent] (3547); Arturo BONUCCI, **La liuteria in rapporto alle esigenze dell'artista esecutore** [String instrument making in relation to the needs of the performing artist] (3552); Cesare CANDI, **Come costruiva il violino Antonio Stradivari—Come lo si costruisce oggi: Se si fosse trovato di fronte ai pianoforti moderni e all'orchestra moderna avrebbe Stradivari usati i medesimi spessori?** [How Antonio Stradivari built the violin—How it is built today: If he had been confronted with modern pianos and the modern orchestra, would Stradivari have used the same thicknesses?] (3554); Mario CORTI, **Liuteria, commercio** [String instrument making and commerce] (3560); Lucien GREILSAMER, **La sonorità in rapporto alla registrazione degli strumenti ad arco** [Sonority in relation to the registration of bowed string instruments] (3574); Guido GUERRINI, **L'eccellenza degli instrumenti ad arco in rapporto al rendimento della orchestra e del quartetto** [The quality of bowed string instruments in relation to performance by orchestra and quartet] (3575); Renato MANCIA, **L'esame scientifico delle opere d'arte applicato alla liuteria in rapporto alla identificazione delle scuole e degli autori e in rapporto al restauro e alla conservazione** [The scientific examination of works of art as applied to string instrument making in relation to the identification of schools and individual makers, and to restoration and conservation] (3590); Lodovico PICCIOLI, **Legni di risonanza: Influenza dei metodi di essicazione sul suono** [Resonant woods: The influence of drying methods on sound] (3595). An appendix includes tables that document the following: Italian imports and exports of string instruments (by country); prices paid for certain instruments over a period of 300 years; prices in effect ca. 1937.

239
bs
[Florence; Cremona] Atti del secondo Congresso internazionale di musica [Proceedings of the Second International Music Congress]. Sponsored by the Maggio Musicale Fiorentino. Ed. by Guido Maria GATTI and Luigi RONGA (Firenze: Le Monnier, 1940) 338 p. *Charts, diagr.* In Italian, German, French, and English; summaries in Italian, German, and French.

The conference was held from 11 through 20 May 1937, in conjunction with the second Maggio Musicale Fiorentino. The following contributions are cited separately: Conrad BECK, **La musique et le public** [Music and the public] (2281); Emmanuel BONDEVILLE, **La radiophonie et la musique contemporaine** [The radio and contemporary music] (5949); Jacques BRILLOUIN, **Éléments psycho-physiologiques du problème de la musique à l'écran** [Psychophysiological elements of the problem of film music] (5743); Alfredo CASELLA, **Musica contemporanea e pubblico** [Contemporary music and the public] (2298); Alberto CAVALCANTI, **Music can provide only interior rhythm** (5115); Paul COLLAER, **La culture musicale par la radiophonie** [Musical cultivation through radio] (2305); Piero COPPOLA, **La funzione educatrice del disco** [The educational function of phonograph records] (2307); Maurice CUVELIER, **Les relations entre la musique contemporaine et le public, considérées avec l'organisation de manifestions musicales** [The relations between contemporary music and the public, considered with the organization of music performances] (2311); Sandro DE FEO, **La musica nel cinematografo** [Music in the cinema] (5130); Giacomo DEBENEDETTI, **In sala o sullo schermo?** [In the hall or on the screen?] (5134); Andrea DELLA CORTE, **I problemi concernenti la rappresentazione delle opere antiche** [Problems connected with the performance of early operas] (5137) and **Il pubblico: Popolo di oggi e di domani** [The public: The people of today and tomorrow] (2789); Maurice EMMANUEL, **La création du violon et ses conséquences** [The creation of the violin and its consequences] (3568); Gianandrea GAVAZZENI, **Il compositore e l'attitudine del pubblico verso la musica moderna** [The composer and the attitude of the public toward modern music] (2321) and **Umanesimo del musicista italiano** [The humanism of Italian musicians] (963); Herbert GERIGK, **Wiedergabepraxis älterer Opern in Deutschland (vom letzten Drittel des 18. Jahrhunderts bis etwa 1830)** [Staging older operas in Germany (from the last third of the 18th century to ca. 1830)] (5156); Paul HINDEMITH, **La viola d'amore** [The viola d'amore] (3579); Paul HÖFFER, **Komponist und Konzertkrise** [The composer and the concert crisis] (2326); Libero INNAMORATI, **I problemi della registrazione musicale** [The problems of music recording] (5760); Ernst KRENEK, **Le point de vue du compositeur contemporain au sujet de** l'attitude du public vis à vis des œuvres modernes [The contemporary composer's point of view on the subject of the public's attitude towards modern works] (2335); László LAJTHA, **La musique d'aujourd'hui et le public** [Today's music and the public] (2337); Michele LESSONA, **Il gusto del pubblico e la musica contemporanea: Funzione educatrice della critica giornalistica** [The public taste and contemporary music: The educational function of journalistic criticism] (5522); Roland Alexis Manuel LÉVY (Roland-Manuel), **La musique prise dans le sujet, élement materiel du film et la musique composée pour le film, élément formel de l'œuvre d'art** [Music taken from within the subject as a material element of the film, and music composed for the film as a formal element of the artwork] (5193); Arturo LORIA, **Il pubblico e la musica** [The public and music] (2348); Sebastiano Arturo LUCIANI, **La musica arte postuma** [Music as a posthumous art] (5528); Gian Francesco MALIPIERO, **I rapporti tra compositore e pubblico** [The relations between composer and public] (2353); Igor MARKEVITCH, **Les musiciens et le public** [Musicians and the public] (2355); Darius MILHAUD, **Wagner, Verdi ed il film** [Wagner, Verdi, and film] (5210); Robert-Aloys MOOSER, **La radio et son influence sur le goût musical** [The radio and its influence on musical taste] (2361); Guido PANNAIN, **Il problema del pubblico: Che cosa è il pubblico—Come si educa il pubblico** [The problem of the public: What is the public? How is the public educated?] (5563); Francesco PASINETTI, **Cenno storico sulla collaborazione della musica col film dalla nascita del cinema a oggi nei diversi paesi europei: Italia** [A historical account of the collaboration of music with film from the birth of the cinema to today in various European countries: Italy] (5221); Henry PRUNIÈRES, **Que doit-il sortir de la crise que traverse actuellement la musique?** [What will be the outcome of the current musical crisis?] (2235); Giulio RAZZI, **La musica lirica e sinfonica nella sua diffusione attraverso la radio** [Operatic and symphonic music as broadcast on radio] (2380); Willi REICH, **Il gusto musicale nella luce della statistica** [Musical taste in the light of statistics] (913); Luigi RONGA, **Creazione dello strumento e creazione della musica** [The creation of the instrument and the creation of music] (998) and **La funzione educatrice della scuola** [The educational function of the school] (4764); Hans ROSBAUD, **Der Rundfunk als Erziehungsmittel für das Publikum** [Radio as a means of educating the public] (2382); Enrico di SAN MARTINO E VALPERGA, **La musica contemporanea e le società dei concerti** [Contemporary music and concert organizations] (2385); André SCHAEFFNER, **Le disque: Sa portée, ses défaillances, ses conséquences** [The phonograph record: Its importance, its weaknesses, its consequences] (5788); Boris de SCHLOEZER, **La fonction sociale du compositeur** [The social function of the composer] (5588); Fausto TORREFRANCA, **Ciò ch'è vivo nella musica del passato** [What is alive in the music of the past] (5615) and **Profonda umanità di una rivoluzione musicale** [The deep humanity of a musical revolution] (1704); Francesco VATIELLI, **Rapporti della musica violinistica con l'ultima letteratura per liuto** [The relations between violin music and the last works for lute] (3607); Antonio VERETTI, **Varie forme di musica nel film** [Different forms of music in film] (5267); Émile VUILLERMOZ, **Les responsabilités de la critique** [The responsibilities of criticism] (5621); Egon WELLESZ, **Der Musiker und sein Publikum** [The musician and his public] (2408) and **Italienische Musiker am österreichischen Hof** [Italian musicians at the Austrian court] (1465).

240 Review by H. BEARD, *The musical times* 4 (1937) 558–59. In
rs Italian.

241 Review by Alfred EINSTEIN, *La rassegna musicale* 4 (1937)
rs 268–69. In Italian.

242 Review by Gianandrea GAVAZZENI, *La rassegna musicale* 4
rs (1937) 181–86. In Italian.

243 Review by Federico GHISI, *Rivista musicale italiana* 4 (1937)
rs 329–34. In Italian.

244 **[Paris] Compte rendu des travaux du Ier**
bs **Congrès international d'art radiophonique**
[Report of the proceedings of the First International Congress on the Art of Broadcasting]. Sponsored by the Bureau International d'Art Radiophonique (Paris: conference, 1938) 24 p. In French.
The meeting was held from 8 through 10 July 1937. The following contributions are cited separately: Manuel BORGUNYO, **La musique, la radio et les enfants** [Music, radio, and children] (4685); BRUSSELMANS,

Musique et micro [Music and microphone] (5745); Jose BRUYR, **Comment on fait des "comprimés" d'œuvres anciennes** [How to make "pills" out of early works] (4499); Paul COLLAER, **L'éducation artistique du public telle que la poursuit la radio belge** [Artistic education of the public as pursued by the Belgian radio] (4509); Roger DÉVIGNE, **Les archives sonores de la radiophonie** [Radio sound archives] (552); R. ELLIS, **La composition des œuvres radiophoniques** [The composition of works for the radio] (5752); Edouard FLAMENT, **La musique radiophonique existe-t-elle? Notes sur l'enregistrement sur film** [Does music for broadcasting exist? Notes on recording on film] (5753); M. GÉRAR, **Psychologie comparée de l'interprète et de l'auditeur** [Comparative psychology of the performer and the listener] (5661); GORIN-FEINBERG, **Les chœurs devant le micro** [Choruses in front of the microphone] (5755); A. KAREL, **La musique devant le micro** [Music in front of the mike] (5764); KEZLER, **La musique synthétique** [Synthetic music] (3668); J. MAIGRET, **Retransmission des spectacles: Opéra, opéra-comique, comédie** [Broadcasting shows: Opera, opéra-comique, comedy] (5772); Madeleine Louise MANSION, **Au sujet de la place des artistes par rapport au micro** [Concerning the placement of artists in relation to the microphone] (5774); MEYROVICZ, **Nécessité de la retouche des partitions pour l'exécution radiophonique** [The necessity of retouching scores for radio performances] (5776); Georges MIGOT, **L'orchestre au micro** [Orchestra at the mike] (5777); Serge MOREUX, **Le mixage en radio et ses nécessités** [Mixing for the radio and its conditions] (5779); J. NOCETI, **La pièce radiophonique musicale** [The musical radio play] (5215); OPDENBERG, **L'accroissement de rendement du travail par la musique** [Work productivity increase through music] (5901); Marcel POOT, **Relations de la musique et du micro** [Music-microphone relations] (5780); SAFRANEC, MANGERET, and ROSENTHAL, **Les échanges de programmes musicaux entre les radios étrangères** [Exchanges of musical programs among foreign radios] (5786); Eric SARNETTE, **Les nouveautés dans la composition des orchestres et leur prise de son radiophonique** [New developments in the composition of orchestras and their recording for the radio] (5787); Alice SAUVREZIS, **Les chœurs d'enfants à la radio** [Children's choruses on the radio] (3318); J. TOMASI, **Apport de la musique dans le théâtre radiophonique** [Contribution of music to theater for radio] (5257).

245 **[Paris] Compte rendu du douzième Congrès de**
bs **la Confédération Internationale des Sociétés**
d'Auteurs et Compositeurs [Proceeding of the Twelfth Congress of the International Confederation of Societies of Authors and Composers] (Paris: conference, 1937) 463 p. In French.
A discussion of the administrative policies of the societies. The conference was held from 14 through 19 July 1937.

246 **[Paris] Congrès international de l'enseigne-**
bs **ment primaire et de l'éducation populaire** [International Congress on Primary Instruction and Public Education]. Sponsored by the Syndicat National des Institutrices et Instituteurs de France et des Colonies (Paris: S.U.D.E.L., 1938) 605 p. *Port., charts, diagr.* In French.
The conference was held from 23 through 31 July 1937. The following contributions are cited separately: František Karel BAKULÉ, **Le chant choral dans l'éducation** [Choral singing in education] (4485); Henri BELLIOT, **Le disque, auxiliaire de l'éducateur** [Recordings as the educator's aid] (4492); Maurice CHEVAIS, **Les instruments de musique du maître et de l'élève** [The musical instruments of the master and the student] (4507); DAVAU, **Les disques d'enseignement** [Instructional recordings] (4513); Gertraud Höfer DESMETTRE, **Choix des disques pour l'enseignement du chant** [Selection of recordings for singing instruction] (3295) and **La radiophonie scolaire** [Educational broadcasting] (4517); Miloslav DISMAN, **Histoire de la radiodiffusion scolaire en Tchécoslovaquie** [History of educational broadcasting in Czechoslovakia] (4518); DRZEWIECKI, **Le théâtre populaire en Pologne** [Public theater in Poland] (5142); Leo KESTENBERG, **La musique dans le plan total de l'éducation** [Music within the integral educational plan] (4568); Lina ROTH, **Le pipeau** [The shawm] (3635); Andre VARAGNAC, **Les loisirs ouvriers, utilisation du folklore pour les fêtes** [Workers' leisure: Uses of folklore in festivals] (3095).

247
bs
[Paris] **Congrès international de musique sacrée: Chant et orgue** [International Congress of Sacred Music: Voice and organ]. Sponsored by the Exposition Internationale des Arts et Techniques de 1937 and Union des Maîtres de Chapelle et Organistes. Ed. by Armand VIVET (Paris: Desclée de Brouwer, 1937) 237 p. *Illus., port., music.* In French.

The conference was held on 24 May and from 19 through 25 July 1937. The following contributions are cited separately: Antoine AUDA, **Ce que sont les modes grégoriens** [What the Gregorian modes are] (6153); AURIOL (abbé), *La musique sacrée* (6154); Paul BERTHIER, **Le cantique et son usage actuel** [The canticle and its current usage] (6166); Joseph BONNET, **Le chant grégorien dans la littérature d'orgue** [Gregorian chant in organ literature] (3343); F. BRUN, **Le clergé et la musique d'église** [The clergy and church music] (6180); Jules DELPORTE, **L'école musicale française des XVᵉ-XVIᵉ siècles** [The French school of music in the 15th to 16th centuries] (6201); Norbert DUFOURCQ, **Les tendances de la facture d'orgues française contemporaine** [Trends in contemporary organ manufacture] (3354); Maurice EMMANUEL, **Le chant liturgique de l'Église romaine ne doit pas être harmonisé** [The liturgical chant of the Roman church must not be harmonized] (6211); Joseph GAJARD, **La chant grégorien** [Gregorian chant] (6218); Amédée GASTOUÉ, **Du style dans l'interprétation du chant grégorien** [On style in the interpretation of Gregorian chant] (3700) and **Les Gildes de Sainte-Cécile** [The Gildes de Sainte-Cécile] (6226); Georges JACOB, **La vie de l'Union des Maîtres de Chapelle et Organistes au cours de ses premières vingt-cinq années** [The life of the Union des Maîtres de Chapelle et Organistes during its first 25 years] (2329); Auguste LE GUENNANT, **La crise des offices solennels et le chant grégorien** [The crisis of the Holy Offices and Gregorian chant] (6282); Guy de LIONCOURT, **Le cantique grégorien** [The Gregorian canticle] (6287); Joseph MEUGÉ, **Communication sur la bibliothèque et le bulletin de l'Union des Maîtres de Chapelle et Organistes** [Report on the library and the bulletin of the Union des Maîtres de Chapelle et Organistes] (3431); Michel OSSORGUINE, **Exposé de l'histoire de la musique religieuse en Russie** [An explanation of the history of religious music in Russia] (6125); Henri POTIRON, **Les équivalences modales dans le chant grégorien** [Modal equivalences in Gregorian chant] (4102); Jean PRIM, **Pour l'application intégrale, sincère et filiale des directives pontificales en matière de musique sacrée** [Towards an integral, sincere, and filial application of the papal directives concerning sacred music] (4888); Félix RAUGEL, **La Commission des Orgues au Service des Monuments Historiques** [The Commission des Orgues of the Service des Monuments Historiques] (3462); René-Pierre ROBLOT (Jacques Debout), **Les cantiques à l'Église** [Canticles in the Church] (6356); Charles TOURNEMIRE, **L'orgue à travers les siècles** [The organ through the centuries] (3497); Maurice TREMBLAY, **Sur les** *scholae* **anciennes et modernes** [The former and current state of parochial schools] (4789); Armand VIVET, **La musique sacrée en France depuis la Révolution** [Religious music in France since the Revolution] (6408).

248
rs
Review by Henri POTIRON, *Musique et liturgie* 4 (1937-1938) 41–45. In French.

249
bs
[Paris] **Deuxième congrès international d'esthétique et de Science de l'art** [Second International Congress on Aesthetics and the Study of Art] (Paris: Librairie Félix Alcan, 1937) 2 v. 371, 528 p. *Illus., charts, diagr.* In French, German, English, Italian, and Spanish.

The conference was held from 7 through 11 August 1937. The following contributions are cited separately: Johannes BIEHLE, **Æsthetik des Orgelklanges und des Orgelspieles** [The aesthetics of the organ's sound and of organ playing] (3337); Franz BRENN, **Das Sein der musikalischen Welt: Eine propädeutische Skizze** [The being of the musical world: A propaedeutic sketch] (5433); Manfred F. BUKOFZER, **Hegel's Musikästhetik** [Hegel's music aesthetics] (5437); Claire CROIZA, **L'art lyrique et l'interprétation** [Lyric art and interpretation] (3293); Marcel Stanislas DUCOUT, **Le chant de la danse: Recherches de synthèse de la danse et de la musique** [The song of dance: The synthetic study of dance and music] (4962); Maurice EMMANUEL, **La polymodie** [Polymodality] (4069); Henri GAGNEBIN, **Les Psaumes huguenots** [Huguenot psalms] (6433); (Mme) HUMBERT-SAUVAGEOT, **Diversité des ambiances crées par les musiques exotiques** [The diversity of atmospheres created by exotic musics] (2641); Arm. J. JANSSENS, **Les fonctions psychologiques de la musique selon Aristote** [The psychological functions of

music according to Aristotle] (5498); Charles KOECHLIN, **Comment compose-t-on?** [How does one compose?] (2332); Rudolf von LABAN, **Wege zur Aesthetik der Tanzkunst** [Toward an aesthetics of the art of dance] (5014); Charles LALO, **Sur les valeurs culturelles et sociales des beaux-arts** [On the cultural and social values of the fine arts] (5519); Vige LANGEVIN, **Causes de la régression de la chanson populaire** [Causes of the decline of traditional song] (2525); Paul LE FLEM, **Les courants de la musique contemporaine** [The directions of contemporary music] (2342); Roland Alexis Manuel LÉVY (Roland-Manuel), **Rythme cinématographique et rythme musical** [Cinematic and musical rhythm] (5194); Serge LIFAR, **Les grands courants de la chorégraphie à travers le XXᵉ siècle** [The major trends of choreography in the 20th century] (5024); Paul LOYONNET, **Étude sur la formation de la langue musicale de Beethoven** [Study on the formation of Beethoven's musical language] (1806); Artur Sergeevič LUR'E (Arthur Vincent Lourié), **De l'harmonie dans la musique contemporaine** [On harmony in contemporary music] (4194); Gian Francesco MALIPIERO, **La musique comme force anti-esthétique** [Music as an anti-aesthetic force] (5532); Claudie MARCEL-DUBOIS, **L'esthétique et la technique des danses populaires** [The aesthetic and technique of traditional dances] (5026); Rolf de MARÉ, **Évolution du ballet, de 1900 à nos jours** [The evolution of the ballet, from 1900 to the present] (5027); Paul-Marie MASSON, **La notion de musicalité** [The idea of musicality] (5679); Raoul Ferraz de MESQUITA, **L'"intuition scientifique" dans les élaborations d'"art pur" manifestée dans les fugues de Bach** [Scientific intuition in the elaborations of pure art manifested in the fugues of Bach] (3952); Henry PRUNIÈRES, **Le symbolisme dans la création musicale** [Symbolism in musical creation] (5934); Vera RJABUČINSKAJA (Véra Riabouchinsky), **Sur la création dans l'interprétation musicale** [On creation in musical performance] (3683); André SCHAEFFNER, **Musique, danse et danse des masques dans une société nègre** [Music, dance, and masked dance in a black society] (2585); Leopold SILBERSTEIN, **Les catégories musicales dans les sciences littéraires** [Musical categories in literary sciences] (5353); Pierre TUGAL, **Pour une méthode de l'histoire de la danse: Le document et les Archives Internationales** [Toward a method of dance history: The document and the Archives Internationales] (767); Henry VALENSI, **La tendance musicaliste en peinture** [The musicalist tendency in painting] (5402); Walter WIORA, **Das musikalische Kunstwerk und die systematische Musikwissenschaft** [The musical work of art and systematic musicology] (933). Includes *discours liminaires* by Paul VALÉRY, Paul CLAUDEL, and Victor BASCH.

250
bs
[Paris] **Onzième Congrès international de psychologie: Rapports et comptes rendus** [Eleventh International Congress of Psychology: Reports and accounts]. Ed. by Henri PIÉRON and Ignace MEYERSON (Agen: Imprimerie Moderne, 1938); (reprint, Nendeln: Kraus, 1974). *Illus., port., tech. drawings.* In French, German, English, and Italian.

The congress was held from 25 through 31 July 1937. The following contributions are cited separately: Julius BAHLE, **Konstruktiver Arbeitstypus und Inspirationstypus im Schaffen der Komponisten** [The constructive working type and the inspirational type in composers' creativity] (5638); Paul FRAISSE, **La structure temporelle des mouvements volontaires rythmés** [The temporal structure of voluntary rhythmic movements] (3992); Charles LALO, **L'invention artistique** [Artistic invention] (5517); Irène MARCUSE, **Il talento musicale nei movimenti della scrittura** [Musical talent in the movements of writing] (5385).

251
bs
[Paris] **Travaux du Iᵉʳ Congrès International de Folklore** [Proceedings of the First International Folklore Congress]. Pref. by Georges Maurice HUISMAN. *Publications du Département et du Musée National des Arts et Traditions Populaires* (Tours: Arrault et Cie, 1938) 448 p. *Maps.* In French, German, English, and Italian.

The conference was held from 23 through 28 August 1937. The following contributions are cited separately: Constantin BRĂILOIU, **Technique des enregistrements sonores** [Technique of sound recording] (527); Maurice CHEVAIS, **Participation de la jeunesse scolaire aux des fêtes et cortèges folkloriques** [Participation of schoolchildren in traditional festivals and processions] (2764); Alexis CHOTTIN, **Le chant et la danse berbères dans le folklore européen** [Berber song and dance in European folklore]

(2766); Émile DAVE, **Fêtes folkloriques de la jeunesse à Namur** [Folkloric youth festivals at Namur] (2787); Paul DELARUE, **Les chants populaires régionaux à l'école et dans les fêtes scolaires et postscolaires** [Traditional regional songs at school and in academic and non-academic festivals] (2788); Roger DÉVIGNE, **Enregistrements sonores** [Sound recordings] (5749); Marguerite GAUTHIER-VILLARS, **Les cantiques populaires de Marie-Madeleine** [Traditional cantiques on Marie-Madeleine] (2824); Georges HAENNI, **La chanson populaire dans la famille et à l'école** [Traditional song in the family and at school] (4546); Wilhelm HEISKE, **Träger, Art der Verbreitung und Wanderung des Volksliedes** [Carriers, means of dissemination, and migration of the folk song] (2851); Maud KARPELES, **The folk dance revival in England, with special reference to folk dancing in school** (4999); Georges de LA FARGE, **Le folklore à l'école: L'instrument musical populaire** [Folklore in the school: The traditional musical instrument] (4578); Claudie MARCEL-DUBOIS, **L'instrument musical populaire en France** [The traditional musical instrument in France] (3260); Louis PINCK, **La circulation des chants, vue de la Lorraine** [The circulation of songs in the Lorraine] (3001); Philippe STERN, **Étude de la musique populaire de tradition orale** [The study of orally transmitted traditional music] (2473); Bence SZABOLCSI, **Die Volksmusik in der Schule und in der Nachschulsbildung** [Traditional music in school and in continuing education] (4656); Marie TEXIER, **Danses et chantes folkloriques dans l'enseignement** [Folkloristic dances and songs in education] (4786); José Gonzalo ZULAICA Y ARREGUI (José Antonio de Donostia), **Quelques observations sur la façon de recueillir les chansons en Pays basque** [Some observations on the manner of collecting songs in the Basque region] (2489).

252
rs
Review in *Revue musicale* 4 (1937) 80–82. In French.

253
bs
[São Paulo] Anais do Primeiro Congresso da Língua Nacional Cantada [Proceedings of the First Congresso da Língua Nacional Cantada] (São Paulo: Departamento Municipal de Cultura, 1938) 786 p. *Illus., music, charts, diagr., maps.* In Portuguese.

The following contributions are cited separately: **A pronúncia cantada e o problema do nasal brasileiro através dos discos** [Singing pronunciation and the problem of the Brazilian nasal sound as found in recordings] (3296); Mário de ANDRADE, **Os compositores e a língua nacional** [Composers and the national language] (2130); Luiz Heitor Corrêa de AZEVEDO, **A Imperial Academia de Música e Ópera Nacional e o canto em vernáculo** [The Imperial Academia de Música e Ópera Nacional and vernacular singing] (1907); Manuel BANDEIRA, **Pronúncias regionais do Brasil** [Regional pronunciations of Brazil] (5919); Carlos Marinho de Paula BARROS, **Reflexões para uma tese** [Reflections for a thesis] (5288); Otávio BEVILACQUA, **Algumas proposições e quesitos** [Some proposals and questions] (4314); J. Lellis CARDOSO, **A fonofotografia e a fonética** [Sound spectrography and phonetics] (3291); Murilo de CARVALHO, **Os compositores e a técnica do canto** [Composers and the technique of singing] (3292); João Itiberê da CUNHA, **Algumas notas para o Congresso da Língua Nacional Cantada** [Some notes for the Congresso da Língua Nacional Cantada] (3196); Enio de FREITAS E CASTRO, **Uma escola brasileira de canto** [A Brazilian school of singing] (3299); Pedro JATOBÁ, **Colisão entre as acentuações verbal e musical no canto** [The conflict between verbal and musical accents in singing] (3309); Cândido JUCÁ FILHO, **Problemas da fonologia carioca** [Problems of the phonology of Rio de Janeiro] (5929); **Mapas folclóricos de variações linguísticas** [Ethnographic maps of linguistic variations] (5938); Francisco MIGNONE, **A pronúncia do canto nacional** [Pronunciation in national song] (3315); **Normas para boa pronúncia da língua nacional no canto erudito** [Norms for the correct pronunciation of the national language in concert singing] (3316).

1938

254
bs
[Bayreuth] Charakter und Erziehung: Bericht über den XVI. Kongress der Deutschen Gesellschaft für Psychologie [Character and education: Report on the 16th congress of the Deutsche

Gesellschaft für Psychologie]. Ed. by Otto KLEMM (Leipzig: Barth, 1939) 288 p. *Illus.* In German.

The congress took place from 2 to 4 July 1938.

255
bs
[Copenhagen] Congrès international des sciences anthropologiques et ethnologiques: Compte rendu de la deuxième session [International Congress of Anthropological and Ethnological Sciences: Report of the second meeting] (København: Munksgaard, 1939) 397 p. *Charts, diagr.* In French, German, Italian, and English.

The conference was held from 1 through 6 August 1938. The following contributions are cited separately: André SCHAEFFNER, **Contribution à l'étude des instruments de musique d'Afrique et d'Océanie** [Contribution to the study of the musical instruments of Africa and Oceania] (2584); G. SMETS, **L'Umuganuro (fête du sorgho) chez les Barundi (territ. belge mandat)** [The Umuganuro (sorghum festival) among the Rundi people (mandated Belgian territory)] (3063); Albert WELLEK, **Zur Vererbung der Musikbegabung und ihrer Typen** [The inheritability of a musical gift and its types] (5719).

256
bs
[Florence] Atti del terzo Congresso internazionale di musica [Proceedings of the Third International Music Congress]. Sponsored by the Maggio Musicale Fiorentino (Firenze: Le Monnier, 1940) viii, 199 p. *Illus., music.* In Italian, French, and German; summary in Italian.

The conference was held from 30 April through 4 May 1938, in conjunction with the third Maggio Musicale Fiorentino. The following contributions are cited separately: Heinrich BESSELER, **Sulla disposizione delle masse orchestrali e corali negli ambienti destinati alle esecuzioni profane e religiose nell'età barocca (con proiezioni)** [On the disposition of orchestral and choral forces in performance spaces for Baroque secular and sacred music (with projections).] (3730); Massimo BONTEMPELLI, **Il nuovo classicismo della musica moderna** [The new classicism of modern music] (2139); Ernst BÜCKEN, **Die Musik als Stil- und Kulturproblem** [Music as a problem of style and culture] (5436); Alfredo CASELLA, **Errori (e pretesi errori) di alcune partiture illustri** [Errors (and alleged errors) in some famous scores] (3811); Paul COLLAER, **Renaissance de la musique ancienne** [Renaissance of early music] (3674); Jacques COPEAU, **L'interprétation des ouvrages dramatiques du passé** [The interpretation of dramatic works of the past] (5124); Piero COPPOLA, **Rievocazioni di un maestro girovago: Dal vecchio repertorio a Maurizio Ravel** [Recollections of a wandering conductor: From the old repertoire to Maurice Ravel] (3890); Giacomo DEBENEDETTI, **L'oratorio di Via Belsiana** [The oratory of Via Belsiana] (5452); Herbert GRAF, **L'opera quale Festspiel** [Opera as festival] (5161); Vittorio GUI, **Letture e interpretazioni delle partiture** [Readings and interpretations of scores] (3784); Jacques HANDSCHIN, **Réflexions dangereuses sur le renouveau de la musique ancienne** [Dangerous reflections on the revival of early music] (881); Knud JEPPESEN, **Palestrina e l'interpretazione** [Palestrina and interpretation] (1347); Arturo LORIA, **Il gusto moderno e la musica del passato** [Modern taste and the music of the past] (985); Darius MILHAUD, **La tradition** [The tradition] (5543); Guido PANNAIN, **La critica e la musica del passato** [Criticism and music of the past] (5561); Alfredo PARENTE, **Musicisti, critici, interpreti e pubblico di fronte alla musica del passato** [Musicians, critics, interpreters, the public, with respect to the music of the past] (996); Luigi RONGA, **La musica senza storia** [The music without history] (2243); Guido SALVINI, **La regia moderna del melodramma** [Modern production of opera] (5236); André SCHAEFFNER, **Musique primitive ou exotique et musique moderne d'occident** [Primitive or exotic music and modern Western music] (1003); Boris de SCHLOEZER, **La musique ancienne et le goût moderne** [Early music and modern taste] (919); Giorgio VENTURINI, **Del modo di rappresentare le opere del passato e dell'*Amfiparnaso* di Orazio Vecchi** [On ways to represent old works and of Orazio Vecchi's *Amfiparnaso*] (5265); Émile VUILLERMOZ, **Le goût moderne et la musique du passé** [Modern taste and music of the past] (1018); Oskar WALLECK, **Die Regie der Oper** [Staging opera] (5269).

257
bs
[Frankfurt am Main] Bericht über den Internationalen Kongreß Singen und Sprechen [Report of the International Congress on Singing and

Speaking] (München: Oldenbourg, 1938) 367 p. *Illus., charts, diagr.* In German and French.

The congress was held from 10 through 15 October 1938. The following contributions are cited separately: Alfred BORUTTAU, **Die Beschaffenheit des harten Gaumens und deren Bedeutung für die Stimmabgabe** [The nature of the hard palate and its significance in vocal production] (3289); Fritz BOSE, **Klangstile als Rassenmerkmale** [Vocal styles as an indication of race] (3290); Helmut BRÄUTIGAM, **Deutsche Volkslieder aus Jugoslawien** [German traditional songs from Yugoslavia] (2748); Alfredo CAIRATI, **Gibt es einen geschmacklichen, technischen oder methodischen Unterschied zwischen dem italienischen und dem deutschen Gesang, oder beruht der Unterschied nur auf dem verschiedenen Aufbau der beiden Sprachen?** [Is there a difference of taste, technique, or method between Italian and German singing, or does the difference lie merely in the different structures of the two languages?] (5921); Hans EMGE, **Die klassischen Schulwerke der Singekunst als Grundlagen für den Sängernachwuchs** [The classic pieces for voice students as a foundation for the next generation of singers] (4523); Jørgen FORCHHAMMER, **Stützen und Stauen** [Support and hindrance] (3298); Viggo FORCHHAMMER, **Die Rutz-Sieversschen Beobachtungen** [The observations of Rutz and Sievers] (5727); Siegfried GOSLICH, **Deklamation und instrumentale Symbolik im begleiteten Kunstgesang** [Declamation and instrumental symbolism in the accompanied art song] (4338); Fritz HÄNDCHEN, **Singen und Stimmbildung in der NS.-Gemeinschaft Kraft durch Freude** [Singing and vocal training in the National Socialist society Kraft durch Freude] (2323); Georg HARTMANN, **Die Erziehung zur Durchgeistigung des Sängerdarstellers** [The education to spirituality of the singer-actor] (5167); Heinrich KÖHLER-HELFFRICH, **Dialog in der Oper** [Dialogue in opera] (5183); Antoni KOHMANN, **Gesangstechnik und Gesangsmethode** [Singing technique and singing method] (3311); Alfons KREICHGAUER, **Akustische Probleme der Opern- und Sprechbühne** [Acoustic problems of the opera and speaking stage] (5832); Isabella MANUCCI DE GRANDIS, **La tecnica di respiro in rapporto all'arte del canto e della parola** [Breathing technique in relation to the arts of singing and speech] (3313); Franziska MARTIENSSEN-LOHMANN, **Übereinstimmung und Abweichung in der Stimmausbildung der männlichen und der weiblichen Stimme** [Commonalities and differences in vocal training for male and for female voices] (4591); Erwin MEYER, **Die raumakustischen Einflüße bei Sprach- und Gesangsdarbietungen** [The influence of room acoustics in spoken and sung performances] (5841); Eugen MICHEL, **Raumakustische Praxis** [Practical room acoustics] (5843); Adolf MOLL, **Wie können wir die Phonetik dem Sing- und Sprechunterricht dienstbar machen?** [How can we make phonetics useful in the teaching of singing and speech?] (4603); MÖSER, **Kulturrecht im Dritten Reich: Rechtsfragen des Sprech- und Gesangunterrichts** [Cultural legislation in the Third Reich: Legal questions in the pedagogy of speech and singing] (2362); Joseph MÜLLER-BLATTAU, **Arie und Lied** [Aria and lied] (2965); Hanns NIEDECKEN-GEBHARD, **Die Aufgaben und Probleme monumentaler Festspielgestaltung** [Responsibilities and problems in the production of monumental festival spectacles] (5213); Helmuth OSTHOFF, **Der Gesangstil der frühdeutschen Oper** [The singing style of early German opera] (5218); Paul PASCHEN, **Stimme und Seele und ihre gemeinsamen Störungen** [Voice and spirit and the disturbances they share] (5735); Gerhard PIETZSCH, **Fragen des Opernnachwuchs** [Questions about the next generation of opera singers] (5223); RICHTER, **Was muß der Kapellmeister von der Behandlung der Stimme des Sängers bei der Einstudierung einer Oper wissen?** [What does a conductor need to know about the treatment of singers' voices in the preparation of an opera?] (3317); Rolf ROENNEKE, **Die Ausdrucksfähigkeit des Gesanges und der Sprache als Grundlage schöpferischer, dramatischer Gestaltung** [The expressive capacity of singing and speech as the foundation of creative, dramatic representation] (5232); RÜHL, **Ausbildung und Schulung des Opernchorsängers im Hinblick auf die Praxis des Repertoiretheaters** [Training and schooling of singers for opera choruses, in view of the experience of the repertory company] (4636); Franz RÜHLMANN, **Ideale Schuleinrichtungen für Opernnachwuchs** [Ideal school arrangements for the next generation of opera] (4637); Walter RUTH, **Das Phonogrammarchiv der Akademie der Wissenschaften in Wien und sein Wirken im Dienste der Sprach- und Musikwissenschaft und der Sprech- und Gesangsausbildung** [The Phonogrammarchiv of the Akademie der Wissenschaften, Vienna, and its effectiveness in the service of linguistics, musicology, and speech and singing training] (752); SCHLENGER, **Gibt es mikrophongeeignete Stimmen, und welches sind ihre Kennzeichen?** [Are there voices suited to microphones, and how are they recognized?] (5791); Heinrich SCHOLE, **Die Vokalität der**

einfachen Töne und das Singen von Vokalen in hoher Stimmlage** [The vocalism of simple tones and the singing of vowels in the high register] (3320); Theobald SCHREMS, **Der Chordirigent als Führerpersönlichkeit** [The choir director as a leader-figure] (3277); Rolf SCHROTH, **Die Bedeutung des Singens in der Kameradschaftserziehung des NSD.-Studentenbundes** [The significance of singing in comradeship training in the NSD-Studentenbund] (2389); Rudolf SCHULZ-DORNBURG, **Das musikalische Wort im Wandel der Zeiten: Grundsätzliches über die unterschiedliche Wortbehandlung in musikalischer Gestalt und Nachgestalt** [The musical word through the ages: A basic discussion of the different treatment of text in the musical conception and reconception] (4381); SCOLARI, **Le due manieri di cantare sorte all'inizio dell'800** [The two styles of singing arising at the beginning of the 19th century] (3321); Otto SOMMER, **Das Singen im Dienste der Volkserziehung** [Singing in the service of educating the people] (4650); Friedrich STICHTENOTH, **Der Gesang in der Kritik der Tagespresse** [Singing in criticism in the daily press] (5605); STRECK, **Die Stimmdiagnose als Grundlage der modernen Stimmbildung und Hilfsmittel gegen pädagogische Pfuscherarbeit** [Vocal diagnosis as a foundation for modern voice training and an aid against pedagogical blunders] (4654); Carl THIEL, **Heimatkunde im Schulgesang** [Local lore in school singing] (4787); Kurt THOMAS, **Über die Aussprache beim chorischen Singen** [Diction in choral singing] (3326); Friedrich TRAUTWEIN, **Die technische Akustik in Schule und Praxis des Singens und Sprechens** [Sound technology in the study and practice of singing and speaking] (5795); Arthur TREUMANN-METTE, **Die anatomisch-physiologischen Leitsätze für Zahnprothetik bei Sprechern und Sängern** [Anatomical and physiological principles for the use of dental prostheses by speakers and singers] (3327); TROMMER, **Reform der Gesangspädagogik** [A reform of the pedagogy of singing] (4659); WARDE, **Die Beziehungen zwischen Sprache und Gesang** [The connections between speech and singing] (3328); Alexis WICART, **La phonation optime pour la parole et le chant: Les contrôles auditifs et visuels pour son enseignement** [Optimal voice production for speech and singing: The auditive and visual controls for teaching it] (4671) and **Les principes d'organisation et de fonctionnement de l'Institut Vocal Universel de Paris** [The organizational and functional principles of the Institut Vocal Universel, Paris] (3330); Walther WÜNSCH, **Grenzgebiete der Musik- und Sprachforschung** [Overlapping areas between musicology and linguistics] (5941); Paul Gerhard WÜSTHOFF, **Die Bedeutung der Vererbung auf dem Gebiet der Sprach- und Stimmheilkunde** [The meaning of heredity in the area of therapy for the speaking and singing voice] (3331); Eberhard ZWIRNER, **Schallplatte und Tonfilm als Quellen sprech- und gesangskundlicher Forschung** [Records and sound film as sources for research in the study of speech and singing] (5799).

258
bs

[Freiburg im Breisgau] Bericht über die zweite Freiburger Tagung für Deutsche Orgelkunst [Report of the second Freiburger Tagung für Deutsche Orgelkunst]. Sponsored by the Universität Freiburg im Breisgau, Musikwissenschaftliches Institut, Arbeitsgemeinschaft für Orgelbau und Glockenwesen, and Arbeitskreis für Hausmusik. Ed. and aftwd. by Joseph MÜLLER-BLATTAU (Kassel: Bärenreiter, 1939) 152 p. *Illus., music, charts, diagr., organ specification.* In German.

The conference, devoted to smaller organs, was held at the Universität Freiburg im Breisgau from 27 through 30 June 1938. The following contributions are cited separately: Wolfgang AULER, **Weltliche Musik auf dem Positiv** [Secular music on the positive] (3335); Arie BOUMAN and P. KLUYVER, **Hausorgeln in Holland** [House organs in Holland] (3346); Wilhelm EHMANN, **Orgel und Volkslied** [Organ and traditional song] (3356); Karl Gustav FELLERER, **Die alte für Kleinorgel bestimmte Orgelmusik** [Early music intended for the small organ] (3358); Gotthold FROTSCHER, **Die Wechselbeziehungen zwischen Orgelmusik und Orgelbau in Geschichte und Gegenwart** [The mutual relation between organ music and organ building in history and in the present] (3366); Herbert HAAG, **Die Orgel im weltlichen Bereich: Geschichtliches und Grundsätzliches** [The organ in the secular realm: History and foundations] (3384); Hans KLOTZ, **Das alte Positiv und die neue Kammerorgel** [The old positive and the new chamber organ] (3401); Christhard MAHRENHOLZ, **Die Kleinorgel: Grundfragen ihres Baues und ihres Klanges** [The small organ: Fundamental questions of its construction and sound] (3420); Johannes G. MEHL, **Die Denkmalpflege auf dem Gebiet der Orgelbaukunst** [Historic conservation in the area of the organ builder's art] (3427); Josef MERTIN, **Erfahrungen mit der Kleinorgel** [Experiences with the small organ] (3430); Traugott MÜLLER-WALT, **Die Toggenburger Bauernorgeln** [Toggenburg peasant organs] (3441); Karl Friedrich RIEBER, **Kleinorgeln in Oberbaden: Zur Geschichte der Orgel am Oberrhein** [Small organs in Upper Baden: Toward a history of organs on the Upper Rhine] (3467); Karl-Ludwig SCHUKE, **Positiv und Kleinorgel vom Standpunkt des Orgelbauers** [Positive and Kleinorgel from the organ builder's point of view] (3477); Walter SUPPER, **Die dreimanualige Übungsorgel: Ein Beitrag zur Kleinorgel** [The three-manual practice organ: A new small organ] (3483); Erich THIENHAUS, **Orgelbaufragen im Lichte der akustischen Forschung** [Issues of organ building in the light of acoustic research] (3495). Descriptions are provided of exhibitions held for the occasion at the University's Musikwissenschaftliches Institut of organ iconography, curated by Walter Supper, and of 13 positive, portative, house, and chamber organs, with dispositions.

259   **[Ghent] Proceedings of the Third Interna-**
bs   **tional Congress of Phonetic Sciences.** Ed. by Edgard BLANCQUAERT and Willem PÉE (Gent: Rijksuniversitet, Fonetisch Laboratorium, 1939) xxiii, 535 p. *Illus., bibliog.* In English, French, German, and Italian.

The conference was held from 18 through 22 July 1938. The following contributions are cited separately: Amaat F.S. BURSSENS, **Le luba, langue à intonation, et la tambour-signal** [Luba, a tonal language, and the talking drum] (5920); Martin GRÜTZMACHER, **Ein neuer Tonhöhenschreiber, seine Anwendung auf mathematische, phonetische und musikalische Probleme** [A new instrument for the graphic representation of pitch, and its use in mathematical, phonetic, and musical problems] (5821); L. LABARRAQUE, **Le science phonétique, base essentielle de l'éducation de la voix chantée** [Phonetic science, essential basis for the training of the singing voice] (3312); Walther WÜNSCH, **Grenzgebiete der Musik- und Sprachforschung** [Overlapping areas between musicology and linguistics] (5942); Cornelis ZWIKKER, **Vues nouvelles sur l'acoustique des salles** [New views on room acoustics] (5864); Eberhard ZWIRNER, **Schwankungen der Mundlage beim Singen einzelner Laute** [Variations in mouth position in the singing of isolated sounds] (3332).

260   **[Namur] Congrès de Namur 1938: Annales**
bs   [Congress of Namur, 1938: Annals]. Sponsored by the Fédération Archéologique et Historique de Belgique. Ed. by J. BALON (Namur: n.p., n.d.). In French.

The following contribution is cited separately: Albert vander LINDEN, **Note sur une ordonnance du Conseil des Finances relatifs aux pianos et aux clavecins (9 janvier 1786)** [Note on an ordinance of the Council of Finances concerning pianos and harpsichords (9 January 1786)] (1802).

261   **[Stockholm] Compte rendu du Treizième**
bs   **Congrès de la Confédération Internationale des Sociétés d'Auteurs et Compositeurs** [Proceedings of the 13th Congress of the International Confederation of the Societies of Authors and Composers] (Paris: conference, 1938) 580 p. In French.

A discussion of the administrative policies of the societies. The conference took place from 27 June through 2 July 1938.

262   **[Zürich] Communications présentées au**
bs   **Congrès de Zurich** [Communications presented at the Zürich congress]. Proceedings of the Eighth International Congress of Historical Sciences (reprint, Nendeln: Kraus, 1976). *Bulletin of the International Committee of Historical Sciences* X/2-3 (Apr-July 1938) 145–739. *Charts, diagr., maps.* In French, German, English, and Italian.

The conference was held from 24 August through 4 September 1938. The following contributions are cited separately: Antoine-Élisée CHERBULIEZ, **Le problème de la périodicité dans l'histoire de l'art musical par rapport aux beaux-arts en général et à la poesie** [The problem of periodicity in the history of musical art in relation to the fine arts in general and poetry] (4918); Jacques HANDSCHIN, **Die Entstehung der Sequenz** [The origins of the sequence] (1113); János HANKISS, **Le drame populaire et la société** [The people's theater and society] (5166).

1939

263   **[Algiers] Sixième Congrès international**
bs   **d'études byzantines: Résumés des rapports et communications** [Sixth International Congress of Byzantine Studies: Summaries of reports and communications]. Sponsored by the International Association of Byzantine Studies. Pref. by Gabriel MILLET (Paris: Comité d'Organisation du Congrés, 1940) v, 289 p.; (reprint, Nendeln: Kraus, 1978). In French.

Report of the contributions for a conference that was to have been held in Algiers, 2-7 October 1939, but was cancelled. The following contribution is cited separately: Egon WELLESZ, **La musique byzantine et ses relations avec le chant grégorien dans la musique du Moyen Âge** [Byzantine music and its relation to Gregorian chant in the music of the Middle Ages] (1212).

264   **[Florence] Atti del secondo Convegno**
bs   **nazionale di studi sul Rinascimento** [Proceedings of the second Convegno nazionale di studi sul Rinascimento]. Sponsored by the Centro Nazionale di Studi sul Rinascimento (Firenze: Arte della Stampa, 1940) xviii, 183 p. *Illus.* In Italian.

The conference was held from 7 through 8 May 1939. The following contribution is cited separately: Federico GHISI, **La musica** [The music] (1314). A **Saggio di bibliografia medicea** [Sampling of bibliographic material on the Medici family] by Sergio CAMERANI is appended.

265   **[Florence] Il IV Congresso internazionale di**
ap   **musica a Firenze** [The Fourth International Music Congress in Florence]. By L. TOMELLERI, *Rivista musicale italiana* (1939) 502–06. In Italian.

Reports on the following papers given at the conference: F. BALLO, **L'opera dei musicisti in rapporto con le polemiche sociali della vita moderna** [Musicians' work in relation to the social polemics of modern life]; A. CASELLA, **Difesa dell' individualismo artistico e della nostra autonomia musicale** [A defense of artistic individualism and of our musical autonomy]; Antoine-Élisée CHERBULIEZ, **Deve il linguaggio essere nazionale o internazionale?** [Should the language be national or international?]; L. CHIARINI, **Supremazia o servitù della musica nella cinematografia?** [Supremacy or servitude of music for the art of cinema]; A. DELLA CORTE, **Nè entusiasmo, nè desinteresse, ma rifugio e svago** [Neither enthusiasm nor disinterest, but refuge and relaxation]; M. LAZZARI, **L'insegnamento musicale in Italia** [Music education in Italy]; A. LUALDI, **Sopra l'ordinamento degli studi musicali** [The regulation of music study]; Ch. VAN DEN BORREN, **La musica antica nella vita contemporanea** [Early music in contemporary life]; and F. VATIELLI, **Valore di una tradizione** [The value of a tradition].

266   **[New York] Papers read at the International**
bs   **Congress of Musicology.** Sponsored by the American Musicological Society. Ed. by Arthur MENDEL, Gilbert CHASE, and Gustave REESE; pref. by Romain ROLLAND, Albert SCHWEITZER, and Carleton Sprague SMITH (New York: Music Educators National Conference, 1944) ix, 301 p. *Illus., facs., music.* In English and French.

The conference was held from 11 through 16 September 1939. The following contributions are cited separately: Samuel P. BAYARD, **Aspects of melodic kinship and variation in British-American folk-tunes** (4416); Annabel Morris BUCHANAN, **Modal and melodic structure in Anglo-American folk music: A neutral mode** (3141); Manfred F. BUKOFZER, **The evolution of Javanese tone-systems** (4054); Jacob Maurice COOPERSMITH, **Concert of unpublished music by Georg Friedrich Händel: Program notes** (1513); Edward Joseph DENT, **La Rappresentazione di anima, e di corpo** [The *Rappresentazione di anima, e di corpo*] (1288); Alfred EINSTEIN, **Mozart's handwriting and the creative process** (1746); Leonard ELLINWOOD, **The French renaissance of the 12th century in music** (1084); Otto GOMBOSI, **New light on ancient Greek music** (3572); Glen HAYDON, **Alfred Day and the theory of harmony** (4176); George HERZOG, **African influences in North**

American Indian music (3155); George Pullen JACKSON, **Some ene-mies of folk-music in North America** (3157); Knud JEPPESEN, **Venetian folk-songs of the Renaissance** (1348); Roy LAMSON, Jr., **English broadside ballad tunes of the 16th and 17th centuries** (2922); Francisco Curt LANGE, **Americanismo musical** (2340); Fernando LIUZZI, **Notes sur les barzelette et les canzoni a ballo du Quattrocento italien, d'après des documents inédits** [Notes on the barzellettas and the canzoni a ballo of fifteenth-century Italy, according to unpublished documents] (4268); Dayton C. MILLER, **Musical tone-color** (4302); Otto ORTMANN, **The psychology of tone-quality** (5686); Dragan PLAMENAC, **Music of the 16th and 17th centuries in Dalmatia** (1407); Gonzalo ROIG, **Some problems confronting musicians in America** (2381); Curt SACHS, **The mystery of the Babylonian notation** (3867); Eduardo SÁNCHEZ DE FUENTES, **The musical folklore of Cuba** (3218); Charles SEEGER, **Music and government: Field for an applied musicology** (5907); Albert SMIJERS, **Music of the Illustrious Confraternity of Our Lady at 's-Hertogenbosch from 1330-1600** (1434); Oliver STRUNK, **Some motet-types of the 16th century** (4287); Davidson TAYLOR, **Music written for radio** (2263).

267   Review by Gilbert CHASE, *Musical America* 4 (1939).
rs

268   **[Siena] Antonio Vivaldi: Note e documenti**
bs   **sulla vita e sulle opere** [Antonio Vivaldi: Notes and documents on his life and works]. Proceedings of the Settimana Musicale; sponsored by the Reale Accademia d'Italia. Ed. by Guido CHIGI SARACINI, Ulderico ROLANDI, and Olga RUDGE (Siena: Accademia Musicale Chigiana, 1939) 7–75. *Illus., port., facs., music, bibliog., list of works, them. cat.* In Italian.

The conference was held from 16 through 21 September 1939. The following contributions are cited separately: Alfredo CASELLA, **Come sono state scelte ed elaborate le musiche della Settimana** [How the music for the Settimana was chosen and planned] (2297) and **Le composizioni sacre e vocali di Antonio Vivaldi** [The sacred vocal compositions of Antonio Vivaldi] (1502); Guido CHIGI SARACINI, ed., **Testimonianze** [Testimonies] (1507); Sebastiano Arturo LUCIANI, **I concerti** [The concertos] (1608); Virgilio MORTARI, *L'Olimpiade* **e il teatro musicale di Antonio Vivaldi** [*L'Olimpiade* and Antonio Vivaldi's musical theater] (1628). Also includes a brief biography of the composer; a list of the original editions of the instrumental works published in his lifetime; lists by genre of the unpublished works in the Foà-Giordano collections of the Biblioteca Nazionale Universitaria, Turin, with first-movement incipits of the instrumental works; and a catalogue of microfilm manuscripts and Venetian prints in the collections of the Accademia Musicale Chigiana, Siena.

1940

269   **[Cleveland] Papers of the American Musico-**
bs   **logical Society.** Sponsored by the American Council of Learned Societies. Ed. by Gustave REESE (Philadelphia: American Musicological Society, 1946) vi, 142 p.

The conference was held from 30 through 31 December 1940; the second day was a joint session with the Music Teachers' National Association. The following contributions are cited separately: Manfred F. BUKOFZER, **The beginnings of polyphonic choral music** (1262); Helen E. BUSH, **The Laborde Chansonnier** (1264); Ernest Thomas FERAND, **Improvisation in music history and education** (4526); Donald N. FERGUSON, **Music and the democratic idea** (5466); Theodore M. FINNEY, **Reproductive versus distributive music teaching at the college level** (4816); Otto GOMBOSI, **The cultural and folkloristic background of the folía** (1318); Erich HERTZMANN, **Trends in the development of the chanson in the early sixteenth century** (1333); Charles HUGHES, **Peter Philips: An English musician in the Netherlands** (1340); Otto KINKELDEY, **The artist and the scholar** (886); Paul Henry LANG, **The influence of political thought on the history of music** (981); Kathi MEYER-BAER, **New facts on the printing of music incunabula** (5979); Isabel POPE, **The musical development and form of the Spanish villancico** (1409); Curt SACHS, **Music history: Two sides of the coin** (914); Leo SCHRADE, **Organ music and the Mass in the fifteenth century** (1428); Carleton Sprague SMITH, **Presidential address** (925).

270   **[Venice] Atti del 4. Congresso nazionale di arti**
bs   **e tradizioni popolari** [Acts of the fourth Congresso nazionale di Arti e Tradizioni Popolari]. Sponsored by the Partito Nazionale Fascista, Reale Accademia d'Italia, and Comitato Nazionale Italiano per le Arti Popolari (Roma: Opera Nazionale Dopolavoro, 1942) 2 v. 619 p. *Illus.* In Italian.

The conference was held in September 1940. The following contributions are cited separately: V. ABIUSO, **I canti e le ninne-nanne popolari sarde** [Sardinian traditional songs and lullabies] (2709); G. BAINCHI, **Valore spirituale ed impronta etnica dei nostri canti di guerra** [Spiritual valor and ethnic imprint of our war songs] (2729); G. BOLLINI, **Il mare nei canti popolari lombardi** [The sea in Lombardian traditional songs] (2740); Giulio FARA, **Etnofonia e civiltà mediterranea** [Mediterranean traditional music and civilization] (2808); S. FARA, **Il ballo tradizionale del popolo di Sardegna** [Traditional dances of the people of Sardinia] (4964); E. PAOLONE, **La musica del popolo nelle sue origini: Caratteri fondamentali e riflessi** [Traditional music in its origins: Fundamental characteristics and reflections] (2987); R. SANTOLLINO, **Il mare nei canti popolari napoletani** [The sea in Neapolitan traditional songs] (3049); Giuseppe SCHIRÓ, **Poesia e musica tradizionali degli italo-albanesi** [Traditional poetry and music of the Italian Albanians] (3053); Enrico SINICROPI, **Canti popolari ennesi** [Traditional songs of Enna] (3061); G. TANCREDI, **Canti e balli garganici** [Songs and dances of the Gargano region] (3079).

271   **[Washington, D.C.] Report of the Committee**
bs   **of the Conference on Inter-American Rela-tions in the Field of Music.** Ed. and intro. by William BERRIEN (Washington, D.C.: United States Department of State, 1940) 151 p. *Bibliog., discog., charts, diagr.*

The following contributions are cited separately: Mário de ANDRADE, **Folk music and folk song in Brazil** (3188); William BERRIEN, **Report of Subcommittee on Recorded Music** (5947); Evans CLARK, **Report on concert interchange in the popular field** (2304); William EARHART, **Report of Subcommittee on Inter-American Exchange in the Field of School Music** (4521); **Report of the activities (to May 23, 1940) of the WPA music program in the diffusion of Latin American music** (2306); Hugh ROSS, **Report of Subcommittee on Music Management and Concert Interchange with Latin America** (2383); Charles SEEGER, **Report of Subcommitte on Research in Comparative Musicology** (2471); Donald SLESINGER, **Memorandum on relation of the film to inter-American relations in the field of music** (5245); Donald SLESINGER, Carl ENGEL, and William SANDERS, **Memorandum on copyright** (5993); Carleton Sprague SMITH, **Report of the Subcommittee on Music Libraries** (684); Davidson TAYLOR, **Report on radio interchange with Latin America** (2398); Burnet C. TUTHILL, **Report of Subcommittee on Interchange of Professors and Students in the Field of Music** (4661); Augustus D. ZANZIG, **Report of suggestions from the Subcommittee on Community and Recreational Music** (2488) and **Some collections of folk songs in the library of the Pan American Union** (769).

1941

272   **[Minneapolis] Papers of the American Musi-**
bs   **cological Society.** Sponsored by the American Council of Learned Societies. Ed. by Gustave REESE; intro. by Otto KINKELDEY (Philadelphia: American Musicological Society, 1946) 170 p.

The conference, held jointly with the Music Teachers' National Association, was held from 29 through 30 December 1941. The following contributions are cited separately: Luiz Heitor Corrêa de AZEVEDO, **Tupynambá melodies in Jean de Léry's** *Histoire d'un voyage faict en la terre du Brésil* (3192); Hans Theodor DAVID, **Ephrata and Bethlehem in Pennsylvania: A comparison** (1740); Donald N. FERGUSON, **What is a musical idea?** (5467); Donald Jay GROUT, **The music of the Italian theatre at Paris, 1682-97** (1565); Raymond KENDALL, **Brahms's knowledge of Bach's music** (2001); Edward E. LOWINSKY, **The concept of physical and musical space in the Renaissance: A preliminary sketch** (1373); William S. NEWMAN, **The recognition of sonata form by theorists of the 18th and 19th centuries** (4276); Abe PEPINSKY,

Geminiani's schematic fingerboard (4099); Yella PESSL, **French patterns and their reading in Bach's secular clavier music** (3762); Dragan PLAMENAC, **An unknown violin tablature of the early 17th century** (1646); Walter H. RUBSAMEN, **Political and ideological censorship of opera** (5235); Benjamin F. SWALIN, **Purcell's masque in *Timon of Athens*** (1693); William Treat UPTON, **Secular music in the United States 150 years ago** (1885); Eric WERNER, **Hebrew music theory of the Middle Ages** (1215).

1942

273
bs

[Siena] G.B. Pergolesi, 1710-1736: Note e documenti, raccolti in occasione della settimana celebrativa [G.B. Pergolesi, 1710-1736: Notes and documents presented on the occasion of the celebratory week]. Sponsored by the Accademia Musicale Chigiana (Siena: Ticci Editore Libraio, 1942) 102 p. *Port., facs., music.* In Italian.

Collection published on the occasion of the 4th Settimana Musicale Senese, held from 15 through 20 September 1942. The following contributions are cited separately: Charles BURNEY, **Un giudizio di Charles Burney** [An appraisal by Charles Burney] (1500); Filippo CAFFARELLI, ***Opera omnia di G.B. Pergolesi*** [*Opera omnia* of G.B. Pergolesi] (804); Adelmo DAMERINI, *La morte di San Giuseppe* (1522); Sebastiano Arturo LUCIANI, *Il geloso schernito* (1609) and **Il presidente de Brosses e Pergolesi** [President de Brosses and Pergolesi] (1611); Elizabeth Jeannette LUIN, **La fama di Pergolesi all'estero** [Pergolesi's fame abroad] (1613); Virgilio MORTARI, *Il Flaminio* (1627); Giuseppe RADICIOTTI, **Il ritratto e la caricatura di Pergolesi** [Portrait and caricature of Pergolesi] (1654); Hugo RIEMANN, **Un giudizio di Hugo Riemann** [An appraisal by Hugo Riemann] (1658); Ulderico ROLANDI, **Contributo alla bibliografia di libretti e di esecuzioni d'opere pergolesiane** [Contribution to the bibliography of libretti and operas by Pergolesi] (1659); Jean-Jacques ROUSSEAU, **Un epigramma di J.J. Rousseau** [An epigram by J.J. Rousseau] (1663); Franco SCHLITZER, **La legenda d'amore di G.B. Pergolesi** [The legend of Pergolesi's love] (1674); **Un autografo firmato di Pergolesi** [An autograph signed by Pergolesi] (1642); Emilia ZANETTI, **Contributo a una bibliografia della musica sacra di G.B. Pergolesi** [Contribution to a bibliography of G.B. Pergolesi's sacred music] (811) and **Il *Guglielmo d'Aquitania*** [The *Guglielmo d'Aquitania*] (1717).

1945

274
bs

[Dakar] Première conférence internationale des Africanistes de l'ouest [Report: First International West African Conference]. Sponsored by the Gouvernement Général de l'Afrique Occidentale Française and Institut Français d'Afrique Noire (Paris: Maisonneuve, 1950-1951) 2 v. 532, 568 p. *Illus., bibliog., charts, diagr., maps, tech. drawings.* In French, English, and Spanish.

The conference was held from 19 through 25 January 1945. The following contribution is cited separately: Georges-Jacques DUCHEMIN, **Autour d'un arc musical du Saloum oriental** [About a musical bow of eastern Saloum] (3565).

1947

275
bs

[Bissau] Conférence internationale des Africanistes de l'Ouest–C.I.A.O.: Programme de la deuxième réunion/Conferência Internacional dos Africanistas Ocidentais: 2a. conferência [International West African Conference: Second conference]. Sponsored by the Junta de Investigações Coloniais (Lisboa: Ministério das Colónias, 1950-1952) 5 v. *Illus., bibliog., maps.* In Portuguese, French, and Spanish.

The conference was held from 8 through 17 December 1947. The following contributions are cited separately: Georges BALANDIER and Paul MERCIER, **Notes sur les théories musicales maures à propos de chants enregistrés** [Notes on Moorish musical theories in relation to recorded songs] (2548); Georges-Jacques DUCHEMIN, **Deux arcs renforcés de Guinée Française** [Two reinforced bows of Guinea] (3566); Gilbert ROUGET, **Note sur les travaux d'ethnographie musicale de la mission Ogooué-Congo** [Note on the work in musical ethnography of the Ogooué-Congo mission] (2579).

276
bs

[Cambridge, Mass.] Music and criticism: A symposium. Ed. by Richard F. FRENCH (Cambridge, MA: Harvard University Press, 1948) viii, 181 p.

The following contributions are cited separately: Huntington CAIRNS, **The future of musical patronage in America** (2295); Edward Morgan FORSTER, **The raison d'être of criticism in the arts** (5471); Lucie HICKENLOOPER (Olga Samaroff Stokowski), **The performer as critic** (5491); Otto KINKELDEY, **Consequences of the recorded performance** (5508); Paul Henry LANG, **The equipment of the musical journalist** (5521); Roger SESSIONS, **The scope of music criticism** (5596); Virgil THOMSON, **The art of judging music** (5612); Edgar WIND, **The critical nature of a work of art** (5629).

277
bs

[Paris] Actes du XXVIIIᵉ Congrès international des américanistes [Proceedings of the 28th International Congress of Americanists] (Paris: Musée de l'Homme, 1948) xlv, 703 p.; (reprint, Nendeln: Kraus, 1976). *Illus., facs., charts, diagr.* In French.

The conference was held from 25 through 30 August 1947. The following contribution is cited separately: Guy STESSER-PÉAN, **Danse des aigles et danse des jaguars chez Indiens Huastèques de la région de Tantoyuca** [Dance of the eagles and dance of the jaguars of the Huastec Indians of the Tantoyuca region] (5066).

278
bs

[Prague] Hudba národů: Sborník přednášek, proslovených na I. mezinárodním sjezdu skladatelů a hudebních kritiků/Musique des nations: Iᵉʳ Congrès international des compositeurs et critiques musicaux [Music of nations: The First International Congress of Composers and Music Critics] (Praha: Syndikát Českých Skladatelů, 1948) 187 p. In Czech and French.

The conference was held from 16 through 26 May 1947. The following contributions are cited separately: Ingmar BENGTSSON, **Skandinávská hudba/Aperçu sur la musique scandinave** [A survey of Scandinavian music] (944); Zdenka BOKESOVÁ, **Slovenská hudba/La musique slovaque** [Slovak music] (947); Alan BUSH, **Britští skladatelé dneška/Compositeurs anglais contemporains** [Contemporary British composers] (2144); Eduardo CAVALLINI, **O nové harmonické řeči/Une nouvelle langue harmonique** [A new harmonic language] (4146); Marcel CUVELIER, **Jeunesses Musicales/Les Jeunesses Musicales** (2310); Alois HÁBA, **Souměrnost evropského tónového systému/Règles du système tonique européen** [Rules of the European tonal system] (4079); Ivan KAMBUROV, **Rytmické zvláštnosti bulharské lidové a umělecké hudby/Les particularités rhythmiques de la musique populaire bulgare et leur répercussion sur l'art musical bulgare** [The rhythmic particularities of Bulgarian traditional music and their repercussions on Bulgarian art music] (4005); Stefania ŁOBACZEWSKA, **Kritika a její vztah k moderní hudbě/La critique et la musique moderne** [Criticism and modern music] (5526); Narayana MENON, **Kam spěje indická hudba?/Où va la musique hindoue?** [Where is Hindu music headed?] (2669); Jan RACEK, **Vznik a počátky barokního hudebního slohu v Čechách/Origine et débuts de la musique baroque en Bohème** [Origin and beginnings of Baroque music in Bohemian lands] (1653); Carleton Sprague SMITH, **Hudba v Severní a Jižní Americe/La musique en Amérique du Nord et en Amérique du Sud** [The music of North and South America] (2250); Dmitrij ŠOSTAKOVIČ, **Svaz sovětských skladatelů/Union des compositeurs soviétiques** [Sojuz Kompozitorov SSSR] (2251); Josef STANISLAV, **O masové písni a jejím dnešním významu/La chanson de masse et son importance actuelle** [Mass song and its present-day importance] (3064); Antonín SYCHRA, **Hudební estetika a kritika/Esthétique et critique musicale** [Aesthetics and music criticism] (5608); Halil Bedi YÖNETKEN, **Turecká hudba/La musique turque** [Turkish music] (2275).

279
bs
[Siena] Fac-simile del Concerto funebre. Proceedings of the 5th Settimana Musicale Senese; sponsored by the Centro di Studi Vivaldiani. Ed. and intro. by Antonio BRUERS. *Quaderni dell'Accademia Chigiana* 15 (Siena: Accademia Musicale Chigiana, 1947) 49 p. *Illus., facs., music.* In Italian.

The following contributions are cited separately: Sebastiano Arturo LUCIANI, **Gli originali di Antonio Vivaldi e le trascrizioni** [Antonio Vivaldi's originals and the transcriptions] (1610), **I violini in tromba marina** [The violins *in tromba marina*] (3760), **La *Juditha* e messa in scena** [*Juditha* and its staging] (3759), and **La visita di Goldoni a Vivaldi** [Goldoni's visit with Vivaldi] (1612); Olga RUDGE, **Note** (1664); Bence SZABOLCSI, **Tre composizioni sconosciute di Antonio Vivaldi** [Three unknown compositions by Antonio Vivaldi] (1695). Includes a facsimile of the MS score of VIVALDI's **Concerto funebre**, RV 579.

1948

280
bs
[Amsterdam] Actes de Xᵐᵉ Congrès international de philosophie/Proceedings of the Tenth International Congress of Philosophy. Sponsored by UNESCO. Ed. by Evert Willem BETH and J.H.A. HOLLAK; ed. and intro. by Hendrik Josephus POS (Amsterdam: North-Holland Publishing Company, 1949) 2 v.; (reprint, Nendeln: Kraus, 1968). *Bibliog.* In English and French.

The conference was held from 11 through 18 August 1948. The following contribution is cited separately: Kurt BLAUKOPF, **The aesthetics of musical humanism from Diderot to Hanslick** (5430).

281
bs
[Basel] International Folk Music Council Conference, *Journal of the International Folk Music Council* I (1949) 5–52.

The first annual conference was held from 13 through 18 September 1948. The following contributions are cited separately: Wilhelm ALTWEGG, **Les Archives Suisses de la Chanson Populaire** [The Schweizerisches Volksliedarchiv] (704); Luiz Heitor Corrêa de AZEVEDO, **L'UNESCO et la musique populaire** [UNESCO and traditional music] (2417); Arnold Adriaan BAKÉ, **Indian folk dances** (4934); Samuel BAUD-BOVY, **La chanson cleftique** [Songs of the kléftis] (2733); Luigi COLACICCHI, **The lament of the maidens** (5121); Robert FRICKER, **The vogel gryff pageant** (2819); Rajna KACAROVA, **Méthodes de préservation et de renaissance du folklore musical** [Methods for the preservation and revival of musical folklore] (2876); Jaap KUNST, **The cultural background of Indonesian music** (2649); Poul LORENZEN, **The revival of folk dancing in Denmark** (5025); Alfons MAISSEN, **The religious and secular folk song of the Romansch people** (2935); Claudie MARCEL-DUBOIS, **Vues sommaires sur les recherches actuelles et le maintien de la tradition musicale populaire française** [Summary views on current research and the maintenance of the French folk music tradition] (2940); Sólōn MICHAÏLÍDĪS, **Greek folk music: Its preservation and traditional practice** (2958); Ole Mørk SANDVIK, **Norwegian folk music and its social significance** (3046); Ahmed Adnan SAYGUN, **Le recueil et la notation de la musique folklorique** [The collection and transcription of folk music] (2466); Armas Otto VÄISÄNEN, **Suggestions for the methodical classification and investigation of folk tunes** (4468); Sándor VERESS, **Folk music in musical and general education** (1017); Karel VETTERL, **Folk song of East Czechoslovakia: Methods of performance and notation** (3100); Walter WIORA, **Concerning the conception of authentic in folk music** (2482).

282
bs
[Brussels] Congrès international des sciences anthropologiques et ethnologiques: Compte rendu de la troisième session [International Congress of Anthropological and Ethnological Sciences: Proceedings of the third meeting]. Sponsored by UNESCO. Ed. by Frans M. OLBRECHTS and Hugette

VAN GELUWE (Tervuren: Musée Royal de l'Afrique Centrale, 1960) xx, 277 p. In French, English, German, Italian, and Spanish.

The following contributions are cited separately: Helen Engel HAUSE, **Terms for musical instruments in the Sudanic languages: A linguistic approach to culture** (5926); Melville J. HERSKOVITS, **Afrobahian cult music** (3201); L.C. van PANHUYS, **Music in Latin America, Surinam, and Curaçao** (2370) and **Some remarks on Dutch song** (2985); Svend SMITH, **On the high resonances of the male voice** (3322).

283
bs
[Dorking] Music and drama in the counties. Proceedings of the third annual meeting of the Standing Conference of County Music Committees. Pref. by W.G. BRIGGS (London: conference, 1949) 119 p. *Illus.*

The meeting was held from 12 through 15 October 1948 at Beatrice Webb House, Pasture Wood, Dorking, Surrey. The report on the third annual meeting of the Standing Conference of Drama Associations, London, held from 14 through 16 September 1948, is also included in this book. The following contributions are cited separately: Gertrude COLLINS and Bernard SHORE, **The teaching of stringed instruments** (3559); R.J. HARRIS, **Care of the piano** (3387); Harold Watkins SHAW, **The schools work of an L.E.A. music adviser** (4777).

284
bs
[Edinburgh] Twelfth International Congress of Psychology. Ed. by James DREVER (London: Oliver and Boyd, 1950) xxviii, 151 p.; (reprint, Nendeln: Kraus, 1974). *Illus.* In English, French, and German.

The conference was held at the University of Edinburgh from 23 through 29 July 1948. The following contribution is cited separately: H.D. WING, **Standardized tests of musical aptitude** (5725).

285
bs
[Florence] Atti del quinto Congresso di musica [Proceedings of the Fifth Music Congress]. Sponsored by the Maggio Musicale Fiorentino. Afterword by Ildebrando PIZZETTI (Firenze: Barbèra, 1948) 172 p. In Italian.

The conference was held from 14 through 17 May 1948, on the occasion of the 11th Maggio Musicale Fiorentino, presided over by Ildebrando Pizzetti. The following contributions are cited separately: Gabriele BIANCHI, **Musica nella realtà della nostra vita** [Music in the reality of our life] (2287); Enzo BORRELLI, **Dal neoclassicismo alla dodecafonia** [From neoclassicism to twelve-tone technique] (4318); Adelmo DAMERINI, **La musica nella vita della scuola contemporanea** [Music in the life of the contemporary school] (4690); Fedele D'AMICO, **Il compositore moderno e il linguaggio musicale** [The contemporary composer and musical language] (2153); Herbert FLEISCHER, **Discutendo il problema linguistico** [Discussing the linguistic problem] (3942); Vito FRAZZI, **Il superamento della tonalità ed il nuovo concetto armonico** [The overcoming of tonality and the new harmonic concept] (4168); Federico GHISI, **Le influenze "ultramontane" e la musica europea** [Ultramontane influences and European music] (2169); Remo GIAZOTTO, **Teatro di provincia e sovvenzioni** [Subsidies and the provinicial theater] (5159); Guido GUERRINI, **Il tramonto di due gloriose espressioni del linguaggio musicale** [The demise of two glorious devices of musical language] (2174); Augusto HERMET, **Musicologia e musica** [Musicology and music] (882); Adriano LUALDI, **La ballata della morte e una parolina di Aristotele** [The ballad of death and a little word of Aristotle] (2208); Sebastiano Arturo LUCIANI, **Inflazione musicale** [Musical inflation] (2349) and **La crisi del sistema temperato** [The crisis of equal temperament] (4091); Roberto LUPI, **Armonia di gravitazione** [Gravitational harmony] (4193); Alberto MANTELLI, **Problemi di linguaggio nell'opera di Strawinsky** [Questions of language in the works of Stravinsky] (2211); Massimo MILA, **La musica e il linguaggio musicale** [Music and musical language] (2214); Virgilio MORTARI, **La crisi del sistema temperato e i problemi del linguaggio musicale** [The crisis of equal temperament and the problems of musical language] (4095); Guido PANNAIN, **Chiarimenti sul concetto di linguaggio** [Clarifications on the concept of language] (5560); Alfredo PARENTE, **Il problema del linguaggio come problema morale** [The problem of language as a moral problem] (2226); Alessandro PIOVESAN, **Offerte e divieti del linguaggio musicale contemporaneo** [Prospects and limits of contemporary musical language] (2230); Ildebrando PIZZETTI, **Discorso di chiusura** [Closing address] (2231); Mario RINALDI, **Funzione della** tecnica nel linguaggio musicale [The function of technique in musical language] (2240); Luigi RONGA, **Aspetti del costume musicale contemporaneo** [Aspects of contemporary musical practice] (2242); Fausto TORREFRANCA, **Perchè non v'è osmosi tra arte e pubblico?** [Why is there no osmosis between art and public?] (2402); Antonio VERETTI, **Il problema del linguaggio nella musica moderna** [The problem of language in modern music] (2268).

286
bs

[New York] Proceedings of the first annual conference: Convention of the Cantors Assembly and the Department of Music of the United Synagogue of America, *Proceedings of the annual convention* I (1948) 35. *Music.* In English, Czech, and French.

The conference was held from 10 through 12 February 1948 at the Jewish Theological Seminary of America, New York. The following contributions are cited separately: Martin ADOLF and Simon GREENBERG, **The cantor's conservatory: To be or not to be?** (6036); Aaron EDGAR, **Systematic planning of a service of worship: Cantor's point of view** (6049); Gershon EPHROS, **The influence of the cantillations on nusah hatefillah** (6051); Harry HALPERN, **Systematic planning of a service of worship: Rabbi's point of view** (6068); Frederick JACOBI, **Synagogue music as I see it** (6073); Siegfried LANDAU, **The history of synagogue music: The role of the cantor in its development** (6076); Frank PELLEG, **Soudobá hudba mezi orientem a okcidentem/La musique contemporaine entre Orient et Occident** [Contemporary music between East and West] (2228); Henry W. SIMON, **Systematic planning of a service of worship: Layman's point of view** (6097); Michael STAVITSKY, Edward SANDROW, and Max WOHLBERG, **The relationship of the congregation, the rabbi, and the cantor: A symposium** (6101); Chemjo VINAVER and Kurt LIST, **Synagogue music: Traditional and modern** (6103).

287
bs

[Paris] Actes du VIᵉ Congrès international d'études byzantines [Proceedings of the Sixth International Congress of Byzantine Studies. Sponsored by the International Association of Byzantine Studies (Paris: Comité Français des Études Byzantines, 1950-1951) 2 v. 413, 426 p.; (reprint, Nendeln: Kraus, 1978). *Illus., bibliog., charts, diagr.* In French.

The conference was held from 27 July through 2 August 1948. The following contribution is cited separately: Raïna PALIKAROVA VERDEIL, **La musique byzantine chez les slaves (Bulgares et Russes) aux IXᵉ-Xᵉ siècles** [The Byzantine music of the Bulgarian and Russian Slavic peoples in the 9th and 10th centuries] (1153).

288
bs

[Turin] V Congresso nazionale delle tradizioni popolari [Fifth Congresso nazionale delle tradizioni popolari]. Sponsored by the Società di Etnografia Italiana, *Lares* XX/1-2 (1954). In Italian.

The conference was held from 9 through 12 September 1948. The following contributions are cited separately: Giovanni Battista BRONZINI, **La canzone della *Finta monacella*: Nuove versioni e loro classificazione** [The canzone *La finta monacella*: New versions and their classification] (2751); Giulio FARA, **Sardegna: Persistenza dell'ethos artistico mediterraneo** [Sardinia: Persistence of the Mediterranean artistic ethos] (2811); Federico GHISI, **Antiche melodie popolari nelle valli valdesi** [Old traditional melodies of the Vaudois valleys] (2831); Emilio TRON, **Canzoni popolari valdesi del risorgimento** [Traditional songs of the Vaudois valleys from the Risorgimento] (3090) and **Cenno sui canti popolari delle Valli Valdesi** [Survey of the traditional songs of the Vaudois valleys] (3091).

1949

289
bs

[Basel] Compte rendu/Kongressbericht/Report. Proceedings of the Fourth Congress of the International Musicological Society; sponsored by the Schweizerische Musikforschende Gesellschaft (Ortsgruppe Basel). Foreword by Ernst MOHR (Basel: Bärenreiter, 1951) 235 p. *Illus., music.* In French, German, English, and Italian.

The conference was held from 9 June through 3 July 1949. The following contributions are cited separately: Hans ALBRECHT, **Zur Frage eines neuen musikalischen Quellenlexikons** [The question of a new dictionary of musical sources] (771); Konrad AMELN, **Die Anfänge der deutschen Passionshistorie** [The beginnings of the German Passion] (1219); Higini ANGLÈS, **Der Rhythmus der monodischen Lyrik des Mittelalters und seine Probleme** [The rhythm of the medieval monodic lyric and its problems] (3886) and **L'œuvre de l'Institut espagnol de musicologie** [The work of the Instituto Español de Musicología] (858); Arnold Adriaan BAKÉ, **Der Begriff *Nâda* in der Indischen Musik** [The concept of *nāda* in Indian music] (2602); Karel Philippus BERNET KEMPERS, **Die Jamisation** [Jamization] (4051); Heinrich BESSELER, **Katalanische Cobla und Alta-Tanzkapelle** [The Catalan cobla and the alta dance ensemble] (2738); Constantin BRĂILOIU, **À propos du jodel** [Concerning the yodel] (2747); Franz BRENN, **Das Wesensgefüge der Musik** [The essential structure of music] (3932) and **Die gregorianischen Modi nach dem *Speculum musicae*** [The Gregorian modes according to the *Speculum musicae*] (1068); Maria Elisabeth BROCKHOFF, **Zur Methodik der musikwissenschaftlichen Analyse** [The methodology of musicological analysis] (3933); Manfred F. BUKOFZER, **The *Caput* Masses and their plainsong** (1263); Hans ENGEL, **Ein Beitrag zur Prosodie im 16. Jahrhundert** [A contribution on the subject of 16th-century prosody] (1294) and **Vom Sinn und Wesen der Musik in Werken und Deutung der Gegenwart** [The meaning and essence of music as seen in contemporary composition and performance] (5462); Ernst Thomas FERAND, **Zufallsmusik und Komposition in der Musiklehre der Renaissance** [Chance music and composition in the music theory of the Renaissance] (1305); Rudolf von FICKER, **Probleme der Editionstechnik mittelalterlicher Musik** [Editing technique and medieval music] (3894); Kurt von FISCHER, **Bemerkungen zu Beethovens Variationenwerken** [Remarks on Beethoven's works in variation form] (4247); Adriaan Daniël FOKKER, **Expériences musicales avec les genres musicaux de Leonhard Euler contenant le septième harmonique** [Musical experiments with Leonhard Euler's genera musica containing the seventh harmonic] (4074); Paul-André GAILLARD, **Petite étude comparée du "note contre note" de Loys Bourgeoys (1547) et du psautier de Jaqui (Goudimel 1565)** [Brief comparative study of the note-against-note style of Loys Bourgeois (1547) and the Jacqui psalter (Goudimel, 1565)] (1310); Arnold GEERING, **Die Nibelungenmelodie in der Trierer Marienklage** [The Nibelungen melody in the Trier Lament of Mary] (1105); Walter GERSTENBERG, **Motetten- und Liedstil bei Ludwig Senfl** [Motet style and song style in Ludwig Senfl] (1558); Federico GHISI, **La musique religieuse de Marco da Gagliano à Santa Maria del Fiore Florence** [The religious music of Marco da Gagliano at Santa Maria del Fiore, Florence] (1559); Franz GIEGLING, **Sinn und Wesen des *concertare*** [The meaning and essence of *concertare*] (4250); Otto GOMBOSI, **Key, mode, species** (1030); Wilibald GURLITT, **Zur Bedeutungsgeschichte von *musicus* und *cantor* bei Isidor von Sevilla** [The etymology of *musicus* and *cantor* in Isidore of Seville] (5925); János HAMMERSCHLAG, **Sigel-Ornamente in ihren harmonischen Relationen** [Unwritten-out ornaments and their harmonic relations] (3677); Jacques HANDSCHIN, **Eine umstrittene Stelle bei Guilelmus Monachus** [A controversial passage in Guilielmus Monachus] (1325) and **Musicologie et musique** [Musicology and music] (880); Hans HICKMANN, **Über den Stand der musikwissenschaftlichen Forschung in Ägypten** [The state of musicological research in Egypt] (2555); Irma HOLST, **Ein Doppelchorwerk mit beziffertem Bass von Claudio Merulo** [A work for double chorus with figured bass by Claudio Merulo] (1339); Knud JEPPESEN, **Zur Kritik der klassischen Harmonielehre** [A critique of classical harmonic theory] (4182); Hermann KELLER, **Über Bachs Bearbeitungen aus dem *Hortus musicus* von Reincken** [Bach's arrangements from Reincken's *Hortus musicus*] (1588); Erika KICKTON, **Die Beziehungen der Tonkunst zur Philosophie (Logik, Ethik, und Metaphysik)** [The relation of music to philosophy (logic, ethics, and metaphysics)] (5507); Hans KLOTZ, **Die Registrierkunst der französischen Organisten des 17. und 18. Jahrhunderts und das Bachspiel** [The art of registration in French organ playing of the 17th and 18th centuries, and Bach performance] (3748); Frank LABHARDT, **Zur st. gallischen Sequenztradition im Spätmittelalter** [The St. Gallen sequence tradition in the late Middle Ages] (1136); Paul Henry LANG, **Stylistic elements in the Classic era** (4358); Jens Peter LARSEN, **Gibt es eine definitive Version von Händels *Messias*?** [Is there a definitive version of Händel's *Messiah*?] (3752); René Bernard LENAERTS, **La missa parodia néerlandaise au 16ᵉ siècle** [The Netherlandish parody Mass during the 16th century] (1365); Paul MIES, **Der Charakter der Tonarten** [The character of the keys] (1624); Walter NEF, **Das mehrsaitige "Monochord"** [The multiple-string "monochord"]

(3592); Marius SCHNEIDER, **Vom ursprünglichen Sinn der Musik** [The original meaning of music] (5589); Joseph SMITS VAN WAESBERGHE, **Das Maastrichter Osterspiel: Beitrag zur Literatur der liturgischen Spiele** [The Maastricht Easter play: A contribution to the literature of liturgical drama] (1182); Bruno STÄBLEIN, **Ambrosianisch—Gregorianisch** [Ambrosian, Gregorian] (1187); Rudolf STEGLICH, **Beethovens "überaus merkwürdige Akzentuation"** [Beethoven's "extremely peculiar accentuation"] (1867); Fausto TORREFRANCA, **Prime ricognizioni sullo stile violoncellistico Plattiano** [Preliminary appraisal of Platti's violoncello style] (1702) and **Problemi Vivaldiani** [Issues in Vivaldi studies] (1703); Walter WIORA, **Die vergleichende Frühgeschichte der europäischen Musik als methodische Forschung** [The comparative history of early European music as methodological research] (1050); Hellmut Christian WOLFF, **Die ethischen Aufgaben der neuen Musik** [The ethical obligations of the new music] (2273); Hermann ZENCK, **Zur Adriaen Willaerts Salmi spezzati** [Adrian Willaert's *salmi spezzati*] (1475).

290
bs
[Cluny, 1949] À Cluny: Congrès scientifique— Fêtes et cérémonies liturgiques en l'honneur des saints abbés Odon et Odilon [At Cluny: Scholarly conference—Festivals and liturgical ceremonies in honor of SS. Abbots Odo and Odilo]. Sponsored by the Centre National de la Recherche Scientifique (CNRS) and Société des Amis de Cluny (Dijon: Bernigaud et Privat, 1950) 342 p. *Illus., facs., bibliog., charts, diagr., maps.* In French.

The conference was held from 9 through 11 July 1949. The following contributions are cited separately: René-Jean HESBERT, **Les témoins manuscripts du culte de Saint Odilon** [The manuscript evidence of the cult of Saint Odilo] (1121); Pierre THOMAS, **Saint Odon de Cluny et son œuvre musicale** [Saint Odo of Cluny and his musical works] (1200).

291
bs
[Florence] Atti del sesto Congresso internazionale di musica [Proceedings of the Sixth International Music Congress]. Sponsored by the Maggio Musicale Fiorentino (Firenze: Barbèra, 1950) 190 p. In Italian, French, and German.

The conference was held from 18 through 21 May 1949. The following contributions are cited separately: Ernest ANSERMET, **Subjectivisme et objectivisme dans l'expression musicale** [Subjectivism and objectivism in musical expression] (5423); Enzo BORRELLI, **Soggetto ed espressione nella musica** [Subject and expression in music] (5432); Valentino BUCCHI, **Solitudine del musicista** [Solitude of the musician] (5435); Luigi DALLAPICCOLA, **Considerazioni sull'insegnamento della composizione** [Considerations on the teaching of composition] (4866); Adelmo DAMERINI, **Di una metodologia storicistica nell'insegnamento della composizione** [On a historicist methodology in the teaching of composition] (4867); Fedele D'AMICO, **Che cos'è l'oggettivismo** [What objectivism is] (5448); Andrea DELLA CORTE, **Storia, cultura e "tendenze" nell'insegnamento della composizione** [History, culture, and trends in the teaching of composition] (4869); Herbert FLEISCHER, **Soggetto e oggetto nell'espressione musicale** [Subject and object in musical expression] (5470); Alberto GENTILI, **L'insegnamento della composizione in rapporto alle tendenze moderne** [The teaching of composition in relation to modern trends] (4872); Federico GHISI, **Per un richiamo alla tradizione umanistica** [Reclaiming the humanist tradition] (4541); Cecil GRAY, **Soggettivismo ed oggettivismo nell'arte musicale** [Subjectivism and objectivism in the musical art] (5480); Guido GUERRINI, **La riforma nelle classi di composizione** [Reform in composition classes] (4823); Augusto HERMET, **Suono come "mistero"** [Sound as "mystery"] (5489); Adriano LUALDI, **Il mantello della miseria** [The cloak of misery] (5527); Massimo MILA, **Sul carattere inconsapevole dell'espressione artistica** [On the unconscious character of artistic expression] (5542); Václav NEUMANN, **La musique en Tchécoslovaquie** [Music in Czechoslovakia] (2365); Guido PANNAIN, **Orientamento storico nell'insegnamento della composizione** [Historical orientation in the teaching of composition] (4612); Alfredo PARENTE, **La favola dell'oggettivismo** [The fable of objectivism] (5565); Goffredo PETRASSI, **L'insegnamento della composizione** [Teaching composition] (4617); Marc PINCHERLE, **De l'enseignement de la composition** [Teaching composition] (4886); Alessandro PIOVESAN, **Attualità dell'oggettivismo musicale** [The reality of musical objectivism] (5568); Mario RINALDI, **Dal sentimento**

individuale alla realtà di tutti [From individual sentiment to the reality of all] (5575); Luigi RONGA, **Soggettivismo e oggettivismo nell'espressione musicale** [Subjectivity and objectivity in musical expression] (5578); Boris de SCHLOEZER, **Expression et création** [Expression and creation] (5587); Heinrich STROBEL, **Lebendiger Kompositionsunterricht!** [Living composition instruction!] (4897); Guido TURCHI, **Cause, effetti ed alcuni rimedi** [Causes, effects, and some remedies] (4660); Mario ZAFRED, **Contributo ad una critica di alcune posizioni formalistiche** [Toward a critique of formalistic positions] (5634).

292
bs
[New York] Selected papers. I: The civilizations of ancient America; II: Acculturation in the Americas—Proceedings and selected papers; III: Indian tribes of aboriginal America. 29th International Congress of Americanists; sponsored by the Wenner-Gren Foundation for Anthropological Research. Ed. by Sol TAX; intro. by Melville J. HERSKOVITS (Chicago: University of Chicago, 1951-1952) 3 v. *Illus., bibliog., maps.* In English, French, and Spanish.

The conference was held from 5 through 12 September 1949. The following contributions are cited separately: John Irvin GAMBLE, **Changing patterns in Kiowa Indian dances** (4968); Willard RHODES, **Acculturation in North American Indian music** (3172); Richard A. WATERMAN, **African influence on the music of the Americas** (3183).

293
bs
[New York] Symposium on local diversity in Iroquois culture. Sponsored by the American Anthropological Association. Ed. by William N. FENTON. *Bureau of American Ethnology Bulletin* 149 (Washington, D.C.: Smithsonian Institution, 1951) v, 187 p. *Illus., music, bibliog.*

The conference was held on 17 November 1949. The following contributions are cited separately: William N. FENTON and Gertrude Prokosch KURATH, **The Feast of the Dead, or ghost dance at Six Nations Reserve, Canada** (3147); Gertrude Prokosch KURATH, **Local diversity in Iroquois music and dance** (3162).

294
bs
[Paris] Actes du XXIᵉ Congrès international des orientalistes [Proceedings of the 21st International Congress of Orientalists] (Paris: Société Asiatique de Paris, 1949) 408 p. *Illus.* In French.

The conference was held from 23 through 31 July 1949. The following contribution is cited separately: Hans HICKMANN, **Sur l'enquête musicologique de la saison 1947-48** [On the musicological inquiry of the 1947-48 season] (3253).

295
bs
[Venice] International Folk Music Council Conference, *Journal of the International Folk Music Council* II (1950) 7–49. *Illus., transcr.* In English and French.

The second annual conference was held from 7 through 11 September 1949. The following contributions are cited separately: Maguy ANDRAL, **Dernières acquisitions phonographiques du Musée National des Arts et Traditions Populaires** [Recent phonographic acquisitions of the Musée National des Arts et Traditions Populaires] (706); Arnold Adriaan BAKÉ, **Some hobby horses in South India** (5587); Francesco BALILLA PRATELLA, **Musica e danza popolare come elemento di rinnovamento artistico** [Traditional music and dance as an element in artistic renewal] (4917); Giuseppe BONOMO, **La contradanza siciliana** [*sic*] [Sicilian contredanse] (4938); Anton Giulio BRAGAGLIA, **Balli popolari e danze d'arte** [Traditional dance and art dance] (4941); François-Joseph BRASSARD, **Chansons d'accompagnement** [Accompaniment songs] (2497); Antoine-Élisée CHERBULIEZ, **Les principes de la musicologie comparée et le folklore musicales** [*sic*] [The principles of comparative musicology and music folklore] (2427); Giuseppe COCCHIARA, **Le siciliane** [Sicilianas] (2770); Hans COMMENDA, **Innviertler Landla dance** (4947); Gianfranco D'ARONCO, **Villotte, canti popolari, poesie popolari contenute nelle pubblicazioni della Società Filologica Friulana (1919-1945)** [Villotte, traditional songs, and traditional poems contained in publications of the Società Filologica Friulana (1919-1945)]

(2786); Bianca Maria GALANTI, **Forms and aspects of the ballo tondo sardo** (4967); Arnold GEERING, **Quelques problèmes touchant la chanson populaire en Suisse** [Some problems concerning traditional song in Switzerland] (2825); Edith GERSON-KIWI, **Wedding dances and songs of the Jews of Bokhara** (2631); Douglas KENNEDY, **England's ritual dances** (5000); Paola LA VALLE, **La musica e i canti popolari in Finlandia** [Traditional music and songs in Finland] (2921); Vige LANGEVIN, **Le style de la danse populaire en France** [The style of popular dance in France] (5016); Claudie MARCEL-DUBOIS, **Quelques formules structurales de la mélodie populaire française** [Some structural formulas of traditional French melody] (4445); Sólōn MICHAĪLĪDĪS, **Regional committees for the comparative study of folk music** (2449); Jean C. MILLIGAN, **Scottish country dancing** (5033); Carmelina NASELI, **Gli strumenti popolari del popolo siciliana** [sic] [Traditional instruments of the people of Sicily] (2968); Sugeng NOTOHADINEGORO, **Some particulars of Indonesian dancing** (5043); Donal Joseph O'SULLIVAN, **Irish dances and songs** (2980); Turi PANDOLFINI, **L'anima musicale dei banditori catanesi** [The musical soul of town criers of Catania] (2984); Herbert PEPPER, **Les problèmes généraux de la musique populaire en Afrique Noire** [General problems of traditional music in sub-Saharan Africa] (2576); Giuseppe PIERSANTELLI, **Lanternette and trallalero in the Genoese popular tradition** (5051); Giulio RAZZI, **Folk music and Italian broadcasting** (3024); Ahmed Adnan SAYGUN, **Des danses d'Anatolie et de leur caractère rituel** [The dances of Anatolia and their ritual character] (5061); Fausto TORREFRANCA, **The** canzoni di alettati matrice **of the court dances and of the filastrocca during the fifteenth century and earlier** (1201); Paolo TOSCHI, **A question about the tarantella** (5078).

1950

296
bs
[Bloomington] International Folk Music Council Conference. Intro. by Evelyn K. WELLS, *Journal of the International Folk Music Council* III (1951) 2–107. *Music, charts, diagr., transcr.*
The third annual conference was held from 17 through 21 July 1950. The following contributions are cited separately: Otto ANDERSSON, **Folk music and art music** (830) and **Revival of folk music and folk dancing in Finland** (2717); Jonas BALYS, **Lithuanian folk songs in the United States** (3134); Marius BARBEAU, **The dragon myths and ritual songs of the Iroquoians** (5286) and **The folk dances of Canada** (4936); Samuel P. BAYARD, **Principal versions of an international folk tune** (4417); Paul G. BREWSTER, **The so-called "folksong" programme of radio: A threat and a challenge** (2499); Bertrand H. BRONSON, **Melodic stability in oral transmission** (4419); Elizabeth BURCHENAL, **Folk dances of the United States: Regional types and origins** (4944); Åke CAMPBELL, **Herdsman's song and yoik in northern Sweden** (2755); Antoine-Élisée CHERBULIEZ, **Interdependence of folk music and art forms in European Romantic music during the nineteenth century** (1935); Ayalah GOREN-KADMAN, **Indigenous and imported elements in the new folk dance in Israel** (4970); Herbert HALPERT, **Vitality of tradition and local songs** (3154); George HERZOG, **Folk song and its social background** (2513) and **The music of Yugoslav heroic epic folk poetry** (2853); George Pullen JACKSON, **Native and imported elements in American religious folk songs** (3156); Maud KARPELES, **Some reflections on authenticity in folk music** (2520); Sarah Gertrude KNOTT, **The National Folk Festival, United States** (3159); Gertrude Prokosch KURATH, **Iroquois midwinter medicine rites** (3161); Alan LOMAX, **The creativity of the folk singer** (2527); Albert B. LORD, **Yugoslav epic poetry** (5329); Ben Gray LUMPKIN, **Traditional folk songs available on commercial phonograph records** (2529); Paul NETTL, **Musical folklore of the Baroque period in Austria** (1633); Sirvart POLADIAN, **Melodic contour in traditional music** (4453); Warren E. ROBERTS, **Comic elements in the traditional English ballad** (5346); J. Olcutt SANDERS, **The Texas cattle country and cowboy square dance** (5060); Ahmed Adnan SAYGUN, **Authenticity in folk music** (2539); Charles SEEGER, **An instantaneous music notator** (3870); Jasim UDDIN, **Folk music of East Pakistan** (2703); Ivan H. WALTON, **Songs of the Great Lakes sailors** (3182); Richard Alan WATERMAN, **Gospel hymns of a negro church in Chicago** (6454).

297
bs
[Florence] La musica nel film [Music in film]. Proceedings of the seventh international conference; sponsored by the Maggio Musicale Fiorentino. Ed. by Luigi CHIARINI. *Quaderni della Mostra Internazionale d'Arte Cinematografica* (Roma: Bianco e Nero, 1950) 147 p. *Illus., facs., music, bibliog., charts, diagr.* In Italian.

The following contributions are cited separately: Daniele AMFITHEATROF, **La musica per film negli Stati Uniti** [Film music in the United States] (5095); Alessandro BLASETTI, Mario SERANDREI, and Sebastiano Arturo LUCIANI, **Il parere del regista, del mentatore e della critica** [The opinion of the director, of the editor, and of criticism] (5105); Enrico CAVAZZUTI, **Problemi della registrazione sonora e del missaggio** [Problems of sound recording and lack of synchronization] (5116); Alessandro CICOGNINI, **Il film musicale** [The musical film] (5118); Nicola COSTARELLI, Gino MARINUZZI, Giuseppe ROSATI, Vincenzo TOMMASINI, and Antonio VERETTI, **Aspetti della musica nel film** [Aspects of music in film] (5125); Franco FERRARA, **La direzione dell'orchestra e la musica cinematografica** [Orchestral direction and film music] (5149); Marius-François GAILLARD, **La musica per film in Francia** [Film music in France] (5153); Rocco GERVASIO and Roman VLAD, **La musica nel documentario** [Music in the documentary] (5157); Tihon Nikolaevič HRENNIKOV, **La musica per film nell'U.R.S.S.** [Film music in the U.S.S.R.] (5171); Ernest IRVING, **La musica per film in Inghilterra** [Film music in England] (5173); Francesco LARAGNINO, **La musica nel disegno animato** [Music in animation] (5190); Achille LONGO, **I musicisti e la critica cinematografica** [Musicians and film criticism] (5197); F.L. LUNGHI, **La musica e il neo-realismo** [Music and neorealism] (5199); Gian Francesco MALIPIERO, Ildebrando PIZZETTI, and Goffredo PETRASSI, **Tre opinioni** [Three opinions] (5203); Enzo MASETTI, **Introduzione ai problemi della musica nel film** [Introduction to the problems of music in film] (5205); Mario VERDONE, **Un breve scenario cinematografico di Alban Berg** [A brief cinematic scenario by Alban Berg] (5266); Adone ZECCHI, **Particolare rilievo della musica in alcuni film** [The particular importance of music in some films] (5275).

298
bs
[Leipzig] Bericht über die Wissenschaftliche Bachtagung [Report on the scholarly Bach conference]. Sponsored by the Gesellschaft für Musikforschung. Ed. by Hans Heinrich EGGEBRECHT; ed. and forew. by Walther VETTER and Ernst Hermann MEYER (Leipzig: Peters, 1951) 503 p. *Illus., music.* In German.

The conference was held from 23 through 26 July 1950. The following contributions are cited separately: Georg ANSCHÜTZ, **Über Aufbauprinzipien in den Werken Johann Sebastian Bachs** [Structural principles in the works of Johann Sebastian Bach] (4306); Dénes BARTHA, **Bemerkungen zur Stilisierung der Volksmusik, besonders der Polonäsen, bei Bach** [Notes on the stylization of traditional music, especially polonaises, in Bach] (4309); Heinrich BESSELER, **Bach und das Mittelalter** [Bach and the Middle Ages] (1488); Walter BLANKENBURG, **Die Bedeutung des Kanons in Bachs Werk** [The meaning of canon in Bach's works] (4139); Siegfried BORRIS, **Johann Sebastian Bachs Unterweisung im Tonsatz** [Johann Sebastian Bach's teaching of composition] (1493); Max DEHNERT, **Neue Aufgaben der biographischen Bachforschung** [New tasks for biographical research on Bach] (1524); Hans-Heinz DRAEGER, **Zur mitteltönigen und gleichschwebenden Temperatur** [Mean-tone and equal-tempered tuning] (4067); Alfred DÜRR, **Stilkritik und Echtheitsprobleme der frühen Kantaten Bachs** [Style criticism and problems of authenticity in the early cantatas of Bach] (4329); Hans Heinrich EGGEBRECHT, **Bach und Leibniz** [Bach and Leibniz] (1535); Rudolf ELLER, **Bruckner und Bach** [Bruckner and Bach] (1951); Ernst FLADE, **Bachs Stellung zum Orgel- und Klavierbau seiner Zeit** [Bach's views on the keyboard instrument construction of his day] (3361); Hans-Heinz DRAEGER Conrad FREYSE, **Unbekannte Jugendbildnisse Friedemann und Emanuel Bachs** [Unknown portraits of the young Friedemann and Emanuel Bach] (5379); Friedrich GRAUPNER, **Johann Sebastian Bach als Musikerzieher** [Johann Sebastian Bach as music teacher] (1564); Wilibald GURLITT, **Johann Sebastian Bach in seiner Zeit und heute** [Johann Sebastian Bach in his time and today] (1568) and **Zu Johann Sebastian Bachs Ostinato-Technik** [Johann Sebastian Bach's ostinato technique] (4339); Harry HAHN, **Der Symmetriebegriff im der Musik Bachs** [The concept of symmetry in Bach's music] (4254); Günter HAUSSWALD, **Zur Sonatenkunst der Bachzeit** [Sonata composition in Bach's time] (4256); Georgij Nikitič HUBOV, **Bach** und die zeitgenössische musikalische Kultur [Bach and the contemporary musical culture] (1579); Georg KNEPLER, Bemerkungen zum Wandel des Bachbildes [Change in the image of Bach] (1591); Karl LAUX, Bach und die deutsche Nation [Bach and the German nation] (1599); Annelise LIEBE, Bachs *Matthäuspassion* in ihrer geschichtlichen Beurteilung [The historical evaluation of Bach's *Matthäuspassion*] (1605); Felix OBERBORBECK, *Vor deinen Thron tret ich hiemit*: Bemerkungen zu Geschichte, Form und Aufführungspraxis von Bachs Lebensepilog [*Vor deinen Thron tret ich hiemit*: Observations on the history, form, and performance practice of Bach's farewell work] (1640); Eberhard REBLING, Der Rationalismus, eine Grundlage des Bachschen Realismus [Rationalism, one of the bases of Bach's realism] (5573); Wolfgang SCHMIEDER, Bemerkungen zur Bachquellenforschung [Observations on Bach source studies] (1675); Eugen SCHMITZ, Bachs h-moll-Messe und die Dresdner katholische Kirchenmusik [Bach's B-minor Mass and Roman Catholic church music in Dresden] (6381); Walter SERAUKY, Zum gegenwärtigen Stande der Bach- und Händelforschung [On the present state of Bach and Händel research] (1679); Heinrich SIEVERS, Friedrich Konrad Griepenkerl und die neu aufgefundene Handschrift von Bachs h-moll Messe [Friedrich Konrad Griepenkerl and the newly discovered manuscript of Bach's B-minor Mass] (1686); Maxim STEMPEL, Bach in Schweden [Bach in Sweden] (3770); Bence SZABOLCSI, Bach, die Volksmusik und das osteuropäische Melos [Bach, folk music, and the Eastern European melos] (4466); Walther VETTER, Bachs Universalität [Bach's universality] (1707); Hellmuth Christian WOLFF, Bach und die Musik der Gegenwart [Bach and the music of today] (2272).

299
bs   [Lüneburg] Kongreß-Bericht: Gesellschaft für Musikforschung [Congress report: Gesellschaft für Musikforschung]. Ed. by Hans ALBRECHT, Helmuth OSTHOFF, and Walter WIORA (Kassel; Basel: Bärenreiter, 1950) 248 p. *Music, bibliog.* In German.
The society's second congress was held from 16 through 20 July 1950. The following contributions are cited separately: Ursula AARBURG, Wechselbeziehungen zwischen Motiv und Tonart im mittelalterlichen Liede, insbesondere im Liede um 1200 [Correlations between motive and mode in medieval song, particularly in song around 1200] (4413); Anna Amalie ABERT, Zum metastasianischen Reformdrama [On Metastasio's reform drama] (5092); Hans von der AU, Frühformen des deutschen Volkstanzes [Early forms of German folk dance] (2727); Arnold Adriaan BAKÉ, Die beiden Tongeschlechter bei Bharata [The two modes in Bharata] (2603); Gerth Wolfgang BARUCH, Musikhistorische Aufgaben und Möglichkeiten des Rundfunks [Musicological tasks and possibilities of broadcasting] (5943); Alfred BERNER, Zum Klavierbau im 17. und 18. Jahrhundert [Keyboard building in the 17th and 18th centuries] (3508); Heinrich BESSELER, Charakterthema und Erlebnisform bei Bach [Character theme and experience form of Bach] (4313); Wolfgang BOETTICHER, Zur Chronologie des Schaffens Orlando di Lassos [Toward a chronology of the works of Roland de Lassus] (1245); Erdmann Werner BÖHME, 150 Lüneburger Musiker-Namen [150 names of Lüneburg musicians] (828); Siegfried BORRIS, Die Widersprüche zwischen älterer Harmonielehre und neueren Tonsatzlehren [The conflicts between traditional theory of harmony and recent theories of composition] (4142); Karl-Eckhardt BRENCHER, Zur Farbe-Ton-Forschung [Concerning research in color-sound relationships] (5643); Hans CONRADIN, Das Problem der Bewegung in der Musik [The problem of movement in music] (5650); Lothar CREMER, Über unser zweifaches Tonhöhenempfinden [Concerning our twofold perception of pitch] (5651); Alfred DÜRR, Zur Chronologie der Weimarer Kantaten J.S. Bachs [Toward a chronology of J.S. Bach's Weimar cantatas] (1534); Hans ECKARDT, Die Ei und Saezuri: Verschollene melismatische Gesangformen im japanischen Tanz [Ei and Saezuri: Forgotten melismatic vocal forms in Japanese dance] (2620); Wilhelm EHMANN, Aufführungspraxis der Bachschen Motetten [Performance practice of Bach's motets] (3739); Ernst EMSHEIMER, Lappischer Kultgesang [Sámi cult singing] (2802) and Schallaufnahmen georgischer Mehrstimmigkeit [Sound recordings of Georgian polyphony] (2621); Hans ENGEL, Soziologisches Porträt Johann Sebastian Bachs [A sociological portrait of Johann Sebastian Bach] (1539) and Über Form und Mosaiktechnik bei Bach, besonders in seinen Arien [Form and mosaic-technique in Bach, particularly in his arias] (4244); Karl Gustav FELLERER, Die Lehre vom Cantus gregorianus im 18. Jahrhundert [Theory of Gregorian chant in the 18th century] (1755); Kurt von FISCHER, Zur Satztechnik von Bachs Klaviersuiten [On compositional

technique in Bach's keyboard suites] (4334); Rudolf GERBER, Die Textwahl in der mehrstimmigen Hymnenkomposition des späten Mittelalters [Choice of text in polyphonic hymn composition of the late Middle Ages] (5316) and Unbekannte Instrumentalwerke von Chr.W. Gluck [Unknown instrumental works by C.W. Gluck] (1762); Walter GERSTENBERG, Zur Verbindung Präludium und Fuge bei J.S. Bach [Concerning the connection between prelude and fugue in J.S. Bach] (4249); Federico GHISI, The oratorios of Giacomo Carissimi in Hamburg Staats-Bibliothek (1560); Kurt GUDEWILL, Die Barform und ihre Modifikationen [The bar form and its modifications] (4251); Robert HAAS, Bach und Wien [Bach and Vienna] (1571); Eta HARICH-SCHNEIDER, Die Gagaku in der Musikabteilung des japanischen Kaiserhofes [Gagaku in the music department of the Japanese imperial court] (2634); Felix HOERBURGER, Zum Problem des Umsingens von Volksliedmelodien [On the problem of re-interpreting traditional songs] (4435); Ernst KLUSEN, César Franck und die Überwindung der Nationalstile im späten 19. Jahrhundert [César Franck and the surmounting of national styles in the late 19th century] (2004); H. KOSCHEL, Hörmängel und ihre audiometrische Feststellung [Hearing deficiencies and their audiometric detection] (5671); Walter KREIDLER, Die Tonleiter als Tonspektrum [The scale as a spectrum of tones] (5833); Walther KRÜGER, Grundbegriffe und Periodizität in der abendländischen Musikgeschichte [Basic principles and periodicity in the history of Western music] (890); Jaap KUNST, Die 2000jährige Geschichte Süd-Sumatras im Spiegel ihrer Musik [The 2000-year history of South Sumatra as reflected in its music] (2652); Walther LIPPHARDT, Die Kyrietropen in ihrer rhythmischen und melodischen Struktur [Rhythmic and melodic structure of the Kyrie tropes] (4010); Paul MOOS, Gehören Gluck, Händel und Bach zur barocken Kunst ihrer Zeit? [Do Gluck, Händel, and Bach belong to the Baroque art of their time?] (1626); Hans Joachim MOSER, Musikalischer Erbgang und seelische Mutation [Musical heredity and psychological change] (5683); Friedrich NEUMANN, Probleme der Mehrklangsbildung [Problems in the formation of chords] (4204); Hans F. REDLICH, Anfänge der Bachpflege in England 1750-1850 [The beginnings of the cultivation of Bach in England, 1750-1850] (1845); Georg REICHERT, Der Passamezzo [The passamezzo] (5058); Jens ROHWER, Zur Überwindung des Formalismus in der musikalischen Tonarten- und Geschlechterlehre [The conquest of formalism in the theory of musical keys and modes] (4214); Walter SALMEN, Vermeintliches und wirkliches Volkslied im späten Mittelalter [Alleged and actual folk song in the late Middle Ages] (3042); Richard SCHAAL, Zur Methodik quellenmässiger Datierung der Werke Pierre de la Rues [Methodology for source-related dating of the works of Pierre de la Rue] (1426); Hans Joachim SCHAEFER, Zur Ästhetik und Dramaturgie bei Wagner [Concerning Wagner's aesthetics and dramaturgy] (5581); Arnold SCHMITZ, Die oratorische Kunst J.S. Bachs: Grundfragen und Grundlagen [The oratorio art of J.S. Bach: Underlying questions and basic principles] (1676); Erich SEEMANN, Mythen vom Ursprung der Musik [Myths about the origin of music] (5351); Heinrich SIEVERS, Die Braunschweiger Tabulaturen [The Braunschweig tablatures] (1433); Joseph SMITS VAN WAESBERGHE, Zur Entstehung der drei Hauptfunktionen in der Harmonik [Concerning the origin of the three primary functions in harmony] (4218); Bruno STÄBLEIN, Alt- und neurömischer Choral [Old and New Roman chant] (1186); Rudolf STEGLICH, Zum Kontrastproblem Johannes Brahms—Hugo Wolf [Viewing Johannes Brahms and Hugo Wolf as opposites] (2104) and Zur Ausdruckskunst des Nürnberger Paumann-Kreises [The art of expression of the Nuremberg Paumann circle] (1442); Rudolf STEPHAN, Einige Hinweise auf die Pflege der Mehrstimmigkeit im frühen Mittelalter in Deutschland [Some indications of the cultivation of polyphony in the early Middle Ages in Germany] (1193); Rudolf STREICH, Das elektrische Musikinstrument im Spiegel der akustischen Forschung [The electric musical instrument as reflected in acoustics research] (3672); Ernst TANZBERGER, Jean Sibelius als Symphoniker [Jean Sibelius as symphonist] (2262); Erich THEINHAUS, Zur Frage der Glockenprüfung und Glockenbegutachtung [Concerning the question of testing and evaluating bells] (3655); Erich THIENHAUS, Vorführung stereophonischer Bandaufnahmen [Demonstration of stereophonic tape recordings] (5794); Ottavio TIBY, La scuola polifonica siciliana dei secc. XVI e XVII [The Sicilian school of polyphony of the 16th and 17th centuries] (1453); Fausto TORREFRANCA, Guido d'Arezzo [Guido of Arezzo] (1202); Erich VALENTIN, Zur Soziologie des Musiklebens [Concerning the sociology of musical life] (5912); René WALLAU, Die kirchliche Bedeutung der Bachschen Musik [The significance of Bach's music in church] (6453); Walter WIORA, Der mittelalterliche Liedkanon [The song canon of the Middle

Ages] (1216); Hellmuth Christian WOLFF, **Der Wert der Geschichte** [The value of history] (935).

300
bs
[Lüneburg] Zweiter Weltkongreß der Musik-bibliotheken [Second World Congress of Music Libraries]. Sponsored by the Association Internationale des Bibliothèques Musicales. Ed. by Hans ALBRECHT (Basel; Kassel: Bärenreiter, 1950; 1951) 72 p. In German, English, and French.

The conference was held from 20 through 22 July 1950. The following contributions are cited separately: Irmgard BECKER-GLAUCH, **Die englischen Musikbibliotheken in Deutschland** [The English music libraries in Germany] (707); Martin CREMER, **Das Schicksal der Musikabteilung der ehemaligen Preußischen Staatsbibliothek** [The fate of the music department of the former Preußische Staatsbibliothek] (711); John Howard DAVIES, **Music librarianship for broadcasting** (542); Valentin DENIS, **Les buts et les moyens des bibliothèques des conservatoires** [The purposes and means of conservatory libraries] (547); Vladimir FÉDOROV, **Échange et prêt entre bibliothèques musicales** [Exchange and lending between music libraries] (568) and **Entente et organisation internationales pour le dépouillement des périodiques musicaux** [An international agreement and organization for the abstracting of music periodicals] (569); Øystein GAUKSTAD, **Registrierung von Volksmusik** [Cataloguing folk music] (578); Robert HAAS, **Einige allgemeine Bemerkungen** [Some general remarks] (721); Hans HALM, **Schallplattenarchiv und öffentliche wissenschaftliche Bibliotheken** [Archives of phonograph records and public scholarly libraries] (587); Helge KRAGEMO, **Konzertprogramme** [Concert programs] (604); Erich Hermann MUELLER VON ASOW, **Der Gesamtkatalog der Musiker-Briefe: Auszug** [Comprehensive catalogue of musicians' letters: Extract] (633); Leopold NOWAK, **Dienst am Leser: Aufgaben, Probleme, Lösungen** [Service to the reader: Tasks, problems, solutions] (639); Alfons OTT, **Wesen und Aufgabe einer musikalischen Volksbibliothek** [The nature and the task of a popular music library] (645); Félix RAUGEL, **La bibliothèque de la maîtrise de la cathédrale d'Aix-en-Provence** [The library in the choir school of the cathedral of Aix-en-Provence] (748); Paul SIEBER, **Die Bibliothek der Allgemeinen Musikgesellschaft Zürich** [The library of the Allgemeine Musikgesellschaft in Zurich] (756); Bruno STÄBLEIN, **Der thematische Katalog der mittelalterlichen einstimmigen Melodien** [The thematic catalogue of monophonic medieval melodies] (797); Henk STAM, **Die Stiftung Donemus** [The Donemus foundation] (694); Hans ZEHNTNER, **Handschriftliche Musiker-nachlässe in schweitzer Bibliotheken** [Manuscript musicians' documents bequeathed to Swiss libraries] (770).

301
bs
[Luxeuil] Mélanges Colombaniens [Columbanian mélange]. Sponsored by the Association des Amis de St. Colomban. Intro. by Patrick O'CONNOR. *Bibliothèque de la Société d'Histoire Ecclésiastique de la France* (Paris: Alsatia, 1951) 418 p. *Illus., facs., music, bibliog., maps.* In French, English, and German.

The conference was held from 20 through 23 July 1950. The following contributions are cited separately: Patrice COUSIN, **La psalmodie chorale dans la règle de Saint Colomban** [Choral psalmody under the rule of Saint Columbanus] (6193); Johannes DUFT, **Saint Colomban dans les manuscrits liturgiques de la bibliothèque abbatiale de Saint-Gall** [Saint Columbanus in liturgical manuscripts at the Stiftsbibliothek of St. Gallen] (6204); René-Jean HESBERT, **Les compositions rhythmiques en l'honneur de Saint Colomban** [Rhythmic compositions in honor of Saint Columbanus] (6250).

302
bs
[Modena] Miscellanea di studi muratoriani [Miscellaneous Muratori studies]. Proceedings of the Convegno di studi storici in onore di L.A. Muratori; sponsored by the Deputazione di Storia Patria per le Antiche Provincie Modenesi. Bibliog. by Tommaso SORBELLI (Modena: Aedes Muratoriana, 1951) 617 p. *Facs., music, bibliog.* In Italian.

The conference was held from 14 through 16 April 1950, in commemoration of the 200th anniversary of the death of the antiquary and historian Locovico Antonio Muratori (1672-1750). The following contribution is cited separately: Guiseppe VECCHI, **S. Geminiano lirica della liturgia Modenese** [St. Geminian in the lyrics of the Modenese liturgy] (6404).

303
bs
[Rome] Atti del [I] Congresso internazionale di musica sacra [Proceedings of the (first) International Congress of Sacred Music]. Sponsored by the Pontificio Istituto di Musica Sacra and Commissione di Musica Sacra per l'Anno Santo. Ed. and intro. by Higini ANGLÈS (Tournai: Desclée, 1952) 420 p. *Music.* In Italian, French, English, German, Latin, and Spanish.

The conference was held from 25 through 30 May 1950. The following contributions are cited separately: Luigi AGUSTONI, **La scomposizione del neuma** [The decomposition of the neume] (3801); Joseph AHRENS, **Die zeitgenössiche Orgelmusik in der katholischen Liturgie** [Contemporary organ music in the Catholic liturgy] (6140); Germano ALBERTI, **Campane "a festa" suonate mediante movimento a rotazione** [Bells for solemn occasions rung with a rotation movement] (3642); Miguel ALTISENT, **Las melodias gregorianas para los *Propios* nuevos** [Gregorian melodies for new Proper chants] (6142); Guglielmo BARBLAN, **Delle influenze del Romanticismo nella musica sacra** [On the influences of Romanticism in sacred music] (1909); Heinrich BESSELER, **Johannes Ciconia: Begründer der Chorpolyphonie** [Johannes Ciconia: A founder of choral polyphony] (1237); Laurence BEVENOT, **L'orgue McClure à tempérament non-égal** [The McClure organ with unequal temperament] (3336); Urbanus BOMM, **Historismus und gregorianischer Vortragstil** [Historicism and Gregorian performance style] (3692); Antony BONNET, **Musique d'orgue et chant grégorien** [Organ music and Gregorian chant] (6174); Louis BROU, **L'antiphonaire wisigothique et l'antiphonaire grégorien au début du VIIIᵉ siècle** [The Visigothic and Gregorian antiphoners at the beginning of the 8th century] (1070); Maurice BUSSON, **De la nécessité d'un graduel à l'usage des petites églises** [The need for a gradual to be used in small churches] (6181); Eugène CARDINE, **De l'édition critique du graduel: Nécessité, avantages, méthode** [On the critical edition of the gradual: Necessity, advantages, method] (3888); Edgardo CARDUCCI-AGUSTINI, **Se i sistemi esclusivisti della musica contemporanea siano conciliabili con lo stile sacro** [Whether the exclusivist systems of contemporary music can be reconciled with sacred style] (5439); Pierre CARRAZ, **L'accent et l'ictus dans la métrique latine** [Accent and ictus in Latin metrics] (3977); Enrico CATTANEO, **Sul canto ambrosiano** [Ambrosian chant] (1072); **Conspectus historicus de cantu in ordine Cisterciensi** [Historical survey of chant in the Cistercian order] (6186); Solange CORBIN, **l'Office en vers *Gaude, Mater Ecclesia* pour la Conception de la Vierge** [The versified Office *Gaude, Mater Ecclesia* for the feast of the Immaculate Conception] (1078); Ernesto DALLA LIBERA, **Nei paesi latini è necessario fomentare il canto del popolo nel tempio; per conseguire ciò dobbiamo cominciare dalla scuola elementare** [In countries where Romance languages are spoken congregations should be encouraged to sing in church; to achieve this we should begin in elementary school] (6196); Leonzio DAYAN, **I canti armeni attraverso la tradizione dei secoli** [Armenian chant over the tradition of the centuries] (6108); Alessandro DE BONIS, **Formazione tecnica dei musicisti di chiesa** [The technical training of church musicians] (4868); Aldhelm DEAN, **The laity and the liturgy** (6198); Simon DELACROIX, **Musique sacrée et pastorale** [Sacred and pastoral music] (6199); Dominique DELALANDE, **L'insuffisance du système d'écriture guidonien, ou l'existence de plusieurs notes mobiles dans le système grégorien** [Inadequacy of the Guidonian system of notation, or, the existence of several movable tones in the Gregorian system] (3816); Valentin DENIS, **La musique et la musicologie dans les universités catholiques** [Music and musicology in Catholic universities] (4814); Bartolomeo DI SALVO, **La notazione paleobizantina e la sua trascrizione** [Paleo-Byzantine notation and its transcription] (3817) and **La tradizione orale dei canti liturgici delle colonie italo-albanesi di Sicilia comparata con quella dei codici antichi bizantini** [The oral tradition of liturgical chants in Italian-Albanian colonies in Sicily, compared with that of the early Byzantine codices] (6007); Celestino ECCHER, **Necessità di formare nei paesi latini cappelle musicali con cantori volontari per l'esecuzione della sacra polifonia** [The need in Romance-speaking countries to train choirs with volunteer singers in the performance of sacred polyphony] (6209); Laurence FEININGER, **Necessità di catalogare la musica esistente nelle cattedrali e negli archivi parrocchiali** [The need for cataloguing music extant in cathedrals and parish archives] (572) and **Orazio Benevoli (1605-1672)** (1544); Karl Gustav FELLERER, **Die kirchliche Monodie um 1600** [Sacred monody around 1600] (1302); Rudolf von FICKER, **Der Choral als symbolische Idee in der mittelalterlichen Mehrstimmigkeit** [Chant as a symbolic idea in medieval polyphony] (1092); Friedrich FREI, **Kirchenmusik mit Orchesterbegleitung, auch wenn sie von grossen Meistern komponiert ist, eignet sich mehr für Konzerte als für liturgische Funktionen** [Church music with orchestral accompaniment, even if it is composed by great masters, is more suitable for concerts than liturgical functions] (6216); Jacques FROGER, **Les divers états du calendrier dans le graduel romain** [The various statuses of the calendar in the Roman gradual] (6217); Joseph GAJARD, **Du rôle des principales familles de manuscrits dans la restauration de la leçon grégorienne authentique** [The role of the principal manuscript families in the restoration of the authentic Gregorian reading] (3896); Alexandre GAZÉ, **L'œuvre de l'Université Catholique d'Ottawa (Canada) au point de vue de la musique sacrée** [The work of the Catholic University of Ottawa (Canada) from the point of view of sacred music] (4817); Fernando GERMANI, **L'organo barocco nell' idea moderna** [The modern concept of the Baroque organ] (3368); Federico GHISI, **L'Ordinarium Missae nel XV secolo ed i primordi della parodia** [The Ordinary of the Mass in the 15th century and the beginnings of parody] (1315); Alberto GHISLANZONI, **Importanza dello studio del canto gregoriano per la formazione dei musicisti di oggi e di domani** [The importance of the study of Gregorian chant for the training of the musicians of today and tomorrow] (4875); Maurice GUILLAUME, **Étude sur le choral** Notre Père au royaume des cieux **de J.S. Bach** [Study of the chorale Vater unser im Himmelreich of J.S. Bach] (1567); Ferdinand HABERL, **Die liturgisch-seelsorgliche und musikalische Notwendigkeit der Schaffung eines kirchlichen und weltlichen Einheitsliederkanons für jede Nation** [The liturgical-pastoral and musical need for the creation of a canon of ecclesiastical and secular standard hymns in every nation] (6246); René-Jean HESBERT, **Groupes neumatiques à signification mélodique** [Neumatic groupings with melodic significance] (3826) and **Les pièces de chant des Messes** Pro defunctis **dans la tradition manuscrite** [The chants of Requiem Masses in the manuscript tradition] (1119); Hans HICKMANN, **Quelques observations sur la musique liturgique des Coptes d'Egypte** [Some observations on the liturgical music of the Copts of Egypt] (6114); Carsten HØEG, **L'Octoechus byzantin** [The Byzantine oktōēchos] (6115); Jacques HOURLIER, **Le domaine de la notation messine** [The territorial reach of Messine (Lorraine) notation] (3829); Michel HUGLO, **Origine de la mélodie du Credo "authentique" de la Vaticane** [Origin of the so-called authentic Credo melody of the Vatican] (1128); Albert IPPEL and Joseph SCHMIDT-GÖRG, **Eine tönende Musikgeschichte** [A history of music in sound] (5761); Simon JARGY, **La musique liturgique syrienne** [Syrian liturgical music] (6117); Knud JEPPESEN, **Die älteste italienische Orgelmusik** [The earliest Italian organ music] (1344); Giuseppe KAFTANGIAN, **Il canto liturgico armeno** [Armenian liturgical chant] (6118); Hermann KELLER, **Die Orgel-Messe im dritten Teil der** Klavier-Übung **von Johann Sebastian Bach** [The organ Mass in the third part of the Clavier-Übung of Johann Sebastian Bach] (1587); Paul-Armand LAILY, **Difficulté de la notation Byzantine et projet de la remplacer par une notation occidentale adaptée** [Difficulty of the Byzantine notation and the project of replacing it with an adapted Western notation] (3842); Auguste LE GUENNANT, **Le mouvement grégorien en France** [The Gregorian movement in France] (2343); René Bernard LENAERTS, **La musique sacrée en Belgique au XVIII**ᵉ **siècle** [Sacred music in Belgium in the 18th century] (1602); Joseph LENNARDS, **L'éducation musicale des enfants** [Musical education of children] (4723); H.W.R. LILLIE, **The vocal training for the clergy** (4833); Walther LIPPHARDT, **Gregor der Grosse und sein Anteil am römischen Antiphonar** [Gregory the Great and his role in the Roman antiphoner] (1142); Renato LUNELLI, **Apologia dell' organo tradizionale** [In defense of the traditional organ] (3418); Fernand MAILLET, **L'apostolat social, artistique et spirituel des manécanteries** [The social, artistic, and spiritual apostolate of boys' choirs] (4731); George MALCOLM, **La musica nell' Ufficiatura liturgica della Cattedrale di Westminster** [Music in the liturgical Office of Westminster Cathedral] (6295); Nicola MARANGOS, **Rito bizantino-greco** [Byzantine-Greek rite] (6121); João Batista da MOTTA E ALBUQUERQUE, **La musica sacra nel Brasile** [Sacred music in Brazil] (6312); Kyriakos MOUSSES, **La musique liturgique chaldéenne** [Chaldean liturgical music] (6124); Paul NEUMANN, **Die Organisation der Kirchenmusikpflege** [The organization of the cultivation of church music] (6320); Jules van NUFFEL, **L'évolution musicale contemporaine et sa répercussion sur la musique sacrée de notre époque: Les possibilités qu'elle offre à celle-ci** [The contemporary musical evolution and its impact on sacred music in our era: The possibilities it offers to the latter] (2222); Raïna PALIKAROVA VERDEIL, **Les notations musicales employées dans les églises slaves au IX**ᵉ **siècle** [Musical notations employed in the Slavic churches in the 9th century] (3858); Rodolfo PAOLI, **L'oratorio nella musica contemporanea** [The oratorio in contemporary music] (4278); Ludwig PICHLER, **Antichi canti bulgari et russi** [Early Bulgarian and Russian chant] (6127); Arthur PIECHLER, **Die Phrasierung der Orgelwerke Bachs** [Phrasing in Bach's organ works] (3763); Nino

PIRROTTA, **Considerazioni sui primi esempi di Missa parodia** [Considerations on the earliest examples of the parody Mass] (1403); Henri POTIRON, **La question modale** [The modal question] (4103); Jean PRIM, **De l'indispensable base juridique et financière de la musique sacrée** [Of the essential legal and financial base of sacred music] (6344); David PUJOL ROCA, **Manuscritos de música neerlandesa conservados en la biblioteca del Monasterio de Montserrat** [Manuscripts of Netherlandish music in the library of the Abbey of Montserrat] (747); Miguel QUEROL GAVALDÁ, **La música religiosa española en el s. XVII** [Spanish religious music in the 17th century] (1650); Rudolf QUOIKA, **Zur Entstehung der italienisch-österriechischen Barockorgel** [The origin of the Italian-Austrian Baroque organ] (3457); Fiorenzo ROMITA, **De studio ac praxi musicae sacrae in seminariis juxta praescripta S. Sedis** [The study and practice of sacred music in seminaries according to the prescriptions of the Holy See] (4891); John Edward RONAN, **Contemporary polyphony for the Proper of the Mass** (2241); Luigi RONGA, **Nota sulla vocalità palestriniana** [A note on Palestrina's vocality] (4379); Carlo ROSSINI, **Necessità delle scuole diocesane di musica sacra** [The need for diocesan schools of sacred music] (6365); Gaston ROUSSEL, **Les maîtrises d'enfants et les Offices liturgiques** [Children's choir schools and the liturgical Offices] (6366); Samuel RUBIO, **Manuscritos musicales de la liturgia bizantina que se conservan en la biblioteca del Monasterio de El Escorial** [Musical manuscripts of the Byzantine liturgy that are preserved in the library of the Monasterio de El Escorial] (751); Heinrich SANDEN, **Neumen ohne Linien: Neuen Forschungen** [Lineless neumes: Recent research] (3869); Carmelo SANGIORGIO, **Le caratteristiche dell' organo liturgico** [Characteristics of the liturgical organ] (3472); Gregor SCHWAKE, **De cantu gregoriano in ore populi** [Gregorian chant in the mouths of the congregation] (6388); John C. SELNER, **Sacred music and art** (5593); Albert SMIJERS, **Il faut unir l'œuvre des diverses Associations de Ste-Cécile et de St-Grégoire, en conservant leur autonomie et leur caractère national** [The work of the various Caecilian and Gregorian associations must be unified, while maintaining their autonomy and national character] (6392); Joseph SMITS VAN WAESBERGHE, **L'évolution des tons psalmodiques au Moyen Âge** [The evolution of psalm tones in the Middle Ages] (1180); Bruno STÄBLEIN, **Zur Frühgeschichte des römischen Chorals** [The early history of Roman chant] (1191); Oliver STRUNK, **The classification and development of the early Byzantine notations** (3874); Franz TACK, **Das zeitgenösische kirchenmusikalische Schrifttum in Deutschland** [Contemporary writing on church music in Germany] (6395); Wilhelm TELEU, **Die Organisation und soziale Stellung der Kirchenmusiker in Deutschland** [The organization and social position of church musicians in Germany] (6397); Pierre THOMAS, **Principes de la théorie modale hexacordale dans les théoriciens médiévaux et principalement dans Guy d'Arezzo** [Principles of hexachordal modal theory in the medieval theorists, especially Guido of Arezzo] (4120); Fausto TORREFRANCA, **Grecia e Occidente: Valor cristiano della polifonia** [Greece and the West: The Christian value of polyphony] (5616); Rudolf WALTER, **Bemerkungen zu Orgelbau und Orgelspiel in Deutschland** [Remarks on organ building and organ playing in Germany] (3502); Egon WELLESZ, **Kontakion and kanōn** (1211); Eric WERNER, **The common ground in the chant of church and synagogue** (6030); Joseph WÖRSCHING, **Die Orgel der Zisterzienserkirche Kaisheim, 1778** [The organ of the Kaisheim Cistercian church, 1778] (3503); Franz ZEHRER, **L'interpretazione moderna della polifonia sacra classica: Difetti da evitare** [Modern interpretation of classic sacred polyphony: Defects to avoid] (3725); José Gonzalo ZULAICA Y ARREGUI (José Antonio de Donostia), **El canto popular religioso en España** [Traditional religious song in Spain] (3128).

1951

304
bs
[Iesi; Maiolati; Fabriano; Ancona] Atti del primo Congresso internazionale di studi spontiniani [Acts of the First International Congress of Spontini Studies] (Fabriano: Arti Grafiche Gentile, 1954) 142 p. *Port., music.* In Italian.

The conference was held from 6 through 9 September 1951. The following contributions are cited separately: Alessandro BELARDINELLI, **Documenti Spontiniani inediti** [The unpublished documents of Spontini] (1912) and **Le Ateniesi di De Jouy** [De Jouy's Le Ateniesi] (5104); Filippo CAFFARELLI, **Documentazioni spontiniane inedite: l'Epistolario** [Unpublished documents of Spontini: The correspondence] (1928), **Il** rapporto di Gaspare Spontini intorno alla riforma della musica sacra [Spontini's relation to the reform of sacred music] (1929), and **Spontini grande italiano e grande europeo** [Spontini: A great Italian and a great European] (1930); Hans ENGEL, **L'opera *Agnese di Hohenstaufen* di Spontini** [Spontini's opera *Agnes von Hohenstaufen*] (1952); Karl Gustav FELLERER, **L'importanza de *La vestale* nella produzione operistica di Spontini** [The importance of *La vestale* among Spontini's operas] (1753); Alberto GHISLANZONI, **Gaspare Spontini e la musica bandistica** [Gaspare Spontini and band music] (1969), **I rapporti fra Spontini e Mendelssohn** [The relationship between Spontini and Mendelssohn] (1970), and **Sintesi della produzione giovanile spontiniana** [Synthesis of Spontini's youthful compositions] (1764); Mateusz GLIŃSKI, **Spontini direttore d'orchestra** [Spontini as orchestral conductor] (1972); Helmuth OSTHOFF, **L'idea drammatica e lo stile musicale nelle opere di Gaspare Spontini** [The dramatic element and the musical style in Spontini's works] (2062); Ulderico ROLANDI, **Tre parodie de *La vestale*** [Three parodies of *La vestale*] (2085); Luigi SERVOLINI, **Inediti Spontiniani a Forlì** [Spontini's unpublished documents in Forlì] (2095); Fausto TORREFRANCA, **Gaspare Spontini e l'opera tedesca** [Gaspare Spontini and German opera] (2111); Gustavo TRAGLIA, **Umiliazioni giovanili e reazioni nell'età matura in Gaspare Spontini** [Youthful humilitations and reactions in Gaspare Spontini's mature period] (2112).

305
bs
[Ochsenhausen] Der Barock: Seine Orgeln und seine Musik in Oberschwaben [The Baroque: Its organs and its music in Upper Swabia]. Proceedings of the Oberschwäbische Barock-, Orgel- und Musiktagung; sponsored by the Kultministerium Stuttgart and Kultministerium Tübingen. Ed. by Walter SUPPER. *Veröffentlichungen der Gesellschaft der Orgelfreunde* 1 (Berlin: Merseburger, 1952) 175 p. *Illus., facs., index, charts, diagr., organ specification.* In German.

The conference was held from 29 July through 5 August 1951. The following contributions are cited separately: Hans BÖHRINGER, **Das Spezifische des "katholischen" Orgelbaus** [The specific character of so-called Catholic organ building] (3341); Franz BÖSKEN, **Der mittelrheinische Orgelbau zur Zeit des Aufenhalts Joseph Gablers in Mainz** [Organ-building in the mid-Rhine region during Joseph Gabler's stays in Mainz] (3345); Corbinian GINDELE, **Der Anteil Beurons an der Rettung der Ottobeurer Orgeln** [Beuron's share in the preservation of the Ottobeuren organs] (3375); Adam GOTTRON, **Joseph Gabler in Mainz** (1562); Rudolf KOPP, **Das Portativ für zeitnahes Schulsingen—Hausmusik und Kammermusik** [A portative organ for up-to-date school singing, Hausmusik, and chamber music] (3405); Hans-Joachim NEUMANN, **Die Elektro-Orgel in der Kirche** [The electric organ in churches] (3671); Rudolf QUOIKA, **Über die österreichische und oberschwäbische Barockorgel: Von der Durchdringung zweier Orgellandschaften** [Austrian and Upper Swabian Baroque organs: On the interpenetration of two organ landscapes] (3455) and **Zur Technologie der süddeutschen Barockorgel** [The technology of the South German Baroque organ] (3458); Félix RAUGEL, **Die Barockorgel in Frankreich** [The Baroque organ in France] (3461); Georg REICHERT, **Beziehungen württembergischer Musiker des 17. Jahrhunderts zum Hamburger Organistenkreis** [Relations of 17th-century Württemberg musicians to the Hamburg organists' circle] (1655); Willi SIEGELE, **Musik des oberschwäbischen Barock** [The music of the Upper Swabian Baroque] (1683); Otto SPÖRRI, **Die neuzeitliche kleine Orgel in der Schweiz** [The contemporary small organ in Switzerland] (3481); Walter SUPPER, ed., **Die oberschwäbische Barockorgel auf württembergischem Boden** [The Upper Swabian Baroque organ in Württemberg territory] (3487); **Dispositionen von ausserwürttembergischen Barockorgeln, die auf die oberschwäbische Barockorgel Bezug nehmen** [Dispositions of Baroque organs from outside Württemberg that relate to Upper Swabian Baroque organs] (3482), and **Oberschwäbische Barock-, Orgel- und Musiktagung** [Meeting on the Baroque, organs, and music in Upper Swabia] (3444).

306
bs
[Opatija] International Folk Music Council Conference, *Journal of the International Folk Music Council* IV (1952) 4–67; VI (1954) 52–55. *Illus., port., transcr.* In English and French.

The fourth annual conference was held from 8 through 14 September 1951. The following contributions are cited separately: Antoine-Élisée

CHERBULIEZ, **Le rythme critère de l'attitude individuelle et collective** [Rhythm as criterion of the individual and collective attitude] (3980); Paul COLLAER, **Importance des musiques ethniques dans la culture musicale contemporaine** [The importance of ethnic musics in contemporary musical culture] (2504); Emanuil ČUČKOV, **Contenu idéologique et procès rythmique de la danse populaire macédonienne** [Ideological content and rhythmic process in Macedonian traditional dance] (4950); Živko FIRFOV, **Les caractères métriques dans la musique populaire macédonienne** [Metric characters in Macedonian traditional music] (3991); Edith GERSON-KIWI, **Migrations and mutations of Oriental folk instruments** (3250); Felix HOERBURGER, **Correspondence between Eastern and Western folk epics** (2514); Radoslav HROVATIN, **Les rapports réciproques du folklore et de la création musicale artistique en Slovénie** [The reciprocal relations of folklore and musical artistic creation in Slovenia] (972); Danica S. JANKOVIĆ and Ljubica S. JANKOVIĆ, **Styles et techniques des danseurs traditionnels serbes** [Styles and techniques of Serbian traditional dancers] (4990); Gurit KADMAN, **Yemenite dances and their influence on the new Israeli folk dances** (4998); Ivo KIRIGIN, **Some theoretical statements on the art of musical folklore based on examples from the National Republic of Croatia** (2894); Leopold KRETZENBACHER, **Folk songs in the folk plays of the Austrian Alpine regions** (5186); France MAROLT (ed. by Valens VODUŠEK), **Slovene folk dance and folk music** (2947); Cvjetko RIHTMAN, **Les formes polyphoniques dans la musique populaire de Bosnie et d'Herzégovine** [Polyphonic forms in the traditional music of Bosnia and Herzegovina] (4211); Walter SALMEN, **Towards the exploration of national idiosyncrasies in wandering song-tunes** (4456); Margaret SARGENT, **Folk and primitive music in Canada** (2465); Patrick SHULDHAM-SHAW, **Folk song and the concert singer** (2541); Miodrag A. VASILJEVIĆ, **Les bases tonales de la musique populaire serbe** [The tonal bases of traditional Serbian music] (4124).

307
bs
[Oxford] The organist and the congregation: Lectures and a sermon delivered at the First Conference of Congregational Organists. Sponsored by the Guild of Congregational Organists. Intro. by Erik ROUTLEY (London: Independent Press, 1952) 62 p.

The conference was held by the Guild of Congregational Organists, an association of church organists in the service of the Congregational Church of England and Wales, at Mansfield College, Oxford, from 22 through 24 June 1951. The following contributions are cited separately: Cyril Stanley CHRISTOPHER, **Playing for a congregation** (6430) and **The work of the organist in a Congregational church** (6431); Jack P.B. DOBBS, **Choir training and repertory** (6432); T. Caryl MICKLEM, **Worship and prophecy: A sermon** (6439); Douglas STEWART, **The organist and his minister** (6450).

308
bs
[Palermo] Atti dello VIII Congresso internazionale di studi bizantini [Acts of the Eighth International Congress of Byzantine Studies] *Studi bizantini e neoellenici* 7-8 (Roma: Associazione Nazionale per gli Studi Bizantini, 1953) 2 v.; (reprint, Nendeln: Kraus, 1978). *Illus., bibliog.* In Italian, French, German, English, and Greek.

The conference was held from 3 through 10 April 1951. The following contribution is cited separately: Bartolomeo DI SALVO, **Lo sviluppo dei modi della musica bizantina dal sec. XIII alla riforma di Chrysanthos** [The development of Byzantine musical modes from the 13th century to the reform of Chrysanthos] (6110). A catalogue of manuscripts exhibited in connection with the conference is cited as no. 779 in this volume.

309
bs
[Paris] Troisième Congrès international des bibliothèques musicales [Third International Congress of Music Libraries]. Sponsored by the Association Internationale des Bibliothèques Musicales and UNESCO. Ed. by Vladimir FÉDOROV; pref. by Julien CAIN, Edward J. CARTER, Luis Heitor Corréa de AZEVEDO, Valentin DENIS, and Louis-Marie MICHON (Kassel: Bärenreiter, 1953) 92 p. *Bibliog.* In French, English, and German.

The conference was held from 22 through 25 July 1951. The following contributions are cited separately: Friedrich BLUME, **Die Frage eines internationalen Quellenlexikons der Musik** [The question of an international lexicon of musical sources] (784); John Howard DAVIES, **Broadcasting music libraries** (539); Valentin DENIS, **Échanges et prêts internationaux de musique** [International exchange and lending of music] (548); Vincent H. DUCKLES, **The place of gramophone recording in a university music library** (562); Renée GIRARDON, **Rapport sur la nécessité d'un nouveau** *Recueil international des sources musicales* [A report on the necessity of a new *International inventory of musical sources*] (788); Richard S. HILL, **Some pros and cons regarding an international code for cataloging practical music** (592) and **The U.S. position on the** *International inventory of musical sources* (789); Alexander Hyatt KING, **An international scheme for publishing summaries of articles in music periodicals** (599); Wilhelm Martin LUTHER, **Die Mikrokopie von Autographen, Unica und sonstigen musikalischen Wertstücken, ihr Austausch innerhalb der Welt und ihre Sicherung gegen Zerfall und Vernichtung** [The microfilming of autographs, unica, and other valuable musical sources, their exchange throughout the world, and their protection against ruin] (615); Kurtz MYERS, **Phonograph records in American public libraries** (634); Nino PIRROTTA, **Fondi musicali non inventariati nè catalogati** [Music collections neither inventoried nor catalogued] (652); Hans ZEHNTNER, **À propos de la refonte d'un** *Répertoire international des sources musicales* [On the refashioning of an *International repertoire of musical sources*] (799).

310 [Santa Isabel] **Conferencia Internacional de**
bs **Africanistas Occidentales: 4a. conferencia** [International West African Conference: Fourth conference] (Madrid: Dirección General de Marruecos y Colonias, 1954) 2 v. *Illus., maps.* In Spanish, French, English, and Polish.

The following contribution is cited separately: Herbert PEPPER, **Considérations sur le langage tambourine et autres langages musicaux d'Afrique centrale: Sur la pensée musicale africaine** [Considerations on drum language and other musical languages of Central Africa: On African musical thought] (2575).

1952

311 [Amsterdam] **Compte rendu du dix-septième**
bs **Congrès de la Confédération Internationale des Sociétés d'Auteurs et Compositeurs** [Report of the 17th congress of the International Confederation of Authors' and Composers' Societies]. Ed. by René JOUGLET (Paris: Confédération Internationale des Sociétés d'Auteurs et Compositeurs, 1952) 386 p. In French.

The conference was held from 16 through 21 June 1952. The following contributions are cited separately: Valerio DE SANCTIS, **L'auteur et la télévision** [The creator and television] (5955); Luis FERNÁNDEZ ARDAVIN, **L'auteur et les pouvoirs publics** [The author and public authorities] (5960); Pál GYÖNGY, **La musique tzigane en dehors de la Hongrie et sa répartition par les sociétés fédérées** [Gypsy music outside Hungary and its distribution among the federated societies] (5962); Marcel HENRION and Léon MALAPLATE, **L'appartenance des auteurs réfugiés aux sociétés d'auteurs** [Refugee authors' membership in copyright collecting societies] (5964); Ludo LANGLOIS, **Les instruments de reproduction mécanique destinés à l'usage privé** [Instruments of mechanical reproduction intended for private use] (5769); Léon MALAPLATE, **Substitution de musique de films** [Substitution of film music] (5978); Cesare Giulio VIOLA, **La collaboration des auteurs nationaux dans l'exploitation des œuvres étrangères sous le signe de la solidarité internationale** [The collaboration of national authors in cases of the exploitation of foreign works in the name of international solidarity] (5998).

312 [Bern] **Bericht über den Internationalen**
bs **Kongress für Kirchenmusik/Compte rendu du Congrès international de musique sacrée** [Report on the International Congress of Sacred Music].

Proceedings of the First International Congress of Church Music *Publikationen der Schweizerischen Musikforschenden Gesellschaft* 2:3 (Bern: Haupt, 1953) 72 p. In German and French.

The conference was held from 30 August through 4 September 1952. The following contributions are cited separately: Walter BLANKENBURG, **Die evangelische Kirchenmusik in Deutschland im Lichte der Liturgie** [Lutheran church music in Germany from the liturgical standpoint] (6425); Karl Gustav FELLERER, **Palestrina** (1303); Wilibald GURLITT, **Die Kirchenorgel in Geschichte und Gegenwart** [The church organ in history and the present] (3379); Jacques HANDSCHIN, **Die Kirchenmusik und die Frage der Wiedervereinigung der Kirchen** [Church music and the question of reunification of the churches] (6015); Anthon van der HORST, **Fragen der Chorerziehung (Zusammenfassung)** [Issues in the training of choral singers (Summary)] (3307); Vladimir IL'IN, **Der gemeinsame Ursprung des gregorianischen und des altrussischen Neumengesangs** [The common origin of Gregorian and Old Russian neumed chants] (1035); Susi JEANS, **Anglikanische Kirchenmusik** [Anglican church music] (6436); Ilmari KROHN, **Errungenschaften und Aussichten der finnischen Kirchenmusik** [Achievements and prospects of Finnish church music] (6016); Edwin NIEVERGELT, **Zeitgenössische evangelische Kirchenmusik (Zusammenfassung)** [Contemporary Protestant church music (Summary)] (6441); Félix RAUGEL, **La musique sacrée à la chapelle des rois de France** [Sacred music at the chapels of the kings of France] (997); Lucien RIMBAULT, **Le psautier huguenot, lien universel d'amitié entre les peuples (Résumé)** [The Huguenot psalter, universal bond of friendship among peoples (Summary)] (6444); Ernst SCHIESS, **Grundzüge des neuen Orgelbaues: Erfahrungen und Erkenntnisse der letzten Jahrzehnte** [Foundations of the new organ building: Experience and findings of the last decades] (3474); Sybrand ZACHARIASSEN, **Aktuelle Orgelbaufragen und Möglichkeiten zu ihrer praktischen Lösung** [Current organ building questions and possibilities of of their practical solution] (3505).

313 [Cambridge] **Proceedings of the Thirtieth In-**
bs **ternational Congress of Americanists** (London: Royal Anthropological Institute, 1955) xxx, 249 p.; (reprint, Nendeln: Kraus, 1976). *Illus., bibliog., charts, diagr.* In English, French, German, and Spanish.

The conference was held from 18 through 23 August 1952. The following contribution is cited separately: Williams YEOMANS, **The musical instruments of pre-Columbian Central America** (3224).

314 [London] **International Folk Music Council**
bs **Conference,** *Journal of the International Folk Music Council* V (1953) 7–64. *Port.* In English and French.

The fifth annual conference was held by invitation of the English Folk Dance and Song Society at Cecil Sharp House, from 16 through 22 August 1952. The following contributions are cited separately: Renato ALMEIDA, **Le folklore et l'enseignement de la musique au Bresil** [Folklore and musical education in Brazil] (2413); Arnold Adriaan BAKÉ, **The impact of Western music on the Indian musical system** (2604); Bertrand Harris BRONSON, **Good and bad in British-American folk song** (2500); **General report** (2439); Frank Stewart HOWES, **The influence of folk music on modern English composition** (2182); Arthur Morris JONES, **Folk music in Africa** (2557); Douglas KENNEDY, **The educational element in folk music and dance** (4566); Vige LANGEVIN, **L'enseignement, en France, de la musique et la danse populaires françaises** [French traditional dance and music instruction in France] (4582); Mohammad MANSOORUDDIN, **Folk songs in East Pakistan** (2660); Takáki (Genjiro) MASU, **The place of folk music in the cultural life of the present day in Japan** (2662); John MAUD, **Address** (2953); Roger PINON, **La chanson folklorique comme introduction à la poésie étrangère** [Traditional song as an introduction to foreign poetry] (4757); Charles SEEGER, **Folk music in the schools of a highly industrialised society** (4774); Ralph VAUGHAN WILLIAMS, **Opening session** (2478).

315 [Pula; Bjelašnica] **Rad kongresa folklorista**
bs **Jugoslavije** [Proceedings of the congresses of Yugoslav folklorists]. Proceedings of the first and second conferences of the Udruženje Folklorista Jugoslavije. Ed. by Vinko ŽGANEC; intro. by Zoran PALČOK;

pref. by Cvjetko RIHTMAN (Zagreb: Savez Udruženja Folklorista Jugoslavije, 1958) 195 p. *Illus., transcr.* In Croatian; summaries in French, German, English, Serbian, Slovene, and Bosnian.

The following contributions are cited separately: Jelena DOPUĐA, **Problemi kinetografije** [Problems of dance notation] (4960); Dragutin M. ĐORĐEVIĆ, **Lazarice u Leskovačkoj Moravi** [Lazarica in Leskovačka Morava] (2794); Vladimir DVORNIKOVIĆ, **Problemi preslovensko, starobalkanskog, elementa u našem muzičkom folkloru** [Problems of pre-Slavonic, or ancient Balkan, elements in our traditional music] (2798); Radoslav HROVATIN, **Intonacijski alfabetar in grafika melodij za leksikografiranje** [The intonational alphabet and graphic representations of melodies in lexicography] (4438); Milica ILIJIN, **Problemi kinetografije: Sistem Ljubice i Danice S. Janković** [Problems of dance notation: The dance notation system of Ljubica and Danica S. Janković] (4988); Zmaga KUMER, **Primitivna instrumentalna glasba in ples v slovenski narodni pesmi** [Primitive instrumental music and dance in Slovene traditional songs] (5325); Pino MLAKAR, **Razvitak plesnog pisma** [The development of dance notation] (5037); Henrik NEUBAUER, **Osnovi kinetografije i njena primjena u folkloristici** [Basic dance notation and its application in ethnochoreology] (5041); Cvjetko RIHTMAN, **O ilirskom porijeklu polifonih oblika narodne muzike Bosne i Hercegovine** [On the Illyric origin of polyphonic genres in the traditional music of Bosnia and Herzegovina] (3033); Vladimir ŠKREBLIN, **Koreograf o kinetografiji** [A choreographer on dance notation] (5063); Onufrij TIMKO, **Ukrajinski muzički folklor u Vojvodini** [Ukrainian traditional music in Vojvodina] (3085); Vinko ŽGANEC, **Autorskopravna zaštita melografskog rada** [Copyright protection for ethnographic transcriptions] (6001) and **Moj sistem koreografije narodnih plesova** [My system of choreography of folk dances] (5087).

316
bs

[Utrecht] **Société Internationale de Musicologie, cinquième congrès/Internationale Gesellschaft für Musikwissenschaft, fünfter Kongreß/International Society for Musical Research, Fifth Congress.** Sponsored by the International Musicological Society (Amsterdam: Vereniging voor Nederlandse Muziekgeschiedenis, 1953) 468 p. *Illus., facs., music, bibliog.* In French, English, German, and Italian.

The conference was held from 3 through 7 July 1952. The following contributions are cited separately: Higini ANGLÈS, **Les musiciens flamands en Espagne et leur influence sur la polyphonie espagnole** [Flemish musicians in Spain and their influence on Spanish polyphony] (1222); Myroslav ANTONOVYČ, **Die Mehrstimmigkeit in den ukrainischen Volksliedern** [Polyphony in Ukrainian traditional songs] (2723); Heinrich BESSELER, **Die Besetzung der Chansons im 15. Jahrhundert** [The instrumentation of chansons in the 15th century] (3691); Erwin BODKY, **New contributions to the problem of the interpretation of Bach's keyboard works** (1490); Charles van den BORREN, **À propos de quelques messes de Josquin** [Concerning some Masses of Josquin] (1248); Maria Elisabeth BROCKHOFF, **Die Kadenz bei Josquin** [The cadence in Josquin] (4144); Manfred F. BUKOFZER, **Interrelations between conductus and clausula** (1071); Jacques CHAILLEY, **Pour une philologie du langage musical** [Toward a philology of musical language] (5922); Suzanne CLERCX-LEJEUNE, **Johannes Ciconia de Leodio** [Johannes Ciconia of Leodio] (1277); Charles CUDWORTH, **Pergolesi, Ricciotti and the Count of Bentinck** (1515); John DANISKAS, **Analytische Studien über die Kompositionstechnik der burgundischen Schule** [Analytic studies on the composition technique of the Burgundian school] (4328); Thurston DART, **English music and musicians in 17th century Holland** (1523); Luther Albert DITTMER, **The ligatures of the Montpellier manuscript** (3818); Hans Heinrich EGGEBRECHT, **Aus der Werkstatt des terminologischen Handwörterbuchs** [From the workshop for the handbook of music terminology] (5407); Hans ENGEL, **Die Entstehung des italienischen Madrigales und die Niederländer** [The development of the Italian madrigal and the Netherlanders] (1295); Karl Gustav FELLERER, **Musikalische Beziehungen zwischen den Niederlanden und Deutschland im 17. Jht** [Musical relationships between the Netherlands and Germany in the 17th century] (1547); Rudolf von FICKER, **Grundsätzliches zur mittelalterlichen Aufführungspraxis** [Basic observations on medieval performance practice] (3696); Kurt von FISCHER, **C.P.E. Bachs Variationenwerke** [C.P.E. Bach's variation works] (1550); Adriaan Daniël FOKKER, **The qualities**

of the equal temperament by 31fifths of a tone in the octave (4075); Paul-André GAILLARD, **Essai sur la rapport des sources mélodiques des *Pseaulmes cinquantes* de Iean Louis (Anvers 1555) et des *Souterliedekens* (Anvers 1540)** [Essay on the relationship of the melodic sources of *Pseaulmes cinquantes* of Jean Louis (Antwerp 1555) and *Souterliedekens* (Antwerp 1540] (4430); Henrik GLAHN, **Entwicklungszüge innerhalb des evangelischen Kirchengesanges des 16. Jhts im Lichte vergleichender Quellenforschung** [Developments in the 16th-century Lutheran hymn in the light of comparative source studies] (1561); Wilibald GURLITT, **Ein begriffsgeschichtliches Wörterbuch der Musik** [A historically oriented dictionary of music terminology] (772); Fred HAMEL, **J.S. Bach als geistesgeschichtliche Erscheinung** [J.S. Bach as phenomenon in intellectual history] (1573); Frank Llewellyn HARRISON, **The Eton College Choirbook (Eton College MS 178)** (1327); Hans HICKMANN, **Quelques nouveaux documents concernant le jeu de la harpe et l'emploi de la chironomie dans l'Egypte pharaonique** [Some new documents concerning harp playing and the use of chironomy in pharaonic Egypt] (1034); Heinrich HUSMANN, **Die mittelniederländischen Lieder der Berliner Handschrift Germ. 8° 190** [Middle Dutch songs in the Berlin manuscript Germ. 8° 190] (1132); Willi KAHL, **Niederländische Werke aus den Bestanden der alten Kölner Jesuitenbibliothek** [Netherlandish works from the collections of the old Jesuit library in Cologne] (728); Walter KOLNEDER, **Das Frühschaffen Antonio Vivaldis** [Antonio Vivaldi's early works] (1592); Arend Johannes Christiaan KOOLE, **Report on the inquiry into the music and instruments of the Basutos in Basutoland** (2559); Jaap KUNST, **Gamelan music** (2650); René Bernard LENAERTS, **Les manuscrits polyphoniques de la Bibliothèque Capitulaire de Tolède** [Polyphonic manuscripts of the Toledo Biblioteca Capitular] (736); Andreas LIESS, **Umdeutung als musikgeschichtlicher Grundbegriff** [Reinterpretation as a basic music historical concept] (894); Albert vander LINDEN, **La place de la Hollande dans l'*Allgemeine musikalische Zeitung* (1798-1848)** [The place of Holland in the *Allgemeine musikalische Zeitung* (1798-1848)] (1803); Paul-Marie MASSON, **Les tâches internationales de la musicologie** [The international tasks of musicology] (898); Hans Joachim MOSER, **Die Niederlande in der Musikgeographie Europas** [The Netherlands in Europe's musical geography] (990); Helmuth OSTHOFF, **Zur Echtheitsfrage und Chronologie bei Josquins Werken** [On authenticity and chronology in Josquin's works] (1394); Dragan PLAMENAC, **New light on Codex Faenza 117** (1162); José QUITIN, **L'intervention du gouvernement hollandais dans la création du Conservatoire Royal de Musique de Liège en 1826** [The intervention of the Dutch government in the creation of the Conservatoire Royal de Musique in Liège in 1826] (4627); Félix RAUGEL, **Anciennes orgues françaises** [Early French organs] (3460); Walter SALMEN, **Das Liederbuch der Anna von Köln und seine Beziehungen zu den Niederlanden** [The songbook of Anna of Cologne and its links to the Netherlands] (1424); Leo SCHRADE, **Renaissance: The historical conception of an epoch** (1429); A.E. SCHRÖDER, **Les origines des Lamentations polyphoniques au XVᵉ siècle dans les Pays-Bas** [The origins of polyphonic Lamentations in the Low Countries in the 15th century] (6387); Charles SEEGER, **Preface to the description of a music** (922); Joseph SMITS VAN WAESBERGHE, **Das niederländische Osterspiel** [The Netherlandish Easter play] (1184); Bruno STÄBLEIN, **Die Tegernseer mensurale Choralschrift aus dem 15. Jahrhundert: Etwas Greifbares zur Rhythmik der mittelalterlichen Monodie** [The Tegernsee mensural chant notation of the 15th century: Something concrete about the rhythm of medieval monophony] (3872); Ulrich TEUBER, **Bemerkungen zur Homophonie im 16. Jh.** [Comments on 16th-century homophony] (1447); Ottavio TIBY, **Emanuele d'Astorga: Aggiunte e correzioni da apportare alle ricerche del Prof. Hans Volkmann** [Emanuele d'Astorga: Addenda and corrections to the research of Hans Volkmann] (1701); Fausto TORREFRANCA, **Origine e significato di repicco, partita, ricercare, sprezzatura** [The origin and meaning of repicco, partita, ricercare, and sprezzatura] (4289); John WARD, **The *folia*** (1020); Egon WELLESZ, **Notes on the Alleluia** (6029); Eric WERNER, **New studies in the history of the early *octoechos*** (6133); Walter WIORA, **Die Melodien der *Souterliedekens* und ihre deutschen Parallelen** [The melodies of the *Souterliedekens* and their German counterparts] (4475); Hellmuth Christian WOLFF, **Der Stilbegriff der *Renaissance* in der Musik der alten Niederländer** [*Renaissance* as a style concept applied to the music of the old Netherlanders] (1473); Franz ZAGIBA, **Die Entstehung des slavischen liturgischen Gesanges im 9. Jahrhundert nach westlichem und östlichem Ritus** [The origin of 9th-century Slavic liturgical chant following the Western and Eastern rites] (1217).

317 [Vienna] Internationaler Musikkongreß:
bs Bericht [International Music Congress: Report].
Sponsored by the Gesellschaft der Musikfreunde im
Wien. Ed. by Fritz RACEK, *Musikerziehung:
Zeitschrift der Musikerzieher Österreichs* special issue
(1953) 164. *Music.* In German.

The following contributions are cited separately: Kurt ATTERBERG,
Verfall der Melodie [Decline of melody] (4414); Karel Philippus
BERNET KEMPERS, **Soziale und asoziale Kunst** [Social and asocial art]
(5868); Kurt BLAUKOPF, **Tonalität und Soziologie** [Tonality and sociol-
ogy] (5869); Vagn BØRGE, **Die Oper im zwischenstaatlichen
Kulturdienst** [Opera in the service of international culture] (5110);
Siegfried BORRIS, **Der Einbruch primitiver Musik in die Musik des
Abendlandes** [The influx of traditional music into Western music] (950);
Jacques CHAILLEY, **Zeitgenössische Musik und das Problem einer
Philologie der Musik** [Contemporary music and the problem of a philology of music] (2302); Antoine-Élisée CHERBULIEZ, **Möglichkeiten und
Auswirkungen des Ethos in der Musik** [Possibilities and consequences
of ethos in music] (5443); Stana ĐJURIĆ-KLAJN, **Gesellschaftsformen
und Musikentwicklung** [Social systems and development of music]
(5876); Gustav DONATH, **Vom Wesen der Oktave** [On the essence of the
octave] (4066); Franz EIBNER, **Mißverständnisse bei der Auseinandersetzung mit dem Werk Heinrich Schenkers** [Misconceptions in
approaching Heinrich Schenker's theories] (3940); Hans ENGEL, **Grundprobleme der Musiksoziologie** [Fundamental problems of music sociol-
ogy] (5878); Karl Gustav FELLERER, **Mensch und Musik** [Man and mu-
sic] (873); Hubert FOSS, **Musik und internationale Kultur** [Music and
international culture] (5408); Rudolf GERBER, **Freiheit und Gesetz in
der älteren und neueren Musik** [Freedom and law in older and newer mu-
sic] (3943); Hugo GLASER, **Musik und Medizin** [Music and medicine]
(5729); Hermann GRABNER, **Die Werkbetrachtung als Zugang zur
zeitgenössischen Musik** [Examination of compositions as access to contemporary music] (3945); Franz GRASBERGER, **Die Sekund als Ausdruckssymbol der neuen Musik** [The second as symbol of expression in
new music] (4174); Fred HAMEL, **Musik und Zeitgeist** [Music and zeit-
geist] (5485); O.T. HARPNER, **Musik im zwischenstaatlichen Kulturaustausch (Mit besonderer Berücksichtigung der englisch-
österreichischen Beziehungen)** [Music in the cultural exchange between
countries (with special emphasis on English-Austrian relations)] (2324); P.
HERZ, **Das mechanisierte Zeitalter der Musik** [The mechanized era of
music] (5490); Hans HICKMANN, **Die Anfänge eines geordneten
Musiklebens im Ägypten der Pharaonen** [The beginnings of an organized musical life in pharaonic Egypt] (1032); G. HUNOLD, **Zur Situation der Musiktheorie** [On the situation of music theory] (3947); André
JURRES, **Donémus** (727); Hermann KELLER, **Die Situation der deutsche Musikhochschulen** [The situation of the German Musikhochschule]
(4829); Hilda KOCHER-KLEIN, **Das Hausmusikmännlein** [The little
Hausmusik man] (979); Andreas LIESS, **Das Geistige in der
zeitgenössischen Musik** [The spiritual in contemporary music] (907);
Ilija MARINKOVIĆ, **Die nationale Richtung der jugoslawischen
Musik und ihre Bedeutung** [The national direction of Yugoslavian music
and its significance] (987); Hans Joachim MOSER, **Diabolus in musica**
(4201); Erich Hermann MUELLER VON ASOW, **Musikerbriefe als
Mittel zur Erweckung und Förderung der Musikliebe** [Musicians' letters as a means to the love of music] (902); Gerhard NESTLER, **Grundbegriffe einer europäischen Musikgeschichte** [Basic concepts for a European music history] (993); Dika NEWLIN, **Zwölftonmusik in Amerika**
[Twelve-tone music in America] (2366); Leopold NOWAK, **Musikwissenschaft und zeitgenössische Musik** [Musicology and contemporary
music] (907); Hermann PFROGNER, **Der Weg der Theorie zwischen
Tonalität und Atonalität** [The path of theory between tonality and atonal-
ity] (4206); Luigi RAIMONDO, **Die Musik als Faktor der Geistesbildung** [Music as a factor in the development of the mind] (5688); Marcel
RUBIN, **Nationale und internationale Musik** [National and international
music] (999); Erich SCHENK, **Ethische Wirkungen der Musik: Ihre
Voraussetzungen** [The ethical power of music and its premises] (5582);
Reinhold SCHMID, **Chorerziehung zur Moderne** [Choral education to
modernity] (4642); Willi SCHUH, **Zur Harmonik Igor Strawinskys** [On
the harmony of Igor Stravinsky] (4217); Alphons SILBERMANN, **Radio
und musikalische Kultur** [Radio and musical culture] (2390); Alexander
SPITZMÜLLER, **Musik im zwischenstaatlichen Kulturaustausch: Ein
der internationalen Lösung harrendes Problem** [Music in the cultural
exchange between nations: A persistent problem awaiting international so-
lution] (1007); Hans THIRRING, **Musik als Faktor der Charakterbildung** [Music as a factor in character formation] (5712); Rudolf von
TOBEL, **Menschliche und künstlerische Probleme des Musikers am**

Beispiel Pablo Casals' [Human and artistic problems of the musician:
Pablo Casals as example] (2401); Imre VINCZE, **Die Hebung der wirt-
schaftlichen Stellung des Sängers** [The improvement of the singer's economic position] (5997); Erik WERBA, **Die österreichische Mittelschule
als Pflegestätte der Musik** [The Austrian secondary school as place for the
cultivation of music] (4795); Alexander WITESCHNIK, **Musik und
Ethos** [Music and ethos] (5631).

1953

318 [Bad Aussee; Salzburg] Internationaler
bs Kongreß für die berufliche Ausbildung der
Musiker: Kongreßbericht [International Congress
on the Professional Training of Musicians: Congress re-
port]. Ed. by Eberhard PREUSSNER, *Musikerziehung:
Zeitschrift der Musikerzieher Österreichs* special issue
(1953) 60. *Music.* In German, French, English, and Italian.

The following contributions are cited separately: Naohiro FUKUI, **Das
Musikschulwesen in Japan** [Music schools in Japan] (4535); Marguerite
HOOD, **Das Musikschulwesen in den USA** [Music schools in the USA]
(4554).

319 [Bamberg] Bericht über den Internationalen
bs musikwissenschaftlichen Kongress [Report on
the International Musicological Congress]. Sponsored
by the Gesellschaft für Musikforschung. Ed. by
Wilfried BRENNECKE, Willi KAHL, and Rudolf
STEGLICH (Kassel: Bärenreiter, 1954) 306 p. *Illus.,
music, bibliog.* In German, French, Italian, and English.

The conference was held from 15 through 19 July 1953. The following contributions are cited separately: Konrad AMELN, **Historische Instrumente
in der gegenwärtigen Musikpraxis** [Historical instruments in the musical
practice of today] (3238); Higini ANGLÈS, **Die Bedeutung des Volksliedes für die Musikgeschichte Europas** [The significance of folk song
for Europe's music history] (941); Arnold Adriaan BAKÉ, **Bemerkungen
zur Entstehungsgeschichte eines Modus** [Observations on the origins of
a mode] (4046); Alfred BERNER, **Die Instrumentenkunde in Wissenschaft und Praxis** [Organology as a science and a practice] (3243); Heinrich BESSELER, **Singstil und Instrumentalstil in der europäischen
Musik** [Vocal and instrumental styles in European music] (945); Friedrich
BLUME, **Musikforschung und Musikleben** [Music research and musical
life] (863); Wolfgang BOETTICHER, **Orlando di Lasso als Demonstrationsobjekt in der Kompositionslehre des 16. und 17. Jahrhunderts** [Roland de Lassus as demonstration object of compositional theory
of the 16th and 17th centuries] (1242); Fritz BOSE, **Instrumentalstile in
primitiver Musik** [Instrumental styles in primitive music] (3193); Carl
DAHLHAUS, **Die *Figurae superficiales* in den Traktaken Christoph
Bernhards** [*Figurae superficiales* in the treatises of Christoph Bernhard]
(1521); Hans-Heinz DRAEGER, **Das Instrument als Träger und
Ausdruck des musikalischen Bewusstseins** [The instrument as vehicle
and expression of musical awareness] (3248); Rudolf ELLER, **Nationale
Bedingtheiten der europäischen Instrumentalstilés** [National factors in
European instrumental style] (1536); Hellmut FEDERHOFER, **Die
Figurenlehre nach Christoph Bernhard und die Dissonanzbehand-
lung in Werken von Heinrich Schütz** [Figural theory according to
Christoph Bernhard and the treatment of dissonance in works by Heinrich
Schütz] (4165); Guy FERCHAULT, **Essai de justification d'une
bibliographie particulière à la philosophie de l'art musical** [An attempt
to justify a special bibliography dedicated to the philosophy of music]
(574); Walter GERSTENBERG, **Generalbasslehre und
Kompositionstechnik in Neidts *Musikalischer Handleitung*** [Basso continuo theory and compositional technique in Neidt's *Musikalischer Handleitung*] (3944); Kurt GUDEWILL, **Vokale und instrumentale Stilmomente in textlosen Kompositionen des Glogauer Liederbuches** [As-
pects of vocal and instrumental style in the textless compositions of the
Glogauer Liederbuch] (1322); Wilibald GURLITT, **Die Kompositionslehre des deutschen 16. und 17. Jahrhunderts** [The theory of composition in 16th- and 17th-century Germany] (1323) and **Musikwissenschaftliche Forschung und Lehre in pädagogischer Sicht** [Teaching and research in musicology, from the standpoint of pedagogy] (4543); Hans
HALM, **Über Verzeichnisse der Werke Beethovens** [Catalogues of

Beethoven's works] (1774); Günter HAUSSWALD, **Instrumentale Züge im Belcanto des 18. Jahrhunderts** [Instrumental characteristics in bel canto of the 18th century] (1575); Lothar HOFFMANN-ERBRECHT, **Grundlagen der Melodiebildung bei Mussorgski** [Musorgskij's principles for structuring melody] (4436); Casper HÖWELER, **Zur internationalen Uniformität der Begriffe *Metrum* und *Rhythmus*** [Regarding the international uniformity of the terms *meter* and *rhythm*] (4001); Heinrich HUSMANN, **Singstil und Instrumentalstil in ihren Voraussetzungen** [The premises of vocal and instrumental styles] (3254); Willi KAHL, **Öffentliche und private Musiksammlungen in ihrer Bedeutung für die musikalische Renaissancebewegung des 19. Jahrhunderts in Deutschland** [Public and private collections of music and their importance for the Renaissance movement in music in Germany during the 19th century] (1996); Georg KARSTÄDT, **Aufführungspraktische Fragen bei Verwendung von Naturtrompeten, Naturhörnern und Zinken** [Performance-practice issues in playing natural trumpets, natural horns, and cornetts] (3624); Karl Michael KOMMA, **Volksmusikalische Grundlagen des Kompositionsstils der letzten Jahrzehnte in Böhmen und Mähren** [The compositional style in Bohemia and Moravia during recent decades, and its roots in traditional music] (2193); Walter KREIDLER, **Der Wert des *Atlas der deutschen Volkskunde* für die Musikgeschichte** [The value of the *Atlas der deutschen Volkskunde* for the history of music] (2911); Walther KRÜGER, **Singstil und Instrumentalstil in der Mehrstimmigkeit der St. Martialepoche** [Vocal and instrumental styles in the polyphony of the St. Martial era] (1135); François LESURE, **La datation des premières editions d'Estienne Roger (1697-1702)** [Dating the first publications of Estienne Roger (1697-1702)] (1603); Werner LOTTERMOSER, **Unterschiede in Klang und Ansprache bei alten und neuen Orgeln** [Differences in sound and speaking qualities between old and new organs] (3416); Willy MAXTON, **Johann Theile als Theoretiker** [Johann Theile as a theorist] (1620); Johannes G. MEHL, **Die Barockorgel in Lahm (Itzgrund) im Zusammenhang des nord- und süddeutschen Orgelbaus ihrer Zeit und die Probleme ihrer Restaurierung** [The Baroque organ in Lahm (Itzgrund) and its connections with North and South German organ building of its time, and issues in its restoration] (3426); Hans Joachim MOSER, **Lage und Ziele der Musikpädagogik aus wissenschaftlicher Schau** [The situation of music pedagogy and its goals, viewed from a scientific standpoint] (4604); Gerhard NESTLER, **Ästhetische Grundlagen des Sing- und Instrumentalstils in der Musik der Gegenwart** [Aesthetic principles of vocal and instrumental style in the music of the present] (2217); Hans NEUPERT, **Kopie und Rekonstruktion: Geschichte und Probleme des Neubaus von besaiteten Tasteninstrumenten** [The copy and the reconstructed instrument: the history of the physical renewal of stringed keyboard instruments, and of the problems encountered] (3535); Alfred OREL, **Die Kontrapunktlehren von Poglietti und Bertali** [The counterpoint treatises of Poglietti and Bertali] (4205); F.W. PAULI, **Phonetische Dokumentation und Musikforschung** [Phonetic documentation and music research] (648); Hermann PFROGNER, **Der Clavis in Andreas Werckmeisters *Nothwendigsten Anmerkungen und Regeln, wie der Bassus continuus oder Generalbass wol könne tractiret werden*** [Key in Andreas Werckmeister's *Die nothwendigste Anmerkungen und Regeln, wie der Bassus continuus oder Generalbass wol könne tractiret werden*] (4100); Rudolf QUOIKA, **Die *Musica* des Jan Blahoslav 1569** [The *Musica* by Jan Blahoslav from 1569] (1414); Félix RAUGEL, **Bernard Jumentier (1749-1829) maître de chapelle de la Collégiate de Saint-Quentin et ses œuvres inédites** [Bernard Jumentier (1749-1829), chapel master of the collegiate church of Saint-Quentin, and his unpublished works] (1844); Gilbert REANEY, **Voices and instruments in the music of Guilleaume de Machaut** (3713); Fritz REUSCH, **Versuch einer Tonraumlehre** [Outline of a theory of tonal space] (4106); Walter SALMEN, **Die altniederländischen Handschriften Berlin 8° 190 und Wien 7970 im Lichte vergleichender Melodienforschung** [The Old Netherlandish manuscripts Berlin 8° 190 and Vienna 7970 in the light of comparative melodic research] (4455); Wolfgang SCHMIEDER, **Musikbibliographische Probleme: Ein Beitrag zur Theorie der Verzeichnung von Büchern über Musik** [Issues in music bibliography: A contribution to the theory of cataloguing books about music] (679); Arnold SCHMITZ, **Die Kadenz als *Ornamentum musicae*** [The cadence as *ornamentum musicae*] (4216); Marius SCHNEIDER, **Arabischer Einfluss in Spanien?** [Arab influence in Spain?] (1174); Walter SENN, **Forschungsaufgaben zur Geschichte des Geigenbaues** [Tasks in researching the history of violin making] (3602); Walter SERAUKY, **Ausgewählte instrumentenkundliche Probleme in einem Musikinstrumenten-Museum** [Some organological issues for a museum of musical instruments] (755); Joseph SMITS VAN WAESBERGHE, **Guido**

von Arezzo als Musikerzieher und Musiktheoretiker [Guido of Arezzo as music pedagogue and theorist] (1181); Ottavio TOBY, **L'origine popolare della siciliana e la sua evoluzione dal Trecento a Bach e ad Haendel** [The traditional origins of the siciliana and its evolution from the trecento to Bach and Händel] (1012); Fausto TORREFRANCA, **Documenti definitivi sulla partita** [Documents defining the partita] (1454); Armas Otto VÄISÄNEN, **Jean Sibelius und die Volksmusik** [Jean Sibelius and folk music] (2114); Nils L. WALLIN, **Zur Deutung der Begriffe *Faburden—Fauxbourdon*** [Interpreting the terms *faburden* and *fauxbourdon*] (1210); Walter WIORA, **Schrift und Tradition als Quellen der Musikgeschichte** [The written and the oral as sources of music history] (2486); Hellmuth Christian WOLFF, **Die Gesangsimprovisationen der Barockzeit** [Singing and improvisation during the Baroque era] (3778); Walther WÜNSCH, **Die südosteuropäische Volksepik, die Ballade und das Tanzlied im Vergleich zu den Frühformen in der abendländischen Musikkultur** [The folk epic of Southeastern Europe, the ballad, and the dance song, compared with the early forms of Western music culture] (3119); Franz ZAGIBA, **Die Funktion des Volksliedgutes in der Entwicklung der südeuropäischen Musikgeschichte** [The role of the folk-song repertoire in the music history of Southern Europe] (1025).

320
bs

[Biarritz; Pamplona] International Folk Music Council Conference, *Journal of the International Folk Music Council* VI (1954) 7–51. *Illus., port., music.*

The sixth annual conference was held from 16 through 22 August 1953. The following contributions are cited separately: Joan AMADES GELAT, **Dances and songs of the Pyrenean shepherds** (2714); Byron ARNOLD, **Some historical folk songs from Alabama** (3133); Marius BARBEAU, **La chanson populaire française en Amerique du Nord** [The French folk song in North America] (3137); Bianca Maria GALANTI, **La danse des spadonari (porte-glaive) dans la province du Piémont (Italie)** [The dance of the *spadonari* (sword-bearers) in provincial Piedmont (Italy)] (4966); Pierre GORON, **La musique folklorique dans l'éducation** [Traditional music in education] (4698); Ragnwald GRAFF, **Music of Norwegian Lapland** (2838); Olav GURVIN, **Three Norwegian dances** (4975); Albert MARINUS, **Chanson populaire—Chanson folklorique** [Popular song—Folk song] (2447); Takāki (Genjiro) MASU, **Music and dances of Japan** (2661); Carmelina NASELLI, **Aspects de la danse rituelle en Italie: Les danses des rites matrimoniaux** [Aspects of ritual dance in Italy: Dances in marriage rites] (5040); Philippe OYHAMBURU, **La danse et la musique en Pays Basque** [Dance and music in the Basque country] (2982); Marion ROSSELLI, **Introduction to studies on Oriental music** (2682); Ruth RUBIN, **Yiddish love songs of the nineteenth century** (2537); Devar SURYA SENA, **Folk songs of Ceylon** (2696); Hugh TRACEY, **The state of folk music in Bantu Africa: A brief survey** (2592); Klaus P. WACHSMANN, **The transplantation of folk music from one social environment to another** (2546); José Gonzalo ZULAICA Y ARREGUI (José Antonio de Donostia), **Les instruments des danse populaires espagnoles** [Instruments of traditional Spanish dance] (3287).

321
bs

[Brussels] Actes du XIème Congrès international de philosophie. IX: Philosophie des valeurs—Éthique, esthétique [Proceedings of the 11th International Congress of Philosophy. IX: Philosophy of values—Ethics, Aesthetics] (Amsterdam: North-Holland Publishing Company, 1953) 286 p.; (reprint, Nendeln: Kraus; Ann Arbor: UMI, 1970). In French, English, German, Italian, and Spanish.

The conference was held from 20 through 26 August 1953. The following contribution is cited separately: H. HARTMANN, **Hauptprobleme der Musikphilosophie** [Principal problems in the philosophy of music] (5488).

322
bs

[Brussels] Music in education. Proceedings of the International Conference on the Role and Place of Music in the Education of Youth and Adults (Paris: UNESCO, 1955) 335 p. *Facs.*

The conference was held from 29 June through 9 July 1953. The following contributions are cited separately: Marcel ANDRIES, **The training of the listener in music appreciation** (4483); Arnold BENTLEY, **The training of specialist teachers of music in the University of Reading in England** (4808); Charles CAPE, **Music in prisons and reformatories in England and Wales** (5871); Antoine-Élisée CHERBULIEZ, **The gramophone** record: An aid in music education (4505); Dragotin CVETKO, **Music education within the reach of all** (4511); Émile DAMAIS, **Musical training of rural school teachers in France** (4811); Valentin DENIS, **Music education in the universities of Europe** (4813); Roger DÉVIGNE, **Sound libraries and their role in music education** (554); Georges DUHAMEL, **The philosophy of music education** (4520); Vladimir FÉDOROV, **The great public music libraries** (571); Guy FERCHAULT, **The libraries of the conservatories** (575); Bengt FRANZÉN, **The educator's point of view** (4530); Naohiro FUKUI, **Individual and private music instruction in Japan** (4534); Lucy GELBER, **The role of music in general education** (4539); Henri GERAEDTS, **The training of music teachers in the Netherlands** (4820); Giorgio Federico GHEDINI, **The composer's point of view** (4873); Fred HAMEL, **A history of music recorded for educational purposes** (970); Yngve HÄRÉN, **Music in the elementary school in Sweden** (4702); Christine HENDRICKX-DUCHAINE, **The curative powers of music** (5731); André HENRY, **Music education, by the specialist or the general teacher?** (4707); J.W. HORTON, **The music specialist in the schools of England** (4825) and **School music education in England** (4711); Mary IBBERSON, **Rural music schools in England** (4907); Tomojirō IKENOUCHI, **School music education in Japan** (4715); Maud KARPELES, **Folk music as a social binding force** (2518); Lucrecia R. KASILAG, **Individual and private instruction in the Philippines** (4565); Douglas KENNEDY, **The importance of audience participation in dancing** (5003); Leo KESTENBERG, **The present state of music education in the occidental world** (4569); Ingeborg Eckhoff KINDEM, **School music education in Norway** (4831); Egon KRAUS, **School music education in Germany** (4721); Egon KRAUS and Wilhelm TWITTENHOFF, **The Orff-Bergese method** (4574); Vanett LAWLER, **New trends in music education** (4583); Joseph LENNARDS, **Music education by the Ward method** (4726); G.J.T. LOHMANN, **A people's school of music in the Netherlands** (4910); Marjorie Jean MALONE, **Music in the elementary schools of the United States** (4732); Maurice MARTENOT, **The Martenot method** (4589); Frank MARTIN, **Eurhythmics: The Jaques-Dalcroze method** (4593); A. MCSHIELDS, **Music in rural schools in Scotland** (4737); Josephine MCVEIGH, **Music in industry: Functional music** (5896); Margarita MENÉNDEZ GARCÍA Y BELTRAN, **The importance of audience participation in singing** (4912); Pietro MONTANI, **The publisher's point of view** (5982); Virgilio MORTARI, **School music education in Italy** (4745); Louta NOUNEBERG, **A new method of instrumental instruction: The film as a means of music education** (3536); Alfons OTT, **The role of popular libraries in music education** (644); Marsi PARIBATRA, **The performer's point of view** (4615); Carl PARRISH, **Music education in the colleges and universities of America** (4840); Jef POELS, **Music in the workers' leisure time** (4913); Eberhard PREUSSNER, **Music education in Europe** (4623); Venkatarama RAGHAVAN, **The present state of music education in the Asiatic continent: India** (4631); Truda REICH-GRBEC, **School music education in Yugoslavia** (4761); Eino ROIHA, **Music education in the universities of the Scandinavian countries** (4843); Heinrich SAMBETH, **A means of education: The making of musical instruments by children and adults** (3275); Domingo SANTA CRUZ, **Music and international understanding** (4639); Charles SEEGER, **A proposal to found an International Society for Music Education** (4644); Harold Watkins SHAW, **Music in the rural schools in England and Wales** (4775); Blanche SOURIAC, **The training of music teachers in France** (4849); Dietrich STOVEROCK, **The training of music teachers in Germany** (4854); María URETA DEL SOLAR, **School music education in Peru** (4791); Miodrag A. VASILJEVIĆ, **The teaching of singing in rural schools of Yugoslavia** (4794); Geoffrey WADDINGTON, **The radio as a means of music education in Canada** (4666); Arnold WALTER, **Music education on the American continent** (4668); I.R. WALTERS, **Individual and private music instruction in England and Wales** (4857); Carl WILLUM HANSEN and Rudolf GRYTTER, **School music education in Denmark** (4798); Harry R. WILSON, **The training of teachers for music in the rural schools of the U.S.A.** (4860); Steuart WILSON, **The role of folk music in education** (4674); Halil Bedi YÖNETKEN, **Music education and folk music** (4801). A French-language version is cited as no. 323 in this volume.

323
bs

[Brussels] **La musique dans l'éducation** [Music in education]. Proceedings of the Conférence Internationale sur le Rôle et la Place de la Musique dans l'Éducation de la Jeunesse et des Adultes; sponsored by UNESCO (Paris: UNESCO; Colin, 1955) 349 p. In French.

The conference was held from 29 June through 9 July 1953. The following contributions are cited separately: Marcel ANDRIES, **La formation du goût musical de l'auditeur** [Formation of the listener's musical taste] (4482); Arnold BENTLEY, **La préparation au professorat de musique à l'Université de Reading, Angleterre** [The training of specialist music teachers at the University of Reading, England] (4807); Charles CAPE, **La musique, moyen de redressement moral des délinquants** [Music as a means of moral rehabilitation of delinquents] (5872); Antoine-Élisée CHERBULIEZ, **Le disque, auxiliaire de l'éducation musicale** [Records as an aid in music education] (4504); Dragotin CVETKO, **L'éducation musicale à la portée de tous** [Music education within the reach of all] (4510); Émile DAMAIS, **La formation de professeurs de musique destinés aux écoles rurales de France** [The training of music teachers destined for rural schools in France] (4810); Valentin DENIS, **L'éducation musicale dans les universités d'Europe** [Music education in European universities] (4812); Roger DÉVIGNE, **Les phonothèques et leur rôle dans l'éducation musicale** [Record libraries and their role in music education] (553); Georges DUHAMEL, **La philosophie de l'éducation musicale** [The philosophy of music education] (4519); Vladimir FÉDOROV, **Les grandes bibliothèques publiques de musique** [The great public music libraries] (570); Guy FERCHAULT, **Les bibliothèques des conservatoires** [The libraries of the conservatories] (573); Bengt FRANZÉN, **Le point de vue de l'éducateur** [The educator's point of view] (4531); Naohiro FUKUI, **L'enseignement musical privé au Japon** [Private music instruction in Japan] (4533); Lucy GELBER, **L'éducation musicale et la formation générale** [Music education and general education] (4538); Henri GERAEDTS, **La formation des spécialistes de musique aux Pays-Bas** [The development of music specialists in the Netherlands] (4819); Giorgio Federico GHEDINI, **Le point de vue du compositeur** [The composer's point of view] (4874); Fred HAMEL, **Une histoire de la musique, enregistrée à des fins éducatives** [A history of music recorded for educational purposes] (969); Yngve HÄRÉN, **La musique à l'école primaire en Suède** [Music in the elementary school in Sweden] (4703); Christine HENDRICKX-DUCHAINE, **La musique et la thérapeutique** [Music and therapy] (5732); André HENRY, **L'enseignement musical doit-il être confié au spécialiste ou à l'instituteur?** [Should music instruction be entrusted to the specialist or to the general teacher?] (4706); J.W. HORTON, **Le spécialiste de musique à l'école en Angleterre** [The music specialist in the schools of England] (4826) and **L'éducation musicale dans les établissements scolaires d'Angleterre** [Music education in the English school system] (4710); Mary IBBERSON, **Les écoles rurales de musique en Angleterre** [Rural music schools in England] (4906); Tomojirō IKENOUCHI, **L'éducation musicale dans les établissements scolaires du Japon** [Music education in the Japanese school system] (4714); Maud KARPELES, **La musique folklorique: Élément de rapprochement social** [Traditional music: The element of social connection] (2519); Lucrecia R. KASILAG, **L'enseignement musical privé aux Philippines** [Private music education in the Philippines] (4564); Douglas KENNEDY, **l'importance de la participation de la communauté à la danse** [The importance of community participation in dance] (5002); Leo KESTENBERG, **L'état actuel de l'éducation musicale dans le monde occidental** [The present state of music education in the Western world] (4567); Ingeborg Eckhoff KINDEM, **L'éducation musicale dans les établissements scolaires de Norvège** [Music education in the Norwegian school system] (4830); Egon KRAUS, **L'éducation musicale dans les établissements scolaires d'Allemagne** [Music education in the German school system] (4719); Egon KRAUS and Wilhelm TWITTENHOFF, **La méthode Orff-Bergese** [The Orff-Bergese method] (4573); Vanett LAWLER, **Nouvelles tendances de l'éducation musicale** [New trends in music education] (4584); Joseph LENNARDS, **L'éducation musicale selon la méthode Ward** [Music education according to the Ward method] (4724); G.J.T. LOHMANN, **Une école populaire de musique aux Pays-Bas** [A popular school of music in the Netherlands] (4909); Marjorie Jean MALONE, **La musique à l'école primaire aux États-Unis** [Music in the elementary schools of the United States] (4733); Maurice MARTENOT, **Le méthode Martenot** [The Martenot method] (4590); Frank MARTIN, **De la rythmique: La méthode Jaques-Dalcroze** [Eurythmics: The Jaques-Dalcroze method] (4592); A. MCSHIELDS, **La musique dans les écoles rurales d'Écosse** [Music in rural schools in Scotland] (4738); Josephine MCVEIGH, **La musique dans l'industrie: Musique fonctionnelle** [Music in industry: Functional music] (5897); Margarita MENÉNDEZ GARCÍA Y BELTRÁN, **L'importance de la participation de la communauté au chant** [The importance of community participation in singing] (4911); Pietro MONTANI, **Le point de vue de l'éditeur** [The publisher's point of view] (5981); Virgilio MORTARI, **L'éducation musicale dans les établissements scolaires d'Italie** [Music education in the Italian school system] (4744); Louta NOUNEBERG, **Une nouvelle méthode d'enseignement instrumental: Le film, auxiliaire de l'éducation musicale** [A new method of instrumental instruction: Film as an aid in music education] (3537); Alfons OTT, **Le rôle des bibliothèques populaires dans l'éducation musicale** [The role of popular libraries in music education] (642); Marsi PARIBATRA, **Le point de vue de l'interprète** [The performer's point of view] (4616); Carl PARRISH, **L'éducation musicale dans les universités des États-Unis** [Music education in the universities of the United States] (4839); Jef POELS, **La musique dans les loisirs des travailleurs** [Music in the leisure time of workers] (4914); Eberhard PREUSSNER, **L'éducation musicale en Europe** [Music education in Europe] (4622); Venkatarama RAGHAVAN, **L'état actuel de l'éducation musicale en Asie: L'example de l'Inde** [The current state of music education in Asia: The example of India] (4630); Truda REICH-GRBEC, **L'éducation musicale dans les établissements scolaires de Yougoslavie** [Music education in the Yugoslav school system] (4760); Eino ROIHA, **L'éducation musicale dans les universités des pays scandinaves** [Music education in universities of the Scandinavian countries] (4842); Heinrich M. SAMBETH, **Un moyen d'éducation: La fabrication d'instruments de musique par les enfants et les adolescents** [A means of education: The making of musical instruments by children and adolescents] (3276); Domingo SANTA CRUZ, **La musique et la compréhension internationale** [Music and international understanding] (4640); Charles SEEGER, **Projet de création d'une société internationale pour l'éducation musicale** [Plan for the creation of an International Society for Music Education] (4643); Harold Watkins SHAW, **La musique dans les écoles rurales d'Angleterre et du pays de Galles** [Music in rural schools in England and Wales] (4776); Blanche SOURIAC, **La préparation au professorat de musique en France** [The training of music teachers in France] (4848); Dietrich STOVEROCK, **La préparation à l'enseignement de la musique en Allemagne** [Preparation for music teaching in Germany] (4853); María URETA DEL SOLAR, **L'éducation musicale dans les établissements scolaires du Pérou** [Music education in the Peruvian school system] (4790); Miodrag A. VASILJEVIĆ, **L'enseignement du chant dans les écoles rurales de Yougoslavie** [The teaching of singing in rural schools of Yugoslavia] (4793); Geoffrey WADDINGTON, **La radio, moyen d'éducation musicale au Canada** [Radio as a means of music education in Canada] (4665); Arnold WALTER, **L'enseignement de la musique sur le continent américain** [Music education on the American continent] (4667); I.R. WALTERS, **L'enseignement musical privé en Angleterre et au pays de Galles** [Private music instruction in England and Wales] (4856); Carl WILLUM HANSEN and Rudolf GRYTTER, **L'éducation musicale dans les établissements scolaires du Danemark** [Music education in the Danish school system] (4797); Harry R. WILSON, **La formation musicale de maîtres destinés aux écoles rurales des États-Unis** [The musical training of teachers destined for rural schools in the United States] (4859); Steuart WILSON, **Le rôle de la musique populaire dans l'éducation** [The role of traditional music in education] (4673); Halil Bedi YÖNETKEN, **L'éducation musicale et la musique folklorique** [Music education and traditional music] (4800). Summary reports of activities, resolutions, and recommendations are provided in appendices. An English-language version is cited as no. 322 in this volume.

324
bs
[Delft] Electro-acoustics: Proceedings of the First ICA-Congress. Sponsored by the International Commission on Acoustics Physical Society of London, Acoustics Group. Ed. by Cornelius Willem KOSTEN and M.L. KASTELEYN, *Acustica: International journal of acoustics/Journal international d'acoustique/Internationale akustische Zeitschrift* IV/1 (1954) 306. *Illus.* In English, French, and German.

The conference was held from 16 through 24 June 1953. The following contributions are cited separately: Richard BIERL, **Neuere Ergebnisse der elektrischen Klangerzeugung und deren Beziehungen zu der mechanischen Klangerzeugung** [Recent results of electronic sound generation and their relation to mechanical sound generation] (3662); Richard FELDTKELLER, **Hörbarkeit nichtlinearer Verzerrungen bei der Übertragung von Instrumentenklängen** [Audible, nonlinear distortions during the transmission of instrumental sounds] (5814); Willi FURRER and Anselm LAUBER, **Die raumakustische Diffusität in Schallaufnahme- und Radiostudios** [The room acoustical diffusion in recording and radio studios] (5817); W.H. GEORGE, **A sound reversal technique applied to the study of tone quality** (5819); Martin GRÜTZMACHER, **Über die Klänge von Glocken und Orgeln** [Concerning the sounds of

bells and organs] (3378); Frederick V. HUNT, **Stylus-groove relations in the phonograph playback process** (5759); Vilhelm Lassen JORDAN, **A system for stereophonic reproduction** (5762); H.S. KNOWLES, **Artificial acoustical environment control** (5827); Willem KOK, **Experimental study of tuning problems** (3404); J.M.A. LENIHAN and S. MCNEIL, **An acoustical study of the Highland bagpipe** (3627); Hermann MEINEL, **Zur Stimmung der Musikinstrumente** [Concerning the tuning of musical instruments] (4094); Derwent M.A. MERCER, **The effect of voicing adjustments on the tone quality of organ flute pipes** (3428); Werner MEYER-EPPLER, **Welche Möglichkeiten bestehen für eine sinnvolle Anwendung elektronischer Musikinstrumente?** [What possibilities exist for a meaningful use of electronic musical instruments?] (4407); J. Rodrigues de MIRANDA, **The radio set as an instrument for the reproduction of music** (5778); André MOLES, **The characterization of sound objects by use of the level recorder in musical acoustics** (5844); Gioacchino PASQUALINI, **Récents résultats obtenus dans l'étude électroacoustique de la caisse harmonique des instruments à archet** [Recent results obtained in the electroacoustic study of the bodies of string instruments] (3594); Auguste C. RAES, **Mesures des coefficients de réflexion en amplitude et phase** [Measurements of coefficients of reflection in amplitude and phase] (5851); Edward Gick RICHARDSON, **Electro-acoustics applied to musical instruments: General review** (3271); H. SCHIESSER, **Die charakteristischen Eigenschaften magnetischer Schallaufzeichnungen in Abhängigkeit von den Betriebsbedingungen und den Tonträgereigenschaften** [The characteristic properties of magnetic sound recording as derived from recording conditions and properties of the medium] (5789); F. SCHLEGEL, **Einige Schallplattenaufnahmeprobleme** [Some sound disc recording problems] (5790); Eugen J. SKUDRZYK, **Betrachtungen zum musikalischen Zusammenklang** [Observations on musical sonority] (5704); Erich THEINHAUS, **Stereophonische Übertragung klangschwacher Instrumente im Konzertsaal** [The use in the concert hall of stereophonic amplification for weak-sounding instruments] (5858); Friedrich TRAUTWEIN, **Elektroakustische Mittel in der aktiven Tonkunst** [Electroacoustic resources in active composition] (4411); Robert William YOUNG, **Inharmonicity of piano strings** (3546).

325
bs
[Ingolstadt; Weltenburg] Altbayern als Orgel-Landschaft [Altbayern as an organ landscape]. Proceedings of the first Orgeltreffen der Gesellschaft der Orgelfreunde; sponsored by the Gesellschaft der Orgelfreunde, Landesgruppe Bayern and Bayerisches Staatsministerium für Unterricht und Kultus. Ed. and intro. by Rudolf QUOIKA; ed. and forew. by Walter SUPPER. *Veröffentlichungen der Gesellschaft der Orgelfreunde* 6 (Berlin: Merseburger, 1954) 32 p. *Illus., index.* In German.

The conference was held from 3 through 5 October 1953. The following contributions are cited separately: Karl BORMANN, **Wie alte und neue Orgeln klingen** [How old and new organs sound] (3344); Max GRÜNZINGER, **Ingolstadt als Kunststadt** [Ingolstadt as a city of the arts] (965); Michael KUNTZ, **Über das zeitgenössische Orgelspiel** [Contemporary organ playing] (3407); Rudolf QUOIKA, **Altbayern als Orgellandschaft** [Altbayern as an organ landscape] (3451); Hans SCHMIDT, **Bayrische Orgelkomponisten in alter und neuer Zeit** [Bavarian composers for organ in former and current times] (3475); Walter SUPPER, **Die Orgel als klingendes Denkmal** [The organ as a sounding monument] (3489).

326
bs
[Paris] Musique et poésie au XVIᵉ siècle [Music and poetry in the 16th century]. Ed. by Jean JACQUOT. *Colloques internationaux du CNRS* (Paris: Centre National de la Recherche Scientifique [CNRS], 1954) 384 p. *Music, bibliog., list of works, charts, diagr.* In French and English.

The conference was held from 30 June through 4 July 1953. The following contributions are cited separately: Nanie BRIDGMAN, **La frottola et la transition de la frottola au madrigal** [The frottola and the transition from the frottola to the madrigal] (4234); Marvin CAMRAS, **Some recent developments in magnetic recording** (5746); Jacques CHAILLEY, **Esprit et technique du chromatisme de la Renaissance** [The spirit and technique of Renaissance chromaticism] (4149); Suzanne CLERCX-LEJEUNE, **L'Espagne XVIᵉ siècle, source d'inspiration du génie héroïque de Monteverdi** [Sixteenth-century Spain: A source of inspiration for

Monteverdi's heroic genius] (1276); Thurston DART, **Rôle de la danse dans l'*ayre* anglais** [The role of dance in the English ayre] (1284); Federico GHISI, **L'*aria di maggio* et la travestissement spirituel de la poésie profane en Italie** [The *aria di maggio* and the spiritual ambiguity of secular poetry in Italy] (5317); Jean JACQUOT, **Lyrisme et sentiment tragique dans les madrigaux d'Orlando Gibbons** [Lyricism and tragic sentiment in the madrigals of Orlando Gibbons] (1342); Raymond LEBÈGUE, **Ronsard et la musique** [Ronsard and music] (5327); François LESURE, **Éléments populaires dans la chanson française au début du XVIᵉ siècle** [Traditional elements in the French chanson at the beginning of the 16th century] (1369); Kenneth J. LEVY, **Vaudeville, vers mesurés, et airs de cour** [Vaudeville, vers mesurés, and airs de cour] (1370); Wilfrid MELLERS, **La mélancolie au début du XVIIᵉ siècle et le madrigal anglais** [Melancholy at the beginning of the 17th century and the English madrigal] (1621); Nino PIRROTTA, **Tragédie et comédie dans la camerata fiorentina** [Tragedy and comedy in the Florentine camerata] (1404); Isabel POPE, **La musique espagnole à la cour de Naples dans la seconde moitié du XVᵉ** [Spanish music at the court of Naples in the second half of the 15th century] (1410); Miguel QUEROL GAVALDÁ, **Importance historique et nationale de romance** [Historical and national importance of the romance] (1413); Verdun L. SAULNIER, **Maurice Scève et la musique** [Maurice Scève and music] (5348); Leo SCHRADE, **L'*Edipo tiranno* d'Andrea Gabrieli et la renaissance de la tragédie grecque** [The *Edipo tiranno* of Andrea Gabrieli and the revival of the Greek tragedy] (5239); Denis STEVENS, **La chanson anglaise avant l'école madrigaliste** [English song before the madrigalist school] (1443); Geneviève THIBAULT DE CHAMBURE, **Musique et poésie en France au XVIᵉ siècle avant les *Amours* de Ronsard** [Music and poetry in France in the 16th century, before Ronsard's *Amours*] (1450); André VERCHALY, **Poésie et air de cour en France jusqu'à 1620** [Poetry and the air de cour in France to 1620] (1459); Daniel Pickering WALKER, **Le chant orphique de Marsile Ficin** [The Orphic songs of Marsilio Ficino] (5624); Jack A. WESTRUP, **L'influence de la musique italienne sur le madrigal anglais** [The influence of Italian music on the English madrigal] (1468); Frances A. YATES, **Poésie et musique dans les *magnificences* au mariage du duc de Joyeuse, Paris, 1581** [Poetry and music in the *magnificences* for the marriage of the Duke of Joyeuse, 1581] (1474).

327 [Salonika] **Pepragmena tou th' diethnous**
bs **byzantinologikou synedriou** [Acts of the Ninth International Byzantine Congress]. Sponsored by the International Association of Byzantine Studies. Ed. by A. KYRIAKIDES, P. XYNGOPOULOS, and P. ZEPOS (Athínai: Typographeion Myrtídē, 1953) 3 v. 516, 632, 350 p.; (reprint, Nendeln: Kraus, 1978). *Music, maps.* In Greek, English, and French.
The conference was held from 12 through 19 April 1953. The following contributions are cited separately: Carsten HØEG, **Quelques remarques sur les rapports entre la musique ecclésiastique de la Russie et la musique byzantine** [Some remarks on the connection between Russian ecclesiastical music and Byzantine music] (6116); Z.I. KARA, **Hē orthē hermēneia kai metagraphiē ton byzantinōn choirigraphōn** [The correct interpretation and transcription of Byzantine musical notation] (3833); Oliver STRUNK, **S. Salvatore di Messina and the musical tradition of Magna Graecia** (1195).

1954

328 [Arras] **La Renaissance dans les provinces du**
bs **Nord: Picardie, Artois, Flandres, Brabant, Hainaut** [The Renaissance in the northern provinces: Picardy, Artois, Flanders, Brabant, Hainaut]. Ed. by François LESURE. *Le chœur des muses* (Paris: Centre National de la Recherche Scientifique [CNRS], 1956) 219 p. *Illus., bibliog.* In French.
The conference was held from 17 through 20 June 1954. The following contributions are cited separately: Anne-Marie BAUTIER-RÉGNIER, **L'édition musicale italienne et les musiciens d'Outremonts au XVIᵉ siècle (1501-1563)** [Italian music publishing and ultramontane musicians in the 16th century (1501-1563)] (1229); Charles van den BORREN, **Musicologie et géographie** [Musicology and geography] (1253); Nanie BRIDGMAN, **Les échanges musicaux entre l'Espagne et les Pays-Bas**

au temps de Philippe le Beau et de Charles V [Musical exchanges between Spain and the Low Countries at the time of Philip the Fair and Charles V] (1259); Paule CHAILLON, **Les musiciens du Nord à la cour de Louis XII** [Northern musicians at the court of Louis XII] (1271); Joseph KREPS, **Le mécénat de la cour de Bruxelles (1430-1559)** [The patronage of the court of Brussels (1430-1559)] (1361); Albert vander LINDEN, **Comment désigner la nationalité des artistes des provinces du Nord à l'époque de la Renaissance** [How to designate the nationalities of artists of northern regions in the epoch of the Renaissance] (1371); Geneviève THIBAULT DE CHAMBURE, **Le concert instrumental dans l'art flamand au XVᵉ siècle et au début du XVIᵉ** [The instrumental concert in Flemish art from the 15th century to the beginning of the 16th] (5401).

329 [Cambridge] **Proceedings of the Twenty-third**
bs **International Congress of Orientalists.** Sponsored by the International Union of Orientalists. Ed. by Denis SINOR (London: Royal Asiatic Society, 1957); (reprint, Nendeln: Kraus, 1968). In English, French, Greek, and Russian.
The conference was held from 21 through 28 August 1954. The following contribution is cited separately: Achot PATMAGRIAN, **L'utilisation des éléments folkoriques dans le chant liturgique arménien au XIIᵉ siècle** [The use of folkloric elements in Armenian liturgical chant of the 12th century] (1155).

330 [Ferrara] **Torquato Tasso.** Sponsored by the
bs Comitato per le Celebrazioni di Torquato Tasso (Milano: Marzorati, 1957). *Illus., facs., bibliog., index.* In Italian.
The conference was held from 16 through 19 September 1954. The following contribution is cited separately: Luigi RONGA, **Tasso e la musica** [Tasso and music] (5347).

331 [Madrid] *V Congreso Nacional de Música Sa-*
bs *grada* [Fifth Congreso Nacional de Música Sagrada]. Ed. by Hipólito VACCHIANO GARCÍA (Madrid: Gráficas Dos de Mayo, 1956) 460 p. *Illus., port., facs., music, index.* In Spanish.
The conference was held from 18 through 22 November 1954. The following contributions are cited separately: Miguel ALTISENT, **Cuestiones prácticas** [Practical questions] (6141); Higini ANGLÈS, **Significado de la polifonía sagrada para la liturgia católica** [The significance of religious polyphony for the Catholic liturgy] (6148); José ARTERO, **Creación de una Escuela Superior de Música Sagrada** [The creation of an Escuela Superior de Música Sagrada] (4862); Francesc de Paula BALDELLÓ, **Cuestiones básicas sobre el *Motu proprio*** [Basic questions on the motu proprio] (6157); **El órgano electrónico, sus cualidades y uso en la sagrada liturgia** [The electronic organ, its qualities, and its use in the liturgy] (6328); Isaac FELIZ, **Necesidad de una formación sólida para los músicos de iglesia** [The necessity of solid training for church musicians] (4871); José María GARCÍA LAHIGUERA, **La Comisión Nacional y las Comisiones Diocesanas de Música Sagrada** [The Comisión Nacional and the Comisiones Diocesanas de Música Sagrada] (6223); Manuel GARCÍA MATOS, **Breve apunte sobre la canción popular religiosa** [A brief report on the religious traditional song] (2821); Manuel GIL ESTEBAN, **Cuestiones prácticas: El canto de las mujeres en la iglesia** [Practical questions: The participation of women in church singing] (6237); Ramón GONZÁLEZ BARRÓN, **Conveniencia de implantar un canon similar a los derechos de autor por las ejecuciones de música sagrada retribuidas** [The propriety of introducing royalties on the model of copyright for paid performances of religious music] (6013) and **Música no santa** [Non-religious music] (6239); Pedro MARTÍNEZ BARREIRO, **Influencia de la música religiosa sobre el hombre medio** [The influence of religious music on the average person] (6300); Antoni MASSANA, **La moderna música sagrada** [Modern religious music] (2212); Jaime MOLL ROQUETA, **Catálogo de los códices, manuscritos y libros musicales expuestos en el V Congreso Nacional de Música Sagrada** [Catalogue of the musical codices, manuscripts, and books exhibited in the fifth Congreso Nacional de Música Sagrada] (778); Beda María MORAGAS, **El canto gregoriano y la ciencia** [Gregorian chant and science] (5415); Nemesio OTAÑO EGUINO, **Razón de mi presencia en este Congreso** [My reasons for attending this Congress] (2369); Vicente PÉREZ-JORGE, **Música contemporánea** [Contemporary music] (6335);

Juan PÉREZ MILLÁN, **Consideraciones acerca del canto popular religioso** [Thoughts on religious traditional song] (6336); Germán PRADO PERAITA, **El repertorio mozárabe** [The Mozarabic repertoire] (6343); Samuel RUBIO, **Música polifónica** [Polyphonic music] (4215); Valentín RUIZ AZNAR, **Cuestiones prácticas** [Practical questions] (6370); José SUBIRÁ, **Importancia de los fondos de música sagrada, impresa e inédita, conservada en archivos y bibliotecas de Madrid** [The significance of the holdings of religious music, published and unpublished, in the archives and libraries of Madrid] (762); José SUSTAETA, **Relaciones esenciales e históricas entre la liturgia y la música** [Fundamental and historical relationships between liturgy and music] (6394); Joan Maria THOMÀS SABATER, **El papel que desempeña el organista en las funciones sagradas** [The role of the organist in the liturgy] (6400); José Gonzalo ZULAICA Y ARREGUI (José Antonio de Donostia), **Cuestiones de canto popular religioso español** [Questions concerning traditional Spanish religious song] (3129).

332
bs
[Palermo] Atti del Congresso internazionale di musiche popolari mediterranee e del Convegno dei bibliotecari musicali [Proceedings of the international congress on Mediterranean traditional music and of the convention of music librarians]. Sponsored by the Ministero della Pubblica Istruzione, Italy, and Assessorato per la Pubblica Istruzione delle Regione Siciliana. Intro. by Fausto TORREFRANCA (Palermo: De Magistris succ. V. Bellotti, 1959) 393 p. *Illus., port., music, transcr.* In Italian, French, German, and English.

The conference was held from 26 through 30 June 1954. The following contributions are cited separately: Joan AMADES GELAT, **La canzone ritmica catalana** [The Catalan rhythmic song] (2713), **Simbolismo delle danze catalane** [The symbolism of Catalan dances] (4928), and **Strumenti di musica popolare in Catalogna** [Traditional music instruments in Catalonia] (3237); Higini ANGLÈS, **La musica sacra medievale in Sicilia** [Medieval sacred music in Sicily] (1055); Luiz Heitor Corrêa de AZEVEDO, **L'UNESCO et la coopération internationale entre les bibliothèques musicales** [UNESCO and international cooperation among music libraries] (517); Samuel BAUD-BOVY, **Sur le rythme de quelques chansons de l'île de Crète** [The rhythm of some songs of the island of Crete] (3967); Eugène BORREL, **À propos du folklore israélite de Salonique** [The folklore of the Salonika Jews] (2743); Constantin BRĂILOIU, **Melodie, ritmi, strumenti e simboli nelle danze mediterranee** [Melodies, rhythms, instruments, and symbols in Mediterranean dance] (2495) and **Un type mélodique méditerranéen** [A Mediterranean song type] (2496); Nanie BRIDGMAN, **Quelques éditions rares de musique italienne du seizième et dix-septième siècle dans les bibliothèques de France** [Some rare editions of 16th- and 17th-century Italian music in French libraries] (710); Luisa CERVELLI, **Polifonia e monodia nel canto religioso popolare del cinquecento** [Polyphony and monody in the religious popular song of the 16th century] (1503); Suzanne CLERCX-LEJEUNE, **Le premier séjour en Italie de Joannes Ciconia (1358-1367)** [Johannes Ciconia's first stay in Italy (1358-1367)] (1076); Paul COLLAER, **À propos de deux chansons bulgares et espagnoles** [Two Bulgarian and Spanish songs] (2773); Adelmo DAMERINI, **Per l'incremento delle biblioteche nei conservatori di musica** [For the expansion of conservatory libraries] (538); Bartolomeo DI SALVO, **Alcune tradizioni musicali liturgiche orientali e la tradizione scritta dei codici bizantini medioevali** [Some eastern liturgical musical traditions and the written tradition of medieval Byzantine manuscripts] (958); Vladimir FÉDOROV, **L'Association Internationale des Bibliothèques Musicales: Son organisation, ses tâches—Ses rapports avec les groupes nationaux et locaux** [The International Association of Music Libraries: Its organization, its tasks, its relationships with national and local groups] (567); Karl Gustav FELLERER, **Probleme der mittelmeerischen Musik in Frühchristlichen Gesang** [Problems of Mediterranean music in early Christian chant] (1029); Bianca Maria GALANTI, **Analogie di forme e ritmi nelle espressioni coreutiche mediterranee: Il ballo tondo sardo e la sardana di Catalogna** [Analogies of form and rhythm in Mediterranean choreutic expression: The Sardinian ballo tondo and Catalan sardana] (4965); Manuel GARCIA MATOS, **Strumenti musicali folkloristici di Ibiza: Gli aerofoni melodici** [Traditional instruments of Ibiza: Melodic aerophones] (3618); Thrasybulos Georges GEORGIADES, **Un esempio di polifonia primordiale della Grecia** [An example of primordial Greek polyphony] (2826); Edith GERSON-KIWI, **Synthesis and symbiosis of styles in Jewish-Oriental folk music** (2630); Alberto GHISLANZONI, **Per un catalogo unico nazionale delle biblioteche musicali** [For a single

national catalogue of music libraries] (579); Jacques HANDSCHIN, **La question du chant "vieux-romain"** [The question of so-called Old Roman chant] (1115); Helmut HUCKE, **Improvvisazione nella Schola Cantorum romana** [Improvisation in the Roman Schola Cantorum] (1125); Manolis KALOMIRIS, **L'évolution de la musique en Grèce** [The evolution of music in Greece] (976); François LESURE, **Bibliothécaires et musicologues** [Librarians and musicologists] (610); Ettore LI GOTTI, **La questione dello strambotto alla luce delle recenti scoperte** [The question of the strambotto in the light of recent discoveries] (5328); Claudie MARCEL-DUBOIS, **Les éléments musicaux et la danse d'une cérémonie rituelle de français méditerranéens** [The musical elements and dance of a ritual ceremony of a Mediterranean French community] (2937); Federico MOMPELLIO, **Le Musiche ad una ed a due voci del palermitano Sigismondo d'India** [The *Musiche* for vocal solo and duet of the Palermo-born Sigismondo d'India] (1625); Hans Joachim MOSER, **De Mari Interno quasi vinculo musico gentium accolentium** [The Mediterranean as a musical tie among neighboring peoples] (2532); Carmelina NASELLI, **Riti prenuziali: Il ballo sul letto, i canti del letto** [Prenuptial rites: Dancing on the bed, songs of the bed] (2969); Giorgio NATALETTI, **I canti greco-albanesi di Sicilia, Calabria e Molise, le melodie liturgiche ebraico-italiane e la musica degli zingari di stanza in Italia** [Greco-Albanian songs of Sicily, Calabria, and Molise, Jewish-Italian liturgical melodies, and the music of Gypsies resident in Italy] (2970); Wolfgang OSTHOFF, **Die frühesten Erscheinungsformen der Passacaglia in der italienischen Musik des 17. Jahrhunderts** [The earliest forms of the passacaglia in Italian music of the 17th century] (4277); Nino PIRROTTA, **Compiti regionali, nazionali, ed internazionali delle biblioteche musicali** [The regional, national, and international tasks of music libraries] (651); Ennio PORRINO, **Per un "corpus" della musiche popolari mediterranee** [For a corpus of traditional Mediterranean music] (2461); Claudio SARTORI, **Uno schedario regionale nella biblioteca musicale del capoluogo della regione** [A regional catalogue in the music library of the region's principal city] (667); Marius SCHNEIDER, **Studi e proposte per un corpus delle musiche popolari mediterranee** [Studies and proposals for a corpus of traditional Mediterranean music] (2469); Bruno STÄBLEIN, **Una sconosciuta sequenza dello stile arcaico in Italia** [A previously unknown archaic-style sequence in Italy] (1188); Gino TANI, **Origini autoctone e paleolitiche della danza italiana** [The indigenous, Paleolithic origins of Italian dance] (5075); Mary TIBALDI CHIESA, **I canti popolari siciliani e la musica greca negli studi de Ettore Romagnoli** [Sicilian traditional songs and Greek music in the scholarship of Ettore Romagnoli] (3080); Ottavio TIBY, **La tradizione del canto popolare in Sicilia e nelle regioni mediterranee** [The tradition of song in Sicily and the Mediterranean regions] (3082); Fausto TORREFRANCA, **La musica siciliana e dei popoli mediterranei nella storia della musica europea** [The music of Sicily and of the Mediterranean peoples in the history of European music] (1013); Paolo TOSCHI, **Etnofonia e musica popolare siciliana e sarda** [*Etnofonia* and the traditional music of Sicily and Sardinia] (3086); Cesare VALABREGA, **La millenaria musica ebraica e Ernest Bloch** [Jewish music over the millennia and Ernest Bloch] (6102); Walter WIORA, **Volks- und Kunstmusik in der griechisch-römischen Antike** [Traditional music and art music in Greco-Roman antiquity] (1051); Hellmuth Christian WOLFF, **Der Siciliano bei J.S. Bach und G.Fr. Haendel** [The siciliano in the works of J.S. Bach and G.F. Händel] (4295).

333
bs
[Paris] La musique instrumentale de la Renaissance [Instrumental music of the Renaissance]. Proceedings of the Journées Internationales d'Études sur la Musique Instrumentale de la Renaissance; sponsored by the Groupe d'Études Musicales de la Renaissance. Ed. and intro. by Jean JACQUOT (Paris: Centre National de la Recherche Scientifique [CNRS], 1955) 390 p. *Music, bibliog., index, charts, diagr.* In French and German.

The conference was held at the Institut de Musicologie of the Université de Paris and in the meeting rooms of the Hôtel de Rohan, Paris, from 28 March through 2 April 1954. The following contributions are cited separately: Flavio BENEDETTI-MICHELANGELI, **Principes d'édition des œuvres de clavier anciennes** [Principles in the editing of early keyboard works] (3887); Wilfried BRENNECKE, **Musique instrumentale d'après un manuscrit allemand** [Instrumental music after a German manuscript] (1258); Safford CAPE, **À propos d'enregistrements de danses du Moyen Âge et de la Renaissance** [Regarding recordings of dances of the Middle Ages and the Renaissance] (5952); Suzanne CLERCX-LEJEUNE,

La toccata, principe du style symphonique [The toccata as the origin of symphonic style] (4237); Elizabeth COLE, **L'anthologie de madrigaux et de musique instrumentale pour ensembles de Francis Tregian** [The anthology of madrigals and instrumental ensemble music by Francis Tregian] (1278); Thurston DART, **Le manuscrit pour le virginal de Trinity College, Dublin** [The virginal manuscript from Trinity College, Dublin] (1282) and **Origines et sources de la musique de chambre en Angleterre (1500-1530)** [Origins and sources of chamber music in England (1500-1530)] (1283); Norbert DUFOURCQ, **Remarques sur le clavier (clavecin et orgue) dans la première moitié du XVIIᵉ siècle** [Remarks on the keyboard (harpsichord and organ) in the first half of the 17th century] (1292); Pierre FROIDEBISE, **Sur quelques éditions de musique d'orgue ancienne** [Some editions of early organ music] (3895); Otto GOMBOSI, **À la recherche de la forme dans la musique de la Renaissance: Francesco da Milano** [In search of form in the music of the Renaissance: Francesco da Milano] (1317); Emil HARASZTI, **Les musiciens de Mathias Corvin et de Béatrice d'Aragon** [The musicians of Matthias Corvinus and Beatrice of Aragon] (1326); Pierre Jean HARDOUIN, **La composition des orgues que pouvaient toucher les musiciens parisiens aux alentours de 1600** [The structure of the organs likely to have been played by Parisian musicians of around 1600] (3386); Daniel HEARTZ, **Les styles instrumentaux dans la musique de la Renaissance** [Instrumental styles in Renaissance music] (1332); Harald HECKMANN, **Influence de la musique instrumentale du XVIᵉ siècle sur la rythmique moderne du XVIIᵉ** [The influence of 16th-century instrumental music on the modern rhythm of the 17th century] (3997); Jean JACQUOT, **Sur quelques formes de la musique de clavier élisabéthaine (d'après des œuvres inédites de John Bull)** [On some forms of Elizabethan keyboard music (based on unpublished pieces by John Bull)] (1343); Macario Santiago KASTNER, **Le "clavecin parfait" de Bartolomeo Jobernardi** [The *cimbalo perfetto* of Bartolomé Jovernardi] (3522) and **Rapports entre Schlick et Cabezón** [Relationships between Schlick and Cabezón] (1355); Denise LAUNAY, **La fantaisie en France jusqu'au milieu du XVIIᵉ siècle** [The fantaisie in France to the middle of the 17th century] (4265); Zofia LISSA, **La formation du style national dans la musique instrumentale polonaise de la Renaissance** [The formation of the national style of Polish instrumental music in the Renaissance] (1372); David LUMSDEN, **De quelques éléments étrangers dans la musique anglaise pour le luth** [On some foreign elements in English lute music] (1374); Ernst Hermann MEYER, **L'élément populaire dans les danses instrumentales allemandes jusqu'à la guerre de Trente Ans** [The popular-music element in German instrumental dances up to the Thirty Years' War] (1383); Richard de MORCOURT, **Le livre de tablature de luth de Domenico Bianchini (1546)** [The lute tablature book of Domenico Bianchini (1546)] (1384); Jeremy NOBLE, **Le répertoire instrumental anglais: 1550-1585** [The English instrumental repertoire: 1550-1585] (1388); Emili PUJOL VILARRUBÍ, **Les ressources instrumentales et leur rôle dans la musique pour vihuela et pour guitare au XVIᵉ siècle et au XVIIᵉ** [Instrumental resources and their role in music for vihuela and guitar in the 16th and 17th centuries] (3599); Claudio SARTORI, **Une pratique des musiciens lombards (1582-1639): L'hommage des chansons instrumentales aux familles d'une ville** [A practice of Lombard musicians (1582-1639): Canzoni strumentali as homages to a city's families] (1425); Theobald SCHREMS, **Rom-Regensburg: Kirchenmusikalische Beziehungen** [Rome-Regensburg: Church music relations] (6386); André SOURIS, **Problèmes d'analyse** [Problems of analysis] (3957); Denis STEVENS, **Les sources de l'In nomine** [The sources of the In nomine] (1444); Geneviève THIBAULT DE CHAMBURE, **Le concert instrumental au XVᵉ siècle** [The instrumental consort in the 15th century] (1448); John M. WARD, **Les sources de la musique pour le clavier en Angleterre** [The sources for keyboard music in England] (1463).

334   **[Paris] Radio, musique et société** [Radio, music,
bs   and society]. Proceedings of the International Congress on the Sociological Aspects of Radio Music; sponsored by the Centre d'Études Radiophoniques, *Cahiers d'études de radio-télévision* 3-4 (1955). In French, German, English, and Italian.

The conference was held from 27 through 30 October 1954. The following contributions are cited separately: Franz ALDER, **Presuppositions of and design for a quantitative study in the sociology of radio music** (5865); Marvin ALISKY, **Mexico's musical microphones: Instruments of cultural integration for the public** (3185); Marcel BELVIANES, **Musique et radio** [Music and radio] (5867); Klaus BLUM, **Plus und minus** [Plus and minus] (2289); Gisèle BRELET, **La radio purifie et confirme la**

musique [Radio purifies and strengthens music] (2292); Michal BRISTIGER, **Le problème de la musique folklorique à la radio polonaise en fonction des changements sociaux et culturels survenus en Pologne.** [The problem of traditional music on Polish radio with regard to social and cultural changes that have occurred in Poland.] (2293); Theodore CAPLOW, **The influence of radio on music as a social institution** (5873); Jacques CHAILLEY, **La radio et le développement de l'instinct harmonique chez les auditeurs** [Radio and the development of the harmonic instinct among listeners] (2301); Edmond COSTÈRE, **Audience de la musique d'aujourd'hui** [Audience of today's music] (2309); Norman DEMUTH, **The music was specially composed** (5138); K. van DIJK, **La musique à la radio: Aspects sociologiques à la suite de quelques recherches hollandaises** [Radio music: Sociological aspects following some Dutch research] (2313); Madame DOSSE, **Place de la musique à la radio dans la vie des candidats bacheliers** [The role of radio music in the life of advanced secondary students] (2314); René DOVAZ, **Nature, développement et champs d'influence des programmes musicaux** [Nature, development, and range of influence of musical programs] (2316); Cedric DUMONT, **La signification sociologique de la musique légère dans le cadre des émissions radiophoniques** [The sociological significance of light music in the design of radio broadcasts] (5877); Carlos A. ECHÁNOVE TRUJILLO, **Remarques sur la qualité artistique de la musique à la radio** [Remarks on the artistic quality of radio music] (2318); Roger GIROD, **Recherches sociologiques et développement de la culture musicale** [Sociological research and the development of musical culture] (5882); Lucien GOUZOU, **Modification de la classe paysanne française par la musique à la radio** [Modification of the French rural class by music on the radio] (5883); Robert HOEBAER, **Extension de la radio en Belgique: Le comportement des auditeurs vis-à-vis de certains programmes musicaux et les possibilités offertes par la radio en matière de culture musicale** [Extension of the radio in Belgium: The behavior of listeners with respect to certain musical programs and possibilities offered by the radio regarding musical culture] (5886); Leonard ISAACS, **The musician in the radio** (5494); Frank E. KNIGHT, **Radio music used therapeutically and the need for research** (5733); René KÖNIG, **Sur quelques problèmes sociologiques de l'émission radiophonique musicale notamment sur les difficultés d'adaptation socio-culturelle à de nouvelles données techniques** [On some sociological problems of musical radio broadcasts and in particular on the difficulties of sociocultural adaptation to new technical ideas] (5891); Mario LABROCA, **Valeur éducative des cycles musicaux illustrés** [Educational value of illustrated musical cycles] (4579); W.L. LANDOWSKI, **Le rôle actuel du disque radiodiffusé dans l'enseignement de la musique** [The current role of record broadcasts in music education] (4581); Rolf LIEBERMANN, **Radio und neue Musik** [Radio and new music] (2344); Edward LOCKSPEISER, **The greed of music** (2347); Gerhard MALETZKE, **Der Mensch im publizistischen Feld** [The human factor in the field of journalism] (5894); Jean-Étienne MARIE, **La radiodiffusion devant le problème de l'initiation à la musique contemporaine** [Radio broadcasting in the face of the problem of initiation to contemporary music] (2354); André MOLES, **Facteurs physiques influençant l'écoute musicale et la cristallisation du groupe auditif** [Physical factors influencing musical hearing and the crystallization of the listening group] (5681); Serge MOREUX, **Réproduction mécanique du son et création musicale** [Mechanical sound reproduction and musical creation] (2215); Edgar MORIN, **"Matérialité" et "magic" de la musique à la radio** [Materiality and magic of radio music] (5682); Frank ONNEN, **Pour une *radio absolue*** [For an absolute radio] (5900); Théodore PONTZEN, **Les émissions musicales en tant qu'objets d'une attention indirecte** [Musical broadcasts as objects of indirect attention] (2374); Jean PORTE, **Problèmes posés par une étude par sondage de l'auditoire radiophonique** [Problems arising from a survey of the radiophonic audience] (2375); Claude ROCHE, **L'attitude de l'auditeur de musique à la radio** [The attitude of the radio music listener] (5697); K. RÖSSEL-MAJDAN, **Das fundamentale Problem der Phonokopie** [The fundamental problem of recording] (5785); Norbert ROUSSEAU, **Sur les responsabilités de la radio dans les rapports musicaux et sociaux** [On radio's responsibility in musical and social connections] (5906); Valérie SOUDÈRES, **Les possiblités d'évolution rapide des jeunes compositeurs grâce à la radio** [The possibilities of rapid evolution of young composers, thanks to radio] (2252); Hans Heinz STUCKENSCHMIDT, **Limitation au sens auditif de l'événement musical** [Limitation to the auditory sense of musical events] (5707); Josef TAL, **Die musiksoziologische Einflusssphäre des israelitischen Radios** [Israeli radio and its influence on music and society] (2397); Jean TEMPREMENT, **La musique à la radio** [Music on the radio] (2399); Robert WANGERMÉE, **La vulgarisation de la musique par la** radio [The vulgarization of music by the radio] (2407); Fritz WINCKEL, **Ueber die Schwankungserscheinungen in der Musik** [On appearances of fluctuation in music] (5723).

335
bs
[Rome] La musica nel XX secolo [Music in the 20th century]. Report of the International Conference of Contemporary Music; sponsored by the Centre Européen de la Culture, Congress for Cultural Freedom, and Radiotelevisione Italiana (RAI). Ed. by Angiola Maria BONISCONTI (Roma: Edizioni RAI Radiotelevisione Italiana, 1954) 79 p. *Illus.* In Italian.
Documentation of a conference held from 4 through 14 April 1954 at the Sala Accademica di Santa Cecilia and other venues in Rome, featuring roundtable discussions by composers, performers, and critics of contemporary music; the international competition "Premi dell'Opera del XX Secolo"; and a series of opera, symphonic, and chamber concerts.

336
bs
[Rouen] Jumièges: Congrès scientifique du XIII. centenaire [Jumièges: Academic congress for the 13th centenary]. Foreword by René-Jean HESBERT; pref. by Georges LANFRY (Rouen: Lecerf, 1955) 2 v. xii, 1070 p. *Illus., facs., music, bibliog., list of works, index, charts, diagr., maps.* In French.
The conference was held from 10 through 12 June 1954, on the occasion of 13th anniversary of the founding of the Abbaye St-Pierre de Jumièges. The following contributions are cited separately: Jacques CHAILLEY, **Jumièges et les séquences aquitaines** [Jumièges and the Aquitanian sequences] (1073); Solange CORBIN, **Valeur et sens de la notation alphabétique, à Jumièges et en Normandie** [The value and meaning of alphabetic notation at Jumièges and in Normandy] (3813); Johannes DUFT, **Le "presbyter de Gimedia" apport son antiphonaire à Saint-Gall** [The "presbyter de Gimedia" brings his antiphoner to St. Gallen] (1081); René-Jean HESBERT, **La composition musicale a Jumièges: Les Offices de S. Philibert et de S. Aycadre** [Musical composition at Jumièges: The Offices of St. Philibert and St. Achard (Aichardus)] (1118), **Les manuscrits liturgiques de Jumièges** [The liturgical manuscripts of Jumièges] (780), **Les manuscrits musicaux de Jumièges** [The musical manuscripts of Jumièges] (781), **Les séquences de Jumièges** [The Jumièges sequences] (1120), **Les tropes de Jumièges** [The tropes of Jumièges] (1122), and **L'hymnologie de St. Philibert: Les hymnes de Tournus et Macon** [The hymnology of St. Philibert: The hymns of Tournus and Macon] (1334); Jean MARILIER, **L'office rythmé de Saint Philibert à Tournus et Dijon** [The versified Offices of Saint Philibert in Tournus and Dijon] (5330).

337
bs
[São Paulo] International Folk Music Council Conference, *Journal of the International Folk Music Council* VII (1955) 1–36. In English, French, and Spanish.
The seventh annual conference was held from 16 through 22 August 1954. The following contributions are cited separately: Renato ALMEIDA, **Origine de la musique folklorique en Amerique** [Origins of traditional music in America] (2491); Renato ALMEIDA, moderator, **Resolutions** (2414); Oneyda ALVARENGA, **Musique folklorique et musique populaire** [Folk music and popular music] (3187); Joan AMADES GELAT, **Musique populaire et musique folklorique** [Popular music and folk music] (2715); Antoine-Élisée CHERBULIEZ, **La base musicologique du folklore musical comparé** [The musicological basis of comparative musical folklore] (2426) and **Le valeur pédagogique du folklore musical dans l'éducation scolaire** [The pedagogical application of traditional music in school] (4506); Monserrate DELIZ, **La danza puertorriqueña** [Puerto Rican dance] (4951); Kikuko KANAI, **The folk music of the Ryūkyūs** (2645); Maud KARPELES, **Definition of folk music** (2517); Douglas KENNEDY, **The folk music revival in England** (2886); Dulce Martins LAMAS, **Folk and popular music in Brazil** (3204); Francisco Curt LANGE, **Investigation and preservation of authentic folk music in Latin America** (3163); Armando LEÇA, **The historical stratification of Portuguese folk music** (2926); Rossini Tavares de LIMA, **La musique folklorique de São Paulo comme point de départ pour une conception de la musique folklorique** [Traditional music of São Paulo as a point of departure for a conception of traditional music] (3205); Vicente T. MENDOZA, **The frontiers between "popular" and "folk"** (3208); José Osório de OLIVEIRA, **Contribution of the Museum of Dundo to the knowledge of African music** (743); Andrew PEARSE,

, **Aspects of change in Caribbean folk music** (3212); José Geraldo de SOUZA, **Rhythmic and modal contribution of Gregorian chant in the folk music of Brazil** (3220); Seihin YAMANOUCHI, **The Ryūkyū Islands as a meeting point of musical cultures in the Pacific area** (4133).

338
bs
[Stade] Orgelbewegung und Historismus: Tagungsberichte. I [The Orgelbewegung and historicism: Congress reports. I]. Proceedings of the second Orgeltreffen der Gesellschaft der Orgelfreunde. Ed. by Walter SUPPER. *Veröffentlichungen der Gesellschaft der Orgelfreunde* 14 (Berlin: Merseburger, 1958) 7–50. *Illus., index, charts, diagr., maps, organ specification.* In German.
The conference was held from 12 through 15 July 1954. The following contributions are cited separately: Hans BÖHRINGER, **Die Orgel als geistliche Aufgabe** [The organ as a spiritual duty] (3340); Gustav FOCK, **Die Hauptepochen des norddeutschen Orgelbaues bis Schnitger** [The major eras of North German organ building up to Schnitger] (3364); Alfred HOPPE, **Die Klassizität des norddeutschen Orgelbaus** [The classic quality of North German organ building] (3390); Hans KLOTZ, **Orgelbewegung und Historismus** [The Orgelbewegung and historicism] (3402); Walter SUPPER, **Die nord- und süddeutsche Barockorgel: Ein stilischer Vergleich—Und eine Synthese?** [The North German and South German organ: A stylistic comparison—And a synthesis?] (3486). Parts II and III are cited as nos. 348 and 346 in this volume.

339
bs
[Vienna] Zweiter internationaler Kongress für katholische Kirchenmusik: Zu Ehren des Heiligen Papstes Pius X [Second International Congress for Catholic Church Music: In Honor of Pope Saint Pius X]. Ed. by Franz KOSCH, Matthias GLATZL, and Leopold NOWAK (Wien: conference, 1955) 422 p. *Illus., music, charts, diagr., transcr., organ specification.* In German, English, French, Italian, Spanish, and Dutch.
The conference was held from 4 through 10 October 1954. The following contributions are cited separately: Júlia d' ALMENDRA, **L'actuel mouvement grégorien au Portugal: Ses origines, sa fondation, son but, son programme et son développement** [The contemporary Gregorian movement in Portugal: Its origins, goals, program, and development] (2278); Higini ANGLÈS, **Die Bedeutung der Vokalpolyphonie für die römische Liturgie** [The significance of vocal polyphony for the Roman liturgy] (940); Eugène CARDINE, **L'interprétation traditionnelle du chant grégorien** [The traditional performance of Gregorian chant] (3694); Edgardo CARDUCCI-AGUSTINI, **Necessità di una valutazione cristiana dell'arte musicale e della sua storia** [The need for a Christian evaluation of the art of music and of its history] (5438); Jacques CHAILLEY, **La musique religieuse contemporaine en France** [Contemporary religious music in France] (6183); Piero DAMILANO, **Le laude filippine: Storia ed interpretazione** [The lauda compositions associated with Filippo Neri: Their history and performance] (1281); Franz EIBNER, **Die Verwendung elektro-akustischer Instrumente beim Gottesdienst** [The use of electroacoustic instruments in divine worship] (6210); Hellmut FEDERHOFER, **Die älteste schriftliche Überlieferung deutscher geistlicher Lieder in Steiermark** [The oldest written transmission of sacred German songs in Styria] (1088); Umberto FRANCA, **Antiphonale-Lectionarium Monasterii Fontis Avellanae** [The antiphoner-lectionary of the Fonte Avellana monastery] (1096); Friedrich GAUGUSCH, **Die Choralpflege auf dem Lande** [Chant cultivation in the countryside] (6230); Adam GOTTRON, **Die Organisation der Kirchenmusik** [The organization of church music] (6241); Theophil HECHT, **Der Primat der Stimme in der katholischen Kirchenmusik** [The primacy of the voice in Catholic church music] (3303); René-Jean HESBERT, **La restitution critique des mélodies grégoriennes et les manuscrits de Klosterneuberg** [The critical restoration of Gregorian melodies and the manuscripts of Klosterneuberg] (3900); Johann Baptist HILBER, **Kirchenmusik als Beruf** [Church music as a profession] (6252); Helmut HUCKE, **Die Tradition des Gregorianischen Gesanges in der römischen Schola Cantorum** [The tradition of Gregorian chant in the Roman Schola Cantorum] (1127); Michel HUGLO, **Vestiges d'un ancien répertoire musical de Haute-Italie** [Remains of an old musical repertoire from Upper Italy] (1129); Josef Andreas JUNGMANN, **Liturgie und Volksgesang** [Liturgy and congregational singing] (6265); Hans KLOTZ, **Tradition und**

Historismus im Orgelbau heute [Tradition and historicism in current organ building] (3403); Fritz KORNFELD, **Chinas katholische Kirchenmusik im Aufbruch einer neuen Zeit** [China's Catholic church music in the dawning of a new era] (6271); Auguste LE GUENNANT, **Le chant grégorien dans l'œuvre pastorale de Pie X** [Gregorian chant in the pastoral work of Pius X] (6281); Heinrich LEMACHER, **Neue Kirchenmusik** [New church music] (2200); Joseph LENNARDS, **Erziehung zur Kirchenmusik an den Grundschulen** [Church music education in elementary schools] (4725); Andreas LIESS, **Das Sakrale in der profanen Gegenwartsmusik** [Sacral qualities in secular contemporary music] (2204); Gaston LITAIZE, **L'improvisation liturgique** [Liturgical improvisation] (6289); Rafael José LÓPEZ GODOY, **La musica sagrada y el canon 1264** [Sacred music and Canon 1264] (6290); Alois MATHÉ, **Beschouwingen over het ritme der gregoriaanse muziek** [Considerations on the rhythm of Gregorian music] (3707); Josef MERTIN, **Über Aufführungspraxis historischer Sakralmusik** [The performance practice of historic sacred music] (3679); Corrado MORETTI, **Definizione di organo** [Definition of the organ] (3437); Johannes OVERATH, **Erziehung zur Kirchenmusik an den höheren Schulen und Seminaren** [Church music education in upper-level schools and seminaries] (4611); Ludwig PICHLER, **Zur Reform der russischen Kirchenmusik** [The reform of Russian church music] (6128); Rudolf QUOIKA, **Die Passauer Orgelbauschule und ihr Wirken in Österreich** [The Passau school of organ building and its influence in Austria] (3453) and **Über den Orgelbaustil Abbate F.X. Chrismans** [The organ building style of P.F.X. Chrisman] (3454); Giuseppe RADOLE, **Richiamo all'interiorità** [The call for a return to interiority] (6349); Erich SCHENK, **Instrumentale Kirchenmusik** [Instrumental church music] (6375); Jean-Pierre SCHMIT, **Liturgie und Volksgesang: Unter besonderer Berücksichtigung der Förderung der lateinischen Sprache** [Liturgy and congregational singing, with particular attention to the furthering of the Latin language] (6379); Joseph SMITS VAN WAESBERGHE, **Neues über die Schola Cantorum zu Rom** [New findings about the Schola Cantorum in Rome] (1183); Walter SUPPER, **Werktreue und heutiger Orgelbau** [Fidelity to the work and contemporary organ building] (3491); Alfred J. SWAN, **Something about the znamenny** (1011); Rudolf WALTER, **Gregorianischer Choral und gottesdienstliches Orgelspiel** [Gregorian chant and organ playing in the worship service] (6412); Egon WELLESZ, **Ein Überblick über die Musik der Ostkirchen: Stand, Aufgaben und Probleme** [A survey of the music of the Eastern churches: State of research, tasks, and problems] (1214); Eric WERNER, **Die Ursprünge der Psalmodie** [The origins of psalmody] (1048); Sybrand ZACHARIASSEN, **Aktuelle Orgelbaufragen** [Current issues in organ building] (3504); Franz ZAGIBA, **Das Studium der Kirchenmusikwissenschaft au den Universitäten und Theologischen Hochschulen** [The musicological study of sacred music in universities and seminaries] (6419), **Probleme, Aufgaben und Organisation der österreichischen Choralforschung** [Problems, tasks, and organization of Austrian chant research] (1218), and **Wie wird die westliche Liturgie in kirchenslawischer Sprache noch heute gepflegt?** [In what ways is the Western liturgy in Church Slavonic still cultivated today?] (6420).

340
bs

[Wégimont] Les colloques de Wégimont. [I: Ethnomusicologie I] [The Wégimont colloquia. [I: Ethnomusicology I]]. Proceedings of the International Colloquium of Music Ethnology; sponsored by the Cercle International d'Études Ethno-musicologiques. Ed. by Paul COLLAER; intro. by Suzanne CLERCX-LEJEUNE (Bruxelles: Elsevier, 1956) 234 p. *Illus., bibliog., discog., transcr.* In French, English, and German.

The conference was held from 19 through 26 September 1954. The following contributions are cited separately: Samuel BAUD-BOVY, **Enregistrements en Crète** [Recordings in Crete] (2734); Constantin BRĂILOIU, **Le rythme enfantin: Notions liminaires** [Children's rhythm: Preliminary notions] (3973); Manfred F. BUKOFZER, **Observations on the study of non-Western music** (2424); Paul COLLAER, **État actuel des connaissances relatives à la perception auditive, à l'émission vocale et à la mémoire musicale: Conséquences relatives à la notation** [The current state of knowledge about auditory perception, vocal production, and musical memory: Consequences for notation] (5649), **Le tambour à friction (rommelpot) en Flandre** [The friction drum (rommelpot) in Flanders] (3646), and **Sixteen Ainu songs** (2613); Liv GRENI, **Über die Vokaltradition in norwegischer Volksmusik** [The vocal tradition in Norwegian folk music] (2839); László LAJTHA, **À propos de l'"intonation fausse"**

dans la musique populaire [So-called faulty intonation in traditional music] (4088); Jean-Noël MAQUET, **La musique chez les Pende et les Tshokwe** [The music of the Pende and Chokwe peoples] (2560); Claudie MARCEL-DUBOIS, **Extensions du domaine d'observations directes en ethnographie musicale française** [Extensions of the scope of direct observation in French ethnomusicology] (2938); Gilbert ROUGET, **À propos de la forme dans les musiques de tradition orale** [On form in musics of oral tradition] (4282); André SCHAEFFNER, **Ethnologie musicale ou musicologie comparée?** [Ethnomusicology or comparative musicology?] (2468); Marius SCHNEIDER, **Les fondements intellectuels et psychologiques du chant magique** [The intellectual and psychological foundations of magical singing] (6459); Walter WIORA, **Gesungene Erzählung als Strophenlied: Zur Problemgeschichte der altdeutschen Ballade und verwandter Gattungen** [Sung narrative as strophic song: The historical problematics of the Old German ballad and related genres] (3116).

1955

341
bs

[Arras] Visages et perspectives de l'art moderne: Peinture, poésie, musique [Aspects and perspectives of modern art: Painting, poetry, music]. Ed. by Jean JACQUOT (Paris: Centre National de la Recherche Scientifique [CNRS], 1956). *Facs., index, charts, diagr.* In French.

The conference was held from 20 through 22 June 1955. The following contributions are cited separately: Robert FRANCÈS, **La musique moderne et l'auditeur** [Modern music and the listener] (2164); André SOURIS, **Les sources sensibles de la musique sérielle** [The sensible sources of serial music] (2253).

342
bs

[Avignon] Actes et mémoires du 1er Congrès international de langue et littérature du Midi de la France [Proceedings and reports of the First International Congress on the Language and Literature of Southern France] *Publications de l'Institut Méditerranéen du Palais du Roure, Avignon* 3 (Avignon: Palais du Roure, 1957). *Illus., music, maps.* In French.

The conference was held from 7 through 10 September 1955. The following contributions are cited separately: Heinrich HUSMANN, **Les époques de la musique provençale au Moyen-Âge** [The epochs of the music of Provence in the Middle Ages] (1131); Michel Paul PHILIPPOT, **Électronique et techniques compositionelles** [Electronics and compositional techniques] (4409).

343
bs

[Bonn] Neue Zusammenarbeit im deutschen Musikleben: Vorträge und Entschließungen [New collaborations in German musical life: Reports and resolutions]. Proceedings of the Bonner Tagung; sponsored by the International Music Council, German Section and Arbeitsgemeinschaft für Musikerziehung und Musikpflege. Ed. by Walter WIORA. *Musikalische Zeitfragen* 1 (Kassel: Bärenreiter, 1956) 80 p. *Bibliog.* In German.

The following contributions are cited separately: Volker ASCHOFF, **Musik und Technik** [Music and technology] (5866); Werner GEIST, **Musik und Gesundheit: Über Mangelerscheinungen im seelischkörperlichen Bereich durch Ausfall musisch-geistiger Eigentätigkeit** [Music and health: Symptoms of deficiency in the psychophysical realm from a deficit in artistic-intellectual activity] (5660); Felix MESSERSCHMID, **Die Schule in der Sicht des musischen Erziehers** [School in the eyes of the humanities educator] (4740); Jost MICHAELS, **Innere Grundlagen des heutigen Orchestermusizierens und ihre Bedeutung für die Nachwuchsfrage** [The inner foundations of current orchestral musicianship, and their bearing on the question of the next generation] (2358); Herbert SASS, **Musikrat und Arbeitsgemeinschaft: Die beiden Organisationen, ihre Entschließungen auf der Bonner Tagung 1955 und deren erste Ergebnisse** [Music Council and Arbeitsgemeinschaft: The two organizations, their resolutions at the 1955 Bonner Tagung, and the first results] (2386); Wilhelm TWITTENHOFF, **Musische Erziehung in Jugendpflege und Jugendsozialarbeit** [Humanities education in social welfare programs for youth] (5911); Walter WIORA, **Das deutsche Musikleben und die Situation der Zeit** [German musical life and the current situation] (5914).

344
bs
[Brussels] **Congrès international des bibliothèques et des centres de documentation** [International Congress of Libraries and Documentation Centers]. Sponsored by the Association Internationale des Bibliothèques Musicales, International Federation for Documentation, and Association Internationale des Bibliothèques Musicales ('s-Gravenhage: Nijhoff, 1955-1958) 3 v. *Bibliog., charts, diagr.* In French, Spanish, German, and English.

The conference was held from 11 through 18 September 1955. The following contributions are cited separately: Ermelinda ACERENZA, **Formación profesional de un bibliotecario de música** [The professional training of a music librarian] (513); Bianca BECHERINI, **Catalogues généraux et catalogues spécialisés dans les bibliothèques musicales** [General and specialized catalogues in music libraries] (520); Friedrich BLUME, **Problèmes musicologiques d'un répertoire des sources musicales** [Musicological problems concerning a repertoire of musical sources] (785); Valentine BRITTEN, Francis F. CLOUGH, and Geoffrey CUMING, **Problems of an international gramophone record catalogue** (826); Gustav C. CHAMRATH, **Die Rechte der Schallplatte und des Tonbandes (International record libraries commission)** [Record and tape copyright laws] (530); Suzanne CLERCX-LEJEUNE, **Le bibliothécaire musical** [The music librarian] (531) and **Le bibliothécaire musical: Sa formation professionnelle** [The music librarian: His professional training] (534); John Howard DAVIES, **The contribution of radio music libraries to national and international musical life** (540); Vincent H. DUCKLES, **The rôle of the public library in modern musical education** (564) and **The role of the public library in modern musical education: An American appraisal** (565); Franz GRASBERGER, **À propos des échanges de musique** [On exchanges of music] (584); J.R. LE COSQUINO DE BUSSY, **Le rôle et la place de la lecture publique dans l'éducation musicale contemporaine** [The role and the place of the public reading in contemporary music education] (605) and **Le rôle et la place de la lecture publique dans l'éducation musicale contemporaine: Quelques nouveaux aspects de la question** [The role and the place of the public reading in contemporary music education: Some new aspects of the question] (608); François LESURE, **Le RISM: Deux ans d'expérience** [RISM: Two years of experience] (796) and **Quelques conséquences bibliographiques et techniques d'un répertoire international des sources musicales** [Some technical and bibliographical consequences of an international repertoire of musical sources] (794); Folke LINDBERG, **A survey of the musical resources of Scandinavia, with particular reference to their use in broadcast performances** (738); Pierre MEYLAN, **Étude comparative sur les bibliothèques musicales publiques dans différents pays (International public music libraries)** [A comparative study of the public music libraries of different countries] (624); Catharine K. MILLER, **Phonograph records in U.S. public libraries** (626); Philip L. MILLER, **Educational and scientific aspects of the record library** (628); Jaime MOLL ROQUETA, **La formation professionnelle d'un bibliothécaire musical** [The professional training of a music librarian] (631) and **Les bibliothèques musicales publiques: Les aspects nationaux du problème** [The public music libraries: The national aspects of the problem] (632); Alfons OTT, **Wirkungsmöglichkeiten in öffentlichen Musikbibliotheken** [Opportunities in public music libraries] (646); F.W. PAULI, **Die deutschen Rundfunk-Musikbibliotheken: Ihre Organisation, ihre internationalen Arbeitsmöglichkeiten** [The music libraries of German broadcasting networks: Their organization and possibilities for international cooperation] (744); Mercedes Reis PEQUENO, **La formation professionnelle du bibliothécaire musicale** [The professional training of the music librarian] (650); Helmut REINHOLD, **Aufbau und Verwendungsmöglichkeiten einer Discothek wertvoller Gesangsaufnahmen im Sendebetrieb** [Collection developments and uses of a radio library of high-quality recordings of singers] (661); Gilbert ROUGET, **Le disque et la bande comme matière d'échanges** [The record and the tape as exchange material] (664); André SCHAEFFNER, **Les tâches scientifiques et pédagogiques des phonothèques musicales** [The scientific and educational tasks of musical sound libraries] (670); Nils SCHIØRRING, **Public music libraries: International co-operation** (673); Enrich STRARAM, **Problèmes relatifs à l'établissement d'un inventaire international des œuvres dont les matériels d'exécution n'existent qu'à de très rares exemplaires** [Problems relating to the

compilation of an international inventory of works whose performing materials have not been mass-produced] (809). A selection of the conference presentations; the full report is cited as no. 345 in this volume.

345
bs
[Brussels] **Quatrième Congrès international des bibliothèques musicales** [Fourth International Congress of Music Libraries]. Sponsored by the Association Internationale des Bibliothèques Musicales. Ed. by Vladimir FÉDOROV, *Fontes artis musicae* III/1 (July 1956) 5–163; III/2 (Dec 1956) 165–272. In French, English, and German.

The conference was held from 11 through 18 September 1955. Another collection of the conference report is cited as no. 344 in this volume. The following contributions are cited separately: Ermelinda ACERENZA, **Formación profesional de un bibliotecario de música** [The professional training of a music librarian] (512); Bianca BECHERINI, **Catalogues généraux et catalogues spécialisés dans les bibliothèques musicales** [General and specialized catalogues in music libraries] (519); Friedrich BLUME, **Problèmes musicologiques d'un répertoire des sources musicales** [Musicological problems concerning a repertoire of musical sources] (786); Valentine BRITTEN, Francis F. CLOUGH, and Geoffrey CUMING, **Problems of an international gramophone record catalogue** (825); Gustav C. CHAMRATH, **Die Rechte der Schallplatte und des Tonbandes** [Record and tape copyright laws] (529); Suzanne CLERCX-LEJEUNE, **Le bibliothécaire musical** [The music librarian] (532) and **Le bibliothécaire musical: Sa formation professionnelle** [The music librarian: His professional training] (533); John Howard DAVIES, **The contribution of radio music libraries to national and international musical life** (541); Roger DECOLLOGNE, **Vers la création d'une phonothèque centrale de prêt** [Establishing a central lending library of recorded sound] (546); Vincent H. DUCKLES, **The rôle of the public library in modern musical education** (563) and **The role of the public library in modern musical education: An American appraisal** (566); Franz GRASBERGER, **À propos des échanges de musique** [On exchanges of music] (583); Arnold von der HALLEN, **Le fonds musical de l'église Saint-Léonard à Zoutleeuw (Belgique)** [The music collection of the St. Leonard church in Zoutleeuw (Belgium)] (782); Roman HAUBENSTOCK-RAMATI, **The Central Library of Music in Tel Aviv, Israel** (723); J.R. LE COSQUINO DE BUSSY, **Le rôle et la place de la lecture publique dans l'éducation musicale contemporaine** [The role and the place of the public reading in contemporary music education] (606) and **Le rôle et la place de la lecture publique dans l'éducation musicale contemporaine: Quelques nouveaux aspects de la question** [The role and the place of the public reading in music education: Some new aspects] (607); François LESURE, **Le RISM: Deux ans d'expérience** [RISM: Two years of experience] (795), **Quelques conséquences bibliographiques et techniques d'un répertoire international des sources musicales** [Some technical and bibliographical consequences of an international catalogue of musical sources] (793), and **Recueils français du XVIIIᵉ siècle: Datations** [Eighteenth-century French compilations: Dating] (807); Folke LINDBERG, **A survey of the musical resources of Scandinavia, with particular reference to their use in broadcast performances** (737); Pierre MEYLAN, **Étude comparative sur les bibliothèques musicales publiques dans différents pays** [A comparative study of the public music libraries of different countries] (623); Catharine K. MILLER, **Phonograph records in U.S. public libraries** (625); Philip L. MILLER, **Educational and scientific aspects of the record library** (627); Jaime MOLL ROQUETA, **La formation professionnelle d'un bibliothécaire musical** [The professional training of a music librarian] (630) and **Les bibliothèques musicales publiques: Les aspects nationaux du problème** [Public music libraries: The national aspects of the problem] (629); Alfons OTT, **Tagung der Arbeitsgemeinschaft für Musikbüchereien** [Conference of the Arbeitsgemeinschaft für Musikbüchereien] (352) and **Wirkungsmöglichkeiten in öffentlichen Musikbibliotheken** [Opportunities in public music libraries] (647); F.W. PAULI, **Die deutschen Rundfunk-Musikbibliotheken: Ihre Organisation, ihre internationalen Arbeitsmöglichkeiten** [The libraries of German broadcasting networks: Their organization and possibilities for international cooperation] (745); Mercedes Reis PEQUENO, **La formation professionnelle du bibliothécaire musical** [The professional training of the music librarian] (649); Hans-Martin PLESSKE, **Musikbibliographie und Deutsche Bücherei** [Music bibliography and the Deutsche Bücherei] (653); Oldřich PULKERT, **The national music institute and its neccessity as a prez-requisite** [*sic*] **for musicological research** (655); Helmut REINHOLD, **Aufbau und Verwendungsmöglichkeiten einer**

Discothek wertvoller Gesangsaufnahmen im Sendebetrieb [Collection development and uses for a radio library of high-quality recordings of singers] (662); Gabriel ROUGET, **Le disque et la bande comme matière d'échanges** [The record and the tape as exchange material] (663); Claudio SARTORI, **I misteri delle biblioteche italiane. II** [The mysteries of Italian libraries. II] (665); Patrick SAUL, **The British Institute of Recorded Sound** (753); André SCHAEFFNER, **Les tâches scientifiques et pédagogiques des phonothèques musicales** [The scientific and educational tasks of musical sound libraries] (669); Nils SCHIØRRING, **Public music libraries: International co-operation** (674); Enrich STRARAM, **Problèmes relatifs à l'établissement d'un inventaire international des œuvres dont les matériels d'exécution n'existent qu'à de très rares exemplaires** [Problems relating to the establishment of an international inventory of works whose performing materials have not been mass-produced] (808). Also includes (p. 5-32) Charles van den BORREN, Edward CARTER, Jack BORNOFF, and Egon KRAUS, **Discours officiels** [Official speeches]; Frits NOSKE, Vladimir Fédorov, Alfons OTT, and F.W. PAULI, **Compte-rendu des travaux de l'Assemblée Générale** [Report of the work of the general assembly]; and Frits NOSKE, John Howard DAVIES, F.W. PAULI, Alfons OTT, and Kaj SCHMIDT-PHISELDECK, **Compte-rendu sommaire des travaux des congrès** [Summary report of the work of the congress].

346
bs

[Hanover] Orgelbewegung und Historismus: Tagungsberichte. III [The Orgelbewegung and historicism: Congress reports. III]. Proceedings of the Internationale Orgeltage; sponsored by the Gesellschaft der Orgelfreunde. Ed. by Walter SUPPER. *Veröffentlichungen der Gesellschaft der Orgelfreunde* 14 (Berlin: Merseburger, 1958) 65–120. *Illus., index, charts, diagr., maps, organ specification.* In German.

The conference was held from 5 through 12 May 1955. The following contributions are cited separately: Susi JEANS, **Orgeln und Orgelmusik in England von 16. bis zum 18. Jahrhundert** [Organs and organ music in England from the 16th to the 18th century] (3396); Ernst Karl RÖSSLER, **Klangfunktion, Orgelsatz und Orgelbau heute** [Sound function, organ writing, and organ building today] (3468); Walter SUPPER, **Wo historisieren wir—Und wo eilen wir im Orgelbau zu sehr voraus?** [Where are we historicizing? And where in organ building are we hurrying too far ahead?] (3492); Rudolf UTERMÖHLEN, **Orgel und Kirchenraum** [The organ and the space of the church] (3499); Finn VIDERØ, **Dietrich Buxtehude** (3925). Parts I and II are cited as nos. 338 and 348 in this volume.

347
bs

[Istanbul] X. Milletlerarası Bizans Tetkikleri Kongresi Tebliğleri/Actes du X. Congrès International d'Études Byzantines [Proceedings of the Tenth International Congress of Byzantine Studies]. Sponsored by the International Association of Byzantine Studies (İstanbul: İstanbul Maatbası', 1957) 344 p.; (reprint, Nendeln: Kraus, 1978). *Illus., maps.* In French, German, English, and Turkish.

The conference was held from 15 through 21 September 1955. The following contributions are cited separately: Giuseppe SCHIRÒ, **Les canons inédits de Joseph l'Hymnographe dans les anciens manuscrits de Grottaferrata** [Unpublished kanōns by Joseph the Hymnographer in the oldest manuscripts of Grottaferrata] (5349); Reinhold SCHLÖTTERER, **Aufgaben und Probleme bei der Erforschung byzantinischen Musiktheorie** [Tasks and problems of research in Byzantine music theory] (1173); Oliver STRUNK, **Two stichera on the death of the Emperor Nicephorus Phocas** (1196); Egon WELLESZ, **The *Akathistos Hymnos*** (5370).

348
bs

[Malmö; Copenhagen] Orgelbewegung und Historismus: Tagungsberichte. II [The Orgelbewegung and historicism: Congress reports. II]. Proceedings of the third Orgeltreffen der Gesellschaft der Orgelfreunde. Ed. by Walter SUPPER. *Veröffentlichungen der Gesellschaft der Orgelfreunde* 14 (Berlin: Merseburger, 1958) 51–64. *Illus., index, charts, diagr., maps, organ specification.* In German.

The conference was held from 12 through 14 April 1955. The following contributions are cited separately: Rudolf QUOIKA, **Warum bauen wir Orgeln mit mechanischer Traktur?** [Why do we build organs with mechanical action?] (3456); Walter SUPPER, **Die Gestaltung des Orgelgehäuses** [The structuring of the organ housing] (3485) and **Über die Pflege von Orgeln mit Denkmalwert** [The maintenance of organs of historical value] (3490). Parts I and III are cited as nos. 338 and 346 in this volume.

349
bs

[Oslo] International Folk Music Council Conference, *Journal of the International Folk Music Council* VIII (1956) 1–56. In English and French.

The eighth conference was held from 29 June through 5 July 1955. The following contributions are cited separately: Marius BARBEAU, **Rondes from French Canada** (4937); Samuel P. BAYARD, **Some folk fiddlers' habits and styles in western Pennsylvania** (3139); Arne BJØRNDAL, **The hardanger fiddle: The tradition, music forms, and style** (3612); Gaston BRENTA, **Collecting and presentation of folk music in television** (2498); Hermann Josef DAHMEN, **Methods and possibilities of presenting folk music in radio** (2508); Erik DAL, **Scandinavian folk music: A survey** (2785); Ernst EMSHEIMER, **Singing contests in Central Asia** (2622); Nikolai Leonida GIOVANNELLI, **Some notes on the adaptation of traditional style and technique by nontraditional performers in respect of Manx songs and dances** (2835); W.S. HUBER, **Swiss dancing songs** (2867); Ernst KLUSEN, **Problems of recording authentic folklore** (2522); Alan LOMAX, **Folk song style** (2528); Claudie MARCEL-DUBOIS, **The relation between broadcasting organizations and specialised folk music institutions** (2446); Sólōn MICHAÏLÍDĪS, **Greek song-dance** (5032); Bruno NETTL, **Communal re-creation as composition technique in primitive culture** (2534); Karel PLICKA, **Songs of the Slovak mountains** (3004); Andreas REISCHEK, **Collecting methods as affected by modern technical equipment** (5783); Patrick SHULDHAM-SHAW, **Scandinavian folk music on British soil** (3058); Olga SKOVRAN and Olivera MLADENOVIĆ, **Problèmes et méthodes de l'adaption scénique des danses populaires dans le cadre des expériences yougoslaves** [Problems and methods of the stage adaptation of traditional dances within the framework of Yugoslavian experience] (5062); Klaus P. WACHSMANN, **Harp songs from Uganda** (2595); Richard WOLFRAM, **European song-dance forms** (5081); Vinko ŽGANEC, **Folklore elements in the Yugoslav Orthodox and Roman Catholic liturgical chant** (6033).

⟶ **[Pula; Bjelašnica] Rad kongresa folklorista Jugoslavije** [Proceedings of the congresses of Yugoslav folklorists]. See no. 315 in this volume.

350
bs

[Royaumont] Les fêtes de la Renaissance [Renaissance festivals]. Proceedings of the Journées Internationales d'Études sur les Fêtes de la Renaissance; sponsored by the Association Internationale des Historiens de la Renaissance et l'Humanisme. Ed. by Jean JACQUOT. *Le chœur des muses* (Paris: Centre National de la Recherche Scientifique [CNRS], 1956) 492 p. *Illus., music, bibliog., index.* In French.

The conference was held from 8 through 13 July 1955. The following contributions are cited separately: Conrad André BEERLI, **Quelques aspects des jeux, fêtes et danses à Berne pendant la première moitié du XVIᵉ** [A few aspects of plays, festivals, and dances at Bern during the first half of the 16th century] (1231); Agne BEIJER, **Visions célestes et infernales dans le théâtre du Moyen Âge et de la Renaissance** [Visions of heaven and hell in the theater of the Middle Ages and the Renaissance] (5102); John P. CUTTS, **Le rôle de la musique dans les masques de Ben Jonson** [The role of music in the masques of Ben Jonson] (5127); Federico GHISI, **Un aspect inédit des intermèdes de 1589 à la cour médicéenne et le développement des courses masquées et des ballets équestres devant les premières décades du XVIIᵉ siècle** [A new aspect of the intermedios of 1589 of the court of the Medicis and the development of masked races and equestrian ballets before the first decades of the 17th century] (5158); Jean JACQUOT, **Joyeuse et triomphante entrée** [Joyous and triumphant entry] (1341); François LESURE, **Le recueil de ballets de Michel Henry (vers 1620)** [The ballet collection of Michel Henry (circa 1620)] (5021); Miguel QUEROL GAVALDÁ, **Le Carnaval à Barcelone au début du XVIIᵉ** [The carnival in Barcelona at the beginning of the 17th century] (5056); Jean ROUSSET, **L'eau et les Tritons dans les fêtes et ballets de** cour **(1580-1640)** [Water and Tritons in festivals and court ballets (1580-1640)] (5059); Leo SCHRADE, **Les fêtes du mariage de Francesco dei Medici et de Bianca Cappello** [The festivals at the marriage of Francesco de' Medici and Bianca Cappello] (1427); Helena M. SHIRE and Kenneth ELLIOTT, **La fricassée en Écosse et ses rapports avec les fêtes de la Renaissance** [The fricassée in Scotland and its relationship to Renaissance festivals] (1432); Frederick William STERNFELD, **Le symbolisme musical dans quelques pièces de Shakespeare présentées à la cour d'Angleterre** [Musical symbolism in some Shakespeare pieces presented at the English court] (5362); Denis STEVENS, **Pièces de théâtre et pageants à l'époque des Tudor** [Theater pieces and pageants during the Tudor era] (5249); Gino TANI, **Le comte d'Aglié et le ballet de cour en Italie** [The count of Aglié and the court ballet in Italy] (5074); Daniel Pickering WALKER, **La musique des intermèdes Florentins de 1589 et l'humanisme** [The music of the Florentine intermedios of 1589 and humanism] (1462); Emanuel WINTERNITZ, **Instruments de musique étranges chez Filippino Lippi, Piero di Cosimo et Lorenzo Costa** [Strange musical instruments in the paintings of Filippino Lippi, Piero di Cosimo, and Lorenzo Costa] (5403).

351
bs

[Wégimont] Les colloques de Wégimont. II: L'ars nova—Recueil d'études sur la musique du XIVe siècle [The Wégimont colloquia. II: The ars nova—Collection of studies on 14th-century music]. Ed. by Paul COLLAER; intro. by Suzanne CLERCX-LEJEUNE. *Bibliothèque de la Faculté de Philosophie et Lettres de l'Université de Liège* 149 (Paris: Belles Lettres, 1959) 274 p. *Music.* In French, Italian, and English.

The conference was held from 19 through 24 September 1955. The following contributions are cited separately: Willi APEL, **Remarks about the isorhythmic motet** (4230); Bianca BECHERINI, **Poesia e musica in Italia ai primi del XV secolo** [Poetry and music in Italy in the early 15th century] (1062); Charles van den BORREN, **L'ars nova** [Ars nova] (1067); Suzanne CLERCX-LEJEUNE, **Johannes Ciconia et la chronologie des mss. italiens, Mod. 568 et Lucca (Mn)** [Johannes Ciconia and the chronology of the Italian manuscripts Modena 568 and Lucca (Mn)] (1075) and **Les accidents sous-entendus et la transcription en notation moderne: Introduction** [Implied accidentals and transcription in modern notation: Introduction] (3889); Kurt von FISCHER, **À propos de la répartition du texte et le nombre de voix dans les œuvres italiennes du trecento** [The layout of texts and the number of voices in Italian works of the trecento] (3697); **Chronologie des manuscrits du trecento** [Chronology of trecento manuscripts] (1093), and **L'influence française sur la notation des manuscrits du trecento** [French influence on the notation of trecento manuscripts] (1095); Federico GHISI, **La persistance du sentiment monodique et l'évolution de la polyphonie italienne du XIVe au XVe siècle** [The persistence of a preference for monody and the evolution of Italian polyphony from the 14th to the 15th centuries] (1107); Alberto GHISLANZONI, **Les formes littéraires et musicales italiennes au commencement du XIVe siècle** [Italian literary and musical forms at the beginning of the 14th century] (1108); Richard H. HOPPIN and Suzanne CLERCX-LEJEUNE, **Notes biographiques sur quelques musiciens français du XIVe siècle** [Biographical notes on several 14th-century French musicians] (1124); Édouard PERROY, **Le point de vue de l'historien** [The historian's point of view] (1156); Nino PIRROTTA, **Cronologia e denominazione dell'ars nova italiana** [The chronology of the Italian ars nova and the question of its designation] (1160); Gilbert REANEY, **Musica ficta in the works of Guillaume de Machaut** (3711); Leo SCHRADE, **The chronology of the ars nova in France** (1175). For each paper, transcriptions of discussion by the colloquium participants, in French, are provided.

1956

352
as

[Berlin] Tagung der Arbeitsgemeinschaft für Musikbüchereien [Conference of the Arbeitsgemeinschaft für Musikbüchereien]. By Alfons OTT, *Fontes artis musicae* III/2 (Dec 1956) 188–91. In German, French, and English. See no. 345 in this volume.

A report on the conference held 23-28 May 1956.

353
bs

[Cagliari; Nuoro; Sassari] Atti del VI Congresso nazionale delle tradizioni popolari [Proceedings of the Sixth Congresso nazionale delle tradizioni popolari]. Sponsored by the Centro per la Documentazione e la Difesa del Folklore Italiano, Centro Etnografico Sardo, and Società di Etnografia Italiana, *Lares* XXII (1956) 222 p. *Illus., maps.* In Italian.

The conference was held from 25 April through 1 May 1956. The following contributions are cited separately: Diego CARPITELLA, **Prospettive e problemi nuovi degli studi di musica popolare in Italia** [New perspectives and problems of the study of traditional music in Italy] (2758); Giovanna DOMPÉ, *Is musicas a Tonara* [Is musicas in Tonnara] (2793); Gavino GABRIEL, **La fonografía del folklore musical** [The recording of musical folklore] (5754).

354
bs

[Florence; Milan] Actes du VIIIe Congrès international d'histoire des sciences [Proceedings of the Eighth International Congress on the History of Science]. Sponsored by the International Union of the History and Philosophy of Science. *Collection des travaux de l'Académie Internationale d'Histoire des Sciences* (Firenze: Gruppo Italiana di Storia delle Scienze; Paris: Hermann, 1958) 1233 p. *Illus.* In French, English, and Italian.

The conference was held from 3 through 9 September 1956. The following contribution is cited separately: Arthur BIREMBAUT, **Les frères Engramelle** [The Engramelle brothers] (3657).

355
bs

[Freising] Altbayerische Orgeltage [Organ days of Altbayern]. Proceedings of the fourth Orgeltreffen der Gesellschaft der Orgelfreunde; sponsored by the Bayerisches Staatsministerium für Unterricht und Kultus. Ed. and intro. by Rudolf QUOIKA; ed. by Walter SUPPER. *Veröffentlichungen der Gesellschaft der Orgelfreunde* 11 (Berlin: Merseburger, 1958) 48 p. *Illus., index, charts, diagr., organ specification.* In German.

The conference was held from 11 through 15 September 1956. The following contributions are cited separately: Hans BÖHRINGER, **Über altitalienische Orgeln** [Early Italian organs] (3342); Josef von GLATTER-GÖTZ, **Die physikalischen und physiologischen Grundlagen der mechanischen Spieltraktur** [The physical and physiological principles of mechanical keyboard action] (3376); Rudolf QUOIKA, **Grundlagen und Grundfragen der altbayerischen Orgelkultur** [Fundamental principles and issues in the organ culture of Altbayern] (3452); Alfred REICHLING, **Frühe Orgelkunst im süddeutschen Raum nach Zeugnissen der Tabulaturen des fünfzehnten Jahrhunderts** [Early organ compositions in the South German region, as evidenced by 15th-century tablatures] (1418); Frumentius RENNER, **Raumakustik und Erdmagnetismus** [Room acoustics and terrestrial magnetism] (5852); Walter SUPPER, **Die Orgel als Ganzheit** [The organ as a totality] (3488).

356
bs

[Hamburg] Bericht über den internationalen musikwissenschaftlichen Kongreß [Report on the international musicological congress]. Sponsored by the Gesellschaft für Musikforschung and Senat der Freien und Hansestadt Hamburg. Ed. by Walter GERSTENBERG, Harald HECKMANN, and Heinrich HUSMANN (Kassel: Bärenreiter, 1957) 258 p. *Illus., music, bibliog., charts, diagr., transcr.* In German.

The conference was held from 17 through 22 September 1956. The following contributions are cited separately: Anna Amalie ABERT, **Wort und Ton** [Word and music] (936); Werner BACHMANN, **Bilddarstellungen der Musik im Rahmen der artes liberales** [Iconographic representation of music as one of the liberal arts] (5373); Karl-Fritz BERNHARDT, **Zur musikschöpferischen Emanzipation der Frau** [The emancipation of woman composers] (861); Siegfried BIMBERG, **Die variable Reagenz des musikalischen Hörens** [Variable reagency in musical hearing] (5642); Wolfgang BOETTICHER, **Die Magnificat-Komposition Orlando di Lassos** [The Magnificat settings of Roland de Lassus] (1240); Carl DAHLHAUS, **Zwei Definitionen der Musik als quadrivialer Disziplin** [Two definitions of music as a discipline of the quadrivium] (5446); Kunz

DITTMER, **Ethnologie und Musikethnologie** [Ethnology and musical ethnology] (2431); Hans-Heinz DRAEGER, **Die "Bedeutung" der Sprachmelodie** [The meaning of speech melody] (5923); Alfred DÜRR, **Gedanken zu J.S. Bachs Umarbeitungen eigener Werke** [Thoughts on J.S. Bach's rearrangements of his own works] (1533); Hans Heinrich EGGEBRECHT, **Zum Wort-Ton-Verhältnis in der** *Musica poetica* **von J.A. Herbst** [On word-to-music relations in the *Musica poetica* of J.A. Herbst] (5461); Rudolf ELLER, **Zur Frage Bach-Vivaldi** [The question of Bach and Vivaldi] (1537); Hans ENGEL, **Zur Italienischen Prosodie** [On Italian prosody] (5313); Christiane ENGELBRECHT, **Eine Sonata con voce von Giovanni Gabrieli** [A sonata with voice by Giovanni Gabrieli] (1540); Hans ERDMANN, **Wesen und Form des Fichtelbarger** [Essence and form of the *Fichtelbarger*] (2804); Heinrich FACK, **Zur Anwendung der Informationstheorie auf Probleme des Hörens** [The application of information theory in issues of hearing] (5654); Georg FEDER, **Das Barocke Wort-Ton-Verhältnis und seine Umgestaltung in den klassizistischen Bach-Bearbeitungen** [The Baroque word-music relationship and its reshaping in Classic Bach arrangements] (1750); Hellmut FEDERHOFER, **Zur Einheit von Wort und Ton im Lied von Johannes Brahms** [The unity of word and music in Johannes Brahms's lieder] (4333); Fritz FELDMANN, **Mattheson und die Rhetorik** [Mattheson and rhetoric] (5464); Kurt HAHN, **Johann Kuhnaus** *Fundamenta compositionis* [Johann Kuhnau's *Fundamenta compositionis*] (5484); Fred HAMEL, **Die Industrieschallplatte als Mittlerin des musikgeschichtlichen Erbes** [The commercial record as transmitter of music history's heritage] (879); Eta HARICH-SCHNEIDER, **Über die Gilden blinder Musiker in Japan** [Guilds of blind musicians in Japan] (2636); Wilhelm HEINITZ, **Hamburg und die vergleichende Musikwissenschaft** [Hamburg and comparative musicology] (2433); Eduard HERZOG, **Sinnbildung und deren Träger in Sprache und Musik** [The vehicles of semiosis in language and music] (5927); Lothar HOFFMANN-ERBRECHT, **Die Rostocker Praetorius-Handschrift (1566)** [The Rostock Praetorius manuscript (1566)] (1338); Helmut HUCKE, **Die beiden Fassungen der Oper** *Didone abbandonata* **von Domenico Sarri** [The two versions of Domenico Sarri's opera *Didone abbandonata*] (5172); Heinrich HÜSCHEN, **Die Musik im Kreise der artes liberales** [Music in the sphere of liberal arts] (5493); Heinrich HUSMANN, **Antike und Orient in ihrer Bedeutung für die europäische Musik** [Antiquity and the East in their significance for European music] (4082); Susi JEANS, **Geschichte und Entwicklung des Voluntary for Double Organ in der englischen Orgelmusik des 17. Jahrhunderts** [History and development of the double organ voluntary in 17th-century English organ music] (1583); Bernhard KAHMANN, **Über Inhalt und Herkunft der Handschrift Cambridge Pepys 1760** [The contents and provenance of the Cambridge Pepys manuscript 1760] (1352); Hans Martin KLINKENBERG, **Der Zerfall des Quadriviums in der Zeit von Boethius bis zu Gerbert von Aurillac** [The disintegration of the quadrivium in the period from Boethius to Gerbert d'Aurillac] (5510); Fritz KOCH, **Moderne Aufnahmetechnik** [Modern recording technique] (5765); Walther KRÜGER, **Wort und Ton in den Notre-Dame-Organa** [Word and music in Notre Dame organa] (3704); Jens Peter LARSEN, **Ein Händel-Requiem: Die Trauerhymne für die Königin Caroline (1737)** [A Händel Requiem: The funeral anthem for Queen Caroline (1737)] (1598); Annelise LIEBE, **Wortforschung als Methode zur Wesensbestimmung des Tones** [Lexical research as a method of determining the nature of musical sound.] (5931); Wolfgang LINHARDT, **Über die Funktionen der verschiedenen Traktursysteme der Orgel** [The functioning of different systems for organ action] (3412); Zofia LISSA, **Semantische Elemente der Musik** [Semantic elements of music] (5932); Werner LOTTERMOSER, **Akustik und Musik** [Acoustics and music] (5837); Carl-Allan MOBERG, **Das Musikleben in Schweden: Musikkulturelle Probleme in einem europäischen Randgebiet** [Musical life in Sweden: Problems of musical culture in a peripheral European area] (989); Wilhelm MOHR, **Wort und Ton** [Text and music] (5334); Hans Joachim MOSER, **Der melodische Mehrterzenverband** [Melodic grouping through stacked thirds] (4450); Ludwig MÜLLER, **Das optische Bild akustische guter Räume** [The optical image of an acoustically good space] (5845); Klaus Wolfgang NIEMÖLLER, **Ars musica—ars poetica—musica poetica** (1386); František POLOCZEK, **Das Räuber-Volkslied in dem Gebiet des Tatra-Gebirges** [Traditional robber songs in the Tatra region] (3009); Jan RAUPP, **"Unsere Krieger ziehen aus dem Kampfe heim": Ein altsorbisches episches Lied** ["Our warriors are coming home from battle": An old Sorb epic song] (3023); Gilbert REANEY, *Quid est musica* **in the** *Quatuor principalia musicae* (5572); Hans-Peter REINECKE, **Akustik und Musik** [Acoustics and music] (5689); Kurt REINHARD, **Tanzlieder der Turkmenen in der Südtürkei** [Dance songs of the Turkmen people in southern Turkey] (2679); Helmut REINHOLD,

Grundverschiedenheiten musikwissenschaftlichen und soziologischen Denkens und Möglichkeiten zu ihrer Überwindung [Fundamental differences between musicological and sociological thinking and possibilities for overcoming them] (5904); Lukas RICHTER, **Platons Stellung zur praktischen und spekulativen Musiktheorie seiner Zeit** [Plato's position in the practical and speculative music theory of his time] (1041); Peter SCHMIEDEL, **Ein unsymmetrisches Tonsystem** [An asymmetric tone system] (4112); Marius SCHNEIDER, **Entstehung der Tonsysteme** [The origin of tonal systems] (4113); Winfried SCHRAMMEK, **Das Buxheimer Orgelbuch als deutsches Liederbuch** [The Buxheimer Orgelbuch as a German songbook] (1176); Walter SENN, **Der Wandel des Geigenklanges seit dem 18. Jahrhundert** [Changes in violin sound since the 18th century] (3603); Walther SIEGMUND-SCHULTZE, **Wort und Ton bei Robert Schumann** [Word and music in works by Robert Schumann] (2097); Joseph SMITS VAN WAESBERGHE, **Matthaei Herbeni Trajectensis** *De natura cantus ac miraculis vocis* **(1496)** [The *De natura cantus ac miraculis vocis* (1496) of Matthaeus Herbenus of Maastricht] (1435); Søren SØRENSEN, **Ein neu gefundene Buxtehude-Kantate** [A newly found Buxtehude cantata] (1690); Georg SOWA, **Eine neu aufgefundene Liederhandschrift mit Noten und Text aus dem Jahre 1544** [A newly found song manuscript, with music and text, from 1544] (1438); Rudolf STEPHAN, **Über sangbare Dichtung in althochdeutscher Zeit** [Poetry for singing in the Old High German period] (5361); Erich STOCKMANN, **Kaukasische und albanische Mehrstimmigkeit** [Caucasian and Albanian polyphony] (3072); Armas Otto VÄISÄNEN, **Yrjö Kilpinens** *Kanteletar*-**Lieder** [Yrjö Kilpinen's *Kanteletar* songs] (2266); Martin VOGEL, **Über die drei Tongeschlechter des Archytas** [Archytas's three tonal genera] (4128); Hellmuth Christian WOLFF, **Rekonstruktion der alten Hamburger Opernbühne** [Reconstruction of the old Hamburg opera stage] (5861); Hans Christoph WORBS, **Eine unbekannte Liederhandschrift aus dem Anfang des 18. Jahrhunderts** [An unknown song manuscript from the beginning of the 18th century] (1716); Walter WÜNSCH, **Die musikalisch-sprachliche Gestaltung des Zehnsilblers im serbokroatischen Volksepos** [The musical and linguistic form of the decasyllable strophe in Serbian-Croatian traditional epic] (5371).

357
bs

[Montenegro] Treći kongres folklorista Jugoslavije [The third Congress of Yugoslav folklorists]. Proceedings of the third congress of the Udruženje Folklorista Jugoslavije. Ed. by Miodrag S. LALEVIĆ; pref. by Jovan VUKMANOVIĆ (Cetinje: Udruženje Folklorista Crne Gore, 1958) 344 p. *Illus., port., transcr., maps, dance notation.* In Serbian, German, Croatian, and Russian.

The conference was held from 1 through 9 September 1956. The following contributions are cited separately: Sergej AKSJUK, **Sovremennaja narodnaja pesnja: Iz opyta russkoj sovetskoj pesni** [Contemporary folk song: About research on Russian Soviet song] (5277); Elly BAŠIĆ, **Brojalica: Melografski problem dječjeg poetskog stvaralaštva** [Counting game: Melographic problems in children's poetry] (2732); Katica BOŠKOVIĆ, **Crnogorski survivali u svadbenim običajima Konavala** [Montenegrin customs in the wedding ceremonies of Konavle] (2745); Olinko DELORKO, **O građi našega pjesničkog folklora i njezinu poznavanju** [Sources for our traditional poetry and their interpretation] (5300); Trifun ĐUKIĆ, **Prvi izvori i razvoj kosovske etike u stvaranju epopeje o Kosovu** [The earliest sources about ethical issues in Kosovo epics] (5304); Felix HOERBURGER, **Wechselbeziehungen im Volkstanz der Slavischen und Germanischen Völker** [Relations between the traditional dance of the Slavic and Germanic peoples] (4982); Radoslav HROVATIN, **Metrični kriteriji za sistematiko jugoslavenskih ljudskih melodij** [Metric criteria for the systematization of Yugoslavian traditional melodies] (4002); Branislav KRSTIĆ, **Postanak i razvoj narodnih pesama o kosovskom boju** [The origin and development of songs about the Battle of Kosovo] (5324); Zmaga KUMER, **Plesni tip "raj" pri Slovencih** [The raj-type dances among the Slovenes] (5009); Niko KURET, **Potreba sodelovanja pri raziskovanju južnoslovanskih mask** [The necessity for collaboration in research on South Slavic Carnival customs] (2920); Jaroslav MARKL, **Písňový typ instrumentální v české lidové písni** [The instrumental type of Czech traditional songs] (2944); Olivera MLADENOVIĆ, **Prilike i mesta za igranje u Srbiji** [Occasions and places for dance in Serbia] (5035); Živomir MLADENOVIĆ, **Topografski elementi narodne pesme** *Ženidba Dušanova* [Topographic elements in the traditional song *Ženidba Dušanova*] (5333); Alija NAMETAK, **Folklorni materijal u deset godišta** *Behara* **(od 1900 do**

1911 godine) [Writings about folklore in ten volumes of *Behar* (1900 to 1911)] (635); Iko OTRIN, **Oblike slovenskih ljudskih plesov** [Slovene traditional dance genres] (5047); Oldřich SIROVÁTKA, **K problematice folkloru charvátské menšiny v Československu** [Issues related to the folklore of the Croatian minority in Czechoslovakia] (3062); Josef STANISLAV, **K otázce významu a hodnoty třídění písní z Bosny a Hercegoviny od L. Kuby** [The significance and value of Ludvík Kuba's classification of songs from Bosnia and Herzegovina] (4462); Miodrag A. VASILJEVIĆ, **Kvalitativne funkcije tonova u tonalnim osnovama našeg muzičkog folklora: Jedan egzaktni metod za tipologiju lestvica** [The qualitative function of pitches and scales in our traditional music: An exact method for determining typology of scales] (4125); Jovan VUKMANOVIĆ, **Opšti pogled na crnogorski folklor** [General survey of Montenegrin folklore] (3110).

358
bs

[Paris] Les influences étrangères dans l'œuvre de W.A. Mozart [Foreign influences in the work of W.A. Mozart]. By André VERCHALY. *Colloques internationaux du CNRS* (Paris: Centre National de la Recherche Scientifique [CNRS], 1958) vii, 273 p. *Illus., port., facs., music, index.* In French.

The conference was held from 10 through 13 October 1956. The following contributions are cited separately: Dénes BARTHA, **Mozart et le folklore musical de l'Europe centrale** [Mozart and the traditional music of central Europe] (1726); Václav DOBIÁŠ, **Wolfgang-Amédée Mozart et la musique tchèque** [Wolfgang Amadeus Mozart and Czech music] (1744); Karl Gustav FELLERER, **Mozart et l'école de Mannheim** [Mozart and the Mannheim school] (1756); Pierre FORTASSIER, **Le récitatif dans l'écriture instrumentale de Mozart** [Recitative in Mozart's instrumental writing] (1759); Ernst HESS, **Remarques sur l'authenticité de l'ouverture KV 311a=Anh. 8** [Remarks on the authenticity of the overture K.311a=Anh. 8] (1778); H.C. Robbins LANDON, **La crise romantique dans la musique autrichienne vers 1770: Quelques précurseurs inconnus de la symphonie en sol mineur (KV 183) de Mozart** [The romantic crisis in Austrian music around 1770: Some unknown precursors of Mozart's symphony in G minor, K.183] (1796); Carl de NYS, **Mozart et les fils de Jean-Sébastien Bach** [Mozart and the sons of Johann Sebastian Bach] (1830); Erich SCHENK, **Mozart incarnation de l'âme autrichienne** [Mozart, the incarnation of the Austrian soul] (1850); Ernst Fritz SCHMID, **L'héritage souabe de Mozart** [Mozart's Swabian heritage] (1854); Antonín SYCHRA, **W.A. Mozart et la musique populaire tchéque** [W.A. Mozart and Czech traditional music] (1873); Luigi Ferdinando TAGLIAVINI, **L'opéra italien du jeune Mozart** [The Italian operas of the young Mozart] (1878); Cesare VALABREGA, **Mozart et le goût italien** [Mozart and the Italian style] (1886); Stig Alfred Ferdinand WALIN, **Sur les conditions générales de l'internationalisme de Mozart** [On the general conditions of Mozart's internationalism] (1891); Helmut WIRTH, **Mozart et Haydn** [Mozart and Haydn] (1898).

359
bs

[Philadelphia] Men and cultures: Selected papers. Proceedings of the Fifth International Congress of Anthropological and Ethnological Sciences; sponsored by the International Union of Anthropological and Ethnological Sciences. Ed. by Anthony F.C. WALLACE (Philadelphia: University of Pennsylvania, 1960) xxxi, 810 p. *Illus., charts, diagr., maps.* In English, French, German, and Spanish.

The conference was held from 1 through 9 September 1956. The following contributions are cited separately: Gertrude Prokosch KURATH and Nadia CHILKOVSKY, **Jazz choreology** (5011); David P. MCALLESTER, **The role of music in western Apache culture** (3167); Willard RHODES, **The Christian hymnology of the North American Indians** (3173).

360
bs

[Prague] Internationale Konferenz über das Leben und Werk W.A. Mozarts [International conference on the life and work of W.A. Mozart]. Ed. by Pavel ECKSTEIN; foreword by Václav DOBIÁŠ; intro. by Antonín SYCHRA (Praha: Svaz Československých Skladatelů, 1956) 291 p. *Illus., port., music.* In German.

The conference was held from 27 through 31 May 1956. The following contributions are cited separately: Maḥmūd Aḥmad AL-ḤIFNĪ, **Ägyptens Verehrung für Mozart** [Egypt's reverence for Mozart] (2277); Walter

BLANKENBURG, **Die Nachwirkung der artes liberales in den reformatorischen Gebieten und deren Auflösungsprozeß** [The influence of the liberal arts in Lutheran areas, and their decline] (6426); Antoine GOLÉA, **Mozart und die französische Revolution** [Mozart and the French Revolution] (1766); Alois HÁBA, **Wolfgang Amadeus Mozart und die weitere Entwicklung der Musik** [Wolfgang Amadeus Mozart and the further development of music] (968); Jelena HOLEČKOVÁ-DOLANSKÁ, **Wie man Mozart singen soll** [How one should sing Mozart] (3745); Antonín HOŘEJŠ, **Die tschechoslowakische Musikwissenschaft und Mozart** [Czechoslovakian musicology and Mozart] (884); Zoltán HRABUSSAY, **Mozartdokumente im Archiv der Stadt Bratislava** [Mozart documents in the Archív Mesta Bratislavy] (1780); Ivan HRUŠOVSKÝ, **Das klassische Musikschaffen der Mozartzeit in der Slowakei** [Classical music production of the Mozart period in Slovakia] (1781); Walter HUMMEL, **Die Mozart-Gedenkstätten Salzburgs: Ihre Betreuung eine Aufgabe der Internationalen Stiftung Mozarteum** [The Mozart memorials of Salzburg: Their maintenance as a task of the Internationale Stiftung Mozarteum] (974); Heinrich HUSMANN, **Zur Entwicklung der Mozartschen Sonatenform** [The development of Mozart's sonata form] (4259); Georg KNEPLER, **Mozart: Eine Gestalt der bürgerlichen Aufklärung** [Mozart: A figure of the bourgeois Enlightenment] (1793); Siegfried KÖHLER, **Instrumentation als Ausdruckskunst im Opernschaffen Wolfgang Amadeus Mozarts** [Instrumentation as an expressive resource in the operas of Wolfgang Amadeus Mozart] (4301); Jiří KRATOCHVÍL, **Betrachtungen über die Urfassung des Konzerts für Klarinette und des Quintetts für Klarinette und Streicher von W.A. Mozart** [Observations on the original version of W.A. Mozart's clarinet concerto and the quintet for clarinet and strings] (3750); Stefania ŁOBACZEWSKA, **Mozarts Sonate F-dur (K.V. 533) als Problem des klassischen Stils** [Mozart's F-major sonata (K.533) as a problem of Classical style] (4396); Olga LOULOVÁ, **Das tschechische Volkslied im Werke von Jan Křtitel Vaňhal** [Czech traditional song in the music of Johann Baptist Vanhal] (1805); Jaroslav MARKL, **Mozart und das tschechische Volkslied** [Mozart and Czech traditional song] (1807); Ivan MARTYNOV, **Mozart und die russische Kunst** [Mozart and Russian art] (1808); Ernst Hermann MEYER, **Mozarts polyphone Tradition** [Mozart's polyphonic tradition] (4200); Guy MOLLAT DU JOURDIN, **Mozart in Paris** (1816); Jan NĚMEČEK, **Das Problem des "Mozartismus" und die tschechischen Dorflehrer** [The problem of so-called Mozartism and the Czech village schoolmasters] (1825); Mirko OČADLÍK, **Voraussetzungen wissenschaftlicher Mozartforschung in Böhmen** [Prerequisites for scholarly research on Mozart in Bohemia] (1832); Zdeňka PILKOVÁ, **Das Melodram Jiří Bendas im Zusammenhang mit der Mozartproblematik** [Jiří Benda's melodramas in connection with Mozart problematics] (5225); Milan POŠTOLKA, **Leopold Koželuh, ein Zeitgenosse Mozarts** [Leopold Koželuh, a contemporary of Mozart] (1839); Jan RACEK, **Beitrag zur Frage des "mozartschen" Stils in der tschechischen vorklassischen Musik** [The question of the so-called Mozartean style in pre-Classic Czech music] (1841); Marcel RUBIN, **Mozart und die Probleme der modernen Musik** [Mozart and the problems of modern music] (1848); Ernst Fritz SCHMID, **Mozarts Lebenswerk: Seine Bergung und Erschliessung** [Mozart's life oeuvre: Its recovery and publication] (920); Walther SIEGMUND-SCHULTZE, **Zur Frage der Beziehungen zwischen Mozarts Vokal und Instrumentalmusik** [The relationships between Mozart's vocal and instrumental art] (1860); Robert SMETANA, **Mozart und das tschechische Volk** [Mozart and the Czech people] (1863); Miloš STÁDNÍK, **W.A. Mozart und neue Betrachtungen über A. Rejcha** [W.A. Mozart and new observations on A. Rejcha] (1865); Bohumír ŠTĚDROŇ, **Mozart und Mähren** [Mozart and Moravia] (1866); Maxim STEMPEL, **Mozart in Schweden** [Mozart in Sweden] (1870); Václav Jan SÝKORA, **František Xaver Dušek** (1874); Bence SZABOLCSI, **Die "Exotismen" Mozarts** [Mozart's exoticisms] (1876); Marie TARANTOVÁ, **Das Echo von Mozarts Werk in der Epoche der Wiedergeburt des tschechischen Volkes** [The echo of Mozart's music in the era of the renaissance of the Czech people] (1880); Cesare VALABREGA, **Mozart und der Geist der italienischen Musik** [Mozart and the spirit of Italian music] (1887); Erich VALENTIN, **Das Kind Mozart** [The child Mozart] (1888); Zeno VANCEA, **Stand und Ergebnisse der rumänischen musikwissenschaftlichen Forschung über die Beziehungen der Werke Mozarts zu Rumänien** [The current status and the findings of Romanian musicological research on the relationships of Mozart's works to Romania] (929); Walther VETTER, **Mozart und Bach** [Mozart and Bach] (4392); Giórgios VÓKOS, **Die Ästhetik der Mozartschen Kompositionen** [The aesthetics of Mozart's compositions] (1890); Jean WITOLD, **Mozarts Humanismus** [Mozart's humanism]

(934); Halil Bedi YÖNETKEN, **Mozart und die türkische Musik** [Mozart and Turkish music] (1902).

361 **[São Tomé] Conferência Internacional dos**
bs **Africanistas Ocidentais: 6a. sessào** [International West African Conference: 6th meeting]. Sponsored by the Conselho Científico para a África ao Sul do Sara (London: C.C.T.A., 1957) 2 v. *Illus., charts, diagr., transcr., maps.* In Portuguese, English, French, and Spanish.

The conference was held from 21 through 8 August 1956. The following contribution is cited separately: M. BARROS, **Folclore musical da Ilha de São Tomé: Velhas danças, suas músicas y cantares** [Traditional music of São Tomé: Old dances and their music and songs] (2549).

362 **[Trossingen; Stuttgart] International Folk**
bs **Music Council Conference,** *Journal of the International Folk Music Council* IX (1957) 4–54. *Music, charts, diagr.* In English and French.

The ninth annual conference was held from 25 through 31 July 1956. The following contributions are cited separately: Abbasuddin AHMAD, **Folk songs of East Pakistan** (2599); Salvador de BARANDIARÁN, **Basque ceremonial dances** (4935); Fritz BOSE, **Folk music research and the cultivation of folk music** (2423); Bertrand Harris BRONSON, **About the commonest British ballads** (2750); Antoine-Élisée CHERBULIEZ, **L'adaptation du folklore brésilien au style de J.S. Bach selon la thèse de Villa-Lobos** [Adapting Brazilian folklore to the style of J.S. Bach according to the thesis of Villa-Lobos] (4321); Francis COLLINSON, **A brief survey of Scottish folk music recordings in the collections of the School of Scottish Studies, Edinburgh University** (2774); Mona DOUGLAS, **The Manx dirk dance as ritual** (4961); Wilfrid FELDHÜTTER, **Bavarian folk songs and folk dances** (2813); Pál JÁRDÁNYI, **The significance of folk music in present-day Hungarian musicology and musical art** (2871); Ernst KLUSEN, **Differences in style between unbroken and revived folk-music traditions** (2521); Viktor KORDA, **Genuine folk polyphony in the Austrian Alps** (2905); Wilhelm KUTTER, **Radio as the destroyer, collector, and restorer of folk music** (2524); Albert MARINUS, **Tradition, évolution, adaptation** [Tradition, evolution, adaptation] (2448); Joseph Hanson Kwabena NKETIA, **Possession dances in African societies** (2571); František POLOCZEK, **Slovakian folk song and folk dance in the present day** (3010); Kurt REINHARD, **Types of Turkmenian songs in Turkey** (2681); Abdel Rahman SAMI, **Folk music and musical trends in Egypt today** (2583); Valens VODUŠEK, **Midsummer ritual songs in Yugoslavia** (3104); Walther WÜNSCH, **The changing shape and the disappearance of Styrian folk song** (3118).

363 **[Venice] Proceedings of the Third International**
bs **Congress on Aesthetics/Actes du troisième Congrès international d'esthétique/Atti del III Congresso internazionale di estetica.** Sponsored by the *Journal of aesthetics & art criticism,* American Society for Aesthetics, Cleveland Museum of Art, *Revue d'esthétique,* and Société Française d'Esthétique. Ed. by Luigi PAREYSON (Torino: Edizioni della Rivista di Estetica, 1957) 732 p. *Illus.* In Italian, English, French, German, and Spanish.

The conference was held from 3 through 5 September 1956. The following contributions are cited separately: Andrea DELLA CORTE, **Preliminari di critica musicale** [Preliminaries to musical criticism] (5453); Cornelio FABRO, **Estetica mozartiana nell'opera di Kierkegard** [Mozartean aesthetics in Kierkegaard's work] (5463); Serge LIFAR, **L'évolution technique et esthétique de la danse académique** [The technical and aesthetic evolution of academic dance] (5023); Elisa OBERTI, **Tecnica e linguaggio musicale** [Musical technique and musical language] (5556); Jeanne PARAIN-VIAL, **L'expérience musicale et l'harmonisation de textes poétiques** [Musical experience and the harmonization of poetic texts] (5564); Luigi ROGNONI, **Tecnica e linguaggio nella musica post-weberniana** [Technique and language in post-Webernian music] (5576); Robert SIOHAN, **Un micro-organisme sonore** [A sonic microorganism] (3956); Henry VALENSI, **De l'art de la musique et de l'art abstrait** [The art of music and abstract art] (5620).

364 **[Vienna] Actes du IVᵉ Congrès international**
bs **des sciences anthropologiques et ethnologiques** [Proceedings of the Fourth International Congress of Anthropology and Ethnology]. Ed. by Robert HEINE-GELDERN, Anna HOHENWART-GERLACHSTEIN, Dorothea KLIMBURG, and Wilhelm KOPPERS (Wien: Holzhausen, 1954-1956) 3 v. *Illus., bibliog., charts, diagr., maps.* In French, English, German, and Italian.

The conference was held from 1 through 8 September 1956. The following contributions are cited separately: Herbert JANSKY, **Vergleichende Volksliederkunde als Hilfsmittel der Völkerspsychologie: Ein Beispiel aus der Turkologie** [The comparative study of traditional song as a resource of ethnopsychology: An example from Turkish studies] (2643); Jean H. SERVIER, **Musique et poésie kabyles** [Kabyle poetry and music] (2589).

365 **[Vienna] Bericht über den internationalen**
bs **musikwissenschaftlichen Kongreß Wien Mozartjahr 1956** [Proceedings of the international musicological congress, Vienna Mozart Year, 1956]. Sponsored by the Gesellschaft zur Herausgabe von Denkmälern der Tonkunst in Österreich, Österreichische Akademie der Wissenschaften, Bundesministerium für Unterricht, and Bundesministerium für Handel und Wiederaufbau. Ed. by Erich SCHENK (Graz; Köln: Böhlau, 1958) xiv, 805 p. *Illus., facs., music, charts, diagr., chronology.* In German, Italian, French, English, and Russian.

The conference was held from 3 through 9 June 1956 in conjunction with celebrations of the 200th anniversary of the birth of Wolfgang Amadeus Mozart. The following contributions are cited separately: Ricardo ALLORTO, **Mozart e Clementi** [Mozart and Clementi] (1721); Cevat Memduh ALTAR, **Wolfgang Amadeus Mozart im Lichte osmanisch-österreichischer Beziehungen** [Wolfgang Amadeus Mozart in the light of Ottoman-Austrian relations] (1722); Higini ANGLÈS, **Die alte spanische Mensuralnotation: Praktische Winke, um den Rhythmus der monodischen Lyrik des Mittelalters besser kennenzulernen** [Old Spanish mensural notation: Practical suggestions toward an improved acquaintance with the rhythm of monodic medieval songs] (3802); Guglielmo BARBLAN, **Le orchestre in Lombardia all'epoca di Mozart** [Orchestras in Lombardy in Mozart's time] (1724); Dénes BARTHA, **Die ungarische Musikforschung des letzten Jahrzehnts: Ein Literaturbericht** [Hungarian music research of the last decade: A bibliographic report] (812); Bianca BECHERINI, **Le sonate per pianoforte di W.A. Mozart: Problemi di esecuzione contemporanea** [W.A. Mozart's piano sonatas: Problems of contemporary performance] (3729); Hermann BECK, **Probleme der venezianischen Messkomposition im 16. Jahrhundert** [Problems of Venetian Mass composition in the 16th century] (4310); Karel Philippus BERNET KEMPERS, **Mahler und Willem Mengelberg** [Mahler and Willem Mengelberg] (2286); Heinrich BESSELER, **Mozart und die deutsche Klassik** [Mozart and German Classicism] (1728); Siegfried BIMBERG, **Die Polarität bei der Rezeption der Tonalitäten** [Polarity in the perception of tonalities] (5641); Wolfgang BOETTICHER, **Die französische Chansonkomposition Orlando di Lassos** [The French chanson compositions of Roland de Lassus] (1239); Werner BOLLERT, **Bemerkungen zu Mozarts Klavierkonzert F-Dur (K.V. 459)** [Comments on Mozart's piano concerto in F major, K.459] (1729); George BREAZUL, **Zu Mozarts Zweihundertjahrfeier** [Regarding Mozart's bicentennial] (1731); Marie BRIQUET, **Contribution à la vie parisienne de Mozart (1764)** [A note on Mozart's life in Paris (1764)] (1732); Jacques CHAILLEY, **A propos de quatre mesures de l'***Entführung***: La renaissance de la modalité dans la musique française avant 1890** [Four measures in the *Entführung*: The rebirth of modality in French music before 1890] (4056); Jósef Michał CHOMIŃSKI, **Der Entwicklungscharakter der Harmonik im Mittelalter und in der Renaissance** [The developmental character of harmony in the Middle Ages and the Renaissance] (4154); Rina di CLEMENTE, **Può la spiritualità di Mozart esercitare una funzione nel caos degli indirizzi musicali di oggi?** [Can Mozart's spirituality have a function in today's chaos of musical trends?] (2148); Giulio COGNI, **Grundzüge einer neuen Musikpsychologie** [Foundations of a new psychology of music] (5648); Dragotin CVETKO, **J.B. Novak: Ein slowenischer Anhänger Mozarts** [J.B. Novak: A Slovenian admirer of Mozart] (1738); Georg von DADELSEN, **Zu den Vorreden des Michael**

Wirkungsweite fahrender Musiker im Dienste der Herzöge von Österreich [The international scope of the influence of itinerant musicians in the service of the Austrian dukes] (1172); Joseph SCHMIDT-GÖRG, **Die besonderen Voraussetzungen zu einer kritischen Gesamtausgabe der Werke Ludwig van Beethovens** [Particular prerequisites for a complete critical edition of Ludwig van Beethoven's works] (3917); Wolfgang SCHMIEDER, **Grenzen und Ziele der Musikdokumentation** [The limits and goals of music documentation] (678); Camillo SCHOENBAUM, **Die Kammermusikwerke des Jan Dismas Zelenka** [The chamber works of Jan Dismas Zelenka] (4380); Ottmar SCHREIBER, **Max Regers musikalischer Nachlaß** [Max Reger's musical legacy] (2093); Willi SCHUH, **Über einige frühe Textbücher zur** *Zauberflöte* [Some early printed librettos of *Die Zauberflöte*] (5240); Walter SERAUKY, **W.A. Mozart und die Musikästhetik des ausklingenden 18. und frühen 19. Jahrhunderts** [W.A. Mozart and the musical aesthetics of the late 18th and early 19th centuries] (5595); Walther SIEGMUND-SCHULTZE, **Zur Frage des Mozartschen Stils** [The question of Mozartean style] (4460); Heinrich SIMBRIGER, **Die heutige Situation der Zwölftonmusik** [The current situation of twelve-tone music] (2249); Joseph SMITS VAN WAESBERGHE, **Die rheno-mosa-mosellanische Neumenschrift** [The neumatic notation of the Rhine/Meuse/Moselle region] (3871); Bohumír ŠTĚDROŇ, **Mozart und Mähren** [Mozart and Moravia] (1008); Kurt STEPHENSON, **Zur Soziologie des Studentenliedes** [The sociology of the student song] (5909); Erich STOCKMANN, **Albanische Volksmusikinstrumente** [Albanian traditional instruments] (3278); Antonín SYCHRA, **Die Bedeutung des Skizzenstudiums für die wissenschaftliche Analyse musikalischer Werke** [The significance of sketch studies in the scholarly analysis of musical works] (928); Bence SZABOLCSI, **Mozart und die Volksbühne** [Mozart and the popular stage] (5256); Franz TACK, **Die musikgeschichtlichen Voraussetzungen der christlichen Kultmusik und ihre Bedeutung für den gregorianischen Vortragsstil** [The music-historical preconditions of music for Christian worship, and their significance for Gregorian performance style] (3717); Willy TAPPOLET, **Le séjour de Wolfgang-Amadé Mozart à Genève en 1766** [Wolfgang Amadeus Mozart's 1766 stay in Geneva] (1879); Roland TENSCHERT, **Der Tonartenkreis in Mozarts Werken** [The range of tonality in Mozart's works] (4220); Vincenzo TERENZIO, **Il problema del preromanticismo e l'arte mozartiana** [The problem of pre-Romanticism in Mozart] (4387); Zeno VANCEA, **Die sozialen Grundlagen der rumänischen Kunstmusik** [The social foundations of Romanian art music] (1015); Walther VETTER, **Mozart im Weltbild Richard Wagners** [Mozart in Richard Wagner's worldview] (2120); Walther R. VOLBACH, **Die Synchronisierung von Aktion und Musik in Mozarts Opern** [The synchronization of action and music in Mozart's operas] (5268); Simone WALLON, **Romances et vaudevilles français dans les variations pour piano et pour piano et violon de Mozart** [French romances and vaudevilles in Mozart's variations for piano and for piano and violin] (1892); Dagmar WEISE, **Zur Gesamtausgabe der Briefe Beethovens durch das Beethoven-Archiv Bonn** [The complete edition of Beethoven's correspondence by the Beethoven-Archiv, Bonn] (3926); Albert WELLEK, **Die ganzheitspsychologischen Aspekte der Musikästhetik** [Musical aesthetics in light of holistic psychology] (5627); Helene WESSELY, **Romanus Weichlein: Ein vergessener österreichischer Instrumentalkomponist des 17. Jahrhunderts** [Romanus Weichlein: A forgotten Austrian composer of instrumental music in the 17th century] (1711); Othmar WESSELY, **Beiträge zur Lebensgeschichte von Johann Zanger** [Contributions to the biography of Johann Zanger] (1467); Fritz WINCKEL, **Die Wirkung der Musik unter dem Gesichtspunkt psychophysiologischer Erscheinungen** [The effects of music from the point of view of psychophysiological phenomena] (5724); Emanuel WINTERNITZ, **Mozarts Raumgefühl** [Mozart's feeling for space] (1897); Hellmuth Christian WOLFF, **Palestrina und Schönberg: Zwei Extreme der europäischen Musik** [Palestrina and Schoenberg: Two extremes of European music] (5632); Hans Christoph WORBS, **Komponist, Publikum und Auftraggeber: Eine Untersuchung an Mozarts Klavierkonzerten** [Composer, audience, and patron: An investigation of Mozart's piano concertos] (1900); Karl Heinrich WÖRNER, **Mozarts Fugenfragmente** [Mozart's fugal fragments] (1901); Walther WÜNSCH, **Volksmusikpflege und Wissenschaft** [Scholarship and the cultivation of traditional music] (2487); Milenko ŽIVKOVIĆ, **Tonale Grundlage in Volksmelodien einiger Gebiete Jugoslawiens** [Tonal foundations of traditional melodies from certain regions of Yugoslavia] (4134); Elsa Margherita von ZSCHINSKY-TROXLER, **Mozarts Violinkonzerte im spieltechnischen Vergleich mit zeitgenössischen italienischen Violinkomponisten** [A comparison of performance technique in

Mozart's violin concertos and the violin music of his Italian contemporaries] (1904).

366
bs
[Wégimont] Les colloques de Wégimont. III: Ethnomusicologie II [The Wégimont colloquia. III: Ethnomusicology II]. Sponsored by the Cercle International d'Études Ethno-musicologiques. Ed. by Paul COLLAER. *Bibliothèque de la Faculté de Philosophie et Lettres de l'Université de Liège* 157 (Paris: Belles Lettres, 1960) 302 p. *Illus., port., music, bibliog., discog., charts, diagr., maps.* In French, German, and English.

The conference was held from 15 through 21 September 1956. The following contributions are cited separately: Paul COLLAER, **Chants et airs des peuples de l'extrême-Nord** [Songs and melodies of the peoples of the far north] (2612) and **Le tambour à friction (II), et idiophones frottés** [The friction drum (II) and rubbed idiophones] (3647); Yvette GRIMAUD, **Note sur la musique vocale des Bochiman !Kung et des Pygmées Babinga** [Notes on the vocal music of the !Kung Bushmen and Babinga Pygmies] (2552); Robert GÜNTHER, **Eine Studie zur Musik in Ruanda** [A study of music in Rwanda] (2553); Ljubica S. JANKOVIĆ and Danica S. JANKOVIĆ, **Sur les traces du plus ancien héritage culturel de la danse et de la musique traditionelles Yougoslaves** [On the track of the oldest cultural heritage in traditional Yugoslav dance and music] (4991); H.E. KAUFMANN and Marius SCHNEIDER, **Lieder aus den Naga-Bergen (Assam)** [Songs from the Naga Hills (Assam)] (2646); Claudie MARCEL-DUBOIS, **Le toulouhou des Pyrénées centrales: Usage rituel et parentés d'un tambour à friction tournoyant** [The toulouhou of the central Pyrénées: Ritual use of a whirling friction drum and related instruments] (3653); Walter SALMEN, **Zur sozialen Schichtung des Berufsmusikertums im mittelalterlichen Eurasien und in Afrika** [The social stratification of professional musicians in medieval Eurasia and in Africa] (2538); André SCHAEFFNER, **Situation des musiciens dans trois sociétés africaines** [The position of musicians in three African societies] (2587); Nils SCHIØRRING, **Musical folklore and ethnomusicology in Denmark** (3052); Marius SCHNEIDER, **Sociologie et mythologie musicales** [The sociology and mythology of music] (2540).

1957

367
bs
[Brussels, etc.] Fêtes et cérémonies au temps de Charles Quint: Fêtes de la Renaissance. II [Festivals and ceremonies at the time of Charles V: Festivals of the Renaissance. II]. Proceedings of the second congress of the Assocation Internationale des Historiens de la Renaissance. Ed. by Jean JACQUOT. *Le chœur des muses* (Paris: Centre National de la Recherche Scientifique [CNRS], 1960) 518 p. *Illus., music.* In French.

The conference was held in Brussels, Antwerp, Ghent, and Liège from 2 through 7 September 1957. The following contributions are cited separately: Hugh BAILLIE, **Les musiciens de la chapelle royale d'Henri VIII au Camp du Drap d'Or** [Musicians of Henry VIII's Chapel Royal at the Field of the Cloth of Gold] (1226); Nanie BRIDGMAN, **La participation musicale à l'entrée de Charles Quint à Cambrai le 20 janvier 1540** [Musical aspects of Charles V's entry into Cambrai, 20 January 1540] (1260); Daniel HEARTZ, **Un divertissement de palais pour Charles Quint à Binche** [A palace entertainment for Charles V at Binche] (1329); Paul KAST, **Remarques sur la musique et les musiciens de la chapelle de François Ier au Camp du Drap d'Or** [Music and the musicians of the chapel of François I at the Field of the Cloth of Gold] (1354).

368
bs
[Cambridge, Mass.] Instrumental music. Sponsored by Harvard University, Department of Music. Ed. by David G. HUGHES; intro. by A. Tillman MERRITT. *Isham Library papers* 1 (Cambridge, MA: Harvard University Press, 1959) vi, 152 p. *Music.*

The conference was held at Isham Memorial Library, Harvard University, on 4 May 1957. The following contributions are cited separately: Otto KINKELDEY, **Dance tunes of the fifteenth century** (1357); H.C. Robbins LANDON, **Problems of authenticity in eighteenth-century music**

(1797); Walter PISTON, **Problems of intonation in the performance of contemporary music** (3797); Eric WERNER, **Instrumental music outside the pale of Classicism and Romanticism** (1896).

369
bs
[Cambridge, Mass.] **Sound and man.** Proceedings of the Second International Congress on Acoustics. Ed. by Robert Bruce LINDSAY (New York: American Institute of Physics, 1957) 199 p. *Illus., music.*
The following contributions are cited separately: E. Power BIGGS, **A musician and his acoustical environment** (3338); Vern O. KNUDSEN, **The acoustics of Symphony Hall, Boston** (5829); Walter KUHL, **Optimal acoustical design of rooms for performing, listening, and recording** (5835); Arnold M. SMALL and Daniel W. MARTIN, **Musical acoustics: Aims, progress, and forecast** (5856).

370
bs
[Chieti] **VII Congresso nazionale delle tradizioni popolari** [Seventh Congresso nazionale delle tradizioni popolari]. Sponsored by the Istituto Italiano di Storia delle Tradizioni e Società di Etnografia Italiana. Ed. by Bianca Maria GALANTI (Firenze: Olschki, 1959) 547 p. *Lares* XXV (1959). *Illus., port., maps.* In Italian.
The conference was held from 4 through 8 September 1957. The following contributions are cited separately: A.M. ALBERTINI, **Studio su nuove versioni della canzone della *Finta monacella*** [Study of new versions of the song *La finta monacella*] (2711); Diego CARPITELLA, **Le registrazioni di cantori popolari in Abruzzo** [The recordings of traditional singers in Abruzzi] (2759); Alberto Mario CIRESE, **Natura e valori del canto popolare secondo Pietro Ercole Visconti (1830)** [The nature and significance of traditional singing according to Pietro Ercole Visconti (1830)] (2767); Federico GHISI, **Le fonti musicali in Piemonte di alcuni canti narrativi popolari** [The musical sources in Piedmont of some narrative traditional songs] (2832); Guido GIULIANTE, **Saltarella: Ritmo vecchio e nuovo** [Saltarella: Old and new rhythm] (4969); Pasquale MARICA and Franz SILESU, **La Settimana Santa a Sanluri** [Holy Week in Sanluri] (2941); M.V. MAYER, **Il canto lirico monostrofico in Abruzzo** [The single-stanza lyric song in the Abruzzi] (2954); D. PICCOLOTTI, **Il canto popolare in rapporto agli usi e costumi del popolo Abruzzese** [Traditional singing in relation to the usages and customs of the people of the Abruzzi] (3000); Romolo TRINCHIERI, **Il canto a braccio tra pastori-poeti nel Monterealese** [The *canto a braccio* among the shepherd-poets in the Montereale area] (3089).

371
bs
[Copenhagen] **International Folk Music Council Conference,** *Journal of the International Folk Music Council* X (1958) 4–51. *Music, charts, diagr., transcr.* In English and French.
The tenth annual conference was held from 23 through 27 August 1957. The following contributions are cited separately: Arnold Adriaan BAKÉ, **Nepalese folk music** (2605); Fritz BOSE, **Law and freedom in the interpretation of European folk epics** (2744); Erik DAL, **The linked stanza in Danish ballads: Its age and its analogues** (5298); Thorkild KNUDSEN, **Structures prémodales et pseudo-grégoriennes dans les mélodies des ballades danoises** [Premodal and pseudo-Gregorian structures in the melodies of Danish ballads] (4084); Rolf MYKLEBUST, **Norwegian folk music records** (2966); Bruno NETTL, **Some linguistic approaches to musical analysis** (3954); Kurt REINHARD, **On the problem of pre-pentatonic scales: Particularly the third-second nucleus** (4105); Willard RHODES, **A study of musical diffusion based on the wandering of the opening peyote song** (3175); Lajos VARGYAS, **Some parallels of rare modal structures in Western and Eastern Europe** (4123); Vinko ŽGANEC, **The tonal and modal structure of Yugoslav folk music** (4476).

372
bs
[Heidelberg] **Stil- und Formprobleme in der Literatur: Vorträge** [Problems of style and form in literature: Report]. Proceedings of the Seventh Congress of the International Federation for Modern Languages and Literatures. Ed. by Paul BÖCKMANN (Heidelberg: Winter, 1959) 524 p. *Bibliog., index.* In German, English, French, and Italian.

The following contributions are cited separately: Stanley Collin ASTON, **The troubadours and the concept of style** (5284); Zygmunt CZERNY, **Contribution à une théorie comparée du motif dans les arts** [Toward a comparative theory of the motive in the arts] (5445).

373
bs
[Kassel] **Die kasseler Tagung der IVMB/La reunion d l'AIBM à Cassel/The Kassel conference of the IAML.** Sponsored by the Association Internationale des Bibliothèque Musicales. Ed. and intro. by Vladimir FÉDOROV, *Fontes artis musicae* IV/2 (Dec 1957) 128. *Bibliog.* In German, French, English, and Italian.
The conference was held from 31 September through 4 October 1957. The following contributions are cited separately: John Howard DAVIES, **Radio music libraries** (544); Kurt GUDEWILL, **Identifizierungen von anonymen und mehrfach zugewiesenen Kompositionen in deutschen Liederdrucken aus der 1. Hälfte des 16. Jahrhunderts** [Identification of anonymous and multi-attributed compositions in German song prints from the first half of the 16th century] (1321); Lionel MCCOLVIN, **Music in public libraries: Why? And what?** (620); Cesare VALABREGA, **Una storia della musica italiana in dischi microsolco** [A history of Italian music in long-playing records] (1014).

374
bs
[Liège] **La technique littéraire des chansons de geste** [The literary technique of chansons de geste]. Proceedings of the Colloque de Liège. *Bibliothèque de la Faculté de Philosophie et Lettres de l'Université de Liège* 150 (Paris: Belles Lettres, 1959) 483 p. In French.
The following contributions are cited separately: André BURGER, **Les deux scènes du cor dans la *Chanson de Roland*** [The two horn scenes in the *Chanson de Roland*] (5294); Jeanne WATHELET-WILLEM, **Les refrains dans la *Chanson de Guillaume*** [Refrains in the *Chanson de Guillaume*] (5369).

375
bs
[London] **Organ and choral aspects and prospects.** Proceedings of the First International Organ Congress. Ed. by Max HINRICHSEN; foreword by John Dykes BOWER. *Hinrichsen's music books* (London: Hinrichsen, 1958) 181 p. *Illus., port., bibliog.*
The conference was held from 27 through 29 May 1957. The following contributions are cited separately: Wilfrid Greenhouse ALLT, **The basic values** (6002); Thomas ARMSTRONG, **The Wesleys: Evangelists and musicians** (942); George DYSON, **The place of the organist in British musical life** (3355); Max HINRICHSEN, **Music for the student of the organ** (806); George LITTLE, **Choral aspects and prospects** (984); **The new Purcell Society Edition and some Purcell music** (1649); Charles PEAKER, **Voice and verse** (6023); Gordon PHILLIPS, **Purcell's organs and organ music** (1644); Leo SOWERBY, **Composition in relation to the church and allied fields in America** (6026); Leslie Pratt SPELMAN, **Organ teaching: Methods and materials** (4651); David WILLIAMS, **The artist in religion** (6031); Franklin B. ZIMMERMAN, **Purcell portraiture** (5406).

376
bs
[Munich] **Akten des vierundzwanzigsten Internationalen Orientalisten-Kongresses** [Proceedings of the 24th International Congress of Orientalists]. Sponsored by the Deutsche Morgenländische Gesellschaft. Ed. by Herbert FRANKE (Wiesbaden: Franz Steiner Verlag, 1959) xii, 776 p. *Illus., bibliog., index.* In German and English.
The conference was held from 28 August through 4 September 1957. The following contribution is cited separately: Ganesh Dutt GAUR, **Folksongs of Kuru Pradesh** (2629).

377
bs
[Neuilly-sur-Seine] **Le luth et sa musique** [The lute and its music]. Sponsored by the Société de Musique d'Autrefois. Ed. and pref. by Jean JACQUOT. *Colloques internationaux du CNRS* (Paris: Centre National de la Recherche Scientifique [CNRS], 1958)

356 p. *Illus., facs., music, index, charts, diagr.* In French.

The conference was held from 10 through 14 September 1957. The following contributions are cited separately: Thomas E. BINKLEY, **Le luth et sa technique** [The lute and its technique] (3550); Wolfgang BOETTICHER, **Les œuvres de Roland de Lassus mises en tablature de luth** [The works of Roland de Lassus transcribed in lute tablature] (1241); Thurston DART, **La méthode de luth de Miss Mary Burwell** [Miss Mary Burwell's lute tutor] (3737) and **La pandore** [The bandora] (3561); Benvenuto DISERTORI, **Contradiction tonale dans la transcription d'un** *strambotto* **célèbre** [Tonal contradiction in the transcription of a famous strambotto] (3695), **Le** *liuto soprano* [The *liuto soprano*] (3563), and **Remarques sur l'évolution du luth en Italie au XVᵉ siècle et au XVIᵉ** [Remarks on the evolution of the lute in 15th- and 16th-century Italy] (3564); Kurt DORFMÜLLER, **La tablature de luth allemande et les problèmes d'édition** [German lute tablature and editing problems] (3892); Daniel HEARTZ, **Les premières "instructions" pour le luth (jusque vers 1550)** [The earliest lute methods (up to ca. 1550)] (1331); Jean JACQUOT, **Objectifs et plan de travail** [Goals and work program] (3901) and **Premiers résultats acquis—Perspectives d'avenir** [First results obtained—Perspectives of the future] (3902); François LESURE, **Recherches sur les luthistes parisiens à l'époque de Louis XIII** [Research on Parisian lutenists of the period of Louis XIII] (1604); David LUMSDEN, **Un catalogue international des sources de la musique pour le luth: Les leçons d'une étude des sources anglais** [An international catalogue of sources of lute music: Lessons from a study of English sources] (613); Lawrence H. MOE, **Le problème des barres de mesure: Étude sur la transcription de la musique de danse des tablatures de luth du XVIᵉ siècle** [The problem of barlines: A study in the transcription of dance music in lute tablatures of the 16th century] (3909); Richard M. MURPHY, **Fantaisie et recercare dans les premières tablatures de luth du XVIᵉ siècle** [Fantasia and ricercare in the first lute tablatures of the 16th century] (4272); Frits NOSKE, **Remarques sur les luthistes des Pays-Bas (1580-1620)** [Lutenists of the Low Countries (1580-1620)] (1390); Michel PODOLSKI, **À la recherche d'une méthode de transcription formelle des tablatures de luth** [In search of a formal transcription method for lute tablatures] (3914); Diana POULTON, **La technique du jeu du luth en France et en Angleterre** [The technique of lute playing in France and England] (3597); Michael PRYNNE, **Comment noter et conserver les mesures des luths anciens** [How to record and preserve the measurements of early lutes] (3598); Karl SCHEIT, **Ce que nous enseignent les traités de luth des environs de 1600** [What can be learned from lute treatises of ca. 1600] (3715); André SOURIS, **Tablature et syntax: Remarques sur le problème de la transcription des tablatures de luth** [Tablature and syntax: Remarks on the problem of transcribing lute tablatures] (3920); Geneviève THIBAULT DE CHAMBURE, **Un manuscrit italien pour luth des premières années du XVIᵉ siècle** [An Italian lute manuscript from the early sixteenth century] (1449); Geneviève THIBAULT DE CHAMBURE and ET AL, **Discussion: Problèmes d'édition** [Discussion: Editing problems] (3923); André VERCHALY, **La tablature dans les recueils français pour chant et luth (1603-1643)** [Tablature in French collections for voice and lute (1603-1643)] (3924); John M. WARD, **Le problème des hauteurs dans la musique pour luth et vihuela au XVIᵉ siècle** [The problem of pitch in lute and vihuela music of the 16th century] (3721); Krystyna WILKOWSKA-CHOMIŃSKA, **À la recherche de la musique pour luth: Expériences polonaises** [In search of lute music: Polish experiences] (932). A second edition, revised and corrected, is cited as RILM ¹⁹⁷⁶1527.

378
bs

[Paris] La musique sacrée [Sacred music]. Proceedings of the third International Congress of Sacred Music. Ed. by Raphael CUTTOLI; pref. by Albert RICHARD, *Revue musicale* 239-240 (1957) 349. *Illus., port.* In French.

Summaries of papers presented at the conference held in July 1957 whose proceedings are cited as no. 379 in this volume. The following contributions are cited separately: Louis T.E. ACHILLE, **Les négros-spirituals, musique populaire sacrée** [African-American spirituals, traditional sacred music] (6135); Joseph AHRENS, **Liturgie et musique d'orgue** [The liturgy and organ music] (6138); BASILE (brother), **Le dilemme de la musique religieuse indigène en Afrique du Sud** [The dilemma of indigenous religious music in South Africa] (6161); Jean BIHAN, **La mouvement grégorien en Europe Occidentale** [The Gregorian movement in Western Europe] (6169) and **Le mouvement grégorien au Canada et en Amérique du Sud** [The Gregorian movement in Canada and

South America] (6167); Émile BLANCHET, **Principes de la musique sacrée** [Principles of sacred music] (6171); Jacques CHAILLEY, **La révision du critère historique dans les problèmes de la musique d'église** [Reconsideration of the historical criterion in problems of church music] (6185); Celso COSTANTINI, **La musique sacrée dans les missions** [Sacred music in missions] (6006); Pierre DENIS, **Le véritable problème des orgues électroniques** [The real problem with electronic organs] (3663); J.-A. DEREUX, **L'"orgue à synthèse"** [The *orgue à synthèse*] (3348); Norbert DUFOURCQ, **Place de M.-R. Delalande dans la musique religieuse occidentale du XVIIᵉᵐᵉ siècle** [The position of M.-R. de Lalande in Western religious music of the 17th century] (1532); Christophe-Jean DUMONT, **Diversité des rites orientaux et enrichissement de la spiritualité catholique** [Diversity in the Eastern rites and the enrichment of Catholic spirituality] (6205); Guillermo FRAILE, **L'orgue électronique** [The electronic organ] (3666); Joseph GAJARD, **La valeur artistique et religieuse toujours actuelle du chant grégorien** [The constantly contemporary artistic and religious value of Gregorian chant] (6221); Johann von GARDNER, **Le rite byzantin** [The Byzantine rite] (6113); Joseph GELINEAU, **La valeur catéchétique du chant populaire** [The catechetic value of congregational singing] (6234); Odette HERTZ, **Pour que les enfants apprennent à l'école comment chanter à l'église** [To the end of having children learn in school how to sing in church] (4708); Jean JEANNETEAU, **L'orgue électronique** [Electronic organs] (6260); Pierre KAELIN, **Qualité musicale et chant populaire** [Musical quality and congregational singing] (6268); Leo LEVI, **Les neumes, les notations bibliques et le chant protochrétien** [Neumes, Biblical notations, and proto-Christian chant] (3844); Cletus MADSEN, **Le mouvement grégorien aux États-Unis** [The Gregorian movement in the United States] (4730); Fernand MAILLET, **La Fédération Internationale des Petits Chanteurs** [The International Federation of Pueri Cantores] (6293); Constant MARTIN, **Les "nouvelles orgues"** [The new organs] (3669); Miguel Darío MIRANDA Y GÓMEZ, **La musique sacrée, art liturgique privilégié** [Sacred music, a privileged liturgical art] (6307); Xavier MORILLEAU, **Valeur pastorale du chant grégorien à la lumière des enseignements pontificaux** [The pastoral value of Gregorian chant in the light of papal teaching] (6310); Carl de NYS, **Les enregistrements de musique sacrée** [Recordings of sacred music] (5983); Jean OBAMA, **L'emploi de la musique indigène dans les chrétientés africaines: Enquête** [The use of indigenous music in African Christianities: Enquiry] (6323) and **Les réussites du chant grégorien au Cameroun** [The successes of Gregorian chant in Cameroon] (6325); René PAROISSIN, **La musique missionaire en Extrême-Orient** [Missionary music in the Far East] (6334); Jean PRIM, **Hommage à Joseph Samson** [Tribute to Joseph Samson] (2377); Félix RAUGEL, Ramón GONZÁLEZ DE AMEZÚA Y NORIEGA, Gaston LITAIZE, Georges ROBERT, and Norbert DUFOURCQ, **L'orgue à tuyaux** [The pipe organ] (3464); Antoine REBOULOT, **L'organiste liturgique au XXᵉ siècle et sa formation** [Liturgical organists in the 20th century and their training] (4890); Aymon-Marie ROGUET, **Valeur pastoral de la musique sacrée** [The pastoral value of sacred music] (6357); Fiorenzo ROMITA, **Les principes de la législation de la musique sacrée d'après l'encyclique** *Musicae sacrae disciplina* [The legislative principles for sacred music according to the encyclical *Musicae sacrae disciplina*] (6363); Gaston ROUSSEL, **Le rôle exemplaire des maîtrises de cathédrales** [The exemplary role of cathedral choir schools] (6367); Robert SASTRE, **Le sacré et la musique négro-africaine** [The sacred, and black African music] (6374); Joseph SMITS VAN WAESBERGHE, **État des recherches scientifiques dans le domaine du chant grégorien** [The state of scientific research in the field of Gregorian chant] (1179); Egon WELLESZ, **Les** *Monumenta musicae Byzantinae* [The *Monumenta musicae Byzantinae*] (3927); Hellmuth Christian WOLFF, **Quelques compositions de l'**Ordinarium missae modernes* [Some modern settings of the Ordinary of the Mass] (6417).

379
bs

[Paris] Perspectives de la musique sacrée à la lumière de l'encyclique *Musicae sacrae disciplina* [Perspectives of sacred music in light of the encyclical *Musicae sacrae disciplina*]. Proceedings of the third International Congress of Sacred Music (Paris: conference, 1959) 738 p. *Illus., port., music.* In French, English, Italian, German, and Spanish.

The conference was held from 1 through 8 July 1957. The following contributions are cited separately: Louis T.E. ACHILLE, **Les négro-spirituals, musique populaire sacrée** [African-American spirituals, traditional sacred music] (6134); Luigi AGUSTONI, **Culte chrétien et chant populaire** [Christian worship services and congregational singing] (6137);

Joseph AHRENS, **Die Liturgie und die Orgelmusik/Liturgie et musique d'orgue** [The liturgy and organ music] (6139); Ilario ALCINI, **L'insegnamento della Musica sacra nei Seminari/L'enseignement de la musique sacrée dans les séminaires** [Sacred music instruction in seminaries] (4805); Higini ANGLÈS, **Organisation internationale de la musique sacrée** [How sacred music is organized at the international level] (6146); Myroslav ANTONOVYČ, **Participation des fidèles d'Ukraine aux chants liturgiques** [The participation of Ukrainian congregations in liturgical singing] (6149); BASILE (brother), **Le dilemme de la musique religieuse indigène en Afrique du Sud** [The dilemma of indigenous religious music in southern Africa] (6162); Marguerite BÉCLARD D'HARCOURT, **Cantiques folkloriques français retrouvés en Louisiane** [Traditional French cantiques found in Louisiana] (3140); Jean BIHAN, **Le mouvement grégorien dans le monde** [The Gregorian movement worldwide] (6168); Bernard BROCKBERND, **La radio au service d'une meilleure musique religieuse** [Radio in the service of a better religious music] (5744); Eugène CARDINE, **Neumes et rythme** [Neumes and rhythm] (3810); Jacques CHAILLEY, **La révision du critère historique dans les problèmes de la musique d'église** [Reconsideration of the historical criterion in problems of church music] (6184); Celso COSTANTINI, **La musique sacrée dans les missions** [Sacred music in missions] (6005); Leonzio DAYAN, **La publication des** Hymnes de l'église arménienne [The publication of the Hymnes de l'église arménienne] (3891); Dominique DELALANDE, **De quelques renseignements mélodiques à tirer de manuscrits purement neumatiques** [Some melodic information that can be retrieved from purely neumatic manuscripts] (3815); Pierre DENIS, **Le véritable problème des orgues électroniques** [The real problem with electronic organs] (3664); Norbert DUFOURCQ, **France et Italie: La place occupée par Michel-Richard Delalande dans la musique occidentale aux XVIIᵉ et XVIIIᵉ siècles** [France and Italy: The position of Michel-Richard de Lalande in Western music of the 17th and 18th centuries] (1530); Christophe-Jean DUMONT, **Diversité des rites orientaux et enrichissement de la spiritualité catholique** [Diversity in the Eastern rites and the enrichment of Catholic spirituality] (6206); Mathias DYKER, **Vestiges d'un style calliphonique dans le chant oriental au XIIIᵉ siècle** [Vestiges of a kalophonic style in Eastern chant of the 13th century] (1082); Raymond FORET, **Les églises d'orient et la musique moderne: Pastorale et musicologie** [Eastern churches and modern music: Pastoral and musicological issues] (6111); Guillermo FRAILE, **El órgano litúrgico/L'orgue liturgique** [The liturgical organ] (3665); Joseph GAJARD, **La valeur artistique et religieuse toujours actuelle du chant grégorien** [The ever-contemporary artistic and religious value of Gregorian chant] (6222); Johann von GARDNER, **Le psautier chanté en slavon au XVIIᵉ siècle** [The psalter sung in Slavonic in the 17th century] (1555); Joseph GELINEAU, **La valeur catéchétique du chant populaire** [The catechetical value of congregational singing] (6235); Ramón GONZÁLEZ DE AMEZÚA Y NORIEGA, **Les orgues électroniques** [Electronic organs] (3667); Francis HAJTAS, **The vernacular religious songs in Hungary since 1932/Le chant religieux populaire en Hongrie depuis 1932** (6248); Odette HERTZ, **Pour que tous nos enfants apprennent à l'école comment chanter à l'église** [To the end of having all our children learn in school how to sing in church] (4709); René-Jean HESBERT, **Structure grégorienne et chant en français** [Gregorian structure and French-language singing] (4433); Helmut HUCKE, **Zum Plan eines Lexikons der katholischen Kirchenmusik/Projet pour un lexique de la musique catholique d'église** [The project of a lexicon of Catholic church music] (6255); Pierre KAELIN, **Qualité musicale et chant populaire** [Musical quality and congregational singing] (6269); Franz KOSCH, **Die Auswirkungen des II. Internationales Kirchenmusikkongresses (Wien, 1954)/Quelques résultats du IIᵉ congrès international de musique sacrée tenu à Vienne en 1954** [Consequences of the second International Congress for Church Music (Vienna, 1954)] (6272); François LESURE, **Les éditions scientifiques de musique polyphonique** [Scholarly editions of polyphonic music] (3905); Leo LEVI, **Les neumes, les notations bibliques et le chant protochrétien** [Neumes, Biblical notations, and proto-Christian chant] (3845); Cletus MADSEN, **Gregorian chant in the United States of America/Mouvement grégorien aux U.S.A.: Incertitudes et espoirs** (4729); Fernand MAILLET, **La Fédération Internationale des** Pueri cantores [The International Federation of Pueri cantores] (6294); Constant MARTIN, **Orgues électroniques d'hier et de demain** [Electronic organs of yesterday and tomorrow] (3670); Hubert MEYERS, **Problèmes actuels de facture d'orgue** [Current problems in organ building] (3433); Miguel Darío MIRANDA Y GÓMEZ, **La encíclica** Musicae sacrae disciplina/**L'encyclique** Musicae sacrae disciplina [The encyclical Musicae sacrae disciplina] (6306); Ernesto MONETA CAGLIO, **Stato attuale delle ricerche concernenti il** canto ambrosiano/**État actuel des recherches concernant le chant ambrosien** [The current state of research on Ambrosian chant] (1150); Xavier MORILLEAU, **Valeur pastorale du chant grégorien à la lumière des enseignements pontificaux** [The pastoral value of Gregorian chant in the light of papal teachings] (6311); Carl de NYS, **Une nouvelle collection de disques** Les archives sonores de la musique sacrée [A new record collection, Archives sonores de la musique sacrée] (5984); Jean OBAMA, **Enquête sur l'emploi de la musique indigène dans les chrétientés africaines** [Enquiry on the use of indigenous music in African Christianities] (6324) and **Les réussites du chant grégorien au Cameroun** [The successes of Gregorian chant in Cameroon] (6326); Johannes OVERATH, **Die** Associatio sub titulo S. Caeciliae pro universis germanicae linguae terris **als Typ einer Landesorganisation für Kirchenmusik /L'Association Sainte-Cécile des pays de langue germanique considérée comme type d'une organisation territoriale pour la musique sacrée** [The Allgemeiner Caecilienverein für Länder Deutscher Zunge as a model of territorial organizations for sacred music] (6330); René PAROISSIN, **Enquête sur la musique missionnaire en Extrême-Orient** [Enquiry on missionary music in the Far East] (6333) and **Musique d'Asie** [Asian music] (2672); Giuseppe PIZZARDO, **L'importance de l'enseignement de la musique dans les séminaires** [The importance of music instruction in seminaries] (4887); José Ignacio PRIETO ARRIZUBIETA, **Orientaciones de la música moderna religiosa en España/Orientations actuelles de la musique religieuse en Espagne** [The directions of modern religious music in Spain] (2234); Jean PRIM, **Hommage à Joseph Samson** [Tribute to Joseph Samson] (2376) and **L'enquête mondiale sur la musique sacrée dans les pays de mission** [Worldwide enquiry on sacred music in countries served by missionaries] (6345); Antoine REBOULOT, **L'organiste liturgique au XXᵉ siècle et sa formation** [Liturgical organists in the 20th century and their training] (4889); Aymon-Marie ROGUET, **Valeur pastorale de la musique sacrée** [The pastoral value of sacred music] (6358); Fiorenzo ROMITA, **I principi della legislazione musicale sacra secondo l'enciclica** Musicae sacrae disciplina/**Les principes de la législation de musique sacrée d'après l'encyclique** Musicae sacrae disciplina [The legislative principles of sacred music according to the encyclical Musicae sacrae disciplina] (6364); Gaston ROUSSEL, **Le rôle exemplaire des maîtrises de cathédrales** [The exemplary role of cathedral choir schools] (6368); Peter ROZING, **Vortrag über indonesische Musik/La musique en Indonésie** [Indonesian music] (6369); Joseph SAMSON, **Propositions sur la qualité** [Propositions on quality] (6372); Robert SASTRE, **Le sacré et la musique négro-africaine** [The sacred, and black African music] (6373); Jean-Pierre SCHMIT, **Une création de l'encyclique: Le responsable diocésain de la musique sacrée** [A creation of the encyclical: The diocesan director of sacred music] (6378); Joseph SMITS VAN WAESBERGHE, **L'état actuel des recherches scientifiques dans le domaine du chant grégorien** [The current state of scientific research in the field of Gregorian chant] (1178); Luigi Ferdinando TAGLIAVINI, **Le rôle liturgique de l'organiste des origines à l'époque classique** [The liturgical role of the organist, from the origins to the Classic era] (6396); Jules VYERMAN, **Le programme des instituts supérieurs de musique sacrée** [The program of tertiary institutions for sacred music] (4900); Egon WELLESZ, **The work done by the editors of** Monumenta musicae Byzantinae/**Les** Monumenta musicae Byzantinae: **Le travail des éditeurs** (3928); Eric WERNER, **Dead Sea scrolls contain musically revealing elements/Les manuscrits de la Mer Morte contiennent des signes intéressant la musique** (1047); Hellmuth Christian WOLFF, **Einige moderne Kompositionen des Ordinarium Missae/Quelques compositions modernes de l'Ordinarium missae** [Some modern settings of the Ordinary of the Mass] (6416). Includes a selected discography of sacred music based on a discography prepared by the Académie du Disque Français. Summaries of papers presented at the conference are cited as no. 378 in this volume.

380
bs
[Remscheid] Musische Jugend und technische Mittler [Youth in the arts and the technological media]. Proceedings of the Möglichkeiten Musisch-technischer Integration. Ed. by Jack BORNOFF and Jörn THIEL; foreword by Bruno TETZNER. Rundbrief 3 (Remscheid: Landesarbeitsgemeinschaft Jugendmusik Nordrhein-Westfalen, 1957) 188 p. Illus., port. In German.

The following contributions are cited separately: Arthur BUNKOWSKI, **Die Jugend und die Macht der Mittler: Bericht über einen Delegiertentag** [Youth and the power of the media: Report on a meeting of delegates] (2294); Gotho von IRMER, **Musik-Schulfunk: Gezielte**

Sendung [Music-educational radio: Targeted broadcasting] (4559); Wolfgang JÄGER, **Jugendfunk: Neue Formen und Ziele** [Youth radio: New forms and goals] (2330); Klaus JUNGK, **Musik und Film** [Music and film] (5177); Ernst KOSTER, **Sinn und Gefahr des Fernsehens für die Jugend** [The meaning and the danger of television for youth] (2334); Egon KRAUS, **Die technischen Mittler in der Westlichen Welt** [Technological media in the Western world] (4572); Adolf LENSING, **Jugend, Film und Bild: Zwischen Pädagogik und Kunst** [Youth, film, and image: Between pedagogy and art] (4586); Hans MERSMANN, **Muse und Technik** [Muse and technology] (2357); Herbert SCHERMALL, **Die Schallplatte: Ein modernes Bildungsmittel** [The record: A modern medium of education] (4641); Wolfgang STRICH, **Wege zu musischem Tun über die technischen Mittler** [Paths to artistic endeavor through the technological media] (4655); Jörn THIEL, **Jugend-, Volks- und Hausmusik im Rundfunk** [Youth music, traditional music, and Hausmusik on radio] (2400); Helmut WERKLE, **"Muse und Technik" aus der sicht der Evangelischen Akademie** [The Muse and technology from the point of view of the Evangelische Akademie] (2409); Johannes Gerhard WIESE, **Filmgestaltung als musische Erziehung** [Film production as arts education] (4796); Walter WIORA, **Musische Gaben in technischer Vermittlung** [Gifts of the arts mediated through technology] (2410); Adolf WULFF, **Musik im Schulfunk, Hilfe im Unterricht** [Music on educational radio, assistance in instruction] (4675).

381 **[Todi] Iacopone e il suo tempo** [Jacopone and his
bs time]. Sponsored by the Centro di Studi sulla Spiritualità Medievale. *Convegni del Centro di Studi sulla Spiritualità Medievale* 1 (Todi: Accademia Tudertina, 1959) 146 p. *Illus., facs., bibliog.* In Italian.
The conference was held from 13 through 15 October 1957. The following contributions are cited separately: Bianca BECHERINI, **La musica italiana dalla laude iacoponica alla laude fiorentina del XV secolo** [Italian music from the lauda of Jacopone to the Florentine lauda of the 15th century] (1061); Mario PERICOLI, **Lauda drammatica e dramma sacro a Todi** [The *lauda drammatica* and sacred drama in Todi] (5222).

382 **[Varaždin] Rad kongresa folklorista**
bs **Jugoslavije** [Proceedings of the congress of Yugoslav folklorists]. Proceedings of the fourth congress of the Savez Udruženja Folklorista Jugoslavije. Ed. by Vinko ŽGANEC (Zagreb: Savez Udruženja Folklorista Jugoslavije, 1959) 351 p. *Illus., transcr.* In Croatian, Slovene, Russian, German, French, and Serbian; summaries in German, French, Croatian, and English.
The following contributions are cited separately: Viktor Mihailovič BELJAEV, **Muzykal'nyj fol'klor narodov dunajskogo basseina** [The musical tradition of the peoples of the Danube basin] (2737); Soňa BURLASOVÁ, **Hudobný folklór Chorvátskeho Grobu a problematika etnických diaspor** [The musical tradition of the village of Chorvátsky Grob and the problematics of ethnic diaspora] (2753); Alberto Mario CIRESE, **O naricaljkama u hrvatskim mjestima pokrajine Molise u Italiji** [Funeral laments in the Croatian villages of Molise, Italy] (2768); Emilia COMIŞEL, **La ballade populaire roumaine** [The traditional Romanian ballad] (2776); Radoslav HROVATIN, **Muzikološka označba pesmi v folklori ob jugoslavensko-avstrijsko-mađarskem tromejniku** [Musicological characterization of song in the tradition of the area where Yugoslavia, Austria, and Hungary meet] (2862); Milica ILIJIN, **Međusobni uticaji narodnih igara raznih etničkih grupa u Prizrenu** [Mutual influences of the traditional dances of the different ethnic groups in Prizren] (4985); Lajos KISS, **Bitne značajke mađarskog muzičkog folklora** [The main characteristics of the Hungarian musical tradition] (4353); Jan RAUPP, **Die Beziehung der sorbischen Musikfolkore zu der des Donauraumes** [The relationship between the Sorb (Wendish) musical tradition and that of the Danube region] (3022); Onufrij TIMKO, **Punktirani ritmovi u muzičkom folkloru vojvođanskih rusina-ukrajinaca** [Punctuated rhythm in the traditional Ruthenian-Ukrainian music of Vojvodina] (3084); Valens VODUŠEK, **Petčetvrtinski takt u slovenskoj narodnoj muzici** [The 5/4 measure in traditional Slovenian music] (3106); Tihamér VUJICSICS, **Narodne pesme i igre jugoslovenskih manjina u Mađarskoj** [Traditional songs and dances of the South Slavic minorities in Hungary] (3108); Vinko ŽGANEC, **Muzički folklor naroda u panonskom bazenu** [Traditional music of the Pannonian basin] (3123).

383 **[Venice] Atti del II° Congresso internazionale**
bs **di storia del teatro** [Acts of the Second International Congress on Theater History]. Sponsored by the Centro Italiano di Richerche Teatrali and International Federation for Theatre Research. Ed. by Francesca ROSELLI and Carla Emilia TANFANI (Venezia: De Luca Storia, 1960) 378 p. *Illus., bibliog., index.* In Italian.
The following contributions are cited separately: Edward Joseph DENT, **La funzione della musica e della danza nel teatro contemporaneo** [The function of music and dance in contemporary theater] (5139); Margret DIETRICH, **La funzione della musica e della danza nel teatro contemporaneo** [The function of music and dance in contemporary theater] (5141); M.V. HEINLEIN, **La funzione della musica e della danza nel teatro contemporaneo** [The function of music and dance in contemporary theater] (5168); Luigi MAGNANI, **La funzione della musica e della danza nel teatro contemporaneo** [The function of music and dance in contemporary theater] (5202); Zeno VANCEA, **La funzione della musica e della danza nel teatro contemporaneo** [The function of music and dance in contemporary theater] (5263).

384 **[Venice] Studi goldoniani** [Goldoni studies]. Pro-
bs ceedings of the International Conference of Goldoni Studies; sponsored by the Comune di Venezia, Fondazione Giorgio Cini, and Istituto Veneto di Scienze, Lettere ed Arti. Ed. by Vittore BRANCA and Nicola MANGINI. *Civiltà veneziana: Studi* 6 (Venezia: Istituto per la Collaborazione Culturale, 1960) 2 v. xxiv, 1002 p. *Illus., port., bibliog., index.* In Italian and French.
The conference was held from 28 September through 1 October 1957. The following contributions are cited separately: Domenico DE' PAOLI, **Il librettista Carlo Goldoni e l'opera comica veneziana** [The librettist Carlo Goldoni and Venetian *opera comica*] (5132); Giovanni Battista DE SANCTIS, **Toni di opera buffa in alcune scene goldoniane** [Opera buffa tones in some scenes by Goldoni] (5133); Andrea DELLA CORTE, **Il libretto e l'influenza di Goldoni** [The libretto and the influence of Goldoni] (5136).

385 **[Washington, D.C.] Music skills.** Proceedings of
bs the workshop on music skills; sponsored by the Catholic University of America. Ed. by Richard H. WERDER (Washington, D.C.: Catholic University of America, 1958) vii, 109 p. *Music, bibliog., charts, diagr.*
The workshop was conducted from 14 through 25 June 1957. The following contributions are cited separately: George BORNOFF, **On developing a string program** (4686); Ernest E. HARRIS, **The music educator today and tomorrow** (4548) and **On conducting and instrumental materials** (3251); Cletus MADSEN, **General and specialized music in our Catholic schools** (4728); Sally MONSOUR, **On developing music reading skills in the elementary school** (4742) and **Some principles of the psychology of learning applied to the teaching of music in the elementary school** (4743); Joseph F. MYTYCH, **On teaching liturgical music in the high school** (4747) and **Singing: Its role and scope in general music** (4748); John B. PAUL, **On piano pedagogy** (4753) and **Principles of piano teaching** (4754); Rose Margaret VANDER ZANDEN, **A review of music education in America** (4792).

386 **[Wégimont] Les colloques de Wégimont. IV:**
bs **Le Baroque musical—Recueil d'études sur la musique du XVIIe siècle** [The Wégimont colloquia. IV: The musical Baroque—Collection of studies on 17th-century music]. Intro. by Suzanne CLERCX-LEJEUNE. *Bibliothèque de la Faculté de Philosophie et Lettres de l'Université de Liège* 171 (Paris: Belles Lettres, 1963) 288 p. In French, English, and German.
Proceedings of a conference held from 9 through 14 September 1957 in conjunction with the 1957 Nuits de septembre program, Liège, Du Baroque au Classique. The following contributions are cited separately: Suzanne CLERCX-LEJEUNE, **Le terme Baroque: Sa signification, son application à la musique** [The term Baroque: Its meaning, its application to music] (1509); Suzanne CLERCX-LEJEUNE *et al.*, **Résolutions** [Resolutions] (1510); Paul COLLAER, **Lyrisme Baroque et tradition populaire**

[Baroque lyricism and the popular culture] (1512); Claude FLAGEL, **Exposé sur la vielle à roue fait à l'occasion du Colloque de Wégimont 1957** [An account of a hurdy-gurdy built on the occasion of the Colloques de Wégimont 1957] (3570); Pierre FROIDEBISE, **Interprétation de la musique d'orgue et réalisation des gloses** [The interpretation of organ music and the realization of *glosas*] (3699); Macario Santiago KASTNER, **Le rôle des tablatures d'orgue au XVIᵉ siècle dans l'avènement du Baroque musical** [The role of 16th-century organ tablatures in the advent of the musical Baroque] (1356); Denise LAUNAY, **À propos d'une Messe de Charles d'Helfer: Le problème de l'exécution des Messes réputées *a cappella* en France, aux XVIIᵉ et XVIIIᵉ siècles** [On a Mass by Charles d'Helfer: The question of the performance of Masses known as *a cappella* in France in the 17th and 18th centuries] (3754); Élisabeth LEBEAU, **La musique des cérémonies célébrées à la mort de Marie-Thérèse, reine de France, 1683: Notes pour servir à la recherche des éléments Baroques dans la musique en France au XVIIᵉ siècle** [The music of the ceremonies held on the death of Marie-Thérèse, Queen of France, 1683: Notes in the service of research on Baroque elements in music in France in the 17th century] (1601); Günther MASSENKEIL, **Zur Frage der Dissonanzbehandlung in der Musik des 17. Jahrhunderts** [The treatment of dissonance in the music of the 17th century] (4197); Floris van der MUEREN, **Limites géographiques du Baroque** [Geographical limits of the Baroque] (1629); Miguel QUEROL GAVALDÁ, **La polyphonie religieuse espagnole au XVIIᵉ siècle** [Spanish sacred polyphony in the 17th century] (1651); Denis STEVENS, **L'interprétation de la musique de Claudio Monteverdi** [Performing the music of Claudio Monteverdi] (3771); Robert WANGERMÉE, **Principes d'interprétation** [Principles of interpretation] (3776); Robert Erich WOLF, **Renaissance, mannerism, Baroque: Three styles, three periods** (1713).

387
bs
[Weilheim/Teck] Richtlinien zum Schutze alter wertvoller Orgeln (Weilheimer Regulativ); Zugleich der kurzgefaßte Bericht über die Arbeitstagung der Orgeldenkmalpfleger [Guidelines for the protection of valuable old organs (Weilheim regulations); together with a summary report of the working meeting of organ conservators]. Proceedings of the Tagung der Orgeldenkmalpfleger in Weilheim/Teck; sponsored by the Vereinigung der Landesdenkmalpfleger in der Bundesrepublik Deutschland. Ed. by Walter SUPPER, Günther GRUNDMANN, and Wolfgang ZÖLLNER; afterword by Rudolf QUOIKA. *Veröffentlichungen der Gesellschaft der Orgelfreunde* 12 (Berlin: Merseburger, 1958) 40 p. *Index, charts, diagr., organ specification.* In German.

The conference was held from 23 through 27 April 1957. The following contributions are cited separately: Hans BÖHRINGER, **Denkmalorgel und Gottesdienst** [Historic organs and divine service] (3339); Günther GRUNDMAN, **Die Orgel: Ein wichtiges Anliegen der Denkmalpflege** [The organ: An important area of concern in cultural conservation] (3377); Wilibald GURLITT, **Der musikgeschichtliche Denkmalwert der alten Orgel** [The value of old organs as cultural monuments from the point of view of historical musicology] (3380); Walter QUOIKA, **Orgeldenkmalpflege in älterer und neuerer Zeit** [Organ conservation in earlier and more recent times] (3459); Rudolf REUTER, **Orgeldenmalpflege in Westfalen** [Conservation of historic organs in Westphalia] (3466); Walter SUPPER, **Der Ertrag der Orgeldenkmalpflege für den Orgelbau der Gegenwart** [Why the conservation of historic organs is valuable for contemporary organ building] (3484); Walter SUPPER and Wolfgang ZÖLLNER, ed., **Die Richtlinien zum Schutze alter wertvoller Orgeln (Weilheimer Regulativ) mit Erläuterungen** [Guidelines for the protection of valuable old organs (Weilheim Regulativ) with explanatory notes] (3493); Rudolf UTERMÖHLEN, **Drei Jahrzehnte Orgeldenkmalpflege in Hannover** [Three decades of organ conservation in Hanover] (3498); Werner WALCKER-MAYER, **Die Wiederherstellung eines Portativs** [The restoration of a portative organ] (3501).

1958

388
bs
[Aix-en-Provence] Actes et mémoires du IIᵉ Congrès international de langue et littérature

du Midi de la France [Proceedings and papers of the second International Congress of Language and Literature of the South of France] (Aix-en-Provence: Centre d'Études Provençales de la Faculté des Lettres, 1961) 448 p. *Bibliog.* In French.

The conference was held from 2 through 8 September 1958. The following contribution is cited separately: André PETIOT, **La musique chez les troubadours** [Music of the troubadours] (1157).

389
bs
[Brno] Leoš Janáček a soudobá hudba [Leoš Janáček and contemporary music]. Ed. by Jaroslav JIRÁNEK and Bohumil KARÁSEK; foreword by Ludvík KUNDERA. *Knižnice Hudebních Rozhledů* A:7 (Praha: Panton, 1963) 430 p. *Music.* In Czech, Russian, German, and Slovak; summaries in Russian and German.

The conference was held from 19 through 26 October 1958. The following contributions are cited separately: Andrej ANDREEV, **Leoš Janáček a Bulharsko** [Janáček and Bulgaria] (2279); Milena ČERNOHORSKÁ, **Význam nápěvků pro Janáčkovu operní tvorbu** [The significance of speech melodies in Janáček's operas] (4320); Osvald CHLUBNA, **Janáčkovy názory na operu a jeho úsilí o nový operní sloh** [Janáček's views on opera and his striving for a new operatic style] (4323); Pavel ECKSTEIN and Walter FELSENSTEIN, **O režijní koncepci a inscenačním slohu v Janáčkových operách** [The concept of direction and style of staging in Janáček's operas] (5145); Marius FLOTHUIS, **Der Widerhall von Janáčeks Musik in Holland und die Möglichkeiten das Interesse für sein Werk zu fördern/O ohlasu Janáčkovy hudby v Holandsku a o možnostech podporovat zájem o jeho dílo** [Reception of Janáček's music in the Netherlands and the possibilities of encouraging an interest in his work] (2320); Čeněk GARDAVSKÝ, **Janáček a psychologie hudební tvorby** [Janáček and the psychology of composition] (5658); Harry GOLDSCHMIDT, **Nochmals: Janáček und Strawinski—Diskussionsbeitrag/Ještě jednou: Janáček a Stravinskij—Diskusní příspěvek** [Once again: Janáček and Stravinsky—Contribution to discussion] (2171); Alois HÁBA, **Hudební sloh Janáčkův a jeho současníků** [The musical style of Janáček and his contemporaries] (4340) and **Janáčkovo pojetí harmonie** [Janáček's concept of harmony] (4175); Everett HELM, **Janáčkovo postavení ve vývoji novodobé hudby** [Janáček's place in the evolution of contemporary music] (2177); Jelena HOLEČKOVÁ-DOLANSKÁ, **K pěveckým problémům Janáčkových oper** [Problems of singing in Janáček's operas] (3793); Hans HOLLÄNDER, **Das monothematische Prinzip der Glagolitischen Messe/Monotematický princip Glagolské Mše** [The monothematic principle in the *Mša glagolskaja*] (4437); František HRABAL, **K otázce hudební tektoniky Výletu pana Broučka do XV. století** [The musical structure of *Výlet pana Broučka do XV. století*] (4258); Karel JANEČEK, **Stavba Janáčkových skladeb** [The structure of Janáček's compositions] (4347); Jaroslav JIRÁNEK, **K některým otázkám vztahu Leoše Janáčka k české a světové hudbě** [Questions on Janáček's relation to Czech and world music] (2185); Bohumil KARÁSEK, **Svět Janáčka dramatika: Rysy kritického realismu v jeho operním díle** [The world of Janáček the dramatist: Traits of critical realism in his operatic works] (5178); Siegfried KÖHLER, **Leoš Janáčeks Progressivität und der musikalische Modernismus in der westlichen Welt/Janáčkova pokrokovost a hudební modernismus v západním světě** [Leoš Janáček's progressiveness and musical modernism in the Western world] (4355); Ernst KRAUSE, **Über Versäumnisse der internationalen Musikkritik/O tom, co mezinárodní hudební kritika zmeškala** [What international music criticism omitted] (5512); Jozef KRESÁNEK, **Tonalita v primitívnej a ľudovej hudbe** [Tonality in primitive music and folk music] (4186); Ludvík KUNDERA, **K otázce interpretace Janáčkových děl** [On the interpretation of Janáček's works] (3794); Vladimír LÉBL, **Diskusní příspěvek k referátům o Janáčkově nápěvkové technice** [Remarks on the papers concerning Janáček's technique of speech melodies] (4360) and **Postavení osobnosti Leoše Janáčka v české hudební kultuře** [The place of Janáček's personality in Czech musical culture] (2197); Josef LOEWENBACH, **Dramatický princip Leoše Janáčka a M.P. Musorgského** [The dramatic principles of Janáček and Musorgskij] (4367); Jaroslav MARKL, **Janáčkova nápěvková teorie a český písňový typ instrumentální** [Janáček's speech melody theory and the instrumental type of Czech song] (4446); Paul MIES, **Skizzen, Fassungen und Ausgabentypen/Skici, verze a typy edic** [Sketches, versions, and types of editions] (3908); Jerzy MŁODZIEJOWSKI, **Janáčkova** hudba v Polsku [Janáček's music in Poland] (2360); Zdeněk NOVÁČEK, **Niektoré podmienky osobitosti u Janáčka, Orffa a Schönberga** [Some conditions of individuality in Janáček, Orff and Schoenberg] (2220); Mirko OČADLÍK, **Janáček a Stravinskij** [Janáček and Stravinsky] (2223); František PALA, **Mladý Janáček a divadlo: Janáčkův poměr k estetickým a etickým otázkám divadla před Šárkou** [The young Janáček and the theater: Janáček's view on aesthetic and ethical issues of theater before Šárka] (5220); Rudolf PEČMAN, **Symfonické dílo Leoše Janáčka v pojetí Břetislava Bakaly** [Janáček's symphonic works interpreted by Břetislav Bakala] (3796); Josef PLAVEC, **Janáčkova tvorba sborová** [Janáček's choral works] (2232); Jan RACEK, **Leoš Janáček a jeho postavení v české a světové hudební kultuře/Leoš Janaček i ego značenie dlja češskoj i mirovoj muzyki/Leoš Janáček und seine Bedeutung in der tschechischen und Welt-Musikkultur** [Janáček and his place in Czech and international musical culture] (2237); Cvjetko RIHTMAN, **O otázce nesoučasnosti přízvuku slova a přízvuku nápěvu v lidové hudbě** [Divergence in word stress and melodic stress in folk music] (4024); Karel RISINGER, **Problém konsonance a disonance v soudobé hudbě** [The problem of consonance and dissonance in contemporary music] (4212); Walter SERAUKY, **Vorläufer in der europäischen Musikgeschichte und Musikästhetik zu Janáčeks Sprachmelodie/Předchůdci Janáčkových "nápěvků" v evropských hudebních dějinách a hudební estetice** [The predecessors of Janáček's speech melodies in European history and aesthetics of music] (5594); Jaroslav SMOLKA, **Příspěvek k poznání vnitřního řádu Janáčkovy melodiky a tematické práce** [Recognition of the inner laws of Janáček's melodic and thematic development] (4382); Bohumír SOBĚSKÝ, **Několik poznámek k referátům o pěveckých problémech Janáčkových oper** [Remarks on the problems of performance in Janáček's operas] (5246); Leo SPIES, **Janáčeks Theorie der Sprachmelodie: Ein Instrument des Naturstudiums, nicht eine Kompositionsmethode/Janáčkova nápěvková teorie: Nástroj studia přírody, nikoliv kompoziční metoda** [Janáček's theory of speech melody as a tool of natural science, not a composition method] (5939); Bohumír ŠTĚDROŇ, **K inspiraci Janáčkových Listů důvěrných** [The inspiration of Janáček's Listy důvěrné] (2254) and **Lidové kořeny Její pastorkyně** [The folk roots of Její pastorkyňa (Jenůfa)] (4383); Theodora STRAKOVÁ, **K problematice Janáčkovy opery Osud** [Problems of Janáček's opera Osud (Fate)] (5251); Věra STŘELCOVÁ, **Několik poznámek k pěvecké interpretaci Janáčkova dramatického slohu** [Remarks on the singer's interpretation of Janáček's dramatic style] (3324); Antonín SYCHRA, **Vztah hudby a slova jako jeden z nejzávažnějších problémů Janáčkova slohu** [The relationship of word and music as one of the most important issues of Janáček's style] (4385); Jiří VÁLEK, **Konkrétnost zobrazení: Základ Janáčkova symfonismu posledního období** [Concrete depiction: The basis of Janáček's symphonism of his last period] (4389); Zeno VANCEA, **Janáček und die führenden Komponisten der südosteuropäischen Schulen: Bartók, Enescu, Kodály/Janáček a čelní skladatelé jihovýchodoevropských škol: Bartók, Enescu, Kodály** [Janáček and the leading composers of the southeastern European schools: Bartók, Enescu, Kodály] (2267); Karel VETTERL, **Otázky tvůrčího a reprodukčního stylu v lidové písni** [Questions of creative and reproductive styles in folk music] (3101); Jaroslav VOLEK, **Živelná dialektika a její klady i nedostatky v teoretických názorech Leoše Janáčka** [Essential dialectics, its pros and cons in Janáček's theoretical views] (3961); Jiří VYSLOUŽIL, **Janáček jako kritik** [Janáček as critic] (5622) and **Janáčkova tvorba ve světle jeho hudební folkloristické teorie** [Janáček's works in light of his theory of musical folklore] (4393); Miloš WASSERBAUER, **K režijnímu pojetí Janáčkových oper** [The director's conception of Janáček's operas] (5270); Albert WELLEK, **Fortschritte in der Theorie der Konsonanz und Dissonanz/Pokrok v teorii konsonance a disonance** [New findings in the theory of consonance and dissonance] (4225); Karl H. WÖRNER, **Katjas Tod: Die Schlußszene der Oper Katja Kabanowa von Leoš Janáček/Kátina smrt: Závěrečná scéna opery Káťa Kabanová Leoše Janáčka** [Káťa's Death: The final scene from the opera Káťa Kabanová by Leoš Janáček] (5273). A discussion of the reception of Janáček's works in Russia by I.V. NEST'EV in Russian and Czech is included (pp. 228-235).

390
bs
[Cologne] Bericht über den siebenten internationalen musikwissenschaftlichen Kongress [Report on the Seventh International Musicological Conference. Sponsored by the International Musicological Society. Ed. by Gerald ABRAHAM, Suzanne CLERCX-LEJEUNE, Hellmut FEDERHOFER,

and Wilhelm PFANNKUCH (Kassel: Bärenreiter, 1959) 366 p. *Illus., music, bibliog.* In German, French, and English.

The conference was held from 23 through 28 June 1958. The following contributions are cited separately: Putnam ALDRICH, **Obligatory improvisation of ornaments** (3726); Higini ANGLÈS, **Die zwei Arten der Mensuralnotation der Monodie des Mittelalters** [The two types of mensural notation used for the monody of the Middle Ages] (1056); Denis ARNOLD, **The influence of ornamentation on the structure of early 17th century church music** (1482); Eva BADURA-SKODA, **Zur Appoggiaturenfrage** [Concerning appoggiaturas] (3728); Arnold Adriaan BAKÉ, **Rhythmischer Kontrapunkt auf einer Rahmentrommel aus Ceylon** [Rhythmic counterpoint on a frame drum of Ceylon] (2606); Mehdi BARKECHLI, **Les rythmes caractéristiques de la musique iranienne** [The characteristic rhythms of Iranian music] (2607); Dénes BARTHA, **Zum Harmoniebegriff in der Musik Béla Bartóks: Ein Beitrag zur theoretischen Erfassung der neuen Musik** [The concept of harmony in the music of Béla Bartók: A contribution to the theory of new music] (4137); Bianca BECHERINI, **Communications sur Antonio Squarcialupi et notes au Cod. Med. Palatino 87** [Communications concerning Antonio Squarcialupi and notes on cod.med.Palatino 87] (1230); Heinz BECKER, **Arbeitsgemeinschaft: Klassifikation der Operngeschichte** [Working group: a classification scheme for opera history] (5100); Alfred BERNER, **Untersuchungsprobleme und Wertungsprinzipien an Musikinstrumenten der Vergangenheit** [Issues in investigating and evaluating musical instruments of the past] (3244); Walter BLANKENBURG, **Kanonimprovisationen im 16. und Anfang des 17. Jahrhunderts** [Canonic improvisations in the 16th and early 17th centuries] (4140); Wolfgang BOETTICHER, **Arbeitsgemeinschaft: Lauten- und Gitarrentabulaturen** [Working group: Lute and guitar tablatures] (523) and **Zum Spätstilproblem im Schaffen Orlando di Lassos** [The problem of a late style in Roland de Lassus] (4316); Fritz BOSE, **Rhythmusprobleme in instrumental begleiteter primitiver Musik** [Questions of the rhythm in instrumentally accompanied primitive music] (2494); David D. BOYDEN, **The violin and its technique: New horizons in research** (3733); Constantin BRĂILOIU, **Musicologie et ethnomusicologie aujourd'hui** [Musicology and ethnomusicology today] (865); Franz BRENN, **Ockeghems spiritueller Rhythmus** [Ockeghem's spiritual rhythm] (3974); Andres BRINER, **Wandlungen des Zeitempfindens im Harmoniebewusstsein** [Shifting temporal sensibility in harmonic consciousness] (3975); Marie BRIQUET, **Deux motets inédits de Montéclair (1667-1737)** [Two unpublished motets by Montéclair (1667-1737)] (1497); Luisa CERVELLI, **Italienische Musikinstrumente in der Praxis des Generalbassspiels: Das Arpichord** [Italian music instruments in the practice of continuo playing: The arpicord] (3509); Jacques CHAILLEY, **Arbeitsgemeinschaft: La révision de la notion traditionelle de tonalité** [Working group: Revising the traditional notion of tonality] (4057) and **Philologie musicale: Principes et premiers résultats** [The philology of music: Principles and first results] (3934); Dieter CHRISTENSEN, **Heterogene Musikstile in dem Dorf Gabela (Herzegowina)** [Heterogenous musical styles in the village of Gabela (Herzegovina)] (4326); Gerhard CROLL, **Zur Vorgeschichte der "Mannheimer"** [The prehistory of the "Mannheimers"] (1514); Dragotin CVETKO, **Ein unbekanntes Inventarium librorum musicalium aus Jahre 1620** [An unknown *Inventarium librorum musicalium* from the year 1620] (1517); Miljenko M. DABO-PERANIĆ, **Le sens de l'harmonie chez les Grecs** [What harmony meant to the Greeks] (1027); Carl DAHLHAUS, **Über den Dissonanzbegriff des Mittelalters** [Concerning the medieval concept of dissonance] (4157); Stana DJURIĆ-KLAJN, **Correspondance inédite de Johannes Brahms** [Unpublished correspondence of Johannes Brahms] (1946); Vincent H. DUCKLES, **The lyrics of John Donne as set by his contemporaries** (5307); Hans Heinrich EGGEBRECHT, **"Diaphonia vulgariter organum"** (1083); Hans ENGEL, **Werden und Wesen des Madrigals** [The madrigal: Evolution and essence] (1296); Christiane ENGELBRECHT, **Die Psalmsätze des Jenaer Chorbuches 34** [Psalm settings in the Jena choirbook 34] (1297); Georg FEDER, **Arbeitsgemeinschaft: Editionsprobleme des späten 18. Jahrhunderts** [Working group: Editorial problems with reference to the late 18th century] (3893); Vladimir FÉDOROV, **B.V. Asaf'ev et la musicologie russe avant et après 1917** [B.V. Asaf'ev and Russian musicology before and after 1917] (872); Arnold FEIL, **Arbeitsgemeinschaft: Die Tradition des "Altrömischen" und des Gregorianischen Chorals** [Working group: The tradition of so-called Old Roman and of Gregorian chant] (1091); Laurence FEININGER, **Raum und Architektur in der vielchörigen römischen Kirchenmusik des 17. Jahrhunderts** [Space and architecture in the polychoral church music of the 17th century] (5813); Marilyn

FELLER, **The new style of Guilio Caccini, member of the Florentine Camerata** (1546); Ernest Thomas FERAND, **Zum Begriff der "compositio" im 15. und 16. Jahrhundert** [The concept of "compositio" during the 15th and 16th centuries] (1306); Kurt von FISCHER, **Neues zur Passionskomposition des 16. Jahrhunderts** [New information on Passion compositions of the 16th century] (1308); Madeleine GARROS, **Les motets à voix seule de Guillaume Gabriel Nivers** [The motets for solo voice by Guillaume Gabriel Nivers] (1556); Karl GEIRINGER, **Unbekannte Werke von Nachkommen J.S. Bachs in amerikanischen Sammlungen** [Unknown works by descendants of J.S. Bach in American collections] (1557); Walter GERSTENBERG, **Grundfragen der Rhythmusforschung** [Basic questions in the study of rhythm] (3994); Harry GOLDSCHMIDT, **Zu einer Neubewertung von Schuberts letzter Schaffenszeit** [Towards a reassessment of Schubert's final creative period] (1974); Kurt GUDEWILL, **Melchior Franck und das geistliche Konzert** [Melchior Franck and the spiritual concerto] (1566); Eta HARICH-SCHNEIDER, **Ein Beitrag zur Quellenkunde Japanischer Musik** [A contribution to the study of Japanese musical sources] (2633); Glen HAYDON, **The Lateran Codex 61** (1328); Hallgrímur HELGASON, **Das Bauerorganum auf Island** [Iceland farmers' organum] (2852); Siegfried HERMELINK, **Zur Geschichte der Kadenz im 16. Jahrhundert** [The history of the cadence during the 16th century] (4177); Eduard HERZOG, **Harmonie und Tonart bei Janáček** [Harmony and key in Janáček] (4179); Hans HICKMANN, **Arbeitsgemeinschaft: Musikalische Stratigraphie Afrikas** [Working group: Musical stratigraphy of Africa] (2554); Lothar HOFFMANN-ERBRECHT, **Neue Dokumente zum Leben Thomas Stoltzers** [New documents concerning the life of Thomas Stoltzer] (1337); Helmut HUCKE, **Zum Problem des Rhythmus im Gregorianischen Gesang** [The problem of rhythm in Gregorian chant] (4003); Heinrich HÜSCHEN, **Der Harmoniebegriff im Musikschrifttum des Altertums und des Mittelalters** [The concept of harmony in the writings on music of antiquity and the Middle Ages] (4181); Jaroslav JIRÁNEK, **Der Beitrag Zdeněk Nejedlýs zur Erforschung des Hussitischen Gesanges** [Zdeněk Nejedlý's contribution to research on Hussite song] (1349); Georg KARSTÄDT, **Neue Ergebnisse zur Buxtehude-Forschung** [New results in Buxtehude research] (1584); Alexander Hyatt KING, **Arbeitsgemeinschaft: Composer and publisher 1500-1850** [Working group: Composer and publisher, 1500-1850] (5973); Percival R. KIRBY, **Physical phenomena which appear to have determined the bases and development of an harmonic sense among Bushmen, Hottentot and Bantu, as I have observed them in southern Africa** (4184); Ernst KLUSEN, **Gregorianischer Choral und frühprotestantisches Kirchenlied: Neue Gesichtspunkte zur Beurteilung ihrer gegenseitigen Beziehungen** [Gregorian chant and early Protestant hymns: New viewpoints on assessing their mutual relations] (1359); Georg KNEPLER, **Über einige geistige Schwierigkeiten der Musikforschung von heute** [Some intellectual difficulties in today's musicological research] (889); Karl-Heinz KÖHLER, **Zwei Grundtypen historischer Musiksammlungen** [Two basic types of historic music collection] (603); Walter KOLNEDER, **Arbeitsgemeinschaft: Dynamik und Agogik in der Musik des Barock** [Working group: Dynamics and agogics in music of the Baroque] (3749); Günther KRAFT, **Thüringisch-sächsische Quellen zur musikphysiologischen Forschung des 17. und 18. Jahrhunderts** [Thuringian and Saxon sources for research in music physiology in the 17th and 18th centuries] (5412); Franz KRAUTWURST, **Grundsätzliches zu einer Filiation geistlicher Musikhandschriften der Reformationszeit** [Basic principles in the filiation of manuscripts of religious music in the Reformation period] (1360); Erwin KROLL, **Die Musikkritiken E.T.A. Hoffmanns** [The music criticism of E.T.A. Hoffmann] (5515); Hans KRÜGER, **Die Verstimmung (scordatura, discordatura) auf Saiten-Instrumenten in Beziehung zur klanglichen Einrichtung der Instrumente und zum Tonsystem und ihre Folgen auf die Aufführungspraxis** [The alternate tuning (scordatura, discordatura) of string instruments in relation to the instruments' acoustic disposition and to the tonal system, and its consequences for performance practice] (3585); Fritz A. KUTTNER, **A "Pythagorean" tone-system in China antedating the early Greek achievements by several centuries** (4087); Jan LARUE, **Harmonic rhythm as an indicator of rhythmic function** (4359); René Bernard LENAERTS, **Improvisation auf der Orgel und der Laute in den Niederlanden (16. und 17. Jahrhundert)** [Improvisation on organ and lute in the Netherlands (16th and 17th centuries)] (3706); Walther LIPPHARDT, **Ein unbekannter karolingischer Tonar und seine Bedeutung für die fränkische Choralüberlieferung** [An unknown Carolingian tonary and its significance for Frankish chant transmission] (1143); Zofia LISSA, **Die Kategorie des Komischen in der Musik** [The category of the comical in music] (5524); Bo LUNDGREN, **Johan Lorentz in**

Kopenhagen: **Organista nulli in Europa secundus** [Johann Lorentz in Copenhagen: *Organista nulli in Europa secundus*] (1615); Franz Jochen MACHATIUS, **Die Tempo-Charaktere** [The tempo characters] (4011); Eric David MACKERNESS, **Mendelssohn and *Charles Auchester*** (2033); Günther MASSENKEIL, **Bemerkungen zum *Compendium musicae* (1618) des René Descartes** [Remarks on René Descartes's *Compendium musicae* (1618)] (5535); René MÉNARD, **Le problème de la mémorisation en musique copte garant de fidélité à la tradition** [The problem of memorization in Coptic music as a guarantee of fidelity to tradition] (6122); Paul MIES, **Die Quellen des op. 61 von Ludwig van Beethoven** [Sources for Ludwig van Beethoven's op. 61] (1813); Francis MULLER, **La technique de la réalisation variée dans la Tablature de Goerlitz (1650) de Samuel Scheidt** [Varied realization technique in Samuel Scheidt's Görlitz tablature (1650)] (4202); Joseph MÜLLER-BLATTAU, **Zur vokalen Improvisation im 16. Jahrhundert** [Vocal improvisation in the 16th century] (3709); Kathleen MUNRO, **Haydn's keyboard arrangement of symphony no. 96 in D** (1822); Giorgio NATALETTI, **Dix ans d'ethno-musicologie en Italie** [Ten years of enthnomusicology in Italy] (2450); Gerhard NESTLER, **Der Rhythmus in der Reihentechnik der Gegenwart** [Rhythm in contemporary serial technique] (4017); Bruno NETTL, **Some historical aspects of ethnomusicology** (2454); Francesco Yosio NOMURA, **Gegenwärtige Probleme der Musikwissenschaft in Japan** [Present-day problems of musicology in Japan] (2367); Frits NOSKE, **Joannes Tollius: Ein niederländische Meister des Frühbarock** [Jan Tollius: A Netherlandish master of the early Baroque] (1638); Irmgard OTTO, **Die instrumentenkundliche Auswertung der deutschen Lexika des 18. Jahrhunderts** [Assessing the discussion of instruments in German lexicons of the 18th century] (3266); Richard PETZOLDT, **Zur sozialen Stellung des Musikers im 17. Jahrhundert** [The social position of the musician in the 17th century] (1643); Hermann PFROGNER, **Zur Definition des Begriffes Atonalität** [The definition of the concept atonality] (4207); Dragan PLAMENAC, **German polyphonic lieder of the 15th century in a little-known manuscript** (1406); Jan RACEK, **Drei unbekannte Autographentorsen W.A. Mozarts** [Three unknown autograph fragments by W.A. Mozart] (1842); Félix RAUGEL, **Saint-Césaire, précepteur du chant gallican** [St. Caesarius, preceptor of Gallican chant] (1166); Gilbert REANEY, **A note on conductus rhythm** (3712); Wolfgang REHM, **Über ein Repertorium der Musik: Anregungen und Vorschläge zu einem neuen Nachschlagewerk** [A repertoire of music: Proposals and suggestions for a new reference work] (658); Hans-Peter REINECKE, **Zum Problem des Hören von Zusammenklängen und Klangfarben im Hinblick auf die akustische Funktion des Ohres** [The problem of hearing simultaneous sounds and sound colors in light of the acoustic functioning of the ear] (5691); Kurt REINHARD, **Eine von der rhythmischen Belebung abhängige Tempobezeichnung** [A system of tempo designations based on rhythmic animation] (4021); Jens ROHWER, **Der Sonanzfaktor im Aufbau von Tonsystemen** [The *Sonanz* factor in the structure of tonal systems] (4213); Walter H. RUBSAMEN, ***The jovial crew*: History of a ballad opera** (5234); Walter SALMEN, **Arbeitsgemeinschaft: Der Musiker in der mittelalterlichen Gesellschaft** [Working group: The musician in medieval society] (1171); Hans Peter SCHANZLIN, **Zur Geschichte der Litanei im 17. Jahrhundert** [Toward a history of the litany in the 17th century] (1669); Hans SCHMID, **Die Kölner Handschrift der *Musica enchiriadis*** [The Cologne manuscript of the *Musica enchiriadis*] (3916); Marius SCHNEIDER, **Arbeitsgemeinschaft: Der Terminus Variation** [Working group: The term *variation*] (4285) and **Prolegomena zu einer Theorie des Rhythmus** [Prolegomena to a theory of rhythm] (4028); Walter SERAUKY, **Zur Neuinterpretation von Richard Wagners Werk** [Toward a reinterpretation of Richard Wagner's work] (5241); Walther SIEGMUND-SCHULTZE, **Probleme der Verdi-Oper** [Problems of Verdian opera] (5244); Joseph SMITS VAN WAESBERGHE, **Zur ursprünglichen Vortragsweise der Prosulen, Sequenzen und Organa** [The original performance style of prosulae, sequences, and organa] (3716); Søren SØRENSEN, **Eine Kantaten-Jahrgang von Christian Ludwig Boxberg (1670-1729)** [A cantata cycle by Christian Ludwig Boxberg (1670-1729)] (1689); Rudolf STEGLICH, **Über die Synkope** [On syncopation] (4031); Fritz STEIN, **Zum Problem der "Jenaer Symphonie"** [The problem of the so-called Jena symphony] (1869); Rudolf STEPHAN, **Zur Cantio-Rhythmik** [Cantio rhythm] (4033); Jan STĘSZEWSKI, **Einige charakteristische Merkmale der Kurpischen Volksmusik** [Some characteristic features of the traditional music of Kurpie] (3067); Denis STEVENS, **Ornamention in Monteverdi's shorter dramatic works** (3772); Antonín SYCHRA, **Das Problem des Rhythmus im Lichte der Beziehungen von Musik und Wort** [The problem of rhythm in light of the relations between music and word] (4035); Bence SZABOLCSI, **Über Form und Improvisation in der Kunst- und Volksmusik** [Form and improvisation in art and traditional music] (3684); Willy TAPPOLET, **Einige prinzipielle Bemerkungen zur Frage der Improvisation** [Initial remarks on the question of improvisation] (3686); Jan van der VEEN, **Problèmes structuraux chez Maurice Ravel** [Structural problems in the works of Maurice Ravel] (4390); Walther VETTER, **Antike Polyphonie?** [Ancient polyphony?] (1046); Ernst Ludwig WAELTNER, **Die *Musica disciplina* des Aurelianus Reomensis** [The *Musica disciplina* of Aurelian of Réôme] (3962); Fritz WINCKEL, **Rekonstruktion historischer Klangstile unter dem Gesichtspunkt von Architektur und Raumakustik** [The reconstruction of historic sonority styles from the standpoint of architecture and room acoustics] (5859); Emanuel WINTERNITZ, **Quattrocento-Intarsien als Quellen der Instrumentengeschichte** [Intarsias of the 15th century as sources for the history of instruments] (5404); Aristide WIRSTA, **Théodore Akimenko: Représentant de l'impressionisme de l'Europe de l'Est** [Fedir Akymenko: A representative of Eastern European impressionism] (2271); Hellmuth Christian WOLFF, **Orientalische Einflüsse in den Improvisationen des 16. und 17. Jahrhunderts** [Asian influences in improvisations of the 16th and 17th centuries] (3724); Karl H. WÖRNER, **Harmoniebewußtsein und Symbolwandel in Schönbergs Oper *Moses und Aron*** [Harmonic consciousness and transformation of symbols in Schoenberg's opera *Moses und Aron*] (4226); Walther WÜNSCH, **Zur Frage der Mehrstimmigkeit des alpenländischen Volksliedes (Steirische Landschaft)** [The question of polyphony in the Alpine traditional song (Styria)] (3121); Percy M. YOUNG, **Some aspects of Handelian research** (5274); Jaroslav ZICH, **Agogische Prinzipe der Wiedergabe** [Agogic principles of performance] (3688); Franklin B. ZIMMERMAN, **Advanced tonal design in the part-songs of William Byrd** (4228).

391 **[Jerusalem] Qybŵṣ galŵyŵt b̲emŵsiqah datyt**
bs [The ingathering of the exiles in sacred music]. Proceedings of the First Israeli Music Congress, *Dŵkan* I (1959). In Hebrew.

The following contributions are cited separately: Mordekay B̲RŴY'ER, **Mŵsiqah datyt b̲etqŵpat qyb̲ŵs galŵyŵt** [Religious music at the time of the ingathering of the exiles] (2610); Me'yr Šim'ŵn GEŠWRY, **Hangŵyn haḥasydy** [The Hasidic nigun] (6059); Leyyb̲ GL'ANṢ, **'Al ḥynŵḥ ḥazanym** [On the training of hazanim] (4876); 'Ezr'a Ṣyŵn MELAMED, **Dbarym 'aḥdym 'al hatpylah b̲esibŵr** [Some thought on congregational prayer] (6078); Yeḥŵšu'a Leyyb̲ NE'EMAN, **'Al ḥynŵḥ ḥazanym** [On the training of hazanim] (4885).

392 **[Liège] International Folk Music Council**
bs **Conference.** Ed. by Maud KARPELES, *Journal of the International Folk Music Council* XI (1959) 7–89. *Music, transcr., dance notation.* In English and French.

The 11th annual conference was held from 28 July through 2 August 1958. The following contributions are cited separately: William R. BASCOM, **The main problems of stability and change in tradition** (2422); Br. BASIL, **A course of study for Bantu musicians** (4489); Fritz BOSE, **Western influences in modern Asian music** (2291); Diego CARPITELLA, **Considérations sur le folklore musical italien dans ses rapports avec la structure sociale du pays** [Thoughts on the relationship between traditional music and social structure in Italy] (2757); Hermann Josef DAHMEN, **Folk music and light music** (2784); Miklós GRABÓCZ, **Folk music developments in the Hungarian radio** (2837); Eta HARICH-SCHNEIDER, **The last remnants of a mendicant musicians' guild: The goze in northern Honshu (Japan)** (2635); Felix HOERBURGER, **The study of folk dance and the need for a uniform method of notation** (4981); Percival R. KIRBY, **The use of European musical techniques by the non-European peoples of southern Africa** (2003); Albrecht KNUST, **An introduction to Kinetography Laban (Labanotation)** (5004); Juana de LABAN, **Rhythm and tempo in dance notation** (5012); Leo LEVI, **Residus grégoriens et byzantins dans le chant des juifs d'Europe occidentale** [Gregorian and Byzantine residues in Western European Jewish song] (2929); Jean-Noël MAQUET, **La tradition du yodel au sud-ouest du Congo belge** [The tradition of yodeling in the southeastern Belgian Congo] (2598); Suiho MATSUMIYA, **Traditional music and dance in Japan today: Its stability and evolution** (2663); Elizabeth MAY, **Japanese children's folk songs before and after contact with the West** (2664); Atta Annan MENSAH, **Problems involved in the arrangement of folk music for Radio Ghana** (2561); Alan P. MERRIAM, **Characteristics of African music** (2562); Tom NABETA,

The place of a music school in Uganda (4835); Giorgio NATALETTI, **Ten years of folk music collecting by the Centro Nazionale Studi di Musica Popolare** (2451); Joseph Hanson Kwabena NKETIA, **Changing traditions of folk music in Ghana** (2566); David RYCROFT, **African music in Johannesburg: African and non-African features** (2581); Winfried SCHRAMMEK, **Birch leaf blowing (Birkenblattblasen)** (3636); Barbara Barnard SMITH, **Folk music in Hawaii** (3230); Josip STOJANOVIĆ, **Some methods applied to broadcasting folk music at the Yugoslav broadcasting stations: Genuine musical folklore and reconstructions** (3074); Mária SZENTPÁL, **Kinetography in the comparative study of folk dance in Hungary** (5073); Hugh TRACEY, **African music within its social setting** (2591); Gerrit Dirk VAN WENGEN, **The study of Creole folk music in Surinam** (3222).

393 **[Marseilles] Acoustique musicale** [Musical
bs acoustics]. Intro. by François CANAC. *Colloques internationaux du CNRS* 84 (Paris: Centre National de la Recherche Scientifique [CNRS], 1959) 259 p. *Illus., music, bibliog., charts, diagr.* In French.

The conference was held from 27 through 29 May 1958. The following contributions are cited separately: Mehdi BARKECHLI, **L'évolution de la gamme dans la musique orientale** [The evolution of the scale in Eastern music] (4048) and **Quelques idées nouvelles sur la consonance** [Some new ideas on consonance] (4135); Benjamin BLADIER, **Contribution à l'étude du violoncelle** [Contribution to the study of the violoncello] (3551); Jacques BRILLOUIN, **Réflexions sur les problèmes dits d'acoustique musicale** [Reflections on the so-called problems of musical acoustics] (5644); Zéphyrin CARRIÈRE, **Entretien d'un tuyau à anche libre** [Examination of a free-reed pipe] (3555); Jacques CHAILLEY, **Le dynamisme des gammes et des accords dans les principaux systèmes acoustiques et son influence sur le développement de la musique** [The dynamism of scales and chords in the principal acoustic systems, and its influence on the development of music] (4058) and **Le problème de l'harmonique 7 devant l'histoire musicale** [The problem of the seventh partial in the face of music history] (4060); Robert DUSSAUT, **Proposition de quelques réformes en théorie acoustico-musicale** [A proposal for some reforms in the theory of musical acoustics] (4068); Adriaan Daniël FOKKER, **Les cinquièmes de ton: Les subtilités des lignes mélodiques et l'enrichissement des harmonies** [Fifth-tones: The subtleties of the melodic lines and the enrichment of harmonies] (4073); Martin GRÜTZMACHER, **Le spectre d'un son de cloche** [The sound spectrum of a bell] (3650); J. GUITTARD, **Calculs et mesures d'impédances acoustiques** [The calculation and measurement of acoustic impedances] (5822); Raoul HUSSON, **La physique du pavillon pharyngo-buccal dans la phonation** [Physics of the pharyngo-buccal cavity in the phonation process] (3308); Joseph KREPS, **Les synthèses sonores de l'orgue à tuyaux** [The sound syntheses of the pipe organ] (3406); Werner LOTTERMOSER, **L'examen acoustique des violons dans la Physikalisch-Technische Bundesanstalt** [The acoustic examination of violins in the Physikalisch-Technische Bundesanstalt] (3589); J. MERCIER, **Étude de la stabilité des oscillations entretenues dans un tuyau sonore couplé à un tuyau mort** [Study of the stability of oscillations maintained in a resonant tube coupled to an inert tube] (5840); Léonid PIMONOW, **La détermination de la qualité des instruments de musique au moyen du spectre sonore transitoire** [The determination of instrument quality by means of the transient sound spectrum] (3269); Edward Gick RICHARDSON, **L'acoustique des cors et des trompes** [The acoustics of horns and trumpets] (3634); P. RIÉTY, **Le vocabulaire d'acoustique musicale d'après la formation du langage musical** [The terminology of musical acoustics, from the standpoint of the formation of musical language] (5417); Andrej Vladimirovič RIMSKIJ-KORSAKOV, **Les recherches sur le timbre des violons et guitares et sur l'excitation des vibrations d'une anche d'harmonium** [Research on the timbre of violins and guitars and on stimulating the vibrations of a harmonium reed] (3600); Robert TANNER, **Le problème des rapports simples: Notion de psycharithme** [The problem of simple ratios: The notion of psycharithm] (5710) and **Le rôle de la fusion dans l'appréciation de justesse des accords** [The role played by fusion in the perception of the justness of chords] (5711); Tamás TARNÓCZY, **Recherches sur le spectre de l'orgue en faisant sonner plusieurs touches à la fois** [Research on the spectrum of the organ when several keys are played simultaneously] (3494); Fritz WINCKEL, **Influence des facteurs psycho-physiologiques sur la sensation de consonance-dissonance** [The influence of psychophysiological factors on the perception of consonance and dissonance] (5721); Robert William YOUNG, **Sur l'intonation de divers instruments de musique,** du U.S. Navy Electronics Laboratory, San Diego 52, California [The intonation of various musical instruments from the U.S. Navy Electronics Laboratory, San Diego 52, California] (3286).

394 [Mexico City] **Miscellanea Paul Rivet**
bs **octogenario dicata** [Miscellany dedicated to Paul Rivet on his eightieth birthday]. Proceedings of the 31st International Congress of Americanists. *Publicaciones del Instituto de Historia* 1:50 (México, D.F.: Universidad Nacional Autónoma de México, 1958) 2 v. *Illus., port., bibliog., transcr., maps.* In Spanish, French, English, German, Italian, and Portuguese.

The following contributions are cited separately: Marius BARBEAU, **Migrations Sibériennes en Amérique** [Siberian migrations in America] (3138); Paulo de CARVALHO NETO, **La rúa: Una danza dramática de moros y cristianos en el folklore paraguayo** [The rúa: A dance-drama of Moors and Christians in Paraguayan folklore] (4946); Melville J. HERSKOVITS, **Some economic aspects of the Afrobahian Candomblé** (6458); Vicente Teódulo MENDOZA, **El ritmo de los cantares mexicanos recolectados por Sahagún** [The rhythm of the Mexican songs collected by Sahagún] (3209).

395 [Munich] **Diskussionsbeiträge zum XI.**
bs **internationalen Byzantinistenkongress** [Report of the discussions at the 11th International Byzantine Congress]. Ed. by Franz Joseph DÖLGER and Hans-Georg BECK (München: Beck, 1961) 105 p.; (reprint, Nendeln: Kraus, 1978). In German.

The following contribution is cited separately: Thrasybulos Georges GEORGIADES, moderator, **Byzantinisches in der Karolingischen Musik** [Byzantine elements in Carolingian music] (1106).

396 [Nuremberg] **Volkskunde-Kongreß: Vorträge**
bs **und Berichte** [Folklore congress: Lectures and reports]. Proceedings of the 11th Deutscher Volkskundetag; sponsored by the Verband der Vereine für Volkskunde. Ed. by Friedrich Heinz SCHMIDT-EBHAUSEN (Stuttgart: Kohlhammer, 1959) 81 p. *Zeitschrift für Volkskunde* (supplement 1959) 81. *Bibliog.* In German.

The following contributions are cited separately: Johannes KÜNZIG, **Authentische Volkslieder auf Schallplatten: Proben aus dem Ton-Bild-Buch** *Ehe sie verklingen...* [Authentic traditional song on record: The test case of the record–illustrated book set *Ehe sie verklingen...*] (5974); Erich SEEMANN, **Das Deutsche Volksliedarchiv und seine Arbeiten: Proben aus einer neuen Schallplattenreihe—*Ältere deutsche Volkslieder in mündlicher Überlieferung*** [The Deutsches Volksliedarchiv and its work: The test case of a new series of recordings—*Ältere deutsche Volkslieder in mündlicher Überlieferung*] (3055).

397 [Paris; Royaumont] **Les théâtres d'Asie** [Asian
bs theatrical genres]. Sponsored by the Centre National de la Recherche Scientifique (CNRS), Groupe de Recherches sur le Théâtre. Ed. by Jean JACQUOT. *Le chœur des muses* (Paris: Centre National de la Recherche Scientifique [CNRS], 1961) viii, 308 p. *Illus., music, bibliog.* In French.

Lectures and essays presented at the Conférences du Théâtre des Nations, Paris, in 1958 and 1959; and at the Journées d'Études de Royaumont, from 28 May through 1 June 1959, Abbaye de Royaumont. The following contributions are cited separately: Jean JACQUOT, **Craig, Yeats et le théâtre d'Orient** [Craig, Yeats, and Asian theater] (5174); Hiao-Ts'iun MA, **Le théâtre de Pékin** [The theater of Beijing] (5200); Gaston RENONDEAU, **L'influence bouddhique sur les Nô** [Buddhist influence on noh] (5231); René SIEFFERT, **Le théâtre japonais** [The Japanese theater] (5243); Van Khê TRÂN, **Le théâtre vietnamien** [Vietnamese theater] (5260); André TRAVERT, **Caractères originaux et évolution actuelle du théâtre pékinoise** [Original character and current evolution of the Beijing theater] (5262).

398 [San José] **Actas del XXXIIIº Congreso**
bs **Internacional de Americanistas** [Proceedings of the 33rd International Congress of Americanists] (San José: Lehmann, 1959) 3 v. In Spanish and English.

The conference was held from 20 through 27 July 1958 in San José, Costa Rica. The following contributions are cited separately: Isabel ARETZ, **Un planteamiento de origenes: El maremare como expresión musical y coreográfica** [Tracing origins: The maremare as musical and choreographic expression] (3190); Alan P. MERRIAM and Robert F.G. SPIER, **Chukchansi Yokuts songs** (3168); Luis Felipe RAMÓN Y RIVERA, **Problemas de la grabación y transcripción musical de los tambores** [Problems in the recording and musical transcription of drums] (2462) and **Supervivencia de la polifonía popular en Venezuela** [The survival of traditional polyphony in Venezuela] (3216); Marjorie B. SMITH, **Progress report on the study of African influences in the music of Panama** (5065).

399 [Todi] **Spiritualità cluniacense** [Cluniac spiritualbs ity] *Convegni del Centro di Studi sulla Spiritualità Medievale* 2 (Todi: Accademia Tudertina, 1960) 349 p. *Illus., bibliog., index.* In Italian.

The conference was held from 12 through 15 October 1958. The following contribution is cited separately: Philibert SCHMITZ, **La liturgie de Cluny** [The liturgy of Cluny] (6382).

400 [Washington, D.C.] **Symposium on Cherokee**
bs **and Iroquois culture.** Sponsored by the American Anthropological Association. Ed. by William N. FENTON and John GULICK. *Bureau of American Ethnology Bulletin* 180 (Washington, D.C.: United States Government Printing Office, 1961) vi, 292 p. *Bibliog.*

The symposium was held on 20 November 1958. The following contributions are cited separately: Gertrude Prokosch KURATH, **Effects of environment on Cherokee-Iroquois ceremonialism, music, and dance** (3160); William C. STURTEVANT, **Comment on Gertrude P. Kurath's** *Effects of environment on Cherokee-Iroquois ceremonialism, music, and dance* (3178).

401 [Wégimont] **Les colloques de Wégimont. IV:**
bs **Ethnomusicologie III** [The Wégimont colloquia. IV: Ethnomusicology III]. Sponsored by the Cercle International d'Études Ethno-musicologiques. Ed. by Paul COLLAER. *Bibliothèque de la Faculté de Philosophie et Lettres de l'Université de Liège* 172 (Paris: Belles Lettres, 1964) 277 p. *Illus., music, discog.* In French, German, English, and Italian.

The conferences were held from 7 through 12 September 1958 and from 7 through 10 September 1960. The following contributions are cited separately: Jacques CHAILLEY, **Ethnomusicologie et harmonie classique** [Ethnomusicology and classical harmony] (4150); Paul COLLAER, **Contributions à la méthode scientifique en ethnomusicologie** [Contributions to scientific method in ethnomusicology] (2428) and **Stratigraphie musicale et structures mélodiques** [Musical stratigraphy and melodic structures] (4062); Emilia COMIŞEL, **La musique de la ballade populaire roumaine** [The music of the traditional Romanian ballad] (2779); Zygmunt ESTREICHER, **Le rythme des Peuls Bororo** [The rhythm of the Bororro Fulße people] (3988); Yvette GRIMAUD, **Étude analytique de la danse** *choma* **des Bochiman !Kung** [Analytical study of the *choma* dance of the !Kung San people] (4973); Giorgio NATALETTI, **Alcuni strumenti di musica populari italiani: Distribuzione geografica** [Some traditional Italian instruments: Their geographic distribution] (3261); Poul Rovsing OLSEN, **Enregistrements faits à Kuwait and Bahrain** [Recordings made in Kuwait and Bahrain] (4098); André SCHAEFFNER, **Le tambour-sur-cadre quadrangulaire chez les Noirs d'Afrique et d'Amérique** [The square frame drum as used by black peoples of Africa and America] (3654); Doris STOCKMANN and Erich STOCKMANN, **Die vokale Bordun-Mehrstimmigkeit in Südalbanien** [Vocal drone polyphony in southern Albania] (3071); Klaus P. WACHSMANN, **Problems of musical stratigraphy in Africa** (2597).

402 [Zaječar; Negotin] **Rad kongresa folklorista**
bs **Jugoslavije** [Proceedings of the congress of Yugoslav folklorists]. Proceedings of the fifth congress of the

CHRONOLOGY AND CONTENTS 1959

Savez Udruženja Folklorista Jugoslavije. Ed. by Miodrag S. LALEVIĆ (Beograd: Naučno Delo, 1960) 307 p. *Illus., bibliog., transcr., maps.* In Serbian, Croatian, Slovene, Bosnian, and Czech; summaries in French, German, and Serbian.

The following contributions are cited separately: Maja BOŠKOVIĆ-STULLI, **Neka suvremena mišljenja o baladi** [Some contemporary views on the ballad] (2746); Tvrtko ČUBELIĆ, **Balada u narodnoj književnosti** [The ballad in traditional literature] (5296); Živko FIRFOV, **Kolektivno vokalno muziciranje u Makedoniji** [Collective vocal music making in Macedonia] (2814); Vasil HADŽIMANOV, **Muzičke balade Makedonije** [The musical ballads of Macedonia] (2846); Radoslav HROVATIN, **Organizacija priprav za kvaliteten program v radijskih emisijah narodne muzike** [Organizing preparations for high-quality programming in the radio broadcast of traditional music] (2863); Milica ILIJIN, **Narodne igre u Timočkoj Krajini** [Traditional dance in the Timočka Krajina] (4987); Zdenka JELÍNKOVÁ, **Lidové tance na Podluží** [Traditional dance of the Podluží region] (4993); Vera KLIČKOVA, **Narodni muzički instrumenti u Makedoniji** [Traditional musical instruments in Macedonia] (3310); Zija KUČUKALIĆ, **Muzički folklor na programima naših radiostanica** [Traditional music in our radio broadcasting centers] (2915); Zmaga KUMER, **Funkcija balade na Slovenskem** [The function of the ballad in Slovenia] (2917); Živomir MLADENOVIĆ, **Narodne pesme Timočke Krajine** [Traditional songs of the Timočka krajina] (2959); Cvjetko RIHTMAN, **Napjev balade u narodnoj tradiciji Bosne i Hercegovine** [Ballad melody in the folk tradition of Bosnia and Herzegovina] (3031); Stjepan STEPANOV, **O nekim načinima pjevanja romanca i balada na području Hrvatske** [Melodic styles in romance and ballad in the territory of Croatia] (3066); Miodrag A. VASILJEVIĆ, **Muzički folklor u zaječarskom kraju** [Traditional music in the Zaječar region] (3098); Valens VODUŠEK, **Neka zapažanja o baladnim napevima na području Slovenije** [Observations on the melodies of ballads in Slovenian territory] (3105); Vinko ŽGANEC, **O muzičkom aspektu narodnih balada na hrvatskom etničkom području** [Musical aspects of the traditional ballad in ethnic-Croatian territory] (3124).

1959

403
bs

[Berlin] *Musica sacra* **in unserer Zeit** [*Musica sacra* in our time]. Proceedings of the first Deutscher Kirchenmusikertag. Foreword by Karl FORSTER and Wolfgang REIMANN. *Edition Merseburger* 1125 (Berlin: Merseburger, 1960) 88 p. *Illus., music.* In German.

The conference was held from 19 through 24 May 1959. The following contributions are cited separately: Urbanus BOMM, **Gregorianischer Choral als Gegenwartskunst** [Gregorian chant as contemporary art] (2290); Arno FORCHERT, **Choralmotette und Choralkonzert: Zur Bedeutung Italiens für die evangelische Kirchenmusik** [Choral motet and vocal concerto: The significance of Italy in Lutheran church music] (1553); Friedrich HÖGNER, **Das Amt des evangelischen Kirchenmusikers heute** [The position of the Protestant church musician today] (6435); Johannes OVERATH, **Der kirchenmusikalische Dienst: Ein wahres Apostolat** [The mission of church music: A true apostolate] (6021); Oskar SÖHNGEN, **Die geistige und künstlerische Situation des neuen Kirchenmusikerstandes** [The spiritual and artistic situation in the new status of the church musician] (6025); Fritz WINCKEL, **Die neue Entwicklung der elektronischen Musik** [The new development of electronic music] (6032); Heinz Werner ZIMMERMAN, **Die Möglichkeiten und Grenzen des Jazz innerhalb der Musiksprache der Gegenwart** [The possibilities and limits of jazz within contemporary musical language] (6034).

404
bs

[Bled] **Rad kongresa folklorista Jugoslavije** [Proceedings of the congress of Yugoslav folklorists]. Proceedings of the sixth congress of the Savez Udruženja Folklorista Jugoslavije. Ed. by Zmaga KUMER (Ljubljana: Savez Udruženja Folkloristov Jugoslavije, 1960) 397 p. *Illus., transcr.* In Croatian, German, Bosnian, and Serbian; summaries in German, English, French, and Croatian.

The following contributions are cited separately: Dragoslav ANTONIJEVIĆ, **Narodnooslobododilačka pesma protiv nečovoštva** [Songs against inhumanity from the time of the War of National Liberation] (2722); Jerko BEZIĆ, **Neki oblici starinskog otegnutog dvoglasnog pjevanja na sjeverozapadnim zadarskim otocima** [Some forms of the old two-voice prolonged song on the islands northwest of Zadar] (2739); Rada BORELI, **Narodna pesma o Partiji i Titu** [Neotraditional songs dedicated to the Party and Tito] (2742); Maja BOŠKOVIĆ-STULLI, **Neki problemi u proučavanju folklora iz Narodnooslobodilačke Borbe** [Some problems in the study of the folklore of the War of National Liberation] (5292); Jelena DOPUDA, **Narodne igre u vremenu Narodnooslobodilačke Borbe u Bosni i Hercegovini** [Traditional dance from the time of the War of National Liberation in Bosnia and Herzegovina] (4958); Živko FIRFOV, **Makedonske narodne pesme iz perioda Narodnooslobodilačke Borbe** [Macedonian traditional songs in the period of the War of National Liberation] (2816); Vladislav HIRŠL, **Pesme Narodnooslobodilačke Borbe iz istočne Srbije** [Songs of the War of National Liberation in eastern Serbia] (2854); Radoslav HROVATIN, **Metrika teksta i melodije na Gorenjskem** [The metrics of texts and melody in Gorenjska] (2861) and **Slovenska partizanska pesem kot predmet znanosti** [Slovene Partisan song as a research subject] (2865); Ivan IVANČAN, **Elementi alpskih plesova u Istri** [Elements of Alpine dance in Istria] (4989); Ernő KIRÁLY and Marija KIRÁLY, **Tragom revolucionarne i borbene pesme kod Mađara, Slovaka, Rusina i Romuna u Vojvodini** [Searching for revolutionary and war songs among the Hungarians, Slovaks, Rusyns, and Romanians of Vojvodina] (2891); Milivoje V. KNEŽEVIĆ, **Tehnika narodne pevane pesme** [Techniques of traditional song] (2899); Mark KRASNIQI, **Naša šiptarska narodna pesma o borbi i izgradnji** [Our neotraditional Albanian songs of war and socialist construction] (2908); Zija KUČUKALIĆ, **Narodne pjesme u Bosni i Hercegovini u doba Narodnooslobodilačke Borbe** [Traditional song in Bosnia and Herzegovina at the time of the War of National Liberation] (2916); Zmaga KUMER, **Življenje ljudske pesmi na Gorenjskem** [The life of the traditional song in Gorenjska] (2919); Niko S. MARTINOVIĆ, **Revolucionarni folklor u periodu šestojanuarske diktature** [Revolutionary folklore in the period of the Dictatorship of Sixth January] (2951); Olivera MLADENOVIĆ, **Opšti pregled na partizanske i druge narodne igre u Oslobodilačkom Ratu** [Survey of Partisan and other neotraditional dances in the War of Liberation] (5034); Živomir MLADENOVIĆ, **Uloga pesme u Narodnooslobodilačkoj Borbi** [The role of songs in the War of National Liberation] (2963); Vidosava NIKOLIĆ, **Naša narodna pesma socialističke izgradnje u pervoj petoletki** [Our neotraditional songs of socialist construction in the first five-year plan] (2975); Shefqet PLLANA, **Šiptarski revolucionarni muzički folklor** [Traditional Albanian revolutionary music] (3006); Cvjetko RIHTMAN, **O odnosu ritma stiha i napjeva u narodnoj tradiciji Bosne i Hercegovine** [The relations between verse rhythm and musical rhythm in the national tradition of Bosnia and Herzegovina] (5344); Branislav RUSIĆ, **Guslarsko tajno sporazumevanje** [The secret communication system of the guslars] (5935); Johann SCHRÖPFER, **Eine unbeachtete Isoglosse der altbalkanischen Folklore: Die Volkslieder der Südslawen und die Orpheussage** [An unrecognized isogloss in Old Balkan folklore: South Slavic traditional songs and the Orpheus myth] (5936); Stjepan STEPANOV, **Problem starosti muzičko-folklorne baštine** [The problem of dating the traditional-music heritage] (4464); Marija ŠUŠTAR, **Oblike plesa štajeriš na Slovenskem** [Forms of the štajeriš dance in Slovenia] (5071); Mitar S. VLAHOVIĆ, **O najstarijim muzičkim instrumentima u Crnoj Gori** [The oldest musical instruments in Montenegro] (3284); Valens VODUŠEK, **Alpske poskočne pesmi v Sloveniji** [Alpine *poskočna* songs in Slovenia] (3102); Sava VUKOSAVLJEV, **Tragom revolucionarne i borbene pesme po Vojvodini** [On the study of revolutionary and war song in Vojvodina] (3111); Jovan VUKOVIĆ, **Akcenat u vokalnoj narodnoj muzici** [Speech stress in traditional vocal music] (4039); Leposava ŽUNIĆ, **Razvitak lika nove žene u pesmi narodne revolucije** [New images of women in revolutionary neotraditional song] (5372).

405
bs

[Budapest] **Bericht über die internationale Konferenz zum Andenken Joseph Haydns** [Report on the International Conference in Memory of Joseph Haydn]. Sponsored by the Magyar Tudományos Akadémia. Ed. by Bence SZABOLCSI and Dénes BARTHA (Budapest: Akadémiai Kiadó, 1961) 186 p. *Illus., facs., music, bibliog.* In German, English, French, Hungarian, and Russian.

The conference was held from 17 through 22 September 1959. The following contributions are cited separately: Dénes BARTHA, **Haydn als Opernkapellmeister** [Haydn as opera kapellmeister] (1725); Heinrich BESSELER, **Einflüsse der Contratanzmuzik auf Joseph Haydn** [Influences of contredanse music on Joseph Haydn] (1727); Karl Gustav FELLERER, **Joseph Haydns Messen** [The Masses of Joseph Haydn] (1754); Karl GEIRINGER, **Sidelights on Haydn's activities in the field of sacred music** (1761); Antonín HOŘEJŠ, **Haydn mit heutigen Augen gesehen** [Haydn seen with today's eyes] (1779); Julij Anatol'evič KREMLĖV, **J. Haydn und die russische Musikkultur** [J. Haydn and Russian musical culture] (3751); H.C. Robbins LANDON, **Survey of Haydn sources in Czechoslovakia** (1798); François LESURE, **Haydn en France** [Haydn in France] (3756); Tamara Nikolaevna LIVANOVA, **Rannie otkliki na iskusstvo Gajdna v Rossii** [Early comments on Haydn's works in Russia] (1804); Paul MIES, **Joseph Haydns Singkanons und ihre Grundidee** [Joseph Haydn's vocal canons and their fundamental idea] (4371); Antal MOLNÁR, **Der gestaltpsychologische Unterschied zwischen Haydn und Mozart** [The difference between Haydn and Mozart according to Gestalt psychology] (1817); Carl de NYS, **À propos du concerto pour deux cors et orchestre en mi bémol majeur** [Regarding the concerto for two horns and orchestra in E♭ major] (1829); Milan POŠTOLKA, **Joseph Haydn und Leopold Koželuh** [Joseph Haydn and Leopold Koželuh] (1838); Ernst Fritz SCHMID, **Joseph Haydn und die vokale Zierpraxis seiner Zeit, dargestellt an einer Arie seines Tobias-Oratoriums** [Joseph Haydn and the vocal ornamentation practice of his time, illustrated by an aria from his *Tobia* oratorio] (1855); Horst SEEGER, **Zur musikhistorischen Bedeutung Albert Christoph Dies' und seiner Haydn-Biographie von 1810** [The musical-historical significance of Albert Christoph Dies and his Haydn biography of 1810] (1858); Walther SIEGMUND-SCHULTZE, **Mozarts *Haydn-Quartette*** [Mozart's "Haydn" quartets] (1859); Antonín SYCHRA, **Über die Bedeutung von Beethovens Skizzen zur IX. Symphonie** [On the meaning of Beethoven's sketches for the ninth symphony] (1872); Bence SZABOLCSI, **Haydn und die ungarische Musik** [Haydn and Hungarian music] (1877); Zeno VANCEA, **Der Einfluß Haydns auf die rumänischen Komponisten des XIX. Jahrhunderts** [The influence of Haydn on 19th-century Romanian composers] (2116).

406 **[Cambridge] Music libraries and instruments.**
bs   Proceedings of the Joint Congress of the Association Internationale des Bibliothèques Musicales and the Galpin Society. Ed. by Unity SHERRINGTON and Guy OLDHAM; foreword by Cecil Bernard OLDMAN. *Hinrichsen's music books* 11 (London: Hinrichsen, 1961) 300 p. *Illus., port., music, charts, diagr., printed index.* In English, French, German, and Italian.

The conference was held from 30 June through 3 July 1959 as the fifth congress of the International Association of Music Libraries (AIBM), held jointly with the Galpin Society, U.K. The following contributions are cited separately: Kenneth ANDERSON, **Public service for music: The use of standard methods in Liverpool's new music library** (705); Anthony BAINES, **Some points in the nomenclature of folk instruments** (3241); Rita BENTON, **The early piano in the United States** (3506); Walter BERGMANN, **Henry Purcell's use of the recorder** (1486); Noel BOSTON, **The barrel organ** (3658); Eric James COATES, **The *British catalogue of music* classification** (535); Dragotin CVETKO, **National sources, their functions and interpretation in musicological research** (537); Jeannine DOUILLEZ, **Collections of musical instruments in Antwerp** (714); Leonard DUCK, **The public provision of music for choirs and orchestras** (558); Vincent H. DUCKLES, **The growth and organization of music research libraries in the western United States** (560); Norbert DUFOURCQ, **Pierre Baillon: Facteur de clavecins, d'orgues, graveur de musique et organiste français** [Pierre Baillon: French maker of harpsichords and organs, music engraver, and French organist] (1531); Roberto GERHARD, **Concrete and electronic sound-composition** (4401); Harald HECKMANN, **Musikalische Quellen auf Mikrofilmen** [Musical sources on microfilm] (590); H. Jean HEDLUND, **James Hook and the patent voice flute** (3622); Ingeborg HEILMAN, **Organization of the music collection of the state library in Aarhus, Denmark** (724); Mantle HOOD, **The Javanese rebab** (3581); Cecil HOPKINSON, moderator, **Towards a definition of certain terms in musical bibliography** (593); Jean JACQUOT, **The international catalogue of music for the lute and kindred instruments** (790); Susi JEANS, **Water organs** (3660); André JURRES, **From microfilm to microphone** (5972); Alexander

Hyatt KING, **The music librarian and his tasks, national and international** (601); Karl-Heinz KÖHLER, **Zur Problematik der Schallplatten-Katalogisierung** [The problematics of record cataloguing] (602); Jan LARUE and Jeanette B. HOLLAND, **Stimmer's women musicians: A unique series of woodcuts** (5383); Folke LINDBERG, **Scandinavian music libraries: Their value for research and broadcasting** (612); Marion LINTON, **Music in Scottish libraries** (739); Victor LUITHLEN, **Musical treasures of the Vienna art museum** (741); James MACGILLIVRAY, **The cylindrical reed pipe from antiquity to the 20th century: Its classification and scope** (3630); C.R. NICEWONGER and Harriet NICEWONGER, **Mediaeval musical instruments sculptured in the decorations of English churches** (5387); Guy OLDHAM, **Two pieces for 5-part shawm band by Louis Couperin** (1641); Cecil Bernard OLDMAN, **Panizzi and the music collection of the British Museum** (742); Alfons OTT, **The role of music in public libraries of medium size** (643); Irmgard OTTO, **Buchschmuck als instrumentenkundliche Quelle** [Book decoration as a source for organology] (5388); Hans-Martin PLESSKE, **Zur Musikalien-Katalogisierung der Deutschen Bücherei** [The cataloguing of musicalia by the Deutsche Bücherei] (654); Kurt REINHARD, **Probleme und Erfahrungen in einem Musikethnologischen Schallarchiv** [Problems and experiences in a sound archive for music ethnology] (660); G.H. ROLLAND, **The music collection in the Mitchell Library** (750); Patrick SAUL, **Preserving recorded sound** (754); Herta SCHETELICH, **Der Gesichtskreis der Musikbüchereiarbeit in einer Großstadt der Deutschen Demokratischen Republik** [The scope of music librarianship in a large city of East Germany] (671); Kenneth SKEAPING, **The Karl Schreinzer collection of violin fittings** (759); Harold SPIVACKE, **The preservation and reference services of sound recordings in a research library** (687); Vincenzo TERENZIO, **Criteri per la classificazione e la catalogazione di una discoteca nelle biblioteche musicali** [Criteria for the classification and cataloguing of a recording collection in a music library] (696); Geneviève THIBAULT DE CHAMBURE, **Les collections privées de livres et d'instruments de musique d'autrefois et d'aujourd'hui** [Private collections of books and musical instruments of yesterday and today] (763); Karl VÖTTERLE, **Musikbibliothek und Musikverlag** [Music libraries and music publishers] (699); Jack A. WESTRUP, **Practical musicology** (3687); Emanuel WINTERNITZ, **The survival of the kithara and the evolution of the cittern: A study in morphology** (3608).

407 **[Certaldo] L'ars nova italiana del Trecento:**
bs   **Primo convegno internazionale** [The Italian ars nova of the 14th century: First international conference]. Sponsored by the International Musicological Society. Ed. by Bianca BECHERINI. *L'ars nova italiana del trecento* 1 (Certaldo: Centro di Studi sull'Ars Nova Italiana del Trecento, 1962) xxi, 208 p. *Illus., facs., music, bibliog.* In Italian, French, and English.

The conference was held from 23 through 26 July 1959. The following contributions are cited separately: Bianca BECHERINI, **Antonio Squarcialupi e il Codice Mediceo Palatino 87** [Antonio Squarcialupi and the Codex Mediceo Palatino 87] (1060) and **L'ars nova italiana del trecento: Strumenti ed espressione musicale** [Italian ars nova of the 14th century: Instruments and musical expression] (3690); Nanie BRIDGMAN, **La musique dans la société française de l'ars nova** [Music in French society at the time of the ars nova] (1069); Suzanne CLERCX-LEJEUNE, **Les débuts de la Messe unitaire et de la *Missa parodia* au XIV siècle et principalement dans l'œuvre de Johannes Ciconia** [The beginnings of the unified Mass and of the parody Mass in the 14th century, especially in the work of Johannes Ciconia] (1074); Fabio FANO, **Punti di vista su l'ars nova** [Points of view on the ars nova] (1087); Karl Gustav FELLERER, **La *Constitutio Docta sanctorum patrum* di Giovanni XXII e la musica nuova del suo tempo** [The *Constitutio Docta sanctorum patrum* of Pope John XXII and the new music of his time] (6213); Kurt von FISCHER, **Les compositions à trois voix chez les compositeurs du trecento** [Compositions for three voices by 14th-century composers] (1094); Federico GHISI, **Rapporti armonici nella polifonia italiana del Trecento** [Harmonic relationships in the Italian polyphony of the 14th century] (4172); Richard H. HOPPIN, **The manuscript J. II. 9. in the Biblioteca Nazionale of Torino** (1123); Nino PIRROTTA, **Piero e l'impressionismo musicale del secolo XIV** [Piero and the musical impressionism of the 14th century] (1161); Albert SEAY, **Paolo da Firenze: A trecento theorist** (1177).

408
bs

[Halle] Händel-Ehrung der Deutschen Demokratischen Republik: Konferenzbericht [Tribute of the German Democratic Republic to Händel: Conference report]. Sponsored by the Händel-Komitee der Deutschen Demokratischen Republik. Ed. by Walther SIEGMUND-SCHULTZE; foreword by Otto GROTEWOHL (Leipzig: VEB Deutscher Verlag für Musik, 1961) 271 p. *Illus., facs., music, charts, diagr.* In German.

The conference was held in conjunction with the Händel-Ehrung festival in Halle from 11 through 19 April 1959, on the occasion of the 200th anniversary of the composer's death. The following contributions are cited separately: Werner BRAUN, **Echtheits- und Datierungsfragen im vokalen Frühwerk Georg Friedrich Händels** [Questions of authenticity and dating in Georg Friedrich Händel's early vocal works] (1494); Hella BROCK, **Händel und die Schulmusik** [Händel and school music] (4687); Alan BUSH, **Zum Problem der Verbreitung von Händels Schaffen unter dem grossen Publikum, besonders bei den Arbeitern und Bauern, durch szenische Aufführungen seiner Oratorien** [The problem of disseminating Händel's works among the larger public, particularly workers and peasants, through staged performances of his oratorios] (3735); Richard ENGLÄNDER, **Händel auf der schwedischen Bühne** [Händel on the Swedish stage] (1541); Werner FELIX, **Händel und Weißenfels** [Händel and Weißenfels] (1545); Günter FLEISCHHAUER, **Händel und die Antike** [Händel and antiquity] (1552); Roman Il'ič GRUBER, **Zur Händel-Pflege in der Sowjetunion** [Händel cultivation in the Soviet Union] (2322); Wilhelm HEINITZ, **Rezitativ-Gestaltung in Händelschen Werken** [The construction of recitative in Händel's works] (3743); Hans HICKMANN, **Instrumentenkundliche und aufführungspraktische Probleme bei der Aufführung und stereofonischen Einspielung Händelscher Werke** [Organological and performance practice problems in the performance and stereophonic recording of Händel's works] (3744); Frederick HUDSON, **Wasserzeichen in Händelschen Manuskripten und Drucken: Wasserzeichen in Verbindung mit anderem Beweismaterial als Mittel zur Datierung der Manuskripte und frühen Drucke Georg Friedrich Händels** [Watermarks in Händel manuscripts and prints: Watermarks together with other evidence as a means of dating Georg Friedrich Händel's manuscripts and early prints] (1581); Georg KNEPLER, **Die motivisch-thematische Arbeit in Händels Oratorien** [Motivic and thematic elaboration in Händel's oratorios] (4440); Siegfried KÖHLER, **Gestaltungsprinzipien Händels in der sozialistischen Vokalsinfonik** [Händelian structural principles in socialist symphonic-vocal music] (2191); Günther KRAFT, **Zur geistigen Umwelt des jungen Händel** [The intellectual environment of the young Händel] (1595); Inge LAMMEL, **Die Pflege Händelscher Oratorien durch die deutsche Arbeiter-Sängerbewegung** [The cultivation of Händel's oratorios by the German workers' choir movement] (2338); Jens Peter LARSEN, **Tempoprobleme bei Händel, dargestellt am Messias** [Tempo problems in Händel as exemplified in *Messiah*] (3753); Ernst Hermann MEYER, **Händels polyphoner Typ** [The typology of Händel's polyphony] (4199); Paul MIES, **Faksimile-Ausgaben von Werken Händels und ihre Bedeutung** [Facimile editions of Händel's works and their significance] (5980); Johanna RUDOLPH, **Über die biblische Gewandung von Händels Oratorien** [The biblical trappings of Händel's oratorios] (1665); Konrad SASSE, **Händels Stellung zu den gesellschaftlichen Problemen in England** [Händel's position on social problems in England] (1668); Horst SEEGER, **Zu Fragen der Aufführungspraxis von Händels Oratorien** [Questions on the performance practice of Händel's oratorios] (3768); Walter SERAUKY, **Georg Friedrich Händels italienische Kantatenwelt** [The world of Georg Friedrich Händel's Italian cantatas] (1678); Walther SIEGMUND-SCHULTZE, **Händels Melodik in Oper und Oratorien** [Händel's melodic style in opera and oratorio] (4458) and **Künftige Aufgaben der Förderung und Pflege des Händelschen Werkes** [Future tasks in the advancement and cultivation of Händel's works] (1685); William Charles SMITH, **Händels Leben in England: Unter besonderer Berücksichtigung seiner Blindheit** [Händel's life in England: With particular attention to his blindness] (1688); Rudolf STEGLICH, **Händels Sprachengebrauch** [Händel's use of languages] (1692); Stephan STOMPOR, **Zu einigen Fragen der Interpretation Händelscher Opern** [Some questions on the staging of Händel's operas] (5250); Antonín SYCHRA, **Romain Rollands Händel-Bild heute gesehen** [Romain Rolland's portrait of Händel from today's perspective] (1694); Hans-Georg USZKOREIT, **Händel und Mendelssohn** [Händel and Mendelssohn-Bartholdy] (2113); Wilhelm WEISMANN, **Choralzitate in Händels Oratorien** [The quotation of chorales in Händel's oratorios] (4472);

Hellmuth Christian WOLFF, **Vom Wesen des alten Belcanto** [The essence of early bel canto] (3779); Percy M. YOUNG, **Zur Interpretation des Saul** [The interpretation of *Saul*] (3780); Frieder ZSCHOCH, **Agrippina—Eine satirische Oper?** [*Agrippina*—A satirical opera?] (5276).

409
bs

[Jerusalem] Mẇsyqah datyt b̈eḥynẇḥ [Sacred music in education]. Proceedings of the Second Israeli Music Congress, *Dẇkan* II (1960). In Hebrew.

The following contributions are cited separately: Bathja BAYER, **Šylẇb hamẇsyqah hadatyt b̈eḥwra'at miqṣẇ'ẇt hayhadẇt wemad'ey** [Incorporating religious music into the teaching of Judaism and the humanities] (4490); Mordekay BRẆY'ER, **Toknyt lymẇdym lemẇsyqah datyt** [Curriculum for the study of religious music] (4500); Me'yr Šim'ẇn G E Š WRY, **Hamẇsyqah haḥasydyt b̈eḥynẇḥ** [Hasidic music in education] (6058); Yẇsep GẆLDŠMYDṬ, **Ḥawayah w'esṭyṭyqah b̈emẇsyqah datyt** [Spiritual experience and aesthetics in religious music] (6065); Me'yr KAṢ, **Yeṣyrẇt mẇsyqalyẇt kepyrẇš leṭeqsṭym miqr'yym** [The use of musical compositions in the interpretations of Biblical texts] (1789); Y. MELAMED, **Hatpylat leyaldey 'edẇt hamizraḥ** [The prayers of the children of the communities of the East] (6080); Yeḥẇšu'a Leyyb NE'EMAN, **Ḥynẇḥ tpylah b̈eḥatey haseper** [Teaching prayer in school] (4749); Dawid PRY-HEN, **Mẇsyqah datyt b̈emesiḱat weḃimḥazah** [Religious music in the school drama] (4758); Yẇsep Q'APAḤ, **Hašyrah wehalaḥnym b̈etpylat yahadẇt teyman** [Song and melody in the prayer of Yemenite Jews] (6090); Eric WERNER, **Qydẇn hamẇsyqah halyṭẇrgyt b̈eḃatey haḱneset b̈eyśra'el** [Promoting liturgical music in Israeli synagogues] (6104).

410
bs

[Kiel] Stilkriterien der neuen Musik [Style criteria for new music]. Proceedings of the Kieler Kongreß des Instituts für Neue Musik und Musikerziehung Darmstadt. Ed. by Siegfried BORRIS. *Veröffentlichungen des Instituts für Neue Musik und Musikerziehung Darmstadt* 1 (Berlin: Merseburger, 1961) 93 p. *Illus., music, bibliog., charts, diagr.* In German.

The 13th annual conference was held from 24 through 28 July 1959. The following contributions are cited separately: Siegfried BORRIS, **Historische Entwicklungslinien der neuen Musik** [Historic tendencies in the development of new music] (2140); Hans-Heinz DRAEGER, **Aesthetische Grundlagen** [Aesthetic foundations] (5456); Wilhelm KELLER, **Tonsatzanalytische Verfahren zur Darstellung von Stilkriterien neuer Musik** [Procedures in compositional analysis for the representation of style criteria of new music] (4352); Walter KOLNEDER, **Pädagogisch-soziologische Betrachtungen zur neuen Musik** [Pedagogical-sociological observations on new music] (2333); Fritz WINCKEL, **Die Psychophysischen Bedingungen des Musikhörens** [The psychophysical conditions of musical hearing] (5722).

411
bs

[Kiel; Copenhagen] Vorträge und Referate [Lectures and reports]. Proceedings of the International Congress of Folk Narrative Research; sponsored by the International Society of Folk Narrative Research. Ed. by Kurt RANKE. *"Fabula": Zeitschrift für Erzählforschung. B: Untersuchungen* 2 (Berlin: Walter de Gruyter, 1961) viii, 474 p. *Fabula* (1961). *Illus., music, bibliog., maps.* In German, English, and French.

The conference was held from 19 through 22 August 1959. The following contribution is cited separately: Zvi SOFER, **Die Verwendung der Volksmusik in der chassidischen Volkserzählung** [The use of traditional music in Hasidic folk narrative] (5359).

412
bs

[Munich] Musik and Musikerziehung in der Reifezeit [Music and music education in adolescence]. Proceedings of the third Bundesschulmusikwoche; sponsored by the Verband Deutscher Schulmusikerzieher. Ed. and pref. by Egon KRAUS (Mainz: Schott, 1959) 323 p. *Illus., music.* In German.

The following contributions are cited separately: Paul AMTMANN, **Spiel im Musikunterricht** [Playing in music classes] (4676); Rudolf Heinz BARTL, **Die Harmonik in der Neuen Musik** [Harmony in the new music] (4679); Hanns BEREKOVEN, **Musikunterricht in der Mittelschule** [Music instruction in middle schools] (4682); Gregor BERGER, **Alban**

Bergs Violinkonzert [Alban Berg's violin concerto] (4683); Friedrich EBERTH, **Lehraufgaben für den Musikunterricht der IV. bis VI. Klasse der Mittelschule** [Teaching responsibilities for music instruction in the fourth through sixth classes of the Mittelschule] (4691); Erich FORNEBERG, **Von Andersens Nachtigallen-Märchen zu Strawinskys Oper** *Le rossignol* [From Andersen's tale of the nightingale to Stravinsky's opera *Solovej*] (4693); Hans Reinhard FRANZKE, **Wege der Musikerziehung in der Berufsschule** [Approaches to music instruction in vocational schools] (4696); Toni GRAD, **Das Lichtbild im Musikunterricht** [Film in music instruction] (4699); Josef HEER, **Persönlichkeit und Werk J. Haydns in den Klassen der Reifejahre (8. bis 10. Schuljahr)** [J. Haydn's personality and works in the years of adolescence (classes 8-10)] (4704); Albert HUTH, **Musik als Lebenshilfe für die 13- bis 16jährigen Jugendlichen** [Music as a counseling technique for young people 13 to 16 years old] (4713); Gotho von IRMER, **Jugend zwischen Volkslied, Schlager, und Jazz** [Youth between traditional song, hit song, and jazz] (5887); Friedrich KLAUSMEIER, **Der Einfluß sozialer Faktoren auf das musikalische Verhalten von Jugendlichen** [The influence of social factors on the musical behavior of young people] (5890); Egon KRAUS, **Musik und Musikerziehung in der Reifezeit** [Music and music education in adolescence] (4720); Hugo LANG, **Musik in göttlicher Ordnung** [Music in the divine order] (5520); Hans MERSMANN, **Das 18. Jahrhundert aus der Sicht unserer Zeit** [The 18th century from the perspective of our time] (1622); Felix MESSERSCHMID, **Musik, Musikerziehung und politische Bildung** [Music, training in music, and political education] (4600); Felix OBERBORBECK, **Das Problem der pädagogischen Verspätung in der Musik** [The problem of pedagogical obsolescence in music] (4751); Heinrich PAPE, **Gedanken zur Musikerziehung in Vorpubertät und Pubertät** [Thoughts on music education in prepuberty and puberty] (4752); Wilhelm PFEIFER, **Das musische Gymnasium in Bayern** [The fine-arts Gymnasium in Bavaria] (4755); Hermann PFROGNER, **Was ist Zwölftonmusik?** [What is 12-tone music?] (4756); Karl REHBERG, **Boris Blachers** *Concertante Musik* **op. 10** [Boris Blacher's *Concertante Musik* op. 10] (4759); Heinrich M. SAMBETH, **Musikerziehung und Muse** [Music education and the Muse] (4768); Hermann SCHIEGL, **Psychologische Grundlagen der Gehörbildung** [Psychological foundations of ear training] (4770); Hans SCHMIDT, **Musikerziehung im Wertfeld der Persönlichkeitsbildung** [Music education and the values of personality development] (4772); Wilhelm SCHWEIZER, **Die Musikerziehung im Bildungsplan der höheren Schulen** [Music instruction in the educational plan of the upper-level schools] (4773); Hermann STOFFELS, **Hermann Reutter** *Die Passion in 9 Inventionen* [*Die Passion in 9 Inventionen* by Hermann Reutter] (4780); Hans TEUSCHER, **Anleitung zum Musikhören (für die Volksschule)** [Instruction in music listening (at the Volksschule level)] (4785); Jörn THIEL, **Die technischen Mittler in der Musikerziehung: Eine Zwischenbilanz** [Mass media in music education: An interim appraisal] (4788); Erich VALENTIN, **Musikwissenschaft und Musikpädagogik** [Musicology and music pedagogy] (4662); Walter WIORA, **Die geschichtliche Sonderstellung der abendländischen Musik** [The special historical position of Western music] (1023).

⟶ **[Paris; Royaumont] Les théâtres d'Asie** [Asian theatrical genres]. See no. 397 in this volume.

413
bs
[Sinaia] International Folk Music Council Conference. Intro. by Anthony BAINES, *Journal of the International Folk Music Council* XII (1960) 3–86. *Illus., music, transcr., tech. drawings.* In English, French, and German.

The 12th annual conference was held from 11 through 17 August 1959. The following contributions are cited separately: Vasile ADĂSCĂLIȚEI, **Some thoughts on the creation of folklore** (2490); Matts ARNBERG, **Recording expedition to the Faroe Islands** (2726); Anthony BAINES, **Organology and European folk music instruments** (3240); Laura BOULTON, **Turkish music** (2608); Antoine-Élisée CHERBULIEZ, **Quelques observations sur le psaltérion (tympanon) populaire Suisse: Hackbrett** [Some observations on the traditional Swiss psaltery (dulcimer): Hackbrett] (3557); Jiří CHLÍBEC, **Some new elements in the folk music of eastern Moravia** (2765); Helen CREIGHTON, **Songs from Nova Scotia** (3144); Sabin V. DRĂGOI, **The production of new songs in the Rumanian People's Republic** (3234); Alica ELSCHEKOVÁ, **A study of central Slovak folk dance** (4963); Vasil HADŽIMANOV, **Instruments folkloriques en Macedoine: Kavalis** [Traditional instruments

in Macedonia: Kavalis] (3621); Felix HOERBURGER, **On relationships between music and movement in folk dancing** (4979); Rajna KACAROVA, **Sur un phénomène concernant le manque de coïncidences entre la figure chorégraphique et la phrase mélodique** [On a phenomenon concerning the lack of correspondence between choreographic figure and melodic phrase] (4995); Gurit KADMAN, **The creative process in present-day Israeli dances** (4997); Leo LEVI, **Jewish folk song in European languages** (2928); MOEURDORJE, **Folk music from Mongolia** (2670); Xuân Khoát NGUYÊN, **Le đàn bầu** [The đàn bầu] (3593); Stojan PETROV, **Bulgarian popular instruments** (3267); Laurence E.R. PICKEN, **Three-note instruments in the Chinese People's Republic** (3268); Mihai POP, **Tradition and innovation in contemporary Rumanian folklore** (3014); Benjamin RAJECZKY, **Old and new singing styles in Hungarian folk song** (3021); Cvjetko RIHTMAN, **Les rapports entre le rythme poétique et le rythme musical dans la tradition populaire de la Bosnie-Herzégovine** [The relationship between poetic and musical rhythm in the folk tradition of Bosnia and Herzegovina] (3035); Ruth RUBIN, **Yiddish folk songs current in French Canada** (3176); Karel SALOMON, **Problems of old songs in a revived language** (2685); Georgios SPYRIDAKIS, **The folklore archive of the Athens Academy** (692); Erich STOCKMANN, **Klarinettentypen in Albanien** [Clarinet types in Albania] (3638) and **Mehrstimmige Gesänge in Südalbanien** [Polyphonic singing in southern Albania] (3073); Alexandru TIBERIU, **The study of folk musical instruments in the Rumanian People's Republic** (3282); Pavel TONKOVIČ, **Some observations on Slovak folk music instruments** (3283); Viktor VINOGRADOV, **The study of folk music in the U.S.S.R.** (2479); Valens VODUŠEK, **The correlation between metrical verse structure, rhythmical and melodic structure in folk songs** (3103); Constantin ZAMFIR, **The instrumental basis of vocal style in Năsăud** (3122).

414
bs
[Stuttgart] Proceedings of the Third International Congress on Acoustics. Sponsored by the International Commission on Acoustics. Ed. by Lothar CREMER (Amsterdam: Elsevier Science, 1961) 2 v. xxvi, 1320 p. *Illus., bibliog.* In English, French, and German.

The following contributions are cited separately: Leo Leroy BERANEK, **Audience absorption and seat absorption in halls for music** (5801); Kurt BLAUKOPF, **Nutzbarmachung neuerer raumakustischer und electroakustischer Erkenntnisse für die Musikwissenschaft** [How recent findings in room acoustics and electroacoustics can be useful for musicology] (5804); Harold BURRIS-MEYER and Vincent MALLORY, **Die Verwendung moderner akustischer Methoden zur Lösung von Problemen des Theaters und der Oper sowohl klassischer wie auch moderner Art** [The use of modern acoustic methods for the solution of problems in theater and opera buildings of classic as well as modern style] (5805); E.E. DAVID, Jr. and G.R. SCHRODDER, **Pitch discrimination of complex sounds** (5808); J.J. GELUK, **Electronic tuners for musical pitch** (5818); E. HIRSCHWEHR, **Raumakustische Messungen an der grossen Wiener Stadthalle** [Room-acoustic measurements in the Wiener Stadthalle] (5823); T. JÁRFÁS and Tamás TARNÓCZY, **Physikalische und Subjektive Nachhallzeit** [Physical and subjective reverberation time] (5824); Vilhelm Lassen JORDAN, **The building-up process of sound pulses in a room and its relation to concert hall quality** (5826); Émile LEIPP and Abraham MOLES, **Objektive Methode zur Bestimmung der Qualität eines Saiteninstruments** [Objective methods for determining the quality of a string instrument] (5587); Alfredo LIETTI, **Activity of the Studio di Fonologia Musicale** (4404); M. LUKÁCS, **Subjektive Untersuchungen über den Zusammenhang zwischen der Nachhallzeit und dem musikalischen Tempo** [Subjective investigations of the relationship between reverberation time and musical tempo] (5838); Max V. MATTHEWS and Newman GUTTMAN, **Generation of music by a digital computer** (4406); Werner MEYER-EPPLER and Hans LEICHER, **Zur Erkennbarkeit gesungener Vokale** [The recognizability of sung vowels] (5842); R.W. MUNCEY and A.F.B. NICKSON, **The acoustics of the Sidney Myer Music Bowl, Melbourne, Australia** (5846) and **The audience and room acoustics** (5847); V.M.A. PEUTZ, **The acoustics of large halls** (5848); Reinier PLOMP and M.A. BOUMAN, **Threshold for tone pulses** (5849); Andrej Vladimirovič RIMSKIJ-KORSAKOV, **Statistische Eigenschaften des Rundfunksignals** [Statistical properties of the radio signal] (5853); W.L. ROSSMAN, **Acoustics and architecture in auditorium design** (5854); W. ZELLER, **Akustik Stuttgarter Kirchen** [The acoustics of Stuttgart's churches] (5863).

1960

415
bs
[Athens] Pepragmena tou 4. diethnous synedriou aisthitikis/Actes du IV Congrès international d'esthétique/Proceedings of the IV International Congress on Aesthetics. Ed. by Panagiōtis A. MICHELĪS (Athínai: conference, 1962) xxiii, 835 p. *Illus., bibliog.* In French, English, Greek, Italian, and German.

The conference was held from 1 through 6 September 1960. The following contributions are cited separately: Otto DERI, **Musical taste and personality** (5653); Robert FRANCÈS, **L'information harmonique et les problèmes d'esthétique** [Harmonic information and aesthetic issues] (5656); Enrico FUBINI, **L'interpretazione musicale** [Musical interpretation] (5473); Jaroslav JIRÁNEK, **About some principal aesthetic problems of further development of musical research** (5499); Jean PUCELLE, **La musique et le temps** [Music and time] (4018); Olivier REVAULT D'ALLONNES, **Techniques modernes et renouvellement esthétique: Le cas de la musique concrète** [Modern techniques and aesthetic renewal: The case of musique concrète] (2239); Herbert M. SCHUELLER, **Musical expression: Research in the last two decades** (821); Robert SIOHAN, **Musique et poésie en quête du hasard** [Music and poetry in search of the aleatoric] (5357); Antonín SYCHRA, **About the problematic of experimental research of musical contents** (5607).

416
bs
[Cologne] Musik in Volksschule und Lehrerbildung [Music at the *Volksschule* level and teacher training]. Sponsored by the Arbeitsgemeinschaft der Musikdozenten an Pädagogischen Hochschulen. Ed. by Kurt SYDOW; intro. by Hans MERSMANN. *Musikalische Zeitfragen* 11 (Kassel; Basel: Bärenreiter, 1961) 110 p. *Bibliog.* In German.

The following contributions are cited separately: Hans Reinhard FRANZKE, **Musik in Volksschule und Lehrerbildung früher und heute** [Music at the Volksschule level and teacher training in the past and today] (4695); Toni GRAD, **Das Musikinstrument in Schule und Lehrerbildung** [Musical instruments in school and in teacher training] (4700); Joseph HEER, **Musikerziehung in Volksschule und Lehrerbildung** [Music education at the Volksschule level and teacher training] (4705); Felix MESSERSCHMID, **Schule und Musik** [School and music] (4741); Felix OBERBORBECK, **Zur Organisation der Musik in der Lehrerbildung** [The organization of music in teacher training] (4837); Hans OTTO, **Die Musik in der neuen Lehrerbildung: Fachegoistischer Anspruch oder Bestandteil grundschichtiger Bildung?** [Music in the new teacher training: A demand based on departmental egoism, or part of a fundamental training?] (4838); Heinrich PAPE, **Zur psychologischen Grundlegung der Musikerziehung** [The psychological foundation of music education] (4613); Gotthard SPEER, **Über Eigenart und Aufbau der musikalischen Oberstufenarbeit in der Volksschule** [Special characteristics and structure of work in music in the upper grades of the Volksschule] (4778); Hildegard TAUSCHER, **Die rhythmisch-musikalische Erziehung in der Grundschule** [Rhythmic-musical training in the Grundschule] (4783); Theodor WARNER, **Didaktik und Methodik des Musikunterrichts** [Didactics and methodology of music instruction] (4669). A comprehensive bibliography of recent literature on the subject is included.

417
bs
[Jerusalem] Mẇsyqah datyt ḥadašah weḥeqer hamẇsyqah datyt [Contemporary religious music and research in religious music]. Proceedings of the Third Israeli Music Congress, *Dẇkan* III (1961). In Hebrew.

The following contributions are cited separately: Me'yr BEN-'WRY, **Parašah bemiqr'a bebytẇy mẇsyqaly** [A chapter of the Bible expressed in music] (6044); 'Ezr'a GABA'Y, **Hasignẇn hamzirahy bemẇsyqah datyt** [The Oriental style of religious music] (6052); Edith GERSON-KIWI, **Nygẇnym šel yehẇdey paras wehašp'atah šel hamẇsyqah haparsyt 'aleyhem** [The influence of Persian music on the niguinm of Persian Jews] (6055); Me'yr Šim'ẇn GEŠWRY, **R' Šlomoh R'abyṣ: Ḥalwš bethyyat haḥazanẇt beyśra'el** [Rabbi Šlomoh R'abyṣ: A pioneer in the revival of hazanut in Israel] (6063); 'Ayleh GRẇSMAN, **He'arẇt 'al hakšaratam hamẇsyqalit šel meḥunakim datyym leganym**

wlekytẇt hanemẇkẇt šel byh"s [Some observations on the musical training of religious educators for kindergarten and lower school grades] (4821); Avigdor HERZOG, **Dereḥ qry'at hatẇrah benẇsaḥ "sfarad-'e"y"** [Torah reading according to the Sephardic-Israel custom] (6069); Yehẇšu'a Leyyb NE'EMAN, **Derakym beḥeqer hamẇsyqah šel haṭa'amym** [Trends in the research of Biblical cantillation] (6081) and **Haẏeṣyrah beḥazanẇt** [Creativity in hazanut] (6082); Re'uben QAŠ'ANY, **Laḥney yehẇdey 'apganystan** [Melodies of Jews in Afghanistan] (2675); Ḥayym QYRŠ, **Šyrat hạsbẇr bemenyyney nẇ'ar** [Congregational singing in youth congregations] (6093); Dawid RẆZẆLYẆ, **'Erneṣṭ Blẇḥ wemip'alẇ** [Ernest Bloch and his work] (2244); Miryam ŠAṬAL, **'Al b'ayẇt hatpylah beṣybẇr** [Problems of public prayer] (6096); Dawid YZR'A'ELY, **Pswqey miqr'a bebytẇy mẇsyqaly** [Biblical verses expressed in music] (6105); Y. ZOHAR, **Haḥynwḥ hamẇsyqaly bebatey haseper** [Music education in state religious schools] (4804).

418
bs
[Los Angeles] Festival of Oriental Music and the Related Arts. Sponsored by the University of California, Los Angeles (Los Angeles: University of California, 1960) 68 p. *Illus., music, bibliog.*

The conference was held from 8 through 22 May 1960. The following contributions are cited separately: Robert E. BROWN, **Introduction to the music of South India** (2609); Hormoz FARHAT, **Persian classical music** (2623); Robert GARFIAS, **Gagaku: Subdivisions of the repertoire** (2627); Mantle HOOD, **Music of the Javanese gamelan** (2640); Claude E. JONES, **Ukiyoye and kabuki** (4919); William P. MALM, **Japanese nagauta music** (2659); Colin MCPHEE, **Music in Bali** (2667); John M. ROSENFIELD, **India: Rasa and raga** (4923).

419
bs
[Ohrid] Rad VII-og kongresa Saveza Folklorista Jugoslavije [Proceedings of the seventh congress of the Savez Folklorista Jugoslavije]. Ed. by Jovan VUKOVIĆ, Dušan NEDELJKOVIĆ, Kiril PENUŠLISKI, and Vinko ŽGANEC (Cetinje: Obod, 1964) 479 p. *Illus., charts, diagr., transcr., maps.* In Serbian, Macedonian, German, Croatian, English, and Slovene; summaries in French, English, German, Italian, and Russian.

The following contributions are cited separately: Dragoslav ANTONIJEVIĆ, **Guslar danas i guslarski podmladak u Užičkom kraju** [Contemporary guslars and those of the next generation in the Užice region] (2721); Jerko BEZIĆ, **Diple s mijehom za zadarskom području** [The diple s mijehom in the Zadar region] (3611); Tvrtko ČUBELIĆ, **Muzički instrumenti u epskoj narodnoj pjesmi** [Musical instruments in traditional epic song] (5297); Dragoslav DEVIĆ, **Okarina (selo Donja Mutnica, Srbija)** [Ocarinas of the village of Donja Mutnica, Serbia] (3615); Jelena DOPUĐA, **Dječje narodne igre u Bosni i Hercegovini (plesne)** [Traditional children's dance-games in Bosnia and Herzegovina] (4954); Trifun ĐUKIĆ, **Gusle kao simboličan spomenik svoje uloge** [The gusle as symbolic monument to its social role] (5378); Živko FIRFOV, **Likot na makedonskata narodna muzika** [Macedonian traditional music] (2815); Evel GASPARINI, **Pjesme pjevane naizmjence i egzogamička odvojenost spolova** [Alternating songs and exogamic separation] (2822); Andrijana GOJKOVIĆ, **O srpskim sviralama-jedinkama** [The Serbian svirala-jedinka] (3619); Marika HADŽI-PECOVA, **Dečje igre u NR Makedoniji** [Children's games in Macedonia] (4976); Vasil HADŽIMANOV, **Triasimetrični taktovi makedonske narodne muzike** [Asymmetrical measures beginning with three-beat groups in traditional Macedonian music] (4920); Radoslav HROVATIN, **Bordunske citre v Sloveniji** [The drone zithers in Slovenia] (3582); Ivan IVANČAN, **Istarska svirala šurla** [An Istrian wind instrument, the šurla] (3623); Ljubica S. JANKOVIĆ and Danica S. JANKOVIĆ, **Tragom našeg najstarijeg orskog kulturnog nasleđa: Izvod** [On the trail of our oldest cultural heritage in the oro genre: Summary] (4992); Slavko JANKOVIĆ, **Upotreba tambure u orkestralne i pedagoške svrhe** [The use of the tambura for orchestral and pedagogical purposes] (4717); Ivan KAČULEV, **Bǎlgarski narodni muzikalni instrumenti** [Traditional Bulgarian instruments] (3256); Ernő KIRÁLY, **Citra kod Mađara u Vojvodini** [The zither among the Hungarians in Vojvodina] (3583); Marija KIRÁLY, **Uticaj društvenog razvitka na Cigane po narodnim pesmama Cigana u naselju Zorka kraj Subotice** [The influence of social development on Gypsy life in the Zorka colony near Subotica, as seen in Gypsy traditional song] (2893); Milivoje V. KNEŽEVIĆ, **Gusle javorove** [The maple-wood gusle] (3584); Nikola KNEŽEVIĆ, **Stvaranje tužbalica, njihovo održavanje i melodijske osobenosti** [The origin of laments, their tradition, and their melodic character] (2901); Leopold KRETZEN-BACHER, **Totentänze in der südostalpinen Volkskultur** [The Dance of Death in southeastern Alpine traditional culture] (5187); Zmaga KUMER, **Panova piščal v Sloveniji** [Panpipes in Slovenia] (3625); Zvonko LOVRENČEVIĆ, **Jedinka i dvojnice u bjelovarskoj okolici** [Jedinka and dvojnice instruments of the Bjelovar region] (3629); Dimče MALENKO, **Kako nastanale nekoi ohridski lirski narodni pesni** [The origin of some traditional lyric songs from Ohrid] (2936); Zagorka MARKOVIĆ, **Izrada frula u Banatu** [Flute making in Banat] (3631); Alija NAMETAK, **Izbegavanje upotrebe muzičkih instrumenata kod bosansko-hercegovačkih muslimana** [The avoidance of using musical instruments among the Muslims of Bosnia and Herzegovina] (2967); Vlastimir NIKOLOVSKI, **Makedonski muzički folklor u kompozicionom tretmanu Stevana Mokranjca** [Traditional Macedonian music in the compositions of Stevan Mokranjac] (2049); Milica OBRADOVIĆ, **Zvučne igračke seoske dece u Bosni i Hercegovini** [Sound-producing toys of village children in Bosnia and Herzegovina] (3263); Roksanda PEJOVIĆ, **Ruganje Hristu, ilustracije Davidova života i 150. Psalma: Scene s muzičkim instrumentima na našim spomenicima** [The Mocking of Christ, illustrations of the the life of David, and the 150th Psalm: Scenes with musical instruments in the art works of our national heritage] (5390); Kiril PENUŠLISKI, **Marko K. Cepenkov, skupljač makedonskih narodnih umotvorina** [Marko K. Cepenkov, a collector of Macedonian folklore] (2991); Kiril PENUŠLISKI, Haralampije POLENAKOVIĆ, and Živko FIRFOV, **Folklor Makedonije** [The folklore of Macedonia] (2992); Herbert PEUKERT, **Der Refrain in der makedonischen Volkslyrik** [The refrain in the Macedonian traditional lyric] (2998); Laurence E.R. PICKEN, **The bagpipe in eastern Turkey** (3632); Shefqet PLLANA, **Tužbalica o Redži, s naročitim osvrtom na jednoglasno i višeglasno pevanje kod Šćiptara u Makedoniji** [The lament for Rexha, with particular reference to monophonic and polyphonic song among the Albanian community in Macedonia] (3007); Haralampije POLENAKOVIĆ, **O narodnoj pesmi *Biljana platno beleše*** [The traditional song *Biljana platno beleše*] (3008); Cvjetko RIHTMAN, **Organološki problemi naše etnomuzikologije** [Organological problems in our ethnomusicology] (3034); Stjepan STEPANOV, **Svirale i bubanj na Baniji** [The svirale and bubanj of Banija] (3637); Miodrag A. VASILJEVIĆ, **Funkcije i vrste glasova u srpskom narodnom pevanju: Objašnjenje reči** [Voice functions and types in traditional Serbian song: An interpretive account] (3097); Tihamér VUJICSICS, **Razvoj srpsko-hrvatske instrumentalne muzike u Mađarskoj** [The development of Serbo-Croatian instrumental music in Hungary] (3109); Jovan VUKMANOVIĆ, **Narodni muzički instrumenti arbanasa u crnogorskom primorju** [Albanian traditional instruments of the Montenegrin coast] (3285); Jovan VUKOVIĆ, **Intonacioni momenti i struktura stiha u tužbalicama** [Elements of intonation and verse structure in laments] (3112); Slobodan ZEČEVIĆ, **Jedan Zlatiborski duvački instrumenat** [A wind instrument from the Zlatibor region] (3641); Vinko ŽGANEC, **Treba li u škole uvesti i učenje netemperirane muzike?** [Should the study of untempered music be introduced into schools?] (4803).

420
bs

[Paris] **La résonance dans les échelles musicales** [*Résonance* in musical scales]. Ed. by Édith WEBER. *Colloques internationaux du CNRS* 516 (Paris: Centre National de la Recherche Scientifique [CNRS], 1963) 402 p. *Music, charts, diagr.* In French; summaries in English and German.

The conference was held from 9 through 14 May 1960. The following contributions are cited separately: Salāh AL-MAHDĪ, **Présence ou absence de la constante de quarte, de quinte et d'octave: Son rôle structurel dans la musique orientale non pentatonique** [Presence or absence of the constant of fourth, fifth, and octave: Its structural role in non-pentatonic Asian music] (4044); Mehdi BARKECHLI, **Les échelles régulières du cycle des quintes et leurs déformations occasionnelles: Dans les cadres non pentatoniques** [Regular scales of the circle of fifths and their occasional deformations in non-pentatonic frameworks] (4047); Dénes BARTHA, **Le développement de la résonance dans les musiques évoluées: Occident au XXᵉ siècle—La musique de Bartók** [The development of overtones in advanced musics: The West in the 20th century—Bartók's music] (4136); François CANAC, **Les éléments de formation des échelles extérieurs à la résonance: Les facteurs de consonance** [Elements of scale formation external to overtones: Factors of consonance] (5646); Jacques CHAILLEY, **Hypothèses de travail** [Working hypotheses]

(4151), **Le développement de la résonance dans les musiques évoluées: Occident du Moyen-Âge au XIXᵉ siècle** [The development of overtone theory in advanced musics: The West, from the Middle Ages to the 19th century] (4148), **Les éléments de formation des échelles extérieurs à la résonance: L'égalisation** [Elements of scale formation external to overtone theory: Equalization] (4059), and **Synthèse et conclusions** [Synthesis and conclusions] (4061); Edmond COSTÈRE, **Les éléments de formation des échelles extérieurs à la résonance: L'attraction** [Elements of scale formation external to overtone theory: Attraction] (4155); Alain DANIÉLOU, **Les éléments de formation des échelles extérieurs à la résonance: Les déformations expressives** [Elements of scale formation external to overtone theory: Expressive deformations] (4064); André DIDIER, **La résonance dans les échelles musicales: Le point de vue des physiciens** [Resonance in musical scales: The viewpoint of physicists] (5811); Yvette GRIMAUD, **Les polysystèmes des musiques de tradition orale peuvent-ils être intégrés à la résonance?** [Can the polysystems of the musics of oral tradition be integrated into overtone theory?] (3946); Hans HICKMANN, **Présence de la constante de quarte, de quinte et d'octave: Son rôle structurel dans l'antiquité pré-hellénique** [Presence of the constant of fourth, fifth, and octave: Its structural role in pre-Hellenic antiquity] (1033); Armand MACHABEY, **Présence ou absence de la constante de quarte, de quinte et d'octave: Son rôle structurel dans la musique grecque antique et la polyphonie occidentale primitive** [Presence or absence of the constant of fourth, fifth, and octave: Its structural role in ancient Greek music and early Western polyphony] (4195); Claudie MARCEL-DUBOIS, **Présence ou absence de la constante de quarte, de quinte et d'octave: Son rôle structurel dans l'ethnomusicologie européenne** [Presence or absence of the constant of fourth, fifth, and octave: Its structural role in European ethnomusicology] (4093); Constantin REGAMEY, **Le développement de la résonance dans les musiques évoluées: Les théories de l'harmonie moderne** [The development of overtones in advanced musics: Theories of modern harmony] (4210); Gilbert ROUGET, **Les éléments de formation des échelles extérieurs à la résonance: Facture instrumentale et résonance** [Elements of scale formation external to overtone theory: Instrument construction and overtone theory] (4107); André SCHAEFFNER, **Les éléments de formation des échelles extérieurs à la résonance: Le timbre** [Elements of scale formation external to overtones: Timbre] (4303); Marius SCHNEIDER, **Présence ou absence de la constante de quarte, de quinte et d'octave: Son rôle structurel dans la consonance polyphonique primitive** [Presence or absence of the constant of fourth, fifth, and octave: Its structural role in primitive polyphonic consonance] (4114); Robert SIOHAN, **Les objections à la résonance** [Objections to overtones] (5703); Robert TANNER, **Critique de la théorie de la résonance** [Critique of the theory of resonance] (5709); Alfred TOMATIS, **La résonance dans les échelles musicales: Le point de vue des physiologistes** [Resonance of musical scales: The viewpoint of physiologists] (5713); Van Khê TRÂN, **Les échelles régulières du cycle des quintes et leurs déformations occasionnelles: Dans le cadre du pentatonique** [Regular scales of the circle of fifths and their occasional deformations in the pentatonic framework] (4122); Walter WIORA, **La résonance dans les échelles musicales: Le point de vue des musicologues** [Overtones in musical scales: The viewpoint of musicologists] (4132) and **Présence ou absence de la constante de quarte, de quinte et d'octave: Son rôle structurel dans l'ethnomusicologie primitive** [Presence or absence of the constant of fourth, fifth, and octave: Its structural role in the ethnomusicology of primitive music] (4131).

421
bs

[Paris] **VIᵉ Congrès international des sciences anthropologiques et ethnologiques. I: Rapport général et anthropologie; II: Ethnologie** [Sixth International Congress of Anthropological and Ethnological Sciences. I: General report and anthropology; II: Ethnology]. Sponsored by the International Union of Anthropological and Ethnological Sciences. Ed. by André LEROI-GOURHAN, Pierre CHAMPION, and Monique de FONTANÈS (Paris: Musée de l'Homme, 1962-1964) 2 v. 664; 666 p. *Illus., bibliog., charts, diagr., maps.* In French, English, German, Italian, Portuguese, and Spanish.

The conference was held from 30 July through 6 August 1960. The following contributions are cited separately: Diego CARPITELLA, **Documenti coreutico-musicali sul *tarantismo* ancora oggi esistente in Puglia** [Choreological-musical documents of the tarantism still extant in Apulia] (4945); Anna CZEKANOWSKA, **Les anciennes mélodies de noce en**

Pologne [Old wedding songs in Poland] (2783); Simone DREYFUS, **Formes de musiques rituelles chez les Indiens d'Amérique du Sud** [Forms of ritual music among the Indians of South America] (3197); K.J. HYE-KERKDAL, **Tanz im Alten China** [Dance in ancient China] (4983); Arcadio de LARREA PALACÍN, **Recherches sur la musique hispano-arabe** [Research on Hispano-Arabic music] (2923); Menashe RAVINA, **Neue israelische Folklore** [New Israeli folklore] (2678); Jacques REVAULT, **Note sur les instruments traditionnels de musique populaire dans le sud tunisien** [Note on traditional music instruments in southern Tunisia] (2577); Gilbert ROUGET, **Musique vodu (Dahomey)** [Vodun music (Dahomey)] (2578); André SCHAEFFNER, **Musiques rituelles Baga** [Baga ritual music] (2586); Carl WIDSTRAND, **Skolt Lapp songs of N.E. Finland** (3115).

422
bs

[Rome] Manierismo, barocco, rococò: Concetti e termini—Convegno internazionale [Mannerism, Baroque, rococo: Concepts and terminology—International conference]. Sponsored by the Accademia Nazionale dei Lincei, Classe di Scienze Morali, Storiche e Filologiche. *Problemi attuali di scienza e di cultura* 52 (Roma: R. Accademia dei Lincei, 1962) 419 p. *Illus., bibliog.* In Italian, German, French, and Spanish.

The conference was held from 21 through 24 April 1960. The following contributions are cited separately: Friedrich BLUME, **Begriff und Grenzen des Barock in der Musik** [The Baroque in music: The concept and its limits] (1489); Andrea DELLA CORTE, **Il Barocco e la musica** [The Baroque and music] (1525); Luigi RONGA, **Il rococò musicale** [The musical rococo] (1847).

423
bs

[Stratford, Ontario] The modern composer and his world. Proceedings of the International Conference of Composers; sponsored by the Canadian League of Composers and Stratford Shakespearean Festival. Ed. by John BECKWITH and Udo KASEMETS; comm. by Marvin DUCHOW, foreword by Louis APPLEBAUM (Toronto: University of Toronto, 1961) xi, 170 p. *Port.*

The conference was held in August 1960. The following contributions are cited separately: Karl-Birger BLOMDAHL and Henk BADINGS, **Opera and ballet** (2137); Václav DOBIÁŠ, Gunther SCHULLER, and Victor FELDBRILL, **Composer and performer** (2156); Henri DUTILLEUX, Zygmunt MYCIELSKI, Constantin REGAMEY, and Gunther SCHULLER, **Some other paths** (2158); Iain HAMILTON, George ROCHBERG, and Ernst KRENEK, **Serialism** (2176); Vagn HOLMBOE and Luciano BERIO, **Form** (2181); Hugh LE CAINE, Josef TAL, and Vladimir USSACHEVSKY, **Synthetic means** (2196); Victor LEGLEY, Vasilij KUHARSKIJ, and Alfred FRANKENSTEIN, **Composer and public** (2199); Heinrich SUTERMEISTER, Jean PAPINEAU-COUTURE, and Aurelio de la VEGA, **Training of composers** (4898).

424
bs

[Vienna] International Folk Music Council Conference. Sponsored by the International Music Council, UNESCO, and Österreichisches Volksliedwerk. Ed. by Maud KARPELES, *Journal of the International Folk Music Council* XIII (1961) 151. In English, German, and French.

The following contributions are cited separately: Marius BARBEAU, **Canadian folk songs** (3136); Mehdi BARKECHLI, **Nécessité d'une coordination des différentes techniques appliquées à la recherche du folklore musical** [The need to coordinate the different techniques applied to research in musical folklore] (2420); Dieter CHRISTENSEN, **Kurdische Brautlieder aus dem vilayet Hakkâri Südost-Türkei** [Kurdish bridal songs from the city of Hakkâri in Southeastern Turkey] (2611); Francis COLLINSON, **Some researches on an obsolete labour song of the Lowland Scottish oyster fishers: Summary** (2775); **Discussion on the preservation of folk music at a meeting of radio representatives** (2515); Donia ETHERINGTON, **A living song-composer in a Scottish-Gaelic oral tradition** (2805); Edith GERSON-KIWI, **Religious chant: A Pan-Asiatic conception of music** (6012); **Importance de la pratique de l'enregistrement sonore en matière de musique populaire** [The importance of the practice of sound recording in the subject of traditional music]

(2472); Josef KLIMA, **Tabulaturen als Quelle der Volksmusik alter Zeiten** [Tablatures as a source of the traditional music of former times] (2897); Vladimír KLUSÁK, **The preservation of folk music traditions in Czechoslovakia** (2440); Claudie MARCEL-DUBOIS, **Principes essentiels de l'enquête ethnomusicologique: Quelques applications françaises** [Essential principles of ethnomusicological inquiry: Some French applications] (2445); Mervyn MCLEAN, **Oral transmission in Maori music** (3228); Takashi OGAWA, **The collection and preservation of folk songs by the Japan Broadcasting Corporation (NHK)** (2671); Kurt REINHARD, **Trommeltänze aus der Süd-Türkei** [Drum dances from southern Turkey] (2680); **Report on the preservation of folk music by means of recordings with special reference to radio organizations** (2516); Winfried SCHRAMMEK, **Die Geschichte des sogenannten Harzspruchs vom Mittelalter bis zur Gegenwart** [The history of the so-called *Harzspruch*, from the Middle Ages to the present] (3054); Ovidiu VARGA, **Le rôle de la radio concernant le recueil, la valorification et la circulation du folklore** [The role of radio with respect to the collection, validation, and circulation of folklore] (2544); Karel VETTERL, **The need for an international select bibliography of folk music summary** (698); László VIKÁR, **Recherches folkloriques en Extrême-Orient et sur les bords de la Volga** [Folkloric research in the Far East and on the banks of the Volga] (2545); Walter WIORA, **Die Natur des Musik und die Musik der Naturvölker** [The nature of music and the music of primitive tribes] (2485); Richard WOLFRAM, **Die Volkstänze in Österreich: Ein Überblick** [Traditional dances in Austria: A survey] (5082).

425
bs

[Warsaw] The book of the first international musicological congress devoted to the works of Frederick Chopin. Sponsored by the Towarzystwo imienia Fryderyka Chopina, Ministerstwo Kultury i Sztuki, and Komitet Roku Chopinowskiego. Ed. by Zofia LISSA; pref. by Tadeusz KOTARBIŃSKI and Leon KRUCZKOWSKI (Warszawa: Państwowe Wydawnictwo Naukowe, 1963) 755 p. *Illus., facs., music.* In English, Russian, French, German, Polish, and Italian.

The conference was held from 16 through 22 February 1960. The following contributions are cited separately: Gerald ABRAHAM, **Chopin and the orchestra** (1906); Aleksandr Dmitrievič ALEKSEEV, **Tradicii ispolnenija Šopena v Rossii i Sovetskom Sojuze** [Chopin performance traditions in Russia and the Soviet Republics] (3781); Willi APEL, **Der Anfang des Präludiums in Deutschland und Polen** [The beginnings of the prelude in Germany and Poland] (1225); Franciszek BARFUSS, **Die polnische historische Oper in den Jugendjahren Chopins** [The Polish historical opera in the years of Chopin's youth] (5099); Alberto BASSO, **Chopin et l'esprit de la musique instrumentale baroque** [Chopin and the spirit of Baroque instrumental music] (1910); Bianca BECHERINI, **Il dissolvimento della tonalità nelle opere di Federico Chopin** [The dissolution of tonality in the works of Frédéric Chopin] (1911); Igor' Fëdorovič BÉLZA, **Nacional'nye istoki tvorčestva Šopena** [National origins of Chopin's music] (1913) and **Rosyjsko-polskie stosunki muzyczne w wieku XVII i XVIII** [Russian-Polish musical relations in the 17th and 18th centuries] (1484); Krzysztof BIEGAŃSKI, **Évolution de l'attitude de Chopin à l'égard du folklore (suivant ses mazurkas)** [The evolution of Chopin's attitude toward folklore in regard to his mazurkas] (1916); Ludwik BIELAWSKI, **Problem krakowiaka w twórczości Chopina** [The problem of the krakowiak in Chopin's work] (1917); Günter BIRKNER, **Das Sequenzrepertoire in Polen und die Stellung des Sequenz Jesu Christe rex superne** [The sequence repertoire in Poland and the place of the sequence *Jesu Christe rex superne*] (1065); Wolfgang BOETTICHER, **Über einige Spätstilprobleme bei Chopin** [Some problems of style in Chopin's late works] (4315); Siegfried BORRIS, **Chopins Bedeutung für den Chromatismus des XIX. Jahrhunderts** [Chopin's significance in 19th-century chromaticism] (4141); Wilfried BRENNECKE, **Johannes Polonus, ein Musiker um 1600** [Johannes Polonus, a musician of the period around 1600] (1257); Jacques CHAILLEY, **L'importance de Chopin dans l'évolution du langage harmonique** [The importance of Chopin in the evolution of harmonic language] (1932) and **Une page d'album de Chopin à Émile Gaillard** [An album page from Chopin to Émile Gaillard] (1933); Suzanne CHAINAYE, **Frédéric Chopin et les apocryphes** [Apocryphal writings attributed to Chopin] (1934); Zofia CHECHLIŃSKA, **Das Problem der Form und die reelle Klanggestalt in Chopins Präludien** [The problem of form and the real sound-shape in Chopin's preludes] (4236); Barbara CHMARA, **Das Problem der Agogik der Nocturni von Field und Chopin** [The problem of agogics in the nocturnes of Field and Chopin] (4324); Józef Michał CHOMIŃSKI, **Die Evolution des Chopinschen Stils** [The evolution of Chopin's style] (4325); Viktor Abramovič CUKKERMAN, **De l'emploi des genres et des formes dans l'œuvre de Chopin** [The use of genres and forms in the works of Chopin] (1940); Dragotin CVETKO, **Chopin chez les Slovènes au XIXe siècle** [Chopin in Slovenia in the 19th century] (1941); Anna CZEKANOWSKA, **Beiträge zum Problem der Modalität und der sogenannten "halbchromatischen Leiter" bei Chopin** [The problem of tonality and the so-called half-chromatic scale in Chopin] (4423); Shande DING, **What makes the Chinese people accept and appreciate Chopin's music** (1945); Janusz DOBROWOLSKI, **Organizacja pola dźwiękowego u Chopina** [Chopin's organization of sound] (1947); Ernst-Jürgen DREYER, **Melodisches Formelgut bei Chopin** [Chopin's repertoire of melodic formulas] (4425); Zbigniew DRZEWIECKI, **Le style d'interprétation de Chopin dans la pédagogie polonaise contemporaine** [The interpretation of Chopin in contemporary Polish pedagogy] (3783); Franz EIBNER, **Die Stimmführung Chopins in der Darstellung Heinrich Schenkers** [Chopin's voice-leading as characterized by Heinrich Schenker] (4160); Jan EKIER, **Le problème d'authenticité de six œuvres de Chopin** [The authenticity problem of six works of Chopin] (1950); Christiane ENGELBRECHT, **Zur Vorgeschichte der Chopinschen Klavierballade** [The prehistory of the Chopinian piano ballade] (4245); Wilm FALCKE, **Zu Chopins Aufenthalt auf Mallorca und zur Chopin-Überlieferung in Palma und Valldemosa** [Chopin's stay in Mallorca and the Chopin tradition in Palma and Valldemosa] (1953); Fabio FANO, **Vertu classique de Chopin** [Chopin's Classic bent] (1954); Hellmut FEDERHOFER, **Musikalische Beziehungen zwischen den Höfen Erzherzog Ferdinands von Innerösterreich und König Sigismunds III von Polen** [Musical relations between the courts of Archduke Ferdinand of Inner Austria and King Sigismund III of Poland] (1298); Hieronim FEICHT, **Zur Entstehung zweier polnischer *carmina patria*** [The origins of two Polish *carmina patria*] (1090); Aleksander FRĄCZKIEWICZ, **Koncerty fortepianowe Chopina jako typ koncertu romantycznego** [Chopin's piano concertos as a model of the Romantic concerto] (1958); Paul-André GAILLARD, **Jugements portés sur Chopin par Mickiewicz d'après le journal de Caroline Olivier** [Mickiewicz's judgments of Chopin as reported in the journal of Caroline Olivier] (1962) and **Le lyrisme pianistique de Chopin et ses antécédents directs** [The pianistic lyricism of Chopin and its direct antecedents] (1963); Franciszek GERMAN, **Chopin im Lichte unbekannter Memoirenquellen gesehen** [Chopin in the light of unknown memoir sources] (1968); Mateusz GLIŃSKI, **Les lettres de Chopin à Delphine Potocki** [Chopin's letters to Delfina Potocka] (1971); Czesław HALSKI, **The Polish origin of the polka** (4977); Arthur HEDLEY, **Some observations on the autograph sources of Chopin's works** (3899); Wilhelm HEINITZ, **Physiologische Beobachtungen zur Werk-Ästhetik F. Chopins** [Physiological observations on the aesthetic character of Frédéric Chopin's works] (3787); Zofia HELMAN, **Wpływ Chopina na wczesną twórczość Karola Szymanowskiego** [Chopin's influence on the early works of Karol Szymanowski] (2178); Lajos HERNÁDI, **Einige charakteristische Züge in dem Chopinschen Klaviersatz** [Some characteristic traits of Chopin's piano writing] (4178); Karol HŁAWICZKA, **Eigentümliche Merkmale Chopins Rhythmik** [Characteristic features of Chopin's rhythm] (4000) and **Ein Beitrag zur Verwandtschaft zwischen der Melodik Chopins und der polnischen Volksmusik** [A study on the relationship between Chopin's melody and Polish folk music] (4434); Alfred HOFFMAN, **Un grand interprète roumain de la musique de Chopin: Dinu Lipatti** [A great Romanian interpretation of the music of Chopin: Dinu Lipatti] (2327); Władysław HORDYŃSKI, **Nieznany list Chopina do Teresy Wodzińskiej** [An unknown letter from Chopin to Teresa Wodzińska] (1985); Heinrich HUSMANN, **Die Stellung der Romantik in der Weltgeschichte der Musik** [The place of Romanticism in universal music history] (3948); Danuta IDASZAK, **Mazurek w polskiej muzyce XVIII wieku** [The mazurka in Polish music of the 18th century] (1782); Jarosław IWASZKIEWICZ, **Styl literacki listów Chopina** [The literary style of Chopin's letters] (1990); Jean JACQUOT, **L'organisation internationale des recherches sur la musique pour luth et les sources polonaises** [The international organization of research on lute music and the Polish sources] (885); Jan Zygmunt JAKUBOWSKI, **Norwid i Chopin** [Norwid and Chopin] (1991); Jaroslav JIRÁNEK, **Beitrag zum Vergleich des Klavierstils von Fryderyk Chopin und Bedřich Smetana** [Toward a comparison between the piano styles of Frédéric Chopin and Bedřich Smetana] (1994); Tadeusz KACZYŃSKI, **Texte poétique en tant que source d'inspiration musicale dans certaines chants de Chopin et de Moniuszko** [Poetic text as the source of musical inspiration in certain songs by Chopin and Moniuszko] (1995); Włodzimierz KAMIŃSKI, **Frühmittelalterliche Musikinstrumente auf polnischem Gebiet** [Early medieval musical instruments in Polish territory] (5741); Józef KAŃSKI, **Über die Aufführungsstile der Werke Chopins: Einige allgemeine Probleme der Aufführung auf Grund von Schallplattenaufnahmen** [Performance styles for Chopin's works: Some general problems of performance, based on sound recordings] (3789); Jurij Vsevolodovič KELDYŠ, **Sovetskaja šopeniana** [Soviet Chopiniana] (2000); Wacław KMICIC-MIELESZYŃSKI, **Sprawa pobytu Chopina w Gdańsku** [Did Chopin visit Gdańsk?] (2007); Georg KNEPLER, **Die Bestimmung des Begriffes "Romantik"** [The definition of the concept of Romanticism] (5511); Krystyna KOBYLAŃSKA, **Sur l'histoire des manuscrits de F. Chopin** [On the history of Chopin's manuscripts] (2008); Andrzej KOSZEWSKI, **Pierwiastek walcowy w twórczości Chopina** [Waltz elements in Chopin's works] (4356); Günther KRAFT, **Polnische Folklore im Lied der Vormärz-Bewegung in Deutschland** [Polish folklore in songs of the Vormärz movement in Germany] (2013); Julij Anatol'evič KREMLËV, **La place historique de l'harmonie de Chopin** [The historical place of Chopin's harmony] (2015) and **L'importance mondiale de l'esthétique de Chopin** [The world importance of Chopin's aesthetic] (5513); György KROÓ, **Einige Probleme des Romantischen bei Chopin und Liszt** [Problems of the Romantic in Chopin and Liszt] (2017); Milada LADMANOVÁ, **Chopin und Smetana** [Chopin and Smetana] (2023); Dieter LEHMANN, **Satztechnische Besonderheiten in den Klavierwerken von Frédéric Chopin und Robert Schumann** [Unusual technical elements in the piano writing of Frédéric Chopin and Robert Schumann] (4362); Heinrich LINDLAR, **Chopin in der deutschen Musikkritik seiner Zeit** [Chopin in the German music criticism of his time] (819); Zofia LISSA, **Die Formenkreuzung bei Chopin** [Hybrid form in Chopin] (4267) and **Über die Verbindungen zwischen der Harmonik von A.N. Skrjabin und der Harmonik von F. Chopin** [Connections between the harmonic practices of A.N. Skrjabin and F. Chopin] (4190); Stefania ŁOBACZEWSKA, **La culture musicale en Pologne au début du XIXᵉ siècle et ses relations avec la musique de Chopin** [Musical culture in Poland at the beginning of the 19th century and its relations with Chopin's music] (2029); Tadeusz MIAZGA, **Prosa pro defunctis *Audi tellus*** (5332); Jakov MIL'ŠTEJN, **Fortep'jannaja faktura Šopena i Lista** [Piano writing in Chopin and Liszt] (2044); Ladislav MOKRÝ, **Zu den Anfängen der Mehrstimmigkeit bei den Westslawen** [The beginnings of polyphony among the West Slavic peoples] (1149); Antal MOLNÁR, **Die Persönlichkeit Chopins** [Chopin's personality] (2045); Otto MORTENSEN, **The Polish dance in Denmark** (5038); Hans Joachim MOSER, **Chopin stilkundlich betrachtet** [Chopin from the point of view of stylistics] (4376); Alina NOWAK-ROMANOWICZ, **Ideologia Józefa Elsnera a Chopin** [Józef Elsner's ideology and Chopin] (2053); Carl de NYS, **Note sur les polonaises de Wilhelm Friedemann Bach** [Note on the polonaises of Wilhelm Friedemann Bach] (1831); Mirko OČADLÍK, **Echa twórczości chopinowskiej u Bedřicha Smetany** [Echoes of Chopin's compositions in Bedřich Smetana] (2055); Maria OTTICH, **Chopin und die Komponisten der nachfolgenden Generationen** [Chopin and the composers of following generations] (2065); Stefania PAWLISZYN, **Elementy melodyki ukraińskiej w twórczości Chopina** [Ukrainian melodic elements in Chopin's works] (2066); Mirosław PERZ, **Handschrift Nr. 1361 der Öffentlichen Städtischen Raczyński-Bibliothek in Poznań: Als neue Quelle zur Geschichte der polnischen Musik in der II. Hälfte des XV. Jahrhunderts** [Manuscript no. 1361 in the Miejska Biblioteka Publiczna im. Edwarda Raczyńskiego, Poznań, as a new source for Polish music history in the second half of the 15th century] (1399); Hans PISCHNER, **Die Bedeutung Chopins für Robert Schumann** [Chopin's significance for Robert Schumann] (2067); Bohdan POCIEJ, **Rola harmoniki w technice przetworzeniowej Chopina** [The role of harmony in Chopin's creative process] (4209); Jaroslav PROCHÁZKA, **The origin of "the Prague mazurka" in G major and Chopin's relations with Václav Hanka** (2074); Maria PROKOPOWICZ, **Musique imprimée à Varsovie en 1800-1830** [Music printed in Warsaw from 1800-1830] (5985); Antoni PROSNAK, **Niektóre zagadnienia wariacyjności etiud Chopina** [Issues of variation technique in Chopin's etudes] (2079); Jan PROSNAK, **Elementy berżeretki francuskiej, "sztajerka" i folkloru ukraińskiego w twórczości Chopina** [Elements of the French bergerette, the sztajerek genre, and Ukrainian folklore in Chopin's works] (2080); Vladimir PROTOPOPOV, **Variacionnost' kak princip razvitija v muzyke Šopena** [Variation technique as a principle of development in Chopin's music] (4280); Jan RACEK, **Les études faites par Leoš Janáček dans les compositions pour piano de Frédéric Chopin** [Leoš Janáček's annotations in his copies of the piano compositions of Frédéric Chopin] (2081); Kurt REINHARD, **Zur Frage des Tempos bei Chopin** [The question of tempo in Chopin] (4022); Witold RUDZIŃSKI, **Źródła stylu** muzycznego Stanisława Moniuszki [Sources of Stanisław Moniuszko's musical style] (2086); Walter SALMEN, **J.F. Reichardt und die osteuropäische Volksmusik** [Johann Friedrich Reichardt and Eastern European traditional music] (1849); Wiarosław SANDELEWSKI, **Les éléments du bel canto italien dans l'œuvre de Chopin** [The elements of Italian bel canto in the works of Chopin] (2092); Walther SIEGMUND-SCHULTZE, **Chopin und Brahms** [Chopin and Brahms] (2096); Jerzy SIENKIEWICZ, **Zapomniany list Chopina (Chopin i Piotr Michałowski)** [A forgotten letter by Chopin (Chopin and Piotr Michałowski)] (2098); Alphons SILBERMANN, **Sozialpsychologische Aspekte im Wandel des Chopin-Idols** [Social-psychological aspects of change in the idolized image of Chopin] (5419); Jaroslav SIMONIDES, **Quelques problèmes relatifs aux traductions de la correspondance de Frédéric Chopin** [Some problems related to the translations of Chopin's correspondence] (5356); Zofia SKORUPSKA, **Chopiniana w zbiorach Biblioteki Kórnickiej** [Chopiniana in the collections of the Biblioteka Kórnicka] (760); Sergej Sergeevič SKREBKOV, **Novatorskie čerty tematičeskogo razvitija v muzyke Šopena** [Innovative features of thematic development in Chopin's music] (4461); Adam SŁAWIŃSKI, **Rytm a harmonia w polonezach Chopina** [Rhythm and harmony in Chopin's polonaises] (4030); Jitka SNÍŽKOVÁ, **Contribution aux relations tchéco-polonaises au XVIᵉ-XVIIᵉ siècle** [Czech-Polish relations in the 16th and 17th centuries] (1436); Jadwiga SOBIESKA and Marian SOBIESKI, **Das Tempo rubato bei Chopin und in der polnischen Volksmusik** [Tempo rubato in Chopin and in Polish traditional music] (3790); Edwin Kornel STADNICKI, **Polski walc fortepianowy przed Chopinem** [The waltz for piano in Poland before Chopin] (2101); Juliusz STARZYŃSKI, **Chopin—Delacroix: Comparaison d'esthétique** [Chopin and Delacroix: An aesthetic comparison] (5604); Bohumír ŠTĚDROŇ, **Janáček und Polen** [Janáček and Poland] (2102); Zofia STĘSZEWSKA and Jan STĘSZEWSKI, **Zur Genese und Chronologie des Mazurkarhythmus in Polen** [The origin and chronology of the mazurka rhythm in Poland] (4034); Adam SUTKOWSKI, **The Pelplin organ tablature (1620-1630): A valuable musical document of Polish music culture in late Renaissance** (1445); Antonín SYCHRA, **Ein Beitrag zur inhaltlichen Deutung von Chopins Schaffen** [Toward an interpretation of the content of Chopin's works] (2108); Václav Jan SÝKORA, **Jan Ladislav Dusík, der älteste Vorgänger Chopins** [Jan Ladislav Dusík, Chopin's earliest precursor] (1875); Maria SZCZEPAŃSKA, **Niektóre zagadnienia polskiej muzyki lutniowej XVI wieku** [Issues in Polish lute music of the 16th century] (1446); Zygmunt Marian SZWEYKOWSKI, **Proces przemian stylistycznych w muzyce wokalno-instrumentalnej epoki saskiej** [The process of stylistic change in the vocal-instrumental music Saxon era] (1696); Władysław TATARKIEWICZ, **Prądy filozoficzne epoki Chopina** [Philosophical currents of Chopin's time] (5610); Mieczysław TOMASZEWSKI, **Verbindungen zwischen den Chopinschen Liederwerken und dem polnischen populären, Volks- und Kunstlied** [Connections between Chopin's song compositions and Polish popular, folk, and art song] (2110); Teresa Dalila TURŁO, **Funkcja harmoniczna figuracji u Chopina** [The function of harmonic figurations in Chopin's music] (4222); Janusz URBAŃSKI, **Das Chopin-Klavier auf der Basis der zeitgenössischen Phonographie** [The Chopin piano, based on contemporary recording technology] (5796); Zeno VANCEA, **Der Chopin-Schüler Carol Mikuli, ein Bindeglied zwischen rumänischer und polnischer Musikkultur** [Chopin's pupil Karol Mikuli, a link between Romanian and Polish musical culture] (2115); Vera VASINA-GROSSMAN, **Šopen i Mogučaja Kučka** [Chopin and the Russian Five] (2117); Waldemar VOISÉ, *Dodecachordon* **d'Henri Glaréan d'après sa correspondance avec Jean Laski (Joannes à Lasco)** [The *Dodecachordon* of Heinrich Glarean, as mentioned in his correspondence with Jan Łaski (Johannes à Lasco)] (1461); Jaroslav VOLEK, **Die Bedeutung Chopins für die Entwicklung der alterierten Akkorde in der Musik des XIX. Jahrhunderts** [Chopin's role in the development of the altered chord in 19th-century music] (4224); Krystyna WILKOWSKA-CHOMIŃSKA, **Nicolas de Cracovie et la musique de la Renaissance en Pologne** [Mikołaj z Krakowa and the music of the Renaissance in Poland] (1469); Walter WIORA, **Chopins préludes und études und Bachs** *Wohltemperiertes Klavier* [Chopin's preludes and etudes and Bach's *Das Wohltemperirtes Clavier*] (2127); Tadeusz Andrzej ZIELIŃSKI, **Forma okresowa w mazurkach Chopina i mazurkach Szymanowskiego** [Periodic form in Chopin's and Szymanowski's mazurkas] (4296).

426
bs

[Warsaw] Poetics/Poetyka/Poetika. Proceedings of the First International Conference of Work-in-Prog-

ress Devoted to Problems of Poetics; sponsored by the Polska Akademia Nauk, Instytut Badań Literackich. Ed. by Donald DAVIE and Kazimierz WYKA (Warszawa: Państwowe Wydawnictwo Naukowe, 1961) xxiii, 893 p. *Illus., music, bibliog., index.* In English, Polish, Russian, French, and German.

The conference was held from 18 through 27 August 1960. The following contributions are cited separately: Ljubomir ANDREJČIN, **O poetike bolgarskih narodnyh pesen** [The poetics of traditional Bulgarian song] (5280); Robert AUSTERLITZ, **The identification of folkloristic genres (based on Gilyak materials)** (2601); Donald DAVIE, **The relation between syntax and music in some modern poems in English** (5299); Petăr DINEKOV, **Nekotorye osobennosti poetiki sovremennoj narodnoj pesni** [Some characteristics of the poetics of contemporary folk song] (5305); Stojan DŽUDŽEV, **Vestiges de la métrique ancienne dans le folklore bulgare** [Vestiges of ancient meter in Bulgarian folklore] (5309); Herbert PEUKERT, **Die Funktion der Formel im Volkslied** [The function of the formula in traditional song] (5341); Pavel TROST, **Das Metrum der litauischen Volkslieder** [The meter of Lithuanian traditional song] (4038).

⟶ **[Wégimont] Les colloques de Wégimont. IV: Ethnomusicologie III** [The Wégimont colloquia. IV: Ethnomusicology III]. See no. 401 in this volume.

1961

427
bs

[Budapest] Liszt—Bartók: Bericht über die zweite Internationale Musikwissenschaftliche Konferenz/Report of the Second International Musicological Conference. Sponsored by the Magyar Tudományos Akadémia. Ed. by Bence SZABOLCSI and Zoltán GÁRDONYI; intro. by Zoltán KODÁLY; pref. by István RUSZNYÁK, *Studia musicologica Academiae Scientiarum Hungaricae* V (1963) 596 p. *Music, transcr.* In German, French, Hungarian, English, and Russian.

The conference was held from 25 through 30 September 1961. The following contributions are cited separately: Gerald ABRAHAM, **Bartók and England** (2129); György BODNÁR, **Bartók et le mouvement** *Nyugat* [Bartók and the *Nyugat* movement] (2138); Ferenc BÓNIS, **Quotations in Bartók's music: A contribution to Bartók's psychology of composition** (4317); Alexandr BUCHNER, **Liszt in Prag** [Liszt in Prague] (1925); Ladislav BURLAS, **Neuerertum und Tradition in Bartók's Formenwelt** [Innovation and tradition in Bartók's formal universe] (4235); József Michał fCHOMIŃSKI, **Einige Probleme der Klangtechnik von Liszt** [Some aspects of sonority technique in Liszt] (4298); János DEMÉNY, **Béla Bartóks Stellung in der Musikgeschichte des 20. Jahrhunderts** [Bela Bartók's position in music history of the 20th century] (2154); Denijs DILLE, **Les problèmes des recherches sur Bartók** [Problems of Bartók research] (2155); Hellmut FEDERHOFER, **Die Diminution in den Klavierwerken von Chopin und Liszt** [Ornamentation in the piano works of Chopin and Liszt] (4332); Werner FELIX, **Liszts Schaffen um 1848: Versuch zur Deutung seiner Programmatik** [Liszt's composition around 1848: Toward an interpretation of his program music] (1956); Čeněk GARDAVSKÝ, **Liszt und seine tschechischen Lehrer** [Liszt and his Czech teacher] (1964); Zoltán GÁRDONYI, **Nationale Thematik in der Musik Franz Liszts bis zum Jahre 1848** [Nationalism in Franz Liszt's music to 1848] (1966) and **Schlußwort der Liszt-Sektion** [Closing remarks of the Liszt session] (1967); Otto GOLDHAMMER, **Liszt, Brahms und Reményi** [Liszt, Brahms, and Reményi] (1973); Monika GORCZYCKA, **Neue Merkmale der Klangtechnik in Bartóks Streichquartetten** [New features of sound technique in Bartók's string quartets] (4337); Everett HELM, **A newly discovered Liszt manuscript** (1982); Alfred HOFFMAN and Nicolae MISSIR, **Sur la tournée de concerts de Ferenc Liszt en 1846-47 dans le Banat, la Transylvanie et les pays roumains** [On the concert tour of Franz Liszt in 1846-47 in Banat, Transylvania, and Romanian territories] (1983); Zoltán HRABUSSAY, **Correspondance de Liszt avec des musiciens de Slovaquie** [Liszt's correspondence with musicians of Slovakia] (1987); Vladimír HUDEC, **Zum Problem des "Lisztartigen" in Smetanas symphonischen Dichtungen** [On the problem of "Lisztishness" in Smetana's symphonic poems] (4346);

Pál JÁRDÁNYI, **Bartók und die Ordnung der Volkslieder** [Bartók and the classification of traditional songs] (4261); Jaroslav JIRÁNEK, **Liszt und Smetana: Ein Beitrag zur Genesis und eine vergleichende Betrachtung ihres Klavierstils** [Liszt and Smetana: On the genesis of their piano styles and a comparative study] (4350); György KERÉNYI and Benjamin RAJECZKY, **Über Bartóks Volksliedaufzeichnungen** [On Bartók's transcription of traditional songs] (2190); Günther KRAFT, **Das Schaffen von Franz Liszt in Weimar** [Franz Liszt's creative work in Weimar] (2014); György KROÓ, **Monothematik und dramaturgie in Bartóks Bühnenwerken** [Monothematicism and dramaturgy in Bartók's stage works] (4443); Dieter LEHMANN, **Bemerkungen zur Liszt-Rezeption in Russland in den vierziger und fünfziger Jahren des 19. Jahrhunderts** [Remarks on Liszt reception in Russia in the 1840s and 1850s] (2025); Lajos LESZNAI, **Realistische Ausdrucksmittel in der Musik Béla Bartóks** [Realistic means of expression in the music of Béla Bartók] (4364); Paul MICHEL, **Franz Liszt als Lehrer und Erzieher** [Franz Liszt as instructor and teacher] (2040); Antal MOLNÁR, **Über Transkriptionen und Paraphrasen von Liszt** [Liszt's transcriptions and paraphrases] (2046); Izrail' Vladimirovič NEST'EV, **Bela Bartok v Rossii** [Béla Bartók in Russia] (2216); Zdeněk NOVÁČEK, **Der entscheidende Einfluß von Liszt auf die fortschrittliche Musikorientation in Pressburg** [Liszt's decisive influence on the progressive musical outlook of Bratislava] (2050); Mirko OČADLÍK, **Die radikalen Demokraten: Liszt und Smetana** [Radical democrats: Liszt and Smetana] (2056); Stojan PETROV, **Bela Bartok i bolgarskaja muzykal'naja kul'tura** [Bartók and Bulgarian musical culture] (2229) and **Proizvedenija Ferenca Lista v Bolgarii** [Liszt's works in Bulgaria] (2371); Milan POŠTOLKA, **Liszt und Böhmen im Spiegel der unveröffentlichten Korrespondenz** [Liszt and Bohemia, as reflected in unpublished correspondence] (2072); Jan RACEK, **Leoš Janáčeks und Béla Bartóks Bedeutung in der Weltmusik** [The international musical significance of Leoš Janáček and Béla Bartók] (2238); Werner RACKWITZ, **Liszts Verhältnis zur Musik Georg Friedrich Händels** [Liszt's relationship to the music of Georg Friedrich Händel] (2082); Ahmed Adnan SAYGUN, **Quelques réflexions sur certaines affinités des musiques folkoriques turque et hongroise** [Some reflections on certain affinities between Turkish and Hungarian traditional music] (3051); Humphrey SEARLE, **Liszt and 20th-century music** (2248); László SOMFAI, **Die Metamorphose der** *Faust-Symphonie* **von Liszt** [The metamorphosis of Liszt's *Faust-Symphonie*] (2099); István SÓTÉR, **Le populisme dans la littérature et la musique** [Populism in literature and music] (5360); Bohumír ŠTĚDROŇ, **Leoš Janáček und Ferenc Liszt** [Leoš Janáček and Franz Liszt] (2255); Wolfgang SUPPAN, **Franz Liszt und die Steiermark** [Franz Liszt and Styria] (2106); Bence SZABOLCSI, **Mensch und Natur in Bartóks Geisteswelt** [Man and nature in Bartók's spiritual world] (2260); István SZELÉNYI, **Der unbekannte Liszt** [The unknown Liszt] (4386); József UJFALUSSY, **Einige inhaltliche Fragen der Brückensymmetrie in Bartóks Werken** [Musical content and arch symmetry in Bartók's works] (4290); Zeno VANCEA, **Einige Beiträge über das erste Manuskript der Colinda-Sammlung von Béla Bartók und über seine einschlägigen Briefe an Constantin Brăiloiu** [Notes on the first manuscript of Béla Bartók's colinda collection and his relevant letters to Constatin Brăiloiu] (3094); Jaroslav VOLEK, **Über einige interessante Beziehungen zwischen thematischer Arbeit und Instrumentation in Bartóks** *Concerto für Orchester* [Some interesting relationships between thematic ideas and instrumentation in Bartók's *Concerto for orchestra*] (4292); John S. WEISSMAN, **On some problems with Bartók research in connection with Bartók's biography** (2269); Feng ZHAO, **Bartók and Chinese musical culture** (2412). The book form of the symposium proceedings is cited as no. 428 in this volume.

428 **[Budapest, 1961] Liszt-Bartók: Bericht über**
bs **die zweite Internationale Musikwissenschaftliche Konferenz/Report of the second International Musicological Conference.** Ed. by Zoltán GÁRDONYI and Bence SZABOLCSI (Budapest: Akadémiai Kiadó, 1963) 596 p. *Music, bibliog.* In German, English, French, and Russian.
The journal form of the symposium proceedings is cited as no. 427 in this volume.

429 **[Cambridge, Mass.] Chanson & madrigal**
bs **1480-1530: Studies in comparison and contrast.** Sponsored by Harvard University, Department of

Music. Ed. by James HAAR. *Isham Library papers* 2 (Cambridge, MA: Harvard University Press, 1964) xiii, 266 p. *Music, index.*
The conference was held at Isham Memorial Library, Harvard University, from 13 through 14 September 1961. The following contributions are cited separately: Howard Mayer BROWN, **The genesis of a style: The Parisian chanson, 1500-1530** (1261); Daniel HEARTZ, **Les goûts réunis, or, The worlds of the madrigal and the chanson confronted** (1330); Walter H. RUBSAMEN, **From frottola to madrigal: The changing pattern of secular Italian vocal music** (1422). Includes a number of previously unavailable complete compositions, in new modern editions.

430 **[Canberra] Australian Aboriginal studies.** Pro-
bs ceedings of the 1961 Conference on Aboriginal Studies; sponsored by the Social Science Research Council of Australia and Australian National University. Ed. by Helen SHEILS (Melbourne: Oxford University, 1963) xx, 505 p. *Bibliog., discog., index, maps.*
The founding conference of the Australian Institute of Aboriginal Studies was held on the campus of the Australian National University in May 1961. The following contribution is cited separately: Trevor A. JONES, **A brief survey of ethnomusicological research in the music of Aboriginal Australia** (3227).

431 **[Cologne] Vorträge zum Urheberrecht/Lec-**
bs **tures on copyright/Conférences sur le droit d'auteur.** Proceedings of the Fourth International Congress on Church Music. *Internationale Gesellschaft für Urheberrecht e.V. Schriftenreihe* 25 (Berlin; Frankfurt am Main: Vahlen, 1961) 69 p. In German, English, and French.
A separate edition of papers on copyright read at the Fourth International Congress on Church Music (see no. 432). The following contributions are cited separately: Ernst Denny HIRSCH BALLIN, **Urheberrecht am Scheideweg** [Copyright at the parting of the ways] (5966); Erich SCHULZE, **Kirchenmusik und Urheberrecht** [Church music and copyright] (5988).

432 **[Cologne] IV. Internationaler Kongress für**
bs **Kirchenmusik in Köln: Dokumente und Berichte** [Fourth International Congress on Church Music in Cologne: Documents and reports]. Ed. by Johannes OVERATH. *Schriftenreihe des Allgemeinen Cäcilien-Verbandes für die Länder der Deutschen Sprache* 4 (Köln: Bachem, 1962) 386 p. *Illus., port.* In German, English, French, Latin, and Italian.
The conference was held from 22 through 30 June 1961. The following contributions are cited separately: Walter ALBUQUERQUE, **Südindische klassische und Volksmusik: Die Ursprünge der indischen Musik in der Legende** [South Indian classical and folk music: The origins of Indian music according to legend] (2600); Vincent ALVARES, **The apostleship of music with regard to a fruitful missionary future in India** (6143); Charles COUTURIER, **Dimensions de l'adaptation/Ausmaße der Adaptation** [Dimensions of adaptation] (6194); Bartolomeo DI SALVO, **Dall'essenza della musica nelle liturgie orientali** [On the essence of music in the Eastern liturgies] (6109); Basilius EBEL, **Grundlagen des Verhältnisses von Kult und Gesang/The basic interdependence of chant and cult/Les bases des relations entre culte et chant/Principi fondamentali del rapporto tra culto e canto** (6208); Ernst Denny HIRSCH BALLIN, **Urheberrecht am Scheideweg/Copyright at the parting of the ways/Le droit d'auteur à la croisée des chemins** (5967); Alfred KRINGS, **Zur Aufführung von Kirchenmusik des Mittelalters und der Renaissance** [On the performance practice of the church music of the Middle Ages and Renaissance] (3703); René Bernard LENAERTS, **Probleme der Messe in ihrer historischen Sicht/Problems of the Mass in their historical perspective/Problèmes de la Messe dans leur perspective historique/Problemi della Messa nella perspettiva storica** (6285); Francesco Yosio NOMURA, **Akkommodation und Kirchenmusikpflege in Japan** [Adaptation and church music cultivation in Japan] (6322); Robert OUÉDRAOGO, **Rapport sur la musique religieuse au Mossi/Bericht über die religiöse Musik im Mossi-Land** [Report on the religious music of the Mossi region] (2573); Fiorenzo

ROMITA, **De Institutis Musicae Sacrae erigendis ad eiusdem musicae sacrae restaurationem juxta S. Pium X/Die Errichtung von Kirchen-musikschulen zur Erneuerung der Kirchenmusik im Sinne des hl. Papstes Pius X.** [The establishment of the Institutum Musicae Sacrae for the restoration of church music with St. Pius X] (6362); John Edward RONAN, **Music education and cathedral choir schools** (4763); Erich SCHULZE, **Kirchenmusik und Urheberrecht/Church music and copy-right/Musique sacrée et droit d'auteur** [Church music and copyright] (5989); Joseph SMITS VAN WAESBERGHE, **Die Ausbildung des Kir-chenmusikers** [The training of the church musician] (4895); Irenäus TOTZKE, **Unsere Verpflichtung gegenüber der ostkirchlichen Musik** [Our obligation to the sacred music of the Eastern church] (6028); Bruno WECHNER, **Die kirchenmusikalische Erziehung des Welt- und Or-densklerus** [Church music education of secular and monastic clergy] (4901). Another publication of the conference is cited as no. 431 in this volume.

433 **[Dakar] The historian in tropical Africa/**
bs **L'historien en Afrique tropicale.** Proceedings of the Fourth International African Seminar; sponsored by the International African Institute and University of Dakar. Ed. and intro. by Jan VANSINA, Raymond MAUNY, and Louis-Vincent THOMAS (London: Ox-ford University, 1964) ix, 428 p. *Charts, diagr., maps.* In English and French.

The following contribution is cited separately: Joseph Hanson Kwabena NKETIA, **Historical evidence in Gã religious music** (2568).

434 **[Herakleion] Pepragmena tou I Diethnous**
bs **Kritologikou Synedriou** [Proceedings of the First International Congress of Cretan Studies]. Sponsored by the Etairia Krītikōn Historikōn Meletōn (Irákleion: Kalokairinos, 1963) 3 v. *Krītika chronika* 15-16 (1961-1962). *Bibliog., index, maps, tech. drawings.* In Greek, Italian, French, English, and German.

The following contributions are cited separately: Samuel BAUD-BOVY, **La place des *rizitika tragoudia* dans la chanson populaire de la Grèce moderne** [The place of rizitika song in traditional song in modern Greece] (2735); Emmanuel DOULGHERAKIS, **I chronologīsis tou kritikou dimotikou tragoudiou** [The dating of the Cretan demotic song] (2795); Demetrios NOTOPOULOS, **Ti epidrasis tou kleftikou tragoudiou eis ta rizitika tragoudia tis Krītis** [The influence of kléftiko on rizitika song in Crete] (2976).

435 **[Jerusalem] Haqŵngres ha'ŵlamy hašlyšy**
bs **lemada'ey hayahadŵt** [Third World Congress of Jewish Studies]. Sponsored by the Hebrew University of Jerusalem, World Union of Jewish Studies (Yerŵšalaym/Al-Quds: Hebrew University/ Ha'unybersytah ha'ibryt, 1965) 379 p. *Bibliog.* In He-brew, English, and French.

The following contributions are cited separately: Israel ADLER, **Le MS Vm¹ de la Bibliothèque Nationale (Cantate pour une circoncision dans le Comtat Venaissin au dix-septième siècle)** [The MS Vm¹ at the Bibliothèque Nationale (a 17th-century cantata for a circumcision in the Comtat Venaissin)] (1477); Hanoch AVENARY, **Who is on Mount Horeb?: A piyyut and its melody from the Geniza** (6038); Hayym BAR-DYYAN, **Music in the life of Vilna Jewry** (6040); Bathja BAYER, **Musical relics in Palestinian archaeology** (5739); Edith GERSON-KIWI, **Halleluia and Jubilus in Oriental Jewish and Chris-tian chant** (6053); Me'yr Sim'ŵn GEŚWRY, **Chants used in the study of the Talmud by Ashkenazi and Oriental Jews** (6056); Avigdor HERZOG, **The Tora readings according to the Israeli Sephardic mode** (6070); Johanna SPECTOR, **Problems of compatibility: Non-Western versus Western tradition in Jewish music** (6098).

436 **[Jerusalem] Mŵsyqah haḥasydŵt** [Hasidic mu-
bs sic]. Proceedings of the Fourth Israeli Music Congress, *Dŵkan* IV (1962). In Hebrew.

The following contributions are cited separately: Alexander Uriah BOSKOVICH, **Hasŵwytah hayehŵdyt** [*Semitic suite*] (2142); Mordekay BRŴY'ER, **BR'ayŵt wederakym beḥeqer hamŵsyqah haḥasydyt**

[Problems and trends in the research of Hasidic music] (6045); Me'yr Sim'ŵn GEŚWRY, **Haḥasydŵt beslyl webezemer** [Hasidism in sound and song] (6057); Yehŵšu'a Leyyb NE'EMAN, **Ṭa'amym wezmyrŵt** [Notation of Hebrew accents and songs] (3856); Yzḥaq Yedydyah PRENQEL, **Hašyrah šebeḥasydŵt** [The song in Hasidic literature] (6087); Y'aqob RŴS, **Hanegynah wehaḥawyah hadatyt** [Music and re-ligious experience] (6094).

437 **[Montreal] Proceedings: The Third World**
bs **Congress of Psychiatry/Comptes rendus: Le troisième Congrès mondial de psychiatrie/ Sitzungsberichte: Der dritte Weltkongress der Psychiatrie/Las actas: El tercer Congreso Mundial de Psiquiatria.** Sponsored by the Cana-dian Psychiatric Association and McGill University (Montréal: McGill University, 1961); (Toronto: Uni-versity of Toronto, 1963) 3 v. In English, French, Ger-man, and Spanish.

The conference was held from 4 through 10 June 1961. The following con-tribution is cited separately: Henry R. ROLLIN, **The therapeutic use of music in a mental hospital with special reference to group treatment** (5736).

438 **[New York] Addresses at the International**
bs **Hymnological Conference.** Sponsored by the Na-tional Council of Churches of Christ. Ed. by James Rawlings SYDNOR. *Papers of the Hymn Society* 24 (New York: Hymn Society of America, 1962) 54 p. *Music.*

The conference was held on 10 and 11 September 1961. The following con-tributions are cited separately: Charles L. ATKINS, **William Billings: His psalm and hymn tunes** (6423); J. Vincent HIGGINSON, **Aspects of American Catholic hymnody** (6251); James Rawlings SYDNOR, **Twen-tieth-century hymnody in the United States** (6452); John W. WORK, **The Negro spiritual** (3184).

439 **[New York] Report of the Eighth Congress of**
bs **the International Musicological Society. I: Pa-pers.** Sponsored by the American Musicological Soci-ety. Ed. by Jan LARUE (Kassel: Bärenreiter, 1961) 472 p. *Illus., facs., music, charts, diagr., transcr.* In English, German, and French.

The conference was held from 5 through 10 September 1961. The follow-ing contributions are cited separately: Anna Amalie ABERT, **Liszt, Wag-ner, und die Beziehungen zwischen Musik und Literatur im 19. Jahr-hundert** [Liszt, Wagner, and the relationship between music and literature in the 19th century] (1905); Higini ANGLÈS, **Der Rhythmus in der Melodik mittelalterlicher Lyrik** [Rhythm in the melody for medieval po-etry] (3803); Myroslav ANTONOVYČ, **The present state of Josquin re-search** (1224); William W. AUSTIN, **Traditional forms in new musical idioms** (4232); Luiz Heitor Corrêa de AZEVEDO, **Survivance et déve-loppement des diverses traditions européennes dans le continent américain** [The survival and development of the various European tradi-tions in the Americas] (943); Milton BABBITT, **Past and present con-cepts of the nature and limits of music** (3930); Wolfgang BOETTICHER, **Zum Parodieproblem bei Orlando di Lasso: Ein spezieller Beitrag zur Frage geistlich-weltlicher Übertragungstechnik** [The parody problem in Roland de Lassus: A special contribution on his technique of transferring secular to sacred] (1243); Allen P. BRITTON, **The singing school movement in the United States** (4905); Solange CORBIN, **Note sur l'ornementation dans le plain-chant grégorien** [Note on ornamentation in Gregorian chant] (1077); Georg von DADELSEN, **Bach-Probleme** [Bach problems] (1518); Thurston DART, **Performance practice in the 17th and 18th centuries: Six problems in instrumental music** (3738); Edward O.D. DOWNES, **The Neapolitan tradition in opera** (1529); Hans Heinrich EGGEBRECHT, **Der Begriff des "Neuen" in der Musik von der Ars nova bis zur Gegenwart** [The concept of the new in music from the ars nova to the present day] (5459); Walter EMERY, **On evidence of derivation** (1538); Hans ENGEL, **Die Quellen des Klassischen Stiles** [Sources of the Classic style] (4330); Georg FEDER, **Bemerkungen über die Ausbildung der Klassischen Tonsprache in der Instrumentalmusik Haydns** [Remarks on the devel-opment of the Classic musical language in Haydn's instrumental music] (4331); Karl Gustav FELLERER, **Beziehungen zwischen geistlicher und** weltlicher Musik im 16. Jahrhundert [Relations between religious and secular music in the 16th century] (1301); Ernest Thomas FERAND, **A history of music seen in the light of ornamentation** (961); Kurt von FISCHER, **Der Begriff des "Neuen" in der Musik von der Ars nova bis zur Gegenwart** [The concept of the new in music from the ars nova to the present day] (5468); Kurt GUDEWILL, **Ursprünge und nationale Aspekte des Quodlibets** [Origins and national aspects of the quodlibet] (4252); Léon GUICHARD, **Liszt, Wagner et les relations entre la musique et la littérature au XIXᵉ siècle** [Liszt, Wagner, and the relationship between music and literature in the 19th century] (5319); Frank Llewellyn HARRISON, **The social position of church musicians in England, 1450-1550** (5885); Helmut HUCKE, **Die neapolitanische Tradition in der Oper** [The Neapolitan tradition in opera] (1580); Heinrich HÜSCHEN, **Frühere und heutige Begriff von Wesen und Grenzen der Musik** [Past and present concepts of the nature and limits of music] (5492); Jean JACQUOT, **La musique pour luth** [Lute music] (595); François LESURE, **Pour une sociologie historique des faits musicaux** [Toward a historical sociology of musical facts] (5893); Edward E. LOWINSKY, **Awareness of tonality in the 16th century** (4192); Claudie MARCEL-DUBOIS, **Remarques sur l'ornementation dans l'ethnomusicologie européenne** [Remarks on ornamentation in European ethnomusicology] (2939); Philip L. MILLER, **Musicology and the phonograph record** (899); Marc PINCHERLE, **Des manières d'exécuter la musique aux XVIIᵉ et XVIIIᵉ siècles** [Performance practice in the 17th and 18th centuries] (3764); Hans-Peter REINECKE, **Musikwissenschaft und Schallplatte** [Musicology and the phonograph record] (5781); Gilbert ROUGET, **Note sur l'ornementation en Afrique noire** [Note on ornamentation in sub-Saharan Africa] (2580); André SCHAEFFNER, **Contribution de l'ethnomusicologie à l'histoire de la musique** [The contribution of ethnomusicology to historical musicology] (2467); Nils SCHIØRRING, **The contribution of ethnomusicology to historical musicology** (4111); Marius SCHNEIDER, **Wurzeln und Anfänge der abendländischen Mehrstimmigkeit** [Origins of Western polyphony] (1005); Charles SEEGER, **The cultivation of various European traditions in the Americas** (1006); Bruno STÄBLEIN, **Die Unterlegung von Texten unter Melismen: Tropus, Sequenz und andere Formen** [Text underlay of melismas: Trope, sequence, and other forms] (1189); Denis STEVENS, **Problems of editing and publishing old music** (3922); Geneviève THIBAULT DE CHAMBURE, **Du rôle de l'ornementation, improvisée ou écrite, dans l'évolution de la musique** [The role of improvised and written ornamentation in the evolution of music] (854) and **L'ornementation dans la musique profane au Moyen Âge** [Ornamentation in secular medieval music] (1199); Van Khê TRÂN, **Note sur l'ornementation au Vietnam** [Note on ornamentation in Vietnam] (2700); André VERCHALY, **La métrique et le rythme musical au temps de l'humanisme** [Verse meter and melodic rhythm in the age of humanism] (1458); Klaus P. WACHSMANN, **Criteria for acculturation** (2480); William G. WAITE, **The era of melismatic polyphony** (1209); Albert WELLEK, **Der gegenwärtige Stand der Musikpsychologie und ihre Bedeutung für die historische Musikforschung** [The present state of music psychology and its significance for historical musicology] (5717); Ernest Glen WEVER, **The physiological basis of musical hearing: Present state and problems of research** (5720); Emanuel WINTERNITZ, **The visual arts as a source for the historian of music** (5405). Part II of the proceedings is cited as no. 440 in this volume.

440
bs
[New York] Report of the Eighth Congress of the International Musicological Society. II: Reports. Sponsored by the American Musicological Society. Ed. by Jan LARUE (Kassel: Bärenreiter, 1962) 184 p. *Music.* In English, French, and German.

The conference was held from 5 through 10 September 1961. The following contributions are cited separately: Gerhard ALBERSHEIM, **The present state of music psychology and its significance for historical musicology** (5635); Putnam ALDRICH, **The role of improvised and written ornamentation in the evolution of musical language** (829); William W. AUSTIN, **Traditional forms in new musical idioms** (4231); Eva BADURA-SKODA, **Liszt, Wagner, and the relations between music and literature in the 19th century** (1908); David D. BOYDEN, **Performance practice in the 17th and 18th centuries** (3732); Nanie BRIDGMAN, **Mécénat et musique** [Patronage and music] (952); Isabelle CAZEAUX, **Le rythme dans la monodie lyrique médiévale** [Rhythm in medieval lyric monody] (3978) and **Verse meter and melodic rhythm in the age of humanism** (1269); Gilbert CHASE, **The cultivation of various European traditions in the Americas** (953); Edward O.D. DOWNES, **The

Neapolitan tradition in opera** (1528); Hans Heinrich EGGEBRECHT, **The concept of the New in music from the ars nova to the present day** (5460); Ludwig FINSCHER, **Origins of Western polyphony** (840); Charles Warren FOX, **The present state of Josquin research** (1309); Henrik GLAHN, **Relations between religious and secular music in the 16th century** (1316); Daniel HEARTZ, **Lute music** (588); Helmut HUCKE, **Modes of underlaying a text to melismas: Trope, sequence, and other forms** (1126); Sylvia W. KENNEY, **Origins and national aspects of the quodlibet** (4262); Alfred MANN, **Sources of the classical idiom** (4369); Arthur MENDEL, **Evidence and explanation** (5539); A. Tillman MERRITT, **Awareness of tonality in the sixteenth century** (4198); Bruno NETTL, **Criteria for acculturation** (2453); Joel NEWMAN, **Problems of editing and publishing old music** (3911); Helmuth OSTHOFF, **Der Durchbruch zum musikalischen Humanismus** [The breakthrough to musical humanism] (1392); Laurence E.R. PICKEN, **The contribution of ethnomusicology to historical musicology** (2458); Hans-Peter REINECKE, **Physiological bases of musical hearing: Present state and problems of research** (5690); Alexander L. RINGER, **The employment of sociological methods in music history** (5905) and **The visual arts as a source for the historian of music** (5394); Denis STEVENS, **Musicology and the phonograph record** (5793); Leo TREITLER, **Bach problems** (1706); Eric WERNER, **Present and past concepts of the nature and limits of music** (5628); Glenn C. WILCOX, **The singing school movement in the United States** (4916). Part I of the proceedings is cited as no. 439 in this volume.

441
bs
[Ohrid] Actes du XIIᵉ Congrès d'études Byzantines [Proceedings of the 12th Congress of Byzantine Studies]. Sponsored by the International Association of Byzantine Studies and Jugoslavenski Odbor za Bizantinske Studije (Beograd: Naučno Delo, 1963-1964) 3 v. 450; 616; 439 p.; (reprint, Nendeln: Kraus, 1978). *Illus., facs., music, charts, diagr., maps.* In French, German, Italian, English, and French.

The conference was held from 10 through 16 September 1961. The following contributions are cited separately: Constantin FLOROS, **Fragen zum musikalischen und metrischen Aufbau der Kontakien** [Questions on the musical and metric structure of kontakia] (4248); Kenneth J. LEVY, **The Byzantine communion cycle and its Slavic counterpart** (1140); Giovanni MARZI, **Martyria e incipit nelle tradizione nomica** [Martyria and incipits in the nomic tradition] (1148); Jelena MILOJKOVIĆ-DJURIĆ, **On the Serbian chant in the eighteenth century after the neumatic manuscripts from Chilandar** (4375); Roksanda PEJOVIĆ, **Instruments de musique dans l'art serbo-macédonien et byzantin** [Musical instruments in Serbo-Macedonian and Byzantine art] (5389); Jørgen RAASTED, **The production of Byzantine musical manuscripts** (1163); Dimitrije STEFANOVIĆ, **Melody construction in Byzantine chant. II** (4463); Oliver STRUNK, **Melody construction in Byzantine chant. I** (4465); Christian THODBERG, **Chromatic alterations in the sticherarium** (3876); Egon WELLESZ, **Melody construction in Byzantine chant** (4473).

442
bs
[Québec] International Folk Music Council Conference. Sponsored by the Université Laval and Canadian Folk Music Society. Ed. by Laurence E.R. PICKEN, *Journal of the International Folk Music Council* XIV (1962) 189. *Illus., port., index, transcr.* In English and French.

The 14th annual conference was held from 28 August through 3 September 1961. The following contributions are cited separately: Maguy ANDRAL, **Permanence de structures élémentaires dans la musique traditionelle française vivante** [The permanence of elementary structures in living traditional French music] (2719); Marius BARBEAU, **Buddhist dirges on the North Pacific coast** (3135); Francis COLLINSON, **The repertoire of a traditional Gaelic singer in the outer Hebrides with reference to versions of her songs known in Canada** (2505); Sidney Robertson COWELL, **The connection between the precenting of psalms on Cape Breton Island and in the Colonial New England churches** (3143); Živko FIRFOV, **Les émigrants macédoniens en Amérique et le folklore macédonien musical** [Macedonian emigrants to America and Macedonian musical folklore] (3149); Graham GEORGE, **Songs of the Salish Indians of British Columbia** (3152); Edith GERSON-KIWI, **Musical sources of the Judaeo-Hispanic romance** (2828); Ida HALPERN, **Kwa-Kiutl music** (3153); Felix HOERBURGER, **Proposals for the work of the IFMC

Dance Commission (4980); Mantle HOOD, **Improvisation on the Java-nese gendèr** (2638); Edward D. IVES, **Satirical songs in Maine and the Maritime provinces of Canada** (5322); Vladimír KLUSÁK, **Songs of Czechs and Slovaks residing in America** (3158); George LIST, **Song in the Hopi culture, past and present** (3164); Claudie MARCEL-DUBOIS, **État présent du répertoire musical traditionnel paysan en France et vues comparées avec le répertoire français au Canada** [The present state of the traditional rural musical repertoire in France, and comparisons with the French repertoire in Canada] (2530); Geneviève MASSIGNON, **Chants de mer de l'ancienne et de la nouvelle France** [Sea songs of old France and French Canada] (2531); Tolia NIKIPROWETZKY, **The music of Mauritania** (2564); Joseph Hanson Kwabena NKETIA, **The hock-et-technique in African music** (2569); Harry OSTER, **Negro French spirituals of Louisiana** (3170); Laurence E.R. PICKEN, **Musical terms in a Chinese dictionary of the first century** (2673); Roger PINON, **Philologie et folklore musical: Les chants de pâtres avant leur émergence folklorique** [Philology and musical folklore: Shepherds' songs before their emergence as folklore] (850); Luis Felipe RAMÓN Y RIVERA, **Rhythmic and melodic elements in Negro music of Venezuela** (3215); Samuel J. SACKETT, **The hammered dulcimer in Ellis County, Kansas** (3601); Charles SEEGER, **The Model B melograph: A progress report** (5792); Barbara B. SMITH, **The bon-odori in Hawaii and in Ja-pan** (5064); Frances Lee UTLEY, **Noah in British and American folksong** (5366); Ovidiu VARGA, **Les variantes folkloriques et les con-ditions de leur survivance** [Folkloric variants and the conditions of their survival] (2477); Walter WIORA, **La musique à l'époque de la peinture paléolithique** [Music at the time of Paleolithic painting] (1049).

443
bs
[Tehran] **The preservation of traditional forms of the learned and popular music of the Orient and the Occident/La préservation des formes traditionelles de la musique savante et populaire dans les pays d'Orient et d'Occident.** Sponsored by the International Music Council and University of Illinois at Urbana-Cham-paign. Ed. by William Kay ARCHER; foreword by Nicolas NABOKOV; intro. by Jack BORNOFF (Ur-bana: Center for Comparative Psycholinguistics, Insti-tute of Communications Research, 1964) vii, 324 p. In English and French.

The conference was held from 6 through 12 April 1961. The following con-tributions are cited separately: William Kay ARCHER, **The musical bride: Some applications of evolution, culture, and tradition** (2492); Mehdi BARKECHLI, **Introduction to the International Congress** (2419); Samuel BAUD-BOVY, **The problems of the preservation of tra-ditional forms** (832); Roger BRAGARD, **Les musées instrumentals, moyens de préservation des formes traditionelles de la musique savante et populaire dans les pays d'Orient et d'Occident** [Instrument museums as a means of preserving traditional forms of art and folk music in Eastern and Western countries] (709); François CANAC, **Faithfulness in the transmission of music as a means of preservation** (5807); Jacques CHAILLEY, **Musique orientale et harmonie européenne** [Oriental mu-sic and European harmony] (4152); Jacques CHARPENTIER, **Les musiques orientales peuvent-elles susciter des formes nouvelles chez les compositeurs occidentaux?** [Can Eastern musics inspire new forms for Western composers?] (2303); Henry COWELL, **The composer's world** (2150); Peter CROSSLEY-HOLLAND, **Music of the Occidental type written by Orientals** (2152); Dragotin CVETKO, **Les transforma-tions sociales ayant une influence sur la vie du musicien et sur sa posi-tion dans la société** [Social transformations that have an influence on the musician's life and on his status in society] (5874); Alain DANIÉLOU, **Es-tablishment of the distinction between the main "families" of music ac-cording to the different fundamental systems** (837); Salah EL MAHDI, **Les problèmes de la préservation des formes traditionelles** [The prob-lems of preserving traditional forms] (2509); Edith GERSON-KIWI, **The integration of Dastgah and Maqam in Oriental-Jewish liturgies** (6054); Zaven HACOBIAN, **La tendance à l'hybridation: L'influence des conceptions a occidentales** [The tendency to hybridization: The influ-ence of Western conceptions] (2512); János KÁRPÁTI, **Quelques notes sur la musique traditionnelle et folklorique dans différentes régions du Maroc** [Some notes on traditional and folk music in different regions of Morocco] (2558); Fumio KOIZUMI, **Contemporary music in Occiden-tal style and its problems in Japan** (2192); Narayana MENON, **Basic principles of music expression as they are found in the music of India**

(2668); Joseph Hanson Kwabena NKETIA, **Continuity of traditional in-struction** (2567); Kurt REINHARD, **Cooperation with the musician: Prospection, conservation, transcription and publication, classifica-tion** (2463); Ahmed Adnan SAYGUN, **Basic principles of musical ex-pression as they are to be found in the modal music of the Middle East** (2687); Marius SCHNEIDER, **Basic principles: The variation, Ori-ent-Occident** (2688); Y. SPIRA, **Developments in Israel** (2695); Josef STANISLAV, **Some remarks on the development of musical creation among African peoples** (2590); Van Khê TRAN, **Basic principles of mu-sical expression as they are found in modal music of the Far East** (2698); Ali Naqi VAZIRI, **Notation: Means for the preservation or de-struction of music traditionally not notated** (3880); Viktor VINOGRADOV, **The experience of applying folk music traditions to professional music in the Eastern republics of the USSR** (2704); Shin'ichi YUIZE, **Means of preservation: Preservation of traditional instruction** (2707).

444
bs
[Todi] **Pellegrinaggi e culto dei santi in Europa fino alla Iª Crociata** [Pilgrimages and the cult of saints in Europe at the end of the First Crusade]. Pro-ceedings of the Convegni del Centro di Studi sulla Spiritualità Medievale. IV; sponsored by the Centro di Studi sulla Spiritualità Medievale (Todi: Accademia Tudertina, 1963) 526 p. *Illus., charts, diagr., tech. drawings.* In Italian, French, and Spanish.

The conference was held from 8 through 11 October 1961. The following contribution is cited separately: Raffaello MONTEROSSO, **Il culto dei santi nella tradizione musicale medievale liturgica ed extraliturgica** [The cult of saints in medieval musical tradition inside and outside the lit-urgy] (1151).

445
bs
[Tokyo] **Music: East and West.** Proceedings of the East-West Music Encounter Conference (Tōkyō: con-ference, 1961) 231 p.

The conference was held from 17 through 22 April 1961. The following contributions are cited separately: Daigoro ARIMA, **Musical education as part of general education** (4677); Sadao BEKKU, **The composer in Japan today** (2135); Vanraj BHATIA, **Western music in India** (3232); Elliott CARTER, **Extending the classical syntax** (2145); Henry COW-ELL, **Oriental influence on Western music** (2151); Peter CROSSLEY-HOLLAND, **Asian music under the impact of Western culture** (2614) and **Operatic and ballet music** (5126); Dragotin CVETKO, **Instruction in music as part of general education** (4689); Alain DANIÉLOU, **The music of India** (2615) and **Problems of Indian music tradition today** (2616); Hans-Heinz DRAEGER, **Liturgical and religious music** (6008); Alfred FRANKENSTEIN, **Instruction in music as part of general edu-cation** (4694); Robert GARFIAS, **Some effects of changing social values on Japanese music** (2628); Yvette GRIMAUD, **Notes on some aesthetic problems of our time** (5482); Lou HARRISON, **Refreshing the auditory perception** (5487); Masao HIRASHIMA, **The composer in Japan today** (2180); Mantle HOOD, **The music of Indonesia** (2639); Milko KELEMAN, **Situation of creative art in the industrial society** (5888); Masakuni KITAZAWA, **Situation of creative art in the industrial society** (5889); George Henry Hubert LASCELLES, Earl of Harewood, **Patron-age of music in the West** (2341); José MACEDA, **Western music in the Philippines** (2658); Colin MCPHEE, **The music crisis in Bali** (2666); M. MIYAGI, **Renewing the musical language: An Eastern view** (5545); Makoto MOROI, **Electronic music** (4408); Francesco Yosio NOMURA, **Religious music** (6020); K. NOMURA, **Problems of music patronage in the East** (2368); R.L. ROY, **Instruction in music as part of general edu-cation** (4766); Keisei SAKKA, **Western music in Japan** (2684); Leo SCHRADE, **Music's place in Western life** (2388); Egon SEEFEHLNER, **Patronage of music in the West: The role of the Maecenas in Europe** (5990); Sukehiro SHIBA, **The music of Japan (gagaku)** (2690); Thakur Jaideva SINGH, **The music of India** (2694); **Patronage of music in India** (2392), and **Presenting the Eastern tradition under conditions of mass distribution** (5908); Hans Heinz STUCKENSCHMIDT, moderator, **Dis-cussion: Music and listener** (5606); Hans Heinz STUCKENSCHMIDT, **Instruction in music as part of general education** (4781); Virgil THOMSON, moderator, **Discussion: Critics' forum** (2264); Virgil THOMSON, **The philosophy of style** (5613); Kazuyuki TOYAMA, **Con-certs in Japan** (2403); Van Khê TRAN, **Presenting the Eastern tradition under conditions of mass distribution** (5910) and **Problems of Sino-Japanese musical tradition today** (2701); Tanjore VISWANATHAN,

Problems of Indian music tradition today (2705); Iannis XENAKIS, **Stochastic music** (5633); Shin'ichi YUIZE, **The music of Japan** (2708).

446
bs

[Užice] Rad VIII-og kongresa folklorista Jugoslavije [Proceedings of the eighth congress of Yugoslavian folklorists]. Proceedings of the 8th congress of the Savez Udruženja Folklorista Jugoslavije. Ed. by Dušan NEDELJKOVIĆ (Beograd: Naučno Delo, 1961) 495 p. *Illus., port., bibliog., transcr., dance notation.* In Serbian, German, Croatian, and Bosnian; summaries in English, French, German, and Russian.

The conference was held from 6 through 10 September 1961. The following contributions are cited separately: Dragoslav ANTONIJEVIĆ, **Narodne pesme poziva na Ustanak** [Folk songs inciting to the Insurrection] (5282); Rada BORELI, **Lirska pesma oblasti Titovog Užiča** [Lyric songs of the Titovo Užice district] (5291); Emilija CEROVIĆ, **Prilog bibliografiji narodnog stvaralaštva u narodnooslobodilačkoj borbi (1941-1945)** [A contribution to the bibliography of music of the People's Revolution (1941-1945)] (805); Olinko DELORKO, **O nekim uspjelim narodnim lirskim pjesmama uz rad** [Some successful traditional lyrical work songs] (5301); Dragoslav DEVIĆ, **Narodne melodije iz perioda Oslobodilačkog rata** [Traditional melodies in the period of the War of National Liberation] (2790); Jelena DOPUĐA, **Narodne igre i njihova povezanost sa motivima i elementima rada u Bosni i Hercegovini** [Folk dances and their connection to motifs and elements of labor in Bosnia and Herzegovina] (4956); Dragutin M. ĐORĐEVIĆ, **Ličnosti narodnog ustanka u partizanskim pesmama leskovačkog kraja** [Heroes of the Insurrection in Partisan songs from the Leskovac region] (5306); Marika HADŽI-PECOVA, **Odraz fašističkih nedela u makedonskim narodnim pesmama** [The reflection of Fascist crimes in Macedonian neotraditional song] (2842); Vasil HADŽIMANOV, **Proces nastajanja makedonskog melosa u Narodnooslobodilačkoj borbi** [The process of Macedonian folk song formation during the Partisan struggle] (2847); Radoslav HROVATIN, **Problemi studija narodnih pesama i igara u vezi sa radom** [Problems in the study of traditional songs and dances related to work] (2438); Milica ILIJIN, **Narodna orska umetnost u oblasti Titovog Užica** [Folk dance in the region of Titovo Užice] (4986); Ernő KIRÁLY, **Rad kao motiv u mađarskim narodnim pesmama** [Work as a motif in Hungarian traditional songs] (2890); Marija KIRÁLY, **Narodni pevači Srema o događajima Drugog svetskog rata** [Srem folk singers on the subject of the Second World War] (2892); Lajos KISS, **O zapevkama, naricanju u okolini Sombora** [The nenia (lament) genre in the vicinity of Sombor] (2895); Mark KRASNIQI, **Motiv heroistva u partizanskoj narodnoj epici** [The motif of heroism in Partisan folk epic] (2907); Niko S. MARTINOVIĆ, **Narodno stvaralaštvo u Ustanku Crne Gore** [The productions of folk culture in the Insurrection in Montenegro] (2950); Živomir MLADENOVIĆ, **Pesma na priredbama kulturnih ekipa u narodnooslobodilačkoj borbi** [Song in the performances of cultural teams during the War of National Liberation] (2961); Ante NAZOR, **Kako se razvijala revolucionarna pjesma oko Mosora** [How the revolutionary song has developed in the Mosor area] (5338); Milica OBRADOVIĆ, **Rad u narodnim društvenim igrama na području Bosne i Hercegovine** [Work in the traditional social games of the Bosnia and Herzegovina region] (5046); Savo J. OROVIĆ, **Narodne pesme u oslobodilačkom ratu i revoluciji** [Folk songs in the War of Liberation and People's Revolution] (2977); Roksanda PEJOVIĆ, **Uticaj folklora narodnooslobodilačke borbe na umetničko stvaralaštvo** [The influence of the folklore of the War of National Liberation on contemporary music] (2227); Đurđica PETROVIĆ, **Put pesme krajinske čete:** *Krajinski smo mladi partizani* [The journey of a song of the Krajina forces: *Krajinski smo mladi partizani*] (2994); Radmila PETROVIĆ, **Narodni melos u oblasti Titovog Užica** [Traditional music melody in the Titovo Užice district] (2996); Shefqet PLLANA, **Rad kao motiv u arbanaškoj narodnoj pesmi** [Work as a motif in Albanian traditional song] (3005); Stevan ROCA, **Užička narodna pesma i pesma** *Junaštvo Janković Stojana* [The traditional song of Užice and the song *Junaštvo Janković Stojana*] (3037); Andrija RŠUMOVIĆ, Vidosava NIKOLIĆ, and Dušan NEDELJKOVIĆ, **Užičke hajdučke pesme, hajdukovanje i hajdučija** [Hajduk ballads of the Užice region, *hajdukovanje* and *hajdučija*] (3040); Milan ŠKRBIĆ, **Problem vrednovanja partizanske narodne pjesme** [The problem of evaluating Partisan folk song] (5599); Doris STOCKMANN, **Zur musikalischen Struktur einiger mehrstimmiger Gesänge der südalbanischen Laben** [The musical structure of some polyphonic songs of the Lab people of southern Albania] (3069); Slobodan ZEČEVIĆ, **Pregled narodnih igara užičkog dela Sandžaka** [Folk dance in the Užice part of the Sandžak]

(5086); Vinko ŽGANEC, **Pjesme uz rad nekad i danas** [Work songs in past and present] (3125); Leposava ŽUNIĆ, **Pesme užičkog partizanskog odreda** [Songs of the Užice Partisan forces] (3132).

1962

447
bs

[Bern] Kirchenmusik in ökumenischer Schau [Church music in an ecumenical perspective]. Proceedings of the Second International Congress of Church Music. Ed. and pref. by Ulrich MÜLLER. *Publikationen der Schweizerischen Musikforschenden Gesellschaft* II:11 (Bern: Haupt, 1964) 101 p. In German and French.

The conference was held from 22 through 29 September 1962. The following contributions are cited separately: Konrad AMELN, **Die Wurzeln des deutschen Kirchenliedes der Reformation** [The roots of the German Reformation hymn] (6422); Higini ANGLÈS, **Das Alte und das Neue in der heutigen Kirchenmusik und die Vereinigung der Christen** [The old and the new in today's church music and the uniting of Christians] (6003); Walter BLANKENBURG, **Offizielle und inoffizielle liturgische Bestrebungen in der Evangelischen Kirche Deutschlands** [Official and unofficial liturgical endeavors in Germany's Protestant church] (6427); Urbanus BOMM, **Gregorianischer Choral als Kultgesang** [Gregorian chant as worship through singing] (6173); Adolf BRUNNER, **Liturgisch-musikalische Möglichkeiten im reformierten Gottesdienst: Zum Vorschlag der Zürcher Liturgiekommission** [Possibilities for liturgical music in the Reformed church service: The proposal of the Zurich Liturgiekommission] (6428); Norbert DUFOURCQ, **Interdépendence de la facture et de la musique d'orgue en France sous la règne de Louis XIV** [The interdependence of organ building and organ music in France during the reign of Louis XIV] (3352); Joseph GELINEAU, **Psalmodie populaire** [Folk psalmody] (6232); Thrasybulos Georges GEORGIADES, **Sprachschichten in der Kirchenmusik** [Language strata in church music] (6011); Friedrich JAKOB, **Tendenzen des heutigen Orgelbaus** [Tendencies in contemporary organ building] (3395); Hans KLOTZ, **À propos de l'orgue de 1500 environ, de l'orgue brabançon de 1550 et de la manière de les jouer** [Organs of ca. 1500, the Brabant organ of 1550, and how they were played] (3400); Maxime KOVALEVSKY, **La musique liturgique orthodoxe russe** [Russian Orthodox liturgical music] (6119); LAURENT (brother), **Neue Formen der Anbetung** [New forms of worship] (6017); Pierre PIDOUX, **Ergebnisse der Forschungen um den Hugenotten-Psalter** [Research findings on the Huguenot Psalter] (1400); Julius SCHWEIZER, **Vom legitimen Ort kirchlicher Musik im Gottesdienst der reformierten Kirchen der deutschen Schweiz** [The legitimate role in worship of church music in the Reformed churches of German-speaking Switzerland] (6447); Oskar SÖHNGEN, **Musik und Theologie** [Music and theology] (5600); Bruno STÄBLEIN, **Das Wesen des Tropus: Ein Beitrag zum Problem Alt und Neu in der Kirchenmusik** [The character of the trope: Contribution to the problem of old versus new in church music] (1190); Heinrich STIRNIMANN, **Ökumenische Gedanken zur Kirchenmusik** [Ecumenical thoughts on church music] (6027); Johannes WAGNER, **Neue Aufgaben der katholischen Kirchenmusik im Zeitalter der pastoralliturgischen Erneuerung** [New obligations of Catholic church music in the age of pastoral-liturgical renewal] (6409); Heinz Werner ZIMMERMANN, **Neue Musik und neues Kirchenlied** [New music and a new hymnody] (6456).

448
bs

[Copenhagen] Fourth International Congress on Acoustics. Sponsored by UNESCO and Statens Teknisk-videnskabelige Fond. Ed. by A. Kjerbye NIELSEN (København: conference, 1962) 2 v. In English, French, and German.

The conference was held from 21 through 28 August 1962. The following contributions are cited separately: Leo Leroy BERANEK, **Rating of acoustic quality of concert halls and opera houses** (5802); Nico V. FRANSSEN, **The mechanism of the human voice and wind instruments** (5815); Vern O. KNUDSEN, **Acoustics of music rooms** (5828); Émile LEIPP, **La cavité buccale, paramètre sensible des spectres rayonnés des instruments à vent** [The oral cavity as a measurable factor in the spectra emitted by wind instruments] (3626); Daniel W. MARTIN, **Musical implications of standardized tuning frequency** (5839); Jürgen MEYER, **Unharmonische Komponenten im Klang der Orgelpfeifen** [Inharmonic components in the sound of organ pipes] (3432); Andrew G.

PIKLER, **Musical transfer functions** (5933); Reinier PLOMP and Willem J.M. LEVELT, **Musical consonance and critical bandwidth** (5850); Fritz WINCKEL, **Über den Einfluß der Deckenhöhe auf die Klangqualität in Konzertsälen** [The influence of ceiling height on sound quality in concert halls] (5860); Robert William YOUNG, **A decade of musical acoustics** (5862).

449
bs
[Crésuz; Wolfsburg] Musique sacrée et langues modernes: Deux colloques internationaux [Sacred music and modern languages: Two international colloquia] *Kinnor; Études* 4 (Paris: Fleurus, 1964) 130 p. *Port., music.* In French.

The conferences were held from 27 through 29 September 1962 in Crésuz, Switzerland, and from 4 through 6 September 1963 in Wolfsburg, Germany. The following contributions are cited separately: Jean BANCAL, **Brèves réflexions sur les éléments techniques propres à "servir" un langue biblique** [Brief reflections on the technical elements appropriate to a Biblical language] (6159); Joseph GELINEAU, **Les chants processionaux: Recherche sur leur structure liturgique** [Processional chants: An investigation of their liturgical structure] (6010) and **Programme musical d'une pastorale liturgique** [The musical program of a pastoral liturgy] (6231); Helmut HUCKE, **Le récitatif liturgique en langue moderne** [Liturgical recitative in modern languages] (6254); Bernard HUIJBERS, **Nouvelles hymnes sur les Évangiles** [New Gospel hymns] (6256); Erhard QUACK, **Facture musical et chants d'assemblée** [Musical composition and congregational songs] (6347).

450
bs
[Hyderabad] Souvenir on Hindustani Music Festival & Seminar. Ed. by T. SESHACHARI, G.N. DANTALE, and M.N. Padma RAO; intro. by S.N. RATANJANKAR. *Andhra Pradesh Sangeeta Nataka Akademi* 7 (Hyderabad: Andhra Pradesh Sangeeta Nataka Akademi, 1966) 71 p. *Port.*

The following contributions are cited separately: G.N. DANTALE, **Personality in music** (2617); S.B. DESHPANDE, **The objective of teaching music** (4516); Pandojirao DHAGE, **The origin of Indian music** (2619); Baburao JOSHI, **Appreciating music** (2644); R.C. MEHTA, **Music and aesthetics** (5538); Kumar PISSAY, **Problems of Indian music** (2674); M.N. Padma RAO, **The long flute** (3633); S.N. RATANJANKAR, **Classicism in Hindustani music** (2677); P. SAMBAMOORTHY, **Influences on Karnatic music** (2686). Photographs and biographies of conference participants and festival performers are included.

451
bs
[Jerusalem] Seper tehylym ḃemẇsyqah [The Book of Psalms in music]. Proceedings of the Fifth Israeli Music Congress, *Dẇkan* V (1963). In Hebrew.

The following contributions are cited separately: Ḥayym ḂAR-DYYAN, **Leḃ'ayẇt haqry'ah lepy haṭa'amym ḃeseper thylym** [On problems of reading psalms according to their Masoretic accents] (6039); Bathja BAYER, **Haḵynẇr hamiqr'ay l'ẇr hamams'aym** [The Biblical kinnor in light of archaeological discoveries] (3549); Alexander Uriah BOSKOVICH, **Dibrey haqdamah la'ereb ha'azunah mitẇḥ yṣyrẇtyw** [Introduction to a night with his own creation] (2141); Mordekay ḂRẄY'ER, **He'arẇt 'al tawey ṭa'amey hamiqr'a ḃeseper šel Y. Rẇyklyn** [Remarks on the Biblical accents in J. Reuchlin's *De accentibus et orthographia*] (6046) and **'Ẅleh weyẇred we'etnaḥt'a ḃeṭa'amey 'em''t** [*'Ẅleh weyẇred* and *'etnaḥt'a* in the Masoretic accents of Job, Ecclesiastes, and Psalms] (6048); Me'yr Šim'ẇn GEŠWRY, **Seper tehylym ḃelaḥn haḥasydym** [Hasidic melodies for the Book of Psalms] (6064); Yẇsep HYYNYMAN, **Seper thylym ḵemaqẇr lenẇsaḥ hatpylah** [The Book of Psalms as the origin of Biblical cantillation] (6072); Zvi KEREN, **Mašma'ẇtah šel hamilah "selah" lepy pyrẇšym yehẇḋym mešẇrtyym** [The meaning of the word *selah* according to traditional Jewish commentaries] (6074); 'Ezr'a Ṣyẇn MELAMED, **Meqẇmẇ šel seper tehylym ḃe'abẇdat h' ḃeḵol yomẇt hašanah** [The place of psalms in daily liturgy throughout the year] (6079); Menaḥem Ṣeby QADARY, **Nytwaḥ taḥḃwry ḃe'ezrat ṭa'amey 'em''t** [Syntactic analysis of Biblical texts with the aid of accents of Job, Ecclesiastes, and Psalms] (6089); Re'uben QAŠ'ANY, **Laḥney seper thylym 'eṣel yehẇdey 'apganysṭan** [Psalm melodies of Jews in Afghanistan] (6092).

452
bs
[Kassel] Bericht über den internationalen musikwissenschaftlichen Kongreß [Report of the International Musicological Conference]. Sponsored by the Gesellschaft für Musikforschung. Ed. by Georg REICHERT and Martin JUST (Kassel: Bärenreiter, 1963) xv, 392 p. *Illus., port., facs., music.* In German, English, and French.

The conference was held from 30 September through 4 October 1962. The following contributions are cited separately: Ernst APPEL, **Über das Verhältnis von Musiktheorie und Kompositionspraxis im späteren Mittelalter (etwa 1200-1500)** [The relation between music theory and compositional practice in the later Middle Ages (ca. 1200-1500)] (1057); Sol BABITZ, **Das Violinspiel im 18. Jahrhundert und heute** [Violin playing in the 18th century and today] (3727); Hermann BECK, **Zur musikalischen Analyse** [Musical analysis] (4311); Heinz BECKER, **Zur Spielpraxis der griechischen Aulos** [The playing technique of the Greek aulos] (3610); Peter BENARY, **Das impressionistische Raumgefühl als Stilfaktor bei Debussy** [The impressionistic sense of space as a stylistic factor in Debussy] (5374) and **Die Stellung der Melodielehre in der Musiktheorie des 18. Jahrhunderts in Deutschland** [The place of the theory of melody in 18th-century German music theory] (1485); Ingmar BENGTSSON, **Über Korrelationen zwischen Durationsvariable und Rhythmuserlebnis** [Correlations between variables of duration and the perception of rhythm] (3969); Robert BERGMANN, **Das Problem der Jazzmusik im heutigen Musikleben** [The problem of jazz in today's musical life] (3231); Karel Philippus BERNET KEMPERS, **Versuch eines vertieften Einblicks in den musikalischen Organismus** [Towards a deeper view into the musical organism] (3931); Günter BIRKNER, **Quellenlage und Katalogisierung des deutschen Volkslied** [The state of the sources and the cataloguing of the German folk song] (522); Friedrich BLUME, **Die Musik von 1830 bis 1914: Strukturprobleme einer Epoche** [Music from 1830 to 1914: Structural problems of an era] (1919); Wolfgang BOETTICHER, **Zum problem der Übergangsperiode der Musik 1580-1620** [The problem of the period of musical transition 1580-1620] (1244); Siegfried BORRIS, **Strukturanalyse von Weberns Symphonie op. 21** [Structural analysis of Webern's symphony op. 21] (4394); Fritz BOSE, **Die Fabrikation der nordischen Bronzeluren** [The production of Nordic bronze lurs] (3613); Lada BRAŠOVANOVA-STANČEVA, **Die Musik von 1830 bis 1914 in Bulgarien** [Music in Bulgaria from 1830 to 1914] (1922); Werner BRAUN, **Zur Parodie im 17. Jahrhundert** [Parody in the 17th century] (1496); Franz BRENN, **Tonsysteme in Equiton und Fawcettzahlen** [Tonal systems in equitone notation and Fawcett numbers] (4053); Jaroslav BUŽGA, **Die soziale Lage des Musikers im Zeitalter des Barocks in den böhmischen Ländern und ihr Einfluss auf seine künstlerischen Möglichkeiten** [The social position of musicians in the Baroque era in the Bohemian lands and its influence on their artistic possibilities] (5870); Dragotin CVETKO, **Die Situation und die Probleme der slowenischen, kroatischen, und serbischen Musik des 19. Jahrhunderts: Die Musik von 1830 bis 1914 in Jugoslawien** [The situation and problems of Slovene, Croatian, and Serbian music in the 19th century: Music in Yugoslavia from 1830 to 1914] (1942); Georg von DADELSEN, **Die Vermischung musikalischer Gattungen als soziologisches Problem** [Mixing together musical genres as a sociological problem] (5875); Carl DAHLHAUS, **Der Tonalitätsbegriff in der neuen Musik** [The concept of tonality in new music] (3938) and **Intervalldissonanz und Akkorddissonanz** [Interval dissonance and chord dissonance] (4156); Louis Helmut DEBES, **Über den Stand der Forschungen zu Claudio Merulo** [The state of research on Claudio Merulo] (1286); Otto Erich DEUTSCH, **Dokumentarische Biographien** [Documentary biographies] (866); Dagmar DROYSEN, **Die Darstellungen von Saiteninstrumenten in der mittelalterlichen Buchmalerei und ihre Bedeutung für die Instrumentenkunde** [The representation of string instruments in medieval book illumination and its organological significance] (5377); Walther DÜRR, **Zur mehrstimmigen Behandlung des chromatischen Schrittes in der Polyphonie des 16. Jahrhunderts** [The multipart treatment of chromatic steps in 16th-century polyphony] (4159); Rudolf ELVERS, **Rudolf Werckmeister: Ein Berliner Musikverleger 1802-1809** [Rudolf Werckmeister: A Berlin music publisher, 1802-1809] (1747); Hans ENGEL, **Die musikalischen Gattungen und ihr sozialer Hintergrund** [Musical genres and their social background] (5879); Hans Ulrich ENGELMANN, **Fragen seriellen Kompositionsverfahren** [Questions of serial compositional procedure] (2160); Georg FEDER, **Zwei Haydn zugeschriebene Klaviersonaten** [Two keyboard sonatas attributed to Haydn] (1751); Hellmut FEDERHOFER, **Historische Musiktheorie: Überblick** [Historical music theory: An overview] (871); Renate FEDERHOFER-KÖNIGS, **Heinrich Saess und seine *Musica plana atque mensurabilis*** [Heinrich Saess and his *Musica plana atque mensurabilis*] (1299); Arnold FEIL, **Zur Rhythmik Schuberts** [Schubert's rhythmics] (3989); Laurence FEININGER, **Die katholische Kirchen-musik in Rom zwischen 1600 und 1800: Eine unfassbare Lacune in der Musikgeschichte** [Catholic church music in Rome between 1600 and 1800: An incomprehensible gap in music history] (1543); Imogen FELLINGER, **Zum Problem der Zeitmasse in Brahms' Musik** [The problem of tempo in Brahms's music] (3990); Ludwig FINSCHER, **Zur Sozialgeschichte des klassischen Streichquartetts** [The social history of the Classic string quartet] (1757); Constantin FLOROS, **Kompositions-technische Probleme der atonalen Musik** [Technical problems of composition in atonal music] (4335); Gerhard FROMMEL, **Tonalitäts-probleme der neuen Musik vom Standpunkt des Komponisten** [Problems of tonality in new music from the standpoint of the composer] (2165); Zoltán GÁRDONYI, **Die Musik von 1830 bis 1914 in Ungarn** [Music in Hungary from 1830 to 1914] (1965); Walter GERSTENBERG, **Andante** (3742); Ursula GÜNTHER, **Das Ende der *ars nova*** [The end of the ars nova] (1111); Fritz HAMANN, **Die Arbeit der Seminar-Musiklehrer und die Bedeutung dieses Standes für die deutsche Musikkultur** [The work of music teachers in the teacher-training institutes and the profession's significance in German music culture] (4824); Heinz Wolfgang HAMANN, **Neue Quellen zur Johann Joseph Fux–Forschung** [New sources for research on Johann Joseph Fux] (1572); Doris HECKLINGER, **Tanzrhythmik als konstitutives Element in Bachs Vokalmusik** [Dance rhythm as a constitutive element of Bach's music] (1576); Harald HECKMANN, **Zur Dokumentation musikalischer Quellen des 16. und 17. Jahrhunderts** [The documentation of musical sources of the 16th and 17th centuries] (591); Wilhelm HEINITZ, **Zeitgemässe Aufführungs-probleme** [Contemporary performance problems] (5666); Ulrich HERDIECKERHOFF, **Die wissenschaftliche Selbstbegründung der Musikpädagogik** [The self-validation of music pedagogy as a science] (4551); Hans Otto HIEKEL, ***Tactus* und Tempo** [*Tactus* and tempo] (1335); Lothar HOFFMANN-ERBRECHT, **Heinrich Finck in Polen** [Heinrich Finck in Poland] (1336); Andreas HOLSCHNEIDER, **Die musikalische Bibliothek Gottfried van Swietens** [Gottfried van Swieten's music library] (725); Marc HONEGGER, **La musique française de 1830 à 1914** [French music from 1830 to 1914] (1984); Oswald JONAS, **Eine private Brahms-Sammlung und ihre Bedeutung für die Brahms-Werkstatt-Erkenntnis** [A private Brahms collection, and its significance in Brahms's working methods] (726) and **Zur realen Antwort in der Fuge bei Bach** [The real answer in the fugues of Bach] (4351); Herta JURISCH, **Zur Dynamik im Klavierwerk Ph.E. Bachs** [Dynamics in the keyboard works of C.P.E. Bach] (1785); Martin JUST, **Ysaac de manu sua** (1350); Fritz KAISER, **Die authentischen Fassungen des D-dur-Konzerts op. 61 von Ludwig van Beethoven** [The authentic versions of Ludwig van Beethoven's D-major concerto, op. 61] (1787); Erhard KARKOSCHKA, **Zur rhythmischen Struktur in der Musik von heute** [Rhythmic structure in the music of today] (4007); Georg KARSTÄDT, **Das Instrument Gottfried Reiches: Horn oder Trompete?** [Gottfried Reiche's instrument: Horn or trumpet?] (5381); Paul KAST, **Die Autographensammlung Campori und ihre musikalischen Schätze** [The Campori autograph collection and its musical treasures] (729); Winfried KIRSCH, **Grundzüge der Te Deum–Vertonungen im 15. und 16. Jahrhundert** [Principles of Te Deum settings in the 15th and 16th centuries] (1358); Ernst KLUSEN, **Gustav Mahler und das böhmisch-mährische Volks-lied** [Gustav Mahler and Bohemian-Moravian folk song] (2005); Walter KOLNEDER, **Zur Frühgeschichte des Solokonzerts** [The early history of the solo concerto] (1593); Siegfried KROSS, **Rhythmik und Sprach-behandlung bei Brahms** [Brahms's rhythmics and treatment of speech] (2018); Ernst LAAFF, **Berufsfragen des jungen Musikwissenschaftlers: Überblick** [Career questions asked by the young musicologist: Overview] (892) and **Berufsfragen des jungen Musikwissenschaftlers: Zusam-menfassung** [Career questions asked by the young musicologist: Summary] (893); János LIEBNER, **Der Einfluß Schillers auf Verdi** [Schiller's influence on Verdi] (5196) and **Ein verschollenes Werk von Béla Bartók** [A forgotten work by Béla Bartók] (2203); Andreas LIESS, **Der junge Debussy und die russiche Musik** [The young Debussy and Russian music] (2028); Heinrich LINDLAR, **Debussysmen beim frühen Strawinsky** [Debussyisms in early Stravinsky] (2205); Irving LOWENS, **Amerikanische Demokratie und die amerikanische Musik von 1830 bis 1914** [American democracy and American music from 1830 to 1914] (2031); Franz Jochen MACHATIUS, ***Eroica*: Das transzendentale Ich** [*Eroica*: The transcendental ego] (5531); Alfred MANN, **Händels Fugenlehre: Ein unveröffentlichtes Manuskript** [Händel's teaching of fugue: An unpublished manuscript] (1617); Günther MASSENKEIL, **Über die Messen Giacomo Carissimis** [The Masses of Giacomo Carissimi] (1618); Willy MAXTON, **Können die *Denkmäler Deutscher Tonkunst* uns heute noch als Quellen zweiter Ordnung dienen?** [Can the *Denkmäler Deutscher*

Tonkunst still serve as secondary sources today?] (3906); John Henry van der MEER, **Zur Geschichte des Klaviziteriums** [The history of the clavicytherium] (3531); Bernhard MEIER, **"Hieroglyphisches" in der Musik des 16. Jahrhunderts** [The concept of the ideographic in music of the 16th century] (1379) and **Musiktheorie und Musik im 16. Jahr-hundert** [Music theory and music in the 16th century] (1380); Fritz METZLER, **Takt und Rhythmus in der freien Melodieerfindung des Grundschulkindes** [Beat and rhythm in the free melodic invention of elementary school children] (4015); Paul MIES, **Über ein besonderes Akzentzeichen bei Joh. Brahms** [A particular accent indication in Brahms] (3854); Wilhelm MOHR, **Über Mischformen und Sonder-bildungen der Variationsform** [Mixed and unique structures in variation form] (4270); Hedwig MUELLER VON ASOW, **Komponierende Frauen** [Women composers] (992); Bernd MÜLLMAN, **Der Musik-wissenschaftler als Redakteur oder Musikkritiker** [The musicologist as editor or music critic] (5553); Friedrich NEUMANN, **Die Zeitgestalt als Grundbegriff der musikalischen Rhythmik** [Time-gestalt as the fundamental principle of musical rhythmics] (3955); Hanns NEUPERT, **Musikwissenschaftler und Instrumentenbau** [Musicologists and instrument making] (3262); Klaus Wolfgang NIEMÖLLER, **Grundzüge einer Neubewertung der Musik an den Lateinschulen des 16. Jahrhunderts** [Principles for a new evaluation of the music of 16th-century Latin schools] (1387); Günther NOLL, **Jean-Jacques Rousseau als Musikerzieher** [Jean-Jacques Rousseau as music educator] (4608); Felix OBERBORBECK, **Pädagogische Berufsmöglichkeiten des Musik-wissenschaftlers** [Career possibilities in teaching for the musicologist] (4609); Alfred OREL, **Die Musik von 1830 bis 1914 in Österreich** [Music in Austria from 1830 to 1914] (2060); Wolfgang OSTHOFF, **Die zwei Fassungen von Verdis *Simon Boccanegra*** [The two versions of Verdi's *Simon Boccanegra*] (2063); Alfons OTT, **Die *Ungarischen Rhapsodien* von Franz Liszt** [Franz Liszt's *Magyar rhapsodiák*] (2064); Irmgard OTTO, **Das Fotografieren von Musikinstrumenten zu wissenschaft-lichen Zwecken** [Photographing musical instruments for scholarly purposes] (3265); Albert PALM, **Mozart und Haydn in der Interpretation Momignys** [Mozart and Haydn in Momigny's interpretation] (1833); Gerhard PÄTZIG, **Heinrich Isaacs *Choralis constantinus*: Eine posthume Werksammlung** [Henricus Isaac's *Choralis constantinus*: A posthumous collection] (1395); Wilhelm PFANNKUCH, **Sonatenform und Sonatenzyklus in den Streichquartetten von Joseph Martin Kraus** [Sonata form and sonata cycle in the string quartets of Joseph Martin Kraus] (4279); Wolfgang PLATH, **Über Skizzen zu Mozarts *Requiem*** [Sketches for Mozart's Requiem] (1837); Gilbert REANEY, **The isorhythmic motet and its social background** (1167) and **Zur Frage der Autorenzuweisung in mittelalterlichen Musiktraktaten** [The attribution of authorship in medieval music treatises] (1168); Wolfgang REHM, **Der Musikwissenschaftler im Musikverlag** [The musicologist and music publishing] (5986); Alfred REICHLING, **Die Präambeln der Hs. Erlangen 554 und ihre Beziehung zur Sammlung Ileborghs** [The preludes of MS Erlangen 554 and their relationship to the Ileborgh Tablature] (1419); Hans-Peter REINECKE, **Der Musikwissenschaftler in der Schallplatten-Industrie** [The musicologist in the recording industry] (5782), **Erläuterungen zur modernen Dokumentations-Technik** [Comments on modern documentation technology] (659), and **Zur Frage der Anwendbarkeit der Informationstheorie auf tonpsychologische Probleme** [The applicability of information theory to problems in the psychology of music] (5692); Friedrich Wilhelm RIEDEL, **Der Reichsstil in der deutschen Musikgeschichte des 18. Jahrhunderts** [The Reichsstil in 18th-century German music history] (1656); Walter H. RUBSAMEN, **Sebastian Festa and the early madrigal** (1423); Martin RUHNKE, **Zum Stand der Telemann-Forschung** [The state of Telemann research] (1666); Walter SALMEN, **Die Auswirkung von Ideen und Kompositionen Reichardts im 19. Jahrhundert** [The effects of Reichardt's ideas and compositions in the 19th century] (2089); Bogusław SCHAEFFER, **Präexistente und inexistente Strukturen** [Preexistent and nonexistent structures] (4283); Reinhold SCHLÖTTERER, **Lehrmethoden des Palestrina-Kontrapunkts** [Teaching methods for Palestrina counterpoint] (4847); Hans SCHMID, **Plan und Durchführung des *Lexicon musicum latinum* I: Erfassung und Erforschung der musikalischen Fachsprache des Mittelalters** [Plan and implementation of the *Lexicon musicum latinum* I: Recording and researching the technical terminology of music in the Middle Ages] (773); Wolfgang SCHMIEDER, **Das Berufs-bild des wissenschaftlichen Musikbibliothekars** [The career of academic music librarian] (676) and **Gedanken über den Begriff, das Wesen und die Aufgaben der Musikdokumentation** [Thoughts on the concept, nature, and tasks of music documentation] (677); Henning SIEDENTOPF, **Zu J.S. Bachs Klaviersatz mit obligaten Stimmen: Instrument und**

Spieltechnik [Bach's writing for keyboard with independent voices: The instrument and playing techique] (1681); Ulrich SIEGELE, **Zur Verbindung von Präludium und Fuge bei J.S. Bach** [The connection between preludes and fugues in J.S. Bach] (1682); Bruno STÄBLEIN, **Erfassung und Erschliessung mittelalterlicher Musikhandschriften** [Inventorying and making available medieval music manuscripts] (693); Joachim STALMANN, **Die reformatorische Musikanschauung des Johann Walter** [Johann Walter's Reformation view of music] (1441); Oskar STOLLBERG, **Die musikalisch-liturgische Bewegung in der zweiten Hälfte de 19. Jahrhunderts im Spiegel unbekannter Briefe und Aufzeichnungen dieser Zeit** [The musical-liturgical movement of the second half of the 19th century as reflected in unknown letters and records of the period] (6451); Hans Heinz STUCKENSCHMIDT, **Musique concrète** (2258); Wolfgang SUPPAN, **Die romantische Ballade als Abbild des Wagnerschen Musikdramas** [The Romantic ballad as a reflection of Wagnerian music drama] (4288); Martin VOGEL, **Die Entstehung der Kirchentonarten** [The origin of the church modes] (4127); Ernst Ludwig WAELTNER, **Plan und Durchführung des** *Lexicon musicum latinum* **II: Archivaufbau mit Hilfe maschineller Datenverarbeitung** [Plan and implementation of the *Lexicon musicum latinum* II: Constructing an archive with the help of machine data processing] (774); Bo WALLNER, **Die Nationalromantik im Norden: Die Musik von 1830 bis 1914 in den skandinavischen Ländern** [National Romanticism in the North: Music in Scandinavian countries from 1830 to 1914] (2123); Liesbeth WEINHOLD, **RISM im Rahmen der Musikdokumentation** [RISM in the framework of music documentation] (798); Josef WENDLER, **Zur Formeltechnik des einstimmigen mittelalterlichen Liedes** [Formulaic technique in the monophonic medieval song] (4474); Eric WERNER, **Mendelssohns Kirchenmusik und ihre Stellung im 19. Jahrhundert** [Mendelssohn-Bartholdy's church music and its status in the 19th century] (2125); Jack A. WESTRUP, **Die Musik von 1830 bis 1914 in England** [Music in England from 1830 to 1914] (2126); Walter WEYLER, **Die Frage der flämischen Musik: Ein Beitrag zur Klärung einer Begriffsverwirrung** [The question of Flemish music: Contribution to the clarification of a concept] (1022); Walter WIORA, **Die musikalischen Gattungen und ihr sozialer Hintergrund** [Musical genres and their social background] (5915); Helmut WIRTH, **Der Musikwissenschaftler beim Rundfunk** [The musicologist in radio] (5798); Walther WÜNSCH, **Über Schallaufnahmen südosteuropäischer Volksepik in der Zeit von 1900 bis 1930** [Sound recordings of southeastern European folk epic in the period 1900-1930] (3120); Percy M. YOUNG, **Johann Christian Bach and his English environment** (1903); Franklin B. ZIMMERMAN, **Social backgrounds of the Restoration anthem** (1718).

453
bs

[Magdeburg] **Beiträge zu einem neuen Telemannbild** [Contributions to a new picture of Telemann]. Proceedings of the Magdeburger Telemann-Festtage; sponsored by the Deutscher Kulturbund and Arbeitskreis Georg Philipp Telemann (Magdeburg: Vorwärts, 1963) 96 p. *Illus., port., music, bibliog.* In German.

The conference was held from 3 through 5 November 1962. The following contributions are cited separately: Günter FLEISCHHAUER, **Einige Gedanken zur Harmonik Telemanns** [Some thoughts on Telemann's harmony] (4167); Wolf HOBOHM, **Verzeichnis des Telemann-Schrifttums: Auswahl** [Catalogue of writings on Telemann: Selections] (816); Willi MAERTENS, **Telemanns Orchestersuite mit Hornquartett: Zu ihrer Deutung und Bedeutung** [Telemann's orchestra suite with four horns: On its interpretation and significance] (1616); Ernst Hermann MEYER, **Zur Telemann-Deutung** [On the significance of Telemann] (1623); Max SCHNEIDER, **Telemannpflege: Eine unserer nationalen Aufgaben** [The cultivation of Telemann: One of our national tasks] (3767); Walther SIEGMUND-SCHULTZE, **Georg Philipp Telemann** [Georg Philipp Telemann] (1684); Krystyna WILKOWSKA-CHOMIŃSKA, **Telemanns Beziehungen zur Polnischen Musik** [Telemann's relation to Polish music] (1712); Hellmut Christian WOLFF, **Telemann und die Hamburger Oper** [Telemann and the Hamburg opera] (1715).

454
bs

[Mexico City] **XXXV Congreso Internacional de Americanistas: Actas y memorias** [35th International Congress of Americanists: Proceedings and reports] (México, D.F.: Editorial Libros de México, 1964) 3 v. *Illus., maps.* In Spanish.

The conference was held from 20 through 25 August 1962. The following contribution is cited separately: José Luis FRANCO, **Sobre un grupo de instrumentos musicales prehispánicos con sistema acústico no conocido** [On a group of pre-Hispanic musical instruments with an unknown acoustic system] (3617).

455
bs

[Mostar; Trebinje] **Rad IX-og kongresa Saveza Folklorista Jugoslavije** [Proceedings of the ninth congress of the Savez Folklorista Jugoslavije]. Proceedings of the ninth congress of the Savez Udruženja Folklorista Jugoslavije. Ed. by Jovan VUKOVIĆ (Sarajevo: Savez Udruženja Folklorista Jugoslavije, 1963) 622 p. *Illus., bibliog., transcr.* In Bosnian, Serbian, Croatian, French, Czech, and Bulgarian; summaries in English, French, German, and Russian.

The following contributions are cited separately: Dragoslav ANTONIJEVIĆ, **Društveni karakter hercegovačkih narodnih pesama izgradnje** [The social character of Herzegovinian neotraditional songs about socialist construction] (5281); Nikola BONIFAČIĆ ROŽIN, **Scenski elementi u proljetnim ophodnim običajima** [Theatrical elements in spring customs] (5109); Đenana BUTUROVIĆ, **Epska narodna tradicija Trebinjske Šume** [The local epic tradition in Trebinjska Šuma] (2754); Emilia COMIŞEL, **Le folklore des coutumes qu'on observe au cours d'une année: Le cycle de la période du printemps** [The folklore of customs observed over the course of a year: The cycle of the spring period] (2778); Tvrtko ČUBELIĆ, **Mogućnosti i osnovne pretpostavke scenskog izvođenja narodnih plesova** [Possibilities of and fundamental requirements for staged performances of folk dances] (4948); Olinko DELORKO, **Rukopisni zbornik narodnih pjesama Ivana Zovka** [Ivan Zovko's manuscript collection of traditional songs] (5302); Dragoslav DEVIĆ, **Nove "narodne" pesme** [New so-called folk songs] (3233); Jelena DOPUĐA, **Pregled narodnih igara Hercegovine** [A survey of the traditional dances of Herzegovina] (4959); Stojan DŽUDŽEV, **Narodnata muzika kato obščestveno javlenie** [Traditional music as a general phenomenon] (2799); Marika HADŽI-PECOVA, **Prvi dan proleća u makedonskim običajima** [The first day of spring in Macedonian customs] (2843); Vasil HADŽIMANOV, **Melodije makedonskih lazaričkih narodnih pesama** [The melodies of traditional Macedonian lazarica songs] (2845); Milica ILIJIN, **Obredno ljuljanje u proleće** [The custom of springtime swinging games] (2869); Živorad JOVANOVIĆ, **Bibliografija o folkloru Bosne i Hercegovine** [Bibliography of the folklore of Bosnia and Herzegovina] (802); Rajna KACAROVA, **Pădarevski kukeri** [The *kukeri* of Pădarevo] (4994); Ernő KIRÁLY, **Pokladno veselje kod Mađara u Vojvodini** [Carnival merrymaking among Vojvodina Hungarians] (2889); Zmaga KUMER, **Vsebina in pomen plesne igre most na Slovenskem** [Meaning and content of the *most* game in Slovenia] (5010); Hannah LAUDOVÁ, **Tradicije i neke crte razvoja savremenog razvoja igračkog folklora u ČSSR** [Traditions and evolutionary traits in the contemporary dance folklore of Czechoslovakia] (5020); Jaroslav MARKL, **Některé soudobé rysy tradiční lidové hudby v Československu** [Some modern features of traditional music in Czechoslovakia] (2943); Radosav MEDENICA, **Hercegovina: Kolevka patrijarhalne kulture i narodne pesme dinaraca** [Herzegovina: Cradle of the patriarchal culture and the traditional songs of the Dinaric people] (2955); Olivera MLADENOVIĆ, **Proigravanje devojaka u okolini Beograda** [Dance initiation rites for girls in the Belgrade vicinity] (5036); Živomir MLADENOVIĆ, **Rukopisne zbirke junačkih narodnih pesama Vuka Vrčevića u Srpskom Učenom Društvu** [Vuk Vrčević's transcriptions of epic songs for the Srpsko Učeno Društvo] (2962); Ante NAZOR, **O nekim pojmovnim i terminološkim problemima suvremenih narodnih pjesama** [On some terminological issues in contemporary traditional songs] (2972); Dušan NEDELJKOVIĆ, **Društvenoistorijska uslovljenost i zakonitost novosti u hercegovačkom pevanju današnje prelazne epohe** [The historical-social conditions and laws of innovation in Herzegovinian traditional song in the current transitional period] (2974); Vlastimir NIKOLOVSKI, **Mogućnost primene folklora i u najsavremenijoj muzičkoj umetnosti** [The possibility of using folk elements in even the most recent art music] (2219); Milica OBRADOVIĆ, **Narodne društvene igre u Hercegovini** [The traditional social games of Herzegovina] (5045); Vlajko PALAVESTRA, **Narodne pripovijetke i predanja u Hercegovini** [Folk tales and local sagas in Herzegovina] (5340); Radmila PETROVIĆ, **Narodne melodije u prolećnim običajima** [Traditional melodies in spring customs] (2995); Miljana RADOVANOVIĆ, **Društvenoistorijski karakter hercegovačkog narodnog pevanja Narodnooslobodilačke Borbe** [The social and historical character of the Herzegovinian traditional song of the War of

National Liberation] (3020); Cvjetko RIHTMAN, **Narodna muzička tradicija istočne Hercegovine** [Music tradition of eastern Herzegovina] (3032); Stevan ROCA, **Gusle kao poklon** [The gusle as gift] (3036); Branislav RUSIĆ, **Pesme sa pevanjem uz ljuljanje kod Makedonaca i susednih južnoslovenskih i neslovenskih naroda** [Songs and customs in swinging games among Macedonians and the neighboring South Slavic and non-Slavic peoples] (3041); Mira SERTIĆ, **Društveni karakter i sadržaj narodne poezije** [The social character and content of traditional poetry] (5352); Ljuba SIMIĆ, **Pripovedne i lirske pesme istočne Hercegovine** [Narrative and lyric songs of eastern Herzegovina] (3060); Marija ŠUŠTAR and Valens VODUŠEK, **Koreografska oblika pomladno-obredne igre most v Sloveniji in njene variante v Jugoslaviji** [Choreographic form of the traditional spring dance game *most* in Slovenia, and its variants in Yugoslavia] (5072).

456
bs
[Paris] **Debussy et l'évolution de la musique au XXᵉ siècle** [Debussy and the evolution of music in the 20th century]. Ed. and aftwd. by Édith WEBER. *Colloques internationaux du CNRS* (Paris: Centre National de la Recherche Scientifique [CNRS], 1965) 365 p. *Music, index.* In French.

The conference was held from 24 through 31 October 1962. The following contributions are cited separately: Júlia d' ALMENDRA, **Debussy et le mouvement modal dans la musique du XXᵉ siècle** [Debussy and the modal movement in 20th-century music] (4045); Ernest ANSERMET, **Debussy et Robert Godet** [Debussy and Robert Godet] (2131) and **Le langage de Debussy** [The language of Debussy] (4307); William W. AUSTIN, **Quelques connaissances et opinions de Schoenberg et Webern sur Debussy** [Some of Schoenberg's and Webern's thoughts and opinions about Debussy] (2132); Luiz Heitor Corrêa de AZEVEDO, **L'influence de Debussy: Amérique Latine** [Debussy's influence: Latin America] (2133); Jean BARRAQUÉ, **Debussy, ou L'approche d'une organisation autogène de la composition** [Debussy, or, The approach of an autogenous compositional organization] (4308); Dénes BARTHA, **L'influence de Debussy: Hongrie** [Debussy's influence: Hungary] (2134); Jacques CHAILLEY, **Apparences et réalités dans le langage de Debussy** [Appearances and realities in the language of Debussy] (4147); Vladimir FÉDOROV, **Debussy, vu par quelques Russes** [Debussy, viewed by some Russians] (2162); Françoise GERVAIS, **Debussy et la tonalité** [Debussy and tonality] (4171) and **L'influence de Debussy: France** [Debussy's influence: France] (2168); Stefan JAROCIŃSKI, **L'influence de Debussy: Pologne** [Debussy's influence: Poland] (2184); Julij Anatol'evič KREMLËV, **Les tendances réalistes dans l'esthétique de Debussy** [Realist tendencies in Debussy's aesthetic] (5514) and **L'influence de Debussy: Russie** [Debussy's influence: Russia] (2194); François LESURE, **Debussy et Edgard Varèse** [Debussy and Edgard Varèse] (2201); Roland Alexis Manuel LÉVY (Roland-Manuel), **Tradition permanente** [Permanent tradition] (2202); Edward LOCKSPEISER, **L'influence de Debussy: Angleterre** [Debussy's influence: England] (2207) and **Quelques problèmes de la psychologie de Debussy** [Some aspects of Debussy's psychology] (2030); Alberto MANTELLI, **L'influence de Debussy: Italie** [Debussy's influence: Italy] (2210); Poul Rovsing OLSEN, **L'influence de Debussy: Pays nordiques** [Debussy's influence: Scandinavian countries] (2224); Frank ONNEN, **L'influence de Debussy: Pays-Bas (Belgique-Hollande)** [Debussy's influence: The Low Countries (Belgium-Holland)] (2225); Virginia RAAD, **L'influence de Debussy: Amérique (États-Unis)** [Debussy's influence: America (United States)] (2236); Henri SAUGUET, **Révolution permanente** [Permanent revolution] (2245); André SCHAEFFNER, **Debussy et ses rapports avec la peinture** [Debussy and his relation to painting] (5396); André SOURIS, **Poétique musicale de Debussy** [Musical poetics of Debussy] (5602); Hans-Heinz STUCKENSCHMIDT, **L'influence de Debussy: Autriche et Allemagne** [Debussy's influence: Austria and Germany] (2257).

457
bs
[Stockholm; Uppsala] **Sixième Congrès international des bibliothèques musicales** [Sixth International Congress of Music Libraries]. Sponsored by the Association Internationale des Bibliothèques Musicales. Ed. by Cari JOHANSSON and Folke LINDBERG, *Fontes artis musicae* XI/1 (Jan-Apr 1964) 70. *Bibliog.* In French, English, and German.

The conference was held from 13 through 18 August 1962. The following contributions are cited separately: Alfons ANNEGARN, **The scientific music librarian and his public** (516); Rita BENTON, **Early musical scholarship in the United States** (859); Åke DAVIDSSON, **Cultural background to collections of old music in Swedish libraries** (712); John Howard DAVIES, moderator, **The training of the music librarian** (545); Kurt DORFMÜLLER, **Der wissenschaftliche Musikbibliothekar und sein Publikum** [The academic music librarian and his public] (556) and **Die bauliche Einrichtung der Musiksammlung der Bayerischen Staatsbibliothek, München** [The architectural dispositions of the music collection of the Bayerische Staatsbibliothek in Munich] (713); Leonard DUCK and Brooks SHEPARD, Jr., **The music librarian and his public** (559); Wolfgang M. FREITAG, **On planning a music library** (576); André JURRES, Maria PROKOPOWICZ, and Hans ZEHNTNER, moderator, **International aspects** (598); Karl-Heinz KÖHLER, **Bauliche und strukturelle Verhältnisse der Musikabteilung der Deutschen Staatsbibliothek, Berlin** [Architectural and structural situation of the music section of the Deutsche Staatsbibliothek in Berlin] (732); Alfons OTT, **Possibilities of musical education in public libraries** (641); Claudio SARTORI, **Le RISM et l'Italie: À l'aventure dans les bibliothèques italiennes** [*RISM* and Italy: In search of adventure in the Italian libraries] (666).

458
bs
[Warsaw] **Karol Szymanowski: Księga sesji Naukowej poświęconej twórczości Karola Szymanowskiego** [Karol Szymanowski: Report of the conference dedicated to the works of Karol Szymanowski]. Ed. by Zofia LISSA; pref. by Henryk GOLAŃSKI (Warszawa: Uniwersytet Warszawski, Instytut Muzykologii, 1964) 383 p. *Illus., music.* In Polish.

The conference was held from 23 through 28 March 1962. The following contributions are cited separately: Ludwik BIELAWSKI, **Karol Szymanowski a muzyka Podhala** [Karol Szymanowski and the Podhale music] (2136); Anna CHOJAK, **Tradycje Szymanowskiego w polskiej muzyce współczesnej** [Szymanowski's traditions in Polish contemporary music] (2146); Józef Michał CHOMIŃSKI, **Szymanowski i muzyka europejska XX wieku** [Szymanowski and 20th-century European music] (2147); Stanisław CZYŻOWSKI, **Problem stylizacji w Królu Rogerze** [Stylization in Szymanowski's *Król Roger*] (4327); Zbigniew DRZEWIECKI, **Kilka uwag o interpretacji utworów fortepianowych Szymanowskiego** [A few remarks on the interpretation of Szymanowski's piano works] (3791); John GŁOWACKI, **Kolorystyka a technika skrzypcowa w twórczości Szymanowskiego** [Coloristic devices in Szymanowski's violin technique] (4299); Monika GORCZYCKA, **Wpływy idealogii twórczej Szymanowskiego na kompoztorów polskich dwudziestolecia międzywojennego** [Szymanowski's influence on Polish composers of the pre-war period] (2172); Zofia HELMAN, **Z zagadnień warsztatu twórczego Karola Szymanowskiego na materiale jego szkiców** [Szymanowski's compositional technique in light of his sketches] (2179); Jarosław IWASZKIEWICZ, **Karol Szymanowski a literatura** [Karol Szymanowski and literature] (2183); Tadeusz KACZYŃSKI, **Zagadnienie autonomiczności i nieautonomiczności muzyki na przkładzie twórczości Karola Szymanowskiego** [Autonomous and non-autonomous music in Szymanowski's output] (2187); Eberhardt KLEMM, **Zagadnienie techniki wariacyjnej u Regera i Szymanowskiego** [Reger's and Szymanowski's variation technique] (4354); Zofia LISSA, **Szymanowski a romantyzm** [Szymanowski and Romanticism] (2206); Stefania ŁOBACZEWSKA, **Sonaty fortepianowe Szymanowskiego a sonaty Skriabina** [Szymanowski's and Skrjabin's piano sonatas] (4366); Izrael NIESTIEV, **Nowe materiały do biografii Karola Szymanowskiego** [New material in Szymanowski's biography] (2218); Kazimierz NOWACKI, **Rola folkloru góralskiego w Harnasiach** [Highlanders' folk art in *Harnasie*] (2221); Bohdan POCIEJ, **Faktura chóralna utworów Szymanowskiego** [Choral texture in Szymanowski's works] (2233); Witold RUDZIŃSKI, **Zagadnienia struktury I Koncertu Skrzypcowego K. Szymanowskiego** [Structural problems in Szymanowski's first violin concerto] (4397); Juliusz STARZYŃSKI, **Szymanowski a problematyka plastyki polskiej w XX-leciu miedzywojennym** [Szymanowski and Polish visual arts between the two World Wars] (5399); Jan STĘSZEWSKI, **Pieśni kurpiowskie w twórczości Karola Szymanowskiego** [The folk songs of the Kurpie regions in Szymanowski's works] (2256); Stefan ŚWIERZEWSKI, **Karol Szymanowski w oczach krytiyki polskiej** [Karol Szymanowski in light of Polish criticism] (2259); Mieczysław TOMASZEWSKI, **Związki słowno-muzyczne w liryce wokalnej Szymanowskiego na materiale Słopiewni** [The relationship between word and music in Szymanowski's lyrical vocal works on the basis of his *Słopiewnie*] (2265); Jadwiga ZABŁOCKA, **Rymy dziecięce Karola Szymanowskiego** [Szymanowski's *Rymy dziecięce* (Children's Rhymes)] (2276); Tadeusz Andrzej ZIELIŃSKI, **Sonorystyka** harmoniczna w trzecim okresie twórczości Szymanowskiego [Harmonic sonorities in Szymanowski's third period output] (4227).

459
bs

[Zlín/Gottwaldov] International Folk Music Council Conference. Ed. by Laurence E.R. PICKEN, *Journal of the International Folk Music Council* XV (1963) 4–83. *Illus., music, bibliog., charts, diagr., transcr.* In English, German, and French; summary in English.

The 15th annual conference was held from 13 through 21 July 1962. The following contributions are cited separately: Viktor Mihailovič BELJAEV, **The formation of folk modal systems** (4050); Alica ELSCHEKOVÁ, **Der mehrstimmige Volksgesang in der Slowakei** [Polyphonic folk song in Slovakia] (4162); Vasil HADŽIMANOV, **The dvotelnik, a Macedonian folk instrument** (3620); Dušan HOLÝ, **Instrumental and vocal performance of dance music in the Horňácko district of south-east Moravia** (2856); Rajna KACAROVA, **La tradition et l'espirit novateur dans la danse populaire** [Tradition and the innovative spirit in folk dance] (4996); Vladimír KARBUSICKÝ and Jaroslav MARKL, **Bohemian folk music: Traditional and contemporary aspects** (2878); Nikolaj KAUFMAN, **Part-singing in Bulgarian folk music** (2880); Lajos KISS, **Über den vokalen und instrumentalen Vortrag der ungarischen Volksweisen** [The vocal and instrumental performance of Hungarian folk tunes] (2896); Ernst KLUSEN, **Gustav Mahler und der Volkslied seiner Heimat** [Gustav Mahler and the folk songs of his homeland] (2006); Dvora LAPSON, **Jewish dances of Eastern and Central Europe** (5017); Hannah LAUDOVÁ, **Sword dances and their parallels in the Č.S.S.R** (5019); Jaroslav MARKL, **Czech bagpipe music** (2942); Tolia NIKIPROWETZKY, **The griots of Senegal and their instruments** (2563); Ernő PESOVÁR, **Der heutige Stand der ungarischen Volkstanzforschung** [The present state of research on Hungarian folk dance] (5048); Radmila PETROVIĆ, **Two styles of vocal music in the Zlatibor region of West Serbia** (2997); Roger PINON, **Contributions nouvelles à l'étude de la danse des sept sauts** [New contributions to the study of the seven-step dance] (5052); Willard RHODES, **North American Indian music in transition: A study of songs with English words as an index of acculturation** (3174); Doris STOCKMANN, **Zur Vokalmusik der südalbanischen Çamen** [The vocal music of the Southern Albanian Çamen] (3070); Wolfgang SUPPAN, **Über die Totenklage im deutschen Sprachraum** [Funeral laments in the German-speaking lands] (3077); Valens VODUŠEK, **Wichtige archaische Funde in den Alpen** [Important archaic finds in the Alps] (3107); Henrietta YURCHENCO, **Survivals of pre-Hispanic music in Mexico** (3225).

1963

460
bs

[Budapest] Europa et Hungaria: Congressus ethnographicus in Hungaria [Europe and Hungary: Ethnographic congress in Hungary]. Proceedings of the Magyar Néprajzi Kongresszus. Ed. by Gyula ORTUTAY and Tibor BODROGI; intro. by Zoltán KODÁLY (Budapest: Akadémiai Kiadó, 1965) 537 p. *Illus., music, bibliog., maps.* In German, English, Hungarian, and Russian.

The conference was held from 16 through 20 October 1963. The following contributions are cited separately: Vladimer V. AHOBADZE, **Forma kollektivnogo truda *nadi* i gruzinskaja chetyrëhgolosnaja pesnja *naduri*** [The form of collective *nadi* work and the Georgian four-part *naduri* song] (2710); Grigol ČHIKVADZE, **Doistoričeskaja gruzinskaja kostjanaja salamuri-flejta** [The prehistoric Georgian salamuri bone flute] (3614); György MARTIN, **East-European relations of Hungarian dance types** (5029); Cvetana Stojanova ROMANSKA, **Bulgarische und mazedonische Heldenlieder und historische Volkslieder über Persönlichkeiten aus der ungarischen Geschichte** [Bulgarian and Macedonian heroic songs and traditional songs on personalities from Hungarian history] (3038); Lajos VARGYAS, **The importance of the Hungarian ballads on the confines of Occident and Orient** (3096).

461
bs

[Cartagena de Indias] Primera Conferencia Interamericana de Etnomusicología [First Inter-American Conference on Ethnomusicology]. Sponsored by the Inter-American Music Council (CIDEM), Pan-American Union, Music Section, and Sociedad Pro-Arte Musical. Ed. by Guillermo ESPINOSA, *Boletín interamericano de música* (supplement 1965) 224. *Illus., charts, diagr., transcr., maps.* In Spanish.

The conference was held from 24 through 28 February 1963. The following contributions are cited separately: Isabel ARETZ, **Cantos navideños en el folklore venezolano** [Christmas songs in Venezuelan folklore] (3189); Lauro AYESTARÁN, **Fétis: Un precursor del criterio etnomusicológico en 1869** [Fétis: A precursor of the ethnomusicological criterion in 1869] (2416); Luis Carlos ESPINOSA and Jesús PINZÓN URREA, **La heterofonía en la música de los indios cunas del Darién** [Heterophony in the music of the Kuna Indians of Darién] (3199); Mantle HOOD, **The quest for norms in ethnomusicology** (2436); MacEdward LEACH, **Collecting techniques with special reference to ballads** (2443); Rossini Tavares de LIMA, **Música folclórica e instrumentos musicais do Brasil** [Traditional music and musical instruments of Brazil] (3259); George LIST, **Music in the culture of the Jíbaro Indians of the Ecuadorian montaña** (3206); Rafael MANZANARES, **Etnomusicología hondureña** [Honduran ethnomusicology] (3207); Andrés PARDO TOVAR, **Proyecciones sociológicas del folklore musical** [Sociological influences on musical folklore] (3211); Luis Felipe RAMÓN Y RIVERA, **Cantos negros de la Fiesta de San Juan** [Black people's songs for the feast of Saint John] (3214); Willard RHODES, **A preliminary study of the Mazatec mushroom ceremony** (3217); Charles SEEGER, **Preface to a critique of music** (2470); Carlos VEGA, **Música de tres notas** [Music of three notes] (3223).

462
bs

[Cetinje] Rad X-og kongresa Saveza Folklorista Jugoslavije [Proceedings of the tenth congress of the Savez Folklorista Jugoslavije]. Proceedings of the tenth congress of the Savez Udruženja Folklorista Jugoslavije. Ed. by Jovan VUKMANOVIĆ (Cetinje: Obod, 1964) 475 p. *Illus., transcr., dance notation.* In Serbian, Bosnian, Croatian, and Slovene; summaries in English, French, German, and Russian.

The following contributions are cited separately: Tvrtko ČUBELIĆ, **Šta je dosad izostavljeno u scenskom izvođenju narodnih plesova** [What has been dropped from stage performances of folk dances] (4949); Dragoslav DEVIĆ, **Naša narodna muzika na gramofonskim pločama** [Our traditional music in phonograph recordings] (2791); Jelena DOPUĐA, **Dramski oblici, elementi i dramski način izvođenja u narodnim igrama-plesovima u Bosni i Hercegovini** [Dramatic forms, elements, and performance techniques in traditional dances of Bosnia and Herzegovina] (4955); Vukoman DŽAKOVIĆ, **Crnogo narodne tužbalice i *Gorski vijenac*** [Traditional Montenegrin laments and *Gorski vijenac*] (5308); Andrijana GOJKOVIĆ, **Narodni muzički instrumenti u Njegoševim delima** [Traditional instruments in Njegoš's works] (5318); Radoslav HROVATIN, **Pentatonika u Jugoslaviji** [Pentatonic scales in Yugoslavia] (2864); Milica ILIJIN, **Narodne igre u Njegoševim delima** [Traditional dance in Njegoš's works] (5321); Nikola KNEŽEVIĆ, **Dramski elementi u izvođenju guslarske pjesme** [Dramatic elements in the performance of guslar song] (2900); Zmaga KUMER, **Prispevek k vrašanju raziskovanja tekstov ljudskih pesmi** [The question of textual research in traditional songs] (5326); Hannah LAUDOVÁ, **Dramski elementi u narodnoj igri** [Dramatic elements in traditional dance] (5018); Jovanka LAZAREVIĆ, **"Vučarska svadba" u Sredačkoj župi** [The "wolf's wedding" in Sredska county] (2925); Aleksandar LININ, **Karakteristične crte gajdarskih melodija u Makedoniji** [Characteristic features of gajdar melodies in Macedonia] (2932); Jaroslav MARKL, **Problematika obrade muzičkog folklora u Čehoslovačkoj** [Problems in the dissemination of musical folklore in Czechoslovakia] (2945); Niko S. MARTINOVIĆ, **Kolo u *Gorskom vijencu*** [Kolo in the *Gorski vijenac*] (5331); Živomir MLADENOVIĆ, **Njegošev doprinos Vukuvoj zbirci narodnih pesama** [Njegoš's contribution to Vuk's collections of traditional songs] (2960); Ljuba SIMIĆ, **Klasifikacija narodnih pesama** [The classification of traditional songs] (5354); Radoš TREBJEŠANIN, **Dramski elementi u dečjim pesmama za igru u leskovačkom kraju** [Dramatic elements in children's singing games in the Leskovac region] (3087); Mitar S. VLAHOVIĆ, **Gusle u Njegoševim delima** [The gusle in Njegoš's works] (5368).

→ **[Crésuz; Wolfsburg] Musique sacrée et langues modernes: Deux colloques internationaux** [Sacred music and modern languages: Two international colloquia] See no. 449 in this volume.

463 **[Jerusalem] East and West in Music.** Proceed-
bs ings of the 16th Annual Conference of the International Folk Music Council; sponsored by the International Music Council, Israel National Commission for UNESCO, and Israel National Council of Culture and Art. Ed. by Maud KARPELES; foreword by Zoltán KODÁLY, *Journal of the International Folk Music Council* XVI (1964) 109. *Illus., music, bibliog., discog., charts, diagr., transcr.* In English and French.

The conference was held from 6 through 9 August 1963. The following contributions are cited separately: Higini ANGLÈS, **Relations of Spanish folk song to the Gregorian chant** (2720); Hanoch AVENARY, **The Hasidic *nigun*: Ethos and melos of a folk liturgy** (6037); Milton BABBITT, **The synthesis, perception, and specification of musical time** (3966); Günter BIRKNER, **Psaume hébraïque et séquence latine** [Jewish psalm and Latin sequence] (6170); Alexander Uriah BOSKOVICH, **La musique israélienne contemporaine et les traditions ethniques** [Contemporary Israeli music and ethnic traditions] (2143); Diego CARPITELLA, **À propos du folklore "reconstruit"** ["Reconstructed" folklore] (2501); Jacques CHAILLEY, **Comment entendre la musique populaire?** [How should one listen to traditional music?] (2502); Dalia COHEN, **An investigation into the tonal structure of the *maqāmāt*** (4420); Paul COLLAER, **La migration du style mélismatique oriental vers l'Occident** [The migration of Eastern melismatic style towards the West] (1026); Peter CROSSLEY-HOLLAND, **Preservation and renewal of traditional music** (2429); Luigi DALLAPICCOLA, **Musique et humanité** [Music and humanity] (5447); Alain DANIÉLOU, **Valeurs éthiques et spirituelles en musique** [Ethical and spiritual values in music] (5449); Ernst EMSHEIMER, **Some remarks on European folk polyphony** (2803); Edith GERSON-KIWI, **The bourdon of the East: Its regional and universal trends** (4170); Zaven HACOBIAN, **L'improvisation et l'ornementation en Orient et en Occident** [Improvisation and ornamentation in the Orient and Occident] (841); Avigdor HERZOG, **Transcription and transnotation in ethnomusicology** (2434); Felix HOERBURGER, **Haphazard assembly as a pre-musical form of polyphony** (4180); Shlomo HOFMAN, **La musique arabe en Israel: Sa préservation, sa rénovation** [Arab music in Israel: Its preservation, its renovation] (2637); Nikolaj KAUFMAN, **Jewish and Gentile folk song in the Balkans and its relation to the liturgical music of the Sephardic Jews in Bulgaria** (2879); Leo LEVI, **Traditions of Biblical cantillation and ekphonetics** (6018); Ehr LIN, **The notation and continuous control of pitch** (3848); George LIST, **Acculturation and musical tradition** (2526); Claudie MARCEL-DUBOIS, **Le tambour bourdonnant** [The friction drum] (3652); Tolia NIKIPROWETZKY, **L'ornementation dans la musique des touareg de l'Aïr** [Ornamentation in the music of the Tuareg people of the Aïr region] (2565); Joseph Hanson Kwabena NKETIA, **Traditional and contemporary idioms of African music** (2572); Spyridon PERISTERIS, **Chansons polyphoniques de l'Épire du nord** [Polyphonic songs of northern Epirus] (2993); Mihai POP, **Continuity and change in traditional folklore** (3013); Bálint SÁROSI, **Les chemins de la culture instrumentale en Hongrie** [The paths of instrument cultivation in Hungary] (3050); Myron SCHAEFFER, **An extension of tone-row techniques through electronic pitch control** (4109); Herzl SHMUELI, **Oriental elements in Israeli song** (2691); Johanna SPECTOR, **Samaritan chant** (6099); Bence SZABOLCSI, **Hebrew recitative-types in Hungary** (3078); Hans TISCHLER, **Remarks on Hindemith's contrapuntal technique** (4221); Hugh TRACEY, **Wood music of the Chopi** (2593); Lajos VARGYAS, **Bartók's melodies in the style of folk songs** (4469); László VIKÁR, **Les parallèles orientaux de l'interprétation des chansons populaires hongroises** [Eastern parallels in the performance practice of Hungarian traditional song] (4471); Klaus P. WACHSMANN, **Human migration and African harps** (2596).

464 **[Jerusalem] Tpylah šel hayamym hanẁra'ym**
bs **wemẁsyqah** [High Holiday prayers and their music]. Proceedings of the Sixth Israeli Music Congress, *Dẁkan* VI (1964). In Hebrew.

The following contributions are cited separately: Bathja BAYER, **Haty'ẁd ha'arky'ẁlẁgy šel hašẁpar ḃe"y** [The archaeological documentation of the shofar in Israel] (6042); Judith R. COHEN, **'Al "Ǩol nidrey" šel 'Arnẁld Šonḃerg** [On Arnold Schoenberg's *Kol nidre*] (4421); 'Ely'ezer 'ELYNER, **Haḃ'yẁṭ šbamaḥzẁr 'ašǩenaz: Haštašlẁtaw wešymwšẁ** [Liturgical poetry in Ashkenazi prayer book: Its development and use] (6050); Me'yr Šim'ẁn GEŠWRY, **Nygẁney hayamym hanẁra'ym eşel haḥasydym** [The Hasidic melodies for the High Holy Days] (6060); 'Abraham Me'yr HABERMAN, **Dbarym 'al hatpylah** [Remarks on prayer] (6066); Yehẁšu'a Leyyḃ NE'EMAN, **Sqyrah 'al nygẁney tpylah šel hayamym hanẁra'ym ḃenẁsaḥ 'eyrẁp̃ah** [A survey of melodies for the prayer of High Holy Days in the Eastern European tradition] (6083).

465 **[Kampala] First Conference on African Traditional Music.** Sponsored by the Makerere University.
bs Ed. and intro. by George Wilberforce KAKOMA; ed. by Gerald MOORE and Okot P'BITEK; intro. by S. Joshua L. ZAKE (Kampala: Uganda Ey'eddembe, 1964) 45 p.

The conference was held from 15 through 18 December 1963. The following contributions are cited separately: Charles DUVELLE, **Opening talk on the music of Africa** (2550); Okot P'BITEK, **Social functions of traditional music in Acholi and Lango** (2574); Aidan William SOUTHALL, **Suggested links between proposed school of African music and the African studies programme at Makerere** (4850). An appendix includes brief abstracts of additional papers and a summary of the closing discussion.

466 **[Katowice] Ryszard Wagner a polska kultura**
bs **muzyczna/Richard Wagner und die polnische Musikkultur** [Richard Wagner and Polish musical culture]. Ed. by Karol MUSIOŁ; intro. by Jan GAWLAS. *Zeszyt naukowy* 5 (Katowice: Panstwowa Wyzsza Szkola Muzyczna, 1964) 146 p. *Music, bibliog.* In Polish; summary in German.

The conference was held at the Biblioteke Panstwowa Wyzsza Szkola Muzyczna in Katowice from 21 through 22 November 1963. The following contributions are cited separately: Mirosław BLIWERT, **Mieczysław Karłowicz a twórczość Ryszarda Wagnera** [Mieczysław Karłowicz and the works of Richard Wagner] (1918); Karol BULA, **Stanisław Moniuszko a reforma Wagnerowska** [Stanisław Moniuszko and the Wagnerian reform of opera] (5113); Zygmunt FOLGA, *Bolesław Śmiały* **Ludomira Różyckiego jako dramat muzyczny** [Ludomir Różycki's *Bolesław Śmiały* and its music dramaturgy] (5150); Franciszek GERMAN, **Powstanie listopadowe w muzyce polskiej** [The November Revolution in Polish music] (2167); Leon MARKIEWICZ, **Ryszard Wagner a Chopinowska myśl harmoniczna** [Richard Wagner and Chopin's harmonic thinking] (4196); Karol MUSIOŁ, **Ryszard Wagner a powstanie listopadowe** [Richard Wagner and the November Revolution] (2048); Szymon NIEMAND, **Wybitni polscy Śpiewacy w repertuarze Wagnerowskim** [Significant Polish signers in productions of Wagner operas] (5214); Lózef POWROŹNIAK, **Spór Karola Lipińskiego z Ryszardem Wagnerem** [The conflict between Karol Lipiński and Richard Wagner] (2073); Józef ŚWIDER, **Stosunek Szymanowskiego do Wagnera** [The relationship between Szymanowski and Wagner] (2107); Maria SZEWCZYK-SKOCZYLAS, **Polskie piśmiennictwo o Wagnerze** [Polish literature about Wagner] (5364).

467 **[Kiel] Norddeutsche und nordeuropäische**
bs **Musik** [Northern German and northern European music]. Sponsored by the Landeskundliche Abteilung des Musikwissenschaftlichen Instituts der Universität Kiel. Ed. by Carl DAHLHAUS and Walter WIORA. *Kieler Schriften zur Musikwissenschaft* 16 (Kassel; New York: Bärenreiter, 1965) 128 p. *Illus., facs., music, maps.* In German.

The conference was held in October 1963. The following contributions are cited separately: Ingmar BENGTSSON, **Romantisch-nationale Strömungen in deutscher und skandinavischer Musik** [Romantic-nationalist trends in German and Scandinavian music] (1914); Werner BRAUN, **Johann Sebastiani (1622-1683) und die Musik in Königsberg** [Johann Sebastiani (1622-83) and music in Königsberg] (1495); Werner BREIG, **Über das Verhältnis von Komposition und Ausführung in der** norddeutschen Orgel-Choralbearbeitung des 17. Jahrhunderts [The relation between composition and performance in North German chorale arrangements for organ in the 17th century] (4319); Carl DAHLHAUS, *Cribrum musicum*: **Der Streit zwischen Scacchi und Siefert** [*Cribrum musicum*: The quarrel of Scacchi and Siefert] (1520); Hans EPPSTEIN, **Aktuelle Tendenzen in der schwedischen Musikpädagogik** [Current tendencies in Swedish music pedagogy] (4524); Bruno GRUSNICK, **Die Datierungen der Dübensammlung** [The datings of the Düben collection] (720); Kurt GUDEWILL, **Musik in der Kieler Universität** [Music at the University of Kiel] (4822); Olav GURVIN, **Über Beziehungen zwischen deutscher und norwegischer Musik** [Links between German and Norwegian music] (966); Gerhard HAHNE, **Musikalische Zusammenhänge zwischen Dänemark und Schleswig-Holstein im 19. Jahrhundert** [Musical connections between Denmark and Schleswig-Holstein in the 19th century] (1978); Dietrich KILIAN, **Buxtehudes *Membra*** [Buxtehude's *Membra*] (1589); Harald KÜMMERLING, **Gottorfer Bestände in der Sammlung Bokemeyer** [Gottorf material in the Bokemeyer collection] (733); Margarete REIMANN, **Zur Editionstechnik von Musik des 17. Jahrhunderts** [The technique of editing 17th-century music] (3915); Friedrich Wilhelm RIEDEL, **Strenger und freier Stil in der nord- und süddeutschen Musik für Tasteninstrumente des 17. Jahrhunderts** [Strict and free style in the North and South German keyboard music of the 17th century] (1657); Nils SCHIØRRING, **Nachwirkungen der Lobwasserpsalter in Dänemark** [Aftereffects of Lobwasser's psalter in Denmark] (6446); Werner SCHWARZ, **Musik und Musikern im deutschen Osten: Nach unveröffentlichten Briefen an Robert Schumann aus den Jahren 1834–1854** [Music and musicians in the German East: On the basis of unpublished letters to Robert Schumann from 1834–1854] (2094); Søren SØRENSEN, **Allgemeines über den dänischen protestantischen Kirchengesang** [General remarks on Danish Protestant hymnody] (6449); Wolfgang WITTROCK, **Volkslieder in Schleswig-Holstein** [Traditional songs in Schleswig-Holstein] (3117).

468
rs
Review by Joseph MÜLLER-BLATTAU, *Die Musikforschung* 4 (July-Sept 1967) 320–21. In German.

469
bs
[Montauban] Actes des Journées internationales d'étude du Baroque [Proceedings of the International Congress on Baroque Studies]. Sponsored by the Festival de Montauban. Intro. by Victor-Lucien TAPIÉ. *Publications de la Faculté des Lettres et Sciences Humaines de Toulouse* A:2 (Toulouse: Faculté des Lettres et Sciences Humaines, 1965) 167 p. *Illus., bibliog.* In French.

The conference was held from 26 through 28 September 1963. The following contributions are cited separately: Macario Santiago KASTNER, **Quelques aspects du Baroque musical espagnol et portugais** [Aspects of Spanish and Portuguese music of the Baroque] (1586); Pierre-Paul LACAS, **Essai sur le Baroque en organologie** [Essay on organological aspects of the Baroque] (3408).

470
bs
[Prague] I. Internationales Seminar Marxistischer Musikwissenschaftler [First International Seminar of Marxist Musicologists], *Beiträge zur Musikwissenschaft* V/4 (1963). In German.
The conference was held from 27 May through 1 June 1963. The following contributions are cited separately: Harry GOLDSCHMIDT, **Musikalische Gestalt und Intonation** [Musical form and intonation] (5479); Jaroslav JIRÁNEK, **Zu einigen Grundbegriffen der marxistischen Ästhetik** [Some fundamental concepts of Marxist aesthetics] (5502); Georg KNEPLER, **Musikgeschichte und Geschichte** [Music history and history] (888); Jozef KRESÁNEK, **Die gesellschaftliche Funktion der Musik** [The social function of music] (5892); János MARÓTHY, **Von der Hagiographie zur Historiographie** [From hagiography to historiography] (897); Günter MAYER, **Zur musiksoziologischen Fragestellung** [On the posing of music-sociological questions] (5895); Ladislav MOKRÝ, **Soziologie und Marxismus** [Sociology and Marxism] (5899); Antonín SYCHRA, **Zur Problemstellung unseres Seminars** [Formulating the problem of our seminar] (5609); József UJFALUSSY, **Zur Dialektik des Wirklichkeitsbildes in der Musik** [The dialectics of the representation of reality in music] (5619). The conference is also cited as no. 471 in this volume.

471
bs
[Prague] Intonation und Gestalt in der Musik: Beiträge und Abhandlungen der Musikwissenschaftler sozialistischer Länder
[*Intonacija* and gestalt in music: Contributions and studies from the musicologists of socialist countries]. Proceedings of the First International Seminar of Marxist Musicologists; sponsored by the Büro Musikwissenschaftler Sozialistischer Länder. Ed. and forew. by Boris Mihajlovič JARUSTOVSKIJ; in collab. with A. ARNOLD and S. MARKUS (Moskva: Muzyka, 1963) 381 p. *Music.* In German.

Collection of essays arising from the work of the First International Seminar of Marxist Musicologists, held in Prague, 1963 (the proceedings are cited as no. 470 in this volume). The following contributions are cited separately: Viktor Abramovič CUKKERMAN and G. BALTER, **Die Komplexanalyse der musikalischen Werke und ihre Methodik** [The complex-analysis of musical works and its methodology] (3937); Harry GOLDSCHMIDT, **Musikalische Gestalt und Intonation** [Musical gestalt and intonation] (5409); Boris Mihajlovič JARUSTOVSKIJ, **"Wie das Leben..."** ["Like life..."] (5411); Jaroslav JIRÁNEK, **Einige Schlüsselprobleme der marxistischen Musikwissenschaft im Lichte der Intonation-theorie Assafjews.** [Some key problems of Marxist musicology in the light of Asaf'ev's intonation theory] (5500); Julij Anatol'evič KREMLËV, **Intonation und Gestalt in der Musik** [Intonation and gestalt in music] (5413); Zofia LISSA, **Über die Prozessualität im Musikwerk** [Processuality in the musical work] (5525); Lev Abramovič MAZEL', **Vom System der musikalischen Ausdruckmittel und einigen Prinzipien der künstlerischen Wirkung der Musik** [The system of musical means of expression and some principles of the artistic effect of music] (5414); Elena ORLOVA, **Die Arbeit Assafjews an der Theorie der Intonation** [Asaf'ev's work on intonation theory] (5416); Josif RYŽKIN, **Bild-Gestaltungskomposition des Musikwerks** [The image-gestalt composition of the musical work] (5418); Walther SIEGMUND-SCHULTZE, **Die Rolle der Melodie in der Musik des sozialistischen Realismus** [The role of melody in the music of socialist realism] (4459); Antonín SYCHRA, **Musikwissenschaft und neue Methode der wissenschaftlichen Analyse** [Musicology and new methods of scientific analysis] (3958). Simultaneously issued by the same publisher in a Russian-language version, under the title *Intonacija i muzykal'nyj obraz: Stat'i i issledovanija muzykovedov Sovetskogo sojuza i drugih socialističeskih stran.*

472
bs
[Royaumont] Le lieu théâtral à la Renaissance
[Theatrical venues in the Renaissance]. Ed. by Jean JACQUOT, Elie KONIGSON, and Marcel ODDON. *Colloques internationaux du CNRS* (Paris: Centre National de la Recherche Scientifique [CNRS], 1964) x, 532 p. *Illus., facs., tech. drawings.* In French and Italian.
The conference was held from 22 through 27 March 1963. The following contributions are cited separately: Charles V. AUBRUN, **Les débuts du drame lyrique en Espagne** [The beginnings of opera in Spain] (5097); Jean JACQUOT, **Les types du lieu théâtral et leurs transformations de la fin du Moyen Âge au milieu du XVIIe siècle** [Theatrical venue types and their transformations from the end of the Middle Ages to the middle of the 17th century] (5175).

473
bs
[Santo Tirso] Actas do Congresso Internacional de Etnografia [Proceedings of the International Congress of Ethnography] (Porto: Imprensa Portuguesa, 1965) 6 v. *Illus., music, maps.* In Portuguese, German, and Spanish.
The conference was held from 10 through 18 July 1963. The following contributions are cited separately: António ALFAIATE MARVÃO, **O folclore musical do Baixo Alentejo nos ciclos litúrgicos da Igreja** [The traditional music of Baixo Alentejo in liturgical cycles of the Church] (2712); Isabel ARTEZ, **Cuentos musicales de Sudamerica** [Musical tales of South America] (3191); Bonifacio GIL, **Panorama de la canción popular andaluza: Consideración preliminar** [Panorama of Andalusian popular song: A preliminary consideration] (2834); Ernst KLUSEN, **Beziehungen zwischen Volksliedforschung und Volksliedpflege** [The connections between folk-song research and folk-song cultivation] (2441); António Maria MOURINHO, **Aspecto e função da música popular Mirandesa profana e religiosa** [Aspects and functions of secular and religious traditional music in Miranda] (2964); Marta Amor MUÑOZ, **Problemas de**

sistematización de las danzas folklóricas [Problems in the systematization of traditional dances] (5039); Afonso do PAÇO, **Sogras e cunhadas no cancioneiro popular e no adagiário** [Mothers-in-law and brothers-in-law in traditional song and in proverbs] (2983); Julián SAN VALERO APARISI, **Las bandas de música en la vida valenciana** [Music bands in Valencian life] (3044).

474   [Venice] **Venezia e la Polonia nei secoli dal**
bs   **XVII al XIX** [Venice and Poland in the 17th to the 19th century]. Sponsored by the Fondazione Giorgio Cini, Polska Akademia Nauk, and Polsko Ministerstwo Szkolnictwa Wyzszego. By Luigi CINI (Venezia: Istituto per la Collaborazione Culturale, 1965) xix, 431 p. *Illus.* In Italian and French.
The conference was held from 28 May through 2 June 1963. The following contributions are cited separately: Józef Michał CHOMIŃSKI, **Le technique polychorale vénitienne en Pologne** [Venetian polychoral technique in Poland] (1508); Nicola MANGINI, **Goldoni e la Polonia** [Goldoni and Poland] (5204).

1964

475   [Amsterdam] **Actes du cinquième Congrès in-**
bs   **ternational d'esthétique/Proceedings of the Fifth International Congress of Aesthetics.** Ed. by Jan ALER ('s-Gravenhage: Mouton, 1964) 1031 p. *Bibliog.* In French, English, German, and Italian.
The conference was held from 24 through 28 August 1964. The following contributions are cited separately: Alphons ASSELBERGS, **"Musical poetry" and organic composition** (5283); J.J. BELJON, **The training of the industrial designer in the Netherlands** (4491); Karel Philippus BERNET KEMPERS, **Die Affektenlehre und die Musikauffassung des neunzehnten Jahrhunderts** [The doctrine of the affections and the concept of music in the nineteenth century] (5429); Daniel CHARLES, **L'esthétique du non finito chez John Cage** [John Cage's aesthetic concept of *non finito*] (5442); G.M.A. CORVER, **Tradition et innovation musicales dans la pensée du compositeur Willem Pijper** [Musical tradition and innovation in the thinking of the composer Willem Pijper] (2149); Pieter FISCHER, **Sa Tendre Majesté la harpe** [Her Tender Majesty, the harp] (3569); Léopold FLAM, **L'art-religion de l'homme moderne** [The art-religion of modern man] (5469); Enrico FUBINI, **Espressione e imitazione della natura nell'estetica musicale del settecento** [Expression and imitation of nature in the musical aesthetic of the 18th century] (5472); Angélique FULIN, **Le langage musical des enfants** [The musical language of children] (5657); François GUILLOT DE RODE, **Fonction mythique et danse** [Mythic function and dance] (4974); Camille JACOBS, **Some psychological remarks concerning the aesthetics of music** (5495); Evgenij Georgievič JAKOVLEV, **Das ästhetische Gefühl, das religiöse Erlebnis und ihre Wechselbeziehung an den verschiedenen Kunstarten** [Aesthetic feeling, religious experience, and their interrelationship in different kinds of art] (5497); André JURRES, **Dutch musical composition in the middle of our century** (2186); Christophe KRAFFT, **L'esthétique du Nouveau Bayreuth** [The aesthetics of the New Bayreuth] (5184); Willem J.M. LEVELT and Reinier PLOMP, **The appreciation of musical intervals** (5675); Serge LIFAR, **Le ballet, synthèse des arts, dans son évolution technique et esthétique** [Ballet, as a sythesis of the arts, in its technical and aesthetic evolution] (5022); Claire MCGLINCHEE, **Shakespeare, Delacroix and Chopin** (2038); Francesco Yosio NOMURA, **On Zen and musical aesthetics** (5555); Carel PORCELIJN, **The position of Alphons Diepenbrock in the Dutch history of music** (2071); Jean PUCELLE, **L'achèvement des "symphonies inachevées"** [The completion of so-called unfinished symphonies] (5570); Herbert M. SCHUELLER, **Artistic greatness as content-material relationship** (5591); Joseph SMITS VAN WAESBERGHE, **Der Niederländer in seinen tänzerischen, sprachlichen, und musikalischen Äusserungen** [The Dutch in their dance, language, and music] (4925); Étienne SOURIAU, **Art et innovation** [Art and innovation] (5601); Hubert Paul Hans TEESING, **Probleme der kunstwissenschaftlichen Wertung** [Problems of evaluation in the study of the arts] (5611).

476   [Berlin] **Bericht der Tagung zu Fragen der**
bs   **Arbeiterliedforschung** [Report of the meeting on issues in research on workers' song]. Sponsored by the Deutsche Akademie der Künste, Abteilung Arbeiterlied. Ed. by Georg KNEPLER; afterword by Frank WERKMEISTER, *Beiträge zur Musikwissenschaft* VI/4 (1964). In German.
The conference was held from 28 through 30 April 1964. The following contributions are cited separately: Jürgen ELSNER, **Der Einfluß der Arbeitermusikbewegung auf die Kampfmusik Hanns Eislers** [The influence of the workers' music movement on Hanns Eisler's songs of struggle] (2159); Radoslav HROVATIN, **Kategorisierung des Partisanenlieds in Jugoslawien** [The categorization of Partisan songs in Yugoslavia] (2860); Vladimír KARBUSICKÝ, **Das Arbeiterlied in der Geschichte und Gesellschaft** [Workers' songs in history and in society] (2877); Karl KLAUDER, **Lehren der deutschen Arbeitersängerbewegung für die heutige Chorpraxis** [Lessons from the German workers' singing movement for contemporary choral practice] (4908); Günther KRAFT, **Stand und Koordinierung der wissenschaftlichen Forschung auf dem Gebiet des Arbeiterliedes in der Deutschen Demokratischen Republik** [The condition and coordination of scholarly research in East Germany in the area of the Arbeiterlied] (2442); Inge LAMMEL, **10 Jahre Arbeiterliedarchiv** [Ten years of the Arbeiterliedarchiv] (734); Sergio LIBEROVICI, **Zur Schaffung neuer politischer Lieder in Italien** [The creation of new political songs in Italy] (2930); Ernst Hermann MEYER, **Aus der Tätigkeit der Kampfgemeinschaft der Arbeitersänger** [Activities of the Kampfgemeinschaft der Arbeitersänger] (5898); Václav PLETKA, **Über einige methodische Probleme der Arbeiterlied-Forschung** [Some methodological problems in research on the workers' song] (2459); Gerd SEMMER, **Über die Ostermarsch-Lieder** [Songs for the Easter marches] (3235); Wolfgang STEINITZ, **Arbeiterlied und Arbeiterkultur** [Workers' songs and the culture of the working class] (3065).

477   [Bratislava] **Anfänge der slavischen Musik**
bs   [Origins of Slavic music]. Ed. by Ladislav MOKRÝ. *Ústav hudobnej vedy: Symposia* 1 (Bratislava: Slovenská Akadémia Vied, 1966) 178 p. *Facs., music.* In German, Russian, and English.
The meeting was held in August 1964. The following contributions are cited separately: Elmar ARRO, **Probleme der Provenienz des altrussischen kirchlich-kultischen Gesanges** [Questions concerning the provenance of Old Russian liturgical chant] (1058); Werner BACHMANN, **Das byzantinische Musikinstrumentarium** [The Byzantine music instrumentarium] (3239); Viktor Mihailovič BELJAEV, **Proishoždenie znamennijja rospeva** [Origins of znamennyj chant] (1063); Alica ELSCHEKOVÁ, **Strukturelle Frühformen slavischer Volksmusik** [Early structural forms of Slavic traditional music] (2801); Jiří FUKAČ, **Zu den Ergebnissen der Forschung über den musikalischen Charakter der Epoche Groß-Mährens** [Research findings on the musical character of the age of Great Moravia] (1098); Włodzimierz KAMIŃSKI, **Beiträge zur Erforschung der frühmittelalterlichen Musikinstrumente der Nordwest- und Ostslaven** [Contributions to research on the early medieval musical instruments of the northwestern and eastern Slavs] (3257); Vladimír KARBUSICKÝ, **Zu den historischen Wurzeln der Metrik der russischen Bylinen** [On the historic roots of the metrics of Russian byliny] (4006); Erwin KOSCHMIEDER, **Wie haben Kyrill und Method zelebriert?** [How did Cyril and Methodius celebrate?] (6274); Stefan LAZAROV, **Die altbulgarische Musik und die Kyrillo-Methodianische Tradition** [Old Bulgarian music and the tradition of Cyril and Methodius] (1138); Kenneth J. LEVY, **Die slavische Kondakarien-Notation** [Slavic *kondakar'* notation] (3846); Ladislav MOKRÝ, **Der Kanon zur Ehre des hl. Demetrius als Quelle für die Frühgeschichte des kirchenslavischen Gesanges** [The kanōn in honor of St. Demetrius as a source for the early history of Church Slavonic chant] (6123); Dimitrije STEFANOVIĆ, **The beginnings of Serbian chant** (1192); Oliver STRUNK, **Zwei Chilandari Chorbücher** [Two Hilandar choirbooks] (1197); Alfred J. SWAN, **O sposobah garmonizacii znamennogo rospeva** [Ways of harmonizing znamennyj chant] (4304); Josef VAŠICA, **Slavische Petrusliturgie** [Slavic liturgy of St. Peter] (6131); Miloš VELIMIROVIĆ, **Preparation of an inventory of sources of old Slavic music** (810).

478   [Budapest] **International Folk Music Council**
bs   **Conference.** Ed. by Zoltán KODÁLY, *Studia*

musicologica Academiae Scientiarum Hungaricae VII (1965) 349. In English, French, and German.

The 17th annual conference was held from 17 through 25 August 1964. The following contributions are cited separately: Jenő ÁDÁM, **The influence of folk music on public musical education in Hungary** (4477); Samuel BAUD-BOVY, **La systématisation des chansons populaires** [The systematization of traditional songs] (4415); Viktor Mihailovič BELJAEV, **Folk music and the history of music** (833); Genovaité ČETKAUS-KAITÉ, **Principes du classement du folklore musical lituanien** [Principles of classification in Lithuanian traditional music] (2762); David CLEGG, **Philaret Kolessa's classification of the Ukrainian recitative songs** (2769); Paul COLLAER, **Lyrisme baroque et tradition populaire** [Baroque lyricism and folk tradition] (1511); Károly CSÉBFALVY, Miklós HAVASS, Pál JÁRDÁNYI, and Lajos VARGYAS, **Systemization of tunes by computers** (4422); Alain DANIÉLOU, **Le folklore et l'histoire de la musique** [Folklore and the history of music] (838); Oskár ELSCHEK, **Problem of variation in eighteenth century Slovak folk music manuscripts** (2800); Alica ELSCHEKOVÁ, **General considerations on the classification of folk tunes** (4426); Edith GERSON-KIWI, **The bards of the Bible** (2827); Vasil HADŽIMANOV, **Les mélodies funèbres du séisme de Skopié** [The funeral melodies of the earthquake at Skopje] (2844); Felix HOERBURGER, **Dance and dance music of the 16th century and their relations to folk dance and folk music** (4978); Dušan HOLÝ, **The classification of ornamental elements in folk dance-music against the background of a metrorhythmical basis** (2855); Volodymyr HOŠOVS'KIJ, **The experiment of systematizing and cataloging folk tunes following the principles of musical dialectology and cybernetics** (5928); Milica ILIJIN, **Influences réciproques des danses urbaines et traditionnelles en Yougoslavie** [Reciprocal influences of urban and traditional dances of Yugoslavia] (4984); Pál JÁRDÁNYI, **Experiences and results in systematizing Hungarian folk-songs** (4439); Rajna KACAROVA, **La classification des mélodies populaires en Bulgarie** [The classification of traditional melodies in Bulgaria] (2875); Leon KNOPOFF, **Some technological advances in musical analysis** (3949); Fumio KOIZUMI, **Towards a systemization of Japanese folk-song** (2648); György MARTIN, **Considérations sur l'analyse des relations entre la danse et la musique de danse populaire** [Considerations on the analysis of the relationship between dance and traditional dance music] (5028); Joseph Hanson Kwabena NKETIA, **The interrelations of African music and dance** (2570); Radmila PETROVIĆ, **The oldest notation of folk tunes in Yugoslavia** (3860); Willard RHODES, **The use of the computer in the classification of folk tunes** (4454); Alexander L. RINGER, **On the question of exoticism in 19th-century music** (2084); Marius SCHNEIDER, **Le rythme de la musique artistique espagnole du XVIe siècle va à travers la chanson populaire** [The rhythm of 16th-century Spanish art music parallels traditional song] (4029); Johanna SPECTOR, **The significance of Samaritan neumes and contemporary practice** (6100); Jan STĘSZEWSKI, **Ébauche de l'histoire des classifications ethnomusicologiques en Pologne** [An outline of the history of ethnomusicological classifications in Poland] (2474); Erich STOCKMANN, **Towards a history of European folk music instruments** (3279); Wolfgang SUPPAN, **A collection of European dances: Breslau 1555** (5068); Bence SZABOLCSI, **Folk music—art music—history of music** (853); Karel VETTERL, **The method of classification and grouping of folk melodies** (4470); Klaus P. WACHSMANN, **The earliest sources of folk music from Africa** (2594); David K. WILGUS, **Fiddler's farewell: The legend of the hanged fiddler** (2547); Walter WIORA, **Ethnomusicology and the history of music** (2483).

479
bs

[Darmstadt] Notation neuer Musik [The notation of new music]. Ed. and forew. by Ernst THOMAS. *Darmstädter Beiträge zur Neuen Musik* 9 (Mainz: Schott, 1965) 116 p. *Illus., facs., music, charts, diagr.* In German.

The symposium was held during the 19th Internationale Ferienkurse für Neue Musik. The following contributions are cited separately: Earle BROWN, **Notation und Ausführung Neuer Musik** [Notation and the performance of new music] (3808); Christoph CASKEL, **Notation für Schlagzeug** [Percussion notation] (3812); Carl DAHLHAUS, **Notenschrift heute** [Music notation today] (3814); Roman HAUBENSTOCK-RAMATI, **Notation: Material und Form** [Notation: Material and form] (3823); Mauricio KAGEL, **Komposition—Notation—Interpretation** [Composition, notation, interpretation] (3832); Aloys KONTARSKY, **Notationen für Klavier** [Notations for piano] (3835); György LIGETI, **Kommunikationsmittel oder Selbstzweck?** [A means of communication

or a goal in itself?] (3847); Siegfried PALM, **Zur Notation für Streichinstrumente** [Notation for string instruments] (3859).

480
bs

[Graz] Die Kirchenmusik und das II. Vatikanische Konzil [Church music and the Vatican Council II]. Sponsored by the Akademie für Musik und Darstellende Kunst in Graz, Abteilung für Kirchenmusik. Ed. and forew. by Philipp HARNONCOURT (Graz: Styria, 1965) 236 p. *Music, charts, diagr.* In German.

The conference was held from 3 through 7 March 1964 during the Kirchenmusikwoche. The following contributions are cited separately: Karl AMON, **Die Funktionsteilung in der Liturgiefeier** [The distribution of responsibilities in the celebration of the liturgy] (6144); Urbanus BOMM, **Choralforschung und Choralpflege in der Gegenwart** [Present-day chant research and chant cultivation] (6172); Paul GUTFLEISCH, **Der Kirchenmusiker als Beruf** [The profession of the church musician] (5884); Philipp HARNONCOURT, **Neue Aufgaben der katholischen Kirchenmusik** [New tasks of Catholic church music] (6249); Hermann KRONSTEINER, **Das deutsche Kirchenlied in der Liturgiefeier** [The German-language hymn in the celebration of the liturgy] (6276); Walther LIPPHARDT, **Möglichkeiten und Grenzen deutscher Gregorianik** [The possibilities and limitations of German-language Gregorian chant] (6288); Erich MARCKHL, **Kirchenmusik, Musikerziehung, Bildung** [Church music, music instruction, education] (4734); Hans NIKLAUS and Heinrich ROHR, **Gesangliche Erziehung der Gemeinde** [The instruction of the congregation in singing] (6321); Franz ZAUNER, **Die liturgische Konstitution und ihre Grundtendenzen** [The liturgical constitution and its fundamental tendencies] (6421).

481
bs

[Hamburg] Zeitgenössisches Musiktheater/ Contemporary music theatre/Théâtre musical contemporain. Proceedings of the Fourth Congress of the International Music Council; sponsored by the International Music Council, International Theater Institute (UNESCO), International Association of Opera Directors, and Internationales Musikzentrum Wien. Ed. by Ernst THOMAS; intro. by Mario LABROCA (Hamburg: Deutscher Musikrat, 1966) 214 p. *Illus., port., list of works.* In German, French, and English.

The conference was held from 16 through 23 June 1964. The following contributions are cited separately: Karl-Birger BLOMDAHL and Erik LINDEGREN, **Fragment of an arctic conversation** (5106); André BOLL, **Le livret: Élément essentiel d'un renouveau du théâtre musical** [The libretto: An essential element of music theater's renewal] (5107); Siegfried BORRIS, **Das neue *dramma per musica*** [The new *dramma per musica*] (5111); Pierre CHEVREUILLE, **La reine verte de Maurice Béjart** [Maurice Béjart's *La reine verte*] (5117); Luigi DALLAPICCOLA, **Livrets et paroles dans l'opéra** [Librettos and words in opera] (5128); Alain DANIÉLOU, **Les influences orientales dans le théâtre musical contemporain** [Eastern influences in contemporary music theater] (5129); Ton DE LEEUW, **Introduction par l'auteur à l'opéra *Alceste*** [Author's introduction to the opera *Alceste*] (5131); Jacques DUPONT, **Le rôle du décorateur dans la mise en scène lyrique** [The role of the designer in opera production] (5143); Werner EGK, **Szenische Darstellung eines für den Funk bestimmten Werkes** [The stage presentation of a work written for radio broadcast] (5146); Wolfgang FORTNER, **Libretto und musikalische Sprache** [Libretto and musical language] (5151); Herbert GRAF, **Training for opera** (4878); Vlado HABUNEK, **Le rôle du metteur en scène** [The role of the stage director] (5165); Everett HELM, **Forms and components: Mixed forms** (5169); Hans Werner HENZE, **Zur Inszenierung zeitgenössischen Musiktheaters** [The staging of contemporary music theater] (5170); Jeanne HÉRICARD, **La formation vocale dans l'opéra contemporain** [Vocal training in contemporary opera] (3304); Boris Mihajlovič JARUSTOVSKIJ, **Probleme des gegenwärtigen Musiktheaters** [Problems of contemporary music theater] (5176); Václav KAŠLÍK, **Die Wiederbelebung der Oper** [The resuscitation of opera] (5179); Shigeo KISHIBE, **The music of the Japanese noh plays** (5180); Ernst KRENEK, **Remarks on the influence of the new technical media (electronics, cinema) on the conception of works for the music stage (opera)** (5185); Li Man KUEI, **Chinese drama** (5188); Diether de LA MOTTE, **Das Verhältnis zwischen Text und Musik** [The relation between text and music] (5189); George Henry Hubert LAS-CELLES, Earl of Harewood, **The place of contemporary music theatre in festivals** (5191); Rolf LIEBERMANN, **Musiktheater oder Stagione**

[Music theater or *stagione*] (5195); Ita MAXIMOWNA, **Die Bühnenbildner im heutigen Musiktheater** [The stage designer and contemporary music theater] (5206); Narayana MENON, **The dance-drama of India** (5207); Massimo MILA, **Stravinski et les nouvelles formes de théâtre musical** [Stravinsky and the new forms of music theater] (5209); Egon MONK, **Der Einfluss Brechts** [Brecht's influence] (5211); Alfred NEUMANN, **The young artists and the contemporary musical theatre** (2364); Carl ORFF, **Das Libretto im zeitgenössischen Musiktheater** [The libretto in contemporary music theater] (5217); Helga PILARCZYK, **Kann man die moderne Oper singen?** [Can one sing modern opera?] (5224); Günther RENNERT, **Zur Regie des zeitgenössischen Musiktheaters** [Directing contemporary music theater] (5229); Wolfgang RENNERT, **Zeitgenössische Oper braucht zeitgenössische Stoffe** [Contemporary opera requires contemporary subjects] (5230); Henri SAUGUET, **Le sujet dans le théâtre musical contemporain** [The subject in contemporary musical theater] (5237); Hans SITTNER, **Ausbildungsprobleme des sängerischen Nachwuchses für das Musiktheater** [Problems in training the rising generation of singers for the music theater] (4894); Hans Heinz STUCKENSCHMIDT, **Stoff und libretto** [Subject-matter and libretto] (5252); Otto TOMEK, **Zur Übernahme neuer musikalischer Bühnenwerke im Hörfunk** [The radio broadcast of new musical stage works] (5258); Van Khê TRẦN, **Le théâtre musical de tradition chinoise** [The music theater of Chinese tradition] (5259); Emilio VEDOVA, **Réalisation scénique de *Intolleranza 60* de Luigi Nono** [The staging of Luigi Nono's *Intolleranza 1960*] (5264); Franz WALTER, **Enquiry on contemporary music theatre in festivals** (2406). Appendices include summaries of discussions, reports on the contemporary music theater scene in member countries of the International Music Council, and lists of film, television, and radio productions of contemporary operas.

482
bs

[Jerusalem] Mẇsyqah hayahdẇt hamišṗahah [Jewish music in the family]. Proceedings of the Seventh Israeli Music Congress, *Dẇkan* VII (1965). In Hebrew.

The following contributions are cited separately: Israel ADLER, **Mẇsyqah 'ẇmanẇtyt miḥẇṣ lema'amad hatpylah bẖyhak"n bẖeqehylẇt hayehẇdẏwt bẖe'eyrẇṗah lipney ha'emansẏṗaṣyah** [Non-liturgical art music in European synagogues before the Emancipation] (6035); Bathja BAYER, **Hašẏr hadaty bẖepy haṣyẖbẇr haḥylẇny** [Religious songs sung by the secular public] (6041); Mordekay BRẆY'ER, **Mẇsyqah 'amamit datyt ḥadašah** [New religious folk music] (6047); Me'yr Šim'ẇn GEŠWRY, **Nygẇney šwlḥan ḥasydyym bẖeyemey šabatẇt weḥagym** [Hasidic tunes sung at the table on Sabbath and holidays] (6062); 'Abraham Me'yr HABERMAN, **Šyrym le'at misẇ'a wehitṗatḥẇtam** [Songs for certain occasions and their development] (6067); Avigdor HERZOG, **Zmirah mesẇrtyt šamḥẇṣ leӄtaay bẖeyt hakneset: Dibrey haqdamah lehadgamẇt mẇsyqalyẇt** [Traditional songs outside the synagogue] (6071); Yehẇšu'a Leyyḃ NE'EMAN, **Zimrat hamišṗahah bẖeyṣyrah haḥazanyt** [Family songs in hazzanut] (6085); Zeby PRYDHABER, **"Ryqẇdey-hamyṣwah": Tẇldẇteyhem wešẇrẇteyhem** [Myṣwah dances: Their history and forms] (5054); Gẇryt QADMAN, **Ryqẇdey ḥagwẇt šel ha'edẇt bẖeyśra'el: Dibrey hesber lesraṭym** [Community dances in Israel: Narration to films] (5055); Yẇsep RẆṬṢYLD, **Zmyrẇt šabʻat šel yehẇdey darẇm germanyah wehaminhagym haqšẇrym bẖehem** [Sabbath songs of South German Jews and customs related to them] (6095).

483
bs

[Kassel] Beiträge zur Geschichte der Musikansschauung im 19. Jahrhundert [Contributions to the history of musical perspectives in the 19th century]. Proceedings of the Musikanschauung im 19. Jahrhundert; sponsored by the Forschungsunternehmen der Fritz-Thyssen-Stiftung, Arbeitskreis Musikwissenschaft. Ed. and forew. by Walter SALMEN; intro. by Karl Gustav FELLERER. *Studien zur Musikgeschichte des 19. Jahrhunderts* 1 (Regensburg: Bosse, 1965) 252 p. *Music, bibliog., index.* In German.

The conference was held from 22 through 24 October 1964. The following contributions are cited separately: Heinz BECKER, **Die historische Bedeutung der Grand Opéra** [The historical significance of grand opera] (5101); Carl DAHLHAUS, **Wagners Begriff der "dichterisch-musikalischen Periode"** [Wagner's concept of the "dichterisch-musikalische Periode"] (4238); Ursula ECKART-BÄCKER, **Die Wiederbelebung von Hector Berlioz: Ein Beitrag zur Musikanschauung in**

Frankreich um 1900 [The resurrection of Hector Berlioz: A contribution to the musical perspective in France ca. 1900] (1948); Arnfried EDLER, **Zur Musikanschauung von Adolf Bernhard Marx** [The musical perspective of Adolf Bernhard Marx] (5458); Imogen FELLINGER, **Grundzüge Brahmsscher Musikauffassung** [The fundamental traits of Brahms's concept of music] (5465); Martin GECK, **E.T.A. Hoffmanns Anschauungen über Kirchenmusik** [E.T.A. Hoffmann's views on church music] (5477); Rudolf HEINZ, **Franz Schubert *An die Musik*: Versuch über ein Musiklied** [Franz Schubert: *An die Musik*—Essay on a song about music] (1981); Jürgen KINDERMANN, **Romantische Aspekte in E.T.A. Hoffmanns Musikanschauung** [Romantic aspects of E.T.A. Hoffmann's perspective on music] (2002); Helmut KIRCHMEYER, **Ein Kapitel Adolf Bernhard Marx: Über Sendungsbewußtsein und Bildungsstand der Berliner Musikkritik zwischen 1824 und 1830** [A chapter of Adolf Bernhard Marx: The sense of mission and the educational attainment of Berlin music critics between 1824 and 1830] (5509); Monika LICHTENFELD, **Gesamtkunstwerk und allgemeine Kunst: Das System der Künste bei Wagner und Hegel** [Gesamtkunstwerk and art in general: The system of the arts in Wagner and Hegel] (5523); Peter RUMMENHÖLLER, **Romantik und Gesamtkunstwerk** [Romanticism and the Gesamtkunstwerk] (4924); Heinrich W. SCHWAB, **Das Musikgedicht als musikologische Quelle** [Poems on music as a source for musicology] (5350); Martin VOGEL, **Nietzsches Wettkampf mit Wagner** [Nietzsche's competition with Wagner] (2121); Walter WIORA, **Die Musik im Weltbild der deutschen Romantik** [Music in the world view of German Romanticism] (2128).

484
rs

Review by Gerald ABRAHAM, *Music & letters* 4 (July 1967) 279–80.

485
rs

Review by Reinhold SIETZ, *Die Musikforschung* 4 (Jan-Mar 1968) 115–16. In German.

486
bs

[Mönchengladbach] Studien zur Musikgeschichte der Stadt Mönchengladbach [Studies on the music history of the city of Mönchengladbach]. Sponsored by the Arbeitsgemeinschaft für Rheinische Musikgeschichte. Ed. and intro. by Karl DREIMÜLLER; in collab. with Peter BLOCH; foreword by Karl Gustav FELLERER. *Beiträge zur rheinischen Musikgeschichte* 61 (Köln: Volk, 1965) 133 p. *Illus., port., facs., music, charts, diagr.* In German.

The following contributions are cited separately: Peter BLOCH, **Bemerkungen zur künstlerischen Ausstattung des Gladbacher Missale** [Remarks on the artistic decoration of the Mönchengladbach Missal] (5375); Karl DREIMÜLLER, **Das neumierte Missale plenarium (Pars hiemalis) Hs. I des Mönchengladbacher Münsterarchivs** [The neumed Missale plenarium (Pars hiemalis) MS 1 of the archive of the Münster, Mönchengladbach] (1080), **Lob des Positivs: Eine zeitgemäße Mönchengladbacher "Orgelpredigt"** [In praise of the positive: A well-timed Mönchengladbach organ sermon] (3350), **Musikerbriefe an einen Gladbacher Musikliebhaber: Aus der Sammlung Ludwig Bisschopinck** [Musicians' letters to a Mönchengladbach music lover: From the Ludwig Bisschopinck collection] (715), **Neumen-Colloquium mit Dom Joseph Kreps, Löwen** [Neume colloquium with Dom Joseph Kreps of Leuven] (900), **Verzeichnis eigener Veröffentlichungen zur Mönchengladbacher Musikgeschichte** [Catalogue of the author's publications on Mönchengladbach music history] (815), and **Zur Geschichte und Soziologie des Mönchengladbacher Musiklebens** [The history and sociology of musical life in Mönchengladbach] (959); Karl FEGERS, **Arbeit im Dienste der Jugend- und Volksmusik: Eine Selbstdarstellung** [Work in the service of youth music and traditional music: A self-portrait] (2163); Gottfried GÖLLER, **Zur Herkunftsbestimmung der liturgischen Handschriften der Abtei St. Vitus** [Determining the provenance of liturgical manuscripts from the abbey of St. Vitus] (1109); Karlheinz HÖFER, **Cornelius Burgh und Mönchengladbach** [Cornelius Burgh and Mönchengladbach] (1578); Ernst KLUSEN, **Das Volkslied im Mönchengladbacher Raum** [Traditional song in the Mönchengladbach region] (2898); Friedrich SCHMIDTMANN, **Selbstbildnis eines Rekonvertiten** [Self-portrait of one who was reconverted] (2246). Simultaneously published by the Kulturamt der Stadt Mönchengladbach under the title *Musik in Mönchengladbach. I.*

487
rs

Review by Johannes AENGENVOORT, *Die Musikforschung* 4 (Jan-Mar 1972) 96–99. In German.

488 **[Münster] Proceedings.** Fifth International Con-
bs gress of Phonetic Sciences. Ed. by Wolfgang BETHGE
and Eberhard ZWIRNER (Basel: S. Karger, 1965)
xxviii, 631 p. *Illus., port., bibliog.* In English, French,
and German.

The conference was held at the University of Münster from 16 through 22
August 1964. The following contribution is cited separately: Iván FÓNAGY,
Zur Gliederung der Satzmelodie [Sentence intonation] (5924).

489 **[New Delhi] Music east and west.** Proceedings of
bs the Conference on the Music of East and West; sponsored by the Sangeet Natak Akademi, Indian Congress
for Cultural Freedom, Max Mueller Bhavan, Delhi Music Society, and Indian Council for Cultural Relations.
Ed. by Roger ASHTON; intro. by Humayun KABIR,
T.T. KRISHNAMACHARI, George Henry Hubert
LASCELLES, Earl of Harewood, Yehudi MENUHIN,
Nicolas NABOKOV, and Dharma VIRA (Nai Dilli: Indian Council for Cultural Relations, 1966) 217 p. *Music.*

The conference was held from 8 through 12 February 1964. The following
contributions are cited separately: Roger ASHTON, **The basic details of
variance between music in India and the West** (831); Peter
CROSSLEY-HOLLAND, **Problems and opportunities in listening to
the music of another civilization** (834); Dragotin CVETKO, **The problem of the process of listening to and of making Western and Indian
music** (835); Alain DANIÉLOU, **Conscious or haphazard evolution in
music** (836); B.R. DEODHAR, **Evolution in Indian music** (2618); Robert
GARFIAS, **Traditional music and the value of education** (2511); Musiri
Subramania IYER, **Classical music under the impact of industrial
change** (2642); Manfred M. JUNIUS, **On the differences and similarities
of structure in Indian and Western music** (842); János KÁRPÁTI, **Béla
Bartók and the East** (2188); Amir KHAN, **The tarānā style of singing**
(2647); Hans-Joachim KOELLREUTTER, **Indian and Western music as
the extension of different attitudes of consciousness** (843);
Hans-Joachim KOELLREUTTER et al., **The structural differences and
similarities of Indian and Western music: The discussion** (844); George
Henry Hubert LASCELLES, Earl of Harewood et al., **The psychology of
the musician and of the listener: The discussion** (845); Lothar LUTZE,
Aspects of Indian music (2657); Geeta MAYOR, **The raag in the twentieth century** (2665); Narayana MENON et al., **Music East and West:
Concluding session** (846); Ernst Hermann MEYER, **Evolution in music**
(848); Nicolas NABOKOV et al., **Traditional music facing industrial
civilization: The discussion** (2533); N.S. RAMACHANDRAN, **Classical music and the mass media (with special reference to South India)**
(2676); Rosette RENSHAW, **Rhythmic structures in Indian and Western music** (4023); R.L. ROY, **Traditional music between a culture and a
civilization** (851); V.V. SADAGOPAN, **Psychology of listening** (2683); P.
SAMBAMOORTHY, **Evolution of music with special reference to musical instruments** (3274); Ravi SHANKAR, **Hindusthani classical music and the demands of today** (2689); Narendrarai N. SHUKLA, **Evolution in Hindusthani music** (2692); Narendrarai N. SHUKLA et al., **Evolution in music: The discussion** (852); Thakur Jaidev SINGH, **Tradition
and the inventive principle** (2693); Hans Heinz STUCKENSCHMIDT,
Trends of improvisation in Western music (1010); Antonín SYCHRA,
Psychology of the listener from the experimental point of view (5708);
Van Khê TRÂN, **Far Eastern musical tradition and the new rhythm**
(2699); Tanjore VISWANATHAN, **Traditional music in South India: A
dynamic force** (2706).

490 **[Novi Vinodolski] Rad XI-og kongresa Saveza**
bs **Folklorista Jugoslavije** [Proceedings of the 11th
congress of the Savez Folklorista Jugoslavije]. Ed. by
Vinko ŽGANEC (Zagreb: Savez Folklorista
Jugoslavije, 1966) 542 p. *Illus., transcr.* In Croatian,
French, English, Serbian, Macedonian, and Slovene.

The following contributions are cited separately: Petar BINGULAC, **O
muzički lepom u folkloru** [On beauty in traditional music] (2493); Emilia
COMIŞEL, **Le folklore des coutumes: L'enterrement, le cérémonial et
le repertoire** [The folklore of customs: The burial, the ceremony, and the
repertoire] (2777); Tvrtko ČUBELIĆ, **Narodna tužbalica, impresivni dio
u pogrebnim običajima i jedan od najstarijih oblika izvorne narodne
pjesme** [Traditional laments, an impressive segment of funeral rituals and
one of the oldest forms of authentic traditional songs] (2780); Jelena

DOPUÐA, **Narodne igre u vezi sa smrti: Primjeri iz Bosne i Hecegovine**
[Traditional dances related to death: Examples from Bosnia and Herze-
govina] (4957); Vladimir FAJDETIĆ, **Narodna glazba Hrvatskog
Primorja, Istre i Kvarnerskih Otoka** [Traditional music of Hrvatsko
Primorje, Istra, and the Kvarner islands] (2806); Ive JELENOVIĆ, **Krčki i
novljanski folklor** [Folklore of Krk and Novi Vinodolski] (2872); Mark
KRASNIQI, **Tužbalica u arbanaškoj narodnoj poeziji** [Laments in Albanian traditional poetry] (2909); Zmaga KUMER, **Smrt v slovenski
ljudski pesmi** [Death in Slovenian folk songs] (2918); Jaroslav MARKL,
**Vuk Stefanović Karadžić i počeci sakupljanja narodnih pesama u
Češkoj** [Vuk Stefanović Karadžić and the beginnings of traditional song
collection in Bohemia] (2946); Niko S. MARTINOVIĆ, **Savo Matov
Martinović saradnik Vuka Karadžića** [Savo Matov Martinović, a collaborator of Vuk Karadžić] (2952); Ante NAZOR, **Običaji i narodno
stvaralaštvo oko smrti u Poljicama** [Death-related customs and traditional arts in Poljice] (2973); Milica OBRADOVIĆ, **"Mrtvac" u nekim
društvenim igrama na području Bosne i Hercegovine** [The deceased in
some social dances of Bosnia and Herzegovina] (5044); Vera PANKOVA,
Narodno stvaralaštvo oko smrti kod Torbeša [Death-related traditional
arts in Torbeš] (2986); Roksanda PEJOVIĆ, **Odnos Miloja Milojevića
prema muzičkom folkloru** [Miloje Milojević's approach to traditional
music] (2990); Radmila POLENAKOVIĆ, **Makedonske narodne
tužbalice** [Macedonian traditional laments] (5342); Boris Nikolaevič
PUTILOV, **Junačkaja pesnja *Marko nahodit sestru* v versijah s Horvatskovo Primor'ja i ostrovov i bylina o kozarine** [The heroic song *Marko
pronalazi sestru* in versions from Hrvatsko Primorje and the islands, and a
bylina about a shepherd] (3018); Cvetana Stojanova ROMANSKA, **Neke
opšte osobine pesama o Kraljeviću Marku koje su zapisane u novije
vreme na dalmatinskim otocima i u Bugarskoj** [Some general characteristics of songs about Prince Marko recently transcribed on the Dalmatian islands and in Bulgaria] (3039); Ljuba SIMIĆ, **Tužbalice ("jaukalice") u
Bosni i Hercegovini** [Laments in Bosnia and Herzegovina] (5355); Doris
STOCKMANN, **Totenklagen der südalbanischen Çamen** [Laments of the
southern Albanian Çam people] (3068); Slobodan ZEČEVIĆ, **Igre nažeg
posmrtnog rituala** [Dances in our funeral rituals] (5085).

491 **[Salzburg] Bericht über den neunten**
bs **internationalen Kongreß** [Report of the ninth international congress]. Proceedings of the ninth congress of the International Musicological Society. Ed. by
Franz GIEGLING (Kassel: Bärenreiter, 1964-1966)
2 v. xii, 67; viii, 286 p. *Facs., music, index, charts,
diagr.* In German, French, English, and Italian.

The conference was held from 30 August through 4 September 1964. The
following contributions are cited separately: Dénes BARTHA, moderator,
Symposium: Idee und Methode "vergleichender" Musikforschung
[Symposium: The concept and method of "comparative" musicology]
(2456); Andres BRINER, **Die moderne Oper: Autoren, Theater,
Publikum** [Modern opera: Authors, theaters, audiences] (5112); Paul
COLLAER, **Structures et domaines expressifs des systèmes musicaux
contemporains** [Structures and expressive domains of contemporary mu-
sical systems] (3936); Dragotin CVETKO et al., **Die Rolle der slawischen
Völker in der Geschichte der europäischen Musik des 18. und 19.
Jahrhunderts** [The role of the Slavic peoples in the history of European
music in the 18th and 19th centuries] (957); Hans-Heinz DRAEGER,
**Analysis and synthesis of musical structures on the basis of informa-
tion theory** (3939); Dagmar DROYSEN, **Die Musikinstrumente in
Europa vom 9. bis 11. Jahrhundert** [Musical instruments in Europe from
the 9th to the 11th centuries] (3249); Vladimir FÉDOROV, **Symposium:
Les origines de l'opéra national en Europe de l'Est au 19ᵉ siècle** [Sym-
posium: The beginnings of national opera in Eastern Europe in the 19th
century] (1955); Ludwig FINSCHER, **Die nationalen Komponenten in
der Musik der ersten Hälfte des 16. Jahrhunderts** [National elements in
the music of the first half of the 16th century] (1307); Walter GERSTEN-
BERG, ed., **Symposium: Der gegenwärtige Stand der Mozart-
Forschung** [Symposium: The present state of Mozart research] (1763);
Ursula GÜNTHER, **Die Rolle Englands, Spaniens, Deutschlands und
Polens in der Musik des 14. Jahrhunderts** [The role of England, Spain,
Germany, and Poland in the music of the 14th century] (1112) and **Round
table der Union Académique Internationale über die geplante
Ausgabe *Corpus des troubadours*** [Roundtable of the Union Académique
Internationale on the planned edition of a *Corpus des troubadours*] (3898);
Heinrich HUSMANN, **Das Organum vor und außerhalb der Notre-
Dame-Schule** [Organum before and outside the Notre Dame School]
(1133); Dietrich KILIAN, **Der Generalbaß um 1600** [Basso continuo

around the year 1600] (1590); René Bernard LENAERTS, **Symposium: Die nationalen Komponenten in der Musik der ersten Hälfte des 16. Jahrhunderts** [Symposium: National elements in the music of the first half of the 16th century] (1367); Walther LIPPHARDT, **Der gegenwärtige Stand der Gregorianik-Forschung** [The current state of research on Gregorian chant] (1141); Zofia LISSA, **Musikalisches Hören in psychologischer Sicht** [Psychological views on musical hearing] (5676); Zofia LISSA and Antonín SYCHRA, moderator, **Symposium: Musikalisches Hören in psychologischer Sicht** [Symposium: Psychological views on musical hearing] (5677); Marie Louise MARTINEZ-GÖLLNER, **Symposium: Das Organum vor und ausserhalb der Notre-Dame-Schule** [Symposium: Organum before and outside the Notre Dame school] (1147); John Henry van der MEER, **Mozarts Hammerflügel** [Mozart's piano] (1811); Massimo MILA, ed., **Die stilistische Einheit in Giuseppe Verdis Werk** [The stylistic unity of Giuseppe Verdi's work] (4374); Alfred OREL, **Österreichs Sendung in der Abendländischen Musik** [Austria's mission in Western music] (908); Bernhard PAUMGARTNER, **Vom Musiktheater Mozarts** [Mozart's music theater] (1834); Wolfgang PLATH, **Der gegenwärtige Stand der Mozart-Forschung** [The present state of Mozart research] (1836); Gilbert ROUGET, moderator, **La musique funéraire en Afrique noire: Fonctions et formes** [Funerary music in black Africa: Functions and forms] (2551); Erich SCHENK, moderator, **Probleme der Schulbildungen in der Musik des 17. und 18. Jahrhunderts im österreichisch-italienischen Raum** [The formation of schools of music in the 17th and 18th centuries in Austrian and Italian territory] (1670); Bence SZABOLCSI, **Die Anfänge der nationalen Oper im 19. Jahrhundert** [The beginnings of national opera in the 19th century] (2109); Luigi Ferdinando TAGLIAVINI, **Musikwissenschaftliche Methode und musikalische Praxis** [Musicological methods and musical practice] (3685); Luigi Ferdinando TAGLIAVINI, Karl GEIRINGER, Alexander L. RINGER, Reinhold SCHLÖTTERER, László SOMFAI, Erwin R. JACOBI, and Eduard REESER, moderator, **Symposium: Musikwissenschaftliche Methode und musikalische Praxis** [Symposium: Musicological methods and musical practice] (3676); Irenäus TOTZKE, **Byzantinische Elemente in der frühen slawischen Kirchenmusik** [Byzantine elements in early Slavic church music] (6130); Leo TREITLER, **Symposium: Structures and expressive contents of contemporary musical systems** (3959); Eric WERNER, moderator, **Mündliche und schriftliche Tradition im Mittelmeerraum** [Oral and written tradition in the Mediterranean region] (1021); Walter WIORA, **Idee und Methode "vergleichender" Musikforschung** [The concept and method of "comparative" musicology] (2484); Hellmuth Christian WOLFF, moderator, **Die Beziehungen zwischen Oper, Oratorium und Instrumentalkusik der Barockzeit** [Relationships among opera, oratorio, and instrumental music of the Baroque period] (1714).

1965

492
bs

[Amsterdam] Acts of the VIIth International Congress of Libraries and Museums of the Performing Arts/Actes du VIIᵉ Congrès international des bibliothèques-musées des arts du spectacle. Sponsored by the International Federation of Library Associations, International Section for Performing Arts Libraries and Museums ('s-Gravenhage: Theater Instituut Nederland/Netherlands Centre of the International Theatre Institute, 1965) 96 p. *Port., charts, diagr.* In French and English.

The following contributions are cited separately: Marthe BESSON, **Une collection théâtre générale et ses fichiers: Intérêt de l'information théâtrale tirée de la presse quotidienne** [A general theater collection and its files: Information concerning the theater drawn from the daily press] (521); L. CALDAGUÈS, **La radio et l'art dramatique** [Radio and dramatic art] (5114); Monique GIRARDIN, **Une collection théâtrale générale et ses fichiers: Fiches d'orientation** [A general theatrical collection and its files: Orientation cards] (580) and **Une source d'information: Les annuaires de théâtre** [A source of information: Theater directories] (5160); Cécile GITEAU, **Les collections générales de théâtre et leurs fichiers** [General theatrical collections and their files] (581); Christoph-Clemens von GLEICH, **Le Répertoire International des Sources Musicales (RISM) et les collections théâtrales** [Répertoire International des Sources Musicales (RISM) and theatrical collections] (582); Siniša JANIĆ, **Rôle de la Section Internationale des Bibliothèques et Musées des Arts du Spectacle en vue de faciliter la création des services de documentation des centres nationaux de L'I.I.T.** [Role of the International Section for Performing Arts Libraries and Museums in facilitating the creation of documentation services of the national centers of the International Theatre Institute] (596); Raško V. JOVANOVIĆ, **Valeur documentaire des enregistrements de pièces ou d'extraits de pièces** [Documentary value of recordings of pieces or extracts of pieces] (5763); François MENNES, **Bibliographie internationale des arts du spectacle** [International bibliography of the performing arts] (621); Milena NIKOLIĆ, **Organisation d'une discothèque: Problèmes de conservation et de catalogage** [Organization of a record library: Problems of conservation and cataloguing] (638); E. ÖHMAN and G.A. LLOYD, **The Universal Decimal Classification (UDC) and theatre** (640); W.J. SUTHERLAND, **Sound and film archives of theatrical performances in the Netherlands** (695); Hellmuth Christian WOLFF, **L'élaboration d'une bibliographie des documents illustrant l'histoire de l'opéra** [Preparation of a bibliography of documents illustrating the history of opera] (701).

493
bs

[Berlin] Artistic values in traditional music. Ed. by Peter CROSSLEY-HOLLAND (Berlin: International Institute for Comparative Music Studies, 1966) 126 p. *Bibliog.* In English and French.

The conference was held from 14 through 16 July 1965. The following contributions are cited separately: William Kay ARCHER, **A quodlibet for Saraswathi: Some observations on the possibilities and limitations of scientific methods applied to the study of artistic values in traditional music** (2415); Peter CROSSLEY-HOLLAND, **Discussion** (2507), **Discussion** (2506), and **Work of the International Institute for Comparative Music Studies during the year 1964-1965** (2430); Alain DANIÉLOU, **Values in music** (839); Mantle HOOD, **Program of the Institute of Enthnomusicology, University of California, Los Angeles** (2435); Yehudi MENUHIN, **Artistic values** (847); Joseph Hanson Kwabena NKETIA, **The dimensions of musical studies** (2455); Willard RHODES, **The new folk music** (2535); Van Khê TRÂN, **Responsabilité des organisations pour la culture et l'éducation dans la préservation des traditions musicales des pays extrême-orientaux** [Responsibility of cultural and educational organizations for the preservation of musical traditions of the Far East] (2702); Fritz WINCKEL, **Aspects of information theory in relation to comparative music studies** (856).

494
bs

[Berlin] Dokumentation [Documentation]. Proceedings of the Europiano-Kongreß. Ed. by Hans Kurt HERZOG; comm. by Franzpeter GOEBELS; in collab. with Georg PREISS and Eckart ROHLFS; foreword by Johann Adolf IBACH; intro. by Siegfried BORRIS (Frankfurt am Main: Fördergemeinschaft Klavier, 1966) 333 p. *Illus., bibliog.* In German, English, French, and Swedish.

Proceedings of the first congress of the Union of European Piano Makers' Associations (Europiano), held from 25 through 30 May 1965. The following contributions are cited separately: **Arbeitsgemeinschaften für Musikerziehung/Study groups/Groupes de travail/Arbetsgrupper** [Study groups for music instruction] (4619); Alfred BERNER, **Co-Referat Arbeitsgemeinschaft Cembalobau** [Supplementary report of the study group on harpsichord building] (3507) and **Die Klavierinstrumente der Musikinstrumenten-Sammlung Berlin** [The keyboard instruments of the Musikinstrumentenmuseum, Berlin] (708); **Colloquium an der Technischen Universität Berlin** [Colloquium at the Technische Universität Berlin] (3513) and **Die Musikinstrumenten-Sammlung Berlin** [The Musikinstrumentenmuseum, Berlin] (719); Franz Rudolf DIETZ, **Das Intonieren von Flügeln** [Toning the hammers of grand pianos] (3511); Karl Gustav FELLERER, **Musikforschung und Klavierinstrumente** [Music research and keyboard instruments] (874); Klaus FENNER, **Unterschiede in der Stimmbarkeit unserer heutigen Klaviere** [Differences in tunability in our contemporary pianos] (3512); Fay Templeton FRISCH, **Neue Wege der Musikerziehung** [New paths of music education] (4532); Helmut V. FUCHS, **Einige akustische und ästhetische Aspekte des Klavierklangs** [Some acoustic and aesthetic aspects of piano sound] (3515); Franzpeter GOEBELS, **Grundbegriffe des Klavierunterrichts** [Basic concepts of piano instruction] (3516); David S. GROVER, **Zusammenarbeit zwischen Klavierherstellern und Erziehungsbehörden/Cooperation between piano manufacturers and educational authorities** (3517); Sumi GUNJI, **Japan und sein Klavierbau** [Japan and its piano builders] (3518); Johann Adolf IBACH, **Generalthema von Berlin: Das Klavier in einer sich wandelnden Welt [General theme from Berlin: The piano in a changing world] (3520); Martin Friedrich JEHLE, **Klavierbauer und Tonkünstler** [Piano makers and composers] (3521); Earle L. KENT, **Influence of irregular patterns in the inharmonicity of piano tone partials upon tuning practice/Der Einfluß von Unregelmässigkeiten in der Obertonverstimmung für die Stimmpraxis** (3523); Adolf Heinrich KÖNIG, **Die Bedeutung der Fachschule für Musikinstrumentenbau für einen fachlich und einheitlich ausgebildeten Klavierbauer** [The significance of the Fachschule für Musikinstrumentenbau for instrument making for a professionally and uniformly trained piano builder] (3524); Lili KROEBER-ASCHE, **Möglichkeiten des Gruppenunterrichts am Klavier** [Possibilities of group piano instruction] (4576); Hans KUNITZ, **Gedanken zur klanglichen Struktur des Klaviers** [Thoughts on the sonic structure of the piano] (3526); Ulrich LAIBLE, **Grenzprobleme des Intonierens von Klavieren und Flügeln** [Side issues in the voicing of pianos and grand pianos] (3527) and **Klavier und Klavierbau 1965: Berufskundliche Ausstellung im Rahmen des Europiano-Kongreß Berlin** [Klavier und Klavierbau 1965: A trade exhibition in the context of the Europiano-Kongreß Berlin] (2336); **Lehrplan für den Klavierunterricht an Musikschulen** [Syllabus for piano instruction at music schools] (4529); Émile LEIPP, **Qu'est-ce qu'un son de piano?/Was ist ein Klavierton?** [What is a piano sound?] (3528); Max MATTHIAS, **Eine betriebswirtschaftliche Betrachtung für die Klavierindustrie** [A business-management perspective on the piano industry] (3530); Jürgen MEYER, **Die Richtcharakteristik des Flügels** [Directional properties in the grand piano] (3532); Hanns NEUPERT, **Aktuelle Probleme des Cembalos und des Cembalobaues** [Current problems: Harpsichords and harpsichord makers] (3534); Georg PREISS, **Das optische Bild des Europiano-Kongresses** [The visual image of the Europiano-Kongreß] (2285); Hermann R. QUEDENFELD, **Der Klavierhändler: Musiker, Psychologe und Verkäufer** [The piano dealer: Musician, psychologist, and salesman] (3539); Martin SASSMANN, **Co-Referat Arbeitsgemeinschaft Cembalobau** [Supplementary report of the study group on harpsichord building] (3540) and **Die Ausstellung Klavier und Klavierbau 1965** [The exhibition Klavier und Klavierbau 1965] (2387); **Schlußberichte** [Closing reports] (3514); Rainer SCHÜTZE, **Die Unterschiede in der akustischen und musikalischen Qualität bei alten und modernen Cembali** [The differences in acoustic and musical quality between old and modern harpsichords] (3541); Hans SITTNER, **Präludium über das Klavier** [Prelude on the piano] (3542); Jürgen SOMMER, **Das elektronische Stimmgerät als Hilfe beim Stimmen von Musikinstrumenten** [The electronic tuning device as an aid in tuning musical instruments] (4115); Alfred STOECKEL, **Der blinde Klavierstimmer: Ein Faktor in der Produktion** [The blind piano tuner: A factor in production] (3543); Lothar THOMMA, **Der Rechenschieber zur Berechnung sämtlicher Saiten für Klaviere und Cembali** [A slide rule for the calculation of all piano and harpsichord strings] (3544); Martin VOGEL, **Tasteninstrumente in reiner Stimmung** [Keyboard instruments in just intonation] (3545); Fritz WINCKEL, **Der Einsatz des Klaviers in der experimentellen Musik** [The use of the piano in experimental music] (2270).

495
bs

[Berlin] II. Internationales Seminar marxistischer Musikwissenschaftler [Second International Seminar of Marxist Musicologists], *Beiträge zur Musikwissenschaft* VII/4 (1965). In German.

The conference was held from 22 through 26 June 1965. The following contributions are cited separately: Siegfried BIMBERG, **Einige Bemerkungen zum Tonalitätsbegriff** [Some remarks on the concept of tonality] (4138); Heinz Alfred BROCKHAUS, **Über einige Probleme und Kriterien des Neuen in der zeitgenössischen Musik** [On some problems and criteria of the new in contemporary music] (5434); Miroslav Karel ČERNÝ, **Über die Kriterien der historischen Wertung der zeitgenössischen Musik** [On the criteria of historical evaluation for contemporary music] (5440); Dimiter CHRISTOFF, **Perspektiven der nationalen musikalischen Tradition** [Perspectives of national musical tradition] (2503); Harry GOLDSCHMIDT, **Gedanken zu einer nichtaristotelischen Musikästhetik** [Thoughts on a non-Aristotelian musical aesthetics] (5478); Jaroslav JIRÁNEK, **Der spezifische Charakter des musikalischen Inhalts in seiner historisch gesellschaftlichen Bedingtheit** [The specific character of musical content as determined by sociohistorical factors] (5501); Václav KUČERA, **Zur Frage der Intonationssemantisierung der Struktur** [On questions of the semanticization of intonation] (5930); János MARÓTHY, József UJFALUSSY, and Dénes ZOLTAI, **Das Verhältnis zwischen ästhetischen und ideologischen Kategorien unter besonderer Berücksichtigung des zeitgenössischen Musikschaffens**

[The relation between aesthetic and ideological categories, with particular consideration of contemporary musical creation] (5533); Günter MAYER, **Zur Dialektik des musikalischen Materials** [On the dialectic of musical materials] (5536); Lev Abramovič MAZEL', **Über die Entwicklung der Sprache (Ausdrucksmittel) der zeitgenössischen Musik** [On the development of the language (means of expression) of contemporary music] (5537); Adrian RATIU, **Aspekte der Ausdrucksmittel im Lichte der Entwicklung der zeitgenössischen Musik** [Aspects of expression in light of the development of contemporary music] (5571); Antonín SYCHRA, **Möglichkeiten der Anwendung der Kybernetik und der Informationstheorie in der marxistischen Musikwissenschaft** [Possible applications of cybernetics and information theory in Marxist musicology] (5420); Vasile TOMESCU, **Beiträge zur dialektischen Behandlung der musikästhetischen Probleme** [Contributions to the dialectic handling of music-aesthetic problems] (5614).

496
bs

[Brno] O interpretaci děl Leoše Janáčka [On the interpretation of Janáček's works]. Ed. by Jiří HADLAČ (Brno: Akademie Věd České Republiky, Ústav pro Etnografii a Folkloristiku, 1966) 103 p. *Sborník Janáčkovy Akademie Múzických Umeni* V (1965). *Port., music, charts, diagr.* In Czech; summaries in Russian, English, French, and German.

The following contributions are cited separately: Bohuš HERAN, **Prstoklady jako výrazový prostředek: Studie k Janáčkově violoncellové Pohádce** [Fingering as a means of expression: A study devoted to Janáček's *Pohádka* for violoncello] (3578); Bedřich JIČÍNSKÝ, **K Brodové interpretaci Janáčkových operních textů** [On Brod's translations of the Janáček opera librettos] (5323); František JÍLEK, **Poznámky k instrumentaci Janáčkových oper** [Observations on the instrumentation of Janáček's operas] (4300); Milan MÁŠA, **K soudobé reprodukci klavírních děl Leoše Janáčka** [Toward a modern interpretation of Leoš Janáček's piano compositions] (3795); Věra STŘELCOVÁ, **V čem vidím modernost pěvecké stránky interpretace Janáčkových oper** [How I see the modern interpretation of vocal parts in Janáček's operas] (3798); Jan TROJAN, **Břetislav Bakala: Janáčkovský interpret** [Břetislav Bakala: An interpreter of Janáček] (3799) and **O některých otázkách teorie a estetiky hudební interpretace** [On some aspects of theory and aesthetics of music interpretation] (5618); Richard TÝNSKÝ, **K problémům soudobé interpretace Janáčka** [Issues in contemporary interpretation of Janáček] (3800); Josef VESELKA, **K slohovým základům Janáčkovské sborové reprodukce** [The stylistic foundations of performance of Janáček's choral music] (4391); Miloš WASSERBAUER, **Otázka soudobosti scénické interpretace Janáčkovy opery Z mrtvého domu** [Question of modernism in stagings of Janáček's opera *Z mrtvého domu*] (5271).

497
bs

[Carbondale] Vision 65: Abstracts of papers. Sponsored by the Southern Illinois University at Carbondale (New York: International Center for the Typographic Arts, 1965) 55 p. *Illus.*

The full conference report is abstracted as no. 498 in this volume.

498
bs

[Carbondale] Vision 65: New challenges for human communications. Sponsored by the Southern Illinois University at Carbondale (New York: International Center for the Typographic Arts, 1965) 280 p. *Illus.*

The conference was held from 21 through 23 October 1965. The following contribution is cited separately: Gottfried Michael KOENIG, **The second phase of electronic music** (4402). A volume of abstracts from the conference is cited as no. 497 in this volume.

499
bs

[Dijon] Septième Congrès international des bibliothèques musicales [Seventh International Congress of Music Libraries]. Sponsored by the Association Internationale des Bibliothèques Musicales. Ed. and intro. by Vladimir FÉDOROV, *Fontes artis musicae* XII/2-3 (May-Dec 1965) 55–230. *Illus., port., music, charts, diagr.* In French, English, and German.

The conference was held from 1 through 6 July 1965. The following contributions are cited separately: Barry S. BROOK, **Le tempo dans l'exécution** de la musique instrumentale à la fin du XVIIIe siècle: Les contributions de C. Mason et William Crotch [Tempo in the performance of instrumental music at the end of the 18th century: The contributions of C. Mason and William Crotch] (3734), **The simplified** *Plaine and easie code system* **for notating music: A proposal for international adoption** (787), and **Utilization of data processing techniques in music documentation** (528); Charles CUDWORTH, **The meaning of** *vivace* **in eighteenth-century England** (3736) and **Un** *Répertoire de Documents Musicaux*: **Secondary report** (536); John Howard DAVIES, **The radio librarian and music documentation techniques** (543); Mariangela DONÀ, **Le bibliothécaire, le documentaliste, le bibliographe musical: Quelques points de contact entre leurs activités respectives** [The librarian, the documentalist, the musical bibliographer: Some points of contact among their respective activities] (555); Vincent H. DUCKLES, **Music librarian—bibliographer—documentalist** (561); Harald HECKMANN, **Geleitwort des Vorsitzenden** [Chairman's introduction] (589); Bernard HUYS, **Réponse au rapport préliminaire de M.A. Jurres** [Reply to the preliminary report by André Jurres] (594); André JURRES, **Les Centres de Documentation Musicale et leurs techniques particulières** [Music Documentation Centers and their particular techniques] (597); Alexander Hyatt KING, **The music librarian, the bibliographer, the documentalist** (600); Denise LAUNAY, **Les rapports de tempo entre mesures binaires et mesures ternaires dans la musique française (1600-1650)** [The relations in tempo between binary and ternary measures in French music (1600-1650)] (3843); Élisabeth LEBEAU, **Le problème des publications originales de musique non imprimées, à propos de la recherche de la musique de film** [The problem of the nonprinted original publication of music, with reference to research on film music] (609); Folke LINDBERG, **Quelques aspects de la documentation musicale audio-visuelle** [Some aspects of audio-visual documentation of music] (611); Claudie MARCEL-DUBOIS, **Instruments de musique ethniques et musées spécialisés d'ethnologie** [Traditional musical instruments and museums specializing in ethnology] (619) and **Le tempo dans les musiques de tradition orale** [Tempo in musics of oral tradition] (4012); Jean-Étienne MARIE, **Musique experimentale** [Experimental music] (4405); Raymond MEYLAN, **Utilisation des calculatrices électroniques pour la comparaison interne du répertoire des basses danses du quinzième siècle** [Use of electronic computers for internal comparison in the repertoire of 15th-century basses danses] (4449); Karl Ludwig NICOL, **Bericht zur ersten** *Table ronde* [Report on the first roundtable] (637); Walter RECKZIEGEL, **Musikbibliographie und Datenspeicher** [Music bibliography and data storage] (657); Patrick SAUL, **A documentation policy for a national sound archive** (668); Herta SCHETELICH, **Nebenbericht** [Secondary report] (672); Nanna SCHIØDT, **Data processing applied to Byzantine chant** (4457); Brooks SHEPARD, Jr., **Secondary report** (683); Geneviève THIBAULT DE CHAMBURE, **Le Te Deum de Lalande: Minutage de l'époque** [Lalande's Te Deum: Contemporary timing] (3773) and **Recherches effectuées au Musée Instrumental du Conservatoire de Paris** [Research carried out at the Musée Instrumental, Conservatoire de Paris, 1962-65] (764); André VERCHALY, **Le tempo dans la** *musique mesurée à l'antique* [Tempo in *musique mesurée à l'antique*] (3719); Simone WALLON, **Rapport secondaire** [Secondary report] (700); Hans ZEHNTNER, **Bibliothekar, Bibliograph und Dokumentalist** [Librarian, bibliographer, and documentalist] (702).

500 **[Florence; Venice; Mantua] Arte pensiero e**
bs **cultura a Mantova nel primo Rinascimento in rapporto con la Toscana e con il Veneto** [Art, thought, and culture in Mantua in the early Renaissance in connection with Tuscany and Veneto]. Proceedings of the VI Convegno internazionale di studi sul Rinascimento; sponsored by the Istituto Nazionale di Studi sul Rinascimento (Firenze: Sansoni, 1965) 257 p. *Illus.* In Italian.

The conference was held from 27 September through 1 October 1965. The following contribution is cited separately: Claudio GALLICO, **Civiltà musicale Mantovana intorno al 1500** [Musical life in Mantua around 1500] (1311).

501 **[Fribourg] La musica nel rinnovamento**
bs **liturgico: Atti della Settimana internazionale di musica sacra** [Music in the liturgical renewal: Proceedings of the International Week of Sacred Music]. Sponsored by the Centro Catechistico Salesiano. Trans.

by Gino STEFANI. *Liturgia e cultura* 2 (Torino: Elle Di Ci, 1966) 271 p. *Music, charts, diagr., gloss.* In Italian.

The following contributions are cited separately: Luigi AGUSTONI, **La cantillazione delle letture e delle preghiere nella messa** [The cantillation of readings and prayers in the Mass] (6136); Joseph GELINEAU, **Salmodia e canti processionali** [Psalmody and processional chant] (6233); Helmut HUCKE, **Il** *munus ministeriale* **della musica nel culto cristiano** [The *munus ministeriale* of music in the Christian religion] (6253); Bernard HUIJBERS, **Valore e limite del lied nella liturgia** [The value and limitations of the lied in the liturgy] (6257); Jean JEANNETEAU, **Il valore attuale del canto gregoriano** [The current value of Gregorian chant] (4348); Jozef JORIS, **Il posto della musica autoctona e contemporanea nella liturgia** [The place of autochthonous and contemporary music in the liturgy] (6264); Josef Andreas JUNGMANN, **Musica sacra e riforma liturgica** [Sacred music and liturgical reform] (6266); Pierre KAELIN, **Coordinamento dell'azione regionale per la musica sacra** [Coordination of regional action for sacred music] (6267); Miguel MANZANO, **I diversi attori del canto liturgico e i rispettivi ruoli** [The various actors in liturgical chant and their respective roles] (6296); Erhard QUACK, **Il ruolo del coro e l'uso della polimelodia** [The role of the choir and the use of polymelody] (6348); René REBOUD, **Gli strumenti musicali e il culto cristiano** [Musical instruments and the Christian liturgy] (6352).

502 **[Geneva] Deuxième Congrès international du**
bs **rythme et de la rythmique** [Second International Congress on Rhythm and Rhythmics] (Genève: Institut Jaques-Dalcroze, 1966) 167 p. In French and German.

Proceedings of a conference held from 9 through 14 August 1965 honoring the 100th anniversary of the birth of Émile Jaques-Dalcroze . The following contributions are cited separately: Ernest ANSERMET, **Les structures du rythme** [The structures of rhythm] (3965); Robert FALLER, **Un esprit nouveau dans l'enseignement du solfège** [A new spirit in the teaching of solfège] (4525); Gisela JAENICKE, **Rhythmik als Mittel zur Ausbildung des Opernsängers** [Rhythmic methods for training opera singers] (4881); Frank MARTIN, **Les sources du rythme musical** [The sources of musical rhythm] (4013); Bernard REICHEL, **L'improvisation** [Improvisation] (4632); Karl Heinz TAUBERT, **Die Beziehungen zwischen den klassischen Tänzen und der Rythmik** [The connections between classic dances and rhythmics] (5076); Fritz WINCKEL, **Rhythmus und Resonanz** [Rhythm and resonance] (4041).

503 **[Jerusalem] Dmŵtam šel mŵ'dey yśra'el:**
bs **Masŵret hašyrah wehitḥašŵtah** [The Seder night and Passover holiday: Musical traditions and contemporary compositions]. Proceedings of the Eighth Israeli Music Congress. Intro. by 'Ezr'a Syŵn MELAMED, Mordekay BRRŴY'ER, Myka'el PRERLMAN, and Amnon SHILOAH, *Dwkan* VIII (1966). In Hebrew.

The following contributions are cited separately: Bathja BAYER, **Seder šel pesaḥ nŵsaḥ yagŵr** [The Passover Seder in the tradition of Yagwr] (6043); Me'yr Šim'ŵn GEŠWYN, **Nygŵney seder šel pesaḥ b̌eḥasydŵt qarlin** [Seder melodies of Karlin's Hasidim] (6061); Ya'aqob KOHEN, **Dibrey haqdamah lehagdamŵt (mehamesŵret hamŵsyqalyt šel ha'edŵt)** [Introduction to representations of Jewish music] (6075); 'Aleksander MALKÝ'EL, **Leyl šby'y šel pesaḥ b̌eb̌eyt haraw Harl"p Zṣ"l** [Eve of the seventh day of Passover at Rabbi Harlap's home] (6077); Yehŵšu'a Leyyb NE'EMAN, **Šyrat pesaḥ b̌emasŵret hangynah ha'aškenazyt** [The Ashkenazi tradition of Passover songs] (6084); Menaḥem Šeby QADARY, **Hašpa'at hahagadah šel pesaḥ 'al hapr'azy'ŵlŵgyah šel ha'ibryt hamŵdernyt** [The Passover Haggadah and its influence on modern Hebrew] (6088); Re'uben QAŠ'ANY, **Hawaey weminhagym b̌eleyl haseder 'eṣel yehŵdey 'apganysṭan** [The Seder night traditions of Afghanistan Jews] (6091); "Yeṣy'at miṣraym": Yŵsep Ṭal—**Dibrey heber šel hamlaḥyn 'al habiṣŵ'a ha'eleqṭrŵny šel hayeṣyrah** [*Exodus*: Electronic music by Josef Tal] (2261).

504 **[Liège] Problèmes d'acoustique.** Proceedings of
bs the Fifth International Congress of Acoustics; sponsored by the International Commission on Acoustics. Ed. by Daniel E. COMMINS. *Les congrès et colloques de l'Université de Liège* 35 (Liège: Université de Liège, 1965) 3 v. *Illus.* In French, German, and English.

The conference was held from 7 through 14 September 1965. The following contributions are cited separately: Richard BIERL, **Musik-Elektronik-praktische: Erfahrungen, Gegenwartsprobleme und Zukunftsfragen** [Electronic music practice: Acquired experience, present-day problems, and future questions] (4398); François CANAC, **Equation canonique des théâtres antiques: Rôle de l'angle d'écoute et de l'orchestre** [Canonic equation of ancient theaters: The role of the angle of listening and of the orchestra] (5806); Michèle CASTELLENGO and Émile LEIPP, **L'acoustique des cloches** [The acoustics of bells] (3645); Henri CHIARUCCI, Guy REIBEL, S. RIST, and B. FERREYRA, **Rapport entre la hauteur et le fondamental d'un son musical** [Relation between the pitch and the fundamental of a musical sound] (5647); Vadim Vladimirovič FURDUEV, **Evaluation objective de l'acoustique des salles** [Objective evaluation of the acoustics of auditoriums] (5816); Hartmut ISING, **Über die Tonbildung in Orgelpfeifen** [Structuring tone in organ pipes] (3391); Tsuneji KOSHIKAWA, Takeshi NAKAYAMA, and Rikuo MIYAGAWA, **On the designing method of reproduced sound quality using the multidimensional sensory and emotional scales** (5768); Cornelis Willem KOSTEN and Pieter Albert DE LANGE, **The new Rotterdam concert hall: Some aspects of the acoustic design** (5831); Émile LEIPP, **Méthode d'appréciation des qualités musicales d'un ensemble orgue-salle** [Method of appreciating the musical qualities of a whole organ-room] (5836); Jean-Sylvain LIENARD, **L'usure des disques** [Wear and tear of records] (5771); Miguel LORENTE, **Physical basis of musical tonality and consonance** (4191); D.M.J.P. MANLEY, **The subjective judgement of liveness and quality of recorded music** (5773); Derwent M.A. MERCER, **Organ pipe adjustments as a guide to theories of the mechanism of the pipe** (3429); Jürgen MEYER, **Die Richtcharakteristiken vom Violoncello** [The directional characteristics of the violoncello] (3591); A. Kjerbye NIELSON, **A direct reading cent-meter: An instrument suitable for the measurement of the tuning inaccuracies of musical instruments** (4097); A. Wayne SLAWSON, **A psychoacoustic comparison between vowel quality and musical timbre** (5705); Tomio YOSHIDA, **An investigation on how industrial music in Japan goes on** (5916).

505
bs

[Ravenna] Dante: Atti della giornata internazionale di studio per il VII centenario [Dante: Proceedings of the international meeting for the 7th centenary]. Sponsored by the Società di Studi Romagnoli (Faenza: Fratelli Lega, 1965) vii, 131 p. *Illus., music, bibliog., maps.* In Italian.

The conference was held from 6 through 7 March 1965. The following contribution is cited separately: Raffaello MONTEROSSO, **Musica e poesia nel *De vulgari eloquentia*** [Music and poetry in *De vulgari eloquentia*] (5335).

1966

506
bs

[Bydgoszcz] Musica antiqua Europae orientalis. Sponsored by the Filharmonia Pomorska imienia Ignacego Paderewskiego and Bydgoskie Towarzystwo Naukowe. Ed. by Zofia LISSA (Warszawa: Państwowe Wydawnictwo Naukowe, 1966). In German, French, English, Polish, and Russian.

The following contributions are cited separately: Ferenc BÓNIS, **Ungarische Musik im XVII.-XVIII. Jahrhundert** [Hungarian music in the 17th-18th centuries] (1492); Maksim V. BRAŽNIKOV, **Russkoe cerkovnoe penie XII-XVIII vekov** [Russian church singing in the 12th to the 18th centuries] (6107); Józef Michał CHOMIŃSKI, **Die Beziehungen der polnischen Musik zu Westeuropa vom XV. bis zum XVII. Jahrhundert** [The relation of Polish music to Western Europe in the 15th through the 17th centuries] (954); Gheorghe CIOBANU, **La culture musicale byzantine sur le territoire de la Roumanie jusqu'au XVIIIᵉ siècle** [Byzantine musical culture in the territory of Romania until the 18th century] (955); Viorel COSMA, **Aspects de la culture musicale sur le territoire de la Roumanie entre le XIVᵉ et le XVIIIᵉ siècle** [Aspects of the musical culture in the territory of Romania between the 14th and 18th centuries] (1279); Dragotin CVETKO, **La musique slovène du XVIᵉ au XVIIIᵉ siècle** [Slovenian music from the 16th to the 18th century] (1280); Stana DJURIC-KLAJN, **Certains aspects de la musique profane serbe de l'époque féodale** [Certain aspects of Serbian secular music of the feudal

era] (1079); Zoltán FALVY, **Musik in Ungarn bis zum Ende des XVI. Jahrhunderts** [Music in Hungary up to the end of the 16th century] (1085); Hieronim FEICHT, **Die polnische Monodie des Mittelalters** [Polish monophony in the Middle Ages] (1300) and **Quellen zur mehrstimmigen Musik in Polen vom späten Mittelalter bis 1600** [Sources of polyphonic music in Poland from the late Middle Ages to 1600] (1089); Romeo GHIRCOIAŞIU, **Les mélodies roumaines du XVIᵉ-XVIIIᵉ siècles** [Romanian melodies between the 16th and 18th centuries] (4431); Jurij Vsevolodovič KELDYŠ, **Voznikovenie i razvitie russkoj opery v XVIII veke** [The emergence and development of Russian opera in the 18th century] (1792); Krešimir KOVAČEVIĆ, **Die kroatische Musik des XVII. und XVIII. Jahrhunderts** [Croatian music of the 17th and 18th centuries] (1594); Venelin KRĂSTEV, **Puti razvitija bolgarskoj muzykal'noj kul'turi v period XII-XVIII stoletii** [Paths of development of Bulgarian musical culture from the 12th to the 18th centuries] (980); Zofia LISSA, **Folk elements in Polish music from the Middle Ages up to the 18th century** (983) and **Ost-West-Probleme in der modernen Musikgeschichtsschreibung** [East-West problems in modern music historiography] (895); Alina NOWAK-ROMANOWICZ, **Musik in den Theaterformen des ehemaligen Polens** [Music in the theatrical forms of former Poland] (5216); Benjamin RAJECZKY, **Mittelalterliche Mehrstimmigkeit in Ungarn** [Medieval polyphony in Hungary] (1164); Richard RYBARIČ, **Die Hauptquellen und Probleme der slowakischen Musikgeschichte bis zum Ende des XVIII Jahrhunderts** [Slovak music history up to the end of the 18th century: Principal sources, topics] (1000); Sergej Sergeevič SKREBKOV, **Èvoljucija stilja v Russkoj horovoj muzyke XVII veka** [The evolution of style in Russian choral music of the 17th century] (1687); Onys'ja Jakovlevna ŠREJER-TKAČENKO, **Razvitie ukrainskoj muzyki XVI-XVII vekah** [The development of Ukrainian music from the 16th to the 18th centuries] (1440); Dimitrije STEFANOVIĆ, **The Serbian chant from the 15th to the 18th centuries** (1009); Zygmunt Marian SZWEYKOWSKI, **Some problems of Baroque music in Poland** (1697); Jaroslav VANICKÝ, **Czech mediaeval and Renaissance music** (1204); Tomislav VOLEK, **Czech music of the seventeenth and eighteenth centuries** (1709); Jan WECOWSKI, **La musique symphonique polonaise du XVIIIᵉ siècle** [Polish symphonic music of the 18th century] (1893).

507
rs

Review by Jan KOUBA, *Hudební věda* 4 (1967) 12–21. In Czech.

508
rs

Review by Walter SALMEN, *Die Musikforschung* 4 (1969) 97–99. In German.

509
rs

Review by Wiarosław SANDELEWSKI, *Rivista italiana di musicologia* 4 (1970) 322–26. In Italian.

510
bs

[New York] American Society of University Composers: Proceedings of the 1966 conference. Ed. by Hubert S. HOWE, Jr. (New York: American Society of University Composers, 1966).

The conference was held from 1 through 3 April 1966. The following contributions are cited separately: Stefan BAUER-MENGELBERG, **Impromptu remarks on new methods of music printing** (5945); Herbert BRUN, **On the conditions under which computers would assist a composer in creating music of contemporary relevance and significance** (4399); Ercolino FERRETTI, **Some research notes on music with the computer** (4400); Iain HAMILTON, **The university and the composing profession: Prospects and problems** (2175); Lejaren HILLER, **Some comments on computer sound synthesis** (5758); Andrew W. IMBRIE, **The University of California series in contemporary music** (5970); David LEWIN, **Is it music?** (4403); Peter WESTERGAARD, moderator, **What do you, as a composer, try to get the student to hear in a piece of music?** (4858); Godfrey WINHAM, **How MUSIC 4B generates formants and non-harmonic partials, and improves loudness control and "quality"** (4412); Charles WUORINEN, **Performance of new music in universities** (2274).

511
bs

[Paris] Stéréophonie et reproduction musicale [Stereophony and music reproduction]. Proceedings of the Eighth International Festival of Sound; sponsored by the Syndicat des Industries Électroniques de Reproduction et d'Enregistrement, Société Française des Électroniciens et Radioélectriciens, and Groupement des Acousticiens de la Langue Française. *Les cahiers* de la *"Revue du Son"* 7 (Paris: Chiron, 1966) 118 p. *Illus., charts, diagr.* In French.

The following contributions are cited separately: Gabriel DECROIX and Jacques DEHASSY, **Stéréaudiométrie, mesure de l'audition binaurale: Possibilités de réhabilitation des malentendants par audioprothèses stéréophoniques** [Stereo-audiometrics, a measurement of binaural hearing: Rehabilitational possibilities for the hearing-impaired by means of stereophonic audioprostheses] (5726); André DIDIER, Jean-Louis LEMONDE, and Joseph LÉON, **Mesures particulières sur les haut-parleurs** [Specialized measurements for loudspeakers] (5750); Claude DUGAS, **Les technologies modernes et leurs applications possibles dans le domaine de la basse fréquence** [The application of modern technology in the area of bass frequencies] (5751); J.W. GARRETT, **Distorsions physiques et psychologiques propres à la stéréophonie** [Physical and psychological distortions inherent in stereophony] (5659); T.S. KORN and J. DEWÈVRE, **Mesures subjectives de la qualité de reproduction sonore et leur correlation avec les mesures physiques** [Subjective measures of sound reproduction quality and their correlation to physical measures] (5767); Émile LEIPP, **Les variables de l'audition musicale** [The variables of musical hearing] (5674); Jean-Sylvain LIENARD, **L'usure des disques** [Wear and tear of records] (5770); H. MERTENS, **L'écoute stéréophonique** [Stereophonic listening] (5775); Michel Paul PHILIPPOT and Charles BRUCK, **Poésie et vérité** [Poetry and truth] (2372); Jean-Claude RISSET, **Synthèse des sons musicaux à l'aide de calculateurs électroniques** [Synthesis of musical sounds with the aid of computers] (4410); M. WERNER, **Critères de qualité de la transmission à modulation de fréquence** [Criteria of quality in FM broadcasting] (5797).

REFERENCE AND RESEARCH MATERIALS

01 Bibliography and librarianship

512 ACERENZA, Ermelinda. **Formación profe-**
as **sional de un bibliotecario de música** [The professional training of a music librarian], *Fontes artis
musicae* III/1 (July 1956) 74–76. In Spanish; summary
in English. See no. 345 in this volume.
Schools of library science, in collaboration with conservatories, should offer a one-year postgraduate program in music librarianship, covering the following disciplines: introduction to music theory and aesthetics; musical sources; musical form and genre; instruments; cataloguing; sound recordings; and practicum. Another version is cited as no. 513 in this volume.

513 ACERENZA, Ermelinda. **Formación profe-**
as **sional de un bibliotecario de música** [The professional training of a music librarian], *Congrès international des bibliothèques et des centres de documentation* ('s-Gravenhage: Nijhoff, 1955-1958) II, 3–4. In
Spanish. See no. 344 in this volume.
Another version is abstracted as no. 512 in this volume.

514 ALTMANN, Wilhelm. **Die geschichtliche Ent-**
as **wicklung der Katalogisierung musikalischer**
Handschriften [The historical development of the
cataloguing of musical manuscripts], *Bericht über den
I. musikwissenschaftlichen Kongress der Deutschen
Musikgesellschaft in Leipzig* (Wiesbaden: Breitkopf &
Härtel, 1926) 49–50. In German. See no. 120 in this
volume.
A catalogue of MS collections would be a useful bibliographic tool. Such a catalogue would best be organized by categories such as theoretical treatises, vocal works, and instrumental works. *(William Renwick)*

515 ALTMANN, Wilhelm. **Die Schaffung einer**
as **internationalen Bibliographie der Musik-**
literatur [The creation of an international bibliography of music literature], *Bericht über den musikwissenschaftlichen Kongreß in Basel* (Leipzig: Breitkopf &
Härtel, 1925) 51–55. In German. See no. 102 in this
volume.
Discusses the strengths and weaknesses of current bibliographies of music literature. Suggestions are given for thorough coverage through French, German, and Italian journals. *(Sylvia Eversole)*

516 ANNEGARN, Alfons. **The scientific music li-**
as **brarian and his public,** *Fontes artis musicae* XI/1
(Jan-Apr 1964) 67. See no. 457 in this volume.
In order to provide the appropriate help to library users, music librarians in research libraries must be well versed in both musicology and music itself. Administrative duties within a library should ideally be handled by another individual, thus freeing the music librarian to deal with other issues.
(Priscilla P. Hodges)

517 AZEVEDO, Luiz Heitor Corrêa de. **L'UNESCO**
as **et la coopération internationale entre les**
bibliothèques musicales [UNESCO and international cooperation among music libraries], *Atti del
Congresso internazionale di musiche popolari
mediterranee e del Convegno dei bibliotecari musicali*
(Palermo: De Magistris succ. V. Bellotti, 1959) 341–48.
In French. See no. 332 in this volume.

518 BARINI, Giorgio. **Sulla opportunità di**
as **compilare una raccolta di indici e cataloghi dei**
codici musicali italiani esistenti negli archivi,
nelle biblioteche e nelle collezioni pubbliche e
private, per servire di base ad una serie di
edizioni critiche delle opere dei nostri classici
[The opportunity of compiling a collection of indexes
and catalogues of Italian musical codices existing in archives, libraries, and in public and private collections,
to serve as a basis for a series of critical editions of our
classical works], *Atti del Congresso internazionale di
scienze storiche. VIII: Atti della sezione IV: Storia dell'-
arte musicale e drammatica* (Roma: R. Accademia dei
Lincei, 1905) 7–9. In Italian. See no. 42 in this volume.
The major obstacle in such a project would be the wide variety of cataloguing systems in Italian musical collections.

519 BECHERINI, Bianca. **Catalogues généraux et**
as **catalogues spécialisés dans les bibliothèques**
musicales [General and specialized catalogues in music libraries], *Fontes artis musicae* III/1 (July 1956)
76–81. In French. See no. 345 in this volume.
Italy is in need of comprehensive catalogues of sources available in general libraries as well as conservatory libraries. Florence is hoping to devote a section of its Biblioteca Nazionale Centrale to Renaissance music. Another version is cited as no. 520 in this volume.

520 BECHERINI, Bianca. **Catalogues généraux et**
as **catalogues spécialisés dans les bibliothèques**
musicales [General and specialized catalogues in music libraries], *Congrès international des bibliothèques
et des centres de documentation* ('s-Gravenhage:
Nijhoff, 1955-1958) II, 5–9. In French. See no. 344 in
this volume.
Another version is abstracted as no. 519 in this volume.

521 BESSON, Marthe. **Une collection théâtre**
as **générale et ses fichiers: Intérêt de l'infor-**
mation théâtrale tirée de la presse quotidienne
[A general theater collection and its files: Information
concerning the theater drawn from the daily press], *Acts
of the VIIth International Congress of Libraries and
Museums of the Performing Arts/Actes du VIIᵉ Congrès
international des bibliothèques-musées des arts du
spectacle* ('s-Gravenhage: Theater Instituut Nederland/
Netherlands Centre of the International Theatre Institute, 1965) 38–45. *Charts, diagr.* In French. See no. 492
in this volume.
Discusses methods of cataloguing.

522 BIRKNER, Günter. **Quellenlage und Katalo-**
as **gisierung des deutschen Volkslied** [The state of
the sources and the cataloguing of the German folk
song], *Bericht über den internationalen musikwissenschaftlichen Kongreß* (Kassel: Bärenreiter, 1963)
345–47. In German. See no. 452 in this volume.
Discusses issues arising from consideration of 18th- and 19th-c. materials in the collections of the Deutsches Volksliedarchiv, Freiburg im Breisgau.

523 BOETTICHER, Wolfgang. **Arbeitsgemein-**
as **schaft: Lauten- und Gitarrentabulaturen**
[Working group: Lute and guitar tablatures], *Bericht
über den siebenten internationalen musikwissenschaftlichen Kongress* (Kassel: Bärenreiter, 1959) 329–32. In
German. See no. 390 in this volume.

Report of a conference workshop reviewing issues in the bibliography, editing, and publishing of early lute and guitar sources discussed at the 1957
Neuilly-sur-Seine conference *Le luth et sa musique* (see no. 377 in this
volume).

524 BONAVENTURA, Arnaldo. **L'archivio delle**
as **voci** [Archive of voices], *Atti del I Congresso
nazionale delle tradizioni popolari* (Firenze:
Rinascimento del Libro, 1930) 215–30. In Italian. See
no. 158 in this volume.

525 BONAVENTURA, Arnaldo. **L'ordinamento**
as **della musica nelle biblioteche italiane e le
relazioni bibliografico-musicali con le altre
nazioni** [The classification of music in Italian libraries
and bibliographic-musical relations with other nations],
*Primo Congresso mondiale delle biblioteche e di
bibliografia* (Roma: Libreria dello Stato, 1931-1933)
II, 188–94. In Italian. See no. 161 in this volume.

Contains suggestions for the organization, classification, and cataloguing
of music-related items in Italian libraries, and discusses the need for music-related information to be shared among libraries on an international
level. *(Susan Poliniak)*

526 BONAVENTURA, Arnaldo. **Sull'ordinamento**
as **della musica e dei libri relativi nelle pubbliche
biblioteche** [On the classification of music and music-related books in public libraries], *Atti del Congresso
internazionale di scienze storiche. VIII: Atti della
sezione IV: Storia dell'arte musicale e drammatica*
(Roma: R. Accademia dei Lincei, 1905) 19–25. In Italian. See no. 42 in this volume.

Proposes a national classification system specifically for musical sources
and discusses new cross-referencing and purchasing methods.

527 BRĂILOIU, Constantin. **Technique des**
as **enregistrements sonores** [Technique of sound re-
cording], *Travaux du Ier Congrès International de Folklore* (Tours: Arrault et Cie, 1938) 286–87. In French.
See no. 251 in this volume.

Focuses on recording and archiving traditional music.

528 BROOK, Barry S. **Utilization of data process-**
as **ing techniques in music documentation,** *Fontes
artis musicae* XII/2-3 (May-Dec 1965) 112–22. See no.
499 in this volume.

A general survey of possible applications. Appended is the text of a proposal, approved by the executive boards of the International Musicological
Society and the International Association of Music Libraries, for the establishment of a computer-indexed Répertoire International de la Littérature
Musicale (RILM). *(David Bloom)*

529 CHAMRATH, Gustav C. **Die Rechte der Schall-**
as **platte und des Tonbandes** [Record and tape copyright laws], *Fontes artis musicae* III/1 (July 1956)
86–95. In German; summary in French. See no. 345 in
this volume.

Public libraries' lending of recorded materials will inevitably lead to illegal, pirated recordings. International agreements should be reached concerning the rights of public music libraries. Another version is cited as no.
530 in this volume.

530 CHAMRATH, Gustav C. **Die Rechte der Schall-**
as **platte und des Tonbandes (International record libraries commission)** [Record and tape copyright laws], *Congrès international des bibliothèques et
des centres de documentation* ('s-Gravenhage: Nijhoff,
1955-1958) II, 15–23. In German. See no. 344 in this
volume.

Another version is abstracted as no. 529 in this volume.

531 CLERCX-LEJEUNE, Suzanne. **Le bibliothé-**
as **caire musical** [The music librarian], *Congrès international des bibliothèques et des centres de documentation* ('s-Gravenhage: Nijhoff, 1955-1958). In French.
See no. 344 in this volume.

Another version is abstracted as no. 532 in this volume.

532 CLERCX-LEJEUNE, Suzanne. **Le bibliothé-**
as **caire musical** [The music librarian], *Fontes artis
musicae* III/1 (July 1956) 155–59. In French. See no.
345 in this volume.

Details the tasks and the educational requirements of music-specialized librarianship. Although there are three major types of music libraries—those
of music schools serving primarily their student population; specialized
collections, which often contain rarities; and the music divisions of large
public or university libraries—the issues faced by the librarian in each are
remarkably similar. Another version is cited as no. 531 in this volume.

533 CLERCX-LEJEUNE, Suzanne. **Le bibliothé-**
as **caire musical: Sa formation professionnelle**
[The music librarian: His professional training], *Fontes
artis musicae* III/1 (July 1956) 51–56. In French. See
no. 345 in this volume.

Not merely a librarian, the music librarian should be trained extensively in
both library and musicological skills. Another version is cited as no. 534 in
this volume.

534 CLERCX-LEJEUNE, Suzanne. **Le bibliothé-**
as **caire musical: Sa formation professionnelle**
[The music librarian: His professional training],
*Congrès international des bibliothèques et des centres
de documentation* ('s-Gravenhage: Nijhoff, 1955-
1958) I, 167–72. In French. See no. 344 in this volume.

Another version is abstracted as no. 533 in this volume.

535 COATES, Eric James. **The** *British catalogue of*
as *music* **classification,** *Music libraries and instruments* (London: Hinrichsen, 1961) 156–65. *Charts,
diagr.* See no. 406 in this volume.

An outline of a new system for the cataloguing of music and books about
music at the British Library, in which subject indexing and classification
are collapsed into a single operation. A complete version is published in
book form, under the same title (London: Council of the British National
Bibliography, 1960); the catalogue itself was published later (London:
Saur, 1988). *(John Berardi)*

536 CUDWORTH, Charles. **Un** *Répertoire de Docu-
as ments Musicaux:* **Secondary report,** *Fontes artis
musicae* XII/2-3 (May-Dec 1965) 145–46. See no. 499
in this volume.

Remarks on the discussion of the roles of music librarian, bibliographer,
and documentalist abstracted as no. 600 in this volume, with particular reference to the need for an international standard documentation of visual
and audiovisual materials analagous to the RISM and RILM projects.
(David Bloom)

537 CVETKO, Dragotin. **National sources, their**
as **functions and interpretation in musicological
research,** *Music libraries and instruments* (London:
Hinrichsen, 1961) 37–39. See no. 406 in this volume.

Issues of national delimitations and international cooperation in documentary historical research are discussed in terms of the author's work with the cataloguing of Yugoslav sources for the Répertoire Internationale des Sources Musicales (RISM).

538
as

DAMERINI, Adelmo. **Per l'incremento delle biblioteche nei conservatori di musica** [For the expansion of conservatory libraries], *Atti del Congresso internazionale di musiche popolari mediterranee e del Convegno dei bibliotecari musicali* (Palermo: De Magistris succ. V. Bellotti, 1959) 349–52. In Italian. See no. 332 in this volume.

539
as

DAVIES, John Howard. **Broadcasting music libraries,** *Troisième Congrès international des bibliothèques musicales* (Kassel: Bärenreiter, 1953) 65. See no. 309 in this volume.

A commission is needed to formulate a list of holdings of radio libraries.

540
as

DAVIES, John Howard. **The contribution of radio music libraries to national and international musical life,** *Congrès international des bibliothèques et des centres de documentation* ('s-Gravenhage: Nijhoff, 1955-1958) I, 178–83. See no. 344 in this volume.

Another version is abstracted as no. 541 in this volume.

541
as

DAVIES, John Howard. **The contribution of radio music libraries to national and international musical life,** *Fontes artis musicae* III/1 (July 1956) 62–67. See no. 345 in this volume.

Radio stations have acquired vast music libraries, rich in performing material. Scores of rare works prepared for singular radio broadcasts should be circulated to performers and ensembles. Another version is cited as no. 540 in this volume.

542
as

DAVIES, John Howard. **Music librarianship for broadcasting,** *Zweiter Weltkongreß der Musikbibliotheken* (Basel; Kassel: Bärenreiter, 1950; 1951) 15–20. See no. 300 in this volume.

Discusses the duties and problems of the music librarian of the BBC, including research necessary to trace and identify music, the preparation of performing material, and the regulation of its use for broadcast performances.

543
as

DAVIES, John Howard. **The radio librarian and music documentation techniques,** *Fontes artis musicae* XII/2-3 (May-Dec 1965) 106–07. See no. 499 in this volume.

The radio librarian's music documentation is likely to be weakest in the contemporary field, simply because standard reference works can never be current, and this is where national Music Documentation Centers can be particularly helpful. In the problem of locating sources for unpublished works, old and modern, Music Documentation Centers are not likely to change things significantly. *(David Bloom)*

544
as

DAVIES, John Howard. **Radio music libraries,** *Fontes artis musicae* IV/2 (Dec 1957) 85–88. See no. 373 in this volume.

Radio music libraries have contributed greatly to musical life. Researchers frequently find access there to material not available elsewhere.

545
as

DAVIES, John Howard, moderator. **The training of the music librarian,** *Fontes artis musicae* XI/1 (Jan-Apr 1964) 53–54. See no. 457 in this volume.

A symposium session with individual contributions on the different skills required for research libraries, record libraries, orchestra libraries, and libraries for mass media such as radio; the training needed in languages and musicology; and the desirable personality characteristics of a music librarian. Participants included Vladimir FÉDOROV, Carl-Gabriel Stellan MÖRNER, Joan PEMBERTON, Helge PETERSEN, Harold SPIVACKE. *(Priscilla P. Hodges)*

546
as

DECOLLOGNE, Roger. **Vers la création d'une phonothèque centrale de prêt** [Establishing a central lending library of recorded sound], *Fontes artis musicae* III/2 (Dec 1956) 174–76. In French. See no. 345 in this volume.

Between 1953 and 1955, the number of sound recordings acquired by the French State through legal deposit has more than doubled. A veritable explosion of these collections is expected during the following few years. A central lending library would satisfy the public's growing interest in sound recordings.

547
as

DENIS, Valentin. **Les buts et les moyens des bibliothèques des conservatoires** [The purposes and means of conservatory libraries], *Zweiter Weltkongreß der Musikbibliotheken* (Basel; Kassel: Bärenreiter, 1950; 1951) 4–7. In French. See no. 300 in this volume.

Suggests a plan for cataloguing rarities kept in conservatory libraries. Such items should be catalogued by a team of qualified librarians, and the complete list should be made available at one central library.

548
as

DENIS, Valentin. **Échanges et prêts internationaux de musique** [International exchange and lending of music], *Troisième Congrès international des bibliothèques musicales* (Kassel: Bärenreiter, 1953) 56–62. In French. See no. 309 in this volume.

Outlines the purposes and needs of organizing an international music loan library and examines the types of materials to be included as well as the supportive agencies. *(Edwin D. Wallace)*

549
as

DEUTSCH, Otto Erich. **Internationale Musikbibliographie der Erstdrucke** [International bibliography of musical first editions], *Primo Congresso mondiale delle biblioteche e di bibliografia* (Roma: Libreria dello Stato, 1931-1933) II, 332–34. In German. See no. 161 in this volume.

Long-standing difficulties in cataloguing the sources of 18th- and 19th-c. music, and in the preparation of complete critical editions of the works of composers of the period, can be alleviated by consultation not only of autograph MSS but also of early and especially first editions, as collected in the Österreichische Nationalbibliothek, Vienna; the Library of Congress, Washington, D.C.; and the private collection of Anthony van Hoboken. *(David Bloom)*

550
as

DEUTSCH, Otto Erich. **Über bibliographische Aufnahme von Originalausgaben unserer Klassiker** [Bibliographic registration of the original editions of our classic composers], *Beethoven-Zentenarfeier: Internationaler musikhistorischer Kongress* (Wien: Universal, 1927) 268–72. In German. See no. 142 in this volume.

The most urgent task in German music bibliography is the cataloguing of original and first editions of the great masters, especially Haydn, with information on locations. Catalogue-card formats are discussed. *(David Bloom)*

551
as

DEUTSCH, Otto Erich. **Zum thematischen Katalog der Werke Schuberts** [On a thematic catalogue of Schubert's work], *Bericht über den internationalen Kongress für Schubertforschung* (Augsburg: Benno Filser, 1929) 175–80. *Illus.* In German. See no. 154 in this volume.

Discusses general cataloguing principles with attention to problematic areas such as dating.

552
as

DÉVIGNE, Roger. **Les archives sonores de la radiophonie** [Radio sound archives], *Compte rendu des travaux du Ier Congrès international d'art radiophonique* (Paris: conference, 1938). In French. See no. 244 in this volume.

553
as

DÉVIGNE, Roger. **Les phonothèques et leur rôle dans l'éducation musicale** [Record libraries and their role in music education], *La musique dans l'éducation* (Paris: UNESCO; Colin, 1955) 230–32. In French. See no. 323 in this volume.

An English-language version is abstracted as no. 554 in this volume.

554
as

DÉVIGNE, Roger. **Sound libraries and their role in music education,** *Music in education* (Paris: UNESCO, 1955) 220–25. See no. 322 in this volume.

Sound archives are particularly important for non-European musics, since no notation adequately represents them. French law has recognized their importance since 1938, requiring that copies of all published recordings be deposited in the Phonothèque Nationale. A French-language version is cited as no. 553. *(Rollin Smith)*

555
as

DONÀ, Mariangela. **Le bibliothécaire, le documentaliste, le bibliographe musical: Quelques points de contact entre leurs activités respectives** [The librarian, the documentalist, the musical bibliographer: Some points of contact among their respective activities], *Fontes artis musicae* XII/2-3 (May-Dec 1965) 137–38. In French. See no. 499 in this volume.

Remarks appended to the discussion abstracted as no. 600 in this volume, with particular attention to the situation of music documentalists in Italy.

556
as

DORFMÜLLER, Kurt. **Der wissenschaftliche Musikbibliothekar und sein Publikum** [The academic music librarian and his public], *Fontes artis musicae* XI/1 (Jan-Apr 1964) 66–67. In German. See no. 457 in this volume.

Visitors to the music divisions of large public libraries—those that are not attached to research or educational institutions—come in two categories: professional researchers and students of musicology, who will consult the librarian only with questions of librarianship and bibliography, and musicians with scientific interests who may have questions about musicology. With the latter, the librarian's responsibility is limited to indicating the sources of an answer, not finding the answer itself. *(David Bloom)*

557
as

DREIMÜLLER, Karl. **Gedanken und Anregungen zur musikalischen Bibliographie und Quellenkunde** [Thoughts and suggestions on music bibliography and source studies], *Bericht über den internationalen musikwissenschaftlichen Kongreß Wien Mozartjahr 1956* (Graz; Köln: Böhlau, 1958) 143–47. In German. See no. 365 in this volume.

Offers proposals for the establishment and maintenance of an international bibliography of musicological writing, issued periodically.

558
as

DUCK, Leonard. **The public provision of music for choirs and orchestras,** *Music libraries and instruments* (London: Hinrichsen, 1961) 53–60. *Port., facs., music.* See no. 406 in this volume.

In order to avoid the high costs of the rental or purchase of parts for performance, many societies and amateur groups utilize the services of music libraries to borrow such materials. The Henry Watson Music Library (Manchester, England) was the first to maintain this practice, and serves as an example of the maintenance of this type of service. The expense involved prohibits smaller libraries from participating. It is important that every single part is accounted for. *(Richard Slapsys)*

559
as

DUCK, Leonard; SHEPARD, Brooks, Jr. **The music librarian and his public,** *Fontes artis musicae* XI/1 (Jan-Apr 1964) 68–69. See no. 457 in this volume.

Issues discussed include multiple function and inadequate funding in public music libraries in England, and the general value of music librarians' training in enabling them to be helpful in different ways. *(Susan Poliniak)*

560
as

DUCKLES, Vincent H. **The growth and organization of music research libraries in the western United States,** *Music libraries and instruments* (London: Hinrichsen, 1961) 47–53. *Facs.* See no. 406 in this volume.

As compared to those in Europe or the eastern U.S., music libraries in California are relatively young, with modest resources, but they are growing. In order to build a good research collection, it is important to seek the advice of scholars, collect current scholarly publications, and acquire a basic reference collection for the study of music history. It is also vital for musicologists to have access to primary sources. The library of the University of California at Berkeley, among other university and state libraries in California, is in the process of developing large collections along these lines. *(Richard Slapsys)*

561
as

DUCKLES, Vincent H. **Music librarian—bibliographer—documentalist,** *Fontes artis musicae* XII/2-3 (May-Dec 1965) 138–41. See no. 499 in this volume.

Remarks appended to the discussion abstracted as no. 600 in this volume, with particular attention to the need for a philosophy of documentation. *(David Bloom)*

562
as

DUCKLES, Vincent H. **The place of gramophone recording in a university music library,** *Troisième Congrès international des bibliothèques musicales* (Kassel: Bärenreiter, 1953) 65–71. See no. 309 in this volume.

Describes the roles that recordings, combined with scores and works of music criticism, have in teaching and research at university libraries.

563
as

DUCKLES, Vincent H. **The rôle of the public library in modern musical education,** *Fontes artis musicae* III/1 (July 1956) 37–38. See no. 345 in this volume.

The so-called "minimum essentials" of public libraries are defined. Exchange relationships between libraries in the same geographical area, and cooperative acquisitions are encouraged. Collecting from the particular region where the library is located is put forth as one of the principal tasks of any public library. Another version is cited as no. 564 in this volume.

564
as

DUCKLES, Vincent H. **The rôle of the public library in modern musical education,** *Congrès international des bibliothèques et des centres de documentation* ('s-Gravenhage: Nijhoff, 1955-1958) I, 153–54. See no. 344 in this volume.

Another version is abstracted as no. 563 in this volume.

565
as

DUCKLES, Vincent H. **The role of the public library in modern musical education: An American appraisal,** *Congrès international des bibliothèques et des centres de documentation* ('s-Gravenhage: Nijhoff, 1955-1958) III. See no. 344 in this volume.

Another version is abstracted as no. 566 in this volume.

566
as

DUCKLES, Vincent H. **The role of the public library in modern musical education: An American appraisal,** *Fontes artis musicae* III/1 (July 1956) 140–43. See no. 345 in this volume.

Nearly 40,000 library outlets, central libraries, branches, and sub-branches serve American communities in the U.S. public library system, each of which is a potential avenue for the dissemination of music education. Another version is cited as no. 565 in this volume.

567
as
FÉDOROV, Vladimir. **L'Association Internationale des Bibliothèques Musicales: Son organisation, ses tâches—Ses rapports avec les groupes nationaux et locaux** [The International Association of Music Libraries: Its organization, its tasks, its relationships with national and local groups], *Atti del Congresso internazionale di musiche popolari mediterranee e del Convegno dei bibliotecari musicali* (Palermo: De Magistris succ. V. Bellotti, 1959) 353–58. In French. See no. 332 in this volume.

568
as
FÉDOROV, Vladimir. **Échange et prêt entre bibliothèques musicales** [Exchange and lending between music libraries], *Zweiter Weltkongreß der Musikbibliotheken* (Basel; Kassel: Bärenreiter, 1950; 1951) 57–61. In French. See no. 300 in this volume.

A stable international agreement would permit each country's central music library to maintain a collection of the essential materials of all countries, through methods including the exchange of unused duplicates and microfilms. Current documentation should be made available through interlibrary loan programs. *(David Bloom)*

569
as
FÉDOROV, Vladimir. **Entente et organisation internationales pour le dépouillement des périodiques musicaux** [An international agreement and organization for the abstracting of music periodicals], *Zweiter Weltkongreß der Musikbibliotheken* (Basel; Kassel: Bärenreiter, 1950; 1951) 49–52. In French. See no. 300 in this volume.

Presents general arguments and proposals for the establishment of an analytic bibliography of music literature, consisting of author and subject indexes and perhaps summaries of particular articles. In addition to the abstracting of current periodicals on a monthly or quarterly basis, the organization should eventually be able to provide country-by-country bibliographies of earlier periodical literature, to as far back as the 17th or 18th c. *(David Bloom)*

570
as
FÉDOROV, Vladimir. **Les grandes bibliothèques publiques de musique** [The great public music libraries], *La musique dans l'éducation* (Paris: UNESCO; Colin, 1955) 217–21. In French. See no. 323 in this volume.

An English-language version is abstracted as no. 571 in this volume.

571
as
FÉDOROV, Vladimir. **The great public music libraries,** *Music in education* (Paris: UNESCO, 1955) 207–12. See no. 322 in this volume.

The major public music libraries have become less concerned with formal education. They remain national repositories, and their temporary and permanent exhibitions arouse the curiosity of laypeople, inciting them to further investigation. A French-language version is cited as no. 570 in this volume. *(Rollin Smith)*

572
as
FEININGER, Laurence. **Necessità di catalogare la musica esistente nelle cattedrali e negli archivi parrocchiali** [The need for cataloguing music extant in cathedrals and parish archives], *Atti del [I] Congresso internazionale di musica sacra* (Tournai: Desclée, 1952) 295–97. In Italian. See no. 303 in this volume.

573
as
FERCHAULT, Guy. **Les bibliothèques des conservatoires** [The libraries of the conservatories], *La musique dans l'éducation* (Paris: UNESCO; Colin, 1955) 227–29. In French. See no. 323 in this volume.

An English-language version is abstracted as no. 575 in this volume.

574
as
FERCHAULT, Guy. **Essai de justification d'une bibliographie particulière à la philosophie de l'art musical** [An attempt to justify a special bibliography dedicated to the philosophy of music], *Bericht über den Internationalen musikwissenschaftlichen Kongreß* (Kassel: Bärenreiter, 1954) 286–89. In French. See no. 319 in this volume.

Provides reasons why engaging with the philosophy and aesthetics of music is important, along with an outline for a future bibliography of the aesthetics of music. Many writings whose titles do not point to music contain valuable discussions on the philosophy of music. *(Carl Skoggard)*

575
as
FERCHAULT, Guy. **The libraries of the conservatories,** *Music in education* (Paris: UNESCO, 1955) 215–20. See no. 322 in this volume.

Only 30 percent of conservatories in France have libraries of value, and these are not open to the public. To integrate conservatory libraries into a general program of music education for young people, adequate premises, equipment, and a lending system are called for. A French-language version is cited as no. 573 in this volume.

576
as
FREITAG, Wolfgang M. **On planning a music library,** *Fontes artis musicae* XI/1 (Jan-Apr 1964) 35–49. *Bibliog.* See no. 457 in this volume.

Planning problems are similar for music departments in large research libraries, music libraries in universities, and music libraries in music departments. Estimations of the number of students served and the prospective increase in readers over a given period (25-50 years), the anticipated growth of the collection, the initial size of the collection, and the number of workers needed now and in future should be considered. Architects and planners should in their designs bear in mind book stacks (open or closed), music and record storage, listening equipment and/or piano practice rooms, tables larger than standard library tables, adequate light and ventilation, and soundproofing. *(Priscilla P. Hodges)*

577
as
GASPERINI, Guido. **Sulle collezioni musicali esistenti presso le pubbliche biblioteche e i loro rapporti con gli studi internazionali di musicologia** [On the existing music collections in public libraries and their relationships with international musicological study], *Primo Congresso mondiale delle biblioteche e di bibliografia* (Roma: Libreria dello Stato, 1931-1933) 241–45. In Italian. See no. 161 in this volume.

Discusses the necessity of music libraries for the study of musicology. Italy is both the originator of and a repository for some of the most important music that is vital to this work.

578
as
GAUKSTAD, Øystein. **Registrierung von Volksmusik** [Cataloguing folk music], *Zweiter Weltkongreß der Musikbibliotheken* (Basel; Kassel: Bärenreiter, 1950; 1951) 38–40. In German. See no. 300 in this volume.

Discusses problems of classification, focusing primarily on Norwegian vocal and instrumental folk music.

579
as
GHISLANZONI, Alberto. **Per un catalogo unico nazionale delle biblioteche musicali** [For a single national catalogue of music libraries], *Atti del Congresso internazionale di musiche popolari mediterranee e del Convegno dei bibliotecari musicali* (Palermo: De Magistris succ. V. Bellotti, 1959) 359–62. In Italian. See no. 332 in this volume.

580
as
GIRARDIN, Monique. **Une collection théâtrale générale et ses fichiers: Fiches d'orientation** [A general theatrical collection and its files: Orientation cards], *Acts of the VIIth International Congress of Libraries and Museums of the Performing Arts/Actes du VIIe Congrès international des bibliothèques-musées*

des arts du spectacle ('s-Gravenhage: Theater Instituut Nederland/Netherlands Centre of the International Theatre Institute, 1965) 46–53. In French. See no. 492 in this volume.

581
as

GITEAU, Cécile. **Les collections générales de théâtre et leurs fichiers** [General theatrical collections and their files], *Acts of the VIIth International Congress of Libraries and Museums of the Performing Arts/Actes du VIIe Congrès international des bibliothèques-musées des arts du spectacle* ('s-Gravenhage: Theater Instituut Nederland/Netherlands Centre of the International Theatre Institute, 1965) 31–37. In French. See no. 492 in this volume.

582
as

GLEICH, Christoph-Clemens von. **Le Répertoire International des Sources Musicales (RISM) et les collections théâtrales** [Répertoire International des Sources Musicales (RISM) and theatrical collections], *Acts of the VIIth International Congress of Libraries and Museums of the Performing Arts/Actes du VIIe Congrès international des bibliothèques-musées des arts du spectacle* ('s-Gravenhage: Theater Instituut Nederland/Netherlands Centre of the International Theatre Institute, 1965) 27–28. In French. See no. 492 in this volume.

Proposes a collaboration with RISM for a resource for theatrical research.

583
as

GRASBERGER, Franz. **À propos des échanges de musique** [On exchanges of music], *Fontes artis musicae* III/1 (July 1956) 68–69. In German and French. See no. 345 in this volume.

Calls for a special commission on interlibrary exchange. What should be exchanged by whom? How should music be exchanged—directly or through a central service? Another version is cited as no. 584 in this volume.

584
as

GRASBERGER, Franz. **À propos des échanges de musique** [On exchanges of music], *Congrès international des bibliothèques et des centres de documentation* ('s-Gravenhage: Nijhoff, 1955-1958) I, 184–85. In German; summary in French. See no. 344 in this volume.

Another version is abstracted as no. 583 in this volume.

585
as

HAAS, Robert. **Die Erhaltung der musikalischen Meisterhandschriften** [The preservation of musical manuscripts of the masters], *Beethoven-Zentenarfeier: Internationaler musikhistorischer Kongress* (Wien: Universal, 1927) 290–91. In German. See no. 142 in this volume.

Little progress was made before World War I in the photographic reproduction of MS sources. This method of making the sources available to the widest possible public while protecting the original documents has made considerable advances since, but needs to be put on a firmer organizational footing. *(David Bloom)*

586
as

HAAS, Robert. **Zur Bibliographie der Operntexte** [On the bibliography of opera librettos], *Bericht über den I. musikwissenschaftlichen Kongress der Deutschen Musikgesellschaft in Leipzig* (Wiesbaden: Breitkopf & Härtel, 1926) 59–61. In German. See no. 120 in this volume.

Reviews the bibliographical work of musicologists such as Josip Mantuani, Oscar G.T. Sonneck, Giovanni and Carlo Salvioli, and Hugo Riemann, comparing the methodologies and suggesting refinements. *(William Renwick)*

587
as

HALM, Hans. **Schallplattenarchiv und öffentliche wissenschaftliche Bibliotheken** [Archives of phonograph records and public scholarly libraries], *Zweiter Weltkongreß der Musikbibliotheken* (Basel; Kassel: Bärenreiter, 1950; 1951) 46–49. In German. See no. 300 in this volume.

Discusses the functions and requirements of maintaining a collection of sound recordings in a general scholarly library.

588
as

HEARTZ, Daniel. **Lute music,** *Report of the Eighth Congress of the International Musicological Society. II: Reports* (Kassel: Bärenreiter, 1962) 72–76. *Music, charts, diagr.* See no. 440 in this volume.

A report on a discussion by Frits NOSKE, Jean JACQUOT, Suzanne BLOCH, Wolfgang BOETTICHER, Thurston DART, Charles Warren FOX, Gusta GOLDSCHMIDT, Daniel HEARTZ, François LESURE, David LUMSDEN, Carol MACCLINTOCK, Geneviève THIBAULT DE CHAMBURE, Giuseppe VECCHI, and André VERCHALY on the paper by Jacquot abstracted as no. 595 in this volume. In addition to questions of the bibliography of lute music, the participants considered issues of dating the earliest manifestations of lutenistic art, music for two or more lutes, and editorial practice in the publication of works originally written in tablature were considered.

589
as

HECKMANN, Harald. **Geleitwort des Vorsitzenden** [Chairman's introduction], *Fontes artis musicae* XII/2-3 (May-Dec 1965) 111. In German. See no. 499 in this volume.

Introduction to a roundtable discussion on the utilization of data-processing techniques in musical documentation.

590
as

HECKMANN, Harald. **Musikalische Quellen auf Mikrofilmen** [Musical sources on microfilm], *Music libraries and instruments* (London: Hinrichsen, 1961) 173–77. In German. See no. 406 in this volume.

Discusses the work of the Deutsches Musikgeschichtliches Archiv, Kassel, in the microform preservation of MS and print sources. *(David Bloom)*

591
as

HECKMANN, Harald. **Zur Dokumentation musikalischer Quellen des 16. und 17. Jahrhunderts** [The documentation of musical sources of the 16th and 17th centuries], *Bericht über den internationalen musikwissenschaftlichen Kongreß* (Kassel: Bärenreiter, 1963) 342–45. In German. See no. 452 in this volume.

Discusses cataloguing problems, with particular attention to classification by incipit.

592
as

HILL, Richard S. **Some pros and cons regarding an international code for cataloging practical music,** *Troisième Congrès international des bibliothèques musicales* (Kassel: Bärenreiter, 1953) 37–45. See no. 309 in this volume.

Recommendations are made for a music cataloguing code that has clarity of outline and articulation of structure. The strengths and weaknesses of past systems are shown. *(Edwin D. Wallace)*

593
as

HOPKINSON, Cecil, moderator. **Towards a definition of certain terms in musical bibliography,** *Music libraries and instruments* (London: Hinrichsen, 1961) 147–55. *Charts, diagr.* See no. 406 in this volume.

Panel discussion on the use of terms such as *edition, impression, Ausgabe, Auflage,* and *édition originale.* Particpants included Otto Erich DEUTSCH, Rudolf ELVERS, Vladimir FÉDOROV, Hans HALM, Albert vander LINDEN, Oliver Wray NEIGHBOUR, Albi ROSENTHAL, Liesbeth WEINHOLD. *(John Berardi)*

594
as
HUYS, Bernard. **Réponse au rapport préliminaire de M.A. Jurres** [Reply to the preliminary report by André Jurres], *Fontes artis musicae* XII/2-3 (May-Dec 1965) 104–06. In French. See no. 499 in this volume.

A response to the conference communication abstracted as no. 597 in this volume. It is possible, and desirable, for a single institution to serve the functions both of a national music library, concerned with the music of the past, and a music information center for contemporary music. *(David Bloom)*

595
as
JACQUOT, Jean. **La musique pour luth** [Lute music], *Report of the Eighth Congress of the International Musicological Society. I: Papers* (Kassel: Bärenreiter, 1961) 75–88. *Facs.* In French. See no. 439 in this volume.

Considerable work has been completed in the bibliography of lute-music sources since the congress *Le luth et sa musique*, Neuilly-sur-Seine, 1957 (see no. 377 in this volume), under the auspices of the International Musicological Society, the Répertoire International des Sources Musicales, and the International Association of Music Libraries. Progress is reported, with particular reference to research in France. *(David Bloom)*

596
as
JANIĆ, Siniša. **Rôle de la Section Internationale des Bibliothèques et Musées des Arts du Spectacle en vue de faciliter la création des services de documentation des centres nationaux de L'I.I.T.** [Role of the International Section for Performing Arts Libraries and Museums in facilitating the creation of documentation services of the national centers of the International Theatre Institute], *Acts of the VIIth International Congress of Libraries and Museums of the Performing Arts/Actes du VIIᵉ Congrès international des bibliothèques-musées des arts du spectacle* ('s-Gravenhage: Theater Instituut Nederland/Netherlands Centre of the International Theatre Institute, 1965) 15–20. In French. See no. 492 in this volume.

Discusses the nature of national centers of the International Theatre Institute.

597
as
JURRES, André. **Les Centres de Documentation Musicale et leurs techniques particulières** [Music Documentation Centers and their particular techniques], *Fontes artis musicae* XII/2-3 (May-Dec 1965) 100–04. In French. See no. 499 in this volume.

Discusses the activities of the 17 national members of the Music Documentation Centers branch of the International Association of Music Libraries, with attention to their role in propagating the music—especially contemporary music—of their respective countries. This task has recently grown to include functioning as an independent publisher of bulletins and scores, and as a producer of recordings. *(David Bloom)*

598
as
JURRES, André; PROKOPOWICZ, Maria. **International aspects.** Moderated by Hans ZEHNTNER, *Fontes artis musicae* XI/1 (Jan-Apr 1964) 60–62. See no. 457 in this volume.

Discusses the profession of the music librarian, with attention to the development of the International Association of Music Information Centres since its founding in 1958 and to efforts in Poland toward exchanging music information on an international basis. *(Priscilla P. Hodges)*

599
as
KING, Alexander Hyatt. **An international scheme for publishing summaries of articles in music periodicals,** *Troisième Congrès international des bibliothèques musicales* (Kassel: Bärenreiter, 1953) 62–64. See no. 309 in this volume.

Describes the feasibility of collecting all musical articles in national periodicals into one international publication.

600
as
KING, Alexander Hyatt. **The music librarian, the bibliographer, the documentalist,** *Fontes artis musicae* XII/2-3 (May-Dec 1965) 135–37. See no. 499 in this volume.

Defines "documentalist" as a person who assembles, handles, and studies documents and makes them available for use and study by others. The tasks and training of documentalists—as opposed to those of music librarians and bibliographers—are discussed. *(David Bloom)*

601
as
KING, Alexander Hyatt. **The music librarian and his tasks, national and international,** *Music libraries and instruments* (London: Hinrichsen, 1961) 40–47. See no. 406 in this volume.

Discusses the work of the International Association of Music Libraries in making improvements and providing standards for music librarianship.

602
as
KÖHLER, Karl-Heinz. **Zur Problematik der Schallplatten-Katalogisierung** [The problematics of record cataloguing], *Music libraries and instruments* (London: Hinrichsen, 1961) 116–19. In German. See no. 406 in this volume.

An explanation of the problems that have been overcome regarding record cataloguing, indexing, and style cataloguing.

603
as
KÖHLER, Karl-Heinz. **Zwei Grundtypen historischer Musiksammlungen** [Two basic types of historic music collection], *Bericht über den siebenten internationalen musikwissenschaftlichen Kongress* (Kassel: Bärenreiter, 1959) 162–64. In German. See no. 390 in this volume.

The first type of collection, generally originating in private hands from before the late 18th c., is marked by the consciousness of its own particular present time, of which the collectors tried to assemble a comprehensive record. The second, historicizing type aims at a record of the musical past. Many great collections of the second type originated, around the turn of the 19th c., when their parent institutions acquired a collection of the first type, as when Sir John Hawkins donated his music collection to the British Museum (1778), when the Königliche Bibliothek Berlin acquired the Bibliothek J.F. Naue (1824), or when Moritz von Dietrichstein organized the Austrian court music archives for the Hofbibliothek in Vienna (1826-29). *(David Bloom)*

604
as
KRAGEMO, Helge. **Konzertprogramme** [Concert programs], *Zweiter Weltkongreß der Musikbibliotheken* (Basel; Kassel: Bärenreiter, 1950; 1951) 31–33. In German. See no. 300 in this volume.

Outlines how various methods of organization of concert programs in libraries can provide tools with which to study the history of a country, of a specific area, or music history in general.

605
as
LE COSQUINO DE BUSSY, J.R. **Le rôle et la place de la lecture publique dans l'éducation musicale contemporaine** [The role and the place of the public reading in contemporary music education], *Congrès international des bibliothèques et des centres de documentation* ('s-Gravenhage: Nijhoff, 1955-1958) I, 151–53. In French. See no. 344 in this volume.

Another version is abstracted as no. 606 in this volume.

606
as
LE COSQUINO DE BUSSY, J.R. **Le rôle et la place de la lecture publique dans l'éducation musicale contemporaine** [The role and the place of the public reading in contemporary music education], *Fontes artis musicae* III/1 (July 1956) 35–36. In French. See no. 345 in this volume.

A definition of the public music library is proposed, and its educational tasks are established. Differences between passive and active learning are pointed out: The former largely involves unguided, often spontaneous, listening (ideally, in a desirable educational climate), while the latter involves a trained educator, such as a librarian. Another version is cited as no. 608 in this volume.

607
as

LE COSQUINO DE BUSSY, J.R. **Le rôle et la place de la lecture publique dans l'éducation musicale contemporaine: Quelques nouveaux aspects de la question** [The role and the place of the public reading in music education: Some new aspects], *Fontes artis musicae* III/1 (July 1956) 138–39. In French. See no. 345 in this volume.

A reprise of the issues raised in no. 605, abstracted in this volume. The responsibilities of the music librarian toward three distinct groups of library users are outlined. The needs of people who come to the library simply to enjoy music are as important as those of people who come with specific or general education goals. To help members of the public develop and broaden their personal tastes is the main goal of the public library. Another version is cited as no. 608 in this volume.

608
as

LE COSQUINO DE BUSSY, J.R. **Le rôle et la place de la lecture publique dans l'éducation musicale contemporaine: Quelques nouveaux aspects de la question** [The role and the place of the public reading in contemporary music education: Some new aspects of the question], *Congrès international des bibliothèques et des centres de documentation* ('s-Gravenhage: Nijhoff, 1955-1958) III. In French. See no. 344 in this volume.

Another version is abstracted as no. 607 in this volume.

609
as

LEBEAU, Élisabeth. **Le problème des publications originales de musique non imprimées, à propos de la recherche de la musique de film** [The problem of the nonprinted original publication of music, with reference to research on film music], *Fontes artis musicae* XII/2-3 (May-Dec 1965) 150–52. In French. See no. 499 in this volume.

Film scores are rarely published in printed form, and obtaining them for research purposes poses a problem, at least in France and presumably elsewhere. The AIMB should address the situation. *(David Bloom)*

610
as

LESURE, François. **Bibliothécaires et musicologues** [Librarians and musicologists], *Atti del Congresso internazionale di musiche popolari mediterranee e del Convegno dei bibliotecari musicali* (Palermo: De Magistris succ. V. Bellotti, 1959) 363–67. In French. See no. 332 in this volume.

Discusses essential principles of the role of music libraries as documentation centers in contemporary scholarship.

611
as

LINDBERG, Folke. **Quelques aspects de la documentation musicale audio-visuelle** [Some aspects of audio-visual documentation of music], *Fontes artis musicae* XII/2-3 (May-Dec 1965) 147–50. In French. See no. 499 in this volume.

Remarks on the concerns of the AIBM in regard to the collection, documentation, classification, dissemination, and use of sound recordings and sound films. *(David Bloom)*

612
as

LINDBERG, Folke. **Scandinavian music libraries: Their value for research and broadcasting,** *Music libraries and instruments* (London: Hinrichsen, 1961) 83–86. See no. 406 in this volume.

There is a major interest in the revival of older music for performance in Scandinavia. Many libraries house excellent collections of music from the 18th and 19th c.; private collections are also repositories. Musicologists use these libraries as bases of research and often turn to radio music libraries. *(Richard Slapsys)*

613
as

LUMSDEN, David. **Un catalogue international des sources de la musique pour le luth: Les leçons d'une étude des sources anglais** [An international catalogue of sources of lute music: Lessons from a study of English sources], *Le luth et sa musique* (Paris: Centre National de la Recherche Scientifique [CNRS], 1958) 297–300. In French. See no. 377 in this volume.

Discusses issues that will arise in the creation of a complete thematic catalogue of all the known sources, on the basis of the author's experience in preparing *The sources of English lute music, 1540-1620* (Ph.D. dissertation, University of Cambridge, 1955). *(David Bloom)*

614
as

LUNGHI, F.L. **Sulla scheda Caravaglios per la raccolta dei canti popolari** [On the Caravaglios index for the collection of traditional songs], *Atti del III Congresso nazionale di arti e tradizioni popolari* (Roma: Opera Nazionale Dopolavoro, 1936) 360–67. In Italian. See no. 218 in this volume.

615
as

LUTHER, Wilhelm Martin. **Die Mikrokopie von Autographen, Unica und sonstigen musikalischen Wertstücken, ihr Austausch innerhalb der Welt und ihre Sicherung gegen Zerfall und Vernichtung** [The microfilming of autographs, unica, and other valuable musical sources, their exchange throughout the world, and their protection against ruin], *Troisième Congrès international des bibliothèques musicales* (Kassel: Bärenreiter, 1953) 48–55. In German. See no. 309 in this volume.

The microfilming and cataloguing of original MSS, incunabula, and unica are underway in all countries. Libraries, musicological societies, and cultural organizations, including UNESCO, have taken up this important work to protect valuable musical sources and to promote ease of exchange among libraries, countries, and individual scholars. *(Sylvia Eversole)*

616
as

MALHERBE, Charles. **Observations relatives à l'établissement d'un catalogue des autographes musicaux dans les principales bibliothèques de l'Europe** [Observations relative to the establishment of a catalogue of musical autographs in the principal libraries of Europe], *Haydn-Zentenarfeier* (Leipzig: Breitkopf & Härtel; Wien: Artaria, 1909) 433–34. In French. See no. 65 in this volume.

617
as

MANTUANI, Josip. **Über die Katalogisierung der katholischen liturgischen Texte** [On the cataloguing of Roman Catholic liturgical texts], *Haydn-Zentenarfeier* (Leipzig: Breitkopf & Härtel; Wien: Artaria, 1909) 437–39. In German. See no. 65 in this volume.

Discusses a system of cataloguing according to text, author, composer, source, and position in the liturgy.

618
as

MANTUANI, Josip. **Über die Katalogisierung des deutschen Liedes** [On the cataloguing of German songs], *Haydn-Zentenarfeier* (Leipzig: Breitkopf & Härtel; Wien: Artaria, 1909) 434–37. *Charts, diagr.* In German. See no. 65 in this volume.

Discusses cataloguing according to title, composer, source, and melody.

619
as

MARCEL-DUBOIS, Claudie. **Instruments de musique ethniques et musées spécialisés d'ethnologie** [Traditional musical instruments and museums specializing in ethnology], *Fontes artis musicae* XII/2-3 (May-Dec 1965) 207–08. In French. See no. 499 in this volume.

In museums devoted to the ethnography of a particular society, group of societies, or culture, the presentation of instruments depends on whether the museum is meant to cater primarily to the general public, to specialists, or both. For the general public, the criteria for exhibiting an instrument should include its quality and beauty and its representative value for the given culture; it may be shown in a strictly musical sector or in sectors of domains (institutions, social life, traditional art) where music plays a role. In museums for specialists, the main criterion is systematization. *(David Bloom)*

620 MCCOLVIN, Lionel. **Music in public libraries:**
as **Why? And what?,** *Fontes artis musicae* IV/2 (Dec 1957) 80–83. See no. 373 in this volume.
Collections of musical works should be made available in public libraries. Librarians must be prepared to acquire a knowledge of music in order to assist library users.

621 MENNES, François. **Bibliographie internatio-**
as **nale des arts du spectacle** [International bibliography of the performing arts], *Acts of the VIIth International Congress of Libraries and Museums of the Performing Arts/Actes du VIIᵉ Congrès international des bibliothèques-musées des arts du spectacle* ('s-Gravenhage: Theater Instituut Nederland/Netherlands Centre of the International Theatre Institute, 1965) 21–26. In French. See no. 492 in this volume.
Discusses the scope and organization of a proposed project.

622 MERLIER, Melpo. **Création à Athènes**
as **d'archives musicales de folklore** [Creation of traditional music archives in Athens], *Congrès de la Societat Internacional de Musicologia* (Barcelona: Casa de Caritat, 1936). In French. See no. 224 in this volume.
The conference report provides only a citation. Neither the text nor a summary of the paper was published here.

623 MEYLAN, Pierre. **Étude comparative sur les**
as **bibliothèques musicales publiques dans différents pays** [A comparative study of the public music libraries of different countries], *Fontes artis musicae* III/1 (July 1956) 116–22. In French. See no. 345 in this volume.
General discussion of the international variety of collections, cataloguing systems, and financial resources. Since most music librarians do not have the time to assist on international source repertoires, it is proposed that an international group of experts be assigned to RISM and a new music literature index. Another version is cited as no. 624 in this volume.

624 MEYLAN, Pierre. **Étude comparative sur les**
as **bibliothèques musicales publiques dans différents pays (International public music libraries)** [A comparative study of the public music libraries of different countries], *Congrès international des bibliothèques et des centres de documentation* ('s-Gravenhage: Nijhoff, 1955-1958) II, 45–50. In French. See no. 344 in this volume.
Another version is abstracted as no. 623 in this volume.

625 MILLER, Catharine K. **Phonograph records in**
as **U.S. public libraries,** *Fontes artis musicae* III/1 (July 1956) 146–47. See no. 345 in this volume.
Summarizes the experiences of public libraries with regard to their holdings of sound recordings, focusing on two aspects of the collections: their organization and use. Organization is concerned with storage, sound equipment, and aspects of cataloguing (e.g., detailed analytics); use entails circulation or in-house playing. It is estimated that 30 to 40 circulations is the lifetime of an American vinyl record. Another version is cited as no. 626 in this volume. *(André Balog)*

626 MILLER, Catharine K. **Phonograph records in**
as **U.S. public libraries,** *Congrès international des bibliothèques et des centres de documentation* ('s-Gravenhage: Nijhoff, 1955-1958) III. See no. 344 in this volume.
Another version is abstracted as no. 625 in this volume.

627 MILLER, Philip L. **Educational and scientific**
as **aspects of the record library,** *Fontes artis musicae* III/1 (July 1956) 41–43. See no. 345 in this volume.
Public collections represent four types: archives, educational collections, public sound libraries (reference or circulation), and broadcasting collections. Weekly record concerts given by the New York Public Library are cited as a popular and useful activity that can be provided by sound libraries. Another version is cited as no. 628 in this volume.

628 MILLER, Philip L. **Educational and scientific**
as **aspects of the record library,** *Congrès international des bibliothèques et des centres de documentation* ('s-Gravenhage: Nijhoff, 1955-1958) I. See no. 344 in this volume.
Another version is abstracted as no. 627 in this volume.

629 MOLL ROQUETA, Jaime. **Les bibliothèques**
as **musicales publiques: Les aspects nationaux du problème** [Public music libraries: The national aspects of the problem], *Fontes artis musicae* III/1 (July 1956) 81–84. In Spanish; summary in French. See no. 345 in this volume.
Spain has no public music libraries other than its principal archives. Provincial music libraries should be established, taking into account respective local music traditions. Another version is cited as no. 632 in this volume.

630 MOLL ROQUETA, Jaime. **La formation**
as **professionnelle d'un bibliothécaire musical** [The professional training of a music librarian], *Fontes artis musicae* III/1 (July 1956) 84–85. In Spanish; summary in French. See no. 345 in this volume.
Music librarians should possess both musical and library skills. Another version is cited as no. 631 in this volume.

631 MOLL ROQUETA, Jaime. **La formation pro-**
as **fessionnelle d'un bibliothécaire musical** [The professional training of a music librarian], *Congrès international des bibliothèques et des centres de documentation* ('s-Gravenhage: Nijhoff, 1955-1958) II, 13–14. In Spanish; summary in French. See no. 344 in this volume.
Another version is abstracted as no. 630 in this volume.

632 MOLL ROQUETA, Jaime. **Les bibliothèques**
as **musicales publiques: Les aspects nationaux du problème** [The public music libraries: The national aspects of the problem], *Congrès international des bibliothèques et des centres de documentation* ('s-Gravenhage: Nijhoff, 1955-1958) II, 10–12. In Spanish; summary in French. See no. 344 in this volume.
Another version is abstracted as no. 629 in this volume.

633 MUELLER VON ASOW, Erich Hermann. **Der**
as **Gesamtkatalog der Musiker-Briefe: Auszug** [Comprehensive catalogue of musicians' letters: Extract], *Zweiter Weltkongreß der Musikbibliotheken* (Basel; Kassel: Bärenreiter, 1950; 1951) 35–38. In German. See no. 300 in this volume.
Discusses methods used since 1945 by the Internationales Musiker-Brief-Archiv in Berlin for the ordering of musicians' letters.

634 MYERS, Kurtz. **Phonograph records in Ameri-**
as **can public libraries,** *Troisième Congrès interna-*
tional des bibliothèques musicales (Kassel: Bärenreiter,
1953) 71–72. See no. 309 in this volume.

Discusses the different services, clientele, and problems encountered regarding record collections in public libraries.

635 NAMETAK, Alija. **Folklorni materijal u deset**
as **godišta** *Behara* **(od 1900 do 1911 godine)** [Writ-
ings about folklore in ten volumes of *Behar* (1900 to
1911)], *Treći kongres folklorista Jugoslavije* (Cetinje:
Udruženje Folklorista Crne Gore, 1958) 65–71. *Illus.* In
Bosnian; summary in French. See no. 357 in this
volume.

The biweekly *Behar*, published in Sarajevo from May 1900 to March 1911,
included 420 contributions about traditional songs, tales, and customs. The
cataloguing of this material for the Institut za Proučavanje Folklora in
Sarajevo is discussed, outlining the indexing methodology for motifs in
traditional tales and songs. *(Zdravko Blažeković)*

636 NETTL, Paul. **Die Notwendigkeit einer Text-**
as **bücherbibliographie** [The need for a bibliography
of librettos], *Beethoven-Zentenarfeier: Internationaler*
musikhistorischer Kongress (Wien: Universal, 1927)
296–97. In German. See no. 142 in this volume.

Discusses the cataloguing requirements for a bibliography of opera and
ballet librettos. Proposals for the cataloguing of visual materials, or iconography, of theater and music are also discussed.

637 NICOL, Karl Ludwig. **Bericht zur ersten** *Table*
as ***ronde*** [Report on the first roundtable], *Fontes artis*
musicae XII/2-3 (May-Dec 1965) 107–08. In German.
See no. 499 in this volume.

Contribution to a roundtable discussion of the music information cen-
ter/music documentation center, from the vantage point of the public music
library. *(David Bloom)*

638 NIKOLIĆ, Milena. **Organisation d'une disco-**
as **thèque: Problèmes de conservation et de cata-**
logage [Organization of a record library: Problems of
conservation and cataloguing], *Acts of the VIIth Inter-*
national Congress of Libraries and Museums of the
Performing Arts/Actes du VIIᵉ Congrès international
des bibliothèques-musées des arts du spectacle
('s-Gravenhage: Theater Instituut Nederland/Nether-
lands Centre of the International Theatre Institute,
1965) 71–74. *Charts, diagr.* In French. See no. 492 in
this volume.

→ NOACK, Friedrich. **Organisation und wissen-**
schaftliche Nutzbarmachung der Arbeit in
den Seminaren [Organizing the work of academic
departments and making it useful]. See no. 906 in this
volume.

639 NOWAK, Leopold. **Dienst am Leser: Auf-**
as **gaben, Probleme, Lösungen** [Service to the reader:
Tasks, problems, solutions], *Zweiter Weltkongreß der*
Musikbibliotheken (Basel; Kassel: Bärenreiter, 1950;
1951) 27–31. In German. See no. 300 in this volume.

Discusses shortcomings and possible improvements to be made in libraries.
Major areas covered include methods of acquisition and retrieval of materials.

640 ÖHMAN, E.; LLOYD, G.A. **The Universal Deci-**
as **mal Classification (UDC) and theatre,** *Acts of the*
VIIth International Congress of Libraries and Museums
of the Performing Arts/Actes du VIIᵉ Congrès interna-
tional des bibliothèques-musées des arts du spectacle

('s-Gravenhage: Theater Instituut Nederland/ Netherlands Centre of the International Theatre Institute, 1965)
59–61. *Charts, diagr.* See no. 492 in this volume.

Describes the general structure of the Universal Decimal Classification
(UDC). Recent revisions in the classification of theatrical subjects are also
discussed.

641 OTT, Alfons. **Possibilities of musical education**
as **in public libraries,** *Fontes artis musicae* XI/1
(Jan-Apr 1964) 63–66. See no. 457 in this volume.

The concept of the public music library began with the founding and en-
dowment of the Musikalische Volksbibliothek in Munich, 1902, by Paul
Marsop. Music libraries ideally should be set up for the lending of books
and scores; should have records and listening equipment available; and
should contain piano practice rooms, archives, iconographies, and periodicals. Music libraries may also serve as performance centers.
(Priscilla P. Hodges)

642 OTT, Alfons. **Le rôle des bibliothèques popu-**
as **laires dans l'éducation musicale** [The role of popular libraries in music education], *La musique dans*
l'éducation (Paris: UNESCO; Colin, 1955) 222–27. In
French. See no. 323 in this volume.

An English-language version is abstracted as no. 644 in this volume.

643 OTT, Alfons. **The role of music in public librar-**
as **ies of medium size,** *Music libraries and instruments*
(London: Hinrichsen, 1961) 79–83. See no. 406 in this
volume.

With a firm conviction of the educational value of music, many general libraries are including music sections; they provide music resources to people living in areas lacking music libraries. The main problems concern the
selection, size, and arrangement of the collection. Enterprising libraries
may include a record collection, piano, and even guest speakers.
(Richard Slapsys)

644 OTT, Alfons. **The role of popular libraries in**
as **music education,** *Music in education* (Paris:
UNESCO, 1955) 212–15. See no. 322 in this volume.

The history of public music libraries in Germany begins with the contribution of the Munich musicologist and cultural philosopher Paul Marsop,
who opened his collection of music books and scores to the public in 1902
and donated it to the municipality in 1907 under the name Musikalische
Volksbibliothek (now incorporated into the Münchner Stadtbibliothek).
The services and range of materials offered in such libraries are outlined in
terms of their social functions. A French-language version is cited as no.
642 in this volume.

645 OTT, Alfons. **Wesen und Aufgabe einer**
as **musikalischen Volksbibliothek** [The nature and
the task of a popular music library], *Zweiter Welt-*
kongreß der Musikbibliotheken (Basel; Kassel: Bärenreiter, 1950; 1951) 24–27. In German. See no. 300 in
this volume.

An overview of priorities, including a reference to the first attempt at such
an institution: the Münchener Musikalische Volksbibliothek, founded in
1902.

646 OTT, Alfons. **Wirkungsmöglichkeiten in**
as **öffentlichen Musikbibliotheken** [Opportunities
in public music libraries], *Congrès international des*
bibliothèques et des centres de documentation
('s-Gravenhage: Nijhoff, 1955-1958) II, 51–60. In German. See no. 344 in this volume.

Another version is abstracted as no. 647 in this volume.

647 OTT, Alfons. **Wirkungsmöglichkeiten in**
as **öffentlichen Musikbibliotheken** [Opportunities in
public music libraries], *Fontes artis musicae* III/1 (July

1956) 122–32. In German; summary in French. See no. 345 in this volume.

Performance is the most essential element of music education and should be the primary focus of the public library. Thus score lending and collaboration with performing ensembles are of great importance. Another version is cited as no. 646 in this volume.

648
as
PAULI, F.W. **Phonetische Dokumentation und Musikforschung** [Phonetic documentation and music research], *Bericht über den Internationalen musikwissenschaftlichen Kongress* (Kassel: Bärenreiter, 1954) 295–99. In German. See no. 319 in this volume.

Sound recordings have become a vital resource for scholars, especially with the development of tape recording. Older sound sources can be transferred onto tape, and then preserved far into the future. Practices in U.S. libraries are described, where holdings in sound recordings have been integrated into university libraries and ample facilities provided. The first meetings of the Commission Internationale des Phonothèques, founded in April 1953, are described. In West Germany, the state radio networks are generating a large quantity of sound recordings in connection with live programming; in 1953 the nonprofit organization Lautarchiv des Deutschen Rundfunks was founded by the networks to make these sound recordings available to researchers and educators. The great historical value of sound recordings in documenting performance practice is stressed. It is hoped that West German copyright law will be modernized in step with developments in sound recording and its uses. *(Carl Skoggard)*

649
as
PEQUENO, Mercedés Reis. **La formation professionnelle du bibliothécaire musical** [The professional training of the music librarian], *Fontes artis musicae* III/1 (July 1956) 57–61. *Charts, diagr.* In Portuguese; summary in French. See no. 345 in this volume.

Although no special program exists in South America, prospective music librarians should attempt to incorporate the training program that exists in the U.S.: B.A. with music major, plus one year M.L.S., plus one year of specialized music librarian studies. Another version is cited as no. 650 in this volume.

650
as
PEQUENO, Mercedes Reis. **La formation professionnelle du bibliothécaire musicale** [The professional training of the music librarian], *Congrès international des bibliothèques et des centres de documentation* ('s-Gravenhage: Nijhoff, 1955-1958) I, 173–77. In Spanish; summary in French. See no. 344 in this volume.

Another version is abstracted as no. 649 in this volume.

651
as
PIRROTTA, Nino. **Compiti regionali, nazionali, ed internazionali delle biblioteche musicali** [The regional, national, and international tasks of music libraries], *Atti del Congresso internazionale di musiche popolari mediterranee e del Convegno dei bibliotecari musicali* (Palermo: De Magistris succ. V. Bellotti, 1959) 331–40. In Italian. See no. 332 in this volume.

652
as
PIRROTTA, Nino. **Fondi musicali non inventariati nè catalogati** [Music collections neither inventoried nor catalogued], *Troisième Congrès international des bibliothèques musicales* (Kassel: Bärenreiter, 1953) 46–47. In Italian. See no. 309 in this volume.

A proposal for an international commission which would develop standards for bibliographic cataloguing.

653
as
PLESSKE, Hans-Martin. **Musikbibliographie und Deutsche Bücherei** [Music bibliography and the Deutsche Bücherei], *Fontes artis musicae* III/2

(Dec 1956) 182–83. In German. See no. 345 in this volume.

Describes the bibliographic activities of the Deutsche Bücherei, Leipzig, which maintains an ongoing, standardized record of music and music-related publications issued in German-speaking countries and regions. The centuries-old bibliographic traditions of the Leipzig music publishers that preceded the comprehensive bibliographic mandate given to the Deutsche Bücherei on 1 January 1943 are traced. *(Carl Skoggard)*

654
as
PLESSKE, Hans-Martin. **Zur Musikalien-Katalogisierung der Deutschen Bücherei** [The cataloguing of musicalia by the Deutsche Bücherei], *Music libraries and instruments* (London: Hinrichsen, 1961) 165–69. In German. See no. 406 in this volume.

Summarizes the cataloguing practices of the music collection at the Deutsche Bücherei in Leipzig.

655
as
PULKERT, Oldřich. **The national music institute and its neccessity as a prez-requisite** [*sic*] **for musicological research,** *Fontes artis musicae* III/2 (Dec 1956) 177–82. See no. 345 in this volume.

Presents an organizational model for establishing a national music center.

656
as
RAELI, Vito. **Collezioni di libretti per musica: Statistica e catalogazione** [Collections of librettos for music: Statistics and cataloguing], *Primo Congresso mondiale delle biblioteche e di bibliografia* (Roma: Libreria dello Stato, 1931-1933) IV, 155–61. In Italian. See no. 161 in this volume.

Discusses the collection and cataloguing of opera librettos, as well as the need for good bibliographies.

657
as
RECKZIEGEL, Walter. **Musikbibliographie und Datenspeicher** [Music bibliography and data storage], *Fontes artis musicae* XII/2-3 (May-Dec 1965) 123–28. In German. See no. 499 in this volume.

Discusses the potential uses of computers in the particular applications of literature lists, incipit catalogues, and data retrieval. *(David Bloom)*

658
as
REHM, Wolfgang. **Über ein Repertorium der Musik: Anregungen und Vorschläge zu einem neuen Nachschlagewerk** [A repertoire of music: Proposals and suggestions for a new reference work], *Bericht über den siebenten internationalen musikwissenschaftlichen Kongress* (Kassel: Bärenreiter, 1959) 221–26. *Music, charts, diagr.* In German. See no. 390 in this volume.

Proposals are offered for a *Repertorium musicae universale* (RMU), or universal musical repertoire, a bibliography of music works, each including a listing for composer, title and alternative titles, instrumentation, and musical and text incipits; data on first performance, MSS, early and modern editions, and sound recordings; remarks on the work's origins; and bibliography. Sample cataloguing for works of the 17th, 18th, and 20th c. is provided, together with a list of proposed abbreviations. *(David Bloom)*

659
as
REINECKE, Hans-Peter. **Erläuterungen zur modernen Dokumentations-Technik** [Comments on modern documentation technology], *Bericht über den internationalen musikwissenschaftlichen Kongreß* (Kassel: Bärenreiter, 1963) 336–37. In German. See no. 452 in this volume.

Discusses the potential uses of electronic data processing in the music library.

660
as
REINHARD, Kurt. **Probleme und Erfahrungen in einem Musikethnologischen Schallarchiv** [Problems and experiences in a sound archive for music ethnology], *Music libraries and instruments*

(London: Hinrichsen, 1961) 119–26. In German. See no. 406 in this volume.

Discusses issues of technical quality in records and tape recordings, cataloguing, copyright, and prioritization, based on the experiences of the Phonogramm-Archiv of the Museum für Völkerkunde, Berlin. *(David Bloom)*

661
as
REINHOLD, Helmut. **Aufbau und Verwendungsmöglichkeiten einer Discothek wertvoller Gesangsaufnahmen im Sendebetrieb** [Collection developments and uses of a radio library of high-quality recordings of singers], *Congrès international des bibliothèques et des centres de documentation* ('s-Gravenhage: Nijhoff, 1955-1958) III. In German. See no. 344 in this volume.

Another version is abstracted as no. 662 in this volume.

662
as
REINHOLD, Helmut. **Aufbau und Verwendungsmöglichkeiten einer Discothek wertvoller Gesangsaufnahmen im Sendebetrieb** [Collection development and uses for a radio library of high-quality recordings of singers], *Fontes artis musicae* III/1 (July 1956) 148–53. In German. See no. 345 in this volume.

There are three basic dimensions to consider in building a library of sound recordings. One may acquire recorded performances of representative works, of representative ensembles, or of specific performers. These three dimensions are not always easy to coordinate. The cultural mandate of state-supported broadcasting stations is to document the significant trends of successive eras. Demonstrating continuity in musical development seems especially important in the wake of the two World Wars. Another version is cited as no. 661 in this volume. *(Carl Skoggard)*

663
as
ROUGET, Gabriel. **Le disque et la bande comme matière d'échanges** [The record and the tape as exchange material], *Quatrième Congrès international des bibliothèques musicales Fontes artis musicae* III/1 (July 1956) 70–71. In French. See no. 345 in this volume.

Another version is cited as no. 664 in this volume.

664
as
ROUGET, Gilbert. **Le disque et la bande comme matière d'échanges** [The record and the tape as exchange material], *Congrès international des bibliothèques et des centres de documentation* ('s-Gravenhage: Nijhoff, 1955-1958) I. In French. See no. 344 in this volume.

Another version is cited as no. 663 in this volume.

665
as
SARTORI, Claudio. **I misteri delle biblioteche italiane. II** [The mysteries of Italian libraries. II], *Fontes artis musicae* III/2 (Dec 1956) 192–202. In Italian. See no. 345 in this volume.

Presents a preliminary survey of Italian collections with holdings that would qualify for RISM cataloguing. Two lists are provided: one by library, and one by composer.

666
as
SARTORI, Claudio. **Le *RISM* et l'Italie: À l'aventure dans les bibliothèques italiennes** [*RISM* and Italy: In search of adventure in the Italian libraries], *Fontes artis musicae* XI/1 (Jan-Apr 1964) 28–33. In French. See no. 457 in this volume.

Although Italy contains some of the richest collections of printed music, theoretical works, and MSS, the state of libraries and archives is notoriously abysmal. The organization of RISM in Italy afforded an opportunity to improve the situation, but even with a well-trained workforce, progress has been problematical because of difficulties in gaining access to some collections, continual financial issues, and the occasional loss of administrative personnel. *(Barbara B. Heyman)*

667
as
SARTORI, Claudio. **Uno schedario regionale nella biblioteca musicale del capoluogo della regione** [A regional catalogue in the music library of the region's principal city], *Atti del Congresso internazionale di musiche popolari mediterranee e del Convegno dei bibliotecari musicali* (Palermo: De Magistris succ. V. Bellotti, 1959) 369–76. In Italian. See no. 332 in this volume.

The cataloging of musical sources, region by region, should be centralized at the region's chief music library, e.g., in Turin for the Piedmont, Milan for Lombardy, etc. *(David Bloom)*

668
as
SAUL, Patrick. **A documentation policy for a national sound archive,** *Fontes artis musicae* XII/2-3 (May-Dec 1965) 152–55. See no. 499 in this volume.

Remarks on the discussion abstracted as no. 611 in this volume, with proposals on the question of what sound documents need to be preserved in archives, and how they are to be classified. *(David Bloom)*

669
as
SCHAEFFNER, André. **Les tâches scientifiques et pédagogiques des phonothèques musicales** [The scientific and educational tasks of musical sound libraries], *Fontes artis musicae* III/1 (July 1956) 39–40. In French. See no. 345 in this volume.

Sound libraries differ from one another according to their equipment, specialization, and recording rights. The system of acquiring recorded documents needs to be reformed. Another version is cited as no. 670 in this volume.

670
as
SCHAEFFNER, André. **Les tâches scientifiques et pédagogiques des phonothèques musicales** [The scientific and educational tasks of musical sound libraries], *Congrès international des bibliothèques et des centres de documentation* ('s-Gravenhage: Nijhoff, 1955-1958) I, 155–56. In French. See no. 344 in this volume.

Another version is abstracted as no. 669 in this volume.

671
as
SCHETELICH, Herta. **Der Gesichtskreis der Musikbüchereiarbeit in einer Großstadt der Deutschen Demokratischen Republik** [The scope of music librarianship in a large city of East Germany], *Music libraries and instruments* (London: Hinrichsen, 1961) 75–78. In German. See no. 406 in this volume.

The perspective is that of the Musikbibliothek der Stadt Leipzig and Musikbibliothek Peters (amalgamated 1953) of the Leipziger Städtische Bibliotheken. *(David Bloom)*

672
as
SCHETELICH, Herta. **Nebenbericht** [Secondary report], *Fontes artis musicae* XII/2-3 (May-Dec 1965) 141–42. In German. See no. 499 in this volume.

Remarks on the discussion of the roles of music librarian, bibliographer, and documentalist abstracted as no. 600 in this volume, with particular reference to public music libraries, where librarians find themselves obliged to serve as bibliographers and documentalists as well. *(David Bloom)*

673
as
SCHIØRRING, Nils. **Public music libraries: International co-operation,** *Congrès international des bibliothèques et des centres de documentation* ('s-Gravenhage: Nijhoff, 1955-1958) II, 61–65. See no. 344 in this volume.

Another version is abstracted as no. 674 in this volume.

674
as
SCHIØRRING, Nils. **Public music libraries: International co-operation,** *Fontes artis musicae* III/1 (July 1956) 132–36. See no. 345 in this volume.

The raising of the musical consciousness of the public must begin at the elementary level, through the aid of the local public library. The commission ought to be regularly informed of public library procedures and capacities in each member country. Another version is cited as no. 673 in this volume.

675 SCHMIDT-PHISELDECK, Josef. **Datierung**
as **der Musikalien** [The dating of music materials], *Beethoven-Zentenarfeier: Internationaler musikhistorischer Kongress* (Wien: Universal, 1927) 279–82. In German. See no. 142 in this volume.
Dates that play a role in cataloguing include the year of publication (sometimes corroborated by checking the plate number from the bottom of the original signature plate), year of composition, date of first performance (especially important for stage works), and copyright date. What is most important to the librarian is often of less interest to the musicologist. *(David Bloom)*

676 SCHMIEDER, Wolfgang. **Das Berufsbild des**
as **wissenschaftlichen Musikbibliothekars** [The career of academic music librarian], *Bericht über den internationalen musikwissenschaftlichen Kongreß* (Kassel: Bärenreiter, 1963) 323. In German. See no. 452 in this volume.
Discusses prospects, qualifications, benefits, and drawbacks of working as a music librarian in an academic library, from the viewpoint of the young musicologist in search of a career. *(David Bloom)*

677 SCHMIEDER, Wolfgang. **Gedanken über den**
as **Begriff, das Wesen und die Aufgaben der Musikdokumentation** [Thoughts on the concept, nature, and tasks of music documentation], *Bericht über den internationalen musikwissenschaftlichen Kongreß* (Kassel: Bärenreiter, 1963) 334–36. In German. See no. 452 in this volume.
Introductory remarks to a conference session.

678 SCHMIEDER, Wolfgang. **Grenzen und Ziele**
as **der Musikdokumentation** [The limits and goals of music documentation], *Bericht über den internationalen musikwissenschaftlichen Kongreß Wien Mozartjahr 1956* (Graz; Köln: Böhlau, 1958) 551. In German. See no. 365 in this volume.
A summary of remarks on the bibliography, cataloguing, and indexing of music sources, recordings, and literature.

679 SCHMIEDER, Wolfgang. **Musikbiblio-**
as **graphische Probleme: Ein Beitrag zur Theorie der Verzeichnung von Büchern über Musik** [Issues in music bibliography: A contribution to the theory of cataloguing books about music], *Bericht über den Internationalen musikwissenschaftlichen Kongress* (Kassel: Bärenreiter, 1954) 282–86. In German. See no. 319 in this volume.
Considers the principles that should underlie a comprehensive bibliography of music literature. Guidelines for inclusion and organization should be based on an understanding of who users of the bibliography are likely to be. The classification of material should be practical, so that material is not unevenly divided into very large and very small categories. A moderate amount of cross-referencing (not indiscriminate cross-referencing) as well as indexing and keywords will help the user. Typography that aids users in scanning is recommended. Personal names, places, and instruments should be the fundamental concepts for grouping material. *(Carl Skoggard)*

680 SCHNEIDER, Constantin. **Musikbibliographie**
as **in Österreich** [Music bibliography in Austria], *Beethoven-Zentenarfeier: Internationaler musikhistorischer Kongress* (Wien: Universal, 1927) 265–67. In German. See no. 142 in this volume.

The most urgent task is the cataloguing of music sources and other documentary materials. Financing and staffing need to be improved, and centralization is desirable.

681 SEIFFERT, Max. **Generalkatalog der in**
as **englischen öffenlichen und privaten Bibliotheken befindlichen älteren Musikalien bis 1800** [General catalogue of musical documents prior to the year 1800 contained in public and private libraries in England], *Report of the Fourth Congress of the International Musical Society* (London: Novello, 1912) 369. In German. See no. 71 in this volume.
Summary of a paper discussing the compilation of the catalogue.

682 SEIFFERT, Max. **Grundaufgaben der Musik-**
as **wissenschaft und das Bückeburger Forschungsinstitut** [Fundamental tasks of musicology and the Bückeburg Forschungsinstitut], *Bericht über den musikwissenschaftlichen Kongreß in Basel* (Leipzig: Breitkopf & Härtel, 1925) 317–20. In German. See no. 102 in this volume.
While great progress has been made during the last 25 years in establishing musicology as an internationally recognized discipline, urgent tasks remain. Many German collections must be catalogued. Bibliography and archival work must be better organized. Though World War I and the subsequent economic chaos destroyed initial hopes for the Fürstliches Institut für Musikforschung in Bückeburg (now the Staatliches Institut für Musikforschung in Berlin), it can still serve as a place for seminars and archival research.

683 SHEPARD, Brooks, Jr. **Secondary report,** *Fontes*
as *artis musicae* XII/2-3 (May-Dec 1965) 108–09. See no. 499 in this volume.
Contribution to a roundtable discussion of the music information center/music documentation center, with attention to the ways in which most music libraries could function as music documentation centers. *(David Bloom)*

684 SMITH, Carleton Sprague. **Report of the Sub-**
as **committee on Music Libraries,** *Report of the Committee of the Conference on Inter-American Relations in the Field of Music* (Washington, D.C.: United States Department of State, 1940) 18–20. See no. 271 in this volume.
Representative sets containing Latin-American music and related studies should be assembled and housed in regional centers in the U.S., and similar sets should be located in Latin-American music capitals. Each set should consist of records, scores, and books. A suggested budget is included. *(Howard Cinnamon)*

685 SMITH, Carleton Sprague. **The service of the li-**
as **brary to musicology,** *Papers read at the Annual Meeting of the American Musicological Society* (New York: American Musicological Society, 1936) 35–41. *Charts, diagr.* See no. 230 in this volume.
A fully functional music library must provide access to quality sound recordings and playback facilities; traditional songs in notated and recorded forms; facsimiles of MSS; photographs of modern dance; a trained director with capable assistants, including a cataloguer who is both a musician and a library school graduate; collections of historic instruments in playable condition; and lectures and concerts pertaining to the unusual items in the collection.

686 SONNECK, Oscar G.T. **Bibliographie, Biblio-**
as **thekswesen: Verhandlungen und Vorträge** [Bibliography and librarianship: Discussions and lectures]. Ed. by Hermann SPRINGER, *Bericht über den zweiten Kongress der Internationalen Musikgesellschaft* (Leipzig: Breitkopf & Härtel, 1907) 6–7. In German. See no. 53 in this volume.

Summarizes two talks: on general principles for the building up of an adequate music library and on the International Musical Society's project of a comprehensive international bibliography of periodical music literature. A summary is appended of discussions generated by the conference's decision to adopt a project to expand and revise Robert Eitner's *Biographisch-bibliographisches Quellen-Lexikon der Musiker und Musikgelehrten* (Leipzig, 1902).

687 SPIVACKE, Harold. **The preservation and ref-**
as **erence services of sound recordings in a re-**
search library, *Music libraries and instruments*
(London: Hinrichsen, 1961) 99–110. See no. 406 in this
volume.

Discusses problems relating to acquisition (amassing too many records, obtaining current publications, issues caused by international embargoes), reference services (the inclusion of sound recordings in national bibliographies), and the improvement of services. Particular attention is paid to concerns regarding the lifespan and preservation of records and tapes, as well as recommendations for storage. There is a need for national collections and the international exchange of live (instantaneous) recordings. *(Susan Poliniak)*

688 SPRINGER, Hermann. **Aufgaben der Gesell-**
as **schaft für Wissenschaftliche Musikbiblio-**
graphie [Tasks of the Gesellschaft für Wissenschaftliche Musikbibliographie], *Beethoven-*
Zentenarfeier: Internationaler musikhistorischer
Kongress (Wien: Universal, 1927) 263–64. In German.
See no. 142 in this volume.

Progress report on the project of a periodical bibliography of music literature in German, with attention to its relation to the international bibliography proposed by the International Musicological Society. *(David Bloom)*

689 SPRINGER, Hermann. **Die jüngsten**
as **Fortschritte der Musikbibliographie** [The most
recent advances in musical bibliography], *Report of the*
Fourth Congress of the International Musical Society
(London: Novello, 1912) 377. In German. See no. 71 in
this volume.

Summary of a paper.

690 SPRINGER, Hermann. **Über den Stand der**
as **musikalischen Bibliographie** [On the current state
of musical bibliography], *Bericht über den zweiten*
Kongress der Internationalen Musikgesellschaft (Leipzig: Breitkopf & Härtel, 1907) 1–6. In German. See no.
53 in this volume.

Brief history and survey of the cataloguing of music libraries in Europe and the U.S.; periodical listing and abstracting of publications; specialized projects such as thematic catalogues for individual composers or chronogically and geographically determined ranges; and proposals for comprehensive bibliographies of MS and print sources.

691 SPRINGER, Hermann. **Wissenschaftliche und**
as **produktive Musikbibliographie** [Scholarly and
productive music bibliography], *Bericht über den I.*
musikwissenschaftlichen Kongress der Deutschen
Musikgesellschaft in Leipzig (Wiesbaden: Breitkopf &
Härtel, 1926) 54–58. In German. See no. 120 in this
volume.

Discusses the role of bibliography in musicology, and suggests ways of ensuring the relevance of bibliography to music.

692 SPYRIDAKIS, Georgios. **The folklore archive**
as **of the Athens Academy,** *Journal of the Interna-*
tional Folk Music Council XII (1960) 75–76. See no.
413 in this volume.

Surveys the activities and holdings of the Laografikon Archeion at the Kentron Ereunis tis Ellinikis Laografias, Akadimia Athinon.

693 STÄBLEIN, Bruno. **Erfassung und Erschlies-**
as **sung mittelalterlicher Musikhandschriften** [In-
ventorying and making available medieval music manu-
scripts], *Bericht über den internationalen musik-*
wissenschaftlichen Kongreß (Kassel: Bärenreiter, 1963)
339–40. In German. See no. 452 in this volume.

Briefly discusses goals and technical issues of microfilm archiving.

694 STAM, Henk. **Die Stiftung Donemus** [The
as Donemus foundation], *Zweiter Weltkongreß der Musik-*
bibliotheken (Basel; Kassel: Bärenreiter, 1950; 1951)
56–57. In German. See no. 300 in this volume.

Description of the aims, methods, and achievements of the Donemus (Dokumentatie Nederlandse Muziek) project to document all compositions from the Netherlands.

695 SUTHERLAND, W.J. **Sound and film archives**
as **of theatrical performances in the Netherlands,**
Acts of the VIIth International Congress of Libraries
and Museums of the Performing Arts/Actes du VIIe
Congrès international des bibliothèques-musées des
arts du spectacle ('s-Gravenhage: Theater Instituut
Nederland/Netherlands Centre of the International
Theatre Institute, 1965) 75–77. See no. 492 in this
volume.

Reports on an ongoing project started by Dutch actors.

696 TERENZIO, Vincenzo. **Criteri per la classi-**
as **ficazione e la catalogazione di una discoteca**
nelle biblioteche musicali [Criteria for the classification and cataloguing of a recording collection in a
music library], *Music libraries and instruments* (London: Hinrichsen, 1961) 126–27. In Italian. See no. 406
in this volume.

Proposes a card cataloguing system for general use. It is important to note recording medium fully (33-rpm disc, 45-rpm disc, and so on) and to distinguish published from unpublished music. Special problems in the cataloguing of duplicate material are addressed. *(Susan Poliniak)*

697 TÉREY-KUTHY, Sándor. **Projet d'archives**
as **internationales de la chanson et de la musique**
populaires [Proposal for international archives of traditional song and music], *Congrès international des*
arts populaires/International congress of popular arts
(Paris: Institut international de coopération
intellectuelle, 1928) 12–13. In French. See no. 153 in
this volume.

The League of Nations should sponsor a formal mechanism of international exchange in the study of traditional music; it might set up a central archive in Paris, Geneva, or Vienna, to further comparative study.

698 VETTERL, Karel. **The need for an interna-**
as **tional select bibliography of folk music sum-**
mary, *Jahrbuch für Philosophie, Kultur, Gesellschaft*
XIII (1961) 68–69. See no. 424 in this volume.

Such a bibliography would be most valuable only if it were truly critical and selective. The International Folk Music Council should organize the project, with the aid of national committees and individual experts.
(Alix Moyer Grunebaum)

699 VÖTTERLE, Karl. **Musikbibliothek und**
as **Musikverlag** [Music libraries and music publishers],
Music libraries and instruments (London: Hinrichsen,
1961) 67–75. In German. See no. 406 in this volume.

Proposals, from the music publisher's point of view, on ways in which librarians and publishers can collaborate.

700 WALLON, Simone. **Rapport secondaire** [Secondary report], *Fontes artis musicae* XII/2-3 (May-Dec 1965) 142–43. In French. See no. 499 in this volume.
as
Remarks on the discussion of the roles of music librarian, bibliographer, and documentalist abstracted as no. 600 in this volume, with particular reference to the situation in France, where specific training for documentalists has existed for some time. The special problems associated with the dissemination of iconographic materials are examined. *(David Bloom)*

701 WOLFF, Hellmuth Christian. **L'élaboration d'une bibliographie des documents illustrant l'histoire de l'opéra** [Preparation of a bibliography of documents illustrating the history of opera], *Acts of the VIIth International Congress of Libraries and Museums of the Performing Arts/Actes du VIIe Congrès international des bibliothèques-musées des arts du spectacle* ('s-Gravenhage: Theater Instituut Nederland/ Netherlands Centre of the International Theatre Institute, 1965) 29–30. In French. See no. 492 in this volume.
Proposes the creation of a bibliography of documents illustrating the history of opera.

702 ZEHNTNER, Hans. **Bibliothekar, Bibliograph und Dokumentalist** [Librarian, bibliographer, and documentalist], *Fontes artis musicae* XII/2-3 (May-Dec 1965) 143–45. In German. See no. 499 in this volume.
as
Remarks on the discussion of the roles of music librarian, bibliographer, and documentalist abstracted as no. 600 in this volume, with particular reference to the documentalist's responsibilities in regard to newer kinds of documents, such as still photographs, films, sound recordings, and electronically stored data. *(David Bloom)*

703 ZOBELEY, Fritz. **Praktische Probleme der Musikbibliographie** [Practical problems of music bibliography], *Beethoven-Zentenarfeier: Internationaler musikhistorischer Kongress* (Wien: Universal, 1927) 276–78. In German. See no. 142 in this volume.
as
The inventories of musical sources in German public libraries are inadequate, and in the case of private collections and those of religious institutions, often nonexistent. Some cataloguing principles are suggested, based on experiences with the Musiksammlung des Grafen von Schönborn-Wiesentheid (Wiesentheid near Würzburg). *(David Bloom)*

02 Libraries, museums, collections

704 ALTWEGG, Wilhelm. **Les Archives Suisses de la Chanson Populaire** [The Schweizerisches Volksliedarchiv], *Journal of the International Folk Music Council* I (1949) 8–12. In French. See no. 281 in this volume.
as
Historical account of the Schweizerische Gesellschaft für Volkskunde/ Société Suisse des Traditions Populaires/Società Svizzera per le Tradizioni Popolari and its archive of traditional song at Basel, instituted 1907. *(David Bloom)*

705 ANDERSON, Kenneth. **Public service for music: The use of standard methods in Liverpool's new music library,** *Music libraries and instruments* (London: Hinrichsen, 1961) 60–61. See no. 406 in this volume.
as
The music library of the University of Liverpool was destroyed in World War II; a new facility was built and opened in 1959. It consists of a combined reference and lending collection, and open access to records. The catalogue is in dictionary form and new shelving allows for easy access to materials. *(Richard Slapsys)*

706 ANDRAL, Maguy. **Dernières acquisitions phonographiques du Musée National des Arts et Traditions Populaires** [Recent phonographic acquisitions of the Musée National des Arts et Traditions Populaires], *Journal of the International Folk Music Council* II (1950) 49. In French. See no. 295 in this volume.
as
The conference report provides only a citation. Neither the text nor a summary of the paper was published here.

707 BECKER-GLAUCH, Irmgard. **Die englischen Musikbibliotheken in Deutschland** [The English music libraries in Germany], *Zweiter Weltkongreß der Musikbibliotheken* (Basel; Kassel: Bärenreiter, 1950; 1951) 20–24. In German. See no. 300 in this volume.
as
Describes services and holdings (with special emphasis on foreign contemporary music) in libraries of Hamburg, Düsseldorf, and Berlin that have received British aid since World War II.

708 BERNER, Alfred. **Die Klavierinstrumente der Musikinstrumenten-Sammlung Berlin** [The keyboard instruments of the Musikinstrumentenmuseum, Berlin], *Dokumentation* (Frankfurt am Main: Fördergemeinschaft Klavier, 1966) 261–72. In German. See no. 494 in this volume.
as
Surveys the pianos, harpsichords, clavichords and other historic keyboard instruments of the Musikinstrumentenmuseum, Berlin, on the occasion of exhibitions mounted in connection with the Europiano-Kongress, Berlin 1965.

709 BRAGARD, Roger. **Les musées instrumentaux, moyens de préservation des formes traditionelles de la musique savante et populaire dans les pays d'Orient et d'Occident** [Instrument museums as a means of preserving traditional forms of art and folk music in Eastern and Western countries], *The preservation of traditional forms of the learned and popular music of the Orient and the Occident/La préservation des formes traditionelles de la musique savante et populaire dans les pays d'Orient et d'Occident* (Urbana: Center for Comparative Psycholinguistics, Institute of Communications Research, 1964) 63–72. In French. See no. 443 in this volume.
as
Preservation work undertaken at the Musée Instrumental, Brussels, is discussed.

710 BRIDGMAN, Nanie. **Quelques éditions rares de musique italienne du seizième et dix-septième siècle dans les bibliothèques de France** [Some rare editions of 16th- and 17th-century Italian music in French libraries], *Atti del Congresso internazionale di musiche popolari mediterranee e del Convegno dei bibliotecari musicali* (Palermo: De Magistris succ. V. Bellotti, 1959) 215–20. *Port.* In French. See no. 332 in this volume.
as
Surveys findings of the French national RISM committee on previously uncatalogued sources in the holdings of the Bibliothèque Municipale, Carcassonne (*F-CC*), Bibliothèque du Conservatoire, Paris (*F-Pc*), Bibliothèque National, Paris (*F-Pn*), Bibliothèque Municipale, Vesoul (*F-VE*), and the private collections of André Meyer and Geneviève Thibault de Chambure. *(David Bloom)*

711 CREMER, Martin. **Das Schicksal der Musikabteilung der ehemaligen Preußischen Staatsbibliothek** [The fate of the music department of the former Preußische Staatsbibliothek], *Zweiter Weltkongreß der Musikbibliotheken* (Basel; Kassel:
as

Bärenreiter, 1950; 1951) 55–56. In German. See no. 300 in this volume.
Briefly traces the history of the library since World War II.

712 DAVIDSSON, Åke. **Cultural background to**
as **collections of old music in Swedish libraries,** *Fontes artis musicae* XI/1 (Jan-Apr 1964) 21–28. See no. 457 in this volume.

Surveys the history of early music collections in Sweden, with particular attention to those of the Universitetsbibliotek, Uppsala, and Kungliga Musikaliska Akademiens Bibliotek, Stockholm. The former include 16th-c. MSS and prints acquired by King Gustavus Adolphus as booty in his campaigns in the Thirty Years' War; MSS of sacred music and instrumental dance music purchased during the rectorship of Olof Rudbeck (from 1661) for the training of students; and the 1500 17th-c. MSS of the Düben collection, donated in 1724 by the composer and organist Gustaf Düben. *(Priscilla P. Hodges)*

713 DORFMÜLLER, Kurt. **Die bauliche Einrich-**
as **tung der Musiksammlung der Bayerischen Staatsbibliothek, München** [The architectural dispositions of the music collection of the Bayerische Staatsbibliothek in Munich], *Fontes artis musicae* XI/1 (Jan-Apr 1964) 34–35. In German. See no. 457 in this volume.

The music collection is part of a centrally organized general library which supervises acquisition, cataloguing, and lending. The library was largely destroyed during World War II, but was restored to its original design; this limited modernization. The music collection includes a spacious reading room, but is lacking in smaller areas for catalogues, periodicals, privileged visitors, and workspace. *(Allen Lott)*

714 DOUILLEZ, Jeannine. **Collections of musical**
as **instruments in Antwerp,** *Music libraries and instruments* (London: Hinrichsen, 1961) 128–31. *Illus.* See no. 406 in this volume.

Focuses on the holdings of the Museum Vleeshuis, the Koninklijk Vlaams Muziekconservatorium, and the Koninklijke Vlaamsche Opera. *(John Berardi)*

715 DREIMÜLLER, Karl. **Musikerbriefe an einen**
as **Gladbacher Musikliebhaber: Aus der Sammlung Ludwig Bisschopinck** [Musicians' letters to a Mönchengladbach music lover: From the Ludwig Bisschopinck collection], *Studien zur Musikgeschichte der Stadt Mönchengladbach* (Köln: Volk, 1965) 111–34. *Illus., facs., music.* In German. See no. 486 in this volume.

The Mönchengladbach import-export trader and amateur pianist Ludwig Bisschopinck (1895-1959) assembled a substantial private collection of musical documents, including a large number of personal letters from contemporary composers. Transcriptions, facsimiles, and facsimile signatures for many of them are provided, together with facsimiles of album-leaf compositions written for Bisschopinck by Josef Matthias Hauer, Walter Niemann, Niels Otto Raasted, Ernst Toch, and Jaromír Weinberger. *(David Bloom)*

716 ÉCORCHEVILLE, Jules. **Sur le catalogue du**
as **fond de musique ancienne de la Bibliothèque Nationale à Paris** [On the catalogue of the early music collection of the Bibliothèque Nationale in Paris], *Haydn-Zentenarfeier* (Leipzig: Breitkopf & Härtel; Wien: Artaria, 1909) 432–33. In French. See no. 65 in this volume.

A description of the collection is followed by a panel discussion.

717 EXPERT, Henry. **Les imprimés d'Attaingnant**
as **conservés à la Bibliothèque Mazarine** [Attaingnant prints in the collections of the Bibliothèque Mazarine], *Actes du Congrès d'histoire de l'art:*

Compte rendu analytique (Paris: Presses Universitaires de France, 1922) 217–18. In French. See no. 95 in this volume.

Summary of a paper.

718 FELLOWES, Edmund Horace. **The Ouseley Li-**
as **brary at Tenbury,** *Société Internationale de Musicologie: Premier Congrès Liège—Compte rendu/ Internationale Gesellschaft für Musikwissenschaft: Erster Kongress Lüttich—Kongressbericht/International Society for Musical Research: First Congress Liège: Report* (London: Plainsong and Mediaeval Music Society, 1930) 112. See no. 178 in this volume.

The Ouseley Library, St. Michael's College, Tenbury, Worcestershire, contains Händel's conducting score of *Messiah* and MSS in the hand of André Danican Philidor, the elder. *(Conrad T. Biel)*

719 [Germany] Die Musikinstrumenten-
as **Sammlung Berlin** [The Musikinstrumentenmuseum, Berlin], *Dokumentation* (Frankfurt am Main: Fördergemeinschaft Klavier, 1966) 260–61. In German. See no. 494 in this volume.

General survey of the Musikinstrumentenmuseum, Berlin, on the occasion of special exhibits held in connection with the Europiano-Kongress, Berlin 1965.

720 GRUSNICK, Bruno. **Die Datierungen der**
as **Dübensammlung** [The datings of the Düben collection], *Norddeutsche und nordeuropäische Musik* (Kassel; New York: Bärenreiter, 1965) 27–31. In German. See no. 467 in this volume.

A preliminary report of research on 17th-c. music materials amassed by the organist Gustaf Düben and his family and donated by his son Anders von Düben to the Universitetsbibliotek Uppsala in 1732. Study of the dating of works by Augustin Pfleger and Johann Philipp Krieger makes it possible to correct gross errors in the accepted dating of certain of their works. A full report is published under the title *Die Dübensammlung: Ein Versuch ihrer chronologischen Ordnung* in *Svensk tidskrift för musikforskning* 46 (1964) and 48 (1966; see RILM [1967] 147). *(David Bloom)*

721 HAAS, Robert. **Einige allgemeine Bemerkun-**
as **gen** [Some general remarks], *Zweiter Weltkongreß der Musikbibliotheken* (Basel; Kassel: Bärenreiter, 1950; 1951) 3–4. In German. See no. 300 in this volume.

States the aims of the International Association of Music Libraries. An assessment of holdings in the Wiener Hofbibliothek with respect to damages caused by World War II is offered.

722 HAAS, Robert. **Mozartforschung und Meister-**
as **archiv** [Mozart research and the Meisterarchiv], *Bericht über die musikwissenschaftliche Tagung der Internationalen Stiftung Mozarteum* (Leipzig: Breitkopf & Härtel, 1932) 298–301. *List of works.* In German. See no. 193 in this volume.

Lists photographic copies of Mozart autographs in the Archiv für Photogramme Musikalischer Meisterhandschriften at the Österreichische Nationalbibliothek, Vienna ("Meisterarchiv"), with notes on the location of the originals. *(David Bloom)*

723 HAUBENSTOCK-RAMATI, Roman. **The Cen-**
as **tral Library of Music in Tel Aviv, Israel,** *Fontes artis musicae* III/2 (Dec 1956) 184–88. In English, French, and German. See no. 345 in this volume.

Documents the genesis of the A.M.L.I. (Americans for a Music Library in Israel) Central Library of Music (later renamed the Felicja Blumental Music Center & Library) in Tel Aviv. Several personal archives—most notably those of Bronislaw Huberman, the founder of the Palestine Symphony Orchestra—as well as collections donated by foreign governments served as the beginnings of the library. *(André Balog)*

724   HEILMAN, Ingeborg. **Organization of the mu-**
as   **sic collection of the state library in Aarhus,**
Denmark, *Music libraries and instruments* (London: Hinrichsen, 1961) 86–88. See no. 406 in this volume.

The Statsbibliotek, Aarhus, contains a comprehensive collection of music printed in Denmark as well as important donations from the Kongelige Bibliotek, Copenhagen. Although it is a general library, the Statsbibliotek's music collection is more extensive than any other in Denmark except that of the Kongelige Bibliotek. Acquisitions are coordinated with the Musikvidenskabeligt Institut, Aarhus Universitet. *(Richard Slapsys)*

725   HOLSCHNEIDER, Andreas. **Die musikalische**
as   **Bibliothek Gottfried van Swietens** [Gottfried van Swieten's music library], *Bericht über den internationalen musikwissenschaftlichen Kongreß* (Kassel: Bärenreiter, 1963) 174–78. In German. See no. 452 in this volume.

Swieten's collection, with its very extensive holdings of MSS by Bach and Händel, was the most important vehicle for the transmission of the German Baroque to the Viennese Classicists; Haydn, Mozart, and Beethoven made frequent use of it, and it also contained many autographs by the former two. The collection was dispersed on his death in 1803, but documentary evidence permits the identification of many of the MSS and of their current locations. *(David Bloom)*

726   JONAS, Oswald. **Eine private Brahms-**
as   **Sammlung und ihre Bedeutung für die**
Brahms-Werkstatt-Erkenntnis [A private Brahms collection, and its significance in Brahms's working methods], *Bericht über den internationalen musikwissenschaftlichen Kongreß* (Kassel: Bärenreiter, 1963) 212–15. In German. See no. 452 in this volume.

The collection, in the author's possession, includes documents with autograph annotations by Brahms: copyists' MSS of the piano reductions of the *Schicksalslied* op. 54 and *Triumphlied* op. 55 (the former copied by Hermann Levi); a print of the *Liebeslieder* op. 52 that was used in the preparation of the reduction for piano four hands; an engraver's copy of the *Neue Liebeslieder* op. 65; copies of the clarinet sonatas op. 120 used in preparing the version for viola; and engravers' copies of the seven-volume *Deutsche Volkslieder* WoO 33. *(David Bloom)*

727   JURRES, André. **Donémus,** *Musikerziehung:*
as   *Zeitschrift der Musikerzieher Österreichs* special issue (1953) 140–42. In German. See no. 317 in this volume.

A discussion of the Donemus foundation (whose name is an abbreviation of Documentatie in Nederland voor Muziek), a Dutch organization based in Amsterdam, from the perspective of its current director. The organization was founded in 1947 with the aim of documenting and publishing modern Dutch music. *(Tina Frühauf)*

728   KAHL, Willi. **Niederländische Werke aus den**
as   **Bestanden der alten Kölner Jesuiten-**
bibliothek [Netherlandish works from the collections of the old Jesuit library in Cologne], *Société Internationale de Musicologie, cinquième congrès/ Internationale Gesellschaft für Musikwissenschaft, fünfter Kongreß/International Society for Musical Research, Fifth Congress* (Amsterdam: Vereniging voor Nederlandse Muziekgeschiedenis, 1953) 252–53. In German. See no. 316 in this volume.

729   KAST, Paul. **Die Autographensammlung**
as   **Campori und ihre musikalischen Schätze** [The Campori autograph collection and its musical treasures], *Bericht über den internationalen musikwissenschaftlichen Kongreß* (Kassel: Bärenreiter, 1963) 226–28. In German. See no. 452 in this volume.

The Raccolta Campori in the holdings of the Biblioteca Estense, Modena, of documents originally collected by the Modena historian Giuseppe Campori (1821-87) includes some 60 autograph compositions, sketches, letters, and other documents by composers, including Haydn, Mozart, Beethoven, Weber, Meyerbeer, Spohr, Andrea Adami, Tartini, Paisiello, Cherubini, Rossini, Donizetti, and Verdi. *(David Bloom)*

730   KING, Alexander Hyatt. **The Mozart bicente-**
as   **nary exhibition in the British Museum: Its his-**
torical and aesthetic significance, *Bericht über den internationalen musikwissenschaftlichen Kongreß Wien Mozartjahr 1956* (Graz; Köln: Böhlau, 1958) 305–08. See no. 365 in this volume.

Report of an exhibit of Mozartiana held at the British Museum, 26 January–10 April 1956. An illustrated guide to the exhibit is published as *Mozart in the British Museum* (London, 1956). *(David Bloom)*

731   KINSKY, Georg. **Schuberthandschriften in**
as   **deutschem Privatbesitz** [Schubert autographs in private possession in Germany], *Bericht über den internationalen Kongress für Schubertforschung* (Augsburg: Benno Filser, 1929) 157–66. In German. See no. 154 in this volume.

Lists major owners and the contents of their collections. The principles of autograph study are also discussed.

732   KÖHLER, Karl-Heinz. **Bauliche und struk-**
as   **turelle Verhältnisse der Musikabteilung der**
Deutschen Staatsbibliothek, Berlin [Architectural and structural situation of the music section of the Deutsche Staatsbibliothek in Berlin], *Fontes artis musicae* XI/1 (Jan-Apr 1964) 49–51. In German. See no. 457 in this volume.

Discusses the facilities of the library's reading room, administrative offices, storage area, record library, and exhibition gallery.

733   KÜMMERLING, Harald. **Gottorfer Bestände**
as   **in der Sammlung Bokemeyer** [Gottorf material in the Bokemeyer collection], *Norddeutsche und nordeuropäische Musik* (Kassel; New York: Bärenreiter, 1965) 92–94. In German. See no. 467 in this volume.

The Bokemeyer music collection, acquired in the mid-19th c. by the then Königliche Bibliothek in Berlin (since 1997 in the Staatsbibliothek Preußischer Kulturbesitz; the author's catalogue of the collection is abstracted as RILM [1970]2815), consists mainly of MSS sold by Georg Österreich to his pupil Heinrich Bokemeyer ca. 1720. It originally included more than 1700 sacred cantatas by German, Italian, and French composers (of which about 850 are still extant) copied by Österreich and his assistants during his tenure as kapellmeister at Schloß Gottorf in Schleswig, 1689-1702, far more music than the ducal chapel could possibly have used; it may be conjectured that Österreich had a clearer recognition of the value of source material than most of his contemporaries, and hoped to preserve a comprehensive record of the music of his time. *(David Bloom)*

734   LAMMEL, Inge. **10 Jahre Arbeiterliedarchiv**
as   [Ten years of the Arbeiterliedarchiv], *Beiträge zur Musikwissenschaft* VI/4 (1964) 255–66. *Bibliog.* In German. See no. 476 in this volume.

The Arbeiterliedarchiv, a unit of the Akademie der Künste, Berlin, is a collection of documentary materials on German workers' songs and the Arbeitermusikbewegung in the 19th-20th c. Its history and holdings are surveyed. *(David Bloom)*

735   LARRINAGA LARRAÑAGA, Juan Ruiz de.
as   **Archivo musical de Aránzazu (Guipúzcoa)** [Musical archive of Aránzazu (Guipúzcoa)], *Crónica del IV Congreso Nacional de Música Sagrada* (Vitoria: Imprenta del Montepío Diocesano, 1930) 202–05. In Spanish. See no. 155 in this volume.

Lists the holdings of the collection in the monastery archive.

736
as

LENAERTS, René Bernard. **Les manuscrits polyphoniques de la Bibliothèque Capitulaire de Tolède** [Polyphonic manuscripts of the Toledo Biblioteca Capitular], *Société Internationale de Musicologie, cinquième congrès/Internationale Gesellschaft für Musikwissenschaft, fünfter Kongreß/International Society for Musical Research, Fifth Congress* (Amsterdam: Vereniging voor Nederlandse Muziekgeschiedenis, 1953) 276–81. In French. See no. 316 in this volume.

737
as

LINDBERG, Folke. **A survey of the musical resources of Scandinavia, with particular reference to their use in broadcast performances,** *Fontes artis musicae* III/1 (July 1956) 109–15. See no. 345 in this volume.

Describes the following music libraries: Musikaliska Akademiens Bibliotek (Stockholm), Uppsala Universitetsbibliotek, Svenska Tonsättares Internationella Musikbyrå (Stockholm); Kongelige Bibliotek (Copenhagen); Sibelius-Akatemian Kirjasto (Helsinki), Radio Suomessa (Helsinki); Universitetsbiblioteket i Oslo. Another version is cited as no. 738 in this volume.

738
as

LINDBERG, Folke. **A survey of the musical resources of Scandinavia, with particular reference to their use in broadcast performances,** *Congrès international des bibliothèques et des centres de documentation* ('s-Gravenhage: Nijhoff, 1955-1958) II, 38–40. See no. 344 in this volume.

Another version is abstracted as no. 737 in this volume in this volume.

739
as

LINTON, Marion. **Music in Scottish libraries,** *Music libraries and instruments* (London: Hinrichsen, 1961) 88–95. *Facs.* See no. 406 in this volume.

The two major music collections in Scotland are at the University of Edinburgh and the University of Glasgow. The Edinburgh collection began with a bequest from John Reid in 1839 and has been subsequently enhanced, most notably by Donald Francis Tovey. The library at the University of Glasgow grew from a collection formed by William Euing in 1874. A third collection exists in the National Library of Scotland, Edinburgh, which includes large collections of Berlioz, Händel, and Scottish composers. Other libraries such as the Mitchell Library, Glasgow, have valuable music collections. *(Richard Slapsys)*

740
as

LIUZZI, Fernando. **Un nuovo schedario di bibliografia musicale romana presso l'Istituto di Studi Romani** [A new index of Roman musical bibliography at the Istituto di Studi Romani], *Congrés de la Societat Internacional de Musicologia* (Barcelona: Casa de Caritat, 1936). In Italian. See no. 224 in this volume.

The conference report provides only a citation. Neither the text nor a summary of the paper was published here.

741
as

LUITHLEN, Victor. **Musical treasures of the Vienna art museum,** *Music libraries and instruments* (London: Hinrichsen, 1961) 244–51. *Illus.* See no. 406 in this volume.

Describes the history, contents, and physical layout of the musical instrument holdings of the Kunsthistorisches Museum, Vienna. The museum aims to maintain a collection of playable instruments. *(Susan Poliniak)*

742
as

OLDMAN, Cecil Bernard. **Panizzi and the music collection of the British Museum,** *Music libraries and instruments* (London: Hinrichsen, 1961) 62–67. *Port., facs.* See no. 406 in this volume.

Until 1840, the music holdings of the British Museum had never been catalogued, although the trustees were harshly criticized for the omission. Antonio Panizzi, Keeper of Printed Books in 1838-56 and Principal Librarian

thereafter, devised the set of rules used by Thomas Oliphant in preparing the first music catalogue, 1841-50. *(Richard Slapsys)*

743
as

OLIVEIRA, José Osório de. **Contribution of the Museum of Dundo to the knowledge of African music,** *Journal of the International Folk Music Council* VII (1955) 36. See no. 337 in this volume.

The conference report provides only a citation. Neither the text nor a summary of the paper was published here. The paper is published in Oliveira's *Uma acção cultural em África* (Lisbon: n.p., 1954).

744
as

PAULI, F.W. **Die deutschen Rundfunk-Musikbibliotheken: Ihre Organisation, ihre internationalen Arbeitsmöglichkeiten** [The music libraries of German broadcasting networks: Their organization and possibilities for international cooperation], *Congrès international des bibliothèques et des centres de documentation* ('s-Gravenhage: Nijhoff, 1955-1958) III. In German. See no. 344 in this volume.

Another version is abstracted as no. 745 in this volume.

745
as

PAULI, F.W. **Die deutschen Rundfunk-Musikbibliotheken: Ihre Organisation, ihre internationalen Arbeitsmöglichkeiten** [The music libraries of German broadcasting networks: Their organization and possibilities for international cooperation], *Fontes artis musicae* III/1 (July 1956) 153–55. In German. See no. 345 in this volume.

Describes some of the library-related problems that have faced German music broadcasting since the end of World War II, and some of the advances that have been made. Many collections were scattered or destroyed, and are in the process of being rebuilt. At the same time, the entire system has been decentralized, so that each regional station is now quasi-independent. The possibilities of sharing or swapping material on the national and the international levels are promising. Another version is cited as no. 744 in this volume. *(Carl Skoggard)*

746
as

PUJOL ROCA, David. **Les archives de musique de l'Abbaye de Montserrat** [The archives of music at the Abbey of Montserrat], *Société Internationale de Musicologie: Premier Congrès Liège—Compte rendu/ Internationale Gesellschaft für Musikwissenschaft: Erster Kongress Lüttich—Kongressbericht/International Society for Musical Research: First Congress Liège: Report* (London: Plainsong and Mediaeval Music Society, 1930) 198–200. *List of works.* In French. See no. 178 in this volume.

Describes the contents and history of the music archives of the library at the Monasterio de Santa María in Montserrat, Catalonia. Information on Spanish music of the 19th c. and earlier is also included. *(Meredith E. Baker)*

747
as

PUJOL ROCA, David. **Manuscritos de música neerlandesa conservados en la biblioteca del Monasterio de Montserrat** [Manuscripts of Netherlandish music in the library of the Abbey of Montserrat], *Atti del [I] Congresso internazionale di musica sacra* (Tournai: Desclée, 1952) 319–22. In Spanish. See no. 303 in this volume.

748
as

RAUGEL, Félix. **La bibliothèque de la maîtrise de la cathédrale d'Aix-en-Provence** [The library in the choir school of the cathedral of Aix-en-Provence], *Zweiter Weltkongreß der Musikbibliotheken* (Basel; Kassel: Bärenreiter, 1950; 1951) 33–35. In French. See no. 300 in this volume.

A brief historical overview mentioning several outstanding items in the collection, including works by Michel-Richard de Lalande and Jean-Joseph Cassanéa de Mondonville.

749 REFARDT, Edgar. **Die Basler Choral-**
as **Inkunabeln** [The Basel incunabula with choral nota-
tion], *Schweizer Jahrbuch für Musikwissenschaft/
Annales suisses de musicologie/Annuario svizzero di
musicologia* I (1924) 118–37. In German. See no. 103
in this volume.

An account of the holdings in this area of the Universität Basel, Öffentliche
Bibliothek, Musikabteilung.

750 ROLLAND, G.H. **The music collection in the**
as **Mitchell Library,** *Music libraries and instruments*
(London: Hinrichsen, 1961) 95–99. See no. 406 in this
volume.

The music room of the Mitchell Library began in 1930 with the purchase of
thousands of items from the estate of the traditional-music collector Frank
Kidson (1855-1926). The Kidson Collection holds a wide range of material
dominated by English traditional music, 17th- and 18th-c. British vocal and
dance music, and the 57-volume index of airs. Other important holdings include the Moody Manners Collection, composed of the scores, parts, and
other materials of an opera company led by Fanny Moody and Charles
Manners in 1898-1916, concert criticism of Robert Turnbull (music critic
of the Glasgow Herald, 1899-1921), and international traditional music
collected by George Gardiner (1853-1910). *(Richard Slapsys)*

751 RUBIO, Samuel. **Manuscritos musicales de la**
as **liturgia bizantina que se conservan en la**
biblioteca del Monasterio de El Escorial [Musi-
cal manuscripts of the Byzantine liturgy that are preserved in the library of the Monasterio de El Escorial],
Atti del [I] Congresso internazionale di musica sacra
(Tournai: Desclée, 1952) 119–22. In Spanish. See no.
303 in this volume.

752 RUTH, Walter. **Das Phonogrammarchiv der**
as **Akademie der Wissenschaften in Wien und**
sein Wirken im Dienste der Sprach- und
Musikwissenschaft und der Sprech- und
Gesangsausbildung [The Phonogrammarchiv of the
Akademie der Wissenschaften, Vienna, and its effectiveness in the service of linguistics, musicology, and
speech and singing training], *Bericht über den Internationalen Kongreß Singen und Sprechen* (München:
Oldenbourg, 1938) 279–93. In German. See no. 257 in
this volume.

Surveys the history of the sound archive (founded 1899) and the value of its
collections in speech research, musicology, and anthropology, together
with facilities for students and teachers, and its central task as an outpost
and defense of German culture in the southeast. *(David Bloom)*

753 SAUL, Patrick. **The British Institute of Re-**
as **corded Sound,** *Fontes artis musicae* III/2 (Dec 1956)
171–73. See no. 345 in this volume.

Describes the Institute, which was expected to move into its refurbished
quarters in the building of the British Museum in late 1956. Plans for concerts and a lecture series are provided in detail.

754 SAUL, Patrick. **Preserving recorded sound,** *Mu-*
as *sic libraries and instruments* (London: Hinrichsen,
1961) 110–16. See no. 406 in this volume.

Describes the aims, collections, rules, and future plans of the British Institute of Recorded Sound, which opened in 1955 on British Museum premises in Russell Square, London. *(John Berardi)*

755 SERAUKY, Walter. **Ausgewählte instrument-**
as **enkundliche Probleme in einem Musikinstru-**
menten-Museum [Some organological issues for a
museum of musical instruments], *Bericht über den
Internationalen musikwissenschaftlichen Kongreß*

(Kassel: Bärenreiter, 1954) 82–85. In German. See no.
319 in this volume.

Discusses the renovation of the Musikinstrumenten-Museum, Leipzig,
which took place in 1952-53. During World War II the premises of the museum were damaged and some 40% of the collection was destroyed. For the
renovation, both the arrangement and classification of the holdings were
reconsidered and updated. Restoration of a war-damaged Gottfried
Silbermann positive organ originally built for Hilbersdorf near Freiberg in
Saxony (1724) is described. *(Carl Skoggard)*

756 SIEBER, Paul. **Die Bibliothek der Allgemeinen**
as **Musikgesellschaft Zürich** [The library of the
Allgemeine Musikgesellschaft in Zurich], *Zweiter
Weltkongreß der Musikbibliotheken* (Basel; Kassel:
Bärenreiter, 1950; 1951) 7–15. In German. See no. 300
in this volume.

Description of the collection, by genre.

757 SIMON, Alicja. **Die Lautenmusikbestände der**
as **Königl. Bibliothek in Berlin** [Lute music holdings
of the Königliche Bibliothek, Berlin],
Haydn-Zentenarfeier (Leipzig: Breitkopf & Härtel;
Wien: Artaria, 1909) 212–20. In German. See no. 65 in
this volume.

The collection is now housed in the Staatsbibliothek Preußischer Kulturbesitz in Berlin.

758 SIMON, Alicja. **Lute music in Berlin libraries,**
as *Report of the Fourth Congress of the International Musical Society* (London: Novello, 1912) 71. See no. 71 in
this volume.

Summary of a paper.

759 SKEAPING, Kenneth. **The Karl Schreinzer col-**
as **lection of violin fittings,** *Music libraries and instruments* (London: Hinrichsen, 1961) 251–53. *Illus.* See
no. 406 in this volume.

The private collection of the Austrian bassist and archivist Karl Schreinzer
includes a comprehensive assortment of violin pegs, bridges, tailpieces,
templates, labels, and silhouettes; violin and viola mutes and buttons; and
violin makers' guild seals and documents. The collection was donated in
1967 to the Germanisches Nationalmuseum, Nuremberg. *(Susan Poliniak)*

760 SKORUPSKA, Zofia. **Chopiniana w zbiorach**
as **Biblioteki Kórnickiej** [Chopiniana in the collections of the Biblioteka Kórnicka], *The book of the first
international musicological congress devoted to the
works of Frederick Chopin* (Warszawa: Państwowe
Wydawnictwo Naukowe, 1963) 488–92. In Polish. See
no. 425 in this volume.

Surveys MSS and prints of the composer and other relevant documents in
the holdings of the library at the Polska Akademia Nauk, Kórnik *(PL-KO)*.

761 SONDHEIMER, Robert. **Sinfonien aus dem 18.**
as **Jahrhundert in den Basler Sammlungen**
Lucas Sarasin und Collegium Musicum [Eigh-
teenth-century symphonies in the Lucas Sarasin and
Collegium Musicum collections in Basel], *Bericht über
den musikwissenschaftlichen Kongreß in Basel* (Leipzig: Breitkopf & Härtel, 1925) 321–25. In German. See
no. 102 in this volume.

The two collections contain pre-Classic works. The Collegium Musicum
collection dates from the 1770s, the collection of Lucas Sarasin
(1730-1802) from the 1760s. Composers represented include Giovanni
Battista Sammartini, Rinaldo di Capua, Andrea Bernasconi, Wenceslaus
Joseph Spourni, Niccolò Jommelli, Pietro Nardini, Niccolò Piccinni,
Gaetano Pugnani, Anton Filz, J.C. Bach, Friedrich Schwindl, Florian
Leopold Gassmann, François-Joseph Gossec, Jan Křtitel Vaňhal, Luigi
Boccherini, Leopold Koželuh, and Christian Cannabich. A longer version
appears in the author's *Die Theorie der Sinfonie und die Beurteilung*

einzelner Sinfoniekomponisten bei den Musikschriftstellern des 18. Jahrhunderts (1925).

762
as
SUBIRÁ, José. **Importancia de los fondos de música sagrada, impresa e inédita, conservada en archivos y bibliotecas de Madrid** [The significance of the holdings of religious music, published and unpublished, in the archives and libraries of Madrid], *V Congreso Nacional de Música Sagrada* (Madrid: Gráficas Dos de Mayo, 1956) 284–91. In Spanish. See no. 331 in this volume.

Offers a brief description of the holdings of the following libraries and archives: Biblioteca Nacional, Biblioteca del Palacio Real, Real Academia de Bellas Artes de San Fernando, Real Conservatorio Superior de Música, Biblioteca Histórica Municipal, Fundación Lázaro Galdiano, Casa Ducal de Medinaceli, Cofradía de Actores (or Cofradía de Cómicos) de Nuestra Señora de la Novena, and some private libraries. *(José López-Calo)*

763
as
THIBAULT DE CHAMBURE, Geneviève. **Les collections privées de livres et d'instruments de musique d'autrefois et d'aujourd'hui** [Private collections of books and musical instruments of yesterday and today], *Music libraries and instruments* (London: Hinrichsen, 1961) 131–47. *Illus., port., facs., music.* In French. See no. 406 in this volume.

Surveys notable historic and current collections of François-Joseph Fétis, James de Rothschild, Jules Écorcheville, Alfred Cortot, Paul Hirsch, André Meyer, Henry Prunières, Anthony van Hoboken, Marc Pincherle, François Lang, and the author. *(John Berardi)*

764
as
THIBAULT DE CHAMBURE, Geneviève. **Recherches effectuées au Musée Instrumental du Conservatoire de Paris (1962-1965)** [Research carried out at the Musée Instrumental, Conservatoire de Paris, 1962-65], *Fontes artis musicae* XII/2-3 (May-Dec 1965) 209–13. *Illus., music, charts, diagr.* In French. See no. 499 in this volume.

For string instruments in the collections, research has been focused on questions relating to preservation and restoration. Wind instruments, particularly recorders, have been subjected to external and internal measurement and their acoustic qualities studied by sound spectrography. A list of the spectrographic properties of 12 recorders is appended. *(David Bloom)*

765
as
THUREN, Hjalmar. **Über die folklorischen Sammlung in Kopenhagen** [On the folklore collection in Copenhagen], *Haydn-Zentenarfeier* (Leipzig: Breitkopf & Härtel; Wien: Artaria, 1909) 303–06. In German. See no. 65 in this volume.

Discusses the Dansk Folkemindesamling in Copenhagen.

766
as
TIERSOT, Julien. **Les autographes de Beethoven à la Bibliothèque du Conservatoire de Paris** [Beethoven autographs in the Bibliothèque du Conservatoire, Paris], *Beethoven-Zentenarfeier: Internationaler musikhistorischer Kongress* (Wien: Universal, 1927) 25. In French. See no. 142 in this volume.

Summary of a paper. The collection preserves complete MSS including that of the sonata in F minor, op. 57, as well as letters, a number of sketches, and some early prints.

767
as
TUGAL, Pierre. **Pour une méthode de l'histoire de la danse: Le document et les Archives Internationales** [Toward a method of dance history: The document and the Archives Internationales], *Deuxième congrès international d'esthétique et de Science de l'art* (Paris: Librairie Félix Alcan, 1937) II, 471–73. In French. See no. 249 in this volume.

Discusses the work of the Archives Internationale de la Danse, Paris, founded in 1933.

768
as
WOLF, Johannes. **Die Schuberthandschriften der Preussischen Staatsbibliothek in Berlin** [The Schubert manuscripts of the Preußische Staatsbibliothek in Berlin], *Bericht über den internationalen Kongress für Schubertforschung* (Augsburg: Benno Filser, 1929) 149–54. *Music, charts, diagr.* In German. See no. 154 in this volume.

The collection includes 46 MSS, 164 first editions (nine with MS annotations), and three letters. Examples of passages that differ from contemporary editions are discussed, and a brief history of the collection is provided.

769
as
ZANZIG, Augustus D. **Some collections of folk songs in the library of the Pan American Union,** *Report of the Committee of the Conference on Inter-American Relations in the Field of Music* (Washington, D.C.: United States Department of State, 1940) 92–93. See no. 271 in this volume.

The collection includes items from Argentina, Brazil, Costa Rica, Ecuador, Mexico, Paraguay, and Peru.

770
as
ZEHNTNER, Hans. **Handschriftliche Musikernachlässe in schweitzer Bibliotheken** [Manuscript musicians' documents bequeathed to Swiss libraries], *Zweiter Weltkongreß der Musikbibliotheken* (Basel; Kassel: Bärenreiter, 1950; 1951) 41–46. *Charts, diagr.* In German. See no. 300 in this volume.

General discussion of collections, focusing on the Universitätsbibliothek Basel and including a list of composers (18th-20th c.) whose MSS are in that library.

03 Encyclopedias and dictionaries

771
as
ALBRECHT, Hans. **Zur Frage eines neuen musikalischen Quellenlexikons** [The question of a new dictionary of musical sources], *Compte rendu/ Kongressbericht/Report* (Basel: Bärenreiter, 1951) 37–38. In German. See no. 289 in this volume.

On the understanding that Robert Eitner's *Biographisch-bibliographisches Quellen-Lexikon* (1900-04) is no longer adequate, proposes the formation of an international committee for the cataloguing of musical MS and print sources through the end of the 18th c. or as far as 1830. *(David Bloom)*

772
as
GURLITT, Wilibald. **Ein begriffsgeschichtliches Wörterbuch der Musik** [A historically oriented dictionary of music terminology], *Société Internationale de Musicologie, cinquième congrès/Internationale Gesellschaft für Musikwissenschaft, fünfter Kongreß/International Society for Musical Research, Fifth Congress* (Amsterdam: Vereniging voor Nederlandse Muziekgeschiedenis, 1953) 211–17. In German. See no. 316 in this volume.

Discusses a major research project on musical terminology (*Handwörterbuch der musikalischen Terminologie*), initiated by the author in 1949.

773
as
SCHMID, Hans. **Plan und Durchführung des *Lexicon musicum latinum* I: Erfassung und Erforschung der musikalischen Fachsprache des Mittelalters** [Plan and implementation of the *Lexicon musicum latinum* I: Recording and researching the technical terminology of music in the Middle Ages], *Bericht über den internationalen musikwissenschaftlichen Kongreß* (Kassel: Bärenreiter, 1963) 349–50. In German. See no. 452 in this volume.

Introductory discussion of the project undertaken by the Bayerische Akademie der Wissenschaften, Munich.

774
as

WAELTNER, Ernst Ludwig. **Plan und Durchführung des** *Lexicon musicum latinum* **II: Archivaufbau mit Hilfe maschineller Datenverarbeitung** [Plan and implementation of the *Lexicon musicum latinum* II: Constructing an archive with the help of machine data processing], *Bericht über den internationalen musikwissenschaftlichen Kongreß* (Kassel: Bärenreiter, 1963) 351–52. In German. See no. 452 in this volume.

Brief account of a punch-card system used in the project at the Bayerische Akademie der Wissenschaften, Munich.

04 Catalogues of libraries, museums, exhibitions

775
as

[Basel, Zurich] **Verzeichnis von Werken der Mannheimer Symphoniker im Besitze der Universitäts-Bibliothek in Basel und der Allgemeinen Musikgesellschaft in Zürich** [Catalogue of works by the Mannheim symphonists in the collections of the Universitätsbibliothek Basel and the Allgemeine Musikgesellschaft Zurich]. By Georg WALTER, *Festschrift zum zweiten Kongreß der Internationalen Musikgesellschaft, verfaßt von Mitgliedern der Schweizerischen Landessektion und den Kongreßteilnehmern* (Basel: Reinhardt, 1906) I, 87–103. In German. See no. 54 in this volume.

776
as

[Basel] **Katalog der Musikinstrumente im Historischen Museum zu Basel** [Catalogue of musical instruments in the Historisches Museum, Basel]. By Karl NEF, *Festschrift zum zweiten Kongreß der Internationalen Musikgesellschaft, verfaßt von Mitgliedern der Schweizerischen Landessektion und den Kongreßteilnehmern* (Basel: Reinhardt, 1906) II, 1–74. *Illus.* In German. See no. 54 in this volume.

777
bm

[Florence] **Mostra bibliografica di musica italiana dalle origini alla fine del secolo XVIII** [Bibliographic exhibition of Italian music from its origins to the end of the 18th century]. By Anita MONDOLFO (Firenze: Olschki, 1937) 102 p. *Illus., facs., music.* In Italian.

A catalogue of an exhibition organized by the R. Biblioteca Nazionale Centrale, on the occasion of the second Congresso Internazionale di Musica (see no. 239 in this volume). The sections of the exhibition were dedicated to ancient MSS, theoretical works, religious music and oratorio, madrigals and chamber music, opera, Monteverdi, and autographs of works performed in Florentine theaters during the 1937 Maggio Musicale.

778
as

[Madrid] **Catálogo de los códices, manuscritos y libros musicales expuestos en el V Congreso Nacional de Música Sagrada** [Catalogue of the musical codices, manuscripts, and books exhibited in the fifth Congreso Nacional de Música Sagrada]. By Jaime MOLL ROQUETA, *V Congreso Nacional de Música Sagrada* (Madrid: Gráficas Dos de Mayo, 1956) 394–432. *Facs.* In Spanish. See no. 331 in this volume.

An exhibition was mounted at the Biblioteca Nacional, Madrid, in conjunction with the Congress. It included Visigothic-Mozarabic and Gregorian MSS (12th-18th c.), medieval monody and polyphony, theory treatises, organ music, Renaissance polyphony, Baroque polyphony in Latin and Spanish, and early and modern editions of religious music. A fuller version of the catalogue is published as *Exposición de música sagrada española: Catálogo* (Madrid: Biblioteca Nacional, 1954). *(José López-Calo)*

779
bc

[Palermo] **Mostra di manoscritti in occasione dell' VIII Congresso Internazionale di Studi Bizantini** [Exhibit of manuscripts on the occasion of the 8th International Congress of Byzantine Studies] (Palermo: Biblioteca Nazionale di Palermo, 1951) 31 p. *Illus., facs.* In Italian.

The congress report is cited as no. 308 in this volume.

780
as

[Rouen] **Les manuscrits liturgiques de Jumièges** [The liturgical manuscripts of Jumièges]. By René-Jean HESBERT, *Jumièges: Congrès scientifique du XIII. centenaire* (Rouen: Lecerf, 1955) 855–72. *Bibliog., charts, diagr.* In French. See no. 336 in this volume.

A catalogue of complete and partial missals, breviaries, ordinals, and rituals confiscated from the library of the Abbaye St.-Pierre in Jumièges during the Revolution, now in the collections of the Bibliothèque Municipale, Rouen.

781
as

[Rouen] **Les manuscrits musicaux de Jumièges** [The musical manuscripts of Jumièges]. By René-Jean HESBERT, *Jumièges: Congrès scientifique du XIII. centenaire* (Rouen: Lecerf, 1955) 901–12. *Illus., facs., charts, diagr.* In French. See no. 336 in this volume.

(1) A brief inventory of the notated music in MSS from the former collection of the Abbaye de Jumièges, confiscated during the Revolution and now in the possession of the Bibliothèque Municipale, Rouen, classified by notational style, liturgical function, and approximate date. (2) Detailed critical examination of the four important MSS in the collection that represent the historic usage in the abbey of Jumièges itself: the 12th-c. missal *F-R* MS 267 (A.401), the later 12th-c. breviary in two volumes of *F-R* MS 209-210 (Y.175), the 13th-c. antiphoner *F-R* MS 248 (A.339), and the 14th-c. gradual-sequentiary-troper *F-R* MS 250 (A.233). *(David Bloom)*

782
as

[Zoutleeuw] **Le fonds musical de l'église Saint-Léonard à Zoutleeuw (Belgique)** [The music collection of the St. Leonard church in Zoutleeuw (Belgium)]. By Arnold von der HALLEN, *Fontes artis musicae* III/2 (Dec 1956) 203–08. In French. See no. 345 in this volume.

Records 16 printed scores (by nine different composers), 22 MSS (by Bailleux, Caraffa, Carpani, Delange, Fiocco, Gregorio, Kerckhofs, Krafft, Martini, and Swillens), and 27 anonymous scores. Incipits for substantial compositions are included.

05 Thematic catalogues

783
as

ALTMANN, Wilhelm. **Über thematische Kataloge** [On thematic catalogues], *Beethoven-Zentenarfeier: Internationaler musikhistorischer Kongress* (Wien: Universal, 1927) 283–89. In German. See no. 142 in this volume.

A brief history of the thematic catalogue, beginning with the sales catalogue published by Breitkopf & Härtel in the years 1762-87. A list of recommendations are provided for the format and content of thematic catalogues compiled for scholarly purposes. *(David Bloom)*

784
as

BLUME, Friedrich. **Die Frage eines internationalen Quellenlexikons der Musik** [The question of an international lexicon of musical sources], *Troisième Congrès international des bibliothèques musicales* (Kassel: Bärenreiter, 1953) 20–24. In German. See no. 309 in this volume.

Eitner's *Biographisch-bibliographisches Quellen-Lexikon der Musik und Musikgelehrten der christlichen Zeitrechnung bis zur Mitte des neunzehten Jahrhunderts* (Leipzig, 1900-1904) must be replaced with a new source which includes data on older monodic, liturgical, and secular music, as well as older theory and literature. The shifting of sources and vast growth of libraries and information have surpassed Eitner's original information up to 1800. The new international music repertoire must include 19th-c. music and must be created by both musicologists and music librarians at national and international levels. *(Sylvia Eversole)*

785
as
BLUME, Friedrich. **Problèmes musicologiques d'un répertoire des sources musicales** [Musicological problems concerning a repertoire of musical sources], *Congrès international des bibliothèques et des centres de documentation* ('s-Gravenhage: Nijhoff, 1955-1958) I, 160–64. In French. See no. 344 in this volume.

Another version is abstracted as no. 786 in this volume.

786
as
BLUME, Friedrich. **Problèmes musicologiques d'un répertoire des sources musicales** [Musicological problems concerning a repertoire of musical sources], *Fontes artis musicae* III/1 (July 1956) 44–48. In German; summary in French. See no. 345 in this volume.

Calls for an overhauling of Robert Eitner's old RISM, expanding the domain of musical sources to include theoretical documents, methods, librettos, and other materials. Making a distinction between printed and manuscript sources is also recommended. Another version is cited as no. 785 in this volume.

787
as
BROOK, Barry S. **The simplified *Plaine and easie code system* for notating music: A proposal for international adoption,** *Fontes artis musicae* XII/2-3 (May-Dec 1965) 156–60. *Music, charts, diagr.* See no. 499 in this volume.

The system proposed by the author and Murray Gould for notating music with ordinary typewriter characters in *Fontes artis musicae* XI/3 (1964) could be used, with some modifications, as an international standard notation for incipits in thematic catalogues. *(David Bloom)*

788
as
GIRARDON, Renée. **Rapport sur la nécessité d'un nouveau *Recueil international des sources musicales*** [A report on the necessity of a new *International inventory of musical sources*], *Troisième Congrès international des bibliothèques musicales* (Kassel: Bärenreiter, 1953) 32–36. In French. See no. 309 in this volume.

There is a need to elaborate and enlarge the original committee working on RISM and to enlarge the scope to include all materials of all countries. *(Edwin D. Wallace)*

789
as
HILL, Richard S. **The U.S. position on the *International inventory of musical sources*,** *Troisième Congrès international des bibliothèques musicales* (Kassel: Bärenreiter, 1953) 28–32. See no. 309 in this volume.

Describes the U.S. participation in the revision of Eitner's *Quellen-Lexikon*, recommending a selective and limited contribution that can be expanded later. *(Edwin D. Wallace)*

790
as
JACQUOT, Jean. **The international catalogue of music for the lute and kindred instruments,** *Music libraries and instruments* (London: Hinrichsen, 1961) 214–17. See no. 406 in this volume.

Progress report on efforts since the congress *Le luth et sa musique* at Neuilly-sur-Seine, 1957 (see no. 377 in this volume). *(Susan Poliniak)*

791
as
KOLLER, Oswald. **Wie könnte ein thematischer Katalog der Messen-, Motetten- und Madrigalliteratur des XV. und XVI. Jahrhunderts eingerichtet werden?** [How could we assemble a thematic catalogue of the Mass, motet, and madrigal literature of the 15th and 16th centuries?], *Bericht über den zweiten Kongress der Internationalen Musikgesellschaft* (Leipzig: Breitkopf & Härtel, 1907) 194. In German. See no. 53 in this volume.

It should be possible for the catalogue to be created in the form of a movable card catalogue. Working principles should be established by a central organ of the International Musical Society, which could prepare a sample catalogue for a single MS and make it available for comment to the society as a whole. *(David Bloom)*

792
as
KROHN, Ilmari. **Über das lexikalische Ordnen von Volksmelodien** [The lexical ordering of traditional-music melodies], *Bericht über den zweiten Kongress der Internationalen Musikgesellschaft* (Leipzig: Breitkopf & Härtel, 1907) 66–74. *Transcr.* In German. See no. 53 in this volume.

Methods used by the author in establishing a thematic-index order for the collection *Suomen kansan sävelmiä* (beginning 1893) are outlined and compared with methods that might be applied to a collection of Sámi melodies. An extended discussion is published in *Welche ist die beste Methode um Volks- und volksmäßige Melodien nach ihrer melodischen (nicht textlichen) Beschaffenheit lexikalisch zu ordnen?* (*Sammelbände der Internationalen Musik-Gesellschaft* 4, 1902-03). *(David Bloom)*

793
as
LESURE, François. **Quelques conséquences bibliographiques et techniques d'un répertoire international des sources musicales** [Some technical and bibliographical consequences of an international catalogue of musical sources], *Fontes artis musicae* III/1 (July 1956) 49–50. In French. See no. 345 in this volume.

RISM cannot possibly be a definitive work, but should simply lead the researcher in the direction of obscure sources. An expanded RISM will lead to far greater international exchange and reprinting. Another version is cited as no. 794 in this volume.

794
as
LESURE, François. **Quelques conséquences bibliographiques et techniques d'un répertoire international des sources musicales** [Some technical and bibliographical consequences of an international repertoire of musical sources], *Congrès international des bibliothèques et des centres de documentation* ('s-Gravenhage: Nijhoff, 1955-1958) I, 165–66. In French. See no. 344 in this volume.

Another version is abstracted as no. 793 in this volume.

795
as
LESURE, François. **Le RISM: Deux ans d'expérience** [RISM: Two years of experience], *Fontes artis musicae* III/1 (July 1956) 144–47. In French. See no. 345 in this volume.

Discusses both conceptual and organizational aspects of the Répertoire International des Sources Musicales, emphasizing cooperation among librarians and musicologists. Another version is cited as no. 796 in this volume.

796
as
LESURE, François. **Le RISM: Deux ans d'expérience** [RISM: Two years of experience], *Congrès international des bibliothèques et des centres de documentation* ('s-Gravenhage: Nijhoff, 1955-1958) III. In French. See no. 344 in this volume.

Another version is abstracted as no. 795 in this volume.

797
as
STÄBLEIN, Bruno. **Der thematische Katalog der mittelalterlischen einstimmigen Melodien** [The thematic catalogue of monophonic medieval melodies], *Zweiter Weltkongreß der Musikbibliotheken* (Basel; Kassel: Bärenreiter, 1950; 1951) 52–54. In German. See no. 300 in this volume.

Discusses the priorities for such a catalogue, including completeness where possible and a means for quickly identifying melodies.

798 WEINHOLD, Liesbeth. **RISM im Rahmen der**
as **Musikdokumentation** [RISM in the framework of
music documentation], *Bericht über den internationalen musikwissenschaftlichen Kongreß* (Kassel:
Bärenreiter, 1963) 341–42. In German. See no. 452 in
this volume.
Discusses the goals and methodology of the Répertoire International des
Sources Musicales.

799 ZEHNTNER, Hans. **À propos de la refonte d'un**
as *Répertoire international des sources musicales*
[On the refashioning of an *International repertoire of
musical sources*], *Troisième Congrès international des
bibliothèques musicales* (Kassel: Bärenreiter, 1953)
24–28. In French. See no. 309 in this volume.
Examines the progress of the revisions made to Eitner's *Bibliographie der
Musik-Sammelwerke des XVI. und XVII. Jahrhunderts* (Berlin, 1877) and
*Biographisch-bibliographisches Quellen-Lexikon der Musiker und Musik-
gelehrten der christlichen Zeitrechnung bis zur Mitte des neunzehnten
Jahrhunderts* (Leipzig, 1900-04), first proposed by Hans Albrecht in 1949,
and proposes various modifications in structure and design of entries.

06 General bibliographies

800 CASTRILLO HERNÁNDEZ, Gonzalo. **Notes**
as **bibliographiques pour l'étude du chant**
populaire en vielle Castille [Bibliographical notes
toward the study of traditional song in old Castile],
*Congrès international des arts populaires/Interna-
tional congress of popular arts* (Paris: Institut international de coopération intellectuelle, 1928) 105. In
French. See no. 153 in this volume.
Summary of the paper abstracted as no. 2760 in this volume.

801 FLOOD, William Henry Grattan. **Irish musical**
as **bibliography,** *Report of the Fourth Congress of the
International Musical Society* (London: Novello, 1912)
359–63. *Bibliog.* See no. 71 in this volume.
Lists sources for Irish traditional music from 1725 to 1905.

802 JOVANOVIĆ, Živorad. **Bibliografija o folkloru**
as **Bosne i Hercegovine** [Bibliography of the folklore
of Bosnia and Herzegovina], *Rad IX-og kongresa
Saveza Folklorista Jugoslavije* (Sarajevo: Savez
Udruženja Folklorista Jugoslavije, 1963) 159–66.
Bibliog. In Serbian. See no. 455 in this volume.
Lists collections and scholarly discussions published in Bosnian, Croatian,
and Serbian from 1882 through 1958.

803 MARTÍNEZ TORNER, Eduardo Fernando.
as **Bibliographie du folklore musical espagnole**
[Bibliography of Spanish musical folklore], *Congrès
international des arts populaires/International congress of popular arts* (Paris: Institut international de
coopération intellectuelle, 1928) 91. In French. See no.
153 in this volume.
Summary of the paper abstracted as no. 820 in this volume.

07 Music bibliographies

804 CAFFARELLI, Filippo. *Opera omnia* **di G.B.**
as **Pergolesi** [*Opera omnia* of G.B. Pergolesi], *G.B.
Pergolesi, 1710-1736: Note e documenti, raccolti in
occasione della settimana celebrativa* (Siena: Ticci

Editore Libraio, 1942) 57–62. In Italian. See no. 273 in
this volume.
A listing of Pergolesi's works as published in the first edition of *Opera omnia di Giov. Batt. Pergolesi* (1939-1942). *(Mark Stevens)*

805 CEROVIĆ, Emilija. **Prilog bibliografiji**
as **narodnog stvaralaštva u narodnooslobodilačkoj borbi (1941-1945)** [A contribution to the
bibliography of music of the People's Revolution
(1941-1945)], *Rad VIII-og kongresa folklorista
Jugoslavije* (Beograd: Naučno Delo, 1961) 309–17.
Port., bibliog., list of works. In Serbian. See no. 446 in
this volume.
A list of collections and individual revolutionary songs, issued in liberated
territories of Yugoslavia.

806 HINRICHSEN, Max. **Music for the student of**
as **the organ,** *Organ and choral aspects and prospects*
(London: Hinrichsen, 1958) 63–95. *List of works.* See
no. 375 in this volume.
A classified checklist culled from the catalogues of Peters and Hinrichsen
editions.

807 LESURE, François. **Recueils français du**
as **XVIIIᵉ siècle: Datations** [Eighteenth-century
French compilations: Dating], *Fontes artis musicae*
III/2 (Dec 1956) 209–19. In French. See no. 345 in this
volume.
Presents a list of 109 publications, from between 1750 and 1790, based on
their press announcements (advertisements).

808 STRARAM, Enrich. **Problèmes relatifs à**
as **l'établissement d'un inventaire international**
des œuvres dont les matériels d'exécution
n'existent qu'à de très rares exemplaires [Prob-
lems relating to the establishment of an international inventory of works whose performing materials have not
been mass-produced], *Fontes artis musicae* III/1 (July
1956) 112–15. *Charts, diagr.* In French. See no. 345 in
this volume.
Radio-France has a large collection of scores available for public loan. A
proposed international radio library cataloguing system is outlined. Another version is cited as no. 809 in this volume.

809 STRARAM, Enrich. **Problèmes relatifs à**
as **l'établissement d'un inventaire international**
des œuvres dont les matériels d'exécution
n'existent qu'à de très rares exemplaires [Prob-
lems relating to the compilation of an international inventory of works whose performing materials have not
been mass-produced], *Congrès international des
bibliothèques et des centres de documentation*
('s-Gravenhage: Nijhoff, 1955-1958) II, 41–44. In
French. See no. 344 in this volume.
Another version is abstracted as no. 808 in this volume.

810 VELIMIROVIĆ, Miloš. **Preparation of an in-**
as **ventory of sources of old Slavic music,** *Anfänge
der slavischen Musik* (Bratislava: Slovenská Akadémia
Vied, 1966) 173–78. See no. 477 in this volume.
A comprehensive catalogue is needed for early Slavic music sources
housed in libraries throughout the world. The major collections should be
microfilmed, and the microfilms housed in a central library. RISM should
possibly be called on for assistance. *(Brian Doherty)*

811 ZANETTI, Emilia. **Contributo a una biblio-**
as **grafia della musica sacra di G.B. Pergolesi**
[Contribution to a bibliography of G.B. Pergolesi's sa-

cred music], *G.B. Pergolesi, 1710-1736: Note e documenti, raccolti in occasione della settimana celebrativa* (Siena: Ticci Editore Libraio, 1942) 89–100. In Italian. See no. 273 in this volume.
A list of MS sources and published editions of religious works.

08 Bibliographies of music literature

812
as
BARTHA, Dénes. **Die ungarische Musikforschung des letzten Jahrzehnts: Ein Literaturbericht** [Hungarian music research of the last decade: A bibliographic report], *Bericht über den internationalen musikwissenschaftlichen Kongreß Wien Mozartjahr 1956* (Graz; Köln: Böhlau, 1958) 22–27. *Bibliog.* In German. See no. 365 in this volume.
Reviews the state of research in ethnomusicology, the history and publication history of art music by composers of Hungarian birth and active in Hungary, source studies particularly for the medieval period, and studies of the influence of traditional Hungarian music on art music. *(Carol K. Baron)*

813
as
COOVER, James B. **A bibliography of east European music periodicals (II),** *Fontes artis musicae* IV/2 (Dec 1957) 97–102. *Bibliog.* See no. 373 in this volume.
Part I is cited as no. 814 in this volume.

814
as
COOVER, James B. **A bibliography of East European music periodicals. I,** *Fontes artis musicae* III/2 (Dec 1956) 219–26. See no. 345 in this volume.
Presents Bulgaria. Part II is cited as no. 813 in this volume.

815
as
DREIMÜLLER, Karl. **Verzeichnis eigener Veröffentlichungen zur Mönchengladbacher Musikgeschichte** [Catalogue of the author's publications on Mönchengladbach music history], *Studien zur Musikgeschichte der Stadt Mönchengladbach* (Köln: Volk, 1965) 35–40. *Bibliog.* In German. See no. 486 in this volume.
Lists periodical articles from 1931 through 1963 in four groups: (1) history of music and of the library at the abbey of St. Vitus in Mönchengladbach; (2) history of organs in Mönchengladbach and vicinity; (3) general music history and musical life; and (4) studies of individual musicians.

816
as
HOBOHM, Wolf. **Verzeichnis des Telemann-Schrifttums: Auswahl** [Catalogue of writings on Telemann: Selections], *Beiträge zu einem neuen Telemannbild* (Magdeburg: Vorwärts, 1963) 83–93. *Bibliog.* In German. See no. 453 in this volume.
Includes biographical materials, writings on the composer's works (by genre), and studies of his reception, in his own time and in the present. *(John Stansell)*

817
as
KINSKY, Georg. **Stand und Aufgaben der neueren Instrumentenkunde: Ein Bibliographischer Überblick** [The current state and the tasks of modern organology: A bibliographic survey], *Bericht über den I. musikwissenschaftlichen Kongress der Deutschen Musikgesellschaft in Leipzig* (Wiesbaden: Breitkopf & Härtel, 1926) 78–79. In German. See no. 120 in this volume.
Includes catalogues of instruments in German museums and Baroque writings on organology.

818
as
KRUTTGE, Eigel. **Zur Musikgeschichte Westfalens** [On the music history of Westphalia], *Bericht über den I. musikwissenschaftlichen Kongress der Deutschen Musikgesellschaft in Leipzig* (Wiesbaden: Breitkopf & Härtel, 1926) 397. In German. See no. 120 in this volume.
A bibliographic survey of music history publications centering on the town of Münster.

819
as
LINDLAR, Heinrich. **Chopin in der deutschen Musikkritik seiner Zeit** [Chopin in the German music criticism of his time], *The book of the first international musicological congress devoted to the works of Frederick Chopin* (Warszawa: Państwowe Wydawnictwo Naukowe, 1963) 334. In German. See no. 425 in this volume.
Summary of a paper, listing some important notices and reviews from the period 1829-50.

820
as
MARTÍNEZ TORNER, Eduardo Fernando. **Bibliographie du folklore musical espagnole** [Bibliography of Spanish musical folklore], *Art populaire: Travaux artistiques et scientifiques du Ier Congrès international des arts populaires* (Paris: Duchartre, 1931) 159–61. In French. See no. 152 in this volume.
Lists publications to 1928: 58 items on theory and 105 collections, including works in Spanish, Catalan, and Basque. A summary is cited as no. 803 in this volume. *(David Bloom)*

821
as
SCHUELLER, Herbert M. **Musical expression: Research in the last two decades,** *Pepragmena tou 4. diethnous synedriou aisthītikīs/Actes du IV Congrès international d'esthétique/Proceedings of the IV International Congress on Aesthetics* (Athínai: conference, 1962) 428–31. See no. 415 in this volume.
A bibliographical overview.

822
as
SÉBILLOT, Paul. **La littérature orale en France: Bibliographie des éditions françaises** [Oral literature in France: Bibliography of French publications], *[I^{e}] Congrès international des traditions populaires* (Paris: Société d'Éditions Scientifiques, 1891). In French. See no. 13 in this volume.

823
as
SPRINGER, Hermann Wilhelm. **Die internationale Verzeichnung der älteren Musikliteratur** [The international cataloguing of early music literature], *Haydn-Zentenarfeier* (Leipzig: Breitkopf & Härtel; Wien: Artaria, 1909) 428–29. In German. See no. 65 in this volume.

824
as
TORREFRANCA, Fausto. **La bibliografia della musica theorica e la necessità di una bibliografia italiana a tutto l'Ottocento** [The bibliography of music theory and the necessity for an Italian bibliography for the entire 19th century], *Primo Congresso mondiale delle biblioteche e di bibliografia* (Roma: Libreria dello Stato, 1931-1933) III, 105–12. *Charts, diagr.* In Italian. See no. 161 in this volume.
There is a need for complete bibliographic resources in the area of Italian music theory—essentially, a national bibliography of music theory. Statistics about the works on theory held in the Biblioteca del Liceo Comunale in Bologna, broken down by era, are supplied.

09 Discographies

825
as
BRITTEN, Valentine; CLOUGH, Francis F.; CUMING, Geoffrey. **Problems of an international gramophone record catalogue,** *Fontes*

artis musicae III/1 (July 1956) 95–108. See no. 345 in this volume.

Outlines the obstacles in collecting a comprehensive international discography, including the difficulties of accurate classification. Another version is cited as no. 826 in this volume.

826
as
BRITTEN, Valentine; CLOUGH, Francis F.; CUMING, Geoffrey. **Problems of an international gramophone record catalogue,** *Congrès international des bibliothèques et des centres de documentation* ('s-Gravenhage: Nijhoff, 1955-1958) II, 24–37. See no. 344 in this volume.

Another version is abstracted as no. 825 in this volume.

827
as
LACHMANN, Robert. **Commission de l'Enregistrement: Rapport** [The Commission on Recording: A report], *Recueil des travaux du Congrès de musique arabe* (Al-Qāhirah: Boulac, 1934) 89–130. *Discog.* In French. See no. 196 in this volume.

Participants at the 1932 Cairo Congress on Arab Music (Mu'tamar al-Mūsīqá al-'Arabiyyah) included musicians from Algeria, Egypt, Iraq, Lebanon, Morocco, Syria, Tunisia, and Turkey. Recordings providing a comprehensive documentation of their performances were made on wax cylinders and subsequently distributed on some 175 78-rpm discs by His Master's Voice UK. The list of recordings is accompanied by a statement of principles of selection and documentation used by the commission on recordings, and a brief analytic report on field recordings made by the author in Egypt subsequent to the conference. *(David Bloom)*

12 Directories

828
as
BÖHME, Erdmann Werner. **150 Lüneburger Musiker-Namen** [150 names of Lüneburg musicians], *Kongreß-Bericht: Gesellschaft für Musikforschung* (Kassel; Basel: Bärenreiter, 1950) 246. In German. See no. 299 in this volume.

Describes a register of Lüneburg musicians from 1532 to 1864 taken from records in the city archives.

UNIVERSAL PERSPECTIVES

19 General

829
as
ALDRICH, Putnam. **The role of improvised and written ornamentation in the evolution of musical language,** *Report of the Eighth Congress of the International Musicological Society. II: Reports* (Kassel: Bärenreiter, 1962) 166–71. *Music.* See no. 440 in this volume.

A report on a roundtable consisting of Putnam ALDRICH, Robert DONINGTON, Edith GERSON-KIWI, Imogene HORSLEY, Erwin R. JACOBI, Otto KINKELDEY, and the authors of the following papers abstracted in this volume, which furnished the basis for the discussion: Solange CORBIN (no. 1077), Ernest FERAND (no. 961), Claudie MARCEL-DUBOIS (no. 2939), Gilbert ROUGET (no. 2580), Geneviève THIBAULT DE CHAMBURE (nos. 854 and 1199), and TRẦN Van Khê (no. 2700).

830
as
ANDERSSON, Otto. **Folk music and art music,** *Journal of the International Folk Music Council* III (1951) 85. See no. 296 in this volume.

Summary of a paper comparing traditional and Western art musics, and discussing their mutual influences.

831
as
ASHTON, Roger. **The basic details of variance between music in India and the West,** *Music east and west* (Nai Dilli: Indian Council for Cultural Relations, 1966) 48–56. See no. 489 in this volume.

Discusses tonality, scales, harmony, rhythm, structure, ornamentation, and social and cultural context.

832
as
BAUD-BOVY, Samuel. **The problems of the preservation of traditional forms,** *The preservation of traditional forms of the learned and popular music of the Orient and the Occident/La préservation des formes traditionelles de la musique savante et populaire dans les pays d'Orient et d'Occident* (Urbana: Center for Comparative Psycholinguistics, Institute of Communications Research, 1964) 58–62. See no. 443 in this volume.

Classical traditions of East and West are valued by audiences, and their preservation can be left to professional musicians and conservatories. Folk traditions cannot strictly be preserved at all, as they are bound to social conditions that inevitably change; they can and should, however, be recorded, notated, taught to schoolchildren, and used as entertainment. *(Judith Drogichen Meyer)*

833
as
BELJAEV, Viktor Mihailovič. **Folk music and the history of music,** *Studia musicologica Academiae Scientiarum Hungaricae* VII (1965) 19–23. See no. 478 in this volume.

Folk songs formed the basis of musical language, and later of professional musical art. In every phase of musical development, folklore has played a determining role. *(David Gagné)*

834
as
CROSSLEY-HOLLAND, Peter. **Problems and opportunities in listening to the music of another civilization,** *Music east and west* (Nai Dilli: Indian Council for Cultural Relations, 1966) 103–11. See no. 489 in this volume.

Discusses what happens when a European listens to Indian music and vice versa. Mutual readjustment is dependent upon understanding. *(Lee James Kotsambas)*

835
as
CVETKO, Dragotin. **The problem of the process of listening to and of making Western and Indian music,** *Music east and west* (Nai Dilli: Indian Council for Cultural Relations, 1966) 112–17. See no. 489 in this volume.

Philosophical and aesthetic views that are very different from those of the Western world have had a direct effect on Indian music.

836 DANIÉLOU, Alain. **Conscious or haphazard**
as **evolution in music,** *Music east and west* (Nai Dilli: Indian Council for Cultural Relations, 1966) 11–15. See no. 489 in this volume.

The main obligation of traditional musicians is to preserve their heritage and avoid hybridization. Contemporary musical practices cannot be taught, since they are still evolving. *(Beverly Eskreis)*

837 DANIÉLOU, Alain. **Establishment of the dis-**
as **tinction between the main "families" of music according to the different fundamental systems,** *The preservation of traditional forms of the learned and popular music of the Orient and the Occident/La préservation des formes traditionelles de la musique savante et populaire dans les pays d'Orient et d'Occident* (Urbana: Center for Comparative Psycholinguistics, Institute of Communications Research, 1964) 132–40. See no. 443 in this volume.

Rather than two great heritages in music, Occidental and Oriental, we should count four: the Indo-Iranian-Byzantine–ancient European modal family, using the tetrachord; the Pythagorean pentatonic family of East and Central Asia; an archaic and completely independent polyphonic system preserved in Cambodia, Thailand, Laos, Java, and Bali; and the predominantly rhythmic system originating in Africa. *(Judith Drogichen Meyer)*

838 DANIÉLOU, Alain. **Le folklore et l'histoire de**
as **la musique** [Folklore and the history of music], *Studia musicologica Academiae Scientiarum Hungaricae* VII (1965) 41–45. In French. See no. 478 in this volume.

In every country and epoch, folklore is the basis upon which more sophisticated musical language rests. Many characteristics of traditional music are too subtle to be measured by standard forms of notation and analysis. *(Daniel Horn)*

839 DANIÉLOU, Alain. **Values in music,** *Artistic val-*
as *ues in traditional music* (Berlin: International Institute for Comparative Music Studies, 1966) 10–18. See no. 493 in this volume.

In addition to their technical differences, musics of various cultures have different philosophical, religious, and intellectual meanings. A thorough study of each musical language will allow comparison of their respective possibilities.

840 FINSCHER, Ludwig. **Origins of Western po-**
as **lyphony,** *Report of the Eighth Congress of the International Musicological Society. II: Reports* (Kassel: Bärenreiter, 1962) 107–11. In German. See no. 440 in this volume.

A report on a discussion by Walter WIORA, William G. WAITE, Gerald ABRAHAM, Higini ANGLÈS, Solange CORBIN, Luther A. DITTMER, Karl Gustav FELLERER, Arnold GEERING, Ewald JAMMERS, Bruno NETTL, Gustave REESE, Klaus P. WACHSMANN, and Joseph SMITS VAN WAESBERGHE of papers by Marius Schneider and by Waite abstracted as nos. 1005 and 1209 in this volume.

841 HACOBIAN, Zaven. **L'improvisation et**
as **l'ornementation en Orient et en Occident** [Improvisation and ornamentation in the Orient and Occident], *Journal of the International Folk Music Council* XVI (1964) 74–76. In French. See no. 463 in this volume.

The term "improvisation" is too general, and can create misunderstandings between Western and Asian musicologists. The performance of the great Eastern musics, with the strictness and detail of its practice and transmission, should perhaps be called "the realization of a mode". There is much in common between ornamentation techniques as used in the great Asian musics and as they were used in 17th- and 18th-c. Europe. *(David Bloom)*

842 JUNIUS, Manfred M. **On the differences and**
as **similarities of structure in Indian and Western**

music, *Music east and west* (Nai Dilli: Indian Council for Cultural Relations, 1966) 66–72. See no. 489 in this volume.

Western music is marked by a linear, additive structure driven by thematic opposition; Indian music is circular, with themes in complementary relation. The same structural difference is to be found in visual arts, dance, and the concept of infinity. *(Beverly Eskreis)*

843 KOELLREUTTER, Hans-Joachim. **Indian and**
as **Western music as the extension of different attitudes of consciousness,** *Music east and west* (Nai Dilli: Indian Council for Cultural Relations, 1966) 43–47. See no. 489 in this volume.

The different attitudes should be seen not as opposite, but as complementary. Increased contact and exchange of ideas are leading to a third, integrating attitude. *(David Bloom)*

844 KOELLREUTTER, Hans-Joachim *et al.* **The**
as **structural differences and similarities of Indian and Western music: The discussion,** *Music east and west* (Nai Dilli: Indian Council for Cultural Relations, 1966) 97–99. See no. 489 in this volume.

A roundtable consisting of Roger ASHTON, Manfred M. JUNIUS, János KÁRPÁTI, Lothar LUTZE, Nicolas NABOKOV, Chandrasekhar PANT, and Rosette RENSHAW.

845 LASCELLES, George Henry Hubert, Earl of
as Harewood et al. **The psychology of the musician and of the listener: The discussion,** *Music east and west* (Nai Dilli: Indian Council for Cultural Relations, 1966) 129–33. See no. 489 in this volume.

A roundtable consisting of Peter CROSSLEY-HOLLAND, Amir KHAN, Hans-Joachim KOELLREUTTER, Yehudi MENUHIN, Nicolas NABOKOV, Chandrasekhar PANT, and Ravi SHANKAR.

846 MENON, Narayana et al. **Music East and West:**
as **Concluding session,** *Music east and west* (Nai Dilli: Indian Council for Cultural Relations, 1966) 197–212. See no. 489 in this volume.

A roundtable consisting of Dragotin CVETKO, Charles Louis FABRI, Nicholas GOLDSCHMIDT, Humayun KABIR, George Henry Hubert LASCELLES (Earl of Harewood), Yehudi MENUHIN, Nicolas NABOKOV, and Hans Heinz STUCKENSCHMIDT.

847 MENUHIN, Yehudi. **Artistic values,** *Artistic val-*
as *ues in traditional music* (Berlin: International Institute for Comparative Music Studies, 1966) 8–9. See no. 493 in this volume.

Artistic value does not reside in the goodness of the object, but in the extent to which the object captures and transfigures a moment of reality. Thus, a very high level of art is to be found among cultures hitherto discounted. *(author)*

848 MEYER, Ernst Hermann. **Evolution in music,**
as *Music east and west* (Nai Dilli: Indian Council for Cultural Relations, 1966) 24–27. See no. 489 in this volume.

Both Western music, in the development of polyphony, and Indian music, in the development of melody, have evolved musical systems that evoke human dilemmas in subtle artistic detail. European musicians can enrich their art through a deeper understanding of the improvisation and inwardness of Indian music. *(Beverly Eskreis)*

849 MYERS, Charles Samuel. **Beitrag zum Studium**
as **der Anfänge der Musik** [Contribution to the study of the origins of music], *Kongress für Ästhetik und allgemeine Kunstwissenschaft: Bericht* (Stuttgart: Enke, 1914) 430–44. In German. See no. 86 in this volume.

850
as

PINON, Roger. **Philologie et folklore musical: Les chants de pâtres avant leur émergence folklorique** [Philology and musical folklore: Shepherds' songs before their emergence as folklore], *Journal of the International Folk Music Council* XIV (1962) 7–15. *Music, charts, diagr., transcr.* In French. See no. 442 in this volume.

Considerable valuable evidence on the ethnographic and musical character of shepherds' and cowherds' calls, songs, and instrumental music exists in the imaginative literature of Egyptian, Greek, and Roman antiquity and that of medieval and Renaissance France. There are even identifiable shepherds' melodies used as compositional material in music of the 12th and 13th c., and directly notated in works such as the 16th-c. *Le traité de vénérie* of Jacques Du Fouilloux. *(David Bloom)*

851
as

ROY, R.L. **Traditional music between a culture and a civilization,** *Music east and west* (Nai Dilli: Indian Council for Cultural Relations, 1966) 171–78. See no. 489 in this volume.

Discusses the contrast between musics of agrarian cultures and urban civilizations, with reference to ancient India, Phoenicia, and Egypt, and modern India, Japan, and England, from sociological, philological, and musicological viewpoints. *(Laurence Morell)*

852
as

SHUKLA, Narendrarai N. *et al.* **Evolution in music: The discussion,** *Music east and west* (Nai Dilli: Indian Council for Cultural Relations, 1966) 38–40. See no. 489 in this volume.

A roundtable consisting of Alain DANIÉLOU, B.R. DEODHAR, Mantle HOOD, George Henry Hubert LASCELLES (Earl of Harewood), Ernst Hermann MEYER, Nicolas NABOKOV, Chandrasekhar PANT, N.S. RAMACHANDRAN, Rosette RENSHAW, P. SAMBAMOORTHY, Thakur Jaidevâ SINGH, and Antonín SYCHRA.

853
as

SZABOLCSI, Bence. **Folk music—art music—history of music,** *Studia musicologica Academiae Scientiarum Hungaricae* VII (1965) 171–79. See no. 478 in this volume.

Although European musicology has tended to focus on the differences between traditional and art musics, they are closely related in many respects. Both represent the taste and style of a community and its evolution. Traditional music interpreters exercise a degree of freedom and variation analagous to the traditions of ornamentation and improvisation in Western art music. In both, a limited number of fundamental musical ideas yield richly varied results. *(David Gagné)*

854
as

THIBAULT DE CHAMBURE, Geneviève. **Du rôle de l'ornementation, improvisée ou écrite, dans l'évolution de la musique** [The role of improvised and written ornamentation in the evolution of music], *Report of the Eighth Congress of the International Musicological Society. I: Papers* (Kassel: Bärenreiter, 1961) 425–27. In French. See no. 439 in this volume.

Introductory remarks to a symposium drawing together ornamentation studies from historical musicology and ethnomusicology. *(David Bloom)*

855
as

VIERKANDT, Alfred. **Prinzipienfragen der ethnologischen Kunstforschung** [Fundamental questions of ethnologically oriented research on art], *Zeitschrift für Ästhetik und allgemeine Kunstwissenschaft* XIX (1925) 338–55. In German. See no. 114 in this volume.

Technological progress may lead to an enrichment of expressive means, as has been the case with music, or the reverse, as with dance. In a response, Richard THURNWALD argues that artistic expression is a permanent feature of all cultures. *(David Bloom)*

856
as

WINCKEL, Fritz. **Aspects of information theory in relation to comparative music studies,** *Artistic values in traditional music* (Berlin: International Institute for Comparative Music Studies, 1966) 124–26. See no. 493 in this volume.

Discusses a search for universal musical laws, analogous to new developments in physics, that would allow translation of content from one musical culture to another.

The International Congress of Musicology, New York, 1939 (see no. 266).
Standing: Harold Spivacke, Otto Kinkeldey, Otto Gombosi, Knud Jeppesen, Fernando Liuzzi, Gustave Reese.
Seated: Edward J. Dent, Carleton Sprague Smith, Curt Sachs, Alfred Einstein, Dayton C. Miller.
Reproduced with permission of the Americal Musicological Society.

HISTORICAL MUSICOLOGY (WESTERN MUSIC)

20 The discipline

857
as
ADLER, Guido. **Zur Periodisierung der Musikgeschichte** [On the periodization of music history], *Report of the Fourth Congress of the International Musical Society* (London: Novello, 1912) 76. In German. See no. 71 in this volume.
Summary of a paper that critiques the concept of style periods; an extended version is published as *Der Stil in der Musik* (Leipzig: Breitkopf & Härtel, 1911).

858
as
ANGLÈS, Higini. **L'œuvre de l'Institut espagnol de musicologie** [The work of the Instituto Español de Musicología], *Compte rendu/Kongressbericht/Report* (Basel: Bärenreiter, 1951) 50–54. In French. See no. 289 in this volume.
The Instituto Español de Musicología is charged with the inventorying and cataloguing of early Spanish music; publishing the series *Monumentos de la música española*; creating an archive of works in photographic and microform reproductions; collecting and publishing traditional dance and songs of the regions of Spain in a *Cancionero popular*; preparing resources for biobibliographical data on Spanish musicians; and publishing monographs and the *Anuario musical*. Topics of particular interest to the Instituto are genres such as instrumental variations, frottola, villancico, and madrigal, and ethnomusicological research in general. *(Scott Fruehwald)*

859
as
BENTON, Rita. **Early musical scholarship in the United States,** *Fontes artis musicae* XI/1 (Jan-Apr 1964) 12–21. *Bibliog.* See no. 457 in this volume.
Surveys the initial development of specialized musical publishing, academic institutions, and libraries, together with the individual contributions of John Sullivan Dwight in criticism, Alexander Wheelock Thayer in biography, Lowell Mason in pedagogy, Oscar Sonneck in U.S. music history and libraries, and Otto Kinkeldey in academic musicology.
(Priscilla P. Hodges)

860
as
BERNET KEMPERS, Karel Philippus. **Das Entstehen von Tonsystemen** [The origin of tonal systems], *Proceedings of the First International Congress of Phonetic Sciences: First meeting of the Internationale Arbeitsgemeinschaft für Phonologie* (Harlem: J. Enschedé, 1933) 39–40. In German. See no. 194 in this volume.

861
as
BERNHARDT, Karl-Fritz. **Zur musikschöpferischen Emanzipation der Frau** [The emancipation of woman composers], *Bericht über den internationalen musikwissenschaftlichen Kongreß* (Kassel: Bärenreiter, 1957) 55–58. *Bibliog.* In German. See no. 356 in this volume.
Briefly discusses the state of research on women composers as it has developed since the mid-19th c.

862
as
BERNOULLI, Eduard. **Über die Schweizerische Musikgesellschaft** [On the Schweizerische Musikgesellschaft], *Haydn-Zentenarfeier* (Leipzig: Breitkopf & Härtel; Wien: Artaria, 1909) 473–84. In German. See no. 65 in this volume.

Presents an overview of the Société de Musique Helvétique/ Schweizerische Musikgesellschaft and activities of the institution, founded in 1808 in Lucern.

863
as
BLUME, Friedrich. **Musikforschung und Musikleben** [Music research and musical life], *Bericht über den Internationalen musikwissenschaftlichen Kongress* (Kassel: Bärenreiter, 1954) 7–23. In German. See no. 319 in this volume.
Surveys the reciprocal relationship between music research and musical life, with particular attention to the German-speaking countries. Since the days of Mozart and Haydn, the two have developed within an organic whole, each nurturing the other. Today there is a danger that specialization in music research will render it irrelevant to the questions posed by modern musical life. *(Carl Skoggard)*

864
as
BOBILLIER, Marie (Michel Brenet). **La musicologie** [Musicology], *Rapport sur la musique contemporaine française* (Roma: Armani & Stein, 1913) 15–19. In French. See no. 76 in this volume.
Surveys French musicology during the 19th c.

865
as
BRĂILOIU, Constantin. **Musicologie et ethnomusicologie aujourd'hui** [Musicology and ethnomusicology today], *Bericht über den siebenten internationalen musikwissenschaftlichen Kongress* (Kassel: Bärenreiter, 1959) 17–29. In French. See no. 390 in this volume.
Long before ethnomusicology was established as a discipline, writers were making ethnomusicological judgments. Today most of these seem absurd; for example, Montaigne's belief that the villanelles of Gascoigne were related to the primitive chants of indigenous Americans. Generally, ethnocentrism has nurtured intolerance, as in the case of Berlioz and his frenetic invectives against Chinese and Indian music, and his conviction that Italians were incapable of producing symphonies. But the advent of ethnomusicology did not banish such nonsense. The same kind of thinking has persisted within the discipline, with its search for mythic origins, its grandiose system-building, its excessive trust in new techologies such as the phonograph, and its myopia toward the traditional music of Europe. As for musicologists, there are signs that they are finally coming to appreciate the contributions that oral tradition can make to their own discipline.
(Carl Skoggard)

866
as
DEUTSCH, Otto Erich. **Dokumentarische Biographien** [Documentary biographies], *Bericht über den internationalen musikwissenschaftlichen Kongreß* (Kassel: Bärenreiter, 1963) 337–39. In German. See no. 452 in this volume.
A general discussion of the genre, its requirements, and its value.

867
as
DWELSHAUVERS, Georges. **Programme des recherches à faire dans les fonds musicaux de la province de Liège** [Program of research to be done in music collections of the province of Liège], *Fédération Archéologique et Historique de Belgique: Annales du XXIᵉ congrès* (Liège: Poncelet, 1909) II, 643f. In French. See no. 64 in this volume.

868
as
DWELSHAUVERS, Georges. **Programme des recherches faites ou à faire dans les fonds musicaux de la province de Liège** [Program of research done or to be done in the music collections of the

province of Liège], *Fédération Archéologique et Historique de Belgique: Annales du XXIIe congrès. I: Documents et compte rendu; II: Rapports & mémoires* (Mechelen: Godenne, 1911) II, 891–98. In French. See no. 73 in this volume.

A summary of the work undertaken between 1 January 1910 and 31 July 1911 by members of the newly formed Société de Musicologie in Liège. *(Albert Dlugasch)*

869 ERGO, Émile. **Des causes et des conséquences**
as **du manque d'unité dans plusieurs branches de la science musicale** [Causes and consequences of the lack of unity among branches of musicology], *Report of the Fourth Congress of the International Musical Society* (London: Novello, 1912) 227. In French. See no. 71 in this volume.
Summary of a paper.

870 FARMER, Henry George. **Rapport général sur**
as **les travaux de la Commission d'Histoire et des Manuscrits** [General report on the work of the Commission on History and Manuscripts], *Recueil des travaux du Congrès de musique arabe* (Al-Qāhirah: Boulac, 1934) 639–46. In French. See no. 196 in this volume.
At the Congress on Arab Music (Mu'tamar al Mūsīqá al-'Arabiyyah) in Cairo (1932), the commission was charged with developing recommendations for the cataloguing of works relevant to the history of Arab music, publication of important MSS, study of iconographic evidence, and institutional support for general research programs; the recommendations are summarized. *(David Bloom)*

871 FEDERHOFER, Hellmut. **Historische Musik-**
as **theorie: Überblick** [Historical music theory: An overview], *Bericht über den internationalen musikwissenschaftlichen Kongreß* (Kassel: Bärenreiter, 1963) 348–49. In German. See no. 452 in this volume.
Introduction to a conference session on the history of music theory, with particular attention to issues of documentation of historic sources and the relation between theory and compositional technique. *(David Bloom)*

872 FÉDOROV, Vladimir. **B.V. Asaf'ev et la musi-**
as **cologie russe avant et après 1917** [B.V. Asaf'ev and Russian musicology before and after 1917], *Bericht über den siebenten internationalen musikwissenschaftlichen Kongress* (Kassel: Bärenreiter, 1959) 99. In French. See no. 390 in this volume.
Places the musicological activities of Boris Asaf'ev in the context of Russian history, with attention to his links to 19th-c. Russian writers on music and to the emergent Soviet regime. Asaf'ev developed intonation theory (*intonacija*) and was a pivotal figure of Russian musicology. *(Carl Skoggard)*

873 FELLERER, Karl Gustav. **Mensch und Musik**
as [Man and music], *Musikerziehung: Zeitschrift der Musikerzieher Österreichs* special issue (1953) 40–42. In German. See no. 317 in this volume.

874 FELLERER, Karl Gustav. **Musikforschung und**
as **Klavierinstrumente** [Music research and keyboard instruments], *Dokumentation* (Frankfurt am Main: Fördergemeinschaft Klavier, 1966) 27–33. In German. See no. 494 in this volume.

875 FERGUSON, Donald N. **The relation of theory**
as **to musicology,** *Papers read at the Annual Meeting of the American Musicological Society* (New York: American Musicological Society, 1936) 17–23. See no. 230 in this volume.

Although physics and psychology have the potential to enhance the knowledge of music, there is currently no tenable theory of music. One may ultimately arise from musicology.

876 GERSTENBERG, Walter. **Spanien in der**
as **deutschen Musikgeschichtsschreibung** [Spain in German music historiography], *Congrés de la Societat Internacional de Musicologia* (Barcelona: Casa de Caritat, 1936). In German. See no. 224 in this volume.
The conference report provides only a citation. Neither the text nor a summary of the paper was published here.

877 GURLITT, Wilibald. **Franz-Joseph Fétis und**
as **seine Rolle in der Geschichte der Musikwissenschaft** [François-Joseph Fétis and his role in the history of musicology], *Société Internationale de Musicologie: Premier Congrès Liège—Compte rendu/Internationale Gesellschaft für Musikwissenschaft: Erster Kongress Lüttich—Kongressbericht/International Society for Musical Research: First Congress Liège: Report* (London: Plainsong and Mediaeval Music Society, 1930) 35–54. In German. See no. 178 in this volume.

878 HAAPANEN, Toivo Elias. **Zur Verbreitung der**
as **romanischen und germanischen Tradition im gregorianischen Gesang** [On the spread of Roman and Germanic tradition in Gregorian chant], *Beethoven-Zentenarfeier: Internationaler musikhistorischer Kongress* (Wien: Universal, 1927) 237–39. In German. See no. 142 in this volume.
Applies the classification of chant traditions into distinct dialects to the transmission of chant in Northern Europe. Whereas in Denmark the tradition of Germanically colored melodies in Roman notation was established at a relatively early point, a similar tradition in Finland was wholly supplanted by the Roman dialect, from the 14th c., apparently under Dominican influence. *(David Bloom)*

879 HAMEL, Fred. **Die Industrieschallplatte als**
as **Mittlerin des musikgeschichtlichen Erbes** [The commercial record as transmitter of music history's heritage], *Bericht über den internationalen musikwissenschaftlichen Kongreß* (Kassel: Bärenreiter, 1957) 105–07. In German. See no. 356 in this volume.
For 20th-c. music, sound recordings provide documentation of a kind that was not possible earlier, of performance practice and of the intentions of composers from Strauss and Pfitzner through Stravinsky and Hindemith. Recording the music of previous eras can be regarded as conservation work, and should be musicologically informed, at least as far as commercial viability allows. *(David Bloom)*

880 HANDSCHIN, Jacques. **Musicologie et**
as **musique** [Musicology and music], *Compte rendu/Kongressbericht/Report* (Basel: Bärenreiter, 1951) 9–22. In French. See no. 289 in this volume.
One can know a great deal about music and not be a musicologist. That which distinguishes a science from simple knowledge is above all the formation of a system. *(Scott Fruehwald)*

881 HANDSCHIN, Jacques. **Réflexions dangereuses**
as **sur le renouveau de la musique ancienne** [Dangerous reflections on the revival of early music], *Atti del terzo Congresso internazionale di musica* (Firenze: Le Monnier, 1940) 40–57. In French; summaries in Italian and German. See no. 256 in this volume.
Music research methods need to be put on a more scientific basis and guidelines should be drawn up to standardize research findings in the field.

882 HERMET, Augusto. **Musicologia e musica** [Musicology and music], *Atti del quinto Congresso di musica* (Firenze: Barbèra, 1948) 157–61. In Italian. See no. 285 in this volume.

Throughout its history, music has been regarded as a derivative of science or a metaphysical experience of mathematical origin. Composition has been an act of unconscious calculation and science a conscious manifestation of art; the balance of science and artistry makes for good musicianship. Laboriously attained artistic truth is the hallmark of perceptive musicology. In appraising 12-tone technique from a historical-theoretical perspective, it becomes apparent that the use of quarter tones can help to define atonal music, just as half steps define tonal music. *(Channan Willner)*

883 HØEG, Carsten. **L'état actuel de l'étude de la musique byzantine** [The current state of the study of Byzantine music], *IIIᵉ Congrès international des études byzantines* (Athínai: Hestia, 1932) 263–65. In French. See no. 163 in this volume.

Our ideas about and knowledge of Byzantine music are vague and incomplete, particularly as regards modes and the history of signs in notational systems. The writings of Georgios Pachymerīs and Manuel Bryennius on the use of modes, and the *Hagiopolitis* treatise on notation, are unjustifiably overlooked, but many important sources are unavailable. There is a need for scholars to have access to libraries in Greek monasteries; for research on phonographic recordings of Greek church music; for research on music derived from Byzantine music; for national committees to supervise research; for facsimile publications of important MSS; and for the publication of catalogues, paleographic albums, and a *Repertorium hymnorum*. *(Barry Salwen)*

884 HOŘEJŠ, Antonín. **Die tschechoslowakische Musikwissenschaft und Mozart** [Czechoslovakian musicology and Mozart], *Internationale Konferenz über das Leben und Werk W.A. Mozarts* (Praha: Svaz Československých Skladatelů, 1956) 236–40. In German. See no. 360 in this volume.

A brief history of musicological research in the Bohemian lands and Slovakia, from the last period of Austrian domination in the mid-19th c. to the period of socialist construction. All Czech musicologists have taken an interest in Mozart and the Czech music of Mozart's time, the most important work being that of the Brno school under Vladimír Helfert in the 1920s and 1930s. *(David Bloom)*

885 JACQUOT, Jean. **L'organisation internationale des recherches sur la musique pour luth et les sources polonaises** [The international organization of research on lute music and the Polish sources], *The book of the first international musicological congress devoted to the works of Frederick Chopin* (Warszawa: Państwowe Wydawnictwo Naukowe, 1963) 547–50. In French. See no. 425 in this volume.

Reviews the state of research on lute music and lute iconography in Poland in the context of developing international cooperation since the 1957 conference at Neuilly-sur-Seine (proceedings published as *Le luth et sa musique*, Paris 1958; and cited as no. 377 in this volume). *(David Bloom)*

886 KINKELDEY, Otto. **The artist and the scholar,** *Papers of the American Musicological Society* (Philadelphia: American Musicological Society, 1946) 126–36. See no. 269 in this volume.

Problems of both categories are explored, including the validity of artistic judgments by nonartists, problems with dogmatic theory, the pretension with which some display academic degrees, and charlatanism within the relatively new field of musicology. Herbert Spencer's essay *What knowledge is of most worth?* is quoted extensively.

887 KINKELDEY, Otto. **Changing relations within the field of musicology,** *Papers read at the Annual Meeting of the American Musicological Society* (New York: American Musicological Society, 1936) 42–57. See no. 230 in this volume.

Ideas of acoustics, theory, and philosophy from ancient Greece are relevant to modern musical scholarship. Today, the fields of physiology, psychology, comparative ethnology, and historiography are changing the nature and scope of musicological inquiry.

888 KNEPLER, Georg. **Musikgeschichte und Geschichte** [Music history and history], *Beiträge zur Musikwissenschaft* V/4 (1963) 291–98. In German. See no. 470 in this volume.

That bourgeois cyclic theories are useless for the periodization of music history or clarification of its driving force is a foregone conclusion among Marxists. In the three style epochs of European music (monodic, polymelodic, and melodic-harmonic styles) we recognize a Hegelian triad: Monody was negated by polymelody, which was negated in turn by melodic-harmonic music—the negation of negation, a synthesis of monody and polyphony. *(Donna Arnold)*

889 KNEPLER, Georg. **Über einige geistige Schwierigkeiten der Musikforschung von heute** [Some intellectual difficulties in today's musicological research], *Bericht über den siebenten internationalen musikwissenschaftlichen Kongress* (Kassel: Bärenreiter, 1959) 160–61. In German. See no. 390 in this volume.

One problem is the lack of awareness in the U.S. and Western Europe of developments in Eastern Europe and Asia; for example Vladimer Ahobadze's field research has found extensive corroboration for Marius Schneider's hypothesis on the historical connection between Georgian and medieval European polyphony. Still more serious is the failure to adopt the perspective of class consciousness, as is being done in the socialist countries, particularly China. *(David Bloom)*

890 KRÜGER, Walther. **Grundbegriffe und Periodizität in der abendländischen Musikgeschichte** [Basic principles and periodicity in the history of Western music], *Kongreß-Bericht: Gesellschaft für Musikforschung* (Kassel; Basel: Bärenreiter, 1950) 200–02. *Charts, diagr.* In German. See no. 299 in this volume.

891 LA LAURENCIE, Lionel de. **Essai d'application des méthodes graphiques à l'étude de la bibliographie musicale** [An application of graphic methods to the study of musical bibliography], *Haydn-Zentenarfeier* (Leipzig: Breitkopf & Härtel; Wien: Artaria, 1909) 526–29. *Charts, diagr.* In French. See no. 65 in this volume.

Provides graphs representing the number of writings appearing in various areas of research (e.g., biography, history, and theory) throughout the 19th c.

892 LAAFF, Ernst. **Berufsfragen des jungen Musikwissenschaftlers: Überblick** [Career questions asked by the young musicologist: Overview], *Bericht über den internationalen musikwissenschaftlichen Kongreß* (Kassel: Bärenreiter, 1963) 321–22. In German. See no. 452 in this volume.

Introductory remarks to a conference session on employment possibilities.

893 LAAFF, Ernst. **Berufsfragen des jungen Musikwissenschaftlers: Zusammenfassung** [Career questions asked by the young musicologist: Summary], *Bericht über den internationalen musikwissenschaftlichen Kongreß* (Kassel: Bärenreiter, 1963) 333. In German. See no. 452 in this volume.

894 LIESS, Andreas. **Umdeutung als musikgeschichtlicher Grundbegriff** [Reinterpretation as a basic music historical concept], *Société Internationale de Musicologie, cinquième congrès/Inter-*

nationale Gesellschaft für Musikwissenschaft, fünfter Kongreß/International Society for Musical Research, Fifth Congress (Amsterdam: Vereniging voor Nederlandse Muziekgeschiedenis, 1953) 282–92. In German. See no. 316 in this volume.

895 LISSA, Zofia. **Ost-West-Probleme in der**
as **modernen Musikgeschichtsschreibung** [East-West problems in modern music historiography], *Musica antiqua Europae orientalis* (Warszawa: Państwowe Wydawnictwo Naukowe, 1966) 19–41. In German. See no. 506 in this volume.

896 MANTUANI, Josip. **Über die Umarbeitung**
as **von Riemanns Opernhandbuch** [The revision of Riemann's *Opern-Handbuch*], *Haydn-Zentenarfeier* (Leipzig: Breitkopf & Härtel; Wien: Artaria, 1909) 439–43. *Charts, diagr.* In German. See no. 65 in this volume.

Discusses the second edition of Hugo Riemann's guidebook to opera (Leipzig, 1893, facsimile published by Olms [Hildesheim and New York, 1979] and cited as RILM[1979]2157; first edition 1887). A summary of a subsequent panel discussion is included.

897 MARÓTHY, János. **Von der Hagiographie zur**
as **Historiographie** [From hagiography to historiography], *Beiträge zur Musikwissenschaft* V/4 (1963) 299–303. In German. See no. 470 in this volume.

Bourgeois thought has held that bourgeois circumstances are in general natural and eternal. Marx and Engels have proven that there is no property in general, no family in general, and no morality in general; rather, societal forms have developed historically, and current conditions and ideas reflect the dominant class. The bourgeois musicology of the 19th c. had a naïve Robinson Crusoe ideal of an unchanging universality in the music of the people. Marxist science showed, however, that musical forms had evolved historically. Bourgeois conservatism cannot successfully battle modern bourgeois decadence. One must replace both with truly modern socialist realism. To that end one must study modern music in aesthetic hindsight. *(Donna Arnold)*

898 MASSON, Paul-Marie. **Les tâches inter-**
as **nationales de la musicologie** [The international tasks of musicology], *Société Internationale de Musicologie, cinquième congrès/Internationale Gesellschaft für Musikwissenschaft, fünfter Kongreß/International Society for Musical Research, Fifth Congress* (Amsterdam: Vereniging voor Nederlandse Muziekgeschiedenis, 1953) 11–18. In French. See no. 316 in this volume.

899 MILLER, Philip L. **Musicology and the phono-**
as **graph record,** *Report of the Eighth Congress of the International Musicological Society. I: Papers* (Kassel: Bärenreiter, 1961) 418–24. See no. 439 in this volume.

Discusses various uses for phonograph records in musicology, including career documentation, anthologies, and analysis of performing styles.

900 [Mönchengladbach, 1964] Neumen-Colloquium
as **mit Dom Joseph Kreps, Löwen** [Neume colloquium with Dom Joseph Kreps of Leuven]. By Karl DREIMÜLLER, *Studien zur Musikgeschichte der Stadt Mönchengladbach* (Köln: Volk, 1965) 65–74. *Illus., facs.* In German. See no. 486 in this volume.

At the meeting of the Arbeitsgemeinschaft für Rheinische Musikgeschichte in Mönchengladbach, June 1964, a group of chant specialists held a colloquium on MSS associated with the Abtei St. Vitus, Mönchengladbach, including the reading of papers abstracted as nos. 1080, 1109, and 5375 in this volume. Joseph Kreps (who died 13 July 1965) spoke on the subject of the role of Charlemagne's capital of Aachen in the development of neumatic

notation; the comparison of the lineless neumed Missale plenarium, MS 1 of the archive of the Münster-Basilika St. Vitus, Mönchengladbach, with the early staffed Gradual of Arnoldus, D-AAd 13; and methodological questions. *(David Bloom)*

901 MOSER, Hans Joachim. **Ziele und Wege der**
as **musikalischen Lokalforschung** [Goals and paths of regional music research], *Bericht über den I. musikwissenschaftlichen Kongress der Deutschen Musikgesellschaft in Leipzig* (Wiesbaden: Breitkopf & Härtel, 1926) 381–84. In German. See no. 120 in this volume.

Discusses the effects of war and inflation on musicology, as well as musicology's main sources of information: libraries, private collections, and publications. The compilation of a lexicon of musicological regional studies from the Middle Ages to 1850 is proposed. *(William Renwick)*

902 MUELLER VON ASOW, Erich Hermann.
as **Musikerbriefe als Mittel zur Erweckung und Förderung der Musikliebe** [Musicians' letters as a means to the love of music], *Musikerziehung: Zeitschrift der Musikerzieher Österreichs* special issue (1953) 143–45. In German. See no. 317 in this volume.

Letters can generate interest in and understanding of music by providing immediate access to the thoughts and ideas of composers as well as insights into their personality and creative process. It is possible to compare the literary and musical styles of a composer as well as to contrast the literary styles of different composers. *(Allen Lott)*

903 MUELLER VON ASOW, Erich Hermann.
as **Musikerepistolographie** [Musicians' epistolography], *Bericht über den internationalen musikwissenschaftlichen Kongreß Wien Mozartjahr 1956* (Graz; Köln: Böhlau, 1958) 430–33. In German. See no. 365 in this volume.

Discusses principles for the study of musicians' correspondence, with particular attention to questions of authentication and cataloguing.

904 MUEREN, Floris van der. **Hoe komen we tot een**
as **geschiedenis der Vlaamsche muziek der 19de eeuw?** [How to arrive at a history of Flemish music in the 19th century?], *Verhandelingen van het Muziekcongres* (Antwerpen: Stad Antwerpen, 1935) 105–06. In Dutch. See no. 210 in this volume.

905 NEF, Karl. **Zur Forschung über die ältere**
as **Instrumentalmusik** [Research on early instrumental music], *Bericht über den zweiten Kongress der Internationalen Musikgesellschaft* (Leipzig: Breitkopf & Härtel, 1907) 195–200. In German. See no. 53 in this volume.

Surveys the state of research on ensemble and orchestral music of the 16th and 17th c., including iconographic and literary studies, social-historical documentation, work on the development of the German and French suite genres and Italian free forms, and issues of performance practice. *(David Bloom)*

906 NOACK, Friedrich. **Organisation und wissen-**
as **schaftliche Nutzbarmachung der Arbeit in den Seminaren** [Organizing the work of academic departments and making it useful], *Beethoven-Zentenarfeier: Internationaler musikhistorischer Kongress* (Wien: Universal, 1927) 273–75. In German. See no. 142 in this volume.

It has been proposed that the period of study leading to the doctorate ought to be lengthened, and include some kind of preliminary examination of the student's preparation in areas such as paleography, the critical study of style, and performance practice. The work could include the performance of important musicological tasks such as the preparation of scores for works that exist only in individual parts or in tablature; the resulting scores could then be listed in a centralized bibliography so that scholars could easily locate them. *(David Bloom)*

907
as
NOWAK, Leopold. **Musikwissenschaft und zeitgenössiche Musik** [Musicology and contemporary music], *Musikerziehung: Zeitschrift der Musikerzieher Österreichs* special issue (1953) 86–90. In German. See no. 317 in this volume.

Explores various musicological pursuits for the development of contemporary music, drawing on examples throughout music history. *(Joseph Giroux)*

908
as
OREL, Alfred. **Österreichs Sendung in der Abendländischen Musik** [Austria's mission in Western music], *Bericht über den neunten internationalen Kongreß* (Kassel: Bärenreiter, 1964-1966) II, 7–19. In German. See no. 491 in this volume.

Brief, informal history of Austria's role in the development of European music, from ca. 1000 B.C. to the present.

909
as
OREL, Alfred. **Zur Quellenkunde für neuere Musikgeschichte** [On the information sources for more recent music history], *Bericht über den I. musikwissenschaftlichen Kongress der Deutschen Musikgesellschaft in Leipzig* (Wiesbaden: Breitkopf & Härtel, 1926) 51–53. In German. See no. 120 in this volume.

Discusses the importance of such bibliographic sources as newspapers, weekly magazines, periodicals, MSS, editions, letters, and thematic catalogues. Problems in working with some of these items are addressed.

(William Renwick)

910
as
ORTMANN, Otto. **The contribution of physiopsychology to musicology,** *Papers read at the Annual Meeting of the American Musicological Society* (New York: American Musicological Society, 1936) 9–13. See no. 230 in this volume.

Physiopsychological methods and theories are relevant to the interpretation of historical data. The perspectives of physiopsychology offer new ways of conceiving performance techniques and systematic investigative procedures.

⟶ PICKEN, Laurence E.R. **The contribution of ethnomusicology to historical musicology.** See no. 2458 in this volume.

911
as
RAUGEL, Félix. **[Paris, 1860] Le Congrès de musique religieuse de Paris (1860)** [The congress of religious music in Paris (1860)]. By Félix RAUGEL, *Comptes rendus, rapports et vœux du Congrès parisien et régional de chant liturgique et de musique d'église* (Paris: Schola Cantorum, 1912) 74–81. In French. See no. 75 in this volume.

912
as
PULIKOWSKI, Julian von. **Probleme und Aufgaben der Musikgeschichte** [Problems and tasks in music history], *Congrés de la Societat Internacional de Musicologia* (Barcelona: Casa de Caritat, 1936). In German. See no. 224 in this volume.

The conference report provides only a citation. Neither the text nor a summary of the paper was published here.

913
as
REICH, Willi. **Il gusto musicale nella luce della statistica** [Musical taste in the light of statistics], *Atti del secondo Congresso internazionale di musica* (Firenze: Le Monnier, 1940) 113–18. In Italian; summaries in French and German. See no. 239 in this volume.

Reviews recent developments in the use of social statistics for music research on composers, performers, and audiences, in work by Leo Wilzin,

Friedrich von Hausegger, and Julius Bahle. Data on opera repertoire in Bavarian theaters from 1871 to 1933 are discussed. *(David Bloom)*

914
as
SACHS, Curt. **Music history: Two sides of the coin,** *Papers of the American Musicological Society* (Philadelphia: American Musicological Society, 1946) 137–42. See no. 269 in this volume.

Two issues must be addressed when considering the nature of musicology as discipline: the first is that music theory is often erroneously thought of as part of the field; the second is that though *music history* is a compound word, most musicologists place far more emphasis on music than history. One remedy is to educate historians to read music; another is to promote understanding of the role of music in general culture.

915
as
SACHS, Curt. **Vers une préhistoire musicale** [Toward a musical prehistory], *Congrés de la Societat Internacional de Musicologia* (Barcelona: Casa de Caritat, 1936). In French. See no. 224 in this volume.

The conference report provides only a citation. Neither the text nor a summary of the paper was published here.

916
as
SALVAGNINI, F. Alberto. **Francesco Caffi: Musicologo veneziano (1778-1874)** [Francesco Caffi: Venetian musicologist (1778-1874)], *Atti del Congresso internazionale di scienze storiche. VIII: Atti della sezione IV: Storia dell'arte musicale e drammatica* (Roma: R. Accademia dei Lincei, 1905) 55–79. *Port.* In Italian. See no. 42 in this volume.

Caffi was noted for his accuracy (especially in the study of Venetian music), for his analysis of a wide range of music, and for his essays on nonmusical subjects. Two samples of his writings are included, a eulogy for Francesco Gardi and a letter on the state of music.

⟶ SCHAEFFNER, André. **Contribution de l'ethnomusicologie à l'histoire de la musique** [The contribution of ethnomusicology to historical musicology]. See no. 2467 in this volume.

917
as
SCHENK, Erich. **Organisation der Mozartforschung** [The organization of Mozart research], *Bericht über die musikwissenschaftliche Tagung der Internationalen Stiftung Mozarteum* (Leipzig: Breitkopf & Härtel, 1932) 302–03. In German. See no. 193 in this volume.

Outlines plans of the Internationale Stiftung Mozarteum in support of Mozart scholarship, as reflected in documents of 1925-26: the revival of the journal *Mozart-Jahrbuch* and the preparation of a completely reliable bibliography; the development of the Mozarteumsbibliothek in Salzburg, with a photographic archive, in collaboration with the Archiv für Photogramme Musikalischer Meisterhandschriften at the Österreichische Nationalbibliothek, Vienna ("Meisterarchiv"); and recruitment of an academically qualified board of directors to aid the Kuratorium in its work. The central headquarters in Salzburg should work to develop the contemporary conscience in things Mozartean, for instance to stop the threatened destruction of Mozart's burial site in the St. Marx cemetery. *(David Bloom)*

918
as
SCHERING, Arnold. **Musikwissenschaft und Kunst der Gegenwart** [Musicology and the art of today], *Bericht über den I. musikwissenschaftlichen Kongress der Deutschen Musikgesellschaft in Leipzig* (Wiesbaden: Breitkopf & Härtel, 1926) 9–20. In German. See no. 120 in this volume.

Discussion of the role of the musicologist in relation to performers, composers, and music lovers. Musicological developments of the preceding half-century (1875-1925) are reviewed, and modern musicology is placed in a historical perspective. *(William Renwick)*

919
as
SCHLOEZER, Boris de. **La musique ancienne et le goût moderne** [Early music and modern taste],

Atti del terzo Congresso internazionale di musica (Firenze: Le Monnier, 1940) 7–16. In French; summaries in Italian and German. See no. 256 in this volume. Discusses priorities in the study of early music and the process of evolution as related to music in general.

920
as

SCHMID, Ernst Fritz. **Mozarts Lebenswerk: Seine Bergung und Erschliessung** [Mozart's life oeuvre: Its recovery and publication], *Internationale Konferenz über das Leben und Werk W.A. Mozarts* (Praha: Svaz Československých Skladatelů, 1956) 15–25. In German. See no. 360 in this volume.

Historical sketch of attempts at the complete cataloguing, recovery, and publication of Mozart's works, from his father's and his own thematic catalogues through the preparation of the Neue Mozart-Ausgabe (of which the author is general editor) beginning in 1954. *(John Stansell)*

921
as

SCHMITZ, Eugen. **Das Verhältnis der Musikwissenschaft zur Populärliteratur und Musikkritik** [The relationship of musicology to popular literature and music criticism], *Haydn-Zentenarfeier* (Leipzig: Breitkopf & Härtel; Wien: Artaria, 1909) 422–28. In German. See no. 65 in this volume.

Offers a cultural overview with attention to the role of the music critic.

⟶   SEEGER, Charles. **Preface to a critique of music.** See no. 2470 in this volume.

922
as

SEEGER, Charles. **Preface to the description of a music,** *Société Internationale de Musicologie, cinquième congrès/Internationale Gesellschaft für Musikwissenschaft, fünfter Kongreß/International Society for Musical Research, Fifth Congress* (Amsterdam: Vereniging voor Nederlandse Muziekgeschiedenis, 1953) 360–70. See no. 316 in this volume.

The musicologist's tasks are to demonstrate how music should be discussed, to free music from the bonds of speech, and to give music the fullest possible autonomy to coexist with language. *(Tsipora Yosselevitch)*

923
as

SEIFFERT, Max. **Zur Forschung über die ältere Klavier- und Orgelmusik** [Research on early keyboard and organ music], *Bericht über den zweiten Kongress der Internationalen Musikgesellschaft* (Leipzig: Breitkopf & Härtel, 1907) 200–04. In German. See no. 53 in this volume.

Reviews historical studies, publication of sources and theoretical works, and the discussion of performance practice (especially with reference to basso continuo accompaniment) for keyboard music of the period from the early 14th c. through C.P.E. Bach. *(David Bloom)*

924
as

SIMON, A. **Das musikwissenschaftliche Studium in der Gegenwart und seine Zukunftsmöglichkeiten** [The study of musicology today, and future possibilities], *Congrés de la Societat Internacional de Musicologia* (Barcelona: Casa de Caritat, 1936). In German. See no. 224 in this volume.

The conference report provides only a citation. Neither the text nor a summary of the paper was published here.

925
as

SMITH, Carleton Sprague. **Presidential address,** *Papers of the American Musicological Society* (Philadelphia: American Musicological Society, 1946) 1–4. See no. 269 in this volume.

A general appeal for cultural tolerance, enlightenment, and democratic scholarship is followed by the identification of three cultural divisions: traditional music of the country, traditional music of the city, and (primarily urban) art music. While these may be of international importance, they must first express the nature of a particular region. *(author)*

926
as

SPIVACKE, Harold. **The place of acoustics in musicology,** *Papers read at the Annual Meeting of the American Musicological Society* (New York: American Musicological Society, 1936) 3–8. See no. 230 in this volume.

Although both are fields that revolve around sound, acoustics and musicology remain largely independent of one another. Generally, musicologists have focused on mathematical acoustics in relation to musical intervals, tonality, and temperament. However, acoustical studies of historic instruments (such as Beethoven's pianos, or 18th- and 19th-c. wind instruments) may shed light on compositional and performance practices. Acoustical studies of 15th- and 16th-c. cathedrals and halls may also reveal new facets of the works for whose performance they were intended. Studies of acoustics may demystify perception's physiological and psychological underpinnings. *(Marilyn Nonken)*

927
as

STRUNK, Oliver. **The historical aspect of musicology,** *Papers read at the Annual Meeting of the American Musicological Society* (New York: American Musicological Society, 1936) 14–16. See no. 230 in this volume.

In 1908, Hugo Riemann outlined the tasks of musicology and historical research. Unlike art or literary historians, who have the actual artworks before them, music historians must work from scores, or sets of instructions. This makes necessary three auxiliary fields of historical study: performance practice, instruments, and notation.

928
as

SYCHRA, Antonín. **Die Bedeutung des Skizzenstudiums für die wissenschaftliche Analyse musikalischer Werke** [The significance of sketch studies in the scholarly analysis of musical works], *Bericht über den internationalen musikwissenschaftlichen Kongreß Wien Mozartjahr 1956* (Graz; Köln: Böhlau, 1958) 616–22. *Music.* In German. See no. 365 in this volume.

A composer's sketches may provide insight into the role of extramusical ideas in the compositional process. Examples are drawn from Mozart's operas and from Dvořák's symphony no. 8. *(David Bloom)*

929
as

VANCEA, Zeno. **Stand und Ergebnisse der rumänischen musikwissenschaftlichen Forschung über die Beziehungen der Werke Mozarts zu Rumänien** [The current status and the findings of Romanian musicological research on the relationships of Mozart's works to Romania], *Internationale Konferenz über das Leben und Werk W.A. Mozarts* (Praha: Svaz Československých Skladatelů, 1956) 112–17. In German. See no. 360 in this volume.

Outlines research (mostly by George Breazul in Bucharest and István Lakatos in Cluj) on the early performance history of Mozart's works in what is now Romanian territory, especially in Sibiu, Timişoara, and Bucharest; on the traditional-music source of the melody of the Janissaries' march in *Die Entführung aus dem Serail* and how it was transmitted to Mozart; and on the authenticity of MSS and prints attributed to Mozart in Romanian collections. *(David Bloom)*

930
as

WELCH, Roy Dickinson. **The bearing of aesthetics and criticism on musicology,** *Papers read at the Annual Meeting of the American Musicological Society* (New York: American Musicological Society, 1936) 24–28. See no. 230 in this volume.

In musicology, analytical rigor and emotional experience are complementary and necessary tools, as Edward J. Dent suggests.

931
as

WERNER, Arno. **Die praktische Durchführung der lokalen Musikforschung in Sachsen-Thüringen** [Carrying out local music research in Saxe-Thuringia], *Bericht über den I. musikwissenschaftlichen Kongress der Deutschen Musikgesellschaft*

in Leipzig (Wiesbaden: Breitkopf & Härtel, 1926) 385–90. In German. See no. 120 in this volume.
Reviews bibliographic work done in Saxony and Thuringia and discusses library holdings.

932 WILKOWSKA-CHOMIŃSKA, Krystyna. **À la**
as **recherche de la musique pour luth: Expériences polonaises** [In search of lute music: Polish experiences], *Le luth et sa musique* (Paris: Centre National de la Recherche Scientifique [CNRS], 1958) 193–208. *Music, transcr.* In French. See no. 377 in this volume.
Summary of research on the Polish lute tradition from the 15th through the 17th c., with particular attention to the transcription and publication of works by Polish composers such as Jakub Reys, Bartłomiej Pękiel, and Wojciech Długoraj and foreign composers active in Poland including Bálint Bakfark and Diomedes Cato. A supplementary list of sources of Polish lute pieces by Wolfgang BOETTICHER is appended. *(David Bloom)*

⟶ WIORA, Walter. **Ethnomusicology and the history of music.** See no. 2483 in this volume.

⟶ WIORA, Walter. **Idee und Methode "vergleichender" Musikforschung** [The concept and method of "comparative" musicology]. See no. 2484 in this volume.

933 WIORA, Walter. **Das musikalische Kunstwerk**
as **und die systematische Musikwissenschaft** [The musical work of art and systematic musicology], *Deuxième congrès international d'esthétique et de Science de l'art* (Paris: Librairie Félix Alcan, 1937) II, 223–26. In German. See no. 249 in this volume.
Systematic musicology can address the structural composition of the musical artwork, its phenomenological status, and the opposition between its autonomy and its connection to life and to symbolic content, together with the way these aspects unfold historically. *(David Bloom)*

⟶ WIORA, Walter. **Schrift und Tradition als Quellen der Musikgeschichte** [The written and the oral as sources of music history]. See no. 2486 in this volume.

934 WITOLD, Jean. **Mozarts Humanismus** [Mo-
as zart's humanism], *Internationale Konferenz über das Leben und Werk W.A. Mozarts* (Praha: Svaz Československých Skladatelů, 1956) 230–35. In German. See no. 360 in this volume.
An appreciation.

935 WOLFF, Hellmuth Christian. **Der Wert der**
as **Geschichte** [The value of history], *Kongreß-Bericht: Gesellschaft für Musikforschung* (Kassel; Basel: Bärenreiter, 1950) 202–04. In German. See no. 299 in this volume.

21 History, general

936 ABERT, Anna Amalie. **Wort und Ton** [Word and
as music], *Bericht über den internationalen musikwissenschaftlichen Kongreß* (Kassel: Bärenreiter, 1957) 43–46. *Charts, diagr.* In German. See no. 356 in this volume.

Considers the possible ways in which composers of Western vocal music have engaged with the texts they set, in terms of four periods of historic change: that from medieval to Renaissance around 1500, that from Renaissance to Baroque around 1600, that from Baroque to Classic ca. 1750, and that around the time of World War I. *(David Bloom)*

937 ADLER, Guido. **Internationalismus in der**
as **Tonkunst** [Internationalism in music], *Bericht über den musikwissenschaftlichen Kongreß in Basel* (Leipzig: Breitkopf & Härtel, 1925) 36–48. In German. See no. 102 in this volume.
The mixture of elements from Asia, antiquity, and Europe in Gregorian chant is the oldest example of internationalism in the art of music. Although nations maintain their individual musical styles through traditional music, most composers in each century combined influences from surrounding lands to develop a newer, higher level of culture. *(Sylvia Eversole)*

938 AERDE, Raymond Joseph Justin van. **Les**
as **ménestrels communaux malinois et joueurs d'instruments divers, établis ou de passage à Malines de 1311 à 1790** [City minstrels of Mechelen and players of different instruments, established at or passing through Mechelen from 1311 to 1790], *Fédération Archéologique et Historique de Belgique: Annales du XXIIᵉ congrès. I: Documents et compte rendu; II: Rapports & mémoires* (Mechelen: Godenne, 1911) II, 507–604. *Illus., port., music, them. cat.* In French. See no. 73 in this volume.
Musicians were hired as watchmen for the city of Mechelen from the 14th to the 18th c. Their salaries, dress, instruments, and functions are described in detail; lists of the names and dates of service of these men are provided. *(Albert Dlugasch)*

939 ALBERT, Karel. **Nationale elementen in het**
as **verloop der muziekgeschiedenis en hun beteekenis voor de huidige muziek** [Nationalist elements in the history of music and their meaning for music today], *Verhandelingen van het Muziekcongres* (Antwerpen: Stad Antwerpen, 1935) 55–61. In Dutch. See no. 210 in this volume.
Discusses the roles of religion, politics, and economics in the development of national styles since the Middle Ages. Nationalism in the 19th c. became associated with the citation of local traditional songs. It is argued that the music of a nation need not be validated through association with the country's traditional music.

940 ANGLÈS, Higini. **Die Bedeutung der Vokal-**
as **polyphonie für die römische Liturgie** [The significance of vocal polyphony for the Roman liturgy], *Zweiter internationaler Kongress für katholische Kirchenmusik: Zu Ehren des Heiligen Papstes Pius X* (Wien: conference, 1955) 154–61. In German. See no. 339 in this volume.
Earlier polyphonic church music, through the beginning of the 17th c., deserves more attention than it has recently received. Pieces by John Dunstable and Guillaume Dufay in particular should be heard more often, as well as Masses of the early 15th c. That the latter often use an instrumental accompaniment, or are based on a secular chanson text, need not be an obstacle. *(David Bloom)*

941 ANGLÈS, Higini. **Die Bedeutung des Volks-**
as **liedes für die Musikgeschichte Europas** [The significance of folk song for Europe's music history], *Bericht über den Internationalen musikwissenschaftlichen Kongress* (Kassel: Bärenreiter, 1954) 181–84. In German. See no. 319 in this volume.
Considers the influence of traditional music on the successive ages and repertoires of Western music from Gregorian chant onward, with special attention to the Iberian Peninsula. *(Carl Skoggard)*

942 ARMSTRONG, Thomas. **The Wesleys: Evange-**
as **lists and musicians,** *Organ and choral aspects and prospects* (London: Hinrichsen, 1958) 95–106. See no. 375 in this volume.
A history of the Wesley family from 1696 to 1876.

943 AZEVEDO, Luiz Heitor Corrêa de. **Survivance**
as **et développement des diverses traditions européennes dans le continent américain** [The survival and development of the various European traditions in the Americas], *Report of the Eighth Congress of the International Musicological Society. I: Papers* (Kassel: Bärenreiter, 1961) 356–64. *Music.* In French. See no. 439 in this volume.
A historical survey of the importation of European church music, dance music, traditional song, opera, and piano playing in South and North America, and their development into new genres. *(David Bloom)*

944 BENGTSSON, Ingmar. **Skandinávská hudba/**
as **Aperçu sur la musique scandinave** [A survey of Scandinavian music], *Hudba národů: Sborník přednášek, proslovených na I. mezinárodním sjezdu skladatelů a hudebních kritiků/Musique des nations: Ier Congrès international des compositeurs et critiques musicaux* (Praha: Syndikát Českých Skladatelů, 1948) 13–15,103–05. In Czech and French. See no. 278 in this volume.
A survey of major Scandinavian composers from the 18th c. to the present; includes Johan Helmich Roman, Franz Berwald, Edvard Grieg, Jean Sibelius, Carl Nielsen, Ture Rangström, Gösta Nystroem, Hilding Rosenberg, Lars-Erik Larsson, Gunnar de Frumerie, Karl-Birger Blomdahl, and Ingvar Lidholm. The work of the Swedish composers' association, Föreningen Svenska Tonsättare, in the publication and distribution of contemporary music is discussed.

945 BESSELER, Heinrich. **Singstil und Instru-**
as **mentalstil in der europäischen Musik** [Vocal and instrumental styles in European music], *Bericht über den Internationalen musikwissenschaftlichen Kongress* (Kassel: Bärenreiter, 1954) 223–40. *Music.* In German. See no. 319 in this volume.
Reviews European music from the origins of Gregorian chant onwards. During two eras, the form-principle of continual unfolding and avoidance of parallelism has been paramount, namely with Gregorian chant during the first millennium and later with Renaissance polyphony. This principle may be regarded, in analogy with literature, as the prose principle, and has been associated with the primacy of vocal music. Three times in European history, the opposing principle, the poetic—structuring by means of parallelism and correspondence—has overcome the prose principle: first with the Notre Dame school, then with the Baroque, and finally with the high Classic and its periodic structure and tonal polarity. On each of these occasions, dance with its inherent accent structure has influenced the shift. Instrumental music emerged as dominant with the latter two developments and today, the instrumental, periodic norms of the Baroque-Classic era are mistakenly assumed to underlie all of European music history. *(Carl Skoggard)*

946 BIEHLE, Herbert. **Die textlichen Grundlagen**
as **als Gesangsproblem** [The text basis as a problem in song], *Société Internationale de Musicologie: Premier Congrès Liège—Compte rendu/Internationale Gesellschaft für Musikwissenschaft: Erster Kongress Lüttich—Kongressbericht/International Society for Musical Research: First Congress Liège: Report* (London: Plainsong and Mediaeval Music Society, 1930) 81–86. In German. See no. 178 in this volume.
Investigates the problem of setting text to music in various periods and concludes that the relationship between text and music has not been constant. *(Scott Fruehwald)*

947 BOKESOVÁ, Zdenka. **Slovenská hudba/La**
as **musique slovaque** [Slovak music], *Hudba národů: Sborník přednášek, proslovených na I. mezinárodním sjezdu skladatelů a hudebních kritiků/Musique des nations: Ier Congrès international des compositeurs et critiques musicaux* (Praha: Syndikát Českých Skladatelů, 1948) 16–21,106–11. In Czech and French. See no. 278 in this volume.
The important Slovak composers of the generation before 1918 were Ján Levoslav Bella, Mikuláš Moyzes, Viliam Figuš Bystrý, and Mikuláš Schneider-Trnavský. After the founding of Czechoslovakia, Slovak composers gathered in Prague around the figure of Vítězslav Novák: Alexander Moyzes, Eugen Suchoň, and Ján Cikker. Their students include Ladislav Holoubek, Tibor Frešo, Dezider Kardoš, Šimon Jurovský, and Andrej Očenáš.

948 BORREN, Charles van den. **Du rôle interna-**
as **tional de la Belgique dans l'histoire musicale** [The international role of Belgium in the history of music], *Société Internationale de Musicologie: Premier Congrès Liège—Compte rendu/Internationale Gesellschaft für Musikwissenschaft: Erster Kongress Lüttich—Kongressbericht/International Society for Musical Research: First Congress Liège: Report* (London: Plainsong and Mediaeval Music Society, 1930) 17–31. In French. See no. 178 in this volume.
Although Belgium has been a politically unified country only since 1831, it has produced a distinctive musical culture since the 14th c.

949 BORREN, Charles van den. **Nationalistische**
as **strekkingen in de musiek** [Nationalist tendencies in music], *Verhandelingen van het Muziekcongres* (Antwerpen: Stad Antwerpen, 1935) 47–54. In Dutch. See no. 210 in this volume.
The notion of national styles in European music and the association of certain genres with particular nations are traced from the early Middle Ages through the 19th c. Peter Benoît's achievement in combining elements of various styles into a single national style is compared with that of other composers in history.

950 BORRIS, Siegfried. **Der Einbruch primitiver**
as **Musik in die Musik des Abendlandes** [The influx of traditional music into Western music], *Musikerziehung: Zeitschrift der Musikerzieher Österreichs* special issue (1953) 51–54. In German. See no. 317 in this volume.

951 BOTTÉE DE TOULMON, Auguste. **Histoire de**
as **l'art musical depuis l'ère chrétienne jusqu'à nos jours** [The history of music from the Christian era to our time], *[Ier] Congrès historique européen* (Paris: P.H. Krabbe, 1835) I, 264–79. In French. See no. 1 in this volume.

952 BRIDGMAN, Nanie. **Mécénat et musique** [Pa-
as tronage and music], *Report of the Eighth Congress of the International Musicological Society. II: Reports* (Kassel: Bärenreiter, 1962) 19–30. In French. See no. 440 in this volume.
A survey of the history of musical patronage, focusing on Italy in the 15th-17th c., and its relation to the flourishing of musical creativity. *(David Bloom)*

953 CHASE, Gilbert. **The cultivation of various Eu-**
as **ropean traditions in the Americas,** *Report of the Eighth Congress of the International Musicological Society. II: Reports* (Kassel: Bärenreiter, 1962) 150–52. See no. 440 in this volume.

A report on a discussion of European influences on the art music and traditional music of the Americas by Isabel ARETZ, Luis Heitor Corrêa de AZEVEDO, Gilbert CHASE, Hans T. DAVID, Mantle HOOD, Irving LOWENS, Albert T. LUPER, David P. MCALLESTER, Eugenio PEREIRA SALAS, Andrés SAS, Charles SEEGER, Carleton Sprague SMITH, and Robert STEVENSON, based on the papers by Azevedo and Seeger abstracted as nos. 943 and 1006, respectively, in this volume.

954 CHOMIŃSKI, Józef Michał. **Die Beziehungen**
as **der polnischen Musik zu Westeuropa vom XV.**
bis zum XVII. Jahrhundert [The relation of Polish music to Western Europe in the 15th through the 17th centuries], *Musica antiqua Europae orientalis* (Warszawa: Państwowe Wydawnictwo Naukowe, 1966). In German. See no. 506 in this volume.

955 CIOBANU, Gheorghe. **La culture musicale**
as **byzantine sur le territoire de la Roumanie**
jusqu'au XVIIIe siècle [Byzantine musical culture in the territory of Romania until the 18th century], *Musica antiqua Europae orientalis* (Warszawa: Państwowe Wydawnictwo Naukowe, 1966). In French. See no. 506 in this volume.

956 CUCLIN, Dimitrie. **Le rôle du chant grégorien**
as **dans le passé jusqu'à nos jours et du chant**
byzantin dans l'avenir [The role of Gregorian chant up to the present day and of Byzantine chant in the future], *Atti del V Congresso internazionale di studi bizantini* (Roma: Associazione Nazionale per gli Studi Bizantini, 1940) II, 474–80. *Music.* In French. See no. 233 in this volume.
Byzantine chant was created via a rigorous system of rules that conformed to the dogmas of the church. The Eastern churches adopted the musical system of the Greeks but eliminated their chromaticism, harmonies, and overactive rhythms, seeing them as not in keeping with that which is holy. However, there is no such thing as "evil" music, only music that is not composed according to certain criteria. The discovery of the true diatonic system (modal, tonal, harmonic) involving the principle of the fifth is neo-Pythagorean. This system made possible the rebirth of Byzantine chant, as well as a wider field of expression and emotion within this music. The division of the octave into 53 commas within the neo-Pythagorean system is discussed. *(Susan Poliniak)*

957 CVETKO, Dragotin *et al.* **Die Rolle der**
as **slawischen Völker in der Geschichte der euro-**
päischen Musik des 18. und 19. Jahrhunderts
[The role of the Slavic peoples in the history of European music in the 18th and 19th centuries], *Bericht über den neunten internationalen Kongreß* (Kassel: Bärenreiter, 1964-1966) 237–48. In German. See no. 491 in this volume.
The roundtable discussion ranges from the figure of Grzegorz Gerwazy Gorczycki (d.1734) to that of Antonín Dvořák. Participants included Hieronim FEICHT, Jaroslav JIRÁNEK, Georg KNEPLER, Dieter LEHMANN, Zofia LISSA, Jan RACEK, Boris SCHWARZ, Irwin SPECTOR, Bohumír ŠTĔDROŇ, Tomislav VOLEK, and Aristide WIRSTA. *(David Bloom)*

958 DI SALVO, Bartolomeo. **Alcune tradizioni**
as **musicali liturgiche orientali e la tradizione**
scritta dei codici bizantini medioevali [Some eastern liturgical musical traditions and the written tradition of medieval Byzantine manuscripts], *Atti del Congresso internazionale di musiche popolari mediterranee e del Convegno dei bibliotecari musicali* (Palermo: De Magistris succ. V. Bellotti, 1959) 229–36. In Italian. See no. 332 in this volume.
The corpus of Byzantine chant has a number of features in common with the extant traditions of Eastern Orthodox and Chaldean churches, the Albanian

churches of Calabria and Sicily, and the Greek tradition of the Badia Greca, Grottaferrata. They include the use of the modal system, most typically the oktōēchos, and its characteristic melodic formulas; further study, incorporating the research of Abraham Zvi Idelsohn on relationships with Jewish liturgical music, may support the hypothesis of musical forms common to the whole of the eastern Mediterranean basin. *(David Bloom)*

959 DREIMÜLLER, Karl. **Zur Geschichte und**
as **Soziologie des Mönchengladbacher Musik-**
lebens [The history and sociology of musical life in Mönchengladbach], *Studien zur Musikgeschichte der Stadt Mönchengladbach* (Köln: Volk, 1965) 17–33. *Illus., port.* In German. See no. 486 in this volume.
An informal survey of notable events and personalities from the 12th c. to the early 1930s, and of research on the subject from the 1920s to the present.

960 FARA, Giulio. **Etnofonia e civiltà mediter-**
as **ranea: Le basi della storia della musica** [Ethnophony and Mediterranean civilization: The bases of music history], *Congrés de la Societat Internacional de Musicologia* (Barcelona: Casa de Caritat, 1936). In Italian. See no. 224 in this volume.
The conference report provides only a citation. Neither the text nor a summary of the paper was published here.

961 FERAND, Ernest Thomas. **A history of music**
as **seen in the light of ornamentation,** *Report of the Eighth Congress of the International Musicological Society. I: Papers* (Kassel: Bärenreiter, 1961) 463–69. See no. 439 in this volume.
Eras in the history of Western music could be recognized by distinctions in the degree of freedom and creativeness vs. standardization and mechanization: free ornamentation up to ca. 1450; standardization from 1535 to ca. 1650; the spread of ornamentation signs in keyboard music ca. 1650-1750; increased tendency to incorporate embellishments into the context and visual appearance of music ca. 1720-1820; and the last phase of pianistic and orchestral ornamentation, 1820-1910. A classification of developmental stages begins with ornamentation as a result of technical or physiological factors (primarily considerations of voice production), followed by structural ornamentation (as in the use of clausula or cadenza in the preparation of a climax), expressive ornamentation, an innovation of the Baroque, and finally, ornamentation for the sake of allegory or symbolism, also an invention of the Baroque. *(David Bloom)*

⟶ FERAND, Ernest Thomas. **Improvisation in**
music history and education. See no. 4526 in this volume.

962 GANDOLFI, Riccardo. **La cappella musicale**
as **della corte di Toscana: 1539-1859** [The music chapel of the Tuscan court: 1539-1859], *Haydn-Zentenarfeier* (Leipzig: Breitkopf & Härtel; Wien: Artaria, 1909) 167–84. *Charts, diagr.* In Italian. See no. 65 in this volume.
Includes lists of musicians and repertoire.

963 GAVAZZENI, Gianandrea. **Umanesimo del mu-**
as **sicista italiano** [The humanism of Italian musicians], *Atti del secondo Congresso internazionale di musica* (Firenze: Le Monnier, 1940) 33–39. In Italian; summaries in French and German. See no. 239 in this volume.
Examines the lifestyles, social positions, and personalities of musicians from the past and present.

964 GIRALDI, R. **La liuteria italiana come arte**
as **popolare** [Italian lute music as traditional art], *Atti del III Congresso nazionale di arti e tradizioni popolari* (Roma: Opera Nazionale Dopolavoro, 1936) 350–51. In Italian. See no. 218 in this volume.

965 GRÜNZINGER, Max. **Ingolstadt als Kunst-**
as **stadt** [Ingolstadt as a city of the arts], *Altbayern als Orgel-Landschaft* (Berlin: Merseburger, 1954) 11–12. In German. See no. 325 in this volume.

966 GURVIN, Olav. **Über Beziehungen zwischen**
as **deutscher und norwegischer Musik** [Links between German and Norwegian music], (Kassel; New York: Bärenreiter, 1965) 37–41. In German. See no. 467 in this volume.
From the 14th through the 16th c. German musical influence was limited to Bergen, where there was a Hanseatic trading settlement, but it became more general thereafter, through Norwegian relations with Copenhagen and Hamburg. German musicians who made careers in Norway include the 18th-c. composers Georg von Bertouch and Johan Daniel Berlin; Friedrich August Reissiger; the 19th-c. composers and pedagogues A.E. Schütze, Carl Arnold, and Friedrich Wilhelm Ferdinand Vogel; the publishers Carl Raabe and Wilhelm Harloff; and the conductors Hugo Kramm and Ernst Glaser. Important German performing groups who visited Norway and Norwegian musicians who studied in Germany in the 19th and 20th c. are listed. *(David Bloom)*

967 GYSI, Fritz. **Alpine Darstellungen in der**
as **Musik** [Alpine representations in music], *Schweizer Jahrbuch für Musikwissenschaft/Annales suisses de musicologie/Annuario svizzero di musicologia* I (1924) 76–91. In German. See no. 103 in this volume.

968 HÁBA, Alois. **Wolfgang Amadeus Mozart und**
as **die weitere Entwicklung der Musik** [Wolfgang Amadeus Mozart and the further development of music], *Internationale Konferenz über das Leben und Werk W.A. Mozarts* (Praha: Svaz Československých Skladatelů, 1956) 56–60. In German. See no. 360 in this volume.
Discusses characteristic features of Mozart's style—the use of especially wide and narrow intervals in melodic construction, the appropriation of sonata, song, and rondo form, the dominance of livelier tempos—in the context of music history in general. An important aspect for contemporary Czech composers is Mozart's role as a champion of bourgeois equal rights and creative freedom. *(Anthony F. Bavota)*

969 HAMEL, Fred. **Une histoire de la musique,**
as **enregistrée à des fins éducatives** [A history of music recorded for educational purposes], *La musique dans l'éducation* (Paris: UNESCO; Colin, 1955) 271–74. In French. See no. 323 in this volume.
An English-language version is abstracted as no. 970 in this volume.

970 HAMEL, Fred. **A history of music recorded for**
as **educational purposes,** *Music in education* (Paris: UNESCO, 1955) 260–63. See no. 322 in this volume.
Outlines the history and function of recorded anthologies of repertoire, such as Curt Sachs's *2000 Jahre Musik* (Parlophon, 1930) and Percy A. Scholes's *Columbia history of music through ear and eye* (Columbia, 1930-38). A French-language version is cited as no. 969 in this volume.

971 HOLMSEN, Borghild. **Les traces les plus**
as **anciennes de la musique en Norvège** [The oldest traces of music in Norway], *Congrès du Millénaire de la Normandie (911-1911)* (Rouen: Léon Gy, 1912) 322–49. *Music.* In French. See no. 77 in this volume.
A history of traditional and art music and poetry in Scandinavia, covering the period 900-1850, citing poets, musicians, and instruments, with some poems quoted, and 30 examples of folk melodies.

972 HROVATIN, Radoslav. **Les rapports réci-**
as **proques du folklore et de la création musicale artistique en Slovénie** [The reciprocal relations of folklore and musical artistic creation in Slovenia], *Journal of the International Folk Music Council* IV (1952) 35–39. *Music, bibliog., transcr.* In French. See no. 306 in this volume.
Art music has drawn on traditional music since the time of the medieval state of Carinthia, whose dukes were enthroned, according to sources of the mid-14th and early 15th c., to the singing of a hymn based on traditional sources. The process can be traced through 16th-c. Protestant hymns, 19th-c. songs by figures such as Josip Hašnik (better known as a poet), and 20th-c. compositions by Anton Lajovic, Matija Bravničar, and Karol Pahor. *(David Bloom)*

973 HUMBERT, Georges. **Les principes naturels de**
as **l'évolution musicale** [The natural principles of the evolution of music], *Congrès international d'histoire de la musique: Documents, mémoires et vœux* (Solesmes: St. Pierre; Paris: Fischbacher, 1901) 221–25. *Charts, diagr.* In French. See no. 32 in this volume.
An introduction to the author's *Notes pour servir à l'étude de l'histoire de la musique* (Neuchâtel: W. Sandoz, 1904). The evolution of music is not due to a series of voluntary acts, but to the evolutionary thrust inherent in the natural properties of music. Music history may be divided into three periods. The fourth one is just beginning.

974 HUMMEL, Walter. **Die Mozart-Gedenkstätten**
as **Salzburgs: Ihre Betreuung eine Aufgabe der Internationalen Stiftung Mozarteum** [The Mozart memorials of Salzburg: Their maintenance as a task of the Internationale Stiftung Mozarteum], *Internationale Konferenz über das Leben und Werk W.A. Mozarts* (Praha: Svaz Československých Skladatelů, 1956) 167–74. In German. See no. 360 in this volume.
Historical accounts of the city's Mozart museums, with their collections, and monuments: Mozarts Geburtshaus on Getreidegasse, the Mozart Wohn-Haus in Makartplatz, the Zauberflötenhäuschen that originally stood near the Theater auf der Wieden in Vienna, the statue of the composer by Ludwig von Schwanthaler in Mozartplatz, and the Mozarteum itself. *(David Bloom)*

975 INDY, Vincent d'. **De la sophistication de**
as **l'œuvre d'art par l'édition** [The refinement of works of art in the editing process], *Haydn-Zentenarfeier* (Leipzig: Breitkopf & Härtel; Wien: Artaria, 1909) 137–41. In French. See no. 65 in this volume.
Discusses examples by various composers, including Haydn, Monteverdi, Gluck, and Rossini.

976 KALOMIRIS, Manolis. **L'évolution de la**
as **musique en Grèce** [The evolution of music in Greece], *Atti del Congresso internazionale di musiche popolari mediterranee e del Convegno dei bibliotecari musicali* (Palermo: De Magistris succ. V. Bellotti, 1959) 75–85. In French. See no. 332 in this volume.
An informal survey of Greek traditional and art music from the Byzantine period to the present.

977 KLEMANTASKI, Louis. **La musique flamande**
as **en Angleterre** [Flemish music in England], *Annales du XXIIIe congrès* (Gent: Siffer, 1914) III, 254–62. In French. See no. 89 in this volume.
Many Flemings emigrated to England during the 14th c., and their musical traditions strongly influenced English composers.

978 KLEMETTI, Heikki. **Aperçu de l'histoire musi-**
as **cale finlandaise** [Outline of Finnish musical history], *Actes du Congrès d'histoire de l'art* (Paris: Presses Universitaires de France, 1923-1924) 922–28. In French. See no. 94 in this volume.

Finland's musical pioneers were two German teachers, Fredrik Pacius (1809-91) and Friedrich Richard Faltin (1835-1918). However, Finland's musical history dates from the beginning of its Christian church. In addition to religious music, secular melodies and dance music were composed before the 19th c. *(Vivian Conejero)*

979 KOCHER-KLEIN, Hilda. **Das Hausmusik-**
as **männlein** [The little Hausmusik man], *Musiker-ziehung: Zeitschrift der Musikerzieher Österreichs* special issue (1953) 145–46. In German. See no. 317 in this volume.

980 KRĂSTEV, Venelin. **Puti razvitija bolgarskoj**
as **muzykal'noj kul'turi v period XII-XVIII stoletii** [Paths of development of Bulgarian musical culture from the 12th to the 18th centuries], *Musica antiqua Europae orientalis* (Warszawa: Państwowe Wydawnictwo Naukowe, 1966). *Music, bibliog.* In Russian. See no. 506 in this volume.

981 LANG, Paul Henry. **The influence of political**
as **thought on the history of music,** *Papers of the American Musicological Society* (Philadelphia: American Musicological Society, 1946) 108–14. See no. 269 in this volume.
Political thought has been an important factor in changes in musical style. The influence of Louis XIV on musical developments in 17th-c. France is a case in point.

982 LEVI, Vito. **Das Schicksal der Mozart-Opern**
as **in Italien** [The fate of the Mozart operas in Italy], *Bericht über den internationalen musikwissenschaft-lichen Kongreß Wien Mozartjahr 1956* (Graz; Köln: Böhlau, 1958) 348–49. In German. See no. 365 in this volume.
Mozart's operas were much more enthusiastically received in their initial Italian appearances (ca. 1797-1807) than has been recognized. Reasons are proposed for the long subsequent period of their neglect and their successful revival in the 20th c. *(David Bloom)*

983 LISSA, Zofia. **Folk elements in Polish music**
as **from the Middle Ages up to the 18th century,** *Musica antiqua Europae orientalis* (Warszawa: Państwowe Wydawnictwo Naukowe, 1966) 354–82. *Music.* See no. 506 in this volume.
Discusses examples from the 11th to the 18th c., including Roman Catholic and Protestant religious music, dance music, and dramatic arts.

984 LITTLE, George. **Choral aspects and prospects,**
as *Organ and choral aspects and prospects* (London: Hinrichsen, 1958) 113–25. See no. 375 in this volume.
A historical survey of choral music from the Middle Ages to the present and a discussion of concerts in Montreal from 1956 to 57.

985 LORIA, Arturo. **Il gusto moderno e la musica**
as **del passato** [Modern taste and the music of the past], *Atti del terzo Congresso internazionale di musica* (Firenze: Le Monnier, 1940) 58–66. In Italian; summaries in French and German. See no. 256 in this volume.
Discusses the effect of audience reception on programming throughout history.

986 LUIN, Elizabeth Jeannette. **Mozarts Opern in**
as **Skandinavien** [Mozart's operas in Scandinavia], *Bericht über den internationalen musikwissenschaft-lichen Kongreß Wien Mozartjahr 1956* (Graz; Köln: Böhlau, 1958) 387–96. *Illus., port.* In German. See no. 365 in this volume.

A survey of productions in Copenhagen, Stockholm, and elsewhere in Scandinavia, from the first Copenhagen staging of *Così fan tutte* (1798) to the Oslo premiere of *Die Zauberflöte* (1930), with particular attention to the Copenhagen director Claus Nielsen Schall (1757-1835) and the singer-director Giuseppe Siboni (1780-1839). *(David Bloom)*

987 MARINKOVIĆ, Ilija. **Die nationale Richtung**
as **der jugoslawischen Musik und ihre Bedeutung** [The national direction of Yugoslavian music and its significance], *Musikerziehung: Zeitschrift der Musik-erzieher Österreichs* special issue (1953) 70–73. In German. See no. 317 in this volume.
The character of Yugoslavian music does not result from the use of folklore as structural material, but from a synthesis of musical and literary content. *(Allen Lott)*

988 MARXER, Otto. **Untergang St. Gallischer**
as **Choralpflege im ausgehenden Mittelalter und in neuer Zeit** [The decline of the St. Gall chant tradition in the late Middle Ages and after], *Acta generalis cantus gregoriani studiosorum conventus, Argentinensis, 16-19 Aug. 1905/Bericht des internationalen Kongresses für gregorianischen Choralgesang/ Compte rendu du Congrès international de plain-chant grégorien* (Strassburg: F.-X. Le Roux, 1905) 123–32. In German. See no. 50 in this volume.

989 MOBERG, Carl-Allan. **Das Musikleben in**
as **Schweden: Musikkulturelle Probleme in einem europäischen Randgebiet** [Musical life in Sweden: Problems of musical culture in a peripheral European area], *Bericht über den internationalen musikwissenschaftlichen Kongreß* (Kassel: Bärenreiter, 1957) 33–40. *Transcr.* In German. See no. 356 in this volume.
Assesses social and historical factors in musical developments from the end of the Middle Ages to the present, in both urban and rural contexts and with reference to political history, church influence, and industrialization. *(David Bloom)*

990 MOSER, Hans Joachim. **Die Niederlande in der**
as **Musikgeographie Europas** [The Netherlands in Europe's musical geography], *Société Internationale de Musicologie, cinquième congrès/Internationale Gesellschaft für Musikwissenschaft, fünfter Kongreß/ International Society for Musical Research, Fifth Congress* (Amsterdam: Vereniging voor Nederlandse Muziekgeschedenis, 1953) 296–303. In German. See no. 316 in this volume.

991 MOSER, Hans Joachim. **Österreich auf der**
as **Musiklandkarte Europas** [Austria on the musical map of Europe], *Bericht über den internationalen musikwissenschaftlichen Kongreß Wien Mozartjahr 1956* (Graz; Köln: Böhlau, 1958) 421–29. In German. See no. 365 in this volume.
Surveys the history of music in the territory of present-day Austria in terms of its relationships with musicians from elsewhere in Europe. *(David Bloom)*

992 MUELLER VON ASOW, Hedwig. **Kom-**
as **ponierende Frauen** [Women composers], *Bericht über den internationalen musikwissenschaftlichen Kongreß* (Kassel: Bärenreiter, 1963) 239–41. In German. See no. 452 in this volume.
Examples of women composers from the Middle Ages through the early 20th c. show that in European art music, as in other kinds of music, creativity is not restricted to men. *(David Bloom)*

993 NESTLER, Gerhard. **Grundbegriffe einer**
as **europäischen Musikgeschichte** [Basic concepts
for a European music history], *Musikerziehung:
Zeitschrift der Musikerzieher Österreichs* special issue
(1953) 79–82. In German. See no. 317 in this volume.

994 OLIVEIRA-LIMA, Manuel de. **La musique au**
as **Brésil au point de vue historique** [Music in Brazil
from a historical point of view], *Haydn-Zentenarfeier*
(Leipzig: Breitkopf & Härtel; Wien: Artaria, 1909)
443–46. In French. See no. 65 in this volume.

995 PAGLICCI-BROZZI, Antonio. **Opportunità di**
as **raccogliere le antiche et tradizionali fanfare**
dei comuni italiani [Opportunities for collecting the
old and traditional fanfares of the Italian municipali-
ties], *Atti del Congresso internazionale di scienze
storiche. VIII: Atti della sezione IV: Storia dell'arte musicale e drammatica* (Roma: R. Accademia dei Lincei,
1905) 51–54. In Italian. See no. 42 in this volume.
Every Italian municipality has always employed a band of trumpeters for
festive occasions. A serious study of Italian fanfare is proposed.

996 PARENTE, Alfredo. **Musicisti, critici,**
as **interpreti e pubblico di fronte alla musica del**
passato [Musicians, critics, interpreters, the public,
with respect to the music of the past], *Atti del terzo
Congresso internazionale di musica* (Firenze: Le
Monnier, 1940) 81–88. In Italian; summaries in French
and German. See no. 256 in this volume.
Discusses the development of conflicting aesthetic perspectives.

997 RAUGEL, Félix. **La musique sacrée à la**
as **chapelle des rois de France** [Sacred music at the
chapels of the kings of France], *Bericht über den Internationalen Kongress für Kirchenmusik/Compte rendu
du Congrès international de musique sacrée* (Bern:
Haupt, 1953) 55–57. In French. See no. 312 in this
volume.
Summary of a paper surveying the history of royal chapel music in France
from the baptism of Clovis (496) to the abdication of Charles X (1830).

998 RONGA, Luigi. **Creazione dello strumento e**
as **creazione della musica** [The creation of the instrument and the creation of music], *Atti del secondo
Congresso internazionale di musica* (Firenze: Le
Monnier, 1940) 324–31. In Italian; summaries in
French and German. See no. 239 in this volume.
Argues against a materialist conception of music history, and for the evolution of a subjective and spiritual character as exemplified in the relationship
between the Italian violin makers and composers of the 17th c. *(David Bloom)*

999 RUBIN, Marcel. **Nationale und internationale**
as **Musik** [National and international music], *Musik-
ziehung: Zeitschrift der Musikerzieher Österreichs* special issue (1953) 65–69. In German. See no. 317 in this
volume.

1000 RYBARIČ, Richard. **Die Hauptquellen und**
as **Probleme der slowakischen Musikgeschichte**
bis zum Ende des XVIII Jahrhunderts [Slovak
music history up to the end of the 18th century: Principal
sources, topics], *Musica antiqua Europae orientalis*
(Warszawa: Państwowe Wydawnictwo Naukowe,
1966) 97–114. In German. See no. 506 in this volume.
Examines topics from the 8th to the 18th c.

1001 SACCHETTI, Liborio. **Le chant religieux de**
as **l'Église orthodoxe russe** [Religious chant of the
Russian Orthodox Church], *Congrès international
d'histoire de la musique: Documents, mémoires et vœux*
(Solesmes: St. Pierre; Paris: Fischbacher, 1901)
134–51. In French. See no. 32 in this volume.
Russian Orthodox chant is an entirely independent musical language,
based on a non-Western system of modes. Its influence on the music of several composers, including Mihail Glinka, Milij Balakirev, and Čajkovskij,
is discussed.

1002 SACCHETTI, Liborio. **Les principaux mo-**
as **ments de l'histoire de la musique profane en**
Russie [The principal moments in the history of secu-
lar music in Russia], *Haydn-Zentenarfeier* (Leipzig:
Breitkopf & Härtel; Wien: Artaria, 1909) 466–73. In
French. See no. 65 in this volume.

1003 SCHAEFFNER, André. **Musique primitive ou**
as **exotique et musique moderne d'occident** [Prim-
itive or exotic music and modern Western music], *Atti
del terzo Congresso internazionale di musica* (Firenze:
Le Monnier, 1940) 176–86. In French; summaries in
Italian and German. See no. 256 in this volume.
Traces the use of exoticisms in Western music.

1004 SCHIEDERMAIR, Ludwig. **Die Musik des**
as **Rheinlandes** [Music of the Rhineland], *Bericht über
den I. musikwissenschaftlichen Kongress der
Deutschen Musikgesellschaft in Leipzig* (Wiesbaden:
Breitkopf & Härtel, 1926) 401. In German. See no. 120
in this volume.

1005 SCHNEIDER, Marius. **Wurzeln und Anfänge**
as **der abendländischen Mehrstimmigkeit** [Ori-
gins of Western polyphony], *Report of the Eighth Congress of the International Musicological Society. I: Papers* (Kassel: Bärenreiter, 1961) 161–78. *Music,
transcr.* In German. See no. 439 in this volume.
The oldest strata within medieval European polyphony are traceable to a
diffusion of late megalithic culture from India through Asia Minor to the
Mediterranean (disseminated eastward as well, to the South Pacific), and a
second diffusion from the Caucasus. Their specific forms include homolo-
gous structures (simultaneous performance of a melody and its variant),
contrary motion, imitation, and drone. Parallel organum is not a fundamental form, but an extreme development of the homologous-structure category. *(David Bloom)*

1006 SEEGER, Charles. **The cultivation of various**
as **European traditions in the Americas,** *Report of
the Eighth Congress of the International Musicological
Society. I: Papers* (Kassel: Bärenreiter, 1961) 364–75.
Music. See no. 439 in this volume.
Sketches the history of the hegemony of European music culture in the New
World in terms of cultural dynamics within European civilizations in the
period of colonization; the transplantation of traditions; the primacy of the
word or text within elite European music traditions; and acculturation
through contact. The only forced imposition of music traditions took place
in the U.S., but neo-Europeanism has been and remains a negative acculturation factor. Trends over the past 30 years, including those stemming from
new technologies, suggest the possibility of a more effective and desirable
interdependence between European and American music.

1007 SPITZMÜLLER, Alexander. **Musik im**
as **zwischenstaatlichen Kulturaustausch: Ein der**
internationalen Lösung harrendes Problem
[Music in the cultural exchange between nations: A persistent problem awaiting international solution], *Musikerziehung: Zeitschrift der Musikerzieher Österreichs*

special issue (1953) 156–59. In German. See no. 317 in this volume.

1008 ŠTĚDROŇ, Bohumír. **Mozart und Mähren**
as [Mozart and Moravia], *Bericht über den internationalen musikwissenschaftlichen Kongreß Wien Mozartjahr 1956* (Graz; Köln: Böhlau, 1958) 603–07. *Bibliog.* In German. See no. 365 in this volume.

Discusses Mozart's stay in Olomouc and Brno, October 1767–January 1768, and the reception of his work in Moravia, with particular reference to the composers Peregrino Gravani (1732-1815), Gotthard Pokorný (1733-1802), Gottfried Rieger (1764-1865), Pavel Křižkovský (1820-85), and Janáček, all active in Brno, and the Olomouc composers Francesco Carlo Müller (1729-1803) and Vilém Hybl (ca. 1751-1824). *(David Bloom)*

1009 STEFANOVIĆ, Dimitrije. **The Serbian chant**
as **from the 15th to the 18th centuries,** *Musica antiqua Europae orientalis* (Warszawa: Państwowe Wydawnictwo Naukowe, 1966). *Facs., music, charts, diagr.* See no. 506 in this volume.

Discusses Serbian chant MSS.

1010 STUCKENSCHMIDT, Hans Heinz. **Trends of**
as **improvisation in Western music,** *Music east and west* (Nai Dilli: Indian Council for Cultural Relations, 1966) 57–65. See no. 489 in this volume.

Improvisational practice was the force behind innovation and progress in Western music from the beginnings of European polyphony through the development of jazz. Now, serial methods of composition and the use of electronically generated sound, working toward the totally predetermined, threaten an end to spontaneity. *(David Bloom)*

1011 SWAN, Alfred J. **Something about the**
as **znamenny,** *Zweiter internationaler Kongress für katholische Kirchenmusik: Zu Ehren des Heiligen Papstes Pius X* (Wien: conference, 1955) 87–88. See no. 339 in this volume.

Surveys the current state of research on Russian znamennyj chant.

1012 TOBY, Ottavio. **L'origine popolare della**
as **siciliana e la sua evoluzione dal Trecento a Bach e ad Haendel** [The traditional origins of the siciliana and its evolution from the trecento to Bach and Händel], *Bericht über den Internationalen musikwissenschaftlichen Kongress* (Kassel: Bärenreiter, 1954) 194–96. In Italian. See no. 319 in this volume.

Traces the literary and musical evidence of the "siciliana" in the centuries before it achieved prominence as a stylized instrumental movement wrought by Bach and Händel. No unbroken thread has been found, either musical or literary. The earliest survivals of poetry so named ("ciciliane"), from the age of Boccaccio, do not point to a literary genre and there is no surviving music from that age which can be linked with Sicily. In the following centuries the Sicilian dialect is often used by poets, but the settings of this poetry show no demonstrable link with Sicily. Alessandro Scarlatti, a native of Palermo, composed two arias titled "aria alla siciliana"; these do not adumbrate the movement type made famous by Bach and Händel. No more Bach-like are examples produced by other 17th-c. composers such as Francesco Antonio Bonporti in Italy and François Rebel in France. It is hypothesized that a certain passionate intensity came to be associated with Sicily over the centuries, and that this general idea is the common denominator for Italian poetry and music (14th-17th c.) which evoke the island by name. There is no good evidence of a dance origin. *(Carl Skoggard)*

1013 TORREFRANCA, Fausto. **La musica siciliana e**
as **dei popoli mediterranei nella storia della musica europea** [The music of Sicily and of the Mediterranean peoples in the history of European music], *Atti del Congresso internazionale di musiche popolari mediterranee e del Convegno dei bibliotecari musicali*

(Palermo: De Magistris succ. V. Bellotti, 1959) 189–204. In Italian. See no. 332 in this volume.

The long-breathed cantilena of traditional Sicilian melody, brought to 19th-c. opera by Bellini, was heard much earlier in Venice and Florence. Evidence of Sicilian influence in northern Italy, in melodic structure and ornamentation, is traced from the 15th through the 18th c.

1014 VALABREGA, Cesare. **Una storia della musica**
as **italiana in dischi microsolco** [A history of Italian music in long-playing records], *Fontes artis musicae* IV/2 (Dec 1957) 83–85. In Italian. See no. 373 in this volume.

The Discoteca di Stato has published a 40-record anthology of the history of Italian music from its origins to the 19th c., known as the *Antologia della storia della musica italiana, dalle origini al secolo XIXo, in 40 dischi microsolco.*

1015 VANCEA, Zeno. **Die sozialen Grundlagen der**
as **rumänischen Kunstmusik** [The social foundations of Romanian art music], *Bericht über den internationalen musikwissenschaftlichen Kongreß Wien Mozartjahr 1956* (Graz; Köln: Böhlau, 1958) 647–52. In German. See no. 365 in this volume.

Social, political, and economic conditions, including the hostility of the Orthodox church to secular music, prevented the emergence of a secular art music in Romania until the mid-19th c. Developments since then include the contributions of George Enescu, the development of a national style inspired by extensive field collection of traditional music, and, since World War II, an aesthetic of realism growing out of the mass movement of the rural and urban working classes at the forefront of social change. *(David Bloom)*

1016 VANDERHAEGE, René (René Lyr). **La**
as **musique en Wallonie** [Music in Wallonia], *Congrès international des Amitiés Françaises* (Mons: Libert, 1911) 135–38. In French. See no. 74 in this volume.

The many accomplishments of Walloon musicians are cited, from Dufay and Binchois through Franck to the Ysaÿes.

1017 VERESS, Sándor. **Folk music in musical and**
as **general education,** *Journal of the International Folk Music Council* I (1949) 40–43. See no. 281 in this volume.

The influence of traditional music on Western music from the mid-19th to the mid-20th c. is comparable to that in the 16th and 17th c. Such developments in Hungarian art music have influenced all levels of education.

1018 VUILLERMOZ, Émile. **Le goût moderne et la**
as **musique du passé** [Modern taste and music of the past], *Atti del terzo Congresso internazionale di musica* (Firenze: Le Monnier, 1940) 21–27. In French; summaries in Italian and German. See no. 256 in this volume.

Discusses differences of style, form, intended audience, and instruments.

1019 WAGNER, Peter. **Ueber den traditionellen**
as **Choral** [On traditional chant], *Acta generalis cantus gregoriani studiosorum conventus, Argentinensis, 16-19 Aug. 1905/Bericht des internationalen Kongresses für gregorianischen Choralgesang/Compte rendu du Congrès international de plain-chant grégorien* (Strassburg: F.-X. Le Roux, 1905) 32–39. In German. See no. 50 in this volume.

Pius X's motu proprio *Tra le sollecitudini* (1903) called for a restoration of "traditional" chant. A developmental view of the history of chant is proposed, excluding the mutilations of the 17th c., but including the earliest MSS from the 9th c. as seen through later medieval codices. Chant reform based in the moderation of an overly scientific "archeological" approach (such as the Solesmes "critical study edition" of 1895) with the practical liturgical requirements of the modern Catholic church is suggested.

1020 WARD, John. **The *folia*,** *Société Internationale de*
as *Musicologie, cinquième congrès/Internationale
Gesellschaft für Musikwissenschaft, fünfter
Kongreß/International Society for Musical Research,
Fifth Congress* (Amsterdam: Vereniging voor
Nederlandse Muziekgeschiedenis, 1953) 415–22.
Bibliog. See no. 316 in this volume.

The Portuguese, Spanish, Italian, and French origins of the *folia* and its development are traced throughout two periods: from the end of the 15th c.
through the 16th c., when its form was variable and appeared under various
names, such as *aria da cantar*, and from the end of the 16th c. to present,
when its form was relatively fixed. *(Tsipora Yosselevitch)*

1021 WERNER, Eric, moderator. **Mündliche und**
as **schriftliche Tradition im Mittelmeerraum**
[Oral and written tradition in the Mediterranean re-
gion], *Bericht über den neunten internationalen
Kongreß* (Kassel: Bärenreiter, 1964-1966) 121–42.
Music, transcr. In German. See no. 491 in this volume.

A roundtable consisting of Hanoch AVENARY, Solange CORBIN,
Fabienne GÉGOU, Edith GERSON-KIWI, Kurt REINHARD, Michal
SMOIRA-ROLL, and Walther WÜNSCH. Topics include a general account of Mediterranean music history through the 12th c.; the significance
of St. Jerome's ability to read silently; mosaic structure in Jewish and
Byzantine monody; the status of Mediterranean tradition in the 13th c.; instruments in Southeast European oral epic and in the Byzantine Empire;
common features of chant rhythm in Romanian, Armenian, Greek, Russian, Georgian, Jewish, and Coptic liturgies; regional issues in the transition from oral to written tradition; and archaic Mediterranean elements in
neotraditional Israeli song. *(David Bloom)*

1022 WEYLER, Walter. **Die Frage der flämischen**
as **Musik: Ein Beitrag zur Klärung einer**
Begriffsverwirrung [The question of Flemish music: Contribution to the clarification of a concept],
*Bericht über den internationalen musikwissenschaft-
lichen Kongreß* (Kassel: Bärenreiter, 1963) 229–33. In
German. See no. 452 in this volume.

Reviews the history of terms meaning "Flanders" and "Flemish" from the
Middle Ages onward. Since the founding of the Belgian state in 1830, the
concept of Flemish music has taken on an increasingly ideological character, which leads to inaccuracy or at least unclearness; "Netherlandish"
would be a less ambiguous designation. *(David Bloom)*

1023 WIORA, Walter. **Die geschichtliche Sonder-**
as **stellung der abendländischen Musik** [The special historical position of Western music], *Musik and
Musikerziehung in der Reifezeit* (Mainz: Schott, 1959)
70–89. *Transcr.* In German. See no. 412 in this volume.

Discussion of the need for pedagogical approaches that assert the unique
historical character and universal appeal of the European musical tradition
without denying the value of non-European cultures. *(David Bloom)*

1024 WOLF, Johannes. **English influence on the evo-**
as **lution of music,** *Report of the Fourth Congress of the
International Musical Society* (London: Novello, 1912)
83–89. See no. 71 in this volume.

Discusses examples from the 16th to the 18th c.

1025 ZAGIBA, Franz. **Die Funktion des Volkslied-**
as **gutes in der Entwicklung der südeuropäischen**
Musikgeschichte [The role of the folk-song repertoire in the music history of Southern Europe], *Bericht
über den Internationalen musikwissenschaftlichen
Kongreß* (Kassel: Bärenreiter, 1954) 197–99. *Music.*
In German. See no. 319 in this volume.

Slavic traditional song has significantly influenced religious music of the
region and still survives in present-day religious practices. For example,
cadences for Lesson recitation tones as preserved in the so-called Lectio-
nary from Trogir (12th-13th c.) are very like the cadences notated for the

melodies used for the Czech hymn *Hospodine pomiluj ny* and also closely
resemble the cadences chanted by modern-day Croatian pilgrims on the
Dalmatian coast. *(Carl Skoggard)*

22 Antiquity (to ca. 500)

1026 COLLAER, Paul. **La migration du style**
as **mélismatique oriental vers l'Occident** [The migration of Eastern melismatic style towards the West],
Journal of the International Folk Music Council XVI
(1964) 70–73. *Transcr.* In French. See no. 463 in this
volume.

The ancestor of a generally Mediterranean musical culture would have
been established ca. 3000 B.C.E. in Mesopotamia, and featured the heptatonic scale and short melodic motifs that could be arranged and rearranged
in longer sequences and also melismatically ornamented in a free rhythm.
Archaeological and ethnomusicological evidence of its spread through migration to Asia Minor, the Caucasus, Europe, and North Africa over the
next two millennia, together with the history of the Dorian invasions, make
it possible to reconstruct an account of the failure of melismatic art in the
West to develop as elaborately as elsewhere. *(David Bloom)*

1027 DABO-PERANIĆ, Miljenko M. **Le sens de**
as **l'harmonie chez les Grecs** [What harmony meant
to the Greeks], *Bericht über den siebenten
internationalen musikwissenschaftlichen Kongress*
(Kassel: Bärenreiter, 1959) 85–86. *Charts, diagr.* In
French. See no. 390 in this volume.

For the Greeks before the Hellenic epoch, the term *harmonia* when applied
to music referred to an entire system of seven scales (the agreement of two
sounds was referred to as *symphonia* or *diaphonia*). The Greek scales corresponded to Western medieval modes. Many innovations of the Hellenic
period are wrongly believed to have been familiar centuries earlier.
(Carl Skoggard)

1028 D'ANGELI, Andrea. **La musica bizantina o**
as **neogreca è il tramite fra la ellenica o classico e**
la gregoriana? [Is Byzantine or neo-Greek music the
path between the Hellenic or classical and the Gregorian?], *Atti del V Congresso internazionale di studi
bizantini* (Roma: Associazione Nazionale per gli Studi
Bizantini, 1940) II, 481–88. In Italian. See no. 233 in
this volume.

Investigates the degree to which aspects of Byzantine chant seeped into
Ambrosian and Gregorian chant. Specific chant examples from these three
areas are mentioned. In chants to the creator from various sources (the ancient Egyptian world, Byzantine chant), the elements of repetition and imitation are present. There is essentially no historical discontinuity from
Greek to Gregorian music. Greater research is needed to determine other
ways in which the Byzantine and Catholic worlds are connected.
(Susan Poliniak)

1029 FELLERER, Karl Gustav. **Probleme der mittel-**
as **meerischen Musik in Frühchristlichen Gesang**
[Problems of Mediterranean music in early Christian
chant], *Atti del Congresso internazionale di musiche
popolari mediterranee e del Convegno dei bibliotecari
musicali* (Palermo: De Magistris succ. V. Bellotti,
1959) 237–42. In German. See no. 332 in this volume.

Programmatic discussion of the value of comparative and ethnomusicological methodology in reconstructing aspects of early Christian liturgical music. Important factors involving the concept of a Mediterranean
culture area are the tensions between classic Greek-style text-centered
forms of hymnody and Asian melismatic forms of psalmody, and between
the quantitative prosody of the region south of the Alps and the qualitative
prosody to the north. *(David Bloom)*

1030
as
GOMBOSI, Otto. **Key, mode, species,** *Compte rendu/Kongressbericht/Report* (Basel: Bärenreiter, 1951) 133–34. See no. 289 in this volume.
Summary of a paper, published in *Journal of the American Musicological Society* IV, 1951, proposing that the Greeks knew no modes; that their octave species were in filial relation to their keys and not conversely; and that, consequently, the octave species were of no importance for the concept of tonality or modality in ancient Greek music. *(Scott Fruehwald)*

1031
as
GRAF, Ernst. **Über den Stand der altgriechischen Musikforschung** [The state of research on ancient Greek music], *Bericht über den zweiten Kongress der Internationalen Musikgesellschaft* (Leipzig: Breitkopf & Härtel, 1907) 154–60. In German. See no. 53 in this volume.
A survey of the literature beginning with the 1890s on musical materials, theoretical writings, and the historical syntheses of Hermann Abert and Hugo Riemann.

1032
as
HICKMANN, Hans. **Die Anfänge eines geordneten Musiklebens im Ägypten der Pharaonen** [The beginnings of an organized musical life in pharaonic Egypt], *Musikerziehung: Zeitschrift der Musikerzieher Österreichs* special issue (1953) 55–57. In German. See no. 317 in this volume.
Explores musical activities under the reign of the pharaohs, drawing on evidence from the graves of the ancient Egyptians. A brief overview of musical life and personalities in the old, middle, and late periods is provided. *(Joseph Giroux)*

1033
as
HICKMANN, Hans. **Présence de la constante de quarte, de quinte et d'octave: Son rôle structurel dans l'antiquité pré-hellénique** [Presence of the constant of fourth, fifth, and octave: Its structural role in pre-Hellenic antiquity], *La résonance dans les échelles musicales* (Paris: Centre National de la Recherche Scientifique [CNRS], 1963) 103–07. In French; summaries in English and German. See no. 420 in this volume.
Two- and three-voice polyphony as early as the third millennium B.C.E. was based on fourth, fifth, and octave, as has been observed from the study of well-preserved wind instruments. Iconographic representations show that lute frets were spaced on the same principles. *(author)*

1034
as
HICKMANN, Hans. **Quelques nouveaux documents concernant le jeu de la harpe et l'emploi de la chironomie dans l'Egypte pharaonique** [Some new documents concerning harp playing and the use of chironomy in pharaonic Egypt], *Société Internationale de Musicologie, cinquième congrès/Internationale Gesellschaft für Musikwissenschaft, fünfter Kongreß/International Society for Musical Research, Fifth Congress* (Amsterdam: Vereniging voor Nederlandse Muziekgeschiedenis, 1953) 233–40. In French. See no. 316 in this volume.

1035
as
IL'IN, Vladimir. **Der gemeinsame Ursprung des gregorianischen und des altrussischen Neumengesangs** [The common origin of Gregorian and Old Russian neumed chants], *Bericht über den Internationalen Kongress für Kirchenmusik/Compte rendu du Congrès international de musique sacrée* (Bern: Haupt, 1953) 38–40. In German. See no. 312 in this volume.

1036
as
LECOMTE. **Différence de la musique des Celtes et de celle des Grecs avec le chant ambrosien et mosarabique et celle du chant ambrosien et mosarbique avec le chant grégorien et celle du chant grégorien avec la musique du Moyen Age** [The difference between the music of the Celts and the Greeks and Ambrosian and Mozarabic chant, and that between Ambrosian and Mozarabic chant and Gregorian chant, and the difference between Gregorian chant and the music of the Middle Ages], *[Ier] Congrès historique européen* (Paris: P.H. Krabbe, 1835) II, 265–92. In French. See no. 1 in this volume.

1037
as
POIRÉE, Élie. **Chant des sept voyelles: Analyse musicale** [Chant of the seven vowels: Musical analysis], *Congrès international d'histoire de la musique: Documents, mémoires et vœux* (Solesmes: St. Pierre; Paris: Fischbacher, 1901) 28–38. *Music.* In French. See no. 32 in this volume.
Applies the ancient Greek theory—that each of the seven planets (Mercury, Venus, the Sun, the Moon, Mars, Jupiter, and Saturn) is associated with a particular musical tone and a particular vowel—to fragments from several MSS.

1038
as
POIRÉE, Élie. **Une nouvelle interprétation rythmique du second hymne à Apollon** [A new rhythmic interpretation of the second hymn to Apollo], *Congrès international d'histoire de la musique: Documents, mémoires et vœux* (Solesmes: St. Pierre; Paris: Fischbacher, 1901) 70–73. *Music.* In French. See no. 32 in this volume.
A proper interpretation must give special attention to the syllabification of the text. The poetic and musical meter of the hymn are discussed.

1039
as
RAMORINO, Felice. **Dell'opportunità di pubblicare in edizione critica gli** *scriptores musici latini* [The opportunity to publish the *scriptores musici latini* in a critical edition], *Atti del Congresso internazionale di scienze storiche. VIII: Atti della sezione IV: Storia dell'arte musicale e drammatica* (Roma: R. Accademia dei Lincei, 1905) 3–5. In Italian. See no. 42 in this volume.
Lists musical treatises from ancient Rome that should be published in modern critical editions, and cites 22 works from Cicero (50 B.C.E.) to Beda (720 C.E.).

1040
as
REINACH, Théodore. **Sur la transcription du premier hymne delphique** [On the transcription of the first Delphic hymn], *Congrès international d'histoire de la musique: Documents, mémoires et vœux* (Solesmes: St. Pierre; Paris: Fischbacher, 1901) 65–69. *Music.* In French. See no. 32 in this volume.
A reply to no. 1044. Discusses a transcription by Albert Thierfelder (1846-1924).

1041
as
RICHTER, Lukas. **Platons Stellung zur praktischen und spekulativen Musiktheorie seiner Zeit** [Plato's position in the practical and speculative music theory of his time], *Bericht über den internationalen musikwissenschaftlichen Kongreß* (Kassel: Bärenreiter, 1957) 196–202. In German. See no. 356 in this volume.
Plato's writings offer the earliest evidence on the relationship between Pythagorean theory and the practical musicianship of the *harmonikoi* in the period before Aristoxenus. He had little respect for the *harmonikoi*, regarding only the mathematical-physical theory of the Pythagoreans as legitimate science. *(David Bloom)*

1042
as
RUELLE, Émile. **Le chant gnostico-magique des sept voyelles grecques** [Gnostic-magic chant of

seven Greek vowels], *Congrès international d'histoire de la musique: Documents, mémoires et vœux* (Solesmes: St. Pierre; Paris: Fischbacher, 1901) 15–27. *Charts, diagr.* In French. See no. 32 in this volume.

The ancient Greeks associated the seven vowels with magical properties. Each vowel was connected with one of the seven planets (Mercury, Venus, the Sun, the Moon, Mars, Jupiter, and Saturn). The vowels were also the bases for the seven degrees of the octave.

1043
as
SUÑOL BAULINAS, Gregori M. **Rapporti tra la musica bizantina e la musica latina liturgica, specialmente il canto ambrosiano** [Connections between Byzantine music and Latin liturgical music, especially Ambrosian chant], *Atti del V Congresso internazionale di studi bizantini* (Roma: Associazione Nazionale per gli Studi Bizantini, 1940) II, 540–41. In Italian. See no. 233 in this volume.

Discusses several modifications to modal theory based on the study of old MSS. For instance, the liturgical modes do not correspond to the Greek modes, and, in relation to Ambrosian chant, modalities have not been assigned to melodies. Ambrosian chant is more Eastern than Gregorian. *(Susan Poliniak)*

1044
as
TIERSOT, Julien. **Le premier hymne delphique** [The first Delphic hymn], *Congrès international d'histoire de la musique: Documents, mémoires et vœux* (Solesmes: St. Pierre; Paris: Fischbacher, 1901) 63–64. *Transcr.* In French. See no. 32 in this volume.

Compares the transcriptions of the hymn by Théodore Reinach and Albert Thierfelder.

1045
as
URSPRUNG, Otto. **Wirklich so viel griechische Einflüsse in der mittelalterlichen Musik?** [Really so much Greek influence on medieval music?], *Bericht über den I. musikwissenschaftlichen Kongress der Deutschen Musikgesellschaft in Leipzig* (Wiesbaden: Breitkopf & Härtel, 1926) 206–08. In German. See no. 120 in this volume.

The extent of Greek influence is clarified by a review of the Greek colony in Rome and the influence of Greek, Byzantine, and Asian culture on Western liturgy. The prevalence of the Greek language in Western liturgy is also discussed. *(William Renwick)*

1046
as
VETTER, Walther. **Antike Polyphonie?** [Ancient polyphony?], *Bericht über den siebenten internationalen musikwissenschaftlichen Kongress* (Kassel: Bärenreiter, 1959) 290–93. In German. See no. 390 in this volume.

A critique of Heinrich Sanden's *Antike Polyphonie* (Heidelberg, 1957). Contrary to Sanden's assertions, the cases of simultaneous pitches in ancient Greek music, as when a pupil sang to the teacher's kithara at a distance of octave, fifth, fourth, etc., do not demonstrate that the music was in any sense polyphonic; as has been understood since the Netherlandish era, polyphony requires that the voices move independently of one another. *(David Bloom)*

1047
as
WERNER, Eric. **Dead Sea scrolls contain musically revealing elements/Les manuscrits de la Mer Morte contiennnent des signes intéressant la musique,** *Perspectives de la musique sacrée à la lumière de l'encyclique* Musicae sacrae disciplina (Paris: conference, 1959) 305–18. In English and French. See no. 379 in this volume.

A survey of evidence on the musical practice of the Essene community and ancient Judaism in general as found in the Dead Sea scrolls discovered at Qumran 1947 and held in the collections of the Muzeon Yisrael, Jerusalem, including their attitudes toward and use of wind instruments and antiphonal singing. Certain marginal signs in the scrolls, not so far successfully interpreted, are shown to have a startling resemblance to neumes of Byzantine

kontakia of the 9th-11th c.: they may represent an attempt at ekphonetic notation. *(David Bloom)*

1048
as
WERNER, Eric. **Die Ursprünge der Psalmodie** [The origins of psalmody], *Zweiter internationaler Kongress für katholische Kirchenmusik: Zu Ehren des Heiligen Papstes Pius X* (Wien: conference, 1955) 82–86. In German. See no. 339 in this volume.

The main distinguishing features of psalmody as a form, the parallelism or varied repetition and the final melisma, are characteristic of ancient polytheistic Hamito-Semitic religious texts (Egyptian, Sumerian-Akkadian, Ugaritic) as well as monotheistic ones, but are not found in Indo-European (e.g. Vedic, Hittite, Lycian) texts. The observation helps in analyzing the musical structure of the Oxyrhynchus Hymn (Oxyrhynchus papyrus 1786 of the Ashmolean Museum, Oxford), in interpreting the different responses to psalmody of the Latin and Eastern church fathers, and in explaining the origins of the antiphon form. *(David Bloom)*

1049
as
WIORA, Walter. **La musique à l'époque de la peinture paléolithique** [Music at the time of Paleolithic painting], *Journal of the International Folk Music Council* XIV (1962) 1–6. *Transcr.* In French. See no. 442 in this volume.

Instruments depicted in the sculpture and painting of the Old Stone Age between 25,000 and 10,000 years ago include whistles, flutes, and musical bows. Common features in the musics of extant hunter-gatherer societies at the greatest possible ethnic distance—the Siberian and Sami peoples of northern Eurasia on the one hand and the Khoisan and Pygmy peoples of southern and central Africa on the other—suggest that Paleolithic music shared the same features, in particular bitonic, tritonic, and tetratonic scale structures. *(David Bloom)*

1050
as
WIORA, Walter. **Die vergleichende Frühgeschichte der europäischen Musik als methodische Forschung** [The comparative history of early European music as methodological research], *Compte rendu/Kongressbericht/Report* (Basel: Bärenreiter, 1951) 212–21. *Music, bibliog.* In German. See no. 289 in this volume.

Discusses the possibility of a comparative reconstruction of early European music history, analogous to the linguistic reconstruction of Proto-Indo-European, by means of a systematic comparison of melodies from both notated and orally transmitted traditions. Examples from an enquiry into the origins of Gregorian chant are provided. *(David Bloom)*

1051
as
WIORA, Walter. **Volks- und Kunstmusik in der griechisch-römischen Antike** [Traditional music and art music in Greco-Roman antiquity], *Atti del Congresso internazionale di musiche popolari mediterranee e del Convegno dei bibliotecari musicali* (Palermo: De Magistris succ. V. Bellotti, 1959) 91–94. In German. See no. 332 in this volume.

Summarizes an analysis of what can be inferred about the genres and functions of music in Greece from the archaic period to the point in late antiquity at which more direct evidence becomes available. An extended version is included in the author's *Europäische Volksmusik und abendländische Tonkunst* (Kassel, 1957). *(David Bloom)*

23 Middle Ages (ca. 500 – 1400)

1052
as
AMELLI, Guerrino Ambrosio Maria. **De Guidonis Aretini, eiusque asseclarum gestis, in conventibus internationalibus oratio Aretii, Romae et Argentinae** [Concerning the deeds of Guido d'Arezzo and his followers: Speech at the international meetings at Arezzo, Rome, and Strasbourg], *Acta generalis cantus gregoriani studiosorum conventus, Argentinensis, 16-19 Aug. 1905/Bericht des*

internationalen Kongresses für gregorianischen Choralgesang/Compte rendu du Congrès international de plain-chant grégorien (Strassburg: F.-X. Le Roux, 1905) 141–45. In Latin. See no. 50 in this volume.

1053
as

ANDOYER, Raphael. **Note sur la chant anté-grégorien** [Note on pre-Gregorian chant], *Comptes rendus, rapports et vœux du Congrès parisien et régional de chant liturgique et de musique d'église* (Paris: Schola Cantorum, 1912) 58–60. In French. See no. 75 in this volume.

1054
as

ANGLÈS, Higini. **Cantors und Ministrers in den Diensten der Könige von Katalonien-Aragonien im 14. Jahrhundert** [Singers and minstrels in the service of the kings of Catalonia and Aragón in the 14th century], *Bericht über den musikwissenschaftlichen Kongreß in Basel* (Leipzig: Breitkopf & Härtel, 1925) 56–66. *Charts, diagr.* In German. See no. 102 in this volume.

Discusses lists of jongleurs, singers, minstrels, and organists taken from account books and government records kept by Jaime II, Alfonso IV, Pedro IV, and Juan I, all kings of Aragón. *(Sylvia Eversole)*

1055
as

ANGLÈS, Higini. **La musica sacra medievale in Sicilia** [Medieval sacred music in Sicily], *Atti del Congresso internazionale di musiche popolari mediterranee e del Convegno dei bibliotecari musicali* (Palermo: De Magistris succ. V. Bellotti, 1959) 205–14. In Italian. See no. 332 in this volume.

A summary of the evidence, particularly from MSS in the collections of the Biblioteca Nacional, Madrid, where they were deposited in the late 18th c. by the viceroy of Sicily, Juan Francisco Pacheco, Duque de Uceda. There is very little documentation of music practice until the period of the Norman kingdom, in the 12th-13th c., from which a rich monophonic repertoire survives. Polyphonic practice can be positively demonstrated for Sicily from no later than the beginning of the 13th c., considerably earlier than for mainland Italy. The music, and its notation, are generally the same as those of France and England in the period. *(David Bloom)*

1056
as

ANGLÈS, Higini. **Die zwei Arten der Mensuralnotation der Monodie des Mittelalters** [The two types of mensural notation used for the monody of the Middle Ages], *Bericht über den siebenten internationalen musikwissenschaftlichen Kongress* (Kassel: Bärenreiter, 1959) 56–57. In German. See no. 390 in this volume.

During the Middle Ages, Europe possessed a unitary tradition of nonmodal rhythm and nonmodal notation, suitable for monody and sometimes applied to polyphony. The fundamentals of this mensural, nonmodal rhythm are explained. *(Carl Skoggard)*

1057
as

APPEL, Ernst. **Über das Verhältnis von Musiktheorie und Kompositionspraxis im späteren Mittelalter (etwa 1200-1500)** [The relation between music theory and compositional practice in the later Middle Ages (ca. 1200-1500)], *Bericht über den internationalen musikwissenschaftlichen Kongreß* (Kassel: Bärenreiter, 1963) 354–56. In German. See no. 452 in this volume.

Discusses discrepancies between surviving compositions and the compositional rules given in medieval treatises.

1058
as

ARRO, Elmar. **Probleme der Provenienz des altrussischen kirchlich-kultischen Gesanges** [Questions concerning the provenance of Old Russian liturgical chant], *Anfänge der slavischen Musik* (Bratislava: Slovenská Akadémia Vied, 1966) 101–15. In German. See no. 477 in this volume.

Early Russian music was based largely on a symmetrical 12-tone scale broken into four equal trichords. The ancient Russian modes are constructed from a trichordal system, and therefore could not have been derived from the Byzantine oktōēchos, which was based on tetrachords. The Russian system also featured whole-tone scale structures and emphasis on the tritone. The system is most likely indigenous, evolving out of folk traditions. *(Brian Doherty)*

1059
as

AUBRY, Pierre. **L'ars mensurabilis et les proses liturgiques au XIIIᵉ siècle** [Ars mensurabilis and liturgical prose in the 13th century], *Haydn-Zentenarfeier* (Leipzig: Breitkopf & Härtel; Wien: Artaria, 1909) 108. In French. See no. 65 in this volume.

Includes a subsequent panel discussion.

1060
as

BECHERINI, Bianca. **Antonio Squarcialupi e il Codice Mediceo Palatino 87** [Antonio Squarcialupi and the Codex Mediceo Palatino 87], *L'ars nova italiana del Trecento: Primo convegno internazionale* (Certaldo: Centro di Studi sull'Ars Nova Italiana del Trecento, 1962) 141–80. *Music, index.* In Italian. See no. 407 in this volume.

Examines documentary evidence relating to the life of the 15th-c. organist known as Antonio degli Organi or Antonio Squarcialupi, an early owner of *I-Fl* MS med.pal.87, now known as the Squarcialupi Codex, and to those of musicians represented in the MS, such as Paolo da Firenze and Francesco Landini. *(Sylvia Eversole)*

1061
as

BECHERINI, Bianca. **La musica italiana dalla laude iacoponica alla laude fiorentina del XV secolo** [Italian music from the lauda of Jacopone to the Florentine lauda of the 15th century], *Iacopone e il suo tempo* (Todi: Accademia Tudertina, 1959) 105–32. In Italian. See no. 381 in this volume.

Laudas from this era, beginning with those of Jacopone da Todi himself, possess a vibrant sense of spirituality that is rarely evident in the form. The histories of the frottola and the lauda in Italy (particularly Florence, as regards the former) in the 15th and 16th c. are discussed, and the permutations and evolutions of the forms and texts are examined. *(Susan Poliniak)*

1062
as

BECHERINI, Bianca. **Poesia e musica in Italia ai primi del XV secolo** [Poetry and music in Italy in the early 15th century], *Les colloques de Wégimont. II: L'ars nova—Recueil d'études sur la musique du XIVᵉ siècle* (Paris: Belles Lettres, 1959) 239–59. *Music.* In Italian. See no. 351 in this volume.

Surveys the continuation of the Italian ars nova style after the death of Francesco Landini (1397) in the texts and music of ballata, madrigal, and the developing caccia and incatenatura (quodlibet) genres. *(David Bloom)*

1063
as

BELJAEV, Viktor Mihailovič. **Proishoždenie znamennogo rospeva** [Origins of znamennyj chant], *Anfänge der slavischen Musik* (Bratislava: Slovenská Akadémia Vied, 1966) 93–99. *Music, charts, diagr.* In Russian. See no. 477 in this volume.

Surveys the modal, melodic, and rhythmic structures in Russian chant of the 11th-12th c. and its development through the polyphonic practice that began in the 16th c.

1064
as

BESSELER, Heinrich. **Erläuterungen zu einer Vorführung ausgewählter Denkmäler der Musik des späten Mittelalters** [Commentary for a performance of selected monuments of late medieval music], *Bericht über die [I] Freiburger Tagung für Deutsche Orgelkunst* (Augsburg: Bärenreiter, 1926) 141–50. *Music.* In German. See no. 122 in this volume.

Historical and analytic remarks preceding a performance of vocal music by Guillaume Dufay, Guillaume de Machaut, Gilles Binchois, Johannes Ockeghem, and Josquin Desprez (with Georg A. Walter, tenor, the boys'

choir of the Rotteck Oberrealschule, and members of the Collegium Musicum of the Universität Freiburg im Breisgau, 29 July 1926).
(David Bloom)

1065
as
BIRKNER, Günter. **Das Sequenzrepertoire in Polen und die Stellung des Sequenz *Jesu Christe rex superne*** [The sequence repertoire in Poland and the place of the sequence *Jesu Christe rex superne*], *The book of the first international musicological congress devoted to the works of Frederick Chopin* (Warszawa: Państwowe Wydawnictwo Naukowe, 1963) 510–13. In German. See no. 425 in this volume.
Examines the melodic structure of the sequence, in honor of St. Stanisław and probably originating in Cracow in the 14th or 15th c.

1066
as
BORGHEZIO, Gino. **Un codice vaticano trecentesio di rime musicale** [A 14th-century Vatican codex of musical rhymes], *Congrès jubilaire* (Brugge: Gruuthuuse, 1925) 231–32. In Italian. See no. 119 in this volume.
Describes a small, Italian, 14th-c. codex of two-voice musical rhymes; a full list of song titles is included.

1067
as
BORREN, Charles van den. **L'ars nova** [Ars nova], *Les colloques de Wégimont. II: L'ars nova—Recueil d'études sur la musique du XIVᵉ siècle* (Paris: Belles Lettres, 1959) 17–26. In French. See no. 351 in this volume.
Discusses the music of the ars nova, in its historical and musicological context, with attention to the current state of research and the quality of available sources. *(Eric Ewazen)*

1068
as
BRENN, Franz. **Die gregorianischen Modi nach dem *Speculum musicae*** [The Gregorian modes according to the *Speculum musicae*], *Compte rendu/Kongressbericht/Report* (Basel: Bärenreiter, 1951) 72–75. In German. See no. 289 in this volume.
In book 6 of his *Speculum musicae*, Jacques de Liège transmits the whole of medieval modal theory in clear form and precise language. Modern musicology may be able to resolve contradictions in his use of the terms *modus* and *tonus*. *(David Bloom)*

1069
as
BRIDGMAN, Nanie. **La musique dans la société française de l'ars nova** [Music in French society at the time of the ars nova], *L'ars nova italiana del Trecento: Primo convegno internazionale* (Certaldo: Centro di Studi sull'Ars Nova Italiana del Trecento, 1962) 83–96. In French. See no. 407 in this volume.
The place of music in people's lives in the 14th c., and the role of the musician in society, are examined through a variety of literary sources and documents, including inventories of musical instruments from people of all classes, and evidence for the uses of music in warfare, religious services, civic events, and amusement. *(John Gordon Morris)*

1070
as
BROU, Louis. **L'antiphonaire wisigothique et l'antiphonaire grégorien au début du VIIIᵉ siècle** [The Visigothic and Gregorian antiphoners at the beginning of the 8th century], *Atti del [I] Congresso internazionale di musica sacra* (Tournai: Desclée, 1952) 183–86. In French. See no. 303 in this volume.
A comparison of the northern Mozarabic and Gregorian-Frankish traditions in the earliest period. Originally published in *Anuário musical 5* (1950).

1071
as
BUKOFZER, Manfred F. **Interrelations between conductus and clausula,** *Société Internationale de Musicologie, cinquième congrès/Internationale Gesellschaft für Musikwissenschaft, fünfter Kongreß/International Society for Musical Re-*

search, Fifth Congress (Amsterdam: Vereniging voor Nederlandse Muziekgeschiedenis, 1953) 96–100. *Bibliog.* See no. 316 in this volume.

1072
as
CATTANEO, Enrico. **Sul canto ambrosiano** [Ambrosian chant], *Atti del [I] Congresso internazionale di musica sacra* (Tournai: Desclée, 1952) 196–98. In Italian. See no. 303 in this volume.

1073
as
CHAILLEY, Jacques. **Jumièges et les séquences aquitaines** [Jumièges and the Aquitanian sequences], *Jumièges: Congrès scientifique du XIII. centenaire* (Rouen: Lecerf, 1955) 937–41. In French. See no. 336 in this volume.
The early sequence of the St. Martial repertoire takes the principle of development and characteristic melodic formulas from the tradition of Notker Balbulus and the St. Gallen chant; but the feature of assonance is from the still earlier Aquitanian prosulas, or adaptation tropes, in which a text was simply underlaid beneath the neumes of a very long melisma. These adaptation tropes may be directly derived from the same Jumièges repertoire that inspired Notker to his own original work. *(David Bloom)*

1074
as
CLERCX-LEJEUNE, Suzanne. **Les débuts de la Messe unitaire et de la *Missa parodia* au XIV siècle et principalement dans l'œuvre de Johannes Ciconia** [The beginnings of the unified Mass and of the parody Mass in the 14th century, especially in the work of Johannes Ciconia], *L'ars nova italiana del Trecento: Primo convegno internazionale* (Certaldo: Centro di Studi sull'Ars Nova Italiana del Trecento, 1962) 97–104. *Facs., music.* In French. See no. 407 in this volume.
The Gloria and Credo movements listed in the author's edition of Ciconia's works as nos. 102 and 143 form a pair, linked by the use of a motive from the part song *Regina gloriosa*, also attributed to Ciconia. The analysis suggests that Ciconia was one of the first composers to attempt to unify the movements of the Mass by experimenting with parody technique. *(John Gordon Morris)*

1075
as
CLERCX-LEJEUNE, Suzanne. **Johannes Ciconia et la chronologie des mss. italiens, Mod. 568 et Lucca (Mn)** [Johannes Ciconia and the chronology of the Italian manuscripts Modena 568 and Lucca (Mn)], *Les colloques de Wégimont. II: L'ars nova—Recueil d'études sur la musique du XIVᵉ siècle* (Paris: Belles Lettres, 1959) 110–30. In French. See no. 351 in this volume.
Pieces by Ciconia in the Modena and Mancini Codices, *I-MOe* MS α.M.5.24 (olim lat.568) and *I-La* MS 184, are examined for biographical evidence on the composer, and especially the chronology of previously misdated works. A fuller version is published as part of the author's *Johannes Ciconia* (Brussels: Académie de Belgique, 1959). *(David Bloom)*

1076
as
CLERCX-LEJEUNE, Suzanne. **Le premier séjour en Italie de Joannes Ciconia (1358-1367)** [Johannes Ciconia's first stay in Italy (1358-1367)], *Atti del Congresso internazionale di musiche popolari mediterranee e del Convegno dei bibliotecari musicali* (Palermo: De Magistris succ. V. Bellotti, 1959) 223–28. In French. See no. 332 in this volume.

1077
as
CORBIN, Solange. **Note sur l'ornementation dans le plain-chant grégorien** [Note on ornamentation in Gregorian chant], *Report of the Eighth Congress of the International Musicological Society. I: Papers* (Kassel: Bärenreiter, 1961) 428–39. *Music, transcr.* In French. See no. 439 in this volume.
Ornamentation by the repetition of formulas is favored in Gregorian chant. Ornamentation by the addition of notes to a melody, and neumes in the

sense of melodic gestures, are developments out of improvised psalmodic practice, related to those still found in Jewish and Muslim cantillation and in some sense rationalized by Gregorianism. The deceleration and reornamentation of an ornamented melody is a phenomenon that has almost disappeared except as a reflex of Mozarabic chant. Ornamentation by vertical superposition is the origin of organum and hence of European polyphony. *(David Bloom)*

1078 CORBIN, Solange. **l'Office en vers *Gaude, Mater Ecclesia* pour la Conception de la Vierge**
as [The versified Office *Gaude, Mater Ecclesia* for the feast of the Immaculate Conception], *Atti del [I] Congresso internazionale di musica sacra* (Tournai: Desclée, 1952) 284–86. In French. See no. 303 in this volume.

An extended account of this 12th-c. Office is given in the author's article *Miracula beatae Mariae semper virginis* (Cahiers de civilisation médiévale X/3-4 [1967]), abstracted as RILM [1968] 167. *(David Bloom)*

1079 DJURIĆ-KLAJN, Stana. **Certains aspects de la musique profane serbe de l'époque féodale**
as [Certain aspects of Serbian secular music of the feudal era], *Musica antiqua Europae orientalis* (Warszawa: Państwowe Wydawnictwo Naukowe, 1966). *Illus.* In French. See no. 506 in this volume.

Examines literary, theatrical, and iconographic sources from the 9th to the 16th c. with attention to instruments and the *skomoroh* (professional entertainer) tradition. A reprint is cited as RILM [1998] 1714.

1080 DREIMÜLLER, Karl. **Das neumierte Missale plenarium (Pars hiemalis) Hs. I des Mönchengladbacher Münsterarchivs** [The neumed Missale plenarium (Pars hiemalis) MS 1 of the archive of the Münster, Mönchengladbach], *Studien zur Musikgeschichte der Stadt Mönchengladbach* (Köln: Volk, 1965) 57–64. *Illus., facs., bibliog.* In German. See no. 486 in this volume.

MS 1 of the Schatzkammer collection at the Münster-Basilika St. Vitus, Mönchengladbach, a well-preserved codex of the 12th c., is the winter section (*pars hiemalis*) of a full missal, containing all the Masses from the first Sunday in Advent to Holy Saturday, together with the baptismal liturgy and the Missa pro defunctis. There is no Ordinary section—individual chants of the Ordinary are introduced into individual Masses according to liturgical position, and not generally provided at all except for more important feasts—and no separation between Temporale and Sanctorale. The music notation, in a German lineless neumatic style, is described in detail. *(David Bloom)*

1081 DUFT, Johannes. **Le "presbyter de Gimedia" apport son antiphonaire à Saint-Gall** [The "presbyter de Gimedia" brings his antiphoner to St. Gallen], *Jumièges: Congrès scientifique du XIII. centenaire* (Rouen: Lecerf, 1955) 925–36. *Illus., facs.* In French. See no. 336 in this volume.

In the preface to the *Liber hymnorum*, Notker Balbulus tells the story of how an antiphoner brought to St. Gallen by a "presbyter de Gimedia" (priest from Jumièges) after the pillage of the Abbaye St.-Pierre by Vikings first inspired him to write sequence texts. Indirect evidence for the plausibility of Notker's story is brought forward. *(David Bloom)*

1082 DYKER, Mathias. **Vestiges d'un style calliphonique dans le chant oriental au XIIIe siècle** [Vestiges of a kalophonic style in Eastern chant of the 13th century], *Perspectives de la musique sacrée à la lumière de l'encyclique* Musicae sacrae disciplina (Paris: conference, 1959) 326–28. In French. See no. 379 in this volume.

Evidence in a MS from the Badia Greca, Grottaferrata (*I-GR* MS Γ.γ.vii) suggests that a kalophonic—i.e., free-form melismatic—style was used in the Byzantine liturgy well before the period in the 14th c. when it has been assumed to have originated. *(David Bloom)*

1083 EGGEBRECHT, Hans Heinrich. **"Diaphonia vulgariter organum"**, *Bericht über den siebenten internationalen musikwissenschaftlichen Kongress* (Kassel: Bärenreiter, 1959) 93–97. In German. See no. 390 in this volume.

An explication of the phrase "diaphonia vulgariter organum dicitur" ("diaphonia, ordinarily called organum") found in Jean d'Afflighem's treatise *De musica*, ca. 1100. This passage contains the first more or less clear discussion of the term *organum*. Afflighem uses it to refer to a second part that accompanies a cantus firmus; in his account the part is sung and resembles an instrument in the way it is sung. The present author observes that whereas *organum* is a common Latin word, used by practicing musicians, *diaphonia* is a term from theory, a learned Greek word applied to the problems of simultaneously sounding voices. In the course of the 12th c. the two terms become associated with related styles of organal composition. "Diaphonation" now refers to a second voice keeping in note-against-note style, while "organum" is applied to an accompanying voice engaging in rhythmic coloration, and behaving like an instrument. *(Carl Skoggard)*

1084 ELLINWOOD, Leonard. **The French renaissance of the 12th century in music**, *Papers read at the International Congress of Musicology* (New York: Music Educators National Conference, 1944) 200–11. *Music.* See no. 266 in this volume.

Discusses the development of polyphony.

1085 FALVY, Zoltán. **Musik in Ungarn bis zum Ende des XVI. Jahrhunderts** [Music in Hungary up to the end of the 16th century], *Musica antiqua Europae orientalis* (Warszawa: Państwowe Wydawnictwo Naukowe, 1966). *Illus., facs., music.* In German. See no. 506 in this volume.

Discusses MSS of religious music and polyphony.

1086 FALVY, Zoltán. **Die neuesten ungarischen Ergebnisse auf dem Gebiete der mitttelalterlichen musikalischen Paläographie** [The most recent Hungarian results in the field of medieval musical paleography], *Bericht über den internationalen musikwissenschaftlichen Kongreß Wien Mozartjahr 1956* (Graz; Köln: Böhlau, 1958) 176–82. *Music, transcr.* In German. See no. 365 in this volume.

A survey of ongoing research, with particular attention to work on the Codex Albensis (*A-Gu* MS 211) and Pray Codex (*H-Bn* MS MNy.1).

1087 FANO, Fabio. **Punti di vista su l'ars nova** [Points of view on the ars nova], *L'ars nova italiana del Trecento: Primo convegno internazionale* (Certaldo: Centro di Studi sull'Ars Nova Italiana del Trecento, 1962) 105–12. In Italian. See no. 407 in this volume.

Defines the ars nova as an artistic state of being and as a time period, in relation to the Renaissance in general and to the technical aspects of melody, harmony, and counterpoint. *(Susan Poliniak)*

1088 FEDERHOFER, Hellmut. **Die älteste schriftliche Überlieferung deutscher geistlicher Lieder in Steiermark** [The oldest written transmission of sacred German songs in Styria], *Zweiter internationaler Kongress für katholische Kirchenmusik: Zu Ehren des Heiligen Papstes Pius X* (Wien: conference, 1955) 208–11. In German. See no. 339 in this volume.

Vernacular hymns in MSS of the 12th through 16th c. in the monasteries of St. Lambrecht, Seckau, Admont, and Vorau provide evidence that the congregation sang in German in the liturgy during the Middle Ages, especially at Easter. The two oldest of the songs, *Christus ist erstanden* and *Es gingen drei Frauen*, are Easter hymns. The Pentecost hymn *Nu biten wir den heiligen Geist* and German versions of several Latin hymns are also discussed. *(David Bloom)*

1089 FEICHT, Hieronim. **Quellen zur mehrstimmigen Musik in Polen vom späten Mittelalter bis 1600** [Sources of polyphonic music in Poland from the late Middle Ages to 1600], *Musica antiqua Europae orientalis* (Warszawa: Państwowe Wydawnictwo Naukowe, 1966). In German. See no. 506 in this volume.

Discusses polyphonic music from the 13th to the 16th c., with background information on monody in the 11th to 12th c.

1090 FEICHT, Hieronim. **Zur Entstehung zweier polnischer *carmina patria*** [The origins of two Polish *carmina patria*], *The book of the first international musicological congress devoted to the works of Frederick Chopin* (Warszawa: Państwowe Wydawnictwo Naukowe, 1963) 527–29. *Music.* In German. See no. 425 in this volume.

Like the 13th-c. *Bogurodzica*, the earliest dated song composed to a Polish text, the 14th-c. Latin St. Stanisław hymn *Gaude mater Polonia* is a medieval work that has attained a status comparable to that of a national anthem. It can be demonstrated that its melody was composed by Italian or French, not Polish, Dominicans. A Polish-language version, with a more extensive discussion of *Bogurodzica*, is included in the collection published as *Studia nad muzyka polskiego sredniowiecza* (Krakow: Polski Wydawnictwo Muzyczne, 1975) and cited as RILM ¹⁹⁷⁵480. *(David Bloom)*

1091 FEIL, Arnold. **Arbeitsgemeinschaft: Die Tradition des "Altrömischen" und des Gregorianischen Chorals** [Working group: The tradition of so-called Old Roman and of Gregorian chant], *Bericht über den siebenten internationalen musikwissenschaftlichen Kongress* (Kassel: Bärenreiter, 1959) 358–63. In German. See no. 390 in this volume.

Summarizes a workshop discussion of issues including the dating of the transition from Old Roman to Gregorian chant, the absence in Rome of Gregorian sources from before the 12th c., the problem of which tradition represents the purest transmission, and the question of identifying specifically Frankish vs. Italian melodic styles. Participants included Joseph SMITS VAN WAESBERGHE (chair), Willi APEL, Eugène CARDINE, Joseph GAJARD, Helmut HUCKE, Walter LIPPHARDT, Bruno STÄBLEIN, and Egon WELLESZ. *(David Bloom)*

⟶ FELLERER, Karl Gustav. **La *Constitutio Docta sanctorum patrum* di Giovanni XXII e la musica nuova del suo tempo** [The *Constitutio Docta sanctorum patrum* of Pope John XXII and the new music of his time]. See no. 6213 in this volume.

1092 FICKER, Rudolf von. **Der Choral als symbolische Idee in der mittelalterlichen Mehrstimmigkeit** [Chant as a symbolic idea in medieval polyphony], *Atti del [I] Congresso internazionale di musica sacra* (Tournai: Desclée, 1952) 303–04. In German. See no. 303 in this volume.

1093 FISCHER, Kurt von. **Chronologie des manuscrits du trecento** [Chronology of trecento manuscripts], *Les colloques de Wégimont. II: L'ars nova—Recueil d'études sur la musique du XIVe siècle* (Paris: Belles Lettres, 1959) 131–36. In French. See no. 351 in this volume.

Transcript of the discussion following a conference paper published as a portion of the author's *Studien zur italienischen Musik des Trecento und frühen Quattrocento* (Bern: Publications de la Société Suisse de Musicologie, sér. II, vol. 5, 1956). MSS particularly considered include *I-Fn* MS Panciatichi 26, the Squarcialupi Codex *I-Fl* MS Mediceo Palatino 87, and *F-Pn* MS it.568. *(David Bloom)*

1094 FISCHER, Kurt von. **Les compositions à trois voix chez les compositeurs du trecento** [Compositions for three voices by 14th-century composers], *L'ars nova italiana del Trecento: Primo convegno internazionale* (Certaldo: Centro di Studi sull'Ars Nova Italiana del Trecento, 1962) 18–31. *Music.* In French. See no. 407 in this volume.

A stylistic analysis of three-part Italian caccia and madrigal compositions of the 14th c. leads to the conclusion that this music did not develop from French models, but from native Italian sources; French influence began to be felt only towards the end of the century. *(John Gordon Morris)*

1095 FISCHER, Kurt von. **L'influence française sur la notation des manuscrits du trecento** [French influence on the notation of trecento manuscripts], *Les colloques de Wégimont. II: L'ars nova—Recueil d'études sur la musique du XIVe siècle* (Paris: Belles Lettres, 1959) 27–34. In French. See no. 351 in this volume.

Transcript of the discussion following a conference paper published as a portion of the author's *Studien zur italienischen Musik des Trecento und frühen Quattrocento* (Bern: Publications de la Société Suisse de Musicologie, sér. II, vol. 5, 1956). MSS particularly considered include the Bologna codex *I-Bc* MS Q15, the Panciatichi Codex *I-Fn* MS Panc.26, the Squarcialupi Codex *I-Fl* MS Mediceo Palatino 87, and *F-Pn* MS it.568. *(David Bloom)*

1096 FRANCA, Umberto. **Antiphonale-Lectionarium Monasterii Fontis Avellanae** [The antiphoner-lectionary of the Fonte Avellana monastery], *Zweiter internationaler Kongress für katholische Kirchenmusik: Zu Ehren des Heiligen Papstes Pius X* (Wien: conference, 1955) 129–37. *Illus., facs.* In Latin. See no. 339 in this volume.

Codex Nn of the Biblioteca Dante Alighieri of the Monastero di Santa Croce in Fonte Avellana is a breviary copied in the monastery's scriptorium in the period of St. Peter Damian (Pier Damiani, 1007-72) or not much later. Its textual and musical contents are described. *(David Bloom)*

1097 FRANQUESA, J. **Darreres troballes sobre el cant visigòtic** [The latest findings about Visigothic chant], *Congrés de la Societat Internacional de Musicologia* (Barcelona: Casa de Caritat, 1936). In Catalan. See no. 224 in this volume.

The conference report provides only a citation. Neither the text nor a summary of the paper was published here.

1098 FUKAČ, Jiří. **Zu den Ergebnissen der Forschung über den musikalischen Charakter der Epoche Groß-Mährens** [Research findings on the musical character of the age of Great Moravia], *Anfänge der slavischen Musik* (Bratislava: Slovenská Akadémia Vied, 1966) 43–48. In German. See no. 477 in this volume.

Study of liturgical music in the 9th-c. kingdom of Great Moravia has been based on meager evidence from scant sources. Approaching the repertoire from the perspective of neighboring contemporary cultures and of what is known about the traditional music of the time may help to construct a more accurate picture of its proper place in the chronological progression from early Byzantine liturgical music to the later Middle Ages. *(Brian Doherty)*

1099 GAISSER, Hugo. **L'origine du *tonus peregrinus*** [The origin of the *tonus peregrinus*], *Congrès international d'histoire de la musique: Documents, mémoires et vœux* (Solesmes: St. Pierre; Paris: Fischbacher, 1901) 127–33. *Music.* In French. See no. 32 in this volume.

The psalm tone, *tonus peregrinus*, though unique, seems not to have originated from a separate source, but also from Byzantine chant, specifically the *tetradus*, the fourth plagal mode.

1100
as

GASTOUÉ, Amédée. **L'*Alarme* de Grimache (vers 1380-1390) et les chansons polyphoniques du Moyen Âge** [Grimace's *À l'arme* (around 1380-1390) and the polyphonic songs of the Middle Ages], *Actes du Congrès d'histoire de l'art* (Paris: Presses Universitaires de France, 1923-1924) 784–89. *Music.* In French. See no. 94 in this volume.

Although there is an abundance of 14th- and 15th-c. MSS of French polyphonic *a cappella* music, the transcriptions are usually inadequate. Grimace's song *À l'arme/À l'arme/Tru tru* is a good example of the style and is also one of the oldest descriptive pieces of music. An edition of the work is included. *(Vivian Conejero)*

1101
as

GASTOUÉ, Amédée. **L'art grégorien: Les origines premières** [Gregorian art: The earliest origins], *Mémoires de Musicologie sacrée, lus aux assises de musique religieuse* (Paris: Schola Cantorum, n.d.) 1–17. *Music.* In French. See no. 34 in this volume.

Gregorian chant was influenced by Judeo-Syrian poetry and language rhythms. Gregorian notation and the use of melodic formulas stem from Hebraic sources; anthems and hymns show Hellenistic influences. The diverse strands of influence were synthesized around the 9th and 10th c. in such places as S. Gallen and Chartres. *(Karen Clute)*

1102
as

GASTOUÉ, Amédée. **Comment on peut s'inspirer des anciens pour l'accompagnement du chant romain** [How to take inspiration from the ancients in accompanying Gregorian chant], *Acta generalis cantus gregoriani studiosorum conventus, Argentinensis, 16-19 Aug. 1905/Bericht des internationalen Kongresses für gregorianischen Choralgesang/ Compte rendu du Congrès international de plain-chant grégorien* (Strassburg: F.-X. Le Roux, 1905) 133–40. *Illus., music.* In French. See no. 50 in this volume.

Discusses performance practice, including vocal as well as instrumental accompaniment.

1103
as

GASTOUÉ, Amédée. **Sur les orgines de la forme sequentia du VIIe-IXe siècles** [The origins of the sequence from the 7th to the 9th century], *Bericht über den zweiten Kongress der Internationalen Musikgesellschaft* (Leipzig: Breitkopf & Härtel, 1907) 165–70. *Music.* In French. See no. 53 in this volume.

Outlines the hypothesis of and evidence for the Byzantine origin of the sequence; a fuller version is published in the author's *Introduction à la paléographie musicale byzantine* (Paris, 1907). *(David Bloom)*

1104
as

GASTOUÉ, Amédée. **Sur l'intérêt de l'étude des traités du Moyen-Âge et de deux traités perdus** [On the reason for studying treatises of the Middle Ages and on two lost treatises], *Acta generalis cantus gregoriani studiosorum conventus, Argentinensis, 16-19 Aug. 1905/Bericht des internationalen Kongresses für gregorianischen Choralgesang/ Compte rendu du Congrès international de plain-chant grégorien* (Strassburg: F.-X. Le Roux, 1905) 80–87. In French. See no. 50 in this volume.

Discusses *De accentibus*, attributed to Censorinus, and *De musica*, attributed to Pope Gregory I.

1105
as

GEERING, Arnold. **Die Nibelungenmelodie in der Trierer Marienklage** [The Nibelungen melody in the Trier Lament of Mary], *Compte rendu/Kongressbericht/Report* (Basel: Bärenreiter, 1951) 118–20. *Music, transcr.* In German. See no. 289 in this volume.

The Trier *Marienklage* (Lament of Mary), in *D-TRs* MS 1973/63, includes five songs to Latin texts and eight to German texts; in the last of these, the stanza form is identical with that of the *Nibelungenlied*, suggesting that its

melody may derive from the melody of the early sung versions of the epic. Further evidence for the thesis is adduced. *(David Bloom)*

1106
as

GEORGIADES, Thrasybulos Georges, moderator. **Byzantinisches in der Karolingischen Musik** [Byzantine elements in Carolingian music], *Diskussionsbeiträge zum XI. internationalen Byzantinistenkongress* (München: Beck, 1961) 70–74. In German. See no. 395 in this volume.

Transcript of a panel discussion on the origins of Byzantine music and its influence on Western chant, by Ewald JAMMERS, Reinhold SCHLÖTTERER, Hans SCHMID, Ernst Ludwig WAELTNER, and Egon WELLESZ. *(Terence Ford)*

1107
as

GHISI, Federico. **La persistance du sentiment monodique et l'évolution de la polyphonie italienne du XIVe au XVe siècle** [The persistence of a preference for monody and the evolution of Italian polyphony from the 14th to the 15th centuries], *Les colloques de Wégimont. II: L'ars nova—Recueil d'études sur la musique du XIVe siècle* (Paris: Belles Lettres, 1959) 217–31. *Music.* In French. See no. 351 in this volume.

A lauda-ballata by Jacopo da Bologna, *Nel mio parlar*, for three voices and two instruments, shows the continuing importance of monody in the flourishing of Italian polyphony at the turn of the 15th c. *(David Bloom)*

1108
as

GHISLANZONI, Alberto. **Les formes littéraires et musicales italiennes au commencement du XIVe siècle** [Italian literary and musical forms at the beginning of the 14th century], *Les colloques de Wégimont. II: L'ars nova—Recueil d'études sur la musique du XIVe siècle* (Paris: Belles Lettres, 1959) 149–63. In French. See no. 351 in this volume.

The early 14th c., a period for which the history of Italian music is not well documented, is in contrast very well known in literary history, as the era of the *dolce stil novo* in poetry. Dante's *De vulgari eloquentia* (ca. 1305); the commentary *De variis inveniendi et rimandi modis* from Francesco da Barberino's Latin glosses to his *Documenti d'amore* (1313-26); the treatise *Summa artis rithmici vulgaris dictaminis* (*I-Vnm* lat.XII, 97 [=4125]) from ca. 1330; and Antonio da Tempo's *Delle rime volgari* (1332) are examined for evidence on terminology, genres, and the Italian preference for monody over polyphony. *(David Bloom)*

1109
as

GÖLLER, Gottfried. **Zur Herkunftsbestimmung der liturgischen Handschriften der Abtei St. Vitus** [Determining the provenance of liturgical manuscripts from the abbey of St. Vitus], *Studien zur Musikgeschichte der Stadt Mönchengladbach* (Köln: Volk, 1965) 41–51. *List of works.* In German. See no. 486 in this volume.

MS 18 in the Schatzkammer collection of the Münster-Basilika St. Vitus, Mönchengladbach, a collectarium dated 1609 and copied by "G.K." (probably Gottfried Kempis), allows the listing of the particular feasts in the liturgical calendar of the Mönchengladbach abbey that distinguished it from the calendar in general use in Cologne. On this basis, a number of 12th-c. MSS can be shown to have been copied at Mönchengladbach, but otherwise none until the end of the 16th c.; apparently the abbey's scriptorium was inactive in the intervening years. *(David Bloom)*

1110
as

GONTIER, Augustin. **Extrait de la dissertation sur le plain-chant et son exécution** [Extract from the dissertation on plainchant and its performance], *Congrès pour la restauration du plain-chant et de la musique d'église* (Paris: De Mourgues, 1862) 77–81. In French. See no. 3 in this volume.

1111
as

GÜNTHER, Ursula. **Das Ende der *ars nova*** [The end of the ars nova], *Bericht über den internationalen* *musikwissenschaftlichen Kongreß* (Kassel: Bärenreiter, 1963) 108–09. In German. See no. 452 in this volume.

The death of Guillaume de Machaut (1377) and the beginning of the Great Schism in the papacy (1378) may be used to date the transition from ars nova to ars subtilior. *(Jeffrey Miller)*

1112 GÜNTHER, Ursula. **Die Rolle Englands,**
as **Spaniens, Deutschlands und Polens in der Musik des 14. Jahrhunderts** [The role of England, Spain, Germany, and Poland in the music of the 14th century], *Bericht über den neunten internationalen Kongreß* (Kassel: Bärenreiter, 1964-1966) II, 188–200. In German. See no. 491 in this volume.

Summary of a roundtable discussion. Particular attention is given to developments in polyphony that were independent of contemporary developments in France and Italy. Participants included Gilbert REANEY, Luther A. DITTMER, Hieronim FEICHT, Kurt von FISCHER, Arnold GEERING, Theodor GÖLLNER, Ursula GÜNTHER, Frank Llewellyn HARRISON, Peter E. PEACOCK, and Denis STEVENS. *(David Bloom)*

1113 HANDSCHIN, Jacques. **Die Entstehung der**
as **Sequenz** [The origins of the sequence], *Bulletin of the International Committee of Historical Sciences* X/2-3 (Apr-July 1938) 604–05. In German. See no. 262 in this volume.

Scholars have preferred to treat the musical aspect of the sequence as a simple and direct evolution of the Gregorian alleluia, but the oldest sequence melodies are quite different from the melismatics of the alleluia, and their ultimate source can only be in secular instrumental music. The sequence's literary aspect is derived from Byzantine hymnody. It is probable that the division of the choir into alternating parts is older than the texting. *(David Bloom)*

1114 HANDSCHIN, Jacques. **Notizen über die Notre**
as **Dame Conductus** [Notes concerning Notre Dame conductus], *Bericht über den I. musikwissenschaftlichen Kongress der Deutschen Musikgesellschaft in Leipzig* (Wiesbaden: Breitkopf & Härtel, 1926) 209–17. *Music.* In German. See no. 120 in this volume.

Various questions pertaining to conductus are discussed, including its sources, its definition according to medieval theory, and its role in the liturgy. *(William Renwick)*

1115 HANDSCHIN, Jacques. **La question du chant**
as **"vieux-romain"** [The question of so-called Old Roman chant], *Atti del Congresso internazionale di musiche popolari mediterranee e del Convegno dei bibliotecari musicali* (Palermo: De Magistris succ. V. Bellotti, 1959) 245–55. *Port.* In French. See no. 332 in this volume.

Reviews evidence on the relationship between Roman and Frankish chant traditions. Many difficulties can be resolved by separation of the questions of liturgical and musical practice, on the understanding that the Catholic unity of chant, and its codification, were not objects of concern to the ecclesiastical authorities until the Carolingian era; earlier sources, such as the Monza Cantatorium (*I-MZ* MS CIX), musically but not liturgically in the Old Roman tradition, should not be interpreted as representing an attempt at codification. *(David Bloom)*

1116 HANDSCHIN, Jacques. **Die Rolle der Nationen**
as **in der mittelaltenlicher Musikgeschichte** [The role of the nations in medieval music history], *Société Internationale de Musicologie: Premier Congrès Liège—Compte rendu/Internationale Gesellschaft für Musikwissenschaft: Erster Kongress Lüttich—Kongressbericht/International Society for Musical Research: First Congress Liège: Report* (London: Plainsong and Mediaeval Music Society, 1930) 138. In German. See no. 178 in this volume.

Summarizes an article discussing the roles of England and Germany in medieval music. The complete article appears in *Schweizerischen Jahrbuch für Musikwissenschaft* V (1931). *(Scott Fruehwald)*

1117 HANDSCHIN, Jacques. **Über frühes und spätes**
as **Mittelalter** [On the early and late Middle Ages], *Beethoven-Zentenarfeier: Internationaler musikhistorischer Kongress* (Wien: Universal, 1927) 149–51. In German. See no. 142 in this volume.

Our picture of the Middle Ages scarcely includes its earlier portion, the period of Romanesque architecture and Johannes Scottus Eriugena. Musically, it was characterized at first by the sequence and trope movement in the Carolingian period, followed by the development of polyphony. *(David Bloom)*

1118 HESBERT, René-Jean. **La composition musi-**
as **cale a Jumièges: Les Offices de S. Philibert et de S. Aycadre** [Musical composition at Jumièges: The Offices of St. Philibert and St. Achard (Aichardus)], *Jumièges: Congrès scientifique du XIII. centenaire* (Rouen: Lecerf, 1955) 959–68. *Music, charts, diagr.* In French. See no. 336 in this volume.

Offices were composed at the Abbaye St.-Pierre in Jumièges for the feasts of St. Philibert, the abbey's founder, and his successor, St. Achard (Aichardus). In each, the choice of modes for the individual pieces appears to be part of a large-scale compositional design, appropriate to the Office's text. Examination of the melodies from a selection of the antiphons and responsories confirms the impression that the composer worked with an expressive range and sensitivity to text that are unusual in Office compositions of the 11th and 12th c. *(David Bloom)*

1119 HESBERT, René-Jean. **Les pièces de chant des**
as **Messes *Pro defunctis* dans la tradition manuscrite** [The chants of Requiem Masses in the manuscript tradition], *Atti del [I] Congresso internazionale di musica sacra* (Tournai: Desclée, 1952) 223–28. In French. See no. 303 in this volume.

1120 HESBERT, René-Jean. **Les séquences de**
as **Jumièges** [The Jumièges sequences], *Jumièges: Congrès scientifique du XIII. centenaire* (Rouen: Lecerf, 1955) 943–58. In French. See no. 336 in this volume.

There are four important MS sources for the sequence repertoire of the Abbaye St.-Pierre in Jumièges: the 12th-c. missal *F-R* MS 267 (A.401), the 14th-c. gradual-sequentiary-troper *F-R* MS 250 (A.233), and the late–15th-c. missals *F-R* MS 301 (Y.58) and MS 302 (Y.89). Cross-comparison of the four fails to provide any solid evidence of the Jumièges repertoire of the 9th c., by which Notker Balbulus is said to have been inspired. On the other hand, certain sequences can be shown conclusively to have been written at Jumièges: those for St. Stephen (*Stephani martyrium*), St. Valentine (*Ad triumphos*), St. Louis (*Ad honorem summi Regis*), and St. Leonard (*Psallat chorus*). Two further sequences, for St. Bathildis (*Benedicta sit beatrix*) and the Tuesday after Pentecost (*Christe salvator*), may also be of Jumièges origin. *(David Bloom)*

1121 HESBERT, René-Jean. **Les témoins manu-**
as **scripts du culte de Saint Odilon** [The manuscript evidence of the cult of Saint Odilo], *À Cluny: Congrès scientifique—Fêtes et cérémonies liturgiques en l'honneur des saints abbés Odon et Odilon* (Dijon: Bernigaud et Privat, 1950) 51–120. *Facs.* In French and Latin. See no. 290 in this volume.

Catalogues and discusses the many liturgical MSS (psalters, hymnals, breviaries, missals, and martyrologies) dating from before the 16th c. and related to the cult of Saint Odilo, Abbot of Cluny (ca. 962-1048). The feasts of the saint are discussed, as are the Église Prieurale at Souvigny and Saint Odilo's relics. Several Masses and Offices are examined in detail. *(Susan Poliniak)*

1122 HESBERT, René-Jean. **Les tropes de Jumièges**
as [The tropes of Jumièges], *Jumièges: Congrès scientifique du XIII. centenaire* (Rouen: Lecerf, 1955) 959–68. *Charts, diagr.* In French. See no. 336 in this volume.

The only generally valuable source of Jumièges tropes is the 14th-c. gradual *F-R* MS 250 (A.233). An analytic account of the tropes in this MS by feast day and Kyriale section is provided, and filiation and provenance are briefly discussed for selected cases. *(Jeanne Halley)*

1123 HOPPIN, Richard H. **The manuscript J. II. 9. in**
as **the Biblioteca Nazionale of Torino,** *L'ars nova italiana del Trecento: Primo convegno internazionale* (Certaldo: Centro di Studi sull'Ars Nova Italiana del Trecento, 1962) 75–82. See no. 407 in this volume.

Gives an account of the contents of the MS, which originated in Cyprus ca. 1413; a fuller account is provided in the author's *The Cypriot-French repertory of the manuscript Torino Biblioteca Nazionale J.II.9, Musica disciplina* XI (1957). *(John Gordon Morris)*

1124 HOPPIN, Richard H.; CLERCX-LEJEUNE, Su-
as zanne. **Notes biographiques sur quelques musiciens français du XIVe siècle** [Biographical notes on several 14th-century French musicians], *Les colloques de Wégimont. II: L'ars nova—Recueil d'études sur la musique du XIVe siècle* (Paris: Belles Lettres, 1959) 63–92. In French. See no. 351 in this volume.

Discusses the identities of 14th-c. French musicians named in the anonymous so-called musicians motets *Musicalis sciencia/Sciencie laudabili* (from *F-Pn* MS Coll. de Picardie 67), *Apollinis eclipsatur/Zodiacum signis lustrantibus* (*I-IV* MS 115 [Ivrea Codex], *F-Sm* MS 222), and *Alma prolis religio/Axe poli* (*F-CH* MS 564), with particular attention to those designated as "Egidius". *(David Bloom)*

1125 HUCKE, Helmut. **Improvvisazione nella**
as **Schola Cantorum romana** [Improvisation in the Roman Schola Cantorum], *Atti del Congresso internazionale di musiche popolari mediterranee e del Convegno dei bibliotecari musicali* (Palermo: De Magistris succ. V. Bellotti, 1959) 259–61. *Port.* In Italian. See no. 332 in this volume.

A comparison among melodies used in the verses of fifth-mode graduals in the Old Roman tradition gives clear evidence of an improvisational practice in the particularly heterogeneous use made of a repertoire of fixed melodic formulas. The Frankish tradition for the same melodies, in contrast, presents a more homogeneous picture. It may be conjectured that the fixing of the melodies took place no later than the separation of the two traditions, not much before the middle of the 8th c.

1126 HUCKE, Helmut. **Modes of underlaying a text**
as **to melismas: Trope, sequence, and other forms,** *Report of the Eighth Congress of the International Musicological Society. II: Reports* (Kassel: Bärenreiter, 1962) 48–52. In German. See no. 440 in this volume.

A report on a discussion by Jacques CHAILLEY, Solange CORBIN, Paul R. EVANS, Helmut HUCKE, Heinrich HUSMANN, Ewald JAMMERS, Georg REICHERT, Joseph SMITS VAN WAESBERGHE, Bruno STÄBLEIN, Rembert WEAKLAND, and Eric WERNER on the paper by Stäblein abstracted as no. 1189 in this volume.

1127 HUCKE, Helmut. **Die Tradition des Gre-**
as **gorianischen Gesanges in der römischen Schola Cantorum** [The tradition of Gregorian chant in the Roman Schola Cantorum], *Zweiter internationaler Kongress für katholische Kirchenmusik: Zu Ehren des Heiligen Papstes Pius X* (Wien: conference, 1955) 120–23. In German. See no. 339 in this volume.

The decisive change from a continuously evolving chant style to a fixed tradition in the Schola would have taken place together with the shift to written transmission of the tradition, a moment for which it is not yet possible to propose an adequate chronology. *(David Bloom)*

1128 HUGLO, Michel. **Origine de la mélodie du**
as **Credo "authentique" de la Vaticane** [Origin of the so-called authentic Credo melody of the Vatican], *Atti del [II] Congresso internazionale di musica sacra* (Tournai: Desclée, 1952) 240–44. In French. See no. 303 in this volume.

The melody of Credo I of the Liber usualis (Solesmes, 1896), presumably chosen for its early 9th-c. Roman authenticity, has important parallels with that of a Greek Credo preserved in *D-KNu* MS W.105, and may in fact be derived from it. The full discussion is published in *Revue grégorienne* XXX (1951). *(David Bloom)*

1129 HUGLO, Michel. **Vestiges d'un ancien réper-**
as **toire musical de Haute-Italie** [Remains of an old musical repertoire from Upper Italy], *Zweiter internationaler Kongress für katholische Kirchenmusik: Zu Ehren des Heiligen Papstes Pius X* (Wien: conference, 1955) 142–45. *Charts, diagr.* In French. See no. 339 in this volume.

The neumatically notated *Ordo scrutiniorum* of *I-Ma* MS T27 suppl. is the only musical survival of pre-Gregorian chant from the patriarchate of Aquileia. Comparison of the choice of texts and musical setting with those of the Old Roman and Ambrosian chants shows it to be a distinct tradition, closer to Milanese than Roman practice. *(David Bloom)*

1130 HUSMANN, Heinrich. **Die Alleluia und**
as **Sequenzen der Mater-Gruppe** [The alleluias and sequences of the *Mater* group], *Bericht über den internationalen musikwissenschaftlichen Kongreß Wien Mozartjahr 1956* (Graz; Köln: Böhlau, 1958) 276–84. *Music.* In German. See no. 365 in this volume.

The Assumption sequences *Congaudent angelorum chori* from St. Gallen and *Alle celeste* from England and France, and the Easter sequence *Fulgens praeclara*, have all been referred to as *Mater* or *Mater sequentiarum*. Their alleluias are compared with each other and with those of a number of other sequences, and the possibility of reconstructing a kind of "ur-alleluia" on the basis of the comparison is entertained. *(David Bloom)*

1131 HUSMANN, Heinrich. **Les époques de la**
as **musique provençale au Moyen-Âge** [The epochs of the music of Provence in the Middle Ages], *Actes et mémoires du 1er Congrès international de langue et littérature du Midi de la France* (Avignon: Palais du Roure, 1957) 197–201. *Music.* In French. See no. 342 in this volume.

Discusses efforts to determine the principles of musical evolution in Provence in the Middle Ages. The modal, mensural, and Gregorian theories, as well as those of Hugo Riemann, regarding rhythm are described. None of these theories is valid for all music in this age, but each contains a kernel of truth and is applicable for a certain time frame of this period. The period can be divided into three epochs, each of which was ruled by a different rhythmic principle. *(Susan Poliniak)*

1132 HUSMANN, Heinrich. **Die mittelniederlän-**
as **dischen Lieder der Berliner Handschrift Germ. 8° 190** [Middle Dutch songs in the Berlin manuscript Germ. 8° 190], *Société Internationale de Musicologie, cinquième congrès/Internationale Gesellschaft für Musikwissenschaft, fünfter Kongreß/International Society for Musical Research, Fifth Congress* (Amsterdam: Vereniging voor Nederlandse Muziekgeschiedenis, 1953) 241–51. In German. See no. 316 in this volume.

A discussion of *D-B* MS Germ.8° 190.

1133
as
HUSMANN, Heinrich. **Das Organum vor und außerhalb der Notre-Dame-Schule** [Organum before and outside the Notre Dame School], *Bericht über den neunten internationalen Kongreß* (Kassel: Bärenreiter, 1964-1966) I, 25–35. In German. See no. 491 in this volume.

The term *organum* in the sense of early vocal polyphony may derive from an analogy between the sound of such music and that of the mixture rank of the organs of the period. The word's frequent use in the texts of early French unrhymed prosas provides clues as to the character of organum before the 11th c. Remarkable similarities between medieval motets and a kind of North African diaphony investigated by André Schaeffner suggest a historical connection to Africa in early organum, perhaps through the Crusades. The St. Victor MS (*F-Pn* MS lat.15139) was demonstrably not composed in Paris. *(David Bloom)*

1134
as
KOSCH, Franz. **Zum Choral der Franciskaner** [*sic*] **im XIII. Jahrhundert** [On the chant of the Franciscans in the 13th century], *Congrés de la Societat Internacional de Musicologia* (Barcelona: Casa de Caritat, 1936). In German. See no. 224 in this volume.

The conference report provides only a citation. Neither the text nor a summary of the paper was published here.

1135
as
KRÜGER, Walther. **Singstil und Instrumentalstil in der Mehrstimmigkeit der St. Martialepoche** [Vocal and instrumental styles in the polyphony of the St. Martial era], *Bericht über den Internationalen musikwissenschaftlichen Kongress* (Kassel: Bärenreiter, 1954) 240–45. *Music.* In German. See no. 319 in this volume.

Hans Spanke has argued for a purely vocal interpretation of the St. Martial pieces; his transcriptions extend the cantus firmus as long as is necessary to accommodate the many notes of the dupla, conceived as a smoothly singable line with uniform values. This repertoire does not seem to represent an authentic vocal style, however. Here the Benedicamus trope *Jubilemus, exultemus* (*F-LG* MS lat.1139) is transcribed with the duplum assigned to a fiddle and with the cantus firmus rendered as a vocal line in strict ternary rhythm, in keeping with the conductus antecedents of the piece. Use of the fiddle is supported by iconographic, literary, and other evidence from the period. Another item in the same MS, the Benedicamus trope *Stirps Jesse*, has an incompletely notated tenor that hints at instrumental performance (its duplum is fully texted). *(Carl Skoggard)*

1136
as
LABHARDT, Frank. **Zur st. gallischen Sequenztradition im Spätmittelalter** [The St. Gallen sequence tradition in the late Middle Ages], *Compte rendu/Kongressbericht/Report* (Basel: Bärenreiter, 1951) 176–77. In German. See no. 289 in this volume.

Discusses the sources and historical significance of the Cuontz Codex (*CH-Sgs* MS 546).

1137
as
LAVOYE, Louis. **Note sur la musique au pays de Liège aux Xe, XIe et XIIe siècles** [On the music of the region of Liège in the 10th, 11th, and 12th centuries], *Fédération Archéologique et Historique de Belgique: Annales du XXIe congrès* (Liège: Poncelet, 1909) II, 746f. In French. See no. 64 in this volume.

1138
as
LAZAROV, Stefan. **Die altbulgarische Musik und die Kyrillo-Methodianische Tradition** [Old Bulgarian music and the tradition of Cyril and Methodius], *Anfänge der slavischen Musik* (Bratislava: Slovenská Akadémia Vied, 1966) 49–53. In German. See no. 477 in this volume.

Kliment and Naum of Ohrid, Macedonian-Bulgarian disciples of SS. Cyril and Methodius in Moravia, having survived the persecution of Slavic missionaries that followed Methodius's death in 885, returned home, where they worked to preserve the Cyrillic tradition, restoring chantbooks destroyed in the persecutions and creating new ones. The specifically Bulgarian repertoire arose from Kliment's teaching of liturgical practice. *(Brian Doherty)*

1139
as
LEMOINE, A. **Plain-chant, texte et exécution** [Plainchant: Text and performance], *Congrès pour la restauration du plain-chant et de la musique d'église* (Paris: De Mourgues, 1862) 117–18. In French. See no. 3 in this volume.

1140
as
LEVY, Kenneth J. **The Byzantine communion cycle and its Slavic counterpart,** *Actes du XIIe Congrès d'études Byzantines* (Beograd: Naučno Delo, 1963-1964) II, 571–74. See no. 441 in this volume.

While the kontakion recensions of the Uspenskij Kondakar (1207) and similar medieval Slavic MSS are very close to those of the well-known Greek recension in liturgical and textual terms, their melodies seem to be unrelated. They are not, however, independent Slavic creations; structural and notational evidence shows that the melodies and texts descend not from the kondakarion but from a Greek asmatikon or choirbook archetype, probably around the year 1100. *(David Bloom)*

1141
as
LIPPHARDT, Walther. **Der gegenwärtige Stand der Gregorianik-Forschung** [The current state of research on Gregorian chant], *Bericht über den neunten internationalen Kongreß* (Kassel: Bärenreiter, 1964-1966) II, 156–66. In German. See no. 491 in this volume.

Report of a roundtable discussion focusing on source studies and the issue of the origins of chant. The participants included Michel HUGLO, Zoltán FALVY, Hieronim FEICHT, Hans-Jörgen HOLMAN, Joseph SMITS VAN WAESBERGHE, Bruno STÄBLEIN, and Oliver STRUNK. *(David Bloom)*

1142
as
LIPPHARDT, Walther. **Gregor der Grosse und sein Anteil am römischen Antiphonar** [Gregory the Great and his role in the Roman antiphoner], *Atti del [I] Congresso internazionale di musica sacra* (Tournai: Desclée, 1952) 248–54. In German. See no. 303 in this volume.

1143
as
LIPPHARDT, Walther. **Ein unbekannter karolingischer Tonar und seine Bedeutung für die fränkische Choralüberlieferung** [An unknown Carolingian tonary and its significance for Frankish chant transmission], *Bericht über den siebenten internationalen musikwissenschaftlichen Kongress* (Kassel: Bärenreiter, 1959) 179–81. *Charts, diagr.* In German. See no. 390 in this volume.

Presents an overview of the earliest extant version of the Metz Tonary, *F-ME* MS 351, of which the author's edition is published as *Der karolingische Tonar von Metz* (Münster, 1965). The absence of antiphons for feasts established after 835 demonstrates that the source used by the copyist was a MS of ca. 830; its author was very probably St. Aldric (800-53), a student of the tradition of Alcuin and the only musician of note in Metz at the relevant time. *(David Bloom)*

1144
as
LIUZZI, Fernando. **Musica e poesia profana del secolo XIV nel ms. Vaticano-Rossiano 215** [Secular music and poetry from the 14th century in the Vatican manuscript Rossi 215], *Congrés de la Societat Internacional de Musicologia* (Barcelona: Casa de Caritat, 1936). In Italian. See no. 224 in this volume.

The conference report provides only a citation. Neither the text nor a summary of the paper was published here.

1145
as
LUDWIG, Friedrich. **Die mehrstimmige Messe des 14. Jahrhunderts** [The polyphonic Mass in the 14th century], *Bericht über den I. musikwissenschaftlichen Kongress der Deutschen Musikgesellschaft in*

Leipzig (Wiesbaden: Breitkopf & Härtel, 1926) 218. In German. See no. 120 in this volume.

Mentions the Tournai Mass, and the important works of Machaut, and lists various sources.

1146 LUDWIG, Friedrich. **Die mehrstimmige Musik**
as **des 11. und 12. Jahrhunderts** [Polyphonic music of the 11th and 12th centuries], *Haydn-Zentenarfeier* (Leipzig: Breitkopf & Härtel; Wien: Artaria, 1909) 101–08. In German. See no. 65 in this volume.

Focuses on the Aquitanian repertoire.

1147 MARTINEZ-GÖLLNER, Marie Louise. **Sym-**
as **posium: Das Organum vor und ausserhalb der Notre-Dame-Schule** [Symposium: Organum before and outside the Notre Dame school], *Bericht über den neunten internationalen Kongreß* (Kassel: Bärenreiter, 1964-1966) II, 68–80. *Music.* In German. See no. 491 in this volume.

Report of the discussion of the conference paper by Heinrich HUSMANN abstracted as no. 1133 in this volume. Participants were Husmann, Solange CORBIN, Arnold GEERING, Thrasybulos Georges GEORGIADES, Theodor GÖLLNER, Frank Llewellyn HARRISON, Joseph SMITS VAN WAESBERGHE, Bruno STÄBLEIN, and Leo TREITLER.

1148 MARZI, Giovanni. **Martyria e incipit nelle**
as **tradizione nomica** [Martyria and incipits in the nomic tradition], *Actes du XIIe Congrès d'études Byzantines* (Beograd: Naučno Delo, 1963-1964) II, 575–82. *Music.* In Italian. See no. 441 in this volume.

Traces of ancient Greek music are to be found in Byzantine chant, for instance in the way the ēchos system reflects the earlier modes and harmoniai, though the formulas vary considerably, especially in transitional passages. The relationship between the *martyria* or neumatic modal signature and the melodic incipit is completely fixed, however, throughout the Byzantine repertoire, as numerous examples show, suggesting the persistence, through the period of Christianization, of the classic concept of *nomos* in the sense of melodic model, with all its ethical implications. *(David Bloom)*

1149 MOKRÝ, Ladislav. **Zu den Anfängen der**
as **Mehrstimmigkeit bei den Westslawen** [The beginnings of polyphony among the West Slavic peoples], *The book of the first international musicological congress devoted to the works of Frederick Chopin* (Warszawa: Państwowe Wydawnictwo Naukowe, 1963) 567–71. In German. See no. 425 in this volume.

Adam Sutkowski has surmised that the earliest known polyphonic compositions from Polish sources, one two-voice and one three-voice setting of the popular trope *Surrexit Christus hodie* in a MS in the collections of the Biblioteka Klasztor pp. Klarysek, Cracow, represent an independent Polish development, from the early 14th c., before polyphony began in Bohemia. Evidence suggests, however, that a Bohemian source, the two-voice setting in the Knihovna Cisterciáckého Kláštera, Vyšší Brod, H 142, is older still, and was known to the composer of the Cracow three-voice setting. *(David Bloom)*

1150 MONETA CAGLIO, Ernesto. **Stato attuale delle**
as **ricerche concernenti il canto ambrosiano/État actuel des recherches concernant le chant ambrosien** [The current state of research on Ambrosian chant], *Perspectives de la musique sacrée à la lumière de l'encyclique* Musicae sacrae disciplina (Paris: conference, 1959) 218–25. In Italian and French. See no. 379 in this volume.

1151 MONTEROSSO, Raffaello. **Il culto dei santi**
as **nella tradizione musicale medievale liturgica ed extraliturgica** [The cult of the saints in medieval musical tradition inside and outside the liturgy],

Pellegrinaggi e culto dei santi in Europa fino alla I^a Crociata (Todi: Accademia Tudertina, 1963) 181–98. In Italian. See no. 444 in this volume.

It is arguable that the chants of the Proper of the Saints (Sanctorale) were warmer and less austere than those of the Proper of the Time (Temporale).

1152 OTT, Karl. **Die Entwicklung des mailändischen**
as **Chorals** [The development of Ambrosian chant], *Acta generalis cantus gregoriani studiosorum conventus, Argentinensis, 16-19 Aug. 1905/Bericht des internationalen Kongresses für gregorianischen Choralgesang/Compte rendu du Congrès international de plain-chant grégorien* (Strassburg: F.-X. Le Roux, 1905) 55–62. In German. See no. 50 in this volume.

The psalmody of the earliest Christianity survives, disguised, in that of the Milanese school. Its hymnody and simple antiphons are traceable to Greek models, while the responsories for Matins and the Offertories bear the stamp of the Gallican liturgy. At the time when the Roman chant was beginning to be written down, the Ambrosian chant had largely stopped developing; it has not yet been possible to show whether the Ambrosian served as a model for the Gregorian. *(author)*

1153 PALIKAROVA VERDEIL, Raïna. **La musique**
as **byzantine chez les slaves (Bulgares et Russes) aux IXe-Xe siècles** [The Byzantine music of the Bulgarian and Russian Slavic peoples in the 9th and 10th centuries], *Actes du VIe Congrès international d'études byzantines* (Paris: Comité Français des Études Byzantines, 1950-1951) II, 321–30. In French. See no. 287 in this volume.

1154 PAPADĪMĪTRIOU, A. **Peri tis Eptanisō**
as **idiorrythmou byzantinis mousikis tis kaloumenis Kritikis** [Concerning the peculiarly rhythmed Byzantine music in the Ionian Islands, the so-called Cretan music], *IIIe Congrès international des études byzantines* (Athínai: Hestia, 1932) 268–69. In Greek. See no. 163 in this volume.

1155 PATMAGRIAN, Achot. **L'utilisation des**
as **éléments folkoriques dans le chant liturgique arménien au XIIe siècle** [The use of folkloric elements in Armenian liturgical chant of the 12th century], *Proceedings of the Twenty-third International Congress of Orientalists* (London: Royal Asiatic Society, 1957) 173f. In French. See no. 329 in this volume.

A 48-page trilingual edition (French, English, and Armenian) was published by Le Soleil (Paris, 1955).

1156 PERROY, Édouard. **Le point de vue de l'his-**
as **torien** [The historian's point of view], *Les colloques de Wégimont. II: L'ars nova—Recueil d'études sur la musique du XIVe siècle* (Paris: Belles Lettres, 1959) 261–69. In French. See no. 351 in this volume.

Contextualizes the musical developments of the ars nova in France and Italy in relation to the political, social, and intellectual history of the period.

1157 PETIOT, André. **La musique chez les trouba-**
as **dours** [Music of the troubadours], *Actes et mémoires du IIe Congrès international de langue et littérature du Midi de la France* (Aix-en-Provence: Centre d'Études Provençales de la Faculté des Lettres, 1961) 105–12. *Illus., music, charts, diagr.* In French. See no. 388 in this volume.

1158 PETRESCU, Ioan Dumitru. **La lecture des**
as **manuscrits musicaux byzantins des Xe, XIe, XIIe siècles** [Reading Byzantine musical manuscripts

of the 10th, 11th, and 12th centuries], *Atti del V Congresso internazionale di studi bizantini* (Roma: Associazione Nazionale per gli Studi Bizantini, 1940) II, 509–20. *Music.* In French. See no. 233 in this volume.

Comparable music MSS from the 10th to the 12th c. essentially agree with each other in terms of notation and the use of symbols. Neumatic notation was equally important in the areas of both vocal modulation and accompaniment. The use of symbols within this notational system is discussed: the meaning of each symbol is not necessarily precise. The choice of modes is examined, as are the conjunct and disjunct constructions of tetrachords, the interpretation of the *apostrophos*, and the rich variety of compositions from this period. *(Susan Poliniak)*

1159 PFAFF, Maurus. **Die Laudes-Akklamationen**
as **des Mittelalters** [The *Laudes* acclamations of the Middle Ages], *Bericht über den internationalen musikwissenschaftlichen Kongreß Wien Mozartjahr 1956* (Graz; Köln: Böhlau, 1958) 457–61. In German. See no. 365 in this volume.

From the time of the imperial crowning of Charlemagne (800), the Frankish *Laudes regiae* were used for the acclamation of kings and emperors. Historical antecedents, texts, music, and transmission are discussed. *(David Bloom)*

1160 PIRROTTA, Nino. **Cronologia e denomina-**
as **zione dell'ars nova italiana** [The chronology of the Italian ars nova and the question of its designation], *Les colloques de Wégimont. II: L'ars nova—Recueil d'études sur la musique du XIVe siècle* (Paris: Belles Lettres, 1959) 93–109. In Italian and French. See no. 351 in this volume.

The appropriateness of the term *ars nova* for Italian music of the 14th c. is critically examined, and questions of the movement's chronology are reviewed, with attention to the problem of the lateness of most preserved sources. *(David Bloom)*

1161 PIRROTTA, Nino. **Piero e l'impressionismo**
as **musicale del secolo XIV** [Piero and the musical impressionism of the 14th century], *L'ars nova italiana del Trecento: Primo convegno internazionale* (Certaldo: Centro di Studi sull'Ars Nova Italiana del Trecento, 1962) 57–74. *List of works, index.* In Italian. See no. 407 in this volume.

Magister Piero, less famous than his compatriots Giovanni da Cascia and Jacopo da Bologna, may be credited with the creation of the caccia, second to the madrigal among the classic forms of the Italian ars nova. His very few identified works, in the Panciatichi and Rossi Codices (*I-Fn* MS Panc. 26 and *I-Rvat* MS Rossi 215), show a highly individual artistry in the use of imitative counterpoint, impressionistic text setting, rhythmic variety, and descriptive harmonic effects. *(Sylvia Eversole)*

1162 PLAMENAC, Dragan. **New light on Codex**
as **Faenza 117,** *Société Internationale de Musicologie, cinquième congrès/Internationale Gesellschaft für Musikwissenschaft, fünfter Kongreß/International Society for Musical Research, Fifth Congress* (Amsterdam: Vereniging voor Nederlandse Muziekgeschiedenis, 1953) 310–26. *Illus., facs., music.* See no. 316 in this volume.

Examines the vocal originals of the collection and identifies the organ Masses.

1163 RAASTED, Jørgen. **The production of Byzan-**
as **tine musical manuscripts,** *Actes du XIIe Congrès d'études Byzantines* (Beograd: Naučno Delo, 1963-1964) II, 601–06. *Illus., music.* See no. 441 in this volume.

In the age of paleo-Byzantine notation, it was common for a single scribe to be responsible for an entire MS, first writing in the hymn text, then inserting the neumes above the lines. After the development of the Middle Byzantine or Round notation in the mid-11th c., it was more likely for a neumator to write in the neumes first and another scribe to underlay the text afterwards; other functions were those of the rubricator and initialist. Evidence for an increasingly complex division of labor in the scriptorium is followed through representative MSS. *(David Bloom)*

1164 RAJECZKY, Benjamin. **Mittelalterliche Mehr-**
as **stimmigkeit in Ungarn** [Medieval polyphony in Hungary], *Musica antiqua Europae orientalis* (Warszawa: Państwowe Wydawnictwo Naukowe, 1966). *Facs.* In German. See no. 506 in this volume.

Discusses developments from the 11th to the 16th c., including Gregorian chant settings.

1165 RAUGEL, Félix. **Le Chant de la Sibylle d'après**
as **un manuscrit du XIIe siècle, conservé aux Ar-**
chives de l'Hérault [The Chant of the Sybil after a 12th-century manuscript preserved at the archives of the Herault], *Actes du Congrès d'histoire de l'art* (Paris: Presses Universitaires de France, 1923-1924) 774–83. *Music.* In French. See no. 94 in this volume.

The MS contains the primitive, D mode version of the Chant of the Sybil. It also offers an unknown variation and comprises one of the oldest known translations in a Romance language from rhymed Latin text. *(Vivian Conejero)*

1166 RAUGEL, Félix. **Saint-Césaire, précepteur du**
as **chant gallican** [St. Caesarius, preceptor of Gallican chant], *Bericht über den siebenten internationalen musikwissenschaftlichen Kongress* (Kassel: Bärenreiter, 1959) 217–18. In French. See no. 390 in this volume.

Caesarius of Arles (470-542), as archbishop of Arles from 502 until his death, played a central role in the development of the monastic cursus and the celebration of the Mass there, including its music, and—Arles being then capital of the Gauls—in the development of Gallican chant as a whole. His surviving writings include more than 100 sermons, a valuable source for musical practice and attitudes toward music during the period. *(David Bloom)*

1167 REANEY, Gilbert. **The isorhythmic motet and**
as **its social background,** *Bericht über den internationalen musikwissenschaftlichen Kongreß* (Kassel: Bärenreiter, 1963) 25–27. See no. 452 in this volume.

The question of performance context is in many ways more important than the elucidation of text in the isorhythmic motet. It is deeply rooted in religious ceremony, and usually remains a paraliturgical work whatever its text; motets written purely for entertainment must have been rare. *(Laurie Appleby)*

1168 REANEY, Gilbert. **Zur Frage der Autoren-**
as **zuweisung in mittelalterlichen Musiktrak-**
taten [The attribution of authorship in medieval music treatises], *Bericht über den internationalen musikwissenschaftlichen Kongreß* (Kassel: Bärenreiter, 1963) 353–54. In German. See no. 452 in this volume.

Summarizes the debate on questionable attributions to Theodonus de Caprio, Magister Lambertus, Simon Tunstede, Johannes de Garlandia, and others. *(David Bloom)*

1169 RIPOLLÉS PÉREZ, Vicente. **Breves anotaciones**
as **a la Epistola Farçida de San Esteban** [Brief annotations to the Epistola farçida of San Esteban], *Bericht über den musikwissenschaftlichen Kongreß in Basel* (Leipzig: Breitkopf & Härtel, 1925) 293–309. *Music.* In Spanish. See no. 102 in this volume.

Two 14th-c. codices in the cathedral of Valencia (codices 68 and 100) contain the epistle *Planchs de Sant Esteve* (*Planctus de S. Stephano*) for St. Stephen's Day (26 December). This epistle had a wide distribution in France, Provence, and Catalonia, with Latin, French, Provençal, patois, and Catalan paraphrases.

1170
as
ROJO, Casiano. **El arte y expresión en el canto gregoriano** [Art and expression in Gregorian chant], *Crónica del IV Congreso Nacional de Música Sagrada* (Vitoria: Imprenta del Montepío Diocesano, 1930) 61–72. In Spanish. See no. 155 in this volume.

Analyzes several expressive and symbolic elements in Gregorian chant, including mode, intervals, and rhythm.

1171
as
SALMEN, Walter. **Arbeitsgemeinschaft: Der Musiker in der mittelalterlichen Gesellschaft** [Working group: The musician in medieval society], *Bericht über den siebenten internationalen musikwissenschaftlichen Kongress* (Kassel: Bärenreiter, 1959) 354–57. In German. See no. 390 in this volume.

Summary report of a workshop on the social, economic, and judicial status of musicians in medieval Europe, with participation by Higini ANGLÈS, Heinrich BESSELER, Suzanne CLERCX-LEJEUNE, Hellmut FEDER-HOFER, Heinrich HÜSCHEN, and Gilbert REANEY. *(David Bloom)*

1172
as
SALMEN, Walter. **Die internationale Wirkungsweite fahrender Musiker im Dienste der Herzöge von Österreich** [The international scope of the influence of itinerant musicians in the service of the Austrian dukes], *Bericht über den internationalen musikwissenschaftlichen Kongreß Wien Mozartjahr 1956* (Graz; Köln: Böhlau, 1958) 544–47. In German. See no. 365 in this volume.

The international musical importance of Vienna was already established in the 12th to 15th c., largely through the prominence of musicians in the service of the Austrian court who traveled throughout Europe, whether on long-term leave from their positions or on official court missions. A preliminary report of research is covered more fully in the author's *Der fahrende Musiker im europäischen Mittelalter* (Kassel, 1960). *(David Bloom)*

1173
as
SCHLÖTTERER, Reinhold. **Aufgaben und Probleme bei der Erforschung byzantinischen Musiktheorie** [Tasks and problems of research in Byzantine music theory], *X. Milletlerarası Bizans Tetkikleri Kongresi Tebliğleri/Actes du X. Congrès International d'Études Byzantines* (İstanbul: İstanbul Maatbası, 1957) 387–89. In German. See no. 347 in this volume.

Theoretical writings apart from the notation manuals or *papadikai* have significance for the study of performance practice, tonal systems, and music history. The study of a single treatise must be based on a comprehensive awareness of all of them, which could be assisted by the production of a terminological lexicon-glossary specifying the interrelated use of each term in the different treatises, general patristic writings, and Roman Catholic theory. An example is provided on the basis of the term *asma*. *(David Bloom)*

1174
as
SCHNEIDER, Marius. **Arabischer Einfluss in Spanien?** [Arab influence in Spain?], *Bericht über den Internationalen musikwissenschaftlichen Kongress* (Kassel: Bärenreiter, 1954) 175–80. In German. See no. 319 in this volume.

Systematically rejects the idea that Arabic music has strongly influenced the music of Spain. The various repertoires of Spanish music do not overlap with music within the Arabic cultural domain. Parallels between Arab and Spanish verse forms and between the medieval European modes and rhythmic formulas mentioned by Arab theorists are not germane, for literary parallels cannot be taken as evidence of musical ones. Compared with material culture and even the plastic arts, music stubbornly resists transplanting from one culture to another. One reason is that the musical expression of a people is racially determined. It is far easier to teach a moderately gifted black African the rudiments of polyphonic performance than a highly gifted Arab, for example, due to the differing musical predispositions of these two races. *(Carl Skoggard)*

1175
as
SCHRADE, Leo. **The chronology of the ars nova in France,** *Les colloques de Wégimont. II:*

L'ars nova—Recueil d'études sur la musique du XIVe siècle (Paris: Belles Lettres, 1959) 37–62. In English and French. See no. 351 in this volume.

Examines sources of French music from the interpolated *La roman de Fauvel* MS *F-Pn* MS fr.146 (1316) to the late 14th- or early 15th-c. compositions of the Chantilly (*F-CH* MS 564) and Turin (*I-Tn* MS J.II.9) codices, in terms of general questions of terminology and chronology and specific issues such as Machaut's personal relation to the ars nova movement and the status of the Mass as a genre. *(David Bloom)*

1176
as
SCHRAMMEK, Winfried. **Das Buxheimer Orgelbuch als deutsches Liederbuch** [The Buxheimer Orgelbuch as a German songbook], *Bericht über den internationalen musikwissenschaftlichen Kongreß* (Kassel: Bärenreiter, 1957) 211–13. In German. See no. 356 in this volume.

Of the 250-odd pieces in the 15th-c. tablature (*D-Mbs* MS Cim.352b [olim Mus.3725]), 117 are derived from German songs; 40 of these can be reconstructed in their original polyphonic Tenorlied versions. *(David Bloom)*

1177
as
SEAY, Albert. **Paolo da Firenze: A trecento theorist,** *L'ars nova italiana del Trecento: Primo convegno internazionale* (Certaldo: Centro di Studi sull'Ars Nova Italiana del Trecento, 1962) 118–40. Music. See no. 407 in this volume.

An edition with commentary and transcribed music examples of the treatise *Ars ad adiscendum contrapunctum*, from the *I-Fl* MS Ashburnham 1119, probably written by Paolo between 1380 and 1410. Its practical style points to an emphasis not on speculative music but on performed music—in particular, the practice of improvised counterpoint—and indicates an independent Italian school in the late 14th c. and early 15th c. about which little is known. *(John Gordon Morris)*

⟶
SMIJERS, Albert. **Music of the Illustrious Confraternity of Our Lady at 's-Hertogenbosch from 1330-1600.** See no. 1434 in this volume.

1178
as
SMITS VAN WAESBERGHE, Joseph. **L'état actuel des recherches scientifiques dans le domaine du chant grégorien** [The current state of scientific research in the field of Gregorian chant], *Perspectives de la musique sacrée à la lumière de l'encyclique* Musicae sacrae disciplina (Paris: conference, 1959) 206–17. In French. See no. 379 in this volume.

A summary is cited as no. 1179 in this volume.

1179
as
SMITS VAN WAESBERGHE, Joseph. **État des recherches scientifiques dans le domaine du chant grégorien** [The state of scientific research in the field of Gregorian chant], *Revue musicale* 239-240 (1957) 87–100. In French. See no. 378 in this volume.

An abridged version of the conference paper is cited as no. 1178 in this volume.

1180
as
SMITS VAN WAESBERGHE, Joseph. **L'évolution des tons psalmodiques au Moyen Âge** [The evolution of psalm tones in the Middle Ages], *Atti del [I] Congresso internazionale di musica sacra* (Tournai: Desclée, 1952) 267–75. In French. See no. 303 in this volume.

1181
as
SMITS VAN WAESBERGHE, Joseph. **Guido von Arezzo als Musikerzieher und Musiktheoretiker** [Guido of Arezzo as music pedagogue and theorist], *Bericht über den Internationalen musikwissenschaftlichen Kongress* (Kassel: Bärenreiter, 1954) 44–47. In German. See no. 319 in this volume.

Guido of Arezzo invented the fundamentals of Western notation as well as solmization. His *Micrologus* was the most widely copied text during the Middle Ages and he is rightly regarded as one of the greatest music pedagogues in European history. His discussions of polyphony and improvisation have particular interest. Guido's exposition of polyphony shows him more in the light of a composer than a theorist. As a chant theorist Guido was conservative. His refusal to accept changes in chant that went beyond the received diatonicism may reflect his desire for clarity in his instructional system. He was a teacher above all. *(Carl Skoggard)*

1182
as
SMITS VAN WAESBERGHE, Joseph. **Das Maastrichter Osterspiel: Beitrag zur Literatur der liturgischen Spiele** [The Maastricht Easter play: A contribution to the literature of liturgical drama], *Compte rendu/Kongressbericht/Report* (Basel: Bärenreiter, 1951) 184–85. In German. See no. 289 in this volume.

A brief account of *NL-DHk* MS 76.F.3.

1183
as
SMITS VAN WAESBERGHE, Joseph. **Neues über die Schola Cantorum zu Rom** [New findings about the Schola Cantorum in Rome], *Zweiter internationaler Kongress für katholische Kirchenmusik: Zu Ehren des Heiligen Papstes Pius X* (Wien: conference, 1955) 111–19. In German. See no. 339 in this volume.

Recent research suggests a clarification of the history of the Schola Cantorum in the 7th-9th c. and its relation to the evolution of Gregorian chant. The singing of the liturgy in Rome in the 7th c. was developing in different ways among two conflicting groups of clergy, the regular clergy of the Benedictine monasteries on the one hand and the secular clergy of the major basilicas on the other. The Schola, arising from an orphanage associated with the basilica of St. John Lateran, initially practiced the secular chant style, what is now known as Old Roman chant, but later adopted the reformed monastic style now known as Gregorian. *(David Bloom)*

1184
as
SMITS VAN WAESBERGHE, Joseph. **Das niederländische Osterspiel** [The Netherlandish Easter play], *Société Internationale de Musicologie, cinquième congrès/Internationale Gesellschaft für Musikwissenschaft, fünfter Kongreß/International Society for Musical Research, Fifth Congress* (Amsterdam: Vereniging voor Nederlandse Muziekgeschiedenis, 1953) 371–76. In German. See no. 316 in this volume.

1185
as
SNOECK, César. **Notes sur les instruments de musiques en usage dans les Flandres au Moyen Âge** [Musical instruments in Flanders during the Middle Ages], *Fédération Archéologique et Historique de Belgique: Congrès de Gand* (Gent: Siffer, 1897) 259–83. In French. See no. 23 in this volume.

A study of the terms used for instruments in the Middle Ages in Flanders and on the misconceptions arising out of the changing terminologies as reflected in theoretical works of the time. *(Albert Dlugasch)*

1186
as
STÄBLEIN, Bruno. **Alt- und neurömischer Choral** [Old and New Roman chant], *Kongreß-Bericht: Gesellschaft für Musikforschung* (Kassel; Basel: Bärenreiter, 1950) 53–56. *Music*. In German. See no. 299 in this volume.

1187
as
STÄBLEIN, Bruno. **Ambrosianisch—Gregorianisch** [Ambrosian, Gregorian], *Compte rendu/Kongressbericht/Report* (Basel: Bärenreiter, 1951) 185–89. *Music*. In German. See no. 289 in this volume.

Ambrosius Kienle noted that the Ambrosian and Gregorian-Roman chant repertoires share several melodies, including a setting of *Ad te, Domine, levavi* in the D mode that was used for an Ingressa in Milan and an Offertory antiphon in Rome. A close comparison shows that the Ambrosian version of this melody is less sharply articulated, more prone to repetition, and more densely melismatic. *(David Bloom)*

1188
as
STÄBLEIN, Bruno. **Una sconosciuta sequenza dello stile arcaico in Italia** [A previously unknown archaic-style sequence in Italy], *Atti del Congresso internazionale di musiche popolari mediterranee e del Convegno dei bibliotecari musicali* (Palermo: De Magistris succ. V. Bellotti, 1959) 289–94. *Music*. In German. See no. 332 in this volume.

Only one melody has previously been known for an archaic sequence, i.e., one from before the time of Notker Balbulus, that of *Rex caeli*; but the melody of *Dulce carmen*, attested only in a defective 9th-c. version in lineless neumes (*D-Mbs* MS clm.19417), can be reconstructed with the help of an 11th-c. contrafactum by St. Pier Damiani, *Caelum terra pontus aethra*. Both it and the *Rex caeli* melody are in the plagal mode on E, connecting them with the extraliturgical cantio repertoire of southern Germany in the 13th to 14th c. *(David Bloom)*

1189
as
STÄBLEIN, Bruno. **Die Unterlegung von Texten unter Melismen: Tropus, Sequenz und andere Formen** [Text underlay of melismas: Trope, sequence, and other forms], *Report of the Eighth Congress of the International Musicological Society. I: Papers* (Kassel: Bärenreiter, 1961) 12–29. *Music*. In German. See no. 439 in this volume.

It is likely that the *jubilare* singing of melismas used nonsense syllables, as is attested in traditional music from the Caucasus to Peru and the liturgies of the Manichaeans, Nestorians, and Syrian and Old Russian churches, until meaningful text underlay became common in the West, in the Carolingian period. The development of the phenomenon is reconstructed from the Old Roman chant (ca. 550-750) to the beginning of the notation of sequences and tropes toward the end of the 9th c. *(David Bloom)*

1190
as
STÄBLEIN, Bruno. **Das Wesen des Tropus: Ein Beitrag zum Problem Alt und Neu in der Kirchenmusik** [The character of the trope: Contribution to the problem of old versus new in church music], *Kirchenmusik in ökumenischer Schau* (Bern: Haupt, 1964) 55–58. In German. See no. 447 in this volume.

A fuller version, with music examples, is published in *Acta musicologica* XXXV (1963).

1191
as
STÄBLEIN, Bruno. **Zur Frühgeschichte des römischen Chorals** [The early history of Roman chant], *Atti del [II] Congresso internazionale di musica sacra* (Tournai: Desclée, 1952) 276. In German. See no. 303 in this volume.

1192
as
STEFANOVIĆ, Dimitrije. **The beginnings of Serbian chant**, *Anfänge der slavischen Musik* (Bratislava: Slovenská Akadémia Vied, 1966) 55–64. *Bibliog*. See no. 477 in this volume.

It is probable that Serbian chant was transmitted orally for a long time before being notated; no Serbian MSS with neumatic notation appear prior to the 15th c., and then only in fragments. A chronological inventory of 14 relevant MSS sheds some light on the earliest period. *(Brian Doherty)*

1193
as
STEPHAN, Rudolf. **Einige Hinweise auf die Pflege der Mehrstimmigkeit im frühen Mittelalter in Deutschland** [Some indications of the cultivation of polyphony in the early Middle Ages in Germany], *Kongreß-Bericht: Gesellschaft für Musikforschung* (Kassel; Basel: Bärenreiter, 1950) 68–71. In German. See no. 299 in this volume.

1194
as
STRAETEN, Edmond vander. **Quels étaient les instruments de musique en usage dans les provinces Belges avant l'avènement de la maison de Bourgogne?** [What were the musical instruments used in the Belgian provinces before the coming of the House of Burgundy?], *Annales de la Fédération Archéolo-*

gique et Historique de Belgique. VII/1 (Bruxelles: Goemaere, 1891) 91–95. In French. See no. 15 in this volume.

A history of instruments played in Belgium during this time is difficult to ascertain because of a lack of documentation. However, it is possible to ascertain the use of string, wind, and percussion instruments, and their association with times of war or peace. *(Albert Dlugasch)*

1195
as

STRUNK, Oliver. **S. Salvatore di Messina and the musical tradition of Magna Graecia,** *Pepragmena tou th' diethnous byzantinologikou synedriou* (Athínai: Typographeion Myrtidē, 1953) II, 274. See no. 327 in this volume.

A volume from the Monastero di S. Salvatore in Messina brings together the contents of two books ordinarily kept separate: the psaltikon, a soloist's book, and the asmatikon, a book for the choir.

1196
as

STRUNK, Oliver. **Two stichera on the death of the Emperor Nicephorus Phocas,** *X. Milletlerarası Bizans Tetkikleri Kongresi Tebliğleri/Actes du X. Congrès International d'Études Byzantines* (İstanbul: İstanbul Maatbası', 1957) 294. See no. 347 in this volume.

A fragmentary sticherarion at the Mone Megistis Lávras on Mt. Athos (*Gr-AOml* MS γ.74) includes stichera for the anniversary of the assassination on 11 December 969 of Nikephoros Phokas, the monastery's patron. The texts and style of notation are discussed. *(David Bloom)*

1197
as

STRUNK, Oliver. **Zwei Chilandari Chorbücher** [Two Hilandar choirbooks], *Anfänge der slavischen Musik* (Bratislava: Slovenská Akadémia Vied, 1966) 65–76. In German. See no. 477 in this volume.

Four conclusions arise from the study of two early Slavonic choirbooks from the Monī Chilandariou on Mt. Athos, the 12th-c. sticherarion *GR-AOh* MS 307 and the early 13th-c. heirmologion *GR-AOh* MS 308: (1) the archaic notation is of Byzantine origin; (2) it was introduced before 1000 and perhaps as early as 950; (3) sometime between 1000 and 1050 the notation was modified and these modifications were of Byzantine origin; and (4) the notational usage was somewhat unlike the Byzantine, and at least one sign was unique to its MS. Comparison of syllabic accents and neumatic structures between the choirbooks and Byzantine sources affirms these conclusions. *(Brian Doherty)*

1198
as

SUÑOL BAULINAS, Gregori M. **État actuel des travaux sur le chant ambrosien** [State of research concerning Ambrosian chant], *Congrés de la Societat Internacional de Musicologia* (Barcelona: Casa de Caritat, 1936). In French. See no. 224 in this volume.

The conference report provides only a citation. Neither the text nor a summary of the paper was published here.

1199
as

THIBAULT DE CHAMBURE, Geneviève. **L'ornementation dans la musique profane au Moyen Âge** [Ornamentation in secular medieval music], *Report of the Eighth Congress of the International Musicological Society. I: Papers* (Kassel: Bärenreiter, 1961) 450–63. *Music.* In French. See no. 439 in this volume.

Considers notated music from France and Italy dating from the 12th through the early 16th c. for evidence of vertical and horizontal ornamentation techniques and their relation to improvisatory practice. The most frequent type is the *battement,* either inside melodies or on cadences; the next most frequent are often purely decorative adjuncts to the melody. The *flores* and *colores* seen from the 13th c. onward demonstrate the continuity of ornamental tradition and its essential role in endowing the melodic line with flexibility. *(David Bloom)*

1200
as

THOMAS, Pierre. **Saint Odon de Cluny et son œuvre musicale** [Saint Odo of Cluny and his musical works], *À Cluny: Congrès scientifique—Fêtes et*

cérémonies liturgiques en l'honneur des saints abbés Odon et Odilon (Dijon: Bernigaud et Privat, 1950) 171–80. *Facs.* In French. See no. 290 in this volume.

Discusses and disputes the authorship of two MSS attributed to Odo of Cluny: a tonary and the treatise *Dialogus de musica.* The attribution of the invention of solmization (traditionally assumed to belong to Guido of Arezzo) is also discussed. *(Susan Poliniak)*

1201
as

TORREFRANCA, Fausto. **The *canzoni di alettali matrice* of the court dances and of the filastrocca during the fifteenth century and earlier,** *Journal of the International Folk Music Council* II (1950) 40–42. See no. 295 in this volume.

Discusses Italian secular songs of the 14th and 15th c. and some of the dances associated with them.

1202
as

TORREFRANCA, Fausto. **Guido d'Arezzo** [Guido of Arezzo], *Kongreß-Bericht: Gesellschaft für Musikforschung* (Kassel; Basel: Bärenreiter, 1950) 60–62. In Italian. See no. 299 in this volume.

1203
as

TORRI, Luigi. **La seule composition musicale connue de Jean d'Arras** [The only known musical composition by Jean d'Arras], *Actes du Congrès d'histoire de l'art* (Paris: Presses Universitaires de France, 1923-1924) 829–32. In Italian. See no. 94 in this volume.

1204
as

VANICKÝ, Jaroslav. **Czech mediaeval and Renaissance music,** *Musica antiqua Europae orientalis* (Warszawa: Państwowe Wydawnictwo Naukowe, 1966). See no. 506 in this volume.

Surveys secular and religious music from the 9th to the 16th c., with references to literature and traditional songs.

1205
as

WAGNER, Peter. **Germanisches und Romanisches im frühmittelalterlichen Kirchengesang** [Germanisms and Romanisms in the chant of the early Middle Ages], *Bericht über den I. musikwissenschaftlichen Kongress der Deutschen Musikgesellschaft in Leipzig* (Wiesbaden: Breitkopf & Härtel, 1926) 21–34. *Music.* In German. See no. 120 in this volume.

Variant readings in German and Italian versions of Gregorian chant are discussed.

1206
as

WAGNER, Peter. **Das *Media vita*** [The *Media vita*], *Schweizer Jahrbuch für Musikwissenschaft/Annales suisses de musicologie/Annuario svizzero di musicologia* I (1924) 18–40. In German. See no. 103 in this volume.

Discusses the Compline antiphon *Media vita in morte sumus.*

1207
as

WAGNER, Peter. **Über den altspanischen, mozarabischen Kirchengesang** [The Old Spanish Mozarabic chant], *Beethoven-Zentenarfeier: Internationaler musikhistorischer Kongress* (Wien: Universal, 1927) 234–36. In German. See no. 142 in this volume.

Offers an account of extant sources and the as yet undeciphered styles of neumatic notation.

1208
as

WAGNER, Peter. **Über den gegenwärtigen Stand der mittelalterlichen Musikforschung** [The current state of research on medieval music], *Bericht über den zweiten Kongress der Internationalen Musikgesellschaft* (Leipzig: Breitkopf & Härtel, 1907) 161–65. In German. See no. 53 in this volume.

Surveys recent studies, including the publication of music and theory sources, and research on notation, history, and theory.

1209 WAITE, William G. **The era of melismatic po-**
as   **lyphony,** *Report of the Eighth Congress of the International Musicological Society. I: Papers* (Kassel:
Bärenreiter, 1961) 178–83. See no. 439 in this volume.

The abundant references to music composition and performance in prosas
of the 11th c., especially those of the St. Martial repertoire, suddenly vanish
around the year 1100. One explanation is that composers' interest had radically shifted from the text-based art of musical troping to that of melismatic
polyphony, and that the texts themselves reflect the shift. *(David Bloom)*

1210 WALLIN, Nils L. **Zur Deutung der Begriffe** *Fa-*
as   *burden—Fauxbourdon* [Interpreting the terms *faburden* and *fauxbourdon*], *Bericht über den Internationalen musikwissenschaftlichen Kongress* (Kassel:
Bärenreiter, 1954) 120–24. In German. See no. 319 in
this volume.

Discusses the etymology of the terms *burden, bourdon, faburden,* and *fauxbourdon,* and how they relate to one another. *Faburden* originated independently of *fauxbourdon,* in England at the beginning of the 14th c. in connection with the carol and improvisatory techniques associated with it.
Whereas *bourdon* is never used to refer to refrains, *burden* is normally so
used. The essential meaning of *faburden* has to do with the improvised performance of verses of carol refrains. *(Carl Skoggard)*

1211 WELLESZ, Egon. **Kontakion and kanōn,** *Atti*
as   *del [I] Congresso internazionale di musica sacra*
(Tournai: Desclée, 1952) 131–33. See no. 303 in this
volume.

1212 WELLESZ, Egon. **La musique byzantine et ses**
as   **relations avec le chant grégorien dans la**
musique du Moyen Âge [Byzantine music and its
relation to Gregorian chant in the music of the Middle
Ages], *Sixième Congrès international d'études
byzantines: Résumés des rapports et communications*
(Paris: Comité d'Organisation du Congrès, 1940) 113f.
In French. See no. 263 in this volume.

1213 WELLESZ, Egon. **Lo stadio attuale delle**
as   **ricerche nel campo della musica sacra**
bizantina [The current state of research in the area of
Byzantine religious music], *Atti del V Congresso
internazionale di studi bizantini* (Roma: Associazione
Nazionale per gli Studi Bizantini, 1940) II, 546–47. In
Italian. See no. 233 in this volume.

In the early part of the 20th c., issues surrounding the notation of Byzantine
music included the proper indication of rhythm and the deciphering of the
melody lines of 13th-c. chant. One method, described briefly, involves the
labeling of different types of rhythm. *(Susan Poliniak)*

1214 WELLESZ, Egon. **Ein Überblick über die**
as   **Musik der Ostkirchen: Stand, Aufgaben und**
Probleme [A survey of the music of the Eastern
churches: State of research, tasks, and problems],
*Zweiter internationaler Kongress für katholische
Kirchenmusik: Zu Ehren des Heiligen Papstes Pius X*
(Wien: conference, 1955) 76–81. In German. See no.
339 in this volume.

Research since World War II has clarified the origins of Byzantine chant in
Jewish synagogal practice, its influence on Western chant, the history of its
notation, its modal composition, and its theological significance. Considerable progress has also been made in the transcription of early Slavic chant.
Work on the transcription of hymnody has not been matched by that on the
chants of the Byzantine Office and Mass, and the music of the Syrian, Armenian, Coptic, and Abyssinian churches has hardly been studied at all.
(David Bloom)

1215 WERNER, Eric. **Hebrew music theory of the**
as   **Middle Ages,** *Papers of the American Musicological
Society* (Philadelphia: American Musicological Society, 1946) 125–36. *Music, charts, diagr.* See no. 272 in
this volume.

A critical inventory of passages on music in Jewish writings of the
10th-14th c. The philosophy of music was a mixture of biblical severity,
Greek logic, and Arabic scholasticism, occasionally flavored by mystic or
kabbalistic speculation. The sources omit musical aesthetics in favor of a
Platonic-style moralistic-theocratic conception of music, and the only evidence of secular music is the statement of Maimonides that it should be
eliminated. Greek ideas in the calculation of intervals were used, and the
well-developed theory of modes may have influenced Western theory
through Byzantium. There was an elementary knowledge of chords and
chromaticism. The few instances of notation used Lombard neumes and
solfège syllables. Rhythmic modes were closely related to those of Arabs,
while melodic ones show a Phrygian or semi-Phrygian structure. *(author)*

⟶   WERNER, Eric. **Die Ursprünge der Psalmodie**
[The origins of psalmody]. See no. 1048 in this volume.

1216 WIORA, Walter. **Der mittelalterliche Lied-**
as   **kanon** [The song canon of the Middle Ages],
Kongreß-Bericht: Gesellschaft für Musikforschung
(Kassel; Basel: Bärenreiter, 1950) 71–75. *Music.* In
German. See no. 299 in this volume.

1217 ZAGIBA, Franz. **Die Entstehung des slavischen**
as   **liturgischen Gesanges im 9. Jahrhundert nach**
westlichem und östlichem Ritus [The origin of
9th-century Slavic liturgical chant following the Western and Eastern rites], *Société Internationale de Musicologie, cinquième congrès/Internationale Gesellschaft für Musikwissenschaft, fünfter Kongreß/Interna-
tional Society for Musical Research, Fifth Congress*
(Amsterdam: Vereniging voor Nederlandse Muziekgeschiedenis, 1953) 456. In German. See no. 316 in this
volume.

1218 ZAGIBA, Franz. **Probleme, Aufgaben und Or-**
as   **ganisation der österreichischen Choral-**
forschung [Problems, tasks, and organization of Austrian chant research], *Zweiter internationaler Kongress
für katholische Kirchenmusik: Zu Ehren des Heiligen
Papstes Pius X* (Wien: conference, 1955) 149–51. In
German. See no. 339 in this volume.

Major tasks include the complete cataloguing of chant MSS and prints in
private and public Austrian collections, the completion of the project of
photocopying the original sources, and the study of sources from the point
of view of establishing the identities of scribal schools and their local and
international relationships. Particularly Austrian chant music, including
the Offices of local saints, treatises, and German-language liturgical texts,
needs to be studied further. The author's *Die ältesten musikalischen
Denkmäler zu Ehren des Heiligen Leopold* (Zürich, 1954) represents a beginning of such efforts. *(David Bloom)*

24 Renaissance (ca. 1400 – 1600)

1219 AMELN, Konrad. **Die Anfänge der deutschen**
as   **Passionshistorie** [The beginnings of the German
Passion], *Compte rendu/Kongressbericht/Report*
(Basel: Bärenreiter, 1951) 39–44. In German. See no.
289 in this volume.

Examines the earliest sources of the Lutheran responsorial Passion, with attention to controversies over dating and attribution, musical characteristics, and the roles of the composer and poet Johann Walter and of Martin
Luther. *(David Bloom)*

1220 ANDRÉ, François. **La vieille chanson française**
as [The old French chanson], *Congrès international des Amitiés Françaises* (Mons: Libert, 1911) 65–70. In French. See no. 74 in this volume.
Examines the origins and conventions of the early French chanson. Many texts are included.

1221 ANGLÈS, Higini. **Die mehrstimmige Musik in**
as **Spanien vor dem 15. Jahrhundert** [Polyphonic music in Spain before the 15th century], *Beethoven-Zentenarfeier: Internationaler musikhistorischer Kongress* (Wien: Universal, 1927) 158–63. *List of works.* In German. See no. 142 in this volume.
A briefly annotated inventory of MS sources and treatises in Spanish collections. The materials are discussed at length in the author's *La música a Catalunya fins al segle XIII* (Barcelona, 1935).

1222 ANGLÈS, Higini. **Les musiciens flamands en**
as **Espagne et leur influence sur la polyphonie espagnole** [Flemish musicians in Spain and their influence on Spanish polyphony], *Société Internationale de Musicologie, cinquième congrès/Internationale Gesellschaft für Musikwissenschaft, fünfter Kongreß/International Society for Musical Research, Fifth Congress* (Amsterdam: Vereniging voor Nederlandse Muziekgeschiedenis, 1953) 47–54. In French. See no. 316 in this volume.

1223 ANGLÈS, Higini. **La polyphonie religieuse**
as **péninsulaire antérieure à la venue des musiciens Flamands en Espagne** [Religious polyphony of the Iberian Peninsula before the arrival of Flemish musicians in Spain], *Société Internationale de Musicologie: Premier Congrès Liège—Compte rendu/Internationale Gesellschaft für Musikwissenschaft: Erster Kongress Lüttich—Kongressbericht/International Society for Musical Research: First Congress Liège: Report* (London: Plainsong and Mediaeval Music Society, 1930) 67–72. In French. See no. 178 in this volume.
Source materials yet to be centralized and organized in a national archive reveal that the peninsular musicians of Spain were acquainted, from the beginning of the 15th c., with the school of Dufay-Binchois and played their compositions. From the second half of the 15th c. through the beginning of the 16th c., Spanish composers studied and sang the music of the Ockeghem-Obrecht-Josquin tradition. Well before the arrival of the Flemish musicians in Spain, in the latter part of the 16th c., they created a national school of polyphonic composition. A list, including sources, is given for 42 composers and their polyphonic religious compositions from the period preceding the flowering of Spanish polyphony in the latter part of the 16th c. *(Nathaniel Rudykoff)*

1224 ANTONOVYČ, Myroslav. **The present state of**
as **Josquin research,** *Report of the Eighth Congress of the International Musicological Society. I: Papers* (Kassel: Bärenreiter, 1961) 53–65. *List of works.* See no. 439 in this volume.
Focuses particularly on questions of attribution. Lists are provided of works identifiable as contrafacta of Josqin's works, and of motets whose attribution to Josquin should be regarded either as proven or discredited.

1225 APEL, Willi. **Der Anfang des Präludiums in**
as **Deutschland und Polen** [The beginnings of the prelude in Germany and Poland], *The book of the first international musicological congress devoted to the works of Frederick Chopin* (Warszawa: Państwowe Wydawnictwo Naukowe, 1963) 496–502. *Music.* In German. See no. 425 in this volume.

Bach's preludes function as an introduction to something—fugue, toccata, suite—while Chopin's do not. The prelude as a genre in Chopin's sense can be traced back as far as the Ileborgh organ tablature, and is found in two 16th-c. Polish sources, the organ tablatures of Jan z Lublina (*PL-Kp* MS 1716) and of the lost MS from Klasztor Sw. Ducha, Crakow (photocopied in *PL-Wn* MS 564). *(David Bloom)*

1226 BAILLIE, Hugh. **Les musiciens de la chapelle**
as **royale d'Henri VIII au Camp du Drap d'Or** [Musicians of Henry VIII's Chapel Royal at the Field of the Cloth of Gold], *Fêtes et cérémonies au temps de Charles Quint: Fêtes de la Renaissance. II* (Paris: Centre National de la Recherche Scientifique [CNRS], 1960) 147–59. In French. See no. 367 in this volume.
Protocol documents from Henry's meeting with François I at the Field of the Cloth of Gold near Calais, June 1520, provide a list of all 19 gentlemen (i.e. adult choristers) of the Chapel Royal who performed during the festivities. Biographical information is provided for William Cornysh, Robert Fayrfax, William Crane, Thomas Farthing, John Lloyd, and others. The organist for the English singers may have been John Giles or the Dutch expatriate Benedictus de Opitiis.

1227 BAL Y GAY, Jesús. **La canción amorosa della**
as **corte de Castilla de fines del siglo XVI y principios del siglo XVII** [The love song at the court of Castile from the end of the 16th and the beginning of the 17th centuries], *Congrés de la Societat Internacional de Musicologia* (Barcelona: Casa de Caritat, 1936). In Spanish. See no. 224 in this volume.
The conference report provides only a citation. Neither the text nor a summary of the paper was published here.

1228 BAS, Giulio. **Une composition d'Ockeghem**
as **conservée dans un manuscrit du Mont-Cassin** [A composition by Ockeghem preserved in a Monte Cassino manuscript], *Actes du Congrès d'histoire de l'art: Compte rendu analytique* (Paris: Presses Universitaires de France, 1922) 68–69. In French. See no. 95 in this volume.
Summary of a conference paper.

1229 BAUTIER-RÉGNIER, Anne-Marie. **L'édition**
as **musicale italienne et les musiciens d'Outre-monts au XVIᵉ siècle (1501-1563)** [Italian music publishing and ultramontane musicians in the 16th century (1501-1563)], *La Renaissance dans les provinces du Nord: Picardie, Artois, Flandres, Brabant, Hainaut* (Paris: Centre National de la Recherche Scientifique [CNRS], 1956) 27–49. *Charts, diagr.* In French. See no. 328 in this volume.
Documents exchanges of influences between Italy and northern France and the Low Countries in the Renaissance by examining statistics regarding music publications.

1230 BECHERINI, Bianca. **Communications sur**
as **Antonio Squarcialupi et notes au Cod. Med. Palatino 87** [Communications concerning Antonio Squarcialupi and notes on cod.med.Palatino 87], *Bericht über den siebenten internationalen musikwissenschaftlichen Kongress* (Kassel: Bärenreiter, 1959) 65. In French. See no. 390 in this volume.
Reviews documents that refer to the Florentine organist now known as Antonio Squarcialupi. He was of humble birth and generally went by the name "Antonio degli Organi"; in several places, however, he is referred to as "Squarcialupis" or "Squarcialupi". The nature of his connection with the prominent Squarcialupi family is not known. The Squarcialupi Codex (*I-Fl* MS Medicео Palatino 87) could not have been assembled by the organist and did not originally belong to the Squarcialupi family; perhaps it entered the family via marriage and was subsequently given to "Antonio Squarcialupi". *(Carl Skoggard)*

1231
as
BEERLI, Conrad André. **Quelques aspects des jeux, fêtes et danses à Berne pendant la première moitié du XVIe** [A few aspects of plays, festivals, and dances at Bern during the first half of the 16th century], *Les fêtes de la Renaissance* (Paris: Centre National de la Recherche Scientifique [CNRS], 1956) 347–70. In French. See no. 350 in this volume.
Examines Helvetic festivals held at Bern in the late 15th c. and early 16th c.

1232
as
BERGMANS, Paul. **Le collegium musicum fondé à Hasselt au XVIe siècle** [The Collegium Musicum founded at Hasselt in the 16th century], *Fédération Archéologique et Historique de Belgique: Annales du XXIe congrès* (Liège: Poncelet, 1909) II, 517f. In French. See no. 64 in this volume.

1233
as
BERNET KEMPERS, Karel Philippus. **Die wallonische und die französische Chanson in der ersten Hälfte des 16. Jahrhunderts** [The Wallonian and the French chanson in the first half of the 16th century], *Société Internationale de Musicologie: Premier Congrès Liège—Compte rendu/Internationale Gesellschaft für Musikwissenschaft: Erster Kongress Lüttich—Kongressbericht/International Society for Musical Research: First Congress Liège: Report* (London: Plainsong and Mediaeval Music Society, 1930) 76–80. In German. See no. 178 in this volume.
The Wallonian chanson, with its avoidance of symmetry and equality of parts, is a Gothic art. The French chanson, with its symmetrical form and sovereignty of a single voice, evinces a new world. *(Scott Fruehwald)*

1234
as
BERNOULLI, Eduard. **Dokumente zur Geschichte des Liedes und Tanzes aus dem 16. und 17. Jahrhundert** [Documents from the history of song and dance of the 16th and 17th centuries], *Bericht über den musikwissenschaftlichen Kongreß in Basel* (Leipzig: Breitkopf & Härtel, 1925) 72–79. In German. See no. 102 in this volume.
Three organ tabulatures from Switzerland are analyzed for content and notation. Types of works include three- and four-voice examples from the Reformation and earlier. The *Kappelerlied* of Ulrich Zwingli is included, as well as works by Desprez, Ludwig Senfl, Hans Zbären, and Heinrich Isaac. *(Sylvia Eversole)*

1235
as
BERNOULLI, Eduard. **Eine Handschrift mit rhythmisierten Meistersängermelodien** [A manuscript containing rhythmic Meistersinger melodies], *Report of the Fourth Congress of the International Musical Society* (London: Novello, 1912) 99. In German. See no. 71 in this volume.
Summary of a paper. Discusses the diverse contents of *D-Mbs* MS Cgm.4999.

1236
as
BESSELER, Heinrich. **Die Anfänge der musikalischen Neuzeit** [The beginnings of musical modernity], *Congrés de la Societat Internacional de Musicologia* (Barcelona: Casa de Caritat, 1936). In German. See no. 224 in this volume.
The conference report provides only a citation. Neither the text nor a summary of the paper was published here.

1237
as
BESSELER, Heinrich. **Johannes Ciconia: Begründer der Chorpolyphonie** [Johannes Ciconia: A founder of choral polyphony], *Atti del [I] Congresso internazionale di musica sacra* (Tournai: Desclée, 1952) 280–83. In German. See no. 303 in this volume.
Ciconia's innovations, particularly in the setting of Mass movements, were of epochal significance. A detailed version of the argument is given in the author's article on Ciconia in *Die Musik in Geschichte und Gegenwart* vol. 2 (Kassel, 1952). *(David Bloom)*

1238
as
BOBILLIER, Marie (Michel Brenet). **Un poète-musicien français du XVe siècle: Eloy d'Amerval** [A French poet-musician of the 15th century: Eloy d'Amerval], *Congrès international d'histoire de la musique: Documents, mémoires et vœux* (Solesmes: St. Pierre; Paris: Fischbacher, 1901) 165–72. In French. See no. 32 in this volume.
The French composer and poet lived from 1455 to 1508 and is considered one of the founders of vocal counterpoint. Portions of his long poem *Le livre de la déablerie* are included. A version of this article appeared in *Revue d'histoire et de critique musicales*, I (1901).

1239
as
BOETTICHER, Wolfgang. **Die französische Chansonkomposition Orlando di Lassos** [The French chanson compositions of Roland de Lassus], *Bericht über den internationalen musikwissenschaftlichen Kongreß Wien Mozartjahr 1956* (Graz; Köln: Böhlau, 1958) 60–65. In German. See no. 365 in this volume.
A survey and chronology of Lassus's output in the genre, in the light of recent discoveries.

1240
as
BOETTICHER, Wolfgang. **Die Magnificat-Komposition Orlando di Lassos** [The Magnificat settings of Roland de Lassus], *Bericht über den internationalen musikwissenschaftlichen Kongreß* (Kassel: Bärenreiter, 1957) 62–64. In German. See no. 356 in this volume.

1241
as
BOETTICHER, Wolfgang. **Les œuvres de Roland de Lassus mises en tablature de luth** [The works of Roland de Lassus transcribed in lute tablature], *Le luth et sa musique* (Paris: Centre National de la Recherche Scientifique [CNRS], 1958) 143–53. In French. See no. 377 in this volume.
The catalogue of Lassus's works can be enriched by a large number of 16th-c. and early 17th-c. lute intabulations, including some of works whose original versions are lost. The inventory, concordances with keyboard transcriptions, style, and handling of polyphony in the context of the growing preference for monodic style are discussed. *(David Bloom)*

1242
as
BOETTICHER, Wolfgang. **Orlando di Lasso als Demonstrationsobjekt in der Kompositionslehre des 16. und 17. Jahrhunderts** [Roland de Lassus as demonstration object for compositional theory of the 16th and 17th centuries], *Bericht über den Internationalen musikwissenschaftlichen Kongress* (Kassel: Bärenreiter, 1954) 124–27. In German. See no. 319 in this volume.
Traces the reception of Lassus in printed theoretical writings and appreciations dating from the 16th and 17th c., with some attention to the 18th c. also. Only those sources that quote passages of his music are considered. References remained sparse during the composer's lifetime. Adrian Le Roy's foreword to the first volume of his edition of Lassus's motets (1564) offered a nuanced evaluation of their style. The French publisher was also the first to discuss the proliferation of instrumental arrangements of Lassus's vocal music, and their unreliability. During the Baroque era, Lassus's music was cited in treatises to demonstrate the correct use of modes and the use of rhetorical figures; during this period, his bicinia were another important didactic resource. *(Carl Skoggard)*

1243
as
BOETTICHER, Wolfgang. **Zum Parodieproblem bei Orlando di Lasso: Ein spezieller Beitrag zur Frage geistlich-weltlicher Übertragungstechnik** [The parody problem in Roland de Lasso: A special contribution on his technique of trans-

ferring secular to sacred], *Report of the Eighth Congress of the International Musicological Society. I: Papers* (Kassel: Bärenreiter, 1961) 214–19. In German. See no. 439 in this volume.

A suvey of Lassus's parody technique, with detailed discussion of particular instances. Lassus's parody compositions employ a brilliant combinatorial art and are models of economy and concentration. The following generation would lack his sense of internal structure, as can be seen in the inferior technique of those many composers who undertook sacred retextings of his secular works. *(Carl Skoggard)*

1244 BOETTICHER, Wolfgang. **Zum problem der**
as **Übergangsperiode der Musik 1580-1620** [The problem of the period of musical transition 1580-1620], *Bericht über den internationalen musikwissenschaftlichen Kongreß* (Kassel: Bärenreiter, 1963) 141–44. In German. See no. 452 in this volume.

The examination of recently discovered works by Giovanni Giacomo Gastoldi and Adriano Banchieri shows that the period bridging the musical Renaissance and the monody of the early Baroque may be counted as a stylistic period in its own right, marked by an anticipation of the continuo principle. *(Daniel Anderson)*

1245 BOETTICHER, Wolfgang. **Zur Chronologie**
as **des Schaffens Orlando di Lassos** [Toward a chronology of the works of Roland de Lassus], *Kongreß-Bericht: Gesellschaft für Musikforschung* (Kassel; Basel: Bärenreiter, 1950) 82–88. *List of works.* In German. See no. 299 in this volume.

1246 BONELLI, L. **Les joueurs de flûte avignonnais**
as **au service de la République de Sienne au XVᵉ siècle** [Avignon flutists in the service of the Republic of Siena during the 15th century], *Actes du Congrès d'histoire de l'art* (Paris: Presses Universitaires de France, 1923-1924) 802–06. In French. See no. 94 in this volume.

1247 BORGHEZIO, Gino. **Poésies latines et fran-**
as **çaises mises en musique conservées dans un manuscrit inconnu de la Bibliothèque capitulaire d'Ivrée** [Latin and French poems set to music in an unknown manuscript in the Biblioteca Capitolare in Ivrea], *Actes du Congrès d'histoire de l'art* (Paris: Presses Universitaires de France, 1923-1924) 790–801. In Italian. See no. 94 in this volume.

1248 BORREN, Charles van den. **À propos de**
as **quelques messes de Josquin** [Concerning some Masses of Josquin], *Société Internationale de Musicologie, cinquième congrès/Internationale Gesellschaft für Musikwissenschaft, fünfter Kongreß/International Society for Musical Research, Fifth Congress* (Amsterdam: Vereniging voor Nederlandse Muziekgeschiedenis, 1953) 79–85. In French. See no. 316 in this volume.

1249 BORREN, Charles van den. **Deux recueils peu**
as **connus d'Orlande de Lassus** [Two little-known collections by Roland de Lassus], *Actes du Congrès d'histoire de l'art* (Paris: Presses Universitaires de France, 1923-1924) 833–45. *List of works, charts, diagr.* In French. See no. 94 in this volume.

Increasingly close relations between Lassus and France are documented by two collections in the Bibliothèque Royale Albert 1ᵉʳ, Brussels. Both the bibliography and the chronology of Lassus's works are to be revised in light of their evidence. *(Vivian Conejero)*

1250 BORREN, Charles van den. **L'esthétique ex-**
as **pressive de Guillaume Dufay dans ses rapports avec la technique musicale du XVᵉ siècle** [The expressive aesthetic of Guillaume Dufay in relation to the musical technique of the 15th century], *Fédération Archéologique et Historique de Belgique: Annales du XXIIᵉ congrès. I: Documents et compte rendu; II: Rapports & mémoires* (Mechelen: Godenne, 1911) II, 899–913. In French. See no. 73 in this volume.

Dufay's *Missa "Se la face ay pale"* is analyzed with respect to its expressive content and compared with the plastic arts of his day. His chansons *Donnés l'assault a la fortresse, Resvelons nous, resvelons, amoureux,* and *La belle se siet au pied de la tour* are likewise analyzed. *(Albert Dlugasch)*

1251 BORREN, Charles van den. **Guillaume Dufay**
as **(avant 1400-1474): Son importance historique** [Guillaume Dufay (before 1400-1474): His historical importance], *Fédération Archéologique et Historique de Belgique: Annales du XXIᵉ congrès* (Liège: Poncelet, 1909) II, 865–70. In French. See no. 64 in this volume.

1252 BORREN, Charles van den. **Hugo et Arnold de**
as **Lantins** [Hugo and Arnold de Lantins], *Congrès de Liège de la Fédération Archéologique et Historique de Belgique, 1932: XXIXᵉ session—Annales* (Liège: n.p., 1932) 263–73. In French. See no. 197 in this volume.

1253 BORREN, Charles van den. **Musicologie et**
as **géographie** [Musicology and geography], *La Renaissance dans les provinces du Nord: Picardie, Artois, Flandres, Brabant, Hainaut* (Paris: Centre National de la Recherche Scientifique [CNRS], 1956) 19–25. In French. See no. 328 in this volume.

Discusses the unusual degree of creative activity in the regions of Bruges, Antwerp, Arras, and Cambrai in the 15th and 16th c.

1254 BORREN, Charles van den. **La musique**
as **pittoresque dans le manuscrit 222 C 22 de la Bibliothèque de Strasbourg (XVᵉ siècle)** [The descriptive music in the manuscript 222 C 22 of the Bibliothèque de Strasbourg (15th century)], *Bericht über den musikwissenschaftlichen Kongreß in Basel* (Leipzig: Breitkopf & Härtel, 1925) 88–105. *Music.* In French. See no. 102 in this volume.

The incomplete notation in the MS, which was burned during the 1870 siege of Strasbourg, provides enough information to locate concordances in other MSS of the period. The Flemish, Italian, German, and French songs have many examples of onomatopoeic writing. Various songs are analyzed for descriptive content, including those of Nicola Zacharie da Brindisi, Guillaume de Machaut, and Oswald von Wolkenstein. *(Sylvia Eversole)*

1255 BORREN, Charles van den. **Sur Benedictus de**
as **Opitiis et deux de ses œuvres recemment publiées en fac simile** [On Benedictus de Opitiis and two of his works recently published in facsimile], *Congrès jubilaire* (Brugge: Gruuthuuse, 1925) 223–23. In French. See no. 119 in this volume.

Discusses in brief the facsimile publication of Jan de Gheet's *Lofzangen ter eere van keizer Maximiliaan en zijn kleinzoon Karel den Vijfde,* which includes Benedictus de Opitiis' *Sub tuum praesidium* and *Summae laudis o Maria. (Susan Poliniak)*

1256 BRAGARD, Roger. **André de Pape,** *Congrès de*
as *Liège de la Fédération Archéologique et Historique de Belgique, 1932: XXIXᵉ session—Annales* (Liège: n.p., 1932) 289f. In French. See no. 197 in this volume.

→ BRANCO, Luís de Freitas. **Les contrepointistes de l'école d'Évora** [The Évora school of contrapuntists]. See no. 4143 in this volume.

1257 BRENNECKE, Wilfried. **Johannes Polonus, ein**
as **Musiker um 1600** [Johannes Polonus, a musician of the period around 1600], *The book of the first international musicological congress devoted to the works of Frederick Chopin* (Warszawa: Państwowe Wydawnictwo Naukowe, 1963) 514–18. *List of works.* In German. See no. 425 in this volume.
Summarizes available information on the composer and violinist's life between 1590 and 1613, and evaluates his status as a composer. An annotated list of his extant works is provided. *(David Bloom)*

1258 BRENNECKE, Wilfried. **Musique instrumen-**
as **tale d'après un manuscrit allemand** [Instrumental music after a German manuscript], *La musique instrumentale de la Renaissance* (Paris: Centre National de la Recherche Scientifique [CNRS], 1955) 127–37. *Music.* In French. See no. 333 in this volume.
A MS in the holdings of the Proske collection of the Bischöfliche Zentralbibliothek, Regensburg (D-Rp MS AR 940-41), written in 1552-60 by Wolfgang Küffer, a student at the University of Wittenberg. The MS contains 314 sacred and secular pieces including French chansons, Italian madrigals, and apparently purely instrumental works; it provides unique evidence of students' musical practice, and of the early development of instrumental ensemble performance of secular vocal music. Attributions and other new information are provided along with incipits of 17 as yet unidentified pieces. *(Susan Poliniak)*

1259 BRIDGMAN, Nanie. **Les échanges musicaux**
as **entre l'Espagne et les Pays-Bas au temps de Philippe le Beau et de Charles V** [Musical exchanges between Spain and the Low Countries at the time of Philip the Fair and Charles V], *La Renaissance dans les provinces du Nord: Picardie, Artois, Flandres, Brabant, Hainaut* (Paris: Centre National de la Recherche Scientifique [CNRS], 1956) 51–61. In French. See no. 328 in this volume.
A historical overview focusing on the early 16th c.

1260 BRIDGMAN, Nanie. **La participation musicale**
as **à l'entrée de Charles Quint à Cambrai le 20 janvier 1540** [Musical aspects of Charles V's entry into Cambrai, 20 January 1540], *Fêtes et cérémonies au temps de Charles Quint: Fêtes de la Renaissance. II* (Paris: Centre National de la Recherche Scientifique [CNRS], 1960) 235–53. *Music.* In French. See no. 367 in this volume.
Music performed for the emperor's *joyeuse entrée* into Cambrai at the beginning of his campaign to suppress the rebellion in Ghent is exceptionally well documented, perhaps indicating the local importance of music. Jean Courtois, the episcopal chapel master, composed a motet for the occasion, *Venite populi terrae*; it is presented in a modern edition.

1261 BROWN, Howard Mayer. **The genesis of a style:**
as **The Parisian chanson, 1500-1530,** *Chanson & madrigal 1480-1530: Studies in comparison and contrast* (Cambridge, MA: Harvard University Press, 1964) 1–50. *Music, index.* See no. 429 in this volume.
The development of the Parisian chanson in 1500-30 began with the chansons of Desprez and reached maturity with Pierre Attaingnant's publication *Chansons nouvelles* in 1528. The latter contains works by Claudin de Sermisy in a new style cantus firmus on popular monophonic tunes is abandoned in favor of a homophonic, chordal style, in which the text is emphasized, and contrpauntal passages minimized. A discussion of the paper by François LESURE, Isabel POPE, and Geneviève THIBAULT DE CHAMBURE is included. *(Alexander G. Smith)*

1262 BUKOFZER, Manfred F. **The beginnings of**
as **polyphonic choral music,** *Papers of the American Musicological Society* (Philadelphia: American Musicological Society, 1946) 23–34. *Music.* See no. 269 in this volume.
Because it was an outgrowth of Gregorian chant sung in unison, polyphonic choral music evolved first within the church at the beginning of the Renaissance. Secular music, traditionally sung by solo voices, developed a choral tradition somewhat later.

1263 BUKOFZER, Manfred F. **The *Caput* Masses**
as **and their plainsong,** *Compte rendu/Kongressbericht/Report* (Basel: Bärenreiter, 1951) 82. See no. 289 in this volume.
Summary of research reported fully in the author's *"Caput": A liturgical-musical study* (New York: Norton, 1950) on the use of the final melisma, on the word *caput*, from the Sarum rite antiphon *Venit ad Petrum*, as a cantus firmus in three 15th-c. Masses. *(Scott Fruehwald)*

1264 BUSH, Helen E. **The Laborde Chansonnier,** *Papers of the American Musicological Society* (Philadelphia: American Musicological Society, 1946) 56–79. *Facs., music, bibliog., list of works.* See no. 269 in this volume.
The MS known as the Laborde Chansonnier (US-Wc MS M2.1L25 case), containing polyphonic settings of French poetry from the 15th c., was first mentioned in Paris in 1857 by Alexandre Joseph Hidulphe Vincent, in a report to the Comité de la Langue, de l'Histoire et des Arts de la France. No trace of the MS can be found prior to that date, and no information about its provenance was offered by Vincent on the occasion of his report. It was only in 1924 that published references to this MS began to appear. In 1936, the Laborde Chansonnier entered the collection of the Library of Congress in Washington, D.C., thus prompting further studies. The origin of its name, physical descriptions, questions of dating, and attempts to identify the name of the family whose coat of arms appears in various places are discussed. *(James Melo)*

1265 CAMETTI, Alberto. **Un nuovo documento sulle**
as **origini di Giovanni Pierluigi da Palestrina: Il testamento di Jacobella Pierluigi (1527)** [A new document on the origins of Giovanni Pierluigi da Palestrina: The testament of Jacobella Pierluigi (1527)], *Atti del Congresso internazionale di scienze storiche. VIII: Atti della sezione IV: Storia dell'arte musicale e drammatica* (Roma: R. Accademia dei Lincei, 1905) 87–92. In Italian. See no. 42 in this volume.
The testament of Jacobella (Palestrina's grandmother) was found in the Archivio di Stato, Rome. A book version is published with the same title (Torino: Fratelli Bocca, 1903).

1266 CAUCHIE, Maurice. **Les chansons à trois voix**
as **de Pierre Cléreau** [The three-voice chansons of Pierre Clereau], *Beethoven-Zentenarfeier: Internationaler musikhistorischer Kongress* (Wien: Universal, 1927) 175–80. In French. See no. 142 in this volume.
Recent discoveries have made it possible to assemble complete versions of 39 of Clereau's (or Cléreau's) *Odes de Ronsard* (1566/75), out of the total 47. Their texts—largely not by Pierre de Ronsard, in spite of the title—and music are briefly discussed. A more extended version is published in *Revue de musicologie* 9 (1927). *(David Bloom)*

1267 CAUCHIE, Maurice. **Les psaumes de Janequin**
as [The psalms of Janequin], *Société Internationale de Musicologie: Premier Congrès Liège—Compte rendu/ Internationale Gesellschaft für Musikwissenschaft: Erster Kongress Lüttich—Kongressbericht/International Society for Musical Research: First Congress Liège: Report* (London: Plainsong and Mediaeval Music Society, 1930) 86–86. In French. See no. 178 in this volume.

Describes two rediscovered (previously believed to be lost) collections of Clément Janequin: 28 psalms in four voices (1549) and 82 psalms in four voices (1559), of which only the bass is extant. *(Conrad T. Biel)*

1268 CAULLET, Gustave. **L'origine malinoise de**
as **Philippe de Monte (Van den Berghe)** [The Mechelen origin of Philippe de Monte (Van den Berghe)], *Fédération Archéologique et Historique de Belgique: Annales du XXIIᵉ congrès. I: Documents et compte rendu; II: Rapports & mémoires* (Mechelen: Godenne, 1911) II, 767–73. In French. See no. 73 in this volume.

A document written in 1555 is presented as evidence that Philippe de Monte was originally from Mechelen.

1269 CAZEAUX, Isabelle. **Verse meter and melodic**
as **rhythm in the age of humanism,** *Report of the Eighth Congress of the International Musicological Society. II: Reports* (Kassel: Bärenreiter, 1962) 67–71. See no. 440 in this volume.

A report on a discussion by Putnam ALDRICH, Nanie BRIDGMAN, Hans ENGEL, Lothar HOFFMANN-ERBRECHT, Knud JEPPESEN, Joseph KERMAN, Edward E. LOWINSKY, Frits NOSKE, Isabel POPE, Miguel QUEROL GAVALDA, Georg REICHERT, and André VERCHALY on the paper by Verchaly abstracted as no. 1458 in this volume.

1270 CESARI, Gaetano. **Die Entwicklung der Mon-**
as **teverdischen Kammermusik** [The development of Monteverdi's chamber music], *Haydn-Zentenarfeier* (Leipzig: Breitkopf & Härtel; Wien: Artaria, 1909) 153–55. In German. See no. 65 in this volume.

Focuses primarily on the works of Monteverdi in the seconda prattica, including *Ah, dolente partita, Ch'io non t'ami,* and *Io mi son giovinetta.*

1271 CHAILLON, Paule. **Les musiciens du Nord à la**
as **cour de Louis XII** [Northern musicians at the court of Louis XII], *La Renaissance dans les provinces du Nord: Picardie, Artois, Flandres, Brabant, Hainaut* (Paris: Centre National de la Recherche Scientifique [CNRS], 1956) 63–69. In French. See no. 328 in this volume.

1272 CHILESOTTI, Oscar. **Gli** *airs de court* **del** *The-*
as *saurus harmonicus* **di J.B. Besard** [The *airs de court* of the *Thesaurus harmonicus* of J.B. Besard], *Atti del Congresso internazionale di scienze storiche. VIII: Atti della sezione IV: Storia dell'arte musicale e drammatica* (Roma: R. Accademia dei Lincei, 1905) 131–34. In Italian. See no. 42 in this volume.

Jean-Baptiste Besard was the only printer of 16th c. airs de cour that display a monodic style foreshadowing the works of the Camerata. Besard's lute tablature is examined and chromatic alterations to the written melodies are suggested.

1273 CHILESOTTI, Oscar. **Le alterazioni croma-**
as **tiche nel secolo XVIᵒ** [Chromatic alterations in the 16th century], *Haydn-Zentenarfeier* (Leipzig: Breitkopf & Härtel; Wien: Artaria, 1909) 128–35. *Music.* In Italian. See no. 65 in this volume.

Discusses examples by several composers, including Jacquet de Berchem (1505-67), Adrian Willaert, and Desprez.

1274 CHILESOTTI, Oscar. **Musiciens français:**
as **Jean-Baptiste Besard et les luthistes du XVIᵉ siècle** [French musicians: Jean-Baptiste Besard and the lutenists of the 16th century], *Congrès international d'histoire de la musique: Documents, mémoires et vœux*

(Solesmes: St. Pierre; Paris: Fischbacher, 1901) 179–90. *Illus., music.* In French. See no. 32 in this volume.

Examples from Besard's collection of lute music, the *Thesaurus harmonicus* (1603), shed light on performers of the time.

1275 CHILESOTTI, Oscar. **Trascrizioni da un codice**
as **musicale di Vincenzo Galilei** [Transcriptions of a musical codex of Vincenzo Galilei], *Atti del Congresso internazionale di scienze storiche. VIII: Atti della sezione IV: Storia dell'arte musicale e drammatica* (Roma: R. Accademia dei Lincei, 1905) 135–38. In Italian. See no. 42 in this volume.

Vincenzo Galilei's *Fronimo* contains a large number of lute transcriptions of polyphonic works by himself, Palestrina, Willaert, Cipriano de Rore, Lassus, and others. The transcriptions can be transposed to within the range of one staff to make them easily playable on the guitar.

⟶ CHOMIŃSKI, Józef Michał. **Die Beziehungen der polnischen Musik zu Westeuropa vom XV. bis zum XVII. Jahrhundert** [The relation of Polish music to Western Europe in the 15th through the 17th centuries]. See no. 954 in this volume.

1276 CLERCX-LEJEUNE, Suzanne. **L'Espagne**
as **XVIᵉ siècle, source d'inspiration du génie héroïque de Monteverdi** [Sixteenth-century Spain: A source of inspiration for Monteverdi's heroic genius], *Musique et poésie au XVIᵉ siècle* (Paris: Centre National de la Recherche Scientifique [CNRS], 1954) 329–43. In French. See no. 326 in this volume.

Discusses the differences between the stile nuovo as practiced by the Florentine Camerata and as practiced by Monteverdi in Mantua, arguing that Mantua and Naples were influenced by the Spanish theater and Jewish musicians from Spain. *(Roy Nitzberg)*

1277 CLERCX-LEJEUNE, Suzanne. **Johannes**
as **Ciconia de Leodio** [Johannes Ciconia of Leodio], *Société Internationale de Musicologie, cinquième congrès/Internationale Gesellschaft für Musikwissenschaft, fünfter Kongreß/International Society for Musical Research, Fifth Congress* (Amsterdam: Vereniging voor Nederlandse Muziekgeschiedenis, 1953) 107–26. In French. See no. 316 in this volume.

1278 COLE, Elizabeth. **L'anthologie de madrigaux**
as **et de musique instrumentale pour ensembles de Francis Tregian** [The anthology of madrigals and instrumental ensemble music by Francis Tregian], *La musique instrumentale de la Renaissance* (Paris: Centre National de la Recherche Scientifique [CNRS], 1955) 115–26. *Music.* In French. See no. 333 in this volume.

Analytic account of the recently discovered *GB-Lbl* MS Egerton 3665, apparently copied by the same hand as that of the Fitzwilliam Virginal Book (*GB-Cfm* MS 32.g.29) and corroborating the hypothesis that Francis Tregian was the copyist of both. *(Susan Poliniak)*

1279 COSMA, Viorel. **Aspects de la culture musicale**
as **sur le territoire de la Roumanie entre le XIVᵉ et le XVIIIᵉ siècle** [Aspects of the musical culture in the territory of Romania between the 14th and 18th centuries], *Musica antiqua Europae orientalis* (Warszawa: Państwowe Wydawnictwo Naukowe, 1966). In French. See no. 506 in this volume.

Discusses traditional, religious, court, and dramatic genres.

1280 CVETKO, Dragotin. **La musique slovène du**
as **XVIᵉ au XVIIIᵉ siècle** [Slovenian music from the
16th to the 18th centuries], *Musica antiqua Europae
orientalis* (Warszawa: Państwowe Wydawnictwo
Naukowe, 1966). *Facs., music, bibliog.* In French. See
no. 506 in this volume.

Examines both sacred and secular music.

1281 DAMILANO, Piero. **Le laude filippine: Storia**
as **ed interpretazione** [The lauda compositions associ-
ated with Filippo Neri: Their history and performance],
*Zweiter internationaler Kongress für katholische
Kirchenmusik: Zu Ehren des Heiligen Papstes Pius X*
(Wien: conference, 1955) 184–86. *Bibliog.* In Italian.
See no. 339 in this volume.

Brief remarks on the history and musical character of the laude sung at and
composed for meetings of the Congregazione dell'Oratorio, Rome,
founded by Filippo Neri in the mid-16th c., with particular attention to
texts, published collections, and the role of Giovenale Ancina. *(David Bloom)*

1282 DART, Thurston. **Le manuscrit pour le virginal**
as **de Trinity College, Dublin** [The virginal manuscript from Trinity College, Dublin], *La musique
instrumentale de la Renaissance* (Paris: Centre National de la Recherche Scientifique [CNRS], 1955)
237–39. In French. See no. 333 in this volume.

Analytic account of the Dublin Virginal MS (*IRL-Dtc* MS D.3.30/i).

1283 DART, Thurston. **Origines et sources de la**
as **musique de chambre en Angleterre (1500-1530)**
[Origins and sources of chamber music in England
(1500-1530)], *La musique instrumentale de la Renaissance* (Paris: Centre National de la Recherche
Scientifique [CNRS], 1955) 77–84. *Music.* In French.
See no. 333 in this volume.

The English instrumental ensemble music that arose in the early 16th c. was
not a more or less arbitrary mixture of elements of traditional music and sacred polyphony, but an independent development of genuinely abstract
music. It was created by a small and exclusive circle with the patronage and
active participation of Henry VIII in the period 1509-25; it was intended for
the enjoyment of the players rather than that of an audience, probably performed on recorders, made frequent use of proportions, and grew on a particularly English taste for speculative as opposed to practical music. An inventory of complete and fragmentary sources is provided. *(David Bloom)*

1284 DART, Thurston. **Rôle de la danse dans l'*ayre***
as ***anglais*** [The role of dance in the English ayre],
Musique et poésie au XVIᵉ siècle (Paris: Centre National de la Recherche Scientifique [CNRS], 1954)
203–09. In French. See no. 326 in this volume.

The ayre and the madrigal developed simultaneously between ca. 1580 and
1630.

1285 DE JONG, Marinus. **Polyphonisten uit de 15ᵉ en**
as **16ᵉ eeuw** [Polyphonists of the 15th and 16th centu-
ries], *Verhandelingen van het Muziekcongres*
(Antwerpen: Stad Antwerpen, 1935) 20–30. In Dutch.
See no. 210 in this volume.

Discusses works of Desprez, Ockeghem, and Obrecht, and their individual
contributions to the development of polyphony.

1286 DEBES, Louis Helmut. **Über den Stand der**
as **Forschungen zu Claudio Merulo** [The state of research on Claudio Merulo], *Bericht über den internationalen musikwissenschaftlichen Kongreß* (Kassel:
Bärenreiter, 1963) 138–41. *Bibliog., list of works.* In
German. See no. 452 in this volume.

Provides supplementary listings to the bibliography and works list of the
Merulo article in the first edition of *Die Musik in Geschichte und Gegenwart.*

1287 DELPORTE, Jules. **La Messe *Christus resurgens***
as **de Louis van Pulaer (d. 1528)** [*Missa "Christus
resurgens"* by Louis van Pullaer (d. 1528)], *Société
Internationale de Musicologie: Premier Congrès
Liège—Compte rendu/Internationale Gesellschaft für
Musikwissenschaft: Erster Kongress Lüttich—
Kongressbericht/International Society for Musical Re-
search: First Congress Liège: Report* (London: Plain-
song and Mediaeval Music Society, 1930) 91–92. In
French. See no. 178 in this volume.

This Mass is the only document by this composer that is known to exist; the
remainder of his works are presumed lost with the rest of the archives at
Cambrai. The work is named after its fundamental theme, taken from the
motet *Christus resurgens* that has been attributed to Heinrich Glarean. The
Mass is in four parts (SATB) except for several five- and three-part sections. *(Meredith E. Baker)*

1288 DENT, Edward Joseph. **La *Rappresentazione di***
as ***anima, e di corpo*** [The *Rappresentatione di anima, et
di corpo*], *Papers read at the International Congress of
Musicology* (New York: Music Educators National
Conference, 1944) 52–61. See no. 266 in this volume.

Outlines the history of Emilio de' Cavalieri's dramatic monody, and discusses its musical and theatrical aspects.

⟶ DJURIĆ-KLAJN, Stana. **Certains aspects de la**
musique profane serbe de l'époque féodale
[Certain aspects of Serbian secular music of the feudal
era]. See no. 1079 in this volume.

1289 DOORSLAER, Georges van. **Aperçu sur la pra-**
as **tique de la musique vocale à Malines au XVᵉ**
siècle [Survey of the performance of vocal music in
Mechelen in the 15th century], *Congrès d'Anvers de la
Fédération Archéologique et Historique de Belgique,
1930: XXVIIIᵉ session—Annales. II: Comptes rendus*
(Antwerpen: Resseler, 1931) 465–84. *Bibliog.* In
French. See no. 162 in this volume.

The practice of discant reached its apogee in the 15th c.; the works performed in Mechelen during this time period are examined and described.
The subgenres examined include chant for within sanctuaries (including
that used at the churches of Sint-Rombout and Notre-Dame and the court
chapel) and outside of churches (e.g., on the feast days of certain saints and
at re-creations of the Nativity). *(Susan Poliniak)*

1290 DOORSLAER, Georges van. **Paul van Winde:**
as **Organiste à la Cour Impériale de Vienne
(1598)** [Paul van Winde: Organist at the Viennese imperial court (1598)], *Société Internationale de Musicologie: Premier Congrès Liège—Compte rendu/Inter-
nationale Gesellschaft für Musikwissenschaft: Erster
Kongress Lüttich—Kongressbericht/International Society for Musical Research: First Congress Liège: Report* (London: Plainsong and Mediaeval Music Society,
1930) 93–99. In French. See no. 178 in this volume.

A biographical study of the Flemish organist and composer.

1291 DOORSLAER, Georges van. **Severin Cornet:**
as **Compositeur-maître de chapelle 1530-1582**
[Séverin Cornet: Composer-choirmaster, 1530-1582],
Congrès jubilaire (Brugge: Gruuthuuse, 1925) 229–29.
In French. See no. 119 in this volume.

A biography of the Flemish musical figure.

1292 DUFOURCQ, Norbert. **Remarques sur le cla-**
as **vier (clavecin et orgue) dans la première moitié
du XVIIᵉ siècle** [Remarks on the keyboard (harpsichord and organ) in the first half of the 17th century], *La*

musique instrumentale de la Renaissance (Paris: Centre National de la Recherche Scientifique [CNRS], 1955) 269–76. *Music*. In French. See no. 333 in this volume.

The differences between the organ, with its capacity for sustained tone, legato, and constant polyphony, and the harpsichord, with its contrasting speed, lightness, and precision, were well understood in the early 17th c. by organist-composers such as Jehan Titelouze, Francisco Correa de Arauxo, and Frescobaldi. In the Netherlandish school of Sweelinck and Scheidt and in France, harpsichord and organ styles interpenetrated one another; Louis Couperin was apparently the first French composer to write in idiomatic and completely distinct styles for both instruments. *(Gregory D'Agostino)*

⟶ DYSON, George. **The place of the organist in British musical life.** See no. 3355 in this volume.

1293
as

EINSTEIN, Alfred. **Filippo di Monte als Madrigalkomponist** [Philippe de Monte as madrigal composer], *Société Internationale de Musicologie: Premier Congrès Liège—Compte rendu/Internationale Gesellschaft für Musikwissenschaft: Erster Kongress Lüttich—Kongressbericht/International Society for Musical Research: First Congress Liège: Report* (London: Plainsong and Mediaeval Music Society, 1930) 102–08. In German. See no. 178 in this volume.

A survey of his works that divides his production into three periods: the time up to his departure for Vienna, from that departure until 1586, and from 1586 to his death in 1603. *(Scott Fruehwald)*

1294
as

ENGEL, Hans. **Ein Beitrag zur Prosodie im 16. Jahrhundert** [A contribution on the subject of 16th-century prosody], *Compte rendu/Kongressbericht/Report* (Basel: Bärenreiter, 1951) 83–95. *Music, charts, diagr.* In German. See no. 289 in this volume.

Developments in the rhythm of art music during the 16th c. are paralleled by developments in contemporary German poetry, where there was a shift to a strict syllable-counting scansion. The relation between musical rhythm and text metrics is discussed in regard to frottole and German polyphonic song. *(David Bloom)*

1295
as

ENGEL, Hans. **Die Entstehung des italienischen Madrigales und die Niederländer** [The development of the Italian madrigal and the Netherlanders], *Société Internationale de Musicologie, cinquième congrès/Internationale Gesellschaft für Musikwissenschaft, fünfter Kongreß/International Society for Musical Research, Fifth Congress* (Amsterdam: Vereniging voor Nederlandse Muziekgeschiedenis, 1953) 166–80. In German. See no. 316 in this volume.

1296
as

ENGEL, Hans. **Werden und Wesen des Madrigals** [The madrigal: Evolution and essence], *Bericht über den siebenten internationalen musikwissenschaftlichen Kongress* (Kassel: Bärenreiter, 1959) 39–52. *Music, charts, diagr.* In German. See no. 390 in this volume.

Traces the evolution of the madrigal against the background of other Italian genres of secular vocal music including the frottola and villanella. Texts, text setting, and the performance of chromatic passages are discussed, and the social and cultural premises of the genre are considered. The madrigal traces a remarkable path from its first flowering via classicism and mannerism to its dissolution with arrival of Baroque style. *(Carl Skoggard)*

1297
as

ENGELBRECHT, Christiane. **Die Psalmsätze des Jenaer Chorbuches 34** [Psalm settings in the Jena choirbook 34], *Bericht über den siebenten internationalen musikwissenschaftlichen Kongress* (Kassel: Bärenreiter, 1959) 97–99. In German. See no. 390 in this volume.

The choirbook Jena 34 was prepared for the court chapel of Torgau during the rule of Friedrich der Weise sometime between 1510 and 1520. The liturgical context of the Allerheiligenstiftskirche in Wittenberg is explained and the difficult problem of attributing the choirbook's fauxbourdon settings is attempted. Comparison with settings by various composers in named Georg Rhau's *Vesperarum precum officia*, 1540, points to the involvement of Adam Rener in the Jena collection. It is probable that Jena 34 was one of the models for Rhau's 1540 publication. *(Carl Skoggard)*

⟶ FALVY, Zoltán. **Musik in Ungarn bis zum Ende des XVI. Jahrhunderts** [Music in Hungary up to the end of the 16th century]. See no. 1085 in this volume.

1298
as

FEDERHOFER, Hellmut. **Musikalische Beziehungen zwischen den Höfen Erzherzog Ferdinands von Innerösterreich und König Sigismunds III von Polen** [Musical relations between the courts of Archduke Ferdinand of Inner Austria and King Sigismund III of Poland], *The book of the first international musicological congress devoted to the works of Frederick Chopin* (Warszawa: Państwowe Wydawnictwo Naukowe, 1963) 522–26. In German. See no. 425 in this volume.

As sovereign of Styria, Carinthia, and Carniola, Archduke Ferdinand kept his court in Graz from 1596 until 1619, when he was installed as the Holy Roman Emperor Ferdinand II. From 1592, when his sister Archduchess Anna married Sigismund III Vasa, relations between the Graz and Cracow courts frequently involved the mostly Italian musical personnel at both. Biographical information on many of these musicians and their interrelations through 1630 is provided. *(David Bloom)*

1299
as

FEDERHOFER-KÖNIGS, Renate. **Heinrich Saess und seine *Musica plana atque mensurabilis*** [Heinrich Saess and his *Musica plana atque mensurabilis*], *Bericht über den internationalen musikwissenschaftlichen Kongreß* (Kassel: Bärenreiter, 1963) 359–61. In German. See no. 452 in this volume.

An account of an early 16th-c. treatise by a contemporary and possibly a countryman of Adam von Fulda.

1300
as

FEICHT, Hieronim. **Die polnische Monodie des Mittelalters** [Polish monophony in the Middle Ages], *Musica antiqua Europae orientalis* (Warszawa: Państwowe Wydawnictwo Naukowe, 1966). In German. See no. 506 in this volume.

Discusses developments from the 9th to the 15th c.

⟶ FEICHT, Hieronim. **Quellen zur mehrstimmigen Musik in Polen vom späten Mittelalter bis 1600** [Sources of polyphonic music in Poland from the late Middle Ages to 1600]. See no. 1089 in this volume.

1301
as

FELLERER, Karl Gustav. **Beziehungen zwischen geistlicher und weltlicher Musik im 16. Jahrhundert** [Relations between religious and secular music in the 16th century], *Report of the Eighth Congress of the International Musicological Society. I: Papers* (Kassel: Bärenreiter, 1961) 203–14. *Music*. In German. See no. 439 in this volume.

Examines the intrusions of the *profanum* into sacred music with which the Council of Trent (concluded 1545) was especially concerned: the secular tunes reused in the parody Masses of Lassus, Palestrina, and others, and the rapid proliferation of extraliturgical instrumental music. Text intelligibility, the central musical problem for the Counter-Reformation, was the criterion for accepting some and rejecting other specific secular techniques in church music. *(David Bloom)*

1302 FELLERER, Karl Gustav. **Die kirchliche**
as **Monodie um 1600** [Sacred monody around 1600],
Atti del [I] Congresso internazionale di musica sacra
(Tournai: Desclée, 1952) 299–302. In German. See no.
303 in this volume.

1303 FELLERER, Karl Gustav. **Palestrina,** *Bericht*
as *über den Internationalen Kongress für Kirchenmusik/*
Compte rendu du Congrès international de musique
sacrée (Bern: Haupt, 1953) 43–50. In German. See no.
312 in this volume.

1304 FELLOWES, Edmund Horace. **The English**
as **madrigal of the sixteenth century,** *Société Inter-*
nationale de Musicologie: Premier Congrès Liège—
Compte rendu/Internationale Gesellschaft für Musik-
wissenschaft: Erster Kongress Lüttich—Kongress-
bericht/International Society for Musical Research:
First Congress Liège: Report (London: Plainsong and
Mediaeval Music Society, 1930) 33–34. See no. 178 in
this volume.

The technique and the genius of English madrigalists differentiate them
from contemporary Italian madrigalists and French chanson composers.
(Scott Fruehwald)

1305 FERAND, Ernest Thomas. *Zufallsmusik* **und**
as *Komposition* **in der Musiklehre der Renais-**
sance [Chance music and composition in the music
theory of the Renaissance], *Compte rendu/Kongress-*
bericht/Report (Basel: Bärenreiter, 1951) 103–08. In
German. See no. 289 in this volume.

A historical account of the concept of *sortisatio* in improvised counterpoint, in theoretical writings from Nicolaus Wollick (*Opus aureum*, 1501)
through Athanasius Kircher (*Musurgia universalis*, 1650). *(David Bloom)*

1306 FERAND, Ernest Thomas. **Zum Begriff der**
as **"compositio" im 15. und 16. Jahrhundert** [The
concept of "compositio" during the 15th and 16th cen-
turies], *Bericht über den siebenten internationalen*
musikwissenschaftlichen Kongress (Kassel: Bärenreiter, 1959) 104–07. In German. See no. 390 in this
volume.

Traces *compositio* and related terms from the Middle Ages up into the 17th
c. During the Middle Ages and the early Renaissance, *compositio* referred
to the literal putting together of elements, whether horizontal or vertical.
Ca. 1500, and deriving from *cantus compositio*, *compositio* comes to mean
the resulting multivoice work (the earliest usage in this sense is by Andreas
Ornithoparchus in 1517). The relationship between *compositio* and *contra-*
punctus is complicated and changing; sometimes they are interchangeable,
and at other times they are used as opposites, with *contrapunctus* referring
to counterpoint that is improvised. *(Carl Skoggard)*

1307 FINSCHER, Ludwig. **Die nationalen Kompo-**
as **nenten in der Musik der ersten Hälfte des 16.**
Jahrhunderts [National elements in the music of the
first half of the 16th century], *Bericht über den neunten*
internationalen Kongreß (Kassel: Bärenreiter,
1964-1966) I, 37–45. In German. See no. 491 in this
volume.

A summary of the social and historical background of and specific local
features in music of the period in the Low Countries, Italy, France, Germany, England, and Spain. *(David Bloom)*

1308 FISCHER, Kurt von. **Neues zur Passionskom-**
as **position des 16. Jahrhunderts** [New information
on Passion compositions of the 16th century], *Bericht*
über den siebenten internationalen musikwissenschaft-

lichen Kongress (Kassel: Bärenreiter, 1959) 107–08. In
German. See no. 390 in this volume.

A list of little-known sources, seven in all.

1309 FOX, Charles Warren. **The present state of**
as **Josquin research,** *Report of the Eighth Congress of*
the International Musicological Society. II: Reports
(Kassel: Bärenreiter, 1962) 64–66. See no. 440 in this
volume.

A report on a discussion by Helmuth OSTHOFF, Myroslav
ANTONOVYČ, Friedrich BLUME, Max van CREVEL, Ludwig
FINSCHER, Charles Warren FOX, Knud JEPPESEN, Gustave REESE,
and Claudio SARTORI on the paper by Antonovyč abstracted as no. 1224
in this volume.

1310 GAILLARD, Paul-André. **Petite étude**
as **comparée du "note contre note" de Loys**
Bourgeoys (1547) et du psautier de Jaqui
(Goudimel 1565) [Brief comparative study of the
note-against-note style of Loys Bourgeois (1547) and
the Jacqui psalter (Goudimel, 1565)], *Compte rendu/*
Kongressbericht/Report (Basel: Bärenreiter, 1951)
115–17. In French. See no. 289 in this volume.

Loys Bourgeois's *Pseaulmes de David* (1547) and Claude Goudimel's
Pseaumes mis en rime françoise (published by the François Jacqui firm,
Geneva, 1565) use the same melodies in 37 psalm settings. Goudimel's set-
tings are often simpler, while Bourgeois uses more modern harmony.
(Scott Fruehwald)

1311 GALLICO, Claudio. **Civiltà musicale**
as **Mantovana intorno al 1500** [Musical life in Mantua
around 1500], *Arte pensiero e cultura a Mantova nel*
primo Rinascimento in rapporto con la Toscana e con il
Veneto (Firenze: Sansoni, 1965) 243–49. In Italian. See
no. 500 in this volume.

Mantua played an important role in the development of Italian secular music in the 16th c. by providing a cultural center where it could flourish, under the patronage of Isabella d'Este. The Italian style moved from an almost
totally improvisatory art form to a written-down one, and it established Italian musicians over their Franco-Flemish counterparts. Frottola texts and
their classification, dissemination, and performance practice are discussed.
(Bill Clemmons)

1312 GASTOUÉ, Amédée. **La musique poly-**
as **phonique: Ses créateurs—L'école franco-**
belge au XVe siècle [Polyphonic music: Its creators—The Franco-Belgian school in the 15th century],
La musique d'église: Compte rendu du Congrès de
musique sacrée (Tourcoing: Duvivier, 1920) 113–42.
Charts, diagr. In French. See no. 93 in this volume.

Offers a historical survey with particular attention to Desprez, Ockeghem,
and Dufay. A list of other 15th-c. musicians of the Flemish school is
included.

1313 GÉROLD, Theodore. **La musique à Strasbourg**
as **dans la première moitié du XVIe siècle** [Music in
Strasbourg in the first half of the 16th century], *Congrés*
de la Societat Internacional de Musicologia (Barcelona: Casa de Caritat, 1936). In French. See no. 224 in
this volume.

The conference report provides only a citation. Neither the text nor a summary of the paper was published here.

1314 GHISI, Federico. **La musica** [The music], *Atti del*
as *secondo Convegno nazionale di studi sul Rinascimento*
(Firenze: Arte della Stampa, 1940) 52–56. In Italian.
See no. 264 in this volume.

Studies of Italian Renaissance literature generally do not acknowledge the
importance of music to literature. The founding of the Istituto Italiano per

la Storia della Musica in Rome and the efforts of the Centro Nazionale di Studi sul Rinascimento to diffuse information and publish works about Renaissance music are discussed. Several relevant publications are mentioned. There is a need for a bibliography of Italian music theory and practice of the period. *(Susan Poliniak)*

1315 GHISI, Federico. **L'Ordinarium Missae nel XV**
as **secolo ed i primordi della parodia** [The Ordinary of the Mass in the 15th century and the beginnings of parody], *Atti del [II] Congresso internazionale di musica sacra* (Tournai: Desclée, 1952) 308–10. In Italian. See no. 303 in this volume.

1316 GLAHN, Henrik. **Relations between religious**
as **and secular music in the 16th century,** *Report of the Eighth Congress of the International Musicological Society. II: Reports* (Kassel: Bärenreiter, 1962) 118–21. In German. See no. 440 in this volume.

A report on a discussion by Konrad AMELN, Karel Philippus BERNET KEMPERS, Wolfgang BOETTICHER, Hellmut FEDERHOFER, Karl Gustav FELLERER, Ludwig FINSCHER, Henrik GLAHN, Erich HERTZMANN, René Bernard LENAERTS, Helmuth OSTHOFF, Claude V. PALISCA, Gustave REESE, and Denis STEVENS of the papers by Fellerer and Boetticher abstracted as nos. 1243 and 1301, respectively, in this volume.

1317 GOMBOSI, Otto. **À la recherche de la forme**
as **dans la musique de la Renaissance: Francesco da Milano** [In search of form in the music of the Renaissance: Francesco da Milano], *La musique instrumentale de la Renaissance* (Paris: Centre National de la Recherche Scientifique [CNRS], 1955) 165–76. *Facs., music, charts, diagr.* In French. See no. 333 in this volume.

The author's method of rebarring Renaissance dance music is also applicable to music of a more abstract character. As illustrated on the example of a ricercar by Francesco da Milano (no. 3 in the Marcolini edition of the *Intovolatura de viola o vero lauto...* Venice 1536), it not only eliminates the awkwardness of the traditional barring technique but also reveals unexpected structural refinements in the pieces. *(David Bloom)*

1318 GOMBOSI, Otto. **The cultural and folkloristic**
as **background of the folía,** *Papers of the American Musicological Society* (Philadelphia: American Musicological Society, 1946) 88–95. See no. 269 in this volume.

The folia and the moresca have several elements in common. Both dances were associated with courtly tournaments and were performed with the dancers riding toy horses and wearing traditional masks. The independent evolution of the folia and the melody of the same name originally associated with the dance are examined.

1319 GOMBOSI, Otto. **Quellenmäßige Belege über**
as **den Einfluß der Chansonkunst auf die deutsche Liedkunst in der zweiten Hälfte des 15. Jahrhunderts** [Source evidence of the influence of the chanson on German song in the second half of the 15th century], *Beethoven-Zentenarfeier: Internationaler musikhistorischer Kongress* (Wien: Universal, 1927) 152–54. In German. See no. 142 in this volume.

Numerous works by Gilles Binchois, Dufay, Ockeghem, and Antoine Busnois are transmitted in German MSS of the 1460s and 1470s, though generally in versions with corrupted titles, no texts, and misspelled or omitted attributions. Detailed study of such MSS may throw considerable light on the role of Netherlandish music in the development of the lied.

(David Bloom)

1320 GRAFCZYŃSKYA, Melania. **Die Polyphonie**
as **am Hofe der Jagellonen** [Polyphony at the Jagiellonian court], *Beethoven-Zentenarfeier: Interna-*

tionaler musikhistorischer Kongress (Wien: Universal, 1927) 164–67. In German. See no. 142 in this volume.

Surveys local and foreign theorists, composers, and performers of polyphonic music in the Jagiellonian capital of Cracow in the 15th and 16th c. *(David Bloom)*

1321 GUDEWILL, Kurt. **Identifizierungen von**
as **anonymen und mehrfach zugewiesenen Kompositionen in deutschen Liederdrucken aus der 1. Hälfte des 16. Jahrhunderts** [Identification of anonymous and multi-attributed compositions in German song prints from the first half of the 16th century], *Fontes artis musicae* IV/2 (Dec 1957) 89–97. *Bibliog.* In German. See no. 373 in this volume.

Presents a bibliography of German song collections, including printers, dates, numbers of voices, and manuscript folios, and attempts to solve the problem of anonymous compositions, as well as those of dubious attribution.

1322 GUDEWILL, Kurt. **Vokale und instrumentale**
as **Stilmomente in textlosen Kompositionen des Glogauer Liederbuches** [Aspects of vocal and instrumental style in the textless compositions of the Glogauer Liederbuch], *Bericht über den Internationalen musikwissenschaftlichen Kongress* (Kassel: Bärenreiter, 1954) 248–52. *Music.* In German. See no. 319 in this volume.

Forty-five mostly three-part untexted works from the Glogauer Liederbuch are analyzed for the degree of instrumental influence shown in their cantus firmus parts. All these works are assumed to represent German songs of ca. 1480 on the basis of indications accompanying them (*Textmarken*). Most of the cantus firmuses are obviously vocal and reflect little or no instrumental influence. However, concluding lines seem more instrumental in character than the rest (secondary voices usually display a more instrumental character than the cantus firmus). *(Carl Skoggard)*

1323 GURLITT, Wilibald. **Die Kompositionslehre**
as **des deutschen 16. und 17. Jahrhunderts** [The theory of composition in 16th- and 17th-century Germany], *Bericht über den Internationalen musikwissenschaftlichen Kongress* (Kassel: Bärenreiter, 1954) 103–13. In German. See no. 319 in this volume.

Surveys sources within a broad historical and cultural context. Former holdings in the monastery of Altzelle are discussed on the basis of an extant catalogue (1514). A detailed outline is given of the contents of Heinrich Faber's MS *Musica poetica* (Braunschweig, 1548), a good example of the instructional material compiled by Wittenberg-trained Lutheran cantors. *(Carl Skoggard)*

1324 GURLITT, Wilibald. **Ein Lütticher Beitrag zur**
as **Adam von Fulda-Frage** [A Liège contribution to the Adam von Fulda question], *Société Internationale de Musicologie: Premier Congrès Liège—Compte rendu/Internationale Gesellschaft für Musikwissenschaft: Erster Kongress Lüttich—Kongressbericht/International Society for Musical Research: First Congress Liège: Report* (London: Plainsong and Mediaeval Music Society, 1930) 125–31. In German. See no. 178 in this volume.

Describes the life and music of this 15th-c. German composer and theorist, and deals with the confusion between him and Adam von Lüttich. *(Scott Fruehwald)*

1325 HANDSCHIN, Jacques. **Eine umstrittene Stelle**
as **bei Guilelmus Monachus** [A controversial passage in Guilielmus Monachus], *Compte rendu/Kongressbericht/Report* (Basel: Bärenreiter, 1951) 145–49. *Music.* In German. See no. 289 in this volume.

In his treatise *De preceptis artis musicae*, Guilielmus distinguishes two basic kinds of fauxbourdon, both of Northern European origin. In one, the cantus firmus is in the tenor, and unembellished; in the other, it lies in the soprano and is embellished. The first type may be related to improvisation. The severe criticism Guilielmus has received for considering both types fauxbourdon and for failing to recognize the opposition between English discant and fauxbourdon is hardly justified. *(David Bloom)*

1326
as

HARASZTI, Emil. **Les musiciens de Mathias Corvin et de Béatrice d'Aragon** [The musicians of Matthias Corvinus and Beatrice of Aragon], *La musique instrumentale de la Renaissance* (Paris: Centre National de la Recherche Scientifique [CNRS], 1955) 35–59. In French. See no. 333 in this volume.

Surveys the musical life of the court at Buda from the marriage of King Matthias Corvinus and Beatrice of Aragon (1476) to the widowed queen's departure from Hungary (1509), from the standpoint of the practice of instrumental music, and with particular attention to Beatrice's musical upbringing; the instrument maker Lorenzo Gusnasco da Pavia and the organ he built for Buda (now in the collections of the Museo Correr, Venice); the identities of the court musicians, with extended biographies of Pietrobono de Burzellis, Jacques Barbireau, Johannes de Stokem, and Erasmus Lapicida; and the evidence of the use of instruments to accompany sacred and secular vocal music. The material is covered at length in the author's *Zene és ünnep Mátyás és Beatrix idejében* (Music and festivities in the time of Matthias and Beatrice), in *Mátyás Király az énekes szinpadon*, ed. I. Lukinich (Budapest, 1940), vol. 2. *(David Bloom)*

1327
as

HARRISON, Frank Llewellyn. **The Eton College Choirbook (Eton College MS 178)**, *Société Internationale de Musicologie, cinquième congrès/ Internationale Gesellschaft für Musikwissenschaft, fünfter Kongreß/International Society for Musical Research, Fifth Congress* (Amsterdam: Vereniging voor Nederlandse Muziekgeschiedenis, 1953) 224–32. *Bibliog.* See no. 316 in this volume.

The most important collection in one of England's most brilliant periods (the last decades of the 15th c.) provides a wealth of material for the study of choral polyphony at this turning point in the history of English church music. *(Tsipora Yosselevitch)*

1328
as

HAYDON, Glen. **The Lateran Codex 61**, *Bericht über den siebenten internationalen musikwissenschaftlichen Kongress* (Kassel: Bärenreiter, 1959) 126–31. *List of works, charts, diagr.* See no. 390 in this volume.

A description of *I-Rsg* MS Codex 61, which contains Costanzo Festa's settings of hymns for the church year as well as 27 hymns by other composers. The MS supplies a survey of polyphonic hymn writing during the first half and extending through the third quarter of the 16th c. A table is appended with information on the non-Festa hymns (MS numbering, folio, liturgical assignment, text, key signature and mensural sign(s), number of voices, composer). *(Carl Skoggard)*

1329
as

HEARTZ, Daniel. **Un divertissement de palais pour Charles Quint à Binche** [A palace entertainment for Charles V at Binche], *Fêtes et cérémonies au temps de Charles Quint: Fêtes de la Renaissance. II* (Paris: Centre National de la Recherche Scientifique [CNRS], 1960) 329–42. *Music.* In French. See no. 367 in this volume.

In August 1549 Mary of Hungary, as regent of the Low Countries, held a series of celebrations at her castle in Binche, Hainaut, in honor of her brother Charles V and his son, the future Philip II; the organist, composer, and courtier Rogier Pathie was charged with organizing the entertainments. One, on the seventh evening, featured a combat dance between savages and *chevaliers* and a staged abduction by the savages of a group of ladies to a purpose-built *castello* which was besieged and bombarded in the following day's entertainment. The political meaning of the spectacle is discussed, and speculation is offered on its choreographical and musical content, on the basis of dance music collected by Thoinot Arbeau (*Orchésographie*, 1588) and Tylman Susato (*Het derde musyck boexken...*, 1551). *(David Bloom)*

1330
as

HEARTZ, Daniel. *Les goûts réunis*, **or, The worlds of the madrigal and the chanson con-**

fronted, *Chanson & madrigal 1480-1530: Studies in comparison and contrast* (Cambridge, MA: Harvard University Press, 1964) 88–138. *Music, index.* See no. 429 in this volume.

The early 16th c. saw close contact between French and Italian musicians, including frequent exchange of prints and MSS, partly in consequence of the French military campaigns of the period. While French chanson composers were influenced by the frottola, the more significant influence was from the northern countries to the southern. Composers discussed in detail include Jacques Arcadelt, Costanzo Festa, Claudin de Sermisy, Philippe Verdelot, and Adrian Willaert. A discussion of this paper by Erich HERTZMANN, Alvin H. JOHNSON, and Claude V. PALISCA is appended. *(Alexander G. Smith)*

1331
as

HEARTZ, Daniel. **Les premières "instructions" pour le luth (jusque vers 1550)** [The earliest lute methods (up to ca. 1550)], *Le luth et sa musique* (Paris: Centre National de la Recherche Scientifique [CNRS], 1958) 77–92. *Music, bibliog., charts, diagr., transcr.* In French. See no. 377 in this volume.

Most publications of lute music in the first half of the 16th c. included instructions for tuning and playing the instrument, and for reading tablatures, as if intended for beginners, even though they contained music that would be much too difficult for beginners to play. The practice ceased at the same time as the polyphonic style of lute playing went into decay, after the deaths of virtuosos like Francesco Canova da Milano (1544) and Alberto da Ripa (1550). *(David Bloom)*

1332
as

HEARTZ, Daniel. **Les styles instrumentaux dans la musique de la Renaissance** [Instrumental styles in Renaissance music], *La musique instrumentale de la Renaissance* (Paris: Centre National de la Recherche Scientifique [CNRS], 1955) 61–76. *Music, charts, diagr.* In French. See no. 333 in this volume.

The early 16th c. saw the creation of an instrumental style independent from the vocal in three basic categories: lute, keyboard, and ensemble. The keyboard style developed especially in genres of imitative counterpoint; the lute style in freer genres, especially dance music. A table of concordances for ensemble, keyboard, and lute dances in the publications of Pierre Attaingnant is appended. *(Susan Poliniak)*

1333
as

HERTZMANN, Erich. **Trends in the development of the chanson in the early sixteenth century,** *Papers of the American Musicological Society* (Philadelphia: American Musicological Society, 1946) 5–10. See no. 269 in this volume.

The differences between religious and secular music—as formulated by Italian theorists in the middle of the 16th c.—apply not only to the Italian madrigal but to the French chanson as well. Through widespread publication, the chanson had a lasting impact on the secularization of music. *(author)*

1334
as

HESBERT, René-Jean. **L'hymnologie de St. Philibert: Les hymnes de Tournus et Macon** [The hymnology of St. Philibert: The hymns of Tournus and Macon], *Jumièges: Congrès scientifique du XIII. centenaire* (Rouen: Lecerf, 1955) 343–46. In French. See no. 336 in this volume.

Of the known hymns in honor of St. Philibert, three (by Jean-Baptiste de Santeul, 1630-97) are not really dedicated to any particular saint. A fourth, in the collection *Piorum carminum libri V* by Louis de Saint-Malachie, or Ludovicus Sancti Malachiae (Paris, 1600), was never used in the liturgy. Finally, there are three hymns specifically devoted to St. Philibert from a single Office, one each for Vespers, Matins, and Lauds, in a lost 16th-c. breviary formerly at the Grand Séminaire, Autun, and in the Mâcon Breviary of the Bibliothèque Municipale, Roanne, MS 21. The texts of the three hymns are transcribed and briefly analyzed. *(David Bloom)*

1335
as

HIEKEL, Hans Otto. *Tactus* **und Tempo** [*Tactus* and tempo], *Bericht über den internationalen musikwissenschaftlichen Kongreß* (Kassel: Bärenreiter, 1963) 145–47. In German. See no. 452 in this volume.

Discusses apparent contradictions in the 16th-c. use of the term *tactus*, particularly in Martin Agricola's *Musica figuralis deudsch*. *(Daniel Anderson)*

1336
as

HOFFMANN-ERBRECHT, Lothar. **Heinrich Finck in Polen** [Heinrich Finck in Poland], *Bericht über den internationalen musikwissenschaftlichen Kongreß* (Kassel: Bärenreiter, 1963) 119–22. In German. See no. 452 in this volume.

Hans Joachim Moser has found records in the Polish royal household accounts of 26 payments made to Finck between 1498 and 1505. Correlating the fluctuating amounts of the payments with events at the courts of Kings Jan I Olbracht and Aleksander I throws considerable light on Finck's Polish career. *(David Bloom)*

1337
as

HOFFMANN-ERBRECHT, Lothar. **Neue Dokumente zum Leben Thomas Stoltzers** [New documents concerning the life of Thomas Stoltzer], *Bericht über den siebenten internationalen musikwissenschaftlichen Kongress* (Kassel: Bärenreiter, 1959) 139–40. In German. See no. 390 in this volume.

Information on Stoltzer is contained in newly examined documents from the archepiscopal archives in Wrocław. The documents confirm his presence in Wrocław between 1519 and 1522, as well as his being invited to become *magister capellae* for the Hungarian court in the latter year. It can be inferred that Stoltzer was most likely born between 1480 and 1485, in Silesia, and that he earned a good income from his Wrocław benefice. It is possible that he and Heinrich Finck traveled together to Hungary in 1491. An annotation on a letter from Stoltzer dated 23 February 1526 refers to him as "the late Thomas...". Since such annotations were usually made shortly after the receipt of a letter, it can be assumed that he was no longer alive in March of that year. *(Carl Skoggard)*

1338
as

HOFFMANN-ERBRECHT, Lothar. **Die Rostocker Praetorius-Handschrift (1566)** [The Rostock Praetorius manuscript (1566)], *Bericht über den internationalen musikwissenschaftlichen Kongreß* (Kassel: Bärenreiter, 1957) 112–13. In German. See no. 356 in this volume.

An overview of the mostly liturgical contents of the MS *Opus musicum, excellens et novum*, D-ROu MS mus.saec.XVI-49 (1-6), copied by Jacob Praetorius the elder (ca. 1530-86). A full discussion, with facsimile reproduction and thematic index, is published as *Das Opus musicum des Jacob Praetorius* in *Acta musicologica* XXVIII (1956). *(David Bloom)*

1339
as

HOLST, Irma. **Ein Doppelchorwerk mit beziffertem Bass von Claudio Merulo** [A work for double chorus with figured bass by Claudio Merulo], *Compte rendu/Kongressbericht/Report* (Basel: Bärenreiter, 1951) 154–59. *Music.* In German. See no. 289 in this volume.

A MS found in 1941, I-Vnm C1.IV.1049 (=10931), bears the title *Memento di Claudio Merulo* and comprises a piece for two four-voice choirs accompanied by string instruments and organ. Its style, with triple rhythms, triad chords, and dissonance, is uncharacteristic for Merulo and seems more reminiscent of Schütz. The MS remains a puzzle. *(David Bloom)*

1340
as

HUGHES, Charles. **Peter Philips: An English musician in the Netherlands,** *Papers of the American Musicological Society* (Philadelphia: American Musicological Society, 1946) 35–48. *Music.* See no. 269 in this volume.

Provides a critical overview of Philips's output, emphasizing the Italian and Flemish elements in his music. Although he is best remembered for his madrigals and motets, his instrumental music seems to have been more widely disseminated through publication in several collections and anthologies during his lifetime. His contemporaries, however, regarded him mostly as a highly accomplished organist rather than as a composer. *(James Melo)*

→ HUSMANN, Heinrich. **Die mittelniederländischen Lieder der Berliner Handschrift Germ. 8° 190** [Middle Dutch songs in the Berlin manuscript Germ. 8° 190]. See no. 1132 in this volume.

1341
as

JACQUOT, Jean. **Joyeuse et triomphante entrée** [Joyous and triumphant entry], *Les fêtes de la Renaissance* (Paris: Centre National de la Recherche Scientifique [CNRS], 1956) 9–19. In French. See no. 350 in this volume.

Discusses the celebrations given in connection with the arrival of royalty in the Renaissance.

1342
as

JACQUOT, Jean. **Lyrisme et sentiment tragique dans les madrigaux d'Orlando Gibbons** [Lyricism and tragic sentiment in the madrigals of Orlando Gibbons], *Musique et poésie au XVIe siècle* (Paris: Centre National de la Recherche Scientifique [CNRS], 1954) 139–51. *Music.* In French. See no. 326 in this volume.

Inspired by melancholy Elizabethan and Jacobean art, Orlando Gibbons reflected this mood in his *First set of madrigals and motetts* (1612). Similar sentiments are found in the works of Byrd, Dowland, Donne, and others. *(Roy Nitzberg)*

1343
as

JACQUOT, Jean. **Sur quelques formes de la musique de clavier élisabéthaine (d'après des œuvres inédites de John Bull)** [On some forms of Elizabethan keyboard music (based on unpublished pieces by John Bull)], *La musique instrumentale de la Renaissance* (Paris: Centre National de la Recherche Scientifique [CNRS], 1955) 241–58. *Music.* In French. See no. 333 in this volume.

A relatively little known source of keyboard music from the English Renaissance is in the holdings of the Bibliothèque Nationale, Paris (F-Pn MS rés.1185, rés.1186, and rés.1186bis). It includes important works by Bull, including three versions of the variations on *Why aske yee*, of which an incomplete version is preserved in the Fitzwilliam Virginal Book (GB-Cf MS 32.g.29). They throw light on the individuality of Bull's compositional technique as compared with those of Morley, Gibbons, Byrd, and others. Editions of the *Why aske yee* variations and of a *Pavin in A re* are included. *(David Bloom)*

1344
as

JEPPESEN, Knud. **Die älteste italienische Orgelmusik** [The earliest Italian organ music], *Atti del [I] Congresso internazionale di musica sacra* (Tournai: Desclée, 1952) 351–53. In German. See no. 303 in this volume.

1345
as

JEPPESEN, Knud. **Die Mehrstimmige italienische Lauda am Anfang des 16. Jahrhunderts** [The polyphonic Italian lauda at the beginning of the 16th century], *Société Internationale de Musicologie: Premier Congrès Liège—Compte rendu/Internationale Gesellschaft für Musikwissenschaft: Erster Kongress Lüttich—Kongressbericht/International Society for Musical Research: First Congress Liège: Report* (London: Plainsong and Mediaeval Music Society, 1930) 155–57. In German. See no. 178 in this volume.

Demonstrates that the lauda, like contemporary Italian secular works, evinces a clear break with the past and breathes the spirit of optimism and courage. *(Scott Fruehwald)*

1346
as

JEPPESEN, Knud. **Eine musiktheoretische Korrespondenz des früheren Cinquecento** [A correspondence concerning music theory, from the early sixteenth century], *Congrés de la Societat Internacional de Musicologia (Barcelona: Casa de Caritat, 1936). In German. See no. 224 in this volume.

The conference report provides only a citation. Neither the text nor a summary of the paper was published here. Another version with the same title is published in *Acta musicologica* VIII (1941), 3-39.

1347
as
JEPPESEN, Knud. **Palestrina e l'interpretazione** [Palestrina and interpretation], *Atti del terzo Congresso internazionale di musica* (Firenze: Le Monnier, 1940) 166–72. In Italian; summaries in French and German. See no. 256 in this volume.

Emphasizes the importance of mastering the musical literature and language of Palestrina's time.

1348
as
JEPPESEN, Knud. **Venetian folk-songs of the Renaissance,** *Papers read at the International Congress of Musicology* (New York: Music Educators National Conference, 1944) 62–75. *Music.* See no. 266 in this volume.

Discusses relationships among Gregorian chant, traditional music, and polyphony.

1349
as
JIRÁNEK, Jaroslav. **Der Beitrag Zdeněk Nejedlýs zur Erforschung des Hussitischen Gesanges** [Zdeněk Nejedlý's contribution to research on Hussite song], *Bericht über den siebenten internationalen musikwissenschaftlichen Kongress* (Kassel: Bärenreiter, 1959) 150–52. In German. See no. 390 in this volume.

Nejedlý's monumental study, originally published in three parts, 1904-13, and recently reissued in five volumes as *Dějiny husitského zpěvu* (Prague, 1954-55) corrected an earlier tendency to minimize the importance of the Hussite Reform in the history and development of Czech music. His mastery of the original source material together with his broad understanding of the revolutionary class character of the Hussite Wars makes him of equal significance as musicologist and as social historian. *(David Bloom)*

1350
as
JUST, Martin. *Ysaac de manu sua,* *Bericht über den internationalen musikwissenschaftlichen Kongreß* (Kassel: Bärenreiter, 1963) 112–14. *Facs.* In German. See no. 452 in this volume.

The codex *D-Bsb* MS Mus.ms. 40021 includes three pieces by Heinrich Isaac with the attribution *"Ysaac de manu sua"*. Analysis of the paper, binding, and handwriting suggests that two of them, four-voice settings of the sequence *Sanctissimae virginis* and the song *In Gottes Namen*, are autographs, while the first piece, a Mass on *Une musque de Biscaye*, was copied by another hand. Isaac may have become acquainted with the collector of the codex during his service with Friedrich III of Saxony. They may be dated 1500 or somewhat later. *(David Bloom)*

1351
as
JUTEN, Gerrit Cornelis Adrianus. **Jacob Obrecht,** *Congrès d'Anvers de la Fédération Archéologique et Historique de Belgique, 1930: XXVIIIᵉ session—Annales. II: Comptes rendus* (Antwerpen: Resseler, 1931) 441–52. In French. See no. 162 in this volume.

1352
as
KAHMANN, Bernhard. **Über Inhalt und Herkunft der Handschrift Cambridge Pepys 1760** [The contents and provenance of the Cambridge Pepys manuscript 1760], *Bericht über den internationalen musikwissenschaftlichen Kongreß* (Kassel: Bärenreiter, 1957) 126–28. In German. See no. 356 in this volume.

The MS *GB-Cmc* MS Pepys 1760, known as Henry VII's Music Book, is part of the collection willed by Samuel Pepys to Magdalene College, Cambridge. The 30 three- and four-voice Latin motets and 27 chansons, all but one with French texts, are largely by composers associated with the court of Louis XII of France, in particular by Antoine de Févin, and may represent a

broadening of the repertoire of both sacred and secular music in England. *(David Bloom)*

1353
as
KAST, Paul. **Biographie und Werk Jean Mouton** [The biography and work of Jean Mouton], *Bericht über den internationalen musikwissenschaftlichen Kongreß Wien Mozartjahr 1956* (Graz; Köln: Böhlau, 1958) 300–03. In German. See no. 365 in this volume.

Recent research indicates that Mouton was born no later than 1459, and that he was probably not, as was previously believed, a pupil of Josquin Desprez. Examination of his works shows him to have been the master of an original compositional style, worthy to be ranked alongside Desprez, Isaac, Obrecht, and Pierre de La Rue. *(David Bloom)*

1354
as
KAST, Paul. **Remarques sur la musique et les musiciens de la chapelle de François Iᵉʳ au Camp du Drap d'Or** [Music and the musicians of the chapel of François I at the Field of the Cloth of Gold], *Fêtes et cérémonies au temps de Charles Quint: Fêtes de la Renaissance. II* (Paris: Centre National de la Recherche Scientifique [CNRS], 1960) 135–46. *Music.* In French. See no. 367 in this volume.

In June 1520 a meeting was held between François I of France and Henry VIII of England, in open country between Guines and Ardres near Calais, in an unsuccessful effort to negotiate an alliance against Emperor Charles V. In emulation of medieval chivalry, the two courts competed in jousting, hospitality, and pageantry; the choirs of the royal chapels drew attention for their elaborate performances. The only musician named in the documentation of the French chapel is the organist, Pierre Mouton; it is likely that Jean Mouton (possibly a relative of Pierre Mouton) was one of them, together with Antonius Divitis (Antoine Le Riche) and Claudin de Sermisy. *(David Bloom)*

1355
as
KASTNER, Macario Santiago. **Rapports entre Schlick et Cabezón** [Relationships between Schlick and Cabezón], *La musique instrumentale de la Renaissance* (Paris: Centre National de la Recherche Scientifique [CNRS], 1955) 217–23. In French. See no. 333 in this volume.

Relatively little is known about the biography of the blind German organist, composer, and theorist Arnolt Schlick (ca. 1460–after 1521), in spite of the historical importance of his work. His possible connections to and influence on Henry Bredemers (1472-1522) and Antonio de Cabezón (1510-66), organists at various times in the service of Prince Carlos of Spain (later Emperor Charles V), are examined. *(Susan Poliniak)*

1356
as
KASTNER, Macario Santiago. **Le rôle des tablatures d'orgue au XVIᵉ siècle dans l'avènement du Baroque musical** [The role of 16th-century organ tablatures in the advent of the musical Baroque], *Les colloques de Wégimont. IV: Le Baroque musical—Recueil d'études sur la musique du XVIIᵉ siècle* (Paris: Belles Lettres, 1963) 131–47. In French. See no. 386 in this volume.

The different styles of notating keyboard music in Spain, France, England, and Italy are surveyed. The Italian style of using two staffs, with a clear marking of the allocation of notes between the two hands, contributed to the development of the vertical, harmonically organized music of the Baroque. *(David Bloom)*

1357
as
KINKELDEY, Otto. **Dance tunes of the fifteenth century,** *Instrumental music* (Cambridge, MA: Harvard University Press, 1959) 3–30. *Music.* See no. 368 in this volume.

By the second half of the 15th c., the upper classes of Italy had developed sophisticated styles of ballroom and drawing room dancing in the bassadanza (basse danse) and the more elaborately choreographed ballo. Famous dancing masters of the period are listed, with discussion of their theoretical and practical writings; French and Italian sources of dance music are examined; and notational questions (mensuration, clefs, key signatures, and accidentals) are addressed. *(Daven Jenkins)*

1358 KIRSCH, Winfried. **Grundzüge der Te**
as **Deum–Vertonungen im 15. und 16. Jahrhundert** [Principles of Te Deum settings in the 15th and 16th centuries], *Bericht über den internationalen musikwissenschaftlichen Kongreß* (Kassel: Bärenreiter, 1963) 117–19. In German. See no. 452 in this volume.

A preliminary attempt at establishing some compositional principles governing polyphonic Te Deum settings in France, Germany, and Italy, in the period from Gilles Binchois through Roland de Lassus. *(author)*

1359 KLUSEN, Ernst. **Gregorianischer Choral und**
as **frühprotestantisches Kirchenlied: Neue Gesichtspunkte zur Beurteilung ihrer gegenseitigen Beziehungen** [Gregorian chant and early Protestant hymns: New viewpoints on assessing their mutual relations], *Bericht über den siebenten internationalen musikwissenschaftlichen Kongress* (Kassel: Bärenreiter, 1959) 157–59. *Music.* In German. See no. 390 in this volume.

Cases in which Protestant composers consciously appropriated Gregorian melodies for their works are well known. The 1544 *Bönnisches Gesangbüchlein* (of which the author's modern edition was published by Kamp-Lintfort [Staufen, 1965] and cited as RILM [1968]22446) provides examples of the unconscious use of Gregorian melodies and melodic formulas, clarifying the significance of the interval of the fourth in early German hymn melody. More examples are provided in a version published in *Rheinisch-Westfälische Zeitschrift für Volkskunde* VI (1960). *(David Bloom)*

1360 KRAUTWURST, Franz. **Grundsätzliches zu**
as **einer Filiation geistlicher Musikhandschriften der Reformationszeit** [Basic principles in the filiation of manuscripts of religious music in the Reformation period], *Bericht über den siebenten internationalen musikwissenschaftlichen Kongress* (Kassel: Bärenreiter, 1959) 166–69. In German. See no. 390 in this volume.

One of the difficulties in establishing the as yet poorly understood filiation of German MSS of the period between ca. 1520 and 1550 is the relatively new factor of printed music. Only in the case of transmission from copyist to copyist can we speak of the dependency of one MS on another; moreover, it is necessary to establish that two or more MSS of a single composition are presenting the same version of that composition—that its variants are largely of a trivial character. *(David Bloom)*

1361 KREPS, Joseph. **Le mécénat de la cour de**
as **Bruxelles (1430-1559)** [The patronage of the court of Brussels (1430-1559)], *La Renaissance dans les provinces du Nord: Picardie, Artois, Flandres, Brabant, Hainaut* (Paris: Centre National de la Recherche Scientifique [CNRS], 1956) 169–95. In French. See no. 328 in this volume.

Discusses Tinctoris, Desprez, Erasmus, and Lassus.

1362 KROYER, Theodor. **Das Orgelbuch Cod.ms.153**
as **der Münchener Universitäts-Bibliothek** [The organbook Cod.ms.153 of the Universitätsbibliothek, Munich], *Bericht über den I. musikwissenschaftlichen Kongress der Deutschen Musikgesellschaft in Leipzig* (Wiesbaden: Breitkopf & Härtel, 1926) 339. In German. See no. 120 in this volume.

Discusses the contents of *D-Mu* MS Cod.ms.153 from the collection of Bishop Johann Egolf von Knöringen (Augsburg). Its main contents are chorales using alternatim practice. *(William Renwick)*

1363 LAVOYE, Louis. **L'art musical belge pendant**
as **la Renaissance** [Belgian musical art during the Re-

naissance], *Fédération Archéologique et Historique de Belgique: Annales du XXIe congrès* (Liège: Poncelet, 1909) II, 953f. In French. See no. 64 in this volume.

1364 LAVOYE, Louis. **Sur une pièce vocale à 4 voix**
as **d'un manuscrit de l'ancienne abbaye de Saint-Trond** [Concerning a four-voice piece in a manuscript from the old abbey of Sint-Truiden], *Société Internationale de Musicologie: Premier Congrès Liège—Compte rendu/Internationale Gesellschaft für Musikwissenschaft: Erster Kongress Lüttich—Kongressbericht/International Society for Musical Research: First Congress Liège: Report* (London: Plainsong and Mediaeval Music Society, 1930) 165–67. *Illus., music.* In French. See no. 178 in this volume.

In the library at the University of Liège, there is a 16th-c. dramatic work by a monk named Christian Fastraets. It exists in two versions, Flemish and Latin: *Het spiel van St. Trudo* and *Comedia una vitam Sancti Trudonis confessoris*, respectively. Act 4, scene 3, contains a four-voice motet in free style composed by D. Joes. Vrancken. A stylistic analysis is included. *(Conrad T. Biel)*

1365 LENAERTS, René Bernard. **La missa parodia**
as **néerlandaise au 16e siècle** [The Netherlandish parody Mass during the 16th century], *Compte rendu/Kongressbericht/Report* (Basel: Bärenreiter, 1951) 179–80. In French. See no. 289 in this volume.

Summary of a paper appearing in English in *The musical quarterly* XXXVI/3 (July 1950), 410-421.

1366 LENAERTS, René Bernard. **Nederlandsche**
as **polifoniese liederen uit de XVe en XVIe eeuwen** [Polyphonic songs of the Low Countries from the 15th and 16th centuries], *Congrès d'Anvers de la Fédération Archéologique et Historique de Belgique, 1930: XXVIIIe session—Annales. II: Comptes rendus* (Antwerpen: Resseler, 1931) 453–64. In Dutch. See no. 162 in this volume.

1367 LENAERTS, René Bernard. **Symposium: Die**
as **nationalen Komponenten in der Musik der ersten Hälfte des 16. Jahrhunderts** [Symposium: National elements in the music of the first half of the 16th century], *Bericht über den neunten internationalen Kongreß* (Kassel: Bärenreiter, 1964-1966) II, 81–87. In German. See no. 491 in this volume.

Report of a discussion of the paper by Ludwig FINSCHER abstracted as no. 1307 in this volume. The participants included Finscher, Daniel HEARTZ, Zofia LISSA, Ernst H. MEYER, Miguel QUEROL GAVALDÁ, Walter H. RUBSAMEN, Geneviève THIBAULT DE CHAMBURE, and Jack A. WESTRUP. *(David Bloom)*

1368 LENAERTS, René Bernard. **Zestiende-euwsche**
as **praalmuziek** [Sixteenth-century ceremonial music], *Verhandelingen van het Muziekcongres* (Antwerpen: Stad Antwerpen, 1935) 15–19. In Dutch. See no. 210 in this volume.

Surveys 16th-c. ceremonial music from Flanders.

1369 LESURE, François. **Éléments populaires dans**
as **la chanson française au début du XVIe siècle** [Traditional elements in the French chanson at the beginning of the 16th century], *Musique et poésie au XVIe siècle* (Paris: Centre National de la Recherche Scientifique [CNRS], 1954) 169–84. *List of works.* In French. See no. 326 in this volume.

Examines works from this period that have survived in oral traditon.

1370 LEVY, Kenneth J. **Vaudeville, vers mesurés, et**
as **airs de cour** [Vaudeville, vers mesurés, and airs de cour], *Musique et poésie au XVIᵉ siècle* (Paris: Centre National de la Recherche Scientifique [CNRS], 1954) 185–201. In French. See no. 326 in this volume.
During the latter part of the 16th c., the aristocratic chanson became a thing of the past, while the air became very popular. *(Scott Fruehwald)*

1371 LINDEN, Albert vander. **Comment désigner la**
as **nationalité des artistes des provinces du Nord à l'époque de la Renaissance** [How to designate the nationalities of artists of northern regions in the epoch of the Renaissance], *La Renaissance dans les provinces du Nord: Picardie, Artois, Flandres, Brabant, Hainaut* (Paris: Centre National de la Recherche Scientifique [CNRS], 1956) 11–17. In French. See no. 328 in this volume.
Offers a historical overview of the problem with special attention given to present-day Belgium and Holland.

1372 LISSA, Zofia. **La formation du style national**
as **dans la musique instrumentale polonaise de la Renaissance** [The formation of the national style of Polish instrumental music in the Renaissance], *La musique instrumentale de la Renaissance* (Paris: Centre National de la Recherche Scientifique [CNRS], 1955) 149–61. In French. See no. 333 in this volume.
Developments in the instrumental music of the Polish Renaissance may be accounted for in terms of several independent ideological currents, moving in parallel: the increasingly autonomous secular stream; the Roman Catholic stream, under the influence of the Netherlandish school and gradually beginning to absorb secular elements; and the music of the Reformation, of an especially democratic and national character. From 1565 the Counter-Reformation, led by the activities of the Jesuits, reinforced the Catholic musical current and the cosmopolitan style, but the secular and national styles were too firmly rooted by this point to be eliminated. *(David Bloom)*

1373 LOWINSKY, Edward E. **The concept of physi-**
as **cal and musical space in the Renaissance: A preliminary sketch,** *Papers of the American Musicological Society* (Philadelphia: American Musicological Society, 1946) 57–84. See no. 272 in this volume.
An idea of tonal space on the analogy of physical space was common around the beginning of the 16th c., and as the European concept of physical space began to change radically with geographical exploration and the development of Copernican astronomy, parallel changes occurred in the understanding of music. These included a massive expansion of vocal and instrumental ranges; the reorganization of polyphony from a system in which the tenor has a separate relation to each of the other voices to one in which all voices are in simultaneous relation to each other, together with the gradual elimination of cantus firmus technique; and the application of circle and sphere analogies to the theory of intervals, leading to equal temperament and modulation technique. Another version is cited as RILM ¹⁹⁹⁵2750. *(David Bloom)*

1374 LUMSDEN, David. **De quelques éléments**
as **étrangers dans la musique anglaise pour le luth** [On some foreign elements in English lute music], *La musique instrumentale de la Renaissance* (Paris: Centre National de la Recherche Scientifique [CNRS], 1955) 197–204. In French. See no. 333 in this volume.
The confluence of foreign musicians from ca. 1540 encouraged young English composers to seek personal ways of expressing their musical thought, for which the lute was an ideal instrument. Particularly French chansons and Italian fantasias were well known; knowledge of German lute music seems to have been limited to chorale arrangements, and there are no references to Spanish lute music at all. Foreign influence diminished from ca. 1570, and in the years 1580-1610 English musicians achieved preeminence on home territory and considerable respect on the continent. *(author)*

1375 LYON, Clément. **Le musicien Philippe de Mons**
as **(de Monte): Est-il malinois ou montois?** [The musician Philippe de Monte: Was he from Mechelen or Mons?], *Annales de la Fédération Archéologique et Historique. III* (Enghien: Spinet, 1899) 369–77. In French. See no. 25 in this volume.
There is insufficient evidence to refute the conclusion that Philippe was from Mons rather than Malines (Mechelen).

1376 MASSON, Paul-Marie. **L'humanisme musical**
as **en France au XVIᵉ siècle: La musique "mesurée à l'antique"** [Musical humanism in France in the 16th century: Music "mesurée à l'antique"], *Bericht über den zweiten Kongress der Internationalen Musikgesellschaft* (Leipzig: Breitkopf & Härtel, 1907) 170–83. *Music.* In French. See no. 53 in this volume.
A survey chiefly of technical issues in the study of the genre of vers mesuré, from the foundation of the Académie de Poésie et Musique by Jean-Antoine de Baïf and Joseph Thibault de Courville in 1570 through the posthumous publication of Claude Le Jeune's settings of Baïf's *Le printemps* in 1603. A more comprehensive treatment is published in *Le Mercure musicale et bulletin français de la S.I.M.* 3 (1907). *(David Bloom)*

1377 MATHIAS, François-Xavier. **Der Choral im**
as **Elsass** [Chant in Alsace], *Acta generalis cantus gregoriani studiosorum conventus, Argentinensis, 16-19 Aug. 1905/Bericht des internationalen Kongresses für gregorianischen Choralgesang/Compte rendu du Congrès international de plain-chant grégorien* (Strassburg: F.-X. Le Roux, 1905) 19–28. In German and French. See no. 50 in this volume.

1378 MEIER, Bernhard. **Glareans *Isagoge in**
as ***musicen* (1516)** [Glarean's *Isagoge in musicen* (1516)], *Bericht über den internationalen musikwissenschaftlichen Kongreß Wien Mozartjahr 1956* (Graz; Köln: Böhlau, 1958) 397–401. In German. See no. 365 in this volume.
Outlines the biographical and historical context of Heinrich Glarean's first treatise on music, its content, and its relation to his later writings. *(David Bloom)*

1379 MEIER, Bernhard. **"Hieroglyphisches" in der**
as **Musik des 16. Jahrhunderts** [The concept of the ideographic in music of the 16th century], *Bericht über den internationalen musikwissenschaftlichen Kongreß* (Kassel: Bärenreiter, 1963) 127–29. In German. See no. 452 in this volume.
Discusses the wide range of word-painting techniques in the second half of the century, with particular reference to the works of Lassus. The argument is presented at length in the author's *Wortausdeutung und Tonalität bei Orlando di Lasso*, in *Kirchenmusikalisches Jahrbuch* XLVII (1963). *(David Bloom)*

1380 MEIER, Bernhard. **Musiktheorie und Musik im**
as **16. Jahrhundert** [Music theory and music in the 16th century], *Bericht über den internationalen musikwissenschaftlichen Kongreß* (Kassel: Bärenreiter, 1963) 356–59. In German. See no. 452 in this volume.
In interpreting the significance of theoretical pronouncements of the Renaissance, it is important to determine whether the author was a working musician, at best a composer, or not; and whether his subject matter is a speculative *musica theorica* or is oriented toward the composition, performance, and criticism of real music. *(David Bloom)*

1381 MERIAN, Wilhelm. **Gregor Meyer**, *Schweizer*
as *Jahrbuch für Musikwissenschaft/Annales suisses de musicologie/Annuario svizzero di musicologia* I (1924) 138–53. In German. See no. 103 in this volume.

An account of the Basel composer and poet (ca. 1510-76).

1382 MERIAN, Wilhelm. **Das Verhältnis von Tabu-**
as **laturtänzen des 16. Jahrhunderts zu vorhandenen Fassungen für mehrere Instrumente** [The relationship of 16th-century tablature dances to extant versions for several instruments], *Beethoven-Zentenarfeier: Internationaler musikhistorischer Kongress* (Wien: Universal, 1927) 189–92. In German. See no. 142 in this volume.

Concordances between dance pieces in German organ tablatures and versions for ensemble performance provide supporting evidence for the author's views (*Der Tanz in den deutschen Tabulaturbüchern*, Leipzig 1927) on the development of a polyphonic keyboard style in the works of Johann Weck (ca.1495-1536), Bernhard Schmid, the elder (1535-92), and Christoph Loeffelholz von Colberg (1572-1619). *(David Bloom)*

1383 MEYER, Ernst Hermann. **L'élément populaire**
as **dans les danses instrumentales allemandes jusqu'à la guerre de Trente Ans** [The popular-music element in German instrumental dances up to the Thirty Years' War], *La musique instrumentale de la Renaissance* (Paris: Centre National de la Recherche Scientifique [CNRS], 1955) 139–47. *Music, list of works.* In French. See no. 333 in this volume.

Between the late 16th c. and ca. 1620 many collections of dance music for instrumental ensemble were published and republished, often representing several different composers. As a close examination of several pieces shows, they shared intonations (in the sense of Boris Asaf'ev's theory) with the music of the petite bourgeoisie and urban working classes of the time, which explains their popularity. *(David Bloom)*

1384 MORCOURT, Richard de. **Le livre de tablature**
as **de luth de Domenico Bianchini (1546)** [The lute tablature book of Domenico Bianchini (1546)], *La musique instrumentale de la Renaissance* (Paris: Centre National de la Recherche Scientifique [CNRS], 1955) 177–95. *Music.* In French. See no. 333 in this volume.

Analytic account of the contents of Bianchini's *Intabolatura de lauto...* (RISM 1546[24]), with particular attention to the relationship between the transcriptions of vocal music and their originals, and to the structural character of the ricercars. Complete editions are provided of the chanson arrangement *Il me souffit de tous mes maulx* and the ricercar no. 6. *(Susan Poliniak)*

1385 MOSER, Hans Joachim. **Paul Hofhaimer als**
as **Orgelkomponist** [Paul Hofhaimer as organ composer], *Beethoven-Zentenarfeier: Internationaler musikhistorischer Kongress* (Wien: Universal, 1927) 181–85. *Music.* In German. See no. 142 in this volume.

Hofhaimer (1459-1537) was perhaps the most celebrated organist of his time. Ironically, it has long been thought that none of his organ compositions have survived. It now seems certain, however, that a Salve Regina in the Fridolin Sicher organ tablature (*CH-SGs* MS 530) is by him. The music is discussed in some detail, and the kinds of organs played by Hofhaimer are characterized. *(David Bloom)*

1386 NIEMÖLLER, Klaus Wolfgang. **Ars musica—**
as **ars poetica—musica poetica**, *Bericht über den internationalen musikwissenschaftlichen Kongreß* (Kassel: Bärenreiter, 1957) 170–71. In German. See no. 356 in this volume.

Documents the ongoing separation of music from the traditional categories of the quadrivium in German theoretical writings in the time of Nicolaus Wollick and his *Opus aureum musicae* (1501). *(David Bloom)*

1387 NIEMÖLLER, Klaus Wolfgang. **Grundzüge**
as **einer Neubewertung der Musik an den Latein-schulen des 16. Jahrhunderts** [Principles for a new evaluation of the music of 16th-century Latin schools], *Bericht über den internationalen musik-wissenschaftlichen Kongreß* (Kassel: Bärenreiter, 1963) 133–35. In German. See no. 452 in this volume.

Other than in the relatively restricted number of court chapels, Latin school choirs were the only significant venues for the cultivation of church music in 16th-c. Germany and the Netherlands. Music was, however, less an academic subject, as it had been in medieval schools, than an *Utilitätsfach* or service unit for the churches, Catholic or Protestant, with which they were associated. *(Daniel Anderson)*

1388 NOBLE, Jeremy. **Le répertoire instrumental**
as **anglais: 1550-1585** [The English instrumental repertoire: 1550-1585], *La musique instrumentale de la Renaissance* (Paris: Centre National de la Recherche Scientifique [CNRS], 1955) 91–114. *Charts, diagr.* In French. See no. 333 in this volume.

A survey of secular instrumental ensemble practice on the basis of *GB-Lbl* MS Add.31390. An analytic account of the contents with all their known concordances is provided. *(Susan Poliniak)*

1389 NORLIND, Tobias. **Die englische Lautenmusik**
as **zur Zeit Shakespeare's** [English lute music in the time of Shakespeare], *Report of the Fourth Congress of the International Musical Society* (London: Novello, 1912) 331. In German. See no. 71 in this volume.

Summary of a paper.

1390 NOSKE, Frits. **Remarques sur les luthistes des**
as **Pays-Bas (1580-1620)** [Lutenists of the Low Countries (1580-1620)], *Le luth et sa musique* (Paris: Centre National de la Recherche Scientifique [CNRS], 1958) 179–92. *Music, transcr.* In French. See no. 377 in this volume.

General remarks on the few extant print and MS sources, with particular attention to the popularity of lute ensembles, as seen in an arrangement of Hubert Waelrant's song *Als ick u vinde* for four lutes and four voices by Emanuel Adriaenssen in the *Pratum musicum...* (Antwerp, 1584; a transcription of the piece is provided); the identification of four dance pieces by Sweelinck in Lord Herbert of Cherbury's lute book (*GB-Cfm* MS mus.689); and the presence of an arrangement of the song *Wilhelmus van Nassouwe* (now the Netherlands national hymn) in the Dallis lute book (*IRL-Dtc* MS D.3.30/i). *(David Bloom)*

1391 OREL, Alfred. **Zur Kompositionstechnik im**
as **Zeitalter der Trienter Codices** [On compositional technique in the age of the Trent Codices], *Bericht über den I. musikwissenschaftlichen Kongress der Deutschen Musikgesellschaft in Leipzig* (Wiesbaden: Breitkopf & Härtel, 1926) 219–24. In German. See no. 120 in this volume.

Discusses the music of Dufay, John Dunstable, Desprez, and Obrecht. Topics covered include coloration, cantus firmus, isorhythm, and faux-bourdon in motets, chansons, and Masses. *(William Renwick)*

1392 OSTHOFF, Helmuth. **Der Durchbruch zum**
as **musikalischen Humanismus** [The breakthrough to musical humanism], *Report of the Eighth Congress of the International Musicological Society. II: Reports* (Kassel: Bärenreiter, 1962) 31–39. In German. See no. 440 in this volume.

An interpretation of the role of Josquin Desprez in the decisive change in polyphony at the beginning of the 16th c. In his motets and Masses, Desprez was able to achieve a harmony between the sacral and the artistic which parallels Erasmian humanism in the world of letters. *(David Bloom)*

1393 OSTHOFF, Helmuth. **Die Psalm-Motetten von**
as **Josquin Deprez** [The psalm motets of Josquin
Desprez], *Bericht über den internationalen musik-*
wissenschaftlichen Kongreß Wien Mozartjahr 1956
(Graz; Köln: Böhlau, 1958) 452–56. In German. See
no. 365 in this volume.

Polyphonic psalm settings are relatively rare before Josquin, and it is
largely through his compositions that the idea of the psalm motet became a
stable concept. Sources, attribution questions, and musical characteristics
are discussed, and works are dated in relation to the composer's biography.
(David Bloom)

1394 OSTHOFF, Helmuth. **Zur Echtheitsfrage und**
as **Chronologie bei Josquins Werken** [On authenticity and chronology in Josquin's works], *Société Inter-*
nationale de Musicologie, cinquième congrès/
Internationale Gesellschaft für Musikwissenschaft,
fünfter Kongreß/International Society for Musical Re-
search, Fifth Congress (Amsterdam: Vereniging voor
Nederlandse Muziekgeschiedenis, 1953) 303–09. In
German. See no. 316 in this volume.

1395 PÄTZIG, Gerhard. **Heinrich Isaacs *Choralis***
as ***constantinus*: Eine posthume Werksammlung**
[Henricus Isaac's *Choralis constantinus*: A posthumous collection], *Bericht über den internationalen*
musikwissenschaftlichen Kongreß (Kassel: Bärenreiter,
1963) 114–16. *Facs.* In German. See no. 452 in this volume.

Isaac's collection of Proper cycles for the cathedral of Konstanz was completed by November 1509, and occupies only volume 2 of the posthumously published *Choralis constantinus*; in spite of the general title
("Chants of Konstanz"), the Propers of volumes 1 and 3 were composed for
the Hofkapelle in Vienna when Isaac was employed by Maximilian I.
(David Bloom)

1396 PEDRELL, Felipe. **Les échanges musicaux en-**
as **tre la France et la Catalogne au Moyen Âge: Le**
français Joan Brudieu, musicien catalan [The
musical exchanges between France and Catalonia during the Middle Ages: The Frenchman Joan Brudieu,
Catalan musician], *Actes du Congrès d'histoire de l'art*
(Paris: Presses Universitaires de France, 1923-1924)
823–28. In French. See no. 94 in this volume.

Master of sacred polyphony and composer of exquisite madrigals, Joan
Brudieu (ca. 1520-91) was born in France, but preferred to live in
Catalonia. Catalan folklore as well as Gregorian chant constituted the cre-
ative source of his work. His masterpiece is the *Missa pro defunctis*.
(Vivian Conejero)

1397 PEDRELL, Felipe. **La música polifónica** [Poly-
as phonic music], *Crónica y actas oficiales del tercer*
Congreso Nacional de Música Sagrada (Barcelona: La
Hormiga de Oro, 1913) 210–20. In Spanish. See no. 78
in this volume.

Polyphony has played a crucial role in the development of Roman Catholic
religious music. The works of Tomás Luis de Victoria are analyzed as paradigms of Spanish polyphony. *(José López-Calo)*

1398 PÉREZ DE VIÑASPRE ORTIZ, Francisco.
as **Consideraciones acerca de los polifonistas**
clásicos españoles [Considerations concerning the
great Spanish polyphonists], *Crónica del IV Congreso*
Nacional de Música Sagrada (Vitoria: Imprenta del
Montepío Diocesano, 1930) 296–304. In Spanish. See
no. 155 in this volume.

Summarizes the history of Spanish sacred polyphony to ca. 1600.

1399 PERZ, Mirosław. **Handschrift Nr. 1361 der**
as **Öffentlichen Städtischen Raczyński-**
Bibliothek in Poznań: Als neue Quelle zur
Geschichte der polnischen Musik in der II.
Hälfte des XV. Jahrhunderts [Manuscript no. 1361
in the Miejska Biblioteka Publiczna im. Edwarda
Raczyńskiego, Poznań, as a new source for Polish music
history in the second half of the 15th century], *The book*
of the first international musicological congress devoted
to the works of Frederick Chopin (Warszawa:
Państwowe Wydawnictwo Naukowe, 1963) 588–92.
Facs., music. In German. See no. 425 in this volume.

The MS, probably from no later than 1500, from a monastery in the Poznań
region, includes some Latin texts from the *Fioretti* of St. Francis and eight
pieces of music in white mensural notation, including six for three voices,
one for two voices, and one mensural monophonic piece, to rhymed Latin
texts of Marian devotion. Only two of the pieces, and part of the text of a
third, can be traced to earlier non-Polish sources. The MS shows that polyphony was established in Poland at that time not only in Cracow but also
in the voivodeship of Poznań. *(David Bloom)*

1400 PIDOUX, Pierre. **Ergebnisse der Forschungen**
as **um den Hugenotten-Psalter** [Research findings on
the Huguenot Psalter], *Kirchenmusik in ökumenischer*
Schau (Bern: Haupt, 1964) 51–55. In German. See no.
447 in this volume.

It is not generally true that the melodies used in the the so-called Geneva
Psalter of 1562 and its precursors were derived from secular songs, though
some may have been, while others clearly stem from Latin hymns. Many,
probably the majority, were original compositions. *(David Bloom)*

1401 PIRRO, André. **Orgues et organistes de**
as **Haguenau de 1491 à 1525** [Organs and organists of
Haguenau from 1491 to 1525], *Compte rendu du*
Congrès d'orgue tenu à l'Université de Strasbourg. IV
(Strasbourg: Société Strasbourgeoise de Librairie
Sostralib, 1934) 182–86. In French. See no. 199 in this
volume.

An annotated list.

1402 PIRRO, André. **Remarques sur l'exécution mu-**
as **sicale de la fin du 14ᵉ au milieu de 15ᵉ siècle** [Re-
marks on musical performance from the end of the 14th
century to the middle of the 15th century], *Société*
Internationale de Musicologie: Premier Congrès
Liège—Compte rendu/Internationale Gesellschaft für
Musikwissenschaft: Erster Kongress Lüttich—
Kongressbericht/International Society for Musical
Research: First Congress Liège: Report (London: Plain-
song and Mediaeval Music Society, 1930) 55–65. In
French. See no. 178 in this volume.

Discusses performance practices in sacred and secular music from 1380 to
1450.

1403 PIRROTTA, Nino. **Considerazioni sui primi**
as **esempi di Missa parodia** [Considerations on the
earliest examples of the parody Mass], *Atti del [I]*
Congresso internazionale di musica sacra (Tournai:
Desclée, 1952) 315–18. In Italian. See no. 303 in this
volume.

1404 PIRROTTA, Nino. **Tragédie et comédie dans la**
as **camerata fiorentina** [Tragedy and comedy in the
Florentine camerata], *Musique et poésie au XVIᵉ siècle*
(Paris: Centre National de la Recherche Scientifique
[CNRS], 1954) 287–97. In French. See no. 326 in this
volume.

Discusses the monodic innovations of Giovanni de' Bardi's Florentine
camerata, the subsequent development of similar styles by Emilio de'

Cavalieri and others, and the historical background of Italian solo song. The wedding of Fernando de' Medici and Cristina di Lorena in 1589 provided the impetus for Bardi to create musical interludes dealing with Greco-Roman myths and allegories of ethical and cosmic significance, translating the expression of poetry into music without obscuring the text. Caccini discussed the new style in *Le nuove musiche* (1602), calling attention to the spontaneity and perfection of execution of the solo songs. The substitution of the chitarrone for the viol as accompaniment is also discussed, and the roles of the villanella, frottola, and mid-16th-c. Italian tragedy and comedy in the development of monody are assessed. *(Roy Nitzberg)*

1405 PLAMENAC, Dragan. **La chanson de *L'homme*** as **armé et MS. VI.E.40 de la Bibliothèque Nationale de Naples** [The song *L'homme armé* and MS VI.E.40 of the Biblioteca Nazionale di Napoli], *Congrès jubilaire* (Brugge: Gruuthuuse, 1925) 229–30. In French. See no. 119 in this volume.

A short survey of the appropriations of *L'homme armé* by various composers, as well as a description of the first couplet of a related song dedicated to Queen Beatrice of Aragon from a 15th-c. collection. *(Susan Poliniak)*

1406 PLAMENAC, Dragan. **German polyphonic lie-** as **der of the 15th century in a little-known manuscript,** *Bericht über den siebenten internationalen musikwissenschaftlichen Kongress* (Kassel: Bärenreiter, 1959) 214–15. *Facs., music.* See no. 390 in this volume.

The so-called Strahov Codex (*CZ-Pst* MS D.G.IV.47, in the Knihovna Kláštera Premonstrátů/Strahovská Knihovna collection of the Národní Muzeum, Prague), well known as a source for Franco-Netherlandish sacred polyphony of the Ockeghem generation, also contains important 15th-c. German works, including previously unknown arrangements of popular German tunes and cantus firmus compositions with German texts, valuable for the construction of the history of the German lied. *(David Bloom)*

1407 PLAMENAC, Dragan. **Music of the 16th and** as **17th centuries in Dalmatia,** *Papers read at the International Congress of Musicology* (New York: Music Educators National Conference, 1944) 21–51. *Music.* See no. 266 in this volume.

The cultural life of the region is compared to that of Italy in the same period, and Andrija Patricij's *Son quest'i bei crin d'oro* and Julije Skjavetić's *Pater noster* are discussed. A Croatian-language translation is cited as RILM [1998]2279 and a French-language version is cited as no. 1408 in this volume.

1408 PLAMENAC, Dragan. **La musique en Dalmatie** as **et sur le littoral croate aux XVIᵉ et XVIIᵉ siècles** [Music in Dalmatia and coastal Croatia in the 16th and 17th centuries], *Congrés de la Societat Internacional de Musicologia* (Barcelona: Casa de Caritat, 1936). In French. See no. 224 in this volume.

The conference report provides only a citation. Neither the text nor a summary of the paper was published here. The original English-language version is abstracted as no. 1407 in this volume and a Croatian-language translation is cited as RILM [1998]2279.

1409 POPE, Isabel. **The musical development and** as **form of the Spanish villancico,** *Papers of the American Musicological Society* (Philadelphia: American Musicological Society, 1946) 11–22. *Music.* See no. 269 in this volume.

The textual and musical elements of the villancicos collected in *Villancicos de diversos autores* (Venice, 1556), better known as the Uppsala Cancionero, make clear that the genre evolved by adapting the Netherlandish polyphony to specifically Spanish melodic features.

1410 POPE, Isabel. **La musique espagnole à la cour** as **de Naples dans la seconde moitié du XVᵉ** [Spanish music at the court of Naples in the second half of the 15th century], *Musique et poésie au XVIᵉ siècle* (Paris:

Centre National de la Recherche Scientifique [CNRS], 1954) 35–61. In French. See no. 326 in this volume.

Examines MSS found in the Archivo de la Corona de Aragón in Barcelona concerning musical life in Naples after its conquest by Spain in 1443, and traces the development of the frottola, villancico, and madrigal in light of the interpretation of Spanish and Italian music. Works by the Spanish composer Johannes Cornago, who served at the Neapolitan court, are discussed. *(Roy Nitzberg)*

1411 PRUSIK, Karl. **Das englische Madrigal um** as **1600** [The English madrigal around 1600], *Beethoven-Zentenarfeier: Internationaler musikhistorischer Kongress* (Wien: Universal, 1927) 186–88. In German. See no. 142 in this volume.

Some 1800 compositions, by 70 different composers, survive from the period, in spite of the losses suffered during the English Civil War and the London fire of 1666. In addition to John Dowland, Thomas Morley, and Orlando Gibbons, composers ranking with the greatest of the Italian madrigalists include John Bennet, John Ward, and John Wilbye. *(David Bloom)*

1412 PUJOL ROCA, David. **Un libre manuscrit amb** as **dotze misses de Pierre de Manchicourt, mestre de capella de Felip II** [A manuscript volume with twelve Masses by Pierre de Manchicourt, chapel master of Philip II], *Congrés de la Societat Internacional de Musicologia* (Barcelona: Casa de Caritat, 1936). In Catalan. See no. 224 in this volume.

The conference report provides only a citation. Neither the text nor a summary of the paper was published here.

1413 QUEROL GAVALDÁ, Miguel. **Importance** as **historique et nationale de romance** [Historical and national importance of the romance], *Musique et poésie au XVIᵉ siècle* (Paris: Centre National de la Recherche Scientifique [CNRS], 1954) 299–327. In French. See no. 326 in this volume.

The romance is the most representative genre of Spanish character.

1414 QUOIKA, Rudolf. **Die *Musica* des Jan** as **Blahoslav 1569** [The *Musica* by Jan Blahoslav from 1569], *Bericht über den Internationalen musikwissenschaftlichen Kongress* (Kassel: Bärenreiter, 1954) 128–31. In German. See no. 319 in this volume.

Places the *Musica* by Blahoslav in the context of the Czech revival sponsored by the Moravian Church. An outline of the treatise is given and parallels with Andreas Ornithoparchus's *Musicae activae micrologus*, 1518, and Venceslas Philomates's *Musicorum libri quatuor, compendiose carmine elucubrati*, 1512, are listed. Blahoslav depended mainly on Ornithoparchus, but his audience was a less learned one and his *Musica* also reflects the influence of more elementary treatises by other writers. It was the aim of the Wittenberg-trained humanist to provide elementary musical instruction to priests, cantors, and singers. *(Carl Skoggard)*

1415 RADOLE, Giuseppe. **Giacomo Gorzanis** as **"leutonista et cittadino della magnifica città di Trieste"** [Giacomo Gorzanis, "lutenist and citizen of the magnificent city of Trieste"], *Bericht über den internationalen musikwissenschaftlichen Kongreß Wien Mozartjahr 1956* (Graz; Köln: Böhlau, 1958) 525–30. *Music, bibliog.* In Italian. See no. 365 in this volume.

An account of documentary evidence on the life of the composer and lutenist Giacomo Garzanis (b. ca. 1520, d. between 1575 and 1579), and a brief evaluation of his compositional output. *(David Bloom)*

⟶ RAJECZKY, Benjámin. **Mittelalterliche Mehr-stimmigkeit in Ungarn** [Medieval polyphony in Hungary]. See no. 1164 in this volume.

1416 RATTAY, Kurt. **Die Musikkultur des deutschen**
as **Ostens im Zeitalter der Reformation** [The music culture of eastern German regions in the age of the Reformation], *Bericht über den I. musikwissenschaftlichen Kongress der Deutschen Musikgesellschaft in Leipzig* (Wiesbaden: Breitkopf & Härtel, 1926) 393–96. In German. See no. 120 in this volume.

Discusses the activities of Johann Walter and Ludwig Senfl in the area of Kaliningrad (formerly Königsberg).

1417 RAUGEL, Félix. **Josquin des Prés à la**
as **Collégiate de Saint-Quentin** [Josquin Desprez at the Saint-Quentin collegiate church], *Actes du Congrès d'histoire de l'art* (Paris: Presses Universitaires de France, 1923-1924) 807–09. In French. See no. 94 in this volume.

Among the most important sources for Desprez's artistic activity in Saint-Quentin are the writings of Claude Hémeré (librarian of Richelieu), who had access to ancient acts and registers and published a history of the collegiate church. Another source, MS 463 of the Saint-Quentin Bibliothèque Municipale, mentions Desprez's sojourn at the collegiate church. *(Vivian Conejero)*

1418 REICHLING, Alfred. **Frühe Orgelkunst im**
as **süddeutschen Raum nach Zeugnissen der Tabulaturen des fünfzehnten Jahrhunderts** [Early organ compositions in the South German region, as evidenced by 15th-century tablatures], *Altbayerische Orgeltage* (Berlin: Merseburger, 1958) 25–29. In German. See no. 355 in this volume.

Reviews sources ranging from the early 15th-c. two-voice Magnificat *D-Mbs* MS Clm 5963, f.248r to the Buxheimer Orgelbuch, *D-Mbs* MS Mus.3752 (also Cim 352b), with remarks on developments in North Germany and on the organist and composer Conrad Paumann. *(David Bloom)*

1419 REICHLING, Alfred. **Die Präambeln der Hs.**
as **Erlangen 554 und ihre Beziehung zur Sammlung Ileborghs** [The preludes of MS Erlangen 554 and their relationship to the Ileborgh Tablature], *Bericht über den internationalen musikwissenschaftlichen Kongreß* (Kassel: Bärenreiter, 1963) 109–11. *Music*. In German. See no. 452 in this volume.

The similarities between the four preludes in the organ tablature *D-ERu* MS 554 (olim 729) and preludes in the 1448 tablature by Adam Ileborgh cannot be coincidental. It is likely that the Erlangen pieces were written in the late 1440s in central Franconia, possibly at the Cistercian monastery of Heilsbronn, whose library formerly held the MS, but earlier than Ileborgh's pieces; it remains unclear whether Ileborgh was directly influenced by them. *(Jeffrey Miller)*

1420 RIHOUËT, Yvonne. **Un motet de Moulu et ses**
as **diverses transcriptions pour orgue** [A motet by Moulu and its various transcriptions for organ], *Bericht über den musikwissenschaftlichen Kongreß in Basel* (Leipzig: Breitkopf & Härtel, 1925) 286–92. *Music*. In French. See no. 102 in this volume.

In 1541, Johann Petreius published a motet by Pierre Moulu, a student of Desprez, in *Trium vocum cantiones centum*. The motet first appeared between 1520 and 1530. In 1531, Pierre Attaingnant published a transcription, unascribed, and another transcription has been found in a MS of Hans Kotter, a Fribourg organist.

1421 RIPOLLÉS PÉREZ, Vicente. **Los ministriles de**
as **los siglos XVI-XVII en la catedral de Valencia** [The ministriles of the cathedral of Valencia in the 16th and 17th centuries], *Congrés de la Societat Internacional de Musicologia* (Barcelona: Casa de Caritat, 1936). In Spanish. See no. 224 in this volume.

The conference report provides only a citation. Neither the text nor a summary of the paper was published here.

1422 RUBSAMEN, Walter H. **From frottola to mad-**
as **rigal: The changing pattern of secular Italian vocal music,** *Chanson & madrigal 1480-1530: Studies in comparison and contrast* (Cambridge, MA: Harvard University Press, 1964) 51–87. *Music, index.* See no. 429 in this volume.

Under the influence of Netherlandish composers such as Isaac and Desprez, Italian vocal music evolved from the accompanied monody, strophic setting, and popular-style text of the frottola to the polyphonic through-composed madrigal, which set texts of high literary quality such as the canzoni of Petrarch and featured imitative counterpoint. The first important composer in this new style was Philippe Verdelot. Includes a discussion of the paper by Nanie BRIDGMAN, Frank A. D'ACCONE, and Nino PIRROTTA. *(Alexander G. Smith)*

1423 RUBSAMEN, Walter H. **Sebastian Festa and**
as **the early madrigal,** *Bericht über den internationalen musikwissenschaftlichen Kongreß* (Kassel: Bärenreiter, 1963) 122–26. *Music.* See no. 452 in this volume.

Evidence in the Medici Codex (*I-Fl* MS 666) shows that Ottobono Fieschi, Bishop of Mondovì in 1519-22, must have been the patron of the composer Sebastiano Festa, providing Festa with the opportunity to participate in the lively cultural life of Rome under Leo X. Festa's historical importance needs to be reevaluated; he was the only composer of the transitional decade in the development from frottola to madrigal, 1520-30, whose works continued to be printed and performed in the era of the madrigal itself. *(David Bloom)*

1424 SALMEN, Walter. **Das Liederbuch der Anna**
as **von Köln und seine Beziehungen zu den Niederlanden** [The songbook of Anna of Cologne and its links to the Netherlands], *Société Internationale de Musicologie, cinquième congrès/Internationale Gesellschaft für Musikwissenschaft, fünfter Kongreß/International Society for Musical Research, Fifth Congress* (Amsterdam: Vereniging voor Nederlandse Muziekgeschiedenis, 1953) 340–51. In German. See no. 316 in this volume.

1425 SARTORI, Claudio. **Une pratique des**
as **musiciens lombards (1582-1639): L'hommage des chansons instrumentales aux familles d'une ville** [A practice of Lombard musicians (1582-1639): Canzoni strumentali as homages to a city's families], *La musique instrumentale de la Renaissance* (Paris: Centre National de la Recherche Scientifique [CNRS], 1955) 305–12. In French. See no. 333 in this volume.

In 1584 the Brescia organist Florentio Maschera published a set of 21 *Canzoni da sonare a quattro voci* written in 1582, of which 11 were untitled, while the others were all named for Brescia's principal families: *La capriola* for the Caprioli, *La martinenga* for the Martinengo, and so forth. The practice became widespread in other Lombard cities (Bergamo, Cremona, Mantua, Milan, and Como) over a period ending with Tarquinio Merula's *Secondo libro delle canzoni da suonare* (1639), dedicated to Bergamo families. Similar titlings were used by Claudio Merulo for Parma and Adriano Banchieri for Bologna, but the custom of organizing an entire collection this way was essentially limited to Lombardy, or to Lombard composers (Giovanni Cavaccio and Biagio Marini) working in Venice; it provides extramusical evidence for the existence of a distinct Lombard school of composition. *(David Bloom)*

1426 SCHAAL, Richard. **Zur Methodik quellen-**
as **mässiger Datierung der Werke Pierre de la Rue** [Methodology for source-related dating of the works of Pierre de la Rue], *Kongreß-Bericht: Gesellschaft für Musikforschung* (Kassel; Basel: Bärenreiter, 1950) 80–82. In German. See no. 299 in this volume.

⟶ SCHMITZ, Arnold. **Die Kadenz als** *Orna-mentum musicae* [The cadence as *ornamentum musicae*]. See no. 4216 in this volume.

1427
as

SCHRADE, Leo. **Les fêtes du mariage de Francesco dei Medici et de Bianca Cappello** [The festivals at the marriage of Francesco de' Medici and Bianca Cappello], *Les fêtes de la Renaissance* (Paris: Centre National de la Recherche Scientifique [CNRS], 1956) 107–32. In French. See no. 350 in this volume.

The series of diverse spectacles at the celebration (Florence, 1579) had a coherent program, with appropriate music for each event. *(Scott Fruehwald)*

1428
as

SCHRADE, Leo. **Organ music and the Mass in the fifteenth century,** *Papers of the American Musicological Society* (Philadelphia: American Musicological Society, 1946) 49–55. See no. 269 in this volume.

Demonstrates that organ compositions of the 15th c. were modeled on 12th-c. organum. The development of the organ Mass is also examined in relation to the survival of organum techniques.

1429
as

SCHRADE, Leo. **Renaissance: The historical conception of an epoch,** *Société Internationale de Musicologie, cinquième congrès/Internationale Gesellschaft für Musikwissenschaft, fünfter Kongreß/International Society for Musical Research, Fifth Congress* (Amsterdam: Vereniging voor Nederlandse Muziekgeschiedenis, 1953) 19–32. See no. 316 in this volume.

The term Renaissance does not pertain to the imitation of antiquity nor its rebirth. It describes a historical conception by which the humanities were established as an epoch, and as a cultural entity. For the first time, humankind reached the stage of admitting comparison with previous civilizations. As introduced by Zarlino, the theory of the cyclical phases of culture include downfall, lacuna, and rebirth. In music, the term refers to the rebirth of standards. *(Tsipora Yosselevitch)*

1430
as

SCHWARTZ, Rudolf. **Zur Akzidentienfrage im 16. Jahrhundert** [The use of accidentals in the 16th century], *Haydn-Zentenarfeier* (Leipzig: Breitkopf & Härtel; Wien: Artaria, 1909) 109–12. *Music.* In German. See no. 65 in this volume.

Discusses an example from Hans Leo Hassler (1564-1612).

1431
as

SCHWARTZ, Rudolf. **Zur Musikkultur der Renaissance** [The musical culture of the Renaissance], *Bericht über den internationalen Kongress für Schubertforschung* (Augsburg: Benno Filser, 1929) 193–95. In German. See no. 154 in this volume.

A speech by Michelangelo Buonarroti the younger dating from the beginning of the 17th c., collected in the *Raccolta di prose fiorentine* (1719-31) under the title *Nella fondazione di un accademia, professante lettere, armi, e musica*, treats music alongside literature and physical exercise as one of the three essential elements in the cultivation of *virtù*. Michelangelo Buonarroti's acknowledgment is a useful corrective to the disdain for music expressed by Baldassare Castiglione, Torquato Tasso, and Benvenuto Cellini. *(David Bloom)*

1432
as

SHIRE, Helena M.; ELLIOTT, Kenneth. **La fricassée en Écosse et ses rapports avec les fêtes de la Renaissance** [The fricassée in Scotland and its relationship to Renaissance festivals], *Les fêtes de la Renaissance* (Paris: Centre National de la Recherche Scientifique [CNRS], 1956) 335–45. *Music.* In French. See no. 350 in this volume.

Discusses a type of popular chanson which possesses a social signifiance and is connected with a festival.

1433
as

SIEVERS, Heinrich. **Die Braunschweiger Tabulaturen** [The Braunschweig tablatures], *Kongreß-Bericht: Gesellschaft für Musikforschung* (Kassel; Basel: Bärenreiter, 1950) 97–102. In German. See no. 299 in this volume.

Describes a MS containing some 70 motets, the earliest datable to 1544, in organ tablature, presumably written down in the years 1585-88 by Magnus Vuinck, first Protestant cantor at the Katharineum, a Latin school. *(Carl Skoggard)*

1434
as

SMIJERS, Albert. **Music of the Illustrious Confraternity of Our Lady at 's-Hertogenbosch from 1330-1600,** *Papers read at the International Congress of Musicology* (New York: Music Educators National Conference, 1944) 184–92. See no. 266 in this volume.

Outlines the history of the Illustre Lieve Vrouwe Broederschap.

1435
as

SMITS VAN WAESBERGHE, Joseph. **Matthaei Herbeni Trajectensis** *De natura cantus ac miraculis vocis* **(1496)** [The *De natura cantus ac miraculis vocis* (1496) of Matthaeus Herbenus of Maastricht], *Bericht über den internationalen musikwissenschaftlichen Kongreß* (Kassel: Bärenreiter, 1957) 219–20. In German. See no. 356 in this volume.

Remarks on Herbenus's treatise, *D-Mbs* MS Clm.10277. The author's edition of the work was published in Cologne by A. Volk in 1957. *(David Bloom)*

1436
as

SNÍŽKOVÁ, Jitka. **Contribution aux relations tchéco-polonaises au XVIᵉ-XVIIᵉ siècle** [Czech-Polish relations in the 16th and 17th centuries], *The book of the first international musicological congress devoted to the works of Frederick Chopin* (Warszawa: Państwowe Wydawnictwo Naukowe, 1963) 608–12. *Charts, diagr.* In French. See no. 425 in this volume.

The closeness in musical matters between Bohemia and Poland in the Renaissance intensified during the years 1471 to 1526. It is exemplified by the late 16th-c. figure Simon Bar Jona Madelka, from Opole in Silesia, who became a master butcher and eminent composer in Plzeň. Six previously unknown motets by him are extant in fragmentary form in the Státní Oblastní Archiv, Klatovy MSS 75-76; together with his published works, the new source shows how Madelka combined personal originality and cohesion with Czech musical culture of the time. *(Susan Poliniak)*

1437
as

SÖHNER, Leo. **Gregorianischen Choral und Orgel in Deutschland von 1500 bis 1700** [Gregorian chant and the organ in Germany, 1500-1700], *Société Internationale de Musicologie: Premier Congrès Liège—Compte rendu/Internationale Gesellschaft für Musikwissenschaft: Erster Kongress Lüttich—Kongressbericht/International Society for Musical Research: First Congress Liège: Report* (London: Plainsong and Mediaeval Music Society, 1930) 208–10. In German. See no. 178 in this volume.

1438
as

SOWA, Georg. **Eine neu aufgefundene Liederhandschrift mit Noten und Text aus dem Jahre 1544** [A newly found song manuscript, with music and text, from 1544], *Bericht über den internationalen musikwissenschaftlichen Kongreß* (Kassel: Bärenreiter, 1957) 223–25. In German. See no. 356 in this volume.

Preliminary report on the discovery in the Varnhagen-Bibliothek, Evangelische Kirchengemeinde, Iserlohn, of a collection of 201 early 16th-c. pieces, songs and dances. A full account is abstracted as RILM [1968] 1752. *(David Bloom)*

1439
as

SQUIRE, William Barclay. **Who was Benedictus?**, *Report of the Fourth Congress of the International Musical Society* (London: Novello, 1912) 152–57. See no. 71 in this volume.

Some musicologists have been confused by the attributions of 16th-c. compositions to various forms of the name "Benedictus". There were three composers: the Fleming Benedictus de Opitiis, who settled in England; the Fleming Benedictus Appenzeller; and the German Benedictus Ducis.

1440
as

ŠREJER-TKAČENKO, Onys'ja Jakovlevna. **Razvitie ukrainskoj muzyki XVI-XVII vekah** [The development of Ukrainian music from the 16th to the 18th centuries], *Musica antiqua Europae orientalis* (Warszawa: Państwowe Wydawnictwo Naukowe, 1966). In Russian. See no. 506 in this volume.

1441
as

STALMANN, Joachim. **Die reformatorische Musikanschauung des Johann Walter** [Johann Walter's Reformation view of music], *Bericht über den internationalen musikwissenschaftlichen Kongreß* (Kassel: Bärenreiter, 1963) 129–32. In German. See no. 452 in this volume.

Walter's poems *Lob und Preis der löblichen Kunst Musica* (1538) and *Lob und Preis der himmlischen Kunst Musica* (1564) express the Reformation theology of music more clearly, and in the first case some four years earlier, than Luther himself. *(Daniel Anderson)*

1442
as

STEGLICH, Rudolf. **Zur Ausdruckskunst des Nürnberger Paumann-Kreises** [The art of expression of the Nuremberg Paumann circle], *Kongreß-Bericht: Gesellschaft für Musikforschung* (Kassel; Basel: Bärenreiter, 1950) 91–93. *Charts, diagr.* In German. See no. 299 in this volume.

1443
as

STEVENS, Denis. **La chanson anglaise avant l'école madrigaliste** [English song before the madrigalist school], *Musique et poésie au XVIe siècle* (Paris: Centre National de la Recherche Scientifique [CNRS], 1954) 121–27. *Music, list of works, charts, diagr.* In French. See no. 326 in this volume.

Describes the difficulty of reconstructing a history of English secular polyphony, due to an extreme lack of sources. Many songs were collected in two MS anthologies that are now in the British Library. They contain a wide range of musical styles, from those of Burgundian influence to those attributed to Henry VIII. There are frequently two lower melismatic passages, suggesting instrumental participation. *(Roy Nitzberg)*

1444
as

STEVENS, Denis. **Les sources de l'In nomine** [The sources of the In nomine], *La musique instrumentale de la Renaissance* (Paris: Centre National de la Recherche Scientifique [CNRS], 1955) 85–90. *Charts, diagr.* In French. See no. 333 in this volume.

The instrumental genre known as In nomine (or sometimes, in keyboard versions, Gloria tibi Trinitas) was a cantus firmus composition based on a part of John Taverner's *Missa "Gloria tibi Trinitas"* (1530), the In nomine Domini section of the Benedictus. Its history from the straightforward keyboard arrangements of the Mulliner Book (*GB-Lbl* MS Add.30513) through the increasingly elaborate consort settings of the 17th c. is surveyed in terms of liturgical meaning and musicological context. An English-language version is published in *Modern musical record* 84 (1954).

1445
as

SUTKOWSKI, Adam. **The Pelplin organ tablature (1620-1630): A valuable musical document of Polish music culture in late Renaissance,** *The book of the first international musicological congress devoted to the works of Frederick Chopin* (Warszawa: Państwowe Wydawnictwo Naukowe,

1963) 628–29. In English and Latin. See no. 425 in this volume.

Preliminary account of six codices of European keyboard music discovered 1957 in the library of the Wyższe Seminarium Duchowne, Pelplin, now catalogued as *PL-PE* MSS 304-08, 308a, with biographical information on the probable copyist, Felix Trzciński, a Cistercian monk in Pelplin (1594-1649). The MSS are analyzed in detail in Polish in *Nieznane polonika muzyczne z XVI i XVII wieku*, *Muzyka* V/1 (1960), and in Italian in A. Sutkowski and O. Mischiati, *Una preziosa fonte di musica strumentale: L'intavolatura di Pelplin*, *L'organo* II (1961). *(Susan Poliniak)*

1446
as

SZCZEPAŃSKA, Maria. **Niektóre zagadnienia polskiej muzyki lutniowej XVI wieku** [Issues in Polish lute music of the 16th century], *The book of the first international musicological congress devoted to the works of Frederick Chopin* (Warszawa: Państwowe Wydawnictwo Naukowe, 1963) 630–32. In Polish. See no. 425 in this volume.

1447
as

TEUBER, Ulrich. **Bemerkungen zur Homophonie im 16. Jh.** [Comments on 16th-century homophony], *Société Internationale de Musicologie, cinquième congrès/Internationale Gesellschaft für Musikwissenschaft, fünfter Kongreß/International Society for Musical Research, Fifth Congress* (Amsterdam: Vereniging voor Nederlandse Muziekgeschiedenis, 1953) 384–97. In German. See no. 316 in this volume.

1448
as

THIBAULT DE CHAMBURE, Geneviève. **Le concert instrumental au XVe siècle** [The instrumental consort in the 15th century], *La musique instrumentale de la Renaissance* (Paris: Centre National de la Recherche Scientifique [CNRS], 1955) 23–33. *Music.* In French. See no. 333 in this volume.

There are hardly any notated sources of ensemble music from before 1500 and none for which the notation is adequate. Literary sources, from the 12th-c. *Roman de Renard* through the poems and other writings of Guillaume de Machaut and the contemporary documentation of performance on various special occasions, provide valuable evidence. In a number of cases it is possible to reconstruct or at least speculate on the instrumental ensemble performance of a piece known in a vocal or keyboard version. *(David Bloom)*

1449
as

THIBAULT DE CHAMBURE, Geneviève. **Un manuscrit italien pour luth des premières années du XVIe siècle** [An Italian lute manuscript from the early sixteenth century], *Le luth et sa musique* (Paris: Centre National de la Recherche Scientifique [CNRS], 1958) 43–76. *Illus., facs., music, index, charts, diagr., transcr.* In French. See no. 377 in this volume.

A MS lute tablature in the author's private collection, acquired in Florence from Leo S. Olschki, was apparently copied in Venice before 1510 and is therefore earlier than the Capirola Lutebook (*US-Cn* Case MS VM C.25), regarded until the present discovery as the oldest Italian MS lute music source. The historical and musical value of the new source are sketched, and a concordance with other sources, index of titles, and transcriptions of several complete pieces into modern notation are provided. The MS, now in the collection of the Bibliothèque Nationale, Paris (*F-Pn* MS rés.vmd 27), is published in facsimile by Éditions Minkoff, Geneva 1981, under the title *Tablature de luth italienne, ca. 1505: 110 pièces pour luth seul et accompagnements pour luth d'œuvres vocales.* *(David Bloom)*

1450
as

THIBAULT DE CHAMBURE, Geneviève. **Musique et poésie en France au XVIe siècle avant les *Amours* de Ronsard** [Music and poetry in France in the 16th century, before Ronsard's *Amours*], *Musique et poésie au XVIe siècle* (Paris: Centre National de la Recherche Scientifique [CNRS], 1954) 79–88. In French. See no. 326 in this volume.

Ronsard's preference for sung poetry with instruments already existed during the first half of the 16th c.

1451
as

THÜRLINGS, Adolf. *Innsbruck, ich muss dich lassen* **(Heinrich Isaac und Cosmas Alder)** [*Innsbruck, ich muss dich lassen* (Heinrich Isaac and Cosmas Alder)], *Festschrift zum zweiten Kongreß der Internationalen Musikgesellschaft, verfaßt von Mitgliedern der Schweizerischen Landessektion und den Kongreßteilnehmern* (Basel: Reinhardt, 1906) I, 54–86. *Illus.* In German. See no. 54 in this volume.

1452
as

THÜRLINGS, Adolf. **Die** *soggetti cavati dalle vocali* **in Huldigungskompositionen und die Herculesmesse des Lupus** [The *soggetti cavati dalle vocali* in Lupus's homage compositions and *Missa Hercules*], *Bericht über den zweiten Kongress der Internationalen Musikgesellschaft* (Leipzig: Breitkopf & Härtel, 1907) 183–94. *Music.* In German. See no. 53 in this volume.

The *soggetto cavato* technique of theme construction, in which the vowels of a title or text incipit are matched to the vowels of the solmization syllables, seems to have been first used in the late 15th c. by Roland de Lassus, as in the *Missa Hercules Dux Ferrariae*, but is most frequent in the 16th c., in musical tributes, especially to Ercole II d'Este (the grandson of Lassus's dedicatee Ercole I), by Jacquet de Berchem, Cipriano de Rore, Lupus, Johannes Lupi, and Johannes de Cleve. The works of Lupus are particularly examined, and biographical evidence on this composer is surveyed. *(David Bloom)*

1453
as

TIBY, Ottavio. **La scuola polifonica siciliana dei secc. XVI e XVII** [The Sicilian school of polyphony of the 16th and 17th centuries], *Kongreß-Bericht: Gesellschaft für Musikforschung* (Kassel; Basel: Bärenreiter, 1950) 89–91. In Italian. See no. 299 in this volume.

⟶
TORREFRANCA, Fausto. **The** *canzoni di alettali matrice* **of the court dances and of the filastrocca during the fifteenth century and earlier.** See no. 1201 in this volume.

1454
as

TORREFRANCA, Fausto. **Documenti definitivi sulla partita** [Documents defining the partita], *Bericht über den Internationalen musikwissenschaftlichen Kongress* (Kassel: Bärenreiter, 1954) 143–48. In Italian. See no. 319 in this volume.

Traces the history of the partita before those of Frescobaldi (1614) and Giovanni Maria Trabaci (1603) and examines the use of the term *partita* and its equivalents in dance manuals. Furthermore, the basis for a distinction between the partita and the suite is considered. A key document is *I-Fn* MS Galilei no. 6, which contains works so titled written by Vincenzo Galilei, presumably between 1563 and 1584. Other examples are known by Carlo Gesualdo, probably composed at Ferrara in ca. 1594 and never published. Several treatises by dancing masters furnish parallel evidence (Prospero Luti, *Opera bellissima nella quale si contengono molte partite...*, 1589, and Livio Lupi di Caravaggio, *Mutanze di gagliarda, tordiglione, passo e mezzo...*, 1600). *(Carl Skoggard)*

1455
as

TORREFRANCA, Fausto. **Le prime villote a quattro e loro importanza storica ed estetica** [The first villottas in four voices and their historic and aesthetic importance], *Atti del III Congresso nazionale di arti e tradizioni popolari* (Roma: Opera Nazionale Dopolavoro, 1936) 182f. In Italian. See no. 218 in this volume.

1456
as

TREND, John Brande. **The madrigal of Pedro Rimonte,** *Congrés de la Societat Internacional de Musicologia* (Barcelona: Casa de Caritat, 1936). See no. 224 in this volume.

The conference report provides only a citation. Neither the text nor a summary of the paper was published here.

1457
as

URSPRUNG, Otto. **Spanische Musik der Vor-Reservata um 1500 und der Früh-Reservata** [Spanish music from before musica reservata, ca. 1500, and the beginnings of musica reservata], *Congrés de la Societat Internacional de Musicologia* (Barcelona: Casa de Caritat, 1936). In German. See no. 224 in this volume.

The conference report provides only a citation. Neither the text nor a summary of the paper was published here. A Spanish-language translation was published in *Anuario musical* XLVI (1991) 263-93, and abstracted as RILM [1991]2153.

⟶
VANICKÝ, Jaroslav. **Czech mediaeval and Renaissance music.** See no. 1204 in this volume.

1458
as

VERCHALY, André. **La métrique et le rythme musical au temps de l'humanisme** [Verse meter and melodic rhythm in the age of humanism], *Report of the Eighth Congress of the International Musicological Society. I: Papers* (Kassel: Bärenreiter, 1961) 66–74. *Music.* In French. See no. 439 in this volume.

Examines the influence on composers of the humanist movement in 16th- and early 17th-c. France, with its program of reviving the aesthetics of classical antiquity as regards the unity of text and music. The work of the Pléiade poets such as Ronsard and Du Bellay had a more durable effect than the *musique mesurée à l'antique* proposed by Baïf, and Italian influence was minimal until Caccini's visit to France in 1604-05. The development of a musical sensitivity to verse rhythm can be traced in the text setting of airs, airs de cour, and particularly the lute songs of Didier Le Blanc, Nicolas de La Grotte, Pierre Guédron, and Gabriel Bataille. *(David Bloom)*

1459
as

VERCHALY, André. **Poésie et air de cour en France jusqu'à 1620** [Poetry and the air de cour in France to 1620], *Musique et poésie au XVIe siècle* (Paris: Centre National de la Recherche Scientifique [CNRS], 1954) 211–24. *Music.* In French. See no. 326 in this volume.

1460
as

VILLANIS, Luigi Alberto. **Alcuni codici manoscritti di musica del secolo XVI** [Some musical codices from the 16th century], *Atti del Congresso internazionale di scienze storiche. VIII: Atti della sezione IV: Storia dell'arte musicale e drammatica* (Roma: R. Accademia dei Lincei, 1905) 319–60. In Italian. See no. 42 in this volume.

Three codices in possession of the Biblioteca Nationale Universitaria, Turin, were written by a certain Languer, Simon Boyleau, and an anonymous composer. The works are analyzed and 16th-c. notation is discussed.

1461
as

VOISÉ, Waldemar. *Dodecachordon* **d'Henri Glaréan d'après sa correspondance avec Jean Laski (Joannes à Lasco)** [The *Dodecachordon* of Heinrich Glarean, as mentioned in his correspondence with Jan Łaski (Johannes à Lasco)], *The book of the first international musicological congress devoted to the works of Frederick Chopin* (Warszawa: Państwowe Wydawnictwo Naukowe, 1963) 638–39. In French. See no. 425 in this volume.

Correspondence of 1528-32 between Heinrich Glarean and the Polish religious reformer Jan Łaski shows that Łaski provided the inspiration for Glarean's *Dodecachordon*. The treatise itself contains no mention of Łaski because by the time it was published, in 1547, Glarean had committed himself to orthodox Catholicism while Łaski had definitively become a Protestant. *(Susan Poliniak)*

1462
as

WALKER, Daniel Pickering. **La musique des intermèdes Florentins de 1589 et l'humanisme** [The music of the Florentine intermedios of 1589 and humanism], *Les fêtes de la Renaissance* (Paris: Centre National de la Recherche Scientifique [CNRS], 1956) 133–44. In French. See no. 350 in this volume.

The only intermedio from the second half of the 16th c. with extant music contains no traces of the stylistic tendencies that led to recitative.

(Scott Fruehwald)

1463
as

WARD, John M. **Les sources de la musique pour le clavier en Angleterre** [The sources for keyboard music in England], *La musique instrumentale de la Renaissance* (Paris: Centre National de la Recherche Scientifique [CNRS], 1955) 225–36. *Music.* In French. See no. 333 in this volume.

On the evidence of a previously unnoted concordance and of general style, the MS Royal Appendix 58 in the collections of the British Library can be dated no earlier than 1540. The Mulliner Book (*GB-Lbl* MS add.30513) was begun around 1560 and completed no more than 10 years later. The Dublin Virginal Book (*IRL-Dtc* MS D.3.30/i) was copied around 1570. The dating clarifies the origins and character of a national English keyboard style based on rich figuration over a mostly chordal accompaniment, gradually coming under the influence first of Italian, later of Franco-Flemish keyboard writing. *(David Bloom)*

1464
as

WEINMANN, Karl. **Palestrina und das Oratorium des hl. Filippo Neri** [Palestrina and the oratory of St. Filippo Neri], *Bericht über den I. musikwissenschaftlichen Kongress der Deutschen Musikgesellschaft in Leipzig* (Wiesbaden: Breitkopf & Härtel, 1926) 323–28. In German. See no. 120 in this volume.

Discusses the style of Palestrina's compositions for the oratory and his direction of music there.

1465
as

WELLESZ, Egon. **Italienische Musiker am österreichischen Hof** [Italian musicians at the Austrian court], *Atti del secondo Congresso internazionale di musica* (Firenze: Le Monnier, 1940) 299–307. *Bibliog.* In German; summaries in Italian and French. See no. 239 in this volume.

Discusses the increasing dominance of Italian musicians and of violins in the Habsburg courts at Graz and Vienna from the late 16th to the early 18th c. *(David Bloom)*

1466
as

WERNER, Theodor Wilhelm. **Anmerkungen zur Motettenkunst Josquins** [Notes concerning Josquin's motet compositions], *Bericht über den musikwissenschaftlichen Kongress in Basel* (Leipzig: Breitkopf & Härtel, 1925) 375. In German. See no. 102 in this volume.

Summarizes a discussion of Desprez's use of both contrapuntal and homophonic styles while testing the hypothesis that motet style does not require a well-balanced form. The sequence *Mittit ad virginem* is discussed in terms of musica reservata. An expanded version appears in *Zeitschrift für Musikwissenschaft* (Oct. 1924).

1467
as

WESSELY, Othmar. **Beiträge zur Lebensgeschichte von Johann Zanger** [Contributions to the biography of Johann Zanger], *Bericht über den internationalen musikwissenschaftlichen Kongreß Wien Mozartjahr 1956* (Graz; Köln: Böhlau, 1958) 708–26. In German. See no. 365 in this volume.

Surveys documentary evidence concerning the life of the Austrian theorist and theologian (1517-87), and his ancestry, works, and descendants. An appendix provides the texts of a biography of Zanger in Latin verse by

Melchior NEUKIRCH (Neofanius) and the will of Zanger's wife, Catharina. *(David Bloom)*

1468
as

WESTRUP, Jack A. **L'influence de la musique italienne sur le madrigal anglais** [The influence of Italian music on the English madrigal], *Musique et poésie au XVIᵉ siècle* (Paris: Centre National de la Recherche Scientifique [CNRS], 1954) 129–38. *Music, bibliog.* In French. See no. 326 in this volume.

While adopting the Italian style, English composers showed equal loyalty to the old traditions of English vocal music as well as other national styles, particularly the French chanson. *(Scott Fruehwald)*

1469
as

WILKOWSKA-CHOMIŃSKA, Krystyna. **Nicolas de Cracovie et la musique de la Renaissance en Pologne** [Mikołaj z Krakowa and the music of the Renaissance in Poland], *The book of the first international musicological congress devoted to the works of Frederick Chopin* (Warszawa: Państwowe Wydawnictwo Naukowe, 1963) 640–45. *Facs., music.* In French. See no. 425 in this volume.

Mikołaj z Krakowa (Nikolaus Cracoviensis) is the Polish composer who best epitomizes the ideal of the Renaissance musician. He was the first Polish composer to write five-voice motets, to use syntactic imitation, and to write polyphonic chansons on Polish texts; the only composer to write isorhythmic motets and madrigals on Polish texts; and the earliest known Polish composer of dance music and other strictly instrumental works. *(Susan Poliniak)*

1470
as

WOLF, Johannes. **Die Akzidentien im 15. und 16. Jahrhundert** [Accidentals in the 15th and 16th centuries], *Haydn-Zentenarfeier* (Leipzig: Breitkopf & Härtel; Wien: Artaria, 1909) 124–26. *Music.* In German. See no. 65 in this volume.

Includes the subsequent panel discussion.

1471
as

WOLF, Johannes. **Altflämische Lieder 14.-15. Jahrhunderts und ihre rhythmische Lesung** [Old Flemish songs of the 14th-15th centuries and their rhythmic interpretation], *Bericht über den musikwissenschaftlichen Kongreß in Basel* (Leipzig: Breitkopf & Härtel, 1925) 376–86. In German. See no. 102 in this volume.

A MS of Croeser de Berges containing 145 Old Flemish (closely related to Plattdeutsch) songs with 137 melodies is considered with respect to rhythm, melody, and instrumentation. The MS appears in modern edition as no. 9 of the series *Maatschappy der vlaemsche Bibliophilen*.

1472
as

WOLF, Johannes. **Ein angebliches Ramos-Manuskript in der Preussischen Staatsbibliothek** [An alleged manuscript of Ramos in the Preußische Staatsbibliothek], *Congrés de la Societat Internacional de Musicologia* (Barcelona: Casa de Caritat, 1936). In German. See no. 224 in this volume.

The conference report provides only a citation. Neither the text nor a summary of the paper was published here.

1473
as

WOLFF, Hellmuth Christian. **Der Stilbegriff der *Renaissance* in der Musik der alten Niederländer** [*Renaissance* as a style concept applied to the music of the old Netherlanders], *Société Internationale de Musicologie, cinquième congrès/Internationale Gesellschaft für Musikwissenschaft, fünfter Kongreß/ International Society for Musical Research, Fifth Congress* (Amsterdam: Vereniging voor Nederlandse Muziekgeschiedenis, 1953) 450–55. In German. See no. 316 in this volume.

1474 YATES, Frances A. **Poésie et musique dans les**
as   *magnificences* **au mariage du duc de Joyeuse,**
         Paris, 1581 [Poetry and music in the *magnificences*
         for the marriage of the Duke of Joyeuse, 1581],
         Musique et poésie au XVIᵉ siècle (Paris: Centre Na-
         tional de la Recherche Scientifique [CNRS], 1954)
         241–64. In French. See no. 326 in this volume.

To honor the marriage of Anne de Joyeuse to the queen's half-sister Marguerite de Lorraine in 1581, Henri III employed all of the artistic resources
of the court to create a glorious two-week festival. The high point was the
Ballet comique de la reine, which marked a new era in the alliance of poetry,
music, and dance. *(Roy Nitzberg)*

1475 ZENCK, Hermann. **Zur Adriaen Willaerts**
as   *Salmi spezzati* [Adrian Willaert's *salmi spezzati*],
         Compte rendu/Kongressbericht/Report (Basel:
         Bärenreiter, 1951) 226–28. In German. See no. 289 in
         this volume.

Discusses Willaert's psalm settings for double chorus in the Venetian *cori
spezzati* style, in the collections published by Antonio Gardane between
1550 and 1557. *(David Bloom)*

1476 ZULAICA Y ARREGUI, José Gonzalo (José An-
as   tonio de Donostia). **La música de Juan**
         Anchieta, siglos XV-XVI [The music of Juan de
         Anchieta (15th-16th century)], *Congrés de la Societat
         Internacional de Musicologia* (Barcelona: Casa de
         Caritat, 1936). In Spanish. See no. 224 in this volume.

The conference report provides only a citation. Neither the text nor a summary of the paper was published here.

25 Baroque (1600 – 1750)

1477 ADLER, Israel. **Le MS Vm¹ de la Bibliothèque**
as   **Nationale (Cantate pour une circoncision dans**
         le Comtat Venaissin au dix-septième siècle)
         [The MS Vm¹ at the Bibliothèque Nationale (a
         17th-century cantata for a circumcision in the Comtat
         Venaissin)], *Haqŵngres ha'ŵlamy hašlyšy lemada'ey
         hayahadŵt* (Yerŵšalaym/Al-Quds: Hebrew Univer-
         sity/Ha'unybersytah ha'ibryt, 1965) 360. In French.
         See no. 435 in this volume.

Explores *F-Pn* MS Vm¹.1307, a cantata based on Hebrew religious poems
for a circumcision ceremony, composed by Louis Saladin (probably not of
Jewish origin) about 1680-1700. The work consists of preludes, dances,
and choruses for three soloists, mixed choir, and orchestra. It includes an
adaptation of a popular song, which might have been part of the traditional
melodic repertoire for circumcisions in the Comtat Venaissin. *(Tina Frühauf)*

1478 AERDE, Raymond Joseph Justin van. **Quelques**
as   **documents inédits concernant la musique dans**
         un village [Some unpublished documents concerning
         music in a village], *Annales du XXIIIᵉ congrès* (Gent:
         Siffer, 1914) III, 285–310. In French. See no. 89 in this
         volume.

Examines 17th- and 18th-c. documents on the musical life of the village of
Kalken in eastern Flanders.

1479 ARNHEIM, Amalie. **Belgische Komponisten**
as   **des 17. und 18. Jahrhunderts und ihre Bezie-**
         hungen zu Deutschland [Belgian composers of the
         17th and 18th centuries and their relations with Ger-
         many], *Annales du XXIIIᵉ congrès* (Gent: Siffer, 1914)
         III, 262–79. In German. See no. 89 in this volume.

Flemish composers, from Lassus to Gretry and Gossec, have strongly influenced musical style in Germany.

1480 ARNHEIM, Amalie. **Englische Suitenkom-**
as   **ponisten des XVII. Jahrhunderts und ihre in**
         Deutschland erschienenen Sammlungen [Eng-
         lish suite composers of the 17th century, and German
         collections of their works], *Report of the Fourth Con-
         gress of the International Musical Society* (London:
         Novello, 1912) 93–99. In German. See no. 71 in this
         volume.

Around 1600, English music and musicians could be found in many German courts. Dance music used by English comedians influenced German
dance music. Many of the English composers represented in German collections were also violists; the most notable were William Brade and
Thomas Simpson, whose influence on the development of the German instrumental music can be traced through the first half of the 17th c. *(author)*

1481 ARNHEIM, Amalie. **Über das Musikleben in**
as   **Bremen im 17. Jahrhundert** [On musical life in
         Bremen in the 17th century], *Haydn-Zentenarfeier*
         (Leipzig: Breitkopf & Härtel; Wien: Artaria, 1909)
         135–36. In German. See no. 65 in this volume.

Includes the subsequent panel discussion.

1482 ARNOLD, Denis. **The influence of ornamenta-**
as   **tion on the structure of early 17th century**
         church music, *Bericht über den siebenten inter-
         nationalen musikwissenschaftlichen Kongress* (Kassel:
         Bärenreiter, 1959) 57–58. See no. 390 in this volume.

After some unsuccessful attempts to mingle decorated solo lines with tutti
parts, Italian composers learned to demarcate the simple massed effects of
the ripieno from material assigned to soloists. The early decades of the 17th
c. saw the establishment of the sectional structure of Baroque church music
that would remain unaltered in its essentials through the era of Mozart and
Haydn. *(Carl Skoggard)*

1483 BAYART, Paul. **Drogon de St. Winnoc et**
as   **quelques autres compositeurs d'offices**
         liturgiques aux XIᵉ et XIIᵉ siècles [Drogon of St.
         Winoc and some other composers of liturgical Offices
         in the 11th and 12th centuries], *Annales du XXIIIᵉ
         congrès* (Gent: Siffer, 1914) III, 280–85. In French. See
         no. 89 in this volume.

Examines MSS found in Bergues of liturgical works composed in honor of
St. Winoc and St. Oswald, patrons of the monastery at Bergues. The style of
the works attributed to the monk Drogon (d. 1080), in particular, is analyzed and compared to that of the Notre Dame school of the same period.

1484 BĖLZA, Igor' Fĕdorovič. **Rosyjsko-polskie**
as   **stosunki muzyczne w wieku XVII i XVIII** [Rus-
         sian-Polish musical relations in the 17th and 18th centu-
         ries], *The book of the first international musicological
         congress devoted to the works of Frederick Chopin*
         (Warszawa: Państwowe Wydawnictwo Naukowe,
         1963) 507–09. In Polish. See no. 425 in this volume.

1485 BENARY, Peter. **Die Stellung der Melodielehre**
as   **in der Musiktheorie des 18. Jahrhunderts in**
         Deutschland [The place of the theory of melody in
         18th-century German music theory], *Bericht über den
         internationalen musikwissenschaftlichen Kongreß*
         (Kassel: Bärenreiter, 1963) 362–64. In German. See no.
         452 in this volume.

Discusses the views of theorists of especially the first half of the 18th c. on
melody in relation to counterpoint, basso continuo, and the style galant.
(David Bloom)

1486 BERGMANN, Walter. **Henry Purcell's use of**
as   **the recorder,** *Music libraries and instruments* (Lon-
         don: Hinrichsen, 1961) 227–33. *Illus., facs., music.* See
         no. 406 in this volume.

Purcell's recorder parts are meant for the three-piece Baroque instrument rather than the one-piece Renaissance variety, and for predominantly treble (alto) instruments. In his incidental stage music the recorder is associated with goddesses such as Venus, and with themes of peace, in opposition to warlike instruments like the trumpet. Because of its pagan associations Purcell did not use it in church music. *(Susan Poliniak)*

1487
as
BERNOULLI, Eduard. **Problem vokaler Kleinkunst aus dem 17. und beginnenden 18. Jahrhundert in der Schweiz** [The problem of minor vocal art from the end of the 17th and beginning of the 18th century in Switzerland], *Festschrift zum zweiten Kongreß der Internationalen Musikgesellschaft, verfaßt von Mitgliedern der Schweizerischen Landessektion und den Kongreßteilnehmern* (Basel: Reinhardt, 1906) I, 104–56. In German. See no. 54 in this volume.

1488
as
BESSELER, Heinrich. **Bach und das Mittelalter** [Bach and the Middle Ages], *Bericht über die Wissenschaftliche Bachtagung* (Leipzig: Peters, 1951) 108–30. In German. See no. 298 in this volume.

Bach is to the age of German music as are Pérotin to the Gothic era and Dufay to the Netherlandish period. Thus, the view of Bach as the culmination of the Middle Ages, becoming an anachronism in his own lifetime, must be revised. Evidence of Bach's relevance to all succeeding generations is seen in *Das wohltemperirte Clavier*. *(James Donald Anderson)*

1489
as
BLUME, Friedrich. **Begriff und Grenzen des Barock in der Musik** [The Baroque in music: The concept and its limits], *Manierismo, barocco, rococò: Concetti e termini—Convegno internazionale* (Roma: R. Accademia dei Lincei, 1962) 377–86. In German. See no. 422 in this volume.

The concept of the Baroque in music can, contrary to some opinions, be used in a musicologically coherent way; but it must be understood that the artistic unity of the Baroque period is built of contrast and contradiction, defined by the inclination to extremes and to contrasts leading to stylistic splits, as in Monteverdi's seconda prattica, which was meant to coexist with, not replace, the prima prattica. *(David Bloom)*

1490
as
BODKY, Erwin. **New contributions to the problem of the interpretation of Bach's keyboard works,** *Société Internationale de Musicologie, cinquième congrès/Internationale Gesellschaft für Musikwissenschaft, fünfter Kongreß/International Society for Musical Research, Fifth Congress* (Amsterdam: Vereniging voor Nederlandse Muziekgeschiedenis, 1953) 73–78. See no. 316 in this volume.

Musicologists have assumed that sound character should not enter into considerations about performance of the keyboard music of Bach's time. When the issue is viewed from the standpoint of playability, however, this assumption seems suspect. Only by assuming the exclusion of a coupler and of terrace dynamics is it possible to argue that Bach wrote fully one half of his keyboard music for clavichord. *(Tsipora Yosselevitch)*

⟶
BOETTICHER, Wolfgang. **Zum problem der Übergangsperiode der Musik 1580-1620** [The problem of the period of musical transition 1580-1620]. See no. 1244 in this volume.

1491
as
BOGHEN, Carlo Felice. **Bernardo Pasquini,** *Actes du Congrès d'histoire de l'art* (Paris: Presses Universitaires de France, 1923-1924) 856–66. In French. See no. 94 in this volume.

1492
as
BÓNIS, Ferenc. **Ungarische Musik im XVII.-XVIII. Jahrhundert** [Hungarian music in the 17th-18th centuries], *Musica antiqua Europae*

orientalis (Warszawa: Państwowe Wydawnictwo Naukowe, 1966). *Illus., facs.* In German. See no. 506 in this volume.

Discusses instruments, composers, MSS, and genres, including opera and dance music.

1493
as
BORRIS, Siegfried. **Johann Sebastian Bachs Unterweisung im Tonsatz** [Johann Sebastian Bach's teaching of composition], *Bericht über die Wissenschaftliche Bachtagung* (Leipzig: Peters, 1951) 210–17. In German. See no. 298 in this volume.

Some modern writers on Bach's compositional principles, including Ernst Kurth and Paul Hindemith, ignore both his own instructional methods and those of contemporaries such as Fux, Rameau, and Friedrich Erhard Niedt. Bach's perspective on music, and his teaching of composition, are rooted in polyphony bound together through harmony. He made his pupils into genuine musicians by retaining the teaching of basso continuo improvisation. His compositional instruction should be regarded as the teaching of musical craft rather than as a system of composition.

⟶
BRANCO, Luís de Freitas. **Les contrepointistes de l'école d'Évora** [The Évora school of contrapuntists]. See no. 4143 in this volume.

1494
as
BRAUN, Werner. **Echtheits- und Datierungsfragen im vokalen Frühwerk Georg Friedrich Händels** [Questions of authenticity and dating in Georg Friedrich Händel's early vocal works], *Händel-Ehrung der Deutschen Demokratischen Republik: Konferenzbericht* (Leipzig: VEB Deutscher Verlag für Musik, 1961) 61–71. *Music.* In German. See no. 408 in this volume.

Discusses the attribution to Händel of a 1704 St. John Passion, the cantata *Ach Herr, mich armen Sünder*, and the Easter dialogue *Triumph, ihr Christen, seid erfreut*, preserved in a MS dated 1714 and signed "G.F.H." in the music archive of the Evangelisch-Lutherisches Pfarramt St. Johannis, Müglen; the first two are almost certainly spurious. The psalm setting *Laudate pueri*, if it was composed in Halle, would have to be from before 1699; it is more likely to have been written in Hamburg. *(David Bloom)*

1495
as
BRAUN, Werner. **Johann Sebastiani (1622-1683) und die Musik in Königsberg** [Johann Sebastiani (1622-83) and music in Königsberg], *Norddeutsche und nordeuropäische Musik* (Kassel; New York: Bärenreiter, 1965) 113–19. In German. See no. 467 in this volume.

Surveys the social, musical, and theological context of Sebastiani's tenure as court kapellmeister in 1663-79, and reevaluates his work as a composer. His knowledge of contemporary Italian practice might have enabled him to make Königsberg a major center of the North German cantata, if not for the disarray caused by the court's and city's theological divisions. His secular music shows some daring, in its rejection of the ideal of full polyphony. *(David Bloom)*

1496
as
BRAUN, Werner. **Zur Parodie im 17. Jahrhundert** [Parody in the 17th century], *Bericht über den internationalen musikwissenschaftlichen Kongreß* (Kassel: Bärenreiter, 1963) 154–55. In German. See no. 452 in this volume.

Georg Quitschreiber's treatise *De parodia* (1611) illustrates the early Baroque notion of parody as style exercise, and an increased sensitivity to the idea of artistic property. *(David Bloom)*

1497
as
BRIQUET, Marie. **Deux motets inédits de Montéclair (1667-1737)** [Two unpublished motets by Montéclair (1667-1737)], *Bericht über den siebenten internationalen musikwissenschaftlichen Kongress* (Kassel: Bärenreiter, 1959) 75–75. In French. See no. 390 in this volume.

Describes the motets *O sacrum convivium* and *Properate huc populi*, written by Michel Pignolet de Montéclair in 1725. Both are preserved in *F-Pn* MS cote Vm.1775 bis (fonds Brossard T.1, n°s 9). Their original destination remains a matter of conjecture. What information is available stems from Sébastien de Brossard's inventory of his library, which dates from 1726. *(Carl Skoggard)*

1498 BRUNHOLD, Paul. **Un livre pièces de clavecin**
as **J.-F. d'Andrieu** [A book of harpsichord pieces by J.-F. Dandrieu], *Actes du Congrès d'histoire de l'art* (Paris: Presses Universitaires de France, 1923-1924) 918–21. In French. See no. 94 in this volume.
The pieces in the volume under discussion were written in the style of the great 18th-c. keyboardists. Jean-François Dandrieu's three later volumes from 1724 and onward break with these traditions, adopting instead the style of François Couperin. *(Vivian Conejero)*

⟶ BÜCKEN, Ernst. **Zur Frage der Begrenzung und Benennung der Stilwandlung im 18. Jahrhundert** [Delimiting and naming the change in style of the 18th century]. See no. 1733 in this volume.

1499 BUNDI, Gian. **Ein musikhistorisches**
as **Kuriosum aus dem Oberengadin** [A historic musical curiosity from the Oberengadin], *Bericht über den musikwissenschaftlichen Kongreß in Basel* (Leipzig: Breitkopf & Härtel, 1925) 106–09. In German. See no. 102 in this volume.
Discusses six music books used in the town of Zuoz, in the upper Engadine, containing sacred and secular works for four to eight voices. Included are madrigals by Monteverdi, Luca Marenzio, Pietro Phillipo Inglesi, Jan Pieterszoon Sweelinck, and Jacob Westerbaen. The high performance level of the choir of Zuoz is also considered. *(Sylvia Eversole)*

1500 BURNEY, Charles. **Un giudizio di Charles**
as **Burney** [An appraisal by Charles Burney], *G.B. Pergolesi, 1710-1736: Note e documenti, raccolti in occasione della settimana celebrativa* (Siena: Ticci Editore Libraio, 1942) 49. In Italian. See no. 273 in this volume.
A brief and favorable commentary on Pergolesi and his works.

1501 CALMUS, Georgy. **Das Théâtre de la Foire des**
as **Lesage (Paris 1712-1738) und seine Bedeutung für die Entwicklung der komischen Oper in Frankreich, England, und Deutschland** [The Théâtre de la Foire of Lesage (Paris 1712-1738) and its significance for the development of comic opera in France, England, and Germany], *Haydn-Zentenarfeier* (Leipzig: Breitkopf & Härtel; Wien: Artaria, 1909) 193–94. In German. See no. 65 in this volume.

1502 CASELLA, Alfredo. **Le composizioni sacre e**
as **vocali di Antonio Vivaldi** [The sacred vocal compositions of Antonio Vivaldi], *Antonio Vivaldi: Note e documenti sulla vita e sulle opere* (Siena: Accademia Musicale Chigiana, 1939) 15–22. In Italian. See no. 268 in this volume.
Critical appreciation of MS works in the Foà-Giordano collections of the Biblioteca Nazionale Universitaria, Turin.

1503 CERVELLI, Luisa. **Polifonia e monodia nel**
as **canto religioso popolare del cinquecento** [Polyphony and monody in the religious popular song of the 16th century], *Atti del Congresso internazionale di musiche popolari mediterranee e del Convegno dei bibliotecari musicali* (Palermo: De Magistris succ. V.

Bellotti, 1959) 63–69. In Italian. See no. 332 in this volume.
Survey of lauda publications of the period of the transition from madrigal to monody, 1563-1600, with particular attention to the composer Giovanni Animuccia. The eventual triumph of the instrumentally accompanied monody may be partly ascribed to its roots in Italian monophonic traditional song. *(David Bloom)*

1504 CHARLIER, Clément. **Un manuscrit musical**
as **mosan de 1728** [A 1728 music manuscript from the Meuse valley], *Congrès de Liège de la Fédération Archéologique et Historique de Belgique, 1932: XXIXe session—Annales* (Liège: n.p., 1932) 273–89. In French. See no. 197 in this volume.

1505 CHERBULIEZ, Antoine-Élisée. **La sarabande,**
as **la chaconne, la passacaille et la folia dans l'œuvre de J.S. Bach** [The saraband, the chaconne, the passacaille, and the folia in J.S. Bach's oeuvre], *Congrés de la Societat Internacional de Musicologia* (Barcelona: Casa de Caritat, 1936). In French. See no. 224 in this volume.
The conference report provides only a citation. Neither the text nor a summary of the paper was published here.

1506 CHIGI SARACINI, Guido. **Un musicien**
as **siennois du XVIIIe siècle: Azzolino Bernardino Della Ciaia, prêtre et chevalier de Saint-Étienne** [A Sienese musician of the 18th century: Azzolino Bernardino Della Ciaja, priest and knight of S. Stefano], *Actes du Congrès d'histoire de l'art* (Paris: Presses Universitaires de France, 1923-1924) 895–917. In Italian. See no. 94 in this volume.

1507 CHIGI SARACINI, Guido, ed. **Testimonianze**
as [Testimonies], *Antonio Vivaldi: Note e documenti sulla vita e sulle opere* (Siena: Accademia Musicale Chigiana, 1939) 37–40. In Italian. See no. 268 in this volume.
A brief collection of documents relating to Vivaldi's life and reception history, including an excerpt on the composer from Carlo Goldoni's *Mémoires* (Paris, 1787); a letter from Vivaldi to Guido Bentivoglio d'Aragona in Ferrara, dated 1737; and the original text of the dedication, to Ferdinand III, Grand Duke of Tuscany, of *L'estro armonico* (Amsterdam, 1711). *(Mark Stevens)*

1508 CHOMIŃSKI, Józef Michał. **Le technique**
as **polychorale vénitienne en Pologne** [Venetian polychoral technique in Poland], *Venezia e la Polonia nei secoli dal XVII al XIX* (Venezia: Istituto per la Collaborazione Culturale, 1965) 179–89. *Music.* In French. See no. 474 in this volume.
Mikołaj Zieleński's *Offertoria totius anni* and *Communiones totius anni* (Venice, 1611) use a polychoral technique indebted to that of Adrian Willaert. Its stylistic traits are analyzed and discussed. *(Sylvia Eversole)*

1509 CLERCX-LEJEUNE, Suzanne. **Le terme Ba-**
as **roque: Sa signification, son application à la musique** [The term Baroque: Its meaning, its application to music], *Les colloques de Wégimont. IV: Le Baroque musical—Recueil d'études sur la musique du XVIIe siècle* (Paris: Belles Lettres, 1963) 17–34. In French. See no. 386 in this volume.
Modern musicology has held that the origins of the Baroque in music, corresponding to that in the visual arts of the 17th c., may be discerned in the development of a new monodic style arising from the disintegration of the edifice of Renaissance polyphony in the later 16th c. But an opposed tendency, toward a continually denser polyphony, can also be seen, particularly in Monteverdi, who was equally comfortable in both styles. The essence of

the musical Baroque is to be found less in one technique or another than in the exploration of new musical materials of all kinds. *(David Bloom)*

1510
as

CLERCX-LEJEUNE, Suzanne *et al.* **Résolutions** [Resolutions], *Les colloques de Wégimont. IV: Le Baroque musical—Recueil d'études sur la musique du XVIIe siècle* (Paris: Belles Lettres, 1963) 267–85. In French. See no. 386 in this volume.

Concluding discussion from a symposium on music of the Baroque. Research on the period should concentrate on the concrete, avoiding overly general, distorting terminology. Musicologists should exercise an influence on the performance practice of Baroque music, through the preparation of practical editions and by involving themselves directly in concert performance. The panelists were Suzanne Clercx-Lejeune, Macario Santiago KASTNER, Denise LAUNAY, Élisabeth LEBEAU, Jean LEJEUNE, Günther MASSENKEIL, Jeremy NOBLE, Miguel QUEROL GAVALDÁ, Robert WANGERMÉE, and Robert Erich WOLF. *(David Bloom)*

1511
as

COLLAER, Paul. **Lyrisme baroque et tradition populaire** [Baroque lyricism and folk tradition], *Studia musicologica Academiae Scientiarum Hungaricae* VII (1965) 25–40. *Music.* In French. See no. 478 in this volume.

For an abstract, see no. 1512.

1512
as

COLLAER, Paul. **Lyrisme Baroque et tradition populaire** [Baroque lyricism and the popular culture], *Les colloques de Wégimont. IV: Le Baroque musical—Recueil d'études sur la musique du XVIIe siècle* (Paris: Belles Lettres, 1963) 109–30. *Music, charts, diagr., transcr.* In French. See no. 386 in this volume.

The novel declamatory style of Monteverdi's *Il combattimento di Tancredi e Clorinda* (1624) is derived from the traditional music of the *cantastorie* of central and southern Italy, who improvise texts in a loose ottava rima to a fixed Hypodorian melodic structure, as shown be examples of ottava singing from Campagna di Roma and Venice, in field recordings in the collections of the Centro Nazionale Studi di Musica Popolare. *(David Bloom)*

1513
as

COOPERSMITH, Jacob Maurice. **Concert of unpublished music by Georg Friedrich Händel: Program notes,** *Papers read at the International Congress of Musicology* (New York: Music Educators National Conference, 1944) 213–25. *Illus., facs., charts, diagr.* See no. 266 in this volume.

The program included *Alla caccia (Diana cacciatrice)* (ca. 1707); *Benchè mi sia crudele,* from *Ottone, re di Germania* (original version 1723; version for contralto possibly 1733); sonata for oboe and continuo (before 1724); *Sarei troppo felice* (cantata for solo soprano and basso continuo, 1707); sonata for violin, violoncello, and continuo (1705); *Hendel, non può mia musa* (1708); sonata for two flutes and continuo (before 1733); *È troppo bella, troppo amorosa,* from *Ho fuggito amore anch'io* (1722-25); *Ero e Leandro* (cantata, ca. 1708); and *Gli dirai,* duet from *Alessandro Severo* (before 1738). *(Michael Adelson)*

⟶

COSMA, Viorel. **Aspects de la culture musicale sur le territoire de la Roumanie entre le XIVe et le XVIIIe siècle** [Aspects of the musical culture in the territory of Romania between the 14th and 18th centuries]. See no. 1279 in this volume.

1514
as

CROLL, Gerhard. **Zur Vorgeschichte der "Mannheimer"** [The prehistory of the "Mannheimers"], *Bericht über den siebenten internationalen musikwissenschaftlichen Kongress* (Kassel: Bärenreiter, 1959) 82–83. In German. See no. 390 in this volume.

Sixteen members of the Mannheim court orchestra as constituted in 1723 came from the Innsbruck court chapel which Karl Philipp had kept before he relocated his court to Neuberg an der Donau and then Mannheim, in 1720; 26 can be traced back to the Düsseldorf ensemble maintained by his

brother, Johann Wilhelm. Most of the string players listed in the 1723 list came from Düsseldorf, whereas most of the wind players came from Innsbruck. The court ensembles of both Innsbruck and Düsseldorf can be traced further back. They share a common origin in the fine chapel that Karl Philipp, then Count Palatinate, maintained in Saxony between 1689 and 1707 (when he moved to Innsbruck). But some of the best-known members of the Mannheim ensemble came from other places, including Brussels, the Romagna region of Italy, and Bohemia. *(Carl Skoggard)*

1515
as

CUDWORTH, Charles. **Pergolesi, Ricciotti and the Count of Bentinck,** *Société Internationale de Musicologie, cinquième congrès/Internationale Gesellschaft für Musikwissenschaft, fünfter Kongreß/International Society for Musical Research, Fifth Congress* (Amsterdam: Vereniging voor Nederlandse Muziekgeschiedenis, 1953) 127–31. See no. 316 in this volume.

Pergolesi was a particularly profitable target for forgers. His six concerts for strings are identical with a set published under the name of Ricciotti, where a dedicatory letter to the count, statesman, and music lover Bentinck is found. *(Tsipora Yosselevitch)*

1516
as

CUMMINGS, William Hayman. **Matthew Locke: Composer for the church and theatre,** *Report of the Fourth Congress of the International Musical Society* (London: Novello, 1912) 100–06. See no. 71 in this volume.

A biography.

⟶

CVETKO, Dragotin. **La musique slovène du XVIe au XVIIIe siècle** [Slovenian music from the 16th to the 18th centuries]. See no. 1280 in this volume.

1517
as

CVETKO, Dragotin. **Ein unbekanntes *Inventarium librorum musicalium* aus Jahre 1620** [An unknown *Inventarium librorum musicalium* from the year 1620], *Bericht über den siebenten internationalen musikwissenschaftlichen Kongress* (Kassel: Bärenreiter, 1959) 84. In German. See no. 390 in this volume.

The *Inventarium librorum muscalium* was prepared in 1620 at the behest of the prince-bishop of Ljubljana, Thomas Hren, and is now in the diocesan archive of Ljubljana. It lists some 300 individual works and collections of numerous composers from the second half of the 16th and the early 17th c. Most of the music is religious, and shows a strong Italian orientation; local composers are nearly absent. Not many of the items listed are known to have survived. *(Carl Skoggard)*

1518
as

DADELSEN, Georg von. **Bach-Probleme** [Bach problems], *Report of the Eighth Congress of the International Musicological Society. I: Papers* (Kassel: Bärenreiter, 1961) 236–49. In German. See no. 439 in this volume.

Outlines the major issues as of ca. 1961 in the chronology and attribution of Bach's works.

1519
as

DADELSEN, Georg von. **Zu den Vorreden des Michael Praetorius** [The prefatory writings of Michael Praetorius], *Bericht über den internationalen musikwissenschaftlichen Kongreß Wien Mozartjahr 1956* (Graz; Köln: Böhlau, 1958) 107–11. In German. See no. 365 in this volume.

The introductions to Praetorius's *Musae Sioniae...ander Theil* (1607), *Terpsichore* (1612), and *Urania* (1613), and other prefatory writings have a more concrete relationship to his musical practice than do his strictly theoretical writings. Examples are adduced of his treatment of rhythmic proportion, note values, and signatures. *(David Bloom)*

1520
as

DAHLHAUS, Carl. *Cribrum musicum*: **Der Streit zwischen Scacchi und Siefert** [*Cribrum musicum*: The quarrel of Scacchi and Siefert], *Norddeutsche und nordeuropäische Musik* (Kassel; New York: Bärenreiter, 1965) 108–12. In German. See no. 467 in this volume.

Marco Scacchi's 1643 polemic against Paul Siefert provides an early example of the term classic (from Latin *classicus*, a taxpayer, as opposed to *proletarius*) to refer both to older and modern composers. His critique of Siefert is on the grounds that Siefert fails to maintain either style. Some of his specific criticisms are ill founded. *(David Bloom)*

1521
as

DAHLHAUS, Carl. **Die *Figurae superficiales* in den Traktaken Christoph Bernhards** [*Figurae superficiales* in the treatises of Christoph Bernhard], *Bericht über den Internationalen musikwissenschaftlichen Kongress* (Kassel: Bärenreiter, 1954) 135–37. In French. See no. 319 in this volume.

Did the recourse of Baroque theorists to the concepts of rhetoric reflect an actual dependence of Baroque music on the rules and forms of poetry and elocution? Alternatively, theorists may have drawn on rhetoric to account for emergent musical phenomena that no longer fit under traditional concepts of music theory. Christoph Bernhard's category *figurae superficiales* was adopted by him to explain emancipated motions within basso continuo voices in terms of conventional contrapuntal theory. Thus the alternative explanation of the relation between Baroque music and rhetorical theory of rhetoric seems valid for Bernhard. As it happens, there is a long history of theorists' making use of the concept of "figures" to fit irregularities into received theories (while failing to identify the principle that would legitimize such phenomena per se). *(Carl Skoggard)*

1522
as

DAMERINI, Adelmo. *La morte di San Giuseppe*, **G.B. Pergolesi, 1710-1736: Note e documenti, raccolti in occasione della settimana celebrativa** (Siena: Ticci Editore Libraio, 1942) 63–70. *Facs., music.* In Italian. See no. 273 in this volume.

Stylistic similarities between the early oratorio and the composer's later music are noted.

1523
as

DART, Thurston. **English music and musicians in 17th century Holland,** *Société Internationale de Musicologie, cinquième congrès/Internationale Gesellschaft für Musikwissenschaft, fünfter Kongreß/International Society for Musical Research, Fifth Congress* (Amsterdam: Vereniging voor Nederlandse Muziekgeschiedenis, 1953) 139–45. *Bibliog.* See no. 316 in this volume.

Johan Thysius's lute book includes English music, some of which is included in Fitzwilliam Virginal Book. Traveling theater companies contributed to the dissemination of English music in Holland. Jigs and other traditional tunes also form part of the English heritage in Holland.

1524
as

DEHNERT, Max. **Neue Aufgaben der biographischen Bachforschung** [New tasks for biographical research on Bach], *Bericht über die Wissenschaftliche Bachtagung* (Leipzig: Peters, 1951) 193–200. In German. See no. 298 in this volume.

Friedrich Blume, in his *J.S. Bach im Wandel der Geschichte* (1947), considered social structure as the parent material of creativity; social history should give new impetus to biographical studies of Bach. Hans Pfitzner's and Ferruccio Busoni's theories of creativity and the insights of Albert Schweitzer retain their usefulness but can now be supplemented with sociological methods of research. *(James Donald Anderson)*

1525
as

DELLA CORTE, Andrea. **Il Barocco e la musica** [The Baroque and music], *Manierismo, barocco, rococò: Concetti e termini—Convegno internazionale* (Roma: R. Accademia dei Lincei, 1962) 361–75. In Italian. See no. 422 in this volume.

A survey of musicologists' views on the application of the term *Baroque* to music of the period 1600-1750 leads to the conclusion that it cannot be given a concrete meaning. Both as a comprehensive generic term and as a specific critical description it covers too much ground to be useful. The analogy between music and the visual arts of the period is largely superficial. *(Susan Poliniak)*

1526
as

DENT, Edward Joseph. **Giuseppe Maria Buini,** *Report of the Fourth Congress of the International Musical Society* (London: Novello, 1912) 106–13. *Charts, diagr.* See no. 71 in this volume.

Discusses the operas of the Bolognese composer Giuseppe Maria Buini (1687-1739, also known as Buina or Bovina).

1527
as

DOORSLAER, Georges van. **Connaît-on des documents relatifs au séjour de Jérôme Frescobaldi à Malines?** [Are there any known documents relating to Girolamo Frescobaldi's stay in Mechelen?], *Fédération Archéologique et Historique de Belgique: Annales du XXIIᵉ congrès. I: Documents et compte rendu; II: Rapports & mémoires* (Mechelen: Godenne, 1911) II, 733–34. In French. See no. 73 in this volume.

Discusses Frescobaldi's relationship to the cathedral of Sint-Rombout at Mechelen.

1528
as

DOWNES, Edward O.D. **The Neapolitan tradition in opera,** *Report of the Eighth Congress of the International Musicological Society. II: Reports* (Kassel: Bärenreiter, 1962) 132–34. See no. 440 in this volume.

A report on a discussion on the concept of a Neapolitan tradition in Italian opera of the early 18th c., by Gerhard CROLL, David DI CHIERA, Edward O.D. DOWNES, Federico GHISI, Donald Jay GROUT, Helmut HUCKE, Oscar MISCHIATI, Sergio PAGANELLI, Nino PIRROTTA, Claudio SARTORI, Luigi Ferdinando TAGLIAVINI, and Hellmuth Christian WOLFF, based on the papers by Hucke and Downes abstracted as nos. 1529 and 1580, respectively, in this volume.

1529
as

DOWNES, Edward O.D. **The Neapolitan tradition in opera,** *Report of the Eighth Congress of the International Musicological Society. I: Papers* (Kassel: Bärenreiter, 1961) 277–84. See no. 439 in this volume.

No evidence justifies the concept of a Neapolitan school of opera. In general, the stylistic and chronological terms applied to general music history are more appropriate to opera than geographic terms and their implication of a *genius loci*; the history of Baroque and pre-Classic opera in Naples is a clear case in point. *(David Bloom)*

1530
as

DUFOURCQ, Norbert. **France et Italie: La place occupée par Michel-Richard Delalande dans la musique occidentale aux XVIIᵉ et XVIIIᵉ siècles** [France and Italy: The position of Michel-Richard de Lalande in Western music of the 17th and 18th centuries], *Perspectives de la musique sacrée à la lumière de l'encyclique* Musicae sacrae disciplina (Paris: conference, 1959) 171–77. In French. See no. 379 in this volume.

The question of musical relations between France and Italy is most acute for the period 1660-1740, the period dominated by the Versailles school and the grand motet, in which Lalande played a central role. A summary is cited as no. 1532 in this volume. *(Meredith A. McCutcheon)*

1531
as

DUFOURCQ, Norbert. **Pierre Baillon: Facteur de clavecins, d'orgues, graveur de musique et organiste français** [Pierre Baillon: French maker of harpsichords and organs, music engraver, and French organist], *Music libraries and instruments* (London: Hinrichsen, 1961) 196–200. In French. See no. 406 in this volume.

A short biography of Pierre Baillon (d. 1681).

1532
as

DUFOURCQ, Norbert. **Place de M.-R. Delalande dans la musique religieuse occidentale du XVIIème siècle** [The position of M.-R. de Lalande in Western religious music of the 17th century], *Revue musicale* 239-240 (1957) 71–72. In French. See no. 378 in this volume.

An abridged version of the conference paper is abstracted as no. 1530 in this volume.

1533
as

DÜRR, Alfred. **Gedanken zu J.S. Bachs Umarbeitungen eigener Werke** [Thoughts on J.S. Bach's rearrangements of his own works], *Bericht über den internationalen musikwissenschaftlichen Kongreß* (Kassel: Bärenreiter, 1957) 75–77. In German. See no. 356 in this volume.

The rearrangements can be divided into three categories: parodies, transcriptions, and new versions. The parodied movements in the B-minor Mass suggest that it was not intended for repeated performances in Leipzig. *(David Bloom)*

1534
as

DÜRR, Alfred. **Zur Chronologie der Weimarer Kantaten J.S. Bachs** [Toward a chronology of J.S. Bach's Weimar cantatas], *Kongreß-Bericht: Gesellschaft für Musikforschung* (Kassel; Basel: Bärenreiter, 1950) 120–21. In German. See no. 299 in this volume.

Summarizes the author's book *Studien über die frühen Kantaten J.S. Bachs* (Leipzig, 1951); an expanded, updated version of the book (Wiesbaden: Breitkopf & Härtel, 1977) is abstracted as RILM ^1977 4520.

1535
as

EGGEBRECHT, Hans Heinrich. **Bach und Leibniz** [Bach and Leibniz], *Bericht über die Wissenschaftliche Bachtagung* (Leipzig: Peters, 1951) 431–43. In German. See no. 298 in this volume.

Discusses parallels between Bach's compositional procedure and Leibniz's thought.

1536
as

ELLER, Rudolf. **Nationale Bedingtheiten des europäischen Instrumentalstiles** [National factors in European instrumental style], *Bericht über den Internationalen musikwissenschaftlichen Kongress* (Kassel: Bärenreiter, 1954) 259–62. In German. See no. 319 in this volume.

During the Baroque era, Italian composers tended to remain within the constraints of the instrumental medium they were using, to "compose out" of the medium. The music of German composers seems less conditioned by the medium being used. One indication of this freedom from the medium is seen in the numerous instrumental transcriptions made by German composers, both of vocal and instrumental works. Sometimes these arrangements demand too much of the instrument for which they are made (whereas the characteristic Italian fault is virtuosity unalloyed with musical substance). This dichotomy between German and Italian attitudes suggests that there are issues that may precede, or be more fundamental than, the question of music's vocal or instrumental character. *(Carl Skoggard)*

1537
as

ELLER, Rudolf. **Zur Frage Bach-Vivaldi** [The question of Bach and Vivaldi], *Bericht über den internationalen musikwissenschaftlichen Kongreß* (Kassel: Bärenreiter, 1957) 80–85. In German. See no. 356 in this volume.

In some of Bach's arrangements for keyboard of Vivaldi's string concertos (BWV 594, 975, and 980), certain movements deviate strongly from Vivaldi's originals and others are altogether new. The changes are discussed in the light of Bach's own developing concerto style. *(David Bloom)*

1538
as

EMERY, Walter. **On evidence of derivation**, *Report of the Eighth Congress of the International Musicological Society. I: Papers* (Kassel: Bärenreiter, 1961) 249–52. *Music, charts, diagr.* See no. 439 in this volume.

Difficulties in determining the genealogical relationships among multiple sources of J.S. Bach's works are illustrated with regard to sources for the canonic variations on *Vom Himmel hoch*, BWV 769.

1539
as

ENGEL, Hans. **Soziologisches Porträt Johann Sebastian Bachs** [A sociological portrait of Johann Sebastian Bach], *Kongreß-Bericht: Gesellschaft für Musikforschung* (Kassel; Basel: Bärenreiter, 1950) 222–26. In German. See no. 299 in this volume.

1540
as

ENGELBRECHT, Christiane. **Eine Sonata con voce von Giovanni Gabrieli** [A sonata with voice by Giovanni Gabrieli], *Bericht über den internationalen musikwissenschaftlichen Kongreß* (Kassel: Bärenreiter, 1957) 88–89. *Music.* In German. See no. 356 in this volume.

A setting for 20 voices of *Dulcis Iesu, patris imago* has much in common with the *Sonata sopra Sancta Maria* of Monteverdi's 1610 Vespers, and provides new evidence for the close relationship between Gabrieli and Monteverdi. *(David Bloom)*

1541
as

ENGLÄNDER, Richard. **Händel auf der schwedischen Bühne** [Händel on the Swedish stage], *Händel-Ehrung der Deutschen Demokratischen Republik: Konferenzbericht* (Leipzig: VEB Deutscher Verlag für Musik, 1961) 251–55. In German. See no. 408 in this volume.

The Stockholm hovkapellmästare Johan Helmich Roman (1694-1758) took an interest in Händel's operas and mounted a Swedish-language concert version of *Acis and Galatea* in 1734; a staging of the same work, again in Swedish, figured prominently in the repertoire of the Kungliga Teater from its first season, 1773, to 1780. Otherwise, the performance of Händel's operas began in 1950, when *Orlando furioso* was staged at the Drottningholm Slottsteater. The success of the 1959 Kungliga Teater production of *Alcina* may mark a new phase. *(David Bloom)*

1542
as

EPSTEIN, Peter. **J.A. Herbsts geistliche Kompositionen** [J.A. Herbst's sacred compositions], *Bericht über den I. musikwissenschaftlichen Kongress der Deutschen Musikgesellschaft in Leipzig* (Wiesbaden: Breitkopf & Härtel, 1926) 368–72. *Music, charts, diagr.* In German. See no. 120 in this volume.

Johann Andreas Herbst developed a distinctive style of through-composition of large portions of scripture, notably in the *Offenbarung Johannis* (1634). He is also significant as a pioneer in the development of the cantata. His use of modes, of cori spezzati, and of instruments is also discussed. *(William Renwick)*

1543
as

FEININGER, Laurence. **Die katholische Kirchenmusik in Rom zwischen 1600 und 1800: Eine unfassbare Lacune in der Musikgeschichte** [Catholic church music in Rome between 1600 and 1800: An incomprehensible gap in music history], *Bericht über den internationalen musikwissenschaftlichen Kongreß* (Kassel: Bärenreiter, 1963) 147–49. In German. See no. 452 in this volume.

A sequence of significant composers whose names are now little known, from Orazio Benevoli to Giuseppe Jannacconi, devoted themselves in Rome to the production of liturgical music that remained entirely independent of the musical trends of the time, in a closed local tradition. *(David Bloom)*

1544
as

FEININGER, Laurence. **Orazio Benevoli (1605-1672)**, *Atti del [I] Congresso internazionale di musica sacra* (Tournai: Desclée, 1952) 298–99. In Italian. See no. 303 in this volume.

1545
as

FELIX, Werner. **Händel und Weißenfels** [Händel and Weißenfels], *Händel-Ehrung der Deutschen*

Demokratischen Republik: Konferenzbericht (Leipzig: VEB Deutscher Verlag für Musik, 1961) 53–60. In German. See no. 408 in this volume.

Weißenfels became known for its intense cultivation of music after the ducal court of Sachsen-Weißenfels relocated there from Halle in 1680, and for cultivation of the German language (Weißenfels was one of the first German courts to replace French with German as the court language); the musical character of the town and court life is exemplified by the career and writings of the court Konzertmeister and librarian Johann Beer (1655-1700). The young Händel, whose childhood visits to Weißenfels are a familiar story, may have been influenced by its atmosphere in a profound way. *(David Bloom)*

1546 FELLER, Marilyn. **The new style of Guilio**
as **Caccini, member of the Florentine Camerata,** *Bericht über den siebenten internationalen musikwissenschaftlichen Kongress* (Kassel: Bärenreiter, 1959) 102–04. See no. 390 in this volume.

Giulio Caccini's earliest surviving monodic song, *Io che da ciel*, dates from 1589. It and his *O benedetto giorno*, a lost monodic song from the same year, represent the first effort by any composer to put ancient Greek theory, long known and already discussed by the Florentine Camerata, seriously into practice. *Io che da ciel* appears crude because Caccini still had to devise notation to convey his new conception. If his monodies of the 1590s are examined in chronological order, one notes an increasing notational command, a clarification and simplification of writing. The later songs also contain new effects, which Caccini was always seeking. His finest and most mature music is preserved in the collection *Nuove musiche e nuova maniera di scriverle* (Venice, 1614). *(Carl Skoggard)*

1547 FELLERER, Karl Gustav. **Musikalische**
as **Beziehungen zwischen den Niederlanden und Deutschland im 17. Jht** [Musical relationships between the Netherlands and Germany in the 17th century], *Société Internationale de Musicologie, cinquième congrès/Internationale Gesellschaft für Musikwissenschaft, fünfter Kongreß/International Society for Musical Research, Fifth Congress* (Amsterdam: Vereniging voor Nederlandse Muziekgeschiedenis, 1953) 181–88. In German. See no. 316 in this volume.

1548 FELLERER, Karl Gustav. **Der Stile antico in der**
as **katholischen Kirchenmusik des 18. Jahrhunderts** [The stile antico in Catholic church music of the 18th century], *Beethoven-Zentenarfeier: Internationaler musikhistorischer Kongress* (Wien: Universal, 1927) 244–46. In German. See no. 142 in this volume.

The *a cappella* polyphonic style of church music associated with Palestrina continued to be used, especially in Italy, throughout the Baroque, by composers many of whom also wrote in stile moderno. *(David Bloom)*

1549 FERAND, Ernest Thomas. **Über verzierte**
as **Parodiekantaten im frühen 18. Jahrhundert** [Embellished parody cantatas in the early 18th century], *Bericht über den internationalen musikwissenschaftlichen Kongreß Wien Mozartjahr 1956* (Graz; Köln: Böhlau, 1958) 216–19. In German. See no. 365 in this volume.

Discusses ornamentation in the duet arrangements of Scarlatti arias in Francesco Durante's XII *duetti da camera*; a variant MS of the work, *I-Rsc* G.302; and embellishments of Giovanni Bononcini's *Divertimenti da camera*, in a MS by Carlo Antonio Benati in the collections of the Liceo Musicale, Bologna. An English-language version is published in *Musical quarterly* XLIX (1958). *(David Bloom)*

1550 FISCHER, Kurt von. **C.P.E. Bachs Variationen-**
as **werke** [C.P.E. Bach's variation works], *Société Internationale de Musicologie, cinquième congrès/Internationale Gesellschaft für Musikwissenschaft, fünfter*

Kongreß/International Society for Musical Research, Fifth Congress (Amsterdam: Vereniging voor Nederlandse Muziekgeschiedens, 1953) 189–90. In German. See no. 316 in this volume.

An earlier version is published in *Revue belge de musicologie* VI (1952).

1551 FISCHER, Wilhelm. **Zur Chronologie der**
as **Klaviersuiten J.S. Bachs** [On the chronology of J.S. Bach's keyboard suites], *Bericht über den musikwissenschaftlichen Kongreß in Basel* (Leipzig: Breitkopf & Härtel, 1925) 127–30. In German. See no. 102 in this volume.

Internal and external evidence suggests that the French suites were composed after the English suites and before the partitas. The contrasting treatment of individual movements (courante, sarabande, and gigue), contrapuntal strictness, and meter show that the French suites could be a transitional phase between the English suites and the partitas, rather than a preliminary study for the English suites.

1552 FLEISCHHAUER, Günter. **Händel und die**
as **Antike** [Händel and antiquity], *Händel-Ehrung der Deutschen Demokratischen Republik: Konferenzbericht* (Leipzig: VEB Deutscher Verlag für Musik, 1961) 87–93. In German. See no. 408 in this volume.

Surveys Händel's operas and choral works whose texts are based on Greek mythology or Hellenistic and Roman history, in the context of the classical-humanist culture of his time in Germany, Italy, and England. An extended discussion of the same topic is abstracted as RILM [1983]4785. *(David Bloom)*

1553 FORCHERT, Arno. **Choralmotette und**
as **Choralkonzert: Zur Bedeutung Italiens für die evangelische Kirchenmusik** [Choral motet and vocal concerto: The significance of Italy in Lutheran church music], *Musica sacra in unserer Zeit* (Berlin: Merseburger, 1960) 68–78. In German. See no. 403 in this volume.

1554 FROTSCHER, Gotthold. **Ein Danziger**
as **Orgelbuch des 18. Jahrhunderts** [A Gdańsk organ book of the 18th century], *Bericht über den I. musikwissenschaftlichen Kongress der Deutschen Musikgesellschaft in Leipzig* (Wiesbaden: Breitkopf & Härtel, 1926) 284–85. In German. See no. 120 in this volume.

This 1747 organ book, from the library of St. John's church, contains chorale variations by Daniel Magnus Gronau. Interesting features are a variation for pedal solo, registration indications, and directions for playing on three manuals at once. *(William Renwick)*

1555 GARDNER, Johann von. **Le psautier chanté en**
as **slavon au XVIIe siècle** [The psalter sung in Slavonic in the 17th century], *Perspectives de la musique sacrée à la lumière de l'encyclique Musicae sacrae disciplina* (Paris: conference, 1959) 346–52. *Music*. In French. See no. 379 in this volume.

In contrast to current practice in the celebration of the morning and evening Offices in the Russian Orthodox church, where the psalms of the kathismata cycle are recited recto tono, they were sung from the late 16th c. up to the reform of Patriarch Nikon a century later. Examples of the melodies used are taken from a MS in the collection of the Bayerische Staatsbibliothek (*D-Mbs* cod.mon.ii). *(David Bloom)*

1556 GARROS, Madeleine. **Les motets à voix seule**
as **de Guillaume Gabriel Nivers** [The motets for solo voice by Guillaume Gabriel Nivers], *Bericht über den siebenten internationalen musikwissenschaftlichen Kongress* (Kassel: Bärenreiter, 1959) 108–10. In French. See no. 390 in this volume.

The 61 motets for solo voice in Nivers's *Motets à voix seule accompagnée de la bass continue...*, issued by Ballard in 1689, are the first such works to be composed in France, with the possible exception of motets by Nicolas-Antoine Lebègue that were advertised in 1687 but do not survive. Nivers would have written his motets for the Offices celebrated at St. Cyr, a royal residence, where he had the principal musical duties. The 1689 publication is described, as is Nivers's style. Little interest was shown in these works outside St. Cyr and some related convents. *(Carl Skoggard)*

1557 GEIRINGER, Karl. **Unbekannte Werke von**
as **Nachkommen J.S. Bachs in amerikanischen Sammlungen** [Unknown works by descendants of J.S. Bach in American collections], *Bericht über den siebenten internationalen musikwissenschaftlichen Kongress* (Kassel: Bärenreiter, 1959) 110–12. In German. See no. 390 in this volume.
Discusses musical sources in the U.S. for members of the Bach family, with particular attention to the holdings of the Moravian Church in Bethlehem, Pennsylvania, and Winston-Salem, North Carolina; the Stellfeld collection at the University of Michigan at Ann Arbor; and the Library of Congress, Washington, D.C. *(Carl Skoggard)*

1558 GERSTENBERG, Walter. **Motetten- und**
as **Liedstil bei Ludwig Senfl** [Motet style and song style in Ludwig Senfl], *Compte rendu/Kongressbericht/Report* (Basel: Bärenreiter, 1951) 121–25. In German. See no. 289 in this volume.
Senfl is the central figure among German musicians born near the end of the 15th c. His Latin motets are more dependent on Netherlandish influence, particularly that of Desprez, than his German-language polyphonic lied compositions, with their reflection of the regular stresses of German speech; the same rhythmic qualities can be found, however, in the motets as well. *(David Bloom)*

1559 GHISI, Federico. **La musique religieuse de**
as **Marco da Gagliano à Santa Maria del Fiore Florence** [The religious music of Marco da Gagliano at Santa Maria del Fiore, Florence], *Compte rendu/Kongressbericht/Report* (Basel: Bärenreiter, 1951) 125–28. In French. See no. 289 in this volume.
Musical documents that were moved from the chapter room of Santa Maria del Fiore to the Museo dell'Opera del Duomo include numerous polyphonic works by Gagliano, many unpublished. *(Scott Fruehwald)*

1560 GHISI, Federico. **The oratorios of Giacomo**
as **Carissimi in Hamburg Staats-Bibliothek,** *Kongreß-Bericht: Gesellschaft für Musikforschung* (Kassel; Basel: Bärenreiter, 1950) 103–07. See no. 299 in this volume.
Discusses Carissimi's unpublished and unknown oratorios, housed at the Staats-Bibliothek Hamburg (now Staats- und Universitätsbibliothek Carl von Ossietzky), drawing on characters, use of chorus, and instrumentation.

1561 GLAHN, Henrik. **Entwicklungszüge innerhalb**
as **des evangelischen Kirchengesanges des 16. Jhts im Lichte vergleichender Quellenforschung** [Developments in the 16th-century Lutheran hymn in the light of comparative source studies], *Société Internationale de Musicologie, cinquième congrès/Internationale Gesellschaft für Musikwissenschaft, fünfter Kongreß/International Society for Musical Research, Fifth Congress* (Amsterdam: Vereniging voor Nederlandse Muziekgeschiedenis, 1953) 199–210. In German. See no. 316 in this volume.

1562 GOTTRON, Adam. **Joseph Gabler in Mainz,**
as *Der Barock: Seine Orgeln und seine Musik in Oberschwaben* (Berlin: Merseburger, 1952) 82–84. *Maps.* In German. See no. 305 in this volume.

Recent research on the life of the Ochsenhausen-born organ builder Joseph Gabler provides information on his life in Mainz in 1719-29 and 1733-37. *(David Bloom)*

1563 GRAESER, Wolfgang. **Joh. Seb. Bachs *Kunst***
as ***der Fuge*** [Johann Sebastian Bach's *Die Kunst der Fuge*], *Bericht über den musikwissenschaftlichen Kongreß in Basel* (Leipzig: Breitkopf & Härtel, 1925) 151–52. In German. See no. 102 in this volume.
Breitkopf & Härtel, together with the Neue Bach-Gesellschaft, have decided to publish *Die Kunst der Fuge* following the new form in the Bach-Gesellschaft edition. A performance edition and a facsimile of the Berlin autograph will follow, with the scholarly notes to be published in the 1924 *Bach-Jahrbuch* XXI (1924), 1-104.

1564 GRAUPNER, Friedrich. **Johann Sebastian**
as **Bach als Musikerzieher** [Johann Sebastian Bach as music teacher], *Bericht über die Wissenschaftliche Bachtagung* (Leipzig: Peters, 1951) 201–09. In German. See no. 298 in this volume.
Bach's limited education made it difficult for him to fulfill the reponsibility of providing his students in Leipzig with a classical background and sometimes led to conflict with Johann Matthias Gesner and Johann August Ernesti, successive rectors of the Thomaskirche. On the other hand, Bach did have success with his private students. Autodidacticism led him to focus less on information than practical skill and personal creativity. His approach recalls the views of Konstantin D. Ušinskij, founder of Russian scientific pedagogy. *(James Donald Anderson)*

1565 GROUT, Donald Jay. **The music of the Italian**
as **theatre at Paris, 1682-97,** *Papers of the American Musicological Society* (Philadelphia: American Musicological Society, 1946) 158–70. *Music.* See no. 272 in this volume.
Evaristo Gherardi, a lead actor with the Comédie-Italienne, Paris, edited a collection of plays performed by the company 1682-97, which was first published in 1698. A definitive six-volume version was issued in 1700, under the title *Le Théâtre Italien de Gherardi ou Recueil général de toutes les Comédies et scènes françaises jouées par les Comédiens*; in this edition 143 Italian arias and duets, French airs, and French chansons used in the performances are appended (out of 340 musical numbers mentioned in the plays' texts). The few identified composers include the veteran Molière actor Philibert Gassaud, a M. de Masse, and the Roman organist and composer Paolo Lorenzini; other composers include almost certainly Jean-Claude Gilliers and probably Marc-Antoine Charpentier. Analysis of this music adds important details to our picture of the early history of opéra comique at the transition point between the comédies-ballets of Molière and Lully and the style of the early 18th c. represented by the Théâtre de la Foire. *(David Bloom)*

1566 GUDEWILL, Kurt. **Melchior Franck und das**
as **geistliche Konzert** [Melchior Franck and the spiritual concerto], *Bericht über den siebenten internationalen musikwissenschaftlichen Kongress* (Kassel: Bärenreiter, 1959) 120–23. In German. See no. 390 in this volume.
An analytic survey of Franck's spiritual concertos, which appear in four collections of his music issued between 1616 and 1636. Franck is a consummate master, and his spiritual concertos make use of nearly every resource then available, including those of the Italian Baroque. However, Franck was slower to adopt Italian features than either Schütz or Johann Hermann Schein. *(Carl Skoggard)*

1567 GUILLAUME, Maurice. **Étude sur le choral**
as ***Notre Père au royaume des cieux* de J.S. Bach** [Study of the chorale *Vater unser im Himmelreich* of J.S. Bach], *Atti del [I] Congresso internazionale di musica sacra* (Tournai: Desclée, 1952) 359–62. In French. See no. 303 in this volume.
Notes by the organist on Bach's treatment of Luther's hymn (1538).

1568 GURLITT, Wilibald. **Johann Sebastian Bach in**
as **seiner Zeit und heute** [Johann Sebastian Bach in his
time and today], *Bericht über die Wissenschaftliche
Bachtagung* (Leipzig: Peters, 1951) 51–80. In German.
See no. 298 in this volume.

Discusses Bach's life and work in their social-historical context, and their
meaning for us today.

1569 GÜTTLER, Hermann. **Die Monumental-**
as **oratorien des Königsberger Kantors Georg
Riedel (1676-1738)** [The monumental oratorios of
the Königsberg cantor Georg Riedel (1676-1738)],
*Bericht über den I. musikwissenschaftlichen Kongress
der Deutschen Musikgesellschaft in Leipzig*
(Wiesbaden: Breitkopf & Härtel, 1926) 373–78. *Facs.,
music.* In German. See no. 120 in this volume.

Includes a short biographical sketch of Riedel and a comparison of his setting of Matthew 28 (1721) with the *Matthäuspassion*, BWV 244 of J.S.
Bach. *(William Renwick)*

1570 HAAPANEN, Toivo Elias. **Eine Introit-**
as **sammlung in finnischen Sprache von Jahre
1605** [An Introit collection in Finnish from 1605],
*Société Internationale de Musicologie: Premier
Congrès Liège—Compte rendu/Internationale Gesellschaft für Musikwissenschaft: Erster Kongress
Lüttich—Kongressbericht/International Society for
Musical Research: First Congress Liège: Report* (London: Plainsong and Mediaeval Music Society, 1930)
132–37. *Music.* In German. See no. 178 in this volume.

Discusses a MS that is unusual in its use of the vernacular.

1571 HAAS, Robert. **Bach und Wien** [Bach and Vi-
as enna], *Kongreß-Bericht: Gesellschaft für Musikforschung* (Kassel; Basel: Bärenreiter, 1950) 129–31.
In German. See no. 299 in this volume.

1572 HAMANN, Heinz Wolfgang. **Neue Quellen zur**
as **Johann Joseph Fux–Forschung** [New sources for
research on Johann Joseph Fux], *Bericht über den
internationalen musikwissenschaftlichen Kongreß*
(Kassel: Bärenreiter, 1963) 158–61. In German. See no.
452 in this volume.

Documentary evidence permits the addition of specific detail to Johann
Friedrich Daube's story (in the *Anleitung zum Selbstunterricht in der
musikalischen Komposition*, 1797-98) of how Fux was discovered as a
composer by Emperor Leopold I. *(David Bloom)*

1573 HAMEL, Fred. **J.S. Bach als geistesgeschicht-**
as **liche Erscheinung** [J.S. Bach as phenomenon in intellectual history], *Société Internationale de Musicologie, cinquième congrès/Internationale Gesellschaft für Musikwissenschaft, fünfter Kongreß/Interna-
tional Society for Musical Research, Fifth Congress*
(Amsterdam: Vereniging voor Nederlandse Muziekgeschiedenis, 1953) 218–23. In German. See no. 316 in
this volume.

1574 HAMMERICH, Angul. **Musical relations be-**
as **tween England and Denmark in the XVII century,** *Report of the Fourth Congress of the International Musical Society* (London: Novello, 1912)
129–33. See no. 71 in this volume.

Christian IV, King of Denmark and Norway (1577-1648), was largely responsible for a period of heightened musical interchange.

1575 HAUSSWALD, Günter. **Instrumentale Züge im**
as **Belcanto des 18. Jahrhunderts** [Instrumental

characteristics in bel canto of the 18th century], *Bericht
über den Internationalen musikwissenschaftlichen
Kongress* (Kassel: Bärenreiter, 1954) 256–58. In German. See no. 319 in this volume.

Solo writing in opera arias from the first half of the 18th c. reveals the growing influence of instrumental idioms. The aria theme itself is often constructed from short motives with pauses between statements, and sometimes is explicitly instrumental in character, as in the case of fanfare motives. The ornamented, melismatic parts of the vocal line are sometimes
disposed in distinct registers, another instrumental characteristic (as in
arias ornamented by the singer Carlo Broschi, known as Farinelli). A close
relationship of the voice with the instrumental accompaniment can also
lend the vocal line an instrumental character, especially if concertante imitation is involved. Many da capo arias borrow from the concerto idiom and
instrumentalize the vocal line as it interacts with ripieno patterns.
(Carl Skoggard)

1576 HECKLINGER, Doris. **Tanzrhythmik als**
as **konstitutives Element in Bachs Vokalmusik**
[Dance rhythm as a constitutive element of Bach's mu-
sic], *Bericht über den internationalen musikwissenschaftlichen Kongreß* (Kassel: Bärenreiter, 1963)
167–70. In German. See no. 452 in this volume.

Dance models enter Bach's work first in instrumental works, then in the
secular cantatas written for Cöthen. In his first two years in Leipzig, he used
a wide range of dance rhythms in sacred cantatas. In 1726-29 he again began restricting the use of dance rhythms to secular music. *(David Bloom)*

⟶ HESBERT, René-Jean. **L'hymnologie de St.
Philibert: Les hymnes de Tournus et Macon**
[The hymnology of St. Philibert: The hymns of Tournus
and Macon]. See no. 1334 in this volume.

1577 HEUSS, Alfred Valentin. **Gedächtnisrede auf**
as **Händel** [Memorial speech for Händel],
Haydn-Zentenarfeier (Leipzig: Breitkopf & Härtel;
Wien: Artaria, 1909) 67–74. In German. See no. 65 in
this volume.

Discusses Händel's importance to German culture.

1578 HÖFER, Karlheinz. **Cornelius Burgh und**
as **Mönchengladbach** [Cornelius Burgh and
Mönchengladbach], *Studien zur Musikgeschichte der
Stadt Mönchengladbach* (Köln: Volk, 1965) 75–81. In
German. See no. 486 in this volume.

Documentary evidence shows that the composer and organist Cornelius
Burgh (ca. 1590–1640) worked as organist for the Abtei St. Vitus,
Mönchengladbach, from 1615 until his marriage in 1618, to a Mönchengladbach native, Eva Aredz or Ulner, after which he settled permanently in
Erkelenz. In 1633 he was invited back to serve as an expert judge of a new
organ, by the Cologne builder Hieronimus Ruprecht, for the parish church
of St. Helena, Mönchengladbach-Rheindahlen. He is also likely to have
worked in Erkelenz with the Mönchengladbach organ builder Johan
Schaden. *(David Bloom)*

1579 HUBOV, Georgij Nikitič. **Bach und die**
as **zeitgenössische musikalische Kultur** [Bach and
the contemporary musical culture]. Trans. from Russian by Viktor GRONFAIN, *Bericht über die
Wissenschaftliche Bachtagung* (Leipzig: Peters, 1951)
81–107. In German. See no. 298 in this volume.

Bach was by nature a dramatist and a realist. These characteristics, combined with his strained relationships with church and state, created for him
a complicated, contradictory form of musical expression. Bach stood on the
side of the people versus both the church and state, and the contradictions
inherent in his position helped to create an art of power and realism which
has been emulated more recently in the works of Russian composers.
(James Donald Anderson)

1580 HUCKE, Helmut. **Die neapolitanische Tradition**
as **in der Oper** [The Neapolitan tradition in opera], *Report of the Eighth Congress of the International Musicological Society. I: Papers* (Kassel: Bärenreiter, 1961) 253–77. *Music.* In German. See no. 439 in this volume.

Outlines the history and musical character of opera in Naples in the Baroque period, focusing on the figures of Alessandro Scarlatti, Leonardo Vinci, Leonardo Leo, and Pergolesi. The notion that Scarlatti was the founder of a specifically Neapolitan school is dismissed; in fact, there is no reason to speak of a Neapolitan school as such. *(David Bloom)*

1581 HUDSON, Frederick. **Wasserzeichen in**
as **Händelschen Manuskripten und Drucken: Wasserzeichen in Verbindung mit anderem Beweismaterial als Mittel zur Datierung der Manuskripte und frühen Drucke Georg Friedrich Händels** [Watermarks in Händel manuscripts and prints: Watermarks together with other evidence as a means of dating Georg Friedrich Händel's manuscripts and early prints], *Händel-Ehrung der Deutschen Demokratischen Republik: Konferenzbericht* (Leipzig: VEB Deutscher Verlag für Musik, 1961) 193–206. *Illus., charts, diagr.* In German. See no. 408 in this volume.

Discusses source studies undertaken in the preparation of the Hallische Händel-Ausgabe edition of the six concerti grossi op. 3. A fuller version, in English, is published in *The music review* (February 1959). *(David Bloom)*

1582 JACHIMECKI, Zdzisław. **Südliche Einflüsse in**
as **der polnischen Musik** [Southern influences in Polish music], *Haydn-Zentenarfeier* (Leipzig: Breitkopf & Härtel; Wien: Artaria, 1909) 156–59. In German. See no. 65 in this volume.

Discusses the work of several composers, including Wojciech Długoraj (ca. 1557–ca. 1619) and Adam Jarzębski (1590-1648).

⟶ JACQUOT, Jean. **Lyrisme et sentiment tragique dans les madrigaux d'Orlando Gibbons** [Lyricism and tragic sentiment in the madrigals of Orlando Gibbons]. See no. 1342 in this volume.

1583 JEANS, Susi. **Geschichte und Entwicklung des**
as **Voluntary for Double Organ in der englischen Orgelmusik des 17. Jahrhunderts** [History and development of the double organ voluntary in 17th-century English organ music], *Bericht über den internationalen musikwissenschaftlichen Kongreß* (Kassel: Bärenreiter, 1957) 123–26. *Music, organ specification.* In German. See no. 356 in this volume.

The voluntary for double organ (organ with two manuals) flourished in England from ca. 1600 to the beginning of the Civil War and the widespread destruction of organs in 1644-50, and again from the Restoration (1660) until the time of John Blow's death in 1708. Examples by John Lugge (ca. 1587-1647) and Blow are examined, and the contributions of Christopher Gibbons (1616-76), Matthew Locke (1622-77), and Purcell are assessed. *(David Bloom)*

1584 KARSTÄDT, Georg. **Neue Ergebnisse zur**
as **Buxtehude-Forschung** [New results in Buxtehude research], *Bericht über den siebenten internationalen musikwissenschaftlichen Kongress* (Kassel: Bärenreiter, 1959) 152–53. In German. See no. 390 in this volume.

Summarizes the state of research in 1957, the 250th anniversary of the composer's death, with particular emphasis on factors in the development of more or less secular concerts in the Abendmusik of the Marienkirche, from the organ recitals of Franz Tunder at mid-century to the immensely scaled, quasi-operatic *rappresentazioni* of Buxtehude's 1705 *Castrum doloris* and *Templum honoris.* *(David Bloom)*

1585 KASTNER, Macario Santiago. **O estilo musical**
as **do Padre Manoel Rodriguez Coelho** [The musical style of Manuel Rodrigues Coelho], *Congrés de la Societat Internacional de Musicologia* (Barcelona: Casa de Caritat, 1936). In Portuguese. See no. 224 in this volume.

The conference report provides only a citation. Neither the text nor a summary of the paper was published here.

1586 KASTNER, Macario Santiago. **Quelques aspects du Baroque musical espagnol et portugais** [Aspects of Spanish and Portuguese music of the Baroque], *Actes des Journées internationales d'étude du Baroque* (Toulouse: Faculté des Lettres et Sciences Humaines, 1965) 85–90. In French. See no. 469 in this volume.

Surveys genres and principal composers of the Iberian Peninsula during the Baroque era, especially of organ music. Sacred music predominated over secular music, due to the strong influence of the church and the lack of elaborate court establishments among the lesser nobility. Particular attention is given to the organist and composer Juan Bautista José Cabanilles and the question of how much he was influenced by French organ music. *(John Gordon Morris)*

1587 KELLER, Hermann. **Die Orgel-Messe im dritten**
as **Teil der *Klavier-Übung* von Johann Sebastian Bach** [The organ Mass in the third part of the *Clavier-Übung* of Johann Sebastian Bach], *Atti del [I] Congresso internazionale di musica sacra* (Tournai: Desclée, 1952) 354–55. In German. See no. 303 in this volume.

Discusses the chorale arrangements for the Mass, BWV 669-77.

1588 KELLER, Hermann. **Über Bachs Bearbeitungen aus dem *Hortus musicus* von Reincken** [Bach's arrangements from Reincken's *Hortus musicus*], *Compte rendu/Kongressbericht/Report* (Basel: Bärenreiter, 1951) 160–61. In German. See no. 289 in this volume.

Three keyboard works, a fugue in B♭ (BWV 954), a sonata in A minor (BWV 965), and a sonata in C (BWV 966), have been recognized as arrangements of trio-sonata movements in Johann Adam Reincken's *Hortus musicus*. The fugue movements, however, are essentially new works, much larger in scale than the originals. Bach probably wrote the works before his famous 1720 meeting with Reincken. *(David Bloom)*

1589 KILIAN, Dietrich. **Buxtehudes *Membra***
as [Buxtehude's *Membra*], (Kassel; New York: Bärenreiter, 1965) 32–35. In German. See no. 467 in this volume.

Discussion of the history, source transmission, and musical character of the seven choral Passion pieces collected as Dietrich Buxtehude's *Membra Jesui*, of which the only extant MS is one acquired by Gustaf Düben after 1680 and held in the Düben collection of the Universitetsbibliotek Uppsala. *(David Bloom)*

1590 KILIAN, Dietrich. **Der Generalbass um 1600**
as [Basso continuo around the year 1600], *Bericht über den neunten internationalen Kongreß* (Kassel: Bärenreiter, 1964-1966) II, 201–11. In German. See no. 491 in this volume.

Topics in the roundtable discussion included homophonic and harmonic texture in sacred vocal music in Italy and South Germany; the origins of basso continuo in Spain; basso continuo in sacred French music; the origins of basso continuo in France; basso continuo and the treatment of dissonance in Monteverdi; the question of the altus voice; the beginnings of basso continuo in Lodovico Viadana's *Cento concerti ecclesiastici* (1602); and sociological aspects of the basso continuo. Participants included Lars Ulrich ABRAHAM, Werner BRAUN, José LOPEZ-CALO, Helmut HAACK,

Denise LAUNAY, Finn MATHIASSEN, Walter H. RUBSAMEN, Søren SØRENSEN, André VERCHALY, and Jack A. WESTRUP. *(David Bloom)*

1591
as
KNEPLER, Georg. **Bemerkungen zum Wandel des Bachbildes** [Change in the image of Bach], *Bericht über die Wissenschaftliche Bachtagung* (Leipzig: Peters, 1951) 308–19. In German. See no. 298 in this volume.

Historical views of Bach's motives need revision. For example, Bach's move from Köthen to Leipzig has been misconstrued, by 19th-c. middle-class historians who projected their own weltanschauung anachronistically onto Bach, as a deliberate choice of sacred music over secular. The evidence shows that Bach moved more for financial reasons, and because of the educational opportunities Leipzig would offer his sons. A more objective view of Bach will place his religious mysticism in context, and balance discussion of the conservative aspects of his compositional practice with that of the progressive aspects. *(James Donald Anderson)*

1592
as
KOLNEDER, Walter. **Das Frühschaffen Antonio Vivaldis** [Antonio Vivaldi's early works], *Société Internationale de Musicologie, cinquième congrès/ Internationale Gesellschaft für Musikwissenschaft, fünfter Kongreß/International Society for Musical Research, Fifth Congress* (Amsterdam: Vereniging voor Nederlandse Muziekgeschiedenis, 1953) 254–62. In German. See no. 316 in this volume.

1593
as
KOLNEDER, Walter. **Zur Frühgeschichte des Solokonzerts** [The early history of the solo concerto], *Bericht über den internationalen musikwissenschaftlichen Kongreß* (Kassel: Bärenreiter, 1963) 149–52. In German. See no. 452 in this volume.

Discusses the evolution of the solo principle in the decades before 1700, with attention to concertos by Torelli and Albinoni and the *Sinfonie*, op. 3, of Giovanni Bononcini, and to the role of the trumpet as leading virtuoso instrument in the orchestras of the period. *(Jeffrey Miller)*

1594
as
KOVAČEVIĆ, Krešimir. **Die kroatische Musik des XVII. und XVIII. Jahrhunderts** [Croatian music of the 17th and 18th centuries], *Musica antiqua Europae orientalis* (Warszawa: Państwowe Wydawnictwo Naukowe, 1966). *Facs.* In German. See no. 506 in this volume.

1595
as
KRAFT, Günther. **Zur geistigen Umwelt des jungen Händel** [The intellectual environment of the young Händel], *Händel-Ehrung der Deutschen Demokratischen Republik: Konferenzbericht* (Leipzig: VEB Deutscher Verlag für Musik, 1961) 45–51. In German. See no. 408 in this volume.

As a student at the University of Halle in 1702, Händel encountered the humanism of the dawn of the German Enlightenment, and its striving for justice, peace, and freedom, themes that are reflected in works such as *Messiah* and *Belshazzar*. *(David Bloom)*

1596
as
LA LAURENCIE, Lionel de. **Les pastorales en musique au XVIIᵉᵐᵉ siècle en France avant Lully et leur influence sur l'opéra** [Musical pastorales in 17th-century France before Lully, and their influence on opera], *Report of the Fourth Congress of the International Musical Society* (London: Novello, 1912) 139–46. In French. See no. 71 in this volume.

1597
as
LANDOWSKA, Wanda. **Bach et les clavecinistes français** [Bach and the French harpsichordists], *Actes du Congrès d'histoire de l'art: Compte rendu analytique* (Paris: Presses Universitaires de France, 1922) 182. In French. See no. 95 in this volume.

Summary of a paper.

1598
as
LARSEN, Jens Peter. **Ein Händel-Requiem: Die Trauerhymne für die Königin Caroline (1737)** [A Händel Requiem: The funeral anthem for Queen Caroline (1737)], *Bericht über den internationalen musikwissenschaftlichen Kongreß* (Kassel: Bärenreiter, 1957) 15–23. *Music.* In German. See no. 356 in this volume.

The anthem *The ways of Zion do mourn* represents a development from Händel's oratorio composition. It is influenced by the English anthem, the Italian duet-chorus, and German church music. *Israel in Egypt* and *Messiah* stem from this work, as do choral techniques of later oratorios.

1599
as
LAUX, Karl. **Bach und die deutsche Nation** [Bach and the German nation], *Bericht über die Wissenschaftliche Bachtagung* (Leipzig: Peters, 1951) 158–80. In German. See no. 298 in this volume.

In 1652, the painter Matthäus Merian vividly described the terrible suffering in Germany caused by the Thirty Years' War. Members of the Bach family were affected by this war. The spirit of peace was to Bach not only a necessity for his life as a musician, but also an affair of the heart that he expressed through music such as the Agnus Dei (the "Dona nobis pacem" section) of the B minor Mass, BWV 232. *(James Donald Anderson)*

1600
as
LAVOYE, Louis. **Le théâtre musical liègeois au XVIIIᵉ siècle** [Musical theater of Liège in the 18th century], *Actes et travaux du Congrés international pour l'étude du XVIIIᵉᵐᵉ siècle en Belgique* (Bruxelles: Editions des Annales Prince de Ligne, 1936) 212–21. In French. See no. 220 in this volume.

By the middle of the 18th c., the people of Liège clamored for their own national theater. Several Belgian opera composers are discussed, with an emphasis on Jean-Noël Hamal's life and four operas. *(Daniel Rosenbaum)*

1601
as
LEBEAU, Élisabeth. **La musique des cérémonies célébrées à la mort de Marie-Thérèse, reine de France, 1683: Notes pour servir à la recherche des éléments Baroques dans la musique en France au XVIIᵉ siècle** [The music of the ceremonies held on the death of Marie-Thérèse, Queen of France, 1683: Notes in the service of research on Baroque elements in music in France in the 17th century], *Les colloques de Wégimont. IV: Le Baroque musical—Recueil d'études sur la musique du XVIIᵉ siècle* (Paris: Belles Lettres, 1963) 200–19. *Illus., facs., music, maps.* In French. See no. 386 in this volume.

An inventory of reports on the music performed throughout France following the queen's death on 31 July. Lully's grand motet settings of the *Dies irae* and *De profundis* were performed at the burial service at St-Denis, 1 September, preceding a funeral oration by Jacques-Bénigne Bossuet; it is not clear when and where Charpentier's motet *Luctus de morte augustissimae Mariae Theresiae Reginae Galliae* (H.331) and histoire sacrée (dramatic motet) *In obitum augustissimae necnon piisimae Gallorum Reginae lamentum* (H.409) were performed. Compositions for the occasion by Guislain Doré (of the Cathédrale de Notre-Dame, Arras), Jean Mignon (of Notre-Dame de Paris), Jean-François Le Sueur, and possibly Michel-Richard de Lalande have not been identified. *(David Bloom)*

1602
as
LENAERTS, René Bernard. **La musique sacrée en Belgique au XVIIIᵉ siècle** [Sacred music in Belgium in the 18th century], *Atti del [I] Congresso internazionale di musica sacra* (Tournai: Desclée, 1952) 311–14. In French. See no. 303 in this volume.

1603
as
LESURE, François. **La datation des premières editions d'Estienne Roger (1697-1702)** [Dating the first publications of Estienne Roger (1697-1702)], *Bericht über den Internationalen musikwissenschaftlichen Kongress* (Kassel: Bärenreiter, 1954) 273–79. *Bibliog., chronology.* In German. See no. 319 in this volume.

Presents a list of more than 150 editions of music issued by the Amsterdam publisher Estienne Roger between 1692 and 1702. The dating is based on five newly examined annual catalogues that Roger sometimes appended to nonmusical publications. *(Carl Skoggard)*

1604 LESURE, François. **Recherches sur les luthistes**
as **parisiens a l'époque de Louis XIII** [Research on Parisian lutenists of the period of Louis XIII], *Le luth et sa musique* (Paris: Centre National de la Recherche Scientifique [CNRS], 1958) 209–23. In French. See no. 377 in this volume.
Summarizes the state of research, with a list of extant tablatures and biographical inventories of all the known lute makers and lutenist-composers active in Paris in the first half of the 17th c. *(David Bloom)*

1605 LIEBE, Annelise. **Bachs *Matthäuspassion* in**
as **ihrer geschichtlichen Beurteilung** [The historical evaluation of Bach's *Matthäuspassion*], *Bericht über die Wissenschaftliche Bachtagung* (Leipzig: Peters, 1951) 331–39. In German. See no. 298 in this volume.
Discusses the position in Bach's oeuvre of the *Matthäuspassion*, the construction of the work, and its position in the history of ideas. Musicological understanding of Bach's use of symbolism supports the views of Wilhelm Dilthey, for whom Bach had brought not simply ritual but religion itself directly into music. *(James Donald Anderson)*

1606 LINDEN, Albert vander. **La musique et la danse**
as **dans les Pays-Bas au XVIIIᵉᵐᵉ siècle** [Music and dance in the Low Countries in the 18th century], *Actes et travaux du Congrés international pour l'étude du XVIIIᵉᵐᵉ siècle en Belgique* (Bruxelles: Editions des Annales Prince de Ligne, 1936) 197–204. In French. See no. 220 in this volume.
A brief overview of ballet in the Low Countries during the 18th c., particularly in Brussels. Specific ballets, dancers, choreographers, types of ballets, and French cultural influences are described. More research is urged. *(Daniel Rosenbaum)*

1607 LONGO, Alessandro. **Observations sur la**
as **valeur historique des compositions pour clavecin de Dominique Scarlatti** [Observations on the historical value of Domenico Scarlatti's compositions for harpsichord], *Congrès international d'histoire de la musique: Documents, mémoires et vœux* (Solesmes: St. Pierre; Paris: Fischbacher, 1901) 213–14. In French. See no. 32 in this volume.
A short introduction to Scarlatti by the editor of a complete works edition.

1608 LUCIANI, Sebastiano Arturo. **I concerti** [The
as concertos], *Antonio Vivaldi: Note e documenti sulla vita e sulle opere* (Siena: Accademia Musicale Chigiana, 1939) 27–31. In Italian. See no. 268 in this volume.
An overview of Vivaldi's works in concerto form, with attention to J.S. Bach's transcriptions of some of them.

1609 LUCIANI, Sebastiano Arturo. *Il geloso*
as *schernito*, *G.B. Pergolesi, 1710-1736: Note e documenti, raccolti in occasione della settimana celebrativa* (Siena: Ticci Editore Libraio, 1942) 71–75. In Italian. See no. 273 in this volume.
A brief history and plot summary of the opera (attributed).

1610 LUCIANI, Sebastiano Arturo. **Gli originali di**
as **Antonio Vivaldi e le trascrizioni** [Antonio Vivaldi's originals and the transcriptions], *Fac-simile del Concerto funebre* (Siena: Accademia Musicale Chigiana, 1947) 31–32. In Italian. See no. 279 in this volume.

The value of facsimile reproductions becomes apparent in view of pieces that have hitherto been available only as transcriptions. *(Mark Stevens)*

1611 LUCIANI, Sebastiano Arturo. **Il presidente de**
as **Brosses e Pergolesi** [President de Brosses and Pergolesi], *G.B. Pergolesi, 1710-1736: Note e documenti, raccolti in occasione della settimana celebrativa* (Siena: Ticci Editore Libraio, 1942) 42–47. *Facs.* In Italian. See no. 273 in this volume.
In his *Lettres familières écrites d'Italie*, which document his tour of Italy 1739-40, Charles de Brosses paid tribute to the music of Pergolesi. *(Mark Stevens)*

1612 LUCIANI, Sebastiano Arturo. **La visita di**
as **Goldoni a Vivaldi** [Goldoni's visit with Vivaldi], *Fac-simile del Concerto funebre* (Siena: Accademia Musicale Chigiana, 1947) 33–37. In Italian. See no. 279 in this volume.
Discusses an excerpt from Goldoni's memoir, which gives a lively account of his meeting with Vivaldi.

1613 LUIN, Elizabeth Jeannette. **La fama di Pergolesi**
as **all'estero** [Pergolesi's fame abroad], *G.B. Pergolesi, 1710-1736: Note e documenti, raccolti in occasione della settimana celebrativa* (Siena: Ticci Editore Libraio, 1942) 50–56. *Facs., music.* In Italian. See no. 273 in this volume.
Pergolesi's reputation in the 18th c., based largely on the Stabat Mater and *La serva padrona*, was considerable. Performances and their reception in various European countries are cited as evidence. *(Mark Stevens)*

1614 LUIN, Elizabeth Jeannette. **L'importanza della**
as **Stabat Mater del Pergolese nei paesi nordici prima della diffusione della *Matthäuspassion*** [The importance of Pergolesi's Stabat Mater in the Nordic countries before the propagation of the *Matthäuspassion*], *Congrés de la Societat Internacional de Musicologia* (Barcelona: Casa de Caritat, 1936). In Italian. See no. 224 in this volume.
The conference report provides only a citation. Neither the text nor a summary of the paper was published here.

1615 LUNDGREN, Bo. **Johan Lorentz in Kopen-**
as **hagen: Organista nulli in Europa secundus** [Johann Lorentz in Copenhagen: *Organista nulli in Europa secundus*], *Bericht über den siebenten internationalen musikwissenschaftlichen Kongress* (Kassel: Bärenreiter, 1959) 183–85. In German. See no. 390 in this volume.
Johann Lorentz (ca. 1610–89), son of the organ builder Johann Lorentz (ca. 1580–1650), is known today primarily as a probable teacher of Buxtehude, but was famous in his time as the organist of the church of St. Nikolaj, Copenhagen, where he served from 1634 until his death in 1689, playing an organ built by his father in regular services and weekday solo concert recitals. Sources of his extant compositions are enumerated. *(David Bloom)*

1616 MAERTENS, Willi. **Telemanns Orchestersuite**
as **mit Hornquartett: Zu ihrer Deutung und Bedeutung** [Telemann's orchestra suite with four horns: On its interpretation and significance], *Beiträge zu einem neuen Telemannbild* (Magdeburg: Vorwärts, 1963) 64–76. In German. See no. 453 in this volume.
Analyzes the suite TWV 55: F11, in terms of the core idea of the contrast between humanity and nature, against the background of the city of Hamburg, with reference to the composer's programmatic movement titles. *(John Stansell)*

1617 MANN, Alfred. **Händels Fugenlehre: Ein**
as **unveröffentlichtes Manuskript** [Händel's teach-

ing of fugue: An unpublished manuscript], *Bericht über den internationalen musikwissenschaftlichen Kongreß* (Kassel: Bärenreiter, 1963) 172–74. In German. See no. 452 in this volume.

The Händel autographs of *GB-Cfm* MS 260, 27-72 seem to represent exercises in thoroughbass and counterpoint prepared for Anne, the Princess Royal, in the early 1720s. The contents, and their relation to other works by Händel, are discussed. *(David Bloom)*

1618
as
MASSENKEIL, Günther. **Über die Messen Giacomo Carissimis** [The Masses of Giacomo Carissimi], *Bericht über den internationalen musikwissenschaftlichen Kongreß* (Kassel: Bärenreiter, 1963) 152–53. In German. See no. 452 in this volume.

In addition to his well-known work as a composer of Latin historiae and oratorios and Italian cantatas, Carissimi was a master of the Mass. The 13 works in the genre that have been attributed to him are surveyed.

1619
as
MASSON, Paul-Marie. **La vie musicale en France, de 1695 à 1730, d'après les recueils périodiques de Ballard** [Musical life in France from 1695 to 1730, on the basis of Ballard's periodically issued collections], *Actes du Congrès d'histoire de l'art: Compte rendu analytique* (Paris: Presses Universitaires de France, 1922) 121. In French. See no. 95 in this volume.

Summary of a paper.

1620
as
MAXTON, Willy. **Johann Theile als Theoretiker** [Johann Theile as a theorist], *Bericht über den Internationalen musikwissenschaftlichen Kongress* (Kassel: Bärenreiter, 1954) 138–40. In German. See no. 319 in this volume.

Both as a theorist and a composer, Theile sought to cleanse church music. Theile's most important treatise, *Das musikalische Kunstbuch*, 1691, is briefly considered and its relation to his church music confirmed. The probable destruction of at least 31 Theile unica held by the Preußische Staatsbibliothek at the outbreak of World War II is compensated for by the present author's copies. *(Carl Skoggard)*

1621
as
MELLERS, Wilfrid. **La mélancolie au début du XVIIᵉ siècle et le madrigal anglais** [Melancholy at the beginning of the 17th century and the English madrigal], *Musique et poésie au XVIᵉ siècle* (Paris: Centre National de la Recherche Scientifique [CNRS], 1954) 153–68. *Music.* In French. See no. 326 in this volume.

The two most important composers of the melancholy madrigal were Ward and Wilbye, who recreated the traditional style of the madrigal in almost symphonic terms. *(Scott Fruehwald)*

1622
as
MERSMANN, Hans. **Das 18. Jahrhundert aus der Sicht unserer Zeit** [The 18th century from the perspective of our time], *Musik and Musikerziehung in der Reifezeit* (Mainz: Schott, 1959) 90–106. In German. See no. 412 in this volume.

A survey of the history of music in Germany from the time of Bach to that of Beethoven in its social, political, and intellectual context. *(David Bloom)*

1623
as
MEYER, Ernst Hermann. **Zur Telemann-Deutung** [On the significance of Telemann], *Beiträge zu einem neuen Telemannbild* (Magdeburg: Vorwärts, 1963) 17–22. In German. See no. 453 in this volume.

When Telemann is dismissed as a prolific but merely transitional composer, his true greatness is missed. Reflecting the significant stylistic changes in the first half of the 18th c., he absorbed Italian influences—emerging with a truly German style—and became the first representative of the early Classical period. *(John Stansell)*

1624
as
MIES, Paul. **Der Charakter der Tonarten** [The character of the keys], *Compte rendu/Kongressbericht/Report* (Basel: Bärenreiter, 1951) 181. In German. See no. 289 in this volume.

Summary of a conference paper applying the framework of the author's *Der Charakter der Tonarten: Eine Untersuchung* (Köln: Staufen, 1948) to key associations in Händel's operas and oratorios. *(David Bloom)*

1625
as
MOMPELLIO, Federico. **Le *Musiche* ad una ed a due voci del palermitano Sigismondo d'India** [The *Musiche* for vocal solo and duet of the Palermo-born Sigismondo d'India], *Atti del Congresso internazionale di musiche popolari mediterranee e del Convegno dei bibliotecari musicali* (Palermo: De Magistris succ. V. Bellotti, 1959) 267–70. In Italian. See no. 332 in this volume.

Notes on the life and work of the Sicilian composer, summarizing from the author's *Sigismondo d'India, musicista palermitano* (Milan, 1957).

1626
as
MOOS, Paul. **Gehören Gluck, Händel und Bach zur barocken Kunst ihrer Zeit?** [Do Gluck, Händel, and Bach belong to the Baroque art of their time?], *Kongreß-Bericht: Gesellschaft für Musikforschung* (Kassel; Basel: Bärenreiter, 1950) 195–97. In German. See no. 299 in this volume.

1627
as
MORTARI, Virgilio. **Il Flaminio,** *G.B. Pergolesi, 1710-1736: Note e documenti, raccolti in occasione della settimana celebrativa* (Siena: Ticci Editore Libraio, 1942) 11–16. *Facs.* In Italian. See no. 273 in this volume.

Almost every component of *Il Flaminio*, a commedia per musica, is stylistically similar to *La serva padrona*.

1628
as
MORTARI, Virgilio. **L'Olimpiade e il teatro musicale di Antonio Vivaldi** [*L'Olimpiade* and Antonio Vivaldi's musical theater], *Antonio Vivaldi: Note e documenti sulla vita e sulle opere* (Siena: Accademia Musicale Chigiana, 1939) 23–26. In Italian. See no. 268 in this volume.

Vivaldi's operas were not received well even in their own time, and have not achieved a position of importance in the history of opera, but their music is bold, expressive, and psychologically penetrating, and some works, including *L'Olimpiade*, deserve revivals. *(Mark Stevens)*

1629
as
MUEREN, Floris van der. **Limites géographiques du Baroque** [Geographical limits of the Baroque], *Les colloques de Wégimont. IV: Le Baroque musical—Recueil d'études sur la musique du XVIIᵉ siècle* (Paris: Belles Lettres, 1963) 83–90. In French. See no. 386 in this volume.

The Baroque style, from Monteverdi through the sons of J.S. Bach, was most suited to the temperament of the Nordic peoples, and reached its climax and most aesthetically satisfying expression in the music of Germany in the early 18th c.

1630
as
MÜLLER-BLATTAU, Joseph. **Zum Verhältnis von Wort und Ton im 17. Jahrhundert** [On the relationship between word and music in the 17th century], *Bericht über den musikwissenschaftlichen Kongreß in Basel* (Leipzig: Breitkopf & Härtel, 1925) 270–75. In German. See no. 102 in this volume.

Christoph Bernhard asserted that singing is always the foundation of musical expression. Two styles are discussed: the *cantar solo* and the *cantar d'affetto*, corresponding to the old (reservata) and new approaches to text.

1631 NAGEL, Wilibald. **Kleine Beiträge zur**
as **Geschichte der Oper in Darmstadt** [Small contributions to the history of opera in Darmstadt], *Haydn-
Zentenarfeier* (Leipzig: Breitkopf & Härtel; Wien:
Artaria, 1909) 184–86. In German. See no. 65 in this
volume.
Covers the period 1673-1719.

1632 NEF, Karl. **Zur Geschichte der Passion** [On the
as history of the Passion], *Société Internationale de Musi-
cologie: Premier Congrès Liège—Compte rendu/
Internationale Gesellschaft für Musikwissenschaft:
Erster Kongress Lüttich—Kongressbericht/Interna-
tional Society for Musical Research: First Congress
Liège: Report* (London: Plainsong and Mediaeval Mu-
sic Society, 1930) 190. In German. See no. 178 in this
volume.
Summarizes an article on the Passion and oratorios of Marc-Antoine
Charpentier. The complete version appears in *Jahrbuch der Musikbibliothek
Peters* (Leipzig, 1931). *(Scott Fruehwald)*

1633 NETTL, Paul. **Musical folklore of the Baroque**
as **period in Austria,** *Journal of the International Folk
Music Council* III (1951) 85–86. See no. 296 in this
volume.
Summary of a paper discussing sources that shed light on traditional musics
of the period and composers who were influenced by traditional music. Another version is abstracted as no. 1634 in this volume.

1634 NETTL, Paul. **La musique populaire du XVIIe**
as **siècle en Autriche** [Traditional music of the 17th
century in Austria], *Congrès international des arts
populaires/International congress of popular arts*
(Paris: Institut international de coopération
intellectuelle, 1928) 101. In French. See no. 153 in this
volume.
Summary of a paper assessing evidence from 17th-c. MSS that the
so-called Austrian dialect of melody known from composers such as Schubert and Johann Strauss already existed during the Baroque, though it was
temporarily eclipsed in the 18th c. by the popularity of Neapolitan songs.
Another version is abstracted as no. 1633 in this volume. *(David Bloom)*

1635 NETTL, Paul. **Spuren des Wiener Liedes in der**
as **zweiten Hälfte des 17. Jahrhunderts** [Traces of
the Vienna lied in the second half of the 17th century],
*Bericht über den I. musikwissenschaftlichen Kongress
der Deutschen Musikgesellschaft in Leipzig*
(Wiesbaden: Breitkopf & Härtel, 1926) 247–49. In German. See no. 120 in this volume.
Discusses lieder by Johann Heinrich Schmelzer, Johann Michael Zächer,
and Adam Krieger. The relatively insignificant production of lieder in Vienna between 1650 and 1700 was the result of the domination of Italian music, particularly opera. *(William Renwick)*

1636 NOACK, Friedrich. **Landgraf Ernst Ludwig**
as **von Hessen-Darmstadt als Komponist** [Ernst
Ludwig, Landgrave of Hessen-Darmstadt, as com-
poser], *Beethoven-Zentenarfeier: Internationaler
musikhistorischer Kongress* (Wien: Universal, 1927)
205–07. *List of works.* In German. See no. 142 in this
volume.
Ernst Ludwig (1667-1739) was not only an important patron of the arts, but
also a musician well above the rank of the talented amateur. His compositions, mostly for string ensembles and written during the period 1709-19
when musical life at the Darmstadt court was at its most brilliant, are evaluated. *(David Bloom)*

1637 NOACK, Friedrich. **Die Opern von Christoph**
as **Graupner in Darmstadt** [The operas of Christoph

Graupner in Darmstadt], *Bericht über den I. musikwissenschaftlichen Kongress der Deutschen Musikgesellschaft in Leipzig* (Wiesbaden: Breitkopf & Härtel,
1926) 252–59. In German. See no. 120 in this volume.
Summarizes Graupner's output, concentrating on the circumstances of his
Darmstadt operas, principally *Berenice und Lucilla* (1710) and *Telemach*
(1711). The influence of Lully is noted. *(William Renwick)*

1638 NOSKE, Frits. **Joannes Tollius: Ein nieder-**
as **ländische Meister des Frühbarock** [Jan Tollius:
A Netherlandish master of the early Baroque], *Bericht
über den siebenten internationalen musikwissenschaft-
lichen Kongress* (Kassel: Bärenreiter, 1959) 203–07.
Music. In German. See no. 390 in this volume.
Surveys the available information on the composer's life, and discusses his
Liber primus motectorum and *Liber secundus motectorum* for five voices
(Venice, 1591) and *Moduli* for three voices (Heidelberg, 1597). Though not
of the rank of, say, Monteverdi, he was a composer of great originality
whose innovations anticipate and in some ways belong to the Baroque.
(David Bloom)

1639 OBERBORBECK, Felix. **Schwäbische Reichs-**
as **städte als Träger deutscher Musikkultur im 18.**
Jahrhundert [Swabian imperial cities as bearers of
German music culture in the 18th century], *Bericht über
den I. musikwissenschaftlichen Kongress der Deutschen
Musikgesellschaft in Leipzig* (Wiesbaden: Breitkopf &
Härtel, 1926) 391–92. In German. See no. 120 in this
volume.
Discusses the musical activities to be found in the princely houses, the imperial city of Augsburg, the collegia musica, and the churches. The activities of the Meistersingers are also mentioned. *(William Renwick)*

1640 OBERBORBECK, Felix. *Vor deinen Thron tret*
as *ich hiemit*: **Bemerkungen zu Geschichte, Form**
und Aufführungspraxis von Bachs Lebens-
epilog [*Vor deinen Thron tret ich hiemit*: Observations
on the history, form, and performance practice of
Bach's farewell work], *Bericht über die Wissenschaftliche Bachtagung* (Leipzig: Peters, 1951) 285–93. *Music.* In German. See no. 298 in this volume.
The chorale prelude BWV 668, said to have been dictated by the dying
Bach to Johann Christoph Altnikol in early July 1750, was published posthumously as the conclusion to *Die Kunst der Fuge* (1751). Issues of quotation, number symbolism, and performance options are considered. Like
Die Kunst der Fuge, BWV 668 can be realized in a number of different
ways: keyboard solo, instrumental ensemble, vocal ensemble, or a combination of these.

1641 OLDHAM, Guy. **Two pieces for 5-part shawm**
as **band by Louis Couperin,** *Music libraries and instruments* (London: Hinrichsen, 1961) 233–38. *Illus.,
facs.* See no. 406 in this volume.
A previously undescribed MS primarily of Couperin's keyboard music in
the author's private collection also includes two fantasias "sur le jeu des
haubois" for five shawms, probably written for the coronation of Louis
XIV in 1654. The MS is more fully described in *Louis Couperin: A new
source of French keyboard music of the mid-17th century, Recherches sur
la musique française classique* I (1960). *(David Bloom)*

1642 [Pergolesi] **Un autografo firmato di Pergolesi**
as [An autograph signed by Pergolesi], *G.B. Pergolesi,
1710-1736: Note e documenti, raccolti in occasione
della settimana celebrativa* (Siena: Ticci Editore
Libraio, 1942) 32–33. In Italian. See no. 273 in this
volume.
Presents facsimiles of pages from Pergolesi's *Lo frate 'nnamorato* found at
Oxford, first published by Don Filippo Caffarelli in volume two of the *Opera omnia*. *(Susan Poliniak)*

1643 PETZOLDT, Richard. **Zur sozialen Stellung des**
as **Musikers im 17. Jahrhundert** [The social position
of the musician in the 17th century], *Bericht über den
siebenten internationalen musikwissenschaftlichen
Kongress* (Kassel: Bärenreiter, 1959) 210–12. In German. See no. 390 in this volume.

Documentary evidence on the social and economic status of Heinrich
Schütz exemplifies the way in which a sociological approach to music history helps us to understand the artist as a part of a concrete time and place.
(David Bloom)

1644 PHILLIPS, Gordon. **Purcell's organs and organ**
as **music,** *Organ and choral aspects and prospects* (London: Hinrichsen, 1958) 133–35. *Port.* See no. 375 in
this volume.

Analyzes and critiques of Purcell's voluntaries; the organs for which they
were written are also described.

1645 PIRRO, André. **Les formes de l'expression dans**
as **la musique de Heinrich Schütz** [Forms of expression in the music of Heinrich Schütz], *Mémoires de
Musicologie sacrée, lus aux assises de musique
religieuse* (Paris: Schola Cantorum, n.d.) 95–104. *Music.* In French. See no. 34 in this volume.

The importance of the text and clearly comprehensible declamation, natural simple rhythms, and harmonic boldness are all characteristics of
Schütz's works that reflect the new spirit of 17th-c. humanism and the influence of Gabrieli and Monteverdi. *(Karen Clute)*

⟶ PLAMENAC, Dragan. **Music of the 16th and
17th centuries in Dalmatia.** See no. 1407 in this
volume.

1646 PLAMENAC, Dragan. **An unknown violin**
as **tablature of the early 17th century,** *Papers of the
American Musicological Society* (Philadelphia: American Musicological Society, 1946) 144–57. *Illus., facs.,
music.* See no. 272 in this volume.

The MS anthology *HR-Zaa* I.a.44, dating from 1625, includes Croatian and
Latin poetry by Croatian authors from Dalmatia. Toward the end are two folios with six dances written in a violin tablature entitled *Intavuolatura del
violino di Sigr. Gabriele Pervaneo da Lesina.* The dances bear the following titles: *Bergamasca, Forze d'Ercole, Ruggiero, Del frate fra Jacupino,
Pass e mezo,* and *Spagnoletta,* and their notation is congruent with concordances in other European MSS. Gabriele Pervaneo (Prvan, Prvanić,
Prvanović) of Hvar was probably an amateur musician. A Croatian-language version is abstracted as RILM [1998]2759. *(Zdravko Blažeković)*

1647 PRUNIÈRES, Henry. **Notes sur les origines de**
as **l'ouverture française, 1640-1660** [Notes on the
origin of the French overture, 1640-1660], *Report of the
Fourth Congress of the International Musical Society*
(London: Novello, 1912) 149–51. In French. See no. 71
in this volume.

Discusses the origin and evolution of the French overture, with attention to
Lully's substitution of a fugato for the traditional second movement. Examples from his ballets *L'amour malade* (1657), *Alcidiane* (1658), and *Xerxes*
(1660) are noted. *(Jenna Orkin)*

1648 PRUNIÈRES, Henry. **Un opéra de Paolo**
as **Lorenzani** [An opera by Paolo Lorenzani], *Actes du
Congrès d'histoire de l'art* (Paris: Presses
Universitaires de France, 1923-1924) 867–73. *Facs.,
music.* In French. See no. 94 in this volume.

The score of Lorenzani's opera *Nicandro et Fileno* was found in the
Bibliothèque Nationale de Paris. Listed in Brossard's catalogue (p. 501),
the score is in Lorenzani's handwriting and contains many detailed performance indications, including clear instructions concerning orchestration.
(Vivian Conejero)

1649 [Purcell Society] **The new Purcell Society Edi-**
as **tion and some Purcell music,** *Organ and choral
aspects and prospects* (London: Hinrichsen, 1958)
149–54. *Port., facs., list of works.* See no. 375 in this
volume.

Includes remarks on the Purcell Society, a list of previously published volumes, and a list of works in Peters and Hinrichsen editions.

1650 QUEROL GAVALDÁ, Miguel. **La música**
as **religiosa española en el s. XVII** [Spanish religious
music in the 17th century], *Atti del [II] Congresso
internazionale di musica sacra* (Tournai: Desclée,
1952) 323–26. In Spanish. See no. 303 in this volume.

1651 QUEROL GAVALDÁ, Miguel. **La polyphonie**
as **religieuse espagnole au XVIIᵉ siècle** [Spanish sacred polyphony in the 17th century], *Les colloques de
Wégimont. IV: Le Baroque musical—Recueil d'études
sur la musique du XVIIᵉ siècle* (Paris: Belles Lettres,
1963) 91–105. *Illus., facs.* In French. See no. 386 in this
volume.

A survey of the main genres—Mass, Vesper and Compline psalms, motet,
and villancico. Typically Baroque features of the Masses and especially
psalms are polychorality, fragmentation of melody and text, and a penchant
for effects, sometimes in less than good taste, of surprise and of pomp.
(David Bloom)

1652 QUITTARD, Henri. **Carissimi et le XVIIᵉ siècle**
as **italien** [Carissimi and the Italian 17th century],
*Mémoires de Musicologie sacrée, lus aux assises de
musique religieuse* (Paris: Schola Cantorum, n.d.)
75–94. In French. See no. 34 in this volume.

Carissimi's oratorios and histoires are used to highlight the stylistic shifts
in the 17th c. The Florentine camerata and the life of church musicians are
also discussed. *(Karen Clute)*

1653 RACEK, Jan. **Vznik a počátky barokního**
as **hudebního slohu v Čechách/Origine et débuts
de la musique baroque en Bohème** [Origin and
beginnings of Baroque music in Bohemian lands],
*Hudba národů: Sborník přednášek, proslovených na I.
mezinárodnim sjezdu skladatelů a hudebních
kritiků/Musique des nations: Iᵉʳ Congrès international
des compositeurs et critiques musicaux* (Praha:
Syndikát Českých Skladatelů, 1948) 51–61,157–67. In
Czech and French. See no. 278 in this volume.

Italian culture in general and the new monodic musical style invaded the
Bohemian lands from the beginning of the 17th c., as represented by
Francesco Stivori, organist of Archduke (later Emperor) Ferdinand II, becoming altogether dominant after the defeat of the insurgent Protestants at
the battle of Bílá Hora in 1620. The dissemination of Italian monody is
demonstrated in a collection of prints assembled in 1604-18 for the Prague
nobleman Franciscus Godefridus Troilus à Lessoth, *CZ-Puk* MS 11B 41. A
biography of Troilus and an analytic discussion of the volume's contents
are provided. The research is fully reported in the author's *Italská monodie
z doby raného baroku v Čechách* (Olomouc, 1945).

1654 RADICIOTTI, Giuseppe. **Il ritratto e la**
as **caricatura di Pergolesi** [Portrait and caricature of
Pergolesi], *G.B. Pergolesi, 1710-1736: Note e
documenti, raccolti in occasione della settimana
celebrativa* (Siena: Ticci Editore Libraio, 1942) 29–31.
Facs. In Italian. See no. 273 in this volume.

An excerpt from the author's posthumously published *Pergolesi* (Milano:
Fratelli Treves, 1935). No verifiable portrait of Pergolesi exists, but a contemporary caricature by Pier Leone Ghezzi provides clues regarding his appearance and deformity. A facsimile of the composer's signature appearing
in the MS of *Lo frate 'nnamorato* is appended. *(Mark Stevens)*

1655 REICHERT, Georg. **Beziehungen württem-**
as **bergischer Musiker des 17. Jahrhunderts zum**
Hamburger Organistenkreis [Relations of
17th-century Württemberg musicians to the Hamburg
organists' circle], *Der Barock: Seine Orgeln und seine*
Musik in Oberschwaben (Berlin: Merseburger, 1952)
70–74. In German. See no. 305 in this volume.

North Germany and South Germany are generally regarded as very distinct
organ cultures, but there were in fact many connections between them. The
Upper Swabian organist Georg Wolfgang Druckenmüller (1628-95)
worked in Colditz in 1647-49 and then studied with Heinrich Scheidemann
in Hamburg in 1649-52 before taking the organist's post at the Hauptkirche
St. Michael in his home town of Schwäbisch Hall. The youngest of his three
sons, Johann Dietrich (1663-97), was organist of St. Ludgeri, Norden,
when that church's famous Arp Schnitger organ was inaugurated; after his
early death, his brother Johann Jakob (1657-1715) succeeded him.
(David Bloom)

1656 RIEDEL, Friedrich Wilhelm. **Der Reichsstil in**
as **der deutschen Musikgeschichte des 18. Jahr-**
hunderts [The Reichsstil in 18th-century German music history], *Bericht über den internationalen musik-*
wissenschaftlichen Kongreß (Kassel: Bärenreiter, 1963)
34–36. In German. See no. 452 in this volume.

The so-called Reichsstil is an architectural style based on a synthesis of
Italian and French architectural elements, invented by the Vienna court architect Johann Bernhard Fischer, that spread from Austria through the areas
of Habsburg influence during the reigns of Leopold I, Joseph I, and Charles
VI. A similar phenomenon may be identified in the Austrian and German
music of the period, with the figure of Johann Joseph Fux corresponding to
Fischer. *(Laurie Appleby)*

1657 RIEDEL, Friedrich Wilhelm. **Strenger und**
as **freier Stil in der nord- und süddeutschen**
Musik für Tasteninstrumente des 17. Jahr-
hunderts [Strict and free style in the North and South
German keyboard music of the 17th century], *Nord-*
deutsche und nordeuropäische Musik (Kassel; New
York: Bärenreiter, 1965) 63–70. In German. See no.
467 in this volume.

In the organ music of North German composers in the generation of
Buxtehude and Johann Adam Reincken, virtuoso pedal passages, simplified harmonies, and ostinato figures were used in fantasia or toccata pieces
alongside passages in strict imitative counterpoint; composers tried to integrate the strict and free styles, whereas in the South they were kept separate.
(David Bloom)

1658 RIEMANN, Hugo. **Un giudizio di Hugo**
as **Riemann** [An appraisal by Hugo Riemann], *G.B.*
Pergolesi, 1710-1736: Note e documenti, raccolti in
occasione della settimana celebrativa (Siena: Ticci
Editore Libraio, 1942) 49. In Italian. See no. 273 in this
volume.

A brief and favorable commentary on Pergolesi and his works.

⟶ RIPOLLÉS PÉREZ, Vicente. **Los ministriles de**
los siglos XVI-XVII en la catedral de Valencia
[The ministriles of the cathedral of Valencia in the 16th
and 17th centuries]. See no. 1421 in this volume.

1659 ROLANDI, Ulderico. **Contributo alla**
as **bibliografia di libretti e di esecuzioni d'opere**
pergolesiane [Contribution to the bibliography of librettos and of performances of operas by Pergolesi],
G.B. Pergolesi, 1710-1736: Note e documenti, raccolti
in occasione della settimana celebrativa (Siena: Ticci
Editore Libraio, 1942) 77–87. *Facs.* In Italian. See no.
273 in this volume.

Descriptions of and commentary on 13 18th-c. librettos, including material
on various pasticcios and *La serva padrona*. *(Mark Stevens)*

1660 ROLLAND, Romain. **An Beethoven: Dankge-**
as **sang** [To Beethoven: Song of thanks], *Beethoven-*
Zentenarfeier: Festbericht (Wien: Otto Maass' Söhne,
1927) 66–74. In German. See no. 141 in this volume.

1661 ROLLAND, Romain. **Notes sur l'***Orfeo* **de Luigi**
as **Rossi, et sur les musiciens italiens à Paris, sous**
Mazarin [Notes on the *Orfeo* of Luigi Rossi, and on
Italian musicians in Paris under Mazarin], *Congrès in-*
ternational d'histoire de la musique: Documents,
mémoires et vœux (Solesmes: St. Pierre; Paris:
Fischbacher, 1901) 191–209. In French. See no. 32 in
this volume.

Discusses Jules Mazarin's relationships with music and musicians, the
Barberini family in France, Rossi's background before his arrival in
France, the first production of Rossi's *L'Orfeo* in Paris (1647), and reli-
gious and political opposition to the work.

1662 ROSENTHAL, Karl August. **Zur Stilistik der**
as **Salzburger Kirchenmusik des 17. Jahr-**
hunderts [The style of Salzburg church music of the
17th century], *Beethoven-Zentenarfeier: Internatio-*
naler musikhistorischer Kongress (Wien: Universal,
1927) 202–04. In German. See no. 142 in this volume.

Brief characterization of the music of the most significant Salzburg
Hofkapellmeisters, Peter Guetfreund (ca.1580-1625), Abraham Megerle
(1607-80), and Andreas Hofer (1629-84). The first half of the century was a
time of late-blooming *a cappella* polyphony.

1663 ROUSSEAU, Jean-Jacques. **Un epigramma di**
as **J.J. Rousseau** [An epigram by J.J. Rousseau], *G.B.*
Pergolesi, 1710-1736: Note e documenti, raccolti in
occasione della settimana celebrativa (Siena: Ticci
Editore Libraio, 1942) 48. In Italian. See no. 273 in this
volume.

Includes excerpts from the *Dictionnaire de musique* and an open letter in
praise of Pergolesi and his works.

1664 RUDGE, Olga. **Note,** *Fac-simile del Concerto*
as *funebre* (Siena: Accademia Musicale Chigiana, 1947)
40–47. In Italian. See no. 279 in this volume.

Includes a critique of Mario Rinaldi's thematic catalogue of Vivaldi's complete works; a glance at a bit of marginalia in one of Vivaldi's concertos;
and notes on editions and library holdings of Vivaldi's works. *(Mark Stevens)*

1665 RUDOLPH, Johanna. **Über die biblische**
as **Gewandung von Händels Oratorien** [The biblical trappings of Händel's oratorios], *Händel-Ehrung*
der Deutschen Demokratischen Republik:
Konferenzbericht (Leipzig: VEB Deutscher Verlag für
Musik, 1961) 181–86. In German. See no. 408 in this
volume.

Händel's choice of biblical subject matter is generally associated with popular struggles against oppression and slavery. The reason he went specifically to the Bible for these themes may be linked to the revolutionary character of radical Protestantism from Luther through the English Civil War.
(David Bloom)

1666 RUHNKE, Martin. **Zum Stand der Telemann-**
as **Forschung** [The state of Telemann research], *Bericht*
über den internationalen musikwissenschaftlichen
Kongreß (Kassel: Bärenreiter, 1963) 161–64. In German. See no. 452 in this volume.

Discusses biographical and musicological studies of the composer since
1920.

1667 SANDBERGER, Adolf. **Neue Forschungen zu**
as **Caccini und Monteverdi** [New research on Caccini
and Monteverdi], *Haydn-Zentenarfeier* (Leipzig:

Breitkopf & Härtel; Wien: Artaria, 1909) 208. In German. See no. 65 in this volume.

Presents recent research on the opera composers Giulio Caccini and Claudio Monteverdi.

1668
as

SASSE, Konrad. **Händels Stellung zu den gesellschaftlichen Problemen in England** [Händel's position on social problems in England], *Händel-Ehrung der Deutschen Demokratischen Republik: Konferenzbericht* (Leipzig: VEB Deutscher Verlag für Musik, 1961) 81–85. In German. See no. 408 in this volume.

Argues that Händel's oratorios show his identification with the progressive forces of the English bourgeoisie: *Saul* and *Israel in Egypt* (both 1739) support the policy of Robert Walpole in the military confrontation with Spain, and *Samson* (1743) refers to Walpole after the collapse of his ministry; while the *Occasional oratorio* (1746) and *Judas Maccabaeus* (1747) are a reaction to the Jacobite uprising of 1745. In *Belshazzar* (1745) and *Jephtha* (1752) Händel transcends the bourgeois point of view to consider its internal contradictions. *(David Bloom)*

1669
as

SCHANZLIN, Hans Peter. **Zur Geschichte der Litanei im 17. Jahrhundert** [Toward a history of the litany in the 17th century], *Bericht über den siebenten internationalen musikwissenschaftlichen Kongress* (Kassel: Bärenreiter, 1959) 259–61. In German. See no. 390 in this volume.

Various litany compositions for Roman Catholic and, in the first quarter of the century, Protestant use were issued by Michael Praetorius, Giovanni Pietro Finatti, Giovanni Francesco Mognossa (identified in a 1673 publication, as maestro di capella at the cathedral of Novara but otherwise unattested), Berthold Hipp, Johann Melchior Gletle, and Heinrich Ignaz Franz von Biber. One musicologically interesting shared feature is a close resemblance to the solo-tutti technique of the concertante style. *(David Bloom)*

1670
as

SCHENK, Erich, moderator. **Probleme der Schulbildungen in der Musik des 17. und 18. Jahrhunderts im österreichisch-italienischen Raum** [The formation of schools of music in the 17th and 18th centuries in Austrian and Italian territory], *Bericht über den neunten internationalen Kongreß* (Kassel: Bärenreiter, 1964-1966) 226–36. In German. See no. 491 in this volume.

Particular topics in the roundtable discussion include the Emilian school, the earlier Viennese school (second half of the 17th c.), the so-called Italian-Austrian organists school, the Dresden school, the school of Montserrat, and the Neapolitan school; the Piedmontese school as the source from which Italian music came to Paris; and Mozart's relation to the Austrian church music tradition. The participants were Barry S. BROOK, Dragotin CVETKO, Richard ENGLÄNDER, Gregori ESTRADA, Constantin FLOROS, Helmut HUCKE, Arend Johannes Christiaan KOOLE, Friedrich Wilhelm RIEDEL, and John G. SUESS. *(David Bloom)*

1671
as

SCHERING, Arnold. **Die Anfänge des Oratoriums** [The beginnings of the oratorio]. Ed. by Ludwig SCHIEDERMAIR, *Bericht über den zweiten Kongress der Internationalen Musikgesellschaft* (Leipzig: Breitkopf & Härtel, 1907) 216–17. In German. See no. 53 in this volume.

The importance of Saint Filippo Neri in the origins of the genre has been exaggerated; his pupil Agostino Manni (author of the text to Emilio de' Cavalieri's *Rappresentatione di Anima, et di Corpo...*, 1600) played a more significant role. The dialogue style of the earliest Italian oratorios is typified by the *Dialogo della samaritana* in Giovanni Francesco Anerio's *Teatro harmonico spirituale* (1619). A complete discussion is provided in the author's Habilitationsschrift (1907, published as *Die Geschichte des Oratoriums*, Leipzig 1911). *(David Bloom)*

1672
as

SCHERING, Arnold. **Die freie Kadenz im Instrumentalkonzert des 18. Jahrhunderts** [The free cadenza in 18th-century instrumental concer-

tos], *Bericht über den zweiten Kongress der Internationalen Musikgesellschaft* (Leipzig: Breitkopf & Härtel, 1907) 204–11. In German. See no. 53 in this volume.

The instrumental cadenza developed chiefly out of the cadenza practice of early Baroque vocal music. Cadenzas, from Torelli through C.P.E. Bach, made little or no systematic use of thematic material from the movement proper, and were therefore quite unlike the cadenzas of the Classical concerto; the more the Baroque cadenza represented a break from the fully composed music, the more successful as an improvisation it was felt to be. No cadenza improvised today is likely to possess the full charm of the free cadenza of the Baroque, because audiences do not any longer perceive the performer as participating in the composition of a work. *(David Bloom)*

1673
as

SCHIEDERMAIR, Ludwig. **Die neapolitanische Oper des 18. Jahrhunderts** [Neapolitan opera of the 18th century], *Bericht über den zweiten Kongress der Internationalen Musikgesellschaft* (Leipzig: Breitkopf & Härtel, 1907) 217. In German. See no. 53 in this volume.

A reevaluation of the previously despised opera traditions of Naples has been sparked by the enthusiasm of Hermann Kretzschmar. The 18th-c. history of the genre and its influence on later composers through Richard Wagner are discussed. *(David Bloom)*

1674
as

SCHLITZER, Franco. **La legenda d'amore di G.B. Pergolesi** [The legend of Pergolesi's love], *G.B. Pergolesi, 1710-1736: Note e documenti, raccolti in occasione della settimana celebrativa* (Siena: Ticci Editore Librario, 1942) 35–41. In Italian. See no. 273 in this volume.

The romantic and tragic story of Pergolesi's love for Maria Spinelli, told in Francesco Florimo's *Cenno storico sulla scuola musicale di Napoli* (1869-71), is shown to be untrue. *(Mark Stevens)*

1675
as

SCHMIEDER, Wolfgang. **Bemerkungen zur Bachquellenforschung** [Observations on Bach source studies], *Bericht über die Wissenschaftliche Bachtagung* (Leipzig: Peters, 1951) 219–30. In German. See no. 298 in this volume.

Direct sources for Bach research (autographs, editions appearing during Bach's lifetime, poetic and other text collections set by Bach, copies from Bach's time and later, and prints made shortly after Bach's death) and indirect sources (death inventories and institutional catalogues, testimony from contemporary private and public writing, acts of religious and secular authorities, and iconographical evidence) are in grave need of systematization, especially since the disruptions of World War II. *(James Donald Anderson)*

1676
as

SCHMITZ, Arnold. **Die oratorische Kunst J.S. Bachs: Grundfragen und Grundlagen** [The oratorio art of J.S. Bach: Underlying questions and basic principles], *Kongreß-Bericht: Gesellschaft für Musikforschung* (Kassel; Basel: Bärenreiter, 1950) 33–49. *Music.* In German. See no. 299 in this volume.

The oratorio combines two of the seven liberal arts: music and rhetoric, bringing together elements from both. Of the elements of rhetoric—inventio, dispositio, decoratio, and elocutio—decoratio is the most directly applicable to music. The classification and function of musical figures in Bach's time and their relation to the interpretation of text are also discussed.

1677
as

SCHNEIDER, Constantin. **Zur Frühgeschichte der Oper in Salzburg (bis 1650)** [On the early history of opera in Salzburg (until 1650)], *Beethoven-Zentenarfeier: Internationaler musikhistorischer Kongress* (Wien: Universal, 1927) 196–201. In German. See no. 142 in this volume.

The three main genres established by 1618—court opera in Italian, staged and semistaged oratorio also largely in Italian, and Latin school drama—were those that survived through the 18th c. Johann Stainhauser's chronicle of the tenures of the prince-archbishops Wolf Dietrich von Raitenau (1587-1612) and Marcus Sitticus von Hohenems (1612-19) provides important evidence. *(David Bloom)*

1678
as
SERAUKY, Walter. **Georg Friedrich Händels italienische Kantatenwelt** [The world of Georg Friedrich Händel's Italian cantatas], *Händel-Ehrung der Deutschen Demokratischen Republik: Konferenzbericht* (Leipzig: VEB Deutscher Verlag für Musik, 1961) 109–13. In German. See no. 408 in this volume.

Händel's work list includes some 72 solo cantatas and 28 cantatas for one or more voices with chamber accompaniment in Italian, together with 22 vocal duets and trios in Italian, mostly composed between 1707 and 1709. Their origins, texts, and musical characteristics are briefly reviewed. *(David Bloom)*

1679
as
SERAUKY, Walter. **Zum gegenwärtigen Stande der Bach- und Händelforschung** [On the present state of Bach and Händel research], *Bericht über die Wissenschaftliche Bachtagung* (Leipzig: Peters, 1951) 295–307. In German. See no. 298 in this volume.

Recent Bach research has produced many bibliographical publications and no comprehensive monographs. Two areas for new research are the clarification of the term *symbol* and, specifically, the role of number symbolism in the light of Bach's mathematical speculations. Händel research is less unified. There is no need for another biography, but Händel's relationships with Hasse and Gluck deserve further study; a closer analysis of the harmonic and structural characteristics of Händel's work is also desirable. *(James Donald Anderson)*

1680
as
SHEDLOCK, John South. **Purcell et Bach** [Purcell and Bach]. Trans. by Fernande SALZEDO, *Congrès international d'histoire de la musique: Documents, mémoires et vœux* (Solesmes: St. Pierre; Paris: Fischbacher, 1901) 210–12. In French. See no. 32 in this volume.

Both Purcell and Bach were strongly influenced by French and Italian music. Both were ignored in the years immediately following their deaths. *(David Bloom)*

1681
as
SIEDENTOPF, Henning. **Zu J.S. Bachs Klaviersatz mit obligaten Stimmen: Instrument und Spieltechnik** [Bach's writing for keyboard with independent voices: The instrument and playing techique], *Bericht über den internationalen musikwissenschaftlichen Kongreß* (Kassel: Bärenreiter, 1963) 170–71. In German. See no. 452 in this volume.

Discusses Bach's contrapuntal writing for keyboard in terms of the limited ambitus (for each manual) of his instruments, the possiblity of using more than one manual, melodic interchange between hands, and single-hand technique. *(David Bloom)*

1682
as
SIEGELE, Ulrich. **Zur Verbindung von Präludium und Fuge bei J.S. Bach** [The connection between preludes and fugues in J.S. Bach], *Bericht über den internationalen musikwissenschaftlichen Kongreß* (Kassel: Bärenreiter, 1963) 164–67. In German. See no. 452 in this volume.

Discusses the pairings of prelude and fugue in *Das wohltemperirte Clavier*, especially in terms of duration and proportion. *(David Bloom)*

1683
as
SIEGELE, Willi. **Musik des oberschwäbischen Barock** [The music of the Upper Swabian Baroque], *Der Barock: Seine Orgeln und seine Musik in Oberschwaben* (Berlin: Merseburger, 1952) 40–58. *Illus.* In German. See no. 305 in this volume.

Musical culture flourished in the region in the 18th c. in its many Benedictine and Premonstratensian monastic foundations, the former in contact with the University of Salzburg and the latter with the abbey of Prémontré in France. In addition to organ music in church services, in which improvisation was the most significant element, there was festive music on important occasions and considerable private music making among the monks. Monastic composers of distinction included Isfrid Kayser, Sixt Bachmann, Conrad Michael Schneider, and Sebastian Sailer, and the theorists Meinrad Spieß and Honorat Goehl. *(David Bloom)*

1684
as
SIEGMUND-SCHULTZE, Walther. **Georg Philipp Telemann** [Georg Philipp Telemann], *Beiträge zu einem neuen Telemannbild* (Magdeburg: Vorwärts, 1963) 9–16. In German. See no. 453 in this volume.

Describes the life and personality of Telemann, who, though perhaps aware of his own shortcomings as a composer, created a large body of useful, pleasant, and accessible music. He often consciously ventured ahead of his time, particularly in the realm of harmony. *(John Stansell)*

1685
as
SIEGMUND-SCHULTZE, Walther. **Küntfige Aufgaben der Förderung und Pflege des Händelschen Werkes** [Future tasks in the advancement and cultivation of Händel's works], *Händel-Ehrung der Deutschen Demokratischen Republik: Konferenzbericht* (Leipzig: VEB Deutscher Verlag für Musik, 1961) 30–38. In German. See no. 408 in this volume.

Closing remarks at a congress on Händel studies. Research areas on the composer that need further work include the study of his relationship to musical traditions of the countries where he was active; his collaboration with his librettists; his use of dramatic characterization with attention to the commonalities and differences between his operas and oratorios; the individual character of his melodic procedure compared to that of his contemporaries; the place of instrumental works within his total output; and the character of his thematic development in relation to the Mannheim school. *(David Bloom)*

1686
as
SIEVERS, Heinrich. **Friedrich Konrad Griepenkerl und die neu aufgefundene Handschrift von Bachs h-moll Messe** [Friedrich Konrad Griepenkerl and the newly discovered manuscript of Bach's B-minor Mass], *Bericht über die Wissenschaftliche Bachtagung* (Leipzig: Peters, 1951) 231–39. In German. See no. 298 in this volume.

The MS, discovered in 1949, measures 24 by 36 cm. and is copied in an 18th-c. hand. It is in two parts, each half-bound in leather. Currently in the possession of the author, it was the property of Friedrich Konrad Griepenkerl (1782-1849), a student in the University of Göttingen from 1805 under Johann Nikolaus Forkel. It resembles the original autograph; some of its important variants match those found in a copy by Johann Philipp Kirnberger. *(James Donald Anderson)*

1687
as
SKREBKOV, Sergej Sergeevič. **Ėvoljucija stilja v Russkoj horovoj muzyke XVII veka** [The evolution of style in Russian choral music of the 17th century], *Musica antiqua Europae orientalis* (Warszawa: Państwowe Wydawnictwo Naukowe, 1966). *Music.* In Russian. See no. 506 in this volume.

1688
as
SMITH, William Charles. **Händels Leben in England: Unter besonderer Berücksichtigung seiner Blindheit** [Händel's life in England: With particular attention to his blindness], *Händel-Ehrung der Deutschen Demokratischen Republik: Konferenzbericht* (Leipzig: VEB Deutscher Verlag für Musik, 1961) 73–79. In German. See no. 408 in this volume.

Factors in Händel's first visits to England, beginning 1710, may have included an acquaintance with John Wych, the resident English minister in Hamburg, as well as his awareness that the Hanover Elector and his court, where Händel was serving as kapellmeister, would eventually move to England on Queen Anne's death. Documentation of his professional and social successes in London, his charitable interest in the Decayed Musicians' Society, and the medical history of his eye ailment are discussed. *(David Bloom)*

1689
as

SØRENSEN, Søren. **Eine Kantaten-Jahrgang von Christian Ludwig Boxberg (1670-1729)** [A cantata cycle by Christian Ludwig Boxberg (1670--1729)], *Bericht über den siebenten internationalen musikwissenschaftlichen Kongress* (Kassel: Bärenreiter, 1959) 254–55. In German. See no. 390 in this volume.

Boxberg, best known for his work for the Leipzig opera as singer, librettist, and composer, left the stage to serve as the organist of the Peter-und-Paul-Kirche, Görlitz, from 1702 until his death, but little of his work as a church musician has survived. A group of 35 cantatas by Boxberg, representing most of a cycle for the liturgical year, has now been located in the holdings of the Akademisk Kapell at the Universitetsbibliotek, Lund (*S-L* MS Saml. Wenster M 1-7, 9-36). The works are briefly described. A complete description is published under the title *Über einen Kantatenjahrgang des Görlitzer Komponisten Christian Ludwig Boxberg* in B. Hjelmborg and S. Sørensen, eds., *Natalicia musicologica Knud Jeppesen septuagenario collegis oblata* (Copenhagen, 1962). *(David Bloom)*

1690
as

SØRENSEN, Søren. **Ein neu gefundene Buxtehude-Kantate** [A newly found Buxtehude cantata], *Bericht über den internationalen musikwissenschaftlichen Kongreß* (Kassel: Bärenreiter, 1957) 221–23. *Music.* In German. See no. 356 in this volume.

A previously unknown cantata on the chorale *Du Friedefürst, Herr Jesu Christ*, for five-part chorus, strings, and continuo, and likely on stylistic grounds to have been written in the 1680s, is in the Düben collection of the Universitetsbibliotek, Uppsala. An edition by the author has been published in Copenhagen by Engstrøm & Sødring (1956). *(David Bloom)*

⟶ SÖHNER, Leo. **Gregorianischen Choral und Orgel in Deutschland von 1500 bis 1700** [Gregorian chant and the organ in Germany, 1500-1700]. See no. 1437 in this volume.

1691
as

SPRINGER, Hermann. **Beziehungen zwischen Oper und Volksmusik im Settecento** [Relationships between opera and traditional music in the 17th century], *Bericht über den musikwissenschaftlichen Kongreß in Basel* (Leipzig: Breitkopf & Härtel, 1925) 326–27. In German. See no. 102 in this volume.

Hermann Kretzschmar recognized the influence of traditional music in the 3/2 meter of Francesco Cavalli's works. The barcaroles have ambiguous historical roots; the term *barcarola*, as used in the 17th c., refers to a piece in regular rhythm that resembles the aria style of Antonio Draghi or Antonio Pietro Cesti. The greatest influx of traditional elements came via opera buffa and intermezzo in the early 18th c., and can be seen in the works of Benedetto Marcello and Salvatore Apolloni.

⟶ ŠREJER-TKAČENKO, Onys'ja Jakovlevna. **Razvitie ukrainskoj muzyki XVI-XVII vekah** [The development of Ukrainian music from the 16th to the 18th centuries]. See no. 1440 in this volume.

1692
as

STEGLICH, Rudolf. **Händels Sprachenge-brauch** [Händel's use of languages], *Händel-Ehrung der Deutschen Demokratischen Republik: Konferenzbericht* (Leipzig: VEB Deutscher Verlag für Musik, 1961) 101–07. In German. See no. 408 in this volume.

Discusses Händel's knowledge of and relative fluency in Latin, French, Italian, and English; multilingual code-switching in his speech, writing, and performance indications; and the particular problems of achieving clarity of diction in the performance of his vocal works. *(David Bloom)*

⟶ STEVENS, Denis. **Les sources de l'In nomine** [The sources of the In nomine]. See no. 1444 in this volume.

1693
as

SWALIN, Benjamin F. **Purcell's masque in Timon of Athens,** *Papers of the American Musicological Society* (Philadelphia: American Musicological Society, 1946) 112–24. *Music, bibliog., charts, diagr.* See no. 272 in this volume.

Thomas Shadwell's 1677-78 adaptation *The history of Timon of Athens, the man-hater* included a masque in the act 2 banquet scene (act 1 in Shakespeare's play), apparently with music by Louis Grabu; in a 1694 revival, the masque used a somewhat different text and an entirely new score by Purcell. Purcell's music is set in the historical context of the English masque, and its structure and style are analyzed. *(David Bloom)*

1694
as

SYCHRA, Antonín. **Romain Rollands Händel-Bild heute gesehen** [Romain Rolland's portrait of Händel from today's perspective], *Händel-Ehrung der Deutschen Demokratischen Republik: Konferenzbericht* (Leipzig: VEB Deutscher Verlag für Musik, 1961) 219–21. In German. See no. 408 in this volume.

Rolland's biography *Haendel* (Paris, 1910), ranking Händel among the realist artists, continues to have relevance, particularly in his understanding of Händel's so-called plagiarism and of the content of his purely instrumental music. *(David Bloom)*

1695
as

SZABOLCSI, Bence. **Tre composizioni sconosciute di Antonio Vivaldi** [Three unknown compositions by Antonio Vivaldi], *Fac-simile del Concerto funebre* (Siena: Accademia Musicale Chigiana, 1947) 24–27. In Italian. See no. 279 in this volume.

Describes three works discovered in the Conservatorio di Musica S. Pietro a Majella in Naples: a concerto in E-flat for violin, viola, and bass; a concerto in G for two violins, viola, violoncello, and bass; and a sinfonia for two violins, viola, and bass. *(Mark Stevens)*

1696
as

SZWEYKOWSKI, Zygmunt Marian. **Proces przemian stylistycznych w muzyce wokalno-instrumentalnej epoki saskiej** [The process of stylistic change in the vocal-instrumental music Saxon era], *The book of the first international musicological congress devoted to the works of Frederick Chopin* (Warszawa: Państwowe Wydawnictwo Naukowe, 1963) 633–37. In Polish. See no. 425 in this volume.

Discusses the history of music in Poland ca. 1697-1763, when the reigning monarchs (Augustus II and Augustus III) were electors of Saxony.

1697
as

SZWEYKOWSKI, Zygmunt Marian. **Some problems of Baroque music in Poland,** *Musica antiqua Europae orientalis* (Warszawa: Państwowe Wydawnictwo Naukowe, 1966). See no. 506 in this volume.

1698
as

TANNERY, Paul. **Lettres inédites adressées au Père Mersenne (celles de Pierre Trichet concernant la musique)** [Unpublished letters addressed to Father Mersenne (those of Pierre Trichet concerning music)], *Annales internationales d'histoire: Congrès de Paris, 1900. V: Histoire des sciences* (Paris: Colin, 1901) V, 311–43. In French. See no. 27 in this volume.

1699
as

TESSIER, André. **Un document sur les répétitions du Triomphe de l'Amour à Saint-Germain-en-Laye (1681)** [A document about the rehearsals of *Le triomphe de l'Amour* at Saint Germain-en-Laye (1681)], *Actes du Congrès d'histoire de l'art* (Paris: Presses Universitaires de France, 1923-1924) 874–94. *Charts, diagr.* In French. See no. 94 in this volume.

Mémoire du pain..., a record of food served at rehearsals for Lully's *Triomphe de l'Amour*, was discovered at the Archives Nationales in Paris under the heading *Pièces justificatives aux comptes des menus-plaisirs*. The document contains a wealth of detailed information concerning the musical life of that time, such as data on the exact compositions of the orchestra and the corps de ballet, and the number of rehearsals undertaken. *(Vivian Conejero)*

1700
as
THOMÀS SABATER, Joan Maria. **La música de órgano** [Organ music], *Crónica del IV Congreso Nacional de Música Sagrada* (Vitoria: Imprenta del Montepío Diocesano, 1930) 220–27. In Spanish. See no. 155 in this volume.

Discusses general characteristics of J.S. Bach's organ works. An analysis of the Roman Catholic Church's rubrics regarding the use of the organ in the liturgy is included. *(José López-Calo)*

1701
as
TIBY, Ottavio. **Emanuele d'Astorga: Aggiunte e correzioni da apportare alle ricerche del Prof. Hans Volkmann** [Emanuele d'Astorga: Addenda and corrections to the research of Hans Volkmann], *Société Internationale de Musicologie, cinquième congrès/Internationale Gesellschaft für Musikwissenschaft, fünfter Kongreß/International Society for Musical Research, Fifth Congress* (Amsterdam: Vereniging voor Nederlandse Muziekgeschiedenis, 1953) 398–403. In Italian. See no. 316 in this volume.

Expands on Volkmann's *Emanuel d'Astorga* (Leipzig: Breitkopf & Härtel, 1911-19), the pioneering biography of the Italian composer (1681-1736).

1702
as
TORREFRANCA, Fausto. **Prime ricognizioni della stile violoncellistico Plattiano** [Preliminary appraisal of Platti's violoncello style], *Compte rendu/Kongressbericht/Report* (Basel: Bärenreiter, 1951) 203–11. *Music*. In Italian. See no. 289 in this volume.

Giovanni Benedetto Platti (before 1692–1763) was a virtuoso on the violoncello as well as the violin, and wrote a number of sonatas and concertos for the instrument, evidently under the patronage of Count Rudolf Franz Erwein von Schönborn. These works, which bear signs of Platti's early stylistic maturity, are precociously modern. They are examined in some detail. *(David Bloom)*

1703
as
TORREFRANCA, Fausto. **Problemi Vivaldiani** [Issues in Vivaldi studies], *Compte rendu/Kongressbericht/Report* (Basel: Bärenreiter, 1951) 195–202. In Italian. See no. 289 in this volume.

Discusses the importance to Vivaldi of the posthumous publication of Corelli's concerti grossi (1714); the failure of Vivaldi's violin concertos to find a lasting success in the 18th c.; Quantz's condemnation of the operatic influence on Vivaldi's style; the importance of Vivaldi's relationship with Crown Prince Friedrich Christian of Poland and Elector of Saxony; and the question of dating the concertos. *(David Bloom)*

1704
as
TORREFRANCA, Fausto. **Profonda umanità di una rivoluzione musicale** [The deep humanity of a musical revolution], *Atti del secondo Congresso internazionale di musica* (Firenze: Le Monnier, 1940) 314–23. In Italian. See no. 239 in this volume.

Argues that the Romantic revolution should be dated to the beginning of the 18th c. so as to include the Italian composers of that period working in the tradition of Italian vocalism with the instruments of Cremona; the Italian violin is the deus ex machina from which it sprang. *(David Bloom)*

1705
as
TORREFRANCA, Fausto. **La sonata italiana per cembalo nella prima metà del Settecento e i concerti di Giovanni Platti (1740)** [The Italian harpsichord sonata in the first half of the 18th century and the concertos of Giovanni Platti (1740)], *Report of the Fourth Congress of the International Musical Society* (London: Novello, 1912) 158. In Italian. See no. 71 in this volume.

Summary of a paper. The discovery of Platti's harpsichord concertos strengthens the argument that the modern concerto style developed among the Venetian composers, before 1740.

1706
as
TREITLER, Leo. **Bach problems,** *Report of the Eighth Congress of the International Musicological Society. II: Reports* (Kassel: Bärenreiter, 1962) 127–31. See no. 440 in this volume.

A report on a discussion by Georg von DADELSEN, Martin BERNSTEIN, Friedrich BLUME, Hans T. DAVID, Alfred DÜRR, Karl GEIRINGER, Arthur MENDEL, William H. SCHEIDE, and Luigi Ferdinando TAGLIAVINI of papers by Dadelsen and Walter Emery abstracted as nos. 1518 and 1538 in this volume.

⟶
TREND, John Brande. **The madrigal of Pedro Rimonte.** See no. 1456 in this volume.

1707
as
VETTER, Walther. **Bachs Universalität** [Bach's universality], *Bericht über die Wissenschaftliche Bachtagung* (Leipzig: Peters, 1951) 131–57. In German. See no. 298 in this volume.

Harmonic, melodic, and rhythmic aspects of the Brandenburg concertos, *Das wohltemperirte Clavier*, and the secular cantatas are seen as evidence of Bach's awareness of life's essential pain. The realities of death and love were known to Bach, who was not embittered by them but instead sweetened death's reality through his *Lebensfreude*. His sense of humor is sometimes evident in the texts he set. *(James Donald Anderson)*

1708
as
VITRY, Paul. **Le tombeau de Henry du Mont, musicien liégeois, établi en France au XVIIᵉ siècle** [The tomb of Henry du Mont, musician of Liège, established in France in the 17th century], *Fédération Archéologique et Historique de Belgique: Annales du XXIᵉ congrès* (Liège: Poncelet, 1909) II, 917–53. In French. See no. 64 in this volume.

1709
as
VOLEK, Tomislav. **Czech music of the seventeenth and eighteenth centuries,** *Musica antiqua Europae orientalis* (Warszawa: Państwowe Wydawnictwo Naukowe, 1966). See no. 506 in this volume.

1710
as
WEINMANN, Karl. **Zur Geschichte der Kirchenmusik im 17. und 18. Jahrhundert** [The history of church music in the 17th and 18th centuries], *Report of the Fourth Congress of the International Musical Society* (London: Novello, 1912) 312. In German. See no. 71 in this volume.

Summary of a paper discussing the state of research on Baroque liturgical music.

1711
as
WESSELY, Helene. **Romanus Weichlein: Ein vergessener österreichischer Instrumentalkomponist des 17. Jahrhunderts** [Romanus Weichlein: A forgotten Austrian composer of instrumental music in the 17th century], *Bericht über den internationalen musikwissenschaftlichen Kongreß Wien Mozartjahr 1956* (Graz; Köln: Böhlau, 1958) 689–707. *Music, charts, diagr.* In German. See no. 365 in this volume.

A brief biography of the Austrian composer and violinist (1652-1706), and an extended discussion of the 12 sonatas for multiple instruments of his *Encaenia musices*, op. 1 (1695). An appendix provides the Latin text of the dedication of this work to Emperor Leopold I. *(David Bloom)*

1712
as
WILKOWSKA-CHOMIŃSKA, Krystyna. **Telemanns Beziehungen zur Polnischen Musik** [Telemann's relation to Polish music], *Beiträge zu einem*

neuen Telemannbild (Magdeburg: Vorwärts, 1963) 23–37. *Music.* In German. See no. 453 in this volume.

Places Telemann's evocations of Polish traditional music in the historical context of Polish-German cultural relations up to his time. His polonaise movements are principally based on mazurka rhythms; he also shows the influence of the music of the Górale (highlanders) of the Polish Carpathians and of the Hanáki region of Moravia. *(John Stansell)*

1713
as
WOLF, Robert Erich. **Renaissance, mannerism, Baroque: Three styles, three periods,** *Les colloques de Wégimont. IV: Le Baroque musical—Recueil d'études sur la musique du XVIIe siècle* (Paris: Belles Lettres, 1963) 35–80. See no. 386 in this volume.

The music of composers such as Caccini, Peri, Monteverdi, Carissimi, and Schütz ought to be regarded not as Baroque but as mannerist, growing out of the political and religious crises of the mid-16th c. and marked by extreme experimentalism and lack of stylistic unity, most characteristically in the setting of a dramatic text. The true Baroque, based on the expression of power and use of closed forms, in a unified, characteristically instrumental style, does not begin until the period 1635-50.

1714
as
WOLFF, Hellmuth Christian, moderator. **Die Beziehungen zwischen Oper, Oratorium und Instrumentalkusik der Barockzeit** [Relationships among opera, oratorio, and instrumental music of the Baroque period], *Bericht über den neunten internationalen Kongreß* (Kassel: Bärenreiter, 1964-1966) II, 212–25. In German. See no. 491 in this volume.

Topics covered in the roundtable discussion include the concept of dialogue as a formal principle; the relations between Giacomo Carissimi's oratorios and the 17th-c. Roman opera; the use of characteristically instrumental forms in 17th-c. opera and oratorio; the Emilian or Bolognese school in the later 17th c.; the Neapolitan School in the early 18th c.; the operatic sources of Vivaldi's solo concertos; Michele Mascitti's sonata op. 5, no. 12, as imitation of opera-ballet; operatic influences on Locatelli; French opera overtures and the early symphony; and clarino style in Baroque opera and oratorio. The participants were J. Murray BARBOUR, Barry S. BROOK, Rudolf ELLER, Hans ENGEL, Karl GEIRINGER, Federico GHISI, Helmut HUCKE, Arend Johannes Christiaan KOOLE, Frits NOSKE, Hans F. REDLICH, John G. SUESS, Giuseppe VECCHI, and Franklin B. ZIMMERMAN. *(David Bloom)*

1715
as
WOLFF, Hellmuth Christian. **Telemann und die Hamburger Oper** [Telemann and the Hamburg opera], *Beiträge zu einem neuen Telemannbild* (Magdeburg: Vorwärts, 1963) 38–49. *Illus.* In German. See no. 453 in this volume.

Surveys Telemann's work as stage composer and librettist, with synopses of seven extant operas written for the Hamburg Gänsemarkt-Oper: *Der geduldige Socrates* (1721), *Sieg der Schönheit* (1722), *Der neumodische Liebhaber Damon* (1724), *Pimpinone* (1725), *Emma und Eginhard* (1728), *Miriways* (1728), and *Flavius Bertaridus, König der Longobarden* (1729). *(John Stansell)*

1716
as
WORBS, Hans Christoph. **Eine unbekannte Liederhandschrift aus dem Anfang des 18. Jahrhunderts** [An unknown song manuscript from the beginning of the 18th century], *Bericht über den internationalen musikwissenschaftlichen Kongreß* (Kassel: Bärenreiter, 1957) 239–41. *Music.* In German. See no. 356 in this volume.

Describes the contents of an 18th-c. MS (*F-Sn* MS sign.no.2490) that includes 101 songs with notated single-voice melody and no accompaniment. Some of the texts treat social and political issues of the time with considerable frankness. *(David Bloom)*

1717
as
ZANETTI, Emilia. **Il *Guglielmo d'Aquitania*** [The *Guglielmo d'Aquitania*], *G.B. Pergolesi, 1710-1736: Note e documenti, raccolti in occasione della settimana celebrativa* (Siena: Ticci Editore Libraio, 1942) 17–27. In Italian. See no. 273 in this volume.

Describes the genesis of the dramma sacro *Guglielmo d'Aquitania* and demonstrates how a persistent motive contributes to musical unity. *(Mark Stevens)*

1718
as
ZIMMERMAN, Franklin B. **Social backgrounds of the Restoration anthem,** *Bericht über den internationalen musikwissenschaftlichen Kongreß* (Kassel: Bärenreiter, 1963) 27–28. See no. 452 in this volume.

The anthem, as it became more secular and popular in the period of the Stuart Restoration, served purposes beyond those intended by the Church of England. For music lovers such as Samuel Pepys, John Evelyn, and Roger North, it was often the most pleasurable part of going to church. Its text, from Psalms or elsewhere in the Bible, could reflect political positions at Court, as in the case of several topical anthems by Purcell. *(Laurie Appleby)*

26 Classic and pre-Classic (ca. 1750 – 1825)

1719
as
ABERT, Hermann. **Beethoven,** *Beethoven-Zentenarfeier: Festbericht* (Wien: Otto Maass' Söhne, 1927) 58–66. In German. See no. 141 in this volume.

1720
as
ADLER, Guido. **Das obligate Akkompagnement der Wiener Klassischen Schule** [Obbligato accompaniment in the Viennese Classic school], *Bericht über den I. musikwissenschaftlichen Kongress der Deutschen Musikgesellschaft in Leipzig* (Wiesbaden: Breitkopf & Härtel, 1926) 35–43. In German. See no. 120 in this volume.

Discusses the gradual shift from basso continuo to keyboard obbligato style in the 18th-c. The importance of textural variety and classical imitation is considered. *(William Renwick)*

⟶
ADLER, Israel. **Mẁsyqah 'ẁmanẁtyt mihẁs lema'amad hatpylah b̊byhak"n b̊eqehylẁt hayehẁdyẁt b̊e'eyrẁpah lipney ha'emansy-p̊aṣyah** [Non-liturgical art music in European synagogues before the Emancipation]. See no. 6035 in this volume.

1721
as
ALLORTO, Ricardo. **Mozart e Clementi** [Mozart and Clementi], *Bericht über den internationalen musikwissenschaftlichen Kongreß Wien Mozartjahr 1956* (Graz; Köln: Böhlau, 1958) 1–4. In Italian. See no. 365 in this volume.

Surveys the attitudes of the two composers toward each other's music, and cases of direct mutual influences, following their famous encounter at the imperial court, Vienna, on 24 December 1781. *(David Bloom)*

1722
as
ALTAR, Cevat Memduh. **Wolfgang Amadeus Mozart im Lichte osmanisch-österreichischer Beziehungen** [Wolfgang Amadeus Mozart in the light of Ottoman-Austrian relations], *Bericht über den internationalen musikwissenschaftlichen Kongreß Wien Mozartjahr 1956* (Graz; Köln: Böhlau, 1958) 5–6. In German. See no. 365 in this volume.

Summary of a paper on the historical-political context of Mozart's use of Turkish elements in his works; the full paper is published in the *Revue belge de musicologie* X (1956). *(David Bloom)*

1723
as
ANDERSSON, Otto. **The introduction of orchestral music into Finland,** *Report of the Fourth*

Congress of the International Musical Society (London: Novello, 1912) 90–93. See no. 71 in this volume.

Discusses orchestras in the late 18th c.

1724
as

BARBLAN, Guglielmo. **Le orchestre in Lombardia all'epoca di Mozart** [Orchestras in Lombardy in Mozart's time], *Bericht über den internationalen musikwissenschaftlichen Kongreß Wien Mozartjahr 1956* (Graz; Köln: Böhlau, 1958) 18–21. In Italian. See no. 365 in this volume.

In 1770, Mozart heard the local orchestras in three cities in Lombardy: Mantua, Cremona, and Milan. Lombardy's central role in the cultivation of instrumental music is demonstrated by the existence of symphony orchestras in these relatively provincial towns, as well as in Bozzolo and Lodi, and by references to them by Leopold Mozart and Sammartini. *(Carol K. Baron)*

1725
as

BARTHA, Dénes. **Haydn als Opernkapellmeister** [Haydn as opera kapellmeister], *Bericht über die internationale Konferenz zum Andenken Joseph Haydns* (Budapest: Akadémiai Kiadó, 1961) 17–23. *List of works, chronology.* In German. See no. 405 in this volume.

A report on Haydn's operas at the Esterházy court between 1776 and 1790 as documented in the collections of the Országos Széchényi Könyvtár, Budapest, including a chronological list of productions. A full account is published in D. Bartha and L. Somfai, *Haydn als Opernkapellmeister: Die Haydn-Dokumente der Esterházy-Versammlung* (Budapest, 1960). *(Jean W. Smith)*

1726
as

BARTHA, Dénes. **Mozart et le folklore musical de l'Europe centrale** [Mozart and the traditional music of central Europe], *Les influences étrangères dans l'œuvre de W.A. Mozart* (Paris: Centre National de la Recherche Scientifique [CNRS], 1958) 157–81. *Music.* In French. See no. 358 in this volume.

Mozart, Dittersdorf, and Haydn incorporated Hungarian traditional melodies into their works. The Hungarian music of the time contained various aspects of Turkish music; these are also reflected in the works of such composers. *(Susan Poliniak)*

⟶ BÉLZA, Igor' Fёdorovič. **Rosyjsko-polskie stosunki muzyczne w wieku XVII i XVIII** [Russian-Polish musical relations in the 17th and 18th centuries]. See no. 1484 in this volume.

1727
as

BESSELER, Heinrich. **Einflüsse der Contratanzmuzik auf Joseph Haydn** [Influences of contredanse music on Joseph Haydn], *Bericht über die internationale Konferenz zum Andenken Joseph Haydns* (Budapest: Akadémiai Kiadó, 1961) 25–40. *Music.* In German. See no. 405 in this volume.

Particular attention is given to the finale movements of Haydn's mature symphonies, and to the mutual influences of Haydn and Mozart on their orchestral works. *(Jean W. Smith)*

1728
as

BESSELER, Heinrich. **Mozart und die deutsche Klassik** [Mozart and German Classicism], *Bericht über den internationalen musikwissenschaftlichen Kongreß Wien Mozartjahr 1956* (Graz; Köln: Böhlau, 1958) 47–54. *Music, charts, diagr.* In German. See no. 365 in this volume.

The Weimar literary period and the Viennese Classic period were closer than is often assumed; examination of Mozart's music in the light of writings on music by Herder, Christian Gottfried Körner, and Schiller demonstrates the connection. A central characteristic of the Weimar writers, also characteristic of Mozart, is a striving for compositional unity. *(Peter Kaliski)*

1729
as

BOLLERT, Werner. **Bemerkungen zu Mozarts Klavierkonzert F-Dur (K.V. 459)** [Comments on

Mozart's piano concerto in F major, K.459], *Bericht über den internationalen musikwissenschaftlichen Kongreß Wien Mozartjahr 1956* (Graz; Köln: Böhlau, 1958) 66–68. In German. See no. 365 in this volume.

⟶ BÓNIS, Ferenc. **Ungarische Musik im XVII.-XVIII. Jahrhundert** [Hungarian music in the 17th-18th centuries]. See no. 1492 in this volume.

1730
as

BORREN, Charles van den. **Quelques manuscripts de Gossec** [Autograph manuscripts of Gossec], *Compte rendu du V*ᵉ *Congrès international des sciences historiques* (Bruxelles: Weissenbruch, 1923) 369–70. In French. See no. 100 in this volume.

The Bibliothèque du Conservatoire Royal de Musique in Brussels has a collection of François-Joseph Gossec's MSS, including those of the operas *Nitrocris*, *Le double déguisement*, and *Le périgourdin*. *(David Nussenbaum)*

1731
as

BREAZUL, George. **Zu Mozarts Zweihundertjahrfeier** [Regarding Mozart's bicentennial], *Bericht über den internationalen musikwissenschaftlichen Kongreß Wien Mozartjahr 1956* (Graz; Köln: Böhlau, 1958) 69–74. *Music.* In German. See no. 365 in this volume.

Discusses the history of Mozart reception in Romania, from the earliest performances of his operas in the late 18th c. In *Die Entführung aus dem Serail*, which was performed in Bucharest in 1790, Mozart quoted Romanian music that was well-known at the time. *(Peter Kaliski)*

1732
as

BRIQUET, Marie. **Contribution à la vie parisienne de Mozart (1764)** [A note on Mozart's life in Paris (1764)], *Bericht über den internationalen musikwissenschaftlichen Kongreß Wien Mozartjahr 1956* (Graz; Köln: Böhlau, 1958) 75–77. In French. See no. 365 in this volume.

Discusses the operas that Mozart might have seen during his first sojourn in Paris (1763-64) and their possible influence on his own earliest theatrical efforts. *(David Bloom)*

1733
as

BÜCKEN, Ernst. **Zur Frage der Begrenzung und Benennung der Stilwandlung im 18. Jahrhundert** [Delimiting and naming the change in style of the 18th century], *Bericht über den I. musikwissenschaftlichen Kongress der Deutschen Musikgesellschaft in Leipzig* (Wiesbaden: Breitkopf & Härtel, 1926) 103–07. In German. See no. 120 in this volume.

Attempts to define the main characteristics of Baroque, galant, rococo, and Classic styles, citing the writings of Johann Mattheson and Johann Adolf Scheibe. Music written in reaction to the Baroque is distinguished from music written in the emerging galant style. *(William Renwick)*

1734
as

CHARLIER, Clément. **L'écho: Périodique musical liégeois du XVIII**ᵉᵐᵉ [*L'écho*: A musical periodical of Liège in the 18th century], *Société Internationale de Musicologie: Premier Congrès Liège—Compte rendu/Internationale Gesellschaft für Musikwissenschaft: Erster Kongress Lüttich—Kongressbericht/International Society for Musical Research: First Congress Liège: Report* (London: Plainsong and Mediaeval Music Society, 1930) 87–90. In French. See no. 178 in this volume.

Several musical gazettes appeared in Liège from the second half of the 18th c. to the beginning of the 19th c. *L'écho, ou Journal de musique françoise, italienne*, one of these publications, appeared regularly from January 1758 to December 1773. It reflected the tastes of its time and their evolution, as well as the Italian influence upon the French and German styles. Lists are supplied that include important composers whose works were included in *L'écho*. Also of interest, particularly from a bibliographic standpoint, are the advertisements that appeared in the publication. *(Nathaniel Rudykoff)*

1735 CHERBULIEZ, Antoine-Élisée. **Zwei Passauer**
as **handschriftliche Klavierauszüge von Mozarts**
***Figaro* und *Don Juan der Schwelger* (1789)**
[Two manuscript piano reductions from Passau of Mozart's *Figaro* and *Don Juan der Schwelger* (1789)],
*Bericht über die musikwissenschaftliche Tagung der
Internationalen Stiftung Mozarteum* (Leipzig:
Breitkopf & Härtel, 1932) 150–57. In German. See no.
193 in this volume.
The collections of the Konservatorium in Zürich contain MS key-
board-vocal scores, traceable to a rare-books dealer in Würzburg, of *Le
nozze di Figaro*, dated Passau, 1789, and *Don Giovanni*, undated but in the
same hand and format, both presumably connected to 1789 productions of
the operas in Passau. The German texts are previously undocumented; that
for *Figaro* is apparently the second oldest German version extant, after that
of the Donaueschingen production of 1787. Musical variants do not seem
to be significant. *(David Bloom)*

1736 CLOSSON, Ernest. **Les particularités**
as **flamandes de Beethoven** [Beethoven's Flemish
characteristics], *Beethoven-Zentenarfeier: Internationaler musikhistorischer Kongress* (Wien: Universal, 1927) 16–18. In French. See no. 142 in this volume.
Argues that Beethoven's personality and style show typical characteristics
of the West Flanders region from which his forebears came.

1737 CURLING, Edward. **Cherubini as a dramatic**
as **composer,** *Report of the Fourth Congress of the International Musical Society* (London: Novello, 1912) 56.
See no. 71 in this volume.
Summary of a paper. Despite the recognition Cherubini received during his
lifetime, his operas are currently underestimated. *(Mei-Mei Meng)*

1738 CVETKO, Dragotin. **J.B. Novak: Ein slowe-**
as **nischer Anhänger Mozarts** [J.B. Novak: A
Slovenian admirer of Mozart], *Bericht über den internationalen musikwissenschaftlichen Kongreß Wien
Mozartjahr 1956* (Graz; Köln: Böhlau, 1958) 103–06.
In German. See no. 365 in this volume.
Until the end of the 18th c., Slovenian musical life was dominated by Italian
Baroque opera. Austrian and German composers were popularized through
the efforts of Janez Krstnik Novak (Johann Baptist, 1756-1833), who
founded an orchestra and played a major part in getting Mozart's operas
performed in Ljubljana. Novak's own opera *Figaro* (1790) attests to Mozart's influence on his musical development. *(Peter Kaliski)*

1739 DANHELOVSKY, Konstantin. **Graf Ferdinand**
as **Troyer: Der Schubertmäzen** [Count Ferdinand
Troyer: Schubert's patron], *Bericht über den inter-
nationalen Kongress für Schubertforschung*
(Augsburg: Benno Filser, 1929) 239–40. In German.
See no. 154 in this volume.
Offers a brief biographical account and comments on the 1826 portrait by
Johann Ender.

1740 DAVID, Hans Theodor. **Ephrata and Bethle-**
as **hem in Pennsylvania: A comparison,** *Papers of
the American Musicological Society* (Philadelphia:
American Musicological Society, 1946) 97–104. See
no. 272 in this volume.
Both towns were founded as German-speaking religious communities;
Ephrata in 1731 by Seventh-Day Baptists and Bethlehem in 1741 by
Moravian Brethren. In Ephrata, musical life was overwhelmingly dominated by the whimsical and erratic personality of the founder, Johann
Conrad Beissel, who lacked formal training in music and did not create a
lasting legacy. By contrast, in 18th-c. Bethlehem music was cultivated on a
more democratic basis and achieved considerable sophistication, featuring
instrumental and vocal performance, secular as well as church music, programming of important works from contemporary Europe, and development of local composers. *(David Bloom)*

1741 DECSEY, Ernst. **Franz Schubert als Tanz-**
as **musiker** [Franz Schubert as dance musician], *Bericht
über den internationalen Kongress für Schubertforschung* (Augsburg: Benno Filser, 1929) 235–38. In
German. See no. 154 in this volume.
An aesthetic and historic evaluation of Schubert's dance music.

1742 DEININGER, Hanz Friedrich. **Zur Genealogie**
as **Wolfgang Amadeus Mozarts: Die ältesten
väterlichen Vorfahren** [The genealogy of
Wolfgang Amadeus Mozart: The earliest paternal an-
cestors], *Bericht über den internationalen musikwissenschaftlichen Kongreß Wien Mozartjahr 1956*
(Graz; Köln: Böhlau, 1958) 116–27. In German. See
no. 365 in this volume.
A report of archival research tracing the composer's ancestry in the paternal
line to 14th-c. Swabia. The full account is published in the *Neues augs-
burger Mozartbuch*, edited by the author, published as a double number of
the *Zeitschrift des Historischen Vereins für Schwaben* 62/63, 1962.
(David Bloom)

1743 DJURIĆ-KLAJN, Stana. **Un contemporain de**
as **Mozart, Ivan-Mane Jarnović** [A contemporary of
Mozart, Giovanni Mane Giornovichi], *Bericht über den
internationalen musikwissenschaftlichen Kongreß
Wien Mozartjahr 1956* (Graz; Köln: Böhlau, 1958)
134–38. In French. See no. 365 in this volume.
Biographical information on the composer (d.1804) with attention to the
question of his Croatian origin. Reprints of the article in Croatian and English were published in *Ivan Mane Jarnović: A Croatian composer/Ivan
Mane Jarnović: Hrvatski skladatelj* (ed. by Stanislav Tuksar; Zagreb:
Koncertna Direkcija, 1978), cited as RILM [1997]3571.

1744 DOBIÁŠ, Václav. **Wolfgang-Amédée Mozart**
as **et la musique tchèque** [Wolfgang Amadeus Mozart
and Czech music], *Les influences étrangères dans
l'œuvre de W.A. Mozart* (Paris: Centre National de la
Recherche Scientifique [CNRS], 1958) 183–88. In
French. See no. 358 in this volume.
The enthusiastic welcome received by Mozart in the Czech countries involved both musical and political factors. His interaction with Czech musical culture may have led to influences on both sides. *(Vivian Conejero)*

1745 DOORSLAER, Georges van. **Connaît-on des**
as **documents relatifs au séjour de Jean-Ladislas
Dussek à Malines?** [Are there any known documents relative to Jan Ladislav Dusík's stay in
Mechelen?], *Fédération Archéologique et Historique
de Belgique: Annales du XXIIᵉ congrès. I: Documents
et compte rendu; II: Rapports & mémoires* (Mechelen:
Godenne, 1911) II, 735–36. In French. See no. 73 in this
volume.
Discusses the relationship of Jan Ladislav Dusík to the cathedral of
Sint-Rombout in Mechelen.

1746 EINSTEIN, Alfred. **Mozart's handwriting and**
as **the creative process,** *Papers read at the International Congress of Musicology* (New York: Music Educators National Conference, 1944) 145–53. *Illus., facs.,
music.* See no. 266 in this volume.
Contradicts the notion that Mozart composed with little or no revision. Examples include MSS of the string quartet K.387 and the piano trio K.542.
(Susan Levine)

1747 ELVERS, Rudolf. **Rudolf Werckmeister: Ein**
as **Berliner Musikverleger 1802-1809** [Rudolf
Werckmeister: A Berlin music publisher, 1802-1809],
Bericht über den internationalen musikwissenschaft-

lichen Kongreß (Kassel: Bärenreiter, 1963) 200–02. In German. See no. 452 in this volume.

Werckmeister, who ran a music lending library in Oranienburg, began to publish music in 1803. In the difficult economic climate of the Napoleonic wars, the enterprise had failed by 1808, though the library continued to thrive. A list of composers whose works Werckmeister issued is appended. *(David Bloom)*

1748
as
ENGEL, Hans. **Mozarts Konzertwerke** [Mozart's concertos], *Bericht über die musikwissenschaftliche Tagung der Internationalen Stiftung Mozarteum* (Leipzig: Breitkopf & Härtel, 1932) 120–28. In German. See no. 193 in this volume.

J.C. Bach, C.P.E. Bach, and Luigi Boccherini provided the most important models for Mozart's instrumental concertos and sinfonie concertanti. His concertos are said to be distinguished from those of his contemporaries by the victorious lyricism of a young generation growing out of rationalism, the healthy folkloric power of his Salzburg origins, and the vital force of the German bourgeoisie, overlapping with the ideals of courtly art. *(David Bloom)*

1749
as
ERDMANN, Hans. **Mozart in norddeutscher Resonanz** [Echoes of Mozart in North Germany], *Bericht über den internationalen musikwissenschaftlichen Kongreß Wien Mozartjahr 1956* (Graz; Köln: Böhlau, 1958) 156–69. *Music, chronology.* In German. See no. 365 in this volume.

Surveys the performance of Mozart's works in North German cities and court venues, from 1786 (when *Die Entführung aus dem Serail* was first performed in Rostock), and evidence of their reception, including a quoted theme from *Don Giovanni* in an early 19th-c. Mecklenburg *Fichtelbook* (itinerant musicians' fakebook). A chronology of Mozart performances at the Mecklenburg-Schwerin court of Ludwigslust from 1803 to 1832 is appended. *(David Bloom)*

1750
as
FEDER, Georg. **Das Barocke Wort-Ton-Verhältnis und seine Umgestaltung in den klassizistischen Bach-Bearbeitungen** [The Baroque word-music relationship and its reshaping in Classic Bach arrangements], *Bericht über den internationalen musikwissenschaftlichen Kongreß* (Kassel: Bärenreiter, 1957) 95–97. In German. See no. 356 in this volume.

Musicians between 1750 and 1829, including W.F. Bach, C.P.E. Bach, Johann Nepomuk Schelble, and Carl Friedrich Zelter, failed to comprehend J.S. Bach's art of interpreting text through music, as is shown by their arrangements of some of his vocal works.

1751
as
FEDER, Georg. **Zwei Haydn zugeschriebene Klaviersonaten** [Two keyboard sonatas attributed to Haydn], *Bericht über den internationalen musikwissenschaftlichen Kongreß* (Kassel: Bärenreiter, 1963) 181–84. *Music.* In German. See no. 452 in this volume.

The MS *CZ-Bm* MS A.12.488 contains five keyboard *Parthien* or sonatas, three of which are known to be by Haydn (Hob.XVI:2, 13, and 14). The other two, both in E♭, can also be attributed to Haydn. *(David Bloom)*

1752
as
FEICHT, Hieronim. **Die Kenntnis Mozarts in Polen** [Knowledge of Mozart in Poland], *Bericht über den internationalen musikwissenschaftlichen Kongreß Wien Mozartjahr 1956* (Graz; Köln: Böhlau, 1958) 191–94. In German. See no. 365 in this volume.

Reviews the performance history of Mozart's works in Poland, from the first Warsaw production of *Die Entführung aus dem Serail*, 1783, through the 19th c. *(David Bloom)*

1753
as
FELLERER, Karl Gustav. **L'importanza de *La vestale* nella produzione operistica di Spontini** [The importance of *La vestale* among Spontini's operas], *Atti del primo Congresso internazionale di studi spontiniani* (Fabriano: Arti Grafiche Gentile, 1954) 33–40. In Italian. See no. 304 in this volume.

La vestale unites traditional idioms with a new national development of dramatic expression.

1754
as
FELLERER, Karl Gustav. **Joseph Haydns Messen** [The Masses of Joseph Haydn], *Bericht über die internationale Konferenz zum Andenken Joseph Haydns* (Budapest: Akadémiai Kiadó, 1961) 41–48. *Illus.* In German. See no. 405 in this volume.

The 1749 encyclical *Annus qui* of Benedict XIV, which established limits on instrumental accompaniments and operatic vocal treatments in the liturgy, was a key factor in the Mass settings of Haydn and Mozart. Haydn's deep personal faith also played a role. *(Jean W. Smith)*

1755
as
FELLERER, Karl Gustav. **Die Lehre vom Cantus gregorianus im 18. Jahrhundert** [Theory of Gregorian chant in the 18th century], *Kongreß-Bericht: Gesellschaft für Musikforschung* (Kassel; Basel: Bärenreiter, 1950) 136–38. In German. See no. 299 in this volume.

1756
as
FELLERER, Karl Gustav. **Mozart et l'école de Mannheim** [Mozart and the Mannheim school], *Les influences étrangères dans l'œuvre de W.A. Mozart* (Paris: Centre National de la Recherche Scientifique [CNRS], 1958) 85–90. In French. See no. 358 in this volume.

Mozart's 1777 visit to Mannheim was of crucial significance to his compositional development. However, the stylistic features of the Mannheim school did not become completely incorporated into Mozart's own style until 1781. *(Vivian Conejero)*

1757
as
FINSCHER, Ludwig. **Zur Sozialgeschichte des klassischen Streichquartetts** [The social history of the Classic string quartet], *Bericht über den internationalen musikwissenschaftlichen Kongreß* (Kassel: Bärenreiter, 1963) 37–39. In German. See no. 452 in this volume.

Discusses the history of the genre from the period of Haydn's op. 1 quartets through Beethoven's op. 59, with attention to the roles of aristocratic dilettanti in the earlier period and, later, of professional quartet concerts and bourgeois *Hausmusik*. *(Laurie Appleby)*

1758
as
FISCHER, Wilhelm. **Die Stetigkeit in Mozarts Schaffen** [The steadiness of Mozart's output], *Bericht über die musikwissenschaftliche Tagung der Internationalen Stiftung Mozarteum* (Leipzig: Breitkopf & Härtel, 1932) 69–71. In German. See no. 193 in this volume.

A bare statistical examination of the Köchel catalogue indicates a considerable slowing of Mozart's compositional output after 1786. A more careful consideration, distinguishing the individual works by genre and ambition, shows that he continued to work at a steady rate except for a relatively brief pause in the depressing period of 1789-90. *(David Bloom)*

1759
as
FORTASSIER, Pierre. **Le récitatif dans l'écriture instrumentale de Mozart** [Recitative in Mozart's instrumental writing], *Les influences étrangères dans l'œuvre de W.A. Mozart* (Paris: Centre National de la Recherche Scientifique [CNRS], 1958) 199–226. *Music.* In French. See no. 358 in this volume.

Mozart included instrumental recitatives in several of his nonvocal works between 1778 and 1780. This type of recitative is similar to a French style, probably due to Mozart's journey to France in 1778; before then his recitatives were more Italian in style. Mozart was not the first composer to use instrumental recitative, but his use of it was most original, and he was constantly reinventing the device for his own purposes. He was adept at reproducing the sense of the human voice in instrumental lines. Mozart's treatment of recitative in his vocal works is also discussed. *(Susan Poliniak)*

1760 FRYKLUND, Daniel. **Eine schwedische Samm-**
as **lung von Briefen von und an Fétis** [A Swedish
collection of letters from and to Fétis], *Société
Internationale de Musicologie: Premier Congrès
Liège—Compte rendu/Internationale Gesellschaft für
Musikwissenschaft: Erster Kongress Lüttich—Kon-
gressbericht/International Society for Musical Research: First Congress Liège: Report* (London: Plainsong and Mediaeval Music Society, 1930) 113–17. In
German. See no. 178 in this volume.

The collection contains approximately 100 letters from and 500 letters to
François-Joseph Fétis. The letters include references to musicians from the
time Fétis lived in Paris until his death, reflections on his work, and writings about music. *(Joan Siegel)*

1761 GEIRINGER, Karl. **Sidelights on Haydn's ac-**
as **tivities in the field of sacred music,** *Bericht über
die internationale Konferenz zum Andenken Joseph
Haydns* (Budapest: Akadémiai Kiadó, 1961) 49–56.
See no. 405 in this volume.

Although most of the Haydn materials in the Esterházy collection were
moved to Budapest after World War I, the Esterházy-Archiv in Eisenstadt
retains fine early copies of some of his religious works. *(Jean W. Smith)*

1762 GERBER, Rudolf. **Unbekannte Instrumental-**
as **werke von Chr. W. Gluck** [Unknown instrumental
works by C.W. Gluck], *Kongreß-Bericht: Gesellschaft
für Musikforschung* (Kassel; Basel: Bärenreiter, 1950)
140. In German. See no. 299 in this volume.

1763 GERSTENBERG, Walter, ed. **Symposium: Der**
as **gegenwärtige Stand der Mozart-Forschung**
[Symposium: The present state of Mozart research],
Bericht über den neunten internationalen Kongreß
(Kassel: Bärenreiter, 1964-1966) II, 88–97. In German.
See no. 491 in this volume.

Discussion of the conference paper abstracted as no. 1836 in this volume.
Participants included Otto Erich DEUTSCH, Hans ENGEL, Klaus
ENGLER, Franz GIEGLING, Heinz Wolfgang HAMANN, Ernst HESS,
Georg KNEPLER, Karl-Heinz KÖHLER, Jan LARUE, Friedrich
NEUMANN, Wolfgang PLATH, Wolfgang REHM, and Walter SENN.

1764 GHISLANZONI, Alberto. **Sintesi della**
as **produzione giovanile spontiniana** [Synthesis of
Spontini's youthful compositions], *Atti del primo
Congresso internazionale di studi spontiniani*
(Fabriano: Arti Grafiche Gentile, 1954) 13–22. In Ital-
ian. See no. 304 in this volume.

Spontini's development as an individual artistic personality is evidenced
by technical and stylistic changes.

1765 GOLDSCHMIDT, Hugo. **Die Reform der**
as **italienischen Oper des 18. Jahrhunderts und**
ihre Beziehungen zur musikalischen Ästhetik
[The reform of 18th-century Italian opera and its relation to musical aesthetics], *Haydn-Zentenarfeier* (Leipzig: Breitkopf & Härtel; Wien: Artaria, 1909) 196–207.
In German. See no. 65 in this volume.

The ideas usually attributed to Gluck's librettist Ranieri De' Calzabigi
(1714-95) were in fact anticipated by such figures as Ludovico Antonio
Muratori, Niccolò Jommelli, and Francesco Algarotti.

1766 GOLÉA, Antoine. **Mozart und die französische**
as **Revolution** [Mozart and the French Revolution],
*Internationale Konferenz über das Leben und Werk
W.A. Mozarts* (Praha: Svaz Československých
Skladatelů, 1956) 156–58. In German. See no. 360 in
this volume.

Mozart's political views are expressed better in his works, especially the
operas, than in his utterances. Before the French Revolution, *Le nozze di
Figaro* and *Don Giovanni* take unambiguously revolutionary positions for
liberty and against tyranny and caste; during the Revolution's first great crisis in 1791, *Die Zauberflöte* is still revolutionary, but more concerned with
justice and order. *(David Bloom)*

1767 GOTTRON, Adam. **Mozart und die musik-**
as **geschichtliche Situation in Mainz zu seiner**
Zeit [Mozart and the music-historical situation in
Mainz in his time], *Bericht über den internationalen
musikwissenschaftlichen Kongreß Wien Mozartjahr
1956* (Graz; Köln: Böhlau, 1958) 230–37. *Music, them.
cat.* In German. See no. 365 in this volume.

A survey of musicians and musical activities in Mainz and its electoral
court in the 18th c., with attention to the situation at the time of Mozart's
visits in 1763 and 1790 and to the importance of a large community of im-
migrant musicians from Bohemia, including Jan Ondráček, the first (in
1724-43) of a series of Bohemian Hofkapellmeisters. Movement incipits
for Ondráček's only surviving composition, a trio sonata (in *F-Pc* MS
rés.f.433.divers.47998), are provided in an appendix. *(David Bloom)*

1768 GÜTTLER, Hermann. **Johann Reichardt: Ein**
as **preussischer Lautenist** [Johann Reichardt: A Prussian lutenist], *Société Internationale de Musicologie:
Premier Congrès Liège—Compte rendu/Internationale
Gesellschaft für Musikwissenschaft: Erster Kongress
Lüttich—Kongressbericht/International Society for
Musical Research: First Congress Liège: Report* (London: Plainsong and Mediaeval Music Society, 1930)
118–24. In German. See no. 178 in this volume.

Biographical study of one of the last guild lutenists and the father of the important theorist Johann Friedrich Reichardt. *(Scott Fruehwald)*

1769 GÜTTLER, Hermann. **Kant und sein**
as **musikalischer Umkreis** [Kant and his musical envi-
ronment], *Beethoven-Zentenarfeier: Internationaler
musikhistorischer Kongress* (Wien: Universal, 1927)
217–21. In German. See no. 142 in this volume.

Surveys the musical life in Königsberg (present-day Kaliningrad in Russia)
during the lifetime of Immanuel Kant (1724-1804). Attention is given to
the philosopher's friendships with the enthusiastic patron and amateur musician, Reichsgraf Heinrich Christian von Keyserlingk, with the young
Johann Friedrich Reichardt, and possibly with the organist-composers
Carl-Gottlieb Richter and Christian Wilhelm Podbielski (both teachers of
E.T.A. Hoffmann); Kant's own views on music are considered. *(David Bloom)*

1770 GÜTTLER, Hermann. **Die Pantomime W.A.**
as **Mozarts und ihre Aufführung** [Mozart's pantomime and its performance], *Report of the Fourth Congress of the International Musical Society* (London:
Novello, 1912) 363. In German. See no. 71 in this
volume.

Summary of a paper discussing efforts to reconstruct *Les petits riens*,
K.a10.

1771 GYSI, Fritz. **Mozart als Kritiker** [Mozart as
as critic], *Bericht über den I. musikwissenschaftlichen
Kongress der Deutschen Musikgesellschaft in Leipzig*
(Wiesbaden: Breitkopf & Härtel, 1926) 266–69. In German. See no. 120 in this volume.

The composer's correspondence reveals his thoughts on instruments, composers, styles, and librettos.

1772 HAAS, Robert. **Zum Kanon im** *Fidelio* [The
as *Fidelio* canon], *Beethoven-Zentenarfeier: Internationaler musikhistorischer Kongress* (Wien: Universal,
1927) 136–37. In German. See no. 142 in this volume.

The quartet in canon form *Mir ist so wunderbar* (*Fidelio*, act 1, no. 4) stands
within a historical Viennese tradition. The form had been a popular genre

for social singing since the Rococo, and appeared on the Vienna opera stage in, among others, Ferdinando Paër's *Camilla, ossia Il sotterraneo* (1799) and Luigi Cherubini's *Faniska* (1806). *(David Bloom)*

1773
as
HAAS, Robert. **Zur Frage der Orchesterbe-setzungen in der zweiten Hälfte des 18. Jahr-hunderts** [Instrumentation in the second half of the 18th century], *Haydn-Zentenarfeier* (Leipzig: Breitkopf & Härtel; Wien: Artaria, 1909) 159–67. In German. See no. 65 in this volume.

Lists the instrumentation of orchestras in the Classic period in various cities, including Berlin, Mannheim, Vienna, Dresden, Munich, Paris, Turin, and Stockholm.

1774
as
HALM, Hans. **Über Verzeichnisse der Werke Beethovens** [Catalogues of Beethoven's works], *Bericht über den Internationalen musikwissenschaft-lichen Kongress* (Kassel: Bärenreiter, 1954) 299–99. In German. See no. 319 in this volume.

Presents a history of Beethoven cataloguing and source studies, beginning with Ernst Ludwig Gerber's entry for Beethoven in his *Neues historisch-biographisches Lexikon der Tonkünstler* (1812). Subsequent landmarks in Beethoven cataloguing have included the thematic catalogue issued by the Hofmeister firm in 1819 and the *Catalogue des œuvres de Louis van Beethoven, que se trouvent chez Artaria & Co.* (provided with opus numbers and said to be revised by the composer himself), issued in the same year and subsequently updated; the list issued during the 1830s by the Cranz firm of Hamburg; the *Thematisches Verzeichnis sämtlicher im Druck erschienenen Werke von Ludwig van Beethoven aus dem Verlag Breitkopf & Härtel* in 1851, which set a new standard for thematic cataloguing (significantly revised by Gustav Nottebohm in 1868 as *Thematisches Verzeichniss der im Druck erschienenen Werke von Ludwig van Beethoven*, with inclusion of much new information on MSS and arrangements); Alexander Wheelock Thayer's *Chronologisches Verzeichnis der Werke Beethovens*; and Wilhelm von Lenz's *Kritischer Katalog sämmtlicher Werke Ludwig van Beethovens mit Analysen derselben*, 1860, important for its analyses and aesthetic evaluations, especially of Beethoven's later works. The present author is completing a catalogue of Beethoven's works undertaken by Georg Kinsky. *(Carl Skoggard)*

1775
as
HAUSLEITHNER, Alexander. **Franz Schuberts Gesänge für Männerstimmen** [Franz Schubert's songs for men's voices], *Bericht über den internationalen Kongress für Schubertforschung* (Augsburg: Benno Filser, 1929) 211–18. In German. See no. 154 in this volume.

Schubert composed over 70 songs for three to eight men's voices. The historical context of this genre is examined.

1776
as
HENNERBERG, Carl Fredrik. **Einige Doku-mente, den Abt Georg Joseph Vogler betreffend** [Documents relating to Abbé Georg Joseph Vogler], *Report of the Fourth Congress of the International Musical Society* (London: Novello, 1912) 134–38. *Port.* In German. See no. 71 in this volume.

Discusses letters and compositions from Vogler's years in Sweden (1786-99).

1777
as
HENNERBERG, Carl Fredrik. **Schwedische Haydn-Handschriften** [Haydn autographs in Sweden], *Haydn-Zentenarfeier* (Leipzig: Breitkopf & Härtel; Wien: Artaria, 1909) 429–32. In German. See no. 65 in this volume.

Discusses several items, including a trio for two violins and bass (in the Universitetsbiblioteket, Uppsala), a symphony in F minor, and several letters (in the Musikaliska Akademiens Bibliotek, Stockholm).

1778
as
HESS, Ernst. **Remarques sur l'authenticité de l'ouverture KV 311a=Anh. 8** [Remarks on the authenticity of the overture K.311a=Anh. 8], *Les influ-*

ences étrangères dans l'œuvre de W.A. Mozart (Paris: Centre National de la Recherche Scientifique [CNRS], 1958) 227–35. In French. See no. 358 in this volume.

Discusses the authenticity issues regarding this overture in B-flat written by Mozart in Paris in 1778 and discovered in 1901. Aspects covered include orchestration, harmony, form, and themes. *(Susan Poliniak)*

1779
as
HOŘEJŠ, Antonín. **Haydn mit heutigen Augen gesehen** [Haydn seen with today's eyes], *Bericht über die internationale Konferenz zum Andenken Joseph Haydns* (Budapest: Akadémiai Kiadó, 1961) 57–60. In German. See no. 405 in this volume.

Haydn's use of traditional materials reflects the social developments of his time.

1780
as
HRABUSSAY, Zoltán. **Mozartdokumente im Archiv der Stadt Bratislava** [Mozart documents in the Archív Mesta Bratislavy], *Internationale Konferenz über das Leben und Werk W.A. Mozarts* (Praha: Svaz Československých Skladatelů, 1956) 253–55. In German. See no. 360 in this volume.

Relatively little is known about Mozart's only trip to Slovakia, for a concert in December 1762. The two Mozart autographs in the possession of the Archív Mesta Bratislavy have nothing to do with his visit: They are a trilingual letter from the composer to his father, dated 2 July 1783 and discussing his involvement in operatic intrigue of the day, and a MS sketch for a sonata movement in G major, possibly from 1786. Bratislava also owns one of the best artistic representations of Mozart, a bust by the Bratislava-born sculptor Viktor Tilgner (1844-96) at the Mestské Múzeum in Bratislava. *(David Bloom)*

1781
as
HRUŠOVSKÝ, Ivan. **Das klassische Musik-schaffen der Mozartzeit in der Slowakei** [Classical music production of the Mozart period in Slovakia], *Internationale Konferenz über das Leben und Werk W.A. Mozarts* (Praha: Svaz Československých Skladatelů, 1956) 256–61. In German. See no. 360 in this volume.

The pre-Classic and Classic styles of Vienna and of Bohemian emigrants to Austria and Germany spread rapidly through the cities of what is now Slovakia among the newly flourishing German, Hungarian, and Slovak bourgeois communities. Social conditions (especially in Bratislava, Trnava, and Banská Bystrica), genres, and the compositions of known and anonymous composers are surveyed. *(David Bloom)*

1782
as
IDASZAK, Danuta. **Mazurek w polskiej muzyce XVIII wieku** [The mazurka in Polish music of the 18th century], *The book of the first international musicological congress devoted to the works of Frederick Chopin* (Warszawa: Państwowe Wydawnictwo Naukowe, 1963) 538–46. *Music.* In Polish. See no. 425 in this volume.

Mazurka rhythms figure prominently in the works of several composers of liturgical music, including Wojciech (Adalbert) Dankowski.

1783
as
IVANOV-BORECKIJ, Mihail. **Ein Moskauer Skizzenbuch von Beethoven** [A Moscow sketch-book by Beethoven], *Beethoven-Zentenarfeier: Internationaler musikhistorischer Kongress* (Wien: Universal, 1927) 88–90. *Facs., music.* In German. See no. 142 in this volume.

A MS notebook used by Beethoven for sketches for the string quartets opp. 130 and 132 was left behind in Moscow by departing émigrés in 1922 and transmitted to the directorate of the Moskovskaja Gosudarstvennaja Konservatorija. It is reproduced in facsimile, with a more extensive commentary, in the conservatory's *Muzykal'noje obrazovanie* (1927). *(David Bloom)*

1784
as
JONAS, Oswald. **Mozart-Handschriften in Amerika** [Mozart manuscripts in America], *Bericht über den internationalen musikwissenschaftlichen*

Kongreß Wien Mozartjahr 1956 (Graz; Köln: Böhlau, 1958) 285–88. *Facs., music.* In German. See no. 365 in this volume.

The musicological value of Mozart autograph MSS in the collections of the Library of Congress, Washington, and the Heinemann Foundation, New York, is considered.

1785 JURISCH, Herta. **Zur Dynamik im Klavierwerk Ph.E. Bachs** [Dynamics in the keyboard works of C.P.E. Bach], *Bericht über den internationalen musikwissenschaftlichen Kongreß* (Kassel: Bärenreiter, 1963) 178–81. *Music.* In German. See no. 452 in this volume.

Bach's dynamic markings display extraordinary variety. When he uses them to emphasize the boundaries of sequences and periods, he shows his attachment to the dialogic tradition of the German Baroque; affective, declamatory dynamic nuances indicate his adherence to the principles of Sturm und Drang. *(David Bloom)*

1786 KAHL, Willi. **Geschichte, Kritik und Aufgaben der K.Ph.E. Bach-Forschung** [The history and tasks, and an assessment, of C.P.E. Bach research], *Beethoven-Zentenarfeier: Internationaler musikhistorischer Kongress* (Wien: Universal, 1927) 211–16. In German. See no. 142 in this volume.

A brief overview, from the critical encomia Bach received during his lifetime, to the state of research ca. 1927, with attention to the need for a revised thematic catalogue and more systematic editing of his works.

1787 KAISER, Fritz. **Die authentischen Fassungen des D-dur-Konzerts op. 61 von Ludwig van Beethoven** [The authentic versions of Ludwig van Beethoven's D-major concerto, op. 61], *Bericht über den internationalen musikwissenschaftlichen Kongreß* (Kassel: Bärenreiter, 1963) 196–98. In German. See no. 452 in this volume.

The MS *GB-Lbl* MS Add.47851 of the concerto, including the solo part in both the violin and piano versions, not copied by Beethoven but featuring autograph annotations by him, served as the engraver's copy for the first print version. It provides evidence that the violinist, composer, and arranger Franz Alexander Pössner (1767-1827) was mainly responsible for the preparation of the piano version; he is also probably responsible for the first edition's corrupted text. *(David Bloom)*

1788 KAMIEŃSKI, Lucjan. **Neue Beiträge zur Entwicklung der Polonaise bis Beethoven** [New contributions on the development of the polonaise up to Beethoven], *Beethoven-Zentenarfeier: Internationaler musikhistorischer Kongress* (Wien: Universal, 1927) 66–74. *Music.* In German. See no. 142 in this volume.

Two early Polish-origin sources of polonaises are a MS in the collections of the Towarzystwo Muzyczne, Warsaw, containing 62 anonymous polonaises arranged for harp, copied by Joseph Sychra in Vilnius, 1772, and one in the Berlin Staatsbibliothek (*D-Bsb* MS 38048) with first-violin parts for 23 polonaises, almost all anonymous, dated 1800. They show clearly that the contrasting trio section was becoming a normal feature of the genre during the period, as reflected by Beethoven's polonaise for piano solo, op. 89. *(David Bloom)*

1789 K̇AŚ, Me'yr. **Yeṣyrŵt mẇsyqalyŵt kepyrẇš leṭeqsṭym miqr'yym** [The use of musical compositions in the interpretations of Biblical texts], *Dẇkan* II (1960) 41–46. *Music.* In Hebrew. See no. 409 in this volume.

Examines three settings of Biblical texts by Bach, Haydn, and Schubert.

1790 KAUFMANN, Paul. **Aus der Bonner Gesellschaft in Beethovens Jugendzeit** [Bonn society at the time of Beethoven's youth], *Beethoven-*

Zentenarfeier: Internationaler musikhistorischer Kongress (Wien: Universal, 1927) 11–15. In German. See no. 142 in this volume.

Includes Beethoveniana and anecdotes of musical life in the city of Bonn and at the court of Archbishop-elector Maximilian Franz (where the author's great-grandfather, Mathias Joseph Kaufmann, served as Hofkammerrat), drawing on the author's *Aus rheinischer Jugendzeit* (Berlin, 1921). *(David Bloom)*

1791 KAUL, Oskar. **Ausstrahlungen der Wiener Vorklassik nach Würzburg** [The influence of the Viennese pre-Classic in Würzburg], *Beethoven-Zentenarfeier: Internationaler musikhistorischer Kongress* (Wien: Universal, 1927) 208–10. In German. See no. 142 in this volume.

The instrumental music of the very prolific, if undistinguished, Würzburg composer Georg Franz Waßmuth in the period 1740-60 exemplifies a tendency in Würzburg, and in Bavaria and Franconia generally, to follow the aesthetic lead of Vienna and Italy rather than Mannheim and North Germany. *(David Bloom)*

1792 KELDYŠ, Jurij Vsevolodovič. **Voznikovenie i razvitie russkoj opery v XVIII veke** [The emergence and development of Russian opera in the 18th century], *Musica antiqua Europae orientalis* (Warszawa: Państwowe Wydawnictwo Naukowe, 1966). *Music.* In Russian. See no. 506 in this volume.

1793 KNEPLER, Georg. **Mozart: Eine Gestalt der bürgerlichen Aufklärung** [Mozart: A figure of the bourgeois Enlightenment], *Internationale Konferenz über das Leben und Werk W.A. Mozarts* (Praha: Svaz Československých Skladatelů, 1956) 98–105. *Music.* In German. See no. 360 in this volume.

When Mozart expresses hostility to the Enlightenment (as in a 1778 letter to his father mentioning Voltaire's recent death) he is parroting the viewpoint of his Catholic upbringing; but his correspondence and works in general show him as an adherent of the Enlightenment, through the values of the bourgeoisie, with which he identified against the conservative aristocracy, culminating in the deeply democratic art of *Die Zauberflöte*. A close analysis of the G minor string quintet K.516 treats it as embodying the Enlightenment theme of victory over pain and sorrow. *(David Bloom)*

1794 KOSCH, Franz. **Florian Leopold Gassmann als Kirchenkomponist** [Florian Leopold Gassmann as composer of church music], *Festschrift den Mitgliedern des Musikhistorischen Kongresses überreicht von der Leitenden Kommission der Denkmäler der Tonkunst in Österreich* (Wien: Universal, 1927) 213–40. *Music.* In German. See no. 147 in this volume.

Presents a biography of Gassmann (1729-74), with attention to the rich Bohemian musical culture into which he was born, and the 20 years spent in Italy, where he acquired fluency in the fashionable Neapolitan style. Gassmann's last church compositions reveal a new direction: a turn to the traditions of the Venetian-Viennese school. Gassmann's relaxed attitude to setting liturgical texts is examined and his church music is surveyed by style parameters (melody, harmony, etc.). His religious works seem to have exerted a fruitful influence both on Haydn and the young Mozart. Several documents (the imperial decree naming him the imperial Hofkapellmeister, dated 1772, and a petition on behalf of his widow, 1774) are reproduced in an appendix. *(Carl Skoggard)*

⟶ KOVAČEVIĆ, Krešimir. **Die kroatische Musik des XVII. und XVIII. Jahrhunderts** [Croatian music of the 17th and 18th centuries]. See no. 1594 in this volume.

1795 KROLL, Erwin. **E.T.A. Hoffmann und Beethoven** [E.T.A. Hoffmann and Beethoven], *Beethoven-Zentenarfeier: Internationaler musikhistorischer*

Kongress (Wien: Universal, 1927) 128–31. In German. See no. 142 in this volume.

Traces Hoffmann's engagement with Beethoven's music as conductor, starting with his 1804 move to Warsaw; as composer, from the piano sonatas of 1807; and as the most perceptive of Beethoven's early critics. *(David Bloom)*

1796
as

LANDON, H.C. Robbins. **La crise romantique dans la musique autrichienne vers 1770: Quelques précurseurs inconnus de la symphonie en sol mineur (KV 183) de Mozart** [The romantic crisis in Austrian music around 1770: Some unknown precursors of Mozart's symphony in G minor, K.183], *Les influences étrangères dans l'œuvre de W.A. Mozart* (Paris: Centre National de la Recherche Scientifique [CNRS], 1958) 27–47. *Music.* In French. See no. 358 in this volume.

Mozart's first symphony in a minor key was written as much under the influence of the contemporary Sturm und Drang movement as out of powerful artistic and personal impulses. *(Vivian Conejero)*

1797
as

LANDON, H.C. Robbins. **Problems of authenticity in eighteenth-century music,** *Instrumental music* (Cambridge, MA: Harvard University Press, 1959) 31–56. See no. 368 in this volume.

Internal stylistic evidence is a less reliable criterion for the attribution of a work than external evidence such as incipit listings, watermarks, or the listing of the composer's name. Examples are drawn from the attribution of works to Haydn, Mozart, Beethoven, Carlo d'Ordonez, and Friedrich Witt. The author's discovery of a Mass in G major apparently identical with Haydn's lost *Missa "Rorate coeli desuper"* is discussed. *(Daven Jenkins)*

1798
as

LANDON, H.C. Robbins. **Survey of Haydn sources in Czechoslovakia,** *Bericht über die internationale Konferenz zum Andenken Joseph Haydns* (Budapest: Akadémiai Kiadó, 1961) 69–79. See no. 405 in this volume.

1799
as

LANSSENS, Martin. **Sur la musique nouvelle de** *Colette et Lucas***: Comédie du Prince de Ligne** [On the new music for *Colette et Lucas*: A comedy by the Prince of Ligne], *Actes et travaux du Congrés international pour l'étude du XVIIIème siècle en Belgique* (Bruxelles: Editions des Annales Prince de Ligne, 1936) 306–08. In French. See no. 220 in this volume.

Colette et Lucas, a pastoral comedy by Prince Charles-Joseph de Ligne, was performed in 1773. In 1914, the Société Royale La Grande Harmonie in Brussels revived the play, with new incidental music composed by Lanssens, as the original score had been lost. *(Daniel Rosenbaum)*

1800
as

LARUE, Jan. **Die Datierung von Wasserzeichen im 18. Jahrhundert** [The dating of watermarks from the 18th century], *Bericht über den internationalen musikwissenschaftlichen Kongreß Wien Mozartjahr 1956* (Graz; Köln: Böhlau, 1958) 318–23. *Illus.* In German. See no. 365 in this volume.

Reviews technical problems in watermark studies, with a list of cases where a watermark is especially liable to misidentification. *(David Bloom)*

⟶   LAVOYE, Louis. **Le théâtre musical liègeois au XVIIIe siècle** [Musical theater of Liège in the 18th century]. See no. 1600 in this volume.

⟶   LENAERTS, René Bernard. **La musique sacrée en Belgique au XVIIIe siècle** [Sacred music in Belgium in the 18th century]. See no. 1602 in this volume.

1801
as

LESURE, François. **L'œuvre de Mozart en France de 1793 à 1810** [The works of Mozart in France from 1793 to 1810], *Bericht über den internationalen musikwissenschaftlichen Kongreß Wien Mozartjahr 1956* (Graz; Köln: Böhlau, 1958) 344–47. In French. See no. 365 in this volume.

A supplement to the research reported in Adolphe Jullien's *Paris dilettante* (1884), focusing on productions of *Die Entführung aus dem Serail* and *Così fan tutte*, concert performances, and the role of the Paris Conservatoire. *(Karen Clute)*

⟶   LINDEN, Albert vander. **La musique et la danse dans les Pays-Bas au XVIIIème siècle** [Music and dance in the Low Countires in the 18th century]. See no. 1606 in this volume.

1802
as

LINDEN, Albert vander. **Note sur une ordonnance du Conseil des Finances relatifs aux pianos et aux clavecins (9 janvier 1786)** [Note on an ordinance of the Council of Finances concerning pianos and harpsichords (9 January 1786)], *Congrès de Namur 1938: Annales* (Namur: n.p., n.d.) 430–40. In French. See no. 260 in this volume.

1803
as

LINDEN, Albert vander. **La place de la Hollande dans l'***Allgemeine musikalische Zeitung* **(1798-1848)** [The place of Holland in the *Allgemeine musikalische Zeitung* (1798-1848)], *Société Internationale de Musicologie, cinquième congrès/Internationale Gesellschaft für Musikwissenschaft, fünfter Kongreß/International Society for Musical Research, Fifth Congress* (Amsterdam: Vereniging voor Nederlandse Muziekgeschiedenis, 1953) 293–95. In French. See no. 316 in this volume.

1804
as

LIVANOVA, Tamara Nikolaevna. **Rannie otkliki na iskusstvo Gajdna v Rossii** [Early comments on Haydn's works in Russia], *Bericht über die internationale Konferenz zum Andenken Joseph Haydns* (Budapest: Akadémiai Kiadó, 1961) 85–92. In Russian. See no. 405 in this volume.

The early impact of Haydn's music in Russia is assessed through reports in the Russian press and comments by Russian writers from the 1790s until the composer's death. Although Haydn's chamber and keyboard music became known first, his oratorios *Die Schöpfung* and *Die Jahreszeiten* enjoyed the greatest success. *(Larry Laskowski)*

1805
as

LOULOVÁ, Olga. **Das tschechische Volkslied im Werke von Jan Křtitel Vaňhal** [Czech traditional song in the music of Johann Baptist Vanhal], *Internationale Konferenz über das Leben und Werk W.A. Mozarts* (Praha: Svaz Československých Skladatelů, 1956) 70–77. *Music.* In German. See no. 360 in this volume.

Elements of Bohemian and Moravian traditional song and dance music, including the use of their melodies as thematic material, can be identified throughout Vanhal's symphonies and piano works. Vanhal's relationship with Mozart, as friend and as fellow musician, may be a major factor in the well-known influence on Mozart of traditional Czech music. *(David Bloom)*

1806
as

LOYONNET, Paul. **Étude sur la formation de la langue musicale de Beethoven** [Study on the formation of Beethoven's musical language], *Deuxième congrès international d'esthétique et de Science de l'art* (Paris: Librairie Félix Alcan, 1937) II, 247–51. In French. See no. 249 in this volume.

Offers programmatic remarks on the concept of Beethoven's musical language, based on the author's study for performance purposes of the solo and chamber piano works, and focusing on the revolutionary development, over the course of his career, of a technique for the symbolic representation of dramatic events and emotions. *(David Bloom)*

1807
as

MARKL, Jaroslav. **Mozart und das tsche-chische Volkslied** [Mozart and Czech traditional song], *Internationale Konferenz über das Leben und Werk W.A. Mozarts* (Praha: Svaz Československých Skladatelů, 1956) 127–34. In German. See no. 360 in this volume.

Czech melodies corresponding to melodic material used by Mozart are to be found in traditional-song collections of the 18th and early 19th c. One such collection, of which an edition is published in the author's *Nejstarší sbírky českých lidových písní* (Prague, 1987; cited as RILM [1988] 6127), is a MS of ca. 1820 from Sadská, near Nymburk, whose principal author was the organist Jan Jakub Němeček, brother of Mozart's friend and biographer Franz Xaver Niemetschek; according to tradition he was also Mozart's host during a visit to the Sadská baths. *(David Bloom)*

1808
as

MARTYNOV, Ivan. **Mozart und die russische Kunst** [Mozart and Russian art], *Internationale Konferenz über das Leben und Werk W.A. Mozarts* (Praha: Svaz Československých Skladatelů, 1956) 106–11. In German. See no. 360 in this volume.

Surveys Russian reception of Mozart's music from the first St. Petersburg production of *Die Zauberflöte* in 1794, with particular attention to the figures of Vladimir Fëdorovič Odoevskij, Turgenev, Aleksandr Ivanovič Gercen, Aleksandr Dmitrievič Ulybišev, Puškin, Glinka, and Čajkovskij. *(David Bloom)*

1809
as

MASSON, Paul-Marie. **Beethoven et Rameau** [Beethoven and Rameau], *Société Internationale de Musicologie: Premier Congrès Liège—Compte rendu/ Internationale Gesellschaft für Musikwissenschaft: Erster Kongress Lüttich—Kongressbericht/International Society for Musical Research: First Congress Liège: Report* (London: Plainsong and Mediaeval Music Society, 1930) 174–81. *Illus., music.* In French. See no. 178 in this volume.

Elements of heroism, martial spirit, and spiritual inspiration found in the dramatic works of Rameau can be seen as foreshadowing the joyous and naturalistic spirit of Beethoven. Musical similarities are shown in various examples: the prelude to the fourth act of *Zoroastre*, and the fourth and fifth acts of *Dardanus* (second version, 1744). The latter exhibits the emotional power of enharmonic modulation and recalls dramatic similarities to the second act of *Fidelio*. *(Meredith E. Baker)*

1810
as

MASSON, Paul-Marie. **Le recueil madrilène des** *Canciones francesas para todos los instrumentos* **vers 1700** [The Madrid anthology *Canciones francesas para todos los instrumentos* from around 1700], *Congrés de la Societat Internacional de Musicologia* (Barcelona: Casa de Caritat, 1936). In French. See no. 224 in this volume.

The conference report provides only a citation. Neither the text nor a summary of the paper was published here. Discusses an anthology of French songs with basso continuo, entitled *Canciones francesas de todos ayres* and published by Joseph de Torres y Martínez Bravo in 1705. It was the first publication of pieces with basso continuo in Spain.

1811
as

MEER, John Henry van der. **Mozarts Hammer-flügel** [Mozart's piano], *Bericht über den neunten internationalen Kongreß* (Kassel: Bärenreiter, 1964-1966) II, 273–80. In German. See no. 491 in this volume.

Discusses the surviving clavichords, harpsichords, and fortepianos Mozart is known to have played.

1812
as

MERSMANN, Hans. **Beethovens Skizzen vom Standpunkt phänomenologischer Musik-betrachtung** [Beethoven's sketches in the light of a

phenomenological view of music], *Bericht über den musikwissenschaftlichen Kongreß in Basel* (Leipzig: Breitkopf & Härtel, 1925) 244–58. *Music.* In German. See no. 102 in this volume.

Gustav Nottebohm's view of the sketches is teleological, romantic, and subjective. The sketches for the quartets, opp. 18, 59, and 74, are used to illustrate a phenomenological approach.

→

MERSMANN, Hans. **Das 18. Jahrhundert aus der Sicht unserer Zeit** [The 18th century from the perspective of our time]. See no. 1622 in this volume.

1813
as

MIES, Paul. **Die Quellen des op. 61 von Ludwig van Beethoven** [Sources for Ludwig van Beethoven's op. 61], *Bericht über den siebenten internationalen musikwissenschaftlichen Kongress* (Kassel: Bärenreiter, 1959) 193–95. In German. See no. 390 in this volume.

A preliminary evaluation of earliest MS and print sources of the violin concerto and its piano version.

1814
as

MIKULICZ, Karl Lothar. **Skizzen zur III. und V. Symphonie und über die Notwendigkeit einer Gesamtausgabe der Skizzen Beethovens** [Sketches for the third and fifth symphonies, and on the need for a complete edition of Beethoven's sketches], *Beethoven-Zentenarfeier: Internationaler musikhistorischer Kongress* (Wien: Universal, 1927) 95–96. In German. See no. 142 in this volume.

Summary of a conference paper.

1815
as

MOLDENHAUER, Hans. **From my autograph collection: C.Ph.E. Bach—Dittersdorf—Mozart,** *Bericht über den internationalen musikwissenschaftlichen Kongreß Wien Mozartjahr 1956* (Graz; Köln: Böhlau, 1958) 412–15. See no. 365 in this volume.

Items of particular historical interest in the author's private collection include (1) a letter of 27 December 1783 from C.P.E. Bach to Johann Gottlob Immanuel Breitkopf, illustrating the composer's notorious thriftiness; (2) a previously uncatalogued minuet by Carl Ditters von Dittersdorf, written for an album in Wrocław, 1779; and (3) Mozart's first- and second-movement cadenzas for his 1772 arrangement as a keyboard concerto of J.C. Bach's sonata op. 5 no. 2 (K.107,1). *(David Bloom)*

1816
as

MOLLAT DU JOURDIN, Guy. **Mozart in Paris,** *Internationale Konferenz über das Leben und Werk W.A. Mozarts* (Praha: Svaz Československých Skladatelů, 1956) 26–33. In German. See no. 360 in this volume.

Biographical information on the composer's stays in Paris in 1764, 1765, and 1778. A fuller account is published in French as *Mozart à Paris* (Paris: Mercure, 1956). *(John Stansell)*

1817
as

MOLNÁR, Antal. **Der gestaltpsychologische Unterschied zwischen Haydn und Mozart** [The difference between Haydn and Mozart according to Gestalt psychology], *Bericht über die internationale Konferenz zum Andenken Joseph Haydns* (Budapest: Akadémiai Kiadó, 1961) 95–103. In German. See no. 405 in this volume.

1818
as

MOOSER, Robert-Aloys. **Un musicien espagnol en Russie à la fin du XVIIIe siècle: Contribution à la biographie de Vincenç Martin i Soler et à la bibliographie de son œuvre** [A Spanish musician in Russia at the end of the 18th century: Contribution to the biography of Vicente Martín y Soler and to the bibliography of his oeuvre], *Congrés de la Societat Internacional de Musicologia* (Barcelona: Casa de Caritat, 1936). In French. See no. 224 in this volume.

The conference report provides only a citation. Neither the text nor a summary of the paper was published here.

1819
as
MORIN, Gösta. **Wolfgang Amadeus Mozart und Schweden** [Wolfgang Amadeus Mozart and Sweden], *Bericht über den internationalen musikwissenschaftlichen Kongreß Wien Mozartjahr 1956* (Graz; Köln: Böhlau, 1958) 416–20. In German. See no. 365 in this volume.

Surveys the performance and publication history of Mozart's works in Sweden, from the performance of an unspecified symphony in Stockholm (1789) through the Swedish premieres of *Der Schauspieldirektor* (1875) and *Bastien und Bastienne* (1893), in the context of a general picture of Swedish concert and opera culture in the late 18th and early 19th c. The only Swedish composer who can be counted as an authentic representative of Viennese Classicism is Johan Wikmanson (1753-1800). *(David Bloom)*

1820
as
MOTTA, José Vianna da. **Beethoven in Portugal,** *Beethoven-Zentenarfeier: Internationaler musikhistorischer Kongress* (Wien: Universal, 1927) 132–35. In German. See no. 142 in this volume.

An overview of Beethoven performance and reception from the symphonic concerts organized in Lisbon in 1822 by João Domingos Bomtempo to the Beethoven influence on certain compositions in classicizing style by Luís de Freitas Branco. The only Portuguese musician Beethoven is certain to have known was the mezzo-soprano Luisa Todi (1753-1833). He may have heard operas by Marcos Antônio Portugal in Vienna between 1794 and 1799. *(David Bloom)*

1821
as
MÜLLER-BLATTAU, Joseph. **Beethovens Mozart-Variationen** [Beethoven's Mozart variations], *Bericht über den internationalen musikwissenschaftlichen Kongreß Wien Mozartjahr 1956* (Graz; Köln: Böhlau, 1958) 434–39. In German. See no. 365 in this volume.

Reviews the biographical context and musical features of Beethoven's variations on themes from *Le nozze di Figaro* (violin and piano, WoO 40) and *Die Zauberflöte* (cello and piano, WoO 46 and 66) and their relation to the variation technique and key choice of the piano variations on original themes, opp. 34 and 35.

1822
as
MUNRO, Kathleen. **Haydn's keyboard arrangement of symphony no. 96 in D,** *Bericht über den siebenten internationalen musikwissenschaftlichen Kongress* (Kassel: Bärenreiter, 1959) 197–19. See no. 390 in this volume.

An autograph piano reduction of the symphony, lacking the second movement, is in the collection acquired by Hans Moldenhauer at the Musicological Institute of the Spokane Conservatory. The MS is described and the history of its ownership traced. *(David Bloom)*

1823
as
NAGEL, Wilibald. **Beethoven Romantiker?** [Beethoven the Romantic?], *Beethoven-Zentenarfeier: Internationaler musikhistorischer Kongress* (Wien: Universal, 1927) 40–42. In German. See no. 142 in this volume.

Elements of Beethoven's music that we call Romantic—defined by influences of Goethe and subjective thought—are individual traits of an accessory rather than fundamental nature; his work considered as a whole is humanistic, active rather than speculative or passive, and therefore Classical in conception. *(David Bloom)*

1824
as
NEF, Karl. **Kleine Beiträge zur Mozartforschung** [Brief reports on Mozart research], *Schweizer Jahrbuch für Musikwissenschaft/Annales suisses de*

musicologie/Annuario svizzero di musicologia I (1924) 1–17. In German. See no. 103 in this volume.

1825
as
NĚMEČEK, Jan. **Das Problem des "Mozartismus" und die tschechischen Dorflehrer** [The problem of so-called Mozartism and the Czech village schoolmasters], *Internationale Konferenz über das Leben und Werk W.A. Mozarts* (Praha: Svaz Československých Skladatelů, 1956) 272–81. *Music.* In German. See no. 360 in this volume.

Musical cultivation in 18th-c. Bohemia was extraordinarily dense, especially in rural districts, among the servant classes, public officials, schoolteachers, and church musicians, who were equally familiar with local music traditions and sophisticated developments elsewhere. This helps to explain the complex interactions between the influence of Czech composers such as Josef Myslivček and Czech traditional music material on Mozart's melodic style, and Mozart's influence, from 1782, on Czech composers including Martin Broulík, Emanuel Jan Faulhaber, Alesius Pařizek, and especially Jakub Jan Ryba. *(David Bloom)*

1826
as
NETTL, Paul. **Mozarts Prager Kontertänze** [Mozart's Prague contredanses], *Bericht über die musikwissenschaftliche Tagung der Internationalen Stiftung Mozarteum* (Leipzig: Breitkopf & Härtel, 1932) 133–35. In German. See no. 193 in this volume.

Georg Nikolaus von Nissen's Mozart biography tells the story of how Count Jan Josef Filip Pachta, who wanted a set of contredanses for a Prague ball from Mozart, maneuvered the composer into writing them before dinner the day of the party. The dances of the story are traditionally associated with the nine contredanses catalogued as K.510, but these are not by Mozart, as an examination of the MS sources, in the holdings of the Univerzita Karlova, Prague, and of the music makes clear. *(David Bloom)*

1827
as
NEWMAN, Sidney. **Mozart's G minor quintet (K. 516) and its relationship to the G minor symphony (K. 550): New evidence from a study of the autograph sources,** *Bericht über den internationalen musikwissenschaftlichen Kongreß Wien Mozartjahr 1956* (Graz; Köln: Böhlau, 1958) 447. See no. 365 in this volume.

Summary of a paper published in *The music review* XVII/4 (1956).

1828
as
NÜTZLADER, Rudolf. **Salieri als Kirchenmusiker** [Salieri as church musician], *Festschrift den Mitgliedern des Musikhistorischen Kongresses überreicht von der Leitenden Kommission der Denkmäler der Tonkunst in Österreich* (Wien: Universal, 1927) 160–78. *Music.* In German. See no. 147 in this volume.

Presents a biography of Antonio Salieri (1750-1825) and then investigates the style of his church music systematically, proceeding by individual parameter (melody, harmony and rhythm, motives, harmony and chordal writing, modulation, counterpoint, double choral writing, instrumentation and orchestration). Taken as a whole, Salieri's church style seems to represent the final phase of Viennese composers' reception of the sweet and attractively theatrical Neapolitan idiom; in this light, Salieri was a fashionable composer but not a significant innovator. The second major influence on his church music stems from the Venetian-Austrian tradition. In conclusion, Salieri's personal relationships with the major masters of Viennese Classicism from Haydn to Schubert are surveyed. *(Carl Skoggard)*

1829
as
NYS, Carl de. **À propos du concerto pour deux cors et orchestre en mi bémol majeur** [Regarding the concerto for two horns and orchestra in E♭ major], *Bericht über die internationale Konferenz zum Andenken Joseph Haydns* (Budapest: Akadémiai Kiadó, 1961) 103–08. *Music.* In French. See no. 405 in this volume.

Haydn's 1805 catalogue mentions a concerto for two horns in E♭ major. The work was considered lost until two solo horn parts plus ripieno parts bearing the name "Heiden" were found in the Fürstlich Oettingen-

Wallterstein'sche Bibliothek in Harburg. Considerations of style and historical data, as well as comparisons with scores of composers contemporary with Haydn, suggest that this is the lost concerto. *(Jean W. Smith)*

1830
as

NYS, Carl de. **Mozart et les fils de Jean-Sébastien Bach** [Mozart and the sons of Johann Sebastian Bach], *Les influences étrangères dans l'œuvre de W.A. Mozart* (Paris: Centre National de la Recherche Scientifique [CNRS], 1958) 91–115. *Music.* In French. See no. 358 in this volume.

Among Bach's sons, it was Wilhelm Friedemann who, through the music of his younger brother Johann Christian, had the greatest influence on Mozart. The latter's expressive chromaticism, tonal instability, and intensity-laden counterpoint are evident in W.F. Bach's works, and both endowed the old forms with new expressiveness. *(Vivian Conejero)*

1831
as

NYS, Carl de. **Note sur les polonaises de Wilhelm Friedemann Bach** [Note on the polonaises of Wilhelm Friedemann Bach], *The book of the first international musicological congress devoted to the works of Frederick Chopin* (Warszawa: Państwowe Wydawnictwo Naukowe, 1963) 578–87. *Music.* In French. See no. 425 in this volume.

The polonaises of Wilhelm Friedemann Bach exhibit some of the same qualities as those composed by Chopin, most notably a melding of form, freedom, and personal expression. There are musical similarities as well. The historical backgrounds of several of Wilhelm Friedemann Bach's pieces are also described. *(Susan Poliniak)*

⟶

OBERBORBECK, Felix. **Schwäbische Reichsstädte als Träger deutscher Musikkultur im 18. Jahrhundert** [Swabian imperial cities as bearers of German music culture in the 18th century]. See no. 1639 in this volume.

1832
as

OČADLÍK, Mirko. **Voraussetzungen wissenschaftlicher Mozartforschung in Böhmen** [Prerequisites for scholarly research on Mozart in Bohemia], *Internationale Konferenz über das Leben und Werk W.A. Mozarts* (Praha: Svaz Československých Skladatelů, 1956) 175–80. In German. See no. 360 in this volume.

In general, Mozart historiography needs to move beyond traditional positivism to an understanding of the relationship between music and society, and Mozart must be recognized, as Beethoven has long been, as a progressive figure; his reception in Prague can be seen in the context of the tensions there between feudalism and Enlightenment. *Don Giovanni* and the symphony no. 38 are interpreted in political terms. *(David Bloom)*

1833
as

PALM, Albert. **Mozart und Haydn in der Interpretation Momignys** [Mozart and Haydn in Momigny's interpretation], *Bericht über den internationalen musikwissenschaftlichen Kongreß* (Kassel: Bärenreiter, 1963) 187–90. In German. See no. 452 in this volume.

Discusses poeticizing analyses of Mozart's string quartet K.421 and Haydn's symphony no. 103 in the *Cours complet d'harmonie et de composition* of Jérôme-Joseph de Momigny, 1806. *(David Bloom)*

1834
as

PAUMGARTNER, Bernhard. **Vom Musiktheater Mozarts** [Mozart's music theater], *Bericht über den neunten internationalen Kongreß* (Kassel: Bärenreiter, 1964-1966) II, 3–6. In German. See no. 491 in this volume.

Remarks on musicological issues in the performance practice of Mozart's operas.

1835
as

PAUMGARTNER, Bernhard. **Zur Synthese der symphonischen Musik Mozarts** [The synthesis

represented by Mozart's symphonic music], *Bericht über die musikwissenschaftliche Tagung der Internationalen Stiftung Mozarteum* (Leipzig: Breitkopf & Härtel, 1932) 72–78. In German. See no. 193 in this volume.

In the comparative-historical approach adopted by Théodore de Wyzewa and Georges de Saint-Foix, Mozart's style is broken into contrasting periods around a so-called Romantic crisis. In contrast to this relatively superficial view, a style-analytic approach shows a deep consistency in, for example, the technique of his thematic development. *(David Bloom)*

1836
as

PLATH, Wolfgang. **Der gegenwärtige Stand der Mozart-Forschung** [The present state of Mozart research], *Bericht über den neunten internationalen Kongreß* (Kassel: Bärenreiter, 1964-1966) I, 47–55. In German. See no. 491 in this volume.

Mozart research is currently in crisis, because of a neglect of the fundamentals; only through systematic, methodical source study can progress be made in the treatment of the basic issues. Problems of Mozart's biography and questionable attributions of his works are discussed. *(David Bloom)*

1837
as

PLATH, Wolfgang. **Über Skizzen zu Mozarts** *Requiem* [Sketches for Mozart's Requiem], *Bericht über den internationalen musikwissenschaftlichen Kongreß* (Kassel: Bärenreiter, 1963) 184–87. *Music.* In German. See no. 452 in this volume.

Two loose autograph leaves, with the accession number 1889.401, in the holdings of the Deutsche Staatsbibliothek, Berlin, have not been fully described; in addition to sketches for *Die Zauberflöte*, they seem to include material Mozart would have used, but Franz Xaver Süssmayr did not, in the completion of the Requiem. *(David Bloom)*

1838
as

POŠTOLKA, Milan. **Joseph Haydn und Leopold Koželuh** [Joseph Haydn and Leopold Koželuh], *Bericht über die internationale Konferenz zum Andenken Joseph Haydns* (Budapest: Akadémiai Kiadó, 1961) 109–15. *Music.* In German. See no. 405 in this volume.

Koželuh was strongly influenced by Haydn. The two composers' works show striking similarities in character of invention and idiom, structure of the sonata cycle, structure of individual movements within the sonata cycle, and choice of genre. *(Larry Laskowski)*

1839
as

POŠTOLKA, Milan. **Leopold Koželuh, ein Zeitgenosse Mozarts** [Leopold Koželuh, a contemporary of Mozart], *Internationale Konferenz über das Leben und Werk W.A. Mozarts* (Praha: Svaz Československých Skladatelů, 1956) 135–45. *Music.* In German. See no. 360 in this volume.

A preliminary sketch of the composer's life and works, with an extended discussion of shared features and structural congruities in his and Mozart's compositional style.

1840
as

PROD'HOMME, Jacques-Gabriel. **Lettres inédites de Le Sueur, Boïeldieu et Cherubini au compositeur anversois Janssens** [Unpublished letters of Le Sueur, Boieldieu, and Cherubini to the Antwerp composer Janssens], *Annales du XXIIIᵉ congrès* (Gent: Siffer, 1914) III, 339–46. In French. See no. 89 in this volume.

Letters to Jan Frans Jozef Janssens from Jean-François Le Sueur, François-Adrien Boieldieu, and Luigi Cherubini.

1841
as

RACEK, Jan. **Beitrag zur Frage des "mozartschen" Stils in der tschechischen vorklassischen Musik** [The question of the so-called Mozartean style in pre-Classic Czech music], *Internationale Konferenz über das Leben und Werk W.A.*

Mozarts (Praha: Svaz Československých Skladatelů, 1956) 34–43. In German. See no. 360 in this volume.

Anticipations of Mozart's style are found in the works of the first Bohemian pre-Classicist, František Václav Míča; important composers who emigrated from Bohemia, including Jan Václav Stamic, Franz Xaver Richter, Johann Anton Fils, Jiří Benda, and Josef Myslivecek; and composers active in Prague at the time of Mozart's maturity, such as František Xaver Brixi, and František Xaver Dušek. *(John Stansell)*

1842 RACEK, Jan. **Drei unbekannte Autographen-**
as **torsen W.A. Mozarts** [Three unknown autograph fragments by W.A. Mozart], *Bericht über den siebenten internationalen musikwissenschaftlichen Kongress* (Kassel: Bärenreiter, 1959) 216–17. In German. See no. 390 in this volume.

The fragments were given by Franz Xaver Mozart to his friend and patron Josephine Baroni-Cavalcabò and eventually collected by the Czech historian and library curator Ferdinand Menčík (d.1916), who left them to the then Kaiserliche und Königliche Hofbibliothek, Vienna, now Österreichische Nationalbibliothek. Hypotheses on their relation to Mozart's completed compositions are briefly discussed. An extended treatment, with facsimile reproductions of the fragments and paleographic analysis, is published as *Unbekannte Autographen-Fragmente von Mozart* in *Deutsches Jahrbuch der Musikwissenschaft* 3, 1958. *(David Bloom)*

1843 RACEK, Jan. **Zur Frage des "Mozart-Stils" in**
as **der tschechischen vorklassischen Musik** [The question of a Mozartean style in pre-Classic Czech music], *Bericht über den internationalen musikwissenschaftlichen Kongreß Wien Mozartjahr 1956* (Graz; Köln: Böhlau, 1958) 493–524. *Music.* In German. See no. 365 in this volume.

Discusses the works of Bohemian composers including František Xaver Brixi, František Antonín Václav Míča, and František Xaver Dušek, as well as emigrants from Bohemia and Moravia to Germany including Jan Václav Stamic, Franz Xaver Richter, Anton Filtz, Franz and Jiří Benda, and Josef Myslivecek. Biographical information is provided for each composer, along with an analysis of stylistic affinities with Mozart's music, and where applicable a consideration of their possible influence on Mozart. *(David Bloom)*

1844 RAUGEL, Félix. **Bernard Jumentier**
as **(1749-1829) maître de chapelle de la Collégiate de Saint-Quentin et ses œuvres inédites** [Bernard Jumentier (1749-1829), chapel master of the collegiate church of Saint-Quentin, and his unpublished works], *Bericht über den Internationalen musikwissenschaftlichen Kongress* (Kassel: Bärenreiter, 1954) 279–81. In French. See no. 319 in this volume.

Outlines the main events in the life of the church musician Bernard Jumentier and discusses his compositions, which remained unpublished. Upon his death, Jumentier's MSS were given to the collegiate church of Saint-Quentin, where he had been in charge of the choir school for many years. The MSS survived World War I but suffered damage in World War II. *(Carl Skoggard)*

1845 REDLICH, Hans F. **Anfänge der Bachpflege in**
as **England 1750-1850** [The beginnings of the cultivation of Bach in England, 1750-1850], *Kongreß-Bericht: Gesellschaft für Musikforschung* (Kassel; Basel: Bärenreiter, 1950) 131–35. In German. See no. 299 in this volume.

1846 ROBERT, Paul-Louis. **Boieldieu et *La dame**
as ***blanche*** [Boieldieu and *La dame blanche*], *Congrès du Millénaire de la Normandie (911-1911)* (Rouen: Léon Gy, 1912) 361–69. In French. See no. 77 in this volume.

Boieldieu's life and the society of his time are illustrated through his unpublished correspondence.

1847 RONGA, Luigi. **Il rococò musicale** [The musical
as rococo], *Manierismo, barocco, rococò: Concetti e termini—Convegno internazionale* (Roma: R. Accademia dei Lincei, 1962) 387–93. In Italian. See no. 422 in this volume.

The era of rococo music is defined as falling between the Baroque and Classic periods (ca. 1725-75). The differences between French and Italian rococo, and the similarities between art forms of the period are outlined. *(Susan Poliniak)*

1848 RUBIN, Marcel. **Mozart und die Probleme der**
as **modernen Musik** [Mozart and the problems of modern music], *Internationale Konferenz über das Leben und Werk W.A. Mozarts* (Praha: Svaz Československých Skladatelů, 1956) 225–29. In German. See no. 360 in this volume.

Mozart presents an example that 20th-c. composers might emulate in important ways. He was an avid experimentalist, but never cut himself off from tradition. In his nationalism, in the anti-feudal tendency of the librettos he chose, and in his adherence to Freemasonry, he showed himself to be a participant in the revolutionary currents of his time, if not as explicitly as Beethoven. His nationalism was expressed positively, in attachment to German linguistic and musical tradition, not negatively, in the form of national prejudices. *(David Bloom)*

1849 SALMEN, Walter. **J.F. Reichardt und die**
as **osteuropäische Volksmusik** [Johann Friedrich Reichardt and Eastern European traditional music], *The book of the first international musicological congress devoted to the works of Frederick Chopin* (Warszawa: Państwowe Wydawnictwo Naukowe, 1963) 601–03. *Music.* In German. See no. 425 in this volume.

Reichardt was exposed to Baltic and Slavic traditional music early in his life in Königsberg. His works show an influence especially of Polish dance rhythms. *(David Bloom)*

1850 SCHENK, Erich. **Mozart incarnation de l'âme**
as **autrichienne** [Mozart, the incarnation of the Austrian soul], *Les influences étrangères dans l'œuvre de W.A. Mozart* (Paris: Centre National de la Recherche Scientifique [CNRS], 1958) 17–26. In French. See no. 358 in this volume.

Austria sits at the intersection of Latin, Germanic, Slavic, and Hungarian cultures, and therefore embodies aspects of each. In the 18th c., Salzburg was filled with musicians from all parts of Europe, which contributed to a sense of internationalism in Mozart's music. Mozart's father possessed a certain urbanity, and his mother a certain serenity, both qualities being typically Austrian. These qualities are apparent in Mozart's music, as are various elements of Austrian traditional music. *(Susan Poliniak)*

1851 SCHENK, Erich. **Mozarts mütterliche Familie**
as [Mozart's maternal relatives], *Bericht über die musikwissenschaftliche Tagung der Internationalen Stiftung Mozarteum* (Leipzig: Breitkopf & Härtel, 1932) 45–68. In German. See no. 193 in this volume.

Summarizes documentary information on Mozart's relatives in the maternal line, from the Pertl, Falter, Schmidpichler, and Göppinger families. His mother's father, Wolfgang Nikolaus Pertl, shows the most evidence of a heritable musical talent. *(David Bloom)*

1852 SCHIEDERMAIR, Ludwig. **Beethoven und das**
as **Rheinland** [Beethoven and the Rhineland], *Beethoven-Zentenarfeier: Internationaler musikhistorischer Kongress* (Wien: Universal, 1927) 7–10. In German. See no. 142 in this volume.

Summarizes the author's argument (in *Der junge Beethoven*, Leipzig, 1925; a reprint is cited as RILM [1978]2810) that the cultural environment of Mainz, Cologne, and Bonn played a decisive role in the young Beethoven's development as a composer. During this time he read works of philosophy (Kant and Rousseau) and German poetry (Schiller and Goethe). *(David Bloom)*

1853
as

SCHIEDERMAIR, Ludwig. **Das deutsche Mozartbild** [The German image of Mozart], *Bericht über die musikwissenschaftliche Tagung der Internationalen Stiftung Mozarteum* (Leipzig: Breitkopf & Härtel, 1932) 1–11. In German. See no. 193 in this volume.

Developing understanding of Mozart since his death has led to an increasing appreciation of the Germanness of his artistic character, and to recognition of the complete integration of Apollonian and Dionysian elements in his works. *(David Bloom)*

1854
as

SCHMID, Ernst Fritz. **L'héritage souabe de Mozart** [Mozart's Swabian heritage], *Les influences étrangères dans l'œuvre de W.A. Mozart* (Paris: Centre National de la Recherche Scientifique [CNRS], 1958) 59–83. *Music.* In French. See no. 358 in this volume.

Mozart's musical and ancestral roots were in Swabia. Mozart's father probably introduced him to traditional and popular Swabian music; their impact can be heard in his works. Swabian musicians such as Johann Gottfried Eckard also had an influence on the composer. *(Susan Poliniak)*

1855
as

SCHMID, Ernst Fritz. **Joseph Haydn und die vokale Zierpraxis seiner Zeit, dargestellt an einer Arie seines Tobias-Oratoriums** [Joseph Haydn and the vocal ornamentation practice of his time, illustrated by an aria from his *Tobia* oratorio], *Bericht über die internationale Konferenz zum Andenken Joseph Haydns* (Budapest: Akadémiai Kiadó, 1961) 117–30. *Facs., music.* In German. See no. 405 in this volume.

The aria *Quando mi dona* from *Il ritorno di Tobia* exists in two forms: an unornamented version from a copy of the score and a shortened, heavily ornamented version from an autograph copy of the vocal part plus figured bass. A comparison of the two versions shows Haydn's training in traditional Italian vocal practice, and sets apart the early oratorios from the later ones, which possess a simpler quality and are more reminiscent of traditional music. *(Larry Laskowski)*

1856
as

SCHMITZ, Arnold. **Beethovens Religiosität** [Beethoven and religion], *Bericht über den I. musikwissenschaftlichen Kongress der Deutschen Musikgesellschaft in Leipzig* (Wiesbaden: Breitkopf & Härtel, 1926) 274–79. In German. See no. 120 in this volume.

Compares the theories regarding Beethoven's religious persuasion—and the influences of deism as opposed to pantheism—based on his music and the evidence of Anton Felix Schindler. Schindler's unreliability is noted, and it is concluded that Beethoven was a Catholic according to the definition of Johann Michael von Sailer. *(William Renwick)*

1857
as

SCHNERICH, Alfred. **Das konfessionelle Element bei Beethoven** [The denominational factor in Beethoven], *Beethoven-Zentenarfeier: Internationaler musikhistorischer Kongress* (Wien: Universal, 1927) 107–10. In German. See no. 142 in this volume.

The relative paucity of liturgical music in Beethoven's output, in comparison to that of Haydn and Mozart on the one hand, and to Liszt and Bruckner on the other, is explained by the circumstances of his career and the general situation of church music in Bonn and Vienna. *(David Bloom)*

1858
as

SEEGER, Horst. **Zur musikhistorischen Bedeutung Albert Christoph Dies' und seiner Haydn-Biographie von 1810** [The musical-historical significance of Albert Christoph Dies and his Haydn biography of 1810], *Bericht über die internationale Konferenz zum Andenken Joseph Haydns* (Budapest: Akadémiai Kiadó, 1961) 131–36. In German. See no. 405 in this volume.

Dies's *Biographische Nachrichten von Joseph Haydn* is firmly rooted in Classical realism; this anti-Romanticism makes his work unique among early Haydn biographies. *(Larry Laskowski)*

1859
as

SIEGMUND-SCHULTZE, Walther. **Mozarts Haydn-Quartette** [Mozart's "Haydn" quartets], *Bericht über die internationale Konferenz zum Andenken Joseph Haydns* (Budapest: Akadémiai Kiadó, 1961) 137–46. *Music.* In German. See no. 405 in this volume.

Mozart's "Haydn" quartets, though heavily influenced by the latter's quartets, also show many traits specific to Mozart, such as the pronounced contrast of themes, the special type of cantabile melody in the slow movements, and the heightening of expression by strong dramatic contrast and less overt humor. They share many stylistic and aesthetic characteristics with the op. 59 quartets of Beethoven; in this sense, Mozart stands alone between Haydn and Beethoven as a great dramatic realist. *(Larry Laskowski)*

1860
as

SIEGMUND-SCHULTZE, Walther. **Zur Frage der Beziehungen zwischen Mozarts Vokal und Instrumentalmusik** [The relationships between Mozart's vocal and instrumental music], *Internationale Konferenz über das Leben und Werk W.A. Mozarts* (Praha: Svaz Československých Skladatelů, 1956) 146–55. *Music.* In German. See no. 360 in this volume.

Discusses vocal-instrumental affinities particularly from Mozart's mature period, analytic comparisons of melodies, and biographical issues. *(David Bloom)*

1861
as

SIMON, Alicja. **Grétry au Théâtre National de Varsovie** [Grétry at the Teatr Wielki in Warsaw], *Société Internationale de Musicologie: Premier Congrès Liège—Compte rendu/Internationale Gesellschaft für Musikwissenschaft: Erster Kongress Lüttich—Kongressbericht/International Society for Musical Research: First Congress Liège: Report* (London: Plainsong and Mediaeval Music Society, 1930) 201–07. *Illus., music.* In French. See no. 178 in this volume.

Opera was introduced to Poland in the early 17th c. and its increasing popularity resulted in the founding of the Teatr Wielki in 1765. The performance of André-Ernest-Modeste Grétry's works in Poland along with other French operas influenced the birth of a national school in 1778. Eventually, opéra comique was replaced in popularity by opera seria and the Polish school, heavily promoted by Wojciech Bogusławski, director of the theater. The performances of Grétry's works, both in French and Polish translations, and their role in late 18th-c. opera in Poland are discussed. *(Conrad T. Biel)*

1862
as

ŠIROLA, Božidar. **Haydn und Beethoven und ihre Stellung zur kroatischen Volksmusik** [Haydn and Beethoven and their relationship to Croatian traditional music], *Beethoven-Zentenarfeier: Internationaler musikhistorischer Kongress* (Wien: Universal, 1927) 111–15. In German. See no. 142 in this volume.

Summarizes the findings of Franjo Ksaver Kuhač on the use of traditional Croatian tunes in symphonies by Haydn and Beethoven, with speculations on their sources. Kuhač published his findings in his essays *Josip Haydn i hrvatske pučke popievke* (1880) and *Beethoven i hrvatske narodne popievke* (1894). Haydn may have been of partly Croatian ancestry.

1863
as

SMETANA, Robert. **Mozart und das tschechische Volk** [Mozart and the Czech people], *Internationale Konferenz über das Leben und Werk W.A. Mozarts* (Praha: Svaz Československých Skladatelů, 1956) 202–09. *Transcr.* In German. See no. 360 in this volume.

The remarkable affinities of Mozart's style with that of Czech music of the period, and the particular openness of Czech audiences to Mozart's music at a time when few Austrians or Germans recognized its value, have been noted. It may also be said that Mozart's experience of feudal and religious oppression in the Salzburg period has parallels in the experience of the Czech nation under Austrian rule, and that his life-affirming, earthly ideals, as contrasted with the heavenly ideals of the Church, are those expressed frequently in 18th-c. Czech traditional music. *(David Bloom)*

1864
as

SONDHEIMER, Robert. **Anfänge des Wiener Stils in der Sinfonie des 18. Jahrhunderts** [Origins of the Viennese style in the 18th-century symphony], *Bericht über den I. musikwissenschaftlichen Kongress der Deutschen Musikgesellschaft in Leipzig* (Wiesbaden: Breitkopf & Härtel, 1926) 260–65. In German. See no. 120 in this volume.

Attempts to distinguish the Viennese style, especially in contrast to the Mannheim school. The historical background of dance suites and folk song characteristic of the Viennese style is noted. *(William Renwick)*

1865
as

STÁDNÍK, Miloš. **W.A. Mozart und neue Betrachtungen über A. Rejcha** [W.A. Mozart and new observations on A. Rejcha], *Internationale Konferenz über das Leben und Werk W.A. Mozarts* (Praha: Svaz Československých Skladatelů, 1956) 79–84. In German. See no. 360 in this volume.

Anton Rejcha was thoroughly acquainted with Mozart's works, whose influence can be traced throughout his own, as well as in his theoretical writings; it may be said of him with more justice than of his friend and colleague Beethoven that he received "Mozart's spirit through Haydn's hands". It may be surmised that in his most important operas, lost except for excerpts quoted in the theoretical works, the Mozartean influence was particularly clear. *(David Bloom)*

1866
as

ŠTĚDROŇ, Bohumír. **Mozart und Mähren** [Mozart and Moravia], *Internationale Konferenz über das Leben und Werk W.A. Mozarts* (Praha: Svaz Československých Skladatelů, 1956) 51–55. In German. See no. 360 in this volume.

Discusses Mozart's visits to Brno and Olomouc in 1767-68, the reception of his works there, and his influence on Moravian composers of his own and later periods. *(Anthony F. Bavota)*

1867
as

STEGLICH, Rudolf. **Beethovens "überaus merkwürdige Akzentuation"** [Beethoven's "extremely peculiar accentuation"], *Compte rendu/ Kongressbericht/Report* (Basel: Bärenreiter, 1951) 190–94. *Music.* In German. See no. 289 in this volume.

The distinctive use of accentuation in Beethoven's works, noted in Schindler's biography of the composer, including the so-called bad accents in his setting of text, is a systematic expressive device. *(David Bloom)*

1868
as

STEIN, Fritz. **Mitteilungen über eine in Jena aufgefundene mutmassliche Jugendsymphonie Beethovens** [A youthful symphony allegedly by Beethoven discovered at Jena], *Report of the Fourth Congress of the International Musical Society* (London: Novello, 1912) 158. In German. See no. 71 in this volume.

Summary of a paper. Describes the work (a symphony in C major) and argues that it is indeed by Beethoven.

1869
as

STEIN, Fritz. **Zum Problem der "Jenaer Symphonie"** [The problem of the so-called Jena symphony], *Bericht über den siebenten internationalen musikwissenschaftlichen Kongress* (Kassel: Bärenreiter, 1959) 279–80. In German. See no. 390 in this volume.

Since the author's discovery in 1909 at the Thüringer Universitätsbibliothek, Jena, of the MS score of a symphony in C major inscribed with the name of Beethoven, evidence has accumulated to suggest that the work was actually by Friedrich Witt; the evidence does not seem conclusive, however. *(David Bloom)*

1870
as

STEMPEL, Maxim. **Mozart in Schweden** [Mozart in Sweden], *Internationale Konferenz über das Leben und Werk W.A. Mozarts* (Praha: Svaz Česko-slovenských Skladatelů, 1956) 189–92. In German. See no. 360 in this volume.

Surveys the history of Mozart reception in Sweden, with emphasis on the period from 1789 to ca. 1850, and the slow acceptance of his operas in the political and aesthetic context of the times. Figures discussed include the MS collector Frederik Samuel Silverstolpe, the anti-Mozart theater director Abraham Niclas Clewberg-Edelcrantz, the composer and conductor Joachim Eggert, the composer and church musician Olof Åhlström, the poet Johan Gabriel Oxenstierna, and the critic Carl Wilhelm Bauck. *(David Bloom)*

1871
as

SUBIRÁ, José. **Un fondo desconocido de música para guitarra** [An unknown stock of guitar music], *Congrés de la Societat Internacional de Musicologia* (Barcelona: Casa de Caritat, 1936). In Spanish. See no. 224 in this volume.

Surveys sources of Spanish guitar music at the Biblioteca Nacional in Madrid. The conference report provides only a citation. Neither the text nor a summary of the paper was published here.

1872
as

SYCHRA, Antonín. **Über die Bedeutung von Beethovens Skizzen zur IX. Symphonie** [On the meaning of Beethoven's sketches for the ninth symphony], *Bericht über die internationale Konferenz zum Andenken Joseph Haydns* (Budapest: Akadémiai Kiadó, 1961) 147–58. *Facs.* In German. See no. 405 in this volume.

The sketches for the ninth symphony illustrate the similarities and differences in the compositional processes for absolute and programmatic music. In the sketches for the first three movements, the subjects are created and developed in a spontaneous way. The sketches for the finale—whose basic idea is programmatic, not vocal—evince a search for an adequate means of expression in purely instrumental music. The sketches for the instrumental recitative are especially revealing, as a dramatic plan evolves in which characteristics of several musical genres play a role. *(Larry Laskowski)*

1873
as

SYCHRA, Antonín. **W.A. Mozart et la musique populaire tchéque** [W.A. Mozart and Czech traditional music], *Les influences étrangères dans l'œuvre de W.A. Mozart* (Paris: Centre National de la Recherche Scientifique [CNRS], 1958) 189–98. *Music.* In French. See no. 358 in this volume.

Mozart was acquainted with Czech traditional songs; he borrowed their motives and general stylistic principles, incorporating them within the framework of the Classic Viennese style. Mozart's music, and the Classic style itself, infiltrated Bohemia's popular music through court orchestras, which were mostly composed of popular musicians. *(Vivian Conejero)*

1874
as

SÝKORA, Václav Jan. **František Xaver Dušek,** *Internationale Konferenz über das Leben und Werk W.A. Mozarts* (Praha: Svaz Československých Skladatelů, 1956) 159–66. In German. See no. 360 in this volume.

Brief account of the Czech composer's life and works, with particular attention to his friendship with and support for Mozart. An extended discussion is published as *František Xaver Dušek: Život a dílo* (Prague, 1958). *(David Bloom)*

1875
as

SÝKORA, Václav Jan. **Jan Ladislav Dusík, der älteste Vorgänger Chopins** [Jan Ladislav Dusík, Chopin's earliest precursor], *The book of the first international musicological congress devoted to the works of Frederick Chopin* (Warszawa: Państwowe Wydawnictwo Naukowe, 1963) 396–98. In German. See no. 425 in this volume.

As a composer and virtuoso pianist of Central European origins who spent most of his career in the West, Dusík (1760-1812) resembles Chopin in many biographical points. Certain features of his compositional style, moreover, anticipate Chopin, and Romanticism in general, in a way that is unique to composers of his generation: in the almost symphonic and yet velvety sound he attained in his piano writing; in the fullness of his harmony and modernity of his modulations; and in his use of elements of the traditional music of his homeland. *(David Bloom)*

1876 SZABOLCSI, Bence. **Die "Exotismen"**
as **Mozarts** [Mozart's exoticisms], *Internationale Konferenz über das Leben und Werk W.A. Mozarts* (Praha: Svaz Československých Skladatelů, 1956) 181–88. *Music, transcr.* In German. See no. 360 in this volume.

A masked dance attested in Hungary as far back as the late 18th c., known as törökös ("Turkish"), presents interesting similarities with Orientalizing passages by Mozart (*Die Entführung aus dem Serail*), Carl Ditters von Dittersdorf, Gluck, and Haydn, as do melodies collected in the *Canzoniere popolare italiano* of Elisabetta Oddone (1917-23) and Eugenia Levi's *Per i vostri bambini* (1906). *(David Bloom)*

1877 SZABOLCSI, Bence. **Haydn und die**
as **ungarische Musik** [Haydn and Hungarian music], *Bericht über die internationale Konferenz zum Andenken Joseph Haydns* (Budapest: Akadémiai Kiadó, 1961) 159–77. In German. See no. 405 in this volume.

1878 TAGLIAVINI, Luigi Ferdinando. **L'opéra**
as **italien du jeune Mozart** [The Italian operas of the young Mozart], *Les influences étrangères dans l'œuvre de W.A. Mozart* (Paris: Centre National de la Recherche Scientifique [CNRS], 1958) 125–56. *Facs., music.* In French. See no. 358 in this volume.

Mozart's Italian sojourns exposed him to the influence of the Italian operatic style, its composers, singers, and texts. Although he developed his own operatic style, Italian traits are always detectable in his works. *(Vivian Conejero)*

1879 TAPPOLET, Willy. **Le séjour de Wolfgang-**
as **Amadé Mozart à Genève en 1766** [Wolfgang Amadeus Mozart's 1766 stay in Geneva], *Bericht über den internationalen musikwissenschaftlichen Kongreß Wien Mozartjahr 1956* (Graz; Köln: Böhlau, 1958) 637–39. In French. See no. 365 in this volume.

Documentary evidence of the itinerary and timetable of Mozart's trip to Geneva, his performances there, his presumed encounter with the young André-Ernest-Modeste Grétry, and his apparent failure to meet with Voltaire are surveyed. *(David Bloom)*

1880 TARANTOVÁ, Marie. **Das Echo von Mozarts**
as **Werk in der Epoche der Wiedergeburt des tschechischen Volkes** [The echo of Mozart's music in the era of the renaissance of the Czech people], *Internationale Konferenz über das Leben und Werk W.A. Mozarts* (Praha: Svaz Československých Skladatelů, 1956) 282–88. In German. See no. 360 in this volume.

Discusses the importance of Mozart to the Czech national movement from the Prague premiere of *Don Giovanni* to the celebrations of its 50th anniversary in 1837 and the Mozart centenary festivities of 1856. Czech-language performing versions of Mozart's operas played a role in the renewal of the language from as early as 1794, and the composers who initiated the national school of composition, including Jan Emanuel Doležálek, Jan Jakub Ryba, and Jan Nepomuk August Vitásek, were among those most influenced by Mozart. An extended Czech-language version is abstracted as RILM [1967]1782). *(David Bloom)*

1881 TORREFRANCA, Fausto. **Influenza di alcuni**
as **musicisti Italiani vissuti a Londra su W.A. Mozart (1764-65)** [Influence of some Italian musicians in London on W.A. Mozart (1764-65)], *Bericht über den musikwissenschaftlichen Kongreß in Basel* (Leipzig: Breitkopf & Härtel, 1925) 336–62. *Music.* In Italian. See no. 102 in this volume.

London provided a pan-European environment in which Mozart could absorb a variety of influences. Italian composers mentioned by Leopold Mozart whose music was known at the time in London included Luigi Borghi and Mattia Vento. Borghi's violin concerto (London, 1774), in a contemporary piano reduction, is seen to have Mozartian characteristics, as are Vento's sonatas for harpsichord with violin accompaniment (1764-77).

1882 TORREFRANCA, Fausto. **Mozart e il quartetto**
as **italiano** [Mozart and the Italian quartet], *Bericht über die musikwissenschaftliche Tagung der Internationalen Stiftung Mozarteum* (Leipzig: Breitkopf & Härtel, 1932) 79–102. In Italian. See no. 193 in this volume.

Argues that the historical origins of the string quartet should be sought not in the German divertimento but as an Italian development out of the Baroque concerto a quattro, in the works of Baldassare Galuppi, Giovanni Battista Sammartini, Luigi Boccherini, Tommaso Giordani, and Giuseppe Maria Cambini, all composers of international reputation. Their possible influence on Mozart's quartet composition is traced in terms of the biographical data on Mozart's interaction with Italian musicians. *(David Bloom)*

1883 UNGER, Max. **Aus Beethovens Werkstatt**
as [From Beethoven's workshop], *Congrés de la Societat Internacional de Musicologia* (Barcelona: Casa de Caritat, 1936). In German. See no. 224 in this volume.

The conference report provides only a citation. Neither the text nor a summary of the paper was published here.

1884 UNGER, Max. **Beethovens Handschrift** [Bee-
as thoven's handwriting], *Bericht über den musikwissenschaftlichen Kongreß in Basel* (Leipzig: Breitkopf & Härtel, 1925) 363. In German. See no. 102 in this volume.

Focuses on Beethoven's alphabetic script. Many so-called mistakes in his published correspondence are the responsibility of his transcribers. An expanded version appears in *Die Musik* (March, 1925).

1885 UPTON, William Treat. **Secular music in the**
as **United States 150 years ago,** *Papers of the American Musicological Society* (Philadelphia: American Musicological Society, 1946) 105–11. *Charts, diagr.* See no. 272 in this volume.

Surveys events of the 1790s in Philadelphia, New York, Boston, Baltimore, and Charleston, with emphasis on important musicians who emigrated from Britain and Europe during the period; the beginnings of secular music publishing in significant volume, including music by local composers and opera librettos; and opera performance. *(David Bloom)*

1886 VALABREGA, Cesare. **Mozart et le goût italien**
as [Mozart and the Italian style], *Les influences étrangères dans l'œuvre de W.A. Mozart* (Paris: Centre National de la Recherche Scientifique [CNRS], 1958) 117–24. In French. See no. 358 in this volume.

The international music scene was Italian-dominated in Mozart's time, so he was exposed to Italian music before he traveled to Italy. Along with its German stylistic elements, Mozart's music is infused with the singing quality of Italian music. Another version is cited as no. 1887 in this volume. *(Vivian Conejero)*

1887 VALABREGA, Cesare. **Mozart und der Geist**
as **der italienischen Musik** [Mozart and the spirit of Italian music], *Internationale Konferenz über das Leben und Werk W.A. Mozarts* (Praha: Svaz Československých Skladatelů, 1956) 44–50. In German. See no. 360 in this volume.

Another version is abstracted as no. 1886 in this volume.

1888 VALENTIN, Erich. **Das Kind Mozart** [The child
as Mozart], *Internationale Konferenz über das Leben und Werk W.A. Mozarts* (Praha: Svaz Československých

Skladatelů, 1956) 196–99. In German. See no. 360 in this volume.

Biographical notes on the composer's early childhood from the perspective of the compositions of 1761-65, edited by Edward J. Dent and the author in the collection published in English as *The earliest compositions of Wolfgang Amadeus Mozart* and in German as *Der früheste Mozart* (Munich: H. Rinn, 1956). *(David Bloom)*

1889
as

VOGL, Hertha. **Zur Geschichte des Oratoriums in Wien von 1725 bis 1740** [The history of the oratorio in Vienna, 1725-40], *Festschrift den Mitgliedern des Musikhistorischen Kongresses überreicht von der Leitenden Kommission der Denkmäler der Tonkunst in Österreich* (Wien: Universal, 1927) 241–64. *Music.* In German. See no. 147 in this volume.

Traces the principal currents in oratorio style in Vienna, with attention to the Venetian-Viennese and the Neapolitan traditions, the former represented chiefly by Johann Joseph Fux. The evolution of the oratorio text, under the influence of Apostolo Zeno and Pietro Metastasio, is described, as is the development of the aria form in oratorio and the emergence of the full-fledged Neapolitan da capo type. The expressive qualities of the Viennese oratorio of these years can be assessed in terms of lyricism and drama as opposed possibilities. Whereas opera remained an entertainment reserved for court society, the oratorio was open to the general public, and thus may be said to have more social significance; however, this wider public was not permitted to express any opinion as to the merits of the music they were being allowed to hear. *(Carl Skoggard)*

1890
as

VÓKOS, Giórgios. **Die Ästhetik der Mozartschen Kompositionen** [The aesthetics of Mozart's compositions], *Internationale Konferenz über das Leben und Werk W.A. Mozarts* (Praha: Svaz Československých Skladatelů, 1956) 193–95. In German. See no. 360 in this volume.

A general appreciation.

⟶

VOLEK, Tomislav. **Czech music of the seventeenth and eighteenth centuries.** See no. 1709 in this volume.

1891
as

WALIN, Stig Alfred Ferdinand. **Sur les conditions générales de l'internationalisme de Mozart** [On the general conditions of Mozart's internationalism], *Les influences étrangères dans l'œuvre de W.A. Mozart* (Paris: Centre National de la Recherche Scientifique [CNRS], 1958) 9–15. In French. See no. 358 in this volume.

As a result of continuous exchanges among composers of different countries, the art music of Europe was international from its inception. It was through the continent's cultivated musical circles that Mozart became exposed to international influences. *(Vivian Conejero)*

1892
as

WALLON, Simone. **Romances et vaudevilles français dans les variations pour piano et pour piano et violon de Mozart** [French romances and vaudevilles in Mozart's variations for piano and for piano and violin], *Bericht über den internationalen musikwissenschaftlichen Kongreß Wien Mozartjahr 1956* (Graz; Köln: Böhlau, 1958) 666–72. *Music.* In French. See no. 365 in this volume.

Investigates the themes for Mozart's variations on *La belle françoise*, K.353; *Ah vous dirai-je, maman*, K.265; *La bergère Célimène*, K.359; and *Hélas, j'ai perdu mon amant*, K.360. All belonged to the repertoire of romance and vaudeville; their sources are enumerated, and variation treatments by other composers are listed. *(David Bloom)*

1893
as

WECOWSKI, Jan. **La musique symphonique polonaise du XVIIIᵉ siècle** [Polish symphonic music of the 18th century], *Musica antiqua Europae*

orientalis (Warszawa: Państwowe Wydawnictwo Naukowe, 1966). *List of works.* In French. See no. 506 in this volume.

Includes a catalogue of symphonies and an index of the libraries where they can be found.

1894
as

WEINMANN, Karl. **Beethovens Verhältnis zur Religion** [Beethoven's relationship to religion], *Beethoven-Zentenarfeier: Internationaler musikhistorischer Kongress* (Wien: Universal, 1927) 19–24. In German. See no. 142 in this volume.

Beethoven was neither atheist, deist, nor pantheist. Biographical evidence including the circumstances of the C major Mass, op. 86, and the *Missa solemnis*, op. 123, shows him to have embraced a true Roman Catholic faith. *(David Bloom)*

1895
as

WEISSENBÄCK, Andreas. **J.G. Albrechtsberger als Kirchenkomponist** [J.G. Albrechtsberger as composer of church music], *Festschrift den Mitgliedern des Musikhistorischen Kongresses überreicht von der Leitenden Kommission der Denkmäler der Tonkunst in Österreich* (Wien: Universal, 1927) 143–59. In German. See no. 147 in this volume.

Offers a biography of Albrechtsberger (1736-1809) and an analytic survey of his religious compositions. Albrechtsberger's treatment of instruments and of liturgical texts is also considered. During his lifetime, Albrechtsberger moved from an elaborately polyphonic, Baroque style to a prevailingly homophonic style; he seems to have been more at home in the former. *(Carl Skoggard)*

1896
as

WERNER, Eric. **Instrumental music outside the pale of Classicism and Romanticism,** *Instrumental music* (Cambridge, MA: Harvard University Press, 1959) 57–69. See no. 368 in this volume.

Between the Viennese school and Schubert and the Berlin-Leipzig-Paris group of early Romantics are the composers who can be considered neither Classic nor Romantic, such as François-Joseph Gossec, Giovanni Battista Viotti, and Anton Rejcha, active in Paris or London between 1790 and 1830. They used conventional forms, polyphonic technique, and cyclical ideas in their music, but were unable to form a definitive tradition of their own; only those with a direct connection to Classicism—Cherubini, Clementi, and the young Mendelssohn—attained a high artistic standard. *(Daven Jenkins)*

1897
as

WINTERNITZ, Emanuel. **Mozarts Raumgefühl** [Mozart's feeling for space], *Bericht über den internationalen musikwissenschaftlichen Kongreß Wien Mozartjahr 1956* (Graz; Köln: Böhlau, 1958) 736–42. *Illus., facs.* In German. See no. 365 in this volume.

A speculative examination of Mozart's handwriting style, and the organization of his score MS pages, suggests a particularly Mozartean sense of space. The insight is connected to Mozart's love of games, especially billiards, and word play. *(David Bloom)*

1898
as

WIRTH, Helmut. **Mozart et Haydn** [Mozart and Haydn], *Les influences étrangères dans l'œuvre de W.A. Mozart* (Paris: Centre National de la Recherche Scientifique [CNRS], 1958) 49–57. In French. See no. 358 in this volume.

Mozart and Haydn musically affected one another throughout their lives. Haydn's influence on Mozart is primarily evident in the latter's symphonies and string quartets; Haydn was influenced by the younger composer in the realms of opera, concerto, and piano music. *(Vivian Conejero)*

1899
as

WOLF, Johannes. **Beethoven Kirchenmusiker?** [Beethoven: Church musician?], *Beethoven-Zentenarfeier: Internationaler musikhistorischer Kongress* (Wien: Universal, 1927) 123–27. *Music.* In German. See no. 142 in this volume.

Beethoven's Masses are not suitable for liturgical use in the Roman Catholic service, but they and much more of his music may certainly be performed to good effect in both Catholic and Protestant churches. His own attitude toward his completed and projected settings of liturgical texts is examined on the basis of sketchbooks and correspondence. *(David Bloom)*

1900
as

WORBS, Hans Christoph. **Komponist, Publikum und Auftraggeber: Eine Untersuchung an Mozarts Klavierkonzerten** [Composer, audience, and patron: An investigation of Mozart's piano concertos], *Bericht über den internationalen musikwissenschaftlichen Kongreß Wien Mozartjahr 1956* (Graz; Köln: Böhlau, 1958) 754–57. In German. See no. 365 in this volume.

Examples of Mozart's accommodation to large concert audiences, and to performers who commissioned concertos from him, are drawn from a comparison of four piano concertos he wrote in 1784, two for Barbara Ployer (K.449 and K.453), and two for himself (K.450 and K.451). *(David Bloom)*

1901
as

WÖRNER, Karl Heinrich. **Mozarts Fugenfragmente** [Mozart's fugal fragments], *Bericht über den internationalen musikwissenschaftlichen Kongreß Wien Mozartjahr 1956* (Graz; Köln: Böhlau, 1958) 743–48. *Music.* In German. See no. 365 in this volume.

Consideration of an inventory of Mozart's MS fugue fragments and their thematic relations with music of J.S. Bach and Händel suggests that they date from 1782, when Mozart was engaged with the counterpoint of Bach and Händel in Vienna. *(David Bloom)*

1902
as

YÖNETKEN, Halil Bedi. **Mozart und die türkische Musik** [Mozart and Turkish music], *Internationale Konferenz über das Leben und Werk W.A. Mozarts* (Praha: Svaz Československých Skladatelů, 1956) 118–20. In German. See no. 360 in this volume.

Turkish lovers of Western music have a special fondness for Mozart, partly because of the composer's own well-attested interest in Turkish music, as expressed in the A-major violin concerto K. 219, the A-major piano sonata K. 33, and the operas *Zaide* and *Die Entführung aus dem Serail*. *(David Bloom)*

1903
as

YOUNG, Percy M. **Johann Christian Bach and his English environment,** *Bericht über den internationalen musikwissenschaftlichen Kongreß* (Kassel: Bärenreiter, 1963) 32–34. See no. 452 in this volume.

Discusses Bach's life in London from 1761 to his death in 1782; his opere serie, ballad operas, and arrangments of Scottish folk songs; and his contributions to the development of the symphony as a form and to the public orchestral concert as an institution. *(Laurie Appleby)*

1904
as

ZSCHINSKY-TROXLER, Elsa Margherita von. **Mozarts Violinkonzerte im spieltechnischen Vergleich mit zeitgenössischen italienischen Violinkomponisten** [A comparison of performance technique in Mozart's violin concertos and the violin music of his Italian contemporaries], *Bericht über den internationalen musikwissenschaftlichen Kongreß Wien Mozartjahr 1956* (Graz; Köln: Böhlau, 1958) 765–72. *Music, charts, diagr.* In German. See no. 365 in this volume.

Mozart's four complete concertos of 1775, considered together with biographical evidence, show signs of the possible influence of Pietro Nardini, Giovanni Battista Viotti, Luigi Boccherini, and others. *(David Bloom)*

27 Romantic and post-Romantic (ca. 1825 – 1910)

1905
as

ABERT, Anna Amalie. **Liszt, Wagner, und die Beziehungen zwischen Musik und Literatur im 19. Jahrhundert** [Liszt, Wagner, and the rela-

tionship between music and literature in the 19th century], *Report of the Eighth Congress of the International Musicological Society. I: Papers* (Kassel: Bärenreiter, 1961) 314–23. In German. See no. 439 in this volume.

Discusses the close relationship of literature and music in Germany in the period of composer-writers from Hoffmann and Weber through Schumann, Otto Nicolai, Gustav Albert Lortzing, Otto Ludwig, and Annette von Droste-Hülshoff to Wagner and Liszt, with particular reference to the concepts of "Tondichtung", "Wort-Ton-Dichtung", and opera.

1906
as

ABRAHAM, Gerald. **Chopin and the orchestra,** *The book of the first international musicological congress devoted to the works of Frederick Chopin* (Warszawa: Państwowe Wydawnictwo Naukowe, 1963) 85–87. *Charts, diagr.* See no. 425 in this volume.

General opinion holds that Chopin was not exceptional as an orchestrator. A reevaluation of this opinion states that Chopin's orchestration was typical of the era, at the very least adequate to the task he had in mind, and was actually quite masterful in isolated sections. *(Susan Poliniak)*

1907
as

AZEVEDO, Luiz Heitor Corrêa de. **A Imperial Academia de Música e Ópera Nacional e o canto em vernáculo** [The Imperial Academia de Música e Ópera Nacional and vernacular singing], *Anais do Primeiro Congresso da Língua Nacional Cantada* (São Paulo: Departamento Municipal de Cultura, 1938) 589–636. In Portuguese. See no. 253 in this volume.

Portuguese-language productions of opera at the Imperial Academia de Música e Ópera Nacional in Rio de Janeiro were common in 1857-63. The revival of this practice is proposed.

1908
as

BADURA-SKODA, Eva. **Liszt, Wagner, and the relations between music and literature in the 19th century,** *Report of the Eighth Congress of the International Musicological Society. II: Reports* (Kassel: Bärenreiter, 1962) 140–45. In German and French. See no. 440 in this volume.

A report on a discussion by Gerald ABRAHAM, Dénes BARTHA, Jacques BARZUN, Otto Erich DEUTSCH, Edward O.D. DOWNES, Hans ENGEL, Léon GUICHARD, Jurij Vsevolodovič KELDYŠ, Karel Philippus BERNET KEMPERS, Joseph KERMAN, Victor LANGE, Wilhelm PFANNKUCH, and Hans F. REDLICH of papers by Anna Amalie Abert and by Guichard abstracted as nos. 1905 and 5319, respectively, in this volume.

1909
as

BARBLAN, Guglielmo. **Delle influenze del Romanticismo nella musica sacra** [On the influences of Romanticism in sacred music], *Atti del [I] Congresso internazionale di musica sacra* (Tournai: Desclée, 1952) 388–91. In Italian. See no. 303 in this volume.

1910
as

BASSO, Alberto. **Chopin et l'esprit de la musique instrumentale baroque** [Chopin and the spirit of Baroque instrumental music], *The book of the first international musicological congress devoted to the works of Frederick Chopin* (Warszawa: Państwowe Wydawnictwo Naukowe, 1963) 271–74. In French. See no. 425 in this volume.

Connecting Chopin to an earlier era helps to control the sentimentalism of regarding him as a unique phenomenon. His affinities with the Baroque—specifically, with Domenico Scarlatti—include an emphasis on keyboard works, sudden changes of harmony and rhythm, dynamic contrasts, and the invention of new expressive devices. *(Susan Poliniak)*

1911
as

BECHERINI, Bianca. **Il dissolvimento della tonalità nelle opere di Federico Chopin** [The dissolution of tonality in the works of Frédéric Chopin], *The book of the first international musicological congress devoted to the works of Frederick Chopin* (Warszawa: Państwowe Wydawnictwo Naukowe, 1963) 88–94. *Music.* In Italian. See no. 425 in this volume.

Describes the instances of chromaticism and atonality in some works of Chopin.

→ BEHREND, William. **Musikalische Länderkunde Dänemarks** [Denmark's musical geography]. See no. 2282 in this volume.

1912 BELARDINELLI, Alessandro. **Documenti**
as **Spontiniani inediti** [The unpublished documents of Spontini], *Atti del primo Congresso internazionale di studi spontiniani* (Fabriano: Arti Grafiche Gentile, 1954) 27–32. In Italian. See no. 304 in this volume.

Discusses the composer's correspondence between 1811 and 1882.

1913 BĚLZA, Igor' Fëdorovič. **Nacional'nye istoki**
as **tvorčestva Šopena** [National origins of Chopin's music], *The book of the first international musicological congress devoted to the works of Frederick Chopin* (Warszawa: Państwowe Wydawnictwo Naukowe, 1963) 23–29. In Russian. See no. 425 in this volume.

1914 BENGTSSON, Ingmar. **Romantisch-nationale**
as **Strömungen in deutscher und skandinavischer Musik** [Romantic-nationalist trends in German and Scandinavian music], *Norddeutsche und nordeuropäische Musik* (Kassel; New York: Bärenreiter, 1965) 42–47. In German. See no. 467 in this volume.

The problem of national Romanticism should be studied in terms of a heterogeneous list of sometimes overlapping attitudinal features: the use of exoticism and of local color; the idealization of the archaic, of the natural, and of the simple; the idea of emancipation from conventions; and conscious nationalism. Style analysis needs to provide finer differentiations, through a methodology that sees stylistic features in terms of their functions. It may be concluded provisionally that the reliance on German models of national style by Scandinavian composers, and their stylistic self-sufficiency, were both greater than has been previously understood. *(David Bloom)*

1915 BERTHA, Sándor de. **Les *Rhapsodies***
as ***hongroises* de Franz Liszt** [Franz Liszt's *Magyar rhapsodiák*], *Report of the Fourth Congress of the International Musical Society* (London: Novello, 1912) 210–24. In French. See no. 71 in this volume.

Examines the number and grouping of the *Magyar rhapsodiák*, their influence on other composers, Wagner's opinion of Hungarian music, and Liszt's views on the history of Hungarian music. The individual rhapsodies are discussed. *(Jenna Orkin)*

1916 BIEGAŃSKI, Krzystof. **Évolution de l'attitude**
as **de Chopin à l'égard du folklore (suivant ses mazurkas)** [The evolution of Chopin's attitude toward folklore in regard to his mazurkas], *The book of the first international musicological congress devoted to the works of Frederick Chopin* (Warszawa: Państwowe Wydawnictwo Naukowe, 1963) 95–99. In French. See no. 425 in this volume.

Some contend that there was no evolution in Chopin's style, that it was fully mature from the outset. However, the mazurkas show an evolution in his relation to traditional music in three stages: the incorporation of traditional elements within the existing idiom of his work, the use of traditional elements changing the idiom melodically and harmonically, and the transformation of traditional material for aesthetic expression. *(Susan Poliniak)*

1917 BIELAWSKI, Ludwik. **Problem krakowiaka w**
as **twórczości Chopina** [The problem of the krakowiak in Chopin's work], *The book of the first international musicological congress devoted to the works of Frederick Chopin* (Warszawa: Państwowe Wydawnictwo Naukowe, 1963) 100–03. *Music.* In Polish. See no. 425 in this volume.

1918 BLIWERT, Mirosław. **Mieczysław Karłowicz a**
as **twórczość Ryszarda Wagnera** [Mieczysław Karłowicz and the works of Richard Wagner], *Ryszard Wagner a polska kultura muzyczna/Richard Wagner und die polnische Musikkultur* (Katowice: Panstwowa Wyzsza Szkola Muzyczna, 1964) 83–94. In Polish; summary in German. See no. 466 in this volume.

1919 BLUME, Friedrich. **Die Musik von 1830 bis**
as **1914: Strukturprobleme einer Epoche** [Music from 1830 to 1914: Structural problems of an era], *Bericht über den internationalen musikwissenschaftlichen Kongreß* (Kassel: Bärenreiter, 1963) 40–50. In German. See no. 452 in this volume.

Discusses problems in the concepts of musical Romanticism, or 19th-c. music, as unitary phenomena. Perhaps it is only in the discussion of national Romanticism, and the nationalist use of folk elements, that the notion of Romanticism is coherent. The contradictions that characterize Romantic music arose in the Classic period, and did not go away after World War I. It may be that Romanticism and Classicism should be regarded as only two stages, or two sides, of a single era. *(Daniel Anderson)*

1920 BOËLLMANN, Marie-Louise. **La pénétration**
as **en France de la musique d'orgue de J.S. Bach au XIXe siècle** [The dissemination of J.S. Bach's organ music in 19th-century France], *Congrés de la Societat Internacional de Musicologia* (Barcelona: Casa de Caritat, 1936). In French. See no. 224 in this volume.

The conference report provides only a citation. Neither the text nor a summary of the paper was published here.

1921 BONNEROT, Jean. **Saint-Saëns en Scan-**
as **dinavie en 1897** [Saint-Saëns in Scandinavia in 1897], *VIe Congrès international des sciences historiques* (Roma: Loescher, 1928) 397–98. In French. See no. 151 in this volume.

1922 BRAŠOVANOVA-STANČEVA, Lada. **Die**
as **Musik von 1830 bis 1914 in Bulgarien** [Music in Bulgaria from 1830 to 1914], *Bericht über den internationalen musikwissenschaftlichen Kongreß* (Kassel: Bärenreiter, 1963) 85–91. *Transcr.* In German. See no. 452 in this volume.

Discusses the preservation of traditional music in the context of the National Renaissance, the development of professional musicians, orchestras, and opera companies, and the composition of the first Bulgarian operas and symphonies. *(David Bloom)*

1923 BRUMARE (abbé). **Extrait d'une dissertation**
as **sur les moyens de restituer le plain-chant, se divisant en deux parties, l'une qui regarde la théorie et l'autre la pratique** [Extract of a dissertation on the means of restoring plainchant, divided into two parts: Theory and practice], *Congrès pour la restauration du plain-chant et de la musique d'église* (Paris: De Mourgues, 1862) 120–23. In French. See no. 3 in this volume.

1924
as

BRUN, F. **Charles Bordes et son école** [Charles Bordes and his following], *Compte rendu du Congrès général de musique sacrée: Aperçu général des préliminaires et du congrès, discours et conférences* (Strasbourg: Alsacien, 1922) 85–94. In French. See no. 96 in this volume.

Bordes (1863-1909) made a crucial contribution to French liturgical music by founding the Schola Cantorum in Paris in 1894, publishing editions of early music, and applying liturgical themes to cantique and motet in his own works. His influence on Vincent d'Indy (1851-1931) is perceptible in certain works. Following Bordes's lead, composition of motets using a 16th-c. classical palette should be encouraged. *(Murat Eyüboğlu)*

1925
as

BUCHNER, Alexandr. **Liszt in Prag** [Liszt in Prague], *Studia musicologica Academiae Scientiarum Hungaricae* V (1963) 27–36. In German. See no. 427 in this volume.

Between 1840 and 1871 Liszt made seven visits to Prague. Only the first two (1840 and 1846) were concert tours. His Prague friends included August Wilhelm Ambros, Jan Bedřich Kittl, and Smetana. A piano piece written by Liszt in Prague, the *Hussitenlied* of 1840, had an important influence on the development of the Czech national style; the melody, thought to have been a 15th-c. Hussite hymn, is actually that of a drinking song composed by Josef Theodor Krov (*Těšme se blahou nadějí*) ca. 1820. *(Gregory L. Fulkerson)*

1926
as

BUCK, Maurits De. **De strijd van Benoit voor zijn kunstautonomie aan de Vlaamsche Muziekschool en aan het Koninklijk Vlaamsch Conservatorium te Antwerpen** [Benoît's battle for artistic autonomy at the Vlaamse Muziekschool and at the Koninklijk Vlaams Muziek Conservatorium in Antwerp], *Verhandelingen van het Muziekcongres* (Antwerpen: Stad Antwerpen, 1935) 93–104. In Dutch. See no. 210 in this volume.

1927
as

BÜCKEN, Ernst. **Schubert und die Klassik** [Schubert and Classicism], *Bericht über den internationalen Kongress für Schubertforschung* (Augsburg: Benno Filser, 1929) 49–53. *Music.* In German. See no. 154 in this volume.

Stylistic features of his lieder indicate that Schubert represents the end of the Classic style.

1928
as

CAFFARELLI, Filippo. **Documentazioni spontiniane inedite: l'Epistolario** [Unpublished documents of Spontini: The correspondence], *Atti del primo Congresso internazionale di studi spontiniani* (Fabriano: Arti Grafiche Gentile, 1954) 48–49. In Italian. See no. 304 in this volume.

Describes how the collection of letters was obtained and notes Spontini's youthful comments.

1929
as

CAFFARELLI, Filippo. **Il rapporto di Gaspare Spontini intorno alla riforma della musica sacra** [Spontini's relation to the reform of sacred music], *Atti del primo Congresso internazionale di studi spontiniani* (Fabriano: Arti Grafiche Gentile, 1954) 59–69. In Italian. See no. 304 in this volume.

Documents kept at the library of the Conservatorio di Musica S. Cecilia in Rome are discussed.

1930
as

CAFFARELLI, Filippo. **Spontini grande italiano e grande europeo** [Spontini: A great Italian and a great European], *Atti del primo Congresso internazionale di studi spontiniani* (Fabriano: Arti Grafiche Gentile, 1954) 7–12. In Italian. See no. 304 in this volume.

Describes national and international aspects of Spontini's works.

1931
as

CARRAUD, Gaston. **La musique symphonique** [Symphonic music], *Rapport sur la musique contemporaine française* (Roma: Armani & Stein, 1913) 77–101. In French. See no. 76 in this volume.

Surveys French orchestral music in the late 19th and early 20th c. Debussy and Vincent d'Indy are seen to represent two opposing aesthetic currents.

1932
as

CHAILLEY, Jacques. **L'importance de Chopin dans l'évolution du langage harmonique** [The importance of Chopin in the evolution of harmonic language], *The book of the first international musicological congress devoted to the works of Frederick Chopin* (Warszawa: Państwowe Wydawnictwo Naukowe, 1963) 30–43. *Music.* In French. See no. 425 in this volume.

Chopin straddled 18th- and 19th-c. styles, and seemed to know that consonance would one day overstep the bounds of tonality. Elements within his music that pushed the boundaries of the harmonic idiom of the time and aided its evolution include his forward-thinking use of the fourth, the seventh, and the pentatonic scale. *(Susan Poliniak)*

1933
as

CHAILLEY, Jacques. **Une page d'album de Chopin à Émile Gaillard** [An album page from Chopin to Émile Gaillard], *The book of the first international musicological congress devoted to the works of Frederick Chopin* (Warszawa: Państwowe Wydawnictwo Naukowe, 1963) 111–13. In French. See no. 425 in this volume.

Three leaves from the album of Chopin's friend and pupil Émile Gaillard contain the autograph of a previously unknown piece by Chopin. The piece is a waltz in Eb, 48 mm. long, headed with the indication "sostenuto", signed and dated at Paris, 20 July 1840. The MS was discovered by Gaillard's son Joseph and donated in 1938 to the collections of the Paris Conservatoire (F-Pc MS 16279). *(Susan Poliniak)*

1934
as

CHAINAYE, Suzanne. **Frédéric Chopin et les apocryphes** [Apocryphal writings attributed to Chopin], *The book of the first international musicological congress devoted to the works of Frederick Chopin* (Warszawa: Państwowe Wydawnictwo Naukowe, 1963) 649–53. In French. See no. 425 in this volume.

A recent addition to the catalogue of writings wrongly attributed to Chopin are the undated letters supposedly written by him to Countess Delfina Potocka and discovered among her papers by Paulina Czernicka in 1945, and used by Kazimierz Wierzyński in *Życie Chopina* (New York 1953; originally published in English as *The life and death of Chopin*, New York 1949). Several proofs of their spuriousness are adduced. *(Susan Poliniak)*

1935
as

CHERBULIEZ, Antoine-Élisée. **Interdependence of folk music and art forms in European Romantic music during the nineteenth century**, *Journal of the International Folk Music Council* III (1951) 107. See no. 296 in this volume.

The conference report provides only a citation. Neither the text nor a summary of the paper was published here.

1936
as

CLAUSS, Emile. **L'Union Sainte-Cécile de Strasbourg** [The Union Sainte-Cécile of Strasbourg], *Compte rendu du Congrès général de musique sacrée: Aperçu général des préliminaires et du congrès, discours et conférences* (Strasbourg: Alsacien, 1922) 1–12. In French. See no. 96 in this volume.

An introduction to the society's history and activities.

1937
as

COEUROY, André. **Gérard de Nerval et la diffusion du sentiment musical en France** [Gérard de Nerval and the diffusion of musical sentiment in France], *Actes du Congrès d'histoire de l'art: Compte*

rendu analytique (Paris: Presses Universitaires de France, 1922) 198. In French. See no. 95 in this volume.
Summary of a paper.

1938
as

COMBARIEU, Jules. **L'état doit-il jouer dans les théâtres et concerts subventionnés un rôle de protecteur à l'égard des œuvres des maîtres tombés dans le domaine public?** [In subsidized theaters and concerts, should the state play the role of protector with regard to works that have come into the public domain?], *Congrès international de musique: Ire session—Exposition Universelle de 1900: Compte rendu, rapports, communications* (Paris: conference, 1901) 21–26. In French. See no. 29 in this volume.
The state should take an interest in the authentic representation of works that are presently given in altered versions. The situation of arts subsidies in several European countries, especially France, is discussed.

1939
as

CORNETTE, Arthur Jacob Hendrik. **Liszt: Le romantique** [Liszt: The romantic], *Compte rendu du Ve Congrès international des sciences historiques* (Bruxelles: Weissenbruch, 1923) 368–69. In French. See no. 100 in this volume.
A discussion of the piano cycles *Années de pèlerinage.*

1940
as

CUKKERMAN, Viktor Abramovič. **De l'emploi des genres et des formes dans l'œuvre de Chopin** [The use of genres and forms in the works of Chopin], *The book of the first international musicological congress devoted to the works of Frederick Chopin* (Warszawa: Państwowe Wydawnictwo Naukowe, 1963) 114–21. *Music.* In French. See no. 425 in this volume.
The strength of Chopin's music emanates in part from his expert employment of accepted forms and genres such as march, mazurka, nocturne, recitative, and barcarole which give his themes unique personal qualities and universality as well. A certain emotional intensity within his works is due in part to structural contrasts. His recapitulations alter the themes in ways that were original during his time, thus enhancing their expressivity. *(Susan Poliniak)*

1941
as

CVETKO, Dragotin. **Chopin chez les Slovènes au XIXe siècle** [Chopin in Slovenia in the 19th century], *The book of the first international musicological congress devoted to the works of Frederick Chopin* (Warszawa: Państwowe Wydawnictwo Naukowe, 1963) 281–87. In French. See no. 425 in this volume.
Slovenian music tastes in the first half of the 19th c. leaned towards Italian and German music; works of French and Slavic composers in concert programs were rare. The first performance of Chopin's works in Ljubljana may have been at a concert in December 1844. After the revolution of March 1848 his music was often performed at the *bésede* soirées of the Slovensko Društvo in Ljubljana; it was seen as "universal," like Mozart's. His influence on Slovenian composers in the early period is attested for emigrant musicians such as Jurij Mihevec in Paris. *(Susan Poliniak)*

1942
as

CVETKO, Dragotin. **Die Situation und die Probleme der slowenischen, kroatischen, und serbischen Musik des 19. Jahrhunderts: Die Musik von 1830 bis 1914 in Jugoslawien** [The situation and problems of Slovene, Croatian, and Serbian music in the 19th century: Music in Yugoslavia from 1830 to 1914], *Bericht über den internationalen musikwissenschaftlichen Kongreß* (Kassel: Bärenreiter, 1963) 80–85. In German. See no. 452 in this volume.
In the first half of the 19th c., under Turkish control, Serbians, Macedonians, Croatians, and Slovenes were limited to church music and traditional music, though Croatia and Slovenia were more susceptible to Austrian influence because of their location. Nationalist movements in music coincided with the struggle for national liberation. By the beginning of World War I developments had begun to parallel those in Western Europe. *(Daniel Anderson)*

1943
as

DELLA CORTE, Andrea. **Il culto di Mozart e la cultura nell'Ottocento italiano** [The cult of Mozart and 19th-century Italian culture], *Bericht über den internationalen musikwissenschaftlichen Kongreß Wien Mozartjahr 1956* (Graz; Köln: Böhlau, 1958) 128–31. In Italian. See no. 365 in this volume.
A miscellany of quotations, in supplement to the information provided in Werner Bollert's *Mozartpflege in Italien (1791-1935)*, in his *Aufsätze zur Musikgeschichte* (Bottrop, 1938). *(David Bloom)*

1944
as

DILLE, Denijs. **Peter Benoit en de nieuwe muziek** [Peter Benoît and the new music], *Verhandelingen van het Muziekcongres* (Antwerpen: Stad Antwerpen, 1935) 63–70. In Dutch. See no. 210 in this volume.
Benoît's works are discussed in relation to those of Debussy, Schoenberg, Stravinsky, Weill, and Hindemith. Benoît's activities in promoting new works through the Koninklijk Vlaams Muziek Conservatorium in Antwerp are outlined.

1945
as

DING, Shande. **What makes the Chinese people accept and appreciate Chopin's music,** *The book of the first international musicological congress devoted to the works of Frederick Chopin* (Warszawa: Państwowe Wydawnictwo Naukowe, 1963) 399–403. *Facs., music.* See no. 425 in this volume.
Chopin's music is popular in China due not only to its artistry, but also to its patriotic bent. His works are imbued with a great deal of national color and a deep love for the motherland. Chopin's use of flexible rhythms, sweeping melodic lines, and repetition also bear similarities to the use of the same devices in Chinese traditional music. *(Susan Poliniak)*

1946
as

DJURIĆ-KLAJN, Stana. **Correspondance inédite de Johannes Brahms** [Unpublished correspondence of Johannes Brahms], *Bericht über den siebenten internationalen musikwissenschaftlichen Kongress* (Kassel: Bärenreiter, 1959) 88–91. In French. See no. 390 in this volume.
Three pieces of correspondence from Brahms to the Serbian violinist Dragomir Krančević (1847-1929) and a card with several autograph measures of music "a la Zingarese" with a dedication to Krančević (then a young pupil of Joseph Hellmesberger) are discussed. A biography of Krančević is provided. *(Carl Skoggard)*

1947
as

DOBROWOLSKI, Janusz. **Organizacja pola dźwiękowego u Chopina** [Chopin's organization of sound], *The book of the first international musicological congress devoted to the works of Frederick Chopin* (Warszawa: Państwowe Wydawnictwo Naukowe, 1963) 127–31. *Facs.* In Polish. See no. 425 in this volume.

1948
as

ECKART-BÄCKER, Ursula. **Die Wiederbelebung von Hector Berlioz: Ein Beitrag zur Musikanschauung in Frankreich um 1900** [The resurrection of Hector Berlioz: A contribution to the musical perspective in France ca. 1900], *Beiträge zur Geschichte der Musikansschauung im 19. Jahrhundert* (Regensburg: Bosse, 1965) 225–46. In German. See no. 483 in this volume.
Berlioz's music was regarded as old-fashioned, Gluckian, by French Wagner enthusiasts such as Auguste de Gasperini (1825-68), but it was reconsidered following the composer's death in 1869 and the French debacle in the war with Prussia. By the time of the celebration of Berlioz's centenary in 1903, politics and patriotism, complete performances of the great vocal and dramatic works, and the sympathies of the French avant-garde led to his being acclaimed as the savior of French music. *(David Bloom)*

1949
as

EISENRING, Carl Jakob. **Karl Greith: Der grösste schweizerische Kirchenmusiker** [Karl Greith: The greatest Swiss church musician], *Akten des fünften internationalen Kongresses katholischer Gelehrten/Compte rendu du Ve Congrès scientifique international des catholiques* (München: Herder, 1901) 338–39. In German. See no. 26 in this volume.

Provides a brief biographical sketch for Carl Greith (1828-87).

1950
as

EKIER, Jan. **Le problème d'authenticité de six œuvres de Chopin** [The authenticity problem of six works of Chopin], *The book of the first international musicological congress devoted to the works of Frederick Chopin* (Warszawa: Państwowe Wydawnictwo Naukowe, 1963) 463–73. *Music.* In French. See no. 425 in this volume.

The authorship of six works attributed to Chopin is called into question: three mazurkas in G, D, and C, a contredanse in G♭, a waltz in E♭, and variations for flute and piano on *Non più mesta* from Rossini's *La Cenerentola*. Only the mazurka in G (from the pair catalogued by Brown as no. 16) seems likely to be authentic. *(Susan Poliniak)*

1951
as

ELLER, Rudolf. **Bruckner und Bach** [Bruckner and Bach], *Bericht über die Wissenschaftliche Bachtagung* (Leipzig: Peters, 1951) 355–66. In German. See no. 298 in this volume.

The importance of Bach in Bruckner's training and compositional technique cannot be denied; but it should be remembered that it was specifically the 19th-c. idea of Bach that influenced Bruckner. Fugal technique in Bruckner is never, as with Bach, absolute; in the finale of the symphony no. 5, for example, it is strictly subordinate to sonata structure. *(David Bloom)*

1952
as

ENGEL, Hans. **L'opera *Agnese di Hohenstaufen* di Spontini** [Spontini's opera *Agnes von Hohenstaufen*], *Atti del primo Congresso internazionale di studi spontiniani* (Fabriano: Arti Grafiche Gentile, 1954) 105–24. In Italian. See no. 304 in this volume.

The opera exemplifies German Romanticism, while demonstrating the expressive problems caused by the language.

1953
as

FALCKE, Wilm. **Zu Chopins Aufenthalt auf Mallorca und zur Chopin-Überlieferung in Palma und Valldemosa** [Chopin's stay in Mallorca and the Chopin tradition in Palma and Valldemosa], *The book of the first international musicological congress devoted to the works of Frederick Chopin* (Warszawa: Państwowe Wydawnictwo Naukowe, 1963) 288–92. In German. See no. 425 in this volume.

Discusses recent research findings relevant to Chopin's biography, with particular attention to Luis Ripoll's *Chopin, su invierno en Mallorca, 1838-1839* (Palma de Mallorca 1955) and various social, cultural, and economic aspects of Chopin tradition on Mallorca since the opening of the Museo de Frédéric Chopin in Valldemosa in 1929. *(David Bloom)*

1954
as

FANO, Fabio. **Vertu classique de Chopin** [Chopin's Classic bent], *The book of the first international musicological congress devoted to the works of Frederick Chopin* (Warszawa: Państwowe Wydawnictwo Naukowe, 1963) 654–58. In French. See no. 425 in this volume.

Chopin is the most Classic of the Romantic composers, in the purity of his form and in his unique ability to take conceptions of a complex, dramatic character akin to the epic concepts of Beethoven and to condense them into the most concise form. *(Susan Poliniak)*

1955
as

FÉDOROV, Vladimir. **Symposium: Les origines de l'opéra national en Europe de l'Est au 19e siècle** [Symposium: The beginnings of national

opera in Eastern Europe in the 19th century], *Bericht über den neunten internationalen Kongreß* (Kassel: Bärenreiter, 1964-1966) II, 98–109. *Music, charts, diagr.* In French. See no. 491 in this volume.

Discussion of the conference paper by Bence SZABOLSCI abstracted as no. 2109 in this volume, with extended remarks on the subject of the rescue opera. Participants included Szabolsci, Gerald ABRAHAM, Dragotin CVETKO, György KROÓ, Rey M. LONGYEAR, Ivan MARTYNOV, Antonín SYCHRA, and Erik TAWASTSTJERNA. Lists of Central and Eastern European opera houses and the languages of their repertoires in the 18th and 19th c. are appended.

⟶   FEICHT, Hieronim. **Die Kenntnis Mozarts in Polen** [Knowledge of Mozart in Poland]. See no. 1752 in this volume.

1956
as

FELIX, Werner. **Liszts Schaffen um 1848: Versuch zur Deutung seiner Programmatik** [Liszt's composition around 1848: Toward an interpretation of his program music], *Studia musicologica Academiae Scientiarum Hungaricae* V (1963) 59–67. *Music.* In German. See no. 427 in this volume.

Liszt's program works of 1848-54 are a response to the Hungarian national uprising of 1848; folk, tragic, and triumphant elements in the music correspond to the history of the revolution and its subsequent collapse. *(William Renwick)*

1957
as

FLEURY, Louis. **De la situation économique des musiciens d'orchestre en France** [On the economic situation of French orchestra musicians], *Haydn-Zentenarfeier* (Leipzig: Breitkopf & Härtel; Wien: Artaria, 1909) 515–26. *Charts, diagr.* In French. See no. 65 in this volume.

Discusses job security, duration of contracts, unemployment, rates of pay, and work regulations.

1958
as

FRĄCZKIEWICZ, Aleksander. **Koncerty fortepianowe Chopina jako typ koncertu romantycznego** [Chopin's piano concertos as a model of the Romantic concerto], *The book of the first international musicological congress devoted to the works of Frederick Chopin* (Warszawa: Państwowe Wydawnictwo Naukowe, 1963) 293–96. In Polish. See no. 425 in this volume.

1959
as

FRIEDLAENDER, Max. **Ansprache zur Einführung** [Inaugural address], *Bericht über den internationalen Kongress für Schubertforschung* (Augsburg: Benno Filser, 1929) 1–26. In German. See no. 154 in this volume.

A general overview and summary of the state of Schubert research.

1960
as

FRIEDLAENDER, Max. **Zur Handschriftenkunde Schuberts** [Schubert autography], *Bericht über den internationalen Kongress für Schubertforschung* (Augsburg: Benno Filser, 1929) 169–72. In German. See no. 154 in this volume.

Discusses MSS including those of *Des Mädchens Klage, Fragment aus dem Aeschylus,* and *Frühlingslied.*

1961
as

GAGNEBIN, Henri. **Divers courants qui se sont manifestes dans la musique suisse romande pendant les cinquante dernières années.** [Various currents in the music of French-speaking Switzerland during the last 50 years], *Bericht über den musikwissenschaftlichen Kongreß in Basel* (Leipzig: Breitkopf & Härtel, 1925) 147–50. In French. See no. 102 in this volume.

The influence of French music during the Reformation, Italian and French music during the 18th c., and German music during the 19th c. created a background for more recent activity. Various 19th-c. Swiss figures are listed.

1962
as

GAILLARD, Paul-André. **Jugements portés sur Chopin par Mickiewicz d'après le journal de Caroline Olivier** [Mickiewicz's judgments of Chopin as reported in the journal of Caroline Olivier], *The book of the first international musicological congress devoted to the works of Frederick Chopin* (Warszawa: Państwowe Wydawnictwo Naukowe, 1963) 659–61. In French. See no. 425 in this volume.

The journal and private papers of the Swiss poet Caroline Olivier, a friend of Adam Mickiewicz, were deposited by her grandson Jean Olivier in the Bibliothèque Cantonale et Universitaire, Lausanne, on the condition that they not be made public until 1980, after the centenary of her death. Meanwhile, excerpts from the journal have been used to demonstrate that Mickiewicz had little respect for Chopin. Other sources, however, including letters by Margaret Fuller and by the poet's brother-in-law Teofil Lenartowicz, suggest a much less negative view. Only when Olivier's journal becomes fully accessible will it be possible to clarify the situation. *(Susan Poliniak)*

1963
as

GAILLARD, Paul-André. **Le lyrisme pianistique de Chopin et ses antécédents directs** [The pianistic lyricism of Chopin and its direct antecedents], *The book of the first international musicological congress devoted to the works of Frederick Chopin* (Warszawa: Państwowe Wydawnictwo Naukowe, 1963) 297–99. In French. See no. 425 in this volume.

Chopin's works were greatly influenced by John Field. Additionally, there are similarities between Chopin's works and those of Schubert and Václav Tomášek. *(Susan Poliniak)*

1964
as

GARDAVSKÝ, Čeněk. **Liszt und seine tschechischen Lehrer** [Liszt and his Czech teacher], *Studia musicologica Academiae Scientiarum Hungaricae* V (1963) 70–76. In German. See no. 427 in this volume.

Teachers of Czech origin played a central role in Liszt's development as a musician. His mastery of piano technique was established in lessons with Carl Czerny in Vienna in 1822-23; much of his compositional technique, particularly in the areas of harmony and thematic development, can be traced to his composition studies with Anton Rejcha in Paris, from 1826 to ca. 1830. *(William Renwick)*

1965
as

GÁRDONYI, Zoltán. **Die Musik von 1830 bis 1914 in Ungarn** [Music in Hungary from 1830 to 1914], *Bericht über den internationalen musikwissenschaftlichen Kongreß* (Kassel: Bärenreiter, 1963) 91–98. In German. See no. 452 in this volume.

An overview, based on the writings of Bence Szabolcsi.

1966
as

GÁRDONYI, Zoltán. **Nationale Thematik in der Musik Franz Liszts bis zum Jahre 1848** [Nationalism in Franz Liszt's music to 1848], *Studia musicologica Academiae Scientiarum Hungaricae* V (1963) 77–88. In German. See no. 427 in this volume.

Liszt's development as a composer is connected with his European travels; French, German, Swiss, Italian, English, Hungarian, Polish, Czech, Russian, Spanish, Romanian, and Ukranian traditional music all had an impact on his work. The themes of cosmopolitanism and nationalism are traced in his career from the move to Vienna in 1822 to the Hungarian revolt of 1848. *(William Renwick)*

1967
as

GÁRDONYI, Zoltán. **Schlußwort der Liszt-Sektion** [Closing remarks of the Liszt session], *Studia musicologica Academiae Scientiarum Hungaricae* V (1963). In German. See no. 427 in this volume.

Summary remarks on the session devoted to Liszt during the International Musicological Society Conference in Budapest (1961).

1968
as

GERMAN, Franciszek. **Chopin im Lichte unbekannter Memoirenquellen gesehen** [Chopin in the light of unknown memoir sources], *The book of the first international musicological congress devoted to the works of Frederick Chopin* (Warszawa: Państwowe Wydawnictwo Naukowe, 1963) 662–68. In German. See no. 425 in this volume.

Heretofore neglected sources of information on Chopin's life include the MS memoirs of his pupil Zofia Rosengardt-Zaleska (in the Biblioteka Jagiellońska, Cracow); correspondence by Aleksander Jełowicki, a participant in the November uprising, friend of Chopin's, and later the monk who heard the composer's dying confession (Muzeum Narodowe, Cracow); the unpublished memoirs of Bogdan Jański, the founder of the Congregatio Resurrectionis (Congregatio archives in Rome); and those of a Polish friend of Chopin's and Václav Hanka's, the scholar and statesman Romuald Hube (Biblioteka Zamoyski, now incorporated into the Biblioteka Narodowa, Warsaw). *(David Bloom)*

1969
as

GHISLANZONI, Alberto. **Gaspare Spontini e la musica bandistica** [Gaspare Spontini and band music], *Atti del primo Congresso internazionale di studi spontiniani* (Fabriano: Arti Grafiche Gentile, 1954) 70–80. In Italian. See no. 304 in this volume.

Spontini's band music is equal in importance to that of his contemporaries.

1970
as

GHISLANZONI, Alberto. **I rapporti fra Spontini e Mendelssohn** [The relationship between Spontini and Mendelssohn], *Atti del primo Congresso internazionale di studi spontiniani* (Fabriano: Arti Grafiche Gentile, 1954) 95–103. In Italian. See no. 304 in this volume.

Spontini, Mendelssohn-Bartholdy, and their respective families met frequently. The composers exchanged letters, and Spontini influenced Mendelssohn-Bartholdy's music considerably.

1971
as

GLIŃSKI, Mateusz. **Les lettres de Chopin à Delphine Potocki** [Chopin's letters to Delfina Potocka], *The book of the first international musicological congress devoted to the works of Frederick Chopin* (Warszawa: Państwowe Wydawnictwo Naukowe, 1963) 669–74. In French. See no. 425 in this volume.

The most distinguished experts have accepted the authenticity of the letters brought to public attention by Paulina Czernicka in 1945 and incorporated into editions of Chopin's correspondence by Zdisław Jachimecki (*Wybór listów*, Wrocław 1945) and recent biographies. Some scholars continue to deny that Chopin wrote them, but their arguments are easily refuted. *(Susan Poliniak)*

1972
as

GLIŃSKI, Mateusz. **Spontini direttore d'orchestra** [Spontini as orchestral conductor], *Atti del primo Congresso internazionale di studi spontiniani* (Fabriano: Arti Grafiche Gentile, 1954) 86–94. In Italian. See no. 304 in this volume.

1973
as

GOLDHAMMER, Otto. **Liszt, Brahms und Reményi** [Liszt, Brahms, and Reményi], *Studia musicologica Academiae Scientiarum Hungaricae* V (1963) 89–100. In German. See no. 427 in this volume.

The violinist Ede Reményi (Hoffmann) engaged the very young Brahms as piano accompanist for a German tour in 1853, when he introduced him to Liszt and to Joseph Joachim. He also influenced the works of Brahms and Liszt, as evidenced by the 1853 MS *Ungarischer Romanzero* (Ch 1 Mappe Liszt 1) in the Richard-Wagner-Museum, Bayreuth. It contains Liszt's settings of verbunkos and csárdás melodies by Antal György Csermák, János Bihari, János Lavotta, and Jozef Zomb, and a set of characteristic pieces by Reményi, dedicated to Liszt. Liszt's and Brahms's appropriations of melodies from the MS are listed. *(William Renwick)*

1974
as

GOLDSCHMIDT, Harry. **Zu einer Neubewertung von Schuberts letzter Schaffenszeit** [Towards a reassessment of Schubert's final creative period], *Bericht über den siebenten internationalen musikwissenschaftlichen Kongress* (Kassel: Bärenreiter, 1959) 118–20. In German. See no. 390 in this volume.

The six settings of Heinrich Heine's lyrics in Schubert's *Schwanengesang*, D.957, offer the key to understanding the other works of his last year, and in particular the final six months. These songs are often cited in the last three piano sonatas and in other late works as well. Self-quotation is therefore an important characteristic of his last creative phase. *Der Atlas*, D.957, no. 8, had the most resonance of all. The programmatic aspect of Schubert's last works needs to be investigated; larger historical changes should be taken into account, i.e., the onset of contradictions in the position of the bourgeois class, a phenomenon that Schubert would have felt in the depths of his heart. *(Carl Skoggard)*

⟶

GUICHARD, Léon. **Liszt, Wagner et les relations entre la musique et la littérature au XIXe siècle** [Liszt, Wagner, and the relationship between music and literature in the 19th century]. See no. 5319 in this volume.

1975
as

GURLITT, Wilibald. **Robert Schumann in seinen Skizzen gegenüber Beethoven** [Robert Schumann in his sketches as compared with Beethoven], *Beethoven-Zentenarfeier: Internationaler musikhistorischer Kongress* (Wien: Universal, 1927) 91–94. In German. See no. 142 in this volume.

Schumann's sketchbooks, in the private Alfred Wiede collection and the holdings of the Robert-Schumann-Haus in Zwickau, show the importance in his compositional process of original inspiration, as opposed to Beethoven's use of sketching to revise and refine an idea. Annotations—dates and commentaries—in Schumann's sketches demonstrate the close connection between his musical ideas and his domestic life. *(David Bloom)*

1976
as

HAAS, Robert. **Schubertforschung und Meisterarchiv** [Schubert research and the Meisterarchiv], *Bericht über den internationalen Kongress für Schubertforschung* (Augsburg: Benno Filser, 1929) 27–36. *Illus., facs.* In German. See no. 154 in this volume.

The Archiv für Photogramme Musikalischer Meisterhandschriften, also known as the Meisterarchiv, is under the auspices of the Österreichische Nationalbibliothek, and houses MSS that would otherwise be inaccessible, including that of Schubert's unfinished symphony in E, D.729.

1977
as

HADOW, William Henry. **Organization of musical life in England,** *Haydn-Zentenarfeier* (Leipzig: Breitkopf & Härtel; Wien: Artaria, 1909) 489–92. See no. 65 in this volume.

Discusses musical institutions, festivals, and performing ensembles, particularly choral societies. Education is addressed, as is the need to bring music to economically depressed areas.

1978
as

HAHNE, Gerhard. **Musikalische Zusammenhänge zwischen Dänemark und Schleswig-Holstein im 19. Jahrhundert** [Musical connections between Denmark and Schleswig-Holstein in the 19th century], *Norddeutsche und nordeuropäische Musik* (Kassel; New York: Bärenreiter, 1965) 48–55. In German. See no. 467 in this volume.

The 19th c. was a time of decline in Schleswig-Holstein (now the German state of Schleswig-Holstein and the Danish county of Sønderjylland), when its cultural life rarely rose above the provincial level; few musicians remained there, whether they opted in the end for Denmark or Germany. Brief biographies are provided for the exemplary cases of Niels W. Gade, Christoph Ernst Friedrich Weyse, Friedrich Kuhlau, Johan Peter Emilius Hartmann, Carl Reinecke, and Cornelius Gurlitt; other locally significant musicians are listed. *(David Bloom)*

1979
as

HANDSCHIN, Jacques. **Die Orgelbewegung in der Schweiz** [The Orgelbewegung in Switzerland], *Bericht über die dritte Tagung für Deutsche Orgelkunst* (Kassel: Bärenreiter, 1928) 116–21. In German. See no. 136 in this volume.

The Swiss organ tradition is not a rich one. Few important instruments of the 17th-18th c. have survived. The central influence in the Swiss Orgelbewegung has been the frequent visits of Albert Schweitzer, much admired there as a theologian. Examples of the current situation are drawn from the restoration by Ernst Schiess, 1923-24, of the organ of the Stadtkirche, Winterthur (an instrument whose 19th-c. form was finalized by the Swiss builder Friedrich Haas in 1843 and the Walcker firm in 1888), and organs in Zürich and Yverdon-les-Bains.

1980
as

HARASZTI, Emil. **Le double aspect de l'art de François Liszt** [The double appearance of Franz Liszt's art], *Congrés de la Societat Internacional de Musicologia* (Barcelona: Casa de Caritat, 1936). In French. See no. 224 in this volume.

The conference report provides only a citation. Neither the text nor a summary of the paper was published here.

1981
as

HEINZ, Rudolf. **Franz Schubert *An die Musik*: Versuch über ein Musiklied** [Franz Schubert: *An die Musik*—Essay on a song about music], *Beiträge zur Geschichte der Musikansschauung im 19. Jahrhundert* (Regensburg: Bosse, 1965) 139–50. In German. See no. 483 in this volume.

Schubert's song is analyzed in terms of the relation between music and text, and in opposition to the analysis of Alfred Einstein in *Schubert: Ein musikalisches Porträt* (Zürich, 1952). In contrast to the ethos of Franz von Schober's poem, Schubert's setting is neither dilettantish nor definitively domesticated. *(David Bloom)*

1982
as

HELM, Everett. **A newly discovered Liszt manuscript,** *Studia musicologica Academiae Scientiarum Hungaricae* V (1963) 101–06. See no. 427 in this volume.

The manuscript was found in a *collection factice*—a selection of sheet music bound into a single volume by a 19th-c. owner—purchased by the author in Europe before World War II and currently part of his private collection. It consists an autograph piano piece entitled *Madrigal*, with a date of 1844 and dedication to the *Intendant* of the Weimar Hoftheater, Ferdinand von Ziegesar; the piece is an early version of *Consolations*, no. 5. *(Alan Garfield)*

1983
as

HOFFMAN, Alfred; MISSIR, Nicolae. **Sur la tournée de concerts de Ferenc Liszt en 1846-47 dans le Banat, la Transylvanie et les pays roumains** [On the concert tour of Franz Liszt in 1846-47 in Banat, Transylvania, and Romanian territories], *Studia musicologica Academiae Scientiarum Hungaricae* V (1963) 107–24. *Illus., chronology.* In French. See no. 427 in this volume.

Between 1 November 1846 and 25 October 1847, in the course of his last concert tour, Liszt traveled through the Romanian-speaking territories of Banat, Transylvania, Wallachia, and Moldavia. The tour is discussed in its historical context, and a detailed chronology is provided. *(William Renwick)*

1984
as

HONEGGER, Marc. **La musique française de 1830 à 1914** [French music from 1830 to 1914], *Bericht über den internationalen musikwissenschaftlichen Kongreß* (Kassel: Bärenreiter, 1963) 66–74. In French. See no. 452 in this volume.

The dates 1830-1914 correspond to a precise phenomenon in the history of German music. In France, on the contrary, no national school of Romanticism existed until the 1860s (the unique figure of Berlioz having exercised no influence until after his death), and as of 1885 it began to be supplanted by an entirely new style that prevailed until long after 1914. *(David Bloom)*

1985
as

HORDYŃSKI, Władysław. **Nieznany list Chopina do Teresy Wodzińskiej** [An unknown letter from Chopin to Teresa Wodzińska], *The book of the first international musicological congress devoted to the works of Frederick Chopin* (Warszawa: Państwowe Wydawnictwo Naukowe, 1963) 675–78. In Polish. See no. 425 in this volume.

1986
as

HOREMANS, Jef. **Minder bekende lyrische drama's van Peter Benoit** [Lesser-known lyric dramas by Peter Benoît], *Verhandelingen van het Muziekcongres* (Antwerpen: Stad Antwerpen, 1935) 39–45. In Dutch. See no. 210 in this volume.

Discussion focuses on *Charlotte Corday* (1876), *De pacificatie van Gent* (1876), and *Karel van Gelderland* (1892).

1987
as

HRABUSSAY, Zoltán. **Correspondance de Liszt avec des musiciens de Slovaquie** [Liszt's correspondence with musicians of Slovakia], *Studia musicologica Academiae Scientiarum Hungaricae* V (1963) 125–29. In French. See no. 427 in this volume.

Musical figures in Slovak lands with whom Liszt corresponded include Ludmila Zamojska (Gizycka-Zamojska), Tadeus Príleský (or Prileszky), and Ján Nepomuk Batka. The contents, historical context, and locations of 29 letters are discussed. *(William Renwick)*

1988
as

HURÉ, Jean. **La musique religieuse et le musique chorale** [Religious music and choral music], *Rapport sur la musique contemporaine française* (Roma: Armani & Stein, 1913) 63–76. In French. See no. 76 in this volume.

Offers brief discussions of composers (including several minor figures) active in French church music in the late 19th and early 20th c.

1989
as

ISTEL, Edgar. **The work and personality of Felipe Pedrell**, *Congrés de la Societat Internacional de Musicologia* (Barcelona: Casa de Caritat, 1936). See no. 224 in this volume.

The conference report provides only a citation. Neither the text nor a summary of the paper was published here.

1990
as

IWASZKIEWICZ, Jarosław. **Styl literacki listów Chopina** [The literary style of Chopin's letters], *The book of the first international musicological congress devoted to the works of Frederick Chopin* (Warszawa: Państwowe Wydawnictwo Naukowe, 1963) 679–83. In Polish. See no. 425 in this volume.

1991
as

JAKUBOWSKI, Jan Zygmunt. **Norwid i Chopin** [Norwid and Chopin], *The book of the first international musicological congress devoted to the works of Frederick Chopin* (Warszawa: Państwowe Wydawnictwo Naukowe, 1963) 684–90. In Polish. See no. 425 in this volume.

The poet and writer Cyprian Kamil Norwid met Chopin at the time of the composer's last illness, and wrote an obituary for him in *Dziennik Polski*; he also wrote at length about Chopin in the memoir *Czarne kwiaty* (Black flowers), the essay on aesthetics *Promethidion*, and the poem *Fortepian Szopena*.

1992
as

JANSEN, H. **L'état de la musique d'église dans les Pays-Bas** [The state of church music in the Low Countries], *La musique d'église: Compte rendu du Congrès de musique sacrée* (Tourcoing: Duvivier, 1920) 225–36. *Charts, diagr.* In French. See no. 93 in this volume.

Discusses the effects in the Low Countries of Pius X's motu proprio *Tra le sollecitudini* (1903). Programs from concerts of religious music given in Utrecht in 1880 and 1912 are included.

1993
as

JÁROSY, Dezső. **Die historische Entwicklung der ungarischen Kirchenmusik** [The historic development of Hungarian church music], *Beethoven-Zentenarfeier: Internationaler musikhistorischer Kongress* (Wien: Universal, 1927) 247–56. In German. See no. 142 in this volume.

A survey of developments in Roman Catholic music during the last quarter of the 19th c., with discussions of the contributions of Liszt and Franz Xaver Witt. Particular attention is drawn to the situation in Timişoara (Temesvár). *(David Bloom)*

1994
as

JIRÁNEK, Jaroslav. **Beitrag zum Vergleich des Klavierstils von Fryderyk Chopin und Bedřich Smetana** [Toward a comparison between the piano styles of Frédéric Chopin and Bedřich Smetana], *The book of the first international musicological congress devoted to the works of Frederick Chopin* (Warszawa: Państwowe Wydawnictwo Naukowe, 1963) 304–12. In German. See no. 425 in this volume.

In his earliest works Smetana was clearly influenced by Chopin, though not so much as to obscure his own folkloric, humorous, and optimistic qualities. The piano writing of his maturity has poetic traits reminiscent of Chopin but is often closer to Liszt, in its orchestral character, or Beethoven, in the carefully thought-out development of thematic material. *(David Bloom)*

1995
as

KACZYŃSKI, Tadeusz. **Texte poétique en tant que source d'inspiration musicale dans certaines chants de Chopin et de Moniuszko** [Poetic text as the source of musical inspiration in certain songs by Chopin and Moniuszko], *The book of the first international musicological congress devoted to the works of Frederick Chopin* (Warszawa: Państwowe Wydawnictwo Naukowe, 1963) 313–18. *Music.* In French. See no. 425 in this volume.

Three of Stanisław Moniuszko's songs set texts also used by Chopin: one by Adam Mickiewicz (*Moja pieszczotka*), and two by Stefan Witwicki (*Hulanka*, *Wiosna*). Similarities and differences in the composers' responses to the poems are outlined. *(David Bloom)*

1996
as

KAHL, Willi. **Öffentliche und private Musiksammlungen in ihrer Bedeutung für die musikalische Renaissancebewegung des 19. Jahrhunderts in Deutschland** [Public and private collections of music and their importance for the Renaissance movement in music in Germany during the 19th century], *Bericht über den Internationalen musikwissenschaftlichen Kongress* (Kassel: Bärenreiter, 1954) 289–94. In German. See no. 319 in this volume.

Traces the beginnings of the restoration of Roman Catholic Renaissance polyphony in Germany, with particular attention to performing and collecting activities undertaken in Munich, Regensberg, and Bonn. Some of the church musicians who contributed the most to this restoration were able to travel to Italy to gather MSS and commission copies from collections there; others were effective without leaving Germany. The powerful urge to undo the effects of the secularization of Roman Catholic institutions motivated German church musicians to achieve as much as they did. Caspar Ett, Johann Caspar Aiblinger, Johann Michael Hauber, Johann Michael Sailer, Carl Proske, Anton Friedrich Justus Thibaut, and Friedrich Heimsoeth are discussed, among others. *(Carl Skoggard)*

1997
as

KAHL, Willi. **Schuberts lyrisches Klavierstück** [Schubert's lyrical piano music], *Bericht über den internationalen Kongress für Schubertforschung* (Augsburg: Benno Filser, 1929) 191–98. In German. See no. 154 in this volume.

Demonstrates the influence of the early Romantic period on the *Impromptus*, D.899 and 935, and the *Moments musicaux*, D.780. Problems of dating and titles superimposed by publishers are also discussed.

1998
as

KAHL, Willi. **Zur Frage nach Schuberts früher Vollendung** [The question of Schubert's early death], *Bericht über den internationalen musikwissenschaftlichen Kongreß Wien Mozartjahr 1956* (Graz; Köln: Böhlau, 1958) 289–93. In German. See no. 365 in this volume.

Surveys contemporaries' and musicologists' attitudes toward and interpretations of Schubert's death, with citations from Schubert's own writings. *(David Bloom)*

1999
as

KALOMIRIS, Manolis. **Die Musik Mozarts in Griechenland** [Mozart's music in Greece], *Bericht über den internationalen musikwissenschaftlichen Kongreß Wien Mozartjahr 1956* (Graz; Köln: Böhlau, 1958) 294–99. In German. See no. 365 in this volume.

Popular works by Mozart were included in the repertoires of the mostly German military bands of the first period of independence (from 1821). Archival materials in Corfu (Kérkyra) show that his music was played there, if rarely, before 1850. Documented performances of specific Mozart works between 1860 and 1955 are surveyed. *(David Bloom)*

2000
as

KELDYŠ, Jurij Vsevolodovič. **Sovetskaja šopeniana** [Soviet Chopiniana], *The book of the first international musicological congress devoted to the works of Frederick Chopin* (Warszawa: Państwowe Wydawnictwo Naukowe, 1963) 478–81. In Russian. See no. 425 in this volume.

Surveys scholarly studies of Chopin and his works in Russia, particularly since 1918.

2001
as

KENDALL, Raymond. **Brahms's knowledge of Bach's music,** *Papers of the American Musicological Society* (Philadelphia: American Musicological Society, 1946) 50–56. See no. 272 in this volume.

The use of style analysis to demonstrate Bach's influence on Brahms is of questionable value unless it can be supported by documentary evidence. Works by Bach that Brahms owned, performed, or conducted are surveyed, and remarks on Bach in Brahms's correspondence are considered. *(David Bloom)*

2002
as

KINDERMANN, Jürgen. **Romantische Aspekte in E.T.A. Hoffmanns Musikanschauung** [Romantic aspects of E.T.A. Hoffmann's perspective on music], *Beiträge zur Geschichte der Musikansschauung im 19. Jahrhundert* (Regensburg: Bosse, 1965) 51–59. In German. See no. 483 in this volume.

Hoffmann failed to realize his ideals of Romantic music in his own compositions, but the same aesthetic is essential to his literary work: in the fictional figure of Kapellmeister Kreisler, in his critical writings on the Viennese Classicists and the church music of the Palestrina period (imitated in his six canzoni of 1808), in the evocation of his love for his Bamberg pupil Julia Marc, and in his identification of music and nature. *(David Bloom)*

2003
as

KIRBY, Percival R. **The use of European musical techniques by the non-European peoples of southern Africa,** *Journal of the International Folk Music Council* XI (1959) 37–40. See no. 392 in this volume.

Surveys religious and secular compositions by black South Africans from the 19th and 20th c., with particular attention to the works of John Knox Bokwe (1855-1922). The reception of Western music by black and Asian ethnic groups is also discussed. *(James R. Cowdery)*

2004
as

KLUSEN, Ernst. **César Franck und die Überwindung der Nationalstile im späten 19. Jahrhundert** [César Franck and the surmounting of national styles in the late 19th century], *Kongreß-Bericht: Gesellschaft für Musikforschung* (Kassel; Basel:

Bärenreiter, 1950) 143–45. In German. See no. 299 in this volume.

Discusses German and French influences on Franck's style.

2005
as

KLUSEN, Ernst. **Gustav Mahler und das böhmisch-mährische Volkslied** [Gustav Mahler and Bohemian-Moravian folk song], *Bericht über den internationalen musikwissenschaftlichen Kongreß* (Kassel: Bärenreiter, 1963) 246–51. *Music.* In German. See no. 452 in this volume.

Though Mahler is said to have known 200 folk songs as a four-year-old in Bohemia, he makes very little direct use of traditional melodic material in his compositions. In contrast, his choice of texts and his harmony often show folk origins. Many of the poems he set from *Des Knaben Wunderhorn* were extant in German-speaking Bohemia as folk songs when he was a child, so that he may have known them before he read the collection. Aspects of his harmonic technique may be derived from the scale and major-minor polarity of traditional Moravian music. *(David Bloom)*

2006
as

KLUSEN, Ernst. **Gustav Mahler und der Volkslied seiner Heimat** [Gustav Mahler and the folk songs of his homeland], *Journal of the International Folk Music Council* XV (1963) 29–37. *Music, bibliog., transcr.* In German; summary in English. See no. 459 in this volume.

Explores the influence of Czech traditional music on Mahler's works.

2007
as

KMICIC-MIELESZYŃSKI, Wacław. **Sprawa pobytu Chopina w Gdańsku** [Did Chopin visit Gdańsk?], *The book of the first international musicological congress devoted to the works of Frederick Chopin* (Warszawa: Państwowe Wydawnictwo Naukowe, 1963) 559. In Polish. See no. 425 in this volume.

Indirect evidence suggests that Chopin may have visited Gdańsk one or more times in the 1820s.

2008
as

KOBYLAŃSKA, Krystyna. **Sur l'histoire des manuscrits de F. Chopin** [On the history of Chopin's manuscripts], *The book of the first international musicological congress devoted to the works of Frederick Chopin* (Warszawa: Państwowe Wydawnictwo Naukowe, 1963) 482–87. In French. See no. 425 in this volume.

A survey of the transmission of autographs, semi-autographs, and authorized copies of Chopin's works in and outside Poland during his lifetime and after his death; includes a list of collections arranged by country. *(Susan Poliniak)*

2009
as

KÖHLER, Franz. **Zur Abstammung Schuberts** [Schubert's ancestry], *Bericht über die I. Tagung der Internationalen Gesellschaft für Experimentelle Phonetik* (Bonn: Scheur, 1930) 79–80. In German. See no. 169 in this volume.

Covers the period from ca. 1590 to the composer's birth in 1797.

2010
as

KÓKAI, Rezső. **Franz Liszt,** *Congrés de la Societat Internacional de Musicologia* (Barcelona: Casa de Caritat, 1936). In German. See no. 224 in this volume.

The conference report provides only a citation. Neither the text nor a summary of the paper was published here.

2011
as

KÖLTZSCH, Hans. **Das Gestaltungsproblem in der Instrumentalmusik Franz Schuberts** [Issues of form in Franz Schubert's instrumental music], *Beethoven-Zentenarfeier: Internationaler musikhistorischer Kongress* (Wien: Universal, 1927) 222–26. In German. See no. 142 in this volume.

The analytic consideration of Schubert's large instrumental works, as opposed to his lied compositions, leads to an entirely different concept of the composer's orientation as being more Classic than Romantic. *(David Bloom)*

2012   KÖLTZSCH, Hans. **Schuberts Sonaten** [Schu-
as   bert's sonatas], *Bericht über die I. Tagung der Internationalen Gesellschaft für Experimentelle Phonetik* (Bonn: Scheur, 1930) 201–08. In German. See no. 169 in this volume.
A stylistic examination focusing on the creative process in the piano sonatas.

2013   KRAFT, Günther. **Polnische Folklore im Lied
as   der Vormärz-Bewegung in Deutschland** [Polish folklore in songs of the Vormärz movement in Germany], *The book of the first international musicological congress devoted to the works of Frederick Chopin* (Warszawa: Państwowe Wydawnictwo Naukowe, 1963) 560–64. *Music.* In German. See no. 425 in this volume.
During the period of the Metternichian Restoration 1815-48, Poland became a symbol of the struggle for freedom to the oppositional Vormärz movement, and traditional Polish melodies are found alongside melodies of a French Revolutionary or Bonapartist connotation in the movement's songs. *(author)*

2014   KRAFT, Günther. **Das Schaffen von Franz Liszt
as   in Weimar** [Franz Liszt's creative work in Weimar], *Studia musicologica Academiae Scientiarum Hungaricae* V (1963) 193–210. *Illus.* In German. See no. 427 in this volume.
Discusses Liszt's impact on the cultural and social life of Weimar from ca. 1841 through his residence there, 1848-61, together with his compositional output from the period. *(William Renwick)*

2015   KREMLËV, Julij Anatol'evič. **La place histo-
as   rique de l'harmonie de Chopin** [The historical place of Chopin's harmony], *The book of the first international musicological congress devoted to the works of Frederick Chopin* (Warszawa: Państwowe Wydawnictwo Naukowe, 1963) 202–06. In French. See no. 425 in this volume.
Chopin used harmonies partly derived from Polish traditional music, giving his style a uniquely Polish character, but one which enriched and informed the development of European music as a whole. Harmony in Chopin's works has a dual function, in the service of melody and in its own right. The innovation instigated a new stage of development in European harmonic thinking. *(Susan Poliniak)*

2016   KRENEK, Ernst. **Franz Schubert und wir**
as   [Franz Schubert and us], *Bericht über den internationalen Kongress für Schubertforschung* (Augsburg: Benno Filser, 1929) 69–76. *Illus., port.* In German. See no. 154 in this volume.
A personal view focusing on historical context.

2017   KROÓ, György. **Einige Probleme des
as   Romantischen bei Chopin und Liszt** [Problems of the Romantic in Chopin and Liszt], *The book of the first international musicological congress devoted to the works of Frederick Chopin* (Warszawa: Państwowe Wydawnictwo Naukowe, 1963) 319–23. In German. See no. 425 in this volume.
Chopin's conception of sonata form is that of a free variation of song form, and the way he uses it, including in the scherzos, leads toward formal breakdown. To Liszt, sonata form was more important; he consciously presents himself as its revolutionary renovator, particularly in the use of monothematicism as a unifying principle. Chopin does, however, prefigure this monothematicism, in a rudimentary form, in works that influenced Liszt. *(David Bloom)*

2018   KROSS, Siegfried. **Rhythmik und Sprachbe-
as   handlung bei Brahms** [Brahms's rhythmics and treatment of speech], *Bericht über den internationalen musikwissenschaftlichen Kongreß* (Kassel: Bärenreiter, 1963) 217–19. In German. See no. 452 in this volume.
Apparent rhythmic faults in Brahms's text setting are not faults at all if melodic contour and harmony are taken into consideration as well as musical rhythm. *(David Bloom)*

2019   KURTHEN, Wilhelm. **Liszt und Bruckner als
as   Messenkomponisten** [Liszt and Bruckner as Mass composers], *Bericht über den I. musikwissenschaftlichen Kongress der Deutschen Musikgesellschaft in Leipzig* (Wiesbaden: Breitkopf & Härtel, 1926) 340. In German. See no. 120 in this volume.
A brief comparative discussion of style, form, and orchestration.

2020   KURTHEN, Wilhelm. **Zur Renaissancebe-
as   wegung des 19. Jahrhunderts im Rheinlande** [On the Renaissance movement of the 19th century in the Rhineland], *Bericht über den I. musikwissenschaftlichen Kongress der Deutschen Musikgesellschaft in Leipzig* (Wiesbaden: Breitkopf & Härtel, 1926) 398–400. In German. See no. 120 in this volume.
Discusses the beginnings of the Caecilian movement, in particular the effect Michael Töpler and Friedrich Heimsoeth had in reawakening an interest in the music of Lassus, Desprez, Palestrina, and Frescobaldi. *(William Renwick)*

2021   LA TOUR DE NOÉ, Gabriel-Marie-Eugène de.
as   **Situation présente des églises des villes et des campagnes sous le rapport du chant et de la musique** [The state of chant and church music in cities and in the provinces], *Congrès pour la restauration du plain-chant et de la musique d'église* (Paris: De Mourgues, 1862) 106–09. In French. See no. 3 in this volume.

2022   LACH, Robert. **Schubert und die Volkslied**
as   [Schubert and folk song], *Bericht über den internationalen Kongress für Schubertforschung* (Augsburg: Benno Filser, 1929) 59–67. *Music.* In German. See no. 154 in this volume.
Features of traditional song are seen in several of Schubert's works, including the eighth and ninth symphonies.

2023   LADMANOVÁ, Milada. **Chopin und Smetana**
as   [Chopin and Smetana], *The book of the first international musicological congress devoted to the works of Frederick Chopin* (Warszawa: Państwowe Wydawnictwo Naukowe, 1963) 324–28. In German. See no. 425 in this volume.
Discusses the biographical evidence of Smetana's reception of Chopin, and compares the two composers in terms of their aesthetic and historical importance. *(David Bloom)*

2024   LANDORMY, Paul. **La musique de chambre**
as   [Chamber music], *Rapport sur la musique contemporaine française* (Roma: Armani & Stein, 1913) 103–16. In French. See no. 76 in this volume.
Surveys French chamber music in the 19th and early 20th c. Categories of compositional schools discussed include the neoclassicists and eclectics, those influenced by César Franck, and the impressionists (primarily Debussy).

2025   LEHMANN, Dieter. **Bemerkungen zur Liszt-
as   Rezeption in Russland in den vierziger und fünfziger Jahren des 19. Jahrhunderts** [Remarks on Liszt reception in Russia in the 1840s and 1850s],

Studia musicologica Academiae Scientiarum Hungaricae V (1963) 211–15. In German. See no. 427 in this volume.

Discusses reactions to Liszt's concert appearances in Russia (in 1842, 1843, and 1847) and to his compositions, focusing on his reception by Glinka, Aleksandr Nikolaevič Serov, and Jurij Karlovič Arnol'd. *(William Renwick)*

2026 LEHMANN, Dieter. **Der russische Komponist**
as **und Musikforscher Alexander Nikolajewitsch Serow und sein Mozart-Bild** [The Russian composer and musicologist Aleksandr Nikolaevič Serov and his image of Mozart], *Bericht über den internationalen musikwissenschaftlichen Kongreß Wien Mozartjahr 1956* (Graz; Köln: Böhlau, 1958) 328–43. In German. See no. 365 in this volume.

As the pioneer of European-style music criticism and research in Russia, Serov understood Mozart's importance in terms of his own particular interests in music drama and in symphonic form. He was among the first to work toward a de-Romanticization of Mozart's image, and played a crucial role in making Mozart's works a living part of Russian musical life. *(David Bloom)*

2027 LEVYSOHN, S. **Die Pflege der Haydnschen**
as **Musik in Dänemark** [The cultivation of Haydn's music in Denmark], *Haydn-Zentenarfeier* (Leipzig: Breitkopf & Härtel; Wien: Artaria, 1909) 529–30. In German. See no. 65 in this volume.

Lists works by Haydn performed by various organizations in the 19th c.

2028 LIESS, Andreas. **Der junge Debussy und die**
as **russiche Musik** [The young Debussy and Russian music], *Bericht über den internationalen musikwissenschaftlichen Kongreß* (Kassel: Bärenreiter, 1963) 241–44. *Music.* In German. See no. 452 in this volume.

The well-known Russian influence on Debussy's compositions is illustrated by previously unnoticed examples drawing on music by Borodin, Balakirev, and Rimskij-Korsakov. *(David Bloom)*

2029 ŁOBACZEWSKA, Stefania. **La culture musi-**
as **cale en Pologne au début du XIX° siècle et ses relations avec la musique de Chopin** [Musical culture in Poland at the beginning of the 19th century and its relations with Chopin's music], *The book of the first international musicological congress devoted to the works of Frederick Chopin* (Warszawa: Państwowe Wydawnictwo Naukowe, 1963) 63–72. *Illus.* In French. See no. 425 in this volume.

Chopin's style evolved through an increasingly individualized assimilation of the musical traditions of Poland and a reinterpretation of Classic forms. The relationship between his style and Polish music of the early 19th c., especially dance music such as the mazurka and the polonaise, is discussed. *(Susan Poliniak)*

2030 LOCKSPEISER, Edward. **Quelques problèmes**
as **de la psychologie de Debussy** [Some aspects of Debussy's psychology], *Debussy et l'évolution de la musique au XX° siècle* (Paris: Centre National de la Recherche Scientifique [CNRS], 1965) 141–50. In French. See no. 456 in this volume.

2031 LOWENS, Irving. **Amerikanische Demokratie**
as **und die amerikanische Musik von 1830 bis 1914** [American democracy and American music from 1830 to 1914]. Trans. from English by Rudolf F. SCHAEFFER, *Bericht über den internationalen musikwissenschaftlichen Kongreß* (Kassel: Bärenreiter, 1963) 74–80. In German. See no. 452 in this volume.

The period 1830-65 was marked by the increasing prestige of folk and popular idioms, and the compositional activities of Foster and Gottschalk. In 1865-1900, a school of professional composers of art music developed, of

whom only MacDowell could be called a genius. Democratizing tendencies at the beginning of the 20th c. were reflected in the works of Sousa, Herbert, Joplin, and Ives. *(David Bloom)*

2032 MACKENZIE, Alexander Campbell. **Gedächt-**
as **nisrede auf Mendelssohn** [Memorial speech for Mendelssohn-Bartholdy], *Haydn-Zentenarfeier* (Leipzig: Breitkopf & Härtel; Wien: Artaria, 1909) 60–66. In German. See no. 65 in this volume.

2033 MACKERNESS, Eric David. **Mendelssohn and**
as ***Charles Auchester,*** *Bericht über den siebenten internationalen musikwissenschaftlichen Kongress* (Kassel: Bärenreiter, 1959) 188. See no. 390 in this volume.

Elizabeth Sara Sheppard's novel *Charles Auchester* (1853) gives a fictionalized portrait of the relation between Felix Mendelssohn-Bartholdy ("Chevalier Seraphael") and the English composer Charles Edward Horsley (the title character). It is immature in style and unconvincing in its portrayal of society, but provides a useful view of Mendelssohn reception in mid-Victorian England. *(David Bloom)*

2034 MAFFIOLETTI, M. **L'aderenza spirituale ed**
as **espressiva della poesia alla musica nei canti del popolo italiano nel Risorgimento** [The spiritual and expressive adherence of the poetry to the music in Italian popular song of the Risorgimento], *Atti del III Congresso nazionale di arti e tradizioni popolari* (Roma: Opera Nazionale Dopolavoro, 1936) 368–82. In Italian. See no. 218 in this volume.

2035 MALHERBE, Charles. **La musique drama-**
as **tique** [Dramatic music], *Rapport sur la musique contemporaine française* (Roma: Armani & Stein, 1913) 21–61. In French. See no. 76 in this volume.

Provides a historical survey of opera in France from 1860 to 1911. Opera, opéra comique, and the repertoire at the Théâtre Lyrique and the Théâtre Italien are discussed.

2036 MARX, Joseph. **Schuberts Lied** [Schubert's lied],
as *Bericht über den internationalen Kongress für Schubertforschung* (Augsburg: Benno Filser, 1929) 113–16. In German. See no. 154 in this volume.

Focuses on the aesthetics of text and music.

2037 MASSON, Paul-Marie. **Préface** [Preface], *Rapport*
as *sur la musique contemporaine française* (Roma: Armani & Stein, 1913) 5–14. In French. See no. 76 in this volume.

Surveys French music during the late 19th and early 20th c.

2038 MCGLINCHEE, Claire. **Shakespeare, Delacroix**
as **and Chopin,** *Actes du cinquième Congrès international d'esthétique/Proceedings of the Fifth International Congress of Aesthetics* ('s-Gravenhage: Mouton, 1964) 187–90. See no. 475 in this volume.

A discussion of Shakespeare's influence on Romanticism includes an interpretation of the programmatic content of Chopin's "Hamlet" nocturne in G minor (op. 15, no. 3). *(Ronnie Gellis)*

2039 MERSMANN, Hans. **Die Lage der abendlän-**
as **dischen Musik um 1900** [The situation of Western music around 1900], *Bericht über den I. musikwissenschaftlichen Kongress der Deutschen Musikgesellschaft in Leipzig* (Wiesbaden: Breitkopf & Härtel, 1926) 289–91. In German. See no. 120 in this volume.

A turning point in Western music occurred around 1900, marked by the advent of impressionism, Symbolism, and internationalism, particularly as manifested in the music of Schoenberg, Mahler, and Debussy. *(William Renwick)*

2040 MICHEL, Paul. **Franz Liszt als Lehrer und**
as **Erzieher** [Franz Liszt as instructor and teacher],
*Studia musicologica Academiae Scientiarum
Hungaricae* V (1963) 217–26. In German. See no. 427
in this volume.

Over a period of some six decades, Liszt devoted a considerable portion of
his time to the teaching of pianists and composers. His pedagogical principles reflected his ideas on the role of music and art in society, which were
strongly influenced by the philosophical, political, and sociological ideas
of Saint-Simon (Claude-Henri de Rouvroy) and Hugues-Félicité-Robert
de Lamennais. *(William Renwick)*

2041 MIES, Paul. **Mehrfache Bearbeitung gleicher**
as **Texte bei Schubert** [Multiple settings of the same
text by Schubert], *Bericht über den internationalen
Kongress für Schubertforschung* (Augsburg: Benno
Filser, 1929) 119–24. *Music.* In German. See no. 154 in
this volume.

Examining different settings of the same text can provide insight into the
compositional process. Alterations can include ornaments, introductions,
and tempo markings. *Rast* from *Die Winterreise*, D.911, is used as an example.

2042 MIES, Paul. **Der zyklische Charakter der**
as **Klaviertänze bei Franz Schubert** [The cyclic
character of Franz Schubert's dances for piano], *Bericht
über den internationalen musikwissenschaftlichen
Kongreß Wien Mozartjahr 1956* (Graz; Köln: Böhlau,
1958) 408–11. *Charts, diagr.* In German. See no. 365 in
this volume.

MSS and early prints show that the collections of dances published during
Schubert's lifetime are not to be regarded as large cycles *(David Bloom)*

2043 MILLET, Lluís. **La chanson populaire et l'art**
as **choral en Catalogne** [Traditional song and choral
art in Catalonia], *Beethoven-Zentenarfeier:
Internationaler musikhistorischer Kongress* (Wien:
Universal, 1927) 351–54. In French. See no. 142 in this
volume.

Traces developments from the first men's choral societies in Catalonia,
founded in the mid-19th c. by Josep Anselm Clavé and offering a popular-style repertoire, to the mixed amateur choirs of the early 20th c. The art
music repertoire of the latter included new works by composers such as
Antoni Nicolau i Parera. *(David Bloom)*

2044 MIL'ŠTEJN, Jakov. **Fortep'jannaja faktura**
as **Šopena i Lista** [Piano writing in Chopin and Liszt],
*The book of the first international musicological con-
gress devoted to the works of Frederick Chopin*
(Warszawa: Państwowe Wydawnictwo Naukowe,
1963) 341–46. In Russian. See no. 425 in this volume.

The essay is reprinted in the author's *Ocerke o Šopena* (Moskva, 1987),
cited as RILM [1988]3594.

2045 MOLNÁR, Antal. **Die Persönlichkeit Chopins**
as [Chopin's personality], *The book of the first interna-
tional musicological congress devoted to the works of
Frederick Chopin* (Warszawa: Państwowe
Wydawnictwo Naukowe, 1963) 701–06. In German.
See no. 425 in this volume.

The defining characteristic of Chopin's originality as a composer is the personal honesty he brought to his work, whether his inspiration was social,
religious, erotic, or humorous. *(David Bloom)*

2046 MOLNÁR, Antal. **Über Transkriptionen und**
as **Paraphrasen von Liszt** [Liszt's transcriptions and
paraphrases], *Studia musicologica Academiae
Scientiarum Hungaricae* V (1963) 227–32. In German.
See no. 427 in this volume.

Discusses the general importance of the genre in 19th-c. European culture,
as a mode of bringing difficult music to lay audiences. An analytic note on
Liszt's paraphrase, ca. 1855, of the act 4 quartet from Verdi's *Rigoletto*
draws attention to its use of advanced harmonies and pianistic refinements.
(William Renwick)

⟶ MORIN, Gösta. **Wolfgang Amadeus Mozart**
und Schweden [Wolfgang Amadeus Mozart and
Sweden]. See no. 1819 in this volume.

2047 MÜLLER, Robert Franz. **Der Körpergrösse**
as **Franz Schuberts: Eine Archivstudie** [Franz
Schubert's height: An archival study], *Bericht über die
I. Tagung der Internationalen Gesellschaft für
Experimentelle Phonetik* (Bonn: Scheur, 1930) 83–86.
In German. See no. 169 in this volume.

Documents Schubert's small physical stature.

2048 MUSIOŁ, Karol. **Ryszard Wagner a powstanie**
as **listopadowe** [Richard Wagner and the November
Revolution], *Ryszard Wagner a polska kultura
muzyczna/Richard Wagner und die polnische
Musikkultur* (Katowice: Panstwowa Wyzsza Szkola
Muzyczna, 1964) 7–22. In Polish; summary in German.
See no. 466 in this volume.

2049 NIKOLOVSKI, Vlastimir. **Makedonski**
as **muzički folklor u kompozicionom tretmanu**
Stevana Mokranjca [Traditional Macedonian music in the compositions of Stevan Mokranjac], *Rad
VII-og kongresa Saveza Folklorista Jugoslavije*
(Cetinje: Obod, 1964) 127–34. *Music, transcr.* In Serbian; summary in French. See no. 419 in this volume.

Mokranjac was not so much an original composer as a good arranger of traditional music. His merit, as a founder of the Yugoslavian national style, is
to have been among the first to draw on traditional-music sources. His technique is analyzed on the basis of the Macedonian song arrangements in the
Rukoveti nos. 10 and 15. *(author)*

2050 NOVÁČEK, Zdeněk. **Der entscheidende**
as **Einfluß von Liszt auf die fortschrittliche**
Musikorientation in Pressburg [Liszt's decisive
influence on the progressive musical outlook of
Bratislava], *Studia musicologica Academiae
Scientiarum Hungaricae* V (1963) 233–39. In German.
See no. 427 in this volume.

Between his 1819 appearance as a child prodigy and his last trip in the year
of his death, 1886, Liszt made altogether 13 visits to Bratislava (then generally known as Pressburg or Pozsony). His crucial impact on musical life in
the city is described. *(William Renwick)*

2051 NOWAK, Leopold. **Franz Schuberts**
as **Kirchenmusik** [Franz Schubert's religious music],
*Bericht über den internationalen Kongress für
Schubertforschung* (Augsburg: Benno Filser, 1929)
183–87. In German. See no. 154 in this volume.

General stylistic features in Schubert's Masses are discussed with regard to
Classic and Romantic influences, orchestration, and text setting.

2052 NOWAK, Leopold. **"Urfassung" und "End-**
as **fassung" bei Anton Bruckner** [The idea of original versions and final versions in Anton Bruckner],
*Bericht über den internationalen musikwissenschaft-
lichen Kongreß Wien Mozartjahr 1956* (Graz; Köln:
Böhlau, 1958) 448–51. In German. See no. 365 in this
volume.

The concept of *Urfassung* should be applied in Bruckner's case to the complete set of drafts preceding the first complete autograph score, which

should be called the "first version". The final version of a Bruckner work is either the latest dated autograph or the latest copy overseen by the composer and including his autograph corrections. *(David Bloom)*

2053 NOWAK-ROMANOWICZ, Alina. **Ideologia**
as **Józefa Elsnera a Chopin** [Józef Elsner's ideology and Chopin], *The book of the first international musicological congress devoted to the works of Frederick Chopin* (Warszawa: Państwowe Wydawnictwo Naukowe, 1963) 713–17. In Polish. See no. 425 in this volume.

2054 NUFFEL, Jules van. **De betrekkingen Benoit-**
as **Tinel** [The connections between Benoît and Tinel], *Verhandelingen van het Muziekcongres* (Antwerpen: Stad Antwerpen, 1935) 87–91. In Dutch. See no. 210 in this volume.

A reprint of an article published in *Dietsche Warande en Belfort* in September 1934 discussing the relationship between Benoît and the Belgian composer Edgar Tinel (1854-1912).

2055 OČADLÍK, Mirko. **Echa twórczości chopinow-**
as **skiej u Bedřicha Smetany** [Echoes of Chopin's compositions in Bedřich Smetany], *The book of the first international musicological congress devoted to the works of Frederick Chopin* (Warszawa: Państwowe Wydawnictwo Naukowe, 1963) 347–49. In Polish. See no. 425 in this volume.

2056 OČADLÍK, Mirko. **Die radikalen Demokraten:**
as **Liszt und Smetana** [Radical democrats: Liszt and Smetana], *Studia musicologica Academiae Scientiarum Hungaricae* V (1963) 241–47. In German. See no. 427 in this volume.

A political examination of the content of Liszt's and Smetana's works, in the context of democratic movements in Hungarian and Bohemian territory in the mid-19th c. and their relation to the situation as it has developed since World War II. *(William Renwick)*

2057 ONTROP, Lodewijk. **Bij de honderdste**
as **verjaring van Peter Benoit's geboortedag** [On the one hundredth anniversary of Peter Benoît's birth], *Verhandelingen van het Muziekcongres* (Antwerpen: Stad Antwerpen, 1935) 31–37. In Dutch. See no. 210 in this volume.

Discusses Benoît's role in the development of a Flemish national style in music during the course of the 19th c.

2058 OPIEŃSKI, Henryk. **Chopins Sonaten und ihr**
as **Verhältnis zum Beethovenschen Stil** [Chopin's sonatas and their relationship to the Beethoven style], *Beethoven-Zentenarfeier: Internationaler musikhistorischer Kongress* (Wien: Universal, 1927) 138–41. In German. See no. 142 in this volume.

Chopin is not likely to have been familiar with Beethoven's works before his first visit to Vienna in 1829. Afterwards his engagement with Beethoven was deeper than is commonly assumed, as is documented in his own correspondence and in Wilhelm von Lenz's *Die großen Pianoforte-Virtuosen unserer Zeit* (Berlin, 1872). The sonatas opp. 35 and 58 exhibit fully thought-through architecture that is not so distant from Beethoven's approach to the free development of sonata form. *(David Bloom)*

2059 OPIEN'SKI, Henryk. **Les premiers opéras**
as **polonais et leur influence sur l'époque de la jeunesse de Chopin** [The first Polish operas and their influence on Chopin's youthful period], *Report of the Fourth Congress of the International Musical Society* (London: Novello, 1912) 146–49. In French. See no. 71 in this volume.

Covers the period from the late 17th to the early 19th c., focusing on the origins of Chopin's concept of musical nationalism.

2060 OREL, Alfred. **Die Musik von 1830 bis 1914 in**
as **Österreich** [Music in Austria from 1830 to 1914], *Bericht über den internationalen musikwissenschaftlichen Kongreß* (Kassel: Bärenreiter, 1963) 54–60. In German. See no. 452 in this volume.

Discusses the influence on the Austrian musical scene of the Metternichian repression, the Revolution of 1848, and the operas of Wagner; and the activities of Brahms, Bruckner, Wolf, Johann Strauß Jr., Franz von Suppé, Carl Millöcker, Mahler, Schoenberg, and Josef Matthias. *(Daniel Anderson)*

2061 OREL, Alfred. **Schubert und Wien** [Schubert and
as Vienna], *Bericht über den internationalen Kongress für Schubertforschung* (Augsburg: Benno Filser, 1929) 39–46. In German. See no. 154 in this volume.

Briefly discusses cultural influences.

2062 OSTHOFF, Helmuth. **L'idea drammatica e lo**
as **stile musicale nelle opere di Gaspare Spontini** [The dramatic element and the musical style in Spontini's works], *Atti del primo Congresso internazionale di studi spontiniani* (Fabriano: Arti Grafiche Gentile, 1954) 53–58. In Italian. See no. 304 in this volume.

Spontini's fame and importance in Europe began with his three operas *La Vestale, Fernand Cortez*, and *Olimpie*.

2063 OSTHOFF, Wolfgang. **Die zwei Fassungen von**
as **Verdis** *Simon Boccanegra* [The two versions of Verdi's *Simon Boccanegra*], *Bericht über den internationalen musikwissenschaftlichen Kongreß* (Kassel: Bärenreiter, 1963) 222. In German. See no. 452 in this volume.

In the 1881 Milan revision of *Simon Boccanegra* the bass line is often unchanged, or fundamentally unchanged, from the 1857 Venice original, while rhythm and melody have been radically rewritten. The changes show that Verdi was chiefly interested in heightening the speechlike, human character of his vocal line rather than responding to the trends and debates of the late 19th c. *(David Bloom)*

2064 OTT, Alfons. **Die** *Ungarischen Rhapsodien* **von**
as **Franz Liszt** [Franz Liszt's *Magyar rhapsodiák*], *Bericht über den internationalen musikwissenschaftlichen Kongreß* (Kassel: Bärenreiter, 1963) 210–12. In German. See no. 452 in this volume.

Liszt wrote, published, revised, republished under different titles, and added to his Hungarian rhapsodies over a very long period, 1839-85. The history of the work, and its relation to the composer's feelings about Hungary, are discussed. *(David Bloom)*

2065 OTTICH, Maria. **Chopin und die Komponisten**
as **der nachfolgenden Generationen** [Chopin and the composers of following generations], *The book of the first international musicological congress devoted to the works of Frederick Chopin* (Warszawa: Państwowe Wydawnictwo Naukowe, 1963) 350–54. In German. See no. 425 in this volume.

Discusses Chopin's influence on composers from Smetana and Brahms through Šostakovič and Françaix. *(David Bloom)*

2066 PAWLISZYN, Stefania. **Elementy melodyki**
as **ukraińskiej w twórczości Chopina** [Ukrainian melodic elements in Chopin's works], *The book of the first international musicological congress devoted to the works of Frederick Chopin* (Warszawa: Państwowe Wydawnictwo Naukowe, 1963) 355–62. *Music, transcr.* In Polish. See no. 425 in this volume.

2067
as

PISCHNER, Hans. **Die Bedeutung Chopins für Robert Schumann** [Chopin's significance for Robert Schumann], *The book of the first international musicological congress devoted to the works of Frederick Chopin* (Warszawa: Państwowe Wydawnictwo Naukowe, 1963) 363–64. In German. See no. 425 in this volume.

Schumann's enthusiasm for Chopin at the beginning of the 1830s is connected with his understanding of the Polish insurrection of 1830-31; he saw the Polish composer, with his deep ties to the folk music of his native land, as a fellow combatant in the struggle against the reactionary establishments of Germany and Austria. *(David Bloom)*

2068
as

POIX, Octave. **Maîtres de chapelle, organistes, orgues, sociétés chorales, cantiques** [Chapel masters, organists, organs, choral societies, hymns], *Congrès pour la restauration du plain-chant et de la musique d'église* (Paris: De Mourgues, 1862) 114. In French. See no. 3 in this volume.

2069
as

POIX, Octave. **Situation présente des églises des villes et des campagnes du diocèse de Soissons, sous le rapport du chant et de la musique** [The state of chant and church music in the cities and the countryside of the diocese of Soissons], *Congrès pour la restauration du plain-chant et de la musique d'église* (Paris: De Mourgues, 1862) 112–13. In French. See no. 3 in this volume.

2070
as

POLS, André M. **De betrekkingen Benoit-Liszt** [The connections between Benoît and Liszt], *Verhandelingen van het Muziekcongres* (Antwerpen: Stad Antwerpen, 1935) 81–85. In Dutch. See no. 210 in this volume.

Discusses the influence of Liszt on several of Benoît's works, including *Rubenscantate* (1877).

2071
as

PORCELIJN, Carel. **The position of Alphons Diepenbrock in the Dutch history of music,** *Actes du cinquième Congrès international d'esthétique/Proceedings of the Fifth International Congress of Aesthetics* ('s-Gravenhage: Mouton, 1964) 201–05. See no. 475 in this volume.

Sets the output of the composer (1862-1921) in the context of Dutch music history from the 1830s through 1960s, with attention to influences on Diepenbrock and to his influence on other Dutch musicians. *(Ronnie Gellis)*

2072
as

POŠTOLKA, Milan. **Liszt und Böhmen im Spiegel der unveröffentlichten Korrespondenz** [Liszt and Bohemia, as reflected in unpublished correspondence], *Studia musicologica Academiae Scientiarum Hungaricae* V (1963) 255–66. In German. See no. 427 in this volume.

Liszt's relations with Bohemia are illustrated by a selection of previously unpublished correspondence in the holdings of the Národní Muzeum and Muzeum Bedřicha Smetany, Prague, including letters to the writer and soldier Prince Friedrich zu Schwarzenberg (1799-1870) and to Prince Friedrich Wilhelm Konstantin von Hohenzollern-Hechingen, together with unpublished or partially published materials concerning Liszt's interactions with the Prague cultural association Umělecka Beseda and its representatives Smetana and Ludevít Procházka. *(William Renwick)*

2073
as

POWROŹNIAK, Lózef. **Spór Karola Lipińskiego z Ryszardem Wagnerem** [The conflict between Karol Lipiński and Richard Wagner], *Ryszard Wagner a polska kultura muzyczna/Richard Wagner und die polnische Musikkultur* (Katowice: Panstwowa Wyzsza Szkola Muzyczna, 1964) 39–45. In Polish; summary in German. See no. 466 in this volume.

2074
as

PROCHÁZKA, Jaroslav. **The origin of "the Prague mazurka" in G major and Chopin's relations with Václav Hanka,** *The book of the first international musicological congress devoted to the works of Frederick Chopin* (Warszawa: Państwowe Wydawnictwo Naukowe, 1963) 365–73. *Music.* In English and Polish. See no. 425 in this volume.

Chopin's Slavic nationalist sentiments began with his contacts in Warsaw with figures such as Kazimierz Brodziński, but intensified when he met the poet and archivist Václav Hanka, a major figure in the Czech national revival, on his first visit to Prague in 1829. Hanka's album, preserved in the Národní Muzeum, Prague, contains a fragmentary autograph piece by Chopin, a mazurka melody in G setting a text by Ignacy Maciejowski (*Jakież kwiaty, jakie wianki*), without accompaniment. *(Susan Poliniak)*

2075
as

PROD'HOMME, Jacques-Gabriel. **Les débuts de Beethoven en France** [The early reception of Beethoven in France], *Beethoven-Zentenarfeier: Internationaler musikhistorischer Kongress* (Wien: Universal, 1927) 116–22. In French. See no. 142 in this volume.

A survey, focusing on the period through the 1830s. Heinrich Simrock, the brother of Beethoven's Bonn publisher Nicolaus Simrock, lived in Paris from the beginning of the Revolution and ran a music dealership there from 1802. The shop would have been the first place in France where Beethoven's music could be purchased. The earliest French-language criticism of Beethoven was in Jérôme-Joseph de Momigny's *Encyclopédie méthodique* (Paris, 1818). The violinist and conductor François-Antoine Habeneck was the central figure in introducing Beethoven's music in concert performance. *(David Bloom)*

2076
as

PROD'HOMME, Jacques-Gabriel. **Fétis, bibliothécaire du Conservatoire de Paris** [Fétis, librarian of the Paris Conservatoire], *Annales du XXIIIᵉ congrès* (Gent: Siffer, 1914) III, 347–60. In French. See no. 89 in this volume.

François-Joseph Fétis served as librarian at the Conservatoire de Paris between 1826 and 1831. Several of his letters from this period are reproduced.

2077
as

PROD'HOMME, Jacques-Gabriel. **La musique et les musiciens en 1848** [Music and musicians in 1848], *Report of the Fourth Congress of the International Musical Society* (London: Novello, 1912) 149. In French. See no. 71 in this volume.

Summary of a paper. Discusses musical life and performing organizations in Paris.

2078
as

PROD'HOMME, Jacques-Gabriel. **Les œuvres de Schubert en France** [The works of Schubert in France], *Bericht über die I. Tagung der Internationalen Gesellschaft für Experimentelle Phonetik* (Bonn: Scheur, 1930) 89–110. In French. See no. 169 in this volume.

Reviews and other publications from 19th-c. Paris attest to a gradually increasing interest in Schubert's work.

2079
as

PROSNAK, Antoni. **Niektóre zagadnienia wariacyjności etiud Chopina** [Issues of variation technique in Chopin's etudes], *The book of the first international musicological congress devoted to the works of Frederick Chopin* (Warszawa: Państwowe Wydawnictwo Naukowe, 1963) 219–23. In Polish. See no. 425 in this volume.

2080
as

PROSNAK, Jan. **Elementy berżeretki francuskiej, "sztajerka" i folkloru ukraińskiego w twórczości Chopina** [Elements of the French bergerette, the sztajerek genre, and Ukrainian folklore in Chopin's works], *The book of the first international mu-*

sicological congress devoted to the works of Frederick Chopin (Warszawa: Państwowe Wydawnictwo Naukowe, 1963) 374–82. *Music.* In Polish. See no. 425 in this volume.

2081 RACEK, Jan. **Les études faites par Leoš**
as **Janáček dans les compositions pour piano de Frédéric Chopin** [Leoš Janáček's annotations in his copies of the piano compositions of Frédéric Chopin], *The book of the first international musicological congress devoted to the works of Frederick Chopin* (Warszawa: Państwowe Wydawnictwo Naukowe, 1963) 383–87. *Music.* In French. See no. 425 in this volume.
Study notes made by Janáček in his copies of the piano works of Chopin are preserved in the Janáčkův Archiv of the Moravské Zemské Muzeum, Brno. They contain not only corrections to typographical errors, but informed ideas on interpretation, as well as personal judgments on the works themselves, showing the Czech composer as a practical musician, and demonstrating his high regard for Chopin. *(Susan Poliniak)*

2082 RACKWITZ, Werner. **Liszts Verhältnis zur**
as **Musik Georg Friedrich Händels** [Liszt's relationship to the music of Georg Friedrich Händel], *Studia musicologica Academiae Scientiarum Hungaricae* V (1963) 267–75. In German. See no. 427 in this volume.
Liszt had a lifelong involvement with the music of Händel, performing Händel's keyboard music and, as conductor, his oratorios, as well as composing an operatic paraphrase, the *Sarabande und Chaconne aus dem Singspiel Almira von Georg Friedrich Händel*, 1879. Documentary evidence of his interest in other Händel works, particularly the anthems, is cited.
(William Renwick)

2083 RILLÉ, Laurent de; BOUTIN, Alfred;
as DUREAU, Théophile; GRIMM, Wilhelm; ROBERT, F.R. **De l'utilité du développement des sociétés orphéoniques (chorales, symphonies, harmonies, fanfares), et des moyens d'améliorer leur répertoire** [The importance of the development of music societies (choruses, symphonies, wind ensembles, brass bands) and the means of improving their repertoire], *Congrès international de musique: Iʳᵉ session—Exposition Universelle de 1900: Compte rendu, rapports, communications* (Paris: conference, 1901) 49–55. In French. See no. 29 in this volume.
The principal function of amateur music societies, such as Orphéon, should be to give recreation to workers. More competent directors should be recruited by means of a competition.

2084 RINGER, Alexander L. **On the question of exot-**
as **icism in 19th-century music,** *Studia musicologica Academiae Scientiarum Hungaricae* VII (1965) 115–23. *Music, bibliog.* See no. 478 in this volume.
Imitated in crude stereotypes by early 18th-c. European composers, music from other cultures (particularly Turkey and Eastern Europe) became a rich source of material for later composers such as Mozart, Beethoven, and Schubert. *(David Gagné)*

2085 ROLANDI, Ulderico. **Tre parodie de *La vestale***
as [Three parodies of *La vestale*], *Atti del primo Congresso internazionale di studi spontiniani* (Fabriano: Arti Grafiche Gentile, 1954) 41–47. In Italian. See no. 304 in this volume.
Briefly describes the plot of the opera and in the scenes in which the parodies occur.

2086 RUDZIŃSKI, Witold. **Źródła stylu muzycz-**
as **nego Stanisława Moniuszki** [Sources of Stanisław Moniuszko's musical style], *The book of the first inter-*

national musicological congress devoted to the works of Frederick Chopin (Warszawa: Państwowe Wydawnictwo Naukowe, 1963) 598–600. In Polish. See no. 425 in this volume.

2087 SABBE, Maurits. **De uitgave der werken van P.**
as **Benoit** [The publication of the works of Peter Benoît], *Verhandelingen van het Muziekcongres* (Antwerpen: Stad Antwerpen, 1935) 108–10. *List of works.* In Dutch. See no. 210 in this volume.

2088 SAKVA, Konstantin Konstantinovič. **Čajkovskij**
as **o Mocarte** [Čajkovskij on Mozart], *Bericht über den internationalen musikwissenschaftlichen Kongreß Wien Mozartjahr 1956* (Graz; Köln: Böhlau, 1958) 537–43. In Russian. See no. 365 in this volume.
Surveys Čajkovskij's lifelong engagement, especially as documented in his own words, with Mozart's works.

2089 SALMEN, Walter. **Die Auswirkung von Ideen**
as **und Kompositionen Reichardts im 19. Jahr-hundert** [The effects of Reichardt's ideas and compositions in the 19th century], *Bericht über den internationalen musikwissenschaftlichen Kongreß* (Kassel: Bärenreiter, 1963) 202–05. In German. See no. 452 in this volume.
The views developed by Johann Friedrich Reichardt in the *Musikalisches Magazin* (1782-91) played a direct role in the origins of German musical Romanticism, along with the less well-known parts he played in the revival of Palestrina and in the preparation of *Des Knaben Wunderhorn*. His stage and choral works continued to be performed well into the middle of the 19th c., and his songs beyond that, particularly in school and Hausmusik contexts. *(David Bloom)*

2090 SAMBETH, Heinrich. **Die Gregorianischen**
as **Melodien in den Werken Franz Liszts mit besonderer Berücksichtigung seiner Kirchenmusik Reformpläne** [The Gregorian melodies in the works of Franz Liszt with special consideration of his plans for the reform of church music], *Bericht über den I. musikwissenschaftlichen Kongress der Deutschen Musikgesellschaft in Leipzig* (Wiesbaden: Breitkopf & Härtel, 1926) 341–42. In German. See no. 120 in this volume.
A summary of an article published in *Musica sacra* LV/8-9 (Aug-Sept 1925). Liszt's use of Gregorian chant in various works, including his Masses, *Totentanz, Eine Symphonie zu Dantes Divina commedia*, and *Christus* is discussed and related to the Cecilian movement. *(William Renwick)*

2091 SANDBERGER, Adolf. **Richard Wagners**
as ***Liebesverbot*** [Richard Wagner's *Das Liebesverbot*], *Haydn-Zentenarfeier* (Leipzig: Breitkopf & Härtel; Wien: Artaria, 1909) 194–96. In German. See no. 65 in this volume.
Discusses Wagner's opera based on Shakespeare's *Measure for measure*.

2092 SANDELEWSKI, Wiarosław. **Les éléments du**
as **bel canto italien dans l'œuvre de Chopin** [The elements of Italian bel canto in the works of Chopin], *The book of the first international musicological congress devoted to the works of Frederick Chopin* (Warszawa: Państwowe Wydawnictwo Naukowe, 1963) 230–35. In French. See no. 425 in this volume.
Common features of Chopin and the bel canto composers include the accompanied monodic style, regular periodic construction, three-part da capo form, and a predilection for particular ornaments such as trills. The influence on Chopin of Muzio Clementi (often referred to as the father of the piano) is much more important in this connection than has been noted.
(Susan Poliniak)

2093 SCHREIBER, Ottmar. **Max Regers musika-**
as **lischer Nachlaß** [Max Reger's musical legacy],
Bericht über den internationalen musikwissenschaft-
lichen Kongreß Wien Mozartjahr 1956 (Graz; Köln:
Böhlau, 1958) 563–70. *Music.* In German. See no. 365
in this volume.

In addition to drafts, variants, fragments, and juvenilia, the musical materials found after Reger's death (May 1916) include some complete movements and near-complete chamber, orchestral, and choral works; these are
briefly reviewed. *(David Bloom)*

2094 SCHWARZ, Werner. **Musik und Musikern im**
as **deutschen Osten: Nach unveröffentlichen**
Briefen an Robert Schumann aus den Jahren
1834-1854 [Music and musicians in the German East:
On the basis of unpublished letters to Robert Schumann
from 1834-1854], *Norddeutsche und nordeuropäische*
Musik (Kassel; New York: Bärenreiter, 1965) 120–25.
In German. See no. 467 in this volume.

Schumann's correspondents in Königsberg included the teacher and con-
ductor Carl Heinrich Saemann and the organist, conductor, and impresario
Fryderyk Edward Sobolewski. The Danzig organist and composer
Friedrich Wilhelm Markull contributed to the *Neue Zeitschrift für Musik.*
Other musicians associated with Königsberg include the English pianist
Anna Robena Laidlaw, dedicatee of the *Fantaisiestücke,* op. 12, and the
composer, piano teacher, and critic Louis Ehlert. *(David Bloom)*

2095 SERVOLINI, Luigi. **Inediti Spontiniani a Forlì**
as [Spontini's unpublished documents in Forlì], *Cahiers*
d'études de radio-télévision 3-4 (1955) 50–51. In Italian. See no. 304 in this volume.

Letters Spontini received while vacationing in Forlì are kept at the Biblioteca Comunale there.

2096 SIEGMUND-SCHULTZE, Walther. **Chopin und**
as **Brahms** [Chopin and Brahms], *The book of the first in-*
ternational musicological congress devoted to the works
of Frederick Chopin (Warszawa: Państwowe
Wydawnictwo Naukowe, 1963) 388–95. *Music.* In German. See no. 425 in this volume.

Three aspects of Chopin's works that particularly attracted Brahms were
his characteristic pianism, his formal construction (both the use of ABA
forms and of techniques such as ostinato), and his national character (especially as seen in the mazurkas). *(David Bloom)*

2097 SIEGMUND-SCHULTZE, Walther. **Wort und**
as **Ton bei Robert Schumann** [Word and music in
works by Robert Schumann], *Bericht über den inter-*
nationalen musikwissenschaftlichen Kongreß (Kassel:
Bärenreiter, 1957) 216–19. In German. See no. 356 in
this volume.

Offers an appreciation of the balance between music and text in
Schumann's vocal music, with reference to the composer's attachment to
German traditional music and the poetic character of his melodic construc-
tion even in strictly instrumental works.

2098 SIENKIEWICZ, Jerzy. **Zapomniany list**
as **Chopina (Chopin i Piotr Michałowski)** [A forgotten letter by Chopin (Chopin and Piotr
Michałowski)], *The book of the first international mu-*
sicological congress devoted to the works of Frederick
Chopin (Warszawa: Państwowe Wydawnictwo
Naukowe, 1963) 718–20. In Polish. See no. 425 in this
volume.

2099 SOMFAI, László. **Die Metamorphose der**
as *Faust-Symphonie* **von Liszt** [The metamorphosis of
Liszt's *Faust-Symphonie*], *Studia musicologica*

Academiae Scientiarum Hungaricae V (1963). *Music.*
In German. See no. 427 in this volume.

An examination of sketches and alternate versions shows how, in the long
period over which the work was composed, from the late 1830s through
1861, much of the thematic material was entirely transformed.
(William Renwick)

2100 SONNECK, Oscar G.T. **Das Musikleben**
as **Amerikas vom Standpunkte der musikalischen**
Länderkunde [America's musical life from the standpoint of musical geography], *Haydn-Zentenarfeier*
(Leipzig: Breitkopf & Härtel; Wien: Artaria, 1909)
446–58. In German. See no. 65 in this volume.

Discusses the position of music in the United States. Orchestras and opera
companies in various major cities are referred to, as are institutions such as
the American Federation of Musicians. Music literature and criticism are
also briefly addressed.

2101 STADNICKI, Edwin Kornel. **Polski walc**
as **fortepianowy przed Chopinem** [The waltz for piano in Poland before Chopin], *The book of the first in-*
ternational musicological congress devoted to the
works of Frederick Chopin (Warszawa: Państwowe
Wydawnictwo Naukowe, 1963) 613–17. In Polish. See
no. 425 in this volume.

Poland saw the development of a specifically local style of piano waltz in
the period 1800-30; its history and influence on Chopin and later composers are surveyed.

2102 ŠTĚDROŇ, Bohumír. **Janáček und Polen**
as [Janáček and Poland], *The book of the first interna-*
tional musicological congress devoted to the works of
Frederick Chopin (Warszawa: Państwowe
Wydawnictwo Naukowe, 1963) 618–23. *Music.* In
German. See no. 425 in this volume.

Janáček's interest in Polish culture was unique among the Czech musicians
of his time. Particular attention is given to his 1901-06 choral work *Otče*
náš, inspired by an exhibition in Brno of paintings by Josef Krzesz-Męcina,
and his abortive candidacy around the same time for the directorship of the
Instytut Muzyczny Warszawski. *(David Bloom)*

2103 STEFAN, Paul. **Schuberts geistige Haltung und**
as **Bedeutung** [Schubert's intellectuality and its signifi-
cance], *Bericht über den internationalen Kongress für*
Schubertforschung (Augsburg: Benno Filser, 1929)
143–46. In German. See no. 154 in this volume.

Offers a general cultural context.

2104 STEGLICH, Rudolf. **Zum Kontrastproblem**
as **Johannes Brahms—Hugo Wolf** [Viewing
Johannes Brahms and Hugo Wolf as opposites],
Kongreß-Bericht: Gesellschaft für Musikforschung
(Kassel; Basel: Bärenreiter, 1950) 140–43. *Music.* In
German. See no. 299 in this volume.

2105 STRAETEN, Edmond vander. **Schuberts**
as **Behandlung der Streichinstrumente mit**
besonder Berücksichtigung der Kammer-
musik [Schubert's treatment of string instruments,
with particular regard to his chamber music], *Bericht*
über den internationalen Kongress für Schubert-
forschung (Augsburg: Benno Filser, 1929) 133–40.
Illus., port. In German. See no. 154 in this volume.

Various works are mentioned, including the string quintet in C, D.956, and
the octet in F, D.803.

2106
as
SUPPAN, Wolfgang. **Franz Liszt und die Steiermark** [Franz Liszt and Styria], *Studia musicologica Academiae Scientiarum Hungaricae* V (1963) 301–10. In German. See no. 427 in this volume.

Discusses the reception of Liszt's visits to Styria as pianist, with sample concert programs; the reception of his compositions in Graz from the 1870s to 1921; and Liszt MSS in the holdings of the Steiermärkisches Landeskonservatorium, Graz. Another version is published in *Mitteilungen des steirischen Tonkünstlerbundes* 53-54 (Jul-Dec 1972) and abstracted as RILM [1973]670. *(William Renwick)*

2107
as
ŚWIDER, Józef. **Stosunek Szymanowskiego do Wagnera** [The relationship between Szymanowski and Wagner], *Ryszard Wagner a polska kultura muzyczna/Richard Wagner und die polnische Musikkultur* (Katowice: Panstwowa Wyzsza Szkola Muzyczna, 1964) 95–103. In Polish; summary in German. See no. 466 in this volume.

2108
as
SYCHRA, Antonín. **Ein Beitrag zur inhaltlichen Deutung von Chopins Schaffen** [Toward an interpretation of the content of Chopin's works], *The book of the first international musicological congress devoted to the works of Frederick Chopin* (Warszawa: Państwowe Wydawnictwo Naukowe, 1963) 732–34. In German. See no. 425 in this volume.

In addition to analyses of harmony, form, and piano style, Chopin's works should be investigated with regard to content, in terms of intonation and genre theory. Even his boldest experimentation is always connected to the concrete expressive function of the composition. *(David Bloom)*

2109
as
SZABOLCSI, Bence. **Die Anfänge der nationalen Oper im 19. Jahrhundert** [The beginnings of national opera in the 19th century], *Bericht über den neunten internationalen Kongreß* (Kassel: Bärenreiter, 1964-1966) I, 57–62. In German. See no. 491 in this volume.

Over a period of less than 70 years, national traditions of music theater developed in Poland, Russia, Slovenia, Hungary, Bohemia, Croatia, and Romania. All these shared certain common traits: a lively consciousness of being behind in relation to Western Europe, with the frank imitation especially of Italian and German models; a national character in all aspects of the work, including language, versification, plot, treatment, and music; national consciousness and a bourgeois-democratic belief in progress; a decisive role for local or folk elements; and the influence of the revolutionary rescue opera. In their use of traditional-music scales, harmonies, and rhythms, declamation and prose texts, and in their close connection with contemporary literary innovation, they anticipated modernity. *(David Bloom)*

→ TARANTOVÁ, Marie. **Das Echo von Mozarts Werk in der Epoche der Wiedergeburt des tschechischen Volkes** [The echo of Mozart's music in the era of the renaissance of the Czech people]. See no. 1880 in this volume.

2110
as
TOMASZEWSKI, Mieczysław. **Verbindungen zwischen den Chopinschen Liederwerken und dem polnischen populären, Volks- und Kunstlied** [Connections between Chopin's song compositions and Polish popular, folk, and art song], *The book of the first international musicological congress devoted to the works of Frederick Chopin* (Warszawa: Państwowe Wydawnictwo Naukowe, 1963) 404–09. In German. See no. 425 in this volume.

Chopin's song output is a marginal part of his work, but very significant in relation to his role in creating a national Polish style. His songs may be classified into categories drawn from everyday Polish musical life: masculine social songs, idyllic folk songs, dumki, romances, ballads, and lyrics. A Polish-language version is included in the collection cited as RILM [1996]5011. *(David Bloom)*

2111
as
TORREFRANCA, Fausto. **Gaspare Spontini e l'opera tedesca** [Gaspare Spontini and German opera], *Atti del primo Congresso internazionale di studi spontiniani* (Fabriano: Arti Grafiche Gentile, 1954) 129–39. In Italian. See no. 304 in this volume.

Spontini's ambition was to create for the world, not only for his country; his ultimate accomplishment was in the German style.

2112
as
TRAGLIA, Gustavo. **Umiliazioni giovanili e reazioni nell'età matura in Gaspare Spontini** [Youthful humiliations and reactions in Gaspare Spontini's mature period], *Cahiers d'études de radio-télévision* 3-4 (1955) 23–26. In Italian. See no. 304 in this volume.

Contrasting characteristics from the music of Spontini's youth and maturity provide insight into the composer's creative mind.

2113
as
USZKOREIT, Hans-Georg. **Händel und Mendelssohn** [Händel and Mendelssohn-Bartholdy], *Händel-Ehrung der Deutschen Demokratischen Republik: Konferenzbericht* (Leipzig: VEB Deutscher Verlag für Musik, 1961) 215–18. In German. See no. 408 in this volume.

Mendelssohn-Bartholdy's work in the cultivation of Händel's music has been overshadowed by his role in the Bach revival of the early 19th c., but is nevertheless important. His enthusiasm for Händel is documented in his correspondence, and he played a leading role in the publication and performance of Händel's oratorios in Germany. Händel's influence on his own works, especially the oratorios, and suggestive biographical parallels between the two musicians are noted. *(David Bloom)*

2114
as
VÄISÄNEN, Armas Otto. **Jean Sibelius und die Volksmusik** [Jean Sibelius and folk music], *Bericht über den Internationalen musikwissenschaftlichen Kongress* (Kassel: Bärenreiter, 1954) 207–09. In German. See no. 319 in this volume.

Distinguishes a primitive layer of Finnish traditional music, associated with the *Kalevala* and the five-stringed kantele, from a Swedish-influenced repertoire of rhymed strophic songs that first appeared in the 16th c. The melodic character of the two layers is quite different. Sibelius was well acquainted with both kinds, and both influenced the melodic character of his music from the early choral symphony *Kullervo* (premiere, 1892) up to *Tapiola*. Sibelius's rhythm, complex and individualized, owes little to traditional Finnish music. *(Carl Skoggard)*

2115
as
VANCEA, Zeno. **Der Chopin-Schüler Carol Mikuli, ein Bindeglied zwischen rumänischer und polnischer Musikkultur** [Chopin's pupil Karol Mikuli, a link between Romanian and Polish musical culture], *The book of the first international musicological congress devoted to the works of Frederick Chopin* (Warszawa: Państwowe Wydawnictwo Naukowe, 1963) 410–12. *Music, bibliog.* In German. See no. 425 in this volume.

Biographical notes on the pianist, composer, pedagogue, and editor of Chopin's work, with particular attention to his piano compositions based on traditional Romanian melodies. *(David Bloom)*

2116
as
VANCEA, Zeno. **Der Einfluß Haydns auf die rumänischen Komponisten des XIX. Jahrhunderts** [The influence of Haydn on 19th-century Romanian composers], *Bericht über die internationale Konferenz zum Andenken Joseph Haydns* (Budapest: Akadémiai Kiadó, 1961) 177–80. In German. See no. 405 in this volume.

In the first half of the 19th c., Romanian composers such as Elena Asachi, Alexandru Flechtenmacher, and Ion Andrei Wachmann sought to unite elements of Romanian traditional music with the Viennese Classical tradition. The model of Haydn, who had already successfully incorporated similar elements into his own music, was decisive. The Romanian composers of the second half of the 19th c., such as Eduard Caudella, George Stephănescu, and Constantin Dimitrescu, though strongly influenced by German Romanticism as well as the Russian and Czech national schools, still looked to the music of Haydn as an example of the synthesis of traditional elements and art music. *(Larry Laskowski)*

2117
as

VASINA-GROSSMAN, Vera. **Šopen i Mogučaja Kučka** [Chopin and the Russian Five], *The book of the first international musicological congress devoted to the works of Frederick Chopin* (Warszawa: Państwowe Wydawnictwo Naukowe, 1963) 413–14. *Music*. In Russian. See no. 425 in this volume.

Discusses the responses to Chopin of Balakirev, Borodin, Kjui, Musorgskij, and Rimskij-Korsakov.

2118
as

VEEN-HIEL, J. De. **Hiel-Benoit—Benoit-Hiel** [Hiel-Benoît—Benoît-Hiel], *Verhandelingen van het Muziekcongres* (Antwerpen: Stad Antwerpen, 1935) 71–79. In Dutch. See no. 210 in this volume.

Discusses the close friendship between Benoît and the Flemish poet Emanuel Hiel. A pair of letters between the two are given in transcription.

2119
as

VERHEYDEN, Prosper. **De muziekhandschriften van P. Benoit** [The music manuscripts of Peter Benoît], *Verhandelingen van het Muziekcongres* (Antwerpen: Stad Antwerpen, 1935) 107. In Dutch. See no. 210 in this volume.

2120
as

VETTER, Walther. **Mozart im Weltbild Richard Wagners** [Mozart in Richard Wagner's worldview], *Bericht über den internationalen musikwissenschaftlichen Kongreß Wien Mozartjahr 1956* (Graz; Köln: Böhlau, 1958) 657–60. In German. See no. 365 in this volume.

A survey of the frequently contradictory views of Mozart expressed in Wagner's critical writings.

2121
as

VOGEL, Martin. **Nietzsches Wettkampf mit Wagner** [Nietzsche's competition with Wagner], *Beiträge zur Geschichte der Musikansschauung im 19. Jahrhundert* (Regensburg: Bosse, 1965) 195–223. *Music, charts, diagr.* In German. See no. 483 in this volume.

In the early 1870s, when the young Nietzsche was an intimate of the Wagner household at Tribschen, he appears to have seen himself as in competition with Wagner as a composer, dramatist, and music critic. His dilettantish, technically inept music did not impress the Wagners, and was received with considerable scorn by Hans von Bülow. His philosophical writings on music, especially the aphorisms directed against Wagner, need to be reexamined in the light of his lack of musical sophistication and personalization of critical issues; for example, evidence from correspondence shows that his praise of *Carmen* (in *Der Fall Wagner*, 1888) was written less out of conviction than spite against Cosima Wagner, who, like her husband, hated Bizet's opera. *(David Bloom)*

2122
as

VRIESLANDER, Otto. **Das organische in Schuberts Himmlischer Länge** [The organic in Schubert's heavenly length], *Bericht über den internationalen Kongress für Schubertforschung* (Augsburg: Benno Filser, 1929) 221–31. *Illus., facs.* In German. See no. 154 in this volume.

Discusses the musical necessity of the unusual length of the first movements of the piano sonatas in A major, D.959, and in B-flat, D.960.

2123
as

WALLNER, Bo. **Die Nationalromantik im Norden: Die Musik von 1830 bis 1914 in den skandinavischen Ländern** [National Romanticism in the North: Music in Scandinavian countries from

1830 to 1914], *Bericht über den internationalen musikwissenschaftlichen Kongreß* (Kassel: Bärenreiter, 1963) 60–66. In German. See no. 452 in this volume.

Discusses the different developments of musical Romanticism in Sweden, Denmark, Norway, and Finland.

2124
as

WALTER, N. **L'évolution de la musique d'orgue française au XIXe siècle sous l'influence de la musique d'orgue de J.S. Bach** [The evolution of French organ music in the 19th century under the influence of the organ music of J.S. Bach], *Congrés de la Societat Internacional de Musicologia* (Barcelona: Casa de Caritat, 1936). In French. See no. 224 in this volume.

The conference report provides only a citation. Neither the text nor a summary of the paper was published here.

⟶

WERNER, Eric. **Instrumental music outside the pale of Classicism and Romanticism.** See no. 1896 in this volume.

2125
as

WERNER, Eric. **Mendelssohns Kirchenmusik und ihre Stellung im 19. Jahrhundert** [Mendelssohn-Bartholdy's church music and its status in the 19th century], *Bericht über den internationalen musikwissenschaftlichen Kongreß* (Kassel: Bärenreiter, 1963) 207–10. In German. See no. 452 in this volume.

Although Mendelssohn-Bartholdy's religious works exerted a powerful influence on the development of church music in the 19th c., both Protestant and Catholic, they found no permanent place in the liturgical repertoire, primarily because changes in Lutheran practice left no room for music so difficult to perform. This is regrettable, as the best of these works have a theological relevance that is lost in the concert hall. *(David Bloom)*

2126
as

WESTRUP, Jack A. **Die Musik von 1830 bis 1914 in England** [Music in England from 1830 to 1914], *Bericht über den internationalen musikwissenschaftlichen Kongreß* (Kassel: Bärenreiter, 1963) 51–54. In German. See no. 452 in this volume.

Discusses the lack of accomplished composers before Elgar, the maintenance of the choral tradition, the light opera of Sullivan, the influence of Wagner, and the late–19th-c. revival of folk song. *(David Bloom)*

2127
as

WIORA, Walter. **Chopins préludes und études und Bachs** *Wohltemperiertes Klavier* [Chopin's preludes and etudes and Bach's *Das Wohltemperirtes Clavier*], *The book of the first international musicological congress devoted to the works of Frederick Chopin* (Warszawa: Państwowe Wydawnictwo Naukowe, 1963) 73–81. In German. See no. 425 in this volume.

Internal evidence suggests that Chopin's 24 etudes were planned as a sequence of pieces in each of the major and minor keys, like his 24 preludes, and in apparent emulation of the design of the *Wohltemperirtes Clavier*. The nature of Bach's influence on Chopin, in the context of Romantic Bach reception and Chopin's own ambitions, is discussed. The article is reprinted in the author's *Historische und systematische Musikwissenschaft: Ausgewahlte Aufsatze* (Saarbrucken, 1972), cited as RILM [1973] 175. *(David Bloom)*

2128
as

WIORA, Walter. **Die Musik im Weltbild der deutschen Romantik** [Music in the world view of German Romanticism], *Beiträge zur Geschichte der Musikansschauung im 19. Jahrhundert* (Regensburg: Bosse, 1965) 11–50. *Bibliog.* In German. See no. 483 in this volume.

A wide-ranging survey of especially literary and musical creators. The views on music of the German Romantics did not develop into an antithesis of Classic views; in spite of differences, they agreed in many ways with those of the other important thinkers of the age of Goethe: Johann Gottfried Herder, Jean Paul, Hegel, and Goethe himself. *(David Bloom)*

28 Twentieth century — Music and composers

2129 ABRAHAM, Gerald. **Bartók and England,**
as *Studia musicologica Academiae Scientiarum Hungaricae* V (1963) 339–46. See no. 427 in this volume.
Bartók first visited England in 1904, by invitation of Hans Richter, for a performance of his *Kossuth* by the Hallé Orchestra at Manchester, and to give a series of piano performances. Letters from Bartók to his mother (Paula Voit Bartók) describe his experiences and attitudes toward the English. Sample newspaper criticism is included, and Bartók's association with the industrialist Robert Mayer and his wife (Dorothy Moulton, a prominent soprano and champion of contemporary music) is examined. *(Alan Garfield)*

2130 ANDRADE, Mário de. **Os compositores e a**
as **língua nacional** [Composers and the national language], *Anais do Primeiro Congresso da Língua Nacional Cantada* (São Paulo: Departamento Municipal de Cultura, 1938) 97–168. In Portuguese. See no. 253 in this volume.
The relationship between text and music in Brazilian art song is discussed, and the influence of the Portuguese language on composition is assessed.

2131 ANSERMET, Ernest. **Debussy et Robert Godet**
as [Debussy and Robert Godet], *Debussy et l'évolution de la musique au XXe siècle* (Paris: Centre National de la Recherche Scientifique [CNRS], 1965) 339–40. In French. See no. 456 in this volume.
Godet, a worldly and knowledgeable journalist for *Le temps*, enjoyed a close relationship with Debussy, who relied on him in difficult situations. Personal recollections of the two men are included. *(Leonard Horowitz)*

2132 AUSTIN, William W. **Quelques connaissances**
as **et opinions de Schoenberg et Webern sur Debussy** [Some of Schoenberg's and Webern's thoughts and opinions about Debussy], *Debussy et l'évolution de la musique au XXe siècle* (Paris: Centre National de la Recherche Scientifique [CNRS], 1965) 319–31. *Bibliog., charts, diagr.* In French. See no. 456 in this volume.
Webern's opinion of Debussy was more modest and expert than Schoenberg's, which involved more general judgments.

2133 AZEVEDO, Luiz Heitor Corrêa de. **L'influence**
as **de Debussy: Amérique Latine** [Debussy's influence: Latin America], *Debussy et l'évolution de la musique au XXe siècle* (Paris: Centre National de la Recherche Scientifique [CNRS], 1965) 233–38. In French. See no. 456 in this volume.
Debussy is highly esteemed in Brazil, but in general his work has had less influence in South America than in North America. Latin American composers have been concerned with acquiring national musical languages reflecting their own traditional musics. Some composers, such as Villa-Lobos, have adapted elements of Debussy's aesthetics. *(Leonard Horowitz)*

2134 BARTHA, Dénes. **L'influence de Debussy:**
as **Hongrie** [Debussy's influence: Hungary], *Debussy et l'évolution de la musique au XXe siècle* (Paris: Centre National de la Recherche Scientifique [CNRS], 1965) 273–87. In French. See no. 456 in this volume.
Although Bartók visited Paris in 1905, it was Kodály who, after his trip to Paris in 1907, introduced Debussy's music to Bartók. In spite of Kodály's admiration for Debussy, only his early piano works exhibit Debussy's

influence. Such influence is more apparent in Bartók's compositions for string quartet and for orchestra. *(Orly Leah Krasner)*

2135 BEKKU, Sadao. **The composer in Japan today,**
as *Music: East and West* (Tōkyō: conference, 1961) 91–98. See no. 445 in this volume.

2136 BIELAWSKI, Ludwik. **Karol Szymanowski a**
as **muzyka Podhala** [Karol Szymanowski and the Podhale music], *Karol Szymanowski: Księga sesji Naukowej poświęconej twórczości Karola Szymanowskiego* (Warszawa: Uniwersytet Warszawski, Instytut Muzykologii, 1964) 8–21. *Music.* In Polish; summary in English. See no. 458 in this volume.
Szymanowski first used a Górals' (Highlanders') melody (in an incorrectly notated version published by Jan Kleczyński) in his piano variations. *Słopiewnie*, settings of Julian Tuwim's poems, show Szymanowski's deepening interest in Podhale music. In *Harnasie*, traditional music becomes the focal point. Authentic versions of Górals' songs, rhythms of their dances, motives from the Tatra region, and the stylization of folk bands (with the prominent solo part of the fiddler) are woven into the fabric of the work. Szymanowski's last works are less dependent on music of the Górals. *(editor)*

2137 BLOMDAHL, Karl-Birger; BADINGS, Henk.
as **Opera and ballet,** *The modern composer and his world* (Toronto: University of Toronto, 1961) 102–08. See no. 423 in this volume.
Blomdahl's opera *Aniara* (1957-58) and Badings's ballets *Kain* (1956) and *Evolutionen* (1958), which make use of electronic materials, are discussed.

2138 BODNÁR, György. **Bartók et le mouvement**
as *Nyugat* [Bartók and the *Nyugat* movement], *Studia musicologica Academiae Scientiarum Hungaricae* V (1963) 347–54. In French. See no. 427 in this volume.
Bartók frequently contributed critical articles to the avant-garde Hungarian review *Nyugat* (West), founded in 1908. He was a friend of the poet Endre Ady, who was the *Nyugat* movement's unofficial leader. Bartók's settings of Ady texts in the song cycle *Öt dal* (Five songs), op. 16 (1916) are discussed. *(William Renwick)*

⟶ BONDEVILLE, Emmanuel. **La radiophonie et**
la musique contemporaine [The radio and contemporary music]. See no. 5949 in this volume.

2139 BONTEMPELLI, Massimo. **Il nuovo**
as **classicismo della musica moderna** [The new classicism of modern music], *Atti del terzo Congresso internazionale di musica* (Firenze: Le Monnier, 1940) 172–76. In Italian; summaries in French and German. See no. 256 in this volume.
Contends that modern taste is always being constructed; an apparent return to an older style is inevitably a step forward.

2140 BORRIS, Siegfried. **Historische Entwicklungs-**
as **linien der neuen Musik** [Historic tendencies in the development of new music], *Stilkriterien der neuen Musik* (Berlin: Merseburger, 1961) 9–34. *Illus.* In German. See no. 410 in this volume.
Traces the development of new music through 1960 with reference to Satie, Stravinsky, Schoenberg, Berg, and Webern, and the aesthetic theories implied by their work. *(Neill Clegg)*

2141 BOSKOVICH, Alexander Uriah. **Dibrey**
as **haqdamah la'ereb ha'azunah mitẇḥ yṣyrẇtyw** [Introduction to a night with his own creation], *Dẇkan* V (1963) 103–08. In Hebrew. See no. 451 in this volume.

2142
as
BOSKOVICH, Alexander Uriah. **Hasẇwytah hayehẇdyt** [*Semitic suite*], *Dẇkan* IV (1962) 48–52. In Hebrew. See no. 436 in this volume.
Describes the use of traditional elements in the *Semitic suite* (1945).

2143
as
BOSKOVICH, Alexander Uriah. **La musique israélienne contemporaine et les traditions ethniques** [Contemporary Israeli music and ethnic traditions], *Journal of the International Folk Music Council* XVI (1964) 39–42. In French. See no. 463 in this volume.
In its first phase, ca. 1940-50, Israeli art music, influenced by the *Sprachmusik* of revived Hebrew and the instrumental music of the local Arab population, used traditional elements for local color. In 1950-59, a more refined use of traditional Asian material developed, under the influence of Bartók and Stravinsky. Since then, it has become possible to imagine a synthesis between the Western, in the form of the universal language of serial technique, and the Eastern, in a form pared down to its most essential and intimate elements. *(David Bloom)*

2144
as
BUSH, Alan. **Britští skladatelé dneška/ Compositeurs anglais contemporains** [Contemporary British composers], *Hudba národů: Sborník přednášek, proslovených na I. mezinárodním sjezdu skladatelů a hudebních kritiků/Musique des nations: Ier Congrès international des compositeurs et critiques musicaux* (Praha: Syndikát Českých Skladatelů, 1948) 22–24,112–15. In Czech and French. See no. 278 in this volume.
An outline of the history of music in Britain, with particular attention to the 20th-c. lineage of the teachers Frederick Corner, Charles Villiers Stanford, and Alexander Mackenzie, notable for their eclecticism and use of traditional-music material.

2145
as
CARTER, Elliott. **Extending the classical syntax,** *Music: East and West* (Tōkyō: conference, 1961) 126–29. See no. 445 in this volume.
Remarks on the question of renewing musical language in 20th-c. music.

2146
as
CHOJAK, Anna. **Tradycje Szymanowskiego w polskiej muzyce współczesnej** [Szymanowski's traditions in Polish contemporary music], *Karol Szymanowski: Księga sesji Naukowej poświęconej twórczości Karola Szymanowskiego* (Warszawa: Uniwersytet Warszawski, Instytut Muzykologii, 1964) 22–36. *Music.* In Polish; summary in English. See no. 458 in this volume.
Szymanowski's influence on modern Polish composers comes from the ideological and artistic outlook expounded in his writings as well as from the music itself. In the first decade after World War II, the works from Szymanowski's national period exerted the strongest influence. After 1956 the modern, experimental threads in his music were seen as more important. *(editor)*

2147
as
CHOMIŃSKI, Józef Michał. **Szymanowski i muzyka europejska XX wieku** [Szymanowski and 20th-century European music], *Karol Szymanowski: Księga sesji Naukowej poświęconej twórczości Karola Szymanowskiego* (Warszawa: Uniwersytet Warszawski, Instytut Muzykologii, 1964) 37–46. In Polish; summary in English. See no. 458 in this volume.
Szymanowski, like many 20th-c. composers, combined traditional forms with new ideas of tonality and modality. This explains his interest in traditional art as a repository of modal structures. *(editor)*

2148
as
CLEMENTE, Rina di. **Può la spiritualità di Mozart esercitare una funzione nel caos degli indirizzi musicali di oggi?** [Can Mozart's spiritual-ity have a function in today's chaos of musical trends?], *Bericht über den internationalen musikwissenschaftlichen Kongreß Wien Mozartjahr 1956* (Graz; Köln: Böhlau, 1958) 132–33. In Italian. See no. 365 in this volume.
Stravinsky's *The rake's progress* is an example of the use of Mozartean inspiration as a corrective influence, not only against the intellectualism or pseudo-intellectualism of contemporary music but also against the late–19th-c. concept of music drama. *(David Bloom)*

2149
as
CORVER, G.M.A. **Tradition et innovation musicales dans la pensée du compositeur Willem Pijper** [Musical tradition and innovation in the thinking of the composer Willem Pijper], *Actes du cinquième Congrès international d'esthétique/Proceedings of the Fifth International Congress of Aesthetics* ('s-Gravenhage: Mouton, 1964) 171–74. In French. See no. 475 in this volume.
Pijper's journalistic criticism ca. 1920-34, written during his most active period as a composer, was based on the idea that works should be judged without reference to their affiliation with one or another compositional school, but strictly in terms of musical qualities and relationships internal to the work. He regarded Debussy as the central figure in the development of possibilities for music after the disappearance of the classical tonal functions, and viewed the greatness of Bartók and Webern as independent of the ethnomusicological inspiration of the one and the atonal technique of the other. *(David Bloom)*

2150
as
COWELL, Henry. **The composer's world,** *The preservation of traditional forms of the learned and popular music of the Orient and the Occident/La préservation des formes traditionelles de la musique savante et populaire dans les pays d'Orient et d'Occident* (Urbana: Center for Comparative Psycholinguistics, Institute of Communications Research, 1964) 99–113. See no. 443 in this volume.
Composers can no longer isolate themselves in the style or developmental methods of one culture, but must study ideas from diverse sources; one absorbs these in the context of one's other experiences until they become part of one's own unconscious resources. *(Judith Drogichen Meyer)*

2151
as
COWELL, Henry. **Oriental influence on Western music,** *Music: East and West* (Tōkyō: conference, 1961) 71–76. See no. 445 in this volume.

2152
as
CROSSLEY-HOLLAND, Peter. **Music of the Occidental type written by Orientals,** *The preservation of traditional forms of the learned and popular music of the Orient and the Occident/La préservation des formes traditionelles de la musique savante et populaire dans les pays d'Orient et d'Occident* (Urbana: Center for Comparative Psycholinguistics, Institute of Communications Research, 1964) 114–24. See no. 443 in this volume.
Western-style art music is now being created successfully in Asia with indigenous materials, particularly in Japan. Asian melody has a modal character and rhythmic freedom that are severely restricted by the application of Western harmony; it is more compatible with the use of modified serial technique. Chamber ensembles are a good medium, and forms reflect a predilection for extemporizing coupled with prescribed forms. *(Michael Collier)*

2153
as
D'AMICO, Fedele. **Il compositore moderno e il linguaggio musicale** [The contemporary composer and musical language], *Atti del quinto Congresso di musica* (Firenze: Barbèra, 1948) 11–23. In Italian. See no. 285 in this volume.
In the past, social function dictated the characteristics of music; today, they are governed by composers living in isolation. The upheavals of the century have fostered tyranny, violence, immorality, and war, leading to an

inevitable decline in artistic excellence. Atonal music causes the disintegration of musical language, while the isolation of the composer precludes innovation. Only social and moral reform can rescue a jeopardized culture. *(Channan Willner)*

2154
as
DEMÉNY, János. **Béla Bartóks Stellung in der Musikgeschichte des 20. Jahrhunderts** [Bela Bartók's position in music history of the 20th century], *Studia musicologica Academiae Scientiarum Hungaricae* V (1963) 403–14. In German. See no. 427 in this volume.

Outlines Bartók's contributions as composer, virtuoso pianist, and ethnomusicologist, with a chronological overview of his most important compositions. Another version is published in *Universitas* XXXIV (1979) and cited as RILM [1979]4899. *(William Renwick)*

⟶
DILLE, Denijs. **Peter Benoit en de nieuwe muziek** [Peter Benoît and the new music]. See no. 1944 in this volume.

2155
as
DILLE, Denijs. **Les problèmes des recherches sur Bartók** [Problems of Bartók research], *Studia musicologica Academiae Scientiarum Hungaricae* V (1963) 415–23. In French. See no. 427 in this volume.

A review of outstanding issues in the study of Bartók's biography, iconography, correspondence, and compositions, with attention to the influence of Hungarian culture on his works. *(William Renwick)*

2156
as
DOBIÁŠ, Václav; FELDBRILL, Victor; SCHULLER, Gunther. **Composer and performer,** *The modern composer and his world* (Toronto: University of Toronto, 1961) 35–46. See no. 423 in this volume.

There should be close links among composers, performers, critics, and musicologists. Composers must always ask themselves whether their music is practical for the performers and whether it is truly adapted to the instrument. *(Dorothy Gray)*

2157
as
DRESDEN, Sem. **L'influence de la musique moderne française aux Pays-Bas** [The influence of modern French music in the Low Countries], *Actes du Congrès d'histoire de l'art: Compte rendu analytique* (Paris: Presses Universitaires de France, 1922) 102. In French. See no. 95 in this volume.

Summary of a paper.

2158
as
DUTILLEUX, Henri; MYCIELSKI, Zygmunt; REGAMEY, Constantin; SCHULLER, Gunther. **Some other paths,** *The modern composer and his world* (Toronto: University of Toronto, 1961) 77–101. See no. 423 in this volume.

Discusses alternatives to serialism in 20th-c. music.

2159
as
ELSNER, Jürgen. **Der Einfluß der Arbeitermusikbewegung auf die Kampfmusik Hanns Eislers** [The influence of the workers' music movement on Hanns Eisler's songs of struggle], *Beiträge zur Musikwissenschaft* VI/4 (1964) 301–06. In German. See no. 476 in this volume.

Eisler's so-called *Kampfmusik* or music of struggle, consisting of songs in popular style on revolutionary and socialist themes written in the 1920s and 1930s, is grounded in the German Arbeitermusikbewegung of the earlier 20th c. *(David Bloom)*

2160
as
ENGELMANN, Hans Ulrich. **Fragen seriellen Kompositionsverfahren** [Questions of serial compositional procedure], *Bericht über den internationalen musikwissenschaftlichen Kongreß*

(Kassel: Bärenreiter, 1963) 374–79. In German. See no. 452 in this volume.

Discusses the wide variation found in the aesthetic and philosophic content of music using serial techniques, according to the goals of the individual composer. *(David Bloom)*

2161
as
ERPF, Hermann. **Orgel und zeitgenössische Musik** [The organ and contemporary music], *Bericht über die [I] Freiburger Tagung für Deutsche Orgelkunst* (Augsburg: Bärenreiter, 1926) 134–38. In German. See no. 122 in this volume.

A new musical style, not yet adopted in church music, is identified by a tense melodic structure using wide intervals; a free chord structure not bound to functional harmony; the free exploitation of tonal space; individualization of color in horizontal and vertical dimensions; liberation of rhythm from regular beat schemes; and the linking of voices on a rhythmic rather than harmonic basis. An appropriate organ for this music is the Oskalyd cinema organ developed by the Walcker firm on the basis of ideas of Hans Luedtke. *(David Bloom)*

2162
as
FÉDOROV, Vladimir. **Debussy, vu par quelques Russes** [Debussy, viewed by some Russians], *Debussy et l'évolution de la musique au XXe siècle* (Paris: Centre National de la Recherche Scientifique [CNRS], 1965) 199–214. In French. See no. 456 in this volume.

Among Russians, there is a certain denial of Debussy's influence on Russian music. A roundtable discussion explores Russian and French influences on each other's music. *(Nanette Jew)*

2163
as
FEGERS, Karl. **Arbeit im Dienste der Jugend- und Volksmusik: Eine Selbstdarstellung** [Work in the service of youth music and traditional music: A self-portrait], *Studien zur Musikgeschichte der Stadt Mönchengladbach* (Köln: Volk, 1965) 105–10. *List of works.* In German. See no. 486 in this volume.

Provides a brief autobiography of the composer and pedagogue, with attention to his work with the Mönchengladbach Stadtarbeitsgemeinschaft für Jugend- und Volksmusik and the 1959 founding of the city's Musikschule. A list of compositions for concert, amateur, and church performance is appended. *(David Bloom)*

2164
as
FRANCÈS, Robert. **La musique moderne et l'auditeur** [Modern music and the listener], *Visages et perspectives de l'art moderne: Peinture, poésie, musique* (Paris: Centre National de la Recherche Scientifique [CNRS], 1956) 163–74. In French. See no. 341 in this volume.

The music-loving public does not in general appreciate modern music. The work of artists, however, must be independent of the public's view of it; composers should believe themselves free to create what they wish. According to the results of psychological tests, the more tonal a piece of music is, the better it is remembered, regardless of the listener's level or type of education. The organizational framework governing a piece of music directly affects the listener's comprehension. *(Susan Poliniak)*

2165
as
FROMMEL, Gerhard. **Tonalitätsprobleme der neuen Musik vom Standpunkt des Komponisten** [Problems of tonality in new music from the standpoint of the composer], *Bericht über den internationalen musikwissenschaftlichen Kongreß* (Kassel: Bärenreiter, 1963) 367–70. In German. See no. 452 in this volume.

Contemporary composers may be divided into two groups on the basis of their attitudes toward tonality. Absolutely atonal composers absolutely reject tonality, leading to a tendency to uniformity in spite of the apparent pluralism in compositional technique. Genuinely pluralistic composers reject dogma and see different kinds of tonality as a rich, not exhausted, field of possibilities. *(David Bloom)*

HISTORICAL MUSICOLOGY

2166
as
GASTOUÉ, Amédée. **La musique religieuse française contemporaine** [Contemporary French religious music], *Congrès régional de liturgie et de musique sacrée* (Moselle: Orphelins-Apprentis Guénange, 1923) 115–34. In French. See no. 98 in this volume.

Discusses the reforms formulated in Pius X's motu proprio *Tra le sollecitudini* (1903), while also addressing 19th-c. proposals for reform, foundational principles of a *schola*, the function of church leaders and composers, and the role of the cantique in church music. *(Murat Eyüboğlu)*

2167
as
GERMAN, Franciszek. **Powstanie listopadowe w muzyce polskiej** [The November Revolution in Polish music], *Ryszard Wagner a polska kultura muzyczna/Richard Wagner und die polnische Musikkultur* (Katowice: Panstwowa Wyzsza Szkola Muzyczna, 1964) 23–38. In Polish; summary in German. See no. 466 in this volume.

The November Revolution (1917) in Europe was an offshoot of the Russian Revolution in that same year. Its impact on Polish music in the 20th c. is traced.

2168
as
GERVAIS, Françoise. **L'influence de Debussy: France** [Debussy's influence: France], *Debussy et l'évolution de la musique au XXᵉ siècle* (Paris: Centre National de la Recherche Scientifique [CNRS], 1965) 269–72. In French. See no. 456 in this volume.

Initially Debussy's influence in France was slight, but eventually the lightness and transparency of his harmony influenced almost all French music. Messiaen's colorings and rhythmic diversity make him Debussy's most direct successor. *(Leonard Horowitz)*

2169
as
GHISI, Federico. **Le influenze "ultramontane" e la musica europea** [Ultramontane influences and European music], *Atti del quinto Congresso di musica* (Firenze: Barbèra, 1948) 153–55. In Italian. See no. 285 in this volume.

Italian music is increasingly subject to continental European influences. While the public favors music that conforms to tradition, musicians prefer sophisticated works that manipulate sounds ingeniously but lack expression. Composers of necessity avail themselves of contemporary techniques, but the means have become an end, and the music has been rendered immobile. Current tendencies are cryptic and sterile; a more human music is called for—with more substantial ideas, greater sincerity, and an expressive simplicity. Italian composers have recently shown an inclination to write expressively. It remains to be seen how influential this trend will be. *(Channan Willner)*

2170
as
GHISLANZONI, Alberto. **Influenze favorevoli e sfavorevoli dei moderni studi storici e musicologici sugli indirizzi estetici e tecnici della creazione musicale di oggi** [Favorable and unfavorable influences of modern historical and musicological studies on the aesthetic and technical directions of contemporary musical creation], *Bericht über den internationalen musikwissenschaftlichen Kongreß Wien Mozartjahr 1956* (Graz; Köln: Böhlau, 1958) 227–29. In Italian. See no. 365 in this volume.

Advancements in the understanding of Eastern musical traditions and of Western art music from Gregorian chant through the Baroque have provided 20th-c. composers with historical reference points for abandoning the tonality of the 18th and 19th c. in favor of a chaotically fragmentary, ultraindividualistic, phenomenological compositional practice. Rightly understood, musicological research would supply a solid basis for reconstructing that which has been destroyed. *(David Bloom)*

2171
as
GOLDSCHMIDT, Harry. **Nochmals: Janáček und Strawinski—Diskussionsbeitrag/Ještě jednou: Janáček a Stravinskij—Diskusní příspěvek** [Once again: Janáček and Stravin-

sky—Contribution to discussion], *Leoš Janáček a soudobá hudba* (Praha: Panton, 1963) 111–16. In German and Czech. See no. 389 in this volume.

Response to the paper abstracted as no. 2223 in this volume.

2172
as
GORCZYCKA, Monika. **Wpływy idealogii twórczej Szymanowskiego na kompoztorów polskich dwudziestolecia międzywojennego** [Szymanowski's influence on Polish composers of the pre-war period], *Karol Szymanowski: Księga sesji Naukowej poświęconej twórczości Karola Szymanowskiego* (Warszawa: Uniwersytet Warszawski, Instytut Muzykologii, 1964) 86–108. *Music.* In Polish; summary in English. See no. 458 in this volume.

Szymanowski's influence on Polish composers between 1919 and 1939 stemmed from his recognized authority on aesthetic problems in composition and from his activities as a composer. He was inspired by the traditional art of the Tatra Highlanders (the Górals) and to a lesser degree by Kurpian folk art. Younger composers were attracted to these and other cultures (including more distant Asian music), but they were mainly interested in their rhythmic peculiarities rather than the melodic elements (as Szymanowski was). Gradually, with the ideology of the new realism and the neoclassicism of Les Six, Polish composers parted from Szymanowski's aesthetic outlook. *(editor)*

2173
as
GRADENWITZ, Peter. **Reihenkomposition im Orient** [Serial composition in Asia], *Bericht über den internationalen musikwissenschaftlichen Kongreß Wien Mozartjahr 1956* (Graz; Köln: Böhlau, 1958) 238–41. In German. See no. 365 in this volume.

Melodic and rhythmic row concepts figure frequently in Asian musical traditions. Modern Asian composers using Western-style serial techniques include Yoritsune Matsudaira in Japan, Roman Haubenstock-Ramati and Yizhak Sadai in Israel, and Cemal Reşit Rey in Turkey. *(David Bloom)*

2174
as
GUERRINI, Guido. **Il tramonto di due gloriose espressioni del linguaggio musicale** [The demise of two glorious devices of musical language], *Atti del quinto Congresso di musica* (Firenze: Barbèra, 1948) 45–51. In Italian. See no. 285 in this volume.

Music can be articulated through the use of cadences and modulations. Their exclusion from 12-tone and polytonal techniques renders compositions incomprehensible to the uninitiated listener. Twelve-tone techniques, therefore, have failed to gain popularity. With the onset of a period of peace and serenity, composers may perhaps write more intelligibly and bring about a renaissance of cadences and modulations. *(Channan Willner)*

2175
as
HAMILTON, Iain. **The university and the composing profession: Prospects and problems,** *American Society of University Composers: Proceedings of the 1966 conference* (New York: American Society of University Composers, 1966). See no. 510 in this volume.

The university composer faces the danger of becoming bogged down. The tenured situation is unnatural and takes one out of the competitive field. In Europe composers make their living from a variety of sources; they have the advantages of publishing and national radio. The American university composer must teach courses at all levels, find time to compose, and maintain contact with the outside music world. *(Judith Drogichen Meyer)*

2176
as
HAMILTON, Iain; KRENEK, Ernst; ROCHBERG, George. **Serialism,** *The modern composer and his world* (Toronto: University of Toronto, 1961) 49–76. See no. 423 in this volume.

Among the topics discussed is the notion that the concept of duration is as much negated in total serialism as it is in aleatory music. *(Dorothy Gray)*

2177
as
HELM, Everett. **Janáčkovo postavení ve vývoji novodobé hudby** [Janáček's place in the evolution of contemporary music], *Leoš Janáček a soudobá hudba*

(Praha: Panton, 1963) 123–23. In Czech. See no. 389 in this volume.

2178
as
HELMAN, Zofia. **Wpływ Chopina na wczesną twórczość Karola Szymanowskiego** [Chopin's influence on the early works of Karol Szymanowski], *The book of the first international musicological congress devoted to the works of Frederick Chopin* (Warszawa: Państwowe Wydawnictwo Naukowe, 1963) 300–03. In Polish. See no. 425 in this volume.

2179
as
HELMAN, Zofia. **Z zagadnień warsztatu twórczego Karola Szymanowskiego na materiale jego szkiców** [Szymanowski's compositional technique in light of his sketches], *Karol Szymanowski: Księga sesji Naukowej poświęconej twórczości Karola Szymanowskiego* (Warszawa: Uniwersytet Warszawski, Instytut Muzykologii, 1964) 109–25. *Facs., music.* In Polish; summary in English. See no. 458 in this volume.

Based on an analysis of the initial sketches of some of the mazurkas, op. 50, the *Métopes*, op. 29, the Stabat Mater, op. 53, and the second violin concerto, op. 61, certain conclusions can be drawn. Szymanowski used the piano during the composition of all works, including orchestral music. Initial ideas were written down and distributed in the composition before the entire plan had been constructed. Materials were usually shaped in the sketch in their ultimate form, with no important changes introduced in the final MS. Melody and harmony play a dominant role in the creative process, while metric and rhythmic schemes are assigned parts of varying importance depending on the character of the composition. Szymanowski made no indications as to agogics, articulation or dynamic stress on the sketches. Nor did he apply any rigid principles to formal construction; the structure of a work evolved during the course of composition. *(editor)*

2180
as
HIRASHIMA, Masao. **The composer in Japan today,** *Music: East and West* (Tōkyō: conference, 1961) 99–106. See no. 445 in this volume.

⟶
HOFMAN, Shlomo. **La musique arabe en Israel: Sa préservation, sa rénovation** [Arab music in Israel: Its preservation, its renovation]. See no. 2637 in this volume.

2181
as
HOLMBOE, Vagn; BERIO, Luciano. **Form,** *The modern composer and his world* (Toronto: University of Toronto, 1961) 134–47. See no. 423 in this volume.

Discusses Holmboe's principle of metamorphosis and Umberto Eco's theory of the open work as applied to Berio's *Thema (Omaggio a Joyce)* (1958). *(Dorothy Gray)*

2182
as
HOWES, Frank Stewart. **The influence of folk music on modern English composition,** *Journal of the International Folk Music Council* V (1953) 52–54. See no. 314 in this volume.

Discusses composers from the 1840s to the present.

2183
as
IWASZKIEWICZ, Jarosław. **Karol Szymanowski a literatura** [Karol Szymanowski and literature], *Karol Szymanowski: Księga sesji Naukowej poświęconej twórczości Karola Szymanowskiego* (Warszawa: Uniwersytet Warszawski, Instytut Muzykologii, 1964) 126–35. In Polish; summary in English. See no. 458 in this volume.

Szymanowski was both a connoisseur of literature and a writer himself. As a reader, his tastes included Schopenhauer and Nietzsche. The texts he selected for his compositions included Vienna Secession literature, Young Poland poets, and, during the last period of his creative life, folk poetry. As a writer, his mastery can best be seen in his essays on music. However, he also wrote a novel, *Ephebos* (unpublished). *(editor)*

2184
as
JAROCIŃSKI, Stefan. **L'influence de Debussy: Pologne** [Debussy's influence: Poland], *Debussy et l'évolution de la musique au XXᵉ siècle* (Paris: Centre National de la Recherche Scientifique [CNRS], 1965) 313–14. In French. See no. 456 in this volume.

After Chopin, Polish music remained under the influence of German traditions. Szymanowski was the first to awaken Polish music from its lethargy; he was strongly influenced by Debussy's music. *(Leonard Horowitz)*

2185
as
JIRÁNEK, Jaroslav. **K některým otázkám vztahu Leoše Janáčka k české a světové hudbě** [Questions on Janáček's relation to Czech and world music], *Leoš Janáček a soudobá hudba* (Praha: Panton, 1963) 155–61. In Czech; summaries in Russian and German. See no. 389 in this volume.

Janáček's new approach to folk music, based on psychological interpretation of traditional song as opposed to its romantic idealization, is compared with that of Smetana, Dvořák, and Musorgskij, and discussed in the context of different social-historical developments in Bohemia and the composer's native Moravia. His specific monothematicism reflects principles of folk variation and figuration technique of Moravian folk bands. *(editors)*

2186
as
JURRES, André. **Dutch musical composition in the middle of our century,** *Actes du cinquième Congrès international d'esthétique/Proceedings of the Fifth International Congress of Aesthetics* ('s-Gravenhage: Mouton, 1964) 15–17. See no. 475 in this volume.

2187
as
KACZYŃSKI, Tadeusz. **Zagadnienie autonomiczności i nieautonomiczności muzyki na przkładzie twórczości Karola Szymanowskiego** [Autonomous and non-autonomous music in Szymanowski's output], *Karol Szymanowski: Księga sesji Naukowej poświęconej twórczości Karola Szymanowskiego* (Warszawa: Uniwersytet Warszawski, Instytut Muzykologii, 1964) 136–41. In Polish; summary in English. See no. 458 in this volume.

Out of 62 opus numbers, only ten of Szymanowski's works are nonprogrammatic (not precluding concealed programmatic elements): the preludes, op. 1; the variations in B-flat minor, op. 3; the studies op. 4; the piano sonatas opp. 8, 21, and 36; the violin sonata, op. 9; the symphony op. 19; and the two string quartets, opp. 37 and 56. Among extramusical associations in his other works, the most important are literary, either in the form of vocal texts, or as the subjects of instrumental program music. The world of the theater also provides ample material, as evidenced by works such as *Król Roger* and *Harnasie*. *(editor)*

2188
as
KÁRPÁTI, János. **Béla Bartók and the East,** *Music east and west* (Nai Dilli: Indian Council for Cultural Relations, 1966) 90–96. See no. 489 in this volume.

Discusses Bartók's encounters with Arab, Turkish, Chinese, and Balinese music. Unlike earlier European composers, he used Eastern elements in his works on the basis of a scientifically cultivated understanding. *(Laurence Morell)*

2189
as
KELLER, Hermann. **Die deutsche Orgelmusik nach Reger** [German organ music after Reger], *Bericht über die [I] Freiburger Tagung für Deutsche Orgelkunst* (Augsburg: Bärenreiter, 1926) 130–33. In German. See no. 122 in this volume.

A Reger tradition has been maintained by some of his pupils, many of whom also studied organ with Karl Straube: Joser Haas, Karl Hasse, Karl Hoyer, and Arno Landmann; others, such as Hermann Grabner and Adolf Busch, avoid Reger's chromaticism. Two paths away from Reger's style are represented by Heinrich Kaminski's rejection of emotionalism and by the symphonic organ style of Franz Schmidt, Friedrich Klose, and Joseph Meßner. Music reflecting the influence of new religious attitudes is composed in the Roman Catholic tradition by Joseph Renner, the younger, and by Franz Philipp; the urgent need for music of similar quality for the Protestant liturgy is not being met. *(David Bloom)*

2190
as
KERÉNYI, György; RAJECZKY, Benjamin. **Über Bartóks Volksliedaufzeichnungen** [On Bartók's transcription of traditional songs], *Studia musicologica Academiae Scientiarum Hungaricae* V (1963) 441–48. *Facs., transcr.* In German. See no. 427 in this volume.

Comments on metronome indications, rhythmic notation, and annotations in Bartók's ethnomusicological field transcriptions. *(William Renwick)*

⟶ KIRBY, Percival R. **The use of European musical techniques by the non-European peoples of southern Africa.** See no. 2003 in this volume.

2191
as
KÖHLER, Siegfried. **Gestaltungsprinzipien Händels in der sozialistischen Vokalsinfonik** [Händelian structural principles in socialist symphonic-vocal music], *Händel-Ehrung der Deutschen Demokratischen Republik: Konferenzbericht* (Leipzig: VEB Deutscher Verlag für Musik, 1961) 265–71. *Mus.* In German. See no. 408 in this volume.

Examples are drawn from Eisler's *Lenin* (1935-37), Šostakovič's *Pesn' o lesah* (1949), and Ernst Hermann Meyer's *Mansfelder Oratorium* (1950). *(David Bloom)*

2192
as
KOIZUMI, Fumio. **Contemporary music in Occidental style and its problems in Japan,** *The preservation of traditional forms of the learned and popular music of the Orient and the Occident/La préservation des formes traditionelles de la musique savante et populaire dans les pays d'Orient et d'Occident* (Urbana: Center for Comparative Psycholinguistics, Institute of Communications Research, 1964) 184–89. See no. 443 in this volume.

In the hundred years since Western music was introduced to Japan, Japanese composers have been making efforts to compose it with Japanese material. The application of Western harmony to Japanese melody destroys the essential character of the latter. Shūkichi Mitsukuri was one of the first composers to avoid this, by the development of new systems of harmony and counterpoint. Meanwhile, the breakdown of major-minor tonality in the West has alleviated the problem; serial and musique concrète techniques are now used in Japan. Traditional music continues to be taught alongside Western music in schools. *(Michael Collier)*

2193
as
KOMMA, Karl Michael. **Volksmusikalische Grundlagen des Kompositionsstils der letzten Jahrzehnte in Böhmen und Mähren** [The compositional style in Bohemia and Moravia during recent decades, and its roots in traditional music], *Bericht über den Internationalen musikwissenschaftlichen Kongress* (Kassel: Bärenreiter, 1954) 203–06. In German. See no. 319 in this volume.

Traces the reception of Czech and German music and traditions by composers in Bohemia and Moravia, and distinguishes the response of the ethnic German composers from that of the Czechs. Until the middle of the 19th c. both ethnic groups shared a compositional style. Thereafter the ethnic Germans continued to follow the avant-garde trends emanating from Germany and Austria; whatever interest they had in local ethnic German traditional music did not influence their composing. On the other hand, ethnic German composers were always influenced by the surrounding Czech traditional music, and this influence remains noticeable in the music of refugees who were driven from their homeland after World War II and settled in Germany. The much more important musical contributions of the Czech composers from Smetana to Janáček and beyond have been directly nurtured by Czech and other Slavic traditional musics. *(Carl Skoggard)*

2194
as
KREMLËV, Julij Anatol'evič. **L'influence de Debussy: Russie** [Debussy's influence: Russia], *Debussy et l'évolution de la musique au XX*ᵉ *siècle* (Paris: Centre National de la Recherche Scientifique [CNRS], 1965) 315–18. In French. See no. 456 in this volume.

2195
as
KROMOLICKI, Josef. **Zum Stil des neuen Kirchenmusikalischen Schaffens** [On the style of new works of sacred music], *Bericht über den I. musikwissenschaftlichen Kongress der Deutschen Musikgesellschaft in Leipzig* (Wiesbaden: Breitkopf & Härtel, 1926) 321. In German. See no. 120 in this volume.

A summary of an article published in *Musica sacra* VIII-IX (Regensburg, 1925), *Musica divina* III (Wien, 1925), *Gregoriusblatt* IX-X (Düsseldorf, 1925), and in *Cäcilienvereinsorgan* (Paderborn, 1925). The effects of the motu proprio *Tra le sollecitudini* (1903) of Pius X and a new interest in Gregorian chant and the style of Palestrina are discussed. *(William Renwick)*

2196
as
LE CAINE, Hugh; TAL, Josef; USSACHEVSKY, Vladimir. **Synthetic means,** *The modern composer and his world* (Toronto: University of Toronto, 1961) 109–33. See no. 423 in this volume.

The potential of electronic music is discussed.

2197
as
LÉBL, Vladimír. **Postavení osobnosti Leoše Janáčka v české hudební kultuře** [The place of Janáček's personality in Czech musical culture], *Leoš Janáček a soudobá hudba* (Praha: Panton, 1963) 198–201. In Czech; summaries in Russian and German. See no. 389 in this volume.

Janáček's position in the history of Czech music is compared with those of his predecessors Smetana and Dvořák and his contemporaries Josef Bohuslav Foerster, Vítězslav Novák, Otakar Ostrčil, and Josef Suk. With the latter four he shares the inspiration of Moravian and Slovak traditional music, and some compositional means, but his personality is incomparable with any other composer in several respects: his deep respect for Moravian culture, his anti-Romanticism, and his extreme striving for the faithful reflection of reality. *(editors)*

2198
as
LECHTHALER, Josef. **Die stilistischen Strömungen in der Kirchenmusik der Nachkriegszeit** [Stylistic currents in the church music of the postwar period], *Beethoven-Zentenarfeier: Internationaler musikhistorischer Kongress* (Wien: Universal, 1927) 257–59. In German. See no. 142 in this volume.

German and Austrian composers writing music for Roman Catholic liturgical use after World War I can be divided into three groups: those influenced primarily by the Cecilian movement and 16th-c. polyphony; those following the lead of composers from the beginning of the 20th c., including Max Reger and Mahler; and those working within the tradition of Viennese Classicism. An extended version is published in *Katholisches Kirchenmusik-Jahrbuch* I (Kronach, Bavaria, 1927). *(David Bloom)*

2199
as
LEGLEY, Victor; FRANKENSTEIN, Alfred; KUHARSKIJ, Vasilij. **Composer and public,** *The modern composer and his world* (Toronto: University of Toronto, 1961) 3–16. See no. 423 in this volume.

The public and the composer are both responsible for the gap between the public and modern music. The music world, including the composer, must try to bridge this gap. Today's critic must remain curious about new music, and must be more concerned with the composition than with the performer. *(Dorothy Gray)*

2200
as
LEMACHER, Heinrich. **Neue Kirchenmusik** [New church music], *Zweiter internationaler Kongress für katholische Kirchenmusik: Zu Ehren des Heiligen Papstes Pius X* (Wien: conference, 1955) 260–64. In German. See no. 339 in this volume.

In recent years many distinguished composers not specializing in church music have written music that is appropriate for the Roman Catholic worship service, including Stravinsky, Hindemith, Messiaen, Kaspar Roeseling, Anton Heiller, Oswald Jaeggi, Johann Baptist Hilber, Franz Krieg, Hermann Schroeder, Ernst Tittel, Joseph Ahrens, Joseph Haas, Georg Trexler, Goffredo Petrassi, Josef Lechthaler, and Leif Kayser. Church music is necessarily different from concert music, but should not be closed to modern developments. *(David Bloom)*

2201 LESURE, François. **Debussy et Edgard Varèse**
as [Debussy and Edgard Varèse], *Debussy et l'évolution de la musique au XXe siècle* (Paris: Centre National de la Recherche Scientifique [CNRS], 1965) 333–38. In French. See no. 456 in this volume.
Discusses correspondence between Debussy and Varèse between 1909 and 1916. Varèse introduced Debussy to the atonal works of Schoenberg.

(Orly Leah Krasner)

2202 LÉVY, Roland Alexis Manuel (Roland-Manuel).
as **Tradition permanente** [Permanent tradition], *Debussy et l'évolution de la musique au XXe siècle* (Paris: Centre National de la Recherche Scientifique [CNRS], 1965) 27–32. In French. See no. 456 in this volume.

2203 LIEBNER, János. **Ein verschollenes Werk von**
as **Béla Bartók** [A forgotten work by Béla Bartók], *Bericht über den internationalen musikwissenschaftlichen Kongreß* (Kassel: Bärenreiter, 1963) 315–17. In German. See no. 452 in this volume.
The suite op. 14 consisted originally of five rather than four movements; a copy of the withdrawn movement, an andante, was made by Bartók's former pupil Irene Egri, and has been found in her possession. Reasons for its withdrawal, in the context of the composer's life circumstances in 1914-18, are discussed. *(David Bloom)*

2204 LIESS, Andreas. **Das Sakrale in der profanen**
as **Gegenwartsmusik** [Sacral qualities in secular contemporary music], *Zweiter internationaler Kongress für katholische Kirchenmusik: Zu Ehren des Heiligen Papstes Pius X* (Wien: conference, 1955) 269–71. In German. See no. 339 in this volume.
The period beginning with works by Stravinsky, Hindemith, Honegger, and Orff of the late 1920s and early 1930s has seen much important concert music of a spiritual, mystical, metaphysical, or general religious inspiration, no less religious than music composed for explicitly liturgical purposes. *(David Bloom)*

2205 LINDLAR, Heinrich. **Debussysmen beim**
as **frühen Strawinsky** [Debussyisms in early Stravinsky], *Bericht über den internationalen musikwissenschaftlichen Kongreß* (Kassel: Bärenreiter, 1963) 252–53. In German. See no. 452 in this volume.
With the possible exception of the first act (1909) of *Le rossignol*, most of the so-called Debussyisms of Stravinsky's early work are really examples of influences that both composers absorbed independently of one another from Russia and from the Far East. Examples of their mutual disrespect and important formal differences in their compositional styles are discussed. *(Leslie B. Dunner)*

2206 LISSA, Zofia. **Szymanowski a romantyzm**
as [Szymanowski and Romanticism], *Karol Szymanowski: Księga sesji Naukowej poświęconej twórczości Karola Szymanowskiego* (Warszawa: Uniwersytet Warszawski, Instytut Muzykologii, 1964) 161–76. In Polish; summary in English. See no. 458 in this volume.
Szymanowski's anti-Romantic artistic credo, expressed in his writings, is at odds with his decidedly Romantic music.

2207 LOCKSPEISER, Edward. **L'influence de De-**
as **bussy: Angleterre** [Debussy's influence: England], *Debussy et l'évolution de la musique au XXe siècle*

(Paris: Centre National de la Recherche Scientifique [CNRS], 1965) 239–40. In French. See no. 456 in this volume.
Debussy influenced English music through the use of chordal ambiguity, particularly involving seventh and ninth chords. Two English composers influenced by Debussy are Cyril Scott and Benjamin Britten.

(Leonard Horowitz)

2208 LUALDI, Adriano. **La ballata della morte e una**
as **parolina di Aristotele** [The ballad of death and a little word of Aristotle], *Atti del quinto Congresso di musica* (Firenze: Barbèra, 1948) 140–46. In Italian. See no. 285 in this volume.
Attempts to define musical ugliness are likened to a question that Aristotle was asked regarding his preference for handsome men. The answer was, in effect, that only the blind would ask such a question; only the insensitive would fail to recognize the severe crisis that has overwhelmed the arts since the turn of the 20th c. *(Channan Willner)*

2209 MAINE, Basil. **Some effects of mechanized**
as **music,** *Atti del primo Congresso internazionale di musica* (Firenze: Le Monnier, 1935) 84–93. Summary in Italian. See no. 203 in this volume.
Offers a critical view of recording technology's influence on performance standards, particularly the concept of virtuosity, and audiences.

2210 MANTELLI, Alberto. **L'influence de Debussy:**
as **Italie** [Debussy's influence: Italy], *Debussy et l'évolution de la musique au XXe siècle* (Paris: Centre National de la Recherche Scientifique [CNRS], 1965) 289–90. In French. See no. 456 in this volume.
Debussy's innovations influenced developments in Italian opera.

2211 MANTELLI, Alberto. **Problemi di linguaggio**
as **nell'opera di Strawinsky** [Questions of language in the works of Stravinsky], *Atti del quinto Congresso di musica* (Firenze: Barbèra, 1948) 97–105. In Italian. See no. 285 in this volume.
The works of Stravinsky entered the European mainstream by 1910. While absorbing the major characteristics of Western music, these works also reached the breaking point of tonality and showed great technical originality: dense chromaticism, organization of hitherto unexplored tonal resources, feverishly animated expressionism, and impressionism. Stylistic diversity and conciseness of expression were also evident. Dissonant elements of popular music and archaic techniques were adventurously transformed. The intellectual and cultural inclinations of Stravinsky's creative process and his use of stylistic transplants for poetic expression characterize his musical language. *(Channan Willner)*

2212 MASSANA, Antoni. **La moderna música sa-**
as **grada** [Modern religious music], *V Congreso Nacional de Música Sagrada* (Madrid: Gráficas Dos de Mayo, 1956) 205–09. In Spanish. See no. 331 in this volume.
Contemporary music, even in religious genres, is excessively dry, in contrast to the emotionality of the old polyphony and Gregorian chant. Modern religious music should return to this emotionality, all the more in that it has more resources than the music of the past. *(José López-Calo)*

2213 MAYUZUMI, Toshiro. **Traditional elements as**
as **a creative source for composition,** *Journal of the International Folk Music Council* XVI (1964) 38–39. See no. 463 in this volume.
An acoustic study of cylindrical Japanese temple bells provided material for the author's *Nehan kōkyōkoku* (Nirvana symphony, 1958) and a tone row for his *Mandala* symphony (1960). It is difficult in practical terms, and unnecessary, to use Japanese traditional instruments in Western-style music. Their characteristic sounds can be reproduced on Western instruments, using slap pizzicato on the cello, for example, to imitate the shamisen, or bowed-string glissandi for the portamento effect of the hichiriki. It will be

particularly important for Japanese composers to develop a precise microtonal notation. *(David Bloom)*

2214 MILA, Massimo. **La musica e il linguaggio musicale** [Music and musical language], *Atti del quinto Congresso di musica* (Firenze: Barbèra, 1948) 25–33. In Italian. See no. 285 in this volume.

Musical language has a syntax through which it brings together harmony, counterpoint, tonality, mode, melody, and rhythm. In examining these components it is necessary to consider the totality of the musical synthesis. René Leibowitz failed to do this in *Schönberg et son école*, a work that otherwise lucidly analyzes the recent history of musical language.

(Channan Willner)

2215 MOREUX, Serge. **Réproduction mécanique du son et création musicale** [Mechanical sound reproduction and musical creation], *Cahiers d'études de radio-télévision* 3-4 (1955) 331–34. In French. See no. 334 in this volume.

A brief critique of the technology's influence on contemporary musical aesthetics.

2216 NEST'EV, Izrail' Vladimirovič. **Bela Bartok v Rossii** [Béla Bartók in Russia], *Studia musicologica Academiae Scientiarum Hungaricae* V (1963) 481–90. In Russian. See no. 427 in this volume.

Discusses Bartók's reception in the Soviet Union on his 1928-29 visit, with particular attention to the response of Boris Asaf'ev.

2217 NESTLER, Gerhard. **Ästhetische Grundlagen des Sing- und Instrumentalstils in der Musik der Gegenwart** [Aesthetic principles of vocal and instrumental style in the music of the present], *Bericht über den Internationalen musikwissenschaftlichen Kongress* (Kassel: Bärenreiter, 1954) 266–69. In German. See no. 319 in this volume.

Musical style of the mid-20th c. represents a synthesis of parameters, such that no one parameter the leading role in determining the style, as has been the case in other eras. An analysis of *Die Darstellung Mariae im Tempel* from the first version of Hindemith's *Das Marienleben* serves to illustrate this synthesis. A similar synthesis of parameters was first achieved in the Baroque era. With both Baroque and mid–20th-c. style, there is no longer a fundamental distinction between vocal and instrumental.

(Carl Skoggard)

2218 NIESTIEV, Izrael. **Nowe materiały do biografii Karola Szymanowskiego** [New material in Szymanowski's biography], *Karol Szymanowski: Księga sesji Naukowej poświęconej twórczości Karola Szymanowskiego* (Warszawa: Uniwersytet Warszawski, Instytut Muzykologii, 1964) 191–208. In Polish; summary in English. See no. 458 in this volume.

The years 1915-20, which Szymanowski spent in the Ukraine, are among the least explored of his life. As evidenced by posters, press notices, and Szymanowski's own articles, he did not turn away from historical events during the Russian Revolution, but took an active part in concert life. The musical life of Elisavetgrad, where Szymanowski and his family spent the years of the revolution, is described, and reminiscences by Henryk Neuhaus about Szymanowski's attitude toward the revolution are included. *(editor)*

2219 NIKOLOVSKI, Vlastimir. **Mogućnost primene folklora i u najsavremenijoj muzičkoj umetnosti** [The possibility of using folk elements in even the most recent art music], *Rad IX-og kongresa Saveza Folklorista Jugoslavije* (Sarajevo: Savez Udruženja Folklorista Jugoslavije, 1963) 429–33. In Serbian; summary in French. See no. 455 in this volume.

Historically, folklore has often been the agent of regeneration for the decomposing human psyche and for decadent aesthetic thinking. In the post-Bartók era, the most rudimentary, primordial elements of traditional music could be adapted to the most radical currents of art music. *(author)*

⟶ NKETIA, Joseph Hanson Kwabena. **Traditional and contemporary idioms of African music.** See no. 2572 in this volume.

2220 NOVÁČEK, Zdeněk. **Niektoré podmienky osobitosti u Janáčka, Orffa a Schönberga** [Some conditions of individuality in Janáček, Orff and Schoenberg], *Leoš Janáček a soudobá hudba* (Praha: Panton, 1963) 236–39. In Slovak; summaries in Russian and German. See no. 389 in this volume.

Only some of the many interrelating factors in a style determine its individuality. Where the peculiarity of Janáček's style is mainly an outcome of his personal temperament, Moravian patriotism, and critical realism, Orff's style was based on his deep knowledge of classical Latin, Old German, and anti-Romantic literary traditions. Schoenberg's distinctive style is characterized by a striving for absolute novelty in the organization of musical material. *(editors)*

2221 NOWACKI, Kazimierz. **Rola folkloru góralskiego w Harnasiach** [Highlanders' folk art in *Harnasie*], *Karol Szymanowski: Księga sesji Naukowej poświęconej twórczości Karola Szymanowskiego* (Warszawa: Uniwersytet Warszawski, Instytut Muzykologii, 1964) 209–25. *Music.* In Polish; summary in English. See no. 458 in this volume.

The native art of the Podhale region was the main source of inspiration for Szymanowski during his last creative period. His use of traditonal music reaches its height in *Harnasie*. Vocal parts are based on authentic material, and in the Górals' (Highlanders') dance music, Szymanowski uses the orchestra to recreate the specific manner of band performances. His technique of uniting two or more melodies or fragments is also a direct recreation of the Górals' manner of performance. *(editor)*

2222 NUFFEL, Jules van. **L'évolution musicale contemporaine et sa répercussion sur la musique sacrée de notre époque: Les possibilités qu'elle offre à celle-ci** [The contemporary musical evolution and its impact on sacred music in our era: The possibilities it offers to the latter], *Atti del [I] Congresso internazionale di musica sacra* (Tournai: Desclée, 1952) 401–04. In French. See no. 303 in this volume.

2223 OČADLÍK, Mirko. **Janáček a Stravinskij** [Janáček and Stravinsky], *Leoš Janáček a soudobá hudba* (Praha: Panton, 1963) 240–43. In Czech; summaries in Russian and German. See no. 389 in this volume.

Stravinsky and Janáček have often been treated as representatives of a unified Slavic trend in contemporary music. However, despite some similarities, they differ from each other in their aspirations and in their approaches to social reality. *(editors)*

2224 OLSEN, Poul Rovsing. **L'influence de Debussy: Pays nordiques** [Debussy's influence: Scandinavian countries], *Debussy et l'évolution de la musique au XXe siècle* (Paris: Centre National de la Recherche Scientifique [CNRS], 1965) 301–11. In French. See no. 456 in this volume.

2225 ONNEN, Frank. **L'influence de Debussy: Pays-Bas (Belgique-Hollande)** [Debussy's influence: The Low Countries (Belgium-Holland)], *Debussy et l'évolution de la musique au XXe siècle* (Paris: Centre

National de la Recherche Scientifique [CNRS], 1965) 291–99. In French. See no. 456 in this volume.

Discusses Debussy's influence on the works of Paul Gilson (1865-1942), Raymond Moulaert (1875-1962), Peter Benoît (1834-1901), Marcel Poot (1901-88), Willem Pijper (1894-1947), and Alphons Diepenbrock (1862-1921).

→ OTTICH, Maria. **Chopin und die Komponisten der nachfolgenden Generationen** [Chopin and the composers of following generations]. See no. 2065 in this volume.

2226 PARENTE, Alfredo. **Il problema del linguaggio**
as **come problema morale** [The problem of language as a moral problem], *Atti del quinto Congresso di musica* (Firenze: Barbèra, 1948) 33–39. In Italian. See no. 285 in this volume.

Musical language, as it unfolds in the act of composition, serves to express private thoughts and feelings, and it is left for the critics to discern and interpret these manifestations in the actual compositions. In order to reverse the growing cleavage between artist and public and make their works more intelligible, composers should cultivate their sensitivity to the world around them. The resultant awareness would enrich their artistic vision, and their enhanced resources would express a wider range of human emotions. *(Channan Willner)*

2227 PEJOVIĆ, Roksanda. **Uticaj folklora**
as **narodnooslobodilačke borbe na umetničko stvaralaštvo** [The influence of the folklore of the War of National Liberation on contemporary music], *Rad VIII-og kongresa folklorista Jugoslavije* (Beograd: Naučno Delo, 1961) 269–74. *Port.* In Serbian; summary in French. See no. 446 in this volume.

Numerous south Slavic composers have been directly inspired by the neotraditional music of the War of National Liberation, in rukoveti and cantatas such as Jovan Bandur's *Jugoslovenska partizanska rapsodija* as well as symphonic works like Josip Slavenski's *Tri Romanije*. Generally the method of using folk melodies is the direct quotation. Oskar Danon's *Kozara* is an example of art music written with folk characteristics, so successfully that one hears it sung spontaneously by the people. *(author)*

2228 PELLEG, Frank. **Soudobá hudba mezi**
as **orientem a okcidentem/La musique contemporaine entre Orient et Occident** [Contemporary music between East and West], *Proceedings of the annual convention* I (1948) 48–50,146–49. In Czech and French. See no. 286 in this volume.

Jewish art-music composers settled in Palestine before 1948 incorporated elements from traditional Sephardic and Ashkenazic music, under influences such as that of the Yemenite singer Braḥa Tsefira into a style modeled on the early 20th-c. art music of France, Russia, and Hungary. Representative composers in this tendency include Israel Brandmann, Yitshak Edel, Joachim Stutschewsky, Paul Ben-Haim, Marc Lavry, Menahem Mahler-Kalkstein (Menahem Avidom), Oedoen Partos, Alexander Uria Boskovitch, Joseph Kaminsky, Erich Walter Sternberg, Hanoch Jacoby, Josef Grünthal (Josef Tal), Marc Starominsky (Mordecai Seter), and Robert Starer.

2229 PETROV, Stojan. **Bela Bartok i bolgarskaja**
as **muzykal'naja kul'tura** [Bartók and Bulgarian musical culture], *Studia musicologica Academiae Scientiarum Hungaricae* V (1963) 491–99. In Russian. See no. 427 in this volume.

Discusses Bartók's involvement with Bulgarian folklore as ethnomusicologist and as composer, with attention to its asymmetrical and other typical rhythmic phenomena.

2230 PIOVESAN, Alessandro. **Offerte e divieti del**
as **linguaggio musicale contemporaneo** [Prospects and limits of contemporary musical language], *Atti del*

quinto Congresso di musica (Firenze: Barbèra, 1948) 119–28. In Italian. See no. 285 in this volume.

Within the framework of the scrutiny to which contemporary values are subject, beauty and intelligence are at odds. Misapplied intelligence has brought about the deformation and disintegration of beauty, and the art of creation has been deprived of emotion. Productivity is now at an ebb; the compositional process, manifesting a preoccupation with minutiae, is slower than ever. Nevertheless, initiative, imagination, and ambition are still prevalent among composers, and with the cultivation and incorporation of 12-tone techniques a unified artistic language may soon develop. *(Channan Willner)*

2231 PIZZETTI, Ildebrando. **Discorso di chiusura**
as [Closing address], *Atti del quinto Congresso di musica* (Firenze: Barbèra, 1948) 161–66. In Italian. See no. 285 in this volume.

The Italian public shows little interest in or understanding of contemporary music because they lack the requisite cultural, theoretical, and practical preparation. The study of music must be added to the curricula of all schools and universities. Music reflects the era in which it is written; in determining whether atonal music is truly representative of our age, one must decide whether it has negated natural musical intuition. It appears that atonal music only seems to be revolutionary; it is organized by a power of attraction that points to an underlying tonal center. *(Channan Willner)*

2232 PLAVEC, Josef. **Janáčkova tvorba sborová**
as [Janáček's choral works], *Leoš Janáček a soudobá hudba* (Praha: Panton, 1963) 254–60. In Czech; summaries in Russian and German. See no. 389 in this volume.

As a chorus master of two Brno singing choirs, Janáček became well acquainted with the Czech choral tradition. Therefore, it was in his choral works that he started to develop his individual composition style. His expressive resources in choral compositions, and the selection and interpretation of poetic texts, focusing on poems by Petr Bezruč, are discussed. *(editors)*

2233 POCIEJ, Bohdan. **Faktura chóralna utworów**
as **Szymanowskiego** [Choral texture in Szymanowski's works], *Karol Szymanowski: Księga sesji Naukowej poświęconej twórczości Karola Szymanowskiego* (Warszawa: Uniwersytet Warszawski, Instytut Muzykologii, 1964) 226–46. *Music.* In Polish; summary in English. See no. 458 in this volume.

Szymanowski's choral works are characterized by three main types of writing: impressionistic-expressionistic; inspired by traditional music; and archaic. These are based on Romantic polyphony, Renaissance polyphony, impressionism, Skrjabin's expressionism, and traditional music. *(editor)*

→ PORCELIJN, Carel. **The position of Alphons Diepenbrock in the Dutch history of music.** See no. 2071 in this volume.

2234 PRIETO ARRIZUBIETA, José Ignacio. **Orien-**
as **taciones de la música moderna religiosa en España/Orientations actuelles de la musique religieuse en Espagne** [The directions of modern religious music in Spain], *Perspectives de la musique sacrée à la lumière de l'encyclique* Musicae sacrae disciplina (Paris: conference, 1959) 447–53. *Music.* In Spanish and French. See no. 379 in this volume.

The modern school of religious music in Spain works under the influence of Vicente Goicoechea Errasti (1854-1916) and includes Nemesio Otaño Eguino, Julio Valdés, Norberto Almandoz Mendizábal, Valentín Ruiz-Aznar, Juan María Thomas Sabater, Antoni Massana Bertrán, Luis Iruarrízaga, José Gonzalo Zulaica y Arregui (José Antonio de Donostia), and the author. *(David Bloom)*

2235 PRUNIÈRES, Henry. **Que doit-il sortir de la**
as **crise que traverse actuellement la musique?** [What will be the outcome of the current musical cri-

sis?], *Atti del secondo Congresso internazionale di musica* (Firenze: Le Monnier, 1940) 78–81. In French; summaries in Italian and German. See no. 239 in this volume.

A brief overview of modern music with speculations on the future importance of electronic instruments.

2236
as
RAAD, Virginia. **L'influence de Debussy: Amérique (États-Unis)** [Debussy's influence: America (United States)], *Debussy et l'évolution de la musique au XXᵉ siècle* (Paris: Centre National de la Recherche Scientifique [CNRS], 1965) 215–32. In French. See no. 456 in this volume.

Edward Burlingame Hill, Louis Gruenberg, Charles Martin Loeffler, Charles Tomlinson Griffes, Deems Taylor, and Mary Howe were influenced by Debussy and impressionism. Debussy also influenced American jazz musicians. *(Nanette Jew)*

2237
as
RACEK, Jan. **Leoš Janáček a jeho postavení v české a světové hudební kultuře/Leoš Janáček i ego značenie dlja češskoj i mirovoj muzyki/Leoš Janáček und seine Bedeutung in der tschechischen und Welt-Musikkultur** [Janáček and his place in Czech and international musical culture], *Leoš Janáček a soudobá hudba* (Praha: Panton, 1963) 37–71. In Czech, Russian, and German. See no. 389 in this volume.

Janáček's idiosyncratic style cannot be likened to any 20th-c. stylistic trends. His affection for Moravian and Slavonic music traditions led to an unprecedented harmonic and rhythmic style, based on his specific interpretation of folk music and speech intonation. His ability to integrate domestic traditions with those of modern world music is comparable to that of Bartók. *(Jadranka Važanová)*

2238
as
RACEK, Jan. **Leoš Janáčeks und Béla Bartóks Bedeutung in der Weltmusik** [The international musical significance of Leoš Janáček and Béla Bartók], *Studia musicologica Academiae Scientiarum Hungaricae* V (1963) 501–13. In German. See no. 427 in this volume.

Places the two composers in a historical context, in terms of their style characteristics, use of nationalistic and traditional-music idioms, and response to the influence of Mahler, Strauss, Debussy, and Stravinsky. *(William Renwick)*

2239
as
REVAULT D'ALLONNES, Olivier. **Techniques modernes et renouvellement esthétique: Le cas de la musique concrète** [Modern techniques and aesthetic renewal: The case of musique concrète], *Pepragmena tou 4. diethnous synedriou aisthītikīs/Actes du IV Congrès international d'esthétique/Proceedings of the IV International Congress on Aesthetics* (Athínai: conference, 1962) 232–35. In French. See no. 415 in this volume.

Argues that research into new forms comes before technical contributions, new techniques cause no upheavals in the language of art music, and new works transform a preexistent sensibility into an aesthetic sensibility. *(author)*

2240
as
RINALDI, Mario. **Funzione della tecnica nel linguaggio musicale** [The function of technique in musical language], *Atti del quinto Congresso di musica* (Firenze: Barbèra, 1948) 109–15. In Italian. See no. 285 in this volume.

The techniques of music are so difficult to master that composers must continuously exercise their skills. Excessive emphasis on technique, however, inhibits good musicianship. Many contemporary composers tackle only the technical challenges of music, thereby bringing about its disintegration. Spontaneous expression and communication depend on the artistic use of a familiar vocabulary, and attempts to effect radical changes lead to mechanical, insipid results. Despite the threats of 12-tone techniques and innovations, tonal music shall prevail. *(Channan Willner)*

2241
as
RONAN, John Edward. **Contemporary polyphony for the Proper of the Mass,** *Atti del [I] Congresso internazionale di musica sacra* (Tournai: Desclée, 1952) 409–10. See no. 303 in this volume.

2242
as
RONGA, Luigi. **Aspetti del costume musicale contemporaneo** [Aspects of contemporary musical practice], *Atti del quinto Congresso di musica* (Firenze: Barbèra, 1948) 66–71. In Italian. See no. 285 in this volume.

While some believe that the simultaneity of technical excellence and personal detachment characteristic of contemporary music are confusing, others contend that it is the novelty of its techniques, as yet unexploited by truly great composers, that disorients the public. There is disagreement as to what constitutes truth, simplicity, and humanity in music. Musicians cannot contain the changes in musical practice, and the public, deprived of new values, is losing its sense of judgment. Neither the influence of jazz and dance, nor the advent of recording, radio, and tape have contributed to musical sensitivity. Only early exposure to contemporary music can counteract the misunderstandings that plague it. *(Channan Willner)*

2243
as
RONGA, Luigi. **La musica senza storia** [The music without history], *Atti del terzo Congresso internazionale di musica* (Firenze: Le Monnier, 1940) 186–93. In Italian; summaries in French and German. See no. 256 in this volume.

Due to the fast pace of its evolution, modern music is becoming a music without a tradition. Consequently, audiences do not understand its language. *(Edwin D. Wallace)*

2244
as
RŴZŴLYŴ, Dawid. **'Erneṣṭ Blŵḥ wemip'alŵ** [Ernest Bloch and his work], *Dŵkan* III (1961) 5–12. In Hebrew. See no. 417 in this volume.

Examines Bloch's contribution to the understanding of Jewish traditions and the Jewish spirit.

2245
as
SAUGUET, Henri. **Révolution permanente** [Permanent revolution], *Debussy et l'évolution de la musique au XXᵉ siècle* (Paris: Centre National de la Recherche Scientifique [CNRS], 1965) 23–26. In French. See no. 456 in this volume.

Debussy's aesthetics are discussed.

2246
as
SCHMIDTMANN, Friedrich. **Selbstbildnis eines Rekonvertiten** [Self-portrait of one who was reconverted], *Studien zur Musikgeschichte der Stadt Mönchengladbach* (Köln: Volk, 1965) 83–85. *Port.* In German. See no. 486 in this volume.

After 20 years of composing first nontonal, then serial, and finally electronic music, the author decided in the mid-1950s that some very serious error had been made in the evolution of the new music. Rather than trying to return to tonality, he submitted to a kind of voluntary quarantine, writing pieces only for mixed or male chorus, a medium in which no sin goes unpunished. *(David Bloom)*

2247
as
SCHÜNEMANN, Georg. **Beziehungen neuer Musik zu exotischer und frühmittelalterlicher Tonkunst** [The relationships of new music to exotic and early medieval music], *Zeitschrift für Ästhetik und allgemeine Kunstwissenschaft* XIX (1925) 411–25. *Music, transcr.* In German. See no. 114 in this volume.

Surveys the conscious use of authentic non-European musical elements in European composition from Saint-Saëns and Franck onward, with particular analysis of Stravinsky's use of primitive rhythm, heterophonic practice in Schoenberg's first serial pieces, and the use of octave divisions other than the conventional 12. The row as a constructional principle is startlingly reminiscent of maqām, rāga, and the ancient Greek *nomos*. Supplementary reports by Philipp JARNACH (noting especially the use of exotic scales and the medieval church modes) and Erich Moritz von HORNBOSTEL are appended. *(David Bloom)*

2248 SEARLE, Humphrey. **Liszt and 20th-century**
as **music,** *Studia musicologica Academiae Scientiarum Hungaricae* V (1963) 277–81. *Music.* See no. 427 in this volume.

Liszt anticipated developments in 20th-c. music through his concepts of the single-movement program piece, the cyclic transformation of thematic material, the use of advanced harmony, and the dissolution of tonality. He particularly influenced Bartók, Schoenberg, Willem Pijper, Karl Amadeus Hartmann, and Nikolaj Mjaskovskij; efforts on behalf of his music in Britain, led by Constant Lambert, are discussed in some detail. *(Alan Garfield)*

2249 SIMBRIGER, Heinrich. **Die heutige Situation**
as **der Zwölftonmusik** [The current situation of twelve-tone music], *Bericht über den internationalen musikwissenschaftlichen Kongreß Wien Mozartjahr 1956* (Graz; Köln: Böhlau, 1958) 593–98. In German. See no. 365 in this volume.

Berg was derided by the orthodox as a conformist whose highest goal was to prevent his 12-tone technique from being noticed. Recent developments such as the author's theory of complementary harmony follow Berg's lead in attempting to break through the isolation of 12-tone music by using the dodecaphonic ordering of tones as a constructional principle that does not necessarily need to be audible. *(David Bloom)*

2250 SMITH, Carleton Sprague. **Hudba v Severní a**
as **Jižní Americe/La musique en Amérique du Nord et en Amérique du Sud** [The music of North and South America], *Hudba národů: Sborník přednášek, proslovených na I. mezinárodním sjezdu skladatelů a hudebních kritiků/Musique des nations: Ier Congrès international des compositeurs et critiques musicaux* (Praha: Syndikát Českých Skladatelů, 1948) 62–63,155–56. In Czech and French. See no. 278 in this volume.

Discusses representative 20th-c. composers including Charles Ives, George Gershwin, Aaron Copland, Virgil Thomson, Carlos Chávez, Heitor Villa-Lobos, Domingo Santa Cruz, and Mozart Camargo Guarnieri.

2251 ŠOSTAKOVIČ, Dmitrij. **Svaz sovětských**
as **skladatelů/Union des compositeurs soviétiques** [Sojuz Kompozitorov SSSR], *Hudba národů: Sborník přednášek, proslovených na I. mezinárodním sjezdu skladatelů a hudebních kritiků/Musique des nations: Ier Congrès international des compositeurs et critiques musicaux* (Praha: Syndikát Českých Skladatelů, 1948) 75–81,123–32. In Czech and French. See no. 278 in this volume.

Traces the history, administrative structure, and activities of the Sojuz Kompozitorov SSSR, founded 1936, with lists of members' important compositions and notes on the contributions of Russian composers, since 1924, to the development of art music composition in Azerbaijan, Georgia, Kyrgyzstan, Tajikistan, Turkmenistan, and Uzbekistan.

2252 SOUDÈRES, Valérie. **Les possiblitiés d'évolu-**
as **tion rapide des jeunes compositeurs grâce à la radio** [The possibilities of rapid evolution of young composers, thanks to radio], *Cahiers d'études de radio-télévision* 3-4 (1955) 391–93. In French. See no. 334 in this volume.

Emphasizes the importance of using the medium to acquaint young composers with earlier masterworks.

2253 SOURIS, André. **Les sources sensibles de la**
as **musique sérielle** [The sensible sources of serial music], *Visages et perspectives de l'art moderne: Peinture, poésie, musique* (Paris: Centre National de la Recherche Scientifique [CNRS], 1956) 175–82. *Facs.* In French. See no. 341 in this volume.

It has been common to view composers of serial music as being too cerebral, but the rules by which their work is governed are neither more nor less complicated than those which govern other, more traditional forms of composition (both in force today and those of the past). Several solutions are offered to the problem that serial composers face regarding the creation of music thoroughly liberated from any tonal systems. *(Susan Poliniak)*

2254 ŠTĚDROŇ, Bohumír. **K inspiraci Janáčkových**
as ***Listů důvěrných*** [The inspiration of Janáček's *Listy důvěrné*], *Leoš Janáček a soudobá hudba* (Praha: Panton, 1963) 313–17. *Bibliog.* In Czech; summaries in Russian and German. See no. 389 in this volume.

An analysis of the string quartet no. 2, *Listy důvěrné* (Intimate letters), composed in January-February 1928, with attention to the compositional process as reflected in Janáček's personal letters to Kamila Stösslová, who inspired the work. *(editors)*

2255 ŠTĚDROŇ, Bohumír. **Leoš Janáček und**
as **Ferenc Liszt** [Leoš Janáček and Franz Liszt], *Studia musicologica Academiae Scientiarum Hungaricae* V (1963) 295–99. In German. See no. 427 in this volume.

In Liszt's compositional output it was church music that exerted the most profound influence on the Czech composer. Janáček's 1901 arrangement for mixed chorus and organ of Liszt's 1879 solo organ Mass *Missa pro organo lectarum celebrationi Missarum adjumento inserviens*, with an original underlay of the Ordinary texts, is discussed in detail. *(William Renwick)*

2256 STĘSZEWSKI, Jan. **Pieśni kurpiowskie w**
as **twórczości Karola Szymanowskiego** [The folk songs of the Kurpie regions in Szymanowski's works], *Karol Szymanowski: Księga sesji Naukowej poświęconej twórczości Karola Szymanowskiego* (Warszawa: Uniwersytet Warszawski, Instytut Muzykologii, 1964) 174–293. *Music, charts, diagr.* In Polish; summary in English. See no. 458 in this volume.

In writing his *Pieśni kurpiowskie* (Kurpie Songs), Szymanowski relied on the collections of Władysław Skierkowski (1886-1941), a local priest and collector of traditional music. Recent scholarship indicates inaccuracies in Skierkowski's notation. To some extent, this undermines the adjective "Kurpian" in Szymanowski's title, without diminishing the value of the compositions. *(editor)*

2257 STUCKENSCHMIDT, Hans-Heinz. **L'influence**
as **de Debussy: Autriche et Allemagne** [Debussy's influence: Austria and Germany], *Debussy et l'évolution de la musique au XXe siècle* (Paris: Centre National de la Recherche Scientifique [CNRS], 1965) 241–61. *Music.* In French. See no. 456 in this volume.

Between 1900 and 1918, the interaction of Debussy and Richard Strauss formed an important musical link between France and Germany. However, Max Reger, Paul Graener, Walter Niemann, and Sigfrid Karg-Elert were more susceptible to Debussy's influence. Schoenberg's attitudes toward Debussy are noted, Debussy's influence on Franz Schreker is discussed, and Berg's *Wozzeck* is compared with Debussy's *Pelléas et Mélisande*. *(Orly Leah Krasner)*

2258 STUCKENSCHMIDT, Hans Heinz. **Musique**
as **concrète,** *Bericht über den internationalen musikwissenschaftlichen Kongreß* (Kassel: Bärenreiter, 1963) 388–89. In German. See no. 452 in this volume.

A brief historical discussion, focusing on the compositions and theoretical writings of Pierre Schaeffer.

2259 ŚWIERZEWSKI, Stefan. **Karol Szymanowski**
as **w oczach krytiyki polskiej** [Karol Szymanowski in light of Polish criticism], *Karol Szymanowski: Księga sesji Naukowej poświęconej twórczości Karola Szymanowskiego* (Warszawa: Uniwersytet Warszawski, Instytut Muzykologii, 1964) 294–304. In Polish; summary in English. See no. 458 in this volume.

Szymanowski's work was a subject of heated debate among Polish music critics from the very beginning. The conflict gained momentum between

1920 and 1923 when representatives of the conservative camp (Piotr Rytel and Stanisław Niewiadomski in particular) claimed that Szymanowski had no individual artistic vision, that he yielded uncritically to foreign influence, and that his work was devoid of essentially Polish features. Adolf Chybiński and Zdzisław Jachimecki were among Szymanowski's defenders, and nearly all Polish music critics took part in the heated polemics. In the 1930s, critics (including Chybiński, Jarosław Iwaszkiewicz, Seweryn Barbag, Józef Michał Chomiński, and Stefania Łobaczewska) began to focus their attention on the national features of Szymanowski's music, his attitude toward folk art, and his technique. *(editor)*

2260 SZABOLCSI, Bence. **Mensch und Natur in**
as **Bartóks Geisteswelt** [Man and nature in Bartók's spiritual world], *Studia musicologica Academiae Scientiarum Hungaricae* V (1963) 525–39. In German. See no. 427 in this volume.

Discusses Bartók the man—his spiritual outlook, his love of nature, and his support of freedom and brotherhood—drawing from his correspondence. *(William Renwick)*

2261 [Tal] **"Yeṣy'at miṣraym": Yŵsep Ṭal—Dibrey**
as **heber šel ḥamlaḥyn 'al habiṣŵ'a ha'eleqṭrŵny šel hayeṣyrah** [*Exodus*: Electronic music by Josef Tal], *Dŵkan* VIII (1965) 87–88. In Hebrew. See no. 503 in this volume.

2262 TANZBERGER, Ernst. **Jean Sibelius als**
as **Symphoniker** [Jean Sibelius as symphonist], *Kongreß-Bericht: Gesellschaft für Musikforschung* (Kassel; Basel: Bärenreiter, 1950) 146–48. In German. See no. 299 in this volume.

2263 TAYLOR, Davidson. **Music written for radio,**
as *Papers read at the International Congress of Musicology* (New York: Music Educators National Conference, 1944) 251–66. *Charts, diagr.* See no. 266 in this volume.

Discusses the medium's effect on composers. Topics include commissions and competitions of broadcasting companies worldwide.

2264 THOMSON, Virgil, moderator. **Discussion:**
as **Critics' forum,** *Music: East and West* (Tōkyō: conference, 1961) 202f. See no. 445 in this volume.

2265 TOMASZEWSKI, Mieczysław. **Związki**
as **słowno-muzyczne w liryce wokalnej Szymanowskiego na materiale** *Slopiewni* [The relationship between word and music in Szymanowski's lyrical vocal works on the basis of his *Slopiewnie*], *Karol Szymanowski: Księga sesji Naukowej poświęconej twórczości Karola Szymanowskiego* (Warszawa: Uniwersytet Warszawski, Instytut Muzykologii, 1964) 305–33. *Music, charts, diagr.* In Polish; summary in German. See no. 458 in this volume.

Provides an analysis of phonetic, structural, expressive, and semantic layers. Szymanowski's work is characterized by avoidance of post-Romantic sound material, constructivism, integration of the principle of montage, expressive unconventionality (e.g., masks of archaic and primitive styles), and semantic ambiguity. *(editor)*

2266 VÄISÄNEN, Armas Otto. **Yrjö Kilpinens**
as *Kanteletar-***Lieder** [Yrjö Kilpinen's *Kanteletar* songs], *Bericht über den internationalen musikwissenschaftlichen Kongreß* (Kassel: Bärenreiter, 1957) 231–32. In German. See no. 356 in this volume.

An appreciation of the composer's op. 100 (1953), 64 settings of texts from Elias Lönnrot's collection *Kanteletar* (1840), the lyrical counterpart to the *Kalevala*.

⟶ VALABREGA, Cesare. **La millenaria musica**
ebraica e Ernest Bloch** [Jewish music over the millennia and Ernest Bloch]. See no. 6102 in this volume.

2267 VANCEA, Zeno. **Janáček und die führenden**
as **Komponisten der südosteuropäischen Schulen: Bartók, Enescu, Kodály/Janáček a čelní skladatelé jihovýchodoevropských škol: Bartók, Enescu, Kodály** [Janáček and the leading composers of the southeastern European schools: Bartók, Enescu, Kodály], *Leoš Janáček a soudobá hudba* (Praha: Panton, 1963) 330–44. In German and Czech. See no. 389 in this volume.

The respect for traditional song and folklore is a common feature linking Janáček with Bartók, Enescu, and Kodály. All four composers expressed their belief that the composer's individual musical language should grow from the deep knowledge of traditional music, though each used different methods of reinterpreting it. *(Jadranka Važanová)*

2268 VERETTI, Antonio. **Il problema del linguaggio**
as **nella musica moderna** [The problem of language in modern music], *Atti del quinto Congresso di musica* (Firenze: Barbèra, 1948) 105–09. In Italian. See no. 285 in this volume.

Whereas contemporary musical language is foreign and inaccessible, the older tonal language, reflecting human values, is understandable. Our civilization, now in crisis, no longer offers the artist any values and principles, and music will be in a state of disarray as long as this situation continues. The artist must nevertheless try to create a human statement, and for this purpose 12-tone techniques must be abandoned. Only direct involvement with society can help to define the stature of the composer. *(Channan Willner)*

2269 WEISSMAN, John S. **On some problems with**
as **Bartók research in connection with Bartók's biography,** *Studia musicologica Academiae Scientiarum Hungaricae* V (1963) 587–96. See no. 427 in this volume.

Research into Bartók's life and work is complicated by the necessity of considering his scientific and ethnomusicological activities, and by the fact that some aspects of his life are connected with persons still living. All Bartók researchers are indebted to János Demény, the editor of Bartók's correspondence. A proposal is made to establish an international Bartók society to collect materials, and a Bartók museum to store them.

2270 WINCKEL, Fritz. **Der Einsatz des Klaviers in**
as **der experimentellen Musik** [The use of the piano in experimental music], *Dokumentation* (Frankfurt am Main: Fördergemeinschaft Klavier, 1966) 33–44. In German. See no. 494 in this volume.

2271 WIRSTA, Aristide. **Théodore Akimenko:**
as **Représentant de l'impressionisme de l'Europe de l'Est** [Fedir Akymenko: A representative of Eastern European impressionism], *Bericht über den siebenten internationalen musikwissenschaftlichen Kongress* (Kassel: Bärenreiter, 1959) 302–05. *Music.* In French. See no. 390 in this volume.

Brief biography of the Ukrainian-born composer Fedir Stepanovyč Akymenko (1876-1945) and critical appreciation of his style, with attention to the predominantly impressionist character of his works of 1902-17 and his increasing use of Ukrainian traditional music from 1917 onwards. *(David Bloom)*

2272 WOLFF, Hellmuth Christian. **Bach und die**
as **Musik der Gegenwart** [Bach and the music of today], *Bericht über die Wissenschaftliche Bachtagung* (Leipzig: Peters, 1951) 375–87. *Music.* In German. See no. 298 in this volume.

Present-day composers frequently turn to the music of Bach for models. Hindemith, Ernst Pepping, Johann Nepomuk David, Wolfgang Fortner, Stravinsky, and Bartók have all consciously imitated Bach, following in the tradition of Schumann, Brahms, Reger, and Franck. Only the harmonic aspect of Bach's music has not been emulated; modern composers have sought new expressive means through the expansion of tonality. *(James Donald Anderson)*

2273
as

WOLFF, Hellmuth Christian. **Die ethischen Aufgaben der neuen Musik** [The ethical obligations of the new music], *Compte rendu/Kongressbericht/Report* (Basel: Bärenreiter, 1951) 221–26. In German. See no. 289 in this volume.

An abridged version of an article published in *Musica* 9 (1949), with attention to the way work by various contemporary composers corresponds to ideas of cultural renewal and creative responsibility advanced by Albert Schweitzer, Hindemith, and Stravinsky. *(David Bloom)*

2274
as

WUORINEN, Charles. **Performance of new music in universities,** *American Society of University Composers: Proceedings of the 1966 conference* (New York: American Society of University Composers, 1966). See no. 510 in this volume.

Contemporary music performance is flourishing in universities. Composers there can directly influence the realization of their works before sophisticated audiences, and university ensembles encourage the composition of chamber music. Performance standards are high, raising those of commercial ensembles. However, financing university ensembles remains a major problem. *(Judith Drogichen Meyer)*

2275
as

YÖNETKEN, Halil Bedi. **Turecká hudba/La musique turque** [Turkish music], *Hudba národů: Sborník přednášek, proslovených na I. mezinárodním sjezdu skladatelů a hudebních kritiků/Musique des nations: I*er *Congrès international des compositeurs et critiques musicaux* (Praha: Syndikát Českých Skladatelů, 1948) 82–88, 180–87. In Czech and French. See no. 278 in this volume.

Turkish music may be divided into three types: classic art music based on maqām and usul, traditional rural and village music, and polyphonic art music drawing on European models. The last dates from 1828, when Sultan Mahmud II brought Giuseppe Donizetti to Istanbul to organize the imperial band. Significant Western-style music began to develop only in the 20th c.; biographies are provided of the composers known as the Turkish Five: Cemil Reşit Rey, Hasan Ferit Alnar, Ahmet Adnan Saygun, Ulvi Cemal Erkin, and Necil Kâzim Akses. *(David Bloom)*

2276
as

ZABŁOCKA, Jadwiga. **Rymy dziecięce Karola Szymanowskiego** [Szymanowski's *Rymy dziecięce* (Children's Rhymes)], *Karol Szymanowski: Księga sesji Naukowej poświęconej twórczości Karola Szymanowskiego* (Warszawa: Uniwersytet Warszawski, Instytut Muzykologii, 1964) 334–44. *Music, charts, diagr.* In Polish; summary in English. See no. 458 in this volume.

Composed during 1922 and 1923, this cycle of 20 short settings of words by Kazimiera Hłakowiczówna recreates not only a child-like psyche, but a child's manner of performance as well. This is achieved by the imitation of a child's speech intonation, the predominance of diatonicism, rhythmic simplicity, a free treatment of meter, recitative-like texture, narrow melodic range, and an interplay of melody with purely coloristic sound effects. *(editor)*

29 Twentieth century — Musical life

2277
as

AL-ḤIFNĪ, Maḥmūd Aḥmad. **Ägyptens Verehrung für Mozart** [Egypt's reverence for Mozart], *Internationale Konferenz über das Leben und Werk W.A. Mozarts* (Praha: Svaz Československých Skladatelů, 1956) 200–01. In German. See no. 360 in this volume.

Mozart's works are performed and studied throughout Egypt; his stage works on Egyptian or generally Arabian themes, from *Thamos, König in Ägypten* through *Die Zauberflöte*, are especially beloved. The bicentenary of his birth was celebrated with various activities, including a festival featuring a production of *Don Giovanni* and a revised edition of the author's *Mutsart qiṣṣat al-ṭifl al-muʿjiz wa-al-mūsīqī al-ʿaqbarī* (Mozart: The story of the miraculous child and the genius musician, Cairo, 1939), and the only book-length study of Mozart to date in Arabic. *(David Bloom)*

2278
as

ALMENDRA, Júlia d'. **L'actuel mouvement grégorien au Portugal: Ses origines, sa fondation, son but, son programme et son développement** [The contemporary Gregorian movement in Portugal: Its origins, goals, program, and development], *Zweiter internationaler Kongress für katholische Kirchenmusik: Zu Ehren des Heiligen Papstes Pius X* (Wien: conference, 1955) 127–28. In French. See no. 339 in this volume.

A survey of organizations and activities, focusing on the Semana Gregoriana festivals in Fátima, beginning 1950, and the Centro de Estudos Gregorianos, Lisbon, founded 1953. *(David Bloom)*

2279
as

ANDREEV, Andrej. **Leoš Janáček a Bulharsko** [Janáček and Bulgaria], *Leoš Janáček a soudobá hudba* (Praha: Panton, 1963) 75–76. In Czech; summaries in Russian and German. See no. 389 in this volume.

Correspondence between Janáček and Dobri Hristov deposited in the archive of the Institut za Muzyka, Bălgarska Akademija na Naukite, shows the composer's interest in Bulgarian folk music. The reception of Janáček's music in Bulgaria is discussed. *(editors)*

2280
as

AUDA, Antoine. **Léonard Terry: Professeur, compositeur, chef d'orchestre et musicologue liégeois** [Léonard Terry: Professor, composer, orchestra conductor, and musicologist of Liège], *Société Internationale de Musicologie: Premier Congrès Liège—Compte rendu/Internationale Gesellschaft für Musikwissenschaft: Erster Kongress Lüttich—Kongressbericht/International Society for Musical Research: First Congress Liège: Report* (London: Plainsong and Mediaeval Music Society, 1930) 73–75. In French. See no. 178 in this volume.

A biography of Léonard Terry (1816-82).

2281
as

BECK, Conrad. **La musique et le public** [Music and the public], *Atti del secondo Congresso internazionale di musica* (Firenze: Le Monnier, 1940) 68–75. In French; summaries in Italian and German. See no. 239 in this volume.

Composers should aim at contact with the world that surrounds them, and at the simplicity that is the fundamental element of art, but not in a facile, banal, or reactionary spirit; at the same time they are obliged to make experiments that can only be clarified by the passage of time, and must be ready to be exposed to misunderstanding and natural resistance. Critics should spend less time criticizing the details of a particular composition or performance and more explaining the richness of expressive possibilities, and demonstrating that the difficulty of understanding a new work is a natural phenomenon, common to all musical periods. *(author)*

2282
as

BEHREND, William. **Musikalische Länderkunde Dänemarks** [Denmark's musical geography], *Haydn-Zentenarfeier* (Leipzig: Breitkopf & Härtel; Wien: Artaria, 1909) 484–89. In German. See no. 65 in this volume.

Provides an overview of the position of musicians in Danish society, concert series, musicological literature, and institutions.

2283 **[Belgium] L'action de l'Orchestre Sym-**
as **phonique Populaire** [The activities of the Orchestre Symphonique Populaire], *La musique et le peuple: Rapports, suggestions, voeux* (Bruxelles: Ministère des Sciences et des Arts, 1932) 83–87. In French. See no. 195 in this volume.

Report on the apparent success of the orchestra, established by law in 1932, in introducing the public to concert life. This success is due in part to low ticket prices. Suggestions are offered for publicity, cost-cutting, and so forth. *(Mark Stevens)*

2284 **[Belgium] Une manifestation d'art musical**
as **populaire à Frameries** [A demonstration of working people's musical art in Frameries], *La musique et le peuple: Rapports, suggestions, voeux* (Bruxelles: Ministère des Sciences et des Arts, 1932) 95–95. In French. See no. 195 in this volume.

Describes the program of a huge concert given by the residents of this town of 14,000, involving six large instrumental and choral ensembles. *(Mark Stevens)*

2285 **[Berlin] Das optische Bild des Europiano-**
as **Kongresses** [The visual image of the Europiano-Kongreß]. By Georg PREISS, *Dokumentation* (Frankfurt am Main: Fördergemeinschaft Klavier, 1966) 272–76. In German. See no. 494 in this volume.

2286 BERNET KEMPERS, Karel Philippus. **Mahler**
as **und Willem Mengelberg** [Mahler and Willem Mengelberg], *Bericht über den internationalen musikwissenschaftlichen Kongreß Wien Mozartjahr 1956* (Graz; Köln: Böhlau, 1958) 41–46. *Charts, diagr.* In German. See no. 365 in this volume.

Reviews the history of the conductor's engagement with Mahler's music from 1902 through 1940. Annotations by both men in Mengelberg's scores of Mahler's works, and the insights that can be gleaned from them, are discussed. *(Carol K. Baron)*

2287 BIANCHI, Gabriele. **Musica nella realtà della**
as **nostra vita** [Music in the reality of our life], *Atti del quinto Congresso di musica* (Firenze: Barbèra, 1948) 55–61. In Italian. See no. 285 in this volume.

It is essential for the proper dissemination of contemporary music that the public be aware of its own preferences, that working conditions permit composers to offer their best, and that performances do justice to new works. Composers must find appreciative listeners, yet neither public nor critics can appraise the new means of composition. Scholars, artists, critics, and public must all be educated differently if working conditions and appreciation are to be improved. A broad humanistic training can help composers tackle the complex values and difficulties of their profession; the study of music in schools and universities, when redirected, can create a more receptive public. *(Channan Willner)*

2288 BLAZIAN, H. **La radiophonie en Roumanie**
as [Broadcasting in Romania], *Procès-verbaux et documents* (Praha: Státní Nakladatelství, 1931) 90–95. In French. See no. 183 in this volume.

2289 BLUM, Klaus. **Plus und minus** [Plus and minus],
as *Cahiers d'études de radio-télévision* 3-4 (1955) 430–31. In German. See no. 334 in this volume.

Discusses categories of radio music, including standard repertoire, functional music, and original compositions for the radio.

2290 BOMM, Urbanus. **Gregorianischer Choral als**
as **Gegenwartskunst** [Gregorian chant as contemporary art], *Musica sacra in unserer Zeit* (Berlin: Merseburger, 1960) 79–88. In German. See no. 403 in this volume.

2291 BOSE, Fritz. **Western influences in modern**
as **Asian music,** *Journal of the International Folk Music Council* XI (1959) 47–50. See no. 392 in this volume.

Discusses Rabindranath Tagore's influence on the development of art songs in India, the popular kroncong music of Java, and the development of Western-influenced art music in China. *(James R. Cowdery)*

2292 BRELET, Gisèle. **La radio purifie et confirme**
as **la musique** [Radio purifies and strengthens music], *Cahiers d'études de radio-télévision* 3-4 (1955) 367–78. In French. See no. 334 in this volume.

Philosophical discussion of the effect of radio on the roles of listener and performer.

2293 BRISTIGER, Michal. **Le problème de la**
as **musique folklorique à la radio polonaise en fonction des changements sociaux et culturels survenus en Pologne.** [The problem of traditional music on Polish radio with regard to social and cultural changes that have occurred in Poland.], *Cahiers d'études de radio-télévision* 3-4 (1955) 462–67. In French. See no. 334 in this volume.

Focuses on radio's role in cultural rebuilding and development since World War II.

2294 BUNKOWSKI, Arthur. **Die Jugend und die**
as **Macht der Mittler: Bericht über einen Delegiertentag** [Youth and the power of the media: Report on a meeting of delegates], *Musische Jugend und technische Mittler* (Remscheid: Landesarbeitsgemeinschaft Jugendmusik Nordrhein-Westfalen, 1957) 83–84. In German. See no. 380 in this volume.

The fifth meeting of representatives of the youth organizations participating in the Landesjugendring Nordrhein-Westfalen, held in Febraty 1955, was devoted to film, organized around a showing of Chaplin's *Limelight* (1952) and a discussion of the concept of film education. *(David Bloom)*

2295 CAIRNS, Huntington. **The future of musical**
as **patronage in America,** *Music and criticism: A symposium* (Cambridge, MA: Harvard University Press, 1948) 163–81. See no. 276 in this volume.

Discusses the economic difficulties of a profession in the creative arts, and includes examples of royalties a composer or scholarly writer might earn. Patronage is considered as a solution to such problems. A historical perspective on musical patronage is presented, indicating that financial difficulties for artists are more prevalent in modern industrialized society than in the past. For today's composers, the world of commerce and the government are two probable sources of funding. However, both can also pose obstacles to creativity. *(William Gilmore)*

2296 **[Cairo, 1932] Séances plénières de la semaine**
as **officiel du Congrès** [Plenary sessions of the Congress's official week], *Recueil des travaux du Congrès de musique arabe* (Al-Qāhirah: Boulac, 1934) 655–710. *Charts, diagr., transcr.* In French. See no. 196 in this volume.

Offers a summary account of the seven sessions, from 28 March to 3 April, at which the work of the individual commissions of the Congress on Arab Music (Mu'tamar al Mūsīqá al-"Arabiyyah) was presented and debated, with extensive transcriptions of discussion.

2297 CASELLA, Alfredo. **Come sono state scelte ed**
as **elaborate le musiche della Settimana** [How the

music for the Settimana was chosen and planned], *Antonio Vivaldi: Note e documenti sulla vita e sulle opere* (Siena: Accademia Musicale Chigiana, 1939) 11–14. In Italian. See no. 268 in this volume.

The musical programming for the first Settimana Musicale Senese consisted of works by Vivaldi chosen for diversity, importance, and infrequency of performance. *(Mark Stevens)*

2298
as
CASELLA, Alfredo. **Musica contemporanea e pubblico** [Contemporary music and the public], *Atti del secondo Congresso internazionale di musica* (Firenze: Le Monnier, 1940) 57–68. In Italian; summaries in French and German. See no. 239 in this volume.

Blame for the indifference of audiences to contemporary music can be shared among composers themselves, performers and concert organizations, and criticism. The great diversity of sometimes irreconcilable tendencies is confusing to the public. Recent statements by Benito Mussolini are cited in favor of the position that composers should be working toward a new social order featuring new relations between music and public and new forms of art. *(David Bloom)*

2299
as
CASELLA, Alfredo. **Scambi musicali** [Musical exchange], *Atti del primo Congresso internazionale di musica* (Firenze: Le Monnier, 1935) 223–26. In Italian. See no. 203 in this volume.

Recent policies—the BBC's tight control and near-exclusion of foreign performers, and the German radio's exclusion of Jewish performers and those from politically hostile countries—exemplify a ruinous protectionist mentality today found even in Italy. Such nationalist campaigns are always the initiative of failed composers and mediocre performers hoping to compensate for their lack of talent. The attention of the world's governments must be directed to a danger that may compromise the existence of musical art. *(David Bloom)*

2300
as
CESARI, Gaetano. **Critica musicale** [Music criticism], *La vita musicale dell'Italia d'oggi* (Torino: Fratelli Bocca, 1921) 139–53. In Italian. See no. 97 in this volume.

Discusses the role of critics in Italian musical life, and the need for them to be thoroughly educated.

2301
as
CHAILLEY, Jacques. **La radio et le développement de l'instinct harmonique chez les auditeurs** [Radio and the development of the harmonic instinct among listeners], *Cahiers d'études de radio-télévision* 3-4 (1955) 401–12. *Music.* In French. See no. 334 in this volume.

Focuses on understanding the extended harmonic vocabulary of the late 19th and early 20th c.

2302
as
CHAILLEY, Jacques. **Zeitgenössische Musik und das Problem einer Philologie der Musik** [Contemporary music and the problem of a philology of music], *Musikerziehung: Zeitschrift der Musikerzieher Österreichs* special issue (1953) 114–18. In German. See no. 317 in this volume.

2303
as
CHARPENTIER, Jacques. **Les musiques orientales peuvent-elles susciter des formes nouvelles chez les compositeurs occidentaux?** [Can Eastern musics inspire new forms for Western composers?], *The preservation of traditional forms of the learned and popular music of the Orient and the Occident/La préservation des formes traditionelles de la musique savante et populaire dans les pays d'Orient et d'Occident* (Urbana: Center for Comparative Psycholinguistics, Institute of Communications Research, 1964) 89–98. In French. See no. 443 in this volume.

Acquaintance with Asian music may inspire Western composers and also help to free Western audiences from a dependence on the tempered scale.

2304
as
CLARK, Evans. **Report on concert interchange in the popular field,** *Report of the Committee of the Conference on Inter-American Relations in the Field of Music* (Washington, D.C.: United States Department of State, 1940) 147–51. See no. 271 in this volume.

Several obstacles make it difficult for Latin Americans to perform in the U.S., including the Immigration Act of 1917 and union laws. The American Federation of Musicians (AFM) enforces a closed shop policy. RCA Victor does as well, although they do make recordings of South American musicians outside of the U.S. Though it is concerned for its many unemployed members, the AFM is interested in broadening the exposure of Latin American music in the U.S. A study is needed to find ways to expose South American countries to music of the U.S. *(Gary Eskow)*

2305
as
COLLAER, Paul. **La culture musicale par la radiophonie** [Musical cultivation through radio], *Atti del secondo Congresso internazionale di musica* (Firenze: Le Monnier, 1940) 145–55. In French; summaries in Italian and German. See no. 239 in this volume.

Discusses the educational functions of radio, for children and for adult music lovers, particularly from the perspective of work done by the Belgian Institut National de Radiodiffusion. Decentralization of radio broadcasts and subsidies from radio organizations to local orchestras and theaters will encourage the maintenance of musical facilities in provincial cities; international cooperation and exchange is needed as well. *(David Bloom)*

2306
as
Committee of the Conference on Inter-American Relations in the Field of Music. **Report of the activities (to May 23, 1940) of the WPA music program in the diffusion of Latin American music,** *Report of the Committee of the Conference on Inter-American Relations in the Field of Music* (Washington, D.C.: United States Department of State, 1940) 49–53. *Charts, diagr.* See no. 271 in this volume.

To celebrate the 50th anniversary of the Pan-American Union, numerous MSS were made available to bands and orchestras throughout the U.S. A distribution list is included. In some cities performances were done from MSS obtained from other sources. Traditional ensembles organized under the Federal Music Project (FMP) in San Antonio, El Paso, and Los Angeles have given many performances of Latin American music; some of these have been recorded. *(Howard Cinnamon)*

2307
as
COPPOLA, Piero. **La funzione educatrice del disco** [The educational function of phonograph records], *Atti del secondo Congresso internazionale di musica* (Firenze: Le Monnier, 1940) 166–72. In Italian; summaries in French and German. See no. 239 in this volume.

A summary of progress in the recording of art music, particularly since the beginning of electrical pressing of records in 1926. Two deplorable problems are the high price of art-music records (which could be eased by a system of public record libraries) and the mentality of the recording companies, which spend freely on publicity for popular musicians but allow the recordings of concert musicians to be virtually unknown. *(David Bloom)*

2308
as
CORIO, Edgardo. **Organizzazioni economiche fra musicisti e loro rapporti** [Economic organizations among musicians and their reports], *La vita musicale dell'Italia d'oggi* (Torino: Fratelli Bocca, 1921) 114–26. In Italian. See no. 97 in this volume.

Lists various organizations, discusses reforms, and argues for coordination and cooperation.

2309
as
COSTÈRE, Edmond. **Audience de la musique d'aujourd'hui** [Audience of today's music], *Cahiers d'études de radio-télévision* 3-4 (1955) 521–25. In French. See no. 334 in this volume.

Briefly discusses listening preferences, and identifies four styles of music: tonal and cardinal (e.g., classic repertoire), tonal and modal (e.g., Debussy), atonal and cardinal (e.g., Schoenberg), and atonal and modal (e.g., musique concrète).

2310
as
CUVELIER, Marcel. **Jeunesses Musicales/Les Jeunesses Musicales,** *Hudba národů: Sborník přednášek, proslovených na I. mezinárodním sjezdu skladatelů a hudebních kritiků/Musique des nations: Ier Congrès international des compositeurs et critiques musicaux* (Praha: Syndikát Českých Skladatelů, 1948) 28–30,116–19. In Czech and French. See no. 278 in this volume.

Summary account by the founder of the youth musical organization, instituted in Belgium as a clandestine organization in the early period of the German occupation, October 1940; focused on its current activities (performing opportunities, classes, and awards) and ongoing efforts to develop an international organization.

2311
as
CUVELIER, Maurice. **Les relations entre la musique contemporaine et le public, considérées avec l'organisation de manifestions musicales** [The relations between contemporary music and the public, considered with the organization of music performances], *Atti del secondo Congresso internazionale di musica* (Firenze: Le Monnier, 1940) 47–56. In French. See no. 239 in this volume.

On the basis of experience in Brussels, and particularly of the Société Philharmonique under the executive direction of Marcel Cuvelier, argues that the public needs to be prepared for the reception in four phases with appropriately informative program notes; with the repetition of difficult new works in the course of a single season; with the inclusion of important repertoire works in all programs; and with the inclusion of a greater proportion of modern works on a very slow and gradual schedule. *(David Bloom)*

2312
as
DENT, Edward Joseph. **International exchange in music,** *Atti del primo Congresso internazionale di musica* (Firenze: Le Monnier, 1935) 226–33. Summary in Italian. See no. 203 in this volume.

Today, international musical exchanges can be promoted for purely artistic motives only among an educated elite. The middle classes of music lovers easily fall prey to nationalism, and people of limited musical understanding are always ready to use patriotism to cover their prejudices. The urgent task is to establish, in all countries, communities of intelligent musical amateurs, who will encourage live performance and active listening, as opposed to the passive listening encouraged by the phonograph and radio.

(David Bloom)

2313
as
DIJK, K. van. **La musique à la radio: Aspects sociologiques à la suite de quelques recherches hollandaises** [Radio music: Sociological aspects following some Dutch research], *Cahiers d'études de radio-télévision* 3-4 (1955) 425–29. *Bibliog., charts, diagr.* In French. See no. 334 in this volume.

Light music has many more radio listeners than opera, chamber, or symphonic music.

2314
as
DOSSE, Madame. **Place de la musique à la radio dans la vie des candidats bacheliers** [The role of radio music in the life of advanced secondary students], *Cahiers d'études de radio-télévision* 3-4 (1955) 479–82. In French. See no. 334 in this volume.

Briefly discusses students' listening habits. For some, music is a distraction, while for others it is central to their experience.

2315
as
DOUILLART, A. **La musique sacrée dans les institutions d'aveugles** [Sacred music in institutions for the blind], *La musique d'église: Compte rendu du Congrès de musique sacrée* (Tourcoing: Duvivier, 1920) 215–19. In French. See no. 93 in this volume.

Briefly outlines the contributions to the restoration of religious music made by institutions in Bordeaux, Nantes, and Poitiers.

2316
as
DOVAZ, René. **Nature, développement et champs d'influence des programmes musicaux** [Nature, development, and range of influence of musical programs], *Cahiers d'études de radio-télévision* 3-4 (1955) 449–57. In French. See no. 334 in this volume.

Depending on artistic quality, radio can develop or degrade music. In Europe, systematic psycho-sociological studies of radio's influence are needed.

2317
as
EBENSTEIN, Julius (Yuval). **Musik und Musiker in Israel, dem Grenzland zwischen Asien und Afrika** [Music and musicians in Israel, the borderland between Asia and Africa], *Bericht über den internationalen musikwissenschaftlichen Kongreß Wien Mozartjahr 1956* (Graz; Köln: Böhlau, 1958) 148–49. In German. See no. 365 in this volume.

A survey of the full range of traditional, neotraditional, and art music. The commemoration of the Mozart bicentenary, under the auspices of the Israel-Mozarteum (founded 1944), marks Israel's full membership in the international music community. *(David Bloom)*

2318
as
ECHÁNOVE TRUJILLO, Carlos A. **Remarques sur la qualité artistique de la musique à la radio** [Remarks on the artistic quality of radio music], *Cahiers d'études de radio-télévision* 3-4 (1955) 318–30. In French. See no. 334 in this volume.

Discusses various cultural influences, with attention to American commercialism.

2319
as
FEDELI, Vito. **Musica da chiesa** [Church music], *La vita musicale dell'Italia d'oggi* (Torino: Fratelli Bocca, 1921) 209–11. In Italian. See no. 97 in this volume.

Discusses the benefits of the wide dissemination of church music and suggests the formation of a singing school.

2320
as
FLOTHUIS, Marius. **Der Widerhall von Janáčeks Musik in Holland und die Möglichkeiten das Interesse für sein Werk zu fördern/O ohlasu Janáčkovy hudby v Holandsku a o možnostech podporovat zájem o jeho dílo** [Reception of Janáček's music in the Netherlands and the possibilities of encouraging an interest in his work], *Leoš Janáček a soudobá hudba* (Praha: Panton, 1963) 94–97. In German and Czech. See no. 389 in this volume.

Because of the tight connection between Janáček's compositional means and Czech language and folk music, the performance and reception of his works abroad, specifically in the Netherlands, encounter some difficulties that need to be overcome. *(editors)*

2321
as
GAVAZZENI, Gianandrea. **Il compositore e l'attitudine del pubblico verso la musica moderna** [The composer and the attitude of the public toward modern music], *Atti del secondo Congresso internazionale di musica* (Firenze: Le Monnier, 1940) 90–97. In Italian; summaries in French and German. See no. 239 in this volume.

If it is true that there is a disagreement between those who write music today and those who listen to it, musicians can also see this disagreement in the opposite way, as a historic starting point, from which they are enabled to escape the disgrace of a musical universal suffrage and address themselves only to those capable of understanding them. *(author)*

2322
as

GRUBER, Roman Il'ič. **Zur Händel-Pflege in der Sowjetunion** [Händel cultivation in the Soviet Union]. Trans. from Russian by Irene WEGGEN, *Händel-Ehrung der Deutschen Demokratischen Republik: Konferenzbericht* (Leipzig: VEB Deutscher Verlag für Musik, 1961) 261–64. In German. See no. 408 in this volume.

Discusses concert and opera performances, exhibitions and publications, and other examples of Händel cultivation in the Russian, Ukrainian, Armenian, and Georgian republics, with particular attention to the commemoration of the 1959 bicentenary of the composer's death. *(David Bloom)*

2323
as

HÄNDCHEN, Fritz. **Singen und Stimmbildung in der NS.-Gemeinschaft Kraft durch Freude** [Singing and vocal training in the National Socialist society Kraft durch Freude], *Bericht über den Internationalen Kongreß Singen und Sprechen* (München: Oldenbourg, 1938) 293–95. In German. See no. 257 in this volume.

⟶

HANDSCHIN, Jacques. **Die Orgelbewegung in der Schweiz** [The Orgelbewegung in Switzerland]. See no. 1979 in this volume.

2324
as

HARPNER, O.T. **Musik im zwischenstaatlichen Kulturaustausch (Mit besonderer Berücksichtigung der englisch-österreichischen Beziehungen)** [Music in the cultural exchange between countries (with special emphasis on English-Austrian relations)], *Musikerziehung: Zeitschrift der Musikerzieher Österreichs* special issue (1953) 154–55. In German. See no. 317 in this volume.

2325
as

HETSCHKO, Alfred. **Die Bedeutung des kulturellen Erbes in Musikerziehung und Musikgestaltung der Deutschen Demokratischen Republik** [The cultural heritage in music pedagogy and music organizing in East Germany], *Bericht über den internationalen musikwissenschaftlichen Kongreß Wien Mozartjahr 1956* (Graz; Köln: Böhlau, 1958) 272–75. In German. See no. 365 in this volume.

A survey of East German cultural policy in music as it corresponds to the cultural interests and needs of the people.

2326
as

HÖFFER, Paul. **Komponist und Konzertkrise** [The composer and the concert crisis], *Atti del secondo Congresso internazionale di musica* (Firenze: Le Monnier, 1940) 75–81. In German; summaries in Italian and French. See no. 239 in this volume.

When concert life began to encounter difficulties ca. 1925-27, musicians and music lovers often said that new music was to blame for the problem; yet now that new music has almost disappeared from subscription concert programs, concerts are no better attended than they were then. In fact, as Eberhard Preußner has shown (*Die bürgerliche Musikkultur*, Hamburg 1935), concert life has always been in crisis; it is the music of amateurs that has historically played the role of bringing musical renewal, and composers should not ignore this. *(author)*

2327
as

HOFFMAN, Alfred. **Un grand interprète roumain de la musique de Chopin: Dinu Lipatti** [A great Romanian interpretation of the music of Chopin: Dinu Lipatti], *The book of the first international musicological congress devoted to the works of Frederick Chopin* (Warszawa: Państwowe Wydaw-

nictwo Naukowe, 1963) 438–43. In French. See no. 425 in this volume.

Dinu Lipatti, a great interpreter of the works of Chopin, advocated abstaining from all artistic artifice and useless tradition in the performance of the works of this composer. Lipatti died in 1950 while still in his early 30s, but left behind several recordings of Chopin's works. *(Susan Poliniak)*

2328
as

HOREMANS, Jef. **Slotwoord** [Closing word], *Verhandelingen van het Muziekcongres* (Antwerpen: Stad Antwerpen, 1935) 121–23. In Dutch. See no. 210 in this volume.

Summarizes discussions and resolutions of the conference.

2329
as

JACOB, Georges. **La vie de l'Union des Maîtres de Chapelle et Organistes au cours de ses premières vingt-cinq années** [The life of the Union des Maîtres de Chapelle et Organistes during its first 25 years], *Congrès international de musique sacrée: Chant et orgue* (Paris: Desclée de Brouwer, 1937) 31–36. In French. See no. 247 in this volume.

As of 1937, there is no diploma designed for those who wish to be organists or maîtres de chapelle.

2330
as

JÄGER, Wolfgang. **Jugendfunk: Neue Formen und Ziele** [Youth radio: New forms and goals], *Musische Jugend und technische Mittler* (Remscheid: Landesarbeitsgemeinschaft Jugendmusik Nordrhein-Westfalen, 1957) 71–80. In German. See no. 380 in this volume.

As director since 1953 of the Jugendfunk division of Norddeutscher Rundfunk, broadcasting to a target audience aged 16 to 25, the author aimed particularly at the active participation of the young people themselves, on both sides of the microphone. *(David Bloom)*

2331
as

JENNISSEN, Émile. **La propagande en chantant** [Propaganda in singing], *Congrès international des Amitiés Françaises* (Mons: Libert, 1911) 97–99. In French. See no. 74 in this volume.

Proposes the formation of a society for the preservation of the French chanson.

2332
as

KOECHLIN, Charles. **Comment compose-t-on?** [How does one compose?], *Deuxième congrès international d'esthétique et de Science de l'art* (Paris: Librairie Félix Alcan, 1937) II, 236–38. In French. See no. 249 in this volume.

Informal remarks. In the vast variety of approaches to composition, from almost purely improvisational creation at the piano to the gradual working through a long series of successive approximations, there is a unity in the concrete and undeniable presence of inspiration. *(David Bloom)*

2333
as

KOLNEDER, Walter. **Pädagogisch-soziologische Betrachtungen zur neuen Musik** [Pedagogical-sociological observations on new music], *Stilkriterien der neuen Musik* (Berlin: Merseburger, 1961) 82–95. In German. See no. 410 in this volume.

Understanding the influence of an artist on society requires an understanding of that society. Problems in the position of new music in contemporary society can be ascribed in part to the lack of concert programming and to the lack of unity among new music composers. *(Neill Clegg)*

2334
as

KOSTER, Ernst. **Sinn und Gefahr des Fernsehens für die Jugend** [The meaning and the danger of television for youth], *Musische Jugend und technische Mittler* (Remscheid: Landesarbeitsgemeinschaft Jugendmusik Nordrhein-Westfalen, 1957) 89–100. *Illus.* In German. See no. 380 in this volume.

A skeptical discussion of the possibilities of educational television, with reference to research in the U.S. by Charles A. Siepmann (*Television and education in the United States*, Paris: Unesco, 1952) and in Germany by Oskar Foerster. *(David Bloom)*

2335 KRENEK, Ernst. **Le point de vue du com-**
as **positeur contemporain au sujet de l'attitude du public vis à vis des œuvres modernes** [The contemporary composer's point of view on the subject of the public's attitude towards modern works], *Atti del secondo Congresso internazionale di musica* (Firenze: Le Monnier, 1940) 108–12. In French; summaries in Italian and German. See no. 239 in this volume.
The elite of music lovers no longer corresponds, as it once did, to the groups that govern society, and is thus unable to open the road to modern composers. Turning to the official authorities, with their necessary conservatism, would not be a solution. What is needed is a new elite, powerful within a private context, that could in part be created through a more serious music education in general schools; this in turn would aid the public in learning to form its own opinion instead of suffering from that inferiority complex that is the true obstacle to an understanding between modern music and the audience. *(author)*

2336 LAIBLE, Ulrich. **Klavier und Klavierbau**
as **1965: Berufskundliche Ausstellung im Rahmen des Europiano-Kongreß Berlin** [Klavier und Klavierbau 1965: A trade exhibition in the context of the Europiano-Kongreß Berlin], *Dokumentation* (Frankfurt am Main: Fördergemeinschaft Klavier, 1966) 278–90. In German. See no. 494 in this volume.
Report of an exhibition of current European piano manufacture held by participant firms at the congress.

2337 LAJTHA, László. **La musique d'aujourd'hui et**
as **le public** [Today's music and the public], *Atti del secondo Congresso internazionale di musica* (Firenze: Le Monnier, 1940) 83–89. In French; summaries in Italian and German. See no. 239 in this volume.
It is not the case that the public is simply uninterested in modern music, but that it has become less interested in art and music in general. One reason is that music education has not kept up with the times but remained excessively devoted to the 18th and 19th c., neglecting earlier and newer music both. Mass audiences have accepted excellent modern music in film scores; jazz has supplanted earlier dance music styles precisely because of its newness. Contemporary composers must abandon the Romantic heroism and redundant phraseology of the last century to create the human face and voice of the present. *(David Bloom)*

2338 LAMMEL, Inge. **Die Pflege Händelscher Ora-**
as **torien durch die deutsche Arbeiter-Sänger-bewegung** [The cultivation of Händel's oratorios by the German workers' choir movement], *Händel-Ehrung der Deutschen Demokratischen Republik: Konferenzbericht* (Leipzig: VEB Deutscher Verlag für Musik, 1961) 229–34. In German. See no. 408 in this volume.
Summarizes material from the dissertation abstracted as RILM [1976]6100. Among the mostly secular works favored by the workers' choir movement in Germany, between its origins at the beginning of the 20th c. and its banning in 1933, Händel's oratorios played a strikingly dominant part. *(David Bloom)*

2339 LANDORMY, Paul. **Des moyens d'organiser, en**
as **France, une ligue pour la protection et le développement de l'art musical** [Of the means of organizing, in France, a league for the protection and development of the musical art], *Congrès international d'histoire de la musique: Documents, mémoires et vœux* (Solesmes: St. Pierre; Paris: Fischbacher, 1901) 246–50. In French. See no. 32 in this volume.

A proposed league should support music education and Parisian performances of the entire classical repertoire, and also publish a music bulletin.

2340 LANGE, Francisco Curt. **Americanismo musi-**
as **cal,** *Papers read at the International Congress of Musicology* (New York: Music Educators National Conference, 1944) 273–83. See no. 266 in this volume.
Description and progress report of a movement dedicated to organizing, promoting, publishing, performing, and teaching Latin American music.

2341 LASCELLES, George Henry Hubert, Earl of
as Harewood. **Patronage of music in the West,** *Music: East and West* (Tōkyō: conference, 1961) 165–69. See no. 445 in this volume.

2342 LE FLEM, Paul. **Les courants de la musique**
as **contemporaine** [The directions of contemporary music], *Deuxième congrès international d'esthétique et de Science de l'art* (Paris: Librairie Félix Alcan, 1937) II, 453–57. In French. See no. 249 in this volume.
After World War I, national schools of music flourished. Composers from some countries borrowed subjects from folklore. Jazz became an important influence. Stravinsky and Schoenberg were examples to younger composers. Ballet gained renewed favor. *(Elizabeth A. Wright)*

2343 LE GUENNANT, Auguste. **Le mouvement**
as **grégorien en France** [The Gregorian movement in France], *Atti del [I] Congresso internazionale di musica sacra* (Tournai: Desclée, 1952) 245–47. In French. See no. 303 in this volume.

2344 LIEBERMANN, Rolf. **Radio und neue Musik**
as [Radio and new music], *Cahiers d'études de radio-télévision* 3-4 (1955) 518–20. In German. See no. 334 in this volume.
Discusses the problem of conservative taste among the listening public, and suggests that the solution is to program good music of all styles from all periods. *(Michael Adelson)*

2345 LIESS, Andreas. **Das Geistige in der**
as **zeitgenössischen Musik** [The spiritual in contemporary music], *Musikerziehung: Zeitschrift der Musikerzieher Österreichs* special issue (1953) 34–36. In German. See no. 317 in this volume.

2346 LIM, Won-sik. **Present status of music in Ko-**
as **rea,** *Bericht über den internationalen musikwissenschaftlichen Kongreß Wien Mozartjahr 1956* (Graz; Köln: Böhlau, 1958) 350–51. See no. 365 in this volume.
Surveys performing organizations, music education facilities, and popular reception of Western art music in South Korea since World War II. *(David Bloom)*

2347 LOCKSPEISER, Edward. **The greed of music,**
as *Cahiers d'études de radio-télévision* 3-4 (1955) 394–95. See no. 334 in this volume.
The 19th c. saw the rise of two tendencies among composers: disintegration, whose casualties were individuals and aesthetic and philosophical principles, and greed, typified by claims to universality. As a democratizer of music, radio both symbolizes and enacts a universalization of aesthetics, allowing the listener to indulge in unlimited greed. *(James R. Cowdery)*

2348 LORIA, Arturo. **Il pubblico e la musica** [The pub-
as lic and music], *Atti del secondo Congresso internazionale di musica* (Firenze: Le Monnier, 1940)
15–24. In Italian; summaries in French and German.
See no. 239 in this volume.

It would be helpful if the lay audience for modern music were to recognize
that it, too, is contemporary, and to take more pride in being called on to
judge new works. There is an unfortunate tendency to discourage young
composers by comparing them unjustly and arbitrarily to those that have
acquired the patina of genius through the passage of time and the love of audiences of the past. *(author)*

2349 LUCIANI, Sebastiano Arturo. **Inflazione musi-
as cale** [Musical inflation], *Atti del quinto Congresso di
musica* (Firenze: Barbèra, 1948) 73–75. In Italian. See
no. 285 in this volume.

The appreciation and practice of art music are in decline. The number of
performing amateurs, who have traditionally constituted a major link between composers and the public, is declining owing to the transmission of
music by radio. Concerts are more numerous but the public finds less time
to attend them. The accessibility of music through broadcasts depreciates
its value and causes the proliferation of poor music, while the inadequate
quality of transmission distorts the music. Recordings, however, are useful.
They make available great performances and unfamiliar works with remarkable fidelity and facilitate the re-creation of the history of music in
sound. *(Channan Willner)*

2350 MACLEAN, Charles. **Questions of musical or-
as ganization,** *Bericht über den zweiten Kongress der
Internationalen Musikgesellschaft* (Leipzig: Breitkopf
& Härtel, 1907) 245. See no. 53 in this volume.

Brief notes on papers on institutional questions read at the conference: by
Ludwig Schiedermair on university music curricula, Jules Écorcheville on
the proposal for the *Bulletin français de la S.I.M.*, William Gray McNaught
on the organization of the eisteddfod revival, and the author on the British
Incorporated Society of Musicians (founded 1882).

2351 MAHY, Alfred. **Le répertoire des sociétés
as d'amateurs** [The repertoire of amateur societies], *La
musique et le peuple: Rapports, suggestions, voeux*
(Bruxelles: Ministère des Sciences et des Arts, 1932)
57–60. In French. See no. 195 in this volume.

Urges more original compositions and transcriptions of classic works for
the use of amateur bands.

2352 MALHERBE, Charles. **L'internationalisme
as dans la musique** [Internationalism in music],
Haydn-Zentenarfeier (Leipzig: Breitkopf & Härtel;
Wien: Artaria, 1909) 56–59. In French. See no. 65 in
this volume.

Discusses the interchange of ideas among nations. Issues of language and
culture are addressed, particularly as they relate to opera.

2353 MALIPIERO, Gian Francesco. **I rapporti tra
as compositore e pubblico** [The relations between
composer and public], *Atti del secondo Congresso
internazionale di musica* (Firenze: Le Monnier, 1940)
103–07. In Italian; summaries in French and German.
See no. 239 in this volume.

The current situation is abnormal. There is an armistice between audiences
and musicians, and few musicians dare to take to the open field; art cannot
live in continuous battle conditions. If composers and public are divided, it
may be appropriate to ask who is "dividing and ruling": it is critics, infatu-
ated with the past, that divide, and virtuoso performers living with the dead
that rule. *(author)*

2354 MARIE, Jean-Étienne. **La radiodiffusion
as devant le problème de l'initiation à la musique
contemporaine** [Radio broadcasting in the face of

the problem of initiation to contemporary music], *Cahiers d'études de radio-télévision* 3-4 (1955) 534–37.
In French. See no. 334 in this volume.

2355 MARKEVITCH, Igor. **Les musiciens et le pub-
as lic** [Musicians and the public], *Atti del secondo
Congresso internazionale di musica* (Firenze: Le
Monnier, 1940) 31–36. In French; summaries in Italian
and German. See no. 239 in this volume.

In the misunderstanding between audiences and musicians, musicians need
to take a greater share of the blame. The public has learned to expect a real
spiritual nourishment and receives instead intellectual games. Moreover,
the continual expansion of knowledge has led to a specialization that sepa-
rates people in their work, opposed to the spirit of synthesis and the need for
universality of which greatness is composed; in the arts we must make the
greatest effort possible toward this spirit of synthesis. *(author)*

2356 MEERENS, Charles. **Réforme du système mu-
as sical** [Reform of the musical system], *Congrès international d'histoire de la musique: Documents, mémoires
et vœux* (Solesmes: St. Pierre; Paris: Fischbacher, 1901)
270–75. *Music, charts, diagr.* In French. See no. 32 in
this volume.

Discusses various topics including the minor mode and its relationship to
the parallel and relative major modes, the clef system, universal pitch standards, tempo classification, and the legal rights of composers.

2357 MERSMANN, Hans. **Muse und Technik** [Muse
as and technology], *Musische Jugend und technische
Mittler* (Remscheid: Landesarbeitsgemeinschaft
Jugendmusik Nordrhein-Westfalen, 1957) 150–61. In
German. See no. 380 in this volume.

Concluding remarks at a conference on the integration of mass-media technology and arts education.

2358 MICHAELS, Jost. **Innere Grundlagen des
as heutigen Orchestermusizierens und ihre
Bedeutung für die Nachwuchsfrage** [The inner
foundations of current orchestral musicianship, and
their bearing on the question of the next generation],
*Neue Zusammenarbeit im deutschen Musikleben:
Vorträge und Entschließungen* (Kassel: Bärenreiter,
1956) 47–57. In German. See no. 343 in this volume.

Discusses the situation in Germany.

2359 MIELANTS, Flor. **Les concerts "De Werker"
as d'Anvers** [The "De Werker" concerts in Antwerp], *La
musique et le peuple: Rapports, suggestions, voeux*
(Bruxelles: Ministère des Sciences et des Arts, 1932)
91–93. In French. See no. 195 in this volume.

The "De Werker" concerts, begun in 1924, have provided inexpensive musical performances for the working people. A short record of concerts, directors, featured performers, and provenance of performed works is given.
(Mark Stevens)

2360 MŁODZIEJOWSKI, Jerzy. **Janáčkova hudba v
as Polsku** [Janáček's music in Poland], *Leoš Janáček a
soudobá hudba* (Praha: Panton, 1963) 226–27. In
Czech; summaries in Russian and German. See no. 389
in this volume.

Janáček's music was introduced in Poland after World War I, when the opera theaters in Poznań, Warsaw, and L'viv performed his opera *Její
pastorkyňa (Jenůfa)*. *(editors)*

2361 MOOSER, Robert-Aloys. **La radio et son influ-
as ence sur le goût musical** [The radio and its influence on musical taste], *Atti del secondo Congresso
internazionale di musica* (Firenze: Le Monnier, 1940)

129–35. In French; summaries in Italian and German.
See no. 239 in this volume.

Certainly radio can be reproved for providing music ready made, and thus discouraging people from bothering to study the art; with force-feeding the audience; and with giving too much time to mediocre works. But it would be wiser to exploit the inevitable phenomenon to the end of forming the public's musical taste, particularly with respect to contemporary works, by introducing them prudently and gradually into the programming. *(David Bloom)*

2362
as

MÖSER. **Kulturrecht im Dritten Reich: Rechtsfragen des Sprech- und Gesangunterrichts** [Cultural legislation in the Third Reich: Legal questions in the pedagogy of speech and singing], *Bericht über den Internationalen Kongreß Singen und Sprechen* (München: Oldenbourg, 1938) 40–43. In German. See no. 257 in this volume.

In the *Führerstaat* as opposed to the liberal state, culture is regarded as a property of the nation; hence all cultural workers, including private voice teachers, must be members of the appropriate subunit of the Reichskulturkammer, which requires them to be morally, personally, and politically trustworthy and professionally qualified. It is illegal to provide private instruction without a written agreement in standard form. Further obligations of the teacher are discussed in detail. *(David Bloom)*

2363
as

MUROI, Mayako. **Der gegenwärtige Stand der Musik in Japan** [The present state of music in Japan], *Bericht über den internationalen musikwissenschaftlichen Kongreß Wien Mozartjahr 1956* (Graz; Köln: Böhlau, 1958) 440–42. In German. See no. 365 in this volume.

Brief survey of the presence of Western art music from 1868 and the political reforms of the Meiji era, with attention to Japanese composers and performers working in Western idioms, in the context of the history of the indigenous musical traditions. *(David Bloom)*

2364
as

NEUMANN, Alfred. **The young artists and the contemporary musical theatre,** *Zeitgenössisches Musiktheater/Contemporary music theatre/Théâtre musical contemporain* (Hamburg: Deutscher Musikrat, 1966) 145–47. See no. 481 in this volume.

The U.S. is currently training more musicians than it can employ. University subsidies encourage music students, even though the professional music world is overcrowded. In order to provide for the future of music theater, programs that support upcoming musical artists must be developed. *(Mary Lou Humphrey)*

2365
as

NEUMANN, Václav. **La musique en Tchécoslovaquie** [Music in Czechoslovakia], *Atti del sesto Congresso internazionale di musica* (Firenze: Barbèra, 1950) 121–24. In French. See no. 291 in this volume.

A plea to establish a rapport between the music communities of Czechoslovakia and the rest of the Western world, as well as a discussion on the nature of subjectivity and objectivity in music (i.e., music includes both qualities, not just one or the other). Music is playing an important role in the social and political changes in Czechoslovakia. *(Susan Poliniak)*

2366
as

NEWLIN, Dika. **Zwölftonmusik in Amerika** [Twelve-tone music in America], *Musikerziehung: Zeitschrift der Musikerzieher Österreichs* special issue (1953) 134–36. In German. See no. 317 in this volume.

The dissemination of Schoenberg's theory in America proceeds through the teaching, concertizing, and recording activities of his successors. *(Joseph Giroux)*

2367
as

NOMURA, Francesco Yosio. **Gegenwärtige Probleme der Musikwissenschaft in Japan** [Present-day problems of musicology in Japan], *Bericht über den siebenten internationalen musikwissenschaftlichen Kongreß* (Kassel: Bärenreiter, 1959) 201–03. In German. See no. 390 in this volume.

The institutionalization of the study of music has been largely confined to the aesthetic viewpoint; practitioners of a more scientific approach such as Tanaka Shōhei, Tanabe Hisao, and Kanetsune Kiyosuke have had to work within natural-science faculties. The establishment of musicology as a discipline in its own right, with chairs at the leading universities, is the most urgent task. The interest in Western music following the Meiji restoration has led to a neglect of Japanese traditional and court music, especially that of periods earlier than the Edo period (1600-1867). Japanese musicology may be able to make a unique contribution through the characteristic Japanese openness to the new trends of 20th-c. European music. *(David Bloom)*

2368
as

NOMURA, K. **Problems of music patronage in the East,** *Music: East and West* (Tōkyō: conference, 1961) 155–58. See no. 445 in this volume.

2369
as

OTAÑO EGUINO, Nemesio. **Razón de mi presencia en este Congreso** [My reasons for attending this Congress], *V Congreso Nacional de Música Sagrada* (Madrid: Gráficas Dos de Mayo, 1956) 153–63. In Spanish. See no. 331 in this volume.

The composer, musicologist, and pedagogue reflects about his role in the reform of Spanish religious music since the 1903 issuing of Pope Pius X's motu proprio *Tra le sollecitudini*. *(José López-Calo)*

2370
as

PANHUYS, L.C. van. **Music in Latin America, Surinam, and Curaçao,** *Congrès international des sciences anthropologiques et ethnologiques: Compte rendu de la troisième session* (Tervuren: Musée Royal de l'Afrique Centrale, 1960) 266. See no. 282 in this volume.

Surveys origins and genres of popular, traditional, and art music in the three places.

2371
as

PETROV, Stojan. **Proizvedenija Ferenca Lista v Bolgarii** [Liszt's works in Bulgaria], *Studia musicologica Academiae Scientiarum Hungaricae* V (1963) 249–54. In Russian. See no. 427 in this volume.

Focuses on Bulgarian reception of the composer's works in the 20th c.

2372
as

PHILIPPOT, Michel Paul; BRUCK, Charles. **Poésie et vérité** [Poetry and truth], *Stéréophonie et reproduction musicale* (Paris: Chiron, 1966) 47–54. In French. See no. 511 in this volume.

The path from composer's intention to listener's judgment often resembles the children's game of "telephone", and the work of acoustic and recording engineers adds new opportunities for distortion, as does the inexperience of today's audiences in active music making, compared with that of 19th-c. audiences. The authors' experiences working together, as conductor and recording engineer respectively, suggests that the difficulties can be overcome. *(David Bloom)*

2373
as

PIRIO, D. **Le chant d'église dans nos patronages de jeunes gens** [Religious song in our youth clubs], *Compte rendu du Congrès général de musique sacrée: Aperçu général des préliminaires et du congrès, discours et conférences* (Strasbourg: Alsacien, 1922) 165–76. In French. See no. 96 in this volume.

Proposes a much greater role for singing in church-sponsored youth clubs and presents the program at the Cathedral of Vannes as a case study.

2374
as

PONTZEN, Théodore. **Les émissions musicales en tant qu'objets d'une attention indirecte** [Musical broadcasts as objects of indirect attention], *Cahiers d'études de radio-télévision* 3-4 (1955) 487–93. In French. See no. 334 in this volume.

Discusses the desire of some listeners for music that creates an emotional atmosphere but demands little attention. The nature and sociological functions of ambient music are explored.

2375 PORTE, Jean. **Problèmes posés par une étude**
as **par sondage de l'auditoire radiophonique**
[Problems arising from a survey of the radiophonic au-
dience], *Cahiers d'études de radio-télévision* 3-4
(1955) 344–47. In French. See no. 334 in this volume.
Discusses methodology and results of two surveys about public taste in music by l'Institut National de la Statistique, commissioned by Radio-Télévision Française (RTF). The first took place in December, 1952;
the second in February, 1954.

⟶ PRÉVOST, A. **Éducation musicale populaire:**
Projet d'utilisation rationnelle de la musique
du 1ᵉʳ Régiment de Guides [Popular music education: A project for rational use of the music of the 1ᵉʳ
Régiment de Guides]. See no. 4624 in this volume.

2376 PRIM, Jean. **Hommage à Joseph Samson** [Trib-
as ute to Joseph Samson], *Perspectives de la musique
sacrée à la lumière de l'encyclique* Musicae sacrae
disciplina (Paris: conference, 1959) 184–85. In French.
See no. 379 in this volume.
An obituary for the French organist, composer, and musicologist
(1888-1957).

2377 PRIM, Jean. **Hommage à Joseph Samson** [Trib-
as ute to Joseph Samson], *Revue musicale* 239-240 (1957)
65–69. In French. See no. 378 in this volume.
Another version is abstracted as no. 2376 in this volume. Includes an
abridged version of SAMSON's conference paper abstracted as no. 6372 in
this volume.

2378 PRUNIÈRES, Henry. **Des rapports artistiques**
as **internationaux considérés du point de vue de**
la musique, de la musicologie et des musiciens
[International artistic relationships from the point of
view of music, musicology, and musicians], *Atti del
primo Congresso internazionale di musica* (Firenze: Le
Monnier, 1935) 239–50. In French; summary in Italian.
See no. 203 in this volume.
The founding of the International Society for Contemporary Music (ISCM)
and the International Musicological Society (IMS), in 1922 and 1927, respectively, signaled an atmosphere of cooperation in performance and
scholarship now threatened by the nationalism of countries including Germany, France, and Italy. Efforts like those of the ISCM and IMS need to be
multiplied and reinforced. Restrictions on international travel and work
permits should be eased for orchestral musicians and soloists.
(Nathaniel Rudykoff)

2379 QUARANTA, Felice. **Mozart fra gli operai**
as [Mozart among the workers], *Bericht über den
internationalen musikwissenschaftlichen Kongreß
Wien Mozartjahr 1956* (Graz; Köln: Böhlau, 1958)
477–80. In Italian. See no. 365 in this volume.
The Università Popolare Don Orione, Turin, was organized in the 1940s by
Giuseppe Pollarolo, under the influence of the philosophy of Luigi Orione,
for impoverished immigrants from the countryside; its series of musical
evenings began in 1949, with the assistance of Filiberto Guala (later man-
aging director of the RAI). A set of five Mozart concerts and concert-
lectures in 1956 was enthusiastically received by the working-class audience. *(David Bloom)*

2380 RAZZI, Giulio. **La musica lirica e sinfonica**
as **nella sua diffusione attraverso la radio** [Oper-
atic and symphonic music as broadcast on radio], *Atti
del secondo Congresso internazionale di musica*
(Firenze: Le Monnier, 1940) 118–25. In Italian; summaries in French and German. See no. 239 in this
volume.
In Italian radio, opera and symphonic music have been successfully broadcast; audiences have shown no difficulty in listening to opera without a

visual stimulus. There are some artistic and technical problems to be overcome. Radio operas and symphonic music written especially for broadcast
will undoubtedly develop; they are not likely to threaten the broadcast of
normal works. *(author)*

2381 ROIG, Gonzalo. **Some problems confronting**
as **musicians in America,** *Papers read at the International Congress of Musicology* (New York: Music Educators National Conference, 1944) 289–91. See no. 266
in this volume.
Emphasizes the need for an exchange of ideas between the Americas on
copyright protection for Latin American composers, as well as the need for
a comprehensive study of Cuban traditional music. *(Susan Levine)*

2382 ROSBAUD, Hans. **Der Rundfunk als Erzie-**
as **hungsmittel für das Publikum** [Radio as a means
of educating the public], *Atti del secondo Congresso
internazionale di musica* (Firenze: Le Monnier, 1940)
135–44. In German; summaries in Italian and French.
See no. 239 in this volume.
The quality of broadcast performances needs to be improved continually
and to respond to the requirements of diverting and distracting the audience, awakening and nourishing its interest, and elevating it spiritually. The
quantity of light music should be expanded, without admitting works of inferior quality; special educational broadcasts should also be prepared. A
well-made mix of music and words in educational programming is capable
not only of refining public taste but also of inciting people to a direct and active involvement with music on their own part. The ability of radio to assist
in the development of a popular engagement with modern music is equally
important. *(David Bloom)*

2383 ROSS, Hugh. **Report of Subcommittee on Mu-**
as **sic Management and Concert Interchange**
with Latin America, *Report of the Committee of the
Conference on Inter-American Relations in the Field of
Music* (Washington, D.C.: United States Department of
State, 1940) 46–48. See no. 271 in this volume.
The possibility of tours of Central and South America and Mexico by great
artists is under study. Jascha Heifetz will make suggestions for younger and
less famous artists. There will also be a South American talent search. Radio stations may be helpful in discovering new artists. There will be contacts between managers from this country and from South America in regard to cultural exchanges. *(Howard Cinnamon)*

2384 RUFFIN. **Communication sur le Comité**
as **Charles Bordes** [Communication on the Charles
Bordes committee], *Compte rendu du Congrès général
de musique sacrée: Aperçu général des préliminaires et
du congrès, discours et conférences* (Strasbourg: Alsacien, 1922) 253–58. In French. See no. 96 in this
volume.
Discusses commemorative activities for Charles Bordes.

2385 SAN MARTINO E VALPERGA, Enrico di. **La**
as **musica contemporanea e le società dei concerti**
[Contemporary music and concert organizations], *Atti
del secondo Congresso internazionale di musica*
(Firenze: Le Monnier, 1940) 25–30. In Italian; summaries in French and German. See no. 239 in this volume.
Argues that programmers in Italy, in the particular opportunities for music
created by the Fascist regime, have been too generous in allowing derivative, insincere, or weak works into concert programs, causing audiences to
lack confidence in new music. *(David Bloom)*

2386 SASS, Herbert. **Musikrat und Arbeits-**
as **gemeinschaft: Die beiden Organisationen, ihre**
Entschließungen auf der Bonner Tagung 1955
und deren erste Ergebnisse [Music Council and
Arbeitsgemeinschaft: The two organizations, their resolutions at the 1955 Bonner Tagung, and the first re-

sults], *Neue Zusammenarbeit im deutschen Musikleben: Vorträge und Entschließungen* (Kassel: Bärenreiter, 1956) 58–73. In German. See no. 343 in this volume.
Concerns the joint work of the German Section of the International Music Council and the Arbeitsgemeinschaft für Musikerziehung und Musikpflege at the Bonn meeting, under the headings of music for youth and laypersons; music in schools; music education outside schools; and the training of a successor generation for art-music orchestras. *(David Bloom)*

2387
as
SASSMANN, Martin. **Die Ausstellung Klavier und Klavierbau 1965** [The exhibition Klavier und Klavierbau 1965], *Dokumentation* (Frankfurt am Main: Fördergemeinschaft Klavier, 1966) 276–78. In German. See no. 494 in this volume.
Report of an exhibition of current European piano manufacture held by participant firms at the Europiano-Kongreß, Berlin, 1965.

2388
as
SCHRADE, Leo. **Music's place in Western life,** *Music: East and West* (Tōkyō: conference, 1961) 40–46. See no. 445 in this volume.

2389
as
SCHROTH, Rolf. **Die Bedeutung des Singens in der Kameradschaftserziehung des NSD.-Studentenbundes** [The significance of singing in comradeship training in the NSD-Studentenbund], *Bericht über den Internationalen Kongreß Singen und Sprechen* (München: Oldenbourg, 1938) 331–36. In German. See no. 257 in this volume.
Argues for group singing as a technique for achieving the triple unity of hard bodies, cultivated minds, and profound souls aimed at by German men's groups in the National Socialist state. *(David Bloom)*

2390
as
SILBERMANN, Alphons. **Radio und musikalische Kultur** [Radio and musical culture], *Musikerziehung: Zeitschrift der Musikerzieher Österreichs* special issue (1953) 107–10. In German. See no. 317 in this volume.

2391
as
SILVA, Giulio. **L'arte del canto** [The art of song], *La vita musicale dell'Italia d'oggi* (Torino: Fratelli Bocca, 1921) 211–17. In Italian. See no. 97 in this volume.
The art song is in decline in modern Italian musical life.

2392
as
SINGH, Thakur Jaideva. **Patronage of music in India,** *Music: East and West* (Tōkyō: conference, 1961) 159–60. See no. 445 in this volume.

2393
as
STANLEY, Albert A. **Provincial music festivals in the United States,** *Report of the Fourth Congress of the International Musical Society* (London: Novello, 1912) 377–84. *Charts, diagr.* See no. 71 in this volume.

2394
as
STEFAN, Paul. **Ein Völkerbund der Musik** [A musical League of Nations], *Atti del primo Congresso internazionale di musica* (Firenze: Le Monnier, 1935) 233–39. In German; summary in Italian. See no. 203 in this volume.
To guarantee the survival and growth of contemporary music, musicians must unite to foster the international performance of works written since the Great War. The activities of the International Society for Contemporary Music, founded in 1922, offer an example. *(Lisa Miller)*

2395
as
STREATFEILD, Richard Alexander. **Concert life in England,** *Haydn-Zentenarfeier* (Leipzig: Breitkopf & Härtel; Wien: Artaria, 1909) 498–507. *Charts, diagr.* See no. 65 in this volume.

Contrasts London's musical life with that of the provinces: In London, choral music has largely lost its hold on the public because of the growing taste for orchestral music. A list of English musical societies is appended.

2396
as
SUÑOL BAULINAS, Gregori M. **Association grégorianiste et cécilienne en Espagne** [Gregorian and Cecilian associations in Spain], *La musique d'église: Compte rendu du Congrès de musique sacrée* (Tourcoing: Duvivier, 1920) 143–47. In French. See no. 93 in this volume.
Briefly outlines the history of the Cecilian association (founded in 1912) and the Gregorian association (founded in 1915).

⟶
SUPPAN, Wolfgang. **Franz Liszt und die Steiermark** [Franz Liszt and Styria]. See no. 2106 in this volume.

2397
as
TAL, Josef. **Die musiksoziologische Einflussphäre des israelitischen Radios** [Israeli radio and its influence on music and society], *Cahiers d'études de radio-télévision* 3-4 (1955) 419–24. In German. See no. 334 in this volume.
Discusses passive vs. active listening, and outlines several types of radio programs that promote the latter, including quiz shows and theme-based programs (e.g., interpretation, instruments, and literature). The importance of radio for shaping a national style among composers is also addressed. *(Michael Adelson)*

2398
as
TAYLOR, Davidson. **Report on radio interchange with Latin America,** *Report of the Committee of the Conference on Inter-American Relations in the Field of Music* (Washington, D.C.: United States Department of State, 1940) 54–85. *Charts, diagr.* See no. 271 in this volume.
As a result of the State Department Conference on Inter-American Relations in the Field of Music during the fall of 1939 and a growing interest in Latin America in general, CBS and NBC have broadcast programs of Latin American composers and performers. Many were broadcast via shortwave to the musicians' homelands. Reports of longwave broadcasts were prepared by Ernest La Prade of NBC and James Fassett of CBS, while reports of shortwave broadcasts were prepared by Elizabeth Tucker of CBS and Charles Bovett of NBC. *(Gary Eskow)*

2399
as
TEMPREMENT, Jean. **La musique à la radio** [Music on the radio], *Cahiers d'études de radio-télévision* 3-4 (1955) 441–45. In French. See no. 334 in this volume.
Discusses radio's responsibility to various types of listeners, including professional musicians, the musically uneducated, and music lovers who do not attend concerts.

2400
as
THIEL, Jörn. **Jugend-, Volks- und Hausmusik im Rundfunk** [Youth music, traditional music, and Hausmusik on radio], *Musische Jugend und technische Mittler* (Remscheid: Landesarbeitsgemeinschaft Jugendmusik Nordrhein-Westfalen, 1957) 53–58. In German. See no. 380 in this volume.
The integration of arts and technology in a positive sense takes place only where their union produces a sense of form and uniqueness for the art in question, enabling the audience to name, judge, localize, and interpret it. *(author)*

2401
as
TOBEL, Rudolf von. **Menschliche und künstlerische Probleme des Musikers am Beispiel Pablo Casals'** [Human and artistic problems of the musician: Pablo Casals as example], *Musikerziehung: Zeitschrift der Musikerzieher Österreichs* special issue (1953) 61–64. In German. See no. 317 in this volume.

2402 TORREFRANCA, Fausto. **Perchè non v'è**
as **osmosi tra arte e pubblico?** [Why is there no osmosis between art and public?], *Atti del quinto Congreso
di musica* (Firenze: Barbèra, 1948) 75–89. In Italian.
See no. 285 in this volume.

Musical language and music's role in society interact. Contemporary composers—aggressive, revolutionary, and undisciplined—have little to offer
the general public. They can control neither the ebb and flow of composition nor the alternation of strong and weak accents, beats, and measures,
nor the coordination of orchestral sonorities and dynamics. Their music
does not cohere; the public finds it unacceptable. The passionate and devoted performing amateurs, proponents of new music since the Middle
Ages, also consider it unacceptable. Only performance by professional musicians is feasible, and the government must provide the requisite funds for
such performances. *(Channan Willner)*

2403 TOYAMA, Kazuyuki. **Concerts in Japan,** *Music:*
as *East and West* (Tōkyō: conference, 1961) 36–39. See
no. 445 in this volume.

2404 **[Vienna] Beethoven und die Wiener Kultur**
as **seiner Zeit** [Beethoven and the Viennese culture of his
time], *Beethoven-Zentenarfeier: Festbericht* (Wien:
Otto Maass' Söhne, 1927) 41–43. In German. See no.
141 in this volume.

A report on an exhibition held in Vienna in conjunction with the centenary
celebration in the year 1927.

2405 VILLALBA, Luis. **La censura de la música**
as **religiosa** [Censorship in religious music], *Crónica del
primer Congreso Nacional de Música Sagrada*
(Valladolid: A. Martín, 1908) 41–50. *Index.* In Spanish.
See no. 57 in this volume.

Censorship of religious music in Spain is discussed in reference to the
guidelines set forth in Pius X's motu proprio *Tra le sollecitudini* (1903).
(José López-Calo)

2406 WALTER, Franz. **Enquiry on contemporary**
as **music theatre in festivals,** *Zeitgenössisches
Musiktheater/Contemporary music theatre/Théâtre
musical contemporain* (Hamburg: Deutscher Musikrat,
1966) 134–37. See no. 481 in this volume.

Presents the results of a questionnaire sent to 28 members of the European
Association of Music Festivals. On the basis of 13 replies the following
conclusions were drawn: (1) festival organizers favor supporting contemporary music; (2) the musical taste of the festival public is decidedly conservative; (3) commissions given by festivals are to be supported; and (4)
though risky, cooperation between festivals to promote contemporary music is worthwhile. Among contemporary operas, works by Berg and Britten
have been relatively well received. *(Mary Lou Humphrey)*

2407 WANGERMÉE, Robert. **La vulgarisation de la**
as **musique par la radio** [The vulgarization of music
by the radio], *Cahiers d'études de radio-télévision* 3-4
(1955) 538–49. In French. See no. 334 in this volume.

Discusses the dangers of passive listening. Particular attention is paid to the
programmers' responsibility for shaping public taste and raising the level
of cultural awareness.

2408 WELLESZ, Egon. **Der Musiker und sein**
as **Publikum** [The musician and his public], *Atti del
secondo Congresso internazionale di musica* (Firenze:
Le Monnier, 1940) 98–103. In German; summaries in
Italian and French. See no. 239 in this volume.

There have always been artists who began with works that could only be
understood by a limited elite group, but they have always been exceptional.
The wider public will accept exceptional works if the composer's idea has
been definitively realized. At the moment, there is too much experimentation, a sign of a transitional era; at its end, it may be hoped that the gap between artists and audience will be bridged. *(author)*

2409 WERKLE, Helmut. **"Muse und Technik" aus**
as **der sicht der Evangelischen Akademie** [The
Muse and technology from the point of view of the
Evangelische Akademie], *Musische Jugend und
technische Mittler* (Remscheid: Landesarbeitsgemeinschaft Jugendmusik Nordrhein-Westfalen,
1957) 28–35. In German. See no. 380 in this volume.

The Lutheran perspective on the question of arts and mass media, as it has
developed since the war and the founding of the Evangelische Akademie
think tank at Loccum near Hanover, is represented by citations from
Werner HESS, Hans-Werner von MEYENN, Hanns LILJE, and Karl
BARTH. *(David Bloom)*

2410 WIORA, Walter. **Musische Gaben in**
as **technischer Vermittlung** [Gifts of the arts mediated through technology], *Musische Jugend und
technische Mittler* (Remscheid: Landesarbeitsgemeinschaft Jugendmusik Nordrhein-Westfalen, 1957)
13–27. In German. See no. 380 in this volume.

Philosophical reflections on the question of how mass media can be used to
communicate, not merely transmit, the gift of a work of art. *(David Bloom)*

2411 WÖRSCHING, Joseph. **Beruf und Bedeutung**
as **des Organistenamtes für den Lehrstand und
das deutsche Volk** [The vocation and significance of
the position of organist for the teaching profession and
for the German people], *Bericht über die dritte Tagung
für Deutsche Orgelkunst* (Kassel: Bärenreiter, 1928)
87–91. In German. See no. 136 in this volume.

Especially since the 1914-18 war, the German Volksschule teacher has become less and less likely to be able to fulfill his traditional role as music
teacher and organist. The tradition is central to the musicality of the German people and, as Schoenberg has lamented, will not survive into the next
century unless urgent measures are taken. *(David Bloom)*

2412 ZHAO, Feng. **Bartók and Chinese musical cul-**
as **ture,** *Studia musicologica Academiae Scientiarum
Hungaricae* V (1963) 393–401. See no. 427 in this
volume.

Increased exposure to Bartók's music in China during the 1950s made him
a model for Chinese composers and music students, some of whom were inspired by his example to take an interest in ethnomusicological research.
Elements of Bartók's biography may be considered in the terms of classical
Chinese philosophy. *(Alan Garfield)*

Mountain Chief listens to his voice as recorded by Frances Densmore
(see nos. 3145, 3146, and 3985) in 1916.
Reproduced with permission of the Smithsonian Institution.

ETHNOMUSICOLOGY

30 The discipline

2413
as
ALMEIDA, Renato. **Le folklore et l'enseigne-ment de la musique au Bresil** [Folklore and musical education in Brazil], *Journal of the International Folk Music Council* V (1953) 44–47. In French. See no. 314 in this volume.

A report on the formulation of a charter at the first Congresso Brasileiro de Folclore (Rio de Janeiro, 1952). The charter understands folklore to be an integral part of anthropological and cultural sciences, considers nontraditional elements that have acquired a collective character to be within its domain, and encourages methodological studies on cultural anthropology, history, and folklore. *(Murat Eyüboğlu)*

2414
as
ALMEIDA, Renato, moderator. **Resolutions,** *Journal of the International Folk Music Council* VII (1955) 23. See no. 337 in this volume.

Outlines two resolutions adopted by the International Folk Music Council on 21 July 1954: (1) A definition of folk music, and (2) a recommendation that traditional music should be a feature of all levels of pedagogy, and should be raised to academic status. *(James R. Cowdery)*

2415
as
ARCHER, William Kay. **A quodlibet for Saraswathi: Some observations on the possibilities and limitations of scientific methods applied to the study of artistic values in traditional music,** *Artistic values in traditional music* (Berlin: International Institute for Comparative Music Studies, 1966) 49–93. *Bibliog.* See no. 493 in this volume.

Discusses the uses and limitations of science as an epistemological tool for investigating music. Special attention is given to the phenomenon of tradition, the question of evolution of different traditions, and the various human purposes music serves.

2416
as
AYESTARÁN, Lauro. **Fétis: Un precursor del criterio etnomusicológico en 1869** [Fétis: A precursor of the ethnomusicological criterion in 1869], *Boletín interamericano de música* (supplement 1965) 15–37. *Facs., music, transcr.* In Spanish. See no. 461 in this volume.

In his *Histoire générale de la musique depuis les temps les plus anciens jusqu'à nos jours* (1869), François-Joseph Fétis was the first to incorporate the musics of the Americas, Asia, Africa, and Oceania into a general music-historical perspective. His wide-ranging discussion of Aztec and Inca/Quechua music is discussed in detail, and a Spanish translation is provided in an appendix, together with a facsimile reproduction of his source for the Quechua *harawi* genre, from the *Antigüidades peruanos* of Johann Jakob Tschudi and Mariano Eduardo de Rivera (Vienna, 1851). *(David Bloom)*

2417
as
AZEVEDO, Luiz Heitor Corrêa de. **L'UNESCO et la musique populaire** [UNESCO and traditional music], *Journal of the International Folk Music Council* I (1949) 19–21. In French. See no. 281 in this volume.

By 1950, the United Nations Educational, Scientific and Cultural Organization plans to institute an Internatonal Music Council or council of international music organizations for the purpose of encouraging the development of national organizations, providing UNESCO with advice in musical matters, mounting festivals and conferences, and founding the international institute of music proposed at UNESCO's 1947 Mexico conference.

Areas in which the International Folk Music Council can assist the new council are outlined. *(David Bloom)*

2418
as
[Azoulay] **Sur les applications du phono-graphe à l'étude des traditions populaires** [On the applications of the phonograph to the study of popular traditions], *Congrès international des traditions populaires* (Paris: E. Lechevalier, E. Leroux, J. Maisonneuve, 1902) 136–37. In French. See no. 31 in this volume.

Describes Léon Azoulay's presentation on the phonograph for the Société d'Anthropologie de Paris. Azoulay had recorded various foreigners in Paris as they sang the traditional songs of their homelands. Mention is made of ethnomusicological recording projects of Hungarian popular songs (by Béla Vikár) and Turkish songs in Hungary. *(Susan Poliniak)*

2419
as
BARKECHLI, Mehdi. **Introduction to the International Congress,** *The preservation of traditional forms of the learned and popular music of the Orient and the Occident/La préservation des formes traditionelles de la musique savante et populaire dans les pays d'Orient et d'Occident* (Urbana: Center for Comparative Psycholinguistics, Institute of Communications Research, 1964) 49–57. See no. 443 in this volume.

Discusses the issue of the endangerment and preservation of tradition; the terminology of the *savant* vs. *populaire* distinction; and the advantages and disadvantages of committing musical traditions to notation. *(Michael Collier)*

2420
as
BARKECHLI, Mehdi. **Nécessité d'une coordination des différentes techniques appliquées à la recherche du folklore musical** [The need to coordinate the different techniques applied to research in musical folklore], *Journal of the International Folk Music Council* XIII (1961) 10–12. In French. See no. 424 in this volume.

2421
as
BARTÓK, Béla. **Les recherches sur le folklore musical en Hongrie** [Music folklore research in Hungary], *Congrès international des arts populaires/International congress of popular arts* (Paris: Institut international de coopération intellectuelle, 1928) 91–94. In French. See no. 153 in this volume.

Summary of the history of collection and classification of traditional music of the Hungarian, Slovak, Romanian, and other peoples of pre-war Hungary from the end of the 19th c. to about 1918. With the continuous extension of urban culture throughout Europe, traditional music is certain to become largely extinct, and international cooperation is needed to preserve as much material as possible in the shortest possible time. Another version is cited as no. 2731 in this volume. The Hungarian original was published as *Zenefloklore-kutatások Magyarországon* in *Zenei szemle* XIII:1 (1929). An English-language version was published in *Béla Bartók: Essays*, edited by Benjamin Suchoff (New York: St. Martin's, 1976). *(David Bloom)*

2422
as
BASCOM, William R. **The main problems of stability and change in tradition,** *Journal of the International Folk Music Council* XI (1959) 7–12. See no. 392 in this volume.

It is time to move beyond mere recording and description of musical items and events: Dynamic processes such as acculturation, innovation, and selectivity must be addressed. Anthropologists can contribute much to our understanding of these processes, since they are in a position to observe the activities of the individuals and groups they study. Musicologists may also make invaluable contributions, since they have the skills for a direct focus on technical musical matters. Processes of selectivity are particularly crucial to understanding the character of individual cultures. *(James R. Cowdery)*

2423 BOSE, Fritz. **Folk music research and the culti-**
as **vation of folk music,** *Journal of the International Folk Music Council* IX (1957) 20–21. See no. 362 in this volume.

The collection and notation of traditional music are laudable pursuits, but researchers need to take care that their efforts do not threaten the survival of traditions in their natural state. *(James R. Cowdery)*

⟶ BRĂILOIU, Constantin. **Musicologie et ethno-**
musicologie aujourd'hui [Musicology and ethnomusicology today]. See no. 865 in this volume.

2424 BUKOFZER, Manfred F. **Observations on the**
as **study of non-Western music,** *Les colloques de Wégimont. [I: Ethnomusicologie I]* (Bruxelles: Elsevier, 1956) 33–36. In English and French. See no. 340 in this volume.

The importance of the study of non-Western music cannot be stressed enough, although some scholars find this shift in emphasis difficult to adopt. Different methods of research are needed for non-Western music, in particular for the distinction between popular and classical music. Comments in French by Constantin BRĂILOIU are appended. *(John R. Metz)*

2425 CARAVAGLIOS, Cesare. **Metodi ed orienta-**
as **menti nelle ricerche delle tradizioni popolari musicale** [Methods and orientations in the search for folk music traditions], *Atti del III Congresso nazionale di arti e tradizioni popolari* (Roma: Opera Nazionale Dopolavoro, 1936) 76–110. In Italian. See no. 218 in this volume.

2426 CHERBULIEZ, Antoine-Élisée. **La base**
as **musicologique du folklore musical comparé** [The musicological basis of comparative musical folklore], *Journal of the International Folk Music Council* VII (1955) 13–14. In French. See no. 337 in this volume.

Summary of a paper describing how the methods and concepts of comparative musicology can be applied to folklore studies.

2427 CHERBULIEZ, Antoine-Élisée. **Les principes**
as **de la musicologie comparée et le folklore musicales** [*sic*] [The principles of comparative musicology and music folklore], *Journal of the International Folk Music Council* II (1950) 49. In French. See no. 295 in this volume.

The conference report provides only a citation. Neither the text nor a summary of the paper was published here.

2428 COLLAER, Paul. **Contributions à la méthode**
as **scientifique en ethnomusicologie** [Contributions to scientific method in ethnomusicology], *Les colloques de Wégimont. IV: Ethnomusicologie III* (Paris: Belles Lettres, 1964) 24–37. In French. See no. 401 in this volume.

In the observation and analysis of musical phenomena, it is important to keep in mind the limitations of our muscles, sense organs, and brains. *(Scott Fruehwald)*

2429 CROSSLEY-HOLLAND, Peter. **Preservation**
as **and renewal of traditional music,** *Journal of the International Folk Music Council* XVI (1964) 15–18. See no. 463 in this volume.

The diffusion of nontraditional forms of music is destroying regional folk and liturgical traditions. Materials must be collected and preserved—giving priority to older traditional music—and the principles of traditional music must be recognized and given new creative outlets, renewing old forms to suit contemporary needs. *(Vivian Conejero)*

2430 CROSSLEY-HOLLAND, Peter. **Work of the In-**
as **ternational Institute for Comparative Music Studies during the year 1964-1965,** *Artistic values in traditional music* (Berlin: International Institute for Comparative Music Studies, 1966) 115–23. See no. 493 in this volume.

Describes field work, research, publication, concerts, and educational activities sponsored by the Berlin organization.

2431 DITTMER, Kunz. **Ethnologie und Musik-**
as **ethnologie** [Ethnology and musical ethnology], *Bericht über den internationalen musikwissenschaftlichen Kongreß* (Kassel: Bärenreiter, 1957) 66–72. In German. See no. 356 in this volume.

Discusses foundational issues in cultural anthropology as they apply to ethnomusicology and comparative musicology.

2432 GABRIEL, Gavino. **Laofonografia** [Laopho-
as nography], *Atti del III Congresso nazionale di arti e tradizioni popolari* (Roma: Opera Nazionale Dopolavoro, 1936) 347–49. In Italian. See no. 218 in this volume.

2433 HEINITZ, Wilhelm. **Hamburg und die ver-**
as **gleichende Musikwissenschaft** [Hamburg and comparative musicology], *Bericht über den internationalen musikwissenschaftlichen Kongreß* (Kassel: Bärenreiter, 1957) 109–11. In German. See no. 356 in this volume.

Research in comparative musicology in Hamburg began at the same time as the founding of the Universität Hamburg in 1919, at the Phonetisches Laboratorium. The Forschungsabteilung für Vergleichende Musikwissenschaft, founded at the phonetics laboratory by the author in 1935, merged with the university's Musik-Institut to form the Musikwissenschaftliches Institut in 1949. The research interest that distinguishes the Hamburg school from those of Vienna and Berlin is in the physical and physiological aspects of music. The term "ethnomusicology" as a replacement for "comparative musicology" is not an improvement: It seems to exclude the music of non-European high cultures. *(David Bloom)*

2434 HERZOG, Avigdor. **Transcription and trans-**
as **notation in ethnomusicology,** *Journal of the International Folk Music Council* XVI (1964) 100–01. *Bibliog., transcr.* See no. 463 in this volume.

Summary of a typological discussion of transcription techniques for traditional music, including established analytic and synthetic techniques, the concise transcription of Béla Bartók, and the amended and didactic techniques developed respectively by the author and Ne'eman, Yehẇšu'a Leyyb at the Hamakẇn hayśra'ely lemẇsyqah datyt. *(David Bloom)*

2435 HOOD, Mantle. **Program of the Institute of**
as **Ethnmusicology, University of California, Los Angeles,** *Artistic values in traditional music* (Berlin: International Institute for Comparative Music Studies, 1966) 108–14. See no. 493 in this volume.

Provides an overview of the curriculum, describes programs of support for research, details laboratory equipment, and lists planned publications.

2436 HOOD, Mantle. **The quest for norms in ethno-**
as **musicology,** *Boletín interamericano de música* (supplement 1965) 67–71. See no. 461 in this volume.

The highly generalized studies of early ethnomusicologists, with their focus on comparative method, and the minute detail of much current work, both fail to promote the comprehension of a musical culture. A quest for the norms of musical style must be situated between these extremes, in terms of the music itself as it is valued in its social context. Actual contact with the society and some performing knowledge of the tradition are essential. *(author)*

2437 HORNBOSTEL, Erich Moritz von. **Über den**
as **gegenwärtigen Stand der vergleichenden Musikwissenschaft** [The current state of comparative musicology], *Bericht über den zweiten Kongress der Internationalen Musikgesellschaft* (Leipzig: Breitkopf & Härtel, 1907) 56–60. In German. See no. 53 in this volume.

Survey of ethnomusicological findings, problems, and tasks from ca. 1885 to 1906, under the headings of tonal system, melody, performance practice (e.g., ornamentation), rhythm, and musical practice (e.g., instruments). *(David Bloom)*

2438 HROVATIN, Radoslav. **Problemi studija**
as **narodnih pesama i igrara u vezi sa radom** [Problems in the study of traditional songs and dances related to work], *Rad VIII-og kongresa folklorista Jugoslavije* (Beograd: Naučno Delo, 1961) 399–404. *Port.* In Serbian; summary in French. See no. 446 in this volume.

Broad discussion of questions of terminology, methodological approach, ideological tendency, and goals.

2439 **[International Folk Music Council] General**
as **report,** *Journal of the International Folk Music Council* V (1953) 9–35. See no. 314 in this volume.

Reports on discussions and resolutions at the fifth conference of the International Folk Music Council concerning (1) the definition of folk music; (2) standards for the dissemination of traditional music; (3) standards for the use of traditional music in pedagogy; (4) the role of traditional music in radio broadcasting; (5) standards for the preservation of traditional music, including archives, sound recordings, films, and publications; (6) the value of national and international festivals; and (7) ways to cultivate official and public support for traditional music. *(James R. Cowdery)*

2440 KLUSÁK, Vladimír. **The preservation of folk**
as **music traditions in Czechoslovakia,** *Journal of the International Folk Music Council* XIII (1961) 90. See no. 424 in this volume.

Summary of a paper. Discusses the activities of Československý Rozhlas (Czechoslovak Radio) in Prague.

2441 KLUSEN, Ernst. **Beziehungen zwischen**
as **Volksliedforschung und Volksliedpflege** [The connections between folk-song research and folk-song cultivation], *Actas do Congresso Internacional de Etnografia* (Porto: Imprensa Portuguesa, 1965) 133–40. In German. See no. 473 in this volume.

Ethnomusicology and folklore have been remarkably focused on past and vanishing works, out of indifference, or ideological blindness, toward the problems of the present. Traditional song repertoires should be analyzed in terms of their capacity to stay alive in the future; newly developing repertoires should be studied; and the relevance of the political viewpoint in the analysis of traditional songs should be acknowledged. *(David Bloom)*

2442 KRAFT, Günther. **Stand und Koordinierung**
as **der wissenschaftlichen Forschung auf dem Gebiet des Arbeiterliedes in der Deutschen Demokratischen Republik** [The condition and coordination of scholarly research in East Germany in the area of the Arbeiterlied], *Beiträge zur Musikwissenschaft* VI/4 (1964) 267–77. In German. See no. 476 in this volume.

2443 LEACH, MacEdward. **Collecting techniques**
as **with special reference to ballads,** *Boletín interamericano de música* (supplement 1965) 179–86. See no. 461 in this volume.

General discussion of the requirements of ethnomusicological fieldwork, in terms of preparation (training and equipment), informant selection, and choice of materials for collection. The field-worker should acquire not only the folklore itself but also a deep personal knowledge of the informant and a complete understanding of the performance context. Harry Belafonte's recording of *The banana boat song (Day-O)* is criticized as joining the textual form of an authentic Jamaican song to an inappropriate Trinidadian-style melody, making it meaningless in relation to its traditional culture matrix. *(David Bloom)*

2444 LINĔVA, Evgenija. **Über neue Methoden des**
as **Folklores in Rußland** [On the new methods of folklore in Russia], *Haydn-Zentenarfeier* (Leipzig: Breitkopf & Härtel; Wien: Artaria, 1909) 233–43. *Transcr.* In German. See no. 65 in this volume.

The use of modern methodology in Russian ethnomusicology began with field studies of polyphonic song in the late 19th c. by Julij Nikolaevič Mel'gunov and Nikolaj Pal'čikov. Beginning in 1897, the author began making phonograph recordings of polyphonic song; transcriptions are published in her *Velikorusskie pesni v narodnoj garmonizacii* (St. Petersburg, 1904-09). The value of these precise documents is illustrated with the analysis of variants of the song *Lučinuška* collected in the Novgorod and Voronež districts. *(David Bloom)*

2445 MARCEL-DUBOIS, Claudie. **Principes**
as **essentiels de l'enquête ethnomusicologique: Quelques applications françaises** [Essential principles of ethnomusicological inquiry: Some French applications], *Journal of the International Folk Music Council* XIII (1961) 13–18. In French. See no. 424 in this volume.

2446 MARCEL-DUBOIS, Claudie. **The relation be-**
as **tween broadcasting organizations and specialised folk music institutions,** *Journal of the International Folk Music Council* VIII (1956) 55. See no. 349 in this volume.

Summary of a paper. Folklore institutions may depend on radio stations for the collection, preservation, and dissemination of traditional music. On the other hand, radio stations need the advice and information that folklorists can provide. *(James R. Cowdery)*

2447 MARINUS, Albert. **Chanson populaire—**
as **Chanson folklorique** [Popular song—Folk song], *Journal of the International Folk Music Council* VI (1954) 21–25. In French. See no. 320 in this volume.

The term "popular song" has taken on the colloquial sense of songs like *La vie en rose* or *Ma petite folie*, created by professional songwriters and acclaimed by whole national populations as opposed to specific local groups. For songs of primary interest to the folklorist—of a particular antiquity, or related to particular performance circumstances, social classes, or geographic regions—it is preferable to use the term "folk song". It is dangerous, however, to insist on providing each term with a definitive meaning, giving the false impression that the field is fully understood. *(David Bloom)*

2448 MARINUS, Albert. **Tradition, évolution, adap-**
as **tation** [Tradition, evolution, adaptation], *Journal of the International Folk Music Council* IX (1957) 15–19. In French. See no. 362 in this volume.

The validity of ethnomusicological research involves a belief in the existence of a fixed, unchanging tradition; but a fixed tradition is a moribund one. The task of ethnomusicology is to determine the modalities and conditions in which traditions adapt themselves to changing circumstances; to the extent that we wish to preserve the folklore that is dear to us, we should perhaps study it under the conditions in which it is best adapted to modern life. *(David Bloom)*

2449
as
MICHAĪLÍDĪS, Sólōn. **Regional committees for the comparative study of folk music,** *Journal of the International Folk Music Council* II (1950) 28–32. See no. 295 in this volume.

A draft proposal for the establishment of regional committees to collect and study traditional musics.

2450
as
NATALETTI, Giorgio. **Dix ans d'ethno-musicologie en Italie** [Ten years of enthnomusicology in Italy], *Bericht über den siebenten internationalen musikwissenschaftlichen Kongress* (Kassel: Bärenreiter, 1959) 198–99. In French. See no. 390 in this volume.

Surveys progress since the 1948 establishment of the Centro Nazionale Studi di Musica Popolare with the support of Radiotelevisione Italiana (RAI) and the Accademia di Santa Cecilia, Rome. *(David Bloom)*

2451
as
NATALETTI, Giorgio. **Ten years of folk music collecting by the Centro Nazionale Studi di Musica Popolare,** *Journal of the International Folk Music Council* XI (1959) 70. See no. 392 in this volume.

Summary of a paper.

2452
as
NEJEDLÝ, Zdeněk. **Les études du prof. O. Hostinsky sur la chanson populaire tchèque** [Professor O. Hostinský's research on Czech traditional song], *Congrès international des arts populaires/International congress of popular arts* (Paris: Institut international de coopération intellectuelle, 1928) 106. In French. See no. 153 in this volume.

Summary of a paper discussing the ethnomusicological work of Otakar Hostinský (1847-1910) as collector, analyst, and theorist, in the context of Romantic thought. Hostinský's method introduced new analytic criteria through the consideration of psychological, sociological, and historical factors. *(David Bloom)*

2453
as
NETTL, Bruno. **Criteria for acculturation,** *Report of the Eighth Congress of the International Musicological Society. II: Reports* (Kassel: Bärenreiter, 1962) 97–100. See no. 440 in this volume.

A report on a discussion by Luiz Heitor Corrêa de AZEVEDO, Klaus P. WACHSMANN, Arnold Adriaan BAKE, Paul COLLAER, Dragotin CVETKO, Edith GERSON-KIWI, Alan LOMAX, Bruno NETTL, Cvjetko RIHTMAN, Charles SEEGER, and Walter WIORA of the paper by Wachsmann abstracted as no. 2480 in this volume.

2454
as
NETTL, Bruno. **Some historical aspects of ethnomusicology,** *Bericht über den siebenten internationalen musikwissenschaftlichen Kongress* (Kassel: Bärenreiter, 1959) 200–01. See no. 390 in this volume.

Surveys theoretical and methodological approaches within ethnomusicology to questions of the origins of musical phenomena, general and specific, and of the nature, causes, and processes of musical change.

(David Bloom)

2455
as
NKETIA, Joseph Hanson Kwabena. **The dimensions of musical studies,** *Artistic values in traditional music* (Berlin: International Institute for Comparative Music Studies, 1966) 34–48. *Bibliog.* See no. 493 in this volume.

Stylistic analysis must be accompanied by awareness of cultural context; however, musical problems will have primarily musical solutions. An analysis of the music of *kwadwom*, an epic song-type performed at Ashanti courts in Ghana, serves as an illustration.

2456
as
OESCH, Hans, intro.; BARTHA, Dénes, moderator. **Symposium: Idee und Methode "vergleichender" Musikforschung** [Symposium: The concept and method of "comparative" musicology], *Bericht über den neunten internationalen Kongreß* (Kassel: Bärenreiter, 1964-1966) II, 23–37. In German. See no. 491 in this volume.

Discussion by Karl Gustav FELLERER, Ernst HEINS, Fritz A. KUTTNER, Claudie MARCEL-DUBOIS, Harold S. POWERS, Marius SCHNEIDER, Eric WERNER, and Walter WIORA of the paper by Walter Wiora abstracted as no. 2484 in this volume.

2457
as
PERNOT, Hubert. **Chants et mélodies populaires: Résolution adoptée par le Congrès des arts populaires** [Traditional songs and melodies: Resolution adopted by the Congress of Popular Arts], *Art populaire: Travaux artistiques et scientifiques du Ier Congrès international des arts populaires* (Paris: Duchartre, 1931) 104. In French. See no. 152 in this volume.

Governments are urged to make recordings of traditional songs.

2458
as
PICKEN, Laurence E.R. **The contribution of ethnomusicology to historical musicology,** *Report of the Eighth Congress of the International Musicological Society. II: Reports* (Kassel: Bärenreiter, 1962) 153–57. In English and French. See no. 440 in this volume.

A report on a discussion by Paul COLLAER, Arnold Adriaan BAKE, Mantle HOOD, Otto KINKELDEY, Claudie MARCEL-DUBOIS, Ivan MARTYNOV, Laurence E.R. PICKEN, Dénes BARTHA, Cvjetko RIHTMAN, Walter SALMEN, Charles SEEGER, and Walter WIORA of papers by André Schaeffner and Nils Schiørring abstracted as nos. 2467 and 4111 in this volume.

2459
as
PLETKA, Václav. **Über einige methodische Probleme der Arbeiterlied-Forschung** [Some methodological problems in research on the workers' song], *Beiträge zur Musikwissenschaft* VI/4 (1964) 332–36. In German. See no. 476 in this volume.

Specific examples are drawn from research in Czechoslovakia. Another version is abstracted as RILM [1977]3329.

2460
as
POLLAK, Hans Wolfgang. **Ausrüstung der von Akademien und Gesellschaften zu entsendenden Reisenden, mit besonderer Rücksicht auf musikwissenschaftliche Zwecke** [The preparation of field researchers from academic institutions and societies, with particular attention to musicological goals], *Haydn-Zentenarfeier* (Leipzig: Breitkopf & Härtel; Wien: Artaria, 1909) 224–26. In German. See no. 65 in this volume.

Includes subsequent panel discussion.

2461
as
PORRINO, Ennio. **Per un "corpus" della musiche popolari mediterranee** [For a corpus of traditional Mediterranean musics], *Atti del Congresso internazionale di musiche popolari mediterranee e del Convegno dei bibliotecari musicali* (Palermo: De Magistris succ. V. Bellotti, 1959) 325–28. In Italian. See no. 332 in this volume.

Proposals for an international commission, preferably with a standing headquarters in Italy, and the recording, transcription, and publication of Mediterranean music. *(David Bloom)*

2462
as
RAMÓN Y RIVERA, Luis Felipe. **Problemas de la grabación y transcripción musical de los tambores** [Problems in the recording and musical transcription of drums], *Actas del XXXIII° Congreso Internacional de Americanistas* (San José: Lehmann, 1959) II, 603–10. In Spanish. See no. 398 in this volume.

The ideal recording medium is moving picture film, with soundtrack; failing this, transcriptions need to show details (e.g., which finger is striking, how far from the drum rim) and pitches of drums, whenever they can be determined. Polyrhythmic music poses special difficulties in transcription. *(Ken Alboum)*

2463 REINHARD, Kurt. **Cooperation with the musi-**
as **cian: Prospection, conservation, transcription and publication, classification,** *The preservation of traditional forms of the learned and popular music of the Orient and the Occident/La préservation des formes traditionelles de la musique savante et populaire dans les pays d'Orient et d'Occident* (Urbana: Center for Comparative Psycholinguistics, Institute of Communications Research, 1964) 214–21. See no. 443 in this volume.

Western musicologists have an obligation to assist in the preservation of non-Western traditional musics, since Western music is largely responsible for their decline. The musicologist and the traditional musician should work together cooperatively in the preservation of the tradition; the musician must refrain from mixing nontraditional forms into the repertoire, and check transcriptions for inaccuracies caused by interference from the Western tradition. *(Michael Collier)*

2464 ROBERTS, Helen Heffron. **The viewpoint of**
as **comparative musicology,** *Papers read at the Annual Meeting of the American Musicological Society* (New York: American Musicological Society, 1936) 29–34. See no. 230 in this volume.

The comparative musicologist evaluates unknown music in relation to other known forms of music, studying it on its own terms and then applying a methodology capable of furnishing bases for comparison. Ideally, comparative musicology will play a larger part in music school curricula.

2465 SARGENT, Margaret. **Folk and primitive mu-**
as **sic in Canada,** *Journal of the International Folk Music Council* IV (1952) 65–68. *Bibliog.* See no. 306 in this volume.

Surveys the history of ethnomusicological research in Canada from the early 17th c., with attention to the role of the National Museum since 1910. *(David Bloom)*

2466 SAYGUN, Ahmed Adnan. **Le recueil et la nota-**
as **tion de la musique folklorique** [The collection and transcription of folk music], *Journal of the International Folk Music Council* I (1949) 27–33. In French. See no. 281 in this volume.

Each item collected should be accompanied by as much information as possible on the details of place, performer, instruments, style, ethnographic context, and so on. Notation of melodies must represent intervals as accurately as possible, particularly in the transcription of music in untempered scales, with attention to the actual frequency ratios. The author's system of five flat symbols and four sharp symbols for the transcription of traditional melodies is offered as an example. *(David Bloom)*

2467 SCHAEFFNER, André. **Contribution de**
as **l'ethnomusicologie à l'histoire de la musique** [The contribution of ethnomusicology to historical musicology], *Report of the Eighth Congress of the International Musicological Society. I: Papers* (Kassel: Bärenreiter, 1961) 376–79. In French. See no. 439 in this volume.

Anthropologists and historians have studied the musician's social position, the circumstances and material conditions of performance, the audience music addresses, and the means by which a music diffuses beyond its place of origin. The principle contribution of ethnomusicology is to cast doubt on a history of our own music based entirely on written documents—theoretical writings and notated scores. *(David Hathwell)*

2468 SCHAEFFNER, André. **Ethnologie musicale ou**
as **musicologie comparée?** [Ethnomusicology or comparative musicology?], *Les colloques de Wégimont. [I: Ethnomusicologie I]* (Bruxelles: Elsevier, 1956) 18–32. In French. See no. 340 in this volume.

Although the two terms have been used as synonyms in the past, they describe separate fields of study, with different subject matter and methodologies. *(Scott Fruehwald)*

2469 SCHNEIDER, Marius. **Studi e proposte per un**
as **corpus delle musiche popolari mediterranee** [Studies and proposals for a corpus of traditional Mediterranean music], *Atti del Congresso internazionale di musiche popolari mediterranee e del Convegno dei bibliotecari musicali* (Palermo: De Magistris succ. V. Bellotti, 1959) 311–24. In French. See no. 332 in this volume.

Discusses particularly the organization of such a project, with attention to the relevance of historical, geographical, linguistic, anthropological, and strictly musical factors in the classification of melodies. *(David Bloom)*

⟶ SEEGER, Charles. **Music and government: Field for an applied musicology.** See no. 5907 in this volume.

2470 SEEGER, Charles. **Preface to a critique of mu-**
as **sic,** *Boletín interamericano de música* (supplement 1965) 41–63. *Charts, diagr.* See no. 461 in this volume.

Musicology and ethnomusicology have developed mainly as descriptive sciences; though subjective value judgments are assumed, they are not explicitly stated, as they must be if the two disciplines are to be made commensurate with each other and the rest of the humanities. The solution will entail regarding the opposition between subjective evaluation and objective fact not as a choice we are forced to make but as a dilemma with which we must live. *(David Bloom)*

2471 SEEGER, Charles. **Report of Subcommitte on**
as **Research in Comparative Musicology,** *Report of the Committee of the Conference on Inter-American Relations in the Field of Music* (Washington, D.C.: United States Department of State, 1940) 21–30. *Charts, diagr.* See no. 271 in this volume.

The subcommittee was divided into three areas of study: primitive music in the Western hemisphere, traditional music in the U.S., and black music. An inter-American musicological society should be established, and existing collections of valuable materials should be saved. Most studies have been in the areas of Anglo-American and African-American music; written and oral traditions from Europe and Africa should also be included. The popularity of traditional music has increased, but training in the collection and study of traditional music lags behind. In the light of the popularity of black traditional music it is surprising that it has not been the subject of more detailed study. While discussions usually center on the extent to which African patterns have been influenced by European music, black music's importance lies in what it reveals about how slaves adapted to white patterns. A memorandum on portable sound recording equipment is included. *(Howard Cinnamon)*

⟶ SMITH, Carleton Sprague. **Presidential address.** See no. 925 in this volume.

2472 Société de Radiodiffusion de la France
as d'Outre-Mer (SORAFOM). **Importance de la pratique de l'enregistrement sonore en matière de musique populaire** [The importance of the practice of sound recording in the subject of traditional music], *Journal of the International Folk Music Council* XIII (1961) 88–89. In French. See no. 424 in this volume.

2473 STERN, Philippe. **Étude de la musique**
as **populaire de tradition orale** [The study of orally
transmitted traditional music], *Travaux du Iᵉʳ Congrès
International de Folklore* (Tours: Arrault et Cie, 1938)
290. In French. See no. 251 in this volume.
Discusses transcription.

2474 STĘSZEWSKI, Jan. **Ébauche de l'histoire des**
as **classifications ethnomusicologiques en**
Pologne [An outline of the history of ethnomusicological classifications in Poland], *Studia
musicologica Academiae Scientiarum Hungaricae* VII
(1965) 345–48. In French. See no. 478 in this volume.
The first ethnomusicological studies in Poland were on song texts; the music itself was studied later. Important 19th-c. studies included those of
Wacław Zaleski and Henryk Oskar Kolberg. After many attemps at classification, coherent methods were developed. *(Daniel Horn)*

2475 STUMPF, Carl. **Vergleichende Musikforschung,**
as **Akustik, Tonpsychologie: Verhandlungen und**
Vorträge [Comparative music research, acoustics,
music psychology: Discussions and lectures], *Bericht
über den zweiten Kongress der Internationalen
Musikgesellschaft* (Leipzig: Breitkopf & Härtel, 1907)
83–85. In German. See no. 53 in this volume.
Notes on conference papers by Pedro Pablo Traversari Salazar, on a proposed history of indigenous and popular music in the Americas; Michel-
Dimitri Calvocoressi, on developments in recent Greek music; A.J. Polak,
on his harmonization of traditional Japanese melodies and correspondence
on the subject with Takamine Hideo of the Tokyo School of Music. A proposal from Gaston Knosp that each branch of the International Musical Society institute a *section exotique* is included. *(David Bloom)*

2476 STUMPF, Carl; HORNBOSTEL, Erich Moritz
as von. **Über die Bedeutung ethnologischer**
Untersuchungen für die Psychologie und
Ästhetik der Tonkunst [The significance of ethno-
logical studies for the psychology and aesthetics of mu-
sic], *Bericht über den IV. Kongress für Experimentelle
Psychologie* (Leipzig: Barth, 1911) 256f. In German.
See no. 70 in this volume.

2477 VARGA, Ovidiu. **Les variantes folkloriques et**
as **les conditions de leur survivance** [Folkloric variants and the conditions of their survival], *Journal of the
International Folk Music Council* XIV (1962) 91–95.
In French. See no. 442 in this volume.
Current ethnomusicological thinking in Romania is based on the idea of the
variant, orally transmitted, as the primary object of study. A very general
conceptual framework for considering variation and transmission in these
terms is outlined, and the activities of various Romanian institutions in the
preservation of traditional music are briefly discussed. *(David Bloom)*

2478 VAUGHAN WILLIAMS, Ralph. **Opening ses-**
as **sion,** *Journal of the International Folk Music Council*
V (1953) 7–8. See no. 314 in this volume.
Collectors who focus on the dissemination of traditional music are tempted
to value quantity over quality, while those who focus on preservation are
too apt to occupy themselves with librarianship while the traditions themselves fall into neglect. A balance must be struck between these extremes: All
that is genuinely traditional should be preserved in collections, and we
should identify and disseminate the most worthy examples. *(James R. Cowdery)*

2479 VINOGRADOV, Viktor. **The study of folk music**
as **in the U.S.S.R.,** *Journal of the International Folk Music Council* XII (1960) 73–75. See no. 413 in this
volume.
A survey of reasearch and publications.

2480 WACHSMANN, Klaus P. **Criteria for accultur-**
as **ation,** *Report of the Eighth Congress of the International Musicological Society. I: Papers* (Kassel:
Bärenreiter, 1961) 139–49. See no. 439 in this volume.
Discusses the implications for musicology of acculturation as a dynamic
process, simultaneously dependent on individuals and on their environment. Topics covered include methods of study (direct observation, interviews, reconstruction from historical testimony, and the use of new technologies); evidence for the hypothesis that music follows general trends of
cultural development; and explanations of musical phenomena based on
contact, as opposed to physical or biological explanations. Examples are
drawn from the author's fieldwork among the Ganda people of Uganda.
(Ruth Herman)

2481 WALLASCHEK, Richard. **Über den Wert**
as **phonographischer Aufnahmen von Gesängen**
der Naturvölker [The value of phonographic recordings of the songs of primitive peoples], *Verhandlungen
des XVI. internationalen Amerikanisten-Kongresses*
(Wien: A. Hartleben, 1910) 557–61. In German. See
no. 61 in this volume.

2482 WIORA, Walter. **Concerning the conception of**
as **authentic in folk music,** *Journal of the International Folk Music Council* I (1949) 14–19. See no. 281
in this volume.
Poets and musicians conceive of traditional music as a *Wertidee* (inspiring
ideal), while scholars must define it as a *Kategorie* (category). The former
is an aesthetic approach; the latter is a more sociological one.

2483 WIORA, Walter. **Ethnomusicology and the his-**
as **tory of music,** *Studia musicologica Academiae
Scientiarum Hungaricae* VII (1965) 187–93. *Bibliog.*
See no. 478 in this volume.
Historical ethnomusicology is an indispensible part of world music history.
Written and oral sources should be researched and compared scientifically
and exhaustively; the constellation of sources can produce a comprehen-
sive outline. The history of German traditional song is a case in point.
(David Gagné)

2484 WIORA, Walter. **Idee und Methode "ver-**
as **gleichender" Musikforschung** [The concept and
method of "comparative" musicology], *Bericht über
den neunten internationalen Kongreß* (Kassel:
Bärenreiter, 1964-1966) I, 3–10. In German, French,
and English. See no. 491 in this volume.
A recent trend has been to reject the term "comparative musicology" now
that it is used for the noncomparative study of non-European musics and
traditional European musics. The original idea, however, of a superregional,
comparative music research as a methodological approach, partly overlapping with but distinct from ethnomusicology, remains valid. The specific
character and general goals of such an approach are outlined. *(Sylvia Eversole)*

2485 WIORA, Walter. **Die Natur der Musik und die**
as **Musik der Naturvölker** [The nature of music and
the music of primitive tribes], *Journal of the International Folk Music Council* XIII (1961) 43–49. *Music.* In
German. See no. 424 in this volume.
The ancient Greek view of music as a natural, timeless realm has been replaced since the early 19th c. by the view that theoretical principles, as well
as genres and styles, are of a time-bound, historical character. Studying the
music of the *Naturvölker* plays an important role in the identification of
musical categories that are indeed universal. *(Alix Moyer Grunebaum)*

2486 WIORA, Walter. **Schrift und Tradition als**
as **Quellen der Musikgeschichte** [The written and the
oral as sources of music history], *Bericht über den
Internationalen musikwissenschaftlichen Kongress*
(Kassel: Bärenreiter, 1954) 159–75. *Music.* In German.
See no. 319 in this volume.

Considers the limitations of written sources and of oral tradition and suggests that the two domains complement each other. Living music of the oral tradition can help scholars imagine how early notated monophonic music may have been performed. The fluidity of form in orally transmitted music can shed light on the evolution of musical forms and genres, and the underlying relationships among them. Finally, orally transmitted music can provide special insight into the roots of music. *(Carl Skoggard)*

2487 WÜNSCH, Walther. **Volksmusikpflege und**
as **Wissenschaft** [Scholarship and the cultivation of traditional music], *Bericht über den internationalen musikwissenschaftlichen Kongreß Wien Mozartjahr 1956* (Graz; Köln: Böhlau, 1958) 758–59. In German. See no. 365 in this volume.
Summary of a programmatic paper. Another version is published in the author's *Beiträge zur Österreichischen Volksliedkunde* (Graz, 1967), cited as RILM [1973]4104.

2488 ZANZIG, Augustus D. **Report of suggestions**
as **from the Subcommittee on Community and Recreational Music,** *Report of the Committee of the Conference on Inter-American Relations in the Field of Music* (Washington, D.C.: United States Department of State, 1940) 86–91. See no. 271 in this volume.
A representative of the U.S. should undertake studies of traditional music in South America. Since many Mexican people live in the West, this area is a testing ground for musical interchanges between Latin Americans and other peoples. Songs should be published, as should a guitar method designed to help people learn South American songs. Furthermore, a clearing house related to music of the U.S. and Latin American countries should be established. It could include information on customs and music festivals; a library of traditional and popular songs and another containing choral and instrumental music; musicological information; films and records; exhibits of instruments and books; and lists of individuals and organizations in the field, including colleges that offer courses in traditional music. *(Gary Eskow)*

2489 ZULAICA Y ARREGUI, José Gonzalo (José An-
as tonio de Donostia). **Quelques observations sur la façon de recueillir les chansons en Pays basque** [Some observations on the manner of collecting songs in the Basque region], *Travaux du Ier Congrès International de Folklore* (Tours: Arrault et Cie, 1938) 290–95. In French. See no. 251 in this volume.
The proper work of the folklorist is not to synthesize theories; rather, it is to provide a collection of facts.

31 General (more than one region)

2490 ADĂSCĂLIȚEI, Vasile. **Some thoughts on the**
as **creation of folklore,** *Journal of the International Folk Music Council* XII (1960) 71–72. See no. 413 in this volume.
In the realm of folklore, creativity involves a dialectic between the individual and the group at each stage of the process. *(James R. Cowdery)*

2491 ALMEIDA, Renato. **Origine de la musique**
as **folklorique en Amerique** [Origins of traditional music in America], *Journal of the International Folk Music Council* VII (1955) 8–10. In French. See no. 337 in this volume.
Traditional music in the Americas is largely the result of cultural adaptation. Due to the enculturation of Native Americans, partially through the church, a great deal of urban and erudite music was absorbed into local traditions, creating cross-influences between traditional and cultivated genres. *(Murat Eyüboğlu)*

2492 ARCHER, William Kay. **The musical bride:**
as **Some applications of evolution, culture, and**

tradition, *The preservation of traditional forms of the learned and popular music of the Orient and the Occident/La préservation des formes traditionelles de la musique savante et populaire dans les pays d'Orient et d'Occident* (Urbana: Center for Comparative Psycholinguistics, Institute of Communications Research, 1964) 27–48. See no. 443 in this volume.
Introductory remarks at a symposium. It is possible that what needs to be discussed is less the preservation of traditional culture than its successful adaptation and hybridization.

2493 BINGULAC, Petar. **O muzički lepom u**
as **folkloru** [On beauty in traditional music], *Rad XI-og kongresa Saveza Folklorista Jugoslavije* (Zagreb: Savez Folklorista Jugoslavije, 1966) 491–503. In Serbian; summary in French. See no. 490 in this volume.
Questions the entrenched assumption that the realm of the aesthetic is the work of art understood in isolation from the society. Traditional music has always been embedded within the texture of society. Accordingly, at a time when art music is encountering difficulties with its public, an aesthetics of traditional music might signal a new direction toward a democratization of art in general, and of music in particular. *(Murat Eyüboğlu)*

2494 BOSE, Fritz. **Rhythmusprobleme in instru-**
as **mental begleiteter primitiver Musik** [Questions of the rhythm in instrumentally accompanied primitive music], *Bericht über den siebenten internationalen musikwissenschaftlichen Kongress* (Kassel: Bärenreiter, 1959) 72–73. In German. See no. 390 in this volume.
Among primitive peoples, three different kinds of instrumental accompaniment are provided for singing and dancing. First there are occasions when instruments are present and are played, without there being an observable musical relationship between the instruments and singers or dancers. In such cases, the instruments are serving a magical function, e.g., the summoning of spirits. Then there is the widespread use of percussion instruments to mark the beat for singing and dancing. Finally, one finds, especially in Africa and among its Negro peoples, highly elaborate, independent accompaniments; the nature of this accompaniment grows out of the characteristics of the instruments themselves. Often wind instruments, having been borrowed from other cultures, do not interact with vocal lines. Horns and trumpets are usually ineffective as accompanying instruments (Western orchestral influence may be suspected for African practices in which they are integrated with singing and dancing). *(Carl Skoggard)*

2495 BRĂILOIU, Constantin. **Melodie, ritmi,**
as **strumenti e simboli nelle danze mediterranee** [Melodies, rhythms, instruments, and symbols in Mediterranean dance], *Atti del Congresso internazionale di musiche popolari mediterranee e del Convegno dei bibliotecari musicali* (Palermo: De Magistris succ. V. Bellotti, 1959) 101–13. *Port.* In French. See no. 332 in this volume.
Wide-ranging examination of the notion of the Mediterranean as a single culture area, with reference to dance and dance music.

2496 BRĂILOIU, Constantin. **Un type mélodique**
as **méditerranéen** [A Mediterranean song type], *Atti del Congresso internazionale di musiche popolari mediterranee e del Convegno dei bibliotecari musicali* (Palermo: De Magistris succ. V. Bellotti, 1959) 59–62. *Port.* In French. See no. 332 in this volume.
The Romanian hora lunga (long song) genre, whose defining feature is improvised construction out of invariant melodic units, was found by Bartók to have cognate forms in Iraq, Turkey, and Ukraine; he gave it a Perso-Arabic provenance. Since his death, similar forms have been identified contrary to his expectations in all the Balkan countries, and indeed throughout the Mediterranean region on both the European and African sides (there is also a single Indochinese example); it should perhaps be thought of as a Mediterranean genre. *(David Bloom)*

2497 BRASSARD, François-Joseph. **Chansons**
as **d'accompagnement** [Accompaniment songs],
Journal of the International Folk Music Council II
(1950) 45–47. In French. See no. 295 in this volume.
Proposes a classificatory distinction between songs sung for their own sake
and songs sung to accompany some other activity. The subtypes of the latter, illustrated by examples from French Canada, include songs accompanying spoken or mimed performance, customs, rituals, work, games, or
dances. In practice, it is common for a non-accompanying song to acquire
an accompaniment function, or for an accompaniment song to enter the
non-accompanying repertoire, and it is not always easy to distinguish between the two. *(David Bloom)*

2498 BRENTA, Gaston. **Collecting and presentation**
as **of folk music in television,** *Journal of the International Folk Music Council* VIII (1956) 55. See no. 349
in this volume.
Summary of a paper. While studio recordings may provide the best technical quality, traditional music is best represented by sound films made in the
field. Recent technical improvements are discussed. *(James R. Cowdery)*

2499 BREWSTER, Paul G. **The so-called "folksong"**
as **programme of radio: A threat and a challenge,**
Journal of the International Folk Music Council III
(1951) 16–18. See no. 296 in this volume.
Folklorists must help radio presenters—and thereby the public—to realize
what real traditional music is. Authentic traditional songs are much more
appealing than the pale imitations that most people hear. *(James R. Cowdery)*

2500 BRONSON, Bertrand Harris. **Good and bad in**
as **British-American folk song,** *Journal of the International Folk Music Council* V (1953) 60–64. See no.
314 in this volume.
As in other areas of artistic endeavor, the gamut of traditional song runs
from the worthless to the precious beyond price. Similarly, performance
practices range from woefully inappropriate arrangements by and for
trained musicians to pure renditions reflecting the best of the genuine tradition. *(James R. Cowdery)*

2501 CARPITELLA, Diego. **À propos du folklore**
as **"reconstruit"** ["Reconstructed" folklore], *Journal of
the International Folk Music Council* XVI (1964)
22–24. In French. See no. 463 in this volume.
The continuity and systematic character of an oral tradition are essential elements of its vitality; when a traditional artistic expression that has become
detached from its historical context and function is presented to an audience in a reconstructed or restored version, it has not in fact been preserved.
Deterioration of the tradition must take place unless, as has happened in
Sardinia, the community itself works to revive it; ethnomusicology can
only study a musical tradition, in as much historical detail as possible, but
cannot arrest its extinction. *(David Bloom)*

2502 CHAILLEY, Jacques. **Comment entendre la**
as **musique populaire?** [How should one listen to traditional music?], *Journal of the International Folk Music Council* XVI (1964) 47–49. In French. See no. 463
in this volume.
There is a fundamental distinction between the way music manifests itself
to the hearer and its substantial reality; what the listener hears is not necessarily what is being performed. Thus, in the case of a traditional vocal polyphony, what the listener experiences may be quite unrelated to what the
performers intend; for example, they may be singing simply for themselves, as individuals, producing the impression of polyphony as a byprod-
uct. It is essential for ethnomusicology to understand such phenomena in
terms of the psychology of each of the performers. *(David Bloom)*

→ CHASE, Gilbert. **The cultivation of various European traditions in the Americas.** See no. 953
in this volume.

2503 CHRISTOFF, Dimiter. **Perspektiven der**
as **nationalen musikalischen Tradition** [Perspec-
tives of national musical tradition], *Beiträge zur
Musikwissenschaft* VII/4 (1965) 359–62. In German.
See no. 495 in this volume.

2504 COLLAER, Paul. **Importance des musiques**
as **ethniques dans la culture musicale contemporaine** [The importance of ethnic musics in contemporary musical culture], *Journal of the International
Folk Music Council* IV (1952) 56–59. In French. See
no. 306 in this volume.
Surveys the burgeoning interest in traditional musics from Europe and elsewhere since the beginning of the 20th c., alongside that in art music from
the 17th c. and earlier. The work of the Institut National de Radiodiffusion
in providing regular broadcasts from its collection of ethnic music recordings, as well as in making its own field recordings in Belgium and Congo,
provides an example that other countries might follow. *(David Bloom)*

2505 COLLINSON, Francis. **The repertoire of a tra-
as ditional Gaelic singer in the outer Hebrides
with reference to versions of her songs known
in Canada,** *Journal of the International Folk Music
Council* XIV (1962) 87–90. See no. 442 in this volume.
Since 1952 James Ross and the author have recorded over 460 Gaelic songs
and more than 1000 proverbs from the singer Nan MacKinnon of Vatersay,
by far the largest collection ever made in Scotland from a single singer.
Only two of the songs seem to be known to Gaelic singers of Nova Scotia:
the piobaireachd song *An tarbh breac dearg* (The red speckled bull), and
the waulking song *Latha dhomh's mi Beinn a Cheathaich*. This is perhaps
because few or no people from Vatersay or her ancestral island, Mingulay,
joined the 19th-c. emigration from the Hebrides to Canada. *(David Bloom)*

2506 CROSSLEY-HOLLAND, Peter. **Discussion,** *Ar-
as tistic values in traditional music* (Berlin: International
Institute for Comparative Music Studies, 1966) 127.
See no. 493 in this volume.
Summarizes a panel discussion on contributions cited as nos. 2535, 2435,
2430, and 856 in this volume.

2507 CROSSLEY-HOLLAND, Peter. **Discussion,** *Ar-
as tistic values in traditional music* (Berlin: International
Institute for Comparative Music Studies, 1966) 94–98.
See no. 493 in this volume.
Summarizes a panel discussion on contributions cited as nos. 847, 839,
2702, 2455, and 2415 in this volume.

2508 DAHMEN, Hermann Josef. **Methods and possi-
as bilities of presenting folk music in radio,** *Journal of the International Folk Music Council* VIII (1956)
53. See no. 349 in this volume.
Summary of a paper discussing ways that radio broadcasts can contribute to
the survival of traditional music. The practice of making and presenting arrangements of traditional music has an honorable 500-year history, and is
not to be rejected out of hand; artistic excellence combined with stylistic
appropriateness may increase public interest in music that many might otherwise consider unworthy of their attention. *(James R. Cowdery)*

2509 EL MAHDI, Salah. **Les problèmes de la**
as **préservation des formes traditionelles** [The
problems of preserving traditional forms], *The preservation of traditional forms of the learned and popular music of the Orient and the Occident/La préservation des
formes traditionelles de la musique savante et populaire
dans les pays d'Orient et d'Occident* (Urbana: Center
for Comparative Psycholinguistics, Institute of Communications Research, 1964) 141–45. In French. See no.
443 in this volume.

Discusses threats to the survival of traditional music brought on by social transformations, and methods of preserving it, with particular reference to the situation in Tunisia. *(Michael Collier)*

2510 FULLER-MAITLAND, John Alexander. **Les in-**
as **fluences réciproques internationales en musique** [International reciprocal influences in music], *Actes du Congrès d'histoire de l'art* (Paris: Presses Universitaires de France, 1923-1924) 735–41. In French. See no. 94 in this volume.

Although music is a universal language, the music of each country has its own individual characteristics that remain peculiar to that country, notwithstanding any outside influences. These idiomatic characteristics are strongest in a country's folk songs. *(Vivian Conejero)*

2511 GARFIAS, Robert. **Traditional music and the**
as **value of education,** *Music east and west* (Nai Dilli: Indian Council for Cultural Relations, 1966) 137–42. See no. 489 in this volume.

Increases in technological development have led to decreases in aesthetic values, and fewer people are willing to spend time undergoing years of training to become first-rate musicians. The public can be sensitized through mass media and education. *(Beverly Eskreis)*

⟶ GASPARINI, Evel. **Pjesme pjevane naizmjence i egzogamička odvojenost spolova** [Alternating songs and exogamic separation]. See no. 2822 in this volume.

2512 HACOBIAN, Zaven. **La tendance à l'hybri-**
as **dation: L'influence des conceptions a occidentales** [The tendency to hybridization: The influence of Western conceptions], *The preservation of traditional forms of the learned and popular music of the Orient and the Occident/La préservation des formes traditionelles de la musique savante et populaire dans les pays d'Orient et d'Occident* (Urbana: Center for Comparative Psycholinguistics, Institute of Communications Research, 1964) 148–62. In French. See no. 443 in this volume.

Hybridization of traditional music can have a negative, impoverishing effect, but also a positive, evolutionary one. The preservation of tradition should be able to guard against the former but not discourage the latter.

2513 HERZOG, George. **Folk song and its social**
as **background,** *Journal of the International Folk Music Council* III (1951) 107. See no. 296 in this volume.

The conference report provides only a citation. Neither the text nor a summary of the paper was published here.

2514 HOERBURGER, Felix. **Correspondence be-**
as **tween Eastern and Western folk epics,** *Journal of the International Folk Music Council* IV (1952) 23–26. See no. 306 in this volume.

Most research on the diffusion history of the epic in Eastern Europe and Western Asia has relied on epic texts; one musical feature on which ample information exists is that of its instrumental accompaniment, which is in all thriving traditions a lute or tanbur, psaltery, or fiddle, and often mentioned in epic texts as being played by the hero. The geographical distribution of the three instrument types follows that of the epic. Interestingly, their terminology is in some cases interchangeable, so that *gusla* or *gusle*, for example, is a fiddle in some languages, psaltery in others, and lute in still others; a functional classification of instruments may correspond better to cultural facts than a structural one. An extended German-language version is published, under the title *Weststöstliche Entsprechungen im Volksepos*, in *Musikforschung* 5 (1954). *(David Bloom)*

2515 International Folk Music Council. **Discussion on**
as **the preservation of folk music at a meeting of radio representatives,** *Journal of the International Folk Music Council* XIII (1961) 91. See no. 424 in this volume.

2516 International Folk Music Council. **Report on the**
as **preservation of folk music by means of recordings with special reference to radio organizations,** *Journal of the International Folk Music Council* XIII (1961) 79–82. See no. 424 in this volume.

2517 KARPELES, Maud. **Definition of folk music,**
as *Journal of the International Folk Music Council* VII (1955) 6–7. See no. 337 in this volume.

According to the IFMC's current definition, folk traditions are those shaped by oral transmission and the circumstances of continuity, variation, and selection. While this implies a time factor, it is difficult to specify exactly how long it takes for a song to become a folk song. For an art song to become a folk song—or vice versa—some form of re-creation is necessary. *(James R. Cowdery)*

2518 KARPELES, Maud. **Folk music as a social**
as **binding force,** *Music in education* (Paris: UNESCO, 1955) 189–92. See no. 322 in this volume.

Traditional music should never be undervalued by the trained musician. It has the capacity to appeal to people in all walks of life. A French-language version is cited as no. 2519 in this volume. *(Elizabeth A. Wright)*

2519 KARPELES, Maud. **La musique folklorique:**
as **Élément de rapprochement social** [Traditional music: The element of social connection], *La musique dans l'éducation* (Paris: UNESCO; Colin, 1955) 197–200. In French. See no. 323 in this volume.

An English-language version is abstracted as no. 2518 in this volume.

2520 KARPELES, Maud. **Some reflections on au-**
as **thenticity in folk music,** *Journal of the International Folk Music Council* III (1951) 10–16. See no. 296 in this volume.

Traditional music involves processes of continuity, variation, and selection; the concept of authenticity, therefore, must reflect this dynamic paradigm. The purest aspects of traditions are those that have survived the test of time. If modern developments merge with these aspects in a satisfying way, they may deserve a claim to authenticity. *(James R. Cowdery)*

2521 KLUSEN, Ernst. **Differences in style between**
as **unbroken and revived folk-music traditions,** *Journal of the International Folk Music Council* IX (1957) 28–29. See no. 362 in this volume.

Summary of a paper. Revival and adaptation are more vital than museum-like preservation, but both approaches have relevant roles to play in the survival of traditional musics. *(James R. Cowdery)*

2522 KLUSEN, Ernst. **Problems of recording au-**
as **thentic folklore,** *Journal of the International Folk Music Council* VIII (1956) 54. See no. 349 in this volume.

Summary of a paper discussing approaches to radio programming of traditional music.

2523 KUBA, Ludvík. **La préesthétique de la chanson**
as **populaire, sa source, son but, ses lois** [The pre-aesthetics of traditional song, its source, goal, and laws], *Congrès international des arts populaires/International congress of popular arts* (Paris: Institut international de coopération intellectuelle, 1928) 104–05. In French. See no. 153 in this volume.

Summary of a paper. The aesthetic sense is a biologically inherent property of the human being, and folk or primitive art is a part of the first stage of human development. The first musical genre is the lyric song, a purely subjective expression which requires no listeners; a more civilized art form is objective, the separation between artist and audience in more civilized arts reflecting the economic division between producers and consumers. The primitive song has a life cycle, like an organism, with a youth, a maturity, and a period when it may be conserved like a dried flower, with a posthumous life as a work of art. *(David Bloom)*

2524 KUTTER, Wilhelm. **Radio as the destroyer, col-**
as **lector, and restorer of folk music,** *Journal of the International Folk Music Council* IX (1957) 34–37. See no. 362 in this volume.

In one generation, newspapers and journals have replaced the personal narration of tales, and radio and sound recordings have replaced home music making. But by recording and disseminating traditional music, radio stations can actually help to reverse the trend whereby traditions are eclipsed by modern developments. *(James R. Cowdery)*

2525 LANGEVIN, Vige. **Causes de la régression de**
as **la chanson populaire** [Causes of the decline of traditional song], *Deuxième congrès international d'esthétique et de Science de l'art* (Paris: Librairie Félix Alcan, 1937) I, 318–22. In French. See no. 249 in this volume.

Traditional song is decaying because of the impact of the phonograph and radio, the noise of farm machinery, the increased speed of transportation, and the evolution of values and ideas. Much of the subject matter is obsolete (wedding customs, children's suffering), and current events are now transmited through the press and radio rather than through ballads. *(David Schiff)*

2526 LIST, George. **Acculturation and musical tra-**
as **dition,** *Journal of the International Folk Music Council* XVI (1964) 18–21. See no. 463 in this volume.

Sketches a theoretical model of transculturation and syncretism. In nonliterate cultures, the music of a dominated group often tends to disintegrate and disappear, particularly if the dominating group disapproves of it on religious grounds. Transfer of function, as when a work song, no longer performed at work, is performed at a festival, may help to preserve traditional musics, but the loss of function may lead to obliteration of the indigenous style. Unacculturated indigenous music may continue alongside imported musics under favorable conditions, including a literacy tradition. The most fruitful outcome is a syncretic hybridization between traditions with common features facilitating cross-fertilization. *(David Bloom)*

2527 LOMAX, Alan. **The creativity of the folk**
as **singer,** *Journal of the International Folk Music Council* III (1951) 107. See no. 296 in this volume.

The conference report provides only a citation. Neither the text nor a summary of the paper was published here.

2528 LOMAX, Alan. **Folk song style,** *Journal of the International Folk Music Council* VIII (1956) 48–50. See no. 349 in this volume.

Presents a typology of world singing styles.

2529 LUMPKIN, Ben Gray. **Traditional folk songs**
as **available on commercial phonograph records,** *Journal of the International Folk Music Council* III (1951) 74–76. See no. 296 in this volume.

The range of songs and performances marketed as "folk music" runs from the authentic to the spurious.

2530 MARCEL-DUBOIS, Claudie. **État présent du**
as **répertoire musical traditionnel paysan en France et vues comparées avec le répertoire français au Canada** [The present state of the traditional rural musical repertoire in France, and compari-

sons with the French repertoire in Canada], *Journal of the International Folk Music Council* XIV (1962) 165. In French. See no. 442 in this volume.

2531 MASSIGNON, Geneviève. **Chants de mer de**
as **l'ancienne et de la nouvelle France** [Sea songs of old France and French Canada], *Journal of the International Folk Music Council* XIV (1962) 74–86. *Music, transcr.* In French. See no. 442 in this volume.

Fieldwork among Acadian informants in Nova Scotia in 1946 yielded examples of maritime laments in which sea battles of the Seven Years' War (1756-63) are recalled in remarkable detail, a *Complainte de la Danaé* and *Complainte du Foudroyant*. They provide the most reliable versions, textually and musically, of songs from France whose identity has been problematic, including one known only from a musico-literary reworking by Gabriel de La Landelle, *Le combat de la Danaé*, first published in 1859. *(David Bloom)*

2532 MOSER, Hans Joachim. **De Mari Interno quasi**
as **vinculo musico gentium accolentium** [The Mediterranean as a musical tie among neighboring peoples], *Atti del Congresso internazionale di musiche popolari mediterranee e del Convegno dei bibliotecari musicali* (Palermo: De Magistris succ. V. Bellotti, 1959) 271–74. In Latin. See no. 332 in this volume.

2533 NABOKOV, Nicolas *et al.* **Traditional music**
as **facing industrial civilization: The discussion,** *Music east and west* (Nai Dilli: Indian Council for Cultural Relations, 1966) 192–95. See no. 489 in this volume.

A roundtable consisting of Alain DANIÉLOU, Robert GARFIAS, Mantle HOOD, Geeta MAYOR, Yehudi MENUHIN, Chandrasekhar PANT, N.S. RAMACHANDRAN, R.L. ROY, Ravi SHANKAR, and Thakur Jaideva SINGH.

2534 NETTL, Bruno. **Communal re-creation as**
as **composition technique in primitive culture,** *Journal of the International Folk Music Council* VIII (1956) 45. See no. 349 in this volume.

The conference report provides only a citation. Neither the text nor a summary of the paper was published here.

2535 RHODES, Willard. **The new folk music,** *Artistic*
as *values in traditional music* (Berlin: International Institute for Comparative Music Studies, 1966) 100–07. See no. 493 in this volume.

Folk music is social behavior expressed through the medium of music; as such, it is always evolving. New folk music represents a connection with the past, and it cannot be studied and validated solely on the basis of aesthetic principles. *(author)*

2536 RIEGLER-DINU, Emil. **Primitivité, évolution**
as **et style de la chanson populaire** [Primitivity, evolution, and style of the traditional song], *Congrès international des arts populaires/International congress of popular arts* (Paris: Institut international de coopération intellectuelle, 1928) 106–07. In French. See no. 153 in this volume.

Summary of a conference paper. Features that have been qualified as primitive (narrow ambitus, monotone repetition of pitches or rhythmic values, free rhythm) may merely be effects of style, as in classical Chinese or liturgical Greek music; a song is only primitive to the extent that its melodic and rhythmic system is capable of evolving in a characteristic direction of greater flexibility over the course of an individual artist's or a community's development. It is foolhardy to treat particular musical tastes as primitive or evolved. Rhythm, melody, and performance also determine the expression of the ethos latently present in the text, but the concept of ethos (Hermann Abert) includes nuances that have not yet been adequately formulated. *(David Bloom)*

2537 RUBIN, Ruth. **Yiddish love songs of the nine-**
as **teenth century,** *Journal of the International Folk Music Council* VI (1954) 48. See no. 320 in this volume.
The conference report provides only a citation. Neither the text nor a summary of the paper was published here.

2538 SALMEN, Walter. **Zur sozialen Schichtung des**
as **Berufsmusikertums im mittelalterlichen Eurasien und in Afrika** [The social stratification of professional musicians in medieval Eurasia and in Africa], *Les colloques de Wégimont. III: Ethnomusicologie II* (Paris: Belles Lettres, 1960) 23–32. In German. See no. 366 in this volume.
Compares the status of musicians in a wide range of anthropologically studied stratified societies throughout the world.

2539 SAYGUN, Ahmed Adnan. **Authenticity in folk**
as **music,** *Journal of the International Folk Music Council* III (1951) 7–10. See no. 296 in this volume.
Discusses aspects of oral traditions and applications of comparative musicology, with examples drawn from Anatolian traditional music.
(James R. Cowdery)

2540 SCHNEIDER, Marius. **Sociologie et mythologie**
as **musicales** [The sociology and mythology of music], *Les colloques de Wégimont. III: Ethnomusicologie II* (Paris: Belles Lettres, 1960) 13–22. In French. See no. 366 in this volume.
In many cultures, creation myths treat sound as the primary creative force. Gods are contacted through sound; the essence of each creature may be a particular sound or song. The power of sound is used to influence other beings or the gods themselves. Musical instruments, often identified with the gods, are capable of giving power to humans. Musicians may have the role of religious contact with gods (high social position) or the role of vagrant (low social position), but either role may have shamanic status. An Italian translation is published in *Il significato della musica* (Milan, 1970), cited as RILM [1973]3047. *(Katharine Fry)*

2541 SHULDHAM-SHAW, Patrick. **Folk song and**
as **the concert singer,** *Journal of the International Folk Music Council* IV (1952) 42–44. See no. 306 in this volume.
Professional singers performing music from traditional-song repertoires should emulate the traditional singer in sincerity, in emphasizing the clarity of words over that of melody, in the choice of tempos that are not too fast or too strict, and in using their own individual personality and diction style. If accompanied by tempered instruments such as pianos they should not try to sing in a natural scale. *(David Bloom)*

2542 STUMPF, Carl. **Vergleichende Musikfor-**
as **schung: Verhandlungen und Vorträge** [Comparative music research: Discussions and lectures], *Bericht über den zweiten Kongress der Internationalen Musikgesellschaft* (Leipzig: Breitkopf & Härtel, 1907) 60–61. In German. See no. 53 in this volume.
Summarizes a talk by Wilhelm SCHMIDT on the general character of the music of primitive peoples, and reports on field studies (including phonographic recordings) of (1) Melanesian peoples of the Bismarck Archipelago, as observed by Emil Stephan (Erich Moritz von HORNBOSTEL); (2) the Monumbo people of Manam Island, northeastern New Guinea, as observed by Rudolf Pöch (Wilhelm SCHMIDT); and (3) Ewe speakers of southern Togo, as observed by Anton Witte (SCHMIDT). The Togo material is published in *Anthropos* I (1906). *(David Bloom)*

2543 TRAVERSARI SALAZAR, Pedro Pablo. **L'arte**
as **in America: Storia dell'arte musicale indigena e popolare** [Art in America: A history of native and traditional music], *Atti del Congresso internazionale di scienze storiche. VIII: Atti della sezione IV: Storia dell'arte musicale e drammatica* (Roma: R. Accademia dei Lincei, 1905) 117–29. *Transcr.* In Italian. See no. 42 in this volume.
American Indian music is divided into three categories: sacred, festive, and war music. Native and newer traditional musics in the Americas are discussed, with an emphasis on South America.

2544 VARGA, Ovidiu. **Le rôle de la radio concernant**
as **le recueil, la valorification et la circulation du folklore** [The role of radio with respect to the collection, validation, and circulation of folklore], *Journal of the International Folk Music Council* XIII (1961) 85–87. In French. See no. 424 in this volume.

2545 VIKÁR, László. **Recherches folkloriques en**
as **Extrême-Orient et sur les bords de la Volga** [Folkloric research in the Far East and on the banks of the Volga], *Journal of the International Folk Music Council* XIII (1961) 54–58. In French. See no. 424 in this volume.

2546 WACHSMANN, Klaus P. **The transplantation**
as **of folk music from one social environment to another,** *Journal of the International Folk Music Council* VI (1954) 41–45. See no. 320 in this volume.
Adaptability may be the key to the survival of traditional musics in modern society. Adaptation or transplantation must involve three considerations: (1) the laws and conventions governing the music, and the latitude allowed in obeying them; (2) the aspects of modern society that cannot be reconciled with these laws and conventions; and (3) the preservation of the essential aspects of the tradition. Ugandan examples are examined, and the Namirembe Music Festival in Kampala is discussed. *(James R. Cowdery)*

2547 WILGUS, David K. **Fiddler's farewell: The leg-**
as **end of the hanged fiddler,** *Studia musicologica Academiae Scientiarum Hungaricae* VII (1965) 194–209. *Bibliog.* See no. 478 in this volume.
Execution ballads—farewell songs reputedly composed and sung by the condemned—have been a part of Western European tradition since the 17th c. Legends in Scotland, Ireland, and Kentucky associate several such ballads with fiddlers who, according to tradition, played the fiddle before being hanged. *(David Gagné)*

32 Africa

2548 BALANDIER, Georges; MERCIER, Paul. **Notes**
as **sur les théories musicales maures à propos de chants enregistrés** [Notes on Moorish musical theories in relation to recorded songs], *Conférence internationale des Africanistes de l'Ouest–C.I.A.O.: Programme de la deuxième réunion/Conferência Internacional dos Africanistas Ocidentais: 2a. conferência* (Lisboa: Ministério das Colónias, 1950-1952) V, 135–92. *Illus., charts, diagr.* In French. See no. 275 in this volume.
Discusses history, theory, performance practice, and instruments. Organological descriptions of the tidinit (a plucked lute) and the ardin (an arched harp) are included.

2549 BARROS, M. **Folclore musical da Ilha de São**
as **Tomé: Velhas danças, suas músicas y cantares** [Traditional music of São Tomé: Old dances and their music and songs], *Conferência Internacional dos Africanistas Ocidentais: 6a. sessào* (London: C.C.T.A., 1957) 101–12. *Transcr.* In Portuguese; summaries in Spanish, French, and English. See no. 361 in this volume.

Presents melodies, rhythmic patterns, and song texts (with Portuguese translations) for four traditional dance genres: lundum, irmandade, ússua, and sôcopé.

2550
as
DUVELLE, Charles. **Opening talk on the music of Africa,** *First Conference on African Traditional Music* (Kampala: Uganda Ey'eddembe, 1964) 7–10. See no. 465 in this volume.

Provides a general overview of ethnomusicological work in Africa, noting issues particularly relevant to African music.

2551
as
GERGELY, Jean, transcript; ROUGET, Gilbert, moderator. **La musique funéraire en Afrique noire: Fonctions et formes** [Funerary music in black Africa: Functions and forms], *Bericht über den neunten internationalen Kongreß* (Kassel: Bärenreiter, 1964-1966) II, 143–55. In French. See no. 491 in this volume.

A roundtable discussion by Robert G. ARMSTRONG, Luiz Heitor Corrêa de AZEVEDO, Charles DUVELLE, Arend Johannes Christiaan KOOLE, Claudie MARCEL-DUBOIS, Roxane Connick MCCOLLESTER, Marius SCHNEIDER, and Klaus P. WACHSMANN on the definition of funerary music as a genre, in terms of its musical traits, instrumental accompaniment, texts, and relations to the representation of death and the expression of emotions; based on field recordings of music from Benin, Mali, Nigeria, Sudan, Burkina Faso, the Republic of the Congo (Brazzaville), Madagascar, and the Afro-Brazilian communities of Brazil. *(David Bloom)*

2552
as
GRIMAUD, Yvette. **Note sur la musique vocale des Bochiman !Kung et des Pygmées Babinga** [Notes on the vocal music of the !Kung Bushmen and Babinga Pygmies], *Les colloques de Wégimont. III: Ethnomusicologie II* (Paris: Belles Lettres, 1960) 105–26. *Music.* In French. See no. 366 in this volume.

Discusses the hypothesis of significant similarities between the musics and dance of Pygmy peoples of the Congo basin and Khoisan speakers of southern Africa. The Babinga people (Cameroon, Equatorial Guinea) and the !Kung (South Africa) share features including developmental technique, polyrhythmic lines, vocal style, and the use of certain intervals that have not been found among other African peoples. The use of nonsense syllables and the ritual functions of !Kung songs are also noted. *(Katharine Fry)*

2553
as
GÜNTHER, Robert. **Eine Studie zur Musik in Ruanda** [A study of music in Rwanda], *Les colloques de Wégimont. III: Ethnomusicologie II* (Paris: Belles Lettres, 1960) 163–86. In German. See no. 366 in this volume.

The research discussed is fully reported in the author's book *Musik in Rwanda* (Tervuren, 1964), cited as RILM [1969]2172. *(David Bloom)*

2554
as
HICKMANN, Hans. **Arbeitsgemeinschaft: Musikalische Stratigraphie Afrikas** [Working group: Musical stratigraphy of Africa], *Bericht über den siebenten internationalen musikwissenschaftlichen Kongress* (Kassel: Bärenreiter, 1959) 334–37. In German and French. See no. 390 in this volume.

At a working session of the conference, Paul COLLAER read a general statement on the concept of stratigraphy as used in geology and archaeology, and its application to ethnomusicology in the discussion of diffusion and change in the oral tradition. Discussion of the state of research on African music from the stratigraphic point of view concluded in favor of a proposal by Fritz BOSE that the stratigraphic analysis should be preceded by a cartographic analysis, mapping the distribution of instruments, styles, usages, and so on within a given temporal moment and in correspondence to other anthropological traits. *(David Bloom)*

2555
as
HICKMANN, Hans. **Über den Stand der musikwissenschaftlichen Forschung in Ägypten** [The state of musicological research in Egypt], *Compte rendu/Kongressbericht/Report* (Basel: Bärenreiter, 1951) 150–53. In German. See no. 289 in this volume.

Topics include the instrument collection of the Egyptian Museum, Cairo, and some of its implications for the music history of ancient Egypt; ethnographic study of present-day instruments and song texts and their correspondences with those of the ancient period; and historical and ethnographic research on Coptic music. *(David Bloom)*

2556
as
HORNBOSTEL, Erich Moritz von. **Über Mehrstimmigkeit in der außereuropäischen Musik** [On polyphony in non-European music], *Haydn-Zentenarfeier* (Leipzig: Breitkopf & Härtel; Wien: Artaria, 1909) 298–303. In German. See no. 65 in this volume.

Offers general observations on several African musics.

2557
as
JONES, Arthur Morris. **Folk music in Africa,** *Journal of the International Folk Music Council* V (1953) 36–40. See no. 314 in this volume.

Discusses musical life in sub-Saharan Africa, with attention to the roles of societies, schools, and radio broadcasting.

2558
as
KÁRPÁTI, János. **Quelques notes sur la musique traditionnelle et folklorique dans différentes régions du Maroc** [Some notes on traditional and folk music in different regions of Morocco], *The preservation of traditional forms of the learned and popular music of the Orient and the Occident/La préservation des formes traditionelles de la musique savante et populaire dans les pays d'Orient et d'Occident* (Urbana: Center for Comparative Psycholinguistics, Institute of Communications Research, 1964) 163–70. In French. See no. 443 in this volume.

Proposes three basic style categories: Andalusian, Berber, and urban.

2559
as
KOOLE, Arend Johannes Christiaan. **Report on the inquiry into the music and instruments of the Basutos in Basutoland,** *Société Internationale de Musicologie, cinquième congrès/Internationale Gesellschaft für Musikwissenschaft, fünfter Kongreß/International Society for Musical Research, Fifth Congress* (Amsterdam: Vereniging voor Nederlandse Muziekgeschiedenis, 1953) 263–70. *Music.* See no. 316 in this volume.

The Basotho people of Lesotho preserve traditional tunes, performance techniques, and instruments.

2560
as
MAQUET, Jean-Noël. **La musique chez les Pende et les Tshokwe** [The music of the Pende and Chokwe peoples], *Les colloques de Wégimont. [I: Ethnomusicologie I]* (Bruxelles: Elsevier, 1956) 169–87. *Illus., charts, diagr., transcr.* In French. See no. 340 in this volume.

Second part of a study based on fieldwork in summer 1954 among groups located in the Kahemba and Tshikapa districts of Congo (Kinshasa), with particular reference to the rich variety of instruments, and to special characteristics of the vocal music, including imitations of birdsong and use of triadic harmony. This part focuses on the Cokwe (Chokwe) people; the first part, on the Pende people, is published in *Problèmes d'Afrique Centrale* 26 (1954). *(David Bloom)*

2561
as
MENSAH, Atta Annan. **Problems involved in the arrangement of folk music for Radio Ghana,** *Journal of the International Folk Music Council* XI (1959) 83–84. See no. 392 in this volume.

Summary of a paper. Unlike popular music, which is easy to record and which many people understand, traditional music presents problems both in recording and in appreciation beyond ethnic boundaries. *(James R. Cowdery)*

2562 MERRIAM, Alan P. **Characteristics of African**
as **music,** *Journal of the International Folk Music Council* XI (1959) 13–19. See no. 392 in this volume.
A survey of the shared features of sub-Saharan music cultures, with particular attention to rhythmic matters.

2563 NIKIPROWETZKY, Tolia. **The griots of Senegal and their instruments,** *Journal of the International Folk Music Council* XV (1963) 79–82. *Illus.* See no. 459 in this volume.

2564 NIKIPROWETZKY, Tolia. **The music of Mauritania,** *Journal of the International Folk Music Council* XIV (1962) 53–55. See no. 442 in this volume.
A preliminary report of the Arab-derived modes; social context of music making and role of the griot caste; and typical instruments. *(June Goldenberg)*

2565 NIKIPROWETZKY, Tolia. **L'ornamentation**
as **dans la musique des touareg de l'Aïr** [Ornamentation in the music of the Tuareg people of the Aïr region], *Journal of the International Folk Music Council* XVI (1964) 81–83. *Transcr.* In French. See no. 463 in this volume.
Summarizes the ethnomusicological situation of the nomadic Tuareg people of the region, with particular attention to the genre of men's songs, sung solo or with the accompaniment of an imzad (single-string fiddle), played by a woman. Their performance features much more ornamentation than is found in the music of neighboring sedentary peoples, some pentatonically organized, some featuring intervals such as the augmented second that seem to have an Asian character. Microintervals are rare. *(David Bloom)*

2566 NKETIA, Joseph Hanson Kwabena. **Changing**
as **traditions of folk music in Ghana,** *Journal of the International Folk Music Council* XI (1959) 31–36. See no. 392 in this volume.
Describes three types of influence on musical change: (1) the dynamics of oral tradition in a given culture, (2) interactions between neighboring cultures, and (3) interactions with non-African cultures. Examples of the third type include influences from Western and Muslim cultures.
(James R. Cowdery)

2567 NKETIA, Joseph Hanson Kwabena. **Continuity**
as **of traditional instruction,** *The preservation of traditional forms of the learned and popular music of the Orient and the Occident/La préservation des formes traditionelles de la musique savante et populaire dans les pays d'Orient et d'Occident* (Urbana: Center for Comparative Psycholinguistics, Institute of Communications Research, 1964) 203–13. See no. 443 in this volume.
Traditional music instruction in Ghana is through slow absorption, beginning at an early age. To preserve the tradition against competition with Western music, more systematic and formalized instructional methods will have to be devised. *(Michael Collier)*

2568 NKETIA, Joseph Hanson Kwabena. **Historical**
as **evidence in Gã religious music,** *The historian in tropical Africa/L'historien en Afrique tropicale* (London: Oxford University, 1964) 265–83. Summary in French. See no. 433 in this volume.
The *kple* or *kpele* cult of the Gã people in coastal Ghana uses songs in Gã, Akan, and Awutu languages or combinations thereof and apparent nonsense syllables. The texts refer to historic events and clan identities, annual rites, migrations, and social upheavals; the music uses heptatonic scales, borrowed from the Akan people, as well as the indigenous pentatonic. A comparison with songs of the *kpa* and *klama* cults suggests that the kple or at least some of its elements was adopted from the Akan-speaking Guang (or Guan) people. *(Susan Poliniak)*

2569 NKETIA, Joseph Hanson Kwabena. **The hock-**
as **et-technique in African music,** *Journal of the International Folk Music Council* XIV (1962) 44–52. *Illus., transcr.* See no. 442 in this volume.
Hocketing—the note-by-note alternation of different voices in the performance of a single tune, rhythm, or tone pattern—is an important part of the repertoire of contrapuntal techniques found in the typically homogeneous instrumental ensemble of Africa, such as the flute ensembles of the Builsa people of northern Ghana and the *ntahera* ivory trumpet ensembles in chiefs' courts of the Ashanti people of southern Ghana, recorded and analyzed by the author. References to cases from other parts of Africa, including those using drums or xylophones, are provided. *(David Bloom)*

2570 NKETIA, Joseph Hanson Kwabena. **The inter-**
as **relations of African music and dance,** *Studia musicologica Academiae Scientiarum Hungaricae* VII (1965) 91–101. *Music.* See no. 478 in this volume.
Discusses aspects of rhythm, tempo, form, phrasing, song texts, and timbre.

2571 NKETIA, Joseph Hanson Kwabena. **Possession**
as **dances in African societies,** *Journal of the International Folk Music Council* IX (1957) 4–9. See no. 362 in this volume.
Discusses West African examples.

2572 NKETIA, Joseph Hanson Kwabena. **Traditional**
as **and contemporary idioms of African music,** *Journal of the International Folk Music Council* XVI (1964) 34–37. See no. 463 in this volume.
The common development in which new idioms of popular and fine art music arise naturally from traditional forms has not taken place in Africa, because professional musicians live in a radically different social setting from that of their ancestors: Tribal frontiers are being broken down and Western-style musical institutions are being introduced. For a long time most Africans accepted Western music as the music of the new age; recently, however, beginning with the development of Christian church music in traditional styles in some countries, a trend toward Africanization in popular and composed art musics has been observable. The latter will be most successful if its composers are versed in a variety of distinct African traditions. *(Vivian Conejero)*

2573 OUEDRAOGO, Robert. **Rapport sur la**
as **musique religieuse au Mossi/Bericht über die religiöse Musik im Mossi-Land** [Report on the religious music of the Mossi region], *IV. Internationaler Kongress für Kirchenmusik in Köln: Dokumente und Berichte* (Köln: Bachem, 1962) 251–86. In French and German. See no. 432 in this volume.
Discusses elements of popular and traditional music among the Mossi people of Burkina Faso and experimentation with their use in the Roman Catholic liturgy.

2574 P'BITEK, Okot. **Social functions of traditional**
as **music in Acholi and Lango,** *First Conference on African Traditional Music* (Kampala: Uganda Ey'eddembe, 1964) 11–23. See no. 465 in this volume.
Focuses on songs and dances of the Acholi and Lango peoples of Uganda, including the dance genres bwola and otole. A discussion of problems of preservation is included.

2575 PEPPER, Herbert. **Considérations sur le**
as **langage tambourine et autres langages musicaux d'Afrique centrale: Sur la pensée musicale africaine** [Considerations on drum language and other musical languages of Central Africa: On African musical thought], *Conferencia Internacional de Africanistas Occidentales: 4a. conferencia* (Madrid: Dirección General de Marruecos y Colonias, 1954) 165f. In French. See no. 310 in this volume.

2576 PEPPER, Herbert. **Les problèmes généraux de**
as **la musique populaire en Afrique Noire** [General
problems of traditional music in sub-Saharan Africa],
Journal of the International Folk Music Council II
(1950) 22–24. In French. See no. 295 in this volume.
Important issues for research include the relation of linguistic tone to phenomena such as drum language, and the correspondence of the many scalar
and modal structures to the intervals of the harmonic series. The latter may
be a result of the use of overtone-scale instruments such as trumpets, but
may also be evidence of an innate human response to mathematically defined intervals. *(David Bloom)*

2577 REVAULT, Jacques. **Note sur les instruments**
as **traditionnels de musique populaire dans le sud**
tunisien [Note on traditional music instruments in
southern Tunisia], *VIᵉ Congrès international des sciences anthropologiques et ethnologiques. I: Rapport
général et anthropologie; II: Ethnologie* (Paris: Musée
de l'Homme, 1962-1964) II, 113–20. In French. See no.
421 in this volume.
Examines the traditional wind, percussion, and string instruments used in
religious ceremonies.

2578 ROUGET, Gilbert. **Musique *vodu* (Dahomey)**
as [Vodun music (Dahomey)], *VIᵉ Congrès international
des sciences anthropologiques et ethnologiques. I:
Rapport général et anthropologie; II: Ethnologie*
(Paris: Musée de l'Homme, 1962-1964) II, 121–22. In
French. See no. 421 in this volume.
Examines the songs performed by female religious initiates at the end of
their seclusion.

2579 ROUGET, Gilbert. **Note sur les travaux**
as **d'ethnographie musicale de la mission**
Ogooué-Congo [Note on the work in musical ethnography of the Ogooué-Congo mission], *Conférence
internationale des Africanistes de l'Ouest–C.I.A.O.:
Programme de la deuxième réunion/Conferência Internacional dos Africanistas Ocidentais: 2a. conferência*
(Lisboa: Ministério das Colónias, 1950-1952)
193–204. In French. See no. 275 in this volume.
Provides general descriptions of instruments and music of the Ba-Benzele
and BaNgombe peoples.

2580 ROUGET, Gilbert. **Note sur l'ornementation en**
as **Afrique noire** [Note on ornamentation in
sub-Saharan Africa], *Report of the Eighth Congress of
the International Musicological Society. I: Papers*
(Kassel: Bärenreiter, 1961) 427–28. In French. See no.
439 in this volume.
Islamic ornamentation techniques, observed especially in griot performance, consist of more or less marked vocal vibrato broadening occasionally into a true melisma. Indigenous sub-Saharan ornamentation is problematic; some cultures definitely reject ornamentation, while others show
what may be called horizontal ornamental forms. The phenomenon that
best deserves the name is the use of a literal ornament in melodic accompaniment, such as bells worn on a singer's wrists, or attached to the curved
neck of a harp.

2581 RYCROFT, David. **African music in Johannes-**
as **burg: African and non-African features,** *Journal of the International Folk Music Council* XI (1959)
25–30. *Transcr.* See no. 392 in this volume.
Traditional music is still heard among the black people of Johannesburg,
but hybrid popular styles are also developing. The African characteristics
of these newer styles include aspects of performance practice and adherence to Bantu speech tones in text settings. *(James R. Cowdery)*

2582 SAFAR, Ali. **Genres de composition musicale**
as **arabe employés en Egypte** [Arab musical genres
practiced in Egypt], *Recueil des travaux du Congrès de
musique arabe* (Al-Qāhirah: Boulac, 1934) 166–70. In
French. See no. 196 in this volume.
Presents 18 vocal and 10 instrumental genres that were proposed as a standard inventory for Egyptian music by the Commission on Modes,
Rhythms, and Composition of the Congress on Arab Music (Mu'tamar al
Mūsīqá al-'Arabiyyah) in Cairo in 1932.

2583 SAMI, Abdel Rahman. **Folk music and musical**
as **trends in Egypt today,** *Journal of the International
Folk Music Council* IX (1957) 11–12. See no. 362 in
this volume.
An overview of Egyptian musical life, focusing on the study and reception
of Arabic music.

2584 SCHAEFFNER, André. **Contribution à l'étude**
as **des instruments de musique d'Afrique et**
d'Océanie [Contribution to the study of the musical
instruments of Africa and Oceania], *Congrès international des sciences anthropologiques et ethnologiques:
Compte rendu de la deuxième session* (København:
Munksgaard, 1939) 268–70. In French. See no. 255 in
this volume.
Describes in very general terms the scraped instruments, wooden drums,
gourd instruments, water drums, musical bows, tubular instruments, and
xylophones of the regions. *(Susan Poliniak)*

2585 SCHAEFFNER, André. **Musique, danse et**
as **danse des masques dans une société nègre** [Mu-
sic, dance, and masked dance in a black society],
*Deuxième congrès international d'esthétique et de Sci-
ence de l'art* (Paris: Librairie Félix Alcan, 1937) I,
308–12. In French. See no. 249 in this volume.
The Dogon people of Mali use music in funeral rites, agrarian rites, circumcisions, and magical rites for purposes of divination and rainmaking; the
role of dance is central. *(David Schiff)*

2586 SCHAEFFNER, André. **Musiques rituelles**
as **Baga** [Baga ritual music], *VIᵉ Congrès international
des sciences anthropologiques et ethnologiques. I:
Rapport général et anthropologie; II: Ethnologie*
(Paris: Musée de l'Homme, 1962-1964) II, 123–26. In
French. See no. 421 in this volume.
Findings from the author's field research with the Baga people of coastal
Guinea.

2587 SCHAEFFNER, André. **Situation des musiciens**
as **dans trois sociétés africaines** [The position of musicians in three African societies], *Les colloques de
Wégimont. III: Ethnomusicologie II* (Paris: Belles Lettres, 1960) 33–49. In French. See no. 366 in this
volume.
The Dogon, a plains people of southwestern Mali, and the Kissi, a forest
people of Guinea, are neighbors. Both reject Islamic culture; their music,
however, shows Islamic influences. The Dogon have no professional musicians; music plays a role only in rituals and is subject to many restrictions of
gender. The Kissi have semiprofessional musicians; in Kissi rituals, restrictions are almost the opposite of the Dogon, and music has a place in Kissi
secular life as well. The Fulбe of Cameroon recognize professional musicians, and foreigners may participate in their rituals. *(Katharine Fry)*

2588 SCHNEIDER, Marius. **Musikethnologische**
as **Kriterien zur Überschichtung von Kultur und**
Rasse in Afrika [Ethnomusicological criteria for the
overlap of cultures and races in Africa], *Congrés de la
Societat Internacional de Musicologia* (Barcelona: Casa

de Caritat, 1936). In German. See no. 224 in this volume.

The conference report provides only a citation. Neither the text nor a summary of the paper was published here.

2589
as
SERVIER, Jean H. **Musique et poésie kabyles** [Kabyle poetry and music], *Actes du IVe Congrès international des sciences anthropologiques et ethnologiques* (Wien: Holzhausen, 1954-1956) III:2, 19–20. In French. See no. 364 in this volume.

Briefly discusses professional singers, instruments, and children's songs.

2590
as
STANISLAV, Josef. **Some remarks on the development of musical creation among African peoples,** *The preservation of traditional forms of the learned and popular music of the Orient and the Occident/La préservation des formes traditionelles de la musique savante et populaire dans les pays d'Orient et d'Occident* (Urbana: Center for Comparative Psycholinguistics, Institute of Communications Research, 1964) 244–50. See no. 443 in this volume.

Discussion of the role of Czech musicologists in the recording of traditional African music since 1945, and of African music itself, with reflections on the vulgarizing influence of third- and sixth-based harmonies from the West. The tradition cannot be preserved without some new form of notation. *(Judith Drogichen Meyer)*

2591
as
TRACEY, Hugh. **African music within its social setting,** *Journal of the International Folk Music Council* XI (1959) 23–24. See no. 392 in this volume.

Summary of a paper surveying the shared features of sub-Saharan music cultures. The full paper was published in *African music* II:1 (1956) 56-58.

2592
as
TRACEY, Hugh. **The state of folk music in Bantu Africa: A brief survey,** *Journal of the International Folk Music Council* VI (1954) 32–36. See no. 320 in this volume.

Bantu traditions are declining and disappearing due to the onslaught of modernity. There is still hope for the development of newer traditions that still reflect Bantu values. *(James R. Cowdery)*

2593
as
TRACEY, Hugh. **Wood music of the Chopi,** *Journal of the International Folk Music Council* XVI (1964) 91. See no. 463 in this volume.

Summary of a paper discussing the history, organology, and performance practice of the *timbila* (xylophones) of the Chopi people of Mozambique. A full account is provided in *Chopi musicians: Their music, poetry, and instruments* (London, 1948). *(David Bloom)*

2594
as
WACHSMANN, Klaus P. **The earliest sources of folk music from Africa,** *Studia musicologica Academiae Scientiarum Hungaricae* VII (1965) 181–86. See no. 478 in this volume.

No collection of African traditional music antedates the 20th c., but sociological factors may make it possible to assess the authenticity of contemporary sources. An example is drawn from the BaGanda people of Uganda. *(David Gagné)*

2595
as
WACHSMANN, Klaus P. **Harp songs from Uganda,** *Journal of the International Folk Music Council* VIII (1956) 23–25. See no. 349 in this volume.

Discusses recorded examples of songs from various parts of Uganda, each accompanied with a local harp.

2596
as
WACHSMANN, Klaus P. **Human migration and African harps,** *Journal of the International Folk Music Council* XVI (1964) 84–88. *Maps.* See no. 463 in this volume.

African harps may be divided into three main types: the "spoon in a cup" type, in which the instrument is held together by the tension of the strings; the tanged type, with the neck jammed into a hole in the small end of the resonator; and the shelf type, with the neck fastened to a shelf projecting from the base of the resonator. Their different distributions can be traced to the historic migrations of the Bantu people around the beginning of the Christian era, the fall of Meroe in the Kush empire in the mid-4th c., and by eastward population pressure around the border between present-day Congo and Uganda during the last two centuries. The "spoon in a cup" harp of Mauretania, played only by women, with its neck resting against the player's body, could be a very old, independent borrowing from Ancient Egypt. *(David Bloom)*

2597
as
WACHSMANN, Klaus P. **Problems of musical stratigraphy in Africa,** *Les colloques de Wégimont. IV: Ethnomusicologie III* (Paris: Belles Lettres, 1964) 19–22. See no. 401 in this volume.

Discusses the stratigraphic issues involved in the creation of a common classificatory terminology; the preparation of a musical inventory on a tribal basis; and the systematic study of the history of intertribal contact. *(Scott Fruehwald)*

⟶
WACHSMANN, Klaus P. **The transplantation of folk music from one social environment to another.** See no. 2546 in this volume.

2598
as
[4] La tradition du yodel au sud-ouest du Congo belge [The tradition of yodeling in the southeastern Belgian Congo]. By Jean-Noël MAQUET, *Journal of the International Folk Music Council* XI (1959) 20–22. In French and English. See no. 392 in this volume.

Examines four examples: a hunting song, two lullabies, and a song that combines instrumental and vocal yodeling, a feat to which the lyrics call attention: "I am the one who can sing and play at the same time." Questions of dissemination and social function are discussed. *(Murat Eyüboğlu)*

33 Asia

2599
as
AHMAD, Abbasuddin. **Folk songs of East Pakistan,** *Journal of the International Folk Music Council* IX (1957) 47–49. See no. 362 in this volume.

Surveys traditional songs from the region (Bangladesh since 1971).

2600
as
ALBUQUERQUE, Walter. **Südindische klassische und Volksmusik: Die Ursprünge der indischen Musik in der Legende** [South Indian classical and folk music: The origins of Indian music according to legend], *IV. Internationaler Kongress für Kirchenmusik in Köln: Dokumente und Berichte* (Köln: Bachem, 1962) 287–303. In German. See no. 432 in this volume.

Discusses theory in the Karnatak tradition and the origin myths of its central concepts.

2601
as
AUSTERLITZ, Robert. **The identification of folkloristic genres (based on Gilyak materials),** *Poetics/Poetyka/Poetika* (Warszawa: Państwowe Wydawnictwo Naukowe, 1961) 505–10. *Illus., charts, diagr.* See no. 426 in this volume.

Discusses the genre classification of epic, folktale, riddle, song, and ditty materials collected in fieldwork among the Giljak (Nivh) people of Sahalin and the Amur Delta in the 1950s.

2602 BAKÉ, Arnold Adriaan. **Der Begriff *Nâda* in**
as **der Indischen Musik** [The concept of *nāda* in Indian music], *Compte rendu/Kongressbericht/Report* (Basel: Bärenreiter, 1951) 55–59. In German. See no. 289 in this volume.

Discusses the philosophical meanings and practical musical applications of the terms *nāda* (sound), *āhatanāda* (sound in its physical aspect, or produced sound), and *anāhatanāda* (sound in its metaphysical aspect, or unrevealed sound). The primary and most direct manifestation of *āhatanāda* is in vocal music. *(David Bloom)*

2603 BAKÉ, Arnold Adriaan. **Die beiden Tonge-**
as **schlechter bei Bharata** [The two modes in Bharata], *Kongreß-Bericht: Gesellschaft für Musikforschung* (Kassel; Basel: Bärenreiter, 1950) 158–60. In German. See no. 299 in this volume.

2604 BAKÉ, Arnold Adriaan. **The impact of Western**
as **music on the Indian musical system,** *Journal of the International Folk Music Council* V (1953) 57–60. See no. 314 in this volume.

While it represents a sincere effort at bridging the gap between East and West, the practice of applying Western harmony to Indian melodies is not promising. Even worse is India's vulgar and obtrusive new popular music, which corrupts Indian folk styles with the addition of Western harmonies and instruments. *(James R. Cowdery)*

2605 BAKÉ, Arnold Adriaan. **Nepalese folk music,**
as *Journal of the International Folk Music Council* X (1958) 50. See no. 371 in this volume.

Summary of a paper.

2606 BAKÉ, Arnold Adriaan. **Rhythmischer**
as **Kontrapunkt auf einer Rahmentrommel aus Ceylon** [Rhythmic counterpoint on a frame drum of Ceylon], *Bericht über den siebenten internationalen musikwissenschaftlichen Kongress* (Kassel: Bärenreiter, 1959) 60–61. *Music*. In German. See no. 390 in this volume.

The principle of sustained rhythmic counterpoint, foreign to Western art music, is essential to the music of India. Rabāna drumming on the coast near Colombo in Sri Lanka (formerly Ceylon) is described as an example. The rabāna is a large frame drum some 25 inches in diameter; a mixed group of men and women seat themselves around it, each performing a variant of the pattern proposed by the lead drummer and displaying his or her own hand gestures. *(Carl Skoggard)*

2607 BARKECHLI, Mehdi. **Les rythmes caracté-**
as **ristiques de la musique iranienne** [The characteristic rhythms of Iranian music], *Bericht über den siebenten internationalen musikwissenschaftlichen Kongress* (Kassel: Bärenreiter, 1959) 61–63. *Charts, diagr*. In French. See no. 390 in this volume.

Iranian meters are elaborated on the basis of a minimal unit of time; the longest meters incorporate 16 of the minimal units. Patterns of units within a meter are either regular or irregular, the latter being more esteemed; the accentual patterns of meters are referred to by means of syllables derived from the word *tana* (for example, *tan tanan tan tanan*). The principal metric patterns from a 12th-c. treatise by Ṣafī al-Dīn (al-Urmawī) are diagrammed. Particular attention is given to those meters associated in Iran for thousands of years with gymnastic exercises. Almost all the old meters continue in use today. *(Carl Skoggard)*

2608 BOULTON, Laura. **Turkish music,** *Journal of the*
as *International Folk Music Council* XII (1960) 83. See no. 413 in this volume.

Brief remarks for a presentation of recordings.

2609 BROWN, Robert E. **Introduction to the music**
as **of South India,** *Festival of Oriental Music and the Related Arts* (Los Angeles: University of California, 1960) 47–53. See no. 418 in this volume.

Outlines the fundamental concepts of rāga, tāla, and ālāpana in Karnatak music, with comparison to related concepts of the Hindustani tradition. *(Jianning You)*

2610 BŔWУ̇'ER, Mordekay. **Mẁsiqah datyt**
as **b̈etqẁpat qybẁṣ galẁуẁt** [Religious music at the time of the ingathering of the exiles], *Dẁkan* I (1959) 11–17. *Music*. In Hebrew. See no. 391 in this volume.

The total separation between secular and sacred music in Israel is unfortunate. The different trends in sacred music caused by exile can be unified. *(Moshe Zorman)*

2611 CHRISTENSEN, Dieter. **Kurdische Braut-**
as **lieder aus dem vilayet Hakkâri Südost-Türkei** [Kurdish bridal songs from the city of Hakkâri in Southeastern Turkey], *Journal of the International Folk Music Council* XIII (1961) 70–72. In German. See no. 424 in this volume.

2612 COLLAER, Paul. **Chants et airs des peuples de**
as **l'extrême-Nord** [Songs and melodies of the peoples of the far north], *Les colloques de Wégimont. III: Ethnomusicologie II* (Paris: Belles Lettres, 1960) 127–47. *Transcr*. In French. See no. 366 in this volume.

Presents music and texts of 21 traditional and modern songs of indigenous Siberian peoples transcribed and translated from recordings and written versions of texts supplied by the Institut Russkoj Literatury of the Rossijskaja Akademija Nauk, Leningrad. A few of the songs are represented only by fragments; texts of three of the songs are summarized rather than fully translated, and those of five others are lacking. *(David Hathwell)*

2613 COLLAER, Paul. **Sixteen Ainu songs,** *Les*
as *colloques de Wégimont. [I: Ethnomusicologie I]* (Bruxelles: Elsevier, 1956) 195–205. *Transcr*. In French and English. See no. 340 in this volume.

Transcriptions of and musical commentaries on a recording of traditional songs collected between 1947 and 1951 on Sahalin and Hokkaidō by NHK broadcasting company and donated by the Japanese Radio Institute to the Institut National Belge de Radiodiffusion. Notes on the song texts and recording conditions, in English, by the Japanese Radio Institute, are included. *(David Bloom)*

2614 CROSSLEY-HOLLAND, Peter. **Asian music**
as **under the impact of Western culture,** *Music: East and West* (Tōkyō: conference, 1961) 50–53. See no. 445 in this volume.

2615 DANIÉLOU, Alain. **The music of India,** *Music:*
as *East and West* (Tōkyō: conference, 1961) 5–8. See no. 445 in this volume.

2616 DANIÉLOU, Alain. **Problems of Indian music**
as **tradition today,** *Music: East and West* (Tōkyō: conference, 1961) 64–66. See no. 445 in this volume.

2617 DANTALE, G.N. **Personality in music,** *Souvenir*
as *on Hindustani Music Festival & Seminar* (Hyderabad: Andhra Pradesh Sangeeta Nataka Akademi, 1966) 19–22. See no. 450 in this volume.

A performer of Hindustani music must project an outstanding personality.

2618 DEODHAR, B.R. **Evolution in Indian music,**
as *Music east and west* (Nai Dilli: Indian Council for Cultural Relations, 1966) 16–21. See no. 489 in this volume.
Discusses the processes of change in various genres and regional traditions.

2619 DHAGE, Pandojirao. **The origin of Indian music,** *Souvenir on Hindustani Music Festival & Seminar* (Hyderabad: Andhra Pradesh Sangeeta Nataka Akademi, 1966) 44–50. See no. 450 in this volume.
Surveys ancient sources for Indian music.

2620 ECKARDT, Hans. **Die Ei und Saezuri: Verschollene melismatische Gesangformen im japanischen Tanz** [Ei and Saezuri: Forgotten melismatic vocal forms in Japanese dance], *Kongreß-Bericht: Gesellschaft für Musikforschung* (Kassel; Basel: Bärenreiter, 1950) 170–72. In German. See no. 299 in this volume.
Discusses two outmoded practices in the music of bugaku. *Ei* are vocal pieces performed between the dances, with fixed percussion patterns; they may also be performed during the dances. *Saezuri* (bird's twittering) is one of the sections of the bugaku dance ryō-wō. The original purpose of saezuri was the recitation of a text (probably ritualistic), which the dancer hummed in a low voice. Fragments of the texts still exist, but the recitation is obsolete. Both ei and saezuri date from the early Heian period (794-897). *(Tina Frühauf)*

2621 EMSHEIMER, Ernst. **Schallaufnahmen georgischer Mehrstimmigkeit** [Sound recordings of Georgian polyphony], *Kongreß-Bericht: Gesellschaft für Musikforschung* (Kassel; Basel: Bärenreiter, 1950) 172–73. In German. See no. 299 in this volume.

2622 EMSHEIMER, Ernst. **Singing contests in Central Asia,** *Journal of the International Folk Music Council* VIII (1956) 26–29. See no. 349 in this volume.
Singing contests in Central Asia are compared with the *agones* depicted in writings from ancient Greece.

2623 FARHAT, Hormoz. **Persian classical music,** *Festival of Oriental Music and the Related Arts* (Los Angeles: University of California, 1960) 58–64. See no. 418 in this volume.
Surveys the history and development of art music in Iran from the late 6th c., with attention to its currently threatened status in the face of the popularity of Western musics, and essential theoretical concepts. *(Jianning You)*

2624 FUJII, Kiyomi. **Aperçu sur la chanson populaire au Japon** [Survey of traditional song in Japan], *Congrès international des arts populaires/International congress of popular arts* (Paris: Institut international de coopération intellectuelle, 1928) 113–17. In French. See no. 153 in this volume.
Summary of a paper treating scales, rhythm, and tempo; work song, minyō, and zokuyō genres; children's song; instruments; and issues of history and preservation. *(David Bloom)*

2625 FUJII, Kiyomi; KODERA, Yukichi; ORIGUCHI, N. **Considérations sur la musique populaire au Japon** [Thoughts concerning traditional music in Japan], *Art populaire: Travaux artistiques et scientifiques du Ier Congrès international des arts populaires* (Paris: Duchartre, 1931) 129–30. In French. See no. 152 in this volume.
Japanese folk songs are generally of religious origin, although the religious character has been lost, and are often concerned with nature. Many archaic songs have been preserved as children's song. Song texts may be classified

according to content as *monozukushi* (enumerations of the enames of objects, originating in the *niimuro no utage* formerly performed to celebrate the completion of a building), *michiyuki* (enumerations of place names), *renka* (love songs), and *home-uta* and *akkutai* (respectively, songs of praise and criticism of individuals); or according to performance occasion as work songs, ceremonial songs, and songs sung for pleasure. Many are accompanied by dance. Very active collection of traditional songs has begun recently under the aegis of a new society, the Nihon Minyō Kyōkai. A summary is cited as no. 2626 in this volume. *(David Bloom)*

2626 FUJII, Kiyomi; KODERA, Yukichi; ORIGUCHI, Nobuo. **Considérations sur la musique populaire au Japon** [Thoughts concerning traditional music in Japan], *Congrès international des arts populaires/International congress of popular arts* (Paris: Institut international de coopération intellectuelle, 1928) 98–101. In French. See no. 153 in this volume.
Summary of the paper abstracted as no. 2625 in this volume.

2627 GARFIAS, Robert. **Gagaku: Subdivisions of the repertoire,** *Festival of Oriental Music and the Related Arts* (Los Angeles: University of California, 1960) 24–32. See no. 418 in this volume.
A survey of history and current practice.

2628 GARFIAS, Robert. **Some effects of changing social values on Japanese music,** *Music: East and West* (Tōkyō: conference, 1961) 18–22. See no. 445 in this volume.
The West prides itself on its contributions to the East, but may be held responsible for the degeneration of Eastern traditions. *(Sylvia Eversole)*

2629 GAUR, Ganesh Dutt. **Folksongs of Kuru Pradesh,** *Akten des vierundzwanzigsten Internationalen Orientalisten-Kongresses* (Wiesbaden: Franz Steiner Verlag, 1959) 573–74. In German. See no. 376 in this volume.
Summary of a paper proposing a classification of attributed and unattributed traditional songs performed in the area of Kurukshetra, on the basis of performance occasions (religious, entertainment). The original English-language version is published in the journal *Shiksha* (Uttar Pradesh Department of Education, Lucknow), January 1958. *(David Bloom)*

2630 GERSON-KIWI, Edith. **Synthesis and symbiosis of styles in Jewish-Oriental folk music,** *Atti del Congresso internazionale di musiche popolari mediterranee e del Convegno dei bibliotecari musicali* (Palermo: De Magistris succ. V. Bellotti, 1959) 153–59. See no. 332 in this volume.
The focus of ethnomusicology has shifted from the consideration of single tribal traditions in their presumably pure form to that of multiple traditions in contact. There is hardly such a thing as a pure tradition in any case; synthesis and symbiosis are the norm. The current situation in Israel provides a wealth of examples suggesting that the authenticity of tradition is threatened not at all by synthesis but by competition with urban musical forms. *(David Bloom)*

2631 GERSON-KIWI, Edith. **Wedding dances and songs of the Jews of Bokhara,** *Journal of the International Folk Music Council* II (1950) 17–18. See no. 295 in this volume.
The week-long Jewish wedding cycle of Bohoro is surveyed.

2632 HANLON, H. **The wedding customs and songs of Ladak,** *Actes du dixième Congrès international des orientalistes* (Leiden: Brill, 1897) IV, 181–84. See no. 20 in this volume.

2633
as
HARICH-SCHNEIDER, Eta. **Ein Beitrag zur Quellenkunde Japanischer Musik** [A contribution to the study of Japanese musical sources], *Bericht über den siebenten internationalen musikwissenschaftlichen Kongress* (Kassel: Bärenreiter, 1959) 123–26. In German. See no. 390 in this volume.

An introduction to the problems encountered by students of Japanese musical sources.

2634
as
HARICH-SCHNEIDER, Eta. **Die Gagaku in der Musikabteilung des japanischen Kaiserhofes** [Gagaku in the music department of the Japanese imperial court], *Kongreß-Bericht: Gesellschaft für Musikforschung* (Kassel; Basel: Bärenreiter, 1950) 168–70. In German. See no. 299 in this volume.

2635
as
HARICH-SCHNEIDER, Eta. **The last remnants of a mendicant musicians' guild: The goze in northern Honshu (Japan),** *Journal of the International Folk Music Council* XI (1959) 56–59. See no. 392 in this volume.

Another version is abstracted as no. 2636 in this volume.

2636
as
HARICH-SCHNEIDER, Eta. **Über die Gilden blinder Musiker in Japan** [Guilds of blind musicians in Japan], *Bericht über den internationalen musikwissenschaftlichen Kongreß* (Kassel: Bärenreiter, 1957) 107–09. In German. See no. 356 in this volume.

Discusses the *goze*—blind female singers and shamisen players—of Takata, Honshu, with particular attention to their centuries-old repertoire of *danmono* (very long ballads), *kudoki* (tragic love stories), and *kouta* (brief, often humorous songs featuring improvisation). *(David Bloom)*

2637
as
HOFMAN, Shlomo. **La musique arabe en Israel: Sa préservation, sa rénovation** [Arab music in Israel: Its preservation, its renovation], *Journal of the International Folk Music Council* XVI (1964) 25–28. In French. See no. 463 in this volume.

Surveys the music of Israel's ethnically complex Arab population, from strictly monophonic maqām music of the oral tradition through large-scale composed music tinged with Occidentalisms; its distribution and reception, including reception in sectors of the Jewish community and academic study. The preservation and renovation of the oral tradition will require training musicians to be *bi-temperamental* in the perception of equally tempered and Arab microtonally tempered scales. *(David Bloom)*

2638
as
HOOD, Mantle. **Improvisation on the Javanese gendèr,** *Journal of the International Folk Music Council* XIV (1962) 163. See no. 442 in this volume.

Describes playing the instrument in the context of Central Javanese gamelan music.

2639
as
HOOD, Mantle. **The music of Indonesia,** *Music: East and West* (Tōkyō: conference, 1961) 23–25. See no. 445 in this volume.

Particular attention is devoted to the gamelan musics of Java and Bali.

2640
as
HOOD, Mantle. **Music of the Javanese gamelan,** *Festival of Oriental Music and the Related Arts* (Los Angeles: University of California, 1960) 17–23. See no. 418 in this volume.

Four considerations contribute to the uniqueness of Central Javanese gamelan sound: the nature of the instruments and tuning systems; a principle of orchestration that might be called stratification; an Eastern sense of time; and the ensemble's relationship with other arts. *(Jianning You)*

2641
as
HUMBERT-SAUVAGEOT, (Mme). **Diversité des ambiances crées par les musiques exotiques** [The diversity of atmospheres created by exotic musics], *Deuxième congrès international d'esthétique et de Science de l'art* (Paris: Librairie Félix Alcan, 1937) I, 315–18. In French. See no. 249 in this volume.

The pace of modern life prevents us from listening to music properly. Eastern music, by contrast, creates a mood of impersonal detachment from the present. Therefore, it can reach many levels of consciousness, moving toward the infinite. *(David Schiff)*

2642
as
IYER, Musiri Subramania. **Classical music under the impact of industrial change,** *Music east and west* (Nai Dilli: Indian Council for Cultural Relations, 1966) 143–45. See no. 489 in this volume.

As a consequence of intense internal migration, Indian culture now arises directly in an urban setting for audiences for whom work and leisure are less integrated, and who are relatively passive consumers of entertainment. Performers need to program music that is easily understood, and children should be introduced to the fundamentals of music appreciation at the earliest possible age. *(Beverly Eskreis)*

2643
as
JANSKY, Herbert. **Vergleichende Volksliederkunde als Hilfsmittel der Völkerspsychologie: Ein Beispiel aus der Turkologie** [The comparative study of traditional song as a resource of ethnopsychology: An example from Turkish studies], *Actes du IVᵉ Congrès international des sciences anthropologiques et ethnologiques* (Wien: Holzhausen, 1954-1956) II:1, 79–84. In German. See no. 364 in this volume.

2644
as
JOSHI, Baburao. **Appreciating music,** *Souvenir on Hindustani Music Festival & Seminar* (Hyderabad: Andhra Pradesh Sangeeta Nataka Akademi, 1966) 7–10. See no. 450 in this volume.

Nonmusicians can learn to appreciate Hindustani music through the efforts of resourceful educators and organizations.

2645
as
KANAI, Kikuko. **The folk music of the Ryūkyūs,** *Journal of the International Folk Music Council* VII (1955) 17–19. See no. 337 in this volume.

Discusses the history of music in the Ryūkyū Islands since the 14th c.

2646
as
KAUFMANN, H.E.; SCHNEIDER, Marius. **Lieder aus den Naga-Bergen (Assam)** [Songs from the Naga Hills (Assam)], *Les colloques de Wégimont. III: Ethnomusicologie II* (Paris: Belles Lettres, 1960) 187–296. In German. See no. 366 in this volume.

Discusses the music of the inhabitants of Naga Hills region of northeast India.

2647
as
KHAN, Amir. **The tarānā style of singing,** *Music east and west* (Nai Dilli: Indian Council for Cultural Relations, 1966) 22–23. See no. 489 in this volume.

Contrary to received opinion, the vocables of tarānā singing are not meaningless.

2648
as
KOIZUMI, Fumio. **Towards a systemization of Japanese folk-song,** *Studia musicologica Academiae Scientiarum Hungaricae* VII (1965) 309–13. *Music.* See no. 478 in this volume.

Great care must be taken in transcribing Japanese traditional songs due to their great elasticity. Most Japanese traditional songs can be classified into four basic tetrachordal types and two basic rhythmic types; still, problems remain to be solved before systematization can be accomplished. *(Daniel Horn)*

2649 KUNST, Jaap. **The cultural background of In-**
as **donesian music,** *Journal of the International Folk Music Council* I (1949) 33. See no. 281 in this volume.
Summary of a paper. Among the many relationships between the cultures of Indonesia and those of neighboring regions, the mutual influences in the realm of instruments are salient.

2650 KUNST, Jaap. **Gamelan music,** *Société Interna-*
as *tionale de Musicologie, cinquième congrès/Internationale Gesellschaft für Musikwissenschaft, fünfter Kongreß/International Society for Musical Research, Fifth Congress* (Amsterdam: Vereniging voor Nederlandse Muziekgeschiedenis, 1953) 271–75. See no. 316 in this volume.
By researching Javanese music—its instruments, performance practices, forms, and complicated tonal systems—the Westerner may come to realize its universal character. *(Tsipora Yosselevitch)*

2651 KUNST, Jaap. **Quelques notes sur la musique**
as **javanaise moderne** [Some notes on modern Javanese music], *Art populaire: Travaux artistiques et scientifiques du Ier Congrès international des arts populaires* (Paris: Duchartre, 1931) 107–17. *Bibliog.* In French. See no. 152 in this volume.

2652 KUNST, Jaap. **Die 2000jährige Geschichte**
as **Süd-Sumatras im Spiegel ihrer Musik** [The 2000-year history of South Sumatra as reflected in its music], *Kongreß-Bericht: Gesellschaft für Musikforschung* (Kassel; Basel: Bärenreiter, 1950) 160–67. *Illus., music, charts, diagr., maps.* In German. See no. 299 in this volume.

2653 LACHMANN, Robert. **Musik and Tonschrift**
as **des Nō** [Music and notation of noh], *Bericht über den I. musikwissenschaftlichen Kongress der Deutschen Musikgesellschaft in Leipzig* (Wiesbaden: Breitkopf & Härtel, 1926) 80–93. *Illus., facs., music.* In German. See no. 120 in this volume.
Includes discussion of noh's harmonic system and melodic style.

2654 LALOY, Louis. **Notes sur la musique**
as **cambodgienne** [Notes on Cambodian music], *Bericht über den zweiten Kongress der Internationalen Musikgesellschaft* (Leipzig: Breitkopf & Härtel, 1907) 61–66. In French. See no. 53 in this volume.
In June 1905, when King Sisowath of Cambodia was visiting Paris, the author had an opportunity to observe and record Khmer court musicians. The observations are summarized, and compared to Thai music as studied by Carl Stumpf (*Tonsystem und Musik der Siamesen*, Leipzig 1901). *(David Bloom)*

2655 LAND, Jan Pieter Nicolaas. **Note sur la musique**
as **de l'île de Java** [Note on the music of the island of Java], *Actes du dixième Congrès international des orientalistes* (Leiden: Brill, 1897) IV, 3–18. *Transcr.* In French. See no. 20 in this volume.
An introduction to Javanese music, with transcribed musical examples.

2656 **[Leiden, 1931] The establishment of schools of**
as **secular music by Ming Huang of the T'ang dynasty.** By Evangeline Dora EDWARDS, *Actes du XVIIIe Congrès international des orientalistes* (Leiden: Brill, 1932) 121f. See no. 189 in this volume.
The emperor Xuanzong (reigned 713-56), commonly known as Minghuang, was an important patron of the arts.

2657 LUTZE, Lothar. **Aspects of Indian music,** *Music*
as *east and west* (Nai Dilli: Indian Council for Cultural Relations, 1966) 73–76. See no. 489 in this volume.
A general discussion, focusing on tāla, cyclicality, improvisation, and listener involvement.

2658 MACEDA, José. **Western music in the Philip-**
as **pines,** *Music: East and West* (Tōkyō: conference, 1961) 86–90. See no. 445 in this volume.

2659 MALM, William P. **Japanese nagauta music,**
as *Festival of Oriental Music and the Related Arts* (Los Angeles: University of California, 1960) 33–36. See no. 418 in this volume.
Summary of research on the love song genre, reported in the author's *Nagauta: The heart of Japanese kabuki music* (Rutland, Vermont, 1963), a reprint of which is cited as RILM ^{1973}4060.

2660 MANSOORUDDIN, Mohammad. **Folk songs in**
as **East Pakistan,** *Journal of the International Folk Music Council* V (1953) 51. See no. 314 in this volume.
Summary of a paper surveying traditional songs from the region (Bangladesh since 1971).

2661 MASU, Takāki (Genjiro). **Music and dances of**
as **Japan,** *Journal of the International Folk Music Council* VI (1954) 40. See no. 320 in this volume.
Brief description of an unscripted lecture-demonstration of classical and traditional genres.

2662 MASU, Takāki (Genjiro). **The place of folk mu-**
as **sic in the cultural life of the present day in Japan,** *Journal of the International Folk Music Council* V (1953) 64–65. See no. 314 in this volume.
Summary of a paper surveying developments in Japanese traditional music in the 20th c.

2663 MATSUMIYA, Suiho. **Traditional music and**
as **dance in Japan today: Its stability and evolution,** *Journal of the International Folk Music Council* XI (1959) 65–66. See no. 392 in this volume.
Summary of a paper.

2664 MAY, Elizabeth. **Japanese children's folk songs**
as **before and after contact with the West,** *Journal of the International Folk Music Council* XI (1959) 59–65. *Music.* See no. 392 in this volume.
In 1879, the Meiji government appointed Izawa Shūji (1851-1917) to head a committee overseeing the introduction of music pedagogy to Japanese public schools. Also appointed to the committee was Luther Whiting Mason (1818-96), the director of music for Boston's primary schools. As part of their undertaking, Izawa, Mason, and others compiled the three-volume *Shōgaku Shōkashu* (*Primary songbook*, 1881-84). These songs, with their fusions of Western and Japanese elements, have had a tremendous impact on Japan's children's song repertoire; examples are compared with older children's songs. *(James R. Cowdery)*

2665 MAYOR, Geeta. **The raag in the twentieth cen-**
as **tury,** *Music east and west* (Nai Dilli: Indian Council for Cultural Relations, 1966) 151–57. See no. 489 in this volume.
Discusses how changes in the social context of performance and teaching have led to changes in rāga; novel uses of rāga in composition; and possibilities for preserving traditional rāga. *(Lee James Kotsambas)*

2666 MCPHEE, Colin. **The music crisis in Bali,** *Mu-*
as *sic: East and West* (Tōkyō: conference, 1961) 60–63. See no. 445 in this volume.

Ancient ensemble types coexist with recently developed instrumental groups in Bali; the Hindu religion and traditions have kept archaic and sacred music alive. *(Sylvia Eversole)*

2667 MCPHEE, Colin. **Music in Bali,** *Festival of Oriental Music and the Related Arts* (Los Angeles: University of California, 1960) 11–16. See no. 418 in this volume.
as

Survey of the different kinds of gamelan in Bali, with reference to the number of musicians, tunings (pélog or sléndro), and social and religious function.

2668 MENON, Narayana. **Basic principles of music expression as they are found in the music of India,** *The preservation of traditional forms of the learned and popular music of the Orient and the Occident/La préservation des formes traditionelles de la musique savante et populaire dans les pays d'Orient et d'Occident* (Urbana: Center for Comparative Psycholinguistics, Institute of Communications Research, 1964) 190–202. See no. 443 in this volume.
as

Discusses the religious origins of Indian music and the *guru-śiṣya* relationship. The close teacher-student communion of the latter must be preserved as music education becomes more institutionalized. *(Michael Collier)*

2669 MENON, Narayana. **Kam spěje indická hudba?/Où va la musique hindoue?** [Where is Hindu music headed?], *Hudba národů: Sborník přednášek, proslovených na I. mezinárodním sjezdu skladatelů a hudebních kritiků/Musique des nations: Ier Congrès international des compositeurs et critiques musicaux* (Praha: Syndikát Českých Skladatelů, 1948) 44–47,150–54. In Czech and French. See no. 278 in this volume.
as

Introductory remarks on the history, structure, and philosophical foundations of music in India's Hindu culture. In current sociopolitical conditions, music is likely to develop into a Western-style art form detached from its religious significance.

2670 MOEURDORJE. **Folk music from Mongolia,** *Journal of the International Folk Music Council* XII (1960) 80. See no. 413 in this volume.
as

Brief remarks for a presentation of recordings.

2671 OGAWA, Takashi. **The collection and preservation of folk songs by the Japan Broadcasting Corporation (NHK),** *Journal of the International Folk Music Council* XIII (1961) 83–84. See no. 424 in this volume.
as

2672 PAROISSIN, René. **Musique d'Asie** [Asian music], *Perspectives de la musique sacrée à la lumière de l'encyclique Musicae sacrae disciplina* (Paris: conference, 1959) 559–63. In French. See no. 379 in this volume.
as

Brief outline of the principles of Indian, Chinese, and Japanese music, with particular attention to their spiritual character. *(David Bloom)*

2673 PICKEN, Laurence E.R. **Musical terms in a Chinese dictionary of the first century,** *Journal of the International Folk Music Council* XIV (1962) 40–43. See no. 442 in this volume.
as

The dictionary *Shuowen jiezi* (Explanation of the written characters) compiled in the Later Han dynasty by Xu Shen (ca. 100 C.E.) includes more than 200 terms relating to music, from which it is possible to construct a general picture of 1st-c. Chinese views of the place of music within the world of sound. Discussed are general terms for sound and music (*yin*, *sheng*, and *yue*); names of instruments, Chinese and foreign, and dance terminology; and a remarkably large list of mostly onomatopoeic names of

sounds made by particular materials, objects, inanimate nature, and animals, humans, ghosts, and demons. *(David Bloom)*

2674 PISSAY, Kumar. **Problems of Indian music,** *Souvenir on Hindustani Music Festival & Seminar* (Hyderabad: Andhra Pradesh Sangeeta Nataka Akademi, 1966) 51–53. See no. 450 in this volume.
as

Once the recipient of royal patronage, Hindustani music now must compete in the public arena.

2675 QAŠ'ANY, Re'uben. **Laḥney yehẇdey 'apganyṣṭan** [Melodies of Jews in Afghanistan], *Dẇkan* III (1961) 73–79. In Hebrew. See no. 417 in this volume.
as

2676 RAMACHANDRAN, N.S. **Classical music and the mass media (with special reference to South India),** *Music east and west* (Nai Dilli: Indian Council for Cultural Relations, 1966) 166–70. See no. 489 in this volume.
as

Discusses the effects of sound recording, cinema, and broadcasting on classical Indian music. The latter has helped to expose people of different regions to one another's traditions. *(Laurence Morell)*

2677 RATANJANKAR, S.N. **Classicism in Hindustani music,** *Souvenir on Hindustani Music Festival & Seminar* (Hyderabad: Andhra Pradesh Sangeeta Nataka Akademi, 1966) 35–40. See no. 450 in this volume.
as

An overview of Hindustani aesthetics.

2678 RAVINA, Menashe. **Neue israelische Folklore** [New Israeli folklore], *VIe Congrès international des sciences anthropologiques et ethnologiques. I: Rapport général et anthropologie; II: Ethnologie* (Paris: Musée de l'Homme, 1962-1964) II, 109–12. In German. See no. 421 in this volume.
as

The coming together of Jews from widely separated geographical regions and the revival of the Hebrew language have led to new songs in which the major-minor system seems to give way to older modal systems (though using tempered scales) and which feature syncopation. *(David Bloom)*

2679 REINHARD, Kurt. **Tanzlieder der Turkmenen in der Südtürkei** [Dance songs of the Turkmen people in southern Turkey], *Bericht über den internationalen musikwissenschaftlichen Kongreß* (Kassel: Bärenreiter, 1957) 189–93. *Transcr.* In German. See no. 356 in this volume.
as

Music collected in 1955 and 1956 in Turkey's small Turkmen community included a number of dance songs that seemed to show a relatively pure Turkic style, less marked by Arabo-Persian influence than most Turkish music. Their scales, rhythms, and other salient characteristics are discussed.

2680 REINHARD, Kurt. **Trommeltänze aus der Süd-Türkei** [Drum dances from southern Turkey], *Journal of the International Folk Music Council* XIII (1961) 19–26. In German. See no. 424 in this volume.
as

2681 REINHARD, Kurt. **Types of Turkmenian songs in Turkey,** *Journal of the International Folk Music Council* IX (1957) 49–54. *Music.* See no. 362 in this volume.
as

Surveys traditional songs from the Turkmen communities in southern Turkey.

2682 ROSSELLI, Marion. **Introduction to studies on Oriental music,** *Journal of the International Folk Music Council* VI (1954) 48. See no. 320 in this volume.
as

The conference report provides only a citation. Neither the text nor a summary of the paper was published here.

2683 SADAGOPAN, V.V. **Psychology of listening,**
as *Music east and west* (Nai Dilli: Indian Council for Cultural Relations, 1966) 118–24. See no. 489 in this volume.
The drone of the tambura, the progression of tones, and rhythmic improvisation present difficulties for the Western listener to classical Indian music.

2684 SAKKA, Keisei. **Western music in Japan,** *Music: East and West* (Tōkyō: conference, 1961) 77–81. See no. 445 in this volume.
Japanese music is not taught in Japanese schools because class consciousness has prohibited the teaching of various types of traditional music. *(Sylvia Eversole)*

2685 SALOMON, Karel. **Problems of old songs in a revived language,** *Journal of the International Folk Music Council* XII (1960) 53–55. See no. 413 in this volume.
When Jews from all over the world moved to Israel, they brought their traditional songs, in whatever local language or dialect they spoke. Singing these songs in modern-day Hebrew presents certain problems, particularly regarding discrepancies between linguistic and melodic accents. As a result, many beautiful old songs are seldom sung now. *(James R. Cowdery)*

2686 SAMBAMOORTHY, P. **Influences on Karnatic music,** *Souvenir on Hindustani Music Festival & Seminar* (Hyderabad: Andhra Pradesh Sangeeta Nataka Akademi, 1966) 41–43. See no. 450 in this volume.
Surveys elements of Hindustani music that have influenced the Karnatak tradition.

→ SAYGUN, Ahmed Adnan. **Authenticity in folk music.** See no. 2539 in this volume.

2687 SAYGUN, Ahmed Adnan. **Basic principles of musical expression as they are to be found in the modal music of the Middle East,** *The preservation of traditional forms of the learned and popular music of the Orient and the Occident/La préservation des formes traditionelles de la musique savante et populaire dans les pays d'Orient et d'Occident* (Urbana: Center for Comparative Psycholinguistics, Institute of Communications Research, 1964) 222–30. See no. 443 in this volume.
The traditional principles of Middle Eastern classical music are undergoing revolutionary change.

2688 SCHNEIDER, Marius. **Basic principles: The variation, Orient-Occident,** *The preservation of traditional forms of the learned and popular music of the Orient and the Occident/La préservation des formes traditionelles de la musique savante et populaire dans les pays d'Orient et d'Occident* (Urbana: Center for Comparative Psycholinguistics, Institute of Communications Research, 1964) 231–39. See no. 443 in this volume.
Discusses the principles of variation and development, with particular reference to classical Japanese music. In Asian music, a musical idea is developed in the course of a performance, according to the composer-performer's inclination, on the basis of continuous variation. Variation in Western music is founded on the principles of opposition and contrast. *(Michael Collier)*

2689 SHANKAR, Ravi. **Hindusthani classical music and the demands of today,** *Music east and west*

(Nai Dilli: Indian Council for Cultural Relations, 1966) 158–65. See no. 489 in this volume.
Discusses problems of performance in and outside India, traditional teaching methods, and innovation.

2690 SHIBA, Sukehiro. **The music of Japan (gagaku),** *Music: East and West* (Tōkyō: conference, 1961) 9–14. See no. 445 in this volume.
Survey of court music and dance (bugaku) from the 7th c., with attention to the distinct schools of Kyoto, Nara, and Osaka. *(Sylvia Eversole)*

2691 SHMUELI, Herzl. **Oriental elements in Israeli song,** *Journal of the International Folk Music Council* XVI (1964) 29. See no. 463 in this volume.
The new indigenous Jewish music traditions developing in Israel is marked, among other things, by an accretion of melodic patterns similar to the motifs of biblical cantillation. Summary of material discussed in the author's *Ha-zemer ha-Yisre'eli* (Tel Aviv, 1971). *(Vivian Conejero)*

2692 SHUKLA, Narendrarai N. **Evolution in Hindusthani music,** *Music east and west* (Nai Dilli: Indian Council for Cultural Relations, 1966) 32–37. See no. 489 in this volume.
A historical account of the development of rāga and tāla in the evolution from dhrupad to khayāl. *(Lee James Kotsambas)*

2693 SINGH, Thakur Jaidev. **Tradition and the inventive principle,** *Music east and west* (Nai Dilli: Indian Council for Cultural Relations, 1966) 179–85. See no. 489 in this volume.
Industrialization and its economic effects have upset the traditional balance between social heritage and innovation, with harmful consequences for Indian music in folk, stage, temple, light, and classical genres. *(Laurence Morell)*

2694 SINGH, Thakur Jaideva. **The music of India,** *Music: East and West* (Tōkyō: conference, 1961) 1–4. See no. 445 in this volume.

2695 SPIRA, Y. **Developments in Israel,** *The preservation of traditional forms of the learned and popular music of the Orient and the Occident/La préservation des formes traditionelles de la musique savante et populaire dans les pays d'Orient et d'Occident* (Urbana: Center for Comparative Psycholinguistics, Institute of Communications Research, 1964) 240–43. See no. 443 in this volume.
In Israel, immigrants bring a wide variety of sacred and secular musical traditions; attempts are being made to preserve them. New folk and classical musics arise as well, in the context of the vernacularization of Hebrew and the kibbutz phenomenon. *(Judith Drogichen Meyer)*

2696 SURYA SENA, Devar. **Folk songs of Ceylon,** *Journal of the International Folk Music Council* VI (1954) 11–14. *Music.* See no. 320 in this volume.
A survey of song types, with an introduction to the raban, a frame drum.

2697 TANABE, Hisao. **Note sur la musique japonaise** [Notes on Japanese music], *Congrès international des arts populaires/International congress of popular arts* (Paris: Institut international de coopération intellectuelle, 1928) 98. In French. See no. 153 in this volume.
Summary of a paper proposing a periodization for the history of music in Japan, into an archaic period to 421 C.E., when the indigenous music reached its highest state of development; 421 to 1221, a period of transformation under Chinese, Korean, and Hindo-Buddhist influence; and a last period beginning with the flourishing of noh theater in the early 14th c. and continuing through the propagation of music by the bourgeois and working classes during the Tokugawa shogunate to the present. *(David Bloom)*

2698 TRẦN, Van Khê. **Basic principles of musical ex-**
as **pression as they are found in modal music of**
the Far East, *The preservation of traditional forms of*
the learned and popular music of the Orient and the
Occident/La préservation des formes traditionelles de
la musique savante et populaire dans les pays d'Orient
et d'Occident (Urbana: Center for Comparative
Psycholinguistics, Institute of Communications Research, 1964) 171–83. See no. 443 in this volume.
Ancient music of East and Southeast Asia derived its principles from cosmological and philosophical conceptions, including the harmony between
Heaven and Earth and the Confucian ideal of inner balance. Contemporary
music, aligned with poetry, stresses improvisation and audience participation. *(Michael Collier)*

2699 TRẦN, Van Khê. **Far Eastern musical tradition**
as **and the new rhythm,** *Music east and west* (Nai
Dilli: Indian Council for Cultural Relations, 1966)
146–50. See no. 489 in this volume.
Discusses the preservation of musical tradition in East Asia, particularly
Vietnam, in the face of innovation in the manufacture of instruments, performing style, and musical idiom, with attention to possible contributions
of Western countries. *(Lee James Kotsambas)*

2700 TRẦN, Van Khê. **Note sur l'ornementation au**
as **Vietnam** [Note on ornamentation in Vietnam], *Report*
of the Eighth Congress of the International Musicologi-
cal Society. I: Papers (Kassel: Bärenreiter, 1961)
445–50. *Transcr.* In French. See no. 439 in this volume.
Vietnamese musicians use ornamentation for linguistic reasons, to imitate
the intonations of Vietnamese speech (with its six phonemic tones); for aesthetic reasons, unornamented sounds being unbeautiful to the Vietnamese
ear; for virtuosic reasons, to display their skill; and for expressive reasons,
to provide a particular nuance. The ornaments may be classified into horizontal types—by added notes or syllables, by unusual sounds or timbres,
and by rhythmic modifications—and the vertical type (polyphony).
(David Bloom)

2701 TRẦN, Van Khê. **Problems of Sino-Japanese**
as **musical tradition today,** *Music: East and West*
(Tōkyō: conference, 1961) 54–59. See no. 445 in this
volume.
The music of Vietnam is the youngest branch of the Sino-Japanese musical
family.

2702 TRẦN, Van Khê. **Responsabilité des organisa-**
as **tions pour la culture et l'éducation dans la**
préservation des traditions musicales des pays
extrême-orientaux [Responsibility of cultural and
educational organizations for the preservation of musical traditions of the Far East], *Artistic values in tradi-*
tional music (Berlin: International Institute for Comparative Music Studies, 1966) 23–33. In French. See
no. 493 in this volume.
Discusses research, conservation and publication of documents, transmission
and perpetuation of traditions, renovation of instruments, and education.

2703 UDDIN, Jasim. **Folk music of East Pakistan,**
as *Journal of the International Folk Music Council* III
(1951) 41–44. See no. 296 in this volume.
Discusses the history of music in the region (now Bangladesh), with attention to the work of the folklorist Dinesh Chandra Sen (1866-1939).
(James R. Cowdery)

2704 VINOGRADOV, Viktor. **The experience of ap-**
as **plying folk music traditions to professional mu-**
sic in the Eastern republics of the USSR, *The*
preservation of traditional forms of the learned and pop-
ular music of the Orient and the Occident/La préser-
vation des formes traditionelles de la musique savante et

populaire dans les pays d'Orient et d'Occident (Urbana:
Center for Comparative Psycholinguistics, Institute of
Communications Research, 1964) 258–78. See no. 443
in this volume.
Central Asian music cultures are localized, and not necessarily corrupted
by stylistic vulgarity. The formation of professional traditional ensembles
is discussed.

2705 VISWANATHAN, Tanjore. **Problems of Indian**
as **music tradition today,** *Music: East and West*
(Tōkyō: conference, 1961) 67–70. See no. 445 in this
volume.
Present-day Indian music is the evolutionary product of the past. The influence of Western methods on Indian music has been relatively insignificant.
(Sylvia Eversole)

2706 VISWANATHAN, Tanjore. **Traditional music**
as **in South India: A dynamic force,** *Music east and*
west (Nai Dilli: Indian Council for Cultural Relations,
1966) 186–91. See no. 489 in this volume.
In the course of its history, Karnatak music has spread from temples to
courts and ultimately to everyday life. Western influence has affected education, performance practice, and instruments. Beginning in the 1920s, the
guru-*śiṣya* system of pedagogy is being replaced by conservatories.
(Laurence Morell)

$\longrightarrow$ YÖNETKEN, Halil Bedi. **Turecká hudba/La**
musique turque [Turkish music]. See no. 2275 in
this volume.

2707 YUIZE, Shin'ichi. **Means of preservation:**
as **Preservation of traditional instruction,** *The*
preservation of traditional forms of the learned and
popular music of the Orient and the Occident/La
préservation des formes traditionelles de la musique
savante et populaire dans les pays d'Orient et
d'Occident (Urbana: Center for Comparative
Psycholinguistics, Institute of Communications Research, 1964) 279–88. See no. 443 in this volume.
Historical discussion of the development of traditional music instruction in
Japan, beginning with the teaching of Buddhist music in the 4th c., the
iemoto master-disciple system, and the development of various music notation systems. Western methods of systematization, now being applied to
traditional Japanese music in Japanese conservatories, may help to solidify
the tradition. *(Judith Drogichen Meyer)*

2708 YUIZE, Shin'ichi. **The music of Japan,** *Music:*
as *East and West* (Tōkyō: conference, 1961) 15–17. See
no. 445 in this volume.

34 Europe

2709 ABIUSO, V. **I canti e le ninne-nanne popolari**
as **sarde** [Sardinian traditional songs and lullabies], *Atti*
del 4. Congresso nazionale di arti e tradizioni popolari
(Roma: Opera Nazionale Dopolavoro, 1942) 357–64.
In Italian. See no. 270 in this volume.

2710 AHOBADZE, Vladimer V. **Forma kollek-**
as **tivnogo truda *nadi* i gruzinskaja chetyrëhgo-**
losnaja pesnja *naduri* [The form of collective *nadi*
work and the Georgian four-part *naduri* song], *Europa*
et Hungaria: Congressus ethnographicus in Hungaria
(Budapest: Akadémiai Kiadó, 1965) 459–68. In Russian. See no. 460 in this volume.

Discusses structural relationships between the Georgian custom of voluntary cooperative harvesting (*nadi*) and the polyphonic singing (*naduri*) that traditionally accompanies it. *(David Bloom)*

2711 ALBERTINI, A.M. **Studio su nuove versioni**
as **della canzone della *Finta monacella*** [Study of new versions of the song *La finta monacella*], *Lares* XXV (1959) 442–49. In Italian. See no. 370 in this volume.

Discusses variants of a traditional Italian ballata about a soldier who tricks his way into his sweetheart's bed by disguising himself as a nun.

2712 ALFAIATE MARVÃO, António. **O folclore mu-**
as **sical do Baixo Alentejo nos ciclos litúrgicos da Igreja** [The traditional music of Baixo Alentejo in liturgical cycles of the Church], *Actas do Congresso Internacional de Etnografia* (Porto: Imprensa Portuguesa, 1965) II, 147–66. In Portuguese. See no. 473 in this volume.

Describes the region's traditional music in general as well as that used in the Church. Musical events of the Christmas season, New Year, Epiphany, Easter, and Pentecost are discussed, and Marian songs are examined.

(Peter S. Bushnell)

2713 AMADES GELAT, Joan. **La canzone ritmica**
as **catalana** [The Catalan rhythmic song], *Atti del Congresso internazionale di musiche popolari mediterranee e del Convegno dei bibliotecari musicali* (Palermo: De Magistris succ. V. Bellotti, 1959) 47–50. In Italian. See no. 332 in this volume.

A preliminary attempt at the classification, formal and functional, of the songs collected in the author's *Folklore de Catalunya* (1950-69), vol. 2 (Barcelona, 1979) (cited as RILM ¹⁹⁷⁹5284). *(David Bloom)*

2714 AMADES GELAT, Joan. **Dances and songs of**
as **the Pyrenean shepherds**, *Journal of the International Folk Music Council* VI (1954) 49–51. *Music.* See no. 320 in this volume.

A survey of genres and practices in the Spanish Pyrenees.

2715 AMADES GELAT, Joan. **Musique populaire et**
as **musique folklorique** [Popular music and folk music], *Journal of the International Folk Music Council* VII (1955) 36. In French. See no. 337 in this volume.

The conference report provides only a citation. Neither the text nor a summary of the paper, which discussed Spanish music, was published here.

2716 ANDERSSON, Otto. **Altertümliche Tonarten**
as **in der Volksmusik mit besonderer Berücksichtigung der finnländischen** [The retention in traditional music of ancient tonalities, with particular attention to that of Finland], *Haydn-Zentenarfeier* (Leipzig: Breitkopf & Härtel; Wien: Artaria, 1909) 259–66. *Transcr.* In German. See no. 65 in this volume.

Focuses primarily on Finnish dance tunes.

2717 ANDERSSON, Otto. **Revival of folk music and**
as **folk dancing in Finland**, *Journal of the International Folk Music Council* III (1951) 6. See no. 296 in this volume.

Summary of a paper. The Finnish folk music and dance movement began as a matter of historical and national interest, it developed as a matter of artistic interest, and it developed further in the realm of the social sciences. *(James R. Cowdery)*

2718 ANDERSSON, Otto. **Violinists and dance-**
as **tunes among the Swedish population in Finland towards the middle of the XIX century,**
Report of the Fourth Congress of the International Musical Society (London: Novello, 1912) 159–66. *Transcr.* See no. 71 in this volume.

Many untutored fiddlers, smiths by trade, were responsible for the abundance of traditional tunes among the Swedish population in Finland. These players picked up virtuoso tricks from trained violinists. *(Mei-Mei Meng)*

2719 ANDRAL, Maguy. **Permanence de structures**
as **élémentaires dans la musique traditionelle française vivante** [The permanence of elementary structures in living traditional French music], *Journal of the International Folk Music Council* XIV (1962) 153–54. In French. See no. 442 in this volume.

The analysis of ethnomusicological documents collected in France ca. 1940-60 yields a number of basic structural traits, formal, rhythmic, and melodic, that may be regarded as elementary units of archaic origin. *(David Bloom)*

2720 ANGLÈS, Higini. **Relations of Spanish folk**
as **song to the Gregorian chant,** *Journal of the International Folk Music Council* XVI (1964) 54–56. *Music, transcr.* See no. 463 in this volume.

The influence of Asian traditional musics dominates the chants of the Proper of the Mass and Office; in the chants of the Ordinary, it is Western traditional music that prevails. Features of Catalan traditional song recalling chant melody include an occasional final melisma (in ploughing songs), recitative-like melodies, and the singing of a melismatic melody with one syllable to each note, analogous to troping. *(Vivian Conejero)*

2721 ANTONIJEVIĆ, Dragoslav. **Guslar danas i**
as **guslarski podmladak u Užičkom kraju** [Contemporary guslars and those of the next generation in the Užice region], *Rad VII-og kongresa Saveza Folklorista Jugoslavije* (Cetinje: Obod, 1964) 427–30. In Serbian; summary in French. See no. 419 in this volume.

The guslar tradition is very much alive in the region, being carried forward by the younger generation. The epic songs they perform are influenced by ongoing social developments. *(author)*

2722 ANTONIJEVIĆ, Dragoslav. **Narodnooslobodo-**
as **dilačka pesma protiv nečoveštva** [Songs against inhumanity from the time of the War of National Liberation], *Rad kongresa folklorista Jugoslavije* (Ljubljana: Savez Udruženja Folkloristov Jugoslavije, 1960) 169–72. In Serbian; summary in English. See no. 404 in this volume.

Examples of songs from the 1941-45 war condemning atrocity and crime, and demanding just punishment for traitors and evildoers, are adduced; their racy couplets always show the bright path toward a renewed socialist humanity. *(author)*

2723 ANTONOVYČ, Myroslav. **Die Mehrstimmig-**
as **keit in den ukrainischen Volksliedern** [Polyphony in Ukrainian traditional song], *Société Internationale de Musicologie, cinquième congrès/Internationale Gesellschaft für Musikwissenschaft, fünfter Kongreß/International Society for Musical Research, Fifth Congress* (Amsterdam: Vereniging voor Nederlandse Muziekgeschiedenis, 1953) 55–64. In German. See no. 316 in this volume.

2724 ARCO Y GARAY, Ricardo del. **La jota arago-**
as **naise** [The Aragonese jota], *Congrès international des arts populaires/International congress of popular arts* (Paris: Institut international de coopération intellectuelle, 1928) 119–20. In French. See no. 153 in this volume.

Summary of the paper abstracted as no. 4933 in this volume.

⟶ ARCO Y GARAY, Ricardo del. **Les couplets et les "Dances" dans le Haut-Aragon (Espagne)** [Coplas and *el dance* in northern Aragón (Spain)]. See no. 4932 in this volume.

2725 ARCO Y GARAY, Ricardo del. **Romances, couplets, danses et autres divertissements dans le Haut-Aragon** [Romances, coplas, and other entertainments in upper Aragon], *Congrès international des arts populaires/International congress of popular arts* (Paris: Institut international de coopération intellectuelle, 1928) 109. In French. See no. 153 in this volume.
as

Summary of a paper surveying sports and games; song genres including alboradas, romances, and coplas addressed to the saints; danza, a mixture of pre-Roman custom (Celtic sword dance) with Reconquista elements (miming of battles between Moors and Christians); and the indigenous dramatic form *el dance*. *(David Bloom)*

2726 ARNBERG, Matts. **Recording expedition to the Faroe Islands,** *Journal of the International Folk Music Council* XII (1960) 82–83. See no. 413 in this volume.
as

2727 AU, Hans von der. **Frühformen des deutschen Volkstanzes** [Early forms of German folk dance], *Kongreß-Bericht: Gesellschaft für Musikforschung* (Kassel; Basel: Bärenreiter, 1950) 178–80. In German. See no. 299 in this volume.
as

2728 AZKÚE, Resurrección María. **La tradición en nuestra música popular y religiosa** [Tradition in our popular religious music], *Crónica del IV Congreso Nacional de Música Sagrada* (Vitoria: Imprenta del Montepío Diocesano, 1930) 282–95. *Music.* In Spanish. See no. 155 in this volume.
as

Offers a comparative analysis of several genres of Spanish traditional sacred music.

2729 BAINCHI, G. **Valore spirituale ed impronta etnica dei nostri canti di guerra** [Spiritual valor and ethnic imprint of our war songs], *Atti del 4. Congresso nazionale di arti e tradizioni popolari* (Roma: Opera Nazionale Dopolavoro, 1942) 365–68. In Italian. See no. 270 in this volume.
as

2730 BARBERÀ, Josep. **Supervivències gregues en la cançó popular catalana** [The survival of Greek elements in Catalan traditional song], *Congrés de la Societat Internacional de Musicologia* (Barcelona: Casa de Caritat, 1936). In Catalan. See no. 224 in this volume.
as

The conference report provides only a citation. Neither the text nor a summary of the paper was published here.

2731 BARTÓK, Béla. **Les recherches sur le folklore musical en Hongrie** [Music folklore research in Hungary], *Art populaire: Travaux artistiques et scientifiques du Ier Congrès international des arts populaires* (Paris: Duchartre, 1931) 127–28. In French. See no. 152 in this volume.
as

Another version is abstracted as 1928-50 in this volume.

2732 BAŠIĆ, Elly. **Brojalica: Melografski problem dječjeg poetskog stvaralaštva** [Counting game: Melographic problems in children's poetry], *Treći kongres folklorista Jugoslavije* (Cetinje: Udruženje Folklorista Crne Gore, 1958) 241–53. *Charts, diagr.,*
as

transcr. In Croatian; summary in French. See no. 357 in this volume.

Counting games represent the most musical aspect of children's creativity, and reflect children's perception of the outside world without their parents' involvement. Research in Montenegro (1955), Istria (1956), and Zagreb (1953-54) indicates that South Slavic counting games are usually recited, while in regions where Romance languages are spoken such games are usually sung. In Italy and Istria, most of the counting games use meaningful phrases, while in South Slavic regions they use nonsense syllables. *(Zdravko Blažeković)*

2733 BAUD-BOVY, Samuel. **La chanson cleftique** [Songs of the kléftïs], *Journal of the International Folk Music Council* I (1949) 44–45. In French. See no. 281 in this volume.
as

Surveys the performance context, verse and musical form, and history of kleftika, the songs of the bandit-guerillas of the Greek anti-Ottoman resistance.

2734 BAUD-BOVY, Samuel. **Enregistrements en Crète** [Recordings in Crete], *Les colloques de Wégimont. [I: Ethnomusicologie I]* (Bruxelles: Elsevier, 1956) 206–07. In French. See no. 340 in this volume.
as

Discusses sound recordings of traditional songs.

2735 BAUD-BOVY, Samuel. **La place des *rizitika tragoudia* dans la chanson populaire de la Grèce moderne** [The place of rizitika song in traditional song in modern Greece], *Krītika chronika* 16 (1961) III,97–105. *Bibliog.* In French. See no. 434 in this volume.
as

The rizitika table songs have a special place in the traditional Cretan repertoire. Their relation to the kleftika of mainland Greece is discussed, with other issues.

2736 BECKING, Gustav. **Der musikalische Bau des montenegrinischen Volksepos** [The musical structure of the folk epic of Montenegro], *Proceedings of the First International Congress of Phonetic Sciences: First meeting of the Internationale Arbeitsgemeinschaft für Phonologie* (Harlem: J. Enschedé, 1933) 53–62. In German. See no. 194 in this volume.
as

Another version is published in *Archives néerlandaises de phonétique* (1933, reprinted in Walter Kramdisch, ed., *Gustav Becking zum Gedächtnis* [Tutzing, 1975], and cited as RILM^{1976}6651).

2737 BELJAEV, Viktor Mihailovič. **Muzykal'nyj fol'klor narodov dunajskogo basseina** [The musical tradition of the peoples of the Danube basin], *Rad kongresa folklorista Jugoslavije* (Zagreb: Savez Udruženja Folklorista Jugoslavije, 1959) 87–94. In Russian; summary in Croatian. See no. 382 in this volume.
as

2738 BESSELER, Heinrich. **Katalanische Cobla und Alta-Tanzkapelle** [The Catalan cobla and the alta dance ensemble], *Compte rendu/Kongressbericht/Report* (Basel: Bärenreiter, 1951) 59–68. *Illus., music.* In German. See no. 289 in this volume.
as

The modern 11-piece cobla ensemble, which accompanies the dancing of the sardana in Catalonia, has historical roots in the Middle Ages. Its core group of instruments, tiple, tenora, and low brass, may be traced to the 15th-c. alta ensemble, also used for dance accompaniment, of two or three shawms and trumpet, trombone, or bagpipe, with the melody in the tenor, as in an alta composition by Francisco de la Torre found in the *Cancionero musical de Palacio* (E-Mp MS 1335). The sardana's rhythmic character is also traceable to the 15th c. *(David Bloom)*

2739 BEZIĆ, Jerko. **Neki oblici starinskog otegnutog dvoglasnog pjevanja na sjeverozapadnim**
as

zadarskim otocima [Some forms of the old two-voice prolonged song on the islands northwest of Zadar], *Rad kongresa folklorista Jugoslavije* (Ljubljana: Savez Udruženja Folkloristov Jugoslavije, 1960) 295–302. *Transcr.* In Croatian; summary in German. See no. 404 in this volume.

A previously unreported phenomenon of the northern Dalmatian islands is the two-voiced melismatic singing on the syllable *oj*, similar to the better-known *ojkanje* singing of Dalmatian hinterland. Its presence may be accounted for by immigration from the Bosnian highland in the 15th and 16th c. *(author)*

2740
as
BOLLINI, G. **Il mare nei canti popolari lombardi** [The sea in Lombardian traditional songs], *Atti del 4. Congresso nazionale di arti e tradizioni popolari* (Roma: Opera Nazionale Dopolavoro, 1942) 369–81. In Italian. See no. 270 in this volume.

2741
as
BOON, Arthur. **La chanson populaire** [Folk song], *La musique et le peuple: Rapports, suggestions, voeux* (Bruxelles: Ministère des Sciences et des Arts, 1932) 19–37. In French. See no. 195 in this volume.

Summarizes what has been done to preserve Belgian traditional songs, what remains to be done, and how the diffusion of traditional song has been furthered. *(Mark Stevens)*

2742
as
BORELI, Rada. **Narodna pesma o Partiji i Titu** [Neotraditional songs dedicated to the Party and Tito], *Rad kongresa folklorista Jugoslavije* (Ljubljana: Savez Udruženja Folkloristov Jugoslavije, 1960) 165–68. In Serbian; summary in English. See no. 404 in this volume.

The collections of the Etnografski Institut at the Srpska Akademija Nauke i Umetnosti include some 20,000 songs, mostly from the War of National Liberation and the period of socialist construction projects, dating from 1919 to the present. Songs dedicated to the Komunistička Partija Jugoslavije and Josip Broz Tito, mostly in easily memorized couplet form, are of historical value for the information they provide on five general topics: the foundation of the Party, the preparation of the Insurrection, the War of National Liberation, socialist construction projects, and the criticism of blunders. *(author)*

2743
as
BORREL, Eugène. **À propos du folklore israélite de Salonique** [The folklore of the Salonika Jews], *Atti del Congresso internazionale di musiche popolari mediterranee e del Convegno dei bibliotecari musicali* (Palermo: De Magistris succ. V. Bellotti, 1959) 57–58. In French. See no. 332 in this volume.

A little-known repertoire of traditional songs is maintained by the Sephardic community of Thessaloníki; with their curious modalities and Spanish-language texts, they deserve careful study, especially comparison with old melodies and texts from Spain. *(David Bloom)*

2744
as
BOSE, Fritz. **Law and freedom in the interpretation of European folk epics,** *Journal of the International Folk Music Council* X (1958) 29–34. *Music.* See no. 371 in this volume.

Discusses the parameters of improvisation in epic song performance in Finland and the Slavic states.

2745
as
BOŠKOVIĆ, Katica. **Crnogorski survivali u svadbenim običajima Konavala** [Montenegrin customs in the wedding ceremonies of Konavle], *Treći kongres folklorista Jugoslavije* (Cetinje: Udruženje Folklorista Crne Gore, 1958) 29–36. *Illus., bibliog.* In Croatian; summary in French. See no. 357 in this volume.

A detailed description of wedding ceremonies in Konavle, a community south of Dubrovnik.

2746
as
BOŠKOVIĆ-STULLI, Maja. **Neka suvremena mišljenja o baladi** [Some contemporary views on the ballad], *Rad kongresa folklorista Jugoslavije* (Beograd: Naučno Delo, 1960) 105–09. In Croatian; summary in German. See no. 402 in this volume.

Discusses writings on traditional ballads by Erich Seemann, Mihail Pavlovič Alekseev, and Olinko Delorko, drawing on examples from the Serbian-Croatian tradition, with particular attention to the relationship between traditional ballads and dances, the importance in the ballad of its musical realization, and cases that are difficult to classify unambiguously as ballad rather than epic. *(author)*

2747
as
BRĂILOIU, Constantin. **À propos du jodel** [Concerning the yodel], *Compte rendu/Kongressbericht/Report* (Basel: Bärenreiter, 1951) 69–71. In French. See no. 289 in this volume.

Hornbostel's conjecture that the yodel represents a vocal imitation of the sound of the alphorn, and that its origins, like the instrument's, are in Asia, cannot be sustained. A reprint appears in the author's collection *Problèmes d'ethnomusicologie* (Geneva, 1973), cited as RILM [1974]3233. *(Scott Fruehwald)*

2748
as
BRÄUTIGAM, Helmut. **Deutsche Volkslieder aus Jugoslawien** [German traditional songs from Yugoslavia], *Bericht über den Internationalen Kongreß Singen und Sprechen* (München: Oldenbourg, 1938) 336–39. In German. See no. 257 in this volume.

A field trip to seven German-speaking communities in the Bačka region of Vojvodina yielded a collection of 450 songs, together with numerous variants. Traditional music thrives there more than in most regions of Germany itself; it is largely maintained by young people, and long song texts are preserved in MS notebooks. Performance style and musical characteristics are briefly sketched. *(David Bloom)*

2749
as
BREDICEANU, Tiberiu. **Historique et état actuel des recherches sur la musique populaire roumaine** [Historical and current research on Romanian traditional music], *Art populaire: Travaux artistiques et scientifiques du Ier Congrès international des arts populaires* (Paris: Duchartre, 1931) 133–40. In French. See no. 152 in this volume.

2750
as
BRONSON, Bertrand Harris. **About the commonest British ballads,** *Journal of the International Folk Music Council* IX (1957) 22–27. *Charts, diagr.* See no. 362 in this volume.

Discusses the most well-known ballads, including versions from England, Scotland, and the U.S., with attention to their shared features.

2751
as
BRONZINI, Giovanni Battista. **La canzone della** *Finta monacella*: **Nuove versioni e loro classificazione** [The canzone *La finta monacella*: New versions and their classification], *Lares* XX/1-2 (1954). In Italian. See no. 288 in this volume.

2752
as
BUKOFZER, Manfred F. **Zur Erklärung des** *Lobetanz* **in der schweizerischen Volksmusik** [Explanation of the *Lobetanz* in Swiss folk music], *Congrés de la Societat Internacional de Musicologia* (Barcelona: Casa de Caritat, 1936). In German. See no. 224 in this volume.

The conference report provides only a citation. Neither the text nor a summary of the paper was published here.

2753
as
BURLASOVÁ, Soňa. **Hudobný folklór Chorvátskeho Grobu a problematika etnických diaspor** [The musical tradition of the village of Chorvátsky Grob and the problematics of ethnic diaspora], *Rad kongresa folklorista Jugoslavije*

(Zagreb: Savez Udruženja Folklorista Jugoslavije, 1959) 133. In Slovak. See no. 382 in this volume.

Discusses the traditional music of Croatian villages in Slovakia. The full version in Slovak is published in *Slovenská etnografia* VI/1-2 (1958).

2754
as
BUTUROVIĆ, Đenana. **Epska narodna tradicija Trebinjske Šume** [The local epic tradition in Trebinjska Šuma], *Rad IX-og kongresa Saveza Folklorista Jugoslavije* (Sarajevo: Savez Udruženja Folklorista Jugoslavije, 1963) 53–58. In Bosnian; summary in English. See no. 455 in this volume.

Performers of traditional epics in the forest district west of Trebinje (Trebinjska Šuma) may be classified by age. Octogenarians were good narrators, but not outstanding as singers and guslars; they had learned their repertoires entirely by oral transmission. Most women performers belonged to this generation. Performers in their 60s were the most proficient singers and guslars, having studied for diplomas and entered competitions in the 1930s and 1940s. The texts they performed were altered from oral tradition to conform with printed versions. Performers aged 30-40 rarely had time to sing, and had no repertoire of their own; their choice of poems often corresponded to that of their children's school texts. *(author)*

2755
as
CAMPBELL, Åke. **Herdsman's song and yoik in northern Sweden,** *Journal of the International Folk Music Council* III (1951) 64–67. See no. 296 in this volume.

Describes the use of instruments and vocal calls in herding by Sámi and Swedish peoples, and discusses the Sámi jojk tradition. *(James R. Cowdery)*

2756
as
CARNOY, Henry. **Le folklore esthonien: Hommage aux travaux de Jacob Hart** [Estonian folklore: Homage to the work of Jakob Hurt], *[Ier] Congrès international des traditions populaires* (Paris: Société d'Éditions Scientifiques, 1891). In French. See no. 13 in this volume.

2757
as
CARPITELLA, Diego. **Considérations sur le folklore musical italien dans ses rapports avec la structure sociale du pays** [Thoughts on the relationship between traditional music and social structure in Italy], *Journal of the International Folk Music Council* XI (1959) 66–70. In French. See no. 392 in this volume.

Examines ideological, economic, and religious influences on traditional music, with attention to the distinct division between Italian urban and rural cultures. *(Murat Eyüboğlu)*

2758
as
CARPITELLA, Diego. **Prospettive e problemi nuovi degli studi di musica popolare in Italia** [New perspectives and problems of the study of traditional music in Italy], *Lares* XXII (1956) 175–78. In Italian. See no. 353 in this volume.

Outlines research issues regarding the assignment of value to traditional music, historical perspective, problems brought to light due to cultural circulation, and the polemic between tonal and modal music (as well as what each term/genre implies in terms of historical placement). *(Susan Poliniak)*

2759
as
CARPITELLA, Diego. **Le registrazioni di cantori popolari in Abruzzo** [The recordings of traditional singers in Abruzzi], *Lares* XXV (1959) 160–64. In Italian. See no. 370 in this volume.

2760
as
CASTRILLO HERNÁNDEZ, Gonzalo. **Le chant populaire de la vieille Castille** [The traditional song of old Castile], *Art populaire: Travaux artistiques et scientifiques du Ier Congrès international des arts populaires* (Paris: Duchartre, 1931) 151–53. In French. See no. 152 in this volume.

An annotated list of publications including recent field collections, art music using traditional-music material, and reproductions and transcriptions of old books, including Mozarabic chant MSS, whose music is related to traditional Castilian song. A summary is cited as no. 800 in this volume. *(David Bloom)*

2761
as
CASTRILLO HERNÁNDEZ, Gonzalo. **Modalité, forme, rythme et harmonie dans les chansons types de la vieille Castille** [Modality, form, rhythm, and harmony in the song types of old Castile], *Congrès international des arts populaires/International congress of popular arts* (Paris: Institut international de coopération intellectuelle, 1928) 107. In French. See no. 153 in this volume.

Medieval modes survive in Castilian songs, which reject the artificial sensibilities of modern melody and lend themselves to the plagal cadence. Their melodic and rhythmic development follows the evolution of the popular *romance*, in three phases: simple recititative form, lightly ornamented melody, and expressive lyric. The influence of Jewish psalmody is detectable. Most songs are inspired by a symmetrical rhythm characteristic of dance melody; the melodic accent governs expressiveness. *(David Bloom)*

2762
as
ČETKAUSKAITÉ, Genovaité. **Principes du classement du folklore musical lituanien** [Principles of classification in Lithuanian traditional music], *Studia musicologica Academiae Scientiarum Hungaricae* VII (1965) 231–46. *Facs., music, bibliog.* In French. See no. 478 in this volume.

Several different types of classification were used in published collections of Lithuanian traditional music in the 19th c. *(William Renwick)*

2763
as
CHERBULIEZ, Antoine-Élisée. **La canción popular en la Suiza Retica** [The traditional songs of the Rhaetia region of Switzerland], *Congrés de la Societat Internacional de Musicologia* (Barcelona: Casa de Caritat, 1936). In Spanish. See no. 224 in this volume.

The conference report provides only a citation. Neither the text nor a summary of the paper was published here.

2764
as
CHEVAIS, Maurice. **Participation de la jeunesse scolaire à des fêtes et cortèges folkloriques** [Participation of schoolchildren in traditional festivals and processions], *Travaux du Ier Congrès International de Folklore* (Tours: Arrault et Cie, 1938) 387–88. In French. See no. 251 in this volume.

2765
as
CHLÍBEC, Jiří. **Some new elements in the folk music of eastern Moravia,** *Journal of the International Folk Music Council* XII (1960) 47–49. See no. 413 in this volume.

A survey of modern developments.

2766
as
CHOTTIN, Alexis. **Le chant et la danse berbères dans le folklore européen** [Berber song and dance in European folklore], *Travaux du Ier Congrès International de Folklore* (Tours: Arrault et Cie, 1938) 154–56. In French. See no. 251 in this volume.

A brief description of Berber dance and songs, focusing on the characteristic quinary rhythms.

2767
as
CIRESE, Alberto Mario. **Natura e valori del canto popolare secondo Pietro Ercole Visconti (1830)** [The nature and significance of traditional singing according to Pietro Ercole Visconti (1830)], *Lares* XXV (1959) 523–35. In Italian. See no. 370 in this volume.

Discusses the views expressed in Visconti's *Saggio de 'canti popolari della provincia di Marittima e Campagna* (Rome: Salviucci, 1830).

2768
as
CIRESE, Alberto Mario. **O naricaljkama u hrvatskim mjestima pokrajine Molise u Italiji** [Funeral laments in the Croatian villages of Molise, Italy], *Rad kongresa folklorista Jugoslavije* (Zagreb: Savez Udruženja Folklorista Jugoslavije, 1959) 143–51. In Croatian. See no. 382 in this volume.

2769
as
CLEGG, David. **Philaret Kolessa's classification of the Ukrainian recitative songs,** *Studia musicologica Academiae Scientiarum Hungaricae* VII (1965) 247–51. See no. 478 in this volume.
Kolessa (1871-1947) developed a classification system for Ukrainian *dumy* (epics) based on one pioneered by Ilmari Krohn (1867-1960). *(Daniel Horn)*

2770
as
COCCHIARA, Giuseppe. **Le siciliane** [Sicilianas], *Journal of the International Folk Music Council* II (1950) 49. In French. See no. 295 in this volume.
The siciliana was a popular Italian song genre during the 15th through 17th c. The conference report provides only a citation. Neither the text nor a summary of the paper was published here.

2771
as
COIRAULT, Patrice. **Quelques exemples de la parenté que montrent des timbres populaires aux XVIIe et XVIIIe siècles avec certaines de nos mélodies folkloriques** [Some examples of the kinship between popular *timbres* of the 17th and 18th centuries and our folkloric melodies], *Congrés de la Societat Internacional de Musicologia* (Barcelona: Casa de Caritat, 1936). In French. See no. 224 in this volume.
The conference report provides only a citation. Neither the text nor a summary of the paper was published here.

2772
as
COLACICCHI, Luigi. **Canti popolari de Ciociaria** [Popular songs of Ciociaria], *Atti del III Congresso nazionale di arti e tradizioni popolari* (Roma: Opera Nazionale Dopolavoro, 1936) 289–334. In Italian. See no. 218 in this volume.

2773
as
COLLAER, Paul. **À propos de deux chansons bulgares et espagnoles** [Two Bulgarian and Spanish songs], *Atti del Congresso internazionale di musiche popolari mediterranee e del Convegno dei bibliotecari musicali* (Palermo: De Magistris succ. V. Bellotti, 1959) 71–74. In French. See no. 332 in this volume.
The lullaby *Nana* from Manuel de Falla's *Siete canciones populares españolas* is so strikingly similar in rhythmic and melodic shape to a lullaby recorded in Bulgaria as to be regarded as a variant of the same song; it may be hypothesized (following theoretical ideas laid down by Marius Schneider) that they are descendants of a single piece from the 3rd millennium B.C.E. There is also a Bulgarian version of *Canción* from the same Falla collection, both featuring an iambic rhythm which probably came from India. *(David Bloom)*

2774
as
COLLINSON, Francis. **A brief survey of Scottish folk music recordings in the collections of the School of Scottish Studies, Edinburgh University,** *Journal of the International Folk Music Council* VII (1957) 39. See no. 362 in this volume.
Summary of a paper.

2775
as
COLLINSON, Francis. **Some researches on an obsolete labour song of the Lowland Scottish oyster fishers: Summary,** *Journal of the International Folk Music Council* XIII (1961) 27. See no. 424 in this volume.

Brief report of the author's collection in 1958-60 of variants of the *Oyster dreg* song, a work song with improvised text.

2776
as
COMIŞEL, Emilia. **La ballade populaire roumaine** [The traditional Romanian ballad], *Rad kongresa folklorista Jugoslavije* (Zagreb: Savez Udruženja Folklorista Jugoslavije, 1959) 135–39. In French. See no. 382 in this volume.
A detailed examination of the musical properties of the *cîntec bătrînesc* ("old song"), or traditional Romanian ballad, in terms of its performance context, melodic style (epic recitative vs. song melody), scale and rhythmic structures, text-music relationship, and instrumental accompaniment, with a view to assisting the investigation of relationships among the musical cultures of the various ethnic groups of the Danube basin. *(David Bloom)*

2777
as
COMIŞEL, Emilia. **Le folklore des coutumes: L'enterrement, le cérémonial et le repertoire** [The folklore of customs: The burial, the ceremony, and the repertoire], *Rad XI-og kongresa Saveza Folklorista Jugoslavije* (Zagreb: Savez Folklorista Jugoslavije, 1966) 443–57. *Transcr.* In French; summary in Croatian. See no. 490 in this volume.
An overview of funeral customs in Romania.

2778
as
COMIŞEL, Emilia. **Le folklore des coutumes qu'on observe au cours d'une année: Le cycle de la période du printemps** [The folklore of customs observed over the course of a year: The cycle of the spring period], *Rad IX-og kongresa Saveza Folklorista Jugoslavije* (Sarajevo: Savez Udruženja Folklorista Jugoslavije, 1963) 299–313. *Bibliog., transcr.* In French. See no. 455 in this volume.
Discusses traditional rituals practiced in Romania in the period around the first full moon after the spring equinox, or from Carnival to Pentecost, with particular attention to the melodies of ritual songs. *(David Bloom)*

2779
as
COMIŞEL, Emilia. **La musique de la ballade populaire roumaine** [The music of the traditional Romanian ballad], *Les colloques de Wégimont. IV: Ethnomusicologie III* (Paris: Belles Lettres, 1964) 39–73. In French. See no. 401 in this volume.
Although popular taste is evolving away from the classic traditional ballad, it continues to occupy an important place in Romanian folklore. *(Scott Fruehwald)*

2780
as
ČUBELIĆ, Tvrtko. **Narodna tužbalica, impresivni dio u pogrebnim običajima i jedan od najstarijih oblika izvorne narodne pjesme** [Traditional laments, an impressive segment of funeral rituals and one of the oldest forms of authentic traditional songs], *Rad XI-og kongresa Saveza Folklorista Jugoslavije* (Zagreb: Savez Folklorista Jugoslavije, 1966) 347–54. In Croatian; summary in German. See no. 490 in this volume.
A general survey of southern Slavic laments and a classification of their characteristics.

2781
as
CUEVAS, Felisa de las. **Les chansons de noce dans la province de Léon** [Wedding songs of the province of León], *Congrès international des arts populaires/International congress of popular arts* (Paris: Institut international de coopération intellectuelle, 1928) 110. In French. See no. 153 in this volume.
Summary of the paper abstracted as no. 2782 in this volume.

2782
as

CUEVAS, Felisa de las. **Les chansons de noce dans la province de Léon** [Wedding songs of the province of León], *Art populaire: Travaux artistiques et scientifiques du Ier Congrès international des arts populaires* (Paris: Duchartre, 1931) 158–59. In French. See no. 152 in this volume.

The typical wedding songs are coplas, in three categories: farewell, welcoming, and congratulatory. Customs of the wedding ceremony and subsequent celebrations are surveyed. A summary is cited as no. 2781 in this volume. *(David Bloom)*

2783
as

CZEKANOWSKA, Anna. **Les anciennes mélodies de noce en Pologne** [Old wedding songs in Poland], *VIe Congrès international des sciences anthropologiques et ethnologiques. I: Rapport général et anthropologie; II: Ethnologie* (Paris: Musée de l'Homme, 1962-1964) II, 97–100. In French. See no. 421 in this volume.

Describes how the wedding songs in several regions of Poland are characterized by seven rhythmic and melodic/modal models: pentatonic with a two-part form and contrasting rhythm, one-part short form in minor mode, pentatonic/major in a mazurka rhythm, recitatival, pentatonic with a two-part form and contrasting rhythm (but resembling a polonaise), melismatic with metric liberties and a form determined by the text, and pentatonic with very slow rhythm. *(Susan Poliniak)*

2784
as

DAHMEN, Hermann Josef. **Folk music and light music,** *Journal of the International Folk Music Council* XI (1959) 84–86. See no. 392 in this volume.

Summary of a paper. Distinctions between traditional and popular musics are discussed, and issues in the programming of traditional music on European radio stations are explored. *(James R. Cowdery)*

2785
as

DAL, Erik. **Scandinavian folk music: A survey.** Trans. from Danish by Lis PIHL, *Journal of the International Folk Music Council* VIII (1956) 6–11. See no. 349 in this volume.

Surveys children's songs, shepherds' calls, ballads, instruments, and dances.

2786
as

D'ARONCO, Gianfranco. **Villotte, canti popolari, poesie popolari contenute nelle pubblicazioni della Società Filologica Friulana (1919-1945)** [Villotte, traditional songs, and traditional poems contained in publications of the Società Filologica Friulana (1919-45)], *Journal of the International Folk Music Council* II (1950) 49. In Italian. See no. 295 in this volume.

The conference report provides only a citation. Neither the text nor a summary of the paper was published here.

2787
as

DAVE, Émile. **Fêtes folkloriques de la jeunesse à Namur** [Folkloric youth festivals at Namur], *Travaux du Ier Congrès International de Folklore* (Tours: Arrault et Cie, 1938) 399–401. In French. See no. 251 in this volume.

Discusses festivals since 1929, with particular attention to festival events of 1933.

2788
as

DELARUE, Paul. **Les chants populaires régionaux à l'école et dans les fêtes scolaires et postscolaires** [Traditional regional songs at school and in academic and non-academic festivals], *Travaux du Ier Congrès International de Folklore* (Tours: Arrault et Cie, 1938) 389–94. In French. See no. 251 in this volume.

Lists several French traditional songs and discusses their use.

2789
as

DELLA CORTE, Andrea. **Il pubblico: Popolo di oggi e di domani** [The public: The people of today and tomorrow], *Atti del secondo Congresso internazionale di musica* (Firenze: Le Monnier, 1940) 27–31. In Italian; summaries in French and German. See no. 239 in this volume.

Discusses the nature and uses of traditional music. Modern perceptions are outlined.

2790
as

DEVIĆ, Dragoslav. **Narodne melodije iz perioda Oslobodilačkog rata** [Traditional melodies in the period of the War of National Liberation], *Rad VIII-og kongresa folklorista Jugoslavije* (Beograd: Naučno Delo, 1961) 263–68. Port., transcr. In Serbian; summary in English. See no. 446 in this volume.

Statistical analysis of the melodies of a sample of 380 Partisan songs shows that they are composed of traditional musical material. *(author)*

2791
as

DEVIĆ, Dragoslav. **Naša narodna muzika na gramofonskim pločama** [Our traditional music in phonograph recordings], *Rad X-og kongresa Saveza Folklorista Jugoslavije* (Cetinje: Obod, 1964) 275–79. In Serbian; summary in French. See no. 462 in this volume.

The recording industry in Yugoslavia since 1949 has produced some 350 traditional-music records in various formats, featuring more than 1500 different melodies, but unfortunately little of this is authentic traditional music; there is a tendency, especially recently, to record new compositions in pseudo-folk style, of dubious artistic quality. *(author)*

2792
as

DOMÍNGUEZ BERRUETA, Juan. **La jota aragonaise** [The Aragonese jota], *Congrès international des arts populaires/International congress of popular arts* (Paris: Institut international de coopération intellectuelle, 1928) 117. In French. See no. 153 in this volume.

Summary of a paper. The jota song genre is said to have been invented by an Arab, but it shows no traces of Asian influence in its purely diatonic melody. Form, accompaniment, and the character of the song texts are briefly described. *(David Bloom)*

2793
as

DOMPÉ, Giovanna. *Is musicas* **a Tonara** [*Is musicas* in Tonnara], *Lares* XXII (1956) 123–24. In Italian. See no. 353 in this volume.

Describes the ancient festival *Is musicas*, which was traditionally presented in Tonnara from the feast day of St. John until the 15th of August (Ferragosto). In general, it involved young lovers asking for the hands of their beloveds, poets and poetry, and singing.

2794
as

ĐORĐEVIĆ, Dragutin M. **Lazarice u Leskovačkoj Moravi** [Lazarica in Leskovačka Morava], *Rad kongresa folklorista Jugoslavije* (Zagreb: Savez Udruženja Folklorista Jugoslavije, 1958) 117–24. Transcr. In Serbian. See no. 315 in this volume.

A detailed description of the Lazarica (Lazarus Saturday) ritual in Leskovačka Morava, in southern Serbia.

2795
as

DOULGHERAKIS, Emmanuel. **I chronologisis tou kritikou dimotikou tragoudiou** [The dating of the Cretan demotic song], *Krītika chronika* 16 (1961) III,66–77. In Greek. See no. 434 in this volume.

Considers the chronology of Cretan traditional song in relation to the *akritikīs* tradition of Cyprus.

2796
as

DRĂGHICEANU, V.I. **Les coutumes d'enterrement des princes roumains** [Burial customs of Romanian princes], *Bulletin de la Section Historique* XI (1924) 110–14. In French. See no. 115 in this volume.

2797 DUYSE, Florimond van. **Chansons populaires**
as [Traditional songs], *IIIe Congrès international de l'art
public* (Liège: n.p., 1905). In French. See no. 49 in this
volume.

Discusses editions of Dutch and Belgian traditional songs by Jan Frans
Willems (1793-1846).

2798 DVORNIKOVIĆ, Vladimir. **Problemi pre-**
as **slovenskog, starobalkanskog, elementa u
našem muzičkom folkloru** [Problems of
pre-Slavonic, or ancient Balkan, elements in our traditional music], *Rad kongresa folklorista Jugoslavije*
(Zagreb: Savez Udruženja Folklorista Jugoslavije,
1958) 91–97. In Serbian; summary in German. See no.
315 in this volume.

Investigates the roots of folklore among the South Slavic peoples.

2799 DŽUDŽEV, Stojan. **Narodnata muzika kato**
as **obščestveno javlenie** [Traditional music as a general
phenomenon], *Rad IX-og kongresa Saveza Folklorista
Jugoslavije* (Sarajevo: Savez Udruženja Folklorista
Jugoslavije, 1963) 490–98. In Bulgarian. See no. 455 in
this volume.

A general definition of the topic.

2800 ELSCHEK, Oskár. **Problem of variation in**
as **eighteenth century Slovak folk music manuscripts,** *Studia musicologica Academiae Scientiarum
Hungaricae* VII (1965) 47–59. *Music, bibliog.* See no.
478 in this volume.

Similarities between some of the traditional melodies in the *Uhrovská
zbierka piesní a tancov z roku 1730* (formerly known as the *Oponická
zbierka piesní a tancov*, held at the Matica Slovenská, Martin) and those in
Anna Szirmay-Keczer's *Melodiarium* (ca. 1730) raise questions of origin
and regional distribution. *(Daniel Horn)*

2801 ELSCHEKOVÁ, Alica. **Strukturelle Frühfor-**
as **men slavischer Volksmusik** [Early structural forms
of Slavic traditional music], *Anfänge der slavischen
Musik* (Bratislava: Slovenská Akadémia Vied, 1966)
147–64. In German. See no. 477 in this volume.

2802 EMSHEIMER, Ernst. **Lappischer Kultgesang**
as [Sámi cult singing], *Kongreß-Bericht: Gesellschaft für
Musikforschung* (Kassel; Basel: Bärenreiter, 1950)
153–57. In German. See no. 299 in this volume.

2803 EMSHEIMER, Ernst. **Some remarks on Euro-**
as **pean folk polyphony,** *Journal of the International
Folk Music Council* XVI (1964) 43–46. *Bibliog.* See
no. 463 in this volume.

Surveys the state of research on vocal part-singing in traditional musics
throughout Europe, with more detailed discussion of its technical features
in the Caucasus, Russia, and the eastern Baltic. *(David Bloom)*

2804 ERDMANN, Hans. **Wesen und Form des**
as **Fichtelbarger** [Essence and form of the
Fichtelbarger], *Bericht über den internationalen
musikwissenschaftlichen Kongreß* (Kassel: Bärenreiter,
1957) 90–91. In German. See no. 356 in this volume.

The *Fichtelbarger* or *Fichtelbööker*, MS collections of dance music for village and town performance in the Mecklenburg region in the 19th c., included polkas, schottisches, mazurkas, polka-mazurkas, rheinländers, and
galops, as well as tunes from popular operas of the period. They were used
by four-piece bands, but only the melody voice is notated; the other players
improvised through the simple eight-bar phrases. These valuable sources
of Mecklenburg traditional practice have become very rare since the 1920s.
The etymology of the terms for these books connects them to the mountain

region of Fichtelgebirge, from whence instrumental bands used to travel to
Mecklenburg at the beginning of the 19th c. *(David Bloom)*

2805 ETHERINGTON, Donia. **A living song-**
as **composer in a Scottish-Gaelic oral tradition,**
Journal of the International Folk Music Council XIII
(1961) 34–38. *Transcr.* See no. 424 in this volume.

Calum Ruadh Iain Uilleam (Red-haired Calum son of Iain son of William,
generally known as Calum Ruadh) is a 58-year-old crofter on the Isle of
Skye; he has been making songs since he was 19. His topics range from local events to personal expressions to mythological and historical narratives, reflecting his functions as both bard and private poet. He does not
compose new melodies; rather, he adapts traditional melodies to his own
texts. However, when he has a particular personal or artistic connection to a
song his adaptation rises to a creative level that approaches composition.
(James R. Cowdery)

2806 FAJDETIĆ, Vladimir. **Narodna glazba**
as **Hrvatskog Primorja, Istre i Kvarnerskih
Otoka** [Traditional music of Hrvatsko Primorje, Istra,
and the Kvarner islands], *Rad XI-og kongresa Saveza
Folklorista Jugoslavije* (Zagreb: Savez Folklorista
Jugoslavije, 1966) 45–54. In Croatian; summary in Italian. See no. 490 in this volume.

Presents the state of research and outlines characteristics of the region's
scales and rhythms.

2807 FARA, Giulio. **Canzone popolare, canto del**
as **popolo etnofonia** [Popular songs, song of the
ethnophonic people], *Atti del III Congresso nazionale
di arti e tradizioni popolari* (Roma: Opera Nazionale
Dopolavoro, 1936) 335–46. In Italian. See no. 218 in
this volume.

2808 FARA, Giulio. **Etnofonia e civiltà mediterranea**
as [Mediterranean traditional music and civilization], *Atti
del 4. Congresso nazionale di arti e tradizioni popolari*
(Roma: Opera Nazionale Dopolavoro, 1942) 106–06.
In Italian. See no. 270 in this volume.

2809 FARA, Giulio. **Il folklore** [Folklore], *La vita musi-*
as *cale dell'Italia d'oggi* (Torino: Fratelli Bocca, 1921)
43–49. In Italian. See no. 97 in this volume.

Italian folk culture could be better preserved through the founding of museums of instruments, the establishment of chairs of ethnography at conservatories, and the teaching of characteristic folk melodies to elementary
school students.

2810 FARA, Giulio. **La musica del popolo** [Music of
as the people], *Atti del I Congresso nazionale delle
tradizioni popolari* (Firenze: Rinascimento del Libro,
1930) 211–15. In Italian. See no. 158 in this volume.

2811 FARA, Giulio. **Sardegna: Persistenza dell'ethos**
as **artistico mediterraneo** [Sardinia: Persistence of the
Mediterranean artistic ethos], *Lares* XX/1-2 (1954)
120–23. In Italian. See no. 288 in this volume.

2812 FAVARA, Alberto. **Le melodie tradizionali di**
as **Val di Mazzara** [The traditional melodies of Val di
Mazzara], *Atti del Congresso internazionale di scienze
storiche. VIII: Atti della sezione IV: Storia dell'arte musicale e drammatica* (Roma: R. Accademia dei Lincei,
1905) 93–105. *Transcr.* In Italian. See no. 42 in this
volume.

Salemi, a small town in Sicily's Mazzara valley, is composed of four ethnic
groups, each with a distinct musical tradition. Melodies depicting nature
are discussed.

2813
as
FELDHÜTTER, Wilfrid. **Bavarian folk songs and folk dances,** *Journal of the International Folk Music Council* IX (1957) 38. See no. 362 in this volume.

Summary of a paper. The Bayerischer Rundfunk has played an important role in the collection and preservation of Bavarian songs, dances, and dance music since 1930, when the organization first collaborated with the collectors Kurt Huber and Kiem Pauli. *(James R. Cowdery)*

2814
as
FIRFOV, Živko. **Kolektivno vokalno muziciranje u Makedoniji** [Collective vocal music making in Macedonia], *Rad kongresa folklorista Jugoslavije* (Beograd: Naučno Delo, 1960) 211–15. In Serbian; summary in French. See no. 402 in this volume.

Discussion of the social context, age and gender distribution, and form of group singing in Macedonian village culture, with particular attention to women's polyphony with and without drone and their use of shouting, shaking, and clucking techniques. *(author)*

2815
as
FIRFOV, Živko. **Likot na makedonskata narodna muzika** [Macedonian traditional music], *Rad VII-og kongresa Saveza Folklorista Jugoslavije* (Cetinje: Obod, 1964) 23–32. *Bibliog.* In Macedonian; summary in French. See no. 419 in this volume.

Macedonian traditional music has its own character that makes it different from neighboring musics; dactyl and trochee dominate in Macedonian music, whereas Bulgarian music prefers the iamb and anapest. The history of music in Macedonia from ancient times is surveyed. *(author)*

2816
as
FIRFOV, Živko. **Makedonske narodne pesme iz perioda Narodnooslobodilačke Borbe** [Macedonian traditional songs in the period of the War of National Liberation], *Rad kongresa folklorista Jugoslavije* (Ljubljana: Savez Udruženja Folkloristov Jugoslavije, 1960) 227–29. In Serbian; summary in English. See no. 404 in this volume.

A corpus of some 150 songs may be classified into three groups: old revolutionary songs with texts topically modified, old songs with new texts, and completely new songs. Particular attention is given to songs transmitted between the various ethnic groups, and to the *vrapci* ("sparrows") genre of satirical texts set to the melodies of well-known songs. *(author)*

2817
as
FLEURY, Jean-François-Bonaventure. **Les génies de l'air en Russie, la divination, la persistance du paganisme dans les chansons et les fêtes, le culte des morts, jeux et danses** [Spirits of air in Russia, soothsaying, the persistence of paganism in songs and festivals, the cult of death, games and dances], *[I^e] Congrès international des traditions populaires* (Paris: Société d'Éditions Scientifiques, 1891). In French. See no. 13 in this volume.

2818
as
FLOOD, William Henry Grattan. **Belgium's musical debt to Ireland,** *Congrès jubilaire* (Brugge: Gruuthuuse, 1925) 228–29. See no. 119 in this volume.

A brief survey of Irish people who influenced musical development in Belgium from the 6th to the 14th c., including missionaries, clerics, and educators. *(Susan Poliniak)*

2819
as
FRICKER, Robert. **The vogel gryff pageant,** *Journal of the International Folk Music Council* I (1949) 7–8. See no. 281 in this volume.

Summary of a paper describing an annual procession in Basel that involves three masked, costumed figures: a savage man, a lion, and a griffin bird (vogel gryff).

2820
as
FRIEDLAENDER, Max. **German folk songs with reference to English and American folk songs,** *Report of the Fourth Congress of the International Musical Society* (London: Novello, 1912) 59. See no. 71 in this volume.

Summary of a paper. The term "folk song" is defined, and German and English songs are compared.

2821
as
GARCÍA MATOS, Manuel. **Breve apunte sobre la canción popular religiosa** [A brief report on the religious traditional song], *V Congreso Nacional de Música Sagrada* (Madrid: Gráficas Dos de Mayo, 1956) 292–303. *Facs., music.* In Spanish. See no. 331 in this volume.

The texts of religious traditional songs are discussed in relation to public preferences, and a Holy Week song from Castile and a Candlemas song from Extremadura are discussed. *(José López-Calo)*

2822
as
GASPARINI, Evel. **Pjesme pjevane naizmjence i egzogamička odvojenost spolova** [Alternating songs and exogamic separation], *Rad VII-og kongresa Saveza Folklorista Jugoslavije* (Cetinje: Obod, 1964) 296–97. In Croatian. See no. 419 in this volume.

Draws on examples from a worldwide range of societies.

2823
as
GAUD, Auguste. **Rondes et chansons du Pays Melois** [Rounds and songs of the Le Mêle region], *La tradition en Poitou et Charentes: Art populaire, ethnographie, folk-lore, hagiographie, histoire* (Paris: Librairie de la Tradition Nationale, 1897) 373–83. *Transcr.* In French. See no. 21 in this volume.

Discusses the function of songs in the daily life of the Le Mêle region.

2824
as
GAUTHIER-VILLARS, Marguerite. **Les cantiques populaires de Marie-Madeleine** [Traditional cantiques on Marie-Madeleine], *Travaux du Ier Congrès International de Folklore* (Tours: Arrault et Cie, 1938) 151–54. In French. See no. 251 in this volume.

Discusses several versions of traditional French songs about Mary Magdalen.

2825
as
GEERING, Arnold. **Quelques problèmes touchant la chanson populaire en Suisse** [Some problems concerning traditional song in Switzerland], *Journal of the International Folk Music Council* II (1950) 37–40. In French. See no. 295 in this volume.

The difficulty of defining popular song, folk song, or traditional song is particularly acute in Switzerland, where the concept is understood somewhat differently in each of the national speech communities. German-speaking Swiss distinguish sharply among the spontaneous *Volkslied*, composed *volkstümliches Lied*, and art song proper; in the francophone cantons the distinction between the first two is blurred, and in Ticino no boundaries at all seem to be recognized. A feature found in the traditional music of all communities is that of polyphonic singing, attested since as early as 1438 and apparently stemming from a natural disposition of the Swiss people; it remains to be discovered whether there is any correlation between this disposition and the atmospheric and geographical conditions of the country. *(David Bloom)*

2826
as
GEORGIADES, Thrasybulos Georges. **Un esempio di polifonia primordiale della Grecia** [An example of primordial Greek polyphony], *Atti del Congresso internazionale di musiche popolari mediterranee e del Convegno dei bibliotecari musicali* (Palermo: De Magistris succ. V. Bellotti, 1959) 243. In Italian. See no. 332 in this volume.

The example of polyphonic dance music performed by the Pontic Greek community with Pontic lyra (short-necked fiddle) and voice can be traced to ancient Greek music and tied to the quantitative meters of classical Greek verse. Issues briefly noted are fully treated in *Musik und Rhythmus bei den Griechen*, Hamburg 1958. *(David Bloom)*

2827 GERSON-KIWI, Edith. **The bards of the Bible,**
as *Studia musicologica Academiae Scientiarum Hungaricae* VII (1965) 61–70. *Music*. See no. 478 in this volume.
The melodies of Hebrew folk epics, ballads, and popular commentaries on chapters or personalities of the Bible are adapted from the patterns of Bible cantillation. This derivation from the intricate, sophisticated liturgical style may provide new evidence of the absorption of art music by traditional idioms. *(David Gagné)*

2828 GERSON-KIWI, Edith. **Musical sources of the**
as **Judaeo-Hispanic romance,** *Journal of the International Folk Music Council* XIV (1962) 158. See no. 442 in this volume.
Summary of a paper. A full version is published in *The musical quarterly* L (1964).

2829 GEUTEBRÜCK, Robert. **Über die Mehr-**
as **stimmigkeit im österreichischen Volksgesang** [On polyphony in Austrian traditional song], *Beethoven-Zentenarfeier: Internationaler musikhistorischer Kongress* (Wien: Universal, 1927) 326–30. *Transcr.* In German. See no. 142 in this volume.
In Carinthia and the mountains of Lower Austria, songs may be sung in three or four parts; otherwise, the only truly polyphonic vocal music of the Alpine region is yodeling, which may be in up to six parts. The formal character of the polyphonic yodel is discussed. The history of polyphonic music in the Alps is as yet poorly understood; it seems certain, however, that it is older than polyphony in European art music. *(David Bloom)*

2830 GHISI, Federico. **Alcune canzoni storiche nelle**
as **valli valdesi del Piemonte** [Some historical songs in the Vaudois valleys of Piedmont], *Bericht über den internationalen musikwissenschaftlichen Kongreß Wien Mozartjahr 1956* (Graz; Köln: Böhlau, 1958) 220–26. *Music*. In Italian. See no. 365 in this volume.
Song texts collected by the author and Emilio Tron from the French-speaking Protestant population of the Chisone and Pellice valleys of the Italian Piedmont preserve stories of local military prowess. French texts and melodies are given for songs about Vaudois combatants in the battles of Salabertrand (1689), Assietta (War of the Austrian Succession, 1747), and Austerlitz (1805). *(David Bloom)*

2831 GHISI, Federico. **Antiche melodie popolari**
as **nelle valli valdesi** [Old traditional melodies of the Vaudois valleys], *Lares* XX/1-2 (1954) 123f. In Italian. See no. 288 in this volume.

2832 GHISI, Federico. **Le fonti musicali in Piemonte**
as **di alcuni canti narrativi popolari** [The musical sources in Piedmont of some narrative traditional songs], *Lares* XXV (1959) 230–37. In Italian. See no. 370 in this volume.
Discusses songs collected by the author and Emilio Tron from Vaudois—French-speaking Protestant—people of the Italian Piedmont.

2833 GIBERT, Vicente Maria de. **Les melodies de les**
as **cançons romancesques a Catalunya** [The melodies of Catalan romances], *Congrés de la Societat Internacional de Musicologia* (Barcelona: Casa de Caritat, 1936). In French. See no. 224 in this volume.
The conference report provides only a citation. Neither the text nor a summary of the paper was published here.

2834 GIL, Bonifacio. **Panorama de la canción popu-**
as **lar andaluza: Consideración preliminar** [Pan-

orama of Andalusian popular song: A preliminary consideration], *Actas do Congresso Internacional de Etnografia* (Porto: Imprensa Portuguesa, 1965) II, 85–99. *Music*. In Spanish. See no. 473 in this volume.
Examines the origins and genres of Andalusian music. There are 55 genres based on five main modes. Lyrics and music are given for Christmas carols, children's songs, lullabies, swing songs, young men's songs, farmers' work songs, religious songs, and vendors' calls. *(Anatole Wieck)*

2835 GIOVANNELLI, Nikolai Leonida. **Some notes**
as **on the adaptation of traditional style and technique by nontraditional performers in respect of Manx songs and dances,** *Journal of the International Folk Music Council* VIII (1956) 45. See no. 349 in this volume.
The conference report provides only a citation. Neither the text nor a summary of the paper was published here.

2836 GÖTZ, Josef. **Stand der Volksliedforschung in**
as **Mähren und Schlesien** [The state of folk song research in Moravia and Silesia], *Haydn-Zentenarfeier* (Leipzig: Breitkopf & Härtel; Wien: Artaria, 1909) 226–27. In German. See no. 65 in this volume.

2837 GRABÓCZ, Miklós. **Folk music developments**
as **in the Hungarian radio,** *Journal of the International Folk Music Council* XI (1959) 81–82. See no. 392 in this volume.
Discusses traditional music programming at the Magyar Rádió és Televízió.

2838 GRAFF, Ragnwald. **Music of Norwegian Lapl-**
as **and,** *Journal of the International Folk Music Council* VI (1954) 29–31. *Transcr.* See no. 320 in this volume.
A survey of Sámi music, with particular attention to the jojk singing tradition.

2839 GRENI, Liv. **Über die Vokaltradition in nor-**
as **wegischer Volksmusik** [The vocal tradition in Norwegian folk music], *Les colloques de Wégimont. [I: Ethnomusicologie I]* (Bruxelles: Elsevier, 1956) 154–68. *Transcr.* In German. See no. 340 in this volume.
Medieval narrative songs have become rare, and can often be collected only in reduced, corrupt versions. Other genres, in contrast, show continuing life, including lullabies and *baadnsull* songs for calming crying children; religious *folketoner*, based on the variation of hymn melodies; and the melodies of improvisational, frequently satirical *stev* quatrains, which have undergone a particularly rich recent development in the areas of Setesdal and Telemark. *(David Bloom)*

2840 GUZMÁN, Antonio. **Deux chansons de la prov-**
as **ince de Palencia** [Two songs of the province of Palencia], *Art populaire: Travaux artistiques et scientifiques du 1er Congrès international des arts populaires* (Paris: Duchartre, 1931) 154. *Music*. In French. See no. 152 in this volume.
Brief report of a presentation of two previously unpublished songs (a cradle song and a song of departure) and two dances (one for children, one for young adults). A summary is cited as no. 2841 in this volume.

2841 GUZMÁN, Antonio. **Deux chansons et deux**
as **danses populaires de la province de Palencia** [Two traditional songs and two traditional dances of the province of Palencia], *Congrès international des arts populaires/International congress of popular arts* (Paris: Institut international de coopération intellectuelle, 1928) 120. In French. See no. 153 in this volume.
Another version is cited as no. 2840 in this volume.

2842 HADŽI-PECOVA, Marika. **Odraz fašističkih**
as **nedela u makedonskim narodnim pesmama**
[The reflection of Fascist crimes in Macedonian
neotraditional song], *Rad VIII-og kongresa folklorista
Jugoslavije* (Beograd: Naučno Delo, 1961) 295–302.
Port. In Serbian; summary in English. See no. 446 in
this volume.

The numerous Macedonian songs referring to fascist terror are perhaps
better remembered than songs on other subjects from the War of National
Liberation. They are in octosyllabic or decasyllabic verse, and sung to traditional melodies, the only new element being the text. *(author)*

2843 HADŽI-PECOVA, Marika. **Prvi dan proleća u**
as **makedonskim običajima** [The first day of spring in
Macedonian customs], *Rad IX-og kongresa Saveza
Folklorista Jugoslavije* (Sarajevo: Savez Udruženja
Folklorista Jugoslavije, 1963) 315–22. *Transcr.* In Ser-
bian; summary in French. See no. 455 in this volume.

In Macedonia, spring begins on 1 March by the Julian calendar (14 March
by the Gregorian). It is traditionally celebrated with rituals to protect the
participants' health, to protect them against snakes and wolves, to protect
the fields and farm animals, and so on; the most important of these observances is the *martenica*, a white and red ribbon tied on the wrist and left
there until the sighting of the first swallow or stork. The customs of the different ethnic communities of Macedonia are compared with those of other
communities, and their functions are discussed. *(author)*

2844 HADŽIMANOV, Vasil. **Les mélodies funèbres**
as **du séisme de Skopié** [The funeral melodies of the
earthquake at Skopje], *Studia musicologica Academiae
Scientiarum Hungaricae* VII (1965) 71–77. *Illus., music.* In French. See no. 478 in this volume.

Discusses women's funeral laments recorded in the wake of the 1963
Skopje earthquake. Although the melodies are spontaneous and often indeterminate in mode and rhythm, they show traces of ancient modality and
polyphony. *(Daniel Horn)*

2845 HADŽIMANOV, Vasil. **Melodije makedonskih**
as **lazaričkih narodnih pesama** [The melodies of traditional Macedonian lazarica songs], *Rad IX-og
kongresa Saveza Folklorista Jugoslavije* (Sarajevo:
Savez Udruženja Folklorista Jugoslavije, 1963)
393–405. *Illus., transcr.* In Serbian; summary in
French. See no. 455 in this volume.

Examines a sample, from various parts of Macedonia, of melodies for the
songs sung by girls in the house-to-house caroling associated with Lazarica
(Lazarus Saturday) festivities. *(author)*

2846 HADŽIMANOV, Vasil. **Muzičke balade**
as **Makedonije** [The musical ballads of Macedonia],
Rad kongresa folklorista Jugoslavije (Beograd:
Naučno Delo, 1960) 151–61. *Transcr.* In Serbian; summary in French. See no. 402 in this volume.

Statistical analysis of 90 Macedonian ballads collected by the author, under
the auspices of the Institut za Folklor, Skopje, on the basis of rhythmic and
melodic features, subject matter, and performance context. Those relating
to Balkan heroes such as Kraljević Marko and Hajduk Veljko Petrović use
more or less the same melodies as versions found throughout the Balkan
peninsula; those on more strictly Macedonian themes feature purely Macedonian musical qualities. New ballads, and new adaptations of old ones,
continue to be created. *(author)*

2847 HADŽIMANOV, Vasil. **Proces nastajanja**
as **makedonskog melosa u Narodnooslobodilačkoj borbi** [The process of Macedonian folk
song formation during the Partisan struggle], *Rad
VIII-og kongresa folklorista Jugoslavije* (Beograd:
Naučno Delo, 1961) 253–62. *Port., transcr.* In Serbian;
summary in French. See no. 446 in this volume.

Statistical analysis of 100 Macedonian Partisan songs, according to the
originality of music and text, revolutionary character, meter, rhythm, tonality, ambitus, structure and length. *(author)*

2848 HADŽIMANOV, Vasil. **Triasimetrični taktovi**
as **makedonske narodne muzike** [Asymmetrical
measures beginning with three-beat groups in traditional Macedonian music], *Rad VII-og kongresa
Saveza Folklorista Jugoslavije* (Cetinje: Obod, 1964)
385–400. *Charts, diagr., transcr.* In Serbian; summary
in English. See no. 419 in this volume.

Statistical comparative analysis of a large number of collections suggests
that the characteristic rhythm of Macedonian song melodies is the
seven-beat bar with the beats always grouped 3+2+2. Possible origins of
the rhythm from ancient Greece, Turkey, and India are considered. *(author)*

2849 HALLÉGUEN, Eugène. **Introduction à**
as **l'histoire littéraire de l'Armorique bretonne
des Vᵉ et VIᵉ siècles jusqu'à nos jours** [Introduc-
tion to the literary history of Breton Armorica from the
5th and 6th century to the present], *[1ᵉʳ] Congrès
celtique international* (Paris: Maisonneuve, 1867;
Saint-Brieuc: Guyon Francisque, 1868) 274–301. In
French. See no. 4 in this volume.

2850 HARASZTI, Emil. **La question Tzigane-**
as **Hongroise au point de vue de l'histoire de la
musique** [The Hungarian Gypsy issue from a musicological perspective], *Société Internationale de
Musicologie: Premier Congrès Liège—Compte
rendu/Internationale Gesellschaft für Musikwissenschaft: Erster Kongress Lüttich—Kongressbericht/In-
ternational Society for Musical Research: First Congress Liège: Report* (London: Plainsong and Mediaeval
Music Society, 1930) 140–45. *Illus., music.* In French.
See no. 178 in this volume.

The historical roots of Hungarian traditional music and Gypsy melody are
inseparable. Liszt contended that Gypsy melody was the primary creative
force behind Hungarian traditional music. Conversely, Bartók headed the
reactionary ideology that Gypsies distorted Hungarian traditional music,
which he believed to be of ancient Asiatic origin since both this music and
that of Eastern cultures use pentatonic scales. Both theories have been exaggerated beyond proof. Ancient traditional melody evolved through sociological changes and has been so fused with Western influences and the
interpretation of the Gypsy in the role of performer, that the product is a result of all of these factors. *(Conrad T. Biel)*

2851 HEISKE, Wilhelm. **Träger, Art der Ver-**
as **breitung und Wanderung des Volksliedes** [Car-
riers, means of dissemination, and migration of the folk
song], *Travaux du Iᵉʳ Congrès International de Folklore*
(Tours: Arrault et Cie, 1938) 140–45. In German. See
no. 251 in this volume.

Discusses sociological influences on traditional songs, focusing on France
and Germany.

2852 HELGASON, Hallgrímur. **Das Bauerorganum**
as **auf Island** [Iceland farmers' organum], *Bericht über
den siebenten internationalen musikwissenschaftlichen
Kongress* (Kassel: Bärenreiter, 1959) 132–32. *Music.*
In German. See no. 390 in this volume.

The tvísöngur of Iceland may have been brought there by the original Vi-
king settlers a thousand years ago. This two-voice singing calls for a group
of male singers to perform a known melody, to which an individual (male)
improvises a second part oriented on the upper and lower fifth (in alternation). There are rules which the improviser should follow. Tvísöngur died
out in the interior of Iceland in the 20th c. *(Carl Skoggard)*

2853
as

HERZOG, George. **The music of Yugoslav heroic epic folk poetry,** *Journal of the International Folk Music Council* III (1951) 62–64. See no. 296 in this volume.

Discusses the use of melodic motives and gusle accompaniment.

2854
as

HIRŠL, Vladislav. **Pesme Narodnooslobodilačke Borbe iz istočne Srbije** [Songs of the War of National Liberation in eastern Serbia], *Rad kongresa folklorista Jugoslavije* (Ljubljana: Savez Udruženja Folkloristov Jugoslavije, 1960) 221–26. In Serbian; summary in French. See no. 404 in this volume.

Describes the typical circumstances in which Partisan songs were created, on the basis of interviews with the original composers, or with people present at the first performance. At the beginning of the war, the Partisan detachments in eastern Serbia sang mainly well-known revolutionary songs, but new songs quickly arose. These included songs sung to Russian and Bulgarian melodies, and songs with new melodies composed together with their texts; some spread to other regions and are still performed today. *(author)*

2855
as

HOLÝ, Dušan. **The classification of ornamental elements in folk dance-music against the background of a metrorhythmical basis,** *Studia musicologica Academiae Scientiarum Hungaricae* VII (1965) 263–72. See no. 478 in this volume.

A quantitative approach to some special charactistics and rules of ornamentation in the dance music of southeastern Moravia. The number of syllables per bar, the location of that bar within a line or song, and the underlying harmonic movement all govern ornamentation. In rhythmic variation, vocalists and instrumentalists differ significantly in their relationship to an overall metrorhythmical plan.

2856
as

HOLÝ, Dušan. **Instrumental and vocal performance of dance music in the Horňácko district of south-east Moravia,** *Journal of the International Folk Music Council* XV (1963) 65–72. *Charts, diagr.* See no. 459 in this volume.

Regional rhythmic and dynamic characteristics of the bowed-string accompaniment style sometimes known as *duvaj* are charted and compared with rhythmic and tempo variations among the singers they are accompanying. *(James R. Cowdery)*

2857
as

HORÁK, Jiří. **L'état actuel de l'étude des chansons populaires en Tchécoslovaquie** [The current state of research on traditional song in Czechoslovakia], *Congrès international des arts populaires/International congress of popular arts* (Paris: Institut international de coopération intellectuelle, 1928) 106. In French. See no. 153 in this volume.

Summary of the paper abstracted as no. 2858 in this volume.

2858
as

HORÁK, Jiří. **L'état actuel de l'étude des chansons populaires en Tchécoslovaquie** [The current state of research on traditional song in Czechoslovakia], *Art populaire: Travaux artistiques et scientifiques du Iᵉʳ Congrès international des arts populaires* (Paris: Duchartre, 1931) 146–48. In French. See no. 152 in this volume.

Focuses on the field collection and publication activities of the Státní Ústav pro Lidovou Píseň, Prague. A summary is cited as no. 2857 in this volume. *(David Bloom)*

2859
as

HOSTINSKÝ, Otakar. **Mitteilungen über das tschechische Volkslied in Böhmen und Mähren** [Information on Czech traditional song in Bohemia and Moravia], *Haydn-Zentenarfeier* (Leipzig: Breitkopf & Härtel; Wien: Artaria, 1909) 268–71. In German. See no. 65 in this volume.

Includes the subsequent panel discussion.

2860
as

HROVATIN, Radoslav. **Kategorisierung des Partisanenlieds in Jugoslawien** [The categorization of Partisan songs in Yugoslavia], *Beiträge zur Musikwissenschaft* VI/4 (1964) 326–31. In German. See no. 476 in this volume.

2861
as

HROVATIN, Radoslav. **Metrika teksta in melodije na Gorenjskem** [The metrics of texts and melody in Gorenjska], *Rad kongresa folklorista Jugoslavije* (Ljubljana: Savez Udruženja Folkloristov Jugoslavije, 1960) 79–82. In Slovene; summary in French. See no. 404 in this volume.

In western Slovenia, especially Gorenjska, most song texts feature a variable number of syllables per line, unlike the isosyllabic line found elsewhere in Yugoslavia. The phenomenon is somewhat less irregular in music for dance. Possible psychological motivations are discussed. *(author)*

2862
as

HROVATIN, Radoslav. **Muzikološka označba pesmi v folklori ob jugoslavensko-avstrijsko-mađarskem tromejniku** [Musicological characterization of song in the tradition of the area where Yugoslavia, Austria, and Hungary meet], *Rad kongresa folklorista Jugoslavije* (Zagreb: Savez Udruženja Folklorista Jugoslavije, 1959) 77–86. *Transcr.* In Slovene; summary in French. See no. 382 in this volume.

The Prekmurje area of Slovenia on the Austrian and Hungarian borders is a transitional zone among Alpine, Pannonian, and Balkan regions. The features of its traditional music include an abundance of rhythmic structures, from isometry to heterometry; construction of melodic stanzas on the basis of a single generally bipartite line of text; pentatonic and diatonic scales (in all modes except Phrygian); vocal monophony in the east, two- and three-voice polyphony, at thirds and fifths, in the west. Many traits are typical of Pannonian music in general. *(author)*

2863
as

HROVATIN, Radoslav. **Organizacija priprav za kvaliteten program v radijskih emisijah narodne muzike** [Organizing preparations for high-quality programming in the radio broadcast of traditional music], *Rad kongresa folklorista Jugoslavije* (Beograd: Naučno Delo, 1960) 207–09. In Slovene. See no. 402 in this volume.

2864
as

HROVATIN, Radoslav. **Pentatonika u Jugoslaviji** [Pentatonic scales in Yugoslavia], *Rad X-og kongresa Saveza Folklorista Jugoslavije* (Cetinje: Obod, 1964) 255–67. *Transcr.* In Croatian and French. See no. 462 in this volume.

Summarizes the geographical region and scale typology of pentatonicism in Yugoslavia, from the Međimurje region of Croatia, where it has long been recognized, through the less familiar cases of Hrvatsko zagorje, Bosnia and Herzegovina, Slovenia, and Macedonia. *(author)*

2865
as

HROVATIN, Radoslav. **Slovenska partizanska pesem kot predmet znanosti** [Slovene Partisan song as a research subject], *Rad kongresa folklorista Jugoslavije* (Ljubljana: Savez Udruženja Folkloristov Jugoslavije, 1960) 255–59. In Slovene; summary in French. See no. 404 in this volume.

The study of Partisan songs has tended to emphasize their social functions, and to treat their aesthetic qualities apologetically, as insignificant, under the influence of an excessive partiality for Western European music; in recent editions they have been modified, and their original melodic, tonal, polyphonic, and especially rhythmic character have been sacrificed in favor of elegant harmonizations and mechanical uniformity. Systematic ethnomusicological study is needed to account for the origin and development of Partisan song as the expression of the revolutionary tendencies of the masses. *(author)*

2866 HUBER, Kurt. **Zur Typologie des Volkslieds im**
as **mittel- und westeuropäischen Raum** [On
folk-song typology in Central and Western Europe],
Congrés de la Societat Internacional de Musicologia
(Barcelona: Casa de Caritat, 1936). In German. See no.
224 in this volume.
The conference report provides only a citation. Neither the text nor a summary of the paper was published here.

2867 HUBER, W.S. **Swiss dancing songs,** *Journal of*
as *the International Folk Music Council* VIII (1956) 36.
See no. 349 in this volume.
Summary of a paper discussing traditional songs that are related to dances or, more generally, to dancing.

2868 HULLEBROECK, Emiel. **Comment faire**
as **chanter les vieilles chansons** [How to keep the old
songs alive], *La musique et le peuple: Rapports, suggestions, voeux* (Bruxelles: Ministère des Sciences et
des Arts, 1932) 39–42. In French. See no. 195 in this
volume.
Criteria for selecting those traditional songs that should be preserved and propagated include melodic simplicity and appropriate texts. Possible methods of diffusion are discussed: through the schools, the armed forces, operettas, street singers, and public gatherings. *(Mark Stevens)*

2869 ILIJIN, Milica. **Obredno ljuljanje u proleće**
as [The custom of springtime swinging games], *Rad IX-og
kongresa Saveza Folklorista Jugoslavije* (Sarajevo:
Savez Udruženja Folklorista Jugoslavije, 1963)
273–86. *Illus., transcr.* In Serbian; summary in French.
See no. 455 in this volume.
Discusses aspects of ritual swinging games practiced in various parts of Yugoslavia, mostly in the context of Christian spring festivals such as St. George's Day and Carnival: timing of the ritual, construction and location of the swing, kinds of tree from which it is hung, the melodies and texts of songs accompanying the event, the festive activities with which it is associated, and its ritual-magical significance, now widely forgotten even by people who continue to practice it. *(author)*

2870 JANICZEK, Julius (Walther Hensel). **La**
as **mélodie et la chanson populaire allemande en
Tchécoslovaquie** [Melody and German traditional
song in Czechoslovakia], *Congrès international des
arts populaires/International congress of popular arts*
(Paris: Institut international de coopération
intellectuelle, 1928) 107–08. In French. See no. 153 in
this volume.
Summary of a paper outlining current views on periodization, regional and ethnic classification, notable features, and the question of Slavic influence.

2871 JÁRDÁNYI, Pál. **The significance of folk music**
as **in present-day Hungarian musicology and
musical art,** *Journal of the International Folk Music
Council* IX (1957) 40–42. See no. 362 in this volume.
A survey of the state of research on Hungarian traditional music. Brief remarks on the role of traditional music in pedagogy and art music are also included. *(James R. Cowdery)*

2872 JELENOVIĆ, Ive. **Krčki i novljanski folklor**
as [Folklore of Krk and Novi Vinodolski], *Rad XI-og
kongresa Saveza Folklorista Jugoslavije* (Zagreb:
Savez Folklorista Jugoslavije, 1966) 55–60. In Croatian; summary in French. See no. 490 in this volume.

2873 JOSÉ, A. **La canción popular burgalesa** [The
as traditional songs of Burgos], *Congrés de la Societat
Internacional de Musicologia* (Barcelona: Casa de
Caritat, 1936). In Spanish. See no. 224 in this volume.
The conference report provides only a citation. Neither the text nor a summary of the paper was published here.

2874 JURJĀNS, Andrejs. **A study on the ligotnes:**
as **Popular songs of St. John's Eve,** *The International Folk-lore Congress of the World's Columbian Exposition. I* (Chicago: Charles H. Sergel, 1898) 374–85.
See no. 18 in this volume.
Ligotnes are songs sung on St. John's Eve in Latvia. Similar musical characteristics among many Indo-European groups may point to a common Aryan ancestor music, and Latvian music may clarify this. Latvian traditional songs may be divided into two categories by form, and may be subdivided further by range. The modes and texts point to ancient origins. *(Ken Alboum)*

2875 KACAROVA, Rajna. **La classification des
as mélodies populaires en Bulgarie** [The classification of traditional melodies in Bulgaria], *Studia
musicologica Academiae Scientiarum Hungaricae* VII
(1965) 293–99. *Bibliog.* In French. See no. 478 in this
volume.
Surveys classifications of traditional songs in published Bulgarian collections from 1842 to 1900, including genre, occasion, melodic traits, locality, length, meter, and tonality. *(William Renwick)*

2876 KACAROVA, Rajna. **Méthodes de préservation
as et de renaissance du folklore musical** [Methods
for the preservation and revival of musical folklore],
Journal of the International Folk Music Council I
(1949) 49–51. In French. See no. 281 in this volume.
Surveys efforts in Bulgaria since the end of World War I.

2877 KARBUSICKÝ, Vladimír. **Das Arbeiterlied in
as der Geschichte und Gesellschaft** [Workers' songs
in history and in society], *Beiträge zur Musikwissenschaft* VI/4 (1964) 317–21. In German. See no. 476 in
this volume.
A discussion with reference to the author's historical study of workers' songs in Bohemia, *Naše dělnické píseň* (Prague, 1953). *(David Bloom)*

2878 KARBUSICKÝ, Vladimír; MARKL, Jaroslav.
as **Bohemian folk music: Traditional and contemporary aspects,** *Journal of the International
Folk Music Council* XV (1963) 25–29. See no. 459 in
this volume.

2879 KAUFMAN, Nikolaj. **Jewish and Gentile folk
as song in the Balkans and its relation to the liturgical music of the Sephardic Jews in Bulgaria,**
Journal of the International Folk Music Council XVI
(1964) 63. See no. 463 in this volume.
Summary of a paper. The synagogal hymns of the Sephardic Jews in Bulgaria resemble traditional urban music of the Balkans, particularly those of Greeks and Bulgarians, including direct melodic borrowings. These relationships may have originated in the Romaniote population of Greek-speaking Jews who lived in the Balkans from the time of the Roman Empire and gradually merged with the Sephardim after the latter arrived from Spain at the end of the 15th c. *(David Bloom)*

2880 KAUFMAN, Nikolaj. **Part-singing in Bulgar-
as ian folk music,** *Journal of the International Folk Music Council* XV (1963) 48–49. *Transcr.* See no. 459 in
this volume.

2881
as
KEEL, Frederick. **Some characteristics of British folk song,** *Report of the Fourth Congress of the International Musical Society* (London: Novello, 1912) 179–84. See no. 71 in this volume.

Comparative discussion of regional characteristics of English, Welsh (north and south), Scottish (Highland and Lowland), and Irish traditional music. *(Mei-Mei Meng)*

2882
as
KENNEDY, Douglas. **Chants populaires anglais** [English traditional songs], *Art populaire: Travaux artistiques et scientifiques du Ier Congrès international des arts populaires* (Paris: Duchartre, 1931) 124–25. In French. See no. 152 in this volume.

An English-language version is abstracted as no. 2884 in this volume.

2883
as
KENNEDY, Douglas. **English folk music,** *Congrès international des arts populaires/International congress of popular arts* (Paris: Institut international de coopération intellectuelle, 1928) 103–04. See no. 153 in this volume.

Summary of a paper. There are no purely musical forms in English traditional music, only those associated with song texts or dance movements; the dance tunes are song tunes modified to suit instrumental performance and choreographic requirements. The music is entirely melodic, based on modal scales, and performers lack a developed harmonic sense. Industrialization, emigration out of the countryside, and mass education have all contributed to a decline in the oral transmission of folklore since the early 19th c.; the traditional songs and dances are now known only to the elderly.

(David Bloom)

2884
as
KENNEDY, Douglas. **English folk songs,** *Congrès international des arts populaires/International congress of popular arts* (Paris: Institut international de coopération intellectuelle, 1928) 110–12. See no. 153 in this volume.

Surveys collections beginning in the late 19th c., focusing on the contributions of Francis James Child, Cecil James Sharp, and the English Folk-Song Society. Authentically preserved versions of many songs are found among rural people of English descent in North America, especially in the southern Appalachians. A French-language version is cited as no. 2882 in this volume. *(David Bloom)*

2885
as
KENNEDY, Douglas. **English singing games,** *Congrès international des arts populaires/International congress of popular arts* (Paris: Institut international de coopération intellectuelle, 1928) 134. See no. 153 in this volume.

Children's singing games represent a composite of primitive forms of drama, music, and dance, for the most part survivals of archaic customs. Research on the subject is briefly noted.

2886
as
KENNEDY, Douglas. **The folk music revival in England,** *Journal of the International Folk Music Council* VII (1955) 15–16. See no. 337 in this volume.

Discusses the efforts of Cecil Sharp and the English Folk Dance and Song Society to foster the reception of traditional music, particularly in the realm of pedagogy. *(James R. Cowdery)*

2887
as
KENNEDY, Douglas. **Folk-song and dance revival,** *Congrès international des arts populaires/International congress of popular arts* (Paris: Institut international de coopération intellectuelle, 1928) 10–11. See no. 153 in this volume.

Following the work of collectors such as Cecil Sharp in establishing a comprehensive corpus of traditional English song and dance, efforts have turned to popularizing these items as potential parts of everyday life; hence the activities of the English Folk Dance Society, founded by Sharp in 1911 and now comprising 51 branches in the United Kingdom and three in the U.S. The relation of the folk revival to the compositions of George Butterworth, Ralph Vaughan Williams, and Gustav Holst is noted. A French-language version is cited as no. 2888 in this volume. *(David Bloom)*

2888
as
KENNEDY, Douglas. **La renaissance de la musique et de la danse populaire en Angleterre** [The rebirth of traditional music and dance in England], *Art populaire: Travaux artistiques et scientifiques du Ier Congrès international des arts populaires* (Paris: Duchartre, 1931) 164–65. In French. See no. 152 in this volume.

An English-language version is abstracted as no. 2887 in this volume.

2889
as
KIRÁLY, Ernő. **Pokladno veselje kod Mađara u Vojvodini** [Carnival merrymaking among Vojvodina Hungarians], *Rad IX-og kongresa Saveza Folklorista Jugoslavije* (Sarajevo: Savez Udruženja Folklorista Jugoslavije, 1963) 383–91. *Illus., transcr.* In Serbian; summary in English. See no. 455 in this volume.

In the village of Vojlovica, southern Banat, many Carnival customs including those with musical elements have been retained that are in decline elsewhere in Vojvodina; they are discussed in detail. *(author)*

2890
as
KIRÁLY, Ernő. **Rad kao motiv u mađarskim narodnim pesmama** [Work as a motif in Hungarian traditional songs], *Rad VIII-og kongresa folklorista Jugoslavije* (Beograd: Naučno Delo, 1961) 409–17. *Port., transcr.* In Serbian; summary in English. See no. 446 in this volume.

Musically, traditional Hungarian work songs in Vojvodina are mostly in new or mixed styles, as opposed to the archaic pentatonic style, and in tempo giusto. Their texts tend to deal with the occupations of agriculture, cattle breeding, and fishery; they do not yet reflect the current mechanization of farm work. A selection of children's, fishermen's, happy, and sad songs is briefly analyzed. *(author)*

2891
as
KIRÁLY, Ernő; KIRÁLY, Marija. **Tragom revolucionarne i borbene pesme kod Mađara, Slovaka, Rusina i Romuna u Vojvodini** [Searching for revolutionary and war songs among the Hungarians, Slovaks, Rusyns, and Romanians of Vojvodina], *Rad kongresa folklorista Jugoslavije* (Ljubljana: Savez Udruženja Folkloristov Jugoslavije, 1960) 209–16. *Transcr.* In Serbian; summary in French. See no. 404 in this volume.

Topics include the Hajduk struggle against injustice; the creation of workers' choirs within the labor movement, and the ideological content of their songs; and the transmission of revolutionary songs between the different ethnic groups. *(author)*

2892
as
KIRÁLY, Marija. **Narodni pevači Srema o događajima Drugog svetskog rata** [Srem folk singers on the subject of the Second World War], *Rad VIII-og kongresa folklorista Jugoslavije* (Beograd: Naučno Delo, 1961) 225–36. *Port., transcr.* In Serbian; summary in English. See no. 446 in this volume.

Songs of the war in Srem used old verse forms, generally octosyllabic or decasyllabic. Each singer used his own characteristic tune, with minor variations and rhythmic accommodations, for any of dozens or hundreds of different texts. All songs could be sung with or without gusle accompaniment. *(author)*

2893
as
KIRÁLY, Marija. **Uticaj društvenog razvitka na Cigane po narodnim pesmama Cigana u naselju Zorka kraj Subotice** [The influence of social development on Gypsy life in the Zorka colony near Subotica, as seen in Gypsy traditional song], *Rad VII-og kongresa Saveza Folklorista Jugoslavije* (Cetinje: Obod, 1964) 175–85. *Illus., transcr.* In Serbian; summary in French. See no. 419 in this volume.

Songs performed by the Zorka Gypsies show evidence of their old beliefs and adventurous lives in former times. Reasons for their slow assimilation among the neighboring populations are discussed. *(author)*

2894 KIRIGIN, Ivo. **Some theoretical statements on**
as **the art of musical folklore based on examples from the National Republic of Croatia,** *Journal of the International Folk Music Council* IV (1952) 54–56. *Transcr.* See no. 306 in this volume.
Traditional music is a reflection of reality, its development dependent on class relations within organized society. For example, in northwestern Croatia songs using traditional structural elements—such as the Istrian scale and two-part polyphony—address contemporary events, opposing Hitler, supporting Tito, and protesting the 1948 expulsion of Yugoslavia from the Cominform agency. *(David Bloom)*

2895 KISS, Lajos. **O zapevkama, naricanju u okolini**
as **Sombora** [The nenia (lament) genre in the vicinity of Sombor], *Rad VIII-og kongresa folklorista Jugoslavije* (Beograd: Naučno Delo, 1961) 439–44. *Port., transcr.* In Serbian; summary in French. See no. 446 in this volume.
Discusses Serbian-language laments from the vicinity of Sombor, Vojvodina, with attention to their unique musical features and to general features of Balkan and Slavic laments. *(author)*

2896 KISS, Lajos. **Über den vokalen und instru-**
as **mentalen Vortrag der ungarischen Volks-weisen** [The vocal and instrumental performance of Hungarian folk tunes], *Journal of the International Folk Music Council* XV (1963) 74–79. *Transcr.* In German. See no. 459 in this volume.
Field researchers elicited vocal and instrumental performances of seven traditional melodies in different regions of Hungary. The melodies belong to various genres, but all are believed to be old. Whenever possible, the same informant provided both the vocal and the instrumental performance of a melody. The traces of an underlying ancient vocal culture are evident from their performances. The old heterophonic tradition has been well preserved in some areas; in others, a feeling for harmony is developing, though in a way completely different from that of professional Gypsy bands. *(Carl Skoggard)*

2897 KLIMA, Josef. **Tabulaturen als Quelle der**
as **Volksmusik alter Zeiten** [Tablatures as a source of the traditional music of former times], *Journal of the International Folk Music Council* XIII (1961) 32–33. In German. See no. 424 in this volume.
Tablature is a highly important source for traditional songs and dances of the period from the end of the 14th c. to 1750, and often the only extant one. Resources for researchers are described. *(Alix Moyer Grunebaum)*

2898 KLUSEN, Ernst. **Das Volkslied im Mönchen-**
as **gladbacher Raum** [Traditional song in the Mönchengladbach region], *Studien zur Musikgeschichte der Stadt Mönchengladbach* (Köln: Volk, 1965) 95–104. *Transcr.* In German. See no. 486 in this volume.
Brief geographical and ethnomusicological survey of the region, with attention to songs traceable to the Middle Ages and earlier, and to the tradition of research beginning with Wilhelm Bäumker (1842-1905) and Peter Norrenberg (1847-94, known also under the pseudonym Hans Zurmühlen). The Niederrheinisches Volksliedarchiv, founded at Viersen in 1938, has been integrated since 1963 into the Institut für Musikalische Volkskunde at the Pädagogische Hochschule, Neuß. *(David Bloom)*

2899 KNEŽEVIĆ, Milivoje V. **Tehnika narodne**
as **pevane pesme** [Techniques of traditional song], *Rad kongresa folklorista Jugoslavije* (Ljubljana: Savez Udruženja Folkloristov Jugoslavije, 1960) 303–12. In Serbian; summary in French. See no. 404 in this volume.

Remarks on the relation between text and melody, with particular attention to refrains, and to the introduction (*pretpev*) and conclusion (*dopev*) of epic songs with gusle accompaniment. *(author)*

2900 KNEŽEVIĆ, Nikola. **Dramski elementi u**
as **izvođenju guslarske pjesme** [Dramatic elements in the performance of guslar song], *Rad X-og kongresa Saveza Folklorista Jugoslavije* (Cetinje: Obod, 1964) 361–68. In Bosnian; summary in Russian. See no. 462 in this volume.
Outlines dramatic, nonmusical elements (acting, body movements) in the performance of South Slav epics.

2901 KNEŽEVIĆ, Nikola. **Stvaranje tužbalica,**
as **njihovo održavanje i melodijske osobenosti** [The origin of laments, their tradition, and their melodic character], *Rad VII-og kongresa Saveza Folklorista Jugoslavije* (Cetinje: Obod, 1964) 419–25. In Bosnian; summary in French. See no. 419 in this volume.
Women's funeral laments (*tužbalice*) in Montenegro and adjacent regions of Serbia and Herzegovina begin at the outset of mourning as improvisation, but talented singers often refine them in form and content, and classic laments, some of great beauty, may be retained and even pass from one locality to another. Their melodic structure is briefly discussed. *(author)*

2902 KOLESSA, Alexandre. **Les motifs mytholo-**
as **giques solaires et lunaires dans les chansons de Noël ukrainiennes** [Solar and lunar mythological motifs in Ukrainian Christmas songs], *Congrès international des arts populaires/International congress of popular arts* (Paris: Institut international de coopération intellectuelle, 1928) 108. In French. See no. 153 in this volume.
Summary of a paper. Ukrainian Christmas songs are survivals from pre-Christian antiquity, as their rhythmic and melodic construction shows, and they retain traces of a mixture of Aryan and Babylonian sun- and moon-worship rituals. *(David Bloom)*

2903 KOLESSA, Filaret. **Les formations anciennes**
as **et nouvelles dans les mélodies populaires ukrainiennes** [Old and new formations in traditional Ukrainian songs], *Art populaire: Travaux artistiques et scientifiques du Ier Congrès international des arts populaires* (Paris: Duchartre, 1931) 150–51. In French. See no. 152 in this volume.

2904 KOLESSA, Filaret. **Über den melodischen und**
as **rhythmischen Aufbau der ukrainischen (kleinrussischen) rezitierenden Gesänge, der sogenannten Kosakenlieder** [The melodic and rhythmic structure of Ukrainian (Little Russian) declamatory songs, the so-called Cossack songs], *Haydn-Zentenarfeier* (Leipzig: Breitkopf & Härtel; Wien: Artaria, 1909) 276–97. *Illus., charts, diagr., transcr.* In German. See no. 65 in this volume.
Provides details of phrase rhythm and overall verse structure of several examples of *dumy*.

2905 KORDA, Viktor. **Genuine folk polyphony in**
as **the Austrian Alps,** *Journal of the International Folk Music Council* IX (1957) 9–10. See no. 362 in this volume.
A survey of polyphonic singing practices.

2906 KOTEK, Georg. **Der Jodler in den öster-**
as **reichischen Alpen** [The yodel in the Austrian Alps],
Beethoven-Zentenarfeier: Internationaler musikhisto-
rischer Kongress (Wien: Universal, 1927) 331–39.
Transcr. In German. See no. 142 in this volume.
Analytic remarks, with attention to geographic variation in yodel forms and
to polyphonic elements including contrary motion, parallel motion, and
canon. Complete transcriptions of eight three-voice yodels from field studies by Josef POMMER and by the author are provided. *(David Bloom)*

2907 KRASNIQI, Mark. **Motiv heroistva u partizan-**
as **skoj narodnoj epici** [The motif of heroism in Partisan folk epic], *Rad VIII-og kongresa folklorista Jugo-*
slavije (Beograd: Naučno Delo, 1961) 287–94. *Port.* In
Serbian; summary in French. See no. 446 in this volume.
Ethnopsychological examination of typical characters shows the new humanism and realism in the portrayal of heroism in epic song of the War of
National Liberation and People's Revolution, as compared to that of traditional epic song in the region. *(David Bloom)*

2908 KRASNIQI, Mark. **Naša šiptarska narodna**
as **pesma o borbi i izgradnji** [Our neotraditional Albanian songs of war and socialist construction], *Rad*
kongresa folklorista Jugoslavije (Ljubljana: Savez
Udruženja Folkloristov Jugoslavije, 1960) 203–08.
Illus. In Serbian; summary in French. See no. 404 in this
volume.
The subject matter of revolutionary songs of ethnic Albanian Yugoslavs includes the national heros of Kosovo and Metohija, the exaltation of Josip
Broz Tito, socialist construction projects, and the new opportunities of Al-
banian-language education. Accompanied by çifteli or sharki, they have
not yet reached the level of artistic development attained by the traditional
Albanian music of the past. *(author)*

2909 KRASNIQI, Mark. **Tužbalica u arbanaškoj**
as **narodnoj poeziji** [Laments in Albanian traditional
poetry], *Rad XI-og kongresa Saveza Folklorista*
Jugoslavije (Zagreb: Savez Folklorista Jugoslavije,
1966) 329–37. In Serbian; summary in German. See no.
490 in this volume.
Surveys funeral laments in various regions of Albania.

2910 KRAUSS, Friedrich S. **Why national epics are**
as **composed: Some reflections illustrated by a**
song of guslars of Bosnia and Herzegovina, *The*
International Folk-lore Congress of the World's Colum-
bian Exposition. I (Chicago: Charles H. Sergel, 1898)
447–65. See no. 18 in this volume.

2911 KREIDLER, Walter. **Der Wert des** *Atlas der*
as *deutschen Volkskunde* **für die Musikgeschichte**
[The value of the *Atlas der deutschen Volkskunde* for
the history of music], *Bericht über den Internationalen*
musikwissenschaftlichen Kongress (Kassel: Bärenreiter,
1954) 209–11. In German. See no. 319 in this volume.
Under the sponsorship of the Notgemeinschaft der Deutschen Wissenschaft (since 1951 Deutsche Forschungsgemeinschaft), data for the mapping project *Atlas der deutschen Volkskunde* was gathered by means of a
survey form with 243 questions (each with subquestions) distributed in
1932 to selected individuals in some 20,000 German-speaking localities
(German-speaking Switzerland was not included); the survey generated 15
million answers to the 243 questions. Several of the questions dealt directly
with traditional music. A map showing the distribution of popular/tradi-
tional music ensembles with at least one viola is reproduced. *(Carl Skoggard)*

2912 KROHN, Ilmari. **De la mesure à 5 temps dans la**
as **musique populaire finnoise** [The five-beat measure in traditional Finnish music], *Congrès interna-*
tional d'histoire de la musique: Documents, mémoires
et vœux (Solesmes: St. Pierre; Paris: Fischbacher, 1901)

241–45. *Music, transcr.* In French. See no. 32 in this
volume.
There are two forms of the five-beat measure in Finnish traditional music:
one that developed from a four-beat measure with the third beat prolonged,
and another (found in traditional religious melodies) stemming from alterations of the end of a four-beat bar.

⟶ KROHN, Ilmari. **Die Kirchentonarten** [The
church modes]. See no. 4086 in this volume.

2913 KROHN, Ilmari. **Über die typischen Merkmale**
as **der finnischen Volksliedmelodien in den**
Abteilungen A I und A II [On typical features of
Finnish folk song melodies in volumes A I and A II],
Haydn-Zentenarfeier (Leipzig: Breitkopf & Härtel;
Wien: Artaria, 1909) 230–33. *Charts, diagr., transcr.* In
German. See no. 65 in this volume.
Discusses rhythmic profiles and incidences of major and minor modes ap-
pearing in the *Suomen kansan sävelmiä. II Laulusävelmiä, Nr. 1-1182.*

2914 KUBA, Ludvík. **Einiges über das istro-**
as **dalmatinische Lied** [Notes on Istrian-Dalmatian
song], *Haydn-Zentenarfeier* (Leipzig: Breitkopf &
Härtel; Wien: Artaria, 1909) 271–75. In German. See
no. 65 in this volume.
Presents observations on melody and rhythm.

2915 KUČUKALIĆ, Zija. **Muzički folklor na**
as **programima naših radiostanica** [Traditional music in our radio broadcasting centers], *Rad kongresa*
folklorista Jugoslavije (Beograd: Naučno Delo, 1960)
201–06. In Bosnian; summary in French. See no. 402 in
this volume.
Production teams responsible for the broadcast of traditional music in Yugoslavia should begin making regular contact with researchers and performers in the field. Performers of traditional music should not be regarded
as artists of an inferior order, and the *narodni orkestri* ("folk ensembles"),
whose performances are more salon music than an authentic interpretation
of tradition, should not be allowed to dominate. Special attention needs to
be paid to song texts, which are often unsuitable for broadcast. *(author)*

2916 KUČUKALIĆ, Zija. **Narodne pjesme u Bosni i**
as **Hercegovini u doba Narodnooslobodilačke**
Borbe [Traditional song in Bosnia and Herzegovina at
the time of the War of National Liberation], *Rad kon-*
gresa folklorista Jugoslavije (Ljubljana: Savez
Udruženja Folkloristov Jugoslavije, 1960). *Transcr.* In
Bosnian; summary in German. See no. 404 in this
volume.
Many of the songs were based on old revolutionary songs, or set to Russian
or other melodies; only some were authentic expressions of a Yugoslav tradition. The main issue with the latter is the relationship between the rural
tradition that served as a starting point and the urban tradition whose influence increased as the insurrection spread to include more and more people
of urban origin. *(author)*

2917 KUMER, Zmaga. **Funkcija balade na Slo-**
as **venskem** [The function of the ballad in Slovenia], *Rad*
kongresa folklorista Jugoslavije (Beograd: Naučno
Delo, 1960) 137–41. In Slovene; summary in French.
See no. 402 in this volume.
Ballads in the most general sense—i.e., sung narrative poems—are preserved in Slovenia largely by elderly women of particular talent, who perform them mostly at wakes. Formerly they were also performed at weddings and in *koledovanje* Christmas caroling. Laments composed on the
occasion of an especially tragic death may develop into true ballads, as examples from the 19th and 20th c. show. Ballads in the etymological
sense—i.e., songs with dance—were found in the Koroška and Gorenjska
regions in the 19th c., but the only one still extant is the wedding kolo
(*svatbeno kolo*) of Bela Krajna. *(author)*

2918 KUMER, Zmaga. **Smrt v slovenski ljudski**
as **pesmi** [Death in Slovenian folk songs], *Rad XI-og
kongresa Saveza Folklorista Jugoslavije* (Zagreb:
Savez Folklorista Jugoslavije, 1966) 309–14. In Slovene; summary in French. See no. 490 in this volume.
Death appears in Slovenian traditional songs in two ways: in narrative
songs it is personified as a woman dressed in white (known as *bela žena* or
bela smrt), while in lyrical songs it is treated as a fact of everyday life.

2919 KUMER, Zmaga. **Življenje ljudske pesmi na**
as **Gorenjskem** [The life of the traditional song in
Gorenjska], *Rad kongresa folklorista Jugoslavije*
(Ljubljana: Savez Udruženja Folkloristov Jugoslavije,
1960) 49–53. In Slovene; summary in German. See no.
404 in this volume.
In the Gorenjska region of Slovenia, traditional songs survive for a wide
variety of reasons. Sad ballads are retained because of the custom of singing at wakes. The *koleda* songs connected with Christmas and New Year
observances are related to the singers' social status. The preferences of individual singers play an important role. The extent to which radio broadcasts will influence song repertoire is not yet clear. *(author)*

2920 KURET, Niko. **Potreba sodelovanja pri**
as **raziskovanju južnoslovanskih mask** [The necessity for collaboration in research on South Slavic Carnival customs], *Treći kongres folklorista Jugoslavije*
(Cetinje: Udruženje Folklorista Crne Gore, 1958)
281–88. *Bibliog.* In Slovene; summary in French. See
no. 357 in this volume.
Surveys masked customs including Carnival, concentrating on the Slovene
regions.

2921 LA VALLE, Paola. **La musica e i canti popolari**
as **in Finlandia** [Traditional music and songs in Fin-
land], *Journal of the International Folk Music Council*
II (1950) 49. In Italian. See no. 295 in this volume.
The conference report provides only a citation. Neither the text nor a summary of the paper was published here.

2922 LAMSON, Roy, Jr. **English broadside ballad**
as **tunes of the 16th and 17th centuries,** *Papers read
at the International Congress of Musicology* (New
York: Music Educators National Conference, 1944)
112–21. *Charts, diagr.* See no. 266 in this volume.
Broadsides can be interpreted as social documents. Their texts and melodies are discussed, and a typology is presented.

2923 LARREA PALACÍN, Arcadio de. **Recherches**
as **sur la musique hispano-arabe** [Research on Hispano-Arabic music], *VIe Congrès international des sciences anthropologiques et ethnologiques. I: Rapport
général et anthropologie; II: Ethnologie* (Paris: Musée
de l'Homme, 1962-1964) II, 107–08. In French. See no.
421 in this volume.
Summary of research reported in the author's *La música hispano-arabe*
(Madrid: Ateneo, 1957).

2924 LAUNIS, Armas. **Die Pentatonik in den**
as **Melodien der Lappen** [The pentatonic scale in the
melodies of the Sámi people], *Haydn-Zentenarfeier*
(Leipzig: Breitkopf & Härtel; Wien: Artaria, 1909)
244–48. *Music.* In German. See no. 65 in this volume.
Includes the subsequent panel discussion.

2925 LAZAREVIĆ, Jovanka. **"Vučarska svadba" u**
as **Sredačkoj župi** [The "wolf's wedding" in Sredska
county], *Rad X-og kongresa Saveza Folklorista
Jugoslavije* (Cetinje: Obod, 1964) 317–21. In Serbian;
summary in Russian. See no. 462 in this volume.

The *vučarska svadba* (wolf's wedding) is an ancient magic winter ritual
performed in villages of Šar Planina to protect them from wolves. In the ritual, costumed characters—two *dedovci* carrying a stuffed wolf on a stick,
the *mlada* or *baba* (a man in rags), the *gočobija*, and a man collecting
gifts—go from house to house singing, dancing, and asking for gifts. Texts
of two songs, transcribed in 1948 in the villages of Rečina and Sredska, are
included. *(Zdravko Blažeković)*

2926 LEÇA, Armando. **The historical stratification**
as **of Portuguese folk music,** *Journal of the International Folk Music Council* VII (1955) 21–22. See no.
337 in this volume.
Summary of a paper discussing developments from the Middle Ages to ca.
1954.

2927 LELAND, Charles Godfrey. **Rapport des**
as **tziganes de l'Europe avec les traditions**
populaires [The relation of European Roma people to
folk traditions], *[I^e] Congrès international des traditions populaires* (Paris: Société d'Éditions Scientifiques, 1891). In French. See no. 13 in this volume.

2928 LEVI, Leo. **Jewish folk song in European lan-**
as **guages,** *Journal of the International Folk Music
Council* XII (1960) 78. See no. 413 in this volume.
Summary of a paper. The influence of local languages on song variants is
noted.

2929 LEVI, Leo. **Résidus grégoriens et byzantins**
as **dans le chant des juifs d'Europe occidentale**
[Gregorian and Byzantine residues in Western European
Jewish song], *Journal of the International Folk Music
Council* XI (1959) 86–88. In French. See no. 392 in this
volume.
Describes interactions between European Jewish and Christian traditions
from the early Middle Ages to the present. Echoes of certain modal and
rhythmic features of early Christian chant can still be heard in Jewish traditional songs. *(James R. Cowdery)*

2930 LIBEROVICI, Sergio. **Zur Schaffung neuer**
as **politischer Lieder in Italien** [The creation of new
political songs in Italy], *Beiträge zur Musikwissenschaft* VI/4 (1964) 337–38. In German. See no. 476 in
this volume.

2931 LINËVA, Evgenija. **Psalms and religious songs**
as **of the Russian sectarians in the Caucasus,** *Report of the Fourth Congress of the International Musical Society* (London: Novello, 1912) 187–201. *Illus.,
transcr.* See no. 71 in this volume.
Describes the close connection between religious and practical life in the
Molokan, Duhobor, and Novyj Izrail' (New Israel) communities. Similarities with Russian peasant songs are discussed. *(Mei-Mei Meng)*

2932 LININ, Aleksandar. **Karakteristične crte**
as **gajdarskih melodija u Makedoniji** [Characteris-
tic features of gajdar melodies in Macedonia], *Rad X-og
kongresa Saveza Folklorista Jugoslavije* (Cetinje:
Obod, 1964) 431–39. *Transcr.* In Serbian; summary in
French. See no. 462 in this volume.
Melodies for the gajdar (bagpiper) are divided into two groups: those for
dancing and those for instrumental-vocal performance. Structurally, their
most prominent feature is the repetition of musical phrases. The musical
phrase exists in one-measure, two-measure, and three-measure forms.
(author)

2933 LIUZZI, Fernando. **Della raccolta dei canti**
as **popolari a cura della commissione tecnica del**
Comitato Nazionale per le Arti Popolari [On the

collection of traditional songs edited by the technical commission of the Comitato Nazionale per le Arte Popolari], *Atti del III Congresso nazionale di arti e tradizioni popolari* (Roma: Opera Nazionale Dopolavoro, 1936) 111–81. In Italian. See no. 218 in this volume.

2934 LOGOTHETI. **La contribution française à**
as **l'étude de la chanson populaire grecque** [The French contribution to the study of the Greek traditional song], *Actes du Congrès d'histoire de l'art* (Paris: Presses Universitaires de France, 1923-1924) 929–34. In French. See no. 94 in this volume.

Greek traditional songs have attracted France's attention as a result of the general interest in Hellenistic culture. Several collections (both musical and literary) have been published in France, the first of which (a literary collection by Claude Charles Fauriel) appeared in 1824. *(Vivian Conejero)*

2935 MAISSEN, Alfons. **The religious and secular**
as **folk song of the Romansch people,** *Journal of the International Folk Music Council* I (1949) 46. See no. 281 in this volume.

Discusses traditional songs of the Romansh-speaking people of Switzerland.

2936 MALENKO, Dimče. **Kako nastanale nekoi**
as **ohridski lirski narodni pesni** [The origin of some traditional lyric songs from Ohrid], *Rad VII-og kongresa Saveza Folklorista Jugoslavije* (Cetinje: Obod, 1964) 17–21. In Macedonian; summary in French. See no. 419 in this volume.

Reviews the history of traditional urban music of Ohrid from about 1850 in terms of celebrated musicians and well-known song texts. *(author)*

2937 MARCEL-DUBOIS, Claudie. **Les éléments**
as **musicaux et la danse d'une cérémonie rituelle de français méditerranéens** [The musical elements and dance of a ritual ceremony of a Mediterranean French community], *Atti del Congresso internazionale di musiche popolari mediterranee e del Convegno dei bibliotecari musicali* (Palermo: De Magistris succ. V. Bellotti, 1959) 161–62. In French. See no. 332 in this volume.

The ritual of the "bull of Barjols" on the feast of St. Marcel (17 January) in the town of Barjols, Var, includes songs, traditional instrumental tunes, special sung Compline and Matins services, and the repeated performance of the tripettes dance. *(David Bloom)*

2938 MARCEL-DUBOIS, Claudie. **Extensions du**
as **domaine d'observations directes en ethnographie musicale française** [Extensions of the scope of direct observation in French ethnomusicology], *Les colloques de Wégimont. [I: Ethnomusicologie I]* (Bruxelles: Elsevier, 1956) 97–119. *Illus., transcr.* In French. See no. 340 in this volume.

Reports on two projects carried out under the auspices of the Musée National des Arts et Traditions Populaires, Paris, exemplifying current trends toward a concept of field observation that goes beyond simple collection. The first is a study of the manufacture of the galoubet (three-holed pipe) and tambourin provençal (double-headed drum) by Marius Fabre, of the village of Barjols (Var); the other concerns work with the oral and instrumental hunting calls of a hunter who has been active in Lorraine, Alsace, the Camargue and the Vosges, and who makes his own instruments. *(David Bloom)*

2939 MARCEL-DUBOIS, Claudie. **Remarques sur**
as **l'ornementation dans l'ethnomusicologie européenne** [Remarks on ornamentation in European ethnomusicology], *Report of the Eighth Congress of the International Musicological Society. I: Papers* (Kassel: Bärenreiter, 1961) 439–45. *Transcr.* In French. See no. 439 in this volume.

Ornamentation in the orally transmitted traditional music of Europe appears to develop out of improvisational practice, as a means for musicians to exteriorize and assert their personalities. Examples of both horizontal and vertical ornamentation from France, Italy, Greece, Hungary, and Norway are examined. *(David Bloom)*

2940 MARCEL-DUBOIS, Claudie. **Vues sommaires**
as **sur les recherches actuelles et le maintien de la tradition musicale populaire française** [Summary views on current research and the maintenance of the French folk music tradition], *Journal of the International Folk Music Council* I (1949) 51–52. In French. See no. 281 in this volume.

A survey, with attention to work done under official auspices since ca. 1939.

2941 MARICA, Pasquale; SILESU, Franz. **La**
as **Settimana Santa a Sanluri** [Holy Week in Sanluri], *Lares* XXV (1959) 237–67. In Italian. See no. 370 in this volume.

2942 MARKL, Jaroslav. **Czech bagpipe music,** *Journal of the International Folk Music Council* XV (1963) 72–74. See no. 459 in this volume.

2943 MARKL, Jaroslav. **Některé soudobé rysy**
as **tradiční lidové hudby v Československu** [Some modern features of traditional music in Czechoslovakia], *Rad IX-og kongresa Saveza Folklorista Jugoslavije* (Sarajevo: Savez Udruženja Folklorista Jugoslavije, 1963) 445–51. In Czech; summaries in French and Croatian. See no. 455 in this volume.

New social and cultural conditions have led to new developments; there are more than 900 traditional music groups, traditional instruments are taught in conservatories, and folk music is part of the general education curriculum. Ensembles are two or three times as large as they were 30 or 50 years ago, with a number of orchestral instruments as well as traditional instruments, and they play with greater force, as required by outdoor performance. Quasi-polyphonic harmony has been replaced by homophony. Tempos are faster, and the beat is treated more flexibly. Free improvisation has given way to a prepared improvisation, which leads to some loss of spontaneity but allows each musical idea to be given its maximum effect. *(author)*

2944 MARKL, Jaroslav. **Písňový typ instrumentální**
as **v české lidové písni** [The instrumental type of Czech traditional songs], *Treći kongres folklorista Jugoslavije* (Cetinje: Udruženje Folklorista Crne Gore, 1958) 255–59. *Transcr.* In Czech; summary in Serbian. See no. 357 in this volume.

Many traditional Czech songs have a clear periodic structure, repetitive rhythmic figures, and major keys. Classical Czech composers (the Stamic brothers, the Benda brothers), as well as Haydn and Mozart, were influenced by songs of this type and introduced their melodic characteristics in art music.

2945 MARKL, Jaroslav. **Problematika obrade**
as **muzičkog folklora u Čehoslovačkoj** [Problems in the dissemination of musical folklore in Czechoslovakia], *Rad X-og kongresa Saveza Folklorista Jugoslavije* (Cetinje: Obod, 1964) 249–53. In Croatian; summary in French. See no. 462 in this volume.

Some 900 amateur ensembles and ten or so professional traditional music and dance groups are active in Czechoslovakia. Music schools and television and radio broadcasting also contribute to the picture, as do recording companies, book publishers, and the organizers of conferences. *(author)*

2946 MARKL, Jaroslav. **Vuk Stefanović Karadžić i**
as **počeci sakupljanja narodnih pesama u Češkoj**
[Vuk Stefanović Karadžić and the beginnings of traditional song collection in Bohemia], *Rad XI-og kongresa
Saveza Folklorista Jugoslavije* (Zagreb: Savez
Folklorista Jugoslavije, 1966) 191–95. In Serbian; summary in German. See no. 490 in this volume.
Outlines collecting activities in Bohemia during the first half of the 19th c.,
particularly the influence of Karadžić on Václav Hanka, Pavel Josef
Šafařik, and František Ladislav Čelakovský, who published the three-
volume collection *Slovanské národní písně* (1822, 1825, and 1827).

2947 MAROLT, France. **Slovene folk dance and folk**
as **music.** Ed. by Valens VODUŠEK, *Journal of the International Folk Music Council* IV (1951) 4–9. *Transcr.*
See no. 306 in this volume.
Dance genres preserve traces of ancient rituals, social structures, and historic events. Musical styles may be divided into five territorial dialects:
Central, Carinthian, Pannonian, Littoral, and Bela Krajina. All feature polyphony, most highly developed in Carinthia, and heptatonic scales, often
with vestiges of pentatonicism. Instruments are generally used alongside
singing to accompany dances. They include shepherd-made wooden and
bark flutes, panpipes (coštimaje), ribbon reed (pisk and pero), idioglot reed
(troba), and bark trumpet (truba or trobila); friction drum (gudalo-dudalo
or muga) made of clay pot and pig's bladder; mouth organ (ustne orglice);
Istrian bagpipes and reed-pipes; and other exogenous instruments such as
violin, cymbals, clarinet, tamburica, and accordion. *(David Bloom)*

2948 MARTÍN GONZÁLEZ, Casto. **Les chansons et**
as **les danses dans un village de Tolède** [The songs
and dances of a village in Toledo], *Art populaire:
Travaux artistiques et scientifiques du I*er *Congrès international des arts populaires* (Paris: Duchartre, 1931)
158. In French. See no. 152 in this volume.
Surveys traditions, feasts, costumes, games, songs, and other local customs
of the village of Las Ventas con Peña Aguilera in the Toledo mountains,
with attention to the soldadesca (militia) confraternity and its festival processions. A summary is cited as no. 2949 in this volume. *(David Bloom)*

2949 MARTÍN GONZÁLEZ, Casto. **Détails folk-**
as **loriques d'un village de Tolède: Chansons et**
danses [Folkloric details of a Toledan village: Songs
and dances], *Congrès international des arts
populaires/International congress of popular arts*
(Paris: Institut international de coopération
intellectuelle, 1928) 110. In French. See no. 153 in this
volume.
Summary of the paper abstracted as no. 2948 in this volume.

2950 MARTINOVIĆ, Niko S. **Narodno stvaralaštvo**
as **u Ustanku Crne Gore** [The productions of folk culture in the Insurrection in Montenegro], *Rad VIII-og
kongresa folklorista Jugoslavije* (Beograd: Naučno
Delo, 1961) 207–20. *Port.* In Serbian; summary in Russian. See no. 446 in this volume.

2951 MARTINOVIĆ, Niko S. **Revolucionarni**
as **folklor u periodu šestojanuarske diktature**
[Revolutionary folklore in the period of the Dictatorship of Sixth January], *Rad kongresa folklorista
Jugoslavije* (Ljubljana: Savez Udruženja Folkloristov
Jugoslavije, 1960) 239–50. In Serbian; summary in
English. See no. 404 in this volume.
During the dictatorship of King Aleksandar of Yugoslavia, 1929-34, inci-
dents of the antifascist struggle in Montenegro were the inspiration for a
number of songs in epic decasyllable, appropriate to be sung in conjunction
with kolo dancing or with gusle accompaniment. *(author)*

2952 MARTINOVIĆ, Niko S. **Savo Matov**
as **Martinović saradnik Vuka Karadžića** [Savo
Matov Martinović, a collaborator with Vuk Karadžić],
Rad XI-og kongresa Saveza Folklorista Jugoslavije
(Zagreb: Savez Folklorista Jugoslavije, 1966) 253–61.
Port. In Serbian; summary in German. See no. 490 in
this volume.
Karadžić first met the Montenegrin guslar Savo Matov Martinović
(1808-96) in Zadar in 1861. Eventually he transcribed songs that
Martinović knew and published them in the fourth and fifth volumes of his
Srpske narodne pjesme (Vienna 1862, 1865). After Karadžić's death,
Martinović published three books with epics: *Ženidba Aleksandra
Aleksandrovića prestolonasljednika ruskog 1866.* (Zagreb, 1868), *Junačke
pjesme kapetana Sava M. Martinovića* (Novi Sad, 1880), and *Viški boj
spjevao Savo M. Martinović 1886. g.* (Zagreb, 1886). His epics were also
transcribed and published by the Croatian folklorists Đuro Deželić and
Velimir Gaj. *(Zdravko Blažeković)*

2953 MAUD, John. **Address,** *Journal of the International*
as *Folk Music Council* V (1953) 51–52. See no. 314 in this
volume.
Summary of a paper. The needs addressed by cultivation of traditional music and dance include aesthetic richness and variety, active leisure, and a
sense of cultural rootedness. *(James R. Cowdery)*

2954 MAYER, M.V. **Il canto lirico monostrofico in**
as **Abruzzo** [The single-stanza lyric song in the
Abruzzi], *Lares* XXV (1959) 449–73. In Italian. See no.
370 in this volume.

2955 MEDENICA, Radosav. **Hercegovina: Kolevka**
as **patrijarhalne kulture i narodne pesme**
dinaraca [Herzegovina: Cradle of the patriarchal culture and the traditional songs of the Dinaric people], *Rad
IX-og kongresa Saveza Folklorista Jugoslavije*
(Sarajevo: Savez Udruženja Folklorista Jugoslavije,
1963) 99–108. In Serbian; summary in French. See no.
455 in this volume.
The characteristic patriarchal culture and the folk epic tradition of the
Dinaric zone originated within the 15th-c. boundaries of Herzegovina,
whence it spread to other regions through migration. Except for the very archaic Macedonian tradition, the Dinaric is the oldest epic tradition of the
area and may be regarded as the ancestor of the others. *(author)*

2956 MERLIER, Melpo. **Les particularités mélo-**
as **diques de la chanson populaire grecque** [The
melodic characteristics of Greek traditional song], *III*e
Congrès international des études byzantines (Athínai:
Hestia, 1932) 267–68. In French. See no. 163 in this
volume.
The traditional music of Greece has little in common with that of Eastern
countries. Greek traditional music differs in its smaller intervals, different
modes, lack of accidentals, and in the types and arrangements of rhythms
and scale degrees. The study of Greek church music and Byzantine music
can provide background. *(Barry Salwen)*

2957 MERSMANN, Hans. **Buts et méthode d'une**
as **étude musical des chants populaires** [Goals and
method of a musical study of traditional songs], *Art
populaire: Travaux artistiques et scientifiques du I*er
Congrès international des arts populaires (Paris:
Duchartre, 1931) 97–100. In French. See no. 152 in this
volume.
The study of German traditional song, begun in the 19th c., has placed more
emphasis on text than on music. Traditional song originates either from a
known singer-composer or from a collective effort. As songs evolve melody changes more rapidly than text.

2958 MICHAÏLÍDÍS, Sólōn. **Greek folk music: Its**
as **preservation and traditional practice,** *Journal of the International Folk Music Council* I (1949) 21–24. See no. 281 in this volume.

Reasons for the survival of traditional music in Greece fall into three main categories: (1) the relative isolation of rural communities from the potentially damaging effects of urban culture; (2) the national personality, which favors the preservation of habits and customs; and (3) the importance of the historical aspects of many songs, particularly the kleftika repertoire.

2959 MLADENOVIĆ, Živomir. **Narodne pesme**
as **Timočke Krajine** [Traditional songs of the Timočka krajina], *Rad kongresa folklorista Jugoslavije* (Beograd: Naučno Delo, 1960) 47–54. *Illus.* In Serbian; summary in French. See no. 402 in this volume.

Songs of the Timok river border between Serbia and Bulgaria are inferior in their texts to those of central Serbia in terms of their content and poetic form; their melodies, on the other hand, are richer and more varied, because of continual interaction with neighboring cultures. According to local tradition the epics *Marko Kraljević i vila* and *Smrt Kraljevića Marka* originated here. *(author)*

2960 MLADENOVIĆ, Živomir. **Njegošev doprinos**
as **Vukuvoj zbirci narodnih pesama** [Njegoš's contribution to Vuk's collections of traditional songs], *Rad X-og kongresa Saveza Folklorista Jugoslavije* (Cetinje: Obod, 1964) 83–90. In Serbian; summary in French. See no. 462 in this volume.

Petar II Petrović Njegoš had recently published his collection *Pévannija cernogorska i hercegovačka* when he met Vuk Stefanović Karadžić, in Vienna in 1833, shortly before the latter's field trip to Montenegro. Unable to complete his study of Montenegrin traditional song because of the climate and the ongoing war with the Turks, Karadžić asked Njegoš to organize his transcriptions for him. Njegoš did this, and also sent Karadžić a collection of Montenegrin epic poems transcribed by Teodor Ikov Piper. Karadžić was interested in publishing only a few of Piper's transcriptions, and Njegoš quarreled with him as a result, finally publishing his own Montenegrin transcriptions in *Ogledalo srbsko* in 1845. *(author)*

2961 MLADENOVIĆ, Živomir. **Pesma na prired-**
as **bama kulturnih ekipa u narodnooslobodi-**
lačkoj borbi [Song in the performances of cultural teams during the War of National Liberation], *Rad VIII-og kongresa folklorista Jugoslavije* (Beograd: Naučno Delo, 1961) 275–85. *Port.* In Serbian; summary in French. See no. 446 in this volume.

Partisan songs grew spontaneously out of the enthusiasm and the sufferings of the participants in the war, but they were also part of organized Partisan life, thanks in part to the cultural teams in the Partisan forces. Political and military leaders gave their full attention to this essential element in reinforcing revolutionary consciousness and morale. *(author)*

2962 MLADENOVIĆ, Živomir. **Rukopisne zbirke**
as **junačkih narodnih pesama Vuka Vrčevića u**
Srpskom Učenom Društvu [Vuk Vrčević's transcriptions of epic songs for the Srpsko Učeno Društvo], *Rad IX-og kongresa Saveza Folklorista Jugoslavije* (Sarajevo: Savez Udruženja Folklorista Jugoslavije, 1963) 109–18. In Serbian; summary in German. See no. 455 in this volume.

In 1867, the Srpsko Učeno Društvo published a volume of Herzegovinian folk tales and games collected by the Austrian vice-consul at Trebinje, Vuk Vrčević. Encouraged by this reception, Vrčević submitted several further MSS containing transcriptions of folk epics, but the society rejected these as aesthetically inferior. Four MS volumes of the collection are kept at the Srpska Akademija Nauka i Umetnosti in Belgrade, etnografska zbirka, 62/I-IV. *(author)*

2963 MLADENOVIĆ, Živomir. **Uloga pesme u**
as **Narodnooslobodilačkoj Borbi** [The role of songs in the War of National Liberation], *Rad kongresa folklorista Jugoslavije* (Ljubljana: Savez Udruženja Folkloristov Jugoslavije, 1960) 161–64. In Serbian; summary in English. See no. 404 in this volume.

At the outset of the war, songs roused and united the population; during the war, they helped to mobilize new fighters and to transmit directives from the insurrectionary leaders. The combatants were not merely listeners and performers; they were also the creators of both text and music. *(author)*

2964 MOURINHO, António Maria. **Aspecto e função**
as **da música popular Mirandesa profana e**
religiosa [Aspects and functions of secular and religious traditional music in Miranda], *Actas do Congresso Internacional de Etnografia* (Porto: Imprensa Portuguesa, 1965) II, 177–78. In Portuguese. See no. 473 in this volume.

Summary of a paper describing musical traditions of Miranda do Douro. Traditional instruments such as the gaita and bass drum are used to initiate festivals at the end of summer or winter. Particularly characterisic is the church music used during two liturgical cycles of the year, commencing with All Saints Day and concluding with Trinity Sunday. *(Peter S. Bushnell)*

2965 MÜLLER-BLATTAU, Joseph. **Arie und Lied**
as [Aria and lied], *Bericht über den Internationalen Kongreß Singen und Sprechen* (München: Oldenbourg, 1938) 17–26. In German. See no. 257 in this volume.

German opera style from Mozart through Wagner shows a polarity between the pure music of the aria and the text-dependent lied.

2966 MYKLEBUST, Rolf. **Norwegian folk music re-**
as **cords,** *Journal of the International Folk Music Council* X (1958) 51. See no. 371 in this volume.

Summary of a paper discussing sound recordings in the collection of Norsk Rikskringkasting (NRK, the Norwegian Broadcasting Corporation) in Oslo.

2967 NAMETAK, Alija. **Izbegavanje upotrebe**
as **muzičkih instrumenata kod bosansko-herce-**
govačkih muslimana [The avoidance of using musical instruments among the Muslims of Bosnia and Herzegovina], *Rad VII-og kongresa Saveza Folklorista Jugoslavije* (Cetinje: Obod, 1964) 359–62. In Bosnian; summary in French. See no. 419 in this volume.

In those parts of Bosnia and Herzegovina where Muslim theologians and ascetics were particularly influential, singers used to use an everyday object—a tobacco pipe (*čibuk*), a piece of wood—to imitate the sound of an accompanying gusle or tambura, due to the belief that instrumental music was sinful. *(author)*

2968 NASELI, Carmelina. **Gli strumenti popolari del**
as **popolo siciliana** [*sic*] [Traditional instruments of the people of Sicily], *Journal of the International Folk Music Council* II (1950) 49. In Italian. See no. 295 in this volume.

The conference report provides only a citation. Neither the text nor a summary of the paper was published here.

2969 NASELLI, Carmelina. **Riti prenuziali: Il ballo**
as **sul letto, i canti del letto** [Prenuptial rites: Dancing on the bed, songs of the bed], *Atti del Congresso internazionale di musiche popolari mediterranee e del Convegno dei bibliotecari musicali* (Palermo: De Magistris succ. V. Bellotti, 1959) 163–80. *Transcr.* In Italian. See no. 332 in this volume.

European customs of dancing and singing on the bed of the wedding chamber represent a pre-Hellenic, or Mediterranean, magical fertility rite, in a jocose, parodistic form. A number of French and Italian cases are considered, and detailed text and music analysis is offered of four French and Wallon songs of a genre in which each verse is in the voice of a part of the bed or an item of bedroom furniture. *(David Bloom)*

2970
as

NATALETTI, Giorgio. **I canti greco-albanesi di Sicilia, Calabria e Molise, le melodie liturgiche ebraico-italiane e la musica degli zingari di stanza in Italia** [Greco-Albanian songs of Sicily, Calabria, and Molise, Jewish-Italian liturgical melodies, and the music of Gypsies resident in Italy], *Atti del Congresso internazionale di musiche popolari mediterranee e del Convegno dei bibliotecari musicali* (Palermo: De Magistris succ. V. Bellotti, 1959) 329. In Italian. See no. 332 in this volume.

Discusses the importance of the music of ethnic-linguistic island populations in the Mediterranean region.

2971
as

NATALETTI, Giorgio. **I poeti a braccio della campagna romana** [The poets' contests of the Roman countryside], *Atti del III Congresso nazionale di arti e tradizioni popolari* (Roma: Opera Nazionale Dopolavoro, 1936) 383–91. In Italian. See no. 218 in this volume.

2972
as

NAZOR, Ante. **O nekim pojmovnim i terminološkim problemima suvremenih narodnih pjesama** [On some terminological issues in contemporary tradititional songs], *Rad IX-og kongresa Saveza Folklorista Jugoslavije* (Sarajevo: Savez Udruženja Folklorista Jugoslavije, 1963) 519–28. *Transcr.* In Croatian. See no. 455 in this volume.

2973
as

NAZOR, Ante. **Običaji i narodno stvaralaštvo oko smrti u Poljicama** [Death-related customs and traditional arts in Poljice], *Rad XI-og kongresa Saveza Folklorista Jugoslavije* (Zagreb: Savez Folklorista Jugoslavije, 1966) 411–19. In Croatian; summary in Russian. See no. 490 in this volume.

A detailed description of funeral customs in Poljica, Croatia, from immediately before death until the first anniversary of death. Partial lament texts are included.

2974
as

NEDELJKOVIĆ, Dušan. **Društvenoistorijska uslovljenost i zakonitost novosti u hercegovačkom pevanju današnje prelazne epohe** [The historical-social conditions and laws of innovation in Herzegovinian traditional song in the current transitional period], *Rad IX-og kongresa Saveza Folklorista Jugoslavije* (Sarajevo: Savez Udruženja Folklorista Jugoslavije, 1963) 169–83. In Serbian; summary in French. See no. 455 in this volume.

In this period of radical social change, particularly in underdeveloped Herzegovina, virtually all neotraditional songs, from the single couplet to the entire epic, are composed from the new point of view of the masses, reflecting socialist construction and enmity to all human exploitation and humiliation. *(author)*

2975
as

NIKOLIĆ, Vidosava. **Naša narodna pesma socijalističke izgradnje u pervoj petoletki** [Our neotraditional songs of socialist construction in the first five-year plan], *Rad kongresa folklorista Jugoslavije* (Ljubljana: Savez Udruženja Folkloristov Jugoslavije, 1960) 269–75. In Serbian; summary in French. See no. 404 in this volume.

Materials collected in a project of the Etnografski Institut, Srpska Akademija Nauka i Umetnosti, include songs of the first Five-Year Plan (1947-52) devoted to the unity of the constituent ethnic groups and leaders in socialist construction; praising the building of railroads, roads, new towns, hydraulic power plants, factories, and mines; expressing the acceptance of socialist forms of labor; celebrating life in work brigades; and dealing with the creation of the new man and new socialist relations among men as an effect of the collective work of the plan. *(author)*

2976
as

NOTOPOULOS, Demetrios. **Ti epidrasis tou kleftikou tragoudiou eis ta rizitika tragoudia tis Krītis** [The influence of kléftiko on rizitika song in Crete], *Krītika chronika* 16 (1961) III,78–92. *Transcr.* In Greek. See no. 434 in this volume.

The kléftiko song genre in Crete shows signs of Dorian origin; it has not replaced traditional Cretan epic song but has had an influence on the rizitika table song genre of the western region of Crete.

2977
as

OROVIĆ, Savo J. **Narodne pesme u oslobodilačkom ratu i revoluciji** [Folk songs in the War of Liberation and People's Revolution], *Rad VIII-og kongresa folklorista Jugoslavije* (Beograd: Naučno Delo, 1961) 195–206. *Illus., port., transcr.* In Serbian; summary in English. See no. 446 in this volume.

Partisan songs were generally short, lyric works, unlike the traditional national epics of Yugoslavia. They included songs of insurrection, youth songs, women's songs, songs about Tito, and songs about particular heroes and specific events. There were also songs with gusle accompaniment, humorous and satirical songs, and laments. *(author)*

2978
as

ORTIZ DÍAZ, Daniel Luis. **Les refrains et chansons de la vallée de Iguna (Santander)** [Refrains and songs of the Iguña valley (Santander)], *Congrès international des arts populaires/International congress of popular arts* (Paris: Institut international de coopération intellectuelle, 1928) 117. In French. See no. 153 in this volume.

Summary of the conference paper abstracted as no. 2979 in this volume.

2979
as

ORTIZ DÍAZ, Daniel Luis. **Refrains et chansons de la vallée de Iguña (Santander)** [Refrains and songs of the Iguña Valley (Santander)], *Art populaire: Travaux artistiques et scientifiques du Ier Congrès international des arts populaires* (Paris: Duchartre, 1931) 159. In French. See no. 152 in this volume.

The traditional music of the Iguña valley in the department of Santander includes a unique genre of unmeasured, free-rhythmed song. A summary is cited as no. 2978 in this volume. *(David Bloom)*

2980
as

O'SULLIVAN, Donal Joseph. **Irish dances and songs,** *Journal of the International Folk Music Council* II (1950) 33–34. See no. 295 in this volume.

Summary of a paper.

2981
as

OTAÑO EGUINO, Nemesio. **Notas sobre el folklore gallego** [Notes on Galician folklore], *Congrés de la Societat Internacional de Musicologia* (Barcelona: Casa de Caritat, 1936). In Spanish. See no. 224 in this volume.

The conference report provides only a citation. Neither the text nor a summary of the paper was published here.

2982
as

OYHAMBURU, Philippe. **La danse et la musique en Pays Basque** [Dance and music in the Basque country], *Journal of the International Folk Music Council* VI (1954) 36–40. In French. See no. 320 in this volume.

A survey of dance and song genres, with discussion of regional differences in the seven Basque provinces of France and Spain.

2983
as

PAÇO, Afonso do. **Sogras e cunhadas no cancioneiro popular e no adagiário** [Mothers-in-law and brothers-in-law in traditional song and in proverbs],

Actas do Congresso Internacional de Etnografia (Porto: Imprensa Portuguesa, 1965) II, 185–213. *Bibliog.* In Spanish. See no. 473 in this volume.

Presents over 100 quatrains from Vila Nova de San Pedro, Portugal. Published sources used were *O Alentejo cem por cento: Subsídios para o estudo dos costumes, tradições, etnografia e folclore regionais* by Joaquim Roque and *Carta de guia de casados* by Francisco Manuel de Melo. *(Peter S. Bushnell)*

2984
as
PANDOLFINI, Turi. **L'anima musicale dei banditori catanesi** [The musical soul of town criers of Catania], *Journal of the International Folk Music Council* II (1950) 49. In Italian. See no. 295 in this volume.

The conference report provides only a citation. Neither the text nor a summary of the paper was published here.

2985
as
PANHUYS, L.C. van. **Some remarks on Dutch song,** *Congrès international des sciences anthropologiques et ethnologiques: Compte rendu de la troisième session* (Tervuren: Musée Royal de l'Afrique Centrale, 1960) 265. See no. 282 in this volume.

Summary of a paper. Surveys Dutch songs and songwriters of the 19th and early 20th c.

2986
as
PANKOVA, Vera. **Narodno stvaralaštvo oko smrti kod Torbeša** [Death-related traditional arts in Torbeš], *Rad XI-og kongresa Saveza Folklorista Jugoslavije* (Zagreb: Savez Folklorista Jugoslavije, 1966) 405–10. In Serbian; summary in Macedonian. See no. 490 in this volume.

Describes funeral rituals among the Torbeš people, ethnically Slavic people in Macedonia who converted to Islam during the Ottoman invasion. Their funeral rituals preserve a number of Christian and even pre-Christian customs.

2987
as
PAOLONE, E. **La musica del popolo nelle sue origini: Caratteri fondamentali e riflessi** [Traditional music in its origins: Fundamental characteristics and reflections], *Atti del 4. Congresso nazionale di arti e tradizioni popolari* (Roma: Opera Nazionale Dopolavoro, 1942) 403–08. In Italian. See no. 270 in this volume.

2988
as
PARTINI, R. **Elementi e sviluppi nel canto popolare** [Elements and development of traditional song], *Atti del III Congresso nazionale di arti e tradizioni popolari* (Roma: Opera Nazionale Dopolavoro, 1936) 393–96. In Italian. See no. 218 in this volume.

2989
as
PEETERS, Theophiel. **Oude Kempische liederen en dansen** [Old Kempish songs and dances], *Fédération Archéologique et Historique de Belgique: Annales du XXIIᵉ congrès. I: Documents et compte rendu; II: Rapports & mémoires* (Mechelen: Godenne, 1911) II, 467–506. *Music.* In Dutch. See no. 73 in this volume.

Songs and dances from Belgium's Kempen region, before and after 1500, are examined from structural and historical viewpoints. Some of these are similar to national melodies and dances of today. The songs examined were derived from church melodies. *(Albert Dlugasch)*

2990
as
PEJOVIĆ, Roksanda. **Odnos Miloja Milojevića prema muzičkom folkloru** [Miloje Milojević's approach to traditional music], *Rad XI-og kongresa Saveza Folklorista Jugoslavije* (Zagreb: Savez Folklorista Jugoslavije, 1966) 481–90. *Music.* In Serbian; summary in Russian. See no. 490 in this volume.

Milojević did fieldwork in southern Serbia and Macedonia and transcribed about 850 traditional songs between 1927 and 1930. He made references to traditional music in his essays, and it influenced his compositions.

2991
as
PENUŠLISKI, Kiril. **Marko K. Cepenkov, skupljač makedonskih narodnih umotvorina** [Marko K. Cepenkov, a collector of Macedonian folklore], *Rad VII-og kongresa Saveza Folklorista Jugoslavije* (Cetinje: Obod, 1964) 63–66. In Serbian; summary in French. See no. 419 in this volume.

Cepenkov (1829-1920), one of Macedonia's most important folklorists, is not fully appreciated by the public, partly because of criticism of his methodology, and partly because so much of his work has remained unpublished, a situation which is currently being rectified. A brief biography is provided. *(author)*

2992
as
PENUŠLISKI, Kiril; FIRFOV, Živko; POLENAKOVIĆ, Haralampije. **Folklor Makedonije** [The folklore of Macedonia], *Rad VII-og kongresa Saveza Folklorista Jugoslavije* (Cetinje: Obod, 1964) 5–13. In Serbian; summary in French. See no. 419 in this volume.

A general discussion. Topics include the history of collection, and creative expressions of traditional culture such as lyric and epic songs, prose, music and dance, customs, and embroidery. *(authors)*

2993
as
PERISTERIS, Spyridon. **Chansons polyphoniques de l'Épire du nord** [Polyphonic songs of northern Epirus], *Journal of the International Folk Music Council* XVI (1964) 51–53. *Transcr.* In French. See no. 463 in this volume.

Ethnic Greeks and Albanians of the Dropolis region in the north of Epirus perform group singing in a polyphonic style that is quite unlike the polyphony of Greeks of neighboring districts. It does share features with a wide range of traditional Mediterranean polyphonic styles from Istria through the Caucasus, and with Byzantine church music, suggesting that it may be a development from Byzantine influence. *(David Bloom)*

⟶
PETROV, Stojan. **Bela Bartok i bolgarskaja muzykal'naja kul'tura** [Bartók and Bulgarian musical culture]. See no. 2229 in this volume.

2994
as
PETROVIĆ, Đurđica. **Put pesme krajinske čete: *Krajinski smo mladi partizani*** [The journey of a song of the Krajina forces: *Krajinski smo mladi partizani*], *Rad VIII-og kongresa folklorista Jugoslavije* (Beograd: Naučno Delo, 1961) 221–24. In Serbian; summary in French. See no. 446 in this volume.

The song *Krajinski smo mladi partizani* ("We are the young Partisans of the Krajina") spread from its origins in Negotinska Krajina among Partisan units as the course of the war brought them into contact with one another. Eventually it was known throughout most of Yugoslavia, with different first lines referring to different localities, and each locality considering it indigenous to their own region. *(author)*

2995
as
PETROVIĆ, Radmila. **Narodne melodije u prolećnim običajima** [Traditional melodies in spring customs], *Rad IX-og kongresa Saveza Folklorista Jugoslavije* (Sarajevo: Savez Udruženja Folklorista Jugoslavije, 1963) 407–16. *Transcr.* In Serbian; summary in English. See no. 455 in this volume.

Discusses melodies from all parts of Serbia associated with spring festivities: songs for swinging games, Lazarica processions, St. George's Day, and Pentecost. *(author)*

2996
as
PETROVIĆ, Radmila. **Narodni melos u oblasti Titovog Užica** [Traditional music melody in the

Titovo Užice district], *Rad VIII-og kongresa folklorista Jugoslavije* (Beograd: Naučno Delo, 1961) 95–106. *Port., transcr.* In Serbian; summary in English. See no. 446 in this volume.

Urban music in the region has assimilated the style features of nearby and more distant regions of Yugoslavia. Rural music consists mainly of two-part vocal music, in two basic styles. The *iz vika* style works with a fixed repertoire of melodies, particular articulation, untempered scales, and harmony based on unisons and seconds. The recently developed *na bas* style features the creation of a new melody for each text, tempered scales, harmony based on thirds (with a fifth at the end of the cadence), and accordion accompaniment. *(author)*

2997 PETROVIĆ, Radmila. **Two styles of vocal music**
as **in the Zlatibor region of West Serbia,** *Journal of the International Folk Music Council* XV (1963) 45–48. *Transcr.* See no. 459 in this volume.

Discusses the older *iz vika* style of two-part singing involving only the intervals of the second and the unison, and the more recent *na bas* style, which mainly involves major and minor thirds and cadential fifths. *(James R. Cowdery)*

2998 PEUKERT, Herbert. **Der Refrain in der**
as **makedonischen Volkslyrik** [The refrain in the Macedonian traditional lyric], *Rad VII-og kongresa Saveza Folklorista Jugoslavije* (Cetinje: Obod, 1964) 37–51. In German; summary in Serbian. See no. 419 in this volume.

An analysis of the typology of the refrains represented in Miodrag Vasiljević's collection, *Jugoslovenski muzički folklor. II: Narodne melodije koje se pevaju u Makedoniji* (Belgrade, 1953). *(David Bloom)*

2999 PHILLIPPE, Jean. **La chanson populaire en**
as **Poitou et dans la Haute-Bretagne** [Traditional songs in Poitou and Upper Brittany], *La tradition en Poitou et Charentes: Art populaire, ethnographie, folk-lore, hagiographie, histoire* (Paris: Librairie de la Tradition Nationale, 1897) 355–71. In French. See no. 21 in this volume.

Local traditional songs are rapidly being forgotten. The occasion for spinning hemp (*filerie*) in Brittany involves the singing of traditional songs. Texts of lullabies, rounds, love songs, laments, legends, and ribald songs are included.

3000 PICCOLOTTI, D. **Il canto popolare in**
as **rapporto agli usi e costumi del popolo Abruzzese** [Traditional singing in relation to the usages and customs of the people of the Abruzzi], *Lares* XXV (1959) 473–523. In Italian. See no. 370 in this volume.

⟶ PIERA GELABERT, Mercedes. **La danse des gitanes du Vallès** [The *Ball de gitanes* of El Valles]. See no. 5050 in this volume.

⟶ PIERSANTELLI, Giuseppe. **Lanternette and trallalero in the Genoese popular tradition.** See no. 5051 in this volume.

3001 PINCK, Louis. **La circulation des chants, vue**
as **de la Lorraine** [The circulation of songs in the Lorraine], *Travaux du Ier Congrès International de Folklore* (Tours: Arrault et Cie, 1938) 145–51. In French. See no. 251 in this volume.

Focuses on 19th- and early 20th-c. traditional song.

3002 PINEAU, Léon. **Les vieux chants populaires**
as **scandinaves** [The old traditional songs of Scandina-

via], *Congrès international des traditions populaires* (Paris: E. Lechevalier, E. Leroux, J. Maisonneuve, 1902) 62–71. In French. See no. 31 in this volume.

During the 12th through the 15th c. in Denmark, Norway, and Sweden, three types of traditional songs were sung: historic songs reflecting on a chivalric age, songs on heroes and myths, and songs that centered around spirits (e.g., of mountains, waters, woods) who interact with humans. The poetic forms of these songs are discussed, and the ways that some of them found into the traditions of other European countries are explored. *(Susan Poliniak)*

3003 PLICKA, Karel. **La musique pastorale et la**
as **chanson populaire slovaque** [Shepherds' music and the Slovak traditional song], *Congrès international des arts populaires/International congress of popular arts* (Paris: Institut international de coopération intellectuelle, 1928) 113. In French. See no. 153 in this volume.

The Slovak shepherd's vertical flute is the basis of the scales and modes used in traditional music and song in the region.

3004 PLICKA, Karel. **Songs of the Slovak moun-**
as **tains,** *Journal of the International Folk Music Council* VIII (1956) 30–31. See no. 349 in this volume.

Summary of a paper discussing songs of the Tatra mountains.

3005 PLLANA, Shefqet. **Rad kao motiv u arba-**
as **naškoj narodnoj pesmi** [Work as a motif in Albanian traditional song], *Rad VIII-og kongresa folklorista Jugoslavije* (Beograd: Naučno Delo, 1961) 425–32. *Port.* In Serbian; summary in English. See no. 446 in this volume.

The earliest Albanian epic songs begin with scenes of brothers building a bridge or a castle. Work motifs are found in songs dealing with cattle breeding, agriculture, and migratory labor, and also in love songs. Contemporary songs treat labor motifs in the building of socialist society, young women freeing themselves from the patriarchal yoke, and the growth of urban industry. *(author)*

3006 PLLANA, Shefqet. **Šiptarski revolucionarni**
as **muzički folklor** [Traditional Albanian revolutionary music], *Rad kongresa folklorista Jugoslavije* (Ljubljana: Savez Udruženja Folkloristov Jugoslavije, 1960) 193–202. *Illus., bibliog., transcr.* In Serbian; summary in German. See no. 404 in this volume.

During the War of National Liberation (1941–45) and the subsequent period of socialist construction, new revolutionary songs were created in the Albanian communities of Yugoslavia, women's songs being of particular interest. Their accompaniment, rhythm, tonality, and use of polyphony are examined, and their geographical distribution is discussed. *(author)*

3007 PLLANA, Shefqet. **Tužbalica o Redži, s**
as **naročitim osvrtom na jednoglasno i višeglasno pevanje kod Šćiptara u Makedoniji** [The lament for Rexha, with particular reference to monophonic and polyphonic song among the Albanian community in Macedonia], *Rad VII-og kongresa Saveza Folklorista Jugoslavije* (Cetinje: Obod, 1964) 431–32. In Serbian. See no. 419 in this volume.

The lament for Rexha concerns an Albanian hero killed by his horse on his wedding day. Among the Gege Albanians the lament is performed in monophonic style; the Tosk Albanians sing it in three voices.

3008 POLENAKOVIĆ, Haralampije. **O narodnoj**
as **pesmi** *Biljana platno beleše* [The traditional song *Biljana platno beleše*], *Rad VII-og kongresa Saveza Folklorista Jugoslavije* (Cetinje: Obod, 1964) 15–16. In Serbian; summary in French. See no. 419 in this volume.

In many of the 30 or so known variants of this traditional Macedonian song, there is a reference to the springs of Ohrid, which are mentioned in literary works as *Biljanini izvori*, "Biljana's springs". It is likely, but cannot be proved, that the song comes from Ohrid. *(author)*

3009 POLOCZEK, František. **Das Räuber-Volkslied**
as **in dem Gebiet des Tatra-Gebirges** [Traditional robber songs in the Tatra region], *Bericht über den internationalen musikwissenschaftlichen Kongreß* (Kassel: Bärenreiter, 1957) 172–74. *Music*. In German. See no. 356 in this volume.
General remarks on the historical background, text, and music of songs about the 18th-c. Slovak outlaw hero Juro Jánošík and his band. *(David Bloom)*

3010 POLOCZEK, František. **Slovakian folk song**
as **and folk dance in the present day,** *Journal of the International Folk Music Council* IX (1957) 13–14. See no. 362 in this volume.

3011 POMMER, Josef. **Juchzer, Rufe und Alm-**
as **schreie aus den österreichischen Alpenländern** [Yodels, calls, and Almschreie from the Austrian alpine countries], *Haydn-Zentenarfeier* (Leipzig: Breitkopf & Härtel; Wien: Artaria, 1909) 248–52. *Music*. In German. See no. 65 in this volume.
Discusses melodic content and harmonic implications of various mountain calls of the region.

3012 POMMER, Josef. *Das Volkslied in Österreich*:
as **Unternehmen des k.k. Ministeriums für Kultus und Unterricht** [*Das Volkslied in Österreich*: An undertaking of the Austro-Hungarian Ministry of Culture and Education], *Haydn-Zentenarfeier* (Leipzig: Breitkopf & Härtel; Wien: Artaria, 1909) 266–68. In German. See no. 65 in this volume.

3013 POP, Mihai. **Continuity and change in tradi-**
as **tional folklore,** *Journal of the International Folk Music Council* XVI (1964) 24–25. See no. 463 in this volume.
Summary of a paper. Social change in Romania has disrupted the earlier oral transmission of music traditions from generation to generation, and has led to many changes in the system of genres. New institutions, radio broadcasts, and specialized academic and publishing activities have served as a protective force. *(David Bloom)*

3014 POP, Mihai. **Tradition and innovation in con-**
as **temporary Rumanian folklore,** *Journal of the International Folk Music Council* XII (1960) 43–46. See no. 413 in this volume.
A survey of modern developments.

3015 PRATO, Stanislas. **Échantillon d'une étude**
as **comparée des chants populaires néo-grecs et des autres, européens et orientaux** [Examples from a study comparing neo-Greek traditional songs and others, European and Eastern], *Congrès international des traditions populaires* (Paris: E. Lechevalier, E. Leroux, J. Maisonneuve, 1902) 107–09. In French. See no. 31 in this volume.
Neo-Greek songs contain subjects dealing with sentiment and fantasy, but not much reflection. Other themes include impossibilties involving love; fanciful images of the sun, moon, and stars; beauty; messengers of love; and botanic images. *(Susan Poliniak)*

3016 PSACHOS, Konstantinos A. **Le chant populaire**
as **hellénique de l'antiquité à nos jours** [Greek traditional song from antiquity to our day], *Art populaire: Travaux artistiques et scientifiques du Ier Congrès international des arts populaires* (Paris: Duchartre, 1931) 126–27. In French. See no. 152 in this volume.

3017 PUJOL PONS, Francisco. **L'œuvre du**
as ***Chansonnier populaire de la Catalogne*** [The *Obra del cançoner popular de Catalunya*], *Beethoven-Zentenarfeier: Internationaler musikhistorischer Kongress* (Wien: Universal, 1927) 355–58. In French. See no. 142 in this volume.
A historical account of the Barcelona organization Orfeó Català and its project of a comprehensive collection of Catalan traditional music (*Obra del cançoner popular de Catalunya*, Barcelona, 1926-29). *(David Bloom)*

3018 PUTILOV, Boris Nikolaevič. **Junačkaja pesnja**
as ***Marko nahodit sestru* v versijah s Horvatskovo Primor'ja i ostrovov i bylina o kozarine** [The heroic song *Marko pronalazi sestru* in versions from Hrvatsko Primorje and the islands, and a bylina about a shepherd], *Rad XI-og kongresa Saveza Folklorista Jugoslavije* (Zagreb: Savez Folklorista Jugoslavije, 1966) 61–68. In Russian. See no. 490 in this volume.
The variant from Hrvatsko Primorje and the islands is the oldest version of the southern Slavic song *Marko pronalazi sestru* (Russian: *Marko nahodit sestru*), which concerns a man finding his sister. This song is compared with an eastern Slavic bylina about a shepherd.

3019 QUELLMALZ, Alfred. **Musikalisches Altgut in**
as **der Volksüberlieferung Südtirols** [Musical heirlooms in the South Tyrol tradition], *Bericht über den internationalen musikwissenschaftlichen Kongreß Wien Mozartjahr 1956* (Graz; Köln: Böhlau, 1958) 481–89. *Transcr*. In German. See no. 365 in this volume.
A brief account of the historical background and fieldwork for the author's *Südtiroler Volkslieder* (Kassel: Bärenreiter, 1968-76), with fully transcribed examples of a range of vocal and instrumental pieces. *(David Bloom)*

3020 RADOVANOVIĆ, Miljana. **Društveno-**
as **istorijski karakter hercegovačkog narodnog pevanja Narodnooslobodilačke Borbe** [The social and historical character of the Herzegovinian traditional song of the War of National Liberation], *Rad IX-og kongresa Saveza Folklorista Jugoslavije* (Sarajevo: Savez Udruženja Folklorista Jugoslavije, 1963) 195–201. In Serbian; summary in French. See no. 455 in this volume.
Considered in its full range from couplets to ballads, Herzegovinian neotraditional song reflects local events in the struggle for liberation with the same evolution and dynamic structure as songs of the period from other parts of Yugoslavia, but with a special expressive richness of its own. *(author)*

3021 RAJECZKY, Benjamin. **Old and new singing**
as **styles in Hungarian folk song,** *Journal of the International Folk Music Council* XII (1960) 56–61. *Music*. See no. 413 in this volume.
The older style is characterized by rich ornamentation and use of different registers; the newer style is simpler, with a more marked rhythm, less ornamentation, and a narrower range. *(James R. Cowdery)*

3022 RAUPP, Jan. **Die Beziehung der sorbischen**
as **Musikfolklore zu der des Donauraumes** [The relationship between the Sorb (Wendish) musical tradition and that of the Danube region], *Rad kongresa folklorista Jugoslavije* (Zagreb: Savez Udruženja

Folklorista Jugoslavije, 1959) 123–32. *Transcr.* In German. See no. 382 in this volume.

Sorb traditional music is closely related to that of the Slavic peoples of the Danube basin, Moravian, Slovak, and South Slavic, as comparisons of song texts and melodies show. *(David Bloom)*

3023 RAUPP, Jan. **"Unsere Krieger ziehen aus dem**
as **Kampfe heim": Ein altsorbisches episches Lied** ["Our warriors are coming home from battle": An old Sorb epic song], *Bericht über den internationalen musikwissenschaftlichen Kongreß* (Kassel: Bärenreiter, 1957) 175–77. *Transcr.* In German. See no. 356 in this volume.

A Sorb (Wendish) war epic published in Ewald Müller's *Das Wendentum in der Niederlausitz* (1893) uses an archaic pre-diatonic scale and textual material that can be dated to the 10th c., suggesting that it is the oldest of all extant Slavic epics. *(David Bloom)*

3024 RAZZI, Giulio. **Folk music and Italian broad-**
as **casting,** *Journal of the International Folk Music Council* II (1950) 47–48. See no. 295 in this volume.

Discusses the ongoing efforts by Italian radio stations to program traditional music.

3025 REPP, Friedrich. **La chanson populaire de l'îlot**
as **linguistique allemand de Spis en Slovaquie** [The traditional song of the German linguistic enclave of Spiš in Slovakia], *Congrès international des arts populaires/International congress of popular arts* (Paris: Institut international de coopération intellectuelle, 1928) 112. In French. See no. 153 in this volume.

Summary of the paper abstracted as no. 3026 in this volume.

3026 REPP, Friedrich. **La chanson populaire de l'îlot**
as **linguistique allemand de Spiz en Slovaquie** [The traditional song of the German linguistic enclave of Spiš in Slovakia], *Art populaire: Travaux artistiques et scientifiques du Ier Congrès international des arts populaires* (Paris: Duchartre, 1931) 150. In French. See no. 152 in this volume.

The Spiš region exemplifies the reciprocal influences of German, Slavic, and Magyar peoples. German song texts of the region, especially long ballads, are old and of high literary quality; in addition to old German folk tunes, they use Slavic and Hungarian tunes, most often in minor keys. The language of the ballads is most likely to be High German, while songs of strictly local origin are in dialect. Most originated in central Germany. A summary is cited as no. 3025 in this volume. *(David Bloom)*

3027 RIEGLER-DINU, Emil. **La hora, la maquam et**
as **la chanson populaire de l'orient européen** [The hora, the maqām, and Eastern European traditional song], *Art populaire: Travaux artistiques et scientifiques du Ier Congrès international des arts populaires* (Paris: Duchartre, 1931) 140–41. In French. See no. 152 in this volume.

The hora lunga genre known in Romania from Maramureş in the north to Dobrogea in the southeast derives, like Ukrainian dumy and the songs of the Crimean Tatars, from Perso-Arabic maqām, in an illustration of the historical continuity of folklore in the formerly Ottoman-ruled parts of Europe. In more urbanized parts of the country, especially in Bucovina, songs reflect the influence of the Western European gassenhauer, with a clear tonic-dominant structure and regular binary and ternary rhythm. In the high Transylvanian plateau and the Carpathians, neither influence has penetrated, and there the hora in the strict sense of the term is marked by a typical tempo giusto or parlando-rubato rhythm, and by pentatonic or Greek modal scales. A summary is cited as no. 3028 in this volume. *(David Bloom)*

3028 RIEGLER-DINU, Emil. **La hora, le maquam et**
as **la chanson populaire de l'orient européen** [The

hora, the maqām, and Eastern European traditional song], *Congrès international des arts populaires/International congress of popular arts* (Paris: Institut international de coopération intellectuelle, 1928) 108–09. In French. See no. 153 in this volume.

Summary of the paper abstracted as no. 3056 in this volume.

3029 RIEGLER-DINU, Emil. **Das rumänische Volks-**
as **lied und die Instrumentalmusik der Bauern** [Romanian traditional song and instrumental music of agricultural communities], *Beethoven-Zentenarfeier: Internationaler musikhistorischer Kongress* (Wien: Universal, 1927) 340–50. *Transcr.* In German. See no. 142 in this volume.

Certain features of melodies in the hora lunga (or doina) genre of traditional Romanian song, especially the cadence formula of the descending fourth, are related to features of the shepherd's flute, tilincă fără dop (ductless flute), and the six-hole fluier. *(David Bloom)*

3030 RIGAU, Antonio P. **Les fêtes de Saint-Roch sur**
as **la place Neuve de Barcelone** [The feast of Saint Roch on Plaça Nova, Barcelona], *Congrès international des arts populaires/International congress of popular arts* (Paris: Institut international de coopération intellectuelle, 1928) 134. In French. See no. 153 in this volume.

Note on the historic origin of the centuries-old Festa Major de Sant Roc, celebrated annually in Barcelona in the week leading up to the feast of St. Roch on 16 August.

3031 RIHTMAN, Cvjetko. **Napjev balade u**
as **narodnoj tradiciji Bosne i Hercegovine** [Ballad melody in the folk tradition of Bosnia and Herzegovina], *Rad kongresa folklorista Jugoslavije* (Beograd: Naučno Delo, 1960) 143–45. In Bosnian; summary in French. See no. 402 in this volume.

In the folk tradition of Bosnia and Herzegovina ballads and other narrative songs often employ short melodies that facilitate the delivery of the verses. Characteristics of the ballad tradition include syllabic singing, emphasis on the text, the use of rests to articulate form, and the manipulation of dynamics to highlight dramatic events. Ballads may be performed by a soloist or by a group of singers, with or without instrumental accompaniment. Another version is cited as RILM ^{1998}8139.

3032 RIHTMAN, Cvjetko. **Narodna muzička**
as **tradicija istočne Hercegovine** [Music tradition of eastern Herzegovina], *Rad IX-og kongresa Saveza Folklorista Jugoslavije* (Sarajevo: Savez Udruženja Folklorista Jugoslavije, 1963) 75–81. *Transcr.* In Bosnian. See no. 455 in this volume.

3033 RIHTMAN, Cvjetko. **O ilirskom porijeklu**
as **polifonih oblika narodne muzike Bosne i Hercegovine** [On the Illyric origin of polyphonic genres in the traditional music of Bosnia and Herzegovina], *Rad kongresa folklorista Jugoslavije* (Zagreb: Savez Udruženja Folklorista Jugoslavije, 1958) 99–104. In Croatian; summary in French. See no. 315 in this volume.

Polyphonic genres that resemble Albanian ones may be remnants of the tradition of ancient Balkan peoples. Originally published in *Zbornik Saveza Folklorista* (Zagreb, 1958). Another version is cited as RILM ^{1998}8141.

3034 RIHTMAN, Cvjetko. **Organološki problemi**
as **naše etnomuzikologije** [Organological problems in our ethnomusicology], *Rad VII-og kongresa Saveza Folklorista Jugoslavije* (Cetinje: Obod, 1964) 201–06. In Bosnian; summary in French. See no. 419 in this volume.

A general survey of instruments in Bosnia and Herzegovina and an outline of problems in their classification. *(author)*

3035 RIHTMAN, Cvjetko. **Les rapports entre le**
as **rythme poétique et le rythme musical dans la tradition populaire de la Bosnie-Herzégovine** [The relationship between poetic and musical rhythm in the folk tradition of Bosnia and Herzegovina], *Journal of the International Folk Music Council* XII (1960) 64–66. In French. See no. 413 in this volume.

Instances in which prosody and musical rhythm come into conflict illuminate processes through which verse and melody influence one another in traditional songs. *(Murat Eyüboğlu)*

3036 ROCA, Stevan. **Gusle kao poklon** [The gusle as
as gift], *Rad IX-og kongresa Saveza Folklorista Jugoslavije* (Sarajevo: Savez Udruženja Folklorista Jugoslavije, 1963) 571–75. In Serbian; summary in French. See no. 455 in this volume.

Various anecdotes illustrate the social importance of the instrument and the artistry of its performers.

3037 ROCA, Stevan. **Užička narodna pesma i pesma**
as ***Junaštvo Janković Stojana*** [The traditional song of Užice and the song *Junaštvo Janković Stojana*], *Rad VIII-og kongresa folklorista Jugoslavije* (Beograd: Naučno Delo, 1961) 447–49. *Port.* In Serbian; summary in English. See no. 446 in this volume.

Discusses three versions of the guslar song *Junaštvo Janković Stojana* (The heroism of Stojan Janković), recorded in Užice, Sarajevo, and Vrlička Krajina (Dalmatia), with emphasis on the beauty of the text. *(author)*

3038 ROMANSKA, Cvetana Stojanova. **Bulgarische**
as **und mazedonische Heldenlieder und historische Volkslieder über Persönlichkeiten aus der ungarischen Geschichte** [Bulgarian and Macedonian heroic songs and traditional songs on personalities from Hungarian history], *Europa et Hungaria: Congressus ethnographicus in Hungaria* (Budapest: Akadémiai Kiadó, 1965) 333f. In German. See no. 460 in this volume.

3039 ROMANSKA, Cvetana Stojanova. **Neke opšte**
as **osobine pesama o Kraljeviću Marku koje su zapisane u novije vreme na dalmatinskim otocima i u Bugarskoj** [Some general characteristics of songs about Prince Marko recently transcribed on the Dalmatian islands and in Bulgaria], *Rad XI-og kongresa Saveza Folklorista Jugoslavije* (Zagreb: Savez Folklorista Jugoslavije, 1966) 231–37. In Serbian; summary in German. See no. 490 in this volume.

3040 RŠUMOVIĆ, Andrija; NEDELJKOVIĆ, Dušan;
as NIKOLIĆ, Vidosava. **Užičke hajdučke pesme, hajdukovanje i hajdučija** [Hajduk ballads of the Užice region, *hajdukovanje* and *hajdučija*], *Rad VIII-og kongresa folklorista Jugoslavije* (Beograd: Naučno Delo, 1961) 121–27. *Port.* In Serbian; summary in French. See no. 446 in this volume.

Hajduk ballads are numerous in the Užice region; the hajduk phenomenon remained there until the end of the People's Revolution of 1941-45, and much can be learned about it through archival research and interviews. The term *hajdučija* for the phenomenon, with the connotation of "banditry", used by scholars of a bourgeois tendency, is inaccurate; *hajdukovanje*, the traditional struggle against all oppression and exploitation, is the only subject of the ballads, which express reactions to the brutal accumulation of capital and the pauperization of the masses. *(authors)*

3041 RUSIĆ, Branislav. **Pesme sa pevanjem uz**
as **ljuljanje kod Makedonaca i susednih južnoslovenskih i neslovenskih naroda** [Songs and customs in swinging games among Macedonians and the neighboring South Slavic and non-Slavic peoples], *Rad IX-og kongresa Saveza Folklorista Jugoslavije* (Sarajevo: Savez Udruženja Folklorista Jugoslavije, 1963) 333–55. *Illus., transcr.* In Serbian; summary in English. See no. 455 in this volume.

Adults and children frequently set up swings on St. George's Day and 1 March, and somewhat less frequently on Shrove Tuesday and the Feast of the Forty Martyrs of Sebaste; as each person swings, girls sing a song suggesting marriage between the person and his or her known or unknown sweetheart. Similar customs and songs are found on St. George's Day in neighboring parts of Bulgaria and Serbia, and on Christmas or Epiphany and then Shrove Tuesday elsewhere in Serbia. Some non-Slav peoples of the region swing on St. George's Day and Shrove Tuesday but, except for the Slav-influenced Meglen Vlach people in northern Greece, they do not sing erotic songs. *(author)*

3042 SALMEN, Walter. **Vermeintliches und**
as **wirkliches Volkslied im späten Mittelalter** [Alleged and actual folk song in the late Middle Ages], *Kongreß-Bericht: Gesellschaft für Musikforschung* (Kassel; Basel: Bärenreiter, 1950) 174–78. *Music.* In German. See no. 299 in this volume.

3043 SAMPER, Baltasar. **El cant de les cançons de**
as **treballada a Mallorca** [The singing of work songs in Majorca], *Congrés de la Societat Internacional de Musicologia* (Barcelona: Casa de Caritat, 1936). In Catalan. See no. 224 in this volume.

The conference report provides only a citation. Neither the text nor a summary of the paper was published here.

3044 SAN VALERO APARISI, Julián. **Las bandas de**
as **música en la vida valenciana** [Music bands in Valencian life], *Actas do Congresso Internacional de Etnografia* (Porto: Imprensa Portuguesa, 1965) II, 337–41. In Spanish. See no. 473 in this volume.

The Valencia region in Spain comprises three provinces, 545 towns. It has 340 bands, in which 15,000 volunteer musicians play each year, and 30,000 to 40,000 young people receive musical instruction under the bands' sponsorship. The bands are typically made up of wind and percussion instruments; their members, mostly manual laborers, perform at all community events. The town of Liria has a much-awarded and thriving band that has been in existence since 1813. The future is uncertain for these organizations, as they compete against radio, records, and the apathy of the young. Some archeological findings in Liria from the Iberian civilization of 2,300 years ago show paintings on vases depicting musicians playing wind and percussion instruments. *(Anatole Wieck)*

3045 SANDVIK, Ole Mørk. **La musique populaire**
as **norvégienne** [Norwegian traditional music], *Art populaire: Travaux artistiques et scientifiques du Ier Congrès international des arts populaires* (Paris: Duchartre, 1931) 130–33. In French. See no. 152 in this volume.

3046 SANDVIK, Ole Mørk. **Norwegian folk music**
as **and its social significance**, *Journal of the International Folk Music Council* I (1949) 12–13. See no. 281 in this volume.

Discusses the roles of traditional music and dance in Norwegian life.

3047 SANNEMANN, Friedrich. **Ueber eine unge-**
as **druckte Sammlung deutscher Volkslieder mit ihren Singweisen in der Altmark und im Magdeburgischen aus Volksmunde gesammelt von Ludolf Parisius** [An unpublished collection of Ger-

man traditional songs with their melodies collected from oral sources in the Altmark and Magdeburg districts by Ludolf Parisius], *Report of the Fourth Congress of the International Musical Society* (London: Novello, 1912) 205. In German. See no. 71 in this volume.

Summary of a paper describing a MS completed in 1879.

3048
as
SANTOLI, Vittorio. **Di una nuova raccolta di canti popolari toscani** [A new collection of popular Tuscan songs], *Atti del I Congresso nazionale delle tradizioni popolari* (Firenze: Rinascimento del Libro, 1930) 66–80. In Italian. See no. 158 in this volume.

3049
as
SANTOLLINO, R. **Il mare nei canti popolari napoletani** [The sea in Neapolitan traditional songs], *Atti del 4. Congresso nazionale di arti e tradizioni popolari* (Roma: Opera Nazionale Dopolavoro, 1942) 409–09. In Italian. See no. 270 in this volume.

3050
as
SÁROSI, Bálint. **Les chemins de la culture instrumentale en Hongrie** [The paths of instrument cultivation in Hungary], *Journal of the International Folk Music Council* XVI (1964) 89–90. In French. See no. 463 in this volume.

The professional performance of traditional Hungarian music has been mostly by Gypsy musicians, favoring the violin, since the beginning of the 19th c. This music is not to be confused with the Gypsies' own traditional music; its origin is Arabo-Persian rather than Gypsy. Amateur Hungarian musicians have tended to replace the traditional homemade flutes, bagpipes, fiddles, etc., with industrially manufactured instruments with similar tuning and playing techniques. *(David Bloom)*

3051
as
SAYGUN, Ahmed Adnan. **Quelques réflexions sur certaines affinités des musiques folkoriques turque et hongroise** [Some reflections on certain affinities between Turkish and Hungarian traditional music], *Studia musicologica Academiae Scientiarum Hungaricae* V (1963) 515–24. *Music.* In German. See no. 427 in this volume.

Compares Turkish and Hungarian traditional musics with respect to modes, cadences, rhythm, and form, and with reference to Bartók's 1936 ethnomusicological field trip to Turkey and research collaboration with the author. *(William Renwick)*

3052
as
SCHIØRRING, Nils. **Musical folklore and ethnomusicology in Denmark,** *Les colloques de Wégimont. III: Ethnomusicologie II* (Paris: Belles Lettres, 1960) 51–53. See no. 366 in this volume.

The Danes' interest in their own traditional vocal music was manifested as early as 1591, with the publication of Anders Sørensen Vedel's *It hundrede vdualde danske viser* (One hundred selected Danish ballads). Ethnomusicological studies have been made by Danes in Greenland (Hjalmar Thuren and William Thalbitzer), the Faroe Islands (Hakon Grüner-Nielsen), Iceland (H. Gad), Mongolia (Henning Haslund-Christensen), Yugoslavia (Birthe Trærup), Afghanistan (Th. Alrad), and Guyana (Jens Yde). *(Katharine Fry)*

3053
as
SCHIRÒ, Giuseppe. **Poesia e musica tradizionali degli italo-albanesi** [Traditional poetry and music of the Italian Albanians], *Atti del 4. Congresso nazionale di arti e tradizioni popolari* (Roma: Opera Nazionale Dopolavoro, 1942) 410–22. In Italian. See no. 270 in this volume.

3054
as
SCHRAMMEK, Winfried. **Die Geschichte des sogenannten Harzspruchs vom Mittelalter bis zur Gegenwart** [The history of the so-called *Harzspruch*, from the Middle Ages to the present], *Jour-*

nal of the International Folk Music Council XIII (1961) 50–53. In German. See no. 424 in this volume.

The couplet "*Es grüne die Tanne, es wachse das Erz,/Gott schenke uns allen ein fröhliches Herz!*" (May the pine tree flourish and the iron ore grow, and may God give us all a happy heart) is sung throughout the Harz mountain region of Niedersachsen and Sachsen-Anhalt. It may be traced to Annaberg in the Erzgebirge district on the Bohemian border, whence miners migrated into the Harz region at the beginning of the 16th c.; it penetrated bourgeois urban culture as a toast in the early 19th c. The couplet alludes to the traditional belief that iron ore grows organically underground. *(David Bloom)*

3055
as
SEEMANN, Erich. **Das Deutsche Volkslied-archiv und seine Arbeiten: Proben aus einer neuen Schallplattenreihe—Ältere deutsche Volkslieder in mündlicher Überlieferung** [The Deutsches Volksliedarchiv and its work: The test case of a new series of recordings—*Ältere deutsche Volkslieder in mündlicher Überlieferung*], *Volkskunde-Kongreß: Vorträge und Berichte* (Stuttgart: Kohlhammer, 1959) 69–72. In German. See no. 396 in this volume.

Discusses an LP recording—*Alte Lieder aus mündlicher Überlieferung* (Old songs from the oral tradition)—of traditional German songs performed by mixed chorus and issued by the Deutsche Grammophon company as vol. 1 of the series *Deutsche Volkslieder: Eine Dokumentation des Deutschen Musikrates.* *(David Bloom)*

3056
as
SERRA Y BOLDÚ, Valerio. **Les goigs ou gozos, poèmes religieux chantés en Catalogne** [The goigs or gozos, religious poems sung in Catalonia], *Art populaire: Travaux artistiques et scientifiques du Ier Congrès international des arts populaires* (Paris: Duchartre, 1931) 155. In French. See no. 152 in this volume.

The goig (*gozo* in Castilian)—a Catalan hymn genre used at the end of religious ceremonies and praising God, the Virgin, or the saints—was created in the 12th c. by the troubadour Guido Fulcodi, later Pope Clement IV. From the 16th c., print editions of goigs, illuminated by fine wood engravings, were disseminated by churches, shrines, and confraternities. A summary is cited as no. 3057. *(David Bloom)*

3057
as
SERRA Y BOLDÚ, Valerio. **Les goigs ou gozos, poèmes religieux chantés en Catalogne** [The goigs or gozos, religious poems sung in Catalonia], *Congrès international des arts populaires/International congress of popular arts* (Paris: Institut international de coopération intellectuelle, 1928) 110. In French. See no. 153 in this volume.

Summary of the paper abstracted as no. 3056 in this volume.

3058
as
SHULDHAM-SHAW, Patrick. **Scandinavian folk music on British soil,** *Journal of the International Folk Music Council* VIII (1956) 11–12. See no. 349 in this volume.

Summary of a paper discussing Scandinavian influences in the traditions of the Scottish islands known as the Hebrides, the Orkneys, and the Shetlands.

3059
as
SIHLEANU, Stefan. **De la musique populaire dans les pays roumains** [Traditional music in Romanian lands], *Report of the Fourth Congress of the International Musical Society* (London: Novello, 1912) 205. In French. See no. 71 in this volume.

Describes traditional music in Romania and in Romanian communities in other parts of Eastern Europe.

3060
as
SIMIĆ, Ljuba. **Pripovedne i lirske pesme istočne Hercegovine** [Narrative and lyric songs of eastern Herzegovina], *Rad IX-og kongresa Saveza*

Folklorista Jugoslavije (Sarajevo: Savez Udruženja Folklorista Jugoslavije, 1963) 63–68. In Bosnian; summary in Russian. See no. 455 in this volume.

3061 SINICROPI, Enrico. **Canti popolari ennesi** [Traas ditional songs of Enna], *Atti del 4. Congresso nazionale di arti e tradizioni popolari* (Roma: Opera Nazionale Dopolavoro, 1942) 423–27. In Italian. See no. 270 in this volume.

3062 SIROVÁTKA, Oldřich. **K problematice folkas loru charvátské menšiny v Československu** [Issues related to the folklore of the Croatian minority in Czechoslovakia], *Treći kongres folklorista Jugoslavije* (Cetinje: Udruženje Folklorista Crne Gore, 1958) 21–27. *Illus., bibliog.* In Czech; summary in Serbian. See no. 357 in this volume.

The Croatian minority in Slovakia is concentrated in the villages of Devínska Nová Ves, Chorvátsky Grob, and Dúbravka (about 3000 people), and in Moravia in Frélichov, Nový Přerov, and Dobré Pole (about 1800 people). Since their settlement there in the 16th c., the Croats lived in a symbiosis with the Slovak and Moravian people in the surrounding villages, and its songs could be traced to Slovak and Moravian melodic formulas. Folklore of the Croatian minority in Slovakia and Moravia has been transcribed and studied since the 19th c. by František Sušil, Alois Vojtěch Šembera, Václav Vážný, and Josef Černík. A bibliography of Czech and Slovak studies about folklore of the Croatian minority in Czechoslovakia is appended. *(Zdravko Blažeković)*

3063 SMETS, G. **L'Umuganuro (fête du sorgho)as chez les Barundi (territ. belge mandat)** [The Umuganuro (sorghum festival) among the Rundi people (mandated Belgian territory)], *Congrès international des sciences anthropologiques et ethnologiques: Compte rendu de la deuxième session* (København: Munksgaard, 1939) 273–74. In French. See no. 255 in this volume.

Discusses the festival celebrated annually around December by the royal court.

3064 STANISLAV, Josef. **O masové písni a jejímas dnešním významu/La chanson de masse et son importance actuelle** [Mass song and its present-day importance], *Hudba národů: Sborník přednášek, proslovených na I. mezinárodním sjezdu skladatelů a hudebních kritiků/Musique des nations: Iᵉʳ Congrès international des compositeurs et critiques musicaux* (Praha: Syndikát Českých Skladatelů, 1948) 64–68,168–73. In Czech and French. See no. 278 in this volume.

Czechoslovak mass song is rooted in traditional Bohemian, Moravian, and Slovak music and in light music such as the slyly anti-Austrian songs of František Kmoch and Rudolf Friml's *Písně Závišovy* (Songs of Záviš) (op. 1, 1906). Since 1934, it has developed through the work of Jaroslav Ježek at the Osvobozené Divadlo (Liberated Theater), and of the author in the music section of Svaz Dělnických Divadelních Ochotníků (Workers' Amateur Theater Union). During World War II, the resistance sang songs by Kmoch and by Karel Hašler, killed at Mauthausen concentration camp in 1941, whose *Ta naše písnička česká* became a kind of informal national anthem. Other notable composers include Ervín Schulhoff, Vít Nejedlý, Jaroslav Teklý, Karel Reiner, Alois Hába, Václav Dobiáš, Albert Pek, Dalibor Vačkář, and Jan Seidel.

3065 STEINITZ, Wolfgang. **Arbeiterlied und Arbeias terkultur** [Workers' songs and the culture of the working class], *Beiträge zur Musikwissenschaft* VI/4 (1964) 279–88. In German. See no. 476 in this volume.

The exact place of workers' songs (*Arbeiterlieder*) within the general body of German folklore is somewhat difficult to define. Many, however, have origins in soldiers' songs. *(Kevin James Harvey)*

3066 STEPANOV, Stjepan. **O nekim načinimaas pjevanja romanca i balada na području Hrvatske** [Melodic styles in romance and ballad in the territory of Croatia], *Rad kongresa folklorista Jugoslavije* (Beograd: Naučno Delo, 1960) 123–35. *Transcr.* In Croatian; summary in German. See no. 402 in this volume.

Older melodic forms found especially in relatively inaccessible parts of southern Croatia feature a narrow range, short melodic units, and recitative style, reflecting the archaic performance situation of a soloist singing for an audience in which, in romance and ballad as in epic song, the intelligibility of the text was the most important consideration. Newer forms found in the plains regions of northern and northeastern Croatia feature wider range, longer phrases, and melismatic ornamentation, sometimes so much so as to threaten the intelligibility of the text, corresponding to the different performance contexts of group singing, accompaniment of dancers, and so on. *(author)*

3067 STĘSZEWSKI, Jan. **Einige charakteristischeas Merkmale der Kurpischen Volksmusik** [Some characteristic features of the traditional music of Kurpie], *Bericht über den siebenten internationalen musikwissenschaftlichen Kongress* (Kassel: Bärenreiter, 1959) 283–84. In German. See no. 390 in this volume.

In the small Kurpie region of northeast Poland, around 100 km north of Warsaw, the musical dialect shows its affinity to Balt and other cultures to the north through the preference for 5/8 meter in tunes associated in the rest of Poland with 6/8, the apocope of stanza-final syllables, and the relatively slow and even rhythmic pulse, as opposed to the quick rubato style of central Poland. These features may be derived from the extinct music of the Prusai (*Pruzzen*, Old Prussian speakers) of Masuria, whence the first Kurpians emigrated in the 16th c. *(David Bloom)*

3068 STOCKMANN, Doris. **Totenklagen deras südalbanischen Çamen** [Laments of the southern Albanian Çam people], *Rad XI-og kongresa Saveza Folklorista Jugoslavije* (Zagreb: Savez Folklorista Jugoslavije, 1966) 433–42. *Music, transcr.* In German; summary in Croatian. See no. 490 in this volume.

An analysis of two laments recorded in 1957 among the Çam people from the Toskëri language group, near the town of Vlorë.

3069 STOCKMANN, Doris. **Zur musikalischenas Struktur einiger mehrstimmiger Gesänge der südalbanischen Laben** [The musical structure of some polyphonic songs of the Lab people of southern Albania], *Rad VIII-og kongresa folklorista Jugoslavije* (Beograd: Naučno Delo, 1961) 445–46. *Port.* In German. See no. 446 in this volume.

Discusses three three-part men's songs (choral drone and two solo voices) of the Lab people, recorded on the southern Albanian coast near Saranda. *(David Bloom)*

3070 STOCKMANN, Doris. **Zur Vokalmusik deras südalbanischen Çamen** [The vocal music of the Southern Albanian Çamen], *Journal of the International Folk Music Council* XV (1963) 38–44. *Transcr.* In German; summary in English. See no. 459 in this volume.

3071 STOCKMANN, Doris; STOCKMANN, Erich.as **Die vokale Bordun-Mehrstimmigkeit in Südalbanien** [Vocal drone polyphony in southern Albania], *Les colloques de Wégimont. IV: Ethnomusicologie III* (Paris: Belles Lettres, 1964) 85–135. *Transcr.* In German. See no. 401 in this volume.

Report on a field expedition.

3072 STOCKMANN, Erich. **Kaukasiche und**
as **albanische Mehrstimmigkeit** [Caucasian and Albanian polyphony], *Bericht über den internationalen
musikwissenschaftlichen Kongreß* (Kassel: Bärenreiter,
1957) 229–31. *Transcr.* In German. See no. 356 in this
volume.

Marius Schneider has drawn parallels between the polyphony of the Caucasus region and that of medieval Europe; similar relations also exist between
Caucasian polyphony and that practiced in the Tosk communities of southern Albania, although in this case no genetic inferences can be made.
(David Bloom)

3073 STOCKMANN, Erich. **Mehrstimmige Gesänge**
as **in Südalbanien** [Polyphonic singing in southern Al-
bania], *Journal of the International Folk Music Council*
XII (1960) 79–80. In German. See no. 413 in this
volume.

Reports on field research among two of the three principal ethnic groups of
the region, the Tosk and the Lab. Women and men of both groups practice
variants of a characteristic polyphonic singing style; the Lab approach
tends to emphasize the text. *(James R. Cowdery)*

3074 STOJANOVIĆ, Josip. **Some methods applied**
as **to broadcasting folk music at the Yugoslav**
broadcasting stations: Genuine musical folk-
lore and reconstructions, *Journal of the International Folk Music Council* XI (1959) 79–81. See no.
392 in this volume.

3075 STRÁNSKÁ, Drahomíra. **L'état actuel de la**
as **chanson populaire dans les montagnes des**
Géants (Krkonose) [The current state of traditional
song in the Riesengebirge (Krkonoše)], *Congrès international des arts populaires/International congress of
popular arts* (Paris: Institut international de
coopération intellectuelle, 1928) 112–13. In French.
See no. 153 in this volume.

Summary of the paper abstracted as no. 3076 in this volume.

3076 STRÁNSKÁ, Drahomíra. **L'état actuel de la**
as **chanson populaire dans les Monts des Géants**
(Krkonose) [The current state of traditional song in
the Riesengebirge (Krkonoše)], *Art populaire: Travaux
artistiques et scientifiques du Ier Congrès international
des arts populaires* (Paris: Duchartre, 1931) 148–50. In
French. See no. 152 in this volume.

Until late in the 19th c., the inhabitants of the Czech portion of the
Riesengebirge were largely occupied in spinning and weaving as a cottage
industry and had little direct contact with the rest of the world. The advent
of textile factories has not caused the disappearance of traditional songs in
the strict sense—ballads and lyric, military, and religious songs—but it has
led to the spread of new songs by broadsheet distribution, as well as lyric
and patriotic songs of urban origin. The question of the relation between
song and work and spiritual needs in contemporary life is examined. A
summary is cited as no. 3075 in this volume. *(David Bloom)*

3077 SUPPAN, Wolfgang. **Über die Totenklage im**
as **deutschen Sprachraum** [Funeral laments in the
German-speaking lands], *Journal of the International
Folk Music Council* XV (1963) 18–24. *Bibliog.,
transcr.* In German; summary in English. See no. 459 in
this volume.

A traditional lament from Siebenbürgen (Transylvania) is discussed and
compared with laments from other parts of Europe and with elements of
Gregorian chant. *(James R. Cowdery)*

3078 SZABOLCSI, Bence. **Hebrew recitative-types**
as **in Hungary,** *Journal of the International Folk Music
Council* XVI (1964) 65. See no. 463 in this volume.

Summary of a survey of Jewish liturgical practice in the Hungarian
Ashkenazic rite, special features found within family ceremony, and Eastern European and Hungarian influence on secular melodies. *(Vivian Conejero)*

3079 TANCREDI, G. **Canti e balli garganici** [Songs
as and dances of the Gargano region], *Atti del 4.
Congresso nazionale di arti e tradizioni popolari*
(Roma: Opera Nazionale Dopolavoro, 1942) 428–28.
In Italian. See no. 270 in this volume.

3080 TIBALDI CHIESA, Mary. **I canti popolari**
as **siciliani e la musica greca negli studi de Ettore**
Romagnoli [Sicilian traditional songs and Greek mu-
sic in the scholarship of Ettore Romagnoli], *Atti del
Congresso internazionale di musiche popolari
mediterranee e del Convegno dei bibliotecari musicali*
(Palermo: De Magistris succ. V. Bellotti, 1959) 95–99.
In Italian. See no. 332 in this volume.

Romagnoli (1871-1938) headed the effort to revive classic Greek drama in
the amphitheater at Syracuse, for which he attempted to create authentic music, with remarkable success. He took an interest in traditional Sicilian music,
in which he saw the traces of the ancient Greek modes, and also supported the
project of compiling a corpus of Mediterranean music. *(David Bloom)*

3081 TIBALDI CHIESA, Mary. **Canzoni popolari**
as **valdostane** [Traditional songs of Valle d'Aosta], *Atti
del III Congresso nazionale di arti e tradizioni popolari*
(Roma: Opera Nazionale Dopolavoro, 1936) 397–97.
In Italian. See no. 218 in this volume.

3082 TIBY, Ottavio. **La tradizione del canto**
as **popolare in Sicilia e nelle regioni mediterranee**
[The tradition of song in Sicily and the Mediterranean
regions], *Atti del Congresso internazionale di musiche
popolari mediterranee e del Convegno dei bibliotecari
musicali* (Palermo: De Magistris succ. V. Bellotti,
1959) 37–46. In Italian. See no. 332 in this volume.

In Sicilian song, the lack of a metric correspondence between text and music suggests that the latter came first. The role of traditional melodic structure in the evolution of a tonal sense is also discussed.

3083 TIERSOT, Julien. **Les chansons populaires de la**
as **France et de la Catalogne** [Traditional songs of
France and Catalonia], *Congrés de la Societat
Internacional de Musicologia* (Barcelona: Casa de
Caritat, 1936). In French. See no. 224 in this volume.

The conference report provides only a citation. Neither the text nor a summary of the paper was published here.

3084 TIMKO, Onufrij. **Punktirani ritmovi u**
as **muzičkom folkloru vojvođanskih rusina-**
ukrajinaca [Punctuated rhythm in the traditional
Ruthenian-Ukrainian music of Vojvodina], *Rad
kongresa folklorista Jugoslavije* (Zagreb: Savez
Udruženja Folklorista Jugoslavije, 1959) 103–12.
Transcr. In Serbian; summary in English. See no. 382 in
this volume.

Before World War I it was common for young people of the Ukrainian minority in what is now Vojvodina to sing traditional Ukrainian songs with a
csárdás rhythm; after the foundation of Yugoslavia, they stopped the practice, as they eliminated lexical borrowings from the Hungarian language.
(author)

3085 TIMKO, Onufrij. **Ukrajinski muzički folklor u**
as **Vojvodini** [Ukrainian traditional music in Vojvodina],
Rad kongresa folklorista Jugoslavije (Zagreb: Savez

Udruženja Folklorista Jugoslavije, 1958) 125–36. In Serbian; summary in English. See no. 315 in this volume.

3086
as
TOSCHI, Paolo. **Etnofonia e musica popolare siciliana e sarda** [*Etnofonia* and the traditional music of Sicily and Sardinia], *Atti del Congresso internazionale di musiche popolari mediterranee e del Convegno dei bibliotecari musicali* (Palermo: De Magistris succ. V. Bellotti, 1959) 89–90. In Italian. See no. 332 in this volume.

The term *etnofonia* (ethnophony) has been fairly widely adopted in the discussion of Italian traditional music, with some unfortunate consequences, suggesting that the music has a primitive, unreflected character, as is not at all the case. It is important to treat the traditional music especially of Sicily and Sardinia in historical terms, with the full range of musicological techniques. *(David Bloom)*

3087
as
TREBJEŠANIN, Radoš. **Dramski elementi u dečjim pesmama za igru u leskovačkom kraju** [Dramatic elements in children's singing games in the Leskovac region], *Rad X-og kongresa Saveza Folklorista Jugoslavije* (Cetinje: Obod, 1964) 413–23. In Serbian; summary in French. See no. 462 in this volume.

Singing games collected in this region lack poetic character, emotion, and picturesque expressions; however, they are rich in rhythm, dialogue, monologue, and acoustic elements. *(author)*

3088
as
TRÉBUCQ, Sylvain. **Les chansons de mariage en Vendée** [Wedding songs of the Vendée], *La tradition en Poitou et Charentes: Art populaire, ethnographie, folk-lore, hagiographie, histoire* (Paris: Librairie de la Tradition Nationale, 1897) 385–96. In French. See no. 21 in this volume.

The courting and wedding tradition in Vendée includes several ceremonial songs.

3089
as
TRINCHIERI, Romolo. **Il canto a braccio tra pastori-poeti nel Monterealese** [The *canto a braccio* among the shepherd-poets in the Montereale area], *Lares* XXV (1959) 267–80. In Italian. See no. 370 in this volume.

Discusses the local version of the central Italian song genre, with its improvised texts.

3090
as
TRON, Emilio. **Canzoni popolari valdesi del risorgimento** [Traditional songs of the Vaudois valleys from the Risorgimento], *Lares* XX/1-2 (1954) 44f. In Italian. See no. 288 in this volume.

3091
as
TRON, Emilio. **Cenno sui canti popolari delle Valli Valdesi** [Survey of the traditional songs of the Vaudois valleys], *Lares* XX/1-2 (1954) 106f. In Italian. See no. 288 in this volume.

3092
as
TURINA, Joaquín. **El cant populár andaluz** [Andalusian traditional song], *Congrés de la Societat Internacional de Musicologia* (Barcelona: Casa de Caritat, 1936). In Catalan. See no. 224 in this volume.

The conference report provides only a citation. Neither the text nor a summary of the paper was published here.

3093
as
VÁCLAVEK, Bedřich. **Les chansons profanes tchèques devenues populaires** [Secular Czech songs that have become folk songs], *Art populaire: Travaux artistiques et scientifiques du Ier Congrès in-*

ternational des arts populaires (Paris: Duchartre, 1931) 140–45. In French. See no. 152 in this volume.

Surveys the concept and history of popular song, from its 19th-c. origins, on the basis of Czech examples. A summary is cited as no. 3236 in this volume.

3094
as
VANCEA, Zeno. **Einige Beiträge über das erste Manuskript der Colinda-Sammlung von Béla Bartók und über seine einschlägigen Briefe an Constantin Brăiloiu** [Notes on the first manuscript of Béla Bartók's colinda collection and his relevant letters to Constatin Brăiloiu], *Studia musicologica Academiae Scientiarum Hungaricae* V (1963) 549–56. In German. See no. 427 in this volume.

An autograph MS of Bartók's *Melodien der rumänischen Colinde (Weihnachtslieder)* (Vienna, 1935) was found among Brăiloiu's papers after his death in 1958. Its annotations include some of Brăiloiu's translations of the colinda texts. *(William Renwick)*

3095
as
VARAGNAC, Andre. **Les loisirs ouvriers, utilisation du folklore pour les fêtes** [Workers' leisure: Uses of folklore in festivals], *Congrès international de l'enseignement primaire et de l'éducation populaire* (Paris: S.U.D.E.L., 1938) 534–35. In French. See no. 246 in this volume.

3096
as
VARGYAS, Lajos. **The importance of the Hungarian ballads on the confines of Occident and Orient,** *Europa et Hungaria: Congressus ethnographicus in Hungaria* (Budapest: Akadémiai Kiadó, 1965) 325–33. *Bibliog.* See no. 460 in this volume.

Hungarian ballads show features from the Central Asian homeland and others adopted from neighboring peoples of Central Europe. Some ballad features originating among Hungarians have been transmitted to other Central European peoples. *(Won-Bin Yim)*

3097
as
VASILJEVIĆ, Miodrag A. **Funkcije i vrste glasova u srpskom narodnom pevanju: Objašnjenje reči** [Voice functions and types in traditional Serbian song: An interpretive account], *Rad VII-og kongresa Saveza Folklorista Jugoslavije* (Cetinje: Obod, 1964) 375–80. *Charts, diagr.* In Serbian; summary in Russian. See no. 419 in this volume.

3098
as
VASILJEVIĆ, Miodrag A. **Muzički folklor u zaječarskom kraju** [Traditional music in the Zaječar region], *Rad kongresa folklorista Jugoslavije* (Beograd: Naučno Delo, 1960) 29–40. *Illus., transcr.* In Serbian; summary in French. See no. 402 in this volume.

The outstanding features of the traditional music of the Zaječar region of eastern Serbia are the great antiquity of the material among the Serb-speaking population (where ritual songs of the pre-Christian Kupalo cult can be found), the richness of rhythm and meter among the Bulgarian speakers, and the perfected scales used by the Vlachs. *(author)*

3099
as
VAUX-PHALIPAU, Marie de. **Moeurs des Serbes de Lusace d'après les chansons populaires** [The customs of the Sorb people of Lusatia as seen in traditional songs], *XVe Congrès international d'anthropologie et d'archéologie préhistorique (suite); V^e session de l'Institut International d'Anthropologie* (Paris: Nourry, 1933) 715–16. In French. See no. 192 in this volume.

Brief remarks on the richness of the Sorb (Wendish) song repertoire and the evidence it provides on typically Sorb traits, such as love of nature (derived from Slavic pre-Christian religion), value placed on sexual fidelity, brother-sister attachment, and oral transmission of folklore from mother to daughter. *(David Bloom)*

3100 VETTERL, Karel. **Folk song of East Czechoslo-**
as **vakia: Methods of performance and notation,**
Journal of the International Folk Music Council I
(1949) 35–37. See no. 281 in this volume.
Discusses aspects of songs from Moravia and Slovakia, including issues regarding rhythmic transcription.

3101 VETTERL, Karel. **Otázky tvůrčího a**
as **reprodukčního stylu v lidové písni** [Questions of
creative and reproductive styles in folk music], *Leoš
Janáček a soudobá hudba* (Praha: Panton, 1963)
345–51. *Music.* In Czech; summaries in Russian and
German. See no. 389 in this volume.
Janáček was one of the first to recognize that a specific performance situation determines the creative variability of melody and rhythm of folk songs,
as in the case of the variants of a given tune being used in dance and
non-dance situations. Dance songs of the Carpathian region of Moravia,
Silesia and Slovakia show an intersection between the archaic
tonal-melodic thinking and the modern harmonic feeling, resulting in interesting tonal-harmonic combinations. *(editors)*

3102 VODUŠEK, Valens. **Alpske poskočne pesmi v**
as **Sloveniji** [Alpine *poskočna* songs in Slovenia], *Rad
kongresa folklorista Jugoslavije* (Ljubljana: Savez
Udruženja Folkloristov Jugoslavije, 1960) 55–78.
Charts, diagr., transcr. In Slovene; summary in English. See no. 404 in this volume.
The *poskočnica* is a Slovene song form, originally consisting of a single
quatrain verse, analogous to the Austrian Schnaderhüpfel. It once was an
improvised accompaniment, alternating with instrumental accompaniment, to the štajriš dance; during the 19th c. it became detached from the
dance and underwent considerable changes in form, varying from region to
region. *(author)*

3103 VODUŠEK, Valens. **The correlation between**
as **metrical verse structure, rhythmical and me-**
lodic structure in folk songs, *Journal of the International Folk Music Council* XII (1960) 67–68. See no.
413 in this volume.
Summary of a paper. Describes findings regarding traditional Slovene
songs.

3104 VODUŠEK, Valens. **Midsummer ritual songs**
as **in Yugoslavia,** *Journal of the International Folk Music Council* IX (1957) 50. See no. 362 in this volume.
The conference report provides only a citation. Neither the text nor a summary of the paper was published here.

3105 VODUŠEK, Valens. **Neka zapažanja o**
as **baladnim napevima na području Slovenije** [Ob-
servations on the melodies of ballads in Slovenian terri-
tory], *Rad kongresa folklorista Jugoslavije* (Beograd:
Naučno Delo, 1960) 109–18. *Transcr.* In Croatian; summary in German. See no. 402 in this volume.
Traditional ballad melodies in Slovenia show the same heterogeneity as the
population; generalizations are difficult to make. One strong common feature seems to be a strict rhythm, unlike the recitativo parlando character of
Yugoslavian epic song. Another is the division of singers into groups, as
between a leader and a chorus; this is inferrable even for the oldest songs,
which lack refrains, in the dominant three-line structure. A rhythmic
typology could be constructed for Slovenian ballad melodies on the basis
of provenance and relative age. *(author)*

3106 VODUŠEK, Valens. **Petčetvrtinski takt u**
as **slovenskoj narodnoj muzici** [The 5/4 measure in
traditional Slovenian music], *Rad kongresa folklorista
Jugoslavije* (Zagreb: Savez Udruženja Folklorista
Jugoslavije, 1959) 87–88. In Croatian; summary in
German. See no. 382 in this volume.

The five-beat unit typical of Slovene music, a regular alternation of a
three-beat and a two-beat measure, was originally tied to dance forms, but
is now most frequently found in ballads and songs associated with traditional customs. Formal comparative analysis indicates its archaic origin,
but it is not found in other Slavic cultures; its relative frequency in western
Alpine Germany and much greater frequency in central France and Brittany
suggests that it may have originated in a Celtic substratum. *(author)*

3107 VODUŠEK, Valens. **Wichtige archaische**
as **Funde in den Alpen** [Important archaic finds in the
Alps], *Journal of the International Folk Music Council*
XV (1963) 25. In German. See no. 459 in this volume.
The inhabitants of Resia, an Alpine community of 3000 in northern Italy
near the Slovenian border, speak an archaic Slovenian dialect. Their music,
very likely the relic of a widely disseminated culture, is also markedly archaic. Its main feature is a two-voice polyphony in which the lower voice is
a drone. Within the confines of this practice are traces of every historical
stage of music from its earliest beginnings to the present. The polyphony of
Resia may provide clues about the origins of present-day Alpine polyphony
and shed light on the preponderance of the major mode in Central European
traditional music. *(Carl Skoggard)*

3108 VUJICSICS, Tihamér. **Narodne pesme i igre**
as **jugoslovenskih manjina u Mađarskoj** [Tradi-
tional songs and dances of the South Slavic minorities
in Hungary], *Rad kongresa folklorista Jugoslavije*
(Zagreb: Savez Udruženja Folklorista Jugoslavije,
1959) 95–101. *Transcr.* In Serbian. See no. 382 in this
volume.

3109 VUJICSICS, Tihamér. **Razvoj srpsko-hrvatske**
as **instrumentalne muzike u Mađarskoj** [The de-
velopment of Serbo-Croatian instrumental music in
Hungary], *Rad VII-og kongresa Saveza Folkloristov
Jugoslavije* (Cetinje: Obod, 1964) 407–08. In Serbian.
See no. 419 in this volume.
Summary of a paper.

3110 VUKMANOVIĆ, Jovan. **Opšti pogled na**
as **crnogorski folklor** [General survey of Montenegrin
folklore], *Treći kongres folklorista Jugoslavije* (Cetinje:
Udruženje Folklorista Crne Gore, 1958) 11–19. *Illus.* In
Serbian; summary in French. See no. 357 in this volume.
Montenegrin folklore is considered in three regions: old Montenegro,
where traditional customs are still preserved in everyday life and folklore is
in its most authentic form; the Montenegrin mountains, where folklore is
influenced by Herzegovina, Sandžak, and Metohija; and the Montenegrin
coast, which has Mediterranean and Albanian influences. In old
Montenegro and the Montenegrin mountains, the characteristic dances are
the udvaje, the zetsko kolo, and the crmničko kolo, which may be performed successively. Dance in Boka Kotorska is significantly influenced
by the West. The most widespread dance is the svatovsko kolo, which has
several regional variants (miljansko kolo, crčanjsko kolo, dobrotsko kolo,
škaljsko kolo). Until World War II, on the feast of St. Tripun (3 February),
Kotor's patron saint, men in Boka Kotorska danced the kolo Bokeljske
Mornarice (kolo of the Navy of Boka Kotorska). The best-known songs are
epics performed with the gusle. *(Zdravko Blažeković)*

3111 VUKOSAVLJEV, Sava. **Tragom revolucio-**
as **narne i borbene pesme po Vojvodini** [On the
study of revolutionary and war song in Vojvodina], *Rad
kongresa folklorista Jugoslavije* (Ljubljana: Savez
Udruženja Folkloristov Jugoslavije, 1960) 217–20. In
Serbian; summary in French. See no. 404 in this
volume.
When the working class was first formed, its songs reflected social-
democratic ideas; new subjects arose from its encounters with the bourgeoisie, as in the case of the 1907 strike song of the agricultural workers at
Melenci, and their number rose rapidly in response to the activities of the
Komunistička Partija Jugoslavije in 1935-41. During the War of National
Liberation they were sung throughout Vojvodina, by members of all ethnic

groups. Partisan songs in Vojvodina are generally 8-12 measures in length, with a richer melodic line than imported songs, a simple rhythmic structure, and a variable line length of 6-13 syllables. *(author)*

3112 VUKOVIĆ, Jovan. **Intonacioni momenti i**
as **struktura stiha u tužbalicama** [Elements of intonation and verse structure in laments], *Rad VII-og kongresa Saveza Folklorista Jugoslavije* (Cetinje: Obod, 1964) 411–17. In Bosnian; summary in French. See no. 419 in this volume.

In the Durmitor region of northern Montenegro, the melodic contours of octosyllabic laments, treated as intonation contours like those of the spoken language, show an alternation between falling, short, accented patterns and rising, long ones accented only on the last syllable. These patterns vary even over a relatively narrow geographical range. *(author)*

3113 VULETIĆ-VUKASOVIĆ, Vid. **A few notes on**
as **the songs of the Southern Slavs,** *The International Folk-lore Congress of the World's Columbian Exposition. I* (Chicago: Charles H. Sergel, 1898) 83–87. See no. 18 in this volume.

The huge repertoire of Southern Slavic traditional songs is divided into four categories: (1) mythical, (2) heroic, (3) love songs, and (4) ballads. The heroic songs are usually about the defeat of the emperor in 1389 at Kosovo, and are accompanied by the gusle. An example from each category is included in English and in the original language. *(Ken Alboum)*

3114 WEBSTER, Wentworth. **Des caractères de**
as **l'improvisation populaire: L'improvisation parmi les Basques et les Béarnais** [Types of traditional improvisation: The improvisation among the Basques and in Béarn], *[I^e] Congrès international des traditions populaires* (Paris: Société d'Éditions Scientifiques, 1891). In French. See no. 13 in this volume.

3115 WIDSTRAND, Carl. **Skolt Lapp songs of N.E.**
as **Finland,** *VIe Congrès international des sciences anthropologiques et ethnologiques. I: Rapport général et anthropologie; II: Ethnologie* (Paris: Musée de l'Homme, 1962-1964) II, 127–27. See no. 421 in this volume.

Discusses the music of a Sámi community in northeastern Finland. Also published in *Journal of the International Folk Music Council* 13 (1961).

3116 WIORA, Walter. **Gesungene Erzählung als**
as **Strophenlied: Zur Problemgeschichte der altdeutschen Ballade und verwandter Gattungen** [Sung narrative as strophic song: The historical problematics of the Old German ballad and related genres], *Les colloques de Wégimont. [I: Ethnomusicologie I]* (Bruxelles: Elsevier, 1956) 120–31. *Transcr.* In German. See no. 340 in this volume.

Strict ballad form, with its multiply repeated stanza melody, seems inappropriate to narrative; hence the through-composed form and recitative in art ballads by composers like Karl Loewe and Schubert. The view of strophic form as central to the German ballad tradition may be a distortion imposed by the collectors of the late 18th and early 19th c.; a broader consideration, including the linguistic enclaves of Lorraine, Russia, and Siebenbürgen and extending back to the 15th c., shows that the tradition makes considerable use of epic melody, recitative and declamation, and melismatic variation. *(David Bloom)*

3117 WITTROCK, Wolfgang. **Volkslieder in**
as **Schleswig-Holstein** [Traditional songs in Schleswig-Holstein], *Norddeutsche und nordeuropäische Musik* (Kassel; New York: Bärenreiter, 1965) 100–07. *Music, transcr.* In German. See no. 467 in this volume.

Historical survey of literary references from as early as the end of the 16th c., of 19th-c. collections, and of 20th-c. studies, with attention to relationships with Danish and West Prussian songs. *(David Bloom)*

3118 WÜNSCH, Walther. **The changing shape and**
as **the disappearance of Styrian folk song,** *Journal of the International Folk Music Council* IX (1957) 45–46. See no. 362 in this volume.

The preservation of authentic singing traditions is a challenge, particularly when watered-down imitations proliferate.

3119 WÜNSCH, Walther. **Die südosteuropäische**
as **Volksepik, die Ballade und das Tanzlied im Vergleich zu den Frühformen in der abendländischen Musikkultur** [The folk epic of Southeastern Europe, the ballad, and the dance song, compared with the early forms of Western music culture], *Bericht über den Internationalen musikwissenschaftlichen Kongress* (Kassel: Bärenreiter, 1954) 200–03. In German. See no. 319 in this volume.

The traditional music of Montenegro and Herzegovina is a self-contained art whose contents and form are distinctive. Undoubtedly this regional music is very ancient. The local epic tradition is described with attention to its music and language, as is the repertoire of unaccompanied songs sung by women, the starine (starice), which are closely related to the epic. Also discussed are latter-day musical phenomena that represent mainly a decaying of older practices. *(Carl Skoggard)*

3120 WÜNSCH, Walther. **Über Schallaufnahmen**
as **südosteuropäischer Volksepik in der Zeit von 1900 bis 1930** [Sound recordings of southeastern European folk epic in the period 1900-1930], *Bericht über den internationalen musikwissenschaftlichen Kongreß* (Kassel: Bärenreiter, 1963) 317–18. In German. See no. 452 in this volume.

The earliest recordings of Serbian and Croatian epics were made at the turn of the 20th c. under the sponsorship of the Vienna Phonogrammarchiv, in the context of language and dialect research. These and later recordings, sound films, and magnetic tape recordings are discussed. *(David Bloom)*

3121 WÜNSCH, Walther. **Zur Frage der Mehr-**
as **stimmigkeit des alpenländischen Volksliedes (Steirische Landschaft)** [The question of polyphony in the Alpine traditional song (Styria)], *Bericht über den siebenten internationalen musikwissenschaftlichen Kongress* (Kassel: Bärenreiter, 1959) 316–18. In German. See no. 390 in this volume.

Monophonic singing has rarely been cultivated in the Alpine region, as represented by Styria. Polyphonic practices include the Liedertafel style of men's group singing, of relatively recent origin and transmitted by notation; the orally transmitted style known as *volksgebundene Polyphonie*, with its two to five voices often including a drone; and multiple-voice yodeling. A reconstruction of the earliest Alpine polyphony might begin by relating it to the art-music techniques of canon, gymel or cantus gemellus, and fauxbourdon. *(David Bloom)*

3122 ZAMFIR, Constantin. **The instrumental basis**
as **of vocal style in Năsăud,** *Journal of the International Folk Music Council* XII (1960) 62–63. *Music.* See no. 413 in this volume.

Summary of a paper. Discusses similarities in vocal and fluier ornamentation among inhabitants of the Năsăud disctict of Romania. *(James R. Cowdery)*

3123 ŽGANEC, Vinko. **Muzički folklor naroda u**
as **panonskom bazenu** [Traditional music of the Pannonian basin], *Rad kongresa folklorista Jugoslavije* (Zagreb: Savez Udruženja Folklorista Jugoslavije, 1959) 71–76. In Croatian; summary in German. See no. 382 in this volume.

All the ethnic groups of the Pannonian basin have at least some traits in common in their traditional music; the larger the group, the more strongly marked these traits are. They may represent survivals of the tradition of the Pannonian Slavs from before the arrival of Magyars in the region. *(author)*

3124
as
ŽGANEC, Vinko. **O muzičkom aspektu narodnih balada na hrvatskom etničkom području** [Musical aspects of the traditional ballad in ethnic-Croatian territory], *Rad kongresa folklorista Jugoslavije* (Beograd: Naučno Delo, 1960) 119–22. In Croatian; summary in German. See no. 402 in this volume.

Discusses rhythm, tempo, melodic structure, scales, textual metrics, and the use of ballads to accompany dance. The latter may be rhythmically synchronized with the dance, polyrhythmically related to it, or wholly independent. Textual repetitions observed in ballad singing used to accompany kolo in Novi Vinodol provide evidence that ballads are not derived from the abridgment of epic songs. The current degeneration of the ballad in Croatian territory is noted. *(author)*

3125
as
ŽGANEC, Vinko. **Pjesme uz rad nekad i danas** [Work songs in past and present], *Rad VIII-og kongresa folklorista Jugoslavije* (Beograd: Naučno Delo, 1961) 347–51. In Croatian; summary in German. See no. 446 in this volume.

The evolution from the archaic communal harvest custom known as *moba* to the new communal work units (whose specific character derives from socialism and from the soldiers of the War of National Liberation) corresponds to an evolution in folkloric expression. *(author)*

3126
as
ZODER, Raimund. **Über den Takt des Ländlers in Oberösterreich** [On the meter of the Ländler in Upper Austria], *Haydn-Zentenarfeier* (Leipzig: Breitkopf & Härtel; Wien: Artaria, 1909) 228–30. *Transcr.* In German. See no. 65 in this volume.

An unusual form of the Ländler in duple meter may be found among samples gathered by the author and presently located in his private collection.

3127
as
ZULAICA Y ARREGUI, José Gonzalo (José Antonio de Donostia). **La canción popular religiosa y artística** [Religious and artistic popular song], *Crónica del IV Congreso Nacional de Música Sagrada* (Vitoria: Imprenta del Montepío Diocesano, 1930) 248–67. In Spanish. See no. 155 in this volume.

Analyzes the tradition of popular songs based on religious topics in the Basque region.

3128
as
ZULAICA Y ARREGUI, José Gonzalo (José Antonio de Donostia). **El canto popular religioso en España** [Traditional religious song in Spain], *Atti del [I] Congresso internazionale di musica sacra* (Tournai: Desclée, 1952) 291–94. In Spanish. See no. 303 in this volume.

3129
as
ZULAICA Y ARREGUI, José Gonzalo (José Antonio de Donostia). **Cuestiones de canto popular religioso español** [Questions concerning traditional Spanish religious song], *V Congreso Nacional de Música Sagrada* (Madrid: Gráficas Dos de Mayo, 1956) 309–21. In Spanish. See no. 331 in this volume.

Religious song in Spain, in its current form, is relatively modern, unlike that of France or Germany. Most of the songs are not of a liturgical character. Regional and occasional genres are surveyed, including the goig or gozo genre of Catalonia and the east, songs praying for rain, songs of catechism, and songs for Easter and Christmas. *(José López-Calo)*

3130
as
ZULAICA Y ARREGUI, José Gonzalo (José Antonio de Donostia). **La musique basque** [Basque music], *Congrès international des arts populaires/International congress of popular arts* (Paris: Institut international de coopération intellectuelle, 1928) 117–18. In French. See no. 153 in this volume.

Summary of the paper abstracted as no. 3131 in this volume.

3131
as
ZULAICA Y ARREGUI, José Gonzalo (José Antonio de Donostia). **La musique populaire basque** [Traditional Basque music], *Art populaire: Travaux artistiques et scientifiques du Iᵉʳ Congrès international des arts populaires* (Paris: Duchartre, 1931) 155–57. In French. See no. 152 in this volume.

Survey of scales and modes, rhythms, genres, instruments, and research and preservation efforts. A summary is cited as no. 3130 in this volume.

3132
as
ŽUNIĆ, Leposava. **Pesme užičkog partizanskog odreda** [Songs of the Užice Partisan forces], *Rad VIII-og kongresa folklorista Jugoslavije* (Beograd: Naučno Delo, 1961) 137–41. In Serbian; summary in French. See no. 446 in this volume.

An overview of songs dealing with the battles, sufferings, heroism, and victories of the Partisans in the Užice region during the War of National Liberation. Some come from the combatants themselves, but most are from the villages, where people enjoyed singing about the participation in the struggle of their own family members. *(author)*

35 North America (north of Mexico)

3133
as
ARNOLD, Byron. **Some historical folk songs from Alabama,** *Journal of the International Folk Music Council* VI (1954) 45–47. See no. 320 in this volume.

Describes fieldwork undertaken in the 1940s.

3134
as
BALYS, Jonas. **Lithuanian folk songs in the United States,** *Journal of the International Folk Music Council* III (1951) 67–70. See no. 296 in this volume.

Discusses song types as well as the more recent songs of emigration.

3135
as
BARBEAU, Marius. **Buddhist dirges on the North Pacific coast,** *Journal of the International Folk Music Council* XIV (1962) 16–21. *Port., transcr.* See no. 442 in this volume.

Remarkable parallels are to be found between funeral songs of the native peoples of British Columbia and Alaska and the music of Buddhist peoples of East Asia, in general melodic style, linguistically similar words, and the use of similar skin drums. It is unlikely that these parallels are coincidental. *(David Bloom)*

3136
as
BARBEAU, Marius. **Canadian folk songs,** *Journal of the International Folk Music Council* XIII (1961) 28–31. *List of works.* See no. 424 in this volume.

A historical survey of ethnomusicological collection activities in Canada, with a list of published, unpublished, and recorded sources for Native, English, and French traditional songs, and an inventory of the holdings of the Archives de Folklore, Université Laval, from 1950 to 1960. *(Alix Moyer Grunebaum)*

3137
as
BARBEAU, Marius. **La chanson populaire française en Amerique du Nord** [The French folk song in North America], *Journal of the International Folk Music Council* VI (1954) 7–10. *Music.* In French. See no. 320 in this volume.

The rich heritage of French traditional music in Canada is exemplified by the boatman's song *Le roi Eugène*, a satire on King François I from not much later than 1526. Wholly unknown in France, it has been collected in Quebec and the Maritime Provinces in some 27 different versions.

(David Bloom)

3138 BARBEAU, Marius. **Migrations Sibériennes en**
as **Amérique** [Siberian migrations in America], *Miscellanea Paul Rivet octogenario dicata* (México, D.F.: Universidad Nacional Autónoma de México, 1958) I, 17–48. *Illus., port.* In French. See no. 394 in this volume.

Explores evidence of the East Asian origins of the native populations of Alaska and British Columbia, including lamentation and funeral songs.

(Murat Eyüboğlu)

3139 BAYARD, Samuel P. **Some folk fiddlers' habits**
as **and styles in western Pennsylvania,** *Journal of the International Folk Music Council* VIII (1956) 15–18. See no. 349 in this volume.

Discusses processes of oral transmission and individual variation.

3140 BÉCLARD D'HARCOURT, Marguerite.
as **Cantiques folkloriques français retrouvés en Louisiane** [Traditional French cantiques found in Louisiana], *Perspectives de la musique sacrée à la lumière de l'encyclique* Musicae sacrae disciplina (Paris: conference, 1959) 509–14. *Transcr.* In French. See no. 379 in this volume.

An account of traditional religious songs collected from French-speaking black Catholics in Louisiana by Elizabeth Brandon. The pieces retain the old diatonic modality lost in traditional song in France itself; with some reworking of the unfortunately corrupted texts, they might be used in the liturgy. Two Passion songs and a *complainte* to the Virgin are given in full.

(David Bloom)

⟶ BRONSON, Bertrand Harris. **About the commonest British ballads.** See no. 2750 in this volume.

3141 BUCHANAN, Annabel Morris. **Modal and me-**
as **lodic structure in Anglo-American folk music: A neutral mode,** *Papers read at the International Congress of Musicology* (New York: Music Educators National Conference, 1944) 84–111. *Music, charts, diagr.* See no. 266 in this volume.

New theories of the modal construction of Anglo-American traditional melodies are contrasted with those of Anne Gilchrist, Cecil Sharp, and Herman Reichenbach. *(Susan Levine)*

3142 CHAPMAN, John W. **Notes on the Tinneh tribe**
as **of Anvik, Alaska,** *Congrès international des américanistes: XVe session* (Québec: Dussault & Proulx, 1907) 32–38. *Illus.* See no. 56 in this volume.

Singing played an important role in the ceremonies of the Koyukon or Ten'a people (formerly known as Tinneh), speakers of an Athapaskan language, of Anvik at the confluence of the Anvik and Yukon rivers. Upon invitation, one village would visit another and a ceremony would take place. Employing a baton decorated with animal skin, a director would lead the guests in the singing of various chants. Unaccompanied solos alternated with full choruses, some of which were introduced by three beats of the drums. In many instances, an antiphonal section would be followed by the chorus ending with caws in imitation of a crow. *(Michael Alterman)*

3143 COWELL, Sidney Robertson. **The connection**
as **between the precenting of psalms on Cape Breton Island and in the Colonial New England churches,** *Journal of the International Folk Mu-*

sic Council XIV (1962) 155–56. See no. 442 in this volume.

Gaelic-speaking Cape Breton Islanders recorded in 1953 performed psalms in a melismatic style, led by a precentor, corresponding exactly to descriptions of psalm singing in Boston in the 17th c., but not deducible from printed psalters of the period. It may be hypothesized that the melismatic style belongs to an orally transmitted tradition from the earliest Calvinist practice. *(David Bloom)*

3144 CREIGHTON, Helen. **Songs from Nova Scotia,**
as *Journal of the International Folk Music Council* XII (1960) 84–85. See no. 413 in this volume.

Brief remarks for a presentation of a film and recordings.

3145 DENSMORE, Frances. **The music of the North**
as **American Indians,** *Actas y trabajos científicos del XXV° Congreso Internacional de Americanistas* (Buenos Aires: Coni; Universidad Nacional de La Plata, 1934) 119–26. *Charts, diagr., transcr.* See no. 198 in this volume.

More than 2000 songs from 20 tribes, transcribed over a period of 25 years, shed light on the creation of this repertoire. A dream would inspire the composition of each song, which was often later completed by two or more individuals. Accompanied by wind and percussion instruments, the songs served functional purposes in medicine, magic, and hunting, and it was common for singers to possess extensive, memorized repertoires.

(Joyce Z. Lindorff)

3146 DENSMORE, Frances. **Recent developments in**
as **the study of Indian music,** *Proceedings of the Nineteenth International Congress of Americanists* (Washington, D.C.: n.p., 1917) 298–301. See no. 91 in this volume.

Reprinted under the title *Study of Indian music* in *Scientific American supplement* 85 (1918), 253-4 and *Etude* 38 (1920), 670.

⟶ DENSMORE, Frances. **Rhythm in the music of the American Indian.** See no. 3985 in this volume.

3147 FENTON, William N.; KURATH, Gertrude
as Prokosch. **The Feast of the Dead, or ghost dance at Six Nations Reserve, Canada,** *Symposium on local diversity in Iroquois culture* (Washington, D.C.: Smithsonian Institution, 1951) 139–65. *Illus., bibliog., transcr., dance notation.* See no. 293 in this volume.

The Feast of the Dead is a constantly recurring feature in the annual ceremonial cycle of the Longhouse or Handsome Lake religion, and is celebrated in some form in all conservative Iroquois communities. Descriptions are furnished of feasts of 1945 (Onondaga Township) and 1949 (Sour Springs Longhouse) in the Six Nations Reserve near Brantford, Ontario. *(Robert Noland)*

3148 FILLMORE, John Comfort. **Primitive scales**
as **and rhythms,** *Memoirs of the International Congress of Anthropology* (Chicago: Schulte, 1894) 158–75. See no. 19 in this volume.

Discusses the Indians of British Columbia, Canada.

3149 FIRFOV, Živko. **Les émigrants macédoniens en**
as **Amérique et le folklore macédonien musical** [Macedonian emigrants to America and Macedonian musical folklore], *Journal of the International Folk Music Council* XIV (1962) 157. In French. See no. 442 in this volume.

The Macedonian community in North America stems largely from emigration following the Ilinden uprising of 1903. Its songs, in typically Macedonian octosyllabic or decasyllabic verse with refrains, treat themes of departure, separation, and return; the music is melodious and sad, but not despairing, thanks to the presence of musical elements of Asian origin. They are characteristically from the southwest of Macedonia, suggesting that this is where most immigrants came from. *(David Bloom)*

3150
as

FLETCHER, Alice Cunningham. **Love songs among the Omaha Indians,** *Memoirs of the International Congress of Anthropology* (Chicago: Schulte, 1894) 153–57. See no. 19 in this volume.

⟶ FRIEDLAENDER, Max. **German folk songs with reference to English and American folk songs.** See no. 2820 in this volume.

3151
as

GAGNON, Ernest. **Les sauvages de l'Amérique et l'art musical** [The savages of America and the musical arts], *Congrès international des américanistes: XVe session* (Québec: Dussault & Proulx, 1907). In French. See no. 56 in this volume.
Report on field observations of music among the Huron people of the Ancienne Lorette region, Quebec, beginning in the 1850s, including discussions of instruments, rhythmic patterns, and ornamentation; transcriptions of songs and dance songs; and commentary. Religious songs such as two Christmas cantiques seem to show evidence of the influence of Gregorian chant. *(David Bloom)*

3152
as

GEORGE, Graham. **Songs of the Salish Indians of British Columbia,** *Journal of the International Folk Music Council* XIV (1962) 22–29. *Transcr.* See no. 442 in this volume.
A formal and statistical analysis of 60 songs collected on wax cylinders in 1912, under the direction of Marius Barbeau, from Salish people of the Thompson and Lillooet groups. Considerations include phrase, scale, and interval structure; percussion-tune relations; and exclamations.
(June Goldenberg)

3153
as

HALPERN, Ida. **Kwa-Kiutl music,** *Journal of the International Folk Music Council* XIV (1962) 159–60. *Transcr.* See no. 442 in this volume.
Summary report on ongoing research among the Kwakiutl (Kwá-kwa-kya-wakw) people of British Columbia. Another version is published in *Proceedings of the centennial workshop on ethnomusicology* (Victoria, 1968) and cited as RILM ¹⁹⁹⁸8388. *(David Bloom)*

3154
as

HALPERT, Herbert. **Vitality of tradition and local songs,** *Journal of the International Folk Music Council* III (1951) 35–40. See no. 296 in this volume.
Discusses traditional songs collected in New Jersey.

3155
as

HERZOG, George. **African influences in North American Indian music,** *Papers read at the International Congress of Musicology* (New York: Music Educators National Conference, 1944) 130–43. *Music.* See no. 266 in this volume.
Discusses possible connections between African-American music and Native American music in the southeastern U.S.

⟶ HERZOG, George. **Musical styles in North America.** See no. 3305 in this volume.

3156
as

JACKSON, George Pullen. **Native and imported elements in American religious folk songs,** *Journal of the International Folk Music Council* III (1951) 70–74. See no. 296 in this volume.
Discusses aspects of older European Protestant songs flourishing in the U.S., as well as those of the newer spirituals that arose there.
(James R. Cowdery)

3157
as

JACKSON, George Pullen. **Some enemies of folk-music in North America,** *Papers read at the International Congress of Musicology* (New York: Music Educators National Conference, 1944) 77–83. See no. 266 in this volume.
Discusses ethnic, geographic, and musical prejudices.

3158
as

KLUSÁK, Vladimír. **Songs of Czechs and Slovaks residing in America,** *Journal of the International Folk Music Council* XIV (1962) 164. See no. 442 in this volume.
Songs collected in Pennsylvania and Ohio by Karel Plicka, George Gershon Korson, and the author illustrate the cultural adaptations of immigrants from Slovakia and southeastern Moravia. *(David Bloom)*

3159
as

KNOTT, Sarah Gertrude. **The National Folk Festival, United States,** *Journal of the International Folk Music Council* III (1951) 27–29. See no. 296 in this volume.
The festival's founder and director discusses its premiere in 1934 and its subsequent development.

3160
as

KURATH, Gertrude Prokosch. **Effects of environment on Cherokee-Iroquois ceremonialism, music, and dance,** *Symposium on Cherokee and Iroquois culture* (Washington, D.C.: United States Government Printing Office, 1961) 173–95. *Bibliog., transcr.* See no. 400 in this volume.

3161
as

KURATH, Gertrude Prokosch. **Iroquois midwinter medicine rites,** *Journal of the International Folk Music Council* III (1951) 96–100. *Charts, diagr., transcr.* See no. 296 in this volume.
Discusses curing ceremonies on Six Nations Reserve, Ontario.

3162
as

KURATH, Gertrude Prokosch. **Local diversity in Iroquois music and dance,** *Symposium on local diversity in Iroquois culture* (Washington, D.C.: Smithsonian Institution, 1951) 109–37. *Illus., music, bibliog.* See no. 293 in this volume.
In Iroquois communities from Ontario to northern New York and northeastern Oklahoma, exposure to modernization, electricity, and modern-day occupations have had an effect on the diffusion and development of ceremonial forms, bringing about divergent local functions. Religious and social conditions have also contributed to these deviations; other local deviations are inherent parts of some songs and dances. *(Robert Noland)*

3163
as

LANGE, Francisco Curt. **Investigation and preservation of authentic folk music in Latin America,** *Journal of the International Folk Music Council* VII (1955) 20–21. See no. 337 in this volume.
Summary of a paper discussing the state of research and the need for more active preservation of traditional music.

3164
as

LIST, George. **Song in the Hopi culture, past and present,** *Journal of the International Folk Music Council* XIV (1962) 30–35. *Transcr.* See no. 442 in this volume.
Hopi culture is undoubtedly in crisis, but certain music and dance traditions have continued vitality, particularly kachina dances. Some songs associated with disappearing religious ceremonies are now sung to children, or used as kachina dance songs. Some attempts have been made to restore traditional ceremony, with the help of anthropological treatises of the turn of the 20th c. Possible signs of missionary influence on melodic structure, and instances of the general Plains phenomenon of the satirical imitation of white people's popular love songs, are noted. *(David Bloom)*

3165
as

LOUDON, E. **Les cérémonies et les poèmes dansés des Indiens Pueblos** [Ceremonies and danced poems of the Pueblo Indians], *Art populaire: Travaux artistiques et scientifiques du Ier Congrès international des arts populaires* (Paris: Duchartre, 1931) 168. In French. See no. 152 in this volume.

3166
as

MATTHEWS, Washington. **Some sacred objects of the Navajo rites,** *The International Folk-lore Congress of the World's Columbian Exposition. I* (Chicago: Charles H. Sergel, 1898) 227–47. See no. 18 in this volume.

3167
as

MCALLESTER, David P. **The role of music in western Apache culture,** *Men and cultures: Selected papers* (Philadelphia: University of Pennsylvania, 1960) 468–72. See no. 359 in this volume.

Attitudes toward and functions of music among the White Mountain Apache people of San Carlos reservation, Arizona, are compared analytically with those of typical white Americans.

3168
as

MERRIAM, Alan P.; SPIER, Robert F.G. **Chukchansi Yokuts songs,** *Actas del XXXIII° Congreso Internacional de Americanistas* (San José: Lehmann, 1959) 611–38. *Transcr.* See no. 398 in this volume.

A discussion of vocal music among the Chukchansi subgroup of the Yokuts people in California. Most of their songs are sung in the context of women's hand games. They feature relatively small range; weak downward movement, with minor third and major second as the most frequent intervals; syncopation, glissando, falling release and rising attack, grace notes, and isometry; pentatonic- and tetratonic-type modes; syllabic settings; an open, nonpulsating style; and a large variety of meters. Transcriptions of 29 songs, with texts and translations, are included. *(Ken Alboum)*

3169
as

MICHELSON, Truman. **Notes on Fox Gens festivals,** *Proceedings of the Twenty-third International Congress of Americanists* (New York: n.p., 1930) 545–46. See no. 149 in this volume.

Describes all of the required gestures and preparations for festivals of the Meshkwahkihaki (Mesquakie/Fox) people of the central U.S., which involve singers, a drummer, rattlers, flutists, and dancers. *(David Nussenbaum)*

3170
as

OSTER, Harry. **Negro French spirituals of Louisiana,** *Journal of the International Folk Music Council* XIV (1962) 166–67. See no. 442 in this volume.

Up until the late 1920s, French-speaking black Catholics in Louisiana sang congregational songs known as cantiques, which involved modal melodies and traces of African or West Indian influence in performance style. Examples collected by Elizabeth Brandon and by the author are deposited in the Archives du Folklore, Université Laval. An example, *Tombeau, tombeau,* is compared with its presumptive original from France, *Madeleine au tombeau,* as collected in the late 19th c. by Achille Millien. *(David Bloom)*

3171
as

PREUSS, Konrad Theodor. **Das Fest des Erwachens (Weinfest) bei den Cora-Indianern** [The festival of awakening (wine festival) among the Cora Indians], *Verhandlungen des XVI. internationalen Amerikanisten-Kongresses* (Wien: A. Hartleben, 1910) 489–512. In German. See no. 61 in this volume.

Discusses customs of the Cora people of Nayarít, Mexico.

3172
as

RHODES, Willard. **Acculturation in North American Indian music,** *Selected papers. I: The civilizations of ancient America; II: Acculturation in the Americas—Proceedings and selected papers; III: Indian tribes of aboriginal America* (Chicago: University of Chicago, 1951-1952) II, 127–32. *Transcr.* See no. 292 in this volume.

Surveys the effects of syncretic religions (Ghost Dance, Native American Church) and Christianity on Native American musical expression. In the

southwestern U.S., where social and ceremonial institutions function comparatively undisturbed by the impact of white culture, cult music genres have remained stable and diverse; in the Plains area, where the secular dance song is the main focus of musical activity, a trend can be observed of uniformization of musical style. Overall remarkably little musical acculturation is found in comparison to other aspects of Indian psychological and material culture. *(David Bloom)*

3173
as

RHODES, Willard. **The Christian hymnology of the North American Indians,** *Men and cultures: Selected papers* (Philadelphia: University of Pennsylvania, 1960) 324–31. *Music, discog.* See no. 359 in this volume.

Discusses the history of hymnody among Indians, with specific examples from Protestant churches among Oglala Sioux and Kiowa people, and syncretic religions such as the Native American Church (peyote cult) and the Indian Shaker Church of the U.S. northwest. The melody in the Oglala case resembles neither those of the established Sioux hymnal (*Dakota Odowan,* New York 1879) nor traditional Sioux music; it may represent a reflex of the Gregorian chant tradition transmitted somehow from the Algonquian northeast.

3174
as

RHODES, Willard. **North American Indian music in transition: A study of songs with English words as an index of acculturation,** *Journal of the International Folk Music Council* XV (1963) 9–14. *Transcr.* See no. 459 in this volume.

English words and phrases are occasionally found in Native American social dance songs and love songs. These songs are lighthearted, and often humorous; there may be a fine line between copying and caricaturing white people's popular songs. Questions concerning the use of such material in studies of acculturation are presented. *(James R. Cowdery)*

3175
as

RHODES, Willard. **A study of musical diffusion based on the wandering of the opening peyote song,** *Journal of the International Folk Music Council* X (1958) 42–49. *Music.* See no. 371 in this volume.

Twelve versions of the first song sung at ceremonies of the peyote cult, drawn from seven tribes in the southwestern U.S., are compared. The farther it has traveled, the more its melodic and rhythmic features have tended to become simplified; however, its structure and personality have remained intact. *(James R. Cowdery)*

3176
as

RUBIN, Ruth. **Yiddish folk songs current in French Canada,** *Journal of the International Folk Music Council* XII (1960) 76–78. See no. 413 in this volume.

Reports on field work undertaken among Jewish communities in Montreal and Toronto.

3177
as

SMITH, C. Alphonso. **Ballads surviving in the United States,** *Proceedings of the Nineteenth International Congress of Americanists* (Washington, D.C.: n.p., 1917) 457–58. See no. 91 in this volume.

Some American ballads continue to evolve, especially in the southeastern United States. There is sometimes little resemblance between American and English ballads (as transcribed by Francis James Child), because they evolved musically in entirely different ways. Another version appeared as *Musical quarterly,* January 1916. *(David Nussenbaum)*

3178
as

STURTEVANT, William C. **Comment on Gertrude P. Kurath's** *Effects of environment on Cherokee-Iroquois ceremonialism, music, and dance,* Symposium on Cherokee and Iroquois culture (Washington, D.C.: United States Government Printing Office, 1961) 197–204. See no. 400 in this volume.

Response to the paper abstracted as no. 3160 in this volume.

3179
as

THALBITZER, William. **Cultic games and festivals in Greenland,** *Congrès international des* américanistes: Compte rendu de la XXIe session, deuxième partie (Göteborg: Museum, 1925) 236–55. See no. 118 in this volume.

Eskimos in Greenland celebrate in large houses resembling those of Alaskan Eskimos. Many of their celebratory games are combined with song and dance.

3180
as
VAN HOOGENHOUCK TULLEKEN, (Mme). **Le chant populaire au Canada** [Traditional song in Canada], *Art populaire: Travaux artistiques et scientifiques du Ier Congrès international des arts populaires* (Paris: Duchartre, 1931) 105–07. In French. See no. 152 in this volume.

An English-language version is abstracted as no. 3181 in this volume.

3181
as
VAN HOOGENHOUCK TULLEKEN, (Mme). **Folk-song in Canada,** *Congrès international des arts populaires/International congress of popular arts* (Paris: Institut international de coopération intellectuelle, 1928) 118. See no. 153 in this volume.

Surveys research on traditional song and dance of Native Canadian, French Canadian, and so-called New Canadian peoples, with attention to the role of the government in the maintenance of archives and mounting of festivals. A French-language version is cited as no. 3180 in this volume. *(David Bloom)*

3182
as
WALTON, Ivan H. **Songs of the Great Lakes sailors,** *Journal of the International Folk Music Council* III (1951) 93–96. See no. 296 in this volume.

Discusses shanties and work songs from the 1890s to the present.

3183
as
WATERMAN, Richard A. **African influence on the music of the Americas,** *Selected papers. I: The civilizations of ancient America; II: Acculturation in the Americas—Proceedings and selected papers; III: Indian tribes of aboriginal America* (Chicago: University of Chicago, 1951-1952) II, 207–18. See no. 292 in this volume.

The relative homogeneity of African-originating groups in the Americas encouraged the retention of values not in conflict with the dominant European culture, and African and European musics are similar enough to permit musical syncretism (one essential factor, the existence of harmony in traditional African music, has only recently been recognized). The various developments within black communities of North and South America and their influence on other communities are surveyed. *(David Bloom)*

3184
as
WORK, John W. **The Negro spiritual,** *Addresses at the International Hymnological Conference* (New York: Hymn Society of America, 1962) 17–27. *Transcr.* See no. 438 in this volume.

The words of the classic spiritual are subordinate to the rhythmic pattern and melodic line of the music. Most spirituals are in duple meter and fall into one of three categories: call and response singing; slow, sustained melody; and syncopated segmented melody. Spirituals were popularized in arrangements by Samuel Coleridge-Taylor, Harry T. Burleigh, and R. Nathaniel Dett, as well as by the earliest concert tours of the Fisk Jubilee Singers in 1871-78. Obstacles to their use in church services include failure to differentiate between spirituals suitable for worship and the highly rhythmic recreational type; the association with the entertainment stage; and the difficulty of establishing an appropriate performance practice.

(Barbara B. Heyman)

36 South and Central America, Caribbean, and Mexico

3185
as
ALISKY, Marvin. **Mexico's musical microphones: Instruments of cultural integration for the public,** *Cahiers d'études de radio-télévision* 3-4 (1955) 446–48. See no. 334 in this volume.

An overview of the cultural importance of traditional music in Mexico, with attention to the role currently played by radio.

3186
as
ALLENDE, U. **La musique populaire chilienne** [Chilean traditional music], *Art populaire: Travaux artistiques et scientifiques du Ier Congrès international des arts populaires* (Paris: Duchartre, 1931) 118–23. In French. See no. 152 in this volume.

3187
as
ALVARENGA, Oneyda. **Musique folklorique et musique populaire** [Folk music and popular music], *Journal of the International Folk Music Council* VII (1955) 36. In French. See no. 337 in this volume.

The conference report provides only a citation. Neither the text nor a summary of the paper, which discussed Brazilian music, was published here.

3188
as
ANDRADE, Mário de. **Folk music and folk song in Brazil.** Trans. by Mary H. PEDROSA, *Report of the Committee of the Conference on Inter-American Relations in the Field of Music* (Washington, D.C.: United States Department of State, 1940) 98–110. *Bibliog., discog.* See no. 271 in this volume.

Because a scientific analysis of Brazilian traditional music has yet to be made, publications on the subject have been of a general nature. In South American countries there are two traditional musics: the national music and that of the Indians. Examples of the former are few, and the latter is almost unknown. However, there are several museums and musical archives housing recordings of Brazilian traditional music. A discography and bibliography relating to the Brazilian Indians are provided, as is a list of some Brazilian musicians and professors interested in traditional music. *(Gary Eskow)*

3189
as
ARETZ, Isabel. **Cantos navideños en el folklore venezolano** [Christmas songs in Venezuelan folklore], *Boletín interamericano de música* (supplement 1965) 75–86. *Illus., charts, diagr., transcr.* In Spanish. See no. 461 in this volume.

Summary of Venezuelan Christmas customs; analysis of the text and musical styles of the different song forms (villancico, romance, aguinaldo, etc.); and description of the instrumental music performed during the season. Observations are based on field recordings from 1947-62 collected by the Instituto Nacional del Folklore, Caracas. Remarks on Venezuelan Christmas songs composed in the 18th and 19th c. are also included. *(David Bloom)*

3190
as
ARETZ, Isabel. **Un planteamiento de origenes: El maremare como expresión musical y coreográfica** [Tracing origins: The maremare as musical and choreographic expression], *Actas del XXXIII° Congreso Internacional de Americanistas* (San José: Lehmann, 1959) 649f. In Spanish. See no. 398 in this volume.

The maremare began in the indigenous Indian culture of Venezuela, as a dance accompanied by panpipes (possibly with a unique tuning), and sometimes vertical reed flute or fiddle. With the extinction of distinct Indian culture, it is now a creole genre. *(Ken Alboum)*

3191
as
ARTEZ, Isabel. **Cuentos musicales de Sudamerica** [Musical tales of South America], *Actas do Congresso Internacional de Etnografia* (Porto: Imprensa Portuguesa, 1965) VI, 45–59. *Music.* In Spanish. See no. 473 in this volume.

Four types of musical tales from different parts of South America are described. These include the imitative tale (from Argentina; the narrator is an instrumentalist who imitates situations in the action), the tale with sung parts (from Venezuela; the narrator tells a story and then occasionally for dramatic effect breaks into song), the tale with one singing character (from Venezuela; the narrator sings the part of just one character), and the sung tale (from Colombia; the whole story is told as a long song). *(Anatole Wieck)*

3192
as
AZEVEDO, Luiz Heitor Corrêa de. **Tupynambá melodies in Jean de Léry's** *Histoire d'un voyage faict en la terre du Brésil,* *Papers of the American Musicological Society* (Philadelphia: American Musicological Society, 1946) 85–96. *Transcr.* See no. 272 in this volume.

The Huguenot pastor Jean de Léry, who traveled to South America in 1556 with a party of Calvinists hoping to establish an "Antarctic France" for the settlement of French Protestants, collected melodies from the Tupinambá people in the vicinity of Rio de Janeiro; he published them in the third edition of his account of the voyage (Geneva, 1585). The melodies are well known in present-day Brazil, but in versions that appear to have been altered—particularly in rhythmic aspects—to make them more singable by Europeans. The source of the corruptions is the Latin version published and illustrated by Theodor de Bry in the *Americae tertia pars* volume (Frankfurt 1592) of *Collectiones peregrinationum in Indiam orientalem et Indiam occidentalem.* *(David Bloom)*

3193
as
BOSE, Fritz. **Instrumentalstile in primitiver Musik** [Instrumental styles in primitive music], *Bericht über den Internationalen musikwissenschaftlichen Kongress* (Kassel: Bärenreiter, 1954) 212–15. In German. See no. 319 in this volume.

Instrumental practices among several Indian peoples of South America are examined. The finger-hole flutes and panpipes in use among the Tukano people living on the Rio Papury, a tributary of the Rio Negro in the Amazon rain forest of Brazil, were not invented by this tribe but imported from higher Indian cultures and ultimately derive from the Chibcha culture. This circumstance fits with the observation that the Tukano do not mix their vocal and instrumental music. Each has its distinct techniques and social uses; their instrumental music, always featuring pairs of instruments, is heard at festivals and has a ritual character. The clear separation of vocal and instrumental music among the Tukano people reflects a practice found among other primitive peoples, and also found in certain European contexts. *(Carl Skoggard)*

3194
as
BRETON, A.C. **Survivals of ceremonial dances among Mexican Indians,** *Verhandlungen des XVI. internationalen Amerikanisten-Kongresses* (Wien: A. Hartleben, 1910) 513–20. See no. 61 in this volume.

3195
as
COMETTANT, Oscar. **La musique en Amérique avant la découverte de Christophe Colomb** [Music in America before Columbus's discovery], *Compte rendu du Ier Congrès international des américanistes* (Nancy: Crépin-Leblond, 1875) 274–301. *Music.* In French. See no. 5 in this volume.

Many instruments have been found in South American archaeological excavations. The kena, an Inca flute, is discussed, and Inca yaraví melodies, arranged for three saxophones by Ambroise THOMAS, are presented. Resemblances between American Indian and northern European traditional musics suggest a common ancestry. *(David Nussenbaum)*

3196
as
CUNHA, João Itiberê da. **Algumas notas para o Congresso da Língua Nacional Cantada** [Some notes for the Congresso da Língua Nacional Cantada], *Anais do Primeiro Congresso da Língua Nacional Cantada* (São Paulo: Departamento Municipal de Cultura, 1938) 565–72. In Portuguese. See no. 253 in this volume.

The importance of dialect phonology in the study of the traditional Portuguese-language songs of Brazil is emphasized.

3197
as
DREYFUS, Simone. **Formes de musiques rituelles chez les Indiens d'Amérique du Sud** [Forms of ritual music among the Indians of South America], *VIe Congrès international des sciences anthropologiques et ethnologiques. I: Rapport général et anthropologie; II: Ethnologie* (Paris: Musée de l'Homme, 1962-1964) II, 101–04. In French. See no. 421 in this volume.

Describes practices among various Amazonian peoples: the instrumental ritual music of the Piaroa (Wothuha) people, the ritual vocal music of the Yaruro and the Kayapó, and the dance rituals of the Kuikuro and the Kayapó. *(Susan Poliniak)*

3198
as
DURÁN, Sixto María. **La musique aborigène et populaire de l'Équateur** [Aboriginal and traditional music of Ecuador], *Art populaire: Travaux artistiques et scientifiques du Ier Congrès international des arts populaires* (Paris: Duchartre, 1931) 117–18. In French. See no. 152 in this volume.

3199
as
ESPINOSA, Luis Carlos; PINZÓN URREA, Jesús. **La heterofonía en la música de los indios cunas del Darién** [Heterophony in the music of the Kuna Indians of Darién], *Boletín interamericano de música* (supplement 1965) 121–29. *Transcr.* In Spanish. See no. 461 in this volume.

Brief ethnographic sketch of the Kuna people of Darién, Panama, and contiguous parts of Colombia, and analytic notes on polyphonic music performed on the double-ranked capador or gamma burui (panpipe), with and without maracas accompaniment, and on paired suara (end-blown notched flutes). *(David Bloom)*

3200
as
GUEVARA, Tomás. **Folklore araucano: Proverbios y refránes** [The Araucano folklore: Proverbs and refránes], *Actas del XVII° Congreso Internacional de Americanistas* (Buenos Aires: Coni, 1912). In Spanish. See no. 68 in this volume.

The *refrán* genre of traditional saying among the Mapuche or Araucano people of Chile, originating from stories, songs, and discourses, reflects Mapuche religion and morals.

3201
as
HERSKOVITS, Melville J. **Afrobahian cult music,** *Congrès international des sciences anthropologiques et ethnologiques: Compte rendu de la troisième session* (Tervuren: Musée Royal de l'Afrique Centrale, 1960) 105. See no. 282 in this volume.

Cult songs of the various Candomblé-type practices of Afro-Brazilian people in Bahia state show that elements of African origin have been retained with considerable purity. *(T. Pierce)*

3202
as
HOUSTON, Elsie. **La musique, la danse et les cérémonies populaires du Brésil** [Traditional music, dance, and ceremonies of Brazil], *Art populaire: Travaux artistiques et scientifiques du Ier Congrès international des arts populaires* (Paris: Duchartre, 1931) 162–63. In French. See no. 152 in this volume.

3203
as
JIMÉNEZ DE LA ESPADA, Marcos. **Yaravíes quiteños** [Yaraví from Quito], *Congreso Internacional de Americanistas: Cuarta reunion* (Madrid: M.G. Hernandez; Fortanet, 1881; 1882) III–LXXX. *Transcr.* In Spanish. See no. 8 in this volume.

Discusses Indian folksongs from a region in modern Ecuador. Transcriptions by Espada include 20 yaravís, eight bailes, 12 tonadas, and five cáchuas and lanchas. Both old and new songs are included, with piano accompaniment. *(David Nussenbaum)*

3204 LAMAS, Dulce Martins. **Folk and popular music in Brazil,** *Journal of the International Folk Music Council* VII (1955) 27–28. See no. 337 in this volume.
as
Summary of a paper surveying traditional song and dance genres.

3205 LIMA, Rossini Tavares de. **La musique folklorique de São Paulo comme point de départ pour une conception de la musique folklorique** [Traditional music of São Paulo as a point of departure for a conception of traditional music], *Journal of the International Folk Music Council* VII (1955) 11–13. In French. See no. 337 in this volume.
as
Surveys features of the traditional music of São Paulo, with attention to origins, dissemination, genres, forms, and composition. Genres such as batuque, samba lenço, samba Pirapora, and jongo are linked to African origins. *(Murat Eyüboğlu)*

3206 LIST, George. **Music in the culture of the Jíbaro Indians of the Ecuadorian montaña,** *Boletín interamericano de música* (supplement 1965) 133–51. *Illus., discog., charts, diagr., transcr., maps.* See no. 461 in this volume.
as
Summary of available ethnomusicological information on the Shuar people (formerly known as Jívaro or Jíbaro) of the mountain region of southeastern Ecuador, along the Peruvian border, including discussion of instruments, vocal and instrumental genres, structural features, and ethnographic performance contexts. *(David Bloom)*

3207 MANZANARES, Rafael. **Etnomusicología hondureña** [Honduran ethnomusicology], *Boletín interamericano de música* (supplement 1965) 199–202. In Spanish. See no. 461 in this volume.
as
Summarizes the state of research on indigenous, creole, and African-derived musical forms of Honduras, and discusses the etymology of the name of the *xike* or *xique* dance genre.

3208 MENDOZA, Vicente T. **The frontiers between "popular" and "folk".** Trans. by Norman FRASER, *Journal of the International Folk Music Council* VII (1955) 24–27. See no. 337 in this volume.
as
Discusses the history of traditional music in Mexico from the 16th c. to the present, differentiating between enduring traditions and transitory fashions. *(James R. Cowdery)*

3209 MENDOZA, Vicente Teódulo. **El ritmo de los cantares mexicanos recolectados por Sahagún** [The rhythm of the Mexican songs collected by Sahagún], *Miscellanea Paul Rivet octogenario dicata* (México, D.F.: Universidad Nacional Autónoma de México, 1958) II, 777–85. *Bibliog., transcr.* In Spanish. See no. 394 in this volume.
as
No music of the Nahua or Aztec people was transcribed during the early Conquest period, but a prosodic analysis of the song texts of the MS *Cantares mexicanos* in the holdings of the Biblioteca Nacional de México, believed to have been copied in the late 16th c. from a compilation made under the direction of Bernardino de Sahagún, shows rhythmic patterns that correspond to those of extant Nahua songs. *(Sylvia Eversole)*

3210 PANHUYS, L.C. van. **Quelques chansons et quelques danses dans la Guyane Néerlandaise** [Some songs and some dances in Dutch Guyana], *Verhandlungen des XXIV. internationalen Amerikanisten-Kongresses* (Hamburg: Friederichsen, De Gruyter, and Co., 1934) 207–11. In French. See no. 176 in this volume.
as
Examines several Creole songs and dances of Suriname (Dutch Guyana) with particular attention to their practice and their linguistic origins.

3211 PARDO TOVAR, Andrés. **Proyecciones sociológicas del folklore musical** [Sociological influences on musical folklore], *Boletín interamericano de música* (supplement 1965) 109–17. *Transcr., maps.* In Spanish. See no. 461 in this volume.
as
A sociological rather than ethnographic approach to musical folklore is sometimes to be preferred. One example from Colombia involves the history of change since the 16th c. in social contexts of performances by the chirimía ensemble of two chirimías (local shawms) and a double-headed drum, and its multiple social functions, in the municipality of Girardota near Medellín; another is that of multiple strata of acculturation from Native, Afro-Colombian, and European sources in traditional songs of the Baudó river valley in southwestern Choco department. *(David Bloom)*

3212 PEARSE, Andrew. **Aspects of change in Caribbean folk music,** *Journal of the International Folk Music Council* VII (1955) 27–28. See no. 337 in this volume.
as
Discusses the role of syncretism in the development of tradtional genres. A list of genres with notes on their roles in musical life is included. *(James R. Cowdery)*

3213 PILET, Raymond. **Mélodies populaires des indiens du Guatemala** [Popular melodies of the Guatemalan Indians], *Congrès International des Américanistes: Compte rendu de la huitième session* (Paris: Leroux, 1892) 16 p. *Transcr.* In French. See no. 14 in this volume.
as
K'iché (Quiché), in addition to describing a Mayan dialect, also refers to Indian music of the province of Verapaz. Six melodies are transcribed: a trumpet call, a shepherd's melody for flute, a zapateado dance, a whistled tune, and two melodies for marimba. Most of the transcriptions have been given piano accompaniments. Also published separately (Paris: Dupont, 1891; 16p.). *(David Nussenbaum)*

3214 RAMÓN Y RIVERA, Luis Felipe. **Cantos negros de la Fiesta de San Juan** [Black people's songs for the feast of Saint John], *Boletín interamericano de música* (supplement 1965) 155–75. *Transcr., maps.* In Spanish. See no. 461 in this volume.
as
Examines the performance context, melodies, and texts of songs performed in the celebration of the feast of St. John the Baptist by the Afro-Venezuelan population of the Barlovento region, Miranda state, on the Caribbean coast of Venezuela, based on field recordings made under the auspices of the Instituto Nacional del Folklore, Caracas. Several complete transcriptions are included. *(David Bloom)*

3215 RAMÓN Y RIVERA, Luis Felipe. **Rhythmic and melodic elements in Negro music of Venezuela,** *Journal of the International Folk Music Council* XIV (1962) 56–60. *Transcr.* See no. 442 in this volume.
as
Research on Afro-Venezuelan music has concentrated on the classification and analysis of toques (rhythmic units) and golpes (songs associated with a particular repertoire of drumming patterns). Examples of several golpes including melodies are transcribed and discussed. *(David Bloom)*

3216 RAMÓN Y RIVERA, Luis Felipe. **Supervivencia de la polifonía popular en Venezuela** [The survival of traditional polyphony in Venezuela], *Actas del XXXIII° Congreso Internacional de Americanistas* (San José: Lehmann, 1959) 647–48. In Spanish. See no. 398 in this volume.
as
An orally transmitted repertoire of polyphonic music has been maintained in Venezuela for two or three centuries, though it is now in danger of extinction. The pieces, in a mixed style, are sung at the *velorios* (wakes) of the Holy Cross. *(Ken Alboum)*

3217 RHODES, Willard. **A preliminary study of the**
as **Mazatec mushroom ceremony,** *Boletín*
interamericano de música (supplement 1965) 189–96.
Transcr. See no. 461 in this volume.
A 1958 field recording by Gordon Wasson, made in Huautla de Jimenez,
Oaxaca, of an all-night curing ceremony of the Mazatec people, in which a
curandera (shaman), her assistants, and the patient eat a certain variety of
mushrooms, features almost continuous chanting by the curandera and
other musical elements. Structural features of music and text are described,
and the musical expression of syncretism between indigenous witchcraft
and Catholicism when the curandera's daughter sings a version of the *Ave
Maria* prayer simultaneously with her mother's chanting is discussed.

3218 SÁNCHEZ DE FUENTES, Eduardo. **The musi-**
as **cal folklore of Cuba,** *Papers read at the Interna-*
tional Congress of Musicology (New York: Music Educators National Conference, 1944) 284–88. See no. 266
in this volume.
A historical overview, including brief descriptions of various songs,
dances, and rhythms.

3219 SAPPER, Karl. **Sitten und Gebräuche der**
as **Pokonchi-Indianer** [Customs and traditions of the
Pocomchí Indians], *Internationaler Amerikanisten-*
Kongress: Vierzehnte Tagung (Stuttgart: Kohlhammer,
1906) 403–17. In German. See no. 47 in this volume.
Discusses the Pocomchí people of Guatemala.

3220 SOUZA, José Geraldo de. **Rhythmic and modal**
as **contribution of Gregorian chant in the folk**
music of Brazil, *Journal of the International Folk*
Music Council VII (1955) 14. See no. 337 in this
volume.
Summary of a paper.

⟶ STRELNIKOV, I.D. **La música y la danza de las**
tribus índias Kaa-Ohwua (Guaraní) y
Botocudo [The music and dance of the Guaraní and
Botocudo Indian tribes]. See no. 5067 in this volume.

3221 TRAVERSARI SALAZAR, Pedro Pablo.
as **Recherches sur la musique des Incas** [Research
on music of the Incas], *Congrès international des arts*
populaires/International congress of popular arts
(Paris: Institut international de coopération intellectuelle, 1928) 97. In French. See no. 153 in this volume.
Summary of a paper reviewing the literature on ca. 1928 on Inca music; on the
history of indigenous music in South America and its relations with that of
the colonizing peoples; and on native instruments and museum collections.

3222 VAN WENGEN, Gerrit Dirk. **The study of**
as **Creole folk music in Surinam,** *Journal of the In-*
ternational Folk Music Council XI (1959) 45–46. See
no. 392 in this volume.
Surveys the state of research on the traditional music and dances of black
people in Suriname.

⟶ VEGA, Carlos. **La flauta de Pan andina** [The
Andean panpipe]. See no. 3639 in this volume.

3223 VEGA, Carlos. **Música de tres notas** [Music of
as three notes], *Boletín interamericano de música* (supplement 1965) 89–106. *Illus., transcr.* In Spanish. See no.
461 in this volume.
Tritonic scales are found in Argentina particularly among rural populations
partly descended from indigenous Andean peoples of the Diaguitan and related language families, no longer extant as distinct groups. They are used
in music for erke (very long side-blown trumpet) and erkencho (clarinet),

and in vocal music such as the baguala song genre. On the basis of a sample
of 20 bagualas, tonality, rhythm, and refrain ("estribillo") structure are
classified and analyzed. *(David Bloom)*

⟶ WATERMAN, Richard A. **African influence on**
the music of the Americas. See no. 3183 in this
volume.

3224 YEOMANS, Williams. **The musical instru-**
as **ments of pre-Columbian Central America,**
Proceedings of the Thirtieth International Congress of
Americanists (London: Royal Anthropological Institute, 1955) 54–57. See no. 313 in this volume.
Information on instruments of Mexican and Mayan cultures from Mexico
City in the north to Nicaragua in the south can be gleaned from surviving
instruments in museum collections and from the iconographic study of
frescoes and codices, as well as from descriptions in Spanish colonial
sources. They include gongs, drums, rattles, whistle-flutes (sometimes im-
precisely known as "flageolets"), conchs, and trumpets. Evidence on performance practice, particularly with reference to rhythm, is summarized.
(David Bloom)

3225 YURCHENCO, Henrietta. **Survivals of**
as **pre-Hispanic music in Mexico,** *Journal of the In-*
ternational Folk Music Council XV (1963) 15–18.
Transcr. See no. 459 in this volume.
In Mexico, pre-Hispanic music is mainly found among native agricultural
tribes. Often such examples coexist with newer traditions associated with
Christianity. *(James R. Cowdery)*

37 Oceania, Australia, New Zealand, New Guinea, the Philippines, and Hawaii

3226 GRAF, Walter. **Zum Inhalt in der Musik der**
as **Naturvölker** [Content in the music of primitive peo-
ples], *Bericht über den internationalen musik-*
wissenschaftlichen Kongreß Wien Mozartjahr 1956
(Graz; Köln: Böhlau, 1958) 242–48. *Transcr.* In German. See no. 365 in this volume.
Examples of the conveying of experiential meaning in non-Western traditional musics are drawn from transcription and analysis of field recordings
made by Rudolf Pöch in the Eastern New Guinea–Bismarck Archipelago
region: (1) flute music in a boys' initiation rite from Wewak (formerly
Dallmannhofen); (2) singing with slit-drum accompaniment in the kanga-
roo dance of the Monumbo people of Manam Island; and (3) a narrative
song, *Lalua botahuam* (Lalua looks out searching), from the Port Moresby
region. *(David Bloom)*

3227 JONES, Trevor A. **A brief survey of ethno-**
as **musicological research in the music of Aborig-**
inal Australia, *Australian Aboriginal studies* (Melbourne: Oxford University, 1963) 280–316. *Bibliog.,*
discog. See no. 430 in this volume.
Aboriginal music is disappearing rapidly, and the only area fully investigated by 1961 was the Arnhem Land Peninsula. An ethnomusicologist
should be present in every related field research party; failing this, anthropologists should make field recordings. Problems of resources for transcription and inadequate supervision must be solved. Ethnomusicology
should aim at a synthesis and comparative reconstruction of Aboriginal
music and that of related peoples, and the dissemination of the music in recorded form. *(Susan Poliniak)*

3228 MCLEAN, Mervyn. **Oral transmission in**
as **Maori music,** *Journal of the International Folk Mu-*
sic Council XIII (1961) 59–62. *Transcr.* See no. 424 in
this volume.

Maori people use traditional song as a record of their history and religious belief. Accurate transmission is governed by *whakaeke*, rules ensuring strict tempo and rhythmic unison, for which a highly trained leader is responsible. Special breathing techniques are taught to maintain a continuous flow, as the briefest pause is an ill omen. Maori melodies and scales are also discussed. *(Alix Moyer Grunebaum)*

→ SCHAEFFNER, André. **Contribution à l'étude des instruments de musique d'Afrique et d'Océanie** [Contribution to the study of the musical instruments of Africa and Oceania]. See no. 2584 in this volume.

3229 SCHMIDT, Wilhelm. **Über Musik und Gesänge**
as **der Karesau-Papuas, Deutsch-Neu-Guinea** [On music and song of Karesau Island Papuans, German New Guinea], *Haydn-Zentenarfeier* (Leipzig: Breitkopf & Härtel; Wien: Artaria, 1909) 297–98. In German. See no. 65 in this volume.
Brief account of research undertaken at the Missionshaus St. Gabriel of the Societas Verbi Divini (Steyler Missionaries) in Mödling bei Wien, Austria, with Bonifaz Tamatai Pritak, an informant from Karesau in the Schouten Islands of East Sepik province. (A full report is published in *Anthropos* 2, 1907.) The subsequent panel discussion is included.

3230 SMITH, Barbara Barnard. **Folk music in Ha-**
as **waii,** *Journal of the International Folk Music Council* XI (1959) 50–55. *Transcr.* See no. 392 in this volume.
Surveys the development of traditional and popular musics from ca. 950 C.E. to the present.

38 Jazz

3231 BERGMANN, Robert. **Das Problem der Jazz-**
as **musik im heutigen Musikleben [The problem of jazz in today's musical life],** *Bericht über den internationalen musikwissenschaftlichen Kongreß* (Kassel: Bärenreiter, 1963) 260–63. See no. 452 in this volume.
The meaning of the word "jazz" has been defined by its etymology, by identifying jazz with race, and in terms of key elements such as improvisation and ostinato; none of these is satisfactory. It would be preferable to abandon the idea of jazz as a genre and refer instead to the music of individual performers and composers as "the music of" Gershwin, Ellington, Bernstein, John Lewis, Billy Taylor, and so on. *(David Bloom)*

39 Popular music

3232 BHATIA, Vanraj. **Western music in India,** *Mu-*
as *sic: East and West* (Tōkyō: conference, 1961) 82–85. See no. 445 in this volume.
Western music was first introduced in India by the British; today, Indian popular music shows the influence of rock, calypso, and cha-cha-chá. *(Sylvia Eversole)*

3233 DEVIĆ, Dragoslav. **Nove "narodne" pesme**
as [New so-called folk songs], *Rad IX-og kongresa Saveza Folklorista Jugoslavije* (Sarajevo: Savez Udruženja Folklorista Jugoslavije, 1963) 545–51. *Music.* In Serbian; summary in German. See no. 455 in this volume.
Newly composed folk songs have been appearing on a virtually daily basis in Yugoslavia since 1944, but only some have the characteristics of authentic traditional music. Those that are adopted by the people are distinguished by easily grasped form, even rhythm, range of between a fifth and an octave, traditional scale, and typical or contemporary lyrical content. The successful examples demonstrate that folklore is no longer to be considered a strictly rural phenomenon. *(author)*

3234 DRĂGOI, Sabin V. **The production of new songs**
as **in the Rumanian People's Republic,** *Journal of the International Folk Music Council* XII (1960) 36–42. *Transcr.* See no. 413 in this volume.
After World War I, changes in social consciousness led to the development of neotraditional songs, characterized by (1) more buoyant, exuberant melodies, with a wider range and less stepwise movement; (2) more vigorous, marked rhythm; (3) scales that are tonal rather than modal; and (4) a less ornamented and more vigorous vocal style. *(James R. Cowdery)*

3235 SEMMER, Gerd. **Über die Ostermarsch-Lieder**
as [Songs for the Easter marches], *Beiträge zur Musikwissenschaft* VI/4 (1964) 339–40. In German. See no. 476 in this volume.
Discusses the songs of the Ostermarschbewegung that developed in West Germany in emulation of the annual Easter marches, since 1958, of the Campaign for Nuclear Disarmament in the U.K. *(David Bloom)*

3236 VÁCLAVEK, Bedřich. **Les chansons tchèques**
as **populaires** [Popularized Czech song], *Congrès international des arts populaires/International congress of popular arts* (Paris: Institut international de coopération intellectuelle, 1928) 113. In French. See no. 153 in this volume.
Summary of the paper abstracted as no. 3093 in this volume.

SOUND SOURCES

40 General (including conducting, organology)

3237
as
AMADES GELAT, Joan. **Strumenti di musica popolare in Catalogna** [Traditional music instruments in Catalonia], *Atti del Congresso internazionale di musiche popolari mediterranee e del Convegno dei bibliotecari musicali* (Palermo: De Magistris succ. V. Bellotti, 1959) 115–22. In Italian. See no. 332 in this volume.

3238
as
AMELN, Konrad. **Historische Instrumente in der gegenwärtigen Musikpraxis** [Historical instruments in the musical practice of today], *Bericht über den Internationalen musikwissenschaftlichen Kongress* (Kassel: Bärenreiter, 1954) 96–99. In German. See no. 319 in this volume.
Discusses the difficulties that hinder the performance of music on historical instruments, especially performance by professional musicians, and describes performances of early music on historical instruments broadcast by the Nordwestdeutscher Rundfunk, Cologne (NWDR; later known as Westdeutscher Rundfunk) in the early 1950s. *(Carl Skoggard)*

3239
as
BACHMANN, Werner. **Das byzantinische Musikinstrumentarium** [The Byzantine music instrumentarium], *Anfänge der slavischen Musik* (Bratislava: Slovenská Akadémia Vied, 1966) 125–38. In German. See no. 477 in this volume.
The study of early Byzantine musical instruments, their nomenclature, and their construction, has thrown light on the interaction between Eastern European and Asian and Arabic cultures and the diffusion of instruments. *(Brian Doherty)*

3240
as
BAINES, Anthony. **Organology and European folk music instruments,** *Journal of the International Folk Music Council* XII (1960) 10–13. See no. 413 in this volume.
An overview of the role of organology in studies of traditional music, with methodological suggestions.

3241
as
BAINES, Anthony. **Some points in the nomenclature of folk instruments,** *Music libraries and instruments* (London: Hinrichsen, 1961) 204–08. See no. 406 in this volume.
The Hornbostel-Sachs nomenclature scheme for European traditional music instruments may imply nonexistent relationships among instruments, and category names may conflict with or belie instruments' actual names and natures. Specific cases are addressed. *(Susan Poliniak)*

3242
as
BERGMANS, Paul. **De l'intérêt qu'il y aurait à dresser un inventaire général des instruments de musique anciens disséminés dans les musées et les collections privées de Belgique** [On the benefit of drawing up a general inventory of the early musical instruments scattered in the museums and private collections of Belgium], *Fédération Archéologique et Historique de Belgique: Annales du XXIᵉ congrès* (Liège: Poncelet, 1909) II, 666f. In French. See no. 64 in this volume.

3243
as
BERNER, Alfred. **Die Instrumentenkunde in Wissenschaft und Praxis** [Organology as a science and a practice], *Bericht über den Internationalen musikwissenschaftlichen Kongress* (Kassel: Bärenreiter, 1954) 57–66. In German. See no. 319 in this volume.
Traces the main historical contours of modern organology from its origins in the latter 19th c. and outlines tasks facing the discipline. *(Carl Skoggard)*

3244
as
BERNER, Alfred. **Untersuchungsprobleme und Wertungsprinzipien an Musikinstrumenten der Vergangenheit** [Issues in investigating and evaluating musical instruments of the past], *Bericht über den siebenten internationalen musikwissenschaftlichen Kongress* (Kassel: Bärenreiter, 1959) 66–68. In German. See no. 390 in this volume.
The investigation of old instruments must seek to establish functional value. Neither the aesthetic merits of an exterior of an instrument nor the pleasingness of its present-day sound are sufficient guides, both being dependent on subjective assessment. The functional value of an instrument is directly related to how true it has remained to its original state, and thus inversely proportional to the interventions and changes that the instrument has undergone over time. A modest, unaltered instrument is of more scientific value than a fine instrument that has been repeatedly altered and whose tone conforms to the taste of our time. However, an instrument that has been actually played and has suffered from practical use is more interesting scientifically than one that was made for only for display or was rarely used. *(Carl Skoggard)*

3245
as
BRICQUEVILLE, Eugène de. **La facture instrumentale** [Instrument building], *Rapport sur la musique contemporaine française* (Roma: Armani & Stein, 1913) 151–56. In French. See no. 76 in this volume.
General historical observations about instrument making in France.

3246
as
BUHLE, Edward. **Über den Stand der Instrumentenkunde** [The state of organology], *Bericht über den zweiten Kongress der Internationalen Musikgesellschaft* (Leipzig: Breitkopf & Härtel, 1907) 217–25. In German. See no. 53 in this volume.
Survey of current research on non-European instruments, instruments of classical antiquity, and more recent European bowed strings, plucked strings, keyboards including organs, and winds. *(David Bloom)*

3247
as
CLOSSON, Ernest. **Les instruments de musique disparus** [Vanished musical instruments], *Compte rendu du Vᵉ Congrès international des sciences historiques* (Bruxelles: Weissenbruch, 1923) 371. In French. See no. 100 in this volume.
Certain instruments have been technically perfected, but in the process have lost their original timbres. Such instruments include the crumhorn, the organ, the clavichord, the lute, and the flute. *(David Nussenbaum)*

3248
as
DRAEGER, Hans-Heinz. **Das Instrument als Träger und Ausdruck des musikalischen Bewusstseins** [The instrument as vehicle and expression of musical awareness], *Bericht über den Internationalen musikwissenschaftlichen Kongress* (Kassel: Bärenreiter, 1954) 67–75. In German. See no. 319 in this volume.
A consideration of methodology to be used in the study of musical instruments. A middle course is outlined that incorporates the taxonomic and

functional outlook as well as interest in the social and cultural contexts of instrumental practice. *(Carl Skoggard)*

3249
as
DROYSEN, Dagmar. **Die Musikinstrumente in Europa vom 9. bis 11. Jahrhundert** [Musical instruments in Europe from the 9th to the 11th centuries], *Bericht über den neunten internationalen Kongreß* (Kassel: Bärenreiter, 1964-1966) II, 176–87. In German. See no. 491 in this volume.

Summary of a roundtable discussion. The focus was on the current state of research with respect to instruments of the period that have been preserved and to the literary and iconographic sources. Participants included Alfred BERNER, Edmund A. BOWLES, Frederick CRANE, Daniel DEVOTO, Hans-Heinz DRAEGER, Reinhold HAMMERSTEIN, John Henry van der MEER, Joseph SMITS VAN WAESBERGHE, Wilhelm STAUDER, Geneviève THIBAULT DE CHAMBURE, and Emanuel WINTERNITZ. *(David Bloom)*

3250
as
GERSON-KIWI, Edith. **Migrations and mutations of Oriental folk instruments,** *Journal of the International Folk Music Council* IV (1952) 16–19. See no. 306 in this volume.

Two contrasting paths characterize the evolution of instruments: that of mutation within a home culture, and that of migration from one culture to another. The development within the Middle East of hand-beaten frame drums such as the biblical *tof* is compared with that of stick-beaten drums, whose diffusion can be traced from Central Asia to China and thence back toward Europe, where the drum has finally become an art rather than folk instrument. *(David Bloom)*

3251
as
HARRIS, Ernest E. **On conducting and instrumental materials,** *Music skills* (Washington, D.C.: Catholic University of America, 1958) 89–90. See no. 385 in this volume.

A short description of a seminar on conducting skills, including score study and a study on the criteria for the selection and use of music materials. A skillful conductor makes for efficient rehearsals and expressive music.
(Susan Poliniak)

3252
as
HASE, Oskar von. **La vente et le prêt de matériel d'orchestre** [The sale and rental of orchestral equipment], *Congrès international des éditeurs: Neuvième session* (Paris: Cercle de la Librairie, 1932) 144–45. In French. See no. 191 in this volume.

3253
as
HICKMANN, Hans. **Sur l'enquête musicologique de la saison 1947-48** [On the musicological inquiry of the 1947-48 season], *Actes du XXIe Congrès international des orientalistes* (Paris: Société Asiatique de Paris, 1949) 71–72. In French. See no. 294 in this volume.

Discusses the state of research on ancient Egyptian instruments. The *Instruments de musique* (nos. 69201-69852, vol. 101 of the *Catalogue général des antiquités Égyptiennes du Musée du Caire*) is a first step toward a general inventory and classification. A study on the two trumpets preserved in the Egyptian Museum in Cairo has already appeared. Another study on rattles, cymbals, and bells is underway. The next phase of the research will focus on percussion instruments. Study of woodwinds and plucked string instruments can only begin when we know more about tuning systems. Recordings of current traditional Egyptian music will be useful for purposes of comparison. *(Murat Eyüboğlu)*

3254
as
HUSMANN, Heinrich. **Singstil und Instrumentalstil in ihren Voraussetzungen** [The premises of vocal and instrumental styles], *Bericht über den Internationalen musikwissenschaftlichen Kongress* (Kassel: Bärenreiter, 1954) 219–23. In German. See no. 319 in this volume.

From a purely systematic analysis of their acoustic properties, speech and instrumental music are polar opposites; singing lies somewhere in between. Whereas instrumental music strives to emancipate itself entirely from noise and sometimes does, vocal music is inevitably compromised by some of the noise character of consonantal speech. But vocal music, like instrumental music, is based on discrete tones; speech intonation continually wavers. It may be asked whether singing originated in imitation of instrumental music (a plausible thought). However, one also sees how it could have been derived directly from speech. Vocal styles can be classified according to whether they seem to have been derived from instrumental idioms or from speech. Three categories of each presumed origin are briefly described. *(Carl Skoggard)*

3255
as
INDY, Vincent d'. **Transformation des instruments dits simples en instruments chromatiques: Définition des instruments chromatiques** [Transformation of so-called simple instruments into chromatic instruments: Definition of chromatic instruments], *Congrès international de musique: Ire session—Exposition Universelle de 1900: Compte rendu, rapports, communications* (Paris: conference, 1901) 31. In French. See no. 29 in this volume.

Chromatic instruments are defined as possessing the 12 tones of the chromatic scale. The only instrument that does not as yet possess a satisfactory sound in its chromatic form is the valve trombone, whose piston mechanism is still inferior to the "natural" slide.

3256
as
KAČULEV, Ivan. **Bălgarski narodni muzikalni instrumenti** [Traditional Bulgarian instruments], *Rad VII-og kongresa Saveza Folklorista Jugoslavije* (Cetinje: Obod, 1964) 319–35. Illus., transcr. In Bulgarian; summary in Russian. See no. 419 in this volume.

3257
as
KAMIŃSKI, Włodzimierz. **Beiträge zur Erforschung der frühmittelalterlichen Musikinstrumente der Nordwest- und Ostslaven** [Contributions to research on the early medieval musical instruments of the northwestern and eastern Slavs], *Anfänge der slavischen Musik* (Bratislava: Slovenská Akadémia Vied, 1966) 139–46. In German. See no. 477 in this volume.

The medieval musical instruments of the northern Slavic peoples display an indigenous amateur tradition of construction and design. *(Brian Doherty)*

3258
as
KLIER, Karl Magnus. **Volkstümliche Querflöten und die Maultrommel in den österreichischen Alpen** [Popular transverse flutes and the jew's harp in the Austrian Alps], *Beethoven-Zentenarfeier: Internationaler musikhistorischer Kongress* (Wien: Universal, 1927) 373–77. Music, transcr. In German. See no. 142 in this volume.

A brief survey of Alpine fifes (*Querpfeife*) and jew's harps, including remarks on history, distribution, manufacture, playing technique, and typical music. *(David Bloom)*

3259
as
LIMA, Rossini Tavares de. **Música folclórica e instrumentos musicais do Brasil** [Traditional music and musical instruments of Brazil], *Boletín interamericano de música* (supplement 1965) 205–24. Illus., bibliog., transcr. In Portuguese. See no. 461 in this volume.

A survey of 51 percussion, wind, and string instruments.

⟶ MARCEL-DUBOIS, Claudie. **Extensions du domaine d'observations directes en ethnographie musicale française** [Extensions of the scope of direct observation in French ethnomusicology]. See no. 2938 in this volume.

3260 MARCEL-DUBOIS, Claudie. **L'instrument**
as **musical populaire en France** [The traditional musical instrument in France], *Travaux du Ier Congrès International de Folklore* (Tours: Arrault et Cie, 1938)
377–81. In French. See no. 251 in this volume.
Discusses regional preferences for instruments such as the accordion and
the clarinet.

3261 NATALETTI, Giorgio. **Alcuni strumenti di**
as **musica populari italiani: Distribuzione**
geografica [Some traditional Italian instruments:
Their geographic distribution], *Les colloques de
Wégimont. IV: Ethnomusicologie III* (Paris: Belles Lettres, 1964) 75–84. *Illus.* In Italian. See no. 401 in this
volume.

3262 NEUPERT, Hanns. **Musikwissenschaftler und**
as **Instrumentenbau** [Musicologists and instrument
making], *Bericht über den internationalen
musikwissenschaftlichen Kongreß* (Kassel: Bärenreiter,
1963) 323–25. In German. See no. 452 in this volume.
Discusses instrument making as a career for the trained musicologist.

3263 OBRADOVIĆ, Milica. **Zvučne igračke seoske**
as **dece u Bosni i Hercegovini** [Sound-producing toys
of village children in Bosnia and Herzegovina], *Rad
VII-og kongresa Saveza Folklorista Jugoslavije*
(Cetinje: Obod, 1964) 363–68. *Illus.* In Bosnian; summary in German. See no. 419 in this volume.
Most of these toys are produced by the children themselves, sometimes
with the help of parents, from natural materials such as wood, bark, grass,
and various fruits. They may be used for their sounds alone, or represent
something after which they are named: *slavić* ("nightingale"), *puhovac*
("blowing wind"). Others still imitate both the shape and the sound of an
object such as a musical instrument: *diple, musike* ("harmonica"), *violina*.
(author)

3264 OBRIST, Alois. **Dürfen oder sollen der Ent-**
as **wicklung der modernen Instrumentation**
Grenzen gezogen werden? [Can and should limits
be set to the development of modern instrumentation?].
Ed. by Karl NEF, *Bericht über den zweiten Kongress
der Internationalen Musikgesellschaft* (Leipzig:
Breitkopf & Härtel, 1907) 211–12. In German. See no.
53 in this volume.
The criticism of expanded instrumental means, from classical antiquity to
the age of Richard Strauss, can be dismissed. As long as new developments
permit an expansion of the contrasts of which an instrument or ensemble is
capable, without a sacrifice of its simple expressive capacities, there can be
no objection to innovation. *(David Bloom)*

3265 OTTO, Irmgard. **Das Fotografieren von**
as **Musikinstrumenten zu wissenschaftlichen**
Zwecken [Photographing musical instruments for
scholarly purposes], *Bericht über den internationalen
musikwissenschaftlichen Kongreß* (Kassel: Bärenreiter,
1963) 309–11. In German. See no. 452 in this volume.
Discusses, from the standpoint of the Musikinstrumenten-Museum des
Staatlichen Instituts für Musikforschung, Berlin, choice of film and format,
and avoidance of shadows; the question of what constitutes the complete
documentation of an instrument; and the value of photographic documentation in organological research. *(David Bloom)*

3266 OTTO, Irmgard. **Die instrumentenkundliche**
as **Auswertung der deutschen Lexika des 18.**
Jahrhunderts [Assessing the discussion of instruments in German lexicons of the 18th century], *Bericht
über den siebenten internationalen musikwissenschaft-*

lichen Kongress (Kassel: Bärenreiter, 1959) 207–09. In
German. See no. 390 in this volume.
Gottlieb Siegmund Corvinus's *Nutzbares, galantes und curiöses
Frauenzimmer-Lexicon* (1715) and Johann Georg Walch's
Philosophisches Lexicon (1726) provide only summary information on
musical instruments; while Benjamin Hederich's *Reales Schul-Lexicon*
(1717) and Christian Schöttgen's *Curiöses Antiquitäten-Lexicon* (1719)
are limited to the instruments of antiquity. More significant sources are
Johann Hübner's *Curieuses und reales Natur- Kunst- Berg- Gewerck- und
Handlungs-Lexicon* (1712) and Johann Theodor Jablonski's *Allgemeines
Lexicon der Künste und Wissenschaften* (1721), in their various editions,
especially in regard to the evolution through the century of a pan-German
terminology. *(David Bloom)*

3267 PETROV, Stojan. **Bulgarian popular instru-**
as **ments,** *Journal of the International Folk Music Council* XII (1960) 34–35. See no. 413 in this volume.
Surveys historical and contemporary sources.

3268 PICKEN, Laurence E.R. **Three-note instru-**
as **ments in the Chinese People's Republic,** *Journal
of the International Folk Music Council* XII (1960)
28–30. See no. 413 in this volume.
Discusses examples from antiquity to the present.

3269 PIMONOW, Léonid. **La détermination de la**
as **qualité des instruments de musique au moyen**
du spectre sonore transitoire [The determination
of instrument quality by means of the transient sound
spectrum], *Acoustique musicale* (Paris: Centre National
de la Recherche Scientifique [CNRS], 1959) 119–34.
Illus., charts, diagr. In French. See no. 393 in this
volume.
Although most harmonic theory deals exclusively with sustained, periodic
sounds, music is largely composed of transient phenomena. Methods of
treating such phenomena are discussed, with particular attention to the
brief transient dissonances caused by unpleasant beats or the absence of fusion and to dissonance-causing characteristics of particular musical instruments. *(David Bloom)*

3270 RADIGUER, Henri. **La situation des chefs de**
as **musique militaire** [The situation of conductors of
military music], *Congrès international de musique: Ire
session—Exposition Universelle de 1900: Compte
rendu, rapports, communications* (Paris: conference,
1901) 62–64. *Charts, diagr.* In French. See no. 29 in this
volume.
Standards of military bandleaders should be improved by establishing in-
spection committees. The salaries of conductors in the area of military music
are discussed.

3271 RICHARDSON, Edward Gick. **Electro-acous-**
as **tics applied to musical instruments: General**
review, *Acustica: International journal of acous-
tics/Journal international d'acoustique/Internationale
akustische Zeitschrift* IV/1 (1954) 212–17. *Illus., port.,
bibliog., charts, diagr.* Summaries in German, French,
and English. See no. 324 in this volume.
Discusses methods of analyzing timbre, factors contributing to the sound
quality of a violin, the physics of brass instruments and organ pipes, and the
international pitch standard.

3272 RODA Y LOPEZ, Cecilio de. **Les instruments**
as **de musique en Espagne au XIIIme siècle** [Musi-
cal instruments in Spain in the 13th century], *Report of
the Fourth Congress of the International Musical Society* (London: Novello, 1912) 332–33. In French. See
no. 71 in this volume.
Summary of a paper.

3273 SACHS, Curt. **Rapport général de la Commis-**
as **sion des Instruments** [General report of the Commission on Instruments], *Recueil des travaux du
Congrès de musique arabe* (Al-Qāhirah: Boulac, 1934)
659–64. In French. See no. 196 in this volume.

At the Congress on Arab Music (Mu'tamar al Mūsīqá al-'Arabiyyah) in
Cairo (1932), the commission was charged with preparing a standard list of
instruments for use in Arab music, and evaluating possible innovations including the adoption of European instruments. Most of the discussion was
devoted to the question of the piano; while the standard piano was clearly
rejected, a majority of members supported the concept of a quarter-tone
tempered instrument. *(David Bloom)*

3274 SAMBAMOORTHY, P. **Evolution of music**
as **with special reference to musical instruments,**
Music east and west (Nai Dilli: Indian Council for Cultural Relations, 1966) 28–31. See no. 489 in this volume.

Discusses the evolution of Indian flutes, lutes, and drums, and the recent
adoption of the European violin.

3275 SAMBETH, Heinrich. **A means of education:**
as **The making of musical instruments by chil-**
dren and adults, *Music in education* (Paris:
UNESCO, 1955) 247–48. See no. 322 in this volume.

Discusses the educational advantages of children making their own musical instruments, with reference to ideas derived from the Orff method. A
French-language version is cited as no. 3276 in this volume.

3276 SAMBETH, Heinrich M. **Un moyen d'éduca-**
as **tion: La fabrication d'instruments de musique**
par les enfants et les adolescents [A means of education: The making of musical instruments by children
and adolescents], *La musique dans l'éducation* (Paris:
UNESCO; Colin, 1955) 257–59. In French. See no. 323
in this volume.

An English-language version is abstracted as no. 3275 in this volume.

3277 SCHREMS, Theobald. **Der Chordirigent als**
as **Führerpersönlichkeit** [The choir director as a
leader-figure], *Bericht über den Internationalen
Kongreß Singen und Sprechen* (München: Oldenbourg,
1938) 191–96. In German. See no. 257 in this volume.

Applies the concept of the *Führerprinzip*, the Nazi leader principle of ultimate authority, to choral conducting.

3278 STOCKMANN, Erich. **Albanische Volksmu-**
as **sikinstrumente** [Albanian traditional instruments],
*Bericht über den internationalen musikwissenschaft-
lichen Kongreß Wien Mozartjahr 1956* (Graz; Köln:
Böhlau, 1958) 612–15. In German. See no. 365 in this
volume.

An informal inventory, with attention to questions of ethnohistorical provenance, from the presumptively oldest stratum of children's instruments
through the modern violin held on the musician's knees, like a lahuta
(gusle). *(David Bloom)*

3279 STOCKMANN, Erich. **Towards a history of**
as **European folk music instruments,** *Studia
musicologica Academiae Scientiarum Hungaricae* VII
(1965) 155–64. See no. 478 in this volume.

Historical research on traditional instruments must be approached comparatively and comprehensively. A systematic typology is needed; instruments
should be studied from morphological, musical, and sociological viewpoints. *(David Gagné)*

3280 STRAETEN, Edmond vander. **Notes sur**
as **quelques instruments de musique en nature ou**
en figuration, trouvés dans la Gaule Belgo-Ro-
maine [Musical instruments, real or depicted, in actuality or in representation, from Belgo-Roman Gaul],
*Annales de la Fédération Archéologique et Historique
de Belgique. VII/2* (Bruxelles: Goemaere, 1892)
374–83. In French. See no. 16 in this volume.

The history of a number of ancient Belgian instruments is discussed: a keyboard and trumpet found on a portion of a mosaic; small bells; fragments of
a curved trumpet; a transverse flute–like instrument on a vase; and a figu-
rine with a sistrum. *(Albert Dlugasch)*

3281 TANABE, Hisao. **Les études récentes con-**
as **cernant les instruments de musique de Japon**
[Recent studies on the musical instruments of Japan],
*Art populaire: Travaux artistiques et scientifiques du Ier
Congrès international des arts populaires* (Paris:
Duchartre, 1931) 130. In French. See no. 152 in this
volume.

Brief account of current views on the origins of the shamisen and biwa and
the history of their introduction into Japan. A summary is cited as no. 3605
in this volume.

3282 TIBERIU, Alexandru. **The study of folk musical**
as **instruments in the Rumanian People's Repub-**
lic, *Journal of the International Folk Music Council*
XII (1960) 13–16. *Illus.* See no. 413 in this volume.

The state of research is surveyed, and a case study of pipe making in the
Transylvanian village of Hodac is presented.

3283 TONKOVIČ, Pavel. **Some observations on Slo-**
as **vak folk music instruments,** *Journal of the International Folk Music Council* XII (1960) 33–34. See no.
413 in this volume.

A survey, with specific notes on the fujara, a duct flute played by shepherds.

3284 VLAHOVIĆ, Mitar S. **O najstarijim muzičkim**
as **instrumentima u Crnoj Gori** [The oldest musical
instruments in Montenegro], *Rad kongresa folklorista
Jugoslavije* (Ljubljana: Savez Udruženja Folkloristov
Jugoslavije, 1960) 313–24. *Illus.* In Serbian; summary
in English. See no. 404 in this volume.

Discusses instruments, including gusle, svirala, duduk, diple, and tepsija
cymbals, mentioned in literary and traditional song texts. *(author)*

3285 VUKMANOVIĆ, Jovan. **Narodni muzički in-**
as **strumenti arbanasa u crnogorskom primorju**
[Albanian traditional instruments of the Montenegrin
coast], *Rad VII-og kongresa Saveza Folklorista Jugoslavije* (Cetinje: Obod, 1964) 297–300. *Illus.* In Serbian; summary in French. See no. 419 in this volume.

Certain localities on the southern Montenegrin coast have Albanian-speak-
ing majorities, descended from Albanian immigrants and assimilated Serb
converts to Islam; their music shows multiple Balkan cultural influences.
In rural districts, they play mainly three instruments: guda (gusle, the most
popular instrument of the Ottoman period), zumare (a wood or metal diple),
and kaval (brass or copper duduk). In the city of Ulcinj, daire and tambura
are also found. *(author)*

3286 YOUNG, Robert William. **Sur l'intonation de di-**
as **vers instruments de musique, du U.S. Navy**
Electronics Laboratory, San Diego 52, Califor-
nia [The intonation of various musical instruments from
the U.S. Navy Electronics Laboratory, San Diego 52,
California], *Acoustique musicale* (Paris: Centre National de la Recherche Scientifique [CNRS], 1959)
169–84. *Charts, diagr.* In French. See no. 393 in this
volume.

Reports observations made with a Stroboconn tuner on the intonation of a
flute, clarinet, alto saxophone, valve trumpet, valve contrabass tuba, and
three models of Steinway piano. Valve instruments suffered from errors in

intonation when valves were used in combination. Pianos were sharp in the highest registers, flat in the lowest, a feature related to the inharmonicity of the strings. Reed instruments showed interval distortion between registers that could be ascribed to the use of the overblowing hole. *(David Bloom)*

3287 ZULAICA Y ARREGUI, José Gonzalo (José Antonio de Donostia). **Les instruments des danse populaires espagnoles** [Instruments of traditional Spanish dance], *Journal of the International Folk Music Council* VI (1954) 26–28. In French. See no. 320 in this volume.
as

An inventory with remarks on construction, playing technique, and geographical distribution.

41 Voice (including choral ensembles)

3288 AIKIN, William Arthur. **Die Phonologie in der Gesangslehre** [Phonology in singing instruction], *Haydn-Zentenarfeier* (Leipzig: Breitkopf & Härtel; Wien: Artaria, 1909) 309–15. *Illus., charts, diagr.* In German. See no. 65 in this volume.
as

Discusses phonetics, diction, and the physiology of vocal production. Anatomical illustrations are provided, as are charts illustrating general tessitura of standard repertoire.

3289 BORUTTAU, Alfred. **Die Beschaffenheit des harten Gaumens und deren Bedeutung für die Stimmabgabe** [The nature of the hard palate and its significance in vocal production], *Bericht über den Internationalen Kongreß Singen und Sprechen* (München: Oldenbourg, 1938) 165–68. In German. See no. 257 in this volume.
as

Argues for a race-based classification of vocal types, according to the configuration of the velum, between the Roman "trumpet" voice produced by a relatively flat velum, and the Nordic "horn" voice associated with a velum at a steep angle. *(David Bloom)*

3290 BOSE, Fritz. **Klangstile als Rassenmerkmale** [Vocal styles as an indication of race], *Bericht über den Internationalen Kongreß Singen und Sprechen* (München: Oldenbourg, 1938) 37–39. In German. See no. 257 in this volume.
as

Voice quality is an inherited characteristic, dependent on race and independent of the cultural environment.

3291 CARDOSO, J. Lellis. **A fonofotografia e a fonética** [Sound spectrography and phonetics], *Anais do Primeiro Congresso da Língua Nacional Cantada* (São Paulo: Departamento Municipal de Cultura, 1938) 516–50. *Illus.* In Portuguese. See no. 253 in this volume.
as

The physiological and psychological aspects of the voice are considered. A comparison of the spectrograms of vowels sung at a particular pitch and of instruments played at the same pitch is proposed as a tool for clarifying singing problems.

3292 CARVALHO, Murilo de. **Os compositores e a técnica do canto** [Composers and the technique of singing], *Anais do Primeiro Congresso da Língua Nacional Cantada* (São Paulo: Departamento Municipal de Cultura, 1938) 647–54. In Portuguese. See no. 253 in this volume.
as

The ways in which a knowledge of singing technique may influence a composer's approach to vocal music are discussed.

3293 CROIZA, Claire. **L'art lyrique et l'interprétation** [Lyric art and interpretation], *Deuxième congrès international d'esthétique et de Science de l'art* (Paris: Librairie Félix Alcan, 1937) II, 256–58. In French. See no. 249 in this volume.
as

There are two kinds of singers, whether in the concert hall or on the stage: those who play a role, and those who live it: only the latter are of interest. To be worthwhile, a musical performance must be imbued with life. Important aspects of musical interpretation for vocalists are listed. The differences between what is required of an opera singer and an actor are discussed. The problems of the concert performer differ from those of the operatic singer. *(Elizabeth A. Wright)*

3294 DELLA CORTE, Andrea. **Ricerca intorno alle "vicende degli stili del canto in rapporto alla cultura musicale e alla pedagogia stilistica"** [Developments in singing styles in relation to musical culture and pedagogy], *Atti del primo Congresso internazionale di musica* (Firenze: Le Monnier, 1935) 203–08. In Italian. See no. 203 in this volume.
as

In the Italian singing tradition, from Caccini through the golden age of bel canto (ca. 1815), vocal pedagogy was unified with larger artistic and cultural movements. This unity was shattered in the era of the conflict between the tenors Adolphe Nourrit and Gilbert-Louis Duprez, and Bellini and Meyerbeer; gradually, the dark sound, chest voice, and declamation came to dominate. Today, singers are poorly prepared for both bel canto roles and the vocal writing of modern composers. The series *Répertoire moderne de vocalises-études*, published by Leduc and Ricordi's *Vocalizzi nello stile moderno*, will help to rectify the latter problem. *(Lisa Miller)*

3295 DESMETTRE, Gertraud Höfer. **Choix des disques pour l'enseignement du chant** [Selection of recordings for singing instruction], *Congrès international de l'enseignement primaire et de l'éducation populaire* (Paris: S.U.D.E.L., 1938) 453–55. In French. See no. 246 in this volume.
as

3296 Discoteca Pública Municipal de São Paulo. **A pronúncia cantada e o problema do nasal brasileiro através dos discos** [Singing pronunciation and the problem of the Brazilian nasal sound as found in recordings], *Anais do Primeiro Congresso da Língua Nacional Cantada* (São Paulo: Departamento Municipal de Cultura, 1938) 189–208. In Portuguese. See no. 253 in this volume.
as

Many recordings of vocal music preserve an inaccurate pronunciation of the nasal vowels that characterize Brazilian Portuguese. The problems involved in the proper rendition of these sounds are discussed.

3297 FORBES, Elena Garnett (Elena Garnetti). **The exercise of voice,** *Proceedings of the Second International Congress of Phonetic Sciences* (Cambridge: Cambridge University Press, 1936) 271–78. See no. 222 in this volume.
as

3298 FORCHHAMMER, Jørgen. **Stützen und Stauen** [Support and hindrance], *Bericht über den Internationalen Kongreß Singen und Sprechen* (München: Oldenbourg, 1938) 168–72. In German. See no. 257 in this volume.
as

General remarks on central principles of voice production.

3299 FREITAS E CASTRO, Enio de. **Uma escola brasileira de canto** [A Brazilian school of singing], *Anais do Primeiro Congresso da Língua Nacional Cantada* (São Paulo: Departamento Municipal de Cultura, 1938) 429–36. In Portuguese. See no. 253 in this volume.
as

A properly Brazilian school of singing must take into consideration the variations in diction among the regional dialects of the Portuguese language.

3300
as

GARSÓ, Siga. **Die Lehre des Kunstgesanges und das Bilden des losen Tones** [The theory of art singing and the development of a relaxed tone], *Zweiter Musikpädagogischer Kongress: Vorträge und Referate* (Berlin: Klavier-Lehrer, 1904) 111–18. In German. See no. 43 in this volume.

3301
as

GASTOUÉ, Lucie. **La formation pratique de la voix** [Practical formation of the voice], *Compte rendu du Congrès général de musique sacrée: Aperçu général des préliminaires et du congrès, discours et conférences* (Strasbourg: Alsacien, 1922) 149–52. In French. See no. 96 in this volume.

Emphasizes the importance of determining vocal range and proposes developmental exercises.

3302
as

GUTTMANN, Alfred. **Kunst und Wissenschaft des Gesanges** [The art and science of singing], *Kongress für Ästhetik und allgemeine Kunstwissenschaft: Bericht* (Stuttgart: Enke, 1914) 511–32. In German. See no. 86 in this volume.

3303
as

HECHT, Theophil. **Der Primat der Stimme in der katholischen Kirchenmusik** [The primacy of the voice in Catholic church music], *Zweiter internationaler Kongress für katholische Kirchenmusik: Zu Ehren des Heiligen Papstes Pius X* (Wien: conference, 1955) 312–15. In German. See no. 339 in this volume.

Scriptural and ecclesiastical authorities on the subject of singing suggest that it must be given more attention; it is particularly important that Roman Catholics receive vocal training at an early age. *(David Bloom)*

3304
as

HÉRICARD, Jeanne. **La formation vocale dans l'opéra contemporain** [Vocal training in contemporary opera], *Zeitgenössisches Musiktheater/Contemporary music theatre/Théâtre musical contemporain* (Hamburg: Deutscher Musikrat, 1966) 143–44. In French. See no. 481 in this volume.

Modern opera is well past the strictly experimental phase, but the hostility of singers toward modern music continues to pose difficulties. Composers must be defended against poorly prepared singers, just as singers must be defended against such dangerous compositional practices as the systematic use of extreme registers. Voices must be prepared progressively and simultaneously for the most advanced music along with other styles; appropriate exercises are suggested. *(David Bloom)*

3305
as

HERZOG, George. **Musical styles in North America,** *Proceedings of the Twenty-third International Congress of Americanists* (New York: n.p., 1930) 455–58. See no. 149 in this volume.

Vocal techniques such as accents, glides, ornaments, shouts, and variations of timbre are all fundamental to the style of Native American music. The music of certain Western tribes does not possess all of these traits.

(David Nussenbaum)

3306
as

HORNBOSTEL, Erich Moritz von. **Die Entstehung des Jodelns** [The rise of yodeling], *Bericht über den musikwissenschaftlichen Kongreß in Basel* (Leipzig: Breitkopf & Härtel, 1925) 203–10. In German. See no. 102 in this volume.

The technique appears to imitate the sudden change of register possible on an instrument such as the alphorn or the shawm. A starting point must have been the appearance of Asian wind instruments in the Alps. In the north

Solomon Islands a parallel technique employing panpipes emerged from Polynesian influence.

3307
as

HORST, Anthon van der. **Fragen der Chorerziehung (Zusammenfassung)** [Issues in the training of choral singers (Summary)], *Bericht über den Internationalen Kongress für Kirchenmusik/Compte rendu du Congrès international de musique sacrée* (Bern: Haupt, 1953) 40–41. In German. See no. 312 in this volume.

Different aspects include psychological training, in which the individual learns to give up some individuality and work for the group; technical training (i.e., vocal technique); musical training (including instruction in pitch and rhythm); and spiritual training, which transforms mere performance into interpretation. *(Larry Laskowski)*

3308
as

HUSSON, Raoul. **La physique du pavillon pharyngo-buccal dans la phonation** [Physics of the pharyngo-buccal cavity in the phonation process], *Acoustique musicale* (Paris: Centre National de la Recherche Scientifique [CNRS], 1959) 253–55. In French. See no. 393 in this volume.

A general account of the acoustics of the pharyngeal-buccal cavity in the production of sung vowels, in terms of the acoustic propagation theory of Yves Rocard. *(David Bloom)*

3309
as

JATOBÁ, Pedro. **Colisão entre as acentuações verbal e musical no canto** [The conflict between verbal and musical accents in singing], *Anais do Primeiro Congresso da Língua Nacional Cantada* (São Paulo: Departamento Municipal de Cultura, 1938) 665–78. In Portuguese. See no. 253 in this volume.

Discusses the problem as it applies to Portuguese-language vocal music.

3310
as

KLIČKOVA, Vera. **Narodni muzički instrumenti u Makedoniji** [Traditional musical instruments in Macedonia], *Rad kongresa folklorista Jugoslavije* (Beograd: Naučno Delo, 1960) 225–40. *Illus., bibliog.* In Serbian; summary in French. See no. 402 in this volume.

A general discussion of percussion, wind, and string instruments, with remarks on their history and manufacture. Plates of representations of the instruments from the 12th through the 19th c. are appended.

3311
as

KOHMANN, Antoni. **Gesangstechnik und Gesangsmethode** [Singing technique and singing method], *Bericht über den Internationalen Kongreß Singen und Sprechen* (München: Oldenbourg, 1938) 172–75. In German. See no. 257 in this volume.

Singing technique cannot be learned from books; a personal relationship between teacher and pupil is required.

3312
as

LABARRAQUE, L. **Le science phonétique, base essentielle de l'éducation de la voix chantée** [Phonetic science, essential basis for the training of the singing voice], *Proceedings of the Third International Congress of Phonetic Sciences* (Gent: Rijksuniversitet, Fonetisch Laboratorium, 1939) 207–20. In French. See no. 259 in this volume.

An understanding of breathing, tongue and larynx movements, and the resonance capacities of the nasal cavities from the standpoint of articulatory phonetics can help singers improve their vocal production. *(Terence Ford)*

3313
as

MANUCCI DE GRANDIS, Isabella. **La tecnica de respiro in rapporto all'arte del canto e della parola** [Breathing technique in relation to the arts of singing and speech], *Bericht über den Internationalen Kongreß Singen und Sprechen* (München: Oldenbourg,

1938) 151–55. In Italian and German. See no. 257 in this volume.

3314 MÉFRAY, Clément. **La formation vocale des**
as **garçons dans les écoles, catéchismes, patron-**
ages, maîtrises [The vocal training of boys in
schools, catechism class, youth clubs, and choir
schools], *La musique d'église: Compte rendu du*
Congrès de musique sacrée (Tourcoing: Duvivier,
1920) 1–13. In French. See no. 93 in this volume.
A choirmaster of Notre-Dame de Bon Port describes how to form and cultivate a boys' choir. Every boy is capable of singing unless he has a physical
deformity or a bad ear, albeit children are inclined to shout (as if they were
playing on the street). Since the term "head voice" is often viewed as pejo-
rative, the term "boy's voice" should be employed instead. A number of vocal exercises and instructions on how to determine the best singers within a
choir are provided. *(Susan Poliniak)*

3315 MIGNONE, Francisco. **A pronúncia do canto**
as **nacional** [Pronunciation in national song], *Anais do*
Primeiro Congresso da Língua Nacional Cantada (São
Paulo: Departamento Municipal de Cultura, 1938)
487–96. In Portuguese. See no. 253 in this volume.
Draws a systematic comparison between the vowels of sung Italian and
Brazilian Portuguese.

3316 [Portuguese singing pronunciation] **Normas**
as **para boa pronúncia da língua nacional no**
canto erudito [Norms for the correct pronunciation
of the national language in concert singing], *Anais do*
Primeiro Congresso da Língua Nacional Cantada (São
Paulo: Departamento Municipal de Cultura, 1938)
49–94. In Portuguese. See no. 253 in this volume.
Proposes a standard singing pronunciation for open and closed vowels,
diphthongs, and consonants in Brazilian Portuguese.

3317 RICHTER. **Was muß der Kapellmeister von**
as **der Behandlung der Stimme des Sängers bei**
der Einstudierung einer Oper wissen? [What
does a conductor need to know about the treatment of
singers' voices in the preparation of an opera?], *Bericht*
über den Internationalen Kongreß Singen und
Sprechen (München: Oldenbourg, 1938) 184–88. In
German. See no. 257 in this volume.
Well-trained opera conductors have studied voice themselves, and have a
thorough knowledge of the voices of singers who work with them. From
the first casting decisions through the performance, opera conductors need
to be personally engaged with the singers, though not in such a way as to
overlap in function with a singer's own teacher. The conductor should play
the piano in the initial solo rehearsals, and ideally should be the stage director as well. *(David Bloom)*

3318 SAUVREZIS, Alice. **Les chœurs d'enfants à la**
as **radio** [Children's choruses on the radio], *Compte*
rendu des travaux du Iᵉʳ Congrès international d'art
radiophonique (Paris: conference, 1938). In French.
See no. 244 in this volume.

3319 SCHMIDT, H. **Über die Registerausbildung**
as **der menschlichen Stimme: Methode**
Nehrlich-Schmidt [Register training for the human
voice: The Nehrlich-Schmidt method], *Bericht über*
den zweiten Kongress der Internationalen Musikgesell-
schaft (Leipzig: Breitkopf & Härtel, 1907) 74–75. In
German. See no. 53 in this volume.
Outline of the author's method of vocal training, based on the work of
Christian Gottfried Nehrlich. An extended version is published as *Register*
der menschlichen Stimme und ihre Behandlung: Anleitung zur Ausbildung
von Singstimmen (Hagen, Westphalia, 1904). *(David Bloom)*

3320 SCHOLE, Heinrich. **Die Vokalität der ein-**
as **fachen Töne und das Singen von Vokalen in**
hoher Stimmlage [The vocalism of simple tones and
the singing of vowels in the high register], *Bericht über*
den Internationalen Kongreß Singen und Sprechen
(München: Oldenbourg, 1938) 301–05. In German. See
no. 257 in this volume.
Reports on an experimental test and explanation in terms of vowel formants
of the difficulty, particularly for sopranos, of making audible distinctions
between vowel sounds. It cannot entirely be corrected, especially since
singers must be concerned first with beauty of tone. Sopranos are advised
to compensate for the problem by the careful articulation of consonants and
stress, by providing visual clues through lip movement and mime, and otherwise to rely on the familiarity or contextuality of the text. *(David Bloom)*

3321 SCOLARI. **Le due manieri di cantare sorte**
as **all'inizio dell'800** [The two styles of singing arising
at the beginning of the 19th century], *Bericht über den*
Internationalen Kongreß Singen und Sprechen
(München: Oldenbourg, 1938) 155–61. In Italian and
German. See no. 257 in this volume.
Remarks on the evolution of bel canto style and the style known in Italian
slang as *canto di fibra* (muscular singing), typified by the use of chest voice
in the upper tenor register. *(David Bloom)*

3322 SMITH, Svend. **On the high resonances of the**
as **male voice,** *Congrès international des sciences*
anthropologiques et ethnologiques: Compte rendu de
la troisième session (Tervuren: Musée Royal de
l'Afrique Centrale, 1960) 225. See no. 282 in this volume.
Reports the results of a comparison in patterning of higher formants between speech and singing.

3323 SOMIGLI, Carlo. **Les mécanismes laryngiens**
as **et les timbres vocaux** [Laryngeal mechanism and
vocal sound quality], *Report of the Fourth Congress of*
the International Musical Society (London: Novello,
1912) 370–72. *Music, charts, diagr.* In French. See no.
71 in this volume.
Outlines normal and abnormal functions.

3324 STŘELCOVÁ, Věra. **Několik poznámek k**
as **pěvecké interpretaci Janáčkova drama-**
tického slohu [Remarks on the singer's interpretation
of Janáček's dramatic style], *Leoš Janáček a soudobá*
hudba (Praha: Panton, 1963) 294–97. In Czech; summaries in Russian and German. See no. 389 in this
volume.
Janáček's new dramatic-melodic style based on psychologically determined speech melodies requires a specific vocal technique based on a balance of the declamatory (dramatic) and the cantilena (lyrical) aspects of vocal interpretation. *(editors)*

3325 TARNEAUD, Jean. **Évolution de nos con-**
as **naissances en pathologie vocale** [The evolution of
our knowledge of vocal pathology], *Proceedings of the*
Second International Congress of Phonetic Sciences
(Cambridge: Cambridge University Press, 1936)
73–75. In French. See no. 222 in this volume.

3326 THOMAS, Kurt. **Über die Aussprache beim**
as **chorischen Singen** [Diction in choral singing],
Bericht über den Internationalen Kongreß Singen und
Sprechen (München: Oldenbourg, 1938) 295–98. In
German. See no. 257 in this volume.
The most important factor in the intelligibility of a sung text is the alterna-
tion of stressed and unstressed syllables of natural speech rhythm. One
technique to help chorus members acquire a feeling for this is through

exercises in group whispering. The whole subject is treated more fully in the author's *Lehrbuch der Chorleitung* (Leipzig, 1935-48). *(David Bloom)*

3327 TREUMANN-METTE, Arthur. **Die anato-**
as **misch-physiologischen Leitsätze für Zahn-prothetik bei Sprechern und Sängern** [Anatomical and physiological principles for the use of dental prostheses by speakers and singers], *Bericht über den Internationalen Kongreß Singen und Sprechen* (München: Oldenbourg, 1938) 47–51. In German. See no. 257 in this volume.
Singers can use correctly placed dental prostheses to correct the position of the teeth and improve voice production.

3328 WARDE. **Die Beziehungen zwischen Sprache**
as **und Gesang** [The connections between speech and singing], *Bericht über den Internationalen Kongreß Singen und Sprechen* (München: Oldenbourg, 1938) 308–11. In German. See no. 257 in this volume.
Just as singers can clearly benefit from training in spoken declamation, so can actors benefit from the study of singing. An example is provided of the use of singing instruction in the vocal training of an actor with a cleft palate. *(David Bloom)*

3329 WERNER, Theodor Wilhelm. **Aus der Frühzeit**
as **des unbegleiteten Männergesangs** [On the origins of the unaccompanied male vocal ensemble], *Bericht über den I. musikwissenschaftlichen Kongress der Deutschen Musikgesellschaft in Leipzig* (Wiesbaden: Breitkopf & Härtel, 1926) 286. In German. See no. 120 in this volume.
From the style's origins in 18th-c. Salzburg (specifically the male quartets of Michael Haydn), it spread to Switzerland, southern Germany, and finally to northern Germany. *(William Renwick)*

3330 WICART, Alexis. **Les principes d'organisation**
as **et de fonctionnement de l'Institut Vocal Universel de Paris** [The organizational and functional principles of the Institut Vocal Universel, Paris], *Bericht über den Internationalen Kongreß Singen und Sprechen* (München: Oldenbourg, 1938) 286–92. In French. See no. 257 in this volume.
At the Congrès Universel de la Voix held in Paris 1937, in connection with the Exposition Internationale, the founding of an international institute in Paris for the purpose of stimulating a renaissance in all the forms of vocal art was proposed. The institute would offer documentary and experimental research facilities, general and specialized instruction, and public events. Details of the various proposed programs are provided. *(David Bloom)*

3331 WÜSTHOFF, Paul Gerhard. **Die Bedeutung der**
as **Vererbung auf dem Gebiet der Sprach- und Stimmheilkunde** [The meaning of heredity in the area of therapy for the speaking and singing voice], *Bericht über den Internationalen Kongreß Singen und Sprechen* (München: Oldenbourg, 1938) 43–47. *Charts, diagr.* In German. See no. 257 in this volume.
Family-tree and twin research shows the heritability of factors in voice quality and vocal pathology. Voice type, for example, is inherited in simple Mendelian fashion, with bass and soprano voices dominant, tenor and alto voices recessive, and baritone and mezzo-soprano heterozygotic. *(Terence Ford)*

3332 ZWIRNER, Eberhard. **Schwankungen der**
as **Mundlage beim Singen einzelner Laute** [Variations in mouth position in the singing of isolated sounds], *Proceedings of the Third International Congress of Phonetic Sciences* (Gent: Rijksuniversiteit,

Fonetisch Laboratorium, 1939) 77–104. *Illus., charts, diagr.* In German. See no. 259 in this volume.
Quantitative analysis shows that different kinds of articulatory movements are involved in speech and singing.

42 Keyboard, organ

3333 AERDE, Raymond Joseph Justin van. **Deux**
as **contrats de facteurs d'orgues belges inconnus jusqu'ici: XVIIe et XVIIIe siècles** [Two contracts of hitherto unknown Belgian organ builders: 17th and 18th centuries], *Annales du XXIIIe congrès* (Gent: Siffer, 1914) III, 243–53. In French. See no. 89 in this volume.
Antoine Bergère and Adrien Rochet built organs in the 17th and 18th c. respectively. Bergère lived in Brussels, Rochet in Nivelles. Their contracts are presented in their entirety.

3334 ANGLÈS, Higini. **Orgelmusik der Schola**
as **Hispanica vom XV. bis XVII. Jahrhundert** [Organ music of the Spanish school from the 15th to the 17th centuries], *Bericht über den I. musikwissenschaftlichen Kongress der Deutschen Musikgesellschaft in Leipzig* (Wiesbaden: Breitkopf & Härtel, 1926) 227–31. In German. See no. 120 in this volume.
Discusses the prominent Spanish organ builders as well as German influences on design. Organists such as those of the Cabezón family, theorists such as Juan Bermudo and Francisco Correa de Arauxo, and various genres of organ music are mentioned. *(William Renwick)*

3335 AULER, Wolfgang. **Weltliche Musik auf dem**
as **Positiv** [Secular music on the positive], *Bericht über die zweite Freiburger Tagung für Deutsche Orgelkunst* (Kassel: Bärenreiter, 1939) 55–62. In German. See no. 258 in this volume.
Relatively few of the problems of contemporary organ building affect the positive; it seems obvious that it should be built with sliding chest and mechanical action. It is suitable for a wide range of early music, especially all sorts of continuo parts. Technical solutions are proposed for special problems in using it as a solo instrument in works by Jan Pieterszoon Sweelinck and Johann Jakob Froberger. *(David Bloom)*

3336 BEVENOT, Laurence. **L'orgue McClure à**
as **tempérament non-égal** [The McClure organ with unequal temperament], *Atti del [I] Congresso internazionale di musica sacra* (Tournai: Desclée, 1952) 342–43. In French. See no. 303 in this volume.
Notes on the extended meantone organ with 19 pipes to the octave designed by A.R. McClure and built 1950 by the Harrison & Harrison firm of Durham, now in the collection of the Faculty of Music, University of Edinburgh, at Alison House. *(David Bloom)*

3337 BIEHLE, Johannes. **Æsthetik des Orgelklanges**
as **und des Orgelspieles** [The aesthetics of the organ's sound and of organ playing], *Deuxième congrès international d'esthétique et de Science de l'art* (Paris: Librairie Félix Alcan, 1937) II, 239–42. In German. See no. 249 in this volume.
Technical discussion, with particular attention to the attainment of *Helligkeit* (clarity).

3338 BIGGS, E. Power. **A musician and his acousti-**
as **cal environment,** *Sound and man* (New York: American Institute of Physics, 1957) 50–52. See no. 369 in this volume.
The acoustics of European churches influenced organ compositions. A study of these churches and organs indicates that American organ builders

and architects have much to learn, particularly in the areas of voicing and proper location of an organ within a building. Open placement of the organ is necessary, as is ample reverberation time. *(author)*

3339 BÖHRINGER, Hans. **Denkmalorgel und**
as **Gottesdienst** [Historic organs and divine service], *Richtlinien zum Schutze alter wertvoller Orgeln (Weilheimer Regulativ); Zugleich der kurzgefaßte Bericht über die Arbeitstagung der Orgeldenkmalpfleger* (Berlin: Merseburger, 1958) 31–32. In German. See no. 387 in this volume.
Argues against the widespread view that organs of the 18th and early 19th c. are unsuitable for use in the Roman Catholic liturgy, with suggested resolutions for some of the practical problems. *(David Bloom)*

3340 BÖHRINGER, Hans. **Die Orgel als geistliche**
as **Aufgabe** [The organ as a spiritual duty], *Orgelbewegung und Historismus: Tagungsberichte. I* (Berlin: Merseburger, 1958) 34–35. In German. See no. 338 in this volume.
The Baroque church organ retained the association with secular power that marked its introduction (along with incense and candles) in the Byzantine and Carolingian period; in the 20th c., with the separation of church and state, the role of the organ is strictly to serve, and a smaller instrument (two or three manuals and 10-35 stops) is adequate. Trying to build an organ suitable for the performance of almost all of the instrument's repertoire is only part of the builder's task; it must also be suitable for its function and space. *(David Bloom)*

3341 BÖHRINGER, Hans. **Das Spezifische des**
as **"katholischen" Orgelbaus** [The specific character of so-called Catholic organ building], *Der Barock: Seine Orgeln und seine Musik in Oberschwaben* (Berlin: Merseburger, 1952) 148–50. In German. See no. 305 in this volume.
The differences between South German and North German organs of the Baroque period have more to do with the different landscapes and associated attitudes than with any difference in the function of the organ in Catholic as opposed to Protestant worship. In today's Catholic churches organs are generally equipped with pedal registers and do not differ essentially from those used in Protestant churches. *(David Bloom)*

3342 BÖHRINGER, Hans. **Über altitalienische**
as **Orgeln** [Early Italian organs], *Altbayerische Orgeltage* (Berlin: Merseburger, 1958) 23–24. *Organ specification.* In German. See no. 355 in this volume.
Notes on the character and current playability of organs from the 15th through early 19th c. in Bologna, Brescia, Treviso, Verona, Calceranica, and Caldonasso, with particular attention to that of the church of San Martino, Bologna (Giovanni Cipri, 1556). *(David Bloom)*

3343 BONNET, Joseph. **Le chant grégorien dans la**
as **littérature d'orgue** [Gregorian chant in organ literature], *Congrès international de musique sacrée: Chant et orgue* (Paris: Desclée de Brouwer, 1937) 76–78. In French. See no. 247 in this volume.
Organists since Léonin and Pérotin have incorporated chant melodies into organ music, among them Titelouze, Frescobaldi, Sweelinck, and Buxtehude. Great organ composers of Bach's time include Couperin and Grigny, from whose *Livre d'orgue* Bach borrowed. Today Gigout, Widor, d'Indy, Chausson, and Hubert Parry, among others, have revived the organ tradition. *(Arthur Maisel)*

3344 BORMANN, Karl. **Wie alte und neue Orgeln**
as **klingen** [How old and new organs sound], *Altbayern als Orgel-Landschaft* (Berlin: Merseburger, 1954) 17–18. In German. See no. 325 in this volume.

3345 BÖSKEN, Franz. **Der mittelrheinische Orgel-**
as **bau zur Zeit des Aufenthalts Joseph Gablers in**

Mainz [Organ-building in the mid-Rhine region during Joseph Gabler's stays in Mainz], *Der Barock: Seine Orgeln und seine Musik in Oberschwaben* (Berlin: Merseburger, 1952) 78–81. *Organ specification.* In German. See no. 305 in this volume.
Examples of important organs that may have influenced the Ochsenhausen-born builder Joseph Gabler during his residences there in 1719-29 and 1733-37 include those of Johann Peter Geißel (such as that of the Pauluskirche, 1631), Johann Friedrich Macrander (Ignazkirche, 1699), Johann Jakob Dahm (Kloster Eberbach, 1707), and Johann Hoffmann (Stephanskirche, 1715). Dispositions for these representative instruments are given and other builders of the time are briefly discussed. *(David Bloom)*

3346 BOUMAN, Arie; KLUYVER, P. **Hausorgeln in**
as **Holland** [House organs in Holland], *Bericht über die zweite Freiburger Tagung für Deutsche Orgelkunst* (Kassel: Bärenreiter, 1939) 125–31. *Illus., bibliog., organ specification.* In German. See no. 258 in this volume.
Though there are some earlier instruments, including examples by Arp Schnitger from around 1700, the house organ flourished in the Netherlands mainly in the period ca. 1750–ca. 1870, as an instrument for home use both in Calvinist devotions and in secular music, at a period when German builders made almost no smaller organs. Provenance, current location, and dispositions are given for a number of representative instruments, and a chronological list of builders is provided. *(David Bloom)*

3347 COUPLEUX, Léon. **L'orgue des ondes** [The bel-
as lows organ], *Compte rendu du Congrès d'orgue tenu à l'Université de Strasbourg. IV* (Strasbourg: Société Strasbourgeoise de Librairie Sostralib, 1934) 139–41. In French. See no. 199 in this volume.
Provides a brief history of the instrument, and discusses its use and technical limitations.

3348 DEREUX, J.-A. **L'"orgue à synthèse"** [The *orgue*
as *à synthèse*], *Revue musicale* 239-240 (1957) 191–98. In French. See no. 378 in this volume.

3349 DOORSLAER, Georges van. **Notes sur les**
as **facteurs d'orgues malinois** [Notes on the organ builders of Mechelen], *Fédération Archéologique et Historique de Belgique: Annales du XXIIᵉ congrès. I: Documents et compte rendu; II: Rapports & mémoires* (Mechelen: Godenne, 1911) II, 605–20. In French. See no. 73 in this volume.
Brief biographical sketches of 28 organ builders of Mechelen from the 16th to the 19th c.

3350 DREIMÜLLER, Karl. **Lob des Positivs: Eine**
as **zeitgemäße Mönchengladbacher "Orgel-predigt"** [In praise of the positive: A well-timed Mönchengladbach organ sermon], *Studien zur Musikgeschichte der Stadt Mönchengladbach* (Köln: Volk, 1965) 87–94. *Illus., organ specification.* In German. See no. 486 in this volume.
Reprint of a festive address at the dedication of a Georg Stahlhuth positive organ in the aula of the Mathematisch-Naturwissenschaftliches Gymnasium, Mönchengladbach, November 1963. *(David Bloom)*

3351 DUFOURCQ, Norbert. **Le grand orgue de la**
as **Chapelle de l'École Royale Militaire** [The great organ of the chapel of the École Royale Militaire], *Compte rendu du Congrès d'orgue tenu à l'Université de Strasbourg. IV* (Strasbourg: Société Strasbourgeoise de Librairie Sostralib, 1934) 187–92. In French. See no. 199 in this volume.
Provides a general description and historical summary of the instrument.

3352 DUFOURCQ, Norbert. **Interdépendence de la**
as **facture et de la musique d'orgue en France sous**
la règne de Louis XIV [The interdependence of organ building and organ music in France during the reign
of Louis XIV], *Kirchenmusik in ökumenischer Schau*
(Bern: Haupt, 1964) 88–90. In French. See no. 447 in
this volume.

Summary of a paper. The full version appeared in *L'organo* III (1962)
149-58.

3353 DUFOURCQ, Norbert. **Le maître franco-**
as **espagnol Aristide Cavaillé-Coll (1811-1899) et**
l'évolution de la musique d'orgue en France
[The Franco-Spanish master Aristide Cavaillé-Coll
(1811-1899) and the evolution of organ music in
France], *Congrés de la Societat Internacional de
Musicologia* (Barcelona: Casa de Caritat, 1936). In
French. See no. 224 in this volume.

The conference report provides only a citation. Neither the text nor a summary of the paper was published here.

3354 DUFOURCQ, Norbert. **Les tendances de la fac-**
as **ture d'orgues française contemporaine** [Trends
in contemporary organ manufacture], *Congrès international de musique sacrée: Chant et orgue* (Paris:
Desclée de Brouwer, 1937) 171–82. In French. See no.
247 in this volume.

The history of organ building, including its current forms. Information on
the important French organists and composers ca. 1937 is included.

3355 DYSON, George. **The place of the organist in**
as **British musical life,** *Organ and choral aspects and
prospects* (London: Hinrichsen, 1958) 24–32. See no.
375 in this volume.

Remarks on the history of the organ in the 14th–16th c., school and church
organists, administrative and amateur organists, and virtuoso organists.

3356 EHMANN, Wilhelm. **Orgel und Volkslied** [Or-
as gan and traditional song], *Bericht über die zweite
Freiburger Tagung für Deutsche Orgelkunst* (Kassel:
Bärenreiter, 1939) 88–97. In German. See no. 258 in
this volume.

Evidence from the late 15th through 17th c. in Germany shows that secular
organ music has always been connected to popular and traditional singing,
improvisational technique, and the character of a handicraft, though it has
never been itself an instrument of the masses. Its history should be noted in
current efforts (ca. 1938) to revive the instrument for Hausmusik and public festivities, marches, political rallies, and so on. *(David Bloom)*

3357 EHRENHOFER, Walther Edmund. **Einheitliche**
as **Gestaltung des Spieltisches unter spezieller**
Berücksichtigung der Pedalfrage [Uniform organization of the console with special consideration of the
pedal question], *Haydn-Zentenarfeier* (Leipzig:
Breitkopf & Härtel; Wien: Artaria, 1909) 607–11. In
German. See no. 65 in this volume.

3358 FELLERER, Karl Gustav. **Die alte für Klein-**
as **orgel bestimmte Orgelmusik** [Early music intended for the small organ], *Bericht über die zweite
Freiburger Tagung für Deutsche Orgelkunst* (Kassel:
Bärenreiter, 1939) 43–54. In German. See no. 258 in this
volume.

From the Middle Ages through the 18th c. large organs began to be used
more exclusively in church music, while secular ensembles increasingly
called for the harpsichord. It is at this period that the smaller organ—positive or portative—developed its own repertoire, separate from that of the
great church organ. Even in the high Baroque, many of Telemann's and J.S.

Bach's organ works, and all of Händel's, are adapted to small instruments.
(David Bloom)

3359 FELLERER, Karl Gustav. **Das Partimentospiel:**
as **Eine Ausgabe des Organisten im 18.**
Jahrhundert [The playing of partimento: A task of the
18th-century organist], *Société Internationale de Musicologie: Premier Congrès Liège—Compte rendu/Inter-
nationale Gesellschaft für Musikwissenschaft: Erster
Kongress Lüttich—Kongressbericht/International Society for Musical Research: First Congress Liège: Report*
(London: Plainsong and Mediaeval Music Society,
1930) 109–12. In German. See no. 178 in this volume.

Describes differences in the treatment of partimento, the practice of improvising melodies and complete pieces above a written bass, to illustrate differences in national styles. *(Scott Fruehwald)*

3360 FISCHER, Wilhelm. **Die konzertierende Orgel**
as **im Orchester des 18. Jahrhunderts** [The concertante organ in the 18th-century orchestra], *Bericht über
die [I] Freiburger Tagung für Deutsche Orgelkunst*
(Augsburg: Bärenreiter, 1926) 68–69. In German. See
no. 122 in this volume.

The recently built Praetorius-Orgel by Oscar Walcker and Wilibald Gurlitt
at the Institut für Musikwissenschaft at the Universität Freiburg (1921)
provides a clue as to what kind of instrument is suitable for the solo parts of
Händel's concertos, the obbligato organ parts in works by Bach and certain
English composers of the late Baroque, and the organ solos in the Masses of
Haydn and Mozart—in particular in its ability to provide a clear articula-
tion of polyphony on a single manual, as modern organs are unable to do.
(David Bloom)

3361 FLADE, Ernst. **Bachs Stellung zum Orgel- und**
as **Klavierbau seiner Zeit** [Bach's views on the keyboard instrument construction of his day], *Bericht über
die Wissenschaftliche Bachtagung* (Leipzig: Peters,
1951) 405–10. In German. See no. 298 in this volume.

Bach's concepts of organ construction were formed in Thuringia, but
through travels he assimilated North German and Netherlandish influences. In his organ dispositions he preferred mutation stops and especially
reed pipes, but also took an interest in string stops. He preferred the clavichord, especially pedal clavichord, to the harpsichord, and was at first un-
enthusiastic, then pleased, with the newly invented pianoforte. He took an
active part in the invention of a lute-harpsichord (*Lautenklavier*). A list by
city of instruments Bach is known to have played, builders with whom he
was acquainted, and so on, is provided.

3362 FLADE, Ernst. **Gottfried Silbermann als**
as **Orgelbauer** [Gottfried Silbermann as organ builder],
*Bericht über die [I] Freiburger Tagung für Deutsche
Orgelkunst* (Augsburg: Bärenreiter, 1926) 59–67. In
German. See no. 122 in this volume.

A brief assessment of the organ builder's life and works, based on the author's *Der Orgelbauer Gottfried Silbermann: Ein Beitrag zur Geschichte
des deutschen Orgelbaues im Zeitalter Bachs* (Leipzig: Kistner & Siegel,
1926). *(David Bloom)*

3363 FLADE, Ernst. **Der Zukunftswert der Silber-**
as **mannorgel** [The value to the future of the Silbermann
organ], *Bericht über die dritte Tagung für Deutsche
Orgelkunst* (Kassel: Bärenreiter, 1928) 103–09. In German. See no. 136 in this volume.

An appreciation of Gottfried Silbermann (1683-1753) and the other builders of the Silbermann family, with particular attention to his organ for the
Freiberg cathedral (1714). The instrument's repertoire of stops, exceptionally appropriate for clear voice-leading in polyphonic music, provides a
valuable model for modern registration.

3364 FOCK, Gustav. **Die Hauptepochen des nord-**
as **deutschen Orgelbaues bis Schnitger** [The major

eras of North German organ building up to Schnitger], *Orgelbewegung und Historismus: Tagungsberichte. I* (Berlin: Merseburger, 1958) 36–47. *Maps, organ specification.* In German. See no. 338 in this volume.

The initial period, ca. 1550-1620, was dominated by builders from or trained in the Netherlandish, especially Brabantine, school, such as Gregorius Vogel, Hendrik Niehoff and Jasper Johansen, Antonius Mors and his sons, Andreas and Marten de Mare, Hermann Raphael Rodensteen, Fabian Peterszoon or Peters, Julius Anton Friese, members of the Slegel family from Zwolle, Jan Graurock, and Gottschalk Burkhard Johansen. A native school flourished in ca. 1535-1630 in Hamburg under Jakob Scherer, his son Hans Scherer the elder, and his grandson Hans Scherer the younger; other German builders included Matthias Mahn, Heinrich Glowatz, and Nikolaus Maass. Gottfried Fritzsche lived in the north from 1629 to his death in 1638, and he and his sons and students provided the transition to Arp Schnitger and his school. Tabular lists of Fritzsche's and Schnitger's students and maps of Schnitger's influence through his students and through his own work are included. *(David Bloom)*

3365 FROTSCHER, Gotthold. **Kult-, Kirchen- und**
as **Konzertorgel** [Devotional, church, and concert organ], *Bericht über die dritte Tagung für Deutsche Orgelkunst* (Kassel: Bärenreiter, 1928) 43–45. In German. See no. 136 in this volume.

A distinction may be drawn within the general concept of the spiritual between churchliness and religiosity. The churchly consists of a repertoire of particular forms and expressive means, connected to a particular historical moment; the religious transcends both the personal and the temporal. The organ of the future will be neither a secular organ nor a church organ in this sense but a *Kultorgel*, a religious organ.

3366 FROTSCHER, Gotthold. **Die Wechselbezie-**
as **hungen zwischen Orgelmusik und Orgelbau in Geschichte und Gegenwart** [The mutual relation between organ music and organ building in history and in the present], *Bericht über die zweite Freiburger Tagung für Deutsche Orgelkunst* (Kassel: Bärenreiter, 1939) 98–103. In German. See no. 258 in this volume.

Notions of ideal organ construction and ideal organ music should not be considered in isolation, but together, in subordination to the concept of *Feier* (celebration and solemnity). Amplifies discussion in the author's *Die Orgel in der politischen Feier, Musik in Jugend und Volk* I/9-10, 1938. *(David Bloom)*

3367 FROTSCHER, Gotthold. **Zur Registrierkunst**
as **des 18. Jahrhunderts** [The art of registration in the 18th century], *Bericht über die [I] Freiburger Tagung für Deutsche Orgelkunst* (Augsburg: Bärenreiter, 1926) 70–75. In German. See no. 122 in this volume.

Among the very few sources of information on registration in 18th-c. organ music are the sets of chorale variations composed by the Danzig organist Daniel Magnus Gronau (d. 1747), all in MS at the Danziger Stadtbibliothek (now the Wojewódzka Biblioteka Publiczna), in which a recommended registration is fully specified for each variation. The registrations for one such work, on *Ach Gott, wie manches Herzeleid*, are discussed in detail. *(David Bloom)*

3368 GERMANI, Fernando. **L'organo barocco nell'**
as **idea moderna** [The modern concept of the Baroque organ], *Atti del [I] Congresso internazionale di musica sacra* (Tournai: Desclée, 1952) 348–50. In Italian. See no. 303 in this volume.

3369 GÉROLD, Theodore. **La section d'orgue, au**
as **congrès de la S.I.M. à Vienne 1909, point de départ du mouvement organal actuel** [The organ section at the S.I.M. congress in Vienna in 1909: The departure point of the current organ movement], *Congrès de la Societat Internacional de Musicologia*

(Barcelona: Casa de Caritat, 1936). In French. See no. 224 in this volume.

The congress mentioned in the title is cited as no. 65 in this volume.

3370 GÉROLD, Theodore. **Strasbourg dans**
as **l'histoire de l'orgue** [Strasbourg in the history of the organ], *Compte rendu du Congrès d'orgue tenu à l'Université de Strasbourg. IV* (Strasbourg: Société Strasbourgeoise de Librairie Sostralib, 1934) 172–77. In French. See no. 199 in this volume.

Covers the period from the 9th to the 20th c., focusing on the years after 1701 when the organ builder Johann Andreas Silbermann settled in Strasbourg.

3371 GEYER, József. **Fautes à éviter dans la disposi-**
as **tion des jeux** [Mistakes to avoid in registration], *Compte rendu du Congrès d'orgue tenu à l'Université de Strasbourg. IV* (Strasbourg: Société Strasbourgeoise de Librairie Sostralib, 1934) 114. *Organ specification.* In French. See no. 199 in this volume.

Summarizes specifications pertaining to organs of 16 and 32 ranks.

3372 GEYER, József. **Un orgue à 52 tuyaux, 4 jeux,**
as **sommier à coulisses, de l'an 228** [An organ with 52 pipes, four ranks, and slider chest, from the year 228], *Compte rendu du Congrès d'orgue tenu à l'Université de Strasbourg. IV* (Strasbourg: Société Strasbourgeoise de Librairie Sostralib, 1934) 164–66. In French. See no. 199 in this volume.

Describes the Roman hydraulis found in 1931 in Aquincum, Hungary, by the archaeologist Lajos Nagy.

3373 GEYER, József. **Schwierigkeiten eines einheit-**
as **lichen Aufbaues der Orgeldispositionen und des Orgelspieltisches** [Difficulties in achieving the uniform construction of organ dispositions and consoles], *Bericht über die dritte Tagung für Deutsche Orgelkunst* (Kassel: Bärenreiter, 1928) 182–88. In German. See no. 136 in this volume.

The idea of a uniform standard for organ building ignores the complexity of the instruments; the different acoustic spaces in which they must be installed; the quite different functions of organs in Catholic worship, Protestant worship, concert hall, and theater; and the artistic personalities of the builder and those responsible for the disposition, without which an instrument will not have a lasting artistic value.

3374 GIBERT, Vicente María. **El canto gregoriano:**
as **Base y fuente de inspiración de la música orgánica** [The Gregorian chant: The basis and inspiration for organ music], *Crónica y actas oficiales del tercer Congreso Nacional de Música Sagrada* (Barcelona: La Hormiga de Oro, 1913) 158–74. In Spanish. See no. 78 in this volume.

The importance of the organ as a religious instrument is highlighted, and the influence of Gregorian chant on the development of organ music is traced. Organ works by Antonio de Cabezón and Bach are analyzed. *(José López-Calo)*

3375 GINDELE, Corbinian. **Der Anteil Beurons an**
as **der Rettung der Ottobeurer Orgeln** [Beuron's share in the preservation of the Ottobeuren organs], *Der Barock: Seine Orgeln und seine Musik in Oberschwaben* (Berlin: Merseburger, 1952) 84–86. *Illus.* In German. See no. 305 in this volume.

The Dreifaltigkeitsorgel and Heilig-Geist-Orgel of the Abtei Ottobeuren, built in 1756-66 by Karl Joseph Riepp, were in need of serious repair by 1903; the Bavarian state government, which was to finance the repairs, planned to modernize the instruments and furnish them with pneumatic actions, against the advice of an official consultant (the Eichstätt Domkapellmeister Wilhelm Widmann). In the end the organs were restored to an almost original state, thanks largely to the efforts of Gregor Molitor, the organist of the Erzabtei St. Martin, Beuron. *(David Bloom)*

3376
as
GLATTER-GÖTZ, Josef von. **Die physikalischen und physiologischen Grundlagen der mechanischen Spieltraktur** [The physical and physiological principles of mechanical keyboard action], *Altbayerische Orgeltage* (Berlin: Merseburger, 1958) 34–40. In German. See no. 355 in this volume.
Pneumatic and electric actions introduce a separation between the fingered key and the sounding pipe, through the transition from one form of energy into another. In mechanical actions, as long as certain rules are followed to maintain the shortest possible spatial and temporal distance between fingering and sound (as the player hears it), attack and sound onset can be altogether merged, for a more alive and creative performance. *(David Bloom)*

3377
as
GRUNDMAN, Günther. **Die Orgel: Ein wichtiges Anliegen der Denkmalpflege** [The organ: An important area of concern in cultural conservation], *Richtlinien zum Schutze alter wertvoller Orgeln (Weilheimer Regulativ); Zugleich der kurzgefaßte Bericht über die Arbeitstagung der Orgeldenkmalpfleger* (Berlin: Merseburger, 1958) 7–11. In German. See no. 387 in this volume.
Discusses the conservation of organs as a specialized domain within the general responsibilities of the cultural conservator. *(David Bloom)*

3378
as
GRÜTZMACHER, Martin. **Über die Klänge von Glocken und Orgeln** [Concerning the sounds of bells and organs], *Acustica: International journal of acoustics/Journal international d'acoustique/Internationale akustische Zeitschrift* IV/1 (1954) 226–29. *Illus., bibliog., charts, diagr.* In German; summaries in English, French, and German. See no. 324 in this volume.
Describes the electroacoustical methods used in the Physikalisch-Technische Bundesanstalt in Braunschweig to obtain data on sonority. *(author)*

3379
as
GURLITT, Wilibald. **Die Kirchenorgel in Geschichte und Gegenwart** [The church organ in history and the present], *Bericht über den Internationalen Kongress für Kirchenmusik/Compte rendu du Congrès international de musique sacrée* (Bern: Haupt, 1953) 23–38. In German. See no. 312 in this volume.

3380
as
GURLITT, Wilibald. **Der musikgeschichtliche Denkmalwert der alten Orgel** [The value of old organs as cultural monuments from the point of view of historical musicology], *Richtlinien zum Schutze alter wertvoller Orgeln (Weilheimer Regulativ); Zugleich der kurzgefaßte Bericht über die Arbeitstagung der Orgeldenkmalpfleger* (Berlin: Merseburger, 1958) 27–29. In German. See no. 387 in this volume.
Evidence of old organs is of particular interest in the historical study of pitch standards—early instruments being generally tuned a major second lower than today's concert pitch—and temperament. Many organ builders refused to adopt equal temperament until the early 19th c., decades after it became standard for other keyboard instruments. *(David Bloom)*

3381
as
GURLITT, Wilibald. **Neue Forschungen über Orgelmusik und Orgelbaukunst** [New research on organ music and the art of organ building], *Congrés de la Societat Internacional de Musicologia* (Barcelona: Casa de Caritat, 1936). In German. See no. 224 in this volume.
The conference report provides only a citation. Neither the text nor a summary of the paper was published here.

3382
as
GURLITT, Wilibald. **Über Prinzipien und zur Geschichte der Registrierkunst in der alten Orgelmusik** [On the principles and history of registration in early organ music], *Bericht über den I. musikwissenschaftlichen Kongress der Deutschen Musikgesellschaft in Leipzig* (Wiesbaden: Breitkopf & Härtel, 1926) 232–36. In German. See no. 120 in this volume.
Discusses organ registration, suggesting a division into three functional categories: characterizing, structural, and symbolic. Five periods are also distinguished on the basis of musical styles and building methods: before 1600, 1600-20, 1620-80, 1680-1740, and after 1740. *(William Renwick)*

3383
as
GURLITT, Wilibald. **Die Wandlungen des Klangideals der Orgel im Lichte der Musikgeschichte** [Changes in the sound ideal of the organ in the light of music history], *Bericht über die [I] Freiburger Tagung für Deutsche Orgelkunst* (Augsburg: Bärenreiter, 1926) 11–42. *Bibliog.* In German. See no. 122 in this volume.
Surveys the history of organ building, organ composition, and organ culture from the 16th to the 19th c., with particular emphasis on the German Baroque, in terms of changing ideals of timbre. *(David Bloom)*

3384
as
HAAG, Herbert. **Die Orgel im weltlichen Bereich: Geschichtliches und Grundsätzliches** [The organ in the secular realm: History and foundations], *Bericht über die zweite Freiburger Tagung für Deutsche Orgelkunst* (Kassel: Bärenreiter, 1939) 78–86. In German. See no. 258 in this volume.
A broad overview of the use of the organ outside the church, from the Roman imperial period onward, with particular attention to its importance in celebratory and solemn occasions in Germany under the National Socialist regime. *(David Bloom)*

3385
as
HAERPFER, Friedrich. **Erfahrungen über Aufstellung und Intonation von modernen Orgeln** [Experiments in the installation and tuning of modern organs], *Haydn-Zentenarfeier* (Leipzig: Breitkopf & Härtel; Wien: Artaria, 1909) 611–16. *Organ specification.* In German. See no. 65 in this volume.
Discusses the restoration of the organ in the Thomaskirche in Strasbourg.

3386
as
HARDOUIN, Pierre Jean. **La composition des orgues que pouvaient toucher les musiciens parisiens aux alentours de 1600** [The structure of the organs likely to have been played by Parisian musicians of around 1600], *La musique instrumentale de la Renaissance* (Paris: Centre National de la Recherche Scientifique [CNRS], 1955) 259–68. In French. See no. 333 in this volume.
In the period 1585-1631 the foundations were laid for the development of the classic Parisian school of organ building through the introduction of Flemish technique by builders such as Jan and Matthijs Langhedul, Nicolas Pescheur and his sons, Valeran de Héman, and Crespin Carlier, as well as by the influence of organists including Charles Racquet at the cathedral of Notre-Dame, Loys Desprez at St-Séverin, Robert Buisson at St-Étienne-du-Mont, and Louis Bourdin at St-Jacques-de-la-Boucherie. *(David Bloom)*

3387
as
HARRIS, R.J. **Care of the piano,** *Music and drama in the counties* (London: conference, 1949). See no. 283 in this volume.

3388
as
HASSE, Karl. **Die geistigen und religiösen Grundlagen der Orgelmusik seit Bach** [The spiritual and religious foundations of organ music since Bach], *Bericht über die dritte Tagung für Deutsche Orgelkunst* (Kassel: Bärenreiter, 1928) 46–57. In German. See no. 136 in this volume.

Musical spirituality developed largely outside the church in the Enlightenment and Romantic periods, while organ music, spurred by technical innovations such as swell mechanism, evolved in a mostly secular direction culminating in the works of Reger. The current revival of the early Baroque organ in the Orgelbewegung signals a renewal of the connection between organ music and spirituality. This renewal will depend, however, on the participation of composers of a wholly personal expressive style. *(David Bloom)*

3389
as

HENNERBERG, Carl Fredrik. **Die schwedischen Orgeln des Mittelalters** [The Swedish organs of the Middle Ages], *Haydn-Zentenarfeier* (Leipzig: Breitkopf & Härtel; Wien: Artaria, 1909) 91–99. *Illus.* In German. See no. 65 in this volume.

Describes several organs throughout the country.

$\longrightarrow$
HINRICHSEN, Max. **Music for the student of the organ.** See no. 806 in this volume.

3390
as

HOPPE, Alfred. **Die Klassizität des norddeutschen Orgelbaus** [The classic quality of North German organ building], *Orgelbewegung und Historismus: Tagungsberichte. I* (Berlin: Merseburger, 1958) 48–50. *Illus., organ specification.* In German. See no. 338 in this volume.

Instruments discussed are the organ of the Schloßkirche Gröningen near Halberstadt, played by Praetorius, with its 26 pedal stops, by David Beck (1592-96); that of the Pfarrgemeinde St. Mauritius und St. Paulus (Moritzkirche) in Halle, by Johann Heinrich Compenius (1624-26); and that of the St. Bartholomäus church in Lamstedt (1692) and other instruments by Arp Schnitger, with regard to their use in performing music of the pre-Baroque era. *(David Bloom)*

3391
as

ISING, Hartmut. **Über die Tonbildung in Orgelpfeifen** [Structuring tone in organ pipes], *Problèmes d'acoustique* (Liège: Université de Liège, 1965) M55. In German. See no. 504 in this volume.

A basic introduction to the specifications of organ pipes and the underlying acoustical rationale. Ideal scalings and construction measurements are proposed. *(Brian Doherty)*

3392
as

JAHNN, Hans Henny. **Entstehung und Bedeutung der Kurvenmensur für die Labialstimmen der Orgel** [Origin and importance of nonlinear scaling for the labial pipes of the organ], *Bericht über den I. musikwissenschaftlichen Kongress der Deutschen Musikgesellschaft in Leipzig* (Wiesbaden: Breitkopf & Härtel, 1926) 71–77. *Illus.* In German. See no. 120 in this volume.

Discusses the scaling and voicing of flue stops on the pipe organ. The practices of organ builders such as Dom François Bédos de Celles OSB, Scherer, Hans Bockelmann, and Schnitger, are compared. *(William Renwick)*

3393
as

JAHNN, Hans Henny. **Gesichtspunkte für die Wahl zweckmässiger Pfeifenmensuren** [Points of view in the choice of appropriate pipe measurements], *Bericht über die [I] Freiburger Tagung für Deutsche Orgelkunst* (Augsburg: Bärenreiter, 1926) 50–58. In German. See no. 122 in this volume.

Principles are proposed for ensuring that a given stop is functionally appropriate, i.e., can be mixed with any other stop, in an organ with reformed registration and mechanical action. *(David Bloom)*

3394
as

JAHNN, Hans Henny. **Monographie der Rohrflöte** [Monograph on the Rohrflöte], *Bericht über die dritte Tagung für Deutsche Orgelkunst* (Kassel: Bärenreiter, 1928) 189–96. *Illus.* In German. See no. 136 in this volume.

Surveys the construction and acoustic properties of half-stopped or *chimney flute* organ stops.

3395
as

JAKOB, Friedrich. **Tendenzen des heutigen Orgelbaus** [Tendencies in contemporary organ building], *Kirchenmusik in ökumenischer Schau* (Bern: Haupt, 1964) 96–100. In German. See no. 447 in this volume.

Summary of a longer article appearing in *Musik und Gottesdienst* I (1963).

3396
as

JEANS, Susi. **Orgeln und Orgelmusik in England von 16. bis zum 18. Jahrhundert** [Organs and organ music in England from the 16th to the 18th century], *Orgelbewegung und Historismus: Tagungsberichte. III* (Berlin: Merseburger, 1958) 97–100. *Organ specification.* In German. See no. 346 in this volume.

The development of the organ in England followed a separate, and slower, path from that of continental Europe. The typically English doubling of the principal choir was established as early as the mid-16th c. Small house organs also existed at this time, known not as organs but single and double regals or even single and double virginals. Important builders included the younger John Howe ("Father" Howe) and John Chappington. The main genre of organ music around 1600 was the cantus firmus fantasia. In the early 17th c. two-manual organs (*double organs*) were introduced—a typical example is the organ of Worcester Cathedral—by Thomas Dallam, 1613-14, and the voluntary for double organ became popular. The organ of St. Paul's Cathedral, London, had pedals from 1720, but pedals remained extremely rare until the 19th c.; the swell box, introduced in the 1712 organ of St. Magnus, London, by Christopher Shrider and the Jordan family, was widely adopted. The organ concerto, often more a chamber than orchestral genre, was very popular in the 18th c. Other well-known 18th-c. builders were Thomas Schwarbrook, John Snetzler, Richard Bridge, John Byfield, and Samuel Green. *(David Bloom)*

3397
as

JORISSENNE, Gustave. **Facteurs d'orgues dans le pays de Liège** [Organ builders in the Liège region], *Fédération Archéologique et Historique de Belgique: Annales du XXIIᵉ congrès. I: Documents et compte rendu; II: Rapports & mémoires* (Mechelen: Godenne, 1911) II, 885–90. In French. See no. 73 in this volume.

Investigates organs and their builders in the region of Liège from 814 to 1805.

3398
as

JUNG, Hermann. **Wege zu einem einheitlichen Aufbau von Disposition und Spieltisch** [Toward a unified construction of disposition and console], *Bericht über die [I] Freiburger Tagung für Deutsche Orgelkunst* (Augsburg: Bärenreiter, 1926) 76–86. *Charts, diagr., organ specification.* In German. See no. 122 in this volume.

Three major factors are involved in the musical and technological success of an organ: the desired function (liturgical, concert, etc.), the available space, and the financial situation. A relatively economical design is proposed for disposition and console of a 60-stop organ that offers a compromise solution between the needs of a modern liturgical organ and an organ adapted to the performance of Baroque music. *(David Bloom)*

3399
as

KELLER, Hermann. **Der Spieltisch** [The console], *Bericht über die dritte Tagung für Deutsche Orgelkunst* (Kassel: Bärenreiter, 1928) 197–203. *Illus., organ specification.* In German. See no. 136 in this volume.

Describes the consoles of a wide range of recent organs (1926-28): at the Dom St. Stefan, Passau, by the G.F. Steinmeyer firm, currently the largest in the world, with 206 stops, designed by Karl Straube; at the Hans-Sachs-Haus, Gelsenkirchen, by the Walcker firm, designed by Hermann Jung; at the Heilandskirche, Hamburg, by the firm P. Furtwängler & Hammer, designed by Christhard Mahrenholz; at the Landeskonservatorium Leipzig (now the Hochschule für Musik), by the firm W. Sauer, designed by Günter Ramin; at the Lichtwarkschule, Hamburg, by K. Kemper & Sohn, designed by Hans Henny Jahnn; at Liverpool Cathedral, England, by the firm of

Henry Willis; and the Theodor Kuhn instrument rebuilt by Ernst Graf and Ernst Thiess for installation in the Stadtkirche, Frauenfeld, Switzerland.

3400 KLOTZ, Hans. **À propos de l'orgue de 1500 en-**
as **viron, de l'orgue brabançon de 1550 et de la manière de les jouer** [Organs of ca. 1500, the Brabant organ of 1550, and how they were played], *Kirchenmusik in ökumenischer Schau* (Bern: Haupt, 1964) 91–96. In French. See no. 447 in this volume.
Typical organs of the turn of the 16th c. are compared with those from the beginning of the so-called North Brabant school (mid-16th c.), associated with the 's-Hertogenbosch builders of the Niehoff, Lampeler van Mill, and Hocque or Hocquet families. *(David Bloom)*

3401 KLOTZ, Hans. **Das alte Positiv und die neue**
as **Kammerorgel** [The old positive and the new chamber organ], *Bericht über die zweite Freiburger Tagung für Deutsche Orgelkunst* (Kassel: Bärenreiter, 1939) 64–77. *Organ specification.* In German. See no. 258 in this volume.
The two geographically distinct schools of organ building in the 15th-17th c., that of East Flanders and Brabant and that of southern Germany from Strasbourg to Vienna, had generally merged by the high Baroque period into a single style, but the positive organ developed entirely within the southern German area, and never acquired any Brabantine characteristics. The contemporary chamber organ, benefiting from the evolution of both schools, has a much wider range of uses, especially as a solo or concertante instrument. Principles for accommodating to the chamber organ's single manual and limited disposition are outlined. *(David Bloom)*

3402 KLOTZ, Hans. **Orgelbewegung und Histo-**
as **rismus** [The Orgelbewegung and historicism], *Orgel-bewegung und Historismus: Tagungsberichte. I* (Berlin: Merseburger, 1958) 25–33. In German. See no. 338 in this volume.
The movement for the renewal of the organ especially in Germany since World War I was bound up with the inner renewal of Christian liturgy, which led first to early music, then to the early organs that were necessary for performing it. The emulation of historical organs carries with it the danger of merely copying the past rather than re-creating it for the present. Principles are suggested for a historically informed, but living, practice of organ building, performance, and composition. *(David Bloom)*

3403 KLOTZ, Hans. **Tradition und Historismus im**
as **Orgelbau heute** [Tradition and historicism in current organ building], *Zweiter internationaler Kongress für katholische Kirchenmusik: Zu Ehren des Heiligen Papstes Pius X* (Wien: conference, 1955) 225–29. In German. See no. 339 in this volume.
Acoustic studies with modern technological means can help organ builders to solutions in line with the great tradition from the medieval through Baroque periods, but can also lead to sterile historicism. Examples are drawn from the disposition of mixture stops and from the dynamic balance among great organ, choir organ, and Brustwerk. *(David Bloom)*

3404 KOK, Willem. **Experimental study of tuning**
as **problems,** *Acustica: International journal of acoustics/Journal international d'acoustique/ Internationale akustische Zeitschrift* IV/1 (1954) 229–30. *Illus., charts, diagr.* Summaries in English, French, and German. See no. 324 in this volume.
Equal temperament in music was a compromise, accepted in a period without electronic equipment. Organ music in particular will recover rich harmony when played with perfect intervals. Methods are described by which this can be done. *(author)*

3405 KOPP, Rudolf. **Das Portativ für zeitnahes**
as **Schulsingen—Hausmusik und Kammermusik** [A portative organ for up-to-date school singing, Hausmusik, and chamber music], *Der Barock: Seine*

Orgeln und seine Musik in Oberschwaben (Berlin: Merseburger, 1952) 141–44. *Charts, diagr.* In German. See no. 305 in this volume.
A portative organ for school use should have an adequate fully chromatic range; a pedal wind system that can be operated by the player; and a pipe rack short enough not to obscure the teacher's view of the classroom. Such an instrument is also well adapted to home music making and chamber performance. A suitable instrument has been built by the Munich firm of Anton Schwenk, under specifications provided by the author and Wilhelm Mitschke of the Institut für Schul- und Volksmusik, Munich. *(David Bloom)*

3406 KREPS, Joseph. **Les synthèses sonores de**
as **l'orgue à tuyaux** [The sound syntheses of the pipe organ], *Acoustique musicale* (Paris: Centre National de la Recherche Scientifique [CNRS], 1959) 145–67. *Illus., charts, diagr.* In French. See no. 393 in this volume.
Discusses the physical parameters of the acoustic character of organ pipes.

⟶ KROHN, Ilmari. **Das akustische Harmonium der Universität zu Helsingfors** [The acoustic harmonium at Helsingin Yliopisto]. See no. 4085 in this volume.

3407 KUNTZ, Michael. **Über das zeitgenössische**
as **Orgelspiel** [Contemporary organ playing], *Altbayern als Orgel-Landschaft* (Berlin: Merseburger, 1954) 18–20. In German. See no. 325 in this volume.

3408 LACAS, Pierre-Paul. **Essai sur le Baroque en**
as **organologie** [Essay on organological aspects of the Baroque], *Actes des Journées internationales d'étude du Baroque* (Toulouse: Faculté des Lettres et Sciences Humaines, 1965) 25–26. In French. See no. 469 in this volume.
Brief survey of the tonal resources of the Baroque organ, 1600-1750.

3409 LAMICHE (abbé). **Les débuts de l'organiste**
as [The beginnings of the organist], *Congrès diocésain de musique religieuse et de plain-chant* (Rodez: Carrère, 1895) 153–56. In French. See no. 22 in this volume.

3410 LEHMANN, Fritz. **Die neue Orgel als Instru-**
as **ment der Volksbildung** [The new organ as a means of mass education], *Bericht über die [I] Freiburger Tagung für Deutsche Orgelkunst* (Augsburg: Bärenreiter, 1926) 110–13. In German. See no. 122 in this volume.
The 1926 organ of the church of St. Marien, Göttingen, designed by Christhard Mahrenholz according to the *Werkprinzip* ideas of the ongoing organ reform movement, has had a remarkable effect on the listening capacity of local audiences. The purity and clarity of its articulation of polyphonic lines arouses an enthusiastic response to music of all sorts, from the normally unpopular early Baroque to Max Reger. The instrument contributes to the musical and indeed moral education of the people as a whole, particularly regarding values of objectivity and communality. *(David Bloom)*

3411 LENK, Alfred. **Etwas vom Rollschweller** [Some-
as thing about the crescendo roller], *Bericht über die dritte Tagung für Deutsche Orgelkunst* (Kassel: Bärenreiter, 1928) 204–05. In German. See no. 136 in this volume.
Argues that current swell mechanisms can be conveniently integrated into a standard console design.

3412 LINHARDT, Wolfgang. **Über die Funktionen**
as **der verschiedenen Traktursysteme der Orgel** [The functioning of different systems for organ action], *Bericht über den internationalen musikwissenschaft-*

lichen Kongreß (Kassel: Bärenreiter, 1957) 142–44. *Charts, diagr.* In German. See no. 356 in this volume.

Simultaneous oscilloscope measurements of key motion, and attack transients in mechanical, pneumatic, and electropneumatic organ actions show that key movement can influence the opening speed of the valve in a pneumatic action with Barker lever. Relatively fast or slow touch can influence attack in mechanical actions or pneumatic actions, while this is obviously impossible with the electric action. Another version is cited as no. 3413 in this volume. *(David Bloom)*

3413
as
LINHARDT, Wolfgang. **Über die Funktionen verschiedener Orgeltraktur-Systeme** [The functioning of different systems of organ action], *Bericht über den internationalen musikwissenschaftlichen Kongreß Wien Mozartjahr 1956* (Graz; Köln: Böhlau, 1958) 352–54. *Illus., charts, diagr.* In German. See no. 365 in this volume.

Another version is abstracted as no. 3412 in this volume.

3414
as
LÖFFLER, Hans. **J.S. Bach und die Orgeln seiner Zeit** [J.S. Bach and the organs of his time], *Bericht über die dritte Tagung für Deutsche Orgelkunst* (Kassel: Bärenreiter, 1928) 122–32. *Organ specification.* In German. See no. 136 in this volume.

Gotthold Frotscher's assertion (see no. 3367 in this volume) that Gottfried Silbermann's organs are the ideal instrument for Bach requires qualification. A survey of all the organs Bach is known to have played, with reference to documentation of his own performance practice and opinions, permits a more nuanced account. Brief biographies of ten organ builders active in Bach's time, and a discussion of typical registration practice of the period, are appended.

3415
as
LOTTERMOSER, Werner. **Der akustische Entwurf und Abgleich moderner Orgeln** [The acoustic design and adjustment of modern organs], *Bericht über den internationalen musikwissenschaftlichen Kongreß Wien Mozartjahr 1956* (Graz; Köln: Böhlau, 1958) 378–83. *Illus., charts, diagr., organ specification.* In German. See no. 365 in this volume.

Describes the work of the musical acoustics laboratory of the Physikalisch-Technische Bundesanstalt, Braunschweig, in helping to attain an optimum Baroque sound quality for three new instruments: the Praetorius-Orgel in the Aula of the Universität Freiburg (E.F. Walcker firm, 1954-55); the Totentanz-Orgel of the Marienkirche, Lübeck (E. Kemper & Sohn, 1954-56); and the main organ of the Nikolaikirche, Siegen (E. Kemper & Sohn, 1954-56). *(David Bloom)*

3416
as
LOTTERMOSER, Werner. **Unterschiede in Klang und Ansprache bei alten und neuen Orgeln** [Differences in sound and speaking qualities between old and new organs], *Bericht über den Internationalen musikwissenschaftlichen Kongress* (Kassel: Bärenreiter, 1954) 75–77. In German. See no. 319 in this volume.

Reports on acoustic measurements of plenum sound produced by the Baroque organs of master builders as compared with measurements for modern instruments. The findings suggest that the Baroque builders exercised all aspects of their craft in combination to control sound quality over the whole range of an instrument. Modern instruments do not show a similar consistency and control of sound quality. On the other hand, Baroque instruments were markedly individual in their sound. The Laboratorium für Musikalische Akustik at the Physikalisch-Technische Bundesanstalt, Braunschweig, is engaged in this research. *(Carl Skoggard)*

3417
as
LUEDTKE, Hans. **Das Oskalyd als neuzeitliche Versuchsorgel** [The Oskalyd as a modern experimental organ], *Bericht über die [I] Freiburger Tagung für Deutsche Orgelkunst* (Augsburg: Bärenreiter, 1926) 139–40. In German. See no. 122 in this volume.

Brief description of an Oskalyd organ, built as a joint venture of the Walcker, P. Furtwängler & Hammer, and W. Sauer firms in consultation with the author; it has two manuals and pedals and a very wide, but compact and easily used, range of stops and stop mixtures, dynamic devices, and percussion. It enables an unusually clear rendering of polyphonic voices, and very rapid changes in tone color, making it ideal for modern music and for the music of Max Reger. *(David Bloom)*

3418
as
LUNELLI, Renato. **Apologia dell' organo tradizionale** [In defense of the traditional organ], *Atti del [I] Congresso internazionale di musica sacra* (Tournai: Desclée, 1952) 356–58. In Italian. See no. 303 in this volume.

Discusses the musical qualities of organs of the Renaissance and Baroque.

3419
as
MAHRENHOLZ, Christhard. **Der gegenwärtige Stand der Orgelfrage im Lichte der Orgelgeschichte** [The current state of the organ question in the light of organ history], *Bericht über die dritte Tagung für Deutsche Orgelkunst* (Kassel: Bärenreiter, 1928) 13–37. *Organ specification.* In German. See no. 136 in this volume.

The Orgelbewegung reform movement originating in the earliest years of the 20th c. aims in the final analysis at a new organ, neither a continuation of the unacceptable instruments of the 19th c. nor a compromise between two different ideals. The new organ must grow out of a full understanding of the instrument's history, through the collegial work of congresses, and above all from a liturgical spirit.

3420
as
MAHRENHOLZ, Christhard. **Die Kleinorgel: Grundfragen ihres Baues und ihres Klanges** [The small organ: Fundamental questions of its construction and sound], *Bericht über die zweite Freiburger Tagung für Deutsche Orgelkunst* (Kassel: Bärenreiter, 1939) 8–19. In German. See no. 258 in this volume.

The Kleinorgel or positive organ of current German manufacture has become something other than the replication of Baroque positives characteristic of the early Orgelbewegung, while also parting ways with the great organ tradition. It is in principle a different instrument, with its own set of problematics. *(David Bloom)*

3421
as
MATHIAS, François-Xavier. **La continuité dans l'évolution de l'expression organale et ses conséquences pour la pédagogie musicale de l'heure présente** [Continuity in the evolution of expressivity in organ music and its consequences for current musical pedagogy], *Compte rendu du Congrès d'orgue tenu à l'Université de Strasbourg. IV* (Strasbourg: Société Strasbourgeoise de Librairie Sostralib, 1934) 146–48. In French. See no. 199 in this volume.

The state of the art of organ playing is examined, and suggestions for its future use in support of the liturgy are offered.

3422
as
MATHIAS, François-Xavier. **L'emplacement des orgues dans les sanctuaires** [The placement of organs in churches], *Compte rendu du Congrès d'orgue tenu à l'Université de Strasbourg. IV* (Strasbourg: Société Strasbourgeoise de Librairie Sostralib, 1934) 134–39. *Illus., charts, diagr.* In French. See no. 199 in this volume.

Liturgical and acoustic factors affecting the location of organs in churches are discussed, focusing on Strasbourg cathedral.

3423
as
MATHIAS, François-Xavier. **L'orgue dans la culture musicale de tous les siècles** [The organ in the musical culture of all centuries], *Compte rendu du Congrès d'orgue tenu à l'Université de Strasbourg. IV* (Strasbourg: Société Strasbourgeoise de Librairie

Sostralib, 1934) 159–62. In French. See no. 199 in this volume.

The organ stands at the very origins of the European musical tradition. In earlier times, it enriched religious monody through rhythm, harmony, and polyphony. Organists were influential in many of the most important stylistic changes in Western music. *(Chang Cho-Hee)*

3424 MATHIAS, François-Xavier. **Die Pragmatik**
as **der Orgelbaugeschichte des 18. Jahrhunderts im Lichte des Pariser Silbermann-Archivs** [The pragmatism of organ building in the 18th century in light of the Paris Silbermann archive], *Société Internationale de Musicologie: Premier Congrès Liège—Compte rendu/Internationale Gesellschaft für Musikwissenschaft: Erster Kongress Lüttich—Kongressbericht/International Society for Musical Research: First Congress Liège: Report* (London: Plainsong and Mediaeval Music Society, 1930) 182–83. In German. See no. 178 in this volume.

This archive of writings of Johann Andreas Silbermann offers an excellent overview of European organ music and organ building in the 18th c. and demonstrates the continuation of certain performance practices since Friedrich Erhard Niedt and Michael Praetorius. *(Scott Fruehwald)*

3425 MATHIAS, François-Xavier. **La Société Inter-**
as **nationale d'Orgue: Son activité au Congrès de Budapest (1930), Strasbourg (1932), Luxemburg (1934)** [The international society of the organ: Its activities at the congresses of Budapest (1930), Strasbourg (1932), Luxembourg (1934)], *Congrés de la Societat Internacional de Musicologia* (Barcelona: Casa de Caritat, 1936). In French. See no. 224 in this volume.

The conference report provides only a citation. Neither the text nor a summary of the paper was published here. The congresses discussed are cited as nos. 171, 199, and 211 in this volume.

3426 MEHL, Johannes G. **Die Barockorgel in Lahm**
as **(Itzgrund) im Zusammenhang des nord- und süddeutschen Orgelbaus ihrer Zeit und die Probleme ihrer Restaurierung** [The Baroque organ in Lahm (Itzgrund) and its connections with North and South German organ building of its time, and issues in its restoration], *Bericht über den Internationalen musikwissenschaftlichen Kongress* (Kassel: Bärenreiter, 1954) 78–82. *Organ specification.* In German. See no. 319 in this volume.

Describes the instrument built for the Lutheran parish church in the village of Lahm (Franconia) by Heinrich Gottlieb Herbst in 1735-36 and restored according to plans of the author in 1934-35. This fine instrument, representative of North German practice, was a fully isolated instance in Franconia. Johann Lorenz Bach (1695-1773; a second cousin of J.S. Bach) served as the organist for the Lahm parish church for 54 years (1719-73). *(Carl Skoggard)*

3427 MEHL, Johannes G. **Die Denkmalpflege auf**
as **dem Gebiet der Orgelbaukunst** [Historic conservation in the area of the organ builder's art], *Bericht über die zweite Freiburger Tagung für Deutsche Orgelkunst* (Kassel: Bärenreiter, 1939) 20–36. In German. See no. 258 in this volume.

Discusses the principles and goals of the conservation of historic organs, and presents Wilibald Gurlitt's viewpoint that conservation should focus primarily on historic sound qualities. Notes on the organization of organ conservation in Germany, which is found wanting, are included. *(David Bloom)*

3428 MERCER, Derwent M.A. **The effect of voicing**
as **adjustments on the tone quality of organ flute**

pipes, *Acustica: International journal of acoustics/Journal international d'acoustique/Internationale akustische Zeitschrift* IV/1 (1954) 237–38. *Illus., bibliog., charts, diagr.* Summaries in English, French, and German. See no. 324 in this volume.

The tonal effects of adjustments that can be made to a pipe are detailed, and the effect of pipe diameter in limiting the number of harmonics is explained. Edge tones are shown to be confined to the initial sounds emitted by a pipe, and a new theory of pipe operation is advanced. *(author)*

3429 MERCER, Derwent M.A. **Organ pipe adjust-**
as **ments as a guide to theories of the mechanism of the pipe,** *Problèmes d'acoustique* (Liège: Université de Liège, 1965) M52. See no. 504 in this volume.

An increase in wind pressure, a decrease in the height of the upper lip, and the fitting of a pipe with a slot increase the presence of harmonics. The roller-beard is used to control a pipe that is speaking unsteadily; it can also affect the harmonic structure. *(Allen Lott)*

3430 MERTIN, Josef. **Erfahrungen mit der**
as **Kleinorgel** [Experiences with the small organ], *Bericht über die zweite Freiburger Tagung für Deutsche Orgelkunst* (Kassel: Bärenreiter, 1939) 118–24. In German. See no. 258 in this volume.

The author's experiences as a conductor of early music with the Wiener Kammerorchester suggest that the transportable chamber positive can play a particularly valuable role as a basso continuo instrument; as an alternative to vocal performance of individual voices in medieval polyphony from Pérotin to Dufay; in the realization of the instrumental parts of Netherlandish music and particularly bringing out imitative structure in Netherlandish motet; in unpedaled keyboard music of J.S. Bach and the so-called organ concertos of Händel; in the Italian ricercar and related forms of the 16th and 17th c.; and as an accompaniment to Gregorian chant. Suggested dispositions and recommendations for equipping the chamber organ with pedals are appended. *(David Bloom)*

3431 MEUGÉ, Joseph. **Communication sur la biblio-**
as **thèque et le bulletin de l'Union des Maîtres de Chapelle et Organistes** [Report on the library and the bulletin of the Union des Maîtres de Chapelle et Organistes], *Congrès international de musique sacrée: Chant et orgue* (Paris: Desclée de Brouwer, 1937) 37–40. In French. See no. 247 in this volume.

Members of the society should take further advantage of these facilities.

3432 MEYER, Jürgen. **Unharmonische Kompo-**
as **nenten im Klang der Orgelpfeifen** [Inharmonic components in the sound of organ pipes], *Fourth International Congress on Acoustics* (København: conference, 1962) I, P53. In German. See no. 448 in this volume.

3433 MEYERS, Hubert. **Problèmes actuels de fac-**
as **ture d'orgue** [Current problems in organ building], *Perspectives de la musique sacrée à la lumière de l'encyclique* Musicae sacrae disciplina (Paris: conference, 1959) 423–27. *Organ specification.* In French. See no. 379 in this volume.

Few builders are adequately prepared from the scientific and musicological viewpoint. Builders should collaborate with musicologist-performers and well qualified voicers (of whom there are very few) in the development of new historical and geographic syntheses. *(David Bloom)*

3434 MIRAMON, Bérenger de. **Les plus récentes**
as **entreprises de la Société Française des Amies de l'Orgue** [The most recent undertakings of the Société Française des Amis de l'Orgue], *Congrés de la*

Societat Internacional de Musicologia (Barcelona: Casa de Caritat, 1936). In French. See no. 224 in this volume.

The conference report provides only a citation. Neither the text nor a summary of the paper was published here.

3435
as

MIRAMON FITZ-JAMES, Bérenger de; DUFOURCQ, Norbert; GONZÁLEZ, V.; MARCHAL, André. **La doctrine parisienne de l'orgue** [The Parisian organ doctrine], *Compte rendu du Congrès d'orgue tenu à l'Université de Strasbourg. IV* (Strasbourg: Société Strasbourgeoise de Librairie Sostralib, 1934) 125–29. *Organ specification.* In French. See no. 199 in this volume.

Compares specifications and qualities of modern organs with older instruments.

3436
as

MOCKERS, F. **La famille franco-suisse Mockers, complétant en France l'œuvre organale d'Aristide Cavaillé-Coll, en continuant celle de Jean André Silbermann (1712-1783)** [The Franco-Swiss Mockers family, completing the organ work of Aristide Cavaillé-Coll in France, and continuing that of Johann Andreas Silbermann (1712-1783)], *Congrés de la Societat Internacional de Musicologia* (Barcelona: Casa de Caritat, 1936). In French. See no. 224 in this volume.

The conference report provides only a citation. Neither the text nor a summary of the paper was published here.

3437
as

MORETTI, Corrado. **Definizione di organo** [Definition of the organ], *Zweiter internationaler Kongress für katholische Kirchenmusik: Zu Ehren des Heiligen Papstes Pius X* (Wien: conference, 1955) 243–45. In Italian. See no. 339 in this volume.

A definition of the organ for liturgical purposes: A musical instrument in which flowing air is caused to vibrate in a system of pipes that emit fundamental pitches and artificial harmonics, intrinsically inert but capable of being combined in synthetic sonorities of variable tone, timbre, and intensity. *(David Bloom)*

3438
as

MOSER, Hans Joachim. **Über deutsche Orgelkunst 1450-1500** [On the art of the German organ, 1450-1500], *Bericht über die dritte Tagung für Deutsche Orgelkunst* (Kassel: Bärenreiter, 1928) 133–38. In German. See no. 136 in this volume.

A survey of composers and building styles for the period. The material is given an extended treatment in the author's book *Paul Hofhaimer: Ein Lied- und Orgelmeister des deutschen Humanismus* (Stuttgart: Cotta, 1929).

3439
as

MULET, Henri. **Étude sur le rôle des mutations et la composition rationnelle du plein-jeu dans un grand-orgue** [The role of mutation stops and the rational composition of the full pleno in the grand organ], *Compte rendu du Congrès général de musique sacrée: Aperçu général des préliminaires et du congrès, discours et conférences* (Strasbourg: Alsacien, 1922) 271–83. In French. See no. 96 in this volume.

3440
as

MULET, Henri. **Les tendances néfastes et antireligieuses de l'orgue moderne** [Harmful and antireligious tendencies in the modern organ], *Compte rendu du Congrès général de musique sacrée: Aperçu général des préliminaires et du congrès, discours et conférences* (Strasbourg: Alsacien, 1922) 259–70. In French. See no. 96 in this volume.

Compares French organs with English and American instruments.

3441
as

MÜLLER-WALT, Traugott. **Die Toggenburger Bauernorgeln** [Toggenburg peasant organs], *Bericht über die zweite Freiburger Tagung für Deutsche Orgelkunst* (Kassel: Bärenreiter, 1939) 132–35. *Illus., organ specification.* In German. See no. 258 in this volume.

Surveys chamber organs built in the period 1754-1821 in the Toggenburg district, St. Gallen canton, by Wendelin Looser, Joseph Looser, Melchior Grob, Heinrich Ammann, and Ulrich Ammann. They were used almost exclusively in the homes of adherents of the Reformed church, for household devotions, but also for secular and even dance music; a typical collection of print music is sketched, representative dispositions are provided, and comparable instruments of neighboring cantons are noted. *(David Bloom)*

3442
as

MUND, Hermann. **Geschichte und Bedeutung des Orgelgehäuses** [The history and significance of the organ case], *Bericht über die [I] Freiburger Tagung für Deutsche Orgelkunst* (Augsburg: Bärenreiter, 1926) 114–21. *Illus., bibliog.* In German. See no. 122 in this volume.

A survey of building styles of cases and facades, particularly in Germany, from the 15th c., and general principles for the restoration of old cases and the design of new ones. *(David Bloom)*

3443
as

MUND, Hermann. **Joachim Wagner, ein Altberliner Orgelbauer** [Joachim Wagner, an organ builder of old Berlin], *Bericht über die dritte Tagung für Deutsche Orgelkunst* (Kassel: Bärenreiter, 1928) 139–48. *Charts, diagr., organ specification.* In German. See no. 136 in this volume.

Provides biographical information on the builder (1690–ca. 1750) and lists 24 organs that can be ascribed with certainty to him, with commentary on individual instruments and a general evaluation of his historical importance.

3444
as

[Ochsenhausen, 1951] Oberschwäbische Barock-, Orgel- und Musiktagung [Meeting on the Baroque, organs, and music in Upper Swabia]. Ed. by Walter SUPPER, *Der Barock: Seine Orgeln und seine Musik in Oberschwaben* (Berlin: Merseburger, 1952) 136–40. *Illus., charts, diagr., organ specification.* In German. See no. 305 in this volume.

An exhibition was held in conjunction with the conference in the library of the Lehrerinnenoberschule (now the Landesakademie für die Musizierende Jugend in Baden-Württemberg) on the premises of the former Reichsabtei Ochsenhausen, 29 July through 5 August 1951. It featured pictures of organs and other documentation relevant to the themes of the conference, and a collection of ten positive, portative, and house organs of recent manufacture, two in original 18th- and 19th-c. cases. Illustrations and dispositions for the small organs are provided. *(David Bloom)*

3445
as

OTAÑO EGUINO, Nemesio. **La organería y los órganos del país vasco** [Organ building and organs in the Basque region], *Congrés de la Societat Internacional de Musicologia* (Barcelona: Casa de Caritat, 1936). In Spanish. See no. 224 in this volume.

The conference report provides only a citation. Neither the text nor a summary of the paper was published here.

3446
as

PEREIRA DE SAMPAIO, José. **Harmonium tessaradécatonique** [Tessaradecatonic harmonium], *Report of the Fourth Congress of the International Musical Society* (London: Novello, 1912) 333. In French. See no. 71 in this volume.

Summary of a paper describing an experimental instrument.

⟶

PHILLIPS, Gordon. **Purcell's organs and organ music.** See no. 1644 in this volume.

3447
as

PIRRO, André. **Orgues et organistes en Alsace et en Lorraine du XIVe au XVIIIe siècle** [Organs and organists in Alsace and in Lorraine from the 14th to the 18th century], *Compte rendu du Congrès d'orgue tenu à l'Université de Strasbourg. IV* (Strasbourg: Société Strasbourgeoise de Librairie Sostralib, 1934) 177–82. In French. See no. 199 in this volume.

An annotated list.

3448 POPPEN, Hermann Meinhard. **Die Ein-**
as **stimmung der heutigen Orgel** [The tuning of the contemporary organ], *Bericht über die dritte Tagung für Deutsche Orgelkunst* (Kassel: Bärenreiter, 1928) 206–10. In German. See no. 136 in this volume.

Although organs are supposed to be tuned at the international standard Kammerton of A4=435, players of other instruments performing music with organ in churches are invariably forced to adopt an uncomfortably low tuning, apparently because the organ tuning is not fully operative above a room temperature of 15° C. In any case orchestral instruments currently tune rather higher. It is proposed that the standard organ tuning be based on A4=440 at 18° C.

3449 PUGH, Robert. **Les Silbermann: Leur œuvre**
as **dans la région alsacienne (projections lumineuses)** [The Silbermanns: Their work in the Alsace region (slides)], *Congrès jubilaire* (Brugge: Gruuthuuse, 1925) 224–25. In French. See no. 119 in this volume.

A very brief survey of the work of the organ builders Andreas and Johann Andreas Silbermann. A journal MS by both artisans regarding organs built, apprentices hired, etc., is discussed, as is a collection of letters by Andreas conserved in the archives of the Église Collégiale St. Martin de Colmar.

(Susan Poliniak)

3450 QUITTARD, Henri. **Les anciennes orgues**
as **françaises** [Early French organs], *Comptes rendus, rapports et vœux du Congrès parisien et régional de chant liturgique et de musique d'église* (Paris: Schola Cantorum, 1912) 110–35. In French. See no. 75 in this volume.

3451 QUOIKA, Rudolf. **Altbayern als Orgelland-**
as **schaft** [Altbayern as an organ landscape], *Altbayern als Orgel-Landschaft* (Berlin: Merseburger, 1954) 23–29. In German. See no. 325 in this volume.

Discusses the organs of the Altbayern region (Niederbayern, Oberbayern, and Oberpfalz).

3452 QUOIKA, Rudolf. **Grundlagen und Grund-**
as **fragen der altbayerischen Orgelkultur** [Fundamental principles and issues in the organ culture of Altbayern], *Altbayerische Orgeltage* (Berlin: Merseburger, 1958) 15–22. In German. See no. 355 in this volume.

A brief historical survey of organ building in the region, from the end of the Thirty Years' War to the present.

3453 QUOIKA, Rudolf. **Die Passauer Orgel-**
as **bauschule und ihr Wirken in Österreich** [The Passau school of organ building and its influence in Austria], *Zweiter internationaler Kongress für katholische Kirchenmusik: Zu Ehren des Heiligen Papstes Pius X* (Wien: conference, 1955) 246–48. *Organ specification.* In German. See no. 339 in this volume.

In that part of the Passau diocese that was under Austrian sovereignty (including the now German territory of Passau itself and the east bank of the river Ilz, together with the present-day dioceses of Linz and St. Pölten) local organ builders in the 17th c. were slow to begin adopting the style dictated by the reforms of the *Caeremoniale episcoporum* (Rome, 1600); most new-style organs in the region were built by firms from Germany. Passau builders working in the new style in the middle third of the century included

Andreas Putz (for the Premonstratensian abbey of Schlägel near Linz, 1634-38), Johann Georg Freundt (Festorgel of the monastery church at Klosterneuburg, 1642), and his son Leopold Freundt (for the Passau cathedral, 1688). *(David Bloom)*

3454 QUOIKA, Rudolf. **Über den Orgelbaustil**
as **Abbate F.X. Chrismanns** [The organ building style of P.F.X. Chrismann], *Zweiter internationaler Kongress für katholische Kirchenmusik: Zu Ehren des Heiligen Papstes Pius X* (Wien: conference, 1955) 249–50. *Bibliog.* In German. See no. 339 in this volume.

The Austrian organ builder and priest Franz Xaver Chrismann (1724-95) developed a personal synthesis between the pragmatic style of his own time and place and the proto-Romantic Italian style of his teacher Pietro Nacchini and of Azzolino Bernardino Della Ciaia, well exemplified by the disposition of his organ for the monastery of St. Florian near Linz (built 1770-74). *(David Bloom)*

3455 QUOIKA, Rudolf. **Über die österreichische**
as **und oberschwäbische Barockorgel: Von der Durchdringung zweier Orgellandschaften** [Austrian and Upper Swabian Baroque organs: On the interpenetration of two organ landscapes], *Der Barock: Seine Orgeln und seine Musik in Oberschwaben* (Berlin: Merseburger, 1952) 59–67. *Illus.* In German. See no. 305 in this volume.

The activities of Austrian organ builders in Swabia and still more those of Swabian builders in Austria played an essential role in the development of the *Reichsstil* or Imperial style that characterizes Baroque organs of the Catholic parts of South Germany and of the Habsburg domains. The evolution of the style from the end of the 15th c. through the dissolution of the monasteries in 1803 is examined in some detail. *(David Bloom)*

3456 QUOIKA, Rudolf. **Warum bauen wir Orgeln**
as **mit mechanischer Traktur?** [Why do we build organs with mechanical action?], *Orgelbewegung und Historismus: Tagungsberichte. II* (Berlin: Merseburger, 1958) 59–64. In German. See no. 348 in this volume.

A historical account of the organ reform movement in the early 20th c. and its advocacy of a historically informed mechanical key action in opposition to the newly developed pneumatic actions. *(David Bloom)*

3457 QUOIKA, Rudolf. **Zur Entstehung der**
as **italienisch-österriechischen Barockorgel** [The origin of the Italian-Austrian Baroque organ], *Atti del [I] Congresso internazionale di musica sacra* (Tournai: Desclée, 1952) 371–79. In German. See no. 303 in this volume.

3458 QUOIKA, Rudolf. **Zur Technologie der süd-**
as **deutschen Barockorgel** [The technology of the South German Baroque organ], *Der Barock: Seine Orgeln und seine Musik in Oberschwaben* (Berlin: Merseburger, 1952) 76–77. In German. See no. 305 in this volume.

Remarks on the variety of forms found in the typical Baroque disposition.

3459 QUOIKA, Walter. **Orgeldenkmalpflege in**
as **älterer und neuerer Zeit** [Organ conservation in earlier and more recent times], *Richtlinien zum Schutze alter wertvoller Orgeln (Weilheimer Regulativ); Zugleich der kurzgefaßte Bericht über die Arbeitstagung der Orgeldenkmalpfleger* (Berlin: Merseburger, 1958) 30. In German. See no. 387 in this volume.

Summary of a discussion of the ideals of conservation of the 19th-c. organ builders Josef Gartner, Carl Eduard Schubert, Max März, and Martin Hechenberger. The full paper is published in *Ars organi* XII (1958). *(David Bloom)*

3460 RAUGEL, Félix. **Anciennes orgues françaises**
as [Early French organs], *Société Internationale de Musicologie, cinquième congrès/Internationale Gesellschaft für Musikwissenschaft, fünfter Kongreß/International Society for Musical Research, Fifth Congress* (Amsterdam: Vereniging voor Nederlandse Muziekgeschiedenis, 1953) 335–39. In French. See no. 316 in this volume.

3461 RAUGEL, Félix. **Die Barockorgel in Frankreich** [The Baroque organ in France], *Der Barock:
as *Seine Orgeln und seine Musik in Oberschwaben* (Berlin: Merseburger, 1952) 87–88. *Illus.* In German. See no. 305 in this volume.
Brief account of instruments and builders of the 15th-17th c., with a characterization of typical dispositions as compared with those of German organs of the same period. *(David Bloom)*

3462 RAUGEL, Félix. **La Commission des Orgues**
as **au Service des Monuments Historiques** [The Commission des Orgues of the Service des Monuments Historiques], *Congrès international de musique sacrée: Chant et orgue* (Paris: Desclée de Brouwer, 1937) 182–84. In French. See no. 247 in this volume.
For a century, the Commission has successfully restored organs in French churches.

3463 RAUGEL, Félix. **Les orgues de Bruckner** [The
as organs of Bruckner], *Compte rendu du Congrès d'orgue tenu à l'Université de Strasbourg. IV* (Strasbourg: Société Strasbourgeoise de Librairie Sostralib, 1934) 193–200. *Illus., bibliog., organ specification.* In French. See no. 199 in this volume.
Provides detailed descriptions of the instruments at the churches of the Augustinian monasteries of Klosterneuburg and of St. Florian, near Linz.

3464 RAUGEL, Félix; DUFOURCQ, Norbert; GON-
as ZÁLEZ DE AMEZÚA Y NORIEGA, Ramón; LITAIZE, Gaston; ROBERT, Georges. **L'orgue à tuyaux** [The pipe organ], *Revue musicale* 239-240 (1957) 199f. In French. See no. 378 in this volume.

3465 REIMANN, Wolfgang. **Die Orgel als Kult- und**
as **Konzertinstrument** [The organ as liturgical and as concert instrument], *Bericht über den Deutschen Kongreß für Kirchenmusik* (Kassel: Bärenreiter, 1928) 112–19. In German. See no. 135 in this volume.
A defense of the technical innovations of the modern organ since the 18th c., with its richly differentiated timbral possibilities and important repertoire from Bach to Reger. If modern instruments fail to offer the ideal sound of the medieval and Renaissance church organ, what is needed is not so much a recreation of the Renaissance organ as an application of the Renaissance artistic and religious spirit, together with good taste and a knowledge of styles, in the building of new ones. *(David Bloom)*

3466 REUTER, Rudolf. **Orgeldenmalpflege in**
as **Westfalen** [Conservation of historic organs in Westphalia], *Richtlinien zum Schutze alter wertvoller Orgeln (Weilheimer Regulativ); Zugleich der kurzgefaßte Bericht über die Arbeitstagung der Orgeldenkmalpfleger* (Berlin: Merseburger, 1958) 32–33. In German. See no. 387 in this volume.
Summary of a congress paper. The problems in Westphalia are similar to those in other regions.

3467 RIEBER, Karl Friedrich. **Kleinorgeln in Ober-**
as **baden: Zur Geschichte der Orgel am Oberrhein** [Small organs in Upper Baden: Toward a history of organs on the Upper Rhine], *Bericht über die zweite Freiburger Tagung für Deutsche Orgelkunst* (Kassel: Bärenreiter, 1939) 136–39. In German. See no. 258 in this volume.
In the countryside of the Rhine valley between the Schwarzwald and the Vosges mountains little physical evidence of the small organs of the 16th c. survives, but extant tablatures, iconography, and literary evidence allow some reconstruction of their use in Hausmusik and in village churches, particularly of the Markgräflerland district between Basel and Freiburg im Breisgau. *(David Bloom)*

⟶ RIMSKIJ-KORSAKOV, Andrej Vladimirovič.
Les recherches sur le timbre des violons et guitares et sur l'excitation des vibrations d'une anche d'harmonium [Research on the timbre of violins and guitars and on stimulating the vibrations of a harmonium reed]. See no. 3600 in this volume.

3468 RÖSSLER, Ernst Karl. **Klangfunktion, Orgel-**
as **satz und Orgelbau heute** [Sound function, organ writing, and organ building today], *Orgelbewegung und Historismus: Tagungsberichte. III* (Berlin: Merseburger, 1958) 82–88. In German. See no. 346 in this volume.
General discussion of organ building in relation to the requirements of 20th-c. music.

3469 RUBARDT, Paul. **Arp Schnitger,** *Bericht über die*
as *dritte Tagung für Deutsche Orgelkunst* (Kassel: Bärenreiter, 1928) 149–75. *Charts, diagr.* In German. See no. 136 in this volume.
An appreciation of the builder (1648-1719), with a brief biography and a technical evaluation of his work under the separate headings bellows and wind pressure, wind trunks and chests, actions and keyboards, pipe materials, tuning and temperament, facades, and dispositions. A chronological list of his organs, with the history of each through 1927, is appended.

3470 RUNG-KELLER, Poul Sophus. **Über Reform**
as **des Orgelbaues** [On the reform of organ building], *Haydn-Zentenarfeier* (Leipzig: Breitkopf & Härtel; Wien: Artaria, 1909) 621–35. *Organ specification, tech. drawings.* In German. See no. 65 in this volume.
Lists specifications for church, concert, and chamber organs.

3471 RUPP, E. **Les sommiers et la traction de l'orgue**
as [The soundboards and action of the organ], *Compte rendu du Congrès d'orgue tenu à l'Université de Strasbourg. IV* (Strasbourg: Société Strasbourgeoise de Librairie Sostralib, 1934) 115–25. In French. See no. 199 in this volume.
Discusses the history of three types of organ actions: mechanical, tubular, and electro-pneumatic.

3472 SANGIORGIO, Carmelo. **Le caratteristiche**
as **dell' organo liturgico** [Characteristics of the liturgical organ], *Atti del [I] Congresso internazionale di musica sacra* (Tournai: Desclée, 1952) 367–70. In Italian. See no. 303 in this volume.

3473 SCHIES, S. **La question professionnelle des**
as **organistes** [The professional question of organists], *Congrès régional de liturgie et de musique sacrée* (Moselle: Orphelins-Apprentis Guénange, 1923) 107–08. In French. See no. 98 in this volume.
Summary of a presentation given originally in German, discussing the need for a professional association of organists addressing moral, religious, aesthetic, and material concerns. *(Murat Eyüboğlu)*

3474
as
SCHIESS, Ernst. **Grundzüge des neuen Orgelbaues: Erfahrungen und Erkenntnisse der letzten Jahrzehnte** [Foundations of the new organ building: Experience and findings of the last decades], *Bericht über den Internationalen Kongress für Kirchenmusik/Compte rendu du Congrès international de musique sacrée* (Bern: Haupt, 1953) 65–67. In German. See no. 312 in this volume.

3475
as
SCHMIDT, Hans. **Bayrische Orgelkomponisten in alter und neuer Zeit** [Bavarian composers for organ in former and current times], *Altbayern als Orgel-Landschaft* (Berlin: Merseburger, 1954) 20–22. In German. See no. 325 in this volume.

3476
as
SCHNORR VON CAROLSFELD, Ernst. **Statistische Mitteilungen über die Orgeln im Bereich der Evangelisch-Lutherischen Landeskirche des Freistaates Sachsen** [Statistics on the organs in the jurisdiction of the Evangelical Lutheran Church of Saxony], *Bericht über die dritte Tagung für Deutsche Orgelkunst* (Kassel: Bärenreiter, 1928) 102. In German. See no. 136 in this volume.

Protestant churches in Saxony contain a total of 1267 organs. A statistical account is given of them by number of manuals, number of stops, action type, chest type, period, and builder.

3477
as
SCHUKE, Karl-Ludwig. **Positiv und Kleinorgel vom Standpunkt des Orgelbauers** [Positive and Kleinorgel from the organ builder's point of view], *Bericht über die zweite Freiburger Tagung für Deutsche Orgelkunst* (Kassel: Bärenreiter, 1939) 37–42. In German. See no. 258 in this volume.

A terminological distinction needs to be maintained between the concept of Kleinorgel or small organ, a small version of the church organ with a similar versatility, and the positive, which is always a single-manual instrument with optional pedal, equipped with slider chest and mechanical action, and notable for its clear, bright, dry sound, especially adapted to early music, as a continuo instrument, and for the Händel organ repertoire, which was not meant for a large organ. *(David Bloom)*

3478
as
SCHWEITZER, Albert. **Die Reform unseres Orgelbaues auf Grund einer allgemeinen Umfrage bei Orgelspielern und Orgelbauern in deutschen und romanischen Ländern** [The reform of our organ building based on a general survey of organ players and organ makers in German and Romance-language countries], *Haydn-Zentenarfeier* (Leipzig: Breitkopf & Härtel; Wien: Artaria, 1909) 581–607. In German. See no. 65 in this volume.

Details various components of organs and their construction.

3479
as
SCHWEITZER, Albert; MATHIAS, François-Xavier. **Internationales Regulativ für Orgelbau** [International regulations for organ building], *Haydn-Zentenarfeier* (Leipzig: Breitkopf & Härtel; Wien: Artaria, 1909) 636–79. *Charts, diagr., organ specification, tech. drawings.* In German. See no. 65 in this volume.

Provides detailed organological specifications.

3480
as
SINCERO, Dino. **L'arte e l'industria organaria** [The art and industry of the organ], *La vita musicale dell'Italia d'oggi* (Torino: Fratelli Bocca, 1921) 230–39. *Charts, diagr., organ specification.* In Italian. See no. 97 in this volume.

Surveys the state of the organ industry in Italy, and discusses construction methods used to obtain the sounds of older instruments.

3481
as
SPÖRRI, Otto. **Die neuzeitliche kleine Orgel in der Schweiz** [The contemporary small organ in Switzerland], *Der Barock: Seine Orgeln und seine Musik in Oberschwaben* (Berlin: Merseburger, 1952) 144–47. *Charts, diagr., organ specification.* In German. See no. 305 in this volume.

A survey of relatively small instruments for church use built in Switzerland in the period 1936-50, including dispositions for organs by the firms Kuhn (Männedorf), Metzler (Dietikon, Zurich), and Ziegler (Geneva). *(David Bloom)*

3482
as
SUPPER, Walter, ed. **Dispositionen von ausserwürttembergischen Barockorgeln, die auf die oberschwäbische Barockorgel Bezug nehmen** [Dispositions of Baroque organs from outside Württemberg that relate to Upper Swabian Baroque organs], *Der Barock: Seine Orgeln und seine Musik in Oberschwaben* (Berlin: Merseburger, 1952) 125–34. *Charts, diagr., organ specification.* In German. See no. 305 in this volume.

Presents the dispositions of typical Baroque organs of Austria and Italy, Alsace, Bavaria and Franconia, Westphalia, and France discussed at a congress on the Baroque organs of Upper Swabia.

3483
as
SUPPER, Walter. **Die dreimanualige Übungsorgel: Ein Beitrag zur Kleinorgel** [The three-manual practice organ: A new small organ], *Bericht über die zweite Freiburger Tagung für Deutsche Orgelkunst* (Kassel: Bärenreiter, 1939) 110–17. *Illus., organ specification.* In German. See no. 258 in this volume.

For the the advanced student with limited access to a large organ, a positive or even a two-manual chamber organ is not adequate. Specifications for a convenient-sized three-manual instrument built according to the *Werkprinzip* of the recent organ-reform movement, and for its construction and housing, are offered. *(David Bloom)*

3484
as
SUPPER, Walter. **Der Ertrag der Orgeldenkmalpflege für den Orgelbau der Gegenwart** [Why the conservation of historic organs is valuable for contemporary organ building], *Richtlinien zum Schutze alter wertvoller Orgeln (Weilheimer Regulativ); Zugleich der kurzgefaßte Bericht über die Arbeitstagung der Orgeldenkmalpfleger* (Berlin: Merseburger, 1958) 33–34. In German. See no. 387 in this volume.

The correct understanding of the early organ, in which all parts are subordinated to the whole, can teach us how to build a new organ that is similarly unified rather than thrown together. *(David Bloom)*

3485
as
SUPPER, Walter. **Die Gestaltung des Orgelgehäuses** [The structuring of the organ housing], *Orgelbewegung und Historismus: Tagungsberichte. II* (Berlin: Merseburger, 1958) 58. In German. See no. 348 in this volume.

Remarks accompanying a slide presentation by the organ architect and builder Poul-Gerhard Andersen, Copenhagen, on the visual aspects of recent Scandinavian organ design. *(David Bloom)*

3486
as
SUPPER, Walter. **Die nord- und süddeutsche Barockorgel: Ein stilischer Vergleich—Und eine Synthese?** [The North German and South German organ: A stylistic comparison—And a synthesis?], *Orgelbewegung und Historismus: Tagungsberichte. I* (Berlin: Merseburger, 1958) 15–24. *Organ specification.* In German. See no. 338 in this volume.

It is unnecessary to try to combine the power of the typical North German instrument (Arp Schnitger, the Hildebrand family) with the range of colors of South German organs (Joseph Gabler, Karl Joseph Riepp, the Holzhey family); good music should be compatible with a less than absolutely authentic disposition (as the Bach revival succeeded with the wholly unsuitable instruments of the 19th c.). In general, historical features (sliding wind chest, mechanical key action) should be used insofar as they serve the music, including both early music and contemporary improvisation; one should not make a *Weltanschauungsfrage* out of every registration. *(David Bloom)*

3487 SUPPER, Walter, ed. **Die oberschwäbische**
as **Barockorgel auf württembergischem Boden** [The Upper Swabian Baroque organ in Württemberg territory], *Der Barock: Seine Orgeln und seine Musik in Oberschwaben* (Berlin: Merseburger, 1952) 89–124. *Illus., facs., charts, diagr., organ specification.* In German. See no. 305 in this volume.

An inventory of historic organs of the 17th and 18th c. in the Oberschwaben region of Baden-Württemberg, with attention to those by the Gabler and Holzhey firms; including brief critical biographies of the builders, directions for visitors, dispositions and measurements for the major instruments discussed, and an account of their acoustic properties by Werner LOTTERMOSER. *(David Bloom)*

3488 SUPPER, Walter. **Die Orgel als Ganzheit** [The
as organ as a totality], *Altbayerische Orgeltage* (Berlin: Merseburger, 1958) 9–14. *Illus., organ specification.* In German. See no. 355 in this volume.

Considerations on the concept of an ideal church organ, with particular attention to the relationship among disposition, case, and acoustic setting, illustrated by old and modern instruments in the Altbayern region. *(David Bloom)*

3489 SUPPER, Walter. **Die Orgel als klingendes**
as **Denkmal** [The organ as a sounding monument], *Altbayern als Orgel-Landschaft* (Berlin: Merseburger, 1954) 13–16. In German. See no. 325 in this volume.

3490 SUPPER, Walter. **Über die Pflege von Orgeln**
as **mit Denkmalwert** [The maintenance of organs of historical value], *Orgelbewegung und Historismus: Tagungsberichte. II* (Berlin: Merseburger, 1958) 56–57. *Illus., charts, diagr.* In German. See no. 348 in this volume.

The most important aspects of restoration are disposition and voicing, if they have been altered in previous repairs. If a historic organ is too small for its church's use, it may be expanded, as long as sliding windchest, mechanical action, etc., are used, but valuable small organs should be transferred to other uses in smaller churches, as choir organs, and so on. *(David Bloom)*

3491 SUPPER, Walter. **Werktreue und heutiger**
as **Orgelbau** [Fidelity to the work and contemporary organ building], *Zweiter internationaler Kongress für katholische Kirchenmusik: Zu Ehren des Heiligen Papstes Pius X* (Wien: conference, 1955) 251–53. *Organ specification.* In German. See no. 339 in this volume.

The ideal of authentic performance is valuable in its place, and concerts on period instruments are desirable, but the progress in organ building since the beginning of the Orgelbewegung has made modern instruments generally the best choice for music of all periods, as long as they are made according to the best current standards (with sliding chest, mechanical key action, and optimal measurements, materials, and voicing), with the most versatile possible disposition. A sample distribution for a relatively large organ and two for relatively small instruments are provided. *(David Bloom)*

3492 SUPPER, Walter. **Wo historisieren wir—Und**
as **wo eilen wir im Orgelbau zu sehr voraus?** [Where are we historicizing? And where in organ building are we hurrying too far ahead?], *Orgelbewegung und Historismus: Tagungsberichte. III* (Berlin: Merseburger, 1958) 89–96. *Illus., organ specification.* In German. See no. 346 in this volume.

Restoration technique has reached a point where it has become permissible to make organic alterations to historic organs, on occasion. In restoring historic housing, simply duplicating an early arrangement may not provide the best solution for a given instrument in a given space; false historicism is also to be avoided in the housing of new organs. The builders of new instruments, and consultants such as the author, should be better prepared technically than those of the past, and their dispositions in particular need not copy earlier ones. Organists can follow similar rules. *(David Bloom)*

3493 SUPPER, Walter; ZÖLLNER, Wolfgang, eds.
as **Die Richtlinien zum Schutze alter wertvoller Orgeln (Weilheimer Regulativ) mit Erläuterungen** [Guidelines for the protection of valuable old organs (Weilheimer Regulativ) with explanatory notes], *Richtlinien zum Schutze alter wertvoller Orgeln (Weilheimer Regulativ); Zugleich der kurzgefaßte Bericht über die Arbeitstagung der Orgeldenkmalpfleger* (Berlin: Merseburger, 1958) 13–26. In German. See no. 387 in this volume.

Formal statement of principles determined at a meeting of organ conservators in Weilheim/Teck in 1957, known thereafter as the Weilheimer Regulativ. *(David Bloom)*

3494 TARNÓCZY, Tamás. **Recherches sur le spectre**
as **de l'orgue en faisant sonner plusieurs touches à la fois** [Research on the spectrum of the organ when several keys are played simultaneously], *Acoustique musicale* (Paris: Centre National de la Recherche Scientifique [CNRS], 1959) 135–43. *Charts, diagr.* In French. See no. 393 in this volume.

Describes a method of ascertaining the timbre of organ stops by means of a spectographic representation of the simultaneous playing of all 12 notes of a given octave. *(David Bloom)*

3495 THIENHAUS, Erich. **Orgelbaufragen im**
as **Lichte der akustischen Forschung** [Issues of organ building in the light of acoustic research], *Bericht über die zweite Freiburger Tagung für Deutsche Orgelkunst* (Kassel: Bärenreiter, 1939) 104–09. *Music, charts, diagr.* In German. See no. 258 in this volume.

A review of recent studies and their implications for organ building: first, on questions of register volume, room acoustics, and pipe materials; second, on tonal onsets and transitions. *(David Bloom)*

3496 THOMÀS SABATER, Joan Maria. **Jordi Bosch,**
as **le plus grand facteur espagnol d'orgues du XVIIIᵉ siècle** [Jordi Bosch: The greatest Spanish organ builder of the 18th century], *Congrés de la Societat Internacional de Musicologia* (Barcelona: Casa de Caritat, 1936). In French. See no. 224 in this volume.

The conference report provides only a citation. Neither the text nor a summary of the paper was published here.

3497 TOURNEMIRE, Charles. **L'orgue à travers les**
as **siècles** [The organ through the centuries], *Congrès international de musique sacrée: Chant et orgue* (Paris: Desclée de Brouwer, 1937) 41–53. In French. See no. 247 in this volume.

Surveys the history of the instrument from the zheng and the syrinx to the first true organ—the hydraulis—its gradual adoption by the Church, and the evolution of the instrument. The literature and the construction of the modern organ are also described. Tasteful improvisation should be encouraged. *(Arthur Maisel)*

3498 UTERMÖHLEN, Rudolf. **Drei Jahrzehnte**
as **Orgeldenkmalpflege in Hannover** [Three decades of organ conservation in Hannover], *Richtlinien zum Schutze alter wertvoller Orgeln (Weilheimer Regulativ); Zugleich der kurzgefaßte Bericht über die*

Arbeitstagung der Orgeldenkmalpfleger (Berlin: Merseburger, 1958) 29–30. In German. See no. 387 in this volume.

Summary of a discussion of the period 1928-57. The complete text is published in *Ars organi* XII (1958).

3499 UTERMÖHLEN, Rudolf. **Orgel und Kir-**
as **chenraum** [The organ and the space of the church], *Orgelbewegung und Historismus: Tagungsberichte. III* (Berlin: Merseburger, 1958) 75–81. In German. See no. 346 in this volume.

The question of the organ is not simply technical-musical; it has to do with the function of space, and hence involves architecture. Since the space is normally that of a church, it is also a spiritual question. The insight has both fundamental and practical consequences. *(David Bloom)*

3500 WALCKER, Oscar. **Zur Geschichte der Orgel-**
as **mensuren und ihrer Bedeutung für die Kunst des Orgelbaues** [The history of organ scaling and its significance for the art of organ building], *Bericht über die [I] Freiburger Tagung für Deutsche Orgelkunst* (Augsburg: Bärenreiter, 1926) 43–49. *Charts, diagr.* In German. See no. 122 in this volume.

Comparative historical account of the development of organ pipe dimensions, especially pipe diameters and their interrelationships, from the earliest documentation (9th-10th c.) to the standard widths of the early 20th c., with attention to their importance in imparting a builder's personal style. *(David Bloom)*

3501 WALCKER-MAYER, Werner. **Die Wiederher-**
as **stellung eines Portativs** [The restoration of a portative organ], *Richtlinien zum Schutze alter wertvoller Orgeln (Weilheimer Regulativ); Zugleich der kurzgefaßte Bericht über die Arbeitstagung der Orgeldenkmalpfleger* (Berlin: Merseburger, 1958) 30. *Organ specification.* In German. See no. 387 in this volume.

Discusses work by the Walcker firm on a 16th-c. baldacchino organ in the collection of the Vorarlberger Landesmuseum, Bregenz. A fuller description is published in the *Walcker-Hausmitteilungen* XVIII August (1957). *(David Bloom)*

3502 WALTER, Rudolf. **Bemerkungen zu Orgelbau**
as **und Orgelspiel in Deutschland** [Remarks on organ building and organ playing in Germany], *Atti del [I] Congresso internazionale di musica sacra* (Tournai: Desclée, 1952) 380–83. In German. See no. 303 in this volume.

3503 WÖRSCHING, Joseph. **Die Orgel der**
as **Zisterzienserkirche Kaisheim, 1778** [The organ of the Kaisheim Cistercian church, 1778], *Atti del [I] Congresso internazionale di musica sacra* (Tournai: Desclée, 1952) 384–87. In German. See no. 303 in this volume.

Discusses the organ of Kloster Kaisheim bei Donauwörth, originally built by Matthias Tretzscher in 1678.

3504 ZACHARIASSEN, Sybrand. **Aktuelle Orgelbau-**
as **fragen** [Current issues in organ building], *Zweiter internationaler Kongreß für katholische Kirchenmusik: Zu Ehren des Heiligen Papstes Pius X* (Wien: conference, 1955) 214–24. In German. See no. 339 in this volume.

Contrasts the excesses and poor design of the Romantic organ at the turn of the 20th c. with an ideal model of an instrument that could be built today. A Danish-language version with English summary is cited as RILM [1988]7513. *(David Bloom)*

3505 ZACHARIASSEN, Sybrand. **Aktuelle Orgel-**
as **baufragen und Möglichkeiten zu ihrer praktischen Lösung** [Current organ building questions and possibilities of of their practical solution], *Bericht über den Internationalen Kongress für Kirchenmusik/Compte rendu du Congrès international de musique sacrée* (Bern: Haupt, 1953) 62–64. In German. See no. 312 in this volume.

43 Keyboard, general

3506 BENTON, Rita. **The early piano in the United**
as **States,** *Music libraries and instruments* (London: Hinrichsen, 1961) 179–89. See no. 406 in this volume.

Describes the history of pianos and piano manufacture in the U.S. between 1771 and 1876.

3507 BERNER, Alfred. **Co-Referat Arbeitsge-**
as **meinschaft Cembalobau** [Supplementary report of the study group on harpsichord building], *Dokumentation* (Frankfurt am Main: Fördergemeinschaft Klavier, 1966) 257–58. In German. See no. 494 in this volume.

3508 BERNER, Alfred. **Zum Klavierbau im 17. und**
as **18. Jahrhundert** [Keyboard building in the 17th and 18th centuries], *Kongreß-Bericht: Gesellschaft für Musikforschung* (Kassel; Basel: Bärenreiter, 1950) 239–43. *Charts, diagr.* In German. See no. 299 in this volume.

3509 CERVELLI, Luisa. **Italienische Musik-**
as **instrumente in der Praxis des General-bassspiels: Das Arpichord** [Italian music instruments in the practice of continuo playing: The arpicordo], *Bericht über den siebenten internationalen musikwissenschaftlichen Kongress* (Kassel: Bärenreiter, 1959) 76–78. *Illus.* In German. See no. 390 in this volume.

The 16th- and 17th-c. sources indicate that the arpicordo was not a kind of harpsichord, but an instrument to be classified with the clavicembalo and the clavichord. It was actually a spinet, but not rectangular, the shape associated with the commonest type of spinet. Rather, it was a five- or six-sided polygon. The arpicordo, whose name derives from *arpa*, was thought of by early writers as a harp laid on its side. A five-sided arpicordo attributed to "Joannis Francisci Brixiani", i.e., Giovan Francesco Antegnati of Brescia, is preserved in the Raccolta Statale di Strumenti Musicali, Roma, Fondo Evan Gorgas. *(Carl Skoggard)*

3510 COON, Leland A. **The distinction between clav-**
as **ichord and harpsichord music,** *Papers read at the Annual Meeting of the American Musicological Society* (New York: American Musicological Society, 1936) 78–87. See no. 230 in this volume.

Discusses the variety and construction of early keyboard instruments, terminology, genres specific to each instrument, distinguishing characteristics of the repertoire, and performance practice.

3511 DIETZ, Franz Rudolf. **Das Intonieren von**
as **Flügeln** [Toning the hammers of grand pianos], *Dokumentation* (Frankfurt am Main: Fördergemeinschaft Klavier, 1966) 183–87. In German. See no. 494 in this volume.

3512 FENNER, Klaus. **Unterschiede in der Stimm-**
as **barkeit unserer heutigen Klaviere** [Differences in

tunability in our contemporary pianos], *Dokumentation* (Frankfurt am Main: Fördergemeinschaft Klavier, 1966) 200–13. In German. See no. 494 in this volume.

⟶ FLADE, Ernst. **Bachs Stellung zum Orgel- und Klavierbau seiner Zeit** [Bach's views on the keyboard instrument construction of his day]. See no. 3361 in this volume.

3513 Fördergemeinschaft Klavier. **Colloquium an der**
as **Technischen Universität Berlin** [Colloquium at the Technische Universität Berlin], *Dokumentation* (Frankfurt am Main: Fördergemeinschaft Klavier, 1966) 176–79. In German. See no. 494 in this volume.
Report on a discussion of piano acoustics, held in connection with the Europiano-Kongreß, Berlin 1965.

3514 Fördergemeinschaft Klavier. **Schlußberichte**
as [Closing reports], *Dokumentation* (Frankfurt am Main: Fördergemeinschaft Klavier, 1966) 296–331. In German. See no. 494 in this volume.
Acts of and responses to the Europiano-Kongreß, Berlin 1965, with the resolutions adopted by the congress; signed remarks by Oswald SASSO, Wilhelm GEBHARDT, and Georg PREISS; press dossier; and a selection of photographs from the proceedings. *(David Bloom)*

3515 FUCHS, Helmut V. **Einige akustische und**
as **ästhetische Aspekte des Klavierklangs** [Some acoustic and aesthetic aspects of piano sound], *Dokumentation* (Frankfurt am Main: Fördergemeinschaft Klavier, 1966) 167–76. In German. See no. 494 in this volume.

3516 GOEBELS, Franzpeter. **Grundbegriffe des**
as **Klavierunterrichts** [Basic concepts of piano instruction], *Dokumentation* (Frankfurt am Main: Fördergemeinschaft Klavier, 1966) 88–94. In German. See no. 494 in this volume.

3517 GROVER, David S. **Zusammenarbeit zwischen**
as **Klavierherstellern und Erziehungsbehörden/ Cooperation between piano manufacturers and educational authorities,** *Dokumentation* (Frankfurt am Main: Fördergemeinschaft Klavier, 1966) 68–82. In German and English. See no. 494 in this volume.
In modern society, the lack of pianist promotion by manufacturers and of consultation with composers about piano improvement has resulted in the alienation of the professional musician from the manufacturer. A standard for school pianos should be created to prevent abuses resulting from competition among manufacturers. Music authorities should be influenced to replace inferior school instruments, to build special music rooms, to encourage music programs in school curricula, and to use the piano instead of the recorder in music appreciation classes. *(Arthur Comegno)*

3518 GUNJI, Sumi. **Japan und sein Klavierbau** [Ja-
as pan and its piano builders], *Dokumentation* (Frankfurt am Main: Fördergemeinschaft Klavier, 1966) 213–17. In German. See no. 494 in this volume.

3519 HARDING, Rosamond E.M. **The pianoforte**
as **from 1709-1851,** *Société Internationale de Musicologie: Premier Congrès Liège—Compte rendu/ Internationale Gesellschaft für Musikwissenschaft: Erster Kongress Lüttich—Kongressbericht/International Society for Musical Research: First Congress Liège: Report* (London: Plainsong and Mediaeval Music Society, 1930) 146–47. See no. 178 in this volume.

Traces the history of the pianoforte. The invention of the instrument was essentially the outcome of an attempt to make the harpsichord more expressive. *(Meredith E. Baker)*

3520 IBACH, Johann Adolf. **Generalthema von**
as **Berlin: Das Klavier in einer sich wandelnden Welt** [General theme from Berlin: The piano in a changing world], *Dokumentation* (Frankfurt am Main: Fördergemeinschaft Klavier, 1966) 20–22. In German. See no. 494 in this volume.

3521 JEHLE, Martin Friedrich. **Klavierbauer und**
as **Tonkünstler** [Piano makers and composers], *Dokumentation* (Frankfurt am Main: Fördergemeinschaft Klavier, 1966) 64–68. In German. See no. 494 in this volume.

3522 KASTNER, Macario Santiago. **Le "clavecin**
as **parfait" de Bartolomeo Jobernardi** [The *cimbalo perfetto* of Bartolomé Jovernardi], *La musique instrumentale de la Renaissance* (Paris: Centre National de la Recherche Scientifique [CNRS], 1955) 293–303. In French. See no. 333 in this volume.
The Italian-born Jovernardi was harpist in the royal chapel of Felipe IV in Madrid from 1633. In *Tratado de la mussica* (*E-Mn* MS 8931) he describes instruments he designed and made himself and brought with him to Spain: a chromatic harp and a single-manual harpsichord that he called perfect, with a reinforced body and an original mechanism allowing the player to change stops rapidly, without stopping the performance. Unfortunately his descriptions are less than precise and the exact nature of his innovations remains unclear. An extended version is published in *Anuario musical* VIII (1952). *(Susan Poliniak)*

3523 KENT, Earle L. **Influence of irregular patterns**
as **in the inharmonicity of piano tone partials upon tuning practice/Der Einfluß von Unregelmässigkeiten in der Obertonverstimmung für die Stimmpraxis,** *Dokumentation* (Frankfurt am Main: Fördergemeinschaft Klavier, 1966) 133–55. In English and German. See no. 494 in this volume.

3524 KÖNIG, Adolf Heinrich. **Die Bedeutung der**
as **Fachschule für Musikinstrumentenbau für einen fachlich und einheitlich ausgebildeten Klavierbauer** [The significance of the Fachschule für Musikinstrumentenbau for instrument making for a professionally and uniformly trained piano builder], *Dokumentation* (Frankfurt am Main: Fördergemeinschaft Klavier, 1966) 223–32. In German. See no. 494 in this volume.

3525 KRAUS, Alexander. **Italian inventions for in-**
as **struments with a keyboard,** *Report of the Fourth Congress of the International Musical Society* (London: Novello, 1912) 324–26. See no. 71 in this volume.
Italian instrument builders invented dampers and pedals for clavichords, spinets, and harpsichords in the 16th c. Cristofori's soft pedal for his clavicembalo col piano e forte engendered the name for the modern piano. *(Mei-Mei Meng)*

3526 KUNITZ, Hans. **Gedanken zur klanglichen**
as **Struktur des Klaviers** [Thoughts on the sonic structure of the piano], *Dokumentation* (Frankfurt am Main: Fördergemeinschaft Klavier, 1966) 44–52. In German. See no. 494 in this volume.

3527
as
LAIBLE, Ulrich. **Grenzprobleme des Into-nierens von Klavieren und Flügeln** [Side issues in the voicing of pianos and grand pianos], *Dokumentation* (Frankfurt am Main: Fördergemeinschaft Klavier, 1966) 180–83. In German. See no. 494 in this volume.

3528
as
LEIPP, Émile. **Qu'est-ce qu'un son de piano?/ Was ist ein Klavierton?** [What is a piano sound?], *Dokumentation* (Frankfurt am Main: Förderge-meinschaft Klavier, 1966) 118–33. In French and Ger-man. See no. 494 in this volume.

3529
as
LUNELLI, Renato. **La fisarmonica e il Trentino** [The accordion and Trentino], *Atti del III Congresso nazionale di arti e tradizioni popolari* (Roma: Opera Nazionale Dopolavoro, 1936) 352–59. In Italian. See no. 218 in this volume.

3530
as
MATTHIAS, Max. **Eine betriebswirtschaft-liche Betrachtung für die Klavierindustrie** [A business-management perspective on the piano indus-try], *Dokumentation* (Frankfurt am Main: Fördergemeinschaft Klavier, 1966) 217–23. In Ger-man. See no. 494 in this volume.

3531
as
MEER, John Henry van der. **Zur Geschichte des Klaviziteriums** [The history of the clavicytherium], *Bericht über den internationalen musikwissenschaft-lichen Kongreß* (Kassel: Bärenreiter, 1963) 305–08. In German. See no. 452 in this volume.

The term "clavicytherium" designated a vertical harpsichord, played from the mid-15th c. until the end of the 18th. It may also have referred to a hy-brid instrument invented ca. 1500 and extant until the mid-18th c. in Ger-many, Italy, France, and England: a keyed harp or harp-piano with gut strings and quill plectra, sometimes equipped with arpichordum. *(David Bloom)*

3532
as
MEYER, Jürgen. **Die Richtcharakteristik des Flügels** [Directional properties in the grand piano], *Dokumentation* (Frankfurt am Main: Fördergemeinschaft Klavier, 1966) 155–67. In Ger-man. See no. 494 in this volume.

3533
as
MOSER, J. **Klavierklang und Resonanzboden-konstruktion** [Piano sound and soundboard construc-tion], *Akten des fünften internationalen Kongresses katholischer Gelehrten/Compte rendu du Ve Congrès scientifique international des catholiques* (München: Herder, 1901) 347–48. In German. See no. 26 in this volume.

3534
as
NEUPERT, Hanns. **Aktuelle Probleme des Cembalos und des Cembalobaues** [Current prob-lems: Harpsichords and harpsichord makers], *Doku-mentation* (Frankfurt am Main: Fördergemeinschaft Klavier, 1966) 240–47. In German. See no. 494 in this volume.

3535
as
NEUPERT, Hans. **Kopie und Rekonstruktion: Geschichte und Probleme des Neubaus von besaiteten Tasteninstrumenten** [The copy and the reconstructed instrument: The history of the physical re-newal of stringed keyboard instruments, and of the prob-lems encountered], *Bericht über den Internationalen musikwissenschaftlichen Kongress* (Kassel: Bärenreiter, 1954) 85–89. In German. See no. 319 in this volume.

Traces the history of harpsichord building and rebuilding during the late 19th and early 20th c. Four states are to be distinguished: the original in-strument, the copy or replica, the newly constructed instrument, and the re-constructed instrument. The copy, which aims to reproduce the weaknesses and limitations of the original, cannot be recommended as an ideal (the way 18th-c. instruments once sounded is no longer even known). The newly constructed instrument, such as the Pleyel harpsichord made for Wanda Landowska, differs from the copy in its degree of recreative freedom. The idea of the copy and of new construction are both typical of the first years of the 20th c. The reconstructed instrument makes free use of modern technol-ogy to re-create a scientifically understood historical model. This method reached its first high point during the 1920s, especially in Germany. The present ideal (1953) of harpsichord builders remains reconstruction, a pro-cess demanding both inspiration and technical finesse. *(Carl Skoggard)*

3536
as
NOUNEBERG, Louta. **A new method of instru-mental instruction: The film as a means of mu-sic education,** *Music in education* (Paris: UNESCO, 1955) 248–52. See no. 322 in this volume.

Discusses the use of filmed recordings of great pianists as a pedagogical tool for analyzing and teaching technique. A French-language version is cited as no. 3537 in this volume.

3537
as
NOUNEBERG, Louta. **Une nouvelle méthode d'enseignement instrumental: Le film, auxiliaire de l'éducation musicale** [A new method of instrumental instruction: Film as an aid in music edu-cation], *La musique dans l'éducation* (Paris: UNESCO; Colin, 1955) 259–62. In French. See no. 323 in this vol-ume.

An English-language version is abstracted as no. 3536 in this volume.

3538
as
PERRACHIO, Luigi. **L'industria dei pianoforti in Italia** [The piano industry in Italy], *La vita musicale dell'Italia d'oggi* (Torino: Fratelli Bocca, 1921) 217–26. In Italian. See no. 97 in this volume.

Provides a brief overview of the piano industry's output and construction materials.

3539
as
QUEDENFELD, Hermann R. **Der Klavier-händler: Musiker, Psychologe und Verkäufer** [The piano dealer: Musician, psychologist, and sales-man], *Dokumentation* (Frankfurt am Main: Fördergemeinschaft Klavier, 1966) 82–86. In German. See no. 494 in this volume.

3540
as
SASSMANN, Martin. **Co-Referat Arbeits-gemeinschaft Cembalobau** [Supplementary report of the study group on harpsichord building], *Doku-mentation* (Frankfurt am Main: Fördergemeinschaft Klavier, 1966) 252–57. In German. See no. 494 in this volume.

3541
as
SCHÜTZE, Rainer. **Die Unterschiede in der akustischen und musikalischen Qualität bei alten und modernen Cembali** [The differences in acoustic and musical quality between old and modern harpsichords], *Dokumentation* (Frankfurt am Main: Fördergemeinschaft Klavier, 1966) 247–52. In German. See no. 494 in this volume.

⟶
SEIFFERT, Max. **Zur Forschung über die ältere Klavier- und Orgelmusik** [Research on early keyboard and organ music]. See no. 923 in this volume.

3542 SITTNER, Hans. **Präludium über das Klavier**
as [Prelude on the piano], *Dokumentation* (Frankfurt am Main: Fördergemeinschaft Klavier, 1966) 16–20. In German. See no. 494 in this volume.

Discusses keyboard literature and the manufactures of keyboard instruments (16th c. to present), the importance of the piano in pedagogy, keyboard technique, and problems of interpretation. Another version is cited as RILM [1970]3943. *(Sibylle Dahms)*

3543 STOECKEL, Alfred. **Der blinde Klavier-**
as **stimmer: Ein Faktor in der Produktion** [The blind piano tuner: A factor in production], *Dokumentation* (Frankfurt am Main: Fördergemeinschaft Klavier, 1966) 232–35. In German. See no. 494 in this volume.

3544 THOMMA, Lothar. **Der Rechenschieber zur**
as **Berechnung sämtlicher Saiten für Klaviere und Cembali** [A slide rule for the calculation of all piano and harpsichord strings], *Dokumentation* (Frankfurt am Main: Fördergemeinschaft Klavier, 1966) 235–39. In German. See no. 494 in this volume.

3545 VOGEL, Martin. **Tasteninstrumente in reiner**
as **Stimmung** [Keyboard instruments in just intonation], *Dokumentation* (Frankfurt am Main: Förderge-meinschaft Klavier, 1966) 52–63. In German. See no. 494 in this volume.

3546 YOUNG, Robert William. **Inharmonicity of pi-**
as **ano strings,** *Acustica: International journal of acoustics/Journal international d'acoustique/Internationale akustische Zeitschrift* IV/1 (1954) 259–62. *Illus., bibliog., charts, diagr.* Summaries in French, German, and English. See no. 324 in this volume.

Inharmonicity, or the departure of the natural frequencies of a piano string from the harmonic series, was measured for bass and treble strings in three sizes of Steinway pianos. The bass strings of the grand piano exhibit less inharmonicity than the corresponding strings of a small upright piano. Tuning is correlated with inharmonicity. *(author)*

44 String (chordophones)

3547 ABBADO, Michelangelo. **Liuteria classica**
as **moderna e decadente** [Classic string instrument making: Modern and decadent], *Congresso internazionale di liuteria: Celebrazioni stradivariane* (Roma: Staderini, 1937). In Italian. See no. 238 in this volume.

Addresses the qualitative decline in string instrument production. After a historical overview, topics include hand craft vs. assembly-line methods, instruments for students, the art of teaching string instrument making, and the need for a new school. *(Mark Stevens)*

3548 ANDERSSON, Otto. **Altnordische Streichin-**
as **strumente** [Old Nordic string instruments], *Haydn-Zentenarfeier* (Leipzig: Breitkopf & Härtel; Wien: Artaria, 1909) 252–59. *Music.* In German. See no. 65 in this volume.

Includes organological descriptions of several instruments, including the Swedish lute and the Norwegian lyra.

3549 BAYER, Bathja. **Haḱynŵr hamiqr'ay l'ŵr**
as **hamamṣ'aym** [The Biblical kinnor in light of archaeological discoveries], *Dwkan* V (1963) 109–22. *Illus.* In Hebrew. See no. 451 in this volume.

Examines archaeological findings related to the origin, shape, and playing techniques of the Biblical instrument the kinnor. *(Moshe Zorman)*

3550 BINKLEY, Thomas E. **Le luth et sa technique**
as [The lute and its technique], *Le luth et sa musique* (Paris: Centre National de la Recherche Scientifique [CNRS], 1958) 25–36. *Bibliog.* In French. See no. 377 in this volume.

Different styles of lute composition reflect technical changes in the lute as it evolved from an ensemble to a solo instrument, as well as changes in playing technique, in three fundamental periods: with plectrum, in the Middle Ages; with alternating thumb and index finger in the early Renaissance; and with thumb for the lower strings and the other fingers for the higher strings from the later Renaissance onwards. Modern lutenists need to use a varied technique to perform a varied repertoire.

3551 BLADIER, Benjamin. **Contribution à l'étude**
as **du violoncelle** [Contribution to the study of the violoncello], *Acoustique musicale* (Paris: Centre National de la Recherche Scientifique [CNRS], 1959) 193–202. *Illus., bibliog., charts, diagr.* In French. See no. 393 in this volume.

Reports on the resonance curves of the bodies of five violoncellos, responding to an electrodynamic stimulus, obtained through a microphone. *(David Bloom)*

3552 BONUCCI, Arturo. **La liuteria in rapporto alle**
as **esigenze dell'artista esecutore** [String instrument making in relation to the needs of the performing artist], *Congresso internazionale di liuteria: Celebrazioni stradivariane* (Roma: Staderini, 1937) 5–7. In Italian. See no. 238 in this volume.

Describes the five criteria for quality string instruments: ease of production, quality of sound throughout the range, uniformity of sound among the four strings, beauty of timbre, and brilliance and clarity of sound. These qualities are ranked from a performer's point of view. *(Mark Stevens)*

3553 BRUGER, Hans Dagobert. **Probleme der**
as **deutschen Lautenmusik des XVIII Jahrhunderts** [Topics in German lute music of the 18th century], *Bericht über den I. musikwissenschaftlichen Kongress der Deutschen Musikgesellschaft in Leipzig* (Wiesbaden: Breitkopf & Härtel, 1926) 237–41. In German. See no. 120 in this volume.

Discusses sources and emphasizes the use of dynamics. The lute as a continuo instrument and its relationship to similar instruments, such as the theorbo and chitarrone, are mentioned. *(William Renwick)*

3554 CANDI, Cesare. **Come costruiva il violino An-**
as **tonio Stradivari—Come lo si costruisce oggi: Se si fosse trovato di fronte ai pianoforti moderni e all'orchestra moderna avrebbe Stradivari usati i medesimi spessori?** [How Antonio Stradivari built the violin—How it is built today: If he had been confronted with modern pianos and the modern orchestra, would Stradivari have used the same thicknesses?], *Congresso internazionale di liuteria: Celebrazioni stradivariane* (Roma: Staderini, 1937) 18–21. In Italian. See no. 238 in this volume.

Discusses the methods of Stradivari that made his instruments distinctive. A brief comparative discussion of the modern violin is included. Topics addressed include form, varnish, decoration, correction of defects, seasoning, choice of woods, and restoration. *(Mark Stevens)*

3555 CARRIÈRE, Zéphyrin. **Entretien d'un tuyau à**
as **anche libre** [Examination of a free-reed pipe], *Acoustique musicale* (Paris: Centre National de la Recherche Scientifique [CNRS], 1959) 215–19. *Illus., charts, diagr.* In French. See no. 393 in this volume.

Describes the test of a simple method of measuring sound pressure with Rudolph Koenig's manometric flame capsule, as proposed by Henri Pierre Maxime Bouasse (*Instruments à vent*, Paris 1929-30). *(David Bloom)*

3556 CAULLET, Gustave. **Simon: Maître de vièle**
as **(1313)** [Simon: Master of the vielle (1313)], *Fédération Archéologique et Historique de Belgique: Annales du XXIIe congrès. I: Documents et compte rendu; II: Rapports & mémoires* (Mechelen: Godenne, 1911) II, 761–66. *Illus.* In French. See no. 73 in this volume.

Discusses the school of vielle playing Simon founded at Ypres in 1313.

3557 CHERBULIEZ, Antoine-Élisée. **Quelques ob-**
as **servations sur le psaltérion (tympanon) populaire Suisse: Hackbrett** [Some observations on the traditional Swiss psaltery (dulcimer): Hackbrett], *Journal of the International Folk Music Council* XII (1960) 23–27. In French. See no. 413 in this volume.

The hackbrett is a dulcimer with a three- or four-octave range, found in parts of the Swiss Alpine region. Its strings, two to five per note, are stretched over a trapezoid sound box; it is played with mallets. Especially in the Appenzell region, the hackbrett is a featured instrument in ensembles. It is a picturesque survivor of the forerunners of the modern piano, and poses problems of typology and terminology for organologists. *(Murat Eyüboğlu)*

3558 CLAUDIUS, Carl. **Die schwedische Nyckelhar-**
as **pa** [The Swedish nyckelharpa], *Bericht über den zweiten Kongress der Internationalen Musikgesellschaft* (Leipzig: Breitkopf & Härtel, 1907) 242–45. *Illus.* In German. See no. 53 in this volume.

Remarks on the Swedish keyed fiddle in supplement to Karl Peter Leffler's *Om nyckelharpospelet på Skansen* (Stockholm, 1899), referring to construction, repertoire, and history. While previous researchers have conjectured that it was brought to Scandinavia by Walloon immigrants early in the Thirty Years' War, iconographic evidence and the testimony of Martin Agricola indicate that it had existed in Sweden more than a century earlier. *(David Bloom)*

3559 COLLINS, Gertrude; SHORE, Bernard. **The**
as **teaching of stringed instruments,** *Music and drama in the counties* (London: conference, 1949). See no. 283 in this volume.

3560 CORTI, Mario. **Liuteria, commercio** [String in-
as strument making and commerce], *Congresso internazionale di liuteria: Celebrazioni stradivariane* (Roma: Staderini, 1937). *Charts, diagr.* In Italian. See no. 238 in this volume.

Discusses the need for an instrument school in order to restore the quality of Italian string instruments, and the problems in obtaining high-quality component parts. *(Mark Stevens)*

3561 DART, Thurston. **La pandore** [The bandora], *Le*
as *luth et sa musique* (Paris: Centre National de la Recherche Scientifique [CNRS], 1958) 225–29. *Illus., bibliog.* In French. See no. 377 in this volume.

Summary of the organology and documentary history of the instrument, a bass cittern popular in Elizabethan England, from its invention by John Rose ca. 1560 through the discussion in Thomas Mace's *Musick's Monument* (1676). A list of MS and print sources of bandora music is appended. *(David Bloom)*

3562 DI DONATO, Vincenzo. **L'industria della**
as **liuteria in Italia** [The string instrument industry in Italy], *La vita musicale dell'Italia d'oggi* (Torino: Fratelli

Bocca, 1921) 226–30. In Italian. See no. 97 in this volume.

Discusses a proposal for uniform physical measurements of instruments.

3563 DISERTORI, Benvenuto. **Le *liuto soprano*** [The
as *liuto soprano*], *Le luth et sa musique* (Paris: Centre National de la Recherche Scientifique [CNRS], 1958) 231–37. *Illus., charts, diagr.* In French. See no. 377 in this volume.

A painting by Pietro Longhi in the Pinacoteca di Brera, Milan, and the organological examination of instruments in the private collections of Ian Harwood and Geneviève Thibault de Chambure as well as the Museo Teatrale alla Scala, Milan, provide evidence of the 18th-c. existence of a soprano lute, to be distinguished from the mandolin, plucked with the fingertips rather than a plectrum; it is probably the instrument for which the solo lute parts in several Vivaldi concertos for multiple instruments were written. *(David Bloom)*

3564 DISERTORI, Benvenuto. **Remarques sur**
as **l'évolution du luth en Italie au XVe siècle et au XVIe** [Remarks on the evolution of the lute in 15th- and 16th-century Italy], *Le luth et sa musique* (Paris: Centre National de la Recherche Scientifique [CNRS], 1958) 19–24. In French. See no. 377 in this volume.

The early 15th-c. lute had nine strings in five courses, all but the highest string being doubled. By the end of the century there were 11 strings in six courses. At the end of the 16th c. there were 16 strings in eight courses.

3565 DUCHEMIN, Georges-Jacques. **Autour d'un**
as **arc musical du Saloum oriental** [About a musical bow of eastern Saloum], *Première conférence internationale des Africanistes de l'ouest* (Paris: Maisonneuve, 1950-1951) II, 248–58. *Illus., bibliog., tech. drawings.* In French. See no. 274 in this volume.

Describes the construction, playing, music, and uses of the bailol, a Fulbe musical bow.

3566 DUCHEMIN, Georges-Jacques. **Deux arcs**
as **renforcés de Guinée Française** [Two reinforced bows of Guinea], *Conférence internationale des Africanistes de l'Ouest– C.I.A.O.: Programme de la deuxième réunion/Conférencia Internacional dos Africanistas Ocidentais: 2a. conferência* (Lisboa: Ministério das Colónias, 1950-1952) V, 127–34. In French. See no. 275 in this volume.

3567 ÉCORCHEVILLE, Jules. **Über die Lauten-**
as **kommission** [On the commission on lute music], *Haydn-Zentenarfeier* (Leipzig: Breitkopf & Härtel; Wien: Artaria, 1909) 211. In German. See no. 65 in this volume.

Discusses the Kommission für Erforschung der Lautenmusik, founded by the author in 1907 under the auspices of the Internationalen Musikgesellschaft.

3568 EMMANUEL, Maurice. **La création du violon**
as **et ses conséquences** [The creation of the violin and its consequences], *Atti del secondo Congresso internazionale di musica* (Firenze: Le Monnier, 1940) 283–91. In French; summaries in Italian and German. See no. 239 in this volume.

Remarks on the history of the violin in the 16th through 18th c. in France and Italy, with particular attention to its important in the evolution of instrumental genres and to the crucial role of the violin makers of Cremona and Brescia. *(David Bloom)*

3569 FISCHER, Pieter. **Sa Tendre Majesté la harpe**
as [Her Tender Majesty, the harp], *Actes du cinquième Congrès international d'esthétique/Proceedings of the*

Fifth International Congress of Aesthetics ('s-Gravenhage: Mouton, 1964) 518–21. In French. See no. 475 in this volume.

The pedal harp, developed around 1720 by Jakob Hochbrucker and introduced to the major European cities primarily by his son Simon, found its way into the modern instrumentarium by an unusual route in the period 1749–ca. 1804, flourishing at first almost exclusively among amateurs, in the restricted circles of the highest social ranks in Paris and Versailles. A sociological and aesthetic analysis of the instrument's attractiveness to this group is advanced in terms of the paired qualities of *majesté* and *tendresse*. *(David Bloom)*

3570
as

FLAGEL, Claude. **Exposé sur la vielle à roue fait à l'occasion du Colloque de Wégimont 1957** [An account of a hurdy-gurdy built on the occasion of the Colloques de Wégimont 1957], *Les colloques de Wégimont. IV: Le Baroque musical—Recueil d'études sur la musique du XVIIᵉ siècle* (Paris: Belles Lettres, 1963) 260–63. In French. See no. 386 in this volume.

Brief remarks on the instrument's history, repertoire, and organology.

3571
as

GALPIN, Francis William. **The origin of the clarsech or Irish harp,** *Report of the Fourth Congress of the International Musical Society* (London: Novello, 1912) 317–24. *Illus.* See no. 71 in this volume.

The development of the instrument is traced from medieval iconography through surviving 18th-c. specimens.

3572
as

GOMBOSI, Otto. **New light on ancient Greek music,** *Papers read at the International Congress of Musicology* (New York: Music Educators National Conference, 1944) 168–83. *Illus., music, charts, diagr.* See no. 266 in this volume.

Discusses the lyre and the kithara, with special emphasis on the tuning of the seven-stringed version of the former. Organological descriptions are provided, along with information about playing techniques.

3573
as

GÖTZ, Josef. **Die Fiedelmusik in der Iglauer Sprachinsel** [Fiddle music in the linguistic enclave of Jihlava], *Haydn-Zentenarfeier* (Leipzig: Breitkopf & Härtel; Wien: Artaria, 1909) 227–28. In German. See no. 65 in this volume.

Provides a basic organological description of the fiddle of Jihlava (Iglau, Czech Republic), with notes on its repertoire.

3574
as

GREILSAMER, Lucien. **La sonorità in rapporto alla registrazione degli strumenti ad arco** [Sonority in relation to the registration of bowed string instruments], *Congresso internazionale di liuteria: Celebrazioni stradivariane* (Roma: Staderini, 1937) 12–18. In Italian. See no. 238 in this volume.

Describes the results of experiments, recent and long past, in which the various components of bowed instruments were varied one by one. *(Mark Stevens)*

3575
as

GUERRINI, Guido. **L'eccellenza degli instrumenti ad arco in rapporto al rendimento della orchestra e del quartetto** [The quality of bowed string instruments in relation to performance by orchestra and quartet], *Congresso internazionale di liuteria: Celebrazioni stradivariane* (Roma: Staderini, 1937) 7–9. In Italian. See no. 238 in this volume.

Discusses the ill effects produced by the use of inferior string instruments in orchestras and quartets.

3576
as

HAMMERICH, Angul. **Bericht über eine alte griechische Lyra von Elfenbein aus der**

Mykenäzeit [Report on an ivory lyre from the Mycenaean period of ancient Greece], *Haydn-Zentenarfeier* (Leipzig: Breitkopf & Härtel; Wien: Artaria, 1909) 99–101. *Illus.* In German. See no. 65 in this volume.

Discusses an instrument found in 1879.

3577
as

HAMMERICH, Angul. **Zur Frage nach dem Ursprung der Streichinstrumente** [The question of the origin of string instruments], *Bericht über den zweiten Kongress der Internationalen Musikgesellschaft* (Leipzig: Breitkopf & Härtel, 1907) 225–30. In German. See no. 53 in this volume.

François-Joseph Fétis has proposed that a rāvaṇāsta-type spike fiddle in ancient India, said to have been invented by Rāvaṇa, the demon king of Lanka in the *Rāmāyaṇa*, was the prototype of all extant bowed string instruments. Most of Fétis's evidence can be dismissed, but a newly noted piece of evidence in support of his hypothesis is the mention by the early 10th-c. geographer Ibn al-Faqīh al-Hamadhānī of a kamānche (Persian spike fiddle) played by the "people in Sind". *(David Bloom)*

3578
as

HERAN, Bohuš. **Prstoklady jako výrazový prostředek: Studie k Janáčkově violoncellové Pohádce** [Fingering as a means of expression: A study devoted to Janáček's *Pohádka* for violoncello], *Sborník Janáčkovy Akademie Múzichých Umeni* V (1965) 18–25. *Music.* In Czech. See no. 496 in this volume.

The seemingly simple matter of fingering is in effect one of the most important elements of the process of interpretation. Through incorrect fingering, the style, character, and understanding of a composition may suffer. Using the *Pohádka* as an example it can easily be shown how these errors are made. *(Jan Trojan)*

3579
as

HINDEMITH, Paul. **La viola d'amore** [The viola d'amore], *Atti del secondo Congresso internazionale di musica* (Firenze: Le Monnier, 1940) 309–13. In Italian; summaries in French and German. See no. 239 in this volume.

Discusses the history and organology of the instrument, the reasons for its near-disappearance in the late 18th c. and its revival today, and its literature, in which the most important works are by Heinrich Ignaz Franz Biber, Attilio Ariosti, Antonio Vivaldi, and Karl Stamic. *(David Bloom)*

3580
as

HOLLINSHEAD, M.T. **The vibrato in violin playing,** *Ninth International Congress of Psychology* (Princeton: Psychological Review Company, 1930) 224. See no. 160 in this volume.

The vibrato rates and amplitudes of 11 famous violinists were compared to vocal vibratos, using Milton Metfessel's method of sonography. No significant differences were found in vibrato rates. However, the average amplitude of a violin vibrato is approximately a quarter-tone, while that of a vocal vibrato is half a tone. *(Ruth Block)*

3581
as

HOOD, Mantle. **The Javanese rebab,** *Music libraries and instruments* (London: Hinrichsen, 1961) 220–26. *Illus., charts, diagr., tech. drawings.* See no. 406 in this volume.

The Arabic word *rabāb* is a general term for bowed lutes diffused through the Islamic world. The Javanese version is called *rebab*; its construction, stringing, tuning, bowing, and hand positions are outlined, and musical and social features of its role as leader of the gamelan are discussed in detail. *(Susan Poliniak)*

3582
as

HROVATIN, Radoslav. **Bordunske citre v Sloveniji** [The drone zithers in Slovenia], *Rad VII-og kongresa Saveza Folklorista Jugoslavije* (Cetinje: Obod, 1964) 301–07. *Illus., transcr.* In Slovene; summary in German. See no. 419 in this volume.

The drone zither, a forerunner of the chord zither, has been known in Slovenia (under the plural designation *citre*) since the 17th c. Its local history, construction, playing technique, and terminology are discussed. *(author)*

3583 KIRÁLY, Ernő. **Citra kod Mađara u Vojvodini**
as [The zither among the Hungarians in Vojvodina], *Rad VII-og kongresa Saveza Folklorista Jugoslavije* (Cetinje: Obod, 1964) 309–17. *Illus., transcr.* In Serbian; summary in German. See no. 419 in this volume.
A more detailed English-language version is abstracted as RILM [1991]817.

3584 KNEŽEVIĆ, Milivoje V. **Gusle javorove** [The
as maple-wood gusle], *Rad VII-og kongresa Saveza Folklorista Jugoslavije* (Cetinje: Obod, 1964) 345–55. *Illus., charts, diagr.* In Serbian; summary in French. See no. 419 in this volume.
A historical discussion of the instrument as used in Serbia, with particular attention to its connection to epic song and its cultural importance, especially during the Ottoman period. *(author)*

3585 KRÜGER, Hans. **Die Verstimmung (scorda-**
as **tura, discordatura) auf Saiten-Instrumenten in Beziehung zur klanglichen Einrichtung der Instrumente und zum Tonsystem und ihre Folgen auf die Aufführungspraxis** [The alternate tuning (scordatura, discordatura) of string instruments in relation to the instruments' acoustic disposition and to the tonal system, and its consequences for performance practice], *Bericht über den siebenten internationalen musikwissenschaftlichen Kongress* (Kassel: Bärenreiter, 1959) 172–74. *Charts, diagr.* In German. See no. 390 in this volume.
The flat-necked construction that dominated bowed instruments until around 1800, when it was replaced with a somewhat angled neck (allowing a higher bridge, increased string tension, and greater volume), favored a performance practice in equal temperament, including the use of adjustable frets (attested for violoncello in Quantz's *Versuch einer Anweisung...*), and an elaborate scordatura practice. There are passages in the works of Bach that must have been intended for scordatura though not marked as such, being much more difficult to play in tune with a normal tuning. *(David Bloom)*

3586 LA LAURENCIE, Lionel de. **Les femmes et le**
as **luth en France aux XVIᵉ et XVIIᵉ siècle** [Women and the lute in France in the 16th and 17th centuries], *Compte rendu du Vᵉ Congrès international des sciences historiques* (Bruxelles: Weissenbruch, 1923) 366–71. In French. See no. 100 in this volume.
The lute was played by several well-known women in the 16th and 17th c. Though the playing of the lute declined in the 18th c., it was still the subject of paintings by Jean-Antoine Watteau. *(David Nussenbaum)*

3587 LEIPP, Émile; MOLES, Abraham. **Objektive**
as **Methode zur Bestimmung der Qualität eines Saiteninstruments** [Objective methods for determining the quality of a string instrument], *Proceedings of the Third International Congress on Acoustics* (Amsterdam: Elsevier Science, 1961) II, 752–55. *Charts, diagr.* In German. See no. 414 in this volume.

3588 LOTTERMOSER, Werner. **Die akustische**
as **Prüfung von Violinen** [Acoustic testing of violins], *Bericht über den internationalen musikwissenschaftlichen Kongreß Wien Mozartjahr 1956* (Graz; Köln: Böhlau, 1958) 384–86. *Illus., charts, diagr.* In German. See no. 365 in this volume.
Testing of violins at the Physikalisch-Technische Bundesanstalt is in two phases: (1) resonance curves for the instrument by pitch and amplitude are taken, and (2) sound spectrographs are made of the chromatic pitches as

performed on the instrument by a trained violinist, and the instrument is judged subjectively. As illustration of the method, data for a mid-range violin and for a Stradivari instrument are compared. *(David Bloom)*

3589 LOTTERMOSER, Werner. **L'examen acous-**
as **tique des violons dans la Physikalisch-Technische Bundesanstalt** [The acoustic examination of violins in the Physikalisch-Technische Bundesanstalt], *Acoustique musicale* (Paris: Centre National de la Recherche Scientifique [CNRS], 1959) 185–91. *Illus., charts, diagr.* In French. See no. 393 in this volume.
Discusses observations of resonance curves, simplified resonance curves (based on dividing the experimental curve into segments corresponding to the formants of vowels in spoken language), and transient phenomena, comparing instruments of various qualities, from old Cremona violins to modern industrial products. A measurement is proposed for the ability of a violin to respond to excitation by different frequency impulses. *(David Bloom)*

3590 MANCIA, Renato. **L'esame scientifico delle**
as **opere d'arte applicato alla liuteria in rapporto alla identificazione delle scuole e degli autori e in rapporto al restauro e alla conservazione** [The scientific examination of works of art as applied to string instrument making in relation to the identification of schools and individual makers, and to restoration and conservation], *Congresso internazionale di liuteria: Celebrazioni stradivariane* (Roma: Staderini, 1937) 10–11. In Italian. See no. 238 in this volume.
Describes how various methods used in dating paintings, such as X rays and microscopic analysis, have been used successfully in dating instruments. *(Mark Stevens)*

3591 MEYER, Jürgen. **Die Richtcharakteristiken**
as **vom Violoncello** [The directional characteristics of the violoncello], *Problèmes d'acoustique* (Liège: Université de Liège, 1965) M54. In German. See no. 504 in this volume.

3592 NEF, Walter. **Das mehrsaitige "Monochord"**
as [The multiple-string "monochord"], *Compte rendu/Kongressbericht/Report* (Basel: Bärenreiter, 1951) 182. In German. See no. 289 in this volume.
Summary of a paper published in English as *The polychord* in *The Galpin Society Journal* IV (1951). Byzantine, Arabic, and European sources from late antiquity through the 15th c. refer to an instrument called the "monochord" but with more than one string. In the only unambiguous references, the instrument can be shown to be a clavichord. *(David Bloom)*

3593 NGUYỄN, Xuân Khoát. **Le đàn bàu** [The đàn
as bàu], *Journal of the International Folk Music Council* XII (1960) 31–33. *Tech. drawings.* In French. See no. 413 in this volume.
An organological study of the Vietnamese monochord, including discussion of performance technique. Use of glissando and trills are linked to the relationship of the instrument's repertoire to traditional songs, and to the fact that Vietnamese is a tone language. A folk tale, according to which a fairy gave the instrument to a young blind woman because of her self-sacrifice on behalf of her husband, is linked to the instrument's association with blind. Several recent variants of the instrument are discussed. *(Murat Eyüboğlu)*

3594 PASQUALINI, Gioacchino. **Récents résultats**
as **obtenus dans l'étude électroacoustique de la caisse harmonique des instruments à archet** [Recent results obtained in the electroacoustic study of the bodies of string instruments], *Acustica: International journal of acoustics/Journal international d'acoustique/Internationale akustische Zeitschrift* IV/1

(1954) 244–49. *Illus., bibliog., charts, diagr.* In French; summaries in English, French, and German. See no. 324 in this volume.

Presents results of tests performed on modern and antique (restored) violins at the Istituto Acoustico O.M. Corbino, Consiglio Nazionale delle Ricerche (CNR), Rome.

3595
as
PICCIOLI, Lodovico. **Legni di risonanza: Influenza dei metodi di essicazione sul suono** [Resonant woods: The influence of drying methods on sound], *Congresso internazionale di liuteria: Celebrazioni stradivariane* (Roma: Staderini, 1937) 9–10. In Italian. See no. 238 in this volume.

The three basic methods of drying woods for the manufacture of instruments (the natural drying of standing timber, the natural drying of cut wood, and several methods of artificial seasoning) are described, with brief comments on their effects. *(Mark Stevens)*

3596
as
PINCHERLE, Marc. **Autour d'une histoire de la harpe** [About a history of the harp], *Actes du Congrès d'histoire de l'art* (Paris: Presses Universitaires de France, 1923-1924) 742–53. In French. See no. 94 in this volume.

Three types of historical documents on the harp exist: musical texts, literary texts, and iconography (which is more dependable than texts). Musical documents are scarce and mostly uninteresting while literary texts abound, but are mostly unreliable. *(Vivian Conejero)*

3597
as
POULTON, Diana. **La technique du jeu du luth en France et en Angleterre** [The technique of lute playing in France and England], *Le luth et sa musique* (Paris: Centre National de la Recherche Scientifique [CNRS], 1958) 107–19. *Music.* In French. See no. 377 in this volume.

A survey of lute tutors from Adrian Le Roy's lost *Instruction d'asseoir toute musique facilement en tablature de luth* in its first English version (1568) through Thomas Mace's *Musick's monument, or, A remembrancer of the best practical musick* (1676), together with iconographic evidence, suggests that major changes in right-hand technique during the period included the alternation of index and middle fingers instead of thumb and index; the restriction of the thumb to bass strings; the liberal use of slurs and slides; and the replacement of chords played with one finger to each note with the "raking play". *(David Bloom)*

3598
as
PRYNNE, Michael. **Comment noter et conserver les mesures des luths anciens** [How to record and preserve the measurements of early lutes], *Le luth et sa musique* (Paris: Centre National de la Recherche Scientifique [CNRS], 1958) 239–41. In French. See no. 377 in this volume.

3599
as
PUJOL VILARRUBÍ, Emili. **Les ressources instrumentales et leur rôle dans la musique pour vihuela et pour guitare au XVIᵉ siècle et au XVIIᵉ** [Instrumental resources and their role in music for vihuela and guitar in the 16th and 17th centuries], *La musique instrumentale de la Renaissance* (Paris: Centre National de la Recherche Scientifique [CNRS], 1955) 205–15. *Music, charts, diagr.* In French. See no. 333 in this volume.

Surveys the history and development of music for the six-course vihuela de mano in 16th-c. Spain, as a generally polyphonic instrument in line with the prevalent style of vocal music, and the rise toward the end of the century of the five-course Spanish guitar, with its rasgado and punteado techniques, more suitable for a melody-and-chord texture. *(David Bloom)*

3600
as
RIMSKIJ-KORSAKOV, Andrej Vladimirovič. **Les recherches sur le timbre des violons et guitares et sur l'excitation des vibrations**

d'une anche d'harmonium [Research on the timbre of violins and guitars and on stimulating the vibrations of a harmonium reed], *Acoustique musicale* (Paris: Centre National de la Recherche Scientifique [CNRS], 1959) 203–13. *Charts, diagr.* In French. See no. 393 in this volume.

(1) Reports on results from an objective method for evaluating violin tone based on the violin's acoustic response curve. A brief stimulus is applied to the instrument's bridge; the acoustic radiation of the vibrating belly is recorded through a microphone and analyzed with a spectroscope. The method was applied to 80 instruments of varying quality. (2) Discusses experimental evidence showing that the vibrations of a harmonium reed are sinusoidal. *(David Bloom)*

3601
as
SACKETT, Samuel J. **The hammered dulcimer in Ellis County, Kansas,** *Journal of the International Folk Music Council* XIV (1962) 61–64. *Charts, diagr.* See no. 442 in this volume.

The instrument, a trapezoidal dulcimer with a mostly diatonic set of 17, 19, or 21 courses of four strings each, is characteristic of the descendants of Volga German immigrants who came to Ellis County in large numbers in the period 1875-78. It was an obligatory part of the band in the community's traditional *hochzeit* or wedding dances, nowadays held in a somewhat attenuated form, and continues to be produced by a few local artisans. Its structure, tuning, performance style, and repertoire are discussed. *(David Bloom)*

3602
as
SENN, Walter. **Forschungsaufgaben zur Geschichte des Geigenbaues** [Tasks in researching the history of violin making], *Bericht über den Internationalen musikwissenschaftlichen Kongress* (Kassel: Bärenreiter, 1954) 89–92. *Illus.* In German. See no. 319 in this volume.

The historian of string instrument making (usually an amateur) has traditionally relied on the evidence of maker's labels and oral tradition. Both kinds of evidence are unreliable, and much wrong information has entered biographical dictionaries and other scholarly literature as a result (egregious errors are cited). New scientific methods are available for making attributions; identifying a specific lot of wood used to make a given instrument can be especially helpful. *(Carl Skoggard)*

3603
as
SENN, Walter. **Der Wandel des Geigenklanges seit dem 18. Jahrhundert** [Changes in violin sound since the 18th century], *Bericht über den internationalen musikwissenschaftlichen Kongreß* (Kassel: Bärenreiter, 1957) 213–16. *Illus.* In German. See no. 356 in this volume.

The members of the violin family are unique in that historic instruments are preferred to new ones. Hardly any violin, however, outside museum collections, remains in its original condition: Alterations that have contributed to a strengthening of tone and change in sound color include the introduction of a stronger bass-bar, the reinforcement of the sound post to the right of the bridge, the use of much thinner bridges and much thicker strings, the replacement of the original neck with a longer one, and the introduction of the modern bow. Such changes improve volume, but at the expense of the earlier, more intimate tonal quality. *(David Bloom)*

3604
as
STAÏS, Valerios. **Un instrument musical du tombeau à coupole de Menidi** [A musical instrument in the domed tomb of Menidi], *Comptes rendus du Congrès international d'archéologie classique: 2ᵉ session* (Al-Qāhirah: Imprimerie Nationale, 1909) 205–06. In French. See no. 63 in this volume.

Discusses the remains of an eight-stringed metal lyre found in the *tholós* tomb at the Mycenaean-era site of Acharnai near Menidi, Greece.

3605
as
TANABE, Hisao. **Les études récentes concernant les instruments de musique de Japon** [Recent studies on the musical instruments of Japan], *Congrès international des arts populaires/In-*

ternational congress of popular arts (Paris: Institut international de coopération intellectuelle, 1928) 94–95. In French. See no. 153 in this volume.
Summary of the paper cited as no. 3281 in this volume.

3606 TESSIER, André. **Quelques sources de l'école**
as **française de luth au XVIIᵉ siècle** [Some sources of the French school of lute playing of the 17th century], *Société Internationale de Musicologie: Premier Congrès Liège—Compte rendu/Internationale Gesellschaft für Musikwissenschaft: Erster Kongress Lüttich—Kongressbericht/International Society for Musical Research: First Congress Liège: Report* (London: Plainsong and Mediaeval Music Society, 1930) 217–24. *List of works.* In French. See no. 178 in this volume.
The French school of lute playing that flourished in France after 1630 is indeed important and its influence was particularly widespread. It is necessary to number and categorize the tablatures from this period that have been collected. The history of this school of playing as well as its principle masters are described. *(Meredith E. Baker)*

3607 VATIELLI, Francesco. **Rapporti della musica**
as **violinistica con l'ultima letteratura per liuto** [The relations between violin music and the last works for lute], *Atti del secondo Congresso internazionale di musica* (Firenze: Le Monnier, 1940) 292–99. In Italian; summaries in French and German. See no. 239 in this volume.
Discusses the relative positions of lute, five-course guitar and chitarriglia, and violin in northern Italy in the 16th to 17th c. *(David Bloom)*

3608 WINTERNITZ, Emanuel. **The survival of the**
as **kithara and the evolution of the cittern: A study in morphology,** *Music libraries and instruments* (London: Hinrichsen, 1961) 209–14. *Illus., facs.* See no. 406 in this volume.
Iconographic evidence, particularly that of the 9th- or 10th-c. Utrecht Psalter (*NL-Uu* MS 32), suggests a continuous line of development from the ancient Greek and Roman kithara through a similar instrument with fingerboard and neck, perhaps as early as the 5th c., to the cittern in its most advanced form in the 16th c.

45 Wind (aerophones)

3609 AERDE, Raymond Joseph Justin van. **Les**
as **Tuerlinckx, facteurs d'instruments de musique à Malines, XVIIIᵉ et XIXᵉ siècles** [The Tuerlinckx family, makers of musical instruments in Mechelen, 18th and 19th centuries], *Annales du XXIIIᵉ congrès* (Gent: Siffer, 1914) III, 311–38. In French. See no. 89 in this volume.
The Tuerlinckx were active as woodwind instrument builders from 1771 to 1840.

3610 BECKER, Heinz. **Zur Spielpraxis der**
as **griechischen Aulos** [The playing technique of the Greek aulos], *Bericht über den internationalen musikwissenschaftlichen Kongreß* (Kassel: Bärenreiter, 1963) 300–02. *Illus.* In German. See no. 452 in this volume.
Evidence from archaeology and iconography, and from comparison of the aulos with instruments that are extant today, suggests that there must have been two different ways of fingering the ancient instrument: using just three holes, with the little finger providing support; and using four holes including one for the thumb. The second pipe must have served as a drone or accompanied the first in parallel intervals. *(David Bloom)*

3611 BEZIĆ, Jerko. **Diple s mijehom na zadarskom**
as **području** [The diple s mijehom in the Zadar region], *Rad VII-og kongresa Saveza Folklorista Jugoslavije* (Cetinje: Obod, 1964) 269–82. *Illus., port., transcr.* In Croatian; summary in Italian. See no. 419 in this volume.
A supplement to the discussion of the instrument in Božidar Širola's *Sviraljke s udarnim jezičkom* (Zagreb, 1937), with particular attention to terminology, manufacture, playing technique, and historical documentation. *(author)*

3612 BJØRNDAL, Arne. **The hardanger fiddle: The**
as **tradition, music forms, and style,** *Journal of the International Folk Music Council* VIII (1956) 13–15. See no. 349 in this volume.
Discusses the Norwegian hardingfele and its repertoire from around 1650 to the present.

3613 BOSE, Fritz. **Die Fabrikation der nordischen**
as **Bronzeluren** [The production of Nordic bronze lurs], *Bericht über den internationalen musikwissenschaftlichen Kongreß* (Kassel: Bärenreiter, 1963) 298–300. In German. See no. 452 in this volume.
Account of an experimental attempt to make a lur in 1938, curtailed because of the outbreak of war.

3614 ČHIKVADZE, Grigol. **Doistoričeskaja**
as **gruzinskaja kostjanaja salamuri-flejta** [The prehistoric Georgian salamuri bone flute], *Europa et Hungaria: Congressus ethnographicus in Hungaria* (Budapest: Akadémiai Kiadó, 1965) 451–58. In Russian. See no. 460 in this volume.
Another version was published in *Pamjati K. Kvitki. 1880-1953* (Moscow, 1983), cited as RILM ¹⁹⁸³2317.

3615 DEVIĆ, Dragoslav. **Okarina (selo Donja**
as **Mutnica, Srbija)** [Ocarinas of the village of Donja Mutnica, Serbia], *Rad VII-og kongresa Folklorista Jugoslavije* (Cetinje: Obod, 1964) 207–15. *Illus., bibliog., transcr., list of pitches.* In Serbian; summary in French. See no. 419 in this volume.
The earthenware instruments, all from a single local maker, come in two variants, cylindrical and flat; a third type, for children, is really a toy whistle imitating the ocarina's sound. *(author)*

3616 DURANT, Félicien. **Instruments en cuivre**
as **omnitoniques à 6 pistons dépendants** [Omnitonic brass instruments with six dependent pistons], *Report of the Fourth Congress of the International Musical Society* (London: Novello, 1912) 314–17. *Charts, diagr.* In French. See no. 71 in this volume.
Discusses design improvements for brass instruments.

3617 FRANCO, José Luis. **Sobre un grupo de instru-**
as **mentos musicales prehispánicos con sistema acústico no conocido** [On a group of pre-Hispanic musical instruments with an unknown acoustic system], *XXXV Congreso Internacional de Americanistas: Actas y memorias* (México, D.F.: Editorial Libros de México, 1964) 369. In Spanish. See no. 454 in this volume.
Summary of a paper describing aerophones from Central America.

3618 GARCIA MATOS, Manuel. **Strumenti musicali**
as **folkloristici di Ibiza: Gli aerofoni melodici** [Traditional instruments of Ibiza: Melodic aerophones], *Atti del Congresso internazionale di musiche popolari mediterranee e del Convegno dei bibliotecari musicali* (Palermo: De Magistris succ. V. Bellotti, 1959) 133–52. *Illus.* In Italian. See no. 332 in this volume.

3619 GOJKOVIĆ, Andrijana. **O srpskim sviralama-**
as **jedinkama** [The Serbian svirala-jedinka], *Rad VII-og kongresa Saveza Folklorista Jugoslavije* (Cetinje: Obod, 1964) 217–22. *Bibliog., transcr.* In Serbian; summary in English. See no. 419 in this volume.

General discussion of the Serbian single flute, known as svirala-jedinka, with attention to terminology, construction, and ornamentation in playing technique. The scales of particular instruments, while they vary widely, are consistent with the musical characteristics of the wider region. *(author)*

3620 HADŽIMANOV, Vasil. **The dvotelnik, a Mace-**
as **donian folk instrument,** *Journal of the International Folk Music Council* XV (1963) 82–83. *Illus.* See no. 459 in this volume.

An organological description of the long-necked Macedonian lute also known as ikitelli.

3621 HADŽIMANOV, Vasil. **Instruments folk-**
as **loriques en Macedoine: Kavalis** [Traditional instruments in Macedonia: Kavals], *Journal of the International Folk Music Council* XII (1960) 21–22. In French. See no. 413 in this volume.

3622 HEDLUND, H. Jean. **James Hook and the pat-**
as **ent voice flute,** *Music libraries and instruments* (London: Hinrichsen, 1961) 239–43. *Illus., music.* See no. 406 in this volume.

The patent voice flute or flauto di voce was an alto transverse flute equipped with an extra hole covered by a membrane, for a mirliton-like distorting effect, made by the English firm of Wigley & McGregor starting 1810. It is featured in a set of trios for two concert flutes and patent voice flute by James Hook, op. 133. *(Susan Poliniak)*

3623 IVANČAN, Ivan. **Istarska svirala šurla** [An
as Istrian wind instrument, the šurla], *Rad VII-og kongresa Saveza Folklorista Jugoslavije* (Cetinje: Obod, 1964) 253–60. *Illus., port., bibliog., transcr.* In Croatian; summary in German. See no. 419 in this volume.

Two hitherto undescribed Istrian instruments are known as šurla: one a single-reed pipe, the other a double-chanter pipe with two independent reeds within a single mouthpiece. Their manufacture is described in detail, and the two-reed instrument is compared to related instruments including diple, svirale (oboe), the sopile of the Kvarner gulf, and the Macedonian zurla. *(author)*

3624 KARSTÄDT, Georg. **Aufführungspraktische**
as **Fragen bei Verwendung von Naturtrompeten, Naturhörnern und Zinken** [Performance-practice issues in playing natural trumpets, natural horns, and cornetts], *Bericht über den Internationalen musikwissenschaftlichen Kongress* (Kassel: Bärenreiter, 1954) 93–95. In German. See no. 319 in this volume.

References in Baroque scores and other written sources to instruments in the horn family are often vague; the physical evidence of old instruments is usually incomplete (mouthpieces are usually missing). Modern players have met the challenge of performing in the clarino register; however, the problem of how Baroque performers produced chromatic notes on natural instruments remains unsolved (stopping was probably not known before ca. 1750). The zink has a very individual sound, and should not be replaced with the modern horn (zink playing is in need of better understanding). *(Carl Skoggard)*

3625 KUMER, Zmaga. **Panova piščal v Sloveniji**
as [Panpipes in Slovenia], *Rad VII-og kongresa Saveza Folklorista Jugoslavije* (Cetinje: Obod, 1964) 261–67. *Illus., transcr., maps.* In Slovene; summary in German. See no. 419 in this volume.

The Slovenian panpipes are known by many names, of which *trstenke* (which also refers to the marsh-reed, *Phragmites communis*, from which they are made), is the most useful. They are made with between six and 26

pipes, sometimes tuned with wax stoppers. They are generally played as a solo instrument, by adults and children, while a reduced version called *coštimaje* may be used in accompaniment. They are made by shepherds, farmhands, and elderly men; it was possible to purchase them at fairs and church festivals up until World War II. *(author)*

3626 LEIPP, Émile. **La cavité buccale, paramètre**
as **sensible des spectres rayonnés des instruments à vent** [The oral cavity as a measurable factor in the spectra emitted by wind instruments], *Fourth International Congress on Acoustics* (København: conference, 1962) I, P51. In French. See no. 448 in this volume.

3627 LENIHAN, J.M.A.; MCNEIL, S. **An acoustical**
as **study of the Highland bagpipe,** *Acustica: International journal of acoustics/Journal international d'acoustique/ Internationale akustische Zeitschrift* IV/1 (1954) 231–32. *Illus., bibliog., charts, diagr.* Summaries in English, French, and German. See no. 324 in this volume.

The frequencies and intervals of the notes in the bagpipe scale were measured with a double beam oscillograph in conjunction with a valve-maintained tuning fork. *(author)*

3628 LIMA, Emirto de. **Las flautas indígenas** [Indige-
as nous flutes], *Congrés de la Societat Internacional de Musicologia* (Barcelona: Casa de Caritat, 1936). In Spanish. See no. 224 in this volume.

The conference report provides only a citation. Neither the text nor a summary of the paper was published here. Discusses the flutes of the Indians of Colombia.

3629 LOVRENČEVIĆ, Zvonko. **Jedinka i dvojnice u**
as **bjelovarskoj okolici** [Jedinka and dvojnice instruments of the Bjelovar region], *Rad VII-og kongresa Saveza Folklorista Jugoslavije* (Cetinje: Obod, 1964) 223–37. *Illus., transcr.* In Croatian; summary in German. See no. 419 in this volume.

The region's wooden flutes—the single-tube jedinka, transverse fajfa or strančica, and double-tube dvojnice—are almost exclusively shepherd's instruments, and rarely or never played in ensembles. The imprecise placement of the holes means that special skills in fingering and breath control are required to play the instrument in tune. With the dvojnice, the six-hole right tube is always used to play the melody, while the five-hole left tube accompanies in slightly flattened parallel thirds and seconds. While the manufacture of these instruments has been in abeyance for several decades, it could easily be resumed. *(author)*

3630 MACGILLIVRAY, James. **The cylindrical reed**
as **pipe from antiquity to the 20th century: Its classification and scope,** *Music libraries and instruments* (London: Hinrichsen, 1961) 218–20. *Illus.* See no. 406 in this volume.

Historical and organological account of cylindrical reed pipe instruments, from the ancient Greek aulos to the family of modern clarinets, classified by reed, shape, and construction. *(Susan Poliniak)*

3631 MARKOVIĆ, Zagorka. **Izrada frula u Banatu**
as [Flute making in Banat], *Rad VII-og kongresa Saveza Folklorista Jugoslavije* (Cetinje: Obod, 1964) 239–42. In Serbian; summary in French. See no. 419 in this volume.

Contrary to received opinion, the frula flute is as popular in Vojvodina as in the mountain regions; players use it to practice fingering technique for bagpipes, which are largely reserved for important public occasions. Observations of Anca Pejakov, a master flute maker in the village of Mokrin, Banat, his teacher, and their pupils, provide a detailed account of the instrument's manufacture. *(author)*

3632 PICKEN, Laurence E.R. **The bagpipe in eastern**
as **Turkey,** *Rad VII-og kongresa Saveza Folklorista Jugoslavije* (Cetinje: Obod, 1964) 245–52. *Charts, diagr., transcr.* Summary in Croatian. See no. 419 in this volume.

An account of the tulum, a bagpipe with double chanter and no separate drone pipe, found in eastern Turkey and used to accompany the horon dance. Data are drawn from field study in the village of Hemşin, Rize province. *(David Bloom)*

3633 RAO, M.N. Padma. **The long flute,** *Souvenir on*
as *Hindustani Music Festival & Seminar* (Hyderabad: Andhra Pradesh Sangeeta Nataka Akademi, 1966) 23–26. See no. 450 in this volume.

The long bamboo flute (bāṅsurī) is one of the most venerable and suitable instruments for Hindustani music.

3634 RICHARDSON, Edward Gick. **L'acoustique**
as **des cors et des trompes** [The acoustics of horns and trumpets], *Acoustique musicale* (Paris: Centre National de la Recherche Scientifique [CNRS], 1959) 245–52. *Illus., charts, diagr.* In French. See no. 393 in this volume.

General remarks on the physics of brass instruments, with an experiment-based account of the timbral differences between trumpet and horn. *(David Bloom)*

3635 ROTH, Lina. **Le pipeau** [The shawm], *Congrès in-*
as *ternational de l'enseignement primaire et de l'éducation populaire* (Paris: S.U.D.E.L., 1938) 308–09. In French. See no. 246 in this volume.

3636 SCHRAMMEK, Winfried. **Birch leaf blowing**
as **(Birkenblattblasen),** *Journal of the International Folk Music Council* XI (1959) 89. See no. 392 in this volume.

Summary of a paper. The instrument—not really a leaf, but a thin plate from the inner bark of a birch tree—and its usage by German shepherds is described. *(James R. Cowdery)*

3637 STEPANOV, Stjepan. **Svirale i bubanj na**
as **Baniji** [The svirale and bubanj of Banija], *Rad VII-og kongresa Saveza Folklorista Jugoslavije* (Cetinje: Obod, 1964) 283–96. *Illus., transcr.* In Croatian; summary in German. See no. 419 in this volume.

The svirale, a primitive shawm of the Banija region on the Bosnian-Croatian border, is a smaller version of the sopile found in the Kvarner gulf. It is invariably played as loudly as possible, in the overblown register, as part of a trio, two svirale players being accompanied by a bubanj, or double-headed cylindrical drum. The svirale is described in detail, with particular attention to the fingering. *(author)*

3638 STOCKMANN, Erich. **Klarinettentypen in**
as **Albanien** [Clarinet types in Albania], *Journal of the International Folk Music Council* XII (1960) 17–20. In German. See no. 413 in this volume.

Distinguishes three categories of clarinet in Albania, according to ergonomic criteria: single clarinets, double clarinets, and clarinets equipped with wind bladders. The methods of construction used for each are described, and terminology is surveyed. *(Carl Skoggard)*

3639 VEGA, Carlos. **La flauta de Pan andina** [The An-
as dean panpipe], *Actas y trabajos científicos del XXV° Congreso Internacional de Americanistas* (Buenos Aires: Coni; Universidad Nacional de La Plata, 1934) 333–46. *Music, bibliog., charts, diagr.* In Spanish. See no. 198 in this volume.

Garcilaso de la Vega provided the earliest (1602) written account of the siringa, or panpipe. These Andean wind instruments, bamboo pipes of graduated lengths attached in a row, are still used by many South American tribes. Since the scale was divided between two instruments, panpipes performed in ensembles, each doubling and providing melody notes. Their characteristics, music, and various names are discussed, and the hypothesis that Polynesians brought their culture to ancient Peru is examined. *(Joyce Z. Lindorff)*

3640 VESSELLA, Alessandro. **Sulla evoluzione**
as **storica della partitura di banda** [On the evolution of the score for band], *Atti del Congresso internazionale di scienze storiche. VIII: Atti della sezione IV: Storia dell'arte musicale e drammatica* (Roma: R. Accademia dei Lincei, 1905) 43–50. In Italian. See no. 42 in this volume.

Although band music dates back to the 17th c., the modern band began in the early 19th c. with the technical perfection of the clarinet. A standardization of instrumentation and the incorporation of recent instruments are proposed.

3641 ZEČEVIĆ, Slobodan. **Jedan Zlatiborski**
as **duvački instrumenat** [A wind instrument from the Zlatibor region], *Rad VII-og kongresa Saveza Folklorista Jugoslavije* (Cetinje: Obod, 1964) 243–44. *Illus.* In Serbian; summary in English. See no. 419 in this volume.

Describes a kind of duduk in three pieces—mouthpiece, tube, and resonator bell—found in the region of Zlatibor mountain in southwestern Serbia. *(author)*

46 Percussion (membranophones and idiophones)

3642 ALBERTI, Germano. **Campane "a festa"**
as **suonate mediante movimento a rotazione** [Bells for solemn occasions rung with a rotation movement], *Atti del [I] Congresso internazionale di musica sacra* (Tournai: Desclée, 1952) 28–29. In Italian. See no. 303 in this volume.

Account of the Veronese or semi-Ambrosian system of mounting church tower bells to swing a full 360° from the initial upside-down vertical position, developed by Verona founders beginning in the later 18th c. *(David Bloom)*

3643 BERGMANS, Paul. **Les carillons belges et la**
as **musique de carillon** [Belgian carillons and carillon music], *Beethoven-Zentenarfeier: Internationaler musikhistorischer Kongress* (Wien: Universal, 1927) 382–84. In French. See no. 142 in this volume.

Surveys the instrument's history, iconography, and repertoire in the Low Countries, from the late 14th c. on.

3644 BOEYNAEMS-PONTUS, H.-J.-L. **À propos du**
as **carillon** [On the carillon], *Fédération Archéologique et Historique de Belgique: Annales du XXII° congrès. I: Documents et compte rendu; II: Rapports & mémoires* (Mechelen: Godenne, 1911) II, 807–08. In French. See no. 73 in this volume.

A short history of the relationship of the words *bam, bem, bim, bom,* and *bum* to the carillon. *(Albert Dlugasch)*

⟶   BURSSENS, Amaat F.S. **Le luba, langue à into-**
      nation, et la tambour-signal [Luba, a tonal language, and the talking drum]. See no. 5920 in this volume.

3645
as
CASTELLENGO, Michèle; LEIPP, Émile. **L'acoustique des cloches** [The acoustics of bells], *Problèmes d'acoustique* (Liège: Université de Liège, 1965) M61. *Illus., bibliog.* In French. See no. 504 in this volume.

Methods for the acoustical analysis of bells are examined, noting their advantages and disadvantages. Sonographs provide the most information. *(Elizabeth A. Wright)*

3646
as
COLLAER, Paul. **Le tambour à friction (rommelpot) en Flandre** [The friction drum (rommelpot) in Flanders], *Les colloques de Wégimont. [I: Ethnomusicologie I]* (Bruxelles: Elsevier, 1956) 188–94. *Illus., transcr.* In French. See no. 340 in this volume.

A survey of information on friction drums in Flemish- and Dutch-speaking regions, as well as in Congo (Kasai region), Spain (Extremadura and Basque country), Italy (Lucania), and Hungary. Particular attention is given to the use of the instrument in Flanders during festivals including Epiphany Eve and Holy Thursday, and to associated songs. *(David Bloom)*

3647
as
COLLAER, Paul. **Le tambour à friction (II), et idiophones frottés** [The friction drum (II) and rubbed idiophones], *Les colloques de Wégimont. III: Ethnomusicologie II* (Paris: Belles Lettres, 1960) 91–104. *Illus.* In French. See no. 366 in this volume.

Summarizes recent findings on friction drums in the strict sense (rubbed membranophones) and on rubbed idiophones (of wood, tortoiseshell, or metal), with emphasis on their construction, playing technique, and cultural significance. Friction instruments are used throughout the world in rituals which are connected with the death and resurrection of humans, gods, or the seasons. Part I, discussing mainly the Flemish rommelpot, is abstracted as no. 3646 in this volume.

(Barbara B. Heyman)

3648
as
DOORSLAER, Georges van. **Le carillon, son origine et son développement** [The carillon, its origin and development], *Fédération Archéologique et Historique de Belgique: Annales du XXIIᵉ congrès. I: Documents et compte rendu; II: Rapports & mémoires* (Mechelen: Godenne, 1911) II, 353–60. In French. See no. 73 in this volume.

The history of 200 years of carillon development in Belgium, from hammer-struck instruments to those incorporating keyboards and more complex mechanisms, is presented. The etymology of the word *carillon* is described.

(Albert Dlugasch)

3649
as
FARCY, Louis de. **La sonnerie de la cathédrale de Rouen** [The bells of the Rouen cathedral], *Congrès du Millénaire de la Normandie (911-1911)* (Rouen: Léon Gy, 1912) 308–21. In French. See no. 77 in this volume.

A list of the bells and their donors, from 644 to 1852, plus historical comments relating to the inscriptions.

3650
as
GRÜTZMACHER, Martin. **Le spectre d'un son de cloche** [The sound spectrum of a bell], *Acoustique musicale* (Paris: Centre National de la Recherche Scientifique [CNRS], 1959) 239–44. *Charts, diagr.* In French. See no. 393 in this volume.

Reports on the experimental study of a modern bronze Gothic-style bell by tape-recording its partial frequencies in isolation from one another.

(David Bloom)

⟶ GRÜTZMACHER, Martin. **Über die Klänge von Glocken und Orgeln** [Concerning the sounds of bells and organs]. See no. 3378 in this volume.

3651
as
JIMÉNEZ DE LA ESPADA, Marcos. **Cloches préhistoriques sud-américaines** [Prehistoric South American bells], *Compte rendu du IIIᵉ Congrès international des américanistes* (Bruxelles: C. Muquardt; Anatole Pamps, 1879) 737–41. In French. See no. 6 in this volume.

The stone bells in a temple on the Peruvian coast much resemble Chinese bells.

3652
as
MARCEL-DUBOIS, Claudie. **Le tambour bourdonnant** [The friction drum], *Journal of the International Folk Music Council* XVI (1964) 90–91. In French. See no. 463 in this volume.

Summary of a general discussion of material given an extended treatment in *Le tambour-bourdon: Son signal et sa tradition*, in *Arts et traditions populaires* XIV (1966).

3653
as
MARCEL-DUBOIS, Claudie. **Le toulouhou des Pyrénées centrales: Usage rituel et parentés d'un tambour à friction tournoyant** [The toulouhou of the central Pyrénées: Ritual use of a whirling friction drum and related instruments], *Les colloques de Wégimont. III: Ethnomusicologie II* (Paris: Belles Lettres, 1960) 55–89. *Illus., charts, diagr.* In French. See no. 366 in this volume.

The toulouhou, a whirling friction drum, is used in Good Friday church services in the French Pyrenees region by male children only; it is never used as a toy and is played by boys up to 15 years old. The meaning and origin of its ritual use, its distribution throughout local villages, and its organology are discussed, with comparison to other instruments used in this ceremony and to whirling friction drums from other localities worldwide. *(Katharine Fry)*

3654
as
SCHAEFFNER, André. **Le tambour-sur-cadre quadrangulaire chez les Noirs d'Afrique et d'Amérique** [The square frame drum as used by black peoples of Africa and America], *Les colloques de Wégimont. IV: Ethnomusicologie III* (Paris: Belles Lettres, 1964) IV, 229–48. *Illus.* In French. See no. 401 in this volume.

3655
as
THEINHAUS, Erich. **Zur Frage der Glockenprüfung und Glockenbegutachtung** [Concerning the question of testing and evaluating bells], *Kongreß-Bericht: Gesellschaft für Musikforschung* (Kassel; Basel: Bärenreiter, 1950) 236–38. *Charts, diagr.* In German. See no. 299 in this volume.

3656
as
TORII, Ryuzo. **Les gongs-cloches au Japan** [The gong-bells of Japan], *XVIᵉ Congrès international d'anthropologie et d'archéologie préhistorique: VIᵉ Assemblée générale de l'Institut International d'Anthropologie* (Bruxelles: Imprimerie Médicale et Scientifique, 1936) 990–93. In French. See no. 221 in this volume.

Describes the construction and ornamental designs (e.g., scenes, motifs) of the three types of gong-bells (i.e., small and relatively plain, large and beautifully adorned, and those that fall in between these two categories) that appeared in Japan between the prehistoric and protohistoric epochs. *(Susan Poliniak)*

47 Mechanical

3657
as
BIREMBAUT, Arthur. **Les frères Engramelle** [The Engramelle brothers], *Actes du VIIIᵉ Congrès international d'histoire des sciences* (Firenze: Gruppo Italiana di Storia delle Scienze; Paris: Hermann, 1958) 149f. In French. See no. 354 in this volume.

Marie Dominique Joseph Engramelle (1727-1805) was a builder of mechanical instruments; his brother Jacques Louis Florentin was an amateur entomologist.

3658
as
BOSTON, Noel. **The barrel organ,** *Music libraries and instruments* (London: Hinrichsen, 1961) 200–04. *Illus.* See no. 406 in this volume.

An appreciation of the instrument, with particular reference to its history in England. Well-preserved instruments of the 18th and 19th c. document performing styles of their periods. The elaborate models once used in churches would be appropriate for use in smaller churches today. *(Susan Poliniak)*

3659
as
ENOCH, W. **Instruments de musique mécanique** [Mechanical musical instruments], *Congrès international des éditeurs: VIᵉ session—Rapports* (Madrid: Asociación de la Librería de España, 1908) 249–51. In French. See no. 60 in this volume.

Calls for the revision of the 1886 Bern agreement, further qualifying the conditions for mechanical instrumentation.

3660
as
JEANS, Susi. **Water organs,** *Music libraries and instruments* (London: Hinrichsen, 1961) 189–95. *Illus., charts, diagr., facs.* See no. 406 in this volume.

The water organ or hydraulic organ originated in ancient Greece and was perfected by Arab scientists. Notable examples are described. *(Susan Poliniak)*

3661
as
OBRIST, Alois. **Sollen Musiker und Musikhistoriker die Entwicklung der Klavierspielapparate fördern, bekämpfen oder zu beeinflussen suchen?** [Should musicians and music historians try to support the development of keyboard playing apparatuses, combat them, or influence them?]. Ed. by Karl NEF, *Bericht über den zweiten Kongress der Internationalen Musikgesellschaft* (Leipzig: Breitkopf & Härtel, 1907) 212. In German. See no. 53 in this volume.

Player pianos, both of the Phonola type in which tempo, dynamics, etc., are manipulated and of the purely mechanical Welte-Mignon type, dishabituate music lovers from making their own music. Therefore their use for pure listening purposes should be discouraged, except perhaps for elderly persons and invalids. For documentation of performance, the objectivity provided by the Mignon type of reproducing piano is to be preferred. *(David Bloom)*

48 Electrophones (synthesized sound)

⟶
ANTONIADES, Sophia. **La musique byzantine rendue par les ondes Martenot** [Byzantine music performed on the ondes Martenot]. See no. 6106 in this volume.

3662
as
BIERL, Richard. **Neuere Ergebnisse der elektrischen Klangerzeugung und deren Beziehungen zu der mechanischen Klangerzeugung** [Recent results of electronic sound generation and their relation to mechanical sound generation], *Acustica: International journal of acoustics/Journal international d'acoustique/ Internationale akustische Zeitschrift* IV/1 (1954) 218–19. *Bibliog.* In German; summaries in German, French, and English. See no. 324 in this volume.

Electronic sound generators without moving parts offer better means of expression than electromechanical generators. The arrangement of timbres along a closed circle of intervals representing the frequency response curves of the system of vibrations (e.g., coupled circuits), as well as some features of the spectrum of oscillations exciting the system, are important

for these new types of instruments and for research on older types as well. *(author)*

3663
as
DENIS, Pierre. **Le véritable problème des orgues électroniques** [The real problem with electronic organs], *Revue musicale* 239-240 (1957) 171–74. In French. See no. 378 in this volume.

An abridged version of the conference paper is abstracted as no. 3664 in this volume.

3664
as
DENIS, Pierre. **Le véritable problème des orgues électroniques** [The real problem with electronic organs], *Perspectives de la musique sacrée à la lumière de l'encyclique* Musicae sacrae disciplina (Paris: conference, 1959) 380–84. In French. See no. 379 in this volume.

A polemic against the use of electronic organs in the Roman Catholic worship service. An abridged version is cited as no. 3663 in this volume. *(David Bloom)*

3665
as
FRAILE, Guillermo. **El órgano litúrgico/ L'orgue liturgique** [The liturgical organ], *Perspectives de la musique sacrée à la lumière de l'encyclique* Musicae sacrae disciplina (Paris: conference, 1959) 385–93. In Spanish and French. See no. 379 in this volume.

The electrostatic organs introduced in 1956 as a joint venture of the Dereux and Múgica firms may well overcome musical objections to the liturgical use of electronic instruments; the theological aspects of the question have been decided in favor of tolerating electronic instruments, in the document *De electrophonicis organis,* issued by the Sacred Congregation of Rites, July 1949. An abridged version is cited as no. 3666 in this volume. *(David Bloom)*

3666
as
FRAILE, Guillermo. **L'orgue électronique** [The electronic organ], *Revue musicale* 239-240 (1957) 175–78. In French. See no. 378 in this volume.

An abridged version of the conference paper, on issues in the liturgical use of electronic organs, is cited as no. 3665 in this volume.

3667
as
GONZÁLEZ DE AMEZÚA Y NORIEGA, Ramón. **Les orgues électroniques** [Electronic organs], *Perspectives de la musique sacrée à la lumière de l'encyclique* Musicae sacrae disciplina (Paris: conference, 1959) 407–11. In French. See no. 379 in this volume.

It is likely that scientific progress in the design of electronic instruments has reached a limit; it may be that an electronic organ will be built one day that is aesthetically, liturgically, and financially adequate for church use, but certainly not for a long time to come. *(David Bloom)*

3668
as
KEZLER. **La musique synthétique** [Synthetic music], *Compte rendu des travaux du Iᵉʳ Congrès international d'art radiophonique* (Paris: conference, 1938). In French. See no. 244 in this volume.

3669
as
MARTIN, Constant. **Les "nouvelles orgues"** [The new organs], *Revue musicale* 239-240 (1957) 183–90. In French. See no. 378 in this volume.

An abridged version of the conference paper is cited as no. 3670 in this volume.

3670
as
MARTIN, Constant. **Orgues électroniques d'hier et de demain** [Electronic organs of yesterday and tomorrow], *Perspectives de la musique sacrée à la lumière de l'encyclique* Musicae sacrae disciplina (Paris: conference, 1959) 412–22. *Organ specification.* In French. See no. 379 in this volume.

The Nouvelles-Orgues of the Martin firm, made in consultation with organists, recreating the precise wave-form and attack of a fairly large number of pipe-organ stops, overcome a good many of the problems of instability and lack of versatility that have characterized typical electronic instruments; they are being used in churches in France, Switzerland and Senegal. An abridged version is cited as no. 3669 in this volume. *(David Bloom)*

3671 NEUMANN, Hans-Joachim. **Die Elektro- Orgel**
as **in der Kirche** [The electric organ in churches], *Der Barock: Seine Orgeln und seine Musik in Oberschwaben* (Berlin: Merseburger, 1952) 155–57. In German. See no. 305 in this volume.

Catholic and Protestant clergy and organists alike should reject electronic instruments for use in worship services.

3672 STREICH, Rudolf. **Das elektrische Musikin-**
as **strument im Spiegel der akustischen Forschung** [The electric musical instrument as reflected in acoustics research], *Kongreß-Bericht: Gesellschaft für Musikforschung* (Kassel; Basel: Bärenreiter, 1950) 233–35. *Charts, diagr.* In German. See no. 299 in this volume.

⟶ TRAUTWEIN, Friedrich. **Über elektrische Synthese von Sprachlauten und musikalischen Tönen (Instruments à ondes)** [On the electric synthesis of speech sound and musical notes (instruments *à ondes*)]. See no. 5940 in this volume.

PERFORMANCE PRACTICE AND NOTATION

50 Performance practice, general (includes improvisation)

3673
as

CELLIER, Alexandre. **L'improvisation** [Improvisation], *Compte rendu du Congrès d'orgue tenu à l'Université de Strasbourg. IV* (Strasbourg: Société Strasbourgeoise de Librairie Sostralib, 1934) 141–46. In French. See no. 199 in this volume.

Offers a historical overview of improvisation in organ music and some of its most famous practitioners. A list of requirements dating from 1727 for the position of organist at the cathedral of Hamburg is provided as an example of the level of ability expected at the time.

3674
as

COLLAER, Paul. **Renaissance de la musique ancienne** [Renaissance of early music], *Atti del terzo Congresso internazionale di musica* (Firenze: Le Monnier, 1940) 147–59. In French; summaries in Italian and German. See no. 256 in this volume.

A short history of the resurgence of pre–18th-c. music, including guidelines for authentic reconstruction and interpretation. *(Edwin D. Wallace)*

3675
as

COMBARIEU, Jules. **Le vandalisme musical** [Musical vandalism], *Congrès international d'histoire de la musique: Documents, mémoires et vœux* (Solesmes: St. Pierre; Paris: Fischbacher, 1901) 298–305. In French. See no. 32 in this volume.

Concert managements take liberties with scores in a manner that is comparable to the defacing of historical monuments. They should be held responsible for such actions.

3676
as

GEIRINGER, Karl; JACOBI, Erwin R.; RINGER, Alexander L.; SCHLÖTTERER, Reinhold; SOMFAI, László; TAGLIAVINI, Luigi Ferdinando. **Symposium: Musikwissenschaftliche Methode und musikalische Praxis** [Symposium: Musicological methods and musical practice]. Moderated by Eduard REESER, *Bericht über den neunten internationalen Kongreß* (Kassel: Bärenreiter, 1964-1966) II, 19–24. *Music.* In German. See no. 491 in this volume.

Discussion of the paper abstracted as RILM 3685 in this volume.

3677
as

HAMMERSCHLAG, János. **Sigel-Ornamente in ihren harmonischen Relationen** [Unwritten-out ornaments and their harmonic relations], *Compte rendu/Kongressbericht/Report* (Basel: Bärenreiter, 1951) 135–44. *Music.* In German. See no. 289 in this volume.

Proposes two basic periods of harmonic style for the interpretation of trills and related signs: a period of consonant ornaments, from sometime before 1500 to ca. 1650, and a period of dissonant ornaments, from 1650 to ca. 1800. *(David Bloom)*

3678
as

HEUSS, Alfred. **Einige grundlegende Begriffe für eine historische Darstellung der musikalischen Dynamik** [Some basic concepts for a historical presentation of musical dynamics], *Haydn-Zentenarfeier* (Leipzig: Breitkopf & Härtel; Wien: Artaria, 1909) 144–47. In German. See no. 65 in this volume.

Provides a brief historical overview of notated and performed dynamics.

3679
as

MERTIN, Josef. **Über Aufführungspraxis historischer Sakralmusik** [The performance practice of historic sacred music], *Zweiter internationaler Kongress für katholische Kirchenmusik: Zu Ehren des Heiligen Papstes Pius X* (Wien: conference, 1955) 188–93. In German. See no. 339 in this volume.

Early music in liturgical use benefits as much from a historical performance practice as does secular music. In particular the use of original instruments clarifies the structure of a non-imitative polyphonic composition. General principles are discussed for the use of instruments that are not specified in the sources for 15th- and 16th-c. vocal music. *(David Bloom)*

3680
as

OBRIST, Alois. **Die historische und künstlerische Bedeutung der Wiederbelebung altertümlicher Musikinstrumente** [The historical and artistic significance of the revival of old musical instruments], *Bericht über den zweiten Kongress der Internationalen Musikgesellschaft* (Leipzig: Breitkopf & Härtel, 1907) 234–42. In German. See no. 53 in this volume.

The movement in favor of early instruments and historical performance practice is of value only insofar as it is based on the strictest historical principles; compromises are ultimately, as in any other art, a dilettantish falsification of the past. It would be helpful to enlist modern composers, who are always interested in new sonorities, to write works for recorder, glass harmonica, crumhorn, and so on. *(David Bloom)*

3681
as

PARENTE, Alfredo. **Il problema dell'interpretazione musicale** [The problem of musical interpretation], *Atti del primo Congresso internazionale di musica* (Firenze: Le Monnier, 1935) 259–67. In Italian. See no. 203 in this volume.

To interpret a musical work is to stimulate the sensibility of the audience in a manner faithful to the composer's original intention. Audiences respond to passive, mnemonic-mechanical, and technical functions; only by abandoning personal impulses and initiatives can the performer achieve the miracle of musical communication while remaining true to the work. *(David Bloom)*

3682
as

PITSCH, Georges. **Sur l'organisation de concerts de musique de chambre** [On the organization of chamber music concerts], *La musique et le peuple: Rapports, suggestions, vœux* (Bruxelles: Ministère des Sciences et des Arts, 1932) 73–77. In French. See no. 195 in this volume.

Describes a project for chamber music performance.

⟶
REICHEL, Bernard. **L'improvisation** [Improvisation]. See no. 4632 in this volume.

3683
as

RJABUČINSKAJA, Vera (Véra Riabouchinsky). **Sur la création dans l'interprétation musicale** [On creation in musical performance], *Deuxième congrès international d'esthétique et de Science de l'art* (Paris: Librairie Félix Alcan, 1937) II, 254–56. In French. See no. 249 in this volume.

Although it is difficult to draw a precise line between a musical performance that is creative and one that is not, the creativity of a performance, especially in singing, is not of an inferior order to that of a composition. *(David Bloom)*

3684 SZABOLCSI, Bence. **Über Form und Improvi-**
as **sation in der Kunst- und Volksmusik** [Form and improvisation in art and traditional music], *Bericht über den siebenten internationalen musikwissenschaftlichen Kongreß* (Kassel: Bärenreiter, 1959) 257–59. In German. See no. 390 in this volume.
Remarks on the nature of improvisation, as a kind of primitive or preparatory phase in the history of a music, as a necessary element of performance, and as an influence on the development of notated art-music forms. *(David Bloom)*

3685 TAGLIAVINI, Luigi Ferdinando. **Musikwissen-**
as **schaftliche Methode und musikalische Praxis** [Musicological methods and musical practice], *Bericht über den neunten internationalen Kongreß* (Kassel: Bärenreiter, 1964-1966) I, 19–24. In Italian. See no. 491 in this volume.
Discusses important issues in the use of research to prepare the authentic performance of early music. It should be remembered that theorists of a particular period may have been inclined to make hard-and-fast rules in areas like ornamentation that stem from improvisational practice and should not be subjected to such precision; that useful-looking theoretical treatises may come from the wrong period to be helpful in the performance of a given work; and that authentic instruments should be used whenever possible. *(David Bloom)*

3686 TAPPOLET, Willy. **Einige prinzipielle Bemer-**
as **kungen zur Frage der Improvisation** [Initial remarks on the question of improvisation], *Bericht über den siebenten internationalen musikwissenschaftlichen Kongress* (Kassel: Bärenreiter, 1959) 287–88. In German. See no. 390 in this volume.
The establishment of improvisation as a distinct field of instruction, under the influence of Émile Jaques-Dalcroze, has led to its being treated as the unification of inspiration and performance, production and reproduction, in contrast to performance on the basis of a written score. Following suggestions of Heinrich Jacoby, it might be preferable to think of improvisation as a particularly confident method of composition, one in which the performer is not afraid to let go, and of composition as the graphic fixing of an improvisation, as Beethoven is said to have practiced it. *(David Bloom)*

3687 WESTRUP, Jack A. **Practical musicology,** *Music*
as *libraries and instruments* (London: Hinrichsen, 1961) 25–30. See no. 406 in this volume.
Practical musicology is defined as the direct relationship between musicology and a practical approach to performance. The puzzles of performance practice through the Baroque era can be dealt with via a mutual understanding between the musicologist and performer with an emphasis on the revival of old instruments and a distinction between transcriptions and originals. Librarians are urged to cooperate. *(Richard Slapsys)*

3688 ZICH, Jaroslav. **Agogische Prinzipe der**
as **Wiedergabe** [Agogic principles of performance], *Bericht über den siebenten internationalen musikwissenschaftlichen Kongress* (Kassel: Bärenreiter, 1959) 319–22. *Music.* In German. See no. 390 in this volume.
Agogic nuances such as rubato are effective as long as listeners experience them as a deformation of an ideal rhythmic shape, and can perceive the ideal through the deformation. Types of deformation are illustrated in their application to performance of works by Smetana, Bach, and Dvořák. *(David Bloom)*

51 Performance practice, to ca. 1600

3689 ANDOYER, Raphael. **Le rythme oratoire, prin-**
as **cipe de la méthode grégorienne** [Oratorical rhythm, principle of the Gregorian method], *Acta*

generalis cantus gregoriani studiosorum conventus, Argentinensis, 16-19 Aug. 1905/Bericht des internationalen Kongresses für gregorianischen Choralgesang/ Compte rendu du Congrès international de plain-chant grégorien (Strassburg: F.-X. Le Roux, 1905) 88–99. In French. See no. 50 in this volume.
Provides insight into performance practice.

3690 BECHERINI, Bianca. **L'ars nova italiana del**
as **trecento: Strumenti ed espressione musicale** [Italian ars nova of the 14th century: Instruments and musical expression], *L'ars nova italiana del Trecento: Primo convegno internazionale* (Certaldo: Centro di Studi sull'Ars Nova Italiana del Trecento, 1962) 40–56. *Music, index.* In Italian. See no. 407 in this volume.
The thesis that the supporting voices of 14th c. vocal music, and even the *superius*, were sometimes performed by instruments, is supported by passages relating to playing and singing in Giovanni di Prato's narrative *Il paradiso degli Alberti* and other literary works by Dante, Boccaccio, and Farinata degli Uberti, as well as in madrigals, frottolas, caccias, and ballatas by Francesco Landini and Magister Piero. *(Sylvia Eversole)*

3691 BESSELER, Heinrich. **Die Besetzung der**
as **Chansons im 15. Jahrhundert** [The instrumentation of chansons in the 15th century], *Société Internationale de Musicologie, cinquième congrès/Internationale Gesellschaft für Musikwissenschaft, fünfter Kongreß/International Society for Musical Research, Fifth Congress* (Amsterdam: Vereniging voor Nederlandse Muziekgeschiedenis, 1953) 65–72. In German. See no. 316 in this volume.

3692 BOMM, Urbanus. **Historismus und gregoria-**
as **nischer Vortragstil** [Historicism and Gregorian performance style], *Atti del [I] Congresso internazionale di musica sacra* (Tournai: Desclée, 1952) 179–82. In German. See no. 303 in this volume.

3693 BOUTROUX, Léon. **Quelques réflexions sur**
as **l'accompagnement du chant grégorien** [Some reflections on the accompaniment of Gregorian chant], *Comptes rendus, rapports et vœux du Congrès parisien et régional de chant liturgique et de musique d'église* (Paris: Schola Cantorum, 1912) 136–42. In French. See no. 75 in this volume.

3694 CARDINE, Eugène. **L'interprétation**
as **traditionnelle du chant grégorien** [The traditional performance of Gregorian chant], *Zweiter internationaler Kongress für katholische Kirchenmusik: Zu Ehren des Heiligen Papstes Pius X* (Wien: conference, 1955) 105–10. *Music.* In French. See no. 339 in this volume.
Neumes form a comprehensive system for the notation of expressive and rhythmic nuances in the performance of Gregorian chant. Examples are drawn from the St. Gallen repertoire. *(Christopher Johnson)*

3695 DISERTORI, Benvenuto. **Contradiction tonale**
as **dans la transcription d'un *strambotto* célèbre** [Tonal contradiction in the transcription of a famous strambotto], *Le luth et sa musique* (Paris: Centre National de la Recherche Scientifique [CNRS], 1958) 37–42. *Music.* In French. See no. 377 in this volume.
Discusses performance problems in the arrangement by Franjo Bosanac of the strambotto *Amando e desiando* by Benedetto Gareth, known as Il Chariteo, in Franciscus's *Tenori e contrabassi intabulati... Libro secundo*, 1511. The absence of accidentals leaves ambiguities that must be resolved at the lutenist's discretion.

3696
as
FICKER, Rudolf von. **Grundsätzliches zur mittelalterlichen Aufführungspraxis** [Basic observations on medieval performance practice], *Société Internationale de Musicologie, cinquième congrès/Internationale Gesellschaft für Musikwissenschaft, fünfter Kongreß/International Society for Musical Research, Fifth Congress* (Amsterdam: Vereniging voor Nederlandse Muziekgeschiedenis, 1953) 33–44. In German. See no. 316 in this volume.

3697
as
FISCHER, Kurt von. **À propos de la répartition du texte et le nombre de voix dans les œuvres italiennes du trecento** [The layout of texts and the number of voices in Italian works of the trecento], *Les colloques de Wégimont. II: L'ars nova—Recueil d'études sur la musique du XIVe siècle* (Paris: Belles Lettres, 1959) 232–38. In French. See no. 351 in this volume.

Transcript of the discussion following a conference paper published as a portion of the author's *Studien zur italienischen Musik des Trecento und frühen Quattrocento* (Bern: Publications de la Société Suisse de Musicologie, sér. II, vol. 5, 1956); explores MS ambiguities in the allocation of parts in a given piece to voices and instruments, and to solo voices as opposed to choirs. *(David Bloom)*

3698
as
FOUCAULT, Alphonse-Gabriel. **Simple observation sur le caractère du rythme grégorien dans la psalmodie** [Simple observation on the character of Gregorian rhythm in psalmody], *Acta generalis cantus gregoriani studiosorum conventus, Argentinensis, 16-19 Aug. 1905/Bericht des internationalen Kongresses für gregorianischen Choralgesang/Compte rendu du Congrès international de plain-chant grégorien* (Strassburg: F.-X. Le Roux, 1905) 29–31. *Music.* In French. See no. 50 in this volume.

Rhythm in Gregorian chant is mixed: it is oratorical in the recitatives, rather declamatory in sung sections, and measured where the character of the music requires such an execution. *(author)*

3699
as
FROIDEBISE, Pierre. **Interprétation de la musique d'orgue et réalisation des gloses** [The interpretation of organ music and the realization of glosas], *Les colloques de Wégimont. IV: Le Baroque musical—Recueil d'études sur la musique du XVIIe siècle* (Paris: Belles Lettres, 1963) 255–59. In French. See no. 386 in this volume.

In conjunction with the author's performance of 16th-c. Spanish organ music at the 1957 Festival de Liège "Les Nuits de Septembre", the principles of melodic variation through ornamentation (*glosa*) as codified by Juan Bermudo and Tomás de Santa María are discussed. *(David Bloom)*

3700
as
GASTOUÉ, Amédée. **Du style dans l'interprétation du chant grégorien** [On style in the interpretation of Gregorian chant], *Congrès international de musique sacrée: Chant et orgue* (Paris: Desclée de Brouwer, 1937) 109–16. In French. See no. 247 in this volume.

Chant must be sung with both force and sensitivity. Tempo and dynamics should not remain fixed.

3701
as
GRASSI LANDI, Bartolomeo. **Observations relatives à l'interprétation des notes neumatiques du chant grégorien** [Observations relative to the interpretation of neumatic notation of Gregorian chant], *Congrès international d'histoire de la musique: Documents, mémoires et vœux* (Solesmes: St. Pierre; Paris: Fischbacher, 1901) 124–26. In French. See no. 32 in this volume.

Music and language are complementary in early music. Thus the rhythm of Gregorian chant is both linguistic and musical. Syllabic accentuation is discussed.

3702
as
KOSCH, Franz. **Der Rhythmus im Choral der Solesmenser** [Rhythm in the chant of the Solesmes monks], *Beethoven-Zentenarfeier: Internationaler musikhistorischer Kongress* (Wien: Universal, 1927) 240–43. In German. See no. 142 in this volume.

Reviews the controversy over the interpretation of Gregorian chant rhythm developed at the abbey of Solesmes. A compromise between André Mocquereau's theory and those of Joseph Pothier and Peter Wagner should be attainable. *(David Bloom)*

3703
as
KRINGS, Alfred. **Zur Aufführung von Kirchenmusik des Mittelalters und der Renaissance** [On the performance practice of church music of the Middle Ages and Renaissance], *IV. Internationaler Kongress für Kirchenmusik in Köln: Dokumente und Berichte* (Köln: Bachem, 1962) 127–29. In German. See no. 432 in this volume.

The music of the Middle Ages and Renaissance is primarily vocal, but was not normally performed a capella. Basic principles for determining instrumentation can be extrapolated from theoretical treatises, paintings, and poetry of the periods.

3704
as
KRÜGER, Walther. **Wort und Ton in den Notre-Dame-Organa** [Word and music in Notre Dame organa], *Bericht über den internationalen musikwissenschaftlichen Kongreß* (Kassel: Bärenreiter, 1957) 135–40. *Illus., music.* In German. See no. 356 in this volume.

Discusses the hypothesis that *sine littera* parts in three- and four-voice organa are meant as instrumental parts; summary of a part of the author's essay *Aufführungspraktische Fragen mittelalterlicher Mehrstimmigkeit*, appearing in consecutive issues of *Musikforschung*, 1956-57. *(David Bloom)*

3705
as
KUNC, Aloys. **Du rhythme qui convient au plain-chant** [Appropriate rhythm for plainchant], *Congrès pour la restauration du plain-chant et de la musique d'église* (Paris: De Mourgues, 1862) 84–86. In French. See no. 3 in this volume.

3706
as
LENAERTS, René Bernard. **Improvisation auf der Orgel und der Laute in den Niederlanden (16. und 17. Jahrhundert)** [Improvisation on organ and lute in the Netherlands (16th and 17th centuries)], *Bericht über den siebenten internationalen musikwissenschaftlichen Kongress* (Kassel: Bärenreiter, 1959) 177–79. In German. See no. 390 in this volume.

Most evidence for improvisation on the organ is indirect, but it is likely to have been intensely practiced, within church services and also, in the Protestant north, in secular music performances. Considerable evidence exists, in contrast, for lute improvisation, from the *Hortus musarum* (1552-53) of Pierre Phalèse the Elder and Emanuel Adriaenssen's *Pratum musicum longe amoenissimum* (1584-1600). *(David Bloom)*

3707
as
MATHÉ, Alois. **Beschouwingen over het ritme der gregoriaanse musiek** [Considerations on the rhythm of Gregorian music], *Zweiter internationaler Kongress für katholische Kirchenmusik: Zu Ehren des Heiligen Papstes Pius X* (Wien: conference, 1955) 146–48. In Dutch. See no. 339 in this volume.

A number of authors, from the earliest period through the 17th c., wrote about the unequal length of notes in Gregorian chant. The performance of chant in equal note values is not supported by these authors; the notion of *cantus planus* is not mentioned by them. They based their ideas about rhythm not only on the rhythm of the text of the chant but also on the configurations of the neumes themselves. *(David Bloom)*

3708
as

MATHIAS, François-Xavier. **Die Choralbegleitung** [Chant accompaniment], *Acta generalis cantus gregoriani studiosorum conventus, Argentinensis, 16-19 Aug. 1905/Bericht des internationalen Kongresses für gregorianischen Choralgesang/ Compte rendu du Congrès international de plain-chant grégorien* (Strassburg: F.-X. Le Roux, 1905) 117–22. In German. See no. 50 in this volume.

Discusses questions of melody and rhythm in Gregorian chant.

3709
as

MÜLLER-BLATTAU, Joseph. **Zur vokalen Improvisation im 16. Jahrhundert** [Vocal improvisation in the 16th century], *Bericht über den siebenten internationalen musikwissenschaftlichen Kongress* (Kassel: Bärenreiter, 1959) 195–96. In German. See no. 390 in this volume.

Enumeration of and brief commentary on German and Italian sources for information on vocal ornamentation from 1522 to ca. 1650. *(David Bloom)*

3710
as

POPULUS, A. **De l'accompagnement du plain-chant** [The accompaniment of plainchant], *Congrès pour la restauration du plain-chant et de la musique d'église* (Paris: De Mourgues, 1862) 119–20. In French. See no. 3 in this volume.

3711
as

REANEY, Gilbert. **Musica ficta in the works of Guillaume de Machaut,** *Les colloques de Wégimont. II: L'ars nova—Recueil d'études sur la musique du XIVe siècle* (Paris: Belles Lettres, 1959) 196–213. In English and French. See no. 351 in this volume.

Machaut frequently wrote his accidentals down, as in the Vogüé MS in the private collection of the Wildenstein Gallery, New York; the variation in his MSS shows the extent to which musica ficta was a decision left to the performer, especially in borderline cases. Particular issues that have not been sufficiently addressed include the identification of Machaut's modes, his use of conflicting signatures, and the tolerance for dissonance in rapid notes off the tactus. *(David Bloom)*

3712
as

REANEY, Gilbert. **A note on conductus rhythm,** *Bericht über den siebenten internationalen musikwissenschaftlichen Kongress* (Kassel: Bärenreiter, 1959) 219–21. *Music.* See no. 390 in this volume.

Principles for interpreting problematic rhythms, on the basis of the assumption that the composer of conductus preferred consonant intervals on the beat, are applied to examples from *GB-Lbl* MS Add.36881 and the somewhat later *Gaude, felix Francia* from the St-Victor MS, *F-Pn* MS lat. 15139. *(David Bloom)*

3713
as

REANEY, Gilbert. **Voices and instruments in the music of Guilleaume de Machaut,** *Bericht über den Internationalen musikwissenschaftlichen Kongress* (Kassel: Bärenreiter, 1954) 245–48. See no. 319 in this volume.

Surveys the categories of Machaut's production with regard to performing media. Generalizations about instrumental vs. vocal performance are mostly unwarranted. Melodic lines with text were not necessarily sung; textless ones were not necessarily meant for instruments. Machaut supplies literary evidence that the *cantus* parts of certain of his ballades could be either sung or performed instrumentally. Iconographic evidence suggests that voices and instruments could be combined. Singers must have simplified or added to *cantus* parts in 14th-c. ballades and rondeaux, since Machaut counsels against this practice in his *Voir dit*. But such elaborate parts seem basically instrumental in conception. Machaut's motets are primarily vocal, though there was a gradual introduction of instrumental performance of motet tenors and contratenors. Tenors and contratenors of works in cantilena style seem well suited for instruments (viols, or perhaps trumpets or bombards). How Machaut's two most unusual works, the Mass and the hoquetus, were realized remains a matter for conjecture. *(Carl Skoggard)*

3714
as

SACHS, Curt. **Problèmes qui se présentent dans l'exécution moderne de la polyphonie du Moyen Age** [Problems concerning the modern performances of medieval polyphony], *Congrés de la Societat Internacional de Musicologia* (Barcelona: Casa de Caritat, 1936). In French. See no. 224 in this volume.

The conference report provides only a citation. Neither the text nor a summary of the paper was published here.

3715
as

SCHEIT, Karl. **Ce que nous enseignent les traités de luth des environs de 1600** [What can be learned from lute treatises of ca. 1600], *Le luth et sa musique* (Paris: Centre National de la Recherche Scientifique [CNRS], 1958) 93–105. *Music.* In French. See no. 377 in this volume.

A comparative study of Matthäus Waissel's *Lautenbuch darinn von der Tabulatur und Application der Lauten gründlicher und voller Unterricht* (Frankfurt an der Oder, 1592); Thomas Robinson's *The Schoole of Musicke* (London, 1603); and other methods published in English, with reference to their use in lute performance today. *(David Bloom)*

3716
as

SMITS VAN WAESBERGHE, Joseph. **Zur ursprünglichen Vortragsweise der Prosulen, Sequenzen und Organa** [The original performance style of prosulae, sequences, and organa], *Bericht über den siebenten internationalen musikwissenschaftlichen Kongress* (Kassel: Bärenreiter, 1959) 251–54. *Illus., facs., music.* In German. See no. 390 in this volume.

Brief account of the hypothesis that prosula and sequence (at least in the French, English, and Spanish repertoires of the original period, in the 9th-10th c.) were performed simultaneously as texted melody (by one or more soloists) and textless melisma (by the choir or schola), and that this practice is the original source of organum and motet. An extended version in Dutch is published as *Over het onstaan van sequens en prosula en beider oorspronkelijke uitvoeringswijze* in *Feestaflevering ter gelegenheid van de zestige verjaardag van Prof. Dr. K. Ph. Bernet Kempers, Orgaan Koninklijke Nederlandse Toonkunstenaars-Vereeniging* 12/2 (1957). *(David Bloom)*

3717
as

TACK, Franz. **Die musikgeschichtlichen Voraussetzungen der christlichen Kultmusik und ihre Bedeutung für den gregorianischen Vortragsstil** [The music-historical preconditions of music for Christian worship, and their significance for Gregorian performance style], *Bericht über den internationalen musikwissenschaftlichen Kongreß Wien Mozartjahr 1956* (Graz; Köln: Böhlau, 1958) 633–36. In German. See no. 365 in this volume.

The early history of church music is bound up with the history of the liturgy: the gradual combination of the Eucharist with synagogue worship in the 1st and 2nd c., and the encounter with Hellenism in the 3rd and 4th c. Correct performance of chant requires the ability to sort out features of a Jewish and generally Asian origin from those that are more Greco-Roman. *(David Bloom)*

3718
as

VALOIS, Jean de. **De la notation mouvement dans le chant grégorien** [The concept of tempo in Gregorian chant], *Compte rendu du Congrès général de musique sacrée: Aperçu général des préliminaires et du congrès, discours et conférences* (Strasbourg: Alsacien, 1922) 285–97. In French. See no. 96 in this volume.

3719
as

VERCHALY, André. **Le tempo dans la *musique mesurée à l'antique*** [Tempo in *musique mesurée à l'antique*], *Fontes artis musicae* XII/2-3 (May-Dec 1965) 202–04. In French. See no. 499 in this volume.

In the *vers mesuré* of the late 16th c.—polyphonic settings of the *vers mesurés à l'antique* by Jean-Antoine de Baïf and his followers—tempo is not clearly indicated. Editorial remarks from the posthumous publication of works by Claude Le Jeune (probably by Cécile Le Jeune), and theoretical discussion by Marin Mersenne and much later Bénigne de Bacilly, suggest that the settings were never to be sung slowly, but always in an imitation of natural spoken declamation, with a light rubato, in accordance with the principle of the primary importance of the text. *(David Bloom)*

3720 WAGNER, Peter. **Der traditionelle Choral-**
as **vortrag und seine geschichtliche Begründung** [Traditional chant performance and its historical foundation], *Acta generalis cantus gregoriani studiosorum conventus, Argentinensis, 16-19 Aug. 1905/Bericht des internationalen Kongresses für gregorianischen Choralgesang/Compte rendu du Congrès international de plain-chant grégorien* (Strassburg: F.-X. Le Roux, 1905) 40–54. In German. See no. 50 in this volume.
Discusses the problem of rhythm in performance practice.

3721 WARD, John M. **Le problème des hauteurs**
as **dans la musique pour luth et vihuela au XVIᵉ siècle** [The problem of pitch in lute and vihuela music of the 16th century], *Le luth et sa musique* (Paris: Centre National de la Recherche Scientifique [CNRS], 1958) 171–78. *Charts, diagr.* In French. See no. 377 in this volume.
Lutenists of the 16th c. often claimed to tune their instruments from *gamma ut* or *a re* in the lowest course, which has led musicologists to assume a tuning from G2 or A2. Evidence suggests that this assumption is at best an oversimplification. *(David Bloom)*

3722 WIDMANN, Wilhelm. **Einrichtung histo-**
as **rischer Musikwerke für Aufführungen** [The arrangement of historical musical works for performance], *Haydn-Zentenarfeier* (Leipzig: Breitkopf & Härtel; Wien: Artaria, 1909) 557–67. *Music.* In German. See no. 65 in this volume.
Discusses the preparation of modern arrangements of older music. Examples from the *Missa "Veni sponsa Christi"* of Palestrina are provided.

3723 WOLF, Johannes. **Über den Wert der Auf-**
as **führungspraxis für die historische Erkenntnis** [On the value of performance practice for historical knowledge], *Bericht über den I. musikwissenschaftlichen Kongress der Deutschen Musikgesellschaft in Leipzig* (Wiesbaden: Breitkopf & Härtel, 1926) 199–202. In German. See no. 120 in this volume.
Discusses various questions of performance practice in Francesco Landini, Pietro Aaron, Gregorian chant, troubadour music, chansons, and music of the Italian trecento. *(William Renwick)*

3724 WOLFF, Hellmuth Christian. **Orientalische**
as **Einflüsse in den Improvisationen des 16. und 17. Jahrhunderts** [Asian influences in improvisations of the 16th and 17th centuries], *Bericht über den siebenten internationalen musikwissenschaftlichen Kongress* (Kassel: Bärenreiter, 1959) 308–15. *Music, transcr.* In German. See no. 390 in this volume.
Ornamentation practice from the recorder treatise *Opera intulata Fontegara* of Sylvestro di Ganassi dal Fontego (1535) to Monteverdi's *L'Orfeo* (1608) yields many parallels with ornamentation of the Muslim world, India, and even farther east. Some such practices may have been transmitted into the European mainstream during the period by Spanish falsetto and then castrato singers. Monteverdi could have been directly influenced by Jewish chant, since Mantua, where *L'Orfeo* was composed, was a center of learned Jewish culture, liberally supported by Duke Vincenzo Gonzaga. *(David Bloom)*

3725 ZEHRER, Franz. **L'interpretazione moderna**
as **della polifonia sacra classica: Difetti da evitare** [Modern interpretation of classic sacred polyphony: Defects to avoid], *Atti del [I] Congresso internazionale*

di musica sacra (Tournai: Desclée, 1952) 336ff. In Italian. See no. 303 in this volume.

52 Performance practice, ca. 1600-1825

3726 ALDRICH, Putnam. **Obligatory improvisation**
as **of ornaments,** *Bericht über den siebenten internationalen musikwissenschaftlichen Kongress* (Kassel: Bärenreiter, 1959) 55–56. See no. 390 in this volume.
Discusses the type of ornamentation associated with French performance style of the late 17th and early 18th c. Context had a bearing on the realization of conventional ornaments, and often suggested the need for one in the absence of notation. Variety in the execution of ornaments was one of the most admired qualities of the French style of singing and playing. To illustrate, different rhythmic interpretations of the trill and their occasions are reviewed. *(Carl Skoggard)*

3727 BABITZ, Sol. **Das Violinspiel im 18. Jahrhun-**
as **dert und heute** [Violin playing in the 18th century and today], *Bericht über den internationalen musikwissenschaftlichen Kongreß* (Kassel: Bärenreiter, 1963) 313–15. In German. See no. 452 in this volume.
Discusses issues in the period performance of 18th-c. music, with particular reference to the qualities of original instruments, and the importance of rubato. *(David Bloom)*

3728 BADURA-SKODA, Eva. **Zur Appoggiaturen-**
as **frage** [Concerning appoggiaturas], *Bericht über den siebenten internationalen musikwissenschaftlichen Kongress* (Kassel: Bärenreiter, 1959) 58–60. In German. See no. 390 in this volume.
Explains the notational conventions for appoggiaturas in the vocal and instrumental music of the 18th c. and discusses the occasions when they are necessary as opposed to merely optional. Singers can learn from instrumental music, where the ornaments are usually indicated; often in arias and recitatives, there are even parallel lines in the instrumental parts that the singer can heed in deciding on appoggiaturas. *(Carl Skoggard)*

3729 BECHERINI, Bianca. **Le sonate per pianoforte**
as **di W.A. Mozart: Problemi di esecuzione contemporanea** [W.A. Mozart's piano sonatas: Problems of contemporary performance], *Bericht über den internationalen musikwissenschaftlichen Kongreß Wien Mozartjahr 1956* (Graz; Köln: Böhlau, 1958) 28–34. In Italian. See no. 365 in this volume.
Mozart's style is misunderstood today and is not being taught properly; it must be treated as something special rather than as an aspect of modern pianism. Old pianos and method books of the time—such as Muzio Clementi's *Gradus ad Parnassum* and Carl Czerny's *Vollständige theoretisch-praktische Pianoforte-Schule*—yield valuable information. Andrea Della Corte's *L'interpretazione musicale e gli interpreti* (1951) exemplifies the correct approach. *(Carol K. Baron)*

3730 BESSELER, Heinrich. **Sulla disposizione delle**
as **masse orchestrali e corali negli ambienti destinati alle esecuzioni profane e religiose nell'età barocca (con proiezioni)** [On the disposition of orchestral and choral forces in performance spaces for Baroque secular and sacred music (with projections).], *Atti del terzo Congresso internazionale di musica* (Firenze: Le Monnier, 1940) 121–29. In Italian; summaries in French and German. See no. 256 in this volume.
Discusses the late 19th-c. practice of using massive orchestral and choral forces for Baroque music and the fact that today, as a result of modern acoustics, its application is inappropriate. *(Edwin D. Wallace)*

3731 BLUME, Friedrich. **Die Orgelbegleitung in der**
as **Musik des 17. Jahrhunderts** [Organ accompaniments in the music of the 17th century], *Bericht über die
dritte Tagung für Deutsche Orgelkunst* (Kassel:
Bärenreiter, 1928) 95–101. In German. See no. 136 in
this volume.

The improvisational character of basso continuo accompaniment cannot be
replaced by a written-out part; the figured basses of the 17th c. do not represent a more primitive stage of development than those of Bach, merely a
different tradition requiring its own performance practice. Some essential
principles for the organ realization of 17th-c. basso continuo are sketched.

3732 BOYDEN, David D. **Performance practice in**
as **the 17th and 18th centuries,** *Report of the Eighth
Congress of the International Musicological Society. II:
Reports* (Kassel: Bärenreiter, 1962) 122–26. See no.
440 in this volume.

A report on a discussion of issues in Baroque performance practice by
Putnam ALDRICH, Sol BABITZ, Eva BADURA-SKODA, David D.
BOYDEN, Thurston DART, Otto Erich DEUTSCH, Robert
DONINGTON, Ralph KIRKPATRICK, Jens Peter LARSEN, Albert van
der LINDEN, Arthur MENDEL, Marc PINCHERLE, and Jack A.
WESTRUP, based on the papers by Pincherle and Dart abstracted as nos.
3738 and 3764, respectively.

3733 BOYDEN, David D. **The violin and its tech-**
as **nique: New horizons in research,** *Bericht über
den siebenten internationalen musikwissenschaftlichen
Kongress* (Kassel: Bärenreiter, 1959) 29–39. *Illus., music.* See no. 390 in this volume.

Reviews the theory and history of the so-called Bach bow, and refutes it.
Recorded performances of the same short passage of solo violin music by
Bach by Yehudi Menuhin, Emil Telmányi, and Kenneth Skeaping are compared. Skeaping's approach calls for performing on a period instrument and
observing guidelines given in 18th-c. treatises. The main contrasts between
the sound of the violin today and in Bach's time involve tone quality, articulation, expression, and the method of realizing three- and four-note chords.
Desiderata for research into historic violin performance are enumerated.

(Carl Skoggard)

3734 BROOK, Barry S. **Le tempo dans l'exécution de**
as **la musique instrumentale à la fin du XVIIIe
siècle: Les contributions de C. Mason et William Crotch** [Tempo in the performance of instrumental music at the end of the 18th century: The contributions of C. Mason and William Crotch], *Fontes artis
musicae* XII/2-3 (May-Dec 1965) 196–201. *Charts,
diagr.* In French. See no. 499 in this volume.

Before the advent of the metronome, *Rules on the times, metres, phrases
and accent of composition* (1806) by the otherwise unknown London pedagogue C. Mason, and writings from 1800 to ca. 1807 by the composer and
theorist William Crotch, recommend the use of a variably weighted pendu-
lum. Both authors regard *vivace* as indicating a faster tempo than *allegro*, in
contradistinction to the view expressed by James Nares in the preface to
Twenty anthems in score, and indeed faster than *vivace* is interpreted today.

(David Bloom)

3735 BUSH, Alan. **Zum Problem der Verbreitung**
as **von Händels Schaffen unter dem grossen
Publikum, besonders bei den Arbeitern und
Bauern, durch szenische Aufführungen seiner
Oratorien** [The problem of disseminating Händel's
works among the larger public, particularly workers and
peasants, through staged performances of his oratorios],
*Händel-Ehrung der Deutschen Demokratischen
Republik: Konferenzbericht* (Leipzig: VEB Deutscher
Verlag für Musik, 1961) 257–60. In German. See no.
408 in this volume.

Authentic period-practice performances of the oratorios are valuable, but
appeal only to a limited elite audience; a wider public is engaged by performances such as the 1938 London staging of *Belshazzar* by the Workers'

Music Association, with a chorus of 350, in which the author served as musical director. *(David Bloom)*

⟶ CELLIER, Alexandre. **L'improvisation** [Impro-
visation]. See no. 3673 in this volume.

⟶ CLERCX-LEJEUNE, Suzanne *et al.* **Résolutions** [Resolutions]. See no. 1510 in this volume.

3736 CUDWORTH, Charles. **The meaning of *vivace***
as **in eighteenth-century England,** *Fontes artis
musicae* XII/2-3 (May-Dec 1965) 194–95. See no. 499
in this volume.

Evidence from the preface to *Twenty anthems in score* by James Nares
(1778) shows that *vivace* indicated a tempo that is lively, but slower than *al-
legretto* or *allegro moderato,* to the generation of English musicians immediately following Händel; the assumption is particularly valuable in determining the tempo of vivace movements by Boyce. *(David Bloom)*

3737 DART, Thurston. **La méthode de luth de Miss**
as **Mary Burwell** [Miss Mary Burwell's lute tutor], *Le
luth et sa musique* (Paris: Centre National de la Recherche Scientifique [CNRS], 1958) 121–26. *Music.* In
French. See no. 377 in this volume.

Brief discussion of a MS lute tutor possibly copied by Mary Burwell between 1665 and 1670, in the private collection of Burwell's descendant Anthony Hammond, of Ingham, Norfolk, UK, with attention to its pedagogical content. A fuller version is published with the author's partial edition of
the work in *The Galpin Society journal* XI (1958); the MS is now in the
Spencer Collection of the Royal Academy of Music (*GB-Lam* MS.604).
(David Bloom)

3738 DART, Thurston. **Performance practice in the**
as **17th and 18th centuries: Six problems in instrumental music,** *Report of the Eighth Congress of
the International Musicological Society. I: Papers*
(Kassel: Bärenreiter, 1961) 231–35. See no. 439 in this
volume.

Especially vexing problems include: (1) determining the intended instruments of early keyboard music and music for instruments of the flute family; (2) interpreting the intended rhythmic and dynamic values and ornamentation practice of the lute tablature repertoire, and of *notes inégales* in
general; and (3) combating the substitution of authentic consort viols with
inappropriate instruments, and the overindulgent use of harpsichord stops.
(Miryam Moscovitz)

3739 EHMANN, Wilhelm. **Aufführungspraxis der**
as **Bachschen Motetten** [Performance practice of
Bach's motets], *Kongreß-Bericht: Gesellschaft für
Musikforschung* (Kassel; Basel: Bärenreiter, 1950)
121–23. In German. See no. 299 in this volume.

3740 FULLER-MAITLAND, John Alexander. **The in-**
as **terpretation of musical ornaments,** *Report of the
Fourth Congress of the International Musical Society*
(London: Novello, 1912) 259–67. *Music.* See no. 71 in
this volume.

Discusses Baroque performance practice, with particular attention to Daniel Gottlob Türk's *Clavierschule* (1789) and the works of Bach.

3741 GÉROLD, Théodore. **De la valeur des petites**
as **notes d'agrément et d'expression** [Of the value of
grace notes and ornament signs], *Congrès international
d'histoire de la musique: Documents, mémoires et vœux*
(Solesmes: St. Pierre; Paris: Fischbacher, 1901) 251–60.
Music. In French. See no. 32 in this volume.

The length of vocal appoggiaturas should be determined by scansion of the
text, as shown by examples from Bach, Mozart, Gluck, and Weber.

3742 GERSTENBERG, Walter. **Andante,** *Bericht über*
as *den internationalen musikwissenschaftlichen Kongreß*
(Kassel: Bärenreiter, 1963) 156–57. In German. See no.
452 in this volume.

Gives an account of the history of the term in the 18th c., from its origins as
an indication of basso continuo playing style to its adoption as a tempo
indication.

3743 HEINITZ, Wilhelm. **Rezitativ-Gestaltung in**
as **Händelschen Werken** [The construction of recitative in Händel's works], *Händel-Ehrung der Deutschen
Demokratischen Republik: Konferenzbericht* (Leipzig:
VEB Deutscher Verlag für Musik, 1961) 135–39. *Music.* In German. See no. 408 in this volume.

An analysis of the recitative *Vain, fluctuating state of human empire*, no. 2
of Händel's oratorio *Belshazzar* (1745), from the point of view of its performance practice. A suitably reworked German-language text corresponds
better to its musical-dramatic structure than the original English text.
(David Bloom)

3744 HICKMANN, Hans. **Instrumentenkundliche**
as **und aufführungspraktische Probleme bei der
Aufführung und stereofonischen Einspielung
Händelscher Werke** [Organological and perfor-
mance practice problems in the performance and ste-
reophonic recording of Händel's works], *Händel-
Ehrung der Deutschen Demokratischen Republik:
Konferenzbericht* (Leipzig: VEB Deutscher Verlag für
Musik, 1961) 207–13. In German. See no. 408 in this
volume.

The performance practice of Händel's instrumental works has received less
attention than that of his vocal works. Problems include vagueness and
contradiction in documentary sources in specifying the instrumental forces
required, and the differences in balance and timbre of 18th-c. instruments
compared to those of the present. Solutions used in the 1959 Archiv recording of the concerti grossi op. 3 by the Cappella Coloniensis under August
Wenzinger are discussed. *(David Bloom)*

3745 HOLEČKOVÁ-DOLANSKÁ, Jelena. **Wie man**
as **Mozart singen soll** [How one should sing Mozart],
*Internationale Konferenz über das Leben und Werk
W.A. Mozarts* (Praha: Svaz Československých
Skladatelů, 1956) 246–52. In German. See no. 360 in
this volume.

Mozart's views on vocal technique, which call especially for taste, musicality, and naturalness, are examined through the documentation of his
comments on and work with Aloysia Weber (Lange) and other singers; the
demands of different operatic roles and the concert arias are surveyed; and
the value of singing Mozart as vocal training is emphasized. *(David Bloom)*

3746 KAUL, Oskar. **Zur Instrumentation Mozarts**
as [Mozart's instrumentation], *Bericht über die
musikwissenschaftliche Tagung der Internationalen
Stiftung Mozarteum* (Leipzig: Breitkopf & Härtel,
1932) 167–71. In German. See no. 193 in this volume.

Sound quality is never an element in its own right, a coloring, in Mozart's
orchestral music; it is always the expression of an immanent property of the
musical gestalt. The development of his instrumentation was organically
connected to the development of his symphonic style. The experience of
the annual Mozartfest, Würzburg, suggests that conductors need an exceptionally strong feeling for his style to achieve the necessary textural transparency. *(David Bloom)*

3747 KELLER, Hermann. **Der Artikulationsstil der**
as **Bachschen Instrumentalwerke** [Articulation
style in Bach's instrumental works], *Bericht über den I.
musikwissenschaftlichen Kongress der Deutschen
Musikgesellschaft in Leipzig* (Wiesbaden: Breitkopf &
Härtel, 1926) 251. In German. See no. 120 in this
volume.

A summary of an article taken from the author's *Die musikalische Artiku-
lation, insbesondere bei Joh. Seb. Bach* (Universität Tubingen, 1924), and
published by Verlag C.F. Schullneiss, Stuttgart, the following year.

3748 KLOTZ, Hans. **Die Registrierkunst der**
as **französischen Organisten des 17. und 18.
Jahrhunderts und das Bachspiel** [The art of registration in French organ playing of the 17th and 18th
centuries, and Bach performance], *Compte
rendu/Kongressbericht/Report* (Basel: Bärenreiter,
1951) 172–76. *Music, organ specification.* In German.
See no. 289 in this volume.

Bach knew, and valued, the French organ school of the Baroque, and it
seems certain that he made use of French registration styles in his own performances. Applying specific French registrations to his works puts them
in a new and persuasive light. *(David Bloom)*

3749 KOLNEDER, Walter. **Arbeitsgemeinschaft:**
as **Dynamik und Agogik in der Musik des Barock**
[Working group: Dynamics and agogics in music of the
Baroque], *Bericht über den siebenten internationalen
musikwissenschaftlichen Kongress* (Kassel:
Bärenreiter, 1959) 343–48. In German. See no. 390 in
this volume.

Summary of contributions to a conference workshop by the author, Heinrich BESSELER, Macario Santiago KASTNER, and Hans-Peter
SCHMITZ on issues of dynamic and tempo modification in the performance of Baroque music, with particular attention to the role of organ and
harpsichord in the concept of terrace dynamics. *(David Bloom)*

3750 KRATOCHVÍL, Jiří. **Betrachtungen über die**
as **Urfassung des Konzerts für Klarinette und des
Quintetts für Klarinette und Streicher von
W.A. Mozart** [Observations on the original version of
W.A. Mozart's clarinet concerto and the quintet for clar-
inet and strings], *Internationale Konferenz über das
Leben und Werk W.A. Mozarts* (Praha: Svaz
Československých Skladatelů, 1956) 262–71. *Music,
bibliog.* In German. See no. 360 in this volume.

The clarinetist Milan Kostohryz has conjectured that the concerto, K.622,
or the quintet, K.581, written for Anton Stadler, were originally intended
for the so-called basset clarinet designed by Stadler with a range extending
through low C, and only later arranged for standard clarinet. There are no
extant autographs for the works, but sufficient internal and external evidence exists to conclude that the hypothesis is correct. A basset clarinet
constructed at the Akademie Múzických Umění in Prague was used for a
performance of the reconstructed score of the concerto in 1951 and of the
quintet at the present conference. A Czech-language version is abstracted
as RILM [1967]436. *(David Bloom)*

3751 KREMLËV, Julij Anatol'evič. **J. Haydn und die**
as **russische Musikkultur** [J. Haydn and Russian musical culture], *Bericht über die internationale
Konferenz zum Andenken Joseph Haydns* (Budapest:
Akadémiai Kiadó, 1961) 61–68. *Illus.* In German. See
no. 405 in this volume.

The three general periods of Haydn reception—great fame, neglect, and a
return of esteem—were paralleled in Russia. Haydn's outstanding quality
is his use of traditional material; the soul of the people was the basis of his
art. *(Jean W. Smith)*

3752 LARSEN, Jens Peter. **Gibt es eine definitive**
as **Version von Händels** *Messias*? [Is there a definitive version of Händel's *Messiah*?], *Compte rendu/
Kongressbericht/Report* (Basel: Bärenreiter, 1951)
178. In German. See no. 289 in this volume.

Summary of a paper. Some of the changes made to *Messiah* between 1741,
the year of its composition, and 1759, the year of Händel's death, are improvements; others were adaptations to the needs of particular singers.

Ongoing study of the sources will make it easier to rectify some of the inadequacies of the performance tradition. *(David Bloom)*

3753 LARSEN, Jens Peter. **Tempoprobleme bei**
as **Händel, dargestellt am** *Messias* [Tempo problems in Händel as exemplified in *Messiah*], *Händel-Ehrung der Deutschen Demokratischen Republik: Konferenzbericht* (Leipzig: VEB Deutscher Verlag für Musik, 1961) 141–53. *Charts, diagr.* In German. See no. 408 in this volume.

Discusses evidence for the original tempos of the numbers of *Messiah*, as well as timings and metronome indications for performances from between ca. 1785 and the present, including a chart of metronome markings for each number of the oratorio in eleven 19th-c. performing versions. The original tempos would perhaps seem startlingly brisk today; excessive slowness is the most widespread violation of Händel's intentions. If we aim not so much at playing the music faster as providing it with an even, flowing movement, it will not seem too fast. *(David Bloom)*

3754 LAUNAY, Denise. **À propos d'une Messe de**
as **Charles d'Helfer: Le problème de l'exécution des Messes réputées** *a cappella* **en France, aux XVIIe et XVIIIe siècles** [On a Mass by Charles d'Helfer: The question of the performance of Masses known as *a cappella* in France in the 17th and 18th centuries], *Les colloques de Wégimont. IV: Le Baroque musical—Recueil d'études sur la musique du XVIIe siècle* (Paris: Belles Lettres, 1963) 177–99. *Illus., facs., music.* In French. See no. 386 in this volume.

A cappella Masses written in the severe *stile antico* counterpoint continued to be sung in French churches long after the style had gone out of date, furnished with basso continuo parts, sometimes even full orchestral accompaniments, by composers such as Sébastien de Brossard, whose score collection in the Bibliothèque National, Paris, provides many examples. Thus a Requiem by Helfer, published by Robert Ballard in 1656, was still being performed in 1774, but in a totally transformed version. Reasons for the practice, and for the failure of French composers to write new Masses in the high Baroque style alongside their motets, are to be sought in the circumstances of the Counter-Reformation French church, as part of an elaborate system of compromises between the austerity demanded by the Tridentine reform and the prevailing preference, especially at court, for more complex and brilliant music. *(David Bloom)*

3755 LEICHTENTRITT, Hugo. **Zur Vortragspraxis**
as **des 17. Jahrhunderts** [Performance practice in the 17th century], *Haydn-Zentenarfeier* (Leipzig: Breitkopf & Härtel; Wien: Artaria, 1909) 147–53. In German. See no. 65 in this volume.

Focuses on questions of instrumentation, primarily in the works of Monteverdi.

3756 LESURE, François. **Haydn en France** [Haydn in
as France], *Bericht über die internationale Konferenz zum Andenken Joseph Haydns* (Budapest: Akadémiai Kiadó, 1961) 79–84. In French. See no. 405 in this volume.

Discusses aspects of Haydn's popularity in France, including homages, performances, and the study of his works in conservatories. *(Jean W. Smith)*

3757 LEWICKI, Ernst. **Die Stimmcharaktere im**
as *Idomeneo* [Voice types of *Idomeneo*], *Bericht über die musikwissenschaftliche Tagung der Internationalen Stiftung Mozarteum* (Leipzig: Breitkopf & Härtel, 1932) 158–60. In German. See no. 193 in this volume.

In the author's performing version of the opera, produced in Karlsruhe in 1917 under Fritz Cortolezis and in Dresden in 1925-28 under Hermann Kutzschbach, the roles of Idomeneo and Idamante are sung by a heroic baritone and lyric tenor respectively. These and other changes can be justified in terms of the record of Mozart's intentions. *(David Bloom)*

3758 LIVANOVA, Tamara Nikolaevna. **Mocart i**
as **russkaja muzykal'naja kul'tura** [Mozart and Russian musical culture], *Bericht über den internationalen musikwissenschaftlichen Kongreß Wien Mozartjahr 1956* (Graz; Köln: Böhlau, 1958) 365–72. In Russian. See no. 365 in this volume.

Surveys the Russian reception of Mozart's music from the first St. Petersburg production of *Die Zauberflöte* (1794) through the early Soviet period. *(David Bloom)*

3759 LUCIANI, Sebastiano Arturo. **La** *Juditha* **e**
as **messa in scena** [*Juditha* and its staging], *Fac-simile del Concerto funebre* (Siena: Accademia Musicale Chigiana, 1947) 38–39. In Italian. See no. 279 in this volume.

The early performances of Vivaldi's *Juditha triumphans devicta Holofernes barbarie*, RV 644, were probably presented with at least rudimentary staging. *(Mark Stevens)*

3760 LUCIANI, Sebastiano Arturo. **I violini in**
as **tromba marina** [The violins *in tromba marina*], *Fac-simile del Concerto funebre* (Siena: Accademia Musicale Chigiana, 1947) 37–38. In Italian. See no. 279 in this volume.

The *due violini in tromba marina* called for in one of Vivaldi's concertos are probably normal violins whose timbres were altered by the use of a parchment device described by Monteverdi. *(Mark Stevens)*

3761 MARSCHNER, Franz. **Zählzeit, Tempo, und**
as **Ausdruck bei Beethoven** [Beat, tempo, and expression in Beethoven], *Beethoven-Zentenarfeier: Internationaler musikhistorischer Kongress* (Wien: Universal, 1927) 100–03. In German. See no. 142 in this volume.

Discusses principles for determining the correct tempos in Beethoven performance, with attention to identifying beat units. The units are not always made clear by the notation, even with the proliferation of time signatures, tempo markings, and phrase markings in the later works. *(David Bloom)*

3762 PESSL, Yella. **French patterns and their read-**
as **ing in Bach's secular clavier music**, *Papers of the American Musicological Society* (Philadelphia: American Musicological Society, 1946) 8–20. *Music.* See no. 272 in this volume.

Evidence shows that Bach was aware of French ornamentation practice and used it. In playing his keyboard pieces molded on French dance forms, performers should always follow the French ornamentation style. *(David Bloom)*

3763 PIECHLER, Arthur. **Die Phrasierung der**
as **Orgelwerke Bachs** [Phrasing in Bach's organ works], *Atti del [I] Congresso internazionale di musica sacra* (Tournai: Desclée, 1952) 363–66. In German. See no. 303 in this volume.

3764 PINCHERLE, Marc. **Des manières d'exécuter**
as **la musique aux XVIIe et XVIIIe siècles** [Performance practice in the 17th and 18th centuries], *Report of the Eighth Congress of the International Musicological Society. I: Papers* (Kassel: Bärenreiter, 1961) 220–31. *Facs., music, bibliog.* In French. See no. 439 in this volume.

A summary of the current understanding of Baroque and Classic bowed instrument practice, with a view to its application in relatively authentic performance. *(David Bloom)*

⟶ POULTON, Diana. **La technique du jeu du luth en France et en Angleterre** [The technique of lute playing in France and England]. See no. 3597 in this volume.

3765
as
QUOIKA, Rudolf. **Die Generalbaßimprovisation nach Josef Seger** [Figured bass improvisation after Josef Seger], *Bericht über den internationalen musikwissenschaftlichen Kongreß Wien Mozartjahr 1956* (Graz; Köln: Böhlau, 1958) 490–92. In German. See no. 365 in this volume.

The Prague organist and composer Josef Seger (1716-82) was noted for his skill in improvising from a figured bass. The transmission of his style in Bohemia into the Romantic era is traced, and the character of the Baroque instruments to which it is suited is discussed. *(David Bloom)*

3766
as
RAUGEL, Félix. **Paris, fidèle au souvenir de Mozart** [Paris, faithful to the memory of Mozart], *Bericht über den internationalen musikwissenschaftlichen Kongreß Wien Mozartjahr 1956* (Graz; Köln: Böhlau, 1958) 535–36. In French. See no. 365 in this volume.

An account of the cultivation of Mozart's music from his departure from the city (1778) through 1956. The first Parisian performances of *Don Giovanni*, *Così fan tutte*, and *Le nozze di Figaro* are noted, and several Mozart societies are discussed. *(Michael Adelson)*

3767
as
SCHNEIDER, Max. **Telemannpflege: Eine unserer nationalen Aufgaben** [The cultivation of Telemann: One of our national tasks], *Beiträge zu einem neuen Telemannbild* (Magdeburg: Vorwärts, 1963) 7–8. In German. See no. 453 in this volume.

3768
as
SEEGER, Horst. **Zu Fragen der Aufführungspraxis von Händels Oratorien** [Questions on the performance practice of Händel's oratorios], *Händel-Ehrung der Deutschen Demokratischen Republik: Konferenzbericht* (Leipzig: VEB Deutscher Verlag für Musik, 1961) 247–50. In German. See no. 408 in this volume.

Our understanding of the deployment of instrumental forces and of the correct use of vocal ornamentation has greatly improved in the last decades; the next essential step is to consider the relation of these factors to the dramaturgical content of each particular work and to the genre of the Händelian oratorio as distinct from opera. *(David Bloom)*

3769
as
STEGLICH, Rudolf. **Das Tempo als Problem der Mozartinterpretation** [Tempo as a problem in Mozart interpretation], *Bericht über die musikwissenschaftliche Tagung der Internationalen Stiftung Mozarteum* (Leipzig: Breitkopf & Härtel, 1932) 172–78. *Music.* In German. See no. 193 in this volume.

Problems of tempo in Mozart's music can be solved only through a sharpened sense of his movement and gestalt qualities, in the sense used by Gustav Becking, Joseph Sievers, Franz Saran, and Josef Rutz. Examples are drawn from the romanze movement of the serenade *Eine kleine Nachtmusik*, K.525, and the andante of the symphony in E♭, K.543. *(David Bloom)*

3770
as
STEMPEL, Maxim. **Bach in Schweden** [Bach in Sweden], *Bericht über die Wissenschaftliche Bachtagung* (Leipzig: Peters, 1951) 367–74. In German. See no. 298 in this volume.

A historical sketch of the reception of Bach's music in Sweden, beginning with the Stockholm Hofkapellmeister and Uppsala music director Johann Christian Friedrich Haeffner (1759-1833), who conducted Bach's orchestral music and performed his organ fugues. Attention is given to the activities of performers and musicologists as well as to cultural figures such as the pedagogues Torsten Fogelquist, August Strindberg, and Nathan Söderblom, all of whom became Bach enthusiasts in Paris at the end of the 19th c. *(David Bloom)*

3771
as
STEVENS, Denis. **L'interprétation de la musique de Claudio Monteverdi** [Performing the music of Claudio Monteverdi], *Les colloques de Wégimont. IV: Le Baroque musical—Recueil d'études sur la musique du XVIIᵉ siècle* (Paris: Belles Lettres, 1963) 241–54. *Music.* In French. See no. 386 in this volume.

Recorded performances of Monteverdi's *Il combattimento di Tancredi e Clorinda* (1624) and the balletto *Volgendo il ciel per l'immortal sentiero* (1636) under the direction of Angelo Ephrikian are compared to recordings by the author (with performers of the British Broadcasting Corporation). Only by making an effort to duplicate the technical aspects of period practice—the instrumentation, realization of basso continuo, tempo, ornamentation, and attitude toward the text—is it possible to create an adequate interpretation. *(David Bloom)*

3772
as
STEVENS, Denis. **Ornamention in Monteverdi's shorter dramatic works,** *Bericht über den siebenten internationalen musikwissenschaftlichen Kongress* (Kassel: Bärenreiter, 1959) 284–87. See no. 390 in this volume.

Italian singers of around the turn of the 17th c. were accustomed to studying the written-out ornaments of how-to publications such as Girolamo dalla Casa's *Il vero modo di diminuir* (Venice 1584), Giovanni Bassano's *Recercate passaggi et cadentie* (Venice 1585), Riccardo Rognoni's *Passaggi per potersi essercitare nel diminuire* (Venice 1592), and especially Giovanni Luca Conforti's *Breve et facile maniera d'essercitarsi ad ogni scolaro* (Rome, 1593). Monteverdi would have expected performers to use such resources to vary the many perfect cadences in *Il ballo delle ingrate* and *Il combattimento di Tancredi e Clorinda*. *(David Bloom)*

3773
as
THIBAULT DE CHAMBURE, Geneviève. **Le Te Deum de Lalande: Minutage de l'époque** [Lalande's Te Deum: Contemporary timing], *Fontes artis musicae* XII/2-3 (May-Dec 1965) 162–65. *Facs., music.* In French. See no. 499 in this volume.

F-Pc MS H.400D provides an exact timing for the last version (before 1711) of Michel-Richard de Lalande's Te Deum. A complete section-by-section timing for the work as published in 1729 is appended. *(David Bloom)*

3774
as
TIRABASSI, Antonio. **Histoire de l'harmonisation à partir de 1600 á 1750** [History of harmonization from 1600 to 1750], *Bericht über den musikwissenschaftlichen Kongreß in Basel* (Leipzig: Breitkopf & Härtel, 1925) 328–33. *Music, charts, diagr.* In French. See no. 102 in this volume.

Presents principles for the realization of figured bass. Galleazzo Sabbatini's *Regola facile e breve per sonare sopra il basso continuo nell'organo, manacordo o altro simile stromento* (Venice, 1628), Francesco Gasparini's *L'armonico pratico al cimbalo* (Venice, 1708), and Michel Corrette's *Le maître de clavecin* (Paris, 1753) are cited. *(David Bloom)*

⟶
TORREFRANCA, Fausto. **Origine e significato di repicco, partita, ricercare, sprezzatura** [The origin and meaning of repicco, partita, ricercare, and sprezzatura]. See no. 4289 in this volume.

3775
as
WALLERSTEIN, Lothar. **Mozarts *Idomeneo* in der Wiener Bearbeitung** [Mozart's *Idomeneo* in the Vienna version], *Bericht über die musikwissenschaftliche Tagung der Internationalen Stiftung Mozarteum* (Leipzig: Breitkopf & Härtel, 1932) 161–66. In German. See no. 193 in this volume.

A defense of the author's textual revisions and of Richard Strauss's additional music for the 1931 Wiener Oper production, which are not meant to be historically accurate but are true to the spirit of the work. *(David Bloom)*

3776
as
WANGERMÉE, Robert. **Principes d'interprétation** [Principles of interpretation], *Les colloques de Wégimont. IV: Le Baroque musical—Recueil d'études sur la musique du XVIIᵉ siècle* (Paris: Belles Lettres, 1963) 223–40. In French. See no. 386 in this volume.

For the 1957 Festival de Liège "Les Nuits de Septembre", the author prepared the music for a pasticcio in 18th-c. style, with a new French text by Jean Le Paillot, under the title *La maîtresse et les deux maestros*, basing the musical numbers and comic plot on a pasticcio traditionally attributed to Pergolesi, *Il maestro di musica* (Paris, 1753), with the addition of other music by Pergolesi and original recitatives. The low priority given to textual authenticity in the project is itself an authentically 18th-c. characteristic. *(David Bloom)*

3777
as

WELLESZ, Egon. **Die Aussetzung des basso continuo in der italienischen Oper** [The realization of the basso continuo in Italian opera], *Report of the Fourth Congress of the International Musical Society* (London: Novello, 1912) 282–85. In German. See no. 71 in this volume.

There are two basic approaches to 17th- and 18th-c. basso continuo: In chamber music, a subtle contrapuntal execution is required, while in dramatic music, the realization can cover whole groups of instruments, with fully harmonized chords. The difficulty of interpreting the sketch-like scores of early operas is considered. *(author)*

3778
as

WOLFF, Hellmuth Christian. **Die Gesangsimprovisationen der Barockzeit** [Singing and improvisation during the Baroque era], *Bericht über den Internationalen musikwissenschaftlichen Kongress* (Kassel: Bärenreiter, 1954) 252–55. In German. See no. 319 in this volume.

In the Renaissance, the singer influenced the player more than the player the singer. The diminution and ornamentation techniques applied to vocal and instrumental genres and their cross-fertilization make this clear. Solo vocal improvisations documented for Farinelli (Carlo Broschi) suggest that instrumental influences were held in check during the Baroque as well. Most of Farinelli's passage work is diatonic, with leaps introduced only occasionally, and rarely does he resort to figures reminiscent of the trumpet or the harpsichord. Johann Adam Hiller's *Anweisung zum musikalisch-zierlichen Gesang* (Leipzig, 1780) shows that this fundamentally vocal approach to improvisation was not the province of a few castratos but was expected of singers in general. The reintroduction of a schooled improvisation into the contemporary performance of Baroque music is urged. *(Carl Skoggard)*

3779
as

WOLFF, Hellmuth Christian. **Vom Wesen des alten Belcanto** [The essence of early bel canto], *Händel-Ehrung der Deutschen Demokratischen Republik: Konferenzbericht* (Leipzig: VEB Deutscher Verlag für Musik, 1961) 95–99. *Music.* In German. See no. 408 in this volume.

Documentary evidence shows how singers improvised ornamentation in performing Händel's solo vocal parts, especially in the da capo repetition of an aria; implications for correct performance practice today are discussed. *(David Bloom)*

3780
as

YOUNG, Percy M. **Zur Interpretation des *Saul*** [The interpretation of *Saul*], *Händel-Ehrung der Deutschen Demokratischen Republik: Konferenzbericht* (Leipzig: VEB Deutscher Verlag für Musik, 1961) 131–34. In German. See no. 408 in this volume.

Discusses the performance history of Händel's oratorio (January 1739), its MS and print sources, its dramaturgy and aesthetic significance, and their implications for musicians today. Just as no two performances of the work were alike in Händel's time, so should there be flexibility in the assembly of a performing version out of its 111 musical numbers now. *(David Bloom)*

53 Performance practice, ca. 1800-1900

3781
as

ALEKSEEV, Aleksandr Dmitrievič. **Tradicii ispolnenija Šopena v Rossii i Sovetskom Sojuze** [Chopin performance traditions in Russia and the Soviet Republics], *The book of the first international musico-logical congress devoted to the works of Frederick Chopin* (Warszawa: Państwowe Wydawnictwo Naukowe, 1963) 421–24. In Russian. See no. 425 in this volume.

3782
as

BIEHLE, Herbert. **Schuberts Lieder als Gesangsproblem** [Schubert's lieder as an issue for singers], *Beethoven-Zentenarfeier: Internationaler musikhistorischer Kongress* (Wien: Universal, 1927) 388–91. In German. See no. 142 in this volume.

Study of the correct performance practice of the lieder should begin with a study of the singers for whom Schubert wrote them, for example Therese Grob and Johann Michael Vogl, both of whom had unusually placed tessituras. An extended version is published in *Musikalisches Magazin* no. 74, 1929. *(David Bloom)*

3783
as

DRZEWIECKI, Zbigniew. **Le style d'interprétation de Chopin dans la pédagogie polonaise contemporaine** [The interpretation of Chopin in contemporary Polish pedagogy], *The book of the first international musicological congress devoted to the works of Frederick Chopin* (Warszawa: Państwowe Wydawnictwo Naukowe, 1963) 430–32. In French. See no. 425 in this volume.

One should balance technical considerations and virtuosity with the emotional considerations necessary for the interpretation of the piece. Contemporary sources help to reconstruct a semblance of how Chopin may have played his own works. A particular problem among Polish and other pedagogues is the treatment of rubato. *(Susan Poliniak)*

3784
as

GUI, Vittorio. **Letture e interpretazioni delle partiture** [Readings and interpretations of scores], *Atti del terzo Congresso internazionale di musica* (Firenze: Le Monnier, 1940) 136–43. In Italian; summaries in French and German. See no. 256 in this volume.

Examples from Wagner, Rossini, and Verdi illustrate discrepancies between various published scores and the original MSS.

3785
as

GÜNTHER, Felix. **Zur Darstellung Schubertscher Lieder** [On the interpretation of Schubert's lieder], *Bericht über den internationalen Kongress für Schubertforschung* (Augsburg: Benno Filser, 1929) 127–30. In German. See no. 154 in this volume.

A brief overview of performance issues. Various songs are mentioned, including *Ganymed*, *Fragment aus dem Aeschylus*, and *Im Frühling*.

3786
as

HASSE, Karl. **Max Reger und die deutsche Orgelkunst** [Max Reger and German organ art], *Bericht über die [I] Freiburger Tagung für Deutsche Orgelkunst* (Augsburg: Bärenreiter, 1926) 122–29. In German. See no. 122 in this volume.

Reger's influence on organ composition, playing, and building in Germany seems less decisive in the late 1920s than it did ten or twenty years earlier; in particular his music seems to demand a Romantic organ, with devices such as the crescendo roller, that is out of step with the times. But in spite of the conservatism of his compositional style he may be said to have gone beyond impressionism and expressionism in his emphasis on the ethical dimension of the German organ, and it is likely that the organ of the future will in fact be appropriate for playing his works. *(David Bloom)*

3787
as

HEINITZ, Wilhelm. **Physiologische Beobachtungen zur Werk-Ästhetik F. Chopins** [Physiological observations on the aesthetic character of Frédéric Chopin's works], *The book of the first international musicological congress devoted to the works of Frederick Chopin* (Warszawa: Państwowe Wydawnictwo Naukowe, 1963) 433–37. In German. See no. 425 in this volume.

Discusses aspects of Chopin's piano writing in terms of the theory of homogeneity, and its implications for performance, with reference to ornamentation, beat, phrasing, dynamics, agogics, fingering, and pulse. *(David Bloom)*

3788
as

INDY, Vincent d'. **Unification de l'orchestration des harmonies et fanfares** [Unification in the orchestration of *harmonies* and *fanfares*], *Congrès international de musique: Ire session—Exposition Universelle de 1900: Compte rendu, rapports, communications* (Paris: conference, 1901) 11–13. *Charts, diagr.* In French. See no. 29 in this volume.

Standardized instrumentation for wind bands (*harmonie*; 65 pieces belonging to six families of instruments) and bands of brass and percussion players (*fanfare*; 49 pieces divided into four sections) would be of advantage to composers and editors.

3789
as

KAŃSKI, Józef. **Über die Aufführungsstile der Werke Chopins: Einige allgemeine Probleme der Aufführung auf Grund von Schallplattenaufnahmen** [Performance styles for Chopin's works: Some general problems of performance, based on sound recordings], *The book of the first international musicological congress devoted to the works of Frederick Chopin* (Warszawa: Państwowe Wydawnictwo Naukowe, 1963) 444–48. *Charts, diagr.* In German. See no. 425 in this volume.

A comparison of agogic, phrasing, and dynamic aspects in 12 recordings of Chopin's A♭ polonaise suggests a classification into three kinds of Chopin performance: classic, romantic, and virtuoso. *(David Bloom)*

3790
as

SOBIESKA, Jadwiga; SOBIESKI, Marian. **Das Tempo rubato bei Chopin und in der polnischen Volksmusik** [Tempo rubato in Chopin and in Polish traditional music], *The book of the first international musicological congress devoted to the works of Frederick Chopin* (Warszawa: Państwowe Wydawnictwo Naukowe, 1963) 247–54. *Music, transcr.* In German. See no. 425 in this volume.

The unique character of Chopin's rubato, the feature of his piano playing that distinguished him from other virtuosos at the time of his arrival in Paris, can be traced to rubato singing and playing in traditional Polish music. *(David Bloom)*

54 Performance practice, Twentieth century

3791
as

DRZEWIECKI, Zbigniew. **Kilka uwag o interpretacji utworów fortepianowych Szymanowskiego** [A few remarks on the interpretation of Szymanowski's piano works], *Karol Szymanowski: Księga sesji Naukowej poświęconej twórczości Karola Szymanowskiego* (Warszawa: Uniwersytet Warszawski, Instytut Muzykologii, 1964) 67–74. In Polish; summary in English. See no. 458 in this volume.

Szymanowzki's keyboard writing went through a continuous evolutionary process. His early and middle works are characterized by great virtuosity, extremes of dynamic and register, massive chords, complex figuration, and rich harmonic color. Examples include *Masques*, *Métopes*, and the third piano sonata. During his nationalistic period, Szymanowski's keyboard writing became simpler, as exemplified by the mazurkas and Polish dances.

3792
as

FLEISCHER, Herbert. **Neue Musik und mechanische Musik** [New music and mechanical music], *Atti del primo Congresso internazionale di musica* (Firenze: Le Monnier, 1935) 68–76. In German; summary in Italian. See no. 203 in this volume.

Contemporary music, as pioneered by Busoni and Schoenberg, appeals to the intellect rather than the emotions. Detached from the performer's

personal talent, it is objectified and to be interpreted with mechanical precision. Ideally, this music would be inscribed directly onto a cylinder, disc, or film, note by note. These techniques are in their first evolutionary stage. *(author)*

3793
as

HOLEČKOVÁ-DOLANSKÁ, Jelena. **K pěveckým problémům Janáčkových oper** [Problems of singing in Janáček's operas], *Leoš Janáček a soudobá hudba* (Praha: Panton, 1963) 124–28. In Czech; summaries in Russian and German. See no. 389 in this volume.

A singer of Janáček's operas has to deal with specific vocal problems, such as dramatic sung speech based on intonation of folk music, clear articulation of a sung word in order to underline its meaning, technical lightness of voice, and the superiority of drama over vocal technique. *(editors)*

3794
as

KUNDERA, Ludvík. **K otázce interpretace Janáčkových děl** [On the interpretation of Janáček's works], *Leoš Janáček a soudobá hudba* (Praha: Panton, 1963) 189–97. *Music.* In Czech; summaries in Russian and German. See no. 389 in this volume.

The performance of Janáček's compositions is made difficult not only by the many typographical errors in editions, but also by the limits of conventional notation with respect to the originality of his musical language, particularly his rubatos. The character of the individual composition is a better guide than its musical notation. *(editors)*

3795
as

MÁŠA, Milan. **K soudobé reprodukci klavírních děl Leoše Janáčka** [Toward a modern interpretation of Leoš Janáček's piano compositions], *Sborník Janáčkovy Akademie Múzichých Umeni* V (1965) 37–41. In Czech. See no. 496 in this volume.

3796
as

PEČMAN, Rudolf. **Symfonické dílo Leoše Janáčka v pojetí Břetislava Bakaly** [Janáček's symphonic works interpreted by Břetislav Bakala], *Leoš Janáček a soudobá hudba* (Praha: Panton, 1963) 250–53. In Czech; summaries in Russian and German. See no. 389 in this volume.

The conductor Břetislav Bakala (1897-1958) developed a specific conducting style for the interpretation of Janáček's symphonic works. *(editors)*

3797
as

PISTON, Walter. **Problems of intonation in the performance of contemporary music,** *Instrumental music* (Cambridge, MA: Harvard University Press, 1959) 70–86. See no. 368 in this volume.

Musical meaning is presently grounded in major-minor tonal feeling, for both performers and audience. It is not clear that this musical meaning, so necessary to playing in tune for conventional tonal music, also applies to nontonal music. In 12-tone music, performers should strive for a precisely equal-tempered intonation. *(Daven Jenkins)*

3798
as

STŘELCOVÁ, Věra. **V čem vidím modernost pěvecké stránky interpretace Janáčkových oper** [How I see the modern interpretation of vocal parts in Janáček's operas], *Sborník Janáčkovy Akademie Múzichých Umeni* V (1965) 43–52. *Music.* In Czech. See no. 496 in this volume.

3799
as

TROJAN, Jan. **Břetislav Bakala: Janáčkovský interpret** [Břetislav Bakala: An interpreter of Janáček], *Sborník Janáčkovy Akademie Múzichých Umeni* V (1965) 91–99. In Czech. See no. 496 in this volume.

Břetislav Bakala, conductor of the Symfonický Orchestr Brněnského Rozhlasu, was Janáček's student and assistant. Bakala's intimate knowledge of original scores gave his interpretations of Janáček's orchestral music a special significance.

3800
as

TÝNSKÝ, Richard. **K problémům soudobé interpretace Janáčka** [Issues in contemporary interpretation of Janáček], *Sborník Janáčkovy Akademie Múzichých Umeni* V (1965) 53–58. In Czech. See no. 496 in this volume.

55 Notation and paleography

3801
as

AGUSTONI, Luigi. **La scomposizione del neuma** [The decomposition of the neume], *Atti del [I] Congresso internazionale di musica sacra* (Tournai: Desclée, 1952) 172–76. In Italian. See no. 303 in this volume.

Notes on the interpretation of neumatic notation of Gregorian-Frankish chant.

3802
as

ANGLÈS, Higini. **Die alte spanische Mensuralnotation: Praktische Winke, um den Rhythmus der monodischen Lyrik des Mittelalters besser kennenzulernen** [Old Spanish mensural notation: Practical suggestions toward an improved acquaintance with the rhythm of monodic medieval songs], *Bericht über den internationalen musikwissenschaftlichen Kongreß Wien Mozartjahr 1956* (Graz; Köln: Böhlau, 1958) 7–17. *Music, charts, diagr., transcr.* In German. See no. 365 in this volume.

The practice of transcribing medieval monody only in rhythmic modes one through three often results in a rhythm that fails to convey the beauty of the melody. Transcriptions using all six rhythmic modes, sometimes in combination, may also be more authentic, as is suggested by evidence from the *Cantigas de Santa María*, the troubadour and trouvère repertoires, and Italian *laudae*. *(Carol K. Baron)*

3803
as

ANGLÈS, Higini. **Der Rhythmus in der Melodik mittelalterlicher Lyrik** [Rhythm in the melody for medieval poetry], *Report of the Eighth Congress of the International Musicological Society. I: Papers* (Kassel: Bärenreiter, 1961) 3–11. *Music, bibliog.* In German. See no. 439 in this volume.

The secret of a rhythmically adequate interpretation of lyric monody from the 12th to the early 14th c. lies not so much in understanding the metrics or accentuation of the texts as in understanding the rhythmic notation, in its sometimes modal and mensural, sometimes mensural but not modal forms. *(David Bloom)*

3804
as

BERNOULLI, Eduard. **Hinweis auf gewisse Alterationszeichen in Drucken des 16. Jahrhunderts** [A note on certain accidental symbols in 16th-century prints], *Haydn-Zentenarfeier* (Leipzig: Breitkopf & Härtel; Wien: Artaria, 1909) 126–27. In German. See no. 65 in this volume.

3805
as

BERNOULLI, Eduard. **Sur la notation de rythmes complexes dans deux imprimés du XVIᵉ siècle** [On the notation of complex rhythms in two 16th-century books], *Actes du Congrès d'histoire de l'art* (Paris: Presses Universitaires de France, 1923-1924) 810–22. In French. See no. 94 in this volume.

Two different song collections dating from the first quarter of the 16th c. provide the opportunity for offering some practical rules concerning the transcription of proportional notation. *(Vivian Conejero)*

3806
as

BERNOULLI, Eduard. **Über die Notation des Meistergesangs** [The notation of Meistergesang], *Bericht über den zweiten Kongreß der Internationalen*

Musikgesellschaft (Leipzig: Breitkopf & Härtel, 1907) 35–37. In German. See no. 53 in this volume.

Discusses principles of rhythmic interpretation with primary reference to the Dresden MS attributed to Adam Puschman (*D-Dl* MS M6) and the Munich *D-Mbs* MS Cgm 4999. *(David Bloom)*

⟶

BOEPPLE, Paul. **Theoretisches und Praktisches zur Rythmik der neuesten Musik** [The theory and practice of rhythm in the newest music]. See no. 3971 in this volume.

⟶

BRENN, Franz. **Tonsysteme in Equiton und Fawcettzahlen** [Tonal systems in equitone notation and Fawcett numbers]. See no. 4053 in this volume.

3807
as

BREZZO, Guido Lorenzo. **Le rythme poétique et sa notation** [Poetic rhythm and its notation], *Compte rendu du Iᵉʳ Congrès du rythme* (Genève: Institut Jaques-Dalcroze, 1926) 244–52. *Music.* In French. See no. 123 in this volume.

Rhythm should be defined in terms of duration and intensity. Verse is precisely metered, but the rules of prosody are necessarily broken when poems are verbally realized. A precise form of prosodic notation can be developed from musical notation.

3808
as

BROWN, Earle. **Notation und Ausführung Neuer Musik** [Notation and the performance of new music], *Notation neuer Musik* (Mainz: Schott, 1965) 64–86. *Music.* In German. See no. 479 in this volume.

Nontraditional notation must be used for works whose sounds cannot possibly be notated in conventional ways. New techniques have a philosophy in common with the flexibility of pre-1600 notations and performance practices; neither should be forced into a traditional mold. The artistic dynamism of Jackson Pollock is a model for combining the mathematical constraints of Schoenberg and Joseph Schillinger with a spontaneous and individual energy. An English-language version is abstracted as RILM [1986]5146. *(Gene W. Leonardi)*

3809
as

CAPELLEN, Georg. **Reformen auf dem Gebiet der Notenschrift** [Reforms in the area of notation], *Zweiter Musikpädagogischer Kongress: Vorträge und Referate* (Berlin: Klavier-Lehrer, 1904) 158–96. In German. See no. 43 in this volume.

3810
as

CARDINE, Eugène. **Neumes et rythme** [Neumes and rhythm], *Perspectives de la musique sacrée à la lumière de l'encyclique* Musicae sacrae disciplina (Paris: conference, 1959) 264–76. *Music.* In French. See no. 379 in this volume.

Surveys principles of the rhythmic interpretation of neumed chant notation.

3811
as

CASELLA, Alfredo. **Errori (e pretesi errori) di alcune partiture illustri** [Errors (and alleged errors) in some famous scores], *Atti del terzo Congresso internazionale di musica* (Firenze: Le Monnier, 1940) 129–35. In Italian; summaries in French and German. See no. 256 in this volume.

Discusses printing errors in Rossini's *Guillaume Tell*, Debussy's *Prélude à l'après-midi d'un faune*, and Arturo Toscanini's erroneous corrections in Beethoven's ninth symphony. *(Edwin D. Wallace)*

3812
as

CASKEL, Christoph. **Notation für Schlagzeug** [Percussion notation], *Notation neuer Musik* (Mainz: Schott, 1965) 110–16. *Music.* In German. See no. 479 in this volume.

A particular problem in percussion notation for contemporary music arises from the fact that one performer is generally expected to play several different instruments, sometimes in very quick succession or simultaneously.

Solutions in particular by Stockhausen and by Pierre Mariétan are discussed. An English-language version is cited as RILM [1971]3066. *(David Bloom)*

3813
as
CORBIN, Solange. **Valeur et sens de la notation alphabétique, à Jumièges et en Normandie** [The value and meaning of alphabetic notation at Jumièges and in Normandy], *Jumièges: Congrès scientifique du XIII. centenaire* (Rouen: Lecerf, 1955) 913–24. *Illus., bibliog.* In French. See no. 336 in this volume.

A comprehensive list of some 40 MS sources containing alphabetic notation, from the 9th through 13th c. Their provenance shows a link in the transmission of the style between Burgundy on one side and Normandy and England on the other: The crucial figure in the process would have been Guillaume de Volpiano, the abbot of St. Bénigne, Dijon, who was active in monastic reform in Normandy at the turn of the 11th c. *(David Bloom)*

3814
as
DAHLHAUS, Carl. **Notenschrift heute** [Music notation today], *Notation neuer Musik* (Mainz: Schott, 1965) 9–34. *Music.* In German. See no. 479 in this volume.

While traditional Western notation is undoubtedly inadequate for contemporary music, its particular inadequacies can be dealt with; the problem of notation in the very broad sense may be really an evasion of the problem of form, which will become obsolete as the problem of form is addressed. *(David Bloom)*

3815
as
DELALANDE, Dominique. **De quelques renseignements mélodiques à tirer de manuscrits purement neumatiques** [Some melodic information that can be retrieved from purely neumatic manuscripts], *Perspectives de la musique sacrée à la lumière de l'encyclique Musicae sacrae disciplina* (Paris: conference, 1959) 277–83. *Music.* In French. See no. 379 in this volume.

Examples of the melodic interpretation of lineless (*campo aperto*) St. Gallen notation.

3816
as
DELALANDE, Dominique. **L'insuffisance du système d'écriture guidonien, ou l'existence de plusieurs notes mobiles dans le système grégorien** [Inadequacy of the Guidonian system of notation, or, the existence of several movable tones in the Gregorian system], *Atti del [I] Congresso internazionale di musica sacra* (Tournai: Desclée, 1952) 202–06. In French. See no. 303 in this volume.

3817
as
DI SALVO, Bartolomeo. **La notazione paleobizantina e la sua trascrizione** [Paleo-Byzantine notation and its transcription], *Atti del [I] Congresso internazionale di musica sacra* (Tournai: Desclée, 1952) 123–28. In Italian. See no. 303 in this volume.

3818
as
DITTMER, Luther Albert. **The ligatures of the Montpellier manuscript,** *Société Internationale de Musicologie, cinquième congrès/Internationale Gesellschaft für Musikwissenschaft, fünfter Kongreß/International Society for Musical Research, Fifth Congress* (Amsterdam: Vereniging voor Nederlandse Muziekgeschiedenis, 1953) 146–54. See no. 316 in this volume.

A study of the ligatures of the motets in the Montpellier Codex (*F-MO* MS H.196) and their comparison with earlier sources permit us to trace the development of the modal concept of notation into the classical mensural notation of the Franconian period. *(Tsipora Yosselevitch)*

3819
as
DREIMÜLLER, Karl. **Neue Neumenfunde** [New neume finds], *Société Internationale de Musicologie: Premier Congrès Liège—Compte rendu/Internationale Gesellschaft für Musikwissenschaft: Erster Kongress Lüttich—Kongressbericht/International Society for Musical Research: First Congress Liège: Report* (London: Plainsong and Mediaeval Music Society, 1930) 100–01. In German. See no. 178 in this volume.

Describes newly discovered medieval and Renaissance MSS from the former abbey Mönchengladbach, now in the cathedral and parish archives. *(Scott Fruehwald)*

3820
as
FELBER, Erwin. **Die orientalischen Notationen und unsere Notenschriftreform** [Eastern notations and our notation reform], *Beethoven-Zentenarfeier: Internationaler musikhistorischer Kongress* (Wien: Universal, 1927) 317–20. *Charts, diagr.* In German. See no. 142 in this volume.

In expanding the European notational system to make it applicable to a wider range of musics, iconic notation, as with the representation of high versus low pitch by high versus low position on the staff, is to be preferred to arbitrary convention. Traditional Asian notations, especially those from India, suggest ways of making notation both simpler and more precise. *(David Bloom)*

3821
as
GEISLER, Christian. **Neue Notation für Gesangsmusik: Vereinfachte a cappella–Gesangsmethode für Schule und Volk—Eine Lösung des Grundgedanken Chevé's** [New notation for vocal music: A simplified *a cappella* method for school and lay singing—A solution based on Chevé's basic idea], *Bericht über den zweiten Kongress der Internationalen Musikgesellschaft* (Leipzig: Breitkopf & Härtel, 1907) 48–55. *Music.* In German. See no. 53 in this volume.

Introduction to the author's figure notation for sight-singing, based on the Galin-Paris-Chevé method, which had been enthusiastically promoted by by Émile Joseph Maurice Chevé, and fully explained in *Lærbog i a cappella sang* (3rd ed., Copenhagen, 1906). *(David Bloom)*

3822
as
GEISLER, Christian. **Der Schulgesang und die Notationsfrage** [School song and the question of notation], *Haydn-Zentenarfeier* (Leipzig: Breitkopf & Härtel; Wien: Artaria, 1909) 368–70. *Illus., music.* In German. See no. 65 in this volume.

Discusses transposition and simplified notation.

3823
as
HAUBENSTOCK-RAMATI, Roman. **Notation: Material und Form** [Notation: Material and form], *Notation neuer Musik* (Mainz: Schott, 1965) 51–54. *Charts, diagr.* In German. See no. 479 in this volume.

There are two immediate causes for the development of new notations: the discovery of new materials (such as those of electronic music), and the invention of new forms. Classic forms, based on repetition, were static closed forms that required an unambiguous notation; the new open forms and dynamic closed forms (an example is the author's *Mobile für Shakespeare*) lead to notational complications. *(David Bloom)*

3824
as
HELLOUIN, Frédéric. **Simplification de la notation musicale** [Simplification of musical notation], *Congrès international de musique: Ire session—Exposition Universelle de 1900: Compte rendu, rapports, communications* (Paris: conference, 1901) 38–39. In French. See no. 29 in this volume.

Music notation should be simplified to the extent that it can easily be understood by the public at large. Transposition is discussed. A response to no. 3993 in this volume.

3825
as
HERMELINK, Siegfried. **Zur Chiavettenfrage** [The question of chiavette], *Bericht über den internationalen musikwissenschaftlichen Kongreß Wien*

Mozartjahr 1956 (Graz; Köln: Böhlau, 1958) 264–71. *Charts, diagr.* In German. See no. 365 in this volume.

A previously unnoticed passage in Thomas Morley's *A plaine and easie Introduction to practicall musicke* sheds light on the late–18th-c. high-clef or chiavette notation. A more detailed account is provided in the author's *Dispositiones modorum* (Tutzing, 1960). *(David Bloom)*

3826
as
HESBERT, René-Jean. **Groupes neumatiques à signification mélodique** [Neumatic groupings with melodic significance], *Atti del [I] Congresso internazionale di musica sacra* (Tournai: Desclée, 1952) 229–35. In French. See no. 303 in this volume.

3827
as
HOUDARD, Georges-Louis. **La notation neumatique** [Neumatic notation], *Congrès international d'histoire de la musique: Documents, mémoires et vœux* (Solesmes: St. Pierre; Paris: Fischbacher, 1901) 103–15. *Music.* In French. See no. 32 in this volume.

Neumatic notation is of Roman origin and has definite rhythmic indications. This rhythm may be considered "musical" (metric) as opposed to "oratorical" (prosodic). A response by Hugo GAISSER is included.

3828
as
HOUDARD, Georges-Louis. **La notation neumatique considérée dans son sens matériel extérieur** [The physical exterior meaning of neumatic notation], *Congrès international d'histoire de la musique: Documents, mémoires et vœux* (Solesmes: St. Pierre; Paris: Fischbacher, 1901) 116–23. *Music.* In French. See no. 32 in this volume.

Discusses the rhythm and meter of Gregorian chant.

3829
as
HOURLIER, Jacques. **Le domaine de la notation messine** [The territorial reach of Messine (Lorraine) notation], *Atti del [I] Congresso internazionale di musica sacra* (Tournai: Desclée, 1952) 236–39. In French. See no. 303 in this volume.

3830
as
INDY, Vincent d'. **Emploi d'un signe distinctif, accompagnant les clefs de fa et de sol dans les partitions vocales et instrumentales pour les parties s'entendant à l'octave** [Use of a distinctive sign, accompanying the F and G clefs in vocal and instrumental scores, for parts heard at the octave], *Congrès international de musique: Ire session—Exposition Universelle de 1900: Compte rendu, rapports, communications* (Paris: conference, 1901) 42–44. *Charts, diagr.* In French. See no. 29 in this volume.

Either a bar or a small figure eight written below the clef indicates that the notes should be performed an octave lower than written; the same indications above the clef may be used for performance an octave higher.

3831
as
INDY, Vincent d'; BAUDOT, Ernest; DUREAU, Théophile; PARÈS, Gabriel. **Y a-t-il utilité à employer la note réelle dans l'écriture musicale?** [Is it useful to employ real pitches in musical notation?], *Congrès international de musique: Ire session—Exposition Universelle de 1900: Compte rendu, rapports, communications* (Paris: conference, 1901) 44–46. In French. See no. 29 in this volume.

All transposing instruments should henceforth be given music to be performed at the pitches written.

3832
as
KAGEL, Mauricio. **Komposition—Notation—Interpretation** [Composition, notation, interpretation], *Notation neuer Musik* (Mainz: Schott, 1965) 55–63. *Charts, diagr.* In German. See no. 479 in this volume.

Discusses the inadequacy of conventional notation for the author's own compositions (e.g., *Transición II*) and examines developments in the relationships among notation, composition, and performance. *(David Bloom)*

3833
as
KARA, Z.I. **Hē orthē hermēneia kai metagraphiē ton byzantinōn choirigraphōn** [The correct interpretation and transcription of Byzantine musical notation], *Pepragmena tou th' diethnous byzantinologikou synedriou* (Athínai: Typographeion Myrtidē, 1953) II, 140–49. *Illus., music.* In Greek. See no. 327 in this volume.

⟶
KASTNER, Macario Santiago. **Le rôle des tablatures d'orgue au XVIe siècle dans l'avènement du Baroque musical** [The role of 16th-century organ tablatures in the advent of the musical Baroque]. See no. 1356 in this volume.

3834
as
KELLER, Hermann. **Die Bedeutung der Artikulationszeichen in den Handschriften und frühen Drucken Mozarts** [The meaning of the articulation signs in Mozart's manuscripts and early prints], *Bericht über den internationalen musikwissenschaftlichen Kongreß Wien Mozartjahr 1956* (Graz; Köln: Böhlau, 1958) 304. In German. See no. 365 in this volume.

Summary of research on Mozart's use of dot and wedge articulation signs. He distinguished between the two in his autographs, which provide a more reliable guide to his intentions than early prints. *(David Bloom)*

3835
as
KONTARSKY, Aloys. **Notationen für Klavier** [Notations for piano], *Notation neuer Musik* (Mainz: Schott, 1965) 92–109. *Music, charts, diagr.* In German. See no. 479 in this volume.

A survey, from the performer's point of view, of innovative signs for the representation of pitch, duration, dynamics, and tone-color (including extended techniques) in piano notation of recent years. Many composers have developed a kind of private notation, and there are too many alternative notations available for a given action. *(David Bloom)*

3836
as
KREPS, Joseph. **Aux sources de notre écriture musicale européenne: XXe siècle (projections lumineuses)** [On the sources of our European musical writing: 20th century (slide projections)], *Congrès jubilaire* (Brugge: Gruuthuuse, 1925) 226–28. In French. See no. 119 in this volume.

A form of musical notation that appears in MSS from the early Middle Ages involves a vertical staff system; another in use in England, Gaul, and Germany involves *campo aperto* and *literae significativae*. The letters disappear with the appearance of diastematic notation, and therefore cannot be interpreted as indicating rhythm. Different methods used to describe rhythm and length values within music (or the apparent lack of such systems) are discussed. *(Susan Poliniak)*

3837
as
KREPS, Joseph. **Le développement des neumes** [The development of the neumes], *Compte rendu du Ve Congrès international des sciences historiques* (Bruxelles: Weissenbruch, 1923) 366–68. In French. See no. 100 in this volume.

Neumatic notation began in the 9th c. The two styles of this type of notation are Greco-Roman and diastematic. A comprehensive glossary of medieval music is needed. *(David Nussenbaum)*

3838
as
KROHN, Ilmari. **Reform der Taktbezeichnung** [Reform of the barline], *Haydn-Zentenarfeier* (Leipzig: Breitkopf & Härtel; Wien: Artaria, 1909) 386–401. In German. See no. 65 in this volume.

Advocates a notational system that indicates the number of metric feet in each phrase.

3839 KROHN, Ilmari. **Zur Einheitlichkeit der**
as **Notenschlüssel** [The unification of clefs], *Bericht über den zweiten Kongress der Internationalen Musikgesellschaft* (Leipzig: Breitkopf & Härtel, 1907) 55–56. *Music.* In German. See no. 53 in this volume.

Report of a proposal for a notation system using only G clefs for piccolo, treble, alto/tenor, and bass registers, by Axel Törnudd, in an article in *Säveletär* 6 (1906), based on original suggestions by Georg Capellen. Unsigned appended notes discuss remarks by Charles Maclean on Walter Hampden Thelwall's system *"Note for note" musical notation* (London, 1897), in which a seven-line staff eliminates the need for accidental signs; and the congress's resolution on the need for a comprehensive modern edition of medieval music sources. *(David Bloom)*

3840 KROHN, Ilmari. **Zweckmässige Notation von**
as **Psalmen und andern rezitativischen Gesängen** [A functional notation for psalms and other chant in recitation tones], *Bericht über den zweiten Kongress der Internationalen Musikgesellschaft* (Leipzig: Breitkopf & Härtel, 1907) 47–48. *Music.* In German. See no. 53 in this volume.

Introduction to the notation employed in the author's collection of unison psalm settings for use in Finnish-speaking Lutheran church services, *Wallittuja Psalmeja* (Helsinki, 1903). An example is provided of a German-language setting, in the first tone, *Warum toben die Heiden—und die Leute reden so vergeblich. (David Bloom)*

3841 KROYER, Theodor. **Zum Akzidentienproblem**
as **im Ausgang des 16. Jahrhunderts** [On problems of accidentals at the end of the 16th century], *Haydn-Zentenarfeier* (Leipzig: Breitkopf & Härtel; Wien: Artaria, 1909) 112–24. *Music, charts, diagr.* In German. See no. 65 in this volume.

Discusses notational inconsistencies in late–16th-c. music.

3842 LAILY, Paul-Armand. **Difficulté de la notation**
as **Byzantine et projet de la remplacer par une notation occidentale adaptée** [Difficulty of the Byzantine notation and the project of replacing it with an adapted Western notation], *Atti del [I] Congresso internazionale di musica sacra* (Tournai: Desclée, 1952) 108–10. In French. See no. 303 in this volume.

3843 LAUNAY, Denise. **Les rapports de tempo entre**
as **mesures binaires et mesures ternaires dans la musique française (1600-1650)** [The relations in tempo between binary and ternary measures in French music (1600-1650)], *Fontes artis musicae* XII/2-3 (May-Dec 1965) 166–94. *Music.* In French. See no. 499 in this volume.

With the decline of proportional notation and the notion of tactus at the end of the 16th c., the notation of French music entered a period of anarchic disarray; for example, ten different mensuration signs were used to mark ternary rhythms in the first half of the 17th c. An analytic interpretation of each of these signs is proposed, as they relate to the binary signs that commonly accompany them. *(David Bloom)*

3844 LEVI, Leo. **Les neumes, les notations bibliques**
as **et le chant protochrétien** [Neumes, Biblical notations, and proto-Christian chant], *Revue musicale* 239-240 (1957) 147ff. In French. See no. 378 in this volume.

An abridged version of the conference paper is cited as no. 3845 in this volume.

3845 LEVI, Leo. **Les neumes, les notations bibliques**
as **et le chant protochrétien** [Neumes, Biblical notations, and proto-Christian chant], *Perspectives de la musique sacrée à la lumière de l'encyclique Musicae*

sacrae disciplina (Paris: conference, 1959) 329–38. *Transcr.* In French. See no. 379 in this volume.

The relationship between the liturgical music practice of the earliest Christians and that of their Jewish contemporaries as recorded in the Palestinian notation should be studied in the context of a wider enquiry, including the study of Babylonian and Tiberian Masoretic MS traditions and the ethnographic analysis of extant oral traditions; examples are drawn from the author's comparative analysis of chant in Syrian Orthodox (Jacobite rite) and Italian Jewish communities. *(David Bloom)*

3846 LEVY, Kenneth J. **Die slavische Kondakarien-**
as **Notation** [Slavic *kondakar'* notation], *Anfänge der slavischen Musik* (Bratislava: Slovenská Akadémia Vied, 1966) 77–92. In German. See no. 477 in this volume.

The notation of the Russian kondakar' repertoire (collections of kondaky or kontakia) probably stems from that of the Byzantine asmatikon or choirbook, as close analysis of the sources suggests. *(Brian Doherty)*

3847 LIGETI, György. **Kommunikationsmittel oder**
as **Selbstzweck?** [A means of communication or a goal in itself?], *Notation neuer Musik* (Mainz: Schott, 1965) 35–50. *Music.* In German. See no. 479 in this volume.

The representative function of the traditional musical score and the aesthetic function of graphic notation need not exclude each other. In general, however, those new notational systems are to be preferred that grow organically from a traditional system, changed and expanded as needed, at least for instrumental and vocal ensembles; for electronic music there is no reason to use traditional notation. Graphic or partially graphic notations used by Friedrich Cerha, Silvano Bussotti, Earle Brown, Franco Evangelisti, Gottfried Michael Koenig, and Mauricio Kagel are discussed. *(David Bloom)*

3848 LIN, Ehr. **The notation and continuous control**
as **of pitch,** *Journal of the International Folk Music Council* XVI (1964) 107–08. *Charts, diagr.* See no. 463 in this volume.

Proposes a system for notating continuous gradual change of pitch within the possibilities of the five-line staff.

3849 LYON, Gustave. **Utilité d'une numération**
as **logique des sons de l'échelle chromatique qui permette à première vue de se rendre compte de la note dont il s'agit et de l'octave où elle se trouve** [Utility of a logical numeration of the sounds of the chromatic scale that allows one to realize at a glance what the note in question is and in what octave it is found], *Haydn-Zentenarfeier* (Leipzig: Breitkopf & Härtel; Wien: Artaria, 1909) 616–21. *Music, charts, diagr.* In French. See no. 65 in this volume.

3850 MAHILLON, Victor-Charles. **Utilité de**
as **désigner les sons de l'échelle chromatique par des numéros** [The use of indicating the sounds of the chromatic scale by numbers], *Congrès international de musique: Ire session—Exposition Universelle de 1900: Compte rendu, rapports, communications* (Paris: conference, 1901) 39–40. *Charts, diagr.* In French. See no. 29 in this volume.

Every chromatic degree of the nine-and-one-half octaves should be assigned a number, especially for the sake of the accurate construction of instruments.

3851 MALHERBE, Charles. **La graphologie dans les**
as **écritures musicales** [Graphology in musical composition], *Haydn-Zentenarfeier* (Leipzig: Breitkopf & Härtel; Wien: Artaria, 1909) 371–74. In French. See no. 65 in this volume.

Discusses MSS of several composers, with special attention to Mozart.

3852 MARTIN, Frank. **La notation du rythme** [The
as notation of rhythm], *Compte rendu du Ier Congrès du
rythme* (Genève: Institut Jaques-Dalcroze, 1926)
82–91. *Music, charts, diagr.* In French. See no. 123 in
this volume.
A new form of rhythmic notation involves the horizontal stacking of two or
three dots next to notes. Metrical notation should be changed so that
stressed notes that fall on weak beats are written as strong beats (i.e., syncopated notes should be written as down beats).

3853 MENCHACA, Angel. **Nouveau système de no-
as tation musicale** [A new system of musical notation],
*Report of the Fourth Congress of the International Mu-
sical Society* (London: Novello, 1912) 267–78. *Music,
charts, diagr.* In French. See no. 71 in this volume.
Describes a graphic system whereby a nine-octave range can be represented in a relatively small space.

3854 MIES, Paul. **Über ein besonderes Akzent-
as zeichen bei Joh. Brahms** [A particular accent indication in Brahms], *Bericht über den internationalen
musikwissenschaftlichen Kongreß* (Kassel: Bärenreiter,
1963) 215–17. *Music.* In German. See no. 452 in this
volume.
Discusses Brahms's use of the diminuendo sign as an indication of accent.

3855 MÜNZER, Georg. **Zur Notation der Meister-
as singer** [The Meistersingers' notation], *Bericht über
den zweiten Kongress der Internationalen Musikgesellschaft* (Leipzig: Breitkopf & Härtel, 1907)
27–33. *Music.* In German. See no. 53 in this volume.
Reviews principles for the interpretation of rhythmic values and *Koloratur*
in the author's edition of Meistergesang MSS, *Das Singebuch des Adam
Puschmann nebst den Originalmelodien des Michel Behaim und Hans
Sachs* (Leipzig, 1906). *(David Bloom)*

3856 NE'EMAN, Yeḥŵšu'a Leyyb'. **Ṭa'amym
as wezmyrŵt** [Notation of Hebrew accents and songs],
Dẇkan IV (1962) 53. In Hebrew. See no. 436 in this
volume.

3857 NOACK, Friedrich. **Die Tabulaturen der
as hessischen Landesbibliothek zu Darmstadt**
[The tablatures in the Hessische Landesbibliothek in
Darmstadt], *Bericht über den musikwissenschaftlichen
Kongreß in Basel* (Leipzig: Breitkopf & Härtel, 1925)
276–85. *Music.* In German. See no. 102 in this volume.
Two obscure MSS in lute tablature and three in organ tablature are found in
the old Hofbibliothek in Darmstadt. Most of the suites, individual pieces,
and dance movements are anonymous. The scarcity of transcriptions of
other tablatures makes comparison difficult. A thematic catalog of all tablatures is a future musicological project that could be coordinated by the
Fürstliches Institut für Musikwissenschaftliche Forschung in Bückeburg.

3858 PALIKAROVA VERDEIL, Raïna. **Les notations
as musicales employées dans les églises slaves au
IXe siècle** [Musical notations employed in the Slavic
churches in the 9th century], *Atti del [I] Congresso
internazionale di musica sacra* (Tournai: Desclée, 1952)
114–18. In French. See no. 303 in this volume.

3859 PALM, Siegfried. **Zur Notation für Streich-
as instrumente** [Notation for string instruments], *Notation neuer Musik* (Mainz: Schott, 1965) 87–91. *Music.*
In German. See no. 479 in this volume.
Practical notes on the needs of performers of new music, in the use of
accidentals, quarter-tone notation, glissandos, and articulation markings.
Purely graphic scores leaving all decisions to the performer do not enable
the performer to realize the composer's intentions. Certain highly graphic

notations, however, like the time-notation in Earle Brown's *Music for cello
and piano* (1954-55), permit a more precise realization than a conventional
notation would. *(David Bloom)*

3860 PETROVIĆ, Radmila. **The oldest notation of
as folk tunes in Yugoslavia,** *Studia musicologica
Academiae Scientiarum Hungaricae* VII (1965)
109–14. *Illus., bibliog.* See no. 478 in this volume.
A Yugoslavian nobleman's letter from 1555 contains two traditional songs
in mensural notation.

3861 PUJOL VILARRUBÍ, Emili. **Le sens instru-
as mental dans la tablature** [Instrumental meaning in
tablatures], *Congrés de la Societat Internacional de
Musicologia* (Barcelona: Casa de Caritat, 1936). In
French. See no. 224 in this volume.
The conference report provides only a citation. Neither the text nor a summary of the paper was published here.

3862 PUJOL VILARRUBÍ, Emili. **La transcription
as de la tablature pour viuhela d'après la technique de l'instrument** [The transcription of the
tablature for vihuela according to the technique of the
instrument], *Congrés de la Societat Internacional de
Musicologia* (Barcelona: Casa de Caritat, 1936). In
French. See no. 224 in this volume.
The conference report provides only a citation. Neither the text nor a summary of the paper was published here.

3863 REYSSCHOOT, Dorsan van. **De quelques
as réformes dans la notation des partitions
d'orchestre d'édition dite *populaire*** [Some reforms in the notation of orchestral scores in popular edi-
tions], *Report of the Fourth Congress of the International Musical Society* (London: Novello, 1912)
366–69. In French. See no. 71 in this volume.
Discusses various simplifications including clefs and transpositions.

3864 ROUSSEAU, Norbert. **Communication sur la
as notation nonantolienne** [Statement on Nonantolan
notation], *La musique d'église: Compte rendu du
Congrès de musique sacrée* (Tourcoing: Duvivier,
1920) 221–23. In French. See no. 93 in this volume.
Evidence of several notations indicates a single and universal rhythmic tradition, thus justifying Pius X's statement in his motu proprio *Tra le
sollecitudini* (1903) that Gregorian chant possesses the beauty of universal
forms.

3865 RUNGE, Paul. **Über die Notation des Mei-
as stergesanges: Berichtigung und Ergänzung
des Referats auf dem Baseler Kongress 1906**
[On the notation of Meistergesang: Correction and supplement to the report given at the Basel congress of
1906], *Haydn-Zentenarfeier* (Leipzig: Breitkopf &
Härtel; Wien: Artaria, 1909) 84–91. *Music.* In German.
See no. 65 in this volume.
Discusses *D-Mbs* MS Cgm.4999. A supplement to no. 3866 in this volume.

3866 RUNGE, Paul. **Über die Notation des Meister-
as gesangs** [The notation of Meistergesang], *Bericht über
den zweiten Kongress der Internationalen Musikgesellschaft* (Leipzig: Breitkopf & Härtel, 1907) 17–26.
Music. In German. See no. 53 in this volume.
An account of the principles for the interpretation of rhythmic values, ligatures, and ornamentation used in the author's editions of the Colmar MS
(*D-Mbs* MS Cgm.4997) and Donaueschingen MS (*D-KA* MS
Donaueschingen.120) in *Die Sangesweisen der Colmarer Handschrift und
die Liederhandschrift Donaueschingen* (Leipzig, 1896). *(David Bloom)*

3867 SACHS, Curt. **The mystery of the Babylonian**
as **notation,** *Papers read at the International Congress of Musicology* (New York: Music Educators National Conference, 1944) 161–67. *Illus.* See no. 266 in this volume.

Discusses interpretations of an inscription on a clay plaque from ca. 800 B.C.E. (preserved as VAT.9307 in the Vorderasiatisches Museum in Berlin; a fragmentary duplicate exists as K.4175-Sm57 in the British Museum).

⟶ SACHS, Melchior Ernst. **Das temperierte 19-tonsystem und eine dafür passende Schrift** [A system for dividing the octave into 19 tones, with appropriate notation]. See no. 4108 in this volume.

3868 SAINT-SAËNS, Camille. **Communication,**
as *Congrès international d'histoire de la musique: Documents, mémoires et vœux* (Solesmes: St. Pierre; Paris: Fischbacher, 1901) 261–63. In French. See no. 32 in this volume.

Discusses the reform of musical notation, including "precautionary" accidentals, a tenor G-clef, and a new triplet notation.

3869 SANDEN, Heinrich. **Neumen ohne Linien:**
as **Neuen Forschungen** [Lineless neumes: Recent research], *Atti del [I] Congresso internazionale di musica sacra* (Tournai: Desclée, 1952) 259–64. In German. See no. 303 in this volume.

3870 SEEGER, Charles. **An instantaneous music**
as **notator,** *Journal of the International Folk Music Council* III (1951) 103–06. *Music, charts, diagr.* See no. 296 in this volume.

Describes a device that converts electronic pitch signals into graphic notation.

3871 SMITS VAN WAESBERGHE, Joseph. **Die**
as **rheno-mosa-mosellanische Neumenschrift** [The neumatic notation of the Rhine/Meuse/Moselle region], *Bericht über den internationalen musikwissenschaftlichen Kongreß Wien Mozartjahr 1956* (Graz; Köln: Böhlau, 1958) 599–603. *Illus.* In German. See no. 365 in this volume.

Matching the characteristic style of 11th- through 13th-c. church architecture in the area west of the Rhine, between the Meuse and Moselle rivers, was a characteristic style of neumatic notation, mixing the Metz and St. Gallen styles with some original features. It is very frequently used in MS copies of Jean d'Afflighem's treatise, suggesting that there may have been an autograph in this style, and also, unexpectedly, in Finland, in chant MSS in the collections of the Helsingin Yliopiston Kirjasto studied by Toivo Haapanen. An inventory of MSS in the style by provenance is provided. *(David Bloom)*

3872 STÄBLEIN, Bruno. **Die Tegernseer mensurale**
as **Choralschrift aus dem 15. Jahrhundert: Etwas Greifbares zur Rhythmik der mittelalterlichen Monodie** [The Tegernsee mensural chant notation of the 15th century: Something concrete about the rhythm of medieval monophony], *Société Internationale de Musicologie, cinquième congrès/ Internationale Gesellschaft für Musikwissenschaft, fünfter Kongreß/International Society for Musical Research, Fifth Congress* (Amsterdam: Vereniging voor Nederlandse Muziekgeschiedenis, 1953) 377–83. In German. See no. 316 in this volume.

3873 STAIGER, Robert. **Über die Notation des**
as **Meistergesangs** [The notation of Meistergesang],

Bericht über den zweiten Kongress der Internationalen Musikgesellschaft (Leipzig: Breitkopf & Härtel, 1907) 34. In German. See no. 53 in this volume.

Clues to the rhythmic interpretation of Meistersinger notation are found especially in MSS from the mid-16th to early 17th c. The mensural notation of the MS from Strasbourg, *D-Mbs* MS Cgm.4999, is perhaps to be explained by the higher educational level of the Strasbourg Meistersinger circle as compared to that of Nuremberg. *(David Bloom)*

3874 STRUNK, Oliver. **The classification and devel-**
as **opment of the early Byzantine notations,** *Atti del [I] Congresso internazionale di musica sacra* (Tournai: Desclée, 1952) 111–13. See no. 303 in this volume.

3875 THIBAUT, Jean-Baptiste. **Les notations**
as **byzantines** [Byzantine notations], *Congrès international d'histoire de la musique: Documents, mémoires et vœux* (Solesmes: St. Pierre; Paris: Fischbacher, 1901) 86–92. *Illus., charts, diagr.* In French. See no. 32 in this volume.

The earliest MSS date from the 10th and 11th c. and employ *constantinopolitaine* notation. From this, other notations evolved. A synoptic table of various notations, including ecphonetic and hagiopolite, is provided.

3876 THODBERG, Christian. **Chromatic alterations**
as **in the sticherarium,** *Actes du XIIᵉ Congrès d'études Byzantines* (Beograd: Naučno Delo, 1963-1964) II, 607–12. *Illus., music, charts, diagr.* See no. 441 in this volume.

The so-called wrong signatures of Psaltikon MSS of the 13th-14th c.—medial signatures that seem to indicate an unexpected pitch—are too numerous to be regarded as simple mistakes. Always associated with a formula that may be regarded as a transposition, they may represent an accommodation with theorists similar to that of the chromatic alterations in Gregorian chant MSS. *(David Bloom)*

3877 TILLYARD, Henry Julius Wetenhall. **Neumes**
as **byzantins primitifs: Systéme Cioslin (sic)—Un nouveau principe de déchiffrement** [Primitive Byzantine neumes: The Coislin system—A new principle of decoding], *Atti del V Congresso internazionale di studi bizantini* (Roma: Associazione Nazionale per gli Studi Bizantini, 1940) II, 542–43. *Illus.* In French. See no. 233 in this volume.

Two concepts aided in the codification of the notation of Byzantine music: melodies that exist in round notation should previously have existed in primitive notation (and can be compared to such), and the signs from round notation should correspond to the Coislin notation. Several issues and rules regarding diastematic notation and hypostatic signs are discussed. *(Susan Poliniak)*

3878 TIRABASSI, Antonio. **Notation mensurelle**
as [Mensural notation], *Compte rendu du Vᵉ Congrès international des sciences historiques* (Bruxelles: Weissenbruch, 1923) 370–71. In French. See no. 100 in this volume.

Modern triple meter transcriptions of *tempus perfectum* vocal polyphony are erroneous. Transcriptions should be in duple meter. *(David Nussenbaum)*

3879 VAN, Guillaume de. **Les neumes et le chant**
as **grégorien** [Neumes and the Gregorian chant], *Congrés de la Societat Internacional de Musicologia* (Barcelona: Casa de Caritat, 1936). In French. See no. 224 in this volume.

The conference report provides only a citation. Neither the text nor a summary of the paper was published here.

3880 VAZIRI, Ali Naqi. **Notation: Means for the**
as **preservation or destruction of music traditionally not notated,** *The preservation of traditional
forms of the learned and popular music of the Orient and
the Occident/La préservation des formes traditionelles
de la musique savante et populaire dans les pays
d'Orient et d'Occident* (Urbana: Center for Comparative Psycholinguistics, Institute of Communications Research, 1964) 251–57. See no. 443 in this volume.
Pitches that lie between the 12 notes of the Western scale, such as those of
an Iranian dastgâh, can be notated with a system using deliberately vague
indications for "less than a sharp" and "less than a flat". Such a system has
been in use in Iran since the early 1920s. Its vagueness does not destroy the
music, since performers can interpret it precisely. *(Judith Drogichen Meyer)*

3881 WAGNER, Peter. **Wie müssen die Melodien der**
as **Vatikanischen Choralausgabe ausgeführt
werden?** [How must the melodies of the Vatican edition of chant be performed?], *Acta generalis cantus
gregoriani studiosorum conventus, Argentinensis,
16-19 Aug. 1905/Bericht des internationalen
Kongresses für gregorianischen Choralgesang/
Compte rendu du Congrès international de plain-chant
grégorien* (Strassburg: F.-X. Le Roux, 1905) 71–79.
Music. In German. See no. 50 in this volume.
Discusses notational questions in the official Vatican edition of chant commissioned by Pius X in 1904.

3882 WOLF, Johannes, ed. **Notationskunde:**
as **Verhandlungen und Vorträge** [The study of notation: Discussions and lectures], *Bericht über den
zweiten Kongress der Internationalen Musikgesellschaft* (Leipzig: Breitkopf & Härtel, 1907) 16–17. In
German. See no. 53 in this volume.
Summarizes conference talks by Hugo GAISSER on the musical and
graphic foundations of ancient Greek notation and its original meaning,
and the musical and graphic origins and values of late Damascene notation;
and by Antoine DECHEVRENS on the rhythmic interpretation of Gregorian chant. The last is published as *Le rhythme du chant grégorien* in *Voix
de St Gall* 5, 6 (1906).

3883 WOLF, Johannes. **Über den Stand der**
as **Notationskunde** [The state of the study of notation],
*Bericht über den zweiten Kongress der Internationalen
Musikgesellschaft* (Leipzig: Breitkopf & Härtel, 1907)
8–16. In German. See no. 53 in this volume.
Surveys the state of research on ancient Greek, neumatic, and mensural no-
tations, instrumental tablature, and proposals for reformed music notation.
(David Bloom)

3884 WOLF, Johannes. **Ueber Guitarren-Tabula-**
as **turen** [On guitar tablatures], *Report of the Fourth Congress of the International Musical Society* (London:
Novello, 1912) 354. In German. See no. 71 in this
volume.
Summary of a paper discussing notational practices from the 16th to the
18th c.

3885 ZAMPIERI, Giusto. **La notazione della par-**
as **titura d'orchestra secondo il sistema Giordano**
[The notation of orchestral scores according to the
Giordano system], *Haydn-Zentenarfeier* (Leipzig:
Breitkopf & Härtel; Wien: Artaria, 1909) 382–84. *Music.* In Italian. See no. 65 in this volume.
Proposes that all transposing instruments be notated at sounding pitch, and
that the categories of instruments be reduced to two: those that read in treble
clef and those that read in bass clef.

58 Editing

3886 ANGLÈS, Higini. **Der Rhythmus der**
as **monodischen Lyrik des Mittelalters und seine
Probleme** [The rhythm of the medieval monodic lyric
and its problems], *Compte rendu/Kongressbericht/Re-
port* (Basel: Bärenreiter, 1951) 45–50. In German. See
no. 289 in this volume.
Examines the difficulties of establishing a correct rhythmic transcription
for Latin hymns and other liturgical monody (sequences, conductus,
tropes, liturgical drama) and for courtly vernacular song of the
Provençal/French repertoire and the Minnesinger. Principles used by the
author in the preparation of his edition of *La música de las Cantigas de
Santa María* are described. *(David Bloom)*

3887 BENEDETTI-MICHELANGELI, Flavio.
as **Principes d'édition des œuvres de clavier
anciennes** [Principles in the editing of early keyboard
works], *La musique instrumentale de la Renaissance*
(Paris: Centre National de la Recherche Scientifique
[CNRS], 1955) 287–91. *Music.* In French. See no. 333
in this volume.
Fernando Germani's edition of Frescobaldi's *Fiori musicali* and *Toccate*
(Rome, 1936-37) exemplifies the qualities needed to ensure the comprehensibility and authentic performance of the work. An edition should have
a table of ornaments or better ornaments written out as realized; a description of the instrument for which the piece was composed, and suggestions
for adapting the registration of a modern instrument; realizations for rhythmic patterns that are to be performed differently from the way they are
notated; and a general consideration of the different dynamism and diapason
of early instruments. The author's edition of the *Canzon a 4* by Luzzasco
Luzzaschi from Alessandro Raverii's anthology *Canzoni per sonare con
ogni sorte di stromenti* (RISM 1608[24]) is appended. *(Susan Poliniak)*

3888 CARDINE, Eugène. **De l'édition critique du**
as **graduel: Nécessité, avantages, méthode** [On the
critical edition of the gradual: Necessity, advantages,
method], *Atti del [I] Congresso internazionale di
musica sacra* (Tournai: Desclée, 1952) 187–91. In
French. See no. 303 in this volume.
Discusses the project inaugurated in 1948 at the Abbaye de St. Pierre,
Solesmes, for a critical edition of the *Graduale romanum*.

3889 CLERCX-LEJEUNE, Suzanne. **Les accidents**
as **sous-entendus et la transcription en notation
moderne: Introduction** [Implied accidentals and
transcription in modern notation: Introduction], *Les
colloques de Wégimont. II: L'ars nova—Recueil
d'études sur la musique du XIVe siècle* (Paris: Belles
Lettres, 1959) 167–95. In French. See no. 351 in this
volume.
Two as yet unresolved problems in the preparation of modern editions of
14th-c. music are its reduction into modern rhythmic values, with the deployment of measure bars, and the supplying of implied accidentals. Correct placement of the accidentals depends on considerations related to the
rules for singing, the rules of counterpoint, and the rules of musica ficta.
(David Bloom)

3890 COPPOLA, Piero. **Rievocazioni di un maestro**
as **girovago: Dal vecchio repertorio a Maurizio
Ravel** [Recollections of a wandering conductor: From
the old repertoire to Maurice Ravel], *Atti del terzo
Congresso internazionale di musica* (Firenze: Le
Monnier, 1940) 143–47. In Italian; summaries in
French and German. See no. 256 in this volume.
Discusses inaccuracies and contradictions in different editions of orches-
tral works by Verdi, Rossini, Bellini, Haydn, Händel, Bach, and Mozart.
Ravel's scores are applauded for their meticulous attention to detail.
(Edwin D. Wallace)

3891
as
DAYAN, Leonzio. **La publication des *Hymnes de l'église arménienne*** [The publication of the *Hymnes de l'église arménienne*], *Perspectives de la musique sacrée à la lumière de l'encyclique* Musicae sacrae disciplina (Paris: conference, 1959) 324–25. In French. See no. 379 in this volume.

Discusses the author's work in the preparation of a Western-notation edition of the Armenian *sharakan* chant repertoire (*Sharakan hayastaneayts ekeghetswoy/Hymnes de l'église arménienne*, Venice, 1954-76).

3892
as
DORFMÜLLER, Kurt. **La tablature de luth allemande et les problèmes d'édition** [German lute tablature and editing problems], *Le luth et sa musique* (Paris: Centre National de la Recherche Scientifique [CNRS], 1958) 245–57. *Music, charts, diagr.* In French. See no. 377 in this volume.

The German tablature, invented for strictly pedagogical purposes in the mid-15th c. and poorly adapted to polyphony, was already inadequate by the 16th c., and there is no reason to preserve it in the preparation of modern editions. It should be permitted to use a variety of modern notation systems, as long as the transcription conforms with the requirements of the instrument on the one hand and clearly shows the polyphonic idea of a piece on the other. Some practical rules are proposed. *(David Bloom)*

3893
as
FEDER, Georg. **Arbeitsgemeinschaft: Editionsprobleme des späten 18. Jahrhunderts** [Working group: Editorial problems with reference to the late 18th century], *Bericht über den siebenten internationalen musikwissenschaftlichen Kongress* (Kassel: Bärenreiter, 1959) 349–54. *Music.* In German. See no. 390 in this volume.

Summarizes a workshop discussion on issues of the critical Gesamtausgabe, with attention to the treatment of variant readings and substantially different published sources for a work, ornamentation, and phrase marking. Participants included Hans ALBRECHT, Eva BADURA-SKODA, Hans ENGEL, Hellmut FEDERHOFER, Karl GEIRINGER, Jens Peter LARSEN (chair), Jan LARUE, Paul MIES, Eduard REESER, Wolfgang REHM, Ernst Fritz SCHMID, Rudolf STEGLICH, Hubert UNVERRICHT, Helmut WIRTH, and Ewald ZIMMERMANN.

(David Bloom)

3894
as
FICKER, Rudolf von. **Probleme der Editionstechnik mittelalterlicher Musik** [Editing technique and medieval music], *Compte rendu/Kongressbericht/Report* (Basel: Bärenreiter, 1951) 109–11. In German. See no. 289 in this volume.

Modern score layout often obscures the structure of medieval music; this can be rectified with the use of divisional dot markings, as in the transcriptions from the Trent Codices published in the *Denkmäler der Tonkunst in Österreich*, vol. 76. *(David Bloom)*

3895
as
FROIDEBISE, Pierre. **Sur quelques éditions de musique d'orgue ancienne** [Some editions of early organ music], *La musique instrumentale de la Renaissance* (Paris: Centre National de la Recherche Scientifique [CNRS], 1955) 277–86. *Music, charts, diagr.* In French. See no. 333 in this volume.

The revival of interest in the qualities of Renaissance and Baroque organs and authentic performance practice in early organ music are traced through the consideration of *Archives des maîtres de l'orgue des XVIᵉ, XVIIᵉ et XVIIIᵉ siècles* (eds. Alexandre Guilmant and André Pirro, Paris, 1898-1914); *Choralvorspiele alter Meister* (ed. Karl Straube, Leipzig, 1907); the Bach edition of Albert Schweitzer and Charles-Marie Widor (New York, 1912-14); *Frühmeister der deutschen Orgelkunst* (ed. Hans Joachim Moser, Leipzig, 1930); *Anthologia pro organo* (ed. Flor Peeters, Brussels, 1949); Macario Santiago Kastner's edition of works by Antonio de Cabezón (Mainz, 1954); *Altenglische Orgelmusik* (ed. Denis Stevens, Kassel, 1953); Pierre Pidoux's edition of the canzoni and ricercars of Andrea Gabrieli (Kassel, 1943-52); and Giacomo Benvenuti's edition of works by Marco Antonio Cavazzoni, Giacomo Fogliano, Julio Segni, *et al.* (Milan, 1941). *(Susan Poliniak)*

3896
as
GAJARD, Joseph. **Du rôle des principales familles de manuscrits dans la restauration de la leçon grégorienne authentique** [The role of the principal manuscript families in the restoration of the authentic Gregorian reading], *Atti del [I] Congresso internazionale di musica sacra* (Tournai: Desclée, 1952) 207–11. In French. See no. 303 in this volume.

3897
as
GEORGIADES, Thrasybulos Georges. **Zur Lasso-Gesamtausgabe** [The complete Lassus edition], *Bericht über den internationalen musikwissenschaftlichen Kongreß Wien Mozartjahr 1956* (Graz; Köln: Böhlau, 1958) 216–19. In German. See no. 365 in this volume.

Discusses the ongoing Breitkopf & Härtel edition of Lassus's works, under the auspices of the Bayerische Akademie der Wissenschaften, with remarks on the desiderata for modern-notation editions of 16th-c. vocal polyphony in general. *(David Bloom)*

3898
as
GÜNTHER, Ursula. **Round table der Union Académie Internationale über die geplante Ausgabe *Corpus des troubadours*** [Roundtable of the Union Académie Internationale on the planned edition of a *Corpus des troubadours*], *Bericht über den neunten internationalen Kongreß* (Kassel: Bärenreiter, 1964-1966) II, 269–72. In German. See no. 491 in this volume.

The project, initiated in 1961 under the direction of Ramon Aramon i Serra, was to produce a philological edition of all extant troubadour texts; the troubadour melodies were to be included in the edition, and the roundtable discussion focused on the undecided question of formats for these, and the desirability of complementing rather than competing with Friedrich Gennrich's editions in the *Summa musica Medii Aevi* series or other ongoing projects. Participants in the discussion included Willi APEL, Heinrich HUSMANN, Raffaello MONTEROSSO, Bruno STÄBLEIN, Oliver STRUNK, and Giuseppe VECCHI. *(David Bloom)*

3899
as
HEDLEY, Arthur. **Some observations on the autograph sources of Chopin's works,** *The book of the first international musicological congress devoted to the works of Frederick Chopin* (Warszawa: Państwowe Wydawnictwo Naukowe, 1963) 474–77. See no. 425 in this volume.

Problems in establishing a definitive text for Chopin's works include errors in his own autographs of a single work—he hated copying—and errors made by his copyist Julian Fontana in publishers' fair copies, which have sometimes been misidentified as the composer's own autographs. *(Susan Poliniak)*

3900
as
HESBERT, René-Jean. **La restitution critique des mélodies grégoriennes et les manuscrits de Klosterneuberg** [The critical restoration of Gregorian melodies and the manuscripts of Klosterneuberg], *Zweiter internationaler Kongress für katholische Kirchenmusik: Zu Ehren des Heiligen Papstes Pius X* (Wien: conference, 1955) 124–26. In French. See no. 339 in this volume.

Summary version of a conference paper, in which examples were drawn from the chant repertoire of the Augustiner-Chorherrenstift, Klosterneuburg. Discusses scientific principles of neumatic restitution (the establishment of the correct grouping of the neumes), melodic restitution, and the problems of clefs and transpositions. *(David Bloom)*

3901
as
JACQUOT, Jean. **Objectifs et plan de travail** [Goals and work program], *Le luth et sa musique* (Paris: Centre National de la Recherche Scientifique [CNRS], 1958) 13–18. In French. See no. 377 in this volume.

Discusses a program of research on the lute music of the Renaissance, with results to be published in the *Choeur des Muses* series of the Centre National de la Recherche Scientifique, Paris, with particular reference to the

Corpus des luthistes français project of a collection of critical editions of French lute music. *(David Bloom)*

3902
as

JACQUOT, Jean. **Premiers résultats acquis— Perspectives d'avenir** [First results obtained—Perspectives of the future], *Le luth et sa musique* (Paris: Centre National de la Recherche Scientifique [CNRS], 1958) 311–42. *Illus., facs., charts, diagr.* In French. See no. 377 in this volume.

Discusses the possibilities of and recommendations for the large-scale international cataloguing and publication of early lute music in tablature and transcription. Remarks on issues of tablature and transcription by Richard de MORCOURT and by Daniel HEARTZ are included, as well as a table of ornamentation and other transcription symbols based on proposals by Michel Podolsky in the paper abstracted as no. 3914 in this volume. *(David Bloom)*

3903
as

JEPPESEN, Knud. **Die Textlegung in der Chansonmusik des späteren 15. Jahrhunderts** [Text underlay in the chanson of the late 15th century], *Beethoven-Zentenarfeier: Internationaler musikhistorischer Kongress* (Wien: Universal, 1927) 155–57. In German. See no. 142 in this volume.

Outlines some principles for the modern edition of works of the period, with regard to determining whether a particular voice is meant to be performed instrumentally or vocally, and the underlaying of text. A more extended version is published in *Juhlakirja Ilmari Krohn'ille* (Ilmari Krohn Festschrift, Helsinki, 1927). *(David Bloom)*

3904
as

KOCZIRZ, Adolf. **Über die Notwendigkeit eines einheitlichen, wissenschaftlichen und instrumentaltechnischen Forderungen entsprechenden Systems in der Übertragung von Lautentabulaturen** [The need for a unified system that meets scientific and organological requirements for lute tablature transcription], *Haydn-Zentenarfeier* (Leipzig: Breitkopf & Härtel; Wien: Artaria, 1909) 220–23. *Music.* In German. See no. 65 in this volume.

Challenges Oscar Chilesotti's mode of single-staff transcription, specifically mentioning his 1890 publication, *Da un codice del cinquecento*. The methodology was faulty because the original tuning of the lute was G2-C3-F3-A3-D4-G4, and Chilesotti raised it by a major sixth to E3-A3-D4-F#4-B4-E5, which is, with the exception of the major third in the middle, the tuning of the guitar. Chilesotti's work was not a true transcription, but rather an arrangement for guitar. Further questions are raised regarding work of the "pseudolutenist" Heinrich Scherrer in Munich, who re-transcribed Chilesotti's work.

3905
as

LESURE, François. **Les éditions scientifiques de musique polyphonique** [Scholarly editions of polyphonic music], *Perspectives de la musique sacrée à la lumière de l'encyclique* Musicae sacrae disciplina (Paris: conference, 1959) 431–36. In French. See no. 379 in this volume.

Surveys progress since the 1920s in the preparation of critical editions, concentrating on religious polyphony from Dufay to the end of the 16th c.

3906
as

MAXTON, Willy. **Können die *Denkmäler Deutscher Tonkunst* uns heute noch als Quellen zweiter Ordnung dienen?** [Can the *Denkmäler Deutscher Tonkunst* still serve as secondary sources today?], *Bericht über den internationalen musikwissenschaftlichen Kongreß* (Kassel: Bärenreiter, 1963) 295–98. In German. See no. 452 in this volume.

The edition of Johann Theile's *Passio nach dem Heiligen Evangelisten Matthäo*, Denkmäler deutscher Tonkunst XVII, 1904, contains no fewer than 333 errors, none of which has been corrected in the so-called critically revised version of 1958. A genuine revision is proposed for the entire series. *(David Bloom)*

3907
as

MAYER-REINACH, Albert. **Vorschläge zur Herausgabe von Vokalmusik des XV.-XVII. Jahrhunderts** [Proposals for editing vocal music of the 15th-17th centuries], *Report of the Fourth Congress of the International Musical Society* (London: Novello, 1912) 365. In German. See no. 71 in this volume.

Summary of a paper.

3908
as

MIES, Paul. **Skizzen, Fassungen und Ausgabentypen/Skici, verze a typy edic** [Sketches, versions, and types of editions], *Leoš Janáček a soudobá hudba* (Praha: Panton, 1963) 220–25. In German and Czech. See no. 389 in this volume.

Methods of editing and publishing should be based on a clear distinction between sketches and drafts, on the one hand, and finished versions approved by the composer, on the other. The problem of compatibility between practical and critical editions requires particular attention. *(Jadranka Važanová)*

3909
as

MOE, Lawrence H. **Le problème des barres de mesure: Étude sur la transcription de la musique de danse des tablatures de luth du XVIe siècle** [The problem of barlines: A study in the transcription of dance music in lute tablatures of the 16th century], *Le luth et sa musique* (Paris: Centre National de la Recherche Scientifique [CNRS], 1958) 259–76. *Music.* In French. See no. 377 in this volume.

The ideal of a music edition reproducing the print or MS original as faithfully as possible, without any deviations at all, is not fully realizable for early music; for 16th-c. lute music, in the absence of a continuous performance tradition, the modern editor is obliged to provide an interpretive transcription that expresses the music's inherent form more clearly than the original tablature did, as in the case of barlines, which tablature did not apply coherently. Dance music, with its regular meter, provides good examples for the establishment of principles for revised barrings. *(David Bloom)*

3910
as

MÜLLER, Hermann. **Zur Editionstechnik bei Kirchenmusikwerken der klassischen Vokalperiode** [On the editing technique for vocal church music of the Classic period], *Bericht über den I. musikwissenschaftlichen Kongreß der Deutschen Musikgesellschaft in Leipzig* (Wiesbaden: Breitkopf & Härtel, 1926) 322. In German. See no. 120 in this volume.

A summary of an article published in *Musica divina* II (Wien, Universal-Edition, 1925), *Musica sacra* VIII-IX (Regensburg, Pustet, 1925), and in *Cäcilienvereinsorgan* II/57 (München-Gladbach, Volksvereinsverlag, 1925). *(William Renwick)*

3911
as

NEWMAN, Joel. **Problems of editing and publishing old music,** *Report of the Eighth Congress of the International Musicological Society. II: Reports* (Kassel: Bärenreiter, 1962) 101–04. See no. 440 in this volume.

A report on a discussion by Konrad AMELN, Eva BADURA-SKODA, Nathan BRODER, Max van CREVEL, Hans T. DAVID, Kurt GUDEWILL, Jean JACQUOT, Alexander Hyatt KING, Ralph KIRKPATRICK, Arthur MENDEL, Dragan PLAMENAC, Gilbert REANEY, Denis STEVENS, and Karl VÖTTERLE on the paper by Stevens abstracted as no. 3922 in this volume.

3912
as

OPIEŃSKI, Henryk. **Le rythme dans l'exécution de la musique vocale** [Rhythm in the performance of vocal music], *Compte rendu du Ier Congrès du rythme* (Genève: Institut Jaques-Dalcroze, 1926) 26–32. *Music.* In French. See no. 123 in this volume.

Modern editions of early polyphony should include bar lines only if they serve to indicate rhythmic groupings.

3913
as

PFANNHAUSER, Karl. **Die Mozart-Gesamtausgabe in Österreich** [The complete edition of Mozart's works in Austria], *Bericht über den internatio-*

nalen musikwissenschaftlichen Kongreß Wien Mozartjahr 1956 (Graz; Köln: Böhlau, 1958) 462–70. In German. See no. 365 in this volume.

Traces the Austrian involvement in the preparation of *Wolfgang Amadeus Mozart's Werke: Kritisch durchgesehene Gesammtausgabe* (Leipzig: Breitkopf & Härtel, 1877-). The early programmatic ideas of Leopold Alexander Zellner and Ferdinand Hiller in the centenary year 1856 and the contributions of Joseph Joachim, Johann Ritter von Herbeck, and Ludwig von Köchel are surveyed. *(David Bloom)*

3914 PODOLSKI, Michel. **À la recherche d'une**
as **méthode de transciption formelle des tablatures de luth** [In search of a formal transcription method for lute tablatures], *Le luth et sa musique* (Paris: Centre National de la Recherche Scientifique [CNRS], 1958) 277–84. *Music*. In French. See no. 377 in this volume.

Formal transcription of tablatures, that is, an untransposed transcription, must be written on two staffs, in the form of a piano score, which makes it difficult to read. In all other respects—in particular that of the ease of reading figured bass parts—it is preferable to the competing systems of modernized tablatures, octave transcriptions, or guitar transcriptions. Information in the tablature that is not present in a piano transcription (ornaments, arpeggiation, notes inégales, etc.) can be added either by running the tablature underneath it or by the use of a standardized set of technical symbols. *(David Bloom)*

3915 REIMANN, Margarete. **Zur Editionstechnik**
as **von Musik des 17. Jahrhunderts** [The technique of editing 17th-century music], *Norddeutsche und nordeuropäische Musik* (Kassel; New York: Bärenreiter, 1965) 83–91. In German. See no. 467 in this volume.

Currently insoluble problems of attribution in the Baroque repertoire, especially in distinguishing textual corruptions from authentic revisions and parody elements in works extant in multiple versions, make the chronological/geographical *Denkmal* edition more useful than the composer-based *Gesamtausgabe*. *(David Bloom)*

3916 SCHMID, Hans. **Die Kölner Handschrift der**
as ***Musica enchiriadis*** [The Cologne manuscript of the *Musica enchiriadis*], *Bericht über den siebenten internationalen musikwissenschaftlichen Kongress* (Kassel: Bärenreiter, 1959) 262–64. In German. See no. 390 in this volume.

The Cologne MS of *Musica enchiriadis* (*D-KNa* MS W 331) is of the same branch in the MS tradition as the Valenciennes MS (*F-VAL* MS 337), of comparable date (early to mid-10th c.), and much less corrupt. The earliest branch is that represented by a fragment in Düsseldorf (*D-DÜmb* MS H3), which can be definitively dated to the 9th c. A Bamberg codex (*D-BAs* MS HS 12) whose text correponds precisely to this fragment is also notable for the correctness of its musical examples, and probably represents, except for its lacunae, the oldest and best text. *(David Bloom)*

3917 SCHMIDT-GÖRG, Joseph. **Die besonderen**
as **Voraussetzungen zu einer kritischen Gesamtausgabe der Werke Ludwig van Beethovens** [Particular prerequisites for a complete critical edition of Ludwig van Beethoven's works], *Bericht über den internationalen musikwissenschaftlichen Kongreß Wien Mozartjahr 1956* (Graz; Köln: Böhlau, 1958) 548–50. In German. See no. 365 in this volume.

Brief remarks on editorial criteria for the project of a new edition by the Beethoven-Archiv, Bonn, to be published by Henle.

3918 SCHNERICH, Alfred. **Die textlichen Versehen**
as **in den Messen Josef Haydns und deren Korrektur** [Textual errors in the Masses of Joseph Haydn and their correction], *Haydn-Zentenarfeier* (Leipzig: Breitkopf & Härtel; Wien: Artaria, 1909) 542–44. In German. See no. 65 in this volume.

3919 SEIFFERT, Max. **Neuausgabe der englischen**
as **Virginalmusik** [New editions of English virginal music], *Report of the Fourth Congress of the International Musical Society* (London: Novello, 1912) 369. In German. See no. 71 in this volume.

Summary of a paper.

3920 SOURIS, André. **Tablature et syntax: Re-**
as **marques sur le problème de la transcription des tablatures de luth** [Tablature and syntax: Remarks on the problem of transcribing lute tablatures], *Le luth et sa musique* (Paris: Centre National de la Recherche Scientifique [CNRS], 1958) 285–95. *Music*. In French. See no. 377 in this volume.

Editors should begin not so much with the graphic image of the tablature as with its realization in sound. The internal relationships that constitute the syntax of lute music, which early lutenists were forced to imagine for themselves, can be captured in modern notation—in particular those related to the duration of notes inadequately specified in tablature, and their curtailment by damping. A parallel transcription and tablature of a set of three allemandes preceded by a *recherche* by François Dufaut, from the 1631 *Tablature de luth de differens autheurs* published by Pierre Ballard, is provided. *(David Bloom)*

3921 SPIRO, Friedrich. **Ueber eine Revision der Bee-**
as **thoven-Gesamtausgabe** [On a revision of the complete works of Beethoven], *Report of the Fourth Congress of the International Musical Society* (London: Novello, 1912) 372–76. In German. See no. 71 in this volume.

Inaccuracies in previous editions are listed.

3922 STEVENS, Denis. **Problems of editing and**
as **publishing old music,** *Report of the Eighth Congress of the International Musicological Society. I: Papers* (Kassel: Bärenreiter, 1961) 150–58. *Music*. See no. 439 in this volume.

There is no agreement on standards for the editing of early music, and hence effectively no standards at all. Some of the resulting problems could be solved if publishers and editors paid sufficient attention to performers' needs. *(Miryam Moscovitz)*

3923 THIBAULT DE CHAMBURE, Geneviève *et al.*
as **Discussion: Problèmes d'édition** [Discussion: Editing problems], *Le luth et sa musique* (Paris: Centre National de la Recherche Scientifique [CNRS], 1958) 303–09. In French. See no. 377 in this volume.

A roundtable discussion of issues pertaining to the preparation of modern editions of lute music. Participants included Thomas E. BINKLEY, Thurston DART, Ian HARWOOD, Jean JACQUOT, Frits NOSKE, Michel PODOLSKI, Diana POULTON, and Frederick William STERNFELD. *(David Bloom)*

3924 VERCHALY, André. **La tablature dans les**
as **recueils français pour chant et luth (1603-1643)** [Tablature in French collections for voice and lute (1603-1643)], *Le luth et sa musique* (Paris: Centre National de la Recherche Scientifique [CNRS], 1958) 155–69. *Music*. In French. See no. 377 in this volume.

Discusses transcription issues encountered in the preparation of the author's edition of a collection of *Airs de cour pour voix et luth (1603-43)* (Paris, 1961). *(David Bloom)*

3925 VIDERØ, Finn. **Dietrich Buxtehude,** *Orgelbewe-*
as *gung und Historismus: Tagungsberichte. III* (Berlin: Merseburger, 1958) 97. In German. See no. 346 in this volume.

Summarizes a discussion of the lack of authentic sources of Buxtehude's organ and other keyboard works, and the many errors of the standard editions. The complete version, published in *Musik und Kirche* 5, 1955, provides exemplification of how these errors can be corrected. *(David Bloom)*

3926 WEISE, Dagmar. **Zur Gesamtausgabe der Briefe**
as **Beethovens durch das Beethoven-Archiv Bonn**
[The complete edition of Beethoven's correspondence by the Beethoven-Archiv, Bonn], *Bericht über den internationalen musikwissenschaftlichen Kongreß Wien Mozartjahr 1956* (Graz; Köln: Böhlau, 1958) 673–77. In German. See no. 365 in this volume.
The editorial principles of a projected complete edition of Beethoven's letters, with remarks on the inadequacies of Ludwig Nohl's edition (1870) are discussed. *(David Bloom)*

3927 WELLESZ, Egon. **Les *Monumenta musicae***
as ***Byzantinae*** [The *Monumenta musicae Byzantinae*], *Revue musicale* 239-240 (1957) 137–41. In French. See no. 378 in this volume.
An abridged version of a conference paper. The original English-language version and a French-language translation are abstracted as no. 3928 in this volume.

3928 WELLESZ, Egon. **The work done by the edi-**
as **tors of *Monumenta musicae Byzantinae*/Les *Monumenta musicae Byzantinae*: Le travail des éditeurs,** *Perspectives de la musique sacrée à la lumière de l'encyclique* Musicae sacrae disciplina (Paris: conference, 1959) 294–304. *Music.* In English and French. See no. 379 in this volume.
An account of the history of the project, from 1932 to 1957, with particular attention to its documentation of the continual influence of Byzantine chant on Western chant during the 6th-9th c. A summary is cited as no. 3927 in this volume. *(Warren A. Bebbington)*

3929 WUSTMANN, Rudolf. **Über Bearbeitung**
as **älterer und ausländischer Gesangstexte** [On the editing of older and foreign song texts], *Haydn-Zentenarfeier* (Leipzig: Breitkopf & Härtel; Wien: Artaria, 1909) 136–37. In German. See no. 65 in this volume.
Includes the subsequent panel discussion.

Anton de Beer plays the 31-tone organ designed by Adriaan Daniël Fokker
(see nos. 3939, 3959, 4073, 4074, and 4075).
Reproduced with permission of the Huygens-Fokker Foundation.

THEORY, ANALYSIS, AND COMPOSITION

60 Theory, general

3930
as

BABBITT, Milton. **Past and present concepts of the nature and limits of music,** *Report of the Eighth Congress of the International Musicological Society. I: Papers* (Kassel: Bärenreiter, 1961) 398–403. See no. 439 in this volume.

Current theory is fundamentally inadequate in stating its empirical domain and choosing its parameters. The limits of coherent musical structure are in no sense to be inferred from the properties of an overtone series. Theories based on the concept of similarity classes of simultaneities have recently begun to prove valuable and reasonable. The introduction of chance methods into composition and the success of 12-tone composition are discussed.

3931
as

BERNET KEMPERS, Karel Philippus. **Versuch eines vertieften Einblicks in den musikalischen Organismus** [Towards a deeper view into the musical organism], *Bericht über den internationalen musikwissenschaftlichen Kongreß* (Kassel: Bärenreiter, 1963) 271–72. In German. See no. 452 in this volume.

Discusses the consequences to analysis of treating the musical work as analogous to a biological organism. Assuming that the motive is the smallest meaningful unit, its constituents may be *talea, color,* and *ordo* as defined and illustrated in the treatise *Ars cantus mensurabilis mensurata per modos iuris* (CoussemakerS, iii, Anon. 5). *(David Bloom)*

3932
as

BRENN, Franz. **Das Wesensgefüge der Musik** [The essential structure of music], *Compte rendu/Kongressbericht/Report* (Basel: Bärenreiter, 1951) 75–80. In German. See no. 289 in this volume.

Discusses prerequisites and preliminary ideas for a structural model of music in terms of its essential distinguishing features and internal and external organization. *(David Bloom)*

3933
as

BROCKHOFF, Maria Elisabeth. **Zur Methodik der musikwissenschaftlichen Analyse** [The methodology of musicological analysis], *Compte rendu/Kongressbericht/Report* (Basel: Bärenreiter, 1951) 80–82. In German. See no. 289 in this volume.

Preliminary ideas on the notion of an objective, exact musical analysis and its potential utility in the context of a broader subjective synthesis are outlined. *(David Bloom)*

3934
as

CHAILLEY, Jacques. **Philologie musicale: Principes et premiers résultats** [The philology of music: Principles and first results], *Bericht über den siebenten internationalen musikwissenschaftlichen Kongress* (Kassel: Bärenreiter, 1959) 78–79. In French. See no. 390 in this volume.

Résonance, the principle of repose or stability, is a fundamental of music. If theories of music do not reflect deductions that can be made concerning this phenomenon, they must be false. Other principles associated with *résonance* include *attraction, tolérance, accoutumance,* and *rationalisation.* The way *résonance* relates to these other principles is discussed. *(Carl Skoggard)*

3935
as

CHERBULIEZ, Antoine-Élisée. **Über die Anwendung der Sieversschen Theorien auf die musikalische Interpretation** [The application of Sievers's theories to musical interpretation], *Bericht über den musikwissenschaftlichen Kongreß in Basel* (Leipzig: Breitkopf & Härtel, 1925) 110–17. In German. See no. 102 in this volume.

Eduard Sievers's theory that every spiritual event is related to a physical action (which he also applied to the phonetic analysis of speech) is applied to text and rhythm in songs, and to the structure and character of melodies. *(Sylvia Eversole)*

3936
as

COLLAER, Paul. **Structures et domaines expressifs des systèmes musicaux contemporains** [Structures and expressive domains of contemporary musical systems], *Bericht über den neunten internationalen Kongreß* (Kassel: Bärenreiter, 1964-1966) I, 62–67. In French. See no. 491 in this volume.

The diatonic system (represented by Prokof'ev, Poulenc, Satie, Stravinsky, Hindemith, and Milhaud) is the expression of the conception of a happy and harmoniously balanced world held by the privileged class of the older agricultural society; the chromatic system (Webern, Berg, Schoenberg, Dallapiccola, and Boulez) expresses the sense of discouragement and impotence felt after the two world wars. The fluctuating or variable scale of electronic music expresses the feelings of a generation brought up in the age of industrial technology and urbanism; it is susceptible of beauty, like the systems that preceded it, but not yet in possession of its own dialectic. *(David Bloom)*

3937
as

CUKKERMAN, Viktor Abramovič; BALTER, G. **Die Komplexanalyse der musikalischen Werke und ihre Methodik** [The complex-analysis of musical works and its methodology], *Intonation und Gestalt in der Musik: Beiträge und Abhandlungen der Musikwissenschaftler sozialistischer Länder* (Moskva: Muzyka, 1963) 283–347. *Music.* In German. See no. 471 in this volume.

Defines and illustrates a method of "total analysis" or complex-analysis on the basis of particular examples: the theme of Beethoven's 32 variations in C minor WoO 80; Chopin's prelude op. 28, no.1; the beginning of the adagio movement in Rahmaninov's piano concerto no. 2, op. 18; and the secondary theme of the opening of Šostakovič's symphony no. 5. Extracted from *Analyz muzykal'nyh proizvedenii* by Lev Abramovič Mazel' and the author (Moscow, 1968). *(David Bloom)*

3938
as

DAHLHAUS, Carl. **Der Tonalitätsbegriff in der neuen Musik** [The concept of tonality in new music], *Bericht über den internationalen musikwissenschaftlichen Kongreß* (Kassel: Bärenreiter, 1963) 370–74. In German. See no. 452 in this volume.

Difficulties in using the term "tonality" with reference to new music can be avoided if the analyst understands tonality as a historical rather than natural phenomenon. Illustrations are drawn from two works in which 12-tone technique coexists with evidently tonal structure, Stravinsky's *Canticum sacrum* and Bartók's violin concerto no. 2. *(David Bloom)*

3939
as

DRAEGER, Hans-Heinz. **Analysis and synthesis of musical structures on the basis of information theory,** *Bericht über den neunten internationalen Kongreß* (Kassel: Bärenreiter, 1964-1966) 261–68. *Charts, diagr.* In English and German. See no. 491 in this volume.

Report of a roundtable discussion of quantitative methods in musical analysis, from the standpoint of the semiotic approach to information theory. It was agreed that methods need to be refined and that the investigation must move beyond syntactics to semantics and pragmatics. Participants included

Gerhard ALBERSHEIM, Mariangela DONÀ, Hans-Heinz DRAEGER, Adriaan Daniël FOKKER, Volker RAHLFS, Jaroslav VOLEK, and Jack M. WATSON, and Fritz WINCKEL. *(David Bloom)*

3940
as
EIBNER, Franz. **Mißverständnisse bei der Auseinandersetzung mit dem Werk Heinrich Schenkers** [Misconceptions in approaching Heinrich Schenker's theories], *Musikerziehung: Zeitschrift der Musikerzieher Österreichs* special issue (1953) 58–60. In German. See no. 317 in this volume.

3941
as
ERLANGER, François Rodolphe d'. **Rapport** [Report], *Recueil des travaux du Congrès de musique arabe* (Al-Qāhirah: Boulac, 1934) 176–398. *Music, charts, diagr., transcr.* In Arabic. See no. 196 in this volume.

Offers a preliminary account of a comprehensive classification of the formal properties of melody, rhythm, and genre in Arab music. A full version is published as vols. 5-6 of *La musique arabe* (Paris: 1930-59). *(David Bloom)*

⟶
FERGUSON, Donald N. **The relation of theory to musicology.** See no. 875 in this volume.

3942
as
FLEISCHER, Herbert. **Discutendo il problema linguistico** [Discussing the linguistic problem], *Atti del quinto Congresso di musica* (Firenze: Barbèra, 1948) 156–57. In Italian. See no. 285 in this volume.

Contemporary musical language and composers' individual means of expression constantly interact. Twelve-tone techniques are genuinely speculative in nature and are historically of secondary importance. Composers, motivated by a need for self-expression, can be successful within a traditional, well-defined framework. In using a new, unorthodox language they must remember that it reflects their musical personality; it cannot be treated as a theoretical abstraction for the initiated and the erudite. Their contributions to the language are essential, but they must not be symbols of a metaphysical, extramusical world. *(Channan Willner)*

3943
as
GERBER, Rudolf. **Freiheit und Gesetz in der älteren und neueren Musik** [Freedom and law in older and newer music], *Musikerziehung: Zeitschrift der Musikerzieher Österreichs* special issue (1953) 12–15. In German. See no. 317 in this volume.

3944
as
GERSTENBERG, Walter. **Generalbasslehre und Kompositionstechnik in Neidts *Musikalischer Handleitung*** [Basso continuo theory and compositional technique in Neidt's *Musikalischer Handleitung*], *Bericht über den Internationalen musikwissenschaftlichen Kongress* (Kassel: Bärenreiter, 1954) 152–55. *Music.* In German. See no. 319 in this volume.

The principle of variation lies at the heart of Friedrich Erhard Niedt's *Musikalischer Handleitung* . The second of its two parts was first issued in 1706 and then reissued in 1721 by Johann Mattheson, having been virtually rewritten by him. This part is concerned with varying the continuo (Andreas Werckmeister had stressed that the bass should not be varied) and offers a wealth of examples as to how the varying is to be done. It marks an important stage in the late Baroque theory of composition. With variation being applied throughout, to the bass as much as to the upper voices, coherence is to be insured through the use of themes or recurring motives in all the parts. Neidt crowns his demonstration of continuo composition by presenting a series of suite movements all of which are elaborated over the same bass. *(Carl Skoggard)*

3945
as
GRABNER, Hermann. **Die Werkbetrachtung als Zugang zur zeitgenössischen Musik** [Examination of compositions as access to contemporary music], *Musikerziehung: Zeitschrift der Musikerzieher*

Österreichs special issue (1953) 119–22. In German. See no. 317 in this volume.

3946
as
GRIMAUD, Yvette. **Les polysystèmes des musiques de tradition orale peuvent-ils être intégrés à la résonance?** [Can the polysystems of the musics of oral tradition be integrated into overtone theory?], *La résonance dans les échelles musicales* (Paris: Centre National de la Recherche Scientifique [CNRS], 1963) 237–48. *Music.* In French; summaries in English and German. See no. 420 in this volume.

Many structural characteristics in orally transmitted music can be discussed in terms of the overtone series, including center of gravity, particular beats as the basis of certain polyphonies, and development of an initial melodic-rhythmic cell.

3947
as
HUNOLD, G. **Zur Situation der Musiktheorie** [On the situation of music theory], *Musikerziehung: Zeitschrift der Musikerzieher Österreichs* special issue (1953) 83–85. In German. See no. 317 in this volume.

3948
as
HUSMANN, Heinrich. **Die Stellung der Romantik in der Weltgeschichte der Musik** [The place of Romanticism in universal music history], *The book of the first international musicological congress devoted to the works of Frederick Chopin* (Warszawa: Państwowe Wydawnictwo Naukowe, 1963) 53–62. In German. See no. 425 in this volume.

In any given period of local music history, either melodic organization, and tendency toward the use of tempered scales, or harmonic organization, with a corresponding tendency away from temperament, dominates over the other. From this dialectical point of view, the Romantic period is part of a longer development in Western music in which melodic organization has come to dominate, beginning with the Renaissance and continuing to atonality. *(David Bloom)*

3949
as
KNOPOFF, Leon. **Some technological advances in musical analysis,** *Studia musicologica Academiae Scientiarum Hungaricae* VII (1965) 301–08. *Illus.* See no. 478 in this volume.

Three new technological aids to analysis are described: (1) a device for notating pieces played on several percussion instruments, (2) a device to record the overtone characteristics of an instrument producing a sustained tone, and (3) a qualitative scheme for determining the rhythmic content and periodicity of a given piece, based on the autocorrelation method. *(Daniel Horn)*

3950
as
KROHN, Ilmari. **Ueber die Methode der musikalischen Analyse** [On the method of musical analysis], *Report of the Fourth Congress of the International Musical Society* (London: Novello, 1912) 250–58. *Charts, diagr.* In German. See no. 71 in this volume.

Discusses meter, harmony, thematic development, rhythm, and the value of objective analysis vs. programmatic speculation.

3951
as
ŁOBACZEWSKA, Stefania. **Die Analyse des musikalischen Kunstwerkes als Problem der Musikwissenschaft** [The analysis of the musical work of art as a problem for musicology], *Bericht über den internationalen musikwissenschaftlichen Kongreß Wien Mozartjahr 1956* (Graz; Köln: Böhlau, 1958) 373–77. In German. See no. 365 in this volume.

Proposes a materialist approach to analysis, treating the musical work as a subjective reflection of objective reality, with particular discussion of the concepts of content, form, methodology, and the importance to analysis of cutural, socioeconomic, and biographical contexts. *(David Bloom)*

3952
as
MESQUITA, Raoul Ferraz de. **L'"intuition scientifique" dans les élaborations d'"art pur"**

manifestée dans les fugues de Bach [Scientific intuition in the elaborations of pure art manifested in the fugues of Bach], *Deuxième congrès international d'esthétique et de Science de l'art* (Paris: Librairie Félix Alcan, 1937) II, 243–47. *Illus.* In French. See no. 249 in this volume.

The transcendent work of musical genius has a logical character that is also found in scientific work, as is most clearly seen in the work of what Étienne Souriau has called "pure art", such as fugues by Bach whose musical structure is directly analogous to the mathematical function of the sinusoidal curve and its derivates. *(David Bloom)*

3953 NADEL, Siegfried. **Sur la structure des**
as **systèmes de gammes et le problème du cycle dans la musique primitive** [On the scale structure and the cycle in primitive music], *Art populaire: Travaux artistiques et scientifiques du Ier Congrès international des arts populaires* (Paris: Duchartre, 1931) 102–04. In French. See no. 152 in this volume.

In the most primitive musics no series of independent pitches is perceived; in the more developed systems of most traditional music scale degrees exist, but only on the basis of pitch. The system of Western art music experiences each pitch in terms of its tension vis-à-vis other pitches. Musical forms may be classified into two main groups: the open or infinite form of primitive music, and the cyclic form of more advanced musics. Precyclic forms are simple projections of the artist's interior life; in cyclic form, the creator achieves a conscious objectification of the work as an independent entity. A summary of the first section is cited as no. 4096 in this volume; a summary of the second section is cited as no. 4273 in this volume.

(David Bloom)

3954 NETTL, Bruno. **Some linguistic approaches to**
as **musical analysis,** *Journal of the International Folk Music Council* X (1958) 37–41. *Charts, diagr.* See no. 371 in this volume.

Methods borrowed from the field of linguistics offer a promising suppliment to standard analytic approaches, particularly for the study of non-Western musics. *(James R. Cowdery)*

3955 NEUMANN, Friedrich. **Die Zeitgestalt als**
as **Grundbegriff der musikalischen Rhythmik** [Time-gestalt as the fundamental principle of musical rhythmics], *Bericht über den internationalen musikwissenschaftlichen Kongreß* (Kassel: Bärenreiter, 1963) 268–70. *Charts, diagr.* In German. See no. 452 in this volume.

From the smallest ornamentation to the broadest formal parameters, the musical artwork is pervaded by time in a gestalt sense; the particular interval becomes a musical event only in the context of a temporal gestalt, and the whole tonal system, understood precisely, is identical to its temporal-rhythmic manifestation. Time-gestalt is the common element through which three currently separate disciplines—harmony, counterpoint, and the study of form—might some day be reunited. *(David Bloom)*

3956 SIOHAN, Robert. **Un micro-organisme sonore**
as [A sonic microorganism], *Proceedings of the Third International Congress on Aesthetics/Actes du troisiéme Congrès international d'esthétique/Atti del III Congresso internazionale di estetica* (Torino: Edizioni della Rivista di Estetica, 1957) 647–50. In French. See no. 363 in this volume.

Proposes the treatment of the interval between two sounds as the fundamental unit of musical structure, vertical and horizontal.

3957 SOURIS, André. **Problèmes d'analyse** [Problems
as of analysis], *La musique instrumentale de la Renaissance* (Paris: Centre National de la Recherche Scientifique [CNRS], 1955) 347–57. *Music.* In French. See no. 333 in this volume.

An open, integrative method of analysis for Renaissance music, one which considers its incipient tonality and chordal structure without neglecting modality and polyphonic movement, enables a clearer understanding of the work's broad character as well as practical conclusions on performance questions such as that of tempo. Examples are taken from a homorhythmic part-song of the mid-16th c. by Jacob Meiland (*Hertzlich tut mich erfrauen*) and William Byrd's pavane *The earle of Salisbury*. *(David Bloom)*

3958 SYCHRA, Antonín. **Musikwissenschaft und**
as **neue Methode der wissenschaflichen Analyse** [Musicology and new methods of scientific analysis]. Trans. by G. BALTER and W. BEYER, *Intonation und Gestalt in der Musik: Beiträge und Abhandlungen der Musikwissenschaftler sozialistischer Länder* (Moskva: Muzyka, 1963) 10–37. In German. See no. 471 in this volume.

Marxist musicology has found it difficult to bridge the gap between sociohistorical conditions and sources of inspiration on one hand, and musical form on the other. A conceptual framework for accomplishing this is provided by a combination of the concept of genre as understood from the Marxist perspective and Asaf'ev's concept of intonation as the minimal complete unit of meaningful form; traditional document-oriented historical study and statistically-based analysis are essential parts of the methodology. Expands on the discussion cited as no. 5609 in this volume. *(David Bloom)*

3959 TREITLER, Leo. **Symposium: Structures and**
as **expressive contents of contemporary musical systems,** *Bericht über den neunten internationalen Kongreß* (Kassel: Bärenreiter, 1964-1966) II, 110–17. See no. 491 in this volume.

Report of discussion of the paper by Paul COLLAER abstracted as no. 3936 in this volume. The participants included Collaer, Milton BABBITT, Adriaan Daniël FOKKER, Karl Heinz FÜSSL, Alexander GOEHR, and Eric SALZMANN. *(David Bloom)*

3960 VILLETARD, Henri. **Odoranne de Sens et son**
as **œuvre musicale** [Odorannus de Sens and his musical oeuvre], *Comptes rendus, rapports et vœux du Congrès parisien et régional de chant liturgique et de musique d'église* (Paris: Schola Cantorum, 1912) 61–67. In French. See no. 75 in this volume.

3961 VOLEK, Jaroslav. **Živelná dialektika a její**
as **klady i nedostatky v teoretických názorech Leoše Janáčka** [Essential dialectics, its pros and cons in Janáček's theoretical views], *Leoš Janáček a soudobá hudba* (Praha: Panton, 1963) 352–60. In Czech; summaries in Russian and German. See no. 389 in this volume.

The usefulness of Janáček's *Úplná nauka o harmonii* (A complete harmony manual) (1920) is compromised by problems of terminology and the lack of exact distinctions among rhythmic-metric, melodic, and harmonic phenomena, in spite of positive achievements such as the account of psychological relations between tones. Janáček's categories of *spletna*—the synthesis of actual perception, feeling and psychological after-effect of the sound—and *dovozování* (inference)—an expectation of the following tone given by the direction of melodic and harmonic movement—are analyzed. *(editors)*

3962 WAELTNER, Ernst Ludwig. **Die *Musica**
as ***disciplina* des Aurelianus Reomensis** [The *Musica disciplina* of Aurelian of Réôme], *Bericht über den siebenten internationalen musikwissenschaftlichen Kongress* (Kassel: Bärenreiter, 1959) 293–95. In German. See no. 390 in this volume.

Summarizes the 9th-c. treatise and its historical significance, particularly in relation to the anonymous *Musica enchiriadis*.

3963 YEKTA, Rauf. **Commission des Modes, des**
as **Rythmes et de la Composition** [The Commission
on Modes, Rhythms, and Composition], *Recueil des
travaux du Congrès de musique arabe* (Al-Qāhirah:
Boulac, 1934) 131–65. In French. See no. 196 in this
volume.

At the Congress on Arab Music (Mu'tamar al-Mūsīká al-'Arabiyyah) in
Cairo (1932), the commission was given the responsibility of establishing
comprehensive standard inventories of modes (maqāmāt), rhythmic units,
and compositional genres for the geographical subdivisions of the Arab
world. The discussions are summarized, and minutes are provided for a selection of the meetings. The results are listed in schematic form in the papers abstracted as no. 2582, 5312, 3941, 3982, 4043, and 4042 in this volume. *(David Bloom)*

3964 ZAMBIASI, Giulio. **Sullo svolgimento**
as **storico-critico dei principii e criteri seguiti nel
dare base scientifica alla musica** [On the historical-critical development of the principles and criteria
following the given scientific basis of music], *Atti del
Congresso internazionale di scienze storiche. VIII: Atti
della sezione IV: Storia dell'arte musicale e
drammatica* (Roma: R. Accademia dei Lincei, 1905)
27–42. In Italian. See no. 42 in this volume.

Presents a general outline of the history of music theory stressing the superiority of enharmonic theory. The notion that melodic pitches are determined by the nature of the harmony is considered.

61 Rhythm, meter, and tempo

3965 ANSERMET, Ernest. **Les structures du rythme**
as [The structures of rhythm], *Deuxième Congrès international du rythme et de la rythmique* (Genève: Institut
Jaques-Dalcroze, 1966) 156–66. *Music.* In French. See
no. 502 in this volume.

Discusses physiological aspects of rhythm, and analyzes examples from
Mozart, Stravinsky, and Debussy.

3966 BABBITT, Milton. **The synthesis, perception,
as and specification of musical time,** *Journal of the
International Folk Music Council* XVI (1964) 92–95.
See no. 463 in this volume.

The experience of composing and realizing music for the RCA Electronic
Music Synthesizer, using punched paper tape as the input control, moti-
vates a rethinking of the nature of sound events and musical structure and
the role of temporal duration. Our understanding of the correspondence between input specification and and perceived output in time-dependent phenomena in general turns out to be critically limited. *(David Bloom)*

⟶ BÆRISWYL, J. **La gymnastique rythmique et
l'école primaire** [Rhythmic gymnastics and the primary school]. See no. 4678 in this volume.

3967 BAUD-BOVY, Samuel. **Sur le rythme de
as quelques chansons de l'île de Crète** [The rhythm
of some songs of the island of Crete], *Atti del Congresso
internazionale di musiche popolari mediterranee e del
Convegno dei bibliotecari musicali* (Palermo: De
Magistris succ. V. Bellotti, 1959) 53–55. *Port.* In
French. See no. 332 in this volume.

A recent ethnomusicological field expedition to Crete sought evidence that
the cretic meter of classical antiquity (long-short-long) was an authentically
Cretan rhythm, which might still be extant on the island in the form of a 5/8
measure. Support was found instead for Brăiloiu's concept of the syllabic
giusto, of which the examples of 5/8 meter seemed to be merely a special
case. *(David Bloom)*

3968 BAUDOT, Ernest. **Utilité d'un appareil
as enregistreur des mouvements des œuvres musicales** [The use of a device for registering the tempi of
musical works], *Congrès international de musique: Ire
session—Exposition Universelle de 1900: Compte
rendu, rapports, communications* (Paris: conference,
1901) 35–38. In French. See no. 29 in this volume.

Registering the exact tempo of a performance will aid the conductor, and
will assure that compositions will always be performed precisely at the
tempo indicated by the composer. A response to no. 3993 in this volume.

3969 BENGTSSON, Ingmar. **Über Korrelationen
as zwischen Durationsvariable und Rhythmuserlebnis** [Correlations between variables of duration and
the perception of rhythm], *Bericht über den internationalen musikwissenschaftlichen Kongreß* (Kassel:
Bärenreiter, 1963) 276–79. In German. See no. 452 in
this volume.

Melodic and harmonic changes have a strong influence on the listener's experience of rhythmic groupings, conditioning the perception of accent.
Sound spectrography data show that perceived rhythmic regularity may not
correspond to the acoustic facts. *(David Bloom)*

3970 BEWERUNGE, Heinrich. **The metrical cursus
as in the antiphon melodies of the Mass,** *Report of
the Fourth Congress of the International Musical Society* (London: Novello, 1912) 54–55. See no. 71 in this
volume.

Summary of a paper. Investigates the antiphon melodies of the Mass for
traces of the metrical cursus found in the prayers of the Leonine and Gelasian
Sacramentaries. Full versions are published in *Irish theological quarterly*,
July 1911 (English) and *Cäcilienvereinsorgan*, July 1911 (German).

3971 BOEPPLE, Paul. **Theoretisches und Prak-
as tisches zur Rythmik der neuesten Musik** [The
theory and practice of rhythm in the newest music],
*Bericht über den musikwissenschaftlichen Kongreß in
Basel* (Leipzig: Breitkopf & Härtel, 1925) 80–87. *Music.* In German. See no. 102 in this volume.

Complex meters and polymeters in 20th-c. music pose unnecessary difficulties due to the traditional notation of time signatures. Music containing
these common rhythmic problems must be studied to understand how
note-grouping relates to the musical phrase. Time signatures must be altered to show various note values, and tempo changes must include
note-value equivalents. *(Sylvia Eversole)*

3972 BOVET, Joseph. **La liberté relative du rythme
as dans le chant grégorien** [The relative freedom of
rhythm in Gregorian chant], *Compte rendu du Ier
Congrès du rythme* (Genève: Institut Jaques-Dalcroze,
1926) 10–14. *Music.* In French. See no. 123 in this
volume.

Though most groupings are either binary or ternary, other rhythmic patterns exist. Proper syllabification of chant text must not be constricted by
repeated rhythmic formulas.

3973 BRĂILOIU, Constantin. **Le rythme enfantin:
as Notions liminaires** [Children's rhythm: Preliminary
notions], *Les colloques de Wégimont. [I: Ethnomusicologie I]* (Bruxelles: Elsevier, 1956) 64–96. *Charts,
diagr., transcr.* In French. See no. 340 in this volume.

Children's rhythm is a particular kind of isochrony, not limited to but characteristic of children's vocal music of an extremely wide segment of the
world's cultures, including almost all of Europe, the Kabyles and Tuaregs
of North Africa, native peoples of Senegal, Benin, and Sudan, indigenous
Taiwanese, Inuit, and so on. Its essential structure is analyzed, with a full
range of examples, as that of a rhythmic series with a value of 8 and a rigorous symmetry akin to that of dance; the question of how it imposes itself on
such a wide typological range of languages is addressed. *(David Bloom)*

3974 BRENN, Franz. **Ockeghems spiritueller**
as **Rhythmus** [Ockeghem's spiritual rhythm], *Bericht über den siebenten internationalen musikwissenschaftlichen Kongress* (Kassel: Bärenreiter, 1959) 73–74. In German. See no. 390 in this volume.

The metrical organization of Ockeghem's music is responsible for its powerful impact on listeners. It suggests multiple perspectives on time; these perspectives engage in a dialogue which ultimately produces the experience of transparency and timelessness. *(Carl Skoggard)*

3975 BRINER, Andres. **Wandlungen des Zeitemp-**
as **findens im Harmoniebewusstsein** [Shifting temporal sensibility in harmonic consciousness], *Bericht über den siebenten internationalen musikwissenschaftlichen Kongress* (Kassel: Bärenreiter, 1959) 74. In German. See no. 390 in this volume.

A rather consistent trend is traced from antiquity through the Romantic era, in which time as subjectively experienced continual change takes the place of a polar dichotomy between eternity and the present. Romantic harmony's connection with a thoroughly subjective sense of time can be demonstrated by taking a succession of characteristic Romantic harmonies and placing them in the regular metrical framework of the Mozart era, which still reflects something of the older objective time-sense. The result will make no musical sense. *(Carl Skoggard)*

3976 CANAT DE CHIZY. **Régularisation des indica-**
as **tions et appareils métronomiques** [Regularization of metronomic indications and devices], *Congrès international de musique: Ire session—Exposition Universelle de 1900: Compte rendu, rapports, communications* (Paris: conference, 1901) 31–33. In French. See no. 29 in this volume.

Audio metronomes are superior to visual ones. The state should regulate the construction of metronomes.

3977 CARRAZ, Pierre. **L'accent et l'ictus dans la**
as **métrique latine** [Accent and ictus in Latin metrics], *Atti del [II] Congresso internazionale di musica sacra* (Tournai: Desclée, 1952) 192–95. In French. See no. 303 in this volume.

Latin prosody has a direct bearing on the correct rhythmic interpretation of Gregorian chant.

3978 CAZEAUX, Isabelle. **Le rythme dans la**
as **monodie lyrique médiévale** [Rhythm in medieval lyric monody], *Report of the Eighth Congress of the International Musicological Society. II: Reports* (Kassel: Bärenreiter, 1962) 43–47. In French. See no. 440 in this volume.

A report on a discussion by Higini ANGLÈS, Jacques CHAILLEY, Luther A. DITTMER, Heinrich HUSMANN, Walter SALMEN, Joseph SMITS VAN WAESBERGHE, and Rembert WEAKLAND of the paper by Anglès abstracted as no. 3803 in this volume.

3979 CHERBULIEZ, Antoine-Élisée. **Polyrythmique**
as **exotique** [Exotic polyrhythm], *Compte rendu du Ier Congrès du rythme* (Genève: Institut Jaques-Dalcroze, 1926) 71–75. In French. See no. 123 in this volume.

Music of primitive peoples is closely related to dance and pantomime. The rhythmic foundations of African and Asian music are either horizontal polyrhythm or paralinear polyrhythm.

3980 CHERBULIEZ, Antoine-Élisée. **Le rythme**
as **critère de l'attitude individuelle et collective** [Rhythm as criterion of the individual and collective attitude], *Journal of the International Folk Music Council* IV (1952) 9–12. In French. See no. 306 in this volume.

The concept of collective rhythm and its connection, through dance, to national musical styles is examined.

3981 CHERBULIEZ, Antoine-Élisée. **L'unité du**
as **temps et sa division: Problème psychologique fondamental du rythme musical** [The unified beat and its divisions: A fundamental psychological problem of musical rhythm], *Compte rendu du Ier Congrès du rythme* (Genève: Institut Jaques-Dalcroze, 1926) 33–38. *Music, charts, diagr.* In French. See no. 123 in this volume.

Rhythm may be defined as variations on a uniform beat. Keeping a uniform beat involves a mental act which is easiest for the performer when the beat resembles the heartbeat.

3982 Commission des Modes, des Rythmes, et de la
as Composition. **Communications sur les rythmes** [Communications on rhythms], *Recueil des travaux du Congrès de musique arabe* (Al-Qāhirah: Boulac, 1934) 399–528. *Transcr.* In French. See no. 196 in this volume.

At the Congress on Arab Music (Mu'tamar al Mūsīqá al-'Arabiyyah), Cairo 1932, standard repertoires of rhythmic units were proposed by the conference's Commission on Modes, Rhythms, and Composition (see no. 3963 in this volume). Transcriptions, without commentary, of 20 simple and compound rhythms for the music of Egypt, 30 for Syria (particularly Aleppo), and a total of 111 for Iraq (particularly Baghdad), Tunisia, Morocco, and Algeria, are included. Sample melodies are given to illustrate the application of the Egyptian and Syrian rhythms.

3983 D'ANGELI, Andrea. **Novità, varietà, necessità**
as **del ritmo** [Novelty, variety, and necessity of rhythm], *Haydn-Zentenarfeier* (Leipzig: Breitkopf & Härtel; Wien: Artaria, 1909) 384–86. In Italian. See no. 65 in this volume.

Provides a historical overview.

3984 DAVID, Lucien. **L'accent d'intensité et le geste**
as **dans l'expression rhythmique de la mélodie grégorienne** [The accent of intensity and gesture in the rhythmic expression of Gregorian melody], *Compte rendu du Ier Congrès du rythme* (Genève: Institut Jaques-Dalcroze, 1926) 15–20. *Music.* In French. See no. 123 in this volume.

Intensity is a function of dynamics and pitch, and is the essence of chant rhythm. Rhythmic considerations demand from the conductor a wide range of physical gestures.

3985 DENSMORE, Frances. **Rhythm in the music of**
as **the American Indian,** *Annaes do XX congresso internacional de americanistas* (Rio de Janeiro: Imprensa Nacional, 1924) 85–89. See no. 99 in this volume.

The distinctive rhythm of Native American music plays a major role, as medicine men associate rhythm with magic. Rhythm is unmeasured, but rhythmic units may be transcribed. Some tribes perform songs with rhythmic accompaniments that are syncopated with the vocal rhythm. *(David Nussenbaum)*

3986 EINSTEIN, Alfred. **Der Tempo-Wechsel im**
as **italienischen Madrigal** [Tempo changes in the Italian madrigal], *Congrés de la Societat Internacional de Musicologia* (Barcelona: Casa de Caritat, 1936). In German. See no. 224 in this volume.

The conference report provides only a citation. Neither the text nor a summary of the paper was published here.

3987 EMMANUEL, Maurice. **Le rythme d'Euripide**
as **à Debussy** [Rhythm from Euripides to Debussy], *Compte rendu du Ier Congrès du rythme* (Genève: Institut Jaques-Dalcroze, 1926) 103–46. In French. See no. 123 in this volume.

The evolution of rhythm is tied to the development of language. Debussy's contribution to the emancipation of rhythm is examined.

3988 ESTREICHER, Zygmunt. **Le rythme des Peuls**
as **Bororo** [The rhythm of the Bororro Fulße people], *Les colloques de Wégimont. IV: Ethnomusicologie III* (Paris: Belles Lettres, 1964) 185–228. *Transcr.* In French. See no. 401 in this volume.
Discusses the diversity of rhythmic patterns in the music of the Bororro, a group of nomadic Fulfulde speakers in Niger.

3989 FEIL, Arnold. **Zur Rhythmik Schuberts** [Schu-
as bert's rhythmics], *Bericht über den internationalen musikwissenschaftlichen Kongreß* (Kassel: Bärenreiter, 1963) 198–200. *Music.* In German. See no. 452 in this volume.
Discusses the dancelike character in the rhythmic structure of Schubert's music, with particular reference to the third movement of the octet D.803.

3990 FELLINGER, Imogen. **Zum Problem der**
as **Zeitmasse in Brahms' Musik** [The problem of tempo in Brahms's music], *Bericht über den internationalen musikwissenschaftlichen Kongreß* (Kassel: Bärenreiter, 1963) 219–22. *Music.* In German. See no. 452 in this volume.
Practically alone among his contemporaries, Brahms generally rejected metronome markings; his tempo indications are, however, carefully thought through and meant to be unambiguous. *(David Bloom)*

3991 FIRFOV, Živko. **Les caractères métriques dans**
as **la musique populaire macédonienne** [Metric characters in Macedonian traditional music], *Journal of the International Folk Music Council* IV (1952) 49–53. *Transcr.* In French. See no. 306 in this volume.
Offers a survey and classification of the metric units of measured (mostly dance) music, with discussion of their possible Indian origins and of the complex rhythmic collaboration between virtuoso drummer and dancer. The metric groups cannot be analyzed into arsis-thesis pairs, providing evidence that this is not a universal category. *(David Bloom)*

3992 FRAISSE, Paul. **La structure temporelle des**
as **mouvements volontaires rythmés** [The temporal structure of voluntary rhythmic movements], *Onzième Congrès international de psychologie: Rapports et comptes rendus* (Agen: Imprimerie Moderne, 1938) 51–56. In French. See no. 250 in this volume.
Describes the results of various experiments on the creation, perception, transmission, and interpretation of rhythm, with special attention to intervals (i.e., of time) and duration. The confusion or misassociation between accentuation and temporal relationships is discussed. *(Susan Poliniak)*

3993 FRÉMONT, Alphonse. **Régularisation des indi-**
as **cations métronomiques** [Regularization of metronomic indications], *Congrès international de musique: Ire session—Exposition Universelle de 1900: Compte rendu, rapports, communications* (Paris: conference, 1901) 34–35. *Charts, diagr.* In French. See no. 29 in this volume.
Proposes a universal scale of tempo indications of 20 degrees, from Grave (36 beats per minute) to Très rapide (240 beats per minute). A response is abstracted as no. 3968 in this volume.

3994 GERSTENBERG, Walter. **Grundfragen der**
as **Rhythmusforschung** [Basic questions in the study of rhythm], *Bericht über den siebenten internationalen musikwissenschaftlichen Kongress* (Kassel: Bärenreiter, 1959) 113–18. In German. See no. 390 in this volume.
A basic quantitative, quadrivial measuring of musical time is fundamental to Western music. A qualitative marking, by means of accentuation or dramatization, sometimes comes to the fore, however. (The absoluteness of the quantitative system disappeared with the loosening of the mensural system.) The accentual concept of rhythm—related to the idea of music as a language of feeling, of the heart—is clearly articulated by Johann Nikolaus

Forkel in the first volume of his *Allgemeine Geschichte der Musik* (1788). In the 20th c., motoric rhythm has succeeded the highly variable and subjective time sense of musical Romanticism. *(Carl Skoggard)*

3995 GIESE, Fritz. **Körperrhythmus in Leben und**
as **Kunst der Völker** [Body rhythm in the life and art of peoples], *Compte rendu du Ier Congrès du rythme* (Genève: Institut Jaques-Dalcroze, 1926) 350–72. In German. See no. 123 in this volume.

3996 GRASERN, Siegfried von. **Das Wesen des**
as **Rhythmus** [The nature of rhythm], *Compte rendu du Ier Congrès du rythme* (Genève: Institut Jaques-Dalcroze, 1926) 373–75. In German. See no. 123 in this volume.
Describes rhythm as the expression of movement.

3997 HECKMANN, Harald. **Influence de la musique**
as **instrumentale du XVIe siècle sur la rythmique moderne du XVIIe** [The influence of 16th-century instrumental music on the modern rhythm of the 17th century], *La musique instrumentale de la Renaissance* (Paris: Centre National de la Recherche Scientifique [CNRS], 1955) 339–45. *Music.* In French. See no. 333 in this volume.
The regular recurring accent and parallel periods of modern music did not exist in the theory or vocal music of the 16th c., but did in instrumental dance music, as outlined in Thoinot Arbeau's *Orchésographie* (1588) and illustrated with dance music by Claude Gervaise, in contrast to vocal works of Obrecht and Heinrich Finck. Dance music appears to be the source of the theory of rhythm in René Descartes's *Compendium musicae* (1618) and the general change in musical style as illustrated by successive rewritings of the Finck melody by Johannes Werlin (1646) and Robert Eitner (1876). *(David Bloom)*

3998 HEINITZ, Wilhelm. **Pulsationsprobleme in**
as **Mozartscher Musik** [Pulse problems in Mozart's music], *Bericht über den internationalen musikwissenschaftlichen Kongreß Wien Mozartjahr 1956* (Graz; Köln: Böhlau, 1958) 261–63. In German. See no. 365 in this volume.
Pulsations, defined as perceived stress on individual notes, provide a homogeneous biological analysis of a composer's style. A comparative analysis of Mozart's and Süssmayr's pulses can be used to identify the latter's contributions to the *Requiem*, K.626. *(David Bloom)*

3999 HÉLOUIN, Frédéric. **Histoire du métronome**
as **en France** [The history of the metronome in France], *Congrès international d'histoire de la musique: Documents, mémoires et vœux* (Solesmes: St. Pierre; Paris: Fischbacher, 1901) 264–69. In French. See no. 32 in this volume.
The government should not standardize metronomes because inventors are still in the midst of altering and perfecting existing models.

4000 HŁAWICZKA, Karol. **Eigentümliche Merk-**
as **male Chopins Rhythmik** [Characteristic features of Chopin's rhythm], *The book of the first international musicological congress devoted to the works of Frederick Chopin* (Warszawa: Państwowe Wydawnictwo Naukowe, 1963) 185–95. *Music.* In German. See no. 425 in this volume.
Sources of inspiration for Chopin's typical rhythms include traditional Polish dance, the French heritage of his father Nicolas Chopin, and the influence of Bach's keyboard writing. *(David Bloom)*

4001 HÖWELER, Casper. **Zur internationalen Uni-**
as **formität der Begriffe *Metrum* und *Rhythmus*** [Regarding the international uniformity of the terms *me-*

ter and *rhythm*], *Bericht über den Internationalen musikwissenschaftlichen Kongress* (Kassel: Bärenreiter, 1954) 47–50. In German. See no. 319 in this volume.

Presents a theory of rhythm and meter based on the distinction between qualitative and quantitative meter. In performance the musician shades both the timing and accentuation of notes. Passages of well-known music are cited to illustrate how the qualitative and quantitative aspects of rhythm, if observed, interact and yield musicality. *(Carl Skoggard)*

4002
as

HROVATIN, Radoslav. **Metrični kriteriji za sistematiko jugoslavenskih ljudskih melodij** [Metric criteria for the systematization of Yugoslavian traditional melodies], *Treći kongres folklorista Jugoslavije* (Cetinje: Udruženje Folklorista Crne Gore, 1958) 211–21. *Charts, diagr., transcr.* In Slovene; summary in French. See no. 357 in this volume.

Compares 19th- and 20th- c. transcriptions of Yugoslavian traditional melodies, with attention to how scholars have determined their metric patterns.

4003
as

HUCKE, Helmut. **Zum Problem des Rhythmus im Gregorianischen Gesang** [The problem of rhythm in Gregorian chant], *Bericht über den siebenten internationalen musikwissenschaftlichen Kongress* (Kassel: Bärenreiter, 1959) 141–42. In German. See no. 390 in this volume.

There is no firm evidence of a specific rhythmic practice of Gregorian chant to be deduced from its notation or from the writings of medieval theorists. Nor is a rhythmic practice deducible from the metric character of the Latin texts of the chants. Nor is it reasonable to argue, as do the members of the Solesmes school, that chant rhythm can be inferred from liturgical form. Perhaps fruitful connections will be found between Gregorian chant and folk song, and the rhythmic character of the former will become clearer as a result. *(Carl Skoggard)*

4004
as

JAQUES-DALCROZE, Émile. **Rythmes d'hier, d'aujourd'hui et de demain et leur enseignement dans les écoles de musique** [Rhythms of yesterday, today, and tomorrow and their teaching in music schools], *Compte rendu du Ier Congrès du rythme* (Genève: Institut Jaques-Dalcroze, 1926) 92–102. *Music.* In French. See no. 123 in this volume.

The basic elements of rhythm are energy, duration, elasticity, and space. It is unfortunate that eurhythmics is not part of conservatory curricula.

4005
as

KAMBUROV, Ivan. **Rytmické zvláštnosti bulharské lidové a umělecké hudby/Les particularités rythmiques de la musique populaire bulgare et leur répercussion sur l'art musical bulgare** [The rhythmic particularities of Bulgarian traditional music and their repercussions on Bulgarian art music], *Hudba národů: Sborník přednášek, proslovených na I. mezinárodním sjezdu skladatelů a hudebních kritiků/Musique des nations: Ier Congrès international des compositeurs et critiques musicaux* (Praha: Syndikát Českých Skladatelů, 1948) 37–40,138–42. In Czech and French. See no. 278 in this volume.

The rhythms of Bulgarian traditional music are based on a constant beat (*chronos prōtos*) of 320-500 units per minute in what may be called hemiolic measures. Composers who have taken inspiration from it include Pančo Vladigerov, Ljubomir Pipkov, Petko Stajnov, Veselin Stojanov, Dimităr Nenov, Bojan Georgiev Ikonomov, Filip Kutev, Marin Goleminov, and especially Svetoslav Obretenov.

4006
as

KARBUSICKÝ, Vladimír. **Zu den historischen Wurzeln der Metrik der russischen Bylinen** [On the historic roots of the metrics of Russian byliny], *Anfänge der slavischen Musik* (Bratislava: Slovenská Akadémia Vied, 1966) 165–71. In German. See no. 477 in this volume.

The musical metrics of the Russian bylina epic must be analyzed in terms of speech prosody as well as musical rhythm; they are deeply rooted in the metrics of medieval Russian verse. *(Brian Doherty)*

4007
as

KARKOSCHKA, Erhard. **Zur rhythmischen Struktur in der Musik von heute** [Rhythmic structure in the music of today], *Bericht über den internationalen musikwissenschaftlichen Kongreß* (Kassel: Bärenreiter, 1963) 379–88. *Music.* In German. See no. 452 in this volume.

The range of developments is illustrated in works by Boris Blacher, Stockhausen, Messiaen, and the author.

4008
as

KOLESSA, Filaret. **Ueber den rhythmischen Aufbau der ukrainischen (kleinrussischen) Volkslieder** [Rhythmic construction of Ukrainian (Little Russian) folk songs], *Report of the Fourth Congress of the International Musical Society* (London: Novello, 1912) 184. In German. See no. 71 in this volume.

Summary of a paper. Discusses the metrical structures of song texts.

4009
as

LÉVY, Ernst. **Métrique et rythmique: Définitions et bases** [Meter and rhythm: Definitions and foundations], *Compte rendu du Ier Congrès du rythme* (Genève: Institut Jaques-Dalcroze, 1926) 76–81. *Charts, diagr.* In French. See no. 123 in this volume.

The human pulse is one common rhythmic tempo. Meter is defined as energy developed according to a principle of order, and rhythm is defined as energy developed according to a principle of cause and effect.

4010
as

LIPPHARDT, Walther. **Die Kyrietropen in ihrer rhythmischen und melodischen Struktur** [Rhythmic and melodic structure of the Kyrie tropes], *Kongreß-Bericht: Gesellschaft für Musikforschung* (Kassel; Basel: Bärenreiter, 1950) 56–59. In German. See no. 299 in this volume.

4011
as

MACHATIUS, Franz Jochen. **Die Tempo-Charaktere** [The tempo characters], *Bericht über den siebenten internationalen musikwissenschaftlichen Kongress* (Kassel: Bärenreiter, 1959) 185–87. In German. See no. 390 in this volume.

Summarizes the author's findings on the typology of tempo in music of the beginning of the Baroque (*Die Tempi in der Musik um 1600*, Ph.D. diss., Freie U., Berlin; the published version is cited as RILM [1977]369) and suggests that the basic inventory of tempo types, or characters, corresponds to an objective inventory of values applicable to music of all periods. *(David Bloom)*

4012
as

MARCEL-DUBOIS, Claudie. **Le tempo dans les musiques de tradition orale** [Tempo in musics of oral tradition], *Fontes artis musicae* XII/2-3 (May-Dec 1965) 204–06. In French. See no. 499 in this volume.

Tempo is an organic part of music in oral transmission, connected to the music's function (lullaby, work song, march) and emotionally expressive character (moderate tempo for joy or love, slow for disgust or fear, fast for courage or anger). Rallentando effects are almost never found, while accelerando is relatively frequent, and tempo doubling is very frequent. *(David Bloom)*

⟶ MARTIN, Frank. **La notation du rythme** [The notation of rhythm]. See no. 3852 in this volume.

4013
as

MARTIN, Frank. **Les sources du rythme musical** [The sources of musical rhythm], *Deuxième Congrès international du rythme et de la rythmique*

(Genève: Institut Jaques-Dalcroze, 1966) 15–21. *Music*. In French. See no. 502 in this volume.

Discusses analogies between poetic and musical meter.

4014
as

MARTÍNEZ TORNER, Eduardo Fernando. **Los ritmos en la música popular castellana** [The rhythms of Spanish traditional music], *Congrés de la Societat Internacional de Musicología* (Barcelona: Casa de Caritat, 1936). In Spanish. See no. 224 in this volume.

The conference report provides only a citation. Neither the text nor a summary of the paper was published here.

4015
as

METZLER, Fritz. **Takt und Rhythmus in der freien Melodieerfindung des Grundschulkindes** [Beat and rhythm in the free melodic invention of elementary school children], *Bericht über den internationalen musikwissenschaftlichen Kongreß* (Kassel: Bärenreiter, 1963) 286–89. *Transcr.* In German. See no. 452 in this volume.

A sample of 1200 melodies improvised by schoolchildren in Reutlingen to set texts reveals a pattern, particularly for prose texts, of free alternation between two-beat and three-beat groupings. *(David Bloom)*

4016
as

MOCQUEREAU, André. **Le rythme libre avant le chant grégorien: Un chapitre de son histoire** [Free rhythm before Gregorian chant: A chapter in its history], *La musique d'église: Compte rendu du Congrès de musique sacrée* (Tourcoing: Duvivier, 1920) 281–321. *Music, charts, diagr.* In French. See no. 93 in this volume.

Analyzes meter, syllabic stress, and verse organization in Greco-Roman poetry and Gregorian chant. The evolution of free rhythm from early strophic construction is traced.

4017
as

NESTLER, Gerhard. **Der Rhythmus in der Reihentechnik der Gegenwart** [Rhythm in contemporary serial technique], *Bericht über den siebenten internationalen musikwissenschaftlichen Kongress* (Kassel: Bärenreiter, 1959) 199–200. In German. See no. 390 in this volume.

Innovative uses of rhythmic values in works by Boulez and Stockhausen signal the introduction of a new kind of subjective time, but also a time that is serially organized.

4018
as

PUCELLE, Jean. **La musique et le temps** [Music and time], *Pepragmena tou 4. diethnous synedriou aisthītikis/Actes du IV Congrès international d'esthétique/Proceedings of the IV International Congress on Aesthetics* (Athínai: conference, 1962) 425–27. In French. See no. 415 in this volume.

Temporally defined categories of analysis include structure, tempo, rhythm, melody, and harmony.

4019
as

PUJOL PONS, Francisco. **Ritme i metrificació de les cançons populars catalanes** [The rhythm and metrics of Catalan traditional songs], *Congrés de la Societat Internacional de Musicología* (Barcelona: Casa de Caritat, 1936). In Catalan. See no. 224 in this volume.

The conference report provides only a citation. Neither the text nor a summary of the paper was published here.

4020
as

REFARDT, Edgar. **Rhythmische Analysen** [Rhythmic analysis], *Compte rendu du Ier Congrès du rythme* (Genève: Institut Jaques-Dalcroze, 1926) 70. In German. See no. 123 in this volume.

Focuses on symphonic adagio themes from the late 18th to early 19th c. A full version appears in the *Bulletin der Union Musicale* III.1, La Haye, 1923.

4021
as

REINHARD, Kurt. **Eine von der rhythmischen Belebung abhängige Tempobezeichnung** [A system of tempo designations based on rhythmic animation], *Bericht über den siebenten internationalen musikwissenschaftlichen Kongress* (Kassel: Bärenreiter, 1959) 229–30. In German. See no. 390 in this volume.

The usual metronomic indications used in ethnomusicological transcription fail to capture the rhythmic intensity of a piece, as in the difference between, for example, two pieces with the same value for a quarter note but one using mostly quarter notes and the other mostly eighths. In *Die Musik der Lolo* (*Baeßler-Archiv* N.F. vol. 3, 1955), the author proposes an alternative, based on the concept of the most frequently occurring note value. Other possibilities proposed by Dieter Christensen in *Die Musik der Kate und Sialum: Beiträge zur Ethnographie Neuguineas* (Ph.D. diss., Freie U., Berlin, 1957) are the notions of an *inner tempo* based on the total number of notes over a fixed period, and a *melic tempo* based on the frequency of pitch change. *(David Bloom)*

4022
as

REINHARD, Kurt. **Zur Frage des Tempos bei Chopin** [The question of tempo in Chopin], *The book of the first international musicological congress devoted to the works of Frederick Chopin* (Warszawa: Państwowe Wydawnictwo Naukowe, 1963) 449–54. *Charts, diagr.* In German. See no. 425 in this volume.

Discusses an attempt to determine the inner tempo of 111 pieces by Chopin, based on ethomusicological analytic methods and the composer's metronome markings. A statistical breakdown of the results is provided, together with full data on 30 mazurkas. *(David Bloom)*

4023
as

RENSHAW, Rosette. **Rhythmic structures in Indian and Western music**, *Music east and west* (Nai Dilli: Indian Council for Cultural Relations, 1966) 77–89. See no. 489 in this volume.

An examination of well-known Western melodies in terms of tāla shows that they have more rhythmically in common with Indian melodies than might be suspected. Western music students would benefit from being liberated from the bondage of the bar-line. *(David Bloom)*

4024
as

RIHTMAN, Cvjetko. **O otázce nesoučasnosti přízvuku slova a přízvuku nápěvu v lidové hudbě** [Divergence in word stress and melodic stress in folk music], *Leoš Janáček a soudobá hudba* (Praha: Panton, 1963) 265–66. In Czech; summaries in Russian and German. See no. 389 in this volume.

Janáček's question whether the verse of a folk song is based on a system of meter, and whether in this case the meter of a verse determines a melodic rhythm of the song, is addressed on the example of Serbian traditional songs. *(editors)*

4025
as

RISLER, Jean. **Le rythme de la musique grecque** [The rhythm of Greek music], *Compte rendu du Ier Congrès du rythme* (Genève: Institut Jaques-Dalcroze, 1926) 5–9. *Music*. In French. See no. 123 in this volume.

Dance, music, and poetry overlap in the area of rhythm. There are six fundamental rhythmic feet, each of which, like the modes, evokes a different effect.

4026
as

ROSENTHAL, Felix. **Auftakt und Abtakt in der Thematik Beethovens** [Upbeat and downbeat in Beethoven's themes], *Beethoven-Zentenarfeier: Internationaler musikhistorischer Kongress* (Wien: Universal, 1927) 97–99. *Music*. In German. See no. 142 in this volume.

Analyzes the characteristic rhythmic structure of Beethoven's themes, from the theoretical perspectives developed by Hugo Riemann, Justus Hermann Wetzel, and Theodor Wiehmayer.

4027 SCHERING, Arnold. **Zur Choralrhythmik** [On
as rhythm in the Protestant chorale], *Bericht über den I.
musikwissenschaftlichen Kongress der Deutschen
Musikgesellschaft in Leipzig* (Wiesbaden: Breitkopf &
Härtel, 1926) 365–67. *Music.* In German. See no. 120 in
this volume.

Discusses metrics, the hemiola, the development of the fermata, and the use
of masculine and feminine endings in the Protestant chorale. *(William Renwick)*

4028 SCHNEIDER, Marius. **Prolegomena zu einer**
as **Theorie des Rhythmus** [Prolegomena to a theory of
rhythm], *Bericht über den siebenten internationalen
musikwissenschaftlichen Kongress* (Kassel:
Bärenreiter, 1959) 264–77. *Charts, diagr., transcr.* In
German. See no. 390 in this volume.

The construction of a theory of musical rhythm begins properly with the
consideration of rhythmic systems as a naturally evolving phenomenon,
excluding phenomena such as magical singing and art music, in which artificial rhythms are frequently used. Far from all of the mathematically possible metric sequences are attested as elements of natural rhythms: those that
are are marked by a balance that permits them to stand on their own and by
their appropriateness to performance with an untrained breathing technique or a technically simple instrument. A preliminary typology is proposed. *(David Bloom)*

4029 SCHNEIDER, Marius. **Le rythme de la**
as **musique artistique espagnole du XVIe siècle**
va à travers la chanson populaire [The rhythm of
16th-century Spanish art music parallels traditional
song], *Studia musicologica Academiae Scientiarum
Hungaricae* VII (1965) 125–40. *Music.* In French. See
no. 478 in this volume.

4030 SŁAWIŃSKI, Adam. **Rytm a harmonia w**
as **polonezach Chopina** [Rhythm and harmony in Chopin's polonaises], *The book of the first international
musicological congress devoted to the works of Frederick Chopin* (Warszawa: Państwowe Wydawnictwo
Naukowe, 1963) 241–46. *Music, charts, diagr.* In Polish. See no. 425 in this volume.

⟶ STÄBLEIN, Bruno. **Die Tegernseer mensurale**
Choralschrift aus dem 15. Jahrhundert:
Etwas Greifbares zur Rhythmik der mittel-
alterlichen Monodie [The Tegernsee mensural
chant notation of the 15th century: Something concrete
about the rhythm of medieval monophony]. See no.
3872 in this volume.

4031 STEGLICH, Rudolf. **Über die Synkope** [On syn-
as copation], *Bericht über den siebenten internationalen
musikwissenschaftlichen Kongress* (Kassel:
Bärenreiter, 1959) 277–78. In German. See no. 390 in
this volume.

In addition to the kind of syncopation familiarly exemplified in jazz, the
shifting of an accent within the given metric scheme of a measure, there is
an essentially different type conveying a literal uplift (*Emporhebung*),
through the strengthening of the rising phase of a phrase, as in the anticipated downbeat of "Alle Menschen werden Brüder" in Beethoven's symphony no. 9 and other 18th- and 19th-c. examples. The latter type, now little
noted, seems from a passage in Sébastien de Brossard's *Dictionnaire de
musique* to have been much better understood in the Baroque. *(David Bloom)*

4032 STEGLICH, Rudolf. **Über Dualismus der**
as *Taktqualität* **im Sonatensatz** [On the dualism of
Taktqualität in sonata movements], *Beethoven-
Zentenarfeier: Internationaler musikhistorischer
Kongress* (Wien: Universal, 1927) 104–06. *Music.* In
German. See no. 142 in this volume.

Proposes a classification of measure types according to parameters of momentum, gravity, and absolute *Taktqualität*. Beethoven uses contrasts in
the latter, under Mozart's influence, as a means of structuring his sonata
themes. *(David Bloom)*

4033 STEPHAN, Rudolf. **Zur Cantio-Rhythmik**
as [Cantio rhythm], *Bericht über den siebenten
internationalen musikwissenschaftlichen Kongress*
(Kassel: Bärenreiter, 1959) 281–82. In German. See no.
390 in this volume.

The cantiones of the 15th c., Latin songs for non-liturgical but religious
use, were notable for their primitive duple and triple rhythms, at a time
when the performance of liturgical song was generally arhythmic. In this
they reflected the same goals as did attempts at rhythmicization of chant
and mensural notation of new compositions, to restore lost rhythms and introduce new ones. *(David Bloom)*

4034 STĘSZEWSKA, Zofia; STĘSZEWSKI, Jan.
as **Zur Genese und Chronologie des Mazurka-**
rhythmus in Polen [The origin and chronology of
the mazurka rhythm in Poland], *The book of the first international musicological congress devoted to the
works of Frederick Chopin* (Warszawa: Państwowe
Wydawnictwo Naukowe, 1963) 624–27. *Music.* In
German. See no. 425 in this volume.

The history of the mazurka rhythm seems tied to the invariant Polish stress
on a word's penultimate syllable, which is believed to have been established between the 15th and early 18th c. Musical sources from the first half
of the 17th c. show the rhythm in a form that is already highly developed,
suggesting that it may have originated as early as 1500. *(author)*

4035 SYCHRA, Antonín. **Das Problem des**
as **Rhythmus im Lichte der Beziehungen von**
Musik und Wort [The problem of rhythm in light of
the relations between music and word], *Bericht über
den siebenten internationalen musikwissenschaftlichen
Kongress* (Kassel: Bärenreiter, 1959) 255–57. *Music,
transcr.* In German. See no. 390 in this volume.

A single melody in its form as a dance tune may be quite different rhythmically from its cantabile form as a texted song; a single rhythm may have entirely different functions in melodies for dance and for song. Melodic
rhythms may be derived from the prosodic forms of a particular language,
as in the case of Czech melodies on the linguistic pattern of a short stressed
syllable followed by a long unstressed syllable. Examples are drawn from
traditional Czech melodies and vocal music by Josef Bohuslav Foerster.
(David Bloom)

4036 TETZEL, Eugen Karl Gottfried. **Rhythmus und**
as **Vortrag** [Rhythm and execution], *Beethoven-Zentenarfeier: Internationaler musikhistorischer
Kongress* (Wien: Universal, 1927) 385–87. In German.
See no. 142 in this volume.

A brief account of the principles of phrasing in musical performance, based
on the opposition between metric stress and rhythmic caesura. An extended
version is provided in the author's *Rhythmus und Vortrag* (Berlin, 1926).
(David Bloom)

4037 TREVES, Marco. **Le rythme dans les phéno-**
as **mènes de la vie** [Rhythm in the phenomena of life],
Compte rendu du Ier Congrès du rythme (Genève:
Institut Jaques-Dalcroze, 1926) 317–44. In French. See
no. 123 in this volume.

A regular rhythmic pattern is a biological necessity for all forms of life.

4038 TROST, Pavel. **Das Metrum der litauischen**
as **Volkslieder** [The meter of Lithuanian traditional
song], *Poetics/Poetyka/Poetika* (Warszawa:

Państwowe Wydawnictwo Naukowe, 1961) 119–25. In German. See no. 426 in this volume.

Discusses characteristics of syllabic stress and poetic meter as they relate to musical meter.

4039 VUKOVIĆ, Jovan. **Akcenat u vokalnoj**
as **narodnoj muzici** [Speech stress in traditional vocal music], *Rad kongresa folklorista Jugoslavije* (Ljubljana: Savez Udruženja Folkloristov Jugoslavije, 1960) 133–35. In Bosnian; summary in English. See no. 404 in this volume.

Accentuation in traditional song is necessarily based in speech stress; nevertheless the degree to which speech stress supports musical rhythm is limited, and is overcome by musical impulses even in the most primary singing. A method of distinguishing between the rhetorical foot and musical foot is illustrated from the decasyllabic line of Yugoslav gusle songs. *(author)*

4040 WIEHMAYER, Theodore. **Über die Grund-**
as **fragen der musikalischen Rhythmik und Metrik** [On the basic questions of musical rhythm and meter], *Bericht über den I. musikwissenschaftlichen Kongress der Deutschen Musikgesellschaft in Leipzig* (Wiesbaden: Breitkopf & Härtel, 1926) 445–62. *Music, charts, diagr.* In German. See no. 120 in this volume.

Contrary to the rhythmic theories of Hugo Riemann and Moritz Hauptmann, musical meter must originate in melodic (tonic) accent. Duple orderings are the most basic metrical structures. A supplementary article by Arnold SCHERING is included. *(William Renwick)*

4041 WINCKEL, Fritz. **Rhythmus und Resonanz**
as [Rhythm and resonance], *Deuxième Congrès international du rythme et de la rythmique* (Genève: Institut Jaques-Dalcroze, 1966) 141–47. *Bibliog.* In German. See no. 502 in this volume.

Discusses physiological rhythms and movement, with attention to the ideas of Émile Jaques-Dalcroze.

62 Tuning, temperament, and scale structures

4042 AL-DARWĪSH, 'Alī. **Maqamates employés**
as **chez les Maures et spécialement en Tunisie** [Maqāmāt used among the Moors, particularly in Tunisia], *Recueil des travaux du Congrès de musique arabe* (Al-Qāhirah: Boulac, 1934) 583–92. *Music.* In French. See no. 196 in this volume.

A repertoire of 18 *tab'* (maqām) scales proposed as a standard inventory for music of the Maghrib region by the Commission on Modes, Rhythms, and Composition (see no. 3963 in this volume) of the Congress on Arab Music (Mu'tamar al Mūsīqá al-'Arabiyyah) in Cairo in 1932. *(David Bloom)*

4043 AL-DARWĪSH, 'Alī. **Maqamates employés en**
as **Egypte et leur décomposition en genres** [Maqāmāt used in Egypt and their analysis into genres], *Recueil des travaux du Congrès de musique arabe* (Al-Qāhirah: Boulac, 1934) 529–81. *Music.* In French. See no. 196 in this volume.

At the Congress on Arab Music (Mu'tamar al Mūsīqá al-'Arabiyyah) in Cairo (1932), a repertoire of 52 maqām scales was proposed as a standard inventory for Egyptian music by the Commission on Modes, Rhythms, and Composition (see no. 3963 in this volume). The maqāmāt are listed by fundamental note, and classified into component trichord, tetrachord, and pentachord clusters. *(David Bloom)*

4044 AL-MAHDĪ, Salāh. **Présence ou absence de la**
as **constante de quarte, de quinte et d'octave: Son rôle structurel dans la musique orientale non**

pentatonique [Presence or absence of the constant of fourth, fifth, and octave: Its structural role in non-pentatonic Asian music], *La résonance dans les échelles musicales* (Paris: Centre National de la Recherche Scientifique [CNRS], 1963) 123–28. In French; summaries in English and German. See no. 420 in this volume.

The earliest Asian music is based on the tetrachord and the pentachord. Later, these played a role analogous to that of the Pythagorean diatonic scale in early Greek music: Two tetrachords separated by a disjunct tone resulted in octaves, fourths, and fifths, the fourth being the last note of the first tetrachord, the fifth the first note of the second tetrachord, and the octave being the last. *(author)*

4045 ALMENDRA, Júlia d'. **Debussy et le mouve-**
as **ment modal dans la musique du XXe siècle** [Debussy and the modal movement in 20th-century music], *Debussy et l'évolution de la musique au XXe siècle* (Paris: Centre National de la Recherche Scientifique [CNRS], 1965) 109–32. In French. See no. 456 in this volume.

Debussy's affinity with Gregorian chant modes stemmed from his early service in the Roman Catholic Church.

4046 BAKÉ, Arnold Adriaan. **Bemerkungen zur**
as **Entstehungsgeschichte eines Modus** [Observations on the origins of a mode], *Bericht über den Internationalen musikwissenschaftlichen Kongress* (Kassel: Bärenreiter, 1954) 184–87. *Music.* In German. See no. 319 in this volume.

Compares the information provided in Bharata's *Nātya-śāstra* with present-day performance of the Vedic liturgical repertoire in southern India (assumed to reflect an little-changed practice thousands of years old) to shed light on the origins of *sa grāma*, the fundamental mode in Bharata's scheme. Even though the Vedic tradition is vocal and Bharata's system is meant for instruments, it is possible to discover congruities between them pointing to the same primary mode. *(Carl Skoggard)*

4047 BARKECHLI, Mehdi. **Les échelles régulières**
as **du cycle des quintes et leurs déformations occasionnelles: Dans les cadres non pentatoniques** [Regular scales of the circle of fifths and their occasional deformations in non-pentatonic frameworks], *La résonance dans les échelles musicales* (Paris: Centre National de la Recherche Scientifique [CNRS], 1963) 173–82. *Charts, diagr.* In French; summaries in English and German. See no. 420 in this volume.

The ratio 4:5:6 for the major perfect chord, as a compromise between the positions of professional musicians and physicists, satisfies nobody. An alternative compromise is offered by the Iranian scale, which is universal, having degrees contained in keeping with the circle of fifths. It accords as well with the Pythagorean melodic scale as with the harmonic scale, since the whole tone is divided into two limmas and one comma. Occasional deformations are due to auditory effects of a psycho-physiological nature giving rise to *attraction* and *tolérance*. Examples are the mechanics of timbre perception and pitch distortion due to volume partials. *(author)*

4048 BARKECHLI, Mehdi. **L'évolution de la gamme**
as **dans la musique orientale** [The evolution of the scale in Eastern music], *Acoustique musicale* (Paris: Centre National de la Recherche Scientifique [CNRS], 1959) 39–45. *Charts, diagr.* In French. See no. 393 in this volume.

Traces links with the theories of Pythagoras, Aristoxenus, and Ṣafī al-Dīn with the scale structures of the Perso-Arabic tradition in its current practice.

4049 BAUDOT, Ernest. **Avantages et inconvénients**
as **du tempérament au point de vue de la pratique musicale** [Advantages and disadvantages of temperament from the perspective of musical practice], *Congrès*

international de musique: Ire session—Exposition Universelle de 1900: Compte rendu, rapports, communications (Paris: conference, 1901) 41–42. In French. See no. 29 in this volume.

Though equally tempered instruments may slightly distort natural intervals, they are still preferable for their tonal diversity. Numerous difficulties face those attempting to construct certain tempered instruments.

4050
as
BELJAEV, Viktor Mihailovič. **The formation of folk modal systems,** *Journal of the International Folk Music Council* XV (1963) 4–9. *Music, charts, diagr.* See no. 459 in this volume.

Modes are best understood as generalized types of melodic movement; they arise from traditional song, and become conceptualized as scales in the making of traditional instruments. Various scales are compared, with intervals expressed in cents, and their usages are briefly characterized. *(James R. Cowdery)*

4051
as
BERNET KEMPERS, Karel Philippus. **Die Jamisation** [Jamization], *Compte rendu/Kongressbericht/Report* (Basel: Bärenreiter, 1951) 162–65. *Charts, diagr.* In German. See no. 289 in this volume.

An introduction to the author's system of pitch nomenclature, using monosyllables to refer unambiguously not only to scale degrees but also to intervals; see *Jamisatie: Voorstel tot een geheel nieuwe, ondubbelzinnige en logische nomenclatur in de muziek* (Rotterdam: Brusse, 1947). *(David Bloom)*

4052
as
BRANDSMA, Engbert. **Über die Tonverhältnisse in der alten und neuen Musik** [Tonal relations in old and new music], *Haydn-Zentenarfeier* (Leipzig: Breitkopf & Härtel; Wien: Artaria, 1909) 353–60. *Music, charts, diagr.* In German. See no. 65 in this volume.

Compares the Pythagorean, just, and equally-tempered tuning systems.

4053
as
BRENN, Franz. **Tonsysteme in Equiton und Fawcettzahlen** [Tonal systems in equitone notation and Fawcett numbers], *Bericht über den internationalen musikwissenschaftlichen Kongreß* (Kassel: Bärenreiter, 1963) 275–76. In German. See no. 452 in this volume.

A brief account of Rodney Fawcett's equitone notation system permitting the easy notation of all scales from the five-note to the 96-note; the scale he developed for the precise measurement of musical intervals (at 100 Fawcetts to the fifth); and their use in comparative musicology. *(Leslie B. Dunner)*

4054
as
BUKOFZER, Manfred F. **The evolution of Javanese tone-systems,** *Papers read at the International Congress of Musicology* (New York: Music Educators National Conference, 1944) 241–50. *Music, charts, diagr.* See no. 266 in this volume.

Analyzes and compares the pelog and slendro tuning systems of the Central Javanese gamelan.

4055
as
BUKOFZER, Manfred F. **Zur Frage der Blasquinte in den exotischen Tonsystemen** [On the question of the blown fifth in exotic tone systems], *Congrés de la Societat Internacional de Musicologia* (Barcelona: Casa de Caritat, 1936). In German. See no. 224 in this volume.

The conference report provides only a citation. Neither the text nor a summary of the paper was published here. Another version is published under the title *Kann die "Blasquintentheorie" zur Erklärung exotischer Ton-Systeme beitragen?*, in *Anthropos* 32 (1937), 402-18.

4056
as
CHAILLEY, Jacques. **A propos de quatre mesures de l'*Entführung*: La renaissance de la modalité dans la musique française avant 1890** [Four measures in the *Entführung*: The rebirth of mo-

dality in French music before 1890], *Bericht über den internationalen musikwissenschaftlichen Kongreß Wien Mozartjahr 1956* (Graz; Köln: Böhlau, 1958) 78–91. *Music.* In French. See no. 365 in this volume.

A chromatic alteration in the Janissary chorus in Act I of *Die Entführung aus dem Serail* was interpreted in the 19th c. as ornamental, and more recently as an instance of the Lydian mode. The revival of the Greek modes is traced, with particular reference to French music, from Gluck and Grétry through Chabrier and Fauré. *(David Bloom)*

4057
as
CHAILLEY, Jacques. **Arbeitsgemeinschaft: La révision de la notion traditionelle de tonalité** [Working group: Revising the traditional notion of tonality], *Bericht über den siebenten internationalen musikwissenschaftlichen Kongress* (Kassel: Bärenreiter, 1959) 332–34. In French. See no. 390 in this volume.

Report of the contributions of the author, Wilhelm HEINITZ, and Jens ROHWER at a conference workshop devoted to a critique of the Rameau-Fétis concept of tonality. It was decided to define tonality as a mode of musical perception in which all tones are understood in relation to a final, unique, conclusive tone, real or virtual. *(David Bloom)*

4058
as
CHAILLEY, Jacques. **Le dynamisme des gammes et des accords dans les principaux systèmes acoustiques et son influence sur le développement de la musique** [The dynamism of scales and chords in the principal acoustic systems, and its influence on the development of music], *Acoustique musicale* (Paris: Centre National de la Recherche Scientifique [CNRS], 1959) 13–18. *Charts, diagr.* In French. See no. 393 in this volume.

A survey of dynamic (Pythagorean), static (Zarlinian), and neutral (temperament) theories of the physics of interval and harmonic structure, and their relation to the evolution of Western music.

4059
as
CHAILLEY, Jacques. **Les éléments de formation des échelles extérieurs à la résonance: L'égalisation** [Elements of scale formation external to overtone theory: Equalization], *La résonance dans les échelles musicales* (Paris: Centre National de la Recherche Scientifique [CNRS], 1963) 191–97. *Music.* In French; summaries in English and German. See no. 420 in this volume.

Draws on examples of pentatonic and heptatonic scales.

4060
as
CHAILLEY, Jacques. **Le problème de l'harmonique 7 devant l'histoire musicale** [The problem of the seventh partial in the face of music history], *Acoustique musicale* (Paris: Centre National de la Recherche Scientifique [CNRS], 1959) 47. In French. See no. 393 in this volume.

Summary of a paper on the historical relation between harmonic theory in terms of overtone ratios and the acceptance of the seventh chord as a consonance.

4061
as
CHAILLEY, Jacques. **Synthèse et conclusions** [Synthesis and conclusions], *La résonance dans les échelles musicales* (Paris: Centre National de la Recherche Scientifique [CNRS], 1963) 293–99. In French. See no. 420 in this volume.

4062
as
COLLAER, Paul. **Stratigraphie musicale et structures mélodiques** [Musical stratigraphy and melodic structures], *Les colloques de Wégimont. IV: Ethnomusicologie III* (Paris: Belles Lettres, 1964) 13–17. In French. See no. 401 in this volume.

Pentatonic and heptatonic scales coexisting within a given culture represent distinct ethnohistorical strata.

4063
as

COLLANGETTES, Xavier Maurice. **Commission de l'Échelle Musicale** [The Commission on the Musical Scale], *Recueil des travaux du Congrès de musique arabe* (Al-Qāhirah: Boulac, 1934) 593–603. *Charts, diagr.* In French. See no. 196 in this volume.

At the Congress on Arab Music (Mu'tamar al Mūsīqá al-'Arabiyyah) in Cairo (1932), the commission was charged with proposing a model of the scale of Arab music to serve as a standard reference for performers; measurements were made for natural and for equal-tempered (quarter-tone) versions of the scale with particular attention to the scale of *maqām rast*. The commission was divided as to the question whether the tempered scale should be adopted for general use, for pedagogical use, or not at all. *(David Bloom)*

4064
as

DANIÉLOU, Alain. **Les éléments de formation des échelles extérieurs à la résonance: Les déformations expressives** [Elements of scale formation external to overtone theory: Expressive deformations], *La résonance dans les échelles musicales* (Paris: Centre National de la Recherche Scientifique [CNRS], 1963) 207–14. In French; summaries in English and German. See no. 420 in this volume.

The concept of expressive deformations implies a mistaken approach: Can expression—the very substance of music—be a deformation? Expressive tonal relations appear deformed only in terms of oversimplified standards stemming from a flawed theory. *(author)*

4065
as

DAYAN, Leonzio. **Il pluricromatismo nella musica armena** [Plurichromaticism in Armenian music], *Bericht über den internationalen musikwissenschaftlichen Kongreß Wien Mozartjahr 1956* (Graz; Köln: Böhlau, 1958) 112–15. In Italian. See no. 365 in this volume.

A general account of the use of microtonal intervals in Armenian traditional music and Armenian Christian sacred music, with reference to the influence of Asian microtonal traditions and to current microtonal experimentation in Western art music. *(David Bloom)*

4066
as

DONATH, Gustav. **Vom Wesen der Oktave** [On the essence of the octave], *Musikerziehung: Zeitschrift der Musikerzieher Österreichs* special issue (1953) 33. In German. See no. 317 in this volume.

The octave is composed of two different but closely related tones that can be viewed as points on a spectrum or as members of an interrupted series. Whether presented successively or simultaneously, the relationship is fundamental to timbre and harmony. *(Joseph Giroux)*

4067
as

DRAEGER, Hans-Heinz. **Zur mitteltönigen und gleichschwebenden Temperatur** [Mean-tone and equal-tempered tuning], *Bericht über die Wissenschaftliche Bachtagung* (Leipzig: Peters, 1951) 389–404. *Music.* In German. See no. 298 in this volume.

Discusses Bach's use of the chromatic ambiguities created by equal temperament, as in *Das wohltemperirte Clavier* and the *Die chromatische Fantasie und Fuge*. *(David Bloom)*

4068
as

DUSSAUT, Robert. **Proposition de quelques réformes en théorie acoustico-musicale** [A proposal for some reforms in the theory of musical acoustics], *Acoustique musicale* (Paris: Centre National de la Recherche Scientifique [CNRS], 1959) 103–10. In French. See no. 393 in this volume.

The scale based on acoustic physics, as proposed by theorists from Aristoxenus through Zarlino, is open to criticism; the Pythagorean scale is more flexible than generally claimed, and is better suited to transposition through early modes and modern keys. If there is to be a single international pitch standard, it would be more logical to base it on G4 (at 384 Hz) than A4, allowing all the frequencies, in both the systems of Zarlino and of Pythagoras, to be expressed in whole numbers.

4069
as

EMMANUEL, Maurice. **La polymodie** [Polymodality], *Deuxième congrès international d'esthétique et de Science de l'art* (Paris: Librairie Félix Alcan, 1937) II, 462–63. In French. See no. 249 in this volume.

The compositional use of a wide variety of modes beyond the conventional major and minor, difficult though it may be to combine with the opulence of modern harmony, is a technique of great promise. *(David Bloom)*

4070
as

FARMER, Henry George. **Histoire abrégée de l'échelle de la musique arabe** [A short history of the scale in Arabic music], *Recueil des travaux du Congrès de musique arabe* (Al-Qāhirah: Boulac, 1934) 647–55. *Charts, diagr.* In French. See no. 196 in this volume.

Provides an account of theoretical writings on the subject, with charts of typical octave divisions, from the 1st c. of the Hegira (7th c. C.E.) through the modern school of the 20th c. and its interest in quarter-tone tempered scales. *(David Bloom)*

4071
as

FELBER, Erwin. **Das Gesetz der Zahlenverschiebung in Märchen und Mythos und sein Einfluss auf die Skalenbildung** [The law of mutation of numbers in fairy tale and myth, and its influence on scale building], *Report of the Fourth Congress of the International Musical Society* (London: Novello, 1912) 178. In German. See no. 71 in this volume.

Summary of a paper. Comparative study of myths and folk tales evinces a pattern whereby the number 9 is replaced by the number 7, while the number 3 is replaced by the number 12: For example, the week of 9 nights was superseded by the week of 7 days, and the original 3 labors of Hercules evolved into 12. Identical developments have occurred in music theory: The number 9 corresponds to the ancient Persian scale, 7 to the diatonic scale, and 12 to the chromatic scale. Similar interactions of these numbers may be found in many regions and cultural domains.

4072
as

FELLERER, Karl Gustav. **Modus und Melodie-Modell** [Mode and melody model], *Congrés de la Societat Internacional de Musicologia* (Barcelona: Casa de Caritat, 1936). In German. See no. 224 in this volume.

The conference report provides only a citation. Neither the text nor a summary of the paper was published here.

4073
as

FOKKER, Adriaan Daniël. **Les cinquièmes de ton: Les subtilités des lignes mélodiques et l'enrichissement des harmonies** [Fifth-tones: The subtleties of the melodic lines and the enrichment of harmonies], *Acoustique musicale* (Paris: Centre National de la Recherche Scientifique [CNRS], 1959) 29–37. *Music, charts, diagr.* In French. See no. 393 in this volume.

The 31-tone scale based on the interval of a fifth of a whole step, originally proposed by Christiaan Huygens in the 17th c., allows composers to use the perfect intervals lost with the adoption of equal temperament. Practical issues—notational standards and the design of a keyboard for a fifth-tone instrument—are discussed.

4074
as

FOKKER, Adriaan Daniël. **Expériences musicales avec les genres musicaux de Leonhard Euler contenant le septième harmonique** [Musical experiments with Leonhard Euler's genera musica containing the seventh harmonic], *Compte rendu/Kongressbericht/Report* (Basel: Bärenreiter, 1951) 113–15. *Charts, diagr.* In French. See no. 289 in this volume.

Leonhard Euler's *Tentamen novae theoriae musicae*, 1739, discusses a musical system capable of incorporating the seventh harmonic. The sound can be heard on an instrument designed by the author—generally known as the "Fokker organ"—kept in Teylers Museum, Haarlem. *(Scott Fruehwald)*

4075
as
FOKKER, Adriaan Daniël. **The qualities of the equal temperament by 31 fifths of a tone in the octave,** *Société Internationale de Musicologie, cinquième congrès/Internationale Gesellschaft für Musikwissenschaft, fünfter Kongreß/International Society for Musical Research, Fifth Congress* (Amsterdam: Vereniging voor Nederlandse Muziekgeschiedenis, 1953) 191–92. See no. 316 in this volume.

Taking the G-sharp to A-flat interval as the elementary step of an equal temperament system may answer the problem of perfect intervals in the performance of Gregorian chant, 17th- and 18th-c. works, and traditional music. *(Tsipora Yosselevitch)*

4076
as
GAISSER, Hugo. **Die acht Kirchentöne in der griechisch-albanesischen Überlieferung** [The eight church modes in Greek-Albanian transmission], *Haydn-Zentenarfeier* (Leipzig: Breitkopf & Härtel; Wien: Artaria, 1909) 83–84. In German. See no. 65 in this volume.

Discusses Byzantine elements surviving in the liturgical and traditional music of the Greek-Albanian people of Sicily.

4077
as
GAISSER, Hugo. **L'origine et la vraie nature du mode dit "chromatique oriental"** [The origin and the true nature of the mode known as "oriental chromatic"], *Congrès international d'histoire de la musique: Documents, mémoires et vœux* (Solesmes: St. Pierre; Paris: Fischbacher, 1901) 93–100. *Music.* In French. See no. 32 in this volume.

The "oriental chromatic" scale is composed of two tetrachords, each identical to the upper tetrachord of the harmonic minor scale. Examples from the repertoire of Byzantine chant are discussed.

4078
as
GRASSI LANDI, Bartolomeo. **Observations sur le genre enharmonique** [Observations on the enharmonic genus], *Congrès international d'histoire de la musique: Documents, mémoires et vœux* (Solesmes: St. Pierre; Paris: Fischbacher, 1901) 57–59. In French. See no. 32 in this volume.

A response to no. 4089, questioning the use of the term "enharmonic".

4079
as
HÁBA, Alois. **Souměrnost evropského tónového systému/Règles du système tonique européen** [Rules of the European tonal system], *Hudba národů: Sborník přednášek, proslovených na I. mezinárodním sjezdu skladatelů a hudebních kritiků/Musique des nations: Ier Congrès international des compositeurs et critiques musicaux* (Praha: Syndikát Českých Skladatelů, 1948) 31–36,133–37. *Charts, diagr.* In Czech and French. See no. 278 in this volume.

A systemic account of the interrelations of the seven Hellenistic modes, on the basis of the compositional practice of Vítězslav Novák, in terms of the relatively major and minor character of the modes themselves and of their constituent intervals. The Lydian mode is the most major of all and should be taken as basic. Spiritual qualities of the intervals are also discussed.

4080
as
HÁBA, Alois. **Welche Aufgaben bietet die Vierteltonmusik der Musikwissenschaft?** [What are the tasks quarter-tone music offers musicology?], *Bericht über den I. musikwissenschaftlichen Kongress der Deutschen Musikgesellschaft in Leipzig* (Wiesbaden: Breitkopf & Härtel, 1926) 304–11. *Charts, diagr.* In German. See no. 120 in this volume.

The potential uses of quarter tones in 20th-c. music are illuminated through examples from ancient Greek, Arab, and east Asian musics, and from the Montpellier Codex (F-MOf MS H196). *(William Renwick)*

4081
as
HEINITZ, Wilhelm. **Asymmetrien in Gebrauchstonleitern** [Asymmetries in functional scales], *Bericht über den I. musikwissenschaftlichen Kongress der Deutschen Musikgesellschaft in Leipzig* (Wiesbaden: Breitkopf & Härtel, 1926) 67–70. *Illus.* In German. See no. 120 in this volume.

Discusses the distribution of tones within melodies, noting the relationships to phrasing and to ascending and descending motions. An analytical method is presented and demonstrated. *(William Renwick)*

4082
as
HUSMANN, Heinrich. **Antike und Orient in ihrer Bedeutung für die europäische Musik** [Antiquity and the East in their significance for European music], *Bericht über den internationalen musikwissenschaftlichen Kongreß* (Kassel: Bärenreiter, 1957) 24–33. In German. See no. 356 in this volume.

The evolution of tempered from pure scale systems, well known in the modern European case, can also be found in the development of ancient Greek music theory, in Javanese pelog and slendro scales, in the seven-tone Thai scale, the 17-tone Near Eastern scale, and the 23-tone Indian scale. Possibilities for a neurophysiological account of these very widely different outcomes are explored. *(David Bloom)*

4083
as
KALLENBACH-GRELLER, Lotte. **Die historischen Grundlagen der Vierteltöne** [The historical foundations of quarter tones], *Beethoven-Zentenarfeier: Internationaler musikhistorischer Kongress* (Wien: Universal, 1927) 359–72. In German. See no. 142 in this volume.

The concept of the quarter-tone has a history in theory from Pythagoras and Aristoxenus to Marchetto da Padova, and in compositional application, from Nicola Vicentino in the 16th c. to Alois Hába in the 20th. *(David Bloom)*

4084
as
KNUDSEN, Thorkild. **Structures prémodales et pseudo-grégoriennes dans les mélodies des ballades danoises** [Premodal and pseudo-Gregorian structures in the melodies of Danish ballads], *Journal of the International Folk Music Council* X (1958) 4–14. *Music.* In French. See no. 371 in this volume.

The corpus of traditional Danish melodies, from medieval ballads through the *skaemteviser* (comic songs) of the 19th c., includes some that are neither tonal nor modal in the traditional sense; they may represent a stratum of what may be called premodal music in which the tonal center is not a fundamental or dominant tone but rather a particular feature of each isolated melodic fragment, within the zone of diatonic or pentatonic intonation. Common features between this structure and that of Gregorian chant can be explained by the hypothesis that chant melodies were originally derived from this generally Germanic premodal stratum before being systematized into the standard Gregorian scales. *(David Bloom)*

4085
as
KROHN, Ilmari. **Das akustische Harmonium der Universität zu Helsingfors** [The acoustic harmonium at Helsingin Yliopisto], *Bericht über den zweiten Kongress der Internationalen Musikgesellschaft* (Leipzig: Breitkopf & Härtel, 1907) 75–83. *Music, charts, diagr.* In German. See no. 53 in this volume.

A four-manual harmonium built for the university at Helsinki by the Kotykiewich firm of Vienna, under the author's direction and on principles developed by Carl Andreas Eitz, is capable of playing in just intonation through a range of keys and church modes. *(David Bloom)*

4086
as
KROHN, Ilmari. **Die Kirchentonarten** [The church modes], *Bericht über den musikwissenschaftlichen Kongreß in Basel* (Leipzig: Breitkopf & Härtel, 1925) 220–30. *Music, charts, diagr.* In German. See no. 102 in this volume.

Discusses the melodic construction of Gregorian chant, and of Protestant and Catholic church song of the 15th and 16th c. with respect to archetypes in the traditional music of various peoples. An essay on harmonic structure is included.

4087 KUTTNER, Fritz A. **A "Pythagorean" tone-**
as **system in China antedating the early Greek**
achievements by several centuries, *Bericht über*
den siebenten internationalen musikwissenschaftlichen
Kongress (Kassel: Bärenreiter, 1959) 174–76. See no.
390 in this volume.

The tuning system ascribed to the minister Ling Lun in accounts of the legendary reign of Huangdi, the Yellow Emperor (26th c. B.C.E.) would have generated intervals somewhat smaller than a perfect fifth; the earliest literary evidence of a properly Pythagorean system in Chinese use comes from the mid-3rd c. B.C.E. in the *Lüshi qunqiu* (Springs and autumns of Master Lü) of Lü Buwei, at a time when the system could have been transmitted from Europe. Nevertheless, a set of stone chimes dating from no later than the mid-6th c. B.C.E. and probably from the 9th c. or even earlier, excavated from Zhou Dynasty tombs at Luoyang, Henan (now in the collections of the Royal Ontario Museum, Toronto) exhibits both Pythagorean (or just) and natural intonations, including the major third, with a deviation of two cents or less. *(David Bloom)*

4088 LAJTHA, László. **À propos de l'"intonation**
as **fausse" dans la musique populaire** [So-called
faulty intonation in traditional music], *Les colloques de*
Wégimont. [I: Ethnomusicologie I] (Bruxelles:
Elsevier, 1956) 145–53. In French. See no. 340 in this
volume.

The criteria classically trained musicians use to determine what is in tune are not applicable for traditional music that does not use a tempered musical system. Ornamentation, regional tradition and style, individual taste, and even the age of the singer or instrumentalist all must be taken into account by those who study comparative folklore and traditional music. A more extended version with musical examples, in Hungarian, is published in the festschrift for Zoltán Kodály's 70th birthday, *Kodály emlékkönyv I* (Akadémiai Kiadó, Budapest 1953). *(Helen-Ursula Katz)*

4089 LALOY, Louis. **Le genre enharmonique des**
as **Grecs** [The Greek enharmonic genus], *Congrès inter-*
national d'histoire de la musique: Documents,
mémoires et vœux (Solesmes: St. Pierre; Paris:
Fischbacher, 1901) 39–56. *Charts, diagr.* In French.
See no. 32 in this volume.

The most primitive enharmonic notions were derived by Olympus the Mysian, who incorporated the quarter tone into the Dorian mode. The construction of the mode and its use in ancient Greek drama are discussed.

4090 LAND, Jan Pieter Nicolaas; ABŪ NAṢR
as MUHAMMAD IBN MUHAMMAD IBN
ṬARKHĀN IBN UZALAGH AL-FĀRĀBĪ.
Recherches sur l'histoire de la gamme arabe
[Research on the history of the Arabic scale], *Actes du*
sixième Congrès international des orientalistes
(Leiden: Brill, 1885) 35–168. In French. See no. 11 in
this volume.

The Arabic scale is not composed of third-tones (17 or 18 scale degrees). The octave contains seven diatonic degrees, analogous to the Western scale. The neutral third, invented in the 8th century, is a compromise betweeen the major and minor thirds. Includes excerpts from Al-Fārābī's *Kitāb al-mūsīqī al kabīr.* *(David Nussenbaum)*

4091 LUCIANI, Sebastiano Arturo. **La crisi del**
as **sistema temperato** [The crisis of equal tempera-
ment], *Atti del quinto Congresso di musica* (Firenze:
Barbèra, 1948) 129–31. In Italian. See no. 285 in this
volume.

Contemporary music, owing to the dictates of form and controls of harmony, is structurally fragmented, melodically asthmatic, and temporally interminable. Stifled by the music's cerebral elements and their complexity, the composer fears clarity, simplicity, and comprehensibility. The intonation of the human voice and orchestral instrument are distorted by equal temperament, and musicians ignore the tuning systems of the past. Quarter-tone instruments, like Hába's piano and Silvestro Baglioni's harmonium, are impractical. Ultrachromaticism is perceptible only when sung, as

in jazz, popular song, and performances by great singers. The purity and quality of just intonation are no longer appreciated by our ears.
(Channan Willner)

4092 LYON, Gustave. **Généralisation de l'emploi du**
as **diapason normal: Étude des moyens de le**
rendre obligatoire [Generalization of the use of *dia-*
pason normal: A study of the means of making it compulsory], *Congrès international de musique: Iʳᵉ ses-*
sion—Exposition Universelle de 1900: Compte rendu,
rapports, communications (Paris: conference, 1901)
28–31. In French. See no. 29 in this volume.

Summarizes attempts to standardize pitch at a universal A4 of 435 vibrations per second, which could be regulated by professors and conductors.

4093 MARCEL-DUBOIS, Claudie. **Présence ou ab-**
as **sence de la constante de quarte, de quinte et**
d'octave: Son rôle structurel dans l'ethnomu-
sicologie européenne [Presence or absence of the
constant of fourth, fifth, and octave: Its structural role in
European ethnomusicology], *La résonance dans les*
échelles musicales (Paris: Centre National de la Recherche Scientifique [CNRS], 1963) 143–48. *Transcr.*
In French; summaries in English and German. See no.
420 in this volume.

Discusses the distribution of intervallic structures in relation to geography, social function, nature of musical expression, and documents considered.

4094 MEINEL, Hermann. **Zur Stimmung der**
as **Musikinstrumente** [Concerning the tuning of musical instruments], *Acustica: International journal of*
acoustics/Journal international d'acoustique/Interna-
tionale akustische Zeitschrift IV/1 (1954) 233–36.
Illus., bibliog., charts, diagr. In German; summaries in
English, French, and German. See no. 324 in this
volume.

Discusses measurements of pitch, the construction of an electro-optical tuning apparatus for musical instruments, and the results obtained with it. The auditory accuracy of the best tuners is astonishingly high. *(author)*

4095 MORTARI, Virgilio. **La crisi del sistema**
as **temperato e i problemi del linguaggio musicale**
[The crisis of equal temperament and the problems of
musical language], *Atti del quinto Congresso di musica*
(Firenze: Barbèra, 1948) 39–45. In Italian. See no. 285
in this volume.

The equilibrium of four elements in music (melody, harmony, rhythm, timbre) is essential. Confused by the repercussions of musical revolutions, and torn between the tonal, atonal, and modal systems, the modern sense of tone has been exhausted. Modal music, owing to just intonation, sounds fresh and natural in its suggestion of ancient and folk music. The unlimited resources of just intonation can help composers to surmount the harmonic constraints of equal temperament, and enable them to write melodic, linear music that is rooted in tradition. *(Channan Willner)*

4096 NADEL, Siegfried. **Sur la structure des**
as **systèmes de gammes** [On the structure of scale systems], *Congrès international des arts populaires/Inter-*
national congress of popular arts (Paris: Institut international de coopération intellectuelle, 1928) 95–96. In
French. See no. 153 in this volume.

Summary of the first section of the paper abstracted as no. 3953 in this volume.

4097 NIELSEN, A. Kjerbye. **A direct reading cent-**
as **meter: An instrument suitable for the measure-**
ment of the tuning inaccuracies of musical in-
struments, *Problèmes d'acoustique* (Liège:

Université de Liège, 1965) J24. *Illus.* See no. 504 in this volume.

Describes an electronic device that measures the logarithmic frequency difference between the nominal and the unknown frequency. *(Allen Lott)*

4098 OLSEN, Poul Rovsing. **Enregistrements faits à**
as **Kuwait and Bahrain** [Recordings made in Kuwait and Bahrain], *Les colloques de Wégimont. IV: Ethnomusicologie III* (Paris: Belles Lettres, 1964) 137–70. *Transcr.* In French. See no. 401 in this volume.

In music of the desert, the tetrachord dominates, while pentachords frequently appear in songs connected with the maritime life of Faylakah island, Kuwait. Some melodies possess a larger ambitus. *(Scott Fruehwald)*

4099 PEPINSKY, Abe. **Geminiani's schematic fin-**
as **gerboard,** *Papers of the American Musicological Society* (Philadelphia: American Musicological Society, 1946) 137–43. *Charts, diagr.* See no. 272 in this volume.

Francesco Geminiani's *The entire new and compleat tutor for the violin* (London, 1747; not to be confused with his better-known writings on violin playing) contains a schematic diagram of a fingerboard marked with frets for all the chromatic tones in a system that does not exactly match any of the known systems of temperament. The interval system implied by the fingerboard is discussed in detail and compared with equal, natural diatonic, meantone, and Pythagorean temperaments together with the result of a 1937 study by Paul C. Greene on the intonational practices of 20th-c. violinists. *(David Bloom)*

4100 PFROGNER, Hermann. **Der Clavis in Andreas**
as **Werckmeisters** *Nothwendigsten Anmerkungen und Regeln, wie der Bassus continuus oder Generalbass wol könne tractiret werden* [Key in Andreas Werckmeister's *Die nothwendigste Anmerkungen und Regeln, wie der Bassus continuus oder Generalbass wol könne tractiret werden*], *Bericht über den Internationalen musikwissenschaftlichen Kongress* (Kassel: Bärenreiter, 1954) 149–51. In German. See no. 319 in this volume.

Werckmeister did not view equal temperament merely as an empirical compromise to bridge the circle of fifths, but as a "musical fiction." This idea borrows something from the older idea of *musica ficta*. Schoenberg's concept of atonality, in which each of the 12 pitches of the equally tempered octave relate to all the rest in the same way, may be understood as an extension of Werckmeister's idea. Werckmeister himself was able to speculate about vast changes in music over time: "Over the past 200 years," he writes in his *Musikalische Paradoxal-Discourse* (1707), "much has changed, and in 100 or 200 years hence musica practica will look and sound entirely different." *(Carl Skoggard)*

4101 PIAZZANO, Geremia. **Le fonotomo: Diviseur**
as **des sons** [The fonotomo: Divider of sounds], *Report of the Fourth Congress of the International Musical Society* (London: Novello, 1912) 332. In French. See no. 71 in this volume.

Summary of a paper that describes a mechanical tuner for equal temperament.

4102 POTIRON, Henri. **Les équivalences modales**
as **dans le chant grégorien** [Modal equivalences in Gregorian chant], *Congrès international de musique sacrée: Chant et orgue* (Paris: Desclée de Brouwer, 1937) 79–84. In French. See no. 247 in this volume.

The modes of a chant are traditionally determined by how it ends, but because identical patterns of intervals can exist in several modes there is often ambiguity. *(Arthur Maisel)*

4103 POTIRON, Henri. **La question modale** [The
as modal question], *Atti del [I] Congresso internazionale di musica sacra* (Tournai: Desclée, 1952) 255ff. In French. See no. 303 in this volume.

4104 REINACH, Théodore. **L'harmonie des sphères**
as [The harmony of the spheres], *Congrès international d'histoire de la musique: Documents, mémoires et vœux* (Solesmes: St. Pierre; Paris: Fischbacher, 1901) 60–62. *Music.* In French. See no. 32 in this volume.

Discusses the Greek modes.

4105 REINHARD, Kurt. **On the problem of pre-**
as **pentatonic scales: Particularly the third-second nucleus,** *Journal of the International Folk Music Council* X (1958) 15–17. See no. 371 in this volume.

Explores questions concerning the origin and function of a three-note melodic neucleus, found in traditional musics worldwide, consisting of a minor third plus a major second. *(James R. Cowdery)*

4106 REUSCH, Fritz. **Versuch einer Tonraumlehre**
as [Outline of a theory of tonal space], *Bericht über den Internationalen musikwissenschaftlichen Kongress* (Kassel: Bärenreiter, 1954) 50–53. In German. See no. 319 in this volume.

The tonal order is based on the interval of the fifth. Two successive fifths along the circle of fifths yield three pitches of the diatonic scale; three fifths along the circle provide five pitches, and four, all seven pitches. These stages of interval generation (the concept of *Quintengeneration* is Robert Lachmann's) correspond to the general historical unfolding of music in successive phases and suggest that a single law underlies all music. *(Carl Skoggard)*

4107 ROUGET, Gilbert. **Les éléments de formation**
as **des échelles extérieurs à la résonance: Facture instrumentale et résonance** [Elements of scale formation external to overtone theory: Instrument construction and overtone theory], *La résonance dans les échelles musicales* (Paris: Centre National de la Recherche Scientifique [CNRS], 1963) 223–34. In French; summaries in English and German. See no. 420 in this volume.

Discusses the generation of overtones by several instruments, including the zither and the xylophone. Scales on the borderline of overtone theory are addressed, and correlations among instrument construction, technique, and tuning are considered. *(author)*

4108 SACHS, Melchior Ernst. **Das temperierte**
as **19-tonsystem und eine dafür passende Schrift** [A system for dividing the octave into 19 tones, with appropriate notation], *Report of the Fourth Congress of the International Musical Society* (London: Novello, 1912) 278–81. *Illus.* In German. See no. 71 in this volume.

Music written for the common 12-tone system can be played in the 19-tone system, and further possibilities are within reach as well. The proposed graphic notation involves the use of color and thickness.

4109 SCHAEFFER, Myron. **An extension of tone-**
as **row techniques through electronic pitch control,** *Journal of the International Folk Music Council* XVI (1964) 95–99. *Charts, diagr.* See no. 463 in this volume.

The use of electronic sounds allows a variety of micro- and macro-tunings, each with its own potential for organization into tone rows, which can be used separately or in combination, in combination with diatonically tuned instruments or voice. Expected consonance values for pairs of notes in various electronically produced octave species, in terms of beats and difference tones, are provided in table form. *(David Bloom)*

4110 SCHÄFER, Oskar. **Das musikalische sehen** [Mu-
as sical seeing], *Bericht über den I. musikwissenschaftlichen Kongress der Deutschen Musikgesellschaft in*

Leipzig (Wiesbaden: Breitkopf & Härtel, 1926) 94–97. *Charts, diagr.* In German. See no. 120 in this volume.

Discusses Karl Laker's acoustical theories, focusing on overtones, interval measurements, temperament, and transposition. *(William Renwick)*

4111
as

SCHIØRRING, Nils. **The contribution of ethnomusicology to historical musicology,** *Report of the Eighth Congress of the International Musicological Society. I: Papers* (Kassel: Bärenreiter, 1961) 380–86. *Transcr.* See no. 439 in this volume.

Examples drawn from Danish traditional music of tunes transcribed from performers from two or three different generations demonstrate the instability of intervals in Western European music.

4112
as

SCHMIEDEL, Peter. **Ein unsymmetrisches Tonsystem** [An asymmetric tone system], *Bericht über den internationalen musikwissenschaftlichen Kongreß* (Kassel: Bärenreiter, 1957) 202–03. In German. See no. 356 in this volume.

The peculiarities of the scales described in Kathleen Schlesinger's *The Greek aulos* (1939) are described in terms of the theory of overtone coincidence, and contrasted with the Pythagorean scale, in which only fifths coincide.

4113
as

SCHNEIDER, Marius. **Entstehung der Tonsysteme** [The origin of tonal systems], *Bericht über den internationalen musikwissenschaftlichen Kongreß* (Kassel: Bärenreiter, 1957) 203–11. *Charts, diagr., transcr.* In German. See no. 356 in this volume.

Discusses the theory that modal systems originate in melodic motives, rather than giving rise to melodies. A classification of scales in these terms is proposed and demonstrated with examples from 26 ethnic groups of North and South America and Africa.

4114
as

SCHNEIDER, Marius. **Présence ou absence de la constante de quarte, de quinte et d'octave: Son rôle structurel dans la consonance polyphonique primitive** [Presence or absence of the constant of fourth, fifth, and octave: Its structural role in primitive polyphonic consonance], *La résonance dans les échelles musicales* (Paris: Centre National de la Recherche Scientifique [CNRS], 1963) 149–58. *Charts, diagr.* In French; summaries in English and German. See no. 420 in this volume.

These intervals play a dominant role in the relatively evolved polyphony of primitive peoples. However, they do not seem to be decisive factors in the genesis of polyphony (which arises from successive or simultaneous variations), nor of tonality. The third is the constitutive element in ancient tone systems. In a given melody, the same third may appear in different sizes. Often the fifth is divided into two equal thirds. But in as much as thirds and fifths become stable, the neutral third begins to assume an entirely new role. It is always to be found at a fixed place in the scale, and it resolves the free intonation of the interval between B and B-flat. *(author)*

4115
as

SOMMER, Jürgen. **Das elektronische Stimmgerät als Hilfe beim Stimmen von Musikinstrumenten** [The electronic tuning device as an aid in tuning musical instruments], *Dokumentation* (Frankfurt am Main: Fördergemeinschaft Klavier, 1966) 187–200. In German. See no. 494 in this volume.

4116
as

STEPHANI, Hermann. **Das Verhältnis von reiner und pythagoreischer Stimmung als psychologisches Problem** [The relationship between pure and Pythagorean tuning as a psychological problem], *Bericht über den I. musikwissenschaftlichen Kongreß der Deutschen Musikgesellschaft in Leipzig* (Wiesbaden: Breitkopf & Härtel, 1926) 417–27. *Charts, diagr.* In German. See no. 120 in this volume.

Reviews the mathematical basis for pure (just) tuning and Pythagorean tuning, then discusses the psychological effects of tempering thirds and fifths. The implications of tuning on music written in different texures (monophony, two-part, three-part), on melody and harmony, and on the understanding of the natural basis of the minor triad are discussed in supplementary papers by Richard WICKE and Wilhelm HEINITZ. *(William Renwick)*

4117
as

SUÑOL BAULINAS, Gregori M. **La modalitat del cant litúrgic llatí** [The modality of Latin liturgical chant], *Congrés de la Societat Internacional de Musicologia* (Barcelona: Casa de Caritat, 1936). In French. See no. 224 in this volume.

The conference report provides only a citation. Neither the text nor a summary of the paper was published here.

4118
as

THELWALL, Walter Hampden. **Mathematical analysis of the tempered chromatic scale,** *Report of the Fourth Congress of the International Musical Society* (London: Novello, 1912) 74. See no. 71 in this volume.

Summary of a paper.

4119
as

THIBAUT, Jean-Baptiste. **Assimilation des échoi byzantins et des modes latins avec les anciens tropes grecs** [Assimilation of Byzantine ēchoi and Latin modes with ancient Greek tropes], *Congrès international d'histoire de la musique: Documents, mémoires et vœux* (Solesmes: St. Pierre; Paris: Fischbacher, 1901) 77–85. *Charts, diagr.* In French. See no. 32 in this volume.

Provides tables of correspondences between Byzantine īchoi and Latin modes.

4120
as

THOMAS, Pierre. **Principes de la théorie modale hexacordale dans les théoriciens médiévaux et principalement dans Guy d'Arezzo** [Principles of hexachordal modal theory in the medieval theorists, especially Guido of Arezzo], *Atti del [I] Congresso internazionale di musica sacra* (Tournai: Desclée, 1952) 276ff. In French. See no. 303 in this volume.

4121
as

TIERSOT, Julien. **Des transformations de la tonalité et du rôle du dièze et du bémol depuis le Moyen Âge jusqu'au XVIIᵉ siècle: Résumé** [On the transformations of tonality and the role of the sharp and the flat from the Middle Ages to the 17th century: Abstract], *Congrès international d'histoire de la musique: Documents, mémoires et vœux* (Solesmes: St. Pierre; Paris: Fischbacher, 1901) 175–78. In French. See no. 32 in this volume.

Though the history of the flat sign may be traced through medieval theoretical writings, the sharp sign's development remains more obscure. Chromatic alterations were employed long before they were notated in the scores.

4122
as

TRẦN, Van Khê. **Les échelles régulières du cycle des quintes et leurs déformations occasionnelles: Dans le cadre du pentatonique** [Regular scales of the circle of fifths and their occasional deformations in the pentatonic framework], *La résonance dans les échelles musicales* (Paris: Centre National de la Recherche Scientifique [CNRS], 1963) 161–71. *Charts, diagr., transcr.* In French; summaries in English and German. See no. 420 in this volume.

Discusses the writings of Lü Buwei and Sima Qian on scales based on progression by fifths. Aspects of ditonic, tritonic, tetratonic, and pentatonic scales are also considered, along with variants of these scales, particularly in the music of Vietnam. *(author)*

4123 VARGYAS, Lajos. **Some parallels of rare**
as **modal structures in Western and Eastern Europe,** *Journal of the International Folk Music Council*
X (1956) 22–28. *Music.* See no. 371 in this volume.
Discusses modal structures that occur rarely in Western European traditional melodies, but are often found in those of Eastern Europe.

4124 VASILJEVIĆ, Miodrag A. **Les bases tonales de**
as **la musique populaire serbe** [The tonal bases of traditional Serbian music], *Journal of the International
Folk Music Council* IV (1952) 19–22. *Transcr.* In
French. See no. 306 in this volume.
Outlines the analysis of traditional Serb melody into three basic scales with
two harmonic functions (those of dominant and subdominant). An extended version is published in *Jugoslavenski muzicki folklor. I: Narodne
melodije koje se pevaju na Kosmetu* (Belgrade, 1950). *(David Bloom)*

4125 VASILJEVIĆ, Miodrag A. **Kvalitativne**
as **funkcije tonova u tonalnim osnovama našeg
muzičkog folklora: Jedan egzaktni metod za
tipologiju lestvica** [The qualitative function of
pitches and scales in our traditional music: An exact
method for determining typology of scales], *Treći
kongres folklorista Jugoslavije* (Cetinje: Udruženje
Folklorista Crne Gore, 1958) 199–209. *Charts, diagr.,
transcr.* In Serbian; summary in French. See no. 357 in
this volume.
Surveys characteristics of 11 traditional Yugoslavian scale types.

4126 VEGA, Carlos. **Escalas con semitonos en la**
as **música de los antiguos peruanos** [Scales with
semitones in ancient Peruvian music], *Actas y trabajos
científicos del XXV° Congreso Internacional de
Americanistas* (Buenos Aires: Coni; Universidad
Nacional de La Plata, 1934) 349–81. *Music, bibliog.,
charts, diagr.* In Spanish. See no. 198 in this volume.
In ancient Peruvian music, scales with semitones may have coexisted with
the pentatonic scale, which was widely believed to be exclusive of other
systems. The tunings of many precolonial and pre-Columbian instruments
created scales resembling the major, Dorian, and Lydian modes. These
tunings may have originated with Andean peoples earlier than the Incas.
Extensive references are made to the research of earlier ethnographers on
the subject, and to theoretical material on the tunings and scales of Andean
panpipes. *(Joyce Z. Lindorff)*

4127 VOGEL, Martin. **Die Entstehung der Kirchen-**
as **tonarten** [The origin of the church modes], *Bericht
über den internationalen musikwissenschaftlichen
Kongreß* (Kassel: Bärenreiter, 1963) 101–06. *Charts,
diagr.* In German. See no. 452 in this volume.
In ancient Greece, the two-octave scale was oriented downward from C4 to
C2; in the Middle Ages, upward from C2 to C4. This change in orientation
helps to explain the development of the four authentic and four plagal
modes of the medieval period from the seven octave species of antiquity.
(Jeffrey Miller)

4128 VOGEL, Martin. **Über die drei Tongeschlechter**
as **des Archytas** [Archytas's three tonal genera], *Bericht
über den internationalen musikwissenschaftlichen
Kongreß* (Kassel: Bärenreiter, 1957) 233–35. *Charts,
diagr.* In German. See no. 356 in this volume.
Building on research reported in the author's dissertation (*Die Zahl Sieben
in der spekulativen Musiktheorie*, Bonn 1955), demonstrates a practical interpretation of the controversial ratios given in Ptolemy's account of the
diatonic, chromatic, and enharmonic genera in the formulations of
Archytas of Tarentum. *(David Bloom)*

4129 WETZEL, Justus Hermann. **Dur und Moll im**
as **diatonischen Tonkreise** [Major and minor in the
diatonic tonal circle], *Kongreß für Ästhetik und allge-*

meine Kunstwissenschaft: Bericht (Stuttgart: Enke,
1914) 501–10. In German. See no. 86 in this volume.

4130 WICKE, Richard. **Untersuchungen zur**
as **Gegensätzlichkeit von Dur und Moll** [Investigations on the opposition of major and minor], *Bericht
über den IX. Kongreß für experimentelle Psychologie*
(Jena: Fischer, 1925) 240f. In German. See no. 121 in
this volume.

4131 WIORA, Walter. **Présence ou absence de la**
as **constante de quarte, de quinte et d'octave: Son
rôle structurel dans l'ethnomusicologie primitive** [Presence or absence of the constant of fourth,
fifth, and octave: Its structural role in the
ethnomusicology of primitive music], *La résonance
dans les échelles musicales* (Paris: Centre National de
la Recherche Scientifique [CNRS], 1963) 129–42.
Transcr. In French; summaries in English and German.
See no. 420 in this volume.
Discusses music before the influence of the three consonant intervals. The
development of scales is considered, and the three intervals are shown to
form a framework which is then filled in.

4132 WIORA, Walter. **La résonance dans les échelles**
as **musicales: Le point de vue des musicologues**
[Overtones in musical scales: The viewpoint of musicologists], *La résonance dans les échelles musicales*
(Paris: Centre National de la Recherche Scientifique
[CNRS], 1963) 37–42. In French; summaries in English and German. See no. 420 in this volume.
Discusses the concept of intention as related to scales, the overtone series,
and psychological musicology.

4133 YAMANOUCHI, Seihin. **The Ryūkyū Islands**
as **as a meeting point of musical cultures in the
Pacific area,** *Journal of the International Folk Music
Council* VII (1955) 22. See no. 337 in this volume.
Summary of a paper comparing the scales of traditional songs from the
Ryūkyū Islands with those of several cultures in East and Southeast Asia.

4134 ŽIVKOVIĆ, Milenko. **Tonale Grundlage in**
as **Volksmelodien einiger Gebiete Jugoslawiens**
[Tonal foundations of traditional melodies from certain
regions of Yugoslavia], *Bericht über den internationalen musikwissenschaftlichen Kongreß Wien
Mozartjahr 1956* (Graz; Köln: Böhlau, 1958) 760–64.
Music, transcr. In German. See no. 365 in this volume.
Song melodies of Bosnia and Herzegovina, Macedonia, Montenegro, and
Serbia belong to five principal modal types: Hypomixolydian, Balkan
(plagal harmonic minor), Aeolian, Phrygian, and Ionian, particularly the
first two. The harmonization of melodies in the traditional modes by Yugoslav art-music composers is briefly discussed. *(David Bloom)*

63 Harmony, counterpoint, and voice-leading

4135 BARKECHLI, Mehdi. **Quelques idées nou-**
as **velles sur la consonance** [Some new ideas on consonance], *Acoustique musicale* (Paris: Centre National
de la Recherche Scientifique [CNRS], 1959) 21–28.
Charts, diagr. In French. See no. 393 in this volume.
Reviews the concepts of classical Greek and medieval Perso-Arabic theorists, Mersenne, and current psychoacoustic research. Particular attention
is given to the phenomenon of the difference-tone illusion and to the perception of consonance in different cultures.

4136
as
BARTHA, Dénes. **Le développement de la résonance dans les musiques évoluées: Occident au XXe siècle—La musique de Bartók** [The development of overtones in advanced musics: The West in the 20th century—Bartók's music], *La résonance dans les échelles musicales* (Paris: Centre National de la Recherche Scientifique [CNRS], 1963) 279–90. *Music.* In French; summaries in English and German. See no. 420 in this volume.

Led by a sure historical instinct, Bartók built his melodies and harmonies on the preferred intervals of ancient tetratonic and pentatonic scales: the octave, fifth, fourth, and minor third, while having a marked antipathy to the major third. Though unaware of Jacques Chailley's theoretical work, Bartók distinguished in his own music between harmonic and melodic realms: The structures he built on the overtone series are always static, in contrast with his personal melodic chromaticism. *(author)*

4137
as
BARTHA, Dénes. **Zum Harmoniebegriff in der Musik Béla Bartóks: Ein Beitrag zur theoretischen Erfassung der neuen Musik** [The concept of harmony in the music of Béla Bartók: A contribution to the theory of new music], *Bericht über den siebenten internationalen musikwissenschaftlichen Kongress* (Kassel: Bärenreiter, 1959) 63–64. In German. See no. 390 in this volume.

A summary of ideas developed by Ernő Lendvai. Bartók's harmony in his chromatic idiom represents an expansion of functional harmony. Each of the three major functions (tonic, dominant, subdominant) are assigned four positions within the 12 notes of the conventional scale, each position being equidistant from its neighbors. The four positions of the subdominant, for example, are *d, f, a♭,* and *b*. Pentatonicism underlies Bartók's melodies and chords and explains his aversion towards major thirds and major sixths in favor of major seconds, minor thirds, and pure fourths (pure fifths are also little used by him). In his late music, Bartók also avoids the layering of pure fourths or pure fifths, either of which would imply a mixing of the harmonic functions. He is partial to assymmetrical divisions of the octave (for example semitone-fourth-semitone-fourth). *(Carl Skoggard)*

4138
as
BIMBERG, Siegfried. **Einige Bemerkungen zum Tonalitätsbegriff** [Some remarks on the concept of tonality], *Beiträge zur Musikwissenschaft* VII/4 (1965) 351–59. In German. See no. 495 in this volume.

4139
as
BLANKENBURG, Walter. **Die Bedeutung des Kanons in Bachs Werk** [The meaning of canon in Bach's works], *Bericht über die Wissenschaftliche Bachtagung* (Leipzig: Peters, 1951) 250–58. In German. See no. 298 in this volume.

The instrumental canon in the 17th and early 18th c. is a rhetorical figure of the composer as creator, in imitation of God. In Bach's work, canon in triple time and featuring prominent thirds, sixths, and octaves denotes completeness. Both in vocal works and in the chorale arrangements of the *Orgelbüchlein,* canon is associated with texts referring to Christmas and Easter.

4140
as
BLANKENBURG, Walter. **Kanonimprovisationen im 16. und Anfang des 17. Jahrhunderts** [Canonic improvisations in the 16th and early 17th centuries], *Bericht über den siebenten internationalen musikwissenschaftlichen Kongress* (Kassel: Bärenreiter, 1959) 68–69. In German. See no. 390 in this volume.

Canonic improvisation "a mente" or "alla mente" during the 16th and early 17th c. called for a soloist to invent a line above a slowly moving cantus firmus so that a second singer could follow in canon. The canonic voices, at the unison, the fifth above or below, or the octave, were to observe the usual rules of consonance and dissonance in relation to the cantus firmus. The cantus firmus was normally borrowed from a religious source. Beginning with Gioseffo Zarlino Italian treatises describe the practice, and treatises written in England and Germany treat it as well. Bach seems to reflect canonic improvisation in the second canon of *Das musikalisches Opfer,*

BWV 1079, and in the first two pieces in his *Canonische Veränderungen über..."Vom Himmel hoch"...,* BWV 769. *(Carl Skoggard)*

⟶
BLAUKOPF, Kurt. **Tonalität und Soziologie** [Tonality and sociology]. See no. 5869 in this volume.

4141
as
BORRIS, Siegfried. **Chopins Bedeutung für den Chromatismus des XIX. Jahrhunderts** [Chopin's significance in 19th-century chromaticism], *The book of the first international musicological congress devoted to the works of Frederick Chopin* (Warszawa: Państwowe Wydawnictwo Naukowe, 1963) 107–10. In German. See no. 425 in this volume.

The great crisis in the history of harmony in the Romantic era is commonly dated from the appearance of Wagner's *Tristan und Isolde,* but is in fact strongly prefigured in Chopin's astonishingly bold chromaticism, particularly in the use of chromatic voice-leading to intensify harmonic tension. *(David Bloom)*

4142
as
BORRIS, Siegfried. **Die Widersprüche zwischen älterer Harmonielehre und neueren Tonsatzlehren** [The conflicts between traditional theory of harmony and recent theories of composition], *Kongreß-Bericht: Gesellschaft für Musikforschung* (Kassel; Basel: Bärenreiter, 1950) 211–13. In German. See no. 299 in this volume.

4143
as
BRANCO, Luís de Freitas. **Les contrepointistes de l'école d'Évora** [The Évora school of contrapuntists], *Actes du Congrès d'histoire de l'art* (Paris: Presses Universitaires de France, 1923-1924) 846–52. In French. See no. 94 in this volume.

The 16th and 17th c. saw the birth and flourishing of a Portuguese school of contrapuntists. Centered in Évora and founded by Manuel Mendes, it reached its apogee in the compositions of Duarte Lobo. The salient feature of the Évora school was the extreme exploitation of dissonance as a means of expression. *(Vivian Conejero)*

4144
as
BROCKHOFF, Maria Elisabeth. **Die Kadenz bei Josquin** [The cadence in Josquin], *Société Internationale de Musicologie, cinquième congrès/ Internationale Gesellschaft für Musikwissenschaft, fünfter Kongreß/International Society for Musical Research, Fifth Congress* (Amsterdam: Vereniging voor Nederlandse Muziekgeschiedenis, 1953) 86–95. In German. See no. 316 in this volume.

4145
as
CAMPO, Conrado del. **La harmonización del canto popular** [The harmonization of traditional song], *Congrés de la Societat Internacional de Musicologia* (Barcelona: Casa de Caritat, 1936). In Spanish. See no. 224 in this volume.

The conference report provides only a citation. Neither the text nor a summary of the paper was published here.

4146
as
CAVALLINI, Eduardo. **O nové harmonické řeči/ Une nouvelle langue harmonique** [A new harmonic language], *Hudba národů: Sborník přednášek, proslovených na I. mezinárodním sjezdu skladatelů a hudebních kritiků/Musique des nations: Ier Congrès international des compositeurs et critiques musicaux* (Praha: Syndikát Českých Skladatelů, 1948) 25–27,120–22. In Czech and French. See no. 278 in this volume.

Discusses developments in plurichromaticism or the use of microtones as they affect harmony, from the proposals in Busoni's *Entwurf einer neuen Ästhetik der Tonkunst* (1907) through the work of Alois Hába and Ivan Vyšnegradskij; Julián Carrillo and Augusto Novaro in Mexico; and in Italy

Silvestro Baglioni, Gustavo Giovanetti, the late Roberto Pelissier, Carlo Petrucci, Emilio Scarani, Amilcare Zanella, and the author.

4147
as

CHAILLEY, Jacques. **Apparences et réalités dans le langage de Debussy** [Appearances and realities in the language of Debussy], *Debussy et l'évolution de la musique au XXe siècle* (Paris: Centre National de la Recherche Scientifique [CNRS], 1965) 47–82. *Music*. In French. See no. 456 in this volume.

In Debussy's time, critics spoke of his violations of the rules of harmony. His new system was developed logically, not by speculations. It included a new use of the seventh degree of the scale, followed by the ninth and the eleventh. This led to an increased use of the whole-tone scale, which was not his invention. There was also an increased use of tones foreign to a chord, such as appogiaturas. *(Alan Kingsley)*

4148
as

CHAILLEY, Jacques. **Le développement de la résonance dans les musiques évoluées: Occident du Moyen-Âge au XIXe siècle** [The development of overtone theory in advanced musics: The West, from the Middle Ages to the 19th century], *La résonance dans les échelles musicales* (Paris: Centre National de la Recherche Scientifique [CNRS], 1963) 267–77. *Music, charts, diagr.* In French; summaries in English and German. See no. 420 in this volume.

The Western scale incorporates a monodic diatonic compass based on overtones 1-4 of the cycle of fifths. Polyphony introduces a new principle: progressive extension of overtone groups superimposed on the pattern given by resonance. Each group appears first as a transient before becoming stable. Currently, groups 11 and 13 are being assimilated. *(author)*

4149
as

CHAILLEY, Jacques. **Esprit et technique du chromatisme de la Renaissance** [The spirit and technique of Renaissance chromaticism], *Musique et poésie au XVIe siècle* (Paris: Centre National de la Recherche Scientifique [CNRS], 1954) 225–39. In French. See no. 326 in this volume.

Discusses the role of humanism in 16th-c. chromaticism.

4150
as

CHAILLEY, Jacques. **Ethnomusicologie et harmonie classique** [Ethnomusicology and classical harmony], *Les colloques de Wégimont. IV: Ethnomusicologie III* (Paris: Belles Lettres, 1964) IV, 249–69. In French. See no. 401 in this volume.

Discusses relationships between harmonies as found in Western art music and in other cultures.

4151
as

CHAILLEY, Jacques. **Hypothèses de travail** [Working hypotheses], *La résonance dans les échelles musicales* (Paris: Centre National de la Recherche Scientifique [CNRS], 1963) 45–48. *Bibliog.* In French. See no. 420 in this volume.

Consonance, or the principle of stability, issues from the overtone series and is characterized most often by octaves, fifths, and fourths. Attraction, or the principle of mobility and dynamism, pertains mainly to the cycle of fifths. *(author)*

4152
as

CHAILLEY, Jacques. **Musique orientale et harmonie européenne** [Oriental music and European harmony], *The preservation of traditional forms of the learned and popular music of the Orient and the Occident/La préservation des formes traditionelles de la musique savante et populaire dans les pays d'Orient et d'Occident* (Urbana: Center for Comparative Psycholinguistics, Institute of Communications Research, 1964) 83–88. In French. See no. 443 in this volume.

Asian musics are not, as Western listeners often suppose, monodic but they do not follow Western polyphonic practice. Many Asian music systems are

based on a consonance at the fourth or fifth without the third, a situation similar to that of an earlier phase of Western music. It is possible to harmonize Asian melodies without destroying their character; Ravel and Bartók have shown the way. *(Judith Drogichen Meyer)*

4153
as

CHERBULIEZ, Antoine-Élisée. **Zur harmonischen Analyse der Einleitung von Mozarts C-Dur Streichquartett (K.V. 465)** [Harmonic analysis of the introduction to Mozart's C-major string quartet (K.465)], *Bericht über die musikwissenschaftliche Tagung der Internationalen Stiftung Mozarteum* (Leipzig: Breitkopf & Härtel, 1932) 103–11. *Music*. In German. See no. 193 in this volume.

A strictly technical view of the famous dissonances in the opening of the quartet K.465 shows that they are analyzable as orthodox cross-relational practice, built on the normal resolution from Neapolitan sixth to dominant seventh, illustrating Mozart's effort to integrate the linear contrapuntal style of Bach and Händel into his personal style. *(David Bloom)*

4154
as

CHOMIŃSKI, Józef Michał. **Der Entwicklungscharakter der Harmonik im Mittelalter und in der Renaissance** [The developmental character of harmony in the Middle Ages and the Renaissance], *Bericht über den internationalen musikwissenschaftlichen Kongreß Wien Mozartjahr 1956* (Graz; Köln: Böhlau, 1958) 92–98. In German. See no. 365 in this volume.

Offers a critical account of attempts to see a prefiguration of major-minor tonality in early polyphony.

4155
as

COSTÈRE, Edmond. **Les éléments de formation des échelles extérieurs à la résonance: L'attraction** [Elements of scale formation external to overtone theory: Attraction], *La résonance dans les échelles musicales* (Paris: Centre National de la Recherche Scientifique [CNRS], 1963) 185–89. *Music*. In French; summaries in English and German. See no. 420 in this volume.

While liberating harmony from the overtone series, contemporary musicians have retained its most elementary concepts: octaves and fifths. In the dodecaphonic system, harmony originates from the intervallic tendency of attraction to octaves, fifths, semitones, and their inversions, based on differences in the power of attraction and on differences in the intrinsic stability to which they give rise. These conform to standards already existing (though interpreted differently) in traditional harmony. *(author)*

4156
as

DAHLHAUS, Carl. **Intervalldissonanz und Akkorddissonanz** [Interval dissonance and chord dissonance], *Bericht über den internationalen musikwissenschaftlichen Kongreß* (Kassel: Bärenreiter, 1963) 272–74. In German. See no. 452 in this volume.

For the analysis of 17th-c. music it is necessary to distinguish two kinds of dissonance: the note-against-note or intervallic dissonance associated with 16th-c. counterpoint, and the note-against-chord dissonance of early chordal harmony. Examples from the history of the transition are discussed. *(Leslie B. Dunner)*

4157
as

DAHLHAUS, Carl. **Über den Dissonanzbegriff des Mittelalters** [Concerning the medieval concept of dissonance], *Bericht über den siebenten internationalen musikwissenschaftlichen Kongress* (Kassel: Bärenreiter, 1959) 87–88. In German. See no. 390 in this volume.

In antiquity, the concept of dissonance was reserved for the out-of-tune individual note. The scholia of the *Musica enchriadis* use the term to mean notes that do not belong in a given tonal order. Subsequently there is a period in which dissonance has a problematic meaning, exemplified by a passage in Jean d'Afflighem, ca. 1100, where "dissonantia" may be referring to simultaneous or nonsimultaneous sounds. The modern usage arises in the 12th and

13th c. Walter Odington confirms it ca. 1300 when he remarks that "concords following prior discords make these bearable." *(Carl Skoggard)*

4158
as

DEUTSCH, Friedrich. **Die Fugenarbeit in den Werken Beethovens** [Fugal technique in Beethoven's works], *Festschrift den Mitgliedern des Musikhistorischen Kongresses überreicht von der Leitenden Kommission der Denkmäler der Tonkunst in Österreich* (Wien: Universal, 1927) 75–106. *Music.* In German. See no. 147 in this volume.

Distinguishes between actual fugues and transient fugal procedures; the former are especially numerous in his late piano sonatas and string quartets, as well as his Missa solemnis, op. 123. The successive elements of a fugue as construed by theorists are considered in relation to Beethoven's practice. Finally, a historical perspective is provided for the development of Beethoven's fugal writing. *(Carl Skoggard)*

4159
as

DÜRR, Walther. **Zur mehrstimmigen Behandlung des chromatischen Schrittes in der Polyphonie des 16. Jahrhunderts** [The multipart treatment of chromatic steps in 16th-century polyphony], *Bericht über den internationalen musikwissenschaftlichen Kongreß* (Kassel: Bärenreiter, 1963) 136–38. *Music.* In German. See no. 452 in this volume.

Particularly in the Italian madrigal from Cesare Tudino to Gesualdo, a chromatic stepwise movement in the melody accompanied by the movement of a third in a lower voice is an indication of an evolution from strictly linear polyphony to the beginnings of functional harmony.

4160
as

EIBNER, Franz. **Die Stimmführung Chopins in der Darstellung Heinrich Schenkers** [Chopin's voice-leading as characterized by Heinrich Schenker], *The book of the first international musicological congress devoted to the works of Frederick Chopin* (Warszawa: Państwowe Wydawnictwo Naukowe, 1963) 145–67. *Music, charts, diagr.* In German. See no. 425 in this volume.

Schenker's analysis, in *Der freie Satz*, of Chopin's scherzo in B♭ minor op. 31 is discussed and expanded with reference to the autograph MS.

4161
as

EINSTEIN, Alfred. **Beethoven und die Polyphonie** [Beethoven and polyphony], *Beethoven-Zentenarfeier: Internationaler musikhistorischer Kongress* (Wien: Universal, 1927) 79–82. *Music.* In German. See no. 142 in this volume.

If Mozart's approach to counterpoint was often a matter of displaying his mastery of an archaic, academic style, Beethoven's fugues were never academically correct, but he used counterpoint for new functions: in the early works as a humoristic device or as a way of disturbing periodicity, and in the later period in the service of an enriched polyphonic concept of melody. *(David Bloom)*

4162
as

ELSCHEKOVÁ, Alica. **Der mehrstimmige Volksgesang in der Slowakei** [Polyphonic folk song in Slovakia], *Journal of the International Folk Music Council* XV (1963) 49–53. *Transcr.* In German. See no. 459 in this volume.

An alanytical survey of traditional polyphonic practices in the western, central, and eastern zones of Slovakia. Contrary to earlier views, such polyphony is known in all three zones. In the west, it has clearly been influenced by art music or popular music, whereas the central zone has distinct centers of indigenous polyphonic practice; the eastern zone does not seem to have any exclusively polyphonic or monophonic areas. Particular attention is given to the features of the polyphony found in the central zone, whose leading centers are considered separately. *(Carl Skoggard)*

4163
as

ERGO, Émile. **Réforme de l'enseignement et de la science de l'harmonie suivant le système des fonctions tonales du Dr. Hugo Riemann** [Reform of the teaching and science of harmony according to the system of tonal functions of Hugo Riemann], *Congrès international de musique: Ire session—Exposition Universelle de 1900: Compte rendu, rapports, communications* (Paris: conference, 1901) 56–62. *Music, charts, diagr.* In French. See no. 29 in this volume.

Outlines Riemann's extensive figured bass notational analysis, which may even be applied to the analysis of counterpoint.

4164
as

ERPF, Hermann. **Einige Begriffe zur Harmonik der neueren Musik** [Some ideas about the harmony of new music], *Bericht über den musikwissenschaftlichen Kongreß in Basel* (Leipzig: Breitkopf & Härtel, 1925) 125–26. In German. See no. 102 in this volume.

Symmetrical, altered, leading-tone, and double–leading-tone chords are listed as new, important functions of atonal music. *(Sylvia Eversole)*

4165
as

FEDERHOFER, Hellmut. **Die Figurenlehre nach Christoph Bernhard und die Dissonanzbehandlung in Werken von Heinrich Schütz** [Figural theory according to Christoph Bernhard and the treatment of dissonance in works by Heinrich Schütz], *Bericht über den Internationalen musikwissenschaftlichen Kongress* (Kassel: Bärenreiter, 1954) 132–35. In German. See no. 319 in this volume.

Schütz's treatment of dissonance stands in a close relationship with Bernhard's figural theory. That Schütz was the intellectual source for his pupil's formulations cannot be doubted. The degree to which Schütz's dissonant *figurae* serve to express an affect and interpret a word of the text depends on the larger context and thus varies from case to case. *(Carl Skoggard)*

4166
as

FEDERHOFER, Hellmut. **Die Funktionstheorie Hugo Riemanns und die Schichtenlehre Heinrich Schenkers** [Hugo Riemann's theory of function and Heinrich Schenker's theory of levels], *Bericht über den internationalen musikwissenschaftlichen Kongreß Wien Mozartjahr 1956* (Graz; Köln: Böhlau, 1958) 183–90. *Music, charts, diagr.* In German. See no. 365 in this volume.

Riemann's illogical conception of minor chords casts doubt on the rest of his theory. Schenker's theory of the major-minor tonal basis of polyphony is preferable, but his work is unsystematic, inconclusive, and contains errors. His idea that the Ursatz exists simultaneously as the fundamental bass of the harmony and as a voice-leading phenomenon is inconsistent. Furthermore, there are no universally acknowledged principles for the application of reduction procedures. *(Carol K. Baron)*

4167
as

FLEISCHHAUER, Günter. **Einige Gedanken zur Harmonik Telemanns** [Some thoughts on Telemann's harmony], *Beiträge zu einem neuen Telemannbild* (Magdeburg: Vorwärts, 1963) 50–63. *Music.* In German. See no. 453 in this volume.

Telemann's use of unusual melodic intervals and chord juxtapositions for dramatic effect is illustrated with works performed at the first Magdeburger Telemann-Festtage, 1962: the secular cantatas *Die Tageszeiten* and *Ino*, the oratorio *Der Tag des Gerichts*, and the opera *Pimpinone*. *(John Stansell)*

4168
as

FRAZZI, Vito. **Il superamento della tonalità ed il nuovo concetto armonico** [The overcoming of tonality and the new harmonic concept], *Atti del quinto Congresso di musica* (Firenze: Barbèra, 1948) 89–95. In Italian. See no. 285 in this volume.

Tonality, in disintegration since 1900, has finally been overcome. Seeking a point of departure and reference, composers have been subscribing to an artificial convention, the tonic triad, while searching for new resources. The nature of tones, however, being mobile, is incompatible with the immobile characteristics of the tonic. Twelve-tone theories being too abstract, a new formulation of tone relationships is called for. The gamut of tones should be organized through the division of the octave into three contextually symmetrical diminished seventh chords. This will furnish tonal, atonal, and polytonal music with a common vocabulary and emancipate chromaticism. *(Channan Willner)*

4169
as

FRERE, Walter Howard. **Key-relationships in early medieval music,** *Report of the Fourth Congress of the International Musical Society* (London: Novello, 1912) 114–28. *Music.* See no. 71 in this volume.

Traces the modal origins of tonal melodies and harmonies.

4170
as

GERSON-KIWI, Edith. **The bourdon of the East: Its regional and universal trends,** *Journal of the International Folk Music Council* XVI (1964) 49–50. See no. 463 in this volume.

Summarizes a discussion of drone styles of India, Persia, and the Maghrib, and their possible influence on the development of fauxbourdon in Spain and Italy. A detailed version of the argument is given in the article abstracted as RILM [1973]3090. *(David Bloom)*

4171
as

GERVAIS, Françoise. **Debussy et la tonalité** [Debussy and tonality], *Debussy et l'évolution de la musique au XXᵉ siècle* (Paris: Centre National de la Recherche Scientifique [CNRS], 1965) 97–108. *Music.* In French. See no. 456 in this volume.

Debussy's innovations included the juxtaposition of tonal and nontonal passages, and the use of initial tones that made the listener unsure of where the piece was going harmonically. Intervals were no longer functional, but melodic. He often used scales that divided the octave into symmetrical parts (such as the whole-tone scale). Most of his systems were temporary, and were soon replaced by others. *(Alan Kingsley)*

4172
as

GHISI, Federico. **Rapporti armonici nella polifonia italiana del Trecento** [Harmonic relationships in the Italian polyphony of the 14th century], *L'ars nova italiana del Trecento: Primo convegno internazionale* (Certaldo: Centro di Studi sull'Ars Nova Italiana del Trecento, 1962) 32–39. *Music, index.* In Italian. See no. 407 in this volume.

The use of certain raised scale degrees in harmonic suspensions and at cadences, derived from the Notre Dame school, recurs frequently in 14th-c. Italian compositions. Musical examples from the Squarcialupi Codex (*I-Fl* MS med.pal.87) and other early MSS show the uses of these major intervals to enhance the descriptive power of the text. *(Sylvia Eversole)*

4173
as

GOW, George C. **Harmonic problems of to-day,** *Haydn-Zentenarfeier* (Leipzig: Breitkopf & Härtel; Wien: Artaria, 1909) 322–30. *Music.* See no. 65 in this volume.

Discusses the expansion of tonality and the meaning of chord color in late–19th-c. music. Included are examples by Debussy, Gabriel Fauré, and Charles Martin Loeffler.

4174
as

GRASBERGER, Franz. **Die Sekund als Ausdruckssymbol der neuen Musik** [The second as symbol of expression in new music], *Musikerziehung: Zeitschrift der Musikerzieher Österreichs* special issue (1953) 123–26. In German. See no. 317 in this volume.

4175
as

HÁBA, Alois. **Janáčkovo pojetí harmonie** [Janáček's concept of harmony], *Leoš Janáček a soudobá hudba* (Praha: Panton, 1963) 121–22. In Czech; summaries in Russian and German. See no. 389 in this volume.

Discusses the theoretical influence of Janáček's teacher at the Varhanická Škola v Praze, František Zdeněk Skuherský, on the composer's concept of harmony. *(editors)*

4176
as

HAYDON, Glen. **Alfred Day and the theory of harmony,** *Papers read at the International Congress of Musicology* (New York: Music Educators National Conference, 1944) 233–40. See no. 266 in this volume.

Outlines the history and reception of the English theorist's work. Day's idea that most of the common chords derive from higher dominant dissonances is also discussed.

4177
as

HERMELINK, Siegfried. **Zur Geschichte der Kadenz im 16. Jahrhundert** [The history of the cadence during the 16th century], *Bericht über den siebenten internationalen musikwissenschaftlichen Kongress* (Kassel: Bärenreiter, 1959) 133–35. *Music.* In German. See no. 390 in this volume.

Presents a systematic review of Gioseffo Zarlino's cadence theory (*Istitutioni harmoniche*, 1558) with attention to its implications for the rise of dominant-tonic harmonic relations. *(Carl Skoggard)*

4178
as

HERNÁDI, Lajos. **Einige charakteristische Züge in dem Chopinschen Klaviersatz** [Some characteristic traits of Chopin's piano writing], *The book of the first international musicological congress devoted to the works of Frederick Chopin* (Warszawa: Państwowe Wydawnictwo Naukowe, 1963) 168–75. *Music.* In German. See no. 425 in this volume.

Chopin's unique handling of passing and changing tones is discussed at length, and compared with that of Liszt.

4179
as

HERZOG, Eduard. **Harmonie und Tonart bei Janáček** [Harmony and key in Janáček], *Bericht über den siebenten internationalen musikwissenschaftlichen Kongress* (Kassel: Bärenreiter, 1959) 136–38. In German. See no. 390 in this volume.

Traces the presence of specific chords in works by Janáček, and of certain chord successions. These chords, whether enharmonically respelled or not, tend to occur at the same pitch in various compositions, in connection with the composer's preferred keys. *(Carl Skoggard)*

4180
as

HOERBURGER, Felix. **Haphazard assembly as a pre-musical form of polyphony,** *Journal of the International Folk Music Council* XVI (1964) 50. See no. 463 in this volume.

Field observations by the author of communal mourning ritual in Romania and kolo singing in Montenegro, and of kolo by Danica S. and Ljubica S. Janković in Yugoslavia, provide instances of a spontaneously occurring polyphony-like phenomenon, when unrelated songs are performed simultaneously by different individuals or groups, creating an unexpected effect of extra-musical or pre-musical unity. *(David Bloom)*

4181
as

HÜSCHEN, Heinrich. **Der Harmoniebegriff im Musikschrifttum des Altertums und des Mittelalters** [The concept of harmony in the writings on music of antiquity and the Middle Ages], *Bericht über den siebenten internationalen musikwissenschaftlichen Kongress* (Kassel: Bärenreiter, 1959) 143–50. In German. See no. 390 in this volume.

Greek *harmonia* derives ultimately from Indo-European **ar-*, denoting the fitting together of different objects into a whole. The word was used by pre-Socratic thinkers, but introduced as a technical term of science and art by Plato and Aristotle. From these until the time of Heinrich Glarean and Gioseffo Zarlino, the Greek term and its Latin equivalent were used in some eight distinct ways, as a synonym for *mousika*, *sýstēma téleion*, *diapasōn*, *trópos*, *génos*, *melodia*, *intervallum*, and *concordantia*. Its modern use begins with the consideration by Franchino Gafori and especially Zarlino of three notes sounding together. *(David Bloom)*

4182
as

JEPPESEN, Knud. **Zur Kritik der klassischen Harmonielehre** [A critique of classical harmonic theory], *Compte rendu/Kongressbericht/Report* (Basel: Bärenreiter, 1951) 23–34. In German. See no. 289 in this volume.

The line of theorizing from Jean-Phillip Rameau to Hugo Riemann is static (concerned with simultaneous sounds, not movement), constructive and speculative rather than empirical, physically rather than psychologically oriented, and deeply concerned with the effort to achieve unity and synthesis. In a new harmonic theory, chords will have to be treated as relative entities, depending on their context and especially voice-leading; as for a unified, objective system of music theory, it is impossible to believe in one. *(David Bloom)*

4183
as
JEPPESON, Knud. **Johann Joseph Fux und die moderne Kontrapunkttheorie** [Johann Joseph Fux and modern contrapuntal theory], *Bericht über den I. musikwissenschaftlichen Kongress der Deutschen Musikgesellschaft in Leipzig* (Wiesbaden: Breitkopf & Härtel, 1926) 187–88. In German. See no. 120 in this volume.

Gradus ad Parnassum remains relevant to modern counterpoint, even though it is recognized to bear little relationship to the style of Palestrina. *(William Renwick)*

4184
as
KIRBY, Percival R. **Physical phenomena which appear to have determined the bases and development of an harmonic sense among Bushmen, Hottentot and Bantu, as I have observed them in southern Africa,** *Bericht über den siebenten internationalen musikwissenschaftlichen Kongress* (Kassel: Bärenreiter, 1959) 154–57. *Transcr.* See no. 390 in this volume.

The pentatonic scale used in vocal music of Khoisan-speaking people of the Kalahari corresponds to the harmonic series available on an instrument made out of a shooting bow and using a calabash or the performer's mouth as a resonator; the scales of instrumental music among all the southern Bantu peoples are likewise based on the harmonic series of a single-string instrument, both with instruments using multiple strings and with the characteristic Zulu flute, umtshingo, which, lacking finger holes, yields a pentatonic scale based on the same series. In the organum-like style of parallel singing that has developed in southern Africa on a pentatonic basis, thirds and sixths naturally occur—unlike that of medieval Europe, on a heptatonic basis, and limited to fourths and fifths—which has hastened the development of a harmonic sense. *(David Bloom)*

4185
as
KLATTE, Wilhelm. **Stimmführung im homophonen Satz und Stufentheorie** [Voice-leading in homophonic music and harmonic theory], *Bericht über den I. musikwissenschaftlichen Kongress der Deutschen Musikgesellschaft in Leipzig* (Wiesbaden: Breitkopf & Härtel, 1926) 171–80. *Music.* In German. See no. 120 in this volume.

Relates voice leading and four-part harmony. A series of examples demonstrates that VII[7] can originate from an underlying IV or V chord, depending on the context. *(William Renwick)*

4186
as
KRESÁNEK, Jozef. **Tonalita v primitívnej a ľudovej hudbe** [Tonality in primitive music and folk music], *Leoš Janáček a soudobá hudba* (Praha: Panton, 1963) 182–88. *Music.* In Slovak; summaries in Russian and German. See no. 389 in this volume.

The tonality of vocal music was developed on the basis of the stenochoric principle, by means of which one central tone pulled toward itself the locally close tones. In contrast, tonality of intrumental music, although developing in parallel with vocal music, was based on the principle of consonance. The mutual interaction of the two principles can be observed in vocal and instrumental genres of traditional music around the world; their dialectical relationship is an important aspect of the study of musical thinking. *(editors)*

4187
as
KROYER, Theodor. **Die threnodische Bedeutung der Quart in der Mensuralmusik** [The threnodic meaning of the fourth in mensural music], *Bericht über den musikwissenschaftlichen Kongreß*

in Basel (Leipzig: Breitkopf & Härtel, 1925) 231–42. *Music.* In German. See no. 102 in this volume.

Adam von Fulda considered the parallel fourth to be harsh when it appeared in fauxbourdon. The parallel motion of fauxbourdon reminded the listener of the parallel organum that accompanied the Office for the Dead and the Requiem. The parallel fourth was used during the 15th c., and later in forms such as the *lamento* madrigal and the *dialogo amoroso*. Over time, its significance has changed: In present-day use its meaning is influenced by the size of the intervals used for expressive ends. In musica reservata of the 17th c., however, the interval and the fauxbourdon technique itself were often used with the goal of rendering the threnodic expression of the text.

4188
as
LACHMANN, Robert. **Zur aussereuropäischen Mehrstimmigkeit** [On non-European polyphony], *Beethoven-Zentenarfeier: Internationaler musikhistorischer Kongress* (Wien: Universal, 1927) - 321–25. *Bibliog.* In German. See no. 142 in this volume.

The variety of polyphonic phenomena seems especially related to the different techniques and characters of different instruments. It is notable that singing with an instrumental ensemble often imitates an instrumental color and technique. In ensemble singing, polyphony is generally a matter of parallel motion, in octaves, fifths, or fourths. The perception of thirds and sixths as consonant, originating in Northern Europe and possibly Russia and the Caucasus, was an exceptional development. *(David Bloom)*

4189
as
LANDÉ, Franz. **Die Dissonanz als harmonisch--melodisches Mischgebilde** [Dissonance as a mixed harmonic-melodic structure], *Bericht über den I. musikwissenschaftlichen Kongress der Deutschen Musikgesellschaft in Leipzig* (Wiesbaden: Breitkopf & Härtel, 1926) 181–86. *Music.* In German. See no. 120 in this volume.

The derivation of dissonance from voice-leading operations in the context of four-part harmony is shown. Passing tones and suspensions are the means by which chromatic chords originate. *(William Renwick)*

4190
as
LISSA, Zofia. **Über die Verbindungen zwischen der Harmonik von A.N. Skrjabin und der Harmonik von F. Chopin** [Connections between the harmonic practices of A.N. Skrjabin and F. Chopin], *The book of the first international musicological congress devoted to the works of Frederick Chopin* (Warszawa: Państwowe Wydawnictwo Naukowe, 1963) 335–40. *Music.* In German. See no. 425 in this volume.

Chopin is the source of several key features of Skrjabin's harmony, including quartal harmony; the "Promethean" chord; figuration with a particular role; independent status of the zone of the Phrygian second; tritonal and semitonal coordination between chords and entire sections; and peculiarities in the structuring of sound in tonal space. A Polish-language version is included in the collection cited as RILM [1971]739. *(author)*

4191
as
LORENTE, Miguel. **Physical basis of musical tonality and consonance,** *Problèmes d'acoustique* (Liège: Université de Liège, 1965) M64. *Illus., bibliog.* See no. 504 in this volume.

In a periodic superposition of sounds, the resultant beat frequency is much less than in a nonperiodic superposition. As the fundamental tones of the component sounds are more closely related, the degrees of both fusion and consonance increase. Since the tonality of a musical passage becomes more pronounced as the relationships of its fundamental tones become simpler, periodicity is the acoustic basis of tonality. A panharmonic scale is constructed via a subdivision into physically equal intervals. *(Anthony Weinfeld)*

4192
as
LOWINSKY, Edward E. **Awareness of tonality in the 16th century,** *Report of the Eighth Congress of the International Musicological Society. I: Papers* (Kassel: Bärenreiter, 1961) 44–52. *Charts, diagr.* See no. 439 in this volume.

Summarizes research on the High Renaissance developments of tonal as opposed to modal harmonic organization, and of extreme, almost atonal, chromaticism. An extended version is published as *Tonality and atonality in 16th-century music* (Berkeley, 1961). *(David Hathwell)*

4193 LUPI, Roberto. **Armonia di gravitazione** [Gravitational harmony], *Atti del quinto Congresso di musica* (Firenze: Barbèra, 1948) 51–54. In Italian. See no. 285 in this volume.

as

Describes a theory of gravitational harmony that relates to tonal, atonal, and modal music. The note of attraction or tonal note, rather than the diatonic scale, is the focus of the composition, and the halo or harmonic atmosphere is the fundamental tonality. The first ten overtones of the note of attraction constitute the harmonic halo; any given halo is related to those containing its note of attraction. The most closely-related are the halos of gravitation that are based on fundamental tones. Modulation is possible; tones are grouped in bimodal scales each containing seven tones and chromatic tonal scales each containing 15 tones. *(Channan Willner)*

4194 LUR'E, Artur Sergeevič (Arthur Vincent Lourié). **De l'harmonie dans la musique contemporaine** [On harmony in contemporary music], *Deuxième congrès international d'esthétique et de Science de l'art* (Paris: Librairie Félix Alcan, 1937) II, 458–62. In French. See no. 249 in this volume.

as

As far as harmony is concerned, expressionism is the only trend of the early 20th c. that continues to exist as a viable school; neoclassicism is exhausted, though there are composers, especially Stravinsky, who continue to seek a new causality in the traditional organization; otherwise young composers are generally disoriented. The genuine evolution of harmony is not an autonomous process but epiphenomenal, dependent on the enrichment of counterpoint. *(David Bloom)*

4195 MACHABEY, Armand. **Présence ou absence de la constante de quarte, de quinte et d'octave: Son rôle structurel dans la musique grecque antique et la polyphonie occidentale primitive** [Presence or absence of the constant of fourth, fifth, and octave: Its structural role in ancient Greek music and early Western polyphony], *La résonance dans les échelles musicales* (Paris: Centre National de la Recherche Scientifique [CNRS], 1963) 109–22. *Music, charts, diagr.* In French; summaries in English and German. See no. 420 in this volume.

as

Variable-tone instruments (e.g., strings) and fixed-tone instruments (e.g., winds) represent the origin of all nonvocal music in Greece. On flutes, fifths and octaves occur spontaneously; on strings, the intervals are chosen. The two types of instruments converge in consonance. In the Middle Ages, this gave rise to the structural cadence as a point of repose. *(author)*

4196 MARKIEWICZ, Leon. **Ryszard Wagner a Chopinowska myśl harmoniczna** [Richard Wagner and Chopin's harmonic thinking], *Ryszard Wagner a polska kultura muzyczna/Richard Wagner und die polnische Musikkultur* (Katowice: Panstwowa Wyzsza Szkola Muzyczna, 1964) 43–68. In Polish; summary in German. See no. 466 in this volume.

as

4197 MASSENKEIL, Günther. **Zur Frage der Dissonanzbehandlung in der Musik des 17. Jahrhunderts** [The treatment of dissonance in the music of the 17th century], *Les colloques de Wégimont. IV: Le Baroque musical—Recueil d'études sur la musique du XVIIᵉ siècle* (Paris: Belles Lettres, 1963) 151–76. *Music.* In German. See no. 386 in this volume.

as

One of the things that distinguishes the *stylus antiquus* from the *stylus modernus*, or the prima prattica from the seconda, in music of the early Baroque is the relatively free use of dissonance in the newer styles; the dissonances are interpreted in the theoretical writings of Christoph Bernhard (a student of Schütz and friend of Giacomo Carissimi) as rhetorical figures. Examples of dissonance from Carissimi's oratorios are analyzed according to Bernhard's concepts. *(David Bloom)*

4198 MERRITT, A. Tillman. **Awareness of tonality in the sixteenth century,** *Report of the Eighth Congress of the International Musicological Society. II: Reports* (Kassel: Bärenreiter, 1962) 58–63. *Charts, diagr.* See no. 440 in this volume.

as

A report on a discussion by Nanie BRIDGMAN, Louise E. CUYLER, Carl DALHAUS, Ludwig FINSCHER, Glen HAYDON, Knud JEPPESEN, Joseph KERMAN, Edward E. LOWINSKY, A. Tillman MERRITT, Helmuth OSTHOFF, and Gustave REESE on the paper by Lowinsky abstracted as no. 4192 in this volume.

4199 MEYER, Ernst Hermann. **Händels polyphoner Typ** [The typology of Händel's polyphony], *Händel-Ehrung der Deutschen Demokratischen Republik: Konferenzbericht* (Leipzig: VEB Deutscher Verlag für Musik, 1961) 22–29. In German. See no. 408 in this volume.

as

Händel's writing for multiple voices ranges from simple blocked chordal accompaniments to strict fugal settings and free, non-imitative counterpoint. He uses polyphonic methods in his vocal works for purposes of characterization and the representation of emotion. His polyphony is less laden with detail than that of Bach, but equally classic in its technical mastery. *(David Bloom)*

4200 MEYER, Ernst Hermann. **Mozarts polyphone Tradition** [Mozart's polyphonic tradition], *Internationale Konferenz über das Leben und Werk W.A. Mozarts* (Praha: Svaz Československých Skladatelů, 1956) 210–24. *Music.* In German. See no. 360 in this volume.

as

Dialogic counterpoint in Mozart's instrumental music, with its simultaneous strictness and expressive spontaneity, is the central example of a generally German or German-Austrian tradition that can be traced from the 16th c. to Brahms, Reger, and Hindemith, and illustrates a specifically German aspect of Mozart's adhesion to Enlightenment. *(David Bloom)*

4201 MOSER, Hans Joachim. **Diabolus in musica,** *Musikerziehung: Zeitschrift der Musikerzieher Österreichs* special issue (1953) 90–92. In German. See no. 317 in this volume.

as

The description of the diabolus in musica as *mi contra fa* involves the interval between two notes from different hexachords. Related intervals, principally the tritone, were carefully avoided throughout the Middle Ages and into the 16th c. In the 18th c. the tritone was recognized for its expressive powers but was still used sparingly. Composers since Bach have used the interval to portray the devil and evil. A longer version appears in *Musikerziehung* VI/3, March 1953, p, 131-47; reprinted in *Musik in Zeit und Raum* (Berlin, 1960), p. 262-80. *(Allen Lott)*

4202 MULLER, Francis. **La technique de la réalisation variée dans la Tablature de Goerlitz (1650) de Samuel Scheidt** [Varied realization technique in Samuel Scheidt's Görlitz tablature (1650)], *Bericht über den siebenten internationalen musikwissenschaftlichen Kongress* (Kassel: Bärenreiter, 1959) 196–97. In French. See no. 390 in this volume.

as

The *Tabulatur-Buch hundert geistlicher Lieder und Psalmen* published by Scheidt at Görlitz (1650) uses a technique Scheidt did not use in the *Tabulatura nova* (1624) of varying the harmonic progression used to accompany a given melody, sometimes within a single realization of the melody, in varied repeats; it may be influenced by Sweelinck. *(David Bloom)*

4203 MÜLLER-BLATTAU, Joseph. **Die deutsche Kontrapunktlehre des 17. Jahrhunderts** [German contrapuntal theory in the 17th century], *Bericht über den I. musikwissenschaftlichen Kongress der Deutschen Musikgesellschaft in Leipzig* (Wiesbaden: Breitkopf & Härtel, 1926) 280–83. In German. See no. 120 in this volume.

as

Discusses mode, counterpoint, dissonance, and intervals in the works of Sethus Calvisius, Johannes Lippius, Henricus Baryphonus, Michael Praetorius, Johannes Crüger, Jan Pieterszoon Sweelinck, Johann Hermann Schein, Johann Andreas Herbst, Matthias Weckmann, Johann Adam Reincken, and Schütz. *(William Renwick)*

4204 NEUMANN, Friedrich. **Probleme der Mehr-**
as **klangsbildung** [Problems in the formation of chords], *Kongreß-Bericht: Gesellschaft für Musikforschung* (Kassel; Basel: Bärenreiter, 1950) 217–19. *Music.* In German. See no. 299 in this volume.

4205 OREL, Alfred. **Die Kontrapunktlehren von**
as **Poglietti und Bertali** [The counterpoint treatises of Poglietti and Bertali], *Bericht über den Internationalen musikwissenschaftlichen Kongress* (Kassel: Bärenreiter, 1954) 140–42. In German. See no. 319 in this volume.
Offers a codicological description of a MS acquired by the author for the Musiksammlung der Stadt Wien, a department of the Stadt- und Landesbibliothek der Stadt Wien. The MS preserves treatises by Alessandro Poglietti (d.1683) and Antoni Bertali (1605-69), the former's inscribed "Regulae compositionis ab Hon Signo Alexandro de Poglietti" and the latter's, "Sequuntur regulae compositionis alterius authoris nempe Domini Antonii Bertalii". The contents of each are outlined. These treatises, forerunners of Johann Joseph Fux's *Gradus ad Parnassum*, reflect the practices of Vienna theorists during the mid-17th c. The MS seems to have once been in a library of a Minorite monastery in Vienna; its contents may originally have been formulated in Latin and then translated into German. *(Carl Skoggard)*

4206 PFROGNER, Hermann. **Der Weg der Theorie**
as **zwischen Tonalität und Atonalität** [The path of theory between tonality and atonality], *Musikerziehung: Zeitschrift der Musikerzieher Österreichs* special issue (1953) 111–14. In German. See no. 317 in this volume.
It is imperative for the future development of music that theorists maintain the distinction between tonality and atonality as being natural opposites. *(Joseph Giroux)*

4207 PFROGNER, Hermann. **Zur Definition des**
as **Begriffes Atonalität** [The definition of the concept atonality], *Bericht über den siebenten internationalen musikwissenschaftlichen Kongress* (Kassel: Bärenreiter, 1959) 212–14. *Charts, diagr.* In German. See no. 390 in this volume.
Atonality is not to be regarded merely as the absence of a tonal center in a system that otherwise remains the same; it asserts a new organization of tonal material, dependent on the equal division of the octave into 12 tones. The issues are discussed in detail in the author's *Die Zwölfordnung der Töne* (Zürich and Vienna, 1953). *(David Bloom)*

4208 PFROGNER, Hermann. **Zur Theorieauffas-**
as **sung der Enharmonik im Zeitalter Mozarts** [The theoretical concept of enharmonics in Mozart's time], *Bericht über den internationalen musikwissenschaftlichen Kongreß Wien Mozartjahr 1956* (Graz; Köln: Böhlau, 1958) 462–70. In German. See no. 365 in this volume.
Discusses the development of the term "enharmonic" in 18th-c. theoretical works with respect to the quarter-tone model of the enharmonic genus in ancient Greek theory and the practical use of enharmonic tones for modulation in equally tempered scales. *(David Bloom)*

4209 POCIEJ, Bohdan. **Rola harmoniki w technice**
as **przetworzeniowej Chopina** [The role of harmony in Chopin's creative process], *The book of the first international musicological congress devoted to the works of Frederick Chopin* (Warszawa: Państwowe Wydawnictwo Naukowe, 1963) 213–18. In Polish. See no. 425 in this volume.

4210 REGAMEY, Constantin. **Le développement de**
as **la résonance dans les musiques évoluées: Les théories de l'harmonie moderne** [The development of overtones in advanced musics: Theories of modern harmony], *La résonance dans les échelles musicales* (Paris: Centre National de la Recherche Scientifique [CNRS], 1963) 251–65. *Music, charts, diagr.* In French; summaries in English and German. See no. 420 in this volume.
The use of the overtone series to justify modern trends in harmony is prefigured in theories of Skrjabin, Hans Kayser, Roberto Lupi, and Hindemith; the application of these theories to scales, and some of their shortcomings, are discussed. *(author)*

4211 RIHTMAN, Cvjetko. **Les formes polypho-**
as **niques dans la musique populaire de Bosnie et d'Herzégovine** [Polyphonic forms in the traditional music of Bosnia and Herzegovina], *Journal of the International Folk Music Council* IV (1952) 30–35. *Transcr.* In French. See no. 306 in this volume.
Takes issue with Guido Adler's claim that traditional multi-part music can never be considered polyphony, only heterophony. Examples from vocal music of Bosnia and Herzegovina show a wide range of properly polyphonic techniques, some of them apparently wholly indigenous. An extended version in Bosnian is published as *Polifoni oblici u narodnoj muzici Bosni i Hercegovine* in *Bilten Instituta za Proučavanje Folklora u Sarajevu* 1 (1951). *(David Bloom)*

4212 RISINGER, Karel. **Problém konsonance a**
as **disonance v soudobé hudbě** [The problem of consonance and dissonance in contemporary music], *Leoš Janáček a soudobá hudba* (Praha: Panton, 1963) 261–64. In Czech; summaries in Russian and German. See no. 389 in this volume.
The phenomenon of consonance and dissonance has psychological and acoustic-physiological aspects. Throughout music history the two aspects interacted with each other in various ways, which resulted in different conceptions of consonance and dissonance. *(editors)*

4213 ROHWER, Jens. **Der Sonanzfaktor im Aufbau**
as **von Tonsystemen** [The *Sonanz* factor in the structure of tonal systems], *Bericht über den siebenten internationalen musikwissenschaftlichen Kongress* (Kassel: Bärenreiter, 1959) 230–40. *Music, charts, diagr.* In German. See no. 390 in this volume.
The experience of listening is divided into the categories of *Kordanz* (sensory impression), *Distanz* (spatial or spatial-like perception), and *Sonanz* (harmonic-tonal nature). A theory of the last is summarized, based on the author's *Der Sonanzfaktor im Tonsystem* (Ph.D. diss., U. Kiel, 1958), published in revised form as *Die harmonischen Grundlagen der Musik* (see RILM [1970]4004). *(David Bloom)*

4214 ROHWER, Jens. **Zur Überwindung des For-**
as **malismus in der musikalischen Tonarten- und Geschlechterlehre** [The conquest of formalism in the theory of musical keys and modes], *Kongreß-Bericht: Gesellschaft für Musikforschung* (Kassel; Basel: Bärenreiter, 1950) 213–16. In German. See no. 299 in this volume.

4215 RUBIO, Samuel. **Música polifónica** [Polyphonic
as music], *V Congreso Nacional de Música Sagrada* (Madrid: Gráficas Dos de Mayo, 1956) 164–69. In Spanish. See no. 331 in this volume.
Discusses specific characteristics of religious polyphony in Spain, as contrasted with that of other nations.

4216 SCHMITZ, Arnold. **Die Kadenz als *Ornamen-**
as ***tum musicae*** [The cadence as *ornamentum musicae*],

Bericht über den Internationalen musikwissenschaft- lichen Kongress (Kassel: Bärenreiter, 1954) 114–20. *Music.* In German. See no. 319 in this volume.

A central topic of composition treatises from the 16th and 17th c. is the management of cadences. Cadences in music are conceived in terms of the theory of rhetoric. They have a grammatical function mirroring the musical text and its sectional structure, and they have an ornamental function that builds on the grammatical function but which has its own significance and rich repertoire of possibilities. The ornamental function is discussed in de- tail, with attention to the many analogies drawn by treatise writers between musical cadences and the uses of ornament in rhetoric, and to the ways in which the grammatical and ornamental function of a cadence can reinforce each other. The terminology used by theorists is examined in detail. *(Carl Skoggard)*

4217
as

SCHUH, Willi. **Zur Harmonik Igor Strawinskys** [On the harmony of Igor Stravinsky], *Musikerziehung: Zeitschrift der Musikerzieher Österreichs* special issue (1953) 127–34. *Music.* In German. See no. 317 in this volume.

Discusses major/minor juxtapositions, polytonality, and tonal centers, drawing on Stravinsky's *The rake's progress* and quotes from *Poétique mu- sicale*. Another version is published in *Schweizerische Musikzeitung* XCII (1952), p. 243-52. *(Robert Taub)*

⟶ SŁAWIŃSKI, Adam. **Rytm a harmonia w polonezach Chopina** [Rhythm and harmony in Cho- pin's polonaises]. See no. 4030 in this volume.

4218
as

SMITS VAN WAESBERGHE, Joseph. **Zur Entstehung der drei Hauptfunktionen in der Harmonik** [Concerning the origin of the three pri- mary functions in harmony], *Kongreß-Bericht: Gesellschaft für Musikforschung* (Kassel; Basel: Bärenreiter, 1950) 209–10. In German. See no. 299 in this volume.

4219
as

STEPHANI, Hermann. **Enharmonik (polare Harmonik) bei Beethoven** [Enharmonics (polar harmony) in Beethoven's works], *Beetho- ven-Zentenarfeier: Internationaler musikhistorischer Kongress* (Wien: Universal, 1927) 83–89. In German. See no. 142 in this volume.

Alternative enharmonic spellings for certain chords resolve to widely sepa- rated keys; the tension set up by such chords may be called polar harmony. Beethoven uses such harmony particularly in vocal music, to express pa- thos, as in a large number of cases from *Fidelio*. It is rare in his later works, and entirely absent from the symphony no. 9, op 125. An annotated list of examples from his works is included. *(David Bloom)*

4220
as

TENSCHERT, Roland. **Der Tonartenkreis in Mozarts Werken** [The range of tonality in Mozart's works], *Bericht über den internationalen musikwiss- schaftlichen Kongreß Wien Mozartjahr 1956* (Graz; Köln: Böhlau, 1958) 640–42. In German. See no. 365 in this volume.

Mozart's key choices show a limited range, compared to those of Haydn, and are often made for practical rather than expressive reasons, as to ac- commodate the needs of a particular instrumental soloist or singer; how- ever, some keys, particularly minor ones, do have a significance in his work. *(David Bloom)*

4221
as

TISCHLER, Hans. **Remarks on Hindemith's contrapuntal technique,** *Journal of the Interna- tional Folk Music Council* XVI (1964) 53. See no. 463 in this volume.

Summary of a paper. Hindemith's approach to counterpoint is conserva- tive, based on consonance, as opposed to one based on independent me- lodic-rhythmic progressions. Dissonance arises, as in the *Ludus tonalis*

(1942), from his use of non-traditional chords, extended application of non-harmonic notes, melodic idiosyncrasies, and polytonality. *(David Bloom)*

4222
as

TURŁO, Teresa Dalila. **Funkcja harmoniczna figuracji u Chopina** [The function of harmonic figu- rations in Chopin's music], *The book of the first interna- tional musicological congress devoted to the works of Frederick Chopin* (Warszawa: Państwowe Wydawnictwo Naukowe, 1963) 255–58. In Polish. See no. 425 in this volume.

4223
as

UNGER, Max. **Die sogenannte Charakteristik der Tonarten** [The so-called key charateristics], *Société Internationale de Musicologie: Premier Congrès Liège—Compte rendu/Internationale Gesellschaft für Musikwissenschaft: Erster Kongress Lüttich—Kongressbericht/International Society for Musical Research: First Congress Liège: Report* (Lon- don: Plainsong and Mediaeval Music Society, 1930) 230. In German. See no. 178 in this volume.

Several contradictions have resulted from discussions regarding the man- ner in which Wagner interpreted keys. For him, the meaning of keys were essential to expressive communication. *(Joan Siegel)*

4224
as

VOLEK, Jaroslav. **Die Bedeutung Chopins für die Entwicklung der alterierten Akkorde in der Musik des XIX. Jahrhunderts** [Chopin's role in the development of the altered chord in 19th-century music], *The book of the first international musicologi- cal congress devoted to the works of Frederick Chopin* (Warszawa: Państwowe Wydawnictwo Naukowe, 1963) 259–68. In German. See no. 425 in this volume.

In the history of altered-chord chromaticism, Wagner, contrary to received opinion, is a less original figure than Chopin and Liszt, and particularly Chopin. *(David Bloom)*

4225
as

WELLEK, Albert. **Fortschritte in der Theorie der Konsonanz und Dissonanz/Pokrok v teorii konsonance a disonance** [New findings in the the- ory of consonance and dissonance], *Leoš Janáček a soudobá hudba* (Praha: Panton, 1963) 387–91. In Ger- man and Czech. See no. 389 in this volume.

Introduction to the concept of the multiplicity of consonance, reconciling Krueger's theory of difference tones with Hornbostel's theory of Tönigkeit. *(Jadranka Važanová)*

4226
as

WÖRNER, Karl H. **Harmoniebewußtsein und Symbolwandel in Schönbergs Oper** *Moses und Aron* [Harmonic consciousness and transformation of symbols in Schoenberg's opera *Moses und Aron*], *Bericht über den siebenten internationalen musik- wissenschaftlichen Kongress* (Kassel: Bärenreiter, 1959) 305–07. *Music.* In German. See no. 390 in this volume.

Schoenberg uses chordal structures in the dodecaphonic technique to en- code meanings of a kind precisely opposed to those of past harmonic prac- tice; selected passages from the opera's first scene show how what was once called dissonance now represents completion, eternity, harmony it- self. *(David Bloom)*

4227
as

ZIELIŃSKI, Tadeusz Andrzej. **Sonorystyka harmoniczna w trzecim okresie twórczości Szymanowskiego** [Harmonic sonorities in Szymanowski's third period output], *Karol Szymanowski: Księga sesji Naukowej poświęconej twórczości Karola Szymanowskiego* (Warszawa: Uniwersytet Warszawski, Instytut Muzykologii, 1964)

345–62. *Music.* In Polish; summary in English. See no. 458 in this volume.

In his third period, Szymanowski broadened his range of chords, proceeding in three directions: chords constructed with intervals of the lower grade (e.g., classic triads and open fifths); chords built in fourths, fifths, and major and minor seconds; and polytonal chords. *(editor)*

4228
as
ZIMMERMAN, Franklin B. **Advanced tonal design in the part-songs of William Byrd,** *Bericht über den siebenten internationalen musikwissenschaftlichen Kongress* (Kassel: Bärenreiter, 1959) 322–26. *Charts, diagr.* See no. 390 in this volume.

Ca. 1600 even the most radical composers, such as Marenzio and Monteverdi, still generally planned the sequence of cadences in a work according to modal regulations. Byrd, in contrast, in his secular songs, organized elaborately integrated structures based on the new tonal principles, and younger English composers followed him. *(David Bloom)*

64 Form and genre

4229
as
ANTCLIFFE, Herbert. **Musical form and the symphonic poem,** *Report of the Fourth Congress of the International Musical Society* (London: Novello, 1912) 206–10. See no. 71 in this volume.

The symphonic poem is a broad category, representing the culmination of polyphonic and homophonic music as well as their relationships to extramusical elements. Ideas for new musical structures are discussed. *(Mei-Mei Meng)*

4230
as
APEL, Willi. **Remarks about the isorhythmic motet,** *Les colloques de Wégimont. II: L'ars nova—Recueil d'études sur la musique du XIVe siècle* (Paris: Belles Lettres, 1959) 139–48. In English and French. See no. 351 in this volume.

Between the motet with isorhythm restricted to the tenor, a 13th-c. development, and the motet with isorhythm in all parts, first found in the Ivrea Codex (*I-IV* MS 115) and not fully established until the 15th c., the ars nova contributed to the structural development of isorhythm with a kind of approximate pan-isorhythm, in motets where the upper parts show isoperiodicity or sectional isorhythm. The structural analysis of isorhythmic motets into colores and taleae is also discussed. *(David Bloom)*

4231
as
AUSTIN, William W. **Traditional forms in new musical idioms,** *Report of the Eighth Congress of the International Musicological Society. I: Papers* (Kassel: Bärenreiter, 1961) 100–08. See no. 439 in this volume.

Discusses older forms in the works of Bartók, Stravinsky, Schoenberg, Berg, and Debussy, with particular attention to sonata form in the music of Webern.

4232
as
AUSTIN, William W. **Traditional forms in new musical idioms,** *Report of the Eighth Congress of the International Musicological Society. II: Reports* (Kassel: Bärenreiter, 1962) 80–83. See no. 440 in this volume.

A report on a discussion by Paul COLLAER, Georg von DADELSEN, Karl Henry ESCHMAN, Kurt von FISCHER, Hans MERSMANN, Hans F. REDLICH, Roger SESSIONS, and Hellmuth Christian WOLFF on the paper by the author abstracted as no. 4231 in this volume.

4233
as
BIENENFELD, Elsa. **Neue Versuche zur Veränderung der klassichen Sinfonieform** [New attempts to modify the Classic symphonic form], *Haydn-Zentenarfeier* (Leipzig: Breitkopf & Härtel; Wien: Artaria, 1909) 141–44. In German. See no. 65 in this volume.

Discusses the number of movements and programmatic vs. abstract music in symphonic form. The works of Mahler are mentioned.

4234
as
BRIDGMAN, Nanie. **La frottola et la transition de la frottola au madrigal** [The frottola and the transition from the frottola to the madrigal], *Musique et poésie au XVIe siècle* (Paris: Centre National de la Recherche Scientifique [CNRS], 1954) 63–77. *Music.* In French. See no. 326 in this volume.

Traces the development of the frottola through the canzone to the madrigal. The influence of the Franco-Flemish contrapuntal tradition cannot fully account for the transition of the homophonic frottola to the more polyphonic madrigal. *(Roy Nitzberg)*

4235
as
BURLAS, Ladislav. **Neuerertum und Tradition in Bartók's Formenwelt** [Innovation and tradition in Bartók's formal universe], *Studia musicologica Academiae Scientiarum Hungaricae* V (1963) 383–91. In German. See no. 427 in this volume.

Investigates the smaller-scale piano pieces, regarded as crystallizations of Bartók's formal design, for classic formal structures, new forms such as those represented in the so-called night music, and traditional-music forms. *(William Renwick)*

4236
as
CHECHLIŃSKA, Zofia. **Das Problem der Form und die reelle Klanggestalt in Chopins Präludien** [The problem of form and the real sound-shape in Chopin's preludes], *The book of the first international musicological congress devoted to the works of Frederick Chopin* (Warszawa: Państwowe Wydawnictwo Naukowe, 1963) 425–29. In German. See no. 425 in this volume.

The real sound-shape of a work includes its agogic and dynamic structure, which is not adequately represented in the score, and varies from performance to performance, as demonstrated by a comparison of recordings of the C-major prelude from Chopin's op. 28 by Alfred Cortot, Artur Rubinstein, and Claudio Arrau. *(David Bloom)*

4237
as
CLERCX-LEJEUNE, Suzanne. **La toccata, principe du style symphonique** [The toccata as the origin of symphonic style], *La musique instrumentale de la Renaissance* (Paris: Centre National de la Recherche Scientifique [CNRS], 1955) 313–26. *Music.* In French. See no. 333 in this volume.

The original use of "toccata," as Otto Gombosi has shown, involved not keyboard but brass instruments, and denoted a festive trumpet fanfare such as was practiced in Spain and Naples as early as the late 14th c., and possibly brought to northern Italy by Johannes Ciconia. The keyboard toccatas of the end of the 16th c. (as compared to intonazioni and preambula) were imitations of this style. The keyboard genre quickly evolved into a prolonged contrapuntal piece, but the original toccata structure in ensemble genres can be traced through works by Giovanni de Macque, Monteverdi, Giovanni Gabrieli, Maurizio Cazzati, Vivaldi, Alessandro Scarlatti, and Giovanni Battista Sammartini as the ancestor of the symphonic style. *(Susan Poliniak)*

4238
as
DAHLHAUS, Carl. **Wagners Begriff der "dichterisch-musikalischen Periode"** [Wagner's concept of the "dichterisch-musikalische Periode"], *Beiträge zur Geschichte der Musikanschauung im 19. Jahrhundert* (Regensburg: Bosse, 1965) 179–94. In German. See no. 483 in this volume.

The term *dichterisch-musikalische Periode* (poetic-musical period) used in Wagner's *Oper und Drama* (1850-51) has been wrongly interpreted by Alfred Lorenz (*Das Geheimnis der Form bei Richard Wagner,* 1924-33) as referring to units of anywhere from 100 to 840 measures; in fact Wagner meant to designate a much smaller unit, what Adolf Bernhard Marx would have recognized as an *erweiterte Periode* (extended period) of 20 to 30 measures. As a formal device, the period is less important in *Der Ring des Nibelungen* than the interweaving of motives in the orchestral writing. *(David Bloom)*

4239 DANCKERT, Werner. **Mozarts Menuettypen**
as [Mozart's minuet types], *Bericht über die musik-wissenschaftliche Tagung der Internationalen Stiftung Mozarteum* (Leipzig: Breitkopf & Härtel, 1932) 129–32. In German. See no. 193 in this volume.

In his serenades and divertimentos, Mozart follows the symmetrical structure and basso continuo sonority of the old Baroque minuet, even when he violates the norm of the eight-measure period. In the sonatas, symphonies, and quartets, structural irregularities contribute to a sharpening of the effect of the conclusion. The broad congruity between his minuets and Haydn's and their deep contrast with Beethoven's scherzos can be understood in terms of the theory of composer personality types developed by Josef Rutz, Hermann Nohl, and Gustav Becking. *(David Bloom)*

4240 DENÉRÉAZ, Alexandre. **Beethoven et les**
as **rythmes cosmiques** [Beethoven and cosmic rhythms], *Beethoven-Zentenarfeier: Internationaler musikhistorischer Kongress* (Wien: Universal, 1927) 45–47. *Illus., charts, diagr.* In French. See no. 142 in this volume.

Beethoven's music exemplifies the ideas of human and cosmic rhythms discussed in the paper abstracted as no. 5810 in this volume. An analysis of dynamic contrasts in the "storm" movement from the symphony no. 6, op. 68, shows a large-scale, frequently asymmetrical form corresponding to the Fibonacci series and to the structural scheme of a tropical hurricane. *(David Bloom)*

4241 DONATH, Gustav. **Gefühlscharaktere in den**
as **Themenkontrasten der klassischen Sonaten-form** [Affective characters in the thematic contrasts of Classic sonata form], *Bericht über den internationalen musikwissenschaftlichen Kongreß Wien Mozartjahr 1956* (Graz; Köln: Böhlau, 1958) 139–42. In German. See no. 365 in this volume.

Discusses thematic contrast in terms of feeling and imagery, following the aesthetic theory of Ludwig Klages.

4242 DWELSHAUVERS, Georges. **La forme musi-**
as **cale, embryon de sonate, adoptée par Jean-Noël Hamal dans son opus I doit-elle être considerée comme une antériorité aux *Sonate a tre* de Stamitz?** [Should the musical form, embryo of sonata form, adopted by Jean-Noël Hamal in his opus 1, be considered an antecedent of the *Sonate a tre* by Stamic?], *Fédération Archéologique et Historique de Belgique: Annales du XXIᵉ congrès* (Liège: Poncelet, 1909) II, 722–29. In French. See no. 64 in this volume.

Compares the form of Hamal's *Six ouvertures de camera*, op. 1, with that of a chamber work by Jan Václav Stamic.

4243 ELLER, Rudolf. **Geschichtliche Stellung und**
as **Wandlung der Vivaldischen Konzertform** [The historical position of and changes in the Vivaldian concerto form], *Bericht über den internationalen musikwissenschaftlichen Kongreß Wien Mozartjahr 1956* (Graz; Köln: Böhlau, 1958) 150–55. In German. See no. 365 in this volume.

If the development of Baroque *Fortspinnung* technique is a key characteristic of Vivaldi's concertos to ca. 1710, the later concertos, especially after ca. 1720, are more marked by their structural use of thematic contrast. Summarizes discussion in the author's Ph.D. dissertation, *Das Formprinzip des Vivaldischen Konzerts* (Leipzig, 1957). *(David Bloom)*

4244 ENGEL, Hans. **Über Form und Mosaiktechnik**
as **bei Bach, besonders in seinen Arien** [Form and mosaic-technique in Bach, particularly in his arias], *Kongreß-Bericht: Gesellschaft für Musikforschung* (Kassel; Basel: Bärenreiter, 1950) 111–19. *Music, charts, diagr.* In German. See no. 299 in this volume.

4245 ENGELBRECHT, Christiane. **Zur Vor-**
as **geschichte der Chopinschen Klavierballade** [The prehistory of the Chopinian piano ballade], *The book of the first international musicological congress devoted to the works of Frederick Chopin* (Warszawa: Państwowe Wydawnictwo Naukowe, 1963) 519–21. In German. See no. 425 in this volume.

Chopin's development of the instrumental ballade as a form has musical origins in the pre-Romantic instrumental romance and the piano rhapsodies of Václav Jan Křtitel Tomášek and Jan Václav Voříšek; its literary origins are in the adoption of the English term "ballad" by Gottfried August Bürger and its transmission through Goethe to Adam Mickiewicz. *(David Bloom)*

4246 FELLERER, Karl Gustav. **Mozarts Litaneien**
as [Mozart's litanies], *Bericht über die musikwissenschaftliche Tagung der Internationalen Stiftung Mozarteum* (Leipzig: Breitkopf & Härtel, 1932) 133–35. In German. See no. 193 in this volume.

Mozart composed two *litaniae lauretanae*, K.109 and 195, and two liturgical litany settings, K.125 and 243, in Salzburg in 1771–76. The later settings are strikingly more worked out than the earlier ones, in terms of counterpoint, instrumental accompaniment, and declamation; they show an important step on the way to the symphonically through-composed Mass. *(David Bloom)*

4247 FISCHER, Kurt von. **Bemerkungen zu**
as **Beethovens Variationenwerken** [Remarks on Beethoven's works in variation form], *Compte rendu/Kongressbericht/Report* (Basel: Bärenreiter, 1951) 111–13. In German. See no. 289 in this volume.

Sketches the evolution of variation form over the three major phases of Beethoven's career, with attention to the early transition to the principle of developing variation, and the late turn from dramatic variation of a theme to variation as an autonomous formal principle. *(David Bloom)*

4248 FLOROS, Constantin. **Fragen zum musika-**
as **lischen und metrischen Aufbau der Kontakien** [Questions on the musical and metric structure of kontakia], *Actes du XIIᵉ Congrès d'études Byzantines* (Beograd: Naučno Delo, 1963-1964) II, 563–69. *Charts, diagr.* In German. See no. 441 in this volume.

Melodic structure in the kontakion genre of Byzantine hymnody provides useful evidence in accounting for apparent structural irregularities in the metric character of the text. *(David Bloom)*

4249 GERSTENBERG, Walter. **Zur Verbindung**
as **Präludium und Fuge bei J.S. Bach** [Concerning the connection between prelude and fugue in J.S. Bach], *Kongreß-Bericht: Gesellschaft für Musikforschung* (Kassel; Basel: Bärenreiter, 1950) 126–29. *Music.* In German. See no. 299 in this volume.

4250 GIEGLING, Franz. **Sinn und Wesen des**
as ***concertare*** [The meaning and essence of *concertare*], *Compte rendu/Kongressbericht/Report* (Basel: Bärenreiter, 1951) 129–32. In German. See no. 289 in this volume.

The Latinizing definition of *concerto/concertare* in the *Syntagma musicum* of Praetorius characterizes the concerto as a kind of conflict between opposed groups of musicians. This definition is based on a false etymology; Italian *concerto* (*conserto* in the 16th and early 17th c.) is derived from Latin *conserere/consertus*, with a connotation of parties coming to agreement. The concerto genre in its current sense originated in northern Italian cities around the turn of the 18th c.; on important festivals, the professional instrumentalists attached to churches would be joined by a large group of less skilled players, a combination that led naturally to the alternation of bravura passages for the former with ritornellos for the latter. *(David Bloom)*

4251
as

GUDEWILL, Kurt. **Die Barform und ihre Modifikationen** [The bar form and its modifications], *Kongreß-Bericht: Gesellschaft für Musikforschung* (Kassel; Basel: Bärenreiter, 1950) 65–68. In German. See no. 299 in this volume.

4252
as

GUDEWILL, Kurt. **Ursprünge und nationale Aspekte des Quodlibets** [Origins and national aspects of the quodlibet], *Report of the Eighth Congress of the International Musicological Society. I: Papers* (Kassel: Bärenreiter, 1961) 30–43. In German. See no. 439 in this volume.

Considers the history of the quodlibet and associated genres (chace, caccia, incatenatura, fricassée, ensalada) in Germany, Italy, France, Spain, and England, from the end of the 15th to the early 18th c. *(David Bloom)*

4253
as

GURLITT, Wilibald. **Burgundische Chanson- und deutsche Liedkunst des 15. Jahrhunderts** [Burgundian chanson and the German art song during the 15th century], *Bericht über den musikwissenschaftlichen Kongreß in Basel* (Leipzig: Breitkopf & Härtel, 1925) 153–76. *Music, charts, diagr.* In German. See no. 102 in this volume.

Research in German songbooks from the second half of the 15th c. reveals the connection between the German lied and the Burgundian chanson. When French melodies were borrowed, the text was omitted and the melody transferred intact to the new piece. Indigenous German lied is, however, fundamentally different from older and contemporary French parallels.

4254
as

HAHN, Harry. **Der Symmetriebegriff in der Musik Bachs** [The concept of symmetry in Bach's music], *Bericht über die Wissenschaftliche Bachtagung* (Leipzig: Peters, 1951) 277–84. *Charts, diagr.* In German. See no. 298 in this volume.

Following Wilhelm Werker's study on symmetry in the structure of Bach's preludes and fugues (1922), four kinds of formal symmetry in Bach's works are distinguished: parallel symmetry by repetition, contrastive symmetry (inversion and mirror effects), dovetailing symmetry (in the proportions, for instance, between alternating parts), and summational symmetry (in the relations among all the sections of a work). *(David Bloom)*

4255
as

HANDSCHIN, Jacques. **Über den Ursprung der Motette** [On the origin of the motet], *Bericht über den musikwissenschaftlichen Kongreß in Basel* (Leipzig: Breitkopf & Härtel, 1925) 189–200. *Music.* In German. See no. 102 in this volume.

Wilhelm Meyer pointed to the parallels between the development of the trope and sequence, and Notre Dame polyphony. However, both he and Friedrich Ludwig were incorrect in assuming that the motet developed from the melismatic sections of the polyphony rather than from the polyphonic settings of a complete chant. An examination of the setting of *Stirps Jesse* from the St. Martial repertoire illustrates the motet's earliest development.

4256
as

HAUSSWALD, Günter. **Zur Sonatenkunst der Bachzeit** [Sonata composition in Bach's time], *Bericht über die Wissenschaftliche Bachtagung* (Leipzig: Peters, 1951) 340–48. In German. See no. 298 in this volume.

Discusses Bach's 30-odd sonata works in relation to those of his contemporaries.

4257
as

HEUSS, Alfred Valentin. **Die genetische Methode, gezeigt an Lied und Arie** [The genetic method, demonstrated in song and aria], *Bericht über den I. musikwissenschaftlichen Kongress der Deutschen Musikgesellschaft in Leipzig* (Wiesbaden: Breitkopf & Härtel, 1926) 442–44. In German. See no. 120 in this volume.

Contends that through-composed aria forms are more organic than strophic lied, and are therefore more advanced. In a supplementary article, Paul

MIES underlines the point that for a technique to be an organic part of music, it must be a means rather than an end. *(William Renwick)*

4258
as

HRABAL, František. **K otázce hudební tektoniky *Výletu pana Broučka do XV. století*** [The musical structure of *Výlet pana Broučka do XV. století*], *Leoš Janáček a soudobá hudba* (Praha: Panton, 1963) 132–39. *Music.* In Czech; summaries in Russian and German. See no. 389 in this volume.

Analyzes a new music-dramatic concept in Janáček's *Výlety páně Broučkovy* (The excursions of Mr. Brouček), focusing on its second part *Výlet pana Broučka do XV. století.* The new concept consists in integrating the artistic gestalt with musical tectonics developing from it and in putting the emphasis on speech melodies (*nápěvek*) and interjections, (*sčasovky*), in both vocal and instrumental parts. *(editors)*

4259
as

HUSMANN, Heinrich. **Zur Entwicklung der Mozartschen Sonatenform** [The development of Mozart's sonata form], *Internationale Konferenz über das Leben und Werk W.A. Mozarts* (Praha: Svaz Československých Skladatelů, 1956) 241–45. In German. See no. 360 in this volume.

In Baroque style more emphasis is placed on the spatial element of form, in Romantic style on the temporal element of expression. Mozart's style displays the typically Baroque feature of terrace dynamics, and the Romantic harmonic effects of chromaticism and modulation by whole steps. In maintaining the three-part sonata structure of exposition, development, and recapitulation, he is strictly Classic, but the microstructure of his themes is highly complex and partly asymmetrical; his work represents the happiest synthesis of the two elements. *(David Bloom)*

4260
as

INDY, Vincent d'. **Quand c'est formée la fugue telle qu'on enseigne actuellement dans les grands conservatoires de l'Europe?** [When did the fugue as currently taught in the great European conservatories take shape?], *Haydn-Zentenarfeier* (Leipzig: Breitkopf & Härtel; Wien: Artaria, 1909) 108–09. In French and German. See no. 65 in this volume.

Includes a subsequent panel discussion.

4261
as

JÁRDÁNYI, Pál. **Bartók und die Ordnung der Volkslieder** [Bartók and the classification of traditional songs], *Studia musicologica Academiae Scientiarum Hungaricae* V (1963) 435–39. In German. See no. 427 in this volume.

Surveys the development of Bartók's tripartite system of isometric, architectonic, and heterometric categories, together with later refinements including those of Kodály. *(William Renwick)*

4262
as

KENNEY, Sylvia W. **Origins and national aspects of the quodlibet,** *Report of the Eighth Congress of the International Musicological Society. II: Reports* (Kassel: Bärenreiter, 1962) 53–57. *Charts, diagr.* See no. 440 in this volume.

A report on a discussion by Isabelle CAZEAUX, Isabel Pope CONANT, Kurt von FISCHER, Federico GHISI, Kurt GUDEWILL, Knud JEPPESEN, Sylvia W. KENNEY, Edward R. LERNER, François LESURE, Dragan PLAMENAC, Geneviève THIBAULT DE CHAMBURE, and Hans TISCHLER of the paper by Gudewill abstracted as no. 4252 in this volume.

4263
as

KROHN, Ilmari. **Die Form des ersten Satzes der *Mondscheinsonate*** [The form of the first movement of the "Moonlight" sonata], *Beethoven-Zentenarfeier: Internationaler musikhistorischer Kongress* (Wien: Universal, 1927) 58–65. *Music, charts, diagr.* In German. See no. 142 in this volume.

Defends the author's analysis, first published in *Zeitschrift der Internationalen Musikgesellschaft* III/6 (1902), according to which the movement is structured on strict principles of sonata form.

4264 KROHN, Ilmari. **Formale und ideelle Einheit-**
as **lichkeit der Symphonien Anton Bruckners**
[The formal and ideal unity of Anton Bruckner's sym-
phonies], *Bericht über den internationalen musikwissenschaftlichen Kongreß Wien Mozartjahr 1956*
(Graz; Köln: Böhlau, 1958) 313–17. *Music.* In German.
See no. 365 in this volume.

Although Bruckner's symphonies give the listener a superficial impression
of formlessness, they merely extend Classic symphonic form with (1) the
use of a third theme, of sublime character; (2) the division of the middle part
of the development into two separate cores, with the transition between
them carrying its own additional significance; (3) the use of sonata form for
the scherzo and its trio; and (4) the introduction of development into the
rondo form. *(David Bloom)*

4265 LAUNAY, Denise. **La fantaisie en France**
as **jusqu'au milieu du XVIIᵉ siècle** [The fantaisie in
France to the middle of the 17th century], *La musique
instrumentale de la Renaissance* (Paris: Centre National de la Recherche Scientifique [CNRS], 1955)
327–38. *Music.* In French. See no. 333 in this volume.

The example of the English *fancy* may have inspired the development from
simple lute or guitar transcriptions of vocal music in the 16th c. to the
fantaisie in the 17th c., a work of imitative counterpoint with a brilliant, improvisational character. Jacques Mauduit's fantaisies for instrumental ensemble, presumably viol consort, now lost, apparently began a vogue
around the turn of the 17th c. among composers such as Eustache Du
Caurroy and Claude Le Jeune, together with Charles Guillet's pieces in the
genre intended for organ. Its history is followed through compositions by
Antoine de Cousu, Charles Racquet, Étienne Moulinié, and Nicolas Métru.
By mid-century, with Marin Marais and Louis Couperin, the term came to
be used less for fugato forms than for free-form capriccios. *(Susan Poliniak)*

4266 LINDGREN, Adolf. **Contribution à l'histoire**
as **de la polonaise** [Contribution to the history of the po-
lonaise], *Congrès international d'histoire de la
musique: Documents, mémoires et vœux* (Solesmes: St.
Pierre; Paris: Fischbacher, 1901) 215–20. *Music.* In
French. See no. 32 in this volume.

The earliest dance compositions that were called polonaises have been discovered in Sweden. The polonaise may have originated from the mazurka.
The works of Franz Magnus Böhme (1827-98) are cited.

4267 LISSA, Zofia. **Die Formenkreuzung bei Cho-**
as **pin** [Hybrid form in Chopin], *The book of the first international musicological congress devoted to the
works of Frederick Chopin* (Warszawa: Państwowe
Wydawnictwo Naukowe, 1963) 207–12. In German.
See no. 425 in this volume.

Chopin's free forms, as seen in three late works—the F-minor fantasy op.
49, the F-minor ballade op. 52, and the A♭-major *Polonaise-fantaisie*, op.
61—may be analyzed as polyformal, using principles of formal development from sonata form, sonata cycle, rondo, and variation forms. In his interest in structural innovation he is closer to Viennese Classicism, particularly to Beethoven, than has been generally realized. A Polish-language
version is included in the collection cited as RILM [1971]739. *(David Bloom)*

4268 LIUZZI, Fernando. **Notes sur les barzelette et**
as **les canzoni a ballo du Quattrocento italien,**
d'après des documents inédits [Notes on the
barzellettas and the canzoni a ballo of fifteenth-century
Italy, according to unpublished documents], *Papers
read at the International Congress of Musicology* (New
York: Music Educators National Conference, 1944)
193–99. In French. See no. 266 in this volume.

Discusses frottola verse forms in MSS including *F-Pn* MS 4917 and fr.
15123.

4269 MERSMANN, Hans. **Beethovens zyklisches**
as **Formprinzip** [Beethoven's principle of cyclic form],
*Beethoven-Zentenarfeier: Internationaler musikhisto-
rischer Kongress* (Wien: Universal, 1927) 52–54. In
German. See no. 142 in this volume.

The striving for cyclic unity is clear in Beethoven's compositions from the
time of the C-major sonata, op. 2, no. 3, through the symphony no. 5, op.67.
From the symphony no. 6, op. 68, onwards unity is accomplished through
the subtler means of tone color and weight. In the late quartets, where the
composer appears to have returned to the loose, suite-like construction of
his earliest works, formal unity gives way to a visionary synthesis of multiplicity and unity. *(David Bloom)*

4270 MOHR, Wilhelm. **Über Mischformen und**
as **Sonderbildungen der Variationsform** [Mixed
and unique structures in variation form], *Bericht über
den internationalen musikwissenschaftlichen Kongreß*
(Kassel: Bärenreiter, 1963) 205–07. In German. See no.
452 in this volume.

Variation form as a genre is essentially of what August Halm calls a monothematic character, but examples of bithematic or polythematic variation
form exist. Particularly interesting cases are Matthias Weckmann's fugue
in D minor; variation no. 14 of Beethoven's Righini variations WoO 65;
Haydn's F-minor variations Hob.XVII:6; Franck's *Variations sym-
phoniques*; and Musorgskij's *Kartinki s vystavki* (Pictures at an exhibition).
(David Bloom)

4271 MÜLLER-BLATTAU, Joseph. **Beethoven und**
as **die Variation** [Beethoven and the variation], *Bericht
über den musikwissenschaftlichen Kongreß in Basel*
(Leipzig: Breitkopf & Härtel, 1925) 55–57. In German.
See no. 102 in this volume.

Beethoven's early works in variation form are based in his improvisational
practice as pianist. In the middle period, he begins writing variation sets in a
more structured, sonata-like fashion, and using them for the first time as
first and last movements in sonatas and symphonies. In the pervasive variation practice of his last compositions, variation becomes the leading principle of creation. *(David Bloom)*

4272 MURPHY, Richard M. **Fantaisie et recercare**
as **dans les premières tablatures de luth du XVIᵉ**
siècle [Fantasia and ricercare in the first lute tablatures
of the 16th century], *Le luth et sa musique* (Paris: Centre
National de la Recherche Scientifique [CNRS], 1958)
127–42. *Music, transcr.* In French. See no. 377 in this
volume.

In the lute music published by Ottaviano Petrucci from 1507 to 1511, the
terms *preludio*, *ricercare*, and *fantasia* are used interchangeably. Critical
remarks on the transcription methods used by Otto Gombosi in his 1955
edition of the Capirola Lutebook (*US-Cn* Case MS VM C.25) are appended.

4273 NADEL, Siegfried. **Le problème du cycle dans**
as **la musique populaire** [The problem of the cycle in
popular music], *Congrès international des arts
populaires/International congress of popular arts*
(Paris: Institut international de coopération
intellectuelle, 1928) 96–97. In French. See no. 153 in
this volume.

Summary of the second section of the paper abstracted as no. 3953 in this
volume.

4274 NEF, Karl. **L'influence de la musique française**
as **sur le développement de la suite** [The influence of
French music on the development of the suite], *Actes du
Congrès d'histoire de l'art* (Paris: Presses Universitaires de France, 1923-1924) 853–55. In French. See
no. 94 in this volume.

The influence of French music on the suite is proven by the universal usage
of the French term *allemande*. Originally a German dance, the *allemande*

has gone through different developmental phases, during which it acquired the particular characteristics for which it is known. *(Vivian Conejero)*

4275
as
NEURATH, Herbert. **Das Violinkonzert in der Wiener klassischen Schule** [The violin concerto in the Viennese Classic school], *Festschrift den Mitgliedern des Musikhistorischen Kongresses überreicht von der Leitenden Kommission der Denkmäler der Tonkunst in Österreich* (Wien: Universal, 1927) 125–42. *Music, charts, diagr.* In German. See no. 147 in this volume.

A survey of the formal and technical characteristics of the violin concerto genre as cultivated by Viennese composers between ca. 1730 and its culmination in Beethoven's hands during the first years of the 19th c. Three periods are distinguished: the pre-Classic, ca. 1730-65, the early Classic, ca. 1765-80, and the high classic, from ca. 1780. Influences from outside the Viennese sphere as well as the influences of various Viennese composers on one another are identified. An appendix diagrams the formal features of concerto rondos in several works by Mozart and Beethoven. *(Carl Skoggard)*

4276
as
NEWMAN, William S. **The recognition of sonata form by theorists of the 18th and 19th centuries,** *Papers of the American Musicological Society* (Philadelphia: American Musicological Society, 1946) 21–29. See no. 272 in this volume.

In the preface to vol. III of his *Vollständige theoretisch-praktische Kompositionslehre* (ca. 1840), Carl Czerny claimed that he was the first to provide a fundamental description of the manner of constructing a sonata. It is true that while 18th-c. theorists make frequent mention of the sonata as a genre, hardly any have anything to say about its formal structure; though Heinrich Christoph Koch's *Versuch einer Anleitung zur Composition* (1793) shows awareness of sonata form in his discussion of the symphony. Not until 1838 does an author come close to disproving Czerny's claim, in a discussion by Adolf Bernhard Marx (*Die Lehre von der musikalischen Komposition*, vol. 2, 1838). *(David Bloom)*

4277
as
OSTHOFF, Wolfgang. **Die frühesten Erscheinungsformen der Passacaglia in der italienischen Musik des 17. Jahrhunderts** [The earliest forms of the passacaglia in Italian music of the 17th century], *Atti del Congresso internazionale di musiche popolari mediterranee e del Convegno dei bibliotecari musicali* (Palermo: De Magistris succ. V. Bellotti, 1959) 275–88. *Music.* In German. See no. 332 in this volume.

The term *passacaglia* in Giovanni Ambrosio Colonna's *Intavolatura di chitarra alla spagnuola...* (Milan 1620), or *passacaglio* in the final scene of Monteverdi's *L'incoronazione di Poppea* (1642), designates something quite different from a set of variations on an ostinato bass as introduced by Frescobaldi in the keyboard version of *Il secondo libro di toccate, canzone...* (1627). The etymology (from Spanish *passacalle*) suggests that it may have originated in Spain as a dance form, and it is likely that many passages in Monteverdi's opera, including the ones so marked, were meant to accompany stylized movements by the performers. *(David Bloom)*

4278
as
PAOLI, Rodolfo. **L'oratorio nella musica contemporanea** [The oratorio in contemporary music], *Atti del [I] Congresso internazionale di musica sacra* (Tournai: Desclée, 1952) 405–08. In Italian. See no. 303 in this volume.

4279
as
PFANNKUCH, Wilhelm. **Sonatenform und Sonatenzyklus in den Streichquartetten von Joseph Martin Kraus** [Sonata form and sonata cycle in the string quartets of Joseph Martin Kraus], *Bericht über den internationalen musikwissenschaftlichen Kongreß* (Kassel: Bärenreiter, 1963) 190–92. In German. See no. 452 in this volume.

Kraus's nine quartets, written between 1773 and 1784, show a developing concept of sonata form and cyclic structure resembling that of Haydn's quartet writing around 1770. *(David Bloom)*

4280
as
PROTOPOPOV, Vladimir. **Variacionnost' kak princip razvitija v muzyke Šopena** [Variation technique as a principle of development in Chopin's music], *The book of the first international musicological congress devoted to the works of Frederick Chopin* (Warszawa: Państwowe Wydawnictwo Naukowe, 1963) 224–29. *Music, charts, diagr.* In Russian. See no. 425 in this volume.

4281
as
ROSENTHAL, Karl August. **Über Vokalformen bei Mozart** [On Mozart's vocal forms], *Festschrift den Mitgliedern des Musikhistorischen Kongresses überreicht von der Leitenden Kommission der Denkmäler der Tonkunst in Österreich* (Wien: Universal, 1927) 5–32. *Bibliog.* In German. See no. 147 in this volume.

Presents a typology of the forms Mozart adopted for his arias and lieder in both his religious and secular music. The main divisions of the typology are (1) sonata form, with or without repetition of the first strophe; (2) a two-part form in which a lesser sonata form is succeeded by a second section, often in quicker tempo; (3) rondo form; (4) three-part song form; and (5) two-part song form. The historical influences on Mozart and his choice of form are traced, and then a more detailed discussion of Mozart's treatment of the different sections of the formal types is given. *(Carl Skoggard)*

4282
as
ROUGET, Gilbert. **À propos de la forme dans les musiques de tradition orale** [On form in musics of oral tradition], *Les colloques de Wégimont. [I: Ethnomusicologie I]* (Bruxelles: Elsevier, 1956) 132–44. In French. See no. 340 in this volume.

Cylinder and disc recordings distort primitive music by not presenting large enough segments of it to show its form. Isolated segments are formless; much ceremonial music finds its form in very large time spans of a day, or even a whole season. Often the action must be observed in order to perceive the form clearly. Reference is made to the Pygmy, Ngoudi, Songhai, Piaroa, Glau, and Tohossou peoples; forms are compared to and contrasted with Western models. *(John R. Metz)*

4283
as
SCHAEFFER, Bogusław. **Präexistente und inexistente Strukturen** [Preexistent and nonexistent structures], *Bericht über den internationalen musikwissenschaftlichen Kongreß* (Kassel: Bärenreiter, 1963) 263–68. *Music, charts, diagr.* In German. See no. 452 in this volume.

Structure is the property of music that permits audible cohesion between form and material; it proceeds from the composer, not from the analysis, and follows from treating the material with an orientation toward form as a goal. Webern's technique of using preexisting structure is illustrated in his *Variationen für Orchester*, op. 30 and in two works by the author (*Model II* for piano, 1956, and *Extrema*, 1957); a concocted example of music that fails to have a structure is also provided. *(David Bloom)*

4284
as
SCHERING, Arnold. **Geschichtliches über das Verhältnis von Oper und Oratorium** [Historical remarks on the relationship between opera and oratorio], *Haydn-Zentenarfeier* (Leipzig: Breitkopf & Härtel; Wien: Artaria, 1909) 207–08. In German. See no. 65 in this volume.

4285
as
SCHNEIDER, Marius. **Arbeitsgemeinschaft: Der Terminus Variation** [Working group: The term *variation*], *Bericht über den siebenten internationalen musikwissenschaftlichen Kongreß* (Kassel: Bärenreiter, 1959) 363–66. In German. See no. 390 in this volume.

Report of a workshop discussion on the concept of variation as technique and as form, in orally transmitted traditional music and notated art music. Participants included Paul COLLAER, Hans Heinrich EGGEBRECHT, Ernest Thomas FERAND, Kurt von FISCHER, Wilhelm MOHR, Klaus P. WACHSMANN, and Walter WIORA. *(David Bloom)*

4286 STEGLICH, Rudolf. **Über das Formhören des**
as **Barock** [On hearing form in the Baroque], *Bericht
über den I. musikwissenschaftlichen Kongress der
Deutschen Musikgesellschaft in Leipzig* (Wiesbaden:
Breitkopf & Härtel, 1926) 430–35. *Music.* In German.
See no. 120 in this volume.
Discusses views on such subjects as meter and rhythm, dynamics, and the
upbeat in the Baroque. The works of Athanasius Kircher, Wolfgang Caspar
Printz, Johann Mattheson, and Johann Adolph Scheibe are quoted, and ex-
amples are taken from the music of Schütz and Johann Hermann Schein.
(William Renwick)

4287 STRUNK, Oliver. **Some motet-types of the 16th**
as **century,** *Papers read at the International Congress of
Musicology* (New York: Music Educators National
Conference, 1944) 155–60. See no. 266 in this volume.
Discusses performance contexts and text setting.

4288 SUPPAN, Wolfgang. **Die romantische Ballade**
as **als Abbild des Wagnerschen Musikdramas**
[The Romantic ballad as a reflection of Wagnerian music drama], *Bericht über den internationalen musikwissenschaftlichen Kongreß* (Kassel: Bärenreiter, 1963)
233–36. *Music.* In German. See no. 452 in this volume.
Discusses the ballad compositions of Martin Plüddemann (1854-97), with
attention to Wagner's influence on their formal character.

4289 TORREFRANCA, Fausto. **Origine e significato**
as **di repicco, partita, ricercare, sprezzatura** [The
origin and meaning of repicco, partita, ricercare, and
sprezzatura], *Société Internationale de Musicologie,
cinquième congrès/Internationale Gesellschaft für
Musikwissenschaft, fünfter Kongreß/International Society for Musical Research, Fifth Congress* (Amsterdam:
Vereniging voor Nederlandse Muziekgeschiedenis,
1953) 404–14. In Italian. See no. 316 in this volume.
Discusses the meaning of terms relating to genres and performance practice
of Italian instrumental music of the Baroque.

4290 UJFALUSSY, József. **Einige inhaltliche Fragen**
as **der Brückensymmetrie in Bartóks Werken**
[Musical content and arch symmetry in Bartók's
works], *Studia musicologica Academiae Scientiarum
Hungaricae* V (1963) 541–47. In German. See no. 427
in this volume.
In addition to the well-known use of arch form in individual movements,
Bartók also frequently used arch form across the whole of a multi-
movement work; the origins of the technique may be found in music of
Haydn, Beethoven, and Liszt. *(William Renwick)*

4291 URBANTSCHITSCH, Victor. **Die Entwicklung**
as **der Sonatenform bei Brahms** [The development
of Brahms's sonata form], *Festschrift den Mitgliedern
des Musikhistorischen Kongresses überreicht von der
Leitenden Kommission der Denkmäler der Tonkunst in
Österreich* (Wien: Universal, 1927) 265–85. *Music.* In
German. See no. 147 in this volume.
A chronological survey of Brahms's cultivation of sonata form is presented
against the background of his emergence from the conservative wing of the
Beethovenian succession. Although the externals of Brahms's sonata
forms do not seem to change from his earliest to his latest works, one notes a
continual refinement of inner technique. Four periods are to be distinguished: 1852-57, 1857-65, 1873-83, and 1884-92. It is significant, perhaps, that Brahms ceased writing independent variation sets in 1873; probably he directed that impetus to vary in the years following to a shaping of
ideas and motives within the sonata form. *(Carl Skoggard)*

4292 VOLEK, Jaroslav. **Über einige interessante**
as **Beziehungen zwischen thematischer Arbeit**
und Instrumentation in Bartóks *Concerto für*
Orchester [Some interesting relationships between
thematic ideas and instrumentation in Bartók's *Concerto for orchestra*], *Studia musicologica Academica
Scientiarum Hungaricae* V (1963) 557–86. *Music.* In
German. See no. 427 in this volume.
Among the form-defining elements of the work, the exposition/develop-
ment structure is less sharply defined than that of the alternation and succession of different instrumental groupings. *(William Renwick)*

4293 WERNER, Theodor Wilhelm. **Über innere**
as **Kriterien für die vokale oder instrumentale**
Bestimmung älterer Musik [On the inner criteria
for the vocal or instrumental determination of early mu-
sic], *Bericht über den I. musikwissenschaftlichen
Kongress der Deutschen Musikgesellschaft in Leipzig*
(Wiesbaden: Breitkopf & Härtel, 1926) 225–26. In German. See no. 120 in this volume.
Compares pieces whose form is derived from their vocal texts with pieces
whose form is derived from melodic motives and themes. *(William Renwick)*

4294 WILLNER, Arthur. **Die innere Einheit der**
as **klassischen Symphonie** [The inner unity of the
Classic symphony], *Beethoven-Zentenarfeier: Internationaler musikhistorischer Kongress* (Wien: Universal,
1927) 43–44. In German. See no. 142 in this volume.
The movements of Beethoven's odd-numbered symphonies are unified by
his motivic economy, so that the contrast between the movements is less
important than the way each contributes functionally to the organic character of the whole. The milder character of the even-numbered symphonies is
partly a consequence of their Romantic-style emphasis on contrast over
unity. *(David Bloom)*

4295 WOLFF, Hellmuth Christian. **Der Siciliano bei**
as **J.S. Bach und G.Fr. Haendel** [The siciliano in the
works of J.S. Bach and G.F. Händel], *Atti del Congresso
internazionale di musiche popolari mediterranee e del
Convegno dei bibliotecari musicali* (Palermo: De
Magistris succ. V. Bellotti, 1959) 301–08. *Music.* In
German. See no. 332 in this volume.
The use of the term *siciliano* to refer to a slow piece of pastoral character in
12/8 or 6/8 meter, with a gentle iambic meter, is traced through its roots in
southern Italian and possibly Venetian traditional music and in Italian art
music from the 17th c., and Bach's and Händel's pieces of this type are analytically enumerated. *(David Bloom)*

4296 ZIELIŃSKI, Tadeusz Andrzej. **Forma okresowa**
as **w mazurkach Chopina i mazurkach**
Szymanowskiego [Periodic form in Chopin's and
Szymanowski's mazurkas], *The book of the first international musicological congress devoted to the works
of Frederick Chopin* (Warszawa: Państwowe
Wydawnictwo Naukowe, 1963) 415–17. *Facs.* In Polish. See no. 425 in this volume.

65 Sound color, texture, and register

4297 BAYER, Friedrich. **Über den Gebrauch der**
as **Instrumente in den Kirchen- und Instrumen-**
talwerken von W.A. Mozart [On the use of instruments in church music and instrumental works by W.A.
Mozart], *Festschrift den Mitgliedern des Musikhistorischen Kongresses überreicht von der Leitenden
Kommission der Denkmäler der Tonkunst in Österreich*
(Wien: Universal, 1927) 33–74. *Music, charts, diagr.* In
German. See no. 147 in this volume.

A systematic discussion of the use of each instrument is followed by discussion of instruments employed in groups. Finally, Mozart's general approach to instrumentation and orchestration is considered, and six phases in his development as an orchestrator are distinguished. *(Carl Skoggard)*

4298 CHOMIŃSKI, Józef Michał. **Einige Probleme**
as **der Klangtechnik von Liszt** [Some aspects of sonority technique in Liszt], *Studia musicologica Academiae Scientiarum Hungaricae* V (1963) 37–47. In German. See no. 427 in this volume.

Liszt's approach to sonority had a central influence on composers of the late 19th and 20th c. His techniques include the use of color to extend dynamic and agogic expressivity; register extremes; and the radical thinning of texture. His orchestral textures alternate between the homogeneous and the heterogeneous, using a homogeneous texture, for example, for references to early music. Characteristic features of his tonal practice such as the use of modal scales and quartal or quintal harmonies also have significant effects on sonority. *(Gregory L. Fulkerson)*

4299 GŁOWACKI, John. **Kolorystyka a technika**
as **skrzypcowa w twórczości Szymanowskiego** [Coloristic devices in Szymanowski's violin technique], *Karol Szymanowski: Księga sesji Naukowej poświęconej twórczości Karola Szymanowskiego* (Warszawa: Uniwersytet Warszawski, Instytut Muzykologii, 1964) 75–85. *Music.* In Polish; summary in English. See no. 458 in this volume.

Technical innovations for the violin can be found in Szymanowski's early compositions: *Notturno e Tarantella* op. 28; the first violin concerto, op. 35; and especially in *Mity*, op.30. Devices such as glissandi in the highest registers, double glissandi, harmonic glissandi, tremolos between different intervals, simultaneous piano and violin tremolos, trills in extreme registers, mixed combinations of parallel intervals and chords, pizzicato, and an extensive treatment of bowing all add to the overall effect. *(editor)*

4300 JÍLEK, František. **Poznámky k instrumentaci**
as **Janáčkových oper** [Observations on the instrumentation of Janáček's operas], *Sborník Janáčkovy Akademie Múzichých Umeni* V (1965) 27–36. In Czech. See no. 496 in this volume.

4301 KÖHLER, Siegfried. **Instrumentation als**
as **Ausdruckskunst im Opernschaffen Wolfgang Amadeus Mozarts** [Instrumentation as an expressive resource in the operas of Wolfgang Amadeus Mozart], *Internationale Konferenz über das Leben und Werk W.A. Mozarts* (Praha: Svaz Československých Skladatelů, 1956) 121–26. In German. See no. 360 in this volume.

In its symphonic, dense color, Mozart's orchestration for his stage works represents a break from pre-Classic tradition; it aims increasingly, as his style matures from *Idomeneo* to *La clemenza di Tito*, at a well-proportioned, extraordinarily differentiated expression of dramatic content. Illustrations are drawn from his handling of wind instruments in operas. *(David Bloom)*

4302 MILLER, Dayton C. **Musical tone-color,** *Papers*
as *read at the International Congress of Musicology* (New York: Music Educators National Conference, 1944) 267–71. *Illus.* See no. 266 in this volume.

Investigative methods using an oscillograph are outlined, and the overtone profiles of various orchestral instruments are briefly described.

4303 SCHAEFFNER, André. **Les éléments de forma-**
as **tion des échelles extérieurs à la résonance: Le timbre** [Elements of scale formation external to overtones: Timbre], *La résonance dans les échelles musicales* (Paris: Centre National de la Recherche Scientifique [CNRS], 1963) 214–21. In French; summaries in English and German. See no. 420 in this volume.

Discusses musical and symbolic reasons why musics of different cultures use such widely varying timbres. Speculations are offered as to a possible parallel between non-Western musical timbres and non-Western masks or costumes: Disguise of the human is common to both.

4304 SWAN, Alfred J. **O sposobah garmonizacii**
as **znamennogo rospeva** [Ways of harmonizing znamennyj chant], *Anfänge der slavischen Musik* (Bratislava: Slovenská Akadémia Vied, 1966) 117–24. *Music.* In Russian. See no. 477 in this volume.

Composers and arrangers incorporating Russian chant melodies into their works should avoid Western-style chromatic harmonization but make use of a modal polyphonic style reflecting the origins of znamennyj, which are to be sought not so much in Byzantine as in traditional Russian music. Examples are drawn from the author's *Liturgical canticles of the Eastern Church* (New York: Boosey & Hawkes, 1956-59).

4305 WLACH, Hans. **Die Oboe bei Beethoven** [The
as oboe in Beethoven's music], *Festschrift den Mitgliedern des Musikhistorischen Kongresses überreicht von der Leitenden Kommission der Denkmäler der Tonkunst in Österreich* (Wien: Universal, 1927) 107–24. *Music.* In German. See no. 147 in this volume.

The evolution of the oboe during Beethoven's lifetime is considered, as is the evidence of his acquaintance with various makes of oboe. Then his treatment of the instrument in his chamber music and in the orchestral music, in particular in relation to each of the other wind instruments, is surveyed. Beethoven demonstrates deep knowledge of the instrument and while he writes adventurously for it, Haydn is reckless in comparison. Another version is published in *Die Oboe: Mitteilungsblatt des Oboisten-Bundes*, no. 3-9 (1928-31). *(Carl Skoggard)*

66 Style analysis

4306 ANSCHÜTZ, Georg. **Über Aufbauprinzipien**
as **in den Werken Johann Sebastian Bachs** [Structural principles in the works of Johann Sebastian Bach], *Bericht über die Wissenschaftliche Bachtagung* (Leipzig: Peters, 1951) 270–76. In German. See no. 298 in this volume.

Bach's use of the structural possibilities of equal temperament through the entire circle of fifths, going well beyond that of contemporary composers including Händel, or indeed any composer before Wagner, is a distinguishing characteristic of his style. Certain patterns of symmetry within the circle of fifths established for Bach's music by Wilhelm Werker correspond to those in a case of color hearing exhibited by the blind organist and pianist Paul Dörken. *(David Bloom)*

4307 ANSERMET, Ernest. **Le langage de Debussy**
as [The language of Debussy], *Debussy et l'évolution de la musique au XXᵉ siècle* (Paris: Centre National de la Recherche Scientifique [CNRS], 1965) 33–46. *Music.* In French. See no. 456 in this volume.

Debussy's impressionist style is discussed in relation to his treatment of harmony, melody, and tonality.

4308 BARRAQUÉ, Jean. **Debussy, ou L'approche**
as **d'une organisation autogène de la composition** [Debussy, or, The approach of an autogenous compositional organization], *Debussy et l'évolution de la musique au XXᵉ siècle* (Paris: Centre National de la Recherche Scientifique [CNRS], 1965) 83–96. *Music.* In French. See no. 456 in this volume.

Debussy's aesthetic principles and creative processes are examined, and the influence of Beethoven is noted.

4309 BARTHA, Dénes. **Bemerkungen zur Stili-**
as **sierung der Volksmusik, besonders der**

Polonäsen, bei Bach [Notes on the stylization of traditional music, especially polonaises, in Bach], *Bericht
über die Wissenschaftliche Bachtagung* (Leipzig: Peters, 1951) 416–19. In German. See no. 298 in this
volume.

Polonaise or *polacca* as a designation in works by Bach, Telemann, and
Sperontes (Johann Sigismund Scholze), and a generation later, Wilhelm
Friedemann Bach, may have served as umbrella terms for Eastern Euro-
pean traditional music of all sorts. *(David Bloom)*

4310 BECK, Hermann. **Probleme der venezianischen
as Messkomposition im 16. Jahrhundert** [Prob-
lems of Venetian Mass composition in the 16th cen-
tury], *Bericht über den internationalen musikwissenschaftlichen Kongreß Wien Mozartjahr 1956* (Graz;
Köln: Böhlau, 1958) 35–40. *Music.* In German. See no.
365 in this volume.

The relatively few Mass settings of Venetian composers from Adrian
Willaert through Giovanni Gabrieli are of the highest artistic quality. Distinguishing features of the Venetian school include the predominance of
duple meters; isolation of the upper voice or upper voice and bass together
from the other voices; instrumental-style elaboration of the polyphonic setting; imitation; articulation of drawn-out lines into matched units; and a
turn toward the rhythmic values of the text. *(author)*

4311 BECK, Hermann. **Zur musikalischen Analyse**
as [Musical analysis], *Bericht über den internationalen
musikwissenschaftlichen Kongreß* (Kassel: Bärenreiter,
1963) 291–92. In German. See no. 452 in this volume.

Discusses the interrelations among the constituent parts of a theme in 18th-
and 19th-c. music, drawing on sonata-exposition examples from Mozart
and Beethoven. *(David Bloom)*

4312 BECKING, Gustav. **Klassik und Romantik**
as [Classic and Romantic], *Bericht über den I. musikwissenschaftlichen Kongress der Deutschen Musikgesellschaft in Leipzig* (Wiesbaden: Breitkopf & Härtel,
1926) 292–96. *Music.* In German. See no. 120 in this
volume.

A discussion of three excerpts attempts to make a distinction between Classic and Romantic styles. A reprint is cited as RILM [1976]5675. *(William Renwick)*

4313 BESSELER, Heinrich. **Charakterthema und
as Erlebnisform bei Bach** [Character theme and experience form of Bach], *Kongreß-Bericht: Gesellschaft
für Musikforschung* (Kassel; Basel: Bärenreiter, 1950)
7–32. In German. See no. 299 in this volume.

Applies the new concept of *Charakterthema* (character theme), whose
traits are segmentation and contrast, to Bach's works.

4314 BEVILACQUA, Otávio. **Algumas proposições
as e quesitos** [Some proposals and questions], *Anais do
Primeiro Congresso da Língua Nacional Cantada* (São
Paulo: Departamento Municipal de Cultura, 1938)
655–62. In Portuguese. See no. 253 in this volume.

The division of words in Portuguese-language vocal music is examined.

4315 BOETTICHER, Wolfgang. **Über einige
as Spätstilprobleme bei Chopin** [Some problems of
style in Chopin's late works], *The book of the first international musicological congress devoted to the works
of Frederick Chopin* (Warszawa: Państwowe
Wydawnictwo Naukowe, 1963) 104–06. In German.
See no. 425 in this volume.

Compositions of the last three years of Chopin's life are marked by style
features of an extreme character, including organ points accompanied by
drastic increases in volume; chromatically ascending chains of trills; use of
ostinato as an organizing principle; and choice of thematic material in terms

of its structural value. His development in this period is to be compared to
that of Beethoven from 1820 to 1826. *(David Bloom)*

4316 BOETTICHER, Wolfgang. **Zum Spätstil-
as problem im Schaffen Orlando di Lassos** [The
problem of a late style in Roland de Lassus], *Bericht
über den siebenten internationalen musikwissenschaftlichen Kongress* (Kassel: Bärenreiter, 1959) 69–71. In
German. See no. 390 in this volume.

The works of Lassus's last years, including the motet cycle for six voices
Musica Dei donum optimi and the cycle of seven-voice spiritual madrigals
Lagrime di S. Pietro, are analyzed for evidence of a definable late style.
These two groups suggest that Lassus was intent on cross-fertilizing the
motet and madrigal genres. Viewed in the light of the rounded achievement
of his middle years, the late compositions do not represent so unified a
style. *(Carl Skoggard)*

4317 BÓNIS, Ferenc. **Quotations in Bartók's music:
as A contribution to Bartók's psychology of composition,** *Studia musicologica Academiae
Scientiarum Hungaricae* V (1963) 355–82. *Music.* See
no. 427 in this volume.

Bartók's works feature quotations from a wide range composers from the
18th to 20th c., including Bach, Beethoven, Liszt, Wagner, Strauss, Debussy, Ravel, Stravinsky, and Kodály. They are used in such a way as to remain inconspicuous to the listener, and appear to encode content of a personal nature. *(Alan Garfield)*

4318 BORRELLI, Enzo. **Dal neoclassicismo alla
as dodecafonia** [From neoclassicism to twelve-tone
technique], *Atti del quinto Congresso di musica*
(Firenze: Barbèra, 1948) 146–52. In Italian. See no. 285
in this volume.

Between the two world wars, the popularity of music that obeys its own laws
was replaced by a preference for music that is subordinate to extramusical
tenets, that is, neoclassical music. Written while self-deception and undue
optimism were covering up a spiritual desert, this music remained out of
touch with reality. Consequently, it is now defunct. Twelve-tone techniques
currently in use manifest a more realistic outlook on the part of composers.
In searching for new modes of expression, they maintain a historical perspective and furnish the public with a courageous response to its demands.
(Channan Willner)

4319 BREIG, Werner. **Über das Verhältnis von Kom-
as position und Ausführung in der norddeutschen Orgel-Choralbearbeitung des 17.
Jahrhunderts** [The relation between composition
and performance in North German chorale arrangements for organ in the 17th century], *Norddeutsche und
nordeuropäische Musik* (Kassel; New York:
Bärenreiter, 1965) 71–82. *Music.* In German. See no.
467 in this volume.

Beginning with Samuel Scheidt's *Tabulatura nova* (1624), the possibilities
of voice crossing, monophonic setting, and the sonority-based form of the
chorale fantasia came to be used consistently as a compositional technique
in the formation of what was perhaps the first organ repertoire based on the
instrument's technical resources. *(author)*

4320 ČERNOHORSKÁ, Milena. **Význam nápěvků
as pro Janáčkovu operní tvorbu** [The significance
of speech melodies in Janáček's operas], *Leoš Janáček
a soudobá hudba* (Praha: Panton, 1963) 77–80. In
Czech; summaries in Russian and German. See no. 389
in this volume.

Janáček based his vocal melodies on the concept of the speech melody
(*nápěvek*), patterns of speech intonation as they relate to psychological
conditions, rather than on a strictly musical basis. He used such melodic
motives, characterizing a specific person in a specific dramatic situation, in
both vocal and orchestral parts, enabling him to integrate the two parts into
a compact unit for the utmost dramatic effect. *(editors)*

4321
as
CHERBULIEZ, Antoine-Élisée. **L'adaptation du folklore brésilien au style de J.S. Bach selon la thèse de Villa-Lobos** [Adapting Brazilian folklore to the style of J.S. Bach according to the thesis of Villa-Lobos], *Journal of the International Folk Music Council* IX (1957) 29–31. In French. See no. 362 in this volume.

An appreciation of the influence of Brazilian traditional music on Villa-Lobos's nine *Bachianas brasileiras* (1930-45). A note by Luis Heitor Corrêa de AZEVEDO discusses the biographical circumstances of the composition. *(David Bloom)*

4322
as
CHERBULIEZ, Antoine-Élisée. **Stilkritischer Vergleich von Mozarts beiden g-moll Sinfonien von 1773 und 1788** [A stylistic comparison between Mozart's two G-minor symphonies, of 1773 and 1778], *Bericht über die musikwissenschaftliche Tagung der Internationalen Stiftung Mozarteum* (Leipzig: Breitkopf & Härtel, 1932) 112–19. In German. See no. 193 in this volume.

The frequently noted emotional affinities between the symphonies K.183 and K.550 correspond to a number of parallels at the technical level.

4323
as
CHLUBNA, Osvald. **Janáčkovy názory na operu a jeho úsilí o nový operní sloh** [Janáček's views on opera and his striving for a new operatic style], *Leoš Janáček a soudobá hudba* (Praha: Panton, 1963) 140–49. In Czech; summaries in Russian and German. See no. 389 in this volume.

The composition of dramatic work should be based on speech; words determine musical rhythm. The composer's task is first to derive a speech melody (*nápěvek*), then add the harmonic aspect, and integrate the vocal motives with orchestral ones. Janáček's views on opera composition are compared with the actual development of his own style. *(editors)*

4324
as
CHMARA, Barbara. **Das Problem der Agogik der Nocturni von Field und Chopin** [The problem of agogics in the nocturnes of Field and Chopin], *The book of the first international musicological congress devoted to the works of Frederick Chopin* (Warszawa: Państwowe Wydawnictwo Naukowe, 1963) 275–80. *Music.* In German. See no. 425 in this volume.

Field fails to find, in harmonic and agogic contrast, a means to the dynamization of form and expression in his nocturnes; the genre is as yet immature. Chopin's concept of the nocturne requires a slow tempo and conscious tying together of agogics with structure and expression, and he is less indebted to Field than has previously been supposed. *(David Bloom)*

4325
as
CHOMIŃSKI, Józef Michał. **Die Evolution des Chopinschen Stils** [The evolution of Chopin's style], *The book of the first international musicological congress devoted to the works of Frederick Chopin* (Warszawa: Państwowe Wydawnictwo Naukowe, 1963) 44–52. *Illus.* In German. See no. 425 in this volume.

In the first period of his stylistic development, to 1830, Chopin largely followed the Classic and Polish-national traditions with which he was brought up. In the second period, to 1839, beginning with the transitional mazurkas (1830-31) and the development of characteristically Romantic single-movement forms, his own individuality as a composer emerged. The third period, from 1839 until his death, saw him synthesizing these two sides as a precursor of a new tendency in European music. An Italian-language version is cited as RILM [1987]2719. *(David Bloom)*

4326
as
CHRISTENSEN, Dieter. **Heterogene Musikstile in dem Dorf Gabela (Herzegovina)** [Heterogenous musical styles in the village of Gabela (Herzegovina)], *Bericht über den siebenten internationalen musikwissenschaftlichen Kongress* (Kassel:

Bärenreiter, 1959) 79–82. *Music.* In German. See no. 390 in this volume.

The song repertoire of 16 Roman Catholic informants was collected during a short stay (10 days) in Gabela, an agricultural village of some 1400 inhabitants near the western border of Herzegovina. Their productions, 55 in total, fell into three distinct groups according to melodic analysis. Those of narrow range, either a minor or a major third, are local (the various genres are briefly discussed); songs belonging in the other groups originated in either Serbia or Bosnia or else the Middle East and were probably learned by the inhabitants of Gabela via radio, though there were neither radios nor electricity in the village at the time of the fieldwork, in 1957. *(Carl Skoggard)*

4327
as
CZYŻOWSKI, Stanisław. **Problem stylizacji w Królu Rogerze** [Stylization in Szymanowski's *Król Roger*], *Karol Szymanowski: Księga sesji Naukowej poświęconej twórczości Karola Szymanowskiego* (Warszawa: Uniwersytet Warszawski, Instytut Muzykologii, 1964) 47–66. *Music.* In Polish; summary in English. See no. 458 in this volume.

In Szymanowski's *Król Roger* (King Roger), the stylized treatment of Byzantine music is found mainly in the first act, where antiphonal psalmody was a starting point for the composer. Here Szymanowski used double choirs, organum technique, fauxbourdon, church modes, and hymns in the Byzantine Kontakion fashion. Asian music is found mainly in two episodes: Roxana's vocalise and the dance of ecstasy. The opera also contains an example of free treatment of an unidentified Asian melody, constructed on maqām patterns. The Shepherd's song and Roxana's lullaby are based on modal scales, recalling old Greek music. The new features of the composer's style are revealed in the third act, particularly in the Shepherd's arias, which are based on elements of Highlanders' music. These reflect the deep stylistic changes that were to take place during Szymanowski's national period. *(editor)*

4328
as
DANISKAS, John. **Analytische Studien über die Kompositionstechnik der burgundischen Schule** [Analytic studies on the composition technique of the Burgundian school], *Société Internationale de Musicologie, cinquième congrès/Internationale Gesellschaft für Musikwissenschaft, fünfter Kongreß/International Society for Musical Research, Fifth Congress* (Amsterdam: Vereniging voor Nederlandse Muziekgeschiedenis, 1953) 132–38. In German. See no. 316 in this volume.

In the 14th and 15th c., the Burgundian court became an important center of musical activity. The importance of the dukes of Burgundy as patrons of music was such that the composers of the period have come to be called the Burgundian school.

4329
as
DÜRR, Alfred. **Stilkritik und Echtheitsprobleme der frühen Kantaten Bachs** [Style criticism and problems of authenticity in the early cantatas of Bach], *Bericht über die Wissenschaftliche Bachtagung* (Leipzig: Peters, 1951) 259–69. In German. See no. 298 in this volume.

Voice exchance, or *Stimmtausch*, is among the most important style elements in Bach's early cantatas. It is seen in the permutation fugues from the cantatas BWV 71 and 169. Other important elements of style are the use of choral interpolation and instrumental ritornello in the arias, and the distinctive relation between the ritornello and the first vocal part to follow it. These, together with some relatively minor style criteria, make it possible to verify the authenticity of BWV 150, and to show that BWV 142 was not composed before 1716, and probably is not by Bach. *(James Donald Anderson)*

4330
as
ENGEL, Hans. **Die Quellen des Klassischen Stiles** [Sources of the Classic style], *Report of the Eighth Congress of the International Musicological Society. I: Papers* (Kassel: Bärenreiter, 1961) 285–304. *Music, charts, diagr.* In German. See no. 439 in this volume.

Traces the sources of structure in Haydn's and Mozart's sonatas and symphonies, including the form of contrasting themes in sonata expositions, distinctive recapitulations, experimental form in the slow movement, introduction of the minuet, contrapuntal finale, and cyclic use of thematic material in a multi-movement work. Particularly influential were Niccolò Jommelli, Giovanni Battista Pescetti, Antonio Maria Sacchini, Giovanni Battista Sammartini, and Baldassare Galuppi.

4331 FEDER, Georg. **Bemerkungen über die**
as **Ausbildung der Klassischen Tonsprache in der Instrumentalmusik Haydns** [Remarks on the development of the Classic musical language in Haydn's instrumental music], *Report of the Eighth Congress of the International Musicological Society. I: Papers* (Kassel: Bärenreiter, 1961) 305–13. *Music.* In German. See no. 439 in this volume.

Haydn's early instrumental music is in a naive divertimento style, rooted in Italy. Under the influence of C.P.E. Bach, in the years around 1770, he achieved an individuality and depth of expression well beyond that of the Mannheim school, notably by means of his *Charakterthemen* and emphatic use of counterpoint. After 1772, and most clearly from 1775-76, Haydn's instrumental style can be called "Classic" without reservations. *(David Bloom)*

4332 FEDERHOFER, Hellmut. **Die Diminution in**
as **den Klavierwerken von Chopin und Liszt** [Ornamentation in the piano works of Chopin and Liszt], *Studia musicologica Academiae Scientiarum Hungaricae* V (1963) 49–57. *Music.* In German. See no. 427 in this volume.

Discusses the various ornamental techniques of Chopin and Liszt, particularly in relation to final cadences; the influence on ornamentation of the two composers' piano performance technique; and the relation of ornamentation to melodic design in their works. *(William Renwick)*

4333 FEDERHOFER, Hellmut. **Zur Einheit von**
as **Wort und Ton im Lied von Johannes Brahms** [The unity of word and music in Johannes Brahms's lieder], *Bericht über den internationalen musikwissenschaftlichen Kongreß* (Kassel: Bärenreiter, 1957) 97–99. *Music.* In German. See no. 356 in this volume.

In Brahms's settings, there is frequently a contradiction between the musical stress of the downbeat and the linguistic stress of the text. Sometimes, as in the case of *Das Mädchen spricht* (op. 107 no. 3), the contradiction is only apparent: In the light of an analysis of tonal structure, it is possible to redraw the barlines in such a way as to eliminate it. *(David Bloom)*

4334 FISCHER, Kurt von. **Zur Satztechnik von**
as **Bachs Klaviersuiten** [On compositional technique in Bach's keyboard suites], *Kongreß-Bericht: Gesellschaft für Musikforschung* (Kassel; Basel: Bärenreiter, 1950) 124–26. In German. See no. 299 in this volume.

4335 FLOROS, Constantin. **Kompositionstechnische**
as **Probleme der atonalen Musik** [Technical problems of composition in atonal music], *Bericht über den internationalen musikwissenschaftlichen Kongreß* (Kassel: Bärenreiter, 1963) 257–60. In German. See no. 452 in this volume.

In the period of so-called free atonality, between the abandonment of tonality and the adoption of the 12-tone method, Schoenberg, Webern, and Berg were forced to organize their compositions according to other principles, including sonority centers *(Klangzentren)*, similar to those used by Skrjabin; sound-surfaces *(Klangfläche)* like those of Debussy, but dissonant; harmony based on the close conjunction, vertical and horizontal, of chromatic neighbors; and primitive rows of as few as three tones. *(David Bloom)*

4336 GEORGIADES, Thrasybulos Georges. **Neue**
as **Quellen zur Theorie der englischen Mehrstimmigkeit bis Dunstable** [New sources for the theory of English polyphony until Dunstable], *Congrés*

de la Societat Internacional de Musicologia (Barcelona: Casa de Caritat, 1936). In German. See no. 224 in this volume.

The conference report provides only a citation. Neither the text nor a summary of the paper was published here.

4337 GORCZYCKA, Monika. **Neue Merkmale der**
as **Klangtechnik in Bartóks Streichquartetten** [New features of sound technique in Bartók's string quartets], *Studia musicologica Academiae Scientiarum Hungaricae* V (1963) 425–33. In German. See no. 427 in this volume.

Bartók's stylistic innovations in the string quartets include new rhythmic and intervallic procedures, some comparable to 12-tone technique and serialism, and novel playing techniques. *(William Renwick)*

4338 GOSLICH, Siegfried. **Deklamation und**
as **instrumentale Symbolik im begleiteten Kunstgesang** [Declamation and instrumental symbolism in the accompanied art song], *Bericht über den Internationalen Kongreß Singen und Sprechen* (München: Oldenbourg, 1938) 27–30. In German. See no. 257 in this volume.

Draws examples from Wagner's operas and Schubert's lieder of how accompaniment supports the text in form, accent, and style. *(Sylvia Eversole)*

4339 GURLITT, Wilibald. **Zu Johann Sebastian**
as **Bachs Ostinato-Technik** [Johann Sebastian Bach's ostinato technique], *Bericht über die Wissenschaftliche Bachtagung* (Leipzig: Peters, 1951) 240–49. *Music.* In German. See no. 298 in this volume.

Analysis of the keyboard sinfonia no. 9 in F minor, BWV 795. Its ostinato figure, a descending, chromatically-filled-in tetrachord, which Christoph Bernhard called a *passus duriusculus* ("harsh passage"), is a figure of the theology of the Cross. The same material is used in Wilhelm Friedemann Bach's F-minor fugue, F.31, no. 8. *(James Donald Anderson)*

4340 HÁBA, Alois. **Hudební sloh Janáčkův a jeho**
as **současníků** [The musical style of Janáček and his contemporaries], *Leoš Janáček a soudobá hudba* (Praha: Panton, 1963) 117–20. In Czech; summaries in Russian and German. See no. 389 in this volume.

Three kinds of compositional styles are distinguished: (1) thematic (repetition and elaboration of melodic ideas); (2) nonthematic; and (3) combination of the first two. Janáček's distinctive use of all three styles is compared with that of his predecessors and contemporaries. *(editors)*

4341 HANDSCHIN, Jacques. **Eine wenig beachtete**
as **Stilrichtung innerhalb der mittelalterlichen Mehrstimmigkeit** [A little-noted stylistic tendency within medieval polyphony], *Schweizer Jahrbuch für Musikwissenschaft/Annales suisses de musicologie/Annuario svizzero di musicologia* I (1924) 56–75. In German. See no. 103 in this volume.

4342 HASSE, Karl. **Art und Wesen der Tonsprache**
as **Beethovens** [Beethoven's musical language as type and essence], *Beethoven-Zentenarfeier: Internationaler musikhistorischer Kongress* (Wien: Universal, 1927) 35–39. In German. See no. 142 in this volume.

Fundamental elements of Beethoven's style include his idiosyncratic use of instrumental tone color, developed out of the techniques of the Mannheim school, and his attachment to the strophic song form of the Berlin school dominated by C.P.E. Bach. *(David Bloom)*

4343 HASSE, Karl. **Palestrina, Schütz, Bach und**
as **Beethoven im Lichte der Stilwandlungen** [Palestrina, Schütz, Bach, and Beethoven in light of

style transformations], *Bericht über den I. musikwissenschaftlichen Kongress der Deutschen Musikgesellschaft in Leipzig* (Wiesbaden: Breitkopf & Härtel, 1926) 245. In German. See no. 120 in this volume.

A summary of an article published in *Neuen Musikzeitung* II (October 1925). The need to distinguish between the personal elements in a composer's style and the universal elements of a style period is discussed. *(William Renwick)*

4344 HEUSS, Alfred Valentin. **Das Orchester-**
as **crescendo bei Beethoven** [The orchestral crescendo in Beethoven], *Bericht über den musikwissenschaftlichen Kongreß in Basel* (Leipzig: Breitkopf & Härtel, 1925) 201–02. In German. See no. 102 in this volume.

The explosive accents in the piano sonata, op. 14, and in the orchestral works find their model in the uncontrolled release that characterized one side of Mannheim dynamics. The other side—the gradual crescendo—is heard in the main theme of the ninth symphony, op. 125.

4345 HILL, Edward Burlingame. **La musique aux**
as **États-Unis** [Music in the United States], *Actes du Congrès d'histoire de l'art* (Paris: Presses Universitaires de France, 1923-1924) 935–36. In French. See no. 94 in this volume.

Serious musical culture in the U.S. is a recent and European-influenced phenomenon. The first generation of American composers was unable to avoid German and French stylistic characteristics, but succeeded in attaining some expression of American traits. *(Vivian Conejero)*

4346 HUDEC, Vladimír. **Zum Problem des**
as **"Lisztartigen" in Smetanas symphonischen Dichtungen** [On the problem of "Lisztishness" in Smetana's symphonic poems], *Studia musicologica Academiae Scientiarum Hungaricae* V (1963) 131–37. *Music.* In German. See no. 427 in this volume.

The impact of Liszt's symphonic poems on Smetana's works in the same genre is outlined in terms of melodic, rhythmic, and harmonic aspects. *(William Renwick)*

4347 JANEČEK, Karel. **Stavba Janáčkových**
as **skladeb** [The structure of Janáček's compositions], *Leoš Janáček a soudobá hudba* (Praha: Panton, 1963) 150–54. In Czech; summaries in Russian and German. See no. 389 in this volume.

Unlike his predecessors, Janáček combined the use of folk melodic material with modern tectonic principles, including abbreviated and concise repetitions and the technique of leaving the previous melodic idea unfinished, so that the new part could start without preparation. *(editors)*

4348 JEANNETEAU, Jean. **Il valore attuale del**
as **canto gregoriano** [The current value of Gregorian chant], *La musica nel rinnovamento liturgico: Atti della Settimana internazionale di musica sacra* (Torino: Elle Di Ci, 1966) 127–44. In Italian. See no. 501 in this volume.

Melody, modality, text underlay, and rhythm all contribute to assessing the aesthetic and spiritual value of Gregorian chant.

4349 JEPPESEN, Knud. **Das *Sprunggesetz* des**
as **Palestrinastils bei betonten Viertelnoten (halben Taktzeiten): Eine vorläufige Mitteilung** [The *law of leaps* in the Palestrina style with respect to accented quarter-notes (in half-measures): A preliminary report], *Bericht über den musikwissenschaftlichen Kongreß in Basel* (Leipzig: Breitkopf & Härtel, 1925) 211–19. *Music.* In German. See no. 102 in this volume.

A study of the relationship between melody and rhythm shows that leaps of a fourth on the second beat and those of a third on the third beat are prohibited. This contributes to a style of fine nuances and gentle motion.

4350 JIRÁNEK, Jaroslav. **Liszt und Smetana: Ein**
as **Beitrag zur Genesis und eine vergleichende Betrachtung ihres Klavierstils** [Liszt and Smetana: On the genesis of their piano styles and a comparative study], *Studia musicologica Academiae Scientiarum Hungaricae* V (1963) 139–92. *Music.* In German. See no. 427 in this volume.

A detailed examination of common features in the piano writing of the two composers, with emphasis on rhythmic freedom and the expansion of texture, colour, and technique. *(William Renwick)*

4351 JONAS, Oswald. **Zur realen Antwort in der**
as **Fuge bei Bach** [The real answer in the fugues of Bach], *Bericht über den internationalen musikwissenschaftlichen Kongreß* (Kassel: Bärenreiter, 1963) 364–66. *Music.* In German. See no. 452 in this volume.

The real answer in fugue construction has generally been regarded as less worthy of discussion than the tonal answer, because of the contribution the latter makes to the unity of the piece as a whole. Yet Bach uses real answers in a third of the fugues of *Das wohltemperirte Clavier*, book I, and nearly half of those of book II. Analysis reveals some of these to be real answers in form but tonal answers in function. *(David Bloom)*

4352 KELLER, Wilhelm. **Tonsatzanalytische**
as **Verfahren zur Darstellung von Stilkriterien neuer Musik** [Procedures in compositional analysis for the representation of style criteria of new music], *Stilkriterien der neuen Musik* (Berlin: Merseburger, 1961) 66–82. In German. See no. 410 in this volume.

Reviews the history of phrase analysis, as a subject of study and as an analytic tool, from the harmonic analysis of Hugo Riemann and Hindemith's *Unterweisung im Tonsatz* (Mainz, 1937), which broke with traditional harmony in order to develop a new foundation for analysis, through works dealing more directly with serial technique. Tone row description, however, is not analysis, and new ways must be found to deal more thoroughly with new music. *(Neill Clegg)*

4353 KISS, Lajos. **Bitne značajke mađarskog**
as **muzičkog folklora** [The main characteristics of the Hungarian musical tradition], *Rad kongresa folklorista Jugoslavije* (Zagreb: Savez Udruženja Folklorista Jugoslavije, 1959) 113–22. *Transcr.* In Serbian; summary in German. See no. 382 in this volume.

The older style of Hungarian music is marked by pentatonicism, not always anhemitonic; a two-part stanza form in which the second part ends with a repetition, at a fifth below, of the ending of the first; isometric stanza structure; parlando rhythm; and rich melismatic ornamentation. The newer style, which has already dominated for several decades, follows the stanza form A-A^5-A^5-A, apparently taken from European models. *(author)*

4354 KLEMM, Eberhardt. **Zagadnienie techniki**
as **wariacyjnej u Regera i Szymanowskiego** [Reger's and Szymanowski's variation technique], *Karol Szymanowski: Księga sesji Naukowej poświęconej twórczości Karola Szymanowskiego* (Warszawa: Uniwersytet Warszawski, Instytut Muzykologii, 1964) 142–60. *Music.* In Polish; summary in English. See no. 458 in this volume.

Szymanowski spent the years 1906-08 mainly in Berlin and Leipzig, where he studied the works of Wagner, Strauss, and Reger. Their influence is evident in Szymanowski's early works. Szymanowski wrote two sets of variations: the first is in his second symphony, op. 19; the second is in his piano sonata, op.21. These are compared with Reger's *Variationen und Fuge über ein Thema von Johann Sebastian Bach*, op. 81. *(editor)*

4355 KÖHLER, Siegfried. **Leoš Janáčeks Progressi-**
as **vität und der musikalische Modernismus in**
der westlichen Welt/Janáčkova pokrokovost a
hudební modernismus v západním světě [Leoš
Janáček's progressiveness and musical modernism in
the Western world], *Leoš Janáček a soudobá hudba*
(Praha: Panton, 1963) 169–75. *Music.* In German and
Czech. See no. 389 in this volume.

Counterposes Janáček's progressive compositional method to serialism
and the constructivist trends of musical modernism. Janáček's technique,
the so-called variability of structural density, is based on a psychological
platform, as demonstrated by the structural analysis of the first piece from
the *Zápisník zmizelého* (The diary of one who disappeared, 1917-19).
(Jadranka Važanová)

4356 KOSZEWSKI, Andrzej. **Pierwiastek walcowy**
as **w twórczości Chopina** [Waltz elements in Chopin's
works], *The book of the first international musicologi-*
cal congress devoted to the works of Frederick Chopin
(Warszawa: Państwowe Wydawnictwo Naukowe,
1963) 196–201. *Music.* In Polish. See no. 425 in this
volume.

4357 KROHN, Ilmari. **Fr. Aug. Gevaerts Stellung**
as **zum gregorianischen Gesang** [François Auguste
Gevaert's views on Gregorian chant], *Société*
Internationale de Musicologie: Premier Congrès
Liège—Compte rendu/Internationale Gesellschaft für
Musikwissenschaft: Erster Kongress Lüttich—Kon-
gressbericht/International Society for Musical Re-
search: First Congress Liège: Report (London: Plainsong and Mediaeval Music Society, 1930) 158–64. *Mu-*
sic. In German. See no. 178 in this volume.

Discusses this 19th-c. scholar's studies of thematic connections, melodic
preservation and variation, syllabic prototypes of hymns, and tonal conceptions. *(Scott Fruehwald)*

4358 LANG, Paul Henry. **Stylistic elements in the**
as **Classic era,** *Compte rendu/Kongressbericht/Report*
(Basel: Bärenreiter, 1951) 22. See no. 289 in this
volume.

Summary of a conference paper. While many scholars assume that an orchestral style must come from orchestral-instrumental sources, some of the
main ingredients in the symphony-like style of C.P.E. Bach's "Prussian"
and "Württemberg" sonatas (W.48-49) can be traced to the animated orchestral fabric of opera. *(Scott Fruehwald)*

4359 LARUE, Jan. **Harmonic rhythm as an indica-**
as **tor of rhythmic function,** *Bericht über den*
siebenten internationalen musikwissenschaftlichen
Kongress (Kassel: Bärenreiter, 1959) 176–77. See no.
390 in this volume.

Harmonic rhythm, the relative speed of chord change, can be determined
with more objectivity than melodic rhythm, and can be used as a reliable index of style period, from the high Renaissance to the breakdown of tonality
toward the end of the 19th c., after which a broader concept of relative consonance and dissonance can be used. *(David Bloom)*

4360 LÉBL, Vladimír. **Diskusní příspěvek k**
as **referátům o Janáčkově nápěvkové technice**
[Remarks on the papers concerning Janáček's technique of speech melodies], *Leoš Janáček a soudobá*
hudba (Praha: Panton, 1963) 202–04. *Music.* In Czech;
summaries in Russian and German. See no. 389 in this
volume.

Comments on the papers abstracted as no. 4320, 4446, 5594, and 5939 in
this volume.

4361 LECHTHALER, Josef. **Die melodische**
as **Nachzeichnungstechnik in den kirchlichen**
Werken Alexander Uttendals [The melodic imita-
tion technique in the religious works of Alexander
Utendal], *Bericht über den I. musikwissenschaftlichen*
Kongress der Deutschen Musikgesellschaft in Leipzig
(Wiesbaden: Breitkopf & Härtel, 1926) 335–38. In Ger-
man. See no. 120 in this volume.

Explains Utendal's melodic variation technique, and the use of rondeau
forms in his motets.

4362 LEHMANN, Dieter. **Satztechnische Besonder-**
as **heiten in den Klavierwerken von Frédéric**
Chopin und Robert Schumann [Unusual technical elements in the piano writing of Frédéric Chopin
and Robert Schumann], *The book of the first interna-*
tional musicological congress devoted to the works of
Frederick Chopin (Warszawa: Państwowe
Wydawnictwo Naukowe, 1963) 329–33. In German.
See no. 425 in this volume.

The polyphonic character of Schumann's early piano writing was a function of his essentially literary inspiration, and changed drastically after his
intensive study of counterpoint; Chopin's polyphony is a function of his
understanding of the instrument, and developed organically through his entire career. *(David Bloom)*

4363 LENAERTS, René Bernard. **Le chanson**
as **polyphonique Néerlandaise aux 15ᵉ et 16ᵉ**
siècles [The Netherlandish polyphonic chanson of the
15th and 16th centuries], *Société Internationale de*
Musicologie: Premier Congrès Liège—Compte rendu/
Internationale Gesellschaft für Musikwissenschaft:
Erster Kongress Lüttich—Kongressbericht/Interna-
tional Society for Musical Research: First Congress
Liège: Report (London: Plainsong and Mediaeval Music Society, 1930) 168–73. *Illus., music.* In French. See
no. 178 in this volume.

Towards the end of the 16th c., the polyphonic chanson became homophonic. Gradually, the old style of contrapuntal writing employing strict
canons or imitative entrances and traditional pre-existing cantus firmi
yielded to a more chordal technique using freely composed themes. The
predominance of the tenor line was replaced by equality among the voices,
then by the predominance of a single-voice melody in the soprano. Analytic
examples illustrate this evolution of style. *(Conrad T. Biel)*

4364 LESZNAI, Lajos. **Realistische Ausdrucks-**
as **mittel in der Musik Béla Bartóks** [Realistic
means of expression in the music of Béla Bartók],
Studia musicologica Academiae Scientiarum
Hungaricae V (1963) 469–79. *Music.* In German. See
no. 427 in this volume.

Elements of Bartók's compositional technique that stem from his environment and his research include the imitation of nature and of traditional-
music melodic form (not only European but also African and Arabic). His
realism is to be construed as a form of social criticism. *(William Renwick)*

4365 LISSA, Zofia. **Über den nationalen Stil von F.**
as **Chopin: Kriterien und Wesensbestimmung** [F.
Chopin's national style: Criteria and essential defini-
tion], *Bericht über den internationalen musikwissen-*
schaftlichen Kongreß Wien Mozartjahr 1956 (Graz;
Köln: Böhlau, 1958) 355–64. *Music.* In German. See
no. 365 in this volume.

Discusses the relationship of Chopin's compositional technique with traditional Polish music and with Polish art music from the standpoint of a systematic definition of "national style". *(David Bloom)*

4366 ŁOBACZEWSKA, Stefania. **Sonaty forte-**
as **pianowe Szymanowskiego a sonaty Skriabina**

[Szymanowski's and Skrjabin's piano sonatas], *Karol Szymanowski: Księga sesji Naukowej poświęconej twórczości Karola Szymanowskiego* (Warszawa: Uniwersytet Warszawski, Instytut Muzykologii, 1964) 177–90. *Music.* In Polish; summary in English. See no. 458 in this volume.

Concentrates on the role of allegro themes in the sonatas of both composers.

4367 LOEWENBACH, Josef. **Dramatický princip**
as **Leoše Janáčka a M.P. Musorgského** [The dramatic principles of Janáček and Musorgskij], *Leoš Janáček a soudobá hudba* (Praha: Panton, 1963) 205–16. In Czech; summaries in Russian and German. See no. 389 in this volume.

The similarities between Janáček and Musorgskij in their stage works include the striving for the faithful reflection of reality; focus on psychological portraiture; balladic character of the plot material; emphasis on dramaturgy; prominence given to the chorus; synchrony between musical and dramatic plan; respect for and inspiration in traditional music; and speech intonation. Nevertheless, Janáček was critical of Musorgskij and not interested in his works. *(editors)*

4368 LUITHLEN, Victor. **Studie zu J. Brahms'**
as **Werken in Variationenform** [A study on variation forms in J. Brahms's works], *Festschrift den Mitgliedern des Musikhistorischen Kongresses überreicht von der Leitenden Kommission der Denkmäler der Tonkunst in Österreich* (Wien: Universal, 1927) 286–320. *Music, charts, diagr.* In German. See no. 147 in this volume.

Surveys Brahms's variation sets and variation-form movements, proceeding by compositional parameter. All in all, Brahms as a composer of variations is the heir of Beethoven; yet undergoing a distinctive development of his own, Brahms's mature variations represent some of his most characteristic, peculiarly Brahmsian, music. This development is summarily traced. *(Carl Skoggard)*

4369 MANN, Alfred. **Sources of the classical idiom,**
as *Report of the Eighth Congress of the International Musicological Society. II: Reports* (Kassel: Bärenreiter, 1962) 135–39. See no. 440 in this volume.

A report on a discussion by Gerald ABRAHAM, J. Murray BARBOUR, Dénes BARTHA, Friedrich BLUME, Gerhard CROLL, Charles CUDWORTH, Erich HERTZMANN, Jens Peter LARSEN, Jan LARUE, Ivan MARTYNOV, William S. NEWMAN, Eduard REESER, and Georg REICHERT of papers by Hans Engel and Georg Feder abstracted as nos. 4330 and 4331 in this volume.

4370 MEYER, Ernst Hermann. **Das Konfliktelement**
as **in Mozarts Instrumentalmusik** [The element of conflict in Mozart's instrumental music], *Bericht über den internationalen musikwissenschaftlichen Kongreß Wien Mozartjahr 1956* (Graz; Köln: Böhlau, 1958) 402–07. In German. See no. 365 in this volume.

Mozart's use of conflicting or mutually contradictory thematic elements as a way of producing dramatic tension has not been sufficiently appreciated. Examples taken from the piano sonatas include cases of conflict between main and secondary themes in the exposition, abrupt shifts in dynamics and accentuation, sharp divergences in emotional character from movement to movement, and sudden harmonic surprises. *(David Bloom)*

4371 MIES, Paul. **Joseph Haydns Singkanons und**
as **ihre Grundidee** [Joseph Haydn's vocal canons and their fundamental idea], *Bericht über die internationale Konferenz zum Andenken Joseph Haydns* (Budapest: Akadémiai Kiadó, 1961) 93–94. In German. See no. 405 in this volume.

The vocal canons are not merely exercises or riddles, but expressions of Haydn's wholly Classic mentality. He often gives the first voice the entire text before bringing in the second voice, thereby preserving the integrity and expressive content of the words. *(Larry Laskowski)*

4372 MIES, Paul. **Stilkundliche Probleme bei Bee-**
as **thoven** [Problems of stylistics in Beethoven's works], *Beethoven-Zentenarfeier: Internationaler musikhistorischer Kongress* (Wien: Universal, 1927) 304–06. In German. See no. 142 in this volume.

Outstanding questions include that of large-scale rhythmic patterns, especially in development sections; the explanation of discrepancies between exposition and recapitulation in certain typical sonata and finale movements; the expressive significance of Beethoven's instrumentation; and the analysis of Beethoven's characteristic theme construction in comparison with that of other composers. *(David Bloom)*

4373 MIES, Paul. **Werdegang und Eigenschaften**
as **der Definition in der musikalischen Stilkunde** [The development and aspects of definition in the theory of musical style], *Bericht über den I. musikwissenschaftlichen Kongress der Deutschen Musikgesellschaft in Leipzig* (Wiesbaden: Breitkopf & Härtel, 1926) 120–23. In German. See no. 120 in this volume.

Discusses various ways of understanding and analyzing musical style, and compares the views of Hermann Abert, Curt Sachs, Harry Goldschmidt, and Paul Moos. *(William Renwick)*

4374 MILA, Massimo, ed. **Die stilistische Einheit in**
as **Giuseppe Verdis Werk** [The stylistic unity of Giuseppe Verdi's work], *Bericht über den neunten internationalen Kongreß* (Kassel: Bärenreiter, 1964-1966) 249–54. In German. See no. 491 in this volume.

A roundtable discussion of the question of unity among the distinct phases of Verdi's career. Participants included Edith Fogl GARRETT, Donald Jay GROUT, William C. HOLMES, Walther SIEGMUND-SCHULTZE, Giovanni UGOLINI, and Lucas UNDERWOOD. *(David Bloom)*

4375 MILOJKOVIĆ-DJURIĆ, Jelena. **On the Serbian**
as **chant in the eighteenth century after the neumatic manuscripts from Chilandar,** *Actes du XIIe Congrès d'études Byzantines* (Beograd: Naučno Delo, 1963-1964) II, 583–87. *Music.* See no. 441 in this volume.

Evidence of an earlier style of chant supplanted in the 18th c. by a Greek-influenced tradition is found in MSS of the Serbian Chilandar monastery (Mone Hilandariou) on Mount Athos (Hagion Oros). Stichera from *GR-AOh* MSS 309, 311, and 312 suggest that both styles existed at the same time. *(David Bloom)*

4376 MOSER, Hans Joachim. **Chopin stilkundlich**
as **betrachtet** [Chopin from the point of view of stylistics], *The book of the first international musicological congress devoted to the works of Frederick Chopin* (Warszawa: Państwowe Wydawnictwo Naukowe, 1963) 707–12. In German. See no. 425 in this volume.

Examines Chopin's style in terms of historical and cultural-geographical context, of typological and biographical aspects of his own character as an artist, and of genre analysis. *(David Bloom)*

4377 RATNER, Leonard G. **Eighteenth century theo-**
as **ries of musical period structure,** *Bericht über den internationalen musikwissenschaftlichen Kongreß Wien Mozartjahr 1956* (Graz; Köln: Böhlau, 1958) 531–34. *Charts, diagr.* In German. See no. 365 in this volume.

Discusses theorists' responses to the change from the uninterrupted flow of Baroque style to the well-defined articulations and balanced phrases and periods of the Classic. A more extended version appeared under the same title in *Musical quarterly* 42 (1956). *(Peter Kaliski)*

4378 RIGLER, Gertrude. **Die Kammermusik**
as **Dittersdorfs** [Dittersdorf's chamber music],
*Festschrift den Mitgliedern des Musikhistorischen
Kongresses überreicht von der Leitenden Kommission
der Denkmäler der Tonkunst in Österreich* (Wien: Universal, 1927) 179–212. *Music.* In German. See no. 147
in this volume.

Part 1: A comparative analysis of Carl Ditters von Dittersdorf's chamber
music leads to the conclusion that it shows far fewer connections to the
Mannhein composers Karl Stamic and Georg Christoph Wagenseil than to
his Viennese contemporaries, including Haydn and Mozart. Part 2: Corrections and additions for Karl Krebs's thematic catalogue for Dittersdorf in
his *Dittersdorfiana* (Berlin, 1900) are provided. Part 3: Dittersdorf's use of
form-sonata form, song and Romanze form, minuet and other dances, variations, rondo form-in his chamber works is systematically surveyed. Part 4:
A synthesis of Dittersdorf's compositional technique is attempted. Part 5:
Dittersdorf's relations with his contemporaries Haydn and Mozart are described. Part 6: The contemporary reception of his music by critics must be
viewed in the broad perspective of diverging styles of North German
(Berlin) and Austrian composers of the period. Berlin critics had little sym-
pathy for Austrian musical "trifling" in a galant vein. *(Carl Skoggard)*

4379 RONGA, Luigi. **Nota sulla vocalità palestri-**
as **niana** [A note on Palestrina's vocality], *Atti del [I]
Congresso internazionale di musica sacra* (Tournai:
Desclée, 1952) 327–29. In Italian. See no. 303 in this
volume.

4380 SCHOENBAUM, Camillo. **Die Kammermusik-**
as **werke des Jan Dismas Zelenka** [The chamber
works of Jan Dismas Zelenka], *Bericht über den internationalen musikwissenschaftlichen Kongreß Wien
Mozartjahr 1956* (Graz; Köln: Böhlau, 1958) 552–62.
Music. In German. See no. 365 in this volume.

The six trio sonatas for winds and continuo, ZWV 181, seem to follow a
large-scale plan like that of Bach's great cyclic works; perhaps the goal was
to explore the contrapuntal capacities of the sonata da chiesa to their utmost
limits, in the manner of Tomaso Albinoni's *Balletti e sonate a tre*, op. 8.
(David Bloom)

4381 SCHULZ-DORNBURG, Rudolf. **Das musika-**
as **lische Wort im Wandel der Zeiten: Grundsätzliches über die unterschiedliche Wortbehandlung in musikalischer Gestalt und Nachgestalt** [The musical word through the ages: A basic
discussion of the different treatment of text in the musical conception and reconception], *Bericht über den
Internationalen Kongreß Singen und Sprechen*
(München: Oldenbourg, 1938) 326–28. In German. See
no. 257 in this volume.

Text settings of different styles and periods (from the 13th-c. English song
Sumer is icumen in to the works of Hans Pfitzner) require different treatments of text articulation and delivery, for which most singers' training
does not equip them very well. *(David Bloom)*

4382 SMOLKA, Jaroslav. **Příspěvek k poznání**
as **vnitřního řádu Janáčkovy melodiky a
tematické práce** [Recognition of the inner laws of
Janáček's melodic and thematic development], *Leoš
Janáček a soudobá hudba* (Praha: Panton, 1963)
275–78. *Music.* In Czech; summaries in Russian and
German. See no. 389 in this volume.

A kind of melodic analogy, frequent in Janáček's work and a part of his tectonic style, is exemplified by three melodically and psychologically similar
motives: that of Jenůfa from *Její pastorkyňa (Jenůfa)* act 2, that of Káťa
from *Káťa Kabanová*, and one from the third part of the quartet *Listy
důvěrné* (Intimate letters). *(editors)*

4383 ŠTĚDROŇ, Bohumír. **Lidové kořeny *Její***
as ***pastorkyně*** [The folk roots of *Její pastorkyňa
(Jenůfa)*], *Leoš Janáček a soudobá hudba* (Praha: Panton, 1963) 317–22. *Music.* In Czech; summaries in Russian and German. See no. 389 in this volume.

Three choral set pieces in *Její pastorkyňa (Jenůfa)* set texts that are known
from collections of Moravian traditional music, but to Janáček's original
melodies. Janáček's sense of the Moravian style was so strong that the composer Jan Kunc included one of them as an authentic Moravian-Slovak
song in his collection *Slovácké* (1912). *(editors)*

4384 SWALIN, Benjamin Franklin. **The Brahms vio-**
as **lin concerto: A stylistic criticism,** *Papers read at
the Annual Meeting of the American Musicological Society* (New York: American Musicological Society,
1936) 65–77. *Music, charts, diagr.* See no. 230 in this
volume.

The violin concerto, op. 77, is distinguished by its organic unity, masculine
character, marked contrasts of mood, floridity (second movement), rhythmic vitality and subtlety, motivic constructions, solid counterpoint, profuse
and facile modulations, sparing use of enharmonicisim and chromaticism
(as compared with Louis Spohr and Karl Goldmark), pedal effects (third
movement), and symphonic dimensions.

4385 SYCHRA, Antonín. **Vztah hudby a slova jako**
as **jeden z nejzávažnějších problémů Janáčkova
slohu** [The relationship of word and music as one of
the most important issues of Janáček's style], *Leoš
Janáček a soudobá hudba* (Praha: Panton, 1963)
298–312. *Music.* In Czech; summaries in Russian and
German. See no. 389 in this volume.

Close examination of Janáček's drafts and fair copies shows the genesis of
gradual changes in individual speech melodies in his works. His motives
are not naturalistic copies or passive imitation of speech, but are artistically
reinterpreted in order to serve his most significant goal: to reflect an immediate emotional expression and the dramatic quality of the moment. His
compositional means, such as intensive chromaticism, frequent changes in
melody, harmony and rhythm, asymmetric and non-periodic structure, all
contribute to the same goal. *(editors)*

4386 SZELÉNYI, István. **Der unbekannte Liszt** [The
as unknown Liszt], *Studia musicologica Academiae
Scientiarum Hungaricae* V (1963) 311–31. *Music.* In
German. See no. 427 in this volume.

Innovative elements in Liszt's compositional technique that anticipate
20th-c. composers include his use of non-Western tetrachordal structures,
bitonality, the tritone, parallel fifths, quartal harmony, ninth chords, and
novel rhythmic effects . *(William Renwick)*

4387 TERENZIO, Vincenzo. **Il problema del prero-**
as **manticismo e l'arte mozartiana** [The problem of
pre-Romanticism in Mozart], *Bericht über den internationalen musikwissenschaftlichen Kongreß Wien
Mozartjahr 1956* (Graz; Köln: Böhlau, 1958) 643–46.
In Italian. See no. 365 in this volume.

Mozart's extraordinary capacity for spiritual synthesis enabled him, in the
continual freshness and luminous clarity of his style, to resolve his uncer-
tainty between the full refinement of 18th-c. Classicism and the first vague,
turbid suggestions of the Romantic sensibility. *(author)*

4388 URSPRUNG, Otto. **Der vokale Grund-**
as **charakter des diskantbetonten figurierten
Stils** [The basic vocal character of the figurative,
discant-emphasized style], *Bericht über den
musikwissenschaftlichen Kongreß in Basel* (Leipzig:
Breitkopf & Härtel, 1925) 364–74. In German. See no.
102 in this volume.

Aspects of text underlay in the *Denkmäler der Tonkunst in Österreich* versions of Dufay and Ockeghem Masses are disputable. Text underlay in the

Dufay period follows the rules for Gregorian chant, except that the last syllable tends to be extended by a melisma. Desprez, in his reservata style, adopted virtuoso singing techniques, such as those later described by Giovanni Luca Conforti in 1593. Alfred Orel's term *verzierte cantus firmus* should be changed to read *cantus figuratus.*

4389
as
VÁLEK, Jiří. **Konkrétnost zobrazení: Základ Janáčkova symfonismu posledního období** [Concrete depiction: The basis of Janáček's symphonism in his last period], *Leoš Janáček a soudobá hudba* (Praha: Panton, 1963) 323–29. *Music, charts, diagr.* In Czech; summaries in Russian and German. See no. 389 in this volume.

Vladimír Helfert suggested in 1926 that Janáček's final orchestral style, represented mainly by the *Sinfonietta*, represents a departure from literary and pictorial inspiration in favor of pure musical thinking. But in the *Sinfonietta* there is a close connection between Janáček's thematic and ideological intentions and his purely musical means. *(editors)*

4390
as
VEEN, Jan van der. **Problèmes structuraux chez Maurice Ravel** [Structural problems in the works of Maurice Ravel], *Bericht über den siebenten internationalen musikwissenschaftlichen Kongress* (Kassel: Bärenreiter, 1959) 289–90. In French. See no. 390 in this volume.

Are Ravel's forms of a psychological, impressionist character, or autonomous and pure? His own comments on his works seem to conflict. A careful style analysis suggests the importance of reticence, what has sometimes been called a certain *pudeur*, which must be conquered by exterior motives such as daring, virtuosity, pastiche and emulation, or pre-established tonal plans. It is the desire for construction that sets his sensibility in motion, creating a unique classicism colored with impressionism. *(David Bloom)*

4391
as
VESELKA, Josef. **K slohovým základům Janáčkovské sborové reprodukce** [The stylistic foundations of performance of Janáček's choral music], *Sborník Janáčkovy Akademie Múzichých Umeni* V (1965) 59–73. In Czech. See no. 496 in this volume.

The late choral works of Janáček mark the beginning of a new era in Czech choral music. The problems of interpretation lie in the structure, in retaining the declamatory aspects of the melody, which gives the melody expression, in retaining the metric patterns, in avoiding all aspects of splitting-up, in making use of agogic accent, and in solving the problems of tone color. *(Jan Trojan)*

4392
as
VETTER, Walther. **Mozart und Bach** [Mozart and Bach], *Internationale Konferenz über das Leben und Werk W.A. Mozarts* (Praha: Svaz Československých Skladatelů, 1956) 61–69. In German. See no. 360 in this volume.

Examines Mozart's string trio arrangements of fugues by Bach in K.404a, with regard to their deviations in ornamentation and phrasing, occasional simplifications, and apparent errors. *(Anthony F. Bavota)*

4393
as
VYSLOUŽIL, Jiří. **Janáčkova tvorba ve světle jeho hudebně folkloristické teorie** [Janáček's works in light of his theory of musical folklore], *Leoš Janáček a soudobá hudba* (Praha: Panton, 1963) 361–76. *Music.* In Czech; summaries in Russian and German. See no. 389 in this volume.

Janáček was the first to provide a comprehensive account of the nature of Moravian traditional music. Twenty years before Bartók, in 1885, he independently came to similar conclusions, that the Moravian repertoire contains the old song types differing substantially from Bohemian traditional music and Western art music in rhythm, tonality, and melody; he also went beyond Bartók and Kodály in his insistence on studying folklore in its original performance context. Examples of his use of the Moravian tradition as a composer are analyzed. *(editors)*

67 Structural analysis

4394
as
BORRIS, Siegfried. **Strukturanalyse von Weberns Symphonie op. 21** [Structural analysis of Webern's symphony op. 21], *Bericht über den internationalen musikwissenschaftlichen Kongreß* (Kassel: Bärenreiter, 1963) 253–57. *Music.* In German. See no. 452 in this volume.

Analysis of sonata structure in the symphony's first movement and variation structure in the second reveals that Webern used simple elements of the tonal system—consonance and imitation—but only as exceptional constellations within the combinatorial method. A later version is cited as RILM [1976]1671. *(Leslie B. Dunner)*

4395
as
BRICKEN, Carl. **Some analytical approaches to musical criticism,** *Papers read at the Annual Meeting of the American Musicological Society* (New York: American Musicological Society, 1936) 58–64. *Music, charts, diagr.* See no. 230 in this volume.

An examination of the first 35 measures of Beethoven's string quartet op. 18, no. 3, reveals how melodic, harmonic, and rhythmic analysis can be used to evaluate a work's quality.

4396
as
ŁOBACZEWSKA, Stefania. **Mozarts Sonate F-dur (K.V. 533) als Problem des klassischen Stils** [Mozart's F-major sonata (K.533) as a problem of Classical style], *Internationale Konferenz über das Leben und Werk W.A. Mozarts* (Praha: Svaz Československých Skladatelů, 1956) 95–97. In German. See no. 360 in this volume.

The history of Classicism is that of the crystallization of the formal technique of pairing a dance-like first theme with a second theme derived from opera and the slow movements of suites, developing in Beethoven's late Classicism into the opposition between the dramatic and the lyrical. Mozart's piano sonata K.533 illustrates the mature pre-Beethoven phase of Classicism, particularly in the first movement, with its typical contrast between a first theme in a comparatively instrumental style and a second theme in vocal style. *(David Bloom)*

4397
as
RUDZIŃSKI, Witold. **Zagadnienia struktury *I Koncertu Skrzypcowego* K. Szymanowskiego** [Structural problems in Szymanowski's first violin concerto], *Karol Szymanowski: Księga sesji Naukowej poświęconej twórczości Karola Szymanowskiego* (Warszawa: Uniwersytet Warszawski, Instytut Muzykologii, 1964) 247–60. *Music, charts, diagr.* In Polish; summary in English. See no. 458 in this volume.

Provides a motivic analysis, demonstrating how the large-scale structure of the work is unified by consistency of motivic material.

68 Computer and electronic composition

4398
as
BIERL, Richard. **Musik-Elektronik-praktische: Erfahrungen, Gegenwartsprobleme und Zukunftsfragen** [Electronic music practice: Acquired experience, present-day problems, and future questions], *Problèmes d'acoustique* (Liège: Université de Liège, 1965) M65. In German. See no. 504 in this volume.

Surveys the current state of electronic music, with graphs of some characteristic sounds. The future of electronic music points towards what is described as an "American" sound. *(Brian Doherty)*

4399
as
BRUN, Herbert. **On the conditions under which computers would assist a composer in creating music of contemporary relevance and significance,** *American Society of University Composers: Proceedings of the 1966 conference* (New York: American Society of University Composers, 1966). See no. 510 in this volume.

A composer's musical thought is a continuous attempt to organize the mind. The mind approaches a system with preconceptions about its implications, and therefore may miss some available content; the computer omits no possibilities. For music to advance, all resources must be used.

(Judith Drogichen Meyer)

4400
as
FERRETTI, Ercolino. **Some research notes on music with the computer,** *American Society of University Composers: Proceedings of the 1966 conference* (New York: American Society of University Composers, 1966). See no. 510 in this volume.

Describes an attempt to codify musical sound mathematically to find a means of notation or storage relevant to electronic music.

(Judith Drogichen Meyer)

4401
as
GERHARD, Roberto. **Concrete and electronic sound-composition,** *Music libraries and instruments* (London: Hinrichsen, 1961) 30–37. See no. 406 in this volume.

The use of magnetic tape in *Symphonie pour un homme seul* (1950) of Pierre Schaeffer and Pierre Henry, Luciano Berio's *Mutazioni* (1955), and Karlheinz Stockhausen's *Gesang der Jünglinge* (1955-56), is used to clarify the distinction and overlap between musique concrète and synthetic electronic music. *(Richard Slapsys)*

4402
as
KOENIG, Gottfried Michael. **The second phase of electronic music,** *Vision 65: New challenges for human communications* (New York: International Center for the Typographic Arts, 1965) 169–83. See no. 498 in this volume.

The first phase of electronic music was characterized by serial compositional techniques and the manipulation of magnetic tape. The second phase involves the transition to automated studios and increasingly complex sound. *(Ralph Hartsock)*

4403
as
LEWIN, David. **Is it music?,** *American Society of University Composers: Proceedings of the 1966 conference* (New York: American Society of University Composers, 1966). See no. 510 in this volume.

Two erroneous views of electronic music are that an electronic piece is an ideal performance of conventional music, and that only unconventional sounds should be used. *(Judith Drogichen Meyer)*

4404
as
LIETTI, Alfredo. **Activity of the Studio di Fonologia Musicale,** *Proceedings of the Third International Congress on Acoustics* (Amsterdam: Elsevier Science, 1961) II, 769–70. See no. 414 in this volume.

The studio, founded in 1954 by Bruno Maderna and Luciano Berio at the Milan studios of RAI (Radio Televisione Italiana), is concerned with the extension of traditional musical experience by means of newer sound recording and other electroacoustic means; the equipment in use is discussed. *(David Bloom)*

4405
as
MARIE, Jean-Étienne. **Musique experimentale** [Experimental music], *Fontes artis musicae* XII/2-3 (May-Dec 1965) 214–22. *Illus., music, discog.* In French. See no. 499 in this volume.

A brief history of post–World War II musique concrète and electronic music.

4406
as
MATTHEWS, Max V.; GUTTMAN, Newman. **Generation of music by a digital computer,** *Proceedings of the Third International Congress on Acous-*

tics (Amsterdam: Elsevier Science, 1961) I, 253–54. *Charts, diagr.* See no. 414 in this volume.

Reports on research in computer-generated music conducted by the authors and John R. Pierce at the Bell Telephone Laboratories, Murray Hill, New Jersey, in the 1950s. *(David Bloom)*

4407
as
MEYER-EPPLER, Werner. **Welche Möglichkeiten bestehen für eine sinnvolle Anwendung elektronischer Musikinstrumente?** [What possibilities exist for a meaningful use of electronic musical instruments?], *Acustica: International journal of acoustics/Journal international d'acoustique/Internationale akustische Zeitschrift* IV/1 (1954) 239–44. *Illus., bibliog., charts, diagr.* In German; summaries in English, French, and German. See no. 324 in this volume.

Due to the choice of tone components, electronic instruments provide composers with a new medium. It is the business of the acoustic expert to educate composers in these possibilities. The Nordwestdeutscher Rundfunk in Cologne has built a special electronic studio for the use of composers. *(author)*

4408
as
MOROI, Makoto. **Electronic music,** *Music: East and West* (Tōkyō: conference, 1961) 130–33. See no. 445 in this volume.

Considers electronic music as a means of renovating musical language.

4409
as
PHILIPPOT, Michel Paul. **Électronique et techniques compositionelles** [Electronics and compositional techniques], *Actes et mémoires du 1er Congrès international de langue et littérature du Midi de la France* (Avignon: Palais du Roure, 1957) 183–88. In French. See no. 342 in this volume.

Discusses the differences between musique concrète and electronic music. Reciprocal influences between the two compositional techniques are examined and the evolution of each is described. In this light, the 12-tone system of Schoenberg appears rather traditional. *(Susan Poliniak)*

4410
as
RISSET, Jean-Claude. **Synthèse des sons musicaux à l'aide de calculateurs électroniques** [Synthesis of musical sounds with the aid of computers], *Stéréophonie et reproduction musicale* (Paris: Chiron, 1966) 93–101. *Illus., bibliog., charts, diagr.* In French. See no. 511 in this volume.

Computerized sound synthesis is already a valuable tool in the study of acoustics, and offers tempting possibilities to musicians as well. The necessary equipment is not yet available in France, but it is in use in several laboratories in the U.S. Examples of computer composition include recent pieces by James C. Tenney (*Dialogue*, 1963) and James Kirtland Randall (*Mudgett: Monologues by a mass murderer*, 1965).

4411
as
TRAUTWEIN, Friedrich. **Elektroakustische Mittel in der aktiven Tonkunst** [Electroacoustic resources in active composition], *Acustica: International journal of acoustics/Journal international d'acoustique/Internationale akustische Zeitschrift* IV/1 (1954) 256–59. *Illus., bibliog., charts, diagr.* In German; summaries in German, French, and English. See no. 324 in this volume.

Standard instruments facilitate only the traditional scale types, limiting melodic and harmonic possibilities. More sharply differentiated timbres can be built up from certain vibrations which by a process of synchronization can be blended in correct phase relationship with each period of the fundamental. *(author)*

4412
as
WINHAM, Godfrey. **How MUSIC 4B generates formants and non-harmonic partials, and improves loudness control and "quality",** *American Society of University Composers: Proceedings of the 1966 conference* (New York: American So-

ciety of University Composers, 1966). See no. 510 in this volume.

Describes a central feature of the Princeton Music 4B System. A number of disadvantages of the OSCIL principle are discussed along with solutions implemented by a unit generator called FORMNT. Understanding of Music 4B and of the principle of sampling a stored function is presumed.

(Judith Drogichen Meyer)

69 Melody and motive

4413
as

AARBURG, Ursula. **Wechselbeziehungen zwischen Motiv und Tonart im mittelalterlichen Liede, insbesondere im Liede um 1200** [Correlations between motive and mode in medieval song, particularly in song around 1200], *Kongreß-Bericht: Gesellschaft für Musikforschung* (Kassel; Basel: Bärenreiter, 1950) 62–65. *Charts, diagr.* In German. See no. 299 in this volume.

Discusses modulation from one mode to another in Provençal Minnesang. Of the four ways of modulating, the preferred at the time was the reinterpretation of a modal motif in a different mode. The *Palästinalied* by Walther von der Vogelweide is analyzed.

4414
as

ATTERBERG, Kurt. **Verfall der Melodie** [Decline of melody], *Musikerziehung: Zeitschrift der Musikerzieher Österreichs* special issue (1953) 151–53. In German. See no. 317 in this volume.

The failure of modern music to appeal to the public can be attributed not to its dissonance but to its lack of melody.

4415
as

BAUD-BOVY, Samuel. **La systématisation des chansons populaires** [The systematization of traditional songs], *Studia musicologica Academiae Scientiarum Hungaricae* VII (1965) 213–29. *Music.* In French. See no. 478 in this volume.

Discusses the methodology and uses of various types of melodic classification.

4416
as

BAYARD, Samuel P. **Aspects of melodic kinship and variation in British-American folk-tunes,** *Papers read at the International Congress of Musicology* (New York: Music Educators National Conference, 1944) 122–29. See no. 266 in this volume.

The repertoire of Anglo-American traditional song is based on a small number of melodies—perhaps around 55 distinct tunes—that may be distinguished through careful study and an understanding of the dynamics of oral tradition. In comparing melodic variants, three factors are salient: (1) consistently parallel melodic contours, even when the scales or modes of variants differ; (2) identical or similar structural tones anchoring these parallel contours; and (3) close resemblances among motives, particularly at cadence points. *(James R. Cowdery)*

4417
as

BAYARD, Samuel P. **Principal versions of an international folk tune,** *Journal of the International Folk Music Council* III (1951) 44–50. *Music.* See no. 296 in this volume.

Discusses variants of a traditional melody that appears in various forms throughout Europe and North America.

4418
as

BREHMER, Fritz. **Untersuchungen über Melodienauffassung und melodische Begabung des Kindes** [Investigations into the child's conception of melodies and the melodic talents of children], *Bericht über den IX. Kongress für experimentelle Psychologie* (Jena: Fischer, 1925) 140f. In German. See no. 121 in this volume.

4419
as

BRONSON, Bertrand H. **Melodic stability in oral transmission,** *Journal of the International Folk Music Council* III (1951) 50–55. *Charts, diagr.* See no. 296 in this volume.

Discusses a methodology for comparing variants of traditional melodies.

4420
as

COHEN, Dalia. **An investigation into the tonal structure of the *maqāmāt*,** *Journal of the International Folk Music Council* XVI (1964) 102–06. *Charts, diagr.* See no. 463 in this volume.

Fundamental-frequency graphs of Arab songs made with a melograph showed that some pitches and melodic intervals are more fixed than others, in consistent and regular patterns of deviation for each maqām, demonstrating empirically that the maqām is a melody type rather than merely a scale.

(Vivian Conejero)

4421
as

COHEN, Judith R. **'Al "Ḳol nidrey" šel 'Arnŵld Šonḅerg** [On Arnold Schoenberg's *Ḳol nidre*], *Dẇkan* VI (1964) 73–83. *Music.* In Hebrew. See no. 464 in this volume.

Analyzes the melody and theme of Schoenberg's *Ḳol nidre*, op. 39, drawing on the relationship to the original tune. His personal views on Judaism and their influence on the work are also considered. *(Moshe Zorman)*

4422
as

CSÉBFALVY, Károly; HAVASS, Miklós; JÁRDÁNYI, Pál; VARGYAS, Lajos. **Systemization of tunes by computers,** *Studia musicologica Academiae Scientiarum Hungaricae* VII (1965) 253–57. See no. 478 in this volume.

A report on activities at the Népzenekutató Csoportj of the Magyar Tudományos Akadémia. Complete tunes are not programmed, but are input either directly by keyboard or by tape, facilitating analysis and systematization. *(David Gagné)*

4423
as

CZEKANOWSKA, Anna. **Beiträge zum Problem der Modalität und der sogenannten "halbchromatischen Leiter" bei Chopin** [The problem of tonality and the so-called half-chromatic scale in Chopin], *The book of the first international musicological congress devoted to the works of Frederick Chopin* (Warszawa: Państwowe Wydawnictwo Naukowe, 1963) 122–26. *Music.* In German. See no. 425 in this volume.

Polish composers before Chopin used the raised fourth scale degree and other modal features of Polish traditional music in instrumental compositions and operas. Chopin took the practice to a higher level, making such features structural as well as purely melodic elements, in his quest for a wholly organic form. *(David Bloom)*

4424
as

DANCKERT, Werner. **Personale Typen des Melodiestils** [Personal types of melodic style], *Bericht über den I. musikwissenschaftlichen Kongress der Deutschen Musikgesellschaft in Leipzig* (Wiesbaden: Breitkopf & Härtel, 1926) 108–12. *Music.* In German. See no. 120 in this volume.

Compares melodic designs, with examples from Dufay and Francesco Landini, with an emphasis on intervals and rhythms.

4425
as

DREYER, Ernst-Jürgen. **Melodisches Formelgut bei Chopin** [Chopin's repertoire of melodic formulas], *The book of the first international musicological congress devoted to the works of Frederick Chopin* (Warszawa: Państwowe Wydawnictwo Naukowe, 1963) 132–44. *Music.* In German. See no. 425 in this volume.

It is an open secret that Chopin often repeats himself, though seldom literally. Rather than seeing these occasions as self-plagiarism, we should regard them as the formulas in which the uniqueness of his style is clearly to be seen. Several examples from the realm of melody are discussed.

(David Bloom)

4426
as
ELSCHEKOVÁ, Alica. **General considerations on the classification of folk tunes**, *Studia musicologica Academiae Scientiarum Hungaricae* VII (1965) 259–62. See no. 478 in this volume.

Classification systems for organizing and evaluating the music of a given culture must be based on the dominant elements of the musical structure, and must unite homogenous musical forms according to their formal and inner relations. This will facilitate objective comparisons and evaluations, and raise the level of our stylistic, comparative, and theoretical knowledge of that culture. *(David Gagné)*

4427
as
FISCHER, Wilhelm. **Zur Geschichte des Fugenthemas** [On the history of fugue subjects], *Bericht über den I. musikwissenschaftlichen Kongress der Deutschen Musikgesellschaft in Leipzig* (Wiesbaden: Breitkopf & Härtel, 1926) 246. In German. See no. 120 in this volume.

Briefly mentions the origins of the fugue subject in the vocal music of the motet and madrigal, and its transformation in the later context of instrumental music. *(William Renwick)*

4428
as
FRIEDLAENDER, Max. **Eigenleben von Volksliedmelodien** [The individual lives of folk-song melodies], *Bericht über den musikwissenschaftlichen Kongreß in Basel* (Leipzig: Breitkopf & Härtel, 1925) 131–46. *Music, charts, diagr.* In German. See no. 102 in this volume.

Two melody types are presented: *Erbarme dich*, with 34 versions from the 17th to the 19th c., and *Wilhelmus van Nassouwe*, with nine versions.

4429
as
FROTSCHER, Gotthold. **Bachs Themenbildung unter dem Einfluß der Affektenlehre** [Bach's thematic construction under the influence of the affections doctrine], *Bericht über den I. musikwissenschaftlichen Kongress der Deutschen Musikgesellschaft in Leipzig* (Wiesbaden: Breitkopf & Härtel, 1926) 436–41. In German. See no. 120 in this volume.

Discusses the expression of affects in fugue subjects. A supplementary article by Moritz BAUER is included.

4430
as
GAILLARD, Paul-André. **Essai sur la rapport des sources mélodiques des *Pseaulmes cinquantes* de Iean Louis (Anvers 1555) et des *Souterliedekens* (Anvers 1540)** [Essay on the relationship of the melodic sources of *Pseaulmes cinquantes* of Jean Louis (Antwerp 1555) and *Souterliedekens* (Antwerp 1540], *Société Internationale de Musicologie, cinquième congrès/Internationale Gesellschaft für Musikwissenschaft, fünfter Kongreß/International Society for Musical Research, Fifth Congress* (Amsterdam: Vereniging voor Nederlandse Muziekgeschiedenis, 1953) 193–98. In French. See no. 316 in this volume.

4431
as
GHIRCOIAŞIU, Romeo. **Les mélodies roumaines du XVIᵉ-XVIIIᵉ siècles** [Romanian melodies between the 16th and 18th centuries], *Musica antiqua Europae orientalis* (Warszawa: Państwowe Wydawnictwo Naukowe, 1966). *Music, charts, diagr.* In French. See no. 506 in this volume.

Focuses on secular melodies, with attention to modal and rhythmic features.

4432
as
HEINITZ, Wilhelm. **Eine Studie zur dynamischen Schichtung in Beethovens Sonatenthemen** [A study of dynamic layering in Beethoven's sonata themes], *Beethoven-Zentenarfeier: Internationaler musikhistorischer Kongress* (Wien: Universal, 1927) 75–78. In German. See no. 142 in this volume.

Statistical methods provide a less subjective approach to the analysis of dynamic layering in music. A comparative analysis of 18 Beethoven sonata themes is discussed.

4433
as
HESBERT, René-Jean. **Structure grégorienne et chant en français** [Gregorian structure and French-language singing], *Perspectives de la musique sacrée à la lumière de l'encyclique* Musicae sacrae disciplina (Paris: conference, 1959) 494–508. *Music.* In French. See no. 379 in this volume.

A method of reducing Gregorian chant melodies to their essential structural schemata allows the melodies to be sung idiomatically to French texts. Such settings, while not permissible in the liturgy, would be useful in the earlier phases of chant pedagogy and in the creation of chant-based songs for nonliturgical use. Examples are given of two Kyries, the Introit *Omnis terra*, and the communion antiphon *Tu es Petrus*. *(David Bloom)*

4434
as
HŁAWICZKA, Karol. **Ein Beitrag zur Verwandschaft zwischen der Melodik Chopins und der polnischen Volksmusik** [A study on the relationship between Chopin's melody and Polish folk music], *The book of the first international musicological congress devoted to the works of Frederick Chopin* (Warszawa: Państwowe Wydawnictwo Naukowe, 1963) 176–84. *Music, transcr.* In German. See no. 425 in this volume.

Chopin's use of ninths in melodic structure is compared to that found in traditional Polish music.

4435
as
HOERBURGER, Felix. **Zum Problem des Umsingens von Volksliedsmelodien** [On the problem of re-interpreting traditional songs], *Kongreß-Bericht: Gesellschaft für Musikforschung* (Kassel; Basel: Bärenreiter, 1950) 181–83. In German. See no. 299 in this volume.

Discusses the technique of varying a tune (*Umsingen*).

4436
as
HOFFMANN-ERBRECHT, Lothar. **Grundlagen der Melodiebildung bei Mussorgski** [Musorgskij's principles for structuring melody], *Bericht über den Internationalen musikwissenschaftlichen Kongress* (Kassel: Bärenreiter, 1954) 262–66. *Music.* In German. See no. 319 in this volume.

Boris Asaf'ev's concept of intonation is richly realized in Musorgskij's music, in particular his opera *Boris Godunov* and his piano cycle *Kartinki s vystavki* (Pictures at an exhibition). Both the vocal lines and the orchestral writing of the opera are inspired by Russian epic folk song, especially that of northern Russia, Musorgskij's homeland. Throughout the opera, Puškin's words are declaimed with the utmost sensitivity. The sixth episode of *Kartinki v vystavki* depicts an encounter between a rich Jew and a poor one; the sources for their contrasting characterization are traced. *(Carl Skoggard)*

4437
as
HOLLÄNDER, Hans. **Das monothematische Prinzip der *Glagolitischen Messe*/Monotematický princip *Glagolské Mše*** [The monothematic principle in the *Mša glagolskaja*], Leoš Janáček a soudobá hudba (Praha: Panton, 1963) 129–31. In German and Czech. See no. 389 in this volume.

Analyzes Janáček's monothematic technique in the *Mša glagolskaja* (Glagolitic Mass). Whereas in his operas the recurrence of certain melodies is motivated by dramatic-psychological expression, in the Mass it is based on the principle of motivic development. *(Jadranka Važanová)*

⟶
HORNBOSTEL, Erich Moritz von. **Über den gegenwärtigen Stand der vergleichenden Musikwissenschaft** [The current state of comparative musicology]. See no. 2437 in this volume.

4438 HROVATIN, Radoslav. **Intonacijski alfabetar in**
as **grafika melodij za leksikografiranje** [The
intonational alphabet and graphic representations of
melodies in lexicography], *Rad kongresa folklorista
Jugoslavije* (Zagreb: Savez Udruženja Folklorista
Jugoslavije, 1958) 181–85. In Slovene; summary in
French. See no. 315 in this volume.
A proposal for the classification of traditional melodies.

4439 JÁRDÁNYI, Pál. **Experiences and results in**
as **systematizing Hungarian folk-songs,** *Studia
musicologica Academiae Scientiarum Hungaricae* VII
(1965) 287–91. See no. 478 in this volume.
An effective method of systematization is essential for understanding a domain of traditional music and determining variants, types, and styles. The
characteristics of the material and varied applications of the systematization often require multiple classification systems. Hungarian folk song collections have been organized by melody type to provide a clear stylistic picture; various indices facilitate finding melodies. *(David Gagné)*

4440 KNEPLER, Georg. **Die motivisch-thematische**
as **Arbeit in Händels Oratorien** [Motivic and thematic
elaboration in Händel's oratorios], *Händel-Ehrung der
Deutschen Demokratischen Republik: Konferenzbericht*
(Leipzig: VEB Deutscher Verlag für Musik, 1961)
155–64. *Music.* In German. See no. 408 in this volume.
Examples of thematic elaboration in Händel's oratorios are found in accompaniment figures and in solo vocal lines; in the transfer of material
from accompaniment to the vocal line; in the development of new melodies
out of given thematic material; and in the cyclic recurrence of thematic material in separate numbers. The phenomenon marks a distinct change from
the style of the operas, and anticipates the developmental techniques of
Classic sonata form. *(David Bloom)*

4441 KOLESSA, Filaret. **Les formations anciennes**
as **et nouvelles dans les mélodies populaires
ukraniennes** [Old and new formations in Ukrainian
folk melodies], *Congrès international des arts
populaires/International congress of popular arts*
(Paris: Institut international de coopération
intellectuelle, 1928) 101–03. In French. See no. 153 in
this volume.
Summary of a paper. The earliest surviving melodies are those of ritual
songs performed by a group singing in unison. They exhibit a relatively
narrow compass and a basis in the church modes; however, their modality
has been greatly changed by the introduction of a chromaticism related to
that of the Southern Slavs. New melodies show a wider compass and clear
major-minor tonality. Musical dialects can be identified corresponding to
language dialects; those of the west represent the more archaic types, those
of the east the more modern. *(David Bloom)*

4442 KROHN, Ilmari. **Methode für Ausbildung zur**
as **Melodik** [Method for training in melodies], *Bericht
über den I. musikwissenschaftlichen Kongress der
Deutschen Musikgesellschaft in Leipzig* (Wiesbaden:
Breitkopf & Härtel, 1926) 190–95. In German. See no.
120 in this volume.
Suggests a method of studying music based on the understanding of melody as the basis of cantus firmus practice, of species and free counterpoint,
and of harmony. *(William Renwick)*

4443 KROÓ, György. **Monothematik und drama-**
as **turgie in Bartóks Bühnenwerken** [Monothema-
ticism and dramaturgy in Bartók's stage works], *Studia
musicologica Academiae Scientiarum Hungaricae* V
(1963) 449–67. *Music.* In German. See no. 427 in this
volume.
Developing variation technique, building motives and themes from single
ideas, is as important a structural principle in *A Kékszakállú herceg vára*

(Duke Bluebeard's castle), *A fából faragott királyfi* (The wooden prince),
and *A csodálatos mandarin* (The miraculous mandarin) as it is in the concert works. The roots of the technique may be traced to Liszt's *Faust-
Symphonie*. *(William Renwick)*

4444 LAUNIS, Armas. **Ueber die Notwendkigeit**
as **einer ein Heitlichen Untersuchungsmethode
der Volksmelodien** [The need for a uniform method
for investigating traditional melodies], *Report of the
Fourth Congress of the International Musical Society*
(London: Novello, 1912) 185–86. In German. See no.
71 in this volume.
Emphasizes the importance of uniformity of fundamental conceptions,
consistent terminology and abbreviations, and comparative procedures
among collections. *(Albert Dlugasch)*

⟶ LIPPHARDT, Walther. **Die Kyrietropen in**
ihrer rhythmischen und melodischen Struktur
[Rhythmic and melodic structure of the Kyrie tropes].
See no. 4010 in this volume.

4445 MARCEL-DUBOIS, Claudie. **Quelques**
as **formules structurales de la mélodie populaire
française** [Some structural formulas of traditional
French melody], *Journal of the International Folk Music Council* II (1950) 49. In French. See no. 295 in this
volume.
The conference report provides only a citation. Neither the text nor a summary of the paper was published here.

4446 MARKL, Jaroslav. **Janáčkova nápěvková**
as **teorie a český písňový typ instrumentální**
[Janáček's speech melody theory and the instrumental
type of Czech song], *Leoš Janáček a soudobá hudba*
(Praha: Panton, 1963) 217–19. In Czech; summaries in
Russian and German. See no. 389 in this volume.
Janáček's theory of speech melody (*nápěvek*) is significant both for the
study of his own compositional style and the ethnomusicological study of
interaction between vocal and instrumental melodic types. *(editors)*

4447 MERSMANN, Hans. **Die Bedeutung der Sub-**
as **stanzgemeinschaft für die Analyse von Instrumentalmusik: Ein Beitrag zur Methodik der
Analyse** [The significance of shared substance for the
analysis of instrumental music: A contribution to the
analytic method], *Bericht über den I. musikwissenschaftlichen Kongress der Deutschen Musikgesellschaft in Leipzig* (Wiesbaden: Breitkopf & Härtel,
1926) 428–29. In German. See no. 120 in this volume.
A summary of an article published in Mersmann's *Angewandten
Musikästhetik* (Verlag Max Hesse, Berlin, 1926). Motivic analysis—specifically criteria for establishing similarity of motives—is the central topic.
In a supplementary article Fritz REUTER dwells on the idea of sec-
ond-theme contrast. *(William Renwick)*

4448 MEYER, Kathi. **Über Melodiebildung in den**
as **geistlichen Spielen des früheren Mittelalters**
[Melody formation in the religious plays of the early
Middle Ages], *Beethoven-Zentenarfeier: Internationaler musikhistorischer Kongress* (Wien: Universal,
1927) 145–48. In German. See no. 142 in this volume.
Melodies in the liturgical dramas of the 11th-12th c. differ according to the
drama's subject matter. Those based on legendary materials or the New
Testament use complete melodies borrowed from secular songs alongside
the original chants; those on subjects from the Old Testament show a development, culminating in the Beauvais *Ludus Danielis* (*GB-Lbl* MS Eg.2615),
of through-composed melody based on fixed melodic motives. *(David Bloom)*

4449 MEYLAN, Raymond. **Utilisation des calculatrices électroniques pour la comparaison interne du répertoire des basses danses du quinzième siècle** [Use of electronic computers for internal comparison in the repertoire of 15th-century basses danses], *Fontes artis musicae* XII/2-3 (May-Dec 1965) 128–35. *Music, charts, diagr.* In French. See no. 499 in this volume.

The incipits of a corpus of basses danses were coded and a program written for an IBM 1620 machine at the Universität Zürich to compare them. Preliminary results and conceptual difficulties of the study are discussed.

(David Bloom)

4450 MOSER, Hans Joachim. **Der melodische Mehrterzenverband** [Melodic grouping through stacked thirds], *Bericht über den internationalen musikwissenschaftlichen Kongreß* (Kassel: Bärenreiter, 1957) 162–68. *Music.* In German. See no. 356 in this volume.

Examines melodic progressions in thirds with the scope of a major or minor seventh or ninth chord, from the 13th c. through Brahms. *(David Bloom)*

4451 ÖHMANN, F. **Melodie und Akzent: Experimentelle Untersuchungen über ihre Beziehungen** [Melody and accent: Experimental investigations on their relationships], *Kongress für Ästhetik und allgemeine Kunstwissenschaft: Bericht* (Stuttgart: Enke, 1914) 476–81. In German. See no. 86 in this volume.

4452 PARISOT, Jean. **Essai d'application de mélodies orientales à des chants d'église** [Trying to match Eastern melodies to Church chants], *Mémoires de Musicologie sacrée, lus aux assises de musique religieuse* (Paris: Schola Cantorum, n.d.) 39–45. In French. See no. 34 in this volume.

Eastern churches have influenced French church music; small melodic ranges, use of melodic formulas, and an equality between text and music are characteristic. Rhythmic organizations are similar, and the Eastern chants are a probable source of five and seven rhythms. *(Karen Clute)*

4453 POLADIAN, Sirvart. **Melodic contour in traditional music,** *Journal of the International Folk Music Council* III (1951) 30–35. *Music.* In English and German. See no. 296 in this volume.

Melodic contour is one of the most enduring characteristics of traditional music, surviving the caprices of oral tradition, the whims of editors, and the fickleness of fads. Examples are drawn from collections of Protestant vocal music—particularly Thomas Ravenscroft's *The Whole Booke of Psalmes* (1621)—and traditional songs recorded in New Jersey. *(James R. Cowdery)*

4454 RHODES, Willard. **The use of the computer in the classification of folk tunes,** *Studia musicologica Academiae Scientiarum Hungaricae* VII (1965) 339–43. See no. 478 in this volume.

The computer has much to offer for international traditional music research, but its use must be accompanied by enlightened aesthetic, intuitive, and musical judgment. *(Daniel Horn)*

4455 SALMEN, Walter. **Die altniederländischen Handschriften Berlin 8° 190 und Wien 7970 im Lichte vergleichender Melodienforschung** [The Old Netherlandish manuscripts Berlin 8° 190 and Vienna 7970 in the light of comparative melodic research], *Bericht über den Internationalen musikwissenschaftlichen Kongress* (Kassel: Bärenreiter, 1954) 187–94. *Music.* In German. See no. 319 in this volume.

Only an ethnomusicological perspective and the comparison of all parallel melodies yields a real understanding of 15th-c. tunes such as those preserved in the Utrecht and Amsterdam songbooks (respectively: *D-Bsb* MS germ.8° 190 and *A-Wn* MS 311-152, olim Fidei-Komißbibliothek MS

7970). Four tunes are considered here, drawing on a wide range of sources.

(Carl Skoggard)

4456 SALMEN, Walter. **Towards the exploration of national idiosyncrasies in wandering songtunes,** *Journal of the International Folk Music Council* VI (1954) 52–55. *Music.* See no. 306 in this volume.

Some traditional song tunes may be found throughout Europe, modified according to local taste and customs. For example, variant forms of a melody first published in France and Germany in the 15th c. have been documented as traditional song tunes in eastern and western Europe in the 20th c.

(James R. Cowdery)

4457 SCHIØDT, Nanna. **Data processing applied to Byzantine chant,** *Fontes artis musicae* XII/2-3 (May-Dec 1965) 122–23. See no. 499 in this volume.

With the help of a programmer at Københavns U., Byzantine hymns in neumatic notation are being coded on paper tape for processing with the GIER (Geodætisk Instituts Elektron-Regnemaskine) computer. The computer helps with tasks that would otherwise be almost impracticable, such as searching several thousand chants for a particular melodic formula; moreover the material, once encoded, will always be available for further inquiry and analysis. *(David Bloom)*

4458 SIEGMUND-SCHULTZE, Walther. **Händels Melodik in Oper und Oratorien** [Händel's melodic style in opera and oratorio], *Händel-Ehrung der Deutschen Demokratischen Republik: Konferenzbericht* (Leipzig: VEB Deutscher Verlag für Musik, 1961) 165–72. *Music.* In German. See no. 408 in this volume.

Discusses Händel's use of melody in dramatic characterization. In the oratorios of the 1730s, it develops, in contrast to the operas, into an expression of a freer humanity—the best side of the bourgeois Enlightenment.

(David Bloom)

4459 SIEGMUND-SCHULTZE, Walther. **Die Rolle der Melodie in der Musik des sozialistischen Realismus** [The role of melody in the music of socialist realism], *Intonation und Gestalt in der Musik: Beiträge und Abhandlungen der Musikwissenschaftler sozialistischer Länder* (Moskva: Muzyka, 1963) 183–99. In German. See no. 471 in this volume.

A concept of melody in the general framework of Asaf'ev's intonation theory, as the discrete *Gestaltwerdung* of a musical inspiration, is elaborated and exemplified in music by Bartók, Prokof'ev, and Hanns Eisler.

(David Bloom)

4460 SIEGMUND-SCHULTZE, Walther. **Zur Frage des Mozartschen Stils** [The question of Mozartean style], *Bericht über den internationalen musikwissenschaftlichen Kongreß Wien Mozartjahr 1956* (Graz; Köln: Böhlau, 1958) 586–92. *Music.* In German. See no. 365 in this volume.

A discussion of distinctive melodic features in Mozart's works. A fuller discussion is published in the author's *Mozarts Melodik und Stil* (Leipzig, 1957). *(David Bloom)*

4461 SKREBKOV, Sergej Sergeevič. **Novatorskie čerty tematičeskogo razvitija v muzyke Šopena** [Innovative features of thematic development in Chopin's music], *The book of the first international musicological congress devoted to the works of Frederick Chopin* (Warszawa: Państwowe Wydawnictwo Naukowe, 1963) 236–40. *Music.* In Russian. See no. 425 in this volume.

4462 STANISLAV, Josef. **K otázce významu a hodnoty třídění písní z Bosny a Hercegoviny**

od L. Kuby [The significance and value of Ludvík Kuba's classification of songs from Bosnia and Herzegovina], *Treći kongres folklorista Jugoslavije* (Cetinje: Udruženje Folklorista Crne Gore, 1958) 223–40. *Charts, diagr., transcr.* In Czech; summary in Serbian. See no. 357 in this volume.

In 1895 Ludvík Kuba donated to the Zemaljski Muzej in Sarajevo a collection of 1125 folk songs that he transcribed in Bosnia and Herzegovina during his four-month stay there in 1893. Most of the songs were published in *Glasnik Zemaljskog Muzeja u Sarajevu* (1906-10), and he also used some of this material in his study *Zpěv a hudba v Bosně a Hercegovině*, published in the collection *Za slovansku písni* (Prague 1933). Kuba classified these songs by comparing their melody types. Melody types for the song *Igrali se vrani konji*, transcribed in Travnik, Stolac, Čajnice, Plevlje, Zvišegrad, Bilek, Visoko, and Maglaj, are compared. *(Zdravko Blažeković)*

4463 STEFANOVIĆ, Dimitrije. **Melody construction**
as **in Byzantine chant. II,** *Actes du XIIᵉ Congrès d'études Byzantines* (Beograd: Naučno Delo, 1963-1964) I, 375–84. *Illus., facs., music.* See no. 441 in this volume.

Examines evidence for the validity of Egon Wellesz's views in the paper abstracted as no. 4473 in this volume in Russian, Bulgarian, and especially Serbian chant traditions. Melodic formulas closely parallel to the heirmologion traditions cited by Wellesz are found in MS traditions of Serbian and Bulgarian stichera. *(David Bloom)*

4464 STEPANOV, Stjepan. **Problem starosti**
as **muzičko-folklorne baštine** [The problem of dating the traditional-music heritage], *Rad kongresa folklorista Jugoslavije* (Ljubljana: Savez Udruženja Folkloristov Jugoslavije, 1960) 285–93. *Transcr.* In Croatian; summary in German. See no. 404 in this volume.

It is more and more frequently supposed that the smaller the inventory of notes in a given melody, the older the melody can be presumed to be, but other factors may be more important: whether the scale is tempered or not, for example, or whether the melody is stable or permits improvised elaboration. In songs of ritual customs and children's songs it should be understood that melodies, like texts, may have changed to reflect changes in general musical practice. Similarities between melodies from different cultures do not prove that they share a single source; the similarities may have arisen by chance. *(author)*

4465 STRUNK, Oliver. **Melody construction in**
as **Byzantine chant. I,** *Actes du XIIᵉ Congrès d'études Byzantines* (Beograd: Naučno Delo, 1963-1964) I, 365–73. *Music, charts, diagr.* See no. 441 in this volume.

The paper by Egon Wellesz abstracted as no. 4473 in this volume tends to underestimate the importance of the influence of poetic structure on musical structure in Christian chant, particulary within the Byzantine tradition. It is also important in the discussion of melodic conservatism to differentiate analytically between melodies fixed by an early notation and those that were transmitted orally in the early period and therefore less stable; for example in accounting for the diversity of melodies in the heirmologion tradition. *(David Bloom)*

4466 SZABOLCSI, Bence. **Bach, die Volksmusik**
as **und das osteuropäische Melos** [Bach, folk music, and the Eastern European melos], *Bericht über die Wissenschaftliche Bachtagung* (Leipzig: Peters, 1951) 411–15. In German. See no. 298 in this volume.

Bach uses traditional songs and dance melodies in various ways, notably for the stylized dance movements of his suites, sonatas, and concertos. Among the most interesting are the Eastern European melodies frequently designated as "polonaise" or "polacca", melody lines evoking *verbunkos* music, and melody types that can be identified as typically Hungarian, Slovak, or Polish. *(David Bloom)*

4467 TOCH, Ernst. **Melodielehre** [Melodic theory],
as *Bericht über den musikwissenschaftlichen Kongreß in*

Basel (Leipzig: Breitkopf & Härtel, 1925) 334–35. *Music.* In German. See no. 102 in this volume.

Briefly discusses parallels between the visual and aural worlds. The theory that melodies with few non-harmonic pitches have a masculine character while those with many are feminine is illustrated with examples by Chopin, Beethoven, Schumann, Mozart, Haydn, and Wagner.

4468 VÄISÄNEN, Armas Otto. **Suggestions for the**
as **methodical classification and investigation of folk tunes,** *Journal of the International Folk Music Council* I (1949) 34–35. See no. 281 in this volume.

Outlines a classification system based on aspects of form and rhythm.

4469 VARGYAS, Lajos. **Bartók's melodies in the**
as **style of folk songs,** *Journal of the International Folk Music Council* XVI (1964) 30–34. *Music.* See no. 463 in this volume.

Bartók's melodies frequently sound like those of authentic traditional songs, although they are in fact entirely original. His technique of applying formal rhythmic and melodic devices taken from traditional music is illustrated by melodies in Hungarian, Slovak, and Bulgarian styles in the piano collections *Tíz könnyű zongoradarab* (1908) and *Mikrokosmos*, vol. 4. *(David Bloom)*

4470 VETTERL, Karel. **The method of classification**
as **and grouping of folk melodies,** *Studia musicologica Academiae Scientiarum Hungaricae* VII (1965) 349–55. *Music.* See no. 478 in this volume.

The classification system developed by the Ústav pro Etnografii a Folkloristiku at the Akademie Věd České Republiky in Brno is similar to the system employed by Bartók. It has distinct advantages over Pál Jardányi's system. *(Daniel Horn)*

4471 VIKÁR, László. **Les parallèles orientaux de**
as **l'interprétation des chansons populaires hongroises** [Eastern parallels in the performance practice of Hungarian traditional song], *Journal of the International Folk Music Council* XVI (1964) 76–80. *Transcr.* In French. See no. 463 in this volume.

Comparative analysis of vocal melodies collected among Mongol (Inner Mongolia), Tatar, Čuvaš, Čeremis, and Hungarian vocal melodies shows that alongside the Finno-Ugrian stratum of Hungarian music is a distinct Turco-Tatar stratum marked by anhemitonic pentatonicism, descending melody, transposition at the fifth, and improvised fioritura. *(David Bloom)*

4472 WEISMANN, Wilhelm. **Choralzitate in**
as **Händels Oratorien** [The quotation of chorales in Händel's oratorios], *Händel-Ehrung der Deutschen Demokratischen Republik: Konferenzbericht* (Leipzig: VEB Deutscher Verlag für Musik, 1961) 173–80. *Music.* In German. See no. 408 in this volume.

Examines melodies from 16th-c. Lutheran hymns quoted in *Israel in Egypt*, *L'allegro ed il penseroso*, *Messiah*, *Samson*, *Joseph and his brethren*, the *Occasional oratorio*, and the anthems HWV 247, 254, 264, and 268. *(David Bloom)*

4473 WELLESZ, Egon. **Melody construction in**
as **Byzantine chant,** *Actes du XIIᵉ Congrès d'études Byzantines* (Beograd: Naučno Delo, 1963-1964) I, 135–51. *Music, charts, diagr.* See no. 441 in this volume.

During the first millennium, the similarities between Eastern and Western chant traditions were greater than the differences; it was probably after the Muslim conquest of large parts of the Eastern empire that the originally diatonic character of Byzantine chant was affected by the abundance of Turkish-influenced ornamental elements. Analysis shows, however, that the fundamental structural principle of constructing melodies from preexisting formulas remains in Byzantine and Serbian traditions as well as the more conservative Western tradition. *(David Bloom)*

4474
as

WENDLER, Josef. **Zur Formeltechnik des einstimmigen mittelalterlichen Liedes** [Formulaic technique in the monophonic medieval song], *Bericht über den internationalen musikwissenschaftlichen Kongreß* (Kassel: Bärenreiter, 1963) 106–07. In German. See no. 452 in this volume.

The attainment of melodic originality for medieval poet-composers required different methods than for melodies based on a chord progression; it consisted above all in the transformation of given melodic models, of playing with formulae. *(Jeffrey Miller)*

4475
as

WIORA, Walter. **Die Melodien der *Souterliedekens* und ihre deutschen Parallelen** [The melodies of the *Souterliedekens* and their German counterparts], *Société Internationale de Musicologie,*

cinquième congrès/Internationale Gesellschaft für Musikwissenschaft, fünfter Kongreß/International Society for Musical Research, Fifth Congress (Amsterdam: Vereniging voor Nederlandse Muziekgeschiedenis, 1953) 438–49. In German. See no. 316 in this volume.

Explores the 16th-c. Dutch Psalter known as *Souterliedekens.*

4476
as

ŽGANEC, Vinko. **The tonal and modal structure of Yugoslav folk music,** *Journal of the International Folk Music Council* X (1958) 18–21. *Music.* See no. 371 in this volume.

The most common melodic type in Yugoslavia is that which ends on the second degree of the scale. The reasons for this development are explored. *(James R. Cowdery)*

Julius Woitinek demonstrates his pedagogical device (see no. 4799).
Public domain.

PEDAGOGY

70 General

4477
as
ÁDÁM, Jenő. **The influence of folk music on public musical education in Hungary,** *Studia musicologica Academiae Scientiarum Hungaricae* VII (1965) 11–18. See no. 478 in this volume.
True Hungarian traditional music was belittled by the upper classes in the early 20th c. It gradually gained acceptance through the efforts of Kodály and others, and became the basis of Hungarian music education.
(David Gagné)

4478
as
ADAMIČ, Emil. **Yougoslavie** [Yugoslavia], *L'éducation musicale trait d'union entre les peuples: Rapports et discours sur l'éducation musicale dans les divers pays* (Praha: Orbis, 1937) 184–85. In French. See no. 232 in this volume.

4479
as
AINAUD, Enrique. **Espagne** [Spain], *L'éducation musicale trait d'union entre les peuples: Rapports et discours sur l'éducation musicale dans les divers pays* (Praha: Orbis, 1937) 37–38. In French. See no. 232 in this volume.

4480
as
AL-ḤIFNĪ, Maḥmūd Aḥmad. **Commission de l'Enseignement** [The Commission on Pedagogy], *Recueil des travaux du Congrès de musique arabe* (Al-Qāhirah: Boulac, 1934) 605–36. *Charts, diagr.* In French. See no. 196 in this volume.
At the Congress on Arab Music (Mu'tamar al Mūsīqá al-'Arabiyyah) in Cairo (1932), the commission prepared a detailed analysis of the state of pedagogy in Egypt and a set of recommendations for the adoption of modern instructional methods. Specific proposals, focused on the need to encourage Arab as opposed to European music, were made for institutional and curricular aspects of music schools, teacher training, and the training of professional musicians. *(David Bloom)*

4481
as
ALALEONA, Domenico. **Educazione musicale del popolo e sua organizzazione nella scuola e nella vita cittadina** [General musical education and its organization in schools and in city life], *La vita musicale dell'Italia d'oggi* (Torino: Fratelli Bocca, 1921) 58–77. In Italian. See no. 97 in this volume.
Discusses various reforms, including the establishment of choral societies and madrigal groups, choral instruction in schools, and the facilitation of orchestra tours.

4482
as
ANDRIES, Marcel. **La formation du goût musical de l'auditeur** [Formation of the listener's musical taste], *La musique dans l'éducation* (Paris: UNESCO; Colin, 1955) 177–81. In French. See no. 323 in this volume.
An English-language version is abstracted as no. 4483 in this volume.

4483
as
ANDRIES, Marcel. **The training of the listener in music appreciation,** *Music in education* (Paris: UNESCO, 1955) 169–73. See no. 322 in this volume.
Addresses how to teach students to hear melody, harmony, rhythm, polyphony, and form, with attention to the ideas of Carl Orff and Émile Jaques-Dalcroze. A French-language version is cited as no. 4482 in this volume.

4484
as
BAILLY, Edmond; LAMPÉRIÈRE, Anna. **La musique et l'éducation sociale** [Music and social education], *Congrès international de l'éducation sociale. I: Rapports présentés; II: Compte rendu des séances* (Paris: Librairie Félix Alcan, 1901) 168–81. In French. See no. 28 in this volume.

4485
as
BAKULE, František Karel. **Le chant choral dans l'éducation** [Choral singing in education], *Congrès international de l'enseignement primaire et de l'éducation populaire* (Paris: S.U.D.E.L., 1938) 305–07. In French. See no. 246 in this volume.

4486
as
BALTZ, Karl von. **Autriche** [Austria], *L'éducation musicale trait d'union entre les peuples: Rapports et discours sur l'éducation musicale dans les divers pays* (Praha: Orbis, 1937) 13–17. In French. See no. 232 in this volume.

4487
as
BANDMANN, Tony. **Welches sind die Grundfehler unserer heutigen Methodik?** [Which are the basic mistakes of our methods today?], *Zweiter Musikpädagogischer Kongress: Vorträge und Referate* (Berlin: Klavier-Lehrer, 1904) 146–57. In German. See no. 43 in this volume.

4488
as
BARINI, Giorgio. **Sulla necessità di render completo e proficuo l'insegnamento della storia della musica negli istituti musicali, ponendo costantemente in relazione la produzione musicale con la storia civile e del costume e con le altre manifestazioni della vita intellettuale nel tempo in cui fiorirono i singoli compositori e si svolsero le varie forme musicali** [The necessity of making instruction in music history in musical institutions complete and useful, always relating musical production to civil and social history and the other manifestations of the intellectual life of the times in which individual composers thrived and various musical styles developed], *Atti del Congresso internazionale di scienze storiche. VIII: Atti della sezione IV: Storia dell'arte musicale e drammatica* (Roma: R. Accademia dei Lincei, 1905) 11–16. In Italian. See no. 42 in this volume.
The quality of musical education can be improved by regarding music's broad social, cultural, and historical relations. Numerous connections between artistic and musical works are cited.

4489
as
BASIL, Br. **A course of study for Bantu musicians,** *Journal of the International Folk Music Council* XI (1959) 44. See no. 392 in this volume.
A proposal for the musical training of black South Africans, emphasizing the importance of indigenous traditions for potential composers.

4490
as
BAYER, Bathja. **Šylwb hamẇsyqah hadatyt beḥwra'at miqṣŵ'ŵt hayhadwt wemad'ey** [Incorporating religious music into the teaching of Judaism and the humanities], *Dwkan* II (1960) 35–40. In Hebrew. See no. 409 in this volume.

The study of liturgical music has many applications to the fields of history, archaeology, and sociology, and should not be treated as a separate discipline. There is a growing need for a research center in this field.
(Moshe Zorman)

4491 BELJON, J.J. **The training of the industrial de-**
as **signer in the Netherlands,** *Actes du cinquième Congrès international d'esthétique/Proceedings of the Fifth International Congress of Aesthetics* ('s-Gravenhage: Mouton, 1964) 961–68. See no. 475 in this volume.
General discussion of a curriculum including training in all the arts; music is mentioned as a source of highly evolved theory and teaching technique, and of valuable metaphors for design issues. *(David Bloom)*

4492 BELLIOT, Henri. **Le disque, auxiliaire de**
as **l'éducateur** [Recordings as the educator's aid], *Congrès international de l'enseignement primaire et de l'éducation populaire* (Paris: S.U.D.E.L., 1938) 448–49. In French. See no. 246 in this volume.

4493 BENEDITO, Rafael. **Le rythme dans la péda-**
as **gogie** [Rhythm in pedagogy], *Compte rendu du Ier Congrès du rythme* (Genève: Institut Jaques-Dalcroze, 1926) 147–51. In French. See no. 123 in this volume.
Too often, a sense of symmetry is taught instead of rhythm. Jaques-Dalcroze's form of rhythmic pedagogy is an ideal educational tool.

4494 BENNEDIK, Frank. **Tonwort und Musik-**
as **erziehung** [Solfège and music education], *Bericht über den I. musikwissenschaftlichen Kongress der Deutschen Musikgesellschaft in Leipzig* (Wiesbaden: Breitkopf & Härtel, 1926) 142–49. *Music, charts, diagr.* In German. See no. 120 in this volume.
The value of solfège is discussed, and an educational curriculum based on solfège is proposed.

4495 BENTZON, Jorgen. **Danemark** [Denmark],
as *L'éducation musicale trait d'union entre les peuples: Rapports et discours sur l'éducation musicale dans les divers pays* (Praha: Orbis, 1937) 33–36. In French. See no. 232 in this volume.

4496 BRĂILOIU, Constantin. **Roumanie** [Romania],
as *L'éducation musicale trait d'union entre les peuples: Rapports et discours sur l'éducation musicale dans les divers pays* (Praha: Orbis, 1937) 118–20. In French. See no. 232 in this volume.

4497 BREAZUL, George. **Roumanie** [Romania],
as *L'éducation musicale trait d'union entre les peuples: Rapports et discours sur l'éducation musicale dans les divers pays* (Praha: Orbis, 1937) 121–26. In French. See no. 232 in this volume.

4498 BRUGNOLI, Attilio. **Proposta di riforma**
as **nell'indirizzo pedagogico e nell'ordinamento degli istituti musicali in Italia** [A proposal for reforming the pedagogical objectives and the regulations of musical institutions in Italy], *La vita musicale dell'Italia d'oggi* (Torino: Fratelli Bocca, 1921) 154–77. *Illus., charts, diagr.* In Italian. See no. 97 in this volume.
Argues for admissions tests that are scientifically designed.

4499 BRUYR, Jose. **Comment on fait des**
as **"comprimés" d'œuvres anciennes** [How to make

"pills" out of early works], *Compte rendu des travaux du Ier Congrès international d'art radiophonique* (Paris: conference, 1938). In French. See no. 244 in this volume.

4500 BRŴY'ER, Mordekay. **Toknyt lymẇdym**
as **lemẇsyqah datyt** [Curriculum for the study of religious music], *Dẇkan* II (1960) 24–34. In Hebrew. See no. 409 in this volume.

4501 CAPELLEN, Georg. **Reformen im musik-**
as **theoretischen Unterricht** [Reforms in music theory instruction], *Zweiter Musikpädagogischer Kongress: Vorträge und Referate* (Berlin: Klavier-Lehrer, 1904) 82–88. In German. See no. 43 in this volume.

4502 CARRILLO, Julián. **La nomenclature des sons**
as [The nomenclature of pitches], *Congrès international d'histoire de la musique: Documents, mémoires et vœux* (Solesmes: St. Pierre; Paris: Fischbacher, 1901) 276–80. *Music, charts, diagr.* In French. See no. 32 in this volume.
Proposes a revised solfège system that would have the advantage of consistent pronunciation in all languages. The new syllables would lend themselves easily to suffixes indicating sharps, flats, double sharps, and double flats.

4503 CHARLIER, Léopold. **Ce qui a été fait au pays**
as **de Liège pour l'éducation populaire par la musique** [What has been done in the area of Liège regarding music education of the populace], *La musique et le peuple: Rapports, suggestions, voeux* (Bruxelles: Ministère des Sciences et des Arts, 1932) 53–56. In French. See no. 195 in this volume.
Describes the success of the cities in the Liège area in music education, by means of early instruction, conservatories, and concerts. In the countryside, choral groups should be organized, and new performing editions of traditional songs should be published expressly for their use. *(Mark Stevens)*

4504 CHERBULIEZ, Antoine-Élisée. **Le disque,**
as **auxiliaire de l'éducation musicale** [Records as an aid in music education], *La musique dans l'éducation* (Paris: UNESCO; Colin, 1955) 266–70. In French. See no. 323 in this volume.
An English-language version is abstracted as no. 4505 in this volume.

4505 CHERBULIEZ, Antoine-Élisée. **The gramo-**
as **phone record: An aid in music education,** *Music in education* (Paris: UNESCO, 1955) 255–59. See no. 322 in this volume.
Examines the advantages and disadvantages of phonograph records on the basis of experience teaching appreciation to adults. A French-language version is cited as no. 4504 in this volume. *(Elizabeth A. Wright)*

4506 CHERBULIEZ, Antoine-Élisée. **Le valeur**
as **pédagogique du folklore musical dans l'éducation scolaire** [The pedagogical application of traditional music in school], *Journal of the International Folk Music Council* VII (1955) 16. In French. See no. 337 in this volume.
Summary of a paper.

4507 CHEVAIS, Maurice. **Les instruments de**
as **musique du maître et de l'élève** [The musical instruments of the master and the student], *Congrès international de l'enseignement primaire et de l'éducation populaire* (Paris: S.U.D.E.L., 1938) 310–12. In French. See no. 246 in this volume.

4508 CLOSSON, Ernest. **Folklore, radio et orphéons**
as [Folklore, radio, and choirs], *La musique et le peuple: Rapports, suggestions, voeux* (Bruxelles: Ministère des Sciences et des Arts, 1932) 79–82. In French. See no. 195 in this volume.

Traditional song must be the basis of music education. Radio is a particularly desirable instrument, as communal listening can strengthen the family unit. Mixed choruses should be fostered. *(Mark Stevens)*

4509 COLLAER, Paul. **L'éducation artistique du**
as **public telle que la poursuit la radio belge** [Artistic education of the public as pursued by the Belgian radio], *Compte rendu des travaux du Iᵉʳ Congrès international d'art radiophonique* (Paris: conference, 1938). In French. See no. 244 in this volume.

4510 CVETKO, Dragotin. **L'éducation musicale à la**
as **portée de tous** [Music education within the reach of all], *La musique dans l'éducation* (Paris: UNESCO; Colin, 1955) 42–47. In French. See no. 323 in this volume.

An English-language version is abstracted as no. 4511 in this volume.

4511 CVETKO, Dragotin. **Music education within**
as **the reach of all,** *Music in education* (Paris: UNESCO, 1955) 41–45. See no. 322 in this volume.

Music education should be regarded as a universal right. Post–World War II educational priorities are discussed, with particular attention to the situation in Slovenia. A French-language version is cited as no. 4510 in this volume. *(Elizabeth A. Wright)*

4512 DAUBRESSE, Mathilde. **Rapport sur**
as **l'enseignement musical en France** [Report on musical teaching in France], *Haydn-Zentenarfeier* (Leipzig: Breitkopf & Härtel; Wien: Artaria, 1909) 507–15. In French. See no. 65 in this volume.

Lists statistics including enrollment figures, organizational structures, and budgets for schools of various types at various levels. Choral societies are also mentioned.

4513 DAVAU. **Les disques d'enseignement** [Instruc-
as tional recordings], *Congrès international de l'enseignement primaire et de l'éducation populaire* (Paris: S.U.D.E.L., 1938) 450–53. In French. See no. 246 in this volume.

4514 DELORT, P. **Plan d'un enseignement pratique**
as **et général du plain-chant et de la musique d'église** [Method of practical and general teaching of plainchant and church music], *Congrès pour la restauration du plain-chant et de la musique d'église* (Paris: De Mourgues, 1862) 89–91. In French. See no. 3 in this volume.

4515 DENT, Edward Joseph. **Grande-Bretagne** [Great
as Britain], *L'éducation musicale trait d'union entre les peuples: Rapports et discours sur l'éducation musicale dans les divers pays* (Praha: Orbis, 1937) 85–87. In French. See no. 232 in this volume.

4516 DESHPANDE, S.B. **The objective of teaching**
as **music,** *Souvenir on Hindustani Music Festival & Seminar* (Hyderabad: Andhra Pradesh Sangeeta Nataka Akademi, 1966) 27–34. See no. 450 in this volume.

Discusses three objectives for education in Hindustani music: discovering talented students, training outstanding performers, and creating appreciative audiences. The qualities of an ideal teacher are outlined.

4517 DESMETTRE, Gertraud Höfer. **La radiophonie**
as **scolaire** [Educational broadcasting], *Congrès international de l'enseignement primaire et de l'éducation populaire* (Paris: S.U.D.E.L., 1938) 463–67. In French. See no. 246 in this volume.

4518 DISMAN, Miloslav. **Histoire de la radio-**
as **diffusion scolaire en Tchécoslovaquie** [History of educational broadcasting in Czechslovakia], *Congrès international de l'enseignement primaire et de l'éducation populaire* (Paris: S.U.D.E.L., 1938) 460–63. In French. See no. 246 in this volume.

4519 DUHAMEL, Georges. **La philosophie de l'édu-**
as **cation musicale** [The philosophy of music education], *La musique dans l'éducation* (Paris: UNESCO; Colin, 1955) 23–34. In French. See no. 323 in this volume.

An English-language version is abstracted as no. 4520 in this volume.

4520 DUHAMEL, Georges. **The philosophy of music**
as **education,** *Music in education* (Paris: UNESCO, 1955) 23–34. See no. 322 in this volume.

Discusses the concept of music education as a means to an end and as an end in itself, the need for higher standards and increased availability of instruction, and the importance of amateur music making. A French-language version is abstracted as no. 4519 in this volume.

4521 EARHART, William. **Report of Subcommittee**
as **on Inter-American Exchange in the Field of School Music,** *Report of the Committee of the Conference on Inter-American Relations in the Field of Music* (Washington, D.C.: United States Department of State, 1940) 31–34. See no. 271 in this volume.

Discusses elementary and secondary instruction, teacher preparation, and various cultural influences on youth including concerts, Christian religious music, and radio. There is currently little exposure in schools to the music of Latin America. Examples suitable for school bands and orchestra should be acquired by obtaining music used in the Latin American countries themselves. The Music Educators National Conference has adopted a resolution in support of this committee. *(Howard Cinnamon)*

4522 EBEL, Arnold. **Einrichtung und Aufgaben der**
as **musikpädagogischen Organisation** [Organization and responsibilities of the music pedagogy association], *Bericht über den I. musikwissenschaftlichen Kongress der Deutschen Musikgesellschaft in Leipzig* (Wiesbaden: Breitkopf & Härtel, 1926) 150–58. In German. See no. 120 in this volume.

Reviews the history and role of music pedagogy associations in Germany, such as the Deutsche Musikpädagogische Verband, the Arbeitsgemeinschaft der Schulmusiker, and the Vereinigte Musikpädagogische Verbände. *(William Renwick)*

4523 EMGE, Hans. **Die klassischen Schulwerke der**
as **Singekunst als Grundlagen für den Sänger-nachwuchs** [The classic pieces for voice students as a foundation for the next generation of singers], *Bericht über den Internationalen Kongreß Singen und Sprechen* (München: Oldenbourg, 1938) 132–37. In German. See no. 257 in this volume.

Argues for a revival of traditional methods of voice pedagogy, particularly the Italian school.

4524 EPPSTEIN, Hans. **Aktuelle Tendenzen in der**
as **schwedischen Musikpädagogik** [Current tendencies in Swedish music pedagogy], *Norddeutsche und nordeuropäische Musik* (Kassel; New York: Bärenreiter, 1965) 56–60. In German. See no. 467 in this volume.

Particular attention is given to the tendency for instrument instruction to be taken over by popular educational associations of a political or religious character, especially the Arbeternas Bildningsförbunde, largely on a group basis, and its consequences, negative and positive. *(David Bloom)*

4525
as
FALLER, Robert. **Un esprit nouveau dans l'enseignement du solfège** [A new spirit in the teaching of solfège], *Deuxième Congrès international du rythme et de la rythmique* (Genève: Institut Jaques-Dalcroze, 1966) 136–40. *Music, charts, diagr.* In French. See no. 502 in this volume.
Discusses the Dalcroze method.

4526
as
FERAND, Ernest Thomas. **Improvisation in music history and education,** *Papers of the American Musicological Society* (Philadelphia: American Musicological Society, 1946) 115–25. See no. 269 in this volume.
Improvisation was an important element in the development of musical forms from the 15th to the 18th c. Modern pedagogy should recognize the value of improvisation and its role in bridging the gap between composers and performers, and between active music making and passive listening.

4527
as
FERRARIA, Luigi Ernesto. **L'educazione del senso ritmico col metodo Jaques-Dalcroze: Ginnastica ritmica** [Education of the rhythmic sense with the Dalcroze method—Rhythmic gymnastics], *La vita musicale dell'Italia d'oggi* (Torino: Fratelli Bocca, 1921) 96–113. In Italian. See no. 97 in this volume.
Reviews the history and general principles of the Dalcroze method, and suggests that it be used systematically in Italian music schools.

4528
as
FISCH, Samuel. **Suisse** [Switzerland], *L'éducation musicale trait d'union entre les peuples: Rapports et discours sur l'éducation musicale dans les divers pays* (Praha: Orbis, 1937) 138–46. In French. See no. 232 in this volume.

4529
as
Fördergemeinschaft Klavier. **Lehrplan für den Klavierunterricht an Musikschulen** [Syllabus for piano instruction at music schools], *Dokumentation* (Frankfurt am Main: Fördergemeinschaft Klavier, 1966) 111–17. In German. See no. 494 in this volume.
Proposals developed in the context of the Europiano-Kongress, Berlin 1965.

4530
as
FRANZÉN, Bengt. **The educator's point of view,** *Music in education* (Paris: UNESCO, 1955) 303–07. See no. 322 in this volume.
Collaborations among educators, composers, and performers must be increased. There is a need for music created for educational purposes. A French-language version is cited as no. 4531 in this volume.
(Elizabeth A. Wright)

4531
as
FRANZÉN, Bengt. **Le point de vue de l'éducateur** [The educator's point of view], *La musique dans l'éducation* (Paris: UNESCO; Colin, 1955) 315–20. In French. See no. 323 in this volume.
An English-language version is abstracted as no. 4530 in this volume.

4532
as
FRISCH, Fay Templeton. **Neue Wege der Musikerziehung** [New paths of music education], *Dokumentation* (Frankfurt am Main: Fördergemeinschaft Klavier, 1966) 106–11. In German. See no. 494 in this volume.
Discusses current developments from the standpoint of piano instruction.

4533
as
FUKUI, Naohiro. **L'enseignement musical privé au Japon** [Private music instruction in Japan], *La musique dans l'éducation* (Paris: UNESCO; Colin, 1955) 164–65. In French. See no. 323 in this volume.
An English-language version is abstracted as no. 4534 in this volume.

4534
as
FUKUI, Naohiro. **Individual and private music instruction in Japan,** *Music in education* (Paris: UNESCO, 1955) 157–58. See no. 322 in this volume.
Outlines the history of Western music instruction since its introduction ca. 1880. The dependence on expatriate teachers from Europe and America has been overcome by the training of Japanese teachers. A French-language version is cited as no. 4533 in this volume.

4535
as
FUKUI, Naohiro. **Das Musikschulwesen in Japan** [Music schools in Japan], *Musikerziehung: Zeitschrift der Musikerzieher Österreichs* special issue (1953) 45–46. In German. See no. 318 in this volume.

4536
as
GARIEL, Eduardo. **De la nécessité de méthodiser l'enseignement de la musique en lui appliquant une base scientifique** [The necessity of systematizing the teaching of music by establishing it on scientific basis], *Congrès international d'histoire de la musique: Documents, mémoires et vœux* (Solesmes: St. Pierre; Paris: Fischbacher, 1901) 281–88. In French. See no. 32 in this volume.
The standardization of pedagogy texts and the mandatory study of pedagogy in music schools and conservatories would be important parts of educational reforms.

4537
as
GEHRELS, W. **Pays-Bas** [The Netherlands], *L'éducation musicale trait d'union entre les peuples: Rapports et discours sur l'éducation musicale dans les divers pays* (Praha: Orbis, 1937) 109–12. In French. See no. 232 in this volume.

→
GEISLER, Christian. **Der Schulgesang und die Notationsfrage** [School song and the question of notation]. See no. 3822 in this volume.

4538
as
GELBER, Lucy. **L'éducation musicale et la formation générale** [Music education and general education], *La musique dans l'éducation* (Paris: UNESCO; Colin, 1955) 181–88. In French. See no. 323 in this volume.
An English-language version is abstracted as no. 4539 in this volume.

4539
as
GELBER, Lucy. **The role of music in general education,** *Music in education* (Paris: UNESCO, 1955) 174–80. See no. 322 in this volume.
Music education aims at disciplining mind and body, awakening creative power and elevating emotions; integrated into the general education syllabus, it plays a useful auxiliary role. A French-language version is cited as no. 4538 in this volume.

4540
as
GENTILI, Alberto. **L'histoire de la théorie dans l'enseignement de la musique** [The history of theory in the teaching of music], *Actes du Congrès d'histoire de l'art* (Paris: Presses Universitaires de France, 1923-1924) 754–58. In Italian. See no. 94 in this volume.

4541
as
GHISI, Federico. **Per un richiamo alla tradizione umanistica** [Reclaiming the humanist tradition], *Atti del sesto Congresso internazionale di musica* (Firenze: Barbèra, 1950) 49–52. In Italian. See no. 291 in this volume.

Discusses how the teaching of composition must be brought into a more humanistic stance, open to the evolution of both technique and musical language. *(Susan Poliniak)*

4542 GILSON, Paul. **La musique et l'éducation des**
as **masses** [Music and the education of the masses], *La musique et le peuple: Rapports, suggestions, voeux* (Bruxelles: Ministère des Sciences et des Arts, 1932) 43–47. In French. See no. 195 in this volume.
Describes the work already done on Belgian traditional songs, lists collections, urges the collection of Congolese songs, and calls for an edition appropriate for use in the schools. *(Mark Stevens)*

4543 GURLITT, Wilibald. **Musikwissenschaftliche**
as **Forschung und Lehre in pädagogischer Sicht** [Teaching and research in musicology, from the standpoint of pedagogy], *Bericht über den Internationalen musikwissenschaftlichen Kongress* (Kassel: Bärenreiter, 1954). In German. See no. 319 in this volume.
Focuses on certain fundamentals of music pedagogy, which are to be upheld even in an era of upheaval such as the present (1953), when the value of musical experience itself is being questioned. Educators must be clear about their own ideals; teaching without conviction, no matter how accomplished such teaching may be technically, is worth very little. The greatest musicologists of the 19th c. drew on passionate ideals and convictions. *(Carl Skoggard)*

4544 HÁBA, Alois. **Tchécoslovaquie** [Czechoslovakia],
as *L'éducation musicale trait d'union entre les peuples: Rapports et discours sur l'éducation musicale dans les divers pays* (Praha: Orbis, 1937) 147–61. In French. See no. 232 in this volume.

4545 HABÖCK, Franz. **Der Gesangsunterricht in**
as **den Schulen** [Singing instruction in schools], *Haydn-Zentenarfeier* (Leipzig: Breitkopf & Härtel; Wien: Artaria, 1909) 333–45. In German. See no. 65 in this volume.
Discusses curricula and graduation requirements for teacher training institutions, middle schools, high schools, and conservatories.

4546 HAENNI, Georges. **La chanson populaire dans**
as **la famille et à l'école** [Traditional song in the family and at school], *Travaux du Ier Congrès International de Folklore* (Tours: Arrault et Cie, 1938) 397–99. In French. See no. 251 in this volume.
Discusses the pedagogical value of traditional songs.

4547 HALOT, Alexandre. **La musique envisagée au**
as **point de vue de l'art public: Ses bienfaits populaires** [Music seen from the point of view of public art: Its popular benefits], *Ier Congrès international de l'art public* (Liège: Bénard, 1900) 95–96. In French. See no. 24 in this volume.
Musical organizations and amateur music groups are beneficial to the general understanding of music.

4548 HARRIS, Ernest E. **The music educator today**
as **and tomorrow,** *Music skills* (Washington, D.C.: Catholic University of America, 1958) 18–28. *Music.* See no. 385 in this volume.
Effective music education is a matter of building concepts; it is the act of being an inventor, not a critic. Rather than attempting to change their students' bad habits, teachers should instill good habits so that the bad ones will die from lack of use. Music teachers must look to the future and the musical education of the masses in an increasingly automated world with more leisure time. *(Susan Poliniak)*

⟶ HARTMANN, Georg. **Die Erziehung zur**
Durchgeistigung des Sängerdarstellers [The education to spirituality of the singer-actor]. See no. 5167 in this volume.

4549 HELFERT, W. **Tchécoslovaquie** [Czechoslova-
as kia], *L'éducation musicale trait d'union entre les peuples: Rapports et discours sur l'éducation musicale dans les divers pays* (Praha: Orbis, 1937) 152–57. In French. See no. 232 in this volume.

4550 HENNIG, Karl Raphael. **Die Musikästhetik und**
as **ihre praktische Einführung** [Music aesthetics and its practical introduction], *Zweiter Musikpädagogischer Kongress: Vorträge und Referate* (Berlin: Klavier-Lehrer, 1904) 59–66. In German. See no. 43 in this volume.

4551 HERDIECKERHOFF, Ulrich. **Die wissen-**
as **schaftliche Selbstbegründung der Musikpädagogik** [The self-validation of music pedagogy as a science], *Bericht über den internationalen musikwissenschaftlichen Kongreß* (Kassel: Bärenreiter, 1963) 284–86. In German. See no. 452 in this volume.
Discusses the prerequisites for a critical music pedagogy in its relation to systematic musicology.

4552 HICKENLOOPER, Lucie (Olga Samaroff
as Stokowski). **États-Unis d'Amérique** [The United States of America], *L'éducation musicale trait d'union entre les peuples: Rapports et discours sur l'éducation musicale dans les divers pays* (Praha: Orbis, 1937) 61–72. In French. See no. 232 in this volume.

4553 HONINCKS, Georges. **Le rôle de la musique**
as **comme élément d'éducation populaire** [The role of music as an element of popular education], *La musique et le peuple: Rapports, suggestions, voeux* (Bruxelles: Ministère des Sciences et des Arts, 1932) 13–18. In French. See no. 195 in this volume.
Discusses the utility of music in creating morality and countering the ill effects of sports and idleness. Methods of bringing music to the people, both in school and out, are described. *(Mark Stevens)*

4554 HOOD, Marguerite. **Das Musikschulwesen in**
as **den USA** [Music schools in the USA], *Musikerziehung: Zeitschrift der Musikerzieher Österreichs* special issue (1953) 47–48. In German. See no. 318 in this volume.

4555 HORN, Michael. **Die Choralfrage in Schule, im**
as **Lehrer- und Priesterseminar** [The chant question in schools, in teacher training institutes, and in seminaries], *Acta generalis cantus gregoriani studiosorum conventus, Argentinensis, 16-19 Aug. 1905/Bericht des internationalen Kongresses für gregorianischen Choralgesang/Compte rendu du Congrès international de plain-chant grégorien* (Strassburg: F.-X. Le Roux, 1905) 100–05. In German. See no. 50 in this volume.
Discusses the pedagogical problem as viewed in Pius X's motu proprio *Tra le sollecitudini* (1903).

4556 HUCH, Robert. **Notenlese-Lehrmethode**
as [Teaching method for reading music], *Zweiter Musikpädagogischer Kongress: Vorträge und Referate* (Berlin: Klavier-Lehrer, 1904) 98–110. In German. See no. 43 in this volume.

4557 IBBERSON, Mary. **Grande-Bretagne** [Great
as   Britain], *L'éducation musicale trait d'union entre les
          peuples: Rapports et discours sur l'éducation musicale
          dans les divers pays* (Praha: Orbis, 1937) 88–90. In
          French. See no. 232 in this volume.

4558 INDY, Vincent d'. **De l'utilité des écoles de chefs
as   d'orchestre et de la généralisation de l'étude
          de l'instrumentation** [On the usefulness of con-
          ducting schools and on the generalization of the study
          of instrumentation], *Congrès international de musique:
          Ire session—Exposition Universelle de 1900: Compte
          rendu, rapports, communications* (Paris: conference,
          1901) 14–15. In French. See no. 29 in this volume.
Students of conducting should be trained in the physical and moral aspects
of conducting, in style interpretation, in the origin and construction of instruments, and in orchestration.

4559 IRMER, Gotho von. **Musik-Schulfunk:
as   Gezielte Sendung** [Music-educational radio: Tar-
          geted broadcasting], *Musische Jugend und technische
          Mittler* (Remscheid: Landesarbeitsgemeinschaft
          Jugendmusik Nordrhein-Westfalen, 1957) 45–50. In
          German. See no. 380 in this volume.
Examples are drawn from the author's experience as director of mu-
sic-educational radio for Radio Bremen.

4560 JAQUES-DALCROZE, Émile. **Une méthode
as   d'éducation par et pour le rythme** [An educa-
          tional method by and for rhythm], *Compte rendu du Ier
          Congrès du rythme* (Genève: Institut Jaques-Dalcroze,
          1926) 196–205. In French. See no. 123 in this volume.
Rhythmic sensitivity is vital not only in music but in other professions
where physical and mental coordination is required. The proposed method
includes gymnastics, rhythmic solfège, and improvisation.

4561 JAQUES-DALCROZE, Émile. **Suisse** [Switzer-
as   land], *L'éducation musicale trait d'union entre les
          peuples: Rapports et discours sur l'éducation musicale
          dans les divers pays* (Praha: Orbis, 1937) 133–37. In
          French. See no. 232 in this volume.

4562 JÖDE, Fritz. **Wege zur Polyphonie in der
as   Erziehung** [The role of polyphony in education],
          *Bericht über den I. musikwissenschaftlichen Kongress
          der Deutschen Musikgesellschaft in Leipzig*
          (Wiesbaden: Breitkopf & Härtel, 1926) 127–33. In Ger-
          man. See no. 120 in this volume.
Focuses on traditional song and contrapuntal choral music from the 16th
through the 19th c., and their use in pedagogy over this same period.
(William Renwick)

4563 KARLYLE, Charles. **International voice train-
as   ing,** *Report of the Fourth Congress of the International
          Musical Society* (London: Novello, 1912) 62. See no. 71
          in this volume.
Summary of a paper. Approaches throughout history in several European
countries are surveyed.

4564 KASILAG, Lucrecia R. **L'enseignement musi-
as   cal privé aux Philippines** [Private music education
          in the Philippines], *La musique dans l'éducation* (Paris:
          UNESCO; Colin, 1955) 169–73. In French. See no. 323
          in this volume.
An English-language version is abstracted as no. 4565 in this volume.

4565 KASILAG, Lucrecia R. **Individual and private
as   instruction in the Philippines,** *Music in education*
          (Paris: UNESCO, 1955) 161–65. See no. 322 in this
          volume.
Surveys the situation in practical music instruction in the Philippines, noting that a musician with university-level training will not necessarily be a
competent teacher. A French-language version is cited as no. 4564 in this
volume. *(Elizabeth A. Wright)*

4566 KENNEDY, Douglas. **The educational element
as   in folk music and dance,** *Journal of the Interna-
          tional Folk Music Council* V (1953) 48–51. See no. 314
          in this volume.
Discusses approaches to teaching traditional music and dance in England at
various age levels.

4567 KESTENBERG, Leo. **L'état actuel de l'édu-
as   cation musicale dans le monde occidental** [The
          present state of music education in the Western world],
          La musique dans l'éducation (Paris: UNESCO; Colin,
          1955) 54–59. In French. See no. 323 in this volume.
An English-language version is abstracted as no. 4569 in this volume.

4568 KESTENBERG, Leo. **La musique dans le plan
as   total de l'éducation** [Music within the integral edu-
          cational plan], *Congrès international de
          l'enseignement primaire et de l'éducation populaire*
          (Paris: S.U.D.E.L., 1938) 303–04. In French. See no.
          246 in this volume.

4569 KESTENBERG, Leo. **The present state of mu-
as   sic education in the occidental world,** *Music in
          education* (Paris: UNESCO, 1955) 52–58. See no. 322
          in this volume.
Music education in Europe should be recognized as a means of synthesizing artistic creation and technical musicianship. The importance of communal activity, and the unity of music education and religious feeling, are
stressed. A French-language version is cited as no. 4567 in this volume.
(Elizabeth A. Wright)

4570 KESTENBERG, Leo. **Tchécoslovaquie** [Czecho-
as   slovakia], *L'éducation musicale trait d'union entre les
          peuples: Rapports et discours sur l'éducation musicale
          dans les divers pays* (Praha: Orbis, 1937) 158–62. In
          French. See no. 232 in this volume.

4571 KJELLSTRÖM, Sven. **Suède** [Sweden],
as   *L'éducation musicale trait d'union entre les peuples:
          Rapports et discours sur l'éducation musicale dans les
          divers pays* (Praha: Orbis, 1937) 127–32. In French.
          See no. 232 in this volume.

4572 KRAUS, Egon. **Die technischen Mittler in der
as   Westlichen Welt** [Technological media in the West-
          ern world], *Musische Jugend und technische Mittler*
          (Remscheid: Landesarbeitsgemeinschaft Jugendmusik
          Nordrhein-Westfalen, 1957) 115–21. In German. See
          no. 380 in this volume.
Reports on the use of broadcast and recording media for pedagogical pur-
poses outside Germany, as observed by the author in the United States, by
John Horton in Great Britain, and by Marie-Jeanne Igot in France.
(David Bloom)

4573 KRAUS, Egon; TWITTENHOFF, Wilhelm. **La
as   méthode Orff-Bergese** [The Orff-Bergese method],
          La musique dans l'éducation (Paris: UNESCO; Colin,
          1955) 252–54. In French. See no. 323 in this volume.
An English-language version is abstracted as no. 4574 in this volume.

4574 KRAUS, Egon; TWITTENHOFF, Wilhelm. **The**
as **Orff-Bergese method,** *Music in education* (Paris:
UNESCO, 1955) 241–44. See no. 322 in this volume.
Brief overview of the Orff method (especially as contrasted with the
Dalcroze method), with attention to the systematization contributed by
Orff's collaborator Hans Bergese. A French-language version is cited as
no. 4573 in this volume.

4575 KRENEK, Ernst. **Autriche** [Austria], *L'éducation*
as *musicale trait d'union entre les peuples: Rapports et*
discours sur l'éducation musicale dans les divers pays
(Praha: Orbis, 1937) 18–21. In French. See no. 232 in
this volume.

4576 KROEBER-ASCHE, Lili. **Möglichkeiten des**
as **Gruppenunterrichts am Klavier** [Possibilities of
group piano instruction], *Dokumentation* (Frankfurt am
Main: Fördergemeinschaft Klavier, 1966) 104–06. In
German. See no. 494 in this volume.

4577 KÜHN, Walter. **Grundlinien zu einer Theorie**
as **der musikalischen Erziehung** [Fundamentals for a
theory of music education], *Bericht über den I. musik-*
wissenschaftlichen Kongress der Deutschen Musik-
gesellschaft in Leipzig (Wiesbaden: Breitkopf & Härtel,
1926) 134–41. In German. See no. 120 in this volume.
Discusses the social and personal importance of music and lists the primary
goals of music education. To meet these goals, the establishment of a school
of music pedagogy is proposed. *(William Renwick)*

4578 LA FARGE, Georges de. **Le folklore à l'école:**
as **L'instrument musical populaire** [Folklore in the
school: The traditional musical instrument], *Travaux du*
Ier Congrès International de Folklore (Tours: Arrault et
Cie, 1938) 401–03. In French. See no. 251 in this
volume.
Presents resolutions for the preservation and dissemination of traditional
music, focusing on the need for education.

4579 LABROCA, Mario. **Valeur éducative des cycles**
as **musicaux illustrés** [Educational value of illustrated
musical cycles], *Cahiers d'études de radio-télévision*
3-4 (1955) 396–400. In French. See no. 334 in this
volume.
An assessment by the codirector of music programming at Radio Audizioni
Italiana (RAI).

4580 LAGUARDA Y FENORELLA, Juan J. **La**
as **enseñanza de la música sagrada** [The teaching of
religious music], *Crónica y actas oficiales del tercer*
Congreso Nacional de Música Sagrada (Barcelona: La
Hormiga de Oro, 1913) 38–50. In Spanish. See no. 78 in
this volume.
The pedagogy of religious music must take into consideration the aesthetic
premises that distinguish it from secular music.

4581 LANDOWSKI, W.L. **Le rôle actuel du disque**
as **radiodiffusé dans l'enseignement de la**
musique [The current role of record broadcasts in music education], *Cahiers d'études de radio-télévision* 3-4
(1955) 458–61. In French. See no. 334 in this volume.
Radio provides frequent opportunities to hear and analyze masterworks. It
also gives young musicians opportunities to listen to great soloists, and it
contributes to music education in general by broadcasting a wide repertoire.

4582 LANGEVIN, Vige. **L'enseignement, en France,**
as **de la musique et la danse populaires françaises**
[French traditional dance and music instruction in

France], *Journal of the International Folk Music Coun-*
cil V (1953) 47–48. In French. See no. 314 in this
volume.
Summary of a paper. Discusses pedagogy for both children and adults, with
attention to the significance of regional styles.

4583 LAWLER, Vanett. **New trends in music educa-**
as **tion,** *Music in education* (Paris: UNESCO, 1955)
87–94. See no. 322 in this volume.
Lists historic and current trends in music education in the U.S., with particular attention to administrative issues. A French-language version is cited
as no. 4584 in this volume. *(Elizabeth A. Wright)*

4584 LAWLER, Vanett. **Nouvelles tendances de**
as **l'éducation musicale** [New trends in music educa-
tion], *La musique dans l'éducation* (Paris: UNESCO;
Colin, 1955) 92–100. In French. See no. 323 in this
volume.
An English-language version is abstracted as no. 4583 in this volume.

4585 LECHNER, Anna. **Autriche** [Austria], *L'éducation*
as *musicale trait d'union entre les peuples: Rapports et*
discours sur l'éducation musicale dans les divers pays
(Praha: Orbis, 1937) 22–25. In French. See no. 232 in
this volume.

⟶ **[Leiden, 1931] The establishment of schools of**
secular music by Ming Huang of the T'ang dy-
nasty. By Evangeline Dora EDWARDS. See no. 2656
in this volume.

4586 LENSING, Adolf. **Jugend, Film und Bild:**
as **Zwischen Pädagogik und Kunst** [Youth, film, and
image: Between pedagogy and art], *Musische Jugend*
und technische Mittler (Remscheid: Landesarbeitsgemeinschaft Jugendmusik Nordrhein-Westfalen,
1957) 85–89. In German. See no. 380 in this volume.
Broad discussion of the potential role of cinema in arts education.

4587 LLONGUERAS BADÍA, Juan. **Espagne** [Spain],
as *L'éducation musicale trait d'union entre les peuples:*
Rapports et discours sur l'éducation musicale dans les
divers pays (Praha: Orbis, 1937) 39–50. In French. See
no. 232 in this volume.

4588 LÖHNER, Ina. **Psycho-physiologischer**
as **Musikunterricht** [Psychophysiological music in-
struction], *Zweiter Musikpädagogischer Kongress:*
Vorträge und Referate (Berlin: Klavier-Lehrer, 1904)
40–48. In German. See no. 43 in this volume.

4589 MARTENOT, Maurice. **The Martenot method,**
as *Music in education* (Paris: UNESCO, 1955) 232–41.
See no. 322 in this volume.
Summarizes the author's pedagogical method; a full discussion is given in
Principes fondamentaux d'éducation musicale et leur application (Paris,
1952). A French-language version is cited as no. 4590 in this volume.

4590 MARTENOT, Maurice. **Le méthode Martenot**
as [The Martenot method], *La musique dans l'éducation*
(Paris: UNESCO; Colin, 1955) 242–51. In French. See
no. 323 in this volume.
An English-language version is abstracted as no. 4589 in this volume.

4591 MARTIENSSEN-LOHMANN, Franziska.
as **Übereinstimmung und Abweichung in der**
Stimmausbildung der männlichen und der

weiblichen Stimme [Commonalities and differences in vocal training for male and for female voices], *Bericht über den Internationalen Kongreß Singen und Sprechen* (München: Oldenbourg, 1938) 143–47. In German. See no. 257 in this volume.

4592 MARTIN, Frank. **De la rythmique: La méthode**
as **Jaques-Dalcroze** [Eurythmics: The Jaques-Dalcroze method], *La musique dans l'éducation* (Paris: UNESCO; Colin, 1955) 235–42. In French. See no. 323 in this volume.
An English-language version is abstracted as no. 4593 in this volume.

4593 MARTIN, Frank. **Eurhythmics: The Jaques-**
as **Dalcroze method,** *Music in education* (Paris: UNESCO, 1955) 225–31. See no. 322 in this volume.
Presents a general account of the eurythmic method of Émile Jaques-Dalcroze. A French-language version is cited as no. 4592 in this volume.

4594 MARTINEAU, A.-Félix. **Enseignement du**
as **plain-chant et de la musique dans les séminaires du diocèse de Nantes** [Teaching of plainchant and music in the seminaries of the diocese of Nantes], *Congrès pour la restauration du plain-chant et de la musique d'église* (Paris: De Mourgues, 1862) 103–05. In French. See no. 3 in this volume.

4595 MATTHAY, Tobias. **Principles of pianoforte**
as **teaching,** *Report of the Fourth Congress of the International Musical Society* (London: Novello, 1912) 326–30. See no. 71 in this volume.
Offers pedagogical suggestions on various topics including practice methods, focusing the student's mind, rubato, shape, time, and pedaling. *(Mei-Mei Meng)*

4596 MAYER, Rudolf. **Grande-Bretagne** [Great Britain],
as *L'éducation musicale trait d'union entre les peuples: Rapports et discours sur l'éducation musicale dans les divers pays* (Praha: Orbis, 1937) 91–95. In French. See no. 232 in this volume.

4597 MÉFRAY, Clément. **La culture vocale** [Vocal
as training], *Compte rendu du Congrès général de musique sacrée: Aperçu général des préliminaires et du congrès, discours et conférences* (Strasbourg: Alsacien, 1922) 137–48. In French. See no. 96 in this volume.
Considers vocal training mainly from a physiological point of view.

4598 MÉFRAY, Clément. **Fondation et organisation**
as **d'une maîtrise** [The foundation and organization of choir schools], *Compte rendu du Congrès général de musique sacrée: Aperçu général des préliminaires et du congrès, discours et conférences* (Strasbourg: Alsacien, 1922) 153–64. In French. See no. 96 in this volume.
Proposes a model and offers practical advice.

4599 MENGEWEIN, Carl. **Die Ausbildung des**
as **musikalischen Gehörs** [The training of musical hearing], *Zweiter Musikpädagogischer Kongress: Vorträge und Referate* (Berlin: Klavier-Lehrer, 1904) 73–81. In German. See no. 43 in this volume.

4600 MESSERSCHMID, Felix. **Musik, Musiker-**
as **ziehung und politische Bildung** [Music, training in music, and political education], *Musik and Musikerziehung in der Reifezeit* (Mainz: Schott, 1959) 61–69. In German. See no. 412 in this volume.

Politics becomes degenerate without a broad nonpolitical foundation, for which the cultivation of the arts among laypersons—particularly music, in Germany—is an effective means: It awakens feelings among the alienated, turns people toward one another, and transcends political borders. The stronger, more vital, and more humane our cultural life is, the better we are enabled to resist totalitarian attempts to politicize it. *(David Bloom)*

4601 MEYER, Kathi. **Zur musikalischen Wissen-**
as **schaftslehre** [Music and scientific knowledge], *Bericht über den I. musikwissenschaftlichen Kongress der Deutschen Musikgesellschaft in Leipzig* (Wiesbaden: Breitkopf & Härtel, 1926) 113–19. In German. See no. 120 in this volume.
A general historical survey of the role of music education in society from the ancient Greeks to modern times. Questions of symbolism, ethos, and the significance of music as a liberal art are discussed, with attention to the ideas of Pythagoras, Plato, and Aristotle. *(William Renwick)*

4602 MILOJEVIĆ, Miloje. **Yougoslavie** [Yugoslavia],
as *L'éducation musicale trait d'union entre les peuples: Rapports et discours sur l'éducation musicale dans les divers pays* (Praha: Orbis, 1937) 175–83. In French. See no. 232 in this volume.

4603 MOLL, Adolf. **Wie können wir die Phonetik**
as **dem Sing- und Sprechunterricht dienstbar machen?** [How can we make phonetics useful in the teaching of singing and speech?], *Bericht über den Internationalen Kongreß Singen und Sprechen* (München: Oldenbourg, 1938) 128–32. In German. See no. 257 in this volume.

4604 MOSER, Hans Joachim. **Lage und Ziele der**
as **Musikpädagogik aus wissenschaftlicher Schau** [The situation of music pedagogy and its goals, viewed from a scientific standpoint], *Bericht über den Internationalen musikwissenschaftlichen Kongress* (Kassel: Bärenreiter, 1954) 27–32. In German. See no. 319 in this volume.
Assesses West German music education (1953). There is an overemphasis on producing piano teachers, and a shortage of teachers for other instruments such as the accordion. Much important research done in foreign countries needs to be introduced, and outreach efforts to develop greater interest in music on the part of the wider public (as pioneered in the U.S.) should be considered. A more nuanced appreciation of the musical training appropriate for a particular type of student is necessary. Lastly, contemporary music must have its place in the curriculum. *(Carl Skoggard)*

4605 MOSER, Hans Joachim. **Die Musikwissenschaft**
as **in der Ausbildung des Kirchenmusikers** [Musicology in the training of the church musician], *Bericht über den Deutschen Kongreß für Kirchenmusik* (Kassel: Bärenreiter, 1928) 48–54. In German. See no. 135 in this volume.
Discusses the ways in which both Catholic and Protestant church musicians are helped by a thorough knowledge of such disciplines as historical musicology (including performance practice), acoustics and perceptual psychology, aesthetics, and ethnomusicology. *(David Bloom)*

4606 MÜNNICH, Richard. **Die Behandlung musik-**
as **ästhetischer Probleme in der höheren Schule** [The handling of problems of musical aesthetics in high school], *Bericht über den I. musikwissenschaftlichen Kongress der Deutschen Musikgesellschaft in Leipzig* (Wiesbaden: Breitkopf & Härtel, 1926) 159–64. In German. See no. 120 in this volume.
Discusses methods for addressing basic questions about the perception and meaning of music.

4607 NEJEDLÝ, Zdeněk. **Tchécoslovaquie** [Czecho-
as   slovakia], *L'éducation musicale trait d'union entre les
         peuples: Rapports et discours sur l'éducation musicale
         dans les divers pays* (Praha: Orbis, 1937) 163–64. In
         French. See no. 232 in this volume.

4608 NOLL, Günther. **Jean-Jacques Rousseau als
as   Musikerzieher** [Jean-Jacques Rousseau as music ed-
         ucator], *Bericht über den internationalen musikwissen-
         schaftlichen Kongreß* (Kassel: Bärenreiter, 1963)
         282–84. In German. See no. 452 in this volume.
Rousseau regarded ear training on the basis of relative pitch perception as
the starting point of all music education. He believed in careful voice training. He held that music education's most important function is aesthetic development, and that it must help children to develop their individual creative power, through improvisation. His ideas continue to be relevant.
(David Bloom)

4609 OBERBORBECK, Felix. **Pädagogische
as   Berufsmöglichkeiten des Musikwissen-
         schaftlers** [Career possibilities in teaching for the mu-
         sicologist], *Bericht über den internationalen musik-
         wissenschaftlichen Kongreß* (Kassel: Bärenreiter,
         1963) 331–32. In German. See no. 452 in this volume.
Lists the types of educational institutions in Germany that offer jobs to musicologists.

4610 OREL, Dobroslav. **Tchécoslovaquie** [Czechoslo-
as   vakia], *L'éducation musicale trait d'union entre les
         peuples: Rapports et discours sur l'éducation musicale
         dans les divers pays* (Praha: Orbis, 1937) 165–66. In
         French. See no. 232 in this volume.

4611 OVERATH, Johannes. **Erziehung zur Kirchen-
as   musik an den höheren Schulen und Seminaren**
         [Church music education in upper-level schools and
         seminaries], *Zweiter internationaler Kongress für
         katholische Kirchenmusik: Zu Ehren des Heiligen
         Papstes Pius X* (Wien: conference, 1955) 303–09. In
         German. See no. 339 in this volume.
Discusses reasons for and methods of providing a thorough education in
church music, and music in general, to Roman Catholic youth, with particular attention to the musical needs of potential priests in Catholic boarding
schools at the secondary and seminary levels. *(David Bloom)*

4612 PANNAIN, Guido. **Orientamento storico
as   nell'insegnamento della composizione** [Histori-
         cal orientation in the teaching of composition], *Atti del
         sesto Congresso internazionale di musica* (Firenze:
         Barbèra, 1950) 70–73. In Italian. See no. 291 in this
         volume.
Examines the classic conflict between the teacher of composition and the
student, between didactics and art. One who studies composition has as a
master not the teacher, but history itself. *(Susan Poliniak)*

4613 PAPE, Heinrich. **Zur psychologischen
as   Grundlegung der Musikerziehung** [The psycho-
         logical foundation of music education], *Musik in Volks-
         schule und Lehrerbildung* (Kassel; Basel: Bärenreiter,
         1961) 75–87. In German. See no. 416 in this volume.

4614 PARENT, Hortense. **De l'enseignement
as   élémentaire du piano en France au point de
         vue de la vulgarisation de la musique** [Elemen-
         tary piano teaching in France from the point of view of
         the popularization of music], *Congrès international
         d'histoire de la musique: Documents, mémoires et vœux*

(Solesmes: St. Pierre; Paris: Fischbacher, 1901)
289–95. In French. See no. 32 in this volume.
Music students should be trained in performance skills, addressing each
type of difficulty separately (e.g., rhythm, reading music, manual dexter-
ity), and piano instructors should have studied pedagogical methods.

4615 PARIBATRA, Marsi. **The performer's point of
as   view,** *Music in education* (Paris: UNESCO, 1955)
         300–03. See no. 322 in this volume.
Discusses the Jeunesses Musicales Thailand, which is organized on principles aiming at overcoming the problems of poorly prepared audiences to
perform an educational function. A French-language version is cited as no.
4616 in this volume. *(David Bloom)*

4616 PARIBATRA, Marsi. **Le point de vue de
as   l'interprète** [The performer's point of view], *La
         musique dans l'éducation* (Paris: UNESCO; Colin,
         1955) 312–15. In French. See no. 323 in this volume.
An English-language version is abstracted as no. 4615 in this volume.

4617 PETRASSI, Goffredo. **L'insegnamento della
as   composizione** [Teaching composition], *Atti del sesto
         Congresso internazionale di musica* (Firenze: Barbèra,
         1950) 116–20. In Italian. See no. 291 in this volume.
Discusses the difficulties in teaching composition to young minds; the issues regarding reaching their innermost sensibilities are discussed, as are
standard methods of doing so. Training that involves the creation of a solid
foundation in technique is necessary to composition students, but students
should not simply repeat the past, so to speak, but should stay in the present
in terms of their own work. Composition students must be taught good in-
stincts that can be used on their own. *(Susan Poliniak)*

4618 PFRIMMER, Albert. **L'utilité de la méthode
as   Jaques-Dalcroze pour le chef d'orchestre et les
         musiciens d'orchestre** [The utility of the
         Jaques-Dalcroze method for conductors and orchestral
         musicians], *Compte rendu du Ier Congrès du rythme*
         (Genève: Institut Jaques-Dalcroze, 1926) 179–95. In
         French. See no. 123 in this volume.
The Dalcroze method is ideal for all orchestra members, as it helps them to
develop a greater sense of melody and harmony, in addition to improving
their sense of rhythm.

4619 **[Piano instruction] Arbeitsgemeinschaften für
as   Musikerziehung/Study groups/Groupes de
         travail/Arbetsgrupper** [Study groups for music in-
         struction], *Dokumentation* (Frankfurt am Main:
         Fördergemeinschaft Klavier, 1966) 94–104. In Ger-
         man, English, French, and Swedish. See no. 494 in this
         volume.
Individual committee reports on piano pedagogy presented at the
Europiano Kongress, Berlin 1965.

4620 PIOTROWSKI, W. **Pologne** [Poland], *L'éducation
as   musicale trait d'union entre les peuples: Rapports et
         discours sur l'éducation musicale dans les divers pays*
         (Praha: Orbis, 1937) 113–17. In French. See no. 232 in
         this volume.

4621 PIZZETTI, Ildebrando. **Gli istituti musicali
as   italiani** [Italian musical institutions], *La vita musicale
         dell'Italia d'oggi* (Torino: Fratelli Bocca, 1921) 78–90.
         In Italian. See no. 97 in this volume.
Suggests various reforms, including a four-year course in literary culture to
be taught in each institution, increased requirements for solfège and dicta-
tion, and a general revision of educational programs and examinations in
view of the needs of modern music and advances in instrument construction. *(Michael Adelson)*

4622 PREUSSNER, Eberhard. **L'éducation musicale**
as **en Europe** [Music education in Europe], *La musique dans l'éducation* (Paris: UNESCO; Colin, 1955) 60–67. In French. See no. 323 in this volume.
An English-language version is abstracted as no. 4623 in this volume.

4623 PREUSSNER, Eberhard. **Music education in**
as **Europe,** *Music in education* (Paris: UNESCO, 1955) 58–65. See no. 322 in this volume.
Presents a historical overview, culminating with the current revival of school music and the use of technology to bridge the gap between popular and art musics. A French-language version is cited as no. 4622 in this volume. *(Elizabeth A. Wright)*

4624 PRÉVOST, A. **Éducation musicale populaire:**
as **Projet d'utilisation rationnelle de la musique du 1ᵉʳ Régiment de Guides** [Popular music education: A project for rational use of the music of the 1ᵉʳ Régiment de Guides], *La musique et le peuple: Rapports, suggestions, voeux* (Bruxelles: Ministère des Sciences et des Arts, 1932) 61–71. In French. See no. 195 in this volume.
The leader of the celebrated military band outlines a project for creating a national symphony orchestra.

4625 PRIEUR, O.S.B. **École d'orgue et de musique**
as **religieuse** [Organ and religious music education], *Compte rendu du Congrès général de musique sacrée: Aperçu général des préliminaires et du congrès, discours et conférences* (Strasbourg: Alsacien, 1922) 231–52. In French. See no. 96 in this volume.
Argues for the establishment of a school of organ and religious music in each diocese, and addresses the practical difficulties that will have to be overcome.

4626 PRINGSHEIM, H.E. **Japon** [Japan], *L'éducation*
as *musicale trait d'union entre les peuples: Rapports et discours sur l'éducation musicale dans les divers pays* (Praha: Orbis, 1937) 102–08. In French. See no. 232 in this volume.

4627 QUITIN, José. **L'intervention du gouverne-**
as **ment hollandais dans la création du Conservatoire Royal de Musique de Liège en 1826** [The intervention of the Dutch government in the creation of the Conservatoire Royal de Musique in Liège in 1826], *Société Internationale de Musicologie, cinquième congrès/Internationale Gesellschaft für Musikwissenschaft, fünfter Kongreß/International Society for Musical Research, Fifth Congress* (Amsterdam: Vereniging voor Nederlandse Muziekgeschiedenis, 1953) 327–34. In French. See no. 316 in this volume.

4628 RABSCH, Edgar. **Instrumentenkunde und ver-**
as **gleichende Musikwissenschaft in der Schule** [Knowledge of instruments and similar musical studies in school], *Bericht über den I. musikwissenschaftlichen Kongress der Deutschen Musikgesellschaft in Leipzig* (Wiesbaden: Breitkopf & Härtel, 1926) 98–100. In German. See no. 120 in this volume.
Presents a method for teaching the development of instruments by family and by cultural region.

4629 RABSCH, Edgar. **Musikwissenschaft in der**
as **Schule: Zum Problem einer Musikbiologie** [Musicology in the school: On the problem of a music biology], *Bericht über den I. musikwissenschaftlichen Kongress der Deutschen Musikgesellschaft in Leipzig*

(Wiesbaden: Breitkopf & Härtel, 1926) 165–67. In German. See no. 120 in this volume.
Suggests a pedagogical approach based on the organic development of music. Common practice music can then be seen as an outgrowth of a longer history. *(William Renwick)*

4630 RAGHAVAN, Venkatarama. **L'état actuel de**
as **l'éducation musicale en Asie: L'example de l'Inde** [The current state of music education in Asia: The example of India], *La musique dans l'éducation* (Paris: UNESCO; Colin, 1955) 76–92. In French. See no. 323 in this volume.
An English-language version is abstracted as no. 4631 in this volume.

4631 RAGHAVAN, Venkatarama. **The present state**
as **of music education in the Asiatic continent: India,** *Music in education* (Paris: UNESCO, 1955) 72–86. See no. 322 in this volume.
Surveys the history of music pedagogy in India from ancient times through the development of modern academic institutions, with attention to the concept in the Carnatic tradition of the *vidvān* or fully accomplished musician as teacher. Indian music needs to be better understood in the West. A French-language version is cited as no. 4630 in this volume.
(Elizabeth A. Wright)

4632 REICHEL, Bernard. **L'improvisation** [Improvi-
as sation], *Deuxième Congrès international du rythme et de la rythmique* (Genève: Institut Jaques-Dalcroze, 1966) 148–53. In French. See no. 502 in this volume.
Discusses improvisation as a pedagogical tool, mentioning the work of Émile Jaques-Dalcroze.

4633 REICHENBACH, Herman. **U.R.S.S.** [The Soviet
as Union], *L'éducation musicale trait d'union entre les peuples: Rapports et discours sur l'éducation musicale dans les divers pays* (Praha: Orbis, 1937) 167–74. In French. See no. 232 in this volume.

4634 RIEMANN, Ludwig. **Die Notwendigkeit der**
as **Einführung der Akustik in den Lehrplan** [The need for the introduction of acoustics into the curriculum], *Zweiter Musikpädagogischer Kongress: Vorträge und Referate* (Berlin: Klavier-Lehrer, 1904) 67–72. In German. See no. 43 in this volume.

4635 ROGER-DUCASSE, Jean Jules. **France** [France],
as *L'éducation musicale trait d'union entre les peuples: Rapports et discours sur l'éducation musicale dans les divers pays* (Praha: Orbis, 1937) 73–79. In French. See no. 232 in this volume.

4636 RÜHL. **Ausbildung und Schulung des Opern-**
as **chorsängers im Hinblick auf die Praxis des Repertoiretheaters** [Training and schooling of singers for opera choruses, in view of the experience of the repertory company], *Bericht über den Internationalen Kongreß Singen und Sprechen* (München: Oldenbourg, 1938) 178–81. In German. See no. 257 in this volume.
Singers need practical experience in choral singing at the student level, vocal training both from the physiological and expressive points of view, knowledge of the choral literature, and training in articulatory phonetics, so that strictly technical issues are never a problem. *(David Bloom)*

4637 RÜHLMANN, Franz. **Ideale Schuleinrich-**
as **tungen für Opernnachwuchs** [Ideal school arrangements for the next generation of opera], *Bericht über den Internationalen Kongreß Singen und Sprechen*

(München: Oldenbourg, 1938) 147–51. In German. See no. 257 in this volume.

In addition to their vocal training, opera singers need to be trained in the functions of theatrical representation. School opera performance by pupils at elementary and secondary levels should receive more support; at the *Hochschule* level there should be a *Reichsakademie* institution bringing dance, theater, and music instruction together under a single roof. *(David Bloom)*

4638 SACHS, Curt. **France** [France], *L'éducation musi-*
as *cale trait d'union entre les peuples: Rapports et discours sur l'éducation musicale dans les divers pays* (Praha: Orbis, 1937) 80–84. In French. See no. 232 in this volume.

4639 SANTA CRUZ, Domingo. **Music and interna-**
as **tional understanding,** *Music in education* (Paris: UNESCO, 1955) 34–40. See no. 322 in this volume.
In addition to its narrow role in the training of professional musicians, music education plays a wider role in the development of international understanding. It should include the study of non-Western musics; contributions that can be made by the International Music Council are outlined. A French-language version is cited as no. 4640 in this volume.

4640 SANTA CRUZ, Domingo. **La musique et la**
as **compréhension internationale** [Music and international understanding], *La musique dans l'éducation* (Paris: UNESCO; Colin, 1955) 35–41. In French. See no. 323 in this volume.
An English-language version is abstracted as no. 4639 in this volume.

4641 SCHERMALL, Herbert. **Die Schallplatte: Ein**
as **modernes Bildungsmittel** [The record: A modern medium of education], *Musische Jugend und technische Mittler* (Remscheid: Landesarbeitsgemeinschaft Jugendmusik Nordrhein-Westfalen, 1957) 58–70. *Illus.* In German. See no. 380 in this volume.
Discusses the educational value of sound recordings of musical and dramatic works. Detailed examples are drawn from school classes' use of the collections, listening booths, and auditorium of the Amerika-Gedenkbibliothek in Berlin's Mitte district, opened 1954. *(David Bloom)*

4642 SCHMID, Reinhold. **Chorerziehung zur**
as **Moderne** [Choral education to modernity], *Musikerziehung: Zeitschrift der Musikerzieher Österreichs* special issue (1953) 26–27. In German. See no. 317 in this volume.

4643 SEEGER, Charles. **Projet de création d'une**
as **société internationale pour l'éducation musi-**
cale [Plan for the creation of an International Society for Music Education], *La musique dans l'éducation* (Paris: UNESCO; Colin, 1955) 339–45. In French. See no. 323 in this volume.
An English-language version is abstracted as no. 4644 in this volume.

4644 SEEGER, Charles. **A proposal to found an In-**
as **ternational Society for Music Education,** *Music in education* (Paris: UNESCO, 1955). See no. 322 in this volume.
A plan for the organization, which was constituted at the conference. A French-language version is cited as no. 4643 in this volume.

4645 SÉRENT, Antoine de. **Rapport sur l'en-**
as **seignement du Latin liturgique** [Report on teaching liturgical Latin], *Compte rendu du Congrès général de musique sacrée: Aperçu général des préliminaires et du congrès, discours et conférences* (Strasbourg:

Alsacien, 1922) 177–84. In French. See no. 96 in this volume.
Proposes practical methods of teaching liturgical Latin to singers without burdening them with complex grammar.

4646 SMITH, Carleton Sprague. **États-Unis**
as **d'Amérique** [The United States of America], *L'éducation musicale trait d'union entre les peuples: Rapports et discours sur l'éducation musicale dans les divers pays* (Praha: Orbis, 1937) 55–60. In French. See no. 232 in this volume.

4647 SMITH, Carleton Sprague. **Grande-Bretagne**
as [Great Britain], *L'éducation musicale trait d'union entre les peuples: Rapports et discours sur l'éducation musicale dans les divers pays* (Praha: Orbis, 1937) 96–101. In French. See no. 232 in this volume.

4648 SOMERVELL, Arthur. **Musical education in**
as **England,** *Haydn-Zentenarfeier* (Leipzig: Breitkopf & Härtel; Wien: Artaria, 1909) 496–98. See no. 65 in this volume.
Discusses primary and secondary schools of the early 20th c.

4649 SOMIGLI, Carlo. **Aus welchen Werken soll die**
as **vollständige Ausbildung der Gesangsorgane**
erreicht werden? [Which works should contribute to a comprehensive training of the voice?], *Zweiter Musikpädagogischer Kongress: Vorträge und Referate* (Berlin: Klavier-Lehrer, 1904) 126–33. In German. See no. 43 in this volume.

4650 SOMMER, Otto. **Das Singen im Dienste der**
as **Volkserziehung** [Singing in the service of educating the people], *Bericht über den Internationalen Kongreß Singen und Sprechen* (München: Oldenbourg, 1938) 181–84. In German. See no. 257 in this volume.
Remarks on the importance of vocal pedagogy in the National Socialist program of total education, with particular attention to the irreplaceable role of singing in the development of breath capacity and control. *(David Bloom)*

4651 SPELMAN, Leslie Pratt. **Organ teaching:**
as **Methods and materials,** *Organ and choral aspects and prospects* (London: Hinrichsen, 1958) 54–62. See no. 375 in this volume.
Beginners' texts, techniques, registration, practicing, the playing of hymn tunes, independence, and artistry are discussed as teaching challenges.

4652 STIEGLITZ, Olga. **Die Musikästhetik und ihre**
as **praktische Einführung** [Music aesthetics and its practical introduction], *Zweiter Musikpädagogischer Kongress: Vorträge und Referate* (Berlin: Klavier-Lehrer, 1904) 49–58. In German. See no. 43 in this volume.

4653 STIVEN, Frederick Benjamin. **États-Unis**
as **d'Amérique** [The United States of America], *L'éducation musicale trait d'union entre les peuples: Rapports et discours sur l'éducation musicale dans les divers pays* (Praha: Orbis, 1937) 51–54. In French. See no. 232 in this volume.

4654 STRECK. **Die Stimmdiagnose als Grundlage**
as **der modernen Stimmbildung und Hilfsmittel**
gegen pädagogische Pfuscherarbeit [Vocal diagnosis as a foundation for modern voice training and an

aid against pedagogical blunders], *Bericht über den Internationalen Kongreß Singen und Sprechen* (München: Oldenbourg, 1938) 140–43. In German. See no. 257 in this volume.

4655 STRICH, Wolfgang. **Wege zu musischem Tun**
as **über die technischen Mittler** [Paths to artistic endeavor through the technological media], *Musische Jugend und technische Mittler* (Remscheid: Landesarbeitsgemeinschaft Jugendmusik Nordrhein-Westfalen, 1957) 121–26. In German. See no. 380 in this volume.
On the basis of the author's experience as an art teacher at the Wannseeheim für Jugendarbeit, Berlin, and director of holiday facilities for apprentices in the spa resort of Scheidegg im Allgäu, evaluates the use in encouraging artistic expression of tape recorder, cinema, record, and opaque projector (epidiascope). *(David Bloom)*

4656 SZABOLCSI, Bence. **Die Volksmusik in der**
as **Schule und in der Nachschulsbildung** [Traditional music in school and in continuing education], *Travaux du Ier Congrès International de Folklore* (Tours: Arrault et Cie, 1938) 394–96. In German. See no. 251 in this volume.
Briefly discusses the applicability of Zoltán Kodály's ideas.

4657 TÉREY-KUTHY, Sándor. **La musique**
as **populaire dans la vie practique et dans l'enseignement** [Traditional music in everyday life and in teaching], *Art populaire: Travaux artistiques et scientifiques du Ier Congrès international des arts populaires* (Paris: Duchartre, 1931) 101–02. In French. See no. 152 in this volume.
Not only should traditional songs continue to be researched, they should be sung—especially in the schools.

4658 TISSIER, Joseph-Marie. **Chant liturgique et**
as **éducation chrétienne** [Liturgical singing and Christian education], *Comptes rendus, rapports et vœux du Congrès parisien et régional de chant liturgique et de musique d'église* (Paris: Schola Cantorum, 1912) 149–60. In French. See no. 75 in this volume.

4659 TROMMER. **Reform der Gesangspädagogik**
as [A reform of the pedagogy of singing], *Bericht über den Internationalen Kongreß Singen und Sprechen* (München: Oldenbourg, 1938) 137–40. In German. See no. 257 in this volume.
With very few exceptions, the literature on vocal pedagogy fails to provide clear guidance, and should be purged. A standard reference is needed, together with a new teaching institution for the transmission of clarified principles. *(David Bloom)*

4660 TURCHI, Guido. **Cause, effetti ed alcuni rimedi**
as [Causes, effects, and some remedies], *Atti del sesto Congresso internazionale di musica* (Firenze: Barbèra, 1950) 59–67. In Italian. See no. 291 in this volume.
Discusses the issues involving the incorporation of contemporary techniques into the teaching of composition and the codification of contemporary music in regards to pedagogy. Compositional pedagogy in Italy in general must take new directions. *(Susan Poliniak)*

4661 TUTHILL, Burnet C. **Report of Subcommittee**
as **on Interchange of Professors and Students in the Field of Music,** *Report of the Committee of the Conference on Inter-American Relations in the Field of Music* (Washington, D.C.: United States Department of State, 1940) 35–36. See no. 271 in this volume.

Topics covered include availability and sources of scholarships for Latin American students and the evaluation of candidates based on a forthcoming survey of Latin American schools by Carleton Sprague Smith. Significantly, no professors applied for exchanges available through the Buenos Aires convention for 1940-41. *(Howard Cinnamon)*

4662 VALENTIN, Erich. **Musikwissenschaft und**
as **Musikpädagogik** [Musicology and music pedagogy], *Musik and Musikerziehung in der Reifezeit* (Mainz: Schott, 1959) 107–12. In German. See no. 412 in this volume.

⟶ VERESS, Sándor. **Folk music in musical and general education.** See no. 1017 in this volume.

4663 VILLA-LOBOS, Heitor. **Brésil** [Brazil],
as *L'éducation musicale trait d'union entre les peuples: Rapports et discours sur l'éducation musicale dans les divers pays* (Praha: Orbis, 1937) 26–32. In French. See no. 232 in this volume.

4664 VUILLERMOZ, Émile. **La musique mécanique**
as **et la culture musicale** [Mechanical music and musical culture], *Atti del primo Congresso internazionale di musica* (Firenze: Le Monnier, 1935) 93–103. In French; summary in Italian. See no. 203 in this volume.
A crisis of taste and musical culture arises from the poor quality of broadcasts, recordings, and sound reproduction. However, if quality improves, sound recordings will contribute to ear training, elementary pedagogy (particularly the teaching of music history), and applied instruction (providing accompaniment for amateur instrumentalists). *(Nathaniel Rudykoff)*

4665 WADDINGTON, Geoffrey. **La radio, moyen**
as **d'éducation musicale au Canada** [Radio as a means of music education in Canada], *La musique dans l'éducation* (Paris: UNESCO; Colin, 1955) 263–65. In French. See no. 323 in this volume.
An English-language version is abstracted as no. 4666 in this volume.

4666 WADDINGTON, Geoffrey. **The radio as a**
as **means of music education in Canada,** *Music in education* (Paris: UNESCO, 1955) 252–55. See no. 322 in this volume.
Surveys the use of radio broadcasts by the Canadian Broadcasting Corporation to promote music appreciation in schools. A French-language version is cited as no. 4665 in this volume. *(Elizabeth A. Wright)*

4667 WALTER, Arnold. **L'enseignement de la**
as **musique sur le continent américain** [Music education on the American continent], *La musique dans l'éducation* (Paris: UNESCO; Colin, 1955) 68–76. In French. See no. 323 in this volume.
An English-language version is abstracted as no. 4668 in this volume.

4668 WALTER, Arnold. **Music education on the**
as **American continent,** *Music in education* (Paris: UNESCO, 1955) 65–72. See no. 322 in this volume.
Discusses the growth in the U.S. of the orchestra, concert life, music camps, and musical training institutions. During the decades from 1920 to 1950, music education in the U.S. progressed further and faster than at any previous time or place. A French-language version is cited as no. 4667 in this volume. *(Elizabeth A. Wright)*

4669 WARNER, Theodor. **Didaktik und Methodik**
as **des Musikunterrichts** [Didactics and methodology of music instruction], *Musik in Volksschule und Lehrerbildung* (Kassel; Basel: Bärenreiter, 1961) 57–68. In German. See no. 416 in this volume.

4670
as

WEBER-BELL, Nana. **Gesangspädagogische Reformen** [Reforms in vocal pedagogy], *Zweiter Musikpädagogischer Kongress: Vorträge und Referate* (Berlin: Klavier-Lehrer, 1904) 134–45. In German. See no. 43 in this volume.

4671
as

WICART, Alexis. **La phonation optime pour la parole et le chant: Les contrôles auditifs et visuels pour son enseignement** [Optimal voice production for speech and singing: The auditive and visual controls for teaching it]. Intro. by Marcelle GÉRAR, *Bericht über den Internationalen Kongreß Singen und Sprechen* (München: Oldenbourg, 1938) 122–27. In French. See no. 257 in this volume.

4672
as

WILLFORT, Egon Stuart. **An encyclopædic method of pianoforte teaching,** *Report of the Fourth Congress of the International Musical Society* (London: Novello, 1912) 346–54. *Illus., music.* See no. 71 in this volume.

The present system of piano teaching is inadequate and would benefit from historical, theoretical, and technical knowledge. An example of a revised teaching process is provided, together with a summary of scales. *(Mei-Mei Meng)*

4673
as

WILSON, Steuart. **Le rôle de la musique populaire dans l'éducation** [The role of traditional music in education], *La musique dans l'éducation* (Paris: UNESCO; Colin, 1955) 47–53. In French. See no. 323 in this volume.

An English-language version is abstracted as no. 4674 in this volume.

4674
as

WILSON, Steuart. **The role of folk music in education,** *Music in education* (Paris: UNESCO, 1955) 46–52. See no. 322 in this volume.

Lists recommendations of the fifth annual conference of the International Folk Music Council, held in London in 1952. A French-language version is cited as no. 4673 in this volume. *(Elizabeth A. Wright)*

⟶ WIORA, Walter. **Die geschichtliche Sonderstellung der abendländischen Musik** [The special historical position of Western music]. See no. 1023 in this volume.

4675
as

WULFF, Adolf. **Musik im Schulfunk, Hilfe im Unterricht** [Music on educational radio, assistance in instruction], *Musische Jugend und technische Mittler* (Remscheid: Landesarbeitsgemeinschaft Jugendmusik Nordrhein-Westfalen, 1957) 50–53. In German. See no. 380 in this volume.

Examples are drawn from the author's work with the educational radio division of Norddeutscher Rundfunk, Hamburg.

71 Preschool, primary, and secondary schools

4676
as

AMTMANN, Paul. **Spiel im Musikunterricht** [Playing in music classes], *Musik and Musikerziehung in der Reifezeit* (Mainz: Schott, 1959) 163–67. In German. See no. 412 in this volume.

Instrument playing as a part of music instruction should not be limited to the use of the Orff instrumentarium in the elementary school classroom, but carried on at the secondary level. The advantages are discussed, and practical solutions to particular problems are offered. *(David Bloom)*

4677
as

ARIMA, Daigoro. **Musical education as part of general education,** *Music: East and West* (Tōkyō: conference, 1961) 119–22. See no. 445 in this volume.

4678
as

BÆRISWYL, J. **La gymnastique rythmique et l'école primaire** [Rhythmic gymnastics and the primary school], *Compte rendu du Ier Congrès du rythme* (Genève: Institut Jaques-Dalcroze, 1926) 220–24. *Music, charts, diagr.* In French. See no. 123 in this volume.

Eurythmics serves as a foundation for mathematical perception.

4679
as

BARTL, Rudolf Heinz. **Die Harmonik in der Neuen Musik** [Harmony in the new music], *Musik and Musikerziehung in der Reifezeit* (Mainz: Schott, 1959) 265–75. In German. See no. 412 in this volume.

Discusses the teaching of 20th-c. harmonic practice to secondary school students, on the basis of examples from the piano literature.

4680
as

BENEDITO, Rafael. **Le folklore musical à l'école** [Musical folklore in school], *Congrès international des arts populaires/International congress of popular arts* (Paris: Institut international de coopération intellectuelle, 1928) 13. In French. See no. 153 in this volume.

Summary of the paper abstracted as no. 4681 in this volume.

4681
as

BENEDITO, Rafael. **Le folklore musical à l'école** [Musical folklore in school], *Art populaire: Travaux artistiques et scientifiques du Ier Congrès international des arts populaires* (Paris: Duchartre, 1931) 102. In French. See no. 152 in this volume.

Folk songs and dances of Spain are now being taught in the elementary schools of Madrid. A summary is cited as no. 4680 in this volume.

4682
as

BEREKOVEN, Hanns. **Musikunterricht in der Mittelschule** [Music instruction in middle schools], *Musik and Musikerziehung in der Reifezeit* (Mainz: Schott, 1959) 174–78. In German. See no. 412 in this volume.

Surveys developments in music instruction at the *Mittelschule* or *Realschule* level in the different West German Bundesländer since World War II.

4683
as

BERGER, Gregor. **Alban Bergs Violinkonzert** [Alban Berg's violin concerto], *Musik and Musikerziehung in der Reifezeit* (Mainz: Schott, 1959) 222–31. *Music, charts, diagr.* In German. See no. 412 in this volume.

Offers specific methodological suggestions for teaching the appreciation and analysis of the work at the lower secondary level of the German school system. *(David Bloom)*

4684
as

BLENSDORF, Charlotte. **Rhythmische Erziehung im Kindergarten: Ausführungen im Anschluss an eine praktische Vorführung mit Kindern im Alter von 4 bis 6 Jahren** [Rhythmic education in kindergarten: Remarks following a practical demonstration with children aged 4 to 6], *Compte rendu du Ier Congrès du rythme* (Genève: Institut Jaques-Dalcroze, 1926) 206–12. *Music.* In German. See no. 123 in this volume.

Includes basic rhythmic analyses of several children's songs.

4685
as

BORGUNYO, Manuel. **La musique, la radio et les enfants** [Music, radio, and children], *Compte rendu des travaux du Ier Congrès international d'art radiophonique* (Paris: conference, 1938). In French. See no. 244 in this volume.

4686
as

BORNOFF, George. **On developing a string program,** *Music skills* (Washington, D.C.: Catholic University of America, 1958) 87–88. See no. 385 in this volume.

Outlines the concepts taught in each level of instruction for violin, viola, violoncello, and double bass. The first level incorporates the teaching of various bowing effects and techniques; the second includes mainly left-hand work (harmonics, double stops, and vibrato). *(Susan Poliniak)*

4687
as

BROCK, Hella. **Händel und die Schulmusik** [Händel and school music], *Händel-Ehrung der Deutschen Demokratischen Republik: Konferenzbericht* (Leipzig: VEB Deutscher Verlag für Musik, 1961) 223–28. In German. See no. 408 in this volume.

Reviews the role of Händel's works in the German elementary and secondary school music curriculum from ca. 1870, when he was regarded almost exclusively as a composer of church music, through the Third Reich, to the present, with attention to the question of approaches to and choice of works for performance and study in the comprehensive secondary schools of the German Democratic Republic. *(David Bloom)*

4688
as

CHÉRION, Augustin. **Y a-t-il utilité à reconstituer les maîtrises? Dans le cas de l'affirmative, quels sont les moyens pratiques pour parvenir à cette reconstitution?** [Is it useful to reconstitute the choir schools? If so, what practical means are there to arrive at this reconstitution?], *Congrès international de musique: Ire session—Exposition Universelle de 1900: Compte rendu, rapports, communications* (Paris: conference, 1901) 46–49. In French. See no. 29 in this volume.

The *maîtrise* (choir school) should offer its students both a theoretical and practical training.

4689
as

CVETKO, Dragotin. **Instruction in music as part of general education,** *Music: East and West* (Tōkyō: conference, 1961) 123–25. See no. 445 in this volume.

4690
as

DAMERINI, Adelmo. **La musica nella vita della scuola contemporanea** [Music in the life of the contemporary school], *Atti del quinto Congresso di musica* (Firenze: Barbèra, 1948) 62–66. In Italian. See no. 285 in this volume.

The public finds contemporary music unintelligible, a judgment that results from ignorance. One must be exposed to music at an early age in order to understand it, but the importance of such study has had little bearing on secondary school curricula. It is proposed that a course of study in music history be offered in junior high schools. An elementary but precise familiarity with the fundamentals of music and an ability to differentiate between styles can help create a musically aware public and can constitute basic training for those intending to pursue graduate studies in music history. *(Channan Willner)*

4691
as

EBERTH, Friedrich. **Lehraufgaben für den Musikunterricht der IV. bis VI. Klasse der Mittelschule** [Teaching responsibilities for music instruction in the fourth through sixth classes of the Mittelschule], *Musik and Musikerziehung in der Reifezeit* (Mainz: Schott, 1959) 178–88. In German. See no. 412 in this volume.

Discusses curricular requirements for music instruction for children in the fourth through sixth years (classes 8-10) of the German Mittelschule (Realschule) program and specific ideas for their implementation. *(David Bloom)*

4692
as

FERRARIA, Luigi Ernesto. **La rythmique en Italie** [Eurythmics in Italy], *Compte rendu du Ier Congrès du rythme* (Genève: Institut Jaques-Dalcroze, 1926) 216–19. In French. See no. 123 in this volume.

The Dalcroze method has been taught in Turin since 1909. Mussolini imposed eurythmics as a required subject in all girls' high schools.

4693
as

FORNEBERG, Erich. **Von Andersens Nachtigallen-Märchen zu Strawinskys Oper** *Le rossignol* [From Andersen's tale of the nightingale to Stravinsky's opera *Solovej*], *Musik and Musikerziehung in der Reifezeit* (Mainz: Schott, 1959) 232–41. *Music, transcr.* In German. See no. 412 in this volume.

An analysis of the literary origins and musical style of the opera from the standpoint of its potential use in music classes in the lower secondary level of the German school system. *(David Bloom)*

4694
as

FRANKENSTEIN, Alfred. **Instruction in music as part of general education,** *Music: East and West* (Tōkyō: conference, 1961) 110–14. See no. 445 in this volume.

4695
as

FRANZKE, Hans Reinhard. **Musik in Volksschule und Lehrerbildung früher und heute** [Music at the Volksschule level and teacher training in the past and today], *Musik in Volksschule und Lehrerbildung* (Kassel; Basel: Bärenreiter, 1961) 91–98. In German. See no. 416 in this volume.

4696
as

FRANZKE, Hans Reinhard. **Wege der Musikerziehung in der Berufsschule** [Approaches to music instruction in vocational schools], *Musik and Musikerziehung in der Reifezeit* (Mainz: Schott, 1959) 168–74. In German. See no. 412 in this volume.

The vocational secondary school (*Berufsschule*) has a shorter tradition in Germany than the *Gymnasium* or *Volksschule*, and its curriculum allows little time for music instruction. Proposals under these limiting conditions are offered for instruction in appreciation and in vocal and instrumental practice, and extracurricular activities including choirs, instrumental ensembles, and organized concert attendance. *(David Bloom)*

4697
as

GLÉYO (church musician). **L'éducation de l'oreille** [Ear training], *Compte rendu du Congrès général de musique sacrée: Aperçu général des préliminaires et du congrès, discours et conférences* (Strasbourg: Alsacien, 1922) 125–35. In French. See no. 96 in this volume.

Considers the vocal training of children from the viewpoints of duration, intonation, and beauty.

4698
as

GORON, Pierre. **La musique folklorique dans l'éducation** [Traditional music in education], *Journal of the International Folk Music Council* VI (1954) 47–48. In French. See no. 320 in this volume.

Summary of a paper discussing the policy initiatives of the Direction de Jeunesse et des Sports (formerly the Direction de la Culture Populaire) of the French Ministère de l'Éducation Nationale (Paris). *(James R. Cowdery)*

4699
as

GRAD, Toni. **Das Lichtbild im Musikunterricht** [Film in music instruction], *Musik and Musikerziehung in der Reifezeit* (Mainz: Schott, 1959) 280–86. In German. See no. 412 in this volume.

Discusses the use of sound films and slide projections in music instruction at the lower secondary level.

4700
as

GRAD, Toni. **Das Musikinstrument in Schule und Lehrerbildung** [Musical instruments in school and in teacher training], *Musik in Volksschule und Lehrerbildung* (Kassel; Basel: Bärenreiter, 1961) 49–56. In German. See no. 416 in this volume.

4701
as
HÄNSSEL, W. **Die Stimmbildung in der Volksschule** [Voice training in the Volksschule], *Zweiter Musikpädagogischer Kongress: Vorträge und Referate* (Berlin: Klavier-Lehrer, 1904) 245–63. In German. See no. 43 in this volume.

4702
as
HÄRÉN, Yngve. **Music in the elementary school in Sweden,** *Music in education* (Paris: UNESCO, 1955) 106–10. See no. 322 in this volume.
Swedish music education on the primary school level aims to strengthen a child's emotional and intellectual contact with music. In addition to providing basic music training in the classroom, most Swedish towns also have community music schools which operate after primary school hours. A French-language version is cited as no. 4703 in this volume.

(Elizabeth A. Wright)

4703
as
HÄRÉN, Yngve. **La musique à l'école primaire en Suède** [Music in the elementary school in Sweden], *La musique dans l'éducation* (Paris: UNESCO; Colin, 1955) 112–16. *Charts, diagr.* In French. See no. 323 in this volume.
An English-language version is abstracted as no. 4702 in this volume.

4704
as
HEER, Josef. **Persönlichkeit und Werk J. Haydns in den Klassen der Reifejahre (8. bis 10. Schuljahr)** [J. Haydn's personality and works in the years of adolescence (classes 8-10)], *Musik and Musikerziehung in der Reifezeit* (Mainz: Schott, 1959) 202–13. *Music.* In German. See no. 412 in this volume.
Illustrates the principle of using biographical discussion of composers to awaken adolescents' interest in the appreciation and analytic discussion of their works with the example of curriculum planning for the study of Haydn's life and compositions. *(David Bloom)*

4705
as
HEER, Joseph. **Musikerziehung in Volksschule und Lehrerbildung** [Music education at the Volksschule level and teacher training], *Musik in Volksschule und Lehrerbildung* (Kassel; Basel: Bärenreiter, 1961) 22–31. In German. See no. 416 in this volume.

4706
as
HENRY, André. **L'enseignement musical doit-il être confié au spécialiste ou à l'instituteur?** [Should music instruction be entrusted to the specialist or to the general teacher?], *La musique dans l'éducation* (Paris: UNESCO; Colin, 1955) 277–80. In French. See no. 323 in this volume.
An English-language version is abstracted as no. 4707 in this volume.

4707
as
HENRY, André. **Music education, by the specialist or the general teacher?,** *Music in education* (Paris: UNESCO, 1955) 267–70. See no. 322 in this volume.
Based on the Belgian experience, it can be concluded that instruction is best left to the regular classroom teacher in early grades, while older children should be taught by musicians with specialized teacher training. A French-language version is cited as no. 4706 in this volume.

4708
as
HERTZ, Odette. **Pour que les enfants apprennent à l'école comment chanter à l'église** [To the end of having children learn in school how to sing in church], *Revue musicale* 239-240 (1957) 267f. In French. See no. 378 in this volume.
Abridged version of the conference paper abstracted as no. 4709 in this volume.

4709
as
HERTZ, Odette. **Pour que tous nos enfants apprennent à l'école comment chanter à l'église** [To the end of having all our children learn in school how to sing in church], *Perspectives de la musique sacrée à la lumière de l'encyclique* Musicae sacrae disciplina (Paris: conference, 1959) 623–25. In French. See no. 379 in this volume.
The Ward method of teaching choral singing to children, developed by Justine Bayard Ward, includes instruction in Gregorian chant; instituting it in the primary school music curriculum would contribute to solving the problem of congregational participation in the sung Mass. An abridged version is cited as no. 4708 in this volume. *(David Bloom)*

4710
as
HORTON, J.W. **L'éducation musicale dans les établissements scolaires d'Angleterre** [Music education in the English school system], *La musique dans l'éducation* (Paris: UNESCO; Colin, 1955) 143–46. In French. See no. 323 in this volume.
An English-language version is abstracted as no. 4711 in this volume.

4711
as
HORTON, J.W. **School music education in England,** *Music in education* (Paris: UNESCO, 1955) 136–39. See no. 322 in this volume.
The process of music education is an unfolding of the power of appreciation. It is not advisable to teach notation before children are exposed to the many sounds of music. A French-language version is cited as no. 4710 in this volume. *(Elizabeth A. Wright)*

4712
as
HUCH, Robert. **Der Schulgesangunterricht auf Grundlage des blossen Intervallesens** [Classes in school singing based on the mere reading of intervals], *Zweiter Musikpädagogischer Kongress: Vorträge und Referate* (Berlin: Klavier-Lehrer, 1904) 241–44. In German. See no. 43 in this volume.

4713
as
HUTH, Albert. **Musik als Lebenshilfe für die 13- bis 16jährigen Jugendlichen** [Music as a counseling technique for young people 13 to 16 years old], *Musik and Musikerziehung in der Reifezeit* (Mainz: Schott, 1959) 41–50. In German. See no. 412 in this volume.
Discusses the value of instruction in instrumental and vocal music and music appreciation as a kind of psychotherapeutic help in the critical adolescent years. *(David Bloom)*

4714
as
IKENOUCHI, Tomojirō. **L'éducation musicale dans les établissements scolaires du Japon** [Music education in the Japanese school system], *La musique dans l'éducation* (Paris: UNESCO; Colin, 1955) 125–28. In French. See no. 323 in this volume.
An English-language version is abstracted as no. 4715 in this volume.

4715
as
IKENOUCHI, Tomojirō. **School music education in Japan,** *Music in education* (Paris: UNESCO, 1955) 118–22. See no. 322 in this volume.
Solfège and percussion instruments are taught from the first year of primary school, while melody instruments are introduced in the third year. There are currently not enough qualified teachers; experimental methods of teacher training are under assessment. A French-language version is cited as no. 4714 in this volume. *(Elizabeth A. Wright)*

4716
as
INGHAM, Gertrude A. **The place of Dalcroze eurhythmics in the school curriculum,** *Compte rendu du I er Congrès du rythme* (Genève: Institut Jaques-Dalcroze, 1926) 162–68. See no. 123 in this volume.
The Dalcroze method strengthens the performance techniques of students.

4717 JANKOVIĆ, Slavko. **Upotreba tambure u**
as **orkestralne i pedagoške svrhe** [The use of the
tambura for orchestral and pedagogical purposes], *Rad
VII-og kongresa Saveza Folklorista Jugoslavije*
(Cetinje: Obod, 1964) 369–73. In Croatian; summary in
German. See no. 419 in this volume.

Over the past century the tambura has become established as a concert instrument. More recently it has been introduced into the Yugoslav school
curriculum as the instrument of choice, on several grounds: (1) it is the most
inexpensive instrument; (2) it is the easiest to learn; (3) it is the most easily
available and transportable; (4) instruction can be on a collective basis, for
groups of up to 20; (5) it is an indigenous instrument; and (6) it can be purchased without foreign currency. Preliminary experiments have been successful, in spite of the lack of materials and trained teachers, but the project
is threatened by opposition on the part of teachers of piano, violin, and harmonica. *(author)*

4718 JOUAN, J.-M.-Joseph. **De l'instituteur**
as **primaire au point de vue de la propagation du**
plain-chant et de la musique religieuse [The primary school teacher from the point of view of the propagation of plainchant and religious music], *Congrès
pour la restauration du plain-chant et de la musique
d'église* (Paris: De Mourgues, 1862) 115–17. In French.
See no. 3 in this volume.

4719 KRAUS, Egon. **L'éducation musicale dans les**
as **établissements scolaires d'Allemagne** [Music
education in the German school system], *La musique
dans l'éducation* (Paris: UNESCO; Colin, 1955)
118–21. In French. See no. 323 in this volume.

An English-language version is abstracted as no. 4721 in this volume.

4720 KRAUS, Egon. **Musik und Musikerziehung in**
as **der Reifezeit** [Music and music education in adoles-
cence], *Musik and Musikerziehung in der Reifezeit*
(Mainz: Schott, 1959) 11–23. In German. See no. 412 in
this volume.

4721 KRAUS, Egon. **School music education in Ger-**
as **many,** *Music in education* (Paris: UNESCO, 1955)
112–15. See no. 322 in this volume.

The curriculum aims at awakening and fostering children's instinctive pleasure in musical self-expression. In addition to singing, the Orff instrumentarium is used. A French-language version is cited as no. 4719 in this volume.

4722 LARSON, William S. **The role of musical apti-**
as **tude in an instrumental music program in a**
public school, *Ninth International Congress of Psychology* (Princeton: Psychological Review Company,
1930) 284–85. See no. 160 in this volume.

The growth of instrumental music in the public schools is responsible for
the admission of large numbers of students with no musical ability into music classes. Using Seashore's Measures of Musical Talent, a rise in percen-
tile averages was found in more advanced classes of a public school system,
indicating a selection of talent. Such testing should be more widely used.

4723 LENNARDS, Joseph. **L'éducation musicale des**
as **enfants** [Musical education of children], *Atti del [I]
Congresso internazionale di musica sacra* (Tournai:
Desclée, 1952) 55–56. In French. See no. 303 in this
volume.

4724 LENNARDS, Joseph. **L'éducation musicale**
as **selon la méthode Ward** [Music education according
to the Ward method], *La musique dans l'éducation*
(Paris: UNESCO; Colin, 1955) 255–57. In French. See
no. 323 in this volume.

An English-language version is abstracted as no. 4726 in this volume.

4725 LENNARDS, Joseph. **Erziehung zur Kirchen-**
as **musik an den Grundschulen** [Church music education in elementary schools], *Zweiter internationaler
Kongress für katholische Kirchenmusik: Zu Ehren des
Heiligen Papstes Pius X* (Wien: conference, 1955)
296–302. In German. See no. 339 in this volume.

It has proven extraordinarily difficult to implement the call, beginning with
the 1903 motu proprio *Tra le sollecitudini* of Pius X, for congregations to
participate in singing the Gregorian chant of the solemn Mass. A better way
to proceed would be to teach chant to children at elementary school level.
Psychological underpinnings for the pedagogical technique are sketched,
and practical proposals for curriculum and technique are offered.
(David Bloom)

4726 LENNARDS, Joseph. **Music education by the**
as **Ward method,** *Music in education* (Paris: UNESCO,
1955) 244–46. See no. 322 in this volume.

Music training should be offered to all children, not just an elite. The pedagogical method developed by Justine Bayard Ward, in which Gregorian
chant instruction plays a central role, is suitable for general primary school
instruction by the regular classroom teacher. A French-language version is
cited as no. 4724 in this volume. *(Elizabeth A. Wright)*

4727 LLONGUERAS BADÍA, Juan. **La rythmique**
as **appliquée à la première éducation des aveugles**
[Eurythmics as applied to the elementary education of
the blind], *Compte rendu du Ier Congrès du rythme*
(Genève: Institut Jaques-Dalcroze, 1926) 169–78. In
French. See no. 123 in this volume.

Blind children should be encouraged to start school early and to engage in
eurythmics, among other disciplines.

4728 MADSEN, Cletus. **General and specialized**
as **music in our Catholic schools,** *Music skills* (Washington, D.C.: Catholic University of America, 1958)
3–17. See no. 385 in this volume.

The concept of music performance in the service of God must be emphasized in Catholic school curricula, so that the student will maintain this idea
throughout adult life. The continuing betterment of performance skills is a
lifelong undertaking, not something to be definitively attained during our
time on this earth. Teachers must know their specific arts well to recognize
great potential (or lack thereof) in their students, so there is a need for improvements in teacher training. There is also a need for school administrators
to recognize the value and place of music in the curriculum. *(Susan Poliniak)*

4729 MADSEN, Cletus. **Gregorian chant in the**
as **United States of America/Mouvement**
grégorien aux U.S.A.: Incertitudes et espoirs,
*Perspectives de la musique sacrée à la lumière de
l'encyclique* Musicae sacrae disciplina (Paris: conference, 1959) 241–59. In English and French. See no. 379
in this volume.

Discusses organizations, with emphasis on the National Catholic Music
Educators Association; and curricula, pedagogical method, types of plain-
chant in use, and questions of quality. A summary is cited as no. 4730 in this
volume. *(Rudolph Palmer)*

4730 MADSEN, Cletus. **Le mouvement grégorien**
as **aux États-Unis** [The Gregorian movement in the
United States], *Revue musicale* 239-240 (1957)
113–18. In French. See no. 378 in this volume.

Abridged version of a conference paper. The original version in English,
and a French-language translation, are abstracted as no. 4729 in this
volume.

4731 MAILLET, Fernand. **L'apostolat social,**
as **artistique et spirituel des manécanteries** [The
social, artistic, and spiritual apostolate of boys' choirs],
Atti del [I] Congresso internazionale di musica sacra

(Tournai: Desclée, 1952) 60–61. In French. See no. 303 in this volume.

Discusses the phenomenon of choir schools doubling as professional performing organizations such as the Manécanterie des Petits Chanteurs à la Croix de Bois.

4732 MALONE, Marjorie Jean. **Music in the elemen-**
as **tary schools of the United States,** *Music in education* (Paris: UNESCO, 1955) 110–11. See no. 322 in this volume.

Music has been added to the daily elementary school program as a means of meeting children's expressive needs. Instruction is provided by the classroom teacher, who introduces music (mainly singing) at any time during the day, and by a music specialist working with the teacher on a fixed schedule. A French-language version is cited as no. 4733 in this volume.

(Elizabeth A. Wright)

4733 MALONE, Marjorie Jean. **La musique à l'école**
as **primaire aux États-Unis** [Music in the elementary schools of the United States], *La musique dans l'éducation* (Paris: UNESCO; Colin, 1955) 116–18. In French. See no. 323 in this volume.

An English-language version is abstracted as no. 4732 in this volume.

4734 MARCKHL, Erich. **Kirchenmusik, Musiker-**
as **ziehung, Bildung** [Church music, music instruction, education], *Die Kirchenmusik und das II. Vatikanische Konzil* (Graz: Styria, 1965) 149–66. In German. See no. 480 in this volume.

Church music, and especially the work of the choir director, can help in some measure to compensate for the inadequacies of music instruction in the public school system. *(David Bloom)*

4735 MARTINEAU, A.-Félix. **Maîtrise de la cathé-**
as **drale de Nantes** [The choir school of the Nantes cathedral], *Congrès pour la restauration du plain-chant et de la musique d'église* (Paris: De Mourgues, 1862) 91–97. In French. See no. 3 in this volume.

4736 MASÓ, R. **La rythmique dans l'enseignement**
as **primaire** [Eurythmics in elementary school education], *Compte rendu du Iᵉʳ Congrès du rythme* (Genève: Institut Jaques-Dalcroze, 1926) 152–61. In French. See no. 123 in this volume.

Eurythmics should become a standard ingredient in primary school curricula.

4737 MCSHIELDS, A. **Music in rural schools in**
as **Scotland,** *Music in education* (Paris: UNESCO, 1955) 97–99. See no. 322 in this volume.

Though rural school resources are severely limited, even single-teacher schools can normally provide basic music instruction, assisted by regional-level field inspectors and BBC educational radio broadcasts. A French-language version is cited as no. 4738 in this volume.

(Elizabeth A. Wright)

4738 MCSHIELDS, A. **La musique dans les écoles**
as **rurales d'Écosse** [Music in rural schools in Scotland], *La musique dans l'éducation* (Paris: UNESCO; Colin, 1955) 103–05. In French. See no. 323 in this volume.

An English-language version is abstracted as no. 4737 in this volume.

4739 MÉFRAY, Clement; PRIEUR, O.S.B.
as **Conférence** [Presentation], *Congrès régional de liturgie et de musique sacrée* (Moselle: Orphelins-Apprentis Guénange, 1923) 140–51. In French. See no. 98 in this volume.

Argues for the superiority of boys over girls and women for the performance of Gregorian chant and presents vocal training methods.

4740 MESSERSCHMID, Felix. **Die Schule in der**
as **Sicht des musischen Erziehers** [School in the eyes of the humanities educator], *Neue Zusammenarbeit im deutschen Musikleben: Vorträge und Entschließungen* (Kassel: Bärenreiter, 1956) 26–38. In German. See no. 343 in this volume.

Considers the situation in Germany.

4741 MESSERSCHMID, Felix. **Schule und Musik**
as [School and music], *Musik in Volksschule und Lehrerbildung* (Kassel; Basel: Bärenreiter, 1961) 11–21. In German. See no. 416 in this volume.

General considerations with particular reference to the *Volksschule* (primary and early secondary) curriculum.

4742 MONSOUR, Sally. **On developing music read-**
as **ing skills in the elementary school,** *Music skills* (Washington, D.C.: Catholic University of America, 1958) 85–86. See no. 385 in this volume.

Steps for building up students' reading skills include demonstrating sound and pitch gradations via the use of recordings, group rhythmic activities, singing familiar songs with both neutral syllables and lyrics, and reading visual notation. *(Susan Poliniak)*

4743 MONSOUR, Sally. **Some principles of the psy-**
as **chology of learning applied to the teaching of music in the elementary school,** *Music skills* (Washington, D.C.: Catholic University of America, 1958) 55–63. See no. 385 in this volume.

The principle of readiness determines that the learning process is affected by experience, motivation, and mental and physical maturity. The principle of need involves motivating students for a more effective learning experience; meaningful material is learned more easily than that which is meaningless. Improvement in one aspect of learning usually results in improvements in other areas as well, and one phase of musical learning can be facilitated by improvement in another. The use of exercises and drills is desirable, as is the learning of a piece of music as a whole as opposed to piecemeal. Emotional stress is detrimental to the learning process. *(Susan Poliniak)*

4744 MORTARI, Virgilio. **L'éducation musicale**
as **dans les établissements scolaires d'Italie** [Music education in the Italian school system], *La musique dans l'éducation* (Paris: UNESCO; Colin, 1955) 129–30. In French. See no. 323 in this volume.

An English-language version is abstracted as no. 4745 in this volume.

4745 MORTARI, Virgilio. **School music education in**
as **Italy,** *Music in education* (Paris: UNESCO, 1955) 122–24. See no. 322 in this volume.

Developments since 1946 include the founding of musical societies at the secondary school and university levels, and government sponsorship of children's concerts, aimed at training the taste of young listeners and, over the long term, restoring direct contact between artist and public. A French-language version is cited as no. 4744 in this volume.

4746 MÜLLER-LIEBENWALDE. **Referat zum**
as **Schulgesang-Unterricht** [Report on classes in school singing], *Zweiter Musikpädagogischer Kongress: Vorträge und Referate* (Berlin: Klavier-Lehrer, 1904) 222–33. In German. See no. 43 in this volume.

4747 MYTYCH, Joseph F. **On teaching liturgical**
as **music in the high school,** *Music skills* (Washington, D.C.: Catholic University of America, 1958) 91–93. See no. 385 in this volume.

Describes a seminar that included discussions on the necessity of teaching the technical features of chant, analytical approaches to chant, psalmody, polyphony, motets, the changing male voice, and appropriate hymns for high school use. *(Susan Poliniak)*

4748 MYTYCH, Joseph F. **Singing: Its role and scope**
as **in general music,** *Music skills* (Washington, D.C.: Catholic University of America, 1958) 64–84. See no. 385 in this volume.

The purposes of singing in general music classes are to add the experience to the student's repertoire, to develop the student's artistic potential, and to encourage the student to learn music through personal benefit. Music in the classroom lays the foundation for a student's use of music in life; assists in the discovery of new musical talent; guides the student towards an intelligible view of music; aids in the development of the student's emotional, spiritual, physical, and mental makeup; and introduces the student to a wide array of different cultures. Care must be exercised in the selection of appropriate songs. Suggestions for involving and engaging students are included. *(Susan Poliniak)*

4749 NE'EMAN, Yehẇšu'a Leyyḇ. **Ḥynẇḥ tpylah**
as **ḇeḇatey haseper** [Teaching prayer in school], *Dẇkan* II (1960) 68–74. In Hebrew. See no. 409 in this volume.

4750 NÖRING, Helene. **Referat über die Arbeiten**
as **der Musiksektion zur Hebung des Schul-gesang-Unterrichts** [Report on the work of the music divison in improving classes in school singing], *Zweiter Musikpädagogischer Kongress: Vorträge und Referate* (Berlin: Klavier-Lehrer, 1904) 215–21. In German. See no. 43 in this volume.

4751 OBERBORBECK, Felix. **Das Problem ´der**
as **pädagogischen Verspätung in der Musik** [The problem of pedagogical obsolescence in music], *Musik and Musikerziehung in der Reifezeit* (Mainz: Schott, 1959) 121–26. In German. See no. 412 in this volume.

Discusses the difficulties with school music instruction when teachers are alienated from the popular music enjoyed by the young.

4752 PAPE, Heinrich. **Gedanken zur Musiker-**
as **ziehung in Vorpubertät und Pubertät** [Thoughts on music education in prepuberty and puberty], *Musik and Musikerziehung in der Reifezeit* (Mainz: Schott, 1959) 24–40. *Charts, diagr.* In German. See no. 412 in this volume.

New efforts should be made to coordinate music pedagogy with the psychology of pupils in the sixth to ninth year of schooling, toward the unhindered growth of the pupil's capacity for musical experience, and from the point of view of the relationship between the instructor's musical values and the developmentally and environmentally conditioned values of the pupil. *(David Bloom)*

4753 PAUL, John B. **On piano pedagogy,** *Music skills*
as (Washington, D.C.: Catholic University of America, 1958) 94. See no. 385 in this volume.

Describes a demonstration class on the teaching of correct rhythm, fingering, pedaling, and good tone quality (which involves relaxation). The seminar included work on the Werder-Paul series of instructional books.

(Susan Poliniak)

4754 PAUL, John B. **Principles of piano teaching,**
as *Music skills* (Washington, D.C.: Catholic University of America, 1958) 29–33. See no. 385 in this volume.

Most piano teachers are part-time class teachers who lack adequate training in the instrument themselves. A child's tendency to play by ear must be encouraged. Group classes are beneficial for beginning students of all levels of talent. The educator must teach music theory and the use of dynamics, and relaxation during playing should be emphasized. *(Susan Poliniak)*

4755 PFEIFER, Wilhelm. **Das musische Gymnasium**
as **in Bayern** [The fine-arts Gymnasium in Bavaria], *Musik and Musikerziehung in der Reifezeit* (Mainz: Schott, 1959) 196–202. In German. See no. 412 in this volume.

Surveys curriculum and administrative practice for music instruction in the fine-arts upper secondary schools of the Bundesland Bavaria (*musische Gymnasien* or *Deutsche Gymnasien* as they are locally known).

(David Bloom)

4756 PFROGNER, Hermann. **Was ist Zwölfton-**
as **musik?** [What is 12-tone music?], *Musik and Musikerziehung in der Reifezeit* (Mainz: Schott, 1959) 213–22. *Music, charts, diagr.* In German. See no. 412 in this volume.

Presents a brief account of the fundamental principles of serial composition, in its aspect as a logical development from 18th- and 19th-c. tonal practice, for the assistance of teachers dealing with the subject at the lower secondary level of the German school system. *(David Bloom)*

4757 PINON, Roger. **La chanson folklorique comme**
as **introduction à la poésie étrangère** [Traditional song as an introduction to foreign poetry], *Journal of the International Folk Music Council* V (1953) 55–57. In French. See no. 314 in this volume.

The advantages of using traditional songs as part of the curriculum of foreign literature and languages in middle and high school education include the modern, simple, and lively language of traditional songs; their narrative rather than descriptive character; and the prominence of themes involving legend and nature. While the anonymous and collective character of such songs focus the student's attention directly on the text, genres such as lullabies and Christmas carols convey the message that poetry responds to fundamental human needs. *(Murat Eyüboğlu)*

4758 ṖRY-ḤEN, Dawid. **Mẇsyqah datyt ḇemesiḱat**
as **weḇimḥazah** [Religious music in the school drama], *Dẇkan* II (1960) 47–55. In Hebrew. See no. 409 in this volume.

4759 REHBERG, Karl. **Boris Blachers *Concertante***
as ***Musik* op. 10** [Boris Blacher's *Concertante Musik* op. 10], *Musik and Musikerziehung in der Reifezeit* (Mainz: Schott, 1959) 250–56. *Music, charts, diagr.* In German. See no. 412 in this volume.

An analysis of the work keyed to its use in music classes in secondary school, with a report of a trial in a sample of Berlin schools, and the students' responses. *(David Bloom)*

4760 REICH-GRBEC, Truda. **L'éducation musicale**
as **dans les établissements scolaires de Yougoslavie** [Music education in the Yugoslav school system], *La musique dans l'éducation* (Paris: UNESCO; Colin, 1955) 121–24. In French. See no. 323 in this volume.

An English-language version is abstracted as no. 4761 in this volume.

4761 REICH-GRBEC, Truda. **School music educa-**
as **tion in Yugoslavia,** *Music in education* (Paris: UNESCO, 1955) 115–18. See no. 322 in this volume.

Presents an ccount of the primary and secondary curricula and of the musical training of primary school teachers, which includes compulsory classes in theory and instrumental performance. A French-language version is cited as no. 4760 in this volume. *(Elizabeth A. Wright)*

4762 ROLLE, Georg. **Referat zur Reform des Schu-**
as **lgesang-Unterrichts** [Report on the reform of classes in school singing], *Zweiter Musikpädagogischer Kongress: Vorträge und Referate* (Berlin: Klavier-Lehrer, 1904) 197–214. In German. See no. 43 in this volume.

4763
as
RONAN, John Edward. **Music education and cathedral choir schools,** *IV. Internationaler Kongress für Kirchenmusik in Köln: Dokumente und Berichte* (Köln: Bachem, 1962) 328–32. See no. 432 in this volume.

Report on the program and curriculum at Roman Catholic choir schools in Canada.

4764
as
RONGA, Luigi. **La funzione educatrice della scuola** [The educational function of the school], *Atti del secondo Congresso internazionale di musica* (Firenze: Le Monnier, 1940) 172–80. In Italian; summaries in French and German. See no. 239 in this volume.

An improved secondary school music education should above all aim at training young people to listen, in the way education in the visual arts now trains them to see, in place of the old abstract study of works and historical data. Sound recordings for classroom use should not be chosen opportunistically as they are now but made expressly for pedagogical purposes. *(author)*

4765
as
ROOTHAM, Cyril Bradley. **Choir-boy training,** *Report of the Fourth Congress of the International Musical Society* (London: Novello, 1912) 307–12. *Music.* See no. 71 in this volume.

Pedagogical suggestions are offered along with criteria for choosing singers.

4766
as
ROY, R.L. **Instruction in music as part of general education,** *Music: East and West* (Tōkyō: conference, 1961) 115–18. See no. 445 in this volume.

4767
as
RUÉ, Miguel. **Scholae cantorum,** *Crónica del primer Congreso Nacional de Música Sagrada* (Valladolid: A. Martín, 1908) 91–96. In Spanish. See no. 57 in this volume.

Proposes new regulations and policies for choir schools in Spain.

4768
as
SAMBETH, Heinrich M. **Musikerziehung und Muse** [Music education and the Muse], *Musik and Musikerziehung in der Reifezeit* (Mainz: Schott, 1959) 126–46. In German. See no. 412 in this volume.

Discusses the concept of a weekly *musische Stunde* (fine-arts hour) in the *Volksschule* curriculum in the first through ninth years of school, organized around songs for instrumental performance, songs for movement, and songs for singing. Examples of the curriculum for each year are provided. *(David Bloom)*

4769
as
SCHIEDERMAIR, Ludwig. **Bemerkungen zum musikhistorischen Unterricht an hohen und mittleren Schulen** [Remarks on music history instruction in secondary schools], *Haydn-Zentenarfeier* (Leipzig: Breitkopf & Härtel; Wien: Artaria, 1909) 306–08. In German. See no. 65 in this volume.

Summarizes the state of affairs at various German schools.

4770
as
SCHIEGL, Hermann. **Psychologische Grundlagen der Gehörbildung** [Psychological foundations of ear training], *Musik and Musikerziehung in der Reifezeit* (Mainz: Schott, 1959) 256–65. In German. See no. 412 in this volume.

Ear training is explained as the production of clear tonal perception. It must begin, because of an inadequate investment at the primary level of the German school system, with the first year of secondary school. Scale-based methods are to be preferred to interval exercises (*Intervalltreffmethode*), and tonality provides the best preparation for free-tonality and atonal works. *(David Bloom)*

4771
as
SCHINZ, Nelly. **La rythmique Jaques-Dalcroze au jardin d'enfants** [The Dalcroze method in kindergarten], *Compte rendu du Ier Congrès du rythme* (Genève: Institut Jaques-Dalcroze, 1926) 213–15. *Music.* In French. See no. 123 in this volume.

The Dalcroze method consists of gymnastic, agogic, metric, and melodic exercises.

4772
as
SCHMIDT, Hans. **Musikerziehung im Wertfeld der Persönlichkeitsbildung** [Music education and the values of personality development], *Musik and Musikerziehung in der Reifezeit* (Mainz: Schott, 1959) 114–20. In German. See no. 412 in this volume.

Discusses the use of instruction in instrumental and vocal music and in music appreciation in the service of educating the whole person. *(David Bloom)*

4773
as
SCHWEIZER, Wilhelm. **Die Musikerziehung im Bildungsplan der höheren Schulen** [Music instruction in the educational plan of the upper-level schools], *Musik and Musikerziehung in der Reifezeit* (Mainz: Schott, 1959) 189–96. In German. See no. 412 in this volume.

Discusses the music curriculum at the Gymnasium level of German secondary education.

4774
as
SEEGER, Charles. **Folk music in the schools of a highly industrialised society,** *Journal of the International Folk Music Council* V (1953) 40–44. See no. 314 in this volume.

Folklorists tend to focus on songs, while educators tend to focus on singers; the former's goal is survival, while the latter's is revival. Both tend to overemphasize the importance of written texts: Revival cannot last if oral tradition is destroyed. *(James R. Cowdery)*

4775
as
SHAW, Harold Watkins. **Music in the rural schools in England and Wales,** *Music in education* (Paris: UNESCO, 1955) 99–102. See no. 322 in this volume.

In England and Wales, music is not a required part of teacher training. In 1953, the combined total of English and Welsh schools with no more than three teachers on staff was 8631; consequently, resources for general primary music educators were extremely limited, though BBC educational broadcasting has been helpful. Isolation and the use of Celtic languages as primary languages posed special problems. A French-language version is cited as no. 4776 in this volume. *(Elizabeth A. Wright)*

4776
as
SHAW, Harold Watkins. **La musique dans les écoles rurales d'Angleterre et du pays de Galles** [Music in rural schools in England and Wales], *La musique dans l'éducation* (Paris: UNESCO; Colin, 1955) 105–08. In French. See no. 323 in this volume.

An English-language version is abstracted as no. 4775 in this volume.

4777
as
SHAW, Harold Watkins. **The schools work of an L.E.A. music adviser,** *Music and drama in the counties* (London: conference, 1949). See no. 283 in this volume.

4778
as
SPEER, Gotthard. **Über Eigenart und Aufbau der musikalischen Oberstufenarbeit in der Volksschule** [Special characteristics and structure of work in music in the upper grades of the Volksschule], *Musik in Volksschule und Lehrerbildung* (Kassel; Basel: Bärenreiter, 1961) 32–41. In German. See no. 416 in this volume.

4779 SPIRO-ROMBRO, Assia. **Proposals for im-**
as **proving elementary violin methods and hints**
for teaching the violin to children, *Report of the*
Fourth Congress of the International Musical Society
(London: Novello, 1912) 337–40. *Illus.* See no. 71 in
this volume.

Present methods of elementary violin teaching are too advanced and do not
focus enough on melody. Teachers must understand the difference between
teaching according to an abstract scheme and using a method based on a
practical system. *(Mei-Mei Meng)*

4780 STOFFELS, Hermann. **Hermann Reutter** *Die*
as *Passion in 9 Inventionen* [*Die Passion in 9*
Inventionen by Hermann Reutter], *Musik and*
Musikerziehung in der Reifezeit (Mainz: Schott, 1959)
241–49. In German. See no. 412 in this volume.

An appreciation and analysis of the work (Reutter's op. 25, for piano solo,
published 1930) in terms of its presentation in music classes at the upper
level of the Gymnasium in the German school system. *(David Bloom)*

4781 STUCKENSCHMIDT, Hans Heinz. **Instruction**
as **in music as part of general education,** *Music:*
East and West (Tōkyō: conference, 1961) 107–09. See
no. 445 in this volume.

4782 SWANN, Mona. **Application de la rythmique à**
as **l'étude du "langage"** [The application of eurythmics to the study of language], *Compte rendu du Ier*
Congrès du rythme (Genève: Institut Jaques-Dalcroze,
1926) 264–69. In French. See no. 123 in this volume.

Eurythmics is an effective means of educating children on the sonic and
structural properties of language.

4783 TAUSCHER, Hildegard. **Die rhythmisch-**
as **musikalische Erziehung in der Grundschule**
[Rhythmic-musical training in the Grundschule], *Musik*
in Volksschule und Lehrerbildung (Kassel; Basel:
Bärenreiter, 1961) 42–48. In German. See no. 416 in
this volume.

4784 TEMPELS, P. **L'influence de l'art sur les**
as **mœurs et l'école primaire** [The influence of art on
customs and the primary school], *Ier Congrès interna-*
tional de l'art public (Liège: Bénard, 1900) 45–49. In
French. See no. 24 in this volume.

Calls for the popularization of artistic education, including the study of
music.

4785 TEUSCHER, Hans. **Anleitung zum**
as **Musikhören (für die Volksschule)** [Instruction in
music listening (at the Volksschule level)], *Musik and*
Musikerziehung in der Reifezeit (Mainz: Schott, 1959)
147–52. *Music.* In German. See no. 412 in this volume.

Two goals of listening instruction in the first through ninth years of schooling are discussed: (1) the taking in, distinguishing, defining, and reproducing of musical tone-sequences; and (2) the application of these narrow
skills to larger musical works. The first is not to be regarded simply as preparation for the second; rather the two should alternate continuously. Detailed examples of pedagogical procedures are provided. *(David Bloom)*

4786 TEXIER, Marie. **Danses et chantes folkloriques**
as **dans l'enseignement** [Folkloristic dances and songs
in education], *Travaux du Ier Congrès International de*
Folklore (Tours: Arrault et Cie, 1938) 403. In French.
See no. 251 in this volume.

Children as young as five benefit from traditional singing and dancing, and
from hearing traditional regional instrumental accompaniment.

4787 THIEL, Carl. **Heimatkunde im Schulgesang**
as [Local lore in school singing], *Bericht über den*
Internationalen Kongreß Singen und Sprechen
(München: Oldenbourg, 1938) 188–91. In German. See
no. 257 in this volume.

Traditional songs, from the pupils' own locality and from all over Germany,
arouse love of country, encourage an understanding of the need to protect
the environment and the nation, and help to improve German pronunciation. *(David Bloom)*

4788 THIEL, Jörn. **Die technischen Mittler in der**
as **Musikerziehung: Eine Zwischenbilanz** [Mass
media in music education: An interim appraisal], *Musik*
and Musikerziehung in der Reifezeit (Mainz: Schott,
1959) 275–80. In German. See no. 412 in this volume.

A review of qualitative progress in audiovisual materials (records, sound
film, television, and radio) for music education at the secondary level since
1955. *(David Bloom)*

4789 TREMBLAY, Maurice. **Sur les *scholae***
as **anciennes et modernes** [The former and current
state of parochial schools], *Congrès international de*
musique sacrée: Chant et orgue (Paris: Desclée de
Brouwer, 1937) 154–56. In French. See no. 247 in this
volume.

Parochial church choirs and music programs, which declined in the 19th c.,
are experiencing a revival.

4790 URETA DEL SOLAR, María. **L'éducation mu-**
as **sicale dans les établissements scolaires du**
Pérou [Music education in the Peruvian school sys-
tem], *La musique dans l'éducation* (Paris: UNESCO;
Colin, 1955) 137–42. In French. See no. 323 in this
volume.

An English-language version is abstracted as no. 4791 in this volume.

4791 URETA DEL SOLAR, María. **School music ed-**
as **ucation in Peru,** *Music in education* (Paris:
UNESCO, 1955) 130–35. See no. 322 in this volume.

Outlines the history of music pedagogy in Peru from the beginning of the
20th c., with emphasis on amateur orchestras and chamber ensembles for
cultural education and the adaptation of pedagogical methods to the needs
of different communities. A French-language version is cited as no. 4790 in
this volume.

4792 VANDER ZANDEN, Rose Margaret. **A review**
as **of music education in America,** *Music skills*
(Washington, D.C.: Catholic University of America,
1958) 34–54. *Bibliog.* See no. 385 in this volume.

Includes a history of music education from the early 19th c. to about 1957.
In Catholic schools, the aim of music education is to give children another
way to love and praise God. Basic teaching practices should include rote
singing (particularly by young children), music reading, and rhythm exercises; the use of simple instruments and recordings is also encouraged.
(Susan Poliniak)

4793 VASILJEVIĆ, Miodrag A. **L'enseignement du**
as **chant dans les écoles rurales de Yougoslavie**
[The teaching of singing in rural schools of Yugoslavia],
La musique dans l'éducation (Paris: UNESCO; Colin,
1955) 109–11. In French. See no. 323 in this volume.

An English-language version is abstracted as no. 4794 in this volume.

4794 VASILJEVIĆ, Miodrag A. **The teaching of sing-**
as **ing in rural schools of Yugoslavia,** *Music in edu-*
cation (Paris: UNESCO, 1955) 103–06. See no. 322 in
this volume.

training)

Instruction is based on popular and traditional songs, supplemented in recent years by solfège at the primary level. A French-language version is cited as no. 4793 in this volume.

4795 WERBA, Erik. **Die österreichische Mittel-**
as **schule als Pflegestätte der Musik** [The Austrian secondary school as place for the cultivation of music], *Musikerziehung: Zeitschrift der Musikerzieher Österreichs* special issue (1953) 77–78. In German. See no. 317 in this volume.

4796 WIESE, Johannes Gerhard. **Filmgestaltung als**
as **musische Erziehung** [Film production as arts education], *Musische Jugend und technische Mittler* (Remscheid: Landesarbeitsgemeinschaft Jugendmusik Nordrhein-Westfalen, 1957) 133–38. *Illus.* In German. See no. 380 in this volume.

Discusses the pedagogical value of collaborative filmmaking projects (including the creation of a musical score), on the example of a project carried out by a group of 12 students at the Gymnasium Raabeschule in Braunschweig between 1953 and 1954. *(David Bloom)*

4797 WILLUM HANSEN, Carl; GRYTTER, Rudolf.
as **L'éducation musicale dans les établissements scolaires du Danemark** [Music education in the Danish school system], *La musique dans l'éducation* (Paris: UNESCO; Colin, 1955) 135–37. In French. See no. 323 in this volume.

An English-language version is abstracted as no. 4798 in this volume.

4798 WILLUM HANSEN, Carl; GRYTTER, Rudolf.
as **School music education in Denmark,** *Music in education* (Paris: UNESCO, 1955) 128–30. See no. 322 in this volume.

Community singing forms the starting point for music education in Denmark. All Danish schools devote at least one period a week to music. A French-language version is cited as no. 4797 in this volume.

(Elizabeth A. Wright)

4799 WOITINEK, Julius. **Eine neuer Schultafel-**
as **Apparat für den Gesangs-Klassen Unterricht** [A new blackboard apparatus for teaching vocal classes], *Report of the Fourth Congress of the International Musical Society* (London: Novello, 1912) 384–85. *Illus.* In German. See no. 71 in this volume.

Summary of a paper describing an invention that provides the sounding of tones as they are indicated with a pointer.

4800 YÖNETKEN, Halil Bedi. **L'éducation musicale**
as **et la musique folklorique** [Music education and traditional music], *La musique dans l'éducation* (Paris: UNESCO; Colin, 1955) 195–97. In French. See no. 323 in this volume.

An English-language version is abstracted as no. 4801 in this volume.

4801 YÖNETKEN, Halil Bedi. **Music education and**
as **folk music,** *Music in education* (Paris: UNESCO, 1955) 187–88. See no. 322 in this volume.

Based on the Turkish experience, traditional music plays a highly important role in music education. Some technical issues, such as those of modality and meter, should be included in the school music curriculum. A French-language version is cited as no. 4800 in this volume.

4802 ZANTEN, Cornelie van. **Referat zum**
as **Schulgesang in Holland** [Report on school singing in Holland], *Zweiter Musikpädagogischer Kongress: Vorträge und Referate* (Berlin: Klavier-Lehrer, 1904) 234–40. In German. See no. 43 in this volume.

4803 ŽGANEC, Vinko. **Treba li u škole uvesti i**
as **učenje netemperirane muzike?** [Should the study of untempered music be introduced into schools?], *Rad VII-og kongresa Saveza Folklorista Jugoslavije* (Cetinje: Obod, 1964) 381–84. In Croatian; summary in German. See no. 419 in this volume.

It is possible to be equally trained in the tempered scale of art music and the untempered scales of our traditional music; many of the singers themselves differentiate clearly between the two systems and can consciously choose to perform a given song in either one. But this capability will die out in the next generation unless the schools intervene by the explicit teaching of the traditional systems. *(author)*

4804 ZOHAR, Y. **Haḥynwḥ hamẇsyqaly ḃeḃatey**
as **haseper** [Music education in state religious schools], *Dẇkan* III (1961) 79–82. In Hebrew. See no. 417 in this volume.

72 Colleges and universities (includes teacher training)

4805 ALCINI, Ilario. **L'insegnamento della Musica**
as **sacra nei Seminari/L'enseignement de la musique sacrée dans les séminaires** [Sacred music instruction in seminaries], *Perspectives de la musique sacrée à la lumière de l'encyclique* Musicae sacrae disciplina (Paris: conference, 1959) 580–98. In Italian and French. See no. 379 in this volume.

Implementation of the goals outlined in the encyclical *Musicae sacrae disciplina* of Pius XII (1955) requires major reforms in musical preparation in the training of Roman Catholic priests. The study of music in seminaries must be obligatory throughout the course, treated as equivalent to other required areas, taught by qualified, adequately paid professors, and cultivated with a serious Cecilian consciousness. *(David Bloom)*

4806 BARGILLIAT, Michael. **Du chant grégorien et**
as **de la musique religieuse dans les collèges et les séminaires** [Concerning Gregorian chant and religious music in colleges and seminaries], *Congrès régional de liturgie et de musique sacrée* (Moselle: Orphelins-Apprentis Guénange, 1923) 154–61. In French. See no. 98 in this volume.

An overview of French pedagogy.

4807 BENTLEY, Arnold. **La préparation au**
as **professorat de musique à l'Université de Reading, Angleterre** [The training of specialist music teachers at the University of Reading, England], *La musique dans l'éducation* (Paris: UNESCO; Colin, 1955) 293–96. In French. See no. 323 in this volume.

An English-language version is abstracted as no. 4808 in this volume.

4808 BENTLEY, Arnold. **The training of specialist**
as **teachers of music in the University of Reading in England,** *Music in education* (Paris: UNESCO, 1955) 282–84. See no. 322 in this volume.

Outlines admissions criteria and curricular requirements of the music education program, which was designed by the author. A French-language version is cited as no. 4807 in this volume. *(Elizabeth A. Wright)*

4809 BORREN, Charles van den. **L'histoire de la**
as **musique dans l'enseignement universitaire** [The history of music in university teaching], *Congrès jubilaire* (Brugge: Gruuthuuse, 1925) 223–23. In French. See no. 119 in this volume.

Music history occupies a negligible place in Belgian university teaching, but its importance merits regard equal to that of other subjects. *(Susan Poliniak)*

4810
as
DAMAIS, Émile. **La formation de professeurs de musique destinés aux écoles rurales de France** [The training of music teachers destined for rural schools in France], *La musique dans l'éducation* (Paris: UNESCO; Colin, 1955) 280–85. In French. See no. 323 in this volume.

An English-language version is abstracted as no. 4811 in this volume.

4811
as
DAMAIS, Émile. **Musical training of rural school teachers in France,** *Music in education* (Paris: UNESCO, 1955) 270–75. See no. 322 in this volume.

Music teachers must be trained equally in music and pedagogy. The musical component should include knowledge of genres and repertoire, solfège, and piano. A French-language version is cited as no. 4810 in this volume.

4812
as
DENIS, Valentin. **L'éducation musicale dans les universités d'Europe** [Music education in European universities], *La musique dans l'éducation* (Paris: UNESCO; Colin, 1955) 151–55. In French. See no. 323 in this volume.

An English-language version is abstracted as no. 4813 in this volume.

4813
as
DENIS, Valentin. **Music education in the universities of Europe,** *Music in education* (Paris: UNESCO, 1955) 144–48. See no. 322 in this volume.

Provides a brief historical summary. Universities as opposed to institutions for professional training should focus on music history and appreciation of the repertoire, but in fact many European universities lack such a curriculum. A French-language version is cited as no. 4812 in this volume.

4814
as
DENIS, Valentin. **La musique et la musicologie dans les universités catholiques** [Music and musicology in Catholic universities], *Atti del [I] Congresso internazionale di musica sacra* (Tournai: Desclée, 1952) 287–90. In French. See no. 303 in this volume.

4815
as
FEDELI, Vito. **La cultura musicale in Italia** [The musical culture in Italy], *La vita musicale dell'Italia d'oggi* (Torino: Fratelli Bocca, 1921) 33–43. In Italian. See no. 97 in this volume.

Focuses on the need for educational reforms, particularly at the university level. A panel discussion is included.

4816
as
FINNEY, Theodore M. **Reproductive versus distributive music teaching at the college level,** *Papers of the American Musicological Society* (Philadelphia: American Musicological Society, 1946) 96–100. See no. 269 in this volume.

Colleges and conservatories offer all the conditions for the technical training of musicians (reproductive teaching), but they must take further steps to develop intelligent responses to music (distributive teaching).

4817
as
GAZÉ, Alexandre. **L'œuvre de l'Université Catholique d'Ottawa (Canada) au point de vue de la musique sacrée** [The work of the Catholic University of Ottawa (Canada) from the point of view of sacred music], *Atti del [I] Congresso internazionale di musica sacra* (Tournai: Desclée, 1952) 304–07. In French. See no. 303 in this volume.

Discusses the Université d'Ottawa, known after 1965 as University of Saint Paul.

4818
as
GENNRICH, Paul. **Die gegenwärtigen Bedingungen für die Vorbildung unserer Kirchenmusiker** [Current conditions for the training of our church musicians], *Bericht über den Deutschen Kongreß für Kirchenmusik* (Kassel: Bärenreiter, 1928) 11–21. In German. See no. 135 in this volume.

Before the World War I, the confessionally based *Lehrerseminar* system of teacher training was the main vehicle for the training of church musicians in Germany. The separation of church and state since the establishment of the Republic in 1918 and the dismantling of the *Lehrerseminare* have led to a crisis. It must be recognized that no separation between church music and school music can be sustained, church music being an essential part of the national musical culture. At the same time, specialized schools for church music must be instituted. *(David Bloom)*

4819
as
GERAEDTS, Henri. **La formation des spécialistes de musique aux Pays-Bas** [The development of music specialists in the Netherlands], *La musique dans l'éducation* (Paris: UNESCO; Colin, 1955) 296–98. In French. See no. 323 in this volume.

An English-language version is abstracted as no. 4820 in this volume.

4820
as
GERAEDTS, Henri. **The training of music teachers in the Netherlands,** *Music in education* (Paris: UNESCO, 1955) 284–86. See no. 322 in this volume.

Improvements are needed in the training of general classroom teachers, who are responsible, under the guidance of a music specialist, for music education at the primary level. A French-language version is cited as no. 4819 in this volume.

4821
as
GRŴSMAN, 'Ayleh. **He'arŵt 'al hakšaratam hamŵsyqalit šel mehunaķim datyym leganym ŵlekytŵt hanemŵkŵt šel byh"s** [Some observations on the musical training of religious educators for kindergarten and lower school grades], *Dŵkan* III (1961) 83–88. In Hebrew. See no. 417 in this volume.

4822
as
GUDEWILL, Kurt. **Musik in der Kieler Universität** [Music at the University of Kiel], *Norddeutsche und nordeuropäische Musik* (Kassel; New York: Bärenreiter, 1965) 95–99. *Illus.* In German. See no. 467 in this volume.

Provides a historical survey, from the founding of the university by Duke Christian Albrecht of Schleswig-Holstein-Gottorf in 1665, through the introduction of music as an academic discipline, under the leadership of the organist and cantor Johann Georg Christian Apel, in 1818, to the 1920s. *(David Bloom)*

4823
as
GUERRINI, Guido. **La riforma nelle classi di composizione** [Reform in composition classes], *Atti del sesto Congresso internazionale di musica* (Firenze: Barbèra, 1950) 74–78. In Italian. See no. 291 in this volume.

Describes problems associated with the teaching of differing compositional practices and philosophies within a university setting (i.e., mixed signals delivered to the students as they pass from one class and one teacher to the next). *(Susan Poliniak)*

4824
as
HAMANN, Fritz. **Die Arbeit der Seminar-Musiklehrer und die Bedeutung dieses Standes für die deutsche Musikkultur** [The work of music teachers in the teacher-training institutes and the profession's significance in German music culture], *Bericht über den internationalen musikwissenschaftlichen Kongreß* (Kassel: Bärenreiter, 1963) 290–91. In German. See no. 452 in this volume.

Through the 19th c. to ca. 1920, the training of singing teachers, organists, and cantors throughout Germany was the almost exclusive province of *Seminarmusiklehrer*, music teachers in the *Lehrerseminar* or teacher-training institutes. The conditions and responsibilities of the job and the reasons for its ultimate disappearance are briefly discussed. *(David Bloom)*

4825
as
HORTON, J.W. **The music specialist in the schools of England,** *Music in education* (Paris: UNESCO, 1955) 291–94. See no. 322 in this volume.

Music specialists are divided into four categories: full-time teachers with tertiary qualifications, part-time teachers with tertiary qualifications, general teachers who took music as a major subject, and teachers with no qualifications in music. A French-language version is cited as no. 4826 in this volume. *(Elizabeth A. Wright)*

4826
as
HORTON, J.W. **Le spécialiste de musique à l'école en Angleterre** [The music specialist in the schools of England], *La musique dans l'éducation* (Paris: UNESCO; Colin, 1955) 303–06. In French. See no. 323 in this volume.

An English-language version is abstracted as no. 4825 in this volume.

→
JORGE, J. **La enseñanza del canto gregoriano en los seminarios** [The teaching of Gregorian chant in the seminaries]. See no. 6263 in this volume.

4827
as
KADEN, Richard. **Musikgeschichte und Formenlehre auf dem Seminar** [Music history and theory of musical form at the teacher-training institute], *Zweiter Musikpädagogischer Kongress: Vorträge und Referate* (Berlin: Klavier-Lehrer, 1904) 89–97. In German. See no. 43 in this volume.

4828
as
KELLER, Hermann. **Die Aufgaben der Musikwissenschaft an den Hochschulen für Musik** [Musicological tasks at Musikhochschulen], *Congrés de la Societat Internacional de Musicologia* (Barcelona: Casa de Caritat, 1936). In German. See no. 224 in this volume.

The conference report provides only a citation. Neither the text nor a summary of the paper was published here.

4829
as
KELLER, Hermann. **Die Situation der deutsche Musikhochschulen** [The situation of the German Musikhochschule], *Musikerziehung: Zeitschrift der Musikerzieher Österreichs* special issue (1953) 74–76. In German. See no. 317 in this volume.

4830
as
KINDEM, Ingeborg Eckhoff. **L'éducation musicale dans les établissements scolaires de Norvège** [Music education in the Norwegian school system], *La musique dans l'éducation* (Paris: UNESCO; Colin, 1955) 131–34. *Charts, diagr.* In French. See no. 323 in this volume.

An English-language version is abstracted as no. 4831 in this volume.

4831
as
KINDEM, Ingeborg Eckhoff. **School music education in Norway,** *Music in education* (Paris: UNESCO, 1955) 124–27. See no. 322 in this volume.

Music education is an obligatory element of the training syllabus for primary school teachers; secondary school teachers offer music classes only if they have university-level qualifications in music, and in fact most secondary music teachers are professional musicians without pedagogical training. A French-language version is cited as no. 4830 in this volume. *(Elizabeth A. Wright)*

4832
as
LEO, Maria. **Die Pädagogik als Lehrgegenstand im Musiklehrer-Seminar** [Pedagogy as subject at the music teachers' seminar], *Zweiter Musikpädagogischer Kongress: Vorträge und Referate* (Berlin: Klavier-Lehrer, 1904) 29–39. In German. See no. 43 in this volume.

4833
as
LILLIE, H.W.R. **The vocal training for the clergy,** *Atti del [I] Congresso internazionale di musica sacra* (Tournai: Desclée, 1952) 59–60. See no. 303 in this volume.

Addresses issues of voice training in Roman Catholic seminaries.

4834
as
MATHIAS, François-Xavier. **La musique liturgique dans le cadre de l'enseignement supérieur** [Liturgical music in the framework of higher education], *La musique d'église: Compte rendu du Congrès de musique sacrée* (Tourcoing: Duvivier, 1920) 323–39. In French. See no. 93 in this volume.

Discusses aesthetic and musical values in light of Pius X's motu proprio *Tra le sollecitudini* (1903). General suggestions for a two-part curriculum covering theory and practice are provided.

4835
as
NABETA, Tom. **The place of a music school in Uganda,** *Journal of the International Folk Music Council* XI (1959) 41–44. See no. 392 in this volume.

A proposal for a teacher-training curriculum that would include topics in both Western and Ugandan musics.

4836
as
NUFFEL, Jules van. **L'école interdiocésaine de Malines et la musique d'Église** [The Interdiocesaan Instituut voor Kerkmuziek in Mechelen and the music of the Catholic Church], *La musique d'église: Compte rendu du Congrès de musique sacrée* (Tourcoing: Duvivier, 1920) 261–79. In French. See no. 93 in this volume.

Briefly outlines the school's history and curricula, with attention to the changes introduced by Pius X's motu proprio *Tra le sollecitudini* (1903).

4837
as
OBERBORBECK, Felix. **Zur Organisation der Musik in der Lehrerbildung** [The organization of music in teacher training], *Musik in Volksschule und Lehrerbildung* (Kassel; Basel: Bärenreiter, 1961) 88–90. In German. See no. 416 in this volume.

4838
as
OTTO, Hans. **Die Musik in der neuen Lehrerbildung: Fachegoistischer Anspruch oder Bestandteil grundschichtiger Bildung?** [Music in the new teacher training: A demand based on departmental egoism, or part of a fundamental training?], *Musik in Volksschule und Lehrerbildung* (Kassel; Basel: Bärenreiter, 1961) 69–74. In German. See no. 416 in this volume.

4839
as
PARRISH, Carl. **L'éducation musicale dans les universités des États-Unis** [Music education in the universities of the United States], *La musique dans l'éducation* (Paris: UNESCO; Colin, 1955) 147–51. In French. See no. 323 in this volume.

An English-language version is abstracted as no. 4840 in this volume.

4840
as
PARRISH, Carl. **Music education in the colleges and universities of America,** *Music in education* (Paris: UNESCO, 1955) 140–44. See no. 322 in this volume.

Undergraduate courses offered to non-music majors include introduction to music for the general student, plus training in the appreciation, history, and literature of music. Opportunities for musical activity include other courses, private instruction in applied music, participation in college performing organizations, and venues for listening to music (student and faculty recitals and access to sound libraries). A French-language version is cited as no. 4839 in this volume. *(Rollin Smith)*

4841
as
POIX, Octave. **De l'enseignement du chant, de la musique et de l'orgue dans les écoles**

normales d'instituteurs, les séminaires et les maîtrises [The teaching of chant, music, and organ in teachers' colleges, seminaries, and choir schools], *Congrès pour la restauration du plain-chant et de la musique d'église* (Paris: De Mourgues, 1862) 113–14. In French. See no. 3 in this volume.

4842 ROIHA, Eino. **L'éducation musicale dans les** **universités des pays scandinaves** [Music education in universities of the Scandinavian countries], *La musique dans l'éducation* (Paris: UNESCO; Colin, 1955) 155–57. In French. See no. 323 in this volume.
as
An English-language version is abstracted as no. 4843 in this volume.

4843 ROIHA, Eino. **Music education in the universi-** **ties of the Scandinavian countries,** *Music in education* (Paris: UNESCO, 1955) 148–50. See no. 322 in this volume.
as
A separation has taken place between performance and academic study, as exemplified by the situation in Helsinki, where historical musicology is the province of the university (Helsingin Yliopisto) and practical music that of the conservatory (Sibelius-Akatemia); there should be greater collaboration between the two bodies. A French-language version is cited as no. 4842 in this volume. *(Elizabeth A. Wright)*

4844 ROLLAND, Romain. **Que l'on doit faire une** **place à l'histoire de la musique dans l'histoire** **de l'art et dans l'enseignement universitaire** [There ought to be a place for music history in art history and in university education], *Troisième Congrès international d'enseignement supérieur* (Paris: A. Chevalier-Marescq, 1902) 517–21. In French. See no. 35 in this volume.
as
Music history can shed light on social history and it should become a standard component of a classical education.

4845 RUÉ, Miguel. **Plan para los diversos cursos de** **la enseñanza del canto gregoriano en los** **seminarios** [A plan for the various courses of Gregorian chant at seminaries], *Crónica y actas oficiales del tercer Congreso Nacional de Música Sagrada* (Barcelona: La Hormiga de Oro, 1913) 64–70. In Spanish. See no. 78 in this volume.
as
Provides an outline of the subjects to be addressed in teaching Gregorian chant at seminaries.

4846 SABLAYROLLES, Mauro. **Importancia de la** **enseñanza del canto gregoriano en los** **seminarios** [The importance of teaching Gregorian chant in seminaries], *Crónica y actas oficiales del tercer Congreso Nacional de Música Sagrada* (Barcelona: La Hormiga de Oro, 1913) 54–60. In Spanish. See no. 78 in this volume.
as
Singing is an important component of a priest's ecclesiastic duties. The impact of music on the congregation cannot be ignored, and the study of Gregorian chant at seminaries should be given the same attention as that devoted to the theological disciplines. *(José López-Calo)*

4847 SCHLÖTTERER, Reinhold. **Lehrmethoden des** **Palestrina-Kontrapunkts** [Teaching methods for Palestrina counterpoint], *Bericht über den internationalen musikwissenschaftlichen Kongreß* (Kassel: Bärenreiter, 1963) 361–62. In German. See no. 452 in this volume.
as
Assuming the desirability of teaching counterpoint in the style of Palestrina, particularly in the university, one could rely on the theories of the composer's contemporaries (Gioseffo Zarlino, Domenico Pietro Cerone), on modern-analytic approaches like that of H.K. Andrews's *An introduction to the technique of Palestrina* (1958), or on Knud Jeppesen's

Kontrapunkt (1935), but each choice is problematic. A fourth possibility, briefly discussed, would begin with the language/rhythm/mensuration problem. *(David Bloom)*

4848 SOURIAC, Blanche. **La préparation au** **professorat de musique en France** [The training of music teachers in France], *La musique dans l'éducation* (Paris: UNESCO; Colin, 1955) 298–303. In French. See no. 323 in this volume.
as
An English-language version is abstracted as no. 4849 in this volume.

4849 SOURIAC, Blanche. **The training of music** **teachers in France,** *Music in education* (Paris: UNESCO, 1955) 286–91. See no. 322 in this volume.
as
Training of specialized music teachers includes practical classroom experience and private study. Teachers are certified by examination at the Centre de Préparation au Professorat de Musique, Paris. A French-language version is cited as no. 4848 in this volume. *(Elizabeth A. Wright)*

4850 SOUTHALL, Aidan William. **Suggested links** **between proposed school of African music and** **the African studies programme at Makerere.** Intro. by Gerald MOORE, *First Conference on African Traditional Music* (Kampala: Uganda Ey'eddembe, 1964) 24–33. See no. 465 in this volume.
as
Report of a discussion about a proposal for funding faculty musicologists.

4851 STANLEY, Albert A. **Music in American uni-** **versities,** *Haydn-Zentenarfeier* (Leipzig: Breitkopf & Härtel; Wien: Artaria, 1909) 459–66. See no. 65 in this volume.
as
After a brief description of the structure of American universities (undergraduate and graduate divisions) as contrasted with European institutions, statistics of music departments, including enrollment figures and courses offered, are provided. The University of Michigan is given special attention.

4852 STANLEY, Albert A. **The value of a collection** **of musical instruments in universities,** *Report of the Fourth Congress of the International Musical Society* (London: Novello, 1912) 341–46. See no. 71 in this volume.
as
Focuses on scientific, sociological, and artistic pedagogical worth.

4853 STOVEROCK, Dietrich. **La préparation à** **l'enseignement de la musique en Allemagne** [Preparation for music teaching in Germany], *La musique dans l'éducation* (Paris: UNESCO; Colin, 1955) 290–93. In French. See no. 323 in this volume.
as
An English-language version is abstracted as no. 4854 in this volume.

4854 STOVEROCK, Dietrich. **The training of music** **teachers in Germany,** *Music in education* (Paris: UNESCO, 1955) 279–81. See no. 322 in this volume.
as
There are no specialized music teachers in primary schools. Secondary-school music teachers are trained at the Hochschule level. Their training program is outlined, with particular attention to training in classroom procedure. A French-language version is cited as no. 4853 in this volume. *(Elizabeth A. Wright)*

4855 SUMMERS, Joseph. **Musical education in Aus-** **tralia, 1863-1911,** *Report of the Fourth Congress of the International Musical Society* (London: Novello, 1912) 73. See no. 71 in this volume.
as
Summary of a paper on Australian universities.

4856 WALTERS, I.R. **L'enseignement musical privé** **en Angleterre et au pays de Galles** [Private music instruction in England and Wales], *La musique dans*
as

l'éducation (Paris: UNESCO; Colin, 1955) 165–68. In French. See no. 323 in this volume.

An English-language version is abstracted as no. 4857 in this volume.

4857
as
WALTERS, I.R. **Individual and private music instruction in England and Wales,** *Music in education* (Paris: UNESCO, 1955) 158–61. See no. 322 in this volume.

A standard training program and certification for private teachers would allow them to have a more dignified status in the community. Specific proposals are offered. A French-language version is cited as no. 4856 in this volume. *(Elizabeth A. Wright)*

4858
as
WESTERGAARD, Peter, moderator. **What do you, as a composer, try to get the student to hear in a piece of music?** *American Society of University Composers: Proceedings of the 1966 conference* (New York: American Society of University Composers, 1966). See no. 510 in this volume.

Problems discussed include students' unfamiliarity with the language of music, the question of intellectual vs. spiritual listening, and the degree of aural understanding that can be expected in contemporary music. Participants included Milton BABBITT, Martin BOYKAN, Robert COGAN, Ross Lee FINNEY, Ben JOHNSTON, Leo KRAFT, Billy Jim LAYTON, Robert Hall LEWIS, Salvatore MARTIRANO, Lawrence MOSS, Louise TALMA, and Roy TRAVIS. *(Judith Drogichen Meyer)*

4859
as
WILSON, Harry R. **La formation musicale de maîtres destinés aux écoles rurales des États-Unis** [The musical training of teachers destined for rural schools in the United States], *La musique dans l'éducation* (Paris: UNESCO; Colin, 1955) 286–89. In French. See no. 323 in this volume.

An English-language version is abstracted as no. 4860 in this volume.

4860
as
WILSON, Harry R. **The training of teachers for music in the rural schools of the U.S.A.,** *Music in education* (Paris: UNESCO, 1955) 275–78. See no. 322 in this volume.

The general philosophy of music teaching in the U.S. emphasizes both good training and the positive attitude of the individual teacher. A French-language version is cited as no. 4859 in this volume. *(Elizabeth A. Wright)*

4861
as
ZANTEN, Cornelie van. **Die Anforderungen des Examens für Kunstgesangspädagogik** [Examination requirements for vocal pedagogy], *Zweiter Musikpädagogischer Kongress: Vorträge und Referate* (Berlin: Klavier-Lehrer, 1904) 119–25. In German. See no. 43 in this volume.

73 Conservatories and other professional training

→
ADOLF, Martin; GREENBERG, Simon. **The cantor's conservatory: To be or not to be?** See no. 6036 in this volume.

4862
as
ARTERO, José. **Creación de una Escuela Superior de Música Sagrada** [The creation of an Escuela Superior de Música Sagrada], *V Congreso Nacional de Música Sagrada* (Madrid: Gráficas Dos de Mayo, 1956) 194–97. In Spanish. See no. 331 in this volume.

The foundation of a conservatory-level school of religious music in Spain, a goal of each of the previous four national congresses of religious music, has finally been achieved with the establishment of the Escuela Superior de Música Sagrada in Madrid (1953), under the direction of Tomás de Manzárraga. Its curriculum is discussed. *(José López-Calo)*

4863
as
BAS, Giulio. **Iniziazione musicale degli esecutori: Precedenza di un'adeguata preparazione artistica a qualsiasi studio tecnico** [The musical initiation of performers: The precedence of an adequate artistic preparation over technical studies], *La vita musicale dell'Italia d'oggi* (Torino: Fratelli Bocca, 1921) 91–95. In Italian. See no. 97 in this volume.

Briefly discusses the need for educational reforms to foster artistic growth.

4864
as
BITTAR, Andre. **La création d'un conservatoire de musique à Beyrouth** [The creation of a music conservatory in Beirut], *Congrès français de la Syrie. III* (Paris: Champion, 1919) 152—153. In French. See no. 92 in this volume.

A proposal to establish an independent music conservatory in Beirut.

4865
as
CARILLO, Julián. **Sur la nécessité d'élever le niveau artistique de la musique militaire** [On the necessity of raising the artistic level of military music], *Report of the Fourth Congress of the International Musical Society* (London: Novello, 1912) 313–14. In French. See no. 71 in this volume.

Conservatories should provide instruction in military band scoring.

4866
as
DALLAPICCOLA, Luigi. **Considerazioni sull'insegnamento della composizione** [Considerations on the teaching of composition], *Atti del sesto Congresso internazionale di musica* (Firenze: Barbèra, 1950) 125–30. In Italian. See no. 291 in this volume.

The conservatory experience for the composition student is changing. Different subjects such as film music are being addressed, and expectations in terms of what the student should be capable of after a certain amount of study have been altered. Composition students must understand that a great deal of their life and work will be conducted in solitude. *(Susan Poliniak)*

4867
as
DAMERINI, Adelmo. **Di una metodologia storicistica nell'insegnamento della composizione** [On a historicist methodology in the teaching of composition], *Atti del sesto Congresso internazionale di musica* (Firenze: Barbèra, 1950) 53–59. In Italian. See no. 291 in this volume.

4868
as
DE BONIS, Alessandro. **Formazione tecnica dei musicisti di chiesa** [The technical training of church musicians], *Atti del [I] Congresso internazionale di musica sacra* (Tournai: Desclée, 1952) 30–33. In Italian. See no. 303 in this volume.

Discusses requirements within the framework of the Roman Catholic church.

4869
as
DELLA CORTE, Andrea. **Storia, cultura e "tendenze" nell'insegnamento della composizione** [History, culture, and trends in the teaching of composition], *Atti del sesto Congresso internazionale di musica* (Firenze: Barbèra, 1950) 39–48. In Italian. See no. 291 in this volume.

Addresses the question of whether the student should study the music theory of the past or the present. The musicological study of the past should not be abandoned. One must distinguish between the studies of theory and practice, and understand how the former affects the latter. In earlier eras, the works of Vincent D'Indy, who recognized the need for knowledge of musical tradition, were used as a framework for study; the views of other prominent educators are also discussed. *(Susan Poliniak)*

4870
as
FEDELI, Vito. **L'insegnamento della composizione negli istituti musicali** [Composition teaching in musical institutes], *Report of the Fourth Congress of the International Musical Society* (London: Novello, 1912) 355–58. In Italian. See no. 71 in this volume.

Suggests a two-part reformed curriculum. Part one would develop technique; harmony and counterpoint would be taught, and students would compose using historical models. Part two would focus on genres and aesthetics.

4871
as

FELIZ, Isaac. **Necesidad de una formación sólida para los músicos de iglesia** [The necessity of solid training for church musicians], *V Congreso Nacional de Música Sagrada* (Madrid: Gráficas Dos de Mayo, 1956) 240–43. In Spanish. See no. 331 in this volume.

If religious music in Spain is to regain some of the splendor of its earlier periods, musicians must be provided with thorough training in their chosen specialties as composers, choir directors, organists, or singers. *(José López-Calo)*

4872
as

GENTILI, Alberto. **L'insegnamento della composizione in rapporto alle tendenze moderne** [The teaching of composition in relation to modern trends], *Atti del sesto Congresso internazionale di musica* (Firenze: Barbèra, 1950) 33–39. In Italian. See no. 291 in this volume.

Discusses, among other issues, the problems of how a conservatory can remain conservative (without burying itself in the past) and yet stay current with the newest developments and techniques; how to determine what is and is not worthy of study; and how to determine the programming of a course of study in composition. *(Susan Poliniak)*

4873
as

GHEDINI, Giorgio Federico. **The composer's point of view,** *Music in education* (Paris: UNESCO, 1955) 297–300. See no. 322 in this volume.

Offers recommendations for instruction in composition, based on the author's experience at the Conservatorio di Musica G. Verdi, Milan. Native musical resources should be used in the training of young composers, to develop national characteristics in opposition to a musical Esperanto; eurythmics and singing should be staple elements in the curriculum; and the teachers should be practicing composers themselves. A French-language version is cited as no. 4874 in this volume. *(Philip Brink)*

4874
as

GHEDINI, Giorgio Federico. **Le point de vue du compositeur** [The composer's point of view], *La musique dans l'éducation* (Paris: UNESCO; Colin, 1955) 309–12. In French. See no. 323 in this volume.

An English-language version is abstracted as no. 4873 in this volume.

4875
as

GHISLANZONI, Alberto. **Importanza dello studio del canto gregoriano per la formazione dei musicisti di oggi e di domani** [The importance of the study of Gregorian chant for the training of the musicians of today and tomorrow], *Atti del [I] Congresso internazionale di musica sacra* (Tournai: Desclée, 1952) 220–22. In Italian. See no. 303 in this volume.

4876
as

GL'ANṢ, Leyyḇ. **'Al ḥynwḥ ḥazanym** [On the training of hazanim], *Dẇkan* I (1959) 57–61. In Hebrew. See no. 391 in this volume.

4877
as

GLORIEUX, Louis. **L'école pontificale de musique sacrée à Rome** [The Pontificio Istituto di Musica Sacra in Rome], *La musique d'église: Compte rendu du Congrès de musique sacrée* (Tourcoing: Duvivier, 1920) 247–59. In French. See no. 93 in this volume.

The school was opened in 1911 by the Associazione Italiana di Santa Cecilia.

4878
as

GRAF, Herbert. **Training for opera,** *Zeitgenössisches Musiktheater/Contemporary music theatre/Théâtre musical contemporain* (Hamburg:

Deutscher Musikrat, 1966) 140–42. See no. 481 in this volume.

Opera houses no longer provide the proper conditions for a young artist interested in gaining professional experience; conservatories and private teachers cannot fulfill this need without a greater connection to opera houses. Opera workshops have been developed in the U.S., and apprenticeship programs have been attempted at the Centro di Avviamento al Teatro Lirico in Florence, the Teatro Lirico in Spoleto, and the Teatro La Fenice in Venice. *(Helena Ross)*

4879
as

GUENYVEAU, J. de. **De la diction dans les écoles de chant** [On diction in chant schools], *La musique d'église: Compte rendu du Congrès de musique sacrée* (Tourcoing: Duvivier, 1920) 237–46. In French. See no. 93 in this volume.

Discusses difficulties in pronunciation when reading Latin from old MSS.

4880
as

GURLITT, Wilibald. **Die musikwissenschaftliche Bildung des Organisten** [The organist's training in musicology], *Bericht über die dritte Tagung für Deutsche Orgelkunst* (Kassel: Bärenreiter, 1928) 110–15. In German. See no. 136 in this volume.

Each period of music history placed a different cultural emphasis on the training of organists: the theological in the Middle Ages, the humanistic in the Renaissance, the organistic in the Baroque, or the historical in the Romantic. The most recent training emphasizes the musicological, which thinks Romanticism through to its conclusions and values all the traditions of the past. An example is provided in the musicological approach to the music of Jan Pieterszoon Sweelinck.

4881
as

JAENICKE, Gisela. **Rhythmik als Mittel zur Ausbildung des Opernsängers** [Rhythmic methods for training opera singers], *Deuxième Congrès international du rythme et de la rythmique* (Genève: Institut Jaques-Dalcroze, 1966) 22–35. In German. See no. 502 in this volume.

Discusses the Dalcroze method.

⟶

JAQUES-DALCROZE, Émile. **Rythmes d'hier, d'aujourd'hui et de demain et leur enseignement dans les écoles de musique** [Rhythms of yesterday, today, and tomorrow and their teaching in music schools]. See no. 4004 in this volume.

4882
as

KOECHLIN, Charles. **La pédagogie musicale** [Music pedagogy], *Rapport sur la musique contemporaine française* (Roma: Armani & Stein, 1913) 139–49. In French. See no. 76 in this volume.

Surveys education in French conservatories, 1850-1911.

4883
as

MERINO, Felipe. **Importancia del estudio del canto gregoriano** [The importance of studying Gregorian chant], *Crónica del primer Congreso Nacional de Música Sagrada* (Valladolid: A. Martín, 1908) 105–12. In Spanish. See no. 57 in this volume.

Celebrates the restoration of Gregorian chant, promoted by Pius X, and proposes a plan of study to be carried out in seminaries in Spain. *(José López-Calo)*

4884
as

MÜLLER-BLATTAU, Joseph. **Über Erziehung: Bildung und Fortbildung der Organisten** [Education: The training and further training of organists], *Bericht über die [I] Freiburger Tagung für Deutsche Orgelkunst* (Augsburg: Bärenreiter, 1926) 99–109. *Music.* In German. See no. 122 in this volume.

A survey of documentary evidence on the history of organ instruction from the early 16th c. through the Prüfungsordnung established in 1910 at the Institut für Kirchenmusik, Berlin-Charlottenburg, for the certification of church organists in Prussia, and an examination of the situation in Germany since the 1918 revolution and separation of church and state. *(David Bloom)*

4885 NE'EMAN, Yehŵšu'a Leyyb. **'Al ḥynẇh**
as **ḥazanym** [On the training of hazanim], *Dẇkan* I
(1959) 46–56. *Music.* In Hebrew. See no. 391 in this
volume.

A detailed description of the program of studies in Jerusalem's school for hazanim that combines musical knowledge with analytical study of the different versions of prayers. *(Moshe Zorman)*

4886 PINCHERLE, Marc. **De l'enseignement de la**
as **composition** [Teaching composition], *Atti del sesto
Congresso internazionale di musica* (Firenze: Barbèra,
1950) 130–37. In French. See no. 291 in this volume.

Discusses a program for the teaching of composition. Education should stress liberalism in terms of form but rigor in terms of the musical contents of the form. Whoever does not possess music within himself is not a composer; similarly, musical innovations come from within, not without, the self. *(Susan Poliniak)*

4887 PIZZARDO, Giuseppe. **L'importance de**
as **l'enseignement de la musique dans les**
séminaires [The importance of music instruction in
seminaries], *Perspectives de la musique sacrée à la
lumière de l'encyclique* Musicae sacrae disciplina
(Paris: conference, 1959) 577–79. In French. See no.
379 in this volume.

Message to the third International Congress of Sacred Music (Paris 1957) from the Congregatio de Seminariis et Studiorum Universitatibus (Congregation of Seminaries and Universities) of the Roman Curia. *(David Bloom)*

4888 PRIM, Jean. **Pour l'application intégrale,**
as **sincère et filiale des directives pontificales en**
matière de musique sacrée [Towards an integral,
sincere, and filial application of the papal directives
concerning sacred music], *Congrès international de
musique sacrée: Chant et orgue* (Paris: Desclée de
Brouwer, 1937) 100–09. In French. See no. 247 in this
volume.

The main directives are the improvement of education in seminaries and an increase in public participation in chant. The Gildes de Sainte-Cécile has a role to play.

4889 REBOULOT, Antoine. **L'organiste liturgique**
as **au XXᵉ siècle et sa formation** [Liturgical organists
in the 20th century and their training], *Perspectives de
la musique sacrée à la lumière de l'encyclique* Musicae
sacrae disciplina (Paris: conference, 1959) 373–79. In
French. See no. 379 in this volume.

Church organists must be liturgists, Gregorianists, and artists. They need a solid foundation in music theory, and thorough knowledge of organ repertoire; it is desirable, but not necessary, for them to be adept at improvisation. A summary is cited as no. 4890 in this volume. *(Rudolph Palmer)*

4890 REBOULOT, Antoine. **L'organiste liturgique**
as **au XXᵉ siècle et sa formation** [Liturgical organists
in the 20th century and their training], *Revue musicale*
239-240 (1957) 165–70. In French. See no. 378 in this
volume.

An abridged version of the conference paper is abstracted as no. 4889 in this volume.

4891 ROMITA, Fiorenzo. **De studio ac praxi musicae**
as **sacrae in seminariis juxta praescripta S. Sedis**
[The study and practice of sacred music in seminaries
according to the prescriptions of the Holy See], *Atti del
[I] Congresso internazionale di musica sacra* (Tournai:

Desclée, 1952) 77–79. In Latin. See no. 303 in this volume.

4892 SALVANY, Gerardo María. **Cómo se debe**
as **ejecutar el canto gregoriano y modo de**
promover la enseñanza de este canto, sobre
todo en los seminarios [The correct way to sing
Gregorian chant and how to promote it, especially in the
seminaries], *Crónica del primer Congreso Nacional de
Música Sagrada* (Valladolid: A. Martín, 1908) 70–77.
In Spanish. See no. 57 in this volume.

Discusses the responsibility of the seminaries for teaching future priests how to read and perform Gregorian chant.

4893 SEIDL, Arthur. **Läßt sich Ästhetik mit Aussicht**
as **auf Erfolg an Konservatorien lehren?** [Can aesthetics be taught in conservatories with a prospect of
success?], *Bericht über den zweiten Kongress der
Internationalen Musikgesellschaft* (Leipzig: Breitkopf
& Härtel, 1907) 129–54. In German. See no. 53 in this
volume.

Argues, largely on the basis of the author's experience as a professor at the Konservatorium Leipzig, that aesthetics is just as appropriate in the conservatory curriculum as in the university's. *(David Bloom)*

4894 SITTNER, Hans. **Ausbildungsprobleme des**
as **sängerischen Nachwuchses für das Musik-**
theater [Problems in training the rising generation of
singers for the music theater], *Zeitgenössisches
Musiktheater/Contemporary music theatre/Théâtre
musical contemporain* (Hamburg: Deutscher Musikrat,
1966) 151–52. In German. See no. 481 in this volume.

Unhealthy aspects of modern life, a lack of attention to care of the voice among schoolchildren, the bad example of popular music, and the inadequate preparation of music teachers at all levels contribute to a crisis in the nurturing of young singers. It would be valuable to have opera studios jointly run by opera houses and prominent conservatories. *(David Bloom)*

4895 SMITS VAN WAESBERGHE, Joseph. **Die**
as **Ausbildung des Kirchenmusikers** [The training
of the church musician], *IV. Internationaler Kongress
für Kirchenmusik in Köln: Dokumente und Berichte*
(Köln: Bachem, 1962) 319–27. In German. See no. 432
in this volume.

General proposals for the curriculum in the musical context of the late 20th c.

4896 STANTON, Hazel Martha. **Psychological tests:**
as **A factor in admission to the Eastman School of**
Music, *Ninth International Congress of Psychology*
(Princeton: Psychological Review Company, 1930)
406–07. See no. 160 in this volume.

The Seashore Measure of Musical Talent has been used as an entrance examination since the establishment of the school in 1921. Scores fall into five categories: safe, probable, possible, doubtful, and discouraged. To attain entrance, a score of possible is required. *(Ruth Block)*

4897 STROBEL, Heinrich. **Lebendiger Komposi-**
as **tionsunterricht!** [Living composition instruction!],
Atti del sesto Congresso internazionale di musica
(Firenze: Barbèra, 1950) 67–70. In German. See no.
291 in this volume.

There are some positive aspects to the teaching of composition at the conservatory level as currently practiced in Europe, particularly its contribution to a sense of historical continuity in today's atmosphere of intergenerational hostility. Nevertheless it is in danger of becoming completely divorced from actual musical practice. Composition instruction should be based not on any theory, historical or dodecaphonic, but on the living contemporary works themselves. *(David Bloom)*

4898
as
SUTERMEISTER, Heinrich; PAPINEAU-COUTURE, Jean; VEGA, Aurelio de la. **Training of composers,** *The modern composer and his world* (Toronto: University of Toronto, 1961) 17–34. See no. 423 in this volume.

Includes brief individual papers and a panel discussion. The composers of today must be strong and exhibit their individuality in their work. They must resist careerist influences. For the gifted, effective study of technique and aesthetics will produce compositions of permanent character. In the study of technique, musical acoustics is the most important concept. In composers' formal education, we should include a comprehensive study of the new forms of music. *(Dorothy Gray)*

4899
as
VANDEWALLE, Charles. **Organisation pratique des scholae grégoriennes** [Practical organization of the chant scholae], *La musique d'église: Compte rendu du Congrès de musique sacrée* (Tourcoing: Duvivier, 1920) 33–43. In French. See no. 93 in this volume.

Discusses curricular structure, and individual areas of study such as solfège and pronunciation, in light of Pius X's motu proprio *Tra le sollecitudini* (1903).

4900
as
VYERMAN, Jules. **Le programme des instituts supérieurs de musique sacrée** [The program of tertiary institutions for sacred music], *Perspectives de la musique sacrée à la lumière de l'encyclique* Musicae sacrae disciplina (Paris: conference, 1959) 626–29. In French. See no. 379 in this volume.

A discussion of curriculum requirements for the upper-level training of church musicians in the light of the encyclical *Musicae sacrae disciplina* of Pius XII (1955), with particular reference to the program of the Lemmensinstituut (Hoger Instituut voor Kerkmuziek), Mechelen. *(David Bloom)*

4901
as
WECHNER, Bruno. **Die kirchenmusikalische Erziehung des Welt- und Ordensklerus** [Church music education of secular and monastic clergy], *IV. Internationaler Kongress für Kirchenmusik in Köln: Dokumente und Berichte* (Köln: Bachem, 1962) 312–19. In German. See no. 432 in this volume.

A historical view, from the wholly unsystematized situation before the Council of Trent to the current high levels of professionalism.

4902
as
ZAMPIERI, Giusto. **L'insegnamento della teoria della musica e del solfeggio nel R. Conservatorio di Milano** [The teaching of music theory and solfège in the Reale Conservatorio di Milano], *Haydn-Zentenarfeier* (Leipzig: Breitkopf & Härtel; Wien: Artaria, 1909) 374–80. *Illus., music.* In Italian. See no. 65 in this volume.

Discusses pedagogical techniques and solfège exercises. The problem of determining vocal range is addressed.

4903
as
ZAMPIERI, Giusto. **I programmi d'insegnamento della storia della musica nel R. Conservatorio di Milano** [The programs of instruction in music history at the Reale Conservatorio di Milano], *Haydn-Zentenarfeier* (Leipzig: Breitkopf & Härtel; Wien: Artaria, 1909) 381. In Italian. See no. 65 in this volume.

Examples of test questions are provided.

4904
as
ZILLINGER, Erwin. **Über die ästhetische Durchbildung der Organisten** [Completing the aesthetic training of organists], *Bericht über die dritte Tagung für Deutsche Orgelkunst* (Kassel: Bärenreiter, 1928) 176–80. In German. See no. 136 in this volume.

A technical education in aesthetics, along with the other aspects of the organist's art, must be supplemented by the education of the artist as a human

being, in the service not so much of church, art, or religion, as life itself. Only thus can a way be found from the backward-looking pessimism of so much current church music to a contemporary equivalent of Buxtehude's "divine cheerfulness" (göttliche Heiterkeit).

74 Music education for amateurs

4905
as
BRITTON, Allen P. **The singing school movement in the United States,** *Report of the Eighth Congress of the International Musicological Society. I: Papers* (Kassel: Bärenreiter, 1961) 89–99. *Facs., music.* See no. 439 in this volume.

The singing school movement in North America grew out of an attempt in the early 18th c. to reform congregational church singing by providing instruction in the rudiments of choral music in the form of evening schools supported by individual rather than government sources. It vanished by the early 20th c., leaving music instruction to the public schools.
(Miryam Moscovitz)

4906
as
IBBERSON, Mary. **Les écoles rurales de musique en Angleterre** [Rural music schools in England], *La musique dans l'éducation* (Paris: UNESCO; Colin, 1955) 158–61. In French. See no. 323 in this volume.

An English-language version is abstracted as no. 4907 in this volume.

4907
as
IBBERSON, Mary. **Rural music schools in England,** *Music in education* (Paris: UNESCO, 1955) 151–53. See no. 322 in this volume.

in this volume The rural music schools movement, which began with the author's founding of the Hertfordshire Rural Music School in 1929 and was formally organized as the Rural Music Schools Association in 1946, aims at providing instrument instruction and performance opportunities for children and adults in English villages remote from urban centers. A French-language version is cited as no. 4906 in this volume. *(Elizabeth A. Wright)*

4908
as
KLAUDER, Karl. **Lehren der deutschen Arbeitersängerbewegung für die heutige Chorpraxis** [Lessons from the German workers' singing movement for contemporary choral practice], *Beiträge zur Musikwissenschaft* VI/4 (1964) 308–16. In German. See no. 476 in this volume.

4909
as
LOHMANN, G.J.T. **Une école populaire de musique aux Pays-Bas** [A popular school of music in the Netherlands], *La musique dans l'éducation* (Paris: UNESCO; Colin, 1955) 161–63. In French. See no. 323 in this volume.

An English-language version is abstracted as no. 4910 in this volume.

4910
as
LOHMANN, G.J.T. **A people's school of music in the Netherlands,** *Music in education* (Paris: UNESCO, 1955) 154–56. See no. 322 in this volume.

The Volksmuziekschool, Amsterdam, founded 1931 by Willem Gehrels, provides instrumental instruction to children unable to afford private lessons. Its methodological principles are described. A French-language version is cited as no. 4909 in this volume.

4911
as
MENÉNDEZ GARCÍA Y BELTRÁN, Margarita. **L'importance de la participation de la communauté au chant** [The importance of community participation in singing], *La musique dans l'éducation* (Paris: UNESCO; Colin, 1955) 188–91. In French. See no. 323 in this volume.

An English-language version is abstracted as no. 4912 in this volume.

4912 MENÉNDEZ GARCÍA Y BELTRAN, Margarita.
as **The importance of audience participation in singing,** *Music in education* (Paris: UNESCO, 1955) 180–83. See no. 322 in this volume.

Music teachers in Cuba should foster the performance of songs by groups of young people and adults. This sort of activity should be an informal pleasure and should not be compared with music teaching at the conservatory level. A French-language version is cited as no. 4911 in this volume.

(Elizabeth A. Wright)

4913 POELS, Jef. **Music in the workers' leisure time,**
as *Music in education* (Paris: UNESCO, 1955) 195–200. See no. 322 in this volume.

Traces the history of workers' musical associations in Europe, particularly Belgium, from the early 19th c. A French-language version is cited as no. 4914 in this volume.

4914 POELS, Jef. **La musique dans les loisirs des**
as **travailleurs** [Music in the leisure time of workers], *La musique dans l'éducation* (Paris: UNESCO; Colin, 1955) 204–09. In French. See no. 323 in this volume.

An English-language version is abstracted as no. 4913 in this volume.

4915 POOT, Marcel. **La radio et les sociétés**
as **instrumentales d'amateurs** [Radio and the amateur instrumental societies], *La musique et le peuple: Rapports, suggestions, voeux* (Bruxelles: Ministère des Sciences et des Arts, 1932) 49–52. In French. See no. 195 in this volume.

Describes the possibilities of radio as an auxiliary educational resource vs. its performance to date. The necessity of a healthy musical life, and the need for the production of competent Belgian conductors, are discussed.

(Mark Stevens)

4916 WILCOX, Glenn C. **The singing school move-**
as **ment in the United States,** *Report of the Eighth Congress of the International Musicological Society. II: Reports* (Kassel: Bärenreiter, 1962) 77–79. See no. 440 in this volume.

A report on a discussion by Irving LOWENS, Allen P. BRITTON, Alan BUECHNER, Gilbert CHASE, H. Wiley HITCHCOCK, Joyce E. MANGLER, Donald M. MCCORKLE, Louis PICHIERRI, Carleton Sprague SMITH, and Glenn C. WILCOX on the paper by Britton abstracted as no. 4905 in this volume.

MUSIC AND OTHER ARTS

75 General

4917 BALILLA PRATELLA, Francesco. **Musica e**
as **danza popolare come elemento di rinnova-**
mento artistico [Traditional music and dance as an
element in artistic renewal], *Journal of the Interna-*
tional Folk Music Council II (1950) 49. In Italian. See
no. 295 in this volume.
The conference report provides only a citation. Neither the text nor a summary of the paper was published here.

4918 CHERBULIEZ, Antoine-Élisée. **Le problème**
as **de la périodicité dans l'histoire de l'art musical**
par rapport aux beaux-arts en général et à la
poesie [The problem of periodicity in the history of
musical art in relation to the fine arts in general and po-
etry], *Bulletin of the International Committee of Histor-*
ical Sciences X/2-3 (Apr-July 1938) 655–57. In French.
See no. 262 in this volume.
It is worth investigating whether the stylistic phases in the evolution of music correspond to similar phases in the other arts wholly, partially, or not at
all, and whether these developments are governed by any general laws. Terminology in this context requires the strictest possible material definitions;
in musicology, terms may need to be reevaluated in a framework of international cooperation. *(Susan Poliniak)*

4919 JONES, Claude E. **Ukiyoye and kabuki,** *Festival*
as *of Oriental Music and the Related Arts* (Los Angeles:
University of California, 1960) 37–40. See no. 418 in
this volume.
The *ukiyo-e* ("pictures of the floating world") style of wood-block printing
originated at the same time as kabuki, in the early 17th c., and the two arts
influenced each other in important ways. Kabuki actors worked with
ukiyo-e artists in the development of costumes and stage design, most effectively in the 19th c. *(Jianning You)*

4920 MOSER, Hans Joachim. **Die Stilverwandtschaft**
as **zwischen der Musik und den anderen Künsten**
[Style relationships between music and the other arts],
Zeitschrift für Ästhetik und allgemeine Kunstwissen-
schaft XIX (1925) 439–45. In German. See no. 114 in
this volume.
Music-historical developments explained in terms of other arts (such as
Curt Sachs's account of the 17th-c. abandonment of isometry as Baroque in
the wider sense) can often be better explained in strictly musical terms; artistic cross-comparisons should be used with caution. The argument is defended in appended remarks by Georg ANSCHÜTZ and SACHS.
(David Bloom)

4921 MUEREN, Floris van der. **L'histoire de la**
as **musique et la comparaison avec les autres arts**
[Music's history and its comparison with other arts],
Bericht über den internationalen musikwissenschaft-
lichen Kongreß Wien Mozartjahr 1956 (Graz; Köln:
Böhlau, 1958) 653–56. In French. See no. 365 in this
volume.
Comparative study of the arts should ask whether they change in analogous
ways at the boundary of each general periodization. The musicologist
should first consider transformations or reorganizations of musical techniques, then enter into comparison with other arts, and finally incorporate
findings into cultural history in its broadest sense. *(David Bloom)*

4922 NATALETTI, Giorgio. **Il disco e il film sonoro**
as **nella ricerca e nelle trascrizioni della musica**
popolare [The record and the sound film in the research and transcription of traditional music], *Atti del*
III Congresso nazionale di arti e tradizioni popolari
(Roma: Opera Nazionale Dopolavoro, 1936) 392–92.
In Italian. See no. 218 in this volume.

4923 ROSENFIELD, John M. **India: Rasa and raga,**
as *Festival of Oriental Music and the Related Arts* (Los
Angeles: University of California, 1960) 54–57. See
no. 418 in this volume.
In India's traditional culture, music, painting, dance, and poetry are all seen
as different pathways to a single devotional goal. The terms *rasa* (for the
emotion expressed) and *rāga* (for the traditional systematization of expression) have application in various art forms. *(Jianning You)*

4924 RUMMENHÖLLER, Peter. **Romantik und**
as **Gesamtkunstwerk** [Romanticism and the Gesamt-
kunstwerk], *Beiträge zur Geschichte der Musikans-*
schauung im 19. Jahrhundert (Regensburg: Bosse,
1965) 161–70. In German. See no. 483 in this volume.
A concept of the Gesamtkunstwerk that was distinct from Wagner's arose
from the inclination of early German Romantic writers to impure genres. It
is discernible in unrealized projects by Philipp Otto Runge ("eine abstracte
mahlerische phantastich-musikalische Dichtung mit Chören...") and
Friedrich Schlegel (a Utopian *Universalpoesie*), and successfully evoked
in the narrative prose of Clemens Brentano (*Godwi*, 1801) and Joseph von
Eichendorff (*Aus dem Leben eines Taugenicht*, 1826). *(David Bloom)*

4925 SMITS VAN WAESBERGHE, Joseph. **Der**
as **Niederländer in seinen tänzerischen, sprach-**
lichen, und musikalischen Äusserungen [The
Dutch in their dance, language, and music], *Actes du*
cinquième Congrès international d'esthétique/Pro-
ceedings of the Fifth International Congress of Aesthet-
ics ('s-Gravenhage: Mouton, 1964) 534–42. In German. See no. 475 in this volume.

76 Dance

4926 ALFORD, Violet. **Dances of the French Basque**
as **country,** *Congrès international des arts*
populaires/International congress of popular arts
(Paris: Institut international de coopération intellectuelle, 1928) 122–23. See no. 153 in this volume.
A brief analytic inventory of dance types of Basse-Navarre, Labourd, and
Soule départements, with attention to thematic content, music, and performance occasion. A French-language version is cited as no. 4927 in this
volume.

4927 ALFORD, Violet. **Quelques danses du Pays**
as **Basque français** [Several dances of the French
Basque region], *Art populaire: Travaux artistiques et*
scientifiques du Ier Congrès international des arts
populaires (Paris: Duchartre, 1931) 177–80. In French.
See no. 152 in this volume.
An English summary is abstracted as no. 4926 in this volume.

4928
as
AMADES GELAT, Joan. **Simbolismo delle danze catalane** [The symbolism of Catalan dances], *Atti del Congresso internazionale di musiche popolari mediterranee e del Convegno dei bibliotecari musicali* (Palermo: De Magistris succ. V. Bellotti, 1959) 123–26. In Italian. See no. 332 in this volume.

4929
as
ANDRADE, Mário de. **A calunga dos mara-catús** [The *calunga* of the maracatu], *Estudos Afro-Brasileiros.* I (Rio de Janeiro: Ariel, 1935) 39–48. In Portuguese. See no. 214 in this volume.
Discusses the role and origins of the *calunga*, a small doll carried by certain participants in the maracatu, a traditional processional dance from north-eastern Brazil.

4930
as
ARAMON I SERRA, Ramon. **Danse et bal du cierge de Castelltersol** [The dansa and ball del ciri of Castelltersol], *Congrès international des arts populaires/International congress of popular arts* (Paris: Institut international de coopération intellectuelle, 1928) 121. In French. See no. 153 in this volume.
Summary of the paper abstracted as no. 4931 in this volume.

4931
as
ARAMON I SERRA, Ramon. **La "Danza" et la danse du cierge de Castelltersol** [The dansa and ball del ciri of Castelltersol], *Art populaire: Travaux artistiques et scientifiques du Ier Congrès international des arts populaires* (Paris: Duchartre, 1931) 191. In French. See no. 152 in this volume.
Typical Catalan dances preserved in the town of Castelltersol in the El Valles region are the dansa and ball del ciri (candle dance) performed at the summer Festa Major. The ball del ciri is danced by couples holding a bouquet of flowers and a vase of scented water; at the end of the dance the vases are broken. Its music consists of a dansa, a sardana, and a pavana. A summary is cited as no. 4930 in this volume. *(James R. Cowdery)*

4932
as
ARCO Y GARAY, Ricardo del. **Les couplets et les "dances" dans le Haut-Aragon (Espagne)** [Coplas and *el dance* in northern Aragón (Spain)], *Art populaire: Travaux artistiques et scientifiques du Ier Congrès international des arts populaires* (Paris: Duchartre, 1931) 189. In French. See no. 152 in this volume.
Discusses el dance, a poetic dialogue with music and dance that accompanies processions for patron saints.

4933
as
ARCO Y GARAY, Ricardo del. **La jota aragonaise** [The Aragonese jota], *Art populaire: Travaux artistiques et scientifiques du Ier Congrès international des arts populaires* (Paris: Duchartre, 1931) 187. In French. See no. 152 in this volume.
Surveys the history, development, and typology of the song genre, and its relation to dance forms and to the cognate genres of Navarre and Valencia. A summary is cited as no. 2724 in this volume.

⟶
ARCO Y GARAY, Ricardo del. **Romances, couplets, danses et autres divertissements dans le Haut-Aragon** [Romances, coplas, and other entertainments in upper Aragon]. See no. 2725 in this volume.

4934
as
BAKÉ, Arnold Adriaan. **Indian folk dances,** *Journal of the International Folk Music Council* I (1949) 47–48. See no. 281 in this volume.
Surveys traditions in India, Nepal, and Sri Lanka.

4935
as
BARANDIARÁN, Salvador de. **Basque cere-monial dances,** *Journal of the International Folk Music Council* IX (1957) 43–44. See no. 362 in this volume.
Summary of a paper describing dances that have both social and civic significance.

4936
as
BARBEAU, Marius. **The folk dances of Can-ada,** *Journal of the International Folk Music Council* III (1951) 29. See no. 296 in this volume.
Summary of a paper discussing Native American, French, and English genres.

4937
as
BARBEAU, Marius. **Rondes from French Can-ada,** *Journal of the International Folk Music Council* VIII (1956) 40. See no. 349 in this volume.
Summary of a paper surveying traditional dances among French-speaking peoples of Canada and the southern U.S.

4938
as
BONOMO, Giuseppe. **La controdanze siciliana** [*sic*] [Sicilian contredanse], *Journal of the International Folk Music Council* II (1950) 49. In Italian. See no. 295 in this volume.
The conference report provides only a citation. Neither the text nor a summary of the paper was published here.

4939
as
BORRELLI, Nicola. **La tarentelle en Campanie** [The tarantella in Campania], *Congrès international des arts populaires/International congress of popular arts* (Paris: Institut international de coopération intellectuelle, 1928) 130. In French. See no. 153 in this volume.
Summary of the paper abstracted as no. 4940 in this volume.

4940
as
BORRELLI, Nicola. **La tarentelle en Campanie** [The tarantella in Campania], *Art populaire: Travaux artistiques et scientifiques du Ier Congrès international des arts populaires* (Paris: Duchartre, 1931) 175–76. In French. See no. 152 in this volume.
Survey of geographic distribution, comparison with other Southern Italian dances, and account of music. The tarantella is a survival of Bacchantic ritual of classical antiquity. A summary is cited as no. 4940 in this volume. *(James R. Cowdery)*

4941
as
BRAGAGLIA, Anton Giulio. **Balli popolari e danze d'arte** [Traditional dance and art dance], *Journal of the International Folk Music Council* II (1950) 49. In Italian. See no. 295 in this volume.
The conference report provides only a citation. Neither the text nor a summary of the paper was published here.

4942
as
BURCHENAL, Elizabeth. **Les danses populaires caractéristiques des États-Unis** [Typical traditional dances of the United States], *Art populaire: Travaux artistiques et scientifiques du Ier Congrès international des arts populaires* (Paris: Duchartre, 1931) 166–67. In French. See no. 152 in this volume.
An English summary is abstracted as no. 4943 in this volume.

4943
as
BURCHENAL, Elizabeth. **Distinctive American country dances which exist in rural communities in the United States,** *Congrès international des arts populaires/International congress of popular arts* (Paris: Institut international de coopération intellectuelle, 1928) 123–24. See no. 153 in this volume.

Traditional dances survive in rural areas of especially stable population. Some are reminiscent of dances of other nationalities, but most appear to be indigenous in origin, and have a distinctly American quality. Much of the music, performed by fiddlers, consists of familiar Irish, Scottish, and English tunes. Jazz, Native American, and African American music and dance should not be regarded as representative of the United States. A French-language version is cited as no. 4942 in this volume. *(David Bloom)*

4944 BURCHENAL, Elizabeth. **Folk dances of the**
as **United States: Regional types and origins,** *Journal of the International Folk Music Council* III (1951) 18–21. See no. 296 in this volume.
The contributions of Scottish and Irish colonists are highlighted, and four regional types—New England country dances, Appalachian mountain dances, play party games, and square dances—are described.
(James R. Cowdery)

4945 CARPITELLA, Diego. **Documenti coreutico-**
as **musicali sul** *tarantismo* **ancora oggi esistente in Puglia** [Choreological-musical documents of the tarantism still extant in Apulia], *VIͤ Congrès international des sciences anthropologiques et ethnologiques. I: Rapport général et anthropologie; II: Ethnologie* (Paris: Musée de l'Homme, 1962-1964) II, 95–96. In Italian. See no. 421 in this volume.
Summary account of research reported in the author's *L'esorcismo coreutico musicale del tarantismo* (in E. de Martino, *La terra del rimorso*, Milan: 1961).

4946 CARVALHO NETO, Paulo de. **La rúa: Una**
as **danza dramática de moros y cristianos en el folklore paraguayo** [The rúa: A dance-drama of Moors and Christians in Paraguayan folklore], *Miscellanea Paul Rivet octogenario dicata* (México, D.F.: Universidad Nacional Autónoma de México, 1958) II, 617–44. Illus., bibliog. In Spanish. See no. 394 in this volume.
Even though the Paraguayan rúa belongs to the group of dramatic dances imported from the Iberian Peninsula into South America, the transformations of its original model were such that later it came to be understood almost as an indigenous genre. The rúa is part of a subgenre of dances that dramatize the struggle between Christians and Moors, an event of great relevance for Iberian culture at the time of colonization, and which undoubtedly played an important role in the process of acculturation. The name of the dance appears in Paraguayan literature as early as 1795, and while the genre continued to flourish in that country, it declined steadily in Spain where it has completely disappeared in modern times. *(James Melo)*

4947 COMMENDA, Hans. **Innviertler Landla**
as **dance,** *Journal of the International Folk Music Council* II (1950) 33. See no. 295 in this volume.
Brief remarks to accompany a demonstration of a Ländler from the Inn region of Austria.

4948 ČUBELIĆ, Tvrtko. **Mogućnosti i osnovne**
as **pretpostavke scenskog izvođenja narodnih plesova** [Possibilities of and fundamental requirements for staged performances of folk dances], *Rad IX-og kongresa Saveza Folklorista Jugoslavije* (Sarajevo: Savez Udruženja Folklorista Jugoslavije, 1963) 435–43. In Croatian; summary in German. See no. 455 in this volume.
After the founding of professional folk dance ensembles in Croatia, starting in 1948, the amateur troupes that had flourished between the wars quickly deteriorated from lack of support; without them, the state-sponsored groups had no source of new ideas, and the quality of their work began to stagnate. The practice, begun around this time, of using fully realized dances as mere building material for original works, is very problematic. *(author)*

4949 ČUBELIĆ, Tvrtko. **Šta je dosad izostavljeno u**
as **scenskom izvođenju narodnih plesova** [What has been dropped from stage performances of folk dances], *Rad X-og kongresa Saveza Folklorista Jugoslavije* (Cetinje: Obod, 1964) 243–48. In Croatian; summary in Russian. See no. 462 in this volume.
Compares performances of folk dances in their authentic rural environment with their stage presentations, which have become popular in Yugoslavia since the 1950s.

4950 ČUČKOV, Emanuil. **Contenu idéologique et**
as **procès rythmique de la danse populaire macédonienne** [Ideological content and rhythmic process in Macedonian traditional dance], *Journal of the International Folk Music Council* IV (1952) 39–41. In French. See no. 306 in this volume.
Many Macedonian dances directly mime work activities, and reflect origins in 19th-c. economic developments, such as those called kalajdžiskoto (tinker), aramijskata (brigand), kopačka (tilling the soil), kako se sadi piperot (how to plant capsicums), and tkaenicata (weaving). The archaic teškoto (heavy dance) is similarly derived from shepherd's movements. The rusalije sword dance used to be performed as a general exorcism for the sick people and animals of a village on the nonfasting days between Christmas and Epiphany (7-19 January); the dancers were initiates of a fraternity dating from pre-Christian times. *(David Bloom)*

⟶ DART, Thurston. **Rôle de la danse dans l'***ayre* **anglais** [The role of dance in the English ayre]. See no. 1284 in this volume.

4951 DELIZ, Monserrate. **La danza puertorriqueña**
as [Puerto Rican dance], *Journal of the International Folk Music Council* VII (1955) 14. See no. 337 in this volume.
Summary of a paper.

4952 DESAIVRE, Léo. **La danse en Poitou** [Dance in
as Poitou], *La tradition en Poitou et Charentes: Art populaire, ethnographie, folk-lore, hagiographie, histoire* (Paris: Librairie de la Tradition Nationale, 1897) 397–404. In French. See no. 21 in this volume.
Several French kings were attracted to the dance known as branle de Poitou. The music featured oboes and cornamuses.

4953 DOMÍNGUEZ BERRUETA, Juan. **Les couplets**
as **et la musique de la jota aragonaise** [The couplets and music of the jota of Aragón], *Art populaire: Travaux artistiques et scientifiques du Iͤʳ Congrès international des arts populaires* (Paris: Duchartre, 1931) 187. In French. See no. 152 in this volume.

4954 DOPUĐA, Jelena. **Dječje narodne igre u Bosni i**
as **Hercegovini (plesne)** [Traditional children's dance-games in Bosnia and Herzegovina], *Rad VII-og kongresa Saveza Folklorista Jugoslavije* (Cetinje: Obod, 1964) 161–67. In Bosnian; summary in English. See no. 419 in this volume.
A preliminary classification of movement-games in the style of traditional dance: fragmentary movements by very small children, hand in hand with or in the lap of an adult; collective dances with mimetic content performed by children aged 3-14, some of which have been taken over from adult dances, but without their symbolic significance; and short and simple movements that accompany singing. *(author)*

4955 DOPUĐA, Jelena. **Dramski oblici, elementi i**
as **dramski način izvođenja u narodnim igrama-plesovima u Bosni i Hercegovini** [Dramatic forms, elements, and performance techniques in traditional dances of Bosnia and Herzegovina], *Rad X-og*

kongresa Saveza Folklorista Jugoslavije (Cetinje: Obod, 1964) 401–12. *Illus., dance notation.* In Bosnian; summary in English. See no. 462 in this volume.

Dances featuring dramatic/mimetic action, usually with sung dialogue, are discussed, with particular attention to the wide range of forms and styles. *(author)*

4956 DOPUĐA, Jelena. **Narodne igre i njihova**
as **povezanost sa motivima i elementima rada u**
Bosni i Hercegovini [Folk dances and their connection to motifs and elements of labor in Bosnia and Herzegovina], *Rad VIII-og kongresa folklorista Jugoslavije* (Beograd: Naučno Delo, 1961) 373–90. *Illus., transcr., dance notation.* In Bosnian; summary in English. See no. 446 in this volume.

Dances of the region relating to work may be categorized into eight groups, according to subject matter: motifs of household activities, of hunting and fishing, of cattle-breeding, of the cultivation of soil, of growing and harvesting food plants, of growing plants for and manufacturing textiles, of miscellaneous everyday activities, and of miscellaneous occupations. They are discussed with reference to historical origin, circumstances of performance, form, and choreographic structure. *(author)*

4957 DOPUĐA, Jelena. **Narodne igre u vezi sa smrti:**
as **Primjeri iz Bosne i Hecegovine** [Traditional dances related to death: Examples from Bosnia and Herzegovina], *Rad XI-og kongresa Saveza Folklorista Jugoslavije* (Zagreb: Savez Folklorista Jugoslavije, 1966) 361–69. In Serbian; summary in German. See no. 490 in this volume.

There are three types of dances related to death in Bosnia and Herzegovina: dances performed after a funeral (žalovito kolo, mrtvačko kolo, posmrtno kolo), dances with the motif of death (most, kapije, kalopero pero), and dances that depict life cycles from birth to death (pletikolo, ljeljenovo kolo).

4958 DOPUĐA, Jelena. **Narodne igre u vremenu**
as **Narodnooslobodilačke Borbe u Bosni i**
Hercegovini [Traditional dance from the time of the War of National Liberation in Bosnia and Herzegovina], *Rad kongresa folklorista Jugoslavije* (Ljubljana: Savez Udruženja Folkloristov Jugoslavije, 1960) 181–92. *Transcr., dance notation.* In Bosnian; summary in English. See no. 404 in this volume.

The dances of the war (1941-45) may be classified into four groups: the cheerful and easily performed Partisan dances, such as the kozaračko kolo; new dances created by analogy with the Partisan dances; traditional dances with new, topical song texts; and dances with no topical content, popular among combatants for purposes of relaxation alone. Some continue to be performed on national holidays and at political meetings; others have been abandoned by adults but are still performed by children. *(author)*

4959 DOPUĐA, Jelena. **Pregled narodnih igara**
as **Hercegovine** [A survey of the traditional dances of Herzegovina], *Rad IX-og kongresa Saveza Folklorista Jugoslavije* (Sarajevo: Savez Udruženja Folklorista Jugoslavije, 1963) 83–94. In Bosnian; summary in English. See no. 455 in this volume.

The oldest dances were performed to the accompaniment of singing, like the kolanje, or to no accompaniment at all; kolanje was the basic form. The generation that is now middle-aged added more elaborate dances and dances accompanied by dvojnice or diple. The younger generation has abandoned most old dances, especially those of the mimetic type, in favor of round dances with instruments and ballroom dance, though kolanje, proleta, and trojanac remain popular. *(author)*

4960 DOPUĐA, Jelena. **Problemi kinetografije** [Problems of dance notation], *Rad kongresa folklorista Jugoslavije* (Zagreb: Savez Udruženja Folklorista Jugoslavije, 1958) 11–38. In Croatian. See no. 315 in this volume.

Classifies systems for dance notation and surveys their application in transcriptions of traditional Yugoslav dances.

4961 DOUGLAS, Mona. **The Manx dirk dance as**
as **ritual,** *Journal of the International Folk Music Council* IX (1957) 31–33. See no. 362 in this volume.

Describes the background and performance of the dance—known locally as the Kirk Maughold sword dance—as taught to the author by its last remaining practitioner, Jack Kermode. *(James R. Cowdery)*

4962 DUCOUT, Marcel Stanislas. **Le chant de la**
as **danse: Recherches de synthèse de la danse et**
de la musique [The song of dance: The synthetic study of dance and music], *Deuxième congrès international d'esthétique et de Science de l'art* (Paris: Librairie Félix Alcan, 1937) II, 251–54. In French. See no. 249 in this volume.

The study of music and dance, which has hitherto been entirely at the analytic level, must now proceed to synthesis. Correspondences between musical sound and dancer's movement are proposed: pitch to the linear or angular distance covered by a motion, or one of its derivates, speed and acceleration; acoustic intensity to the distance between a moving body and stable mass; timbre to a less homogeneous set of modalities. *(David Bloom)*

4963 ELSCHEKOVÁ, Alica. **A study of central Slo-**
as **vak folk dance,** *Journal of the International Folk Music Council* XII (1960) 81. See no. 413 in this volume.

Brief remarks for a presentation of a film and recordings.

4964 FARA, S. **Il ballo tradizionale del popolo di**
as **Sardegna** [Traditional dances of the people of Sardinia], *Atti del 4. Congresso nazionale di arti e tradizioni popolari* (Roma: Opera Nazionale Dopolavoro, 1942) 382–402. In Italian. See no. 270 in this volume.

4965 GALANTI, Bianca Maria. **Analogie di forme e**
as **ritmi nelle espressioni coreutiche mediter-**
ranee: Il ballo tondo sardo e la sardana di
Catalogna [Analogies of form and rhythm in Mediterranean choreutic expression: The Sardinian ballo tondo and Catalan sardana], *Atti del Congresso internazionale di musiche popolari mediterranee e del Convegno dei bibliotecari musicali* (Palermo: De Magistris succ. V. Bellotti, 1959) 127–31. In Italian. See no. 332 in this volume.

There are no direct connections between the two round dances; the name of the Catalan dance, *sardana*, which sounds as if it ought to mean "Sardinian", is actually a modern derivate of an earlier *cerdana*. Both, however, are likely to have origins in ancient Greece.

4966 GALANTI, Bianca Maria. **La danse des**
as ***spadonari* (porte-glaive) dans la province du**
Piémont (Italie) [The dance of the *spadonari* (sword-bearers) in provincial Piedmont (Italy)], *Journal of the International Folk Music Council* VI (1954) 17–20. In French. See no. 320 in this volume.

The dance of the *spadonari di San Giorio* is performed over three days, beginning on St. George's Day, in San Giorgio (Turin). It dramatizes the legend of a wicked feudal lord who asserted the *jus primae noctis* over the brides of the local peasantry until he was assassinated by a young bridegroom and his friends. Other sword dances, such as those of St. Blaise at Venaus and St. Vincent at Giaglione (both Val di Susa), seem to have a principally religious significance, though in one figure in the latter the dancers pretend to use their sword blades as plows, evoking an origin in a primitive agricultural society. In general the most important aspect of the sword dance may be its aesthetic value, as a tribute and gift to the local patron saint. *(David Bloom)*

4967 GALANTI, Bianca Maria. **Forms and aspects of**
as **the ballo tondo sardo,** *Journal of the International Folk Music Council* II (1950) 14–16. See no. 295 in this volume.

Discusses variants of the Sardinian round dance also known as ballu sardu, ballu tundu, duru-duru, or boroboboi.

4968 GAMBLE, John Irvin. **Changing patterns in**
as **Kiowa Indian dances,** *Selected papers. I: The civilizations of ancient America; II: Acculturation in the Americas—Proceedings and selected papers; III: Indian tribes of aboriginal America* (Chicago: University of Chicago, 1951-1952) II, 94–104. See no. 292 in this volume.

Since the turn of the 20th c., the religious ceremony of the Sun Dance, which Kiowa people in Oklahoma used to gather to perform three times a year, has vanished. People continue to dance at small-scale rural singing and large-scale dance or powwow events, but the religious element is much diminished. Inventories are given of dances known from prior to 1900 and those of ca. 1949. The material is discussed at length in the author's M.A. thesis, *Kiowa dance gatherings and costumed dancers* (Washington U., 1952). *(David Bloom)*

⟶ GIOVANNELLI, Nikolai Leonida. **Some notes**
on the adaptation of traditional style and technique by nontraditional performers in respect of Manx songs and dances. See no. 2835 in this volume.

4969 GIULIANTE, Guido. **Saltarella: Ritmo vecchio**
as **e nuovo** [Saltarella: Old and new rhythm], *Lares* XXV (1959) 164–230. In Italian. See no. 370 in this volume.

Discusses the Abruzzi version of the saltarello, known locally as *saltarella*.

4970 GOREN-KADMAN, Ayalah. **Indigenous and**
as **imported elements in the new folk dance in Israel,** *Journal of the International Folk Music Council* III (1951) 55–57. See no. 296 in this volume.

Traditional Israeli dance is a blend of elements from Middle Eastern and Eastern European Jewish traditions.

4971 GRASES GONZÁLEZ, Pedro. **Les danses du**
as **Panadés** [The dansas of Penedès], *Congrès international des arts populaires/International congress of popular arts* (Paris: Institut international de coopération intellectuelle, 1928) 121–22. In French. See no. 153 in this volume.

Summary of the paper abstracted as no. 4972 in this volume.

4972 GRASES GONZÁLEZ, Pedro. **Les danses du**
as **Panadés (Los bailes del Panadès)** [The dansas of Penedès], *Art populaire: Travaux artistiques et scientifiques du Iᵉʳ Congrès international des arts populaires* (Paris: Ducharte, 1931) 192. In French. See no. 152 in this volume.

The Penedès region of Barcelona province is noted for outdoor dance-dramas (*balls*) representing historical or biblical events, by anonymous authors. A brief account of their content is provided. A summary is cited as no. 4971 in this volume. *(James R. Cowdery)*

4973 GRIMAUD, Yvette. **Étude analytique de la**
as **danse *choma* des Bochiman !Kung** [Analytical study of the *choma* dance of the !Kung San people], *Les colloques de Wégimont. IV: Ethnomusicologie III* (Paris: Belles Lettres, 1964) 171–83. *Transcr.* In French. See no. 401 in this volume.

Analysis of the continuous dancing performed by !Kung boys during the period of their *choma* or initiation ritual.

4974 GUILLOT DE RODE, François. **Fonction**
as **mythique et danse** [Mythic function and dance], *Actes du cinquième Congrès international d'esthétique/Proceedings of the Fifth International Congress of Aesthetics* ('s-Gravenhage: Mouton, 1964) 822–25. In French. See no. 475 in this volume.

From the first step, the movements of a dance create an unreal space-time by canceling the normal movements with which real space-time is defined; in this way dance emanates from mythic function in a way that is both immediate and primordially abstract. *(David Bloom)*

4975 GURVIN, Olav. **Three Norwegian dances,** *Journal of the International Folk Music Council* VI (1954) 48. See no. 320 in this volume.

The conference report provides only a citation. Neither the text nor a summary of the paper was published here.

⟶ GUZMÁN, Antonio. **Deux chansons et deux**
danses populaires de la province de Palencia. See no. 2841 in this volume.

4976 HADŽI-PECOVA, Marika. **Dečje igre u NR**
as **Makedoniji** [Children's games in Macedonia], *Rad VII-og kongresa Saveza Folklorista Jugoslavije* (Cetinje: Obod, 1964) 53–61. *Bibliog., transcr.* In Serbian. See no. 419 in this volume.

Remarks on the parameters of analyzing children's games in Macedonia; on the ways in which they reflect history and current events; and on their relations with similar games found in other parts of Yugoslavia. *(author)*

4977 HALSKI, Czesław. **The Polish origin of the**
as **polka,** *The book of the first international musicological congress devoted to the works of Frederick Chopin* (Warszawa: Państwowe Wydawnictwo Naukowe, 1963) 530–37. *Music, bibliog.* See no. 425 in this volume.

According to persistent mythology, the polka was invented in 1830 by a farm-maid in Kostelec nad Labem, the name a corruption of Czech *půlka* (half) on the basis of the dance's short steps. Research shows, however, that it is certainly of Polish origin, a form of krakowiak that became popular in Bohemia in the 1830s; the name is simply Czech for "Polish woman". It was transmitted to Western Europe through Bohemia, whence the belief that it originated there. *(Susan Poliniak)*

4978 HOERBURGER, Felix. **Dance and dance music**
as **of the 16th century and their relations to folk dance and folk music,** *Studia musicologica Academiae Scientiarum Hungaricae* VII (1965) 79–83. See no. 478 in this volume.

There was much mutual influence between peasantry and aristocracy in dance and dance music in the 16th c. Many traditional dances such as the galliard and branle were stylized and standardized in the courts. *(David Gagné)*

4979 HOERBURGER, Felix. **On relationships be-**
as **tween music and movement in folk dancing,** *Journal of the International Folk Music Council* XII (1960) 70. See no. 413 in this volume.

The notion of direct correspondence between traditional dance and music is oversimplified: Sometimes the relations between traditional music and dance resemble those in polyphonic music. *(James R. Cowdery)*

4980 HOERBURGER, Felix. **Proposals for the work**
as **of the IFMC Dance Commission,** *Journal of the International Folk Music Council* XIV (1962) 161–62. See no. 442 in this volume.

The International Folk Music Council should institute a special commission on traditional dance, charged with standardizing terminology and notation and assessing the dance situation in various countries. Eventually it might undertake the preparation of a large-scale bibliography and handbook. *(David Bloom)*

4981 HOERBURGER, Felix. **The study of folk dance**
as **and the need for a uniform method of notation,**
Journal of the International Folk Music Council XI
(1959) 71–73. See no. 392 in this volume.
Outlines the issues and problems involved in transcultural dance notation.
Labanotation offers the best solution available so far. *(James R. Cowdery)*

4982 HOERBURGER, Felix. **Wechselbeziehungen**
as **im Volkstanz der Slavischen und Germanischen Völker** [Relations between the traditional
dance of the Slavic and Germanic peoples], *Treći
kongres folklorista Jugoslavije* (Cetinje: Udruženje
Folklorista Crne Gore, 1958) 297–302. In German;
summary in Croatian. See no. 357 in this volume.

⟶ HROVATIN, Radoslav. **Problemi studija
narodnih pesama i igrara u vezi sa radom**
[Problems in the study of traditional songs and dances
related to work]. See no. 2438 in this volume.

4983 HYE-KERKDAL, K.J. **Tanz im Alten China**
as [Dance in ancient China], *VIe Congrès international
des sciences anthropologiques et ethnologiques. I:
Rapport général et anthropologie; II: Ethnologie*
(Paris: Musée de l'Homme, 1962-1964) II, 105–06. In
German. See no. 421 in this volume.
Summary version of a paper published under the same title in *Archiv für
Völkerkunde* 16 (1961).

4984 ILIJIN, Milica. **Influences réciproques des
as danses urbaines et traditionnelles en
Yougoslavie** [Reciprocal influences of urban and traditional dances of Yugoslavia], *Studia musicologica
Academiae Scientiarum Hungaricae* VII (1965) 85–89.
In French. See no. 478 in this volume.
The 19th-c. influx of foreign traditional and social dances produced varying results in different parts of Yugoslavia. In Serbia, traditional dance remained the dominant force, though it became more elaborate through contact with outside genres. Elsewhere, foreign dances replaced traditional
dances, or merged with them to create hybrid forms. *(Daniel Horn)*

4985 ILIJIN, Milica. **Međusobni uticaji narodnih
as igara raznih etničkih grupa u Prizrenu** [Mutual
influences of the traditional dances of the different ethnic groups in Prizren], *Rad kongresa folklorista
Jugoslavije* (Zagreb: Savez Udruženja Folklorista
Jugoslavije, 1959) 153–57. In Serbian; summary in
German. See no. 382 in this volume.
Influences in traditional dance from one ethnic group to another in Prizren,
Kosovo are never one-sided but always mutual, as is shown by the examples of the lako kolo ("light" kolo) and dances derived from the Turkish
kılıç sword dance. The latter are danced not only by Turks but also by Serbs
(who call their version *kaladžone*), Albanians, Vlachs, and Gypsies, all of
whom deny its Turkish origins and claim to have invented it themselves.
(author)

4986 ILIJIN, Milica. **Narodna orska umetnost u
as oblasti Titovog Užica** [Folk dance in the region of
Titovo Užice], *Rad VIII-og kongresa folklorista
Jugoslavije* (Beograd: Naučno Delo, 1961) 107–15.
Port. In Serbian; summary in French. See no. 446 in this
volume.
Although the very old local dances, unlike songs, seem not to be performed
by young people, some survive among the elderly. These are listed and discussed in terms of their relation to dances from elsewhere in Serbia and
Montenegro, vocal and instrumental accompaniment, and the occasions of
their performance, in particular *sabor* lamenting assemblies. *(author)*

4987 ILIJIN, Milica. **Narodne igre u Timočkoj
as Krajini** [Traditional dance in the Timočka Krajina],
Rad kongresa folklorista Jugoslavije (Beograd:
Naučno Delo, 1960) 41–45. In Serbian; summary in
French. See no. 402 in this volume.
The very rich, ethnically complex situation of dance traditions on the
Timok river border between Serbia and Bulgaria is now giving way to an
urbanized folklore, as a result of recent economic and cultural progress.
(author)

4988 ILIJIN, Milica. **Problemi kinetografije: Sistem
as Ljubice i Danice S. Janković** [Problems of dance
notation: The dance notation system of Ljubica and
Danica S. Janković], *Rad kongresa folklorista
Jugoslavije* (Zagreb: Savez Udruženja Folklorista
Jugoslavije, 1958) 39–44. In Serbian; summary in
French. See no. 315 in this volume.
Ljubica and Danica S. Janković published 637 transcriptions of folk dances
in Yugoslavia, applying their own tablature notation system.

4989 IVANČAN, Ivan. **Elementi alpskih plesova u
as Istri** [Elements of Alpine dance in Istria], *Rad
kongresa folklorista Jugoslavije* (Ljubljana: Savez
Udruženja Folkloristov Jugoslavije, 1960) 97–101. In
Croatian; summary in French. See no. 404 in this
volume.
Affinities between Istrian dances and those of the Alpine region include the
formation of couples within the circle; the leadership of the baton-carrying
Tanzführer or *promena*; stomping with one leg while the free leg is extended forward; and the use of teasing verses in sung accompaniment.
Other traits suggest more recent Austrian and Slovene influences. *(author)*

4990 JANKOVIĆ, Danica S.; JANKOVIĆ, Ljubica S.
as **Styles et techniques des danseurs traditionnels
serbes** [Styles and techniques of Serbian traditional
dancers], *Journal of the International Folk Music
Council* IV (1952) 12–15. In French. See no. 306 in this
volume.
Surveys the history and stylistic range of ethnic-Serb dance in Serbia
proper, Kosovo, and Vojvodina, and discusses the outlook for its preservation. *(David Bloom)*

4991 JANKOVIĆ, Ljubica S.; JANKOVIĆ, Danica S.
as **Sur les traces du plus ancien héritage culturel
de la danse et de la musique traditionelles
Yougoslaves** [On the track of the oldest cultural heritage in traditional Yugoslav dance and music], *Les
colloques de Wégimont. III: Ethnomusicologie II*
(Paris: Belles Lettres, 1960) 149–61. In French. See no.
366 in this volume.
According to research on traditional dance undertaken between the two
world wars, the regions of Kosovo and Metohija in Serbia preserve the oldest rituals, the oldest ritual melodies used to accompany ritual dance, the
oldest traditional relationships between music and dance (notably, the practice by which the drummer takes the beat from the principal dancer), and the
oldest surviving form of *čalgija* (a traditional orchestra of Turkish origin).
Poreč on the Istrian peninsula preserves the next oldest traditions, followed
by villages of the Mijac subgroup of Macedonians. Certain Yugoslav traditions have parallels in traditions of southern India; their relationships remain to be studied. *(David Hathwell)*

4992 JANKOVIĆ, Ljubica S.; JANKOVIĆ, Danica S.
as **Tragom našeg najstarijeg orskog kulturnog
nasleđa: Izvod** [On the trail of our oldest cultural heritage in the oro genre: Summary], *Rad VII-og kongresa
Saveza Folklorista Jugoslavije* (Cetinje: Obod, 1964)
159–60. In Serbian. See no. 419 in this volume.
Discusses the history and development of the oro dance tradition in
Kosovo, Serbia and in Macedonia.

4993 JELÍNKOVÁ, Zdenka. **Lidové tance na Podluží**
as [Traditional dance of the Podluží region], *Rad kongresa folklorista Jugoslavije* (Beograd: Naučno Delo, 1960) 217–24. In Czech; summary in Serbian. See no. 402 in this volume.

4994 KACAROVA, Rajna. **Pădarevski kukeri** [The
as *kukeri* of Pădarevo], *Rad IX-og kongresa Saveza Folklorista Jugoslavije* (Sarajevo: Savez Udruženja Folklorista Jugoslavije, 1963) 499–508. *Illus., transcr.* In Bulgarian; summary in German. See no. 455 in this volume.
In the village of Pădarevo, Bulgaria, masked *kukeri* dancers used to perform on Shrove Tuesday but have shifted the celebration to the feast of St. Simeon Senex (celebrated by the Orthodox on 16 February in the Gregorian calendar), just after the Trifon Zarezan vintners' festival. The song-melody, costumes, rituals, and historical significance of the phenomenon are discussed. *(author)*

4995 KACAROVA, Rajna. **Sur un phénomène**
as **concernant le manque de coïncidences entre la figure chorégraphique et la phrase mélodique** [On a phenomenon concerning the lack of correspondence between choreographic figure and melodic phrase], *Journal of the International Folk Music Council* XII (1960) 68–69. In French. See no. 413 in this volume.
Some traditional dances involve melodic and choreographic figures that do not correspond metrically; for example, Bulgarian horos where four-measure choreographic patterns are danced to three-measure melodic phrases (and other non-matching combinations) are common. One of the explanations of this phenomenon is the evolution of the music and the dance in relative independence from one another. In such instances, the underlying rhythm is the binding element between the music and dance, rather than the periodicity of figures. *(Murat Eyüboğlu)*

4996 KACAROVA, Rajna. **La tradition et l'espirit**
as **novateur dans la danse populaire** [Tradition and the innovative spirit in folk dance], *Journal of the International Folk Music Council* XV (1963) 63–64. *Transcr.* In French. See no. 459 in this volume.
Descriptions of traditional dances from 150 years ago correspond closely to their current performance. Still, traditional dances evolve. Different movements and accents are introduced when a new melody is used; and without any change in the melody, individual dancers may introduce new steps, movements, and gestures. Also, modifications to melody and to choreography may occur simultaneously. Modifications to traditional dances always occur within the parameters of the prototype to which they originally belong. Two versions of the *Ronde des brigades*, sung by railroad workers of the Lovetch-Troyan line, are discussed. *(Murat Eyüboğlu)*

4997 KADMAN, Gurit. **The creative process in pres-**
as **ent-day Israeli dances,** *Journal of the International Folk Music Council* XII (1960) 85–86. See no. 413 in this volume.
Brief remarks for a presentation of films.

4998 KADMAN, Gurit. **Yemenite dances and their**
as **influence on the new Israeli folk dances,** *Journal of the International Folk Music Council* IV (1952) 27–29. See no. 306 in this volume.
The Yemeni Jewish community represents the oldest continuous settlement of Jews in the world. Its members began emigrating to Palestine some time before 1900. Yemeni Jewish dance has an essentially religious function, particularly that of men, which is more interesting, creative, and tradition-bound than that of the women. Its Asian character has provided an essential counterbalance to the European style with which Israeli neotraditional dance began at the 1944 Shavuot festival at Kibbutz Dalia. *(David Bloom)*

4999 KARPELES, Maud. **The folk dance revival in**
as **England, with special reference to folk dancing in school,** *Travaux du Ier Congrès International de Folklore* (Tours: Arrault et Cie, 1938) 382–85. See no. 251 in this volume.
Discusses the contributions of Cecil Sharp (1859-1924) to the English folk dance revival, which include collection and notation as well as the founding of the English Folk Dance Society in 1911.

5000 KENNEDY, Douglas. **England's ritual dances,**
as *Journal of the International Folk Music Council* II (1950) 8–10. See no. 295 in this volume.
Discusses morris and other seasonal and ceremonial genres.

5001 KENNEDY, Douglas. **English folk-dance,**
as *Congrès international des arts populaires/International congress of popular arts* (Paris: Institut international de coopération intellectuelle, 1928) 124–27. See no. 153 in this volume.
Ritual dances include sword dance, Morris dance, and ceremonial processions such as the Furry dance of Helston, Cornwall; the Horn dance of Abbots Bromley, Staffordshire; and the Hobby Horse of Padstow, Cornwall, and Minehead, Somerset. The country dance, purely social in character, is found with a wide variety of steps and figures in all parts of England, lowland Scotland, and rural communities of North America. *(David Bloom)*

5002 KENNEDY, Douglas. **l'importance de la par-**
as **ticipation de la communauté à la danse** [The importance of community participation in dance], *La musique dans l'éducation* (Paris: UNESCO; Colin, 1955) 191–95. In French. See no. 323 in this volume.
An English-language version is abstracted as no. 5003 in this volume.

5003 KENNEDY, Douglas. **The importance of audi-**
as **ence participation in dancing,** *Music in education* (Paris: UNESCO, 1955) 183–87. See no. 322 in this volume.
Laypeople's enjoyment of music depends on their ability to enter actively into the music. The best way to teach traditional dancing seems to be for skilled dancers to demonstrate and for unskilled persons to follow their demonstration. A French-language version is cited as no. 4800 in this volume. *(Elizabeth A. Wright)*

→ KENNEDY, Douglas. **La renaissance de la musique et de la danse populaire en Angleterre** [The rebirth of traditional music and dance in England]. See no. 2888 in this volume.

5004 KNUST, Albrecht. **An introduction to**
as **Kinetography Laban (Labanotation),** *Journal of the International Folk Music Council* XI (1959) 73–76. *Dance notation.* In English, German, and French. See no. 392 in this volume.

5005 KODERA, Yukichi; KITANO, H.; ORIGUCHI,
as Nobuo. **Les danses populaires japonaises** [Japanese traditional dances], *Art populaire: Travaux artistiques et scientifiques du Ier Congrès international des arts populaires* (Paris: Duchartre, 1931) 185–86. In French. See no. 152 in this volume.
A classificatory survey under the headings kagura, animal dances (such as the lion dance shishi-mai), bon, erotic dance, and dances associated with religious processions such as rendō, furyū, and hayashi. From the choreographic point of view there are two basic genres: slow dances accompanied by song, and fast dances with only instrumental accompaniment. Efforts to preserve the heritage of traditional dance in Japan are noted. A summary is cited as no. 5006 in this volume. *(James R. Cowdery)*

5006
as
KODERA, Yukichi; KITANO, H.; ORIGUCHI, Nobuo. **Les danses populaires japonaises** [Japanese traditional dances], *Congrès international des arts populaires/International congress of popular arts* (Paris: Institut international de coopération intellectuelle, 1928) 130–33. In French. See no. 153 in this volume.

Summary of the paper abstracted as no. 5005 in this volume.

5007
as
KUBA, Ludvík. **La danse slave: Ses principales formes et leur signification** [Slavic dance: Its principal forms and their significance], *Congrès international des arts populaires/International congress of popular arts* (Paris: Institut international de coopération intellectuelle, 1928) 133–34. In French. See no. 153 in this volume.

Summary of the paper abstracted as no. 5008 in this volume.

5008
as
KUBA, Ludvík. **La danse slave: Ses principales formes et leur signification** [Slavic dance: Its principal forms and their significance], *Art populaire: Travaux artistiques et scientifiques du Ier Congrès international des arts populaires* (Paris: Duchartre, 1931) 166. In French. See no. 152 in this volume.

Dance is the art form representing that system of the universe that is founded on the principle of the ego. Slavic dance may be subclassified in this way into individual dances (glorifying the ego itself), couple dances (glorifying the union of two individuals toward the perpetuation of the species), and collective dances (glorifying the social ideal). A summary is cited as no. 5007 in this volume. *(David Bloom)*

5009
as
KUMER, Zmaga. **Plesni tip "raj" pri Slovencih** [The raj-type dances among the Slovenes], *Treći kongres folklorista Jugoslavije* (Cetinje: Udruženje Folklorista Crne Gore, 1958) 289–95. In Slovene; summary in German. See no. 357 in this volume.

5010
as
KUMER, Zmaga. **Vsebina in pomen plesne igre most na Slovenskem** [Meaning and content of the *most* game in Slovenia], *Rad IX-og kongresa Saveza Folklorista Jugoslavije* (Sarajevo: Savez Udruženja Folklorista Jugoslavije, 1963) 471–79. In Slovene; summary in French. See no. 455 in this volume.

The *most* (bridge) game is a ritual dance-game practiced in Easter or Pentecost celebrations in Bela Krajina, and formerly known throughout the rest of Slovenia, where it survives as a children's game. It is accompanied by songs describing a bridge's construction and a sacrifice required of those who want to cross it. Only five rather primitive tunes are used, and the heptasyllabic verse is of an archaic Slovene style. The significance of the ritual is unclear: it may descend from sacrifices on the occasion of building a bridge to water and fertility deities, and it may symbolize regeneration. *(author)*

5011
as
KURATH, Gertrude Prokosch; CHILKOVSKY, Nadia. **Jazz choreology,** *Men and cultures: Selected papers* (Philadelphia: University of Pennsylvania, 1960) 152–60. *Illus., bibliog., discog., dance notation.* See no. 359 in this volume.

An ethnochoreological approach to popular dance forms in North America based on jazz rhythm, with separate brief communications by Kurath on the evolution from the two-step to the various forms of jitterbug—fox trot, duck walk, double lindy, etc.—and by Chilkovsky on the use of Labanotation in recording such dances.

5012
as
LABAN, Juana de. **Rhythm and tempo in dance notation,** *Journal of the International Folk Music Council* XI (1959) 76–77. See no. 392 in this volume.

Summary of a paper.

5013
as
LABAN, Rudolf von. **Der Tanz als Eigenkunst** [Dance as an art in its own right], *Zeitschrift für Ästhetik und allgemeine Kunstwissenschaft* XIX (1925) 356–64. *Dance notation.* In German. See no. 114 in this volume.

What moves us in dance is neither the accompanying music nor any dramatic scenario, but the movement of the human body, in a regular rhythm, inscribed in the surrounding space. An analysis of this type has always been available for the higher forms of dance; its history is connected to the history of dance notation. *(David Bloom)*

5014
as
LABAN, Rudolf von. **Wege zur Aesthetik der Tanzkunst** [Toward an aesthetics of the art of dance], *Deuxième congrès international d'esthétique et de Science de l'art* (Paris: Librairie Félix Alcan, 1937) II, 474–77. In German. See no. 249 in this volume.

5015
as
LAJTHA, László. **Les jeux et les danses populaires en Hongrie** [Traditional games and dances in Hungary], *Art populaire: Travaux artistiques et scientifiques du Ier Congrès international des arts populaires* (Paris: Duchartre, 1931) 172–74. In French. See no. 152 in this volume.

5016
as
LANGEVIN, Vige. **Le style de la danse populaire en France** [The style of popular dance in France], *Journal of the International Folk Music Council* II (1950) 24–28. In French. See no. 295 in this volume.

Popular dance may be defined as that cultivated among and transmitted by urban and rural working people, whether or not it originates among them rather than in courtly, bourgeois, or intellectual circles. Its classification in France must be made on the basis not of morphological analysis but of style. The repertoire of styles is surveyed briefly by geographic region. *(David Bloom)*

5017
as
LAPSON, Dvora. **Jewish dances of Eastern and Central Europe,** *Indiana theory review* XV (1963) 58–61. See no. 459 in this volume.

5018
as
LAUDOVÁ, Hannah. **Dramski elementi u narodnoj igri** [Dramatic elements in traditional dance], *Rad X-og kongresa Saveza Folklorista Jugoslavije* (Cetinje: Obod, 1964) 395–99. In Serbian; summary in French. See no. 462 in this volume.

If traditional dance is to continue to exist, it must be presented in staged performances. Contemporary ensembles have understood that dances, customs, and rituals offer a naturally dramatic basis for staging, allowing them to distance themselves from strange bourgeois hybrid forms. *(author)*

5019
as
LAUDOVÁ, Hannah. **Sword dances and their parallels in the C.S.S.R,** *Indiana theory review* XV (1963) 62–63. See no. 459 in this volume.

Summary of a paper.

5020
as
LAUDOVÁ, Hannah. **Tradicije i neke crte razvoja savremenog razvoja igračkog folklora u CSSR** [Traditions and evolutionary traits in the contemporary dance folklore of Czechoslovakia], *Rad IX-og kongresa Saveza Folklorista Jugoslavije* (Sarajevo: Savez Udruženja Folklorista Jugoslavije, 1963) 515–18. In Serbian; summary in French. See no. 455 in this volume.

The folk-dance revival in Bohemia toward the end of the 19th c. took place at the same time as patriarchal institutions in rural life began to disintegrate; amateur ensembles played an important role in national efforts to democratize social relations. The creative work of contemporary professional ensembles can hardly be called folk dance, but it does make a contribution to the continuity of the tradition of folk performance. *(author)*

5021
as

LESURE, François. **Le recueil de ballets de Michel Henry (vers 1620)** [The ballet collection of Michel Henry (circa 1620)], *Les fêtes de la Renaissance* (Paris: Centre National de la Recherche Scientifique [CNRS], 1956) 205–20. *Bibliog.* In French. See no. 350 in this volume.

Contains a list of ballet performances at the French court, 1580-1620 in chronological order as they appear in the MS of Michel Henry. The list includes titles, dates, musical instruments used, numbers of airs, names of artists or singers, and other details.

5022
as

LIFAR, Serge. **Le ballet, synthèse des arts, dans son évolution technique et esthétique** [Ballet, as a sythesis of the arts, in its technical and aesthetic evolution], *Actes du cinquième Congrès international d'esthétique/Proceedings of the Fifth International Congress of Aesthetics* ('s-Gravenhage: Mouton, 1964) 106–09. In French. See no. 475 in this volume.

Dance, as an incarnation of rhythm, is art par excellence, using the body to inscribe poetry in space, and transmitting a metaphysical message as the source of life, love, and unreal visions. It may be speculated that dancers created religion out of aesthetics. *(David Bloom)*

5023
as

LIFAR, Serge. **L'évolution technique et esthétique de la danse académique** [The technical and aesthetic evolution of academic dance], *Proceedings of the Third International Congress on Aesthetics/Actes du troisiéme Congrès international d'esthétique/Atti del III Congresso internazionale di estetica* (Torino: Edizioni della Rivista di Estetica, 1957) 664–68. In French. See no. 363 in this volume.

Brief account of the history and basic principles of ballet as an intellectually founded art, from the ballet de cour of the 17th c. through the reforms introduced by the author in his work at the Paris Opéra and at the Institut Chorégraphique (founded 1947, renamed Université de la Danse in 1957). The staging of *Icare* (1935, score by Arthur Honegger) and the publication of *Le manifeste du chorégraphe* (Paris, 1935) are also discussed. *(David Bloom)*

5024
as

LIFAR, Serge. **Les grands courants de la chorégraphie à travers le XXᵉ siècle** [The major trends of choreography in the 20th century], *Deuxième congrès international d'esthétique et de Science de l'art* (Paris: Librairie Félix Alcan, 1937) II, 478–83. In French. See no. 249 in this volume.

5025
as

LORENZEN, Poul. **The revival of folk dancing in Denmark,** *Journal of the International Folk Music Council* I (1949) 24–27. See no. 281 in this volume.

Aspects of the preservation of Danish traditional dance are discussed, with attention to the efforts of the Foreningen til Folkedansens Fremme (the Danish Folk Dance Society, founded in 1901).

⟶

LOUDON, E. **Les cérémonies et les poèmes dansés des Indiens Pueblos** [Ceremonies and danced poems of the Pueblo Indians]. See no. 3165 in this volume.

5026
as

MARCEL-DUBOIS, Claudie. **L'esthétique et la technique des danses populaires** [The aesthetic and technique of traditional dances], *Deuxième congrès international d'esthétique et de Science de l'art* (Paris: Librairie Félix Alcan, 1937) I, 322–25. In French. See no. 249 in this volume.

The aesthetics of traditional dance is a consequence of its functional origin in the attainment of practical goals through magic; the direct and instinctive mode of transmission; and the performer's freedom within the basic rules of a particular dance. Note is made of the efforts of the Archives Internationales de la Danse to familiarize the public with a range of European dance traditions through its diorama exhibits. *(David Schiff)*

5027
as

MARÉ, Rolf de. **Évolution du ballet, de 1900 à nos jours** [The evolution of the ballet, from 1900 to the present], *Deuxième congrès international d'esthétique et de Science de l'art* (Paris: Librairie Félix Alcan, 1937) II, 466–70. In French. See no. 249 in this volume.

5028
as

MARTIN, György. **Considérations sur l'analyse des relations entre la danse et la musique de danse populaire** [Considerations on the analysis of the relationship between dance and traditional dance music], *Studia musicologica Academiae Scientiarum Hungaricae* VII (1965) 315–38. *Illus., music, bibliog.* In French. See no. 478 in this volume.

Rhythm is the guiding and unifying factor in the relationship between dance and dance music.

5029
as

MARTIN, György. **East-European relations of Hungarian dance types,** *Europa et Hungaria: Congressus ethnographicus in Hungaria* (Budapest: Akadémiai Kiadó, 1965) 469–515. *Illus., bibliog.* See no. 460 in this volume.

The old Hungarian dance types generally stem from the same stock as those of Slovakia, Romania, and Poland. Strong Balkan influences may be detected in the Hungarian weapon dances. *(Won-Bin Yim)*

5030
as

MASOLIVER MARTÍNEZ, Juan. **La "dance" de Híjar (province de Teruel)** [The *dance* of Híjar (Teruel province)], *Art populaire: Travaux artistiques et scientifiques du Iᵉʳ Congrès international des arts populaires* (Paris: Duchartre, 1931) 188. In French. See no. 152 in this volume.

The form of the Aragonese *dance* practiced in the town of Híjar in Teruel province is a sacred drama venerating the Virgin Mary. One group of performers represents an invasion of infidels attempting to steal a statue of the Virgin; they are opposed by a group of Christian soldiers. A battle is enacted, after which the soldiers perform a sequence of dances. A summary is cited as no. 5031 in this volume. *(James R. Cowdery)*

5031
as

MASOLIVER MARTÍNEZ, Juan. **La danse de Híjar** [The *dance* of Híjar], *Congrès international des arts populaires/International congress of popular arts* (Paris: Institut international de coopération intellectuelle, 1928) 121. In French. See no. 153 in this volume.

Summary of the paper abstracted as no. 5030 in this volume.

⟶

MASU, Takāki (Genjiro). **Music and dances of Japan.** See no. 2661 in this volume.

⟶

MATSUMIYA, Suiho. **Traditional music and dance in Japan today: Its stability and evolution.** See no. 2663 in this volume.

5032
as

MICHAĪLĪDĪS, Sólōn. **Greek song-dance,** *Journal of the International Folk Music Council* VIII (1956) 37–39. See no. 349 in this volume.

Surveys Greek traditional dances from antiquity to the present, with references to accompanying songs.

5033
as

MILLIGAN, Jean C. **Scottish country dancing,** *Journal of the International Folk Music Council* II (1950) 32. See no. 295 in this volume.

Brief remarks to accompany a demonstration.

5034
as

MLADENOVIĆ, Olivera. **Opšti pregled na partizanske i druge narodne igre u Oslobodilačkom Ratu** [Survey of Partisan and other neotraditional dances in the War of Liberation], *Rad* *kongresa folklorista Jugoslavije* (Ljubljana: Savez Udruženja Folkloristov Jugoslavije, 1960) 177–80. In Serbian; summary in French. See no. 404 in this volume.

Partisan dances from the Yugoslav War of National Liberation (1941-45) are a possibly unique case of traditional dance arising from war conditions. They were performed not only by cultural teams but also by the combatants themselves, or by the combatants with the inhabitants of liberated regions. Dances included the local ones, and some known throughout Yugoslavia such as the kozaračko kolo and the crnogorsko kolo; they were accompanied by topical songs mostly in octosyllabic or decasyllabic couplets. Most are now disappearing, though the kozaračko kolo continues to be performed. *(author)*

5035
as
MLADENOVIĆ, Olivera. **Prilike i mesta za igranje u Srbiji** [Occasions and places for dance in Serbia], *Treći kongres folklorista Jugoslavije* (Cetinje: Udruženje Folklorista Crne Gore, 1958) 263–80. *Illus., bibliog.* In Serbian; summary in French. See no. 357 in this volume.

Dances are usually performed in Serbia on church and secular holidays. They usually start early in the evening and last all night, sometimes even until noon the following day, but on specific occasions (as in the custom called *ranilo*) they could begin in the middle of the night. Dances on regular days could be held in the center of the village, on its edge, or distanced from it; on church holidays they are usually performed near the church; and during family celebrations (such as weddings) dances are held in homes.

5036
as
MLADENOVIĆ, Olivera. **Proigravanje devojaka u okolini Beograda** [Dance initiation rites for girls in the Belgrade vicinity], *Rad IX-og kongresa Saveza Folklorista Jugoslavije* (Sarajevo: Savez Udruženja Folklorista Jugoslavije, 1963) 463–70. In Serbian; summary in German. See no. 455 in this volume.

In the villages of the Belgrade vicinity, girls join the kolo dance for the first time at the age of 16 or 17, at one of the important spring festivals, with ceremonies that may be survivals of an old pubertal initiation rite; being admitted to the kolo is a sign of the girl's marriageability. *(author)*

5037
as
MLAKAR, Pino. **Razvitak plesnog pisma** [The development of dance notation], *Rad kongresa folklorista Jugoslavije* (Zagreb: Savez Udruženja Folklorista Jugoslavije, 1958) 55–60. In Croatian. See no. 315 in this volume.

Outlines the history of music notation since its beginnings, and recommends Labanotation as the most appropriate system of dance notation for traditional dance.

5038
as
MORTENSEN, Otto. **The Polish dance in Denmark,** *The book of the first international musicological congress devoted to the works of Frederick Chopin* (Warszawa: Państwowe Wydawnictwo Naukowe, 1963) 572–77. See no. 425 in this volume.

In the 16th c., the traditional outdoor chain dances of Denmark began to be replaced by indoor pair dancing, first among the nobility and then among other classes; a dance genre of Polish origin (polskdans, polonesse, or polonaise) became extremely popular in spite of a reputation for being immoral, violent, and even on occasion lethal (three accounts of death by dancing are attested in documents of 1579-90). The history of the dance and its nomenclature through the 19th c. are surveyed; biographical information is provided on Polish musicians active in Denmark in the 17th c. *(Susan Poliniak)*

5039
as
MUÑOZ, Marta Amor. **Problemas de sistematización de las danzas folklóricas** [Problems in the systematization of traditional dances], *Actas do Congresso Internacional de Etnografia* (Porto: Imprensa Portuguesa, 1965) II, 179–84. In Spanish. See no. 473 in this volume.

In Argentina, ethnomusicologists and ethnochoreologists including Carlos Vega, Isabel Artez, and Antonio R. Barceló have adapted Curt Sachs's classification system. The three-year curriculum of the Escuela Nacional de Danzas de Argentina is discussed. *(Peter S. Bushnell)*

5040
as
NASELLI, Carmelina. **Aspects de la danse rituelle en Italie: Les danses des rites matrimoniaux** [Aspects of ritual dance in Italy: Dances in marriage rites], *Journal of the International Folk Music Council* VI (1954) 15–17. In French. See no. 320 in this volume.

The purpose of wedding dances today appears to be a simple expression of good wishes, but they were originally meant to emphasize the couple's change of social status. Some, such as the lachera in Piedmont, have become elaborated from a single figure, while others consist of a fragment of a more complex dance; for example, the laccio d'amore in Abruzzi is the last figure of a traditional sword dance, in which the dancers leave aside their swords to dance around a pole, carrying the end of a ribbon fixed to the top of the pole. Along with other plait dances, ribbon dances, and Maypole celebrations proper to various calendar occasions in different parts of Italy, the laccio d'amore retains a symbolic reference to fecundity in the presence of women dancing around a pole, reminiscent of the Lucania betrothal custom in which the man presents the woman with a long staff wrapped in ribbon and hung with gifts of jewelry. *(David Bloom)*

5041
as
NEUBAUER, Henrik. **Osnovi kinetografije i njena primjena u folkloristici** [Basic dance notation and its application in ethnochoreology], *Rad kongresa folklorista Jugoslavije* (Zagreb: Savez Udruženja Folklorista Jugoslavije, 1958) 61–78. In Croatian; summary in English. See no. 315 in this volume.

Describes the Labanotation system and its application in transcribing traditional dances.

⟶ NKETIA, Joseph Hanson Kwabena. **The interrelations of African music and dance.** See no. 2570 in this volume.

5042
as
NORLIND, Tobias. **Die polnischen Tänze ausserhalb Polens** [Polish dances outside Poland], *Report of the Fourth Congress of the International Musical Society* (London: Novello, 1912) 201–04. *Music.* In German. See no. 71 in this volume.

The mazurka, the polonaise, and the Swedish polska were all derived from 16th-c. Polish dance.

5043
as
NOTOHADINEGORO, Sugeng. **Some particulars of Indonesian dancing,** *Journal of the International Folk Music Council* II (1950) 35–36. See no. 295 in this volume.

Focuses on the *wayang wong* genre of Java, with brief remarks on other Indonesian genres.

5044
as
OBRADOVIĆ, Milica. **"Mrtvac" u nekim društvenim igrama na području Bosne i Hercegovine** [The deceased in some social dances of Bosnia and Herzegovina], *Rad XI-og kongresa Saveza Folklorista Jugoslavije* (Zagreb: Savez Folklorista Jugoslavije, 1966) 371–74. In Bosnian; summary in German. See no. 490 in this volume.

Dances about the deceased or those impersonating them, often with humorous references, are found throughout Bosnia and Herzegovina. The most common are celivati mrca (kissing the dead), mrca (the dead), živi mrca (the living dead), and zadužbina (the legacy). In upper Herzegovina, particularly in Gacka, dizanje mrca (waking the dead) is popular. Umro čo'ek (the man died) and mrtvac (the dead), are danced by young women in Bosanska Posavina. *(Zdravko Blažeković)*

5045
as
OBRADOVIĆ, Milica. **Narodne društvene igre u Hercegovini** [The traditional social games of

Herzegovina], *Rad IX-og kongresa Saveza Folklorista Jugoslavije* (Sarajevo: Savez Udruženja Folklorista Jugoslavije, 1963) 95–98. In Bosnian; summary in German. See no. 455 in this volume.

Adults of both sexes, and girls, participate in indoor games of satirical-humorous content, most of which are now regarded as outmoded; formerly, men played all the roles, male and female, in masks, and the games involved the tricking or punishing of the uninitiated. Boys and younger married men play outdoor games, largely contests of strength and agility. Children's games have changed with the times in form and content, but retain their old names. *(author)*

5046 OBRADOVIĆ, Milica. **Rad u narodnim**
as **društvenim igrama na području Bosne i Hercegovine** [Work in the traditional social games of the Bosnia and Herzegovina region], *Rad VIII-og kongresa folklorista Jugoslavije* (Beograd: Naučno Delo, 1961) 391–98. *Illus., port.* In Bosnian; summary in German. See no. 446 in this volume.

Work motifs in children's games and dances, illustrated by examples from the region, can be identified in (1) gestures imitative of work elements, used by adults playing with infants; (2) imitation of the construction of household and outdoor equipment and objects by preschool children; (3) playing with toy tools; (4) imitations of specific jobs through movement; (5) work-gestures used in particular games to deceive other players, "like a fox"; (6) comical work-gestures imposed as a penalty on players who are "out"; (7) comical, sometimes masked, dramatizations of particular jobs; and (8) games connected to particular jobs only by their names ("killing bees", "shooting ducks"), and not through any element of the game's content or performance. *(author)*

5047 OTRIN, Iko. **Oblike slovenskih ljudskih plesov**
as [Slovene traditional dance genres], *Treći kongres folklorista Jugoslavije* (Cetinje: Udruženje Folklorista Crne Gore, 1958) 303–19. *Dance notation.* In Slovene; summary in German. See no. 357 in this volume.

⟶ OYHAMBURU, Philippe. **La danse et la musique en Pays Basque** [Dance and music in the Basque country]. See no. 2982 in this volume.

5048 PESOVÁR, Ernő. **Der heutige Stand der**
as **ungarischen Volkstanzforschung** [The present state of research on Hungarian folk dance], *Journal of the International Folk Music Council* XV (1963) 53–57. *Bibliog.* In German. See no. 459 in this volume.

Reviews scholarly activities of the previous 15 years. During this time, dance research has been undertaken in the hope of providing the basis for a national dance art; there is great interest in traditional dance as it is being practiced today. Research is now planned systematically, and trained scholars are being deployed. Modern methods of documentation are being used. The introduction of Labanotation has been of particular value. Modern research, instead of focusing on folk customs, seeks to understand dance as such and to develop a typology of Hungarian traditional dance. *(Carl Skoggard)*

5049 PIERA GELABERT, Mercedes. **La danse des**
as **gitanes du Vallès** [The ball de gitanes of El Valles], *Art populaire: Travaux artistiques et scientifiques du Ier Congrès international des arts populaires* (Paris: Duchartre, 1931) 192. In French. See no. 152 in this volume.

Among the important dances of the El Valles region in Barcelona province is the ball de gitanes, a dramatic performance staged at Carnival in village main squares; its performers, instrumental accompaniment, and musical form are described. A summary is cited as no. 5050 in this volume. *(James R. Cowdery)*

5050 PIERA GELABERT, Mercedes. **La danse des**
as **gitanes du Vallès** [The *Ball de gitanes* of El Valles],

Congrès international des arts populaires/International congress of popular arts (Paris: Institut international de coopération intellectuelle, 1928) 120–21. In French. See no. 153 in this volume.

Summary of the paper abstracted as no. 5049 in this volume.

5051 PIERSANTELLI, Giuseppe. **Lanternette and**
as **trallalero in the Genoese popular tradition,** *Journal of the International Folk Music Council* II (1950) 19–22. See no. 295 in this volume.

Discusses dances typical of the traditional Renaissance social event known as *lanternette* or *lucernetta*, and sketches the history of the polyphonic trallalero song genre. *(James R. Cowdery)*

5052 PINON, Roger. **Contributions nouvelles à**
as **l'étude de la danse des sept sauts** [New contributions to the study of the seven-step dance], *Journal of the International Folk Music Council* XV (1963) 61–62. In French. See no. 459 in this volume.

Summary of a paper. The seven-step dance is widespread across France, Wallonia, Holland, the Basque region, and the German-speaking Lorraine, and it has a number of different local appellations and variants. The melody of the dance is very old, and the dance itself is impossible to date. *(Murat Eyüboğlu)*

5053 POSPÍŠIL, František. **The present condition of**
as **choreographic research in northern, central, and southern America,** *Verhandlungen des XXIV. internationalen Amerikanisten-Kongresses* (Hamburg: Friederichsen, De Gruyter, and Co., 1934) 212–13. See no. 176 in this volume.

Calls for the use of film in the study of choreography and lists institutions that possess films of dance.

5054 PRYDHABER, Zeby. **"Ryqẇdey-hamyṣwah":**
as **Tẇldẇteyhem weṣẇrẇteyhem** [Myṣwah dances: Their history and forms], *Dẇkan* VII (1965) 75–85. In Hebrew. See no. 482 in this volume.

Explores the tradition of dances for and with the bride and groom at the wedding, which fulfill the mitzvah or commandment of bringing joy to the newly married couple on their wedding day.

5055 QADMAN, Gẇryt. **Ryqẇdey ḥagyẇt šel**
as **ha'edẇt b̌eyśra'el: Dibrey hesber lesraṭym** [Community dances in Israel: Narration to films], *Dẇkan* VII (1965) 87–98. In Hebrew. See no. 482 in this volume.

5056 QUEROL GAVALDÁ, Miguel. **Le Carnaval à**
as **Barcelone au début du XVIIe** [The carnival in Barcelona at the beginning of the 17th century], *Les fêtes de la Renaissance* (Paris: Centre National de la Recherche Scientifique [CNRS], 1956) 371–78. In French. See no. 350 in this volume.

Deals with the content of the Carnival that took place in Barcelona in 1633. Included is a description of the characters along with some extracts from the poetry, as well as a discussion of the Carnival of 1616 with reference to the dances that characterized it.

5057 RÉGNIER, Henriette. **Les danses populaires**
as **françaises** [Traditional French dances], *Art populaire: Travaux artistiques et scientifiques du Ier Congrès international des arts populaires* (Paris: Duchartre, 1931) 169–71. In French. See no. 152 in this volume.

5058 REICHERT, Georg. **Der Passamezzo** [The
as passamezzo], *Kongreß-Bericht: Gesellschaft für*

Musikforschung (Kassel; Basel: Bärenreiter, 1950) 94–97. *Music.* In German. See no. 299 in this volume.

Discusses the passamezzo, an Italian dance popular from the mid-16th c. to about 1650.

5059
as
ROUSSET, Jean. **L'eau et les Tritons dans les fêtes et ballets de cour (1580-1640)** [Water and Tritons in festivals and court ballets (1580-1640)], *Les fêtes de la Renaissance* (Paris: Centre National de la Recherche Scientifique [CNRS], 1956) 235–45. In French. See no. 350 in this volume.

Examines this theme in France, at the court of Savoy, and at Florence to show the convergence of different types of arts. *(Scott Fruehwald)*

5060
as
SANDERS, J. Olcutt. **The Texas cattle country and cowboy square dance,** *Journal of the International Folk Music Council* III (1951) 22–26. See no. 296 in this volume.

Discusses developments from the 1880s to the present.

5061
as
SAYGUN, Ahmed Adnan. **Des danses d'Anatolie et de leur caractère rituel** [The dances of Anatolia and their ritual character], *Journal of the International Folk Music Council* II (1950) 10–14. *Transcr.* In French. See no. 295 in this volume.

Dances with mimetic content show evidence of thematic material that might be traced as far back as the mythology of the Sumerians; the repetition of melodic fragments in the music of others represents the survival of archaic magic formulas. Only intensive comparative study of the dances of different regions will permit the reconstruction of their lost meanings. *(David Bloom)*

5062
as
SKOVRAN, Olga; MLADENOVIĆ, Olivera. **Problèmes et méthodes de l'adaption scénique des danses populaires dans le cadre des expériences yougoslaves** [Problems and methods of the stage adaptation of traditional dances within the framework of Yugoslavian experience], *Journal of the International Folk Music Council* VIII (1956) 41–45. In French. See no. 349 in this volume.

In Yugoslavia, traditional dances are increasingly being adapted for the stage; such adaptations raise questions about the preservation of some of the dances' essential characteristics. Dancers who do not have a background in traditional dancing need to develop the capacity to feel and assimilate the stylistic and technical details of the traditional dances. Ensembles are in a position to negotiate authenticity when combining variants of a dance into a single version, or when choreographing new dances in traditional styles. The Serbian performing group Kolo is discussed. *(Murat Eyüboğlu)*

5063
as
ŠKREBLIN, Vladimir. **Koreograf o kinetografiji** [A choreographer on dance notation], *Rad kongresa folklorista Jugoslavije* (Zagreb: Savez Udruženja Folklorista Jugoslavije, 1958) 49–54. In Croatian; summary in German. See no. 315 in this volume.

A proposal for a system for notation of folk dances.

5064
as
SMITH, Barbara B. **The bon-odori in Hawaii and in Japan,** *Journal of the International Folk Music Council* XIV (1962) 36–39. See no. 442 in this volume.

The Japanese version of the Buddhist festival at the full moon of the seventh lunar month is known as *bon* and marked by festive dancing after the performance of rituals for the comforting of the souls of the dead. The dancing, bon-odori, is also practiced in the Japanese communities of Hawaii, with some differences: it is typically held on weekends, incorporates *ryūkōka* popular songs, and has recently featured movements of right foot together with right hand, in opposition to the traditional Japanese technique of moving right hand together with left foot. The participation of Hawaiians of other ethnicities is on the increase. *(David Bloom)*

5065
as
SMITH, Majorie B. **Progress report on the study of African influences in the music of Panama,** *Actas del XXXIIIº Congreso Internacional de Americanistas* (San José: Lehmann, 1959) 639–46. See no. 398 in this volume.

Particular attention is given to dance genres, tamborito, punto, mejorano, and especially cumbia, and the role of the Cimarrón people, descendants of Afro-Panamanians who escaped from slavery. *(Ken Alboum)*

5066
as
STESSER-PÉAN, Guy. **Danse des aigles et danse des jaguars chez Indiens Huastèques de la région de Tantoyuca** [Dance of the eagles and dance of the jaguars of the Huastec Indians of the Tantoyuca region], *Actes du XXVIIIᵉ Congrès international des américanistes* (Paris: Musée de l'Homme, 1948) 335–38. *Illus.* In French. See no. 277 in this volume.

Although these nocturnal dances are considered to be entertainments, they are imbued with a certain religious character.

5067
as
STRELNIKOV, I.D. **La música y la danza de las tribus índias Kaa-Ohwua (Guaraní) y Botocudo** [The music and dance of the Guaraní and Botocudo Indian tribes], *Proceedings of the Twenty-third International Congress of Americanists* (New York: n.p., 1930) 796–802. In Spanish. See no. 149 in this volume.

Describes a funeral dance of the indigenous people of Paraguay that is sung to the name of the dead man. The São Paulo Vespers service combines both European and traditional music elements. *(David Nussenbaum)*

5068
as
SUPPAN, Wolfgang. **A collection of European dances: Breslau 1555,** *Studia musicologica Academiae Scientiarum Hungaricae* VII (1965) 165–69. *Illus., bibliog.* See no. 478 in this volume.

The collection *Viel feiner lieblicher Stucklein, Spanischer, Welscher, Englischer, Frantzösischer composition u. tentz*, published in Breslau in 1555, includes prefaces and other comments by the brothers Bartholomäus and Paul Hessen regarding the pieces and their performance. *(David Gagné)*

5069
as
SUROTO, Noto. **Le caractère de la danse javanaise** [The nature of Javanese dance], *Art populaire: Travaux artistiques et scientifiques du Iᵉʳ Congrès international des arts populaires* (Paris: Duchartre, 1931) 181–83. In French. See no. 152 in this volume.

A survey of the forms and history of Javanese dance, with particular attention to the Hindu religious aspect of its origins and to its aesthetic development. A summary is cited as no. 5070 in this volume.

5070
as
SUROTO, Noto. **Le caractère de la danse javanaise** [The nature of Javanese dance], *Congrès international des arts populaires/International congress of popular arts* (Paris: Institut international de coopération intellectuelle, 1928) 127–30. In French. See no. 153 in this volume.

Summary of the paper abstracted as no. 5069 in this volume.

5071
as
ŠUŠTAR, Marija. **Oblike plesa štajeriš na Slovenskem** [Forms of the štajeriš dance in Slovenia], *Rad kongresa folklorista Jugoslavije* (Ljubljana: Savez Udruženja Folkloristov Jugoslavije, 1960) 83–90. *Transcr., dance notation.* In Croatian; summary in German. See no. 404 in this volume.

The štajeriš (from German *steierisch*, "Styrian") is one of the few dances extant in Slovenia in which the traces of an older sung dance can be discerned. It is danced either by couples or in a circle of three or more dancers. *(author)*

5072
as
ŠUŠTAR, Marija; VODUŠEK, Valens. **Koreografska oblika pomladno-obredne igre most v**

Sloveniji in njene variante v Jugoslaviji [Choreographic form of the traditional spring dance game *most* in Slovenia, and its variants in Yugoslavia], *Rad IX-og kongresa Saveza Folklorista Jugoslavije* (Sarajevo: Savez Udruženja Folklorista Jugoslavije, 1963) 481–87. In Slovene; summary in German. See no. 455 in this volume.

The *most* or "bridge" dance-game is performed on Easter Monday in Črnomelj, Metlika, and Predgrad in Bela Krajina, with a different choreography in each place. Correspondents to each of the forms, also in Easter Monday dances, can be found in South Serbia, Herzegovina, and Croatia, as well as two recently discovered *most* variants in northwestern Slovenia. The oldest forms are apparently those danced only by women and girls. *(authors)*

5073 SZENTPÁL, Mária. **Kinetography in the com-**
as **parative study of folk dance in Hungary,** *Journal of the International Folk Music Council* XI (1959) 77–79. See no. 392 in this volume.
Summary of a paper. Labanotation has been used in Hungarian ethnochoreology since 1945.

⟶ TANCREDI, G. **Canti e balli garganici** [Songs and dances of the Gargano region]. See no. 3079 in this volume.

5074 TANI, Gino. **Le comte d'Aglié et le ballet de**
as **cour en Italie** [The count d'Aglié and the court ballet in Italy], *Les fêtes de la Renaissance* (Paris: Centre National de la Recherche Scientifique [CNRS], 1956) 235–58. In French. See no. 350 in this volume.
Reexamines the history of ballet, claiming that French ballet is a manifestation of the Italian spirit. The court of Turin maintained artistic and cultural exchanges with Paris. Biographical information on Filippo d'Aglié, including his activities as both a soldier and an artist, is presented, as well as descriptions of ballet plots and names of artists who contributed to ballet history. The works of d'Aglié are listed in chronological order, including detailed descriptions of content and critical observations.

5075 TANI, Gino. **Origini autoctone e paleolitiche**
as **della danza italiana** [The indigenous, Paleolithic origins of Italian dance], *Atti del Congresso internazionale di musiche popolari mediterranee e del Convegno dei bibliotecari musicali* (Palermo: De Magistris succ. V. Bellotti, 1959) 183–87. In Italian. See no. 332 in this volume.
Discusses the significance of the representations of dancing in the cave graffiti of the Grotte dell'Addaura, near Palermo, excavated in 1950, in comparison with dance images in other Stone Age cave paintings. *(David Bloom)*

5076 TAUBERT, Karl Heinz. **Die Beziehungen**
as **zwischen den klassischen Tänzen und der Rythmik** [The connections between classic dances and rhythmics], *Deuxième Congrès international du rythme et de la rythmique* (Genève: Institut Jaques-Dalcroze, 1966) 154–55. In German. See no. 502 in this volume.
Discusses the ideas of Émile Jaques-Dalcroze.

5077 THOMAS, Northcote Whitridge. **La danse**
as **totémique en Europe** [Totemic dance in Europe], *Congrès international des traditions populaires* (Paris: E. Lechevalier, E. Leroux, J. Maisonneuve, 1902) 71–76. In French. See no. 31 in this volume.
Describes how dances imitative of chickens and other fowl relate to marriage ceremonies in various European cultures. What began as sacrificing chickens at weddings hundreds of years ago evolved into priests wearing costumes indicative of chickens and/or performing dances imitative of

their movements at the ceremony; this was further transformed into the French tradition of serving chicken at wedding feasts. *(Susan Poliniak)*

5078 TOSCHI, Paolo. **A question about the taran-**
as **tella,** *Journal of the International Folk Music Council* II (1950) 19. See no. 295 in this volume.
Summary of a paper discussing two different dances in Italy that are both called *tarantella*: an elegant courtship dance and an agitated curative ritual. Both dances derive their name from the city of Taranto. *(James R. Cowdery)*

5079 TRÉBUCQ, Sylvain. **Danses maraichines**
as [Maraichine dances], *La tradition en Poitou et Charentes: Art populaire, ethnographie, folk-lore, hagiographie, histoire* (Paris: Librairie de la Tradition Nationale, 1897) 405–10. In French. See no. 21 in this volume.
Presents descriptions and musical transcriptions of the following dances of the Vendée: maraichine à deux; maraichine à trois; barienne; and branle.

5080 VULETIĆ-VUKASOVIĆ, Vid. **La moreška et**
as **le juge gras (le roi du village) dans l'île de Cuozola (Dalmatie)** [The moreška and the fat judge (the king of the village) on the island of Korčula (Dalmatia)], *Congrès international des traditions populaires* (Paris: E. Lechevalier, E. Leroux, J. Maisonneuve, 1902) 77–78. In French. See no. 31 in this volume.
The moreška and *The king of the village* are two theatrical works with music performed on the island of Korčula. The moreška involves a cast of armed men plus simple music (tambours, flutes, etc.). *The king of the village* involves a cast consisting of a king, his entourage, his soldiers, and a band of musicians; the assemblage enters a church and participates at Mass, and afterwards dances the mostra and feasts at a royal dinner. *(Susan Poliniak)*

5081 WOLFRAM, Richard. **European song-dance**
as **forms,** *Journal of the International Folk Music Council* VIII (1956) 32–36. See no. 349 in this volume.
Surveys examples of traditional dances accompanied only by singing.

5082 WOLFRAM, Richard. **Die Volkstänze in**
as **Österreich: Ein Überblick** [Traditional dances in Austria: A survey], *Journal of the International Folk Music Council* XIII (1961) 5–9. In German. See no. 424 in this volume.
Draws on the author's *Die Volkstänze in Österreich und verwandte Tänze in Europa* (Salzburg, 1951).

5083 ZALDÍVAR, José. **Les danses populaires**
as **catalanes** [Catalan traditional dances], *Art populaire: Travaux artistiques et scientifiques du Iᵉʳ Congrès international des arts populaires* (Paris: Duchartre, 1931) 190. In French. See no. 152 in this volume.
Provides a typological survey. A summary is cited as no. 5084 in this volume.

5084 ZALDÍVAR, José. **Les danses populaires**
as **catalanes** [Catalan traditional dances], *Congrès international des arts populaires/International congress of popular arts* (Paris: Institut international de coopération intellectuelle, 1928) 120. In French. See no. 153 in this volume.
Summary of the article abstracted as no. 5083 in this volume.

5085 ZEČEVIĆ, Slobodan. **Igre našeg posmrtnog**
as **rituala** [Dances in our funeral rituals], *Rad XI-og kongresa Saveza Folklorista Jugoslavije* (Zagreb: Savez Folklorista Jugoslavije, 1966) 375–83. In Serbian; summary in English. See no. 490 in this volume.

The žalosno kolo (sad kolo) is performed around the hat or another piece of clothing of the deceased. The kolo naopako (kolo upside-down) is performed in the direction opposite to the usual one. *(Zdravko Blažeković)*

5086
as

ZEČEVIĆ, Slobodan. **Pregled narodnih igara užičkog dela Sandžaka** [Folk dance in the Užice part of the Sandžak], *Rad VIII-og kongresa folklorista Jugoslavije* (Beograd: Naučno Delo, 1961) 117–20. *Port.* In Serbian; summary in English. See no. 446 in this volume.

The southern part of the Titovo Užice district belonged, in the period of Turkish dominance, to the administrative district known as the Sandžak. Historical developments have given it a marked ethnic and religious pluralism, which accounts for its extraordinary variety of dance forms and styles, including ritual dances of great antiquity. A list of local dances is provided. *(author)*

5087
as

ŽGANEC, Vinko. **Moj sistem koreografije narodnih plesova** [My system of choreography of folk dances], *Rad kongresa folklorista Jugoslavije* (Zagreb: Savez Udruženja Folklorista Jugoslavije, 1958) 45–48. *Transcr., dance notation.* In Croatian. See no. 315 in this volume.

The Croatian ethnomusicologist describes his own system of dance notation, which is used in publications of the Institut za Narodnu Umjetnost in Zagreb. The system is simple, and it enables very basic notation. *Zdravko Blažeković)*

5088
as

ZICH, Otákar. **Les particularités rythmiques des danses populaires tchécoslovaques** [The rhythmic characteristics of Czechoslovakian traditional dances], *Art populaire: Travaux artistiques et scientifiques du Ier Congrès international des arts populaires* (Paris: Duchartre, 1931) 184. In French. See no. 152 in this volume.

5089
as

ZULAICA Y ARREGUI, José Gonzalo (José Antonio de Donostia). **Les danses basques** [Basque dances], *Congrès international des arts populaires/International congress of popular arts* (Paris: Institut international de coopération intellectuelle, 1928) 122. In French. See no. 153 in this volume.

Summary of the paper abstracted as no. 5090 in this volume.

5090
as

ZULAICA Y ARREGUI, José Gonzalo (José Antonio de Donostia). **Les danses basques** [Basque dances], *Art populaire: Travaux artistiques et scientifiques du Ier Congrès international des arts populaires* (Paris: Duchartre, 1931) 193. In French. See no. 152 in this volume.

A great variety of dances is found in the Basque country, each province having its own special forms. They are performed almost exclusively by men, notable more for athleticism than grace, and known as "staff dance", "shield dance", and so on, according to the dancers' accessories. Dances are performed on Sundays and feast days, in municipal and religious processions, and inside churches. Preservation efforts are described. A summary is cited as no. 5089 in this volume. *(James R. Cowdery)*

77 Dramatic arts

5091
as

ABER, Adolf. **Das Problem der Stilbühne bei den Werken Richard Wagners** [*Stilbühne* and staging the works of Richard Wagner], *Bericht über den I. musikwissenschaftlichen Kongress der Deutschen Musikgesellschaft in Leipzig* (Wiesbaden: Breitkopf & Härtel, 1926) 312–13. In German. See no. 120 in this volume.

Briefly discusses two approaches to staging: one in which the clarity of the text is paramount; the other in which dramatic expression is more important. Reference is made to the work of Adolphe Appia. *(William Renwick)*

5092
as

ABERT, Anna Amalie. **Zum metastasianischen Reformdrama** [On Metastasio's reform drama], *Kongreß-Bericht: Gesellschaft für Musikforschung* (Kassel; Basel: Bärenreiter, 1950) 138–39. In German. See no. 299 in this volume.

The poet and librettist Pietro Metastasio (1698-1782) established the conventions of the opera seria.

5093
as

ABERT, Hermann. **Grundprobleme der Operngeschichte** [Basic issues in opera history], *Bericht über den musikwissenschaftlichen Kongreß in Basel* (Leipzig: Breitkopf & Härtel, 1925) 22–35. In German. See no. 102 in this volume.

Gesamtkunstwerk—far from being a 19th-c. idea—is as old as opera itself. Still, the vast aesthetic differences between Wagner's and Ottavio Rinuccini's solutions to the problem of words and music must be analyzed thoroughly. *(Sylvia Eversole)*

5094
as

ABERT, Hermann. **Zur Geschichte der Oper in Württemberg** [On the history of opera in Württemberg], *Haydn-Zentenarfeier* (Leipzig: Breitkopf & Härtel; Wien: Artaria, 1909) 186–93. In German. See no. 65 in this volume.

Particular attention is given to the influence of French opera.

5095
as

AMFITHEATROF, Daniele. **La musica per film negli Stati Uniti** [Film music in the United States], *La musica nel film* (Roma: Bianco e Nero, 1950) 118–28. *Illus., facs., music, charts, diagr.* In Italian. See no. 297 in this volume.

Describes the process of creating a film score for an American studio and discusses the state of film music and the works of composers currently active, including Bernard Herrmann, Franz Waxman, Johnny Green, and Alfred Newman. Film composers of this era attempt to emulate Max Steiner's style as closely as possible. The use of musical clichés is unfortunately quite common. Production budgets, composers' fees, microphones, copyrights, and the importance of good orchestrations are discussed. *(Susan Poliniak)*

5096
as

APPIA, Adolphe. **Das Problem der Stilbühne den Werken Richard Wagners: Mitreferat** [*Stilbühne* and staging the works of Richard Wagner: A report], *Bericht über den I. musikwissenschaftlichen Kongress der Deutschen Musikgesellschaft in Leipzig* (Wiesbaden: Breitkopf & Härtel, 1926) 314–17. In German. See no. 120 in this volume.

Distinguishes two different approaches to production in Wagner's music dramas: one in which pageant and spectacle are stressed, and another in which dramatic expression is most important. Fidelity to the score and the role of music in bringing the characters to life are cited in support of the latter approach. *(William Renwick)*

5097
as

AUBRUN, Charles V. **Les débuts du drame lyrique en Espagne** [The beginnings of opera in Spain], *Le lieu théâtral à la Renaissance* (Paris: Centre National de la Recherche Scientifique [CNRS], 1964) 423–44. In French. See no. 472 in this volume.

Describes activities beginning in 1622.

5098
as

BAKÉ, Arnold Adriaan. **Some hobby horses in South India,** *Journal of the International Folk Music Council* II (1950) 43–45. *Transcr.* See no. 295 in this volume.

Presents examples of hobby horses in various dramatic genres.

5099 BARFUSS, Franciszek. **Die polnische**
as **historische Oper in den Jugendjahren Chopins** [The Polish historical opera in the years of Chopin's youth], *The book of the first international musicological congress devoted to the works of Frederick Chopin* (Warszawa: Państwowe Wydawnictwo Naukowe,
1963) 503–06. In German. See no. 425 in this volume.

Discusses the background to the substantial number of Polish-language
works in the operatic repertoire of the Teatr Narodowy, Warsaw, in the early
19th c., with particular attention to librettists' use of Polish history and
composers' use of traditional-music elements. *(David Bloom)*

5100 BECKER, Heinz. **Arbeitsgemeinschaft: Klassi-
as fication der Operngeschichte** [Working group: a
classification scheme for opera history], *Bericht über
den siebenten internationalen musikwissenschaftlichen
Kongress* (Kassel: Bärenreiter, 1959) 338–39. In German. See no. 390 in this volume.

A working session of the conference began with a discussion by Donald J.
GROUT of the difficulties of an exact periodization of operatic styles: the
ambiguity of the term *opera*, especially with regard to music theater earlier
than 1600; the question of whether the special sociological conditions of
opera—its extremely high production costs—should be taken into consideration; and the lack of fit between the style periodizations of its two constituent elements of literature and music. A relatively narrow classification
into 12 periods from early Baroque to neoclassicism was proposed.

5101 BECKER, Heinz. **Die historische Bedeutung
as der Grand Opéra** [The historical significance of
grand opera], *Beiträge zur Geschichte der Musikansschauung im 19. Jahrhundert* (Regensburg: Bosse,
1965) 151–59. In German. See no. 483 in this volume.

Grand opera, from Auber's *La muette de Portici* (1828) through
Meyerbeer's *L'africaine* (1865), was less a genre than a set of external criteria (through-composition, length of three to five acts, star singers, large
chorus and ballet, spectacular staging) created by the superior technical capacities of the Paris Opéra. While critics such as Heine complained that it
pandered to the vulgarity of the audience, it was meant seriously, both as
drama (with the convention of the tragic ending) and musically, as
Meyerbeer's correspondence shows. Grand opera provided an essential
model for later developments in music theater, especially the music dramas
of Wagner. *(David Bloom)*

5102 BEIJER, Agne. **Visions célestes et infernales
as dans le théâtre du Moyen Âge et de la Renaissance** [Visions of heaven and hell in the theater of the
Middle Ages and the Renaissance], *Les fêtes de la Renaissance* (Paris: Centre National de la Recherche
Scientifique [CNRS], 1956) 405–17. In French. See no.
350 in this volume.

Examines the depiction of supernatural scenes in a wide variety of genres,
including early opera.

5103 BEKKER, Paul. **Organisation des Opern-
as theaters** [The organization of opera theaters], *Atti del
primo Congresso internazionale di musica* (Firenze: Le
Monnier, 1935) 194–203. *Charts, diagr.* In German;
summary in Italian. See no. 203 in this volume.

The organization of an opera theater should be neither in conflict with nor
dependent on artistic factors but rather another aspect of a single creative
impulse. Administrative design depends on local conditions. Publicly subsidized opera has the advantage of being treated as a public good, but it is
susceptible to the harmful influences of funding bodies and political
groups. Participation of the general public is to be encouraged, so that opera
may become a genuinely popular theater. *(author)*

5104 BELARDINELLI, Alessandro. *Le Ateniesi* di De
as **Jouy** [De Jouy's *Le Ateniesi*], *Atti del primo Congresso
internazionale di studi spontiniani* (Fabriano: Arti

Grafiche Gentile, 1954) 81–85. In Italian. See no. 304
in this volume.

This libretto has never been found, and perhaps was never written at all.

5105 BLASETTI, Alessandro; LUCIANI, Sebastiano
as Arturo; SERANDREI, Mario. **Il parere del
regista, del mentatore e della critica** [The opinion of the director, of the editor, and of criticism], *La
musica nel film* (Roma: Bianco e Nero, 1950) 91–96. In
Italian. See no. 297 in this volume.

Remarks on film music from a director, a film editor, and a critic. Blasetti
comments that film and music have much in common; music can determine
the success or failure of a film, and a good theme can render a film unforget-
table. Serandrei notes that film composers are often expected to rescue
films from their inadequacies, but music often distracts the audience from
the film instead of serving as a complement. Luciani asserts that music is
necessary to film. Film music is often written on a tight schedule, but
should still be written with as much care and passion as music for the stage
(i.e., opera). *(Susan Poliniak)*

5106 BLOMDAHL, Karl-Birger; LINDEGREN, Erik.
as **Fragment of an arctic conversation,**
*Zeitgenössisches Musiktheater/Contemporary music
theatre/Théâtre musical contemporain* (Hamburg:
Deutscher Musikrat, 1966) 59–60. See no. 481 in this
volume.

The composer and librettist discuss their operatic collaborations.

5107 BOLL, André. **Le livret: Élément essentiel d'un
as renouveau du théâtre musical** [The libretto: An
essential element of music theater's renewal],
*Zeitgenössisches Musiktheater/Contemporary music
theatre/Théâtre musical contemporain* (Hamburg:
Deutscher Musikrat, 1966) 48–51. In French. See no.
481 in this volume.

A composer in search of a libretto is less in need of a great poet than of a
playwright willing to bend to the requirements of sung theater. The libretto
must be constructed dramatically, whatever the subject matter. It must take
into account the prosodic character of the language in which it is written to
facilitate intelligibility. It may allow the composer (and stage designer) the
chance to make use of new technical discoveries. Following these principles, it has been possible to create masterpieces in any musical language,
whether modal, tonal, polytonal, or dodecaphonic. *(David Bloom)*

5108 BONAVIA, Ferruccio. **L'opera in Inghilterra**
as [Opera in England], *Atti del primo Congresso
internazionale di musica* (Firenze: Le Monnier, 1935)
183–88. In Italian. See no. 203 in this volume.

Considers works by Rutland Boughton, Gustav Holst, Ethel Smyth, Frederick Delius, and Ralph Vaughan Williams.

5109 BONIFAČIĆ ROŽIN, Nikola. **Scenski elementi
as u proljetnim ophodnim običajima** [Theatrical elements in spring customs], *Rad IX-og kongresa Saveza
Folklorista Jugoslavije* (Sarajevo: Savez Udruženja
Folklorista Jugoslavije, 1963) 323–31. In Croatian;
summary in German. See no. 455 in this volume.

Discusses motifs, personification, mimetic dancing, costume, and choral
song in springtime mendication rituals practiced in villages of northern and
eastern Croatia during religious festivals. *(author)*

5110 BÖRGE, Vagn. **Die Oper im zwischenstaat-
as lichen Kulturdienst** [Opera in the service of international culture], *Musikerziehung: Zeitschrift der Musikerzieher Österreichs* special issue (1953) 150–51. In
German. See no. 317 in this volume.

Because of its ability to express common values, opera is an instrument in
developing understanding among nations. International tours of leading
opera companies are invaluable cultural exchange programs. *(Allen Lott)*

5111 BORRIS, Siegfried. **Das neue _dramma per_**
as **_musica_** [The new _dramma per musica_],
_Zeitgenössisches Musiktheater/Contemporary music
theatre/Théâtre musical contemporain_ (Hamburg:
Deutscher Musikrat, 1966) 66–69. In German. See no.
481 in this volume.

The concept of the _dramma per musica_ is central to the origin of opera at the
end of the 16th c., and to Gluck's and Wagner's reforms in the 18th and 19th
c. In the 20th c., partly under the influence of Busoni's young classicism,
many opera composers, including Berg, Hindemith, Milhaud, Honegger,
Stravinsky, Weill, Schoenberg, Einem, Blacher, Britten, and Busoni himself, have a tendency to use autonomous musical structures. _(David Bloom)_

5112 BRINER, Andres. **Die moderne Oper: Autoren,**
as **Theater, Publikum** [Modern opera: Authors, theaters, audiences], _Bericht über den neunten internationalen Kongreß_ (Kassel: Bärenreiter, 1964-1966)
255–60. In German. See no. 491 in this volume.

Topics in the roundtable discussion include the relations between compos-
ers and audiences in the U.S.; the relation between plot materials and cur-
rent events in librettos since ca. 1920; the use of passacaglia form in works
by Berg, Busoni, Hindemith, and Britten; and the dramaturgy of
Prokof'ev's early operas in relation to the ideas of Vsevolod Mejerhol'd.
The participants were Willi SCHUH, Ladislav BURLAS, Karl
GEIRINGER, Irving LOWENS, Wilhelm PFANNKUCH, Ivan
VOJTĚCH, and LeRoy WEIL. _(David Bloom)_

5113 BULA, Karol. **Stanisław Moniuszko a reforma**
as **Wagnerowska** [Stanisław Moniuszko and the Wagnerian reform of opera], _Ryszard Wagner a polska
kultura muzyczna/Richard Wagner und die polnische
Musikkultur_ (Katowice: Panstwowa Wyzsza Szkola
Muzyczna, 1964) 69–81. In Polish; summary in German. See no. 466 in this volume.

5114 CALDAGUÈS, L. **La radio et l'art dramatique**
as [Radio and dramatic art], _Acts of the VIIth International
Congress of Libraries and Museums of the Performing
Arts/Actes du VIIe Congrès international des biblio-
thèques-musées des arts du spectacle_ ('s-Gravenhage:
Theater Instituut Nederland/Netherlands Centre of the
International Theatre Institute, 1965) 78–83. _Charts,
diagr._ In French. See no. 492 in this volume.

Programming ideas are discussed, and the holdings of the theater archive of
the Office de Radiodiffusion-Télévision Française (ORTF) are described.

5115 CAVALCANTI, Alberto. **Music can provide**
as **only interior rhythm,** _Atti del secondo Congresso
internazionale di musica_ (Firenze: Le Monnier, 1940)
265–70. Summaries in Italian, French, and German.
See no. 239 in this volume.

Other than in the American musical comedy, which has achieved a perfection that demands respect, film music is as a rule mediocre. Exceptional
cases are those of the composers Maurice Jaubert and Benjamin Britten
(who have collaborated on films directed by the author), and Darius
Milhaud. Film music must be written for the film, and for an audience that
has little relation, in size and in mentality, to a concert audience. The musician and the director must understand that film is a collective work in which
they form only two parts of an intricate machinery. _(author)_

5116 CAVAZZUTI, Enrico. **Problemi della registra-**
as **zione sonora e del missaggio** [Problems of sound
recording and lack of synchronization], _La musica nel
film_ (Roma: Bianco e Nero, 1950) 97–106. _Illus.,
charts, diagr._ In Italian. See no. 297 in this volume.

The quality of sound recording for a film depends on the acoustic qualities of
the space in which the sound was originally recorded; optimal recording conditions are discussed. The number, types, and placement of microphones, as
well as electronic sound manipulation techniques, are examined, and the

achievement of Joseph Maxfield is explored. Issues surrounding the synchronization (and lack thereof) of music with dialogue and sound effects are
discussed; compositional techniques to avoid various problems, such as music interfering with the intelligibility of spoken dialogue because of timbral
similarities, are suggested. _(Susan Poliniak)_

5117 CHEVREUILLE, Pierre. **La reine verte de**
as **Maurice Béjart** [Maurice Béjart's _La reine verte_],
_Zeitgenössisches Musiktheater/Contemporary music
theatre/Théâtre musical contemporain_ (Hamburg:
Deutscher Musikrat, 1966) 82–84. In French. See no.
481 in this volume.

Béjart's artistic synthesis of the elements of ballet, mime, singing, declamation, cinema, staging, and so on, culminates in the spectacle _La reine verte_
(1963), which was staged to music by Pierre Henry. _(David Bloom)_

5118 CICOGNINI, Alessandro. **Il film musicale** [The
as musical film], _La musica nel film_ (Roma: Bianco e
Nero, 1950) 61–62. In Italian. See no. 297 in this
volume.

There are two types of musical film: those that revolve partially around music, and those that revolve entirely around music. Of the first type, there are
three subdivisions: the film revue with musical scenes on a real or imagined
stage; the operetta film in which the frequent transitions from spoken to
sung text have no justification within the story; and the musical film in
which the presentation of an excerpt from an opera or symphony in a room
or parlor is justified within the story. Of the second type, there are two subdivisions: the operatic film and the animated film. _(Susan Poliniak)_

5119 CIERNIAK, Jędrzej. **Le théâtre populaire an-**
as **cien et moderne en Pologne** [Historical and contemporary folk theater in Poland], _Art populaire:
Travaux artistiques et scientifiques du Ier Congrès international des arts populaires_ (Paris: Duchartre, 1931)
200f. In French. See no. 152 in this volume.

Polish theatrical traditions date from a very early period of performances
solemnizing life-cycle and calendrical events in the lives of working and
peasant families and communities. The medieval liturgical theater, beginning in the 14th c., quickly acquired so many profane elements that it must
be regarded as secular; it continues to exist in the forms of pastorals, _chopka_
(mystery plays concluded with a satirical revue), and brief comedy performances followed by the singing of a canticle. In recent years the rural theater has become moribund, or reduced to a crude copy of the urban theater;
attempts to recreate a popular theater on a strictly ethnographic basis are described. A summary is cited as no. 5120 in this volume. _(James R. Cowdery)_

5120 CIERNIAK, Jędrzej. **Le théâtre populaire an-**
as **cien et moderne en Pologne** [Early and contemporary folk theater in Poland], _Congrès international des
arts populaires/International congress of popular arts_
(Paris: Institut international de coopération intellectuelle, 1928) 137–38. In French. See no. 153 in this
volume.

Summary of the paper abstracted as no. 5119 in this volume.

5121 COLACICCHI, Luigi. **The lament of the maid-**
as **ens,** _Journal of the International Folk Music Council_ I
(1949) 38–40. See no. 281 in this volume.

Describes the _Pianto delle zitelle_, a traditional Passion play performed at
the Santuario della Santissima Trinità in Vallepietra, Italy.

5122 COMBARIEU, Jules. **De l'évolution du drame**
as **lyrique** [On the evolution of lyric drama], _Congrès international de musique: Ire session—Exposition
Universelle de 1900: Compte rendu, rapports, commu-
nications_ (Paris: conference, 1901) 19–21. In French.
See no. 29 in this volume.

Some aesthetic guidelines for post-Wagnerian opera might include: a synthesis of continuous melody and anti-dramatic melody, a reevaluation of
the sublimation of the ballet in opera, the incorporation of local and national

themes into operas, and the reduction of instrumentation for the sake of the comprehension of the text. Questions of staging are also considered.

5123
as
Commission Nationale Japonaise pour la Coopération Intellectuelle. **Le théâtre au Japon et ses relations avec l'art dramatique populaire** [Japanese theater and its relations with traditional dramatic arts], *Congrès international des arts populaires/International congress of popular arts* (Paris: Institut international de coopération intellectuelle, 1928) 136–37. In French. See no. 153 in this volume.

Brief history of Japanese art theater forms, with particular attention to kabuki.

5124
as
COPEAU, Jacques. **L'interprétation des ouvrages dramatiques du passé** [The interpretation of dramatic works of the past], *Atti del terzo Congresso internazionale di musica* (Firenze: Le Monnier, 1940) 73–78. In French; summaries in Italian and German. See no. 256 in this volume.

Discusses the need for careful interpretations of operas of the past.

5125
as
COSTARELLI, Nicola; MARINUZZI, Gino; ROSATI, Giuseppe; TOMMASINI, Vincenzo; VERETTI, Antonio. **Aspetti della musica nel film** [Aspects of music in film], *La musica nel film* (Roma: Bianco e Nero, 1950) 30–48. In Italian. See no. 297 in this volume.

Film music is not the same as music that is to be performed in the concert hall, and should not be treated as such by classical composers. Film music should encapsulate and possibly advance the action occurring on the screen; there should be collaboration between the director and the composer. The film *Fantasia* points to the possiblities of the musical film. Music expands the expressive and communicative capabilities of film. The technical constraints film imposes on the composer and the application of the concept of program music to film are discussed, and film music is compared with music for operas and ballets. *(Susan Poliniak)*

5126
as
CROSSLEY-HOLLAND, Peter. **Operatic and ballet music,** *Music: East and West* (Tōkyō: conference, 1961) 30–35. See no. 445 in this volume.

Remarks on music for stage performances in Asian and European traditions.

5127
as
CUTTS, John P. **Le rôle de la musique dans les masques de Ben Jonson** [The role of music in the masques of Ben Jonson], *Les fêtes de la Renaissance* (Paris: Centre National de la Recherche Scientifique [CNRS], 1956) 285–318. *Music, bibliog.* In French. See no. 350 in this volume.

Concerns the masques of Ben Jonson and the role of music as a secondary element within them; includes a comparison of *The masque of the queen* (1609-1610) and *Oberon* (1610-1611) accompanied by Jonson's observations regarding these works. The masques of Ben Jonson were the basis for the development of English opera.

5128
as
DALLAPICCOLA, Luigi. **Livrets et paroles dans l'opéra** [Librettos and words in opera], *Zeitgenössisches Musiktheater/Contemporary music theatre/Théâtre musical contemporain* (Hamburg: Deutscher Musikrat, 1966) 52–56. In French. See no. 481 in this volume.

Discusses the process of writing librettos for the operas *Volo di notte* (1940) and *Il prigioniero* (1949).

5129
as
DANIÉLOU, Alain. **Les influences orientales dans le théâtre musical contemporain** [Eastern influences in contemporary music theater], *Zeitgenössisches Musiktheater/Contemporary music theatre/Théâtre musical contemporain* (Hamburg:

Deutscher Musikrat, 1966) 116–20. In French. See no. 481 in this volume.

The separation of Eastern and Western forms of music theater is a relatively recent historical development; numerous points of contact existed from the beginning of the Christian era until the end of the Middle Ages. In the first European operas, Caccini and Monteverdi used techniques remarkably similar to those of the ancient Iranian *ta'ziye* drama. Composers from Händel to Schoenberg and his disciples have used Asian musical effects. In contemporary music theater, Asian concepts that could be applied include the framing prologue of Kālidāsa; alternation between natural and supernatural or comic and dramatic situations; double casting of actors and singers in the same role; the different emotional, symbolic, and atmospheric uses of music; and many others. *(David Bloom)*

5130
as
DE FEO, Sandro. **La musica nel cinematografo** [Music in the cinema], *Atti del secondo Congresso internazionale di musica* (Firenze: Le Monnier, 1940) 232–38. In Italian; summaries in French and German. See no. 239 in this volume.

Strictly speaking, music is not necessary to film; but historically, the purely silent film is something like Rousseau's state of nature, to which society can never return. Aesthetically, the musical score provides film with a desirable dimensionality and cohesion. Scores cited include those of Erich Wolfgang Korngold for *A midsummer night's dream* (William Dieterle and Max Reinhardt, 1934) and *Captain Blood* (Michael Curtiz, 1935); Herbert Stothart for *Mutiny on the Bounty* (Frank Lloyd, 1935); Arthur Lange for *The great Ziegfeld* (Robert Z. Leonard, 1935); and Gerard Carbonara for *Trail of the lonesome pine* (Henry Hathaway, 1936). *(author)*

5131
as
DE LEEUW, Ton. **Introduction par l'auteur à l'opéra** *Alceste* [Author's introduction to the opera *Alceste*], *Zeitgenössisches Musiktheater/Contemporary music theatre/Théâtre musical contemporain* (Hamburg: Deutscher Musikrat, 1966) 114. In French. See no. 481 in this volume.

The opera *Alceste* (1963), with music and libretto (after Euripides) by the author, was conceived for both stage and television performance. It features a relatively less experimental score than in his other works, the doubling of roles by actors and dancers, and simple, highly symbolic sets inspired by engravings by Anton Heyboer. *(David Bloom)*

5132
as
DE' PAOLI, Domenico. **Il librettista Carlo Goldoni e l'opera comica veneziana** [The librettist Carlo Goldoni and Venetian *opera comica*], *Studi goldoniani* (Venezia: Istituto per la Collaborazione Culturale, 1960) 571–91. In Italian. See no. 384 in this volume.

Goldoni's innovations in the mature comedies are all anticipated in his texts for music, in particular his psychological realism and his blend of sentiment and pathos with more purely comic elements. The features are traced in an examination of the intermezzi, *drammi seri*, and *drammi giocosi* through *La buona figliuola* (music by Egidio Duni, 1756), based on Samuel Richardson's novel *Pamela*, which, in the setting by Niccolò Piccinni, marks the definitive moment of transition from the relatively crude Neapolitan opera buffa to what may be called the Italian *opera comica*. *(Susan Poliniak)*

5133
as
DE SANCTIS, Giovanni Battista. **Toni di opera buffa in alcune scene goldoniane** [Opera buffa tones in some scenes by Goldoni], *Studi goldoniani* (Venezia: Istituto per la Collaborazione Culturale, 1960) 593–602. In Italian. See no. 384 in this volume.

Just as the pathetic elements of Goldoni's great comedies are partly inspired by the librettos of Metastasio, so is the buffo character, in the technical sense, traceable to opera buffa librettos, both Neapolitan and Goldoni's own. Analysis of dialogue and monologue in a range of his plays provides many examples of operatic rhythm, dynamics, parallelisms, and repetitions. *(Susan Poliniak)*

5134
as
DEBENEDETTI, Giacomo. **In sala o sullo schermo?** [In the hall or on the screen?], *Atti del secondo Congresso internazionale di musica* (Firenze:

Le Monnier, 1940) 245–51. In Italian; summaries in French and German. See no. 239 in this volume.

Film music collaborates in keeping the audience's attention, as a kind of substitute for the physical environment. It belongs more to the subjective time of the spectator than the objective time of the action, signifying the audience's, not the characters', state of mind. It reaches into the narrative only when it announces something that is not present to the eye (like the bagpipes signaling Bothwell's approach in John Ford's *Mary of Scotland*, 1936). *(author)*

5135
as

DEINHARDT, Hans. **Übersetzungsfragen im besonderen Hinblick auf die Oper Mozarts** [Questions of translation, with a special view to the operas of Mozart], *Bericht über den I. musikwissenschaftlichen Kongress der Deutschen Musikgesellschaft in Leipzig* (Wiesbaden: Breitkopf & Härtel, 1926) 270–73. In German. See no. 120 in this volume.

Issues discussed include the role of the libretto in recitatives, the vocal sounds of the bel canto aria, and the original intentions of the composer. *(William Renwick)*

5136
as

DELLA CORTE, Andrea. **Il libretto e l'influenza di Goldoni** [The libretto and the influence of Goldoni], *Studi goldoniani* (Venezia: Istituto per la Collaborazione Culturale, 1960) 567–70. In Italian. See no. 384 in this volume.

Goldoni's librettos mark the first appearance of a distinctly Italian sensibility in opera, in the way words are made to serve music, and in the highlighting of contrasts, such as those between young and old, and noble and plebeian. Though he apparently regarded them as artistically unimportant compared to his plays, they exercised an influence on the musical styles of Baldassare Galuppi and Niccolò Piccinni. *(Susan Poliniak)*

5137
as

DELLA CORTE, Andrea. **I problemi concernenti la rappresentazione delle opere antiche** [Problems connected with the performance of early operas], *Atti del secondo Congresso internazionale di musica* (Firenze: Le Monnier, 1940) 210–17. In Italian; summaries in French and German. See no. 239 in this volume.

Beyond the strictly musicological problems of the revival of operas from the 17th and 18th c., there is the more or less economic problem of persuading the public to accept works that are so distant from current tastes. They should be accompanied, or better preceded, by a broad-based, calm, and assiduous propaganda effort to prepare the public to listen with understanding. *(author)*

5138
as

DEMUTH, Norman. **The music was specially composed,** *Cahiers d'études de radio-télévision* 3-4 (1955) 413–18. See no. 334 in this volume.

Examines the issues involved in composing background music for radio.

5139
as

DENT, Edward Joseph. **La funzione della musica e della danza nel teatro contemporaneo** [The function of music and dance in contemporary theater], *Atti del II° Congresso internazionale di storia del teatro* (Venezia: De Luca Storia, 1960) 305–11. In Italian. See no. 383 in this volume.

Discusses historical influences on Berlioz's *Les troyens* and describes its premiere.

5140
as

DENT, Edward Joseph. **Henry Purcell and his opera *Dido and Aeneas*,** *Beethoven-Zentenarfeier: Festbericht* (Wien: Otto Maass' Söhne, 1927) 74–80. See no. 141 in this volume.

5141
as

DIETRICH, Margret. **La funzione della musica e della danza nel teatro contemporaneo** [The function of music and dance in contemporary theater], *Atti*

del *II° Congresso internazionale di storia del teatro* (Venezia: De Luca Storia, 1960) 312–23. In Italian. See no. 383 in this volume.

Discusses the roles of music and dance in Austrian theater since the Baroque era.

5142
as

DRZEWIECKI. **Le théâtre populaire en Pologne** [Public theater in Poland], *Congrès international de l'enseignement primaire et de l'éducation populaire* (Paris: S.U.D.E.L., 1938) 321–23. In French. See no. 246 in this volume.

5143
as

DUPONT, Jacques. **Le rôle du décorateur dans la mise en scène lyrique** [The role of the designer in opera production], *Zeitgenössisches Musiktheater/ Contemporary music theatre/Théâtre musical contemporain* (Hamburg: Deutscher Musikrat, 1966) 96–97. In French. See no. 481 in this volume.

A successful opera set allows spectators to be fully receptive to the sound and action of the piece. The designer must work closely with the director, know and love the music, and efface his or her personality in favor of the finished production. *(David Bloom)*

5144
as

EBERT, Carl. **Moderne Opernregie** [Modern opera direction], *Atti del primo Congresso internazionale di musica* (Firenze: Le Monnier, 1935) 105–08. In German; summary in Italian. See no. 203 in this volume.

Focuses on staging's relation to music and dramatic pacing.

5145
as

ECKSTEIN, Pavel; FELSENSTEIN, Walter. **O režijní koncepci a inscenačním slohu v Janáčkových operách** [The concept of direction and style of staging in Janáček's operas], *Leoš Janáček a soudobá hudba* (Praha: Panton, 1963) 81–89. In Czech; summaries in Russian and German. See no. 389 in this volume.

An interchange between the head dramaturge at the Národní Divadlo, Prague, and the intendant at the Komische Oper, Berlin. Whereas Janáček's ideas concerning the directing of his operas were clearly articulated, their staging is a more complex problem, because the style of staging determines whether the composer's message reaches the contemporary audience. *(editors)*

5146
as

EGK, Werner. **Szenische Darstellung eines für den Funk bestimmten Werkes** [The stage presentation of a work written for radio broadcast], *Zeitgenössisches Musiktheater/Contemporary music theatre/Théâtre musical contemporain* (Hamburg: Deutscher Musikrat, 1966) 112–13. In German. See no. 481 in this volume.

An account of the composition of the author's radio opera *Columbus: Bericht und Bildnis* (1932; broadcast on Bayrischer Rundfunk, 1933) and its transferral to the stage by the Städtische Bühnen, Frankfurt, in 1942. *(David Bloom)*

5147
as

EINSTEIN, Alfred. **Le tendenze attuali dell'opera tedesca** [Current trends in German opera], *Atti del primo Congresso internazionale di musica* (Firenze: Le Monnier, 1935) 169–81. In Italian. See no. 203 in this volume.

A survey of active theater composers considers the economic crisis and absence of a coherent German opera tradition. Hopeful trends may be represented by Berg's *Wozzeck*, Weill's *Die Bürgschaft*, and certain works of Richard Strauss. *(David Bloom)*

5148
as

FELIX, Werner. **Die Entwicklung des dramatischen Konfliktes in den Opern Mozarts als Ausdruck der gesellschaftlichen Auseinandersetzungen seiner Zeit** [The development of dramatic conflicts in Mozart's operas as the expression of social confrontations of his time], *Bericht über den internationalen musikwissenschaftlichen Kongreß Wien Mozartjahr 1956* (Graz; Köln: Böhlau, 1958) 195–98. In German. See no. 365 in this volume.

Considers the influence of the reforms of Joseph II, and the Enlightenment in general, on Mozart's choice of librettos as well as their musical treatment. *(Peter Kaliski)*

5149 FERRARA, Franco. **La direzione dell'orchestra**
as **e la musica cinematografica** [Orchestral direction and film music], *La musica nel film* (Roma: Bianco e Nero, 1950) 78–79. In Italian. See no. 297 in this volume.

The conductor of film music must direct the music in such a way as to maximize its relevance to the on-screen action; additionally, the conductor must be able to divide his attention between the screen and the instrumentalists during a recording session. The composer must indicate the tempos and film timings within the score; if the tempo and timing indications are faulty, the conductor must be able to vary the tempos indicated to make the music fit the action on the screen. Special attention must be paid to the balance of timbres and dynamics, and the relative volumes of instruments. Collaboration among the conductor, composer, technicians, and musicians can ensure successful recordings. *(Susan Poliniak)*

5150 FOLGA, Zygmunt. *Bolesław Śmiały* **Ludomira**
as **Różyckiego jako dramat muzyczny** [Ludomir Różycki's *Bolesław Śmiały* and its music dramaturgy], *Ryszard Wagner a polska kultura muzyczna/Richard Wagner und die polnische Musikkultur* (Katowice: Panstwowa Wyzsza Szkola Muzyczna, 1964) 105–22. In Polish; summary in German. See no. 466 in this volume.

5151 FORTNER, Wolfgang. **Libretto und musi-**
as **kalische Sprache** [Libretto and musical language], *Zeitgenössisches Musiktheater/Contemporary music theatre/Théâtre musical contemporain* (Hamburg: Deutscher Musikrat, 1966) 62. In German. See no. 481 in this volume.

In the operas *Die Bluthochzeit* (1956) and *In seinem Garten liebt Don Perlimplin Belisa* (1962), based on plays by Federico García Lorca, musical form grows directly from the text. *(David Bloom)*

5152 FÜRST, Leonhard. **Prinzipien musikalischer**
as **Gestaltung im Tonfilm** [Principles of musical organization in the sound film], *Atti del primo Congresso internazionale di musica* (Firenze: Le Monnier, 1935) 216–22. In German; summary in Italian. See no. 203 in this volume.

Neither the silent film nor the staged genres of theater, opera, and dance offer a model for the sound film as a work of art. In the world of the sound film, visual and musical aspects should not be separated. Ultimately, formal unity will be based on an equivalence between the rhythms of music and image, functioning as interdependent components of the work as a whole. *(David Bloom)*

5153 GAILLARD, Marius-François. **La musica per**
as **film in Francia** [Film music in France], *La musica nel film* (Roma: Bianco e Nero, 1950) 107–13. In Italian. See no. 297 in this volume.

Discusses the importance of music for film, including silent pictures. The process of composing for film is described and difficulties are pointed out. The author's music for Marcel L'Herbier's 1921 silent drama *El Dorado* is discussed in detail, and a number of classical composers who have written for film, such as Honegger and Ravel, are mentioned. *(Susan Poliniak)*

5154 GASCO, Alberto. **La scenografia** [Scenography],
as *La vita musicale dell'Italia d'oggi* (Torino: Fratelli

Bocca, 1921) 204–08. In Italian. See no. 97 in this volume.

Discusses problems with various opera houses.

5155 GASCO, Alberto. **Il teatro lirico in Italia** [Opera
as houses in Italy], *La vita musicale dell'Italia d'oggi* (Torino: Fratelli Bocca, 1921) 184–96. In Italian. See no. 97 in this volume.

Discusses finances and proposed tax reforms as they affect theaters.

5156 GERIGK, Herbert. **Wiedergabepraxis älterer**
as **Opern in Deutschland (vom letzten Drittel des 18. Jahrhunderts bis etwa 1830)** [Staging older operas in Germany (from the last third of the 18th century to ca. 1830)], *Atti del secondo Congresso internazionale di musica* (Firenze: Le Monnier, 1940) 205–10. In German; summaries in Italian and French. See no. 239 in this volume.

For operas with Italian texts, it is better to try to improve the old German versions than to prepare entirely new ones, because the former, in spite of their poor quality, represent the spirit of the time in which the music was written. *Parlando* style represents insuperable difficulties to German singers, especially in ensemble numbers; the *recitativo secco* parts can be replaced with spoken dialogue. Cuts are otherwise to be avoided, as are exaggerated staging effects, transpositions of the vocal parts, and excessively large instrumental forces. *(author)*

5157 GERVASIO, Rocco; VLAD, Roman. **La musica**
as **nel documentario** [Music in the documentary], *La musica nel film* (Roma: Bianco e Nero, 1950) 69–77. In Italian. See no. 297 in this volume.

Discusses the differences between music for documentaries and music for other types of films. In dramatic films, themes often revolve around individual characters, whereas in documentaries themes can concern not just people but concepts. There are special problems to be addressed regarding the relation of music to narration; documentaries often require longer individual music cues than other types of films. In certain instances, music can be substituted for narration. Generally, the degree to which the music is suited to the film is inversely proportional to the value of the music in an absolute sense. Different cinematic tactics within documentaries and how music can serve them are described. *(Susan Poliniak)*

5158 GHISI, Federico. **Un aspect inédit des**
as **intermèdes de 1589 à la cour médicéenne et le développement des courses masquées et des ballets équestres devant les premières décades du XVIIᵉ siècle** [A new aspect of the intermedios of 1589 of the court of the Medicis and the development of masked races and equestrian ballets before the first decades of the 17th century], *Les fêtes de la Renaissance* (Paris: Centre National de la Recherche Scientifique [CNRS], 1956) 145–204. *Music.* In French. See no. 350 in this volume.

Discusses late–16th-c. intermedio music as a source of the bel canto style, and examines an intermedio with music by Caccini. A description of the scenography can be found in the Biblioteca Marucelliana in Florence.

5159 GIAZOTTO, Remo. **Teatro di provincia e**
as **sovvenzioni** [Subsidies and the provinicial theater], *Atti del quinto Congresso di musica* (Firenze: Barbèra, 1948) 133–40. In Italian. See no. 285 in this volume.

Swift measures must be taken to reverse the neglect that opera has suffered in the provinces in recent years. Provincial theaters, built during the 18th c., are small and accommodate few paying patrons; standing room generates little revenue. The government must subsidize the construction of modern opera houses in all urban centers. This can sustain the operatic tradition and facilitate the apprenticeship of young singers and conductors. The country's vocal resources can thereby be cultivated and contemporary opera can flourish. *(Willner Channan)*

5160 GIRARDIN, Monique. **Une source d'infor-**
as **mation: Les annuaires de théâtre** [A source of information: Theater directories], *Acts of the VIIth International Congress of Libraries and Museums of the Performing Arts/Actes du VIIe Congrès international des bibliothèques-musées des arts du spectacle* ('s-Gravenhage: Theater Instituut Nederland/Netherlands Centre of the International Theatre Institute, 1965) 54–58. *Charts, diagr.* In French. See no. 492 in this volume.

Discusses various types of data to be found, including personnel, admission prices, audience numbers, histories of theater companies, and chronological lists of productions.

5161 GRAF, Herbert. **L'opera quale Festspiel** [Opera
as as festival], *Atti del terzo Congresso internazionale di musica* (Firenze: Le Monnier, 1940) 161–65. In Italian; summaries in French and German. See no. 256 in this volume.

Discusses the basic principles and origins of opera festivals, with examples from the ancient Greeks to the present time. *(Edwin D. Wallace)*

5162 GRASBERGER, Franz. **Zur Symbolik der**
as ***Zauberflöte*** [The symbolism of *Die Zauberflöte*], *Bericht über den internationalen musikwissenschaftlichen Kongreß Wien Mozartjahr 1956* (Graz; Köln: Böhlau, 1958) 249–52. *Music.* In German. See no. 365 in this volume.

Die Zauberflöte should not be regarded as a story at all, but as a purely symbolic construct, and concerned with the opposition not of good and evil but of male and female, conveyed as much by Mozart's music as by Schikaneder's text. Mozart, in his symbolic characterization, uses the skills of the absolute musician as much as those of the dramatist, in the cyclical and contrapuntal deployment of symbolic musical material. *(David Bloom)*

5163 GREGOR, Joseph. **Die historische Drama-**
as **turgie in der Geschichte der Oper** [Historical dramaturgy in the history of opera], *Haydn-Zentenarfeier* (Leipzig: Breitkopf & Härtel; Wien: Artaria, 1909) 208–10. In German. See no. 65 in this volume.

Refers to the works of Heinrich Alfred Bulthaupt (1849-1905) and Eduard Hanslick.

5164 GREGOR, Joseph. **Typen der Regie der Oper**
as **im 20. Jahrhundert** [Types of opera direction in the 20th century], *Bericht über den internationalen musikwissenschaftlichen Kongreß Wien Mozartjahr 1956* (Graz; Köln: Böhlau, 1958) 253–60. In German. See no. 365 in this volume.

The 20th-c. revolution in stage design has allowed innovations in stage direction that approach the aesthetic quality of the previous high point of opera staging, in the late Baroque, though it is not clear whether any of the current experiments can add up to a single stable style. Examples are drawn from contrasted stagings of scenes from *Fidelio*, *Die Walküre*, and other works, based on research materials for the author's *Die Theaterregie in der Welt unseres Jahrhunderts* (1958). *(David Bloom)*

5165 HABUNEK, Vlado. **Le rôle du metteur en scène**
as [The role of the stage director], *Zeitgenössisches Musiktheater/Contemporary music theatre/Théâtre musical contemporain* (Hamburg: Deutscher Musikrat, 1966) 94–95. In French. See no. 481 in this volume.

Discusses the staging of operas in Yugoslavia. The director has a greater responsibility in the production of less-accessible works. Stylization can provide fascinating results, but most often superimposes the director's personality over that of the composer. Realistic sets and acting can, with precision and purity, achieve the needed grandeur. For an opera to achieve a definitive, noble form, singers must be trained in terms of the entire body, not just the voice. *(David Bloom)*

5166 HANKISS, János. **Le drame populaire et la**
as **société** [The people's theater and society], *Bulletin of the International Committee of Historical Sciences* X/2-3 (Apr-July 1938) 650–53. In French. See no. 262 in this volume.

A brief discussion of the people's theater, including theater created and performed by working-class actors, plays with working-class protagonists, the *Volksstück*, and the *commedia in dialetto*. Their associations with music are discussed, from the satirical couplets of 17th- and 18th-c. Italian comedy to melodrama and peasant tragedy. The use of music follows the idealization in such dramas of the people themselves. *(Susan Poliniak)*

5167 HARTMANN, Georg. **Die Erziehung zur**
as **Durchgeistigung des Sängerdarstellers** [The education to spirituality of the singer-actor], *Bericht über den Internationalen Kongreß Singen und Sprechen* (München: Oldenbourg, 1938) 211–13. In German. See no. 257 in this volume.

Few singers are adequately trained in the art of representing a character onstage. They need to study movement, speech, and possibly the visual arts, since it is a visual impression that they must create. *(David Bloom)*

5168 HEINLEIN, M.V. **La funzione della musica e**
as **della danza nel teatro contemporaneo** [The function of music and dance in contemporary theater], *Atti del II° Congresso internazionale di storia del teatro* (Venezia: De Luca Storia, 1960) 341–52. In Italian. See no. 383 in this volume.

Traces the history of musical comedy as it evolved in the U.S.

5169 HELM, Everett. **Forms and components:**
as **Mixed forms,** *Zeitgenössisches Musiktheater/Contemporary music theatre/Théâtre musical contemporain* (Hamburg: Deutscher Musikrat, 1966) 75–77. See no. 481 in this volume.

Composers have always avoided the idea of opera as a monolithic genre. Monteverdi called the *L'incoronazione di Poppea* a *dramma per musica*, and Bellini, Donizetti, and Verdi used the terms *tragedia lirica*, *dramma tragico*, and *melodramma* (which has different connotations in France, England, Italy, and the U.S.). Wagner's legacy demands that 20th-c. opera be good drama. Attempts at new approaches have not yet yielded a solution; Strauss's and Stravinsky's works attest to this. It is possible that new genres will arise from the use of the spoken word, dance, and electronics; whether or not they will be considered operas remains to be seen. *(Helena Ross)*

5170 HENZE, Hans Werner. **Zur Inszenierung**
as **zeitgenössischen Musiktheaters** [The staging of contemporary music theater], *Zeitgenössisches Musiktheater/Contemporary music theatre/Théâtre musical contemporain* (Hamburg: Deutscher Musikrat, 1966) 101–02. In German. See no. 481 in this volume.

Most stage directors think of the opera score as a helpless, sickly, alien thing that needs to be aided, usually with significant cuts. Balanchine's work with ballet exemplifies a better approach to staging musical works. *(David Bloom)*

5171 HRENNIKOV, Tihon Nikolaevič. **La musica**
as **per film nell'U.R.S.S.** [Film music in the U.S.S.R.], *La musica nel film* (Roma: Bianco e Nero, 1950) 129–34. In Italian. See no. 297 in this volume.

Discusses the film music of Isaak Dunaevskij (one of the first Soviet classical composers to write for film), Daniil and Dmitrij Pokrass, Dmitrij Šostakovič, Dmitrij Kabalevskij, Venedikt Puškov, Aram Hačaturjan, Nikolaj Krjukov, and Sergej Prokof'ev; a number of other film composers are mentioned in passing. *(Susan Poliniak)*

5172 HUCKE, Helmut. **Die beiden Fassungen der**
as **Oper *Didone abbandonata* von Domenico Sarri** [The two versions of Domenico Sarri's opera *Didone abbandonata*], *Bericht über den internationalen musik-*

wissenschaftlichen Kongreß (Kassel: Bärenreiter, 1957) 113–17. *Music.* In German. See no. 356 in this volume.

The opera, written for a Naples production of 1724, is the earliest setting of Metastasio's first original libretto. Sarri's revision of the score for Venice, 1730, provides a wealth of examples of changing fashions in Neapolitan theater music. *(David Bloom)*

5173
as

IRVING, Ernest. **La musica per film in Inghilterra** [Film music in England], *La musica nel film* (Roma: Bianco e Nero, 1950) 114–17. In Italian. See no. 297 in this volume.

Describes aspects of film scores by Ralph Vaughan Williams, Anton Karas, John Greenwood, William Alwin, Constant Lambert, Ian Whyte, William Walton, Sir Arnold Bax, Georges Auric, and others. British film music is better than U.S. film music, which is too stereotypical and full of musical jokes. The beginnings of the London Symphony Orchestra, the London Philharmonic Orchestra, and the Royal Philharmonic Orchestra are described. Sir Thomas Beecham's conducting work on Brian Easdale's score to *The red shoes* and on the opera film *The tales of Hoffman* is discussed. *(Susan Poliniak)*

5174
as

JACQUOT, Jean. **Craig, Yeats et le théâtre d'Orient** [Craig, Yeats, and Asian theater], *Les théâtres d'Asie* (Paris: Centre National de la Recherche Scientifique [CNRS], 1961) 271–83. In French. See no. 397 in this volume.

In his work as a playwright, William Butler Yeats was strongly engaged with Asian theatrical traditions. He was influenced by the writings on Asian masks and puppetry of the stage director and designer Edward Gordon Craig, who contributed designs to productions of Yeats's plays at the Abbey Theater, and by Ezra Pound, who introduced him to the Japanese noh.

5175
as

JACQUOT, Jean. **Les types du lieu théâtral et leurs transformations de la fin du Moyen Âge au milieu du XVIIᵉ siècle** [Theatrical venue types and their transformations from the end of the Middle Ages to the middle of the 17th century], *Le lieu théâtral à la Renaissance* (Paris: Centre National de la Recherche Scientifique [CNRS], 1964) 473–509. In French. See no. 472 in this volume.

Examines resources for the accurate restoration of theaters, theatrical machinery, and stage sets from the 15th to the 17th c. Aspects of presenting Achillini and Monteverdi's *Mercurio e Marte* (1628) and similar works—particularly regarding the placement and usage of musicians—are discussed, and Italian styles and techniques that were applied in other European countries are examined. The contexts of court masques, ballets, and other entertainments are explored. *(Susan Poliniak)*

5176
as

JARUSTOVSKIJ, Boris Mihajlovič. **Probleme des gegenwärtigen Musiktheaters** [Problems of contemporary music theater], *Zeitgenössisches Musiktheater/Contemporary music theatre/Théâtre musical contemporain* (Hamburg: Deutscher Musikrat, 1966) 37–42. In German. See no. 481 in this volume.

Experimentation is essential to progress, but the experimental work itself may be most significant as a preparation for a later one. For example, in writing *Nos*, Šostakovič was developing techniques that he would later use for the more mature *Katerina Izmajlova*. Experimentation must be a part of developing national traditions. *(David Bloom)*

5177
as

JUNGK, Klaus. **Musik und Film** [Music and film], *Musische Jugend und technische Mittler* (Remscheid: Landesarbeitsgemeinschaft Jugendmusik Nordrhein-Westfalen, 1957) 101–11. In German. See no. 380 in this volume.

Broad discussion from the composer's point of view.

5178
as

KARÁSEK, Bohumil. **Svět Janáčka dramatika: Rysy kritického realismu v jeho operním**

díle [The world of Janáček the dramatist: Traits of critical realism in his operatic works], *Leoš Janáček a soudobá hudba* (Praha: Panton, 1963) 162–68. In Czech; summaries in Russian and German. See no. 389 in this volume.

Critical realism is conceived as a product of the historical period of intensified class conflicts during early imperialism, oscillating between classical realism and naturalism. The features of critical realism are identified in Janáček's librettos and compared with operatic works of other Czech and European composers of the late 19th and early 20th c. *(editors)*

5179
as

KAŠLÍK, Václav. **Die Wiederbelebung der Oper** [The resuscitation of opera], *Zeitgenössisches Musiktheater/Contemporary music theatre/Théâtre musical contemporain* (Hamburg: Deutscher Musikrat, 1966) 86–89. In German. See no. 481 in this volume.

Discusses the author's stagings of operas from the standard repertoire for television and at the Tylovo Divadlo and Laterna Magica in Prague. The stagings are designed to bring new life to the music theater through highly stylized production and multimedia techniques. *(David Bloom)*

5180
as

KISHIBE, Shigeo. **The music of the Japanese noh plays,** *Zeitgenössisches Musiktheater/Contemporary music theatre/Théâtre musical contemporain* (Hamburg: Deutscher Musikrat, 1966) 124–25. See no. 481 in this volume.

Noh encompasses theater, the visual arts, dance, and music. The music consists of solo singing, choral singing in unison, and an ensemble of three or four instruments. Each actor, musical event, and section has a specific name and function. The melodies serve the words and are therefore severe and rarely melismatic. The words are made to fit a predetermined eight-beat pattern. The modal system is built around three tones separated by perfect fourths. *(Helena Ross)*

5181
as

KODERA, Yukichi. **Les kagura, les représentations populaires bouddhiques et les nouvelles représentations populaires au Japon** [The kagura, traditional Buddhist performances, and contemporary folk theater in Japan], *Congrès international des arts populaires/International congress of popular arts* (Paris: Institut international de coopération intellectuelle, 1928) 138–40. In French. See no. 153 in this volume.

Summary of the paper abstracted as no. 5182 in this volume.

5182
as

KODERA, Yukichi. **Les kagura, les représentations populaires bouddhiques et les nouvelles représentations populaires au Japon** [The kagura, traditional Buddhist performances, and contemporary folk theater in Japan], *Art populaire: Travaux artistiques et scientifiques du Iᵉʳ Congrès international des arts populaires* (Paris: Duchartre, 1931) 194–99. In French. See no. 152 in this volume.

The folk theater of Japan includes sacred Shinto drama (kagura pieces of dramatic content, as opposed to abstract kagura) and activities surrounding Buddhist temple processions, now becoming relatively rare. Recent innovations include kabuki-style performances by the kagura actors, normally on the evening following a daytime kagura performance, and amateur kabuki performances. The most original development is hakata niwaka, a comic improvisational genre originating in Hakata, Fukuoka prefecture; during the peak of their popularity in the 1820s, these were satires of the Japanese government, but they no longer have a political aspect. A summary is cited as no. 5181 in this volume. *(James R. Cowdery)*

5183
as

KÖHLER-HELFFRICH, Heinrich. **Dialog in der Oper** [Dialogue in opera], *Bericht über den Internationalen Kongreß Singen und Sprechen* (München: Oldenbourg, 1938) 225–26. In German. See no. 257 in this volume.

Opera with spoken dialogue is more suitable for German audiences after a working day than the masterpieces of Wagner, Pfitzner, and Strauss, which should perhaps be reserved for holidays. In repertoire works such as *Carmen* and *Prodaná nevěsta* (The bartered bride) the dialogue should be better written and more musically performed; and new operas with spoken dialogue are needed. *(David Bloom)*

5184
as

KRAFFT, Christophe. **L'esthétique du Nouveau Bayreuth** [The aesthetics of the New Bayreuth], *Actes du cinquième Congrès international d'esthétique/Proceedings of the Fifth International Congress of Aesthetics* ('s-Gravenhage: Mouton, 1964) 570–73. In French. See no. 475 in this volume.

The nonrealistic stagings since 1951 of the annual Bayreuther Festspiele, inspired by the aesthetics of directors like Alphonse Appia and taking advantage of technological advances in the use of the cyclorama, lighting, and projected images, differ from the literalist stagings of Wagner himself, but are faithful to the composer's prophetic vision. *(David Bloom)*

5185
as

KRENEK, Ernst. **Remarks on the influence of the new technical media (electronics, cinema) on the conception of works for the music stage (opera),** *Zeitgenössisches Musiktheater/Contemporary music theatre/Théâtre musical contemporain* (Hamburg: Deutscher Musikrat, 1966) 108. See no. 481 in this volume.

Electronic music has influenced the concept of music in general. Many composers are using the percussion section of the orchestra (including the piano) to create effects inspired by electronic sounds. Stage productions are also incorporating electronic sounds to enhance or contrast with the orchestra, or to replace the orchestra altogether. Problems with synchronization between tape and stage demand further experimentation. *(Mary Lou Humphrey)*

5186
as

KRETZENBACHER, Leopold. **Folk songs in the folk plays of the Austrian Alpine regions,** *Journal of the International Folk Music Council* IV (1952) 45–49. See no. 306 in this volume.

The repertoire includes large-scale open-air *Großspiele*, especially Passion play; smaller-scale indoor *Stubenspiele* on subjects relating to church festivals, and brief *Umzugsspiele* or procession plays for holiday mendication customs. They originated in strictly liturgical gestures in the Middle Ages, as narratives of the Creation and of the life of Jesus; added secondary biblical themes and morality tales in the Renaissance; and took on their current form in the Counter-Reformation. Singing is an essential feature. The music, which often has an elaborate operetta-like dramaturgical function, is transmitted orally, even in cases where the text is written down; it is never accompanied by instruments. *(David Bloom)*

5187
as

KRETZENBACHER, Leopold. **Totentänze in der südostalpinen Volkskultur** [The Dance of Death in southeastern Alpine traditional culture], *Rad VII-og kongresa Saveza Folklorista Jugoslavije* (Cetinje: Obod, 1964) 299–309. *Transcr.* In German. See no. 419 in this volume.

The Dance of Death is well known as a motif in visual art of the late Middle Ages and Renaissance, and as a subject of poetry, in parts of Europe including the southeastern Alps; it is also an actual sung dance-drama genre of German- and Slovene-speaking peoples in the southeastern Alps, still extant in Styria and Carinthia, performed by amateurs of the agricultural classes in their homes or in the public rooms of inns. Text and music from a Styrian example collected by the author (*Schäferspiel*) are quoted at length. *(David Bloom)*

5188
as

KUEI, Li Man. **Chinese drama,** *Zeitgenössisches Musiktheater/Contemporary music theatre/Théâtre musical contemporain* (Hamburg: Deutscher Musikrat, 1966) 130. *Illus.* See no. 481 in this volume.

Chinese classical drama, a combination of music, literature, and dance, originated in the Tang dynasty (618-907 C.E.) and reached full development during the Song dynasty (960-1279). The drama *Changsheng dian* (The palace of eternal youth) by Hong Sheng (1645-1704) is discussed.

5189
as

LA MOTTE, Diether de. **Das Verhältnis zwischen Text und Musik** [The relation between text and music], *Zeitgenössisches Musiktheater/Contemporary music theatre/Théâtre musical contemporain* (Hamburg: Deutscher Musikrat, 1966) 43–45. In German. See no. 481 in this volume.

As a result of Wagner's influence, there has been an increasing dominance of note-to-syllable settings and a rarity of coloratura and textual repetition. The balance between text and music that characterized opera from Monteverdi to Verdi has been reweighted in favor of text. Carl Orff and Hans Werner Henze have demonstrated ways to restore the role of singing. *(David Bloom)*

5190
as

LARAGNINO, Francesco. **La musica nel disegno animato** [Music in animation], *La musica nel film* (Roma: Bianco e Nero, 1950) 63–68. In Italian. See no. 297 in this volume.

Describes several musical issues surrounding the live-action film *Yellow sky* (score by Alfred Newman), especially the problem of film music for live action being filled with clichés, both compositional and instrumental (such as the use of trombones to indicate stupor and the use of oboes for pathetic scenes). In live-action film, the music serves the picture; in animation, the picture serves the music, since the music is chosen before the animation work is begun. The role of the narrator is discussed, as well as various animated films from the Walt Disney studio, including *Fantasia* and *Make mine music. (Susan Poliniak)*

5191
as

LASCELLES, George Henry Hubert, Earl of Harewood. **The place of contemporary music theatre in festivals,** *Zeitgenössisches Musiktheater/Contemporary music theatre/Théâtre musical contemporain* (Hamburg: Deutscher Musikrat, 1966) 132–33. See no. 481 in this volume.

Music festivals must feature new music. While orchestras tend toward conservatism to preserve their reputations, opera companies are more likely to take risks. Unfortunately, productions of contemporary opera are rarely repeated. Edinburgh has featured a number of first performances, but has never commissioned a new work or staged operas by unknown composers. In 1959, Blomdahl's *Aniara* and Berg's *Wozzeck* were poorly attended. Because of its well-known suite, Prokof'ev's *Ljubov' k trëm apel'sinam* (The love for three oranges) was sold out, but his *Igrok* (The gambler) was only half-full. The festival director must program such works, thereby increasing and encouraging knowledge of them. *(Helena Ross)*

5192
as

LEICHTENTRITT, Hugo. **On the prologue in early opera,** *Papers read at the Annual Meeting of the American Musicological Society* (New York: American Musicological Society, 1936) 88–95. See no. 230 in this volume.

Explores the prologue's roots in Greek drama, its significance in 17th-c. opera, and its absence from the modern repertoire, focusing on the operas of Monteverdi and Francesco Cavalli.

5193
as

LÉVY, Roland Alexis Manuel (Roland-Manuel). **La musique prise dans le sujet, élement materiel du film et la musique composée pour le film, élément formel de l'œuvre d'art** [Music taken from within the subject as a material element of the film, and music composed for the film as a formal element of the artwork], *Atti del secondo Congresso internazionale di musica* (Firenze: Le Monnier, 1940) 253–56. In French; summaries in Italian and German. See no. 239 in this volume.

Spontaneously recorded music and natural noise, once they are chosen and ordered in a film's soundtrack, acquire a dignity that was at first unexpected, entering into harmony, rivalry, and sometimes even conflict with the score composed for the film. Between fake bad music created by a competent composer and real bad music appropriated in its raw state from the popular muse, between an impressionist nocturne for large orchestra and the authentic concerto of the crickets and frogs, among all these realities of first, second, or third degree, the artificial music does not necessarily win out over the natural. *(author)*

5194 LÉVY, Roland Alexis Manuel (Roland-Manuel).
as **Rythme cinématographique et rythme musical** [Cinematic and musical rhythm], *Deuxième congrès international d'esthétique et de Science de l'art* (Paris: Librairie Félix Alcan, 1937) II, 364–66. In French. See no. 249 in this volume.

The organization of movement in a film, through its succession of images, its rhythm, is what makes cinema an art. The advent of the sound film, in 1928, has led to possibilities of synchronization between music and film, generally more successful when the movement is composed to the music rather than the other way around, and also to disjunctions between the two, which can create a strange and subtle poetry. Also published in *Le cinéma* 2, 1945; a reprint is cited as RILM [1989]10967. *(David Bloom)*

5195 LIEBERMANN, Rolf. **Musiktheater oder**
as **Stagione** [Music theater or *stagione*], *Zeitgenössisches Musiktheater/Contemporary music theatre/Théâtre musical contemporain* (Hamburg: Deutscher Musikrat, 1966) 29–32. In German. See no. 481 in this volume.

There are three prerequisites for the presentation of a contemporary opera as a Gesamtkunstwerk: the enlisting of first-class stage directors and designers; the availability of suitable singers in the context of a real repertory company rather than a two-month *stagione*; and consistently demanding critical standards. *(David Bloom)*

5196 LIEBNER, János. **Der Einfluß Schillers auf**
as **Verdi** [Schiller's influence on Verdi], *Bericht über den internationalen musikwissenschaftlichen Kongreß* (Kassel: Bärenreiter, 1963) 222–25. In German. See no. 452 in this volume.

Verdi wrote four operas with librettos drawn directly from Schiller (*Giovanna d'Arco, I masnadieri, Luisa Miller*, and *Don Carlos*). Simon Boccanegra shares historical subject matter with Schiller's early *Die Verschwörung des Fiesco in Genua*. The text of *La forza del destino* uses an entire scene from *Wallensteins Lager* and seems to have a more profound relationship with *Die Braut von Messina*. *(David Bloom)*

5197 LONGO, Achille. **I musicisti e la critica**
as **cinematografica** [Musicians and film criticism], *La musica nel film* (Roma: Bianco e Nero, 1950) 86–90. In Italian. See no. 297 in this volume.

In Italy, film music is not expected to do as much for a film as, say, costumes and sets do. Film editors do not respect the music written for a film, thinking it dispensable and transposable from one part of a film to another. Music is, on the contrary, a vital part of the film. It is the job of the listening public and the film critic to recognize good film music and praise it. Several general statements made by critics about film music are cited, and the assumptions behind these statements are analyzed. *(Susan Poliniak)*

5198 LUALDI, Adriano. **Due nuove vie per la**
as **musica: Radio e film sonoro** [Two new roads for music: Radio and film with sound], *Atti del primo Congresso internazionale di musica* (Firenze: Le Monnier, 1935) 43–52. In Italian. See no. 203 in this volume.

In the silent cinema, music occupied an ancillary position. Now, in the era of sound film, music has been emancipated. On the radio, music plays a similarly central role, making propaganda acceptable to the masses. *(Lisa Miller)*

5199 LUNGHI, F.L. **La musica e il neo-realismo** [Mu-
as sic and neorealism], *La musica nel film* (Roma: Bianco e Nero, 1950) 56–60. In Italian. See no. 297 in this volume.

Neorealistic films are not so much commentary as they are a means for vision and understanding; the inner lives of characters are stressed. Music for films of this genre should share these qualities and reflect the action, tone, and message being conveyed on the screen. *(Susan Poliniak)*

5200 MA, Hiao-Ts'iun. **Le théâtre de Pékin** [The the-
as ater of Beijing], *Les théâtres d'Asie* (Paris: Centre National de la Recherche Scientifique [CNRS], 1961) 89–97. *Transcr.* In French. See no. 397 in this volume.

Surveys the yuanqu, kunqu, jingju (Beijing opera) styles, in terms of their characteristic association with specific emotional states and the jingju system of color symbolism. The yuanqu (late 13th-late 14th c.) was the earliest complete Chinese theatrical genre, comprising three elements: song, declamation, and action. Only the protagonist sings; the other actors declaim. Inspired by the yuanqu, the kunqu originated in the 14th c. and was an intermediary between yuanqu and jingju. Its music has 17 tones divided into four modes, each having a distinct character. The kunqu decayed in the 19th c. but did not disappear altogether. Jingju originated in the province of Hubei. Its singing is very simple compared with its instrumental music, and has only four principal modes. *(Donna Arnold)*

5201 MACHABEY, Armand. **Rapport sur le théâtre**
as **musical en France** [Report on music theater in France], *Atti del primo Congresso internazionale di musica* (Firenze: Le Monnier, 1935) 139–69. In French; summary in Italian. See no. 203 in this volume.

Examines representative stage works: Milhaud's *Maximilien*, Jacques Ibert's *Angélique* and *Le roi d'Yvetot*, Alfred Bachelet's *Un jardin sur l'Oronte*, and Henry Février's *La femme nue*. The public's indifference to contemporary opera should not be attributed to the rise of modernism but rather the failure of librettists to adapt to the audience's evolving psychology. *(author)*

5202 MAGNANI, Luigi. **La funzione della musica e**
as **della danza nel teatro contemporaneo** [The function of music and dance in contemporary theater], *Atti del II° Congresso internazionale di storia del teatro* (Venezia: De Luca Storia, 1960) 324–29. In Italian. See no. 383 in this volume.

Music has the power to heighten the effects of drama, poetry, and acting in opera and theater.

5203 MALIPIERO, Gian Francesco; PETRASSI,
as Goffredo; PIZZETTI, Ildebrando. **Tre opinioni** [Three opinions], *La musica nel film* (Roma: Bianco e Nero, 1950) 80–85. In Italian. See no. 297 in this volume.

Three composers discuss the issues involved in creating film music.

5204 MANGINI, Nicola. **Goldoni e la Polonia**
as [Goldoni and Poland], *Venezia e la Polonia nei secoli dal XVII al XIX* (Venezia: Istituto per la Collaborazione Culturale, 1965) 203–15. In Italian. See no. 474 in this volume.

Surveys the history of operatic settings and incidental music on Polish stages, including information on the composers and musicians involved. *(Sylvia Eversole)*

5205 MASETTI, Enzo. **Introduzione ai problemi**
as **della musica nel film** [Introduction to the problems of music in film], *La musica nel film* (Roma: Bianco e Nero, 1950) 7–29. In Italian. See no. 297 in this volume.

Considers whether or not film music is an art, and what is involved in the creation of music for film. Film imposes limits on music, but these limits can be overcome. Composing for film can be technically challenging, as it involves the creation of music within an allotted time frame to correspond to a visual sequence; the director and composer in essence collaborate on the music, as the composer must interpret the director's wishes. The composer's work can be crucial to the film's sense of artistic unity. Film music involves a union of visual and musical rhythms. Issues surrounding asynchronization, the functions and importance of themes, the uses of particular instruments, and instrumental effects are also discussed. *(Susan Poliniak)*

5206 MAXIMOWNA, Ita. **Die Bühnenbildner im**
as **heutigen Musiktheater** [The stage designer and
contemporary music theater], *Zeitgenössisches
Musiktheater/Contemporary music theatre/Théâtre musical contemporain* (Hamburg: Deutscher Musikrat,
1966) 98–100. In German. See no. 481 in this volume.
General remarks on set design; productions of Blacher's *Preussisches
Märchen* and Henze's *Der Prinz von Homburg* are cited as examples.
(David Bloom)

5207 MENON, Narayana. **The dance-drama of In-**
as **dia,** *Zeitgenössisches Musiktheater/Contemporary
music theatre/Théâtre musical contemporain* (Hamburg: Deutscher Musikrat, 1966) 126–29. See no. 481
in this volume.
South India's dance-dramas involve codified forms of communication
through language, gesture, and facial expression. Sanskrit temple dramas are
discussed, and the kathakaḷi and bhāgavata mēḷā traditions are examined.

5208 MILA, Massimo. **Musica e ritmo nel cinema-**
as **tografo** [Music and rhythm in the cinema], *Atti del
primo Congresso internazionale di musica* (Firenze: Le
Monnier, 1935) 209–16. In Italian. See no. 203 in this
volume.
Music in films should be used as a functional device to enhance the film's
rhythm. Examples are taken from René Clair's *Cinéma* (1924), a filmed
entr'acte with music by René Clair designed to complement Satie's ballet
Relâche; W. (Woodbridge) S. Van Dyke's *White shadows in the South Seas*
(1928), for which no composer was credited; Josef von Sternberg's *Blonde
Venus* (1932), with music by Oskar Potoker; and Edmund Goulding's
Grand Hotel (1932), with music by William Axt. *(Lisa Miller)*

5209 MILA, Massimo. **Stravinski et les nouvelles**
as **formes de théâtre musical** [Stravinsky and the new
forms of music theater], *Zeitgenössisches Musik-
theater/Contemporary music theatre/Théâtre musical
contemporain* (Hamburg: Deutscher Musikrat, 1966)
78–81. In French. See no. 481 in this volume.
With the exceptions of *Mavra* and *The rake's progress*, Stravinsky never
accepted music theater forms that were inherited from the past, but established a unique approach for each new work. He used new forms in hopes of
demystifying the theater and purging it of the suspect element of interpretation. *(David Bloom)*

5210 MILHAUD, Darius. **Wagner, Verdi ed il film**
as [Wagner, Verdi, and film], *Atti del secondo Congresso
internazionale di musica* (Firenze: Le Monnier, 1940)
257–61. In Italian; summaries in French and German.
See no. 239 in this volume.
In the beginning of the sound film, music attempted to address the public in
a popular and simplistic way, and pushed the infantile idea of the leitmotiv
beyond what even Wagner might have imagined, making entire scores out
of a single song. Fortunately the Wagnerian point of departure has been
abandoned in favor of the elements of surprise and imagination. Film
scores should follow the dramatic or psychological evolution of the scenario, intervening sparingly but in an indispensable way, and always with a
stylistic unity. *(author)*

5211 MONK, Egon. **Der Einfluss Brechts** [Brecht's in-
as fluence], *Zeitgenössisches Musiktheater/Contempo-
rary music theatre/Théâtre musical contemporain*
(Hamburg: Deutscher Musikrat, 1966) 70–74. In German. See no. 481 in this volume.
Brecht wrote no opera librettos after *Aufstieg und Fall der Stadt
Mahagonny* (1930). It seems that 34 years later, his ideas on the music theater have not been fully explored. *(David Bloom)*

5212 NETTL, Paul. *Sethos* **und die freimauerische**
as **Grundlage der** *Zauberflöte* [*Sethos* and the
Masonic foundation of *Die Zauberflöte*], *Bericht über
die musikwissenschaftliche Tagung der Internationalen
Stiftung Mozarteum* (Leipzig: Breitkopf & Härtel,
1932) 142–49. In German. See no. 193 in this volume.
Adduces evidence supporting the view that Emanuel Schikaneder was the
sole author of the *Zauberflöte* libretto, including documentation of his
membership in the lodge Carl zu den drei Schlüsseln in Regensburg,
1788-89. Carl Ludwig Gieseke may have introduced Schikaneder to
Christoph Martin Wieland's *Dschinnistan*, as he is said to have claimed,
but Wieland's tales are less important as a source than Matthias Claudius's
German version, 1777-78, of the novel *Sethos*, by Jean Terrasson. Another
neglected source is the libretto by Caterino Mazzolà, assisted by Lorenzo
da Ponte, for Johann Gottlieb Naumann's opera *Osiride* (Dresden, 1781).
(David Bloom)

5213 NIEDECKEN-GEBHARD, Hanns. **Die Auf-**
as **gaben und Probleme monumentaler Festspiel-**
gestaltung [Responsibilities and problems in the production of monumental festival spectacles], *Bericht
über den Internationalen Kongreß Singen und
Sprechen* (München: Oldenbourg, 1938) 213–18. In
German. See no. 257 in this volume.
Argues for the political value, under National Socialism, of staging music
theater in very large open-air spaces such as the Dietrich-Eckart-Bühne in
Berlin, which was used in 1936-37, during the Olympic games and the festivities in honor of the city's 700th anniversary, for monumental productions of Händel's *Hercules* and Gluck's *Orpheus*. Unsolved difficulties are
the placement of microphones and the perceptual discrepancy between apparently very small singers and greatly amplified sound. *(David Bloom)*

5214 NIEMAND, Szymon. **Wybitni polscy Śpiewacy**
as **w repertuarze Wagnerowskim** [Significant Polish singers in productions of Wagner operas], *Ryszard
Wagner a polska kultura muzyczna/Richard Wagner
und die polnische Musikkultur* (Katowice: Panstwowa
Wyzsza Szkola Muzyczna, 1964) 123–32. In Polish;
summary in German. See no. 466 in this volume.

5215 NOCETI, J. **La pièce radiophonique musicale**
as [The musical radio play], *Compte rendu des travaux du
Ier Congrès international d'art radiophonique* (Paris:
conference, 1938). In French. See no. 244 in this
volume.

5216 NOWAK-ROMANOWICZ, Alina. **Musik in**
as **den Theaterformen des ehemaligen Polens**
[Music in the theatrical forms of former Poland],
Musica antiqua Europae orientalis (Warszawa:
Państwowe Wydawnictwo Naukowe, 1966). *Music*. In
German. See no. 506 in this volume.
Discusses topics from the 15th to the 17th c., including liturgical dramas,
jugglers, and jesters.

5217 ORFF, Carl. **Das Libretto im zeitgenössischen**
as **Musiktheater** [The libretto in contemporary music
theater], *Zeitgenössisches Musiktheater/Contemporary
music theatre/Théâtre musical contemporain* (Hamburg: Deutscher Musikrat, 1966) 61. In German. See no.
481 in this volume.
Discusses the librettos for *Die Kluge* (1943) and *Die Bernauerin* (1947),
and the use of ancient and medieval texts in *Carmina burana* (1937),
Antigonae (1949), *Catulli Carmina* (1943), and *Trionfo di Afrodite* (1953).
(David Bloom)

5218
as
OSTHOFF, Helmuth. **Der Gesangstil der früh-deutschen Oper** [The singing style of early German opera], *Bericht über den Internationalen Kongreß Singen und Sprechen* (München: Oldenbourg, 1938) 11–17. In German. See no. 257 in this volume.

Whereas in Italy a highly specialized professional approach was the norm, it was a prized attribute for German singers in the period from 1627 to ca. 1740 to be flexible, able to sing in several different languages and in different vocal registers (especially for men, who sometimes, for instance, sang tenor roles in one opera and alto roles in another, no castrati being available). Many major opera composers began as singers. Johann Sigismund Kusser's *Erindo* (ca. 1693-94) provides an example of a work from the transitional period, when German composers began incorporating virtuoso elements into their style. *(David Bloom)*

5219
as
OZAWA, Y. **Le théâtre de marionnettes et d'ombres au Japon** [The puppet and shadow theaters of Japan], *Congrès international des arts populaires/International congress of popular arts* (Paris: Institut international de coopération intellectuelle, 1928) 134–36. In French. See no. 153 in this volume.

Japanese puppet theater ranges from a relatively primitive form provided for children at temple festivals to the sophisticated art known now as bunraku, which originated in Ōsaka in the late 17th c. There is also a theater of marionettes called *ito-ayatsuri* or *nankin-ayatsuri*, said to be of Chinese origin, which has recently been revived and used in the performance of modern Japanese plays, works by Maurice Maeterlinck, and so on. The traditional shadow play, *utsushi-e*, is extinct. *(David Bloom)*

5220
as
PALA, František. **Mladý Janáček a divadlo: Janáčkův poměr k estetickým a etickým otázkám divadla před *Šárkou*** [The young Janáček and the theater: Janáček's view on aesthetic and ethical issues of theater before *Šárka*], *Leoš Janáček a soudobá hudba* (Praha: Panton, 1963) 244–49. In Czech; summaries in Russian and German. See no. 389 in this volume.

After his studies in Prague, Leipzig, and Vienna, the young Janáček became fully involved in pedagogy, performing, and organizational work in Brno. He was particularly keen as a critic; as editor of the journal *Hudební listy* (1884-88), he formulated his ideas about musical drama well before the creation of his first opera, *Šárka*. His anti-Wagnerian views were influenced by Robert Zimmermann's *Allgemeine Ästhetik als Formwissenschaft* (Vienna, 1868) and Josef Durdík's *Všeobecná aesthetika* (General aesthetics, 1875). *(editors)*

5221
as
PASINETTI, Francesco. **Cenno storico sulla collaborazione della musica col film dalla nascita del cinema a oggi nei diversi paesi europei: Italia** [A historical account of the collaboration of music with film from the birth of the cinema to today in various European countries: Italy], *Atti del secondo Congresso internazionale di musica* (Firenze: Le Monnier, 1940) 239–42. In Italian; summaries in French and German. See no. 239 in this volume.

Summary of music in Italian film production including composers, scores to be performed in the screening of silent films of the period ca. 1913-1930, and soundtracks through ca. 1937.

5222
as
PERICOLI, Mario. **Lauda drammatica e dramma sacro a Todi** [The *lauda drammatica* and sacred drama in Todi], *Iacopone e il suo tempo* (Todi: Accademia Tudertina, 1959) 133–41. In Italian. See no. 381 in this volume.

Traces the documentary history of the lauda and other forms of sacred drama in Todi from the works of Jacopone da Todi through ca. 1600.

5223
as
PIETZSCH, Gerhard. **Fragen des Opern-nachwuchs** [Questions about the next generation of opera singers], *Bericht über den Internationalen Kongreß Singen und Sprechen* (München: Oldenbourg, 1938) 116–19. In German. See no. 257 in this volume.

Proposes remedies to the shortage of operatic vocal types—other than the lyric soprano and the baritone—and of stage directors in the generation raised during the World War and the subsequent period of economic privation.

5224
as
PILARCZYK, Helga. **Kann man die moderne Oper singen?** [Can one sing modern opera?], *Zeitgenössisches Musiktheater/Contemporary music theatre/Théâtre musical contemporain* (Hamburg: Deutscher Musikrat, 1966) 148–50. In German. See no. 481 in this volume.

The author's predilection for Schoenberg's and Berg's soprano roles is primarily intuitive rather than intellectual: It is based as much on her feeling for the psychological reality of the roles as on their variety of expressive vocal techniques. The approach of the director Günther Rennert makes it possible for singers to develop these techniques without compromising their emotional identification with a part. It is not true that modern music destroys the voice. *(David Bloom)*

5225
as
PILKOVÁ, Zdeňka. **Das Melodram Jiří Bendas im Zusammenhang mit der Mozartproblematik** [Jiří Benda's melodramas in connection with Mozart problematics], *Internationale Konferenz über das Leben und Werk W.A. Mozarts* (Praha: Svaz Československých Skladatelů, 1956) 85–94. In German. See no. 360 in this volume.

Benda was the most important early practitioner of the melodrama genre, in which a musical accompaniment is provided for spoken text. His *Ariadne auf Naxos* and *Medea* (both 1775) were applauded by Mozart, who used the form himself in *Zaide* and *Thamos, König in Ägypten*. Benda's melodramas influenced the general development of serious opera, in the development of alternatives to the mechanical alternation between secco recitative and aria, prefiguring the arioso passages in *Idomeneo*. *(David Bloom)*

5226
as
RADICIOTTI, Giuseppe. **Teatro e musica in Roma nel secondo quarto del secolo XIX** [Theater and music in Rome during the second quarter of the 19th century], *Atti del Congresso internazionale di scienze storiche. VIII: Atti della sezione IV: Storia dell'arte musicale e drammatica* (Roma: R. Accademia dei Lincei, 1905) 157–318. In Italian. See no. 42 in this volume.

Rome had three major opera houses and many minor ones, but the quality of operatic performances was very poor. Toward 1850, standards began to improve. During those years revivals became increasingly common while Risorgimento references frequently found their way into libretto. Lists of repertoire, casts, and performances at the Valle, Argentina, and Apollo theaters from 1823-1849 are included.

5227
as
RASI, Luigi. **Della costruzione di un museo dell'arte drammatica italiana. I** [On the construction of a museum of Italian dramatic art. I], *Atti del Congresso internazionale di scienze storiche. VIII: Atti della sezione IV: Storia dell'arte musicale e drammatica* (Roma: R. Accademia dei Lincei, 1905) 17–18. In Italian. See no. 42 in this volume.

Calls for the establishment of a national museum devoted to the dramatic arts, including prints, drawings, paintings, and sculptures relating to the history of Italian theater.

5228
as
RASI, Luigi. **Della costruzione di un museo dell'arte drammatica italiana. II** [On the construction of a museum of Italian dramatic art. II], *Atti del Congresso internazionale di scienze storiche. VIII:*

Atti della sezione IV: Storia dell'arte musicale e drammatica (Roma: R. Accademia dei Lincei, 1905) 139–55. In Italian. See no. 42 in this volume.

Proposes that the museum should include portraits of Italian actors, masks, costumes, and monographs from the 16th to the 19th c., primarily concerning the commedia dell'arte.

5229 RENNERT, Günther. **Zur Regie des zeit-**
as **genössischen Musiktheaters** [Directing contemporary music theater], *Zeitgenössisches Musiktheater/Contemporary music theatre/Théâtre musical contemporain* (Hamburg: Deutscher Musikrat, 1966) 90–93. In German. See no. 481 in this volume.

Unlike the operas of the 18th and 19th c., which tend to be integrated into a typological schema, many 20th-c. music theater pieces are written according to their own unique stylistic laws. They tend to share a distanced character related to that of Brecht's epic theater, as evidenced in works by Stravinsky (*Oedipus rex* and *The flood*) and Dallapiccola (*Il prigioniero*). The lessons learned in staging such works can be applied, to some extent, to the standard repertoire, thus bringing surprising new life to works that had been paralyzed by convention. *(David Bloom)*

5230 RENNERT, Wolfgang. **Zeitgenössische Oper**
as **braucht zeitgenössische Stoffe** [Contemporary opera requires contemporary subjects], *Zeitgenössisches Musiktheater/Contemporary music theatre/Théâtre musical contemporain* (Hamburg: Deutscher Musikrat, 1966) 63–64. In German. See no. 481 in this volume.

Many contemporary opera composers show a tendency to adapt material from literature, especially from the 19th c. Timeless material as used by Stravinsky, Orff, and Honegger fits contemporary musical styles, as does contemporary writing; an example of the latter is Humphrey Searle's *The photo of the colonel* (1964), based on a play by Ionesco. *(David Bloom)*

5231 RENONDEAU, Gaston. **L'influence boudd-**
as **hique sur les Nô** [Buddhist influence on noh], *Les théâtres d'Asie* (Paris: Centre National de la Recherche Scientifique [CNRS], 1961) 163–92. In French. See no. 397 in this volume.

Includes a historical overview, discussion of the veneration in noh of the Bodhisattva Kwannon, and analytic remarks on a play from the *shura noh* (warrior-ghost noh) repertoire, *Tomonagi*. A French-language translation of *Tomonagi* is appended.

5232 ROENNEKE, Rolf. **Die Ausdrucksfähigkeit**
as **des Gesanges und der Sprache als Grundlage schöpferischer, dramatischer Gestaltung** [The expressive capacity of singing and speech as the foundation of creative, dramatic representation], *Bericht über den Internationalen Kongreß Singen und Sprechen* (München: Oldenbourg, 1938) 218–22. In German. See no. 257 in this volume.

5233 ROSSI-DORIA, Gastone. **Tendenze dell'odierno**
as **teatro musicale italiano** [Trends in today's Italian music theater], *Atti del primo Congresso internazionale di musica* (Firenze: Le Monnier, 1935) 125–39. In Italian. See no. 203 in this volume.

Considers dramatic works by the Italian modernists Ildebrando Pizzetti, Francesco Malipiero, Franco Alfano, Ottorino Respighi, and Alfredo Casella. *(David Bloom)*

5234 RUBSAMEN, Walter H. ***The jovial crew*: His-**
as **tory of a ballad opera**, *Bericht über den siebenten internationalen musikwissenschaftlichen Kongress* (Kassel: Bärenreiter, 1959) 240–43. *Music.* See no. 390 in this volume.

Surveys the performance history, text, and music of *The jovial crew* (first performed Drury Lane, 1731), adapted from Richard Brome's 1641 play *A jovial crew, or, The merry beggars*, by Edward Roome, Matthew Concanen, and Sir William Yonge. The work appeared in some 12 different versions between its premiere and the last production in 1813 (with a revised book by Samuel James Arnold and some lyrics by Thomas Moore). Particular note is taken of the sources, structural features, and use of Aeolian, transposed Dorian, and Mixolydian modes in some of the published tunes used in the work. *(David Bloom)*

5235 RUBSAMEN, Walter H. **Political and ideologi-**
as **cal censorship of opera**, *Papers of the American Musicological Society* (Philadelphia: American Musicological Society, 1946) 30–42. See no. 272 in this volume.

Whenever in European history a ruling clique has brooked no opposition to its doctrines, then the freedom of musical creation and performance has also been abolished, opera being the most affected form. Examples are drawn particularly from the history of the French Revolution, of Soviet Russia, and of National Socialist Germany. From a musical point of view, the suppression of an opera can only be effective if there is nothing of lasting value in the work itself. If Berg's *Wozzeck* is a masterpiece, it will continue to be performed in Germany long after the Nazi regime has disappeared. *(David Bloom)*

5236 SALVINI, Guido. **La regia moderna del**
as **melodramma** [Modern production of opera], *Atti del terzo Congresso internazionale di musica* (Firenze: Le Monnier, 1940) 114–19. In Italian; summaries in French and German. See no. 256 in this volume.

Discusses the responsibility of the opera producer to achieve balance between music and dramatic action. Verdi's operas are mentioned as examples. *(Edwin D. Wallace)*

5237 SAUGUET, Henri. **Le sujet dans le théâtre mu-**
as **sical contemporain** [The subject in contemporary musical theater], *Zeitgenössisches Musiktheater/Contemporary music theatre/Théâtre musical contemporain* (Hamburg: Deutscher Musikrat, 1966) 57–58. In French. See no. 481 in this volume.

In the opera repertoire developed between 1814 and 1914, the works that best represented the tastes or aesthetics of the time were not necessarily the ones that survived. Rather, the ones that have lasted are works of a certain essential musical quality that makes them relevant to many generations. Composers should recall Verdi's aphorism that a theater musician needs to forget that he is a musician to make good opera. *(David Bloom)*

5238 SCHIEDERMAIR, Ludwig. **Über den Stand**
as **der Operngeschichte** [The state of historical research on opera], *Bericht über den zweiten Kongress der Internationalen Musikgesellschaft* (Leipzig: Breitkopf & Härtel, 1907) 212–16. In German. See no. 53 in this volume.

A broad survey of research since the late 19th c. on the origins of opera, on music and librettos of particular works, and on genres and national schools. *(David Bloom)*

5239 SCHRADE, Leo. **L'*Edipo tiranno* d'Andrea**
as **Gabrieli et la renaissance de la tragédie grecque** [The *Edipo tiranno* of Andrea Gabrieli and the revival of the Greek tragedy], *Musique et poésie au XVIe siècle* (Paris: Centre National de la Recherche Scientifique [CNRS], 1954) 275–85. In French. See no. 326 in this volume.

Discusses Orsatto Giustiniani's translation of Sophocles' *Oidipous tyrannos* and the choruses written for it by Andrea Gabrieli.

5240 SCHUH, Willi. **Über einige frühe Textbücher**
as **zur *Zauberflöte*** [Some early printed librettos of *Die Zauberflöte*], *Bericht über den internationalen musik-*

wissenschaftlichen Kongreß Wien Mozartjahr 1956 (Graz; Köln: Böhlau, 1958) 571–78. In German. See no. 365 in this volume.

Librettos printed for sale at performance venues include that for the Theater auf der Wieden (Vienna, 1791), presumably Emanuel Schikaneder's original text; that for the Kärntnertortheater (Vienna, 1801), in a revision by Peter von Braun; and an Italian-language translation by Giovanni De Gamerra for the Dresdner Oper, 1794, which provides valuable information on staging practice for the work. The revision by Christian Vulpius for the Weimar Hoftheater (1794) and popular reprints, *Arienbücher*, illustrated versions, and prompt books are also briefly discussed. *(David Bloom)*

5241 SERAUKY, Walter. **Zur Neuinterpretation von**
as **Richard Wagners Werk** [Toward a reinterpretation of Richard Wagner's work], *Bericht über den siebenten internationalen musikwissenschaftlichen Kongress* (Kassel: Bärenreiter, 1959) 244–47. In German. See no. 390 in this volume.

The negative evaluation of Wagner's music that was a consequence of its misuse by the National Socialist regime from 1933 has been to some extent overcome, thanks partly to Wieland and Wolfgang Wagner's stagings of the operas at Bayreuth since 1951; but the critical interpretation of Wagner is still in need of renewal. Topics for reconsideration include the psychological content expressed through his fusion of drama and music; his disposition toward early music, especially that of J.S. Bach; and the supremacy of music, poetry, and dance, and relatively minor status of the static visual arts (lighting, sets, and costumes), in the concept of the Gesamtkunstwerk. *(David Bloom)*

5242 SESSIONS, Roger. **L'opera negli Stati Uniti**
as [Opera in the United States], *Atti del primo Congresso internazionale di musica* (Firenze: Le Monnier, 1935) 188–94. In Italian. See no. 203 in this volume.

Opera in the U.S. is devoted almost exclusively to European works. George Antheil's *Transatlantic* is the first attempt an American composer has made to free himself from false Romantic theatrical conventions. Louis Gruenberg's *Emperor Jones*, which lacks musical originality, exhibits an undeniable instinct for the requirements of theater. *(Lisa Miller)*

5243 SIEFFERT, René. **Le théâtre japonais** [The Japa-
as nese theater], *Les théâtres d'Asie* (Paris: Centre National de la Recherche Scientifique [CNRS], 1961) 133–61. *Bibliog.* In French. See no. 397 in this volume.

Historical and genre survey of noh, jōruri, kabuki, and contemporary Japanese theater.

5244 SIEGMUND-SCHULTZE, Walther. **Probleme**
as **der Verdi-Oper** [Problems of Verdian opera], *Bericht über den siebenten internationalen musikwissenschaftlichen Kongress* (Kassel: Bärenreiter, 1959) 247–50. *Music.* In German. See no. 390 in this volume.

It is not the case that the national and political function disappeared from Verdi's operas from the 1850s onward. The new quality of these works is rather in the currency of their dramatic material; their realism in the sense of Friedrich Engels ("particular characters under particular circumstances"); the development of new forms in which dance, chorus, and the structure of large-scale solo or ensemble *scena* have a social-critical significance; and the characteristic melodic gestures (the terse repeated phrase, the sweeping tuneful cadence, and the great four-part melodic arch). *(David Bloom)*

5245 SLESINGER, Donald. **Memorandum on rela-**
as **tion of the film to inter-American relations in the field of music,** *Report of the Committee of the Conference on Inter-American Relations in the Field of Music* (Washington, D.C.: United States Department of State, 1940) 37. See no. 271 in this volume.

Many contemporary films contain music worthy of being preserved separately. Films of American countries should be studied in this regard. Film may enhance the appreciation of music and facilitate the exchange of musical materials. *(Howard Cinnamon)*

5246 SOBĚSKÝ, Bohumil. **Několik poznámek k**
as **referátům o pěveckých problémech Janáčkových oper** [Remarks on the problems of performance in Janáček's operas], *Leoš Janáček a soudobá hudba* (Praha: Panton, 1963) 279–80. In Czech; summaries in Russian and German. See no. 389 in this volume.

A response to the papers abstracted as no. 3793 and 3324 in this volume.

5247 **Société des Historiens du Théâtre: Organisa-**
as **tion internationale des recherches d'histoire théâtrale** [Société des Historiens du Théâtre: International organization for theater history research], *VIIe Congrès international des sciences historiques* (Warszawa: conference, 1933) 116–18. In French. See no. 209 in this volume.

5248 SONNECK, Oscar G.T. **Ciampi's** *Bertoldo,*
as ***Bertoldino e Cacasenno*: A contribution to the history of pasticcio,** *Report of the Fourth Congress of the International Musical Society* (London: Novello, 1912) 71. See no. 71 in this volume.

Summary of a paper. The earliest extant versions of Goldoni's libretto for Ciampi's opera show that different performances included different arias, some of which were made to order while others were interpolations from other operas. A full version is published in *Quarterly magazine*, July 1911.

5249 STEVENS, Denis. **Pièces de théâtre et** *pageants*
as **à l'époque des Tudor** [Theater pieces and pageants during the Tudor era], *Les fêtes de la Renaissance* (Paris: Centre National de la Recherche Scientifique [CNRS], 1956) 259–84. In French. See no. 350 in this volume.

The tradition of theatrical representations began during the reign of Henry VII and continued until the time of the Stuarts, when masques replaced spectacles at court. *(Scott Fruehwald)*

5250 STOMPOR, Stephan. **Zu einigen Fragen der In-**
as **terpretation Händelscher Opern** [Some questions on the staging of Händel's operas], *Händel-Ehrung der Deutschen Demokratischen Republik: Konferenzbericht* (Leipzig: VEB Deutscher Verlag für Musik, 1961) 235–40. In German. See no. 408 in this volume.

Productions of operas by Händel at the Landestheater, Halle, in the mid-1950s suggest viable solutions to the problems of staging Baroque opera in the 20th c., in particular the free German-language adaptations of the original Italian texts, the effort to maintain a continuously developing narrative line over the alternation between recitative and aria, and the use of stylized, but not abstract, sets. *(David Bloom)*

5251 STRAKOVÁ, Theodora. **K problematice**
as **Janáčkovy opery** *Osud* [Problems of Janáček's opera *Osud* (Fate)], *Leoš Janáček a soudobá hudba* (Praha: Panton, 1963) 289–93. In Czech; summaries in Russian and German. See no. 389 in this volume.

From the depiction of village life in *Její pastorkyňa (Jenůfa)*, the composer turned to urban realism in the spa setting of Luhačovice in his fourth opera, *Osud* (Fate). As with *Jenůfa*, its music is based on speech melodies, and its individual acts are characterized by the typical melodic motives. A new element is the precise monothematicism. The libretto, the circumstances of creation, and the problems of reception are discussed. *(editors)*

5252 STUCKENSCHMIDT, Hans Heinz. **Stoff und li-**
as **bretto** [Subject-matter and libretto], *Zeitgenössisches Musiktheater/Contemporary music theatre/Théâtre musical contemporain* (Hamburg: Deutscher Musikrat, 1966) 34–36. In German. See no. 481 in this volume.

Opera has always benefited from composers' awareness of the literary avant-garde of the day. For opera to be completely renewed as a genre, modern composers and writers must overcome feelings of mutual reserve that many seem to have recently experienced. *(David Bloom)*

5253
as
SUBIRÁ, José. **La chanson et la danse populaires dans le Théâtre espagnol du XVIIIᵉ siècle** [Traditional song and dance in the Spanish theater of the 18th century], *Congrès international des arts populaires/International congress of popular arts* (Paris: Institut international de coopération intellectuelle, 1928) 119. In French. See no. 153 in this volume.

The MS collections of the Biblioteca Histórica Municipal, Madrid (*ES-Mm*), document music for more than 1,500 tonadillas, comedies, brief scenes, monologues, and other items by scarcely known authors from the Madrid theater of the 18th c. Their folkloric character is manifested in melodic and rhythmic aspects; the use of genre names such as fandango and folía; the use of traditional instruments like the guitar, or their imitation by bowed instruments; and the use of well-known traditional tunes. A brief account of genres represented in the collection is provided. *(David Bloom)*

5254
as
SUBIRÁ, José. **La música instrumental al servicio de las obras dramáticas declamadas** [Instrumental music at the service of dramatic declamations], *Congrés de la Societat Internacional de Musicologia* (Barcelona: Casa de Caritat, 1936). In Spanish. See no. 224 in this volume.

The conference report provides only a citation. Neither the text nor a summary of the paper was published here.

5255
as
SUBIRÁ, José. **Le théâtre lyrique espagnol au 18ᵉ siècle** [The Spanish lyric theater in the 18th century], *Société Internationale de Musicologie: Premier Congrès Liège—Compte rendu/Internationale Gesellschaft für Musikwissenschaft: Erster Kongress Lüttich—Kongressbericht/International Society for Musical Research: First Congress Liège: Report* (London: Plainsong and Mediaeval Music Society, 1930) 214–16. *Illus., music.* In French. See no. 178 in this volume.

Spanish theatrical genres of the 18th c., including entremeses, sainetes, bailes, tonadillas, and zarzuelas, are discussed, drawing on sources. *(Conrad T. Biel)*

5256
as
SZABOLCSI, Bence. **Mozart und die Volksbühne** [Mozart and the popular stage], *Bericht über den internationalen musikwissenschaftlichen Kongreß Wien Mozartjahr 1956* (Graz; Köln: Böhlau, 1958) 623–32. *Transcr.* In German. See no. 365 in this volume.

Mozart's awareness of Italian, French, and German traditions of popular comedy is unarguable. His use of Hanswurst and commedia dell'arte elements in his dramatic works is explored, with an incidental remark on popular exoticism in the employment of Turkish and Hungarian musical motives. *(David Bloom)*

5257
as
TOMASI, J. **Apport de la musique dans le théâtre radiophonique** [Contribution of music to theater for radio], *Compte rendu des travaux du Iᵉʳ Congrès international d'art radiophonique* (Paris: conference, 1938). In French. See no. 244 in this volume.

5258
as
TOMEK, Otto. **Zur Übernahme neuer musikalischer Bühnenwerke im Hörfunk** [The radio broadcast of new musical stage works], *Zeitgenössisches Musiktheater/Contemporary music theatre/Théâtre musical contemporain* (Hamburg: Deutscher Musikrat, 1966) 109–11. In German. See no. 481 in this volume.

Radio operas such as Werner Egk's *Columbus* (1932) and Winfried Zillig's *Die Verlobung in San Domingo* (1957) have been successfully transferred to the stage, but no adequate format has yet been developed for the broadcast of stage operas. Radio productions by the Westdeutscher Rundfunk, Cologne, of Giselher Klebe's *Alkmene* and Luigi Nono's *Intolleranza 1960* in 1962 prove, however, that difficulties can be overcome. *(David Bloom)*

5259
as
TRÂN, Van Khê. **Le théâtre musical de tradition chinoise** [The music theater of Chinese tradition], *Zeitgenössisches Musiktheater/Contemporary music theatre/Théâtre musical contemporain* (Hamburg: Deutscher Musikrat, 1966) 121–23. In French. See no. 481 in this volume.

Summarizes elements of staging, acting, and music in traditional Chinese and Vietnamese music drama.

5260
as
TRÂN, Van Khê. **Le théâtre vietnamien** [Vietnamese theater], *Les théâtres d'Asie* (Paris: Centre National de la Recherche Scientifique [CNRS], 1961) 203–19. In French. See no. 397 in this volume.

Disucsses traditional and modern trends, including vocal and gestural techniques, with comparison to Chinese theatrical tradition.

5261
as
TRAVERSARI SALAZAR, Pedro Pablo. **Les représentations dramatiques populaires de l'Équateur** [Traditional dramatic performanc ein Ecuador], *Congrès international des arts populaires/International congress of popular arts* (Paris: Institut international de coopération intellectuelle, 1928) 134. In French. See no. 153 in this volume.

Survey of the indigenous tradition, currently undergoing a revival, and its religious, warrior, rustic, and fantastical dances.

5262
as
TRAVERT, André. **Caractères originaux et évolution actuelle du théâtre pékinoise** [Original character and current evolution of the Beijing theater], *Les théâtres d'Asie* (Paris: Centre National de la Recherche Scientifique [CNRS], 1961) 99–132. In French. See no. 397 in this volume.

Today, authentic traditional Beijing opera (*jingju*) survives only in Taipei, Taiwan, where it has been called *guoju* since 1949. In Hong Kong, it is presented rarely and at great expense. The "new China" has successfully sent performances on tour to foreign countries, but at the cost of renouncing traditional principles and customs. *(Donna Arnold)*

5263
as
VANCEA, Zeno. **La funzione della musica e della danza nel teatro contemporaneo** [The function of music and dance in contemporary theater], *Atti del IIᵒ Congresso internazionale di storia del teatro* (Venezia: De Luca Storia, 1960) 330–38. In Italian. See no. 383 in this volume.

Traces trends through various periods in the history of opera.

5264
as
VEDOVA, Emilio. **Réalisation scénique de *Intolleranza 60* de Luigi Nono** [The staging of Luigi Nono's *Intolleranza 1960*], *Zeitgenössisches Musiktheater/Contemporary music theatre/Théâtre musical contemporain* (Hamburg: Deutscher Musikrat, 1966) 103–06. In French. See no. 481 in this volume.

Describes the creation of collages, images, and costumes for the premiere of Nono's *Intolleranza 1960* at the Teatro La Fenice, Venice, 1961. *(David Bloom)*

5265
as
VENTURINI, Giorgio. **Del modo di rappresentare le opere del passato e del l'*Amfiparnaso* di Orazio Vecchi** [On ways to represent old works and of Orazio Vecchi's *Amfiparnaso*], *Atti del terzo Congresso internazionale di musica* (Firenze: Le

Monnier, 1940) 108–14. In Italian; summaries in French and German. See no. 256 in this volume.

It is inappropriate to stage old operas in modern style. Works should be placed in historical context.

5266 VERDONE, Mario. **Un breve scenario**
as **cinematografico di Alban Berg** [A brief cinematic scenario by Alban Berg], *La musica nel film* (Roma: Bianco e Nero, 1950) 135–38. *Charts, diagr.* In Italian. See no. 297 in this volume.

Sergej Mihailovič Ėjzenštejn believed in an intimate correspondence of film with the other arts. The rhythms of film music should match the rhythms of the film. Alban Berg saw the artistic possibilities for film; his ideas for a screen adaptation of *Lulu* are described. *(Susan Poliniak)*

5267 VERETTI, Antonio. **Varie forme di musica nel**
as **film** [Different forms of music in film], *Atti del secondo Congresso internazionale di musica* (Firenze: Le Monnier, 1940) 228–32. In Italian; summaries in French and German. See no. 239 in this volume.

With some exceptions, film music today tends to comment on, rather than completing, the film. In the accompaniment of silent scenes, a piece may be out of synchrony with the action: an apparent independence of the music from the visual stimulus can resolve itself into a broader expression of the film's content. From a formal point of view, a film score should be regarded as a suite made up of theme-and-variation, rondo, song, and dance forms. *(author)*

5268 VOLBACH, Walther R. **Die Synchronisierung**
as **von Aktion und Musik in Mozarts Opern** [The synchronization of action and music in Mozart's operas], *Bericht über den internationalen musikwissenschaftlichen Kongreß Wien Mozartjahr 1956* (Graz; Köln: Böhlau, 1958) 661–65. In German. See no. 365 in this volume.

An examination of problem cases in the coordination of movement to music in the staging of the Mozart canon, at the level of the small detail, with particular attention to difficulties of the strictly instrumental passages. *(David Bloom)*

5269 WALLECK, Oskar. **Die Regie der Oper** [Staging
as opera], *Atti del terzo Congresso internazionale di musica* (Firenze: Le Monnier, 1940) 94–102. In German; summaries in Italian and French. See no. 256 in this volume.

Opera directors must be careful not to apply a 19th-c. Romantic style indiscriminately; operas should be produced in a style appropriate to the period of composition. *(Edwin D. Wallace)*

5270 WASSERBAUER, Miloš. **K režijnímu pojetí**
as **Janáčkových oper** [The director's conception of Janáček's operas], *Leoš Janáček a soudobá hudba* (Praha: Panton, 1963) 381–86. In Czech; summaries in Russian and German. See no. 389 in this volume.

Notes by the Brno director on issues of staging *Její pastorkyně (Jenůfa)*, *Výlety páně Broučkovy*, *Příhody Lišky Bystroušky* (The cunning little vixen) *Věc Makropulos*, and *Z mrtvého domu*.

5271 WASSERBAUER, Miloš. **Otázka soudobosti**
as **scénické interpretace Janáčkovy opery *Z mrtvého domu*** [Question of modernism in stagings of Janáček's opera *Z mrtvého domu*], *Sborník Janáčkovy Akademie Múzichých Umeni* V (1965) 75–80. In Czech. See no. 496 in this volume.

5272 WELLESZ, Egon. **Die dramaturgische**
as **Bedeutung des *Fidelio*** [The dramaturgical significance of *Fidelio*], *Beethoven-Zentenarfeier: Internationaler musikhistorischer Kongress* (Wien:

Universal, 1927) 48–51. In German. See no. 142 in this volume.

In its position between the Baroque-Rococo tradition and the Romantic style, Beethoven's only opera is neither one nor the other, and has no true heirs until the 20th-c. reaction against the exaggerated focus on plot dynamics in late Romantic opera. *(David Bloom)*

5273 WÖRNER, Karl H. **Katjas Tod: Die Schluß-**
as **szene der Oper *Katja Kabanowa* von Leoš Janáček/Kátina smrt: Závěrečná scéna opery *Káťa Kabanová* Leoše Janáčka** [Káťa's Death: The final scene from the opera *Káťa Kabanová* by Leoš Janáček], *Leoš Janáček a soudobá hudba* (Praha: Panton, 1963) 392–403. *Music.* In German and Czech. See no. 389 in this volume.

Offers a musical and dramaturgical analysis of act 3, scene 2.

5274 YOUNG, Percy M. **Some aspects of Handelian**
as **research,** *Bericht über den siebenten internationalen musikwissenschaftlichen Kongress* (Kassel: Bärenreiter, 1959) 318–19. See no. 390 in this volume.

Among the important antecedents of the English oratorio were stage plays on biblical themes, including themes later used by Händel; a particularly significant example is that of *The tragedy of Saul*, published without ascription by Henry Playford in 1703 (now generally ascribed to Roger Boyle, Earl of Orrery). The playwright Aaron Hill, who famously advised Händel to set English texts, attempted his own *Saul, a Tragedy*, probably in the same decade as Händel's 1738 oratorio. *(David Bloom)*

5275 ZECCHI, Adone. **Particolare rilievo della**
as **musica in alcuni film** [The particular importance of music in some films], *La musica nel film* (Roma: Bianco e Nero, 1950) 49–55. In Italian. See no. 297 in this volume.

Film music in general is worthy of the attention of critics. In many American films, there is no personal responsibility for the music or artistic originality; much American film music is too commercial or is bland background noise. E.F. Burian's music for Karel Steklý's 1947 film *Siréna* is examined. Stravinsky's thoughts on film music are discussed. Film music and the film itself should coexist as in a marriage. *(Susan Poliniak)*

5276 ZSCHOCH, Frieder. *Agrippina*—**Eine**
as **satirische Oper?** [*Agrippina*—A satirical opera?], *Händel-Ehrung der Deutschen Demokratischen Republik: Konferenzbericht* (Leipzig: VEB Deutscher Verlag für Musik, 1961) 241–43. In German. See no. 408 in this volume.

Discusses Händel's second Italian opera (1709, libretto by Vincenzo Grimani), with particular reference to its 1959 production at the Opernhaus Leipzig, staged by Klaus Dreyer. *(David Bloom)*

78 Poetry and other literature

→ ABERT, Anna Amalie. **Liszt, Wagner, und die Beziehungen zwischen Musik und Literatur im 19. Jahrhundert** [Liszt, Wagner, and the relationship between music and literature in the 19th century]. See no. 1905 in this volume.

5277 AKSJUK, Sergej. **Sovremennaja narodnaja**
as **pesnja: Iz opyta russkoj sovetskoj pesni** [Contemporary folk song: About research on Russian Soviet songs], *Treći kongres folklorista Jugoslavije* (Cetinje: Udruženje Folklorista Crne Gore, 1958) 75–82. *Illus.* In Russian; summary in Serbian. See no. 357 in this volume.

An analysis of motifs about Soviet life in contemporary Russian folk songs.

5278
as
ALTWEGG, Wilhelm. **Die Entwicklung des Rhythmus in Goethes Lyrik** [The development of rhythm in Goethe's lyric poetry], *Compte rendu du Ier Congrès du rythme* (Genève: Institut Jaques-Dalcroze, 1926) 270–85. In German. See no. 123 in this volume.
Presents an overview of metric characteristics of several poems, including *Mailied* and *Herbstgefühl*.

5279
as
ALTWEGG, Wilhelm. **Die Rhythmen der deutschen Verskunst** [The rhythm of German verse], *Compte rendu du Ier Congrès du rythme* (Genève: Institut Jaques-Dalcroze, 1926) 225–35. *Music, charts, diagr.* In German. See no. 123 in this volume.
Includes partial metrical analyses of several poems, including Goethe's *Wanderers Sturmlied* and Gottfried Keller's *Unter Sternen*.

5280
as
ANDREJČIN, Ljubomir. **O poetike bolgarskih narodnyh pesen** [The poetics of traditional Bulgarian song], *Poetics/Poetyka/Poetika* (Warszawa: Państwowe Wydawnictwo Naukowe, 1961) 501–04. In Russian. See no. 426 in this volume.

5281
as
ANTONIJEVIĆ, Dragoslav. **Društveni karakter hercegovačkih narodnih pesama izgradnje** [The social character of Herzegovinian neotraditional songs about socialist construction], *Rad IX-og kongresa Saveza Folklorista Jugoslavije* (Sarajevo: Savez Udruženja Folklorista Jugoslavije, 1963) 203–10. In Serbian; summary in French. See no. 455 in this volume.
Songs collected during 1949-53 in field research sponsored by the Etnografski Institut of the Srpska Akademija Nauke i Umetnosti included the songs of Herzegovinian work brigades; many of these songs were about the construction projects themselves. They served as a kind of verse chronicle of local events and also had a mobilizing function, from appeals at the beginning of a project to the proclamation of its completion. *(author)*

5282
as
ANTONIJEVIĆ, Dragoslav. **Narodne pesme poziva na Ustanak** [Folk songs inciting to the Insurrection], *Rad VIII-og kongresa folklorista Jugoslavije* (Beograd: Naučno Delo, 1961) 187–93. *Port.* In Serbian; summary in English. See no. 446 in this volume.
The first Partisan songs arose immediately after the Central Committee of the Komunistička Partija Jugoslavije issued its manifesto calling the people to revolt; in a sense they transmitted the Party's decisions throughout the country. Their texts constantly bring into relief the roles of the Party and of Tito in preparing, organizing, and directing the Insurrection. *(author)*

5283
as
ASSELBERGS, Alphons. **"Musical poetry" and organic composition,** *Actes du cinquième Congrès international d'esthétique/Proceedings of the Fifth International Congress of Aesthetics* ('s-Gravenhage: Mouton, 1964) 745–49. See no. 475 in this volume.
Jan Pieter Heije (1809-76), an Amsterdam physician, poet, and music enthusiast (especially as general secretary of the Maatschappij tot Bevordering der Toonkunst, from 1843), published his *Eenige gedichten, geschikt...op muziek gebragt te worden*, a collection of 57 verse texts intended for musical settings, in the *Nieuwe werken der Hollandsche Maatschappij van Fraaije Kunsten en Wetenschappen* II/1 (1841). A consideration of the poems as opposed to his purely literary poems suggests that his thinking anticipated 20th-c. notions of organic unity. *(David Bloom)*

5284
as
ASTON, Stanley Collin. **The troubadours and the concept of style,** *Stil- und Formprobleme in der Literature: Vorträge* (Heidelberg: Winter, 1959) 142–47. See no. 372 in this volume.
The gradual shift in the 12th c. from the *trobar clus* to *trobar ric* style, marked by the pursuit of virtuosity and elegance for their own sake and the cult of language, signaled the end of troubadour poetry as a living art. *(Terence Ford)*

5285
as
AUBRY, Pierre. **La légende dorée du jongleur** [The golden legend of the jongleur], *Congrès international d'histoire de la musique: Documents, mémoires et vœux* (Solesmes: St. Pierre; Paris: Fischbacher, 1901) 155–64. In French. See no. 32 in this volume.
Stories about itinerant musicians of the Middle Ages reveal important aspects of their social status.

5286
as
BARBEAU, Marius. **The dragon myths and ritual songs of the Iroquoians,** *Journal of the International Folk Music Council* III (1951) 81–85. See no. 296 in this volume.
Discusses folklore about dragons as depicted in song texts from the Iroquois and Wyandot peoples.

5287
as
BARBI, M. **Poesia e musica popolare** [Poetry and traditional music], *Atti del III Congresso nazionale di arti e tradizioni popolari* (Roma: Opera Nazionale Dopolavoro, 1936) 511–11. In Italian. See no. 218 in this volume.

5288
as
BARROS, Carlos Marinho de Paula. **Reflexões para uma tese** [Reflections for a thesis], *Anais do Primeiro Congresso da Língua Nacional Cantada* (São Paulo: Departamento Municipal de Cultura, 1938) 320–27. In Portuguese. See no. 253 in this volume.
Discusses the question of correspondence between linguistic accent and musical accent in text setting, on the basis of examples ranging from Gregorian chant to Brazilian traditional song.

⟶
BECKING, Gustav. **Der musikalische Bau des montenegrinischen Volksepos** [The musical structure of the folk epic of Montenegro]. See no. 2736 in this volume.

5289
as
BLÉMONT, Émile. **La tradition poétique** [The poetic tradition], *Congrès international des traditions populaires* (Paris: E. Lechevalier, E. Leroux, J. Maisonneuve, 1902) 44–61. In French. See no. 31 in this volume.
There are certain elements that characterize traditional poetry (i.e., that which is both recited and sung), including anonymity of the author, simple rhymes, and well-accented song rhythms. Thematic elements of traditional verse may include love, war, individuals of high social class, saints, historical events, and the exotic or foreign. Certain characters are peculiar to each country's verse, and may reappear later in other literature of that same country (e.g., King Arthur in England); often, these figures are inhabitants of enchanted worlds. Traditional poetry led to and contributed to various song forms such as the virelai and the ballade. Traditional verse in France, although existent, was eclipsed by other forms of expression from roughly the 17th c. through the 19th c. *(Susan Poliniak)*

5290
as
BÖHME, Erdmann Werner. **Mozart in der schönen Literatur** [Mozart in *belles lettres*], *Bericht über die musikwissenschaftliche Tagung der Internationalen Stiftung Mozarteum* (Leipzig: Breitkopf & Härtel, 1932) 179–297. *Bibliog.* In German. See no. 193 in this volume.
An extended critical survey of the use of Mozart's life and works as topics in literary works. A bibliography of dramatic works, novels and short fiction, poetry, and literary criticism, from 1762 (with a poem by one Puffendorf *Auf den kleinen sechsjährigen Claviristen aus Salzburg*) through 1932, is appended. *(David Bloom)*

5291
as
BORELI, Rada. **Lirska pesma oblasti Titovog Užica** [Lyric songs of the Titovo Užice district], *Rad VIII-og kongresa folklorista Jugoslavije* (Beograd: Naučno Delo, 1961) 129–35. In Serbian; summary in French. See no. 446 in this volume.

An overview of song texts, drawing a distinction between the older ones, linked to traditional customs, and new ones tied to the War of National Liberation and People's Revolution in Yugoslavia. *(author)*

5292
as

BOŠKOVIĆ-STULLI, Maja. **Neki problemi u proučavanju folklora iz Narodnooslobodi-lačke Borbe** [Some problems in the study of the folklore of the War of National Liberation], *Rad kongresa folklorista Jugoslavije* (Ljubljana: Savez Udruženja Folkloristov Jugoslavije, 1960) 251–54. In Croatian; summary in English. See no. 404 in this volume.

Briefly discusses textual issues, including sources, transmission, form, structure, and literary quality.

5293
as

BUGIEL, V. **Quelles sont les premières phases de la poésie des peuples primitifs** [What are the first phases in the poetry of primitive peoples?], *XVe Congrès international d'anthropologie et d'archéologie préhistorique (suite); V^e session de l'Institut International d'Anthropologie* (Paris: Nourry, 1933) 793–804. In French. See no. 192 in this volume.

In most cases, primitive songs are of a reflexive origin, corresponding to a need to respond to some excitation of the interior life: work songs, laments, and other spontaneous songs. Examples are provided from a wide range of field studies from Asia, Africa, and the Americas, as well as Europe. Their character allows them to be considered as an independent and interesting literary category. *(David Bloom)*

5294
as

BURGER, André. **Les deux scènes du cor dans la *Chanson de Roland*** [The two horn scenes in the *Chanson de Roland*], *La technique littéraire des chansons de geste* (Paris: Belles Lettres, 1959) 105ff. In French. See no. 374 in this volume.

Discusses the imagery of the oliphant, or horn, with which Roland tries to summon help in the dénouement of the poem.

⟶

COEUROY, André. **Gérard de Nerval et la diffusion du sentiment musical en France** [Gérard de Nerval and the diffusion of musical sentiment in France]. See no. 1937 in this volume.

5295
as

COUILLAUT, Camille. **La réforme de la prononciation du latin** [Reforming Latin pronunciation], *Comptes rendus, rapports et vœux du Congrès parisien et régional de chant liturgique et de musique d'église* (Paris: Schola Cantorum, 1912) 82–87. In French. See no. 75 in this volume.

5296
as

ČUBELIĆ, Tvrtko. **Balada u narodnoj književnosti** [The ballad in traditional literature], *Rad kongresa folklorista Jugoslavije* (Beograd: Naučno Delo, 1960) 83–104. *Bibliog.* In Croatian; summary in German. See no. 402 in this volume.

Traditional European ballads, including those of Yugoslavia, have been characterized as abridgments of previously existing epics, as an outgrowth of courtly poetic performance, and as a collective product of the folk. Rather, they should be regarded as a distinct literary form, the work of a single author and an individual creative personality. The stylistic character of a given work can be described in terms of its emotional content, its architectonic use of suspense, and its metrical features. *(author)*

5297
as

ČUBELIĆ, Tvrtko. **Muzički instrumenti u epskoj narodnoj pjesmi** [Musical instruments in traditional epic song], *Rad VII-og kongresa Saveza Folklorista Jugoslavije* (Cetinje: Obod, 1964) 401–05. In Croatian; summary in German. See no. 419 in this volume.

In the text of the epic, the mention of musical instruments never serves to establish the epic mood or to perform a plot function but is always strictly ornamental, subordinate to the presentation of the hero. The gusle, as the instrument of highest prestige for accompanying epic song, serves the function best; this includes the frequent use of women guslars as characters, invariably praised as masters of their art. Second in importance, especially in epics sung by Muslims, is the tambura, generally with two strings, with a more lyrical connotation. Wind instruments are mentioned only in connection with ensembles also including percussion instruments. *(author)*

5298
as

DAL, Erik. **The linked stanza in Danish ballads: Its age and its analogues,** *Journal of the International Folk Music Council* X (1958) 35–36. See no. 371 in this volume.

The linked stanza type (Danish *gentagelsesstrofe*, Swedish *upprepningsstrofe*) involves repeating the end of a stanza's text at the beginning of the next stanza.

5299
as

DAVIE, Donald. **The relation between syntax and music in some modern poems in English,** *Poetics/Poetyka/Poetika* (Warszawa: Państwowe Wydawnictwo Naukowe, 1961) 203–14. See no. 426 in this volume.

Discusses ways in which manipulation of syntax contributes to the musicality of poetry particularly by T.S. Eliot, with attention to the inspiration of the Symbolist movement and Paul Valéry. *(Susan Poliniak)*

5300
as

DELORKO, Olinko. **O građi našega pjesničkog folklora i njezinu poznavanju** [Sources for our traditional poetry and their interpretation], *Treći kongres folklorista Jugoslavije* (Cetinje: Udruženje Folklorista Crne Gore, 1958) 173–78. In Croatian; summary in French. See no. 357 in this volume.

Surveys published and unpublished collections of Croatian and Serbian traditional poetry from the 19th and 20th c.

5301
as

DELORKO, Olinko. **O nekim uspjelim narodnim lirskim pjesmama uz rad** [Some successful traditional lyrical work songs], *Rad VIII-og kongresa folklorista Jugoslavije* (Beograd: Naučno Delo, 1961) 405–08. *Port.* In Croatian; summary in German. See no. 446 in this volume.

Songs from different regions of Croatia provide rare examples of traditional song texts in which a positive attitude toward work is successfully integrated with lyrical motifs. *(author)*

5302
as

DELORKO, Olinko. **Rukopisni zbornik narodnih pjesama Ivana Zovka** [Ivan Zovko's manuscript collection of traditional songs], *Rad IX-og kongresa Saveza Folklorista Jugoslavije* (Sarajevo: Savez Udruženja Folklorista Jugoslavije, 1963) 119–25. In Croatian; summary in German. See no. 455 in this volume.

The Jugoslavenska Akademija Znanosti i Umjetnosti, Zagreb, owns the MS collection of song texts *Tisuću hrvatskih narodnih ženskih pjesama* (1000 Croatian women's folk songs), which was collected in Bosnia and Herzegovina by the Mostar-born writer and folklorist Ivan Zovko (1864-1900). The material is largely in decasyllabic verse, comes from both Catholic and Muslim sources, and features a very wide range of subject matter. Only a few of the texts have been published in anthologies. *(author)*

5303
as

DESPARMET, Joseph. **La poésie arabe actuelle à Blida et sa métrique** [Contemporary Arab poetry in Blida, and its metrics], *Actes du XIVe Congrès international des orientalistes. III: Langues musulmanes (arabe, persan et turc)* (Paris: Leroux, 1905) 437–602. In French. See no. 48 in this volume.

Based on the author's fieldwork in Blida near Algiers, discusses the metric structure of popular Maghreb Arab poetry and song texts, with a large number of transliterated and translated examples. Also published in book form by E. Leroux, Paris 1907. *(David Nussenbaum)*

5304 ĐUKIĆ, Trifun. **Prvi izvori i razvoj kosovske**
as **etike u stvaranju epopeje o Kosovu** [The earliest
sources about ethical issues in Kosovo epics], *Treći
kongres folklorista Jugoslavije* (Cetinje: Udruženje
Folklorista Crne Gore, 1958) 101–05. *Illus.* In Serbian;
summary in French. See no. 357 in this volume.
Discusses historical sources for songs about the Battle of Kosovo in 1489.

5305 DINEKOV, Petăr. **Nekotorye osobennosti**
as **poetiki sovremennoj narodnoj pesni** [Some
characteristics of the poetics of contemporary folk
song], *Poetics/Poetyka/Poetika* (Warszawa:
Państwowe Wydawnictwo Naukowe, 1961) 487–99. In
Russian. See no. 426 in this volume.
Discusses Bulgarian neotraditional song.

5306 ĐORĐEVIĆ, Dragutin M. **Ličnosti narodnog**
as **ustanka u partizanskim pesmama lesko-**
vačkog kraja [Heroes of the Insurrection in Partisan
songs from the Leskovac region], *Rad VIII-og kongresa
folklorista Jugoslavije* (Beograd: Naučno Delo, 1961)
237–44. *Port.* In Serbian; summary in Russian. See no.
446 in this volume.
Summarizes texts of songs about Partisan heroes from the area around
Leskovac, Serbia.

5307 DUCKLES, Vincent H. **The lyrics of John**
as **Donne as set by his contemporaries,** *Bericht über
den siebenten internationalen musikwissenschaftlichen
Kongress* (Kassel: Bärenreiter, 1959) 91–92. *List of
works.* See no. 390 in this volume.
In all, 17th-c. English composers made ten settings of eight lyrics by John
Donne, a very small number in consideration of the greatness of this poet.
Six of the lyrics that were set are love poems and two are divine poems.
When lyrics that have sometimes been assigned to Donne are also taken
into account, the total number of 17th-c. settings rises to 29 and involves 17
different texts. Most are ayres with lute accompaniment; few if any can be
said to do justice to the concentration and complexity of Donne's poetry. A
list of the 29 settings and their sources is appended. *(Carl Skoggard)*

5308 DŽAKOVIĆ, Vukoman. **Crnogo narodne**
as **tužbalice i *Gorski vijenac*** [Traditional Montenegrin
laments and *Gorski vijenac*], *Rad X-og kongresa Saveza
Folklorista Jugoslavije* (Cetinje: Obod, 1964) 203–10.
In Serbian; summary in French. See no. 462 in this
volume.
All the Montenegrin folklore genres are woven into the text of Petar II
Petrović Njegoš's verse drama *Gorski vijenac* (The mountain wreath,
1847)—epic song, wedding song, kolo, anecdote, and proverb—but in
stylized form, except for the *tužbalica* lament, which is presented with its
subject matter and form intact. *(author)*

5309 DŽUDŽEV, Stojan. **Vestiges de la métrique**
as **ancienne dans le folklore bulgare** [Vestiges of an-
cient meter in Bulgarian folklore], *Poetics/Poetyka/
Poetika* (Warszawa: Państwowe Wydawnictwo
Naukowe, 1961) 537–58. *Illus., music, charts, diagr.* In
French. See no. 426 in this volume.
Poetic meters in Bulgarian folklore show traces of the classical Greek
styles of Sophocles and Aeschylus.

5310 EICKHOFF, Paul. **Die Bedeutung des Vier-**
as **takters als herrschenden Prinzips in der**
griechisch-römischen Metrik und Rythmik
[The significance of four-four time as a governing principle in Greco-Roman meter and rhythm], *Bericht über
den I. musikwissenschaftlichen Kongress der Deutschen
Musikgesellschaft in Leipzig* (Wiesbaden: Breitkopf &

Härtel, 1926) 203–05. *Music.* In German. See no. 120 in
this volume.
Discusses the relationship between poetic meter and 4/4 time, and suggests
that common time underlies many of the ancient Greek and Roman poetic
meters. *(William Renwick)*

5311 EICKHOFF, Paul. **Nach welchem Rhythmus**
as **müssen die Melodien der deutschen evan-**
gelischen Kirchenlieder gesungen werden? [To
which rhythms must the melodies of the German
Protestant hymns be sung?], *Bericht über den I. musikwissenschaftlichen Kongress der Deutschen Musikgesellschaft in Leipzig* (Wiesbaden: Breitkopf & Härtel,
1926) 360–64. *Music, charts, diagr.* In German. See no.
120 in this volume.
Compares examples of settings in 4/4, 3/4, and 3/2 meters, considering the
relationship of meter to hymn texts.

5312 EL GAREM, Ali. **Rapport sur la composition**
as [Report on composition], *Recueil des travaux du
Congrès de musique arabe* (Al-Qāhirah: Boulac, 1934)
171–75. In French. See no. 196 in this volume.
Poetic genres such as qaṣīdah and mūwaššaḥ, used for the texts of Arab
songs, are discussed.

⟶ ENGEL, Hans. **Ein Beitrag zur Prosodie im 16.**
Jahrhundert [A contribution on the subject of
16th-century prosody]. See no. 1294 in this volume.

5313 ENGEL, Hans. **Zur Italienischen Prosodie** [On
as Italian prosody], *Bericht über den internationalen
musikwissenschaftlichen Kongreß* (Kassel: Bärenreiter,
1957) 85–87. *Music.* In German. See no. 356 in this volume.
During the 17th c., the older German poetic meter, with its relatively free
number of unaccented syllables in a foot, was giving way to a stricter kind
of meter. A similar development was occurring in music throughout Europe; its effects may be seen in a more refined handling of text meter in Italian song compositions of the period, in which composers distinguished between word-accent and verse-accent. Examples are drawn from Arcadelt,
Rore, and Mozart. *(David Bloom)*

5314 ESPIAU DE LA MAESTRE, André. **Mozarts**
as **weltanschauliche Bedeutung in der modernen**
französischen Literatur [The significance of Mozart in the world views of modern French authors],
*Bericht über den internationalen musikwissenschaft-
lichen Kongreß Wien Mozartjahr 1956* (Graz; Köln:
Böhlau, 1958) 170–75. In German. See no. 365 in this
volume.
Surveys philosophical aspects of the Mozart reception by writers including
André Gide, Paul Claudel, Henri Ghéon, François Mauriac, and in particular Pierre-Jean Jouve. *(David Bloom)*

⟶ FELBER, Erwin. **Das Gesetz der Zahlenver-**
schiebung in Märchen und Mythos und sein
Einfluss auf die Skalenbildung [The law of mutation of numbers in fairy tale and myth, and its influence
on scale building]. See no. 4071 in this volume.

5315 FELBER, Erwin. **Die Musik in den Märchen**
as **und Mythen der verschiedenen Völker** [Music
in the fairy tales and myths of various peoples], *Report
of the Fourth Congress of the International Musical Society* (London: Novello, 1912) 167–78. In German. See
no. 71 in this volume.
Since folk tales tend to be untouched by foreign influence, their descriptions of musical character and affect is especially valuable. *(Jenna Orkin)*

5316 GERBER, Rudolf. **Die Textwahl in der mehr-**
as **stimmigen Hymnenkomposition des späten**
Mittelalters [Choice of text in polyphonic hymn
composition of the late Middle Ages], *Kongreß-*
Bericht: Gesellschaft für Musikforschung (Kassel;
Basel: Bärenreiter, 1950) 75–79. In German. See no.
299 in this volume.

5317 GHISI, Federico. **L'*aria di maggio* et la**
as **travestissement spirituel de la poésie profane**
en Italie [The *aria di maggio* and the spiritual ambiguity of secular poetry in Italy], *Musique et poésie au XVIᵉ*
siècle (Paris: Centre National de la Recherche
Scientifique [CNRS], 1954) 265–73. In French. See no.
326 in this volume.

The poetry of the Renaissance evinces a dualistic vision of spiritual truth:
one side exalts pleasure and licentiousness, while the other punishes the
body with repentance. *(Scott Fruehwald)*

5318 GOJKOVIĆ, Andrijana. **Narodni muzički**
as **instrumenti u Njegoševim delima** [Traditional instruments in Njegoš's works], *Rad X-og kongresa*
Saveza Folklorista Jugoslavije (Cetinje: Obod, 1964)
119–23. *Illus.* In Serbian; summary in English. See no.
462 in this volume.

In his poems, Petar II Petrović Njegoš mentions most of the instruments
used in Montenegrin traditional music: gusle, diple, tambura, truba (bark
reedpipe), bubanj and doboš (double-headed drums), and talambas (kettle-
drum). The gusle and its players are singled out in particular as representing
the heroic spirit of the population. *(author)*

5319 GUICHARD, Léon. **Liszt, Wagner et les rela-**
as **tions entre la musique et la littérature au XIXᵉ**
siècle [Liszt, Wagner, and the relationship between
music and literature in the 19th century], *Report of the*
Eighth Congress of the International Musicological So-
ciety. I: Papers (Kassel: Bärenreiter, 1961) 323–32. In
French. See no. 439 in this volume.

Liszt in Paris in the 1830s was greatly influenced by French Romantic literature, especially that of Hugues-Félicité-Robert de Lamennais. He wrote
articles in collaboration with Marie d'Agoult and was himself an inspiration to French writers, notably George Sand. From 1860, Wagner had many
supporters among French writers, including Champfleury (Jules-
François-Félix Husson), Baudelaire, Édouard Schuré, and Édouard
Dujardin; the *Revue wagnérienne* was begun in 1885. Wagner's influence
on the French novel is evident from around 1885 (e.g., in works by Élémir
Bourges, Henry Céard, and Théodore de Wyzewa) and reached a climax in
the years 1896-1910. His incontestable influence on French theater (Paul
Claudel especially) is visible in the *théâtre idéaliste* of the 1890s. His influence on Symbolist poetry has perhaps been exaggerated.

5320 HEUSS, Alfred Valentin. **Der geistige Zusam-**
as **menhang zwischen Text und Musik im**
Strophenlied [The intellectual connection between
text and music in strophic song], *Kongress für Ästhetik*
und allgemeine Kunstwissenschaft: Bericht (Stuttgart:
Enke, 1914) 444–55. In German. See no. 86 in this
volume.

5321 ILIJIN, Milica. **Narodne igre u Njegoševim**
as **delima** [Traditional dance in Njegoš's works], *Rad*
X-og kongresa Saveza Folklorista Jugoslavije (Cetinje:
Obod, 1964) 147–53. In Serbian; summary in French.
See no. 462 in this volume.

Nearly all of the works of Petar II Petrović Njegoš refer to kolo, oro, and
traditional knightly dance. In his use of the kolo dancers as a chorus in the
verse dramas *Gorski vijenac* and *Šćepan Mali* (both 1847), Njegoš was not
so much elevating them to the level of an ancient Greek chorus as responding to the way in which kolo in traditional Montenegrin culture has always
served as a collective expression of the community's feelings. *(author)*

5322 IVES, Edward D. **Satirical songs in Maine and**
as **the Maritime provinces of Canada,** *Journal of*
the International Folk Music Council XIV (1962)
65–69. See no. 442 in this volume.

A rich tradition of Maine, New Brunswick, and Prince Edward Island was
the composition of satirical song texts to popular tunes, mocking particular
local factory bosses and similarly offensive individuals, by working-class
writers such as the woodsman Lawrence ("Larry") Gorman (1846-1917).
Some of Gorman's texts are offered, along with the stories of how they were
originally written, which are in some cases better remembered than the
songs. *(David Bloom)*

5323 JIČÍNSKÝ, Bedřich. **K Brodové interpretaci**
as **Janáčkových operních textů** [On Brod's translations of the Janáček opera librettos], *Sborník Janáčkovy*
Akademie Múzichých Umeni V (1965) 81–89. In
Czech. See no. 496 in this volume.

Max Brod is among the foremost of Janáček's translators. His results are,
however, not always successful. One can speak of a Brod paradox that can
be explained by their different creative personalities. *(Jan Trojan)*

5324 KRSTIĆ, Branislav. **Postanak i razvoj**
as **narodnih pesama o kosovskom boju** [The origin
and development of songs about the Battle of Kosovo],
Treći kongres folklorista Jugoslavije (Cetinje:
Udruženje Folklorista Crne Gore, 1958) 83–99. *Illus.* In
Serbian; summary in French. See no. 357 in this
volume.

Discusses historical sources for songs about the Battle of Kosovo in 1489.

5325 KUMER, Zmaga. **Primitivna instrumentalna**
as **glasba in ples v slovenski narodni pesmi** [Primi-
tive instrumental music and dance in Slovene traditional songs], *Rad kongresa folklorista Jugoslavije*
(Zagreb: Savez Udruženja Folklorista Jugoslavije,
1958) 79–90. In Slovene; summary in English. See no.
315 in this volume.

Considers references to instruments and dance in Slovenian traditional
songs. The gosli mentioned in the variants of one of the oldest medieval
Slovene folk songs from the Orpheus cycle *Godec pred peklom* (The fiddler
in hell) is probably the gusle. In two variants of the Bluebeard ballad, the se-
ducer is playing the lajna, which is probably the medieval hurdy-gurdy
(from the German Leier). Narrative songs mention playing the peró (a leaf
from a pear tree, walnut tree, or fern that produces a clarinet-like sound);
the drumlica (jew's harp) appears in love songs. Surprisingly, the oprekelj,
a portable dulcimer, is mentioned only twice in variants of the song about
the animals' wedding. A string is often mentioned to refer to a string instrument, and it is also used as a symbol of a girl's beauty. The double bass, the
clarinet, and the accordion are mentioned only incidentally. The trumpet
appears mainly in songs about death, the drum in soldiers' songs.
(Zdravko Blažeković)

5326 KUMER, Zmaga. **Prispevek k vrašanju**
as **raziskovanja tekstov ljudskih pesmi** [The question of textual research in traditional songs], *Rad X-og*
kongresa Saveza Folklorista Jugoslavije (Cetinje:
Obod, 1964) 269–73. In Croatian; summary in German.
See no. 462 in this volume.

Examples from Slovene song texts show the value of style analysis in identifying their origin and national character.

5327 LEBÈGUE, Raymond. **Ronsard et la musique**
as [Ronsard and music], *Musique et poésie au XVIᵉ siècle*
(Paris: Centre National de la Recherche Scientifique
[CNRS], 1954) 105–19. In French. See no. 326 in this
volume.

Examines Ronsard's ideas on the union of poetry and music and discusses
the influences that led to their formation.

5328 LI GOTTI, Ettore. **La questione dello stram-**
as **botto alla luce delle recenti scoperte** [The question of the strambotto in the light of recent discoveries], *Atti del Congresso internazionale di musiche popolari mediterranee e del Convegno dei bibliotecari musicali* (Palermo: De Magistris succ. V. Bellotti, 1959) 263–65. In Italian. See no. 332 in this volume.

The strambotto song text genre has roots in French and Spanish *estribot* or *estribote*, and ultimately in the Arabic *mūwaššaḥ* of the 9th–11th c. It may have originated in Sicily, during the multilingual period of the Norman kingdom, taking its lyric as opposed to satirical content from a local love poetry, and diffused from there to northern Italy. *(David Bloom)*

5329 LORD, Albert B. **Yugoslav epic poetry**, *Journal*
as *of the International Folk Music Council* III (1951) 57–61. See no. 296 in this volume.

Texts of epic performances collected in the 1930s are compared with more recent performances by the same singers, showing a high degree of stability over time. *(James R. Cowdery)*

5330 MARILIER, Jean. **L'office rythmé de Saint**
as **Philibert à Tournus et Dijon** [The versified Offices of Saint Philibert in Tournus and Dijon], *Jumièges: Congrès scientifique du XIII. centenaire* (Rouen: Lecerf, 1955) I, 335–42. *Illus.* In French. See no. 336 in this volume.

Comparison of the texts of a 14th-c. Office of St. Philibert as celebrated in the 14th c. at the Abbaye de St-Philibert, Tournus (as published in the *Analecta hymnica* of Guido Maria Dreves, vol. 18) and that in a breviary, dated 1404, of the Église de St-Philibert in Dijon, suggests that the Dijon Office is the earlier of the two; and that the Tournus monk who adapted it to the monastic cursus did so by adding sections from a still earlier Office in rhymed hexameters. *(David Bloom)*

5331 MARTINOVIĆ, Niko S. **Kolo u *Gorskom***
as ***vijencu*** [Kolo in the *Gorski vijenac*], *Rad X-og kongresa Saveza Folklorista Jugoslavije* (Cetinje: Obod, 1964) 137–45. *Illus.* In Serbian; summary in French. See no. 462 in this volume.

In Montenegro, the kolo dance traditionally served to incite people to combat in the struggle for independence. In Petar II Petrović Njegoš's epic verse drama *Gorski vijenac* (The mountain wreath, 1847), the group of kolo dancers acting as a kind of chorus is in effect the principal character, representing the invincibility of the people. Remarks on the etymology of the term *oro*, sometimes used in Montenegro to mean *kolo*, are appended. *(author)*

5332 MIAZGA, Tadeusz. **Prosa pro defunctis *Audi***
as ***tellus*,** *The book of the first international musicological congress devoted to the works of Frederick Chopin* (Warszawa: Państwowe Wydawnictwo Naukowe, 1963) 565–66. *Charts, diagr.* In Polish. See no. 425 in this volume.

An account of a version of the Requiem prosa *Audi tellus* found in the gradual of the former Konwent Kanoników Regularnych Lateraneńsych of Kraśnik, now in the MS collection of the Metropolitalne Seminarium Duchowne, Lublin.

5333 MLADENOVIĆ, Živomir. **Topografski elementi**
as **narodne pesme *Ženidba Dušanova*** [Topographic elements in the traditional song *Ženidba Dušanova*], *Treći kongres folklorista Jugoslavije* (Cetinje: Udruženje Folklorista Crne Gore, 1958) 149–61. *Illus., port.* In Serbian; summary in French. See no. 357 in this volume.

A textual analysis of the epic *O ženidbi sprskoga cara Stefana*, first published in 1815 by Vuk Stefanović Karadžić and later known as *Ženidba Dušanova*.

5334 MOHR, Wilhelm. **Wort und Ton** [Text and music],
as *Bericht über den internationalen musikwissenschaftlichen Kongreß* (Kassel: Bärenreiter, 1957) 157–62. *Music.* In German. See no. 356 in this volume.

Examines questions of metrics and meaning in poetry, music, and musical settings of poetic texts, from the literary scholar's point of view. *(David Bloom)*

5335 MONTEROSSO, Raffaello. **Musica e poesia nel**
as ***De vulgari eloquentia*** [Music and poetry in *De vulgari eloquentia*], *Dante: Atti della giornata internazionale di studio per il VII centenario* (Faenza: Fratelli Lega, 1965) 83–100. *Facs., music, charts, diagr.* In Italian. See no. 505 in this volume.

Discusses the relationship between Dante's work and medieval philosophies of music. His aesthetics are compared with those of Bernart de Ventadorn and Pierre Vidal, and his reference to Arnaut Daniel is noted.

5336 MÓRIN, Germain. **Les AOI de la *Chanson de***
as ***Roland*** [The AOI of the *Chanson de Roland*], *Congrès de Dinant: Compte rendu* (Namur: Wesmael-Charlier, 1904) 565–80. In French. See no. 41 in this volume.

The letters "AOI" appear in the margin throughout the MS of the *Chanson de Roland*.

5337 MOSER, Hans Joachim. **Musikalische**
as **Probleme des deutschen Minnesangs** [Musical problems of the German Minnesang], *Bericht über den musikwissenschaftlichen Kongreß in Basel* (Leipzig: Breitkopf & Härtel, 1925) 259–69. *Music.* In German. See no. 102 in this volume.

Textual criticism can play a role in the study of rhythmic and melodic problems in medieval secular monophony. Examples show that even when there is no second version of the music, the literary text can offer clues as to an accurate reading.

5338 NAZOR, Ante. **Kako se razvijala revolu-**
as **cionarna pjesma oko Mosora** [How the revolutionary song has developed in the Mosor area], *Rad VIII-og kongresa folklorista Jugoslavije* (Beograd: Naučno Delo, 1961) 245–52. *Port.* In Croatian; summary in English. See no. 446 in this volume.

Revolutionary poetry has been developing in the Mosor mountain region of Dalmatia, inland from Split, alongside industrial development and the strengthening of the working class. Most poems are shorter song lyrics of decasyllabic couplets. Original works, and larger works that would reflect the Mosor tradition of epic, are both rare. *(author)*

5339 NEF-LAVATER, L. **Les principaux mètres du**
as **vers français** [The principal meters of French verse], *Compte rendu du Ier Congrès du rythme* (Genève: Institut Jaques-Dalcroze, 1926) 236–39. In French. See no. 123 in this volume.

Includes examples of poems composed in twelve, ten, nine, eight, and seven feet, and also free verse.

5340 PALAVESTRA, Vlajko. **Narodne pripovijetke i**
as **predanja u Hercegovini** [Folk tales and local sagas in Herzegovina], *Rad IX-og kongresa Saveza Folklorista Jugoslavije* (Sarajevo: Savez Udruženja Folklorista Jugoslavije, 1963) 59–62. In Bosnian; summary in German. See no. 455 in this volume.

Discusses the style characteristics, motifs, and transmission of Herzegovinian traditional narrative.

5341 PEUKERT, Herbert. **Die Funktion der Formel**
as **im Volkslied** [The function of the formula in traditional song], *Poetics/Poetyka/Poetika* (Warszawa:

Państwowe Wydawnictwo Naukowe, 1961) 525–36. In German. See no. 426 in this volume.

An examination of the role of textual formulas in the creation of various traditional genres.

5342 POLENAKOVIĆ, Radmila. **Makedonske**
as **narodne tužbalice** [Macedonian traditional laments], *Rad XI-og kongresa Saveza Folklorista Jugoslavije* (Zagreb: Savez Folklorista Jugoslavije, 1966) 323–27. In Macedonian; summary in French. See no. 490 in this volume.

Discusses the texts of laments, which are usually performed by women.

5343 PRATO, Stanislao. **Quelques images poétiques**
as **des chants populaires rapprochés de la littérature artistique** [Selected imagery of traditional songs related to literature], *[Iᵉ] Congrès international des traditions populaires* (Paris: Société d'Éditions Scientifiques, 1891). In French. See no. 13 in this volume.

5344 RIHTMAN, Cvjetko. **O odnosu ritma stiha i**
as **napjeva u narodnoj tradiciji Bosne i Hercegovine** [The relations between verse rhythm and musical rhythm in the national tradition of Bosnia and Herzegovina], *Rad kongresa folklorista Jugoslavije* (Ljubljana: Savez Udruženja Folkloristov Jugoslavije, 1960) 129–32. In Bosnian; summary in French. See no. 404 in this volume.

Contrary to received opinion, syllable-count alone cannot provide an adequate account of the rhythmic structure of Bosnian song texts; they should be analyzed into trochaic and dactylic feet. *(author)*

5345 RIZA NUR. **Keuroghlou, poète populaire turc**
as [Köroğlu, Turkish traditional poet], *XVᵉ Congrès international d'anthropologie et d'archéologie préhistorique (suite); Vᵉ session de l'Institut International d'Anthropologie* (Paris: Nourry, 1933) 725–26. In French. See no. 192 in this volume.

Köroğlu, the aşık-hero of the Turkish epic cycle, was a historical person, and an author of written poetry, of which two examples have been found in *F-Pn* supp. turc. MS 109. The poems identify him as having lived in the reign of Murad III (1574-94) and served in the army led against Persia by Özdemiroğlu Osman Paşa. He was an important military chief—not, as has been said, a bandit—as well as poet and musician; his verses, with a characteristic music also called Köroğlu, are still orally transmitted in Anatolia. *(David Bloom)*

5346 ROBERTS, Warren E. **Comic elements in the**
as **traditional English ballad,** *Journal of the International Folk Music Council* III (1951) 76–81. See no. 296 in this volume.

Discusses English and Scottish ballad texts.

5347 RONGA, Luigi. **Tasso e la musica** [Tasso and mu-
as sic], *Torquato Tasso* (Milano: Marzorati, 1957) 187–207. In Italian. See no. 330 in this volume.

Discusses the musicality of Tasso's poetic works, as well as his musical life (acquaintances, musical background and training, opinions on music, and the role of and references to music in his works). *(Susan Poliniak)*

5348 SAULNIER, Verdun L. **Maurice Scève et la**
as **musique** [Maurice Scève and music], *Musique et poésie au XVIᵉ siècle* (Paris: Centre National de la Recherche Scientifique [CNRS], 1954) 89–103. In French. See no. 326 in this volume.

The poet's relationship to the music and musicians of his period is discussed in terms of his aesthetics (his musical curiosity, music as a source of inspiration and decorative details, music and poetic techniques, and the

problem of banality) and his oeuvre (his success and reputation, and the dating and state of his texts). *(Roy Nitzberg)*

5349 SCHIRÒ, Giuseppe. **Les canons inédits de Jo-**
as **seph l'Hymnographe dans les anciens manuscrits de Grottaferrata** [Unpublished kanōns by Joseph the Hymnographer in the oldest manuscripts of Grottaferrata], *X. Milletlerarası Bizans Tetkikleri Kongresi Tebliğleri/Actes du X. Congrès International d'Études Byzantines* (İstanbul: İstanbul Maatbası', 1957) 286. In French. See no. 347 in this volume.

St. Joseph the Hymnographer (816-86) was the most prolific author of kanōn texts. In addition to his works known from the various editions of the mēnaion and paraklētikē, some 60 unpublished texts are extant in the collections of the Biblioteca Statale del Monumento Nazionale (Badia Greca), Grottaferrata (*I-GR*). His poetic style, while always elegant, is somewhat formulaic. *(David Bloom)*

5350 SCHWAB, Heinrich W. **Das Musikgedicht als**
as **musikologische Quelle** [Poems on music as a source for musicology], *Beiträge zur Geschichte der Musikanschauung im 19. Jahrhundert* (Regensburg: Bosse, 1965) 127–38. In German. See no. 483 in this volume.

Poems on the subject of music can provide valuable evidence on the history of music and its social functions, from the godlike status awarded to Beethoven to the erotic character of *Hausmusik* performance. Poems by Clemens Brentano, Wilhelm Müller, Friedrich August von Stägemann, Christian Gottlieb Lieberkühn, Detlev von Liliencron, Ferdinand Freiligrath, Ferdinand von Saar, and Adolf Wurmbach are discussed. *(David Bloom)*

5351 SEEMANN, Erich. **Mythen vom Ursprung der**
as **Musik** [Myths about the origin of music], *Kongreß-Bericht: Gesellschaft für Musikforschung* (Kassel; Basel: Bärenreiter, 1950) 151–53. In German. See no. 299 in this volume.

5352 SERTIĆ, Mira. **Društveni karakter i sadržaj**
as **narodne poezije** [The social character and content of traditional poetry], *Rad IX-og kongresa Saveza Folklorista Jugoslavije* (Sarajevo: Savez Udruženja Folklorista Jugoslavije, 1963) 185–94. In Croatian; summary in German. See no. 455 in this volume.

Discussion of the texts of songs sung in the performance of certain ritual customs in Yugoslavia, Germany, and England shows traditional verse to have a social character that is lacking from artistically intended verse. *(author)*

5353 SILBERSTEIN, Leopold. **Les catégories musi-**
as **cales dans les sciences littéraires** [Musical categories in literary sciences], *Deuxième congrès international d'esthétique et de Science de l'art* (Paris: Librairie Félix Alcan, 1937) II, 213–17. In French. See no. 249 in this volume.

Applying the concept of leitmotiv to literary texts from before and after Wagner can be valuable, but must take account of the difference between music and literature in general. *(David Bloom)*

5354 SIMIĆ, Ljuba. **Klasifikacija narodnih pesama**
as [The classification of traditional songs], *Rad X-og kongresa Saveza Folklorista Jugoslavije* (Cetinje: Obod, 1964) 463–68. In Serbian; summary in French. See no. 462 in this volume.

For a collection of narratives and lyric poems from the village of Imljani in the Skender Vakuf municipality (sponsored by the Zemaljski Muzej, Sarajevo, and published in *Glasnik Zemaljskog Muzeja* new series 17, 1962), conventional classification systems seemed inadequate, particularly for songs with both lyric and epic elements. It would be preferable to classify all, except for laments and couplet songs, according to content. The classificatory work in Wolfram Eberhard and Pertev Naili Boratav's *Typen türkischer Volksmärchen* (Wiesbaden, 1953) provides a helpful example. *(author)*

5355
as

SIMIĆ, Ljuba. **Tužbalice ("jaukalice") u Bosni i Hercegovini** [Laments in Bosnia and Herzegovina], *Rad XI-og kongresa Saveza Folklorista Jugoslavije* (Zagreb: Savez Folklorista Jugoslavije, 1966) 315–22. In Serbian; summary in Russian. See no. 490 in this volume.

A discussion and comparison of lament texts.

5356
as

SIMONIDES, Jaroslav. **Quelques problèmes relatifs aux traductions de la correspondance de Frédéric Chopin** [Some problems related to the translations of Chopin's correspondence], *The book of the first international musicological congress devoted to the works of Frederick Chopin* (Warszawa: Państwowe Wydawnictwo Naukowe, 1963) 721–24. In French. See no. 425 in this volume.

Critique of literary tone and factual correctness in German versions by Bernard Scharlitt (Leipzig, 1911) and Alexander von Guttry (Munich, 1928), and the French-language version edited by Henryk Opieński and translated by Stéphane Danysz (Paris, 1933). *(Susan Poliniak)*

5357
as

SIOHAN, Robert. **Musique et poésie en quête du hasard** [Music and poetry in search of the aleatoric], *Pepragmena tou 4. diethnous synedriou aisthītikīs/Actes du IV Congrès international d'esthétique/Proceedings of the IV International Congress on Aesthetics* (Athínai: conference, 1962) 432–34. In French. See no. 415 in this volume.

Discusses philosophical difficulties in the concept of chance in art.

5358
as

SMEND, Julius. **Die Synthese von Text und Ton im deutschen Choral und deren Bedeutung für das Orgelspiel** [The synthesis of text and music in the German chorale and its significance for organ playing], *Bericht über die dritte Tagung für Deutsche Orgelkunst* (Kassel: Bärenreiter, 1928) 83–86. In German. See no. 136 in this volume.

The best of the traditional Lutheran chorales are remarkable for their text-music unity, at least in their first stanzas, though there are also many failures, especially among the cases of retexting. Organists cannot do justice to the music of chorales or chorale arrangements without paying close attention to the texts.

5359
as

SOFER, Zvi. **Die Verwendung der Volksmusik in der chassidischen Volkserzählung** [The use of traditional music in Hasidic folk narrative], *Vorträge und Referate* (Berlin: Walter de Gruyter, 1961) 406–13. *Transcr.* In German. See no. 411 in this volume.

Discusses the *nigun* style of vocalization and other musical features of storytelling.

5360
as

SŐTÉR, István. **Le populisme dans la littérature et la musique** [Populism in literature and music], *Studia musicologica Academiae Scientiarum Hungaricae* V (1963) 11–23. In French. See no. 427 in this volume.

The poetry of 19th-c. Hungary and the 20th-c. Hungarian music that was greatly influenced by it, specifically that of Bartók and Kodály, may be regarded as parts of a single generally populist cultural superstructure.

5361
as

STEPHAN, Rudolf. **Über sangbare Dichtung in althochdeutscher Zeit** [Poetry for singing in the Old High German period], *Bericht über den internationalen musikwissenschaftlichen Kongreß* (Kassel: Bärenreiter, 1957) 225–29. In German. See no. 356 in this volume.

Little can be said about the musical character of the extant Frankish texts of the 8th c. For the 9th and early 10th c., valuable sources include the notated *Petruslied* (*D-Mbs* MS lat.6260, f.158v), the *Galluslied* of Ratpert of St. Gallen, and especially the *Evangeliorum liber* of Otfried von Weißenburg. *(David Bloom)*

5362
as

STERNFELD, Frederick William. **Le symbolisme musical dans quelques pièces de Shakespeare présentées à la cour d'Angleterre** [Musical symbolism in some Shakespeare pieces presented at the English court], *Les fêtes de la Renaissance* (Paris: Centre National de la Recherche Scientifique [CNRS], 1956) 319–33. In French. See no. 350 in this volume.

Suggests that the music used in Shakespeare's plays symbolized contemporary political events.

5363
as

SWANN, Mona. **The rhythms of English verse,** *Compte rendu du Ier Congrès du rythme* (Genève: Institut Jaques-Dalcroze, 1926) 240–43. See no. 123 in this volume.

Contrasts examples of iambic pentameter—and more "natural" meters—by Geoffrey Chaucer, Shakespeare, and John Milton with ballads, nursery rhymes, and poems in other meters.

5364
as

SZEWCZYK-SKOCZYLAS, Maria. **Polskie piśmiennictwo o Wagnerze** [Polish literature about Wagner], *Ryszard Wagner a polska kultura muzyczna/Richard Wagner und die polnische Musikkultur* (Katowice: Panstwowa Wyzsza Szkola Muzyczna, 1964) 133–43. In Polish; summary in German. See no. 466 in this volume.

5365
as

TREND, John Brande. **A note on Spanish madrigals,** *Société Internationale de Musicologie: Premier Congrès Liège—Compte rendu/Internationale Gesellschaft für Musikwissenschaft: Erster Kongress Lüttich—Kongressbericht/International Society for Musical Research: First Congress Liège: Report* (London: Plainsong and Mediaeval Music Society, 1930) 225–29. *Illus., music.* See no. 178 in this volume.

A villancico is a poem, derived from Moorish poetic forms in Arabic but written by Christians in Spanish vernacular, that had a direct influence on the music to which it was set. Previously unknown madrigal settings of lute songs are found in the Biblioteca Medinaceli, and the Palacio Real in Madrid. Late 16th-c. secular pieces were titled villancicos regardless of verse form. Composers mentioned are Cristóbal de Morales; Tomás Luis de Victoria; Pedro Rimonte; Mateo Flecha, the younger; Sebastián Raval; Pedro Valenzuela; Joan Brudieu; Francisco and Pedro Guerrero; Rodrigo de Ceballos; Juan Navarro; and Juan Vásquez. Poets mentioned are Ausiàs March; Juan Boscán Almogáver; Garcilaso de la Vega; Gutierre de Cetina; Baltazar de Alcázar; Gaspar de Aguilar; Luís de Camões; Lope de Vega; Gil Vicente; and Iñigo López de Mendoza, Marqués de Santillana. *(Conrad T. Biel)*

5366
as

UTLEY, Frances Lee. **Noah in British and American folksong,** *Journal of the International Folk Music Council* XIV (1962) 70–73. *List of works.* See no. 442 in this volume.

Interim report on a survey of traditional songs making reference to the biblical story of Noah, particularly non-narrative songs from Britain and the United States and including a significant number of African-American songs. First-line classification proved inadequate; a more elaborate system was developed, organized around a "Census of Noah stanzas" on the basis of phrasal formulas and rhyme-pairs. *(David Bloom)*

5367 VEKOVIĆ, Divna. **Chants populaires de**
as **femmes serbes** [Traditional songs of Serbian
women], *XVᵉ Congrès international d'anthropologie et
d'archéologie préhistorique (suite); Vᵉ session de
l'Institut International d'Anthropologie* (Paris: Nourry,
1933) 710–15. In French. See no. 192 in this volume.

Volumes 2 and 5 of *Narodna srbska pesnarica* (1815) by Vuk Stefanović
Karadžić contain songs sung particularly by women. French versions of
eight song texts are presented and their themes are briefly surveyed. *(David Bloom)*

5368 VLAHOVIĆ, Mitar S. **Gusle u Njegoševim**
as **delima** [The gusle in Njegoš's works], *Rad X-og
kongresa Saveza Folklorista Jugoslavije* (Cetinje:
Obod, 1964) 199–201. *Illus.* In Serbian; summary in
French. See no. 462 in this volume.

Petar II Petrović Njegoš learned singing to gusle accompaniment as a child
from his father, an accomplished player; one of his instruments is on display at the Njegošev Muzej in Biljarda palace, Cetinje. The gusle is introduced in many of his works, notably *Gorski vijenac* (The mountain
wreath). *(author)*

5369 WATHELET-WILLEM, Jeanne. **Les refrains**
as **dans la *Chanson de Guillaume*** [Refrains in the
Chanson de Guillaume], *La technique littéraire des
chansons de geste* (Paris: Belles Lettres, 1959) 457f. In
French. See no. 374 in this volume.

Analysis of the structure and function of the refrain is the key to understanding the *Chanson de Guillaume*. The relationship of the refrain to musical composition and performance of the chanson de geste in general, and
the origins of the musical material, are discussed. *(Barbara B. Heyman)*

5370 WELLESZ, Egon. **The *Akathistos Hymnos*,** *X.*
as *Milletlerarası Bizans Tetkikleri Kongresi Tebliğleri/
Actes du X. Congrès International d'Études Byzantines*
(İstanbul: İstanbul Maatbası', 1957) 297. In Greek. See
no. 347 in this volume.

Only one complete transmission of the music of the celebrated kontakion
Akathistos, for all 24 stanzas, is extant, in the 13th-c. Ashburnham Codex
(*I-Fl* Ashburnham 64), and its text varies from that of the standard versions.
The melodic line can be demonstrated to derive from an earler, less orna-
mented version. *(David Bloom)*

5371 WÜNSCH, Walter. **Die musikalisch-**
as **sprachliche Gestaltung des Zehnsilblers im
serbokroatischen Volksepos** [The musical and linguistic form of the decasyllabic strophe in Serbian-
Croatian traditional epic], *Bericht über den internationalen musikwissenschaftlichen Kongreß* (Kassel:
Bärenreiter, 1957) 241–42. In German. See no. 356 in
this volume.

An introduction to the characteristic epic of Montenegro and the Dinaric
basin, with particular attention to the verse form.

5372 ŽUNIĆ, Leposava. **Razvitak lika nove žene u**
as **pesmi narodne revolucije** [New images of women
in revolutionary neotraditional song], *Rad kongresa
folklorista Jugoslavije* (Ljubljana: Savez Udruženja
Folkloristov Jugoslavije, 1960) 265–68. In Serbian;
summary in German. See no. 404 in this volume.

In the song tradition of the War of National Liberation women are portrayed
as combatants for freedom and for equal rights, as heroic caretakers of
wounded soldiers, as dedicated partners to the revolutionaries, and as
self-sacrificing mothers and sisters; these figures show an affinity with the
legendary women of South Slavic epic. *(author)*

79 Visual arts (including iconography)

5373 BACHMANN, Werner. **Bilddarstellungen der**
as **Musik im Rahmen der artes liberales** [Icono-
graphic representation of music as one of the liberal
arts], *Bericht über den internationalen musikwissenschaftlichen Kongreß* (Kassel: Bärenreiter, 1957)
46–55. *Facs.* In German. See no. 356 in this volume.

Discusses personified representations of music in illustrations and miniatures in MSS from the 11th to 13th c.

5374 BENARY, Peter. **Das impressionistische**
as **Raumgefühl als Stilfaktor bei Debussy** [The impressionistic sense of space as a stylistic factor in De-
bussy], *Bericht über den internationalen
musikwissenschaftlichen Kongreß* (Kassel: Bärenreiter,
1963) 244–46. In German. See no. 452 in this volume.

Aspects of form, melody, and the treatment of the individual note in Debussy's compositions correspond to the techniques used by impressionist
painters to communicate a particular sense of space. *(David Bloom)*

5375 BLOCH, Peter. **Bemerkungen zur künst-**
as **lerischen Ausstattung des Gladbacher Missale**
[Remarks on the artistic decoration of the Mönchen-
gladbach Missal], *Studien zur Musikgeschichte der
Stadt Mönchengladbach* (Köln: Volk, 1965) 53–56.
Illus., facs. In German. See no. 486 in this volume.

MS 1 of the Schatzkammer collection in the Münster-Basilika St. Vitus,
Mönchengladbach, a Missale plenarium copied at the Abtei St. Vitus
around the mid-12th c., contains two miniatures, of the Crucifixion and of
the Nativity; a ligatured illumination of the capitals in "Vere Dignum" in
the Preface of the Mass; and numerous illuminated single capitals. Technique and style, presumably those of illuminators at the abbey's scriptorium, are the same as those of the dedication leaf (the only extant part of
the MS) of a copy of Ambrosius Autpertus's *Commentarium in
Apocalypsim* in the Germanisches Nationalmuseum, Nürnberg, and of the
MS of Albertus Aquensis's *Historia Hierosolymitana* in *D-Bs* MS
lat.fol.677. *(David Bloom)*

5376 BOVY, Adrien. **Rythme et arts plastiques**
as [Rhythm and the plastic arts], *Compte rendu du Iᵉʳ
Congrès du rythme* (Genève: Institut Jaques-Dalcroze,
1926) 376–83. In French. See no. 123 in this volume.

All plastic arts that depict movement naturally involve rhythm as well.

5377 DROYSEN, Dagmar. **Die Darstellungen von**
as **Saiteninstrumenten in der mittelalterlichen
Buchmalerei und ihre Bedeutung für die
Instrumentenkunde** [The representation of string
instruments in medieval book illumination and its organological significance], *Bericht über den internationalen musikwissenschaftlichen Kongreß* (Kassel:
Bärenreiter, 1963) 302–05. In German. See no. 452 in
this volume.

From the pre-Carolingian period until the 11th c. illuminations had a primarily symbolic rather than literal function, and their organological value
is limited. The most realistic representations began in the 11th c. in An-
glo-Saxon MSS, and became general in the 12th c. The 13th and early 14th
c. saw a retreat to a relatively crude schematism. *(David Bloom)*

5378 ĐUKIĆ, Trifun. **Gusle kao simboličan spomenik**
as **svoje uloge** [The gusle as symbolic monument to its
social role], *Rad VII-og kongresa Saveza Folklorista
Jugoslavije* (Cetinje: Obod, 1964) 357–58. In Serbian;
summary in German. See no. 419 in this volume.

The gusle was originally a simple, primitive instrument; after centuries as the essential accompaniment to epic song, it became an inspiration for paintings depicting famous moments in Serbian history. *(author)*

5379 FREYSE, Conrad. **Unbekannte Jugendbildnisse**
as **Friedemann und Emanuel Bachs** [Unknown portraits of the young Friedemann and Emanuel Bach], *Bericht über die Wissenschaftliche Bachtagung* (Leipzig: Peters, 1951) 349–54. *Illus., port.* In German. See no. 298 in this volume.

Two pastel portraits said to be of W.F. and C.P.E. Bach and datable to ca. 1730 are in the collections of the Bachhaus, Eisenach. Evidence suggests they are authentic, painted by Gottlieb Friedrich Bach (1714-85), son of J.S. Bach's cousin Johann Ludwig Bach, during his visit to Leipzig in 1733.

5380 GEIRINGER, Karl. **Gaudenzio Ferraris Engel-**
as **konzert im Dome von Saronno: Ein Beitrag zur Instrumentenkundes des 16. Jahrhunderts** [Gaudenzio Ferrari's angel concert in the cathedral of Saronno: A contribution to organology of the 16th century], *Beethoven-Zentenarfeier: Internationaler musikhistorischer Kongress* (Wien: Universal, 1927) 378–81. *Illus.* In German. See no. 142 in this volume.

Many representations of musicians in the early Renaissance are carefully naturalistic, and thus of great value to the musicologist. In the late Renaissance, artists present a more schematic view. Ferrari's fresco (1534-36) at S. Maria dei Miracoli, Saronno, depicts a total of 52 different kinds of instruments within organological family relationships. *(David Bloom)*

5381 KARSTÄDT, Georg. **Das Instrument Gottfried**
as **Reiches: Horn oder Trompete?** [Gottfried Reiche's instrument: Horn or trumpet?], *Bericht über den internationalen musikwissenschaftlichen Kongreß* (Kassel: Bärenreiter, 1963) 311–13. *Illus.* In German. See no. 452 in this volume.

In an oil portrait by Elias Gottlob Haussmann, and an engraving made from it in 1727 by Johann Friedrich Rosbach, the Leipzig *Stadtmusikant* Gottfried Reiche is shown with an instrument shaped like a horn but with structural features suggesting it belongs to the trumpet family. It can in fact be identified as a hunting horn of the type called for, as *corno di caccia*, in the scores of Bach's Brandenburg concerto no. 1, in the cantata *Was mir behagt, ist nur die muntre Jagd!*, BWV 208, and some other cantatas. *(David Bloom)*

5382 KVĚT, Jindrich. **L'antiphonaire de Sedlec**
as **conservé à la Bibliothèque de l'Université de Prague** [The antiphonary of Sedlec kept at the library of the Univerzita Karlova v Praze], *Deuxième Congrès international des études byzantines* (Beograd: Državna Štamparija, 1929) 155–56. In French. See no. 131 in this volume.

Investigates the Byzantine influences shown in the miniatures in the book, which date from the end of the Roman age in Bohemia. The notation shows elements of Czech and northern Italian influences. *(Susan Poliniak)*

5383 LARUE, Jan; HOLLAND, Jeanette B. **Stimmer's**
as **women musicians: A unique series of woodcuts,** *Music libraries and instruments* (London: Hinrichsen, 1961) 261–68. *Facs.* See no. 406 in this volume.

A series of ten woodcuts from the 1570s by the Swiss artist Tobias Stimmer, of which there are exemplars in the Prints Division of the New York Public Library Research Collections, depict women playing instruments, with descriptive text. The instruments exhibited are the lute; viol; quintern; positive organ; transverse flute; psaltery; cornett; clarion; bass shawm; and pot, lid and spoon. A more extended version is published in the *Bulletin of the New York Public Library* 64 (1960). *(Susan Poliniak)*

5384 LEICHTENTRITT, Hugo. **Ältere Bildwerke als**
as **Quellen der musikgeschichtlichen Forschung** [Early sculptures as research sources for music history],

Bericht über den zweiten Kongress der Internationalen Musikgesellschaft (Leipzig: Breitkopf & Härtel, 1907) 230–34. In German. See no. 53 in this volume.

Proposals for the organization of research in music iconography in Europe, on a country-by-country basis, beginning with the cataloguing of sculpture and carvings of music-historical value. *(David Bloom)*

5385 MARCUSE, Irène. **Il talento musicale nei**
as **movimenti della scrittura** [Musical talent in the movements of writing], *Onzième Congrès international de psychologie: Rapports et comptes rendus* (Agen: Imprimerie Moderne, 1938) 397–98. In Italian. See no. 250 in this volume.

Describes the differences in hand gestures among different types of musicians (i.e., violinists, cellists, pianists, conductors, and singers) while writing. Writing with much movement is the sign of a great force of artistic fantasy; change in direction can signify creative inspiration. The writing of musicians is a sort of poetry in motion which is never static, but always dynamic. *(Susan Poliniak)*

5386 NEF, Karl. **Seb. Virdungs** *Musica getutscht*
as [Sebastian Virdung's *Musica getutscht*], *Bericht über den musikwissenschaftlichen Kongreß in Basel* (Leipzig: Breitkopf & Härtel, 1925) 7–21. In German. See no. 102 in this volume.

The woodcuts depicting instruments in Virdung's instruction book of 1511 raise questions about their realism, the identity of their creators, and Virdung's main source of information. Errors in the text and illustrations are identified and discussed. *(Sylvia Eversole)*

5387 NICEWONGER, C.R.; NICEWONGER, Har-
as riet. **Mediaeval musical instruments sculptured in the decorations of English churches,** *Music libraries and instruments* (London: Hinrichsen, 1961) 253–55. *Illus.* See no. 406 in this volume.

Most depictions are of angels and their instruments, though one devil bagpiper was discovered.

5388 OTTO, Irmgard. **Buchschmuck als instrumen-**
as **tenkundliche Quelle** [Book decoration as a source for organology], *Music libraries and instruments* (London: Hinrichsen, 1961) 256–61. *Illus., facs.* In German. See no. 406 in this volume.

Discusses printed or engraved title-page vignettes and illustrations in which representations of kithara, harp, organ, trumpet, lute, panpipes, shawm, and percussion instruments serve a purely decorative function, from the 17th through the beginning of the 20th c. *(David Bloom)*

5389 PEJOVIĆ, Roksanda. **Instruments de musique**
as **dans l'art serbo-macédonien et byzantin** [Musical instruments in Serbo-Macedonian and Byzantine art], *Actes du XIIe Congrès d'études Byzantines* (Beograd: Naučno Delo, 1963-1964) II, 589–601. *Illus.* In French. See no. 441 in this volume.

Surveys typical motifs in the representation of instruments in frescos, miniatures, decorative carvings, and architectural details, of the region of Byzantine influence in the Middle Ages, with attention to references to classical mythology, biblical imagery, and secular life of the period. *(David Bloom)*

5390 PEJOVIĆ, Roksanda. **Ruganje Hristu,**
as **ilustracije Davidova života i 150. Psalma: Scene s muzičkim instrumentima na našim spomenicima** [The Mocking of Christ, illustrations of the the life of David, and the 150th Psalm: Scenes with musical instruments in the art works of our national heritage], *Rad VII-og kongresa Saveza Folklorista Jugoslavije* (Cetinje: Obod, 1964) 337–43. *Illus.* In Serbian; summary in Russian. See no. 419 in this volume.

5391
as

RHEINWALD, Albert. **Les rythmes de l'activité créatrice** [The rhythms of creative activity], *Compte rendu du Ier Congrès du rythme* (Genève: Institut Jaques-Dalcroze, 1926) 384–87. In French. See no. 123 in this volume.

In addition to perceiving physical motion, the painter must be able to capture a sense of interior rhythm in the subject.

5392
as

RICART MATAS, Josep. **Els instruments musicals en la iconografia hispànica de l'Edat mitjana** [Musical instruments in Spanish iconography of the Middle Ages], *Congrés de la Societat Internacional de Musicologia* (Barcelona: Casa de Caritat, 1936). In Catalan. See no. 224 in this volume.

The conference report provides only a citation. Neither the text nor a summary of the paper was published here.

5393
as

RIEZLER, Walter. **Das neue Raumgefühl in bildender Kunst und Musik** [The new feeling for space in graphic art and music], *Zeitschrift für Ästhetik und allgemeine Kunstwissenschaft* XXV (supplement 1931) 179–205. In German. See no. 177 in this volume.

5394
as

RINGER, Alexander L. **The visual arts as a source for the historian of music,** *Report of the Eighth Congress of the International Musicological Society. II: Reports* (Kassel: Bärenreiter, 1962) 84–87. See no. 440 in this volume.

A report on a discussion by Geneviève THIBAULT DE CHAMBURE, Emanuel WINTERNITZ, Patricia EGAN, Karl GEIRINGER, Jean JACQUOT, Albert van DER LINDEN, Claudie MARCEL-DUBOIS, Floris van DER MUEREN, Marc PINCHERLE, and Wolfgang STECHOW of the paper by Winternitz abstracted as no. 5405 in this volume.

5395
as

SACHS, Curt. **Die Musik im Rahmen der Schwesterkunste** [Music in the milieu of the sister arts], *Bericht über den musikwissenschaftlichen Kongreß in Basel* (Leipzig: Breitkopf & Härtel, 1925) 310–10. In German. See no. 102 in this volume.

In various times and cultures, music and the visual arts are respectively more and less important relative to each other. A full version appears in *Archiv für Musikwissenschaft* (October, 1924).

5396
as

SCHAEFFNER, André. **Debussy et ses rapports avec la peinture** [Debussy and his relation to painting], *Debussy et l'évolution de la musique au XXe siècle* (Paris: Centre National de la Recherche Scientifique [CNRS], 1965) 151–66. In French. See no. 456 in this volume.

Debussy admired the paintings of Édouard Manet, Eugène-Louis Boudin, and Johan Barthold Jongkind, and his works suggest the influence of impressionist art.

5397
as

SCHEURLEER, Daniel François. **Iconography of musical instruments,** *Report of the Fourth Congress of the International Musical Society* (London: Novello, 1912) 334–37. See no. 71 in this volume.

Because the compilation of the extant iconographies of musical instruments is uneven and incomplete, an international committee has been set up to prepare as complete an inventory as possible. *(Mei-Mei Meng)*

5398
as

SQUIRE, Willian Barclay. **L'iconographie musical** [Musical iconography], *Actes du Congrès d'histoire de l'art* (Paris: Presses Universitaires de France, 1923-1924) 731–34. In French. See no. 94 in this volume.

The classification of portraiture by subject has suffered from a lack of attention. In music, the sources of reference are even scarcer. An international

collection of detailed descriptions of pictures and drawings of musicians would make a valuable reference work. *(Vivian Conejero)*

5399
as

STARZYŃSKI, Juliusz. **Szymanowski a problematyka plastyki polskiej w XX-leciu miedzywojennym** [Szymanowski and Polish visual arts between the two World Wars], *Karol Szymanowski: Księga sesji Naukowej poświęconej twórczości Karola Szymanowskiego* (Warszawa: Uniwersytet Warszawski, Instytut Muzykologii, 1964) 261–73. In Polish; summary in English. See no. 458 in this volume.

Szymanowski felt that all arts of his day were linked by an inner relationship stemming from social and psychological transformations. These were characterized by a departure from nationalism and the subsequent view of artworks as autonomous formal constructions; a radical revision of attitudes toward artistic traditions, leading to a departure from the influence of German music and post-Romantic expression; a view of national art as an independent manifestation of universal values; and an understanding of Góral art as representing an essentially Polish folk art. In his outlook, Szymanowski showed a close affinity to the philosophy of Leon Chwistek (1884-1944). *(editor)*

5400
as

STECHOW, Wolfgang. **Raum und Zeit in der graphischen und musikalischen Illustration** [Space and time in graphic and musical illustration], *Zeitschrift für Ästhetik und allgemeine Kunstwissenschaft* XXV (supplement 1931) 118–27. In German. See no. 177 in this volume.

5401
as

THIBAULT DE CHAMBURE, Geneviève. **Le concert instrumental dans l'art flamand au XVe siècle et au début du XVIe** [The instrumental concert in Flemish art from the 15th century to the beginning of the 16th], *La Renaissance dans les provinces du Nord: Picardie, Artois, Flandres, Brabant, Hainaut* (Paris: Centre National de la Recherche Scientifique [CNRS], 1956) 197f. In French. See no. 328 in this volume.

5402
as

VALENSI, Henry. **La tendance musicaliste en peinture** [The musicalist tendency in painting], *Deuxième congrès international d'esthétique et de Science de l'art* (Paris: Librairie Félix Alcan, 1937) II, 402–05. In French. See no. 249 in this volume.

Axiomatic account of the school of musicalism as formalized by the author in 1913; not to be considered as a translation of music into other media but as a nonmusician's response to the evolution of music as the predominant art of the 20th c. *(David Bloom)*

5403
as

WINTERNITZ, Emanuel. **Instruments de musique étranges chez Filippino Lippi, Piero di Cosimo et Lorenzo Costa** [Strange musical instruments in the paintings of Filippino Lippi, Piero di Cosimo, and Lorenzo Costa], *Les fêtes de la Renaissance* (Paris: Centre National de la Recherche Scientifique [CNRS], 1956) 379–95. *Illus.* In French. See no. 350 in this volume.

Concludes that the instruments represented in the paintings were actual stage instruments, and demonstrates that the interest in antiquity extended to the reconstruction of ancient instruments and their depiction in paintings. *(Scott Fruehwald)*

5404
as

WINTERNITZ, Emanuel. **Quattrocento-Intarsien als Quellen der Instrumentengeschichte** [Intarsias of the 15th century as sources for the history of instruments], *Bericht über den siebenten internationalen musikwissenschaftlichen Kongress* (Kassel: Bärenreiter, 1959) 300–02. *Illus.* In German. See no. 390 in this volume.

Musical iconography of the short-lived fashion of intarsia decoration in Italy is particularly valuable because instruments are shown at or nearly at life size. Examples include the representations of clavichord and lira da braccio of the celebrated studiolo of Federico da Montefeltro's residence in Urbino; of positive organ, vielle, lira da braccio, lute, and zink (cornett) in the studiolo of his residence at Gubbio, and 11-string lute, probably by Damiano da Bergamo, from Bologna, both in the collections of the Metropolitan Museum of Art, New York; of an early harpsichord in the choir stalls of the Genoa cathedral; of a cittern in decorations by Giovanni da Verona for the monastery of Monte Oliveto Maggiore near Siena; and of lutes, viola da gamba, recorders, crumhorns, and spinettino in the doors of the Stanza della Segnatura in the Vatican. A revised version is included in the book abstracted as RILM [1969]241. *(David Bloom)*

5405
as
WINTERNITZ, Emanuel. **The visual arts as a source for the historian of music,** *Report of the*

Eighth Congress of the International Musicological Society. I: Papers (Kassel: Bärenreiter, 1961) 109–20. *Illus.* See no. 439 in this volume.

The study of music iconography begins with the Renaissance, when painters such as Raphael used representations of instruments from Greek sculpture and Roman sarcophagi as models for their own works. Its use for musicological purposes is surveyed, from Vincenzo Galilei and Michael Praetorius through the present, and critically evaluated. *(David Bloom)*

5406
as
ZIMMERMAN, Franklin B. **Purcell portraiture,** *Organ and choral aspects and prospects* (London: Hinrichsen, 1958) 136–49. *Port.* See no. 375 in this volume.

A table of 37 paintings, drawings, and engravings with analytical commentaries.

MUSIC AND RELATED DISCIPLINES

80 General

5407
as
EGGEBRECHT, Hans Heinrich. **Aus der Werkstatt des terminologischen Handwörterbuchs** [From the workshop for the handbook of music terminology], *Société Internationale de Musicologie, cinquième congrès/Internationale Gesellschaft für Musikwissenschaft, fünfter Kongreß/International Society for Musical Research, Fifth Congress* (Amsterdam: Vereniging voor Nederlandse Muziekgeschiedenis, 1953) 155–65. In German. See no. 316 in this volume.
Discusses the author's work on the *Handwörterbuch der musikalischen Terminologie*.

5408
as
FOSS, Hubert. **Musik und internationale Kultur** [Music and international culture], *Musikerziehung: Zeitschrift der Musikerzieher Österreichs* special issue (1953) 147–50. In German. See no. 317 in this volume.
Draws parallels between the artistic and societal roles of composers and poets. Works from various time periods are cited to support the hypothesis that art (specifically music) inevitably reflects upon the culture from which it originates. *(Robert Taub)*

5409
as
GOLDSCHMIDT, Harry. **Musikalische Gestalt und Intonation** [Musical gestalt and intonation], *Intonation und Gestalt in der Musik: Beiträge und Abhandlungen der Musikwissenschaftler sozialistischer Länder* (Moskva: Muzyka, 1963) 145–58. In German. See no. 471 in this volume.
Offers a broad consideration of the concept of gestalt and Asaf'ev's intonation theory as essential features of the way in which music reflects social reality from the historical-dialectical point of view. Based on the conference paper cited as RILM 5479 in this volume. *(David Bloom)*

5410
as
HALOT, Alexandre. **La bonne musique pour le peuple** [Good music for the public], *IIIe Congrès international de l'art public* (Liège: n.p., 1905) 4. In French. See no. 49 in this volume.
Musical compositions should be easily understood by the public.

5411
as
JARUSTOVSKIJ, Boris Mihajlovič. **"Wie das Leben..."** ["Like life..."]. Trans. by G. BALTER, *Intonation und Gestalt in der Musik: Beiträge und Abhandlungen der Musikwissenschaftler sozialistischer Länder* (Moskva: Muzyka, 1963) 100–44. In German. See no. 471 in this volume.
Draws on examples from European, especially Russian, art music of the 19th-20th c. to illustrate the ways in which what Asaf'ev called *intonacija* is a reflection of material reality in the sense of Lenin's aesthetic theory. *(David Bloom)*

5412
as
KRAFT, Günther. **Thüringisch-sächsische Quellen zur musikphysiologischen Forschung des 17. und 18. Jahrhunderts** [Thuringian and Saxon sources for research in music physiology in the 17th and 18th centuries], *Bericht über den siebenten internationalen musikwissenschaftlichen Kongress* (Kassel: Bärenreiter, 1959) 164–66. In German. See no. 390 in this volume.

Provides information on the life and work of theorists from academic centers in southeastern Germany in the Baroque period, primarily Jena, including the mathematician Erhard Weigel, the Coburg professor of medicine Johann Christian Frommann, the physiologist Georg Wolfgang Wedel, and the organist Johann Nicolaus Bach (1669-1753), with brief bibliographical notes on a number of other figures. *(David Bloom)*

5413
as
KREMLËV, Julij Anatol'evič. **Intonation und Gestalt in der Musik** [Intonation and gestalt in music]. Trans. by A. ARNOLD, *Intonation und Gestalt in der Musik: Beiträge und Abhandlungen der Musikwissenschaftler sozialistischer Länder* (Moskva: Muzyka, 1963) 37–55. In German. See no. 471 in this volume.
Provides a general account of Asaf'ev's intonation theory in terms of the interpretation of *intonacija* as a reflection (*Wiederspiegelung*) of material reality. *(David Bloom)*

5414
as
MAZEL', Lev Abramovič. **Vom System der musikalischen Ausdrucksmittel und einigen Prinzipien der künstlerischen Wirkung der Musik** [The system of musical means of expression and some principles of the artistic effect of music]. Trans. by G. BALTER, *Intonation und Gestalt in der Musik: Beiträge und Abhandlungen der Musikwissenschaftler sozialistischer Länder* (Moskva: Muzyka, 1963) 241–82. In German. See no. 471 in this volume.
A unified materialist theory of music drawing on Asafev's concept of *intonacija* that accounts for music's emotional power will work in terms of the extreme heterogeneity of musical means and the multilayered, concentrated character of its effects, on a principle of the cumulation of functions. *(David Bloom)*

5415
as
MORAGAS, Beda María. **El canto gregoriano y la ciencia** [Gregorian chant and science], *V Congreso Nacional de Música Sagrada* (Madrid: Gráficas Dos de Mayo, 1956) 136–45. In Spanish. See no. 331 in this volume.
The study of Gregorian chant is important not only for the history of the liturgy, but also for disciplines such as philology and paleography, to which it provides valuable material. *(José López-Calo)*

5416
as
ORLOVA, Elena. **Die Arbeit Assafjews an der Theorie der Intonation** [Asaf'ev's work on intonation theory]. Trans. by A. ARNOLD, *Intonation und Gestalt in der Musik: Beiträge und Abhandlungen der Musikwissenschaftler sozialistischer Länder* (Moskva: Muzyka, 1963) 159–82. In German. See no. 471 in this volume.
Presents a summary report from a biographical perspective of the development of Boris Asaf'ev's thinking on the concept of *intonacija* from 1917 through the 1940s; a more extended account is available in Russian in the author's *B.V. Asaf'ev: Put' issledovatelja i publicista* (Leningrad, 1964) and in the books abstracted as RILM [1984]5660 and [1984]3796. *(David Bloom)*

5417
as
RIÉTY, P. **Le vocabulaire d'acoustique musicale d'après la formation du langage musical** [The terminology of musical acoustics, from the standpoint of the formation of musical language], *Acoustique musicale* (Paris: Centre National de la Recherche Scientifique [CNRS], 1959) 111–15. In French. See no. 393 in this volume.

The French national standards agency, Association Française de Normalisation, envisages the publication of a standard terminology of musical acoustics. Problems will have to be faced in reconciling objective criteria with the usage of musicians, including the problem of historical change in the values of interval frequencies from the ratio-based Pythagorean scale to harmony-based equal temperament.

5418
as
RYŽKIN, Josif. **Bild-Gestaltungskomposition des Musikwerks** [The image-gestalt composition of the musical work]. Trans. by G. BALTER, *Intonation und Gestalt in der Musik: Beiträge und Abhandlungen der Musikwissenschaftler sozialistischer Länder* (Moskva: Muzyka, 1963) 200–40. In German. See no. 471 in this volume.
Offers a typological study of the ways in which musical works manifest the concept of the image-gestalt, the dialectical unity of form and content, regarded as the means whereby a work of art constitutes an objectified reflection of social reality, with particular reference to the evolution of different genres in European art music. *(David Bloom)*

5419
as
SILBERMANN, Alphons. **Sozialpsychologische Aspekte im Wandel des Chopin-Idols** [Social-psychological aspects of change in the idolized image of Chopin], *The book of the first international musicological congress devoted to the works of Frederick Chopin* (Warszawa: Państwowe Wydawnictwo Naukowe, 1963) 604–07. In German. See no. 425 in this volume.
The image of Chopin changes alongside social change. Romantic aspects of his music, Classic aspects, his character as a Romantic revolutionary, or his ironic diffidence are variously emphasized. Throughout, his figure in music history remains idolized. *(David Bloom)*

5420
as
SYCHRA, Antonín. **Möglichkeiten der Anwendung der Kybernetik und der Informationstheorie in der marxistischen Musikwissenschaft** [Possible applications of cybernetics and information theory in Marxist musicology], *Beiträge zur Musikwissenschaft* VII/4 (1965) 402–32. In German. See no. 495 in this volume.

81 Philosophy, aesthetics, criticism

5421
as
ABERT, Hermann. **Geistlich und Weltlich in der Musik** [The sacred and the secular in music], *Zeitschrift für Ästhetik und allgemeine Kunstwissenschaft* XIX (1925) 397–411. In German. See no. 114 in this volume.
Offers a historical critique of the idea that sacred and secular musics are of aesthetically different categories. Supporting reports by Gerhard von KEUSSLER and Arnold SCHERING are appended. *(David Bloom)*

5422
as
ANON. (a critic). **Musical criticism in England,** *Haydn-Zentenarfeier* (Leipzig: Breitkopf & Härtel; Wien: Artaria, 1909) 492–96. See no. 65 in this volume.
Provides a brief historical synopsis and then surveys the state of the discipline in London and the provinces.

5423
as
ANSERMET, Ernest. **Subjectivisme et objectivisme dans l'expression musicale** [Subjectivism and objectivism in musical expression], *Atti del sesto Congresso internazionale di musica* (Firenze: Barbèra, 1950) 138–46. In French. See no. 291 in this volume.
Music is born from a rapport between subject and object; it is impossible to separate the subjective from the objective in music. Music is essentially expression. Within subjectivity there exists freedom in music. The problem of subjectivity vs. objectivity in 20th-c. music is particularly grave if one denies that music is a transmitter of the culture in which it was created. *(Susan Poliniak)*

5424
as
ANTCLIFFE, Herbert. **Inductive and comparative criticism as applied to the art of music,** *Haydn-Zentenarfeier* (Leipzig: Breitkopf & Härtel; Wien: Artaria, 1909) 364–68. See no. 65 in this volume.
Compares two approaches to criticism as exemplified in the work of Jacques-Anatole-François Thibault (Anatole France) and Arthur Symons.

5425
as
BAENSCH, Otto. **Rhythmus in allgemein philosophischer Betrachung** [Rhythm as seen from a general philosophical perspective], *Dritter Kongress für Ästhetik und allgemeine Kunstwissenschaft: Bericht* (Stuttgart: Enke, 1927) 202f. In German. See no. 137 in this volume.

5426
as
BAUER, Moritz. **Symbol in der Musik** [Symbol in music], *Dritter Kongress für Ästhetik und allgemeine Kunstwissenschaft: Bericht* (Stuttgart: Enke, 1927) 388–92. In German. See no. 137 in this volume.
Offers a supplement to a contribution by Arnold Schering (cited as RILM 5584 in this volume).

5427
as
BAUM, O. **Der Blinde als Kritiker** [The blind as critics], *Procès-verbaux et documents* (Praha: Státní Nakladatelství, 1931) 87–89. In German. See no. 183 in this volume.

5428
as
BECKING, Gustav. **Zur Typologie des musikalischen Schaffens** [On the typology of musical works], *Bericht über den musikwissenschaftlichen Kongreß in Basel* (Leipzig: Breitkopf & Härtel, 1925) 67–71. In German. See no. 102 in this volume.
The similarities in the philosophies of Goethe and Kant originate in basic constants in their personalities that underlies their beliefs. Differences arise due to individual experiences and expressions. This type of study is applied to an analysis of rhythm, harmony, and melody in the works of composers such as Mozart, Beethoven, Schumann, and Brahms. *(Sylvia Eversole)*

5429
as
BERNET KEMPERS, Karel Philippus. **Die Affektenlehre und die Musikauffassung des neunzehnten Jahrhunderts** [The doctrine of the affections and the concept of music in the nineteenth century], *Actes du cinquième Congrès international d'esthétique/Proceedings of the Fifth International Congress of Aesthetics* ('s-Gravenhage: Mouton, 1964) 969–71. In German. See no. 475 in this volume.
While professional philosophy abandoned the concept of the affections in the 19th c., it continued to be relevant to working musicians and poets, and audiences. The role of writers was a determining factor throughout the Romantic, realistic, and impressionist eras. A fuller version is included in the author's *Die Dichter und die romantische Musik* in the *Festschrift Hans Engel* (Kassel, 1964). *(David Bloom)*

5430
as
BLAUKOPF, Kurt. **The aesthetics of musical humanism from Diderot to Hanslick,** *Actes de Xme Congrès international de philosophie/Proceedings of the Tenth International Congress of Philosophy* (Amsterdam: North-Holland Publishing Company, 1949) I, 534–36. *Bibliog.* See no. 280 in this volume.
The humanist aesthetics of the Viennese Classic school were foreshadowed by the French Encyclopedists, particularly Diderot, despite Berlioz's low opinion of their musical competence. Although some Encyclopedists—such as Jean le Rond d'Alembert—rejected the notion of absolute music, Diderot and Friedrich Melchior von Grimm did not. There is a direct line from Diderot's ideas about the equality of words and music to the development of the concept of absolute music and the writings of Hanslick.

5431 BONAVENTURA, Arnaldo. **Progrès et**
as **nationalité dans la musique** [Progress and nationality in music], *Congrès international d'histoire de la
musique: Documents, mémoires et vœux* (Solesmes: St.
Pierre; Paris: Fischbacher, 1901) 226–40. In French.
See no. 32 in this volume.

Throughout the history of Italian opera, critics have panned new works for
being too instrumental, i.e., too German. Though ethnic traits often distinguish different compositions, all Western music is based on a single tonal
language. The works of several composers, including Rossini, Verdi, and
Wagner, are mentioned.

5432 BORRELLI, Enzo. **Soggetto ed espressione**
as **nella musica** [Subject and expression in music], *Atti
del sesto Congresso internazionale di musica* (Firenze:
Barbèra, 1950) 153–61. In Italian. See no. 291 in this
volume.

Discusses noumens and phenomenalism (in particular as pertaining to the
ideas of Schopenhauer) in relation to musical expression, focusing on the
Romantic era. Wagner's *Tristan und Isolde* is analyzed at length. The problem of objectivity as regards opera librettos is examined. *(Susan Poliniak)*

5433 BRENN, Franz. **Das Sein der musikalischen**
as **Welt: Eine propädeutische Skizze** [The being of
the musical world: A propaedeutic sketch], *Deuxième
congrès international d'esthétique et de Science de
l'art* (Paris: Librairie Félix Alcan, 1937) II, 506–09. In
German. See no. 249 in this volume.

Provides an outline of a phenomenological approach to music aesthetics.

5434 BROCKHAUS, Heinz Alfred. **Über einige**
as **Probleme und Kriterien des Neuen in der
zeitgenössischen Musik** [On some problems and
criteria of the new in contemporary music], *Beiträge
zur Musikwissenschaft* VII/4 (1965) 328–37. In German. See no. 495 in this volume.

5435 BUCCHI, Valentino. **Solitudine del musicista**
as [Solitude of the musician], *Atti del sesto Congresso
internazionale di musica* (Firenze: Barbèra, 1950)
161–66. In Italian. See no. 291 in this volume.

Discusses the differences between objectivist and subjectivist viewpoints
on the act of composition, as well as problems concerning the determination of audience or purpose intended by the composer for a work, and the
justification of the 12-tone system. The abandonment of traditional musical
values coincides with the end of a culture and a social structure.

(Susan Poliniak)

5436 BÜCKEN, Ernst. **Die Musik als Stil- und**
as **Kulturproblem** [Music as a problem of style and cul-
ture], *Atti del terzo Congresso internazionale di musica*
(Firenze: Le Monnier, 1940) 67–73. In German; summaries in Italian and French. See no. 256 in this volume.

Discusses beliefs about older music and the means of correcting misconceptions.

5437 BUKOFZER, Manfred F. **Hegel's Musik-**
as **ästhetik** [Hegel's music aesthetics], *Deuxième
congrès international d'esthétique et de Science de
l'art* (Paris: Librairie Félix Alcan, 1937) II, 32–34. In
German. See no. 249 in this volume.

The debate as to whether Hegel's views on music should be regarded as Romantic or Classic, or whether they pertain to the aesthetics of content or that
of form, is based on a misunderstanding of his terminology. Hegel's position is that music is autonomously and immanently structured, and that its
symbolic character is to be understood monistically rather than
dualistically, in that its meaning cannot be separated from its material manifestation; in this respect he should be considered neither Classic nor Romantic but modern. *(David Bloom)*

5438 CARDUCCI-AGUSTINI, Edgardo. **Necessità di**
as **una valutazione cristiana dell'arte musicale e
della sua storia** [The need for a Christian evaluation
of the art of music and of its history], *Zweiter internationaler Kongress für katholische Kirchenmusik: Zu
Ehren des Heiligen Papstes Pius X* (Wien: conference,
1955) 274–78. In Italian. See no. 339 in this volume.

It is a properly Christian characteristic to have a unique point of reference
for all the operations of mental life, including those involved in aesthetics
and in music history. The vitality and greatness of a particular music, for instance, correlates with the degree of intensity and urgency in its intuitive
communication of the great drama of which we are all part. Pure Romanticism shows the consciousness of humanity's immanent wound; Beethoven
and Wagner join the Adamic motif of the Fall to the genuinely Christic motif of Redemption. *(David Bloom)*

5439 CARDUCCI-AGUSTINI, Edgardo. **Se i sistemi**
as **esclusivisti della musica contemporanea siano
conciliabili con lo stile sacro** [Whether the exclusivist systems of contemporary music can be reconciled
with sacred style], *Atti del [I] Congresso internazionale
di musica sacra* (Tournai: Desclée, 1952) 395–97. In
Italian. See no. 303 in this volume.

5440 ČERNÝ, Miroslav Karel. **Über die Kriterien**
as **der historischen Wertung der zeitgenössischen
Musik** [On the criteria of historical evaluation for contemporary music], *Beiträge zur Musikwissenschaft*
VII/4 (1965) 325–28. In German. See no. 495 in this
volume.

5441 CESARI, Gaetano. **Le funzione, i metodi, gli**
as **scopi della critica musicale** [The function, methods, and purposes of music criticism], *Atti del primo
Congresso internazionale di musica* (Firenze: Le
Monnier, 1935) 11–17. In Italian. See no. 203 in this
volume.

In Italy, young composer-critics are keeping the public appraised of the activities and intentions of the compositional avant-garde. In so doing, they
are pressuring journalist-critics to update their knowledge and spurring traditional composers to broaden their horizons. *(Lisa Miller)*

5442 CHARLES, Daniel. **L'esthétique du *non finito***
as **chez John Cage** [John Cage's aesthetic concept of
non finito], *Actes du cinquième Congrès international
d'esthétique/Proceedings of the Fifth International
Congress of Aesthetics* ('s-Gravenhage: Mouton, 1964)
219–21. In French. See no. 475 in this volume.

Discusses the *Dances for prepared piano* (1946) and *Concert* (1958) in
terms of the concept of the *non finito* (Donatello's term for the sculpture
technique, most famously used by Michelangelo, of carving a subject as if it
were emerging from an uncarved block of marble) as an aesthetic category.
An earlier version of the article is abstracted as RILM [1973]2712.

5443 CHERBULIEZ, Antoine-Élisée. **Möglichkeiten**
as **und Auswirkungen des Ethos in der Musik**
[Possibilities and consequences of ethos in music],
*Musikerziehung: Zeitschrift der Musikerzieher Öster-
reichs* special issue (1953) 46–50. In German. See no.
317 in this volume.

5444 CUCLIN, Dimitrie. **Musique: Art, science, et**
as **philosophie** [Music: Art, science, and philosophy],
*Actes du huitième Congrès international de
philosophie* (Praha: conference, 1936) 1073–77. In
French. See no. 213 in this volume.

Musical science is composed of four elements: expansion, digression,
force, and sensitivity. The diatonic systems have strict and irreproachable
laws which parallel metaphysical laws. D'Indy marks the end of the first era

of music. After him, music can be perfectly understood as a science, and open to free creation. *(David Nussenbaum)*

5445
as
CZERNY, Zygmunt. **Contribution à une théorie comparée du motif dans les arts** [Toward a comparative theory of the motive in the arts], *Stil- und Formprobleme in der Literatur: Vorträge* (Heidelberg: Winter, 1959) 38–50. In French. See no. 372 in this volume.

Each of the three groups of arts—musical, plastic, and literary—has its own unifying force, from which it is inseparable, in the use respectively of musical, figurative, and intellectual motives. *(Terence Ford)*

5446
as
DAHLHAUS, Carl. **Zwei Definitionen der Musik als quadrivialer Disziplin** [Two definitions of music as a discipline of the quadrivium], *Bericht über den internationalen musikwissenschaftlichen Kongreß* (Kassel: Bärenreiter, 1957) 64–66. In German. See no. 356 in this volume.

Music theory is ranked in the quadrivium because of its mathematical character, but this means different things in different classical traditions. The thesis of Aurelian of Réôme in the *Musica disciplina* is in a Pythagorean/Platonic tradition, based on the theory of ideal numbers; those of Boethius and Jehan des Murs treat numbers in the Aristotelian tradition, as abstractions. *(David Bloom)*

5447
as
DALLAPICCOLA, Luigi. **Musique et humanité** [Music and humanity], *Journal of the International Folk Music Council* XVI (1964) 8–10. In French. See no. 463 in this volume.

Remarks on the philosophical concept of humanity as applied to composers, and the origin of the author's *Canti di prigionia* (1938-41), *Volo di notte* (1940), *Marsia* (1942-43), and *Il prigioniero* (1944-48) in response to the 1938 adoption of racist policies in Fascist Italy and the 1940 bombing of London. *(David Bloom)*

5448
as
D'AMICO, Fedele. **Che cos'è l'oggettivismo** [What objectivism is], *Atti del sesto Congresso internazionale di musica* (Firenze: Barbèra, 1950) 17–26. In Italian. See no. 291 in this volume.

Subjectivism and objectivism are viewed as polar opposites. So-called objective music is governed by its own laws, and is, in essence, the renunciation of the spirit (of art); so-called subjective music is the expression of the sole thing that a person can truly express, the self. The factors that brought about the end of Romantic (i.e., truly subjective) music are discussed. In a sense, a great deal of Romantic music was also fully objective in its universal themes and appeal. Objectivism can be said to embody a strong attention to language. The issue of determining who comprises the audience for modern music is discussed. *(Susan Poliniak)*

5449
as
DANIÉLOU, Alain. **Valeurs éthiques et spirituelles en musique** [Ethical and spiritual values in music], *Journal of the International Folk Music Council* XVI (1964) 11–14. In French. See no. 463 in this volume.

Music played an important ethical and spiritual role in all the ancient civilizations, as it still does in most non-Western cultures. To understand this role, and perhaps return to it, we should begin studying sound phenomena on a new basis, with particular attention to their psychophysiological effects. Study of the technical means of music in other cultures, as an essential element of such a program, is a goal of the International Institute for Comparative Music Studies, founded in 1963 in Berlin. *(David Bloom)*

5450
as
DAURIAC, Lionel Alexandre. **Note sur l'inspiration musicale** [Note on musical inspiration], *Haydn-Zentenarfeier* (Leipzig: Breitkopf & Härtel; Wien: Artaria, 1909) 402–07. In French. See no. 65 in this volume.

Discusses creativity and originality.

5451
as
DAURIAC, Lionel Alexandre. **Le pensée musicale** [Musical thought], *Congrès international d'histoire de la musique: Documents, mémoires et vœux* (Solesmes: St. Pierre; Paris: Fischbacher, 1901) 296–97. In French. See no. 32 in this volume.

Music displays "thoughts" or "ideas" stemming from the musical phrase.

5452
as
DEBENEDETTI, Giacomo. **L'oratorio di Via Belsiana** [The oratory of Via Belsiana], *Atti del terzo Congresso internazionale di musica* (Firenze: Le Monnier, 1940) 102–07. In Italian; summaries in French and German. See no. 256 in this volume.

Examines why modern music is difficult to understand while older music is not.

5453
as
DELLA CORTE, Andrea. **Preliminari di critica musicale** [Preliminaries to musical criticism], *Proceedings of the Third International Congress on Aesthetics/Actes du troisième Congrès international d'esthétique/Atti del III Congresso internazionale di estetica* (Torino: Edizioni della Rivista di Estetica, 1957) 660–63. In Italian. See no. 363 in this volume.

Presents a brief analytic account of the concept of criticism of the musical work, based on definitions of the individual terms, and emphasizing the distinction between the essential components of academic understanding and aesthetic response. *(David Bloom)*

5454
as
DIMIER, Charles. **Prolégomènes à l'esthétique** [Prolegomena to aesthetics], *[Ier] Congrès international de philosophie: Procès-verbaux, sommaires* (Paris: Imprimerie Nationale, 1901) 38–39. In French. See no. 37 in this volume.

Summary of a conference paper. A publication of the full version is abstracted as RILM 5455 in this volume.

5455
ap
DIMIER, Charles. **Prolégomènes à l'esthétique** [Prolegomena to aesthetics], *Revue de métaphysique et de morale* (1900) 622–26. In French.

Imitation is perceived differently from the object. Art may be defined as the reduction of heterogeneity (nature) into homogeneity. A summary of the paper is cited as RILM 5454 in this volume.

5456
as
DRAEGER, Hans-Heinz. **Aesthetische Grundlagen** [Aesthetic foundations], *Stilkriterien der neuen Musik* (Berlin: Merseburger, 1961) 34–44. In German. See no. 410 in this volume.

Earlier approaches to musical aesthetics are not suitable for new music. Research in the psychology of musical hearing may help to identify ways of making new music accessible to more people. *(Neill Clegg)*

5457
as
ÉCORCHEVILLE, Jules. **L'internationalisme dans la musique** [Internationalism in music], *Report of the Fourth Congress of the International Musical Society* (London: Novello, 1912) 76–77. In French. See no. 71 in this volume.

Summary of a paper. Nationalism and originality are based on spontaneity of feeling, while internationalism is the result of intelligence and reflection.

5458
as
EDLER, Arnfried. **Zur Musikanschauung von Adolf Bernhard Marx** [The musical perspective of Adolf Bernhard Marx], *Beiträge zur Geschichte der Musikansschauung im 19. Jahrhundert* (Regensburg: Bosse, 1965) 103–12. In German. See no. 483 in this volume.

Marx's *Die Lehre von der musikalischen Komposition, praktisch-theoretisch* (1837) is best understood in the context of his general ideas on music and on theory. His attempt to bring together the so-called rational theology of the Hegelian dialectic with the Romantic idea of identity-expression is not a success; recognizing the impossibility of creating an original and coherent system with eclectic methods on a syncretic foundation, he takes refuge in pragmatism. *(David Bloom)*

5459
as

EGGEBRECHT, Hans Heinrich. **Der Begriff des "Neuen" in der Musik von der Ars nova bis zur Gegenwart** [The concept of the new in music from the ars nova to the present day], *Report of the Eighth Congress of the International Musicological Society. I: Papers* (Kassel: Bärenreiter, 1961) 195–202. In German. See no. 439 in this volume.

Examines the points of view of the individual musicians and theorists who have championed or rejected ideas of the new. Each so-called new music since the beginning of the 14th c. has perceived itself in terms of progress in a sense that may, with the music of Schoenberg and Webern, have come to an end. A companion piece to the essay by Kurt von Fischer abstracted as RILM 5468 in this volume. *(David Bloom)*

5460
as

EGGEBRECHT, Hans Heinrich. **The concept of the New in music from the ars nova to the present day,** *Report of the Eighth Congress of the International Musicological Society. II: Reports* (Kassel: Bärenreiter, 1962) 112–17. In German and English. See no. 440 in this volume.

A report on a discussion by William W. AUSTIN, Milton BABBITT, Jacques CHAILLEY, Hans Heinrich EGGEBRECHT, Kurt von FISCHER, Heinrich HÜSCHEN, Jurij Vsevolodovič KELDYŠ, Paul Henry LANG, Hans MERSMANN, Nino PIRROTTA, Gilbert REANEY, Hans REDLICH, and Walter SALMEN of the papers by Fischer and Eggebrecht abstracted as RILM 5468 and 5459 in this volume.

5461
as

EGGEBRECHT, Hans Heinrich. **Zum Wort-Ton-Verhältnis in der *Musica poetica* von J.A. Herbst** [On word-to-music relations in the *Musica poetica* of J.A. Herbst], *Bericht über den internationalen musikwissenschaftlichen Kongreß* (Kassel: Bärenreiter, 1957) 77–80. In German. See no. 356 in this volume.

Johann Andreas Herbst's *Musica poetica* (1643) exemplifies the 17th-c. view of the Protestant Kantorei tradition in several ways: in the threefold division of the *ars compositionis* into *musica theoretica*, *practica*, and *poetica*; in the treatment of composition theory as *poetica*; in the association of music composition with rhetoric, as an *explicatio textus*; and in the fundamental character given to expression. *(David Bloom)*

5462
as

ENGEL, Hans. **Vom Sinn und Wesen der Musik in Werken und Deutung der Gegenwart** [The meaning and essence of music as seen in contemporary composition and performance], *Compte rendu/Kongressbericht/Report* (Basel: Bärenreiter, 1951) 96–103. In German. See no. 289 in this volume.

Presents a general discussion of 20th-c. philosophical orientations in music and musicology, with attention to changing views on expressivity, mysticism, and the role of physical movement; and reactions to World War II–era catastrophes. *(David Bloom)*

5463
as

FABRO, Cornelio. **Estetica mozartiana nell'opera di Kierkegard** [Mozartean aesthetics in Kierkegaard's work], *Proceedings of the Third International Congress on Aesthetics/Actes du troisième Congrès international d'esthétique/Atti del III Congresso internazionale di estetica* (Torino: Edizioni della Rivista di Estetica, 1957) 706–10. In Italian. See no. 363 in this volume.

Summary account of the philosophical response to Mozart's operas in Søren Kierkegaard's *Enten/Eller* (Copenhagen, 1843).

5464
as

FELDMANN, Fritz. **Mattheson und die Rhetorik** [Mattheson and rhetoric], *Bericht über den*

internationalen musikwissenschaftlichen Kongreß (Kassel: Bärenreiter, 1957) 99–103. In German. See no. 356 in this volume.

Attempts to place Mattheson's concept of musical rhetoric in the context of philosophical theories of rhetoric from Aristotle to the Baroque.

5465
as

FELLINGER, Imogen. **Grundzüge Brahmsscher Musikauffassung** [The fundamental traits of Brahms's concept of music], *Beiträge zur Geschichte der Musikansschauung im 19. Jahrhundert* (Regensburg: Bosse, 1965) 113–26. *Music.* In German. See no. 483 in this volume.

Brahms frequently toyed with the project of setting his ideas on music down in literary form, like so many other composers of his time, but he never carried it through. Nevertheless, his correspondence, especially from the critical period of the 1850s, provides evidence of his views on literature, compositional technique, music history, and the notion of the fully realized work. *(David Bloom)*

⟶

FERCHAULT, Guy. **Essai de justification d'une bibliographie particulière à la philosophie de l'art musical** [An attempt to justify a special bibliography dedicated to the philosophy of music]. See no. 574 in this volume.

5466
as

FERGUSON, Donald N. **Music and the democratic idea,** *Papers of the American Musicological Society* (Philadelphia: American Musicological Society, 1946) 101–07. See no. 269 in this volume.

Music is not completely abstract; it is an expressive art that bears reference to human passions born of ordinary experience. As such, it may serve as a metaphoric utterance of humanistic and democratic ideals. *(author)*

5467
as

FERGUSON, Donald N. **What is a musical idea?,** *Papers of the American Musicological Society* (Philadelphia: American Musicological Society, 1946) 43–49. See no. 272 in this volume.

Visual and literary media of expression set forth things themselves, and from this delineation or image we deduce our own valuations. Music sets forth something very like the valuations of our images, from which we may deduce the concrete image of the experience; this may be what gives music its unique power to illuminate the values of experience. *(David Bloom)*

5468
as

FISCHER, Kurt von. **Der Begriff des "Neuen" in der Musik von der Ars nova bis zur Gegenwart** [The concept of the new in music from the ars nova to the present day], *Report of the Eighth Congress of the International Musicological Society. I: Papers* (Kassel: Bärenreiter, 1961) 184–202. In German. See no. 439 in this volume.

The drive to create something new is of decisive importance in the history of Western music. It should be seen in the framework of a nonlinear development proceeding on many different levels. Critical periods include those of the ars nova, the 1420s, the age of Josquin Desprez, the monody of ca. 1600, the Enlightenment, Romanticism, the period of 1910-20, and the development of dodecaphony and serialism. A companion piece to the essay by Hans Heinrich Eggebrecht abstracted as RILM 5459 in this volume. *(David Bloom)*

5469
as

FLAM, Léopold. **L'art-religion de l'homme moderne** [The art-religion of modern man], *Actes du cinquième Congrès international d'esthétique/Proceedings of the Fifth International Congress of Aesthetics* ('s-Gravenhage: Mouton, 1964) 812–21. In French. See no. 475 in this volume.

Hegel's idea of a *Kunstreligion*, intended as a characterization of ancient Greek religion, may be applied to modern aesthetics; the theory of the death of God leads to the cult of the semidivine creative genius, including musicians such as Beethoven and Wagner. *(David Bloom)*

5470
as
FLEISCHER, Herbert. **Soggetto e oggetto nell'espressione musicale** [Subject and object in musical expression], *Atti del sesto Congresso internazionale di musica* (Firenze: Barbèra, 1950) 9–17. In Italian. See no. 291 in this volume.

Subjectivism and objectivism are seen as polar opposites. Twentieth-century music and issues surrounding the conflicts between objective and subjective aspects and constructs are examined, including the forces of personality and passion, of logic, and of spirituality. Hanslick's thoughts on the unity of emotive and constructive elements in music are also discussed. The so-called pre-Classical music of Italy contains a complete unity of expression and form, and reveals a quintessential sense of humanity; contemporary music aspires to these goals. *(Susan Poliniak)*

5471
as
FORSTER, Edward Morgan. **The raison d'être of criticism in the arts,** *Music and criticism: A symposium* (Cambridge, MA: Harvard University Press, 1948) 9–34. See no. 276 in this volume.

For the general public, criticism can educate and stimulate by precise transmission of works of art. For the creative artist, however, it is less helpful: Unlike creative processes, the critical mind is entirely conscious and unsentimental. *(William Gilmore)*

5472
as
FUBINI, Enrico. **Espressione e imitazione della natura nell'estetica musicale del settecento** [Expression and imitation of nature in the musical aesthetic of the 18th century], *Actes du cinquième Congrès international d'esthétique/Proceedings of the Fifth International Congress of Aesthetics* ('s-Gravenhage: Mouton, 1964) 626–30. In Italian. See no. 475 in this volume.

The concept of art as the imitation of nature, prevalent in the thinking of the French Enlightenment, was so poorly suited to music that it seemed possible to deny that music was an art at all. Rameau's way around the difficulty was to assimilate music to reason itself, emphasizing its intimate, covert, austere logicality; Diderot's still more radical alternative (especially in *Le neveu de Rameau*) was to treat music as able to express that which logic cannot: obscure emotions, powerful and instinctive passions, private values. *(David Bloom)*

5473
as
FUBINI, Enrico. **L'interpretazione musicale** [Musical interpretation], *Pepragmena tou 4. diethnous synedriou aisthītikīs/Actes du IV Congrès international d'esthétique/Proceedings of the IV International Congress on Aesthetics* (Athínai: conference, 1962) 555–58. In Italian. See no. 415 in this volume.

Philosophical problems in the relationship between notation and interpretation are discussed. An extended version of the argument is published in *Notazione musicale e interpretazione*, in *Rassegna musicale* XXXI (1961).

5474
as
GANDILLOT, Maurice. **Base rationiste du système musical** [The rationist basis of the system of music], *Haydn-Zentenarfeier* (Leipzig: Breitkopf & Härtel; Wien: Artaria, 1909) 407–22. In French. See no. 65 in this volume.

Extrapolates the rationist theory as detailed in the author's *Théorie de la musique* (Paris, 1907). Also extracted in *Revue scientifique* 30 March and 6 April 1907.

5475
as
GANDILLOT, Maurice. **Sur la langage musicale** [On musical language], *Report of the Fourth Congress of the International Musical Society* (London: Novello, 1912) 228–37. *Music, charts, diagr.* In French. See no. 71 in this volume.

Discusses the logic and emotional meaning of successive parts of musical phrases.

5476
as
GATTI, Guido Maria. **Dell'interpretazione musicale** [Musical interpretation], *Atti del primo Congresso internazionale di musica* (Firenze: Le

Monnier, 1935) 268–76. In Italian. See no. 203 in this volume.

The musical work lives not in the score but only in performance, itself a creative, or recreative, act. In *Aesthetica in nuce* (1928), Benedetto Croce proposes that the image and its expression—the creation and recreation—are to be regarded equally as works of art. *(David Bloom)*

5477
as
GECK, Martin. **E.T.A. Hoffmanns Anschauungen über Kirchenmusik** [E.T.A. Hoffmann's views on church music], *Beiträge zur Geschichte der Musikanschauung im 19. Jahrhundert* (Regensburg: Bosse, 1965) 61–71. In German. See no. 483 in this volume.

Hoffmann's history of church music, based on the veneration of a few particular composers, especially Palestrina, is not sustainable. However, the practical ideas he drew from his research were of great importance in the 19th-c. renewal of church music. *(David Bloom)*

5478
as
GOLDSCHMIDT, Harry. **Gedanken zu einer nichtaristotelischen Musikästhetik** [Thoughts on a non-Aristotelian musical aesthetics], *Beiträge zur Musikwissenschaft* VII/4 (1965) 387–401. In German. See no. 495 in this volume.

5479
as
GOLDSCHMIDT, Harry. **Musikalische Gestalt und Intonation** [Musical form and intonation], *Beiträge zur Musikwissenschaft* V/4 (1963) 283–90. In German. See no. 470 in this volume.

In order to articulate the aesthetic relation of music to society, Marxist aesthetics has developed the concepts of *gestalt* and *intonacija* as a central concern. The boundary between musical and speech-governed thought is fluid: Thinking in tones and verbal thinking both build on the historical development of socially based consciousness. The maturity of musical art manifests itself in the abundance and distinctiveness of musical thought. *(Donna Arnold)*

5480
as
GRAY, Cecil. **Soggettivismo ed oggettivismo nell'arte musicale** [Subjectivism and objectivism in the musical art], *Atti del sesto Congresso internazionale di musica* (Firenze: Barbèra, 1950) 104–07. In Italian. See no. 291 in this volume.

The best in art embraces both the subjective and the objective and cannot easily be defined. Music is the art form that best embodies the era in which it was created. *(Susan Poliniak)*

5481
as
GREEN, L. Dunton. **Situation actuelle de la critique en Angleterre** [The current situation of criticism in England], *Procès-verbaux et documents* (Praha: Státní Nakladatelství, 1931) 115–20. In French. See no. 183 in this volume.

5482
as
GRIMAUD, Yvette. **Notes on some aesthetic problems of our time,** *Music: East and West* (Tōkyō: conference, 1961) 152–54. See no. 445 in this volume.

Remarks on the issue of renewing musical language.

5483
as
GRIVEAU, Maurice. **Le sens et l'expression de la musique pure** [Meaning and expression of pure music], *Report of the Fourth Congress of the International Musical Society* (London: Novello, 1912) 238–50. *Music, charts, diagr.* In French. See no. 71 in this volume.

Discusses graphic, gestural, and linguistic analogies.

5484
as
HAHN, Kurt. **Johann Kuhnaus *Fundamenta compositionis*** [Johann Kuhnau's *Fundamenta compositionis*], *Bericht über den internationalen musik-*

wissenschaftlichen Kongreß (Kassel: Bärenreiter, 1957) 103–05. In German. See no. 356 in this volume.

The MS treatise (the first part of a collection of four treatises, *D-B* MS Mus.ms.autogr.theor.Kuhnau, that also includes two by Christoph Bernhard and one by Johann Theile) shares a number of elements, including identical passages of text and even musical examples, with Johann Gottfried Walther's *Praecepta der musicalischen Composition* (Weimar 1708), but it was apparently written earlier, in 1703. Kuhnau and Walther may, however, both have been referring to a common source. Errors in the text make it clear that the copyist may have been one of Kuhnau's students but was not Kuhnau himself. *(David Bloom)*

5485 HAMEL, Fred. **Musik und Zeitgeist** [Music and
as zeitgeist], *Musikerziehung: Zeitschrift der Musikerzieher Österreichs* special issue (1953) 28–32. In German. See no. 317 in this volume.

5486 HANDSCHIN, Jacques. **Zur Musikästhetik des**
as **19. Jahrhunderts** [The aesthetics of music of the 19th century], *Société Internationale de Musicologie: Premier Congrès Liège—Compte rendu/Internationale Gesellschaft für Musikwissenschaft: Erster Kongress Lüttich—Kongressbericht/International Society for Musical Research: First Congress Liège: Report* (London: Plainsong and Mediaeval Music Society, 1930) 139. *Bibliog.* In French. See no. 178 in this volume.

Romantic-era music deals with feelings, but essentially maintains Classical form. Musorgskij connected the feelings of the Romantics with objectivity, which led to Romantic realism. Musorgskij's music influenced Stravinsky, who in turn linked the former's ideas to Bach. *(Joan Siegel)*

5487 HARRISON, Lou. **Refreshing the auditory per-**
as **ception,** *Music: East and West* (Tōkyō: conference, 1961) 141–43. See no. 445 in this volume.

Remarks on the issue of renewing musical language in the 20th c.

5488 HARTMANN, H. **Hauptprobleme der**
as **Musikphilosophie** [Principal problems in the philosophy of music], *Actes du XIème Congrès international de philosophie. IX: Philosophie des valeurs—Éthique, esthétique* (Amsterdam: North-Holland Publishing Company, 1953) 271. In German. See no. 321 in this volume.

5489 HERMET, Augusto. **Suono come "mistero"**
as [Sound as "mystery"], *Atti del sesto Congresso internazionale di musica* (Firenze: Barbèra, 1950) 173–75. In Italian. See no. 291 in this volume.

Music is dependent on sound for existence. The essential principle of art is the rendering of the sensible and intelligible as mystery; music works with silence to render sound as mystery. Music operates subjectively through a rigorous system of syntactic norms within traditional models. *(Susan Poliniak)*

5490 HERZ, P. **Das mechanisierte Zeitalter der**
as **Musik** [The mechanized era of music], *Musikerziehung: Zeitschrift der Musikerzieher Österreichs* special issue (1953) 18–21. In German. See no. 317 in this volume.

5491 HICKENLOOPER, Lucie (Olga Samaroff
as Stokowski). **The performer as critic,** *Music and criticism: A symposium* (Cambridge, MA: Harvard University Press, 1948) 73–100. See no. 276 in this volume.

Personal recollections of writing music criticism for one newspaper (the New York *Evening post*) are used to illustrate the critic's role in the larger community. Guidelines for critics are offered, as well as suggestions for improving standards of criticism, including an exchange program whereby critics could rotate among different cities. *(William Gilmore)*

5492 HÜSCHEN, Heinrich. **Frühere und heutige**
as **Begriffe von Wesen und Grenzen der Musik** [Past and present concepts of the nature and limits of music], *Report of the Eighth Congress of the International Musicological Society. I: Papers* (Kassel: Bärenreiter, 1961) 386–98. In German. See no. 439 in this volume.

Surveys Western concepts of music and its functions from ancient Greece to modern times.

5493 HÜSCHEN, Heinrich. **Die Musik im Kreise der**
as **artes liberales** [Music in the sphere of liberal arts], *Bericht über den internationalen musikwissenschaftlichen Kongreß* (Kassel: Bärenreiter, 1957) 117–23. In German. See no. 356 in this volume.

In the tradition of the seven *artes liberales* from antiquity through the mid-16th c., the position of music was ambiguous; it was ranked as one of the speculative/mathematical disciplines of the quadrivium but conceived by many authorities, even in the earliest period, in basically perceptual terms, and later in rhetorical terms, which would make it appear logically part of the trivium. In practice it was gradually emancipated from the framework of the liberal arts altogether, as is seen from the superiority accorded it by both Aquinas and Luther. *(David Bloom)*

5494 ISAACS, Leonard. **The musician in the radio,**
as *Cahiers d'études de radio-télévision* 3-4 (1955) 507–14. See no. 334 in this volume.

Discusses artistic integrity in broadcasting.

5495 JACOBS, Camille. **Some psychological re-**
as **marks concerning the aesthetics of music,** *Actes du cinquième Congrès international d'esthétique/Proceedings of the Fifth International Congress of Aesthetics* ('s-Gravenhage: Mouton, 1964) 760–64. See no. 475 in this volume.

A scientifically valid aesthetics of music should integrate psychological with philosophical foundations. Nico H. Frijda's concept of the *expressive radical* in the expression of feeling through bodily activity provides an interpretation of Julius Bahle's experimental results on the musical expression of emotion; the role of what Adriaan D. de Groot calls *collateral meanings* might be examined through the investigation of program music. *(David Bloom)*

5496 JACOBY, Heinrich. **Voraussetzungen und**
as **Grundlagen einer lebendigen Musikkultur** [Prerequisites and foundations for a living musical culture], *Zeitschrift für Ästhetik und allgemeine Kunstwissenschaft* XIX (1925) 281–337. In German. See no. 114 in this volume.

Provides an introduction to the theory of the musical and unmusical as a category of ordinary experience rather than a specifically artistic concept, with application to general aesthetic and pedagogical problems. *(David Bloom)*

5497 JAKOVLEV, Evgenij Georgievič. **Das**
as **ästhetische Gefühl, das religiöse Erlebnis und ihre Wechselbeziehung an den verschiedenen Kunstarten** [Aesthetic feeling, religious experience, and their interrelationship in different kinds of art], *Actes du cinquième Congrès international d'esthétique/Proceedings of the Fifth International Congress of Aesthetics* ('s-Gravenhage: Mouton, 1964) 826–28. In German. See no. 475 in this volume.

Discusses the dialectic through which the essentially materialist aesthetic emancipates itself from the irrationality of religious faith in the domains of painting, literature, architecture, and music; the last exemplified historically by a general rejection of religious influence as in Beethoven and Musorgskij, or by the adaptation of religious themes to bourgeois realism, as in the Requiems of Mozart, Berlioz, and Verdi. *(David Bloom)*

5498
as
JANSSENS, Arm. J. **Les fonctions psychologiques de la musique selon Aristote** [The psychological functions of music according to Aristotle], *Deuxième congrès international d'esthétique et de Science de l'art* (Paris: Librairie Félix Alcan, 1937) II, 18–22. In French. See no. 249 in this volume.

Aristotle defines four functions for music: biological, moral, aesthetic, and a cathartic function, to be distinguished from that of tragedy. A bibliographical study of his ideas in terms of their sources in earlier Greek philosophy is published as *Aristoteles en de oudere muziekaesthetiek* in *Philologische Studiën* (Leuven) VI, 1934-35. *(Elizabeth A. Wright)*

5499
as
JIRÁNEK, Jaroslav. **About some principal aesthetic problems of further development of musical research**, *Pepragmena tou 4. diethnous synedriou aisthītikīs/Actes du IV Congrès international d'esthétique/Proceedings of the IV International Congress on Aesthetics* (Athínai: conference, 1962) 422–24. See no. 415 in this volume.

The unrepeatable nature of music presents musicology with fundamental epistemological difficulties.

5500
as
JIRÁNEK, Jaroslav. **Einige Schlüsselprobleme der marxistischen Musikwissenschaft im Lichte der Intonation-theorie Assafjews.** [Some key problems of Marxist musicology in the light of Asaf'ev's intonation theory]. Trans. by W. BEYER and A. LANGER, *Intonation und Gestalt in der Musik: Beiträge und Abhandlungen der Musikwissenschaftler sozialistischer Länder* (Moskva: Muzyka, 1963) 56–99. In German. See no. 471 in this volume.

The fundamental methodological task of Marxist musicology is to solve the problem of the relationship between the aesthetic and the social in musical composition. It should aim at the methodological unity of history, theory, and aesthetics. A recognition-theoretical analysis of the phenomenon of intonation as conceptualized by Asaf'ev reveals a complex of specific underlying laws of music. *(David Bloom)*

5501
as
JIRÁNEK, Jaroslav. **Der spezifische Charakter des musikalischen Inhalts in seiner historischgesellschaftlichen Bedingtheit** [The specific character of musical content as determined by socio-historical factors], *Beiträge zur Musikwissenschaft* VII/4 (1965) 343–47. In German. See no. 495 in this volume.

5502
as
JIRÁNEK, Jaroslav. **Zu einigen Grundbegriffen der marxistischen Ästhetik** [Some fundamental concepts of Marxist aesthetics], *Beiträge zur Musikwissenschaft* V/4 (1963) 261–74. In German. See no. 470 in this volume.

A central problem for Marxist musicologists, formulating the relation between, and the unity of, the artistic and the social, has also been confronted by bourgeois scholars, such as Deryck Cooke in *The language of music* (Oxford, 1959). Very little progress has been made in the solution of fundamental problems since Hanslick. *(Donna Arnold)*

5503
as
JOSZ, René; ROCHELLE, Ernest. **Essai d'une théorie de l'évolution de l'art musical, conforme aux conceptions scientifiques modernes de l'évolution** [Attempt at a theory of the evolution of the musical art according to modern scientific conceptions on evolution], *Actes du Congrès d'histoire de l'art* (Paris: Presses Universitaires de France, 1923-1924) 759–73. In French. See no. 94 in this volume.

Eternal nature and mortal human beings are the two creators of form; motion and form are the two characteristics of life and evolution. The evolution of form consists of five stages. It begins with a period of formation,

goes through periods of idealism and individualism, and culminates in a period of materialism. During a back-to-nature period, the cycle starts all over again. *(Vivian Conejero)*

5504
as
KALLENBACH-GRELLER, Lotte. **Die Klangwerte der modernen Musik** [The sound values of modern music], *Bericht über den I. musikwissenschaftlichen Kongress der Deutschen Musikgesellschaft in Leipzig* (Wiesbaden: Breitkopf & Härtel, 1926) 297–303. In German. See no. 120 in this volume.

Schoenberg's atonality is criticized for its lack of true historical development as well as its lack of relationship to the overtone series and to a concept of consonance and dissonance. An abridged version of *Klangwerte der modernen Musik mit einer allgemeinen Einleitung über Musik als Weltanschauung* (Verlag Kahnt, Leipzig). *(William Renwick)*

5505
as
KEUSSLER, Gerhard von. **Rhythmus in der Musik** [Rhythm in music], *Dritter Kongress für Ästhetik und allgemeine Kunstwissenschaft: Bericht* (Stuttgart: Enke, 1927) 270–72. In German. See no. 137 in this volume.

A supplement to the essay abstracted as RILM 5625 in this volume.

5506
as
KEUSSLER, Gerhard von. **Sinnestäuschungen und Musikästhetik** [Illusions and music aesthetics], *Bericht über den I. musikwissenschaftlichen Kongress der Deutschen Musikgesellschaft in Leipzig* (Wiesbaden: Breitkopf & Härtel, 1926) 416. In German. See no. 120 in this volume.

A summary of an article published in *Zeitschrift für Musikwissenschaft* VIII (1925). Music's ability to produce illusory effects—as distinct from hallucinations—is discussed. *(William Renwick)*

5507
as
KICKTON, Erika. **Die Beziehungen der Tonkunst zur Philosophie (Logik, Ethik, und Metaphysik)** [The relation of music to philosophy (logic, ethics, and metaphysics)], *Compte rendu/Kongressbericht/Report* (Basel: Bärenreiter, 1951) 166–71. In German. See no. 289 in this volume.

Offers a broad overview, with attention to the emotions and the mathematical character of cognition.

5508
as
KINKELDEY, Otto. **Consequences of the recorded performance,** *Music and criticism: A symposium* (Cambridge, MA: Harvard University Press, 1948) 115–36. See no. 276 in this volume.

Since music is a temporal art and performances are ephemeral, recordings serve the critic by allowing repeated hearings.

5509
as
KIRCHMEYER, Helmut. **Ein Kapitel Adolf Bernhard Marx: Über Sendungsbewußtsein und Bildungsstand der Berliner Musikkritik zwischen 1824 und 1830** [A chapter of Adolf Bernhard Marx: The sense of mission and the educational attainment of Berlin music critics between 1824 and 1830], *Beiträge zur Geschichte der Musikanschauung im 19. Jahrhundert* (Regensburg: Bosse, 1965) 73–101. In German. See no. 483 in this volume.

Examines Marx's views during his editorship of the *Berliner allgemeine musikalische Zeitung* in their relation to the social and music-historical context of the period. No other periodical of the 19th c.—except in the time around 1848—worked with such intensity on critical issues and the development of a systematic critical stance. *(David Bloom)*

5510
as
KLINKENBERG, Hans Martin. **Der Zerfall des Quadriviums in der Zeit von Boethius bis zu Gerbert von Aurillac** [The disintegration of the quadrivium in the period from Boethius to Gerbert d'Aurillac], *Bericht über den internationalen musik-*

wissenschaftlichen Kongreß (Kassel: Bärenreiter, 1957) 129–33. In German. See no. 356 in this volume.

The system of the *artes liberales* could not survive the 10th-c. change in the understanding of music differentiating it from the other, mathematically oriented disciplines of the quadrivium. A fuller version, with references, is published in Josef Koch, ed., *Artes liberales in der antiken Bildung zur Wissenschaft des Mittelalters* (Leiden: Brill, 1959). *(David Bloom)*

5511 KNEPLER, Georg. **Die Bestimmung des**
as **Begriffes "Romantik"** [The definition of the concept of Romanticism], *The book of the first international musicological congress devoted to the works of Frederick Chopin* (Warszawa: Państwowe Wydawnictwo Naukowe, 1963) 691–95. In German. See no. 425 in this volume.

Chopin, Liszt, and other contemporaries greeted every new musical advance as "Romantic", but it can be seen from a 20th-c. vantage point that Romanticism was not progressive but reactionary, Metternichian, medievalizing and orientalizing, opposed to Enlightenment and to the revolutionary character of early capitalism. Chopin's music is in this sense not Romantic but realistic, as are the works of Schubert and even Schumann. *(David Bloom)*

5512 KRAUSE, Ernst. **Über Versäumnisse der inter-**
as **nationalen Musikkritik/O tom, co mezinárodní hudební kritika zmeškala** [What international music criticism omitted], *Leoš Janáček a soudobá hudba* (Praha: Panton, 1963) 176–81. In German and Czech. See no. 389 in this volume.

Until the first performance of *Její pastorkyňa (Jenůfa)* in Berlin in 1924, the musical world outside the Czech lands paid little attention to Janáček; international music critics failed to recognize the value of Janáček's style. *(Jadranka Važanová)*

5513 KREMLËV, Julij Anatol'evič. **L'importance**
as **mondiale de l'esthétique de Chopin** [The world importance of Chopin's aesthetic], *The book of the first international musicological congress devoted to the works of Frederick Chopin* (Warszawa: Państwowe Wydawnictwo Naukowe, 1963) 696–700. In French. See no. 425 in this volume.

Outlines Chopin's essentially realist aesthetics as communicated through his music: the universal and democratic character of his patriotism, the almost verbal quality of his expressiveness, the synthesis of Romantic and Classic elements. *(Susan Poliniak)*

5514 KREMLËV, Julij Anatol'evič. **Les tendances**
as **réalistes dans l'esthétique de Debussy** [Realist tendencies in Debussy's aesthetic], *Debussy et l'évolution de la musique au XXᵉ siècle* (Paris: Centre National de la Recherche Scientifique [CNRS], 1965) 189–98. In French. See no. 456 in this volume.

Debussy's aesthetics are not simply those of impressionism. Symbolist influences are found in *Pelléas et Mélisande*, and expressionism influenced *La chute de la maison Usher*. Neoclassicism also plays a role in his works, and some commentators find evidence of constructivism, and even surrealism. These seeming contradictions are resolved when his oeuvre is examined in depth. *(Alan Kingsley)*

5515 KROLL, Erwin. **Die Musikkritiken E.T.A.**
as **Hoffmanns** [The music criticism of E.T.A. Hoffmann], *Bericht über den siebenten internationalen musikwissenschaftlichen Kongress* (Kassel: Bärenreiter, 1959) 169–71. In German. See no. 390 in this volume.

A survey of the state of research since the author's dissertation (*E.T.A. Hoffmanns musikalische Anschauungen*, U. Königsberg, 1909) and appreciation of Hoffmann's status as the father of modern criticism, between his teacher Johann Friedrich Reichardt and his follower Robert Schumann. *(David Bloom)*

5516 LACH, Robert. **Mozart und die Gegenwart**
as [Mozart and the present], *Bericht über die musikwissenschaftliche Tagung der Internationalen Stiftung Mozarteum* (Leipzig: Breitkopf & Härtel, 1932) 12–21. In German. See no. 193 in this volume.

In light of a distinction between pathos, expressed aesthetically in terms of content, and ethos, expressed in terms of form, Mozart counts on the side of ethos. Modern humanity turns to the work of Mozart as toward the figure of Parsifal or Siegfried, the childlike genius joyously affirming life and the world. *(David Bloom)*

5517 LALO, Charles. **L'invention artistique** [Artistic
as invention], *Onzième Congrès international de psychologie: Rapports et comptes rendus* (Agen: Imprimerie Moderne, 1938) 293–95. In French. See no. 250 in this volume.

Artistic invention involves the creation of a new complex structure in a heterogeneous milieu; the unity within an artistic creation is of a heterogeneous sort, not that which involves the joining of separate elements. Passion, catharsis, and related states give impulse and direction to creative evolution. *(Susan Poliniak)*

5518 LALO, Charles. **La philosophie de la musique**
as [Philosophy of music], *Rapport sur la musique contemporaine française* (Roma: Armani & Stein, 1913) 117–26. *Bibliog.* In French. See no. 76 in this volume.

Surveys various speculations on the state of musical philosophy in France in the late 19th c.

5519 LALO, Charles. **Sur les valeurs culturelles et**
as **sociales des beaux-arts** [On the cultural and social values of the fine arts], *Deuxième congrès international d'esthétique et de Science de l'art* (Paris: Librairie Félix Alcan, 1937) I, 358–63. In French. See no. 249 in this volume.

All artistic beauty results from the quasi-contrapuntal interplay of voices, parts, sides, which puts them in the same problem-family as games and sports. A general science of art must remain above the confusion of schools differentiated by their views of social functions, from the Romantic treatment of beauty as a religious cult object to the ranking of art by the Classic *honnête homme* as just a little superior to the game of darts, and focus on the strictly aesthetic. *(David Bloom)*

5520 LANG, Hugo. **Musik in göttlicher Ordnung**
as [Music in the divine order], *Musik and Musikerziehung in der Reifezeit* (Mainz: Schott, 1959) 51–60. In German. See no. 412 in this volume.

An Augustinian theology of music recognizes a value in music of all kinds, including contemporary experimental works, as long as it manifests an elementary structure of which the listener can be aware. *(David Bloom)*

5521 LANG, Paul Henry. **The equipment of the musi-**
as **cal journalist,** *Music and criticism: A symposium* (Cambridge, MA: Harvard University Press, 1948) 137–61. See no. 276 in this volume.

Musical journalism is distinguished from music criticism by its emphasis on the recreative as opposed to the creative artist. Both roles require scholarship, practical musical experience, knowledge of musical literature, and independent thought. Alfred Einstein is cited as an example of an outstanding critic. *(William Gilmore)*

5522 LESSONA, Michele. **Il gusto del pubblico e la**
as **musica contemporanea: Funzione educatrice della critica giornalistica** [The public taste and contemporary music: The educational function of journalistic criticism], *Atti del secondo Congresso internazionale di musica* (Firenze: Le Monnier, 1940) 185–93. In Italian; summaries in French and German. See no. 239 in this volume.

Reviewers can educate the public particularly on the subject of contemporary music by means of the interpretive commentary on a work, its appreciation, and a discreet use of comparison with other works, designed to lead the reader from the known to the less known. It would be useful for newspapers to present a kind of preemptive criticism before the first hearing of a new work. *(David Bloom)*

5523
as
LICHTENFELD, Monika. **Gesamtkunstwerk und allgemeine Kunst: Das System der Künste bei Wagner und Hegel** [Gesamtkunstwerk and art in general: The system of the arts in Wagner and Hegel], *Beiträge zur Geschichte der Musikansschauung im 19. Jahrhundert* (Regensburg: Bosse, 1965) 171–77. In German. See no. 483 in this volume.

Though Wagner appears to have known Hegel's philosophy only indirectly, if at all, his idea of a musical realization of the totality of the arts may be regarded as antithetical to—but dependent on—Hegel's ideas. They agree on the essential oneness of art, and on the critique of the one-sidedness of the individual arts, but for Hegel the totality of art resides in the idea, where for Wagner it can be brought into being in the perceptual present of the Gesamtkunstwerk. *(David Bloom)*

5524
as
LISSA, Zofia. **Die Kategorie des Komischen in der Musik** [The category of the comical in music], *Bericht über den siebenten internationalen musikwissenschaftlichen Kongress* (Kassel: Bärenreiter, 1959) 181–83. In German. See no. 390 in this volume.

Contrary to widespread opinion, music is highly capable of a *vis comica*, though only in a relative degree, only in brief phases of larger works, and never so strong as to evoke actual laughter. Three types can be distinguished: an autonomous type, based on the incongruity of strictly musical elements within a structure; a heteronomous type, based on the musical imitation of visually or acoustically incongruous elements such as animal sounds or comical human behavior, often found in stage works; and a complex type, based on the incongruous synchronization of musical and nonmusical elements. Examples for the first two categories are discussed; the third is a relatively new type, made possible by the development of sound film. *(David Bloom)*

5525
as
LISSA, Zofia. **Über die Prozessualität im Musikwerk** [Processuality in the musical work]. Trans. by K. WEINTRAUB, *Intonation und Gestalt in der Musik: Beiträge und Abhandlungen der Musikwissenschaftler sozialistischer Länder* (Moskva: Muzyka, 1963) 348–82. In German. See no. 471 in this volume.

Considers the character of objective time and represented time in relation to the development of musical theories of the reflection of social reality, intonation theory, and gestalt. *(David Bloom)*

5526
as
ŁOBACZEWSKA, Stefania. **Kritika a její vztah k moderní hudbě/La critique et la musique moderne** [Criticism and modern music], *Hudba národů: Sborník přednášek, proslovených na I. mezinárodním sjezdu skladatelů a hudebních kritiků/Musique des nations: Ier Congrès international des compositeurs et critiques musicaux* (Praha: Syndikát Českých Skladatelů, 1948) 41–43,143–45. In Czech and French. See no. 278 in this volume.

The modern music critic should keep the public fully informed on new developments, comment on new works, and form the public's taste. Criticism needs to be informed by the understanding that audiences today are animated by a curiosity to know about everything, with the same intensity as that with which our ancestors around 1830 wanted to be moved.

5527
as
LUALDI, Adriano. **Il mantello della miseria** [The cloak of misery], *Atti del sesto Congresso internazionale di musica* (Firenze: Barbèra, 1950) 166–72. In Italian. See no. 291 in this volume.

Discusses the aesthetics of ugliness as regards mainly post–World War II composers and their works. Music is essentially subjective in nature, and

expresses human sentiment. In considering the act of the cerebral fabrication of an artistic, musical work, however, it is impossible to separate the subjective from the objective. Various opera composers (e.g., Stravinsky, Verdi) are discussed in relation to objectivism and the portrayal of reality. *(Susan Poliniak)*

5528
as
LUCIANI, Sebastiano Arturo. **La musica arte postuma** [Music as a posthumous art], *Atti del secondo Congresso internazionale di musica* (Firenze: Le Monnier, 1940) 42–45. In Italian; summaries in French and German. See no. 239 in this volume.

Preference for the music of the past is based in the nature of musical pleasure itself, which consists, as noted in the *Problemata physica* attributed to Aristotle, more in deepening than in learning, that is in rehearing; music needs aging in order to be appreciated. *(author)*

5529
as
LUSSY, Mathis. **De la culture du sentiment musical** [The cultivation of musical feeling], *Festschrift zum zweiten Kongreß der Internationalen Musikgesellschaft, verfaßt von Mitgliedern der Schweizerischen Landessektion und dem Kongreßteilnehmern* (Basel: Reinhardt, 1906) I, 5–53. In French. See no. 54 in this volume.

The article is also published separately in book form by Heugel (Paris, 1906).

5530
as
LUZZATO, G.L. **Essenza e funzione della critica d'arte** [Essence and function of art criticism], *Congrès international d'histoire de l'art (XIIIème)* (Stockholm: A.B. Hasse, 1933) 249–50. In Italian. See no. 208 in this volume.

5531
as
MACHATIUS, Franz Jochen. ***Eroica*: Das transzendentale Ich** [*Eroica*: The transcendental ego], *Bericht über den internationalen musikwissenschaftlichen Kongreß* (Kassel: Bärenreiter, 1963) 193–96. In German. See no. 452 in this volume.

Discusses Beethoven's style from the symphony no. 3 onward in connection with the transcendental idealism of Johann Gottlieb Fichte (1762-1814).

5532
as
MALIPIERO, Gian Francesco. **La musique comme force anti-esthétique** [Music as an anti-aesthetic force], *Deuxième congrès international d'esthétique et de Science de l'art* (Paris: Librairie Félix Alcan, 1937) II, 464–65. In French. See no. 249 in this volume.

The development of music performance for a paying audience, beginning with the opera in 17th-c. Venice, has come in the 20th c. to have a deleterious effect, with the spread of bad music through loudspeakers in factories and cafés and through phonograph records, radio, and sound films, on the mores and spirituality of Western civilization as a whole. *(David Bloom)*

5533
as
MARÓTHY, János; UJFALUSSY, József; ZOLTAI, Dénes. **Das Verhältnis zwischen ästhetischen und ideologischen Kategorien unter besonderer Berücksichtigung des zeitgenössischen Musikschaffens** [The relation between aesthetic and ideological categories, with particular consideration of contemporary musical creation], *Beiträge zur Musikwissenschaft* VII/4 (1965) 257–77. In German. See no. 495 in this volume.

5534
as
MARSCHNER, Franz. **Wertbegriff als Grundlage der Musikästhetik** [The concept of value as the foundation of musical aesthetics], *Bericht über den zweiten Kongress der Internationalen Musikgesellschaft* (Leipzig: Breitkopf & Härtel, 1907) 86–87. In German. See no. 53 in this volume.

Offers brief programmatic remarks on the notion of value as a mediating principle between the subjective and objective, and between content and form, allowing an aesthetic system that unifies the standpoints of creator, work, and receiver. *(David Bloom)*

5535 MASSENKEIL, Günther. **Bemerkungen zum** **as** ***Compendium musicae (1618) des René Descartes*** [Remarks on René Descartes's *Compendium musicae (1618)*], *Bericht über den siebenten internationalen musikwissenschaftlichen Kongress* (Kassel: Bärenreiter, 1959) 188–91. *Charts, diagr.* In German. See no. 390 in this volume.

Descartes's music treatise, unpublished until after his death in 1650, is derivative of Zarlino, and its use of axiomatic deductive method is not as fully developed as it was to be in his later philosophical and mathematical work. Nevertheless he was the first to treat the beat and sequence of beats in geometrical terms, as analogous to line segments. *(David Bloom)*

5536 MAYER, Günter. **Zur Dialektik des musika-** **as** **lischen Materials** [On the dialectic of musical materials], *Beiträge zur Musikwissenschaft* VII/4 (1965) 363–76. In German. See no. 495 in this volume.

5537 MAZEL', Lev Abramovič. **Über die Entwick-** **as** **lung der Sprache (Ausdrucksmittel) der zeitgenössischen Musik** [On the development of the language (means of expression) of contemporary music], *Beiträge zur Musikwissenschaft* VII/4 (1965) 278–324. In German. See no. 495 in this volume.

5538 MEHTA, R.C. **Music and aesthetics,** *Souvenir on* **as** *Hindustani Music Festival & Seminar* (Hyderabad: Andhra Pradesh Sangeeta Nataka Akademi, 1966) 11–18. See no. 450 in this volume.

Surveys topics in Indian musical aesthetics.

5539 MENDEL, Arthur. **Evidence and explanation,** **as** *Report of the Eighth Congress of the International Musicological Society. II: Reports* (Kassel: Bärenreiter, 1962) 3–18. *Charts, diagr.* See no. 440 in this volume.

Presents a wide-ranging examination of the epistemological questions in historical musicology, of empirical validity, explanatory power, and descriptive thickness in Isaiah Berlin's sense. *(David Bloom)*

5540 MERSMANN, Hans. **Zeit und Musik** [Time and **as** music], *Zeitschrift für Ästhetik und allgemeine Kunstwissenschaft* XXV (supplement 1931) 216–30. In German. See no. 177 in this volume.

5541 MERSMANN, Hans. **Zur Phänomenologie der** **as** **Musik** [The phenomenology of music], *Zeitschrift für Ästhetik und allgemeine Kunstwissenschaft* XIX (1925) 372–98. *Charts, diagr.* In German. See no. 114 in this volume.

Offers a general statement of the viewpoint, object, and analytic technique of a phenomenological (as opposed to psychological) approach to music aesthetics, drawing on a more extended treatment, *Versuch einer Phänomenologie der Musik*, in *Zeitschrift für Musikwissenschaft* V (1922-23). Supporting reports by Gustav BECKING and Helmut PLESSNER are appended. *(David Bloom)*

5542 MILA, Massimo. **Sul carattere inconsapevole** **as** **dell'espressione artistica** [On the unconscious character of artistic expression], *Atti del sesto Congresso internazionale di musica* (Firenze: Barbèra, 1950) 97–103. In Italian. See no. 291 in this volume.

The study of aesthetics is in a critical period right now; there are issues to be addressed regarding the usage of the term objectivity with regard to music.

Expression is the fundamental characteristic of our conception of music; artistic expression is the manifestation of the being who created it. *(Susan Poliniak)*

5543 MILHAUD, Darius. **La tradition** [The tradition], **as** *Atti del terzo Congresso internazionale di musica* (Firenze: Le Monnier, 1940) 89–94. In French; summaries in Italian and German. See no. 256 in this volume.

There is a gap between modern music and audience comprehension. To have meaning, music must be based on tradition.

5544 MILLIET, Paul. **Étant donné l'influence que la** **as** **critique peut exercer sur le développement de l'art musical, n'y a-t-il pas lieu d'émettre un vœu relatif à la manière dont elle s'exerce?** [Given the influence criticism can exercise on the development of the musical art, should not a standard be established with respect to the way it operates?], *Congrès international de musique: Ire session—Exposition Universelle de 1900: Compte rendu, rapports, communications* (Paris: conference, 1901) 15–19. In French. See no. 29 in this volume.

The critic should not attempt to judge new compositions. The profession should be regulated by a competitive system.

5545 MIYAGI, M. **Renewing the musical language:** **as** **An Eastern view,** *Music: East and West* (Tōkyō: conference, 1961) 147–51. See no. 445 in this volume.

5546 MOOS, Paul. **Die Ästhetik des Rhythmus bei** **as** **Theodor Lipps** [The aesthetics of rhythm of Theodor Lipps], *Haydn-Zentenarfeier* (Leipzig: Breitkopf & Härtel; Wien: Artaria, 1909) 345–53. In German. See no. 65 in this volume.

Presents the ideas of the German philosopher. A summary of a subsequent panel discussion is included.

5547 MOOS, Paul. **Beziehungen der jüngsten** **as** **Musikwissenschaft zur Ästhetik** [The relationship of the new musicology to aesthetics], *Bericht über den I. musikwissenschaftlichen Kongress der Deutschen Musikgesellschaft in Leipzig* (Wiesbaden: Breitkopf & Härtel, 1926) 405–15. In German. See no. 120 in this volume.

Discusses the contributions of Manfred F. Bukofzer, Paul Mies, and Ernst Kurth to aesthetics through musicology. Supplementary papers by Hans MERSMANN, who invokes Hugo Riemann, and Hermann ERPF, who discusses music analysis in terms of form, content, and value, are included. *(William Renwick)*

5548 MOOS, Paul. **Hermann Siebeck als Musik-** **as** **ästhetiker** [Hermann Siebeck as aesthetician of music], *Beethoven-Zentenarfeier: Internationaler musikhistorischer Kongress* (Wien: Universal, 1927) 312–16. In German. See no. 142 in this volume.

In his general approach to aesthetics Siebeck (1842-1921) adopted the idealistic concept of the beautiful, based on the representational function in each of the arts and incorporating the concept of aesthetic perception of the unreal. His views on music, given an extended treatment in the author's *Die deutsche Ästhetik der Gegenwart: Versuch einer kritischen Darstellung*, Berlin 1931, are summarized. *(David Bloom)*

5549 MOOS, Paul. **Symbol in der Musik** [Symbol in **as** music], *Dritter Kongress für Ästhetik und allgemeine Kunstwissenschaft: Bericht* (Stuttgart: Enke, 1927) 379f. In German. See no. 137 in this volume.

A supplement to the essay cited as RILM 5584 in this volume.

5550 MOOS, Paul. **Theodor Lipps als Musik-**
as **ästhetiker** [Theodor Lipps as a music aesthetician],
*Bericht über den zweiten Kongress der Internationalen
Musikgesellschaft* (Leipzig: Breitkopf & Härtel, 1907)
87–111. In German. See no. 53 in this volume.

Presents a critical account of the psychologizing aesthetics of Lipps (1851-1914), contrasted with the philosophical approach adopted by Karl Robert Eduard von Hartmann. An extended version forms part of the author's *Die deutsche Ästhetik der Gegenwart: Mit besonderer Berücksichtigung der Musikästhetik* (Berlin: Schuster & Loeffler, 1919). *(David Bloom)*

5551 MOOS, Paul. **Über den gegenwärtigen Stand**
as **der Musikästhetik** [On the present status of music
aesthetics], *Kongress für Ästhetik und allgemeine
Kunstwissenschaft: Bericht* (Stuttgart: Enke, 1914)
416–30. In German. See no. 86 in this volume.

5552 MOOSER, Robert-Aloys. **Le contrôle de la cri-**
as **tique musicale sur les auditions radiopho-**
niques [Music criticism as a way of monitoring radio
programs], *Atti del primo Congresso internazionale di
musica* (Firenze: Le Monnier, 1935) 61–68. In French;
summary in Italian. See no. 203 in this volume.

The music critics of the daily press are in a position to exercise a valuable influence on radio broadcasts, supervising them and directing their efforts, calling questionable activities to the attention of their management, and judging their quality as they do for concerts and theater. *(author)*

5553 MÜLLMAN, Bernd. **Der Musikwissenschaftler**
as **als Redakteur oder Musikkritiker** [The musicologist as editor or music critic], *Bericht über den internationalen musikwissenschaftlichen Kongreß* (Kassel:
Bärenreiter, 1963) 327–28. In German. See no. 452 in
this volume.

Discusses the possibilities of a career in journalism for the young musicologist.

5554 NESTLER, Gerhard. **Über den Begriff der**
as **Mannigfaltigkeit im Einfachen (J.J. Winckel-**
mann) in der Musik der Wiener Klassik [The
concept of multiplicity within the simple (J.J.
Winckelmann) in the music of Viennese Classicism],
*Bericht über den internationalen musikwissenschaft-
lichen Kongreß Wien Mozartjahr 1956* (Graz; Köln:
Böhlau, 1958) 443–46. In German. See no. 365 in this
volume.

The Classicism of Haydn and Mozart, as opposed to that of Gluck, has little to do with notions of a return to the values of classical antiquity; it is better analyzed in terms of Winckelmann's doctrines of simplicity and unity.
(David Bloom)

5555 NOMURA, Francesco Yosio. **On Zen and musi-**
as **cal aesthetics,** *Actes du cinquième Congrès international d'esthétique/Proceedings of the Fifth International Congress of Aesthetics* ('s-Gravenhage: Mouton,
1964) 843–46. See no. 475 in this volume.

Briefly describes the liturgical shōmyō chant (with its accompaniment of bells, drums, wooden gongs, and so on) and the shakuhachi playing (with a function like that of meditation) of the Fuke sect. Aspects of Zen aesthetics that might contribute toward a wider aesthetics of music include the view that the seat of feeling is the abdomen, as opposed to the heart; the rejection of dualism between mind and body, self and non-self; and the eschatological attitude. *(Ronnie Gellis)*

5556 OBERTI, Elisa. **Tecnica e linguaggio musicale**
as [Musical technique and musical language], *Proceedings
of the Third International Congress on Aesthetics/Actes
du troisiéme Congrès international d'esthétique/Atti del
III Congresso internazionale di estetica* (Torino:

Edizioni della Rivista di Estetica, 1957) 642–46. In Italian. See no. 363 in this volume.

Outlines the phenomenological ramifications of the argument that the musical art is a language, documented in sounds that are organized according to specific technical means. *(David Bloom)*

5557 OREL, Alfred. **Mozart in der Kunstanschau-**
as **ung Franz Grillparzers** [Mozart in Franz
Grillparzer's view of art], *Bericht über die musik-
wissenschaftliche Tagung der Internationalen Stiftung
Mozarteum* (Leipzig: Breitkopf & Härtel, 1932) 39–44.
In German. See no. 193 in this volume.

The preeminent Austrian writer Grillparzer (1791-1872) knew and respected Beethoven, but regarded Mozart as the greatest of all composers; he was musically a conservative, and had little understanding of the concept of the Gesamtkunstwerk. A century later, his judgment seems false in several respects, but is consistent with his view that poetry gives a corporal form to the spiritual, music a spiritual form to the sensual. *(David Bloom)*

5558 OREL, Alfred. **Rhythmus in der Musik** [Rhythm
as in music], *Dritter Kongress für Ästhetik und allgemeine
Kunstwissenschaft: Bericht* (Stuttgart: Enke, 1927)
273f. In German. See no. 137 in this volume.

A supplement to the essay cited as RILM 5625 in this volume.

5559 OREL, Alfred. **Zum Begriff der Wiener**
as **Klassik** [The concept of Viennese Classicism], *Beethoven-Zentenarfeier: Internationaler musikhistorischer Kongress* (Wien: Universal, 1927) 29–31. In
German. See no. 142 in this volume.

The music of Haydn, Mozart, and Beethoven shares important technical features and ideas characteristic of the whole of the 18th and early 19th c., but their specific period is to be regarded as one of transition between Classic and Romantic. *(David Bloom)*

5560 PANNAIN, Guido. **Chiarimenti sul concetto di**
as **linguaggio** [Clarifications on the concept of lan-
guage], *Atti del quinto Congresso di musica* (Firenze:
Barbèra, 1948) 115–19. In Italian. See no. 285 in this
volume.

Musical language, a means of expressing and communicating imagination, creativity, and sensitivity, is continuously in a state of flux. At best a manifestation of both emotional and intellectual processes, it is currently pervaded by elements of logic. Since music must be understood on its own terms, the ill-disguised presence of mathematicians, philosophers, and orators among musicians is to be discouraged. Only erudite critics can justly appraise contemporary procedures; musicians must use their natural inclination and imagination in interpreting them. *(Channan Willner)*

5561 PANNAIN, Guido. **La critica e la musica del**
as **passato** [Criticism and music of the past], *Atti del terzo
Congresso internazionale di musica* (Firenze: Le
Monnier, 1940) 16–21. In Italian; summaries in French
and German. See no. 256 in this volume.

Understanding critical responses to older music is essential for modern interpreters.

5562 PANNAIN, Guido. **La critica musicale come**
as **critica d'arte** [Music criticism as art criticism], *Atti
del primo Congresso internazionale di musica* (Firenze:
Le Monnier, 1935) 18–30. In Italian. See no. 203 in this
volume.

Critics must understand a work's technical features to interpret its spiritual aspects. The writings of the theorist Ernst Kurth, the critic Paul Bekker, and the musicologists Ernst Bücken and Heinrich Besseler are examined.
(Lisa Miller)

5563 PANNAIN, Guido. **Il problema del pubblico:**
as **Che cosa è il pubblico—Come si educa il**
pubblico [The problem of the public: What is the pub-

lic? How is the public educated?], *Atti del secondo Congresso internazionale di musica* (Firenze: Le Monnier, 1940) 36–41. In Italian; summaries in French and German. See no. 239 in this volume.

Discusses the importance of criticism in the cultivation of the audience's taste and spiritual capacity.

5564 PARAIN-VIAL, Jeanne. **L'expérience musicale**
as **et l'harmonisation de textes poétiques** [Musical experience and the harmonization of poetic texts], *Proceedings of the Third International Congress on Aesthetics/Actes du troisiéme Congrès international d'esthétique/Atti del III Congresso internazionale di estetica* (Torino: Edizioni della Rivista di Estetica, 1957) 657–59. In French. See no. 363 in this volume.

Whether a given phrase in a Schumann lied, for example, can be objectively experienced constitutes a philosophical problem. Its strictly objective properties (the rhythm and interval properties of the phrase) can only be verified by someone with a specific technical expertise, but the meaning of the phrase, and its resultant emotion, are in no way explained by such an analysis. This argument leads to a fundamentally metaphysical concept of musical experience, which relates to the rich polyvalence existing between text and melody. *(David Bloom)*

5565 PARENTE, Alfredo. **La favola dell'oggetti-**
as **vismo** [The fable of objectivism], *Atti del sesto Congresso internazionale di musica* (Firenze: Barbèra, 1950) 78–86. In Italian. See no. 291 in this volume.

Subjectivity can be a sort of slavery. Objectivism has nothing to do with fantasy; it is in opposition to Romanticism, and carries with it a negative connotation (albeit one good point is that objectivity is synonymous with universalism). One can live a life of sentimentalism or a life of imagination, but not both at once. *(Susan Poliniak)*

5566 PARRY, Charles Hubert Hastings. **The meaning**
as **of ugliness in art,** *Report of the Fourth Congress of the International Musical Society* (London: Novello, 1912) 77–83. See no. 71 in this volume.

Wholesome ugliness is distinguished from the unwholesome variety by its ability to act as an aesthetic challenge.

5567 PENKERT, Anton. **Die musikalische Formung**
as **von Witz und Humor** [The musical forming of wit and humor], *Kongress für Ästhetik und allgemeine Kunstwissenschaft: Bericht* (Stuttgart: Enke, 1914) 482–89. In German. See no. 86 in this volume.

5568 PIOVESAN, Alessandro. **Attualità dell'oggetti-**
as **vismo musicale** [The reality of musical objectivism], *Atti del sesto Congresso internazionale di musica* (Firenze: Barbèra, 1950) 146–52. In Italian. See no. 291 in this volume.

The terms objectivity and subjectivity are in opposition to each other. The issue of whether music suggests or describes is addressed, and Stravinsky's views on the subject are discussed. Objectivism can be seen as a product of intellectual rationalism; the artist should not be reduced to the role of an automaton or a tool that mechanically churns out soulless work. *(Susan Poliniak)*

5569 PRATT, Carroll C. **Schopenhauer's theory of**
as **music,** *Ninth International Congress of Psychology* (Princeton: Psychological Review Company, 1930) 350–51. See no. 160 in this volume.

The will consists almost exclusively of ideas of movements that have been deposited in the memory from previous involuntary actions. Hence music, more nearly than the other arts, may be seen as a copy of the will itself.

5570 PUCELLE, Jean. **L'achèvement des "sympho-**
as **nies inachevées"** [The completion of so-called unfin-

ished symphonies], *Actes du cinquième Congrès international d'esthétique/Proceedings of the Fifth International Congress of Aesthetics* ('s-Gravenhage: Mouton, 1964) 256–59. In French. See no. 475 in this volume.

In the context of a general philosophical discussion of the aesthetic concepts of the finished and the unfinished, musical examples discussed include Mozart's Requiem, Guillaume Lekeu's cello sonata (completed by Vincent d'Indy), and Musorgskij's *Boris Godunov*. *(Ronnie Gellis)*

5571 RATIU, Adrian. **Aspekte der Ausdrucksmittel**
as **im Lichte der Entwicklung der zeitgenös-sischen Musik** [Aspects of expression in light of the development of contemporary music], *Beiträge zur Musikwissenschaft* VII/4 (1965) 337–42. In German. See no. 495 in this volume.

5572 REANEY, Gilbert. *Quid est musica* **in the**
as *Quatuor principalia musicae,* *Bericht über den internationalen musikwissenschaftlichen Kongreß* (Kassel: Bärenreiter, 1957) 177–79. See no. 356 in this volume.

Discusses the classification of music as one of the *artes liberales*, along with other terminology and classificatory issues, in the 13th-c. English treatise *Quatuor principalia musice* (Coussemaker S, iv, 200–298, now attributed to John of Tewkesbury) and its primary source, the *Tractatus de musica* of Magister Lambertus.

5573 REBLING, Eberhard. **Der Rationalismus, eine**
as **Grundlage des Bachschen Realismus** [Rationalism, one of the bases of Bach's realism], *Bericht über die Wissenschaftliche Bachtagung* (Leipzig: Peters, 1951) 420–30. In German. See no. 298 in this volume.

Only a musicology informed by dialectical materialism is capable of providing a scientific and objective account of Bach's greatness. Just as Descartes, Spinoza, and Leibniz prepared the ground for materialistic philosophy, so did Bach, through the brilliant synthesis and progressiveness of his work, open the way to the complete individualization and embourgeoisement of music in the second half of the 18th c. *(David Bloom)*

5574 RIEMANN, Hugo. *Gignomenon* **und** *Gegonos*
as **beim Musikhören** [*Gignomenon* and *gegonos* in hearing music], *Kongress für Ästhetik und allgemeine Kunstwissenschaft: Bericht* (Stuttgart: Enke, 1914) 533–35. In German. See no. 86 in this volume.

5575 RINALDI, Mario. **Dal sentimento individuale**
as **alla realtà di tutti** [From individual sentiment to the reality of all], *Atti del sesto Congresso internazionale di musica* (Firenze: Barbèra, 1950) 107–15. In Italian. See no. 291 in this volume.

Discusses the idea of the language of music as an expression of emotion and how this relates to having a personal style of composition; the notion of the subjectivity or objectivity of music is also examined. Imagination provokes emotion, which in turn provokes the creative impulse. *(Susan Poliniak)*

5576 ROGNONI, Luigi. **Tecnica e linguaggio nella**
as **musica post-weberniana** [Technique and language in post-Webernian music], *Proceedings of the Third International Congress on Aesthetics/Actes du troisiéme Congrès international d'esthétique/Atti del III Congresso internazionale di estetica* (Torino: Edizioni della Rivista di Estetica, 1957) 651–56. In Italian. See no. 363 in this volume.

The need for a so-called return to nature exists only when a dangerous step away from nature has been taken; remounting to the origins of the world of sounds, to the pure perception of the acoustic fact, in the way open to post-Webernian composition in general and especially to electronic music, may be a way of renewing contact with nature. *(David Bloom)*

5577
as
RONGA, Luigi. **Nuove tendenze nella critica musicale europea** [New tendencies in European music criticism], *Atti del primo Congresso internazionale di musica* (Firenze: Le Monnier, 1935) 31–42. In Italian. See no. 203 in this volume.

Reviews the methods and theories of the theorist Ernst Kurth, the critic Paul Bekker, and the musicologists Ernst Bücken and Heinrich Besseler in relation to contempory Italian aesthetics. *(David Bloom)*

5578
as
RONGA, Luigi. **Soggettivismo e oggettivismo nell'espressione musicale** [Subjectivity and objectivity in musical expression], *Atti del sesto Congresso internazionale di musica* (Firenze: Barbèra, 1950) 27–31. In Italian. See no. 291 in this volume.

Romantic aesthetic thought has given back to the artist a sense of creative liberty. The difference between the composer-as-artist and composer-as-artisan is discussed, as are the conditions that should be met for music to be considered objective (e.g., universal meaning and existence on a superior spiritual plane). *(Susan Poliniak)*

5579
as
RUCKMICK, Christian A. **Musical appreciation: A study of the higher emotions,** *Ninth International Congress of Psychology* (Princeton: Psychological Review Company, 1930) 372–73. See no. 160 in this volume.

Aesthetic evaluation in music is composed of three categories: analytic, perceptual, and affective. Since artistic temperament often bases its judgment largely on general feelings, affect is considered to be the most important. *(Ruth Block)*

5580
as
SANBORN, Herbert Charles. **The problem of music,** *Ninth International Congress of Psychology* (Princeton: Psychological Review Company, 1930) 379. See no. 160 in this volume.

In contrast to the Wagnerian focus on emotional communication, Hanslick contends that music consists primarily of formal patterns. Though the artist's and listener's feelings are real, they are aesthetically irrelevant. *(Ruth Block)*

5581
as
SCHAEFER, Hans Joachim. **Zur Ästhetik und Dramaturgie bei Wagner** [Concerning Wagner's aesthetics and dramaturgy], *Kongreß-Bericht: Gesellschaft für Musikforschung* (Kassel; Basel: Bärenreiter, 1950) 192–95. In German. See no. 299 in this volume.

5582
as
SCHENK, Erich. **Ethische Wirkungen der Musik: Ihre Voraussetzungen** [The ethical power of music and its premises], *Musikerziehung: Zeitschrift der Musikerzieher Österreichs* special issue (1953) 37–39. In German. See no. 317 in this volume.

A reprint is cited as RILM [1976]8828.

5583
as
SCHERING, Arnold. **Das Probleme einer Philosophie der Musikgeschichte** [The problem of a philosophy of music history], *Bericht über den musikwissenschaftlichen Kongreß in Basel* (Leipzig: Breitkopf & Härtel, 1925) 311–16. In German. See no. 102 in this volume.

Music's creation of its own world and forms along with its transitory nature ensures its uniqueness, phenomenologically, and makes a philosophy of music history problematic.

5584
as
SCHERING, Arnold. **Symbol in der Musik** [Symbol in music], *Dritter Kongress für Ästhetik und allgemeine Kunstwissenschaft: Bericht* (Stuttgart: Enke, 1927) 379–87. In German. See no. 137 in this volume.

A supplement is cited as RILM 5549 in this volume.

5585
as
SCHERING, Arnold. **Zur Grundlegung der musikalische Hermeneutik** [On the foundation of musical hermeneutics], *Kongress für Ästhetik und allgemeine Kunstwissenschaft: Bericht* (Stuttgart: Enke, 1914) 490–500. In German. See no. 86 in this volume.

5586
as
SCHLOEZER, Boris de. **Comprendre la musique** [Understanding music], *Atti del primo Congresso internazionale di musica* (Firenze: Le Monnier, 1935) 250–58. In French; summary in Italian. See no. 203 in this volume.

Music offers the most complete and pure manifestation of the immanent relation of form to content that characterizes all the arts. The difficulty in defining the meaning of a musical work stems not from vagueness or abstraction but rather from its very concreteness: the content is of the same substance as the expression. To understand a musical work is to grasp the singular unity of a given system of sounds. *(David Bloom)*

5587
as
SCHLOEZER, Boris de. **Expression et création** [Expression and creation], *Atti del sesto Congresso internazionale di musica* (Firenze: Barbèra, 1950) 94–97. In French. See no. 291 in this volume.

Defines the term *expression* as it applies to the conveyance of ideas and the conveyance of emotion, and to how they differ. Music expresses emotions and contains psychological meaning; inexpressive music is an impossibility. *(Susan Poliniak)*

5588
as
SCHLOEZER, Boris de. **La fonction sociale du compositeur** [The social function of the composer], *Atti del secondo Congresso internazionale di musica* (Firenze: Le Monnier, 1940) 9–14. In French; summaries in Italian and German. See no. 239 in this volume.

With the enormous expansion of audiences in the age of the radio and phonograph it might be supposed that the role of the composer would become much more important, but this is not the case; to serve the amorphous and anonymous new public, composers are forced to renounce self-expression. They are reduced to the choice between an arrogant, isolated individualism and a degrading accommodation to a conformism deprived of any moral or religious foundation. *(David Bloom)*

5589
as
SCHNEIDER, Marius. **Vom ursprünglichen Sinn der Musik** [The original meaning of music], *Compte rendu/Kongressbericht/Report* (Basel: Bärenreiter, 1951) 183–84. *Bibliog.* In German. See no. 289 in this volume.

Offers a philosophical interpretation of the symbolism in the Vedic myth of the origin of music.

5590
as
SCHRADE, Leo. **Mozart und die Romantiker** [Mozart and the Romantics], *Bericht über die musikwissenschaftliche Tagung der Internationalen Stiftung Mozarteum* (Leipzig: Breitkopf & Härtel, 1932) 22–38. In German. See no. 193 in this volume.

In the first decade of the 19th c., German writers of the Romantic school, starting with Mozart's operas and then considering his instrumental works, began to develop an interpretation of Mozart's music as Romantic; as E.T.A. Hoffmann said, with some justice, Mozart can only be understood from a Romantic point of view. *(David Bloom)*

5591
as
SCHUELLER, Herbert M. **Artistic greatness as content-material relationship,** *Actes du cinquième Congrès international d'esthétique/Proceedings of the Fifth International Congress of Aesthetics* ('s-Gravenhage: Mouton, 1964) 470–73. See no. 475 in this volume.

The concept of greatness as the outcome of a struggle between the content of a work and its material expression is illustrated by works of poetry, film, sculpture, and music, including Mozart's *Don Giovanni* and Beethoven's "Hammerklavier" sonata, op. 106. *(David Bloom)*

5592 SEIDL, Arthur. **Hermann Abert: Die**
as **spätantike Musikästhetik und ihre Bedeutung für das Mittelalter** [Hermann Abert: The musical aesthetics of late antiquity and its significance for the Middle Ages], *Bericht über den zweiten Kongress der Internationalen Musikgesellschaft* (Leipzig: Breitkopf & Härtel, 1907) 128–29. In German. See no. 53 in this volume.

Summary of Abert's conference paper on the influence of neo-Pythagorean, Judeo-Alexandrian, and Neoplatonic thinking on the musical attitudes of early Christianity. A full account of Abert's views is published in his *Die Musikanschauung des Mittelalters und ihre Grundlagen* (Halle, 1904). *(David Bloom)*

5593 SELNER, John C. **Sacred music and art,** *Atti del*
as *[I] Congresso internazionale di musica sacra* (Tournai: Desclée, 1952) 411–15. See no. 303 in this volume.

5594 SERAUKY, Walter. **Vorläufer in der euro-**
as **päischen Musikgeschichte und Musikästhetik zu Janáčeks Sprachmelodie/Předchůdci Janáčkových "nápěvků" v evropských hudebních dějinách a hudební estetice** [The predecessors of Janáček's speech melodies in European history and aesthetics of music], *Leoš Janáček a soudobá hudba* (Praha: Panton, 1963) 267–74. In German and Czech. See no. 389 in this volume.

The writings of Jean-Jacques Rousseau, Johann Gottfried Herder, Wagner, Herbert Spencer, and Musorgskij anticipate Janáček's theory of speech melody (*nápěvek*); nevertheless, Janáček was the first composer to study melodic aspects of speech systematically and apply the results to music-dramatic works. *(Jadranka Važanová)*

5595 SERAUKY, Walter. **W.A. Mozart und die**
as **Musikästhetik des ausklingenden 18. und frühen 19. Jahrhunderts** [W.A. Mozart and the musical aesthetics of the late 18th and early 19th centuries], *Bericht über den internationalen musikwissenschaftlichen Kongreß Wien Mozartjahr 1956* (Graz; Köln: Böhlau, 1958) 579–85. In German. See no. 365 in this volume.

Surveys Mozart criticism by the writers of his time, including Heinrich Boßler (1744-1812), Carl Friedrich Cramer (1752-1807), Johann Friedrich Reichardt (1752-1814), Christian Friedrich Daniel Schubart (1739-91), Wilhelm Heinrich Wackenroder (1773-98), and Johann Friedrich Rochlitz (1769-1842). *(David Bloom)*

5596 SESSIONS, Roger. **The scope of music criti-**
as **cism,** *Music and criticism: A symposium* (Cambridge, MA: Harvard University Press, 1948) 35–52. See no. 276 in this volume.

In order to have a living relationship with the products of other times and places, the critic must first understand his or her own musical time and place. With this understanding, a critic's primary concern must be the work itself; any other frames of reference are secondary. *(William Gilmore)*

5597 SIEBECK, Hermann. **Über musikalische**
as **Einfühlung** [On musical empathy], *Bericht über den I. Kongress für Experimentelle Psychologie* (Leipzig: Barth, 1904) 93. In German. See no. 44 in this volume.

5598 SIMONETTI, A. **Il linguaggio della musica** [The
as language of music], *7° Congresso di musica sacra* (Torino: author, 1905) 70–76. In Italian. See no. 52 in this volume.

Offers an overview of the development of the aesthetics of music, with references to the ideals of Wagner and the principles of other composers and aestheticians. *(André Balog)*

5599 ŠKRBIĆ, Milan. **Problem vrednovanja**
as **partizanske narodne pjesme** [The problem of evaluating Partisan folk song], *Rad VIII-og kongresa folklorista Jugoslavije* (Beograd: Naučno Delo, 1961) 307–08. In Croatian; summary in German. See no. 446 in this volume.

Partisan song arose spontaneously, without regard to questions of artistic value. It nevertheless frequently attains pure beauty, in its concise, original expression. It is a duty to discover, through objective analysis, the lasting value of some of the poems. *(author)*

5600 SÖHNGEN, Oskar. **Musik und Theologie** [Mu-
as sic and theology], *Kirchenmusik in ökumenischer Schau* (Bern: Haupt, 1964) 15–21. In German. See no. 447 in this volume.

The relationship between music and theology has historically taken three forms: a cosmological form, based on the discoveries attributed to Pythagoras; a pragmatic form, concerned with the effects of music, especially in the liturgical context, on the state of the soul; and an aesthetic form, developed by Luther, inspired by wonder at music's beauty and apparent meaningfulness. A theology of music following Luther's conception is sketched. *(David Bloom)*

5601 SOURIAU, Étienne. **Art et innovation** [Art and
as innovation], *Actes du cinquième Congrès international d'esthétique/Proceedings of the Fifth International Congress of Aesthetics* ('s-Gravenhage: Mouton, 1964) 25–32. In French. See no. 475 in this volume.

Presents philosophical reflections on the concepts of innovation and modernity, drawing on ideas of Plato, Baruch Spinoza, Eugène Delacroix, Charles Baudelaire, and Henri Bergson, and including references to movements of the musical avant-garde from Monteverdi through Webern and Messiaen.

5602 SOURIS, André. **Poétique musicale de Debussy**
as [Musical poetics of Debussy], *Debussy et l'évolution de la musique au XXᵉ siècle* (Paris: Centre National de la Recherche Scientifique [CNRS], 1965) 133–40. In French. See no. 456 in this volume.

Maurice Merleau-Ponty undertook a philosophical analysis of the works of Mallarmé and Cézanne. For a similar analysis of Debussy, the complexities of his music must be examined. Some guidelines and definitions must be found to discuss topics such as intervals and form. A traditional analysis will not work, since the various musical elements must not be separated from their context. *(Alan Kingsley)*

5603 SPRINGER, Hermann. **Beethoven und die**
as **Musikkritik** [Beethoven and music criticism], *Beethoven-Zentenarfeier: Internationaler musikhistorischer Kongress* (Wien: Universal, 1927) 32–34. In German. See no. 142 in this volume.

Contemporary critics who showed an ability to understand Beethoven's music included E.T.A. Hoffmann, the somewhat limited Amadeus Wendt, and Adolf Bernhard Marx. *(David Bloom)*

5604 STARZYŃSKI, Juliusz. **Chopin—Delacroix:**
as **Comparaison d'esthétique** [Chopin and Delacroix: An aesthetic comparison], *The book of the first international musicological congress devoted to the works of Frederick Chopin* (Warszawa: Państwowe Wydawnictwo Naukowe, 1963) 725–31. In French. See no. 425 in this volume.

Delacroix was an informed and enthusiastic admirer of the music of his friend Chopin; Chopin is said to have been signally insensitive to Delacroix as a painter, but this judgment comes largely from the testimony of George Sand, which is not free of malice. Other evidence suggests that Chopin was interested in painting in general, and the work of Delacroix in particular, especially toward the end of his life. They shared an understanding of the work of art that was neither Classic nor Romantic, but based on the independence and integrity of the work's internal logic. *(Susan Poliniak)*

5605
as
STICHTENOTH, Friedrich. **Der Gesang in der Kritik der Tagespresse** [Singing in criticism in the daily press], *Bericht über den Internationalen Kongreß Singen und Sprechen* (München: Oldenbourg, 1938) 322–26. In German. See no. 257 in this volume.

The relativity of critical criteria (which apply differently in different situations), the vagueness of technical terminology, and the attitude of readers all make vocal music more prone to critical misinterpretation than instrumental music. There can be no single curriculum for the critic's training, which must bring together endlessly different and often completely unrelated experiences. *(David Bloom)*

5606
as
STUCKENSCHMIDT, Hans Heinz, moderator. **Discussion: Music and listener,** *Music: East and West* (Tōkyō: conference, 1961) 183–201. See no. 445 in this volume.

5607
as
SYCHRA, Antonín. **About the problematic of experimental research of musical contents,** *Pepragmena tou 4. diethnous synedriou aisthītikīs/ Actes du IV Congrès international d'esthétique/Proceedings of the IV International Congress on Aesthetics* (Athínai: conference, 1962) 435–39. See no. 415 in this volume.

Offers a critique of Leonard B. Meyer's theory of musical meaning. Examples are drawn from Janáček's treatment of speech rhythm in *Jenůfa*.

5608
as
SYCHRA, Antonín. **Hudební estetika a kritika/Esthétique et critique musicale** [Aesthetics and music criticism], *Hudba národů: Sborník přednášek, proslovených na I. mezinárodním sjezdu skladatelů a hudebních kritiků/Musique des nations: Ier Congrès international des compositeurs et critiques musicaux* (Praha: Syndikát Českých Skladatelů, 1948) 69–74,174–79. In Czech and French. See no. 278 in this volume.

Criticism makes the connection between art and social conditions, between art and musicological scholarship, and most importantly between the artwork and the audience. It relies on musicology for facts, but should not expect science to provide one general formula to account for the problems of artistic creation and judgment.

5609
as
SYCHRA, Antonín. **Zur Problemstellung unseres Seminars** [Formulating the problem of our seminar], *Beiträge zur Musikwissenschaft* V/4 (1963) 245–61. In German. See no. 470 in this volume.

In connection with the current sharpening of ideological battles, art-historical and consequently music-historical questions are moving to the center of public interest. Marxist science is sometimes presented as merely the application of an already given doctrine, but the door has been opened to modern searching and experimentation; understanding Marxism as a process, we no longer slight pre-Marxist and non-Marxist traditions. *(Donna Arnold)*

5610
as
TATARKIEWICZ, Władysław. **Prądy filozoficzne epoki Chopina** [Philosophical currents of Chopin's time], *The book of the first international musicological congress devoted to the works of Frederick Chopin* (Warszawa: Państwowe Wydawnictwo Naukowe, 1963) 735–37. In Polish. See no. 425 in this volume.

5611
as
TEESING, Hubert Paul Hans. **Probleme der kunstwissenschaftlichen Wertung** [Problems of evaluation in the study of the arts], *Actes du cinquième Congrès international d'esthétique/Proceedings of the Fifth International Congress of Aesthetics* ('s-Gravenhage: Mouton, 1964) 486–91. In German. See no. 475 in this volume.

Addresses particularly the difficulty of establishing standards that apply to a very heterogeneous body of work (as in the confrontation, among others, of Classic and modern or of Eastern and Western musics), appealing to Roman Ingarden's theory of value and to general notions of mimesis and harmony. A system of values must be open, susceptible to change, as each generation writes its own art history. *(David Bloom)*

5612
as
THOMSON, Virgil. **The art of judging music,** *Music and criticism: A symposium* (Cambridge, MA: Harvard University Press, 1948) 101–13. See no. 276 in this volume.

Discusses the methods and responsibilities of a professional music critic. A three-stage procedure is suggested to ensure fair judgment: listening, score analysis, and reflection. *(William Gilmore)*

5613
as
THOMSON, Virgil. **The philosophy of style,** *Music: East and West* (Tōkyō: conference, 1961) 144–46. See no. 445 in this volume.

Remarks on the issue of renewing musical language in the 20th c.

5614
as
TOMESCU, Vasile. **Beiträge zur dialektischen Behandlung der musikästhetischen Probleme** [Contributions to the dialectic handling of music-aesthetic problems], *Beiträge zur Musikwissenschaft* VII/4 (1965) 347–50. In German. See no. 495 in this volume.

5615
as
TORREFRANCA, Fausto. **Ciò ch'è vivo nella musica del passato** [What is alive in the music of the past], *Atti del secondo Congresso internazionale di musica* (Firenze: Le Monnier, 1940) 195–205. In Italian; summaries in French and German. See no. 239 in this volume.

Considers the question of what has survived from the Italian tradition beginning with the Camerata Fiorentina in the 16th c. Opera has been the subject of much empty controversy, and is currently in a somewhat sleepy state. Sacred music, in a continuing tradition from the 17th c., is less in need of renewal than of an inner strengthening, which will have to originate in a strengthening of religiosity itself. The 18th-c. Italian tradition of instrumental music involves the renewal of expressive means in the directions of architectonic order, melodic inflection, and harmonic-contrapuntal substance, and eventually the enrichment of instrumental color. *(David Bloom)*

5616
as
TORREFRANCA, Fausto. **Grecia e Occidente: Valor cristiano della polifonia** [Greece and the West: The Christian value of polyphony], *Atti del [I] Congresso internazionale di musica sacra* (Tournai: Desclée, 1952) 330–35. In Italian. See no. 303 in this volume.

5617
as
TORREFRANCA, Fausto. **L'intuizione musicale quale sintesi a priori estetica** [Musical intuition as a priori aesthetic synthesis], *Atti del IV Congresso internazionale di filosofia* (Genova: A.F. Formíggini, 1911) III, 513–21. In Italian. See no. 69 in this volume.

Discusses the relation of music to intuition and spiritual harmony, with references to Kant, Croce, Leibniz, and Bergson. Music is an atypical, a-logical art. *(David Nussenbaum)*

5618
as
TROJAN, Jan. **O některých otázkách teorie a estetiky hubdební interpretace** [On some aspects of theory and aesthetics of music interpretation], *Sborník Janáčkovy Akademie Múzichých Umeni* V (1965) 7–15. In Czech. See no. 496 in this volume.

5619
as
UJFALUSSY, József. **Zur Dialektik des Wirklichkeitsbildes in der Musik** [The dialectics of the representation of reality in music], *Beiträge zur*

Musikwissenschaft V/4 (1963) 275–82. In German. See no. 470 in this volume.

Is the application of technical terminology for materialistic cognitive theory also warranted for music? Underlying this issue is one of the basic dilemmas of Marxist aesthetics. Either music is an art, art is a method of cognition, and in this trap the reflection of reality in music is a copy; or in music there exists no copy, no reflection of reality, and in this trap either music is no art or art has nothing to do with cognition. Application of the scientific terms *picture*, *copy*, *gestalt* in the aesthetic, gnoseological sense is justified for music, but not for literature and the visual arts. *(Donna Arnold)*

5620
as

VALENSI, Henry. **De l'art de la musique et de l'art abstrait** [The art of music and abstract art], *Proceedings of the Third International Congress on Aesthetics/Actes du troisiéme Congrès international d'esthétique/Atti del III Congresso internazionale di estetica* (Torino: Edizioni della Rivista di Estetica, 1957) 638–41. In French. See no. 363 in this volume.

What is commonly called *abstract* art might better be called *musicalized* art, avoiding the confused opposition between the abstract and reality. Music and abstraction have in common their constructivism, foundation in the scientific spirit, subjectivity, and psychological rhythmicality. *(David Bloom)*

5621
as

VUILLERMOZ, Émile. **Les responsabilités de la critique** [The responsibilities of criticism], *Atti del secondo Congresso internazionale di musica* (Firenze: Le Monnier, 1940) 180–85. In French; summaries in Italian and German. See no. 239 in this volume.

The daily press bears some blame for the gulf that exists between contemporary composers and the audience, in its employment of critics who lack a technical knowledge of the foundations of music and in insisting that reviews be short and hurried in tone. *(David Bloom)*

5622
as

VYSLOUŽIL, Jiří. **Janáček jako kritik** [Janáček as critic], *Leoš Janáček a soudobá hudba* (Praha: Panton, 1963) 377–80. In Czech; summaries in Russian and German. See no. 389 in this volume.

In 1884, the Družstvo Českého Národního Divadla (Society for a Czech National Theater) inaugurated Brno's first permanent professional Czech-language theater in the Prozatímní Divadlo (Provisional Theater), and Janáček began publishing the journal *Hudební listy* (1884-88) specifically to review its opera productions. As a music critic, he had significant influence on the new theater's growth and artistic direction. *(editors)*

5623
as

WAGNER, Peter. **Ästhetik des gregorianischen Gesanges** [The aesthetics of Gregorian chant], *Bericht über den Deutschen Kongreß für Kirchenmusik* (Kassel: Bärenreiter, 1928) 71–80. In German. See no. 135 in this volume.

The artistic quality of chant in its context in the celebration of the High Mass is derived from its origins in synagogal psalmody, notable in the variety of structural uses of repetition and alternation, the feature of melodic rhyme, and the modern-sounding modal scales and free rhythms. *(David Bloom)*

5624
as

WALKER, Daniel Pickering. **Le chant orphique de Marsile Ficin** [The Orphic songs of Marsilio Ficino], *Musique et poésie au XVIᵉ siècle* (Paris: Centre National de la Recherche Scientifique [CNRS], 1954) 17–33. In French. See no. 326 in this volume.

The neo-Platonist Florentine philosopher (1433-99) was known for his singing of Orphic hymns. Relationships among the affections doctrine, Platonic theory, and ancient religious beliefs are explored.

5625
as

WALTERSHAUSEN, Hermann Wolfgang von. **Rhythmus in der Musik** [Rhythm in music], *Dritter Kongress für Ästhetik und allgemeine Kunstwissenschaft: Bericht* (Stuttgart: Enke, 1927) 260–70. In German. See no. 137 in this volume.

Supplements are cited as RILM 5505 and RILM 5558 in this volume.

5626
as

WARSCHAUER, Frank. **Kritik neuer Gebiete** [Criticism of new areas], *Procès-verbaux et documents* (Praha: Státní Nakladatelství, 1931) 152–63. In German. See no. 183 in this volume.

⟶

WELCH, Roy Dickinson. **The bearing of aesthetics and criticism on musicology.** See no. 930 in this volume.

5627
as

WELLEK, Albert. **Die ganzheitpsychologischen Aspekte der Musikästhetik** [Musical aesthetics in light of holistic psychology], *Bericht über den internationalen musikwissenschaftlichen Kongreß Wien Mozartjahr 1956* (Graz; Köln: Böhlau, 1958) 678–88. In German. See no. 365 in this volume.

The distinction between formal and expressive aesthetic orientations is a false one; a synthetic aesthetics of form and expression as a single gestalt is needed. Strict atonality, 12-tone and 24-tone serialism, tempered quarter-tones, and the principle of nonrepetition are all unsustainable on psychological grounds. *(author)*

5628
as

WERNER, Eric. **Present and past concepts of the nature and limits of music,** *Report of the Eighth Congress of the International Musicological Society. II: Reports* (Kassel: Bärenreiter, 1962) 158–62. See no. 440 in this volume.

A report on a discussion by Milton BABBITT, Jacques CHAILLEY, Hans-Heinz DRAEGER, Karl Gustav FELLERER, Allen FORTE, Heinrich HÜSCHEN, Zofia LISSA, Leonart B. MEYER, Hans-Peter REINECKE, Charles SEEGER, Fritz WINCKEL, and Walter WIORA of papers by Hüschen and Babbitt abstracted as RILM 5492 and RILM 3930, respectively, in this volume.

5629
as

WIND, Edgar. **The critical nature of a work of art,** *Music and criticism: A symposium* (Cambridge, MA: Harvard University Press, 1948) 53–72. See no. 276 in this volume.

Plato's view of art is rational: Because of its transformative power, it is to be worshiped, feared, and ultimately controlled. Although nobody possesses the omniscience Plato felt would be necessary to regulate art responsibly, the critic is best qualified for the task in the modern world. Furthermore, an open dialogue among critics, the public, and artists themselves would create a self-correcting system.

5630
as

WITASEK, Stephan. **Zur allgemeinen Analyse des musikalischen Genusses** [Toward a general analysis of musical pleasure], *Bericht über den zweiten Kongress der Internationalen Musikgesellschaft* (Leipzig: Breitkopf & Härtel, 1907) 111–28. In German. See no. 53 in this volume.

Outlines the application to music of the author's theory of general aesthetics as published in *Grundzüge der allgemeinen Ästhetik* (Leipzig: Barth, 1904). The state of pleasure induced by music is predicated on the association between the perception of the musical structures and the fantasy feelings that the musical structures call forth; there is no need to bring metaphysical ideas into the analysis. *(David Bloom)*

5631
as

WITESCHNIK, Alexander. **Musik und Ethos** [Music and ethos], *Musikerziehung: Zeitschrift der Musikerzieher Österreichs* special issue (1953) 43–45. In German. See no. 317 in this volume.

5632
as

WOLFF, Hellmuth Christian. **Palestrina und Schönberg: Zwei Extreme der europäischen Musik** [Palestrina and Schoenberg: Two extremes of European music], *Bericht über den internationalen musikwissenschaftlichen Kongreß Wien Mozartjahr 1956* (Graz; Köln: Böhlau, 1958) 749–53. In German. See no. 365 in this volume.

Contrasts between the two composers in aesthetic orientation, compositional technique, and personality are drawn in terms inspired by Eduard Spranger's psychology of types. *(David Bloom)*

5633
as
XENAKIS, Iannis. **Stochastic music,** *Music: East and West* (Tōkyō: conference, 1961) 134–40. See no. 445 in this volume.

Remarks on the question of renewing musical language in the 20th c.

5634
as
ZAFRED, Mario. **Contributo ad una critica di alcune posizioni formalistiche** [Toward a critique of formalistic positions], *Atti del sesto Congresso internazionale di musica* (Firenze: Barbèra, 1950) 87–93. In Italian. See no. 291 in this volume.

Discusses the difference between subjectivity and objectivity regarding musical expression and composition itself, freedom (i.e., of composition and technique) in musical art, and 12-tone systems. *(Susan Poliniak)*

82 Psychology and hearing

5635
as
ALBERSHEIM, Gerhard. **The present state of music psychology and its significance for historical musicology,** *Report of the Eighth Congress of the International Musicological Society. II: Reports* (Kassel: Bärenreiter, 1962) 88–92. In English and German. See no. 440 in this volume.

A report on a discussion by Gerhard ALBERSHEIM, Rudolf ARNHEIM, Carl DALHAUS, Hans-Heinz DRAEGER, Heinrich HUSMANN, Zofia LISSA, Carroll C. PRATT, Antonín SYCHRA, Albert WELLEK, and Fritz WINCKEL of the paper by Wellek abstracted as RILM 5717 in this volume.

5636
as
BAHLE, Julius. **Gefühl und Wille im musikalischen Schaffen** [Feeling and will in musical creation], *Gefühl und Wille: Bericht über den XV. Kongress der Deutschen Gesellschaft für Psychologie* (Jena: Fischer, 1937) 194–96. In German. See no. 231 in this volume.

Presents a schematic outline of the role of emotion and will in an experimentally based account of the psychology of composition, drawing on ideas of environmental and internal stimulus and the influence of the working process itself, in opposition to Hans Pfitzner's theory of ex nihilo inspiration. An extended version is published in the journal *Industrielle Psychotechnik*, July 1936, and a complete account in the author's *Der musikalische Schaffensprozeß* (Leipzig: S. Hirzel, 1936). *(David Bloom)*

5637
as
BAHLE, Julius. **Die Gestaltübertragung im vokalen Schaffen zeitgenössischer Komponisten** [Shape translation in the vocal work of contemporary composers], *Bericht über den XIII. Kongress der Deutschen Gesellschaft für Psychologie* (Jena: Fischer, 1934) 112–32. In German. See no. 207 in this volume.

5638
as
BAHLE, Julius. **Konstruktiver Arbeitstypus und Inspirationstypus im Schaffen der Komponisten** [The constructive working type and the inspirational type in composers' creativity], *Onzième Congrès international de psychologie: Rapports et comptes rendus* (Agen: Imprimerie Moderne, 1938) 285–86. In German. See no. 250 in this volume.

Proposes a basic division of composers' psychological styles into the working type (analogous to Jung's introverted personality type), focused on the conditions of creation, and the inspirational type (analogous to Jung's extraverted type), focused on the end product. *(David Bloom)*

5639
as
BAHLE, Julius. **Persönlichkeit und Kunstwerk im zeitgenössischen Musikschaffen: Ein psychologisch-pädagogischer Beitrag zum Verständnis neuer Musik** [Personality and the work of art in contemporary composition: A psychological and pedagogical contribution to the understanding of new music], *Psychologie des Gemeinschaftslebens: Bericht über den XIV. Kongress der Deutschen Gesellschaft für Psychologie* (Jena: Fischer, 1935) 315–25. In German. See no. 219 in this volume.

5640
as
BEATTY, R.T. **The sensation of pitch in listening to vibrato singing,** *Bericht über die I. Tagung der Internationalen Gesellschaft für Experimentelle Phonetik* (Bonn: Scheur, 1930) 15–16. See no. 169 in this volume.

The pitch variation in vibrato singing, which may amount to as much as a semitone, is experienced by the listener as an intensity variation. A mathematical model is proposed to account for the fact. *(L. Poundie Burstein)*

5641
as
BIMBERG, Siegfried. **Die Polarität bei der Rezeption der Tonalitäten** [Polarity in the perception of tonalities], *Bericht über den internationalen musikwissenschaftlichen Kongreß Wien Mozartjahr 1956* (Graz; Köln: Böhlau, 1958) 55–59. *Music, charts, diagr.* In German. See no. 365 in this volume.

From 1950 to 1954 the Institut für Musikwissenschaft und Musikerziehung of the University of Halle tested children in the first through eighth years of school in their perception of and ability to sing in major and minor keys. The concept of polarity was found not to be symbolic (i.e., the association of dark with minor and light with major) but is based on different leading-tone tendencies.

5642
as
BIMBERG, Siegfried. **Die variable Reagenz des musikalischen Hörens** [Variable reagency in musical hearing], *Bericht über den internationalen musikwissenschaftlichen Kongreß* (Kassel: Bärenreiter, 1957) 58–59. In German. See no. 356 in this volume.

Groups of singers trained in tonal and modal traditions were tested for their deviation from a theoretical tuning model. The character of the music itself played the determining role in the results, while singers' tradition was a conditioning factor. *(David Bloom)*

5643
as
BRENCHER, Karl-Eckhardt. **Zur Farbe-Ton-Forschung** [Concerning research in color-sound relationships], *Kongreß-Bericht: Gesellschaft für Musikforschung* (Kassel; Basel: Bärenreiter, 1950) 187–89. In German. See no. 299 in this volume.

Investigates the extent to which color-sound associations contribute to the capacity for visual memories in the blind.

5644
as
BRILLOUIN, Jacques. **Réflexions sur les problèmes dits d'acoustique musicale** [Reflections on the so-called problems of musical acoustics], *Acoustique musicale* (Paris: Centre National de la Recherche Scientifique [CNRS], 1959) 75–82. *Music.* In French. See no. 393 in this volume.

Music is organized in a psychological world of two dimensions: duration and pitch. Each type of music proposes a way of exploring this world, on an itinerary characterized by a kind of fundamental function which may assign preeminence to duration or to pitch but always includes both. To cut music up into segments, whether horizontal or vertical, is to destroy it. *(author)*

5645
as
CALVOCORESSI, Michel D. **Psychophysiology: The true road to necessary reforms in musical aesthetics,** *Report of the Fourth Congress of the International Musical Society* (London: Novello, 1912) 224–27. See no. 71 in this volume.

Modern research refutes the theory that music is the only truly abstract art; rather, it demonstrates the physiological basis of music. Writers on music and on psychophysiology should cooperate to supply the missing aesthetic link. *(Mei-Mei Meng)*

5646 CANAC, François. **Les éléments de formation**
as **des échelles extérieurs à la résonance: Les facteurs de consonance** [Elements of scale formation external to overtones: Factors of consonance], *La résonance dans les échelles musicales* (Paris: Centre National de la Recherche Scientifique [CNRS], 1963) 199–205. In French; summaries in English and German. See no. 420 in this volume.
Consonance factors may be classified into two groups. First are those closely linked to the source, being perceived by the brain as a nondeformed image of that which is received by the ear. The brain thereby discerns certain relations different from those produced by noise. Second are those linked to the operation of the ear, independent of aesthetic sensations. These modify reception and are mainly of a physiological nature. *(author)*

5647 CHIARUCCI, Henri; FERREYRA, B.; REIBEL,
as Guy; RIST, S. **Rapport entre la hauteur et le fondamental d'un son musical** [Relation between the pitch and the fundamental of a musical sound], *Problèmes d'acoustique* (Liège: Université de Liège, 1965) M53. *Illus.* In French. See no. 504 in this volume.
Summarizes new information on pitch perception and its relationship to acoustical considerations.

5648 COGNI, Giulio. **Grundzüge einer neuen**
as **Musikpsychologie** [Foundations of a new psychology of music], *Bericht über den internationalen musikwissenschaftlichen Kongreß Wien Mozartjahr 1956* (Graz; Köln: Böhlau, 1958) 99–102. In German. See no. 365 in this volume.
Summarizes key concepts from the author's *Che cosa è la musica?— Elementi di psicologia della musica* (Milan, 1956).

5649 COLLAER, Paul. **État actuel des connaissances**
as **relatives à la perception auditive, à l'émission vocale et à la mémoire musicale: Conséquences relatives à la notation** [The current state of knowledge about auditory perception, vocal production, and musical memory: Consequences for notation], *Les colloques de Wégimont. [I: Ethnomusicologie I]* (Bruxelles: Elsevier, 1956) 37–55. *Bibliog., charts, diagr.* In French. See no. 340 in this volume.
Precise pitches and small intervals (e.g., half steps) are characteristic of music in advanced cultures. The smallest intervals appear at low intensity and in higher frequencies, as in the music of Gypsy violinists and flamenco singers. Vibrato (pitch fluctuation) is similarly related to pitch and intensity. These facts can be studied in relation to Ohm's law, to the shape of the cochlea, and to the specific characteristics of the aural nerve endings. Musical memory is dependent on the first, last, and essential inner notes of a melody. Ethnomusicologists must use electronic equipment to measure pitch and rhythm phenomena. Mathematical analysis of seemingly careless rhythms in traditional music demonstrates subtle and controlled rhythmic patterns that few trained Western musicians can perceive. *(John R. Metz)*

5650 CONRADIN, Hans. **Das Problem der Bewe-**
as **gung in der Musik** [The problem of movement in music], *Kongreß-Bericht: Gesellschaft für Musikforschung* (Kassel; Basel: Bärenreiter, 1950) 189–92. In German. See no. 299 in this volume.
Discusses the psychology of sound and music.

5651 CREMER, Lothar. **Über unser zweifaches**
as **Tonhöhenempfinden** [Concerning our twofold perception of pitch], *Kongreß-Bericht: Gesellschaft für Musikforschung* (Kassel; Basel: Bärenreiter, 1950) 230–31. In German. See no. 299 in this volume.
The two-components theory of pitch divides pitch into two autonomous perceptual components: (1) brightness, a quantitatively measurable property of musical tones and noises, and (2) the chroma, a color characteristic of tones which correlates to pitch classes based on the octave. *(Tina Frühauf)*

5652 DENÉRÉAZ, Alexandre. **L'harmonie moderne**
as **et les phénomènes d'ordre "complémentaire"** [Modern harmony and the phenomena of the so-called complementary type], *Bericht über den musikwissenschaftlichen Kongreß in Basel* (Leipzig: Breitkopf & Härtel, 1925) 118–214. *Illus., music.* In French. See no. 102 in this volume.
The theory of complementary colors associated with corresponding tones is particularly relevant to the music of Chopin, Liszt, Wagner, and Franck.

5653 DERI, Otto. **Musical taste and personality,**
as *Pepragmena tou 4. diethnous synedriou aisthītikīs/ Actes du IV Congrès international d'esthétique/Proceedings of the IV International Congress on Aesthetics* (Athínai: conference, 1962) 257–60. See no. 415 in this volume.
Presents results of two studies. The first shows that people who prefer Classic music are more controlled and abstract in their emotional life than those who prefer Romantic music. The second indicates that sensitivity to serious (complex) music is correlated with visual aesthetic sensitivity. *Michael Adelson*)

5654 FACK, Heinrich. **Zur Anwendung der Infor-**
as **mationstheorie auf Probleme des Hörens** [The application of information theory in issues of hearing], *Bericht über den internationalen musikwissenschaftlichen Kongreß* (Kassel: Bärenreiter, 1957) 91–95. *Charts, diagr.* In German. See no. 356 in this volume.
Proposes a mathematical model of the information capacity of the human ear, on the basis of recent experiments.

5655 FEUCHTWANGER, Erich. **Das Musische in**
as **der Sprache und seine Pathologie** [The artistic aspect of language and its pathology], *Proceedings of the First International Congress of Phonetic Sciences: First meeting of the Internationale Arbeitsgemeinschaft für Phonologie* (Harlem: J. Enschedé, 1933) 114–18. In German. See no. 194 in this volume.

⟶ FRAISSE, Paul. **La structure temporelle des mouvements volontaires rythmés** [The temporal structure of voluntary rhythmic movements]. See no. 3992 in this volume.

5656 FRANCÈS, Robert. **L'information harmo-**
as **nique et les problèmes d'esthétique** [Harmonic information and aesthetic issues], *Pepragmena tou 4. diethnous synedriou aisthītikīs/Actes du IV Congrès international d'esthétique/Proceedings of the IV International Congress on Aesthetics* (Athínai: conference, 1962) 353–55. In French. See no. 415 in this volume.
Briefly discusses acculturation of the ear and psychological aspects of harmonic structures.

5657 FULIN, Angélique. **Le langage musical des en-**
as **fants** [The musical language of children], *Actes du cinquième Congrès international d'esthétique/Proceedings of the Fifth International Congress of Aesthetics* ('s-Gravenhage: Mouton, 1964) 885–89. *Music, charts, diagr.* In French. See no. 475 in this volume.

A sample of 112 Parisian schoolgirls ages 6-16 improvised sung versions of their given names, imitated the call of a cuckoo and the sound of bells, and improvised a melody on a set verse text. In spite of their wide experience of tempered scales, they often used untempered intervals comparable to the natural third and the Pythagorean third. Tritonic and tetratonic scales dominated especially in the younger children (6-9); for older children heptatonic scales had evolved, but could be used modally, without a necessary tonic final. *(David Bloom)*

5658
as
GARDAVSKÝ, Čeněk. **Janáček a psychologie hudební tvorby** [Janáček and the psychology of composition], *Leoš Janáček a soudobá hudba* (Praha: Panton, 1963) 98–107. *Music.* In Czech; summaries in Russian and German. See no. 389 in this volume.
Janáček was the first Czech composer interested in psychological phenomena of music composition and perception. Working from ideas of Hermann Helmholtz and Wilhelm Wundt, he articulated a theory of affect in chord connections in his *O skladbě souzvuků a jejich spojů* (Praha, 1897) and *Úplná nauka o harmonii* (Brno, 1912-13). His ideas on the compositional process are an important component of his theory of harmony. *(editors)*

5659
as
GARRETT, J.W. **Distorsions physiques et psychologiques propres à la stéréophonie** [Physical and psychological distortions inherent in stereophony], *Stéréophonie et reproduction musicale* (Paris: Chiron, 1966) 40–46. In French. See no. 511 in this volume.
Particular attention is given to those subjective distortions that create illusions of localization and spatiality and their value in therapy for the hearing-impaired, in music recording, and such live amplified performance as *son et lumière* spectacles.

5660
as
GEIST, Werner. **Musik und Gesundheit: Über Mangelerscheinungen im seelisch-körperlichen Bereich durch Ausfall musisch-geistiger Eigentätigkeit** [Music and health: Symptoms of deficiency in the psychophysical realm from a deficit in artistic-intellectual activity], *Neue Zusammenarbeit im deutschen Musikleben: Vorträge und Entschließungen* (Kassel: Bärenreiter, 1956) 22–25. In German. See no. 343 in this volume.
The situation in Germany is discussed.

5661
as
GÉRAR, M. **Psychologie comparée de l'interprète et de l'auditeur** [Comparative psychology of the performer and the listener], *Compte rendu des travaux du Ier Congrès international d'art radiophonique* (Paris: conference, 1938). In French. See no. 244 in this volume.

5662
as
GRAESER, Wolfgang. **Neue Bahnen in der Musikforschung** [New directions in music research], *Beethoven-Zentenarfeier: Internationaler musikhistorischer Kongress* (Wien: Universal, 1927) 301–03. In German. See no. 142 in this volume.
Outlines a broad program of research on the perception and cognition of hearing, incorporating ideas from current mathematics and physics, treating auditory space as a functional space of unlimited dimensionality. Preliminary formulations are found in the author's *Bachs "Kunst der Fuge"*, in *Bach-Jahrbuch XXI*, 1924, and *Körpersinn—Gymnastik/ Tanz/Sport* (Munich, 1927). *(David Bloom)*

5663
as
GUTTMANN, Alfred. **Das Tempo und seine Variationsbreite** [Tempo and its range of variability], *Bericht über den XII. Kongreß der Deutschen Gesellschaft für Psychologie* (Jena: Fischer, 1932) 341–42. In German. See no. 188 in this volume.
The general psychological concept of a personal immanent tempo was investigated through a musical manifestation, the tempos chosen by conductors for particular pieces from the symphonic repertoire, as measured

somewhat crudely by the total time of each movement. Timings from a period of nearly 25 years, representing thousands of performances, were used. The results are fully reported in *Archiv für die gesamte Psychologie* 85 (1932) p. 331-350. *(David Bloom)*

5664
as
GYSI, Fritz. **Über Zusammenhänge zwischen Ton und Farbe** [On the relationship between pitch and color], *Bericht über den musikwissenschaftlichen Kongreß in Basel* (Leipzig: Breitkopf & Härtel, 1925) 177–83. *Charts, diagr.* In German. See no. 102 in this volume.
Curiosity about synaesthesia dates from antiquity. Attempts to relate color to pitch from the 18th c. to the present have yielded contradictory results. The work of various researchers including Bainbridge Bishop and Alexander Wallace Rimington is discussed.

5665
as
HANDSCHIN, Jacques. **La notion de "qualité" dans la psychologie du son** [The concept of quality in the psychology of sound], *Congrés de la Societat Internacional de Musicologia* (Barcelona: Casa de Caritat, 1936). In French. See no. 224 in this volume.
The conference report provides only a citation. Neither the text nor a summary of the paper was published here.

5666
as
HEINITZ, Wilhelm. **Zeitgemässe Aufführungsprobleme** [Contemporary performance problems], *Bericht über den internationalen musikwissenschaftlichen Kongreß* (Kassel: Bärenreiter, 1963) 293–95. In German. See no. 452 in this volume.
Discusses the use of the author's homogeneity theory and the phonic personality formula in the interpretation of scores.

5667
as
HEINLEIN, Christian Paul. **The effect of the musical modes on amplitude of tapping and on the nature of pianoforte performance,** *Ninth International Congress of Psychology* (Princeton: Psychological Review Company, 1930) 217–18. See no. 160 in this volume.
The results of an experiment are summarized. Conservatory-trained pianists tend to play unfamiliar compositions in major keys more rapidly, loudly and staccato than those in minor keys. No definite conclusions are drawn from the tapping component of the experiment.

5668
as
JONES, Llewellyn Wynn. **Experimental studies in consonance and rhythm,** *VIIIth International Congress of Psychology: Proceedings and papers* (Groningen: Noordhoff, 1927) 448–51. See no. 125 in this volume.
The Seashore Measure of Musical Talent furnishes excellent material in the laboratory or school, but experimental studies show that the test's method of paired comparison, judging time, and tapping in time need considerable modification. The results obtained by the comparison method naturally lead to the study of harmony, which has been minimally investigated by musicians, but may furnish a valuable basis for psychological tests. *(Mi-Sook Han)*

5669
as
JUHÁSZ, A. **Wiedererkennungsversuche auf musikalischem Gebiete** [Recognition experiments in music], *Bericht über den VIII. Kongress für experimentelle Psychologie* (Jena: Fischer, 1924) 182f. In German. See no. 101 in this volume.

5670
as
KATZ, D. **Über einige Versuche im Anschluss an die Tonwortmethode von Karl Eitz** [On some experiments following the solmization method of Carl Eitz], *Bericht über den VI. Kongress für Experimentelle Psychologie* (Leipzig: Barth, 1914) 86,141. In German. See no. 90 in this volume.

5671 KOSCHEL, H. **Hörmängel und ihre audio-**
as **metrische Feststellung** [Hearing deficiencies and
their audiometric detection], *Kongreß-Bericht: Gesellschaft für Musikforschung* (Kassel; Basel: Bärenreiter,
1950) 231–33. In German. See no. 299 in this volume.

5672 KRUEGER, Felix. **Die psychologischen**
as **Grundlagen der Konsonanz und Dissonanz**
[The psychological foundations of consonance and dis-
sonance], *Haydn-Zentenarfeier* (Leipzig: Breitkopf &
Härtel; Wien: Artaria, 1909) 330–33. In German. See
no. 65 in this volume.
Includes the subsequent panel discussion.

5673 LANGELÜDDEKE, Albrecht. **Über rhyth-**
as **mische Defekte** [Rhythmic defects], *Bericht über
den XII. Kongreß der Deutschen Gesellschaft für
Psychologie* (Jena: Fischer, 1932) 377. In German. See
no. 188 in this volume.
Presents a brief report of an experiment series on the concepts of rhythm
and beat as understood by Ludwig Klages, in which rhythmic disturbances
in normal subjects were compared to those in patients with manic depres-
sion, schizophrenia, and chronic encephalitis. *(David Bloom)*

5674 LEIPP, Émile. **Les variables de l'audition musi-**
as **cale** [The variables of musical hearing], *Stéréophonie
et reproduction musicale* (Paris: Chiron, 1966) 30–39.
Bibliog., charts, diagr. In French. See no. 511 in this
volume.
The process of musical listening is discussed in terms of communication
theory. Listeners tend to isolate those elements of performed music that correspond to their musical memory; critical judgment depends on a balance between perception and memory, mediated by cognitive processing, and varies
infinitely. Broad outlines of good and bad taste can thus be defined only for a
community with a shared auditory experience over the long term.

5675 LEVELT, Willem J.M.; PLOMP, Reinier. **The**
as **appreciation of musical intervals,** *Actes du
cinquième Congrès international d'esthétique/Pro-
ceedings of the Fifth International Congress of Aesthetics* ('s-Gravenhage: Mouton, 1964) 901–04. See no.
475 in this volume.
Musical laypersons do not often distinguish "consonant" from "beautiful",
and they are likely to say that the third and sixth sound more "consonant"
than fourth, fifth, and octave. Experimental data shows that the aesthetic
evaluation of an interval is correlated to the distance between the pitches
(and partials), and that the responsible mechanism is part of the physiology
of the ear, not of the cognitive system. *(David Bloom)*

5676 LISSA, Zofia. **Musikalisches Hören in psycho-**
as **logischer Sicht** [Psychological views on musical
hearing], *Bericht über den neunten internationalen
Kongreß* (Kassel: Bärenreiter, 1964-1966) I, 11–18. In
German. See no. 491 in this volume.
A recognition-theoretical analysis of musical genres would have to account, for example, for the way genres differ in regard to the experience of
subjective time. Abstract instrumental music has the temporal structure
simply of the subjective time it occupies, but the temporal character of genres of a cyclic type may be suspended or even open. In stage works, the additional level of the time represented in the dramatic action may be further
complicated by narrators, chorus, etc., outside the action, and by its continuous or discontinuous character. More subtle problems are found in the
consideration of program music, particularly when it has a historical reference. *(David Bloom)*

5677 LISSA, Zofia. **Symposium: Musikalisches**
as **Hören in psychologischer Sicht** [Symposium:
Psychological views on musical hearing]. Moderated

by Antonín SYCHRA, *Bericht über den neunten internationalen Kongreß* (Kassel: Bärenreiter, 1964-1966)
II, 38–50. In German. See no. 491 in this volume.
Discusses the conference paper abstracted as RILM 5676 in this volume;
includes a more formal communication by Marija BLINOVA, *Die zeitliche
Natur der Musik im Lichte der Lehre über die höhere Nerventätigkeit* (The
temporal nature of music in the light of theories of the activities of the
higher nervous system). Participants included Gerhard ALBERSHEIM,
Ingmar BENTSSON, Hans CONRADIN, Harry GOLDSCHMIDT,
Hans-Peter REINECKE, and József UJFALUSSY.

5678 MALL, G.D. **Wirkungen der Musik auf**
as **verschiedene Persönlichkeitstypen** [The effects
of music on different personality types], *Psychologie
des Gemeinschaftslebens: Bericht über den XIV.
Kongress der Deutschen Gesellschaft für Psychologie*
(Jena: Fischer, 1935) 310–15. In German. See no. 219
in this volume.

5679 MASSON, Paul-Marie. **La notion de musicalité**
as [The idea of musicality], *Deuxième congrès international d'esthétique et de Science de l'art* (Paris:
Librairie Félix Alcan, 1937) II, 227–31. In French. See
no. 249 in this volume.
The perception of musicality is based on the relations of analogy between
successive moments (through total or partial repetition) and differentiation
between simultaneous sounds (harmonic and polymelodic); passing harmonies bring simultaneity into the realm of succession, imitative counterpoint brings succession into the realm of simultaneities. More generally,
musicality is simply the happy effect of a musician's skill and fluency in the
use of procedures specific to music, a species of what might be called
artiality. *(David Bloom)*

5680 MCNAUGHT, William Gray. **Introductory to**
as **tonic sol-fa,** *Report of the Fourth Congress of the International Musical Society* (London: Novello, 1912)
364–65. See no. 71 in this volume.
The psychological phenomenon of the temporary memory of absolute pitch
is the basis of all musical perception. The association of syllables with this
effect is essential. *(Mei-Mei Meng)*

5681 MOLES, André. **Facteurs physiques influen-**
as **çant l'écoute musicale et la cristallisation du
groupe auditif** [Physical factors influencing musical
hearing and the crystallization of the listening group],
Cahiers d'études de radio-télévision 3-4 (1955)
379–90. *Charts, diagr.* In French. See no. 334 in this
volume.
Discusses the psychological effects of musical sound in general and of radio broadcasts in particular.

⟶ MOLNÁR, Antal. **Der gestaltpsychologische
Unterschied zwischen Haydn und Mozart** [The
difference between Haydn and Mozart according to
Gestalt psychology]. See no. 1817 in this volume.

5682 MORIN, Edgar. **"Matérialité" et "magic" de la**
as **musique à la radio** [Materiality and magic of radio
music], *Cahiers d'études de radio-télévision* 3-4 (1955)
483–86. In French. See no. 334 in this volume.
Briefly discusses affective, psychological, and sociological effects.

5683 MOSER, Hans Joachim. **Musikalischer Erb-**
as **gang und seelische Mutation** [Musical heredity
and psychological change], *Kongreß-Bericht: Gesellschaft für Musikforschung* (Kassel; Basel: Bärenreiter,
1950) 197–99. In German. See no. 299 in this volume.

5684
as

MYERS, Charles Samuel. **Individuelle Unterschiede in der Auffassung von Tönen** [Individual differences in the concept of tones], *Bericht über den V. Kongress für experimentelle Psychologie* (Leipzig: Barth, 1912) 148–50. In German. See no. 79 in this volume.

5685
as

NADEL, Siegfried. **Die Hauptprobleme der neueren Musikpsychologie** [Leading issues in recent music psychology], *Beethoven-Zentenarfeier: Internationaler musikhistorischer Kongress* (Wien: Universal, 1927) 307–11. In German. See no. 142 in this volume.

It has become clear that the characterization of tone color involves factors other than that of the overtone series. The notion of pitch as a single continuous dimension must be supplemented by one of tone quality that accounts for the perception of identity between pitches at the remove of an octave. The two theories of consonance, as a lack of disturbance (beats, difference tones) and as a coincidence of partials, have not been reconciled. Research is only beginning on the profound question of melody as the carrier of a sign function. *(David Bloom)*

⟶

ORTMANN, Otto. **The contribution of physiopsychology to musicology.** See no. 910 in this volume.

5686
as

ORTMANN, Otto. **The psychology of tone-quality,** *Papers read at the International Congress of Musicology* (New York: Music Educators National Conference, 1944) 227–32. See no. 266 in this volume.

Discusses the physical properties, perception, and description of sound.

5687
as

PETERSON, Joseph; SMITH, W.F. **Habituation effects of the equally tempered musical scale,** *Ninth International Congress of Psychology* (Princeton: Psychological Review Company, 1930) 338–39. See no. 160 in this volume.

Thirty-six college students (half with and half without musical training) were tested to determine if habituation to the equally tempered scale results in tolerance for mistuned intervals in just temperament. The musically trained students were able to detect changes in both scales more consistently than the untrained students. *(Ruth Block)*

5688
as

RAIMONDO, Luigi. **Die Musik als Faktor der Geistesbildung** [Music as a factor in the development of the mind], *Musikerziehung: Zeitschrift der Musikerzieher Österreichs* special issue (1953) 22–24. In German. See no. 317 in this volume.

As the highest of all art forms, music can help people to become aware of themselves and their creative abilities and to discover their innermost life. *(Allen Lott)*

5689
as

REINECKE, Hans-Peter. **Akustik und Musik** [Acoustics and music], *Bericht über den internationalen musikwissenschaftlichen Kongreß* (Kassel: Bärenreiter, 1957) 179–89. *Charts, diagr., tech. drawings.* In German. See no. 356 in this volume.

Discusses the physical and neurological aspects of musical hearing, with particular attention to the perception of consonance and tempered scales. *(David Bloom)*

5690
as

REINECKE, Hans-Peter. **Physiological bases of musical hearing: Present state and problems of research,** *Report of the Eighth Congress of the International Musicological Society. II: Reports* (Kassel: Bärenreiter, 1962) 93–96. In German. See no. 440 in this volume.

A report on a discussion by Melville CLARK, Jr., Paul COLLAER, Hans-Heinz DRAEGER, Heinrich HUSMANN, Hans-Peter REINECKE,

Charles SHACKFORD, Antonín SYCHRA, Albert WELLEK, Ernest Glen WEVER, and Fritz WINCKEL of the paper by Wever abstracted as RILM 5720 in this volume.

5691
as

REINECKE, Hans-Peter. **Zum Problem des Hören von Zusammenklängen und Klangfarben im Hinblick auf die akustische Funktion des Ohres** [The problem of hearing simultaneous sounds and sound colors in light of the acoustic functioning of the ear], *Bericht über den siebenten internationalen musikwissenschaftlichen Kongress* (Kassel: Bärenreiter, 1959) 227–29. In German. See no. 390 in this volume.

The physical-mechanical properties of the ear and its consequent distortion of sound input must be understood in order to arrive at an empirical account of the phenomena of consonance, dissonance, and blending, and the question of tone-color perception. *(David Bloom)*

5692
as

REINECKE, Hans-Peter. **Zur Frage der Anwendbarkeit der Informationstheorie auf tonpsychologische Probleme** [The applicability of information theory to problems in the psychology of music], *Bericht über den internationalen musikwissenschaftlichen Kongreß* (Kassel: Bärenreiter, 1963) 279–81. In German. See no. 452 in this volume.

The physiological, acoustic, and psychological aspects of musical hearing can be treated as closed communication systems in information-theoretical terms, but operate on very different structural principles. They must be investigated separately before the relations among them can be established. *(David Bloom)*

5693
as

RÉVÉSZ, Géza. **Neue Versuche über binaurale Tonmischung** [New research on binaural sound mixture], *Bericht über den VI. Kongress für Experimentelle Psychologie* (Leipzig: Barth, 1914) 90f. In German. See no. 90 in this volume.

5694
as

RÉVÉSZ, Géza. **Über die hervorragenden akustischen Eigenschaften und musikalischen Fähigkeiten des siebenjährigen Komponisten Erwin Nyiregyházy** [The outstanding acoustic capacities and musical abilities of the seven-year-old composer Ervin Nyíregyházi], *Bericht über den IV. Kongress für Experimentelle Psychologie* (Leipzig: Barth, 1911) 224f. In German. See no. 70 in this volume.

5695
as

RÉVÉSZ, Géza. **Über musikalische Begabung** [On musical talent], *Bericht über den VI. Kongress für Experimentelle Psychologie* (Leipzig: Barth, 1914) 88,134. In German. See no. 90 in this volume.

5696
as

RÉVÉSZ, Géza. **Über Orthosymphonie: Eine merkwürdige parakustische Erscheinung** [On Orthosymphonie: A strange para-acoustic phenomenon], *Bericht über den III. Kongress für experimentalle Psychologie* (Leipzig: Barth, 1909) 243f. In German. See no. 59 in this volume.

5697
as

ROCHE, Claude. **L'attitude de l'auditeur de musique à la radio** [The attitude of the radio music listener], *Cahiers d'études de radio-télévision* 3-4 (1955) 437–40. In French. See no. 334 in this volume.

Discusses the psychological differences between listening to music on the radio and in a concert hall.

5698
as

ROSENTHAL, Felix. **Die Musik als Eindruck. II** [Music as impression. II], *Haydn-Zentenarfeier*

(Leipzig: Breitkopf & Härtel; Wien: Artaria, 1909) 315–22. In German. See no. 65 in this volume.

Discusses the psychology of hearing.

5699 SCHNEIDER, Max. **Raumtiefenhören in der**
as **Musik** [Spatial depth hearing in music], *Zeitschrift für Ästhetik und allgemeine Kunstwissenschaft* XXV (supplement 1931) 207–15. In German. See no. 177 in this volume.

5700 SCHOEN, Max. **The nature of the musical**
as **mind,** *Ninth International Congress of Psychology* (Princeton: Psychological Review Company, 1930) 383. See no. 160 in this volume.

An investigation into the constituent elements of the music lover's mentality is needed.

5701 SCHOLE, Heinrich. **Experimentelle Unter-**
as **suchungen an höchsten und an kürzesten Tönen** [Experimental investigations into the highest and shortest tones], *Psychologie des Gemeinschaftslebens: Bericht über den XIV. Kongress der Deutschen Gesellschaft für Psychologie* (Jena: Fischer, 1935) 309–10. In German. See no. 219 in this volume.

5702 SEASHORE, Carl E. **The role of experimental**
as **psychology in the science of art and music,** *Ninth International Congress of Psychology* (Princeton: Psychological Review Company, 1930) 384–85. See no. 160 in this volume.

Identifies areas for additional research, including aesthetics, genetics, anthropology, and education.

5703 SIOHAN, Robert. **Les objections à la résonance**
as [Objections to overtones], *La résonance dans les échelles musicales* (Paris: Centre National de la Recherche Scientifique [CNRS], 1963) 51–61. *Music*. In French; summaries in English and German. See no. 420 in this volume.

The perfect major chord—the basis of the entire harmonic system—is supposedly justified by the natural overtones of strings and pipes; but are the overtones of plates and bells any less natural? If, moreover, one seeks in overtones some educative principle for the ear, then the overtones of bells, accessible since the 9th c. at least, would have played this role much more readily than that of strings. *(author)*

5704 SKUDRZYK, Eugen J. **Betrachtungen zum**
as **musikalischen Zusammenklang** [Observations on musical sonority], *Acustica: International journal of acoustics/Journal international d'acoustique/Internationale akustische Zeitschrift* IV/1 (1954) 249–53. *Illus., bibliog., charts, diagr.* In German; summaries in English, French, and German. See no. 324 in this volume.

Owing to the limited time constant and the nonlinear distortion of the human ear, sound impressions depend not only upon amplitudes, but also upon phases of harmonics—that is, on the envelope of the sound phenomena. This envelope is not only important for the sensation of distance and direction, but also plays a fundamental role in musical acoustics; for example, it is the cause of numerous acoustic illusions. The hearing of the envelope and the frequency dependence on internal friction of wood used to make musical instruments offer a natural explanation for the quality of old violins. *(author)*

5705 SLAWSON, A. Wayne. **A psychoacoustic com-**
as **parison between vowel quality and musical timbre,** *Problèmes d'acoustique* (Liège: Université de Liège, 1965) M66. See no. 504 in this volume.

It is possible that a listener categorizes the quality of human vowel sounds and certain musical timbres on the basis of the same psychoacoustical process, since both vowel quality and musical timbre are similar functions of their acoustical correlates. A series of eight experiments demonstrated that the spectrum envelope of a sound must be held constant or shifted only slightly in order to maintain minimal differences in timbre when the fundamental frequency is changed. *(Brian Doherty)*

⟶ STEPHANI, Hermann. **Das Verhältnis von reiner und pythagoreischer Stimmung als psychologisches Problem** [The relationship between pure and Pythagorean tuning as a psychological problem]. See no. 4116 in this volume.

5706 STÖHR, Adolf. **Das psychophysiologische**
as **Problem der Klangfarbe** [The psycho-physiological problem of tone color], *Haydn-Zentenarfeier* (Leipzig: Breitkopf & Härtel; Wien: Artaria, 1909) 360–63. In German. See no. 65 in this volume.

Refers to the resonance hypothesis of Hermann von Helmholtz.

5707 STUCKENSCHMIDT, Hans Heinz. **Limitation**
as **au sens auditif de l'événement musical** [Limitation to the auditory sense of musical events], *Cahiers d'études de radio-télévision* 3-4 (1955) 473–78. In French. See no. 334 in this volume.

Unlike the concert hall, where one's listening experience is affected by other sensory stimuli (such as the visual decor), radio broadcasts provide opportunities for total concentration on the music. However, due to passivity among listeners, these opportunities are rarely used to full advantage. *(Michael Adelson)*

⟶ STUMPF, Carl. **Vergleichende Musikforschung, Akustik, Tonpsychologie: Verhandlungen und Vorträge** [Comparative music research, acoustics, music psychology: Discussions and lectures]. See no. 2475 in this volume.

5708 SYCHRA, Antonín. **Psychology of the listener**
as **from the experimental point of view,** *Music east and west* (Nai Dilli: Indian Council for Cultural Relations, 1966) 125–28. See no. 489 in this volume.

The perceptual experience of music should not be confused with its scientific analysis.

5709 TANNER, Robert. **Critique de la théorie de la**
as **résonance** [Critique of the theory of resonance], *La résonance dans les échelles musicales* (Paris: Centre National de la Recherche Scientifique [CNRS], 1963) 63–100. *Charts, diagr.* In French; summaries in English and German. See no. 420 in this volume.

A scientific theory of musical aesthetics cannot be based on a correlation of resonance properties to the auditive phenomenon. The fusion theory, excellent though it is with respect to auditory perception, cannot explain music: Its development leads to insoluble experimental contradictions, and its physical principles have no correspondence to the psychological phenomenon of music. The resonance theory posits a causal link between harmonics and intervals, but fails to explain how this could be established. Furthermore, it is based only on a numerical similarity between acoustic data of harmonics and musical data of intervals. *(author)*

5710 TANNER, Robert. **Le problème des rapports**
as **simples: Notion de psycharithme** [The problem of simple ratios: The notion of psycharithm], *Acoustique musicale* (Paris: Centre National de la Recherche Scientifique [CNRS], 1959) 83–101. *Music, charts, diagr.* In French. See no. 393 in this volume.

An introductory account of psycharithm theory, with examples of its application to the analysis of ancient Greek music.

5711 TANNER, Robert. **Le rôle de la fusion dans**
as **l'appréciation de justesse des accords** [The role
played by fusion in the perception of the justness of
chords], *Acoustique musicale* (Paris: Centre National
de la Recherche Scientifique [CNRS], 1959) 49–59. In
French. See no. 393 in this volume.
Experiments at the Centre de Recherches Scientifiques de Marseille, using
a device that produces continuously variable intervals and chords to a precision level of 0.1 savarts, show that fusion is responsible for the perception
of justness in chords, but not that it has any role whatever in their genesis,
structure, or musical properties. *(David Bloom)*

5712 THIRRING, Hans. **Musik als Faktor der**
as **Charakterbildung** [Music as a factor in character
formation], *Musikerziehung: Zeitschrift der
Musikerzieher Österreichs* special issue (1953) 16–17.
In German. See no. 317 in this volume.

5713 TOMATIS, Alfred. **La résonance dans les**
as **échelles musicales: Le point de vue des**
physiologistes [Resonance of musical scales: The
viewpoint of physiologists], *La résonance dans les
échelles musicales* (Paris: Centre National de la Recherche Scientifique [CNRS], 1963) 33–35. In French;
summaries in English and German. See no. 420 in this
volume.
Music, as defined by its physical substrate, appears in acoustical architecture as the exploitation of a medium's resonance. Though its possibilities
are therefore infinite, they are subordinate to the listener's psycho-
physiological reactions. From the accord between the two springs the adaptation of the senses that motivate psychoacoustic conditioning. *(author)*

5714 VERNON, Phillip Elwart. **The psychology of**
as **music: Its scope and methodology,** *Ninth International Congress of Psychology* (Princeton: Psychological Review Company, 1930) 461–62. See no. 160 in this
volume.
Emphasizes the importance of a common language for scientists and musicians.

5715 WALLASCHEK, Richard. **Natural selection**
as **and music,** *International Congress of Experimental
Psychology: Second session* (London: Williams &
Norgate, 1892) 73–77. See no. 17 in this volume.

5716 WALTHER, Léon. **Le rythme dans le travail**
as **professionnel** [Rhythm in professional work],
Compte rendu du Ier Congrès du rythme (Genève:
Institut Jaques-Dalcroze, 1926) 299–306. *Charts,
diagr.* In French. See no. 123 in this volume.
Rhythmic sensitivity may improve both psychological and physical performance.

⟶ WELLEK, Albert. **Die ganzheitspsychologischen**
Aspekte der Musikästhetik [Musical aesthetics in
light of holistic psychology]. See no. 5627 in this
volume.

5717 WELLEK, Albert. **Der gegenwärtige Stand der**
as **Musikpsychologie und ihre Bedeutung für die**
historische Musikforschung [The present state of
music psychology and its significance for historical
musicology], *Report of the Eighth Congress of the International Musicological Society. I: Papers* (Kassel:
Bärenreiter, 1961) 121–32. In German. See no. 439 in
this volume.

Surveys the literature up to 1961, beginning with Ernst Kurth's proposals
in *Musikpsychologie* (1931) for a psychology of music in the strict sense, as
distinct from the psychologies of sound and audition. *(David Bloom)*

5718 WELLEK, Albert. **Zur Typologie der Musi-**
as **kalität der Deutschen Stämme** [A typology of
musicality among the Germanic tribes], *Psychologie
des Gemeinschaftslebens: Bericht über den XIV.
Kongress der Deutschen Gesellschaft für Psychologie*
(Jena: Fischer, 1935) 130–37. In German. See no. 219
in this volume.
Considers the genealogy of social types.

5719 WELLEK, Albert. **Zur Vererbung der Musik-**
as **begabung und ihrer Typen** [The inheritability of a
musical gift and its types], *Congrès international des
sciences anthropologiques et ethnologiques: Compte
rendu de la deuxième session* (København:
Munksgaard, 1939) 133–55. In German. See no. 255 in
this volume.

5720 WEVER, Ernest Glen. **The physiological basis**
as **of musical hearing: Present state and prob-**
lems of research, *Report of the Eighth Congress of
the International Musicological Society. I: Papers*
(Kassel: Bärenreiter, 1961) 133–38. *Illus., charts,
diagr.* See no. 439 in this volume.
Reviews current (as of 1961) theories of consonance and of aural distortion.

5721 WINCKEL, Fritz. **Influence des facteurs psy-**
as **cho-physiologiques sur la sensation de conso-**
nance-dissonance [The influence of psychophysiological factors on the perception of consonance and dis-
sonance], *Acoustique musicale* (Paris: Centre National
de la Recherche Scientifique [CNRS], 1959) 61–74.
Bibliog., charts, diagr. In French. See no. 393 in this
volume.
Reviews experimental research applicable to the study of intervals from a
physiological rather than mathematical point of view. *(David Bloom)*

5722 WINCKEL, Fritz. **Die Psychophysischen**
as **Bedingungen des Musikhörens** [The psychophysical conditions of musical hearing], *Stilkriterien
der neuen Musik* (Berlin: Merseburger, 1961) 45–65. In
German. See no. 410 in this volume.
Research at the Groupe de Recherches Musicales, under the auspices of the
Radiodiffusion-Télévision Française, concentrating on two primary areas—the scientific analysis of musical language, and musical acoustics—is
reviewed, from the standpoint of the needs of composers and performers.
(Neill Clegg)

5723 WINCKEL, Fritz. **Ueber die Schwankungs-**
as **erscheinungen in der Musik** [On appearances of
fluctuation in music], *Cahiers d'études de radio-
télévision* 3-4 (1955) 526–33. In German. See no. 334 in
this volume.
Briefly discusses psychoacoustics as related to radio broadcasts of music.

5724 WINCKEL, Fritz. **Die Wirkung der Musik**
as **unter dem Gesichtspunkt psychophysiolo-**
gischer Erscheinungen [The effects of music from
the point of view of psychophysiological phenomena],
*Bericht über den internationalen musikwissenschaft-
lichen Kongreß Wien Mozartjahr 1956* (Graz; Köln:
Böhlau, 1958) 727–35. *Charts, diagr.* In German. See
no. 365 in this volume.

Surveys experimental results on limits in the perception of frequency, dynamics, pitch, timbre, and connection and articulation across the time dimension, with comparisons between music and speech. *(David Bloom)*

5725 WING, H.D. **Standardized tests of musical apti-**
as **tude,** *Twelfth International Congress of Psychology* (London: Oliver and Boyd, 1950) 129f. See no. 284 in this volume.

83 Physiology, therapy, and medicine

5726 DECROIX, Gabriel; DEHASSY, Jacques.
as **Stéréaudiométrie, mesure de l'audition binaurale: Possibilités de réhabilitation des malentendants par audioprothèses stéréophoniques** [Stereo-audiometrics, a measurement of binaural hearing: Rehabilitational possibilities for the hearing-impaired by means of stereophonic audioprostheses], *Stéréophonie et reproduction musicale* (Paris: Chiron, 1966) 3–16. *Illus., bibliog., charts, diagr.* In French. See no. 511 in this volume.
The advantage of binaural over monaural hearing is particularly important in three areas: the perception of sound intensity, the perception of the direction and distance of a sound, and the discrimination of speech in noisy environments. Research confirms that the development of stereophonic hearing aids offers significant improvement in these areas, except in the case of patients with symmetrical hearing loss who have become habituated to monophonic devices over a relatively long period. *(David Bloom)*

5727 FORCHHAMMER, Viggo. **Die Rutz-Sievers-**
as **schen Beobachtungen** [The observations of Rutz and Sievers], *Bericht über den Internationalen Kongreß Singen und Sprechen* (München: Oldenbourg, 1938) 175–78. In German. See no. 257 in this volume.
The research of Joseph Rutz (1837-95) led to the hypothesis that composers work in one of four characteristic sound-types, each associated with a particular body posture; Eduard Sievers (1850-1932) added two further types to the list. The analyses are discussed, with remarks on the use of the associated postures in authentic performance. *(David Bloom)*

5728 FOREL, Oscar Louis. **Le rôle du rythme en**
as **physiologie et psycho-pathologie** [The role of rhythm in physiology and psycho-pathology], *Compte rendu du Ier Congrès du rythme* (Genève: Institut Jaques-Dalcroze, 1926) 307–16. In French. See no. 123 in this volume.
Many of the body's organs function in regular rhythms. Since basic acquired rhythms are the foundation for all rhythms of human life, rhythmic distortions of people's lives can have a pathological effect.

⟶ GEIST, Werner. **Musik und Gesundheit: Über Mangelerscheinungen im seelisch-körperlichen Bereich durch Ausfall musisch-geistiger Eigentätigkeit** [Music and health: Symptoms of deficiency in the psychophysical realm from a deficit in artistic-intellectual activity]. See no. 5660 in this volume.

5729 GLASER, Hugo. **Musik und Medizin** [Music and
as medicine], *Musikerziehung: Zeitschrift der Musikerzieher Österreichs* special issue (1953) 24–26. In German. See no. 317 in this volume.
Discusses various aspects of a presumed relationship between medicine and music, including the doctor's strong interest in music, the relation between rhythmic sensation and biology, and music as therapy. *(Robert Taub)*

5730 HEINITZ, Wilhelm. **Die Erfassung des**
as **subjectiv-motorischen Elements in der musikalischen Produktion des Primitiven** [A survey of subjective motoric elements in the musical production of primitive cultures], *Société Internationale de Musicologie: Premier Congrès Liège—Compte rendu/Internationale Gesellschaft für Musikwissenschaft: Erster Kongress Lüttich—Kongressbericht/International Society for Musical Research: First Congress Liège: Report* (London: Plainsong and Mediaeval Music Society, 1930) 148–53. In German. See no. 178 in this volume.

5731 HENDRICKX-DUCHAINE, Christine. **The cu-**
as **rative powers of music,** *Music in education* (Paris: UNESCO, 1955) 200–04. See no. 322 in this volume.
The experience of using music in the institutional treatment of mental illness in Belgian sanatoria shows that it has both psychotherapeutic and social-educational value. A French version is cited as RILM 5732 in this volume.

5732 HENDRICKX-DUCHAINE, Christine. **La**
as **musique et la thérapeutique** [Music and therapy], *La musique dans l'éducation* (Paris: UNESCO; Colin, 1955) 210–14. In French. See no. 323 in this volume.
An English version is abstracted as RILM 5731 in this volume.

5733 KNIGHT, Frank E. **Radio music used therapeu-**
as **tically and the need for research,** *Cahiers d'études de radio-télévision* 3-4 (1955) 468–72. See no. 334 in this volume.
Describes results of informal experiments in children's therapy. Suggestions for further research are offered.

5734 ORLANDINI, Icilio. **Il dattilapero** [The finger
as stretcher], *Report of the Fourth Congress of the International Musical Society* (London: Novello, 1912) 331–32. In Italian. See no. 71 in this volume.
Summary of a paper describing an invention that increases finger strength and independence.

5735 PASCHEN, Paul. **Stimme und Seele und ihre**
as **gemeinsamen Störungen** [Voice and spirit and the disturbances they share], *Bericht über den Internationalen Kongreß Singen und Sprechen* (München: Oldenbourg, 1938) 34–37. In German. See no. 257 in this volume.
Discusses the effects of emotional disturbance on voice production in regard to neck, mouth, and resonating chambers.

5736 ROLLIN, Henry R. **The therapeutic use of mu-**
as **sic in a mental hospital with special reference to group treatment,** *Proceedings: The Third World Congress of Psychiatry/Comptes rendus: Le troisième Congrès mondial de psychiatrie/Sitzungsberichte: Der dritte Weltkongress der Psychiatrie/Las actas: El tercer Congreso Mundial de Psiquiatria* (Montréal: McGill University, 1961) I, 556–59. See no. 437 in this volume.
Discusses the experience from 1955 of a therapy program at Horton Hospital, Epsom, England.

5737 SEASHORE, Robert Holmes. **Individual differ-**
as **ences in rhythmic motor coordinations,** *Ninth International Congress of Psychology* (Princeton: Psychological Review Company, 1930) 385–86. See no. 160 in this volume.
Trained instrumental musicians scored higher than a randomly selected group on a University of Iowa test for motor rhythms. However, some

students without musical training also scored well. Specific practice on the motor rhythm tests have resulted in only moderate gains in precision. These findings have led to a tentative description of a basic motor capacity. *(Ruth Block)*

⟶ SOMIGLI, Carlo. **Les mécanismes laryngiens et les timbres vocaux** [Laryngeal mechanism and vocal sound quality]. See no. 3323 in this volume.

⟶ STRECK. **Die Stimmdiagnose als Grundlage der modernen Stimmbildung und Hilfsmittel gegen pädagogische Pfuscherarbeit** [Vocal diagnosis as a foundation for modern voice training and an aid against pedagogical blunders]. See no. 4654 in this volume.

5738 WEBER-BAULER, Léon. **Le rôle du geste**
as **rythmé dans la pratique psychothérapique** [The role of the rhythmic gesture in psychotherapeutic practice], *Compte rendu du Ier Congrès du rythme* (Genève: Institut Jaques-Dalcroze, 1926) 345–49. In French. See no. 123 in this volume.
Regular rhythmic patterns are effective and soothing to those undergoing treatment for nervous disorders. The therapeutic benefits of massage therapy and detailed awareness of gesture are noted.

84 Archaeology

5739 BAYER, Bathja. **Musical relics in Palestinian**
as **archaeology**, *Haqŵngres ha'ŵlamy hašlyšy lemada'ey hayahadŵt* (Yerŵšalaym/Al-Quds: Hebrew U./Ha'unybersytah ha'ibryt, 1965) 364–64. See no. 435 in this volume.

5740 BERNOULLI, Eduard. **Der Archäologe**
as **Bianchini über Musikinstrumente in alten Volks- und Kultgebräuchen** [The archaeologist Bianchini on music instruments in early folk and religious customs], *Schweizer Jahrbuch für Musikwissenschaft/Annales suisses de musicologie/Annuario svizzero di musicologia* I (1924) 41–55. In German. See no. 103 in this volume.
Discusses the work of the polymath Francesco Bianchini (Franciscus Blanchinus, 1662-1729) and his treatise *De tribus generibus instrumentorum musicae veterum organicae.* *(David Bloom)*

5741 KAMIŃSKI, Włodzimierz. **Frühmittelalterliche**
as **Musikinstrumente auf polnischem Gebiet** [Early medieval musical instruments in Polish territory], *The book of the first international musicological congress devoted to the works of Frederick Chopin* (Warszawa: Państwowe Wydawnictwo Naukowe, 1963) 551–58. *Illus.* In German. See no. 425 in this volume.
The findings of archaeological research sponsored by the Muzeum Instrumentów Muzycznych, Poznań, beginning in 1956, including the remains of two chordophones, three recorders, four recorder mouthpieces, and a scraper, are discussed in connection with early medieval written sources. *(David Bloom)*

5742 TARACENA AGUIRRE, Blas. **Numancia**
as [Numantia], *IV Congreso Internacional de Arqueología* (Barcelona: Exposición Internacional, 1929). In Spanish. See no. 156 in this volume.
Discusses archaeological findings at the Roman settlement of Numantia in Spain.

85 Engineering and sound recording

5743 BRILLOUIN, Jacques. **Éléments psycho-**
as **physiologiques du problème de la musique à l'écran** [Psychophysiological elements of the problem of film music], *Atti del secondo Congresso internazionale di musica* (Firenze: Le Monnier, 1940) 219–28. *Charts, diagr.* In French; summaries in Italian and German. See no. 239 in this volume.
Considers acoustic requirements for the recording of film music. Balances must be adjusted in relation to the volume at which the music is to be played back. Reverberation and the proportion between higher and lower frequencies can be regulated—particularly in the mixing process—to provide effects of room reverberation, open-air ambience, and distancing. *(author)*

5744 BROCKBERND, Bernard. **La radio au service**
as **d'une meilleure musique religieuse** [Radio in the service of a better religious music], *Perspectives de la musique sacrée à la lumière de l'encyclique* Musicae sacrae disciplina (Paris: conference, 1959) 630–32. In French. See no. 379 in this volume.
Outlines practical proposals for using broadcasts on Roman Catholic radio, both of worship services and of religious music in concert format, as a tool for educating listeners in the appreciation of quality in religious music. *(David Bloom)*

5745 BRUSSELMANS. **Musique et micro** [Music and
as microphone], *Compte rendu des travaux du Ier Congrès international d'art radiophonique* (Paris: conference, 1938). In French. See no. 244 in this volume.

5746 CAMRAS, Marvin. **Some recent developments**
as **in magnetic recording**, *Acustica: International journal of acoustics/Journal international d'acoustique/Internationale akustische Zeitschrift* IV/1 (1954) 26–29. *Illus., bibliog., charts, diagr.* Summaries in English, French, and German. See no. 326 in this volume.
Trends in magnetic recording take advantage of its erasability, fast response, and high resolution. Recent developments include high-output magnetic tapes, the magnetic modulator head, the time compressor, half-track recording, and magnetic contact printing. *(author)*

⟶ CANAC, François. **Faithfulness in the transmission of music as a means of preservation.** See no. 5807 in this volume.

5747 COEUROY, André. **Problèmes intérieurs et**
as **extérieurs de radio** [Radio's internal and external problems], *Atti del primo Congresso internazionale di musica* (Firenze: Le Monnier, 1935) 52–61. *Charts, diagr.* In French; summary in Italian. See no. 203 in this volume.
Internal policies must be established to give radio programs a balance of educational and entertainment content. Radio must take advantage of the developmental potential sound recordings offer and also continue to broadcast live orchestral, operatic, and dramatic productions. Above all, the central problem confronting radio producers is how to bring art to a largely uncultivated public. *(author)*

5748 COLACICCHI, Luigi. **Il disco e la musica** [Re-
as cords and music], *Atti del primo Congresso internazionale di musica* (Firenze: Le Monnier, 1935) 76–83. In Italian. See no. 203 in this volume.
Sound recording technology has made a large quantity of music available and has given music a newly independent, abstract status. In the future, recordings will influence pedagogy and the creation of new music. *(Lisa Miller)*

5749 DÉVIGNE, Roger. **Enregistrements sonores**
as [Sound recordings], *Travaux du Ier Congrès International de Folklore* (Tours: Arrault et Cie, 1938) 287–89.
In French. See no. 251 in this volume.
Discusses problems in making field recordings of traditional music, including availability of electrical power and microphone choice.

5750 DIDIER, André; LEMONDE, Jean-Louis;
as LÉON, Joseph. **Mesures particulières sur les
haut-parleurs** [Specialized measurements for loud-
speakers], *Stéréophonie et reproduction musicale*
(Paris: Chiron, 1966) 55–61. *Charts, diagr.* In French.
See no. 511 in this volume.
Discusses methods for bridging the gap between objective measures of
speaker quality (tests in an echo-proof environment) and subjective tests,
through a procedure that eliminates the distortions of phase rotation.
(David Bloom)

5751 DUGAS, Claude. **Les technologies modernes et
as leurs applications possibles dans le domaine de
la basse fréquence** [The application of modern technology in the area of bass frequencies], *Stéréophonie et
reproduction musicale* (Paris: Chiron, 1966) 84–92. In
French. See no. 511 in this volume.
Particular attention is given to microelectronic techniques including integrated circuits and hybrid circuits.

5752 ELLIS, R. **La composition des œuvres radio-
as phoniques** [The composition of works for the radio],
*Compte rendu des travaux du Ier Congrès international
d'art radiophonique* (Paris: conference, 1938). In
French. See no. 244 in this volume.

5753 FLAMENT, Edouard. **La musique radiopho-
as nique existe-t-elle? Notes sur l'enregistrement
sur film** [Does music for broadcasting exist? Notes on
recording on film], *Compte rendu des travaux du Ier
Congrès international d'art radiophonique* (Paris: conference, 1938). In French. See no. 244 in this volume.

5754 GABRIEL, Gavino. **La fonografía del folklore
as musical** [The recording of musical folklore], *Lares*
XXII (1956) 120–22. In Spanish. See no. 353 in this
volume.
Discusses the technical challenges faced in the recording of traditional vocal music. One must be both a discriminating scholar and a competent recording engineer to do the work properly.

5755 GORIN-FEINBERG. **Les chœurs devant le mi-
as cro** [Choruses in front of the microphone], *Compte
rendu des travaux du Ier Congrès international d'art
radiophonique* (Paris: conference, 1938). In French.
See no. 244 in this volume.

5756 HANLEY, Miles Laurence. **Phonographic re-
as cording,** *Proceedings of the Second International
Congress of Phonetic Sciences* (Cambridge: Cambridge University Press, 1936) 75–82. See no. 222 in
this volume.

5757 HARTMANN, C.V. **The photographones,** *Ver-
as handlungen des XVI. internationalen Amerikanisten-
Kongresses* (Wien: A. Hartleben, 1910) 563–68. See
no. 61 in this volume.

5758 HILLER, Lejaren. **Some comments on com-
as puter sound synthesis,** *American Society of University Composers: Proceedings of the 1966 conference*
(New York: American Society of University Composers, 1966). See no. 510 in this volume.
Analog-to-digital conversion is useful for finding and analyzing all possible sounds, and for building up nontape archives of electronic music. In the
future analog and digital components will both be necessary.
(Judith Drogichen Meyer)

5759 HUNT, Frederick V. **Stylus-groove relations in
as the phonograph playback process,** *Acustica: International journal of acoustics/Journal international
d'acoustique/Internationale akustische Zeitschrift* IV/1
(1954) 33–35. *Bibliog., charts, diagr.* Summaries in
English, French, and German. See no. 324 in this
volume.
The motion of a phonograph pickup stylus in a lateral-cut record groove is
analyzed with due regard for the first-order effects of elastic deformation of
the groove walls. The relative response at any frequency is governed in part
by a groove-pickup response function embodying the effect of resonance
between the compliance of the groove and the effective mass of the stylus.
A translation-loss function further controls the response at fundamental
frequency only, and imposes a sharp cut-off at a recorded wavelength
which is a function of the stylus and record parameters. The distortion response at harmonic frequencies is effectively controlled by a scanning-loss
function, which also varies with the recorded wavelength and which imposes its own cut-off at a somewhat shorter wavelength. Experimental
measurements with special test recordings confirm the theoretical predic-
tions. *(author)*

5760 INNAMORATI, Libero. **I problemi della
as registrazione musicale** [The problems of music re-
cording], *Atti del secondo Congresso internazionale di
musica* (Firenze: Le Monnier, 1940) 261–65. In Italian;
summaries in French and German. See no. 239 in this
volume.
Discusses the special theoretical and practical difficulties faced by the recording engineer in preparing film soundtracks. *(author)*

5761 IPPEL, Albert; SCHMIDT-GÖRG, Joseph. **Eine
as tönende Musikgeschichte** [A history of music in
sound], *Atti del [I] Congresso internazionale di musica
sacra* (Tournai: Desclée, 1952) 55–56. In German. See
no. 303 in this volume.
Discusses an educational recording series to be produced by the Institut für
Film und Bild in Wissenschaft und Unterricht, Munich, under the general
title *Tönende Musikgeschichte*. *(David Bloom)*

5762 JORDAN, Vilhelm Lassen. **A system for stereo-
as phonic reproduction,** *Acustica: International journal of acoustics/Journal international d'acoustique/
Internationale akustische Zeitschrift* IV/1 (1954)
36–38. *Bibliog., charts, diagr.* Summaries in English,
French, and German. See no. 324 in this volume.
When two loudspeakers transmit the same sound signal, the relation between the angular displacement of the virtual sound source and the difference in intensity level of the two sources is linear within a certain range, and
a mean value of the slope of the curve may be fixed at 0.5 decibels per degree of angle. This implies the use of microphones with suitable directional
characteristics. The stereophonic impression of a two channel system arranged according to this principle is satisfactory, although the level is a little too low for sounds originating close to the axis of symmetry. *(author)*

5763 JOVANOVIĆ, Raško V. **Valeur documentaire
as des enregistrements de pièces ou d'extraits de
pièces** [Documentary value of recordings of pieces or
extracts of pieces], *Acts of the VIIth International Congress of Libraries and Museums of the Performing*

Arts/Actes du VIIe Congrès international des bibliothèques-musées des arts du spectacle ('s-Gravenhage: Theater Instituut Nederland/Netherlands Centre of the International Theatre Institute, 1965) 84–90. *Charts, diagr.* In French. See no. 492 in this volume.

Offers a general appreciation of old recordings, specifically those of opera. A brief discussion of physical media is included (e.g., 78-rpm records, magnetic tape).

5764 KAREL, A. **La musique devant le micro** [Music
as   in front of the mike], *Compte rendu des travaux du Ier Congrès international d'art radiophonique* (Paris: conference, 1938). In French. See no. 244 in this volume.

5765 KOCH, Fritz. **Moderne Aufnahmetechnik**
as   [Modern recording technique], *Bericht über den internationalen musikwissenschaftlichen Kongreß* (Kassel: Bärenreiter, 1957) 133–35. In German. See no. 356 in this volume.

In the early days, sound engineers aimed at the most natural possible sound. Special effects of multiple microphones, echo chambers, and overdubbing were introduced first for dance music, later for entertainment music and operetta. Hans Werner Henze's radio opera *Das Ende einer Welt* (1952) provides an example of art music written with special recording effects in mind. *(David Bloom)*

5766 KOCH, Ludwig. **Schallplattenmusik** [Recorded
as   music], *Atti del primo Congresso internazionale di musica* (Firenze: Le Monnier, 1935) 109–17. In German; summary in Italian. See no. 203 in this volume.

A historical and statistical overview emphasizes the recording industry's traditional commitment to recording art music in relation to more profitable ventures.

5767 KORN, T.S.; DEWÈVRE, J. **Mesures subjec-**
as   **tives de la qualité de reproduction sonore et leur correlation avec les mesures physiques** [Subjective measures of sound reproduction quality and their correlation to physical measures], *Stéréophonie et reproduction musicale* (Paris: Chiron, 1966) 76–83. *Bibliog., charts, diagr.* In French. See no. 511 in this volume.

Report of an experiment in the use of musical logatoms, by analogy with the verbal logatoms used in testing telephone systems.

5768 KOSHIKAWA, Tsuneji; MIYAGAWA, Rikuo;
as   NAKAYAMA, Takeshi. **On the designing method of reproduced sound quality using the multidimensional sensory and emotional scales,** *Problèmes d'acoustique* (Liège: Université de Liège, 1965) M67. See no. 504 in this volume.

Discusses the subjective evaluation of sound quality according to which the physical characteristics of acoustical products—such as stereos and radios—are designed. A scaling model and a new evaluating process of sound quality are proposed. *(Elizabeth A. Wright)*

5769 LANGLOIS, Ludo. **Les instruments de repro-**
as   **duction mécanique destinés à l'usage privé** [Instruments of mechanical reproduction intended for private use], *Compte rendu du dix-septième Congrès de la Confédération Internationale des Sociétés d'Auteurs et Compositeurs* (Paris: Confédération Internationale des Sociétés d'Auteurs et Compositeurs, 1952) 273. In French. See no. 311 in this volume.

Recommends revisions of the definitions of the terms public domain and private domain as the means of controlling the fraudulent use of mechanical reproduction; summarizes resolutions passed by societies in Switzerland, Germany, France, Belgium, Denmark, and Austria. *(Marilyn S. Bliss)*

5770 LIENARD, Jean-Sylvain. **L'usure des disques**
as   [Wear and tear of records], *Stéréophonie et reproduction musicale* (Paris: Chiron, 1966) 17–29. *Illus., charts, diagr.* In French. See no. 511 in this volume.

Discusses physical and perceptual aspects of wear. Adequate care can increase a record's lifespan to as many as 300 playings.

5771 LIENARD, Jean-Sylvain. **L'usure des disques**
as   [Wear and tear of records], *Problèmes d'acoustique* (Liège: Université de Liège, 1965) M63. *Illus.* In French. See no. 504 in this volume.

Discusses efforts to determine the lifespan of a vinyl disk, to illustrate what sort of deterioration the reproduced sound undergoes, and to relate this information to acoustical criteria. *(Elizabeth A. Wright)*

⟶   LUALDI, Adriano. **Due nuove vie per la musica: Radio e film sonoro** [Two new roads for music: Radio and film with sound]. See no. 5198 in this volume.

5772 MAIGRET, J. **Retransmission des spectacles:**
as   **Opéra, opéra-comique, comédie** [Broadcasting shows: Opera, opéra-comique, comedy], *Compte rendu des travaux du Ier Congrès international d'art radiophonique* (Paris: conference, 1938). In French. See no. 244 in this volume.

5773 MANLEY, D.M.J.P. **The subjective judgement**
as   **of liveness and quality of recorded music,** *Problèmes d'acoustique* (Liège: Université de Liège, 1965) M62. *Illus.* In French. See no. 504 in this volume.

Through two experiments using recorded organ and choir music, it was determined that a combination of microphone positioning and a keen ear and judgment on the part of the listener were the most important factors in evaluation of the recordings. *(Brian Doherty)*

5774 MANSION, Madeleine Louise. **Au sujet de la**
as   **place des artistes par rapport au micro** [Concerning the placement of artists in relation to the microphone], *Compte rendu des travaux du Ier Congrès international d'art radiophonique* (Paris: conference, 1938). In French. See no. 244 in this volume.

5775 MERTENS, H. **L'écoute stéréophonique** [Ste-
as   reophonic listening], *Stéréophonie et reproduction musicale* (Paris: Chiron, 1966) 102–16. *Illus., charts, diagr.* In French. See no. 511 in this volume.

Discusses the physics of stereophonic sound reproduction in its relation to the theory of directional and spatial hearing.

5776 MEYROVICZ. **Nécessité de la retouche des**
as   **partitions pour l'exécution radiophonique** [The necessity of retouching scores for radio performances], *Compte rendu des travaux du Ier Congrès international d'art radiophonique* (Paris: conference, 1938). In French. See no. 244 in this volume.

5777 MIGOT, Georges. **L'orchestre au micro** [Orches-
as   tra at the mike], *Compte rendu des travaux du Ier Congrès international d'art radiophonique* (Paris: conference, 1938). In French. See no. 244 in this volume.

5778 MIRANDA, J. Rodrigues de. **The radio set as an**
as   **instrument for the reproduction of music,** *Acustica: International journal of acoustics/Journal international d'acoustique/Internationale akustische Zeitschrift* IV/1 (1954) 38–41. *Charts, diagr.* Summa-

ries in English, French, and German. See no. 324 in this volume.

It is important to be able to adjust bass response, to cut off or gradually attenuate the treble, and to reduce distortion as high frequency range increases. The electroacoustical engineer and the designer should cooperate closely. The cabinet must be rigid, the loudspeaker chosen in accordance with the acoustical properties of the cabinet, placed forward, and its cloth chosen carefully. *(author)*

5779
as

MOREUX, Serge. **Le mixage en radio et ses nécessités** [Mixing for the radio and its conditions], *Compte rendu des travaux du Ier Congrès international d'art radiophonique* (Paris: conference, 1938). In French. See no. 244 in this volume.

5780
as

POOT, Marcel. **Relations de la musique et du micro** [Music-microphone relations], *Compte rendu des travaux du Ier Congrès international d'art radiophonique* (Paris: conference, 1938). In French. See no. 244 in this volume.

5781
as

REINECKE, Hans-Peter. **Musikwissenschaft und Schallplatte** [Musicology and the phonograph record], *Report of the Eighth Congress of the International Musicological Society. I: Papers* (Kassel: Bärenreiter, 1961) 404–18. In German. See no. 439 in this volume.

Discusses the technological and artistic changes in the musical world brought about by recording. Topics include modifications in sound through recording technique, effects on sound and interpretation, standardization and perfectionism, and the idea of the recording as a document.

5782
as

REINECKE, Hans-Peter. **Der Musikwissenschaftler in der Schallplatten-Industrie** [The musicologist in the recording industry], *Bericht über den internationalen musikwissenschaftlichen Kongreß* (Kassel: Bärenreiter, 1963) 330–31. In German. See no. 452 in this volume.

Discusses career possibilities for musicologists as producers, marketing specialists and press relations personnel, writers/editors, and engineers. *(David Bloom)*

5783
as

REISCHEK, Andreas. **Collecting methods as affected by modern technical equipment,** *Journal of the International Folk Music Council* VIII (1956) 53–54. See no. 349 in this volume.

Summary of a paper. Scientists—including folklorists—ought to use the most up-to-date equipment available, except when practical considerations, such as portability, are factors. *(James R. Cowdery)*

5784
as

ROSBAUD, Hans. **Probleme der Programmgestaltung und der künstlerisch-technischen Wiedergabe im deutschen Rundfunk** [Issues in programming and artistic and technical reproduction in German radio], *Atti del primo Congresso internazionale di musica* (Firenze: Le Monnier, 1935) 118–23. In German; summary in Italian. See no. 203 in this volume.

With an eye toward educating the public, radio programmers face the challenge of balancing light music with the works of great Classical, Romantic, and modern composers, while avoiding music in truly bad taste. Technical issues include the size of broadcast studios and the placement, number, and quality of microphones. *(author)*

5785
as

RÖSSEL-MAJDAN, K. **Das fundamentale Problem der Phonokopie** [The fundamental problem of recording], *Cahiers d'études de radio-télévision* 3-4 (1955) 302–09. In German. See no. 334 in this volume.

A brief overview of technical and aesthetic limitations.

5786
as

SAFRANEC; MANGERET; ROSENTHAL. **Les échanges de programmes musicaux entre les radios étrangères** [Exchanges of musical programs among foreign radios], *Compte rendu des travaux du Ier Congrès international d'art radiophonique* (Paris: conference, 1938). In French. See no. 244 in this volume.

5787
as

SARNETTE, Eric. **Les nouveautés dans la composition des orchestres et leur prise de son radiophonique** [New developments in the composition of orchestras and their recording for the radio], *Compte rendu des travaux du Ier Congrès international d'art radiophonique* (Paris: conference, 1938). In French. See no. 244 in this volume.

5788
as

SCHAEFFNER, André. **Le disque: Sa portée, ses défaillances, ses conséquences** [The phonograph record: Its importance, its weaknesses, its consequences], *Atti del secondo Congresso internazionale di musica* (Firenze: Le Monnier, 1940) 156–65. In French; summaries in Italian and German. See no. 239 in this volume.

The record has contributed greatly to the education of the public and of performers and scholars, particularly in the case of non-European and traditional European musics, for which our conventional notation is not adequate. The lack of creativity in the recording process as compared, say, with photography, and the distortions records make in the sound of a performance are well known. It is possible that these distortions will find an echo in the compositions of the future; or, equally likely, that composers will detach themselves from what is realized on records and direct themselves toward new expressions, as has happened to painting in the face of photography. *(author)*

5789
as

SCHIESSER, H. **Die charakteristischen Eigenschaften magnetischer Schallaufzeichnungen in Abhängigkeit von den Betriebsbedingungen und den Tonträgereigenschaften** [The characteristic properties of magnetic sound recording as derived from recording conditions and properties of the medium], *Acustica: International journal of acoustics/Journal international d'acoustique/Internationale akustische Zeitschrift* IV/1 (1954) 41–44. *Bibliog., charts, diagr.* In German; summaries in English, French, and German. See no. 324 in this volume.

Discusses sensitivity, level, frequency response, nonlinear distortion, background noise, print-through, and erasure.

5790
as

SCHLEGEL, F. **Einige Schallplattenaufnahmeprobleme** [Some sound disc recording problems], *Acustica: International journal of acoustics/Journal international d'acoustique/Internationale akustische Zeitschrift* IV/1 (1954) 45–47. *Bibliog., charts, diagr.* In German; summaries in English, French, and German. See no. 324 in this volume.

Certain problems in phonograph disc recording are discussed with special reference to cutting heads damped by countercoupling only. *(author)*

5791
as

SCHLENGER. **Gibt es mikrophongeeignete Stimmen, und welches sind ihre Kennzeichen?** [Are there voices suited to microphones, and how are they recognized?], *Bericht über den Internationalen Kongreß Singen und Sprechen* (München: Oldenbourg, 1938) 339–41. In German. See no. 257 in this volume.

Voices suited to radio are those that are well placed, thoroughly trained from a technical standpoint, and especially those whose owners have something to say. It is certainly not the case that weak, whispery voices work best. *(David Bloom)*

5792
as

SEEGER, Charles. **The Model B melograph: A progress report,** *Journal of the International Folk Music Council* XIV (1962) 168. See no. 442 in this volume.

5793
as

STEVENS, Denis. **Musicology and the phonograph record,** *Report of the Eighth Congress of the International Musicological Society. II: Reports* (Kassel: Bärenreiter, 1962) 163–65. See no. 440 in this volume.

A report on a discussion by Gerald ABRAHAM, Ludwig FINSCHER, Irving KOLODIN, George LIST, Carl de NYS, Harold SPIVACKE, and Denis STEVENS of the papers by Hans-Peter Reinecke and Philip L. Miller abstracted as RILM 5781 and RILM 899 respectively, in this volume.

5794
as

THIENHAUS, Erich. **Vorführung stereophonischer Bandaufnahmen** [Demonstration of stereophonic tape recordings], *Kongreß-Bericht: Gesellschaft für Musikforschung* (Kassel; Basel: Bärenreiter, 1950) 243–45. *Charts, diagr.* In German. See no. 299 in this volume.

5795
as

TRAUTWEIN, Friedrich. **Die technische Akustik in Schule und Praxis des Singens und Sprechens** [Sound technology in the study and practice of singing and speaking], *Bericht über den Internationalen Kongreß Singen und Sprechen* (München: Oldenbourg, 1938) 298–301. In German. See no. 257 in this volume.

Defends technology against the charge of being in some sense opposed to art and creativity, and surveys some of the uses of sound recording and amplification in music pedagogy and performance. *(David Bloom)*

5796
as

URBAŃSKI, Janusz. **Das Chopin-Klavier auf der Basis der zeitgenössischen Phonographie** [The Chopin piano, based on contemporary recording technology], *The book of the first international musicological congress devoted to the works of Frederick Chopin* (Warszawa: Państwowe Wydawnictwo Naukowe, 1963) 455–60. In German. See no. 425 in this volume.

Particular attention is given to the project of the Nagrania Polskie/Muza recording company, beginning 1959, of recording Chopin's complete works as performed by Polish artists. *(David Bloom)*

5797
as

WERNER, M. **Critères de qualité de la transmission à modulation de fréquence** [Criteria of quality in FM broadcasting], *Stéréophonie et reproduction musicale* (Paris: Chiron, 1966) 62–75. *Illus., charts, diagr.* In French. See no. 511 in this volume.

FM transmission needs to overcome the problems of poor-quality speakers and the very unpleasant crackling caused by overload; some solutions are proposed.

5798
as

WIRTH, Helmut. **Der Musikwissenschaftler beim Rundfunk** [The musicologist in radio], *Bericht über den internationalen musikwissenschaftlichen Kongreß* (Kassel: Bärenreiter, 1963) 328–29. In German. See no. 452 in this volume.

Discusses careers in radio for the young musicologist.

5799
as

ZWIRNER, Eberhard. **Schallplatte und Tonfilm als Quellen sprech- und gesangskundlicher Forschung** [Records and sound films as sources for research in the study of speech and singing], *Bericht über den Internationalen Kongreß Singen und Sprechen* (München: Oldenbourg, 1938) 30–34. In German. See no. 257 in this volume.

A brief history of the development of sound recording in the record and film industries, from the perspective of the student of phonetic change and change in singing technique. *(Sylvia Eversole)*

86 Physics, mathematics, acoustics, architecture

5800
as

ANGLAS, Jules Philippe Louis. **La science des sons dans ses rapports avec la musique** [The science of sound in relation to music], *Rapport sur la musique contemporaine française* (Roma: Armani & Stein, 1913) 127–38. *Bibliog., charts, diagr.* In French. See no. 76 in this volume.

Surveys the state of research in the first decade of the 20th c.

5801
as

BERANEK, Leo Leroy. **Audience absorption and seat absorption in halls for music,** *Proceedings of the Third International Congress on Acoustics* (Amsterdam: Elsevier Science, 1961) II, 913–17. *Bibliog., charts, diagr.* See no. 414 in this volume.

Preliminary report of research discussed in the author's *Music, acoustics and architecture* (New York, 1962).

5802
as

BERANEK, Leo Leroy. **Rating of acoustic quality of concert halls and opera houses,** *Fourth International Congress on Acoustics* (København: conference, 1962) II, 15–29. *Illus.* See no. 448 in this volume.

Factors considered include reverberation time, intensity of direct sound, diffusion, balance and blend, and presence of acoustical blemishes, such as echo, noise, tonal distortion, and hall nonuniformity. A more detailed account is provided in the author's *Music, Acoustics, and Architecture*, New York 1962. *(Allen Lott)*

5803
as

BIEHLE, Johannes. **Theorie des Kirchenbaues vom Standpunkte des Kirchenmusikers** [Architecture in Protestant churches from the standpoint of the church musician], *Report of the Fourth Congress of the International Musical Society* (London: Novello, 1912) 286–302. *Illus., charts, diagr., tech. drawings.* In German. See no. 71 in this volume.

Offers suggestions for architectural designs for Protestant chuches.

⟶

BIGGS, E. Power. **A musician and his acoustical environment.** See no. 3338 in this volume.

5804
as

BLAUKOPF, Kurt. **Nutzbarmachung neuerer raumakustischer und electroakustischer Erkenntnisse für die Musikwissenschaft** [How recent findings in room acoustics and electroacoustics can be useful for musicology], *Proceedings of the Third International Congress on Acoustics* (Amsterdam: Elsevier Science, 1961) II, 983–86. *Bibliog.* In German. See no. 414 in this volume.

5805
as

BURRIS-MEYER, Harold; MALLORY, Vincent. **Die Verwendung moderner akustischer Methoden zur Lösung von Problemen des Theaters und der Oper sowohl klassischer wie auch moderner Art** [The use of modern acoustic methods for the solution of problems in theater and opera buildings of classic as well as modern style], *Proceedings of the Third International Congress on Acoustics* (Amsterdam: Elsevier Science, 1961) II, 967–71. *Illus., charts, diagr.* In German. See no. 414 in this volume.

5806 CANAC, François. **Equation canonique des**
as **théâtres antiques: Rôle de l'angle d'écoute et**
de l'orchestre [Canonic equation of ancient theaters:
The role of the angle of listening and of the orchestra],
Problèmes d'acoustique (Liège: Université de Liège,
1965) G13. In French. See no. 504 in this volume.
Ancient theaters were constructed using similar geometric proportions that
can be related to a common equation.

5807 CANAC, François. **Faithfulness in the trans-**
as **mission of music as a means of preservation,**
The preservation of traditional forms of the learned and
popular music of the Orient and the Occident/La
préservation des formes traditionelles de la musique
savante et populaire dans les pays d'Orient et
d'Occident (Urbana: Center for Comparative
Psycholinguistics, Institute of Communications Research, 1964) 73–82. See no. 443 in this volume.
Discusses the physical effects of performance spaces, and of recording
techniques, on the perception of musical works, and the role of physics in
correcting problems. *(Judith Drogichen Meyer)*

5808 DAVID, E.E., Jr.; SCHRODDER, G.R. **Pitch dis-**
as **crimination of complex sounds,** *Proceedings of*
the Third International Congress on Acoustics (Amsterdam: Elsevier Science, 1961) I, 106–09. *Bibliog.,*
charts, diagr. See no. 414 in this volume.

5809 DENÉRÉAZ, Alexandre. **De la musique à**
as **l'"Harmonie des spheres"** [From music to the
"harmony of the spheres"], *Congrès jubilaire* (Brugge:
Gruuthuuse, 1925) 221–22. In French. See no. 119 in
this volume.
Cosmic and physical phenomena (e.g., planetary orbits, human anatomy,
the sequence of the four seasons) may have a certain concordance with music theory as regards the tempered scale. *(Susan Poliniak)*

5810 DENÉRÉAZ, Alexandre. **Rythmes humains et**
as **rythmes cosmiques** [Human and cosmic rhythms],
Compte rendu du Ier Congrès du rythme (Genève:
Institut Jaques-Dalcroze, 1926) 39–69. *Charts, diagr.*
In French. See no. 123 in this volume.
Rhythmic and harmonic properties are closely related to the Fibonacci se-
ries, specifically the ratio 618/1000 (n/n+1, as n increases). The ratios of
human anatomy and planet distances also relate to musical ratios.

5811 DIDIER, André. **La résonance dans les échelles**
as **musicales: Le point de vue des physiciens** [Res-
onance in musical scales: The viewpoint of physicists],
La résonance dans les échelles musicales (Paris: Centre
National de la Recherche Scientifique [CNRS], 1963)
21–32. *Charts, diagr.* In French; summaries in English
and German. See no. 420 in this volume.
Discusses the nature of resonance as a concept in acoustics, optics, and
electricity; the notion of the musical instrument as frequency oscillator; and
the problem of scales.

5812 DILLENSEGER, R.P. **La puissance organale**
as **mise en proportion avec le cubage des**
sanctuaires et des salles de concert [The sound
volume of organs in proportion to the area of churches
and concert halls], *Compte rendu du Congrès d'orgue*
tenu à l'Université de Strasbourg. IV (Strasbourg:
Société Strasbourgeoise de Librairie Sostralib, 1934)
129–34. *Charts, diagr.* In French. See no. 199 in this
volume.
Outlines various acoustic factors affecting the performance of organs according to the size of venues, and presents statistics pertaining to the
Strasbourg cathedral.

5813 FEININGER, Laurence. **Raum und Architek-**
as **tur in der vielchörigen römischen Kirchen-**
musik des 17. Jahrhunderts [Space and architecture in the polychoral church music of the 17th century],
Bericht über den siebenten internationalen musik-
wissenschaftlichen Kongress (Kassel: Bärenreiter,
1959) 100–01. In German. See no. 390 in this volume.
The Venetian and Roman schools of polychoral writing differ fundamentally. The former employs choirs of contrasting register and involves a great
simplification of harmony and bass line; its effects are coloristic. The Roman school, which absorbed the technique of the Netherlandish composers
resident in Rome via Palestrina, deploys several choirs in a single register.
The counterpoint resists simplification. This art animates the architectural
spaces for which it was conceived, the great Baroque churches of Rome; at
St. Peter's the four choirs, elevated some 25 meters and distant from one another some 40 meters, answer one another across the altar, which becomes
the focal point for listening. Since the Roman polychoral idiom exists only
to set space to music, musical expression per se is foreign to it. Orazio
Benevoli is its great master. *(Carl Skoggard)*

5814 FELDTKELLER, Richard. **Hörbarkeit nicht-**
as **linearer Verzerrungen bei der Übertragung**
von Instrumentenklängen [Audible, nonlinear
distortions during the transmission of instrumental
sounds], *Acustica: International journal of acoustics/*
Journal international d'acoustique/Internationale
akustische Zeitschrift IV/1 (1954) 70–72. *Illus., charts,*
diagr. In German; summaries in English, French, and
German. See no. 324 in this volume.
A timbre poor in overtones is much more sensitive to nonlinear distortion
than one rich in overtones. The causes and the extent of this difference are
discussed. *(author)*

5815 FRANSSEN, Nico V. **The mechanism of the hu-**
as **man voice and wind instruments,** *Fourth Inter-*
national Congress on Acoustics (København: conference, 1962) I, G12. *Illus.* See no. 448 in this volume.
Sound production with a continuous air stream is compared to the functioning of an electric motor with a continuous direct current supply. As with the
case of the motor, a tuning element and an amplifier must be present in wind
instruments. Formant frequencies as well as pitch frequencies are generated, not filtered. *(Allen Lott)*

5816 FURDUEV, Vadim Vladimirovič. **Evaluation**
as **objective de l'acoustique des salles** [Objective
evaluation of the acoustics of auditoriums], *Problèmes*
d'acoustique (Liège: Université de Liège, 1965) 41–45.
In French. See no. 504 in this volume.
Presents techniques for evaluating the acoustics of concert halls and audi-
toriums and describing these evaluations mathematically. *(Brian Doherty)*

5817 FURRER, Willi; LAUBER, Anselm. **Die**
as **raumakustische Diffusität in Schallaufnahme-**
und Radiostudios [The room acoustical diffusion in
recording and radio studios], *Acustica: International*
journal of acoustics/Journal international
d'acoustique/Internationale akustische Zeitschrift IV/1
(1954) 29–33. *Illus., charts, diagr.* In German; summaries in English, French, and German. See no. 324 in this
volume.
Diffuseness, or the homogeneity of a room's sound field, plays an important part in radio and recording studios. Earlier investigations showed that
the mean height of a frequency response peak of a room is a suitable index
of diffuseness. However, the determination of this quantity from the frequency response is so laborious that a special apparatus had to be developed to ensure quick and easy measurement. *(author)*

5818 GELUK, J.J. **Electronic tuners for musical**
as **pitch,** *Proceedings of the Third International Con-*
gress on Acoustics (Amsterdam: Elsevier Science,

1961) I, 220–23. *Bibliog., charts, diagr.* See no. 414 in this volume.

5819
as
GEORGE, W.H. **A sound reversal technique applied to the study of tone quality,** *Acustica: International journal of acoustics/Journal international d'acoustique/Internationale akustische Zeitschrift* IV/1 (1954) 224–25. *Bibliog.* Summaries in English, French, and German. See no. 324 in this volume.

Reversal of magnetic-tape sound recordings is used to investigate the influence upon tone quality of growth and decay of sounds. If the instantaneous overtone structure changes with time, reversal of the sound profoundly alters the tone quality. The idea of tone quality as the overtone structure of the steady state of a note modified by transients is abandoned for the idea of tone quality as a pattern property. *(author)*

5820
as
GOSSET, Alphonse. **Le théâtre populaire** [Popular theater], *IIIᵉ Congrès international de l'art public* (Liège: n.p., 1905) 15. In French. See no. 49 in this volume.

Discusses the architecture of a popular theater.

5821
as
GRÜTZMACHER, Martin. **Ein neuer Tonhöhenschreiber, seine Anwendung auf mathematische, phonetische und musikalische Probleme** [A new instrument for the graphic representation of pitch, and its use in mathematical, phonetic, and musical problems], *Proceedings of the Third International Congress of Phonetic Sciences* (Gent: Rijksuniversitet, Fonetisch Laboratorium, 1939) 105–09. *Illus.* In German. See no. 259 in this volume.

A device developed in joint work by the author and Werner Lottermoser uses the technology of the oscilloscope, cathode rays, and photo cells to produce a continuous graphic representation of pitch on light-sensitive paper. It can be used for the study of speech or of music; in the latter case staff notation can be superimposed on the graph. *(Terence Ford)*

5822
as
GUITTARD, J. **Calculs et mesures d'impédances acoustiques** [The calculation and measurement of acoustic impedances], *Acoustique musicale* (Paris: Centre National de la Recherche Scientifique [CNRS], 1959) 221–29. *Charts, diagr.* In French. See no. 393 in this volume.

Proposes a mathematical account of variable impedance in resonant tubes, as observed with the aid of the manometric flame capsule. *(David Bloom)*

5823
as
HIRSCHWEHR, E. **Raumakustische Messungen an der grossen Wiener Stadthalle** [Room-acoustic measurements in the Wiener Stadthalle], *Proceedings of the Third International Congress on Acoustics* (Amsterdam: Elsevier Science, 1961) II, 243–47. *Charts, diagr.* In German. See no. 414 in this volume.

5824
as
JÁRFÁS, T.; TARNÓCZY, Tamás. **Physikalische und Subjektive Nachhallzeit** [Physical and subjective reverberation time], *Proceedings of the Third International Congress on Acoustics* (Amsterdam: Elsevier Science, 1961) II, 974–78. *Charts, diagr.* In German. See no. 414 in this volume.

Discusses the relation between reverberation as a physical phenomenon and the listener's perception of reverberation in concert halls and recordings.

5825
as
JONES, Stephen. **Two methods of measuring intonation,** *Bericht über die I. Tagung der Internationalen Gesellschaft für Experimentelle Phonetik* (Bonn: Scheur, 1930) 49–52. *Illus.* See no. 169 in this volume.

Describes experimental approaches to the kymographic notation of melodic curves in speech or singing, with a logarithmic protractor, and with a

scaled array of metal reeds that vibrate sympathetically with a voice produced through an attached mouth funnel. *(L. Poundie Burstein)*

5826
as
JORDAN, Vilhelm Lassen. **The building-up process of sound pulses in a room and its relation to concert hall quality,** *Proceedings of the Third International Congress on Acoustics* (Amsterdam: Elsevier Science, 1961) II, 922–25. *Charts, diagr.* See no. 414 in this volume.

Discusses solutions arrived at in the acoustic design of Tivolis Koncertsal, Copenhagen, inaugurated 1956.

5827
as
KNOWLES, H.S. **Artificial acoustical environment control,** *Acustica: International journal of acoustics/Journal international d'acoustique/Internationale akustische Zeitschrift* IV/1 (1954) 80–82. *Bibliog., charts, diagr.* Summaries in German, French, and English. See no. 324 in this volume.

The acoustic field of a concert hall differs markedly from that of an outdoor amphitheater. To provide a sound field outdoors approximating that of a hall an array of loudspeakers was suspended over and around an area and supplied with multiply delayed, attenuated, and spectrally modified signals. Listeners showed a significant preference for the simulated indoor acoustical environment even when presented with a visible outdoor environment. *(author)*

5828
as
KNUDSEN, Vern O. **Acoustics of music rooms,** *Fourth International Congress on Acoustics* (København: conference, 1962) I, M27. See no. 448 in this volume.

5829
as
KNUDSEN, Vern O. **The acoustics of Symphony Hall, Boston,** *Sound and man* (New York: American Institute of Physics, 1957) 109–10. See no. 369 in this volume.

Boston's Symphony Hall's designer, Wallace Clement Ware Sabine, did pioneering work in architectural acoustics. The hall has good timing, blending, and distribution of reflected sound, and is free from noise, echoes, and undesirable reflections. *(Allen Lott)*

5830
as
KÖHLER, Wolfgang. **Akustische Untersuchungen** [Acoustic investigations], *Bericht über den V. Kongress für experimentelle Psychologie* (Leipzig: Barth, 1912) 151. In German. See no. 79 in this volume.

⟶
KOSCHEL, H. **Hörmängel und ihre audiometrische Feststellung** [Hearing deficiencies and their audiometric detection]. See no. 5671 in this volume.

5831
as
KOSTEN, Cornelis Willem; DE LANGE, Pieter Albert. **The new Rotterdam concert hall: Some aspects of the acoustic design,** *Problèmes d'acoustique* (Liège: Université de Liège, 1965) G43. In French. See no. 504 in this volume.

Discusses the acoustical rationale for various constructional aspects of the Concertgebouw de Doelen. Mathematical justifications for figures on absorption coefficients are given. *(Brian Doherty)*

5832
as
KREICHGAUER, Alfons. **Akustische Probleme der Opern- und Sprechbühne** [Acoustic problems of the opera and speaking stage], *Bericht über den Internationalen Kongreß Singen und Sprechen* (München: Oldenbourg, 1938) 319–22. In German. See no. 257 in this volume.

Stage sets affect room acoustics, and it is important for the set designer, performers, and particularly the director to take this into account. Lighting has an acoustic significance, in that performers will be more intelligible if their mouths are well lit. Conductors, who have the ultimate responsibility for sound quality, are poorly placed to judge it from a position in the pit; they ought to make a point of listening at least to crucial passages from the house. Authors and composers should understand that not all desirable dynamic effects can be achieved. *(David Bloom)*

5833 KREIDLER, Walter. **Die Tonleiter als Ton-**
as **spektrum** [The scale as a spectrum of tones], *Kongreß-Bericht: Gesellschaft für Musikforschung* (Kassel; Basel: Bärenreiter, 1950) 229–30. In German. See no. 299 in this volume.

5834 KREPS, Joseph. **Le "nombre musical" chez**
as **saint Augustin et au Moyen Âge** [The musical number of St. Augustine and during the Middle Ages], *Compte rendu du Ier Congrès du rythme* (Genève: Institut Jaques-Dalcroze, 1926) 21–25. In French. See no. 123 in this volume.

In his treatise *De musica*, St. Augustine defines music as a combination of the arts of movement. *Numerus musicalis* indicates not rhythm, but the mathematical proportions of the intervals.

5835 KUHL, Walter. **Optimal acoustical design of**
as **rooms for performing, listening, and record-ing,** *Sound and man* (New York: American Institute of Physics, 1957) 53–58. See no. 369 in this volume.

The complex nature of the optimal room acoustical design is stressed. Optimal reverberation time values are given for rooms used for different purposes. The effects of first reflections from the boundaries are discussed, with attention to diffusors of various types. *(author)*

5836 LEIPP, Émile. **Méthode d'appréciation des**
as **qualités musicales d'un ensemble orgue-salle** [Method of appreciating the musical qualities of a whole organ-room], *Problèmes d'acoustique* (Liège: Université de Liège, 1965) M51. *Illus.* In French. See no. 504 in this volume.

Extant methods are insufficient for measuring the acoustics of a room and obtaining a satisfactory correlation between what is heard by the musician and what is heard by the listener. A method is proposed that uses a sonograph for measuring the musical quality of a room containing an organ (churches are used as examples). *(Elizabeth A. Wright)*

5837 LOTTERMOSER, Werner. **Akustik und Musik**
as [Acoustics and music], *Bericht über den internationalen musikwissenschaftlichen Kongreß* (Kassel: Bärenreiter, 1957) 148–56. *Illus., facs., charts, diagr., tech. drawings.* In German. See no. 356 in this volume.

Overview of research from 1955-56, particularly in Germany, including discussion of sound reproduction, tuning issues, spatial acoustics, issues in organ building, and neurophysiological questions.

5838 LUKÁCS, M. **Subjektive Untersuchungen**
as **über den Zusammenhang zwischen der Nach-hallzeit und dem musikalischen Tempo** [Subjective investigations of the relationship between reverberation time and musical tempo], *Proceedings of the Third International Congress on Acoustics* (Amsterdam: Elsevier Science, 1961) II, 977–82. *Bibliog., charts, diagr.* In German. See no. 414 in this volume.

5839 MARTIN, Daniel W. **Musical implications of**
as **standardized tuning frequency,** *Fourth International Congress on Acoustics* (København: conference, 1962) I, P52. See no. 448 in this volume.

Some of the most outstanding orchestras deviate intentionally from internationally established tuning frequency standards, for musical reasons.

Experiments are needed to discover the nature of the perception and identification of such deviations and explore the possibility of and basis for a musically optimum reference frequency. *(Allen Lott)*

5840 MERCIER, J. **Étude de la stabilité des oscilla-**
as **tions entretenues dans un tuyau sonore couplé à un tuyau mort** [Study of the stability of oscillations maintained in a resonant tube coupled to an inert tube], *Acoustique musicale* (Paris: Centre National de la Recherche Scientifique [CNRS], 1959) 231–37. *Charts, diagr.* In French. See no. 393 in this volume.

5841 MEYER, Erwin. **Die raumakustischen Ein-**
as **flüße bei Sprach- und Gesangsdarbietungen** [The influence of room acoustics in spoken and sung performances], *Bericht über den Internationalen Kongreß Singen und Sprechen* (München: Oldenbourg, 1938) 100–08. *Charts, diagr.* In German. See no. 257 in this volume.

Discusses the effects of reverberation time, room size, and the use of fabric wall covering on sound output and intelligibility.

5842 MEYER-EPPLER, Werner; LEICHER, Hans.
as **Zur Erkennbarkeit gesungener Vokale** [The recognizability of sung vowels], *Proceedings of the Third International Congress on Acoustics* (Amsterdam: Elsevier Science, 1961) I, 236–38. *Bibliog., charts, diagr.* In German. See no. 414 in this volume.

5843 MICHEL, Eugen. **Raumakustische Praxis**
as [Practical room acoustics], *Bericht über den Internationalen Kongreß Singen und Sprechen* (München: Oldenbourg, 1938) 98–99. In German. See no. 257 in this volume.

One of the best ways to design a room acoustically, large or small, is to follow established practice.

5844 MOLES, André. **The characterization of sound**
as **objects by use of the level recorder in musical acoustics,** *Acustica: International journal of acoustics/Journal international d'acoustique/Internationale akustische Zeitschrift* IV/1 (1954) 241–44. *Illus., bibliog., charts, diagr.* Summaries in English, French, and German. See no. 324 in this volume.

A musical sound is a quasi-periodic phenomenon, best expressed by a three-dimensional representation in terms of level, pitch, and duration; its perception follows the Weber-Fechner law. Because the logarithmic bathymeter is subject to various restrictions, and only gives recordings of the level-time plane, a method of signal classification was developed that can be applied to both noises and musical sounds. *(author)*

5845 MÜLLER, Ludwig. **Das optische Bild akustisch**
as **guter Räume** [The optical image of an acoustically good space], *Bericht über den internationalen musikwissenschaftlichen Kongreß* (Kassel: Bärenreiter, 1957) 168–69. *Charts, diagr.* In German. See no. 356 in this volume.

An acoustically optimal hall can be recognized visually by the quantity and proportion of wood and soft fabric in the interior surfaces. Special characteristics that may or may not be desirable in a particular case are provided by the use of baffles on the walls or by smooth walls and ceiling. *(David Bloom)*

5846 MUNCEY, R.W.; NICKSON, A.F.B. **The acous-**
as **tics of the Sidney Myer Music Bowl, Melbourne, Australia,** *Proceedings of the Third International Congress on Acoustics* (Amsterdam: Elsevier Science, 1961) II, 948–50. *Illus., bibliog.* See no. 414 in this volume.

The structure, set in a natural amphitheater, was opened in 1959 as the largest purpose-built permanent outdoor performance venue in Australia.

5847 MUNCEY, R.W.; NICKSON, A.F.B. **The audi-**
as **ence and room acoustics,** *Proceedings of the Third International Congress on Acoustics* (Amsterdam: Elsevier Science, 1961) II, 936–38. *Bibliog.* See no. 414 in this volume.

5848 PEUTZ, V.M.A. **The acoustics of large halls,**
as *Proceedings of the Third International Congress on Acoustics* (Amsterdam: Elsevier Science, 1961) II, 941–43. *Charts, diagr.* See no. 414 in this volume.

5849 PLOMP, Reinier; BOUMAN, M.A. **Threshold**
as **for tone pulses,** *Proceedings of the Third International Congress on Acoustics* (Amsterdam: Elsevier Science, 1961) I, 119–21. *Bibliog., charts, diagr.* See no. 414 in this volume.

5850 PLOMP, Reinier; LEVELT, Willem J.M. **Musi-**
as **cal consonance and critical bandwidth,** *Fourth International Congress on Acoustics* (København: conference, 1962) I, P55. See no. 448 in this volume.
For complex tones (fundamental frequency plus overtones), consonance is related to simple frequency ratios, as Hermann von Helmholtz originally suggested, but for pure tones, consonance is a function of the difference in frequency between the tones. *(Allen Lott)*

5851 RAES, Auguste C. **Mesures des coefficients de**
as **réflexion en amplitude et phase** [Measurements of coefficients of reflection in amplitude and phase], *Acustica: International journal of acoustics/Journal international d'acoustique/Internationale akustische Zeitschrift* IV/1 (1954) 123–25. *Illus., charts, diagr.* In French; summaries in English, French, and German. See no. 324 in this volume.
Describes three methods which proved to be useful in architectural acoustics. The main principle is to separate the incident and the reflected waves in time and space so they can be measured independently, reducing calculations to a minimum. Acoustical transmission line tests are convenient for testing small samples under normal incidence with great operational speed. A direct reading reflection coefficient meter is described. Free room tests are designed to test absorbing materials, including vibrating panels and curtains, in situ and without touching them, under normal incidence. Oblique incidence tests are also discussed. *(author)*

5852 RENNER, Frumentius. **Raumakustik und Erd-**
as **magnetismus** [Room acoustics and terrestrial magnetism], *Altbayerische Orgeltage* (Berlin: Merseburger, 1958) 30–33. *Charts, diagr.* In German. See no. 355 in this volume.
Many cases of pervasive acoustic distortion in large rooms can be blamed primarily on local disturbances in the terrestrial magnetic field. The phenomenon is explained, and ways of mitigating it, in terms of the room-acoustic properties of church organs, are briefly discussed. *(David Bloom)*

5853 RIMSKIJ-KORSAKOV, Andrej Vladimirovič.
as **Statistische Eigenschaften des Rundfunk-signals** [Statistical properties of the radio signal], *Proceedings of the Third International Congress on Acoustics* (Amsterdam: Elsevier Science, 1961) II, 779–81. *Charts, diagr.* In German. See no. 414 in this volume.

5854 ROSSMAN, W.L. **Acoustics and architecture in**
as **auditorium design,** *Proceedings of the Third International Congress on Acoustics* (Amsterdam: Elsevier Science, 1961) II, 938–40. See no. 414 in this volume.

5855 SELMER, E.W. **Vorschläge zu Zeitnormungen**
as **bei Melodieaufnahmen** [Proposals for standardizing the time representation in intonation records], *Bericht über die I. Tagung der Internationalen Gesellschaft für Experimentelle Phonetik* (Bonn: Scheur, 1930) 31–32. In German. See no. 169 in this volume.
The time dimension in kymographic representation of melodic curves in speech and singing should be standardized, so that curves for different languages and dialects can be directly compared. A good standard would be a horizontal extension of 300mm/sec.

5856 SMALL, Arnold M.; MARTIN, Daniel W. **Musi-**
as **cal acoustics: Aims, progress, and forecast,** *Sound and man* (New York: American Institute of Physics, 1957) 68–75. *Music.* See no. 369 in this volume.
An attempt to delineate the broad areas and objectives of the science of musical acoustics and point up current problems, progress, and outlook. *(author)*

———→ SPIVACKE, Harold. **The place of acoustics in musicology.** See no. 926 in this volume.

———→ STREICH, Rudolf. **Das elektrische Musikinstrument im Spiegel der akustischen Forschung** [The electric musical instrument as reflected in acoustics research]. See no. 3672 in this volume.

5857 STUMPF, Carl. **Über neuere Untersuchungen**
as **zur Tonlehre** [On new studies of musical acoustics], *Bericht über den VI. Kongress für Experimentelle Psychologie* (Leipzig: Barth, 1914) 305f. In German. See no. 90 in this volume.

———→ STUMPF, Carl. **Vergleichende Musikforschung, Akustik, Tonpsychologie: Verhandlungen und Vorträge** [Comparative music research, acoustics, music psychology: Discussions and lectures]. See no. 2475 in this volume.

5858 THEINHAUS, Erich. **Stereophonische Über-**
as **tragung klangschwacher Instrumente im Konzertsaal** [The use in the concert hall of stereophonic amplification for weak-sounding instruments], *Acustica: International journal of acoustics/Journal international d'acoustique/Internationale akustische Zeitschrift* IV/1 (1954) 253–56. *Illus., bibliog., charts, diagr.* In German; summaries in French, English, and German. See no. 324 in this volume.
Due to intrinsic properties or unfavorable placement in the concert hall, certain instruments may sound weaker than desired. In both cases the live sound may be mixed with stereophonic amplification. An electroacoustic device that does not change the natural timbre, thus keeping the listener unaware of the use of amplification, is discussed. *(author)*

5859 WINCKEL, Fritz. **Rekonstruktion historischer**
as **Klangstile unter dem Gesichtspunkt von Architektur und Raumakustik** [The reconstruction of historic sonority styles from the standpoint of architecture and room acoustics], *Bericht über den siebenten internationalen musikwissenschaftlichen Kongress* (Kassel: Bärenreiter, 1959) 295–300. *Illus., charts, diagr.* In German. See no. 390 in this volume.
Some particular developments in music history can be traced to developments in architecture, and the evolution of the spaces in which music is performed. In general, the longer the reverberation time in a typical space, the slower the prevailing tempo of music performed there is likely to be. The columns of Greek and Egyptian temples and Gothic cathedrals, and the

cylindrical projections on the walls of modern radio studios, favor the diffusion of reverberation and hence clarity of sound; this factor influenced the medieval development of organum. In the Baroque, the rich deployment of decoration, particularly of wood, provided bright, radiant timbres. *(David Bloom)*

5860
as
WINCKEL, Fritz. **Über den Einfluß der Deckenhöhe auf die Klangqualität in Konzertsälen** [The influence of ceiling height on sound quality in concert halls], *Fourth International Congress on Acoustics* (København: conference, 1962) I, M37. In German. See no. 448 in this volume.

5861
as
WOLFF, Hellmuth Christian. **Rekonstruktion der alten Hamburger Opernbühne** [Reconstruction of the old Hamburg opera stage], *Bericht über den internationalen musikwissenschaftlichen Kongreß* (Kassel: Bärenreiter, 1957) 235–39. *Tech. drawings.* In German. See no. 356 in this volume.
Contemporary evidence permits an exact description of the stage layout of the old opera house in the Gänsemarkt during its first flowering in 1678-1738. *(David Bloom)*

5862
as
YOUNG, Robert William. **A decade of musical acoustics,** *Fourth International Congress on Acoustics* (København: conference, 1962) II, 231–50. *Illus., bibliog.* See no. 448 in this volume.
A survey of recent research in the areas of electronic music, musical instruments, and scales and intonation, with attention to the relation of academic publications to the field as a whole. *(Allen Lott)*

5863
as
ZELLER, W. **Akustik Stuttgarter Kirchen** [The acoustics of Stuttgart's churches], *Proceedings of the Third International Congress on Acoustics* (Amsterdam: Elsevier Science, 1961) II, 1950–55. *Charts, diagr.* In German. See no. 414 in this volume.

5864
as
ZWIKKER, Cornelis. **Vues nouvelles sur l'acoustique des salles** [New views on room acoustics], *Proceedings of the Third International Congress of Phonetic Sciences* (Gent: Rijksuniversitet, Fonetisch Laboratorium, 1939) 148–52. In French. See no. 259 in this volume.
Factors affecting room acoustics include room size and shape, and the material of wall covering. Recording studios in particular would benefit from advances in the field. *(Terence Ford)*

87 Sociology

5865
as
ALDER, Franz. **Presuppositions of and design for a quantitative study in the sociology of radio music,** *Cahiers d'études de radio-télévision* 3-4 (1955) 550–58. See no. 334 in this volume.
Focuses on possible correlations between various types of radio audiences and their preferred musics.

5866
as
ASCHOFF, Volker. **Musik und Technik** [Music and technology], *Neue Zusammenarbeit im deutschen Musikleben: Vorträge und Entschließungen* (Kassel: Bärenreiter, 1956) 19–21. In German. See no. 343 in this volume.
Surveys the role of technology in German musical life.

5867
as
BELVIANES, Marcel. **Musique et radio** [Music and radio], *Cahiers d'études de radio-télévision* 3-4 (1955) 432–36. In French. See no. 334 in this volume.
Discusses the social benefits of broadcasting a wide range of musics.

5868
as
BERNET KEMPERS, Karel Philippus. **Soziale und asoziale Kunst** [Social and asocial art], *Musikerziehung: Zeitschrift der Musikerzieher Österreichs* special issue (1953) 101–03. In German. See no. 317 in this volume.

5869
as
BLAUKOPF, Kurt. **Tonalität und Soziologie** [Tonality and sociology], *Musikerziehung: Zeitschrift der Musikerzieher Österreichs* special issue (1953) 104–06. In German. See no. 317 in this volume.

5870
as
BUŽGA, Jaroslav. **Die soziale Lage des Musikers im Zeitalter des Barocks in den böhmischen Ländern und ihr Einfluss auf seine künstlerischen Möglichkeiten** [The social position of musicians in the Baroque era in the Bohemian lands and its influence on their artistic possibilities], *Bericht über den internationalen musikwissenschaftlichen Kongreß* (Kassel: Bärenreiter, 1963) 28–32. In German. See no. 452 in this volume.
Musical life flourished in Bohemia and Moravia in the period ca. 1622–ca. 1740, though hindered by the economic and social problems resulting from the Thirty Years' War. Few musicians could be regarded as professionals, other than town trumpeters; most were employees of churches or schools, with other duties beyond music making, or members of the lower classes, servants and *muzikaři* or minstrels. Considerable data exists on the social position of individual performers and performer-composers. *(Laurie Appleby)*

5871
as
CAPE, Charles. **Music in prisons and reformatories in England and Wales,** *Music in education* (Paris: UNESCO, 1955) 205–07. See no. 322 in this volume.
Music facilities have been provided in Welsh and English prisons and Borstal institutions since about 1920. Both music appreciation and active music-making are encouraged. A French version is cited as RILM 5872 in this volume. *(Elizabeth A. Wright)*

5872
as
CAPE, Charles. **La musique, moyen de redressement moral des délinquants** [Music as a means of moral rehabilitation of delinquents], *La musique dans l'éducation* (Paris: UNESCO; Colin, 1955) 214–17. In French. See no. 323 in this volume.
An English version is abstracted as RILM 5871 in this volume.

5873
as
CAPLOW, Theodore. **The influence of radio on music as a social institution,** *Cahiers d'études de radio-télévision* 3-4 (1955) 279–91. See no. 334 in this volume.
Offers historical perspectives on the selection and training of musicians, the selection and training of audiences, models of performance, economic aspects of performance and listening, and the formation of attitudes.

5874
as
CVETKO, Dragotin. **Les transformations sociales ayant une influence sur la vie du musicien et sur sa position dans la société** [Social transformations that have an influence on the musician's life and on his status in society], *The preservation of traditional forms of the learned and popular music of the Orient and the Occident/La préservation des formes traditionelles de la musique savante et populaire dans les pays d'Orient et d'Occident* (Urbana: Center for Comparative Psycholinguistics, Institute of Communi-

cations Research, 1964) 125–31. In French. See no. 443 in this volume.

Artists will always be dependent on the influences of their social environment.

5875 DADELSEN, Georg von. **Die Vermischung**
as **musikalischer Gattungen als soziologisches**
Problem [Mixing together musical genres as a sociological problem], *Bericht über den internationalen musikwissenschaftlichen Kongreß* (Kassel: Bärenreiter, 1963) 23–24. In German. See no. 452 in this volume.

A particular genre begins with the need to maintain its distinction from other genres, but must ultimately revitalize itself by borrowing from or combining with genres at the same social level, higher-ranking, or lower-ranking ones; the last is the most important. The methodological relationship between historical musicology and sociology as a whole is discussed. *(Laurie Appleby)*

5876 ĐJURIĆ-KLAJN, Stana. **Gesellschaftsformen**
as **und Musikentwicklung** [Social systems and development of music], *Musikerziehung: Zeitschrift der Musikerzieher Österreichs* special issue (1953) 136–39. In German. See no. 317 in this volume.

5877 DUMONT, Cedric. **La signification sociolo-**
as **gique de la musique légère dans le cadre des**
émissions radiophoniques [The sociological significance of light music in the design of radio broadcasts], *Cahiers d'études de radio-télévision* 3-4 (1955) 559–62. In French. See no. 334 in this volume.

In contrast with earlier periods, the general public today is alienated from art music. Light music serves to bridge this gap.

5878 ENGEL, Hans. **Grundprobleme der Musik-**
as **soziologie** [Fundamental problems of music sociology], *Musikerziehung: Zeitschrift der Musikerzieher Österreichs* special issue (1953) 96–100. In German. See no. 317 in this volume.

5879 ENGEL, Hans. **Die musikalischen Gattungen**
as **und ihr sozialer Hintergrund** [Musical genres and their social background], *Bericht über den internationalen musikwissenschaftlichen Kongreß* (Kassel: Bärenreiter, 1963) 1–14. In German. See no. 452 in this volume.

Discusses the concept of genre in the context of the requirements of a sociology of music.

5880 ENGEL, Hans. **Musiksoziologie und musika-**
as **lische Volkskunde** [The sociology of music and musical folkore], *Bericht über die musikwissenschaftliche Tagung der Internationalen Stiftung Mozarteum* (Leipzig: Breitkopf & Härtel, 1932) 304–12. In German. See no. 193 in this volume.

Sociological approaches to music include the sociology of music, which studies the mutual relations between music and people in communities, and is of particular interest to music historians; the application of sociological methods to music history, as yet not consistently attempted; and folklore studies, as a branch of anthropology, which may have more relevance than sociology to the analysis of art music. *(David Bloom)*

5881 ENGEL, Hans. **Soziologische Betrachtung des**
as **Madrigales** [Sociological perspective on the madrigal], *Congrés de la Societat Internacional de Musicologia* (Barcelona: Casa de Caritat, 1936). In German. See no. 224 in this volume.

The conference report provides only a citation. Neither the text nor a summary of the paper was published here.

⟶ ENGEL, Hans. **Soziologisches Porträt Johann**
Sebastian Bachs [A sociological portrait of Johann Sebastian Bach]. See no. 1539 in this volume.

5882 GIROD, Roger. **Recherches sociologiques et**
as **développement de la culture musicale** [Sociological research and the development of musical culture], *Cahiers d'études de radio-télévision* 3-4 (1955) 338–43. In French. See no. 334 in this volume.

Discusses social factors that prevent entire social groups from benefiting from radio broadcasts of art music.

5883 GOUZOU, Lucien. **Modification de la classe**
as **paysanne française par la musique à la radio**
[Modification of the French rural class by music on the radio], *Cahiers d'études de radio-télévision* 3-4 (1955) 310–17. In French. See no. 334 in this volume.

Offers psychological and sociological speculations.

5884 GUTFLEISCH, Paul. **Der Kirchenmusiker als**
as **Beruf** [The profession of the church musician], *Die Kirchenmusik und das II. Vatikanische Konzil* (Graz: Styria, 1965) 167–72. *Charts, diagr.* In German. See no. 480 in this volume.

Outlines the duties and compensation of the fully trained church musician in Roman Catholic churches, based on the example of conditions for full-time and freelance musicians in the diocese of Limburg, Germany. *(David Bloom)*

5885 HARRISON, Frank Llewellyn. **The social posi-**
as **tion of church musicians in England,**
1450-1550, *Report of the Eighth Congress of the International Musicological Society. I: Papers* (Kassel: Bärenreiter, 1961) 346–55. *Charts, diagr.* See no. 439 in this volume.

Examines documentary evidence regarding strength of choral establishments, stipends, careers, recruitment and education, and the supplying of polyphonic music.

5886 HOEBAER, Robert. **Extension de la radio en**
as **Belgique: Le comportement des auditeurs**
vis-à-vis de certains programmes musicaux et
les possibilités offertes par la radio en matière
de culture musicale [Extension of the radio in Belgium: The behavior of listeners with respect to certain musical programs and possibilities offered by the radio regarding musical culture], *Cahiers d'études de radio-télévision* 3-4 (1955) 494–506. *Charts, diagr.* In French. See no. 334 in this volume.

Presents geographic and demographic statistics on listening habits in the early 1950s.

5887 IRMER, Gotho von. **Jugend zwischen Volks-**
as **lied, Schlager, und Jazz** [Youth between traditional song, hit song, and jazz], *Musik and Musikerziehung in der Reifezeit* (Mainz: Schott, 1959) 157–62. In German. See no. 412 in this volume.

Summary of commentary and ensuing discussion at a conference session on the attitudes toward pop music of German secondary-school students, based on taped interviews with the students. *(David Bloom)*

5888 KELEMAN, Milko. **Situation of creative art in**
as **the industrial society,** *Music: East and West* (Tōkyō: conference, 1961) 181–82. See no. 445 in this volume.

5889
as
KITAZAWA, Masakuni. **Situation of creative art in the industrial society,** *Music: East and West* (Tōkyō: conference, 1961) 178–80. See no. 445 in this volume.

5890
as
KLAUSMEIER, Friedrich. **Der Einfluß sozialer Faktoren auf das musikalische Verhalten von Jugendlichen** [The influence of social factors on the musical behavior of young people], *Musik and Musikerziehung in der Reifezeit* (Mainz: Schott, 1959) 152–57. In German. See no. 412 in this volume.

A survey of secondary-school students of ages 14-20, including students in vocational schools, in the city of Cologne, showed a discrepancy between the goals of music pedagogy and the interests of the students. Few students have experienced the kind of social environment of small town or organized group in which traditional songs and young people's songs flourish. If we are to win our students away from pop and jazz music, a new kind of song will be be needed. *(David Bloom)*

5891
as
KÖNIG, René. **Sur quelques problèmes sociologiques de l'émission radiophonique musicale notamment sur les difficultés d'adaptation socio-culturelle à de nouvelles données techniques** [On some sociological problems of musical radio broadcasts and in particular on the difficulties of sociocultural adaptation to new technical ideas], *Cahiers d'études de radio-télévision* 3-4 (1955) 348–66. In French. See no. 334 in this volume.

5892
as
KRESÁNEK, Jozef. **Die gesellschaftliche Funktion der Musik** [The social function of music], *Beiträge zur Musikwissenschaft* V/4 (1963) 304–07. In German. See no. 470 in this volume.

Problems concerning the reflection of reality in music are often handled by mechanically applying perceptions drawn from literature and the visual arts. Marxist musicology opposes this. Precise physical, physiological, and psychological elements furnish the societal function of music, in particular collectivity and the so-called infection of feeling. In modern times musical collectivity has been destroyed by the division between artists and listeners. *(Donna Arnold)*

5893
as
LESURE, François. **Pour une sociologie historique des faits musicaux** [Toward a historical sociology of musical facts], *Report of the Eighth Congress of the International Musicological Society. I: Papers* (Kassel: Bärenreiter, 1961) 333–46. *Charts, diagr.* In French. See no. 439 in this volume.

The use of documentary evidence to define the relations between creators and consumers of music—the role of artists in society—is exemplified by short studies of (1) the role of choir schools (*maîtrises ecclésiastiques*) and the question of the supremacy of Paris in French music of the 16th-18th c.; (2) the importance of minstrels' guilds and their *escolles* in the training of French musicians of the 14th-15th c.; and (3) the significance of print run statistics for French music publishing of the 16th-17th c. *(David Bloom)*

5894
as
MALETZKE, Gerhard. **Der Mensch im publizistischen Feld** [The human factor in the field of journalism], *Cahiers d'études de radio-télévision* 3-4 (1955) 292–301. In German. See no. 334 in this volume.

A sociological overview, with attention to the medium of radio.

5895
as
MAYER, Günter. **Zur musiksoziologischen Fragestellung** [On the posing of music-sociological questions], *Beiträge zur Musikwissenschaft* V/4 (1963) 311–20. In German. See no. 470 in this volume.

In the conquest of dogmatism in Marxist sociology, clarification of sociological problems plays a special role. Research institutions have existed for a long time, and preliminary results of sociological research have been put forward. For aesthetics, however, claims derived from research have not been forthcoming. We Marxist musicologists must ask why we have held back, what we understand from music sociology, and what relationship music sociology and musical aesthetics have. Theodor W. Adorno, influenced by the dialectic of Hegel and Marx, stressed both the necessity and difficulty of social mediation in referring to the dialectical analysis of music. *(Donna Arnold)*

5896
as
MCVEIGH, Josephine. **Music in industry: Functional music,** *Music in education* (Paris: UNESCO, 1955) 192–95. See no. 322 in this volume.

Functional music in the workplace is intended to relieve workers' tensions and boredom, and to restimulate them. A detailed account of the compilation of industrial music programs is included. A French version is cited as RILM 5897 in this volume. *(Elizabeth A. Wright)*

5897
as
MCVEIGH, Josephine. **La musique dans l'industrie: Musique fonctionnelle** [Music in industry: Functional music], *La musique dans l'éducation* (Paris: UNESCO; Colin, 1955) 200–04. In French. See no. 323 in this volume.

An English version is abstracted as RILM 5896 in this volume.

5898
as
MEYER, Ernst Hermann. **Aus der Tätigkeit der Kampfgemeinschaft der Arbeitersänger** [Activities of the Kampfgemeinschaft der Arbeitersänger], *Beiträge zur Musikwissenschaft* VI/4 (1964) 289–94. In German. See no. 476 in this volume.

The Kampfgemeinschaft was founded in 1931, as a Communist-oriented equivalent of the socialist Deutscher Arbeiter-Sängerbund.

5899
as
MOKRÝ, Ladislav. **Soziologie und Marxismus** [Sociology and Marxism], *Beiträge zur Musikwissenschaft* V/4 (1963) 307–11. In German. See no. 470 in this volume.

In Western European music sociology, especially German, music sociology is considered a subordinate science to historiography. As Kurt Blaukopf has said, a separate music sociology would not be needed if musicology were being fair to all sides, but since that is not the case, supplementary sociological work is needed to make a sociological and historical discipline out of musicology, even though it contradicts Marxist musicology. No critical analysis is possible without analyzing the theoretical concepts of bourgeois music sociology. *(Donna Arnold)*

5900
as
ONNEN, Frank. **Pour une *radio absolue*** [For an absolute radio], *Cahiers d'études de radio-télévision* 3-4 (1955) 515–17. In French. See no. 334 in this volume.

Briefly discusses various viewpoints of radio's cultural mission.

5901
as
OPDENBERG. **L'accroissement de rendement du travail par la musique** [Work productivity increase through music], *Compte rendu des travaux du Ier Congrès international d'art radiophonique* (Paris: conference, 1938). In French. See no. 244 in this volume.

→
PETZOLDT, Richard. **Zur sozialen Stellung des Musikers im 17. Jahrhundert** [The social position of the musician in the 17th century]. See no. 1643 in this volume.

5902
as
PIÉRARD, Louis; DEPASSE, Charles. **Avant-propos** [Opening remarks], *La musique et le peuple: Rapports, suggestions, voeux* (Bruxelles: Ministère des Sciences et des Arts, 1932) 5–9. In French. See no. 195 in this volume.

Restates the statutory purposes of the Conseil Supérieur de l'Éducation Populaire: primarily, the governmental promotion of moral and useful employments of the people's spare time. *(Mark Stevens)*

5903 PIRRO, André. **La musique sur les galères du**
as **roi** [Music on the royal galleys], *Actes du Congrès d'histoire de l'art: Compte rendu analytique* (Paris: Presses Universitaires de France, 1922) 121. In French. See no. 95 in this volume.

Summary of a paper. An extended version is published in Italian under the title *La musica delle antiche galee francesi* in *Cultura musicale*, I (1922).

5904 REINHOLD, Helmut. **Grundverschieden-**
as **heiten musikwissenschaftlichen und soziologischen Denkens und Möglichkeiten zu ihrer Überwindung** [Fundamental differences between musicological and sociological thinking and possibilities for overcoming them], *Bericht über den internationalen musikwissenschaftlichen Kongreß* (Kassel: Bärenreiter, 1957) 193–96. In German. See no. 356 in this volume.

For the sociology of music to go beyond programmatic notions to active research, sociologists must resist their traditional reluctance to consider the longitudinal, the specific, and the judgmental; the social component of aesthetic things will be visible only if the researcher has the courage to consider their significance and value. The musicological approach to the aesthetic object must also acknowledge its pre-aesthetic and extra-aesthetic aspects. *(David Bloom)*

5905 RINGER, Alexander L. **The employment of so-**
as **ciological methods in music history,** *Report of the Eighth Congress of the International Musicological Society. II: Reports* (Kassel: Bärenreiter, 1962) 146–49. See no. 440 in this volume.

A report on a discussion by Edmund A. BOWLES, Dragotin CVETKO, Hans ENGEL, Jurij Vsevolodovič KELDYŠ, François LESURE, Leonard B. MEYER, Alexander L. RINGER, Walter SALMEN, Emanuel WINTERNITZ, and Walter WIORA of the papers by Lesure and by Frank Llewellyn Harrison abstracted as RILM 5893 and RILM 5885 in this volume.

5906 ROUSSEAU, Norbert. **Sur les responsabilités**
as **de la radio dans les rapports musicaux et sociaux** [On radio's responsibility in musical and social connections], *Cahiers d'études de radio-télévision* 3-4 (1955) 335–37. In French. See no. 334 in this volume.

Discusses the place of radio in debates over elitism vs. populism.

5907 SEEGER, Charles. **Music and government:**
as **Field for an applied musicology,** *Papers read at the International Congress of Musicology* (New York: Music Educators National Conference, 1944) 11–20. See no. 266 in this volume.

The U.S. government has no particular policies regarding music; musicologists should play a role in developing such policies.

5908 SINGH, Thakur Jaideva. **Presenting the East-**
as **ern tradition under conditions of mass distribution,** *Music: East and West* (Tōkyō: conference, 1961) 170–72. See no. 445 in this volume.

5909 STEPHENSON, Kurt. **Zur Soziologie des**
as **Studentenliedes** [The sociology of the student song], *Bericht über den internationalen musikwissenschaftlichen Kongreß Wien Mozartjahr 1956* (Graz; Köln: Böhlau, 1958) 608–11. In German. See no. 365 in this volume.

Programmatic and methodological remarks on the framework of ongoing research on German student songs in the early 19th c. *(David Bloom)*

5910 TRẦN, Van Khê. **Presenting the Eastern tradi-**
as **tion under conditions of mass distribution,** *Music: East and West* (Tōkyō: conference, 1961) 173–77. See no. 445 in this volume.

Widespread distribution through film, TV, records, and radio has brought music to everyone; there are advantages and disadvantages to this. *(Sylvia Eversole)*

5911 TWITTENHOFF, Wilhelm. **Musische Er-**
as **ziehung in Jugendpflege und Jugendsozialarbeit** [Humanities education in social welfare programs for youth], *Neue Zusammenarbeit im deutschen Musikleben: Vorträge und Entschließungen* (Kassel: Bärenreiter, 1956) 39–46. In German. See no. 343 in this volume.

Discusses the situation in Germany.

5912 VALENTIN, Erich. **Zur Soziologie des Musik-**
as **lebens** [Concerning the sociology of musical life], *Kongreß-Bericht: Gesellschaft für Musikforschung* (Kassel; Basel: Bärenreiter, 1950) 220–22. In German. See no. 299 in this volume.

5913 WALDSBURGER, Jean. **Les applications du**
as **rythme à l'organisation du travail professionnel** [The applications of rhythm to the organization of professional work], *Compte rendu du Iᵉʳ Congrès du rythme* (Genève: Institut Jaques-Dalcroze, 1926) 286–98. *Charts, diagr.* In French. See no. 123 in this volume.

Eurhythmic exercise may contribute to the productivity and humanization of the workforce.

5914 WIORA, Walter. **Das deutsche Musikleben und**
as **die Situation der Zeit** [German musical life and the current situation], *Neue Zusammenarbeit im deutschen Musikleben: Vorträge und Entschließungen* (Kassel: Bärenreiter, 1956) 9–18. In German. See no. 343 in this volume.

5915 WIORA, Walter. **Die musikalischen Gattungen**
as **und ihr sozialen Hintergrund** [Musical genres and their social background], *Bericht über den internationalen musikwissenschaftlichen Kongreß* (Kassel: Bärenreiter, 1963) 15–23. In German. See no. 452 in this volume.

The history of genres, moving from their original social performance contexts of church, court, and home to an autonomous existence in concert halls and broadcasts, will be an important aspect of a new historical musicology. *(David Bloom)*

5916 YOSHIDA, Tomio. **An investigation on how in-**
as **dustrial music in Japan goes on,** *Problèmes d'acoustique* (Liège: Université de Liège, 1965) M56–60. *Bibliog.* See no. 504 in this volume.

In controlled experiments, the introduction of background music into the workplace has not produced any measurable increase in production efficiency. However, there has been a notable effect on worker morale: music has alleviated some of the dullness inherent in the workplace. Specific types of music elicit different emotional effects. *(Brian Doherty)*

88 Linguistics, semiotics

5917 AUBRY, Pierre. **Les raisons historiques du**
as **rythme oratoire** [The historical reasons for oratorical rhythm], *Mémoires de Musicologie sacrée, lus aux*

assises de musique religieuse (Paris: Schola Cantorum, n.d.) 19–28. *Bibliog.* In French. See no. 34 in this volume.

The rhythm of chant is inextricably tied to the rhythms of "Latin vulgare", which was accented, ignored classical poetic metrics, and distinguished vowels by quality instead of duration. Includes a brief history of the Latin language with special emphasis on its introduction into the Church. *(Karen Clute)*

5918 BALLY, Charles. **Le rythme linguistique et sa**
as **signification sociale** [Linguistic rhythm and its social significance], *Compte rendu du Ier Congrès du rythme* (Genève: Institut Jaques-Dalcroze, 1926) 253–63. In French. See no. 123 in this volume.
Discusses how features such as syllabic stress can be used to determine the degree of evolution of a language and its social function.

5919 BANDEIRA, Manuel. **Pronúncias regionais do**
as **Brasil** [Regional pronunciations of Brazil], *Anais do Primeiro Congreso da Língua Nacional Cantada* (São Paulo: Departamento Municipal de Cultura, 1938) 181–86. *Charts, diagr.* In Portuguese. See no. 253 in this volume.
Regional variations in the pronunciation of vowels and consonants in Brazilian Portuguese are tabulated.

5920 BURSSENS, Amaat F.S. **Le luba, langue à into-**
as **nation, et la tambour-signal** [Luba, a tonal language, and the talking drum], *Proceedings of the Third International Congress of Phonetic Sciences* (Gent: Rijksuniversitet, Fonetisch Laboratorium, 1939) 503–07. *Illus., transcr.* In French. See no. 259 in this volume.
The transmission of linguistic tone and rhythm in drumming is exemplified from the author's fieldwork on speakers of the Luba or Tshiluba language in the Kasai district, Congo (Kinshasa); organological data on Luba drums is included. *(Terence Ford)*

5921 CAIRATI, Alfredo. **Gibt es einen geschmack-**
as **lichen, technischen oder methodischen Unterschied zwischen dem italienischen und dem deutschen Gesang, oder beruht der Unterschied nur auf dem verschiedenen Aufbau der beiden Sprachen?** [Is there a difference of taste, technique, or method between Italian and German singing, or does the difference lie merely in the different structures of the two languages?], *Bericht über den Internationalen Kongreß Singen und Sprechen* (München: Oldenbourg, 1938) 161–65. In German. See no. 257 in this volume.
Contrastive analysis of the articulatory phonetics of German and Italian suggests that German really does present singers with special problems which can, however, be overcome with training. *(David Bloom)*

5922 CHAILLEY, Jacques. **Pour une philologie du**
as **langage musical** [Toward a philology of musical language], *Société Internationale de Musicologie, cinquième congrès/Internationale Gesellschaft für Musikwissenschaft, fünfter Kongreß/International Society for Musical Research, Fifth Congress* (Amsterdam: Vereniging voor Nederlandse Muziekgeschiedenis, 1953) 96–106. In French. See no. 316 in this volume.

→ CUNHA, João Itiberê da. **Algumas notas para o Congreso da Língua Nacional Cantada** [Some notes for the Congreso da Língua Nacional Cantada]. See no. 3196 in this volume.

5923 DRAEGER, Hans-Heinz. **Die "Bedeutung" der**
as **Sprachmelodie** [The meaning of speech melody], *Bericht über den internationalen musikwissenschaftlichen Kongreß* (Kassel: Bärenreiter, 1957) 73–75. In German. See no. 356 in this volume.
The meaning of a pitch contour, sung or spoken, depends on the effect of its final note; to the extent that the final effect is associated with a particular meaning, the speech melody may be said to be linguistically meaningful. There is no absolute relation between the sense and construction of a sentence on the one hand and the final effect and mental associations of the intervals used on the other. *(David Bloom)*

5924 FÓNAGY, Iván. **Zur Gliederung der Satz-**
as **melodie** [Sentence intonation], *Proceedings* (Basel: S. Karger, 1965) 281–86. *Music, bibliog., charts, diagr.* In German. See no. 488 in this volume.

→ GRÜTZMACHER, Martin. **Ein neuer Tonhöhenschreiber, seine Anwendung auf mathematische, phonetische und musikalische Probleme** [A new instrument for the graphic representation of pitch, and its use in mathematical, phonetic, and musical problems]. See no. 5821 in this volume.

5925 GURLITT, Wilibald. **Zur Bedeutungs-**
as **geschichte von** *musicus* **und** *cantor* **bei Isidor von Sevilla** [The etymology of *musicus* and *cantor* in Isidore of Seville], *Compte rendu/Kongressbericht/Report* (Basel: Bärenreiter, 1951) 134–35. In German. See no. 289 in this volume.
Summary of a paper published in *Abhandlungen der Akademie der Wissenschaften und der Literatur in Mainz, Geistes- und sozialwissenschaftliche Klasse* 7 (1950). Isidore's compendium *Etymologiarum sive Originum libri XX* treats the Greek-derived term *musica* in book 3, among the liberal arts. The Latin *cantor* is in book 7, chapter 12 (*De clericis*). The dialectical tension between theory (*musica/musicus*) in the Hellenistic spirit and practice (*cantus/cantor*) in the Roman-Christian spirit continues to be fruitful today. *(David Bloom)*

5926 HAUSE, Helen Engel. **Terms for musical in-**
as **struments in the Sudanic languages: A linguistic approach to culture,** *Congrès international des sciences anthropologiques et ethnologiques: Compte rendu de la troisième session* (Tervuren: Musée Royal de l'Afrique Centrale, 1960) 103. See no. 282 in this volume.
Lexicographical investigation of the instrument vocabulary of the Western Sudanic branch of the Niger-Congo language family shows correspondences with the history of cultural diffusion through the spread of Islam and the influence of the great West African kingdoms. A full version is published as Supplement no. 7 of the *Journal of the American Oriental Society*, 1948. *(T. Pierce)*

5927 HERZOG, Eduard. **Sinnbildung und deren**
as **Träger in Sprache und Musik** [The vehicles of semiosis in language and music], *Bericht über den internationalen musikwissenschaftlichen Kongreß* (Kassel: Bärenreiter, 1957) 111–12. In German. See no. 356 in this volume.
In music as in speech, meaning is conveyed by the elements of articulation and intonation. Articulation provides the fundamental expression units of speech, while intonation, in the form of a continuous melodic line, does this for music. The consequences for the kinds of meanings expressed in these situations are explored. *(David Bloom)*

5928 HOŠOVS'KIJ, Volodymyr. **The experiment of**
as **systematizing and cataloging folk tunes following the principles of musical dialectology and cybernetics,** *Studia musicologica Academiae*

Scientiarum Hungaricae V (1965) 273–86. See no. 478 in this volume.

Approaching traditional tunes as grammatical constructions within a particular musical dialect, a method is proposed for conducting syntactical, morphological, and phonetic analysis with the aid of a computer. The modeling techniques discussed establish melodic and rhythmic prototypes that could assist in mapping ethnic territories and codifying their features.

5929
as
JUCÁ FILHO, Cândido. **Problemas da fonologia carioca** [Problems of the phonology of Rio de Janeiro], *Anais do Primeiro Congresso da Língua Nacional Cantada* (São Paulo: Departamento Municipal de Cultura, 1938) 330–40. In Portuguese. See no. 253 in this volume.

Questions of diction relating to both vowels and consonants in the singing of texts in the Rio de Janeiro dialect of Brazilian Portuguese are addressed.

5930
as
KUČERA, Václav. **Zur Frage der Intonationssemantisierung der Struktur** [On questions of the semanticization of intonation], *Beiträge zur Musikwissenschaft* VII/4 (1965) 377–86. In German. See no. 495 in this volume.

5931
as
LIEBE, Annelise. **Wortforschung als Methode zur Wesensbestimmung des Tones** [Lexical research as a method of determining the nature of musical sound.], *Bericht über den internationalen musikwissenschaftlichen Kongreß* (Kassel: Bärenreiter, 1957) 140–42. In German. See no. 356 in this volume.

Standard German includes some 1600 words designating features of sound, only 450 of which are found in writings on music from the 16th through the beginning of the 19th c. Such words can be divided into four groups: those characterizing a sound as an object, those referring to intensity, those describing relative pleasantness or unpleasantness, and those designating a value judgment on the part of a musician or listener.

5932
as
LISSA, Zofia. **Semantische Elemente der Musik** [Semantic elements of music], *Bericht über den internationalen musikwissenschaftlichen Kongreß* (Kassel: Bärenreiter, 1957) 145–48. In German. See no. 356 in this volume.

Not all music has an intentional semantic function; when it does, as in works from the Romantic through expressionist periods, it may be regarded as a presentation function, in the sense of the direct communication of an otherwise incommunicable value. Music is inherently polysemic, and its value is never foregrounded in the ways that value is in the representational arts. *(David Bloom)*

5933
as
PIKLER, Andrew G. **Musical transfer functions,** *Fourth International Congress on Acoustics* (København: conference, 1962) I, P54. See no. 448 in this volume.

The conventional transfer process, i.e., composition, production of a score, performance, and perception of a musical work, may be expanded (addition of more performance levels and remote or delayed audiences), contracted (combination or elimination of a step in the transfer process, e.g., improvisation), or modified (as in the combination of man and machine in processed music). *(Allen Lott)*

5934
as
PRUNIÈRES, Henry. **Le symbolisme dans la création musicale** [Symbolism in musical creation], *Deuxième congrès international d'esthétique et de Science de l'art* (Paris: Librairie Félix Alcan, 1937) II, 232–35. In French. See no. 249 in this volume.

Surveys the ways in which music has a representative function, in terms of philosophical background (Goethe, Hegel, Bergson); direct analogical associations between particular sound-qualities and meanings; and conventionalized associations. Music is, however, too indeterminate an art to convey more than a generalized idea of its content. *(David Bloom)*

5935
as
RUSIĆ, Branislav. **Guslarsko tajno sporazumevanje** [The secret communication system of the guslars], *Rad kongresa folklorista Jugoslavije* (Ljubljana: Savez Udruženja Folkloristov Jugoslavije, 1960) 351–55. In Serbian; summary in English. See no. 404 in this volume.

Macedonian guslars, mostly blind itinerant musicians in groups of three or four men, make use of a secret language, known as *gegavska skošinjalka*; a related argot, *gegavački jezik*, is used by the guslars of Srem and Slavonia. Both feature a vocabulary of Slavic (Macedonian and Serbian-Croatian) words with changed meanings, and Latin-derived words borrowed through Albanian, and are not related to any other known argot. *(author)*

5936
as
SCHRÖPFER, Johann. **Eine unbeachtete Isoglosse der altbalkanischen Folklore: Die Volkslieder der Südslawen und die Orpheussage** [An unrecognized isogloss in Old Balkan folklore: South Slavic traditional songs and the Orpheus myth], *Rad kongresa folklorista Jugoslavije* (Ljubljana: Savez Udruženja Folkloristov Jugoslavije, 1960) 123–28. In German; summary in Croatian. See no. 404 in this volume.

A grammatical peculiarity of South Slavic traditional song texts is the use of the *dativus sympatheticus* construction, describing an action as if it were consciously "received" by an inanimate object. The construction, very rare in Indo-European altogether, is certainly not Slavic in origin; it may not be too fanciful to suppose that it originated among the ancient Thracians, who inhabited the Balkans before the coming of the Slavs, and this in turn suggests a possible interpretation of the myth of the Thracian culture-hero Orpheus, who was said to be able to "move" trees, rocks, and other objects, with his singing. *(David Bloom)*

5937
as
SIEVERS, Eduard. **Demonstrationen zur Lehre von den klanglichen Konstanten in Rede und Musik** [Demonstration of the theory of sonic constants in speech and music], *Kongress für Ästhetik und allgemeine Kunstwissenschaft: Bericht* (Stuttgart: Enke, 1914) 456–75. In German. See no. 86 in this volume.

5938
as
Sociedade de Etnografia e Folclore; Divisão de Expansão Cultural. **Mapas folclóricos de variações linguísticas** [Ethnographic maps of linguistic variations], *Anais do Primeiro Congresso da Língua Nacional Cantada* (São Paulo: Departamento Municipal de Cultura, 1938) 172–78. *Maps.* In Portuguese. See no. 253 in this volume.

A collection of isogloss maps of São Paulo state, Brazil, showing dialectal variations in the pronunciation of Brazilian Portuguese.

5939
as
SPIES, Leo. **Janáčeks Theorie der Sprachmelodie: Ein Instrument des Naturstudiums, nicht eine Kompositionsmethode/Janáčkova nápěvková teorie: Nástroj studia přírody, nikoliv kompoziční metoda** [Janáček's theory of speech melody as a tool of natural science, not a composition method], *Leoš Janáček a soudobá hudba* (Praha: Panton, 1963) 281–88. *Music.* In German and Czech. See no. 389 in this volume.

It was a scientifically based analysis of the intonation patterns of spoken Czech that led Janáček to the theory of speech melody (*nápěvek*) embodied in the declamatory style of his operas.

5940
as
TRAUTWEIN, Friedrich. **Über elektrische Synthese von Sprachlauten und musikalischen Tönen (Instruments à ondes)** [On the electric synthesis of speech sound and musical notes (instruments *à ondes*)], *Proceedings of the First International Congress of Phonetic Sciences: First meeting of the Internationale Arbeitsgemeinschaft für Phonologie* (Harlem:

J. Enschedé, 1933) 200–01. In German. See no. 194 in this volume.

Discusses the practical application of speech sounds and their synthesis with music to instruments *à ondes* (based on waves). The principle of these instruments is to set up the tune and the volume by reading the difference between the frequencies from two oscillators. *(Tina Frühauf)*

5941 WÜNSCH, Walther. **Grenzgebiete der Musik-**
as **und Sprachforschung** [Overlapping areas between musicology and linguistics], *Bericht über den Internationalen Kongreß Singen und Sprechen* (München: Oldenbourg, 1938) 315–19. In German. See no. 257 in this volume.

Another version is abstracted as RILM 5942 in this volume.

5942 WÜNSCH, Walther. **Grenzgebiete der Musik-**
as **und Sprachforschung** [Overlapping areas between musicology and linguistics], *Proceedings of the Third International Congress of Phonetic Sciences* (Gent: Rijksuniversitet, Fonetisch Laboratorium, 1939) 72–77. In German. See no. 259 in this volume.

Studies in music and linguistics often concentrate on similar parameters such as rhythm, pitch, and timbre. Traditional Serbian and Croatian songs show how the two fields can benefit from cross-fertilizing their methodologies. Another version is cited as RILM 5941 in this volume. *(Terence Ford)*

89 Printing, publishing, and music business

5943 BARUCH, Gerth Wolfgang. **Musikhistorische**
as **Aufgaben und Möglichkeiten des Rundfunks** [Musicological tasks and possibilities of broadcasting], *Kongreß-Bericht: Gesellschaft für Musikforschung* (Kassel; Basel: Bärenreiter, 1950) 204–06. In German. See no. 299 in this volume.

5944 BAUDIN, Georges. **La législation** [Legislation],
as *Rapport sur la musique contemporaine française* (Roma: Armani & Stein, 1913) 157–67. In French. See no. 76 in this volume.

Discusses French copyright law from the late 18th c. to 1911.

5945 BAUER-MENGELBERG, Stefan. **Impromptu**
as **remarks on new methods of music printing,** *American Society of University Composers: Proceedings of the 1966 conference* (New York: American Society of University Composers, 1966). See no. 510 in this volume.

Soon it will be feasible to photograph graphic materials such as scores. Composers must make the most legible scores possible; their works will then be more likely to be performed, require less rehearsal time, and be more easily computer-scanned. Columbia University is developing a system for encoding musical notation on computer punch cards.

(Judith Drogichen Meyer)

5946 BERGMANS, Paul. **L'imprimeur Gérard de**
as **Lisa, chantre maître de chapelle à Trevise (1463-1496)** [The printer Gerard de Lisa, cantor choirmaster at Treviso], *Congrès jubilaire* (Brugge: Gruuthuuse, 1925) 222–22. In French. See no. 119 in this volume.

This Belgian printer, who introduced typography to Treviso, was originally from Ghent. Belgian musicians who were established in Treviso in the 15th c. and the beginning of the 16th c. include Jan Nasco. *(Susan Poliniak)*

5947 BERRIEN, William. **Report of Subcommittee**
as **on Recorded Music,** *Report of the Committee of the Conference on Inter-American Relations in the Field of Music* (Washington, D.C.: United States Department of State, 1940) 111–46. *Discog.* See no. 271 in this volume.

After its January meetings, the parent committee authorized its chairman to recommend to the leading U.S. recording companies that more Latin American records manufactured outside the U.S. be made available in this country, and that representations of U.S. music be circulated throughout South American countries. Two commercial discographies of Brazilian popular music, prepared by Mário de Andrade and Oneyda Alvarenga are included, as is one of American folk songs, compiled by Alan Lomax. *(Gary Eskow)*

5948 BERTRAND, Paul. **Les contrefaçons au Can-**
as **ada** [Counterfeiting in Canada], *Congrès international des éditeurs: VIe session—Rapports* (Madrid: Asociación de la Libreria de España, 1908) 256–68. In French. See no. 60 in this volume.

Calls for the Canadian government to regulate the importation of illicitly published scores, and favor the sale of union editions.

5949 BONDEVILLE, Emmanuel. **La radiophonie et**
as **la musique contemporaine** [The radio and contemporary music], *Atti del secondo Congresso internazionale di musica* (Firenze: Le Monnier, 1940) 125–28. In French; summaries in Italian and German. See no. 239 in this volume.

Radio can be a powerful force for popularization of contemporary music, allowing a particular piece to be heard and reheard until it is understood. It is interesting to note that the contemporary composer's preference for small ensembles and pure timbres corresponds in some sense to the exigencies of the microphone. The radio is a new instrument in its own right, which may stimulate the creation of new works. *(author)*

5950 BOOSEY, Arthur. **L'appropriation du droit**
as **d'auteur sur les œuvres musicales par les fabricants d'instruments mécaniques, tels que les éoliennes, etc.** [The appropriation of copyrights on musical works by manufacturers of mechanical instruments, such as aeolian instruments, etc.], *IVe Congrès international des éditeurs: Rapports* (Leipzig: F.A. Brockhaus, 1901) 143–48. In French. See no. 38 in this volume.

Proposes national and international regulations of musical compositions performed by mechanical instruments.

5951 BRETON, Paul. **La propriété artistique au**
as **Brésil** [Artistic property in Brazil], *Congrès international des éditeurs: VIe session—Rapports* (Madrid: Asociación de la Libreria de España, 1908) 269–72. In French. See no. 60 in this volume.

Suggests that Brazil should sign the Montevideo and Bern agreements, since it has no music publishers union.

5952 CAPE, Safford. **À propos d'enregistrements de**
as **danses du Moyen Âge et de la Renaissance** [Regarding recordings of dances of the Middle Ages and the Renaissance], *La musique instrumentale de la Renaissance* (Paris: Centre National de la Recherche Scientifique [CNRS], 1955) 163–64. In French. See no. 333 in this volume.

Remarks accompanying a hearing of recordings by the Brussels Pro Musica Antiqua (directed by the author) of 13th- and 14th-c. dances by anonymous composers, pieces from the *Danseryes* of Tylman Susato, and solo lute dances performed by Michel Podolski. New dance compositions broadly declined during the 15th c., partly because of the preference for more learned musical forms, and reemerged at the beginning of the 16th c., with the spread of printing technology and the popularity of the lute. *(David Bloom)*

5953
as

CLAUSETTI, Carlo. **La diminution de la vente des éditions musicales et ses causes** [The decline of music publication sales and its causes], *Congrès international des éditeurs: Neuvième session* (Paris: Cercle de la Librairie, 1932) 115–19. In French. See no. 191 in this volume.

The decline in music sales is due to moral, artistic, and technical problems. In addition, sound films are undermining the market for live performances.

5954
as

CLAYTON, Henry. **La subdivision territoriale du droit d'auteur** [The territorial subdivision of copyrights], *IVe Congrès international des éditeurs: Rapports* (Leipzig: F.A. Brockhaus, 1901) 129–35. In French. See no. 38 in this volume.

Because music is an international language, composers' rights are often abused by unauthorized foreign editions. More stringent international regulations are proposed. Foreign agents should publicize the copyrights they acquire. *(David Nussenbaum)*

5955
as

DE SANCTIS, Valerio. **L'auteur et la télévision** [The creator and television], *Compte rendu du dix-septième Congrès de la Confédération Internationale des Sociétés d'Auteurs et Compositeurs* (Paris: Confédération Internationale des Sociétés d'Auteurs et Compositeurs, 1952) 33–37. In French. See no. 311 in this volume.

Television is a valuable way of bringing concert works and theatrical works to a wide public, but authors must be properly paid. *(Marilyn S. Bliss)*

5956
as

DOMMANGE, René. **Le régime de la licence obligatoire en matière de reproduction musico-mécanique** [Mandatory licensing regulations concerning mechanically reproduced music], *Congrès international des éditeurs: Neuvième session* (Paris: Cercle de la Librairie, 1932) 129–37. In French. See no. 191 in this volume.

5957
as

DOTESIO, Louis. **La musique et les droits d'auteur** [Music and the rights of the author], *Congrès international des éditeurs: VIe session—Rapports* (Madrid: Asociación de la Librería de España, 1908) 280–82. In French. See no. 60 in this volume.

Suggests that Haiti, Switzerland, and Spain should abolish customs duties on imported music as the other members of the Berne convention have.

5958
as

ENOCH, W. **De la contrefaçon musicale en Europe (Belgique, Pays-Bas, Roumanie, Turquie, Grèce) et en Égypte** [On musical counterfeiting in Europe (Belgium, Low Countries, Romania, Turkey, Greece) and in Egypt], *Congrès international des éditeurs: VIe session—Rapports* (Madrid: Asociación de la Librería de España, 1908) 252–55. In French. See no. 60 in this volume.

Proposes that a special commission on counterfeiting be established.

5959
as

ENOCH, W. **Des instruments de musique mécaniques** [Mechanical musical instruments], *Congrès international des éditeurs: 5e session—Rapports* (Milano: Associazione Tipografico-Libraria Italiana, 1907) 114–16. In French. See no. 55 in this volume.

In the Berlin conference for the revision of the Bern Convention scheduled for 1908, each delegation should have its country's permission to revise the international protocol on mechanical reproduction rights.

5960
as

FERNÁNDEZ ARDAVIN, Luis. **L'auteur et les pouvoirs publics** [The author and public authorities], *Compte rendu du dix-septième Congrès de la*

Confédération Internationale des Sociétés d'Auteurs et Compositeurs (Paris: Confédération Internationale des Sociétés d'Auteurs et Compositeurs, 1952) 141–45. In French. See no. 311 in this volume.

Presents a short history of composers' and authors' financial and legal situations from ancient Greece to the present. Changing views of artists by the 18th- and 19th-c. public led to a demand for protective societies, for which there is a continuing need. *(Marilyn S. Bliss)*

5961
as

GASCO, Alberto. **I diritti d'autore** [Copyrights], *La vita musicale dell'Italia d'oggi* (Torino: Fratelli Bocca, 1921) 198–204. In Italian. See no. 97 in this volume.

Briefly discusses performing rights as they pertain to opera houses.

5962
as

GYÖNGY, Pál. **La musique tzigane en dehors de la Hongrie et sa répartition par les sociétés fédérées** [Gypsy music outside Hungary and its distribution among the federated societies], *Compte rendu du dix-septième Congrès de la Confédération Internationale des Sociétés d'Auteurs et Compositeurs* (Paris: Confédération Internationale des Sociétés d'Auteurs et Compositeurs, 1952) 212–17. In French. See no. 311 in this volume.

Presents a short history of Gypsy music and composers in Hungary since the 16th c. Beginning with Berlioz and Liszt, art music composers have exploited the music of popular musicians of Hungarian Gypsy or Jewish origin such as János Bihari (who created the modern form of the traditional tune known as the Rákóczy march) and Márk Rózsavölgyi. CISAC member organizations should make efforts to protect the rights of Gypsy composers. *(Marilyn S. Bliss)*

5963
as

HASE, Oskar von. **Entente internationale entre les marchands de musique** [International agreement among music dealers], *IVe Congrès international des éditeurs: Rapports* (Leipzig: F.A. Brockhaus, 1901) 149–55. In French. See no. 38 in this volume.

An outline of the goals of the International Association of Music Dealers.

5964
as

HENRION, Marcel; MALAPLATE, Léon. **L'appartenance des auteurs réfugiés aux sociétés d'auteurs** [Refugee authors' membership in copyright collecting societies], *Compte rendu du dix-septième Congrès de la Confédération Internationale des Sociétés d'Auteurs et Compositeurs* (Paris: Confédération Internationale des Sociétés d'Auteurs et Compositeurs, 1952) 247–71. In French. See no. 311 in this volume.

Refugee composers and authors need to know their rights for just remuneration in foreign countries; a summary of the rights is given. *(Marilyn S. Bliss)*

5965
as

HINRICHSEN, Henri. **Prix fort et rabais dans le commerce de la musique** [Full price and discounts in the sale of music], *IVe Congrès international des éditeurs: Rapports* (Leipzig: F.A. Brockhaus, 1901) 136–42. In French. See no. 38 in this volume.

Wholesalers' price alterations must be regulated by publishers.

5966
as

HIRSCH BALLIN, Ernst Denny. **Urheberrecht am Scheideweg** [Copyright at the parting of the ways], *Vorträge zum Urheberrecht/Lectures on copyright/Conférences sur le droit d'auteur* (Berlin; Frankfurt am Main: Vahlen, 1961) 14–22. In German. See no. 431 in this volume.

An early edition of the congress paper abstracted as no. 5967 in this volume.

5967 HIRSCH BALLIN, Ernst Denny. **Urheberrecht**
as **am Scheideweg/Copyright at the parting of the
ways/Le droit d'auteur à la croisée des
chemins,** *IV. Internationaler Kongress für Kirchenmusik in Köln: Dokumente und Berichte* (Köln:
Bachem, 1962) 87–101. In German, English, and
French. See no. 432 in this volume.
Modern copyright laws allow individual authors and composers to lose the
rights to their own works. Property and mass rights are overtaking individual rights. Another version is cited as RILM 5966 in this volume. *(T. Pierce)*

5968 HITZIG, Wilhelm. **Bedeutung der Verlags-**
as **archive für die Musikforschung** [The significance of publishing house archives for music research],
*Beethoven-Zentenarfeier: Internationaler musik-
historischer Kongress* (Wien: Universal, 1927)
292–95. In German. See no. 142 in this volume.
Documents of musicological significance found by the author in the preparation of *Katalog des Archivs Breitkopf & Härtel Leipzig* (Leipzig, 1925)
included records of payments to composers, including Beethoven; editorial
files of the *Allgemeine musikalische Zeitung* and *Leipziger Literaturzeitung*, which have made it possible to identify the authors of anonymous
articles; editorial files from the complete editions of works by sundry composers; the fair copies of works used by engravers, whose annotations may,
as in the case of works by Prince Louis Ferdinand of Prussia and Jan
Ladislav Dusík, be of great musicological interest; and the copybooks of
letters sent by the firm. *(David Bloom)*

5969 HULLEBROECK, Emiel. **Het vraagstuk der**
as **auteursrechten** [The question of copyright],
Verhandelingen van het Muziekcongres (Antwerpen:
Stad Antwerpen, 1935) 111–19. In Dutch. See no. 210
in this volume.
Authors' rights protections are surveyed from the International Convention
for the Protection of Literary and Artistic Works held in Bern in 1886
(known as the Bern convention) to the founding of the Genootschap van
Nederlandse Componisten in 1922.

5970 IMBRIE, Andrew W. **The University of Califor-**
as **nia series in contemporary music,** *American Society of University Composers: Proceedings of the 1966
conference* (New York: American Society of University
Composers, 1966). See no. 510 in this volume.
Problems of distribution and advertising have been solved; the first three
scores of this series are about to be issued. Only scores of faculty and students of this university are acceptable, and royalties cannot be paid. It is
hoped that other university presses will follow suit. *(Judith Drogichen Meyer)*

5971 JESPERSEN, Einar. **Le maintien du prix fort**
as **ou prix du catalogue dans le commerce de la
musique** [Maintaining full or catalogue prices in the
sale of music], *Congrès international des éditeurs:
Huitième session—Conclusion des rapports* (Budapest:
Athenaeum, 1913) 9. In French. See no. 88 in this
volume.
National music dealers' unions should be internationally coordinated, and
they should standardize the price of editions.

5972 JURRES, André. **From microfilm to micro-**
as **phone,** *Music libraries and instruments* (London:
Hinrichsen, 1961) 169–73. See no. 406 in this volume.
Describes the functions of the Amsterdam-based Donemus foundation,
which acts as an alternative to music publishers for its affiliated Dutch composers. The foundation reproduces scores and parts for perusal and rental,
publishes an English-language magazine entitled *Key notes* (previously
Sonorum speculum) and various books, and presents concerts. The foundation also possesses an extensive Dutch music and recording library.
(Susan Poliniak)

5973 KING, Alexander Hyatt. **Arbeitsgemeinschaft:**
as **Composer and publisher 1500-1850** [Working
group: Composer and publisher, 1500-1850], *Bericht
über den siebenten internationalen musikwissenschaftlichen Kongress* (Kassel: Bärenreiter, 1959) 340–43.
Charts, diagr. See no. 390 in this volume.
Summarizes brief remarks by Eva BADURA-SKODA on first editions of
the Viennese Classic; John Howard DAVIES on English publishing from
ca. 1580 to 1625; Vincent DUCKLES on early important publishers in the
United States; Vladimir FÉDOROV on the firms of Pierre Attaingnant and
Le Roy & Ballard; Anthony van HOBOKEN on Haydn's relations with his
publishers; Willi KAHL on publishing in Cologne, and Macario Santiago
KASTNER on publishing in Spain, in the 16th-17th c.; Albert van der LIN-
DEN on the Plantin-Moretus firm 1577-1639; Anna MONDOLFI on the
role of Ottaviano Petrucci in the publication of part songs in the early 16th
c., and on the failure to develop a system of publishing operas in Italy in the
17th-18th c.; Frits NOSKE on issues of tablature and basso continuo notation in the 17th-18th c.; and Kay SCHMIDT-PHISELDECK on the delayed
development of Scandinavian music publishing. *(David Bloom)*

5974 KÜNZIG, Johannes. **Authentische Volkslieder**
as **auf Schallplatten: Proben aus dem Ton-Bild-
Buch *Ehe sie verklingen*...** [Authentic traditional
song on record: The test case of the record–illustrated
book set *Ehe sie verklingen*...], *Volkskunde-Kongreß:
Vorträge und Berichte* (Stuttgart: Kohlhammer, 1959)
65–68. In German. See no. 396 in this volume.
Discusses the author's book-and-recording set of songs of German emigrant communities in Eastern Europe *Ehe sie verklingen...: Alte deutsche
Volksweisen vom Böhmerwald bis zur Wolga* (Freiburg im Breisgau:
Herder, 1958). *(David Bloom)*

5975 LEBEAU, Élisabeth. **Une succursale officieuse**
as **de Johann Anton André à Paris, de 1802 à
1806: Ses éditions mozartiennes** [An unofficial
branch of Johann Anton André in Paris, from 1802 to
1806: Its Mozart editions], *Bericht über den internationalen musikwissenschaftlichen Kongreß Wien
Mozartjahr 1956* (Graz; Köln: Böhlau, 1958) 324–27.
Charts, diagr. In French. See no. 365 in this volume.
Plates from the firm of Johann Anton André (Offenbach am Main) are
used for editions of German music published by the firm Imprimerie
Lithographique (Charenton, 1802-04; Paris, 1804-06), edited either anon-
ymously or by "Mme Vernay" or "Mme Duhan". The state of research on
the Imprimerie Lithographique and its relation to the André firm is summa-
rized, with particular attention to the former's catalogue of Mozart works.
(Karen Clute)

5976 LEDUC, Émile. **Les contrefaçons dans la**
as **République Argentine (et dans les États
sud-américains de langue espagnole)** [Counter-
feiting in the Argentine Republic (and in the Spanish-speaking South American states)], *Congrès international des éditeurs: VIᵉ session—Rapports* (Madrid:
Asociación de la Librería de España, 1908) 273–79. In
French. See no. 60 in this volume.
Suggests that new efforts should be made to secure the rights of composers
and publishers.

5977 LEDUC, Émile. **La protection des droits**
as **d'auteur dans les républiques latines de
l'Amérique du Sud** [The protection of an author's
rights in the Latin republics of South America],
*Congrès international des éditeurs: VIᵉ session—Rap-
ports* (Madrid: Asociación de la Librería de España,
1908) 283–88. In French. See no. 60 in this volume.
Outlines the conditions in eight South American countries, and calls for the
general improvement of the protection of the composer's rights.

→ LESURE, François. **La datation des premières éditions d'Estienne Roger (1697-1702)** [Dating the first publications of Estienne Roger (1697-1702)]. See no. 1603 in this volume.

5978
as
MALAPLATE, Léon. **Substitution de musique de films** [Substitution of film music], *Compte rendu du dix-septième Congrès de la Confédération Internationale des Sociétés d'Auteurs et Compositeurs* (Paris: Confédération Internationale des Sociétés d'Auteurs et Compositeurs, 1952) 217–18. In French. See no. 311 in this volume.

The practice of replacing music composed for a particular film with other music without the original composer's consent, should be eliminated. *(Marilyn S. Bliss)*

5979
as
MEYER-BAER, Kathi. **New facts on the printing of music incunabula,** *Papers of the American Musicological Society* (Philadelphia: American Musicological Society, 1946) 80–87. See no. 269 in this volume.

Offers general information about early music printing and outlines a project to list and describe all the music incunabula available in European libraries.

5980
as
MIES, Paul. **Faksimile-Ausgaben von Werken Händels und ihre Bedeutung** [Facimile editions of Händel's works and their significance], *Händel-Ehrung der Deutschen Demokratischen Republik: Konferenzbericht* (Leipzig: VEB Deutscher Verlag für Musik, 1961) 187–91. *Facs., music.* In German. See no. 408 in this volume.

Discusses the Sacred Harmonic Society edition of the *Messiah* autograph, London 1868; Friedrich Chrysander's editions of the *Jephtha* and *Messiah* scores, 1885; and a 1923 publication of the duet *Quel fior che all'alba ride*, HWV 200, by the Drei-Masken Verlag, Munich. *(David Bloom)*

5981
as
MONTANI, Pietro. **Le point de vue de l'éditeur** [The publisher's point of view], *La musique dans l'éducation* (Paris: UNESCO; Colin, 1955) 320–22. In French. See no. 323 in this volume.

An English version is abstracted as RILM 5982 in this volume.

5982
as
MONTANI, Pietro. **The publisher's point of view,** *Music in education* (Paris: UNESCO, 1955) 307–09. See no. 322 in this volume.

Music publishing and education share important links, including the printing of etude books and critical editions. Publishers should maintain close contact with conservatories to exchange information on new musical trends. A French version is cited as RILM 5981 in this volume.

→ NEWMAN, Joel. **Problems of editing and publishing old music.** See no. 3911 in this volume.

5983
as
NYS, Carl de. **Les enregistrements de musique sacrée** [Recordings of sacred music], *Revue musicale* 239-240 (1957) 315–26. *Discog.* In French. See no. 378 in this volume.

Abridged version of the conference paper abstracted as RILM 5984 in this volume.

5984
as
NYS, Carl de. **Une nouvelle collection de disques** *Les archives sonores de la musique sacrée* [A new record collection, *Archives sonores de la musique sacrée*], *Perspectives de la musique sacrée à la lumière de l'encyclique* Musicae sacrae disciplina (Paris: conference, 1959) 656–58. *Discog.* In French. See no. 379 in this volume.

A series of recordings representing the whole of the tradition of Roman Catholic church music, in line with the principles of the encyclical *Musicae sacrae disciplina* of Pius XII (1955), is to be issued by the Lumen label, Paris. A summary is cited as RILM 5983 in this volume. *(Warren A. Bebbington)*

5985
as
PROKOPOWICZ, Maria. **Musique imprimée à Varsovie en 1800-1830** [Music printed in Warsaw from 1800-1830], *The book of the first international musicological congress devoted to the works of Frederick Chopin* (Warszawa: Państwowe Wydawnictwo Naukowe, 1963) 593–97. In French. See no. 425 in this volume.

Music publishing began to be put on a professional basis from 1803-06, when Józef Elsner and Abbé Izydor Józef Cybulski set up their own studios for the purpose of engraving music by Polish composers. In 1820-30, the quantity of music published in Warsaw greatly increased, and included considerable foreign music of a relatively light character. The print shops also functioned as dealers, selling imported scores by Haydn, Mozart, Beethoven, Hummel, and Field. *(Susan Poliniak)*

5986
as
REHM, Wolfgang. **Der Musikwissenschaftler im Musikverlag** [The musicologist and music publishing], *Bericht über den internationalen musikwissenschaftlichen Kongreß* (Kassel: Bärenreiter, 1963) 325–27. In German. See no. 452 in this volume.

Discusses the possibility of a career in music publishing for the young musicologist.

5987
as
SCALA, Stefano. **La stampa e la restaurazione della musica sacra** [The publishing and restoration of sacred music], *7° Congresso di musica sacra* (Torino: author, 1905) 67–69. In Italian. See no. 52 in this volume.

Pays tribute to Pope Pius X, identifying him as "the Saint Francis of Assisi of liturgical chant and sacred music". *(André Balog)*

5988
as
SCHULZE, Erich. **Kirchenmusik und Urheberrecht** [Church music and copyright], *Vorträge zum Urheberrecht/Lectures on copyright/Conférences sur le droit d'auteur* (Berlin; Frankfurt am Main: Vahlen, 1961) 23–32. In German. See no. 431 in this volume.

An early edition of the congress paper abstracted as RILM 5989 in this volume.

5989
as
SCHULZE, Erich. **Kirchenmusik und Urheberrecht/Church music and copyright/Musique sacrée et droit d'auteur** [Church music and copyright], *IV. Internationaler Kongress für Kirchenmusik in Köln: Dokumente und Berichte* (Köln: Bachem, 1962) 102–19. In German, English, and French. See no. 432 in this volume.

A critique of present laws, which allow performance of church music without remunerating composers, since performances in church are by nature free and not-for-profit. Another version is cited as RILM 5988 in this volume. *(T. Pierce)*

5990
as
SEEFEHLNER, Egon. **Patronage of music in the West: The role of the Maecenas in Europe,** *Music: East and West* (Tōkyō: conference, 1961) 161–64. See no. 445 in this volume.

5991
as
SEITZ, A. **Rapport sur la possibilité d'une confédération internationale** [Report on the possibility of an international federation], *Troisième Congrès de la Fédération des Artistes Musiciens de France (Deuxième Congrès international)* (Paris: Fédération des Artistes Musiciens de France, 1904) 76–84. In French. See no. 46 in this volume.

5992 SIMON, Alicja. **Über einige amerikanische**
as **Beethoven-Ausgaben** [On some American Beethoven editions], *Beethoven-Zentenarfeier: Internationaler musikhistorischer Kongress* (Wien: Universal, 1927) 26–28. In German. See no. 142 in this volume.

Presents an interim report of research on Beethoven reception in the U.S. during the 19th c., with attention to the publication of his works and of spurious works under his name, performance history, and critical responses. The ongoing work at the Library of Congress is described. *(David Bloom)*

5993 SLESINGER, Donald; ENGEL, Carl;
as SANDERS, William. **Memorandum on copyright,** *Report of the Committee of the Conference on Inter-American Relations in the Field of Music* (Washington, D.C.: United States Department of State, 1940) 38–45. See no. 271 in this volume.

The U.S. has copyright relations with 18 Latin American countries under 14 different treaties; their provisions should be unified. An inter-American copyright union should be formed, and laws should be passed to encourage publishers to exploit their properties for the cultural benefit of all nations. *(Howard Cinnamon)*

5994 SPRINGER, Hermann. **Die musikalischen**
as **Blockdrucke des 15. und 16. Jahrhunderts** [Musical block printing in the 15th and 16th centuries], *Bericht über den zweiten Kongress der Internationalen Musikgesellschaft* (Leipzig: Breitkopf & Härtel, 1907) 37–46. In German. See no. 53 in this volume.

The earliest music prints, possibly as early as 1480, were made with woodblocks. This technique continued to be used long after the introduction of movable type for music printing in the late 1490s, and reached its peak, functionally and artistically, in the edition cut by Andrea Antico, 1539, for the Scotto firm in Venice, of the second book of Adrian Willaert's four-voice motets. *(David Bloom)*

⟶ STEVENS, Denis. **Problems of editing and publishing old music.** See no. 3922 in this volume.

5995 URSPRUNG, Otto. **Der kunst- und handels-**
as **politische Gang der Musikdrucke von 1462-1600** [The development of artistic and commercial policy in music printing from 1462 to 1600], *Bericht über den internationalen Kongress für Schubertforschung* (Augsburg: Benno Filser, 1929) 168–74. *Charts, diagr.* In German. See no. 154 in this volume.

Surveys the history of the printed publication of music treatises and sources in Europe, with emphasis on structural differences between the centralization of the industry in Italy and France and its extremely productive decentralization in Germany. *(David Bloom)*

5996 VATIELLI, Francesco. **L'edizione: Musica e**
as **letteratura musicale** [Publishing: Music and musical literature], *La vita musicale dell'Italia d'oggi*

(Torino: Fratelli Bocca, 1921) 49–57. In Italian. See no. 97 in this volume.

Argues for the centralization of publications in order to ensure uniform goals, methods, and quality.

5997 VINCZE, Imre. **Die Hebung der wirtschaft-**
as **lichen Stellung des Sängers** [The improvement of the singer's economic position], *Musikerziehung: Zeitschrift der Musikerzieher Österreichs* special issue (1953) 93–95. In German. See no. 317 in this volume.

5998 VIOLA, Cesare Giulio. **La collaboration des**
as **auteurs nationaux dans l'exploitation des œuvres étrangères sous le signe de la solidarité internationale** [The collaboration of national authors in cases of the exploitation of foreign works in the name of international solidarity], *Compte rendu du dix-septième Congrès de la Confédération Internationale des Sociétés d'Auteurs et Compositeurs* (Paris: Confédération Internationale des Sociétés d'Auteurs et Compositeurs, 1952) 24–26. In French. See no. 311 in this volume.

Discusses the need for safeguards against the exploitation of authors' and composers' works in foreign countries.

5999 VOLKMANN, Ludwig. **Conventions interna-**
as **tionales pour les remises dans le commerce de la musique** [International conventions for the sorting-out of the music business], *Congrès international des éditeurs: VIe session—Rapports* (Madrid: Asociación de la Libreria de España, 1908) 289–98. In French. See no. 60 in this volume.

Discusses the major music publisher's associations, which differ widely from country to country, and calls for the pursuit of international accords.

6000 WEINBERGER, Joseph. **La réglementation**
as **internationale du droit d'exécution des œuvres musicales** [The international regulation of performing rights of musical works], *Congrès international des éditeurs: 5e session—Rapports* (Milano: Associazione Tipografico-Libraria Italiana, 1907) 228–37. In French. See no. 55 in this volume.

Performance rights should be the responsibility of the publisher. Germany especially needs to advance its activity in this area, if a successful international regulation of performance rights is to be established.

6001 ŽGANEC, Vinko. **Autorskopravna zaštita**
as **melografskog rada** [Copyright protection for ethnographic transcriptions], *Rad kongresa folklorista Jugoslavije* (Zagreb: Savez Udruženja Folklorista Jugoslavije, 1958) 187–95. In Croatian. See no. 315 in this volume.

An outline of the situation in Yugoslavia during the 1950s.

MUSIC IN LITURGY AND RITUAL

90 General

6002
as
ALLT, Wilfrid Greenhouse. **The basic values,** *Organ and choral aspects and prospects* (London: Hinrichsen, 1958) 46–53. See no. 375 in this volume.
Serial techniques, as well as the use of traditional music idioms, jazz, and other music of sensual appeal have no place in church music.

6003
as
ANGLÈS, Higini. **Das Alte und das Neue in der heutigen Kirchenmusik und die Vereinigung der Christen** [The old and the new in today's church music and the uniting of Christians], *Kirchenmusik in ökumenischer Schau* (Bern: Haupt, 1964) 9–14. In German. See no. 447 in this volume.
The rich musical heritage of Christianity is discussed from an ecumenical point of view, and contemporary problems are reviewed. The increasing use of vernacular texts in Catholic liturgy endangers the survival of Gregorian chant; that of folk melodies in Catholic and Protestant churches threatens sacred polyphony; the traditional organ, too, is threatened, by electronic instruments; and the encouragement of new compositions for liturgical use is an urgent task. *(David Bloom)*

6004
as
CHERBULIEZ, Antoine-Élisée. **Zum Problem der religiösen Musik** [The problem of religious music], *Schweizer Jahrbuch für Musikwissenschaft/Annales suisses de musicologie/Annuario svizzero di musicologia* I (1924) 92–117. In German. See no. 103 in this volume.

6005
as
COSTANTINI, Celso. **La musique sacrée dans les missions** [Sacred music in missions], *Perspectives de la musique sacrée à la lumière de l'encyclique* Musicae sacrae disciplina (Paris: conference, 1959) 523–25. In French. See no. 379 in this volume.
Other than Gregorian chant, with its special character as the official music of the Roman Catholic church, Western music in the liturgy in mission churches in Africa and Asia should be partly or wholly replaced by music in an indigenous tradition. An example of a successful adaptation is the *Messe des savanes* of Abbé Robert Ouedraogo of Upper Volta (Burkina Faso). The traditionally religious understanding of music in East Asia, especially China, is discussed. A summary is cited as no. 6006 in this volume. *(Warren A. Bebbington)*

6006
as
COSTANTINI, Celso. **La musique sacrée dans les missions** [Sacred music in missions], *Revue musicale* 239-240 (1957) 231–34. In French. See no. 378 in this volume.
An abridged version of the conference paper is abstracted as no. 6005 in this volume.

6007
as
DI SALVO, Bartolomeo. **La tradizione orale dei canti liturgici delle colonie italo-albanesi di Sicilia comparata con quella dei codici antichi bizantini** [The oral tradition of liturgical chants in Italian-Albanian colonies in Sicily, compared with that of the early Byzantine codices], *Atti del [I] Congresso internazionale di musica sacra* (Tournai: Desclée, 1952) 129–30. In Italian. See no. 303 in this volume.

6008
as
DRAEGER, Hans-Heinz. **Liturgical and religious music,** *Music: East and West* (Tōkyō: conference, 1961) 47–49. See no. 445 in this volume.

6009
as
ELWART, Antoine-Amable-Élie. **Quelles sont les causes qui ont donné naissance à la musique religieuse? Pourquoi s'est-elle écartée de son but? Et quels seraient les moyens de l'y ramener?** [What gave birth to religious music? Why has it veered from its goal? How could it be brought back to it?], *Congrès historique* (Paris: A. Le Gallois, 1839) 387–99. In French. See no. 2 in this volume.
Delivered at the 13th session of the Congrès Historique, 1838.

6010
as
GELINEAU, Joseph. **Les chants processionaux: Recherche sur leur structure liturgique** [Processional chants: An investigation of their liturgical structure], *Musique sacrée et langues modernes: Deux colloques internationaux* (Paris: Fleurus, 1964) 105–18. In French. See no. 449 in this volume.
Discusses Roman, Byzantine, and Syrian or Chaldean styles in the genre.

6011
as
GEORGIADES, Thrasybulos Georges. **Sprachschichten in der Kirchenmusik** [Language strata in church music], *Kirchenmusik in ökumenischer Schau* (Bern: Haupt, 1964) 24–32. In German. See no. 447 in this volume.
Summary of a paper treating prose and verse as different strata of liturgical language; the full version is published in *Musik und Kirche* I (1963).

6012
as
GERSON-KIWI, Edith. **Religious chant: A Pan-Asiatic conception of music,** *Journal of the International Folk Music Council* XIII (1961) 64–67. Transcr. See no. 424 in this volume.
Unlike traditional song, which tends to be differentiated according to ethnic and geographical regions, the cantillation styles of sacred and heroic chant show pervasively common Asian features. Draws on examples from Shinto, Buddhist, Tibetan, Brahman, Muslim, and Jewish rituals. *(Alix Moyer Grunebaum)*

6013
as
GONZÁLEZ BARRÓN, Ramón. **Conveniencia de implantar un canon similar a los derechos de autor por las ejecuciones de música sagrada retribuidas** [The propriety of introducing royalties on the model of copyright for paid performances of religious music], *V Congreso Nacional de Música Sagrada* (Madrid: Gráficas Dos de Mayo, 1956) 245–49. In Spanish. See no. 331 in this volume.
On the one hand, the Church prohibits liturgical performance of works by composers who insist on author's rights; religious music is made for God, and its reward is to be expected only from God. On the other hand, composers of religious music need to be compensated for their training and their work. From a practical point of view the question is extremely complex. *(José López-Calo)*

6014
as
HADOW, William Henry. **The influence of secular idiom upon English church music,** *Report of the Fourth Congress of the International Musical Society* (London: Novello, 1912) 61. See no. 71 in this volume.
Summary of a paper. Surveys trends from the 15th to the early 20th c.

6015
as
HANDSCHIN, Jacques. **Die Kirchenmusik und die Frage der Wiedervereinigung der Kirchen** [Church music and the question of reunification of the churches], *Bericht über den Internationalen Kongress für Kirchenmusik/Compte rendu du Congrès international de musique sacrée* (Bern: Haupt, 1953) 9–23. In German. See no. 312 in this volume.

6016
as
KROHN, Ilmari. **Errungenschaften und Aussichten der finnischen Kirchenmusik** [Achievements and prospects of Finnish church music], *Bericht über den Internationalen Kongress für Kirchenmusik/Compte rendu du Congrès international de musique sacrée* (Bern: Haupt, 1953) 41–42. In German. See no. 312 in this volume.

⟶ LAGUARDA Y FENORELLA, Juan J. **La enseñanza de la música sagrada** [The teaching of religious music]. See no. 4580 in this volume.

6017
as
LAURENT (brother). **Neue Formen der Anbetung** [New forms of worship], *Kirchenmusik in ökumenischer Schau* (Bern: Haupt, 1964) 84–87. In German. See no. 447 in this volume.
Discusses the theology of music in liturgy from the standpoint of the Taizé Community; a fuller version is published in *Liturgisches Jahrbuch* 13 (1963):2ff.

6018
as
LEVI, Leo. **Traditions of Biblical cantillation and ekphonetics,** *Journal of the International Folk Music Council* XVI (1964) 64–65. See no. 463 in this volume.
Within Judaism from the 2nd to 9th c. the ekphonetic notation for Bible reading developed into an increasingly intricate system and then stopped, while the oral tradition of cantillation in different parts of the diaspora began adapting under various local influences. In the Syrian and Byzantine churches, in contrast, notated music continued to evolve toward a fixed hymnody and diastematic chant notation and cantillation practice ceased developing. Reasons for these different outcomes should perhaps be sought in cultural differences. *(David Bloom)*

6019
as
MATHIAS, François-Xavier. **L'orgue dans l'antiquité chrétienne: Probabilité de sa part médiate et indirecte à l'évolution du chant cultuel, à partir du 5ᵉ siècle** [The organ in Christian antiquity: The probability that it played a mediate and indirect role in the evolution of liturgical chant from the 5th century onwards], *Compte rendu du Congrès d'orgue tenu à l'Université de Strasbourg. IV* (Strasbourg: Société Strasbourgeoise de Librairie Sostralib, 1934) 166–71. In French. See no. 199 in this volume.
A historical overview including a summary of the early, pre-Christian development of the instrument.

6020
as
NOMURA, Francesco Yosio. **Religious music,** *Music: East and West* (Tōkyō: conference, 1961) 26–29. See no. 445 in this volume.
Remarks comparing Asian and European religious musics.

6021
as
OVERATH, Johannes. **Der kirchenmusikalische Dienst: Ein wahres Apostolat** [The mission of church music: A true apostolate], *Musica sacra in unserer Zeit* (Berlin: Merseburger, 1960) 36–42. In German. See no. 403 in this volume.

6022
as
PARISOT, Jean. **La chant grégorien et les mélodies de la synagogue** [Gregorian chant and synagogue melodies], *Compte rendu du Congrès général de musique sacrée: Aperçu général des préliminaires et du congrès, discours et conférences* (Strasbourg: Alsacien, 1922) 185–205. *Music.* In French. See no. 96 in this volume.
Explores modal, melodic, and rhythmic resemblances between Jewish and Christian chant traditions.

6023
as
PEAKER, Charles. **Voice and verse,** *Organ and choral aspects and prospects* (London: Hinrichsen, 1958) 125–31. See no. 375 in this volume.
Discusses the marriage of language and music in Christian vocal genres, with notes on usage in Canadian churches.

6024
as
QUOIKA, Rudolf. **Gregorianischer Choral und Orgel** [Gregorian chant and the organ], *Bericht über die dritte Tagung für Deutsche Orgelkunst* (Kassel: Bärenreiter, 1928) 78–82. In German. See no. 136 in this volume.
The sound quality of the organ resembles that of chant, with its freedom from passion and hurry, and a trust in God, manifested in sound. The history of the organ's liturgical use is bound up with that of chant, from the 9th c. to the cantus firmus settings (including Protestant ones, e.g., by Michael Praetorius, Samuel Scheidt, and J.S. Bach) of the 17th and early 18th c. The revival of chant since Pius X's motu proprio *Tra le sollecitudini* (1903) requires a renewal of Roman Catholic organ music as well, with which the movement for organ reform can play an essential part.

6025
as
SÖHNGEN, Oskar. **Die geistige und künstlerische Situation des neuen Kirchenmusikerstandes** [The spiritual and artistic situation in the new status of the church musician], *Musica sacra in unserer Zeit* (Berlin: Merseburger, 1960) 16–26. In German. See no. 403 in this volume.

6026
as
SOWERBY, Leo. **Composition in relation to the church and allied fields in America,** *Organ and choral aspects and prospects* (London: Hinrichsen, 1958) 33–46. See no. 375 in this volume.
Remarks on the history of church music, choirs, influences, and composers.

6027
as
STIRNIMANN, Heinrich. **Ökumenische Gedanken zur Kirchenmusik** [Ecumenical thoughts on church music], *Kirchenmusik in ökumenischer Schau* (Bern: Haupt, 1964) 21–23. In German. See no. 447 in this volume.
Discusses elements of the theology of music common to Catholic, Eastern, and Protestant thinking.

6028
as
TOTZKE, Irenäus. **Unsere Verpflichtung gegenüber der ostkirchlichen Musik** [Our obligation to the sacred music of the Eastern church], *IV. Internationaler Kongress für Kirchenmusik in Köln: Dokumente und Berichte* (Köln: Bachem, 1962) 161–62. In German. See no. 432 in this volume.
After the Great Schism of 1054, the Western church lost its Eastern tradition and the East its Western influence; Western ears frequently hear authentic music of the Eastern church without understanding it. Research on and performance of the Eastern liturgy in Western Europe should be encouraged.

6029
as
WELLESZ, Egon. **Notes on the Alleluia,** *Société Internationale de Musicologie, cinquième congrès/ Internationale Gesellschaft für Musikwissenschaft, fünfter Kongreß/International Society for Musical Research, Fifth Congress* (Amsterdam: Vereniging voor Nederlandse Muziekgeschiedenis, 1953) 423–27. See no. 316 in this volume.
Comparison of Byzantine and Latin Alleluias provides insights on the question of the rise of the sequence; the technique illustrates the value of

comparative research on the formal development of the melodies of the Eastern and Western churches. *(Tsipora Yosselevitch)*

6030
as
WERNER, Eric. **The common ground in the chant of church and synagogue,** *Atti del [I] Congresso internazionale di musica sacra* (Tournai: Desclée, 1952) 134–48. See no. 303 in this volume.

6031
as
WILLIAMS, David. **The artist in religion,** *Organ and choral aspects and prospects* (London: Hinrichsen, 1958) 106–13. See no. 375 in this volume.
Both visual and aural art can lead one to a higher spiritual realm.

6032
as
WINCKEL, Fritz. **Die neue Entwicklung der elektronischen Musik** [The new development of electronic music], *Musica sacra in unserer Zeit* (Berlin: Merseburger, 1960) 43–48. *Illus.* In German. See no. 403 in this volume.
Addresses the issue of using electroacoustic music in worship services.

6033
as
ŽGANEC, Vinko. **Folklore elements in the Yugoslav Orthodox and Roman Catholic liturgical chant,** *Journal of the International Folk Music Council* VIII (1956) 19–22. See no. 349 in this volume.
Includes discussions of modality and singing style.

6034
as
ZIMMERMAN, Heinz Werner. **Die Möglichkeiten und Grenzen des Jazz innerhalb der Musiksprache der Gegenwart** [The possibilities and limits of jazz within contemporary musical language], *Musica sacra in unserer Zeit* (Berlin: Merseburger, 1960) 49–67. In German. See no. 403 in this volume.
Addresses the use of jazz idioms in church music, from the composer's point of view.

91 Jewish

6035
as
ADLER, Israel. **Mẇsyqah 'ẇmanẇtyt miḥẇṣ lema'amad hatpylah b̉b̉yhak"n b̉eqehylẇt hayeḥẇdyẇt b̉e'eyrẇp̉'ah lipney ha'-emanṣypaṣyah** [Non-liturgical art music in European synagogues before the Emancipation], *Dẇkan* VII (1965) 7–10. In Hebrew. See no. 482 in this volume.
Discusses the role of art music in the cultural life of Jewish communities, including 17th- and 18th-c. Italian works.

6036
as
ADOLF, Martin; GREENBERG, Simon. **The cantor's conservatory: To be or not to be?,** *Proceedings of the annual convention* I (1948) 25–28. See no. 286 in this volume.
Discusses cantorial training, schools, financial support for students, and libraries for research.

6037
as
AVENARY, Hanoch. **The Hasidic *nigun*: Ethos and melos of a folk liturgy,** *Journal of the International Folk Music Council* XVI (1964) 60–63. *Bibliog., transcr.* See no. 463 in this volume.
The Hasidic nigun is a wordless vocal melody used as an extension of the liturgy, as prelude or postlude to the traditional prayers. Different melodic types are found in the rabbi's solo singing, individuals praying on their own, and congregational song; varying between strict rhythm and recitative character, they bear less resemblance to synagogal recitative than to Walachian farmer and shepherd songs. A fourth type is the dance-nigun, marked by taut rhythm, syncopation, rather long bridge passages, and varied repetitions. *(Vivian Conejero)*

6038
as
AVENARY, Hanoch. ***Who is on Mount Horeb?*: A piyyut and its melody from the Geniza,** *Haqẇngres ha'ẇlamy hašlyšy lemada'ey hayahadẇt* (Yerẇšalaym/Al-Quds: Hebrew University/Ha'unybersytah ha'ibryt, 1965) 362–63. See no. 435 in this volume.

6039
as
B̉AR-DYYAN, Ḥayym. **Leb̉'ayẇt haqry'ah lepy haṭa'amym b̉eseper thylym** [On problems of reading psalms according to their Masoretic accents], *Dẇkan* V (1963) 95–102. In Hebrew. See no. 451 in this volume.

6040
as
B̉AR-DYYAN, Ḥayym. **Music in the life of Vilna Jewry,** *Haqẇngres ha'ẇlamy hašlyšy lemada'ey hayahadẇt* (Yerẇšalaym/Al-Quds: Hebrew University/Ha'unybersytah ha'ibryt, 1965) 360–61. See no. 435 in this volume.

6041
as
BAYER, Bathja. **Hašyr hadaty b̉epy haṣyb̉ẇr haḥylẇny** [Religious songs sung by the secular public], *Dẇkan* VII (1965) 11–30. In Hebrew. See no. 482 in this volume.

6042
as
BAYER, Bathja. **Haty'ẇd ha'arky'ẇlẇgy šel hašẇp̉ar b̉e"y** [The archaeological documentation of the shofar in Israel], *Dẇkan* VI (1964) 15–34. *Illus.* In Hebrew. See no. 464 in this volume.
Discusses shofar performance practice and the instrument's importance in religious services through an examination of archaeological documentation from the 2nd c. to the present. *(Moshe Zorman)*

6043
as
BAYER, Bathja. **Seder šel p̉esaḥ nẇsaḥ yagẇr** [The Passover Seder in the tradition of Yagẇr], *Dẇkan* VIII (1966) 89–98. In Hebrew. See no. 503 in this volume.

6044
as
B̉EN-'W̉RY, Me'yr. **P̉arašah b̉emiqr'a b̉ebyṭẇy mẇsyqaly** [A chapter of the Bible expressed in music], *Dẇkan* III (1961) 13–20. In Hebrew. See no. 417 in this volume.

6045
as
B̉RW̉Y'ER, Mordekay. **B̉'ayẇt wederakym b̉eḥeqer hamẇsyqah haḥasydyt** [Problems and trends in the research of Hasidic music], *Dẇkan* IV (1962) 38–47. In Hebrew. See no. 436 in this volume.

6046
as
B̉RW̉Y'ER, Mordekay. **He'arẇt 'al tawey ṭa'amey hamiqr'a b̉eseper šel Y. Rẇyklyn** [Remarks on the Biblical accents in J. Reuchlin's *De accentibus et orthographia*], *Dẇkan* V (1963) 44–46. *Music.* In Hebrew. See no. 451 in this volume.
Johannes Reuchlin's *De accentibus et orthographia linguae Hebraicae* (Hagenau, 1518), was the first publication of notated Jewish cantillation. Relationships between cantillation and ecclesiastical music of that period are examined. *(Moshe Zorman)*

⟶ B̉RW̉Y'ER, Mordekay. **Mẇsiqah datyt b̉etqẇpat qyb̉ẇṣ galẇyẇt** [Religious music at the time of the ingathering of the exiles]. See no. 2610 in this volume.

6047
as
B̉RW̉Y'ER, Mordekay. **Mẇsyqah 'amamit datyt ḥadašah** [New religious folk music], *Dẇkan* VII (1965) 31–38. In Hebrew. See no. 482 in this volume.

6048 BRŴY'ER, Mordekay. **'Ŵleh weyŵred**
as **we'etnaḥt'a beṭa'amey 'em"t** ['Ŵleh weyŵred
and 'etnaḥt'a in the Masoretic accents of Job, Ecclesiastes, and Psalms], *Dŵkan* V (1963) 53–66. In Hebrew.
See no. 451 in this volume.

6049 EDGAR, Aaron. **Systematic planning of a ser-
as vice of worship: Cantor's point of view,** *Proceedings of the annual convention* I (1948) 11. See no.
286 in this volume.
Congregations must be trained to understand and participate in the Jewish
service. The balance between cantorial recitative, choral compositions, and
congregational singing must be maintained.

6050 'ELYNER, 'Ely'ezer. **Haṗywṭ šbamaḥzŵr
as 'ašḱenaz: Haštašlŵtaw wešymŵšŵ** [Liturgical
poetry in Ashkenazi prayer books: Its development and
use], *Dŵkan* VI (1964) 35–48. In Hebrew. See no. 464
in this volume.

6051 EPHROS, Gershon. **The influence of the
as cantillations on nusah hatefillah,** *Proceedings of
the annual convention* I (1948) 8–9. See no. 286 in this
volume.
The nusahim (traditional Jewish prayer modes) were preserved from early
times, first by oral transmissions, then by publication.

6052 GABA'Y, 'Ezr'a. **Hasignŵn hamzirahy
as bemŵsyqah datyt** [The Oriental style of religious
music], *Dŵkan* III (1961) 49–59. In Hebrew. See no.
417 in this volume.

6053 GERSON-KIWI, Edith. **Halleluia and Jubilus
as in Oriental Jewish and Christian chant,**
Haqŵngres ha'ŵlamy hašlyšy lemada'ey hayahadŵt
(Yerŵšalaym/Al-Quds: Hebrew University/
Ha'unybersyṭah ha'ibryt, 1965) 371–71. See no. 435 in
this volume.

6054 GERSON-KIWI, Edith. **The integration of
as Dastgah and Maqam in Oriental-Jewish liturgies,** *The preservation of traditional forms of the
learned and popular music of the Orient and the
Occident/La préservation des formes traditionelles de
la musique savante et populaire dans les pays d'Orient
et d'Occident* (Urbana: Center for Comparative
Psycholinguistics, Institute of Communications Research, 1964) 146–47. See no. 443 in this volume.
Summary of a conference paper. The Jewish communities of Iran and the
Arab countries have incorporated the dastgāh and maqām systems into
their liturgical music. *(Judith Drogichen Meyer)*

6055 GERSON-KIWI, Edith. **Nygŵnim šel yehŵdey
as ṗaras wehašṗ'atah šel hamŵsyqah haṗarsyt
'aleyhem** [The influence of Persian music on the
nigunim of Persian Jews], *Dŵkan* III (1961) 60–62. In
Hebrew. See no. 417 in this volume.

6056 GEŠWRY, Me'yr Šim'ŵn. **Chants used in the
as study of the Talmud by Ashkenazi and Oriental
Jews,** *Haqŵngres ha'ŵlamy hašlyšy lemada'ey
hayahadŵt* (Yerŵšalaym/Al-Quds: Hebrew University/
Ha'unybersyṭah ha'ibryt, 1965) 366–68. See no. 435 in
this volume.

6057 GEŠWRY, Me'yr Šim'ŵn. **Haḥasydŵt beṣlyl
as webezemer** [Hasidism in sound and song], *Dŵkan* IV
(1962) 20–37. In Hebrew. See no. 436 in this volume.
Surveys the evolution of Hasidic music and discusses its significance in
prayer.

6058 GEŠWRY, Me'yr Šim'ŵn. **Hamŵsyqah haas ḥasydyt behynŵh** [Hasidic music in education],
Dŵkan II (1960) 75–78. In Hebrew. See no. 409 in this
volume.

6059 GEŠWRY, Me'yr Šim'ŵn. **Hanygŵn haḥasydy**
as [The Hasidic nigun], *Dŵkan* I (1959) 62–70. *Music.* In
Hebrew. See no. 391 in this volume.
Analyzes transcriptions of orally transmitted nigunim to evaluate the originality of this music. Though growing from the traditional Eastern European
musical background, Hasidic music is unique because of its new spiritual
essence. *(Moshe Zorman)*

6060 GEŠWRY, Me'yr Šim'ŵn. **Nygŵney hayamym
as hanŵra'ym eṣel haḥasydym** [The Hasidic melodies for the High Holy Days], *Dŵkan* VI (1964) 49–62.
In Hebrew. See no. 464 in this volume.

6061 GEŠWRY, Me'yr Šim'ŵn. **Nygŵney seder šel
as ṗesaḥ behasydŵt qarlin** [Seder melodies of
Karlin's Hasidim], *Dŵkan* VIII (1966) 61–74. In Hebrew. See no. 503 in this volume.

6062 GEŠWRY, Me'yr Šim'ŵn. **Nygŵney šŵlḥan
as ḥasydyym beyemey šabatŵt wehagym** [Hasidic
tunes sung at the table on Sabbath and holidays],
Dŵkan VII (1965) 39–50. In Hebrew. See no. 482 in
this volume.

6063 GEŠWRY, Me'yr Šim'ŵn. **R' Šlomoh R'abyṣ:
as Halŵṣ bethyyat haḥazanŵt beyśra'el** [Rabbi
Šlomoh R'abyṣ: A pioneer in the revival of hazanut in
Israel], *Dŵkan* III (1961) 31–38. In Hebrew. See no.
417 in this volume.
Surveys the life and career of Israel's first professional hazan.

6064 GEŠWRY, Me'yr Šim'ŵn. **Seper tehylym
as belahn haḥasydym** [Hasidic melodies for the Book
of Psalms], *Dŵkan* V (1963) 122–28. In Hebrew. See
no. 451 in this volume.

6065 GŴLDŠMYDṬ, Yŵsep. **Ḥawayah w'estyṭyqah
as bemŵsyqah datyt** [Spiritual experience and aesthetics in religious music], *Dŵkan* II (1960) 5–14. In Hebrew. See no. 409 in this volume.

6066 HABERMAN, 'Abraham Me'yr. **Dbarym 'al
as hatpylah** [Remarks on prayer], *Dŵkan* VI (1964)
7–14. In Hebrew. See no. 464 in this volume.

6067 HABERMAN, 'Abraham Me'yr. **Šyrym le'at
as misŵ'a wehitṗathŵtam** [Songs for certain occasions and their development], *Dŵkan* VII (1965)
51–58. In Hebrew. See no. 482 in this volume.

6068 HALPERN, Harry. **Systematic planning of a
as service of worship: Rabbi's point of view,** *Proceedings of the annual convention* I (1948) 11. See no.
286 in this volume.

The reading of the Torah should be limited to seven or eight people. Long solo chants must be avoided, and English prayers should be included in the service.

6069
as
HERZOG, Avigdor. **Dereḥ qry'at hatŵrah b̌enŵsaḥ "sfarad-'e"y""** [Torah reading according to the Sephardic-Israel custom], *Dŵkan* III (1961) 63–72. In Hebrew. See no. 417 in this volume.

6070
as
HERZOG, Avigdor. **The Tora readings according to the Israeli Sephardic mode,** *Haqŵngres ha'ŵlamy hašlyšy lemada'ey hayahadŵt* (Yerŵšalaym/Al-Quds: Hebrew University/Ha'unybersytah ha'ibryt, 1965) 369–70. See no. 435 in this volume.

6071
as
HERZOG, Avigdor. **Zmirah mesŵrtyt šamḥŵs leK̇taley b̌eyt haK̇neset: Dibrey haqdamah lehadgamŵt mŵsyqalyŵt** [Traditional songs outside the synagogue], *Dŵkan* VII (1965) 59–64. In Hebrew. See no. 482 in this volume.

6072
as
HYYNYMAN, Yŵsep. **Seper thylym K̇emaqŵr lenŵsaḥ hatpylah** [The Book of Psalms as the origin of Biblical cantillation], *Dŵkan* V (1963) 35–43. In Hebrew. See no. 451 in this volume.

6073
as
JACOBI, Frederick. **Synagogue music as I see it,** *Proceedings of the annual convention* I (1948) 3–5. See no. 286 in this volume.
The exclusive use of traditional sources, including Jewish folk material, limits the composer. Jewish music must be universal rather than nationalistic.

6074
as
KEREN, Zvi. **Mašma'ŵtah šel hamilah "selah" lepy p̌yrŵšym yehŵdyym mesŵrtyym** [The meaning of the word *selah* according to traditional Jewish commentaries], *Dŵkan* V (1963) 47–52. In Hebrew. See no. 451 in this volume.
The connotation of the Hebrew term *selah* has led to much conjecture and speculation by scholars. Some believe that the original Hebrew meaning has been lost, others agree it stands for *forever.* The traditional Jewish interpretation is discussed.

6075
as
K̇OHEN, Ya'aqob. **Dibrey haqdamah lehagdamŵt (mehamesŵret hamŵsyqalyt šel ha'edŵt)** [Introduction to representations of Jewish music], *Dŵkan* VIII (1965) 51–54. In Hebrew. See no. 503 in this volume.

6076
as
LANDAU, Siegfried. **The history of synagogue music: The role of the cantor in its development,** *Proceedings of the annual convention* I (1948) 6–8. See no. 286 in this volume.
Secular songs and dances have been gradually accepted, with necessary modifications, into synagogue music.

6077
as
MALK̇Y'EL, 'Alek̇sander. **Leyl šby'y šel p̌esaḥ b̌eb̌eyt haraw Ḥarl"p Zṣ"l** [Eve of the seventh day of Passover at Rabbi Ḥarlap's home], *Dŵkan* VIII (1966) 55–60. In Hebrew. See no. 503 in this volume.

6078
as
MELAMED, 'Ezr'a Ṣyŵn. **Dbarym 'aḥdym 'al hatpylah b̌eṣibŵr** [Some thought on congregational prayer], *Dŵkan* I (1959) 6–10. In Hebrew. See no. 391 in this volume.

6079
as
MELAMED, 'Ezr'a Ṣyŵn. **Meqŵmŵ šel seper tehylym b̌e'abŵdat h' b̌ekol yomŵt hašanah** [The place of psalms in daily liturgy throughout the year], *Dŵkan* V (1963) 7–34. In Hebrew. See no. 451 in this volume.

6080
as
MELAMED, Y. **Hatpylat leyaldey 'edŵt hamizraḥ** [The prayers of the children of the communities of the East], *Dŵkan* II (1960) 61–67. *Music.* In Hebrew. See no. 409 in this volume.
Surveys the theoretical and artistic output of Rabbi Israel Najara (ca. 1555-ca. 1628), creator of the liturgical music of the Sephardic community. Differences between Sephardic and Ashkenazic cantillation are also discussed. *(Moshe Zorman)*

6081
as
NE'EMAN, Yehŵšu'a Leyyb̌. **Derakym b̌eheqer hamŵsyqah šel hata'amym** [Trends in the research of Biblical cantillation], *Dŵkan* III (1961) 23–30. In Hebrew. See no. 417 in this volume.
Discusses three books dealing with Biblical cantillation: *Tŵldŵt haneaynah ha'iwryt* by Abraham Zvi Idelsohn (Berlin, 1924); *The cantillation of the Bible* by Solomon Rosowsky (New York, 1957); and a book by the author. *(Moshe Zorman)*

6082
as
NE'EMAN, Yehŵšu'a Leyyb̌. **Hayeṣyrah b̌ehazanŵt** [Creativity in hazanut], *Dŵkan* III (1961) 39–43. In Hebrew. See no. 417 in this volume.

6083
as
NE'EMAN, Yehŵšu'a Leyyb̌. **Sqyrah 'al nygŵney tpylah šel hayamym hanŵra'ym b̌enŵsaḥ 'eyrŵp̌ah** [A survey of melodies for the prayer of High Holy Days in the Eastern European tradition], *Dŵkan* VI (1964) 63–72. In Hebrew. See no. 464 in this volume.

6084
as
NE'EMAN, Yehŵšu'a Leyyb̌. **Šyrat p̌esaḥ b̌emasŵret hangynah ha'ašk̇enazyt** [The Ashkenazi tradition of Passover songs], *Dŵkan* VIII (1966) 75–86. *Music.* In Hebrew. See no. 503 in this volume.
Analyzes Askenazi Passover songs and their relationships to the Haggadah. Examples from Abraham Baer's *Ba'al tpylah* (Göteborg, 1877) and Abraham Idelson's *'Ŵṣar negynŵt yśra'el* (Jerusalem, 1922-28) are included. *(Moshe Zorman)*

→
NE'EMAN, Yehŵšu'a Leyyb̌. **Ṭa'amym wezmyrŵt** [Notation of Hebrew accents and songs]. See no. 3856 in this volume.

6085
as
NE'EMAN, Yehŵšu'a Leyyb̌. **Zimrat hamišp̌aḥah b̌eyṣyrah hahazanyt** [Family songs in hazzanut], *Dŵkan* VII (1965) 65–74. In Hebrew. See no. 482 in this volume.

6086
as
PAPAGEŌRGIOS, Spyridōn K. **Merkwürdige in der Synagogen von Corfu in Gebrauch befindliche Hymnen** [Curious hymns used in the synagogue of Corfu], *Verhandlungen des fünften Internationalen Orientalisten-Congresses* (Berlin: A. Asher, 1882) II,1, 226–32. In German. See no. 7 in this volume.
Corfu was, for centuries, home to a dynamic Jewish community. The earliest Jewish settlers arrived during the 13th c. while the island was still under Byzantine rule. These Jews, known as Romaniot, readily adapted many elements of the dominant Greek culture and language. The Romaniot maintained a separate congregation and attempted to preserve their liturgical rites and customs. *(Tina Frühauf)*

6087
as
PRENQEL, Yẓḥaq Yedydyah. **Hašyrah šeḇeḥasydẇt** [The song in Hasidic literature], *Dẇkan* IV (1962) 7–14. In Hebrew. See no. 436 in this volume.

6088
as
QADARY, Menaḥem Ṣeby. **Hašpa'at ha-hagadah šel pesaḥ 'al hapr'azy'ẇlẇgyah šel ha'ibryt hamẇdernyt** [The Passover Haggadah and its influence on modern Hebrew], *Dẇkan* VIII (1966) 23–46. In Hebrew. See no. 503 in this volume.

6089
as
QADARY, Menaḥem Ṣeby. **Nytwaḥ taḥbẇry ḇe'ezrat ṭa'amey 'em"t** [Syntactic analysis of Biblical texts with the aid of accents of Job, Ecclesiastes, and Psalms], *Dẇkan* V (1963) 67–94. In Hebrew. See no. 451 in this volume.

6090
as
Q'APAḤ, Yẇsep. **Hašyrah wehalaḥnym ḇetpylat yahadẇt teyman** [Song and melody in the prayer of Yemenite Jews], *Dẇkan* II (1960) 56–60. *Music.* In Hebrew. See no. 409 in this volume.
The Yemenite Jews' religious music can be traced back to Biblical times and has not been influenced by its changing environment since. *(Moshe Zorman)*

6091
as
QAŠ'ANY, Re'uben. **Hawaey weminhagym ḇeleyl haseder 'eṣel yehẇdey 'apganysṭan** [The Seder night traditions of Afghanistan Jews], *Dẇkan* VIII (1966) 47–50. In Hebrew. See no. 503 in this volume.

6092
as
QAŠ'ANY, Re'uben. **Laḥney seper thylym 'eṣel yehẇdey 'apganysṭan** [Psalm melodies of Jews in Afghanistan], *Dẇkan* V (1963) 129–32. In Hebrew. See no. 451 in this volume.

6093
as
QYRŠ, Ḥayym. **Šyrat haṣbẇr ḇemenyyney nẇ'ar** [Congregational singing in youth congregations], *Dẇkan* III (1961) 89–93. In Hebrew. See no. 417 in this volume.

6094
as
RẆS, Y'aqob. **Hanegynah wehaḥawyah hadatyt** [Music and religious experience], *Dẇkan* IV (1962) 15–19. In Hebrew. See no. 436 in this volume.

6095
as
RẆṬŠYLD, Yẇsep. **Zmyrẇt šaḇ'at šel yehẇdey darẇm germanyah wehaminhagym haqšẇrym ḇehem** [Sabbath songs of South German Jews and customs related to them], *Dẇkan* VII (1965) 99–104. In Hebrew. See no. 482 in this volume.

6096
as
ŠATAL, Miryam. **'Al ḇ'ayẇt hatpylah ḇeṣybẇr** [Problems of public prayer], *Dẇkan* III (1961) 44–48. In Hebrew. See no. 417 in this volume.

6097
as
SIMON, Henry W. **Systematic planning of a service of worship: Layman's point of view,** *Proceedings of the annual convention* I (1948) 9–10. See no. 286 in this volume.
Personal participation, congregational singing, and timing are important for a synagogue service.

6098
as
SPECTOR, Johanna. **Problems of compatibility: Non-Western versus Western tradition in Jewish music,** *Haqẇngres ha'ẇlamy hašlyšy lemada'ey hayahadẇt* (Yerwšalaym/Al-Quds: Hebrew University/Ha'unybersyṭah ha'ibryt, 1965) 365–65. See no. 435 in this volume.

6099
as
SPECTOR, Johanna. **Samaritan chant,** *Journal of the International Folk Music Council* XVI (1964) 66–69. *Facs., bibliog., transcr.* See no. 463 in this volume.
Summary of the controversial history of the Samaritan people now consisting of two small communities in Nablus and Holon (Tel Aviv), and an account of their liturgical practice in contrast to Jewish practice. Samaritan music is exclusively religious and exclusively vocal, except for hand-clapping on joyous occasions, and sung only by men (Samaritan women sing the traditional music of other local groups). Examples of their synagogal cantillation tradition are discussed. *(David Bloom)*

6100
as
SPECTOR, Johanna. **The significance of Samaritan neumes and contemporary practice,** *Studia musicologica Academiae Scientiarum Hungaricae* VII (1965) 141–53. *Music, charts, diagr.* See no. 478 in this volume.
The Samaritan religion, which shares common ancestry with Judaism, uses a form of cantillation that may be similar to ancient Jewish cantillation. Their neumatic notation is also related to that used in Judaism, though it is less sophisticated. Contemporary Samaritan cantillation may have deviated in some ways from older practices. *(David Gagné)*

6101
as
STAVITSKY, Michael; SANDROW, Edward; WOHLBERG, Max. **The relationship of the congregation, the rabbi, and the cantor: A symposium,** *Proceedings of the annual convention* I (1948) 16–20. See no. 286 in this volume.
A discussion on synagogue services; topics include tradition, types of chant, and group participation.

6102
as
VALABREGA, Cesare. **La millenaria musica ebraica e Ernest Bloch** [Jewish music over the millennia and Ernest Bloch], *Atti del Congresso internazionale di musiche popolari mediterranee e del Convegno dei bibliotecari musicali* (Palermo: De Magistris succ. V. Bellotti, 1959) 295–99. In Italian. See no. 332 in this volume.
A brief summary of the history of Jewish music and appreciation of Bloch's religious-themed compositions.

6103
as
VINAVER, Chemjo; LIST, Kurt. **Synagogue music: Traditional and modern,** *Proceedings of the annual convention* I (1948) 20–24. See no. 286 in this volume.
Two composers discuss the use of traditional Jewish melodies. A deeply religious composer who wants to create new music with spiritual and aesthetic values is faced with certain problems.

6104
as
WERNER, Eric. **Qydẇn hamẇsyqah halyṭẇrgyt ḇeḇatey haḵneset ḇeyśra'el** [Promoting liturgical music in Israeli synagogues], *Dẇkan* II (1960) 79–82. In Hebrew. See no. 409 in this volume.
Liturgical music should only serve prayer and has to remain pure and simple. A return to ancient psalmodic chant is recommended. *(Moshe Zorman)*

6105
as
YZR'A'ELY, Dawid. **Pswqey miqr'a ḇeḇytwy mẇsyqaly** [Biblical verses expressed in music], *Dẇkan* III (1961) 21–22. In Hebrew. See no. 417 in this volume.

92 Byzantine (and other Eastern)

6106
as
ANTONIADES, Sophia. **La musique byzantine rendue par les ondes Martenot** [Byzantine music performed on the ondes martenot], *IIIᵉ Congrès interna-*

tional des études byzantines (Athínai: Hestia, 1932) 265–66. In French. See no. 163 in this volume.

The ondes Martenot, an instrument operating on electrical and acoustical wave principles, can play very small intervals. This makes it useful in the study and performance of Byzantine music. *(Barry Salwen)*

6107 BRAŽNIKOV, Maksim V. **Russkoe cerkovnoe**
as **penie XII-XVIII vekov** [Russian church singing in the 12th to the 18th centuries], *Musica antiqua Europae orientalis* (Warszawa: Państwowe Wydawnictwo Naukowe, 1966). *Music.* In Russian. See no. 506 in this volume.

6108 DAYAN, Leonzio. **I canti armeni attraverso la**
as **tradizione dei secoli** [Armenian chant over the tradition of the centuries], *Atti del [I] Congresso internazionale di musica sacra* (Tournai: Desclée, 1952) 152–54. In Italian. See no. 303 in this volume.

6109 DI SALVO, Bartolomeo. **Dall'essenza della**
as **musica nelle liturgie orientali** [On the essence of music in the Eastern liturgies], *IV. Internationaler Kongress für Kirchenmusik in Köln: Dokumente und Berichte* (Köln: Bachem, 1962) 155–61. In Italian. See no. 432 in this volume.

Issues of the history of ekphonetic notation and of the sticherarion in early Byzantine liturgical practice are discussed on the basis of evidence in the anonymous treatise *Hagiopolitīs* (probably originating in Jerusalem; the most importance source, *F-Pn* gr.360, is from the early 14th c.).

6110 DI SALVO, Bartolomeo. **Lo sviluppo dei modi**
as **della musica bizantina dal sec. XIII alla**
riforma di Chrysanthos [The development of Byzantine musical modes from the 13th century to the reform of Chrysanthos], *Atti dello VIII Congresso internazionale di studi bizantini* (Roma: Associazione Nazionale per gli Studi Bizantini, 1953) II, 405 fiche. In Italian. See no. 308 in this volume.

6111 FORET, Raymond. **Les églises d'orient et la**
as **musique moderne: Pastorale et musicologie** [Eastern churches and modern music: Pastoral and musicological issues], *Perspectives de la musique sacrée à la lumière de l'encyclique Musicae sacrae disciplina* (Paris: conference, 1959) 339–45. In French. See no. 379 in this volume.

Attempts to introduce Western-style harmony to the liturgical chant of Eastern churches have been successful, encouraging a wide participation on the part of the congregation, when they have been compatible with the melodies and their traditional-music roots, as happened particularly early with Russian Orthodox church music, but only recently and to a limited extent with Greek Orthodox chant. *(David Bloom)*

6112 GAÏSSER, P. Ugo. **I canti ecclesiastici italo-**
as **greci** [Greco-Italian ecclesiastical songs], *Atti del Congresso internazionale di scienze storiche. VIII: Atti della sezione IV: Storia dell'arte musicale e drammatica* (Roma: R. Accademia dei Lincei, 1905) 107–16. *Transcr.* In Italian. See no. 42 in this volume.

Greek Orthodox churches in Calabria and Sicily maintain certain melodies of ancient Greek origin. A wide range of hymns in various modes and meters are discussed and transcriptions of some are included.

6113 GARDNER, Johann von. **Le rite byzantin** [The
as Byzantine rite], *Revue musicale* 239-240 (1957) 143–46. In French. See no. 378 in this volume.

A discussion of Greek, Romanian, and Slavic liturgical music, with particular attention to the Russian monodic chant styles. *(Meredith A. McCutcheon)*

6114 HICKMANN, Hans. **Quelques observations sur**
as **la musique liturgique des Coptes d'Egypte** [Some observations on the liturgical music of the Copts of Egypt], *Atti del [II] Congresso internazionale di musica sacra* (Tournai: Desclée, 1952) 100–06. In French. See no. 303 in this volume.

6115 HØEG, Carsten. **L'Octoechus byzantin** [The
as Byzantine oktōēchos], *Atti del [I] Congresso internazionale di musica sacra* (Tournai: Desclée, 1952) 107–08. In French. See no. 303 in this volume.

6116 HØEG, Carsten. **Quelques remarques sur les**
as **rapports entre la musique ecclésiastique de la**
Russie et la musique byzantine [Some remarks on the connection between Russian ecclesiastical music and Byzantine music], *Pepragmena tou th' diethnous byzantinologikou synedriou* (Athínai: Typographeion Myrtidē, 1953) II, 120–24. In French. See no. 327 in this volume.

A general comparison of music from the 11th and 12th c.

6117 JARGY, Simon. **La musique liturgique**
as **syrienne** [Syrian liturgical music], *Atti del [I] Congresso internazionale di musica sacra* (Tournai: Desclée, 1952) 166–71. In French. See no. 303 in this volume.

6118 KAFTANGIAN, Giuseppe. **Il canto liturgico**
as **armeno** [Armenian liturgical chant], *Atti del [I] Congresso internazionale di musica sacra* (Tournai: Desclée, 1952) 149–51. In Italian. See no. 303 in this volume.

6119 KOVALEVSKY, Maxime. **La musique**
as **liturgique orthodoxe russe** [Russian Orthodox liturgical music], *Kirchenmusik in ökumenischer Schau* (Bern: Haupt, 1964) 32–38. *Bibliog., discog.* In French. See no. 447 in this volume.

A brief historical account covering the period from the 10th c. to 1945. A German-language version is abstracted as RILM [1970]4192.

6120 **[Manuscripts] Sezione speciale: Manoscritti**
ac **miniati e con notazione musicali** [Special section: Manuscripts with illustrations and musical notation], *Mostra di manoscritti in occasione dell'VIII Congresso Internazionale di Studi Bizantini* (Palermo: Biblioteca Nazionale di Palermo, 1951) 21–26. In Italian. See no. 779 in this volume.

Lists and describes MSS from the 7th to the 16th c., with information on their locations.

6121 MARANGOS, Nicola. **Rito bizantino-greco**
as [Byzantine-Greek rite], *Atti del [I] Congresso internazionale di musica sacra* (Tournai: Desclée, 1952) 155–57. In Italian. See no. 303 in this volume.

6122 MÉNARD, René. **Le problème de la mémo-**
as **risation en musique copte garant de fidélité à**
la tradition [The problem of memorization in Coptic music as a guarantee of fidelity to tradition], *Bericht über den siebenten internationalen musikwissenschaftlichen Kongress* (Kassel: Bärenreiter, 1959) 191–93. In French. See no. 390 in this volume.

The large repertoire of chants of the Coptic liturgy, from Masses of at least two hours in length to Offices such as those of Holy Week lasting up to six or seven hours, is transmitted entirely orally; there are reasons for supposing, nevertheless, that the tradition is well preserved. *(David Bloom)*

6123
as

MOKRÝ, Ladislav. **Der Kanon zur Ehre des hl. Demetrius als Quelle für die Frühgeschichte des kirchenslavischen Gesanges** [The kanōn in honor of St. Demetrius as a source for the early history of Church Slavonic chant], *Anfänge der slavischen Musik* (Bratislava: Slovenská Akadémia Vied, 1966) 35–42. In German. See no. 477 in this volume.

The kanōn to St. Demetrius of Thessaloníkī, attributed to St. Methodius and first transmitted in the Novgorod menaia of the late 11th c., is the most well known and influential text of the Old Church Slavonic repertoire. It is derived from the Byzantine rite, and particularly important for understanding how Eastern and Western elements contributed to the formation of the Slavic liturgy. *(Brian Doherty)*

6124
as

MOUSSES, Kyriakos. **La musique liturgique chaldéenne** [Chaldean liturgical music], *Atti del [I] Congresso internazionale di musica sacra* (Tournai: Desclée, 1952) 164–65. In French. See no. 303 in this volume.

6125
as

OSSORGUINE, Michel. **Exposé de l'histoire de la musique religieuse en Russie** [An explanation of the history of religious music in Russia], *Congrès international de musique sacrée: Chant et orgue* (Paris: Desclée de Brouwer, 1937) 122–28. In French. See no. 247 in this volume.

Russian chant derived from Greek sources, both directly and via Bulgaria. Its ultimate source is Byzantine chant. Russia's isolation from the West accounts for the differences between the music styles of the two regions. *(Arthur Maisel)*

6126
as

PETRESCU, Ioan Dumitru. **Les principes du chant d'église byzantin** [Principles of chant in the Byzantine church], *Actes du IVe Congrès des études byzantines* (Sofija: Imprimerie de la Cour, 1935) 242–57. In French. See no. 215 in this volume.

6127
as

PICHLER, Ludwig. **Antichi canti bulgari et russi** [Early Bulgarian and Russian chant], *Atti del [I] Congresso internazionale di musica sacra* (Tournai: Desclée, 1952) 158–63. In Italian. See no. 303 in this volume.

6128
as

PICHLER, Ludwig. **Zur Reform der russischen Kirchenmusik** [The reform of Russian church music], *Zweiter internationaler Kongress für katholische Kirchenmusik: Zu Ehren des Heiligen Papstes Pius X* (Wien: conference, 1955) 93–97. In German. See no. 339 in this volume.

The original chant melodies of the Russian Orthodox liturgy had fallen into almost complete disuse by the time Dmytro Stepanovyč Bortnjans'ky (1751-1825) began producing harmonized versions of them. Many distinguished composers have followed Bortnjans'ky's lead in this (notably Aleksandr Dmitrievič Kastal'skij, 1856-1926), and in the composition of new settings of the Orthodox liturgical texts. Since the 1917 Revolution, little can be reported about the cultivation of church music in the Soviet Union; among Russian émigré communities the most important development is the maintenance of monophonic chant at the Institut de Théologie Orthodoxe Saint-Serge, Paris (founded 1925). *(David Bloom)*

6129
as

PSACHOS, Konstantinos A. **Histoire, art, parasémantique et tradition de la musique byzantine** [The history, art, parasemantics, and tradition of Byzantine music], *IIIe Congrès international des études byzantines* (Athínai: Hestia, 1932) 266–67. In French. See no. 163 in this volume.

Ancient Byzantine music is closely related to ancient Greek music, from which its modal system is derived, as well as to Eastern music. It was developed for use in sacred settings; secular use was considered profane. Modern Greek music demonstrates the continuity of the tradition through the centuries, communicated by priestly performers of sacred music and the oral transmission of folk melodies. *(Barry Salwen)*

6130
as

TOTZKE, Irenäus. **Byzantinische Elemente in der frühen slawischen Kirchenmusik** [Byzantine elements in early Slavic church music], *Bericht über den neunten internationalen Kongreß* (Kassel: Bärenreiter, 1964-1966) II, 156–66. In German. See no. 491 in this volume.

Report of a wide-ranging roundtable discussion, beginning with the question of identity between Byzantine and Slavic neumatic systems. Participants included Myroslav ANTONOvyč, Constantin FLOROS, Johann von GARDNER, Jerzy GOŁOS, Heinrich HUSMANN, Jurij Vsedolodovič KELDYŠ, Erwin KOSCHMIEDER, José MALI, Ladislav MOKRÝ, Dimitrije STEFANOVIĆ, Oliver STRUNK, Miloš VELIMIROVIĆ, Eric WERNER, and Walther WÜNSCH. *(David Bloom)*

6131
as

VAŠICA, Josef. **Slavische Petrusliturgie** [Slavic liturgy of St. Peter], *Anfänge der slavischen Musik* (Bratislava: Slovenská Akadémia Vied, 1966) 23–34. In German. See no. 477 in this volume.

The Greek liturgy of St. Peter originated as an amalgam of Byzantine and Roman traditions in Macedonia in the 8th and 9th c. Evidence of the early Glagolitic liturgical sources indicates that it was the basis for the Slavonic liturgy created by SS. Cyril and Methodius in their mission to Great Moravia. A detailed version of the argument, in Czech, is published as *Slovanská liturgie sv. Petra* in *Byzantinoslavica* VIII (1946). *(Brian Doherty)*

6132
as

WELLESZ, Egon. **Stand der byzantinischen Forschung** [The state of Byzantine research], *Congrés de la Societat Internacional de Musicologia* (Barcelona: Casa de Caritat, 1936). In German. See no. 224 in this volume.

The conference report provides only a citation. Neither the text nor a summary of the paper was published here.

6133
as

WERNER, Eric. **New studies in the history of the early *octoechos*,** *Société Internationale de Musicologie, cinquième congrès/Internationale Gesellschaft für Musikwissenschaft, fünfter Kongreß/International Society for Musical Research, Fifth Congress* (Amsterdam: Vereniging voor Nederlandse Muziekgeschiedenis, 1953) 428–37. See no. 316 in this volume.

A short historical survey of the eight *modi* shows that the idea of one universal oktōēchos is a fiction. *(Tsipora Yosselevitch)*

93 Roman Catholic

6134
as

ACHILLE, Louis T.E. **Les négro-spirituals, musique populaire sacrée** [African-American spirituals, traditional sacred music], *Perspectives de la musique sacrée à la lumière de l'encyclique* Musicae sacrae disciplina (Paris: conference, 1959) 530–37. In French. See no. 379 in this volume.

The history and development of the spiritual as an expression of Protestant faith among enslaved Africans in North America offers valuable lessons to those who wish to work toward an indigenous Catholic music in Africa: Spirituals developed spontaneously, from within the community, rather than being fostered from outside, and made use of cultural characteristics that were not Christian in origin but were religious in character and compatible with Christianity. A musical expression might find itself more easily if instruction, prayer, and praise meetings were to be held in outdoor venues. A summary is cited as no. 6135 in this volume. *(David Bloom)*

6135
as
ACHILLE, Louis T.E. **Les négros-spirituals, musique populaire sacrée** [African-American spirituals, traditional sacred music], *Revue musicale* 239-240 (1957) 239–45. In French. See no. 378 in this volume.

An abridged version of the conference paper is abstracted as no. 6134 in this volume.

6136
as
AGUSTONI, Luigi. **La cantillazione delle letture e delle preghiere nella messa** [The cantillation of readings and prayers in the Mass], *La musica nel rinnovamento liturgico: Atti della Settimana internazionale di musica sacra* (Torino: Elle Di Ci, 1966) 91–125. *Music.* In Italian. See no. 501 in this volume.

Discusses phrasing, rhythm, and declamation of text in Gregorian chant and modern liturgical practice.

6137
as
AGUSTONI, Luigi. **Culte chrétien et chant populaire** [Christian worship services and congregational singing], *Perspectives de la musique sacrée à la lumière de l'encyclique* Musicae sacrae disciplina (Paris: conference, 1959) 469–75. In French. See no. 379 in this volume.

Numerous papal pronouncements, especially the encyclical *Musicae sacrae disciplina* of Pius XII, clarify that it is both the right and the duty of the congregation to participate musically in the celebration of the Roman Catholic Mass. Principles are discussed for the use of Gregorian chant repertoire and new settings of the Latin texts of the Ordinary for solemn sung Masses, and vernacular songs in the *Missa lecta*. *(David Bloom)*

6138
as
AHRENS, Joseph. **Liturgie et musique d'orgue** [The liturgy and organ music], *Revue musicale* 239-240 (1957) 159–64. In French. See no. 378 in this volume.

Abridged version of a conference paper. The original German-language version and a French-language translation are abstracted as no. 6139 in this volume.

6139
as
AHRENS, Joseph. **Die Liturgie und die Orgelmusik/Liturgie et musique d'orgue** [The liturgy and organ music], *Perspectives de la musique sacrée à la lumière de l'encyclique* Musicae sacrae disciplina (Paris: conference, 1959) 355–72. In German and French. See no. 379 in this volume.

A historical overview from the introduction of the organ into the Latin liturgy during the papacy of St. Vitalian (657-72) to the critical situation since World War II, when the relevance of the organ in both Catholic and Protestant services has become increasingly unclear. Its renewal will succeed only if electronic instruments are rejected. A summary is cited as no. 6138 in this volume. *(Warren A. Bebbington)*

6140
as
AHRENS, Joseph. **Die zeitgenössiche Orgelmusik in der katholischen Liturgie** [Contemporary organ music in the Catholic liturgy], *Atti del [I] Congresso internazionale di musica sacra* (Tournai: Desclée, 1952) 388–91. In German. See no. 303 in this volume.

⟶ ALFAIATE MARVÃO, António. **O folclore musical do Baixo Alentejo nos ciclos litúrgicos da Igreja** [The traditional music of Baixo Alentejo in liturgical cycles of the Church]. See no. 2712 in this volume.

6141
as
ALTISENT, Miguel. **Cuestiones prácticas** [Practical questions], *V Congreso Nacional de Música Sagrada* (Madrid: Gráficas Dos de Mayo, 1956) 250–55. In Spanish. See no. 331 in this volume.

Two fundamental needs of Roman Catholic religious music are the creation of new *scholae cantorum* and the encouragement of congregational singing.

6142
as
ALTISENT, Miguel. **Las melodias gregorianas para los *Propios* nuevos** [Gregorian melodies for new Proper chants], *Atti del [I] Congresso internazionale di musica sacra* (Tournai: Desclée, 1952) 177–78. In Spanish. See no. 303 in this volume.

6143
as
ALVARES, Vincent. **The apostleship of music with regard to a fruitful missionary future in India,** *IV. Internationaler Kongress für Kirchenmusik in Köln: Dokumente und Berichte* (Köln: Bachem, 1962) 304–11. See no. 432 in this volume.

Indian religious worship is expressed via song and dance. The differences between Western and Indian musical systems raise the issue of which musical language should be used by missionaries in India; a comparison of rāgas and church modes may serve as a means of bridging the sacred music gap.

6144
as
AMON, Karl. **Die Funktionsteilung in der Liturgiefeier** [The distribution of responsibilities in the celebration of the liturgy], *Die Kirchenmusik und das II. Vatikanische Konzil* (Graz: Styria, 1965) 33–49. *Bibliog.* In German. See no. 480 in this volume.

Summary theological discussion of the roles of the different participants in the celebration of the Roman Catholic Mass after the reforms of Vatican Council II, with particular attention to the different contributions of the congregation, the cantor, and the choir, as well as the organist and other instrumentalists. *(David Bloom)*

6145
as
ANGLÈS, Higini. **Nécessité d'un catalogue détaillé des manuscrits grégoriens du Moyen Age** [The necessity for a detailed catalogue of Gregorian manuscripts of the Middle Ages], *Congrés de la Societat Internacional de Musicologia* (Barcelona: Casa de Caritat, 1936). In French. See no. 224 in this volume.

The conference report provides only a citation. Neither the text nor a summary of the paper was published here.

6146
as
ANGLÈS, Higini. **Organisation internationale de la musique sacrée** [How sacred music is organized at the international level], *Perspectives de la musique sacrée à la lumière de l'encyclique* Musicae sacrae disciplina (Paris: conference, 1959) 646–49. In French. See no. 379 in this volume.

Reviews the history of, and outlook for, proposals for the foundation of an International Society of Sacred Music under the auspices of the Pontificio Istituto di Musica Sacra, together with the development of national associations. *(David Bloom)*

6147
as
ANGLÈS, Higini. **La polyphonie de la Court pontificale d'Avignon de la seconde moitié du XIVe siècle en Catalogne** [Polyphony at the papal court of Avignon during the second half of the 14th century in Catalunya], *Congrés de la Societat Internacional de Musicologia* (Barcelona: Casa de Caritat, 1936). In French. See no. 224 in this volume.

The conference report provides only a citation. Neither the text nor a summary of the paper was published here.

6148
as
ANGLÈS, Higini. **Significado de la polifonía sagrada para la liturgia católica** [The significance of religious polyphony for the Catholic liturgy], *V Congreso Nacional de Música Sagrada* (Madrid: Gráficas Dos de Mayo, 1956) 95–112. In Spanish. See no. 331 in this volume.

Summarizes the case for polyphony in the liturgy, beginning with papal proclamations on the subject, and proposes a plan for the training of choirs. *(José López-Calo)*

6149
as

ANTONOVYČ, Myroslav. **Participation des fidèles d'Ukraine aux chants liturgiques** [The participation of Ukrainian congregations in liturgical singing], *Perspectives de la musique sacrée à la lumière de l'encyclique* Musicae sacrae disciplina (Paris: conference, 1959) 319–23. *Transcr.* In French. See no. 379 in this volume.

An account of polyphonic congregational singing in Uniate churches of Western Ukraine (formerly eastern Galicia).

6150
as

ARTERO, José. **Pío X y su motu proprio en la historia musical de España** [Pius X and his motu proprio in Spain's musical history], *Crónica del IV Congreso Nacional de Música Sagrada* (Vitoria: Imprenta del Montepío Diocesano, 1930) 56–60. In Spanish. See no. 155 in this volume.

Discusses the Spanish reaction to Pius X's motu proprio *Tra le sollecitudini* (1903).

6151
as

Association Française Sainte-Cécile. **Séances d'études dans l'après-midi du Mardi 6 juin** [Study session on the afternoon of Tuesday, 6 June], *Congrès régional de liturgie et de musique sacrée* (Moselle: Orphelins-Apprentis Guénange, 1923) 87–101. In French. See no. 98 in this volume.

Includes a discussion of three presentations: (1) Father ALARDO, **La liturgie et le prêtre** [The liturgy and the priest]; (2) Dom DAVID, O.S.B., **Le prêtre et le chant paroissial** [The priest and parish singing]; and (3) Amédée GASTOUÉ, **L'influence féminine dans la réforme de la musique d'église** [Women's influence on the reform of church music]. *(Murat Eyüboğlu)*

6152
as

AUBRY, Pierre. **Les jongleurs dans l'histoire: Saint-Julien-des-Ménétriers** [Minstrels in history: Saint-Julien-des-Ménétriers], *Mémoires de Musicologie sacrée, lus aux assises de musique religieuse* (Paris: Schola Cantorum, n.d.) 57–74. In French. See no. 34 in this volume.

Summarizes the evolution of *jonglerie* from the 2nd to 18th c. with emphasis on the chapel and hospital Saint-Julien-des-Ménétriers, which was founded by ministrels in the Middle Ages and destroyed during the Revolution. Includes extensive citations of historical documents. *(Karen Clute)*

6153
as

AUDA, Antoine. **Ce que sont les modes grégoriens** [What the Gregorian modes are], *Congrès international de musique sacrée: Chant et orgue* (Paris: Desclée de Brouwer, 1937) 140–47. In French. See no. 247 in this volume.

Remarks on modal theory from antiquity through the Middle Ages and the Renaissance.

6154
as

AURIOL (abbé). *La musique sacrée*, *Congrès international de musique sacrée: Chant et orgue* (Paris: Desclée de Brouwer, 1937) 191–94. In French. See no. 247 in this volume.

A report on the journal, published in Toulouse under the author's editorship.

6155
as

AVY, M. **Actes épiscopaux concernant la musique d'église: Deux observations** [Episcopal acts on church music: Two observations], *Congrès pour la restauration du plain-chant et de la musique d'église* (Paris: De Mourgues, 1862) 118. In French. See no. 3 in this volume.

6156
as

BAIXAULI, Mariano. **Necesidad del estudio de nuestra polifonía religiosa** [The necessity of studying our religious polyphonic music], *Crónica del primer Congreso Nacional de Música Sagrada* (Valladolid: A. Martín, 1908) 87–90. In Spanish. See no. 57 in this volume.

Following the renewed interest in religious music sparked by Pius X's motu proprio *Tra le sollecitudini* (1903), advocates the study of Spanish polyphony from the Renaissance as a means of improving the repertoire in Spanish churches. *(José López-Calo)*

6157
as

BALDELLÓ, Francesc de Paula. **Cuestiones básicas sobre el *Motu proprio*** [Basic questions on the motu proprio], *V Congreso Nacional de Música Sagrada* (Madrid: Gráficas Dos de Mayo, 1956) 219–23. In Spanish. See no. 331 in this volume.

Pius X was profoundly interested in the reform of church music even before he became pope, and worked assiduously for it after his promulgation of the motu proprio *Tra le sollecitudini* (1903). Pius XII's *Mediator Dei* (1947) brings the ecclesiastical legislation on religious music up to date; one of its important points that has not yet been fulfilled is its recommendations on the liturgical use of national traditional music styles. *(José López-Calo)*

6158
as

BALLMANN, Willibrord. **Vom Wesen der liturgischen Musik** [On the nature of liturgical music], *Bericht über den I. musikwissenschaftlichen Kongress der Deutschen Musikgesellschaft in Leipzig* (Wiesbaden: Breitkopf & Härtel, 1926) 343–49. In German. See no. 120 in this volume.

Proposes that chant is the ideal style of liturgical music: it is free of secular rhythm, it is vocal rather than instrumental, and it suitably enhances text. *(William Renwick)*

6159
as

BANCAL, Jean. **Brèves réflexions sur les éléments techniques propres à "servir" un langue biblique** [Brief reflections on the technical elements appropriate to a Biblical language], *Musique sacrée et langues modernes: Deux colloques internationaux* (Paris: Fleurus, 1964) 119–25. In French. See no. 449 in this volume.

Texts for modern-language sacred music in the Roman Catholic liturgy may expand the direct use of Biblical material, but the traditional vocabulary and sentence structure should be retained.

6160
as

BARBRY, Winoc. **Beauté musical et beauté liturgique** [Musical beauty and liturgical beauty], *La musique d'église: Compte rendu du Congrès de musique sacrée* (Tourcoing: Duvivier, 1920) 177–90. In French. See no. 93 in this volume.

Gregorian chant exemplifies religious beauty in music for three reasons: It renounces mathematical rhythm, thus freeing the perception of time from the present moment and evoking eternity; it has the strength of a unified utterance (in contrast with polyphony); and it appeals to reason.

6161
as

BASILE (brother). **Le dilemme de la musique religieuse indigène en Afrique du Sud** [The dilemma of indigenous religious music in South Africa], *Revue musicale* 239-240 (1957) 255ff. In French. See no. 378 in this volume.

An abridged version of the conference paper is cited as no. 6162 in this volume.

6162
as

BASILE (brother). **Le dilemme de la musique religieuse indigène en Afrique du Sud** [The dilemma of indigenous religious music in southern Africa], *Perspectives de la musique sacrée à la lumière de l'encyclique* Musicae sacrae disciplina (Paris: conference, 1959) 567–74. In French. See no. 379 in this volume.

A discussion of conflicts between indigenous African music and European traditions in the creation of a suitable music for African celebration of the Roman Catholic liturgy; an extended version is offered in the author's *Aux rythmes des tambours: Le musicien chez les noirs d'Afrique* (Montréal, 1949). *(David Bloom)*

6163 BAYART, Paul. **Les fins de la musique sacrée**
as [The goals of sacred music], *Compte rendu du Congrès général de musique sacrée: Aperçu général des préliminaires et du congrès, discours et conférences* (Strasbourg: Alsacien, 1922) 13–21. In French. See no. 96 in this volume.

Music enhances worship and deepens the meaning of the textual content when correctly used. It also creates a bond within the congregation.

6164 BELDA, Juan. **Caracteres de la música orgánica litúrgica** [The characteristics of liturgical organ
as music], *Crónica y actas oficiales del tercer Congreso Nacional de Música Sagrada* (Barcelona: La Hormiga de Oro, 1913) 122–26. In Spanish. See no. 78 in this volume.

Although religious music is primarily vocal, the organ is allowed in the liturgy. Liturgical organ music must take advantage of the expressive and technical resources of the instrument (such as its capacity for continuously sustained sounds and its variety of registers) and put them exclusively at the service of the liturgy. *(José López-Calo)*

6165 BERRONE, Antonio. **Restaurazione della musica sacra secondo il *Motu proprio* di S.S. il
as Papa Pio X** [The restoration of sacred music according to the motu proprio of His Holiness Pope Pius X], *7° Congresso di musica sacra* (Torino: author, 1905) 54–59. In Italian. See no. 52 in this volume.

Discusses the implications of the motu proprio, *Tra le sollecitudini*, issued on 22 November 1903, and the successive Decree *Urbis et orbis* of the Sacrorum Rituum Congregationem issued on 8 January 1904. *(André Balog)*

6166 BERTHIER, Paul. **Le cantique et son usage actuel** [The canticle and its current usage], *Congrès in-*
as *ternational de musique sacrée: Chant et orgue* (Paris: Desclée de Brouwer, 1937) 163–71. In French. See no. 247 in this volume.

New canticles should be composed and admitted into the liturgy.

6167 BIHAN, Jean. **Le mouvement grégorien au Canada et en Amérique du Sud** [The Gregorian
as movement in Canada and South America], *Revue musicale* 239-240 (1957) 119–23. In French. See no. 378 in this volume.

An abridged version of part of the conference paper is abstracted as no. 6168 in this volume.

6168 BIHAN, Jean. **Le mouvement grégorien dans le monde** [The Gregorian movement worldwide], *Per-*
as *spectives de la musique sacrée à la lumière de l'encyclique* Musicae sacrae disciplina (Paris: conference, 1959) 226–40. In French. See no. 379 in this volume.

Focuses on the history and current situation of the chant revival in Britain, France, Hungary, Italy, the Netherlands, Poland, Portugal, Spain, Sweden, and Switzerland; Belgium and Germany, where interest levels have been relatively low; Canada; and Argentina, Brazil, and Uruguay. A summary of the section on Europe is cited as no. 6169 in this volume; a summary of the section on Canada and South America is cited as no. 6167 in this volume. *(Meredith A. McCutcheon)*

6169 BIHAN, Jean. **La mouvement grégorien en Europe Occidentale** [The Gregorian movement in
as Western Europe], *Revue musicale* 239-240 (1957) 101–12. In French. See no. 378 in this volume.

An abridged version of part of the paper is abstracted as no. 6168 in this volume.

6170 BIRKNER, Günter. **Psaume hébraïque et séquence latine** [Jewish psalm and Latin sequence],
as *Journal of the International Folk Music Council* XVI (1964) 56–60. *Charts, diagr.* In French. See no. 463 in this volume.

Evidence from the melodic choices of Notker Balbulus, at the beginning of the recorded history of the sequence, and from analogies between the structural features of psalm texts and sequence texts, suggests that the origin of the Alleluia-based sequence may have been much earlier than Notker, through an unbroken evolution from the practice of the synagogue to that of the early church. *(David Bloom)*

6171 BLANCHET, Émile. **Principes de la musique sacrée** [Principles of sacred music], *Revue musicale*
as 239-240 (1957) 33–36. In French. See no. 378 in this volume.

6172 BOMM, Urbanus. **Choralforschung und Choralpflege in der Gegenwart** [Present-day
as chant research and chant cultivation], *Die Kirchenmusik und das II. Vatikanische Konzil* (Graz: Styria, 1965) 91–119. In German. See no. 480 in this volume.

The essential liturgical status of the Roman chant tradition, as affirmed in the 1903 motu proprio of Pius X, *Tra le sollecitudini*, is reaffirmed in the new liturgical constitution promulgated by the Vatican Council II (*Sacrosanctum concilium*, December 1963). The problematics of chant research, however, in its relation to actual liturgical practice, need to be reformulated in light of particular recommendations for the maximum employment of vernacular languages, for the furnishing of simpler melodies for the use of smaller congregations, and for the completion of *editiones typicae* as well as improved critical editions of Gregorian chants. *(David Bloom)*

6173 BOMM, Urbanus. **Gregorianischer Choral als Kultgesang** [Gregorian chant as worship through
as singing], *Kirchenmusik in ökumenischer Schau* (Bern: Haupt, 1964) 38–42. In German. See no. 447 in this volume.

Chant is to be regarded theologically not as a miracle, but nevertheless as a truthful expression of divine glory, a humanly cultivated testimony to the *sensa animi Christiani*. *(David Bloom)*

6174 BONNET, Antony. **Musique d'orgue et chant grégorien** [Organ music and Gregorian chant], *Atti*
as *del [I] Congresso internazionale di musica sacra* (Tournai: Desclée, 1952) 344–47. In French. See no. 303 in this volume.

6175 BORDES, Charles. **De l'emploi de la musique figurée spécialement de la musique pale-
as strinienne dans les offices liturgiques** [The use of figured-bass music, especially that of Palestrina, in liturgical Offices], *Congrès diocésain de musique religieuse et de plain-chant* (Rodez: Carrère, 1895) 146–52. In French. See no. 22 in this volume.

6176 BÖSER, Fidelis. **Orgel und Liturgie** [Organ and liturgy], *Bericht über die [I] Freiburger Tagung für
as Deutsche Orgelkunst* (Augsburg: Bärenreiter, 1926) 92–98. In German. See no. 122 in this volume.

An introduction to the theology of the organ, from a Roman Catholic stand-point, and the priestly status of the church organist. Asserts that the Baroque organ is the only kind of organ suitable for liturgical use. *(David Bloom)*

6177 BOYER, Louis. **La musique moderne à l'église**
as   [Modern music in church], *Compte rendu du Congrès général de musique sacrée: Aperçu général des préliminaires et du congrès, discours et conférences* (Strasbourg: Alsacien, 1922) 95–106. In French. See no. 96 in this volume.

The church demands music that is saintly, truthful, and universal. Modern music, as exemplified by Debussy's detestable chromaticism and harmony, is not suitable for the church. Composers must face the hard labor that the craft of composition demands and develop a musical language that features chant as its central element. *(Murat Eyüboğlu)*

6178 BOYER, Louis. **La musique religieuse en**
as   **Dordogne** [Religious music in Dordogne], *La musique d'église: Compte rendu du Congrès de musique sacrée* (Tourcoing: Duvivier, 1920) 45–53. In French. See no. 93 in this volume.

Discusses regional musical priorities in light of Pius X's motu proprio *Tra le sollecitudini* (1903).

6179 BRUN, F. **Le cantique d'inspiration**
as   **grégorienne** [Gregorian-inspired canticle], *Comptes rendus, rapports et vœux du Congrès parisien et régional de chant liturgique et de musique d'église* (Paris: Schola Cantorum, 1912) 161–65. In French. See no. 75 in this volume.

6180 BRUN, F. **Le clergé et la musique d'église** [The
as   clergy and church music], *Congrès international de musique sacrée: Chant et orgue* (Paris: Desclée de Brouwer, 1937) 135–40. In French. See no. 247 in this volume.

Comments on methods for the improvement and expansion of the performance of religious music.

6181 BUSSON, Maurice. **De la nécessité d'un**
as   **graduel à l'usage des petites églises** [The need for a gradual to be used in small churches], *Atti del [I] Congresso internazionale di musica sacra* (Tournai: Desclée, 1952) 34–36. In French. See no. 303 in this volume.

6182 CAPRA, Marcello. **Breve cronaca del Con-**
as   **gresso** [Brief chronicle of the congress], *7° Congresso di musica sacra* (Torino: author, 1905) 5–12. In Italian. See no. 52 in this volume.

Lists the events of the conference. Officials of the conference are named, including its president, Monsignore Angelo Nasoni, the director of the Milanese periodical *Musica sacra*. The secretary of the conference was Marcello Capra, editor in chief of the Turin periodical *Santa Cecilia*. *(André Balog)*

6183 CHAILLEY, Jacques. **La musique religieuse**
as   **contemporaine en France** [Contemporary religious music in France], *Zweiter internationaler Kongress für katholische Kirchenmusik: Zu Ehren des Heiligen Papstes Pius X* (Wien: conference, 1955) 162–71. In French. See no. 339 in this volume.

Surveys French religious music of the first half of the 20th c. from the point of view of its possible use in Roman Catholic liturgy. Composers need to be better prepared to understand the Church's requirements, but the musical direction within particular churches must also be educated to understand contemporary music in a less haphazard way. *(David Bloom)*

6184 CHAILLEY, Jacques. **La révision du critère**
as   **historique dans les problèmes de la musique d'église** [Reconsideration of the historical criterion in problems of church music], *Perspectives de la musique sacrée à la lumière de l'encyclique* Musicae sacrae disciplina (Paris: conference, 1959) 156–67. In French. See no. 379 in this volume.

Chant performance has been greatly improved by the work of the Benedictines of the Abbaye de St-Pierre, Solesmes, but erroneous notions of a single original, supposedly pure form of Gregorian chant, of a formal modal system analagous to that of the Byzantine oktōēchos, of the active participation of Gregory I in the creation of chant, persist. A more historically aware approach is needed to deal with the doctrinal issues of other types of music in the liturgy, from the old questions of polyphony and instrumental music to that of the musical avant-garde of our own time. A summary is cited as no. 6185 in this volume. *(David Bloom)*

6185 CHAILLEY, Jacques. **La révision du critère**
as   **historique dans les problèmes de la musique d'église** [Reconsideration of the historical criterion in problems of church music], *Revue musicale* 239-240 (1957) 55–62. In French. See no. 378 in this volume.

Summary of the paper abstracted as no. 6184 in this volume.

6186 **[Cistercian order] Conspectus historicus de**
as   **cantu in ordine Cisterciensi** [Historical survey of chant in the Cistercian order], *Atti del [I] Congresso internazionale di musica sacra* (Tournai: Desclée, 1952) 199–201. In Latin. See no. 303 in this volume.

6187 CLERVAL, J.A. **La musique religieuse à No-**
as   **tre-Dame de Chartres** [Religious music at the Cathedral of Notre-Dame in Chartres], *Mémoires de Musicologie sacrée, lus aux assises de musique religieuse* (Paris: Schola Cantorum, n.d.) 47–56. In French. See no. 34 in this volume.

A brief history of the *maîtres de musique* of Chartres between the 6th and 18th c., including the role of church musical personnel and the introduction of instruments into the service. Special emphasis on Fulbert of Chartres and *Musica enchiriadis* concerning paleography and notation. *(Karen Clute)*

6188 COLLARD, E. **Le cantique populaire** [The popu-
as   lar canticle], *Congrès régional de liturgie et de musique sacrée* (Moselle: Orphelins-Apprentis Guénange, 1923) 68–84. In French. See no. 98 in this volume.

Although Pope Pius X encouraged their use in his motu proprio *Tra le sollecitudini* (1903), canticles remain peripheral to church repertoire. Existing in two sources, *Cantiques spirituels à l'usage des retraites* (1750) and Louis Lambillotte's *Chants à Marie pour le mois de mai et les fêtes de la Sainte Vierge* (1854), the canticle repertoire was created by writing religious texts to popular melodies. While some examples of the canticle might be inappropriate for church use, the repertoire should nevertheless be carefully sifted for a more complete integration into the sung liturgy. *(Murat Eyüboğlu)*

6189 COLLARD, E. **La musique palestrinienne** [The
as   music of Palestrina], *Compte rendu du Congrès général de musique sacrée: Aperçu général des préliminaires et du congrès, discours et conférences* (Strasbourg: Alsacien, 1922) 55–70. In French. See no. 96 in this volume.

Due to false preconceptions about its aesthetic merit and technical difficulty, Palestrina's music does not occupy the place it deserves in the church. This situation can be remedied by training church musicians and the public in the subtleties of Palestrina's music with the help of good editions.

6190 **[Congregational singing] L'étude du chant**
as   **religieux** [The study of religious singing]. *Congrès diocésain de musique religieuse et de plain-chant*

(Rodez: Carrère, 1895) 63–64. In French. See no. 22 in this volume.

6191
as
[Congregational singing] Lettre d'un organiste de campagne [Letter from a country organist]. *Congrès diocésain de musique religieuse et de plain-chant* (Rodez: Carrère, 1895) 65–67. In French. See no. 22 in this volume.

6192
as
[Congregational singing] Si j'étais vicaire! [If I were a vicar!], *Congrès diocésain de musique religieuse et de plain-chant* (Rodez: Carrère, 1895) 68–73. In French. See no. 22 in this volume.

6193
as
COUSIN, Patrice. **La psalmodie chorale dans la règle de Saint Colomban** [Choral psalmody under the rule of Saint Columbanus], *Mélanges Colombaniens* (Paris: Alsatia, 1951) 179–92. *Bibliog.* In French. See no. 301 in this volume.
Choral psalmody under the rule of St. Columbanus is examined from these aspects: the restoration of the psalms in the choral Office; the spirit of the Office; the origin of the organization of Columbanus's Office; and the Office known as the *Laus perennis*. A short comparison is made between the Offices of St. Columbanus and St. Benedict. *(Albert Dlugasch)*

6194
as
COUTURIER, Charles. **Dimensions de l'adaptation/Ausmaße der Adaptation** [Dimensions of adaptation], *IV. Internationaler Kongress für Kirchenmusik in Köln: Dokumente und Berichte* (Köln: Bachem, 1962) 236–47. In French and German. See no. 432 in this volume.
Certain customs, such as the kissing of the consecrated objects during communion, may need to be modified in missionary work among cultures where they are objectionable.

6195
as
CRISPOLTI, Filippo. **Il pensiero cattolico nella riforma delle arti colle sue necessarie attinenze alla musica sacra** [Catholic thinking regarding the reform of the arts and its inevitable bearing on sacred music], *7° Congresso di musica sacra* (Torino: author, 1905) 59–61. In Italian. See no. 52 in this volume.
Acknowledges the potentially threatening influences of modern art, but affirms the enduring message of beauty in religious music. *(André Balog)*

6196
as
DALLA LIBERA, Ernesto. **Nei paesi latini è necessario fomentare il canto del popolo nel tempio; per conseguire ciò dobbiamo cominciare dalla scuola elementare** [In countries where Romance languages are spoken congregations should be encouraged to sing in church; to achieve this we should begin in elementary school], *Atti del [I] Congresso internazionale di musica sacra* (Tournai: Desclée, 1952) 37–40. In Italian. See no. 303 in this volume.

6197
as
DAVID, D.L. **L'art dans la psalmodie** [Art in psalmody], *Compte rendu du Congrès général de musique sacrée: Aperçu général des préliminaires et du congrès, discours et conférences* (Strasbourg: Alsacien, 1922) 31–54. *Music.* In French. See no. 96 in this volume.
Discusses the theory of psalm tones, vocal technique, and cadences.

6198
as
DEAN, Aldhelm. **The laity and the liturgy,** *Atti del [I] Congresso internazionale di musica sacra* (Tournai: Desclée, 1952) 41–43. See no. 303 in this volume.

6199
as
DELACROIX, Simon. **Musique sacrée et pastorale** [Sacred and pastoral music], *Atti del [I] Congresso internazionale di musica sacra* (Tournai: Desclée, 1952) 44–48. In French. See no. 303 in this volume.

6200
as
DELPORTE, Jules. **Le cantique populaire d'après les principes du *Motu proprio* et d'après la tradition** [The popular canticle according to the principles of the motu proprio and of the tradition], *Compte rendu du Congrès général de musique sacrée: Aperçu général des préliminaires et du congrès, discours et conférences* (Strasbourg: Alsacien, 1922) 107–24. In French. See no. 96 in this volume.
Traces the origins of the popular canticle to the Second Empire and considers the revivalist efforts of Charles Bordes and Vincent d'Indy following Pius X's motu proprio *Tra le sollecitudini* (1903).

6201
as
DELPORTE, Jules. **L'école musicale française des XVᵉ-XVIᵉ siècles** [The French school of music in the 15th to 16th centuries], *Congrès international de musique sacrée: Chant et orgue* (Paris: Desclée de Brouwer, 1937) 130–34. In French. See no. 247 in this volume.
The revival of the religious music of the French Renaissance is long overdue and well worth the effort, particularly considering that it includes the music of Josquin Desprez. *(Arthur Maisel)*

6202
as
DELPORTE, Jules. **La restauration du chant unanime à l'Église: Question capitale** [The restoration of unison chant in the Church: Crucial question], *La musique d'église: Compte rendu du Congrès de musique sacrée* (Tourcoing: Duvivier, 1920) 341–51. In French. See no. 93 in this volume.
Discusses Pius X's motu proprio *Tra le sollecitudini* (1903), and lists various advantages of unison chant, including its broad communicative power and the unification of religious taste. A call for educational reforms is included.

6203
as
DOREN, Rombaut van. **Le rôle joué par l'Abbay de Saint-Gall dans la diffusion du chant romain** [The role played by the abbey of St. Gallen in the diffusion of Roman chant], *Congrès jubilaire* (Brugge: Gruuthuuse, 1925) 225–26. In French. See no. 119 in this volume.
A 13th-c. document implies that the most important center of musical study in the Carolingian empire was the St. Gallen canton; details regarding the evidence for such an assumption are discussed. *(Susan Poliniak)*

6204
as
DUFT, Johannes. **Saint Colomban dans les manuscrits liturgiques de la bibliothèque abbatiale de Saint-Gall** [Saint Columbanus in liturgical manuscripts at the Stiftsbibliothek of St. Gallen], *Mélanges Colombaniens* (Paris: Alsatia, 1951) 317–26. *Music, musical facsimiles.* In French. See no. 301 in this volume.
MSS honoring St. Columbanus in the church and library of St. Gallen fall into four classes: litanies, breviaries, missals, and sequences. Some texts are included. *(Albert Dlugasch)*

6205
as
DUMONT, Christophe-Jean. **Diversité des rites orientaux et enrichissement de la spiritualité catholique** [Diversity in the Eastern rites and the enrichment of Catholic spirituality], *Revue musicale* 239-240 (1957) 131–36. In French. See no. 378 in this volume.
An abridged version of the conference paper is cited as no. 6206 in this volume.

6206
as
DUMONT, Christophe-Jean. **Diversité des rites orientaux et enrichissement de la spiritualité catholique** [Diversity in the Eastern rites and the enrichment of Catholic spirituality], *Perspectives de la musique sacrée à la lumière de l'encyclique* Musicae sacrae disciplina (Paris: conference, 1959) 287–93. In French. See no. 379 in this volume.

Introductory remarks on the theological character of liturgical music in the Syrian, Maronite, Armenian, Coptic/Ethiopian, and Byzantine traditions, in terms of their relation to the Latin liturgy and the importance accorded to them in the encyclical *Musicae sacrae disciplina* of Pius XII. *(David Bloom)*

6207
as
DUTOIT, H. **Tradition et progrès dans l'Église et dans l'art religieux** [Tradition and progress in the Church and in religious art], *La musique d'église: Compte rendu du Congrès de musique sacrée* (Tourcoing: Duvivier, 1920) 149–54. In French. See no. 93 in this volume.

Though as a human creation religious art will perpetually change, it must always express the eternal mysteries of Christianity.

6208
as
EBEL, Basilius. **Grundlagen des Verhältnisses von Kult und Gesang/The basic interdependence of chant and cult/Les bases des relations entre culte et chant/Principi fondamentali del rapporto tra culto e canto,** *IV. Internationaler Kongress für Kirchenmusik in Köln: Dokumente und Berichte* (Köln: Bachem, 1962) 163–202. In German, English, French, and Italian. See no. 432 in this volume.

Chant is sung prayer and prayerful song, the melodious expression of holy words sung within a ritual. In the early Church, the melodious presentation of specific lessons and traditions served as mnemonic aids. In the absence of written language, musical form has kept the text, philosophies, and legends of the faith intact.

6209
as
ECCHER, Celestino. **Necessità di formare nei paesi latini cappelle musicali con cantori volontari per l'esecuzione della sacra polifonia** [The need in Romance-speaking countries to train choirs with volunteer singers in the performance of sacred polyphony], *Atti del [I] Congresso internazionale di musica sacra* (Tournai: Desclée, 1952) 49–52. In Italian. See no. 303 in this volume.

6210
as
EIBNER, Franz. **Die Verwendung elektroakustischer Instrumente beim Gottesdienst** [The use of electroacoustic instruments in divine worship], *Zweiter internationaler Kongress für katholische Kirchenmusik: Zu Ehren des Heiligen Papstes Pius X* (Wien: conference, 1955) 230–38. In German. See no. 339 in this volume.

The decree of 13 July 1949 of the Sacred Congregation of Rites allowing the use of electronic instruments as a substitute for the pipe organ should not be understood as a simple permission. Bishops are required to grant special permission for each individual case. The rule is meant specifically for congregations that cannot afford to replace organs lost during World War II, although it is mostly quite wealthy congregations that are using such instruments; and is conditional on the electronic instrument's being worthy of a role in divine worship, which is never the case. In fact a positive, or at worst a harmonium, is a much more adequate substitute. *(David Bloom)*

6211
as
EMMANUEL, Maurice. **Le chant liturgique de l'Église romaine ne doit pas être harmonisé** [The liturgical chant of the Roman church must not be harmonized], *Congrès international de musique sacrée: Chant et orgue* (Paris: Desclée de Brouwer, 1937) 66–72. In French. See no. 247 in this volume.

In the West, there are two general types of music: linear (Pythagorean) and harmonic. Chant belongs to the former category. Antiphonal chant may be accompanied by instruments but must not be harmonized. *(Arthur Maisel)*

6212
as
EVRARD (canon). **Rapport de M. le Chanoine Evrard** [Report by the canon Evrard], *Congrès régional de liturgie et de musique sacrée* (Moselle: Orphelins-Apprentis Guénange, 1923) 176–86. In French. See no. 98 in this volume.

Compares examples from the Kyriale and the catechism in terms of dogma, morals, and means of sanctification.

→ FELLERER, Karl Gustav. **Beziehungen zwischen geistlicher und weltlicher Musik im 16. Jahrhundert** [Relations between religious and secular music in the 16th century]. See no. 1301 in this volume.

6213
as
FELLERER, Karl Gustav. **La *Constitutio Docta sanctorum patrum* di Giovanni XXII e la musica nuova del suo tempo** [The *Constitutio Docta sanctorum patrum* of Pope John XXII and the new music of his time], *L'ars nova italiana del Trecento: Primo convegno internazionale* (Certaldo: Centro di Studi sull'Ars Nova Italiana del Trecento, 1962) 9–17. In Italian. See no. 407 in this volume.

The papal decree against the use of complex polyphony in sacred music (1324-25) could be viewed as an attempt to stem the invasion of the seemingly profane into the liturgical realm. Trends in the secular ars nova stood in opposition to the qualities of traditional church music (e.g., major/minor tonality in opposition to modal tonality), and were also thought to threaten the gravity of the liturgy and the musical identity of particular church festivals. *(Susan Poliniak)*

6214
as
FELLERER, Karl Gustav. **Kirche und Musik in frühen Mittelalter** [Church and music in the early Middle Ages], *Bericht über den internationalen musikwissenschaftlichen Kongreß Wien Mozartjahr 1956* (Graz; Köln: Böhlau, 1958) 199–202. In German. See no. 365 in this volume.

Surveys the developments in western European church music from the papacy of Damasus (366-84) through that of Leo IV (847-55), with attention to the role played by ecclesiastical authorities in the cultivation of Gregorian chant and attitudes toward secular music. *(David Bloom)*

6215
as
FORT (abbé). **Moyens pratiques de réorganisation du chant grégorien dans les paroisses rurales** [Practical means of reorganizing Gregorian chant in rural parishes], *Congrès diocésain de musique religieuse et de plain-chant* (Rodez: Carrère, 1895) 59–62. In French. See no. 22 in this volume.

6216
as
FREI, Friedrich. **Kirchenmusik mit Orchesterbegleitung, auch wenn sie von grossen Meistern komponiert ist, eignet sich mehr für Konzerte als für liturgische Funktionen** [Church music with orchestral accompaniment, even if it is composed by great masters, is more suitable for concerts than liturgical functions], *Atti del [I] Congresso internazionale di musica sacra* (Tournai: Desclée, 1952) 398–400. In German. See no. 303 in this volume.

6217
as
FROGER, Jacques. **Les divers états du calendrier dans le graduel romain** [The various statuses of the calendar in the Roman gradual], *Atti del [I] Congresso internazionale di musica sacra* (Tournai:

Desclée, 1952) 207–11. In French. See no. 303 in this volume.

6218
as
GAJARD, Joseph. **La chant grégorien** [Gregorian chant], *Congrès international de musique sacrée: Chant et orgue* (Paris: Desclée de Brouwer, 1937) 55–66. In French. See no. 247 in this volume.

An introduction to Gregorian chant. The structure of this type of chant was determined by its function as prayer. Its rhythmic freedom expressed freedom from the material world. *(Arthur Maisel)*

6219
as
GAJARD, Joseph. **L'interprétation du chant grégorien** [Performance of Gregorian chant], *Congrés de la Societat Internacional de Musicologia* (Barcelona: Casa de Caritat, 1936). In French. See no. 224 in this volume.

The conference report provides only a citation. Neither the text nor a summary of the paper was published here.

6220
as
GAJARD, Joseph. **La restitution mélodique du chant grégorien** [The melodic reconstruction of Gregorian chant], *Congrés de la Societat Internacional de Musicologia* (Barcelona: Casa de Caritat, 1936). In French. See no. 224 in this volume.

The conference report provides only a citation. Neither the text nor a summary of the paper was published here.

6221
as
GAJARD, Joseph. **La valeur artistique et religieuse toujours actuelle du chant grégorien** [The constantly contemporary artistic and religious value of Gregorian chant], *Revue musicale* 239-240 (1957) 83–86. In French. See no. 378 in this volume.

Abridgment of the conference paper abstracted as no. 6222 in this volume.

6222
as
GAJARD, Joseph. **La valeur artistique et religieuse toujours actuelle du chant grégorien** [The ever-contemporary artistic and religious value of Gregorian chant], *Perspectives de la musique sacrée à la lumière de l'encyclique* Musicae sacrae disciplina (Paris: conference, 1959) 198–205. In French. See no. 379 in this volume.

There is an objective reason for the preference given by the Church to Gregorian chant as the essential music of the Roman Church: The art is identical to its goal of liturgical prayer, existing of and for itself. A summary is cited as no. 6221 in this volume. *(David Bloom)*

6223
as
GARCÍA LAHIGUERA, José María. **La Comisión Nacional y las Comisiones Diocesanas de Música Sagrada** [The Comisión Nacional and the Comisiones Diocesanas de Música Sagrada], *V Congreso Nacional de Música Sagrada* (Madrid: Gráficas Dos de Mayo, 1956) 118–25. In Spanish. See no. 331 in this volume.

The recommendations of the four previous national congresses of religious music in Spain have not been successfully implemented, partly because of the lack of a national committee to coordinate the work of the Comisiones Diocesanas de Música Sagrada. *(José López-Calo)*

6224
as
GASTOUÉ, Amédée. **Documents latins du moyen-âge sur le chant byzantins** [Latin documents from the Middle Ages on Byzantine chant], *Deuxième Congrès international des études byzantines* (Beograd: Državna Štamparija, 1929) 157–61. In French, Latin, and Greek. See no. 131 in this volume.

Latin chant books contain pieces written and sung in Greek (e.g., *Kyrie eleison*). A number of antiphons and other types of sacred music, as well as various musical terms (e.g., the names of certain neumes), show evidence of Byzantine influences. Evidently, an appreciable number of Byzantine sources (i.e., for the study of Byzantine religious music) were available to

the authors of many Latin MSS, which were in part transformed for use in the Roman liturgy. *(Susan Poliniak)*

6225
as
GASTOUÉ, Amédée. **Essai sur le passé et l'avenir de la polyphonie sacrée** [Essay on the past and the future of sacred polyphony], *Compte rendu du Congrès général de musique sacrée: Aperçu général des préliminaires et du congrès, discours et conférences* (Strasbourg: Alsacien, 1922) 71–84. In French. See no. 96 in this volume.

Discusses performance practice questions such as the assignment of singers per part and instrumental doubling of voices. Issues of modern liturgical music, such as the reconciliation of chromatic harmony and new genres with the traditional paradigms of Roman Catholic church music, are also addressed. *(Murat Eyüboğlu)*

6226
as
GASTOUÉ, Amédée. **Les Gildes de Sainte-Cécile** [The Gildes de Sainte-Cécile], *Congrès international de musique sacrée: Chant et orgue* (Paris: Desclée de Brouwer, 1937) 94–100. In French. See no. 247 in this volume.

Founded in 1924, the Gildes de Sainte-Cécile contributes broadly to religious music activity in France.

6227
as
GASTOUÉ, Amédée. **Les proses parisiennes du XIIe siècle et l'œuvre d'Adam de Saint-Victor** [The Parisian prosae of the 12th century and the works of Adam de St. Victor], *Comptes rendus, rapports et vœux du Congrès parisien et régional de chant liturgique et de musique d'église* (Paris: Schola Cantorum, 1912) 68–73. In French. See no. 75 in this volume.

6228
as
GASTOUÉ, Amédée. **Quelques aspects variés de la question grégorienne** [Various aspects of the Gregorian question], *Compte rendu du Congrès général de musique sacrée: Aperçu général des préliminaires et du congrès, discours et conférences* (Strasbourg: Alsacien, 1922) 23–29. In French. See no. 96 in this volume.

Discusses the coordination between chant and ceremony and explores performance practice issues, arguing that they cannot be solved through reference to Oriental traditions.

6229
as
GASTOUÉ, Amédée. **Les récitatifs liturgiques du codex espagnol Rés. F. 967 de la Bibliothèque du Conservatore Nationale** [*sic*] **de Musique à Paris** [The liturgical recitatives of the Spanish codex rés.F.967 at the library of the Conservatoire National de Musique in Paris], *Congrés de la Societat Internacional de Musicologia* (Barcelona: Casa de Caritat, 1936). In French. See no. 224 in this volume.

The conference report provides only a citation. Neither the text nor a summary of the paper was published here.

6230
as
GAUGUSCH, Friedrich. **Die Choralpflege auf dem Lande** [Chant cultivation in the countryside], *Zweiter internationaler Kongress für katholische Kirchenmusik: Zu Ehren des Heiligen Papstes Pius X* (Wien: conference, 1955) 138–41. In German. See no. 339 in this volume.

In the context of its recommendation of Gregorian chant in the Catholic liturgy, Pius X's motu proprio *Tra le sollecitudini* (1903) mentions particularly that the congregation should be prepared to participate in the singing, even in smaller village churches. General suggestions are offered on the sequence in which pieces should be learned, the role of young people, the question of traditional vs. modern notation, and the pedagogical value of vernacular translations of the Ordinary and Proper texts. *(David Bloom)*

6231
as
GELINEAU, Joseph. **Programme musical d'une pastorale liturgique** [The musical program of a pastoral liturgy], *Musique sacrée et langues modernes: Deux colloques internationaux* (Paris: Fleurus, 1964) 17–37. In French. See no. 449 in this volume.

Discusses questions of form, performance practice, and text translation in the musical setting of the vernacular Roman Catholic liturgy.

6232
as
GELINEAU, Joseph. **Psalmodie populaire** [Folk psalmody], *Kirchenmusik in ökumenischer Schau* (Bern: Haupt, 1964) 74–79. In French. See no. 447 in this volume.

Discusses psalmody in the Roman Catholic liturgy in terms of the issue of congregational participation, with historical, theological, and musical considerations. Poetic modern-language paraphrases of psalm texts sung by the congregation are, strictly speaking, not psalmody but hymnody; the congregation's role in the liturgy proper is to sing the interpolated refrains between verses. While the verses should be as faithful to tradition as possible, textually and musically, the refrains may be adapted somewhat to popular needs; it is not necessary, however, to give them a popular-song tonality instead of the traditional ecclesiastical mode. *(David Bloom)*

6233
as
GELINEAU, Joseph. **Salmodia e canti processionali** [Psalmody and processional chant], *La musica nel rinnovamento liturgico: Atti della Settimana internazionale di musica sacra* (Torino: Elle Di Ci, 1966) 145–68. In Italian. See no. 501 in this volume.

Discusses the genesis, structure, and function of psalmody. Particular attention is given to responsory psalms and to modern reforms instituted by the Vatican Council II.

6234
as
GELINEAU, Joseph. **La valeur catéchétique du chant populaire** [The catechetic value of congregational singing], *Revue musicale* 239-240 (1957) 211–21. In French. See no. 378 in this volume.

An abridged version of the conference paper is abstracted as no. 6235 in this volume.

6235
as
GELINEAU, Joseph. **La valeur catéchétique du chant populaire** [The catechetical value of congregational singing], *Perspectives de la musique sacrée à la lumière de l'encyclique* Musicae sacrae disciplina (Paris: conference, 1959) 476–83. In French. See no. 379 in this volume.

The use of congregational singing as a means of teaching the Roman Catholic doctrine, established in the history of the early church, is particularly crucial at the current moment, as the encyclical *Musicae sacrae disciplina* (1955) of Pius XII makes clear, in view of the widespread ignorance or misunderstanding of the tenets of the faith among Catholics and non-Catholics alike. A summary is cited as no. 6234 in this volume. *(Warren A. Bebbington)*

6236
as
GHIGNONI, Alessandro. **La musica sacra e religiosa del popolo** [Sacred and religious music of the people], *7° Congresso di musica sacra* (Torino: author, 1905) 61–66. In Italian. See no. 52 in this volume.

Argues for the wider acceptance of traditional music in church, citing the benediction Pope Pius X extended to the Società Italiana per la Musica Religiosa Popolare on 29 November 1904. *(André Balog)*

⟶
GIBERT, Vicente María. **El canto gregoriano: Base y fuente de inspiración de la música orgánica** [The Gregorian chant: The basis and inspiration for organ music]. See no. 3374 in this volume.

6237
as
GIL ESTEBAN, Manuel. **Cuestiones prácticas: El canto de las mujeres en la iglesia** [Practical questions: The participation of women in church singing], *V Congreso Nacional de Música Sagrada* (Madrid:

Gráficas Dos de Mayo, 1956) 270–76. In Spanish. See no. 331 in this volume.

Ecclesiastical law permits women to sing within the congregation, and on an exceptional basis to form a separate choir; they are not allowed to sing in mixed choirs. *(José López-Calo)*

6238
as
GLORIEUX, Louis. **Excellence de la Messe solennelle** [Excellence of the solemn Mass], *La musique d'église: Compte rendu du Congrès de musique sacrée* (Tourcoing: Duvivier, 1920) 55–66. In French. See no. 93 in this volume.

The musical character and spectacular nature of the Solemn Mass are key factors that communicate its religious meaning.

6239
as
GONZÁLEZ BARRÓN, Ramón. **Música no santa** [Non-religious music], *V Congreso Nacional de Música Sagrada* (Madrid: Gráficas Dos de Mayo, 1956) 231–36. In Spanish. See no. 331 in this volume.

In the motu proprio *Tra le sollecitudini* (1903) Pius X condemned the use of operatic music in churches. Symphonic music, however, although it is equally secular, is still performed in churches; this is an abuse that should be rooted out, as in the view of the first Congresso Internazionale di Musica Sacra (Rome, 1950) and of church musicians in general. *(José López-Calo)*

6240
as
GONZÁLEZ GARCÍA-VALLADOLID, Casimiro. **La música sagrada y los concilios españoles** [Religious music and the Spanish councils], *Crónica del primer Congreso Nacional de Música Sagrada* (Valladolid: A. Martín, 1908) 112–16. In Spanish. See no. 57 in this volume.

A summary of the main policies regarding religious music in Spain, as established in several councils.

6241
as
GOTTRON, Adam. **Die Organisation der Kirchenmusik** [The organization of church music], *Zweiter internationaler Kongress für katholische Kirchenmusik: Zu Ehren des Heiligen Papstes Pius X* (Wien: conference, 1955) 320–28. In German. See no. 339 in this volume.

(1) It would be valuable for each church to have two distinct groups of singers: the *schola* of men and boys singing the monophonic chants of the Ordinary in alternation with the congregation, fulfilling the liturgical function of the choir in the sense of Pius X's motu proprio *Tra le sollecitudini* (1903); and a *capella* that could include women, singing polyphonic compositions of the Proper. (2) All bishops should establish a diocesan commission for church music, with thoroughly knowledgeable members; there should also be administrative entities for church music at the state or national levels. (3) The Pontificio Istituto di Musica Sacra in Rome should found a comprehensive collection of books, journals, and recordings that could be made available to researchers around the world in microfilm and tape formats. *(David Bloom)*

6242
as
GRAVIER (canon). **Le cantique français: Son importance dans les exercices religieux et dans l'enseignement** [The French canticle: Its importance in religious practices and in teaching], *Congrès diocésain de musique religieuse et de plain-chant* (Rodez: Carrère, 1895) 126–41. In French. See no. 22 in this volume.

6243
as
GROSJEAN, M. **De l'état actuel de la musique religieuse dans le diocèse de Saint-Dié** [The state of religious music in the diocese of Saint-Dié], *Congrès pour la restauration du plain-chant et de la musique d'église* (Paris: De Mourgues, 1862) 118–19. In French. See no. 3 in this volume.

6244
as
GUILMANT, Alexandre. **Du rôle de l'orgue dans les offices liturgiques** [The role of the organ in

liturgical Offices], *Congrès diocésain de musique religieuse et de plain-chant* (Rodez: Carrère, 1895) 157–59. In French. See no. 22 in this volume.

6245
as
HAAPANEN, Toivo Elias. **Denkmäler des gregorianischen Gesanges in Finnland** [Monuments of Gregorian chant in Finland], *Bericht über den musikwissenschaftlichen Kongreß in Basel* (Leipzig: Breitkopf & Härtel, 1925) 184–88. In German. See no. 102 in this volume.

Research in Finnish music has, in the past, been limited to the collection and control of sources. Examples of Gregorian chant, including collections for the Mass and Office, as well as miscellaneous liturgical books, give evidence of musical cultivation during the Middle Ages.

6246
as
HABERL, Ferdinand. **Die liturgisch-seelsorgliche und musikalische Notwendigkeit der Schaffung eines kirchlichen und weltlichen Einheitsliederkanons für jede Nation** [The liturgical-pastoral and musical need for the creation of a canon of ecclesiastical and secular standard hymns in every nation], *Atti del [I] Congresso internazionale di musica sacra* (Tournai: Desclée, 1952) 53–54. In German. See no. 303 in this volume.

6247
as
HABERL, Franz Xaver. **Was ist im XIX. Jahrhundert für die Kenntnis altklassischer Werke kirchlicher Tonkunst geschehen** [Nineteenth-century contributions to our knowledge of the classic church music], *Akten des fünften internationalen Kongresses katholischer Gelehrten/Compte rendu du Vᵉ Congrès scientifique international des catholiques* (München: Herder, 1901) 331–33. In German. See no. 26 in this volume.

Discusses the early–19th-c. interest in 16th-c. religious music.

6248
as
HAJTAS, Francis. **The vernacular religious songs in Hungary since 1932/Le chant religieux populaire en Hongrie depuis 1932,** *Perspectives de la musique sacrée à la lumière de l'encyclique* Musicae sacrae disciplina (Paris: conference, 1959) 515–22. In English and French. See no. 379 in this volume.

Hungarian-language Catholic hymnody dates from around the 11th c., but it was largely orally transmitted until the 17th c. In the 18th and 19th c., the melodies were corrupted under German and Slavic influence. Restoration was begun in 1927, culminating with the publication of the hymnal *Szent vagy Uram* (1932). The role of the hymnal in the current Hungarian community is discussed. *(David Bloom)*

6249
as
HARNONCOURT, Philipp. **Neue Aufgaben der katholischen Kirchenmusik** [New tasks of Catholic church music], *Die Kirchenmusik und das II. Vatikanische Konzil* (Graz: Styria, 1965) 51–75. In German. See no. 480 in this volume.

Outlines consequences for church music practice of the new Roman Catholic liturgical constitution (*Sacrosanctum concilium*, December 1963): the priority of liturgical function over aesthetic value; the priority of sung over spoken liturgy; the necessity of congregational as opposed to choir singing; the renewal of the office of the cantor; and the introduction of liturgical music with vernacular texts for Mass and Office. *(David Bloom)*

6250
as
HESBERT, René-Jean. **Les compositions rhythmiques en l'honneur de Saint Colomban** [Rhythmic compositions in honor of Saint Columbanus], *Mélanges Colombaniens* (Paris: Alsatia, 1951) 327–58. *Facs., music, musical facsimiles.* In French. See no. 301 in this volume.

Examines 21 hymns and sequences written in honor of St. Columbanus from the 7th to the 18th c.; texts are included as well as MS locations when possible. *(Albert Dlugasch)*

6251
as
HIGGINSON, J. Vincent. **Aspects of American Catholic hymnody,** *Addresses at the International Hymnological Conference* (New York: Hymn Society of America, 1962) 42–54. See no. 438 in this volume.

The features of Catholic hymnody in North America are traced through early missionary work, the influence of European immigration, and the development of English, American, and German hymnals in the 19th and 20th c. The high standards of current hymnals have been shaped by a number of Papal decrees of 1947-58, all permitting greater congregational participation, and an increased focus on pedagogy and professional training. *(Barbara B. Heyman)*

6252
as
HILBER, Johann Baptist. **Kirchenmusik als Beruf** [Church music as a profession], *Zweiter internationaler Kongress für katholische Kirchenmusik: Zu Ehren des Heiligen Papstes Pius X* (Wien: conference, 1955) 282–87. In German. See no. 339 in this volume.

Discusses the concept of church music within Roman Catholicism as a *vocatio Dei*, and the responsibilities of musicians, pastors, and congregations from this perspective. Musicians must be treated with respect, given adequate compensation, and, as composers, enjoy copyright protection. *(David Bloom)*

6253
as
HUCKE, Helmut. **Il *munus ministeriale* della musica nel culto cristiano** [The *munus ministeriale* of music in the Christian religion], *La musica nel rinnovamento liturgico: Atti della Settimana internazionale di musica sacra* (Torino: Elle Di Ci, 1966) 45–64. In Italian. See no. 501 in this volume.

Discusses various aspects of the *Sacrosanctum concilium* of Vatican Council II, including the notions of *praecipua ancilla* (first among servants) and *munus ministeriale* (eternal gift), as well as modes of singing, call and response, and cantillation.

6254
as
HUCKE, Helmut. **Le récitatif liturgique en langue moderne** [Liturgical recitative in modern languages], *Musique sacrée et langues modernes: Deux colloques internationaux* (Paris: Fleurus, 1964) 59–76. In French. See no. 449 in this volume.

With vernacular texts, liturgical recitatives need to be more varied in style, more dramatic, and clearly audible. Examples of German recitative in folkloric style are discussed.

6255
as
HUCKE, Helmut. **Zum Plan eines Lexikons der katholischen Kirchenmusik/Projet pour un lexique de la musique catholique d'église** [The project of a lexicon of Catholic church music], *Perspectives de la musique sacrée à la lumière de l'encyclique* Musicae sacrae disciplina (Paris: conference, 1959) 650–55. In German and French. See no. 379 in this volume.

6256
as
HUIJBERS, Bernard. **Nouvelles hymnes sur les Évangiles** [New Gospel hymns], *Musique sacrée et langues modernes: Deux colloques internationaux* (Paris: Fleurus, 1964) 77–95. In French. See no. 449 in this volume.

Discusses hymns composed by the author, with old or original melodies, to Dutch-language texts by the poet Huub Oosterhuis, to be sung in the Roman Catholic liturgy before or after the sermon.

6257
as
HUIJBERS, Bernard. **Valore e limite del lied nella liturgia** [The value and limitations of the lied in the liturgy], *La musica nel rinnovamento liturgico: Atti della Settimana internazionale di musica sacra*

(Torino: Elle Di Ci, 1966) 187–205. *Music*. In Italian. See no. 501 in this volume.

Discusses strophic structure and aesthetics as criteria.

6258
as
INRY, G. **L'état de la musique religieuse dans le diocèse de Rennes et spécialement à la métropole** [The state of liturgical music in the diocese of Rennes and especially in the metropolitan area], *La musique d'église: Compte rendu du Congrès de musique sacrée* (Tourcoing: Duvivier, 1920) 353–60. In French. See no. 93 in this volume.

Presents a report by a church organist regarding changes in response to Pius X's motu proprio *Tra le sollecitudini* (1903).

⟶ JACOB, Georges. **La vie de l'Union des Maîtres de Chapelle et Organistes au cours de ses premières vingt-cinq années** [The life of the Union des Maîtres de Chapelle et Organistes during its first 25 years]. See no. 2329 in this volume.

6259
as
JANSSENS, Laurent. **Le chant officiel de l'Église** [The official chant of the Church], *La musique d'église: Compte rendu du Congrès de musique sacrée* (Tourcoing: Duvivier, 1920) 191–207. In French. See no. 93 in this volume.

Gregorian chant has several advantages over other forms of religious music including simplicity, calm, and the fact that as sung prayer it is clearly not concert music.

6260
as
JEANNETEAU, Jean. **L'orgue électronique** [Electronic organs], *Revue musicale* 239-240 (1957) 179–82. In French. See no. 378 in this volume.

Remarks on the liturgical use of electronic organs.

6261
as
JOHNER, Dominicus. **Der Dialog im liturgischen Gesang** [Dialogue in liturgical chant], *Congrés de la Societat Internacional de Musicologia* (Barcelona: Casa de Caritat, 1936). In German. See no. 224 in this volume.

The conference report provides only a citation. Neither the text nor a summary of the paper was published here. Another version was published in *Benediktinische Monatsschrift* XVIII (1936) 241-53.

6262
as
JOHNER, Dominicus. **Wie gelangen wir zu einem würdigen Vortrag des gregorianischen Chorals?** [How should we arrive at a worthy performance of Gregorian chant?], *Bericht über den Deutschen Kongreß für Kirchenmusik* (Kassel: Bärenreiter, 1928) 81–101. *Music*. In German. See no. 135 in this volume.

Inadequacies in the chant performance of Roman Catholic church choirs have to do largely with the lack of rehearsal time (in comparison to that given to polyphonic music), the exclusive focus on rhythmic issues, and a tendency to avoid personal expression. Choir directors should aim for legato singing and rhythmic clarity. Good effects can be derived from a varied deployment of forces—choir, boys' choir, and congregation—including the use of small choral groups. The performance can be expressive without falling into the error of subjectivity if it is based on the expressivity of the text. Also published in *Musica sacra* LVII (1927) and *Gregorius-Blatt* LI (1927). *(David Bloom)*

6263
as
JORGE, J. **La enseñanza del canto gregoriano en los seminarios** [The teaching of Gregorian chant in the seminaries], *Crónica del primer Congreso Nacional de Música Sagrada* (Valladolid: A. Martín, 1908) 50–58. In Spanish. See no. 57 in this volume.

In his motu proprio *Tra le sollecitudini* (1903), Pope Pius X advocated a return to the practice of singing Gregorian chant regularly during the liturgical service as a means of recapturing the original purity of religious music.

Consistent with this recommendation, Gregorian chant became a required discipline for seminarie throughout Spain. *(José López-Calo)*

6264
as
JORIS, Jozef. **Il posto della musica autoctona e contemporanea nella liturgia** [The place of autochthonous and contemporary music in the liturgy], *La musica nel rinnovamento liturgico: Atti della Settimana internazionale di musica sacra* (Torino: Elle Di Ci, 1966) 169–85. In Italian. See no. 501 in this volume.

Provides an historical overview and discusses the three criteria given in Pius X's motu proprio *Tra le sollecitudini* (1903): sanctity, universality, and artistic quality.

6265
as
JUNGMANN, Josef Andreas. **Liturgie und Volksgesang** [Liturgy and congregational singing], *Zweiter internationaler Kongress für katholische Kirchenmusik: Zu Ehren des Heiligen Papstes Pius X* (Wien: conference, 1955) 194–202. In German. See no. 339 in this volume.

The increased interest in congregational participation in the musical part of the Roman Catholic liturgy is evidenced in newer diocesan hymnals as well as on a national basis in Austria and Germany. This is part of the religious renewal begun by Pius X in his motu proprio *Tra le sollecitudini* (1903). The innovation is discussed from a theological perspective. *(David Bloom)*

6266
as
JUNGMANN, Josef Andreas. **Musica sacra e riforma liturgica** [Sacred music and liturgical reform], *La musica nel rinnovamento liturgico: Atti della Settimana internazionale di musica sacra* (Torino: Elle Di Ci, 1966) 27–44. In Italian. See no. 501 in this volume.

The priorities for church music, following *Sacrosanctum concilium* issued by the Vatican Council II on 4 December 1963, include primacy of text, the importance of a unified community voice, and an appropriately solemn aesthetic. Historical background is included.

6267
as
KAELIN, Pierre. **Coordinamento dell'azione regionale per la musica sacra** [Coordination of regional action for sacred music], *La musica nel rinnovamento liturgico: Atti della Settimana internazionale di musica sacra* (Torino: Elle Di Ci, 1966) 245–65. *Charts, diagr*. In Italian. See no. 501 in this volume.

Presents a four-part plan: organization, education, creation and preservation of repertoire, and dissemination of doctrine and repertoire.

6268
as
KAELIN, Pierre. **Qualité musicale et chant populaire** [Musical quality and congregational singing], *Revue musicale* 239-240 (1957) 223ff. In French. See no. 378 in this volume.

An abridged version of the conference paper is abstracted as no. 6269 in this volume.

6269
as
KAELIN, Pierre. **Qualité musicale et chant populaire** [Musical quality and congregational singing], *Perspectives de la musique sacrée à la lumière de l'encyclique* Musicae sacrae disciplina (Paris: conference, 1959) 484–93. In French. See no. 379 in this volume.

Congregational singing in the Roman Catholic liturgy should be of high artistic quality. Principles for achieving this are discussed. An abridged version is cited as no. 6268 in this volume. *(David Bloom)*

6270
as
KIENLE, Ambrosius. **Über den Choral bei den Cisterciensern** [On the chant of the Cistercians], *Akten des fünften internationalen Kongresses katholischer Gelehrten/Compte rendu du Ve Congrès scientifique international des catholiques* (München:

Herder, 1901) 328–29. In German. See no. 26 in this volume.

6271 KORNFELD, Fritz. **Chinas katholische Kirchenmusik im Aufbruch einer neuen Zeit**
as [China's Catholic church music in the dawning of a new era], *Zweiter internationaler Kongress für katholische Kirchenmusik: Zu Ehren des Heiligen Papstes Pius X* (Wien: conference, 1955) 265–68. *Music.* In German. See no. 339 in this volume.

The tonal structure of traditional Chinese music, together with the phonological structure of the Chinese languages, make Gregorian chant virtually impossible for Chinese congregations to perform; chants of a similar character, however, can be composed by using Chinese scales and by breaking up the Latin syllables, with their consonant clusters and final consonants, into more pronounceable units. Two of the author's attempts, a *Tantum ergo* in Latin and an *Ave Maria* in Chinese, are reproduced in the standard cipher notation. *(David Bloom)*

6272 KOSCH, Franz. **Die Auswirkungen des II.**
as **Internationales Kirchenmusikkongresses (Wien, 1954)/Quelques résultats du IIe congrès international de musique sacrée tenu à Vienne en 1954** [Consequences of the second International Congress for Church Music (Vienna, 1954)], *Perspectives de la musique sacrée à la lumière de l'encyclique Musicae sacrae disciplina* (Paris: conference, 1959) 635–42. In German and French. See no. 379 in this volume.

The conference under discussion is cited as no. 339 in this volume.

6273 KOSCH, Franz. **Die Enzyklika *Musicae sacrae***
as ***disciplina* Pius' XII. und die Vota des Wiener Kirchenmusikkongresses** [Pius XII's encyclical *Musicae sacrae disciplina* and the decisions of the Vienna congress of church music], *Bericht über den internationalen musikwissenschaftlichen Kongreß Wien Mozartjahr 1956* (Graz; Köln: Böhlau, 1958) 309–12. In German. See no. 365 in this volume.

The second International Congress of Church Music, Vienna 1954 (see no. 339 in this volume), concluded, among other things, that the sung Mass should be celebrated exclusively in Latin; that the vernacular should be permitted in the *Missa lecta*, but not in literal translations of liturgical texts; and that only the sung Latin Mass should be used on important feast days and as much as possible Sundays. These recommendations are examined in the light of the encyclical of December 1955. *(David Bloom)*

6274 KOSCHMIEDER, Erwin. **Wie haben Kyrill**
as **und Method zelebriert?** [How did Cyril and Methodius celebrate?], *Anfänge der slavischen Musik* (Bratislava: Slovenská Akadémia Vied, 1966) 7–22. In German. See no. 477 in this volume.

A lack of contemporary sources that contain decipherable neumes has hindered research into the liturgical practices of Cyril and Methodius, the Greek missionaries who established Catholicism in Slavic regions. Much evidence is gleaned from later Greek and Latin sources, particularly those from the 11th c., which show faithful translations from liturgical books of the Greek Orthodox church and neumes closely allied with earlier Byzantine neumes. It is likely that the liturgical rites celebrated by the early missionaries had Greek and Latin origins. *(Brian Doherty)*

6275 KREPS, Joseph. **Le rôle unificateur de**
as **l'organiste liturgique** [The unifying role of the liturgical organist], *La musique d'église: Compte rendu du Congrès de musique sacrée* (Tourcoing: Duvivier, 1920) 95–111. In French. See no. 93 in this volume.

In light of Pius X's motu proprio *Tra le sollecitudini* (1903), the responsibilities of the organist include those of providing appropriate music for each service and of establishing a general atmosphere of unified style and thought.

6276 KRONSTEINER, Hermann. **Das deutsche**
as **Kirchenlied in der Liturgiefeier** [The German-language hymn in the celebration of the liturgy], *Die Kirchenmusik und das II. Vatikanische Konzil* (Graz: Styria, 1965) 77–90. In German. See no. 480 in this volume.

The need for Roman Catholic church music using vernacular texts following the new constitution on the liturgy (*Sacrosanctum concilium*, December 1963) can be partly satisfied in German-speaking congregations by the use of the German heritage, including the appropriation of the best Lutheran hymns. New hymns must also be composed. It is possible that a jazz or pop style may be used though no suitable models for congregational (as opposed to solo) singing in such styles exist. Only strict translations from the Latin liturgy may be used for the pieces of the Ordinary and Proper; paraphrases may be used in general hymnody. *(David Bloom)*

6277 LA TOMBELLE, Fernand de. **Le répertoire**
as **moderne** [Modern repertoire], *La musique d'église: Compte rendu du Congrès de musique sacrée* (Tourcoing: Duvivier, 1920) 155–76. In French. See no. 93 in this volume.

Discusses the Church's position regarding progressive repertoire as stated in Pius X's motu proprio *Tra le sollecitudini* (1903).

6278 LA TOUR DE NOÉ, Gabriel-Marie-Eugène de.
as **Véritable caractère de la musique d'église** [The true character of church music], *Congrès pour la restauration du plain-chant et de la musique d'église* (Paris: De Mourgues, 1862) 88–89. In French. See no. 3 in this volume.

6279 LAFFON (abbé). **Les livres liturgiques et les**
as **décrets du St-Siège** [The liturgical books and the decrees of the Holy See], *Congrès diocésain de musique religieuse et de plain-chant* (Rodez: Carrère, 1895) 53–58. In French. See no. 22 in this volume.

6280 LAIR DE BEAUVAIS, Alfred. **De l'état actuel**
as **de la musique sacrée dans le diocèse de Bayeux** [The state of religious music in the diocese of Bayeux], *Congrès pour la restauration du plain-chant et de la musique d'église* (Paris: De Mourgues, 1862) 105–06. In French. See no. 3 in this volume.

6281 LE GUENNANT, Auguste. **Le chant grégorien**
as **dans l'œuvre pastorale de Pie X** [Gregorian chant in the pastoral work of Pius X], *Zweiter internationaler Kongress für katholische Kirchenmusik: Zu Ehren des Heiligen Papstes Pius X* (Wien: conference, 1955) 98–104. In French. See no. 339 in this volume.

Pius X reestablished Gregorian chant as the musical standard for Roman Catholic worship in his motu proprio *Tra le sollecitudini* (1903). This may be seen as an exercise of Pius's pastoral duties, to the spiritual benefit of all Catholics. *(Christopher Johnson)*

6282 LE GUENNANT, Auguste. **La crise des offices**
as **solennels et le chant grégorien** [The crisis of the Holy Offices and Gregorian chant], *Congrès international de musique sacrée: Chant et orgue* (Paris: Desclée de Brouwer, 1937) 72–75. In French. See no. 247 in this volume.

Among the faithful in major French cities, especially Paris, there is a growing disaffection with the Offices. This has resulted from the congregation's passing from an active to a passive role, and a resulting indifference. If the congregation were to be given an active part to play in the services, interest could be resurrected. *(Arthur Maisel)*

6283
as

LE GUENNANT, Auguste. **La crise du recrutement des chanteurs professionels d'Église** [The crisis of recruitment of professional singers of the Church], *La musique d'église: Compte rendu du Congrès de musique sacrée* (Tourcoing: Duvivier, 1920) 209–14. In French. See no. 93 in this volume.

Discusses several causes of the situation, including budgetary constraints and the relative isolation of the job.

6284
as

LECHTHALER, Josef. **Der katholische Organist als Baumeister des liturgischen Gesamtkunstwerkes** [The Catholic organist as architect of the liturgical Gesamtkunstwerk], *Bericht über den Deutschen Kongreß für Kirchenmusik* (Kassel: Bärenreiter, 1928) 62–70. In German. See no. 135 in this volume.

The organ in the sung Mass has a double function: as accompaniment and as a linking agent between the chants of the choir and the priest. The latter task requires a creative bringing together of the different style characteristics of songs from different periods and of the style of the day's particular feast, through which the liturgy takes on the structure, articulation, and finish of a Gesamtkunstwerk. Skills the organist must bring to bear on the task are outlined. *(David Bloom)*

6285
as

LENAERTS, René Bernard. **Probleme der Messe in ihrer historischen Sicht/Problems of the Mass in their historical perspective/Problèmes de la Messe dans leur perspective historique/Problemi della Messa nella perspettiva storica**, *IV. Internationaler Kongress für Kirchenmusik in Köln: Dokumente und Berichte* (Köln: Bachem, 1962) 202–36. In German, English, French, and Italian. See no. 432 in this volume.

The coexistence of traditional and modern music became a special problem as polyphonic technique began to unfold. Safeguarding both the liturgical function of the music and its artistic development will require a redefinition of the role of sacred music.

6286
as

LHOUMEAU, Antonin. **La musique populaire à l'Église** [Folk music in the Church], *La tradition en Poitou et Charentes: Art populaire, ethnographie, folk-lore, hagiographie, histoire* (Paris: Librairie de la Tradition Nationale, 1897) 115–23. In French. See no. 21 in this volume.

Gregorian chant, parts of which are sung by the congregation, contributes to the popularization of music. The proper rhythms of the texts should not be altered by a fixed meter. Modern popular chant should not be overly influenced by secular music.

6287
as

LIONCOURT, Guy de. **Le cantique grégorien** [The Gregorian canticle], *Congrès international de musique sacrée: Chant et orgue* (Paris: Desclée de Brouwer, 1937) 184–90. In French. See no. 247 in this volume.

Discusses the vernacular music that has evolved from Gregorian chant.

6288
as

LIPPHARDT, Walther. **Möglichkeiten und Grenzen deutscher Gregorianik** [The possibilities and limitations of German-language Gregorian chant], *Die Kirchenmusik und das II. Vatikanische Konzil* (Graz: Styria, 1965) 121–48. In German. See no. 480 in this volume.

On the basis of the constitution of the liturgy promulgated by the Vatican Council II (*Sacrosanctum concilium*, December 1963), summarizes arguments for and against the preparation and use of chant in German, with particular regard to readings, psalms, antiphons, and hymns. *(David Bloom)*

6289
as

LITAIZE, Gaston. **L'improvisation liturgique** [Liturgical improvisation], *Zweiter internationaler*

Kongress für katholische Kirchenmusik: Zu Ehren des Heiligen Papstes Pius X (Wien: conference, 1955) 241–42. In French. See no. 339 in this volume.

General principles, based on the author's experience as church organist and as director of religious programming for the Office de Radiodiffusion-Télévision Française. The organ's function is to complement, not contrast with, the calm fervor of Gregorian chant; improvisation should be inspired by the music that has just been or is about to be sung, maintaining its rhythmic and modal character. The composed repertoire, and virtuoso display, are not unsuited to the beginning and end of the service. *(David Bloom)*

6290
as

LÓPEZ GODOY, Rafael José. **La musica sagrada y el canon 1264** [Sacred music and Canon 1264], *Zweiter internationaler Kongress für katholische Kirchenmusik: Zu Ehren des Heiligen Papstes Pius X* (Wien: conference, 1955) 288–94. In Spanish. See no. 339 in this volume.

Analytic account of papal and other official positions on the status of sacred music within the Roman Catholic Church as codified in Canon 1264 of the 1917 Code of Canon Law, with particular reference to its prohibition on church premises of music with any tinge of the lascivious or impure. *(David Bloom)*

6291
as

MAC CREA, Dan. **Gregorian music in our churches**, *Akten des fünften internationalen Kongresses katholischer Gelehrten/Compte rendu du Vᵉ Congrès scientifique international des catholiques* (München: Herder, 1901) 330–31. In English and German; summary in Latin. See no. 26 in this volume.

Discusses interpretive problems of Gregorian chant.

6292
as

MAHIEU, Léon. **La soumission à l'Église: Condition essentielle de la musique sacrée** [Submission to the Church: An essential condition of sacred music], *La musique d'église: Compte rendu du Congrès de musique sacrée* (Tourcoing: Duvivier, 1920) 15–25. In French. See no. 93 in this volume.

Emphasizes the need for musical aesthetics to reflect Roman Catholic church doctrine.

6293
as

MAILLET, Fernand. **La Fédération Internationale des Petits Chanteurs** [The International Federation of Pueri Cantores], *Revue musicale* 239-240 (1957) 273ff. In French. See no. 378 in this volume.

An abridged version of the conference paper is cited as no. 6294 in this volume.

6294
as

MAILLET, Fernand. **La Fédération Internationale des *Pueri cantores*** [The International Federation of Pueri Cantores], *Perspectives de la musique sacrée à la lumière de l'encyclique* Musicae sacrae disciplina (Paris: conference, 1959) 643–45. In French. See no. 379 in this volume.

The movement of boys' choirs inspired by the motu proprio *Tra le sollecitudini* of Pius X (1903), beginning with the 1907 founding in Paris of the Manécanterie des Petits Chanteurs à la Croix de Bois, has been formally organized at an international level since 1947-51. The Federation is represented in 92 countries by some 2,800 groups. An abridged version of this paper is cited as no. 6293 in this volume. *(David Bloom)*

6295
as

MALCOLM, George. **La musica nell' Ufficiatura liturgica della Cattedrale di Westminster** [Music in the liturgical Office of Westminster Cathedral], *Atti del [I] Congresso internazionale di musica sacra* (Tournai: Desclée, 1952) 62–65. In Italian. See no. 303 in this volume.

Notes on liturgical music at Westminster Cathedral (Metropolitan Church of the Most Precious Blood), London, from the author's point of view as its master of music from 1947.

6296
as
MANZANO, Miguel. **I diversi attori del canto liturgico e i rispettivi ruoli** [The various actors in liturgical chant and their respective roles], *La musica nel rinnovamento liturgico: Atti della Settimana internazionale di musica sacra* (Torino: Elle Di Ci, 1966) 65–89. *Music.* In Italian. See no. 501 in this volume.

According to the Vatican Council II, namely *Sacrosanctum concilium*, priests, deacons, readers, and musicians all have appropriate musical duties in liturgical services.

6297
as
MARTINEAU, A.-Félix. **De l'accompagnement du plain-chant** [The accompaniment of plain-chant], *Congrès pour la restauration du plain-chant et de la musique d'église* (Paris: De Mourgues, 1862) 102–03. In French. See no. 3 in this volume.

6298
as
MARTINEAU, A.-Félix. **Du plain-chant dans le diocèse de Nantes** [Plainchant in the diocese of Nantes], *Congrès pour la restauration du plain-chant et de la musique d'église* (Paris: De Mourgues, 1862) 97–102. In French. See no. 3 in this volume.

6299
as
MARTINEAU, A.-Félix. **Le maître de chapelle** [The choirmaster], *Congrès pour la restauration du plain-chant et de la musique d'église* (Paris: De Mourgues, 1862) 103. In French. See no. 3 in this volume.

6300
as
MARTÍNEZ BARREIRO, Pedro. **Influencia de la música religiosa sobre el hombre medio** [The influence of religious music on the average person], *V Congreso Nacional de Música Sagrada* (Madrid: Gráficas Dos de Mayo, 1956) 243–44. In Spanish. See no. 331 in this volume.

6301
as
MARTY. **Les journées grégoriennes de Lourdes** [The conference in Lourdes on Gregorian chant], *La musique d'église: Compte rendu du Congrès de musique sacrée* (Tourcoing: Duvivier, 1920) 361–66. In French. See no. 93 in this volume.

The 1920 conference included religious services, presentations of polyphonic music, and lectures.

6302
as
MASSART, M. **Note sur l'état du chant dans la collégiale de Saint-Quentin** [The state of chant in the Collegiate church of Saint-Quentin], *Congrès pour la restauration du plain-chant et de la musique d'église* (Paris: De Mourgues, 1862) 114–15. In French. See no. 3 in this volume.

6303
as
MATHIAS, François-Xavier. **L'orgue au service du culte catholique** [The role of the organ in the Catholic religion], *Compte rendu du Congrès d'orgue tenu à l'Université de Strasbourg. IV* (Strasbourg: Société Strasbourgeoise de Librairie Sostralib, 1934) 162–64. In French. See no. 199 in this volume.

Discusses the organ's role in supporting and amplifying the Catholic liturgy, and the spiritual connotations acquired by the instrument.

6304
as
MATHIAS, François-Xavier. **L'orgue dans le culte** [The organ in the liturgy], *Compte rendu du Congrès d'orgue tenu à l'Université de Strasbourg. IV* (Strasbourg: Société Strasbourgeoise de Librairie Sostralib, 1934) 157–59. In French. See no. 199 in this volume.

Focuses on the Catholic liturgy.

6305
as
MATHIAS, François-Xavier. **Sujektivität und Objektivität in der katholischen Kirchenmusik** [Subjectivity and objectivity in Catholic church music], *Report of the Fourth Congress of the International Musical Society* (London: Novello, 1912) 303. In German. See no. 71 in this volume.

Summary of a paper discussing theological perspectives on the role of church music; the full version is published in *Kirchenmusikalisches Jahrbuch*, 1911.

6306
as
MIRANDA Y GÓMEZ, Miguel Darío. **La encíclica *Musicae sacrae disciplina*/L'encyclique *Musicae sacrae disciplina*** [The encyclical *Musicae sacrae disciplina*], *Perspectives de la musique sacrée à la lumière de l'encyclique* Musicae sacrae disciplina (Paris: conference, 1959) 121–30. In Spanish and French. See no. 379 in this volume.

Pius XII's encyclical letter on sacred music (1955) reinforces the principles of Pius X's motu proprio *Tra le sollecitudini* (1903), which marked the beginning of the restoration of liturgical music, establishing Gregorian chant as superior to all other forms, and the apostolic constitution *Divini cultus sanctitatem* (1928) of Pius XI. A summary is cited as no. 6307 in this volume. *(Meredith A. McCutcheon)*

6307
as
MIRANDA Y GÓMEZ, Miguel Darío. **La musique sacrée, art liturgique privilégié** [Sacred music, a privileged liturgical art], *Revue musicale* 239-240 (1957) 37–40. In French. See no. 378 in this volume.

Summary of a discussion of the encyclical *Musicae sacrae disciplina* (1955) of Pius XII. The original version, in Spanish with a French-language translation, is abstracted as no. 6306 in this volume.

⟶
MOBERG, Carl-Allan. **Zur Geschichte des schwedischen Kirchen-Gesangs** [On the history of Swedish church songs]. See no. 6440 in this volume.

6308
as
MOCQUEREAU, André. **La psalmodie romaine et l'accent tonique latin** [Roman psalmody and the Latin tonic accent], *Congrès diocésain de musique religieuse et de plain-chant* (Rodez: Carrère, 1895). In French. See no. 22 in this volume.

6309
as
MOISSL, Franz. **Über die Notwendigkeit unterbehördlicher Durchführungsvorschriften zum *motu propio* vom 22 November 1903** [The necessity of regulations from the lesser hierarchy for the implementation of the motu proprio of 22 November 1903], *Haydn-Zentenarfeier* (Leipzig: Breitkopf & Härtel; Wien: Artaria, 1909) 567–75. In German. See no. 65 in this volume.

Discusses changes in procedures of Roman Catholic Church music.

6310
as
MORILLEAU, Xavier. **Valeur pastorale du chant grégorien à la lumière des enseignements pontificaux** [The pastoral value of Gregorian chant in the light of papal teaching], *Revue musicale* 239-240 (1957) 75–81. In French. See no. 378 in this volume.

An abridged version of the conference paper is abstracted as no. 6311 in this volume.

6311
as
MORILLEAU, Xavier. **Valeur pastorale du chant grégorien à la lumière des enseignements pontificaux** [The pastoral value of Gregorian chant in the light of papal teachings], *Perspectives de la musique sacrée à la lumière de l'encyclique* Musicae

sacrae disciplina (Paris: conference, 1959) 187–97. In French. See no. 379 in this volume.

Discusses the value of Gregorian chant, in Latin, with the congregational responses, from the standpoint of its liturgical effectiveness as the pastor sees it, and as Pius XII discusses it in the encyclical *Musicae sacrae disciplina*. A summary is cited as no. 6310 in this volume. *(Warren A. Bebbington)*

6312 MOTTA E ALBUQUERQUE, João Batista da.
as **La musica sacra nel Brasile** [Sacred music in Brazil], *Atti del [I] Congresso internazionale di musica sacra* (Tournai: Desclée, 1952) 66–68. In Italian. See no. 303 in this volume.

⟶ MOURINHO, António Maria. **Aspecto e função da música popular Mirandesa profana e religiosa** [Aspects and functions of secular and religious traditional music in Miranda]. See no. 2964 in this volume.

6313 MÜLLER, Hermann. **Beethovens *Missa** as **solemnis** und das *Motu proprio* des Papstes Pius X. über Kirchenmusik** [Beethoven's *Missa solemnis* and Pope Pius X's motu proprio on church music], *Beethoven-Zentenarfeier: Internationaler musikhistorischer Kongress* (Wien: Universal, 1927) 229–31. In German. See no. 142 in this volume.

Properly understood, the 1903 papal declaration *Tra le sollecitudini* does not rule out the liturgical use of Beethoven's Mass in D major, op. 123. *(David Bloom)*

6314 MÜLLER, Hermann. **Einiges über klassische** as **kirchliche Polyphonie** [On classical church polyphony], *Bericht über den Deutschen Kongreß für Kirchenmusik* (Kassel: Bärenreiter, 1928) 102–09. In German. See no. 135 in this volume.

Remarks keyed to the selection of music at the celebration of a solemn evening Mass at the Hedwigskirche, Berlin—under the musical direction of Pius Kalt, including *a cappella* works by composers from Dufay through Giovanni Gabrieli—on the artistic and liturgical value of Renaissance polyphony. *(David Bloom)*

6315 MÜLLER, Hermann. **Das katholische deutsche** as **Kirchenlied** [The German Catholic hymn], *Bericht über den Deutschen Kongreß für Kirchenmusik* (Kassel: Bärenreiter, 1928) 110–11. In German. See no. 135 in this volume.

Brief remarks on the character and quality of German hymnody from before the Reformation, in the context of a performance with audience participation of hymns from the author's *Kyrioleis: Kleiner Psalter geistlicher Lieder dem jungen Deutschland* (originally published under the title *Kyrioleis: Kleiner Psalter geistlicher Lieder dem jungen Deutschland dargereicht*, Burg Rothenfels: Deutsches Quickbornhaus, 1923; based on Michael Vehe's *Ein new Gesangbüchlin geystlicher Lieder*, Leipzig, 1537). *(David Bloom)*

6316 MÜLLER, Hermann. **Neue Bestrebungen auf** as **dem Gebiete des katholischen deutschen Kirchenliedes** [New endeavors in the field of Catholic German hymns], *Bericht über den I. musikwissenschaftlichen Kongress der Deutschen Musikgesellschaft in Leipzig* (Wiesbaden: Breitkopf & Härtel, 1926) 350. In German. See no. 120 in this volume.

A summary of an article published in *Musica Divina* II (1925).

6317 MÜLLER, Hermann. **Prinzipielles zur** as **katholischen Kirchenmusik** [Principles of Catholic church music], *Report of the Fourth Congress of the International Musical Society* (London: Novello, 1912) 303–06. In German. See no. 71 in this volume.

Modern idioms are potentially worthy of adaptation to liturgical purposes. The situation in German-speaking countries is assessed.

6318 MÜLLER, Hermann. **Zur Urgeschichte des** as **deutschen Kirchenliedes** [On the early history of German hymns], *Haydn-Zentenarfeier* (Leipzig: Breitkopf & Härtel; Wien: Artaria, 1909) 532–36. In German. See no. 65 in this volume.

Reviews relevant scholarship, focusing on Kyrie tropes.

6319 NASONI, A.; SIZIA, Giacomo; TEBALDINI, as Giovanni. **Considerandi, deliberazioni e voti esratti dai verbali e sinteticamente disposti** [Summaries of the considerations, deliberations, and votes of the congress], *7° Congresso di musica sacra* (Torino: author, 1905) 47–53. In Italian. See no. 52 in this volume.

Discusses issues regarding *scholae cantorum*, Gregorian chant, religious music in general, organs, bells, other instruments (including bands and orchestras), propaganda, and organization. *(André Balog)*

6320 NEUMANN, Paul. **Die Organisation der** as **Kirchenmusikpflege** [The organization of the cultivation of church music], *Atti del [I] Congresso internazionale di musica sacra* (Tournai: Desclée, 1952) 69–72. In German. See no. 303 in this volume.

Discusses administrative structures within the Roman Catholic Church.

6321 NIKLAUS, Hans; ROHR, Heinrich. **Gesang-** as **liche Erziehung der Gemeinde** [The instruction of the congregation in singing], *Die Kirchenmusik und das II. Vatikanische Konzil* (Graz: Styria, 1965) 173–213. *Music*. In German. See no. 480 in this volume.

The diocese of Mainz, Germany, has considerable experience, antedating the decisions of the Vatican Council II, with the preparation of congregations to sing German-language Gregorian chant at Mass and at Vespers. General principles and specific practical methods are outlined. *(David Bloom)*

6322 NOMURA, Francesco Yosio. **Akkommodation** as **und Kirchenmusikpflege in Japan** [Adaptation and church music cultivation in Japan], *IV. Internationaler Kongress für Kirchenmusik in Köln: Dokumente und Berichte* (Köln: Bachem, 1962) 247–51. In German. See no. 432 in this volume.

Music in the Catholic church in Japan has used Western musical chant and hymn forms with Japanese texts. Musical elements from Asian traditions have also begun to be introduced.

⟶ NUFFEL, Jules van. **L'école interdiocésaine de Malines et la musique d'Église** [The Interdiocesaan Instituut voor Kerkmuziek in Mechelen and the music of the Catholic Church]. See no. 4836 in this volume.

⟶ NUFFEL, Jules van. **L'évolution musicale contemporaine et sa répercussion sur la musique sacrée de notre époque: Les possibilités qu'elle offre à celle-ci** [The contemporary musical evolution and its impact on sacred music in our era: The possibilities it offers to the latter]. See no. 2222 in this volume.

6323 OBAMA, Jean. **L'emploi de la musique** as **indigène dans les chrétientés africaines: Enquête** [The use of indigenous music in African Christianities: Enquiry], *Revue musicale* 239-240 (1957) 247–50. In French. See no. 378 in this volume.

An abridged version of the conference paper is abstracted as no. 6324 in this volume.

6324
as
OBAMA, Jean. **Enquête sur l'emploi de la musique indigène dans les chrétientés africaines** [Enquiry on the use of indigenous music in African Christianities], *Perspectives de la musique sacrée à la lumière de l'encyclique* Musicae sacrae disciplina (Paris: conference, 1959) 547–51. In French. See no. 379 in this volume.

A questionnaire sent to Roman Catholic missions in connection with the third International Congress of Sacred Music (Paris 1957) received some 40 responses from Africa, which are summarized, with particular attention to different experiences with Gregorian chant and with attempts at the creation of indigenous liturgical musics. Another version is cited as no. 989 in this volume. *(David Bloom)*

6325
as
OBAMA, Jean. **Les réussites du chant grégorien au Cameroun** [The successes of Gregorian chant in Cameroon], *Revue musicale* 239-240 (1957) 125–27. In French. See no. 378 in this volume.

An abridged version of the conference paper is abstracted as no. 6326 in this volume.

6326
as
OBAMA, Jean. **Les réussites du chant grégorien au Cameroun** [The successes of Gregorian chant in Cameroon], *Perspectives de la musique sacrée à la lumière de l'encyclique* Musicae sacrae disciplina (Paris: conference, 1959) 260–62. In French. See no. 379 in this volume.

Gregorian chant and African dance music display a strong modal relationship. The history of Roman Catholic church music in Cameroon from 1904 to 1951 is summarized, and the author's own Ewondo-language hymn texts and settings are discussed. A summary is cited as no. 6325 in this volume. *(Meredith A. McCutcheon)*

6327
as
OLMEDA, Federico. **La música sagrada en las parroquias** [Religious music in the parishes], *Crónica del primer Congreso Nacional de Música Sagrada* (Valladolid: A. Martín, 1908) 78–87. In Spanish. See no. 57 in this volume.

Discusses the lack of musical knowledge among priests in small, rural parishes in Spain. Congregations should benefit from the renewed interest in music advocated by Pius X in his motu proprio *Tra le sollecitudini* (1903), and through the implementation of systematic programs for teaching Gregorian chant. *(José López-Calo)*

6328
as
Organería Española, S.A. **El órgano electrónico, sus cualidades y uso en la sagrada liturgia** [The electronic organ, its qualities, and its use in the liturgy], *V Congreso Nacional de Música Sagrada* (Madrid: Gráficas Dos de Mayo, 1956) 177–81. In Spanish. See no. 331 in this volume.

6329
as
OTAÑO EGUINO, Nemesio. **Música litúrgica moderna** [Modern liturgical music], *Crónica y actas oficiales del tercer Congreso Nacional de Música Sagrada* (Barcelona: La Hormiga de Oro, 1913) 87–109. In Spanish. See no. 78 in this volume.

The practice of liturgical music is under the complete jurisdiction of the church, which determines that it is not an end in itself but an instrument of religious indoctrination. The guidelines for the practice of modern liturgical music were outlined in Pius X's motu proprio *Tra le sollecitudini* (1903), where the characteristics of Gregorian chant are taken as the ultimate standard for Roman Catholic liturgical music. *(José López-Calo)*

6330
as
OVERATH, Johannes. **Die** *Associatio sub titulo S. Caeciliae pro universis germanicae linguae terris* **als Typ einer Landesorganisation für Kirchenmusik/L'Association Sainte-Cécile des pays de langue germanique considérée comme type d'une organisation territoriale pour la musique sacrée** [The Allgemeiner Caecilienverein für Länder Deutscher Zunge as a model of territorial organizations for sacred music], *Perspectives de la musique sacrée à la lumière de l'encyclique* Musicae sacrae disciplina (Paris: conference, 1959) 599–612. In German and French. See no. 379 in this volume.

Surveys the history of the umbrella organization of the Caecilian movement among German-speaking Catholics of Austria, Germany, Luxembourg, and Switzerland, from its founding in 1867; its organization and function; and its status within the Roman Catholic Church. *(David Bloom)*

6331
as
PARISOT, Jean. **L'accompagnement du chant grégorien** [Accompanying Gregorian Chant], *Congrès régional de liturgie et de musique sacrée* (Moselle: Orphelins-Apprentis Guénange, 1923) 102–08. In French. See no. 98 in this volume.

Discusses problems associated with providing melodic and harmonic organ accompaniment to Gregorian chant.

6332
as
PARISOT, Jean. **De l'harmonisation du chant grégorien** [On the harmonization of Gregorian chant], *Compte rendu du Congrès général de musique sacrée: Aperçu général des préliminaires et du congrès, discours et conférences* (Strasbourg: Alsacien, 1922) 207–30. *Music.* In French. See no. 96 in this volume.

Adrien de la Fage introduced organ accompaniment to Gregorian chant in 1829. The subsequent religious and aesthetic debates are brought into focus in a discussion of published accompaniments.

6333
as
PAROISSIN, René. **Enquête sur la musique missionnaire en Extrême-Orient** [Enquiry on missionary music in the Far East], *Perspectives de la musique sacrée à la lumière de l'encyclique* Musicae sacrae disciplina (Paris: conference, 1959) 564–66. *Music.* In French. See no. 379 in this volume.

Brief report of responses to a survey conducted in connection with the third International Congress of Sacred Music (Paris 1957), from India, Burma, Indonesia, Vietnam, Laos, China, and Japan. A setting of the Ave Maria in Mandarin is appended. Another version of this paper is cited as no. 6334 in this volume. *(David Bloom)*

6334
as
PAROISSIN, René. **La musique missionaire en Extrême-Orient** [Missionary music in the Far East], *Revue musicale* 239-240 (1957) 251–54. In French. See no. 378 in this volume.

Another version of this paper is cited as no. 6333 in this volume.

6335
as
PÉREZ-JORGE, Vicente. **Música contemporánea** [Contemporary music], *V Congreso Nacional de Música Sagrada* (Madrid: Gráficas Dos de Mayo, 1956) 182–90. In Spanish. See no. 331 in this volume.

As long as modern religious music maintains the necessary qualities of holiness, formal goodness, and universality, the Church accepts it, with no further restrictions on the expressive freedom of the composer, as stated by Pius X in the motu proprio *Tra le sollecitudini* (1903). Some recent works by Spanish and non-Spanish composers are given as examples. *(José López-Calo)*

6336
as
PÉREZ MILLÁN, Juan. **Consideraciones acerca del canto popular religioso** [Thoughts on religious traditional song], *V Congreso Nacional de Música Sagrada* (Madrid: Gráficas Dos de Mayo, 1956) 321–31. In Spanish. See no. 331 in this volume.

The furthering of congregational singing has been a goal of popes beginning with Pius X. Some ways of attaining it include providing a good repertoire of songs; publishing those that are already well known; having church music directors try them out; and training seminary students and priests to work with them. *(José López-Calo)*

6337 PIUS X, Pope. *Motu proprio* **sur la musique**
as **sacrée** [Motu proprio on sacred music], *Comptes rendus, rapports et vœux du Congrès parisien et régional de chant liturgique et de musique d'église* (Paris: Schola Cantorum, 1912) 166–75. In French. See no. 75 in this volume.

A French-language translation of *Tra le sollecitudini* (1903).

6338 POIVET, Henry. *Una fides, unus cantus, una*
as *lingua,, Comptes rendus, rapports et vœux du Congrès parisien et régional de chant liturgique et de musique d'église* (Paris: Schola Cantorum, 1912) 88–93. In French. See no. 75 in this volume.

6339 POTHIER, Joseph. **La catholicité du chant de**
as **l'église romaine** [The catholicity of the chant of the Roman church], *Acta generalis cantus gregoriani studiosorum conventus, Argentinensis, 16-19 Aug. 1905/Bericht des internationalen Kongresses für gregorianischen Choralgesang/Compte rendu du Congrès international de plain-chant grégorien* (Strassburg: F.-X. Le Roux, 1905) 13–18. In French. See no. 50 in this volume.

Plainchant has a universal quality; it adapts to all situations: simple chants for the masses, more elaborate chants for priests and professional singers. Its high aesthetic quality pleases the artist while helping the people understand the tone of the prayers. Medieval theoreticians viewed music as a science based on mathematics, almost completely ignoring the interpretive aspect of chant. But being a living art, chant was passed down by generations. While theoretical study is important, now that we are starting to know much about plainchant, let us remember that chant is for all persons to praise their God.

6340 POUNIAU (abbé). **Du chant dans les paroisses**
as **rurales** [Chant in rural parishes], *Congrès diocésain de musique religieuse et de plain-chant* (Rodez: Carrère, 1895) 123–25. In French. See no. 22 in this volume.

6341 PRADO PERAITA, Germán. **El canto litúrgico**
as **como medio de apostolado** [Liturgical chant as a medium for apostolate], *Crónica del IV Congreso Nacional de Música Sagrada* (Vitoria: Imprenta del Montepío Diocesano, 1930) 229–33. In Spanish. See no. 155 in this volume.

Discusses the edifying influence of religious vocal music, particularly in rural areas.

6342 PRADO PERAITA, Germán. **Participación**
as **activa en el culto por medio del canto** [Active participation in the Mass through song], *Crónica del IV Congreso Nacional de Música Sagrada* (Vitoria: Imprenta del Montepío Diocesano, 1930) 233–37. In Spanish. See no. 155 in this volume.

Opportunities for active involvement in religious services have increased following Pius X's motu proprio *Tra le sollecitudini* (1903).

6343 PRADO PERAITA, Germán. **El repertorio**
as **mozárabe** [The Mozarabic repertoire], *V Congreso Nacional de Música Sagrada* (Madrid: Gráficas Dos de Mayo, 1956) 128–35. In Spanish. See no. 331 in this volume.

Argues that the praise of Gregorian chant by Pope Pius X in the motu proprio *Tra le sollecitudini* (1903) could equally be applied to Mozarabic chant. *(José López-Calo)*

6344 PRIM, Jean. **De l'indispensable base juridique**
as **et financière de la musique sacrée** [Of the essential legal and financial base of sacred music], *Atti del [I]*

Congresso internazionale di musica sacra (Tournai: Desclée, 1952) 73–76. In French. See no. 303 in this volume.

Discusses the administration of sacred music within the Roman Catholic Church.

6345 PRIM, Jean. **L'enquête mondiale sur la**
as **musique sacrée dans les pays de mission** [World-wide enquiry on sacred music in countries served by missionaries], *Perspectives de la musique sacrée à la lumière de l'encyclique* Musicae sacrae disciplina (Paris: conference, 1959) 538–45. In French. See no. 379 in this volume.

In preparation for the third International Congress of Sacred Music (Paris 1957) a questionnaire on issues of sacred music in Roman Catholic missions was sent to missions in Africa, Asia, Oceania, and Native Canadian communities. A list of respondents is appended, and particular responses are discussed in some detail in the conference papers abstracted as no. 2672, 6324, and 6333 in this volume. *(David Bloom)*

6346 PUJOL ROCA, David. **El canto litúrgico de los**
as **fieles** [The liturgical chant of the faithful], *Crónica del IV Congreso Nacional de Música Sagrada* (Vitoria: Imprenta del Montepío Diocesano, 1930) 239–47. In Spanish. See no. 155 in this volume.

The musical participation of the congregation in the liturgy was promoted by Pius X in his motu propio *Tra le sollecitudini* (1903). *(José López-Calo)*

6347 QUACK, Erhard. **Facture musical et chants**
as **d'assemblée** [Musical composition and congregational songs], *Musique sacrée et langues modernes: Deux colloques internationaux* (Paris: Fleurus, 1964) 39–52. In French. See no. 449 in this volume.

In Roman Catholic churches in the diocese of Speyer, as of 1962, the Mass was mostly sung in German, though good German verse translations of psalm texts are lacking. Some modern solutions are suggested.

6348 QUACK, Erhard. **Il ruolo del coro e l'uso della**
as **polimelodia** [The role of the choir and the use of polymelody], *La musica nel rinnovamento liturgico: Atti della Settimana internazionale di musica sacra* (Torino: Elle Di Ci, 1966) 207–23. In Italian. See no. 501 in this volume.

An historical overview of the tensions between artistic and liturgical priorities. The structure of the Mass is also discussed.

6349 RADOLE, Giuseppe. **Richiamo all'interiorità**
as [The call for a return to interiority], *Zweiter internationaler Kongress für katholische Kirchenmusik: Zu Ehren des Heiligen Papstes Pius X* (Wien: conference, 1955) 279–80. In Italian. See no. 339 in this volume.

Composers of sacred music are often accused of a conformist attitude toward tradition and ecclesiastical prescriptions; the complaint has some foundation. Pius X's motu proprio *Tra le sollecitudini* (1903) is a call not for composers to return to C major, nor for some new prescribed liturgical style, but rather a call to the elimination of exteriorities, such as the second-hand theatrical conventions that threatened sacred music at that time, in favor of the sanctity of inspiration. *(David Bloom)*

6350 RAILLARD, F. **De la restauration du chant**
as **grégorien** [The restoration of Gregorian chant], *Congrès pour la restauration du plain-chant et de la musique d'église* (Paris: De Mourgues, 1862) 87–88. In French. See no. 3 in this volume.

6351 RAUGEL, Félix. **La cantique français** [The
as French canticle], *La musique d'église: Compte rendu du Congrès de musique sacrée* (Tourcoing: Duvivier,

1920) 67–94. *Music.* In French. See no. 93 in this volume.

Presents an historical survey of primarily liturgical music covering the period from the 9th c. to the late 19th c. Particular attention is given to the trouvère Gautier de Coincy (1177 or 1178-1236) and his work *Miracles de Nostre-Dame* (part one dating from 1214 to1222, part two from 1222 to 1233).

6352
as
REBOUD, René. **Gli strumenti musicali e il culto cristiano** [Musical instruments and the Christian liturgy], *La musica nel rinnovamento liturgico: Atti della Settimana internazionale di musica sacra* (Torino: Elle Di Ci, 1966) 225–44. In Italian. See no. 501 in this volume.

Provides an historical overview, focusing primarily on the organ, and discussing Pius X's motu proprio *Tra le sollecitudini* (1903) and the instruction *De musica sacra* (3 September 1958).

6353
as
RIPOLLÉS PÉREZ, Vicente. **Importancia de la polifonía en la liturgia y poder expresivo** [The use of polyphony in the liturgy and its expressive power], *Crónica del IV Congreso Nacional de Música Sagrada* (Vitoria: Imprenta del Montepío Diocesano, 1930) 329–248. In Spanish. See no. 155 in this volume.

Pius X's motu proprio *Tra le sollecitudini* (1903) states that Gregorian chant is the official music of the church, but sacred polyphony is also regarded as an important genre. Works by Palestrina as well as several Spanish polyphonists (including Francisco Guerrero, Tomás Luis de Victoria, and Cristóbal de Morales) are cited in support of this statement. *(José López-Calo)*

6354
as
RIPOLLÉS PÉREZ, Vicente. **La cultura litúrgica-musical del clero** [The musical and liturgical culture of the clergy], *Crónica del primer Congreso Nacional de Música Sagrada* (Valladolid: A. Martín, 1908) 59–62. In Spanish. See no. 57 in this volume.

In order to avoid the increasing presence of secular music in Spanish churches, the clergy should follow Pius X's motu proprio *Tra le sollecitudini* (1903) in deciding what to sing. *(José López-Calo)*

6355
as
ROBERT DU BOTNEAU, Gustave. **Une maîtrise grégorienne** [A Gregorian choir school], *Comptes rendus, rapports et vœux du Congrès parisien et régional de chant liturgique et de musique d'église* (Paris: Schola Cantorum, 1912) 143–48. In French. See no. 75 in this volume.

6356
as
ROBLOT, René-Pierre (Jacques Debout). **Les cantiques à l'Église** [Canticles in the Church], *Congrès international de musique sacrée: Chant et orgue* (Paris: Desclée de Brouwer, 1937) 158–63. In French. See no. 247 in this volume.

Latin is the true living language, and vernacular canticles deserve a secondary place in the liturgy.

6357
as
ROGUET, Aymon-Marie. **Valeur pastoral de la musique sacrée** [The pastoral value of sacred music], *Revue musicale* 239-240 (1957) 41–43. In French. See no. 378 in this volume.

Summary of the conference paper abstracted as no. 6358 in this volume.

6358
as
ROGUET, Aymon-Marie. **Valeur pastorale de la musique sacrée** [The pastoral value of sacred music], *Perspectives de la musique sacrée à la lumière de l'encyclique* Musicae sacrae disciplina (Paris: conference, 1959) 131–36. In French. See no. 379 in this volume.

Pius XII's encyclical *Musicae sacrae disciplina* (1955) holds that the purpose of all religious art is to assist the faithful in their worship. Sacred music, an integral part of the liturgy, has a pastoral, or nourishing, value because it develops religious virtue in the faithful by uniting them with God. An abridged version is cited as no. 6357 in this volume. *(Meredith A. McCutcheon)*

6359
as
ROJO, Casiano. **Le chant grégorien en Espagne** [Gregorian chant in Spain], *Acta generalis cantus gregoriani studiosorum conventus, Argentinensis, 16-19 Aug. 1905/Bericht des internationalen Kongresses für gregorianischen Choralgesang/ Compte rendu du Congrès international de plain-chant grégorien* (Strassburg: F.-X. Le Roux, 1905) 63–70. In French. See no. 50 in this volume.

Discusses religious music in Spain following Pius X's motu proprio *Tra le sollecitudini* (1903).

6360
as
ROJO, Casiano. **Lección práctica de canto gregoriano** [A practical lesson on Gregorian chant], *Crónica del primer Congreso Nacional de Música Sagrada* (Valladolid: A. Martín, 1908) 99–105. In Spanish. See no. 57 in this volume.

Discusses the similarities between spoken language and Gregorian chant, and offers some recommendations for singing the chant accordingly. The relationship between text and music is considered from the perspectives of recitatives, syllabic chants, and melismatic chants. *(José López-Calo)*

6361
as
ROMEU, Luis. **El canto gregoriano: Supremo modelo y fuente de inspiración de la música religiosa** [Gregorian chant: The ultimate model and inspiration for religious music], *Crónica y actas oficiales del tercer Congreso Nacional de Música Sagrada* (Barcelona: La Hormiga de Oro, 1913) 113–18. In Spanish. See no. 78 in this volume.

The Roman Catholic Church has favored Gregorian chant as the ultimate model for liturgical music because of its natural rhythm, its diatonicism, and its choral qualities. *(José López-Calo)*

6362
as
ROMITA, Fiorenzo. **De Institutis Musicae Sacrae erigendis ad eiusdem musicae sacrae restaurationem juxta S. Pium X/Die Errichtung von Kirchenmusikschulen zur Erneuerung der Kirchenmusik im Sinne des hl. Papstes Pius X.** [The establishment of the Institutum Musicae Sacrae for the restoration of church music with St. Pius X], *IV. Internationaler Kongress für Kirchenmusik in Köln: Dokumente und Berichte* (Köln: Bachem, 1962) 132–41. In Latin and German. See no. 432 in this volume.

The founding of the Pontificium Institutum Musicae Sacrae in Rome in 1911 through the efforts of Pope Pius X is a culmination of the history of papally administered music education from before the reforms of Gregory I, whose organization of the liturgy for the church year provided its formal basis.

6363
as
ROMITA, Fiorenzo. **Les principes de la législation de la musique sacrée d'après l'encyclique** *Musicae sacrae disciplina* [The legislative principles for sacred music according to the encyclical *Musicae sacrae disciplina*], *Revue musicale* 239-240 (1957) 45–53. In French. See no. 378 in this volume.

Summary of a paper. The original Italian-language version and a French-language translation are abstracted as no. 6364 in this volume.

6364
as
ROMITA, Fiorenzo. **I principi della legislazione musicale sacra secondo l'enciclica** *Musicae sacrae disciplina*/**Les principes de la législation de la musique sacrée d'après l'encyclique** *Musicae sacrae disciplina* [The legislative princi-

ples for sacred music according to the encyclical
Musicae sacrae disciplina], *Perspectives de la musique
sacrée à la lumière de l'encyclique* Musicae sacrae
disciplina (Paris: conference, 1959) 137–55. In Italian
and French. See no. 379 in this volume.

The encyclical (1955) avoids the formulation of an aesthetic or technical
law for musical composition; Pius XII considers the true source of sacred
music to be the committed Christian artist's soul. Apparent legislative conflicts between the encyclical and Pius X's motu proprio *Tra le sollecitudini*
(1903) are owing to different historical and aesthetic situations. A summary
is cited as no. 6363 in this volume. *(Meredith A. McCutcheon)*

6365 ROSSINI, Carlo. **Necessità delle scuole
as** **diocesane di musica sacra** [The need for diocesan
schools of sacred music], *Atti del [I] Congresso
internazionale di musica sacra* (Tournai: Desclée,
1952) 80–81. In Italian. See no. 303 in this volume.

6366 ROUSSEL, Gaston. **Les maîtrises d'enfants et
as** **les Offices liturgiques** [Children's choir schools and
the liturgical Offices], *Atti del [I] Congresso
internazionale di musica sacra* (Tournai: Desclée,
1952) 82–85. In French. See no. 303 in this volume.

6367 ROUSSEL, Gaston. **Le rôle exemplaire des
as** **maîtrises de cathédrales** [The exemplary role of
cathedral choir schools], *Revue musicale* 239-240
(1957) 263–66. In French. See no. 378 in this volume.

An abridged version of the conference paper is abstracted as no. 6368 in
this volume.

6368 ROUSSEL, Gaston. **Le rôle exemplaire des
as** **maîtrises de cathédrales** [The exemplary role of
cathedral choir schools], *Perspectives de la musique
sacrée à la lumière de l'encyclique* Musicae sacrae
disciplina (Paris: conference, 1959) 618–22. In French.
See no. 379 in this volume.

Cathedral choir schools rank with seminaries as the most important centers
of Catholic education. They must insist on a liturgical life together with
their pedagogical responsibilities, and must produce a liturgy that will be a
living symbol of the permanence of worship, in line with the cathedral's
moral influence on the diocese. A summary is cited as no. 6367 in this volume. *(Warren A. Bebbington)*

6369 ROZING, Peter. **Vortrag über indonesische
as** **Musik/La musique en Indonésie** [Indonesian mu-
sic], *Perspectives de la musique sacrée à la lumière de
l'encyclique* Musicae sacrae disciplina (Paris: conference, 1959) 552–58. In German and French. See no. 379
in this volume.

Brief account, with particular attention to the developing repertoires of Roman Catholic liturgical music—both through the retexting of old melodies
and new compositions—in local idioms in Java and Flores. *(David Bloom)*

6370 RUIZ AZNAR, Valentín. **Cuestiones prácticas
as** [Practical questions], *V Congreso Nacional de Música
Sagrada* (Madrid: Gráficas Dos de Mayo, 1956)
237–39. In Spanish. See no. 331 in this volume.

For the correct performance of religious music in Roman Catholic
churches, the conception of the choir must change: among other things
choirs need more members, professionally trained in a wide range of genres. *(José López-Calo)*

⟶ SABLAYROLLES, Maur. **Importancia de la
enseñanza del canto gregoriano en los
seminarios** [The importance of teaching Gregorian
chant in seminaries]. See no. 4846 in this volume.

6371 SABLAYROLLES, Mauro. **Un regard sur mon
as** *Iter hispanicum* [A look at my *Iter hispanicum*],
Congrés de la Societat Internacional de Musicologia
(Barcelona: Casa de Caritat, 1936). In French. See no.
224 in this volume.

Describes Gregorian chant research undertaken in Spain. The conference
report provides only a citation. Neither the text nor a summary of the paper
was published here.

6372 SAMSON, Joseph. **Propositions sur la qualité**
as [Propositions on quality], *Perspectives de la musique
sacrée à la lumière de l'encyclique* Musicae sacrae
disciplina (Paris: conference, 1959) 178–86. In French.
See no. 379 in this volume.

A polemic. No art of any sort is necessary to the efficacy of the Roman
Catholic Mass, but if there is to be art it should be of the highest quality; this
was better understood at the time of the Reformation by Protestant than
Catholic theologians, but also well understood in the motu proprio *Tra le
sollecitudini* (1903) of Pius X. The point of view is not mere aestheticism,
because when one speaks of art, especially sacred art, spiritual values are
always at issue. *(David Bloom)*

6373 SASTRE, Robert. **Le sacré et la musique
as** **négro-africaine** [The sacred, and black African mu-
sic], *Perspectives de la musique sacrée à la lumière de
l'encyclique* Musicae sacrae disciplina (Paris: conference, 1959) 526–30. In French. See no. 379 in this
volume.

African traditional music responds to a vision of the sacred and of humanity
that may conflict with that of Cartesian dualism, but is not at all in conflict
with that of the Bible; and its monophonic, strongly text-bound melodies
are highly comparable with those of Gregorian chant. Pius XII's recommendations in the encyclical *Musicae sacrae disciplina* for the use of indigenous music traditions by missionaries working in non-Christian societies
should be implemented in the light of this understanding. An abridged version is cited as no. 6374 in this volume. *(David Bloom)*

6374 SASTRE, Robert. **Le sacré et la musique
as** **négro-africaine** [The sacred, and black African mu-
sic], *Revue musicale* 239-240 (1957) 235–38. In
French. See no. 378 in this volume.

An abridged version of the conference paper is abstracted as no. 6373 in
this volume.

6375 SCHENK, Erich. **Instrumentale Kirchenmusik**
as [Instrumental church music], *Zweiter internationaler
Kongress für katholische Kirchenmusik: Zu Ehren des
Heiligen Papstes Pius X* (Wien: conference, 1955)
174–83. In German. See no. 339 in this volume.

In the context of the old controversy on the use of instruments other than the
organ in the Roman Catholic liturgy, considers primarily developments in
Austria since the issuing of Pius X's motu proprio *Tra le sollecitudini*
(1903) in the liturgical use of Mass settings by Classic and Romantic composers, and the creation of new settings by 32 composers of the 20th c.
(David Bloom)

6376 SCHERING, Arnold. **Zur Frage de Orgelmit-
as** **wirkung in der Kirchenmusik des 15. Jahrhunderts** [The question of organ participation in
church music of the 15th century], *Bericht über die [I]
Freiburger Tagung für Deutsche Orgelkunst*
(Augsburg: Bärenreiter, 1926) 87–91. *Music.* In German. See no. 122 in this volume.

Iconographic evidence from the altarpiece by Hubert and Jan van Eyck in
the cathedral of St. Bavon, Gent, and from the transmitted vocal music and
organ music of the period, suggests that the organ's part in church singing
was taken by a positive organ whose range did not exceed the ranges of the
voices. The fundamental tenor line was played with the left hand and the
discantus with the right, in the manner of a bicinium, not as a chord-playing
support instrument, but as a substitute for paired groups of monodic wind
instruments. *(David Bloom)*

6377 SCHMID, Andreas. **Kirchengesang nach den**
as **Liturgikern des Mittelalters** [Church singing according to the liturgists of the Middle Ages], *Akten des fünften internationalen Kongresses katholischer Gelehrten/Compte rendu du Ve Congrès scientifique international des catholiques* (München: Herder, 1901) 327–28. In German. See no. 26 in this volume.
Mentions Isidore of Seville, Amalarius of Metz, Walafrid Strabo, and Rabanus Maurus.

6378 SCHMIT, Jean-Pierre. **Une création de**
as **l'encyclique: Le responsable diocésain de la musique sacrée** [A creation of the encyclical: The diocesan director of sacred music], *Perspectives de la musique sacrée à la lumière de l'encyclique* Musicae sacrae disciplina (Paris: conference, 1959) 613–17. In French. See no. 379 in this volume.
Discusses changes in church music administration at the diocesan level resulting from Pius XII's encyclical *Musicae sacrae disciplina* (1955). *(David Bloom)*

6379 SCHMIT, Jean-Pierre. **Liturgie und Volks-**
as **gesang: Unter besonderer Berücksichtigung der Förderung der lateinischen Sprache** [Liturgy and congregational singing, with particular attention to the furthering of the Latin language], *Zweiter internationaler Kongress für katholische Kirchenmusik: Zu Ehren des Heiligen Papstes Pius X* (Wien: conference, 1955) 203–07. In German. See no. 339 in this volume.
The congregation's singing during the solemn Mass should be in Latin. Difficult melismatic and neumatic chant should be left to the choir. Vernacular hymns should be encouraged outside the liturgy itself, to fill out the *Missa lecta* and in nonliturgical services. Neotraditional vernacular songs must satisfy the requirements of good church music with respect both to texts and melody. *(David Bloom)*

6380 SCHMITT, Antonius. **Propositions sur le chant**
as **grégorien, d'après les faits universellement admis par les archéologues** [Propositions on Gregorian chant on the basis of facts that have been universally accepted by archaeologists], *Del congresso europeo di canto liturgico in Arezzo e della restaurazione del canto gregoriano: Memoria* (Lucca: author, 1882). In French. See no. 10 in this volume.

6381 SCHMITZ, Eugen. **Bachs h-moll-Messe und**
as **die Dresdner katholische Kirchenmusik** [Bach's B-minor Mass and Roman Catholic church music in Dresden], *Bericht über die Wissenschaftliche Bachtagung* (Leipzig: Peters, 1951) 320–30. In German. See no. 298 in this volume.
Argues that Bach's Mass BWV 232 was conceived for Roman Catholic liturgical use at the Dresden court, on the basis of historical evidence, liturgical style, tonality, overall form, choice and treatment of small forms, and orchestral and choral technique. *(James Donald Anderson)*

6382 SCHMITZ, Philibert. **La liturgie de Cluny** [The
as liturgy of Cluny], *Spiritualità cluniacense* (Todi: Accademia Tudertina, 1960) 83–99. In French. See no. 399 in this volume.
Surveys the contents, especially biblical texts, and performance practice of the Mass and Office chants of the Cluniac reform in the Benedictine monastic order. *(Susan Poliniak)*

6383 SCHNABL, Karl. **Charakteristik der Kirchen-**
as **musik** [Characteristic of church music], *Haydn-Zentenarfeier* (Leipzig: Breitkopf & Härtel; Wien: Artaria, 1909) 531–32. In German. See no. 65 in this volume.
The comments on Roman Catholic church music includes the subsequent panel discussion.

6384 SCHNERICH, Alfred. **Kirchenmusikalische**
as **Denkmalpflege** [Preservation of monuments of church music], *Haydn-Zentenarfeier* (Leipzig: Breitkopf & Härtel; Wien: Artaria, 1909) 546–50. In German. See no. 65 in this volume.
Discusses appropriate criteria for liturgical compositions in the Roman Catholic rite.

6385 SCHNERICH, Alfred. **Die Wiener Kirchen-**
as **musikvereine** [Vienna church music associations], *Haydn-Zentenarfeier* (Leipzig: Breitkopf & Härtel; Wien: Artaria, 1909) 544–46. In German. See no. 65 in this volume.
Associations formed in Vienna dedicated to the promotion of Roman Catholic church music.

6386 SCHREMS, Theobald. **Rom-Regensburg:**
as **Kirchenmusikalische Beziehungen** [Rome-Regensburg: Church music relations], *La musique instrumentale de la Renaissance* (Paris: Centre National de la Recherche Scientifique [CNRS], 1955) 90–92. In German. See no. 333 in this volume.

6387 SCHRÖDER, A.E. **Les origines des Lamenta-**
as **tions polyphoniques au XVe siècle dans les Pays-Bas** [The origins of polyphonic Lamentations in the Low Countries in the 15th century], *Société Internationale de Musicologie, cinquième congrès/Internationale Gesellschaft für Musikwissenschaft, fünfter Kongreß/International Society for Musical Research, Fifth Congress* (Amsterdam: Vereniging voor Nederlandse Muziekgeschiedenis, 1953) 352–59. In French. See no. 316 in this volume.

6388 SCHWAKE, Gregor. **De cantu gregoriano in**
as **ore populi** [Gregorian chant in the mouths of the congregation], *Atti del [II] Congresso internazionale di musica sacra* (Tournai: Desclée, 1952) 265–66. In Latin. See no. 303 in this volume.

6389 SÉGUY (abbé). **La musique d'église dans le**
as **diocèse de Valence** [Church music in the diocese of Valence], *Congrès pour la restauration du plain-chant et de la musique d'église* (Paris: De Mourgues, 1862) 118. In French. See no. 3 in this volume.

6390 SERRANO, Luciano. **Los tres géneros de**
as **música sagrada y su situación canónica en el santuario** [The three genres of religious music and their canonical status in the churches], *Crónica del primer Congreso Nacional de Música Sagrada* (Valladolid: A. Martín, 1908) 96–99. In Spanish. See no. 57 in this volume.
The Roman Catholic Church accepts three types of musical genres: Gregorian chant, classical polyphony, and modern religious music. According to Pius X's motu proprio *Tra le sollecitudini* (1903), Gregorian chant is the highest form of religious music. *(José López-Calo)*

6391
as

SERVIÈRES (abbé). **À travers l'histoire du chant religieux** [Across the history of religious singing], *Congrès diocésain de musique religieuse et de plain-chant* (Rodez: Carrère, 1895) 113–22. In French. See no. 22 in this volume.

6392
as

SMIJERS, Albert. **Il faut unir l'œuvre des diverses Associations de Ste-Cécile et de St-Grégoire, en conservant leur autonomie et leur caractère national** [The work of the various Caecilian and Gregorian associations must be unified, while maintaining their autonomy and national character], *Atti del [I] Congresso internazionale di musica sacra* (Tournai: Desclée, 1952) 87–88. In French. See no. 303 in this volume.

6393
as

SUÑOL BAULINAS, Gregori M. **Características generales del canto gregoriano** [The general characteristics of Gregorian chant], *Crónica y actas oficiales del tercer Congreso Nacional de Música Sagrada* (Barcelona: La Hormiga de Oro, 1913) 132–51. In Spanish. See no. 78 in this volume.

Gregorian chant, as the paradigmatic form of religious music in the Roman Catholic Church, has also a universal character that stems from its melodic richness, its natural rhythm, and the simplicity of its forms. *(José López-Calo)*

6394
as

SUSTAETA, José. **Relaciones esenciales e históricas entre la liturgia y la música** [Fundamental and historical relationships between liturgy and music], *V Congreso Nacional de Música Sagrada* (Madrid: Gráficas Dos de Mayo, 1956) 280–83. In Spanish. See no. 331 in this volume.

The historical development of Roman Catholic liturgical music is examined.

6395
as

TACK, Franz. **Das zeitgenösische kirchenmusikalische Schrifttum in Deutschland** [Contemporary writing on church music in Germany], *Atti del [I] Congresso internazionale di musica sacra* (Tournai: Desclée, 1952) 93–95. In German. See no. 303 in this volume.

6396
as

TAGLIAVINI, Luigi Ferdinando. **Le rôle liturgique de l'organiste des origines à l'époque classique** [The liturgical role of the organist, from the origins to the Classic era], *Perspectives de la musique sacrée à la lumière de l'encyclique* Musicae sacrae disciplina (Paris: conference, 1959) 367–72. In French. See no. 379 in this volume.

The role of the organ in the Roman Catholic liturgy has developed since the Middle Ages in three main directions, defined as accompaniment of, supplementation to, and alternation with the choir. Its history from the 15th to the 17th c. is presented in some detail, especially with regard to liturgical factors in the evolution of new musical forms such as ricercar, prelude, and toccata. *(David Bloom)*

6397
as

TELEU, Wilhelm. **Die Organisation und soziale Stellung der Kirchenmusiker in Deutschland** [The organization and social position of church musicians in Germany], *Atti del [I] Congresso internazionale di musica sacra* (Tournai: Desclée, 1952) 96–99. In German. See no. 303 in this volume.

6398
as

THELLIER DE PONCHEVILLE, Charles. **Le bienfait social de la liturgie** [The social benefit of the liturgy], *La musique d'église: Compte rendu du Congrès de musique sacrée* (Tourcoing: Duvivier, 1920) 27–32. In French. See no. 93 in this volume.

Music can emphasize the moral teachings of the church and enhance good will among people.

6399
as

THINOT (abbé). **Les chœurs d'église de Reims** [Church choirs of Reims], *Comptes rendus, rapports et vœux du Congrès parisien et régional de chant liturgique et de musique d'église* (Paris: Schola Cantorum, 1912) 94–109. In French. See no. 75 in this volume.

→

THOMÀS SABATER, Joan Maria. **La música de órgano** [Organ music]. See no. 1700 in this volume.

6400
as

THOMÀS SABATER, Joan Maria. **El papel que desempeña el organista en las funciones sagradas** [The role of the organist in the liturgy], *V Congreso Nacional de Música Sagrada* (Madrid: Gráficas Dos de Mayo, 1956) 172–76. In Spanish. See no. 331 in this volume.

The duties of the organist are parallel to those of the officiant priest and his assistant as well as those of the choirmaster. The organist's performance must be accommodated to the goals of the congregation, which are to pray and to worship. The organ is compared with the less noble harmonium. *(José López-Calo)*

6401
as

URSPRUNG, Otto. **Das Wesen des Kirchenstils** [The nature of the church style], *Bericht über den internationalen Kongress für Schubertforschung* (Augsburg: Benno Filser, 1929) 232–33. In German. See no. 154 in this volume.

Briefly discusses the conflict between compositional and liturgical priorities.

6402
as

VANDEWALLE, Charles. **La schola paroissiale et le chant collectif** [The parish schola and congregational singing], *Congrès régional de liturgie et de musique sacrée* (Moselle: Orphelins-Apprentis Guénange, 1923) 58–67. In French. See no. 98 in this volume.

Church services can be greatly enhanced by collective participation in the sung liturgy. Following Pope Pius X's suggestions in his motu proprio *Tra le sollecitudini* (1903), the formation of *scholae cantorum* in large churches and *scholae* in small churches is necessary to ensure such participation. *(Murat Eyüboğlu)*

6403
as

VANSON, Charles-Victor. **Sur une association canoniquement érigée en la paroisse Saint-Pierre de Nancy pour l'exécution du chant dans les offices paroissiaux** [On a canonical association erected in the parish of Saint-Pierre in Nancy for the performance of chant in the parochial ceremonies], *Congrès pour la restauration du plain-chant et de la musique d'église* (Paris: De Mourgues, 1862) 81–84. In French. See no. 3 in this volume.

6404
as

VECCHI, Guiseppe. **S. Geminiano lirica della liturgia Modenese** [St. Geminian in the lyrics of the Modenese liturgy], *Miscellanea di studi muratoriani* (Modena: Aedes Muratoriana, 1951) 524–36. *Music.* In Italian. See no. 302 in this volume.

Lodovico Antonio Muratori was the first to make known one of the oldest poetic-musical monuments of the Middle Ages, the Song of the Modenese Sentries, which contains a prayer to St. Geminian, patron saint of Modena. The discussion of the MS includes a textual and rhythmic analysis of this sequence-like song; another liturgy for St. Geminian is also included. *(Sylvia Eversole)*

6405 VIGOUREL (abbé). **Du chant ecclésiastique**
as   [On ecclesiastical singing], *Congrès diocésain de musique religieuse et de plain-chant* (Rodez: Carrère, 1895) 44–52. In French. See no. 22 in this volume.

6406 VILLETARD, Henri. **Recherche et étude de**
as   **fragments de manuscrits de plain-chant** [Research and study of fragments of plainchant manuscripts], *Mémoires de Musicologie sacrée, lus aux assises de musique religieuse* (Paris: Schola Cantorum, n.d.) 29–38. In French. See no. 34 in this volume.
The complete MSS conserved in public depositories are abundant sources needing reexamination. Musical paleography and intensive field work will lead to new comprehensive hypotheses. *(Karen Clute)*

6407 VIÑASPRE Y ORTIZ, Francisco Pérez de.
as   **Significado del *motu proprio*** [The significance of the motu proprio], *Crónica del primer Congreso Nacional de Música Sagrada* (Valladolid: A. Martín, 1908) 62–69. In Spanish. See no. 57 in this volume.
In his motu proprio *Tra le sollecitudini* (1903), Pius X attempted to reestablish the Gregorian chant and the old polyphony as the only legitimate Catholic music. The religious works of Spanish composers such as Tomás Luis de Victoria, Francisco Guerrero, and Cristóbal de Morales became part of the project of reforming religious music in Spain. *(José López-Calo)*

6408 VIVET, Armand. **La musique sacrée en France**
as   **depuis la Révolution** [Religious music in France since the Revolution], *Congrès international de musique sacrée: Chant et orgue* (Paris: Desclée de Brouwer, 1937) 147–53. In French. See no. 247 in this volume.
The rebirth of religious music began in the time of Napoléon, and reached its peak by the late 19th c.

6409 WAGNER, Johannes. **Neue Aufgaben der**
as   **katholischen Kirchenmusik im Zeitalter der pastoralliturgischen Erneuerung** [New obligations of Catholic church music in the age of pastoral-liturgical renewal], *Kirchenmusik in ökumenischer Schau* (Bern: Haupt, 1964) 60–64. In German. See no. 447 in this volume.
Summary of a paper. The full version is published in *Liturgisches Jahrbuch* XIII (1963) 22-29.

6410 WAGNER, Peter. **Über gregorianischen Choral**
as   [On Gregorian chant], *Haydn-Zentenarfeier* (Leipzig: Breitkopf & Härtel; Wien: Artaria, 1909) 550–56. In German. See no. 65 in this volume.
Discusses the musical character of sections of the Roman Catholic Mass. Pius X's motu proprio *Tra le sollecitudini* (1903) is also addressed.

6411 WAGNER, Peter. **Ueber die Zweckmässigkeit**
as   **der Choralrestauration und ihre praktische Durchführung** [On the advisability of the chant revival and its practical realization], *Acta generalis cantus gregoriani studiosorum conventus, Argentinensis, 16-19 Aug. 1905/Bericht des internationalen Kongresses für gregorianischen Choralgesang/ Compte rendu du Congrès international de plain-chant grégorien* (Strassburg: F.-X. Le Roux, 1905) 106–16. In German. See no. 50 in this volume.
Discusses Pius X's motu proprio *Tra le sollecitudini* (1903).

⟶ WAGNER, Peter. **Wie müssen die Melodien der Vatikanischen Choralausgabe ausgeführt werden?** [How must the melodies of the Vatican edi-

tion of chant be performed?]. See no. 3881 in this volume.

6412 WALTER, Rudolf. **Gregorianischer Choral**
as   **und gottesdienstliches Orgelspiel** [Gregorian chant and organ playing in the worship service], *Zweiter internationaler Kongress für katholische Kirchenmusik: Zu Ehren des Heiligen Papstes Pius X* (Wien: conference, 1955) 254–57. In German. See no. 339 in this volume.
It is desirable—following the motu proprio *Tra le sollecitudini* (1903) of Pius X—to use music based on chant melodies for the organ solo portions of the Roman Catholic worship service, but few organists are well prepared to improvise such music, and not enough composed music is being written for the purpose, especially for the preludes and interludes, an exception being music by Corbinian Gindele. Composers such as Johann Nepomuk David and Hermann Schroeder have been discouraged by organists' poor response to their initial efforts in this direction. It would help if organists were given an allowance for the purchase of new sheet music instead of having to buy it themselves. *(David Bloom)*

6413 WEINMANN, Karl. **Alte und moderne**
as   **Kirchenmusik: Historisch-kritische Bemerkungen zur Theorie und Praxis** [Old and modern church music: Historical-critical remarks on theory and practice], *Haydn-Zentenarfeier* (Leipzig: Breitkopf & Härtel; Wien: Artaria, 1909) 537–42. In German. See no. 65 in this volume.
Discusses liturgical music in light of Pius X's motu proprio *Tra le sollecitudini* (1903).

6414 WEISSENBÄCK, Andreas. **Was bedeutet die**
as   **neue liturgische Bewegung für die Kirchenmusik?** [What is the meaning of the new liturgical movement for church music?], *Bericht über den I. musikwissenschaftlichen Kongress der Deutschen Musikgesellschaft in Leipzig* (Wiesbaden: Breitkopf & Härtel, 1926) 329–34. In German. See no. 120 in this volume.
Discusses the effects of the moto proprio *Tra le sollecitudini* (1903) of Pius X on the Church. The use of the vernacular is addressed, and the importance of folk elements in worship is discussed. *(William Renwick)*

6415 WEYLAND, François-Anatole. **Rapport de M.**
as   **l'abbé Weyland** [Report by abbé Weyland], *Congrès régional de liturgie et de musique sacrée* (Moselle: Orphelins-Apprentis Guénange, 1923) 161–75. In French. See no. 98 in this volume.
Reviews writings by former church leaders regarding the crucial role of music in liturgy and offers guidance to raise the current standards. *(Murat Eyüboğlu)*

6416 WOLFF, Hellmuth Christian. **Einige moderne**
as   **Kompositionen des Ordinarium Missae/ Quelques compositions modernes de l'Ordinarium missae** [Some modern settings of the Ordinary of the Mass], *Perspectives de la musique sacrée à la lumière de l'encyclique* Musicae sacrae disciplina (Paris: conference, 1959) 437–46. In German and French. See no. 379 in this volume.
Settings include those that, like Stravinsky's 1948 Mass, are appropriate for liturgical use and others, like Janáček's *Mša glagolskaja* (Glagolitic Mass, 1926-27), that are subjectively expressive of the text and not liturgical in spirit. Works by younger German and Swiss composers, Catholic and Protestant, such as Benno Ammann's *Missa "Defensor pacis"* (1946), evoke the linear polyphony of the 16th c. Purely instrumental settings include Hermann Schroeder's *Orgel-Ordinarium "Cunctipotens genitor Deus"* (published 1964) and the author's orchestral *Sinfonia da missa* (1949). A summary is cited as no. 6417 in this volume. *(Warren A. Bebbington)*

6417 WOLFF, Hellmuth Christian. **Quelques compo-**
as **sitions de l'*Ordinarium missae* modernes** [Some
modern settings of the Ordinary of the Mass], *Revue
musicale* 239-240 (1957) 205–08. In French. See no.
378 in this volume.

Abridged version of a conference paper. The original German-language
version, and a French-language translation, are abstracted as no. 6416 in
this volume.

6418 YUNG, Alfred. **Note sur la musique d'église**
as **dans le diocèse de Verdun** [Church music in the diocese of Verdun], *Congrès pour la restauration du
plain-chant et de la musique d'église* (Paris: De
Mourgues, 1862) 117. In French. See no. 3 in this
volume.

6419 ZAGIBA, Franz. **Das Studium der Kirchen-**
as **musikwissenschaft au den Universitäten und
Theologischen Hochschulen** [The musicological
study of sacred music in universities and seminaries],
*Zweiter internationaler Kongress für katholische
Kirchenmusik: Zu Ehren des Heiligen Papstes Pius X*
(Wien: conference, 1955) 316–18. In German. See no.
339 in this volume.

Briefly surveys the history of the musicology of church music as an independent discipline, from Peter Wagner's establishment of an Académie
Grégorienne at the Université de Fribourg in 1901. *(David Bloom)*

6420 ZAGIBA, Franz. **Wie wird die westliche**
as **Liturgie in kirchenslawischer Sprache noch
heute gepflegt?** [In what ways is the Western liturgy
in Church Slavonic still cultivated today?], *Zweiter
internationaler Kongress für katholische
Kirchenmusik: Zu Ehren des Heiligen Papstes Pius X*
(Wien: conference, 1955) 89–92. In German. See no.
339 in this volume.

The Glagolitic liturgy created by Sts. Cyril and Methodius has been in continuous use among Roman Catholic speakers of Slavic languages, particularly in Croatia, since the 9th c., under a privilege granted (except in
885-1248) from Rome. The privilege has been renewed and in some ways
extended in the 20th c.; a new official edition of the missal in 1927 inspired
modern composers such as Janáček. On the island of Krk in Croatia the
Glagolitic liturgy preserves a very old polyphonic practice, which is now
being intensively studied. *(David Bloom)*

6421 ZAUNER, Franz. **Die liturgische Konstitution**
as **und ihre Grundtendenzen** [The liturgical constitution and its fundamental tendencies], *Die Kirchenmusik
und das II. Vatikanische Konzil* (Graz: Styria, 1965)
13–32. In German. See no. 480 in this volume.

Summary remarks on the theology of the new Roman Catholic liturgical
charter, *Sacrosanctum concilium*, promulgated by the Vatican Council II in
December 1963. *(David Bloom)*

94 Protestant

6422 AMELN, Konrad. **Die Wurzeln des deutschen**
as **Kirchenliedes der Reformation** [The roots of the
German Reformation hymn], *Kirchenmusik in
ökumenischer Schau* (Bern: Haupt, 1964) 47–51.
Bibliog. In German. See no. 447 in this volume.

Gregorian chant, cantio, and orally transmitted sacred and secular traditional song all contributed to the origin of Lutheran hymnody. *(David Bloom)*

6423 ATKINS, Charles L. **William Billings: His**
as **psalm and hymn tunes,** *Addresses at the International Hymnological Conference* (New York: Hymn
Society of America, 1962) 3–16. See no. 438 in this
volume.

Billings has been little appreciated since his death in 1800, but he had a de-
cisively unifying influence on the chaotic state of New England church
singing as it was ca. 1770. His life, works, and influence are surveyed.
(Michael Adelson)

6424 BALTHASAR, Karl. **Kirchenmusik und**
as **neuere evangelische Liturgik** [Church music and
the new Lutheran liturgy], *Bericht über den I.
musikwissenschaftlichen Kongress der Deutschen
Musikgesellschaft in Leipzig* (Wiesbaden: Breitkopf &
Härtel, 1926) 353–58. In German. See no. 120 in this
volume.

Discusses contemporary reform in Lutheran worship, focusing on the re-
discovery of traditional Lutheran music, the role of the organ, and the significance of J.S. Bach. *(William Renwick)*

6425 BLANKENBURG, Walter. **Die evangelische**
as **Kirchenmusik in Deutschland im Lichte der
Liturgie** [Lutheran church music in Germany from the
liturgical standpoint], *Bericht über den Internationalen
Kongress für Kirchenmusik/Compte rendu du Congrès
international de musique sacrée* (Bern: Haupt, 1953)
42–43. In German. See no. 312 in this volume.

6426 BLANKENBURG, Walter. **Die Nachwirkung**
as **der artes liberales in den reformatorischen
Gebieten und deren Auflösungsprozeß** [The influence of the liberal arts in Lutheran areas, and their
decline], *Internationale Konferenz über das Leben und
Werk W.A. Mozarts* (Praha: Svaz Československých
Skladatelů, 1956) 60–62. In German. See no. 360 in this
volume.

Luther tended in some ways to hold music outside of the medieval tradition
of the seven liberal arts, as being closer to theology and therefore higher
than the others. In other ways, he and his early followers tended to the reck-
oning of music as of the trivium instead of the quadrivium, with their insistence on its expressive, hence rhetorical value. The struggle between onto-
logical and ethical understandings of music was to last into the 18th c.
(David Bloom)

6427 BLANKENBURG, Walter. **Offizielle und**
as **inoffizielle liturgische Bestrebungen in der
Evangelischen Kirche Deutschlands** [Official
and unofficial liturgical endeavors in Germany's
Protestant church], *Kirchenmusik in ökumenischer
Schau* (Bern: Haupt, 1964) 64–67. In German. See no.
447 in this volume.

Summary of a conference paper. The full version appears in *Liturgisches
Jahrbuch* XIII (1963)70-83.

6428 BRUNNER, Adolf. **Liturgisch-musikalische**
as **Möglichkeiten im reformierten Gottesdienst:
Zum Vorschlag der Zürcher Liturgie-
kommission** [Possibilities for liturgical music in the
Reformed church service: The proposal of the Zurich
Liturgiekommission], *Kirchenmusik in ökumenischer
Schau* (Bern: Haupt, 1964) 68–73. In German. See no.
447 in this volume.

The Zurich Cantonal Synod of the Reformed Church has set up a Commission on the Liturgy to carry out a revision of all its liturgical books; musical
aspects of the project and their theological underpinnings are discussed.
(David Bloom)

6429
as
CELLIER, Alexandre. **Le rôle de l'orgue dans le culte protestant** [The role of the organ in the Protestant religion], *Compte rendu du Congrès d'orgue tenu à l'Université de Strasbourg. IV* (Strasbourg: Société Strasbourgeoise de Librairie Sostralib, 1934) 148–51. In French. See no. 199 in this volume.

6430
as
CHRISTOPHER, Cyril Stanley. **Playing for a congregation,** *The organist and the congregation: Lectures and a sermon delivered at the First Conference of Congregational Organists* (London: Independent Press, 1952) 24–30. See no. 307 in this volume.

As regards Congregational parishes, includes rules and guidelines for music choice (which depends on the size and communal disposition of the congregation, as well as the instrument to be played) and for the direction and accompaniment of hymns. *(Susan Poliniak)*

6431
as
CHRISTOPHER, Cyril Stanley. **The work of the organist in a Congregational church,** *The organist and the congregation: Lectures and a sermon delivered at the First Conference of Congregational Organists* (London: Independent Press, 1952) 9–23. See no. 307 in this volume.

The factors over which an organist in a member church of the Congregational Church of England and Wales has control are the choice of music, the standard of performances, and the contribution to the fellowship of the church. Music itself in Congregational services serves to allow the congregation to take an active part in the service, to emphasize an aspect of Christian teaching, and to assist in creating and maintaining a spiritual atmosphere. The organist must have good technique, good taste in worthy music, and a musical sensibility that never oversteps the bounds of good taste. Guidelines for the performance of anthem accompaniments, voluntaries, and extemporizations are supplied. *(Susan Poliniak)*

6432
as
DOBBS, Jack P.B. **Choir training and repertory,** *The organist and the congregation: Lectures and a sermon delivered at the First Conference of Congregational Organists* (London: Independent Press, 1952) 41–55. See no. 307 in this volume.

Provides guidelines on how to choose music for worship in Congregational churches and how to perform it in the most worthy manner. The music must be performed for God, not the worshipers, but should stir the individual to devotion and act as a channel for worship itself. The elements of rhythm, melody, harmony, and form must all be appropriate to the setting and occasion. Music for children's choirs must be suitable without being cloying. Detailed guidelines for preparation (including how to conduct rehearsals) and performance are supplied. *(Susan Poliniak)*

⟶
EICKHOFF, Paul. **Nach welchem Rhythmus müssen die Melodien der deutschen evangelischen Kirchenlieder gesungen werden?** [To which rhythms must the melodies of the German Protestant hymns be sung?]. See no. 5311 in this volume.

6433
as
GAGNEBIN, Henri. **Les Psaumes huguenots** [Huguenot psalms], *Deuxième congrès international d'esthétique et de Science de l'art* (Paris: Librairie Félix Alcan, 1937) II, 510–15. In French. See no. 249 in this volume.

Brief historical account of 16th-c. French-language Protestant psalmody, and its revival, 1902-37.

6434
as
GÖLZ, Richard. **Die heutige Lage der evangelischen Kirche auf dem Gebiete des Gottesdienstes** [The current situation of the Protestant church vis-à-vis the church service], *Bericht über den Deutschen Kongreß für Kirchenmusik* (Kassel: Bärenreiter, 1928) 55–61. In German. See no. 135 in this volume.

Among the many urgent problems facing Lutheran church music today there are also positive factors, in particular the involvement of young people in the Singbewegung. It is hoped that Lutheran youth will become more active in church choirs and in helping to renovate the dismal state of congregational singing as well. *(David Bloom)*

6435
as
HÖGNER, Friedrich. **Das Amt des evangelischen Kirchenmusikers heute** [The position of the Protestant church musician today], *Musica sacra in unserer Zeit* (Berlin: Merseburger], 1960) 27–35. In German. See no. 403 in this volume.

6436
as
JEANS, Susi. **Anglikanische Kirchenmusik** [Anglican church music], *Bericht über den Internationalen Kongress für Kirchenmusik/Compte rendu du Congrès international de musique sacrée* (Bern: Haupt, 1953) 57–61. In German. See no. 312 in this volume.

6437
as
MAHRENHOLZ, Christhard. **Orgel und Liturgie** [Organ and liturgy], *Bericht über die dritte Tagung für Deutsche Orgelkunst* (Kassel: Bärenreiter, 1928) 58–71. In German. See no. 136 in this volume.

Theological discussion, from the Lutheran standpoint, of the organ's liturgical function, which is to serve the divine word, in cantus firmus and chorale, as an independent part of the service. Recognizing the separateness of the organ's function is a necessary precondition to any new flourishing of organ playing, building, and composition.

6438
as
MENDELSSOHN, Arnold. **Die Orgel im Gottesdienst** [The organ in church services], *Bericht über die dritte Tagung für Deutsche Orgelkunst* (Kassel: Bärenreiter, 1928) 72–77. In German. See no. 136 in this volume.

The Lutheran divine service is to be regarded as a Gesamtkunstwerk in which the functions of the musician and of the pastor must be subordinated to the function of the service as a whole. Practical methods for instituting these principles in the work of the organist (including registration), the choir, and the singing congregation are discussed.

6439
as
MICKLEM, T. Caryl. **Worship and prophecy: A sermon,** *The organist and the congregation: Lectures and a sermon delivered at the First Conference of Congregational Organists* (London: Independent Press, 1952) 56–61. See no. 307 in this volume.

Organists in Congregational churches are instruments of worship whose purpose is to spread the word of their faith. Within the discipline of the Gospel, organists must do their best and come prepared to services not just in a musical capacity, but as worshipers as well. None but the best will do for God, and all must be done with the Gospel in mind. *(Susan Poliniak)*

6440
as
MOBERG, Carl-Allan. **Zur Geschichte des schwedischen Kirchen-Gesangs** [On the history of Swedish church songs], *Société Internationale de Musicologie: Premier Congrès Liège/Compte rendu/ Internationale Gesellschaft für Musikwissenschaft: Erster Kongress Lüttich—Kongressbericht/International Society for Musical Research: First Congress Liège: Report* (London: Plainsong and Mediaeval Music Society, 1930) 184–90. *Music.* In German. See no. 178 in this volume.

Roman Catholic church music played an important role in Sweden during the Reformation, as the reformers wanted to revise only the texts, not the music itself. *(Scott Fruehwald)*

6441
as
NIEVERGELT, Edwin. **Zeitgenössische evangelische Kirchenmusik (Zusammenfassung)** [Contemporary Protestant church music (Summary)], *Bericht über den Internationalen Kongress für Kirchenmusik/Compte rendu du Congrès international*

de musique sacrée (Bern: Haupt, 1953) 50–52. In German. See no. 312 in this volume.

Important changes in the course of the 20th c. include the change from Romantic to modern style, the renaissance of older music (especially Schütz), the change in the nature and use of the organ, the change in the use of the human voice, and changes in the liturgy itself. The use of Protestant chorales, return to the Baroque concept of the word-tone relationship, and free interpretation of Schützian compositional forms are also discussed. *(Larry Laskowski)*

6442 PIZOT-MONNIER, Madame Pierre. **De l'orgue**
as **dans le culte protestant** [The organ in the Protestant religion], *Compte rendu du Congrès d'orgue tenu à l'Université de Strasbourg. IV* (Strasbourg: Société Strasbourgeoise de Librairie Sostralib, 1934) 151–57. In French. See no. 199 in this volume.

The desirable attributes of an instrument, the training and functions of organists, and the choice of repertoire are discussed.

6443 PLATH, Johannes. **Die liturgischen Aufgaben**
as **des Organisten und Chordirigenten** [The liturgical duties of the organist and choir director], *Bericht über den Deutschen Kongreß für Kirchenmusik* (Kassel: Bärenreiter, 1928) 32–40. In German. See no. 135 in this volume.

Outlines the responsibilities of Lutheran church musicians to the liturgical service itself, the community, and the intellectual tradition, with reference to the question of how these can be reflected in their training. In the state-sponsored Lehrerseminar system before the 1918 Revolution, the focus was on music, and liturgy was not studied systematically. State and church should collaborate to make liturgy an obligatory examinable subject in institutions where church music is taught. *(David Bloom)*

6444 RIMBAULT, Lucien. **Le psautier huguenot,**
as **lien universel d'amitié entre les peuples**
(Résumé) [The Huguenot psalter, universal bond of friendship among peoples (Summary)], *Bericht über den Internationalen Kongress für Kirchenmusik/ Compte rendu du Congrès international de musique sacrée* (Bern: Haupt, 1953) 52–54. In French. See no. 312 in this volume.

The Huguenot psalter, in its many translations, has appealed to a wide diversity of ethnic and economic groups. It may be one of the most precious of the Reformed Church's offerings to the ecumenical movement. *(Larry Laskowski)*

6445 SANNEMANN, Friedrich. **Grundsätze**
as **evangelischer Kirchenmusik** [Principles of Protestant church music], *Haydn-Zentenarfeier* (Leipzig: Breitkopf & Härtel; Wien: Artaria, 1909) 576–80. In German. See no. 65 in this volume.

Discusses the effect of church reforms from 1800 to 1830.

6446 SCHIØRRING, Nils. **Nachwirkungen der**
as **Lobwasserpsalter in Dänemark** [Aftereffects of Lobwasser's psalter in Denmark], *Norddeutsche und nordeuropäische Musik* (Kassel; New York: Bärenreiter, 1965) 22–26. *Facs., music.* In German. See no. 467 in this volume.

Around the beginning of the 1570s the thinking of the Danish preacher Niels Hemmingsen began to take a Calvinist turn, and shortly afterward the Geneva Psalter, in the German translation of Ambrosius Lobwasser, arrived. The earliest Danish translations of Lobwasser's texts date from 1600, in MS sources; relatively few printed Danish versions exist, and there is evidence that some spread by oral transmission. Signs of Lobwasser influence become much rarer after ca. 1620, when a purely Lutheran doctrine had begun to prevail. *(David Bloom)*

6447 SCHWEIZER, Julius. **Vom legitimen Ort kirch-**
as **licher Musik im Gottesdienst der reformierten**

Kirchen der deutschen Schweiz [The legitimate role in worship of church music in the Reformed churches of German-speaking Switzerland], *Kirchenmusik in ökumenischer Schau* (Bern: Haupt, 1964) 43–47. In German. See no. 447 in this volume.

Since the Baroque period, it has been understood that Zwingli's theology permits music in Reformed church services, though Zwingli himself rejected it. A still more central role could be given to music in worship, as long as it is performed by the congregation, with appropriate melodies that do not overwhelm the text, and choir and organ serving strictly accessory functions. *(David Bloom)*

6448 SMEND, Julius. **Die notwendige Beziehung**
as **zwischen dem Kirchenmusiker und dem Vertreter des Predigtamts** [The necessary relation between the church musician and the person who holds the office of preacher], *Bericht über den Deutschen Kongreß für Kirchenmusik* (Kassel: Bärenreiter, 1928) 22–31. In German. See no. 135 in this volume.

Close cooperation and friendship between pastor and musician in the Lutheran church may be modeled on the relationship between Luther himself and Johann Walter. General principles for their joint work are examined in historical, theological, and practical dimensions. *(David Bloom)*

6449 SØRENSEN, Søren. **Allgemeines über den**
as **dänischen protestantischen Kirchengesang** [General remarks on Danish Protestant hymnody], *Norddeutsche und nordeuropäische Musik* (Kassel; New York: Bärenreiter, 1965) 11–21. In German. See no. 467 in this volume.

The monophonic melodies of the first Danish hymnal, Hans Thomissøn's *Den danske psalmbog* (1569), are derived largely from the German Reformation, but well over two-thirds of them are different enough from the German models to be regarded as original; others are tied directly to Danish traditional music. The further history and musical character of Danish hymnody are briefly traced from Thomas Kingo's *Den voordnede ny kirke-psalme-bog* (1699) through Thomas Laub's *Dansk kirkesang* (1918). *(David Bloom)*

6450 STEWART, Douglas. **The organist and his min-**
as **ister,** *The organist and the congregation: Lectures and a sermon delivered at the First Conference of Congregational Organists* (London: Independent Press, 1952) 31–40. See no. 307 in this volume.

The organist and minister in a Congregational church must each understand what worship is and what it demands of the worshipers. Organists should not indulge in self-glorification through their music, but must also realize that religion cannot be served by bad art. Organists should educate their ministers in musical matters, when needed. Overall, good technique, appropriate musical taste, and a lack of musical snobbishness are required of an organist, who must also understand that the music cannot overshadow spiritual aspects. *(Susan Poliniak)*

6451 STOLLBERG, Oskar. **Die musikalisch-**
as **liturgische Bewegung in der zweiten Hälfte de 19. Jahrhunderts im Spiegel unbekannter Briefe und Aufzeichnungen dieser Zeit** [The musical-liturgical movement of the second half of the 19th century as reflected in unknown letters and records of the period], *Bericht über den internationalen musikwissenschaftlichen Kongreß* (Kassel: Bärenreiter, 1963) 236–38. In German. See no. 452 in this volume.

Documents left by participants in the Romantic restoration of Protestant church music in Germany show that, contrary to common belief, the movement was not merely a revival of old practice but involved the creation of new work; that it attained a wide influence; that its aims were not vague and mystical; and that it was not complacent. *(David Bloom)*

6452 SYDNOR, James Rawlings. **Twentieth-century**
as **hymnody in the United States,** *Addresses at the In-*

ternational Hymnological Conference (New York: Hymn Society of America, 1962) 28–41. See no. 438 in this volume.

Protestant hymnody in the U.S. has been shaped by the work of British and American hymnologists, organizations such as the Hymn Society of America, and the influence of the gospel song movement. American hymnals are characterized by eclecticism, with an active search for fresh contemporary, international, and traditional-music sources. Congregational singing has been stimulated by efforts in the church school; the composition of organ preludes based on hymns; musical training offered by theological seminaries, conferences and workshops; the awareness of the importance of acoustics in church architecture; and the revival of the pipe organ. *(Barbara B. Heyman)*

6453 WALLAU, René. **Die kirchliche Bedeutung der**
as **Bachschen Musik** [The significance of Bach's music in church], *Kongreß-Bericht: Gesellschaft für Musikforschung* (Kassel; Basel: Bärenreiter, 1950) 107–11. In German. See no. 299 in this volume.

6454 WATERMAN, Richard Alan. **Gospel hymns of a**
as **negro church in Chicago,** *Journal of the International Folk Music Council* III (1951) 87–93. See no. 296 in this volume.

Details the sequence of musical events at a typical Sunday service, and discusses other church events that involve music. The name of the church is not provided. *(James R. Cowdery)*

6455 WOLF, Johannes. **Die Aufgaben des evan-**
as **gelischen Kirchenmusikers in geschichtlicher Beleuchtung** [The duties of the Lutheran church musician in a historical light], *Bericht über den Deutschen Kongreß für Kirchenmusik* (Kassel: Bärenreiter, 1928) 41–47. In German. See no. 135 in this volume.

A survey. The concept of the professionally trained church singer arose in the earliest period of the church, and has continued through the development of the roles of choir, organ, and congregational singing. Church music performance and especially composition should represent the best of contemporary music, as it did in the medieval, Reformation, and Baroque periods. *(David Bloom)*

6456 ZIMMERMANN, Heinz Werner. **Neue Musik**
as **und neues Kirchenlied** [New music and a new hymnody], *Kirchenmusik in ökumenischer Schau* (Bern: Haupt, 1964) 79–83. In German. See no. 447 in this volume.

Summarizes a discussion of the possibilities of hymns in contemporary idioms from an Protestant perspective. A full version appeared in *Musik und Gottesdienst* VI (1962), and an expanded version in *Musik und Kirche* II (1963).

95 Buddhist

6457 GROOT, Jan Jakob Maria de. **Buddhist masses**
as **for the dead at Amoy: An ethnological essay,** *Actes du sixième Congrès international des orientalistes* (Leiden: Brill, 1885) 120. See no. 11 in this volume.

99 Other

6458 HERSKOVITS, Melville J. **Some economic as-**
as **pects of the Afrobahian Candomblé,** *Miscellanea Paul Rivet octogenario dicata* (México, D.F.: Universidad Nacional Autónoma de México, 1958) II, 227–48. See no. 394 in this volume.

6459 SCHNEIDER, Marius. **Les fondements**
as **intellectuels et psychologiques du chant magique** [The intellectual and psychological foundations of magical singing], *Les colloques de Wégimont. [I: Ethnomusicologie I]* (Bruxelles: Elsevier, 1956) 56–63. In French. See no. 340 in this volume.

The world was originally created by sound. Emanating from the primordial abyss (the Tao) and becoming suffused with light, it was gradually converted into matter. The materialization, however, cannot be said to have been completed since all objects retain some of the sound-light substance by which they were formed. Creation-chants, which came from these primordial spaces, are from gods who created beings from parts of themselves in an act of sacrifice. Magicians believe that the hunger of the gods is satisfied by returning the chants to them. Chant that alternates between heaven and earth is the most substantial form of mutual sacrifice and maintains life in the universe. Music is the essence of heaven and earth. *(Helen-Ursula Katz)*

Conference of the International Folk Music Council, Bloomington, 1950 (see no. 296).

Reproduced with permission of the Indiana University Archives (PS50-1612).

1. Reidar Thoralf Christiansen **2.** E. Eddy Nadel **3.** V. Dolan **4.** Sam Eskin **5.** Ahmed Saygun **6.** Bertrand Harris Bronson **7.** J. Olcutt Sanders **8.** Joseph Raben **9.** Ruth Crawford Seeger **10.** Charles Seeger **11.** J. Mickey **12.** B. Lattimer **13.** H. Reeves **14.** L. Austen **15.** Sidney Robertson Cowell **16.** George Pullen Jackson **17.** Evelyn K. Wells **18.** Mrs. La Farge **19.** Jonas Balys **20.** Duncan Emrich **21.** May Gadd **22.** A. Kaufman **23.** H. Darington **24.** Seán Ó Súilleabháin **25.** Sirvart Poladian **26.** Laurits Bødker **27.** Albert Lord **28.** Samuel P. Bayard **29.** Nilufer Saygun **30.** Herbert Halpert **31.** Elizabeth Burchenal **32.** Åke Campbell **33.** Otto Andersson **34.** Mrs. Lumpkin **35.** Ben Gray Lumpkin **36.** Sigurd Emanuel Erixon **37.** Jasim Uddin **38.** George Herzog **39.** Maud Karpeles **40.** Marius Barbeau **41.** Walter Anderson **42.** Stith Thompson.

CONFERENCE LOCATIONS

Algeria
Al-Jazā'ir, Asian studies, 1905: 48bs
  Byzantine studies, 1939 (not held), 263bs

Argentina
Buenos Aires, American studies, 1910: 68bs
La Plata, American studies, 1932: 198bs

Australia
Canberra, Aboriginal studies, 1961: 430bs

Austria
Bad Aussee and Salzburg, professional training,
  1953: 318bs
Graz, on Vatican Council II, 1964: 480bs
Innsbruck, experimental psychology, 1911: 70bs
Salzburg, Mozart, 1931: 193bs
  musicology, 1964: 491bs
Wien, American studies, 1908: 61bs
  anthropology, 1956: 364bs
  Beethoven-Zentenarfeier, 1927: 141bs
  copyright, 1932: 200bs
  musicology, 1927: 142bs: 147bs
  musicology, 1952: 317bs
  musicology, 1956: 365bs
  Roman Catholic church music, 1954: 339bs
  Schubert, 1928: 154bs
  traditional music, 1960: 424bs

Belgium
Antwerpen, archaeology, 1930: 162bs
  copyright, 1885: 12bs
  Flemish music, 1934: 210bs
Brugge, culture, 1925: 119bs
Bruxelles, American studies, 1879: 6bs
  anthropology, 1948: 282bs
  anthropology and archaeology, 1935: 221bs
  archaeology, 1892: 16bs
  cultural policies, 1932: 195bs
  historiography, 1923: 100bs
  librarianship, 1955: 344bs, 345bs
  pedagogy, 1953: 322bs, 323bs
  philosophy, 1953: 321bs
  public art, 1898: 24bs
  Renaissance court music, 1957: 367bs
  18th-c. studies, 1936: 220bs
Dinant, Soc. Archéologique de Namur, 1903: 41bs
Enghien, archaeology and history, 1898: 25bs
Gent, archaeology and history, 1896: 23bs
  Belgian culture, 1913: 89bs
  phonetics, 1938: 259bs
Liège, acoustics, 1965: 504bs
  archaeology and history, 1909: 64bs
  archaeology and history, 1932: 197bs
  chanson de geste, 1957: 374bs
  public art, 1905: 49bs
  traditional music, 1958: 392bs
Mechelen, archaeology and history, 1911: 73bs
Mons, francophone unity, 1911: 74bs
Namur, 1938: 260bs
Wégimont, ars nova, 1955: 351bs
  Baroque, 1957: 386bs
  ethnomusicology, 1954: 340bs
  ethnomusicology, 1956: 366bs
  ethnomusicology, 1958: 401bs
  ethnomusicology, 1960: 401bs

Bosnia and Herzegovina
Bjelašnica, folklore, 1955: 315bs
Mostar and Trebinje, folklore, 1962: 455bs

Brazil
Recife, traditional music, 1934: 214bs
Rio de Janeiro, American studies, 1922: 99bs
São Paulo, singing in Portuguese, 1937: 253bs
  traditional music, 1954: 337bs

Bulgaria
Sofija, Byzantine studies, 1934: 215bs

Canada
Ontario, Stratford, 20th-c. music, 1960: 423bs
Québec, Montreal, psychiatry, 1961: 437bs
  Québec, American studies, 1906: 56bs
  Québec, traditional music, 1961: 442bs

Colombia
Cartagena de Indias, ethomusicology: 1963: 461bs

Costa Rica
San José, American studies, 1958: 398bs

Croatia
Novi Vinodolski, folklore, 1964: 490bs
Opatija, folklore, 1951: 306bs
Pula, folklore, 1952: 315bs
Varaždin, folklore, 1957: 382bs

Czech Republic
Brno, Janáček, 1958: 389bs
  Janáček, 1965: 496bs
Praha, composers and critics, 1947: 278bs
  criticism, 1930: 183bs
  folk arts, 1928: 152bs
  intonation theory and Gestalt psychology, 1963:
    471bs
  Marxism, 1963: 470bs
  Mozart, 1956: 360bs
  pedagogy, 1936: 232bs
  philosophy, 1934: 213bs
Zlín, traditional music, 1962: 459bs

Denmark
København, acoustics, 1962: 448bs
  anthropology, 1939: 255bs
  copyright, 1933: 202bs
  Orgelbewegung, 1955: 348bs
  traditional music, 1957: 371bs
  traditional narrative, 1959: 411bs

Egypt
Al-Qāhirah, archaeology, 1909: 63bs
  Arab music, 1932: 196bs

Equatorial Guinea
Malabo, West African studies, 1951: 310bs

France
Aix-en-Provence, language and literature of
  southern France, 1958: 388bs
Arras, Renaissance, 1954: 328bs
  20th-c. arts, 1955: 341bs
Avignon, language and literature of southern
  France, 1955: 342bs

Biarritz, traditional music, 1953: 320bs
Cluny, St. Odo and St. Odilo, 1949: 290bs
Dijon, librarianship, 1965: 499bs
Liège, musicology, 1930: 178bs
Luxeuil, Columbanus, 1950: 301bs
Marseille, acoustics, 1958: 393bs
  Syria, 1919: 92bs
Metz, Roman Catholic church music, 1922: 98bs
Montauban, Baroque, 1963: 469bs
Nancy, American studies, 1875: 5bs
Neuilly-sur-Seine, lute music, 1957: 377bs,
Niort, ethnography, 1896: 21bs
Paris, aesthetics, 1937: 249bs
  American studies, 1890: 14bs
  American studies, 1947: 277bs
  anthropology, 1960: 421bs
  anthropology and archaeology, 1931: 192bs
  Asian drama, 1958-59: 397bs
  Asian studies, 1949: 294bs
  Byzantine studies, 1948: 287bs
  Christian religious music, 1957: 378bs, 379bs
  copyright, 1926: 130bs
  copyright, 1937: 245bs
  Debussy, 1962: 456bs
  dramatic arts, 1927: 138bs
  film, 1926: 129bs
  folklore, 1900: 31bs
  folklore, 1937: 251bs
  higher education, 1900: 35bs
  history, 1835: 1bs
  history, 1838: 2bs
  history, 1900: 27bs
  history of art, 1921: 94bs, 95bs
  intervals and scales, 1960: 420bs
  librarianship, 1951: 309bs
  mass media, 1937: 244bs
  Mozart, 1956: 358bs
  musicians, 1904: 46bs
  musicology, 1900: 32bs
  musicology, 1912: 80ap
  pedagogy, 1937: 246bs
  philosophy, 1900: 36bs, 37bs
  psychology, 1937: 250bs
  publishing and printing, 1931: 191bs
  Renaissance instrumental music, 1954: 333bs
  Roman Catholic church music, 1860: 3bs
  Roman Catholic church music, 1900: 34bs
  Roman Catholic church music, 1911: 75bs
  Roman Catholic church music, 1937: 247bs
  social education, 1900: 28bs
  sociological aspects of radio, 1954: 334bs
  sound recording and reproduction, 1965: 511bs
  Western music, 1900: 29bs, 33bs
  16th-c. music and poetry, 1953: 326bs
Rodez, Gregorian chant, 1895: 22bs
Rouen, Normandie millennium, 1912: 77bs
  13th centenary of the Abbaye St-Pierre de
    Jumièges, 1954: 336bs
Royaumont, Asian drama, 1959: 397bs
  Renaissance drama, 1963: 472bs
  Renaissance festivals, 1955: 350bs
Saint-Brieuc, Celtic people, 1867: 4bs
Strasbourg, Gregorian chant, 1905: 50bs
  Roman Catholic church music, 1921: 96bs
Tourcoing, Roman Catholic church music, 1919:
  93bs

Slovenia
Bled, folklore, 1959: 404bs

Spain
Barcelona, archaeology, 1929: 156bs
   musicology, 1936: 224bs
   Roman Catholic church music, 1912: 78bs
Madrid, American studies, 1881: 8bs
   copyright, 1929: 159bs
   publishing, 1908: 1908: 60bs
   Roman Catholic church music, 1954: 331bs
Pamplona, traditional music, 1953: 320bs
Sevilla, copyright, 1935: 223bs
Valladolid, Roman Catholic church music, 1907:
   57bs
Vitoria, Roman Catholic church music, 1928:
   155bs

Sweden
Göteborg, American studies, 1924: 118bs
Malmö, Orgelbewegung, 1955: 348bs
Stockholm, art history, 1931: 208bs
   copyright, 1938: 261bs
Stockholm and Uppsala, librarianship, 1962:
   457bs

Switzerland
Basel, musicology, 1906: 53bs, 54bs
   musicology, 1924: 102bs, 103bs
   musicology, 1949: 289bs
   traditional music, 1948: 281bs
Bern, church music, 1952: 312bs
   church music, 1962: 447bs

Crésuz, Roman Catholic church music and
   modern languages, 1962: 449bs
Fribourg, Roman Catholic church music, 1965:
   501bs
Genève, Asian studies, 1894: 20bs
   rhythm, 1926: 123bs
   rhythm, 1965: 502bs
Zürich, historical sciences, 1938: 262bs

Turkey
İstanbul, Byzantine studies, 1955: 347bs

Uganda
Kampala, African traditional music, 1963: 465bs

United Kingdom — England
Cambridge, American studies, 1952: 313bs
   Asian studies, 1954: 329bs
   librarianship and instruments, 1959: 406bs
Dorking, music in the counties, 1948: 283bs
London, copyright, 1931: 190bs
   drama in the counties, 1948: 283bs
   musicology, 1911: 71bs
   organ and choral music, 1957: 375bs
   phonetics, 1935: 222bs
   psychology, 1892: 17bs
   traditional music, 1952: 314bs
Oxford, Congregational organists, 1951: 307bs

United Kingdom — Scotland
Edinburgh, psychology, 1948: 284bs

United States of America
California, Los Angeles, Asian music and related
   arts, 1960: 418bs
Connecticut, New Haven, psychology, 1930:
   160bs
Illinois, Carbondale, communication, 1965: 497bs,
   498bs
   Chicago, anthropology, 1893: 19bs
   Chicago, folklore, 1893: 18bs
   Chicago, musicology, 1936: 230bs
Indiana, Bloomington, traditional music, 1950:
   296bs

Massachusetts, Cambridge, acoustics, 1956: 369bs
   Cambridge, chanson and madrigal, 1961: 429bs
   Cambridge, instrumental music, 1957: 368bs
   Cambridge, music and criticism, 1947: 276bs
Minnesota, Minneapolis, musicology, 1941: 272bs
New York, New York, American studies, 1928:
   149bs
   American studies, 1949: 292bs
   hymnology, 1961: 438bs
   Iroquois culture, 1949: 293bs
   Jewish liturgical music, 1948: 286bs
   musicology, 1939: 266bs
   musicology, 1961: 439bs, 440bs
   20th-c. music, 1966: 510bs
Ohio, Cleveland, musicology, 1940: 269bs
Pennsylvania, Philadelphia, anthropology, 1956:
   359bs
Washington, D.C., American studies, 1915: 91bs
   Cherokee and Iroquois culture, 1958: 400bs
   inter-American relations in music, 1940: 271bs
   pedagogy, 1957: 385bs

CONFERENCE SPONSORS

AUSTRALIA

Australian National University
Aboriginal studies conference, 1961: 430bs
Social Science Research Council of Australia
Aboriginal studies conference, 1961: 430bs

AUSTRIA

Akademie für Musik und Darstellende Kunst in Graz, Abteilung für Kirchenmusik
Roman Catholic church music conference, 1964: 480bs
Bundesministerium für Unterricht
Mozart conference, 1956: 365bs
Gesellschaft zur Herausgabe von Denkmälern der Tonkunst in Österreich
Mozart conference, 1956: 365bs
Österreichische Akademie der Wissenschaften
Mozart conference, 1956: 365bs
Österreichisches Volksliedwerk
IFMC conference, 1960: 424bs

BELGIUM

Cercle Archéologique et Historique de Gand
Belgian history conference, 1896: 23bs
Cercle International d'Études Ethno-musicologiques
ethnomusicology conference, 1954: 340bs
ethnomusicology conference, 1956:366bs
ethnomusicology conference, 1960: 401bs
Brugge, municipality
history conference, 1925: 119bs
Exposition Internationale de Liège
public art conference, 1905: 49bs
Fédération Archéologique et Historique de Belgique
conference, 1892: 16bs
conference, 1896: 23bs
conference, 1898: 25bs
conference, 1911: 73bs
conference, 1913: 89bs
conference, 1930: 162bs
conference, 1932: 197bs
conference, 1938: 260bs
Institut Archéologique Liégeois
history conference, 1909: 64bs
Léopold II, King of Belgium
public art conference, 1898: 24bs
Ministère des Affaires Étrangères
history conference, 1925: 119bs
Ministère des Sciences et des Arts
history conference, 1925: 119bs
Œuvre Nationale Belge
public art conference, 1898: 24bs
Société Archéologique de Namur
history conference, 1903: 41bs
Société d'Art et d'Histoire du Diocèse de Liège
history conference, 1909: 64bs

CANADA

Canadian Folk Music Society
IFMC conference, 1961: 442bs
Canadian League of Composers
20th-c. music conference, 1960: 423bs
Canadian Psychiatric Association
psychiatry conference, 1961: 437bs
McGill University
psychiatry conference, 1961: 437bs
Stratford Shakespearean Festival
20th-c. music conference, 1960: 423bs
Université Laval
IFMC conference, 1961: 442bs

CUBA

Sociedad Pro-Arte Musical
ethnomusicology conference, 1963: 461bs

CZECHOSLOVAKIA

Ministerstvo Školství a Národní Osvěty
criticism conference, 1930: 183bs

DENMARK

Statens Teknisk-videnskabelige Fond
acoustics, 1962: 448bs

EGYPT

Fu'ād , King of Egypt
Arab music conference, 1932: 196bs
Ministry of Education
Arab music conference, 1932: 196bs

EUROPE

Union of European Piano Makers Association (Europiano)
1st conference, 1965: 494bs

FRANCE

Amitiés Françaises
conference, 1911: 74bs
Association des Amis de St. Colomban
Colombanian liturgy conference, 1950: 301bs
Association Française Sainte-Cécile
AIBM conference, 1957: 98bs
Association Internationale des Historiens de la Renaissance
2nd conference, 1957: 367bs
Centre d'Études Radiophoniques
broadcasting conference, 1954: 334bs
Centre National de la Recherche Scientifique (CNRS)
Cluny conference, 1949: 290bs
Centre National de la Recherche Scientifique (CNRS), Groupe de Recherches sur le Théâtre
Asian theater conference, 1958-59: 397bs
Chambre de Commerce de Marseille
Middle Eastern culture conference, 1919: 92bs
Exposition Universelle de 1900
musicology conference, 1900: 32bs
philosophy conference, 1900: 37bs
Festival de Montauban
Baroque conference, 1963: 469bs
Gouvernement Général de l'Afrique Occidentale Française
West African studies conference, 1945: 274bs
Groupe d'Études Musicales de la Renaissance
Renaissance conference, 1954: 333bs
Groupement Acousticiens des la Langue Française
sound recording and reproduction conference, 1966: 511bs
Institut Français d'Afrique Noire
West African studies conference, 1945: 274bs
Institut Historique
history conference, 1835: 1bs

Ministère du Commerce, de l'Industrie et des Colonies
folklore conference, 1889: 13bs
Ministère du Commerce, de l'Industrie, des Postes et des Télégraphes
musicology conference, 1900: 33bs
philosophy conference, 1900: 37bs
Revue d'esthétique
aesthetics conference, 1956: 363bs
Société d'Émulation des Côtes-du-Nord
Celtic history, 1867: 4bs
Société de l'Histoire de l'Art Français
art history conference, 1921: 94bs, 95bs
Société de Musique d'Autrefois
lute conference, 1957: 377bs
Société des Amis de Cluny
Cluny conference, 1949: 290bs
Société des Amis du Prince de Ligne
18th-c. Belgium conference, 1935: 220bs
Société Française d'Esthétique
aesthetics conference, 1956: 363bs
Société Française des Électroniciens et Radioélectriciens
sound recording and reproduction conference, 1966: 511bs
Société Union Musicologique
conference, 1926: 126ap, 127ap, 128ap
Société Universelle du Théâtre
dramatic arts conference, 1927: 138bs
Syndicat des Industries Électroniques de Reproduction et d'Enregistrement
sound recording and reproduction conference, 1966: 511bs
Syndicat National des Institutrices et Instituteurs de France et des Colonies
pedagogy conference, 1937: 246bs
Union des Maîtres de Chapelle et Organistes
Roman Catholic church music conference, 1937: 247bs

GERMANY

Arbeitsgemeinschaft der Musikdozenten an Pädagogischen Hochschulen
pedagogy conference, 1960: 416bs
Arbeitsgemeinschaft für Musikerziehung und Musikpflege
German musical life conference, 1955: 343bs
Arbeitsgemeinschaft für Orgelbau und Glockenwesen
organ conference, 1938: 258bs
Arbeitsgemeinschaft für Rheinische Musikgeschichte
Mönchengladbach history conference, 1964: 486bs
Arbeitskreis für Hausmusik
organ conference, 1938: 258bs
Arbeitskreis Georg Philipp Telemann
Telemann conference, 1962: 453bs
Bayerisches Staatsministerium für Unterricht und Kultus
organ conference, 1953: 325bs
organ conference, 1956: 355bs
Büro Musikwissenschaftler Sozialistischer Länder
Marxist musicology conference, 1963: 471bs
Bundesministerium für Handel und Wiederaufbau
Mozart conference, 1956: 365bs

Deutsche Akademie der Künste, Abteilung Arbeiterlied
mass song conference, 1964: 476bs
Deutsche Gesellschaft für Psychologie
12th conference, 1931: 188bs
13th conference, 1933: 207bs
14th conference, 1934: 219bs
15th conference, 1936: 231bs
16th conference, 1938: 254bs
Deutsche Morgenländische Gesellschaft
Asian studies conference, 1957: 376bs
Deutsche Musikgesellschaft
1st conference, 1925: 120bs
Deutscher Kulturbund
Telemann conference, 1962: 453bs
Forschungsunternehmen der Fritz-Thyssen-Stiftung, Arbeitskreis Musikwissenschaft
19th-c. music conference, 1964: 483bs
Freiburger Tagung für Deutsche Orgelkunst
2nd conference, 1938: 258bs
Gesellschaft der Musikfreunde im Wien
musicology conference, 1952: 317bs
Gesellschaft der Orgelfreunde
organ conference, 1955: 346bs
Gesellschaft der Orgelfreunde, Landesgruppe Bayern
organ conference, 1953: 325bs
Gesellschaft für Ästhetik und Allgemeine Kunstwissenschaft
2nd conference, 1924: 114bs
3rd conference, 1927: 137bs
4th conference, 1930: 177bs
Gesellschaft für Experimentalle Psychologie
1st conference, 1904: 44bs
3rd conference, 1908: 59bs
4th conference, 1911: 70bs
5th conference, 1912: 79bs
6th conference, 1914: 90bs
8th conference, 1923: 101bs
9th conference, 1925: 121bs
Gesellschaft für Musikalische Aufführungs- und Mechanische Vervielfältigungsrechte
CISAC conference, 1928: 148bs
Gesellschaft für Musikforschung
Bach conference, 1950: 298bs
conference, 1950: 299bs
conference, 1953: 319bs
conference, 1956: 356bs
conference, 1962: 452bs
Händel-Komitee der Deutschen Demokratischen Republik
Händel conference, 1959: 408bs
Kultministerium Stuttgart
organ conference, 1951: 305bs
Kultministerium Tübingen
organ conference, 1951: 305bs
Landeskundliche Abteilung des Musikwissenschaftlichen Instituts der Universität Kiel
Northern European music conference, 1963: 467bs
Landesverein der Kirchenmusiker Sachsens
organ conference, 1927: 136bs
Musikpädagogischer Verband
pedagogy conference, 1904: 43bs
Preußisches Ministerium für Wissenschaft, Kunst und Volksbildung
church music conference, 1927: 135bs
Senat der Freien und Hansestadt Hamburg
musicology conference, 1956: 356bs
Staatliche Akademie für Kirchen- und Schulmusik in Charlottenburg
church music conference, 1927: 135bs
Universität Freiburg im Breisgau, Musikwissenschaftliches Institut
organ conference, 1926: 122bs
organ conference, 1938: 258bs

Verband der Vereine für Volkskunde
11th conference, 1958: 396bs
Verband Deutscher Schulmusikerzieher
pedagogy conference, 1959: 412bs
Vereinigung der Landesdenkmalpfleger in der Bundesrepublik Deutschland
organ conference, 1957: 387bs
Vorstande des Deutschen Musikpädagogischen Verbandes
pedagogy conference, 1913: 87bs

GREECE
Etairia Kritikōn Historikōn Meletōn
Cretan studies conference, 1961: 434bs

HUNGARY
Magyar Tudományos Akadémia
Haydn conference, 1959: 405bs
Liszt and Bartók conference, 1961: 427bs

INDIA
Delhi Music Society
world music conference, 1964: 489bs
Indian Congress for Cultural Freedom
world music conference, 1964: 489bs
Indian Council for Cultural Relations
world music conference, 1964: 489bs
Max Mueller Bhavan
world music conference, 1964: 489bs
Sangeet Natak Akademi
world music conference, 1964: 489bs

INTERNATIONAL
Association Internationale des Historiens de la Renaissance
Renaissance conference, 1955: 350bs
Bureau International d'Art Radiophonique
broadcasting conference, 1937: 244bs
Congress for Cultural Freedom
20th-c. music conference, 1954: 335bs
Exposition Internationale des Arts et Techniques de 1937
Roman Catholic church music conference, 1937: 247bs
Inter-American Music Council (CIDEM)
ethnomusicology conference, 1963: 461bs
International African Institute
African studies conference, 1961: 433bs
International Association of Byzantine Studies (AIEB)
2nd conference, 1927: 131bs
3rd conference, 1930: 163bs
4th conference, 1934: 215bs
5th conference, 1936: 233bs
6th conference (cancelled), 1939: 263bs
6th conference, 1948: 287bs
9th conference, 1953: 327bs
10th conference, 1955: 347bs
12th conference, 1961: 441bs
International Association of Music Libraries (AIBM)
conference, 1950: 300bs
conference, 1951: 309bs
conference, 1955: 344bs, 345bs
conference, 1957: 373bs
conference, 1959: 406bs
conference, 1962: 457bs
conference, 1965: 499bs
International Association of Opera Directors
20th-c. opera conference, 1964: 481bs
International Commission on Acoustics
1st conference, 1953: 324bs
3rd conference, 1959: 414bs
5th conference, 1965: 504bs
International Committee of Historical Sciences
8th conference, 1938: 262bs

International Confederation of Societies of Authors and Composers (CISAC)
1st conference, 1926: 130bs
2nd conference, 1927: 140bs
3rd conference, 1928: 148bs
4th conference, 1929: 159bs
5th conference, 1930: 170bs
6th conference, 1931: 190bs
7th conference, 1932: 200bs
8th conference, 1933: 202bs
10th conference, 1935: 223bs
11th conference, 1936: 229bs
12th conference, 1937: 245bs
13th conference, 1938: 261bs
17th conference, 1952: 311bs
International Congress of Phonetic Sciences
5th conference, 1931: 192bs
6th conference, 1935: 221bs
International Federation for Documentation
AIBM conference, 1955: 344bs
International Federation for Theatre Research
theater history conference, 1957: 383bs
International Federation of Library Associations
7th conference, 1965: 492bs
International Folk Music Council
1st conference, 1948: 281bs
2nd conference, 1949: 295bs
3rd conference, 1950: 296bs
4th conference, 1951: 306bs
5th conference, 1952: 314bs
6th conference, 1953: 320bs
7th conference, 1954: 337bs
8th conference, 1955: 349bs
9th conference, 1956: 362bs
10th conference, 1957: 371bs
11th conference, 1958: 392bs
12th conference, 1959: 413bs
13th conference, 1960: 424bs
14th conference, 1961: 442bs
15th conference, 1962: 459bs
16th conference, 1963: 463bs
17th conference, 1964: 478bs
International Institute for Anthropology (IIA)
1st conference, 1932: 194bs
International Literary and Artistic Association (ALAI)
8th conference, 1885: 12bs
International Music Council
German musical life conference, 1955: 343bs
IFMC conference, 1960: 424bs
world music preservation conference, 1961: 443bs
IFMC conference, 1963: 463bs
20th-c. opera conference, 1964: 481bs
International Musical Society
1st conference, 1904: 45ap
2nd conference, 1906: 53bs, 54bs
3rd conference, 1909: 65bs
4th conference, 1911: 71bs
International Musicological Society
1st conference, 1930: 178bs
3rd conference, 1936: 224bs
4th conference, 1949: 289bs
5th conference, 1952: 316bs
7th conference, 1958: 390bs
14th-c. Italian music conference, 1959: 407bs
8th conference, 1961: 439bs, 440bs
9th conference, 1964: 491bs
International Publishers' Association (UIE)
4th conference, 1901: 38bs
5th conference, 1906: 55bs
6th conference, 1908: 60bs
8th conference, 1913: 88bs
9th conference, 1931: 191bs
International Society of Folk Narrative Research
traditional narrative conference, 1959: 411bs

International Union of Anthropological and Ethnological Sciences
5th conference, 1956: 359bs
6th conference, 1960: 421bs
International Union of Orientalists
23rd conference, 1954: 329bs
International Union of the History and Philosophy of Science
history of science conference, 1956: 354bs
Internationale Gesellschaft für Experimentelle Phonetik
1st conference, 1930: 169bs
Internationale Stiftung Mozarteum
conference, 1931: 193bs
Internationales Musikzentrum Wien
20th-c. opera conference, 1964: 481bs
League of Nations, International Institute of Intellectual Cooperation
cinematography conference, 1926: 129bs
folklore conference, 1928: 152bs
Pan-American Union, Music Section
ethnomusicology conference, 1963: 461bs
Scientific Council for Africa South of the Sahara
6th conference, 1956: 361bs
UNESCO
philosophy conference, 1948: 280bs
anthropology conference, 1948: 282bs
AIBM conference, 1951: 309bs
pedagogy conference, 1953: 323bs
IFMC conference, 1960: 424bs
acoustics, 1962: 448bs
International Theater Institute, 20th-c. opera conference, 1964: 481bs

ISRAEL
Hebrew University of Jerusalem, World Union of Jewish Studies
Jewish studies conference, 1961: 435bs
Israel National Commission for UNESCO
IFMC conference, 1963: 463bs
National Council of Culture and Art
IFMC conference, 1963: 463bs

ITALY
Accademia Musicale Chigiana
Pergolesi conference, 1942: 273bs
Accademia Nazionale dei Lincei, Classe di Scienze Morali, Storiche e Filologiche
musicology conference, 1960: 422bs
Assessorato per la Pubblica Istruzione delle Regione Siciliana
Mediterranean music conference, 1954: 332bs
Centro Catechistico Salesiano
Roman Catholic church music conference, 1965: 501bs
Centro di Studi sulla Spiritualità Medievale
Jacopone conference, 1957: 381bs
Middle Ages conference, 1961: 444bs
Centro di Studi Vivaldiani
Vivaldi conference, 1947: 279bs
Centro Etnografico Sardo
folklore conference, 1956: 353bs
Centro Italiano di Richerche Teatrali
theater history conference, 1957: 383bs
Centro Nazionale di Studi sul Rinascimento
Renaissance conference, 1939: 264bs
Centro per la Documentazione e la Difesa del Folklore Italiano
folklore conference, 1956: 353bs
Comitato Nazionale Italiano per le Arti Popolari
folklore conference, 1934: 218bs
folklore conference, 1940: 270bs
Comitato Nazionale per le Tradizioni Popolari
folklore conference, 1929:158bs
Comitato per le Celebrazioni di Torquato Tasso
Tasso conference, 1954: 330bs

Comitato per le Celebrazioni Stradivariane
string instrument making conference, 1937: 238bs
Commissione di Musica Sacra per l'Anno Santo
Roman Catholic church music conference, 1950: 303bs
Deputazione di Storia Patria per le Antiche Provincie Modenesi
Muratori conference, 1950: 302bs
Fondazione Giorgio Cini
Goldoni conference, 1957: 474bs
Venice and Poland conference, 1963: 384bs
Istituto Italiano di Storia delle Tradizioni
folklore conference, 1957: 370bs
Istituto Nazionale di Studi sul Rinascimento
Renaissance conference, 1965: 500bs
Istituto Veneto di Scienze Lettere ed Arti
Goldoni conference, 1957: 384bs
Maggio Musicale Fiorentino
2nd conference, 1937: 239bs
3rd conference, 1938: 256bs
5th conference, 1948: 285bs
6th conference, 1949: 291bs
7th conference, 1950: 297bs
Ministero della Educazione Nazionale: Direzione Generale delle Accademie e Biblioteche
librarianship conference, 1929: 161bs
Ministero della Pubblica Istruzione, Italy
Mediterranean music conference, 1954: 332bs
Il pianoforte
Italian music conference, 1921: 97bs
Pontificio Istituto di Musica Sacra
Roman Catholic church music conference, 1950: 303bs
Radiotelevisione Italiana (RAI)
20th-c. music conference, 1954: 335bs
Reale Accademia d'Italia
Vivaldi conference, 1939: 268bs
folklore conference, 1940: 270bs
Rivista musicale italiana
Italian music conference, 1921: 97bs
Santa Cecilia
Italian music conference, 1921: 97bs
Section d'Histoire Musicale de L'Institut Français de Florence
musicology conference, 1911: 76bs
Società di Etnografia Italiana
folklore conference, 1948: 288bs
folklore conference, 1956: 353bs
folklore conference, 1957: 370bs
Società di Studi Romagnoli
Dante conference, 1965: 505bs
Società Italiana degli Autori ed Editori
CISAC conference, 1927: 140bs
Venezia, municipality
Goldoni conference, 1957: 384bs
Vittorio Emmanuele III, King of Italy
philosophy conference, 1911: 69bs

POLAND
Bydgoskie Towarzystwo Naukowe
Eastern European music conference, 1966: 506bs
Filharmonia Pomorska imienia Ignacego Paderewskiego
Eastern European music conference, 1966: 506bs
Komitet Roku Chopinowskiego
Chopin conference, 1960: 425bs
Ministerstwo Kultury i Sztuki
Chopin conference, 1960: 425bs
Polska Akademia Nauk
Venice and Poland conference, 1963: 474bs
Polska Akademia Nauk, Instytut Badań Literackich
poetics conference, 1960: 426bs

Polsko Ministerstwo Szkolnictwa Wyzszego
Venice and Poland conference, 1963: 474bs
Towarzystvo imienia Fryderyka Chopina
Chopin conference, 1960: 425bs

PORTUGAL
Conselho Científico para a África ao Sul do Sara
West African studies conference, 1956: 361bs
Junta de Investigações Coloniais
West African studies conference, 1947: 275bs

SENEGAL
University of Dakar
African studies conference, 1961: 433bs

SPAIN
Sociedad General de Autores y Editores
CISAC conference, 1935: 223bs

SWITZERLAND
Centre Européen de la Culture
20th-c. music conference, 1954: 335bs
Historisches Museum Basel
IMS conference, 1906: 54bs
Institut de Rythmique de Genève
rhythm and meter conference, 1926: 123bs
Neue Schweizerische Musikgesellschaft
conference, 1924: 102bs
Neue Schweizerische Musikgesellschaft, Ortsgruppe Basel
musicology conference, 1924: 102bs
musicology conference, 1924: 103bs
Schweizerische Musikforschende Gesellschaft, Ortsgruppe Basel
IMS conference, 1949: 289bs

UGANDA
Makerere University
African music conference, 1963: 465bs

UNITED KINGDOM
English Folk Dance and Song Society
IFMC conference, 1952: 314bs
Performing Right Society
CISAC conference, 1931: 190bs
Physical Society of London, Acoustics Group
acoustics conference, 1953: 324bs
Standing Conference of County Music Committees
3rd annual meeting, 1948: 283bs
Standing Conference of Drama Associations
3rd annual meeting, 1948: 283bs

UNITED KINGDOM — ENGLAND AND WALES
Guild of Congregational Organists
Congregational church music, 1951: 307bs

UNITED STATES OF AMERICA
American Anthropological Association
Iroquois culture conference, 1949: 293bs
Iroquois and Cherokee cultures conference, 1958: 400bs
American Council of Learned Societies
AMS conference, 1940: 269bs
AMS conference, 1941: 272bs
American Musicological Society
2nd conference, 1936: 230bs
5th conference, 1939: 266bs
6th conference, 1940: 269bs
7th conference, 1941: 272bs
IMS conference, 1961: 439bs, 440bs
American Society for Aesthetics
aesthetics conference, 1956: 363bs
American Society of University Composers
1st conference, 1966: 510bs
Cantors Assembly
1st annual convention, 1948: 286bs

Catholic University of America
 pedagogy conference, 1957: 385bs
Cleveland Museum of Art
 aesthetics conference, 1956: 363bs
Harvard University, Department of Music
 chanson and madrigal conference, 1961: 368bs
 instrumental music conference, 1957: 429bs
Journal of aesthetics & art criticism
 aesthetics conference, 1956: 363bs
Music Teachers National Association
 musicology conference, 1936: 230bs
 conference, 1940: 269bs
 conference, 1941: 272bs
National Council of Churches of Christ
 hymnology conference, 1961: 438bs

Southern Illinois University at Carbondale
 communication conference, 1965: 497bs, 498bs
United Synagogue of America
 Department of Music, 1st annual convention,
  1948: 286bs
University of California, Los Angeles
 Asian music conference, 1960: 418bs
University of Illinois at Urbana-Champaign
 world music preservation conference, 1961:
  443bs
**Wenner-Gren Foundation for Anthropological
 Research**
 American studies conference, 1949: 292bs

YUGOSLAVIA
Jugoslavenski Odbor za Bizantinske Studije
 Byzantine studies conference, 1961: 441bs
**Udruženje Folklorista Jugoslavije/Savez
 Udruženja Folklorista Jugoslavije**
 1st and 2nd conferences, 1952 and 1955: 315bs
 3rd conference, 1956: 357bs
 4th conference, 1957: 382bs
 5th conference, 1958: 402bs
 6th conference, 1959: 404bs
 7th conference, 1960: 419bs
 8th conference, 1961: 446bs
 9th conference, 1962: 455bs
 10th conference, 1963: 462bs
 11th conference, 1964: 490bs

AUTHORS AND SUBJECTS

A

AARBURG, Ursula, 4413as[69]

Aaron, Pietro
performance practice, 3723as[51]

ABBADO, Michelangelo, 3547as[44]

ABER, Adolf, 104rs[16], 5091as[77]

ABERT, Anna Amalie, 936as[21], 1905as[27], 5092as[77]

Abert, Anna Amalie
writings, 19th-c. music and literature, 1908as[27]

ABERT, Hermann, 66rs[16], 127ap[16], 1719as[26], 5093as[77], 5094as[77], 5421as[81]

Abert, Hermann
writings, concept of ethos, applied to traditional song, 2536as[31]
___ Greek antiquity, 1031as[22]
___ on style, 4373as[66]
___ medieval aesthetics, 5592as[81]

ABIUSO, V., 2709as[34]

Aboriginal music, *see* **Australia**

ABRAHAM, Gerald, 390bs, 484rs[16], 840as[19], 1906as[27], 1908as[27], 1955as[27], 2129as[28], 4369as[66], 5793as[85]

ABRAHAM, Lars Ulrich, 1590as[25]

absolute music
England, 1500-30, 1283as[24]
humor, 5524as[81]
relation to humanism, 18th-19th c., 5430as[81]
Szymanowski, K., 2187as[28]

abstract music, *see* **absolute music**

ABŪ NAṢR MUḤAMMAD IBN MUḤAMMAD IBN ṬARKHĀN IBN UZALAGH AL-FĀRĀBĪ, 4090as[62]

academic institutions, *see also* **choir schools; instruments — collections; libraries, museums, collections; pedagogy** headwords; **religious institutions**
Argentina, Buenos Aires, Escuela Nac. de Danzas de Argentina, 5039as[76]
Belgium, Antwerpen, Koninklijk Vlaams Muziek Conservatorium, activities of Benoît, 1926as[27], 1944as[27]
___ ___ Vlaamse Muziekschool, activities of Benoît, 1926as[27]
___ Liège, Conservatoire Royal de Musique, establishment, 4627as[70]
___ Mechelen, Interdiocesaan Inst. voor Kerkmuziek, 4836as[72]
___ ___ Lemmensinst., curriculum, 4900as[73]
Bosnia and Herzegovina, Sarajevo, Inst. za Proučavanje Folklora, cataloguing of *Behar*, 635as[1]
Canada, Ontario, Ottawa, U., role of religious music, to 1950, 4817as[72]
Croatia, Zagreb, Inst. za Narodnu Umjetnost, dance transcriptions, 5087as[76]
Czech Republic, Brno, Akademie Věd České Republiky, Ústav pro Etnografii a Folkloristiku, classification of traditional melodies, 4470as[69]
___ Praha, Akademie Múzických Umění, basset clarinet making, 3750as[52]
___ ___ Varhanická Škola, relation to Janáček, 4175as[63]

Denmark, Aarhus, U., Musikvidenskabeligt Inst., relation to Aarhus Statsbibl., 724as[2]
___ København, U., Byzantine chant database, 4457as[69]
England, Hitchin, Hertfordshire Rural Music School, 4906as[74], 4907as[74]
___ Reading, U., teacher training program, ca. 1953, 4807as[72], 4808as[72]
Finland, Helsinki, Sibelius-Akatemia, 4842as[72], 4843as[72]
___ ___ Yliopisto, 4842as[72], 4843as[72]
France, Nantes, cathedral, choir school, 4735as[71]
___ Paris, Centre de Préparation au Professorat de Musique, 4848as[72], 4849as[72]
___ ___ Centre Nat. de la Recherche Scientifique (CNRS), Renaissance lute music project, 3901as[58]
___ ___ Conservatoire, relation to Mozart reception, 1793-1810, 1801as[26]
___ ___ Inst. Chorégraphique, activities of Lifar, 5023as[76]
___ ___ Inst. de Théologie Orthodoxe Saint-Serge, cultivation of Russian Orthodox chant, 6128as[92]
___ ___ Inst. Vocal Universel, proposed, 1937, 3330as[41]
___ ___ Schola Cantorum, activities of Bordes, 1924as[27]
___ ___ U. de la Danse, 5023as[76]
Germany, Berlin, Internat. Inst. for Comparative Music Studies, relation to ethical and spiritual values, 5449as[81]
___ ___ Königliches Inst. für Kirchenmusik, organ pedagogy, 4884as[73]
___ Braunschweig, Gymnasium Raabeschule, filmmaking project, 1953-54, 4796as[71]
___ ___ Katharineum, activities of Vuinck, 1433as[24]
___ ___ Physikalisch-Technische Bundesanstalt, Laboratorium für Musikalische Akustik, 3415as[42]
___ ___ Physikalisch-Technische Bundesanstalt, Laboratorium für Musikalische Akustik, organ acoustics measurements, 3416as[42]
___ ___ Physikalisch-Technische Bundesanstalt, Laboratorium für Musikalische Akustik, sonority research methods, 3378as[42]
___ Freiburg im Breisgau, U., Inst. für Musikwissenschaft, Praetorius-Orgel, 3360as[42], 3415as[42]
___ Halle, U., activities of Händel, 1595as[25]
___ ___ U., Instit. für Musikwissenschaft und Musikerziehung, tonality perception experiment, 5641as[82]
___ Hamburg, Lichtwarkschule, organ, 3399as[42]
___ Kiel, U., history of music, 1665-1920s, 4822as[72]
___ Leipzig, Conservatorium, aesthetics as subject, 4893as[73]
___ ___ Hochschule für Musik, organ, 3399as[42]
___ Ludwigsburg, Fachschule für Musikinstrumentenbau, training for piano builders, 3524as[43]
___ Mönchengladbach, Musikschule, relation to Fegers, 2163as[28]
___ München, Bayerische Akademie der Wissenschaften, *Lexicon musicum latinum*, use of electronic data processing, 774as[3]
___ ___ Bayerische Akademie der Wissenschaften, *Lexicon musicum latinum*, ca. 1962, 773as[3]

___ ___ Bayerische Akademie der Wissenschaften, sponsorship of Breitkopf & Härtel Lassus edition, 3897as[58]
___ ___ Inst. für Film und Bild in Wissenschaft und Unterricht (IWU), *Tönende Musikgeschichte* project, 1950, 5761as[85]
Israel, Jerusalem, Hamakẇn hayśra'ely lemẇsyqah datyt, transcription techniques, 2434as[30]
Italy, Milano, Reale Conservatorio, pedagogical methods, 4902as[73]
___ ___ Reale Conservatorio, teaching of music history, 4903as[73]
___ Roma, Accademia di Santa Cecilia, relation to ethnomusicology, 1948-58, 2450as[30]
___ ___ Centro Naz. di Studi sul Rinascimento, 1314as[24]
___ ___ Centro Naz. Studi di Musica Popolare, 2451as[30]
___ ___ Centro Naz. Studi di Musica Popolare, 1948-58, 2450as[30]
___ ___ Consiglio Naz. delle Ricerche (CNR), violin acoustics tests, 3594as[44]
___ ___ Ist. Italiano per la Storia della Musica, 1314as[24]
___ ___ Ist. Naz. di Studi Romani, Roman musical publications, index, 740as[2]
___ Torino, U. Popolare Don Orione, concert series, 2379as[29]
Netherlands, Amsterdam, Volksmuziekschool, 1931-53, 4909as[74], 4910as[74]
Poland, Warszawa, Inst. Muzyczny, relation to Janáček, 2102as[27]
Portugal, Lisboa, Centro de Estudos Gregorianos, 2278as[29]
Spain, Barcelona, Inst. Español de Musicología, 858as[20]
___ Madrid, Escuela Superior de Música Sagrada, 4862as[73]
Switzerland, Fribourg, U., Académie Grégorienne, relation to history of church music research, 6419as[93]
___ Zürich, U., database of basses danses, 4449as[69]
Uganda, Kampala, Makerere U., African studies program, 4850as[72]
USA, California, U., publication of contemporary music, ca. 1966, 5970as[89]
___ ___ U. of, Los Angeles, ethnomusicology, ca. 1966, 2435as[30]
___ Iowa, U. of, Iowa City, test for motor coordination, 5737as[83]
___ Michigan, U. of, Ann Arbor, pedagogy, 4851as[72]
___ New York, New York, Columbia U., computerized notation encoding system, ca. 1966, 5945as[89]
___ ___ Rochester, U. of, Eastman School of Music, entrance requirements, 4896as[73]
Vatican, Pontificio Ist. di Musica Sacra, founding of Internat. Soc. of Sacred Music, 6146as[93]
___ ___ history and development, 4877as[73], 6362as[93]
___ ___ organizational proposals, 1954, 6241as[93]

academies, *see* **academic institutions; performing organizations; societies, associations, fraternities, etc.** headwords

accent, *see* **interpretation** headwords; **rhythm and meter**

Altnikol, Johann Christoph
  life, relation to Bach *Vor deinen Thron tret ich hiermit*, 1640as[25]
ALTWEGG, Wilhelm, 704as[2], 5278as[78], 5279as[78]
ALVARENGA, Oneyda, 3187as[36]
Alvarenga, Oneyda
  writings, discography of Brazilian popular music, 5947as[89]
ALVARES, Vincent, 6143as[93]
Alwin, William
  works, film music, 5173as[77]
AMADES GELAT, Joan, 2713as[34], 2714as[34], 2715as[34], 3237as[40], 4928as[76]
Amalarius of Metz
  writings, church singing, 6377as[93]
amateurs, *see also* **performers** headwords
  art music, relation to appreciation, 20th c., 2349as[29]
  associations, influence on appreciation, 4547as[70]
  audiences, influenced by phonograph and radio, 2312as[29]
  Austria, string quartets, 1762-1806, 1757as[26]
  Belgium, bands, repertoire, 2351as[29]
  ___ instrumental societies, relation to radio, ca. 1932, 4915as[74]
  ___ pedagogy, 4553as[70]
  Czech Republic, Bohemia, role in traditional dance revival, from late 19th c., 5020as[76]
  ___ traditional music and dance ensembles, ca. 1963, 2945as[34]
  England, pedagogy, rural music schools, 4906as[74], 4907as[74]
  ___ relation to libraries, 558as[1]
  Ernst Ludwig, Landgrave of Hessen-Darmstadt, 1636as[25]
  France, music societies, ca. 1900, 2083as[27]
  Germany, choral performers, 1960s, relation to earlier Arbeitermusikbewegung, 4908as[74]
  ___ Hausmusik, audiences, radio, ca. 1957, 2400as[29]
  ___ Singbewegung, activities of youth, 6434as[94]
  Hausmusik, 979as[21]
  Heinrich Christian, Imperial Count of Keyserlingk, 1769as[26]
  instrument building, northern Slavic states, early Middle Ages, 3257as[40]
  instrumental playing, accompaniment, use of sound recordings, 4664as[70]
  organists, England, 14th-16th c., 3355as[42]
  pedagogy, choral singing, 4911as[74], 4912as[74]
  ___ traditional dance, 5002as[76], 5003as[76]
  ___ viewed by Duhamel, 4519as[70], 4520as[70]
  Peru, ensembles, role in pedagogy, 4790as[71], 4791as[71]
  Pervaneo, G., 1646as[25]
  reception of new music, 20th c., 2402as[29]
  Romance-speaking countries, Roman Catholic church choirs, performance of polyphony, 6209as[93]
  Slovakia, traditional music and dance ensembles, ca. 1963, 2945as[34]
  Spain, Valencia, bands, 3044as[34]
Ambros, August Wilhelm
  life, relation to Liszt, 1925as[27]
Ambrosian chant, *see* **chant — Christian (Western)**
AMELLI, Guerrino Ambrosio Maria, 1052as[23]
AMELN, Konrad, 1219as[24], 1316as[24], 3238as[40], 3911as[58], 6422as[94]
American Indians, *see* **Indians and Inuits**
Americas, *see also* **Central America**; **Latin American studies**; **North America**; **South America**; **West Indies**
  cultural policies, copyright, ca. 1939, 2381as[29]
  culture, conferences, 1875, 5bs
  ___ ___ 1879, 6bs
  ___ ___ 1881, 8bs
  ___ ___ 1890, 14bs
  ___ ___ 1904, 47bs
  ___ ___ 1906, 56bs
  ___ ___ 1908, 61bs
  ___ ___ 1910, 68bs
  ___ ___ 1915, 91bs
  ___ ___ 1922, 99bs
  ___ ___ 1924, 118bs
  ___ ___ 1928, 149bs
  ___ ___ 1930, 176bs
  ___ ___ 1932, 198bs
  ___ ___ 1947, 277bs
  ___ ___ 1949, 292bs
  ___ ___ 1952, 313bs
  ___ ___ 1958, 394bs, 398bs
  ___ ___ 1962, 454bs
  dance, state of research, ca. 1934, 5053as[76]
  history of music, film music, 5245as[77]
  ___ influenced by Europe, 943as[21], 953as[21], 1006as[21]
  ___ 1900-1947, 2250as[28]
  musical life, influenced by African music, 3183as[35]
  pedagogy, exchange of professors and students, 1940s, 4661as[70]
  traditional music, 2491as[31], 2543as[31]
  ___ influenced by Europe, 953as[21]
  ___ state of research, ca. 1906, 2475as[30]
  ___ ca. 1940, 2471as[30]
Amerval, Eloy d'
  writings, *Le livre de la déablerie*, 1238as[24]
AMFITHEATROF, Daniele, 5095as[77]
Ammann, Benno
  works, *Missa "Defensor pacis"*, 6416as[93], 6417as[93]
Ammann, Heinrich
  instruments, chamber organs, 3441as[42]
Ammann, Ulrich
  instruments, chamber organs, 3441as[42]
AMON, Karl, 6144as[93]
AMTMANN, Paul, 4676as[71]
analysis, *see also* **information theory**; **Schenkerian theory**; **semantics**; **semiotics**; **set theory**; specific composers and genres; **style**; **theory**
  Baroque music, classification of dissonances, 4156as[63]
  Classic, theme structure, 4311as[66]
  compared with psychology of listening, 5708as[82]
  complex-analysis, 3937as[60]
  as discipline, materialist approach, 3951as[60]
  functional, applied to Scandinavian national Romantic styles, 1914as[27]
  genre theory, applied to Chopin, 2108as[27]
  Gregorian chant, 4348as[66]
  ___ structural schemata, relation to French-language texts, 4433as[69]
  harmonic, 20th-c. music, based on overtone series, 4210as[63]
  melodic, ethnomusicological perspective, 4455as[69]
  methodology, 3950as[60]
  ___ influenced by linguistics, 3954as[60]
  ___ interval as fundamental unit, 3956as[60]
  ___ objective vs. subjective aspects, 3933as[60]
  ___ organicism, 3931as[60]
  ___ relation to criticism, 4395as[67]
  motivic, instrumental music, 4447as[69]
  music symbolism, 5934as[88]
  musical meaning, experimental issues, 5607as[81]
  ___ scientific approach, 5722as[82]
  open analysis, applied to Renaissance music, 3957as[60]
  quantitative methods, use in semiotic approach, 3939as[60]
  relation to aesthetics, 5547as[81]
  rhythmic, adagio themes, late 18th-early 19th c., 4020as[61]
  statistical, applied to Beethoven sonata themes, 4432as[69]
  style, use of harmonic rhythm concept, 4359as[66]
  time, temporally defined categories, 4018as[61]

  traditional music, problems, 838as[19]
  use of typology, 5428as[81]
  20th-c. music, 5560as[81]
  ___ methodologies, 4352as[66]
  ___ relation to composition, 3945as[60]
ANASTASIJEVIĆ, Dragutin N., 131bs, *132rs[16], 132rs[16], *133rs[16]
Anchieta, Juan de
  works, 1476as[24]
Ancina, Giovenale
  life, influence on lauda, 1281as[24]
Andersen, Poul-Gerhard
  instruments, organ building, case design, 3485as[42]
ANDERSON, Kenneth, 705as[2]
ANDERSSON, Otto, 830as[19], 1723as[26], 2716as[34], 2717as[34], 2718as[34], 3548as[44]
Andes region, *see* **South America**; specific countries
ANDOYER, Raphael, 1053as[23], 3689as[51]
ANDRADE, Mário de, 2130as[28], 3188as[36], 4929as[76]
Andrade, Mário de
  writings, discography of Brazilian popular music, 5947as[89]
ANDRAL, Maguy, 706as[2], 2719as[34]
ANDRÉ, François, 1220as[24]
ANDREEV, Andrej, 2279as[29]
ANDREJČIN, Ljubomir, 5280as[78]
Andrews, Herbert Kennedy
  writings, *An introduction to the technique of Palestrina*, use in counterpoint instruction, 4847as[72]
ANDRIES, Marcel, 4482as[70], 4483as[70]
anecdotes, reminiscences, etc., *see also* **autobiographies, diaries, etc.**; **correspondence**; **humor**
  Ansermet, E., on Debussy and Godet, 2131as[28]
  Beethoven, L. von, by Bonn contemporaries, 1790as[26]
  Brosses, C. de, on Pergolesi, 1611ac[25]
  Debussy, C., by Ansermet, 2131as[28]
  Godet, R., by Ansermet, 2131as[28]
  Goldoni, C., on Vivaldi, 1612as[25]
  Neuhaus, H., on Szymanowski, 2218as[28]
  Pergolesi, G.B., by Brosses, 1611ac[25]
  Slavic states, southern, gusle playing, 3036as[34]
  Szymanowski, K., by Neuhaus, 2218as[28]
  Vivaldi, A., by Goldoni, 1612as[25]
Anerio, Giovanni Francesco
  works, *Teatro harmonico spirituale, Dialogo della samaritana*, 1671as[25]
angels
  iconography, Ferrari, G., 5380as[79]
ANGLAS, Jules Philippe Louis, 76bs, 5800as[86]
ANGLÈS, Higini, 303bs, 840as[19], 858as[20], 940as[21], 941as[21], 1054as[23], 1055as[23], 1056as[23], 1171as[23], 1221as[24], 1222as[24], 1223as[24], 2720as[34], 3334as[42], 3802as[55], 3803as[55], 3886as[58], 3978as[61], 6003as[90], 6145as[93], 6146as[93], 6147as[93], 6148as[93]
Angola
  ethnomusicology, activities of Museu do Dundo, 743as[2]
animals, *see also* **nature**; **science**
  birds, Congo, Democratic Republic, Cokwe people, birdcall imitations, 2560as[32]
  cattle, Bosnia and Herzegovina, relation to traditional dance, 4956as[76]
  chickens, Europe, role in marriage ceremonies, 5077as[76]
  China, sound terminology, Later Han dynasty, 2673as[33]
  crows, USA, Alaska, Koyukon (Ten'a) people, imitated in singing, 3142as[35]
  cuckoos, imitated by children, 5657as[82]
  dragons, North America, Iroquois and Wyandot peoples, subject of traditional songs, 5286as[78]
  France, hunting calls, 2938as[34]

horses, India, South, hobby horses, 5098as[77]
___ Italy, Firenze, equestrian ballets, late 16th c.,
   5158as[77]
___ ___ represented in dances, 1318as[24]
Macedonia, relation to spring festival rituals,
   2843as[34]
sheep, Scandinavia, shepherd's calls, 2785as[34]
Sweden, northern, herding, 2755as[34]
Switzerland, Basel, vogel gryff pageant, 2819as[34]
wolves, Serbia, Kosovo, Šar Planina, vučarska
   svadba ritual, 2925as[34]

Animuccia, Giovanni
   works, lauda compositions, relation to monody
      form, 1503as[25]

Anna of Cologne
   manuscripts, songbook, relation to Netherlands,
      1424as[24]

**Anna von Habsburg, Queen of Sigismund III
   Vasa**
   life, relation to Graz and Kraków history of music,
      1298as[24]

Anne, Princess of England
   life, studies with Händel, 1617as[25]

ANNEGARN, Alfons, 516as[1]

anniversaries, *see* **ceremonies; congresses, conferences, symposia; festivals**

ANON. (COUNTRY ORGANIST), 6191as[93]
ANON. (CRITIC), 5422as[81]
ANON. (PARISH PRIEST), 6190as[93]

Anonymous V
   writings, *Ars cantus mensurabilis mensurata per
      modos iuris*, relation to organicist analysis,
      3931as[60]

ANSCHÜTZ, Georg, 4306as[66], 4920as[75]
ANSERMET, Ernest, 2131as[28], 3965as[61], 4307as[66],
   5423as[81]
ANTCLIFFE, Herbert, 4229as[64], 5424as[81]

Antegnati, Giovan Francesco
   life, arpicordo building, 3509as[43]

Antheil, George
   works, *Transatlantic*, 5242as[77]

anthem, *see also* **choral music; national anthem;
   religion and religious music — Christianity
   (Protestant)**
   England, influence on Händel *The ways of Zion do
      mourn*, 1598as[25]
___ social context, late 17th c., 1718as[25]
Händel, G.F., quotation of Lutheran hymns,
   4472as[69]

anthologies, *see also* **hymnals; manuscripts and
   prints** headwords; **songbooks**
   Besard, J.-B., *Thesaurus harmonicus*, 1274as[24]
   Bulgaria, traditional songs, 1842-1900, 2875as[34]
   Czech Republic, traditional songs, 18th-early 19th
      c., 1807as[26]
   France, 1750-90, 807as[7]
   Germany, English composers, 17th c., 1480as[25]
   Gherardi, E., *Le Théâtre Italien de Gherardi...*,
      1565as[25]
   history of music, sound recordings, 969as[21],
      970as[21]
   Krohn, I., *Suomen kansan sävelmiä*, melodic
      analysis, 2913as[34]
   Künzig, J., *Ehe sie verklingen...: Alte deutsche
      Volksweisen von Böhmerwald bis zur
      Wolga*, 5974as[89]
   Linëva, E., *Velikorusskie pesni v noradnoj
      garmonizacii*, 2444as[30]
   Lithuania, traditional music, 19th c., 2762as[34]
   Quellmalz, A., *Südtiroler Volkslieder*, 3019as[34]
   Raverii, A., *Canzoni per sonare con ogni sorte di
      stromenti*, 3887as[58]
   Torres y Martínez Bravo, J. de, *Canciones
      francesas de todos ayres*, 1810as[26]

anthropology, *see also* **cultural studies;
   ethnomusicology; sociology**
   archeology, instruments, viewed by Bianchini,
      5740as[84]
   conferences, 1893, 19bs
___ 1931, 192bs
___ 1935, 221bs
___ 1939, 255bs
___ 1948, 282bs
___ 1956, 359bs, 364bs
___ 1960, 421bs
   as discipline, relation to ethnomusicology, ca.
      1958, 2422as[30]
___ relation to music, 873as[20]
   ethnography, conference, 1963, 473bs
___ conference,1963, 460bs
___ museums, instrument collections, 619as[1]
   relation to experimental psychology, 5702as[82]

Antico, Andrea
   life, block printing, 5994as[89]

antiphon, *see* **Mass**

antiphoners, *see* **liturgical books**

antiphony, *see also* **polychoral style; space; texture**
   Palestine, antiquity, relation to Qumran Scrolls,
      1047as[22]
   Szymanowski, K., *Król Roger*, 4327as[66]

antiquity, *see also* **archaeology**; specific countries,
   names, topics
   aesthetics, influence on Middle Ages, 5592as[81]
   Africa, instruments, harp family, 2596as[32]
   agrarian vs. urban cultures, 851as[19]
   Asia, intervals, 4044as[62]
   Babylonia, notation, 3867as[55]
   Celtic people, history of music, relation to
      Ambrosian and Mozarabic chant, 1036as[22]
   Central America, instruments, 3224as[36]
___ wind instruments, 3617as[45]
   China, instruments, three-tone scales, 3268as[40]
___ scales, relation to circle of fifths, 4122as[62]
   Egypt, instruments, state of research, ca. 1949,
      3253as[40]
___ musical life, 1032as[22]
___ state of research, ca. 1949, 2555as[32]
   Europe, state of research, ca. 1949, 1050as[22]
   Gaul, instruments, iconography, 3280as[40]
   Greco-Roman, depicted in Händel vocal music,
      1552as[25]
   Greece, competitions, compared with Central
      Asian singing contests, 2622as[33]
___ concept of nomos, influence on Byzantine
      music, 1148as[23]
___ dance, 5032as[76]
___ ___ relation to sardana and ballo tondo gen-
      res, 4965as[76]
___ Delphi, hymns, 1044as[22]
___ ___ hymns, transcription, 1040as[22]
___ ___ dramatic arts, prologues, influence on 17th-c.
      opera, 5192as[77]
___ history of music, polyphony, 1046as[22]
___ ___ psycharithmic analysis, 5710as[82]
___ ___ relation to Ambrosian and Mozarabic
      chant, 1036as[22]
___ influence on Catalunya traditional songs,
      2730as[34]
___ influence on Gregorian chant, 3717as[51]
___ instruments, aulos, performance technique,
      3610as[45]
___ ___ lyre family, 3572as[44]
___ ___ variable and fixed-tone instruments, re-
      lation to origins of cadence, 4195as[63]
___ linguistics, vowels, relation to music,
      1042as[22]
___ melody, influence on Greek Orthodox church,
      6112as[92]
___ modality, relation to Byzantine music,
      6129as[92]
___ ___ relation to Sicilian traditional music,
      3080as[34]

___ musical life, traditional vs. art music,
      1051as[22]
___ notation, 3882as[55]
___ pedagogy, 4601as[70]
___ poetry, cretic meter, relation to Krítī
      traditional song, 3967as[61]
___ ___ meter, relation to Bulgarian folklore,
      5309as[78]
___ scales, relation to Western music, 4082as[62]
___ state of research, 1031as[22]
___ theory, concept of enharmonics, 4208as[63]
___ ___ genera, 4128as[62]
___ ___ influenced by planets, 1037as[22]
___ ___ modality, 4104as[62]
___ ___ modality, compared with Byzantine
      oktōēchos, 4119as[62]
___ ___ scales, 4112as[62]
___ ___ viewed by Plato, 1041as[22]
___ traditional music, songs, 3016as[34]
___ views on music, 2485as[30]
   history of music, use of microtones, 4080as[62]
   India, 2619as[33]
___ modality, concept of sa grāma, 4046as[62]
   influence on Gregorian chant, role of Byzantine
      chant, 1028as[22]
   instruments, organ, role in Christian liturgical
      chant, 5th c. and after, 6019as[90]
___ viewed by Bianchini, 5740as[84]
   Italy, dance, relation to tarantella, 4939as[76],
      4940as[76]
   literature, depiction of shepherd songs, 850as[19]
   Mediterranean region, culture, influence on
      Christian chant, 1029as[22]
   Paleolithic era, musical behavior, 1049as[22]
   Palestine, Jewish music, Qumran Scrolls, 1047as[22]
   philosophy, influence on Ficino, 5624as[81]
   poetry, meter, influence on Gregorian chant,
      4016as[61]
___ ___ use of common time, 5310as[78]
   polytheistic cultures, religious texts, relation to
      psalmody, 1048as[22]
   relation to 20th-c. dance music, 2826as[34]
   Roman Empire, literature, poetic meters, 5310as[78]
___ treatises, 1039as[22]
   sculpture, basis of Renaissance iconography,
      5405as[79]
   Serbia, Kupalo cult, 3098as[34]
   South America, instruments, 3195as[36]
___ scales, 4126as[62]
   Spain, instruments, iconography, 3044as[34]
___ Numancia settlement, 5742as[84]
   Sumeria, culture, influence on Anatolian dance,
      5061as[34]
   theory, consonance and dissonance, 4135as[63]
   Ukraine, relation to Christmas songs, 2902as[34]

ANTONIADES, Sophia, 6106as[92]
ANTONIJEVIĆ, Dragoslav, 2721as[34], 2722as[34],
   5281as[78], 5282as[78]

Antonio da Tempo
   writings, *Delle rime volgari*, 1108as[23]

ANTONOVYČ, Myroslav, 1224as[24], 1309as[24],
   2723as[34], 6130as[92], 6149as[93]
ANTZE, Gustav Wilhelm Otto, 176bs

anzad (=imzad), *see* **instruments — string (violin
   family)**

Aotearoa, *see* **New Zealand**

Apel, Johann Georg Christian
   life, cantorship at U. Kiel, from 1818, 4822as[72]

APEL, Willi, 1091as[23], 1225as[24], 3898as[58], 4230as[64]

Apolloni, Salvatore
   works, operas, influenced by traditional music,
      1691as[25]

APPEL, Ernst, 1057as[23]

Appenzeller, Benedictus
   life, state of research, 1439as[24]

APPIA, Adolphe, 5096as[77]

Appia, Adolphe
   works, art, scenography, 5091as[77]

works, directing, influence on Bayreuth
  Festspiele, 1951-64, 5184as[77]
APPLEBAUM, Louis, 423bs
appoggiatura, *see* **ornamentation**
appreciation, *see also* **audiences**; **pedagogy** headwords
  Belgium, influenced by radio, ca. 1937, 2305as[29]
  Canada, influenced by Canadian Broadcasting
    Corporation (CBC), ca. 1953, 4665as[70],
    4666as[70]
  children, relation to ear training, 4785as[71]
  early, role of public libraries, 674as[1]
  India, Hindustani tradition, 2644as[33], 4516as[70]
  influenced by mass media, 2349as[29]
  influenced by radio, 2382as[29], 2407as[29]
  influenced by sound recordings, ca. 1937,
    2307as[29], 5788as[85]
  influenced by study of composer correspondence,
    902as[20]
  listening, pedagogy, 4482as[70], 4483as[70]
  ___ radio, 5707as[82]
  ___ ___ compared with live performance,
    5697as[82]
  ___ relation to communication theory, 5674as[82]
  ___ ca. 1961, 5606as[81]
  pedagogy, Germany, role of radio, 5784as[85]
  ___ recorded anthologies, 969as[21]
  ___ secondary, ca. 1937, 4764as[71]
  ___ use of phonograph records, 4504as[70],
    4505as[70]
  ___ ___ recorded anthologies, 970as[21]
  psychology, 5579as[81], 5700as[82]
  ___ relation to 20th-c. music, 5456as[81]
  religious music, Roman Catholic, influenced by
    radio, 5744as[85]
  role of amateur associations, 4547as[70]
  role of criticism, 5471as[81]
  role of public libraries, 607as[1], 608as[1], 673as[1]
  20th-c. music, influenced by criticism, ca. 1937,
    5621as[81]
  ___ relation to pedagogy, 4690as[71]
aptitude and ability, *see also* **perception**; **testing**
  instrumental playing, relation to public schools,
    4722as[71]
  mathematics, relation to eurythmics, 4678as[71]
  musicality, 5679as[82]
  ___ typology, 5718as[82]
  relation to handwriting, 5385as[79]
  relation to heredity, 5683as[82]
  talent, 5695as[82]
  ___ relation to heredity, 5719as[82]
Aquileian chant, *see* **chant — Christian (Western)**
Aquinas, Thomas
  writings, views on music, 5493as[81]
Aquitanian repertoire, *see also* **chant — Christian
  (Western)**; **conductus**; **discant**; **organum**
  sequence, influenced by Jumièges repertoire,
    1073as[23]
  11th-12th c., 1146as[23]
Arab studies, *see also* **Islamic studies**; **maqām**;
  Middle East; specific countries
  antiquity, use of microtones, 4080as[62]
  discography, Congress on Arab Music
    performances, Al-Qāhirah, 1932, 827as[9]
  instruments, influence on Byzantine instruments,
    3239as[40]
  ___ traditional, 3273as[40]
  Israel, traditional music, ca. 1964, 2637as[33]
  literature, mūwaššaḥ, relation to strambotto,
    5328as[78]
  musicology, research policies, 1932, 870as[20]
  Spain, Hispano-Arabic music, 2923as[34]
  ___ musical heritage, 1174as[23]
  theory, 3941as[60]
  ___ scales, 4063as[62], 4090as[62]
  ___ 7th-20th c., 4070as[62]
  traditional music, conference, 1932, 196bs,
    2296as[29]
  ___ influence on Bartók, 4364as[66]

influence on Israeli art music, 1940-63,
  2143as[28]
___ rhythmic patterns, 3982as[61]
___ song texts, poetic genres, 5312as[78]
___ structural patterns, 3963as[60]
ARAMON I SERRA, Ramon, 4930as[76], 4931as[76]
Aramon i Serra, Ramon
  editions, *Corpus des troubadours*, 3898as[58]
Arbeau, Thoinot, *see* **Tabourot, Jehan (Thoinot
  Arbeau)**
Arcadelt, Jacques
  works, Italian songs, 5313as[78]
  ___ relation to French-Italian cultural exchange,
    1330as[24]
archaeology, *see also* **antiquity**
  conferences, 1892, 16bs
  ___ 1898, 25bs
  ___ 1909, 63bs
  ___ 1929, 156bs
  ___ 1930, 162bs
  ___ 1931, 192bs
  ___ 1935, 221bs
  Georgia, instruments, flute, prehistoric times,
    3614as[45]
  Greece, Acharnai, instruments, lyre, 3604as[44]
  ___ instruments, aulos, relation to performance
    technique, 3610as[45]
  instruments, viewed by Bianchini, 5740as[84]
  Israel, instruments, kinnor, 3549as[44]
  Italy, Sicilia, Grotte dell'Addaura, Stone Age cave
    graffiti, representations of dance, 5075as[76]
  Middle East, Palestine, ca. 1961, 5739as[84]
  Poland, instruments, early Middle Ages, research,
    1956-60, 5741as[84]
  Spain, Numancia, 5742as[84]
ARCHER, William Kay, 443bs, 2415as[30], 2492as[31]
architecture, *see also* **acoustics**; **performance
  venues**
  acoustics, relation to auditorium design, 5854as[86]
  ___ relation to history of music, 5859as[86]
  churches, Protestant, viewed by church musicians,
    5803as[86]
  ___ relation to organ building, 3499as[42]
  Europe, Romanesque, 1117as[23]
  France, 11th-13th c., 3871as[55]
  Germany, East Berlin, Deutsche Staatsbibl., music
    section, 732as[2]
  Italy, Roma, Baroque churches, relation to
    polychoral style, 5813as[86]
  music libraries, 576as[1]
  theaters, early 20th c., 5820as[86]
archives, *see* **catalogues — library, museum, collection**; **libraries, museums, collections**
Archytas
  writings, genera rations, 4128as[62]
ARCO Y GARAY, Ricardo del, 2724as[34], 2725as[34],
  4932as[76], 4933as[76]
ardin, *see* **instruments — string (harp family)**
Aredz (Ulner), Eva
  life, relation to Burgh, 1578as[25]
ARETZ, Isabel, 953as[21], 3189as[36], 3190as[36]
Argentina
  dance, traditional, state of research, 5039as[76]
  economics, counterfeit scores, 5976as[89]
  traditional music, role in storytelling, 3191as[36]
aria, *see also* **opera** headwords; **song** headwords
  Bach, J.S., form, 4244as[64]
  Ciampi, V.L., *Bertold, Bertoldino e Cacasenno*,
    5248as[77]
  form, through-composed, compared with strophic
    lied, 4257as[64]
  Händel, G.F., ornamentation, 3779as[52]
  solo parts, instrumental characteristics, ca.
    1700-50, 1575as[25]
ARIMA, Daigoro, 4677as[71]
arioso, *see* **aria**

Ariosti, Attilio
  works, viola d'amore, 3579as[44]
Aristotle
  writings, aesthetics, 5498as[81]
  ___ *Problemata physica* (attributed), 5528as[81]
  ___ relation to pedagogy, 4601as[70]
  ___ rhetoric, 5464as[81]
Aristoxenus
  writings, scale theory, 4048as[62]
Armenia
  musical life, Händel reception, 2322as[29]
  religious music, editions, *Sharakan hayastaneayts
    ekeghetswoy/Hymnes de l'église
    arménienne*, 3891as[58]
  ___ folkloric elements, 12th c., 1155as[23]
  traditional music, microtonality, 4065as[62]
ARMSTRONG, Robert G., 2551as[32]
ARMSTRONG, Thomas, 942as[21]
Arnaut Daniel
  writings, viewed by Dante, 5335as[78]
ARNBERG, Matts, 2726as[34]
ARNHEIM, Amalie, 1479as[25], 1480as[25], 1481as[25]
ARNHEIM, Rudolf, 5635as[82]
Arnim, Ludwig Achim von
  editions, *Des Knaben Wunderhorn*, influence on
    Mahler, 2005as[27]
  ___ ___ role of Reichardt, 2089as[27]
ARNOLD, A., 471bs, 5413as[80], 5416as[80]
ARNOLD, Byron, 3133as[35]
Arnold, Carl
  life, Norway, 966as[21]
ARNOLD, Denis, 1482as[25]
Arnol'd, Jurij Karlovič
  life, views on Liszt, 1840s-50s, 2025as[27]
Arnold, Samuel James
  writings, revisions of *The jovial crew* (1813),
    5234as[77]
Arnold de Lantins, *see* **Lantins, Arnold de**
Aron, Pietro, *see* **Aaron, Pietro**
Arouet, François Marie (Voltaire)
  life, Genève, relation to Mozart, 1879as[26]
arrangements, *see also* **instrumentation and
  orchestration**; **intabulation**; **paraphrase
  (19th c.)**
  Bach, J.C., sonatas, keyboard, op. 5 no. 2, by
    Mozart, as concerto, 1815as[26]
  Bach, J.S., fugues, by Mozart, for string trio,
    4392as[66]
  ___ of Luther *Vater unser im Himmelreich*,
    1567as[25]
  ___ of own works, 1533as[25]
  ___ of Reincken trio sonata movements, 1588as[25]
  ___ of Vivaldi concertos, 1608as[25]
  ___ of Vivaldi string concertos, for keyboard,
    1537as[25]
  ___ vocal music, by Classic composers, 1750as[26]
  Beethoven, L. van, concertos, violin, by Pössner,
    as piano concerto, 1787as[26]
  Bosanac, F., of Gareth *Amando e desiando*,
    3695as[51]
  Burleigh, H.T., of spirituals, 3184as[35]
  chanson, as lied, 15th c., 4253as[64]
  Chant of the Sybil, 12th c., 1165as[23]
  Classic, of Bach vocal works, 1750as[26]
  Coleridge-Taylor, S., of spirituals, 3184as[35]
  Dett, R.N., of spirituals, 3184as[35]
  Durante, F., of Scarlatti arias, for duet, 1549as[25]
  Germany, of vocal and instrumental works, for
    instruments, Baroque era, 1536as[25]
  harp, of polonaises, 1788as[25]
  Janáček, L., of Liszt *Missa pro organo...*, 2255as[28]
  Lassus, R. de, of vocal music, for instruments,
    viewed by Le Roy, 1242as[25]
  Liszt, F., *Missa pro organo...*, 1879, by Janáček,
    2255as[28]
  Luther, M., *Vater unser im Himmelreich*, by Bach,
    1567as[25]

B

USA, 3177as[35]
___ relation to UK versions, 3177as[35]
___ shared features, 2750as[34]
ballad opera, *see* **opera** headwords
ballade (medieval)
relation to traditional poetry, 5289as[78]
ballade (19th-20th c.), *see* **instruments — keyboard (piano family)**
Ballard, Pierre
editions, *Tablature de luth de differens autheurs*, Dufaut lute dances, 3920as[58]
Ballard, Robert
life, publication of Helfer Requiem, 3754as[52]
ballata
Italy, use of instruments, 14th c., 3690as[51]
___ 15th c., 1062as[23]
ballet, *see* **choreographers**; **dance — ballet**; **dance — by place**; **dance — notation**; **dance music** headwords
ballet de cour, *see* **dance — ballet**
ballet music, *see* **dance music** headwords
BALLMANN, Willibrord, 6158as[93]
BALLY, Charles, 5918as[88]
BALON, J., 260bs
BALTER, G., 3937as[60], 3958as[60], 5411as[80], 5414as[80], 5418as[80]
BALTHASAR, Karl, 6424as[94]
Baltic states, *see also* specific countries
traditional music, influence on Reichardt, 1849as[26]
___ relation to Kurpie traditional music, 3067as[34]
BALTZ, Karl von, 4486as[70]
BALYS, Jonas, 3134as[35]
BANCAL, Jean, 6159as[93]
Banchieri, Adriano
works, canzoni strumentali, dedications, 1425as[24]
___ relation to Baroque, 1244as[24]
band, *see also* **ensemble playing**; **orchestra**; **performing organizations**
Belgium, amateurs, repertoire, 2351as[29]
___ 1er Régiment de Guides, 4624as[70]
Germany, Mecklenburg, 19th c., 2804as[34]
Greece, performances of Mozart, 19th c., 1999as[27]
instrumentation, history and development, 3640as[45]
instrumentation and orchestration, 3788as[53]
Spain, Valencia, 3044as[34]
band music, *see also* **fanfare**; **instruments — wind**; **military music**; **orchestral music**; specific genres
Czech Republic, Moravia, traditional, influence on Janáček, 2185as[28]
Poland, Podhale, depicted in Szymanowski *Harnasie*, 2221as[28]
Spontini, G., 1969as[27]
BANDEIRA, Manuel, 5919as[88]
BANDMANN, Tony, 4487as[70]
bandora, *see* **instruments — string (cittern family)**
Bandur, Jovan
works, *Jugoslavenska partizanska rapsodija*, influenced by War of National Liberation songs, 2227as[28]
Bangladesh
history of music, 2703as[33]
traditional music, songs, 2599as[33], 2660as[33]
bāṅsuri, *see* **instruments — wind (woodwind, flute family)**
bar form, *see* **form**
BARANDIARÁN, Salvador de, 4935as[76]
Barbag, Seweryn Eugeniusz
writings, on Szymanowski, 2259as[28]
BARBEAU, Marius, 3135as[35], 3136as[35], 3137as[35], 3138as[35], 4936as[76], 4937as[76], 5286as[78]
Barbeau, Marius
collections, Salish songs, 3152as[35]

BARBERÀ, Josep, 2730as[34]
Barberini family
lives, relation to Mazarin, 1661as[25]
BARBI, M., 5287as[78]
Barbireau, Jacques
life, at Hungarian court, 1326as[24]
BARBLAN, Guglielmo, 1724as[26], 1909as[27]
BARBOUR, J. Murray, 1714as[25], 4369as[66]
BARBRY, Winoc, 6160as[93]
barcarole
Italy, relation to opera, early 18th c., 1691as[25]
Barceló, Antonio R.
writings, on Argentinian folk dances, 5039as[76]
Bardi, Giovanni, *see* **De' Bardi, Giovanni**
bards, *see* **epic**; **performers — traditional and neotraditional music**
BAR-DYYAN, Ḥayym, 6039as[91], 6040as[91]
BARFUSS, Franciszek, 5099as[77]
BARGILLIAT, Michael, 4806as[72]
BARINI, Giorgio, 518as[1], 4488as[70]
BÆRISWYL, J., 4678as[71]
BARKECHLI, Mehdi, 2419as[30], 2420as[30], 2607as[33], 4047as[62], 4048as[62], 4135as[63]
Baroni-Cavalcabò, Josephine
collections, W.A. Mozart autograph fragments, 1842as[26]
Baroque, *see also* **performance practice — by topic**; **rococo**; **visual and plastic arts**
architecture, influence on instrumental style, 5859as[86]
as concept, 1489as[25]
conferences, 1957, 386bs
___ 1960, 422bs
___ 1963, 469bs
Czech Republic, 1653as[25]
editions, Denkmäler vs. Gesamtausgaben, 3915as[58]
form, perception, 4286as[64]
history of music, influenced by traditional music, 1017as[21]
instruments, organology, 817as[8]
as musicological concept, critique, 1525as[25]
opera and oratorio, relation to instrumental genres, 1714as[25]
Poland, 1697as[25]
religious music, state of research, ca. 1911, 1710as[25]
rhetoric, 5464as[81]
___ relation to counterpoint, 1521as[25]
rhythm and meter, relation to dance music, 3997as[61]
singing, improvisation, 3778as[52]
state of research, ca. 1957, 1510as[25]
style, 1626as[25]
___ compared with 20th-c. style, 2217as[28]
___ concept of parody, 1496as[25]
___ geographical distribution, 1629as[25]
___ periodization, 1244as[24]
___ relation to mannerism, 1713as[25]
___ relation to visual and plastic arts, 1509as[25]
___ stile antico, 1548as[25]
___ use of dissonance, rhetorical value, 4197as[63]
___ vertical texture, influenced by Italian organ tablature, 1356as[24]
___ viewed by theorists, 1733as[26]
theory, classification of dissonances, 4156as[63]
___ form, 4377as[66]
BARRAQUÉ, Jean, 4308as[66]
barrel organ, *see* **instruments — mechanical**
BARROS, Carlos Marinho de Paula, 5288as[78]
BARROS, M., 2549as[32]
BARTH, Karl, 2409as[29]
BARTHA, Dénes, 405bs, 812as[8], 1725as[26], 1726as[26], 1908as[27], 2134as[28], 2456as[30], 2458as[30], 4136as[63], 4137as[63], 4309as[66], 4369as[66]
BARTL, Rudolf Heinz, 4679as[71]

BARTÓK, Béla, 2421as[30], 2731as[34]
Bartók, Béla
correspondence, edited by Demény, 2269as[28]
___ to Brăiloiu, 3094as[34]
editions, traditional music, 2190as[28]
festivals and conferences, Hungary, Budapest, 1961, 427bs
___ Budapest, 1963, 428bs
life, 2154as[28]
___ England visits, 2129as[28]
___ personality, 2260as[28]
___ state of research, 2269as[28]
___ 1961, 2155as[28]
___ transcriptions, 2434as[30]
___ Turkey, 3051as[34]
___ views on Gypsy music, 2850as[34]
manuscripts, *Melodien der rumänischen Colinde (Weihnachtslieder)*, Brăiloiu annotations, 3094as[34]
reception, China, 1950s, 2412as[29]
___ Russia, 1928-29, 2216as[28]
works, compared with Janáček, 2237as[28], 2238as[28], 2267as[28]
___ *Concerto for orchestra*, BB 123, form and instrumentation, 4292as[64]
___ concertos, violin, no. 2, BB 117, use of 12-tone technique with tonal structure, 3938as[60]
___ harmony, 4137as[63]
___ ___ influenced by Asian melodies, 4152as[63]
___ influence on Israeli art music, 1950-59, 2143as[28]
___ influenced by Bach, 2272as[28]
___ influenced by Bulgarian traditional music, 2229as[28]
___ influenced by Debussy, 2134as[28]
___ influenced by Eastern music, 2188as[28]
___ influenced by Liszt, 2248as[28]
___ influenced by 19th-c. Hungarian poetry, 5360as[78]
___ melodies, relation to intonation theory, 4459as[69]
___ *Öt dal*, BB 72, 2138as[28]
___ piano music, form, 4235as[64]
___ ___ influenced by traditional song, 4469as[69]
___ quartets, string, style innovations, 4337as[66]
___ realism, 4364as[66]
___ relation to overtones, 4136as[63]
___ stage works, use of developing variation, 4443as[69]
___ state of research, 1961, 2155as[28]
___ suites, piano, BB 70, withdrawn andante movt., 2203as[28]
___ use of arch form, 4290as[64]
___ use of older forms, 4231as[64]
___ use of quotation, psychological meaning, 4317as[66]
___ viewed by Pijper, 2149as[28]
writings, Bulgarian traditional music, 2229as[28]
___ classification of traditional melodies, 4470as[69]
___ classification of traditional songs, 4261as[64]
___ criticism, in *Nyugat*, 2138as[28]
___ ethnomusicology, compared with Janáček, 4393as[64]
___ views on long song genre, 2496as[31]
Bartók, Paula Voit
correspondence, from B. Bartók, 2129as[28]
BARTOŠ, Josef, 183bs
BARUCH, Gerth Wolfgang, 5943as[89]
Baryphonus, Henricus
works, counterpoint, 4203as[63]
Barzellis, Pietrobono de, *see* **Pietrobono de Burzellis**
BARZUN, Jacques, 1908as[27]
BAS, Giulio, 51as[16], 1228as[24], 4863as[73]
BASCH, Victor, 249bs
BASCOM, William R., 2422as[30]

Belarus

Karlin, Hasidic people, religious music, Seder melodies, 6061as[91]

BELDA, Juan, 6164as[93]

Belgique, *see* **Belgium**

Belgium, *see also* **Low Countries**

Antwerpen, collections, instruments, 714as[2]

___ musical life, "De Werker" concerts, 2359as[29]

___ ___ publishing and printing, Plantin-Moretus firm, 5973as[89]

___ religious music, psalters, 4430as[69]

Binche, musical life, festivities for Felipe II, 1549, 1329as[24]

Bruxelles, musical life, concerts, 20th-c. music, ca. 1937, 2311as[29]

___ ___ court patronage, 1430-1559, 1361as[24]

cultural policies, Conseil Supérieur de l'Éducation Populaire, 5902as[87]

___ national symphony orchestra, projected, 1932, 4624as[70]

___ pedagogy, 4553as[70]

___ therapy, institutionalized mental patients, ca. 1953, 5731as[83], 5732as[83]

___ ca. 1932, 4915as[74]

culture, conferences, 1913, 89bs

___ ___ 1925, 119bs

___ 18th c., conference, 1936, 220bs

Dinant, history, conference, 1903, 41bs

ethnomusicology, activities of Inst. de la Radiodiffusion Nationale Belge, 2504as[31]

Flanders, history of music, conference, 1934, 210bs

___ ___ 19th c., 904as[20]

___ instruments, Middle Ages, terminology, 1185as[23]

___ traditional music, religious festivals, 3646as[46]

___ western, culture, influence on Beethoven, 1736as[26]

Frameries, musical life, mass concert, 2284as[29]

Hasselt, musical life, 16th c., 1232as[24]

history of music, birthplace of Philippe de Monte, 1375as[24]

___ influence on Germany, 17th-18th c., 1479as[25]

___ Old Flemish songs, 1471as[24]

___ Renaissance, 1363as[24]

___ 15th-16th c., 1253as[24]

___ 14th c. to present, 948as[21]

instruments, carillon, 18th-20th c., 3648as[46]

___ early music, inventories, proposed, 1909, 3242as[40]

___ iconography, antiquity, 3280as[40]

___ Middle Ages, 1194as[23]

___ organ builders, 17th-18th c., 3333as[42]

Kalken, musical life, 17th-18th c., 1478as[25]

Kempen, dance, 2989as[34]

___ traditional music, songs, 2989as[34]

Liège, history of music, conference, 1909, 64bs

___ ___ 10th-12th c., 1137as[23]

___ instruments, organ, 814-1805, 3397as[42]

___ musical life, national theatre and opera, 18th c., 1600as[25]

___ musicology, state of research, ca. 1909, 867as[20]

___ ___ 1910-11, 868as[20]

___ pedagogy, Conservatoire Royal de Musique, establishment, 4627as[70]

___ periodicals, *L'écho, ou Journal de musique françoise, italienne,* 1734as[26]

Liège area, pedagogy, 1930s, 4503as[70]

mass media, radio, audiences, ca. 1954, 5886as[87]

___ ___ influence on appreciation, ca. 1937, 2305as[29]

Mechelen, history of music, discant, 15th c., 1289as[24]

___ instruments, organ builders, 16th-19th c., 3349as[42]

___ ___ Tuerlinckx family, 18th-19th c., 3609as[45]

___ musical life, minstrels as watchmen, 1311-1790, 938as[21]

musical life, chamber music concerts, 3682as[50]

___ Jeunesses Musicales, 2310as[29]

___ Middle Ages, influenced by Ireland, 2818as[34]

___ role of Orchestre Symphonique Populaire, 2283as[29]

___ workers' music associations, 19th-20th c., 4913as[74], 4914as[74]

Namur, culture, conference, 1938, 260bs

___ musical life, youth festivals, 1929-33, 2787as[34]

pedagogy, music history as subject, 4809as[72]

religious music, 18th c., 1602as[25]

traditional music, preservation, 2741as[34], 2868as[34]

___ relation to pedagogy, 4542as[70]

Wallonie, history of music, 1016as[21]

___ ___ chansons, early 16th c., 1233as[24]

___ traditional music, songs, prenuptial bed rituals, 2969as[34]

BELJAEV, Viktor Mihailovič, 833as[19], 1063as[23], 2737as[34], 4050as[62]

BELJON, J.J., 4491as[70]

Bella, Ján Levoslav

works, 947as[21]

Bellini, Vincenzo

performance practice, operas, 3294as[41]

works, operas, concept of genre, 5169as[77]

___ use of Sicilian traditional melodic style, 1013as[21]

BELLIOT, Henri, 4492as[70]

bells, *see* **instruments — percussion (bells)**

Belorussia, *see* **Belarus**

BELVIANES, Marcel, 5867as[87]

BÊLZA, Igor' Fëdorovič, 1484as[25], 1913as[27]

BENARY, Peter, 1485as[25], 5374as[79]

Benati, Carlo Antonio

manuscripts, embellishment of Bononcini *Duetti da camera,* 1549as[25]

Benda, Franz

works, influenced by Czech traditional songs, 2944as[34]

___ relation to Mozart, 1843as[26]

Benda, Georg, *see* **Benda, Jiří**

Benda, Jiří

works, influenced by Czech traditional songs, 2944as[34]

___ melodramas, influence on Mozart, 5225as[77]

___ relation to Mozart, 1843as[26]

BENEDETTI-MICHELANGELI, Flavio, 3887as[58]

Benedict, Saint

writings, Office regulations, compared with Columbanus Office, 6193as[93]

Benedict XIV, Pope

writings, *Annus qui,* influence on Haydn and Mozart, 1754as[26]

BENEDITO, Rafael, 4493as[70], 4680as[71], 4681as[71]

Benevoli, Orazio

life, 1544as[25]

works, polychoral music, 5813as[86]

BENGTSSON, Ingmar, 944as[21], 1914as[27], 3969as[61], 5677as[82]

Ben-Haim, Paul

works, to 1947, 2228as[28]

Benin

traditional music, Vodun music, female initiation songs, 2578as[32]

BENNEDIK, Frank, 4494as[70]

Bennet, John

works, madrigals, 1411as[24]

Benoît, Peter

aesthetics, nationalism, 949as[21], 2057as[27]

festivals and conferences, Belgium, Antwerpen, 1934, 210bs, 2328as[29]

life, Antwerpen, 1926as[27]

___ relation to Hiel, 2118as[27]

___ relation to Tinel, 2054as[27]

manuscripts, 2119as[27]

works, influenced by Debussy, 2225as[28]

___ influenced by Liszt, 2070as[27]

___ operas, 1986as[27]

___ publication, 2087as[27]

___ relation to 20th-c. music, 1944as[27]

Bentinck, Willem

life, relation to Pergolesi, 1515as[25]

Bentivoglio d'Aragona, Guido

correspondence, from Vivaldi, 1507as[25]

BENTLEY, Arnold, 4807as[72], 4808as[72]

BENTON, Rita, 859as[20], 3506as[43]

BENTZON, Jorgen, 4495as[70]

Benvenuti, Giacomo

editions, early Italian organ music, 3895as[58]

BEN-'WRY, Me'yr, 6044as[91]

Berchem, Jacquet de, *see* **Jacquet de Berchem**

works, use of soggetti cavati, 1452as[24]

BEREKOVEN, Hanns, 4682as[71]

Berg, Alban

performances, *Wozzeck,* at Edinburgh Internat. Festival, 1959, 5191as[77]

reception, operas, 2406as[29]

___ *Wozzeck,* relation to Nazi censorship, 5235as[77]

works, atonal music, formal organization, 4335as[66]

___ concertos, violin, use in pedagogy, 4683as[71]

___ operas, role of libretto, 5111as[77]

___ ___ use of passacaglia form, 5112as[77]

___ ___ viewed by Pilarczyk, 5224as[77]

___ relation to history of 20th-c. music, 2140as[28]

___ serialism, 2249as[28]

___ use of older forms, 4231as[64]

___ *Wozzeck,* 5147as[77]

___ ___ compared with Debussy *Pelléas et Mélisande,* 2257as[28]

writings, film scenario for *Lulu,* 5266as[77]

BERGER, Gregor, 4683as[71]

Bergère, Antoine

life, organ building, 3333as[42]

Bergese, Hans

writings, contributions to Orff method, 4573as[70], 4574as[70]

Berghe, Philippe van den, *see* **Monte, Philippe de**

BERGMANN, Robert, 3231as[38]

BERGMANN, Walter, 1486as[25]

BERGMANS, Paul, 1232as[24], 3242as[40], 3643as[46], 5946as[89]

Bergson, Henri-Louis

aesthetics, 5617as[81]

writings, aesthetic innovation, 5601as[81]

___ music symbolism, 5934as[88]

BERIO, Luciano, 2181as[28]

Berio, Luciano

life, founding of Studio di Fonologia Musicale, 4404as[68]

works, *Mutazioni,* 4401as[68]

Berlin, Isaiah

writings, thick description concept, applied to historical musicology, 5539as[81]

Berlin, Johan Daniel

life, Norway residence, 966as[21]

Berlioz, Hector

reception, France, late 19th-early 20th c., 1948as[27]

works, appropriation of Gypsy themes, 5962as[89]

___ in holdings of Nat. Lib. of Scotland, 739as[2]

___ influence on history of French music, 1984as[27]

___ Requiem, relation to bourgeois realism, 5497as[81]

___ *Les troyens,* 5139as[77]

writings, relation to ethnomusicology, 865as[20]

___ views on Encyclopedists, 5430as[81]

Bermudo, Juan

writings, on glosa, 3699as[51]

history of music, World War II songs, 2916as[34]
instruments, children's instruments, 3263as[40]
___ traditional, research issues, 3034as[34]
literature, song texts, metric analysis, 5344as[78]
Muslim people, instruments, surrogate
___ instruments, 2967as[34]
periodicals, *Behar*, writings on folklore, 635as[1]
Skender Vakuf, Imljani, literature, traditional,
___ 5354as[78]
traditional music, ballads, 3031as[34]
___ epics, relation to nationalism, 2910as[34]
___ laments, 5355as[78]
___ polyphony, 4211as[63]
___ ___ relation to Albanian music, 3033as[34]
___ rhythm, 3035as[34]
___ songs, 3119as[34]
___ ___ melody types, 4462as[69]
Trebinjska Šuma, musical life, epic performance,
___ ca. 1962, 2754as[34]

Bossuet, Jean-Bénigne
writings, funeral orations, for Queen
___ Marie-Thérèse, 1683, 1601as[25]
BOSTON, Noel, 3658as[47]
BOTTAZZO, Luigi, 51as[16]
BOTTÉE DE TOULMON, Auguste, 951as[21]

Bouasse, Henri Pierre Maxime
writings, *Instruments à vent*, 3555as[44]

Boudin, Eugène-Louis
works, art, viewed by Debussy, 5396as[79]

Boughton, Rutland
works, operas, 5108as[77]

Boulez, Pierre
works, serialism, rhythmic features, 1950s,
___ 4017as[61]
BOULTON, Laura, 2608as[33]
BOUMAN, Arie, 3346as[42]
BOUMAN, M.A., 5849as[86]
BOURDELLÉS (ABBÉ), 4bs

Bourdin, Louis
life, organ playing, relation to Paris organ building
___ school, 3386as[42]

Bourgeois, Loys
works, *Pseaulmes de David*, compared with
___ Goudimel *Pseaumes mis en rime françoise*,
___ 1310as[24]

Bourges, Élémir
writings, influenced by Wagner, 5319as[78]
BOUTIN, Alfred, 2083as[27]
BOUTROUX, Léon, 3693as[51]
BOVET, Joseph, 3972as[61]

Bovett, Charles
writings, on broadcasts of Latin American music,
___ 2398as[29]
BOVY, Adrien, 5376as[79]
bow, *see* **instruments — string** headwords
bow, musical (=musical bow), *see* **instruments —
___ string (musical bow)**
bowed instruments, *see* **instruments — string** head-
___ words
BOWER, John Dykes, 375bs
BOWLES, Edmund A., 3249as[40], 5905as[87]

Boxberg, Christian Ludwig
life, 1689as[25]
manuscripts, cantata cycles, at U. Bibl. Lund,
___ 1689as[25]

Boyce, William
performance practice, vivace movements,
___ 3736as[52]
BOYDEN, David D., 3732as[52], 3733as[52]
BOYER, Louis, 6177as[93], 6178as[93]
BOYKAN, Martin, 4858as[72]

Boyle, Roger, Earl of Orrery
writings, *The tragedy of Saul* (attributed), relation
___ to Händel oratorios, 5274as[77]

Boyleau, Simon
works, secular, 1460as[24]
boys' voices, *see* **choir schools**

Brade, William
works, influence on Germany, 1480as[25]
BRAGAGLIA, Anton Giulio, 4941as[76]
BRAGARD, Roger, 709as[2], 1256as[24]

Brahms, Johannes
aesthetics, 5465as[81]
collections, MSS and prints, O. Jonas collection
___ (private), 726as[2]
correspondence, to Krančević, 1946as[27]
life, relation to Wolf, 2104as[27]
___ views on Bach, 2001as[27]
performance practice, diminuendo sign, 3854as[55]
___ tempo indications, 3990as[61]
performances, as accompanist, Germany, 1853,
___ 1973as[27]
works, concertos, violin, op. 77, 4384as[66]
___ influenced by Bach, 2272as[28]
___ influenced by Chopin, 2065as[27], 2096as[27]
___ lieder, text setting, 4333as[66]
___ relation to typology, 5428as[81]
___ settings of verbunkos and csárdás, influenced
___ by Reményi, 1973as[27]
___ sonata form, 4291as[64]
___ text setting, apparent rythmic flaws, 2018as[27]
___ variations, 4368as[66]
BRĂILOIU, Constantin, 527as[1], 865as[20], 2424as[30],
___ 2495as[31], 2496as[31], 2747as[34], 3973as[61],
___ 4496as[70]

Brăiloiu, Constantin
life, relation to Bartók, 3094as[34]
writings, syllabic giusto concept, applied to Krítí
___ traditional song, 3967as[61]
BRANCA, Vittore, 384bs
BRANCO, Luís de Freitas, 4143as[63]

Branco, Luís de Freitas
works, influenced by Beethoven, 1820as[26]
BRANDÃO, Paulo José Pires, 99bs

Brandmann, Israel
works, 2228as[28]

Brandon, Elizabeth
collections, Louisiana cantiques, 3140as[35],
___ 3170as[35]
BRANDSMA, Engbert, 4052as[62]
branle, *see* **dance — by genre**
Brasil, *see* **Brazil**
BRAŠOVANOVA-STANČEVA, Lada, 1922as[27]
brass bands, *see* **band**; **performing organizations**
BRASSARD, François-Joseph, 2497as[31]
BRASSINNE, Jacques, 64bs

Braun, Peter von
writings, revision of Schikaneder *Die Zauberflöte*
___ libretto, 5240as[77]
BRAUN, Werner, 1494as[25], 1495as[25], 1496as[25],
___ 1590as[25]
BRÄUTIGAM, Helmut, 2748as[34]

Bravničar, Matija
works, influenced by Slovenian traditional music,
___ 972as[21]

Brazil
Bahia, economics, relation to Candomblé,
___ 6458as[99]
___ religious music, Candomblé songs, African
___ origins, 3201as[36]
black people, funeral music, 2551as[32]
cultural policies, copyright law, relation to
___ Montevideo and Bern agreements, 5951as[89]
culture, Portuguese language, pronunciation,
___ regional dialects, 5919as[88]
ethnomusicology, ca. 1940, 3188as[36]
___ ca. 1952, 2413as[30]
folklore, 3202as[36]
history of music, 994as[21]
___ songs, 20th c., 2130as[28]

instruments, traditional, 3259as[40]
northeastern, dance, maracatu, role of calunga,
___ 4929as[76]
pedagogy, singing, relation to regional dialects,
___ 3299as[41]
religious music, Roman Catholic, ca. 1950,
___ 6312as[93]
Rio de Janeiro, musical life, Imperial Academia de
___ Música e Ópera Nac., Portuguese-language
___ productions, 1857-63, 1907as[27]
São Paulo state, culture, Portuguese dialects,
___ 5938as[88]
___ traditional music, 3205as[36]
traditional music, 3187as[36], 3204as[36]
___ conference, 1934, 214bs
___ influence on Villa-Lobos *Bachianas
___ brasileiras*, 4321as[66]
___ influenced by Tupinambá melodies, 3192as[36]
___ songs, Portuguese regional dialects, 3196as[36]
Tukano people, traditional music, instrumental
___ music, 3193as[36]
BRAŽNIKOV, Maksim V., 6107as[92]
BREAZUL, George, 1731as[26], 4497as[70]

Brecht, Bertolt
aesthetics, influence on 20th-c. opera, 5229as[77]
writings, librettos, 5211as[77]

Bredemers, Henry
life, 1355as[24]
BREDICEANU, Tiberiu, 2749as[34]
BRÉHIER, L., 116rs[16]
BREHMER, Fritz, 4418as[69]
BREIG, Werner, 4319as[66]

Breitkopf, Johann Gottlob Immanuel
correspondence, from C.P.E. Bach, 1815as[26]
BRELET, Gisèle, 2292as[29]
BRENCHER, Karl-Eckhardt, 5643as[82]
Brenet, Michel, *see* **Bobillier, Marie (Michel
___ Brenet)**
BRENN, Franz, 1068as[23], 3932as[60], 3974as[61],
___ 4053as[62], 5433as[81]
BRENNECKE, Wilfried, 319bs, 1257as[24], 1258as[24]
BRENTA, Gaston, 2498as[31]

Brentano, Clemens
editions, *Des Knaben Wunderhorn*, influence on
___ Mahler, 2005as[27]
___ role of Reichardt, 2089as[27]
writings, poetry, music as subject, 5350as[78]
BRETON, A.C., 3194as[36]
BRETON, Paul, 5951as[89]
breviaries, *see* **liturgical books**
BREWSTER, Paul G., 2499as[31]
BREZZO, Guido Lorenzo, 3807as[55]
BRICKEN, Carl, 4395as[67]
BRICQUEVILLE, Eugène de, 3245as[40]

Bridge, Richard
instruments, organs, 3396as[42]
BRIDGMAN, Nanie, 710as[2], 952as[21], 1069as[23],
___ 1259as[24], 1260as[24], 1269as[24], 1422as[24],
___ 4198as[63], 4234as[64]
BRIGGS, W.G., 283bs
BRILLOUIN, Jacques, 5644as[82], 5743as[85]
BRINER, Andres, 3975as[61], 5112as[77]
BRIQUET, Marie, 1497as[25], 1732as[26]
BRISTIGER, Michal, 2293as[29]

Britten, Benjamin
reception, operas, 2406as[29]
works, film music, 5115as[77]
___ influenced by Debussy, 2207as[28]
___ operas, role of libretto, 5111as[77]
___ ___ use of passacaglia form, 5112as[77]
BRITTEN, Valentine, 825as[9], 826as[9]
BRITTON, Allen P., 4905as[74], 4916as[74]

Brixi, František Xaver
works, relation to Mozart, 1843as[26]

broadcasting, *see* **mass media**

broadside ballad, *see* **ballad**

Broadway musical, *see* **musical theater — popular**

BROCK, Hella, 4687as[71]

BROCKBERND, Bernard, 5744as[85]

BROCKHAUS, Heinz Alfred, 5434as[81]

BROCKHOFF, Maria Elisabeth, 3933as[60], 4144as[63]

BRODER, Nathan, 3911as[58]

Brodziński, Kazimierz
life, nationalism, influence on Chopin, 2074as[27]

Brome, Richard
writings, *A jovial crew, or, The merry beggars*, basis of ballad opera *The jovial crew*, 5234as[77]

BRONSON, Bertrand Harris, 2500as[31], 2750as[34], 4419as[69]

BRONZINI, Giovanni Battista, 2751as[34]

BROOK, Barry S., 528as[1], 787as[5], 1670as[25], 1714as[25], 3734as[52]

Broschi, Carlo (Farinelli)
performance practice, improvisation, 3778as[52]
___ ornamentation, 1575as[25]

Brossard, Sébastien de
catalogues, thematic, 1648as[25]
collections, in Bibl. Nat., Paris, 3754as[52]
works, Mass accompaniments, 3754as[52]
writings, *Dictionnaire de musique*, discussion of uplift syncopation, 4031as[61]
___ Montéclair motets, 1497as[25]

Brosses, Charles de
writings, *Lettres familières écrites d'Italie*, 1739-40, relation to Pergolesi, 1611ac[25]

BROU, Louis, 1070as[23]

BROUARDEL, Paul-Camille-Hippolyte, 35bs

Broulík, Martin
works, influenced by Mozart, 1825as[26]

BROWN, Earle, 3808as[55]

Brown, Earle
works, *Music for cello and piano*, 3859as[55]
___ notation, 3847as[55]

BROWN, Howard Mayer, 1261as[24]

BROWN, Robert E., 2609as[33]

Broz, Josip (Tito)
life, depicted in Partisan songs, 2977as[34], 5282as[78]
tributes, ethnic-Albanian mass songs, 2908as[34]
___ songs, 1919-60, 2742as[34]

BRUCK, Charles, 2372as[29]

Bruckner, Anton
life, organ playing, 3463as[42]
manuscripts, original vs. final versions, 2052as[27]
works, influenced by Bach, 1951as[27]
___ Masses, compared with Liszt, 2019as[27]
___ religious music, compared with Beethoven, 1857as[26]
___ symphonies, form, 4264as[64]

Brudieu, Joan
life, 1396as[24]
works, 5365as[78]

BRUERS, Antonio, 279bs

BRUGER, Hans Dagobert, 3553as[44]

BRUGNOLI, Attilio, 4498as[70]

BRUMARE (ABBÉ), 1923as[27]

BRUN, F., 1924as[27], 6179as[93], 6180as[93]

BRUN, Herbert, 4399as[68]

BRUNHOLD, Paul, 1498as[25]

BRUNNER, Adolf, 6428as[94]

BRUSSELMANS, 5745as[85]

BRUYR, Jose, 4499as[70]

BRWY'ER, Mordekay, 503bs, 2610as[33], 4500as[70], 6045as[91], 6046as[91], 6047as[91], 6048as[91]

Bry, Theodor de
writings, *Collectiones peregrinationum in Indiam orientalem et Indiam occidentalem*,
corruption of Tupinambá melodies, 3192as[36]

Bryennius, Manuel
writings, 883as[20]

BUCCHI, Valentino, 5435as[81]

BUCHANAN, Annabel Morris, 3141as[35]

Büchel (=alphorn), *see* **instruments — wind (brass)**

BUCHNER, Alexandr, 1925as[27]

BUCK, Maurits De, 1926as[27]

BÜCKEN, Ernst, 1733as[26], 1927as[27], 5436as[81]

Bücken, Ernst
writings, 5562as[81]
___ relation to Italian aesthetics, 5577as[81]

Buddhist music, *see* **chant — Buddhist; religion and religious music — Buddhism**

BUECHNER, Alan C., 4916as[74]

bugaku, *see* **dance — by genre**

BUGIEL, V., 5293as[78]

BUHLE, Edward, 3246as[40]

BÜHLER, Karl, 101bs, 121bs, 188bs

Buini, Giuseppe Maria
works, operas, 1526as[25]

Buisson, Robert
life, organ playing, relation to Paris organ building school, 3386as[42]

BUKOFZER, Manfred F., 1071as[23], 1262as[24], 1263as[24], 2424as[30], 2752as[34], 4054as[62], 4055as[62], 5437as[81]

Bukofzer, Manfred F.
aesthetics, 5547as[81]

BULA, Karol, 5113as[77]

Bulgaria, *see also* **Slavic states**
dance, horo, relation to dance music, 4995as[76]
ethnomusicology, song classification, 1842-1900, 2875as[34]
folklore, poetic meters, relation to classical Greek meters, 5309as[78]
history of music, Byzantine, 9th-10th c., 1153as[23]
___ role of Kliment and Naum of Ohrid, 1138as[23]
___ 12th-18th c., 980as[21]
___ 1830-1914, 1922as[27]
instruments, traditional, 3256as[40], 3267as[40]
musical life, reception of Janáček, 2279as[29]
___ reception of Liszt, 20th c., 2371as[29]
Pădarevo, dance, kukeri mummers performances, 4994as[76]
Sephardic Jewish people, religious music, hymns, relation to Balkan traditional music, 2879as[34]
Timok river region, dance, history and development, 4987as[76]
___ traditional music, songs, 2959as[34]
traditional music, influence on Bartók, 2229as[28]
___ influence on Serbian World War II songs, 2854as[34]
___ preservation and revival, ca. 1948, 2876as[34]
___ rhythm and meter, influence on Bulgarian art music, 4005as[61]
___ songs, Hungarian history as subject, 3038as[34]
___ ___ Marko Kraljević as subject, 3039as[34]
___ ___ melodies, influence on Bartók piano music, 4469as[69]
___ ___ poetics, 5280as[78]
___ ___ relation to Falla *Siete canciones populares españolas*, 2773as[34]
___ ___ viewed by Janáček, 2279as[29]
___ vocal polyphony, 2880as[34]

Bulgarian music (outside Bulgaria)
Serbia, Zaječar region, 3098as[34]

Bulgarian Orthodox chant, *see* **chant — Eastern Orthodox; religion and religious music — Christianity (Eastern Orthodox)**

Bull, John
works, keyboard music, in Paris MS sources, 1343as[24]

Bülow, Hans von
life, relation to Nietzsche, 2121as[27]

Bulthaupt, Heinrich Alfred
writings, 5163as[77]

BUNDI, Gian, 1499as[25]

BUNKOWSKI, Arthur, 2294as[29]

Buonarroti, Michelangelo, *see* **Michelangelo Buonarroti**

BURCHENAL, Elizabeth, 4942as[76], 4943as[76], 4944as[76]

BURGER, André, 5294as[78]

Bürger, Gottfried August
writings, ballads, relation to piano ballade, 4245as[64]

Burgh, Cornelius
life, Mönchengladbach, 1578as[25]

Burian, Emil František
works, film music, for Steklý *Siréna*, 5275as[77]

Burkina Faso
Mossi people, traditional music, 2573as[32]

BURLAS, Ladislav, 4235as[64], 5112as[77]

BURLASOVÁ, Soňa, 2753as[34]

Burleigh, Henry Thacker (Harry)
works, arrangements, spirituals, 3184as[35]

burlesque (20th c.), *see* **musical revue, cabaret, etc.**

BURNEY, Charles, 1500ac[5]

BURRIS-MEYER, Harold, 5805as[86]

BURSSENS, Amaat F.S., 5920as[88]

Burundi
Rundi people, musical life, Umuganuro festival, 3063as[34]

Burwell, Mary
life, relation to Burwell Lute Tutor, 3737as[52]

BUSH, Alan, 2144as[28], 3735as[52]

BUSH, Helen E., 1264as[24]

business, *see* **careers; economics; management**

Busnois, Antoine
manuscripts, chansons, German sources, 1319as[24]

Busnoys, Antoine, *see* **Busnois, Antoine**

Busoni, Ferruccio
aesthetics, 3792as[54]
works, operas, role of libretto, 5111as[77]
___ use of passacaglia form, 5112as[77]
writings, concept of creativity, 1524as[25]
___ *Entwurf einer neuen Ästhetik der Tonkunst*, relation to microtonal harmony, 4146as[63]

BUSSON, Maurice, 6181as[93]

Bussotti, Sylvano
works, notation, 3847as[55]

BUSUISCEANU, A., 117rs[16]

BUTUROVIĆ, Đenana, 2754as[34]

BUXTEHUDE, Dietrich, 122bs

Buxtehude, Dietrich
editions, keyboard music, critique, 3925as[58]
life, relation to Lorentz, 1615as[25]
___ state of research, ca. 1957, 1584as[25]
manuscripts, *Du Friedefürst, Herr Jesu Christ*, BuxWV 20, 1690as[25]
works, *Membra Jesu*, BuxWV 75, 1589as[25]
___ organ music, influenced by Gregorian chant, 3343as[42]
___ ___ integration of strict and free styles, 1657as[25]

BUŽGA, Jaroslav, 5870as[87]

Byelarus, *see* **Belarus**

Byelorussia, *see* **Belarus**

Byfield, John
instruments, organs, 3396as[42]

Byrd, William
aesthetics, melancholia, 1342as[24]
works, *The earle of Salisbury*, open analysis, 3957as[60]
___ form, advanced tonal design, 4228as[63]

spiritual and artistic situation, ca. 1959, 6025as[90]
Stoltzer, T., 1337as[24]
theological value, 6021as[90]

Chybiński, Adolf
writings, on Szymanowski, 2259as[28]

Ciampi, Vincenzo Legrenzio
performances, *Bertoldo, Bertoldino e Cacasenno*, role of pasticcio, 5248as[77]

CICOGNINI, Alessandro, 5118as[77]

Ciconia, Johannes
life, 1277as[24]
___ Italy sojourn, 1358-67, 1076as[23]
manuscripts, 1075as[23]
works, Mass movements, parody technique, 1074as[23]
___ *Regina gloriosa*, attribution, 1074as[23]
___ relation to toccata, 4237as[64]
___ vocal music, polyphonic innovation, 1237as[24]

CIERNIAK, Jędrzej, 5119as[77], 5120as[77]

Cikker, Ján
works, 947as[21]

cinema, *see* film

CINI, Luigi, 474bs

CIOBANU, Gheorghe, 955as[21]

Cipri, Giovanni
instruments, organs, at S. Martino, Bologna, 3342as[42]

CIRESE, Alberto Mario, 2767as[34], 2768as[34]

cithara (=kithara), *see* instruments — string (lyre family)

cittern, *see* instruments — string (cittern family)

Clair, René
works, directing, *Cinéma*, 5208as[77]

clàirseach (=Irish harp), *see* instruments — string (harp family)

clarinet, *see* instruments — wind (woodwind, reed family)

clarino, *see* instruments — wind (brass)

CLARK, Evans, 2304as[29]

CLARK, Melville, Jr., 5690as[82]

clàrsach (=Irish harp), *see* instruments — string (harp family)

Classic, *see also* **Enlightenment; Mannheim school; performance practice — by topic; rococo; Viennese school (18th c.)**
aesthetics, 5554as[81]
___ social functions of art, 5519as[81]
editions, critical editions, 3893as[58]
history and development, state of research, 1961, 4369as[66]
motive and theme, 4396as[67]
relation to Romanticism, 1919as[27], 4312as[66]
Slovakia, 1781as[26]
style, exoticism, 1876as[26]
___ sources, 4330as[66]
___ viewed by theorists, 1733as[26]
theory, form, 4377as[66]

Classicism, *see* **aesthetics; Classic; visual and plastic arts**

classification, *see* cataloguing, classification, indexing, etc.

CLAUDEL, Paul, 249bs

Claudel, Paul
writings, influenced by Wagner, 5319as[78]
___ Mozart, W.A., 5314as[78]

Claudin de Sermisy, *see* **Sermisy, Claudin de**

CLAUDIUS, Carl, 3558as[44]

Claudius, Matthias
writings, translation of Terrasson *Sethos*, relation to Mozart *Die Zauberflöte*, 5212as[77]

CLAUSETTI, Carlo, 5953as[89]

CLAUSS, Emile, 1936as[27]

clausula, *see also* **Notre Dame school**
relation to conductus, 1071as[23]

Clavé, Josep Anselm
life, Catalunya, founding of choral societies, 2043as[27]

clavecin (=harpsichord), *see* instruments — keyboard (harpsichord family)

clavichord, *see* instruments — keyboard (clavichord family)

clavicytherium, *see* instruments — keyboard (harpsichord family)

CLAYTON, Henry, 5954as[89]

CLEGG, David, 2769as[34]

Clement IV, Pope
works, goigs, 3056as[34], 3057as[34]

CLEMENTE, Rina di, 2148as[28]

Clementi, Muzio
life, relation to Mozart, 1721as[26]
works, *Gradus ad Parnassum*, 3729as[52]
___ piano music, influence on Chopin, 2092as[27]
___ style, relation to Classic, 1896as[26]

CLERCX-LEJEUNE, Suzanne, 340bs, 351bs, 386bs, 390bs, 531as[1], 532as[1], 533as[1], 534as[1], 1074as[23], 1075as[23], 1076as[23], 1124as[23], 1171as[23], 1276as[24], 1277as[24], 1509as[25], 1510as[25], 3889as[58], 4237as[64]

Clereau, Pierre
works, *Odes de Ronsard*, 1266as[24]

CLÉROT, Léon Francisco R., 99bs

CLERVAL, J.A., 6187as[93]

Cleve, Johannes de
works, use of soggetti cavati, 1452as[24]

Clewberg-Edelcrantz, Abraham Niclas
life, views on Mozart, 1870as[26]

CLOSSON, Ernest, 1736as[26], 3247as[40], 4508as[70]

CLOUGH, Francis F., 825as[9], 826as[9]

COATES, Eric James, 535as[1]

COCCHIARA, Giuseppe, 2770as[34]

codices, *see* manuscripts and prints headwords; notation and paleography

codicology, *see* source studies

Coelho, Manuel Rodrigues
works, style, 1585as[25]

COEUROY, André, 1937as[27], 5747as[85]

COGAN, Robert, 4858as[72]

COGNI, Giulio, 5648as[82]

COHEN, Dalia, 4420as[69]

COHEN, Judith R., 4421as[69]

COIRAULT, Patrice, 2771as[34]

COLACICCHI, Luigi, 2772as[34], 5121as[77], 5748as[85]

COLE, Elizabeth, 1278as[24]

Coleridge-Taylor, Samuel
works, arrangements, spirituals, 3184as[35]

COLLAER, Paul, 340bs, 351bs, 366bs, 401bs, 1026as[22], 1511as[25], 1512as[25], 2305as[29], 2428as[30], 2453as[30], 2458as[30], 2504as[31], 2554as[32], 2612as[33], 2613as[33], 2773as[34], 3646as[46], 3647as[46], 3674as[50], 3936as[60], 3959as[60], 4062as[62], 4232as[64], 4285as[64], 4509as[70], 5649as[82], 5690as[82]

COLLANGETTES, Xavier Maurice, 4063as[62]

COLLARD, E., 6188as[93], 6189as[93]

collections, *see* instruments — collections; libraries, museums, collections

colleges, *see* academic institutions

COLLINS, Gertrude, 3559as[44]

COLLINSON, Francis, 2505as[31], 2774as[34], 2775as[34]

colloquium proceedings, *see* congresses, conferences, symposia

Colombia
Baudó river valley, traditional music, acculturation, 3211as[36]
Girardota, musical life, chirimía ensemble, 16th-20th c., 3211as[36]
Indians, instruments, flutes, 3628as[45]

Kuna people, traditional music, instrumental polyphony, 3199as[36]
traditional music, role in storytelling, 3191as[36]

Colonna, Giovanni Ambrosio
works, *Intavolatura di chitarra all spagnuola...*, relation to passacaglia, 4277as[64]

color, *see* perception; rhythm and meter

Columbanus, Saint
festivals and conferences, France, Luxeuil, 1950, 301bs
tributes, St. Gallen MSS, 6204as[93]
___ 7th-18th c., 6250as[93]
writings, monastic regulations, Office, 6193as[93]

COMBARIEU, Jules, 32bs, 1938as[27], 3675as[50], 5122as[77]

comedy, *see* humor

COMETTANT, Oscar, 3195as[36]

comic opera, *see* opera buffa; opéra comique; operetta; other opera headwords

COMIŞEL, Emilia, 2776as[34], 2777as[34], 2778as[34], 2779as[34]

COMMENDA, Hans, 4947as[76]

COMMINS, Daniel E., 504bs

communication theory, *see* semiotics

Communion, *see* Mass

communism, *see* socialism and communism

Compenius, Johann Heinrich
instruments, organs, at Moritzkirche Halle, 3390as[42]

competitions, awards, and prizes
Asia, Central, singing contests, 2622as[33]

Compline (Divine Office), *see* **Office**

composers, *see* autobiographies, diaries, etc.; biographies — collective; composition; individual names

composition, *see also* **aleatory music; avant-garde; creative process; instrumentation and orchestration; set theory; specific composers; specific forms, genres, media, styles, techniques, etc.; twentieth-century music**
aesthetics, subjectivism vs. objectivism, 5634as[81]
Badings, H., 2137as[28]
Beck, C., 2281as[29]
Blomdahl, K.-B., 2137as[28]
Bulgaria, 1830-1914, 1922as[27]
Cavallini, E., 4146as[63]
computer applications, 4399as[68]
___ Music 4B, 1960s, 4412as[68]
Dallapiccola, L., 5447as[81]
Europe, freedom and rules, 3943as[60]
___ women composers, 992as[21]
Fegers, K., 2163as[28]
film music, 5177as[77], 5203as[77]
Franco-Burgundian, Burgundian school, 4328as[66]
Guttman, N., 4406as[68]
Holmboe, V., 2181as[28]
Huijbers, B., hymns, use in Roman Catholic liturgy, 6256as[93]
influenced by sound recordings, 5748as[85]
Kagel, M., 3832as[55]
Karkoschka, E., 4007as[61]
Matthews, M.V., 4406as[68]
Mayuzumi, T., 2213as[28]
Middle Ages, relation to theory, 1057as[23]
motive and theme, as unifying force, 5445as[81]
Norway, 19th-20th c., influenced by Germany training, 966as[21]
Obama, J., 6325as[93], 6326as[93]
organicism, 4257as[64]
pedagogy, conservatory, late 1940s, 4866as[73]
___ historicism, 4867as[73]
___ inner vs. outer resources, 4886as[73]
___ principles, 4612as[70]
___ proposed reform, 1911, 4870as[73]
___ relation to humanism, 4541as[70]
___ relation to psychology, 4617as[73]
___ role of historical study, 4869as[73], 4897as[73]

Webern, A., symponies, op. 21, use of consonance, 4394as[67]

20th-c. music, psychology and physiology, 4212as[63]

contemporary music, *see* **aleatory music;
avant-garde; electronic music and computer
music; serialism;** *specific names, places;* **twentieth-century music**

contests, *see* **competitions, awards, and prizes**

continuo, *see* **basso continuo**

contrafactum, *see also* **parody**

Damiani, P., of 9th-c. *Dulce carmen* sequence, 1188as[23]

Desprez, J., 1224as[24]

history and development, early 17th c., 1496as[25]

conventions, *see* **congresses, conferences, symposia**

Cooke, Deryck

writings, *The language of music,* 5502as[81]

COON, Leland A., 3510as[43]

COOPERSMITH, Jacob Maurice, 1513as[25]

COPEAU, Jacques, 5124as[77]

Copland, Aaron

works, to 1947, 2250as[28]

COPPOLA, Piero, 2307as[29], 3890as[58]

Coptic chant, *see* **chant — Coptic**

copyists

Fontana, J., 3899as[58]

Kempis, G., 1109as[23]

Küffer, W., 1258as[24]

Levi, H., 726as[2]

Philidor, A.D., 718as[2]

Praetorius, J., the elder, 1338as[24]

Sychra, J., 1788as[26]

Trzciński, F., 1445as[24]

copyright and patents, *see also* **law; publishing
and printing**

Americas, internat. treaties, 5993as[89]

___ ca. 1939, 2381as[29]

Brazil, counterfeit scores, 5976as[89]

___ relation to Montevideo and Bern agreements, 5951as[89]

Canada, union editions of scores, 5948as[89]

conferences, 1885, 12bs

___ 1926, 130bs

___ 1927, 140bs

___ 1928, 148bs

___ 1929, 159bs

___ 1930, 170bs

___ 1931, 190bs

___ 1932, 200bs

___ 1933, 202bs

___ 1935, 223bs

___ 1936, 229bs

___ 1937, 245bs

___ 1938, 261bs

___ 1952, 311bs

___ 1961, 431bs

copyright collecting societies, history and development, antiquity to 1950s, 5960as[89]

Europe, mechanical reproduction rights, ca. 1952, 5769as[85]

France, late 18th to early 20th c., 5944as[89]

Germany, sound recordings, ca. 1953, 648as[1]

Hungary, Roma people, 5962as[89]

individual authors, compared with institutional rights, ca. 1961, 5966as[89], 5967as[89]

internat., 5954as[89]

___ Bern Convention, relation to mechanical instruments, 3659as[47]

___ ___ relation to mechanical instruments, ca. 1906, 5959as[89]

___ ___ relation to tariffs, 5957as[89]

___ performing rights, ca. 1906, 6000as[89]

___ refugees, 5964as[89]

___ relation to mechanical instruments, ca. 1901, 5950as[89]

___ sound recordings, 529as[1]

___ ___ ethnomusicological material, 660as[1]

___ television royalties, 5955as[89]

___ 1886-1922, 5969as[89]

___ ca. 1952, 5998as[89]

Italy, performing rights, relation to opera houses, 5961as[89]

licensing of mechanical reproduction, 5956as[89]

performing rights, relation to church music, 6013as[90]

___ ___ ca. 1961, 5988as[89], 5989as[89]

Slavic states, southern, ethnographic transcriptions, 1950s, 6001as[89]

sound recordings, 530as[1]

South America, 5977as[89]

USA, film music, 5095as[77]

CORBIN, Solange, 829as[19], 840as[19], 1021as[21], 1077as[23], 1078as[23], 1126as[23], 1147as[23], 3813as[55]

Corelli, Arcangelo

works, concerti grossi, influence on Vivaldi, 1703as[25]

Corfu (=Kérkyra), *see* **Greece**

CORIO, Edgardo, 2308as[29]

Cornago, Johannes

works, 1410as[24]

cornamusa (=cornamuse), *see* **instruments — wind
(woodwind, reed family)**

cornamuse, *see* **instruments — wind (woodwind,
reed family)**

Corner, Frederick

life, teaching, relation to 20th-c. British composition, 2144as[28]

Cornet, Séverin

life, 1291as[24]

corneta (=erke), *see* **instruments — wind (brass)**

cornett, *see* **instruments — wind (brass)**

CORNETTE, Arthur Jacob Hendrik, 1939as[27]

cornetto (=cornett), *see* **instruments — wind (brass)**

corno da caccia (= horn), *see* **instruments — wind
(brass)**

Cornysh, William

life, as Chapel Royal singer, 1226as[24]

Correa de Arauxo, Francisco

works, keyboard music, organ vs. harpsichord styles, 1292as[24]

writings, organ, 3334as[42]

correspondence, *see also* **anecdotes, reminiscences,
etc.; autobiographies, diaries, etc.**

Bach, C.P.E., to Breitkopf, 1815as[26]

Bartók, B., edited by Demény, 2269as[28]

___ evidence of personality, 2260as[28]

___ to Brăiloiu, 3094as[34]

___ to P.V. Bartók, 2129as[28]

Bartók, P.V., from B. Bartók, 2129as[28]

Batka, J.N., with Liszt, 1987as[27]

Beethoven, L. van, 766as[2]

___ editions, 3926as[58]

___ handwriting, 1884as[26]

___ on religious music, 1899as[26]

Benoît, P., with Hiel, 2118as[27]

Bentivoglio d'Aragona, G., from Vivaldi, 1507as[25]

Boieldieu, F.-A., 1846as[26]

___ to Janssens, 1840as[26]

Brahms, J., on aesthetics, 5465as[81]

___ on Bach, 2001as[27]

___ to Krančević, 1946as[27]

Brăiloiu, C., from Bartók, 3094as[34]

Breitkopf, J.G.I., from C.P.E. Bach, 1815as[26]

Breitkopf & Härtel, 5968as[89]

Cherubini, L., to Janssens, 1840as[26]

Chopin, F., literary style, 1990as[27]

___ on Beethoven, 2058as[27]

___ to Michałowski, 2098as[27]

___ to Potocka, authenticity, 1971as[27]

___ to Wodzińska, 1985as[27]

composers, influence of study on appreciation, 902as[20]

Debussy, C., with Varèse, 2201as[28]

Fétis, F.-J., 1760as[26], 2076as[27]

Fuller, M., views on Mickiewicz and Chopin, 1962as[27]

Glarean, H., with Łaski, on *Dodecachordon,* 1461as[24]

Haydn, J., Sweden collections, 1777as[26]

Hiel, E., with Benoît, 2118as[27]

Hristov, D., with Janáček, 2279as[29]

Janáček, L., to Stösslová, 2254as[28]

___ with Hristov, 2279as[29]

Janssens, J.F.J., from Boieldieu, 1840as[26]

___ from Cherubini, 1840as[26]

___ from Le Sueur, 1840as[26]

Jelowicki, A., views on Chopin, 1968as[27]

Krančević, D., from Brahms, 1946as[27]

Łaski, J., with Glarean, 1461as[24]

Lenartowicz, T., views on Mickiewicz and Chopin, 1962as[27]

Liszt, F., with Slovak musicians, 1987as[27]

Mendelssohn-Bartholdy, F., with Spontini, 1970as[27]

Mersenne, M., from Trichet, 1698as[25]

Meyerbeer, G., on grand opera, 5101as[77]

Michałowski, P., from Chopin, 2098as[27]

Mozart, L., from W.A. Mozart, 1780as[26]

Mozart, W.A., as criticism, 1771as[26]

___ to L. Mozart, 1780as[26]

musicians, cataloguing methods, 633as[1]

on theory, early 16th c., 1346as[24]

Polak, A.J., with Takamine, 2475as[30]

Potocka, D., from Chopin (attributed), 1971as[27]

Príleský, T., with Liszt, 1987as[27]

principles of study, 903as[20]

Schubert, F., autographs, 768as[2]

Silbermann, A., 3449as[42]

Spontini, G., 1928as[27]

___ at Bibl. Comunale, Forlì, 2095as[27]

___ with Mendelssohn-Bartholdy, 1970as[27]

___ 1811-82, 1912as[27]

Stoltzer, T., relation to date of death, 1337as[24]

Stösslová, K., from Janáček, 2254as[28]

Le Sueur, J.-F., to Janssens, 1840as[26]

Takamine, H., with Polak, 2475as[30]

Trichet, P., to Mersenne, 1698as[25]

use in musicology, 909as[20]

Varèse, E., with Debussy, 2201as[28]

Vivaldi, A., to Bentivoglio d'Aragona, 1507as[25]

Vogler, G.J., 1776as[26]

Wodzińska, T., from Chopin, 1985as[27]

Zamojska, L., with Liszt, 1987as[27]

Corrette, Michel

writings, *Le maître de clavecin,* 3774as[52]

CORTI, Mario, 3560as[44]

Cortolezis, Fritz

performances, Mozart *Idomeneo, re di Creta,* 3757as[52]

Cortot, Alfred

collections, 763as[2]

sound recordings, Chopin prelude op. 28 no. 1, 4236as[64]

CORVER, G.M.A., 2149as[28]

Corvinus, Gottlieb Siegmund

writings, *Nutzbares, galantes und curiöses
Frauenzimmer-Lexicon* (1715), treatment of instruments, 3266as[40]

COSMA, Viorel, 1279as[24]

Costa, Lorenzo

works, art, depiction of musical instruments, 5403as[79]

COSTANTINI, Celso, 6005as[90], 6006as[90]

COSTARELLI, Nicola, 5125as[77]

COSTÈRE, Edmond, 2309as[29], 4155as[63]

costumes

masks, non-Western, compared with non-Western timbre, 4303as[65]

Nono, L., *Intolleranza 1960,* 5264as[77]

criticism — general, *see also* aesthetics; other criticism headwords; reception
Asia, ca. 1961, 2264as[28]
concept of work, principles of criticism, 5453as[81]
conference, 1930, 183bs
___ 1947, 276bs, 278bs
as discipline, relation to musicology, 930as[20]
England, to 1909, 5422as[81]
___ ca. 1930, 5481as[81]
Europe, 5577as[81]
___ ca. 1961, 2264as[28]
France, proposed standards, 1901, 5544as[81]
influenced by blindness, 5427as[81]
Italy, 5577as[81]
___ relation to avant-garde, ca. 1935, 5441as[81]
___ role in culture, 2300as[29]
methodology, 5562as[81]
practice of criticism, 5491as[81], 5612as[81]
___ journalism, 5521as[81]
___ ___ ca. 1937, 5621as[81]
___ relation to contemporary music, 5596as[81]
___ role of sound recordings, 5508as[81]
relation to creativity, 5471as[81]
relation to musicology, 921as[20], 5608as[81]
responsibilities, 2281as[29]
role of critic in society, 5629as[81]
USA, ca. 1909, 2100as[27]
value judgments, relation to analysis, 4395as[67]
visual and plastic arts, 5530as[81]
20th-c. music, 2226as[28], 5560as[81]
ca. 1930, 5626as[81]
Crna Gora (=Montenegro), *see* Serbia and Montenegro
Croatia, *see also* Slavic states
Banija, instruments, svirale, 3637as[45]
Bjelovar, instruments, jedinka and dvojnice, 3629as[45]
coastal, history of music, 16th-17th c., 1408as[24]
cultural policies, professional folkloric dance ensembles, 1948-63, 4948as[76]
Dalmatia, history of music, 16th-17th c., 1407as[24]
___ northern islands, traditional music, ojkanje, 2739as[34]
___ traditional music, songs, Marko Kraljević as subject, 3039as[34]
dance, traditional, staged, performances, 1948-63, 4948as[76]
folklore, children, counting games, 2732as[34]
history of music, 17th-18th c., 1594as[25]
Hrvatsko Primorje, traditional music, *Marko pronalazi sestru*, 3018as[34]
Istra, dance, influenced by Alpine region, 4989as[76]
___ instruments, šurla, 3623as[45]
Istra and Dalmatia, traditional music, songs, 2914as[34]
Istra and Kvarner, traditional music, 2806as[34]
Konavle, folklore, weddings, 2745as[34]
Korčula, dramatic arts, 5080as[76]
Krk, religious music, polyphonic practice, 6420as[93]
Krk and Novi Vinodolski, folklore, 2872as[34]
Kvarner, instruments, sopile, compared with Banija svirale, 3637as[45]
literature, poetry, traditional, 5300as[78]
Mosor, folklore, revolutionary song texts, 5338as[78]
northern and eastern, folklore, spring mendication rituals, 5109as[77]
Poljica, folklore, funerals, 2973as[34]
traditional music, ballads, 3124as[34]
___ epics, field recordings, ca. 1900, 3120as[34]
___ influence on Haydn and Beethoven, 1862as[26]
___ mass songs, 1940s, 2894as[34]
___ songs, melodies, 3066as[34]
___ ___ phonetic aspects, 5941as[88], 5942as[88]
___ work songs, use of lyrical motifs, 5301as[78]
Zadar region, instruments, diple s mijehom, 3611as[45]

Croatian music (outside Croatia)
Bosnia and Herzegovina, song texts, women's songs, 19th c., 5302as[78]
Czech Republic, Moravia, folklore, 3062as[34]
Italy, Molise, funeral laments, 2768as[34]
Slovakia, Chorvátsky Grob, 2753as[34]
___ folklore, 3062as[34]
Croce, Benedetto
aesthetics, 5617as[81]
writings, *Aesthetica in nuce*, 5476as[81]
Croeser de Berges
manuscripts, Old Flemish songs, 14th-15th c., 1471as[24]
CROIZA, Claire, 3293as[41]
CROLL, Gerhard, 1514as[25], 1528as[25], 4369as[66]
CROSSLEY-HOLLAND, Peter, 493bs, 834as[19], 845as[19], 2152as[28], 2429as[30], 2430as[30], 2506as[31], 2507as[31], 2614as[33], 5126as[77]
Crotch, William
writings, on performance practice, 3734as[52]
Crüger, Johannes
works, counterpoint, 4203as[63]
cryptography, *see* notation and paleography; symbolism
CSÉBFALVY, Károly, 4422as[69]
Csermák, Antal György
works, dance music, influence on Liszt and Brahms, 1973as[27]
ČSSR, *see* Czech Republic; Slovakia
Cuba, *see also* West Indies
pedagogy, amateurs, choral singing, 4911as[74], 4912as[74]
traditional music, 3218as[36]
___ state of research, ca. 1939, 2381as[29]
ČUBELIĆ, Tvrtko, 2780as[34], 4948as[76], 4949as[76], 5296as[78], 5297as[78]
ČUČKOV, Emanuil, 4950as[76]
CUCLIN, Dimitrie, 956as[21], 5444as[81]
CUDWORTH, Charles, 536as[1], 1515as[25], 3736as[52], 4369as[66]
CUEVAS, Felisa de las, 2781as[34], 2782as[34]
Cui, César, *see* Kjui, Cezar'
CUKKERMAN, Viktor Abramovič, 1940as[27], 3937as[60]
cultural policies, *see also* economics; politics; sociology; urban studies
Austria, relation to traditional music, 3012as[34]
Belgium, conference, 1932, 195bs
___ Conseil Supérieur de l'Éducation Populaire, 5902as[87]
___ establishment of Orchestre Symphonique Populaire, 2283as[27]
___ national symphony orchestra, project, 1932, 4624as[70]
___ pedagogy, 4553as[70]
___ ___ 1930s, 4503as[70]
___ ___ ca. 1932, 4508as[70]
___ traditional song, 2741as[34], 2868as[34], 4542as[70]
___ ca. 1932, 4915as[74]
Canada, traditional music, ca. 1928, 3180as[35], 3181as[35]
Croatia, professional folkloric dance ensembles, 1948-63, 4948as[76]
cultural exchange programs, role of opera, 5110as[77]
Egypt, pedagogy, 1932, 4480as[70]
Europe, art music subventions, relation to authenticity, 1938as[27]
___ broadcasting, 661as[1]
___ ___ relation to sound libraries, 662as[1]
___ nationalism, 1930s, 2299as[29]
France, reign of Louis XIV, influence on style, 981as[21]
___ relation to metronome, 3976as[61]
___ ___ ca. 1900, 3999as[61]
___ Revolution, opera censorship, 5235as[77]
___ traditional music, 4698as[71]

___ ___ research and preservation, ca. 1939-1948, 2940as[34]
Germany, East, 2325as[29]
___ Nazism, choral conducting, 3277as[40]
___ ___ music pedagogy, 2362as[29]
___ ___ open-air music theater, 5213as[77]
___ ___ opera censorship, 5235as[77]
___ ___ relation to Wagner reception, post-Nazi era, 5241as[77]
___ ___ singing and vocal training, 2323as[29]
___ ___ singing as comradeship training, 2389as[29]
___ ___ vocal pedagogy, 4650as[70]
___ relation to youth welfare programs, ca. 1955, 5911as[87]
___ training of church musicians, after 1918, 4818as[72]
internat., music education as universal right, 4510as[70], 4511as[70]
___ public art, conference, 1898, 24bs
Italy, children's concerts, mid-20th c., 4744as[71], 4745as[71]
___ fascism, relation to Dallapiccola vocal music, 5447as[81]
___ provincial opera houses, 5159as[77]
refugees, copyright issues, 5964as[89]
Romania, traditional music, 1960s, 3013as[34]
Russia, Soviet era, opera censorship, 5235as[77]
Slavic states, southern, mass songs, 3125as[34]
___ ___ socialist construction projects, brigade songs, 5281as[78]
Spain, pedagogy, choir schools, 4767as[71]
___ religious music, censorship, 2405as[29]
___ ___ councils, 6240as[93]
___ ___ relation to Pius X *Tra le sollecitudini*, 6407as[93]
traditional music, 2439as[30]
___ sound recordings, 2457as[30]
USA, Federal Music Project (FMP), sponsorship of Latin American music performances, 1940, 2306as[29]
___ Immigration Act of 1917, relation to Latin American musicians, 2304as[29]
___ musicology, 5907as[87]
___ Works Progress Administration (WPA), sponsorship of Latin American music performances, 1940, 2306as[29]
cultural studies, *see also* anthropology; sociology
England, melancholia, ca. 1600, 1342as[24]
Europe, recreational activities, workers' music associations, 19th-20th c., 4914as[74]
___ workers' music associations, 19th-20th c., 4913as[74]
France, 14th c., role of music, 1069as[23]
Germany, Ingolstadt, artistic heritage, 965as[21]
Hungary, populist culture, 19th and 20th c., relation to poetry and music, 5360as[78]
Italy, concept of virtù, early 17th c., 1431as[24]
___ madrigal, 1296as[24]
___ program booklets, 604as[1]
songs, relation to exogamy, 2822as[34]
CUMING, Geoffrey, 825as[9], 826as[9]
CUMMINGS, William Hayman, 1516as[25]
CUNHA, João Itiberê da, 3196as[36]
CURLING, Edward, 1737as[26]
CUTTOLI, Raphael, 378bs
CUTTS, John P., 5127as[77]
CUVELIER, Marcel, 2310as[29]
Cuvelier, Marcel
life, management of Société Philharmonique de Bruxelles, 2311as[29]
CUVELIER, Maurice, 2311as[29]
CUYLER, Louise E., 4198as[63]
CVETKO, Dragotin, 537as[1], 835as[19], 846as[19], 957as[21], 1171as[23], 1280as[24], 1517as[25], 1670as[25], 1738as[26], 1941as[27], 1942as[27], 1955as[27], 2453as[30], 4510as[70], 4511as[70], 4689as[71], 5874as[87], 5905as[87]

Cybulski, Izydor Józef
life, publishing activities, early 19th c., 5985as[89]

Cyprus
history of music, early 14th c., MS evidence, 1123as[23]
traditional music, akritikīs tradition, relation to Cretan songs, 2795as[34]

Cyril, Saint
life, development of Glagolitic liturgy, 6420as[93]
___ liturgical practice, source evidence, 6274as[93]
___ relation to Old Bulgarian music, 1138as[23]
writings, Glagolitic liturgy, influenced by liturgy of St. Peter, 6131as[92]

Czech music (outside Czech Republic)
USA, songs, 3158as[35]

Czech Republic
Bohemia, cultural policies, post–World War II, relation to Smetana, 2056as[27]
___ dance, traditional, revival, late 19th c. to mid-20th c., 5020as[76]
___ ethnomusicology, early 19th c., 2946as[34]
___ history of music, relation to Mozart, 1825as[26]
___ musical life, reception of Mozart, 1832as[26]
___ ___ relation to Liszt, 2072as[27]
___ musicology, Mozart studies, 884as[20]
___ politics, mid-19th c., relation to Smetana, 2056as[27]
___ popular music, mass song, 2877as[34]
___ traditional music, stability and change, 2878as[34]
Croatian people, folklore, 3062as[34]
dance, polka, 4977as[76]
___ traditional, rhythm, 5088as[76]
ethnomusicology, activities of Hostinský, 2452as[30]
___ activities of Státní Ústav pro Lidovou Píseň, Praha, 2857as[34], 2858as[34]
___ research in Africa, 1945-61, 2590as[32]
German-speaking people, traditional music, songs, melodies, 2870as[34]
___ ___ texts, influence on Mahler works, 2005as[27]
history, Hussite Wars, 1349as[24]
___ national revival, early 19th c., influence on Chopin, 2074as[27]
history of music, Czech vs. ethnic German composers, ca. 1850-1950, 2193as[28]
___ Italy, early 17th c., 1653as[25]
___ polyphony, 14th c., 1149as[23]
___ relation to Mozart, 968as[21], 1841as[26], 1843as[26], 1863as[26]
___ ___ 1787-1856, 1880as[26]
___ relation to Poland, Renaissance, 1436as[24]
___ role of Janáček, 2197as[28]
___ 9th-16th c., 1204as[23]
___ 17th-18th c., 1709as[25]
___ late 1940s, 2365as[29]
Horňácko, traditional music, dance music, rhythmic and dynamic variations, 2856as[34]
Jihlava, instruments, fiddle, 3573as[44]
Krkonoše, musical life, influenced by industrialization, 3075as[34], 3076as[34]
mass media, radio, relation to pedagogy, 4518as[70]
Moravia, dance, sword dances, 5019as[76]
___ eastern, traditional music, innovations, mid-20th c., 2765as[34]
___ Hanáki region, traditional music, influence on Telemann, 1712as[25]
___ history of music, influenced by Mozart, 1866as[26]
___ musical life, reception of Mozart, 1008as[21]
___ Podluží region, dance, 4993as[76]
___ southeastern, traditional music, dance music, 2855as[34]
___ traditional music, influence on Czech composers, 2197as[28]
___ ___ influence on Janáček, 2237as[28]
___ ___ relation to Janáček *Její pastorkyňa* choruses, 4383as[66]

___ ___ songs, 3100as[34]
___ ___ state of research, ca. 1909, 2836as[34]
___ ___ used by Janáček, 2185as[28]
___ ___ viewed by Janáček, 4393as[66]
musical life, reception of Mozart, late 18th c., 1744as[26]
___ relation to traditional music, ca. 1962, 2943as[34]
___ relation to traditional music and dance, ca. 1963, 2945as[34]
___ social position of musicians, 1620s-ca. 1740, 5870as[87]
pedagogy, activities of Moravian Brethren, 16th c., 1414as[24]
popular music, mass song, history and development, to 1947, 3064as[34]
___ ___ state of research, 1964, 2459as[30]
___ 19th-early 20th c., 3093as[34], 3236as[39]
Praha, musical life, Liszt visits, 1840-71, 1925as[27]
___ ___ opera, activities of Kašlík, 5179as[77]
traditional music, bagpipe music, 2942as[34]
___ influence on Janáček, 2320as[29]
___ influence on Mahler, 2006as[27]
___ influence on Vaňhal, 1805as[26]
___ instrumental music, relation to Janáček speech melody theory, 4446as[69]
___ preservation, role of Československý Rozhlas, ca. 1961, 2440as[30]
___ relation to Mozart, 1807as[26], 1873as[26]
___ songs, 2878as[34]
___ ___ influence on Classic composers, 2944as[34]
___ ___ rhythmic features, relation to Czech prosody, 4035as[61]

Czechoslovakia, *see* **Czech Republic**; **Slovakia**
CZEKANOWSKA, Anna, 2783as[34], 4423as[69]

Czernicka, Paulina
life, discovery of Chopin-Potocka correspondence, 1934as[27], 1971as[27]

Czerny, Carl
life, teaching of Liszt, 1964as[27]
writings, on sonata form, 4276as[64]
___ *Vollständige theoretisch-praktische Pianoforte-Schule*, 3729as[52]
CZERNY, Zygmunt, 5445as[81]
CZYŻOWSKI, Stanisław, 4327as[66]

D

Da Ponte, Lorenzo
writings, libretto for Naumann *Osiride*, relation to Mozart *Die Zauberflöte*, 5212as[77]
DABO-PERANIĆ, Miljenko, 1027as[22]
D'ACCONE, Frank A., 1422as[24]
DADELSEN, Georg von, 1518as[25], 1519as[25], 1706as[25], 4232as[64], 5875as[87]
DAGNINO, Eduardo, 51as[16]
DAHLHAUS, Carl, 467bs, *468rs[16], 1520as[25], 1521as[25], 3814as[55], 3938as[60], 4156as[63], 4157as[63], 4198as[63], 4238as[64], 5446as[81], 5635as[82]

Dahm, Johann Jakob
instruments, organs, influence on J. Gabler, 3345as[42]
DAHMEN, Hermann Josef, 2508as[31], 2784as[34]

Dahomey, *see* **Benin**
DAL, Erik, 2785as[34], 5298as[78]

Dalcroze, Émile-Jaques, *see* **Jaques-Dalcroze, Émile**

Dalcroze method, *see* **movement and gesture**; **pedagogy** headwords

Dalla Casa, Girolamo
writings, *Il vero modo di diminuir*, 3772as[52]
DALLA LIBERA, Ernesto, 6196as[93]

Dallam, Thomas
instruments, organs, at Worcester Cathedral, 3396as[42]
DALLAPICCOLA, Luigi, 4866as[73], 5128as[77], 5447as[81]

Dallapiccola, Luigi
works, *Il prigioniero*, 5229as[77]

Dalmatia, *see* **Croatia**
DAMAIS, Émile, 4810as[72], 4811as[72]
DAMERINI, Adelmo, 538as[1], 1522ac[25], 4690as[71], 4867as[73]

Damiano da Bergamo
works, art, intarsia decorations (attributed), instrument iconography, 5404as[79]
D'AMICO, Fedele, 2153as[28], 5448as[81]
DAMILANO, Piero, 1281as[24]

dance — ballet, *see also* **choreographers**; **dance music** headwords; **movement and gesture**; other **dance** headwords
aesthetics, relation to religion, 5022as[76]
France, ballet de cour, performances, listed by Henry, 5021as[76]
___ ___ water and Tritons as themes, 1580-1640, 5059as[76]
___ Paris, Joyeuse-Lorraine marriage festivities, 1585, 1474as[24]
history and development, viewed by Lifar, 5023as[76]
___ 1900-1930s, 5027as[76]
Italy, ballet de cour, relation to France, 17th c., 5074as[76]
___ ___ water and Tritons as themes, 1580-1640, 5059as[76]
Lifar, S., *Icare*, 5023as[76]
Low Countries, 17th c., 1606as[25]
performance venues, 15th-17th c., 5175as[77]
revival, 1920s-30s, 2342as[29]

dance — by genre, *see also* **choreographers**; **dance music** headwords; other **dance** headwords
ballo, Italy, late 15th c., 1357as[24]
ballo tondo, 4965as[76]
barienne, 5079as[76]
basse danse, Italy, late 15th c., 1357as[24]
bhāgavata mēḷā, 5207as[77]
branle, France, Vendée, 5079as[76]
branle de Poitou, 4952as[76]
bugaku, ei and saezuri, 2620as[33]
bwola, 2574as[32]
crnogorsko kolo, 5034as[76]
csárdás, rhythm, influence on Vojvodina Ukrainian traditional music, 3084as[34]
el dance, Spain, Híjar, 5030as[76], 5031as[76]
double lindy, ethnochoreological analysis, 5011as[76]
duck walk, ethnochoreological analysis, 5011as[76]
folia, relation to moresca, 1318as[24]
foxtrot, ethnochoreological analysis, 5011as[76]
horo, Bulgaria, relation to dance music, 4995as[76]
jitterbug, ethnochoreological analysis, 5011as[76]
jota, Spain, Aragón, 2724as[34], 4933as[76]
kalađojne, Serbia, Kosovo, relation to Turkish kılıç, 4985as[76]
kathakali, 5207as[77]
kılıç, Serbia, Kosovo, relation to Kosovo traditional dances, 4985as[76]
kolo, Croatia, Novi Vinodol, 3124as[34]
___ Montenegro, portrayed in Njegoš *Gorski vijenac*, 5331as[78]
___ ___ portrayed in Njegoš verse dramas, 5321as[78]
___ Serbia, Beograd region, role in girls' initiation rite, 5036as[76]
kolo naopako, 5085as[76]
kozaračko kolo, 4958as[76], 5034as[76]
lako kolo, Serbia, Kosovo, interethnic influences, 4985as[76]
Ländler, Austria, Innviertl, 4947as[76]
maracatú, Brazil, role of calunga, 4929as[76]

maraichine, 5079as[76]
maremare, Venezuala, 3190as[36]
mazurka, influence on Telemann, 1712as[25]
___ outside Poland, 5042as[76]
moresca, relation to folia, 1318as[24]
moreška, Croatia, Korčula, 5080as[76]
morris, England, 5000as[76]
mostra, Croatia, Korčula, 5080as[76]
oro, 4992as[76]
otole, 2574as[32]
passamezzo, 5058as[76]
polka, history and development, 4977as[76]
polonaise, outside Poland, 5042as[76]
polska, Sweden, 5042as[76]
polskdans, 16th-19th c., 5038as[76]
saltarella, 4969as[76]
sardana, history and etymology, 4965as[76]
seven-step dance, Europe, variants, 5052as[76]
square dance, USA, Texas, history and
    development, 5060as[76]
štajeriš, 5071as[76]
sword dance, Italy, Piemonte, 4966as[76]
___ survey, 5019as[76]
tarantella, Italy, 5078as[76]
___ ___ Campania, 4939as[76], 4940as[76]
___ ___ Puglia, ca. 1960, 4945as[76]
tripettes, France, Barjols, 2937as[34]
two-step, origin of jitterbug forms, 5011as[76]
xique, Honduras, 3207as[36]
žalosno kolo, 5085as[76]

dance — by place, *see also* **choreographers**; **dance
    music** headwords; **movement and gesture**;
    other **dance** headwords
Africa, Mali, Dogon people, 2585as[32]
___ relation to music, 2570as[32]
___ Southern, !Kung people, choma, 4973as[76]
___ West, spirit possession, 2571as[32]
Austria, Innviertl, Ländler, 4947as[76]
___ traditional, 5082as[76]
___ 18th c. to mid-20th c., 5141as[77]
Belgium, Binche, festivities, 1549, 1329as[24]
___ Kempen, history and development, 2989as[34]
Bosnia and Herzegovina, children's dance games,
    classification, 4954as[76]
___ children's dances, work as subject, 5046as[76]
___ traditional, 4959as[76]
___ ___ death as subject, 4957as[76], 5044as[76]
___ ___ relation to work, 4956as[76]
___ traditional dance-drama, 4955as[76]
___ World War II, 4958as[76]
Brazil, 3202as[36]
Bulgaria, horo, relation to dance music, 4995as[76]
___ Pădarevo, traditional dance, kukeri mummers
    performances, 4994as[76]
___ Timok river region, traditional, 4987as[76]
Cameroon, Babinga people, compared with !Kung
    dance, 2552as[32]
Canada, French-speaking people, traditional,
    4937as[76]
___ Iroquois people, Feast of the Dead, 3147as[35]
___ traditional, 4936as[76]
China, antiquity, 4983as[76]
___ terminology, Later Han dynasty, 2673as[33]
Croatia, Istra, influenced by Alpine region,
    4989as[76]
___ Korčula, relation to dramatic arts, 5080as[76]
___ northern and eastern, spring mendication
    rituals, 5109as[77]
___ Novi Vinodol, kolo, relation to ballads,
    3124as[34]
___ traditional, staged, performances, 1948-63,
    4948as[76]
___ ___ staged performances, 1948-63, 4948as[76]
Cuba, 3218as[36]
Czech Republic, Bohemia, traditional, revival, late
    19th to mid-20th c., 5020as[76]
___ Moravia, Podluží region, 4993as[76]
___ ___ sword dances, 5019as[76]
___ polka, Polish origin, 4977as[76]
___ traditional, rhythm, 5088as[76]

___ traditional performing groups, ca. 1963,
    2945as[34]
Denmark, polskdans, history and development,
    5038as[76]
___ traditional, preservation, 5025as[76]
Ecuador, traditional, relation to dramatic arts,
    5261as[77]
England, relation to ayre, ca. 1580-1630, 1284as[24]
___ ritual dances, 5000as[76]
___ traditional, 5001as[76]
___ ___ pedagogy, 4566as[70]
___ ___ revival, influenced by Sharp, 4999as[76]
Equatorial Guinea, Babinga people, compared
    with !Kung dance, 2552as[32]
Europe, Alpine region, influence on Istra,
    4989as[76]
___ ___ southeastern, Dance of Death traditional
    dance-drama, 5187as[77]
___ Basque region, 5089as[76], 5090as[76]
___ ___ ceremonial, 4935as[76]
___ Eastern and Central, Jewish people, 5017as[76]
___ Germanic people, compared with Slavic
    people, 4982as[76]
___ influenced by Poland, 16th c., 5042as[76]
___ relation to Berber dance, 2766as[34]
___ seven-step dance, variants, 5052as[76]
___ traditional, accompanied by song, 5081as[76]
___ weddings, imitation of birds, 5077as[76]
___ 16th c., 4978as[76]
Finland, traditional, revival, 20th c., 2717as[34]
France, Barjols, St. Marcel bull ritual, 2937as[34]
___ Basque region, 2982as[34], 4926as[76], 4927as[76]
___ Poitou, branle de Poitou, 4952as[76]
___ traditional, 5016as[76], 5057as[76]
___ ___ pedagogy, 4582as[70]
___ Vendée, maraichines, 5079as[76]
Germany, Bayern, traditional, collected by
    Bayerischer Rundfunk, 2813as[34]
___ early forms, 2727as[34]
Greece, antiquity to present, 5032as[76]
Honduras, xique, 3207as[36]
Hungary, south Slavic people, 3108as[34]
___ törökös, 1876as[26]
___ traditional, 5015as[76], 5029as[76]
Iberian Peninsula, dramatic dances, influence on
    South America, 4946as[76]
India, bhāgavata mēḷā, 5207as[77]
___ kathakaḷi, 5207as[77]
___ South, dance-dramas, 5207as[77]
___ traditional, 4934as[76]
Indonesia, 5043as[76]
___ Java, 5069as[76], 5070as[76]
___ ___ wayang wong, 5043as[76]
Ireland, traditional, 2980as[34]
Israel, creative process, 4997as[76]
___ neotraditional, influenced by Yemeni Jewish
    dance, 4998as[76]
___ social, 5055as[76]
___ traditional, syncretism, 4970as[76]
Italy, Abruzzi, saltarella, 4969as[76]
___ Campania, tarantella, 4939as[76], 4940as[76]
___ Gargano region, 3079as[34]
___ Genova, traditional, Renaissance, 5051as[76]
___ Piemonte, sword dances, 4966as[76]
___ Puglia, tarantella, as therapy, ca. 1960,
    4945as[76]
___ relation to siciliana, 1012as[21]
___ Sardegna, ballo tondo, historic origins,
    4965as[76]
___ ___ ballo tondo sardo, 4967as[76]
___ ___ traditional, 4964as[76]
___ Sicilia, Stone Age, represented in Grotte
    dell'Addaura cave graffiti, 5075as[76]
___ ___ traditional, 4938as[76]
___ tarantella, 5078as[76]
___ wedding rituals, 5040as[76]
___ 14th-15th c., 1201as[23]
___ late 15th c., 1357as[24]
Japan, 2661as[33], 5005as[76], 5006as[76]
___ bugaku, 2690as[33]

___ relation to traditional songs, 2625as[33],
    2626as[33]
___ to 1958, 2663as[33]
Macedonia, 2992as[34]
___ relation to drumming, 3991as[61]
___ relation to sociology, 4950as[76]
___ traditional, oro, 4992as[76]
Mediterranean region, 2495as[31]
Mexico, Indians, ceremonial dances, 3194as[36]
___ Tantoyuca, Huastec people, 5066as[76]
Montenegro, 3110as[34]
___ kolo, portrayed in Njegoš *Gorski vijenac*,
    5331as[78]
___ ___ portrayed in Njegoš verse dramas,
    5321as[78]
Nepal, traditional, 4934as[76]
Netherlands, 4925as[75]
North America, Iroquois people, influenced by
    environment, 3160as[35], 3178as[35]
___ local diversity, 3162as[35]
___ jazz-based popular dance, ethnochoreological
    analysis, 5011as[76]
Norway, traditional, 3046as[34], 4975as[76]
Papua New Guinea, 3226as[37]
Paraguay, Guaraní and Botocudo people, 5067as[76]
___ rúa, 4946as[76]
Poland, influence on Europe, 16th c., 5042as[76]
___ krakowiak, relation to polka, 4977as[76]
Puerto Rico, 4951as[76]
Russia, traditional, 2817as[34]
Scandinavia, 2785as[34]
Scotland, traditional, 5033as[76]
Serbia, 5035as[76]
___ Beograd region, kolo, role in girls' initiation
    rite, 5036as[76]
___ funerals, 5085as[76]
___ Kosovo, Šar Planina, vučarska svadba ritual,
    2925as[34]
___ ___ traditional, interethnic influences,
    4985as[76]
___ ___ traditional, oro, 4992as[76]
___ Timočka Krajina, traditional, 4987as[76]
___ traditional, history and classification,
    4990as[76]
___ Užice region, 4986as[76]
___ southern, traditional, 5086as[76]
Slavic states, compared with Germanic people,
    4982as[76]
___ southern, masked, 2920as[34]
___ ___ Partisan dances, 5034as[76]
___ ___ relation to ballads, 2746as[34]
___ ___ traditional, historical strata, 4991as[76]
___ ___ traditional, stage adaptations, 5062as[76]
___ ___ traditional, staged performances,
    4949as[76]
___ ___ traditional, transcription systems,
    4960as[76], 4988as[76]
___ ___ traditional, urban influences, 4984as[76]
___ ___ traditional, 5007as[76], 5008as[76]
Slovakia, 3010as[34]
___ sword dances, 5019as[76]
___ traditional, 4963as[76]
___ traditional performing groups, ca. 1963,
    2945as[34]
Slovenia, raj types, 5009as[76]
___ references in traditional songs, 5325as[78]
___ relation to ballads, 2917as[34]
___ štajeriš, 5071as[76]
___ ___ relation to poskočnica, 3102as[34]
___ traditional, 2947as[34], 5047as[76]
___ ___ most game, 5010as[76], 5072as[76]
South Africa, !Kung people, compared with
    Babinga dance, 2552as[32]
Spain, Aragón, jota, 2724as[34], 4933as[76]
___ northern, el dance, 4932as[76]
___ northern, traditional, 2725as[34]
___ Barcelona, Carnival, 17th c., 5056as[76]
___ Basque region, 2982as[34]
___ Castelltersol, 4930as[76], 4931as[76]
___ Catalunya, 5083as[76], 5084as[76]

_____ _____ sardana, historic origins, 4965as[76]

_____ _____ traditional, symbolism, 4928as[76]

_____ _____ Híjar, el dance, 5030as[76], 5031as[76]

_____ Madrid, dramatic arts, 18th c., 5253as[77]

_____ Palencia, 2840as[34], 2841as[34]

_____ Penedès, dance-dramas, 4971as[76], 4972as[76]

_____ Pyrenees region, 2714as[34]

_____ role in elementary pedagogy, 4680as[71], 4681as[71]

_____ El Vallès, ball de gitanes, 5049as[76], 5050as[76]

_____ Las Ventas con Peña Aguilera, 2948as[34], 2949as[34]

Sri Lanka, traditional, 4934as[76]

Suriname, black people, state of research, ca. 1958, 3222as[36]

_____ Creole people, 3210as[36]

Sweden, polska, 5042as[76]

Turkey, Anatolia, ritual character, 5061as[76]

_____ southern, 2680as[33]

Uganda, Acholi people, 2574as[32]

_____ Lango people, 2574as[32]

UK, Isle of Man, adaptation by nontraditional performers, 2835as[34]

_____ _____ Kirk Maughold sword dance, 4961as[76]

USA, central, Meshkwahkihaki people, 3169as[35]

_____ Cherokee people, influenced by environment, 3160as[35], 3178as[35]

_____ Oklahoma, Kiowa people, ca. 1900-49, 4968as[76]

_____ South, French-speaking people, 4937as[76]

_____ Texas, square dance, history and development, 5060as[76]

_____ traditional, 4942as[76], 4943as[76], 4944as[76]

Uzbekistan, Bohoro, Jewish people, wedding cycle, 2631as[33]

Venezuela, maremare, history and development, 3190as[36]

Yemen, Jewish people, traditional, influence on Israeli neotraditional dance, 4998as[76]

dance — choreography, _see_ **choreographers; dance** headwords; **dance music** headwords

dance — general, _see also_ **choreographers; dance music** headwords; **ethnochoreologists; ethnochoreology; movement and gesture;** other **dance** headwords; **performers — dance**

aesthetics, relation to mythic function, 4974as[76]

_____ relation to 20th-c. music, 2242as[28]

_____ viewed by Laban, 5013as[76], 5014as[76]

choreography, 1900-1930s, 5024as[76]

collections, _Intavuolature del violino di Sigr. Gabriele Pervaneo da Lesina,_ early 17th c., 1646as[25]

historiography, relation to Archives Internationales de la Dance, 767as[2]

history and development, effects of technology, 855as[19]

influence on Western music, 945as[21]

Jewish people, secular influence, 6076as[91]

_____ wedding, 5054as[76]

nationalism, relation to collective rhythm, 3980as[61]

opera, history and development, 5263as[77]

pedagogy, for opera singers, 4637as[70]

_____ preschool, 4786as[71]

relation to sound, 4962as[76]

relation to theater, mid-20th c., 5202as[77]

rhythm, relation to Dalcroze method, 5076as[76]

traditional, aesthetics, 5026as[76]

_____ conservation, use of staged performances, 5018as[76]

_____ relation to art dance, 4941as[76]

_____ relation to dance music, 4979as[76], 4995as[76], 5028as[76]

_____ relation to labor, ethnomusicological approaches, 2438as[30]

_____ role in artistic renewal, 4917as[75]

_____ stability and change, 4996as[76]

traditional cultures, instrumental accompaniment, 2494as[31]

_____ relation to rhythm, 3979as[61]

dance — modern, _see_ **dance — by genre; dance — by place; dance — general; movement and gesture; performers — dance**

dance — notation, _see also_ **ethnochoreology;** other **dance** headwords

history and development, 5037as[76]

_____ relation to aesthetics, 5013as[76]

Labanotation, 5004as[76], 5012as[76], 5037as[76], 5041as[76]

_____ applied to ethnochoreology, 4981as[76]

_____ applied to Hungarian traditional dance, 1945-58, 5073as[76]

_____ applied to jazz-based popular dance, 5011as[76]

_____ applied to traditional dance, 5037as[76], 5041as[76]

_____ use in Hungarian ethnochoreology, 5048as[76]

Sharp, C.J., 4999as[76]

Škreblin system, 5063as[76]

Slavic states, southern, traditional dances, 4960as[76], 4988as[76]

traditional dance, role of proposed IFMC Dance Commission, 1961, 4980as[76]

transcultural, 4981as[76]

Žganec system, 5087as[76]

dance — popular and traditional, _see_ **dance — by genre; dance — by place; dance — general; dance music** headwords

dance music, _see_ **dance music — by composer; dance music — by genre; dance music — by place; dance music — general**

dance music — by composer, _see also_ **dance** headwords; **dance music — by genre; dance music — by place; dance music — general; minuet; suite**

Bach, J.S., saraband, 1505as[25]

Bach, W.F., polonaises, 1831as[26]

Badings, H., electronic ballets, 2137as[28]

Böhme, F.M., polonaises, 4266as[64]

Bull, J., _Pavin in A re_, 1343as[24]

Chopin, F., mazurkas, compared with Szymanowski, 4296as[64]

_____ _____ influence on Brahms, 2096as[27]

_____ _____ inner tempo analysis, 4022as[61]

_____ polonaises, 1831as[26]

_____ waltzes, piano, influenced by Polish piano waltzes, 1800-23, 2101as[27]

Henry, P., _La reine verte_, 5117as[77]

Honegger, A., _Icare_, 5023as[76]

Lully, J.-B., ballets, overtures, 1647as[25]

Mikołaj z Krakowa, 1469as[24]

Mozart, W.A., contredanses, 1826as[26]

Satie, E., relation to Clair _Cinéma_, 5208as[77]

Schubert, F., 1741as[26], 2042as[27]

Szymanowski, K., mazurkas, compared with Chopin, 4296as[64]

dance music — by genre, _see also_ **dance** headwords; **dance music — by composer; dance music — by place; dance music — general; minuet**

ballet, compared with film music, 5125as[77]

basse danse, analysis, computer applications, 4449as[49]

contredanse, influence on Haydn, 1727as[26]

_____ Mozart, W.A., 1826as[26]

cumbia, 5065as[76]

folia, history and development, 1318as[24]

_____ 16th c. to present, 1020as[21]

hora, Romania, local influences, 3027as[34], 3028as[34]

horo, Bulgaria, relation to dance, 4995as[76]

jig, Netherlands, relation to English sources, 1523as[25]

jota, 4953as[76]

_____ Spain, Aragón, 2724as[34], 4933as[76]

krakowiak, relation to Chopin, 1917as[27]

Ländler, Austria, Oberösterreich, 3126as[34]

maremare, Venezuela, 3190as[36]

mazurka, Poland, rhythm, 15th-18th c., 4034as[61]

_____ relation to Chopin stylistic evolution, 1916as[27]

_____ relation to polonaise, 4266as[64]

_____ rhythmic patterns, used in 18th-c. Polish religious music, 1782as[26]

_____ Szymanowski, K., piano music, 3791as[54]

mejorano, 5065as[76]

passacalle, 4277as[64]

polonaise, 4266as[64]

_____ Bach, W.F., 1831as[26]

_____ Chopin, F., 1831as[26]

_____ relation to Eastern Europe, 4309as[66]

_____ late 18th-early 19th c., 1788as[26]

punto, 5065as[76]

sardana, cobla, 2738as[34]

tamborito, 5065as[76]

tarantella, Italy, Campania, 4939as[76], 4940as[76]

traditional dance, hochzeit (Volga German), use of dulcimer, 3601as[44]

waltz, piano waltz, Poland, 1800-30, 2101as[27]

_____ role in Chopin style, 4356as[66]

dance music — by place, _see also_ **dance music — by composer; dance music — by genre; dance music — general; suite**

Africa, 2570as[32]

_____ compared with Roman Catholic church music, 6325as[93], 6326as[93]

_____ Mali, Dogon people, 2585as[32]

Austria, Oberösterreich, Ländler, 3126as[34]

Brazil, traditional, 3204as[36]

Bulgaria, horo, relation to dance, 4995as[76]

Canada, Québec, Ancienne Lorette, Huron people, 3151as[35]

Czech Republic, Horňácko, rhythmic and dynamic variations, 2856as[34]

_____ Moravia, ornamentation, 2855as[34]

Denmark, Greenland, Inuit people, 3179as[35]

England, traditional, 2883as[34]

Europe, Carpathian region, traditional dance music, tonal-melodic vs. harmonic feeling, 3101as[34]

_____ collections, 1555, 5068as[76]

_____ Eastern, Hasidic people, relation to nigun, 6037as[91]

_____ history and development, 13th-16th c., 5952as[89]

_____ Renaissance, 1332as[24]

_____ traditional, songs, 5081as[76]

_____ 16th c., 4978as[76]

_____ _____ relation to 17th-c. rhythmic theory, 3997as[61]

Finland, 978as[21]

_____ Swedish people, mid-19th c., 2718as[34]

_____ traditional, 2716as[34]

France, Basque region, 4926as[76], 4927as[76]

Germany, Bayern, traditional, collected by Bayerischer Rundfunk, 2813as[34]

_____ Darmstadt, tablatures, 3857as[55]

_____ influenced by England, 17th c., 1480as[25]

_____ instrumental dances, influenced by popular music, late 16th-early 17th c., 1383as[24]

_____ Mecklenburg, 19th c., 2804as[34]

_____ 16th c., 1382as[24], 1438as[24]

Greece, antiquity, rhythm and meter, 4025as[61]

_____ Pontic people, 2826as[34]

_____ songs, antiquity to present, 5032as[76]

Hungary, verbunkos and csárdás, influence on Liszt and Brahms, 1973as[27]

_____ 17th-18th c., 1492as[25]

Italy, Campania, tarantella, 4939as[76], 4940as[76]

_____ partitas, 16th c., 1454as[24]

_____ late 15th c., 1357as[24]

Japan, 5005as[76], 5006as[76]

_____ bugaku, ei and saezuri, 2620as[33]

Macedonia, 2992as[34]

Mediterranean region, 2495as[31]

North America, Indians, use of English words and phrases, 3174as[35]

Panama, traditional, influenced by African dance, 5065as[76]

Poland, influence on Chopin, 2029as[27]
___ influenced by traditional music, 983as[21]
___ krakowiak, relation to Chopin, 1917as[27]
___ mazurka, relation to Chopin stylistic
    evolution, 1916as[27]
___ ___ rhythm, 15th-18th c., 4034as[61]
___ ___ rhythmic patterns, used in 18th-c. reli-
    gious music, 1782as[26]
___ Podhale, influence on Szymanowski
    Harnasie, 2221as[28]
___ sztajerek, influence on Chopin, 2080as[27]
___ traditional dance, influence on Chopin
    rhythm, 4000as[61]
___ waltz, piano, 1800-30, 2101as[27]
Romania, hora, local influences, 3027as[34],
    3028as[34]
São Tomé and Príncipe, 2549as[32]
Slavic states, southern, women's round dance,
    3119as[34]
Spain, Aragón, jota, 2724as[34], 4933as[76], 4953as[76]
___ Castelltersol, ball del ciri, 4930as[76], 4931as[76]
___ instruments, 3287as[40]
___ Madrid, dramatic arts, 18th c., 5253as[77]
___ passacalle, 4277as[64]
___ El Vallès, ball de gitanes, 5049as[76], 5050as[76]
Switzerland, Toggenburg, use of chamber organs,
    3441as[42]
___ traditional, songs, 2867as[34]
Turkey, southern, Turkmen people, 2679as[33]
USA, Kansas, Ellis County, Volga German
    immigrants, use of dulcimer, 3601as[44]
___ Southwest, Hopi people, kachina songs,
    3164as[35]
___ ___ Pueblo people, 3165as[35]
___ traditional, 4942as[76], 4943as[76]
Venezuela, maremare, history and development,
    3190as[36]

dance music — general, *see also* **dance** headwords;
    dance music — by composer; **dance music —
    by genre**; **dance music — by place**; **suite**
history and development, comparison of Asian
    and European genres, 5126as[77]
melody, rhythmic aspects, relation to texted song
    melodies, 4035as[61]
rhythm, Bach, J.S., 1576as[25]
___ influence on Schubert, 3989as[61]
Switzerland, organ tablatures, 16th-17th c.,
    1234as[24]
traditional, relation to dance, 4979as[76], 4995as[76],
    5028as[76]

dance music — popular and traditional, *see* **dance
    music — by genre**; **dance music — by place**
dance-drama, *see* **dance — by place**; **dramatic
    arts**
dancers, *see* **performers — dance**
DANCKERT, Werner, 4239as[64], 4424as[69]
Dandrieu, Jean-François
works, harpsichord music, 1498as[25]
D'ANGELI, Andrea, 1028as[22], 3983as[61]
DANHELOVSKY, Konstantin, 1739as[26]
Daniel, Arnaut, *see* **Arnaut Daniel**
DANIÉLOU, Alain, 836as[19], 837as[19], 838as[19],
    839as[19], 852as[19], 2533as[31], 2615as[33], 2616as[33],
    4064as[62], 5129as[77], 5449as[81]
DANISKAS, John, 4328as[66]
Dankowski, Wojciech
works, religious music, use of mazurka rhythms,
    1782as[26]
Danmark, *see* **Denmark**
Danon, Oskar
works, *Kozara*, influenced by War of National
    Liberation songs, 2227as[28]
DANTALE, G.N., 450bs, 2617as[33]
Dante Alighieri
festivals and conferences, Italy, Ravenna, 1965,
    505bs
writings, *De vulgari eloquentia*, 1108as[23],
    5335as[78]

___ references to performance practice, 3690as[51]
Danysz, Stéphane
writings, translations, Chopin correspondence,
    critique, 5356as[78]
D'ARONCO, Gianfranco, 2786as[34]
DART, Thurston, 588as[1], 1282as[24], 1283as[24],
    1284as[24], 1523as[25], 3561as[44], 3732as[52],
    3737as[52], 3738as[52], 3923as[58]
data processing, *see* **computer applications**
databases, *see* **academic institutions**
dating, *see also* **editing**; **notation and paleography**;
    publishing and printing; **watermarks**
Desprez, J., psalm motets, 1393as[24]
France, ars nova, 1175as[23]
Händel, G.F., early vocal works, 1494as[25]
instruments, 3590as[44]
Italy, ars nova, 1160as[23]
___ MSS, 14th c., 1093as[23]
Krieger, J.P., works in Düben collection, 720as[2]
Laborde Chansonnier (Washington, D.C.),
    1264as[24]
Pfleger, A., works in Düben collection, 720as[2]
relation to cataloguing, 675as[1]
Scève, M., 5348as[78]
Schubert, F., piano music, 1997as[27]
___ relation to thematic catalogue, 551as[1]
Daube, Johann Friedrich
writings, *Anleitung zum Selbstunterricht in der
    musikalischen Komposition*, Fux anecdotes,
    1572as[25]
DAUBRESSE, Mathilde, 4512as[70]
DAURIAC, Lionel Alexandre, 5450as[81], 5451as[81]
DAVAU, 4513as[70]
DAVE, Émile, 2787as[34]
DAVID, D.L., 6197as[93]
DAVID, E.E., Jr., 5808as[86]
DAVID, Hans T., 953as[21], 1706as[25], 1740as[26],
    3911as[58]
David, Johann Nepomuk
works, influenced by Bach, 2272as[28]
___ organ music, 6412as[93]
David, King of Judah and Israel
life, depicted in Serbian art works, 5390as[79]
DAVID, Lucien, 3984as[61]
DAVID, O.S.B., 6151as[93]
DAVIDSSON, Åke, 712as[2]
DAVIE, Donald, 426bs, 5299as[78]
DAVIES, John Howard, 345bs, 539as[1], 540as[1],
    541as[1], 542as[1], 543as[1], 544as[1], 545as[1],
    5973as[89]
Day, Alfred
writings, harmony, 4176as[63]
DAYAN, Leonzio, 3891as[58], 4065as[62], 6108as[92]
De' Bardi, Giovanni
aesthetics, relation to melody, 1404as[24]
De Betto di Bardi, Donato (Donatello)
aesthetics, non finito concept, 5442as[81]
DE BONIS, Alessandro, 4868as[73]
De' Calzabigi, Ranieri
writings, librettos, relation to opera reform,
    1765as[26]
De' Cavalieri, Emilio
works, monody, 1404as[24]
___ *Rappresentatione di Anima, et di Corpo*,
    1288as[24]
___ ___ libretto, 1671as[25]
DE FEO, Sandro, 5130as[77]
De Gamerra, Giovanni
translations, Schikaneder *Die Zauberflöte* libretto,
    5240as[77]
DE JONG, Marinus, 1285as[24]
DE LANGE, Pieter Albert, 5831as[86]
DE LEEUW, Ton, 5131as[77]
DE' PAOLI, Domenico, 5132as[77]

De' Rossi, Luigi, *see* **Rossi, Luigi**
DE SANCTIS, Giovanni Battista, 5133as[77]
DE SANCTIS, Valerio, 5955as[89]
dealers, *see also* **advertising and marketing**; **pub-
    lishers and printers**
Europe, piano, 3539as[43]
Olschki, L., 1449as[24]
printed music, 5963as[89]
___ international cooperation, 5971as[89]
___ relation to publishers, ca. 1901, 5965as[89]
Simrock, H., 2075as[27]
DEAN, Aldhelm, 6198as[93]
death and dying
ballads, hanging of fiddler as subject, 2547as[31]
Bosnia and Herzegovina, subject of traditional
    dances, 4957as[76], 5044as[76]
Denmark, late 16th c., role of polskdans, 5038as[76]
Romania, funeral customs, 2777as[34], 2796as[34]
Russia, role in folklore, 2817as[34]
Schubert, F., 1998as[27]
Slovenia, subject of traditional songs, 2918as[34]
symbolism, use of parallel fourths, 4187as[63]
DEBENEDETTI, Giacomo, 5134as[77], 5452as[81]
DEBES, Louis Helmut, 1286as[24]
Debussy, Claude
aesthetics, 2202as[28], 2245as[28], 4307as[66], 5602as[81]
___ impressionism, 5396as[79]
___ influence on France, 2168as[28]
___ influence on Germany and Austria, 2257as[28]
___ influence on Hungary, 2134as[28]
___ influence on Italian opera, 2210as[28]
___ influence on Latin America, 2133as[28]
___ influence on Netherlands, 2225as[28]
___ influence on Poland, 2184as[28]
___ influence on Russia, 2194as[28]
___ influence on Scandinavia, 2224as[28]
___ influence on USA, 2236as[28]
___ influences, 5514as[81]
___ modality, 4045as[62]
___ relation to creative process, 4308as[66]
___ viewed by Schoenberg and Webern, 2132as[28]
correspondence, with Varèse, 2201as[28]
festivals and conferences, France, Paris, 1962,
    456bs
life, psychology, 2030as[27]
___ relation to Godet, 2131as[28]
reception, Russia, 2162as[28]
works, chamber music, 2024as[27]
___ early, influenced by Russian composers,
    2028as[27]
___ harmony, 4147as[63], 4173as[63]
___ influence on England, 2207as[28]
___ influence on Janáček and Bartók, 2238as[28]
___ orchestral music, compared with Indy,
    1931as[27]
___ *Prélude à l'après-midi d'un faune*, printing
    errors, 3811as[55]
___ quoted by Bartók, 4317as[66]
___ relation to Benoît, 1944as[27]
___ relation to pictorial impressionism, 5374as[79]
___ relation to Stravinsky, 2205as[28]
___ rhythm and meter, 3987as[61]
___ sound-surfaces, influence on atonal
    composers, 4335as[66]
___ tonality, 4171as[63]
___ unsuitable for liturgy, 6177as[93]
___ use of older forms, 4231as[64]
___ viewed by Pijper, 2149as[28]
___ ca. 1900, 2039as[27]
DECHEVRENS, Antoine, 3882as[55]
declamation and diction, *see also* **articulation**;
    singing
choral singing, 3326as[41]
foundation of dramatic representation, 5232as[77]
German, relation to traditional songs, 4787as[71]
German vs. Italian, influence on singing, 5921as[88]
Mass, prayers and readings, 6136as[93]
pedagogy, chant scholae, 4899as[73]

___ Congress on Arab Music performances, Al-Qāhirah, 1932, 827as[9]
Brazil, popular music, 5947as[89]
___ traditional music, 3188as[36]
USA, traditional music, 5947as[89]

discography (as discipline), *see* **cataloguing, classification, indexing, etc.**

DISCOTECA PÚBLICA MUNICIPAL DE SÃO PAULO, 3296as[41], 5919as[88]

discs, *see* **sound recordings**

diseases, *see* **medicine — by name; medicine — by topic**

DISERTORI, Benvenuto, 3563as[44], 3564as[44], 3695as[51]

DISMAN, Miloslav, 4518as[70]

Disney, Walter (Walt)
works, directing, *Fantasia*, 5125as[77]

dissonance, *see* **consonance and dissonance**

Dittersdorf, Carl Ditters von
manuscripts, minuet (uncatalogued), 1815as[26]
works, chamber music, 4378as[66]
___ influenced by Hungarian traditional music, 1726as[26]

DITTMER, Kunz, 2431as[30]

DITTMER, Luther Albert, 840as[19], 1112as[23], 3818as[55], 3978as[61]

Divine Liturgy (Byzantine), *see* **Byzantine studies; chant — Byzantine; religion and religious music — Christianity (Eastern Orthodox)**

Divitis, Antonius
life, relation to Field of Cloth of Gold, 1520, 1354as[24]

DJURIĆ-KLAJN, Stana, 1079as[23], 1743as[26], 1946as[27]

Długoraj, Wojciech
editions, ca. 1957, 932as[20]
works, 1582as[25]

DOBBS, Jack P.B., 6432as[94]

DOBIÁŠ, Václav, 360bs, 1744as[26], 2156as[28]

Dobiáš, Václav
works, mass song, 3064as[34]

DOBROWOLSKI, Janusz, 1947as[27]

dodecaphony, *see* **serialism**

Doležálek, Jan Emanuel
works, influenced by Mozart, 1880as[26]

DÖLGER, Franz Joseph, 395bs

DOMÍNGUEZ BERRUETA, Juan, 2792as[34], 4953as[76]

DOMMANGE, René, 5956as[89]

DOMPÉ, Giovanna, 2793as[34]

DONÀ, Mariangela, 555as[1], 3939as[60]

Donatello, *see* **De Betto di Bardi, Donato (Donatello)**

DONATH, Gustav, 4066as[62], 4241as[64]

DONINGTON, Robert, 829as[19], 3732as[52]

Donizetti, Gaetano
works, operas, concept of genre, 5169as[77]

Donizetti, Giuseppe
life, Istanbul, 2275as[28]

Donne, John
aesthetics, melancholia, 1342as[24]
writings, poetry, settings, 17th-c., 5307as[78]

Donostia, José Antonio de, *see* **Zulaica y Arregui, José Gonzalo (José Antonio de Donostia)**

DOORSLAER, Georges van, 1289as[24], 1290as[24], 1291as[24], 1527as[25], 1745as[26], 3349as[42], 3648as[46]

DOPUĐA, Jelena, 4954as[76], 4955as[76], 4956as[76], 4957as[76], 4958as[76], 4959as[76], 4960as[76]

ĐORĐEVIĆ, Dragutin M., 2794as[34], 5306as[78]

Doré, Guislain
works, for funeral of Queen Marie-Thérèse, 1683, 1601as[25]

DOREN, Rombaut van, 6203as[93]

DORFMÜLLER, Kurt, 556as[1], 713as[2], 3892as[58]

Dörken, Paul
life, color hearing, relation to Bach, 4306as[66]

DOSSE, Madame, 2314as[29]

DOTESIO, Louis, 5957as[89]

DOUGLAS, Mona, 4961as[76]

DOUILLART, A., 2315as[29]

DOUILLEZ, Jeannine, 714as[2]

DOULGHERAKIS, Emmanuel, 2795as[34]

DOVAZ, René, 2316as[29]

Dowland, John
aesthetics, melancholia, 1342as[24]
works, madrigals, 1411as[24]

DOWNES, Edward O.D., 1528as[25], 1529as[25], 1908as[27]

DRAEGER, Hans-Heinz, 3248as[40], 3249as[40], 3939as[60], 4067as[62], 5456as[81], 5628as[81], 5635as[82], 5690as[82], 5923as[88], 6008as[90]

Draghi, Antonio
works, operas, influenced by traditional music, 1691as[25]

DRĂGHICEANU, V.I., 2796as[34]

DRĂGOI, Sabin V., 3234as[39]

dramatic arts, *see also* **costumes; dramaturgy; film; incidental music; literature; liturgical drama; masque; melodrama; musical revue, cabaret, etc.; musical theater — popular; opera** headwords; **pantomime**
acting, compared with singing, 3293as[41]
___ pedagogy, benefit of vocal training, 3328as[41]
Asia, conference, 1958-59, 397bs
___ masks and puppet theater, viewed by Craig, influence on Yeats, 5174as[77]
Austria, Salzburg, early 17th c., 1677as[25]
___ 18th c. to mid-20th c., 5141as[77]
bibliographies, 582as[1]
Bosnia and Herzegovina, traditional dance-drama, 4955as[76]
China, 5188as[77], 5259as[77]
___ Beijing, 5200as[77]
___ compared with Vietnam, 5260as[77]
___ jingju, 5262as[77]
conferences, 1903, 42bs
___ 1927, 138bs
___ 1957, 383bs
Croatia, Korčula, 5080as[76]
___ northern and eastern, spring mendication rituals, 5109as[77]
Czech Republic, Praha, Osvobozené Divadlo, influence on mass song, 3064as[34]
declamation, use of instrumental music, 5254as[77]
Ecuador, traditional, 5261as[77]
England, stage plays on biblical themes, relation to Händel oratorios, 5274as[77]
___ Tudor era, court masques and spectacles, 5249as[77]
Europe, Alpine region, southeastern, Dance of Death traditional dance-dramas, 5187as[77]
France, influenced by Wagner, 5319as[78]
Greece, antiquity, prologues, influence on 17th-c. opera, 5192as[77]
___ ___ use of enharmonic genus, 4089as[62]
history and development, comparison of Asian and European genres, 5126as[77]
___ state of research, ca. 1933, 5247as[77]
India, South, dance-dramas, 5207as[77]
___ ___ hobby horses, 5098as[77]
influenced by singing and speech, 5232as[77]
Italy, Firenze, Medici wedding entertainments, late 16th c., 1427as[24], 1462as[24], 5158as[77]
___ relation to monody, late 16th c., 1404as[24]
___ Todi, sacred drama, 13th-16th c., 5222as[77]
Japan, 5123as[77], 5181as[77], 5182as[77]
___ kabuki, nagauta, 2659as[33]
___ ___ relation to ukiyo-e, 4919as[75]
___ noh, 2653as[33], 5180as[77]
___ ___ influenced by Buddhism, 5231as[77]
___ puppet theaters, 5219as[77]

___ ca. 1958, 5243as[77]
librarianship, cataloguing, 580as[1], 581as[1]
___ press articles, 521as[1]
___ Internat. Theatre Inst., 596as[1]
___ Universal Decimal Classification, 640as[1]
Locke, M., 1516as[25]
Netherlands, librarianship, 695as[1]
___ traveling English theaters, 17th c., 1523as[25]
people's theater, relation to music, 5166as[77]
performance venues, 15th-17th c., 5175as[77]
Poland, influenced by traditional music, 983as[21]
___ public theater, ca. 1937, 5142as[77]
___ 14th-20th c., 5119as[77], 5120as[77]
___ 15th-17th c., 5216as[77]
radio, plays, musical, 5215as[77]
___ ___ role of music, 5257as[77]
relation to radio, 5114as[77]
Renaissance, conference, 1963, 472bs
Romania, 14th-18th c., 1279as[24]
Serbia, 9th-16th c., 1079as[23]
Shakespeare, W., use of music, relation to politics, 5362as[78]
societies, conference, 1926, 130bs
Spain, Aragón, northern, el dance, 2725as[34], 4932as[76]
___ Híjar, el dance, 5030as[76], 5031as[76]
___ influence on Italy, 16th c., 1276as[24]
___ Madrid, relation to traditional music, 18th c., 5253as[77]
___ 18th c., 5255as[77]
Szymanowski, K., 2187as[28]
Taiwan, Taipei, guoju, 5262as[77]
traditional dance staging, use in conservation of traditional dance, 5018as[76]
tragedy, cathartic function, relation to music, 5498as[81]
Vietnam, 5259as[77], 5260as[77]
20th c., conference, 1964, 481bs

dramaturgy, *see also* **dramatic arts; film; libretto** headwords; **opera** headwords
Austria, Alpine region, traditional drama, use of songs, 5186as[77]
___ Wien, oratorios, 1725-40, 1889as[26]
Bartók, B., use of developing variation, 4443as[69]
Beethoven, L. van, *Fidelio*, 5272as[77]
De' Cavalieri, E., *Rappresentatione di anima, et di corpo*, 1288as[24]
film music, ca. 1937, 5210as[77]
grand opera, 19th c., 5101as[77]
Händel, G.F., *Belshazzar*, recitative, no. 2, 3743as[52]
___ oratorios, 3768as[52]
___ use of melody, comparison of operas and oratorios, 4458as[69]
Janáček, L., 4385as[66]
___ compared with Musorgskij, 4367as[66]
___ *Káťa Kabanová*, act 3, scene 2, 5273as[77]
___ operas, speech melodies, 4320as[66]
___ *Výlety páně Broučkovy*, part 2, 4258as[64]
Musorgskij, M.P., compared with Janáček, 4367as[66]
opera, relation to singing, 5224as[77]
___ use of history, 5163as[77]
___ mid-20th c., 5202as[77]
___ 20th c., 5144as[77]
Prokof'ev, S.S., early operas, influenced by Mejerhol'd, 5112as[77]
Różychi, L., *Bolesław Śmiały*, 5150as[77]
Telemann, G.P., harmonic devices, 4167as[63]
Verdi, G., *Simon Boccanegra*, 1881 revision, 2063as[27]
Wagner, R., relation to aesthetics, 5581as[81]
___ relation to psychology, 5241as[77]

dramma per musica, *see* **libretto** headwords; **opera** headwords

DREIMÜLLER, Karl, 486bs, *487rs[16], 557as[1], 715as[2], 815as[8], 900as[20], 959as[21], 1080as[23], 3350as[42], 3819as[55]

DRESDEN, Sem, 2157as[28]

E

Gilson, Paul
works, influenced by Debussy, 2225as[28]

GINDELE, Corbinian, 3375as[42]

Gindele, Corbinian
works, organ music, 6412as[93]

Giocondo, Fra, *see* **Giovanni da Verona (Fra Giocondo)**

Giordani, Tommaso
works, influence on Mozart string quartets, 1882as[26]

Giornovichi, Giovanni Mane
life, 1743as[26]

Giovanetti, Gustavo
works, microtonal music, 4146as[63]

GIOVANNELLI, Nikolai Leonida, 2835as[34]

Giovanni da Cascia
works, compared with Piero, 1161as[23]

Giovanni da Firenze, *see* **Giovanni da Cascia**

Giovanni da Prato
writings, *Il paradiso degli Alberti*, references to performance practice, 3690as[51]

Giovanni da Verona (Fra Giocondo)
works, art, intarsia decorations, instrument iconography, 5404as[79]

GIRALDI, R., 964as[21]

GIRARDIN, Monique, 580as[1], 5160as[77]

GIRARDON, Renée, 788as[5]

GIROD, Roger, 5882as[87]

GITEAU, Cécile, 581as[1]

GIULIANTE, Guido, 4969as[76]

Giustiniani, Orsatto
writings, *Edipo tiranno*, 5239as[77]

Gizycka-Zamojska, Ludmila, *see* **Zamojska, Ludmila**

GLAHN, Henrik, 1316as[24], 1561as[25]

GL'ANS, Leyyb, 4876as[73]

Glarean, Heinrich
correspondence, with Łaski, on *Dodecachordon*, 1461as[24]
works, *Christus resurgens*, basis of Pullaer Mass, 1287as[24]
writings, *Isagoge in musicen*, 1378as[24]

Glareanus, Henricus, *see* **Glarean, Heinrich**

GLASER, Curt, 86bs

Glaser, Ernst
life, Norway, 966as[21]

GLASER, Hugo, 5729as[83]

GLATTER-GÖTZ, Josef von, 3376as[42]

GLATZL, Matthias, 339bs

Glebov, Igor, *see* **Asaf'ev, Boris (Igor Glebov)**

GLEICH, Christoph-Clemens von, 582as[1]

Gletle, Johann Melchior
works, litanies, 1669as[25]

GLÉYO (CHURCH MUSICIAN), 4697as[71]

Glinka, Mihail Ivanovič
life, views on Liszt, 1840s-50s, 2025as[27]
works, influenced by Russian Orthodox chant, 1001as[21]

GLIŃSKI, Mateusz, 1971as[27], 1972as[27]

globalization, *see* **syncretism; transculturation**

GLORIEUX, Louis, 4877as[73], 6238as[93]

GŁOWACKI, John, 4299as[65]

Glowatz, Heinrich
instruments, organs, 3364as[42]

Gluck, Christoph Willibald
aesthetics, 5554as[81]
life, relation to Händel, 1679as[25]
performance practice, vocal appoggiaturas, 3741as[52]
performances, *Orfeo ed Euridice*, at Dietrich-Eckart-Buhne, Berlin, 1936-37, 5213as[77]
works, editing, 975as[21]
___ instrumental music, 1762as[26]

___ operas, relation to opera reform, 1765as[26]
___ ___ role of libretto, 5111as[77]
___ ___ relation to Baroque style, 1626as[25]

Godet, Robert
life, relation to Debussy, 2131as[28]

GOEBELS, Franzpeter, 494bs, 3516as[43]

Goehl, Honorat
writings, theory, 1683as[25]

GOEHR, Alexander, 3959as[60]

GOEJE, Michael Johan de, 11bs

Goethe, Johann Wolfgang von
aesthetics, compared with German Romanticism, 2128as[27]
___ influence on Beethoven, 1823as[26]
writings, ballads, relation to piano ballade, 4245as[64]
___ influence on Beethoven, 1852as[26]
___ philosophy, compared with Kant, 5428as[81]
___ poetry, rhythm and meter, 5278as[78]
___ views on music symbolism, 5934as[88]
___ *Wanderers Sturmlied*, 5279as[78]

Goicoechea Errasti, Vicente
life, relation to 20th-c. Spanish religious music, 2234as[28]

GOJKOVIĆ, Andrijana, 3619as[45], 5318as[78]

GOLAŃSKI, Henryk, 458bs

GOLDHAMMER, Otto, 1973as[27]

Goldmark, Karl
works, harmony, compared with Brahms, 4384as[66]

Goldoni, Carlo
festivals and conferences, Italy, Venezia, 1957, 384bs
life, relation to Vivaldi, 1612as[25]
performances, Poland, 5204as[77]
writings, comedies, relation to opera librettos, 5133as[77]
___ libretto for *La buona figliuola*, relation to opera comica genre, 5132as[77]
___ librettos, influence on Italian opera, 5136as[77]
___ *Mémoires*, views on Vivaldi, 1507as[25]

GOLDSCHMIDT, Gusta, 588as[1]

GOLDSCHMIDT, Harry, 1974as[27], 2171as[28], 5409as[80], 5478as[81], 5479as[81], 5677as[82]

Goldschmidt, Harry
writings, on style, 4373as[66]

GOLDSCHMIDT, Hugo, 1765as[26]

GOLDSCHMIDT, Nicholas, 846as[19]

GOLÉA, Antoine, 1766as[26]

Goleminov, Marin
works, influenced by Bulgarian traditional rhythm, 4005as[61]

GÖLLER, Gottfried, 1109as[23]

GÖLLNER, Theodor, 1112as[23], 1147as[23]

GOŁOS, Jerzy, 6130as[92]

GÖLZ, Richard, 6434as[94]

GOMBOSI, Otto, 1030as[22], 1317as[24], 1318as[24], 1319as[24], 3572as[44]

Gombosi, Otto Johannes
editions, *Capirola lutebook*, 1955, critique, 4272as[64]
writings, origins of toccata, 4237as[64]

GONTIER, Augustin, 1110as[23]

Gonzaga, Vincenzo I, Duke of Mantua
life, relation to Jewish culture, 3724as[51]

GONZALEZ, V., 3435as[42]

GONZÁLEZ BARRÓN, Ramón, 6013as[90], 6239as[93]

GONZÁLEZ DE AMEZÚA Y NORIEGA, Ramón, 3464as[42], 3667as[48]

GONZÁLEZ GARCÍA-VALLADOLID, Casimiro, 6240as[93]

GORCZYCKA, Monika, 2172as[28], 4337as[66]

Gorczycki, Grzegorz Gerwazy
works, influence on European music, 957as[21]

GOREN-KADMAN, Ayalah, 4970as[76]

GORIN-FEINBERG, 5755as[85]

Gorman, Lawrence
writings, satirical song texts, 5322as[78]

GORON, Pierre, 4698as[71]

Gorzanis, Giacomo
life, 1415as[24]

GOSLICH, Siegfried, 4338as[66]

gospel music
USA, influence on US Protestant hymnody, 6452as[94]

Gossec, François-Joseph
collections, symphonies, 761as[2]
manuscripts, at Bibl. du Conservatoire Royal de Musique, Bruxelles, 1730as[26]
works, relation to Classicism, 1896as[26]

GOSSET, Alphonse, 5820as[86]

GOTTRON, Adam, 1562as[25], 1767as[26], 6241as[93]

GÖTZ, Josef, 2836as[34], 3573as[44]

Goudimel, Claude
works, *Pseaumes mises en rime françoise*, compared with Bourgeois *Pseaulmes de David*, 1310as[24]

Gould, Murray
life, developing of *Plaine and easie* code, 787as[5]

Goulding, Edmund
works, directing, *Grand Hotel*, 5208as[77]

GOUZOU, Lucien, 5883as[87]

GOW, George C., 4173as[63]

GRABNER, Hermann, 3945as[60]

GRABÓCZ, Miklós, 2837as[34]

Grabu, Louis
works, incidental music for Shadwell *The history of Timon of Athens, the man-hater*, 1693as[25]

GRAD, Toni, 4699as[71], 4700as[71]

GRADENWITZ, Peter, 2173as[28]

Gradual, *see* **Mass**

graduals, *see* **liturgical books**

Graener, Paul
works, influenced by Debussy, 2257as[28]

GRAESER, Wolfgang, 1563as[25], 5662as[82]

GRAF, Ernst, 1031as[22]

Graf, Ernst
instruments, organs, at Stadtkirche, Frauenfeld, 3399as[42]

GRAF, Herbert, 4878as[73], 5161as[77]

GRAF, Walter, 3226as[37]

GRAFCZYŃSKYA, Melania, 1320as[24]

GRAFF, Ragnwald, 2838as[34]

gramophone, *see* **sound recording and reproduction**

GRANIĆ, Philaret, 131bs, *132rs[16], *133rs[16]

GRASBERGER, Franz, 583as[1], 584as[1], 4174as[63], 5162as[77]

GRASERN, Siegfried von, 3996as[61]

GRASES GONZÁLEZ, Pedro, 4971as[76], 4972as[76]

GRASSI LANDI, Bartolomeo, 3701as[51], 4078as[62]

Graupner, Christoph
works, operas, for Darmstadt, 1637as[25]

GRAUPNER, Friedrich, 1564as[25]

Graurock, Jan
instruments, organs, 3364as[42]

Gravani, Peregrino
works, influenced by Mozart, 1008as[21]

gravicembalo (=harpsichord), *see* **instruments — keyboard (harpsichord family)**

GRAVIER (CANON), 6242as[93]

GRAY, Cecil, 5480as[81]

Great Britain, *see* **United Kingdom**

Greece, *see also* **Balkan states**
Acharnai, instruments, lyre, 3604as[44]
antiquity, competitions, compared with Central Asian singing contests, 2622as[33]
___ concept of harmonia, 1027as[22]

Guilmant, Alexandre
  editions, *Archives des maîtres de l'orgue...*, 3895as[58]

Guinea
  Baga people, traditional music, ceremonies, 2586as[32]
  instruments, musical bows, 3566as[44]
  Kissi people, musical life, compared with Dogon and Fulɓe, 2587as[32]

Guinée, *see* **Guinea**

guitar, *see* **instruments — string (guitar family)**

GUITTARD, J., 5822as[86]

GULICK, John, 400bs

Gunasco da Pavia, Lorenzo
  instruments, organs, 1326as[24]

GUNJI, Sumi, 3518as[43]

GÜNTHER, Felix, 3785as[53]

GÜNTHER, Robert, 2553as[32]

GÜNTHER, Ursula, 1111as[23], 1112as[23], 3898as[58]

Gurlitt, Cornelius
  life, Schleswig-Holstein, 1978as[27]

GURLITT, Wilibald, 122bs, 772as[3], 877as[20], 1323as[24], 1324as[24], 1568as[25], 1975as[27], 3379as[42], 3380as[42], 3381as[42], 3382as[42], 3383as[42], 4253as[70], 4339as[66], 4543as[70], 4880as[73], 5925as[88]

Gurlitt, Wilibald
  instruments, organs, Praetorius-Orgel, 3360as[42]
  writings, conservation of organs, 3427as[42]

GURVIN, Olav, 966as[21], 4975as[76]

gusle, *see* **instruments — string (violin family)**

Gustavus II Adolphus, King of Sweden
  collections, 16th-c. MSS and prints, 712as[2]

GUTFLEISCH, Paul, 5884as[87]

GÜTTLER, Hermann, 1569as[25], 1768as[26], 1769as[26], 1770as[26]

GUTTMAN, Newman, 4406as[68]

GUTTMANN, Alfred, 3302as[41], 5663as[82]

Guttry, Alexander von
  writings, on Chopin correspondence, 5356as[78]

GUZMÁN, Antonio, 2840as[34], 2841as[34]

GWLDŠMYDṬ, Yŵsep, 6065as[91]

GYÖNGY, Pál, 5962as[89]

Gypsy studies, *see* **Roma studies**

GYSI, Fritz, 967as[21], 1771as[26], 5664as[82]

H

HAACK, Helmut, 1590as[25]

HAAG, Herbert, 3384as[42]

HAAPANEN, Toivo Elias, 878as[20], 1570as[25], 6245as[93]

Haapanen, Toivo Elias
  writings, Helsinki chant MSS, 3871as[55]

HAAR, James, 429bs

Haas, Friedrich
  instruments, organs, 1979as[27]

Haas, Joseph
  works, used in Roman Catholic liturgy, 2200as[28]

HAAS, Robert, 585as[1], 586as[1], 721as[2], 722as[2], 1571as[25], 1772as[26], 1773as[26], 1976as[27]

HÁBA, Alois, 968as[21], 4079as[62], 4080as[62], 4175as[63], 4340as[66], 4544as[70]

Hába, Alois
  instruments, quarter-tone piano, 4091as[62]
  works, mass song, 3064as[34]
  ___ microtonal music, 4146as[63]

Habeneck, François-Antoine
  life, Paris, relation to Beethoven reception, 2075as[27]

HABERL, Ferdinand, 6246as[93]

HABERL, Franz Xaver, 6247as[93]

HABERMAN, 'Abraham Me'yr, 6066as[91], 6067as[91]

HABÖCK, Franz, 4545as[70]

Habsburg family
  lives, patronage of Italian musicians, 16th-18th c., 1465as[24]

HABUNEK, Vlado, 5165as[77]

Hačaturjan, Aram
  works, film music, 5171as[77]

HACOBIAN, Zaven, 841as[19], 2512as[31]

HADLAČ, Jiří, 496bs

HADOW, William Henry, 1977as[27], 6014as[90]

HADŽIMANOV, Vasil, 2844as[34], 2845as[34], 2846as[34], 2847as[34], 2848as[34], 3620as[45], 3621as[45]

HADŽI-PECOVA, Marika, 2842as[34], 2843as[34], 4976as[76]

Haeffner, Johann Christian Friedrich
  performances, Bach orchestral and organ works, 3770as[52]

HAENNI, Georges, 4546as[70]

HAERPFER, Friedrich, 3385as[42]

HAHN, Harry, 4254as[64]

HAHN, Kurt, 5484as[81]

HAHNE, Gerhard, 1978as[27]

Hajduk Veljko, *see* **Petrović, Veljko (Hajduk Veljko)**

HAJTAS, Francis, 6248as[93]

HALLÉGUEN, Eugène, 2849as[34]

HALLEN, Arnold von der, 782as[4]

Halm, August Otto
  writings, variation form, 4270as[64]

HALM, Hans, 587as[1], 593as[1], 1774as[26]

HALOT, Alexandre, 4547as[70], 5410as[80]

HALPERN, Harry, 6068as[91]

HALPERN, Ida, 3153as[35]

HALPERT, Herbert, 3154as[35]

HALSKI, Czesław, 4977as[76]

Hamal, Jean-Noël
  works, operas, 1600as[25]
  ___ *Six ouvertures de camera*, op. 1, compared with Stamic *Sonate a tre*, 4242as[64]

HAMANN, Fritz, 4824as[72]

HAMANN, Heinz Wolfgang, 1572as[25], 1763as[26]

HAMEL, Fred, 879as[20], 969as[21], 970as[21], 1573as[25], 5485as[81]

HAMILTON, Iain, 2175as[28], 2176as[28]

hammer dulcimer (=dulcimer), *see* **instruments — string (dulcimer family)**

HAMMERICH, Angul, 1574as[25], 3576as[44], 3577as[44]

HAMMERSCHLAG, János, 3677as[50]

HAMMERSTEIN, Reinhold, 3249as[40]

Hammond, Anthony
  collections, Burwell Lute Tutor, 3737as[52]

HÄNDCHEN, Fritz, 2323as[29]

Händel, Georg Friedrich
  collections, in Nat. Lib. of Scotland, 739as[2]
  editions, vocal music, facsimile editions, 1868-1923, 5980as[89]
  festivals and conferences, Germany, Halle, 1959, 408bs
  life, England, 1688as[25]
  ___ influenced by German Enlightenment, 1595as[25]
  ___ multilingualism, 1692as[25]
  ___ relation to Weißenfels culture, 1545as[25]
  ___ state of research, 1950, 1679as[25]
  ___ viewed by Rolland, 1694as[25]
  manuscripts, concerti grossi, op. 3, watermarks, 1581as[25]
  ___ *Messiah*, HWV 56, at Ouseley Lib., Tenbury, 718as[2]
  performance practice, *Belshazzar*, recitative, no. 2, 3743as[52]
  ___ instrumental music, 3744as[52]
  ___ operas, 20th c., 5250as[77]
  ___ oratorios, state of research, 1959, 3768as[52]
  ___ use of positive organ, 3430as[42]
  ___ vocal music, ornamentation, 3779as[52]
  performances, *Agrippina*, by Opernhaus Leipzig, 1959, 5276as[77]
  ___ *Hercules*, at Dietrich-Eckart-Buhne, Berlin, 1936-37, 5213as[77]
  ___ operas, by Landestheater, Halle, mid-1950s, 5250as[77]
  ___ ___ Sweden, 18th-20th c., 1541as[25]
  ___ oratorios, staged productions, 20th c., 3735as[52]
  ___ unpublished works, ca. 1939, 1513as[25]
  reception, Europe, Eastern, Soviet era, 2322as[29]
  ___ Germany, in school curriculum, 1870-1959, 4687as[71]
  ___ oratorios, Germany, 20th c., 2338as[29]
  ___ role of Mendelssohn-Bartholdy, 2113as[27]
  sound recordings, concerti grossi, op. 3, relation to performance practice, 3744as[52]
  tributes, 1577as[25]
  works, cantatas, Italian texts, 1678as[25]
  ___ circle of fifths, compared with Bach, 4306as[66]
  ___ counterpoint and basso continuo exercises, 1617as[25]
  ___ dramatic works, use of melody, 4458as[69]
  ___ early vocal music, attribution and dating, 1494as[25]
  ___ influence on Mozart, 1901as[26]
  ___ influence on socialist vocal-symphonic music, 2191as[28]
  ___ key character, 1624as[25]
  ___ *Messiah*, HWV 56, revisions, 3752as[52]
  ___ ___ tempos, 3753as[52]
  ___ oratorios, biblical themes, relation to English stage plays, 5274as[77]
  ___ ___ political themes, 1665as[25]
  ___ ___ relation to English politics, 1668as[25]
  ___ ___ thematic elaboration, 4440as[69]
  ___ oratorios and anthems, quotation of Lutheran hymns, 4472as[69]
  ___ organ music, adapted for small organs, 3358as[42]
  ___ ___ relation to positive, 3477as[42]
  ___ polyphony, 4199as[63]
  ___ relation to Baroque style, 1626as[25]
  ___ *Saul*, 3780as[52]
  ___ sicilianas, 1012as[21], 4295as[64]
  ___ state of research, 1959, 1685as[25]
  ___ viewed by Liszt, 2082as[27]
  ___ vocal music, themes from antiquity, 1552as[25]
  ___ *The ways of Zion do mourn*, HWV 264, 1598as[25]

HANDSCHIN, Jacques, 179rs[16], 880as[20], 881as[20], 1113as[23], 1114as[23], 1115as[23], 1116as[23], 1117as[23], 1325as[24], 1979as[27], 4255as[64], 4341as[66], 5486as[81], 5665as[82], 6015as[90]

Hanka, Václav
  collections, Bohemian traditional music, 2946as[34]
  life, nationalism, influence on Chopin, 2074as[27]
  ___ relation to Chopin and Hube, 1968as[27]

HANKEL, Marie, 58bs

HANKISS, János, 5166as[77]

HANLEY, Miles Laurence, 5756as[85]

HANLON, H., 2632as[33]

Hanslick, Eduard
  aesthetics, compared with Wagner, 5580as[81]
  ___ concept of absolute music, 5430as[81]
  writings, 5163as[77]
  ___ on emotive and constructive elements, 5470as[81]

Hanslund-Christensen, Henning
  writings, on Mongolia, 3052as[34]

HÄNSSEL, W., 4701as[71]

HARASZTI, Emil, 1326as[24], 1980as[27], 2850as[34]

___ influence on Romanian composers, 19th c., 2116as[27]

___ influenced by contredanse, 1727as[26]

___ influenced by Czech traditional songs, 2944as[34]

___ influenced by Gassmann, 1794as[26]

___ influenced by Hungarian traditional music, 1726as[26]

___ influenced by traditional music, 1779as[26]

___ instrumental music, relation to Classic style, 4331as[66]

___ key choices, compared with Mozart, 4220as[63]

___ Masses, influenced by Benedict XIV *Annus qui*, 1754as[26]

___ minuets, 4239as[64]

___ *Missa "Rorate coeli desuper"*, Hob.XXII:3, attribution, 1797as[26]

___ operas, 1776-90, 1725as[26]

___ quartets, string, influence on Mozart, 1859as[26]

___ ca. 1770, compared with Kraus quartets, 4279as[64]

___ relation to Classic style, 5559as[81]

___ relation to Hungary, 1877as[26]

___ relation to Mozart, 1898as[26]

___ relation to Warszawa dealers, 5985as[89]

___ religious music, compared with Beethoven, 1857as[26]

___ sonatas, keyboard, attribution, 1751as[26]

___ style, sources, 4330as[66]

___ symphonies, use of Croatian melodies, 1862as[26]

___ symphonies, Hob.I:103, viewed by Momigny, 1833as[26]

___ use in pedagogy, 4704as[71]

___ use of oboe, compared with Beethoven, 4305as[65]

___ variations, piano, Hob.XVII:6, use of polythematic form, 4270as[64]

Haydn, Michael, *see* Haydn, Johann Michael

HAYDON, Glen, 1328as[24], 4176as[63], 4198as[63]

hazanim, *see* prayer leaders — **Judaism**

hearing, *see* **physiology**

HEARTZ, Daniel, 588as[1], 1329as[24], 1330as[24], 1331as[24], 1332as[24], 1367as[24], 3902as[58]

Hebrew chant, *see* **chant — Jewish**

Hebrew music, *see* **Jewish studies**; **religion and religious music — Judaism**

Hechenberger, Martin

life, views on organ conservation, 3459as[42]

HECHT, Theophil, 3303as[41]

HECKLINGER, Doris, 1576as[25]

HECKMANN, Harald, 356bs, 589as[1], 590as[1], 591as[1], 3997as[61]

Hederich, Benjamin

writings, *Reales Schul-Lexicon* (1717), treatment of instruments, 3266as[40]

HEDLEY, Arthur, 3899as[58]

HEDLUND, H. Jean, 3622as[45]

HEER, Josef, 4704as[71]

HEER, Joseph, 4705as[71]

Hegel, Georg Wilhelm Friedrich

aesthetics, 5437as[81]

___ compared with German Romanticism, 2128as[27]

___ relation to Wagner, 5523as[81]

writings, dialectical analysis, relation to sociology of music, 5895as[87]

___ Kunstreligion concept, relation to aesthetic modernism, 5469as[81]

___ views on music symbolism, 5934as[88]

HEGER, Franz, 61bs, *62rs[16]

Heifetz, Jascha

life, advice to young artists, 2383as[29]

Heije, Jan Pieter

writings, song texts, 5283as[78]

Heiller, Anton

works, use in Roman Catholic liturgy, 2200as[28]

HEILMAN, Ingeborg, 724as[2]

Heimsoeth, Friedrich

life, 1996as[27]

___ relation to Caecilianism, 2020as[27]

Heine, Heinrich

writings, on grand opera, 5101as[77]

___ poetry, set by Schubert, 1974as[27]

HEINE-GELDERN, Robert, 364bs

HEINITZ, Wilhelm, 107rs[16], 2433as[30], 3743as[52], 3787as[53], 3998as[61], 4057as[62], 4081as[62], 4116as[62], 4432as[69], 5666as[82], 5730as[83]

HEINLEIN, Christian Paul, 5667as[82]

HEINLEIN, M.V., 5168as[77]

Heinrich Christian, Imperial Count of Keyserlingk

life, relation to Kant, 1769as[26]

HEINS, Ernst, 2456as[30]

HEINZ, Rudolf, 1981as[27]

HEISKE, Wilhelm, 2851as[34]

Helfer, Charles d'

works, Requiem, 3754as[52]

Helfert, Vladimír

writings, on Janáček late orchestral style, 4389as[66]

___ on Mozart, 884as[20]

HELFERT, W., 4549as[70]

HELGASON, Hallgrímur, 2852as[34]

Hellmesberger, Joseph

life, teaching of Krančević, 1946as[27]

HELLOUIN, Frédéric, 3824as[55]

HELM, Everett, 1982as[27], 2177as[28], 5169as[77]

HELMAN, Zofia, 2178as[28], 2179as[28]

Helmholtz, Hermann von

writings, on consonance, 5850as[86]

___ psychology, influence on Janáček, 5658as[82]

___ resonance hypothesis, 5706as[82]

HÉLOUIN, Frédéric, 3999as[61]

Héman, Valeran de

instruments, organs, relation to Paris school, 3386as[42]

Hémeré, Claude

writings, on Desprez, 1417as[24]

Hemmingsen, Niels

life, 6446as[94]

HENDRICKX-DUCHAINE, Christine, 5731as[83], 5732as[83]

HENNERBERG, Carl Fredrik, 1776as[26], 1777as[26], 3389as[42]

HENNIG, Karl Raphael, 4550as[70]

HENNINGS, C.R., 128ap[16]

Henri III, King of France

life, Joyeuse-Lorraine marriage festivities, 1585, 1474as[24]

HENRION, Marcel, 5964as[89]

HENRY, André, 4706as[71], 4707as[71]

Henry, Michel

chronologies, list of ballet performances, 1580-1620, 5021as[76]

Henry, Pierre

works, *La reine verte*, Béjart choreography, 5117as[77]

___ *Symphonie pour un homme seul*, 4401as[68]

Henry VIII, King of England

life, Field of Cloth of Gold, 1520, 1354as[24]

___ patronage, chamber music, 1283as[24]

___ ___ Chapel Royal, 1520, 1226as[24]

HENZE, Hans Werner, 5170as[77]

Henze, Hans Werner

performances, *Der Prinze von Homburg*, scenography, 5206as[77]

works, *Das Ende einer Welt*, special recording effects, 5765as[85]

___ operas, 5189as[77]

HERAN, Bohuš, 3578as[44]

Herbeck, Johann Ritter von

life, relation to Mozart, 3913as[58]

Herbenus, Matthaeus

writings, *De natura cantus ac miraculis vocis*, 1435as[24]

Herbst, Heinrich Gottlieb

instruments, organs, at parish church, Lahm, 3426as[42]

Herbst, Johann Andreas

works, counterpoint, 4203as[63]

___ religious music, 1542as[25]

writings, *Musica poetica*, 5461as[81]

Herder, Johann Gottfried

aesthetics, compared with German Romanticism, 2128as[27]

writings, relation to Janáček speech melody theory, 5594as[81]

___ relation to Mozart, 1728as[26]

HERDIECKERHOFF, Ulrich, 4551as[70]

HÉRICARD, Jeanne, 3304as[41]

HERMELINK, Siegfried, 3825as[55], 4177as[63]

hermeneutics, *see also* **phenomenology**; **symbolism**

as discipline, history and development, 5585as[81]

form, relation to content, 5586as[81]

HERMET, Augusto, 882as[20], 5489as[81]

HERNÁDI, Lajos, 4178as[63]

Herrmann, Bernard

works, film music, 5095as[77]

HERSKOVITS, Melville J., 292bs, 3201as[36], 6458as[99]

HERTZ, Odette, 4708as[71], 4709as[71]

HERTZMANN, Erich, 180rs[16], 1316as[24], 1330as[24], 1333as[24], 4369as[66]

HERZ, P., 5490as[81]

HERZOG, Avigdor, 2434as[30], 6069as[91], 6070as[91], 6071as[91]

HERZOG, Eduard, 4179as[63], 5927as[88]

HERZOG, George, 2513as[31], 2853as[34], 3155as[35], 3305as[41]

HERZOG, Hans Kurt, 494bs

HESBERT, René-Jean, 336bs, 780as[4], 781as[4], 1118as[23], 1119as[23], 1120as[23], 1121as[23], 1122as[23], 1334as[24], 3826as[55], 3900as[58], 4433as[69], 6250as[93]

HESS, Ernst, 1763as[26], 1778as[26]

HESS, Werner, 2409as[29]

Hessen, Bartholomäus

collections, dance music, 5068as[76]

Hessen, Paul

collections, dance music, 5068as[76]

heterophony, *see also* **texture**

Bosnia and Herzegovina, compared with polyphony, 4211as[63]

Schoenberg, A., 2247as[28]

HETSCHKO, Alfred, 2325as[29]

HEUSS, Alfred Valentin, 67rs[16], 108rs[16], 1577as[25], 3678as[50], 4257as[64], 4344as[66], 5320as[78]

Heyboer, Anton

works, art, influence on De Leeuw, 5131as[77]

HEYMANS, Gerard, 125bs

HICKENLOOPER, Lucie (Olga Samaroff Stokowski), 4552as[70], 5491as[81]

HICKMANN, Hans, 1032as[22], 1033as[22], 1034as[22], 2554as[32], 2555as[32], 3253as[40], 3744as[52], 6114as[92]

HIEKEL, Hans Otto, 1335as[24]

Hiel, Emanuel

life, relation to Benoît, 2118as[27]

HIGGINSON, J. Vincent, 6251as[93]

HILBER, Johann Baptist, 6252as[93]

Hilber, Johann Baptist

works, used in Roman Catholic liturgy, 2200as[28]

Hildebrand family

instruments, organs, 3486as[42]

___ Purcell, H., 1486as[25]
salamuri, Georgia, prehistoric, 3614as[45]
shakuhachi playing, Fuke sect, aesthetics, 5555as[81]
suara, Latin America, Kuna people, 3199as[36]
svirala, Montenegro, references in song texts, 3284as[40]
svirala-jedinka, Serbia, 3619as[45]
tilincă fără dop, Romania, influence on song melodies, 3029as[34]
umtshingo, Africa, pentatonicism, 4184as[63]
vertical reed flute, Venezuela, Indians, use in maremare accompaniment, 3190as[36]

instruments — wind (woodwind, reed family)
aulos playing, technique, state of research, 3610as[45]
bagpipe, Scotland, temperament and tuning, 3627as[45]
bagpipe music, Czech Republic, 2942as[34]
basset clarinet making, Czech Republic, Praha, Akademie Múzických Umění, 3750as[52]
chirimía, Colombia, Girardota, social functions, 3211as[45]
clarinet, Albania, traditional, 3638as[45]
___ France, regional preferences, 3260as[40]
clarinet music, Mozart, W.A., relation to basset clarinet, 3750as[52]
cornamuse music, France, branle de Poitou, 4952as[76]
diple, Montenegro, references in song texts, 3284as[40]
___ use in accompanying Herzegovina dance, 4959as[76]
diple s mijehom, Croatia, Zadar region, 3611as[45]
erkencho, Argentina, 3223as[36]
free-reed instruments, acoustics, 3555as[44]
gajdar music, Macedonia, melodic typology, 2932as[34]
oboe music, Beethoven, L. van, 4305as[65]
___ France, branle de Poitou, 4952as[76]
reed instruments, history and development, antiquity to 20th c., 3630as[45]
shawm music, Couperin, L., fantasias, 1641as[25]
shawm playing, influence on yodeling, 3306as[41]
single-reed and double-chanter šurla, Croatia, Istra, 3623as[45]
sopile, Croatia, Kvarner gulf, 3637as[45]
svirale, Slavic states, southern, Banija, 3637as[45]
tulum, Turkey, Rize province, Hemşin, 3632as[45]

intabulation, *see also* **arrangements**; **tablatures**
lute, of Lassus works, inventory, 1241as[24]

intermedio, *see* **intermezzo**

intermezzo (vocal), *see* **intermezzo (vocal)**

intermezzo (vocal), *see also* **pastorale**
Italy, Firenze, late 16th c., 5158as[77]

interpretation, *see* **interpretation — by performer or topic**

interpretation — by composer, *see also* **articulation; dynamics; ensemble playing; improvisation; interpretation — by performer or topic; ornamentation; performance practice** headwords; **tempo; vibrato**
Bach, J.S., agogic nuance, 3688as[50]
___ organ works, phrasing, 3763as[52]
Brahms, J., use of diminuendo sign, 3854as[55]
Chopin, F., by Lipatti, 2327as[29]
___ piano music, by Janáček, 2081as[27]
___ ___ role of homogeneity theory, 3787as[53]
___ Polish pedagogy, 3783as[53]
___ polonaises, op. 53, 3789as[53]
___ preludes, 4236as[64]
___ Russian Federation, to 1960, 3781as[53]
Dvořák, A., agogic nuance, 3688as[50]
Händel, G.F., operas, 20th c., 5250as[77]
Janáček, L., by Bakala, 3799as[54]
___ choral music, 4391as[66]
___ operas, 3793as[54], 5246as[77]
___ ___ staging, 5270as[77]
___ ___ vocal parts, 3798as[54]
___ ___ vocal technique, 3324as[41]

___ orchestral music, by Bakala, 3796as[54]
___ piano music, 3795as[54]
___ relation to notation, 3794as[54]
Mozart, W.A., orchestral music, 3746as[52]
Schubert, F., lieder, 3785as[53]
Smetana, B., agogic nuance, 3688as[50]
Szymanowski, K., piano music, 3791as[54]

interpretation — by performer or topic, *see also* **articulation; dynamics; ensemble playing; improvisation; instrumental playing; interpretation — by composer; ornamentation; performance practice** headwords; **tempo; vibrato**
aesthetics, 5476as[81], 5618as[81]
___ role of performer, 3681as[50]
Arrau, C., Chopin prelude, op. 28, no. 1, 4236as[64]
Bakala, B., Janáček orchestral music, 3796as[54], 3799as[54]
Chopin, F., rubato, influenced by Polish traditional music, 3790as[53]
___ ___ viewed by Polish pedagogy, 3783as[53]
Cortot, A., Chopin prelude, op. 28, no. 1, 4236as[64]
Gregorian chant, 6262as[93], 6291as[93]
___ role of historicism, 3692as[51]
___ Vatican edition, 1904, 3881as[55]
Janáček, L., Chopin piano music, 2081as[27]
Lipatti, D., Chopin piano music, 2327as[29]
notation, philosophical issues, 5473as[81]
piano music, 16th-20th c., 3542as[43]
polyphony, Middle Ages and Renaissance, 3725as[51]
rhythm and meter, agogics, Chopin, F., 4236as[64]
Rubinstein, A., Chopin prelude, op. 28, no. 1, 4236as[64]
vocal music, 3293as[41]
Western music, relation to criticism, 5561as[81]
20th-c. music, intellect vs. emotion, 3792as[54]

intervals, *see also* **modality; scales; tonality**
analysis, interval as fundamental unit, 3956as[60]
antiquity, pre-Hellenic, relation to resonance theory, 1033as[22]
Armenia, microtonality, 4065as[62]
Asia, antiquity, 4044as[62]
Augustine of Hippo, Saint, relation to movement, 5834as[86]
Bartók, B., chromatic idiom, 4137as[63]
___ relation to overtones, 4136as[63]
Chopin, F., in melodic structure, compared with Polish traditional music, 4434as[69]
___ influence on evolution of harmonic language, 1932as[27]
Denmark, traditional music, 4111as[62]
Dufay, G., relation to melodic design, 4424as[69]
Europe, classification and distribution, 4093as[62]
fifth, basis of diatonic scale, 4106as[62]
Gregorian chant, 1170as[23]
history and development, evolutionary approach, 4131as[62]
___ relation to polyphony, 4114as[62]
Iran, dastgāh, notation, 3880as[55]
Laker, K., 4110as[62]
Landini, F., relation to melodic design, 4424as[69]
measurement, Fawcett system, 4053as[62]
microtonality, relation to harmony, to 1947, 4146as[63]
nomenclature, 4051as[62]
octave, 4066as[62]
perception, relation to overtones theory, 4151as[63]
___ relation to psychoacoustics, 5709as[82]
second, use in 20th-c. music, 4174as[63]
Serbia, Zlatibor, traditional polyphony, 2997as[34]
singing, children, pedagogy, 4712as[71]
theory, intervallic attraction, 4155as[63]
third, melodic, 13th-19th c., 4450as[69]
traditional music, third-second nucleus, 4105as[62]
tritone, symbolism, Middle Ages to present, 4201as[63]
universals, 5649as[82]

intonation, *see* **pitch; psalmody; temperament and tuning**

intonation theory, *see also* **theory**
analysis, applied to Chopin, 2108as[27]
___ applied to German Renaissance dance tunes, 1383as[24]
Asaf'ev, B., 872as[20]
___ 1917-40, 5416as[80]
Musorgskij, M., 4436as[69]
relation to Gestalt psychology, 5409as[80], 5413as[80]
___ conference, 1963, 471bs
relation to Marxism, 3958as[60], 5411as[80], 5414as[80], 5479as[81], 5500as[81]
relation to melody, 4459as[69]
relation to semiotics, 5930as[88]
relation to time, 5525as[81]

Introit, *see* **Mass**

Inuits, *see* **Indians and Inuits**

inventories, *see* **catalogues and indexes** headwords

Ionesco, Eugène
writings, *La photo du colonel*, relation to Searle *The photo of the colonel*, 5230as[77]

Īpeiros, *see* **Greece**

IPPEL, Albert, 5761as[85]

Iran
history of music, 6th c. to present, 2623as[33]
Jewish people, religious music, nigunim, influenced by Persian music, 6055as[91]
theory, dastgāh, notation of intervals, 3880as[55]
___ rhythm and meter, 2607as[33]
___ scale, relation to circle of fifths, 4047as[62]

Iraq
antiquity, notation, 3867as[55]

Ireland
bibliographies, traditional music, 1725-1905, 801as[6]
dance, traditional, 2980as[34]
___ influence on USA traditional dance, 4944as[76]
instruments, harp, history and development, 3571as[44]
musical life, Middle Ages, influence on Belgium, 2818as[34]
traditional music, ballads, hanging of fiddler as subject, 2547as[31]
___ songs, 2980as[34]
___ ___ regional characteristics, 2881as[34]

Irish harp, *see* **instruments — string (harp family)**

IRMER, Gotho von, 4559as[70], 5887as[87]

Iruarrízaga, Luis
works, religious music, 2234as[28]

IRVING, Ernest, 5173as[77]

Isaac, Heinrich
manuscripts, Swiss organ tablature, 1234as[24]
works, *Choralis constantinus*, 1395as[24]
___ in Berlin MS 40021, 1350as[24]
___ *Innsbruck, ich muss dich lassen*, 1451as[24]
___ vocal polyphony, influence on Italian madrigal, 1422as[24]

ISAACS, Leonard, 5494as[81]

Isawa, Syuji, *see* **Izawa, Shūji**

Isidore of Seville
writings, church singing, 6377as[93]

ISING, Hartmut, 3391as[42]

Islamic studies, *see also* **Arab studies**
Africa, West, influence on non-Muslim music, 2587as[32]
___ influence on Western Sudanic instrument terminology, 5926as[88]
Bosnia and Herzegovina, Muslim people, surrogate instruments, 2967as[34]
Ghana, 2566as[32]
languages, conference, 1905, 48bs
Macedonia, Torbeš people, funerals, 2986as[34]
ornamentation, influence on European art music, 16th-17th c., 3724as[51]

Ísland, *see* **Iceland**

Isle of Man, *see* **United Kingdom**

J

___ ___ style, 4391as[66]
___ compared with Bartók, 2238as[28]
___ compared with Stravinsky, 2171as[28]
___ creative process, 4340as[66]
___ form, tectonic analysis, 4347as[66]
___ harmony, preferred chords, 4179as[63]
___ influence on 20th-c. music, 2177as[28]
___ influenced by Glagolitic liturgy, 6420as[93]
___ influenced by Moravian traditional music, 4393as[66]
___ influenced by Mozart, 1008as[21]
___ influenced by traditional music, 2267as[28]
___ *Její pastorkyňa (Jenůfa)*, choruses, relation to Moravian traditional music, 4383as[66]
___ ___ meaning analysis, 5607as[81]
___ *Kát'a Kabanová*, act 3, scene 2, 5273as[77]
___ melody, melodic analogy, 4382as[66]
___ *Mša glagolskaja (Glagolitic Mass)*, monothematicism, 4437as[69]
___ ___ relation to liturgy, 6416as[93], 6417as[93]
___ nationalism and internationalism, 2237as[28]
___ operas, compared with Musorgskij, 4367as[66]
___ ___ critical realism, 5178as[77]
___ ___ instrumentation, 4300as[65]
___ ___ libretto translations by Brod, 5323as[78]
___ ___ speech melodies, 4320as[66]
___ ___ speech-based structure, 4323as[66]
___ *Osud*, 5251as[77]
___ *Otče náš*, influenced by Krzesz-Męcina paintings, 2102as[27]
___ *Pohádka*, interpretation, 3578as[44]
___ quartets, string, no. 2, creative process, 2254as[28]
___ role in Czech music history, 2197as[28]
___ *Sinfonietta*, 4389as[66]
___ speech melody, 4360as[66]
___ style, 2220as[28]
___ use of traditional music, 2185as[28]
___ vocal music, dramaturgy, 4385as[66]
___ *Výlety páně Broučkovy*, part 2, tectonic analysis, 4258as[64]
___ *Zápisník zmizelého (The diary of one who disappeared)*, progressive character, 4355as[66]
___ writings, concept of harmony, influenced by Skuherský, 4175as[63]
___ criticism, 1884-88, 5622as[81]
___ ethnomusicology, compared with Bartók and Kodály, 4393as[66]
___ psychology of composition and perception, 5658as[82]
___ speech melody theory, 4446as[69], 5594as[81]
___ ___ relation to opera, 5939as[88]
___ traditional music metrics, 4024as[61]
___ *Úplná nauka o harmonii*, evaluation, 3961as[60]
JANEČEK, Karel, 4347as[66]

Janequin, Clément
collections, psalms, 1267as[24]
JANIC, Sinisa, 596as[1]
JANICZEK, Julius (Walther Hensel), 2870as[34]
JANKOVIĆ, Danica S., 4990as[76], 4991as[76], 4992as[76]

Janković, Danica S.
transcriptions, traditional dance, 4988as[76]
writings, Yugoslavian spontaneous polyphony, 4180as[63]
JANKOVIĆ, Ljubica S., 4990as[76], 4991as[76], 4992as[76]

Janković, Ljubica S.
transcriptions, traditional dance, 4988as[76]
writings, Yugoslavian spontaneous polyphony, 4180as[63]
JANKOVIĆ, Slavko, 4717as[71]

Jánošík, Juro
life, basis of traditional songs, 3009as[34]
JANSEN, H., 1992as[27]

Jański, Bogdan
manuscripts, memoirs, views on Chopin, 1968as[27]

JANSKY, Herbert, 2643as[33]
JANSSENS, Arm. J., 5498as[81]

Janssens, Jan Frans Jozef
correspondence, 1840as[26]
JANSSENS, Laurent, 6259as[93]

Japan
aesthetics, variation, compared with Western music, 2688as[33]
Ainu people, traditional music, songs, 2613as[33]
Buddhism, influence on noh, 5231as[77]
___ Zen, aesthetics, 5555as[81]
court music, gagaku, 2627as[33], 2634as[33], 2690as[33]
dance, 5005as[76], 5006as[76]
___ bon-odori, compared with bon-odori in Hawaii, 5064as[76]
___ bugaku, ei and saezuri, 2620as[33]
___ to 1958, 2663as[33]
dramatic arts, 5123as[77], 5181as[77], 5182as[77]
___ kabuki, relation to ukiyo-e, 4919as[75]
___ noh, 2653as[33], 5180as[77]
___ ___ influence on Yeats, 5174as[77]
___ ___ influenced by Buddhism, 5231as[77]
___ puppet theaters, 5219as[77]
___ ca. 1958, 5243as[77]
ethnomusicology, melody classification, 2648as[33]
history of music, composers, ca. 1961, 2135as[28], 2180as[28]
___ influenced by traditional instruments, ca. 1963, 2213as[28]
___ nagauta song, 2659as[33]
___ periodization, 2697as[33]
___ source studies, 2633as[33]
___ 20th c., 2192as[28]
___ to 1958, 2663as[33]
instruments, bells, antiquity, 3656as[46]
___ biwa, history and development, 3281as[40], 3605as[44]
___ influence on 20th-c. music, 2213as[28]
___ piano building, ca. 1965, 3518as[43]
___ shamisen, history and development, 3281as[40], 3605as[44]
musical life, 2661as[33], 2708as[33]
___ background music, 5916as[87]
___ concerts, 2403as[29]
___ influenced by Western music, 2628as[33]
___ Western vs. Japanese music, 2684as[33]
___ 1868-1958, 2363as[29]
musicology, 20th c., 2367as[29]
pedagogy, elementary, ca. 1953, 4714as[71], 4715as[71]
___ music schools, 4535as[70]
___ private instruction, Western music, 1880-1953, 4533as[70], 4534as[70]
___ traditional music, 4th-20th c., 2707as[33]
religious music, Roman Catholic, use of Western and traditional elements, 6322as[93]
Ryūkyū Islands, history of music, 14th-20th c., 2645as[33]
___ traditional music, scales, 4133as[62]
Takata, musical life, goze, 2635as[33], 2636as[33]
traditional music, 2624as[33]
___ children's songs, history and development, 2664as[33]
___ influence on composers, ca. 1961, 2192as[28]
___ songs, typology, 2625as[33], 2626as[33]
___ 20th c., 2662as[33]
visual and plastic arts, ukiyo-e, relation to kabuki, 4919as[75]

Japanese music (outside Japan)
USA, Hawaii, ryūkōka songs, used in bon-odori dancing, 5064as[76]
JAQUES-DALCROZE, Émile, 4004as[61], 4560as[70], 4561as[70]

Jaques-Dalcroze, Émile
festivals and conferences, Switzerland, Genève, 1965, 502bs
writings, 5076as[76]
___ appreciation pedagogy, 4482as[70], 4483as[70]
___ eurythmics, 4592as[70], 4593as[70]

___ improvisation pedagogy, 3686as[50], 4632as[70]
JÁRDÁNYI, Pál, 2871as[34], 4261as[64], 4422as[69], 4439as[69]

Járdányi, Pál
writings, classification of traditional melodies, 4470as[69]
JÁRFÁS, T., 5824as[86]
JARGY, Simon, 6117as[92]
JARNACH, Philipp, 2247as[28]
Jarnović, Ivan Mane, *see* **Giornovichi, Giovanni Mane**
JAROCIŃSKI, Stefan, 2184as[28]
JÁROSY, Dezső, 1993as[27]
JARUSTOVSKIJ, Boris Mihajlovič, 471bs, 5176as[77], 5411as[80]

Jarzębski, Adam
works, 1582as[25]
JATOBÁ, Pedro, 3309as[41]

Jaubert, Maurice
works, film music, 5115as[77]
Java, *see* **Indonesia**
jazz
aesthetics, relation to 20th-c. music, 2242as[28]
definitions, ca. 1962, 3231as[38]
improvisation, 1010as[21]
influence on Christian liturgical music, 6034as[90]
influence on 20th-c. music, 2342as[29]
North America, relation to popular dance, 5011as[76]
USA, influenced by Debussy, 2236as[28]

Jean d'Afflighem
manuscripts, notation, 3871as[55]
writings, concept of dissonance, 4157as[63]
___ *De musica*, concept of organum, 1083as[23]

Jean de Muris, *see* **Jehan des Murs**
JEANNETEAU, Jean, 4348as[66], 6260as[93]
JEANS, Susi, 1583as[25], 3396as[42], 3660as[47], 6436as[94]

Jehan des Murs
writings, relation to quadrivium, 5446as[81]
JEHLE, Martin Friedrich, 3521as[43]
JELENOVIĆ, Ive, 2872as[34]
JELÍNKOVÁ, Zdenka, 4993as[76]

Jelowicki, Aleksander
correspondence, views on Chopin, 1968as[27]
JENNISSEN, Émile, 2331as[29]
JEPPESEN, Knud, 226rs[16], 1269as[24], 1309as[24], 1344as[24], 1345as[24], 1346as[24], 1347as[24], 1348as[24], 3903as[58], 4182as[63], 4183as[63], 4198as[63], 4262as[64], 4349as[66]

Jeppesen, Knud
writings, *Kontrapunkt*, use in counterpoint instruction, 4847as[72]

Jerome, Saint
life, silent reading, 1021as[21]
JERPHANION, P. de, 166rs[16]
JESPERSEN, Einar, 5971as[89]

Jesus of Nazareth
life, Mocking of Christ, depicted in Serbian art works, 5390as[79]

Jewish chant, *see* **chant — Jewish**
Jewish studies, *see also* **chant — Jewish; religion and religious music — Judaism**
Afghanistan, melodies, 2675as[33]
antiquity, Qumran Scrolls, 1047as[22]
Canada, Yiddish songs, 3176as[35]
conference, 1961, 435bs
dance, wedding, history and development, 5054as[76]
Europe, Eastern and Central, dance, 5017as[76]
___ traditional music, relation to history of music, 2929as[34]
___ traditional songs, relation to language, 2928as[34]

Germany, radio, nationalist policies, 1930s, 2299as[29]
Greece, Thessalonikī, Sephardic people, traditional songs, 2743as[34]
Hasidic people, songs, 6087as[91]
___ storytelling, use of music, 5359as[78]
history of music, 6102as[91]
Israel, dance, social, 5055as[76]
___ ___ syncretism, 4970as[76]
___ Jerusalem, school for hazanim, 4885as[73]
___ traditional songs, relation to Hebrew language, 2685as[33]
Italy, Italian-Jewish liturgical music, 2970as[34]
___ musical life, synagogues, 17th-18th c., 6035as[91]
___ stile nuovo, 1276as[24]
Lithuania, Vilnius, 6040as[91]
Middle East, Jewish liturgical music, influenced by maqām and dastgāh systems, 6054as[91]
Musorgskij, M., *Kartniki v vystavki* (Pictures at an exhibition), 4436as[69]
relation to Bloch, 2244as[28]
Schoenberg, A., *Kol nidre*, op. 39, 4421as[69]
selah, 6074as[91]
Spain, Castilla, psalm, influence on traditional songs, 2761as[34]
___ Sephardic people, romance, 2828as[34]
theory, 10th-14th c., 1215as[23]
traditional music, influence on Israel art music, to 1947, 2228as[28]
___ relation to ritual, 6047as[91]
___ representations, 6075as[91]
___ songs, Yiddish, 19th c., 2537as[31]
___ Western vs. non-Western, 6098as[91]
Uzbekistan, Bohoro, wedding cycle, 2631as[33]
jew's harp, *see* **instruments — percussion (jew's harp family)**
Ježek, Jaroslav
works, mass song, 3064as[34]
JIČÍNSKÝ, Bedřich, 5323as[78]
jig, *see* **dance music — by genre**
JÍLEK, František, 4300as[65]
JIMÉNEZ DE LA ESPADA, Marcos, 3203as[36], 3651as[46]
jingju (Beijing opera), *see* **dramatic arts**
JIRÁNEK, Jaroslav, 389bs, 957as[21], 1349as[24], 1994as[27], 2185as[28], 4350as[66], 5499as[81], 5500as[81], 5501as[81], 5502as[81]
Joachim, Joseph
life, relation to Mozart, 3913as[58]
JÖDE, Fritz, 4562as[70]
Johann Wilhelm, Elector of the Palatinate
life, Düsseldorf, chapel, 1514as[25]
Johannes Afflighemensis, *see* **Jean d'Afflighem**
Johannes de Florentia, *see* **Giovanni da Cascia**
Johannes de Garlandia
writings, treatises, attribution, 1168as[23]
Johannes de Muris, *see* **Jehan des Murs**
Johannes of Lublin, *see* **Jan z Lublina**
Johannes Scottus Eriugena
life, 1117as[23]
Johansen, Gottschalk Burkhard
instruments, organs, 3364as[42]
Johansen, Jasper
instruments, organs, 3364as[42]
JOHANSSON, Cari, 457bs
John of Tewkesbury
writings, *Quatuor principalia musice*, 5572as[81]
John XXII, Pope
writings, *Docta sanctorum patrum*, relation to ars nova, 6213as[93]
JOHNER, Dominicus, 6261as[93], 6262as[93]
JOHNSON, Alvin H., 1330as[24]
JOHNSTON, Ben, 4858as[72]
Jommelli, Niccolò
collections, symphonies, 761as[2]

works, influence on Classic style, 4330as[66]
___ operas, relation to opera reform, 1765as[26]
JONAS, Oswald, 726as[2], 1784as[26], 4351as[66]
JONES, Arthur Morris, 2557as[32]
JONES, Claude E., 4919as[75]
JONES, Daniel, 222bs
JONES, Llewellyn Wynn, 5668as[82]
JONES, Stephen, 5825as[86]
JONES, Trevor A., 3227as[37]
Jongkind, Johan Barthold
works, art, viewed by Debussy, 5396as[79]
jongleurs, *see* **minstrels**
Jonson, Ben
writings, *The masque of the queen*, compared with *Oberon*, 5127as[77]
JORDAN, Vilhelm Lassen, 5762as[85], 5826as[86]
Jordan family
instruments, organs, at St. Magnus, London, 3396as[42]
JORGE, J., 6263as[93]
JORIS, Jozef, 6264as[93]
JORISSENNE, Gustave, 3397as[42]
JOSÉ, A., 2873as[34]
Joseph II, Holy Roman Emperor
life, reforms, relation to Mozart operas, 5148as[77]
Joseph the Hymnographer, Saint
manuscripts, kanōn texts, 5349as[78]
JOSHI, Baburao, 2644as[33]
Josquin, *see* **Desprez, Josquin**
Josquin Desprez, *see* **Desprez, Josquin**
JOSZ, René, 5503as[81]
jota, *see* **dance — by genre; dance music — by genre**
JOUAN, J.-M.-Joseph, 4718as[71]
JOUGLET, René, 31bs
journals, *see* **periodicals**
Jouve, Pierre-Jean
writings, Mozart, W.A., 5314as[78]
Jouy, Étienne de
writings, libretto for *Le Ateniesi*, lost, 5104as[77]
JOVANOVIĆ, Raško V., 5763as[85]
JOVANOVIĆ, Živorad, 802as[6]
Jovernardi, Bartolomé
instruments, harpsichords and harps, 3522as[43]
Joyeuse, Anne de
life, marriage to Marguerite de Lorraine, 1474as[24]
Juan I, King of Aragón
life, patronage, 1054as[23]
JUCÁ FILHO, Cândido, 5929as[88]
Judaism, *see* **Jewish studies; religion and religious music — Judaism**
judgment, *see* **aesthetics; criticism — general**
JUHÁSZ, A., 5669as[82]
Jumentier, Bernard
life, 1844as[26]
Jung, Carl Gustav
writings, personality types, applied to composers, 5638as[82]
JUNG, Hermann, 3398as[42]
Jung, Hermann
instruments, organs, at Hans-Sachs-Haus, Gelsenkirchen, 3399as[42]
JUNGK, Klaus, 5177as[77]
JUNGMANN, Josef Andreas, 6265as[93], 6266as[93]
JUNIUS, Manfred M., 842as[19], 844as[19]
JURISCH, Herta, 1785as[26]
JURJÁNS, Andrejs, 2874as[34]
Jurovský, Šimon
works, 947as[21]
JURRES, André, 597as[1], 598as[1], 727as[2], 2186as[28], 5972as[89]

Jurres, André
writings, *Les centres de documentation musicale et leurs techniques particulières*, 594as[1]
JUST, Martin, 452bs, 1350as[24]
just intonation, *see* **temperament and tuning**
JUTEN, Gerrit Cornelis Adrianus, 1351as[24]
juvenile music, *see* **children; pedagogy** headwords

K

Kabalevskij, Dmitrij Borisovič
works, film music, 5171as[77]
KABIR, Humayun, 489bs, 846as[19]
kabuki, *see* **dramatic arts; Japan**
KACAROVA, Rajna, 2875as[34], 2876as[34], 4994as[76], 4995as[76], 4996as[76]
KAČULEV, Ivan, 3256as[40]
KACZYŃSKI, Tadeusz, 1995as[27], 2187as[28]
KADEN, Richard, 4827as[72]
KADMAN, Gurit, 4997as[76], 4998as[76]
KAELIN, Pierre, 6267as[93], 6268as[93], 6269as[93]
KAFKA, Gustav, 188bs
KAFTANGIAN, Giuseppe, 6118as[92]
KAGEL, Mauricio, 3832as[55]
Kagel, Mauricio
works, notation, 3847as[55]
KAHL, Willi, 319bs, 728as[2], 1786as[26], 1996as[27], 1997as[27], 1998as[27], 5973as[89]
KAHMANN, Bernhard, 1352as[24]
KAISER, Fritz, 1787as[26]
KAKOMA, George Wilberforce, 465bs
Kālidāsa
writings, techniques, application to 20th-c. music theater, 5129as[77]
KALLENBACH-GRELLER, Lotte, 4083as[62], 5504as[81]
KALOMIRIS, Manolis, 976as[21], 1999as[27]
Kalt, Pius
performances, for solemn Mass, use of polyphony, 6314as[93]
kamancha (=kamānche), *see* **instruments — string (violin family)**
kamānche, *see* **instruments — string (violin family)**
KAMBUROV, Ivan, 4005as[61]
KAMIEŃSKI, Lucjan, 1788as[26]
KAMIŃSKI, Włodzimierz, 3257as[40], 5741as[84]
Kaminsky, Joseph
works, to 1947, 2228as[28]
Kampuchea, *see* **Cambodia**
KANAI, Kikuko, 2645as[33]
Kanetsune, Kiyosuke
writings, musicology, 2367as[29]
kanōn, *see* **chant — Byzantine; hymn**
KAŃSKI, Józef, 3789as[53]
Kant, Immanuel
aesthetics, 5617as[81]
life, Kaliningrad, 1769as[26]
writings, influence on Beethoven, 1852as[26]
___ philosophy, compared with Goethe, 5428as[81]
KARA, Z.I., 3833as[55]
Karadžić, Vuk Stefanović
collections, Bohemian traditional music, 2946as[34]
___ *Narodna srbska pesnarica*, women's songs, 5367as[78]
editions, *Ženidba Dušanova*, 5333as[78]
life, relation to Petar II, 2960as[34]
transcriptions, Martinović epics, 2952as[34]
Karas, Anton
works, film music, 5173as[77]
KARÁSEK, Bohumil, 389bs, 5178as[77]

KARBUSICKÝ, Vladimír, 2877as[34], 2878as[34], 4006as[61]

Kardoš, Dezider
works, 947as[21]

KAREL, A., 5764as[85]

Karg-Elert, Sigfrid
works, influenced by Debussy, 2257as[28]

KARKOSCHKA, Erhard, 4007as[61]

Karl Philipp, Elector of the Palatinate
life, court chapels, 1514as[25]

Karłowicz, Mieczysław
works, influenced by Wagner, 1918as[27]

KARLYLE, Charles, 4563as[70]

KÁRPÁTI, János, 844as[19], 2188as[28], 2558as[32]

KARPELES, Maud, 392bs, 424bs, 463bs, 2517as[31], 2518as[31], 2519as[31], 2520as[31], 4999as[76]

KARSTÄDT, Georg, 1584as[25], 3624as[45], 5381as[79]

ĶAŠ, Me'yr, 1789as[26]

KASCHNER, G., 211ap[16]

KASEMETS, Udo, 423bs

KASILAG, Lucrecia R., 4564as[70], 4565as[70]

KAŠLÍK, Václav, 5179as[77]

KAST, Paul, 729as[2], 1353as[24], 1354as[24]

Kastal'skij, Aleksandr Dmitrievič
works, Russian Orthodox chant harmonizations, 6128as[92]

KASTELEYN, M.L., 324bs

KASTNER, Macario Santiago, 1355as[24], 1356as[24], 1510as[25], 1585as[25], 1586as[25], 3522as[43], 3749as[52], 5973as[89]

Kastner, Macario Santiago
editions, Cabezón organ music, 3895as[58]

KATZ, D., 5670as[82]

KAUFMAN, Nikolaj, 2879as[34], 2880as[34]

KAUFMANN, H.E., 2646as[33]

Kaufmann, Mathias Joseph
life, 1790as[26]

KAUFMANN, Paul, 1790as[26]

KAUL, Oskar, 1791as[26], 3746as[52]

kaval, *see* **instruments — wind (woodwind, flute family)**

Kayser, Hans
writings, harmony, relation to overtone series, 4210as[63]

Kayser, Isfrid
works, 1683as[25]

Kayser, Leif
works, used in Roman Catholic liturgy, 2200as[28]

KEEL, Frederick, 2881as[34]

KELDYŠ, Jurij Vsevolodovič, 957as[21], 1792as[26], 1908as[27], 2000as[27], 5460as[81], 5905as[87], 6130as[92]

KELEMAN, Milko, 5888as[87]

Keller, Gottfried
writings, *Unter Sternen*, 5279as[78]

KELLER, Hermann, 1587as[25], 1588as[25], 2189as[28], 3399as[42], 3747as[52], 3834as[55], 4828as[72], 4829as[72]

KELLER, Wilhelm, 4352as[66]

Kempis, Gottfried
manuscripts, Mönchengladbach collectarium, attributed, 1109as[23]

kena, *see* **instruments — wind (woodwind, flute family)**

KENDALL, Raymond, 2001as[27]

KENNEDY, Douglas, 2882as[34], 2883as[34], 2884as[34], 2885as[34], 2886as[34], 2887as[34], 2888as[34], 4566as[70], 5000as[76], 5001as[76], 5002as[76], 5003as[76]

KENNEY, Sylvia W., 4262as[64]

KENT, Earle L., 3523as[43]

KEREN, Zvi, 6074as[91]

KERÉNYI, György, 2190as[28]

KERMAN, Joseph, 1269as[24], 1908as[27], 4198as[63]

Kermode, Jack
life, dancing of Kirk Maughold sword dance, 4961as[76]

KESTENBERG, Leo, 4567as[70], 4568as[70], 4569as[70], 4570as[70]

KEUSSLER, Gerhard von, 5421as[81], 5505as[81], 5506as[81]

key, *see* **tonality**

keyboard harmony, *see* **counterpoint**; **harmony**

keyboard instruments, *see* **instruments — keyboard**

keyed fiddle (=nyckelharpa), *see* **instruments — string (hurdy-gurdy family)**

KEZLER, 3668as[48]

KHAN, Amir, 845as[19], 2647as[33]

Khatchaturian, Aram, *see* **Hačaturjan, Aram**

Kibris, *see* **Cyprus**

KICKTON, Erika, 5507as[81]

Kidson, Frank
collections, British traditional and art music, 750as[2]

KIENLE, Ambrosius, 6270as[93]

Kienle, Ambrosius
writings, Gregorian chant, 1187as[23]

Kierkegaard, Søren
writings, *Enten/Eller*, views on Mozart operas, 5463as[81]

KILIAN, Dietrich, 1589as[25], 1590as[25]

Kilpinen, Yrjö
works, *Kanteletar*, op. 100, 2266as[28]

KINDEM, Ingeborg Eckhoff, 4830as[72], 4831as[72]

KINDERMANN, Jürgen, 2002as[27]

kinesthetics, *see* **pedagogy** headwords; **sports and games**

KING, Alexander Hyatt, 345bs, 599as[1], 600as[1], 601as[1], 730as[2], 3911as[58], 5973as[89]

Kingo, Thomas
editions, *Den vorordnede ny kirke-psalme-bog*, 6449as[94]

KINKELDEY, Otto, 272bs, 829as[19], 886as[20], 887as[20], 1357as[24], 2458as[30], 5508as[81]

Kinkeldey, Otto
writings, musicology, 859as[20]

kinnor, *see* **instruments — string (lyre family)**

KINSKY, Georg, 731as[2], 817as[8]

Kinsky, Georg
writings, Beethoven works project, 1774as[26]

KIRÁLY, Ernő, 2889as[34], 2890as[34], 2891as[34], 3583as[44]

KIRÁLY, Marija, 2891as[34], 2892as[34], 2893as[34]

KIRBY, Percival R., 2003as[27], 4184as[63]

Kircher, Athanasius
writings, Baroque form, 4286as[64]
___ *Musurgia universalis*, sortisatio, 1305as[24]

KIRCHMEYER, Helmut, 5509as[81]

KIRIGIN, Ivo, 2894as[34]

KIRKPATRICK, Ralph, 3732as[52], 3911as[58]

Kirnberger, Johann Philipp
manuscripts, copy of Bach Mass, BWV 232, 1686as[25]

KIRSCH, Winfried, 1358as[24]

KISHIBE, Shigeo, 5180as[77]

KISS, Lajos, 2895as[34], 2896as[34], 4353as[66]

KITANO, H., 5005as[76], 5006as[76]

KITAZAWA, Masakuni, 5889as[87]

kithara, *see* **instruments — string (lyre family)**

Kittl, Jan Bedřich
life, relation to Liszt, 1925as[27]

KJELLSTRÖM, Sven, 4571as[70]

Kjui, Cezar'
life, views on Chopin, 2117as[27]

Klages, Ludwig
writings, psychology, rhythm and beat, 5673as[82]
___ sonata form, 4241as[64]

KLATTE, Wilhelm, 4185as[63]

KLAUDER, Karl, 4908as[74]

KLAUSMEIER, Friedrich, 5890as[87]

Klebe, Giselher
performances, *Alkmene*, on Westdeutscher Rundfunk, 1962, 5258as[77]

Kleczyński, Jan
editions, Polish traditional music, relation to Szymanowski piano variations, 2136as[28]

KLEMANTASKI, Louis, 977as[21]

KLEMETTI, Heikki, 978as[21]

KLEMM, Eberhardt, 4354as[66]

KLEMM, Otto, 207bs, 219bs, 231bs, 254bs

KLIČKOVA, Vera, 3310as[41]

KLIER, Karl Magnus, 3258as[40]

KLIMA, Josef, 2897as[34]

KLIMBURG, Dorothea, 364bs

Kliment of Ohrid, Saint
life, relation to Old Bulgarian music, 1138as[23]

KLINKENBERG, Hans Martin, 5510as[81]

KLOTZ, Hans, 3400as[42], 3401as[42], 3402as[42], 3403as[42], 3748as[52]

KLUSÁK, Vladimír, 2440as[30], 3158as[35]

KLUSEN, Ernst, 1359as[24], 2004as[27], 2005as[27], 2006as[27], 2441as[30], 2521as[31], 2522as[31], 2898as[34]

KLUYVER, P., 3346as[42]

KMICIC-MIELESZYŃSKI, Wacław, 2007as[27]

Kmoch, František
works, songs, influence on Czech and Slovak mass song, 3064as[34]

KNEPLER, Georg, 476bs, 888as[20], 889as[20], 957as[21], 1591as[25], 1763as[26], 1793as[26], 4440as[69], 5511as[81]

KNEŽEVIĆ, Milivoje V., 2899as[34], 3584as[44]

KNEŽEVIĆ, Nikola, 2900as[34], 2901as[34]

KNIGHT, Frank E., 5733as[83]

KNOPOFF, Leon, 3949as[60]

Knöringen, Johann Egolf von
collections, organ music, 1362as[24]

Knosp, Gaston
writings, on Internat. Musical Soc., 2475as[30]

KNOTT, Sarah Gertrude, 3159as[35]

KNOWLES, H.S., 5827as[86]

KNUDSEN, Thorkild, 4084as[62]

KNUDSEN, Vern O., 5828as[86], 5829as[86]

KNUST, Albrecht, 5004as[76]

KOBYLAŃSKA, Krystyna, 2008as[27]

KOCH, Fritz, 5765as[85]

Koch, Heinrich Christoph
writings, on sonata form, 4276as[64]

KOCH, Ludwig, 5766as[85]

Köchel, Ludwig von
life, relation to Mozart, 3913as[58]

KOCHER-KLEIN, Hilda, 979as[21]

KOCZIRZ, Adolf, 3904as[58]

KODÁLY, Zoltán, 427bs, 460bs, 463bs, 478bs

Kodály, Zoltán
life, influence on Hungarian pedagogy, 4477as[70]
___ relation to Debussy, 2134as[28]
works, compared with Janáček, 2267as[28]
___ influenced by 19th-c. Hungarian poetry, 5360as[78]
___ quoted by Bartók, 4317as[66]
writings, ethnomusicology, compared with Janáček, 4393as[66]
___ pedagogy, 4656as[70]

Kodály method, *see* **pedagogy — general**

KODERA, Yukichi, 2625as[33], 2626as[33], 5005as[76], 5006as[76], 5181as[77], 5182as[77]

KUTTER, Wilhelm, 2524as[31]
KUTTNER, Fritz A., 2456as[30], 4087as[62]
Kutzschbach, Hermann
   performances, Mozart *Idomeneo, re di Creta*, 3757as[52]
Kuwait
   traditional music, scales, 4098as[62]
KVĚT, Jindrich, 5382as[79]
Kypros, *see* **Cyprus**
KYRIAKIDES, A., 327bs
Kyriale, *see* **liturgical books**
Kyrie, *see* **Mass**

L

LA FAGE, Adrien de, 3bs
La Fage, Adrien de
   works, accompaniment to chant, 6332as[93]
LA FARGE, Georges de, 4578as[70]
La Grotte, Nicolas de
   works, songs, lute, 1458as[24]
La Landelle, Gabriel de
   works, *Le combat de la Danaé*, relation to Acadian laments, 2531as[31]
LA LAURENCIE, Lionel de, 891as[20], 1596as[25], 3586as[44]
LA MOTTE, Diether de, 5189as[77]
La Prade, Ernest
   writings, on broadcasts of Latin American music, 2398as[29]
La Rue, Pierre de
   works, 1426as[24]
LA TOMBELLE, Fernand de, 6277as[93]
LA TOUR DE NOÉ, Gabriel-Marie-Eugène de, 2021as[27], 6278as[93]
LA VALLE, Paola, 2921as[34]
LAAFF, Ernst, 892as[20], 893as[20]
LABAN, Juana de, 5012as[76]
LABAN, Rudolf von, 5013as[76], 5014as[76]
Labanotation, *see* **dance — notation**
LABARRAQUE, L., 3312as[41]
LABHARDT, Frank, 1136as[23]
LABROCA, Mario, 481bs, 4579as[70]
Labrunie, Gérard (Gérard de Nerval)
   writings, influence on French musical life, 1937as[27]
LACAS, Pierre-Paul, 3408as[42]
LACH, Robert, 2022as[27], 5516as[81]
LACHMANN, Robert, 827as[9], 2653as[33], 4188as[63]
Lachmann, Robert
   writings, generation of fifths, 4106as[62]
Ladakh, *see* **India**
LADMANOVÁ, Milada, 2023as[27]
LAFENESTRE, G., 21bs
LAFFON (ABBÉ), 6279as[93]
LAGUARDA Y FENORELLA, Juan J., 4580as[70]
LAIBLE, Ulrich, 2336as[29], 3527as[43]
Laidlaw, Anna Robena
   life, relation to Schumann, 2094as[27]
LAILY, Paul-Armand, 3842as[55]
LAIR DE BEAUVAIS, Alfred, 6280as[93]
Lajovic, Anton
   works, influenced by Slovenian traditional music, 972as[21]
LAJTHA, László, 2337as[29], 4088as[62], 5015as[76]
Laker, Karl
   writings, 4110as[62]
Lalande, Michel-Richard de
   collections, cathedral choir school, Aix-en-Provence, 748as[2]

life, relation to French-Italian musical relations, 1530as[25], 1532as[25]
   manuscripts, Te Deum, 3773as[52]
   works, for funeral of Queen Marie-Thérèse, 1683, 1601as[25]
LALEVIĆ, Miodrag S., 357bs, 402bs
LALO, Charles, 5517as[81], 5518as[81], 5519as[81]
LALOY, Louis, 2654as[33], 4089as[62]
LAMAS, Dulce Martins, 3204as[36]
Lambert, Constant
   life, promoting of Liszt, 2248as[28]
   works, film music, 5173as[77]
Lambert, Master, *see* **Lambertus, Magister (Pseudo-Aristoteles)**
Lambertini, Prospero, *see* **Benedict XIV, Pope**
Lambertus, Magister (Pseudo-Aristoteles)
   writings, *Tractatus de musica*, 5572as[81]
   ___ treatises, attribution, 1168as[23]
Lambillotte, Louis
   collections, *Chants à Marie pour le mois de mai et les fêtes de la Sainte Vierge*, 6188as[93]
Lamennais, Hugues-Félicité-Robert de
   writings, influence on Liszt, 5319as[78]
   ___ influence on Liszt pedagogy, 2040as[27]
lament
   Albania, 2909as[34]
   ___ southern, Çam people, 3068as[34]
   Balkan states, 2895as[34]
   Bosnia and Herzegovina, 5355as[78]
   Canada, Nova Scotia, Acadian people, maritime laments, 2531as[31]
   Croatia, Poljica, 2973as[34]
   Italy, Molise, Croatian people, funeral music, 2768as[34]
   ___ Vallepietra, *Pianto delle zitelle*, 5121as[77]
   Macedonia, 5342as[78]
   ___ Skopje, earthquake victims, 1963, 2844as[34]
   madrigal, use of parallel fourths, 4187as[63]
   Montenegro, Durmitor region, 3112as[34]
   ___ tužbalica genre, use in Njegoš *Gorski vijenac*, 5308as[78]
   North America, northwestern, Indians, relation to East Asian music, 3138as[35]
   Romania, Transylvania, German-speaking people, 3077as[34]
   Serbia, Sombor region, 2895as[34]
   Slavic states, southern, 2780as[34], 2901as[34]
   ___ Partisan songs, 2977as[34]
   Slovenia, relation to ballad, 2917as[34]
Lamentations of Jeremiah, *see also* **Bible**
   Low Countries, polyphonic settings, 15th c., 6387as[93]
LAMICHE (ABBÉ), 3409as[42]
LAMMEL, Inge, 734as[2], 2338as[29]
Lampeler van Mill family
   instruments, organs, 3400as[42]
LAMPÉRIÈRE, Anna, 4484as[70]
LAMSON, Roy, Jr., 2922as[34]
LAND, Jan Pieter Nicolaas, 2655as[33], 4090as[62]
LANDAU, Siegfried, 6076as[91]
LANDÉ, Franz, 4189as[63]
Landini, Francesco
   life, 1062as[23]
   ___ relation to Squarcialupi, 1060as[23]
   performance practice, 3723as[51]
   works, melodic design, 4424as[69]
   ___ secular, relation to performance practice, 3690as[51]
Ländler, *see* **dance — by genre; dance music — by genre**
LANDON, H.C. Robbins, 1796as[26], 1797as[26], 1798as[26]
LANDORMY, Paul, 2024as[27], 2339as[29]
LANDOWSKA, Wanda, 1597as[25]
Landowska, Wanda
   life, Pleyel harpsichord, 3535as[43]

LANDOWSKI, W.L., 4581as[70]
LANFRY, Georges, 336bs
Lang, François
   collections, 763as[2]
LANG, Hugo, 5520as[81]
LANG, Paul Henry, 981as[21], 4358as[66], 5460as[81], 5521as[81]
Lange, Aloysia Weber
   life, relation to Mozart, 3745as[52]
Lange, Arthur
   works, film music, for Leonard *The great Ziegfeld*, 5130as[77]
LANGE, Francisco Curt, 2340as[29], 3163as[35]
LANGE, Victor, 1908as[27]
LANGELÜDDEKE, Albrecht, 5673as[82]
LANGER, A., 5500as[81]
LANGEVIN, Vige, 2525as[31], 4582as[70], 5016as[76]
Langhedul, Jan
   instruments, organs, relation to Paris school, 3386as[42]
Langhedul, Matthijs
   instruments, organs, relation to Paris school, 3386as[42]
LANGLOIS, Ludo, 5769as[85]
language, *see also* **encyclopedias and dictionaries; linguistics; philology; rhetoric; semantics; terminology; text setting; translation; vers mesuré**
   Africa, drum language, 2575as[32]
   ___ sub-Saharan, relation to drumming, 2576as[32]
   Bantu languages, South Africa, Johannesburg, influence on popular songs, 2581as[32]
   Celtic languages, England and Wales, relation to music pedagogy, 4775as[71], 4776as[71]
   Chinese languages, use in Gregorian chant, 6271as[93]
   compared with music, 5483as[81]
   Creole, Suriname, relation to songs and dances, 3210as[36]
   Czech, influence on Janáček, 2320as[29]
   ___ prosody, relation to Czech song melody, 4035as[61]
   ___ viewed by Janáček, 5939as[88]
   Dutch, hymn texts, use in Roman Catholic liturgy, 6256as[93]
   English, North America, Indians, use in traditional songs, 3174as[35]
   Esperanto, songbooks, 58bs
   Europe, Jewish people, traditional songs, 2928as[34]
   Ewondo, Obama hymns, 6325as[93], 6326as[93]
   Finnish, use in Introits, 1605, 1570as[25]
   French, use in Gregorian chant, ca. 1957, 4433as[69]
   German, cultivation, late 17th c., 1545as[25]
   ___ instrument terms, standardization, 18th c., 3266as[40]
   ___ recitative texts, use in Roman Catholic liturgy, ca. 1963, 6254as[93]
   ___ relation to singing, 5921as[88]
   ___ religious music, Roman Catholic Church, influenced by *Sacrosanctum concilium*, 6276as[93]
   ___ set by Spontini, 1952as[27]
   ___ sound quality terms, 16th-19th c., 5931as[88]
   ___ use in Gregorian chant, 6321as[93]
   ___ ___ late 20th c., 6288as[93]
   ___ use in Roman Catholic liturgy, 12th-16th c., 1088as[23]
   ___ use in Slovakian traditional songs, 3025as[34]
   Ghana, kple cult song texts, 2568as[32]
   Greek, use in Roman Catholic liturgy, 1045as[22]
   Händel, G.F., multilingualism, 1692as[25]
   Hebrew, Israel, relation to traditional songs, 2685as[33]
   ___ modern, influence on Israeli art music, 1940-50, 2143as[28]
   ___ ___ influenced by Haggadah, 6088as[91]

history and development, relation to rhythm, 3987as[61]

India, tarānā singing, relation to vocables, 2647as[33]

Italian, Sicilian dialect, relation to siciliana, 1012as[21]

___ vowels, compared with Portuguese, 3315as[41]

Japanese, use in Roman Catholic liturgy, 6322as[93]

Latin, Gregorian chant, relation to pastoral value, 6310as[93], 6311as[93]

___ ___ rhythm, 5917as[88]

___ ___ use of rhythm, 3701as[51]

___ influence on Macedonian guslar argot, 5935as[88]

___ liturgical, pedagogy, 4645as[70]

___ ___ pronunciation reform, ca. 1911, 5295as[78]

___ ___ role of congregational singing, 6379as[93]

___ medieval, music lexicography, 773as[3]

___ prosody, relation to rhythmic interpretation of Gregorian chant, 3977as[61]

___ relation to cantiques, 6356as[93]

___ relation to Christian unity, 6338as[93]

Macedonia, guslar argot, 5935as[88]

modern languages, use in liturgical music, conferences, 1962-63, 449bs

Muslim people, conference, 1905, 48bs

Niger-Congo family, Western Sudanic branch, instrument vocabularies, 5926as[88]

Old Church Slavonic, use in Roman Catholic liturgy, 6420as[93]

pathology, 5655as[82]

pedagogy, children, use of eurythmics, 4782as[71]

___ use of traditional songs, 4757as[71]

Polish, prosody, relation to mazurka rhythm, 4034as[61]

___ use in Teatr Narodowy opera librettos, early 19th c., 5099as[77]

Portuguese, Brazil, influence on composition, 20th c., 2130as[28]

___ ___ pronunciation, 3316as[41]

___ ___ pronunciation, nasal vowels, 3296as[41]

___ ___ pronunciation, regional dialects, 5919as[88]

___ ___ regional dialects, relation to singing, 3299as[41]

___ ___ regional dialects, relation to traditional songs, 3196as[36]

___ ___ Rio de Janeiro, diction, 5929as[88]

___ ___ São Paulo state, dialects, 5938as[88]

___ ___ singing, conference, 1937, 253bs

___ ___ vowels, compared with Italian, 3315as[41]

___ ___ stress patterns, relation to singing, 3309as[41]

___ ___ text setting, word division, 4314as[66]

South Slavic languages, grammar, sympathetic dative construction, use in song texts, 5936as[88]

Spanish, Greece, Thessaloníkī, Sephardic Jewish people, traditional songs, 2743as[34]

speech, compared with melody, 5923as[88]

___ intonation, relation to Janáček speech melodies, 4320as[66]

___ melodic curves, comparison of languages, 5855as[86]

___ perception, 5724as[82]

___ relation to Gregorian chant, 6360as[93]

___ relation to singing styles, 3254as[40]

___ sound, relation to electronic instruments, 5940as[88]

Ukrainian, Serbia, Vojvodina, influenced by Hungarian music, 3084as[34]

vernacular, Roman Catholic liturgy, 6249as[93]

___ use in Gregorian chant, late 20th c., 6172as[93]

Vietnamese, tones, relation to Vietnamese music, 2700as[33]

Languer (16th-c. composer)
works, 1460as[24]

LANSSENS, Martin, 1799as[26]

Lantins, Arnold de
works, 1252as[24]

Lantins, Hugo de
works, 1252as[24]

Lapicida, Erasmus
life, at Hungarian court, 1326as[24]

LAPSON, Dvora, 5017as[76]

LARAGNINO, Francesco, 5190as[77]

LARNAUDE, Ferdinand, 35bs

LARREA PALACÍN, Arcadio de, 2923as[34]

LARRINAGA LARRAÑAGA, Juan Ruiz de, 735as[2]

LARSEN, Jens Peter, 1598as[25], 3732as[52], 3752as[52], 3753as[52], 3893as[58], 4369as[66]

LARSON, William S., 4722as[71]

Larsson, Lars-Erik
works, 944as[21]

LARUE, Jan, 439bs, 440bs, 1763as[26], 1800as[26], 3893as[58], 4359as[66], 4369as[66], 5383as[79]

LASCELLES, George Henry Hubert, Earl of Harewood, 489bs, 845as[19], 846as[19], 852as[19], 2341as[29], 5191as[77]

Łaski, Jan
correspondence, with Glarean, on *Dodecachordon*, 1461as[24]

Lasso, Orlando di, *see* **Lassus, Roland de**

Lassus, Roland de
editions, complete works, Breitkopf & Härtel, ca. 1958, 3897as[58]

life, relation to court at Bruxelles, 1361as[24]

reception, Germany, Rheinland, 19th c., 2020as[27]

___ treatises and appreciations, 16th-17th c., 1242as[24]

works, chansons, 1239as[24]

___ chronology, 1245as[24]

___ in lute intabulations, 16th-early 17th c., inventory, 1241as[24]

___ late, style, 4316as[66]

___ Magnificats, 1240as[24]

___ Masses, parody, 1301as[24]

___ *Missa Hercules Dux Ferrariae*, soggetto cavato, 1452as[24]

___ parody technique, 1243as[24]

___ relation to France, 1249as[24]

___ word painting, 1379as[24]

Latin American music (outside Latin America)
USA, band and orchestra performances, 1940, 2306as[29]

___ radio broadcasts, 2398as[29]

___ use in pedagogy, ca. 1940, 4521as[70]

Latin American studies, *see also* **Americas**; **Central America**; **South America**; specific countries; **West Indies**

history of music, influenced by Debussy, 2133as[28]

___ use of documentation, 684as[1]

mass media, sound recordings, US distribution, ca. 1940, 5947as[89]

musical life, Americanismo movement, 2340as[29]

___ USA performers, 2383as[29]

___ 1948, 2370as[29]

pedagogy, survey, 4661as[70]

religious music, Gregorian chant, 20th-c. revival, 6167as[93], 6168as[93]

traditional music, in Pan-American Union library, Washington, D.C., 769as[2]

___ state of research, ca. 1940, 2488as[30]

___ state of research, ca. 1954, 3163as[35]

Latvia, *see also* **Baltic states**
traditional music, origins, 2874as[34]

Latvijah, *see* **Latvia**

Laub, Thomas
works, *Dansk kirkesang*, 6449as[94]

LAUBER, Anselm, 5817as[86]

lauda, *see also* **religion and religious music — Christianity (Roman Catholic)**
Italy, rhythm and meter, transcription, 3802as[55]

___ Roma, Congregazione dell'Oratorio performance, history and development, 1281as[24]

___ Todi, lauda drammatica, 13th-16th c., 5222as[77]

___ transition to monody form, 1563-1600, 1503as[25]

___ 13th-16th c., 1061as[23]

___ early 16th c., 1345as[24]

Laudes regiae
history and development, 1159as[23]

LAUDOVÁ, Hannah, 5018as[76], 5019as[76], 5020as[76]

LAUNAY, Denise, 1510as[25], 1590as[25], 3754as[52], 3843as[55], 4265as[64]

LAUNIS, Armas, 2924as[34], 4444as[69]

LAURENT, V., 236rs[16]

LAURENT (BROTHER), 6017as[90]

LAUX, Karl, 1599as[25]

Lavotta, János
works, dance music, influence on Liszt and Brahms, 1973as[27]

LAVOYE, Louis, 1137as[23], 1363as[24], 1364as[24], 1600as[25]

Lavry, Marc
works, to 1947, 2228as[28]

law, *see also* **copyright and patents**
Belgium, organ building contracts, 17th-18th c., 3333as[42]

composers, rights, viewed by Meerens, 2356as[29]

counterfeit scores, proposed commission, 1908, 5958as[89]

Europe, travel and work permits, 2378as[29]

Middle Ages, status of musicians, 1171as[23]

Roman Catholic Church, canon law, sacred music, 1917, 6290as[93]

___ foundations of church music administration, 6344as[93]

___ liturgical music legislation, use of electronic organ, 1949, 3665as[48], 3666as[48]

___ regulation, viewed by Pius XII, 6363as[93], 6364as[93]

LAWLER, Vanett, 4583as[70], 4584as[70]

LAYTON, Billy Jim, 4858as[72]

LAZAREVIĆ, Jovanka, 2925as[34]

LAZAROV, Stefan, 1138as[23]

Le Blanc, Didier
works, songs, lute, 1458as[24]

LE CAINE, Hugh, 2196as[28]

LE COSQUINO DE BUSSY, J.R., 605as[1], 606as[1], 607as[1], 608as[1]

LE FLEM, Paul, 2342as[29]

LE GUENNANT, Auguste, 2343as[29], 6281as[93], 6282as[93], 6283as[93]

LE JEAN, Jean-Marie, 4bs

Le Jeune, Cécile
editions, Claude Le Jeune works, 3719as[51]

Le Jeune, Claude
performance practice, vers mesuré, 3719as[51]

works, fantaisies, 4265as[64]

___ *Le printemps*, as settings of vers mesuré, 1376as[24]

Le Paillot, Jean
writings, libretto for Wangermée *La maîtresse et les deux maestros*, 3776as[52]

Le Roy, Adrian
writings, *Instruction d'asseoir toute musique facilement*, right-hand lute technique, 3597as[44]

___ on Lassus, 1242as[24]

Le Sueur, Jean-François
correspondence, to Janssens, 1840as[26]

works, for funeral of Queen Marie-Thérèse, 1683, 1601as[25]

LEACH, MacEdward, 2443as[30]

Lebanon
Bayrūt, pedagogy, conservatory, proposed, 1919, 4864as[73]

culture, conference, 1919, 92bs

library catalogues, see **catalogues — library, museum, collection**

libretto — by librettist, see also **dramaturgy**; **literature**; **opera** headwords

___ harmony, altered chords, compared with Wagner, 4224as[63]

___ *Hussitenlied* (1840), influenced by Krov *Těšme se blahou naději*, 1925as[27]

___ influence on Benoît, 2070as[27]

___ influence on 20th-c. music, 2248as[28]

___ innovative techniques, 4386as[66]

___ *Madrigal* MS (1844), relation to *Consolations* no. 5, 1982as[27]

___ *Magyar rhapsodiák*, 1915as[27]

___ ___ history and development, 1839-85, 2064as[27]

___ Masses, compared with Bruckner, 2019as[27]

___ *Missa pro organo...*, 1879, arranged by Janáček, 2255as[28]

___ paraphrases, influence on 19th-c. European culture, 2046as[27]

___ piano music, compared with Chopin, 2044as[27]

___ ___ compared with Smetana, 4350as[66]

___ ___ harmony, compared with Chopin, 4178as[63]

___ ___ influence on Smetana, 1994as[27]

___ ___ ornamentation, 4332as[66]

___ program music, 1848-54, relation to 1848 Hungarian uprising, 1956as[27]

___ quoted by Bartók, 4317as[66]

___ relation to color, 5652as[82]

___ relation to Hungarian and Bohemian politics, 2056as[27]

___ relation to 19th-c. literature, 1908as[27]

___ religious music, 1993as[27]

___ ___ compared with Beethoven, 1857as[26]

___ ___ influence on Janáček, 2255as[28]

___ *Rigoletto: Paraphrase de concert*, 2046as[27]

___ settings of verbunkos and csárdás, influenced by Reményi, 1973as[27]

___ sonata form, compared with Chopin, 2017as[27]

___ sonority, 4298as[65]

___ symphonic poems, influence on Smetana, 4346as[66]

___ use of Gregorian chant, 2090as[27]

LITAIZE, Gaston, 3464as[42], 6289as[93]

litany, *see also* **religion and religious music** headwords

Europe, history and development, 17th c., 1669as[25]

Mozart, W.A., 4246as[64]

Switzerland, St. Gallen, Columbanus tributes, 6204as[93]

literature, *see also* **dramatic arts; libretto** headwords; **poetry; song texts; text setting**

aesthetics, conference, 1959, 372bs

antiquity, depiction of shepherd songs, 850as[19]

Brome, R., *A jovial crew, or, The merry beggars*, 5234as[77]

Caesarius of Arles, sermons, evidence of Gallican chant practice, 1166as[23]

Czech Republic, 16th-19th c., 1204as[23]

Europe, 19th c., relation to affections doctrine, 5429as[81]

___ relation to music, 1908as[27]

Fastraets, C., *Het spiel van St. Trudo/Comedia una vitam Sancti Trudonis confessoris*, 1364as[24]

France, Bretagne, history and development, 2849as[34]

___ *Chanson de Guillaume*, refrains, 5369as[78]

___ *Chanson de Roland*, oliphant imagery, 5294as[78]

___ depiction of shepherd songs, Middle Ages and Renaissance, 850as[19]

___ influenced by Mozart, 5314as[78]

___ oral, bibliography, 1891, 822as[8]

___ relation to Liszt and Wagner, 5319as[78]

___ southern, conference, 1958, 388bs

García Lorca, F., *Amor de Don Perlimplín con Belisa en su jardín*, basis of Fortner *In seinem Garten liebt Don Perlimplin Belisa*, 5151as[77]

___ *Bodas de sangre*, basis of Fortner *Die Bluthochzeit*, 5151as[77]

Germany, Oberbaden, references to small organs, 16th c., 3467as[42]

___ relation to music, 19th c., 1905as[27]

___ Weimar, relation to Mozart, 1728as[26]

Giustiniani, O., *Edipo tiranno*, 5239as[77]

Goldoni, C., comedies, relation to opera librettos, 5133as[77]

___ plays, Polish performances, 5204as[77]

harp as subject, 3596as[44]

Hasidic, use of songs, 6087as[91]

history and development, periodization, relation to periodization of opera history, 5100as[77]

Hoffmann, E.T.A., Romanticism, 2002as[27]

imagery, relation to traditional song, 5343as[78]

India, *Rāmāyaṇa*, 3577as[44]

influence on Szymanowski, 2183as[28]

Italy, role in pedagogy, 4621as[70]

___ early 14th c., 1108as[23]

Jonson, B., masques, relation to opera, 5127as[77]

Middle Ages, depiction of jongleurs, 5285as[78]

motive concept, compared with music, 5445as[81]

Mozart as subject, 5290as[78]

Netherlands, 4925as[75]

Njegoš, P. II P., dramas, portrayal of kolo dancers, 5321as[78]

___ *Gorski vijenac*, portrayal of kolo dancers, 5331as[78]

___ *Gorski vijenac* (The mountain wreath), references to gusle, 5368as[78]

___ ___ use of Montenegrin folklore, 5308as[78]

oral narrative, conference, 1959, 411bs

___ depictions of music, 5315as[78]

___ numerology, relation to scales, 4071as[62]

Poland, relation to Wagner reception, 5364as[78]

relation to 20th-c. opera, 5230as[77]

Richardson, S., *Pamela*, basis of Goldoni *La buona figliuola*, 5132as[77]

Rolland, R., 4844as[72]

Serbia, 9th-16th c., 1079as[23]

Shakespeare, W., influence on Chopin and Delacroix, 2038as[27]

Sheppard, E.S., *Charles Auchester*, depiction of Horsley and Mendelssohn-Bartholdy, 2033as[27]

Sophocles, *Oidipous tyrannos*, translated by Giustiniani, 5239as[77]

Spain, Valencia, *Planchs de Sant Esteve*, 1169as[23]

Symbolism, influence on Eliot, 5299as[78]

theory, relation to music, 5353as[78]

viewed by Brahms, 5465as[81]

Lithuania, *see also* **Baltic states**

ethnomusicology, classification, 19th c., 2762as[34]

traditional music, songs, meter, 4038as[61]

Vilnius, Jewish people, musical life, 6040as[91]

Lithuanian music (outside Lithuania)

USA, songs, 3134as[35]

LITTLE, George, 984as[21]

liturgical books, *see also* **chant — general; hymnals; psalters; religion and religious music** headwords

antiphoners, Czech Republic, Sedlec, 5382as[79]

___ Gregorian, early 8th c., 1070as[23]

___ Mozarabic, early 8th c., 1070as[23]

___ Roman, role of Gregory I, 1142as[23]

asmatika, Italy, Messina, Monastero di S. Salvatore, 1195as[23]

breviaries, France, Autun, Grand Séminaire, hymn tributes to St. Philibert, 1334as[24]

___ Italy, Fonte Avellana, Monastero di Santa Croce, 11th c., 1096as[23]

France, Jumièges, Abbaye St.-Pierre, at Bibl. Mun., Rouen, catalogue, 780as[4], 781as[4]

graduals, for small churches, 6181as[93]

___ *Graduale romanum*, calendar, 6217as[93]

___ ___ Solesmes edition, 3888as[58]

___ Liber usualis, Credo I, use of Greek melody, 1128as[23]

___ Poland, Kraśnik, Konwent Kanoników Regularnych Lateraneńskych, *Audi tellus prosa*, 5332as[78]

Haggadoth, influence on modern Hebrew, 6088as[91]

heirmologia, oral vs. notated traditions, 4465as[69]

___ Slavonic MSS, early 13th-c., 1197as[23]

kondakars, relation to Byzantine asmatikon, 3846as[55]

Kyriales, early 20th c., compared with catechism, 6212as[93]

lectionaries, Croatia, Trogir, cadences, 1025as[21]

missals, Germany, Mönchengladbach Missale plenarium, illumination, 5375as[79]

___ Glagolitic liturgy, 6420as[93]

___ Mönchengladbach Missale plenarium, 1080as[23]

psaltika, chromatic alterations, 3876as[55]

___ Italy, Messina, Monastero di S. Salvatore, Byzantine liturgical volume, 1195as[23]

Russia, Novgorod, menaia, late 11th c., kanōn to Demetrius of Thessalonikī, 6123as[92]

sacramentaries, Gelasian Sacramentary, metrical cursus, 3970as[61]

___ Leonine Sacramentary, metrical cursus, 3970as[61]

stichēraria, history and development, evidenced in *Hagiopolitēs* treatise, 6109as[92]

___ Slavonic MSS, 12th-c., 1197as[23]

Switzerland, St. Gallen, Columbanus tributes, 6204as[93]

tonaries, Metz Tonary, dating and attribution, 1143as[23]

Vatican, relation to the Holy See, 6279as[93]

liturgical drama, *see also* **dramatic arts; trope**

Italy, Vallepietra, *Pianto delle zitelle*, 5121as[77]

melody, 11th-12th c., 4448as[69]

Netherlands, Easter play, 1184as[23]

___ Maastricht, Easter play, 1182as[23]

Spain, Penedès, 4971as[76], 4972as[76]

liturgy, *see* **religion and religious music** headwords; **theology**

LIUZZI, Fernando, 740as[2], 1144as[23], 2933as[34], 4268as[64]

LIVANOVA, Tamara Nikolaevna, 1804as[26], 3758as[52]

LLONGUERAS BADÍA, Juan, 4587as[70], 4727as[71]

LLOYD, G.A., 640as[1]

Lloyd, John

life, as Chapel Royal singer, 1226as[24]

ŁOBACZEWSKA, Stefania, 2029as[27], 3951as[60], 4366as[66], 4396as[67], 5526as[81]

Łobaczewska, Stefania

writings, on Szymanowski, 2259as[28]

Lobo, Duarte

works, 4143as[63]

Lobwasser, Ambrosius

writings, German translation of Geneva Psalter, role in Danish psalmody, 6446as[94]

Locatelli, Pietro Antonio

works, sonatas, violin, influenced by opera, 1714as[25]

Locke, Matthew

life, 1516as[25]

works, voluntaries, organ, 1583as[25]

LOCKSPEISER, Edward, 2030as[27], 2207as[28], 2347as[29]

Loeffelholz von Colberg, Christoph

works, organ music, 1382as[24]

Loeffler, Charles Martin

works, harmony, 4173as[63]

___ influenced by Debussy, 2236as[28]

LOEWENBACH, Josef, 4367as[66]

LÖFFLER, Hans, 3414as[42]

LOGOṬHETI, 2934as[34]

LOHMANN, G.J.T., 4909as[74], 4910as[74]

LÖHNER, Ina, 4588as[70]

LOMAX, Alan, 2453as[30], 2527as[31], 2528as[31]

Lomax, Alan
writings, discography of American traditional songs, 5947as[89]

Longhi, Pietro
works, art, representation of soprano lute, 3563as[44]

LONGO, Achille, 5197as[77]

LONGO, Alessandro, 1607as[25]

LONGYEAR, Rey M., 1955as[27]

Lönnrot, Elias
collections, *Kanteletar*, set by Kilpinen, 2266as[28]

Looser, Joseph
instruments, chamber organs, 3441as[42]

Looser, Wendelin
instruments, chamber organs, 3441as[42]

LÓPEZ CALO, José, 1590as[25]

López de Mendoza, Iñigo, Marqués de Santillana
writings, villancicos, 5365as[78]

LÓPEZ GODOY, Rafael José, 6290as[93]

Lorca, Federico García, *see* **García Lorca, Federico**

LORD, Albert B., 5329as[78]

LORENTE, Miguel, 4191as[63]

Lorentz, Johann (organ builder)
life, relation to Lorentz (organist), 1615as[25]

Lorentz, Johann (organist)
catalogues, extant compositions, 1615as[25]
life, København, 1634-89, 1615as[25]

Lorenz, Alfred
writings, *Das Geheimnis der Form bei Richard Wagner*, concept of poetic-musical period, 4238as[64]

Lorenzani, Paolo
works, *Nicandro et Fileno*, 1648as[25]

LORENZEN, Poul, 5025as[76]

Lorenzini, Paolo
works, Comédie-Italienne repertoire, 1565as[25]

LORIA, Arturo, 985as[21], 2348as[29]

Loris, Heinrich, *see* **Glarean, Heinrich**

Lorraine, Marguerite de
life, marriage to Anne de Joyeuse, 1474as[24]

Lortzing, Albert, *see* **Lortzing, Gustav Albert**

Lortzing, Gustav Albert
aesthetics, literature and music, 1905as[27]

LOTTERMOSER, Werner, 3415as[42], 3416as[42], 3487as[42], 3588as[44], 3589as[44], 5837as[86]

Lottermoser, Werner
life, electronic pitch transcription research, 5821as[86]

LOUDON, E., 3165as[35]

Louis, Jean
editions, *Pseaulmes cinquantes*, 4430as[69]

Louis Ferdinand, Prince of Prussia
manuscripts, at Breitkopf & Härtel arch., Leipzig, 5968as[89]

Louis XII, King of France
life, patronage, court musicians, 1271as[24]

Louis XIV, King of France
life, influence on music, 981as[21]

LOULOVÁ, Olga, 1805as[26]

LOVRENČEVIĆ, Zvonko, 3629as[45]

Low Countries, *see also* **Belgium**; **Europe**; **Netherlands**
dance, ballet, 18th c., 1606as[25]
Flanders, history of music, ceremonial music, 16th c., 1368as[24]
history, nationality issues, 1371as[24]
___ Renaissance, conference, 1954, 328bs
___ 1540 rebellion, 1260as[24]
history of music, early music, performance practice, use of positive organ, 3430as[42]
___ ethnic-terminology issues, 1022as[21]
___ Franco-Flemish school, 15th c., 1312as[24]

___ influence on French court music, ca. 1498-1515, 1271as[24]
___ influence on Italian madrigals, 1295as[24]
___ influence on Polish instrumental music, 16th c., 1372as[24]
___ lute music, sources, 1580-1620, 1390as[24]
___ Middle Dutch songs, manuscripts, 1132as[23]
___ polyphony, 15th-16th c., 1285as[24]
___ relation to Italy, 16th c., 1229as[24]
___ relation to Renaissance, 1473as[24]
___ relation to Spain, early 16th c., 1259as[24]
iconography, musicians, 15th-early 16th c., 5401as[79]
instruments, carillons, late 14th-20th c., 3643as[46]
___ friction drums, 3646as[46]
religious music, Lamentations of Jeremiah, polyphonic settings, 15th c., 6387as[93]
___ polyphony, 15th c., 1406as[24]
___ late 19th-early 20th c., 1992as[27]
traditional music, songs, 19th c., 2797as[34]

LOWENS, Irving, 953as[21], 2031as[27], 4916as[74], 5112as[77]

LOWINSKY, Edward E., 1269as[24], 1373as[24], 4192as[63], 4198as[63]

LOYONNET, Paul, 1806as[26]

Lü, Buwei
writings, *Lüshi qunqiu* (Springs and autumns of Master Lü), relation to Pythagorean tuning, 4087as[62]
___ views on scales, 4122as[62]

LUALDI, Adriano, 2208as[28], 5198as[77], 5527as[81]

Lubnan, *see* **Lebanon**

LUCIANI, Sebastiano Arturo, 1608as[25], 1609ac[25], 1610as[25], 1611ac[25], 1612as[25], 2349as[29], 3759as[52], 3760as[52], 4091as[62], 5105as[77], 5528as[81]

LUDWIG, Friedrich, 1145as[23], 1146as[23]

Ludwig, Friedrich
writings, motet origins, 4255as[64]

Ludwig, Otto
aesthetics, literature and music, 1905as[27]

LUEDTKE, Hans, 3417as[42]

Luedtke, Hans
instruments, organs, influence on Walcker firm, 2161as[28]

Lugge, John
works, voluntaries, organ, 1583as[25]

LUIN, Elizabeth Jeannette, 986as[21], 1613ac[25], 1614as[25]

LUITHLEN, Victor, 741as[2], 4368as[66]

LUKÁCS, M., 5838as[86]

Lully, Jean-Baptiste
performances, rehearsals for *Le triomphe de l'Amour*, 1699as[25]
works, grands motets, for funeral of Queen Marie-Thérèse, 1683, 1601as[25]
___ operas, influence on Graupner, 1637as[25]
___ overtures, 1647as[25]

LUMPKIN, Ben Gray, 2529as[31]

LUMSDEN, David, 588as[1], 613as[1], 1374as[24]

LUNDGREN, Bo, 1615as[25]

LUNELLI, Renato, 3418as[42], 3529as[43]

LUNGHI, F.L., 614as[1], 5199as[77]

LUPER, Albert T., 953as[21]

Lupi, Johannes
works, use of soggetti cavati, 1452as[24]

LUPI, Roberto, 4193as[63]

Lupi, Roberto
writings, harmony, relation to overtone series, 4210as[63]

Lupi da Caravaggio, Livio
writings, *Mutanze di gagliarda, tordiglione, passo e mezzo...*, 1454as[24]

Lupus
works, use of soggetti cavati, 1452as[24]

lur, *see* **instruments — wind (brass)**

LUR'E, Artur Sergeevič (Arthur Vincent Lourié), 4194as[63]

LUSSY, Mathis, 5529as[81]

lute, *see* **instruments — string (lute family)**

Luther, Martin
life, relation to responsorial Passions, 1219as[24]
___ relation to Walter, 6448as[94]
___ views on music, 6426as[94]
works, *Vater unser im Himmelreich*, arranged by Bach, 1567as[25]
writings, music, 5493as[81]
___ music aesthetics, 5600as[81]
___ theology of music, compared with Walter poems, 1441as[24]

LUTHER, Wilhelm Martin, 615as[1]

Luti, Prospero
writings, *Opera bellissima nella quale si contengono molte partite...*, 1454as[24]

LUTZE, Lothar, 844as[19], 2657as[33]

Luzzaschi, Luzzasco
editions, *Canzon a 4*, 3887as[58]

LUZZATO, G.L., 5530as[81]

LYON, Clément, 1375as[24]

LYON, Gustave, 80ap[16], *81ra[16], *82ra[16], *83ra[16], *84ra[16], *85ra[16], 171ap[16], 3849as[55], 4092as[62]

lyra, *see* **instruments — string (violin family)**

lyre, *see* **instruments — string (lyre family)**

lyric drama, *see* **opera** headwords

lyrics, *see* **song texts**

M

MA, Hiao-Ts'iun, 5200as[77]

Maass, Nikolaus
instruments, organs, 3364as[42]

MAC CREA, Dan, 6291as[93]

MACCLINTOCK, Carol, 588as[1]

Mace, Thomas
writings, *Musick's monument, or, A remembrancer of the best practical musick*, bandora, 3561as[44]
___ ___ right-hand lute technique, 3597as[44]

MACEDA, José, 2658as[33]

Macedonia, *see also* **Greece**; **Slavic states**
Albanian people, traditional music, lament for Rexha, 3007as[34]
dance, traditional, oro, 4992as[76]
___ ___ relation to sociology, 4950as[76]
ethnomusicology, activities of Cepenkov, 2991as[34]
___ activities of Milojević, 2990as[34]
folklore, 2992as[34]
___ children's games, 4976as[76]
___ spring festival rituals, 2843as[34]
history of music, Partisan songs, 2847as[34]
___ revolutionary songs, 2816as[34]
___ role of Kliment and Naum of Ohrid, 1138as[23]
___ World War II songs, Fascism as subject, 2842as[34]
iconography, instruments, Middle Ages, 5389as[79]
instruments, dvotelnik, 3620as[45]
___ kaval, 3621as[45]
___ 12th-19th c., 3310as[41]
musical life, guslars, use of secret argot, 5935as[88]
Ohrid, traditional music, songs, ca. 1850-1960, 2936as[34]
Skopje, traditional music, funeral laments, 2844as[34]
Torbeš people, folklore, funeral customs, 2986as[34]
traditional music, 2815as[34]
___ ballads, 2846as[34]
___ gajdar music, melodic typology, 2932as[34]
___ group singing, 2814as[34]

___ laments, 5342as[78]

___ Lazarica songs, 2845as[34]

___ melodies, use in Mokranjac *Rukoveti*, 2049as[27]

___ rhythm and meter, 2848as[34], 3991as[61]

___ song refrains, typology, 2998as[34]

___ songs, *Biljana platno beleše*, relation to Ohrid, 3008as[34]

___ ___ Hungarian history as subject, 3038as[34]

Macedonian music (outside Macedonia)

USA, traditional music, 3149as[35]

MACGILLIVRAY, James, 3630as[45]

MACHABEY, Armand, 4195as[63], 5201as[77]

MACHATIUS, Franz Jochen, 4011as[61], 5531as[81]

Machaut, Guillaume de, see Guillaume de Machaut

Maciejowski, Ignacy

writings, *Jakież kwiaty, jakie wianki*, set by Chopin, 2074as[27]

Mackenzie, Alexander

life, teaching of British composers, 2144as[28]

MACKENZIE, Alexander Campbell, 2032as[27]

MACKERNESS, Eric David, 2033as[27]

MacKinnon, Nan

life, repertoire, 2505as[31]

MACLEAN, Charles, 71bs, *72rs[16], 2350as[29]

Maclean, Charles

writings, notation, 3839as[55]

Macque, Giovanni de

works, instrumental music, relation to toccata, 4237as[64]

Macrander, Johann Friedrich

instruments, organs, influence on J. Gabler, 3345as[42]

Madelka, Simon Bar Jona

works, relation to Czech music, 1436as[24]

Maderno, Bruno

life, founding of Studio di Fonologia Musicale, 4404as[68]

madrigal, see also frottola

aesthetics, relation to lauda, 1563-1600, 1503as[25]

Brudieu, J., 1396as[24]

cataloguing, proposal, 1906, 791as[5]

conference, 1961, 429bs

England, melancholia, early 17th c., 1621as[25]

___ relation to ayre, 1284as[24]

___ relation to national style, 1468as[24]

___ 16th c., 1304as[24]

___ ca. 1600, 1411as[24]

Gibbons, O., melancholia, 1342as[24]

history and development, relation to chanson, 1333as[24]

role of Festa, 1423as[24]

influence on fugue, 4427as[69]

Italy, compared with England, 16th c., 1304as[24]

___ harmonization of chromatic melodies, 16th c., 4159as[63]

___ history and development, 1296as[24], 1422as[24]

___ ___ relation to Netherlands composers, 1295as[24]

___ tempo, 3986as[61]

___ three-part, relation to French models, 14th c., 1094as[23]

___ use of instruments, 14th c., 3690as[51]

___ 15th c., 1062as[23]

___ 16th c., in Küffer MS, 1258as[24]

laments, use of parallel fourths, 4187as[63]

Lassus, R. de, *Lagrime di S. Pietro*, 4316as[66]

Mikołaj z Krakowa, 1469as[24]

Monte, P. de, 1293as[24]

Monteverdi, C., as chamber music, 1270as[24]

Philips, P., 1340as[24]

relation to frottola, 4234as[64]

Rimonte, P., 1456as[24]

sociology, 5881as[87]

MADSEN, Cletus, 4728as[71], 4729as[71], 4730as[71]

MAERTENS, Willi, 1616as[25]

MAFFIOLETTI, M., 2034as[27]

magazines, see periodicals

magic

Africa, Mali, Dogon people, 2585as[32]

Americas, Indians, role of rhythm, 3985as[61]

Greece, relation to vowels, antiquity, 1042as[22]

Macedonia, spring festival rituals, 2843as[34]

Mediterranean region, fertility rites, pre-Hellenic period, 2969as[34]

North America, Indians, songs, 3145as[35]

primitive peoples, instrumental accompaniments, 2494as[31]

relation to traditional dance aesthetics, 5026as[76]

singing, use of non-natural rhythms, 4028as[61]

Slavic states, southern, swinging games, 2869as[34]

MAGNANI, Luigi, 5202as[77]

Magnificat, see canticle

Magyarország, see Hungary

MAHIEU, Léon, 6292as[93]

MAHILLON, Victor-Charles, 3850as[55]

Mahler, Gustav

life, relation to Mengelberg, 2286as[29]

works, influence on Janáček and Bartók, 2238as[28]

___ influence on Roman Catholic music, 2198as[28]

___ influenced by Czech traditional songs, 2005as[27], 2006as[27]

___ symphonies, 4233as[64]

___ ca. 1900, 2039as[27]

Mahmud II, Sultan of the Ottoman Empire

life, influence on Turkish Western-style art music, 2275as[28]

Mahn, Matthias

instruments, organs, 3364as[42]

MAHRENHOLZ, Christhard, 136bs, 3419as[42], 3420as[42], 6437as[94]

Mahrenholz, Christhard

instruments, organs, at Heilandskirche, Hamburg, 3399as[42]

___ ___ at St. Marien church, Göttingen, 3410as[42]

MAHY, Alfred, 2351as[29]

MAIGRET, J., 5772as[85]

MAILLET, Fernand, 4731as[71], 6293as[93], 6294as[93]

Maimonides, see Moses ben Maimon (Maimonides)

MAINE, Basil, 2209as[28]

MAISSEN, Alfons, 2935as[34]

makam, see maqām

Makedonija, see Macedonia

maladies, see medicine — by name; medicine — by topic; therapy

MALAPLATE, Léon, 5964as[89], 5978as[89]

MALCOLM, George, 6295as[93]

MALENKO, Dimče, 2936as[34]

MALETZKE, Gerhard, 5894as[87]

MALHERBE, Charles, 616as[1], 2035as[27], 2352as[29], 3851as[55]

Mali

Dogon people, culture, ceremonies, 2585as[32]

___ musical life, compared with Kissi and Fulɓe, 2587as[32]

MALI, José, 6130as[92]

MALIPIERO, Gian Francesco, 2353as[29], 5203as[77], 5532as[81]

Malipiero, Gian Francesco

works, operas, 5233as[77]

MALḰY'EL, 'Aleksander, 6077as[91]

MALL, G.D., 5678as[82]

Mallarmé, Stéphane

writings, viewed by Merleau-Ponty, 5602as[81]

mallet instruments, see instruments — percussion (mallet)

MALLORY, Vincent, 5805as[86]

MALM, William P., 2659as[33]

MALONE, Marjorie Jean, 4732as[71], 4733as[71]

management, see also careers; performing organizations

Americas, role in cultural exchange, 2383as[29]

liberties with scores, responsibility, 3675as[50]

opera companies, 5103as[77]

Roman Catholic church music, administration, financial and legal foundations, 6344as[93]

___ cultivation responsibilities, 6320as[93]

___ organizational proposals, 1954, 6241as[93]

Manchicourt, Pierre de

manuscripts, Masses, 1412as[24]

MANCIA, Renato, 3590as[44]

mandolin, see instruments — string (lute family)

Manet, Edouard

works, art, viewed by Debussy, 5396as[79]

MANGERET, 5786as[85]

MANGINI, Nicola, 384bs, 5204as[77]

MANGLER, Joyce E., 4916as[74]

MANLEY, D.M.J.P., 5773as[85]

MANN, Alfred, 1617as[25], 4369as[66]

mannerism, see also musica reservata

conference, 1960, 422bs

style, relation to European history, 1713as[25]

Manners, Charles

collections, Moody-Manners Opera Company materials, 750as[2]

Mannheim school, see also Classic

catalogues, symphonic works, in Basel and Zürich collections, 775as[4]

dynamics, influence on Beethoven, 4344as[66]

influence on Mozart, 1756as[26]

instrumentation and orchestration, influence on Beethoven, 4342as[66]

style, compared with Haydn, 4331as[66]

___ thematic development, compared with Händel, 1685as[25]

symphonies, compared with Viennese symphonies, 1864as[26]

Manni, Agostino

life, relation to oratorio, 1671as[25]

MANSION, Madeleine Louise, 5774as[85]

MANSOORUDDIN, Mohammad, 2660as[33]

MANTELLI, Alberto, 2210as[28], 2211as[28]

Mantova, Alberto da, see Ripa, Alberto da

MANTUANI, Josip, 617as[1], 618as[1], 896as[20]

Mantuani, Josip

bibliographies, operas, 586as[1]

MANUCCI DE GRANDIS, Isabella, 3313as[41]

manuscripts and prints — by author, see also other manuscripts and prints headwords; source studies; tablatures

Albertus Aquensis, *Historia Hierosolymitana*, illumination, 5375as[79]

Aldric, tonary, 1143as[23]

Autpertus, A., *Commentarium in Apocalypsim*, dedication leaf, 5375as[79]

Bach, J.S., Masses, BWV 232, Griepenkerl copy, 1686as[25]

Bartók, B., *Melodien der rumänischen Colinde (Weihnachtslieder)*, Brăiloiu annotations, 3094as[34]

___ suites, piano, op. 14, withdrawn andante movt. Egri copy, 2203as[28]

Beethoven, L. van, 766as[2]

___ concertos, violin, engraver's copy, 1787as[26]

___ quartets, string, opp. 18, 59, and 74, sketches, 1812as[26]

___ sketchbook for string quartets, opp. 130 and 132, 1783as[26]

___ sketchbooks, 1975as[27]

Benati, C.A., embellishment of Bononcini *Duetti da camera*, 1549as[25]

Benoît, P., 2119as[27]

Bertali, A., *Sequuntur regulae compositionis...*, 4205as[63]

Boxberg, C.L., cantata cycle, 1689as[25]

rhythm and meter, accent, 4040as[61], 4451as[69]
role in pedagogy, 4442as[69]
Romania, cîntec bătrînesc, 2776as[34]
___ spring festival songs, 2778as[34]
___ traditional songs, influenced by traditional flutes, 3029as[34]
___ 16th-18th c., 4431as[69]
Russian Orthodox chant, kondakarion repertoire, relation to Byzantine asmatikon tradition, 1140as[23]
Scandinavia, Gregorian chant, dialects, 878as[20]
___ Sámi people, use of pentatonic scale, 2924as[34]
Schoenberg, A., Kol nidre, op. 39, 4421as[69]
Schumann, R., relation to poetry, 2097as[27]
semiotics, 5927as[88]
Serbia, spring festival rituals, 2995as[34]
___ Srem, World War II songs, 2892as[34]
___ Timok river region, compared with central Serbia, 2959as[34]
___ Užice region, 2996as[34]
Sibelius, J., influenced by Finnish traditional music, 2114as[27]
siciliano, used by Händel and Bach, 4295as[64]
Slavic states, southern, rhythm and meter, 4002as[61]
___ ___ traditional songs, relation to texts, 2899as[34]
Slavonic chant, melodic construction, 4463as[69]
Slovakia, German-speaking people, traditional songs, 2870as[34]
___ oral tradition, early 18th-c. sources, 2800as[34]
___ Spiš, German-speaking people, traditional songs, 3025as[34]
Slovenia, ballad, rhythmic typology, 3105as[34]
___ Gorenjska, rhythm and meter, 2861as[34]
___ traditional songs, most game, 5010as[76]
___ ___ relation to texts, 3103as[34]
song, rhythmic aspects, relation to dance melody, 4035as[61]
Spain, Madrid, dramatic arts, relation to traditional music, 18th c., 5253as[77]
___ villancicos, 16th c., 1409as[24]
structure, relation to scale, 4081as[62]
Switzerland, Genève, Geneva Psalter, 1562, 1400as[24]
Telemann, G.P., vocal music, unusual intervals, 4167as[63]
traditional music, analysis, computer applications, 5928as[88]
___ cataloguing, 792as[5]
___ classification, 4468as[69], 4470as[69]
___ dating, 4464as[69]
___ relation to overtone series, 3946as[60]
___ research methodology, 4444as[69]
___ stability, 4419as[69], 4453as[69]
traditional songs, relation to texts, 3035as[34]
trope, Kyrie, 4010as[61]
UK, traditional music, modality, 3141as[35]
___ traditional songs, kinship and variation, 4416as[69]
Ukraine, dumy, 2904as[34]
___ traditional music, 4441as[69]
USA, Southwest, Hopi people, influenced by missionaries, 3164as[35]
___ traditional music, modality, 3141as[35]
___ traditional songs, kinship and variation, 4416as[69]
Utendal, A., 4361as[66]
Venezuela, black people, relation to rhythm, 3215as[36]
Verdi, G., from 1850s, 5244as[77]
Western music, primacy over harmony, 3948as[60]

memoirs, see **anecdotes, reminiscences, etc.; autobiographies, diaries, etc.; correspondence**
memory, see **psychology**
MÉNARD, René, 6122as[92]
MENCHACA, Angel, 3853as[55]
Menčík, Ferdinand
collections, W.A. Mozart autograph fragments, 1842as[26]

MENDEL, Arthur, 266bs, *267rs[16], 1706as[25], 3732as[52], 3911as[58], 5539as[81]
MENDELSSOHN, Arnold, 6438as[94]
Mendelssohn, Felix, see **Mendelssohn-Bartholdy, Felix**
Mendelssohn-Bartholdy, Felix
life, depicted in Sheppard Charles Auchester, 2033as[27]
___ relation to Spontini, 1970as[27]
___ role in Händel revival, 2113as[27]
tributes, 2032as[27]
works, influenced by Händel, 2113as[27]
___ religious music, 2125as[27]
___ style, relation to Classic, 1896as[26]
Mendes, Manuel
life, Évora, 4143as[63]
MENDOZA, Vicente Teódulo, 3208as[36], 3209as[36]
MENÉNDEZ GARCÍA Y BELTRÁN, Margarita, 4911as[74], 4912as[74]
Mengelberg, Willem
life, relation to Mahler, 2286as[29]
MENGEWEIN, Carl, 4599as[70]
MENNES, François, 621as[1]
MENON, Narayana, 846as[19], 2668as[33], 2669as[33], 5207as[77]
MENSAH, Atta Annan, 2561as[32]
mensural notation, see **notation and paleography**
mental illness, see **psychology; therapy**
MENUHIN, Yehudi, 489bs, 845as[19], 846as[19], 847as[19], 2533as[31]
Menuhin, Yehudi
sound recordings, Bach solo violin music, 3733as[52]
MENZERATH, Paul, 169bs
MERCER, Derwent M.A., 3428as[42], 3429as[42]
MERCIER, J., 5840as[86]
MERCIER, Paul, 2548as[32]
Merian, Matthäus
writings, on Thirty Years' War, 1599as[25]
MERIAN, Wilhelm, 109rs[16], 181rs[16], 1381as[24], 1382as[24]
MERINO, Felipe, 4883as[73]
Merleau-Ponty, Maurice
writings, on Mallarmé and Cézanne, 5602as[81]
MERLIER, Melpo, 622as[1], 2956as[34]
MERRIAM, Alan P., 2562as[32], 3168as[35]
MERRITT, A. Tillman, 368bs, 4198as[63]
Mersenne, Marin
correspondence, from Trichet, 1698as[25]
writings, consonance and dissonance, 4135as[63]
___ vers mesuré, 3719as[51]
MERSMANN, Hans, 416bs, 1622as[25], 1812as[26], 2039as[27], 2357as[29], 2957as[34], 4232as[64], 4269as[64], 4447as[69], 5460as[81], 5540as[81], 5541as[81], 5547as[81]
MERTENS, H., 5775as[85]
MERTIN, Josef, 3430as[42], 3679as[50]
Merula, Tarquinio
works, Secondo libro delle canzoni da suonare..., dedications, 1425as[24]
Merulo, Claudio
bibliographies, 1286as[24]
works, canzoni strumentali, dedications, 1425as[24]
___ double choruses, attribution, 1339as[24]
MESQUITA, Raoul Ferraz de, 3952as[60]
MESSERSCHMID, Felix, 4600as[70], 4740as[71], 4741as[71]
Messiaen, Olivier
aesthetics, influenced by Debussy, 2168as[28]
works, rhythmic structure, 4007as[61]
___ use in Roman Catholic liturgy, 2200as[28]
Metastasio, Pietro
writings, libretto for Sarri Didone abbandonata, 5172as[77]

___ librettos, influence on Goldoni comedies, 5133as[77]
___ ___ influence on opera seria, 5092as[77]
meter, see **rhythm and meter**
Methodius, Saint
life, development of Glagolitic liturgy, 6420as[93]
___ liturgical practice, source evidence, 6274as[93]
___ relation to Old Bulgarian music, 1138as[23]
writings, Glagolitic liturgy, influenced by liturgy of St. Peter, 6131as[92]
___ kanōn to St. Demetrius of Thessaloníkī, attribution, 6123as[92]
metronome, see also **tempo**
France, history and development, 3999as[61]
___ regularization, 3976as[61]
markings, regularization, 3993as[61]
Métru, Nicolas
works, fantaisies, 4265as[64]
METZLER, Fritz, 4015as[61]
MEUGÉ, Joseph, 3431as[42]
Mexico, see also **Latin America**
Aztec people, traditional music, viewed by Fétis, 2416as[30]
history of music, 20th c., microtonal music, 4146as[63]
Indians, traditional music, pre-Hispanic elements, 3225as[36]
mass media, radio, broadcasting of traditional music, 3185as[36]
Mazatec people, culture, mushroom ceremony, 3217as[36]
Nayarít, Cora people, culture, festivals, 3171as[35]
Tantoyuca, Huastec people, dance, 5066as[76]
traditional music, 16th-20th c., 3208as[36]
MEYENN, Hans-Werner von, 2409as[29]
MEYER, 110rs[16]
Meyer, André
collections, 763as[2]
___ 16th- and 17th-c. Italian sources, 710as[2]
MEYER, Ernst Hermann, 298bs, 848as[19], 852as[19], 1367as[24], 1383as[24], 1623as[25], 4199as[63], 4200as[63], 4370as[66], 5898as[87]
Meyer, Ernst Hermann
works, Mansfelder Oratorium, influenced by Händel, 2191as[28]
MEYER, Erwin, 5841as[86]
Meyer, Gregor
life, 1381as[24]
MEYER, Jürgen, 3432as[42], 3532as[43], 3591as[44]
MEYER, Kathi, 4448as[69], 4601as[70]
MEYER, Leonard B., 5628as[81], 5905as[87]
Meyer, Leonard B.
writings, musical meaning, 5607as[81]
Meyer, Wilhelm
writings, motet origins, 4255as[64]
MEYER-BAER, Kathi, 5979as[89]
Meyerbeer, Giacomo
aesthetics, grand opera, 5101as[77]
performance practice, operas, 3294as[41]
MEYER-EPPLER, Werner, 4407as[68], 5842as[86]
MEYERS, Hubert, 3433as[42]
MEYERSON, Ignace, 250bs
MEYLAN, Pierre, 623as[1], 624as[1]
MEYLAN, Raymond, 4449as[69]
MEYROVICZ, 5776as[85]
Miaskovsky, Nikolai, see **Mjaskovskij, Nikolaj**
MIAZGA, Tadeusz, 5332as[78]
MICHAELS, Jost, 2358as[29]
MICHAĪLĪDĪS, Sólōn, 2449as[30], 2958as[34], 5032as[76]
Michałowski, Piotr
correspondence, from Chopin, 2098as[27]
MICHEL, André Paul Charles, 94bs
MICHEL, Eugen, 5843as[86]
MICHEL, Paul, 2040as[27]

Iran, dastgāh, influence on Jewish liturgical music, 6054as[91]

Israel, neotraditional songs, 2678as[33]

Italy, traditional music, influence on Monteverdi *Il combattimento di Tancredi e Clorinda*, 1511as[25], 1512as[25]

Japan, noh, 5180as[77]

Jewish music, nusah, influenced by cantillation, 6051as[91]

___ 10th-14th c., 1215as[23]

Latvia, Ligotnes, 2874as[34]

Macedonia, Skopje, funeral laments, 2844as[34]

Mauritania, traditional music, relation to Arab music, 2564as[32]

Mediterranean region, eastern, Christian chant traditions, 958as[21]

Minnesang, Middle Ages, relation to motif, 4413as[69]

Mozart, W.A., *Die Entführung aus dem Serail*, Act I, Janissary chorus, 4056as[62]

polymodality, 4069as[62]

relation to melodic motives, 4113as[62]

relation to melody, 4072as[62]

relation to ornamentation, 841as[19]

Renaissance, open analysis, 3957as[60]

Romania, 16th-18th c., 4431as[69]

Russia, traditional music, relation to znamennyj chant, 4304as[65]

___ znamennyj chant, 1063as[23]

Russian Orthodox chant, 1001as[21]

Slavic states, southern, Christian religious music, influenced by traditional music, 6033as[90]

___ ___ traditional music, 4134as[62], 4476as[69]

Spain, Andalucía, 2834as[34]

___ Castilla, traditional songs, 2761as[34]

___ Szymanowski, K., influenced by traditional music, 2147as[28]

___ *Król Roger*, 4327as[66]

traditional music, 4050as[62]

___ pedagogy, 4800as[71], 4801as[71]

UK, traditional music, 3141as[35]

USA, Louisiana, French-speaking black people, cantiques, 3140as[35]

___ traditional music, 3141as[35]

Western chant, Christian, antiquity, 4117as[62]

___ ___ history and development, 4127as[62]

___ Christian and Jewish traditions, 6022as[90]

20th-c. music, relation to temperament and tuning, 4095as[62]

Modena, Iulio da, *see* **Segni, Julio (Iulio da Modena)**

modern dance, *see* **choreographers**; **dance** head-words; **movement and gesture**

modernism, *see also* **aesthetics**; **avant-garde**; **twentieth-century music**
France, relation to opera, 5201as[77]
Italy, opera, 5233as[77]
Szymanowski, K., 2146as[28]

modes, *see* **intervals**; **modality**; **scales**

MOE, Lawrence H., 3909as[58]

MOEURDORJE, 2670as[33]

Mognossa, Giovanni Francesco
works, litanies, 1669as[25]

MOHR, Ernst, 289bs

MOHR, Wilhelm, 4270as[64], 4285as[64], 5334as[78]

MOISSL, Franz, 6309as[93]

Mokranjac, Stevan
works, *Rukoveti*, nos. 10 and 15, use of Macedonian melodies, 2049as[27]

MOKRÝ, Ladislav, 477bs, 1149as[23], 5899as[87], 6123as[92], 6130as[92]

Moldavia, *see* **Moldova**

MOLDENHAUER, Hans, 1815as[26]

Moldova
musical life, Liszt concert tour, 1846-47, 1983as[27]

MOLES, Abraham, 3587as[44]

MOLES, André, 5681as[82], 5844as[86]

Molinier, Étienne, *see* **Moulinié, Étienne**

Molitor, Gregor
life, role in restoration of Ottobeuren organs, 3375as[42]

MOLL, Adolf, 4603as[70]

MOLL ROQUETA, Jaime, 629as[1], 630as[1], 631as[1], 632as[1], 778as[4]

MOLLAT DU JOURDIN, Guy, 1816as[26]

MOLNÁR, Antal, 1817as[26], 2045as[27], 2046as[27]

Momigny, Jérôme-Joseph de
writings, *Cours complet d'harmonie et de composition*, analyses of Haydn and Mozart works, 1833as[26]
___ on Beethoven, 2075as[27]

MOMPELLIO, Federico, 1625as[25]

Monachus, Guilielmus, *see* **Guilielmus Monachus**

monasteries, *see* **religious institutions**; **religious orders**

MONDOLFI, Anna, 5973as[89]

MONDOLFO, Anita, 777bm[4]

Mondonville, Jean-Joseph Cassanéa de
collections, cathedral choir school, Aix-en-Provence, 748as[2]

MONETA CAGLIO, Ernesto, 1150as[23]

MONFLIER, Georges, 77bs

Mongolia
traditional music, 2670as[33]

Moniuszko, Stanisław
works, influences, 2086as[27]
___ operas, influenced by Wagner, 5113as[77]
___ songs, text setting, 1995as[27]

MONK, Egon, 5211as[77]

monochord, *see* **instruments — string (zither family)**

monody, *see also* **song** headwords
Caccini, G., 1589-1614, 1546as[25]
Europe, ca. 1600, 1302as[24]
Italy, Firenze, Camerata monodic style, anticipated by air de cour, 1272as[24]
___ late 16th c., 1404as[24]
Poland, 11th-12th c., 1089as[23]
relation to Renaissance polyphony, 1509as[25]

monophony, *see also* **texture**
Middle Ages, lied, use of melodic formulas, 4474as[69]
___ notation, 1056as[23]
___ rhythm and meter, 3886as[58]
___ thematic cataloguing, 797as[5]
___ vocal music, rhythmic analysis, 3978as[61]
Poland, 9th-15th c., 1300as[24]
rhythm, 15th c., 3872as[55]
Spain, rhythm and meter, transcription, 3802as[55]

MONSOUR, Sally, 4742as[71], 4743as[71]

Montaigne, Michel Eyquem de
writings, relation to ethnomusicology, 865as[20]

MONTANI, Pietro, 5981as[89], 5982as[89]

Monte, Filippo di, *see* **Monte, Philippe de**

Monte, Philippe de
life, 1293as[24]
___ birth, 1375as[24]
___ relation to Mechelen, 1268as[24]

Montéclair, Michel Pignolet de
works, *O sacrum convivium* and *Properate huc populi*, 1497as[25]

Montefeltro, Federico, *see* **Federico da Montefeltro, Duke of Urbino**

Montenegrin music (outside Montenegro)
Croatia, Konavle, wedding ceremonies, 2745as[34]

Montenegro, *see* **Serbia and Montenegro**

MONTEROSSO, Raffaello, 1151as[23], 3898as[58], 5335as[78]

Monteverdi, Claudio
exhibitions, Italy, Firenze, 1937, 777bm[4]
life, 1667as[25]
performance practice, dramatic works, 3771as[52]

___ ___ ornamentation, 3772as[52]

___ instrumentation and orchestration, 3755as[52]

___ *Mercurio e Marte*, staging, 5175as[77]

performances, madrigals, in Zuoz, 1499as[25]

works, *Il combattimento di Tancredi e Clorinda*, influenced by traditional music, 1511as[25], 1512as[25]

___ compared with Tollius, 1638as[25]

___ dissonance, relation to basso continuo, 1590as[25]

___ editing, 975as[21]

___ form, modal design, 4228as[63]

___ *L'incoronazione di Poppea*, concept of genre, 5169as[77]

___ ___ relation to passacaglia, 4277as[64]

___ influence on Schütz, 1645as[25]

___ influenced by Spain, 1276as[24]

___ instrumental music, relation to toccata, 4237as[64]

___ madrigals, as chamber music, 1270as[24]

___ monophonic and polyphonic styles, relation to Baroque, 1509as[25]

___ operas, compared with ta'ziye drama, 5129as[77]

___ ___ prologues, 5192as[77]

___ *L'Orfeo*, ornamentation, influenced by Asia, 3724as[51]

___ seconda prattica, relation to concept of Baroque, 1489as[25]

___ *Sonata sopra Sancta Maria*, SV 206/11, compared with Gabrieli *Dulcis Iesu, patris imago*, 1540as[25]

___ style, viewed as mannerist, 1713as[25]

writings, applied to Vivaldi performance practice, 3760as[25]

Moody, Fanny
collections, Moody-Manners Opera Company materials, 750as[2]

MOORE, Gerald, 465bs, 4850as[72]

Moore, Thomas
writings, contributions to *The jovial crew* (1813), 5234as[77]

MOOS, Paul, 1626as[25], 5546as[81], 5547as[81], 5548as[81], 5549as[81], 5550as[81], 5551as[81]

Moos, Paul
writings, on style, 4373as[66]

MOOSER, Robert-Aloys, 1818as[26], 2361as[29], 5552as[81]

MORAGAS, Beda María, 5415as[80]

Morales, Cristóbal de
works, relation to Pius X *Tra le sollecitudini*, 6353as[93], 6407as[93]
___ villancicos, 5365as[78]

morals, *see* **ethics and morals**

Moravia, *see* **Czech Republic**

MORCOURT, Richard de, 1384as[24], 3902as[58]

MORETTI, Corrado, 3437as[42]

MOREUX, Serge, 2215as[28], 5779as[85]

MORILLEAU, Xavier, 6310as[93], 6311as[93]

MORIN, Edgar, 5682as[82]

MÓRIN, Germain, 5336as[78]

MORIN, Gösta, 1819as[26]

Morley, Thomas
works, madrigals, 1411as[24]
writings, *A plaine and easie introduction to practicall musick*, relation to chiavette notation, 3825as[55]

MÖRNER, Carl-Gabriel Stellan, 545as[1]

Morocco
traditional music, classification, 2558as[32]

MOROI, Makoto, 4408as[68]

Mors family
instruments, organs, 3364as[42]

MORTARI, Virgilio, 1627ac[25], 1628as[25], 4095as[62], 4744as[71], 4745as[71]

MORTENSEN, Otto, 5038as[76]

MÖSER, 2362as[29]

MOSER, Hans Joachim, 901as[20], 990as[21], 991as[21], 1385as[24], 2532as[31], 3438as[42], 4201as[63], 4376as[66], 4450as[69], 4604as[70], 4605as[70], 4920as[75], 5337as[78], 5683as[82]

Moser, Hans Joachim
    editions, *Frühmeister der deutschen Orgelkunst*, 3895as[58]
    life, research on Finck, 1336as[24]

MOSER, J., 3533as[43]

Moses ben Maimon (Maimonides)
    writings, 1215as[23]

Moslem music, *see* **Islamic studies; religion and religious music — Islam**

MOSS, Lawrence, 4858as[72]

motet
    Bordes, C., influenced by Renaissance, 1924as[27]
    Braunschweig Organ Tablature, 1433as[24]
    composition, 15th c., 1391as[24]
    Desprez, J., attribution issues, 1224as[24]
    ___ psalm settings, 1393as[24]
    ___ relation to humanism, 1392as[24]
    ___ style, 1466as[24]
    France, as funeral music, late 17th c., 1601as[25]
    ___ grands motets, relation to Italian music, 1530as[25], 1532as[25]
    ___ musicians' motets, 14th c., 1124as[23]
    history and development, relation to prosula and sequence, 3716as[51]
    ___ viewed by Meyer and Ludwig, 4255as[64]
    influence on fugue, 4427as[69]
    isorhythmic, Middle Ages, 4230as[64]
    ___ relation to performance context, 1167as[23]
    Lassus, R. de, *Musica Dei donum optimi*, 4316as[66]
    ___ viewed by Le Roy, 1242as[24]
    Low Countries, performance practice, use of positive organ, 3430as[42]
    Mikołaj z Krakowa, 1469as[24]
    Montéclair, M.P. de, 1497as[25]
    Montpellier Codex, notation, 3818as[55]
    Nivers, G. B., 1556as[25]
    Philips, P., 1340as[24]
    Senfl, L., style, 1558as[25]
    Spain, 17th c., 1651as[25]
    Tollius, J., appreciation, 1638as[25]
    typology, 16th c., 4287as[64]
    Utendal, A., 4361as[66]
    Willaert, A., editions, block printing, 5994as[89]
    15th-16th c., thematic cataloguing proposal, 1906, 791as[5]

motif, *see* **leitmotiv; motive and theme**

motion pictures, *see* **film**

motive and theme, *see also* **leitmotiv; melody**
    analysis, 18th- and 19th-c. music, 4311as[66]
    atonal music, use of primitive rows, 4335as[66]
    Bach, J.S., Charakterthemem, 4313as[66]
    ___ fugues, influenced by affections doctrine, 4429as[69]
    ___ relation to rhetoric, 1676as[25]
    Bartók, B., stage works, developing variation, 4443as[69]
    Beethoven, L. van, 4372as[66]
    ___ influenced by Mozart, 4032as[61]
    ___ rhythm, 4026as[61]
    ___ sonatas, dynamics, 4432as[69]
    ___ symphonies, 4294as[64]
    Brahms, J., concertos, violin, op. 77, 4384as[66]
    Chopin, F., late style, 4315as[66]
    ___ thematic development, 4461as[69]
    ___ variation technique, 4280as[64]
    Classic, 4396as[67]
    composition, as unifying device, 5445as[81]
    concertos, 4243as[64]
    early music, relation to form, 4293as[64]
    film music, 5205as[77]
    fugue, history and development, relation to medium, 4427as[69]
    Haydn, J., Charakterthemen, 4331as[66]

instrumental music, analysis, 4447as[69]
Janáček, L., dramaturgy, 4385as[66]
    ___ *Glagolská mše*, monothematicism, 4437as[69]
lied, Middle Ages, melodic formulas, 4474as[69]
Lupus, soggetti cavati, 1452as[24]
Minnesang, Middle Ages, relation to modality, 4413as[69]
motive, relation to organicist analysis, 3931as[60]
Mozart, W.A., overtures, K.311a, 1778as[26]
    ___ sonata form, 4259as[64]
    ___ sonatas, piano, 4370as[66]
Niedt, F.E., 3944as[60]
relation to modality, 4113as[62]
Slavic states, southern, epics, 2853as[34]
sonata form, 4241as[64]
symphony, rhythm and meter, late 18th-early 19th c., 4020as[61]
Szymanowski, K., concertos, violin, no. 1, op. 35, 4397as[67]

MOTTA, José Vianna da, 1820as[26]

MOTTA E ALBUQUERQUE, João Batista da, 6312as[93]

motto, *see* **motive and theme**

Moulaert, Raymond
    works, influenced by Debussy, 2225as[28]

Moulinié, Étienne
    works, fantaisies, 4265as[64]

Moulton, Dorothy
    life, relation to Bartók, 2129as[28]

Moulu, Pierre
    works, motet, 1420as[24]

MOURINHO, António Maria, 2964as[34]

MOUSSES, Kyriakos, 6124as[92]

Moussorgsky, Modest, *see* **Musorgskij, Modest Petrovič**

Mouton, Jean
    life, 1353as[24]
    ___ relation to Field of Cloth of Gold, 1520, 1354as[24]

Mouton, Pierre
    performances, organ, at Field of Cloth of Gold, 1520, 1354as[24]

movement and gesture, *see also* **dance — general; physiology; sports and games**
    compared with music, 5483as[81]
    Dalcroze method, 4041as[61], 4716as[71]
    ___ compared with Orff method, 4573as[70], 4574as[70]
    ___ conference, 1926, 123bs
    ___ relation to conducting and orchestral playing, 4618as[70]
    ___ use in opera singer training, 4881as[73]
    ___ viewed by Martin, 4592as[70], 4593as[70]
    depicted in visual and plastic arts, relation to rhythm and meter, 5376as[79]
    eurythmics, blind children, 4727as[71]
    ___ children, relation to language, 4782as[71]
    ___ pedagogy, role in composition pedagogy, 4874as[73]
    ___ relation to mathematics, 4678as[71]
    ___ role in composition pedagogy, 4873as[73]
    ___ role in pedagogy, 4736as[71]
    ___ use in work, 5913as[87]
    film, rhythm, 5194as[77]
    handwriting, relation to creativity, 5385as[79]
    Italy, use of Dalcroze method, 4527as[70], 4692as[71]
    Mozart, W.A., relation to tempo, 3769as[52]
    relation to music, 5650as[82]
    relation to rhythm, 3996as[61]
    relation to therapy, 5738as[83]
    relation to vocal training, 5167as[77]
    relation to 20th-c. music, 5462as[81]

Moyzes, Alexander
    works, 947as[21]

Moyzes, Mikuláš
    works, 947as[21]

Mozambique
    Chopi people, traditional music, timbila music, 2593as[32]

Mozarabic chant, *see* **chant — Christian (Western)**

Mozart, Franz Xaver Wolfgang
    collections, W.A. Mozart autograph fragments, 1842as[26]

Mozart, Leopold
    correspondence, views on London sojourn, 1764-65, 1881as[26]
    life, relation to Lombardia orchestras, 1724as[26]

Mozart, Wolfgang Amadeus
    aesthetics, 5554as[81]
    ___ Classic vs. Romantic, 4387as[66]
    ___ humanism, 934as[20]
    ___ influence on Stravinsky *The rake's progress*, 2148as[28]
    catalogues, 920as[20]
    correspondence, as criticism, 1771as[26]
    editions, 920as[20]
    ___ *Gesamtausgabe*, Austrian involvement, 3913as[58]
    ___ Imprimerie Lithographique, 1802-06, 5975as[89]
    ___ operas, problem of translation, 5135as[77]
    exhibitions, England, London, British Lib., 1956, 730as[2]
    festivals and conferences, Austria, Salzburg, 1931, 193bs
    ___ Wien, 1956, 365bs
    ___ Czech Republic, Praha, 1956, 360bs
    ___ France, Paris, 1956, 358bs
    iconography, Tilgner bust, 1780as[26]
    life, genealogy, 1742as[26]
    ___ Genève, 1879as[26]
    ___ Lombardia, 1724as[26]
    ___ Mainz, 1767as[26]
    ___ maternal relatives, 1851as[26]
    ___ Moravia, 1008as[21]
    ___ 1767-68, 1866as[26]
    ___ Paris, 1816as[26]
    ___ 1763-64, 1732as[26]
    ___ psychology, compared with Haydn, 1817as[26]
    ___ rate of compositional output, 1758as[26]
    ___ relation to Clementi, 1721as[26]
    ___ relation to Dittersdorf, 4378as[66]
    ___ relation to Dušek, 1874as[26]
    ___ relation to Enlightenment, 1793as[26]
    ___ relation to Vaňhal, 1805as[26]
    ___ state of research, 1925-26, 917as[20]
    ___ as subject in literature, 5290as[78]
    ___ 1761-65, 1888as[26]
    manuscripts, articulation signs, 3834as[55]
    ___ at Arch. Mesta, Bratislava, 1780as[26]
    ___ autograph fragments, collected by Menčík, 1842as[26]
    ___ *Don Giovanni*, keyboard reductions, 1735as[26]
    ___ facsimiles, at Österreichische Natbibl., Wien, 722as[2]
    ___ fugue fragments, 1901as[26]
    ___ graphology, 3851as[55]
    ___ *Le nozze di Figaro*, keyboard reductions, 1735as[26]
    ___ operas, sketch studies, 928as[20]
    ___ relation to creative process, 1746as[26]
    ___ sense of space, 1897as[26]
    ___ US collections, 1784as[26]
    performance practice, operas, relation to research, 1834as[26]
    ___ piano music, 3729as[52]
    ___ vocal appoggiaturas, 3741as[52]
    ___ vocal music, 3745as[52]
    performances, France, Paris, 1793-1810, 1801as[26]
    ___ Germany, North, 1749as[26]
    ___ Greece, 19th-20th c., 1999as[27]
    ___ *Idomeneo, re di Creta*, by Wiener Oper, 1931, 3775as[52]
    ___ ___ Germany, 1917-28, 3757as[52]
    ___ operas, Scandinavia, 986as[21]

N

Navarro, Juan
   works, 5365as[78]
NAZOR, Ante, 2972as[34], 2973as[34], 5338as[78]
Near East, *see* **Middle East**
NEDELJKOVIĆ, Dušan, 419bs, 446bs, 2974as[34], 3040as[34]
Nederland, *see* **Netherlands**
NE'EMAN, Yehŵŝu'a Leyyb, 3856as[55], 4749as[71], 4885as[73], 6081as[91], 6082as[91], 6083as[91], 6084as[91], 6085as[91]
Ne'eman, Yehŵŝu'a Leyyb
   transcriptions, 2434as[30]
NEF, Karl, 776as[4], 905as[20], 1632as[25], 1824as[26], 3264as[40], 3661as[47], 4274as[64], 5386as[79]
NEF, Walter, 3592as[44]
NEF-LAVATER, L., 5339as[78]
Nehrlich, Christian Gottfried
   life, voice teaching, 3319as[41]
NEIGHBOUR, Oliver Wray, 593as[1]
Nejedlý, Vít
   works, mass song, 3064as[34]
NEJEDLÝ, Zdeněk, 2452as[30], 4607as[70]
Nejedlý, Zdeněk
   writings, *Dějiny husitského zpěvu* (History of Hussite song), 1349as[24]
Němeček, František Xaver, *see* **Niemetschek, Franz Xaver**
NĚMEČEK, Jan, 1825as[26]
Němeček, Jan Jakub
   manuscripts, Czech traditional songs, 1807as[26]
Nenov, Dimităr
   works, influenced by Bulgarian traditional rhythm, 4005as[61]
neoclassicism, *see also* **aesthetics**; **twentieth-century music**
   compared with serialism, 4318as[66]
   Debussy, C., 5514as[81]
   France, chamber music, late 19th-early 20th c., 2024as[27]
neotraditional music, *see* **performers — traditional and neotraditional music; performing groups — traditional and neotraditional music; popular music** headwords
Nepal
   dance, 4934as[76]
   traditional music, 2605as[33]
Neri, Filippo, Saint
   life, influence on lauda history and development, 1281as[24]
   ___ relation to oratorio, 1671as[25]
   ___ relation to Palestrina, 1464as[24]
NERICI, Luigi, 10bs
Nerval, Gérard de, *see* **Labrunie, Gérard (Gérard de Nerval)**
NEST'EV, Izrail' Vladimirovič, 389bs, 2216as[28]
NESTLER, Gerhard, 993as[21], 2217as[28], 4017as[61], 5554as[81]
Netherlands, *see also* **Low Countries**
   dramatic arts, Easter plays, 1184as[23]
   history of music, composition, mid-20th c., 2186as[28]
   ___ influenced by Debussy, 2225as[28]
   ___ influenced by England, 17th c., 1523as[25]
   ___ influenced by France, 20th c., 2157as[28]
   ___ MSS, at Monasterio de S. María, Montserrat, 747as[2]
   ___ polyphonic songs, 15th-16th c., 1366as[24]
   ___ polyphony, influence on Philips, 1340as[24]
   ___ influence on Spanish villancico, 16th c., 1409as[24]
   ___ relation to Diepenbrock, 2071as[27]
   ___ represented in *Allgemeine musikalische Zeitung*, 1798-1848, 1803as[26]
   ___ songbooks, 15th c., 4455as[69]
   instruments, chamber organ, 1750-1870, 3346as[42]

   librarianship, dramatic arts, 695as[1]
   musical life, 4925as[75]
   ___ Donemus Foundation, 5972as[89]
   ___ Latin schools, 16th c., 1387as[24]
   ___ reception of Janáček, 2320as[29]
   ___ relation to Anna of Cologne songbook, 1424as[24]
   ___ relation to Europe, 990as[21]
   ___ relation to Germany, 17th c., 1547as[25]
   ___ 20th c., 727as[2]
   Netherlands Antilles, Curaçao, musical life, 1948, 2370as[29]
   pedagogy, school singing, 4802as[71]
   ___ teacher training, 4819as[72], 4820as[72]
   religious music, parody Masses, 16th c., 1365as[24]
   's-Hertogenbosch, musical life, Illustre Lieve Vrouwe Broederschap, 1330-1600, 1434as[24]
   's-Hertogenbosch, instruments, organs, mid-16th c., compared with organs of ca. 1500, 3400as[42]
   traditional music, songs, 2985as[34]
NETTL, Bruno, 840as[19], 2453as[30], 2454as[30], 2534as[31], 3954as[60]
NETTL, Paul, 636as[1], 1633as[25], 1634as[25], 1635as[25], 1826as[26], 5212as[77]
NEUBAUER, Henrik, 5041as[76]
Neue Einfachheit, *see* **twentieth-century music**
Neue Sachlichkeit, *see* **aesthetics; twentieth-century music**
Neuhaus, Henryk
   writings, on Szymanowski, 2218as[28]
NEUKIRCH, Melchior (Neofanius), 1467as[24]
NEUMANN, Alfred, 2364as[29]
NEUMANN, Friedrich, 1763as[26], 3955as[60], 4204as[63]
NEUMANN, Hans-Joachim, 3671as[48]
NEUMANN, Paul, 6320as[93]
NEUMANN, Václav, 2365as[29]
neumatic notation, *see* **notation and paleography**
NEUPERT, Hanns, 3262as[40], 3534as[43], 3535as[43]
NEURATH, Herbert, 4275as[64]
New Zealand, *see also* **Oceania**
   Maori people, musical life, song transmission, 3228as[37]
NEWLIN, Dika, 2366as[29]
Newman, Alfred
   works, film music, 5095as[77]
   ___ for Wellman *Yellow sky*, 5190as[77]
NEWMAN, Joel, 3911as[58]
NEWMAN, Sidney, 1827as[26]
NEWMAN, William S., 4276as[64], 4369as[66]
newspapers, *see* **periodicals**
NGUYỄN, Xuân Khoát, 3593as[44]
NICEWONGER, C.R., 5387as[79]
NICEWONGER, Harriet, 5387as[79]
NICKSON, A.F.B., 5846as[86], 5847as[86]
NICOL, Karl Ludwig, 637as[1]
Nicolai, Otto
   aesthetics, literature and music, 1905as[27]
Nicolau i Parera, Antoni
   works, choral music, 2043as[27]
Nicolaus Cracoviensis, *see* **Mikołaj z Krakowa**
NIEDECKEN-GEBHARD, Hanns, 5213as[77]
Niedt, Friedrich Erhard
   writings, instructional methods, 1493as[25]
   ___ *Musikalischer Handleitung* II, continuo composition, 3944as[60]
   ___ on organ performance practice, 3424as[42]
Niehoff, Hendrik
   instruments, organs, 3364as[42]
Niehoff family
   instruments, organs, 3400as[42]
NIELSEN, A. Kjerbye, 448bs, 4097as[62]

Nielsen, Carl
   works, 944as[21]
NIEMAND, Szymon, 5214as[77]
Niemann, Walter
   manuscripts, in Bisschopinck collection (private), 715as[2]
   works, influenced by Debussy, 2257as[28]
Niemetschek, Franz Xaver
   life, relation to Mozart, 1807as[26]
NIEMÖLLER, Klaus Wolfgang, 1386as[24], 1387as[24]
NIESTIEV, Izrael, 2218as[28]
Nietzsche, Friedrich Wilhelm
   life, relation to Wagner, 2121as[27]
   writings, viewed by Szymanowski, 2183as[28]
NIEVERGELT, Edwin, 6441as[94]
Niewiadomski, Stanisław
   writings, on Szymanowski, 2259as[28]
Niger
   Aïr region, Tuareg people, traditional music, ornamentation, 2565as[32]
   Bororro people, traditional music, rhythmic patterns, 3988as[61]
Nihon, *see* **Japan**
NIKIPROWETZKY, Tolia, 2563as[32], 2564as[32], 2565as[32]
NIKLAUS, Hans, 6321as[93]
NIKOLIC, Milena, 638as[1]
NIKOLIĆ, Vidosava, 2975as[34], 3040as[34]
NIKOLOVSKI, Vlastimir, 2049as[27], 2219as[28]
Nikon, Patriarch of Moscow and All Russia
   life, church music reforms, relation to melodic psalmody, 1555as[25]
Nippon, *see* **Japan**
Nissen, Georg Nikolaus von
   writings, *Biographie W.A. Mozarts...*, 1826as[26]
Nivers, Guillaume Gabriel
   works, solo motets, 1556as[25]
Njegoš, Petar II Petrović (Petar II, Prince-Bishop of Montenegro)
   life, relation to gusle playing, 5368as[78]
   ___ relation to Karadžić, 2960as[34]
   writings, *Gorski vijenac*, portrayal of kolo dancers, 5331as[78]
   ___ *Gorski vijenac* (The mountain wreath), use of Montenegrin folklore, 5308as[78]
   ___ poems, instrument references, 5318as[78]
   ___ verse dramas, portrayal of Montenegrin dance, 5321as[78]
NKETIA, Joseph Hanson Kwabena, 2455as[30], 2566as[32], 2567as[32], 2568as[32], 2569as[32], 2570as[32], 2571as[32], 2572as[32]
nō (=noh), *see* **dramatic arts; Japan**
NOACK, Friedrich, 906as[20], 1636as[25], 1637as[25], 3857as[55]
NOACK, Hermann, 177bs
NOBLE, Jeremy, 1388as[24], 1510as[25]
NOCETI, J., 5215as[77]
nocturne
   Chopin, F., compared with Field, 4324as[66]
   Field, J., compared with Chopin, 4324as[66]
noël, *see* **carol; Christmas music**
noh, *see* **dramatic arts; Japan**
Nohl, Hermann
   writings, composer personality types, 4239as[64]
Nohl, Ludwig
   editions, Beethoven correspondence, 3926as[58]
noise
   film music, use of recorded sound, ca. 1937, 5193as[77]
   speech, relation to singing, 3254as[40]
NOLL, Günther, 4608as[70]
NOMURA, Francesco Yosio, 2367as[29], 5555as[81], 6020as[90], 6322as[93]
NOMURA, K., 2368as[29]

Portugal, M.A., performances, Austria, Wien, 1794-99, 1820as[26]

Rameau, J.-P., compared with Beethoven, 1809as[26]

Rejcha, A., influenced by Mozart, 1865as[26]

Šostakovič, D., 5176as[77]

Spontini, G., 2062as[27]

___ influenced by German opera, 2111as[27]

Strauss, R., 5147as[77]

Stravinsky, I., 5209as[77]

___ aesthetics, 5527as[81]

Verdi, G., 5236as[77]

___ aesthetics, 5527as[81]

Vivaldi, A., 1628as[25]

Wagner, R., Gesamtkunstwerk concept, 5241as[77]

___ scenography, 5096as[77]

___ staging, 5091as[77]

opera — by place, *see also* **aria; bel canto; costumes; dance — ballet; directors, producers, etc.; dramatic arts; dramaturgy; intermezzo (vocal); libretto** headwords; **masque; melodrama; operetta;** other **opera** headwords; **pastorale; performance venues; performers** headwords; **performing organizations; recitative; scenography**

Austria, Wien, use of canons, ca. 1800, 1772as[26]

Belgium, Liège, 18th c., 1600as[25]

Brazil, Rio de Janeiro, Imperial Academia de Música e Ópera Nac., Portuguese-language productions, 1857-63, 1907as[27]

Czech Republic, Brno, role of Janáček as critic, 1884-88, 5622as[81]

___ Praha, activities of Kašlík, 5179as[77]

England, ballad opera, *The jovial crew* (1731), performance history, 5234as[77]

___ 1930s, 5108as[77]

Europe, Central, national opera, 19th c., 1955as[27], 2109as[27]

___ Eastern, national opera, 19th c., 1955as[27], 2109as[27]

___ influenced by Théâtre de la Foire, 1712-38, 1501as[25]

___ Western, influence on Central and Eastern European national opera, 19th c., 2109as[27]

France, influenced by pastorale, 17th c., 1596as[25]

___ lyric drama, 5122as[77]

___ Paris, influence on Mozart, 1732as[26]

___ ___ performances of Mozart, 3766as[52]

___ ___ performances of Mozart, 1793-1810, 1801as[26]

___ 1860-1911, 2035as[27]

___ 1930s, 5201as[77]

Germany, aesthetics, 19th c., 1905as[27]

___ Bayern, statistical data, 1871-1933, 913as[20]

___ Bayreuth, Bayreuth Festspiele, aesthetics, 1951-64, 5184as[77]

___ Darmstadt, 1673-1719, 1631as[25]

___ Hamburg, relation to Telemann, 1715as[25]

___ perception of dialogue, 5183as[77]

___ revivals, ca. 1937, 5156as[77]

___ Württemberg, French influence, 5094as[77]

___ 1930s, 5147as[77]

___ ca. 1938, 5223as[77]

Hungary, 17th-18th c., 1492as[25]

Italy, basso continuo, performance practice, 3777as[52]

___ government support, 5159as[77]

___ history and development, early 18th c., 1528as[25]

___ influence on Mozart, 1878as[26]

___ influenced by Debussy, 2210as[28]

___ influenced by economics, ca. 1921, 5155as[77]

___ influenced by Goldoni librettos, 5136as[77]

___ influenced by traditional music, early 18th c., 1691as[25]

___ modernism, 5233as[77]

___ Napoli, concept of Neapolitan school, 1529as[25]

___ ___ 18th c., 1580as[25], 1673as[25]

___ ___ ca. 1730, 5172as[77]

___ opera houses, relation to copyright, 5961as[89]

___ performance practice, 3294as[41]

___ performances of Mozart, 982as[21]

___ publishing and printing, 17th-18th c., 5973as[89]

___ radio broadcasts, reception, ca. 1937, 2380as[29]

___ Roma, repertoire and cast, 1823-49, 5226as[77]

___ 16th c., reception, ca. 1937, 5615as[81]

Poland, Warszawa, historical operas, early 19th c., 5099as[77]

___ late 17th-early 19th, influence on Chopin, 2059as[27]

___ 18th c., 1861as[26]

Russia, 18th c., 1792as[26]

Scandinavia, performances of Mozart, 986as[21]

Slavic states, southern, 20th c., 5165as[77]

Spain, 17th c., 5097as[77]

Sweden, performances of Mozart, 18th-19th c., 1819as[26]

USA, composer-audience relations, 20th c., 5112as[77]

___ pedagogy, relation to professional opportunities, ca. 1966, 2364as[29]

___ 1790s, 1885as[26]

___ 1930s, 5242as[77]

opéra — by place

France, Paris, Comédie-Italienne, musical repertoire, ca. 1700, 1565as[25]

opera — general, *see also* **aria; bel canto; burlesque (17th-19th c.);** costumes; **directors, producers, etc.; dramatic arts; dramaturgy; intermezzo (vocal); libretto** headwords; **masque; melodrama; operetta;** other **opera** headwords; **pastorale; performers** headwords; **recitative; scenography**

aesthetics, viewed by Janáček, to 1888, 5220as[77]

___ words and music, history and development, 5093as[77]

ballad opera, England, exemplified by *The jovial crew*, 5234as[77]

Baroque, performance practice, 20th c., 5250as[77]

___ relation to instrumental music, 1714as[25]

bibliography, 701as[1]

broadcasts, 5258as[77], 5772as[85]

censorship, 5235as[77]

chorus, singers, training, 4636as[70]

compared with film music, 5125as[77]

conducting, 3317as[41]

directing, 5170as[77]

___ 20th c., 5165as[77], 5229as[77]

early, depiction of the supernatural, 5102as[77]

early music movement, interpretation, 5124as[77]

festivals, antiquity to 20th c., 5161as[77]

films, 5118as[77]

German, influence on Spontiti, 2111as[27]

___ text-music relation, 18th-19th c., 2965as[34]

grand opera, reception, 19th c., 5101as[77]

handbook, Riemann, H., 1893, 896as[20]

history and development, 5263as[77]

___ concept of genre, 5169as[77]

___ periodization issues, 5100as[77]

___ relation to Beethoven *Fidelio*, 5272as[77]

___ relation to oratorio, 4284as[64]

influenced by Asian drama, 5129as[77]

influenced by electronic music and computer music, 5185as[77]

management, administration, 5103as[77]

national characteristics, 5431as[81]

national opera, Central and Eastern Europe, 19th c., 1955as[27], 2109as[27]

opera comica, compared with opera buffa, 5132as[77]

opera seria, history and development, influenced by Metastasio, 5092as[77]

orchestral music, influence on C.P.E. Bach keyboard sonatas, 4358as[66]

performance practice, 5265as[77]

___ acoustic issues, state of research, ca. 1959, 5805as[86]

___ pre-19th c., 5269as[77]

professional training, 20th c., 4878as[73]

prologues, 17th c., 5192as[77]

reception, 17th- and 18th-c. works, ca. 1937, 5137as[77]

___ 19th-c. works, 5237as[77]

___ 20th-c. works, 2406as[29], 5191as[77]

relation to internationalism, 2352as[29]

rescue opera, Central and Eastern Europe, 19th c., 1955as[27], 2109as[27]

role in cultural exchange programs, 5110as[77]

singers, pedagogy, 4637as[70]

___ ___ acting and singing, 5167as[77]

___ ___ use of Dalcroze method, 4881as[73]

___ ___ 20th c., 3304as[41], 4894as[73]

sound recordings, early, 5763as[85]

staging, 20th c., 5144as[77], 5164as[77]

___ 20th-c. works, 5195as[77]

state of research, ca. 1906, 5238as[77]

20th c., influenced by Wagner, 5189as[77]

___ role of experimentation, 5176as[77]

opera buffa, *see* **aria; bel canto; directors, producers, etc.; dramatic arts; dramaturgy; intermezzo (vocal); libretto** headwords; **musical revue, cabaret, etc.; musical theater — popular; opera** headwords; **operetta; performers** headwords; **recitative**

opéra comique, *see* **aria; bel canto; directors, producers, etc.; dramatic arts; dramaturgy; libretto** headwords; **musical revue, cabaret, etc.; musical theater — popular; opera** headwords; **operetta; performers** headwords; **recitative**

opera houses, *see* **architecture; performance venues**

opera seria, *see* **aria; bel canto; costumes; directors, producers, etc.; dramatic arts; dramaturgy; intermezzo (vocal); libretto** headwords; **masque; opera** headwords; **performers** headwords; **recitative; scenography**

operetta, *see also* **aria; directors, producers, etc.; dramaturgy; musical theater — popular; opera** headwords; **performers** headwords; **recitative**

films, 5118as[77]

Opieński, Henryk

editions, Chopin correspondence, critique, 5356as[78]

OPIEŃSKI, Henryk, 2058as[27], 2059as[27], 3912as[58]

Opitiis, Benedictus de

life, presence at Field of Cloth of Gold, 1520, 1226as[24]

___ state of research, 1439as[24]

works, *Sub tuum presidium* and *Summae laudis o Maria*, 1255as[24]

oral tradition, *see also* **folklore**

Bosnia and Herzegovina, *Igrali se vrani konji*, melody types, 4462as[69]

Byzantine chant, influence on melodic construction, 4465as[69]

Canada, French-speaking people, *Le roi Eugène*, 3137as[35]

compared with written transmission, 2486as[30], 4774as[71]

concept of authenticity, 2520as[31], 2539as[31]

dance, stability and change, 4996as[76]

definitions, 2517as[31]

Egypt, Coptic Christian people, chant, accuracy of transmission, 6122as[92]

Europe, melodies, 4417as[69]

___ songs, Bulgarian vs. Spanish versions, 2773as[34]

France, songs, 2851as[34]

Germany, songs, 2851as[34], 2957as[34]

Ghana, 2566as[32]

Italy, *La finta monacella*, 2711as[34], 2751as[34]

Mediterranean region, transition to written tradition, 1021as[21]

Grob, T., 3782as[53]
Lange, A.W., 3745as[52]
Nourrit, A., 3294as[41]
Pilarczyk, H., 5224as[77]
Poland, Wagner opera performances, 5214as[77]
Roman Catholic Church, careers, 6283as[93]
Siboni, G., 986as[21]
Spain, Aragón, 14th c., 1054as[23]
___ falsettists and castratos, 16th-17th c., influenced by Asian ornamentation practice, 3724as[51]
Todi, L., 1820as[26]
Vogl, J.M., 3782as[53]

performers — wind
Spain, Valencia, cathedral, ministriles, 16th-17th c., 1421as[24]

performing groups — traditional and neotraditional music, see also **performers — traditional and neotraditional music; performing organizations**
Czech Republic, ca. 1962, 2943as[34]
Serbia, čalgija ensembles, history and development, 4991as[76]
Slovakia, ca. 1962, 2943as[34]

performing organizations, see also **band; church musicians; management; opera — by place; performance venues; performers** headwords above; **societies, associations, fraternities, etc.** headwords
Austria, Wien, Wiener Kammerorchester, use of positive organ, 3430as[42]
Belgium, Bruxelles, Pro Musica Antiqua, sound recordings, 5952as[89]
___ ___ Société Philharmonique, 20th-c. music, ca. 1937, 2311as[29]
___ Hasselt, collegium musicum, 16th c., 1232as[24]
___ Orchestre Symphonique Populaire, 2283as[29]
Brazil, Rio de Janeiro, Imperial Academia de Música e Ópera Nac., Portuguese-language opera productions, 1857-63, 1907as[27]
choirs, boys, manécanterie model, 4731as[71]
___ pedagogy, 4765as[71]
___ Roman Catholic churches, 6370as[93]
___ ___ participation by women, 6237as[93]
___ ___ relation to congregational singing, 6141as[93]
___ ___ training, 6148as[93]
Czech Republic, Praha, Laterna Magica, activities of Kašlík, 5179as[77]
___ ___ Tylovo Divadlo, activities of Kašlík, 5179as[77]
England, Chapel Royal, at Field of Cloth of Gold, 1520, 1226as[24]
___ London, BBC, Monteverdi dramatic works, 3771as[52]
___ ___ Moody-Manners Opera Company, collections, at Mitchell Lib., Glasgow, 750as[2]
___ ___ Philharmonic Orchestra, 5173as[77]
___ ___ Royal Philharmonic, 5173as[77]
___ ___ Symphony Orchestra, 5173as[77]
___ ___ Workers' Music Assoc., Händel *Belshazzar*, 1938, 3735as[52]
___ ca. 1909, 1977as[27]
Europe, Central, opera companies, 18th-19th c., 1955as[27]
___ Eastern, opera companies, 18th-19th c., 1955as[27]
France, Cambrai, episcopal chapel, 1540, 1260as[24]
___ music societies, history and development, 2083as[27]
___ Paris, Comédie-Italienne, musical repertoire, ca. 1700, 1565as[25]
___ ___ Manécanterie des Petits Chanteurs à la Croix de Bois, relation to Internat. Federation of Pueri Cantores, 6293as[93], 6294as[93]
___ ___ Opéra, activities of Lifar, 5023as[76]
___ ___ Opéra, influence on 19th-c. opera, 5101as[77]

___ ___ Théâtre Italien, repertoire, 1860-1911, 2035as[27]
___ ___ Théâtre Lyrique, repertoire, 1860-1911, 2035as[27]
___ ___ ___ 1848, 2077as[27]
___ Reims, church choirs, 6399as[93]
___ royal chapel, at Field of Cloth of Gold, 1520, 1354as[24]
Germany, Frankfurt, Städtische Bühnen, Egk *Columbus* performance, 1942, 5146as[77]
___ Halle, Landestheater, Händel opera productions, mid-1950s, 5250as[77]
___ Köln, Cappella Coloniensis, 3744as[52]
___ Leipzig, Opernhaus, Händel *Agrippina* production, 1959, 5276as[77]
___ Mannheim, court orchestra, relation to earlier orchestras, 1514as[25]
___ Schwaben, collegia musica, 18th c., 1639as[25]
___ Torgau, court chapel of Friedrich der Weise, 1297as[24]
___ 19th-20th c., Norway performances, 966as[21]
Italy, opera companies, apprenticeship programs, 4878as[73]
___ relation to 20th-c. music, 2385as[29]
___ role in pedagogy, 1921, 4481as[70]
___ Roma, Schola Cantorum, relation to Gregorian chant, Middle Ages, 1127as[23]
___ ___ Schola Cantorum, relation to Gregorian chant, 7th-9th c., 1183as[23]
___ Toscana, court music chapel, 1539-1859, 962as[21]
___ Venezia, Teatro La Fenice, premiere of Nono *Intolleranza 1960*, 5264as[77]
Korea (South), 1945-58, 2346as[29]
Middle East, Palestine Symphony Orchestra, 723as[2]
Poland, Warszawa, Teatr Narodowy, historical operas, early 19th c., 5099as[77]
relation to Roman Catholic music, 6319as[93]
Roman Catholic Church, choirs, liturgical role, 6348as[93]
___ scholae, relation to participation, 6402as[93]
Serbia, Beograd, Ansambl Kolo, 5062as[76]
Spain, Barcelona, Orfeó Català, 3017as[34]
___ Catalunya, choirs, 19th-20th c., 2043as[27]
Sweden, Drottningholm, Slottsteater, Händel *Orlando furioso* production, 1950, 1541as[25]
___ Stockholm, Kungliga Teater, Händel opera productions, 1773 and 1959, 1541as[25]
Switzerland, Basel, Collegium Musicum, symphonies, mid-18th c., 761as[2]
___ Zuoz, choir, 1499as[25]
USA, relation to geography, ca. 1909, 2100as[27]
___ relation to WPA, 1940, 2306as[29]
___ Tennessee, Nashville, Fisk U., Jubilee Singers, 3184as[35]

Pergolesi, Giovanni Battista
aesthetics, viewed by Burney, 1500ac[25]
___ viewed by Rousseau, 1663ac[25]
catalogues, MSS and editions, 811ac[7]
editions, *Opera omnia*, 1939-42, list of works, 804ac[7]
festivals and conferences, Italy, Siena, 1942, 273bs
iconography, caricature by Ghezzi, 1654as[25]
life, relation to Ricciotti, 1515as[25]
___ relation to Spinelli, 1674ac[25]
manuscripts, *Lo frate 'nnamorato*, signed autograph, 1642as[25]
reception, Stabat Mater, Scandinavia, relation to Bach *Matthäuspassion*, 1614as[25]
___ 18th c., 1613as[25]
works, *La fenice sul rogo, ovvero La morte di S Giuseppe*, compared with later works, 1522ac[25]
___ *Il Flaminio*, compared with *La serva padrona*, 1627ac[25]
___ *Il geloso schernito* (attributed), 1609as[25]
___ *Il maestro di musica* (attributed), 3776as[52]
___ operas, 1580as[25]

___ *Li prodigi della divina grazia nella conversione di S Guglielmo Duca d'Aquitania*, 1717ac[25]
___ *La serva padrona*, 1659as[25]
___ viewed by Brosses, 1611ac[25]
___ viewed by Riemann, 1658ac[25]

Peri, Jacopo
works, style, viewed as mannerist, 1713as[25]
PERICOLI, Mario, 5222as[77]

periodicals
Allgemeine musikalische Zeitung, editorial files, 5968as[89]
___ representation of Netherlands, 1798-1848, 1803as[26]
Bach-Jahrbuch, notes on *Die Kunst der Fuge* edition, 1563as[25]
Behar, writings on folklore, 1900-11, 635as[1]
Berliner allgemeine musikalische Zeitung, 1824-30, 5509as[81]
Bulletin trimestriel de l'Union des Maîtres de Chapelle et Organistes, 3431as[42]
Europe, use in bibliographic coverage, 515as[1]
France, Ballard music collections, 1695-1730, 1619as[25]
Glasnik Zemaljskog Muzeja u Sarajevu, Kuba transcriptions, 4462as[69]
Hudební listy, activities of Janáček, 5220as[77]
___ 1884-88, 5622as[81]
Key notes, relation to Donemus Foundation, 5972as[89]
L'écho, ou Journal de musique françoise, italienne, 1734as[26]
Leipziger Literaturzeitung, editorial files, 5968as[89]
Mozart-Jahrbuch, 917as[29]
Musikalisch Magazin, 1782-91, role in history of Romanticism, 2089as[27]
La musique sacrée, 6154as[93]
Muzykal'noje obrazovanie, 1783as[26]
newspapers, criticism, 20th-c. music, influence on appreciation, ca. 1937, 5522as[81], 5621as[81]
Nyugat, Bartók contributions, 2138as[28]
Revue wagnérienne, 5319as[78]
Sonorum speculum, relation to Donemus, 5972as[89]
use in musicology, 909as[20]
PERISTERIS, Spyridon, 2993as[34]
PERLMAN, Myka'el, 503bs
PERNOT, Hubert, 2457as[30]

Pérotin
performance practice, use of positive organ, 3430as[42]
works, compared with Bach, 1488as[25]
___ organ music, influenced by Gregorian chant, 3343as[42]
PERRACHIO, Luigi, 3538as[43]
PERROY, Édouard, 1156as[23]
Persia, see **Iran**
personality, see **psychology**

Pertl, Wolfgang Nikolaus
life, relation to Mozart, 1851as[26]

Peru
antiquity, scales, 4126as[62]
coastal region, instruments, stone bells, antiquity, 3651as[46]
pedagogy, history and development, 1900-53, 4790as[71], 4791as[71]
Quechua people, traditional music, viewed by Fétis, 2416as[30]

Pervaneo, Gabriele
life, 1646as[25]
PERZ, Mirosław, 1399as[24]

Pescetti, Giovanni Battista
works, influence on Classic style, 4330as[66]

Pescheur, Nicolas
instruments, organs, relation to Paris school, 3386as[24]
PESOVÁR, Ernő, 5048as[76]

Europe, German-speaking lands, meter, 17th c., 5313as[78]

France, Paris, Joyeuse-Lorraine marriage festivities, 1585, 1474as[24]

___ performance practice, early 16th c., 1450as[24]

___ relation to air de cour, to 1620, 1459as[24]

___ rhythm and meter, 5339as[78]

German-language, prosody, 16th c., 1294as[24]

Germany, influence on Beethoven, 1852as[26]

___ music as subject, 19th c., 5350as[78]

___ rhythm and meter, 5279as[78]

Goethe, J.W. von, rhythm and meter, 5278as[78]

Greece, antiquity, relation to 20th-c. dance music, 2826as[34]

___ ___ rhythm and meter, 4025as[61]

___ ___ rhythm and meter, relation to Bulgarian folklore, 5309as[78]

Heine, H., set by Schubert in *Schwanengesang* D.957, 1974as[27]

Hungary, 19th c., influence on 20th-c. Hungarian music, 5360as[78]

Italy, Albanian people, 3053as[34]

___ Campagna, traditional contests, 2971as[34]

___ Friuli, traditional, bibliography, 2786as[34]

___ relation to siciliana, 1012as[21]

___ Renaissance, 5317as[78]

___ settings, Risorgimento, 2034as[27]

___ ___ 15th c., 1062as[23]

___ Tonnaro, *Is musicas* festival, 2793as[34]

___ 14th c., 1144as[23]

Latin and French, settings, 1247as[24]

Mallarmé, S., viewed by Merleau-Ponty, 5602as[81]

Mickiewicz, A.B., set by Chopin and Moniuszko, 1995as[27]

Middle Ages, references to instrument ensembles, 1448as[24]

Middle Ages and Renaissance, depiction of vocal religious music, 3703as[51]

Njegoš, P. II P., instrument references, 5318as[78]

Norway, 900-1850, 971as[21]

origins, relation to song, 5293as[78]

Oxenstierna, J.G., 1870as[26]

poetics, conference, 1960, 426bs

Poland, viewed by Szymanowski, 2183as[28]

relation to music, 5334as[78]

relation to traditional music, 5287as[78]

Renaissance, references to instrument ensembles, 1448as[24]

rhythm and meter, compared with music, 4013as[61]

___ notation, 3807as[55]

Ronsard, P. de, aesthetics, 5327as[78]

Scandinavia, 12th-15th c., 3002as[34]

Scève, M., 5348as[78]

Serbia, traditional, 5300as[78]

Spain, Barcelona, Carnival, 17th c., 5056as[76]

___ villancicos, late 16th c., 5365as[78]

stylistic phases, periodicity, 4918as[75]

Syria, Jewish people, relation to Gregorian chant, 1101as[23]

Tasso, T., relation to music, 5347as[78]

traditional, characteristics, 5289as[78]

Tuwim, J., basis of Szymanowski *Słopiewnie*, 2136as[28]

Witwicki, S., set by Chopin and Moniuszko, 1995as[27]

16th c., conference, 1953, 326bs

Poglietti, Alessandro

manuscripts, *Regulae compositionis...*, at Stadt- und Landesbibl., Wien, 4205as[63]

POIRÉE, Élie, 1037as[22], 1038as[22]

POIVET, Henry, 6338as[93]

POIX, Octave, 2068as[27], 2069as[27], 4841as[72]

Pokorný, Gotthard

works, influenced by Mozart, 1008as[21]

Pokrass, Daniil Jakovlevič

works, film music, 5171as[77]

Pokrass, Dmitrij Jakovlevič

works, film music, 5171as[77]

POLADIAN, Sirvart, 4453as[69]

Polak, A.J.

writings, harmonization of Japanese melodies, 2475as[30]

Polak, Jakub, *see* Reys, Jakub

Poland

culture, relation to Venezia, 17th-19th c., 474bs

dance, influence on Europe, 16th c., 5042as[76]

___ krakowiak, relation to polka, 4977as[76]

___ traditional, relation to Danish polskdans, 5038as[76]

___ ___ relation to Hungarian dance, 5029as[76]

dramatic arts, public theater, ca. 1937, 5142as[77]

___ 14th-20th c., 5119as[77], 5120as[77]

___ 15th-17th c., 5216as[77]

Gdańsk, musical life, Chopin visits, 1820s, 2007as[27]

___ early 19th c., relation to Schumann, 2094as[27]

history, 1830s, viewed by Schumann, 2067as[27]

history of music, Baroque, 1697as[25]

___ influence on Chopin, 1913as[27]

___ influenced by Debussy, 2184as[28]

___ influenced by Polish traditional music, 4423as[69]

___ influenced by traditional music, 11th-18th c., 983as[21]

___ instrumental music, Renaissance, 1372as[24]

___ lute music, state of research, ca. 1960, 885as[20]

___ ___ 15th-17th c., state of research, 932as[20]

___ ___ 16th c., 1446as[24]

___ monophons, 9th-15th c., 1300as[24]

___ opera, late 17th-early 19th c., influence on Chopin, 2059as[27]

___ ___ 18th c., 1861as[26]

___ piano music, waltzes, 1800-30, 2101as[27]

___ polyphony, 13th-16th c., 1089as[23]

___ ___ 14th c., 1112as[23], 1149as[23]

___ relation to Bolshevik revolution, 2167as[28]

___ relation to Chopin songs, 2110as[27]

___ relation to Czech Republic, Renaissance, 1436as[24]

___ relation to Russia, 17th-18th c., 1484as[25]

___ relation to Western Europe, 15th-17th c., 954as[21]

___ role of Finck, 1498-1505, 1336as[24]

___ southern influences, 1582as[25]

___ symphonies, 18th c., 1893as[26]

___ early 19th c., relation to Chopin style, 2029as[27]

___ 1697-1763, 1696as[25]

instruments, early Middle Ages, archaeological research, 1956-60, 5741as[84]

Kraków, history of music, *Jesu Christe rex superne* sequence, melodic structure, 1065as[23]

___ ___ 1592-1630, 1298as[24]

___ ___ musical life, 15th-16th c., 1320as[24]

Kurpie, traditional music, rhythm and meter, 3067as[34]

librarianship, internat. exchange, 598as[1]

mass media, radio, influence on musical life, 1945-54, 2293as[29]

musical life, performances of Mozart, 1752as[26]

___ reception of Janáček, 2360as[29]

___ reception of Wagner, 466bs

___ ___ relation to November Revolution, 2048as[27]

___ early 20th c., influence on Janáček, 2102as[27]

Podhale, Góral people, folklore, influence on Szymanowski, 5399as[79]

___ traditional music, influence on Szymanowski, 2136as[28], 2221as[28]

Poznań region, history of music, polyphony, 15th c., 1399as[24]

religious music, nationalism, 13th-14th c., 1090as[23]

traditional music, dance music, influence on Chopin rhythm, 4000as[61]

___ harmony, influence on Chopin, 2015as[27]

___ influence on Chopin, 4365as[66]

___ influence on Szymanowski, 2172as[28]

___ influence on Szymanowski choral music, 2233as[28]

___ influence on Telemann, 1712as[25]

___ melodic style, compared with Chopin, 4434as[69]

___ melody, use in Vormärz songs, 2013as[27]

___ relation to Chopin songs, 2110as[27]

___ rubato, influence on Chopin, 3790as[53]

___ sztajerek, influence on Chopin, 2080as[27]

___ use in Polish opera, early 19th c., 5099as[77]

___ wedding songs, 2783as[34]

Warszawa, history of music, opera, historical operas, early 19th c., 5099as[77]

___ musical life, publishing and printing, 1800-30, 5985as[89]

POLENAKOVIĆ, Haralampije, 2992as[34], 3008as[34]

POLENAKOVIĆ, Radmila, 5342as[78]

politics, *see also* **cultural policies; economics; nationalism; socialism and communism; sociology; urban studies; wars and catastrophes**

Austria, influence on history of music, 1830-1914, 2060as[27]

Bohemia, influence on Mozart reception, late 18th c., 1744as[26]

democracy, relation to aesthetics, 5466as[81]

England, influence on anthems, late 17th c., 1718as[25]

___ reflected in Händel oratorios, 1668as[25]

___ relation to music used in Shakespeare plays, 5362as[78]

Europe, early Middle Ages, association of organ with secular power, 3340as[42]

___ Western, early 16th c., 1307as[24]

France, Paris, relation to Rossi *L'Orfeo* premiere, 1661as[25]

Germany, influence on musicology, 1920s, 901as[20]

___ Vormärz movement, 1815-48, use of Polish melodies, 2013as[27]

___ 20th c., role of music pedagogy, 4600as[70]

India, relation to Westernization, ca. 1947, 2669as[33]

Italy, propaganda, radio, 5198as[77]

___ Risorgimento, influence on librettos, 1823-49, 5226as[77]

___ ___ traditional songs, 3090as[34]

___ songs, ca. 1964, 2930as[34]

Lamennais, H.-F.-R. de, influence on Liszt pedagogy, 2040as[27]

Mozart, W.A., 1832as[26]

___ operas, 1766as[26]

Russia, Bolshevik revolution, influence on Polish music, 2167as[28]

___ ___ relation to Wagner reception in Poland, 2048as[27]

Slavic states, southern, World War II, relation to mass songs, 2722as[34]

___ ___ World War II, relation to Partisan songs, 2961as[34], 5282as[78]

Sweden, late Middle Ages to present, 989as[21]

___ political educational associations, relation to instrumental instruction, 4524as[70]

___ relation to Mozart reception, 1789-1850, 1870as[26]

Symanowski, K., views on Russian Revolution, 2218as[28]

USA, relation to history of music, 1830-1914, 2031as[27]

Pollack, Jackson

works, art, relation to notation, 3808as[55]

POLLAK, Hans Wolfgang, 2460as[30]

Pollarolo, Giuseppe

life, founding of U. Popolare Don Orione, 2379as[29]

POLLERI, Giovanni B., 51as[16]

POLOCZEK, František, 3009as[34], 3010as[34]

psychiatry, *see* **medicine — by topic; psychology; therapy**

psychoacoustics, *see* **acoustics; psychology**

psychology, *see also* **information theory; perception; physiology; science; therapy**
 children, melodic ability, 4418as[69]
 cognitive, 5648as[82]
 ___ genre recognition, role of subjective experience of time, 5676as[82]
 ___ relation to appreciation, 5700as[82]
 ___ relation to listening, 2502as[31]
 ___ state of research, 1927, 5685as[82]
 ___ terminology, applied to realist aesthetics, 5619as[81]
 comparative, relation to performer and audience, 5661as[82]
 concept of quality, relation to sound, 5665as[82]
 conferences, 1892, 17bs
 ___ 1908, 59bs
 ___ 1914, 90bs
 ___ 1921, 79bs
 ___ 1923, 101bs
 ___ 1925, 121bs
 ___ 1927, 125bs
 ___ 1930, 160bs
 ___ 1931, 188bs
 ___ 1933, 207bs
 ___ 1936, 231bs
 ___ 1937, 250bs
 ___ 1938, 254bs
 ___ 1948, 284bs
 creativity, development, 5688as[82]
 ___ role of emotion and will, 5636as[82]
 ___ role of improvisation, viewed by Rousseau, 4608as[70]
 Debussy, C., 2030as[27]
 development, character formation, role of music, 5712as[82]
 ___ preadolescents and adolescents, relation to pedagogy, 4752as[71]
 as discipline, 5702as[82]
 ___ relation to church musicians, 4605as[70]
 ___ relation to ethnomusicology, 2476as[30]
 ___ relation to musicology, 887as[20], 910as[20]
 ___ relation to theory, 875as[20]
 ___ role in Janáček theory of harmony, 5658as[82]
 ___ survey of literature, 1931-61, 5717as[82]
 emotions, musical feeling, 5529as[81]
 ___ relation to appreciation, 5579as[81]
 ___ relation to composition, 5575as[81]
 ___ relation to music, 5507as[81]
 ___ role in aesthetics, 5580as[81]
 experimental psychology, conferences, 1904, 44bs
 ___ ___ 1911, 70bs
 Gestalt psychology, analysis, applied to Haydn and Mozart, 1817as[26]
 ___ concept of time, 5525as[81]
 ___ ___ relation to rhythm, 3955as[60]
 ___ relation to intonation theory, 5409as[80], 5413as[80]
 ___ ___ conference, 1963, 471bs
 hallucination, compared with musical illusion, 5506as[81]
 holistic, relation to aesthetics, 5627as[81]
 learning, applied to elementary pedagogy, 4743as[71]
 listening, compared with analysis, 5708as[82]
 ___ effects of radio, 5681as[82], 5682as[82]
 ___ ___ compared with live performance, 5697as[82], 5707as[82]
 ___ relation to ethical and spiritual values, 5449as[81]
 ___ relation to performers, 845as[19]
 memory, melodies, 5649as[82]
 ___ recognition experiments, 5669as[82]
 ___ relation to judgment, 5674as[82]
 ___ relation to tonality and reception of 20th-c. music, 2164as[28]
 motivation, use of rhythm, 5716as[82]

 performance, relation to listeners, 845as[19]
 personality, conference, 1934, 219bs
 ___ influenced by pedagogy, 4772as[71]
 ___ relation to composition, 20th c., 5639as[82]
 ___ relation to musical taste, 5653as[82]
 ___ typology, influence on creative process, 5428as[81]
 ___ ___ Jungian, applied to composers, 5638as[82]
 ___ ___ ___ relation to musicality, 5678as[82], 5718as[82]
 psychoacoustics, 5644as[82], 5830as[86]
 ___ consonance and dissonance, 20th c., 4212as[63]
 ___ perceived reverberation time, relation to physical reverberation time, 5824as[86]
 ___ ___ relation to tempo, 5838as[86]
 ___ pitch discrimination, complex sounds, 5808as[86]
 ___ radio broadcasts, 5723as[82]
 ___ relation to overtones theory, 4151as[63]
 ___ threshold of tone pulse perception, 5849as[86]
 ___ timbre, 5705as[82]
 psychomusicology, applied to scales, 4132as[62]
 ___ state of research, 1961, 5635as[82]
 ___ terminology, 5714as[82]
 psychopathology, relation to voice production, 5735as[83]
 psychophysiology, relation to aesthetics, 5645as[82]
 relation to aesthetics, 5466as[81], 5495as[81]
 relation to pedagogy, 4588as[70], 4613as[70]
 ___ composition, 4617as[70]
 relation to sonority, 5706as[82]
 Spranger, E., 5632as[81]

Ptolemy, Claudius
 writings, genera ratios, 4128as[62]

publishers and printers, *see also* **catalogues — publisher; dealers; publishing and printing**
 AIBM, Music Documentation Centers, 597as[1]
 André firm, 5975as[89]
 Attaingnant, P., 717as[2], 1332as[24], 1420as[24], 5973as[89]
 Baillon, P., 1531as[25]
 Ballard, R., 3754as[25]
 Ballard firm, 1619as[25]
 Breitkopf & Härtel, 783as[5], 1563as[25], 1774as[26], 3897as[58], 3913as[58], 5968as[89]
 Centre Nat. de la Recherche Scientifique (CNRS), 3901as[58]
 Chrysander, F., 5980as[89]
 Cranz firm, 1774as[26]
 Donemus, 727as[2], 5972as[89]
 Drei-Masken Verlag, 5980as[89]
 Gardane, A., 1475as[24]
 Harloff, W., 966as[21]
 Henle firm, 3917as[58]
 Hinrichsen firm, 1649as[25]
 Hofmeister firm, 1774as[26]
 Imprimerie Lithographique, 5975as[89]
 Jacqui firm, 1310as[24]
 Peters firm, 1649as[25]
 Petreius, J., 1420as[24]
 Petrucci, O., 5973as[89]
 Plantin-Moretus firm, 5973as[89]
 Playford, H., 5274as[77]
 Raabe, C., 966as[21]
 Roger, E., 1603as[25]
 Le Roy, A., 1242as[24]
 Le Roy & Ballard firm, 5973as[89]
 Sacred Harmonic Society, 5980as[89]
 Scotto firm, 5994as[89]
 U. of California, 5970as[89]
 Werckmeister, R., 1747as[26]

publishers' catalogues, *see* **catalogues — publisher**

publishing and printing, *see also* **copyright and patents; dating; publishers and printers**
 Argentina, counterfeit scores, 5976as[89]
 Austria, Wien, Classic period, 5973as[89]
 Belgium, Antwerpen, Plantin-Moretus firm, 1577-1639, 5973as[89]
 Benoît, P., 2087as[27]
 block printing, 15th-16th c., 5994as[89]

 Brazil, relation to Montevideo and Bern agreements, 5951as[89]
 Canada, counterfeit and union-edition scores, 5948as[89]
 careers, ca. 1962, 5986as[89]
 chanson, relation to secularization of music, 16th c., 1333as[24]
 conferences, 1901, 38bs, 39bs, 40bs
 ___ 1906, 55bs
 ___ 1908, 60bs
 ___ 1913, 88bs
 ___ 1931, 191bs
 counterfeit scores, proposed commission, 1908, 5958as[89]
 early music, standards, 3922as[58]
 England, ca. 1580-1625, 5973as[89]
 Europe, facsimile editions, Händel vocal music, 1868-1923, 5980as[89]
 ___ incunabula and early prints, 5979as[89]
 ___ 16th c., relation to popularity of dance genres, 5952as[89]
 ___ to 1600, 5995as[89]
 forgeries, 18th c., 1515as[25]
 France, Ballard music collections, 1695-1730, 1619as[25]
 ___ Greek traditional songs, 19th c., 2934as[34]
 ___ lute music, *Corpus des luthistes français* project, 3901as[58]
 ___ print runs, 16th-17th c., 5893as[87]
 Germany, Köln, 16th-17th c., 5973as[89]
 ___ Leipzig, history and development, relation to Deutsche Bücherei, 653as[1]
 ___ lied collections, early 16th c., 1321as[24]
 ___ ca. 1520-50, influence on church music MS transmission, 1360as[24]
 Hungary, art music, 812as[8]
 Italy, music and music literature, centralization, proposed, 1921, 5996as[89]
 ___ relation to Low Countries and northern France, 16th c., 1229as[24]
 ___ Treviso, 15th-16th c., 5946as[89]
 ___ 16th-18th c., 5973as[89]
 marketing, negative influences, ca. 1932, 5953as[89]
 music editor associations, ca. 1906, 5999as[89]
 Netherlands, 20th c., activities of Donemus, 5972as[89]
 Poland, Warszawa, 1800-30, 5985as[89]
 printed book ornamentation, depiction of instruments, 17th-20th c., 5388as[79]
 relation to librarianship, 20th c., 699as[1]
 relation to pedagogy, 5981as[89], 5982as[89]
 relation to source studies, 3908as[58]
 religious music, Roman Catholic, relation to Pius X, 5987as[89]
 Scandinavia, history and development, 5973as[89]
 Spain, Barcelona, Inst. Español de Musicologia, 858as[20]
 ___ 16th-17th c., 5973as[89]
 Sweden, activities of the Föreningen Svenska Tonsättare, to 1947, 944as[21]
 ___ Mozart works, 18th-19th c., 1819as[26]
 USA, Beethoven editions, 19th c., 5992as[89]
 ___ California, U. of California series in contemporary music, ca. 1966, 5970as[89]
 ___ early period, 5973as[89]
 ___ music literature, 19th c., 859as[20]
 ___ secular music, 1790s, 1885as[26]
PUCELLE, Jean, 4018as[61], 5570as[81]
Puerto Rico, *see* **United States of America**
Puffendorf
 writings, *Auf den kleinen sechsjährigen Claviristen aus Salzburg*, 5290as[78]
PUGH, Robert, 3449as[42]
Pugnani, Gaetano
 collections, symphonies, 761as[2]
PUJOL PONS, Francisco, 3017as[34], 4019as[61]
PUJOL ROCA, David, 746as[2], 747as[2], 1412as[24], 6346as[93]

___ Illinois, Chicago, black people, 6454as[94]
___ Pennsylvania, German-speaking religious communities, 18th c., 1740as[26]
___ singing school movement, 18th-early 20th c., 4905as[74]
___ ___ 18th-19th c., 4916as[74]
___ traditional, history and development, 3156as[35]
___ West, Indians, 3173as[35]
religion and religious music — Christianity (Roman Catholic), *see also* **Caecilianism; chant** headwords; **church documents; church musicians; Counter-Reformation; lauda; litany; liturgical books; Mass; Office;** specific genres
academic institutions, Pontificio Ist. di Musica Sacra, 6362as[93]
administration, cultivation responsibilities, 6320as[93]
___ legal and financial foundations, 6344as[93]
___ organizational proposals, 1954, 6241as[93]
aesthetics, 5593as[81], 5598as[81], 6163as[93], 6195as[93]
___ concept of artistic quality, 2377as[29], 6372as[93]
___ Gregorian chant as model, 6329as[93]
___ relation to doctrine, 6207as[93], 6292as[93]
Africa, missions, questionnaire survey, 1957, 6323as[93], 6324as[93]
___ relation to African traditional music, 6161as[93], 6162as[93]
___ relevance of North American spiritual, 6134as[93], 6135as[93]
___ use of indigenous musical traditions, 6005as[90]
___ ___ proposal, 1957, 6006as[90]
Albrechtsberger, J.G., 1895as[26]
appreciation, role of Catholic radio broadcasts, 5744as[85]
Asia, missions, questionnaire survey, 1957, 6333as[93], 6334as[93]
___ use of indigenous musical traditions, 6005as[90]
___ ___ proposal, 1957, 6006as[90]
associations, unity vs. autonomy, 6392as[93]
Austria, Salzburg, 17th c., 1662as[25]
___ use of instruments in liturgy, 20th c., 6375as[93]
___ Wien, associations, 6385as[93]
Baroque, late, stile antico, 1548as[25]
Beethoven, L. van, 1899as[26]
___ influenced by career, 1857as[26]
Belgium, Flanders, festivals, 3646as[46]
___ Mechelen, Interdiocesaan Inst. voor Kerkmuziek, 4836as[72]
___ ___ 18th c., 1602as[25]
Bordes, C., 1924as[27]
Brazil, ca. 1950, 6312as[93]
Burkina Faso, Mossi people, 2573as[32]
Canada, Ottawa, U., to 1950, 4817as[72]
canon law, 1917, 6290as[93]
canticles, 20th c., 6166as[93]
cantiques, history and development, 6188as[93]
___ role in liturgy, 6356as[93]
characteristics, 6278as[93], 6383as[93]
China, proposed chant style, 6271as[93]
choirs, formation and training, 6370as[93]
choral music, women singers, 6237as[93]
Classic, vocal music, editing, 3910as[58]
conferences, 1860, 3bs, 911as[20]
___ 1882, 9bs, 10bs
___ 1900, 26bs, 34bs
___ 1905, 52bs, 6319as[93]
___ 1907, 57bs
___ 1911, 75bs
___ 1912, 78bs
___ 1919, 93bs
___ 1921, 96bs
___ 1922, 98bs
___ 1928, 155bs
___ 1937, 247bs
___ 1950, 303bs
___ 1954, 331bs, 339bs, 6273as[93]
___ 1957, 378bs, 379bs
___ 1961, 432bs
___ 1965, 501bs

congregational singing, aesthetic assessment, 6268as[93], 6269as[93]
___ catechetical value, 6234as[93], 6235as[93]
___ role of elementary education, ca. 1950, 6196as[93]
coordination of regional activities, 6267as[93]
Croatia, influenced by traditional songs, 1025as[21]
Czech Republic, 9th-16th c., 1204as[23]
Ecuador, traditional dances, 5261as[77]
England, Eton Choirbook, 1327as[24]
episcopal acts, 6155as[93]
Europe, Basque region, dances, 5089as[76], 5090as[76]
___ German-speaking lands, after World War I, 2198as[28]
___ ___ early 20th c., 6317as[93]
___ German-speaking people, role of Allgemeiner Caecilienverein für Länder Deutscher Zunge, 6330as[93]
___ Middle Ages, church singing, 6377as[93]
___ monody, ca. 1600, 1302as[24]
___ use of basso continuo, ca. 1600, 1590as[25]
France, Bayeux diocese, 6280as[93]
___ cities vs. provinces, 2021as[27]
___ Dordogne, influenced by Pius X *Tra le sollecitudini*, 6178as[93]
___ institutions for the blind, 2315as[29]
___ Nantes diocese, pedagogy, 4594as[70]
___ parochial programs, 19th c. to 1930s, 4789as[71]
___ pedagogy, 4806as[72]
___ ___ elementary, mid-19th c., 4718as[71]
___ ___ proposal, 1921, 4625as[70]
___ relation to papal directives, ca. 1937, 4888as[73]
___ Renaissance, 6201as[93]
___ Rennes, influenced by Pius X *Tra le sollecitudini*, 6258as[93]
___ role of congregation, ca. 1937, 6282as[93]
___ Saint-Dié diocese, mid-19th c., 6243as[93]
___ Soissons, mid-19th c., 2069as[27]
___ Valence diocese, mid-19th c., 6389as[93]
___ Verdun diocese, mid-19th c., 6418as[93]
___ 9th-19th c., 6351as[93]
___ early 14th c., relation to ars nova, 6213as[93]
___ late 18th c. to 1930s, 6408as[93]
___ mid-19th c., 2068as[27]
___ late 19th to early 20th c., 1988as[27]
___ early 20th c., 2166as[28]
___ 20th c., use in liturgy, 6183as[93]
Gagliano, M. da, 1559as[25]
Gassmann, F.L., 1794as[26]
Germany, cantio repertoire, 13th-14th c., relation to 9th-c. sequence, 1188as[23]
___ depicted in journalism, ca. 1950, 6395as[93]
___ organ music, early 20th c., 2189as[28]
___ Regensburg, relation to Roma, 6386as[93]
___ restoration of Renaissance polyphony, 19th c., 1996as[27]
___ Speyer diocese, German-language Mass, ca. 1962, 6347as[93]
Haydn, J., collections, Esterházy-Arch., Eisenstadt, 1761as[26]
history and development, relation to Eastern Orthodox music, 6028as[90]
___ relation to Pius X *Tra le sollecitudini*, 6413as[93]
___ 20th c., 2222as[28]
___ 1954-57, role of 2nd International Congress of Sacred Music, 6272as[93]
Huijbers, B., hymns, 6256as[93]
Hungary, hymnody, 11th-20th c., 6248as[93]
___ MSS, to late 16th c., 1085as[23]
___ late 19th c., 1993as[27]
Hussites, Hussite song, viewed by Nejedlý, 1349as[24]
___ hymns, relation to Liszt *Hussitenlied*, 1925as[27]
hymns, pre-Reformation, 6315as[93]
India, use of traditional and Western idioms, 6143as[93]
Indonesia, use of local idioms, 6369as[93]

influenced by Pius X *Tra le sollecitudini*, 1019as[21]
internat., administration, dioceses, from 1955, 6378as[93]
___ missions, questionnaire survey, 1957, 6345as[93]
___ Pontificio Ist. di Musica Sacra, relation to proposed Internat. Soc. of Sacred Music, 6146as[93]
___ small churches, gradual, 6181as[93]
Italy, dissemination, 2319as[29]
___ influence on traditional music, 2757as[34]
___ influenced by ornamentation, Baroque era, 1482as[25]
___ Modena, Song of the Modenese Sentries, prayer to St. Geminian, 6404as[93]
___ relation to sword dances, 4966as[76]
___ Roma, relation to Regensburg, 6386as[93]
___ ___ 17th-18th c., 1543as[25]
___ Sicilia, Middle Ages, 1055as[23]
___ 17th c., reception, ca. 1937, 5615as[81]
Japan, use of Asian musical elements, 6322as[93]
Jumentier, B., 1844as[26]
Latin pronunciation, reform, ca. 1911, 5295as[78]
liturgical texts, cataloguing, 617as[1]
liturgy, 6171as[93], 6394as[93]
___ antiquity, Greek influences, 1045as[22]
___ composition, 20th c., 6177as[93]
___ congregational singing, 6141as[93]
___ ___ influenced by Pius X *Tra le sollecitudini*, 6265as[93], 6346as[93]
___ use of Latin, 6379as[93]
___ ecclesiastical instructions, 6415as[93]
___ organ playing, 6176as[93]
___ ___ improvisation, 6289as[93]
___ ___ use of improvisations and compositions, 6412as[93]
___ participation, role of schola, 6402as[93]
___ pastoral value, viewed by Pius XII, 6357as[93], 6358as[93]
___ repertoire, relation to Pius X *Tra le sollecitudini*, 6390as[93]
___ role of artistic goals, 6348as[93]
___ role of laity, 6198as[93]
___ role of organist, 6275as[93], 6400as[93]
___ role of priests, 6151as[93]
___ state of research, 1957, 6184as[93], 6185as[93]
___ style, relation to 20th-c. compositional systems, 5439as[81]
___ use of conductus, 1114as[23]
___ use of electronic organ, 3664as[48], 3667as[48], 6210as[93], 6260as[93], 6328as[93]
___ use of instruments, 6352as[93]
___ use of modern languages, 6231as[93]
___ ___ conferences, 1962-63, 449bs
___ use of orchestra, 6216as[93]
___ use of organ, 1700as[25], 3472as[42], 6164as[93]
___ use of polyphony, 6148as[93]
___ use of secular elements, 6239as[93]
___ use of 20th-c. compositions, 2200as[28]
___ use of 20th-c. organ music, 6140as[93]
___ viewed by Pius XII, 6306as[93], 6307as[93]
Low Countries, late 19th-early 20th c., 1992as[27]
Middle Ages, 6214as[93]
___ aesthetics, 5592as[81]
___ chant standardization, Roman vs. Frankish, 1115as[23]
___ cult of the saints, 1151as[23]
___ liturgical monody, rhythmic interpretation, 3886as[58]
Netherlands, Maastricht, Easter play, 1182as[23]
organ music, 3497as[42], 6304as[93]
___ Germany, South, relation to organ building, 3341as[42]
___ use of electronic organ, critique, 3663as[48]
organ playing, as career, 3473as[42]
___ historic instruments, 3339as[42]
___ Middle Ages to 17th c., 6396as[93]
___ pedagogy, 20th c., 4889as[73], 4890as[73]
Palestrina, G.P. da, reception, early 20th c., 6189as[93]

___ Mechelen, Sint-Rombout cathedral, activities
of Frescobaldi, 1527as[25]
___ ___ Sint-Rombout cathedral, relation to
Dusík, 1745as[26]
___ Sint-Truiden, abbey, motet MS, 1364as[24]
churches, organ specifications, 3470as[42]
___ relation to organ building, 3373as[42], 3499as[42]
Denmark, København, St. Nikolaj, Lorentz organ
recitals, 1615as[25]
England, Liverpool, cathedral, organ, 3399as[42]
___ London, St. Magnus Church, organ, 3396as[42]
___ ___ St. Paul's Cathedral, organ, 3396as[42]
___ ___ Westminster Cathedral, Office, ca. 1950,
6295as[93]
___ Worcester, cathedral, organ, 3396as[42]
France, Bergues, abbey, 1483as[25]
___ Chartres, Notre-Dame cathedral, 6th-18th c.,
6187as[93]
___ Dijon, Église de St-Philibert, versified Office
of St. Philibert, 5330as[78]
___ Jumièges, Abbaye St.-Pierre, antiphoner,
influence on Notker Balbulus, 1081as[23]
___ ___ Abbaye St.-Pierre, conference, 1954,
336bs
___ ___ Abbaye St.-Pierre, liturgical books, at
Bibl. Mun., Rouen, catalogue, 780as[4]
___ ___ Abbaye St.-Pierre, music MSS, at Bibl.
Mun., Rouen, catalogue, 781as[4]
___ ___ Abbaye St.-Pierre, Offices, 1118as[23]
___ ___ Abbaye St.-Pierre, prosula repertoire, in-
fluence on Aquitanian sequence, 1073as[23]
___ ___ Abbaye St.-Pierre, sequences, 1120as[23]
___ ___ Abbaye St.-Pierre, tropes, 1122as[23]
___ Nancy, Saint-Pierre, Gregorian chant,
6403as[93]
___ Paris, Saint-Julien-des-Ménétriers, 6152as[93]
___ Reims, Roman Catholic Church, choirs,
6399as[93]
___ Rouen, cathedral, bells, 3649as[46]
___ Saint-Quentin, collegiate church, activities of
Desprez, 1417as[24]
___ ___ collegiate church, Jumentier MSS,
1844as[26]
___ ___ collegiate church, mid-19th c., 6302as[93]
___ Solesmes, Abbaye de Saint Pierre, chant
rhythm, 3702as[51]
___ ___ Abbaye de Saint Pierre, Graduale
romanum edition, 3888as[58]
___ Souvigny, Église Prieurale, relics of Odilo of
Cluny, 1121as[23]
___ St. Cyr, royal chapel, performance of Nivers
motets, 1556as[25]
___ Strasbourg, cathedral, acoustics, 5812as[86]
___ ___ cathedral, organ, 3422as[42]
___ St.-Thomas church, organ, 3385as[42]
___ Tournus, Abbaye de St.-Philibert, versified
Office of St. Philibert, 5330as[78]
___ Vannes, cathedral, youth club, 2373as[29]
Germany, Altzelle, monastery, library, 1323as[24]
___ Berlin, Hedwigskirche, 6314as[93]
___ Beuron, archabbey, relation to Ottobeuren
organs, 3375as[42]
___ Dresden, Hofkirche, relation to Bach Mass,
BWV 232, 6381as[93]
___ Freiberg, cathedral, organ, 3363as[42]
___ Görlitz, Peter-und-Paul-Kirche, role of
Boxberg, 1689as[25]
___ Göttingen, St. Marien church, organ, 3410as[42]
___ Hamburg, cathedral, organist position, 1727,
3673as[50]
___ Heilandskirche, organ, 3399as[42]
___ Kaisheim, monastery, organ, 3503as[42]
___ Lahm, parish church, organ, 3426as[42]
___ Leipzig, Thomaskirche, activities of Bach as
teacher, 1564as[25]
___ Lübeck, Marienkirche, Abendmusik concerts,
17th c., 1584as[25]
___ ___ Marienkirche, Totentanz-Orgel, 3415as[42]
___ Mönchengladbach, Münster-Basilika St.
Vitus, 815as[8]

___ ___ Münster-Basilika St. Vitus, MSS,
3819as[55]
___ ___ Münster-Basilika St. Vitus, relation to
Burgh, 1578as[25]
___ ___ Münster-Basilika St. Vitus, scriptorium,
12th-17th c., 1109as[23]
___ Mönchengladbach-Rheindahlen, St. Helena
church, relation to Burgh, 1578as[25]
___ North, churches, typical organs, 3390as[42]
___ Oberschwaben, 18th c., 1683as[25]
___ Passau, cathedral, organ, 3453as[42]
___ Sachsen, Protestant churches, organs,
3476as[42]
___ Schwaben, 18th c., 1639as[25]
___ Siegen, Nikolaikirche, organ, 3415as[42]
___ Stuttgart, churches, acoustics, 5863as[86]
___ Wittenberg, Allerheiligenstiftskirche, liturgy,
1297as[24]
Italy, Genova, cathedral, intarsia decoration,
instrument iconography, 5404as[79]
___ Grottaferrata, Badia Greca, chant tradition,
958as[21]
___ Messina, Monastero di S. Salvatore di
Messina, Byzantine liturgical book,
1195as[23]
___ Monte Oliveto Maggiore, abbey, intarsia
decorations, instrument iconography,
5404as[79]
___ Novara, cathedral, relation to Mognossa,
1669as[25]
___ Roma, basilicas, sponsorship of Schola
Cantorum, 7th-9th c., 1183as[23]
___ Saronno, S. Maria del Miracoli church,
Ferrari frescoes, 5380as[79]
___ Vallepietra, Santuario della Santissima
Trinità, Pianto delle zitelle, 5121as[77]
seminaries, Gregorian chant pedagogy, ca. 1913,
4845as[72], 4846as[72]
Spain, Aránzazu, Franciscan monastery, arch.,
735as[2]
___ Montserrat, Monasterio de S. María, archives,
746as[2]
___ Roman Catholic churches, liturgical
repertoire, relation to Pius X Tra le
sollecitudini, 6354as[93]
___ seminaries, Gregorian chant pedagogy,
4883as[73], 6263as[93]
___ Valencia, cathedral, ministriles, 16th-17th c.,
1421as[24]
Switzerland, Frauenfeld, Stadtkirche, organ,
3399as[42]
___ St. Gallen, MSS, Columbanus tributes,
6204as[93]
___ Winterthur, Stadtkirche, organ, 1979as[27]
Vatican, S. Pietro basilica, polychoral music
performance, 5813as[86]

religious orders, see also **religion and religious
music** headwords
Benedictine, France, Cluny, activities of Odilo,
1121as[23]
___ ___ Cluny, conference, 1949, 290bs
___ ___ Cluny, conference, 1958, 399bs
___ ___ Cluny, liturgical practice, 6382as[93]
___ ___ Solesmes, Abbaye de Saint Pierre, influ-
ence on liturgical music, 6184as[93], 6185as[93]
___ Italy, Roma, Gregorian chant, 7th-9th c.,
1183as[23]
Cistercian, Gregorian chant, 6186as[93], 6270as[93]
Dominican, Finland, 14th c., 878as[20]
___ Poland, 14th c., authorship of Gaude mater
Polonia, 1090as[23]
Franciscan, Austria, Wien, theory treatises,
mid-17th c., 4205as[63]
___ Gregorian chant, 13th c., 1134as[23]
Society of Jesus, Poland, influence on
instrumental music, 16th c., 1372as[24]

Reményi, Ede
performances, Germany, 1853, relation to Brahms
and Liszt, 1973as[27]

works, Ungarischer Romanzero segment, relation
to Liszt and Brahms, 1973as[27]
reminiscences, see anecdotes, reminiscences, etc.;
autobiographies, diaries, etc.
Renaissance, see also **Counter-Reformation**; humanism; performance practice — by topic;
Reformation
aesthetics, relation to concept of space, 1373as[24]
choral music, polyphony, 1262as[24]
chromaticism, relation to humanism, 4149as[63]
concept of history, 1429as[24]
conferences, 1953, 326bs
___ 1955, 350bs
court music, royal entrances, 1341as[24]
dramatic arts, conference, 1963, 472bs
___ depiction of the supernatural, 5102as[77]
France, religious music, 6201as[93]
history of music, ensemble music, 1448as[24]
___ influenced by traditional music, 1017as[21]
improvisation, 1305as[24]
instrumental music, conference, 1954, 333bs
___ style, 1332as[24]
Italy, conference, 1939, 264bs
___ state of research, 1314as[24]
Poland, national style, 1372as[24]
___ role of Mikołaj z Krakowa, 1469as[24]
polyphony, influence on Szymanowski choral
music, 2233as[28]
relation to ars nova, 1087as[23]
religious music, polyphony, editions, 1920-57,
3905as[58]
___ viewed by Hoffmann, 2002as[27]
Spain, polyphony, influenced by Flanders,
1223as[24]
as style concept, 1473as[24]
text setting, relation to humanism, 1269as[24]
tonality, 4192as[63]
RENARD-GRENSON, Lucien, 64bs
Rener, Adam
works, psalm settings, attribution, 1297as[24]
RENNER, Frumentius, 5852as[86]
RENNERT, Günther, 5229as[77]
Rennert, Günther
works, directing, operas, 5224as[77]
RENNERT, Wolfgang, 5230as[77]
RENONDEAU, Gaston, 5231as[77]
RENSHAW, Rosette, 844as[19], 852as[19], 4023as[61]
REPP, Friedrich, 3025as[34], 3026as[34]
République Centrafricaine, see **Central African Re-
public**
Requiem, see Mass
resonance, see acoustics
Respighi, Ottorino
works, operas, 5233as[77]
Reuchlin, Johannes
writings, De accentibus et orthographia linguae
Hebraicae, on cantillation, 6046as[91]
REUSCH, Fritz, 4106as[62]
REUTER, Fritz, 4447as[69]
REUTER, Rudolf, 3466as[42]
Reutter, Hermann
works, Die Passion in 9 Inventionen, use in
pedagogy, 4780as[71]
REVAULT, Jacques, 2577as[32]
REVAULT D'ALLONNES, Olivier, 2239as[28]
reverberation, see acoustics
RÉVÉSZ, Géza, 5693as[82], 5694as[82], 5695as[82],
5696as[82]
reviews, see **criticism** headwords; reception
revue, see musical revue, cabaret, etc.
Rey, Cemal Reşit
works, 2275as[28]
___ serialism, 2173as[28]
Reys, Jakub
editions, ca. 1957, 932as[20]

RUHNKE, Martin, 1666as[25]
Ruimonte, Pedro, *see* **Rimonte, Pedro**
RUIZ AZNAR, Valentín, 6370as[93]
Ruiz-Aznar, Valentín
   works, religious music, 2234as[28]
Rumania, *see* **Romania**
rummelpot (=friction drum), *see* **instruments — percussion (drum)**
RUMMENHÖLLER, Peter, 4924as[75]
RUNGE, Paul, 3865as[55], 3866as[55]
RUNG-KELLER, Poul Sophus, 3470as[42]
RUPP, E., 3471as[42]
Ruprecht, Hieronimus
   life, organ building,
      Mönchengladbach-Rheindahlen organ,
      1578as[25]
   ___ ___ relation to Burgh, 1578as[25]
Rus', *see* **Ukraine**
RUSIĆ, Branislav, 3041as[34], 5935as[88]
Russia, *see also* **USSR**
   Caucasus Mountains region, religious music,
      sectarian communities, 2931as[34]
   Čeremis people, traditional music, vocal melodies,
      compared with Hungarian melodies,
      4471as[69]
   Čuvaš people, traditional music, vocal melodies,
      compared with Hungarian melodies,
      4471as[69]
   ethnomusicology, ca. 1900, 2444as[30]
   folklore, 2817as[34]
   history of music, Byzantine, 9th-10th c., 1153as[23]
   ___ choral music, 17th c., 1687as[25]
   ___ influence on Debussy and Stravinsky,
      2205as[28]
   ___ opera, 18th c., 1792as[26]
   ___ relation to France, 2162as[28]
   ___ relation to Poland, 17th-18th c., 1484as[25]
   ___ secular music, 1002as[21]
   ___ znammenyj chant, 11th-16th c., 1063as[23]
   Kaliningrad, history of music, Sebastiani tenure as
      court kapellmeister, 1495as[25]
   ___ musical life, activities of Walter and Senfl,
      1416as[24]
   ___ ___ relation to Kant, 1769as[26]
   ___ ___ early 19th c., relation to Schumann,
      2094as[27]
   ___ traditional music, influence on Reichardt,
      1849as[26]
   literature, byliny, 4006as[61]
   musical life, activities of Martín y Soler, 1818as[26]
   ___ Chopin performance tradition, 3781as[53]
   ___ Händel reception, 2322as[29]
   ___ reception of Chopin, 19th c., 2117as[27]
   ___ reception of Haydn, ca. 1790-1809, 1804as[26]
   ___ reception of Liszt, 1840s-50s, 2025as[27]
   ___ reception of Mozart, 1808as[26], 3758as[52]
   ___ ___ influenced by Serov, 2026as[27]
   religious music, history and development,
      6125as[92]
   ___ liturgy, 10th-20th c., 6119as[92]
   ___ znamennyj chant, state of research, 1954,
      1011as[21]
   ___ 11th-12th c., 6116as[92]
   ___ 12th-18th c., 6107as[92]
   Siberia, indigenous peoples, traditional music,
      songs, collection, 2612as[33]
   ___ traditional music, relation to Paleolithic
      music, 1049as[22]
   traditional music, influence on Serbian World War
      II songs, 2854as[34]
   ___ relation to znamennyj chant, 4304as[65]
   ___ scale structures, relation to Orthodox chant,
      1058as[23]
   Volga region, folklore, 2545as[31]
Russian chant, *see* **chant — Eastern Orthodox**
Russian Federation, *see* **Russia; USSR**

Russian Orthodox chant, *see* **chant — Eastern Orthodox**
RUSZNYÁK, István, 427bs
RUTH, Walter, 752as[2]
Rutz, Josef
   writings, 3769as[52]
   ___ composer personality types, applied to Haydn,
      Mozart, and Beethoven, 4239as[64]
Rutz, Joseph
   writings, sound-types and body posture, 5727as[83]
Rwanda
   traditional music, 2553as[32]
RŴS, Y'aqob, 6094as[91]
RŴṬŠYLD, Yŵsep, 6095as[91]
RŴZŴLYŴ, Dawid, 2244as[28]
Ryba, Jakub Jan
   works, influenced by Mozart, 1825as[26], 1880as[26]
RYBARIČ, Richard, 1000as[21]
RYCROFT, David, 2581as[32]
Rytel, Piotr
   writings, on Szymanowski, 2259as[28]
Ryūkyū Islands, *see* **Japan**
RYŽKIN, Josif, 5418as[80]

S

Saar, Ferdinand von
   writings, poetry, music as subject, 5350as[78]
Sabbatini, Galeazzo
   writings, *Regola facile e breve per sonare sopra il
      basso continuo nell'organo, manacordo o
      altro simile stromento,* 3774as[52]
SABBE, Maurits, 2087as[27]
Sabine, Wallace Clement Ware
   works, architecture, Symphony Hall, Boston,
      5829as[86]
SABLAYROLLES, Mauro, 4846as[72], 6371as[93]
SACCHETTI, Liborio, 1001as[21], 1002as[21]
Sacchini, Antonio Maria
   works, contribution to Classic style, 4330as[66]
SACHS, Curt, 914as[20], 915as[20], 3273as[40], 3714as[51],
      3867as[55], 4638as[70], 4920as[75], 5395as[79]
Sachs, Curt
   editions, *2000 Jahre Musik,* 969as[21], 970as[21]
   writings, on dance, 5039as[76]
   ___ on style, 4373as[66]
   ___ organology, European traditional music
      instruments, 3241as[40]
SACHS, Melchior Ernst, 4108as[62]
SACKETT, Samuel J., 3601as[44]
sacramentaries, *see* **liturgical books**
sacred music, *see* **chant** headwords; **religion and religious music** headwords; specific genres and
   services
SADAGOPAN, V.V., 2683as[33]
Sadai, Yizhak
   works, serialism, 2173as[28]
Saemann, Carl Heinrich
   correspondence, with Schumann, 2094as[27]
Saess, Heinrich
   writings, *Musica plana atque mensurabilis,*
      1299as[24]
SAFAR, Ali, 2582as[32]
Šafařik, Pavel Josef
   collections, Bohemian traditional music, 2946as[34]
Ṣafi al-Din
   writings, meter, 2607as[33]
   ___ scale theory, 4048as[62]
SAFRANEC, 5786as[85]
saga, *see* **epic; folklore; literature; myth and legend;
   mythology; poetry**

Sahagún, Bernardino de
   collections, Mexican Indian songs, late 16th c.,
      3209as[36]
Sailer, Johann Michael
   life, restoration of Renaissance polyphony,
      1996as[27]
   writings, relation to Beethoven, 1856as[26]
Sailer, Sebastian
   works, 1683as[25]
SAINTENOY, Paul, 15bs, 16bs
Saint-Foix, Georges de
   writings, on Mozart, 1835as[26]
Saint-Malachie, Louis de
   writings, *Piorum carminum,* tributes to St.
      Philibert, 1334as[24]
SAINT-SAËNS, Camille, 3868as[55]
Saint-Saëns, Camille
   life, Scandinavia, 1897, 1921as[27]
Saint-Simon, Claude-Henri, Comte de, *see*
   **Rouvroy, Claude-Henri de, Comte de
   Saint-Simon**
Sakartvelo, *see* **Georgia**
SAKKA, Keisei, 2684as[33]
SAKVA, Konstantin Konstantinovič, 2088as[27]
Saladin, Louis
   manuscripts, cantata, 1477as[25]
salamuri, *see* **instruments — wind (woodwind, flute
   family)**
salaries, pensions, etc., *see also* **economics**
   composers, royalties, mid-20th c., 2295as[29]
   France, military bandleaders, ca. 1900, 3270as[40]
   Germany, Limburg, church musicians, Roman
      Catholic, ca. 1965, 5884as[87]
Salieri, Antonio
   life, 1828as[26]
   works, religious music, 1828as[26]
SALMEN, Walter, 483bs, *484rs[16], *485rs[16],
      508rs[16], 1171as[23], 1172as[23], 1424as[24], 1849as[26],
      2089as[27], 2458as[30], 2538as[31], 3042as[34],
      3978as[61], 4455as[69], 4456as[69], 5460as[81],
      5905as[87]
SALOMON, Karel, 2685as[33]
SALVAGNINI, F. Alberto, 916as[20]
SALVANY, Gerardo María, 4892as[73]
SALVINI, Guido, 5236as[77]
Salvioli, Carlo
   bibliographies, opera, 586as[1]
Salvioli, Giovanni
   bibliographies, opera, 586as[1]
SALZEDO, Fernande, 1680as[25]
SALZMAN, Eric, 3959as[60]
Samaroff, Olga, *see* **Hickenlooper, Lucie (Olga
   Samaroff Stokowski)**
SAMBAMOORTHY, P., 852as[19], 2686as[33],
      3274as[40]
SAMBETH, Heinrich M., 2090as[27], 3275as[40],
      3276as[40], 4768as[71]
SAMI, Abdel Rahman, 2583as[32]
Sámi people, *see* **Finland; Norway; Scandinavia**
samisen (=shamisen), *see* **instruments — string (lute
   family)**
Sammartini, Giovanni Battista
   collections, symphonies, 761as[2]
   life, relation to Lombardia orchestras, 1724as[26]
   works, contribution to Classic style, 4330as[66]
   ___ influence on Mozart string quartets, 1882as[26]
   ___ instrumental music, relation to toccata,
      4237as[64]
SAMPER, Baltasar, 3043as[34]
SAMSON, Joseph, 2377as[29], 6372as[93]
Samson, Joseph
   obituaries, 2376as[29]
SAN MARTINO E VALPERGA, Enrico di,
      2385as[29]

SCHAAL, Richard, 1426as[24]

Schaden, Johan
 instruments, organ building, relation to Burgh, 1578as[25]

SCHAEFER, Hans Joachim, 5581as[81]

SCHAEFFER, Bogusław, 4283as[64]

SCHAEFFER, Myron, 4109as[62]

Schaeffer, Pierre
 works, musique concrète, 2258as[28]
 ___ *Symphonie pour un homme seul*, 4401as[68]
 writings, musique concrète, 2258as[28]

SCHAEFFER, Rudolf F., 2031as[27]

SCHAEFFNER, André, 669as[1], 670as[1], 1003as[21], 2467as[30], 2468as[30], 2584as[32], 2585as[32], 2586as[32], 2587as[32], 3654as[46], 4303as[65], 5396as[79], 5788as[85]

Schaeffner, André
 writings, North African diaphony, relation to organum, 1133as[23]

SCHÄFER, Oskar, 4110as[62]

Schall, Claus Nielsen
 works, directing, Mozart operas, 986as[21]

schalmei (=shawm), *see* **instruments — wind (woodwind, reed family)**

SCHANZLIN, Hans Peter, 1669as[25]

Scharlitt, Bernard
 writings, translations, Chopin correspondence, 5356as[78]

Scheibe, Johann Adolph
 writings, Baroque form, 4286as[64]
 ___ mid-18th c. styles, 1733as[26]

SCHEIDE, William H., 1706as[25]

SCHEIDEMANN, Heinrich, 122bs

Scheidt, Samuel
 works, keyboard music, organ vs. harpsichord styles, 1292as[24]
 ___ *Tabulatura nova*, relation to organ technical resources, 4319as[66]
 ___ *Tabulatur-Buch hundert geistlicher Lieder und Psalmen*, variation technique, 4202as[63]
 ___ use of cantus firmus, 6024as[90]

Schein, Johann Hermann
 works, 4286as[64]
 ___ counterpoint, 4203as[63]
 ___ spiritual concertos, compared with Franck, 1566as[25]

SCHEIT, Karl, 3715as[51]

SCHENK, Erich, 193bs, 365bs, 917as[20], 1670as[25], 1850as[26], 1851as[26], 5582as[81], 6375as[93]

Schenker, Heinrich
 writings, *Der freie Satz*, views on Chopin scherzo op. 31, 4160as[63]

Schenkerian theory, *see also* **analysis**; **theory**
 approaches, 3940as[60]
 critique, 4166as[63]

Scherer family
 instruments, organs, 3364as[42], 3392as[42]

SCHERING, Arnold, 918as[20], 1671as[25], 1672as[25], 4027as[61], 4040as[61], 4284as[64], 5421as[81], 5583as[81], 5584as[81], 5585as[81], 6376as[93]

SCHERMALL, Herbert, 4641as[70]

Scherrer, Heinrich
 transcriptions, lute music, 3904as[58]

scherzo
 Beethoven, L. van, compared with Haydn and Mozart minuets, 4239as[64]

SCHETELICH, Herta, 671as[1], 672as[1]

SCHEURLEER, Daniel François, 5397as[79]

Schiavetto, Giulio, *see* **Skjavetić, Julije**

SCHIEDERMAIR, Ludwig, 1004as[21], 1671as[25], 1673as[25], 1852as[26], 1853as[26], 4769as[71], 5238as[77]

Schiedermair, Ludwig
 writings, university music curricula, 2350as[29]

SCHIEGL, Hermann, 4770as[71]

SCHIES, S., 3473as[42]

SCHIESS, Ernst, 3474as[42]

Schiess, Ernst
 instruments, organs, Switzerland, 1979as[27]

SCHIESSER, H., 5789as[85]

Schikaneder, Emanuel
 editions, libretto for Mozart *Die Zauberflöte*, 5240as[77]
 writings, libretto for Mozart *Die Zauberflöte*, 5212as[77]
 ___ ___ symbolism, 5162as[77]

Schiller, Johann Christoph Friedrich von
 writings, basis of Verdi librettos, 5196as[77]
 ___ influence on Beethoven, 1852as[26]
 ___ relation to Mozart, 1728as[26]

Schillinger, Joseph
 works, notation, 3808as[55]

Schindler, Anton Felix
 writings, Beethoven theology, 1856as[26]
 ___ *Biographie von Ludwig von Beethoven*, Beethoven accentuation practice, 1867as[26]

SCHINZ, Nelly, 4771as[71]

SCHIØDT, Nanna, 4457as[69]

SCHIØRRING, Nils, 673as[1], 674as[1], 3052as[34], 4111as[62], 6446as[94]

SCHIRÒ, Giuseppe, 3053as[34], 5349as[78]

SCHLEGEL, F., 5790as[85]

SCHLENGER, 5791as[85]

Schlesinger, Kathleen
 writings, *The Greek aulos*, 4112as[62]

Schlick, Arnolt
 life, 1355as[24]

SCHLITZER, Franco, 1674ac[25]

SCHLOEZER, Boris de, 919as[20], 5586as[81], 5587as[81], 5588as[81]

SCHLÖTTERER, Reinhold, 1106as[23], 1173as[23], 3676as[50], 4847as[72]

Schmelzer, Johann Heinrich
 works, lieder, 1635as[25]

SCHMID, Andreas, 6377as[93]

Schmid, Bernhard, the elder
 works, organ music, 1382as[24]

SCHMID, Ernst Fritz, 920as[20], 1854as[26], 1855as[26], 3893as[58]

SCHMID, Hans, 773as[3], 3916as[58]

SCHMID, Reinhold, 4642as[70]

SCHMIDT, H., 3319as[41]

SCHMIDT, Hans, 3475as[42], 4772as[71]

SCHMIDT, Wilhelm, 2542as[31], 3229as[37]

SCHMIDT-EBHAUSEN, Friedrich Heinz, 396bs

SCHMIDT-GÖRG, Joseph, 3917as[58], 5761as[85]

SCHMIDTMANN, Friedrich, 2246as[28]

SCHMIDT-PHISELDECK, Josef, 675as[1]

SCHMIDT-PHISELDECK, Kay, 345bs, 5973as[89]

SCHMIEDEL, Peter, 4112as[62]

SCHMIEDER, Wolfgang, 676as[1], 677as[1], 678as[1], 679as[1], 1675as[25]

SCHMIT, Jean-Pierre, 6378as[93], 6379as[93]

SCHMITT, Antonius, 6380as[93]

SCHMITZ, Arnold, 1676as[25], 1856as[26], 4216as[63]

SCHMITZ, Eugen, 921as[20], 6381as[93]

SCHMITZ, Hans-Peter, 3749as[52]

SCHMITZ, Philibert, 6382as[93]

SCHNABL, Karl, 6383as[93]

Schneider, Conrad Michael
 works, 1683as[25]

SCHNEIDER, Constantin, 680as[1], 1677as[25]

SCHNEIDER, Marius, 947as[21], 1174as[23], 2456as[30], 2469as[30], 2540as[31], 2551as[32], 2588as[32], 2646as[33], 2688as[33], 4028as[61], 4029as[61], 4113as[62], 4114as[62], 4285as[64], 5589as[81], 6459as[99]

Schneider, Marius
 writings, Caucasus traditional polyphony, 3072as[34]
 ___ comparative melody reconstruction, applied to Spanish and Bulgarian songs, 2773as[34]
 ___ origins of polyphony, 889as[20]

SCHNEIDER, Max, 3767as[52], 5699as[82]

Schneider-Trnavský, Mikuláš
 works, 947as[21]

SCHNERICH, Alfred, 1857as[26], 3918as[58], 6384as[93], 6385as[93]

Schnitger, Arp
 instruments, organ building, Lamstedt St. Bartholomäus, 3390as[42]
 ___ organs, 3364as[42], 3469as[42], 3486as[42]
 ___ ___ played by J.D. Druckenmüller, 1655as[25]

Schnitger family
 instruments, organs, 3392as[42]

SCHNORR VON CAROLSFELD, Ernst, 3476as[42]

Schober, Franz von
 writings, *An die Musik*, set by Schubert, 1981as[27]

SCHOEN, Max, 5700as[82]

SCHOENBAUM, Camillo, 4380as[66]

Schoenberg, Arnold
 aesthetics, 3792as[54]
 ___ compared with Palestrina, 5632as[81]
 ___ serialism, 4409as[68]
 life, views on Debussy, 2132as[28], 2257as[28]
 works, atonal music, formal organization, 4335as[66]
 ___ atonality, relation to Werckmeister, 4100as[62]
 ___ critique, 5504as[81]
 ___ heterophony, 2247as[28]
 ___ influence on younger composers, 2342as[29]
 ___ influenced by Liszt, 2248as[28]
 ___ *Kol nidre*, op. 39, 4421as[69]
 ___ *Moses und Aron*, harmonic symbolism, 4226as[63]
 ___ notation, 3808as[55]
 ___ operas, role of libretto, 5111as[77]
 ___ ___ viewed by Pilarczyk, 5224as[77]
 ___ relation to Benoît, 1944as[27]
 ___ relation to history of 20th-c. music, 2140as[28]
 ___ style, compared with Janáček, 2220as[28]
 ___ use of older forms, 4231as[64]
 ___ viewed by Debussy and Varèse, 2201as[28]
 ___ ca. 1900, 2039as[27]
 writings, theory, influence on USA, 2366as[29]
 ___ views on Volksschule teachers, 2411as[29]

SCHOLE, Heinrich, 3320as[41], 5701as[82]

SCHOLES, Percy A., 206rs[16]

Scholes, Percy A.
 works, editing, *Columbia history of music through ear and eye*, 969as[21], 970as[21]

Scholze, Johann Sigismund (Sperontes)

Schönberg, Arnold, *see* **Schoenberg, Arnold**

Schönborn, Rudolf Franz Erwein von
 life, patronage of Platti, 1702as[25]

schools, *see* **academic institutions**; **choir schools**; **pedagogy** headwords

Schopenhauer, Arthur
 aesthetics, views on music, 5569as[81]
 writings, relation to Romantic aesthetics, 5432as[81]
 ___ viewed by Szymanowski, 2183as[28]

Schöttgen, Christian
 writings, *Curiöses Antiquitäten-Lexicon* (1719), treatment of instruments, 3266as[40]

SCHRADE, Leo, 1175as[23], 1427as[24], 1428as[24], 1429as[24], 2388as[29], 5239as[77], 5590as[81]

SCHRAMMEK, Winfried, 1176as[23], 3054as[34], 3636as[45]

SCHREIBER, Ottmar, 2093as[27]

Schreinzer, Karl
 collections, violin and viola fittings, 759as[2]

Schreker, Franz
 works, influenced by Debussy, 2257as[28]

___ *Pesn' o lesah* (Song of the forest), influenced by Händel, 2191as[28]
SŐTÉR, István, 5360as[78]
SOUDÈRES, Valérie, 2252as[28]
SOUGUENET, Léon, 74bs
sound recording and reproduction, *see also* **computer applications**; **mass media**; **sound recordings**
acoustics, state of research, 1956, 5837as[86]
amplification, instruments, 5858as[86]
analog vs. digital, 5758as[85]
bass frequencies, 5751as[85]
choruses, 5755as[85]
conference, 1965, 511bs
copyright, Bern Convention, ca. 1906, 5959as[89]
ethnomusicology, 2472as[30]
___ drummming, 2462as[30]
___ field recordings, 5754as[85]
___ ca. 1908, 2481as[30]
___ ca. 1955, 5783as[85]
Europe, mechanical reproduction rights, issue of private domain, 1952, 5769as[85]
evaluation, 5768as[85], 5773as[85]
___ objective vs. subjective, 5750as[85], 5767as[85]
film music, 5116as[77]
___ engineering, ca. 1937, 5760as[85]
___ microphones, ca. 1950, 5095as[77]
___ ca. 1937, 5743as[85]
film soundtracks, use of spontaneous sound, ca. 1937, 5193as[77]
history and development, 5748as[85]
___ influence on culture, 5781as[85]
___ influence on musical life, 2209as[28]
___ influence on reception, 2242as[28]
___ influence on 20th-c. music, 2215as[28]
___ limitations, ca. 1948, 5785as[85]
___ relation to economics, 5766as[85]
___ relation to musicology, 5793as[85]
___ relation to radio, 5747as[85]
___ early 20th c., 3792as[54]
___ ca. 1954, 5778as[85]
___ to 1957, 5765as[85]
Italy, Milano, Studio di Fonologia Musicale, 4404as[68]
melograph, Model B, 5792as[85]
microphones, 5780as[85]
___ placement, 5774as[85]
___ relation to music, 5745as[85]
___ ca. 1938, 5764as[85]
open-air music theater, 5213as[77]
orchestras, 5777as[85]
phonographs, stylus-groove relations, 5759as[85]
___ use in musicology, 899as[20]
___ ca. 1935, 5756as[85]
___ ca. 1953, 5790as[85]
photographphone, 5757as[85]
radio, 5784as[85]
___ mixing, 5779as[85]
___ relation to composition of orchestra, 5787as[85]
recording industry, careers, 5782as[85]
___ marketing priorities, ca. 1937, 2307as[29]
relation to vocal pedagogy and performance, 5795as[85]
stereo, 5762as[85], 5775as[85]
___ hearing aids, 5726as[83]
___ subjective distortions, 5659as[82]
studio, acoustics, 5817as[86], 5835as[86], 5864as[86]
tape, stereo, 5794as[85]
___ ca. 1953, 5746as[85], 5789as[85]
tape recorders, use in pedagogy, ca. 1957, 4655as[70]
traditional music, relation to preservation, 5807as[86]
___ ca. 1938, 5749as[85]
voice, relation to radio, 5791as[85]
sound recordings, *see also* **discographies**; **sound recording and reproduction**
AIBM, Music Documentation Centers, 597as[1]
anthologies, history of music, 969as[21], 970as[21]

___ Italy, 1014as[21]
___ Künzig, J., *Ehe sie verklingen...: Alte deutsche Volksweisen von Böhmerwald bis zur Wolga*, 5974as[89]
Archiv-Produktion, *Pro musica antiqua* historical series, dance music, 5952as[89]
art music, assessment, 1926-37, 2307as[29]
___ influence on appreciation, 2349as[29]
Austria, Vienna, Österreichische Akademie der Wissenschaften, Phonogrammarch., 752as[2]
Azoulay, L., traditional songs, 2418as[30]
Brazil, vocal music, pronunciation of nasal vowels, 3296as[41]
Brussels Pro Musica Antiqua, medieval and Renaissance dance music, 5952as[89]
cataloguing, 696as[1]
Chopin, F., 5796as[85]
___ polonaises, op. 53, 3789as[53]
Columbia Records, *Columbia history of music through ear and eye*, 969as[21], 970as[21]
Deutsche Grammophon, *Deutsche Volkslieder* series, 3055as[34]
England, London, British Inst. of Recorded Sound, 754as[2]
___ ___ British Inst. of Recorded Sound, 1956, 753as[2]
France, Paris, Musée Nat. des Arts et Traditions Populaires, acquisitions, ca. 1949, 706as[2]
___ ___ Phonothèque Nat. collection, relation to pedagogy, 553as[1], 554as[1]
___ public libraries, mid-1950s, 546as[1]
Georgia, traditional polyphony, 2621as[33]
Germany, *Tönende Musikgeschichte* project, 1950, 5761as[85]
Greece, Crete, traditional music, 2734as[34]
Händel, G.F., concerti grossi, op. 3, 3744as[52]
His Master's Voice, ca. 1932, 827as[9]
influence on concert audiences, 2312as[29]
influence on reception, 2372as[29]
Italy, Abruzzi, traditional songs, 2759as[34]
Japan, Ainu people, 2613as[33]
laofonografia, 2432as[30]
librarianship, 611as[1], 627as[1], 628as[1], 638as[1], 668as[1], 702as[1]
___ copyright, 529as[1], 530as[1]
___ exchange aspects, 663as[1], 664as[1]
___ USA, public libraries, 1950s, 625as[1], 634as[1]
___ ___ public libraries, mid-1950s, 626as[1]
___ ca. 1953, 648as[1]
___ ca. 1961, 687as[1]
Lumen, *Les archives sonores de la musique sacrée* series, 5983as[89], 5984as[89]
Monteverdi, C., dramatic works, 3771as[52]
Nagrania Polskie/Muza, Chopin complete works, 5796as[85]
Netherlands, dramatic arts, librarianship, 695as[1]
Norway, traditional music, at Norsk Rikskringkasting, Oslo, 2966as[34]
opera, early, 5763as[85]
Parlophon, *2000 Jahre Musik*, 969as[21], 970as[21]
phonograph records, assessment, ca. 1937, 5788as[85]
___ relation to popular music research, ca. 1934, 4922as[75]
___ use in pedagogy, 4505as[70]
___ ___ ca. 1957, 4655as[70]
___ vinyl, conservation and restoration, 5770as[85]
___ ___ deterioration, 5771as[85]
RCA Victor, relation to Latin American musicians, 2304as[29]
Scotland, traditional music, School of Scottish Studies, Edinburgh, 2774as[34]
singing, as a source for research on phonetic change, 5799as[85]
Slavic states, southern, epics, 1900-30, 3120as[34]
___ ___ traditional and neotraditional music, 1949-63, 2791as[34]
sociology, relation to moral decline, 5532as[81]
sound archives, broadcasting stations, development and uses, 661as[1], 662as[1]

___ documentation issues, ca. 1961, 602as[1]
___ ethnomusicological material, technical issues, ca. 1959, 660as[1]
___ university, role in pedagogy, 562as[1]
traditional music, 527as[1], 2457as[30]
___ activities of Inst. Nat. de Radiodiffusion, Belgium, 2504as[31]
___ authenticity, 2529as[31]
___ distortion of forms, 4282as[64]
___ songs, ca. 1937, 2525as[31]
___ standards, 2439as[30]
use in criticism, 5508as[81]
use in pedagogy, 4492as[70], 4504as[70], 4572as[70], 4641as[70], 4664as[70]
___ secondary, ca. 1937, 4764as[71]
___ ___ 1955-58, 4788as[71]
___ vocal, 3295as[41]
___ ca. 1937, 4513as[70]
Vikár, B., Hungarian traditional songs, 2418as[30]
20th-c. music, as musicological resources, 879as[20]
sound space, *see* **space**
source studies, *see also* **manuscripts and prints — by author; notation and paleography**
Austria, traditional music, Baroque, 1633as[25], 1634as[25]
Bach, J.S., *Canonische Veränderungen über..."Vom Himmel hoch..."*, BWV 769, 1538as[25]
___ 1950, 1675as[25]
Bach family, MSS in US collections, 1557as[25]
Beethoven, L. van, concertos, violin, op. 61, 1813as[26]
___ religious music, 1899as[26]
___ symphonies, no. 3, op. 55, and no. 5, op. 67, sketches, 1814as[26]
___ symphonies, no. 9, op. 125, sketches, 1872as[26]
brass music, performance practice, Baroque era, 3624as[45]
Bruckner, A., original vs. final versions, 2052as[27]
Buxtehude, D., keyboard music, 3925as[58]
___ *Membra Jesu*, BuxWV 75, 1589as[25]
Byzantine music, 883as[20]
Chopin, F., variant readings, 3899as[58]
conductus, Notre Dame school, 1114as[23]
Desprez, J., psalm motets, 1393as[24]
as discipline, relation to Schubert autographs, 731as[2]
Dusík, J.L., 1745as[26]
France, dance music, late 15th c., 1357as[24]
Frescobaldi, G., relation to Mechelen, 1527as[25]
Germany, lute music, 18th c., 3553as[44]
___ Protestant church music, ca. 1520-50, MS filiation, 1360as[24]
___ vocal improvisation, 1522-ca. 1650, 3709as[51]
Gregorian chant, filiation, 3896as[58]
Händel, G.F., *Messiah*, 3752as[52]
___ *Saul*, 3780as[52]
harp, 3596as[44]
Hungary, Middle Ages, 812as[8]
hymns, Lutheran, 16th c., 1561as[25]
Italy, dance music, late 15th c., 1357as[24]
___ vocal improvisation, 1522-ca. 1650, 3709as[51]
Janáček, L., vocal music, 4385as[66]
Japan, issues, 2633as[33]
Minnesang, use of textual criticism, 5337as[78]
Mozarabic chant, 1207as[23]
Mozart, W.A., state of research, 1964, 1836as[26]
Netherlandish school, chansons, German MSS, 1319as[24]
Passions, 16th c., 1308as[24]
Requiem, chant movements, 1119as[23]
La Rue, P. de, works, dating, 1426as[24]
sketches, relation to editing, 3908as[58]
sound recordings, 5781as[85]
Spain, polyphony, to ca. 1400 c., 1221as[24]
Squarcialupi, A., 1230as[24]
Stoltzer, T., 1337as[24]

___ religious music, 1929as[27]
___ *La vestale*, 1753as[26]
___ ___ parodies, 2085as[27]
SPÖRRI, Otto, 3481as[42]

sports and games, *see also* **dance** headwords;
movement and gesture
Bosnia and Herzegovina, children, dance games,
4954as[76]
___ ___ work as subject of games, 5046as[76]
___ Herzegovina, collected by Vrčević, 2962as[34]
___ ___ social games, 5045as[76]
England, children, singing games, 2885as[34]
gymnastics, kindergarten, relation to Dalcroze
method, 4771as[71]
___ relation to Dalcroze method, 4560as[70]
Hungary, traditional games, 5015as[76]
Iran, gymnastics, rhythmic accompaniment,
2607as[33]
Israel, radio quiz shows, 2397as[29]
Italy, Firenze, Medici court, late 16th c., 5158as[77]
Macedonia, children, 4976as[76]
Mozart, W.A., 1897as[26]
play, relation to art, 5519as[81]
Russia, 2817as[34]
Serbia, swinging games, songs, 2995as[34]
Slavic states, southern, ritual swinging games,
2869as[34]
Slovenia, children, most game, 5010as[76]
___ most game, 5072as[76]
Spain, Aragón, northern, 2725as[34]
___ Las Ventas con Peña Aguilera, 2948as[34],
2949as[34]
USA, California, Chukchansi Yokuts people,
women's game songs, 3168as[35]

Spourni, Wenceslaus Joseph
collections, symphonies, 761as[2]

Spranger, Eduard
writings, psychology of types, 5632as[81]
SPRINGER, Hermann Wilhelm, 686as[1], 688as[1],
689as[1], 690as[1], 691as[1], 823as[8], 1691as[25],
5603as[81], 5994as[89]

spurious works, *see* **attribution and authenticity**
SPYRIDAKIS, Georgios, 692as[1]

Squarcialupi, Antonio
life, documentary evidence, 1060as[23], 1230as[24]

Squarcialupi family
lives, relation to A. Squarcialupi, 1230as[24]
SQUIRE, William Barclay, 1439as[24], 5398as[79]

Srbija (=Serbia), *see* **Serbia and Montenegro**
ŠREJER-TKAČENKO, Onys'ja Jakovlevna,
1440as[24]

Sri Lanka
dance, traditional, 4934as[76]
musical life, rabāna playing, 2606as[33]
traditional music, songs, 2696as[33]
STÄBLEIN, Bruno, 693as[1], 797as[5], 1091as[23],
1126as[23], 1141as[23], 1147as[23], 1186as[23],
1187as[23], 1188as[23], 1189as[23], 1190as[23],
1191as[23], 3872as[55], 3898as[58]

Stadler, Anton
life, relation to Mozart, 3750as[52]
STADNICKI, Edwin Kornel, 2101as[27]
STÁDNÍK, Miloš, 1865as[26]

stage directors, *see* **directors, producers, etc.**

Stägemann, Friedrich August von
writings, poetry, music as subject, 5350as[78]

Stahlhuth, Georg
tributes, 3350as[42]
STAIGER, Robert, 3873as[55]

Stainhauser, Johann
writings, Salzburg dramatic arts, 1677as[25]
STAÏS, Valerios, 3604as[44]

Stajnov, Petko
works, influenced by Bulgarian traditional rhythm,
4005as[61]
STALMANN, Joachim, 1441as[24]

STAM, Henk, 694as[1]

Stamic, Jan Václav
works, influenced by Czech traditional songs,
2944as[34]
___ relation to Mozart, 1843as[26]
___ *Sonate a tre*, compared with Hamal *Six
ouvertures de camera,* op. 1, 4242as[64]

Stamic, Karl
works, influenced by Czech traditional songs,
2944as[34]
___ viola d'amore, 3579as[44]

Stanford, Charles Villiers
life, teaching of British composers, 2144as[28]
STANISLAV, Josef, 2590as[32], 3064as[34], 4462as[69]
STANLEY, Albert A., 2393as[29], 4851as[72], 4852as[72]
STANTON, Hazel Martha, 4896as[73]

Starer, Robert
works, to 1947, 2228as[28]

Starominsky, Marc, *see* **Seter, Mordecai**
STARR, Frederick, 18bs
STARZYŃSKI, Juliusz, 5399as[79], 5604as[81]

statistical analysis, *see* **analysis; information theory**
STAUDER, Wilhelm, 3249as[40]
STAVITSKY, Michael, 6101as[91]
STECHOW, Wolfgang, 5394as[79], 5400as[79]
ŠTĚDROŇ, Bohumír, 957as[21], 1008as[21], 1866as[26],
2102as[27], 2254as[28], 2255as[28], 4383as[66]
STEFAN, Paul, 2103as[27], 2394as[29]
STEFANI, Gino, 501bs
STEFANOVIĆ, Dimitrije, 1009as[21], 1192as[23],
4463as[69], 6130as[92]
STEGLICH, Rudolf, 319bs, 1442as[24], 1692as[25],
1867as[26], 2104as[27], 3769as[52], 3893as[58],
4031as[61], 4032as[61], 4286as[64]
STEIN, Fritz, 1868as[26], 1869as[26]

Steiner, Max
works, film music, influence, 5095as[77]
STEINITZ, Wolfgang, 3065as[34]
STELLFELD, Jean Auguste, 210bs
STEMPEL, Maxim, 1870as[26], 3770as[52]
STEPANOV, Stjepan, 3066as[34], 3637as[45], 4464as[69]

Stephan, Emil
writings, Bismarck Archipelago traditional music,
2542as[31]
STEPHAN, Rudolf, 1193as[23], 4033as[61], 5361as[78]

Stephănescu, George
works, influenced by Haydn, 2116as[27]
STEPHANI, Hermann, 4116as[62], 4219as[63]
STEPHENSON, Kurt, 5909as[87]
STERN, Philippe, 2473as[30]

Sternberg, Erich Walter
works, to 1947, 2228as[28]

Sternberg, Josef von
works, directing, *Blonde Venus*, 5208as[77]
STERNFELD, Frederick William, 3923as[58],
5362as[78]
STESSER-PÉAN, Guy, 5066as[76]
STĘSZEWSKA, Zofia, 4034as[61]
STĘSZEWSKI, Jan, 2256as[28], 2474as[30], 3067as[34],
4034as[61]
STEVENS, Denis, 1112as[23], 1316as[24], 1443as[24],
1444as[24], 3771as[52], 3772as[52], 3911as[58],
3922as[58], 5249as[77], 5793as[85]

Stevens, Denis
editions, early English organ music, 3895as[58]
STEVENSON, Robert, 953as[21]
STEWART, Douglas, 6450as[94]

stichēraria, *see* **liturgical books**
STICHTENOTH, Friedrich, 5605as[81]
STIEGLITZ, Olga, 4652as[70]

stile antico, *see* **Baroque**

Stimmer, Tobias
works, art, depiction of women musicians,
5383as[79]
STIRNIMANN, Heinrich, 6027as[90]
STIVEN, Frederick Benjamin, 4653as[70]

Stivori, Francesco
life, relation to history of Czech music, 1653as[25]

Stockhausen, Karlheinz
works, *Gesang der Jünglinge,* 4401as[68]
___ rhythmic structure, 4007as[61]
___ serialism, rhythmic features, 1950s, 4017as[61]
STOCKMANN, Doris, 3068as[34], 3069as[34],
3070as[34], 3071as[34]
STOCKMANN, Erich, 3071as[34], 3072as[34], 3073as[34],
3278as[40], 3279as[40], 3638as[45]
STOECKEL, Alfred, 3543as[43]
STOFFELS, Hermann, 4780as[71]
STÖHR, Adolf, 5706as[82]

Stojanov, Veselin
works, influenced by Bulgarian traditional rhythm,
4005as[61]
STOJANOVIĆ, Josip, 3074as[34]

Stokem, Johannes de
life, at Hungarian court, 1326as[24]
STOLLBERG, Oskar, 6451as[94]

Stoltzer, Thomas
life, 1337as[24]
STOMPOR, Stephan, 5250as[77]

Stösslová, Kamila
correspondence, from Janáček, relation to string
quartet no. 2, 2254as[28]

Stothart, Herbert
works, film music, for Lloyd *Mutiny on the
Bounty,* 5130as[77]
STOVEROCK, Dietrich, 4853as[72], 4854as[72]

Stradivari, Antonio
festivals and conferences, Italy, Cremona, 1937,
238bs
instruments, violin making, 3554as[44]
STRAETEN, Edmond vander, 1194as[23], 2105as[27],
3280as[40]
STRAKOVÁ, Theodora, 5251as[77]

strambotto, *see* **song texts**
STRÁNSKÁ, Drahomíra, 3075as[34], 3076as[34]
STRARAM, Enrich, 808as[7], 809as[7]

Straube, Karl
editions, *Choralvorspiele alter Meister,* 3895as[58]
instruments, organs, at cathedral, Passau, 3399as[42]
life, teaching of organ composers, 2189as[28]

Strauss, Richard
life, relation to Debussy, 2257as[28]
works, additional music for Mozart *Idomeneo, re
di Creta,* 3775as[52]
___ influence on Janáček and Bartók, 2238as[28]
___ influence on Szymanowski, 4354as[66]
___ operas, 5147as[77]
___ ___ concept of genre, 5169as[77]
___ quoted by Bartók, 4317as[66]

Stravinsky, Igor
aesthetics, compared with Janáček, 2223as[28]
___ influenced by Musorgskij, 5486as[81]
___ subjectivism vs. objectivism, 5568as[81]
life, views on film music, 5275as[77]
works, *Canticum sacrum,* 3938as[60]
___ compared with Janáček, 2171as[28]
___ concert music, spiritual inspiration, from late
1920s, 2204as[28]
___ early, 2211as[28]
___ ___ relation to Debussy, 2205as[28]
___ *The flood,* influenced by Brecht, 5229as[77]
___ harmony, to 1937, 4194as[63]
___ influence on Israeli art music, 1950-59,
2143as[28]
___ influence on Janáček and Bartók, 2238as[28]
___ influence on younger composers, 2342as[29]

U

Pennsylvania, musical life, German-speaking religious communities, 18th c., 1740as[26]
___ western, musical life, fiddle playing, 3139as[35]
popular music, film musicals, ca. 1937, 5115as[77]
Puerto Rico, dance, 4951as[76]
religious music, Christian, history and development, 6026as[90]
___ Gregorian chant, ca. 1957, 4729as[71], 4730as[71]
___ Protestant hymnody, 20th c., 6452as[94]
___ Roman Catholic hymnody, 6251as[93]
___ traditional, history and development, 3156as[35]
South, Appalachia, traditional music, relation to English traditional music, 2884as[34]
___ French-speaking people, dance, 4937as[76]
southeastern, Indians, traditional music, influenced by African-American music, 3155as[35]
Southwest, Hopi people, traditional music, songs, 3164as[35]
___ Indians, traditional music, peyote songs, diffusion, 3175as[35]
___ Navajo people, culture, 3166as[35]
___ Omaha people, traditional music, love songs, 3150as[35]
___ Pueblo people, musical life, 3165as[35]
Texas, dance, square dance, history and development, 5060as[76]
traditional music, ballads, 3177as[35]
___ ___ hanging of fiddler as subject, 2547as[31]
___ ___ shared features, 2750as[34]
___ song texts, Noah motive, 5366as[78]
___ song tunes, kinship and variation, 4416as[69]
___ songs, compared with Germany, 2820as[34]
___ value distinctions, 2500as[31]
West, Indians, religious music, hymnody, 3173as[35]

universal harmony, see harmony

universals, see also ethnomusicology; world music
aesthetics, 5483as[81]
artistic expression, 855as[19]
Bach, J.S., 1707as[25]
chant, 6459as[99]
harmony, 4150as[63]
intervals, 5649as[82]
origins of music, 849as[19]
ornamentation, 829as[19], 841as[19], 854as[19]
relation to information theory, 856as[19]
relation to radio, 2347as[29]
rhythm and meter, children, 3973as[61]
scales and intervals, experimental study, 5657as[82]
traditional music, 2485as[30]

universities, see academic institutions
UNVERRICHT, Hubert, 3893as[58]

Upper Volta, see Burkina Faso
UPTON, William Treat, 1885as[26]

urban studies, see also cultural policies; economics; geography; politics; sociology
agrarian vs. urban cultures, 851as[19]
Austria, Salzburg, Mozart monuments and museums, 974as[21]
Bosnia and Herzegovina, World War II songs, 2916as[34]
Czech Republic, Krkonoše, influenced by industrialization, 3075as[34], 3076as[34]
Italy, influence on traditional music, 2757as[34]
public art, conference, 1905, 49bs
URBAŃSKI, Janusz, 5796as[85]
URBANTSCHITSCH, Victor, 4291as[64]
URETA DEL SOLAR, María, 4790as[71], 4791as[71]
URSPRUNG, Otto, 1045as[22], 1457as[24], 4388as[66], 5995as[89], 6401as[93]

USA, see United States of America
Ušinskij, Konstantin D.
writings, pedagogy, 1564as[25]
USSACHEVSKY, Vladimir, 2196as[28]
USSR, see also Russia
aesthetics, relation to Bach, 1579as[25]
cultural policies, opera censorship, 5235as[77]

eastern, Nivh people, folklore, genre classification, 2601as[33]
ethnomusicology, ca. 1959, 2479as[30]
history of music, film music, to 1950, 5171as[77]
___ influenced by Debussy, 2194as[28]
musical life, activities of Sojuz Kompozitorov SSSR, 1936-47, 2251as[28]
___ reception of Bartók, 1928-29, 2216as[28]
___ reception of Haydn, 3751as[52]
musicology, activities of Asaf'ev, 872as[20]
___ Chopin studies, 1918 to present, 2000as[27]
Tatar people, traditional music, vocal melodies, compared with Hungarian melodies, 4471as[69]
traditional music, songs, references to Soviet life, 5277as[78]
USZKOREIT, Hans-Georg, 2113as[27]

Utendal, Alexander
works, melodic variation, 4361as[66]
UTERMÖHLEN, Rudolf, 3498as[42], 3499as[42]
UTLEY, Frances Lee, 5366as[78]

Uzbekistan
Bohoro, Jewish people, culture, wedding cycle, 2631as[33]

V

VACCHIANO GARCÍA, Hipólito, 331bs
Vačkář, Dalibor
works, mass songs, 3064as[34]
VÁCLAVEK, Bedřich, 3093as[34], 3236as[39]
VÄISÄNEN, Armas Otto, 2114as[27], 2266as[28], 4468as[69]
VALABREGA, Cesare, 1014as[21], 1886as[26], 1887as[26], 6102as[91]
Valdés, Julio
works, religious music, 2234as[28]
VÁLEK, Jiří, 4389as[66]
VALENSI, Henry, 5402as[79], 5620as[81]
VALENTIN, Erich, 1888as[26], 4662as[70], 5912as[87]
Valenzuela, Pedro
works, 5365as[78]
VALÉRY, Paul, 249bs
Valéry, Paul
writings, influence on Eliot musicality, 5299as[78]
VALOIS, Jean de, 3718as[51]
VAN, Guillaume de, 3879as[55]
VAN DEN GHEYN, Gabriel Edmond Guillaume, 23bs
Van Dyke, Woodbridge S.
works, directing, White shadows in the South Seas, 5208as[77]
VAN GELUWE, Hugette, 282bs
VAN HOOGENHOUCK TULLEKEN (MME), 3180as[35], 3181as[35]
VAN WENGEN, Gerrit Dirk, 3222as[36]
VANCEA, Zeno, 929as[20], 1015as[21], 2115as[27], 2116as[27], 2267as[28], 3094as[34], 5263as[77]
VANDER ZANDEN, Rose Margaret, 4792as[71]
VANDERHAEGE, René (René Lyr), 1016as[21]
VANDEWALLE, Charles, 4899as[73], 6402as[93]
Vaňhal, Jan Křtitel
collections, symphonies, 761as[2]
life, relation to Mozart, 1805as[26]
VANICKÝ, Jaroslav, 1204as[23]
VANSINA, Jan, 433bs
VANSON, Charles-Victor, 6403as[93]
VARAGNAC, Andre, 3095as[34]
Varèse, Edgard
correspondence, with Debussy, 2201as[28]
VARGA, Ovidiu, 2477as[30], 2544as[31]

VARGYAS, Lajos, 3096as[34], 4123as[62], 4422as[69], 4469as[69]

variation, see also ostinato; passacaglia and chaconne; quotation
aesthetics, compared with Japanese music, 2688as[33]
Bach, C.P.E., 1550as[25]
Bach, J.S., Canonische Veränderungen über..."Vom Himmel hoch...", BWV 769, 1538as[25]
Beethoven, L. van, 4247as[64], 4271as[64]
___ use of Mozart themes, 1821as[26]
Brahms, J., 4368as[66]
___ relation to sonata form, 4291as[64]
Bull, J., Why ask you?, 1343as[24]
Chopin, F., based on Rossini Non più mesta, attributed, 1950as[27]
___ etudes, 2079as[27]
Gronau, J.M., chorale variations, 1747, 1554as[25]
Italy, partitas, 16th c., 1454as[24]
Mozart, W.A., theme sources, 1892as[26]
Niedt, F.E., basso continuo, 3944as[60]
polythematic types, 4270as[64]
Reger, M., Variationen und Fuge über ein Thema von Johann Sebastian Bach, op. 81, compared with Szymanowski, 4354as[66]
Scheidt, S., Tabulatur-Buch hundert geistlicher Lieder und Psalmen, varied harmonic progression, 4202as[63]
Spain, organ music, glosas, 16th c., 3699as[51]
Szymanowski, K., compared with Reger, 4354as[66]
traditional vs. art music, 4285as[64]
VAŠICA, Josef, 6131as[92]
VASILJEVIĆ, Miodrag A., 3097as[34], 3098as[34], 4124as[62], 4125as[62], 4793as[71], 4794as[71]
Vasiljević, Miodrag A.
collections, Jugoslovenski muzički folklor. II, refrain typology, 2998as[34]
VASINA-GROSSMAN, Vera, 2117as[27]
Vásquez, Juan
works, 5365as[78]
Vatican
religious music, liturgical books and decrees, 6279as[93]
VATIELLI, Francesco, 157bs, 3607as[44], 5996as[89]
vaudeville (16th c.), see air de cour
vaudeville (17th-18th c.), see opera — general; opéra comique
VAUGHAN WILLIAMS, Ralph, 2478as[30]
Vaughan Williams, Ralph
works, film music, 5173as[77]
___ operas, 5108as[77]
VAUX-PHALIPAU, Marie de, 3099as[34]
VAZIRI, Ali Naqi, 3880as[55]
Vážný, Václav
writings, Croatian folklore, 3062as[34]
VECCHI, Giuseppe, 588as[1], 1714as[25], 3898as[58], 6404as[93]
Vecchi, Orazio
performance practice, Amfiparnaso, 5265as[77]
Vedel, Anders Sørensen
writings, It hundrede vdualde danske viser (One hundred selected Danish ballads), 1591, 3052as[34]
VEDOVA, Emilio, 5264as[77]
VEEN, Jan van der, 4390as[66]
VEEN-HIEL, J. De, 2118as[27]
VEGA, Aurelio de la, 4898as[73]
VEGA, Carlos, 3223as[36], 3639as[45], 4126as[62]
Vega, Carlos
writings, Argentinian folk dances, 5039as[76]
Vega, Lope de
writings, villancicos, 5365as[78]
Vehe, Michael
writings, Ein new Gesangbüchlin geystlicher Lieder, 6315as[93]

___ ___ form, 4243as[64]
___ ___ influenced by opera, 1714as[25]
___ ___ use of soprano lute, 3563as[44]
___ concertos, string, arranged by Bach, 1537as[25]
___ early, 1592as[25]
___ instrumental music, relation to toccata, 4237as[64]
___ *L'Olimpiade*, appreciation, 1628as[25]
___ viola d'amore, 3579as[44]
VIVET, Armand, 247bs, *248rs[16], 6408as[93]
VLAD, Roman, 5157as[77]

Vladigerov, Pančo
works, influenced by Bulgarian traditional rhythm, 4005as[61]
VLAHOVIĆ, Mitar S., 3284as[40], 5368as[78]

vocal music, *see also* **choral music**; specific genres
Albania, southern, Çamen people, 3070as[34]
Bach, J.S., arranged by Classic composers, 1750as[26]
Beethoven, L. van, harmony, 4219as[63]
Belgium, Mechelen, discant, 15th c., 1289as[24]
Canada, Christian, 6023as[90]
Classic, religious music, editing, 3910as[58]
composition, influenced by knowledge of singing technique, 3292as[41]
Congo, Democratic Republic, Cokwe people, 2560as[32]
ensembles, male, Europe, German-speaking lands, history and development, 3329as[41]
form, through-composed vs. strophic, relation to organicism, 4257as[64]
Franck, M., spiritual concertos, 1566as[25]
Händel, G.F., early, attribution and dating, 1494as[25]
Haydn, J., canons, 4371as[66]
India, concept of anāhatanāda, 2602as[33]
Italy, Napoli, influenced by Spain, late 15th c., 1410as[24]
___ Tonnaro, *Is musicas* festival, 2793as[34]
Japan, bugaku, ei and saezuri, 2620as[33]
Middle Ages, 1064as[23]
Mozart, W.A., compared with instrumental music, 1860as[26]
___ form typology, 4281as[64]
___ performance practice, 3745as[52]
___ recitatives, 1759as[26]
Palestrina, G.P. da, style, 4379as[66]
Portuguese language, text setting, word division, 4314as[66]
relation to instrumental ensemble music, to 1500, 1448as[24]
relation to pedagogy, 4649as[70]
Renaissance, relation to instrumental music, 1332as[24]
___ rhythm and meter, compared with dance music, 3997as[61]
___ viewed by 19th c., 6247as[93]
rhythm and meter, accent, 5288as[78]
Schumann, R., text setting, 2097as[27]
Serbia, Zlatibor, traditional polyphony, 2997as[34]
shape translation, 20th c., 5637as[82]
Sweden, northern, relation to herding, 2755as[34]
Switzerland, minor works, late 17th to early 18th c., 1487as[25]
Szymanowski, K., 2187as[28]
text setting, Middle Ages to early 20th c., 936as[21]
traditional, polyphony, state of research, ca. 1964, 2803as[34]
15th-17th c., editing, 3907as[58]

vocal pedagogy, *see* **singing**
Vodun religious music, *see* **religion and religious music — Vodun**
VODUŠEK, Valens, 2947as[34], 3102as[34], 3103as[34], 3104as[34], 3105as[34], 3106as[34], 3107as[34], 5072as[76]

Vogel, Friedrich Wilhelm Ferdinand
life, Norway residence, 966as[21]

Vogel, Gregorius
instruments, organs, 3364as[42]
VOGEL, Martin, 2121as[27], 3545as[43], 4127as[62], 4128as[62]
VOGL, Hertha, 1889as[26]

Vogl, Johann Michael
performances, Schubert lieder, 3782as[53]

Vogler, Georg Joseph
life, Sweden, 1786-99, 1776as[26]

voice, *see also* **bel canto**; **singing**
acoustics, compared with wind instruments, 5815as[86]
influenced by race, 3289as[41], 3290as[41]
male, formant analysis, 3322as[41]
Mozart, W.A., *Idomeneo, re di Creta*, voice types, 3757as[52]
pathology, state of research, ca. 1936, 3325as[41]
physiology, larynx, relation to sound quality, 3323as[41]
___ pharyngo-buccal cavity, 3308as[41]
production, relation to ethnomusicology, 5649as[82]
___ relation to radio, 5791as[85]
Schubert, F., lieder, tessituras, 3782as[53]
therapy, relation to heredity, 3331as[41]
vibrato, compared with violin, 3580as[44]

voice flute (=recorder), *see* **instruments — wind (woodwind, flute family)**
voice leading, *see* **counterpoint**
VOISÉ, Waldemar, 1461as[24]

voix de ville, *see also* **air de cour**; **chanson (14th-16th c.)**
VOJTĚCH, Ivan, 5112as[77]
VÓKOS, Giórgios, 1890as[26]
VOLBACH, Walther R., 5268as[77]
VOLEK, Jaroslav, 3939as[60], 3961as[60], 4224as[63], 4292as[64]
VOLEK, Tomislav, 957as[21], 1709as[25]

Volkmann, Hans
writings, *Emanuel d'Astorga*, critique, 1701as[25]
VOLKMANN, Ludwig, 5999as[89]

Voltaire, *see* **Arouet, François Marie (Voltaire)**
voodoo, *see* **religion and religious music — Vodun**
Vořísek, Jan Václav
works, rhapsodies, piano, relation to ballade, 4245as[64]
VÖTTERLE, Karl, 699as[1], 3911as[58]

Vrancken, D. Joes.
works, motets, 1364as[24]

Vrčević, Vuk
collections, Herzegovinian folklore, 2962as[34]
VRIESLANDER, Otto, 2122as[27]
VUILLERMOZ, Émile, 1018as[21], 4664as[70], 5621as[81]

Vuinck, Magnus
manuscripts, Braunschweig Organ Tablature, 1433as[24]
VUJICSICS, Tihamér, 3108as[34], 3109as[34]
VUKMANOVIĆ, Jovan, 357bs, 462bs, 3110as[34], 3285as[40]
VUKOSAVLJEV, Sava, 3111as[34]
VUKOVIĆ, Jovan, 419bs, 455bs, 3112as[34], 4039as[61]
VULETIĆ-VUKASOVIĆ, Vid, 3113as[34], 5080as[76]
VULIĆ, N., 133rs[16]

Vulpius, Christian
writings, revision of Schikaneder *Die Zauberflöte* libretto, 5240as[77]
VYERMAN, Jules, 4900as[73]

Vyshnegradsky, Ivan, *see* **Vyšnegradskij, Ivan Aleksandrovič**
VYSLOUŽIL, Jiří, 4393as[66], 5622as[81]

Vyšnegradskij, Ivan Aleksandrovič
works, microtonal music, 4146as[63]

W

Wachmann, Ion Andrei
works, influenced by Haydn, 2116as[27]
WACHSMANN, Klaus P., 840as[19], 2453as[30], 2480as[30], 2546as[31], 2551as[32], 2594as[32], 2595as[32], 2596as[32], 2597as[32], 4285as[64]

Wackenroder, Wilhelm Heinrich
writings, on Mozart, 5595as[81]

Wacław z Oleska, *see* **Zaleski, Wacław**
WADDINGTON, Geoffrey, 4665as[70], 4666as[70]

Waelrant, Hubert
works, *Als ick u vinde*, arranged by Adriaenssen, 1390as[24]
WAELTNER, Ernst Ludwig, 774as[3], 1106as[23], 3962as[60]

Wagner, Cosima
life, relation to Nietzsche, 2121as[27]

Wagner, Joachim
instruments, organs, 3443as[42]
WAGNER, Johannes, 6409as[93]
WAGNER, Peter, 1019as[21], 1205as[23], 1206as[23], 1207as[23], 1208as[23], 3720as[51], 3881as[55], 5623as[81], 6410as[93], 6411as[93]

Wagner, Peter
life, founding of Académie Grégorienne, 6419as[93]
writings, on chant rhythm, 3702as[51]

Wagner, Richard
aesthetics, 5598as[81]
___ compared with Hanslick, 5580as[81]
___ concept of Gesamtkunstwerk, relation to Hegel, 5523as[81]
___ concept of poetic-musical period, 4238as[64]
___ harmony, relation to Chopin, 4196as[63]
___ influence on Moniuszko, 5113as[77]
___ influenced by grand opera, 5101as[77]
___ key characteristics, 4223as[63]
___ literature and music, 1905as[27]
___ opera, words and music, 5093as[77]
___ relation to dramaturgy, 5581as[81]
festivals and conferences, Poland, Katowice, 1963, 466bs
life, relation to French literature, 5319as[78]
___ relation to Lipiński, 2073as[27]
___ relation to Nietzsche, 2121as[27]
___ views on Hungarian music, 1915as[27]
___ views on Mozart, 2120as[27]
manuscripts, compared with published scores, 3784as[53]
performances, by Polish singers, 5214as[77]
___ operas, Bayreuth, 1951-64, 5184as[77]
reception, cult of creative genius, 5469as[81]
___ Poland, 5364as[78]
___ relation to November Revolution, 2048as[27]
___ 1950s, 5241as[77]
works, circle of fifths, compared with Bach, 4306as[66]
___ harmony, altered chords, compared with Chopin and Liszt, 4224as[63]
___ influence on Austrian music, 2060as[27]
___ influence on English music, 2126as[27]
___ influence on film music, ca. 1937, 5210as[77]
___ influence on Karłowicz, 1918as[27]
___ influence on Szymanowski, 2107as[27], 4354as[66]
___ influence on 20th-c. opera, 5189as[77]
___ leitmotivs, relation to literature, 5353as[78]
___ *Das Liebesverbot*, 2091as[27]
___ national characteristics, 5431as[81]
___ operas, concept of genre, 5169as[77]
___ ___ influence on Plüddemann ballads, 4288as[64]
___ ___ influenced by Neapolitan opera, 1673as[25]
___ ___ role of libretto, 5111as[77]

GUIDO ADLER HIGINI ANGLÈS
JACQUES BARZUN LUCIANO BER
HENRY COWELL FEDELE D'AMICO C
GEORGES DUHAMEL HENRI DUTI
ALOIS HÁBA PAUL HINDEMITH AN
VON HORNBOSTEL ERNST KRENE
WANDA LANDOWSKA FRANÇOIS
LIFAR GYÖRGY LIGETI ALAN LOMA
GIAN FRANCESCO MALIPIERO IG
MASSIMO MILA DARIUS MILHAUD
VÁCLAV NEUMANN CARL ORFF
GABRIEL PIERNÉ NINO PIRROT
PRUNIÈRES ROMAIN ROLLAND
SCHWEITZER CHARLES SEEGER
NICOLAS SLONIMSKY VIRGIL THOM
RALPH VAUGHAN WILLIAMS HE
EMANUEL WINTERNITZ IANNIS XE
ERNEST ANSERMET BÉLA BARTÓ
FRANZ BOAS ALFREDO CASELLA